FAMILY LAW:
CASES, MATERIALS AND PROBLEMS

SECOND EDITION

Peter N. Swisher
Professor of Law
University of Richmond

Anthony Miller
Professor of Law
Pepperdine University

Jana B. Singer
Associate Professor of Law
University of Maryland

CASEBOOK SERIES

1998

QUESTIONS ABOUT THIS PUBLICATION?

For questions about the **Editorial Content** or reprint permission, please call:
Dennis Leski, J.D. .... (800) 424-0651 ext. 240
David Youngsmith, J.D. .... (800) 424-0651 ext. 263
Outside the United States and Canada please call .... (415) 908-3200

To order a copy of this book, or for assistance with shipments, billing or other customer service matters, please call:

Customer Services Department at .... (800) 533-1646
Outside the United States and Canada, please call .... (518) 487-3000
Fax number .... (518) 487-3584

For information on other Matthew Bender publications, please call
Your account manager or .... (800) 223-1940
Outside the United States and Canada, please call .... (518) 487-3000

This publication is designed to provide accurate and authoritative information in regard to the subject matter covered. It is sold with the understanding that the publisher is not engaged in rendering legal, accounting, or other professional services. If legal advice or other expert assistance is required, the services of a competent professional should be sought.

Copyright © 1998 By Matthew Bender & Company Incorporated
All Rights Reserved. Printed in United States of America.
No copyright is claimed in the text of statutes, regulations, and excerpts from court opinions quoted within this work. Permission to copy material exceeding fair use, 17 U.S.C. § 107, may be licensed for a fee of $ .25 per page per copy from the Copyright Clearance Center, 222 Rosewood Drive, Danvers, Mass. 01923, telephone (978) 750-8400.

Library of Congress Card Number: 98-33819

ISBN 0-8205-3128-6

LIBRARY OF CONGRESS CATALOGING IN PUBLICATION DATA

Swisher, Peter N., 1944–
    Family law: case, materials, and problems / Peter N. Swisher, H. Anthony Miller, Jana B. Singer. — 2nd ed.
    p. cm. — (Casebook series)
    Includes bibliographical references and index.
    ISBN 0-8205-3128-6
    1. Domestic relations—United States—Cases. I. Miller, H. Anthony. II. Singer, Jana B. III. Title. IV. Series: Casebook series (New York, N.Y.)
    KF504.S95 1998
    346.7301′5—dc21

98-33819
CIP

MATTHEW BENDER

MATTHEW BENDER & CO., INC.
Editorial Offices
Two Park Avenue, New York, NY 10016-5675 (212) 448-2000
201 Mission Street, San Francisco, CA 94105-1831 (415) 908-3200

PREFACE TO THE SECOND EDITION

Over the past three decades, both the scope and content of American family law have changed dramatically. Traditionally, the study of family law—also known as domestic relations law—focused on the regulation of marriage and divorce, and on the legal relationship between (married) parents and their children. Contemporary family law includes these subjects, but it has expanded to encompass such topics as the legal and economic relationships between unmarried cohabitants; the rights and obligations of unmarried parents; the regulation of reproductive decision-making and technology; and the appropriate role of the state in mediating between parental authority and child protection. In many areas, most notably divorce, the primary focus of family law has shifted from moral to economic issues, and the general practitioner or business lawyer must understand important family law concepts and principles in order to represent her clients adequately. At the same time, the legal principles governing family relationships have come to incorporate significant elements of constitutional law, criminal law, contract law, tort law, corporate law, and employee benefits and tax law. The modern family law practitioner must be aware of these elements and understand their impact on a wide range of family law doctrines and principles.

Family law scholarship has also flourished over the past 25 years. Leading law reviews and other journals are filled with articles on family law topics—from divorce to domestic violence, from gestational surrogacy to open adoption. Contemporary family law scholars have applied a variety of theories and jurisprudential approaches to the study of family law—from feminist theory to economic analysis, from empirical research to therapeutic jurisprudence and family systems theory. In many instances, this scholarship has contributed to significant changes in traditional family law doctrines and practice. In addition, both the study and the practice of family law has become increasingly inter-disciplinary; a full understanding of many family law topics now requires the integration of knowledge from a variety of disciplines and perspectives. For example, lawyers and mediators who handle child custody disputes routinely draw upon psychological theory and methodology; adjudications of paternity rest on principle of genetics and statistical techniques; and social science evidence regarding the incidence and causes of intimate violence is central to developing effective legal and policy responses to such violence.

This Casebook seeks to integrate the theory and practice of family law. Our goal is to give students a solid grounding in contemporary family law doctrines and practice, while at the same time situating that practice within a broader theoretical and historical framework. We focus on those areas of family law that are most important to the modern practitioner and that are the subject of ongoing public debate, both within the legal profession and in society at large—topics such as the economic and parenting consequences of divorce; the appropriate role of the state in regulating access to and exit from marriage; the legal and social meaning of parenthood; and state's role in protecting children. We want students both to understand and to be able to think critically about contemporary family law doctrines and practice. To that end, the Casebook uses an extensive set of problems—many based on recent court decisions—to apply and extend the doctrines introduced in the principal cases. Through these problems, combined with principal cases and substantial Notes and Questions, we challenge students to define what American family law presently is and what it should be, now and in the future.

The Casebook is divided into three main parts. Part I focuses on the formation of family relationships. Chapter 1 addresses entry into marriage. It examines both traditional state regulation of marriage and the development of a constitutionally protected right to marry. The chapter also uses contemporary litigation over same-sex marriage to examine the contours of the right to marry and to explore the tension between marriage as a state-defined and protected status and marriage as a matter of private contract.

Chapter 2 explores the legal and economic consequences of marriage. It examines the property rights and support obligations that have traditionally accompanied marriage and considers the ways in which those rights and obligations have been transformed by contemporary notions of spousal autonomy, partnership marriage and gender equality. The Chapter also examines the effect of changes in marital and parenting roles on the structure of the workplace and on the legal relationship between the work and family responsibilities.

Chapter 3 examines consensual alternatives to marriage as another means of family formation. Starting with the landmark *Marvin* case, these materials explore the law's evolving response to adult, non-marital cohabitation. The chapter uses the legal rights and obligations of unmarried cohabitants to explore the role of contract and partnership principles in structuring and regulating intimate relationships, as well as the advantages and disadvantages of formal versus functional definitions of family. The final section of the chapter examines legislative responses to cohabitation, including recent domestic partnership legislation.

Chapters 4 and 5 focus on the formation of parent-child relationships. Chapter 4 explores the legal regulation of procreation and reproductive decision-making. It begins with the Supreme Court's reproductive rights jurisprudence and examines the application of that jurisprudence to new reproductive alternatives such as surrogacy, in vitro fertilization and human cloning. Chapter 5 focuses on the establishment of legal parenthood, with an emphasis on the legal relationship between unmarried parents and their children. This chapter examines the effect of advances in scientific techniques, such as DNA testing, on the establishment of paternity and the assignment of parental rights and obligations. It also explores the law's shifting treatment of biology as a basis for parenthood, and highlights the tension between treating parenthood as a biological fact and treating it as a matter of social and legal construction.

Part II of the Casebook focuses on the legal regulation of ongoing family relationships. Chapter 6 examines domestic violence and intra-family torts. It explores the changing legal response to violence within families and highlights contemporary debates over the appropriate state response to such violence. The chapter includes an examination of the federal Violence Against Women Act, as well as state civil and criminal remedies for domestic violence, including mandatory arrest and no-drop prosecution policies. The final section of the chapter considers the appropriate role of the tort system as a means of addressing conflicts between family members.

Chapter 7 focuses on the care and supervision of children. The chapter first explores the constitutional framework for allocating authority and responsibility for children's welfare among parents, children, and the state. It then uses that framework to examine contemporary legal responses to child abuse and neglect, medical and educational decision-making on behalf of children, disagreements between parents and children, the foster care system and the grounds for termination of parental rights.

Chapter 8 focuses on contemporary adoption law and practice. The cases and materials highlight the changing nature of adoption and explore the requirements of parental consent and the role of the unwed father in the adoption process. The chapter also explores the relevance of race, ethnicity and religion in adoption. Finally, the chapter examines current debates regarding the legal and social consequences of adoption, with a focus on issues of confidentiality, information disclosure and open adoption.

Part III of the Casebook focuses on the process of divorce and parental separation, along with its economic and parenting consequences. Chapter 9 addresses divorce grounds and jurisdiction. It discusses both traditional and contemporary grounds for divorce, and highlights the contemporary debate over the appropriate role of fault and the desirability of unilateral, no-fault divorce. The chapter also explores a number of important ethical issues faced by the family law practitioner, including the unique ethical issues faced by attorneys who represent children. The chapter concludes with an examination of alternative processes for resolving divorce-related disputes, with an emphasis on the advantages and disadvantages of mediation and non-adversary dispute resolution techniques.

Chapter 10 focuses on the economic consequences of divorce. It emphasizes the theoretical and the practical connections between property division and spousal support, as alternatives means of apportioning the economic gains and losses that result from participation in a marriage. The chapter uses a combination of problems and principal cases to examine comprehensively the valuation and distribution of property upon divorce, under both equitable distribution and community property principles. The materials on spousal support focus on alternative rationales for post-divorce income sharing, and on the relationship between support obligations and property distribution.

Chapters 11 and 12 turn to the parenting consequences of divorce. Chapter 11 examines the contemporary law of child support. The focus of this chapter is on the ways in which support guidelines and enforcement mechanisms actually function. The chapter includes an examination of state and federal enforcement mechanisms, as well as contemporary approaches to jurisdictional issues, including the new Uniform Interstate Family Support Act.

Chapter 12 focuses on the allocation of residential and decision-making responsibility for children. It explores the contemporary application of the best interest of the child standard for resolving custody disputes between parents, as well as alternative approaches such as joint custody, parenting plans and the primary caretaker standard. The chapter highlights the current debate over parental relocation and modification of custody arrangements, and includes a detailed examination of child custody jurisdiction, in both the national and international contexts.

Chapter 13 focuses on marital and divorce agreements. It explores the extent to which prospective, current and separating spouses may fix by agreement the economic and other consequences of their union. In addition to the practical importance of these issues, these materials afford students (and teachers) the opportunity to revisit several of the thematic questions raised in the opening chapters of the Casebook: What are the relative roles of contract and status principles in family law? What is the appropriate balance between public and private ordering in the formation and dissolution of family relationships? To what extent have the answers to these questions changed over the past quarter century, and why?

Finally, Chapter 14 examines the tax and bankruptcy consequences of divorce. Tax topics discussed include the prerequisites to the deduction of support payments and attorneys' fees, to a claim of the child dependency exemption, and to the entitlement to a favorable filing status. The chapter concludes by identifying relevant bankruptcy provisions and examining their impact on family law proceedings.

While the Casebook is intended for a basic course in Family Law, it may also be used for a separate course in Parents, Children and the State. A professor teaching such a course may wish to begin with Chapter 5 (Establishing Legal Parenthood), followed by Chapter 7 (Care and Supervision of Children); Chapter 8 (Adoption) and Chapter 12 (Child Custody and Visitation).

Most of the principal cases and excerpts have been edited, often quite extensively. We have used ellipses to indicate where text has been deleted. Some footnotes and citations within cases have also been eliminated, as have some concurring and dissenting opinions. Throughout the book, footnotes to the text and to opinions and other quoted material are numbered consecutively from the beginning of each chapter.

Peter N. Swisher,
UNIVERSITY OF RICHMOND

Anthony Miller,
PEPPERDINE UNIVERSITY

Jana B. Singer,
UNIVERSITY OF MARYLAND

ACKNOWLEDGMENTS

The authors wish to thank the following authors and copyright holders for granting permission to reprint excerpts from the following copyrighted works:

American Law Institute (ALI), *Principles of the Law of Family Dissolution: Analysis and Recommendations, Proposed Final Draft, Part I* (1997):

—§ 403 Comment *c*,

—§ 405, illustration 1,

—§ 4.18,

—§ 5.02, Comment *d*,

—§ 5.05 Comments. Copyright 1997 by the ALI. All rights reserved.

American Bar Association, Commission on Domestic Violence, *When Will They Ever Learn? Educating to End Domestic Violence: A Law School Report* 26 (1997).

Gary S. Becker, *Nobel Lecture: The Economic Way of Looking at Behavior*, 101 J. of Political Economy 385, 397–98 (1993). Copyright 1992 by The Nobel Foundation.

David Blankenhorn, *The State of the Family and the Family Policy Debate*, 36 Santa Clara L. Rev. 431, 436–37 (1996).

June Carbone, *Morality, Public Policy and the Family: The Role of Marriage and the Public/Private Divide*, 36 Santa Clara L. Rev. 265, 267–69, 275–78 (1996).

Clare Dalton, *Domestic Violence, Domestic Torts and Divorce Constraints and Possibilities*, 31 New Eng. L. Rev. 319 (1997).

Ira M. Ellman, *The Theory of Alimony*, 77 Cal. L. Rev. 1, 46–51 (1989).

L. Jean Emery, *The Case for Agency Adoption*, 3(1), The Future of Children 139, 140–44 (1993) (Adopted from L. Jean Emery, CWLA Standards for Adoption Services, Revised). Copyright 1988 by the Child Welfare League of America, Washington, D.C.

Lucinda M. Finley, *Transcending Equality Theory: A Way Out of the Maternity and the Workplace Debate*, 86 Colum. L. Rev. 1118, 1124–27 (1986).

Sally F. Goldfarb, *Marital Partnership and the Case For Permanent Alimony*, 27 J. Fam. L. 351, 354–55 (1988–89).

S. Green & J. Long, Marriage and Family Law Agreements 213 (McGraw-Hill 1984) (further reproduction strictly prohibited).

John De Witt Gregory, Peter N. Swisher, & Sheryl L. Scheible-Wolf, Understanding Family Law (Matthew Bender 2d ed. 1995).

Cheryl Hanna, *No Right to Choose: Mandated Victim Participation in Domestic Violence Prosecutions*, 109 Harv. L. Rev. 1849 (1996).

Arlie Hochschild with Anne Machung, The Second Shift 11–13 (1989). Copyright 1989 by Arlie Hochschild. Used by permission of Penguin-Putnam, Inc.

Jon Jeter, *Covenant Marriages Tie the Knot Tightly*, The Washington Post, August 15, 1997 at A1 and A18–A19.

Martin H. Malin, *Fathers and Parental Leave*, Texas L. Rev. 1047, 1049–52, 1055–57, 1071–78 (1994).

Mark T. McDermott, Agency Versus Independent Adoption: The Case for Independent Adoption, 3(1), *The Future of Children* 146–52 (Spring 1993). Adapted with permission of The David and Lucile Packard Foundation. (*The Future of Children* journals and executive summaries are available free of charge by faxing mailing information to: Circulation Department, 650-948-6498.)

Lisa Mundy, *Fault Line*, The Washington Post Magazine, October 26, 1997. Copyright 1997, The Washington Post. Reprinted with permission.

National Conference of Commissioners on Uniform State Laws:

—Uniform Child Custody Jurisdiction Act, 9 U.L.A. 123 (1988).

—Uniform Status of Children of Assisted Conception Act, Alternatives A and B, 9B U.L.A. (1998 Supp. at 190, 197).

—Uniform Premarital Agreement Act, 9B U.L.A. 369 (1983).

Twila L. Perry, *The Transracial Adoption Controversy: An Analysis of Discourse and Subordination*, 21 N.Y.U. Rev. L. & Soc. Change 33, 34, 41–44, 53, 65–66 (1993–94).

Jana B. Singer, *The Privatization of Family Law,* 1992 Wis. L. Rev. 1443, 1540–48.

Scott Stanley & Howard Markman, Can Government Rescue Marriages?, The University of Denver Center for Marital and Family Studies 1–2 (1997).

United Press Syndicate, *Dear Abby* (1988).

D. Kelly Weisberg, *Professional Women and the Professionalization of Motherhood: Marcia Clark's Double Bind*, 6 Hastings Women's L.J. 295 (1995). Copyright 1995 by the University of California, Hastings College of the Law.

Joan Williams, *Is Coverture Dead? Beyond A New Theory of Alimony*, 82 Georgetown L.J. 2227, 2236–41, 2245–46 (1994).

TABLE OF CONTENTS

FAMILY LAW: CASES, MATERIALS AND PROBLEMS

SECOND EDITION

PART I: FORMATION OF FAMILY RELATIONSHIPS

CHAPTER 1
ENTERING MARRIAGE

§ 1.01	Introduction	1
§ 1.02	Marriage as a Contract or Status?	2
	Maynard v. Hill	3
	Notes and Questions	4
§ 1.03	Formalities of Marriage: The Statutory Requirements	10
	Nelson v. Marshall	10
	Notes and Questions	12
§ 1.04	Informal Marriages	14
	[A] Common Law Marriages	14
	Crosson v. Crosson	15
	Notes and Questions	17
	[B] Putative Marriage	19
	Rebouche v. Anderson	20
	Notes and Questions	22
	[C] Marriage by Proxy	23
	Torres v. Torres	23
	Notes and Questions	25
	[D] "Marriage" by Estoppel	26
	In re Marriage of Recknor	26
	Notes and Questions	30
§ 1.05	The Last-in-Time Marriage Presumption	32
	Hewitt v. Firestone Tire & Rubber Co.	32
	Notes and Questions	37
§ 1.06	State Regulation of Marriage Versus an Individual's Constitutional Right to Marry	39
	Zablocki, Milwaukee County Clerk v. Redhail	39
	Notes and Questions	43
§ 1.07	Capacity and Intent to Marry	44
	[A] Introduction	44
	[B] Same-Sex Marriage	46
	Baehr v. Lewin	46

		Notes and Questions	53
	[C]	Plural Marriage	57
		Potter v. Murray City	58
		Notes and Questions	61
	[D]	Prohibited Degrees of Kinship	63
		In re Estate of Stiles	65
		Etheridge v. Shaddock	67
		Notes and Questions	68
	[E]	Age Restrictions	69
		Moe v. Dinkins	70
		Notes and Questions	73
	[F]	Mental and Physical Incapacity	73
		Geitner v. Geitner	74
		Notes and Questions	76
	[G]	Consent Requirements: Fraud	77
		V.J.S. v. M.J.B.	78
		Notes and Questions	79
	[H]	Consent Requirements: Duress	80
		Stakelum v. Terral	81
		Notes and Questions	82
	[I]	Limited-Purpose Marriages	83
		Roe v. Immigration & Naturalization Service	83
		Notes and Questions	86
§ 1.08	Conflict of Laws: Which Marriage Law Governs?		88
	Seizer v. Sessions		89
	Notes and Questions		92
	Randall v. Randall		93
	Notes and Questions		95
§ 1.09	Annulment of Marriage		96
	[A]	Annulment Jurisdiction	96
	[B]	Annulment Grounds and Defenses	97
	[C]	Property and Support Rights on Annulment	98
		MacPherson v. MacPherson	98
		Notes and Questions	101
§ 1.10	Summary: A Marriage and Annulment Problem		102

CHAPTER 2
LEGAL AND ECONOMIC CONSEQUENCES OF MARRIAGE

§ 2.01	Introduction		105
§ 2.02	Roles and Responsibilities during Marriage		106
	[A]	The Traditional View	106
		Bradwell v. Illinois	107

		Graham v. Graham 108
		Notes and Questions 110
	[B]	The Modern Theory—Marriage as a Partnership of Equals 111
	[C]	Testing the Theory Against Reality: Contemporary Perspectives on Marriage 112
		Notes and Questions 118
§ 2.03	Marital Property Rights 119
	[A]	The Married Women's Property Acts 119
	[B]	Tenancy by the Entirety 121
	[C]	Property Rights on the Death of a Spouse 121
	[D]	The Community Property System 123
§ 2.04	Support Obligations During Marriage 124
	[A]	The Nonintervention Principle 124
		McGuire v. McGuire 124
		Notes and Questions 126
	[B]	The Common Law Doctrine of Necessaries 127
		Connor v. Southwest Florida Regional Medical Center 127
		Notes and Questions 130
	[C]	Spousal and Child Support Statutes 131
		Notes and Questions 133
	[D]	Enforcement of Support Obligations 135
	[E]	Relative Responsibility Statutes 135
		Notes and Questions 136
§ 2.05	Economic Transactions Between Spouses 139
	Borelli v. Brusseau 139
	Notes and Questions 144
§ 2.06	Third-Party Interference With Marriage 146
	[A]	Intentional Torts 146
		Hoye v. Hoye 146
		Notes and Questions 149
	[B]	Rights of Consortium 150
		Notes and Questions 150
	[C]	Evidentiary and Testimonial Privileges 151
§ 2.07	Integrating Family and Work 153
	[A]	Dual Career Couples 153
		Parks v. City of Warner Robbins 153
		Notes and Questions 157
	[B]	Pregnancy, Childbearing and Employment 161
		California Federal Savings & Loan Association v. Guerra ... 161
		Notes and Questions 167
	[C]	Working and Caring for Children 172
		Kelly v. Crosfield Catalysts 174
		Notes and Questions 177

Pricket v. Circuit Science, Inc. 181
Notes and Questions 183
Notes and Questions (Parental Leave) 188

CHAPTER 3
CONSENSUAL ALTERNATIVES TO MARRIAGE

§ 3.01 Introduction 189
§ 3.02 Disputes Between Unmarried Cohabitants 191
    [A]   The Role of Contract 191
           Marvin v. Marvin, California Supreme Court (1976) ... 191
           Notes and Comments 195
           Marvin v. Marvin, California Superior Court (1979) ... 196
           Notes and Comments 200
           Thomas v. LaRosa 202
           Notes and Questions 206
    [B]   Property and Partnership Theories 206
           Connell v. Francisco 207
           Davis v. Davis (Miss. 1994) 210
           Notes and Questions 213
§ 3.03 Disputes Between Cohabitants and Third Parties 216
        Davis v. Department of Employment Security 216
        Notes and Comments 218
        Braschi v. Stahl Associates Company 218
        Notes and Questions 222
§ 3.04 Domestic Partnership Legislation 228
        Notes and Comments 229

CHAPTER 4
HAVING CHILDREN: THE ALTERNATIVE CHOICES

§ 4.01 Contraception 235
        Griswold v. Connecticut 235
        Notes and Questions 239
§ 4.02 Abortion 243
        Roe v. Wade 243
        Notes and Questions 252
        Planned Parenthood v. Casey 256
        Notes and Questions 266
§ 4.03 Sterilization 270
        In re Grady 273
        Notes and Questions 280
§ 4.04 Surrogacy 284

		In the Matter of Baby M	285
		Notes and Questions	294
		Johnson v. Calvert	297
		Notes and Questions	301
		Notes and Questions (Uniform Act)	307
§ 4.05		New Reproductive Technology	309
	[A]	Artificial Insemination	309
		In re Baby Doe	309
		Jhordan C. v. Mary K.	310
		Notes and Questions	315
	[B]	In Vitro Fertilization and the Status of the Embryo	317
		Davis v. Davis (Tenn. 1992)	317
		Notes and Questions	326
	[C]	Cloning	329
		Notes and Questions	330

CHAPTER 5
ESTABLISHING LEGAL PARENTHOOD

§ 5.01		Introduction	331
	[A]	Historical Background	331
	[B]	Current Perspectives	332
§ 5.02		Nonmarital Children and the Constitution	334
	[A]	Inheritance Rights	334
		Trimble v. Gordon	334
		Parham v. Hughes	339
		Notes and Questions	342
	[B]	Limitation of Paternity Actions	343
		Clark v. Jeter	343
		Notes and Questions	346
§ 5.03		Establishing Paternity	347
	[A]	Scientific Testing	347
		In re Paternity of M.J.B.	348
		Notes and Questions	353
	[B]	Res Judicata and Relitigation	358
		Tandra S. v. Tyronne W.	358
		Notes and Questions	365
		Jessica G. v. Hector M.	365
		Notes and Questions	369
	[C]	Procedural Issues in Paternity Cases	369
§ 5.04		Imposing Parental Support Obligations	371
		Murphy v. Meyers	371
		Notes and Questions	373

		Pietros v. Pietros	375
		Notes and Questions	378
§ 5.05		Establishing Parental Rights	378
	[A]	Presumptive Parents	379
		Michael H. v. Gerald D.	379
		Notes and Questions	385
	[B]	Non-Presumptive Parents	389
		Lehr v. Robertson	390
		Notes and Questions	397
		In re Adoption of Kelsey S.	402
		In re Adoption of Michael H.	410
		Notes and Questions	415

PART II: REGULATION OF ONGOING FAMILY RELATIONSHIPS

CHAPTER 6
DOMESTIC VIOLENCE AND INTRAFAMILY TORTS

§ 6.01			Introduction	419
	[A]		Nature and Extent of the Problem	420
	[B]		Why Doesn't She Leave?	422
§ 6.02			Legal Responses to Domestic Violence	423
	[A]		The Traditional View	423
			State v. Rhodes	424
			Notes and Questions	425
	[B]		Contemporary Approaches to Domestic Violence	426
		[1]	Criminal Prosecution: Mandatory Arrest and No-Drop Prosecution Policies	426
			Notes and Questions	433
		[2]	The Civil Protection Order Process	435
			Baker v. Baker	436
			Notes and Questions	442
		[3]	Marital Rape	443
			Warren v. State	444
			Notes and Questions	446
		[4]	Federal Involvement: The Violence Against Women Act	447
			Seaton v. Seaton	449
			Notes and Questions	456
§ 6.03			Intrafamily Tort Liability	457
	[A]		Tort Claims Between Spouses	457
			Twyman v. Twyman	457
			Notes and Questions	467

		Pickering v. Pickering 469

                Pickering v. Pickering 469
                Notes and Questions 472
       [B]   Parent-Child Tort Actions 473
              Broadbent v. Broadbent 473
              Notes and Questions 481

CHAPTER 7
CARE AND SUPERVISION OF CHILDREN

§ 7.01 Introduction 485
§ 7.02 The Constitutional Framework 486
           Meyer v. Nebraska 486
           Pierce v. Society of Sisters 487
           Notes and Questions 488
           Prince v. Commonwealth of Massachusetts 491
           Wisconsin v. Yoder 494
           Notes and Questions 504
§ 7.03 Child Abuse and Neglect 507
       [A]   Abuse or Discipline? 507
              In the Interest of J.P. 508
              Notes and Questions 517
       [B]   Parental Failure to Protect 522
              Rice v. State 523
              Notes and Questions 532
       [C]   Defining and Responding To Child Neglect 534
              In the Interests of N.M.W. 534
              Notes and Questions 537
       [D]   Abuse or Neglect of A Fetus? 540
              Whitner v. State 540
              Notes and Questions 549
       [E]   Government Responsibility to Protect Children 553
              Deshaney v. Winnebago County Dep't of Social Services 553
              Notes and Questions 561
§ 7.04 Medical Decision-Making On Behalf of Children 562
       [A]   Criminal Prosecution for Parental Failure to Seek Medical Care 563
              Commonwealth v. Twitchell 563
              Notes and Questions 568
       [B]   Medical Neglect 569
              Newmark v. Williams/DCPS 569
              In re Sampson 577
              Notes and Questions 581
       [C]   Children As Decision-Makers 582
              In re E.G. 582

		Notes and Questions	587
§ 7.05		When Parent and Child Disagree: What Role for the State?	588
	[A]	Decisions About Reproduction	588
		Bellotti v. Baird	588
		Notes and Questions	593
	[B]	Children Beyond Parental Control	597
		R. J. D. v. Vaughan Clinic, P.C.	597
		Notes and Questions	601
§ 7.06		The Foster Care System	604
	[A]	The Foster Family	605
		Smith v. O.F.F.E.R.	605
		Notes and Questions	611
		In the Matter of B.	612
		Notes and Questions	622
	[B]	Kinship Care	624
		Notes and Questions	625
	[C]	Permanent Dispositions and Foster Care Reform: From Family Preservation to Termination of Parental Rights	627
		Bush v. State	630
		Recodo v. State	636
		Notes and Questions	643

CHAPTER 8
ADOPTION

§ 8.01		Introduction	647
§ 8.02		Consent to Adoption	650
	[A]	Timing and Validity of Consent	650
		Doe v. Clark	650
		Notes and Questions	652
		Yopp v. Batt	653
		Notes and Questions	661
	[B]	Consequences of Invalid Consent	664
		Lemley v. Barr	664
		Notes and Questions	667
§ 8.03		Unwed Fathers, Due Process and Involuntary Termination of Parental Rights	668
		In re Adoption of Baby E.A.W.	669
		In re Baby Boy C., D.C. Court of Appeals (1990)	678
		In re Baby Boy C., D.C. Superior Court (1992)	689
		Notes and Questions	692
§ 8.04		The Adoption Process	695
	[A]	Agency Adoption	696
		Notes and Questions	699

	[B]	Independent Adoption and the Lawyer's Role	699
		In re Petrie	702
		Notes and Questions	709
	[C]	Stepparent and Second-Parent Adoption	713
		Adoptions of B.L.V.B. and E.L.V.B.	713
		Notes and Questions	717
	[D]	Procedural Requirements	718
		Notes and Questions	719
§ 8.05		Selecting an Adoptive Family: The Relevance of Race, Ethnicity and Religion	720
	[A]	The Role of Race in Adoption	720
		Dewees v. Stevenson	723
		Notes and Questions	727
	[B]	The Indian Child Welfare Act	729
		In re Bridget R.	730
		Notes and Questions	740
	[C]	Religion	741
		Orzechowski v. Perales	741
		Notes and Questions	744
§ 8.06		Legal Consequences of Adoption	746
	[A]	Confidentiality and Access to Adoption Records	747
		Doe v. Sundquist	747
		Notes and Questions	750
	[B]	"Open Adoption" and Post-adoption Visitation	752
		Groves v. Clark	752
		Notes and Questions	756
	[C]	Disclosure Requirements and "Wrongful Adoption"	758
		McKinney v. State	758
		Notes and Questions	764

PART III: DISSOLUTION OF FAMILY RELATIONSHIPS

CHAPTER 9
DIVORCE OR DISSOLUTION OF MARRIAGE

§ 9.01		Introduction	768
	[A]	Historical Background	768
	[B]	Historical Fault Grounds for Divorce and the No-Fault Revolution	769
	[C]	Current Divorce Statistics and Concerns	770
§ 9.02		Divorce Jurisdiction	772
	[A]	The Domiciliary Requirement	772
		Sosna v. Iowa	774
		Notes and Questions	779

	[B]	Migratory Divorces	782
		[1] Sister State Migratory Divorces	783
		Notes and Questions	785
		[2] Foreign Country Migratory Divorces	786
		Mayer v. Mayer	787
		Notes and Questions	793
	[C]	Collateral Attack on a Void Divorce	795
	[D]	The Divisible Divorce Doctrine	797
		Vanderbilt v. Vanderbilt	798
		Notes and Questions	799
§ 9.03	Divorce Grounds and Defenses		801
	[A]	Fault Grounds for Divorce	801
		[1] Overview	801
		[2] Adultery, Cruelty, and Desertion	802
		Williams v. Williams	802
		Notes and Questions	804
	[B]	No-Fault Divorce Grounds	809
		[1] Living Separate and Apart	809
		Sinha v. Sinha	810
		Notes and Questions	813
		[2] Irreconcilable Differences	813
		Grosskopf v. Grosskopf	814
		Notes and Questions	818
§ 9.04	The Relevance—If Any—of Fault Factors in No-Fault Divorces		821
	[A]	Arguments for Rejecting Fault Factors in No-Fault Divorces	821
	[B]	Arguments for Retaining Fault Factors in No-Fault Divorces	822
	[C]	Can Nonfinancial Factors Viably Coexist With Financial Factors in Determining Financial Issues in Divorce?	823
	[D]	Problem	825
§ 9.05	Ethical Issues for the Family Lawyer		826
	[A]	Dual Representation in Divorce Proceedings: Is It Ethical?	827
		Coulson v. Coulson	829
		Notes and Questions	832
	[B]	Problems With Confidential Information	834
		Woods v. Superior Court of Tulare County	834
		Notes and Questions	838
	[C]	Sexual Relations With a Divorce Client	840
		Committee on Professional Ethics and Conduct of the Iowa State Bar v. Hill	841
		Notes and Questions	843
	[D]	Candor Toward the Court and Withdrawal from the Case	843
		Matza v. Matza	844
		Notes and Questions	846

§ 9.06	Representing Children			847
	Clark v Alexander			847
	Notes and Questions			852
§ 9.07	Alternative Dispute Resolution			856
	[A]	Divorce Mediation		856
		[1]	Overview and Current Status	856
		[2]	Concerns About Mediation	858
			Notes and Questions	860
	[B]	Binding Arbitration		864
		Miller v. Miller		865
		Notes and Questions		868

CHAPTER 10
ECONOMIC CONSEQUENCES OF DIVORCE

§ 10.01	Introduction				870
§ 10.02	Distribution of Property on Divorce or Dissolution of Marriage				872
	[A]	General Introduction			872
		[1]	Community Property States		872
		[2]	Equitable Distribution States		873
			[a]	"Dual Property" Equitable Distribution States	874
			[b]	"All Property" Equitable Distribution States	875
			[c]	A Comparison of Dual Property and All Property Regimes	875
	[B]	Equitable Distribution and Community Property Overview			876
	[C]	Marital or Separate Property—Or Both?			877
		Harper v. Harper			878
		Notes and Questions			882
	[D]	"Tracing" and Transmutation of Property			885
		Chenault v. Chenault			886
		Notes and Questions			889
	[E]	Passive versus Active Appreciation of Separate Property			890
		Notes and Questions			891
	[F]	Property Acquired by Gift or Inheritance			893
		Notes and Questions			894
	[G]	Pensions and Retirement Benefits			895
		[1]	Complexity of Dividing Benefits		895
		[2]	Qualified Domestic Relations Orders (QDROs)		897
		[3]	Valuing and Dividing Retirement Benefits		898
			In re Rolfe v. Rolfe		899
			Notes and Questions		900
	[H]	Deferred Compensation Benefits: Separate or Marital Property?			901
	[I]	Personal Injury and Workers' Compensation Awards			902
		Notes and Questions			905

TABLE OF CONTENTS

- [J] Professional Degrees and Licenses 906
  - *O'Brien v. O'Brien* 907
  - Notes and Questions 911
- [K] The Family Residence 915
- [L] Classifying and Valuing Professional Goodwill 918
  - *Dugan v. Dugan* 919
  - Notes and Questions 926
- [M] Valuing Businesses and Professional Practices 927
- [N] Distribution of Property 930
  - [1] General Introduction 930
  - [2] Statutory Factors for Distributing Marital Property 931
  - [3] An Equal Division Presumption versus an Equal Division "Starting Point" 933
  - [4] Recharacterization and Distribution of Property Based Upon Long-Term Marriages 935
- [O] The Role of Fault in the Distribution of Marital Property 938
  - [1] "Economic Fault": The Dissipation or Waste of Marital Assets 938
  - [2] Marital Misconduct as a Factor in Dividing Marital Property 941
    - [a] Arguments for Rejecting Marital Misconduct Fault Factors in Equitable Distribution Proceedings 940
    - [b] Arguments for Retaining Marital Misconduct Fault Factors in Equitable Distribution Proceedings 941
      - *Sparks v. Sparks* 943
      - Notes and Questions 947
- [P] The Role of Judicial Discretion in Distributing Property on Divorce 950
- [Q] Selected Research Biography on Equitable Distribution of Marital Property 952
  - [1] Treatises 952
  - [2] Looseleaf Services and Reporters 952
  - [3] Selected Law Review Articles on Equitable Distribution 952

§ 10.03 Spousal Support 953

- [A] Need and Gender: The Traditional Rationales 954
  - *Orr v. Orr* 954
  - Notes and Questions 956
- [B] Rehabilitation and Self-Sufficiency 956
  - *In re Marriage of Otis* 956
  - *Van Klootwyk v. Van Klootwyk* 960
  - Notes and Questions 966
- [C] Alimony as Compensation for Loss 969
  - *In re Marriage of Williams* 969
  - Notes and Questions 972
- [D] Alimony as Income Sharing 977
  - *Delozier v Delozier* 977
  - Notes and Questions 981

[E]	The Intersection of Alimony and Property Theory	983
	In re Marriage of Francis	983
	Notes and Questions	989
[F]	Modification of Support Awards	991
	Gilman v. Gilman	991
	Notes and Questions	998

CHAPTER 11
CHILD SUPPORT

§ 11.01 Introduction 1003
§ 11.02 Federal Mandate 1004
    P.O.P.S. v. Gardner 1004
    Notes and Questions 1007
§ 11.03 Guidelines 1010
    [A] Income Shares Model 1010
        Voishan v. Palma 1010
        Notes and Questions 1013
    [B] Percentage of Income 1016
        Eklund v. Eklund 1016
        Notes and Questions 1019
§ 11.04 Income 1022
    [A] Gross or Net? 1022
        Notes and Questions 1024
    [B] Actual Income or Capacity to Earn? 1025
        Henderson v. Smith 1025
        In re the Marriage of Paulin 1026
        Harvey v. Robinson 1028
        Goldberger v. Goldberger 1030
        Notes and Questions 1032
    [C] Spousal Income 1032
        In re the Marriage Of Wood 1032
        Notes and Questions 1035
    [D] Support for other children 1036
        Hasty v. Hasty 1036
        Notes and Questions 1039
    [E] Extraordinarily High Income 1040
        Estevez v. Superior Court 1040
        Notes and Questions 1044
§ 11.05 Duration of Support 1045
    [A] Majority/Emancipation 1045
        Stanton v. Stanton 1045
        Baril v. Baril 1048

		Notes and Questions	1050
	[B]	Support for College	1053
		Childers v. Childers	1053
		In re Marriage of Plummer	1054
		Notes and Questions	1056

§ 11.06 Modification of Support 1057
    In re the Marriage of McCord 1057
    Notes and Questions 1060

§ 11.07 Enforcement of Support Orders 1063

	[A]	State Remedies	1063
		Hicks v. Feiock	1063
		Notes and Questions	1068
	[B]	Federal Enforcement.	1071
		United States v. Hampshire	1071
		Notes and Questions	1074

§ 11.08 Jurisdiction for Support and Interstate Enforcement 1077

	[A]	Personal Jurisdiction	1077
		Kulko v. Superior Court	1077
		Notes and Questions	1082
	[B]	Interstate Enforcement	1083
		Welsher v. Rager	1083
		Notes and Questions	1085

CHAPTER 12
PARENTING AFTER DIVORCE: CHILD CUSTODY AND VISITATION

§ 12.01 Introduction 1091
§ 12.02 Factors In Disputed Cases 1093

	[A]	The Best Interest Standard	1093
		Maxfield v. Maxfield	1093
		Notes and Questions	1097
	[B]	The Gender of the Parents	1099
		Pusey v. Pusey	1099
		Notes and Questions	1101
	[C]	The Primary Caretaker	1103
		Pikula v. Pikula	1103
		Notes and Questions	1107
	[D]	Child's Preference	1108
		Yates v. Yates	1108
		Notes and Questions	1111
	[E]	Religion	1112
		Pater v. Pater	1112
		Notes and Questions	1115

	[F]	Race	1116
		Palmore v. Sidoti	1116
		Notes and Questions	1119
	[G]	Parental Fitness	1120
		[1] Sexual Conduct	1120
		Hanhart v. Hanhart	1120
		Notes and Questions	1123
		[2] Sexual Preference	1125
		Bottoms v. Bottoms	1125
		Notes and Questions	1130
	[H]	Physical and Mental Health	1133
		In re Marriage of Carney	1133
		Schumm v. Schumm	1138
		Notes and Questions	1141
	[I]	Working Parents	1142
		Ireland v. Smith	1142
		Notes and Questions	1145
	[J]	Child Abuse and Domestic Violence	1148
		Allen v. Farrow	1148
		Notes and Questions	1152

§ 12.03 Visitation ... 1155
Sterbling v. Sterbling ... 1155
Notes and Questions ... 1157

§ 12.04 Joint Custody and Parenting Plans ... 1163
Squires v. Squires ... 1163
Notes and Questions ... 1168

§ 12.05 Modification ... 1175

	[A]	Changed Circumstances or Best Interest?	1175
		Burchard v. Garay	1175
		Notes and Questions	1181
	[B]	Relocation	1184
		Tropea v. Tropea	1184
		Notes and Questions	1189

§ 12.06 Child Custody Jurisdiction ... 1193

	[A]	Introduction	1193
	[B]	Traditional Jurisdiction	1193
	[C]	State Legislation	1195
		Notes and Questions	1197
		Matter of Custody of Ross	1199
		Notes and Questions	1204
		Greenlaw v. Smith	1205
		Notes and Questions	1209
	[D]	Federal Legislation	1212

		Notes and Questions	1213
		Atkins v. Atkins	1214
		Notes and Questions	1217
	[E]	International Law	1221
		Feder v. Evans-Feder	1221
		Notes and Questions	1228

CHAPTER 13
MARITAL CONTRACTS: PREMARITAL AND SEPARATION AGREEMENTS

§ 13.01	Introduction			1231
§ 13.02	Breach of Promise-to-Marry Contracts and Premarital Gifts			1234
	Brown v. Thomas			1234
	Notes and Questions			1238
§ 13.03	Premarital Agreements			1242
	[A]	Introduction		1242
	[B]	Traditional Premarital Agreements: Estate Planning		1243
		In re Estate of Benker		1243
		Notes and Questions		1246
	[C]	Divorce Planning in Premarital Agreements		1248
		Osborne v. Osborne		1248
		Notes and Questions		1251
	[D]	Waiver of Spousal Support		1252
		Rider v. Rider		1252
		Notes and Questions		1255
	[E]	The Uniform Premarital Agreement Act		1256
		Notes and Questions		1259
§ 13.04	Separation or Property Settlement Agreements			1263
	[A]	Introduction		1263
	[B]	Necessary Elements for a Valid Separation Agreement		1264
		Golder v. Golder		1264
		Notes and Questions		1268
	[C]	Subsequent Attack on a Separation Agreement Based Upon Nondisclosure of Marital Assets: Intrinsic vs. Extrinsic Fraud		1270
		Cerniglia v. Cerniglia		1271
		Notes and Questions		1273
	[D]	Drafting a Separation Agreement		1276
		[1]	A Recommended Checklist Approach	1276
		[2]	Separation Agreement Problem	1281
§ 13.05	State Recognition of Religious Contracts			1283
	Avitzur v. Avitzur			1284
	Notes and Questions			1286

CHAPTER 14
TAX CONSEQUENCES AND BANKRUPTCY

§ 14.01 Introduction 1289
§ 14.02 Tax Consequences of Marriage and Divorce 1289
    [A]   Child and Spousal Support 1289
        Roosevelt v. Commissioner 1289
        Fosberg v. Commissioner 1291
        Notes and Questions 1292
    [B]   Tax Aspects of Property Division 1298
        Arnes v. United States [Arnes I] 1298
        Notes and Questions 1301
§ 14.03 Bankruptcy and Divorce 1305
    In re Osterberg 1305
    In re Patterson 1309
    Notes and Questions 1311

CHAPTER 1

ENTERING MARRIAGE

SYNOPSIS

§ 1.01 Introduction
§ 1.02 Marriage as a Contract or Status?
§ 1.03 Formalities of Marriage: The Statutory Requirements
§ 1.04 Informal Marriages
    [A] Common Law Marriages
    [B] Putative Marriage
    [C] Marriage by Proxy
    [D] "Marriage" by Estoppel
§ 1.05 The Last-in-Time Marriage Presumption
§ 1.06 State Regulation of Marriage Versus an Individual's Constitutional Right to Marry
§ 1.07 Capacity and Intent to Marry
    [A] Introduction
    [B] Same-Sex Marriage
    [C] Plural Marriage
    [D] Prohibited Degrees of Kinship
    [E] Age Restrictions
    [F] Mental and Physical Incapacity
    [G] Consent Requirements: Fraud
    [H] Consent Requirements: Duress
    [I] Limited-Purpose Marriages
§ 1.08 Conflict of Laws: Which Marriage Law Governs?
§ 1.09 Annulment of Marriage
    [A] Annulment Jurisdiction
    [B] Annulment Grounds and Defenses
    [C] Property and Support Rights on Annulment
§ 1.10 Summary: A Marriage and Annulment Problem

§ 1.01 Introduction

Despite the growing diversity of family relationships and alternative family forms in contemporary American society, marriage still remains an important legal and social institution. A significant majority of Americans will marry at some point in their lives, and most Americans still regard marriage as an important part of their life plan. *See, e.g.* Homer Clark, The Law of Domestic Relations in the United States 26 (1988) ("Notwithstanding these developments, a majority of Americans still marry in the traditional way and continue to regard marriage as the most important relationship in their lives"). Moreover, the law continues to use marriage as an important criterion for allocating a wide range of social and economic benefits and burdens. *See, e.g.* David Chambers, *What If? The Legal Consequences of Marriage and the Legal Needs of Lesbian and Gay Male Couples*, 95 Mich. L. Rev. 447 (1996); and Jana Singer, *The Privatization of Family Law*, 1992 Wis. L. Rev. 1446–56 (1992). Thus, decisions about who may marry, and about what relationships will be recognized as valid marriages, continue to be of significant theoretical and practical importance to family law practitioners and scholars.

Indeed, contemporary debates over "family values often center on the question of who may marry, as well as on what legal and economic consequences should follow from the decision to marry. *See, e.g.,* Walter Weyrauch, *Metamorphoses of Marriage,* 13 Fam. L. Q. 415 (1980) (discussing the changing role of formal and informal marriages in the United States); Same Sex Marriage: Pro and Con (Andrew Sullivan, ed. 1997); Barbara DeFoe Whitehead, The Divorce Culture (1997); and *Symposium: Law and the New American Family*, 73 Ind. L. J. 393 (1998). Historical evidence also suggests that access to marriage was at the core of the values that motivated those who fought for, and framed, the Fourteenth Amendment. *See* Peggy Cooper Davis, Neglected Stories: Family Values and the Constitution (1997).

The materials in this Chapter focus on entry into marriage. They examine both substantive state regulation of the capacity and intent to marry, as well as statutory marriage formalities and a number of exceptions to these statutory formalities. This examination highlights the tension between marriage as a *public status* and marriage as a *private contract*. It also illuminates the crucial interplay between state authority to regulate marriage and individual decision making about marriage as a fundamental constitutional right. *See, e.g.* Janet Dolgin, *The Family in Transition: From Griswold to Eisenstadt and Beyond*, 82 Geo. L.J. 1519 (1994); and Anne C. Dailey, *Constitutional Privacy and the Just Family*, 67 Tulane L. Rev. 955 (1993). Moreover, in resolving disputes involving the access to marriage, courts and legislatures increasingly have been required to articulate both the public and private purposes of marriage. These decisions thus provide an opportunity to examine the extent to which traditional and contemporary legal regulation of marriage serves the public and private purposes of the institution of marriage *per se*.

§ 1.02 Marriage as a Contract or Status?

One of the most enduring questions concerning marriage is whether marriage is a status relationship, or a private contract. The prevailing view today seems to be that marriage has elements of *both* status and contract, but that the balance between these two significant elements has shifted over time. For example, marital partners today have considerably more contractual freedom than in the past to determine privately the terms of their relationship, and to decide whether or not their relationship will continue. On the other hand, even where a court is faced with purely economic or contractual questions regarding marital support and property division, there is a recognition of the relevance of martial status, and the state's power to regulate such a relationship. As you read the following case, consider the extent to which its characterization of marriage as a status relationship, based upon contract, continues to hold true today.

MAYNARD v. HILL
United States Supreme Court
125 U.S. 190 (1888)

[Husband and Wife were married in Vermont in 1828 and lived there until 1850, when they moved to Ohio. Husband then left Wife without support, and journeyed to the West Coast, promising to send for his wife later, or alternately promising that he would return within two years. Wife never heard again from Husband until she learned that their marriage had been dissolved and that Husband had remarried in Oregon, where he lived with his second wife until his death. This case was brought by Husband's children by his first marriage to claim their share of property acquired under the auspices of a federal statute that provided for donations of land to settlers of the Oregon territory. The trial and appellate courts both concluded that the children had failed to state a valid cause of action or any ground for relief in equity.]

MR. JUSTICE FIELD

. . .

[Was the Oregon legislative act, declaring the bonds of matrimony between Husband and Wife to be dissolved, valid?]

Marriage, as creating the most important relation in life, as having more to do with the morals and civilization of a people than any other institution, has always been subject to the control of the [state] legislature. That body prescribes the age at which parties may contract to marry, the procedure or form essential to constitute marriage, the duties and obligations it creates, its effects upon the property rights of both, and the acts which may constitute grounds for its dissolution.

When this country was settled, the power to grant a divorce was exercised by the Parliament of England. The ecclesiastical courts [of England] were limited to the granting of divorces from bed and board. . . . The legislative assemblies of the colonies followed the example of Parliament and treated the object as one within their province. And until a recent period legislative divorces have been granted in all of the States.

In *Craine v. Meginnis*, 1 G. & J. 463, 474, the Supreme Court of Maryland said: "Divorces in this State from the earliest times have emanated from the General Assembly and can now be viewed in no other light than as regular exertions of the legislative power." . . .

The weight of authority . . . is decidedly in favor of the position that the power over divorces remains with the [state] legislature. We are compelled to hold that the granting of divorces was a rightful subject of legislation. . . . [W]e cannot inquire into [the legislature's] motives in passing the act granting the divorce.

[Complainants] allege that no cause existed for the divorce and that it was obtained without the knowledge of the wife . . . . Knowledge or ignorance of parties of intended legislation does not affect its validity.

. . . [While] marriage is often termed by text writers and in decisions of courts a civil contract generally to indicate that it must be founded upon the agreement of the parties, and does not require any religious ceremony for its solemnization—it is something more than a contract. The consent of the parties is of course essential to its existence, but when the contract to marry is executed by the marriage, a relation between the parties is created which they cannot change. The relation once formed, the law steps in and holds the parties to various obligations and liabilities. It is an institution in the maintenance of which in its purity the public is deeply interested, for it is the foundation of the family and of society, without which, there would be neither civilization nor progress. . . .

NOTES AND QUESTIONS

(1) Implicit throughout *Maynard* is the traditional view that marriage is a *status* relationship involving three parties—Husband, Wife and the State—and that the State may validly regulate such a relationship. *See, e.g. Sosna v. Iowa*, 419 U.S. 393, 404 (1975) (the inception and termination of marriage has "long been regarded as a virtually exclusive province of the State," within constitutional limitations); Stephen Sugarman, Divorce Reform at the Crossroads, 138 (1990) ("Marriage, at least in this century, is typically said to be best understood as a status, rather than as a contractual relationship.").

However, the *Maynard* rationale has not been universally adopted by all states. For example, in *Ponder v. Graham*, 4 Fla. 23 (Fla. 1851), the Florida Supreme Court relied on the view that marriage is a *contract*, rather than a *status* relationship, and thus state legislation regulating marriage might arguably impair the parties' contractual obligations if it affected their vested property rights. *See also Ryan v. Ryan*, 277 So. 2d 266 (Fla. 1973). *And see Seizer v. Sessions*, 915 P.2d 553, 561 (Wash. Ct. App. 1996), *rev'd on other grounds* 940 P.2d 261 (Wash. 1997) (comparing Washington and Texas law, and pointing out that under Washington law "the spouses by mutual consent can terminate a marriage, or can mutually treat the community property presumptions as terminated by agreeing to live separate and apart" whereas under Texas law "the institution of marriage is a status, more than a mere contract"). *See also* Luvern V. Ricke, *The [Washington] Dissolution [of Marriage] Act of 1973: From Status to Contract?* 49 Wash. L. Rev. 375 (1974); Wright, *Marriage: From Status to Contract?*, 13 Anglo-Am. L. Rev. 17 (1984). *Query:* What are the strengths and weaknesses of each approach?

(2) In *Maynard* the complainants argued that the husband's divorce "was obtained without the knowledge of the wife." It is now recognized in most states that the defendant in a divorce action must be given due process notice of the divorce suit and an opportunity to be heard, and if the defendant's whereabouts are unknown and cannot be discovered by reasonable diligence, notice by publication is required. *See, e.g., Atherton v. Atherton*, 181 U.S. 155 (1901); *Williams v. North Carolina [I]*, 317 U.S. 287 (1942); Restatement (Second) of Conflict of Laws § 69 (1971). What underlying public policy argument would be the basis for such a requirement?

(3) The current statutory regulation of marriage has a number of critics. Professor Lenore Weitzman, for example, in *Legal Regulation of Marriage: Tradition and Change, A Proposal for Individual Contracts and Contracts in Lieu of Marriage*, 62 Cal. L. Rev. 1169, 1170 (1974), argues that "Prospective spouses are neither informed of the terms of a [marriage] contract, nor are they allowed any options about these terms. . . . [O]ur society has undergone profound transformations in the past century, and the long-standing legal

structure of marriage may now be anachronistic. The state's interest in preserving the traditional family may not be important enough to offset new societal and individual needs which require more flexibility and choice in family forms." *See also* Lenore Weitzman, The Marriage Contract: Spouses, Lovers, and the Law (1981).

Query: What is the probability that many state legislatures will abolish or amend these "anachronistic" marriage requirements in the foreseeable future? And if the parties are able to privately contract free from all state regulation of marriage, what protection will be afforded to prevent the possible exploitation of one of the contracting parties by the other contracting party? Finally, is present state family law only a "patchwork attempt" stretching at "old law to deal with modern realities" as Professor Weitzman argues, or can American family law adequately address, rectify, and realistically subsume many of Professor Weitzman's legitimate concerns? *See also* Chapter 3, *below* and Mary Ann Glendon, *Marriage and the State: The Withering Away of Marriage*, 62 Va. L. Rev. 663, 666 (1976) ("If the state is now in the process of divesting itself of its marriage regulation business, then, of course, it is not likely to set up shop as an enforcer to heretofore unenforceable contracts.").

(4) Marriage and the traditional nuclear family structure, however, have been battered by current social and economic factors, and some commentators argue that "our society is moving in the direction of a post-marriage or post-nuclear family system, where the married couple, father-mother unit will no longer be held up as a dominant cultural ideal and will no longer reflect the empirical reality for all, or even most, children." David Blankenhorn, *The State of the Family and the Family Policy Debate*, 36 Santa Clara L. Rev. 431, 431–32 (1996). Indeed, some commentators are now arguing for the uncoupling of marriage and childrearing. *See, e.g.* June Carbone and Margaret Brinig, *Rethinking Marriage: Feminist Ideology, Economic Change, and Divorce*, 65 Tulane L. Rev. 953 (1991); Martha Fineman, The Neutered Mother (1995). Other commentators argue that many of these social ills are caused in large part by father absence. *See, e.g.* David Blankenhorn, Fatherless America (1995). And Professor Barbara Bennett Woodhouse posits that

> women's situation can and will be improved by a legal framework that supports marriage (same sex as well as heterosexual), asks both partners (not just women) to do their share of the nurture work, and expects both to treat each other with respect and concern. As long as the law seeks to bring both private and public responsibilities into play, it will have to grapple with defining what conduct and what responsibilities trigger individual obligations and claims.

Barbara Woodhouse, and Katharine Bartlett, *Sex, Lies, and Dissipation: The Discourse of Fault in a No-Fault Era*, 82 Georgetown L.J. 2525, 2564 (1994).

Writes David Blankenhorn:

> What is society going to do about this state of affairs? Given the increasing recognition of the trend toward the post-marriage, post-nuclear family and the obviously negative consequences of this trend, especially for children, a new family debate is now emerging. . . . There are two fault lines that I believe will characterize this new debate in the coming months and years. On one side of the fault line will be those who argue that we cannot reverse the trend—that is, that we cannot reinstitutionalize marriage. Therefore, we must instead deal with the consequences of the weakening of marriage, especially the economic consequences, recognizing the reality that more and more of

our children are simply not going to be growing up with their two married parents. . . . Those on the other side of this fault line will insist that we must seek to reverse the trend. They will direct their efforts to strengthening the institution of marriage and seeking to create cultural change in favor of the idea that unwed childbearing is wrong, that our divorce rate is far too high, and that every child deserves a father. . . .

Blankenhorn, *supra*, at 436–37. *Query:* Which side of this family law public policy debate is more persuasive to you? Why? Based upon what underlying public policy rationales? Other commentators, however, do not believe that these two so-called "fault lines" realistically define the parameters of contemporary marriage in America, which today involves *both* private and public ordering. *See, e.g.* Jana Singer, *The Privatization of Family Law*, 1992 Wis. L. Rev. 1446, and *Symposium: Opportunities for and Limitations of Private Ordering in Family Law*, 73 Ind. L.J. 453 (1998).

(5) The Louisiana legislature, in an attempt to strengthen and reinstitutionalize marriage, enacted, effective in 1997, a so-called "covenant" marriage statute as an alternative to "regular" marriage. Under a "covenant" marriage, the parties agree not to obtain a no-fault divorce, and can only dissolve their marriage based on traditional fault grounds such as adultery, cruelty, desertion, conviction of a felony, or separation for two years or more. The couple must also agree to obtain premarital counseling from a clergy member or other marital counselor prior to marriage. Louisiana House Bill 756 (1997). Other states have expressed interest in this Louisiana approach:

A covenant marriage bill in Indiana was defeated earlier this year, but lawmakers say it is all but certain to reemerge in the next legislative session. In June, officials of Lenawee County, Michigan, began mandating premarital counseling for any couple who wanted a wedding ceremony performed by a local judge or magistrate. And experts say that at least nine other states are considering measures to beef up requirements for marriage licenses. . . .

"People are beginning to realize that broken families are the source of many, many problems that our children are facing," said state Rep. Tony Perkins, the Baton Rouge Republican who sponsored the bill, "and ideas like this seem to represent kind of a middle ground for people who are against repealing no-fault divorce laws out and out."

"I don't think there's any question that you're going to see a lot of activity around the country as other state legislatures will be studying the concept and trying to adopt it," said Jeff Atkinson, a University of Chicago law professor and a member of the American Bar Association's Family Law Council. "I think you'll see more and more state legislatures around the country saying through force of law: "We the state do not want you to get divorced." . . .

The real catalyst behind the anti-divorce campaign, however, is emerging—if disputed—research suggesting that children are profoundly harmed by divorce and that the emotional trauma can stay with them into adulthood. Statistics indicate that children raised by single parents are more likely than children from two-parent households to be poor, drop out of high school, bear out-of-wedlock off-spring and use drugs.

"This myth that marriage and divorce is purely a private matter is blithering nonsense," said James Sheridan, the Michigan judge who spearheaded the effort in that state to require premarital counseling. "All we ask is that you get to know the person you're marrying before your marry them. Who pays when these children drop out of high school and go on welfare? Who pays when these children engage in criminal behavior? The taxpayer pays."

The notion that the public has a vested interest in seeing families succeed is hardly a point of contention. Rather, the issue for opponents of measures like the ones enacted in Michigan and Louisiana is whether discouraging divorce is enough to improve the quality of marriage, either for parents or their children.

"Are children any better off when they're forced to remain in a hostile household?" said Joe Cook, executive director of the American Civil Liberties Union in Louisiana.

"It's a laudable goal," said Atkinson of the ABA. "But is divorce automatically worse than every alternative? I don't think these kinds of measures are going to be adding to the happiness or longevity of marriage."

Jon Jeter, *Covenant Marriages Tie the Knot Tightly*, The Washington Post, August 15, 1997 at A1 and A18-A19. *And see* Mary Corey, *States Explore Making Breaking Up Hard to Do*, Baltimore Sun, May 19, 1997 at A1 (stating that legislators in at least 20 states have introduced bills to modify no-fault divorce). *But see* Laura Bradford, *The Counterrevolution: A Critique of Recent Proposals to Reform No-Fault Divorce Laws*, 49 Stan. L. Rev. 607 (1997) (predicting that such proposals "will not increase moral behavior", and arguing that fault-based divorce regimes have a negative impact on women). *See also* J. Herbie DiFonzo, *Covenant Marriage and the Limits of Law* (draft manuscript, 1998) (observing that state covenant marriage acts, the Uniform Premarital Agreement Act, and other prenuptial variations all "converge in the direction of customized marriage" and the question "of whether the prenuptial contract is drafted by the legislature or by the parties themselves is actually of less moment" than the reality "that family law has shifted into a recognition of a range of enforceable marriage contracts.").

(6) Other legislators, sociologists, and clergy have argued that the states should require premarital counseling prior to marriage. *See, e.g.* Time, October 7, 1996, at 84 ("Marriage is a commitment," says Brian Willats, a spokesman for the Michigan Family Forum, which supports premarital counseling. "It's not just notarized dating.") In an August, 1997 Time Magazine/CNN national poll, over two-thirds of those Americans polled favored mandatory premarital counseling.

A number of states, therefore, are now considering making marriages better and more stable by mandating premarital counseling as a requirement for obtaining a marriage license. Some states are considering an incentive model, with longer delays for getting a marriage license unless a couple gets premarital counseling (e.g. Maryland and Michigan) or by giving the parties a tax break (e.g. Iowa) while other states are considering an outright mandate for premarital counseling (e.g. Minnesota and Mississippi). The intention is to help couples increase their odds for successful marriages from the start. *See e.g.* Scott Stanley & Howard Markman, *Can Government Rescue Marriages?* (The University of Denver Center for Marital and Family Studies, 1997) at 1-2:

> There is a trend sweeping the country to make changes in legal codes to strengthen and stabilize marriages. There are two key thrusts emerging in states legislatures: the first involves changes in laws that would make it harder for couples to divorce; the

second involves efforts to encourage or mandate couples to participate in premarital counseling. . . . While strange bedfellows, there is a growing consensus among both liberal and conservative political and religious leaders that something must be done. . . .

Our studies show that marital failure is predictable to a surprising degree—with up to 90 percent accuracy in some research samples using premarital data. Hence, for many couples the seeds of divorce are present prior to marriage. The factors that predict marital failure range from relatively static dimensions, such as a history of parental divorce and differences in religion, to more dynamic dimensions such as communication and conflict management patterns. The dynamic factors make the most attractive targets for premarital counseling because these factors are both highly predictive of divorce and amenable to change. In essence, it is not how much couples love each other, but how they handle conflict that best predicts future marital distress or divorce—and conflict is inevitable. . . .

[Recent empirical studies] strongly suggest that couples can learn skills and enhance ways of thinking—prior to marriage—that significantly improves their odds of having good marriages. We and our colleagues in Germany have tracked the positive effects of such training for years following the marriage ceremony, with better communication, greater satisfaction, 50% lower break-up rates, and 50% lower incidence of physical aggression. . . .

Trying to prevent marital distress is hardly controversial. The controversy is whether or not governments should force it on a broad scale. Government mandated premarital counseling may have serious negative effects that are not being considered. . . . First, many segments of society are averse to increasing governmental intervention in family life. . . . Second, mandating premarital counseling would be a bureaucratic nightmare. There would be endless debates about what should be required and who is qualified to provide the training. . . . Third, we are concerned that there are virtually no data on the effectiveness of mandated programs while there is steadily growing evidence on the effectiveness when couples volunteer for such programs. We do hope, over time, to have better data on the effects of mandating premarital and marital training within both religious and military institutions. . . . Given the possible negatives of various initiatives to strengthen the institution of marriage, we argue for a less complicated path until we have had more discussion and research on the effects of the alternatives.

This does not mean that we, as a society, have no means to begin tackling these problems. The most immediately effective strategies may lie in the field of education rather than legislation. With a growing national consensus, a large scale public health education campaign could bring together educators, clergy, mental health professionals, and politicians to focus on two key goals: 1) To extol strong and happy marriages as a high value and a high priority, and 2) to encourage couples to take advantage of effective tools to make their marriages not just more stable, but truly better. . . .

We are talking about values here. Values that say marriage is important. Values that say working to resolve differences is good. Values that say preparing for marriage is wise. Values that lead to increased dedication for the task of building strong and happy marriages. These things can be done if we have the collective will. Let's get to it. *Id.*

Recent Legislation. The Florida Legislature in 1998 by a vote of 91 to 16 in the Florida House, and a unanimous vote in the Senate, enacted Florida's Marriage Preparation and Preservation Act of 1998. The preamble and rationale for this new legislation reads as follows:

> Just as the family is the foundation of society, the marital relationship is the foundation of a family. Consequently, strengthening marriages can only lead to stronger families, children and communities, as well as a stronger economy. An inability to cope with stress from both internal and external sources leads to significantly higher incidents of domestic violence, child abuse, absenteeism, medical costs, learning and social deficiencies, and divorce. Relationship skills can be learned. Once learned, relationship skills can facilitate communication between parties to a marriage and assist couples in avoiding conflict. . . . By reducing conflict and increasing communication, stressors can be diminished and coping can be furthered. When effective coping exists, domestic violence, child abuse, and divorce and its effect on children . . . are diminished. . . . The state has a compelling interest in educating its citizens with regard to marriage and, if contemplated, the effects of divorce. . . .

This new Florida legislation provides that: (1) all Florida high school students must take a required course in "marriage and relationship skill based education"; (2) engaged couples are encouraged to take a "premarital preparation course" of at least four hours in length, which may include instruction in conflict resolution, communication skills, financial responsibilities, children and parenting, and data on problems married couples face. Those who take such a premarital preparation course from a religious or secular marriage counselor are entitled to a $32.50 reduction in the cost of their marriage license, which normally costs between $88 and $200, depending on the county where they are married [Originally, the bill required mandatory premarital counseling, but this was objected to by a number of conservative and liberal legislators alike as constituting unwarranted governmental interference in marriage, although these voluntary incentives were generally supported by the legislature]; (3) each couple applying for a marriage license will also be given a handbook prepared by the Florida Bar Association informing couples of "the rights and responsibilities under Florida law of marital partners to each other and to their children, both during a marriage and upon dissolution"; and (4) couples with children who file for divorce must take a "Parent Education and Family Stabilization Course" that covers the legal and emotional impact of divorce on adults and children, financial responsibility, laws regarding child abuse and neglect, and conflict resolution skills. *See* Michael McManus, "Florida Passes Nation's Most Sweeping Reform of Marriage Laws", *Ethics and Religion Advance* (May 16, 1998) (predicting that this law will inspire many other states to pass similar laws).

Query: What are the strengths and weaknesses of these approaches? Are these proposals realistic means to strengthen or reinstitutionalize marriage in today's contemporary society? Why or why not? What should be the proper role of the State *vis-a-vis* the parties themselves with regard to the institution of marriage?

(7) The current trend in America and Western Europe appears to favor lessening formal state regulation over marriage and the family. In contrast, various Marxist and former Marxist societies that were once committed to radically changing and weakening these same marital institutions based upon historical perceptions of their oppressiveness have been unable to alter the pattern significantly. *See, e.g.* J. Eekelaar, Family Law and Social Policy,

22–23 (2d ed. 1984) (discussing the former Soviet Union experience and public policy after World War II of strengthening marriage and discouraging divorce). *See also* Dyuzheva, *International Marriage and Divorce Regulation and Recognition in Russia*, 29 Fam. L.Q. 645 (1995); Palmer, *The People's Republic of China: New Marriage Regulations*, 26 J. Fam. L. 39 (1987–88); Soltesz, *Hungary: Toward a Strengthening of Marriage*, 26 J. Fam. L. 113 (1987-88). These social experiments in Eastern Europe and Asia arguably demonstrate the remarkable social and cultural resilience of the traditional nuclear family and its continuing importance both in the raising and socialization of children and in providing for the economic and social support and interdependence of its members.

§ 1.03 Formalities of Marriage: The Statutory Requirements

For formal statutory marriages, each state requires that the parties obtain a license prior to marriage, and be married by a priest, rabbi, minister, or another statutorily authorized religious, judicial, or civil officer. A blood test for sexually transmitted diseases is required in many states, and in other states, a test for rubella (German measles) is also required for women of child-bearing years. Depending upon the particular state, marriage licenses are valid from 30 to 60 days before they must be renewed; and there is normally a waiting-period in the majority of states, averaging from three to five days before the parties can be married.

If the parties wish to have a religious wedding ceremony in a denomination that does not have an acknowledged "minister," such as the Society of Friends or Ba'hai, so-called "Quaker statutes" in many states will recognize such a marriage if performed according to the tenets of the particular religious denomination. A number of state statutes also recognize marriages of native American Indians if performed according to tribal custom or law.

A marriage license is normally issued by a clerk of court or a county clerk where the parties, or either of them, reside, or where the marriage ceremony is to be celebrated. But since a residency or domiciliary requirement is not required for marriage in a vast majority of states, the parties may also be married in another state of their choice. Marriage license statutes generally require that certain information be furnished by the applicant under oath, such as the applicant's age, prior marital status, and prior divorces, if any. *See generally* 1 Homer H. Clark, Jr., Law of Domestic Relations 85–100 (2d ed. 1987).

According to Professor Clark, this statutory regulation of marriage, in addition to the collection of vital statistics, also helps prevent hasty and ill-advised marriages. "Both license and ceremony [also] serve the additional purpose of providing objective proof that the marriage has occurred, avoiding the problems of evidence and accusations of fraud which often arise out of informal marriages." *Id.* at 86. *See also* Samuel Green & John Long, Marriage and Family Law Agreements (1984).

But what happens when there is an imperfection or lack of a marriage license? The following case discusses this problem.

NELSON v. MARSHALL
Missouri Court of Appeals
869 S.W.2d 132 (1993)

LOWENSTEIN, JUDGE.

This appeal from a bench trial involves the question of whether a valid, legal marriage can occur pursuant to [Mo. Rev. Stat.] 451.041 . . . where a ceremonial marriage occurred without application for, or issuance of, a marriage license, and the "groom" died the following day, negating any opportunity for successful application or issuance of a marriage license. Appellant Linda Nelson (Linda), asks to be declared the widow of Samuel Marshall (Sam). She asserts the trial court erred as a matter of law in holding there was no valid marriage due to their failure to obtain a marriage license.

Linda and the decedent Sam had a twelve and a half year relationship. Linda and Sam lived together from December 1991 until Sam's hospitalization in February, 1992. During the course of their relationship, they discussed the issue of marriage.

On February 12, 1992, while Sam was in a Columbia, Missouri hospital, Sam and Linda attempted to get married. At Sam's request, Linda discussed with the hospital chaplain, Reverend Jensen, the procedure of how they could get married under their current circumstances. Reverend Jensen called the Boone County Recorder that day to find out the procedure for obtaining a marriage license for someone in the hospital. He was told the parties would have to get a waiver for the three day waiting period from a judge before the marriage certificate could be issued. . . . Jensen relayed this information to Linda. He noted it would be difficult to get both the waiver and the license because it was a legal holiday, Lincoln's birthday.

A "marriage" ceremony conducted by Jensen was held February 12, in Sam's room despite the absence of a marriage license. Linda believed the paperwork could be completed after the ceremony. Following the ceremony, Sam and Linda both believed they were married.

The following day, February 13, Jensen told Linda that both she and Sam needed to sign some papers to obtain the license [in accordance with Mo. Rev. Stat. 451.040.2]. . . . The papers were never signed because of Sam's worsening condition. That evening Sam died. No marriage license was ever obtained.

Linda filed for letters of administration in the Probate Court of Howard County seeking to be appointed Personal Representative of Sam's estate. Respondents, Marion Marshall and Elma Lou Davis (Sam's brother and sister) also filed a joint application for letters of administration declaring they were the only heirs-at-law and that Sam had no surviving spouse. . . . This suit was instituted by Linda after the existence of the marriage was questioned by respondents in the probate proceeding. . . .

The general rule is that marriage is a contract as well as a status or a legal condition and the state has a legitimate and rightful concern with the persons domiciled in its borders in relation to this status. *State ex rel Miller v. Jones*, 349 S.W.2d 534, 537 (Mo. App. 1961). . . To further the state's interest in the marital relationship, it may implement "reasonable regulations that do not interfere in a significant manner with decisions to enter into marital relationships." People v. Schuppert, 217 Ill. App. 3d 715, 577 N.E.2d 828, 830 (Ill. App. Ct. 1991). . . [citing Zablocki v. Redhail, 434 U.S. 374, 98 S.Ct. 673, 54 L.Ed.2d 618 (1978)]. Requiring a marriage license is an appropriate regulation. A rational relationship exists between "the requirement that marriages be licensed and the strong continuing interest of the State in the institution of marriage . . . ." Id. As part of Missouri's laws regulating marriage, and the statute at the heart of this appeal, § 451.040.1 requires a marriage license for a marriage to be considered valid. . . . The question before this court is whether, under these facts, there was a valid marriage between Sam and Linda. . . .

While this court recognizes that the doctrine of ab initio nullity of marriages is looked upon with disfavor, *In re Guthery's Estate*, 205 Mo. App. 664, 226 S.W.2d 626 (Mo. Ct. App. 1920), Missouri is among the states whose "licensing statute plainly makes an unlicensed marriage invalid." Carabetta v. Carabetta, 182 Conn. 344, 438 A.2d 109 (Conn. 1980). *Accord Lopez v. Lopez*, 102 N.J. Super. 253, 245 A.2d 771, 772 (N.J. Super. Ct. 1968); *State v. Lard*, 86 N.M. 71, 519 P.2d 307, 310 (N.M. Ct. App. 1974) (marriage as a civil contract requires a license); the court declines to follow those states which have declared their licensing provision as merely directory, and holds the absence of a marriage license as a fatal flaw. . . . *DeMedio v. DeMedio*, 215 Pa. Super. 255, 257 A.2d 290, 301-302 (Pa. Super. 1969); *Picarella v. Picarella*, 20 Md. App. 499, 316 A.2d 826, 834 (Md. 1974); *Wright v. Vales*, 1 Ark. App. 175, 613 S.W.2d 850, 852 (Ark. App. 1981) (Arkansas has no statute providing a marriage is void when no license is obtained); *Maxwell v. Maxwell*, 51 Misc.2d 687, 273 N.Y.S.2d 728 (N.Y. Sup. 1966); *Johnson v. Johnson*, 235 S.C. 542, 112 S.E.2d 647 (S.C. 1960) (marriage solemnized pursuant to a defective license or without any license does not affect its validity.)

This court recognizes that while this decision requires a marriage license for a marriage to be valid, this does not preclude the long established doctrine of proving the existence of a valid marriage with circumstantial evidence. . . . *Smith v. Smith*, 361 Mo. 894, 237 S.W.2d 84 (Mo. 1951) (parole evidence of ceremony and marriage certificate [was] sufficient). . . . Here, there never was, nor ever will be, a license application or a certificate issued; hence no valid marriage. . . .

. . . This case stands for the proposition that a marriage will not be declared valid in this state without the parties having first obtained, or ever having obtained, a license. . . . A contrary result here would lead to the legal problems the courts faced with proving common law marriages, which the legislature sought to avoid by enacting the requirements set forth in Chapter 451 [Mo. Rev. Stat.].

. . . The judgment is affirmed. . . .

NOTES AND QUESTIONS

(1) The *Nelson* court, *supra*, conceded that, in a number of other states, an imperfection in the marriage license would not necessarily affect the validity of such a marriage. *See, e.g., Johnson v. Johnson*, 112 S.E.2d 647 (S.C. 1960); *DeMedio v. DeMedio*, 257 A.2d 290 (Pa. Super. Ct. 1969); *Picarella v. Picarella*, 316 A.2d 826 (Md. Ct. App. 1974). Why then did the *Nelson* court expressly decline to follow such precedent? Which is the better-reasoned judicial approach, in your opinion? Why?

(2) A majority of American states today have *directory* marriage statutes, requiring only *substantial compliance* with state statutory requirements for a valid marriage in order to validate the parties' good faith marital expectations. However, a minority of jurisdictions have *mandatory* statutory requirements for marriage, such as Missouri in the *Nelson* case, *above*, under which, if every marital statute is not strictly complied with, there is no valid marriage. However, many mandatory jurisdictions also have a "curative" or "savings"

provision in order to prevent possible hardship to the parties. For example, Va. Code Ann. § 20-31 provides: "No marriage solemnized under a license issued in this state by any person professing to be authorized to solemnize [it] shall be deemed or adjudged to be void on account of any want of authority in such person, or any defect, omission, or imperfection in such license, if the marriage be in all other respects lawful, and be consummated with the full belief on the part of the persons so married, or either of them, that they have been lawfully joined in marriage."

"Consummation" of a marriage normally means the physical act of sexual intercourse, although some confused courts have held that "consummation" refers to the marriage ceremony itself. The general view is that a ceremonial marriage is valid even though it is not consummated; but various "curative" statutes still require that a questionable marriage be "consummated" nevertheless. *See generally* 1 Homer H. Clark, Jr., Law of Domestic Relations 92–93 (2d ed. 1987).

(3) The *Nelson* court recognized "the long-established doctrine of proving the existence of a valid marriage with circumstantial evidence." *Query:* How would an attorney go about proving the existence of a valid marriage affecting his or her client? According to Wigmore on Evidence, a valid marriage may be proven by: (1) offering a valid marriage certificate or a record of the marriage; (2) offering testimony of eyewitnesses who were present at the marriage ceremony; or (3) offering evidence of matrimonial cohabitation and community repute, which raises at least a rebuttable presumption of a valid marriage. *See* 5 Wigmore on Evidence § 1645; 7 Wigmore on Evidence §§ 2082–88; and 9 Wigmore on Evidence § 2505. *See also* Swisher, *Proving the Validity of Marriage*, 43 Virginia Lawyer 29 (December 1994).

(4) **Problem.** Dick and Jane plan to be married in the State of Marshall (the 51st state of the United States), which has mandatory marriage formalities. Dick, a third-year law student, does not believe the state should have any right to infringe on his fundamental right to marry, but he and Jane apply for a state marriage license and take the required blood test anyway. Dick tells Jane that they will be married in Marshall by Dick's Uncle Fred, a Presbyterian minister who lives in the neighboring state of Holmes. Unknown to Jane, but known to Dick, Uncle Fred is not a bona fide ordained Presbyterian minister who is authorized by the State to perform marriages, but he is someone who has obtained a mail-order "theological degree" from the Universal Life Church, Inc., of Modesto, California. Uncle Fred then marries Dick and Jane in a ceremony at the home of Jane's parents in the state of Marshall.

To make matters worse, unknown to both Dick and Jane, the clerk of court apparently misplaced their marriage license data in an obsolete file that was later incinerated by a janitor; and Dick lost his copy of the marriage license and certificate when he left it in the pocket of his rented tuxedo after the marriage. Two years later, Dick and Jane's application for passports to visit Europe is returned to them with a letter stating that "we can find no record that you have ever been married, and we must therefore conclude that you are not married."

Are Dick and Jane legally married? If you were representing Dick and Jane in a suit to affirm their marriage in the state of Marshall, what arguments could be made in support of their marriage? What arguments against?

§ 1.04 Informal Marriages

An alternative to a formal statutory marriage—or to nonmarital cohabitation—is an "informal" marriage, which generally includes: common law marriage, putative marriage, marriage by proxy, *de facto* "marriage", and "marriage" by estoppel.

Although various courts traditionally have viewed informal marriages with suspicion and mistrust, other courts have recognized the validity of such marriages under the public policy rationale of promoting marriage in general, and of validating the present expectations of the parties, especially concerning marital property and support rights. *See generally* Walter Weyrauch, *Informal and Formal Marriage An Appraisal of Trends in Family Organization*, 28 U. Chi. L. Rev. 88 (1960); Walter Weyrauch, *Metamorphoses of Marriage*, 13 Fam. L.Q. 415 (1980).

[A] Common Law Marriages

A common law marriage need not be formally solemnized, but there must be a present intent and agreement to enter into a matrimonial relationship. These can be inferred through cohabitation and community repute as husband and wife. Thus, common law marriages are as fully valid as ceremonial marriages in those jurisdictions where common law marriages are recognized. *See, e.g., Renshaw v. Heckler*, 787 F.2d 50 (2d Cir. 1986) (applying Pa. law). *See also Weaver v. State*, 855 S.W.2d 116 (Tex. Ct. App. 1993) (holding that once a common law marriage has been established, it is generally given the same legal significance as a ceremonial marriage, and this includes the privilege not to testify against the other spouse). However, the intent to be married under a common law marriage cannot be inferred from mere cohabitation alone, and the courts normally require that proof of a common law marriage be established by clear and convincing evidence to prevent any fraudulent claims. *See, e.g., In re Estate of Fischer* 176 N.W.2d 801 (Iowa 1970). *See generally* Stein, *Common Law Marriage: Its History and Certain Contemporary Problems*, 9 J. Fam. L. 271 (1969), and Hall, *Common Law Marriage*, 46 Cambridge L.J. 106 (1987).

Until recently, the recognition of common law marriages in the United States seemed to be on the decline. However, with more cohabiting couples and alternative lifestyles, the recognition of common law marriages by various courts and commentators may reverse this trend. *See, e.g.* Note, *Common Law Marriage and Unmarried Cohabitators: An Old Solution to a New Problem*, 39 U. Pitt. L. Rev. 579 (1978); Reppy, *Property and Support Rights of Unmarried Cohabitants: A Proposal for Creating a New Legal Status*, 44 La. L. Rev. 1677, 1678 (1984), where the author supports a revival in the recognition of common law marriage throughout the United States since "contract law cannot provide adequate solutions to the problems raised by a large number of cohabiting couples." *See also* Caudill, *Legal Recognition of Unmarried Cohabitation: A Proposal to Update and Reconsider Common Law Marriage*, 49 Tenn. L. Rev. 537 (1982). *And see* Cynthia Grant Bowman, *A Feminist Proposal to Bring Back Common Law Marriage*, 75 Or. L. Rev. 709 (1996).

Query: How would you characterize common law marriage: Is it marriage as a status relationship or marriage as a contract?

The following case discusses the necessary elements for a valid common law marriage.

CROSSON v. CROSSON
Alabama Civil Court of Appeals
668 So. 2d 868 (1995)

CRAWLEY, JUDGE.

Bruce Crosson and Barbara Crosson were married in February, 1982, in a ceremonial marriage. The Crossons were divorced in June, 1993. It is undisputed that after the divorce Mr. Crosson asked his former wife to come back and be his wife. Mrs. Crosson (the "wife") accepted the invitation to move back in with Mr. Crosson ("the husband"). They began living together in August 1993.

Unknown to the wife, the husband married another woman in October, 1994. Upon discovering that fact, the wife immediately sued for a divorce from the husband, contending that she was his common law wife, and that he had committed adultery, and bigamy, and that there was an irretrievable breakdown of the marriage. . . .

The first issue is whether the parties entered into a common law marriage.

"This Court has recently reaffirmed the requirements for a common law marriage in Alabama in *Etheridge v. Yeager*, 465 So. 2d 378 (Ala. 1985). In that opinion, citing various cases as precedent, we held that while no ceremony or particular words are necessary, there are common elements which must be present, either explicitly expressed or implicitly inferred from the circumstances, in order for a common law marriage to exist. These elements are: 1) capacity; 2) present mutual agreement to permanently enter the marriage relationship to the exclusion of all other relationships; and 3) public recognition of the relationship as a marriage and public assumption of marital duties and cohabitation." *Boswell v. Boswell*, 497 So. 2d 479, 480 (Ala. 1986) (citations omitted). . . .

I. *The Boswell Criteria*

1. Capacity

Both parties testified that immediately after their divorce, neither party married anyone else and that there was no other impediment to their remarriage. Therefore, both parties had the capacity to enter into the marital relationship.

2. Present Mutual Agreement

The wife testified that she and the husband intended to enter into a marital relationship when "Bruce told me that he loved me and that he knew that he had made some mistakes, that I had taught him a very valuable lesson and that he loved me and *he wanted me to come back and be his wife and I did*." (Emphasis added) . . .

The husband's only contradictory testimony as to their mutual assent to be married is his testimony that he dated others and that he and the others were seen together at restaurants. He did not tell the wife, and he contends that he did not intend to enter into an agreement to get married when the wife replied "maybe" to his proposal of marriage; however, the wife moved in and began living with him on the same day. The husband's subjective intent, i.e., any unexpressed intent he may have had not to be married, must yield to the reasonable conclusion to be drawn by his objective acts such as his failure to dispute what appeared to be a marital relationship. These acts speak for themselves. *McGiffert v. State ex rel. Stowe*, 366 So. 2d 680 (Ala. 1978). . . .

3. Public Recognition

The husband admitted that after she moved back to his home, she kept her clothes, personal belongings, furnishings, etc., at the house, and that they shared household duties. The wife did not remove her wedding band when she was divorced. In April, 1994, the parties filed a federal tax return for the year 1993, stating that their status was "married filing joint return." . . .

The parties lived together until the wife's job required her to move to Mississippi in March, 1994. The wife took an apartment in Mississippi, listing her husband as her "husband" on the application for utilities. Upon the husband's first visit to the wife's apartment, he went to the office where she worked to obtain a key to the apartment, and the office manager asked him if he was "Barbara's husband" to which he replied "Yes." . . . On several social occasions the wife introduced him as her husband, and he made no comment regarding that introduction, but now contends that he made no comment because he did not want to embarrass his wife by correcting her. . . .

These facts meet the required elements, stated in *Boswell, supra*, of capacity, present mutual agreement, and public recognition of the relationship as a marriage and public assumption of marital duties and cohabitation, thereby inferring consent to enter a matrimonial relationship to the exclusion of all other relationships. . . .

II. *Issues in Rebuttal*. . .

The husband contends that the relationship did not amount to a common law marriage because they discussed having a ceremonial marriage, which never occurred. We disagree. . . . "The intent to participate in a marriage ceremony in the future does not prove a couple's nonmarriage." *Mattison v. Kirk*, 497 So. 2d 120, 123 (Ala. 1986). . . . In *Mattison* . . . the court noted: "It is not uncommon even for ceremonially married couples to have a second marriage ceremony—a sort of celebration and renewal of marriage vows." [Id.] The fact that two people are planning a wedding ceremony does not mean that they are not presently married. . . .

The husband contends that he could not be found to have intended to be in a marital relationship, permanent and exclusive of all others, because he had dated other women and had been seen with them in public places, although the wife had no knowledge of these actions. We disagree. . . . When asked why he did not tell the wife he was dating others, the husband stated "Why should I? I don't have no ties with her. She is not—I'm not married to her."

> "Once there is a marriage, common law or ceremonial, it is *not* "transitory ephemeral, or conditional." Once married, by common law or by ceremony, the spouses are married. There is no such thing as being a "little bit" married; and once married, one spouse's *liaison amoureuse* does not end the marital status, whether that status was created by common law or by ceremony, though it may afford the other spouse a ground for judicially terminating the legal relationship."

Adams v. Boan, 559 So. 2d 1084, 1087 (Ala. 1990). . . .

The husband contends that his ceremonial marriage on October 1, 1994, to Cheryl Gaddy Rollings was evidence that could be considered by the trial court to rebut the presumption of an actual marriage between the husband and wife, based upon their cohabitation, etc. We disagree. . . .

"A subsequent asserting 'we knew we were not married' by a party to such an agreement [to enter into a marital relationship] will hardly vitiate a valid marriage where the *original* understanding was to presently enter into a marriage relationship, followed by public recognition of the relationship." *Huffmaster [v. Huffmaster]* 279 Ala. 594, 595, 188 So. 2d 552, 554 (Ala. 1966) (emphasis added). . . . .

III. *Conclusion*

The arguments raised to rebut the contention that these parties had a common law marriage—(1) their discussion of a ceremonial marriage, (2) the husband dating others, and (3) the husband's subsequent marriage to another—are, as discussed above—insufficient to rebut the facts suggesting a common law marriage. . . .

NOTES AND QUESTIONS

(1) *Query.* What if a purported husband and wife attempt to contract a common law marriage at a time when a legal impediment to their common law marriage does in fact exist—for example, when one of the parties was not yet legally divorced from a prior spouse? Some courts will recognize that the parties' common law marriage still exists after the legal impediment is subsequently removed, under a "continuing-agreement" rationale. *See, e.g., Rickard v. Trousdale*, 508 So. 2d 260 (Ala. 1987); Parker v. Parker, 265 S.E.2d 237 (N.C. Ct. App. 1980). Other courts, however, have held that an initial meretricious relationship cannot ripen into a valid common law marriage absent proof of a new agreement to marry after the impediment is removed. *See, e.g., Dandy v. Dandy*, 234 So. 2d 728 (Fla. Dist. Ct. App. 1970); Byers v. Mount Vernon Mills, Inc., 231 S.E.2d 699 (S.C. 1977). Which underlying theory is more persuasive to you? Why?

(2) According to Samuel Green & John Long, Marriage and Family Law Agreements 80–86 (1984), the following jurisdictions still recognize common law marriages if contracted within that state: Alabama, Colorado, Georgia [until 1997], Idaho, Iowa, Kansas, Montana, Ohio [until 1991], Oklahoma, Pennsylvania, Rhode Island, South Carolina, Texas, and the District of Columbia. *See also* 1 Homer H. Clark, Jr., Law of Domestic Relations 100–24 (2d ed. 1987).

(3) Most other jurisdictions will not recognize common law marriages if contracted within their own state, but *will* nevertheless recognize common law marriages if contracted in one of the jurisdictions mentioned above. *See, e.g., In the Matter of the Estate of Burroughs*, 486 N.W.2d 113 (Mich. Ct. App. 1992); *Blaw-Knox Construction Co. v. Morris*, 596 A.2d 679 (Md. 1991); *Farah v. Farah*, 429 S.E.2d 626 (Va. Ct. App. 1993). *See also Chatman v. Ribicoff*, 196 F. Supp. 931 (N.D. Calif. 1961); Weisel v. National. Transp. Co., 218 N.Y.S.2d 725 (N.Y. App. Div. 1961). What is the underlying public policy rationale? *See* Restatement (Second) Conflict of Laws 283(2) (1971) (stating that a marriage valid where contracted would be valid everywhere unless it violates the strong public policy of another

state). *Cf. Enlow v. Fire Protection Sys., Inc.*, 803 S.W.2d 148 (Mo. Ct. App. 1991) (holding that Missouri will not recognize a common law marriage between Missouri residents even if the marriage occurred in a state that legally recognizes common law marriages).

(4) Assuming that a sister state will recognize a common law marriage from another state, what evidence should warrant such recognition? Visits of short duration to the common law marriage state? *See, e.g., Metropolitan Life Ins. Co. v. Holding*, 293 F. Supp. 854 (E.D. Va. 1968); *Renshaw v. Heckler*, 787 F.2d 50 (2d Cir. 1986); *Ventura v. Ventura*, 280 N.Y.S.2d 5 (N.Y. Sup. Ct. 1967). Or must the parties have established a more significant relationship with the common law marriage state? *Compare Grant v. Superior Court*, 555 P.2d 895 (Ariz. Ct. App. 1976) *with Mission Ins. Co. v. Industrial Comm'n*, 559 P.2d 1085 (Ariz. Ct. App. 1976). *See also Hesington v. Estate of Hesington*, 640 S.W.2d 824 (Mo. Ct. App. 1982); *Kelderhaus v. Kelderhaus*, 467 S.E.2d 303 (Va. Ct. App. 1996).

For example, assume that Herb and Wendy are ceremonially married in Arizona, but, unknown to either of them, their formal marriage is invalid due to an imperfection in the marriage license, with the result that the marrying official did not have proper authorization from the State of Arizona to marry Herb and Wendy. They then decide to move to Virginia, where Herb has a new job in Richmond. On their way to Virginia, Herb and Wendy travel through Texas and Oklahoma, states that both recognize common law marriage. They register in an overnight motel and hotel in each state as husband and wife. Wendy tells the manager of one hotel that Herb and Wendy are newlyweds. The manager offers them his congratulations, and he sends a bottle of champagne to their room. They eat dinner that night at a local restaurant, and tell the waiter and the restaurant manager that they are husband and wife.

A year later, Herb and Wendy discover that due to irreconcilable differences they can no longer live together as husband and wife. Wendy sues Herb for divorce, requesting spousal support and a division of the parties' marital property. Herb, however, discovers that their Arizona marriage was invalid, and he argues therefore that he owes Wendy no spousal support and has no other marital obligations. *Query:* Do Herb and Wendy have a valid common law marriage? Why or why not? What if Herb and Wendy had lived in Virginia as husband and wife for over twenty years, and had made week-long visits each summer to Corpus Christi, Texas, to visit Wendy's sister, where they held themselves out to Wendy's sister and her friends as husband and wife? A valid common law marriage? *Compare Kelderhaus v. Kelderhaus*, 467 S.E.2d 303 (Va. Ct. App. 1996) *with Metropolitan Life Ins. Co. v. Holding*, 293 F. Supp. 854 (E.D. Va. 1968). What underlying public policy arguments are involved here?

(5) **Problem: A Valid Common Law Remarriage?** Harry and Wilma were ceremonially married in the state of Marshall, which recognizes both ceremonial and common law marriages. Five years later they were divorced in Marshall, but shortly thereafter they began living together. During their post-divorce cohabitation period, Harry and Wilma maintained their property separately, and executed various legal documents as single individuals. However, they purchased two insurance policies as husband and wife. Wilma told various neighbors that she was Harry's wife, but her old friends still knew her as Harry's girlfriend. Most of their neighbors considered them married, but not Harry's family. Because of their uncertain legal status, Harry and Wilma planned a second formal marriage ceremony in December, but Harry died unexpectedly in October. Did Harry and Wilma have a valid

common law remarriage? Why or why not? *Compare Skipworth v. Skipworth,* 360 So. 2d 975 (Ala. 1978) *with Ward v. Terriere,* 386 P.2d 352 (Colo. 1963) *and Brack v. Brack,* 329 N.W.2d 432 (Mich. Ct. App. 1982). *See also Crosson v. Crosson, above*; B. Glenn, Annotation, *Common-law Marriage between Parties Previously Divorced,* 82 A.L.R. 2d 688 (1962) and Later Case Service.

What if Wilma told you, as her attorney, that although she and Harry had cohabited, and held themselves out to the community as husband and wife, that they never in fact had any mutual intent and agreement to be remarried? Do you have an ethical responsibility to divulge this information to a probate court in a subsequent legal dispute between Wilma and Harry's brothers and sisters? Why or why not? *See* ABA Code of Professional Responsibility DR 7-102(b)(1) and ABA Model Rule 3.3.

(6) Can the parties to a common law marriage later negate their legal status through a "common law divorce"? *See Chivers v. Couch Motor Lines,* 159 So. 2d 544 (La. Ct. App. 1964) (applying Florida law); *Crosson v. Crosson, above.*

(7) The common law marriage theory received national attention in two well-publicized cases. In a New York case, actor William Hurt was sued by his alleged common law wife Sandra Jennings for a share of his estimated ten million dollars. Although Hurt and Jennings shared a three-year relationship, Jennings claimed that their common law marriage was legally established when the couple lived together for five weeks in 1982-83 while Hurt was filming the movie *The Big Chill* in South Carolina. Hurt, however, claimed that although they were living together, he never intended to marry Jennings. What result? *See Jennings v. Hurt,* 554 N.Y.S.2d 220 (N.Y. App. Div. 1990).

In a second common law marriage dispute, Sandra Renfro sued New York Yankee outfielder Dave Winfield in a Texas court, arguing that a valid common law marriage existed between them, and she also requested support for the parties' six-year-old daughter. A Houston jury voted 10 to 2 to recognize this common law marriage, and the court ordered Winfield to pay Renfro $210,000 in attorneys' fees, and $10,000 a month temporary alimony until the parties' divorce claim is settled. Newsweek, July 24, 1989, at 46-47.

Query: With the dramatic increase of unmarried cohabitation in recent years, does an informal common law marriage now constitute a viable alternative remedy to a nonmarital cohabitation agreement defining the (typically financial) rights and obligations of the cohabitants? Are other equitable remedies available (*see* Chapter 3 *below*)? Why or why not? *See* Gregory, Swisher & Scheible, Understanding Family Law § 1.02 *Nonmarital Cohabitation* (2nd ed., Matthew Bender 1995).

[B] Putative Marriage

A putative marriage is a "curative" marriage when one or both of the parties were ignorant of an impediment that made their ceremonial marriage invalid. *See, e.g., Hicklin v. Hicklin,* 509 N.W.2d 627 (Neb. 1994). The putative marriage concept is most often found in those states following a French or Spanish civil law tradition, such as California, Louisiana, and Texas. Various other states following an English common law tradition have also adopted the putative marriage concept by statute, including Alaska, Illinois, Minnesota, Nebraska, and Wisconsin. The Uniform Marriage and Divorce Act § 209 also recognizes putative marriages.

A putative marriage must be contracted with a good faith belief that the ceremonial marriage was valid, but unlike common law marriages, cohabitation of the parties is not always required. Like a spouse by any other marriage, a putative spouse may claim various marital property and support rights and wrongful death and social security benefits and may inherit from the other putative spouse. *See generally* Note, *Rights of the Putative Spouse*, 1978 S. Ill. U. L.J. 423 (1978); Luther & Luther, *Support and Property Rights of the Putative Spouse*, 24 Hastings L.J. 311 (1973); Blakesley, *The Putative Marriage Doctrine*, 60 Tulane L. Rev. 1 (1985).

But what constitutes a "good faith belief" that the prior marriage was valid? The following case discusses this question.

REBOUCHE v. ANDERSON
Louisiana Court of Appeal
505 So. 2d 808 (1987)

LINDSAY, JUDGE.

The plaintiff, Doris D. Rebouche, filed suit against Charles E. Anderson, Bob L. Kightlinger, B & B Medical, Inc. & SciMed Life Systems, Inc., for the wrongful death of her alleged husband, Joseph Y. Rebouche. Plaintiff claimed the decedent underwent open heart surgery on November 6, 1984, and that Anderson and Kightlinger, employed by B & B, were operating a heart-lung machine. Plaintiff claimed that the wrong valve was opened, causing the decedent to suffer an air embolism to the brain and brain damage. As a result, the decedent died on January 4, 1985.

B & B Medical filed an exception of no cause or right of action, claiming that Kightlinger and Anderson were not employed by the company and that the plaintiff was not the lawful widow of the decedent. Kightlinger and Anderson also filed an exception of no cause or right of action, asserting that plaintiff was not the lawful widow of the decedent.

A hearing on the exceptions was held and the plaintiff argued she was the putative spouse of the decedent.

FACTS

The record indicates that the plaintiff has a sixth grade education and is below normal intelligence. Experts indicated at trial that plaintiff has a mental age of 12 years.

The plaintiff testified that in 1945, when she was 15 years old, she married Johnny Malcolm Wheeler. Two children were born of that marriage. Plaintiff testified the marriage with Wheeler deteriorated, she left Wheeler, and she and the children lived with her parents in Shreveport while plaintiff worked as a waitress in a local eatery. Plaintiff testified that a divorce was obtained from Wheeler, but that her mother took care of everything. Plaintiff's mother was awarded custody of plaintiff's two children.

Plaintiff then married Thomas J. Ramsey around 1955. The couple moved to Baton Rouge, and one child was born of the marriage, Thomas J. Ramsey, Jr. Plaintiff testified that Ramsey treated her cruelly and failed to provide the necessities of life. In 1959, plaintiff left Ramsey and returned to live with her parents in Shreveport. Plaintiff testified that at the time she left, she asked Ramsey if he would get a divorce and claimed he said that he would. However, Ramsey took no action to secure a divorce and in fact the parties did not divorce.

Plaintiff and her son testified that around 1963, Ramsey called Thomas J. Ramsey, Jr., and told him that he had remarried, and he invited the boy to return to Baton Rouge to live with Ramsey and his new wife. The record indicates that Ramsey did not in fact remarry until 1972.

Plaintiff claims she had no communication with Ramsey between the time she left Baton Rouge and her marriage to the decedent, Joseph Y. Rebouche in 1967. The record indicates that the couple and Thomas J. Ramsey, Jr., went to Oklahoma to look at a coon dog and while there decided to get married.

Plaintiff claimed that because Ramsey told her he would obtain a divorce, because Ramsey indicated he had remarried, and because a long period of time had elapsed without communication with Ramsey, she assumed they were divorced and that she was free to marry Rebouche.

GOOD FAITH

The plaintiff argues that the trial court erred in failing to properly apply Louisiana law in determining whether she was entitled to putative spouse status. The plaintiff claims the trial court used an objective analysis rather than the subjective analysis required by Louisiana law. For the following reasons, we conclude that the trial court was not in error in denying the plaintiff putative spouse status. . . .

The good faith required for putative spouse status has been defined as an honest and reasonable belief that the marriage was valid and that no legal impediment to it existed. *Hart v. Hart*, 427 So. 2d 1341 (La. Ct. App. 1983) *Galbraith v. Galbraith*, 396 So. 2d 1364 (La. Ct. App. 1981).

Good faith consists of being ignorant of the cause which prevents the formation of the marriage, or being ignorant of the defects in the celebration which caused the nullity. *Succession of Davis*, 142 So. 2d 481 (La. Ct. App. 1962). The question of whether a party is in good faith is subjective and depends on all the circumstances presented in any given case. *Galbraith v. Galbraith, supra*; *Hart v. Hart, supra*. Although the good faith analysis incorporates the objective elements of reasonableness, the inquiry is essentially a subjective one. *Hart v. Hart, supra*; . . . .

There are several factors weighing in favor of plaintiff's claim that she honestly and reasonably believed she was divorced from Ramsey. Plaintiff offered extensive expert testimony to establish that she had an extremely low level of intelligence and has a mental age of approximately 12 years. Plaintiff has worked as a waitress most of her adult life and her tasks were limited to writing down orders and submitting them to the kitchen. She was not required to total the customer's checks. Plaintiff argued that due to her limited education and intelligence she was honest and reasonable in believing that she was divorced from Ramsey. Plaintiff also urged that Ramsey told her he would obtain a divorce and that when Ramsey called the couple's son in 1963 and told him he had remarried, the plaintiff assumed that Ramsey had obtained the divorce. Plaintiff also argued that because such a long period of time passed with no communication from Ramsey, she assumed they were divorced. Plaintiff admitted having undergone a divorce from her first husband, Johnny Wheeler, but argued that her mother took care of the details in those proceedings. There are also numerous factors weighing against plaintiff's claim that she had an honest and reasonable belief that she was divorced from Ramsey. The plaintiff was 30 years old when she left Ramsey and was the mother of several children. Plaintiff had previously been divorced and in spite of her claim that her mother took care of the divorce proceedings, the record indicates that plaintiff accepted personal service of the divorce petition which was filed against her and signed the affidavit attached to her answer. Plaintiff testified that when she married, she knew that a marriage license was required and that she also knew that a divorce was necessary from Ramsey when she left him. . . .

Plaintiff made much of her lack of education and intelligence at trial; however plaintiff was not illiterate. She worked much of her adult life as a waitress. Her neighbors and Ramsey testified that they did not notice any limited intellectual ability on the part of the plaintiff.

Given all these factors, it must be determined whether this plaintiff under these circumstances had an honest and reasonable belief that she was divorced from Ramsey. The trial court found that she did not and that finding is entitled to great weight and is not to be overturned unless shown to be clearly wrong. The decision in this case turns largely on the credibility determinations of the trial judge, and those determinations appear to be correct.

Even though this plaintiff had limited education and intelligence, she was acquainted with divorce proceedings and knew that it was necessary to obtain one from Ramsey. She did not personally take action to obtain a divorce. It is disputed whether Ramsey actually said he would obtain a divorce, but in light of plaintiff's distrust of Ramsey, she was unreasonable in relying on any indication he may have offered that he would obtain a divorce. The record also calls into question whether Ramsey relayed to plaintiff in 1963 that he had remarried. In his reasons for judgment, the trial judge indicated that this part of the conversation probably did not occur. In spite of plaintiff's low intelligence, she knew a divorce was necessary, she was distrustful of Ramsey, and she had the ability to contact Ramsey in Baton Rouge to determine whether she and Ramsey were in fact divorced before she married Rebouche. She failed to do this. . . .

From our review of the record and the applicable law, we agree with the trial court that plaintiff did not have an honest and reasonable belief that there was no impediment to her marriage to Rebouche. We must affirm the trial court judgment finding that plaintiff did not have the requisite good faith to entitle her to putative spouse status.

NOTES AND QUESTIONS

(1) If a good faith belief in the validity of a ceremonial marriage and ignorance of any defects to that marriage is a subjective test, and if the plaintiff in *Rebouche* had a mental age of 12 and believed that her marriage to Rebouche was valid, why then did the court refuse to find that she was a putative spouse? Are you persuaded by the court's reasoning? Why or why not? *See also Weaver v. State*, 855 S.W.2d 116, 121 (Tex. Ct. App. 1993) ("If a putative spouse is unaware of the previous undissolved marriage or other impediment, good faith is presumed"); Hicklin v. Hicklin, 509 N.W.2d 627, 631 (Neb. 1994) ("Good faith, in the context of a putative marriage, means an honest and reasonable belief that the marriage was valid at the time of the ceremony").

(2) The Federal government applies a putative spouse test for social security benefits. 42 U.S.C. § 416(h)(1)(B) provides in part that if an applicant "in good faith went through

a marriage ceremony resulting in a purported marriage between them which, but for a legal impediment not known to the applicant at the time of such ceremony, would have been a valid marriage, and such applicant and the insured individual were living in the same household at the time of the death of such insured individual such purported marriage shall be deemed to be a valid marriage."

(3) *Query.* What other remedies might be available to a purported spouse in those states that do not recognize the concept of putative marriage? *See* Chapter 3, *below*. What about sister-state and foreign-country recognition of a putative marriage? *See generally* Fine, *The Rights of Putative Spouses: Choice of Law Issues and Comparative Insights*, 32 Int'l. & Comp. L.Q. 708 (1983).

(4) Should a state be required to recognize a bigamous or polygamous putative marriage? Why or why not? On the impact of specific facts bringing the party's good faith belief into question, *see, e.g., Batey v. Batey*, 1997 WL 47156 (Alaska 1997) (holding that a party's good faith belief in his or her putative spouse status "must be present at all times, and must precede the removal of a marital impediment" and that allowing a person "who knowingly enters into a bigamous marriage to claim that he or she eventually developed a good faith belief in the validity of that marriage would vitiate [the purpose of the putative-marriage doctrine]"). *Cf. In re Dalip Singh Bir's Estate*, 188 P.2d 499 (Cal. Ct. App. 1948) (recognizing a bigamous putative marriage for intestate succession purposes). *See also* § 1.07[C] *below*.

[C] Marriage by Proxy

A marriage by proxy is an attempt to comply with statutory marriage requirements by designating a "stand-in" who appears for the absent prospective spouse or by having the absent party participate in the ceremony via telephone. The validity of a marriage by proxy is normally governed by the law of the jurisdiction where the ceremony takes place.

Explorers Christopher Columbus and Vasco de Balboa were each married by proxy, though not while enroute to America. Poet W. H. Auden also contracted a proxy marriage to help his spouse escape from Nazi Germany, and some Russian emigrants to the United States have entered into proxy marriages with spouses back in Russia.

However, current federal immigration law will not recognize "a spouse, wife, or husband by reason of any marriage ceremony where the contracting parties thereto are not physically present in the presence of each other, unless the marriage shall have been consummated." 8 U.S.C. § 1101(a)(35). *Query:* Why not?

Although proxy marriages are still utilized today, the literature on marriage by proxy is limited and dated. *See* Howery, *Marriage by Proxy and Other Informal Marriages*, 13 U.M.K.C. L. Rev. 48 (1944); Moore, *The Case for Marriage by Proxy*, 11 Clev. Marshall L. Rev. 313 (1962); and Comment, *Validity of Proxy Marriages*, 25 S. Cal. L. Rev. 181 (1952). *See also* M. L. Cross, Annotation, *Proxy Marriages*, 170 A.L.R. 947 (1947). The following case, however, illustrates its possible application.

TORRES v. TORRES
New Jersey Superior Court, Chancery Division
366 A.2d 713 (1976)

HECKMAN, J.S.C.

The matter comes before the court on plaintiff's motion for summary judgment to annul a marriage contracted by proxy in Cuba. The material facts are not in dispute and lend themselves to resolution by summary judgment. Plaintiff, a Cuban national at the time of the marriage, had known defendant in Cuba for some time before escaping to the United States on May 8, 1967. Defendant, also a Cuban national, remained domiciled in Cuba, and plaintiff took up residence in New Jersey. Plaintiff states by way of affidavit that he sent his proxy to Cuba on October 28, 1967, where a ceremony of marriage took place. A copy of the Cuban certificate of marriage was produced by defendant. The authenticity of the certificate is not in issue. Some months after the marriage defendant came to the United States to live with plaintiff. A child was born to the couple on April 7, 1969. The parties resided together in New Jersey until January 1975.

The sole issue presented is whether a proxy marriage will be recognized by the State of New Jersey. Research has failed to disclose any precedent in this State, although the issue has been raised in other trial courts of this State.

Plaintiff in his trial brief relies upon *Lopez v. Lopez*, 102 N.J. Super. 253 (N.J. Super Ct. Ch. Div. 1968), which involved a plaintiff-husband who was a resident of New Jersey and a defendant-wife who was a resident of Cuba. These people were purportedly married by proxy on or about May 4, 1966. The entire problem arose as a result of defendant's repeated refusal to join her husband in New Jersey. The court found as a fact that the wife fraudulently induced plaintiff to enter into the proxy marriage, never intending to reside in New Jersey with her husband. *Lopez, supra*, at 257. The court therein, by way of *obiter dictum*, declared all proxy marriages subject to annulment on the ground that they failed to comply with the statutory requirement of solemnization,. The court utilized the definition of "solemnization" as found in *Respole v. Respole*, 70 N.E.2d 465, 170 A.L.R. 942 (Ohio C.P. 1946): Solemnization of marriage, or the celebration of the marriage ceremony or rites comprehends a personal appearance together by the contracting parties before one authorized by law to celebrate marriage ceremonies, and that the marriage ceremonies or rites be entered into and performed by the parties to such marriage together with the minister or other person authorized to perform such in the presence of each other and one or more witnesses, in order that the fact of the marriage contract may have due publication for the sake of notoriety and the certainty of its being made.

This interpretation of the word "solemnization" need not be accepted by the State of New Jersey. Justice Pashman, in *Parkinson v. J & S Tool Co.*, 64 N.J. 159 (N.J. 1974), dealing with a *de facto* spouse claiming under workmen's compensation dependent status, spoke of the intent of N.J.S.A. 37:1-10. The purpose of the statute was to invalidate common law marriages and any other marriage in which there was a lack of legal process and lack of commitment. The intent of the statute is to prevent illegitimate common law unions which are marked by this lack of commitment and which union may dissolve at any moment. The uncertainty as to economic support and dependency are the primary concerns of the State.

The interest of the State, as evidenced by this statute, is not diminished by recognizing a proxy marriage. The marriage in this case occurred on October 28, 1967, in a country recognizing such ceremonies of marriage. Plaintiff husband complied with the necessary legal processes of the Cuban statute in that he specifically named a person to stand in his stead in Cuba, by executing a special power of attorney. The marriage was recorded by the proper authorities in Havana, Cuba, and a certificate of marriage was issued by the Register of Vital Statistics of Havana, Cuba. The requirement of New Jersey that there be a recognition of legal process has thus been met by the parties.

The only other requirement of the statute is that there be a showing of commitment. This requirement is evidenced by the facts in this case. Plaintiff husband went to great lengths to become married, a certificate of marriage was issued, defendant came to the United States, the couple used the same surname, they lived together as man and wife in the same house for seven years, and a child was born to them. In the eyes of the public, these people constituted a family unit.

The requirement of solemnization can thus be met by both a showing of legal process and a showing of commitment. I find no reason in the law to justify the conclusion that all proxy marriages are void. *Lopez, supra,* by *obiter dictum* declared proxy marriages to be void, but the decision is based on an alternative ground—fraud.

There is nothing in the facts at bar nor in New Jersey law so strongly indicative of any inflexible and unyielding conviction as to warrant setting aside this marriage.

In addition, I find plaintiff husband barred by the doctrines of collateral estoppel and unclean hands from attacking the marriage of which he was the prime beneficiary and primarily responsible for its creation. *Dacunzo v. Edgye*, 19 N.J. 443 (N.J. 1955); *Hansen v. Fredo*, 123 N.J. Super. 388 (N.J. Super. Ct. Ch. Div. 1973).

Thus, to effect equity and justice and in good conscience, I must deny plaintiff's motion.

NOTES AND QUESTIONS

(1) As noted in *Torres*, some courts construe state marriage statutes to require both parties to be present in person, either at the time the marriage license is obtained or at the time of the ceremony. *See, e.g., Respole v. Respole*, 34 Ohio Ops. 1, 70 N.E.2d 465 (Ohio C.P. 1946) (applying W. Va. law). *But see Hardin v. Davis,* 30 Ohio Ops. 524, 16 Ohio Supp. 19 (Ohio C.P. 1945) (stating that although Ohio law does not authorize a marriage by proxy due to Ohio statutory requirements of personal presence of the parties at the ceremony, Ohio courts will nevertheless recognize proxy marriages when performed in a state where such marriages are valid). How did the *Torres* court, *above* address this problem?

Many states have not dealt with this issue, and as Professor Clark points out, "There is remarkably little case authority on the validity of proxy marriages contracted in American states." 1 Homer H. Clark, Jr., Law of Domestic Relations 124–27 (2d ed. 1987). Recent judicial recognition of proxy marriages contracted in various American states, however, seems to be on the rise. *See, e.g., Blankenship v. Blankenship*, 133 B.R. 398 (N. D. Ohio 1991); *Landrum v. Gomez*, 37 F.3d 1505 (9th Cir. 1994) (applying Cal. law). What is the underlying public policy reason for the recognition of proxy marriages? What is the argument against recognizing a marriage by proxy?

(2) Proxy marriages in America and Europe have been utilized most often in time of war, primarily to legitimize children and to provide the civilian spouse with military allotments, insurance, and death benefits. *See* Comment, *Validity of Proxy Marriages*, 25 S. Cal. L. Rev. 181, 183 (1952); Howery, *Marriage by Proxy and Other Informal Marriages*, 13 UMKC L. Rev. 48, 54 (1944).

(3) **Problem.** Lieutenant William Barrons, subsequent to his departure overseas in April of 1944, learned that his girlfriend June was pregnant and took immediate steps to do all within his power to rectify the situation by contacting the Red Cross to perform a proxy marriage.

William and June were domiciliaries of Texas and California, but their marriage by proxy was celebrated on July 20, 1944, in Reno, Nevada, because the parties were under a mistaken belief that Nevada recognized such marriages. A Red Cross official acted as the "stand-in" for William at the marriage ceremony, and Nevada marriage statutes were otherwise complied with. (Nevada had abolished common law marriage in 1943.)

A week later, on July 27, 1944, Lieutenant Barrons was killed in action. His brother and June were now contesting the right to his National Service Life Insurance Policy, and June can only qualify if she is the legal widow of William, but Nevada has no case law on marriages by proxy. Section 4054 of the Nevada statutes provided in part that: "The parties shall declare, in the presence of the judge, minister, or magistrate, and the attending witnesses, that they take each other as husband and wife."

Was this a valid proxy marriage? Why or why not? *See Barrons v. United States*, 191 F.2d 92 (9th Cir. 1951) (purportedly applying Texas, California, Nevada, West Virginia, and District of Columbia law.)

(4) Section 206(b) of the Uniform Marriage and Divorce Act recognizes proxy marriage, providing in part:

> If a party to a marriage is unable to be present at the solemnization, he [or she] may authorize in writing a third person to act as his [or her] proxy. If the person solemnizing the marriage is satisfied that the absent party is unable to be present and has consented to the marriage, he [or she] may solemnize the marriage by proxy.

[D] "Marriage" by Estoppel

A so-called marriage by estoppel or marriage by quasi-estoppel is most frequently found when a husband or wife has obtained an invalid divorce from a prior spouse, and then remarries. Since the prior divorce is legally invalid, so is the second bigamous marriage. But if the parties knew about, or had participated in, the invalid prior divorce and invalid second marriage, then they may be estopped by their conduct from questioning the legal validity of this second marriage. Thus, they are still "married" under estoppel principles, even though they are not legally married. *See generally* Clark, *Estoppel Against Jurisdictional Attack on Decrees of Divorce*, 70 Yale L.J. 45 (1960); Phillips, *Equitable Preclusion of Jurisdictional Attacks on Void Divorces*, 37 Fordham L. Rev. 355 (1969); and Rosenberg, *How Void is a Void Decree, or the Estoppel Effect of Invalid Divorce Decrees*, 8 Fam. L.Q. 207 (1974). *See also* Gregory G. Sarno, Annotation, *Estoppel or Laches Precluding Lawful Spouse From Asserting Rights in Decedent's Estate as Against Putative Spouse*, 81 A.L.R.3d 110 (1977). The following case demonstrates this principle of a "marriage" by estoppel.

IN RE MARRIAGE OF RECKNOR
California Court of Appeal
138 Cal. App. 3d 539 (1982)

DANIELSON, J.

Ralph W. Recknor has appealed from an order that he pay Eve Lynn Recknor spousal support pendente lite and pay her attorney fees.

FACTS

Eve Lynn Recknor was formerly married to Gerard Cautero. On May 4, 1965, a complaint for divorce was filed in Los Angeles by Eve Lynn Cautero against Gerard Cautero, on the ground of extreme cruelty.

Eve and Ralph Recknor were married on May 19, 1965.

On October 4, 1965, an interlocutory judgment was entered in the Cautero divorce action.

On July 6, 1966, the Cautero divorce became final.

On November 26, 1980, Eve Lynn petitioned for dissolution of her marriage to Ralph W. Recknor. She requested custody of their two children, child support, spousal support, and attorney fees.

On March 30, 1981, Ralph filed an "amended response" and requested dissolution on the ground of irreconcilable differences and a declaration of nullity of the marriage. The nullity was requested on the ground that the marriage was void because on the date of marriage, neither the interlocutory nor the final decree had been entered dissolving Eve's prior marriage, and on the ground that the marriage was voidable because of a prior existing marriage.

On April 2, 1981, a hearing was held on the issues of spousal support and attorney fees. The evidence was in conflict as to whether Ralph knew of Eve's preexisting marriage before their wedding.

Ralph testified at the hearing that he had gone through a formal wedding ceremony with Eve on May 19, 1965, but that he had not known about the prior marriage before he and Eve got married. He said that he found out from a third party, about a year after the wedding. He admitted, however, that after he found out that Eve's prior marriage had not been dissolved, he continued to live with Eve and fathered another child.

Eve testified that he did know about the prior marriage, as follows:

THE WITNESS: Number One, I was pregnant. I told [Ralph] that I was married, and I said—well, he wanted to go through with a marriage ceremony.

THE COURT: How did he know you were married?

THE WITNESS: Because I told him that I was married; and when he said, "I want to have a marriage ceremony before the baby was born," I said, "I don't want to go through the ceremony, because it is not legal. It doesn't mean anything. I am married." He said, "I will feel better if you do." I said, "It doesn't mean anything. I don't want to do it." He said, "Just do it, because it will make me feel better."

Q. BY MR. ESENSTEN [attorney for Eve]: In relationship to the date of marriage of May, 1965, when did that conversation take place?

A. The conversation about the marriage ceremony?

Q. Yes.

A. Well, I am sure it took place a couple of months prior to that, because we went back and forth on it, and I kept saying, I didn't want to do it.

At the time of the wedding ceremony, Eve and Ralph had been living together for about six months. When she had discovered that she was pregnant, Ralph had had a marriage announcement printed, dated January 1 or 2, 1965.

However, Eve also testified that she knew that the marriage to Ralph was not valid. . . .

DISCUSSION

It is contended by appellant that Civil Code §§ 4455 and 4456 [repealed and reenacted in 1994 as California Family Code §§ 2254 and 2255] preclude the award of support and attorney fees to Eve on an estoppel theory, because she admitted that she knew that she was not free to marry. We agree that Eve is not a "putative spouse," but we find that she can properly receive support and attorney fees, as in an ordinary dissolution proceeding, because Ralph was estopped to deny the validity of their marriage. . . .

The status of "putative spouse" requires innocence or good faith belief. "An innocent participant who has duly solemnized a matrimonial union which is void because of some legal infirmity acquires the status of putative spouse." (*Estate of Vargas*, 36 Cal.App.3d 714, 717, 111 Cal.Rptr. 779, 81 A.L.R.3d 1 (Cal. Ct. App. 1974).)

A finding that one or both parties to a void or voidable marriage entered the marriage in good faith may be deemed to be implied by the trial court's judgment. (*See In re Marriage of Trantafello*, 94 Cal.App.3d 533, 539-540, 156 Cal.Rptr. 556 (Cal. Ct. App. 1979).) However, there could be no such finding of good faith in this case, conferring the status of putative spouse, because Eve knew that her final judgment of divorce had not been entered, and of its effect. Thus, Eve could not receive support under §§ 4455 or 4456.

However, the award may be upheld on the independent, equitable ground of estoppel.

In *Spellens v. Spellens, supra*, 49 Cal.2d 210, 222 (Cal. 1957) the court expressly rejected the "putative spouse" doctrine as the basis for its holding and used instead the theory of equitable estoppel to uphold an award of temporary support. The court held that when the husband is estopped to deny the validity of the marriage, the wife need not also obtain status as a putative spouse.

In *Spellens v. Spellens*, the facts were as follows: While Annelen was unhappily married to Robert, Sol Spellens said that he wanted to marry her and promised to take care of her if she would. Annelen finally decided to marry Sol, and she sought a divorce from Robert. After the interlocutory judgment, but before the final judgment, she married Sol in Mexico, on Sol's representation that the marriage would be valid. About a year later, Sol left, saying that the marriage was not valid. Annelen filed an action to have the marriage declared valid, asking that Sol be estopped to question its validity, or that she be awarded damages for fraud, and that she be declared a putative spouse. Sol asserted that their marriage was void. (*Id.*, at pp. 213-216.)

The trial court found that the marriage was invalid and that no estoppel could exist, but that Annelen was Sol's putative spouse. (*Id.*, at p. 216.) Annelen sought support and attorney fees pendente lite, but they were denied because no marriage had existed. (*Id.*, at p. 217.)

In *Spellens*, our Supreme Court reviewed the case law on estoppel in marital cases. The court noted that estoppel to deny the validity of a divorce decree exists where the party denying validity procured the decree, or remarried in reliance on the decree, or aided the other party in procuring the decree so that the latter would be free to marry. (*Id.*, at pp. 217-218, citing *Rediker v. Rediker*, 35 Cal.2d 796, 805, 220 P.2d 1, 20 A.L.R.2d 1152 (Cal. 1950).). . . .

After reviewing the case law, the *Spellens* court expressly held that the same policy which prevents a spouse from denying the validity of a prior foreign divorce decree also prevents denial of the validity of the second marriage. (*Id.*, at p. 220.)

The court said the following: "It is not the marriage which is found valid. . . and thus the policy [against bigamous marriages] is not thwarted. Rather it is that defendant by reason of his conduct will not be permitted to question its validity or the divorce; so far as he is concerned, he and plaintiff are husband and wife." (*Id.*, at pp. 220-221.)

The court held that because the husband could not deny the validity of the marriage, the wife was entitled to attorney fees, costs and support during trial, as if she had been validly married. (*Id.*, at p. 222.)

A distinction between the present case and *Spellens* is that in this case, Eve did not believe that her marriage ceremony to Ralph was valid, because she knew that she did not have a final divorce from her prior husband. (*Id.*, at p. 226.)

The question remains whether the doctrine of estoppel applies, nevertheless, to the present case, to prevent Ralph from denying the validity of this marriage.

As the court said in *Estate of Vargas*, supra, 36 Cal.App.3d 714, 718 (Cal. Ct. App. 1974) " 'Equity or chancery law has its origin in the necessity for exceptions to the application of rules of law in those cases where the law, by reason of its universality, would create injustice in the affairs of men.' [Citations.] Equity acts 'in order to meet the requirements of every case, and to satisfy the needs of progressive social condition, in which new primary rights and duties are constantly arising, and new kinds of wrongs are constantly committed.' [Citation.] Equity need not wait upon precedent 'but will assert itself in those situations where right and justice would be defeated but for its intervention.' "

Thus, we need not confine the doctrine of estoppel to the precise facts found in the *Spellens* case. The present case cries out for application of that equitable doctrine.

The doctrine has been stated as follows:

> Whenever a party has, by his own statement or conduct, intentionally and deliberately led another to believe a particular thing true and to act upon such belief, he is not, in any litigation arising out of such statement or conduct, permitted to contradict it.

(Ev. Code, § 623.)

The elements of estoppel are representation or promise; made with knowledge of the facts; to a party ignorant of the truth; with the intent that the other party act on it; when the other party has, in fact been induced to rely on it. (*See Seymour v. Oelrichs*, 156 Cal. 782, 795, 122 P. 847 (Cal. 1909); 7 Witkin, Summary of Cal. Law (8th ed. 1974) Equity, § 132.)

Estoppel applies to prevent a person from asserting a right where his conduct or silence makes it unconscionable for him to assert it. (*See Brown v. Brown*, 274 Cal.App.2d 178, 188, 82 Cal.Rptr. 238 (Cal. Ct. App. 1969).)

In this case, Ralph was properly estopped to deny that he was validly married to Eve. He went through a formal marriage ceremony with her, knowing that her divorce was not final, and continued to live with her as her husband for 15 years, during which time they had two children. Further, Ralph waited almost 15 years to attempt to assert the invalidity of his marriage to Eve. . . .

Appellant's contention that a valid marriage must exist to support an award of support pendente lite under the statutes is not determinative, because we have found that Ralph is estopped to deny the validity of the marriage. . . . *The order is affirmed.*

NOTES AND QUESTIONS

(1) If you were legal counsel representing Eve in the *Recknor* case, *above*, how would you advise her regarding her legal status as Ralph's "wife"? Is she now "married"? Can either spouse bring a suit for divorce to terminate their "marriage"? Can Eve bring a suit to affirm their "marriage"? Must Eve and Ralph now file separate tax returns, in the absence of a recognized filing status such as "unmarried filing jointly"? How will they determine their future property and support rights? These troubling problems are just some of complications resulting from a so-called "marriage" by estoppel.

(2) Application of the doctrine of equitable estoppel in family law is a way to validate the parties' marital expectations in the contested "marriage." It is based upon a personal disability of the party attacking the void divorce decree and the subsequent invalid remarriage under the theory that one who has taken a prior position regarding a divorce and subsequent marriage, and who has obtained a benefit from it, cannot later take an inconsistent position which would prejudice the other party.

This family law estoppel or quasi-estoppel doctrine is broader than a traditional estoppel theory in that one party does not necessarily have to rely to his or her detriment upon factual representations made by the other party. It is sufficient, in some cases, that a court find only that it would be unfair to let a party take advantage of the legal invalidity of the divorce decree and the invalidity of the subsequent remarriage. *See* Clark, *Estoppel Against Jurisdictional Attack on Decrees of Divorce,* 70 Yale L.J. 45, 46–49 (1960); and Rosenberg, *How Void is a Void Decree, or the Estoppel Effect of Invalid Divorce Decrees,* 8 Fam. L.Q. 207, 208–09 (1974).

(3) There are three different rules regarding the validity or invalidity of a "marriage" by estoppel—especially when it involves a void migratory divorce— in which the parties improperly attempted to exploit the more liberal divorce laws of another state. *See* Swisher, *Foreign Migratory Divorces: A Reappraisal,* 21 J. Fam. L. 9, 37–48 (1982-83). The courts are often split as to which rule should govern, even within the same jurisdiction.

(i) Under a "traditional" rule, the domiciliary state and the parties are not bound by any estoppel defense in collaterally attacking a void divorce and subsequent "remarriage." The rationale behind this rule is that estoppel, even for a limited purpose, results in the recognition of a void divorce granted by a court lacking any jurisdiction whatever, and therefore violates the domiciliary state's strong public policy. *See, e.g., Ainscow v. Alexander,* 39 A.2d 54 (Del. Super. Ct. 1944); *Everett v. Everett,* 345 So. 2d 586 (La. Ct. App. 1977); *In Re Estate of Steffke,* 222 N.W.2d 628 (Wis. 1974); *Prudential Ins. Co. v. Lewis,* 306 F. Supp. 1177 (N.D. Ala. 1969).

(ii) Under the "sociological" rule affecting a "marriage" by estoppel with an invalid prior divorce and remarriage, a court will attempt to validate the parties' "real" expectations of divorce and remarriage, rather than relying on a purely theoretical and perhaps "unreal" legal basis. *See* Clark, *above*, 70 Yale L.J. 45, 56–57 (1960). Thus, the Second Restatement of Conflict of Laws § 74 (1971), largely influenced by Professor Clark's article, states the general rule that: "A person may be precluded from attacking the validity of a foreign divorce decree if, under the circumstances, it would be inequitable for him [or her] to do so." Although this "sociological" rule appears to be the law in a growing number of American jurisdictions, it has been criticized by Professor Phillips for resulting in "uncertainty and ambiguity as to a person's marital status and his capacity to marry. Then, too, estoppel can prevent a valid dissolution of a prior dead marriage and, consequently, the regularization of a bigamous marriage that has been attempted." Phillips, *Equitable Preclusion of Jurisdictional Attacks on Void Divorces*, 37 Fordham L. Rev. 355, 365–66 (1969).

(iii) A third rule of "marriage" by estoppel resulting from an invalid prior divorce is called the "status-versus-property-right" rule. If the action deals with marital *status*, including actions to declare the nullity of a void marriage, separation, or divorce, then estoppel is deemed to be inappropriate. But if the action deals with a *property right*, such as taking against a deceased spouse's will, or enforcing an alleged right to support, then estoppel may apply. *See, e.g., Caldwell v. Caldwell*, 298 N.Y. 146, 81 N.E.2d 60 (N.Y. 1948); *Rabourn v. Rabourn*, 385 P.2d 581 (Alaska. 1963); *Brown v. Brown*, 274 Cal. App. 2d 178 (Cal. App. Ct. 1969); *Romanski's Estate*, 47 A.2d 233 (Pa. 1946).

On the other hand, the Michigan Court of Appeals in *Harris v. Harris*, 506 N. W.2d 3, 5 (Mich. Ct. App. 1993) refused to apply the doctrine of equitable estoppel to preclude annulment of a bigamous marriage when both parties knew of the marriage's invalidity:

> We appreciate the circuit court's concern regarding granting relief when both parties are alleged to have known at the outset that the marriage was bigamous and therefore both did not have clean hands. While we find no case in Michigan discussing this precise point, other jurisdictions are apparently split on the resolution of the issue. Although equitable concerns may come into play where a marriage is merely "voidable," [a number of] courts appear to hold that equitable principles of estoppel and clean hands do not prevent a party to a void marriage [such as a bigamous marriage] from seeking and obtaining an annulment in court. . . .[R]efusing to grant an annulment would contravene [Michigan] public policy because it could be construed as essentially condoning bigamy.

Which estoppel "rule" is most persuasive to you? Why? *See also* Swisher, *Foreign Migratory Divorces: A Reappraisal*, 21 J. Fam. L. 9, 37–48 (1982-83).

(4) Whichever estoppel rule a specific court utilizes, "the application of the principles of equitable estoppel cannot be subjected to fixed and settled rules of universal application, but rests largely on the facts and circumstances of each particular case." *Weber v. Weber*, 200 Neb. 659, 265 N.W.2d 436, 441 (Neb. 1978).

(5) If a husband and wife may be estopped from collaterally attacking a void migratory divorce and a subsequent "marriage," should the State also be estopped? *Compare* Ehrenzweig, Conflict of Laws 253 (1963), and Goodrich, Handbook of the Conflict of Laws, 259 (4th ed. 1964) *with* Von Mehren, *The Validity of Foreign Divorces*, 45 Mass. L.Q. 23, 29 (1960) *and* Currie, *Suitcase Divorce in the Conflict of Laws*, 34 U. Chi. L. Rev. 26, 54–55 (1966).

(6) Unfortunately, the existing literature regarding the concept of "marriage" by estoppel is relatively dated, and a new empirical study of the current effects of "marriage" by estoppel on contemporary American society would be welcome.

§ 1.05 The Last-in-Time Marriage Presumption

The typical scenario for a last-in-time marriage presumption is not as uncommon as one might suppose: A husband [or wife] has unexpectedly died, and the bereaved surviving spouse is in the process of bringing a legal proceeding, which might include a wrongful death action; a suit for social security, workers' compensation, or other insurance benefits; an action to recover for loss of consortium; or an intestate succession action. During the pendency of this litigation, however, a former wife turns up, claiming that she has never been divorced from the deceased husband, and that she, rather than the subsequent wife, should recover any proceeds from her husband's death. Which wife should prevail?

To a lay person, and to many lawyers, the conclusion might be that since American law generally prohibits bigamy and other plural marriages (*see* § 1.07[C] *below*), the first-in-time wife should recover all the proceeds. But this conclusion would be erroneous. The last-in-time marriage presumption is based upon "one of the strongest presumptions of law"—that an existing marriage, once shown, is valid. *See, e.g., Hewitt v. Firestone Tire & Rubber Co*, 490 F. Supp. 1358 (E.D. Va, 1980), *below*. A subsequent marriage therefore raises a very strong, but rebuttable, presumption that the earlier marriage was terminated by death, divorce, or annulment, and the *former* spouse therefore has the burden of proving that there was in fact no death, divorce, or annulment. Normally this means that the former spouse, in order to rebut the last-in-time marriage presumption, must make a search of the divorce records where the deceased spouse resided, or where the deceased spouse *might* reasonably have resided, and show that there was no divorce in those jurisdictions. If the former spouse fails to rebut the last-in-time marriage presumption, the subsequent spouse will prevail. *See generally* J.E. Keefe, Jr., Annotation, *Presumption as to Validity of Second Marriage*, 14 A.L.R.2d 7 (1950) and Later Case Service; and Swisher & Jones, *The Last-in-Time Marriage Presumption*, 29 Fam. L. Q. 409 (1995).

The following case illustrates these problems of proof.

HEWITT v. FIRESTONE TIRE & RUBBER CO.
United States District Court
490 F. Supp. 1358 (E.D. Va.1980)

WARRINER, District Judge.

This diversity action is before the Court for approval of a settlement pursuant to Virginia's Death by Wrongful Act statute, Va. Code § 8.01-55. Two questions are raised. The first requires the Court to determine which of two claimants is the decedent's surviving spouse. The second, which in part is dependent upon the first, requires the Court to determine whether the amount of the settlement is fair and just and, if so, how the settlement funds should be distributed and apportioned among the several beneficiaries.

I.

On 14 June 1966 John Carthel Hewitt, a twenty-year-old soldier in the United States Army, married Barbara Anne Cullum, also twenty, in Texas. John and Barbara resided together as husband and wife through December, 1966, but thereafter were separated when John was confined in a penitentiary....

Upon his release from prison in December, 1967, John was sent to South Vietnam by the Army. He returned to the United States on thirty days' leave in March of 1968, and spent that leave with his wife in Paris, Texas. During this time John and Barbara's first child was conceived; John Carthel Hewitt, Jr., was born on 27 November 1968.

John returned to South Vietnam in April, 1968, and remained there until a new duty assignment in January, 1969, brought him stateside. John and Barbara lived together in Aberdeen, Maryland, from March, 1969, until August, 1969, when they returned to Texas. The couple stayed in Texas until September, 1969, when John suddenly deserted his wife and family. When John left Barbara she was several months pregnant with their second child, Larry Dwayne Hewitt, who subsequently was born on 3 March 1970.

Barbara next heard from John in December, 1969, when he telephoned from an unspecified location. In this conversation John stated that he cared for Barbara but that he would not return home. John further told Barbara, falsely, that financial support would be forthcoming. Neither Barbara Hewitt nor any of her children ever received financial support, emotional support, or any other form of support from John after September, 1969.

The last time Barbara talked to John was in August of 1973 when she called him about a divorce. [Footnote omitted.] ... In the course of the telephone call, John, according to Barbara, assented to a divorce. John allegedly told Barbara to have a lawyer "draw up the papers" and send them to him. He said he would then "sign the papers" and return them to the lawyer with his fee. Barbara stated that she saw a lawyer, that the lawyer drafted pleadings and mailed them to John, but that John never returned either the papers or the fee. Barbara could not recall the name or location of the office of the attorney she purportedly visited.

In October, 1969, John had met Nancy Anne Threatt. She was single, twenty-four years old, living and working in Aberdeen, Maryland. On 26 December, 1969, after a brief courtship, John and Nancy were married in Fayetteville, North Carolina, at the home of Nancy's parents. Nancy and her parents were aware of John's previous marriage and of his child, John, Jr. John represented to Nancy and her family, however, that his first marriage had ended in divorce. Nancy Threatt married John in good faith, unaware of any legal impediment that prohibited John from entering a second marriage.....

John and Nancy lived together continuously from the time of their marriage until John's death some eight years later. They lived first in Aberdeen, Maryland, and then in Hopewell, Virginia. They had three children. Ronald Wayne Hewitt was born sometime in 1972, William David Hewitt in July, 1973. A third child died of accidental drowning. Although the first years of the marriage were trying, in time the relationship grew secure and John proved to be an attentive, faithful, and devoted husband and father. He provided well for his family out of his earnings as an over-the-road truck driver.

On 17 November 1977, John Carthel Hewitt was killed when his tractor-trailer truck left the road and overturned near Woodbridge, Virginia, in Prince William County. At the time of his death John Hewitt was thirty-one years of age, in good health, and gainfully employed as a truck driver by Great Coastal Transport Corporation, a trucking concern located in Richmond, Virginia.

Barbara learned of John's death and immediately, within a month, filed an application for social security benefits as his widow. Cognizant of John Hewitt's later marriage to Nancy, the Social Security Administration sought information as to the existence of a decree of divorce dissolving the marriage of John and Barbara Hewitt. No decree was located. On this basis, the Administration awarded widow's, as well as surviving children's benefits, to Barbara Hewitt and her family. She currently receives $823.00 per month in social security benefits.

In March, 1979, suit for damages for the wrongful death of John Carthel Hewitt was commenced in this Court. The complaint was filed by Nancy Anne Hewitt and Jerome L. Lonnes as co-administrators of the Estate of John Carthel Hewitt. After extensive discovery and negotiations the parties reached a settlement. Pursuant to Virginia statute, the parties tendered the terms of the settlement to the Court for its approval. Va. Code § 8.01-55. By its terms, the defendant Firestone Tire and Rubber Company, while denying liability, agreed to pay $400,000 to the administrators for a release of all claims against Firestone arising from John's death.

After reaching and submitting the settlement to the Court, counsel for the co-administrators learned and informed the Court about John's earlier marriage to Barbara and of his children by that marriage. Thus advised that there might be conflicting claimants to the settlement proceeds, the Court appointed guardians ad litem for the two sets of children, ordered notice by publication, and set the matter for an evidentiary hearing to determine the rightful beneficiaries, the propriety of the settlement, and the fair distribution of the funds. The $400,000 previously placed in the registry of the Court was deposited into an interest-bearing account.

A hearing was held on 31 March 1980. All parties were represented by counsel except Nancy Hewitt in her individual capacity. All parties, including Nancy, sought approval of the $400,000 settlement notwithstanding the existence of the additional claimants not contemplated when the settlement was reached. The parties also sought a judicial determination of the rightful beneficiaries and how the settlement funds should be distributed.

II.

Virginia's Death by Wrongful Act statute, a direct descendant of Lord Campbell's Act, provides that damages shall be distributed to "the surviving spouse . . . [and] children of the deceased . . ." Va. Code § 8.01-53. This statute serves also as a guide for a court disbursing funds after a claim for death by wrongful act is compromised. Va. Code § 8.01-55. The classes of beneficiaries named in the statute are exclusive; a court is not at liberty to consider additional or alternative beneficiaries.

In the case at bar two women, Barbara Hewitt and Nancy Hewitt, claim to be the surviving spouse of John Carthel Hewitt. Both cannot be. *See Reynolds v. United States*, 98 U.S. 145 (1878); Va. Code § 20-38.1. Accordingly, the Court must determine which of the two claimants is the surviving spouse and rightful beneficiary.

In Virginia, as in most jurisdictions, a presumption exists that a marriage last-in-time is valid, and that any prior marriage was terminated by death or divorce. . . . This presumption is strong but rebuttable. While the party challenging the legality of the second union need not "make plenary proof of a negative averment," he must, in order to shift the burden, introduce such evidence as, in the absence of all counter testimony, will afford reasonable grounds for presuming that the former marriage was not dissolved. *De Ryder v. Metropolitan Life Ins. Co.*, 206 Va. 602, 607-608, 145 S.E.2d 177, 181 (Va. 1965); *Parker v. American Lumber Corp.*, 190 Va. 181, 186, 56 S.E.2d 214, 216 (Va. 1949). . . .

In an effort to rebut the presumption favoring the validity of John Hewitt's second marriage, Barbara Hewitt makes two factual arguments. Barbara states, first, that she talked to John about a divorce in 1973—four years after his marriage to Nancy. Barbara asserts that during a telephone conversation John assented to a divorce, and instructed Barbara to have a lawyer "draw up the papers" and forward them to him. Barbara has testified that in fact she saw a lawyer and that the lawyer drafted divorce papers and mailed them to John. The implication is that John, by agreeing to a divorce, recognized that he was still married to Barbara—and thus that his second marriage was bigamous and void.

The Court acknowledges that recognition of a continuing marriage by both parties thereto, subsequent to a second marriage by one of the parties, may amount to evidence sufficient to overcome the presumption that the first marriage was terminated. *E.g.*, *Jones v. Case*, 266 Ala. 498, 97 So. 2d 816 (Ala. 1957); *Travelers Ins. Co. v. Lester*, 73 Ga.App. 465, 36 S.E.2d 880 (Ga. Ct. App. 1946) [or evidence of a divorce between the parties obtained after a second marriage by one of those parties]. . . . Indeed, if the Court had evidence which would lend credibility to Barbara's testimony about the 1973 phone call, the Court might conclude that the presumption had been rebutted and the burden transferred. But no evidence is before the Court which corroborates Barbara's claim. . . .Barbara testified that she saw a lawyer about a divorce, and that he prepared divorce papers. Barbara, however, is unable to remember the lawyer's name, or the location of his office. . . . She did not produce the papers or copies of them. She had not recontacted the lawyer for his corroborative evidence. The Court cannot be persuaded by the uncorroborated, though easily corroborated, testimony of interested witnesses who make claims that are practically incapable of contradiction.

The second point made by Barbara to rebut the presumption of the validity of the second marriage is that John *could not* have obtained a divorce during the three months that lapsed from September, 1969, when he left Barbara, to December, 1969, when he married Nancy. This claim cannot be supported. Divorce laws existing in the fifty States in 1969 demonstrate that John could have obtained an *ex parte* divorce in at least six jurisdictions, including Texas. . . . The possibility of a foreign divorce, though not decisive here, also must be acknowledged. . . . Counsel for Barbara, however, in their efforts to rebut the presumption, have failed to come forward with any documentary evidence from any jurisdiction which establishes that no divorce decree was entered dissolving the marriage of John and Barbara Hewitt. [In a footnote, the Court acknowledged that Barbara testified that after John's death she filed for Social Security Benefits as John's widow, and it is uncontroverted that an investigation conducted by the Social Security Administration in parts of Texas, North Carolina, Maryland, and New Jersey failed to find any record of a divorce between John and Barbara Hewitt, and Barbara was named John Hewitt's widow and receives monthly benefits for his death. "For several reasons, the Court must discount arguments based on the documents of the Social Security Administration. First and foremost, the documents were not introduced and have not been admitted in evidence. . . . [I]t is plain to the Court that it would be unfair to consider the records now. Counsel for Nancy Hewitt has had no opportunity to challenge the documents. Moreover, even assuming the documents had been properly offered and admitted, the Court would regard them—with nothing more—as unpersuasive. None of the information contained in the records has been verified or authenticated. What is more, the records themselves do not indicate that those who conducted the search were qualified to conduct a competent search."]

Counsel for Barbara explain their failure to offer any documentary evidence of the absence of a divorce by arguing that a litigant seeking to overcome the presumption favoring the validity of the second marriage "is not put to the test of proving a negative." Counsel argue, further, that the presumption favoring the second marriage is "simply a rule of evidence" that may be rebutted by a showing of little more than the legality of the first marriage. Because this Court believes that the positions advanced by Barbara fundamentally misperceive the nature and strength of the presumption favoring the second marriage—as that presumption has been established by Virginia decisional law—as well as the nature and sufficiency of the evidence necessary to rebut that presumption, the Court will answer the arguments in some detail.

Virginia adopted the generally accepted rule that presumes the validity of the second marriage by the decision rendered for a unanimous court in *Parker v. American Lumber Corp.*, 190 Va. 181, 56 S.E.2d 214 (Va. 1949). The language used in *Parker* to define the presumption was quoted with approval by the Virginia Supreme Court twenty years later in *De Ryder v. Metropolitan Life Ins. Co.*, 206 Va. 602, 145 S.E.2d 177 (Va. 1965). In both opinions the Court quoted the same language to describe the strength and nature of the presumption: The presumption arising in favor of the validity of a second marriage is not a conclusive presumption, but a rebuttable presumption, and the one contending against the legality of the second marriage is not required to make plenary proof of a negative averment. It is enough that he introduce such evidence as, in the absence of all counter testimony, will afford reasonable grounds for presuming that the allegation is true, and when it is done the *onus probandi* will be thrown on his adversary. . . .[The presumptions supporting the validity of the second marriage arise "because the law presumes morality and legitimacy, not immorality and bastardy." *Parker v. American Lumber Corp.*, 190 Va. 181, 195, 56 S.E. 2d 214, 216 (Va. 1949). Another reason given for presuming the validity of the second marriage is that it is more equitable to require the party attacking the second marriage to prove its invalidity than to put the innocent party thereto to proof of the capacity of the other contracting party. *See Lampkin v. Travelers' Ins. Co.*, 11 Colo. App. 249, 52 P. 1040 (Colo. Ct. App. 1898).] . . .

The nature and the amount of evidence that will provide reasonable grounds for finding that the first marriage has not been dissolved will vary in each case. As a rule, however, the contesting party must attempt to document in every reasonable manner the absence of a divorce. In *Parker*, the first wife established a valid marriage, and testified that she had not divorced the deceased nor received notice of a divorce obtained by him. The Virginia Supreme Court was unpersuaded, observing that "[there] was no other attempt to prove there had been no divorce." *Parker v. American Lumber Corp.*, 190 Va. 181, 187, 56 S.E. 2d 214, 216 (Va. 1949). Similarly, in *De Ryder* the first wife by competent evidence proved that her former husband had not secured a divorce in several places where he lived: Orange County, New York, and Norfolk, Hampton, and Elizabeth City counties, Virginia. Nonetheless, the Court ruled that the first wife failed to rebut the presumption favoring the last marriage because the evidence did not show that divorce records were searched in other places where the deceased had resided, or could have resided. *DeRyder v. Metropolitan Life Ins.*, 206 Va. 602, 606-607, 145 S.E.2d 177, 182 (Va. 1965). . . .

The Court does not suggest that it is incumbent upon the party seeking to overcome the presumption of the validity of the second marriage to document the absence of a divorce dissolving the first marriage in every jurisdiction where a divorce could possibly have been obtained. Were such a rule recognized in this day of divorce-on-demand the presumption favoring the second marriage would not be rebuttable, but effectively irrebuttable. The Virginia litigant seeking to negate the existence of a divorce generally does have a burden, however, of showing that no divorce was entered in jurisdictions where the parties resided or where on any reasonable basis a decree might have been obtained.

In the case at bar, Barbara Hewitt, John Hewitt's first wife, has failed to introduce evidence that affords reasonable grounds for presuming that her marriage to John was not dissolved. Barbara's claim that John recognized his marriage to her subsequent to his marriage to Nancy is insufficiently substantiated. Barbara's contention that John could not have obtained a divorce during the three-month period between the time he left Barbara and married Nancy is erroneous. Barbara has introduced no documentary evidence that indicates the absence of a divorce between John and Barbara. . . . Not being successfully rebutted, the presumption of the validity of John Hewitt's second marriage must prevail. The Court finds, accordingly, that Nancy Anne Hewitt is John Hewitt's surviving spouse, and is thus a beneficiary pursuant to Virginia's Death by Wrongful Act statute, Va. Code § 8.01-53.

III. [The court went on to discuss distribution among the beneficiaries.]

NOTES AND QUESTIONS

(1) The *Hewitt* court, *supra*, followed the majority view in most states that the last-in-time marriage presumption "is one of the strongest presumptions known to the law." It also applies with equal force to valid common law marriages. *See, e.g., In Re Estate of Leonard* 207 N.W. 2d 166, 168 (Mich. Ct. App. 1973) (the presumption of the validity of a second marriage, even a common law marriage, predominates over the continuance of a prior marriage "because the law presumes morality of the parties, and also that parties to the marriage are not bigamists or their children bastards"). The *Hewitt* court also held with the majority of jurisdictions that in order to rebut this last-in-time marriage presumption, the prior spouse must come forward with documentary evidence that no annulment or divorce was entered in any jurisdiction where the parties (or either of them) resided, or where they *might* have reasonably resided. *See also In Re Estate of Lee*, 360 So. 2d 1111 (Fla. Dist. Ct. App. 1978); *Fishman v. Fishman*, 369 N.Y.S.2d 756 (N.Y. App. Div. 1975); *Compton v. Davis Oil Co.*, 607 F. Supp. 1221 (D. Wyo. 1985). However, if the prior wife does present evidence that no divorce proceedings were instituted in any jurisdiction where the husband might reasonably have pursued them, then the presumption would be properly rebutted. *See, e.g., Davis v. Davis*, 521 S.W.2d 603 (Tex. 1975). Two commentators argue that the last-in-time marriage presumption continues to serve an important legal and social function since its underlying public policy bases are premised on presuming the innocence

and morality of the parties, protecting the legitimacy of their offspring, validating the reasonable marital expectations of the subsequent spouses, and generally strengthening and stabilizing the social and moral standards of the community. *See generally* Swisher & Jones, *The Last-in-Time Marriage Presumption*, 29 Fam. L. Q. 409, 443 (1995).

Query: If the Social Security Administration could find no prior divorce records in *Hewitt*, why was the presumption NOT rebutted in that case?

(2) There is a minority view in some states that all a prior spouse has to do to rebut the last-in-time marriage presumption is offer evidence of a valid mariage, and then the burden of proof shifts to the subsequent spouse to demonstrate that there was a divorce. *See, e.g., Tatum v. Tatum*, 241 F.2d 401 (9th Cir. 1957) (purportedly applying California law); *Dibble v. Dibble* 100 N.E.2d 451 (Ohio Ct. App. 1950) (refusing to recognize the presumption); *Glover v. Glover*, 172 Ga. App. 278, 322 S.E. 2d 755 (Ga. App. Ct. 1984). But this minority rule has been criticized for its inequitable application to the innocent subsequent spouse and family. *See, e.g.* Taylor, *Repeal of the Presumption of the Validity of Subsequent Marriages: Another Irrational Step Toward Increasing the Welfare Rolls*, 21 Mercer L. Rev. 465 (1970) (criticizing a Georgia statute that restricts the applicability of the last-in-time marriage presumption).

(3) **Problem.** Curtis Martin, a Virginia resident, was killed in an automobile accident on June 14, 1986, in Nash County, North Carolina. He had a group life insurance policy written in Milford, Delaware, on February 28, 1986, with the Continental Casualty Company providing for the payment of the policy proceeds "to the surviving spouse of the decedent." However, three women made the claim that each was the surviving spouse of the decedent: Josephine Martin, Joyce Martin, and Sally Richardson. Consequently, the Continental Casualty Company filed an interpleader action pursuant to 28 U.S.C. § 1335 in federal district court to determine which of the three claimants was Curtis Martin's legal spouse and thus was entitled to his life insurance proceeds.

Sally Richardson, a Delaware resident, claimed to be the common law wife of Curtis Martin at the time of his death. However, neither Delaware nor Virginia recognize common law marriage if celebrated in that state. As evidence of such a "marriage" in North Carolina, Sally Richardson's attorney submitted a North Carolina traffic-accident report, which listed Curtis Martin and Sally Richardson as residing at the same address. (Richardson killed Curtis Martin and two minor children in the North Carolina automobile accident, and was subsequently convicted on three counts of felony death by motor vehicle.) Josephine Martin, a Virginia resident, also claimed to be the surviving spouse of Curtis Martin. She entered into a marriage ceremony with Curtis on December 23, 1969, in Richmond, Virginia; and the existence of that ceremony is documented by an appropriate marriage certificate. Finally, Joyce Martin, a Maryland resident, also filed a claim for the insurance proceeds, claiming to be the wife of the deceased. Joyce Martin also submitted a marriage certificate demonstrating that she and Curtis Martin participated in a marriage ceremony in South Carolina on April 21, 1984.

Josephine Martin argued that the 1984 marriage of Curtis and Joyce Martin was void *ab initio* because of its bigamous nature since Josephine's attorney had searched the divorce records in Virginia and South Carolina from 1970 to the time of Curtis Martin's death, and those searches revealed no divorce between Josephine and Curtis Martin in those states.

(a) Which state law should be applied in this case?

(b) Which wife should recover the insurance proceeds as the legal wife of Curtis Martin? *See Continental Casualty Co. v. Martin*, Civil Action No. 87-0206-R (E.D.Va. July 17, 1987).

§ 1.06 State Regulation of Marriage Versus an Individual's Constitutional Right to Marry

The United States Supreme Court case of *Maynard v. Hill* (*see* § 1.02, *above*) emphasized the state's strong interest in regulating marriage. More recent Supreme Court decisions, however, have tended to emphasize the importance of marriage to individuals, and have suggested that an individual's decision regarding marriage has important constitutional dimensions, as illustrated in the following case.

ZABLOCKI, MILWAUKEE COUNTY CLERK v. REDHAIL
United States Supreme Court
434 U. S. 374 (1978)

Mr. Justice Marshall delivered the opinion of the Court.

At issue in this case is the constitutionality of a Wisconsin statute, Wis. Stat. §§ 245.10(1), (4), (5) (1973), which provides that members of a certain class of Wisconsin residents may not marry, within the State or elsewhere, without first obtaining a court order granting permission to marry. The class is defined by the statute to include any "Wisconsin resident having minor issue not in his custody and which he is under obligation to support by any court order or judgment." The statute specifies that court permission cannot be granted unless the marriage applicant submits proof of compliance with the support obligation and, in addition, demonstrates that the children covered by the support order "are not then and are not likely thereafter to become public charges." . . .

I.

Appellee Redhail is a Wisconsin resident who, under the terms of § 245.10, is unable to enter into a lawful marriage in Wisconsin or elsewhere so long as he maintains his Wisconsin residency. The facts, according to the stipulation filed by the parties in the District Court, are as follows. In January, 1972, when appellee was a minor and a high school student, a paternity action was instituted against him in Milwaukee County Court, alleging that he was the father of a baby girl born out of wedlock on July 5, 1971. After he appeared and admitted that he was the child's father, the court entered an order on May 12, 1972 adjudging appellee the father and ordering him to pay $109.00 per month as support for the child until she reached 18 years of age. From May 1972 until August 1974 appellee was unemployed and indigent and unable to make any support payments.

On September 27, 1974, appellee filed an application for a marriage license with appellant Zablocki, and a few days later the application was denied on the sole ground that the appellee had not obtained a court order granting him permission to marry, as required by § 245.10. Although appellee did not petition a state court thereafter, it is stipulated that he would not have been able to satisfy either of the statutory prerequisites for an order granting permission to marry. First, he had not satisfied his support obligations to his illegitimate child, and as of December 1974 there was an arrearage in excess of $3,700. Second, the child had been a public charge since her birth, receiving benefits under the Aid to Families with Dependent Children program. It is stipulated that the child's benefit payments were such that she would have been a public charge even if appellee had been current in his support payments.

II.

In evaluating §§ 245.10 (1), (4), (5) under the Equal Protection Clause, "we must first determine what burden of justification the classification created thereby must meet, by looking to the nature of the classification and the individual interests affected." *Memorial Hosp. v. Maricopa County*, 415 U.S. 250, 253 (1974). Since our past decisions make clear that the right to marry is of fundamental importance, and since the classification at issue here significantly interferes with the exercise of that right, we believe that "critical examination" of the state interests advanced in support of the classification is required. . . .

The leading decision of this court on the right to marry is *Loving v. Virginia*, 388 U.S. 1 (1967). In that case, an interracial couple who had been convicted of violating Virginia's miscegenation laws challenged the statutory scheme on both equal protection and due process grounds. The Court's opinion could have rested solely on the ground that the statutes discriminated on the basis of race in violation of the Equal Protection Clause. But the Court went on to hold that the laws arbitrarily deprived the couple of a fundamental liberty protected by the Due Process Clause, the freedom to marry. . . .

[R]ecent decisions have established that the right to marry is part of the fundamental "right of privacy" implicit in the Fourteenth Amendment's Due Process Clause. . . .Cases subsequent to *Griswold* [*v. Connecticut*, 381 U.S. 479 (1965)] and *Loving* have routinely categorized the decision to marry as among the personal decisions protected by the right of privacy . . . .

It is not surprising that the decision to marry has been placed on the same level of importance as decisions relating to procreation, childbirth, child rearing, and family relationships. As the facts of this case illustrate, it would make little sense to recognize a right to privacy with respect to other matters of family life and not with respect to the decision to enter the relationship that is the foundation of the family in our society. The woman whom appellee desired to marry had a fundamental right to seek an abortion of their expected child or to bring the child into life to suffer the myriad of social, if not economic, disabilities that the status of illegitimacy brings. Surely, a decision to marry and raise the child in a traditional family setting must receive equivalent protection. . . .

Under the challenged statute, no Wisconsin resident in the affected class may marry in Wisconsin or elsewhere without a court order, and marriages contracted in violation of the statute are both void and punishable as criminal offenses. Some of those in the affected class, like appellee, will never be able to obtain the necessary court order because they either lack the financial means to meet their support obligations or cannot prove that their children will not become charges. These persons are absolutely prevented from getting married. Many others, able in theory to satisfy the statute's requirements will be sufficiently burdened by having to do so that they will in effect be coerced into foregoing their right to marry. . . . [E]ven those who can meet the statute's requirements suffer a serious intrusion into their freedom of choice. . . .

III.

When a statutory classification significantly interferes with the exercise of a fundamental right, it cannot be upheld unless it is supported by sufficiently important state interests and is closely tailored to effectuate only those interests. Appellant asserts that two interests are served by the challenged statute: the permission-to-marry proceeding furnishes an opportunity to counsel the applicant as to the necessity of fulfilling his prior support obligations and the welfare of the out-of-custody children is protected. . . .

With regard to safeguarding the welfare of the out-of-custody children, appellant's brief does not make clear the connection between the State's interest and the statute's requirements. . . . [A]ppellant's counsel suggested that . . . the statute provides incentive for the applicant to make support payments to his children. . . . This "collection device" rationale cannot justify the statute's broad infringement on the right to marry.

First, with respect to individuals who are unable to meet the statutory requirements, the statute merely prevents the applicant from getting married, without delivering any money at all into the hands of the applicant's prior children. . . . [T]he State already has numerous other means for exacting compliance with support obligations, means that are at least as effective as the instant statute's and yet do not impinge upon the right to marry. . . .

Since the support obligation is the same whether the child is born in or out wedlock, the net result of preventing the marriage is simply illegitimate children. The statutory classification created by § 245.10 (1),(4),(5) thus cannot be justified by the interests advanced in support of it. The judgment of the District Court is, accordingly, *Affirmed.*

MR. JUSTICE STEWART, concurring in the judgment.

I cannot join the opinion of the Court. To hold, as the Court does, that the Wisconsin statute violates the Equal Protection Clause seems to me to misconceive the meaning of that constitutional guarantee. The Equal Protection Clause deals not with substantive rights or freedoms but with invidiously discriminatory classification. The paradigm of its violation is, of course, classification by race.

Like almost any law, the Wisconsin statute now before us affects some people and does not affect others. But to say that it thereby creates "classifications" in the equal protection sense strikes me as little short of fantasy. The problem in this case is not one of discriminatory classifications but of unwarranted encroachment upon a constitutionally protected freedom. I think that the Wisconsin statute is unconstitutional because it exceeds the bounds of permissible state regulation of marriage and invades the sphere of liberty protected by the Due Process Clause of the Fourteenth Amendment.

I do not agree with the court that there is a "right to marry" in the constitutional sense. That right, or more accurately that privilege, is under our federal system peculiarly one to be defined and limited by state law. A State may not only "significantly interfere with decisions to enter into the marital relationship," but may in many circumstances absolutely prohibit it. Surely a State may legitimately say that no one can marry his or her sibling, that no one can marry who is not at least 14 years old, that no one can marry without first passing an examination for venereal disease, or that no one can marry who has a living husband or wife. But just as surely in regulating the intimate human relationship of marriage, there is a limit beyond which a State may not constitutionally go. . . .

Mr. Justice POWELL, concurring in the judgment.

I concur in the judgment of the Court that Wisconsin's restrictions . . . cannot meet applicable constitutional standards. I write separately because the majority's rationale sweeps too broadly in an area which traditionally has been subject to pervasive state regulation. The court apparently would subject all state regulation which "directly and substantially" interferes with the decision to marry in a traditional family setting to "critical examination" or "compelling state interest" analysis. . . .

[I]t is fair to say that there is a right of marital and familial privacy which places some substantive limits on the regulatory power of government. But the court has yet to hold that all regulation touching upon marriage implicates a "fundamental right" triggering the most exacting judicial scrutiny. . . .

In my view analysis must start from the recognition of domestic relations as "an area that has long been regarded as a virtually exclusive province of the States." *Sosna v. Iowa*, 419 U.S. 393, 404 (1975). The marriage relation traditionally has been subject to regulation, initially by the ecclesiastical authorities, and later by the secular state. . . .

State power over domestic relations is not without constitutional limits. The Due Process Clause requires a showing of justification "when the government intrudes on choices concerning family living arrangements" in a manner which is contrary to deeply rooted traditions. Due process constraints also limit the extent to which the State may monopolize the process of ordering certain human relationships while excluding the truly indigent from that process. Furthermore under the Equal Protection Clause, the means chosen by the State in this case must bear "a fair and substantial relation" to the object of the legislation. . . .

The Wisconsin measure in this case does not pass muster under either due process or equal protection standards. . . .

Mr. Justice REHNQUIST, dissenting.

I substantially agree with my Brother Powell's reasons for rejecting the Court's conclusion that marriage is the sort of "fundamental right" which must invariably trigger the strictest judicial scrutiny. I disagree with his imposition of an "intermediate" standard of review, which leads him to conclude that the statute though generally valid as an "additional collection mechanism" offends the Constitution by its "failure to make provision for those without the means to comply with the child-support obligations." . . .

[T]he Wisconsin Legislature has "adopted this rule in the course of constructing a complex social welfare system that necessarily details with the intimacies of family life." Because of the limited amount of funds available for support of needy children, the State has an exceptionally strong interest in securing as much support as their parents are able to pay. . . .

In the case of some applicants, this statute makes the proposed marriage legally impossible for financial reasons; in a similar number of extreme cases, the Social Security Act makes the proposed marriage practically impossible for the same reasons. I cannot conclude that such a difference justifies the application of a heightened standard of review to the statute in question here.

NOTES AND QUESTIONS

(1) What does the *Zablocki* case actually hold? Does *Zablocki* now recognize the principle that marriage, although regulated by state law, is a fundamental constitutional right that is protected by the Due Process Clause against arbitrary and unreasonable state action? Must the state now demonstrate a "compelling state interest" to prohibit certain marriages and to regulate other marriages, or should state regulation of marriage be based upon a "rational reason" test, or upon an "intermediate level of scrutiny" test? What less onerous means could Wisconsin have utilized against Redhail instead of prohibiting his marriage *per se* for failure to pay child support?

In a concurring opinion in *Zablocki* Mr. Justice Powell was troubled that "the majority's rationale sweeps too broadly in an area which traditionally has been subject to pervasive state regulation," and Mr. Justice Rehnquist questions exactly when a compelling state interest analysis should be applied to any state regulation which may "directly and substantially" interfere with the decision to marry.

Query: What other state marital regulations may arguably "directly and substantially" interfere with the constitutional right to marry? According to Mr. Justice Stewart's concurring opinion, "a State may legitimately say that no one can marry his or her sibling" and that "no one can marry without first passing an examination for venereal disease." What compelling state interests would justify these prohibitions regarding an individual's right to marry? *See, e.g., Israel v. Allen*, 577 P.2d 762 (Colo. 1978) (holding that a state statute prohibiting marriage "between a brother and sister, whether the relationship is by half or whole blood *or by adoption*" was unconstitutional). What is the distinction between state *regulation* of marriage and a state's *prohibition* of certain marriages?

(2) **Problem.** Donald is a prison inmate who is serving a sentence of 20 years to life. Donald wishes to marry Susan, and be allowed to participate in conjugal visits under the state's family reunion program, but he is prohibited from marrying Susan under the state's civil death statute that holds an incarcerated prisoner sentenced to life is in the situation of civil death, which precludes him or her from marriage. Donald appeals his marriage prohibition. What legal arguments can be made on his behalf? What arguments on behalf of the state? How should the court rule? *See, e.g., Ferrin v. New York Dep't of Correctional Servs.*, 517 N.E.2d 1370 (N.Y. 1987). *Cf. Doe v. Commissioner of Corrections*, 518 N.E.2d 536 (N.Y. 1987), *cert. denied*, 488 U.S. 879 (1988), (holding that "certain constitutional rights, including the right to marry, survive incarceration" and an inmate "does not forfeit all constitutional protection upon conviction and incarceration; but retains those rights that are not inconsistent with his status as a prisoner or with the legitimate penological objectives of the corrections system.") *Query:* What would constitute legitimate penological objectives in allowing or prohibiting inmate marriages? *See Turner v. Safley*, 482 U.S. 78 (1987) (holding that although marriage is subject to substantial restrictions as a result of incarceration, sufficient important attributes of marriage remain to form a constitutionally protected relationship).

(3) **Problem.** What if a state prohibition of marriage did not relate to the right to marry *per se*, but instead affected the right to engage in a licensed business activity if the applicant was married, and the applicant's spouse had engaged in prohibited activities? In the case

of *Levinson v. Washington Horse Racing Comm'n*, 740 P.2d 898 (Wash. Ct. App. 1987), a state agency refused to grant applicant wife a license to race horses on the basis of state regulations providing for disqualification if either spouse had engaged in a violation of Washington State racing rules. (Husband had been convicted of narcotics violations.) The trial court affirmed the action. The wife appealed on the ground that the regulations represented an infringement on her constitutional fundamental right to marry. The Commission argued that the goal of maintaining integrity in horse racing was a sufficiently important state interest to justify the prohibition of spouses of narcotics felons from owning and racing horses, and the Commission cited a similar decision from Louisiana which upheld the same rule in order to maintain honesty and integrity in horse racing. What should be the result on appeal?

Query: What about state anti-nepotism policies that prohibit spouses from working in the same office do such policies unconstitutionally infringe on the fundamental right to marry under *Zablocki*? Why or why not? *See generally* Chapter 2.07[A], *below*. What about the rules at the United States military academies that prohibit cadets from marrying?

(4) **Problem.** Ralph has been ordered to attend a chemical dependency program which is operated by the State of Holmes. Under the terms of this program, Ralph must attend daily sessions for a period of six months, during which time he must live in a dormitory on the grounds of the facility. He is allowed to go home on Friday evening and must return by 5:00 p.m. on Sunday evening. This chemical dependency program places heavy emphasis on therapy and on compliance with all the rules of the program. Minor infractions of the rules are dealt with quite severely, and since Ralph was ordered to attend the program by a court he cannot quit it.

Ralph has been dating Sally for some time, and on Saturday evening he asked Sally to marry him, and the couple made plans to marry each other on the following Saturday. In accordance with the rules of the Holmes Chemical Dependency Program, Ralph had to secure the permission of the Resident Director to get married. The Resident Director, however, told Ralph informally that the Director felt in his professional and clinical judgment that Ralph and Sally's plans to marry at this time would detrimentally interfere with Ralph's treatment, and that he would not consent to the marriage.

Ralph now comes to your law office for advice as to whether or not he can successfully challenge the Director's decision. Based on the decisions cited above, what advice would you give to Ralph? *See generally* Reich, *Individual Rights and Social Welfare: The Emerging Legal Issues*, 74 Yale L.J. 1245 (1965); 1 Homer H. Clark, Jr., Law of Domestic Relations 76, 83–84, 88; Vol. 2, p. 114 (2d ed. 1987).

§ 1.07 Capacity and Intent to Marry

Assuming the parties have met the legal requirements for a valid formal or informal marriage, they must also possess the legal *capacity* and *intent* to marry. If either the husband or the wife lacks this legal capacity or intent to marry, then their marriage may be *void* or *voidable* depending upon the seriousness of the marital impediment.

[A] Introduction

The historical distinction between void and voidable marriages, based upon a lack of capacity or intent to marry, arose as a result of jurisdictional conflicts between English ecclesiastical and civil courts: If the marriage could be attacked after the death of one of the spouses, then it was a void *ab initio* marriage. But if the marriage could not be attacked after the death of one of the spouses, even though it was canonically invalid, then in the civil courts the marriage was voidable only, and the surviving spouse was entitled to all appropriate marital property rights. Under present-day American family law, a defective marriage is classified as either *void* or *voidable*, based upon the seriousness of its defect. See Goda, *The Historical Evolution of the Concepts of Void and Voidable Marriages*, 7 J. Fam. L. 297 (1967).

A void or void *ab initio* marriage is a legal nullity, incapable of possessing any marital consequences. Thus, the parties to a void *ab initio* marriage can never ratify it, and void *ab initio* marriages can be collaterally attacked by any interested party or by the State, even after the death of either "spouse." Examples of void *ab initio* marriages in the vast majority of states are: same-sex marriage, bigamous or polygamous marriage, and incestuous marriage. In a minority of states underage marriage is also void *ab initio*. Since a void *ab initio* marriage is a legal nullity from its inception, no formal annulment action is necessary, but an annulment action may still be brought to establish a legal record of the void *ab initio* marriage.

A voidable marriage, on the other hand, is a *valid* marriage for all civil purposes unless it is annulled in a direct legal proceeding by either the husband or the wife. The marital defect in a voidable marriage therefore may be ratified by the parties, and when one of the spouses dies, an annulment action cannot be brought by the other spouse. Likewise, interested third parties and the state generally cannot attack a voidable marriage. Examples of voidable marriages in most jurisdictions are underage marriages; marriage to a mental incompetent; fraudulent marriage; marriage under duress; and marriage in jest. In some states, a voidable marriage may also be annulled for natural and incurable impotency; marriage to a felon or prostitute; or marriage to a spouse who is pregnant by another man, or who has at a time close to the marriage impregnated another woman. When a voidable marriage is annulled in a formal legal proceeding, this voidable marriage then becomes a void marriage, though not void *ab initio*. *See, e.g. Arnelle v. Fisher*, 647 So. 2d 1047, 1048–49 (Fla. Dist. Ct. App. 1994) (recognizing that although the invalidity of a void *ab initio* marriage may be asserted in either a direct or collateral proceeding at any time, a voidable marriage is good for every purpose, and can only be attacked in a direct proceeding by either husband or wife during the life of the parties).

The traditional common law distinctions between void *ab initio* and voidable marriages is therefore of crucial importance in determining any spousal support or marital property rights: with a void *ab initio* marriage there are no marital rights; but with a voidable marriage, in the absence of a formal annulment action, both spouses still retain all property and support rights that normally devolve upon them by reason of their marriage. Moreover, in many jurisdictions today, by state statutory authority, in an annulment proceeding involving a voidable marriage, the spouses generally have the same spousal support and marital property rights that spouses have in a divorce action. *See generally* Note, *The Void and Voidable Marriage: A Study in Judicial Method*, 7 Stan. L. Rev. 529 (1955); Wade, *Void and De Facto Marriages*, 9 Sydney L. Rev. 356 (1981); Wrenn, *In Search of a Balanced Procedural Law for Marriage and Nullity Cases*, 46 Jurist 602 (1986).

[B] Same-Sex Marriage

Historically, marriage has been defined as the voluntary union of one man and one woman to the exclusion of all others. States have therefore refused to permit marriages between two persons of the same sex. *See generally* Homer Clark, The Law of Domestic Relations in the United States 75–80 (1988). In recent years, however, this definition of marriage has been challenged on a variety of constitutional grounds. The following case considers one such constitutional challenge.

BAEHR v. LEWIN
Supreme Court of Hawaii
852 P.2d 44 (1993)

LEVISON, JUDGE, in which MOON, CHIEF JUDGE, joins.

The plaintiff-appellants Ninia Baehr (Baehr), Genora Dancel (Dancel), Tammy Rodrigues (Rodrigues), Antoinette Pregil (Pregil), Pat Lagon (Lagon), and Joseph Melilio (Melilio) (collectively "the plaintiffs") appeal the circuit court's order . . . granting the motion of the defendant-appellee John C. Lewin (Lewin) in his official capacity as Director of the Department of Health (DOH), State of Hawaii, for judgment on the pleadings, resulting in the dismissal of the plaintiff's action with prejudice for failure to state a claim against Lewin upon which relief can be granted. . . .

I. BACKGROUND

On May 1, 1991, the plaintiffs filed a complaint for injunctive and declaratory relief in the Circuit Court of the First Circuit, State of Hawaii, seeking, inter alia: (1) a declaration that Hawaii Revised Statutes (HRS) Sec. 572-1 (1985)—the section of the Hawaii Marriage Law enumerating the requisites of a valid marriage contract—is unconstitutional insofar as it is construed and applied by the DOH to justify refusing to issue a marriage license on the sole basis that the applicant couple is of the same sex; and (2) preliminary and permanent injunctions prohibiting the future withholding of marriage licenses on that sole basis.

The plaintiffs' complaint avers that: (1) the DOH's interpretation and application of HRS Sec. 572-1 to deny same-sex couples access to marriage licenses violates the plaintiffs' right to privacy, as guaranteed by article I, section 6 of the Hawaii Constitution, as well as to the equal protection of the laws and due process of law, as guaranteed by article I, section 5 of the Hawaii Constitution; (2) the plaintiffs have no plain, adequate, or complete remedy at law to redress their alleged injuries; and (3) the plaintiffs are presently suffering and will continue to suffer irreparable injury from the DOH's acts, policies, and practices in the absence of declaratory and injunctive relief. . . .

On July 9, 1991, Lewin filed his motion for judgment on the pleadings, pursuant to Hawaii Rules of Civil Procedure . . . and memorandum in support thereof in the circuit court. . . . The memorandum was unsupported by and contained no references to any affidavits, depositions, answers to interrogatories, or admissions on file. Indeed, the record in this case suggests that the parties have not conducted any formal discovery.

In his memorandum, Lewin urged that the plaintiffs' complaint failed to state a claim upon which relief could be granted for the following reasons: (1) the state's marriage laws "contemplate marriage as a union between a man and a woman"; (2) because the only legally recognized right to marry "is the right to enter a heterosexual marriage, plaintiffs do not have a cognizable right, fundamental or otherwise, to enter into state-licensed homosexual marriages"; (3) the state's marriage laws do not "burden, penalize, infringe, or interfere in any way with the [plaintiff's] private relationships"; (4) the state is under no obligation "to take affirmative steps to provide homosexual unions with its official approval"; (5) the state's marriage laws "protect and foster and may help to perpetuate the basic family unit, regarded as vital to society, that provides status and a nurturing environment to children born to married persons" and, in addition, "constitute a statement of moral values of the community in a manner that is not burdensome to [the] plaintiffs." . . .

The plaintiffs filed a memorandum in opposition to Lewin's motion for judgment on the pleadings on August 29, 1991. . . . [T]hey argued that, for purposes of Lewin's motion, the circuit court was bound to accept all the facts alleged in their complaint as true and that the complaint therefore could not be dismissed for failure to state a claim unless it appeared beyond doubt that they could prove no set of facts that would entitle them to the relief sought. Proclaiming their homosexuality and asserting a fundamental constitutional right to sexual orientation, the plaintiffs reiterated their position that the DOH's refusal to issue marriage licenses to the applicant couples violated their rights to privacy, equal protection of the laws, and due process of law under article I, sections 5 and 6 of the Hawaii Constitution.

The circuit court heard Lewin's motion on September 3, 1991, and, on October 1, 1991, filed its order granting Lewin's motion for judgment on the pleadings on the basis that Lewin "was entitled to judgment in his favor as a matter of law" and dismissing the plaintiff's complaint with prejudice. The plaintiffs' timely appeal followed.

II. JUDGMENT ON THE PLEADINGS WAS ERRONEOUSLY GRANTED

A complaint should not be dismissed for failure to state a claim unless it appears beyond doubt that the plaintiff can prove no set of facts in support of his or her claim that would entitle him or her to relief. . . . We must therefore view a plaintiff's complaint in a light most favorable to him or her in order to determine whether the allegations contained therein could warrant relief under any alternative theory. . . . For this reason, in reviewing the circuit court's order dismissing the plaintiff's complaint in this case, our consideration is strictly limited to the allegations of the complaint, and we must deem those allegations to be true. . . .

We conclude that the circuit court's order runs aground on the shoals of the Hawaii Constitution's equal protection clause and that, on the record before us, unresolved factual questions preclude entry of judgment, as a matter of law, in favor of Lewin and against the plaintiffs. Before we address the plaintiffs' equal protection claim, however, it is necessary as a threshold matter to consider their allegations regarding the right to privacy (and, derivatively, due process of the law). . . .

It is now well established that "a right to personal privacy, or a guarantee of certain areas or zones of privacy" is implicit in the United States Constitution. . . . And article I, section 6, of the Hawaii Constitution expressly states that "[t]he right of the people to privacy is recognized and shall not be infringed without the showing of a compelling state interest." Hawaii Const. art. I Sec. 6 (1978). . . . This right is similar to the privacy right discussed in cases such as *Griswold v. Connecticut* [381 U.S. 479 (1965)], *Eisenstadt v. Baird* [405 U.S. 438 (1972)], *Roe v. Wade* [410 U.S. 113 (1973)], etc. It is a right that, though unstated in the federal Constitution, emanates from the penumbra of several guarantees of the Bill of Rights. Because of this, there has been some confusion as to the source of the right and the importance of it. As such, it is treated as a fundamental right subject to interference only when a compelling state interest is demonstrated. . . .

Accordingly, there is no doubt that, at a minimum, article I, section 6 of the Hawaii Constitution encompasses all of the fundamental rights expressly recognized as being subsumed within the privacy protections of the United States Constitution. . . . [The court then discusses in depth the case of *Zablocki v. Redhail*, appearing in § 1.06 *supra*, and the fundamental right to marry]. . . .

The foregoing case law demonstrates that the federal construct of the fundamental right to marry—subsumed within the right to privacy implicitly protected by the United States Constitution—presently contemplates unions between men and women. (Once again, this is hardly surprising inasmuch as such unions are the only state-sanctioned marriages currently acknowledged in this country). . . .

Applying the foregoing standards to the present cases, we do not believe that a right to same-sex marriage is so rooted in the traditions and collective conscience of our people that failure to recognize it would violate the fundamental principles of liberty and justice that lie at the base of all our civil and political institutions. Neither do we believe that a right to same-sex marriage is implicit in the concept of ordered liberty. . . . Accordingly, we hold that the applicant couples do not have a fundamental constitutional right to same-sex marriage arising out of the right to privacy or otherwise.

Our holding, however, does not leave the applicant couples without a potential remedy in this case. As we will discuss below, the applicant couples are free to press their equal protection claim. If they are successful, the State of Hawaii will no longer be permitted to refuse marriage licenses to couples merely on the basis that they are of the same sex. But there is no fundamental right to marriage for same-sex couples under article I, section 6 of the Hawaii Constitution. . . .

The power to regulate marriage is a sovereign function reserved exclusively to the respective states. . . . By its very nature, the power to regulate the marriage relation includes the power to determine the requisites of a valid marriage contract and to control the qualifications of the contracting parties, the forms and procedures necessary to solemnize the marriage, the duties and obligations it creates, its effect upon property and other rights, and the grounds for marital dissolution [citing *Salisbury v. List*, 501 F. Supp. 105, 107 (D. Nev. 1980), and *Maynard v. Hill*, § 1.02, *above*]. . . .

The applicant couples correctly contend that the DOH's refusal to allow them to marry on the basis that they are members of the same sex deprives them of access to a multiplicity of [state] rights and benefits that are contingent upon that status . . . [including] (1) a variety of state income tax advantages, including deductions, credits, rates, exemptions, and estimates . . . (2) public assistance from and exemptions relating to the Department of Human Services . . . (3) control, division, acquisition, and disposition of community property . . . (4) rights relating to dower, curtesy, and inheritance . . . (5) rights to notice, protection, benefits, and inheritance under the Uniform Probate Code . . . (6) award of child custody and support payments in divorce proceedings . . . (7) the right to spousal support . . . (8) the right to enter into premarital agreements . . . (9) the right to change of name . . . (10) the right to file a nonsupport action . . . (11) post-divorce rights relating to support and property division . . . (12) the benefit of the spousal privilege and confidential marital communications . . . (13) the benefit of the exemption of real property from attachment or execution . . . and (14) the right to bring a wrongful death action . . . For present purposes, it is not disputed that the applicant couples would be entitled to all of these marital rights and benefits, but for the fact that they are denied access to the state-conferred legal status of marriage.

. . . Notwithstanding the state's acknowledged stewardship over the institution of marriage, the extent of permissible state regulation of the right of access to the marital relationship is subject to constitutional limitations or constraints. . . . It has been held that a state may deny the right to marry only for compelling reasons. *Salisbury*, 501 F. Supp. 105, 107 (D. Nev. 1980). . . . [S]tates, including Hawaii, may and do prohibit marriage for such 'compelling' reasons as consanguinity (to prevent incest). . . , immature age (to protect the welfare of children). . . , presence of venereal disease (to foster public health). . . , and to prevent bigamy. . . .

The equal protection clauses of the United States and Hawaii Constitutions are not mirror images of one another. The fourteenth amendment to the United States Constitution somewhat concisely provides, in relevant part, that a state may not "deny to any person within its jurisdiction the equal protection of the laws." Hawaii's counterpart is more elaborate. Article I, section 5 of the Hawaii Constitution provides in relevant part that "[n]o person shall. . . be denied the equal protection of the laws, nor be denied the enjoyment of the person's civil rights or be discriminated against in the exercise thereof because of race, religion, *sex*, or ancestry" (Emphasis added). Thus, by its plain language, the Hawaii Constitution prohibits state-sanctioned discrimination against any person in the exercise of his or her civil rights on the basis of sex.

"The freedom to marry has long been recognized as one of the vital personal rights essential to the orderly pursuit of happiness by free [people]." *Loving [v. Virginia]*, 388 U.S. 1, 12, 87 S. Ct. 1817, 1824 (1967). So "fundamental" does the United States Supreme Court consider the institution of marriage that it has deemed marriage to be "one of the basic civil rights of [men and women]" *Id.* [quoting *Skinner v. Oklahoma*, 316 U.S. 535, 541, 62 S. Ct. 1110, 1113 (1942)].

Rudimentary principles of statutory construction render manifest the fact that, by its plain language, HRS Sec. 572-1 restricts the marital relation to a male and a female. . . .Accordingly, on its face. . . HRS Sec. 572-1 denies same-sex couples access to the marital status and its concomitant rights and benefits. It is the state's regulation of access to the status of married persons, on the basis of the applicant's sex, that gives rise to the question whether the applicant couples have been denied the equal protection of the laws in violation of article I, section 5 of the Hawaii Constitution.

Relying primarily on four decisions construing the law of other jurisdictions [*Jones v. Hallahan*, 501 S.W.2d 588 (Ky. Ct. App. 1973); *Baker v. Nelson*, 191 N.W.2d 185 (Minn. 1971) *appeal dismissed* 409 U.S. 810 (1972); *De Santo v. Barnsley*, 476 A.2d 952 (Pa. Super. Ct. 1984); *Singer v. Hara*, 522 P.2d 1187 (Wash. Ct. App. 1974)] . . ., Lewin proposes that "the right of persons of the same sex to marry one another does not exist because marriage, by definition and usage, means a special relationship between a man and a woman". . . . We believe Lewin's argument to be circular and unpersuasive.

Two of the decisions upon which Lewin relies are demonstrably inapposite to the appellant couples' claim. In *Baker v. Nelson*, 291 Minn. 310, 191 N.W.2d 185 (1971), *appeal dismissed* 409 U.S. 810 . . . (1972), the questions for decision were whether a marriage of two persons of the same sex was authorized by state statutes and, if not, whether state authorization was compelled by various provisions of the United States Constitution, including the fourteenth amendment. Regarding the first question, the *Baker* court arrived at the same conclusion as have we with respect to HRS 572-1: by their plain language, the Minnesota marriage statutes precluded same-sex marriages. Regarding the second question, however, the court merely held that the United States Constitution was not offended; apparently, no state constitutional questions were raised and none were addressed.

De Santo v. Barnsley, 328 Pa. Super. 181, 476 A.2d 952 (1984) also is distinguishable. In *De Santo*, the court held only that common law same-sex marriage did not exist in Pennsylvania, a result irrelevant to the present case. . . .

Jones v. Hallahan, 501 S.W.2d 588 (Ky. Ct. App. 1973) and *Singer v. Hara*, 11 Wash. App. 247, 522 P.2d 1187, *review denied* 84 Wash. 2d 1008 (1974) warrant more in-depth analysis. In *Jones*, the appellants, both females, sought review of a judgment that held that they were not entitled to have a marriage license issued to them, contending that refusal to issue the license deprived them of the basic constitutional rights to marry, associate, and exercise religion freely. . . .

Significantly, the appellants' equal protection rights—federal and state—were not asserted in *Jones*, and, accordingly, the appeals court was relieved of the necessity of addressing and attempting to distinguish the decision of the United States Supreme Court in *Loving*. *Loving* involved the appeal of a black woman and a Caucasian man (the Lovings) who were married in the District of Columbia and thereafter returned to their home state of Virginia to establish their marital abode. 388 U.S. at 2. . . . The Lovings were duly indicted for and convicted of violating Virginia's miscegenation laws, which banned interracial marriages. *Id.* In his sentencing decision, the trial judge stated, in substance, that Divine Providence had not intended that the marriage state extend to interracial unions. . . .

The Lovings appealed the constitutionality of the state's miscegenation laws to the Virginia Supreme Court of Appeals, which upheld their constitutionality and affirmed the Lovings conviction. . . . The Lovings then pressed their appeal to the United States Supreme Court. . . .

In a landmark decision, the United States Supreme Court, through Chief Justice Warren, struck down the Virginia miscegenation laws on both equal protection and due process grounds. The Court's holding as to the former is pertinent for present purposes:

> [T]he Equal Protection Clause requires the consideration of whether the classification drawn by any statute constitute an arbitrary and invidious discrimination. . . .
>
> There can be no question but that Virginia's miscegenation statutes rest solely upon distinctions drawn according to race. *The statutes proscribe generally accepted conduct if engaged in by members of different races.* . . . At the very least, the Equal Protection Clause demands that racial classifications . . . be subjected to the "most rigid scrutiny," . . . and, if they are ever to be upheld, *they must be shown to be necessary to the*

accomplishment of some permissible state objective, independent of the racial discrimination which it was the object of the Fourteenth Amendment to eliminate.

There is patently no legitimate overriding purpose independent of invidious discrimination which justifies this classification. . . . We have consistently denied the constitutionality of measures which restrict the rights of citizens on account of race. There can be no doubt that restricting the freedom to marry solely because of racial classifications violates the central meaning of the Equal Protection Clause. *Id.* At 10-12, 87 S. Ct. At 1823 (emphasis added and citation omitted).

The facts of *Loving* and the respective reasoning of the Virginia courts, on one hand, and the United States Supreme Court on the other, both discredit the reasoning of *Jones* and unmask the tautological and circular nature of Lewin's argument that HRS 572-1 does not implicate article I, section 5 of the Hawaii Constitution because same sex marriage is an innate impossibility. . . . With all due respect to the Virginia courts of a bygone era, we do not believe that trial judges are the ultimate authorities on the subject of Divine Will, and, as *Loving* amply demonstrates, constitutional law may mandate, like it or not, that customs change with an evolving social order.

Singer v. Hara, 11 Wash. App. 247, 522 P.2d 1187 . . . suffers the same fate as does *Jones*. In *Singer*, two males appealed from a trial court's order denying their motion to show cause by which they sought to compel the county auditor to issue them a marriage license. On appeal, the unsuccessful applicants argued that: (1) the trial court erred in concluding that the Washington state marriage laws prohibited same-sex marriage; (2) the trial court's order violated the equal rights amendment to the state constitution; and (3) the trial court's order violated various provisions of the United States Constitution, including the fourteen amendment. . . .

Regarding the appellants' federal and state claims, the court specifically "[did] not take exception to the proposition that *the Equal Protection Clause of the Fourteenth Amendment requires strict judicial scrutiny of legislative attempts at sexual discrimination" Id.* At 261, 522 P.2d at 1196 (emphasis added). Nevertheless, the *Singer* court found no defect in the state's marriage laws, under either the United States Constitution or the state constitution's equal rights amendment, based upon the rationale of *Jones*: "[a]ppellants were not denied a marriage license because of their sex; rather, they were denied a marriage license because of the nature of marriage itself." *Id.* As in *Jones,* we reject this exercise in tortured and conclusory sophistry. . . .

"Whenever a denial of equal protection of the laws is alleged, as a rule our initial inquiry has been whether the legislation in question should be subjected to 'strict scrutiny' or to a 'rational basis' test." . . . This court has applied "strict scrutiny" analysis to "laws classifying on the basis of suspect categories or impinging upon fundamental rights expressly or impliedly granted by the Constitution," in which case the laws are "presumed to be unconstitutional unless the state shows compelling state interests which justify such classifications." . . .

As we have indicated, HRS Sec. 572-1, on its face and as applied, regulates access to the marital status and its concomitant rights and benefits on the basis of the applicant's sex. As such, HRS Sec. 572-1 establishes a sex-based classification. . . .

. . . Accordingly, we hold that sex is a "suspect category" for purposes of equal protection analysis under article I, section 5 of the Hawaii Constitution and that HRS Sec. 572-1 is subject to a "strict scrutiny" test. It therefore follows, and we so hold, that . . . HRS Sec. 572-1 is presumed to be unconstitutional . . . unless Lewin, as an agent of the State of Hawaii, can show that (a) the statute's sex-based classification is justified by compelling state interests and (b) the statute is narrowly drawn to avoid unnecessary abridgements of the applicant couples' constitutional rights. . . .

Vacated and remanded.

. . . [A concurring opinion by Judge James S. Burns is omitted.]

WALTER M. HEEN.

I dissent. Although the lower court judge may have engaged in "verbal overkill" in arriving at his decision, the result he reached was correct and should be affirmed. I agree with the plurality's holding that Appellants do not have a fundamental right to a same sex marriage protected by article I section 6 of the Hawaii Constitution. However, I cannot agree with the plurality that: (1) Appellants have a "civil right" to a same sex marriage; (2) Hawaii Revised Statutes (HRS) Sec. 572-1 unconstitutionally discriminates against Appellants who seek a license to enter into a same sex marriage; (3) Appellants are entitled to an evidentiary hearing that applies a "strict scrutiny" standard of review to the statute; and (4) HRS Sec. 572-1 is presumptively unconstitutional. Moreover, in my view, Appellants' claim that they are being discriminatorily denied statutory benefits accorded to spouses in a legalized marriage should be addressed by the legislature. . . .

Citing *Loving v. Virginia*, 388 U.S. 1, 87 S. Ct. 1817, 18 L. Ed. 2d 1010 (1967), the plurality holds that Appellants have a civil right to marriage. I disagree. "It is axiomatic . . . that a decision does not stand for a proposition not considered by the court." . . .

Loving is simply not authority for the plurality's proposition that the civil right to marriage must be accorded to same sex couples. *Loving* points out that the right to marriage occupies an extremely venerated position in our society. So does every other case discussing marriage. However, the plaintiff in *Loving* was not claiming a right to a same sex marriage. *Loving* involved a marriage between a white male and a black female whose marriage, which took place in Washington D.C., was refused recognition in Virginia under that state's miscegenation laws. . . .

Loving and *Zablocki* neither establish the right to a same sex marriage nor limit a state's power to prohibit any person from entering into such a marriage. The plurality's conclusion here that Appellants have a right to a same sex marriage. . . is completely contrary to the clear import of *Zablocki* and *Loving*. Although appellants suggest an analogy between the racial classification involved in *Loving*. . . and the alleged sexual classification involved in the case at bar, we do not find such an analogy. The operative distinction lies in the relationship which is described by the term "marriage" itself, and that relationship is the legal union of one man and one woman. . . .

The issue of a right to a same sex marriage has been considered by the courts in four other states. Those courts arrive at the opposite conclusion from the plurality here. . . . I do not agree with the plurality's contention that those cases are not precedent for this case. The basic issue in each of those four cases, as in this one, was whether any person has the right to legally marry another person of the same sex. Neither do I agree with the plurality that *Loving* refutes the reasoning of the courts in those four cases. . . .

In my view, the purpose of HRS 572-1 is analogous to the purpose of Washington's marriage license statute as stated in *Singer, supra*.

> In the instant case, it is apparent that the *state's refusal to grant a license allowing the appellants to marry one another is not based upon appellants' status as males, but rather it is based upon the state's recognition that our society as a whole views marriage as the appropriate and desirable forum for procreation and the rearing of children. . . . [M]arriage exists as a protected legal institution primarily because of societal values associated with the propagation of the human race. . . . Thus the refusal of the state to authorize same sex marriage results from such impossibility of reproduction rather than from an invidious discrimination "on account of sex".* Therefore, the definition of marriage as the legal union of one man and one woman is permissible as applied to appellants, notwithstanding the prohibition contained in the ERA, because it is founded upon the unique physical characteristics of the sexes and appellants are not being discriminated against because of their status as males per se.

Id. 11 Wash. App. at 259-260, 522 P.2d at 1195 (emphasis added). . . . The Washington court's reasoning is pertinent, in my view, to Appellants' claim in the case at hand, and supports the constitutionality of the statute.

Appellants complain that because they are not allowed to legalize their relationships, they are denied a multitude of statutory benefits conferred upon spouses in a legal marriage. However, redress for those deprivations is a matter for the legislature, which can express the will of the populace in deciding whether such benefits should be extended to persons in Appellants' circumstances. Those benefits can be conferred without rooting out the very essence of a legal marriage. This court should not manufacture a civil right which is unsupported by any precedent, and whose legal incidents—the entitlement to those statutory benefits—will reach beyond the right to enter into a legal marriage and overturn long standing public policy encompassing other areas of public concern. This decision will have far-reaching and grave repercussions on the finances and policies of the governments and industry of this state and all the other states in the country.

NOTES AND QUESTIONS

(1) The case of *Baehr v. Lewin* was remanded back to the trial court, which in *Baehr et al. v. Miike*, No. 91-1394, 1996 WL 694235 (Haw. Cir. Ct. Dec. 3, 1996) found that the defendant State of Hawaii did not establish a compelling state interest to prohibit same-sex marriage and "failed to establish or prove any adverse consequences to the public resulting from same-sex marriage" and "failed to establish or prove the legal significance of the institution of traditional marriage and the need to protect traditional marriage as a fundamental structure of society." Thus, the trial court recognized the validity of same-sex marriage in Hawaii. This trial court decision is being appealed to the Hawaiian Supreme Court. *Query:* What arguments can be made in *support* of the legal recognition of same-sex marriage? What public policy arguments can be made *against* recognizing same-sex marriage? Which arguments are more persuasive to you? Why? *See also* David O. Coolridge, *Same-sex Marriage? Baehr v. Miike and the Meaning of Marriage*, 38 S. Tex. L. Rev. 1 (1997). *But see* Lynn Wardle, *The Potential Impact of Homosexual Parenting on Children*,

1997 U. Ill. L. Rev. 8, 884–91 (1997) (arguing that this 1996 decision ". . . leaves much to be desired in terms of fair summarization of the evidence, and thorough legal analysis."). For a spirited dialogue, pro and con, on the issue of same-sex marriage, see Kathryn Dean Kendall, *Principles and Prejudice: Lesbian and Gay Civil Marriage and the Realization of Equality,* 22 J. Comp. L. 81 (1996); Lynne Marie Kohm, *A Reply to "Principles and Prejudice": Marriage and the Realization that Principles Win Over Political Will,* 22 J. Comp. L. 293 (1996).

(2) In the wake of the *Baehr* decision, a number of Hawaiian state legislators in February of 1997 were calling for a state constitutional amendment to ban same-sex marriages in Hawaii, but at the same time the Hawaii legislature also was considering another legislative proposal that would give gay and lesbian couples many of the same benefits of married heterosexual couples. The first legislative bill would put before Hawaii's voters in 1998 as a constitutional amendment giving the state the power to approve only opposite-sex marriages, while the second bill would spell out alternative marriage-like benefits for which same-sex couples would be eligible, similar to marriage-like benefits already enacted in a number of Scandinavian countries. *See, e.g.* Fawcett, *Taking the Middle Path: Recent Swedish Legislation Grants Property Rights to Unmarried Cohabitants,* 24 Fam. L. Q. 179 (1990); Bradley, *Unmarried Cohabitation in Sweden: A Renewed Social Institution?* 11 J. Legal History 300 (1990). *And see* Foley, *The State of Gay Marriage: Will Hawaii Lead the Way?* 20 Family Advocate 39 (Summer, 1997).

In July of 1997, the Hawaii Legislature was the first state legislature to pass a comprehensive statewide domestic partnership statute. *See generally* § 3.04, Note (3), *below.*

Query: Which branch of government should determine whether same-sex marriages are legally valid or invalid the legislature or the courts? Do you agree with Judge Levison in the *Baehr* majority opinion that "constitutional law may mandate, like it or not, that customs change with an evolving social order"? Or do you agree with Judge Heen in his dissenting opinion that "marriage exists as a protected legal institution primarily because of societal values associated with the propagation of the human race"? Is a state's legislative prohibition against same sex marriage unconstitutional under a "strict scrutiny" standard of review, or does it serve a compelling state interest? What compelling state interest, if any, is involved? *See generally Same-Sex Marriage: Pro and Con* (Andrew Sullivan, ed. 1997); and William Eskridge Jr., *The Case for Same Sex Marriage: From Sexual Liberty to Civilized Commitment* (1997). *See also* Richard Posner, *Should There Be Homosexual Marriage? And If So, Who Should Decide?* 95 Mich. L. Rev. 1578 (1997) (critiquing William Eskridge's treatise advocating state statutory reforms to permit same-sex marriage. Judge Posner finds Eskridge's argument for state legislative reform to be persuasive and compelling, but he rejects Eskridge's contention that the Constitution should be interpreted as granting the right to same-sex marriage).

(3) An earlier argument in favor of same-sex marriages was made in Note, *The Legality of Homosexual Marriage,* 82 Yale L.J. 573 (1973), where the author concluded that state equal rights amendments providing that equality of rights "shall not be denied or abridged on account of sex" mandated that same-sex relationships be protected under state marriage laws, similar to the argument made by the court in *Baehr v. Lewin*. But the court in *Singer v. Hara,* 522 P.2d 1187, 1193–94 (Wash. Ct. App. 1974), took issue with this contention, and concluded, "We do not believe that approval of the ERA by the people of this state

reflects any intention on their part to offer couples involved in same-sex relationships the protection of our marriage laws."

Likewise, in *Baker v. Nelson*, 191 N.W.2d 185 (Minn. 1971) the Minnesota Supreme Court concluded that "The Equal Protection Clause of the Fourteenth Amendment, like the Due Process Clause, is not offended by the state's classification of persons authorized to marry. There is no irrational or invidious discrimination. . . . *Loving v. Virginia*, 388 U. S. 1 (1967), upon which petitioners additionally rely, does not militate against this conclusion. . . . *Loving* does indicate that not all state restrictions upon the right to marry are beyond the reach of the Fourteenth Amendment. But in a common-sense and in a constitutional sense, there is a clear distinction between a marital restriction based merely upon race and one based upon the fundamental difference in sex." *Query:* Can *Baehr* be reconciled with or distinguished from cases such as *Baker* and *Singer*?

(4) Not all gay and lesbian rights advocates support the concept of same-sex marriage. For example, Professor Nancy Polikoff has been critical of the efforts by gay and lesbian advocates to pursue legalized homosexual marriage. She writes

> For those who support lesbian and gay marriage because it would allow us access to the package of benefits now associated with heterosexual marriage, . . . advocating lesbian and gay marriage is an obvious choice. I do not share that vision. Advocating lesbian and gay marriage will detract from, even contradict, efforts to unhook economic benefits from marriage and make basic health care and other necessities available to all. Nancy Polikoff, *We Will Get What We Ask For: Why Legalizing Gay and Lesbian Marriage Will Not Dismantle the Legal Structure of Gender in Every Marriage*, 79 Va. L. Rev. 1535, 1549 (1993). *See also* Steven Homer, *Against Marriage*, 29 Harv. C. R.-C. L. L. Rev. 505, 515–16 (1994).

See also Paula Ettelbrick, *Wedlock Alert: A Comment on Lesbian and Gay Family Recognition*, 5 J. L. & Policy 107 (1996). Ms. Ettelbrick favors the attempt to broaden a definition of family to include gay and lesbian relationships, but she rejects any efforts to bring such relationships within a marriage rubric: "By questioning the building of an entire system on marriage and biology, when so many, gay and straight alike, do not fit that particular model, we create a vision of family that would encompass the way in which most citizens live their lives as family." In an earlier article, "Since When is Marriage a Path to Liberation?" in *Out/Look* (Fall 1989), Ms. Ettelbrick wrote:

> Marriage will not liberate us lesbians and gay men. In fact, it will constrain us, make us more invisible, force our assimilation into the mainstream and undermine the goals of gay liberation. . . . Marriage runs contrary to two of the primary goals of the lesbian and gay movement: the affirmation of gay identity and culture; and the validation of many forms of relationships. . . . The moment we argue, as some among us insist on doing, that we should be treated as equals because we are really just like married couples and hold the same values to be true, we undermine the very purpose of our movement and begin the dangerous process of silencing our different voices. . . . We will be liberated only when we are respected and accepted for our differences and the diversity we provide to this society. Marriage is not a path to that liberation. *Id.* at 9.

But see contra Barbara J. Cox, *The Lesbian Wife: Same Sex Marriage as an Expression of Radical and Plural Democracy*, 33 Cal. West. L. Rev. 155 (1997). Professor Cox disagrees with Paula Ettelbrick's position regarding same sex marriage, and she takes issue with Nancy Polikoff's statement that "the desire to marry in the lesbian and gay community is an attempt to mimic the worst of mainstream society". Professor Cox argues instead that the legal recognition of same sex marriage would not negatively impact any efforts to reform society, and could have "more potential to transform society progressively than any other redefinition [of marriage or alternatives to marriage] could".

(5) Currently the vast majority of American jurisdictions do not recognize same-sex marriage and hold such marriages to be *void ab initio. See, e.g. Dean v. District of Columbia*, 653 A.2d 307 (D.C. Ct. App. 1995) (holding that under District of Columbia marriage statutes, the definition of "marriage" does not include same-sex unions); *Jones v. Hallahan*, 501 S.W. 2d 588 (Ky. Ct. App. 1973) (refusing to recognize a homosexual marriage under Kentucky law); *Baker v. Nelson* 191 N.W.2d 185 (Minn. 1971) (refusing to recognize a same-sex marriage under Minnesota law); *De Santo v. Barnsley,* 476 A.2d 952 (Pa. Super. Ct. 1984) (holding that same-sex common law marriages do not exist in Pennsylvania); *Slayton v. State*, 633 S.W.2d 934, 937 (Tex. Ct. App. 1982) ("In this state, it is not possible for a marriage to exist between persons of the same sex"); *Weaver v. G. D. Searle Co.*, 558 F. Supp. 720, 723 (N.D. Ala. 1983) ("This court, and the common law, holds that parties are not married unless they are of the opposite sex and go through a marriage ceremony").

(6) *Query*. Must sister states recognize a Hawaiian same-sex marriage under the full faith and credit requirement of Article IV Section 1 of the United States Constitution? In the wake of the *Baehr* decision, a number of states enacted statutes providing that these states would not recognize same-sex marriages if validly contracted in another state, such as Hawaii, since a same-sex marriage would be against the forum state's strong public policy. *See, e.g.* Ariz. Rev. Stat. Ann. § 25-101[C] (1996); Conn. Gen. Stat. Ann. § 46a-81r (1995); Ill. Comp. Stat. Ann. § 5/213.1 (1996); Utah Code Ann. § 30-1-2 (1995); Va. Code Ann. § 20-45.2 (1997).

Congress enacted the so-called Defense of Marriage Act, 110 Stat. 2419 (1996) which amends 28 U.S.C. Section 1738C to provide that "No State, territory, or possession of the United States, or Indian tribe, shall be required to give effect to any public act, record, or judicial proceeding of any other State, territory, possession, or tribe respecting a relationship between persons of the same sex that is treated as a marriage.. . . or a right or claim arising from such a relationship." The Act also amended 1 U.S.C. § 7 by adding a definition of "marriage" and "spouse" which would affect any ruling, regulation, or interpretation made by any federal bureau or administrative agency in the United States. The term *marriage* under this statute means only a legal union between one man and one woman as husband and wife, and the word "spouse" refers only to a person of the opposite sex who is a husband or wife. However, some commentators question whether these state and federal legislatures have the constitutional power to enact such laws. *See, e.g.*, Larry Kramer, *Same Sex Marriage, Conflict of Laws, and the Unconstitutional Public Policy Exception*, 106 Yale L.J. 1965, 2008 (1997) (arguing that "if states cannot selectively discriminate against each others' laws, Congress cannot authorize them to do it"). *See also* Diane Guillerman, *Comment, The Defense of Marriage Act: The Latest Maneuver in the Continuing Battle to Legalize Same-Sex Marriage*, 34 Houston L. Rev. 425 (1997), and Note, *The Defense of Marriage Act and the Overextension of Congressional Authority*, 97 Colum. L. Rev. 1435 (1997).

A majority of legal scholars and commentators therefore appear to support the legal recognition of same-sex marriage, and question why state and federal law prohibit such marriages. However, a majority of state legislatures and courts continue to prohibit same-sex marriage. Why this apparent dichotomy? Professor William Galston, speaking of American family law reform generally, observes that:

> [I]n a democratic society, we are compelled to reflect on the public culture of that society. We can, of course, draw moral principles from our scholarly work and from our philosophical speculation, which is entirely appropriate. But, there are also moral principles at work in the culture as a whole. The balance that is to be struck between our private philosophical and scholarly conceptions of what is just, or where responsibility lies, for example, and what the public culture of society believes about those same issues is an important question. I would submit that in a democracy, we are not free to ignore the public culture in which people believe. We cannot end our moral and practical reflection with that, but we must take it into account. William Galston, *Public Morality and Public Policy: The Case of Children and Family Policy*, 36 Santa Clara L. Rev. 313, 314–15 (1996).

Query: Do you find Professor Galston's observation persuasive? Why or why not? What *is* the proper role and function of the state legislatures, the courts, legal commentators, and family law practitioners in American family law regulation and reform?

(7) **Transsexual Marriage**. The facts in *Anonymous v. Anonymous*, 67 Misc. 2d 982, 325 N.Y.S. 2d 499 (N.Y. Sup. Ct. 1971), were that the morning after the marriage ceremony, plaintiff husband, a noncommissioned Army officer who thought he had married a female, reached over for his bride and made the discovery that s/he had male sexual organs. His "wife" argued that subsequently s/he could have an operation to remove her male sex organs, but the court concluded that the marriage ceremony was a nullity. *See also B. v. B.*, 355 N.Y.S. 2d 712 (N.Y. Sup. Ct. 1974) (holding that sex reassignment surgery cannot achieve the legal result of making one sex into another for the purpose of marriage). However, in the case of *M.T. v. J.T.*, 140 N.J. Super. 77, 355 A.2d 204 (N.J. Super. Ct. App. Div. 1976), the wife was born with male genitals, but s/he underwent sex-change surgery which the husband was aware of at the time of the marriage. *Held*: She was considered a female for marital and legal purposes, and the husband had the duty to support her under their valid marriage. *See generally* Peter G. Guthrie, Annotation, *Marriage Between Persons of the Same Sex*, 63 A.L.R. 3d 1199 (1975). *Query:* What should be the legal test for determining a person's sex for purposes of establishing a valid marriage? *See* Note, *Transsexuals in Limbo: The Search for a Legal Definition of Sex*, 31 Md. L. Rev. 236, 244-247 (1971); Comment, *Transsexualism, Sex Reassignment Surgery, and the Law*, 56 Cornell L. Rev. 963 (1971); Dewar, *Transsexualism and Marriage*, 15 Kingston L. Rev. 58 (1985); Note, 16 Sw. U. L. Rev. 505 (1986).

[C] Plural Marriage

Bigamous, polygamous, or plural marriages are void *ab initio* marriages in the vast majority of American jurisdictions, and they are proscribed by state bigamy statutes. Such statutes provide criminal penalties for plural marriages ranging from one to seven years in prison, but these bigamy statutes, though on the books, are seldom enforced. *See, e.g.*, Slovenko, *Legal Essay: The De Facto Decriminalization of Bigamy*, 17 J. Fam. L. 297 (1978).

It has been estimated by various commentators that there are more than 30,000 polygamous marriages in the United States, and an untold number of intentional and unintentional bigamous relationships. Thus the legal problem of plural marriage, as the next case demonstrates, is still with us.

POTTER v. MURRAY CITY
United States Court of Appeals
760 F.2d 1065 (10th Cir.1985)

HOLLOWAY, CHIEF JUDGE.

In this suit the plaintiff-appellant Royston E. Potter (plaintiff) challenges Utah's proscription against polygamy or plural marriage.

His principal claim is that the termination of his employment as a city police officer for the practice of plural marriage violated his rights to the free exercise of his religion and his right to privacy. On cross-motions for summary judgment, the district court ruled in favor of defendants, explaining its reasoning in a scholarly opinion. *Potter v. Murray City*, 585 F. Supp. 1126 (D. Utah 1984). Plaintiff appeals.

I

Plaintiff is a former police officer of Murray City, Utah. The City terminated plaintiff's employment after it learned that he practiced plural marriage. The basis for the discharge was that by his plural marriage plaintiff failed to support, obey and defend Article III of the Constitution of the State of Utah.

Plaintiff brought suit under 42 U.S.C. § 1983 and the First and Fourteenth Amendments. He sought monetary damages against the City, its Chief of Police, and the Murray City Civil Service Commission. He also sought declaratory and injunctive relief against the State of Utah and its Governor and Attorney General to determine that Utah's laws prohibiting plural marriage were invalid and to enjoin their enforcement. *Id.* Because of the claim that Utah's proscription against plural marriages was mandated by Congress in Utah's Enabling Act as a condition for admission into the Union, the trial court on motion of the State of Utah ordered the United States to be joined as a party.

On appeal, plaintiff argues that (1) the portion of Utah's enabling act requiring that Utah forever prohibit polygamy is void by reason of the equal footing doctrine; (2) plaintiff's termination for practicing plural marriage violated his First Amendment right to the free exercise of religion; (3) his termination infringed on his fundamental right of privacy; and (4) his termination violated the constitutional guarantees of due process and equal protection because Utah's laws prohibiting plural marriage have long been in desuetude. Defendants disagree and also assert a number of defenses. We need not reach any of these arguments because we conclude that plaintiff's constitutional claims lack merit.

II. *Analysis*

A. The Equal Footing Doctrine

Plaintiff argues that Utah's Enabling Act providing that polygamy will be forever prohibited violates the equal footing doctrine. Assuming, arguendo, that the Enabling Act does violate the doctrine, it would not entitle the plaintiff to any relief.

The equal footing doctrine embraces the precept that each state is "equal in power, dignity, and authority," and that a state's sovereign power may not be constitutionally diminished by any conditions in the acts under which the State was admitted to the Union. . . .

Assuming, *arguendo*, that the Enabling Act does violate the equal footing doctrine, as the district court recognized, the State of Utah had full power since statehood to enact or amend in the manner provided by its own laws, any constitutional or statutory provisions dealing with the subject of marriage consistently with the Constitution of the United States as the supreme law of the land. The prohibition of polygamy as provided by its Constitution and laws, continues to be its settled public policy as does its commitment to monogamy as the cornerstone of its regulation of marriage.

B. The Free Exercise Clause

In *Reynolds v. United States*, 98 U.S. 145 (1878), the Supreme Court affirmed a criminal conviction of a Mormon for practicing polygamy and rejected the argument that Congress' prohibition of polygamy violated the defendant's right to the free exercise of religion. Plaintiff argues that *Reynolds* is no longer controlling because later cases have "in effect" overturned the decision. We disagree. Plaintiff principally relies on *Wisconsin v. Yoder*, 406 U.S. 205 (1972). There the Supreme Court held that the religious belief of the Amish that their salvation requires life in a church community apart from the world necessitated that they be exempted from a state law requirement that children attend public school beyond the eighth grade. *Yoder* explained that for a state to compel school attendance beyond the eighth grade when there is a claim that it "interferes with the practice of a legitimate religious belief, it must appear either that the State does not deny the free exercise of religious belief by its requirement, or that there is a state interest of sufficient magnitude to override the interest claiming protection under the Free Exercise Clause." *Id.* at 214. As Chief Justice Burger stated, "[t]he essence of all that has been said and written on the subject [of the Free Exercise Clause] is that only those interests of the highest order and those not otherwise served can overbalance legitimate claims to the free exercise of religion." *Id.* at 215.

The parties have stipulated here for the purpose of the motions for summary judgment that plaintiff's practice of plural marriage is the result of a good faith religious belief. The plaintiff has made an undisputed showing that his two wives consented to the plural marriage, and that the wives and five children of the marriages receive love and adequate care and attention and do not want for any necessity of life. Plaintiff points out that the State defendants have not presented any empirical evidence that monogamy is superior to polygamy, nor has the Utah legislature ever considered whether its anti-polygamy laws are wise. Hence plaintiff argues that under *Yoder*, summary judgment should have been entered in his favor rather than for the defendants.

We cannot disregard *Reynolds*, however, because in *Yoder* and afterwards the Supreme Court has recognized the continued validity of *Reynolds*. In *Yoder*, *Reynolds* was one of the four cases that the Court cited in support of the proposition that "[i]t is true that activities of individuals, even when religiously based, are often subject to regulation by the States in the exercise of their undoubted power to promote the health, safety, and general welfare, or the Federal Government in the exercise of its delegated powers." 406 U.S. at 220; *see also id.* at 230. Since *Yoder*, the Court has said that "[s]tatutes making bigamy a crime surely cut into an individual's freedom to associate, but few today seriously claim such statutes violate the First Amendment or any other constitutional provision." *Paris Adult Theatre I v. Slaton,* 413 U.S. 49, 68 n.15 (1973); *see also Zablocki v. Redhail,* 434 U.S. 374, 392 (1978) (Stewart, J., concurring in the judgment) (state may legitimately say that no one who has a living husband or wife can marry); *id.* at 399 (Powell, J., concurring in the judgment) (state has undeniable interest in insuring that its rules of domestic relations reflect widely held values of its people, and state regulation has included bans on incest, bigamy and homosexuality as well as various preconditions to marriage). Moreover, *Reynolds* has been cited with approval since *Yoder.* . . .

We are in agreement with the district court that the State of Utah

> beyond the declaration of policy and public interest implicit in the prohibition of polygamy under criminal sanction, has established a vast and convoluted network of other laws clearly establishing its compelling state interest in and commitment to a system of domestic relations based exclusively upon the practice of monogamy as opposed to plural marriage.

585 F. Supp. at 1138. Monogamy is inextricably woven into the fabric of our society. It is the bedrock upon which our culture is built. *Cf. Zablocki v. Redhail,* 434 U.S. 374, 384 (1978) (marriage is foundation of family and society; "a bilateral loyalty"). In light of these fundamental values, the State is justified, by a compelling interest, in upholding and enforcing its ban on plural marriage to protect the monogamous marriage relationship.

C. The right to privacy

Plaintiff argues that his constitutional right to privacy prohibits the State of Utah sanctioning him for entering into a polygamous marriage. Again we disagree.

We find no authority for extending the constitutional right of privacy so far that it would protect polygamous marriages. We decline to do so. *Cf. Paris Adult Theatre I v. Slaton,* 413 U.S. 49, 68 n.15 (1973) (few today seriously claim that making bigamy a crime violates the First Amendment or any other constitutional provision).

D. Laws in desuetude

Plaintiff further argues that Utah's laws prohibiting polygamy have fallen into desuetude. He says that there have been fewer than 25 prosecutions in Utah since 1952 for such offenses, that there are at least 5,000 to 10,000 polygamist family members in the State, and that during Chief Gillen's thirty-year tenure he had never arrested anyone nor seen anyone arrested or prosecuted for violating Utah's anti-bigamy statute. Thus he says that invoking laws which have long been in disuse to sanction him is a violation of the constitutional guarantees of due process and equal protection, citing *Yick Wo v. Hopkins,* 118 U.S. 356 (1886), and *People v. Acme Markets, Inc.,* 334 N.E.2d 555 (N.Y. 1975). *See also United States v. Elliott,* 266 F. Supp. 318, 326 (S.D.N.Y. 1967). We disagree.

Polygamy has been prohibited in our society since its inception. *See Reynolds,* 98 U.S. 145, 164-165 (1878). The prohibitions continue in full force today. We cannot agree that the discharge of plaintiff for engaging in bigamy violated any constitutional guarantee. The showing made did not establish the enforcement of a "basically obsolete or an empty law whose function has long since passed." *United States v. Elliott, supra,* 266 F. Supp. 318,

326 (S.D.N.Y. 1967). The showing of minimal numbers of prosecutions does not establish an abandonment of the State's laws and an irrational revival of them here.

"[M]ere failure to prosecute other offenders is no basis for a finding of denial of equal protection." [numerous citations omitted.] Selectivity in the enforcement of council laws is subject to constitutional constraints. Nevertheless, the conscious exercise of some selectivity in enforcement is not in itself a federal constitutional violation so long as the selection was not deliberately based upon an unjustifiable standard such as race, religion, or other arbitrary classification [citing *United States v. Amon*, 669 F.2d 1351, 1355-1356 (10th Cir. 1981), *cert. denied*, 459 U.S. 825 (1982)].

III. *Conclusion*

In sum, we find no error in the conclusions of the district court and uphold the summary judgment on the merits for the defendants. . . .

NOTES AND QUESTIONS

(1) *Potter, above*, is one of a long line of cases prohibiting bigamous and polygamous marriages in America. *See* 1 Homer H. Clark, Law of Domestic Relations in the United States 64–70 (2d ed. 1987). Thus, the crime of bigamy is committed when an attempt is made to contract a second marriage while a valid first marriage is still in existence, and this offense is punishable even though it was committed under the influence of a strong religious belief. *See, e.g. Reynolds v. United States*, 98 U.S. 145 (1878). *See also* Davis, *Plural Marriage and Religious Freedom: The Impact of Reynolds v. United States*, 15 Ariz. L. Rev. 287 (1973).

Nevertheless, subsequent cases have upheld an individual's fundamental right to the free exercise of religion. *See, e.g., Sherbert v. Verner*, 374 U.S. 398 (1963) (involving the wrongful discharge of a Seventh Day Adventist from her state job for refusing to work on Saturdays, the Sabbath Day of her faith); *Wisconsin v. Yoder*, 406 U.S. 205 (1972) (involving Amish whose religious beliefs exempted them from attending public schools beyond the eighth grade). In a concurring and dissenting opinion to *Yoder*, Justice Douglas noted that *Yoder* opened the way to give religious beliefs a broader base than previously recognized, and he opined that in time *Reynolds* would be overruled. 406 U.S. 205, 247 (1972). And Professor Lawrence Tribe has suggested that after *Sherbert v. Verner* the *Reynolds* case may be a candidate for reconsideration. L. Tribe, American Constitutional Law 853-854 (1978). To date, however, few courts have seriously questioned the *Reynolds* decision.

Query: Should the same equal-protection arguments applied by the Hawaiian Supreme Court to same-sex marriage in *Baehr v. Lewin, above*, also apply to plural marriages? Why or why not?

(2) Polygamy has been defined as having several spouses at the same time; where bigamy has been defined as contracting a second marriage while the first marriage is still subsisting. Traditionally, state bigamy statutes did not require any specific intent for a conviction, but the Model Penal Code and some recent cases now require a guilty intent for a bigamy

conviction. *See generally* Green & Long, Marriage and Family Law Agreements, 37–40 (1984).

(3) What happens if husband and wife divorce their first spouses and then remarry, but the prior divorce was invalid? A bigamous marriage? *See Williams v. North Carolina [II]*, 325 U.S. 226 (1945) (refusing to recognize a bigamous Nevada marriage after an invalid divorce based on a sham domicile in Nevada); *Hager v. Hager*, 349 S.E.2d 908 (Va. Ct. App. 1986) (refusing to recognize a bigamous South Carolina marriage after a prior invalid divorce). *See also* M.C. Dranfield, Annotation, *Bigamy—Mistaken Belief as to Divorce*, 56 A.L.R. 2d 915 (1957) and Later Case Service.

(4) Polygamous marriages are legally recognized in many African, Asian, and Muslim countries, and although the practice of polygamy is in a decline throughout the Muslim world due to social and economic factors, arguments for and against its legality and morality are still being made. Four most commonly advanced arguments supporting polygamy are as follows: the Qur'an (like the Old Testament of the Bible) gives religious authority to a man having more than one wife; polygamy is justified when the wife is barren or unwell, allowing the husband to have children without divorcing his first wife or leaving her ill-provided for; polygamy helps to prevent immorality, such as prostitution, rape, fornication, adultery, and the high divorce rate found in many Western monogamous societies; and polygamy protects widows and orphans by responding to the excess of women over men in time of war or other disasters. *See* Hodkinson, Muslim Family Law: A Sourcebook, 107-108 (1984). Recent commentators have argued, however, that the patriarchial culture that has influenced Islamic jurisprudence in family law matters for centuries should now yield to the Qur'anic Principle of Equality. *See, e.g.* Azizah al-Hibri, *Islam, Law and Custom: Redefining Muslim Women's Rights*, 12 Amer. U. J. of Int'l L. & Pol. 1 (1997). *See also* Leila P. Sayeh & Adrian Morse Jr., *Islam and the Treatment of Women: An Incomplete Understanding of Gradualism*, 30 Tex. Int'l L.J. 311 (1995).

Similar arguments have been made supporting plural marriages in America, including the rising incidence of extramarital sex and a soaring divorce rate. *See, e.g.* Nedrow, *Polygamy and the Right to Marry: New Life for an Old Lifestyle*, 11 Mem. St. U.L. Rev. 303 (1981). *See also* Elizabeth Joseph, *My Husband's Nine Wives*, New York Times, May 23, 1991 at A31 (an opinion piece by a female lawyer describing her own polygamous marriage, and arguing that polygamy offers women a viable solution for "successfully juggling career, motherhood, and marriage").

(5) Suppose the husband, a Muslim, validly marries two wives in Saudi Arabia, and then becomes a legal resident of California. Should California recognize these marriages? Why or why not? *See* 1 Homer H. Clark, Jr., Law of Domestic Relations 134–35 (2d ed. 1987). *Cf. In Re Dalip Singh Bir's Estate*, 188 P.2d 499 (Cal. Ct. App. 1948).

Can bigamous or polygamous marriages, contracted in the United States, ever be validated? Consider the following fact situation.

On February 5, 1972, James Shippy executed his last will and testament, leaving his entire estate to his then wife Marion, if she survived him. Otherwise his estate would go to his two children, Dorothy and Thomas Shippy. On January 9, 1973, Marion Shippy obtained an interlocutory divorce decree from James in Alameda County, California. In that proceeding, both parties relinquished all claims to the other's estate. A final decree of divorce, however, was not entered until eight years later, in 1981, and pursuant to a

California statute, the final divorce decree was then entered *nunc pro tunc* to take effect as of May 14, 1973.

In the interim, however, in 1976, James Shippy married Inge in Valdez, Alaska, and on July 15, 1981 James Shippy died in an airplane crash in Alaska. At the time of his death, James and Inge were residents of Kitsap County, Washington, and Inge commenced probate proceedings in Washington. James' children, Dorothy and Thomas Shippy, intervened, asking that their father's will be admitted into probate.

The trial court judge held that since Marion, the first wife, had relinquished all claims to James' estate, and since James' marriage to Inge, the second wife, during the interlocutory divorce period was bigamous and void under Alaska law, all of James' property should pass to his two children. However, Washington state law also recognizes the retroactive effect of a *nunc pro tunc* divorce decree from a sister state on an intervening second marriage. What should be the result on appeal? Based upon which state's law and public policy? Does this, in effect, validate a *de facto* sister-state bigamous marriage? Why or why not? *See In re Estate of Shippy*, 678 P.2d 848 (Wash. Ct. App. 1984). *See also* C.P. Jhong, Annotation, *Entering Judgment or Decree of Divorce Nunc Pro Tunc*, 19 A.L.R. 3d 648 (1968). What validates a sister-state bigamous marriage? Would reversing the trial court because of the retroactive divorce decree allow one state to validate what was a bigamous marriage in another?

(6) **Enoch Arden Statutes.** A legal dilemma is found in Alfred Lord Tennyson's 1864 poem *Enoch Arden*. Enoch Arden, a rough sailor's lad, married Annie Lee, the prettiest damsel in the port, much to the distress of the noble Phillip Ray, the miller's only son, who had loved Annie Lee in silence. Enoch went to sea, but did not return. Annie then married Phillip Ray, thinking Enoch was dead. But ten years later, Enoch returned. *Query:* Can Annie and Phillip now be prosecuted for bigamy? In order to alleviate this potential hardship, many states have passed so-called "Enoch Arden statutes" that establish a time period (normally five to seven years) after which a spouse with a good faith belief that the absent spouse is dead may remarry. However, it is important to note that these statutes do not validate the second marriage; they only prevent a criminal prosecution for bigamy.

Query: What advice would you give your client who was in Annie Lee's predicament, and who was about to remarry Phillip Ray? *See Anonymous v. Anonymous*, 186 Misc. 772, 62 N.Y.S. 2d 130 (N.Y. Sup. Ct. 1946); and Fenton & Kaufman, *Enoch Arden Revisited*, 13 J. Fam. L. 245 (1973-74).

[D] Prohibited Degrees of Kinship

Incestuous marriages, or marriages within prohibited degrees of kinship, are prohibited in most states. The problem, however, is ascertaining what particular degrees of kinship are prohibited by state statute, and what are not.

Incestuous marriages traditionally were prohibited by consanguinity (such as marrying one's parent or one's sibling); or by affinity (such as marrying one's mother-in-law). An example of a traditional statute is Ann. Laws of Mass. C. 207 §§ 1-2 (1983), which was first enacted in 1785:

> § 1: No man shall marry his mother, grandmother, daughter, granddaughter, sister, stepmother, grandfather's wife, grandson's wife, wife's mother, wife's grandmother,

wife's daughter, wife's granddaughter, brother's daughter, sister's daughter, father's sister, or mother's sister. [In 1983, "son's wife" was deleted.]

§ 2: No woman shall marry her father, grandfather, son, grandson, brother, stepfather, grandmother's husband, daughter's husband, granddaughter's husband, husband's grandfather, husband's son, husband's grandson, brother's son, sister's son, father's brother, or mother's brother. [In 1983 "husband's father" was deleted.]

In approximately half the states, first cousin marriages are also prohibited. *See, e.g., In Re Marriage of Adams*, 604 P.2d 332 (Mont. 1979). *But see also* Moore, *A Defense of First Cousin Marriage*, 10 Cle.-Marshall L. Rev. 139 (1961). *Query:* What constitutes a legitimate state interest, if any, in prohibiting first-cousin marriages?

A growing number of states have adopted a less restrictive approach to incestuous marriage based upon § 207 of the Uniform Marriage and Divorce Act. With minor amendments, these statutes generally provide that a marriage is incestuous and void only if it is between: (1) an ancestor and a descendant; (2) a brother and sister of half or whole blood or by adoption; or (3) an uncle and niece, or aunt and nephew. *See, e.g.* Cal. Fam. Code § 2200, Va. Code Ann. § 20-38.1 (1975); and N.Y. Dom. Rel. Law § 5 (1971).

In addition to its religious proscription, incest prohibitions have also been justified based upon genetic and eugenics grounds, but this rationale has been questioned by various writers. *See, e.g.* C. Stern, Principles of Human Genetics (3d ed. 1973) and H. Maisch, Incest (1972). Perhaps the strongest basis for justifying a prohibition against such marriages is the historical and sociological "incest taboo," where the survival of family harmony is dependent on prohibiting sexual rivalries-which also protects younger children against exploitation. *See, e.g.* Murdock, Social Structure 292-313 (1949). For a legal overview on incestuous marriage; *see generally* 1 Homer H. Clark, Jr., Law of Domestic Relations 149-159 (2d ed. 1987); Storke, *The Incestuous Marriage: Relic of the Past*, 36 U. Colo. L. Rev. 473 (1964); Bratt, *Incest Statutes and the Fundamental Right to Marry: Is Oedipus Free to Marry?*, 18 Fam. L. Q. 257 (1984); W.R. Habeeb, Annotation, *Sexual Intercourse Between Persons Related by Half Blood as Incest*, 72 A.L.R. 2d 706 (1960) and Later Case Service.

These moral and legal difficulties in defining and justifying statutory prohibitions against incestuous marriages are aptly described by Professor Carolyn Bratt in *Incest Statutes and the Fundamental Right to Marry: Is Oedipus Free to Marry?*, 18 Fam. L. Q. 257, 257–58:

> The U.S. Supreme Court has found that the right to marry is a constitutionally protected right [citing in a footnote *Zablocki v. Redhail*, 434 U.S. 374 (1978) and *Loving v. Virginia*, 388 U.S. 1 (1967)]. That right is restricted, however, by making some choices of a marriage partner illegal. The constitutional validity of modern state incest statutes is difficult to analyze because of shifting definitions, reflexive fears, ambivalent attitudes, and underlying facile generalizations.
>
> The mere word "incest" triggers strong feelings of revulsion in most people. Therefore, any *a priori* labeling of a marriage as incestuous tends to preclude objective thought about the permissibility of the particular form of the marriage prohibition at issue. Such revulsion stems largely from the confusion of incest with sexual abuse of children. This confusion is not limited to the general public, but extends to the courts as well. . . .
>
> . . . Nevertheless, one must understand the distinction between state incest statutes as a vehicle for prohibiting and punishing sexual abuse of minors and state incest

statutes as a marriage prohibition for adults. The rightful condemnation of the intrinsically abusive nature of adult-child sexual relationships must not be used to shield incest statutes prohibiting marriage between certain adults from an objective evaluation.

Another major obstacle to any attempt to analyze the constitutional validity of state incest statutes is the lack of a constant definition for the incest concept. Although the incest taboo is present in almost every society, the precise relationships within which marriage is prohibited vary not only state to state but also crossculturally and transhistorically. The most common nucleus of forbidden relationships is parent-child and sibling-sibling marriage, but beyond that generalization, the content of the taboo lacks uniformity. . . .

The incest motif persists as a tradition. Alleged public horror combined with obvious fascination for the theme extends in an unbroken line from the myths of preliterate peoples [including Greek mythology, Egyptian myths, Japanese mythology, and Sophocles' version of the Oedipus Rex legend] to contemporary literature [such as subconscious incest in Tennessee Williams' *Cat on a Hot Tin Roof*, Eugene O'Neill's *Mourning Becomes Electra*, and D.H. Lawrence's *Sons and Lovers*.]. . . .

Finally, myths and half-truths about the genetic effects of incestuous matings on the offspring represent another impediment to an analysis of the constitutional validity of contemporary incest statutes as marriage prohibitions. Although directly contradicted by current scientific knowledge of genetic inheritance, common knowledge continues to teach that incestuous unions cause mentally and/or physically defective offspring.

Once one recognizes these analytical difficulties—reflexive fears, shifting definitions of incest itself, ambivalent attitudes, and facile underlying generalizations—one can begin to rationally evaluate the validity of state incest statutes in the light of the constitutional right to marry. After making such an analysis, this author has concluded that neither the civil marriage bar nor the criminal bar against incestuous acts serves any valid purpose which cannot be better served by statutes which do not impinge on the constitutional right to marry. *Id.*

The next two cases illustrate some of these problems related to incestuous marriages.

IN RE ESTATE OF STILES
Ohio Supreme Court
391 N.E.2d 1026 (1979)

MAHONEY, J.

The singular issue before us is whether a common law marriage between an uncle and his niece is void or voidable. If it is merely voidable, then it can not be collaterally attacked after the death of one of the parties.

Statutory law clearly prohibits the marriage of an uncle to his niece. R.C. § 3101.01 reads as follows: Male persons of the age of eighteen years, and female persons of the age of sixteen years, not nearer of kin than second cousins, and not having a husband or wife living, may be joined in marriage. Prior to 1974, former R.C. § 2905.07 and its predecessors, G.C. § 13023 and R.C. § 7019, treated sexual intercourse between a niece and her uncle as incestuous and criminally punishable.

R.C. § 2905.07 reads as follows: No persons, being nearer of kin, by consanguinity or affinity, than cousins, having knowledge of such relationship, shall commit adultery or fornication together. Whoever violates this section shall be imprisoned not less than one nor more than ten years.

We find from the case law that the courts in Ohio which have considered this question prior to 1974 held the uncle and niece marriage to be void *ab initio*. See *State v. Brown*, 47 Ohio St. 102 (Ohio 1890); *Heyse v. Michalske*, 31 Ohio Law Abs. 484 (Ohio Prob. 1940); *Basickas v. Basickas*, 93 Ohio App. 531 (Ohio Ct. App. 1953).

Appellee urges us to apply the reasoning of this court in *Mazzolini v. Mazzolini*, 168 Ohio St. 357 (Ohio 1958). The majority opinion in *Mazzolini* adopted what they considered to be the modern trend, that unless a prohibitory marriage statute expressly declared such marriage void, they were merely voidable. The opinion further noted that sexual intercourse between first cousins was not incest in Ohio. By a 4 to 3 decision, the court held in paragraph three of the syllabus: Although a marriage in Ohio between first cousins is not approved by law, it is not expressly prohibited and made void by any statutory enactment, and, where first cousins by blood, one a resident of Massachusetts and the other a resident of Ohio, are lawfully married in Massachusetts and remove to Ohio to live, such marriage is not void in Ohio, and an action by the Ohio resident instituted in Ohio to annul the marriage on the ground that it is void *ab initio* cannot be maintained.

Mazzolini, supra, involved the doctrine of *lex loci contractus* and a unique Massachusetts statute. We decline to adopt its reasoning, and we confine its holding to the peculiar fact situation that confronted this court at that time.

We hold that the marriage of an uncle to his niece is incestuous and void *ab initio*. To hold otherwise would be a mockery of the statute and emasculate the purpose of marriage laws. Such incestuous marriages "are shocking to good morals, [and are] unalterably opposed to a well defined public policy." (*See Mazzolini, supra*, at page 358.) They are meretricious in their conception and can never ripen into anything better. Were we to hold to the contrary, these parties would be permitted to profit and take advantage of their violation of the law. The state has an interest in all marriages and is virtually a party to them. The state's interest can only be protected properly by treating such meretricious relationships as void *ab initio*.

Appellee correctly points out that under the new Criminal Code, effective January 1, 1974, R.C. § 2905.07 was repealed and sexual intercourse between an uncle and his niece was no longer criminally punishable. She argues that this was a new expression of the public policy.

One of the purposes of the new Criminal Code (H.B. No. 511) was to decriminalize certain unlawful sexual behavior and leave the parties to whatever chastisement society would impose without making them criminally liable. It was supposedly an enlightened approach to "social crimes." We do not believe that the General Assembly intended to change the state's public policy so as to favor fornication, adultery, rape of one spouse by the other, sodomy, fellatio, homosexuality and some forms of incest.

Accordingly, we reverse the judgment of the Court of Appeals.

ETHERIDGE v. SHADDOCK
Arkansas Supreme Court
706 S.W.2d 395 (1986)

GEORGE ROSE SMITH, J.

This is a petition by the appellant, now Eva Jean Etheridge, for a change of custody of the parties' two children. The chancellor denied the petition, finding that there had been no change of conditions calling for the requested modification of the divorce decree. Mrs. Etheridge's appeal comes to this court under Rule 29(1)(c).

The parties were married in 1971 and divorced in April, 1984. The court granted custody of the children to the father, subject to specified visitation privileges. In the latter part of 1984 Shaddock began living with his first cousin, Anna Frank Delozier, who was getting a divorce. After the divorce was granted the two cousins married in Arkansas, not knowing that such a marriage is prohibited by Arkansas law. Ark. Stat. Ann. § 55-103 (Repl. 1971).

In July, 1985, the present petition was filed, alleging the incestuous marriage as a ground for a change of custody. Shaddock and his cousin promptly had their marriage annulled in Arkansas and made a trip to Texas for the sole purpose of remarrying there, such marriages not being prohibited by Texas law. The appellant's arguments are presented as three points for reversal, but essentially the single contention is that the appellee's marriage was sufficient basis for a change of custody.

We have no doubt that the Arkansas policy against incest is so strong that we would not recognize the validity of a marriage, even if performed in another state, between very close blood relatives, such as a father and daughter or a brother and sister. The majority view, however, in states forbidding a marriage between first cousins, is that such a marriage does not create "much social alarm," so that the marriage will be recognized if it was valid by the law of the state in which it took place. Leflar, American Conflicts Law, § 221 (3d ed. 1977).

In the case at bar the chancellor was right in relying on our decision in *State v. Graves*, 228 Ark. 378, 307 S.W.2d 545 (Ark. 1957). That case involved a marriage between a 17-year-old boy and a 13-year-old girl, which was then declared by statute to be "absolutely void." Act 32 of 1941. The young couple, accompanied by the boy's father and the girl's parents, had gone to Mississippi for the marriage, where it was valid. After their return to Arkansas a charge of contributing to the delinquency of the minor girl was filed against the boy and against the girl's parents. The trial court, without a jury, found the defendants not guilty. The State appealed.

In affirming the judgment we emphasized the fact that we had no statute declaring such an underage marriage to be void when performed elsewhere. To the contrary, our policy is ordinarily to give effect to a marriage that was valid in the state where it was performed. The heart of our decision is to be found in the closing paragraph of the majority opinion: The celebration of a marriage gives rise to many ramifications, including questions of legitimacy, inheritance, property rights, dower and homestead, and causes of action growing out of the marital statutes. We have no statute which provides that marriages such as the one involved here, celebrated in another state, are void in the State of Arkansas. We see no reason to elaborate upon a line of reasoning that is still good. The chancellor was right. *Affirmed.*

NOTES AND QUESTIONS

(1) The *Stiles* and *Etheridge* cases discuss two interrelated issues dealing with incestuous marriages: (i) should certain prohibited degrees of kinship be void *ab initio*, or merely voidable; and (ii) should the forum domiciliary state recognize evasionary sister-state marriages?

Query: What was Justice Mahoney's rationale for holding an uncle-niece marriage to be void *ab initio* in the *Stiles* case? Is this a persuasive rationale in your opinion? Or is Justice Mahoney's opinion another telling example of what Professor Bratt describes as "typical judicial condemnation of incest" including emotion laden phrases such as incest "violating the voice of nature, degrading the family, and offending decency and morals"? Bratt, *above*, at 259. Is the *Etheridge* case a better reasoned decision? Why or why not?

In the later case of *Soley v. Soley*, 655 N.E.2d 1381 (Ohio Ct. App. 1995) the court refused to apply the reasoning of *Stiles* to a marriage between first cousins. *Query:* What is the significant difference, if any, between a uncle-niece marriage and a first cousin marriage?

(2) *Stiles* illustrates the traditional view that uncle-niece marriages are void *ab initio*, even if celebrated in a jurisdiction recognizing such marriages as valid. *See also Sclamberg v. Sclamberg*, 41 N.E. 2d 801 (Ind. 1942); *Catalano v. Catalano*, 170 A.2d 726 (Conn. 1961); *Weeks v. Weeks*, 654 So. 2d 33 (Miss. 1995). However, in the case of *In re May's Estate*, 305 N.Y. 486, 114 N.E.2d 4 (N.Y. 1953), an uncle and niece, both members of the Jewish faith and New York domiciliaries, were married in Rhode Island under applicable Rhode Island law which recognized such a marriage. The New York Court of Appeals also recognized this marriage, even though N. Y. Dom. Rel. Law § 5 specifically declared that any marriage between an uncle and niece in New York was "incestuous and void." The majority opinion in *May* stated that this statute only applied to New York marriages, and sister-state marriages should be determined by the *lex loci contractus*. But Judge Desmond, in dissent, stated the traditional view that it "is fundamental that every State has the right to determine the marital status of its own citizens," and the Restatement of Conflict of Laws § 121 (1934), stating the general rule that "a marriage valid where celebrated is valid everywhere," would not apply if such a marriage were "contrary to the prohibitions of natural law or the express prohibitions of a [state] statute." Which rationale is more persuasive to you? Why? *See also Leszinske v. Poole*, 798 P.2d 1049 (N.M. Ct. App. 1990), cert. denied, 797 P.2d 983 (N.M. 1990) (holding that New Mexico would recognize an uncle-niece marriage if validly performed in another jurisdiction). See also R. Leflar, American Conflicts of Law 448 (3d ed. 1977) ("The weight of domiciliary law on uncle-niece [marriages] looks to the law of the place of celebration, and treats a marriage valid there as valid at the domicile also.").

(3) The *Etheridge* case, *above*, discussed the recognition of an evasionary incestuous marriage between first cousins. How did the *Etheridge* court distinguish first-cousin and underage evasionary marriages from a marriage "between very close blood relatives"? *Cf. In Re Marriage of Adams*, 604 P.2d 332 (Mont. 1979) (holding that a first-cousin marriage is void *ab initio*).

(4) As discussed in Note (2) above, the Restatement of Conflict of Laws § 121 (1934) generally provides that a marriage valid where celebrated will be valid everywhere unless

it is contrary "to the prohibitions of natural law" or violates the express prohibitions of a state statute. The Restatement (Second) of Conflict of Laws § 283(2) (1971) likewise provides that a marriage valid where contracted will everywhere be recognized as valid "unless it violates a strong public policy of another state which had the most significant relationship to the spouses and the marriage at the time of the marriage." Also, a minority of states have enacted the Uniform Marriage Evasion Act which applies to sister-state evasionary marriages that are prohibited in the state of domicile. (Note: This act was subsequently withdrawn by the National Conference of Commissioners on Uniform State Laws.) How were these concepts addressed in the *Etheridge* case?

(5) **Problem.** Martin Israel and Tammy Israel were brother and sister by adoption. Prior to their respective parents' marriage in 1975, Martin, then age 18, was living in the State of Washington with his father; and Tammy, then age 13, was living with her mother in the State of Colorado. Subsequent to their parents' marriage, Martin and Tammy desired to marry each other, with their parents' consent. They also had an affidavit filed by Bishop Evans of the Roman Catholic Archdiocese of Denver stating that the Church had no objections to this marriage. The State of Colorado, however, refused to grant Martin and Tammy a marriage license based upon the state's incest statute, promulgated under the Uniform Marriage and Divorce Act, that prohibits the marriage of a brother or sister "whether the relationship is by half or whole blood or by adoption". Martin and Tammy argue that marriage is a fundamental constitutional right, and the State of Colorado cannot show any compelling state interest for prohibiting the marriage of a brother and sister by adoption. The State of Colorado, however, argues that the underlying purpose of the state incest prohibition is to preserve family harmony, and that family law incest prohibitions can be based upon affinity relationships as well as consanguinity. What should be the result on appeal? Explain your reasoning. *See Israel v. Allen*, 577 P.2d 762 (Colo. 1978).

[E] Age Restrictions

Under the early common law, marrying before the age of discretion rendered the marriage void. However, a majority of American jurisdictions now treat an underage marriage as merely voidable rather than void *ab initio*. *See, e.g. Holbert v. West*, 730 F. Supp. 50 (E.D. Ky. 1990) (applying Ky. law). *But see* Va. Code § 20-45.1, apparently overriding *Needham v. Needham*, 183 Va. 681, 33 S.E.2d 288 (Va. 1945).

Statutory age restrictions for marriage are widely considered necessary to prevent minor, immature persons from entering into unstable marriages that are likely to fail. Accordingly, in almost all jurisdictions, a man and woman are free to marry without parental consent at the age of 18 or older. The consent of a parent or parent substitute, however, is required for certain underage marriages—most often for 16-and 17-year-olds—and a majority of states also provide for additional "exceptional circumstances," such as when the would-be bride is pregnant. *See generally* Lynn Wardle, *Rethinking Marital Age Restrictions*, 22 J. Fam. L. 1 (1983-84); and Comment, *Capacity, Parental Power, and a Minor's Right to Remain Married*, 22 Santa Clara L. Rev. 447 (1982). Are such age restrictions to marriage constitutional? The following case addresses this issue.

MOE v. DINKINS
United States District Court
533 F. Supp. 623 (1981), *aff'd*, 669 F.2d 67 (2d Cir.), *cert. denied*, 459 U.S. 827 (1982)

CONSTANCE BAKER MOTLEY, D. J.

Plaintiffs Maria Moe, Raoul Roe and Ricardo Roe seek a judgment declaring unconstitutional, and enjoining the enforcement of, the parental consent requirement of New York Domestic Relations Law §§ 15.2 and 15.3. Section 15.2 provides that all male applicants for a marriage license between ages 16 and 18 and all female applicants between ages 14 and 18 must obtain "written consent to the marriage from both parents of the minor or minors or such as shall then be living." Section 15.3 requires that a woman between ages 14 and 16 obtain judicial approval of the marriage, as well as the parental consent required by § 15.2.

This action is now before the court on plaintiffs' motion for summary judgment declaring § 15 unconstitutional and enjoining its enforcement.

The plaintiff class consists of: persons who wish to marry in New York State but cannot obtain a marriage license or judicial approval to obtain a marriage license because they, or the persons whom they seek to marry, lack parental consent as required by New York Dom. Rel Law §§ 15.2 and 15.3. The plaintiff class is represented by Maria Moe and Raoul Roe.

The defendant class consists of: All town and city clerks in New York State. All such clerks are required by New York State law to enforce the parental consent provisions of New York Dom. Rel. Law §§ 15.2 and 15.3.

The defendant class is represented by David Dinkins, City Clerk of New York City. David Axelrod, New York State Commissioner of Health, is also a defendant in this action.

Plaintiff Raoul Roe was eighteen years old when this action was commenced. Plaintiff Maria Moe was fifteen years old. Plaintiff Ricardo Roe is their one-year old son who was born out of wedlock. Plaintiffs live together as an independent family unit. In late November, 1978, Maria became pregnant by Raoul and in April, 1979, they moved into an apartment together. Maria requested consent from her mother, a widow, to marry Raoul, but Mrs. Moe refused, allegedly because she wishes to continue receiving welfare benefits for Maria. Maria and Raoul continue to be prevented from marrying because of Mrs. Moe's failure to give consent to the marriage as required by § 15. Maria and Raoul allege that they wish to marry in order to cement their family unit and to remove the stigma of illegitimacy from their son, Ricardo. . . .

The Merits

Plaintiffs contend that § 15 of the New York Dom. Rel. Law, requiring parental consent for the marriage of minors between the ages of fourteen and eighteen, deprives them of the liberty which is guaranteed to them by the Due Process Clause of the Fourteenth Amendment to the Federal Constitution.

A review of Supreme Court decisions defining liberties guaranteed by the Fourteenth Amendment reveals that activities relating to child-rearing and education of children, *Pierce v. Society of Sisters*, 268 U.S. 510 (1925), procreation, *Skinner v. Oklahoma*, 316 U.S. 535 (1942), abortion, *Roe v. Wade*, 410 U.S. 113 (1973), family relations, *Moore v. City of East Cleveland*, 431 U.S. 494 (1977), contraception, *Carey v. Population Servs. Int'l*, 431 U.S. 678 (1977), and, most recently, marriage, *Zablocki v. Redhail*, 434 U.S. 374 (1978), are constitutionally protected rights of individual privacy embodied within the concept of liberty which the Due Process Clause of the Fourteenth Amendment was designed to protect.

However, neither *Zablocki* nor its predecessors, *Loving v. Virginia*, 388 U.S. 1 (1967), *Griswold v. Connecticut*, 381 U.S. 479 (1965), arose in the context of state regulation of marriages of minors. In that respect, this is a case of first impression.

While it is true that a child, because of his minority, is not beyond the protection of the Constitution, *In re Gault*, 387 U.S. 1 (1967), the Court has recognized the State's power to make adjustments in the constitutional rights of minors. *Ginsberg v. New York*, 390 U.S. 629 (1968) (criminal statute prohibiting the sale of obscene material to minors whether or not obscene to adults upheld despite First Amendment challenge); *Prince v. Massachusetts*, 321 U.S. 158 (1944) (child labor law prohibiting minors from selling merchandise on the streets upheld despite Jehovah Witness' challenge based on religious freedom). "The power of the State to control the conduct of children reaches beyond the scope of authority over adults." *Id.* at 168. This power to adjust minors' constitutional rights flows from the State's concern with the unique position of minors. In *Bellotti v. Baird*, 443 U.S. 622 (1979), the Court noted "three reasons justifying the conclusion that the constitutional rights of children cannot be equated with those of adults: the peculiar vulnerability of children; their inability to make critical decisions in an informed and mature manner; and the importance of the parental role in child-rearing." *Id.* at 634.

Likewise, marriage occupies a unique position under the law. It has been the subject of extensive regulation and control, within constitutional limits, in its inception and termination and has "long been regarded as a virtually exclusive province of the State." *Sosna v. Iowa*, 419 U.S. 393, 404 (1975).

While it is evident that the New York law before this court directly abridges the right of minors to marry, *in the absence of parental consent*, the question is whether the State interests that support the abridgement can overcome the substantive protection of the Constitution. The unique position of minors and marriage under the law leads this court to conclude that § 15 should not be subjected to strict scrutiny, the test which the Supreme Court has ruled must be applied whenever a state statute burdens the exercise of a fundamental liberty protected by the Constitution. Applying strict scrutiny would require determination of whether there was a compelling state interest and whether the statute had been closely tailored to achieve that state interest. *See, e.g., Carey v. Population Servs. Int'l*, 431 U.S. 678 (1977). The compelling state purpose necessitated by application of the strict scrutiny test "would cast doubt on a network of restrictions that the States have fashioned to govern marriage and divorce." *Zablocki v. Redhail*, 434 U.S. 374, 399 (1978) (Powell, J., concurring). It is this court's view that § 15 should be looked at solely to determine whether there exists a rational relation between the means chosen by the New York legislature and the legitimate state interests advanced by the State. *Cf. Ginsberg v. New York*, 390 U.S. 629, 629 (1968) (rationality test employed in area of protected freedom). Section 15 clearly meets this test.

The State interests advanced to justify the parental consent requirement of § 15 include the protection of minors from immature decision-making and preventing unstable marriages.

The State possesses paternalistic power to protect and promote the welfare of children who lack the capacity to act in their own best interest. *See Addington v. Texas*, 441 U.S. 418, 426 (1979). The State interests in mature decision-making and in preventing unstable marriages are legitimate under its *parens patriae* power.

Plaintiffs also contend that § 15 denied them the opportunity to make an individualized showing of maturity and denies them the only means by which they can legitimize their children and live in the traditional family unit sanctioned by law. On the other hand, New York's § 15 merely delays plaintiffs' access to the institution of marriage. *Cf. Sosna v. Iowa*, 419 U.S. at 393, 406 (1975)(durational residency requirement of one year for divorce proceedings held constitutional). Moreover, the prohibition does not bar minors whose parents consent to their child's marriage. Assuming *arguendo* that the illegitimacy of plaintiff Moe's child and plaintiff Coe's yet unborn child is a harm, it is not a harm inflicted by § 15. It is merely an incidental consequence of the lawful exercise of State power. The illegitimacy of plaintiffs' children, like the denial of marriage without parental consent, is a temporary situation at worst. A subsequent marriage of the parents legitimatizes the child, thereby erasing the mark of illegitimacy. *Estate of Elson*, 94 Misc. 2d 983, 405 N.Y.S.2d 984 (N.Y. Sur. Ct. 1978). The rights or benefits flowing from the marriage of minors are only temporarily suspended by § 15. Any alleged harm to these rights and benefits is not inflicted by § 15, but is simply an incidental consequence of the valid exercise of State power. . . .

An age attainment requirement for marriage is established in every American jurisdiction. The requirement of parental consent ensures that at least one mature person will participate in the decision of a minor to marry. That the State has provided for such consent in § 15 is rationally related to the State's legitimate interest in light of the fact that minors often lack the "experience, perspective and judgment" necessary to make "important, affirmative choices with potentially serious consequences." *Bellotti v. Baird, supra*, 443 U.S. 622, 635-636 (1979).

Plaintiffs' reliance on the abortion and contraception cases is misplaced. These cases can be distinguished from the instant case in that:

> a pregnant minor's options are much different than those facing a minor in other situations, *such as deciding whether to marry*. A minor not permitted to marry before the age of maturity is required simply to postpone her decision. She and her intended spouse may preserve the opportunity for a later marriage should they continue to desire it.

Bellotti v. Baird, supra, 443 U.S. 622, 642 (1979) (emphasis added).

Giving birth to an unwanted child involves an irretrievable change in position for a minor as well as for an adult, whereas the temporary denial of the right to marry does not. Plaintiffs are not irretrievably foreclosed from marrying. The gravamen of the complaint, in the instant case, is not total deprivation but only delay.

This court concludes that § 15's requirement of parental consent is rationally related to the State's legitimate interests in mature decision-making with respect to marriage by minors and preventing unstable marriages. It is also rationally related to the State's legitimate interest in supporting the fundamental privacy right of a parent to act in what the parent perceives to be the best interest of the child free from state court scrutiny. Section 15, therefore, does not offend the constitutional rights of minors but represents a constitutionally valid exercise of state power.

Accordingly, plaintiffs' motion for summary judgment in their favor is denied and summary judgment is entered in favor of defendants.

NOTES AND QUESTIONS

(1) The *Moe* decision reiterated that the right to marry is a fundamental constitutional right and subject to strict scrutiny, so a state must demonstrate a compelling interest in prohibiting certain marriages. *See, e.g., Loving v. Virginia*, 388 U.S. 1 (1967); *Zablocki v. Redhail*, 434 U.S. 374 (1978). Why, then, did Judge Motley apply a rational relationship test to the New York statute prohibiting underage marriages rather than a compelling state interest test?

(2) **Problem.** Assume that Alice and Jerry, 17-year-old domiciliaries of the state of Holmes, desire to marry each other, but they cannot obtain parental consent as required by the Holmes statute. Alice and Jerry therefore travel to the sister state of Marshall, where 17-year-olds may validly marry without parental consent. After their marriage in Marshall, Alice and Jerry return to Holmes. Should Holmes recognize this evasionary underage marriage? Why or why not? Based upon what underlying public policy arguments? *Compare Wilkins v. Zelichowski*, 140 A.2d 65 (N.J. 1958) (refusing to recognize an evasionary underage marriage of New Jersey domiciliaries in Indiana on public policy grounds); *with State v. Graves*, 307 S.W.2d 545 (Ark. 1957) (recognizing a sister-state evasionary underage marriage of Arkansas domiciliaries since such a marriage was not against Arkansas' strong public policy). *See also Husband v. Pierce*, 800 S.W.2d 661 (Tex. Ct. App. 1990) (holding that the Mexican marriage of a 15-year-old minor without parental consent would be recognized in Texas, since the validity of a marriage is generally determined by the law of the place where it is celebrated).

(3) **Problem.** Raymond and Judy were married when Raymond was only 17 years old. However, Raymond misrepresented himself to the licensing official as being 18 years old. Five months after the marriage, but still before Raymond attained the age of 18, he filed an annulment action through his mother as guardian *ad litem*. Should Raymond be able to procure a valid annulment from Judy, or should his fraudulent misrepresentation regarding his age bar this action based upon an estoppel or "unclean hands" doctrine? *Compare Ruiz v. Ruiz*, 6 Cal. App. 3d 58 (Cal. Ct. App. 1970) *with Duley v. Duley*, 151 A.2d 255 (D.C. 1959) *and Picarella v. Picarella*, 316 A.2d 826 (Md. 1974).

[F] Mental and Physical Incapacity

Under the common law, marriage to a person lacking the mental capacity to consent was held to be void *ab initio*, and this view is still recognized in some states. An increasing number of jurisdictions by statutory and case law, however, have treated marriage to a mentally incapacitated person as voidable rather than void. Physical incapacity, such as natural and incurable impotency of the body, is also treated as creating a voidable marriage. For example, § 208(a) of the Uniform Marriage and Divorce Act provides the following:

> The . . . court shall enter its decree declaring the invalidity of a marriage entered into under the following circumstances: (1) a party lacked capacity to consent to the

marriage at the time the marriage was solemnized, either because of mental incapacity or infirmity or because of the influence of alcohol, drugs, or other incapacitating substances [or] (2) a party lacks the physical capacity to consummate the marriage by sexual intercourse, and at the time the marriage was solemnized the other party did not know of the incapacity.

The test for mental capacity to consent when the marriage is solemnized has been defined as a capacity to understand the nature of the marital contract as well as understand the duties and responsibilities of marriage. *See, e.g., Forbis v. Forbis*, 274 S.W. 2d 800 (Mo. Ct. App. 1955); Homan v. Homan, 147 N.W.2d 630 (Neb. 1967). Other courts, however, have held that the only requirement is the ability to consent at the time of marriage, without any additional duties and responsibilities test. *See, e.g. Young v. Colorado Nat'l. Bank*, 148 Colo. 104, 365 P.2d 701 (Colo. 1961). For discussions of marriage and mental incompetency generally, *see* 1 Homer H. Clark, Law of Domestic Relations 182–88 (2d ed. 1987); Note, *The Right of the Mentally Disabled to Marry*, 15 J. Fam. L. 463 (1977); Linn & Bowers, *Historical Fallacies Behind Legal Prohibitions of Marriage Involving Mentally Retarded Persons*, 13 Gonzaga L. Rev. 625 (1978); and Shaman, *Persons Who Are Mentally Retarded: Their Right to Marry and Have Children*, 12 Fam. L.Q. 61 (1978).

Query: If a person has already been adjudged to be legally incompetent, should his or her capacity to marry be based upon an "ordinary business" test, or should the capacity to marry be based upon a lesser test than transacting normal day-to-day business affairs? The following case addresses this question.

GEITNER v. GEITNER
North Carolina Court of Appeals
312 S.E.2d 236 (1984)

This is an annulment action initiated by plaintiff, First National Bank of Catawba County, purporting to act on behalf of its ward, David Royer Geitner, against Marcia Townsend Geitner, to have declared void *ab initio* or the marriage between David Royer Geitner and Marcia Townsend Geitner which took place on 29 May 1980.

David Royer Geitner is 49 years old and is an adjudicated incompetent with a long history of mental illness. Mr. Geitner has been diagnosed as a chronic paranoid schizophrenic and has received extensive psychiatric treatment. Mr. Geitner has been a patient at various mental institutions for much of his adult life.

In May of 1961, First National Bank of Catawba County filed an Application for Guardianship of Mr. Geitner's estate, listing the total value of that estate as $45,000.00. On 19 May 1961, Letters of Guardianship, appointing First National Bank of Catawba County as Guardian, were issued by the Clerk of Superior Court of Catawba County. Since that time, Mr. Geitner has inherited approximately $900,000.00 from his father, which became part of the estate managed by the guardian bank.

In June of 1975, Mr. Geitner was conditionally released from confinement at Broughton Hospital at Morganton, North Carolina, pursuant to a judicial finding that he was not imminently dangerous to himself or others. The conditions of his release, as recommended by his physician and the court, included provision for a structured environment with attendants to do his cooking, cleaning, driving, etc. Mr. Geitner has lived in that environment in a house purchased by the guardian bank with funds from his estate and has continued to receive psychiatric treatment since his release from Broughton Hospital in 1975.

Mr. Geitner met Marcia Townsend in April of 1980 at the Carolina Friendship House, an outpatient mental health facility in Boone, North Carolina. Marcia Townsend suffers from no mental disability but is confined to a wheelchair as a victim of Friedreich's Ataxia, a disease of the nervous system resulting in the loss of muscular coordination and control. She attended Friendship House to take cooking lessons. The couple found themselves attracted to each other and spent a great deal of time together. On 28 May 1980, Mr. Geitner proposed to Marcia Townsend. She accepted the next day. Mr. Geitner arranged transportation to Watauga Hospital where the couple had blood tests and physical examinations. They then went to the Register of Deeds Office to obtain a marriage license. They were married that day, 29 May 1980, at the magistrate's office.

Since their marriage, David Royer Geitner and Marcia Townsend Geitner have continued to live together in the house purchased by the guardian bank for Mr. Geitner, with certain domestic duties being provided by an attendant employed by the guardian bank. The guardian bank has refused to provide any funds for the benefit of Marcia Townsend Geitner and, in fact, reduced David Royer Geitner's allowance from $160.00 per week to $50.00 per week in May of 1980.

This annulment action was initiated by the guardian bank on 23 October 1980. At that time, David Royer Geitner's only surviving relatives were an elderly aunt and several cousins, among whom were the chairman of the board and the wife of a member of the trust committee of the bank.

Upon Mr. Geitner's application, a guardian ad litem was appointed on 28 May 1981 to represent Mr. Geitner's interests. Mr. Geitner, through his guardian ad litem, was permitted to intervene in this action as a party defendant. The case came on for trial, and on 22 March 1982, a jury returned a verdict finding that David Royer Geitner had sufficient mental capacity and understanding on 29 May 1980 to enter into a marriage contract with Marcia Townsend Geitner. Judgment was entered accordingly. Plaintiff appeals.

EAGLES, JUDGE.

Plaintiff guardian bank asks us to find that the trial judge erred in denying its motions for directed verdict, judgment notwithstanding the verdict, and a new trial. Plaintiff contends that a marriage with a legally declared incompetent is void as a matter of law. We do not agree.

A voidable marriage is valid "for all civil purposes until annulled by a competent tribunal in a direct proceeding, but a void marriage is a nullity and may be impeached at any time." *Ivery v. Ivery*, 258 N.C. 721, 726, 129 S.E. 2d 457, 461 (N.C. 1963). Our Supreme Court has held that, under the common law as modified by G.S. § 51-3 and G.S. § 50-4, a marriage of a person incapable of contracting for want of understanding is not void, but voidable. *Id.* at 730, 129 S.E. 2d at 463. We find that prior adjudication of incompetency is not conclusive on the issue of later capacity to marry and does not bar a party from entering a contract to marry.

The mental capacity of a party at the precise time when the marriage is celebrated controls its validity or invalidity. 1 Lee, North Carolina Family Law § 24 (4th ed. 1979). As to what constitutes mental capacity or incapacity to enter into a contract to marry, "the general rule is that the test is the capacity of the person to understand the special nature of the contract of marriage, and the duties and responsibilities which it entails, which is to be determined from the facts and circumstances of each case." *Ivery*, 258 N.C. 721, 732, 129 S.E.2d 457, 464-465 (N.C. 1963) (quoting 55 C.J.S. *Marriage* § 12). In Lee's treatise on North Carolina family law, it is noted that "unlike other transactions, an insane person's capacity to marry is not necessarily affected by guardianship. . . .[R]easons why guardianship removes from the insane person all capacity to contract do not apply to marriage." 1 Lee, *supra* § 24 n. 119 (quoting McCurdy, *Insanity as a Ground for Annulment or Divorce in English or American Law*, 29 Va. L. Rev. 771 (1943).) In fact, "tests judicially applied for a determination of incompetency in guardianship matters differ markedly from those applied for the determination of mental capacity to contract a marriage, for even though under guardianship as an incompetent, a person may have in fact sufficient mental capacity to validly contract marriage." 4 Am. Jur. 2d Annulment of Marriage § 28.

We find that, here, sufficient evidence was presented to support a jury's verdict. Defendants presented both expert and lay witnesses who testified that Mr. Geitner did have, on 29 May 1980, adequate mental capacity and understanding of the special nature of a contract to marry. The fact that plaintiff guardian bank offered conflicting evidence merely required the jury to consider the credibility of the witnesses and evidence on each side. The fact that there was conflicting evidence does not require a directed verdict, judgment notwithstanding the verdict, or a new trial.

Plaintiff guardian bank also assigns as error the trial judge's charge to the jury that the burden of proof was on the plaintiff to prove that David Royer Geitner lacked the mental capacity and understanding sufficient to contract a valid marriage. We find no error. When the fact of marriage has been established by evidence, "the burden of persuasion on the issue of invalidity is on the party asserting such." 2 Brandis, N.C. Evidence § 244 (2d rev. ed. 1982). And even if a party's insanity is proved to be of such a chronic nature that it is presumed to continue, it does not shift the burden of the issue. 2 Brandis, N.C. Evidence § 238 (2d rev. ed. 1982). The plaintiff had the burden of proof on Mr. Geitner's capacity to contract a valid marriage.

The rest of plaintiff's assignments of error concern the admissibility of certain evidence. Several of these assignments of error concern testimony to the effect that Mr. Geitner had the capability to understand the nature of marriage. We note that both expert and lay witnesses may testify as to mental capacity or condition. . . . We hold that since the testimony complained of by plaintiff was based on the witnesses' observations and reasonable opportunities to form opinions as to Mr. Geitner's mental condition, there was no error in admitting this testimony. We have carefully examined the remaining assignments of error and find them to be without merit. No error.

NOTES AND QUESTIONS

(1) The *Geitner* court held that a prior adjudication of mental incompetency was not conclusive on the issue of David Geitner's subsequent capacity to marry. *See also Edmund v. Edwards*, 287 N.W. 2d 420 (Neb. 1980). *Query:* Why not? But in *May v. Leneair*, 297 N.W. 2d 882 (Mich. Ct. App. 1980), a Michigan appellate court held that a prior adjudication of mental incompetency would bar a subsequent marriage, under a Michigan statute

requiring a doctor's certificate filed that an incompetent person wishing to marry had been "cured" of his or her disability. What happens if marriage to a mental incompetent is contracted during a party's "lucid interval," even though the party was still mentally ill, and was not "curable"? *See, e.g., Larson v. Larson*, 192 N.E. 2d 594 (Ill. App. Ct. 1963).

(2) Assume hypothetically that the guardian *ad litem* for David Geitner had brought the annulment action after the death of David Geitner. What result? What if David Geitner had died during the appellate process?

(3) **Impotency of the Body.** Would "incurable physical impotency, or incapacity for copulation" under a state annulment statute include psychological as well as physical impotency? *See Rickards v. Rickards*, 166 A.2d 425 (Del. 1960). What if the couple had lived together for over three years, but the wife was still a virgin? *See Tompkins v. Tompkins*, 111 A. 599 (N.J. Ch. 1920). Or what if there was a persistent refusal to consummate the marriage? *See* M.L. Cross, Annotation, *Refusal of Sexual Intercourse as Ground for Annulment*, 28 A.L.R. 2d 499 (1953) and Later Case Service. Can a wife be impotent, even though she had become pregnant and miscarried? *See T. v. M.*, 242 A.2d 670 (N.J. Super. Ct. Ch. Div. 1968). Or can a plaintiff, who knew of defendant's impotence, but continued to live with the defendant for a long period of time thereafter, bring an annulment action? Why or why not? *See D. v. D.*, 20 A.2d 139 (Del. 1941). *See generally* David B. Perlmutter, Annotation, *Incapacity for Sexual Intercourse as Ground for Annulment*, 52 A.L.R. 3d 589 (1973).

[G] Consent Requirements: Fraud

A marriage procured by fraud is a voidable marriage according to decisional and statutory law in many states. The problem, however, is to ascertain the *degree* of fraud necessary to annul such a marriage. The influential Massachusetts case of *Reynolds v. Reynolds*, 85 Mass. 605 (Mass. 1862), commented upon in 13 Harv. L. Rev. 110 (1899), defined a two-pronged traditional test for determining a fraudulent marriage: (1) it must be material fraud; and (2) it must affect the essentials of the marriage. Material fraud generally means "but for" the fraud, there would have been no marriage. But the "essentials of the marriage" test is harder to define, and according to one commentator, it must adversely affect "the *possibility* of normal marital cohabitation." *See* Kingsley, *What are the Proper Grounds for Granting Annulments?*, 18 Law & Contemp. Probs. 39 (1953) (emphasis added). Thus, examples of material fraud that do affect the "essentials" of the marriage have included lying about an intent not to have sexual intercourse or not to have children during the marriage; concealment of impotency or venereal disease; concealment of pregnancy by another person; and lying about one's religious beliefs. However, examples of material fraud that do not affect the essentials of the marriage under this traditional test, except in "extreme cases," have included lying about a party's character, chastity, age, health, wealth, citizenship and ancestry; number or prior marriages and divorces; and lack of love and affection. *See generally* the earlier classic studies of Vanmeman, *Annulment of Marriage for Fraud*, 9 Minn. L. Rev. 497 (1925); Kingsley, *Fraud as a Ground for Annulment of Marriage*, 18 S. Cal. L. Rev. 213 (1945). *Query:* What is the state public policy rationale behind this traditional view?

A more modern approach to fraudulent marriage, adopted by other courts, encompasses the "material fraud" test, but rejects the "essentials of the present marriage" requirement.

See, e.g., Kober v. Kober, 211 N.E. 2d 817 (N.Y. 1965) (husband was anti-Semitic and a member of the Nazi Party during World War II). Other grounds for annulment based upon material fraud alone have included: misrepresentation of love and affection, *Schinker v. Schinker*, 68 N.Y.S. 2d 470 (N.Y. App. Div. 1947); misrepresentation of a prior marital status, *Smith v. Smith*, 77 N.Y.S.2d 902 (N.Y. App. Div. 1948); misrepresentation of age, *Tacchi v. Tacchi*, 195 N.Y.S.2d 892 (N.Y. Sup. Ct. 1959); and husband's membership in the Deutsche Bund, *Siecht v. Siecht*, 41 N.Y.S.2d 393 (N.Y. Sup. Ct. 1943).

Most of these cases following the "modern" approach to fraudulent marriages have come from New York, and some commentators have pointed out that due to the difficulties of obtaining a New York divorce before 1970, far more New Yorkers sued for annulment to end their marriages, or obtained migratory divorces in other jurisdictions, than in those states having more liberal divorce laws. *See, e.g.* Note, *Annulments for Fraud—New York's Answer to Reno?*, 48 Colum. L. Rev. 900 (1948). *And see generally* 1 Homer H. Clark, Jr., Law of Domestic Relations 191–212 (2d ed. 1987).

The following case applies the "essentials of the marriage" test to an allegedly fraudulent marriage.

V.J.S. v. M.J.B.
Superior Court of New Jersey, Chancery Division
592 A.2d 328 (1991)

KRAFTE, J. S.C. . . . There is inherent jurisdiction in a court of equity to annul fraudulent contracts, including a contract of marriage. *Costello v. Porzelt*, 282 A.2d 432 (N.Y. Ch. 1971). . . . Where the marriage has been consummated, the fraud of defendant will entitle plaintiff to an annulment only when the fraud is of an extreme nature, going to one of the essentials of marriage [citations omitted]. . . . Under the annulment statute, a judgment may be granted where there was a "fraud as to the essentials of the marriage." *N.J.S.A.* 2A:34-1(d).

In *Yearn v. Horter*, 110 A. 31 (N.J. Ch. 1920), the court addressed the nature and quantum of fraud which would justify annulment of a consummated marriage in the following excerpt:

> What is fraud in respect to the "essentials" of marriage, or, to use the broader term, what is "sufficient fraud," I think remains today the subject of ascertainment in every case brought before this court in which the complaining spouse alleges that his or her consent to a marriage was induced by the defendant's fraud. Id. at 198, 110 A. at 34. What is essential to the relationship of the parties in one marriage may be of considerably less significance in another. Therefore, a determination of whether a fraud goes to the essentials of the marriage must be decided on a case-by-case basis.

Here plaintiff [wife] testified that she did not want to have children. Her conviction was communicated to defendant [husband] and he, representing that he was in agreement with her wish not to have children, agreed prior to the marriage not to have children and to only have sexual intercourse with the use of contraception. After the consummation of the marriage and despite the parties' agreement, defendant expressed a desire to have children, and refused to engage in sexual intercourse utilizing any form of contraception. Plaintiff had and maintains no desire to have children, a fact made clearly known to defendant prior to the marriage.

In *Williams v. Witt*, 235 A.2d 902 (N.J. Super. Ct. App. Div. 1967), the court held that an annulment may be granted where one of the parties prior to the marriage forms a fixed determination *never* to have children and does not communicate that intention to his intended spouse. The court explained that an annulment in such a case is granted on the theory that since procreation is considered to be an essential element of the marriage, there exists an implied promise at the time of the marriage to raise a family. An undisclosed contrary intention, therefore, constitutes a fraud going to an essential of the marriage. *Id.* at 3, 235 A.2d at 903. The intention *never* to have children must antedate the marriage, for it is the implied promise to have children, coupled with the intent not to fulfill it, that constitutes the fraud. *Ibid.*

The facts presented to this court are the antithesis of the facts in *Williams v. Witt, supra.* This court finds that there was an express agreement between the parties prior to the marriage *not* to have children. After the wedding ceremony, defendant, in direct contradiction of the agreement, expressed his desire to have children. Since defendant's premarital uncommunicated intention to have children constitutes the essential element of plaintiff's cause of action, it was incumbent on her to prove her charge of fraud by clear and convincing evidence. *Id.* At 4, 235 A.2d 902.

Defendant interposed no defense at the trial. After evaluating the uncontroverted proofs and credibility of plaintiff's testimony, this court is satisfied that plaintiff clearly and convincingly proved that there was, in fact, a premarital fraudulent intent on the part of the defendant to have children in direct opposition to the express agreement between the parties prior to marriage not to have children. . . . If defendant's true intention to have children was made known to plaintiff, she would not have married defendant. . . .

The granting of an annulment on the ground that defendant possessed a premarital uncommunicated intent to have children in contradiction to an expressed antenuptial agreement not to have children is not against public policy. Public policy encourages full disclosure of pertinent facts, especially in contemplation of entering a bond as significant as marriage. Here plaintiff relied on defendant's expressed agreement not to have children. By declaring this marriage null and void . . . this court is acting in full compliance with public policy. Public policy dictates against the use of fraud to encourage a party to enter a marriage. . . .

. . . [T]he alleged marriage between the parties is hereby declared null and void.

NOTES AND QUESTIONS

(1) In the case of *Sanderson v. Sanderson*, 186 S.E.2d 84 (Va. 1972), the wife fraudulently concealed from her husband the fact that she had been married and divorced five times, telling him instead that she had only been married and divorced one time before. The court held there could be no annulment, since this fact did not affect the "essentials" of the Sandersons' present marriage, citing authority in J. Evans, Annotation, *Concealment of or Misrepresentation as to Prior Marital Status as Ground for Annulment of Marriage*, 15 A.L.R. 3d 759 (1967). However, in *Wolfe v. Wolfe*, 389 N.E.2d 1143 (Ill. 1979) the Illinois Supreme Court granted husband's suit for annulment based upon fraud and the fact that his wife had lied to him about her prior divorce, insisting instead that her former husband

was dead, when the husband, a Roman Catholic, testified that due to his strong religious convictions, he would not have married had he not believed his wife was a widow. *Query:* Can *Sanderson* be distinguished from *Wolfe*? How should a court determine what is "essential" to the marriage?

(2) It is generally held by most courts that any alleged fraud must be proved by clear and convincing evidence. *See, e.g., Bilowit v. Dolitsky*, 124 N.J. Super. 101, 304 A.2d 774 (N.J. Ch. 1973). Thus, although a premarital fraudulent intent not to have children is grounds to annul a marriage, the evidence must clearly and convincingly establish that the defendant's intention not to father children with the plaintiff was fixed prior to the marriage. *See, e.g., Tobon v. Sanchez*, 517 A.2d 885 (N.J. Ch. 1986).

(3) Most courts have consistently held that misrepresentations about premarital chastity do not generally constitute fraud that goes to the "essentials of the marriage". *See, e.g. DuPont v. DuPont*, 90 A.2d 468 (Del. 1952), *cert. denied*, 344 U.S. 836 (1952). However, many states will grant an annulment to a husband if a pregnant wife fraudulently misrepresents the paternity of the child she is carrying. *See, e.g. Arndt v. Arndt*, 82 N.E.2d 908 (Ill. App. Ct. 1948). What accounts for this result? Should a misrepresentation of pregnancy affect the "essentials of the marriage"? Why or why not? *Compare Mobley v. Mobley*, 16 So.2d 5 (Ala. 1943) *and Husband v. Wife*, 262 A.2d 656 (Del. Super. 1970) *with Masters v. Masters*, 108 N.W.2d 674 (Wis. 1961) *and Parks v. Parks*, 418 S.W.2d 726 (Ky. 1967).

(4) **Problem.** Wilma brings an action against Eugene in the State of Holmes, alleging that Eugene fraudulently concealed the existence of his prior marital status to another spouse at the time of their marriage, and therefore Eugene is liable to Wilma in tort for a "fraudulent inducement into a marriage contract." Wilma's attorney seeks compensatory and punitive damages for her mental pain and suffering, as well as for lost wages and retirement pay, totaling over $200,000. Eugene's attorney, however, argues that such a suit is barred by the state's "anti-heart balm" statutes that have abrogated the common law breach-of-promise-to-marry action. Should Wilma's action succeed? Why or why not? *See, e.g. Holcomb v. Kincaid*, 406 So. 2d 650 (La. Ct. App. 1981); *Buckley v. Buckley*, 133 Cal. App. 3d 927 (Cal. Ct. App. 1982); *Morris v. MacNab*,135 A.2d 657 (N.J. 1957); *Tuck v. Tuck*, 200 N.E.2d 554 (N.J. App. Div. 1964); *McGhee v. McGhee*, 353 P.2d 760 (Idaho 1960); *Humphreys v. Baird*, 90 S.E.2d 796 (Va. 1956). *See also* C.T. Foster, Annotation, *Liability of Putative Spouse to Other for Wrongfully Inducing Entry Into or Cohabitation Under Illegal, Void, or Nonexistent Marriage*, 72 A.L.R. 2d 956, 981 (1960) and Later Case Service.

[H] Consent Requirements: Duress

In most states, according to case or statutory law, a marriage where the consent of one of the parties was obtained by duress is a voidable marriage. Such duress must have existed at the time of the marriage, where the complaining party could not act as a free agent in entering the marriage due to coercive force or fear from another person. *See generally* Kingsley, *Duress as a Ground for Annulment of Marriage*, 33 S. Cal. L. Rev. 1 (1959); Brown, *The Shotgun Marriage*, 42 Tulane L. Rev. 837 (1968); Davies, *Duress and Nullity of Marriage*, 88 Law Q. Rev. 549 (1972); and Bradley, *Duress and Arranged Marriages*, 46 Mod. L. Rev. 499 (1983). *See also* M.L. Cross, Annotation, *What Constitutes Duress*

Sufficient to Warrant Divorce or Annulment of Marriage, 16 A.L.R. 2d 1430 (1951), and Later Case Service. The evidentiary burden of proving duress, however, may be a problem, as the following case illustrates.

STAKELUM v. TERRAL
Louisiana Court of Appeals
126 So. 2d 689 (1961)

YARRUT, JUDGE.

Plaintiff and defendant were students attending medical school in New Orleans. Both are in their early "twenties." She hails from a small Texas town, and he is a life-long resident of New Orleans. Having fallen in love and believing he would marry her, she engaged in premarital sexual intercourse on many occasions. As they sowed, they reaped. She became pregnant and promptly advised him. He promised to marry her, and made several voluntary dates for the ceremony, but, on each occasion, found some excuse for postponement. When the pregnancy developed to its sixth month, she became panicky and advised her sister in Texas, who was married to a detective on the police force of a large Texas city. Defendant's sister and brother-in-law came to New Orleans to attend the wedding after plaintiff fixed the ceremony for Friday, November 29th. They arrived in New Orleans on Wednesday (27th). Defendant and her brother-in-law spoke to plaintiff over the telephone and asked that he advance the ceremony to the 28th (Thanksgiving Day) because they had to return to Texas on the 29th, but wanted to be present for the wedding. Plaintiff, at first reluctant, was persuaded to agree to the 28th.

Plaintiff contends he agreed only because defendant and her brother-in-law threatened him and his parents with death. On the morning of the 28th, plaintiff and defendant, with their relatives, embarked by automobile for Mississippi; plaintiff and his parents in one automobile; defendant, her sister and husband (police-detective) in the other. Plaintiff suggested Mississippi as the place for the ceremony. They stopped at Picayune at the office of the Justice of the Peace. He agreed to perform the ceremony, but advised them first to go to Bay St. Louis for a license. Plaintiff and defendant went to Bay St. Louis, obtained the license, returned to Picayune and were there married by the same Justice of the Peace. After the ceremony an unsettled argument ensued between plaintiff and defendant over financial support for herself and the expected baby. All then left the scene of the wedding, plaintiff with his parents for New Orleans; defendant with her sister and husband for Texas. They have been separated ever since. . . .Because defendant's brother-in-law usually carried a pistol as a police officer in Texas, plaintiff sought to prove he carried a pistol in New Orleans, concealed on his person at all times, as a constant threat to plaintiff. The officer, his wife and defendant, all swore positively he carried no pistol at any time. Neither plaintiff nor his parents saw a pistol or heard threats on the way to, or during, the wedding ceremony.

The Justice of the Peace testified that, during the ceremony, everything was normal, nobody was frightened, and no threats were made. After the wedding, however, as the parties did not embrace and kiss, he remarked he did not know whether the ceremony was a wedding or a wake. He spoke to plaintiff and his parents in their automobile outside his office. When he repeated the above remark to them, one of them replied they would rather not discuss the matter. When plaintiff's parents were asked why they did not notify the police when threatened, they said they did not have time. All they need have done was to refrain from accompanying their son to Mississippi; alerted the New Orleans or Bay St. Louis authorities; or informed the Justice of the Peace before the ceremony, or when he came to their automobile, after the ceremony, to remark that the ceremony appeared to be a wake. Neither defendant nor her brother-in-law was present at that time, so any one of them could have spoken freely, even if previously silent under fear of duress. The whole story, as developed by the testimony, convinces us, as it did the District Judge, that no threats of bodily harm or death were ever made; that everything said or done was to appeal to plaintiff's manhood and decency; that plaintiff and his parents had every opportunity to notify the New Orleans or Bay St. Louis police, or the Justice of the Peace. It is apparent this annulment suit is plaintiff's delayed answer to defendant's demands for financial assistance for herself and baby, with the hope of avoiding that responsibility. Plaintiff has failed to carry the burden of proving his case by a preponderance of the evidence. We can find no error in the judgment of the District Court and it is affirmed, at the cost of plaintiff. *Affirmed.*

NOTES AND QUESTIONS

(1) The courts have generally held that the test for duress is a subjective one, and is based upon an individual's particular fear of force or coercion, rather than being based on an objective "reasonable person of ordinary prudence" standard. *Query:* Was the husband in the *Stakelum* case *above* subjectively under duress? Why or why not?

In a similar case, *Worthington v. Worthington*, 352 S.W.2d 80 (Ark. 1961), the husband Paul claimed that his pregnant wife Judith's stepfather threatened to shoot him if he did not marry Judith, and when the parties traveled to Idabel, Oklahoma to be married, Paul conveyed these threats against his life to the Idabel, Oklahoma Chief of Police. The Chief of Police later testified: "I told the boy he didn't have to marry the girl and the choice was strictly up to him. I said that I didn't know what the Arkansas statutes were but that I could tell him what they are in Oklahoma and I said "you do as you please, you don't have to marry her." Paul went ahead with the wedding, later claiming that Judith's stepfather also threatened to return to Little Rock, Arkansas, and kill Paul's parents as well. A marriage under duress? Why or why not? What would happen, hypothetically, if Judith Worthington's stepfather was accidentally killed in an automobile accident three days after the marriage, but Paul waited an additional year after the automobile accident before he brought his annulment proceeding based on duress?

Query: What public policy rationale—if any—is served by denying annulments in both the *Worthington* and *Stakelum* cases?

(2) Note that the *Stakelum* and *Worthington* cases, *supra*, were decided prior to the widespread adoption of no-fault divorce, and at a time when the stigma for women bearing a child out of wedlock was considerably greater than it is today. Courts of that era might also give a young man the "choice" of marrying his "wronged" girlfriend or going to jail. *See, e.g.* Walter Waddlington, *Shotgun Marriage by Operation of Law,* 1 Ga. L. Rev. 183 (1967). Again, with greater societal acceptance of no-fault divorce and single parenthood, marriage under duress actions are not as common as they once were a number of years ago.

[I] Limited-Purpose Marriages

A *sham marriage* is a marriage for a limited purpose and with a limited intent, such as a man marrying a pregnant woman only to legitimize their child, but without intending to consent to any of the other normal incidents of marriage. In this situation, some courts have held that such a marriage with limited intent and for a limited purpose is valid for *all* purposes, regardless of the parties' motive for marriage, and no annulment may be granted. *See, e.g. Campbell v. Moore*, 1 S.E.2d 784 (S.C. 1939); *Schibi v. Schibi*, 69 A.2d 831 (Conn. 1949); *Bishop v. Bishop*, 308 N.Y.S.2d 998 (N.Y. Sup. Ct. 1970) *And see generally* Wade, *Limited Purpose Marriages*, 45 Mod. L. Rev. 259 (1982); Comment, *Sham Marriages*, 20 U. Chi. L. Rev. 710 (1953); A. Della Porta, Annotation, *Validity of the Marriage as Affected by the Parties Intention That it Should Be Only a Matter of Form or Jest*, 14 A.L.R.2d 624 (1950) and Later Case Service.

Sham marriages have also been frequently used by some foreign nationals who marry American citizens in order to circumvent American immigration laws. The possibility of this limited-purpose marriage has resulted in Immigration and Naturalization Service investigatory procedures covering all marriages where one party is a foreign national. *See* Note, *The Constitutionality of the I.N.S. Sham Marriage Investigation Policy*, 99 Harv. L. Rev. 1238 (1986). Various courts have held that sham marriages for immigration purposes are invalid marriages. *See, e.g., United States v. Rubenstein*, 151 F.2d 915 (2d Cir. 1945), *cert. denied*, 326 U.S. 766 (1945); United States v. Lutwak, 195 F.2d 748 (7th Cir. 1952), *aff'd* 344 U.S. 604 (1953). *See also* Note, *Immigration Marriage Fraud Amendments of 1986: Till Congress Do Us Part*, 41 U. Miami L. Rev. 1087 (1987).

A marriage in jest, on the other hand, although it is based upon apparent consent of the parties, actually involves no consent, since the parties realize the marriage is no more than a "joke." Because a marriage is presumed to be valid and possess the necessary element of mutual consent, however, the burden is on the party attempting to annul the marriage to demonstrate that it was a marriage in jest. Nevertheless, "where two people go through a ceremony of marriage having no object whatever, but simply as the result of youthful exuberance, dare, and jest, and no cohabitation follows, the courts in most [but not all] cases have reasoned that it would not be in the interest of society to declare such a marriage valid, since there is not even a minimum objective to be attained by compelling two people to accept the responsibilities of their inconsiderate and foolhardy experience, except, perhaps, the doubtful purpose of deterring other young people from tampering lightly with a relationship of such fundamental importance." *See* A. Della Porta, Annotation, *Validity of the Marriage as Affected by the Parties' Intention That it Should Be Only a Matter of Form or Jest*, 14 A.L.R.2d 624 (1950) and Later Case Service.

The following case demonstrates some of the problems involving a sham marriage for limited immigration purposes.

ROE v. IMMIGRATION & NATURALIZATION SERVICE
United States Court of Appeals
771 F.2d 1328 (9th Cir. 1985)

WIGGINS, CIRCUIT JUDGE.

Hurn Bu Roe invokes our jurisdiction under 8 U.S.C. § 1105(a) to review a decision of the Board of Immigration Appeals (BIA). The BIA found him deportable for failure to fulfill his marital agreement and as an alien who was excludable at the time of entry for lack of a valid labor certification and a valid visa. The BIA also denied Roe's application for suspension of deportation. We affirm.

BACKGROUND

Hurn Bu Roe is a native and citizen of South Korea who entered the United States in April 1971 as the spouse of a fifth preference immigrant, Yong Cha Kang. Shortly before his entry into the United States, Roe divorced his first wife, Sook Hee Song, and married Yong. Within a few weeks after his entry into the United States, Roe divorced Yong. Roe returned to Korea and reentered the United States in October 1971 along with his first wife and their child. In December 1971, Roe remarried his first wife. In March 1972, Roe filed a second preference visa petition on behalf of his first wife.

On August 23, 1974, the INS initiated deportation proceedings against Roe. He was charged as deportable under 8 U.S.C. §§ 1251(a)(2) and (c), for entry into the United States with an immigrant visa procured by fraud on the basis of a marriage which was judicially annulled or terminated within two years of entry. Subsequently, the INS amended its original charge. Roe was also charged as deportable under 8 U.S.C. § 1251(c)(2), for failure or refusal to fulfill his marital agreement with Yong, and under 8 U.S.C. § 1251(a)(1) as an alien who was excludable at the time of entry for lack of a valid labor certification [8 U.S.C.§ 1182(a)(14)] and for lack of a valid visa [8 U.S.C. § 1182(a)(20)]. Roe denied the allegations of a sham marriage but admitted that he entered the United States with the purpose of performing skilled or unskilled labor and lacked a valid labor certification at the time of his entry. Roe also applied for suspension of deportation under 8 U.S.C. § 1254(a)(1).

In January 1982, the IJ held that the INS met its burden of demonstrating that Roe failed to fulfill his marital agreement which he made solely for the purpose of procuring his entry as an immigrant, *i.e.*, that Roe's marriage was a sham entered into solely for immigration purposes. Accordingly, the IJ found Roe deportable as charged under 8 U.S.C. § 1251(c)(2). The IJ also concluded that Roe was deportable as charged under 8 U.S.C. § 1251(a)(1) because he was excludable at the time of entry under 8 U.S.C. §§ 1182(a)(14) and (20). The IJ rejected Roe's application for suspension of deportation on the ground that Roe failed to establish extreme hardship. On appeal, the BIA affirmed the IJ's decision. Roe timely filed the present petition for review.

DISCUSSION

Roe contends that: (1) the BIA's finding of a sham marriage is not supported by substantial evidence; (2) the INS violated its own regulation and denied him due process by preventing him from rebutting adverse evidence and presenting evidence on his behalf; (3) he was inadequately represented by counsel at his deportation hearing; (4) the BIA abused its discretion in denying his request for suspension of deportation; and (5) the immigration judge violated 8 C.F.R. § 242.17 (1985) by failing to notify him of his alleged eligibility for relief from deportation under 8 U.S.C. § 1251(f). We address each contention in turn.

1. Sham Marriage

Roe contends that the BIA's determination that his marriage to Yong was a sham is not supported by substantial evidence. We disagree.

We must sustain the BIA's finding of a sham marriage if it is supported by substantial and probative evidence. *Garcia-Jaramillo v. INS*, 604 F.2d 1236, 1238 (9th Cir. 1979), *cert. denied*, 449 U.S. 828 (1980). Although a marriage may be legally valid under the laws of the country where the marriage took place, the INS is free to conduct an inquiry to determine whether the marriage was entered into for the purpose of circumventing the immigration laws. *Id.* "A marriage is a sham if the bride and groom did not intend to establish a life together at the time they were married." *Id.* (*quoting Bark v. INS*, 511 F.2d 1200, 1201 (9th Cir. 1975)).

Based on the record before us, we are satisfied that substantial evidence supports the determination that Roe's marriage to Yong was a sham. We agree with the IJ that the sequence of events demonstrates that Roe married Yong solely for the purpose of securing an immigrant visa for himself and eventually for his first wife and their child.

The record reveals that on December 30, 1966, Roe married Sook Hee Song. The following year Sook gave birth to their oldest daughter.

In 1970, Roe was introduced to Yong Cha Kang and met with her on several occasions. Shortly after Yong informed Roe that she would soon be immigrating to the United States as the beneficiary of a fifth preference visa, Roe proposed to Yong. Roe and Yong were married on December 7, 1970. That same day Roe divorced his first wife.

Yong testified that she learned of Roe's previous marriage only after submitting a visa petition on his behalf. Yong also testified that she and Roe did not live together in Korea or in the United States after their marriage.

Yong immigrated to the United States on December 19, 1970, as a permanent resident. She settled in Columbus, Georgia, to live with her sister and brother-in-law.

On the basis of his marriage to Yong, Roe was issued an "Immigrant Visa and Alien Registration" on March 16, 1971. Although the visa indicated that Roe's final address in the United States was the home of Yong in Columbus, Georgia and that Roe's intended port of entry was Los Angeles, California, Roe entered the United States on April 3, 1971, through Honolulu, Hawaii. Upon his arrival in Honolulu, Roe was greeted by a long-time friend, Barney Kim, whom he had contacted prior to leaving Korea. Roe stayed with Mr. Kim and secured employment from him. Within a few days after his arrival, Roe obtained a business license in Hawaii.

After ascertaining that Yong had received his "green card," Roe flew to Georgia on a round-trip ticket. In Georgia, Roe did not stay with Yong; he registered at the YMCA for the duration of his sojourn.

Yong testified that she asked Roe to stay with her in Georgia but he refused. She also testified that Roe never sought employment in Georgia. After obtaining his green card from Yong, and before returning to Hawaii, Roe initiated divorce proceedings through the Korean Consulate's office in Houston, Texas. Roe's divorce from Yong was finalized on May 11, 1971.

Roe returned to Honolulu and on May 9, 1971, departed for Korea. He returned to the United States on October 9, 1971, again through Honolulu, Hawaii. Roe's first wife and his daughter also arrived in Honolulu that same day. Roe's first wife entered the United States as a non-immigrant student. Roe and his first family proceeded to settle in southern California where Roe and his first wife remarried on December 22, 1971. Although Roe testified that he found employment opportunities and good living conditions in Hawaii and for that reason did not want to live in Columbus with Yong, he relinquished these opportunities to settle in southern California with his first wife. As the BIA noted, "the resourcefulness with which [Roe] established himself in California is notably missing with regard to his intentions and efforts to live with [Yong] in Columbus."

Roe and his defense witnesses disputed Yong's testimony. Roe claimed that he sought employment in Georgia but could not find any and that he wanted Yong to return to Hawaii with him where he had a job and could provide for their needs. Roe also testified that he divorced Yong because she would "not obey." Roe's defense witnesses claimed that Yong was aware of Roe's first marriage when she married him. The IJ found them not credible. The immigration judge is in a better position to assess the credibility of a witness than are we. *See Espinoza Ojeda v. INS*, 419 F.2d 183, 186 (9th Cir. 1969). Because the IJ's credibility determinations are grounded upon reasonable, substantial and probative evidence, we will not disturb them. *Garcia-Jaramillo v. INS*, 604 F.2d 1236, 1238 (9th Cir. 1979).

Based on our review of the record as a whole, we conclude that the BIA's determination that Roe's marriage to Yong was a sham was amply supported by substantial evidence. . . .[Roe's other contentions, which the court also rejected, have been omitted.]

CONCLUSION

The BIA's order of deportation is Affirmed and the petition for review is denied.

NOTES AND QUESTIONS

(1) The courts are widely split on the validity of sham marriages for a limited purpose. On one hand, the slightest limited consent has resulted in a binding marriage for *all* purposes, especially in cases where children are legitimized through a sham marriage. *See, e.g., Bishop v. Bishop*, 308 N.Y.S.2d 998 (N.Y. Sup. Ct. 1970); *Schibi v. Schibi*, 69 A.2d 831 (Conn. 1949).

On the other hand, a number of sham marriages for immigration purposes have been held to be invalid. *See, e.g., United States v. Rubenstein*, 151 F.2d 915, 919 (2d Cir. 1945), *cert. denied*, 326 U.S. 766 (1945) ("It is quite true that a marriage without subsequent consummation will be valid; but if the spouses agree to a marriage . . . with the understanding that they will put an end to it as soon as it has served its purpose to deceive, they have never really agreed to be married at all."); *United States v. Lutwak*, 195 F.2d 748, 753 (7th Cir. 1952), *aff'd* 344 U.S. 604 (1953) ("A sham marriage, void under the law of this country as against public policy, can have no validity.")

In evaluating two marriages alleged to be shams, the court in *United States v. Diogo*, 320 F.2d 898 (2d Cir. 1963) held that the two consummated marriages were valid because the immigrant spouses apparently contracted these marriages in good faith. And in *Johl v. United States*, 370 F.2d 174 (9th Cir. 1966), the court held that the validity or invalidity of the marriage was irrelevant, since the government was concerned with the parties' *fraudulent purpose* in deceiving the INS, rather than determining the validity or invalidity of the marital relationship itself. *See also United States v. Tagalicud*, 84 F.3d 1180 (9th Cir. 1996) (holding that marriage to an immigrant for financial gain is not necessarily a sham marriage); *Kleinfield v. Veruki*, 372 S.E.2d 407 (Va. Ct. App. 1988) (applying New Jersey law) (holding that a "green-card" sham marriage for immigration purposes was a voidable marriage, and not void *ab initio*). *Query:* Which approach did the *Roe* court, *above*, adopt? Which approach is most persuasive to you? Why?

(2) Professor Clark criticizes these inconsistent judicial decisions, arguing that a marriage must be based upon the consent and agreement of husband and wife to be married, rather than turning upon various external governmental policies, such as immigration law or tax law. A marriage, in other words, should be valid for all purposes, or invalid for all purposes. *See generally* 1 Homer H. Clark, Jr., Law of Domestic Relations 212–18 (2d ed. 1987), and Green & Long, Marriage and Family Law Agreements 66–74 (1984).

(3) Since marriage to an American citizen normally exempts an alien from the quota restrictions of the federal Immigration and Naturalization Act, 8 U.S.C.A. Sec. 1151, so-called "green card" marriages, or sham marriages for immigration purposes, have constituted a major problem for the Immigration and Naturalization Service (INS). *See, e.g. Kleinfield v. Veruki,* 372 S.E.2d 407 (Va. Ct. App. 1988) (involving a New Jersey "green card" marriage entered into to avoid INS quota restrictions). Accordingly, in 1986, Congress enacted the Immigration Marriage Fraud Amendments Act, 8 U.S.C.A. Sec. 1154(b) which basically creates a two year "conditional" status for certain alien spouses who become permanent resident aliens by virtue of a marriage entered into less than two years before obtaining such conditional status. This conditional status is removed if after two years the marriage is again determined to be "genuine" at the time the spouse obtained permanent resident status. However, this conditional status can be revoked if the Attorney General determines that the marriage has been judicially terminated within the conditional two year period. If deportation proceedings have been initiated at the time of the marriage, however, then Section 5 of the Immigration Marriage Fraud Amendments Act requires that the alien spouse leave the United States for two years before any further adjustment of status can be made by the INS. Although some federal courts have upheld the constitutionality of Section 5 of the Act, *see, e.g. Almario v. Attorney General*, 872 F.2d 147 (6th Cir. 1989) and *Anetekhai v. INS,* 876 F.2d 1218 (5th Cir. 1989), the District of Columbia Federal Circuit Court in the case of *Escobar v. INS*, 896 F.2d 564 (D.C. Cir. 1990), *appeal dismissed*, 925 F.2d 488 (D.C. Cir. 1991) held that Sec. 5 of the Act violated the citizen *wife's* constitutional due process rights and privacy interests by depriving her of her alien husband for such a two year period. Largely based upon these constitutional concerns raised in the *Escobar* case, the Immigration Act of 1990, 8 U.S.C.A. Sec. 1255(e)(3) amended existing law under the Immigration Fraud Amendments Act that the two year deportation provision shall not apply if the alien spouse establishes by clear and convincing evidence that his or her marriage to an American citizen was entered into in good faith, without any fee or other consideration paid by the alien spouse, and was not for the purpose of procuring the alien's entry into the United States in circumvention of immigration quota restrictions. *See generally* Note, *Immigration Marriage Fraud Amendments of 1986: Till Congress Do Us Part*, 41 U. Miami L. Rev. 1087 (1987); Note, *The Constitutionality of the INS Sham Marriage*

Investigation Policy, 99 Harv. L. Rev. 1238 (1986); Carol Sanger, *Immigration Reform and Control of the Undocumented Family*, 2 Georgetown Immigration L.J. 295 (1987).

(4) **Marriage in Jest.** The fact situation involving marriages in jest typically involves young people, who, after a tennis match, dance, or another social engagement, dare each other to get married, and do so. In a relatively small number of reported cases, if such marriages remain unconsummated, and the parties do not cohabit after the marriage, a court may grant an annulment based upon the lack of voluntary consent, and based upon the parties' relative immaturity. *See, e.g., Davis v. Davis* 175 A. 574 (Conn. 1934); Meredith v. Shakespeare, 122 S.E. 520 (W.Va. 1924). *See also* A. Della Porta, Annotation, *Validity of the Marriage as Affected by the Parties Intention That it Should Be Only a Matter of Form or Jest,* 14 A.L.R.2d 624 (1950) and Later Case Service. However, in the case of *Hand v. Berry*, 170 Ga. 743, 154 S.E. 239, 239 (Ga. 1930), a young couple dared each other to marry "in a spirit of hilarity and without serious intent," "in a spirit of fun, braggadocio, and levity," and "in a spirit of misguided fun and jest." The Georgia court was not amused, found no fraud, and held that the marriage was valid. *See also Lannamann v. Lannamann*, 171 Pa. Super. 147, 89 A.2d 897, 898 (Pa. Super. Ct. 1952) ("since there was no fraud, duress, or lack of mental capacity, the marriage is valid."). *See generally* Green & Long, Marriage and Family Law Agreements 64–66 (1984). *Query:* Can these marriage-in-jest cases be reconciled? If not, what is the underlying public policy rationale for each decision?

§ 1.08 Conflict of Laws: Which Marriage Law Governs?

Americans, as a migratory people, often move from state to state, and occasionally move between foreign countries. Due to the large number and variety of state statutes that regulate marriage and divorce, it thus becomes necessary to determine which particular state's law will govern the solemnization of marriage under applicable conflict-of-laws principles.

The traditional *lex loci contractus* rule states that the law of the place of celebration governs the legal requirements for marriage. That is to say, a marriage valid where it was celebrated is valid everywhere, unless such marriage violates the forum state's strong public policy. *See, e.g.*, Restatement, Conflict of Laws, §§ 121-123 (1934). The more recent *Second Restatement* of Conflict of Laws approach, which has been adopted by a majority of states, holds that the validity of a marriage is to be determined by the local law of the state which has the "most significant relationship" to the spouses and the marriage. Restatement (Second) Conflict of Laws, § 283(1) (1971). Section 283(2) of the *Second Restatement* also provides that "A marriage which satisfies the requirements of the state where the marriage was contracted will everywhere be recognized as valid unless it violates the strong public policy of another state which has the most significant relationship to the spouses and the marriage."

What constitutes a "significant relationship" to the spouses and the marriage? Restatement (Second) Conflict of Laws § 6 (1971), states that relevant factors in choosing the applicable rule of law would include: (a) the needs of the interstate and international systems; (b) the relevant policies of the forum; (c) the relevant policies of other interested states and the relative interests of those states in the determination of the particular issue; (d) the protection of justified expectations; (e) the basic policies underlying the particular field of law; (f) certainty, predictability, and uniformity of result; and (g) ease in the determination and application of the law to be applied.

Since conflict of laws problems often result in unexpected "land mines" for the unwary family law practitioner, both student and attorney are strongly urged to do collateral reading in this area before litigating a questionable marriage with any related conflict of laws issue. A recommended bibliography should include Taintor, *Marriage in the Conflicts of Law*, 9 Vand. L. Rev. 607 (1956) (a classic older work); Baade, *Marriage and Divorce in American Conflicts of Law*, 72 Colum. L. Rev. 329 (1972) (criticizing the *Second Restatement* position); and Reese, *Marriage in American Conflicts of Law*, 26 Int'l. & Comp. L.Q. 952 (1977) (defending the *Second Restatement* position). *See also* Gotlieb, *The Incidental Question Revisited*, 26 Int'l. & Comp. L.Q. 734 (1977); Fine, *The Application of Issue Analysis to Choice of Law Involving Family Law Matters in the United States*, 26 Loy. L. Rev. 31, 295 (1980); Smart, *Interest Analysis, False Conflicts, and the Essential Validity of Marriage*, 14 Anglo-Am. L. Rev. 225 (1985); and Richman & Reynolds, Understanding Conflict of Laws, Chapter 6, *Family Law* §§ 117–22 (2nd ed., Matthew Bender 1995).

How do the courts apply these conflict of laws principles in order to determine the validity of a marriage? The following case is an illustration.

SEIZER v. SESSIONS
Washington Court of Appeals
915 P.2d 553 (1996), *rev'd*, 940 P.2d 261 (Wash. 1997)

CHARLES K. WIGGINS, JUDGE PRO TEM.

Rosalie Sessions, first wife of the late Elmer Sessions, and Barbara Sessions, Elmer's third wife, each claims a portion of lottery proceeds won by Elmer before his death. Elmer abandoned Rosalie in Texas almost 40 years ago, and later married Barbara while living in Washington. Rosalie claims that Elmer never divorced her. Ownership of the lottery proceeds depends on the choice of law. Under Texas law, Rosalie might be entitled to one-quarter of the proceeds if she can prove that Elmer never divorced her. Under Washington law, Barbara might be entitled to the entire proceeds if Barbara can prove that Rosalie's marriage with Elmer was defunct. . . .

FACTS

Elmer and Rosalie Sessions married on November 21, 1941, in Houston, Texas. Their daughter Bonnie, now Bonnie Seizer (Seizer) was born in 1942. Rosalie and Elmer lived in Houston until approximately 1948. From 1948 until 1954 the family traveled throughout the country, living in eight cities during these 5 years. Elmer's work in the oil business required frequent moves.

In 1954, while living in New York State, Rosalie Sessions was hospitalized for the treatment of mental illness. After the hospital released Rosalie, Elmer moved the family back to Houston. Rosalie became ill again during the drive back. In Houston, Elmer left Rosalie and [Bonnie] living with Rosalie's parents. . . .Then Elmer "just announced he was leaving." No one knew where he was going. . . .

While separated from Rosalie, Elmer married Mary Anastos in July 1955; Elmer and Mary divorced in 1982. In 1984, Elmer and Barbara Sessions married. Barbara was unaware of his pre-existing marriage to Rosalie. The couple lived in Washington during their marriage.

In September, 1989, Elmer and Barbara visited Tucson, Arizona, on an extended business trip. On September 27, 1989, either Barbara or Elmer purchased a ticket in the Arizona State Lottery and won $2,576,908.30, with a net annual payment to Elmer of $97,922.53 for 20 years. The beneficiary of the annuity is Barbara M. Sessions.

Elmer died on August 19, 1991. . . . In 1992, Seizer, as Rosalie's guardian, filed this action seeking Rosalie's community property interest in the Arizona lottery proceeds. Seizer sought a partial summary judgment that the law of Texas applied. Barbara Sessions moved for summary judgment dismissing the case. On March 18, 1994 the trial court granted summary judgment in favor of Barbara, holding that as a matter of Washington law, the marriage was defunct and that RCW 26.16.140 precluded recovery [to Rosalie]. Seizer appeals. . . .

ANALYSIS

Seizer argues that the trial court erred in determining as a matter of law that Washington law applies. . . . We must first determine whether Texas and Washington law actually conflict. When the parties dispute choice of law, an actual conflict between the law of Washington and the law of another state must be shown to exist before Washington courts will engage in a conflict of laws analysis. . . .

Texas law differs from Washington law. Under Washington's separate and apart statute, after a marriage becomes defunct, earnings and accumulations are the acquiring spouse's separate property. . . . RCW 26.16.140 and *Aetna Life Ins. Co. v. Bunt*, 110 Wash. 2d 368, 754 P.2d 993 (Wash. 1988). . . . A marriage is considered defunct when both parties to the marriage no longer have the will to continue the marital relationship. . . . A finding that a marriage is defunct will defeat the presumption that all property acquired during the marriage is community property. . . .

The Family Code of Texas does not treat marriages as defunct even if the spouses live separate and apart. Once a marriage exists, under Texas law, it is terminated only by death or court decree. . . . Estate of Claveria v. Claveria, 615 S.W.2d 164, 167 (Tex. 1981). . . . Under Texas law, the first spouse and the subsequent putative spouse each has an interest in assets acquired by the twice-married spouse. . . . *Caruso v. Lucius* 448 S.W.2d 711, 712 n. 1 (Tex. Ct. App. 1970). . . .

The differences in Washington and Texas law lead to differing results in this case. Under Washington law, if the trial court found the marriage defunct, Rosalie would have no interest in the lottery proceeds since Elmer acquired this asset after their separation, and Elmer could freely dispose of his separate property by designating Barbara as his beneficiary. Under Texas law, if Rosalie demonstrates that Elmer did not obtain a divorce, she would recover one-quarter of the lottery proceeds. Under Texas law, Barbara would be entitled to half of the community property acquired by herself and Elmer plus a further one-quarter as Elmer's beneficiary if she proves that she innocently entered into a valid marriage with Elmer with no knowledge of his pre-existing marriage. . . .

Since an actual conflict in laws exists that could lead to differing results, we proceed to decide which state's law applies. Washington state has adopted the "most significant relationship rule" as developed by the Restatement (Second) of Conflict of Laws. Section 6 of the Restatement sets forth seven factors relevant to a determination of the state having the most significant relationship to the issue:

(a) the needs of the interstate and international systems,

(b) the relevant policies of the forum,

(c) the relevant polices of other interested states and the relative interests of those states in the determination of the particular issue,

(d) the protection of justified expectations,

(e) the basic policies underlying the particular field of law,

(f) certainty, predictability and uniformity of result, and

(g) ease in the determination and application of the law applied. . . .

Both Washington and Texas are community property states, with similar law relating to community property. . . . But the precise issue in this case turns, not so much on community property law, as on the nature of the marital relationship. . . . The laws of Washington and Texas spring from different views of the nature of marriage, and we find this difference significant to this case. Washington law has regarded marriage as a "civil contract" from the earliest territorial days. . . . [Under] the Dissolution Act of 1973, which eliminated "fault" as a ground for divorce. . . "[t]he determination to dissolve a marriage rests with the spouses, not with the state." Professor [Luvern] Ricke [in 49 Wash. L. Rev. 375, 378 (1974)] points out that the 1973 Act also changed the role of the parties, giving them a much larger role in negotiating the economic aspects of the dissolution of their marriage, much as contracting parties can negotiate the end of a contract. . . . Even before the 1973 Act, Washington's "separate and apart" statute, RCW 26.16.140, allowed the parties to end the community property aspects of their marriage by living separate and apart. . . . The significant point for our purposes is that under Washington law, the spouses by mutual consent can terminate the marriage or can mutually treat the community property presumptions as terminated by agreeing to live separate and apart. . . .

Texas law does not have a "separate and apart" statute. To the contrary, its settled law favors the sanctity of the marital relationship. As one Texas court stated, "[t]he institution of marriage is a status, more than a mere contract, and has been defined as the voluntary union for life of one man and one woman as husband and wife, to the exclusion of all others." . . . Simpson v. Simpson, 380 S.W.2d 855, 858 (Tex. Ct. App. 1964). Under Texas law, even if the spouses have been separated for great lengths of time and even if one spouse has remarried without divorcing, the first spouse still may recover a portion of the decedent's estate. . . . *Caruso v. Lucius, supra* 448 S.W.2d 711, 712-713 (Tex. Ct. App. 1970). . . .

Consideration of these relevant policies of the two interested states strongly favors the application of Texas law to this case. Texas was the last domicil of Elmer and Rosalie and remains Rosalie's home. Texas law does not permit Elmer to terminate the marital status without formal proceedings, and Texas has a strong interest in providing for the abandoned spouse, who is disabled. Although Washington allows spouses to agree to live separate and apart, Washington has no interest in allowing deserting spouses from other states to seek refuge under Washington's separate and apart statute. This is especially true when the abandoned spouse is mentally incompetent. . . .

The basic policy underlying the marital property laws of both Texas and Washington is to provide fairly and equitably for both spouses when the marriage terminates in separation, dissolution, or death. Texas law more fairly and equitably protects an abandoned spouse such as Rosalie. . . .

CONCLUSION

After considering all relevant factors, we hold that Texas has the most significant relationship to the determination of ownership of Elmer's lottery proceeds. Accordingly, we reverse the summary judgment and remand for a determination of Rosalie's interest in the lottery proceeds under Texas law. . . .

NOTES AND QUESTIONS

(1) The Court of Appeals opinion in *Seizer v. Sessions* reprinted above was subsequently reversed by the Washington Supreme Court. The higher court adopted the Restatement (2d) of Conflict of Laws Section 258 presumption that the character of personal property should be determined under the law of the state where the spouse who acquired that property was domiciled (in this case Washington):

> The Restatement comments contain two presumptions. "[T]he local law of the state where the spouses were domiciled at the time the movable was acquired will usually be applied to determine marital property interests. . . ." Sec. 258, cmt. b. And "[w]hen the spouses have separate domiciles at the time of the acquisition of the movable, the local law of the state where the spouse who acquired the movable was domiciled at the time will usually be applied. . . ." Sec. 258 cmt. c. If we apply the presumption in comment c, Washington law should be applied because Rosalie and Elmer had separate domiciles when he acquired the [lottery] winnings and he was domiciled in Washington at that time. *Seizer v. Sessions*, 940 P.2d 261, 265 (Wash. 1997) *reversing* 915 P.2d 553 (Wash. Ct. App. 1996).

But query: If the local law where the spouse who acquires the personal property will "usually" be applied, does this necessarily mandate that local law will "always" be applied? Are there any special circumstances involved in this case that suggest a different outcome? Why or why not? Will this case arguably encourage deserting spouses to "forum shop" in states like Washington that recognizes the contractual concept of a "defunct marriage"? Or is the Washington Supreme Court decision the better-reasoned view in providing needed uniformity and predictability in interstate conflict-of-laws disputes?

(2) Marital conflict of laws controversies are not limited to legal disputes between American states, as their scope can be international as well. *See, e.g. Schwebel v. Unger*, 42 D.L.R. 2d 622 (Ontario Ct. App.), *aff'd*, 48 D.L.R.2d 644 (Supreme Ct. of Canada) (1964), where an Ontario court held that a woman was free to marry even though a prior Italian divorce decree from her previous husband was not recognized under Ontario law, since at the time of her remarriage she had been domiciled in Israel, where an Italian divorce *would* be recognized.

(3) **Problem.** Ralph is an American citizen, born in Seattle, Washington, but he is also a "habitual resident" of the United Kingdom. Ralph first met Maria—a Brazilian citizen—in St. Moritz, Switzerland, where she was vacationing while she was separated from her former husband, and where Ralph worked temporarily as an artistic director. Maria had been granted a decree of desquite in Brazil from her first husband, but this did not entitle her under Brazilian law to remarry. After living in Las Vegas, Nevada for seven weeks, Maria obtained a Nevada divorce from her first husband, and the next day Maria married Ralph in Las

Vegas. Ralph and Maria then moved to London, England, where Ralph worked and lived. Ralph has sought a petition from an English court that his marriage celebrated in Las Vegas to Maria is a valid and subsisting marriage. In her answer, Maria has alleged that at all material times, she was a citizen of and domiciled in Brazil, where the status of her former marriage was regarded as indissoluble. Accordingly, Maria alleges that she lacked the legal capacity to enter into their Nevada marriage, and Maria therefore prays that her marriage to Ralph be declared null and void.

How should the English court decide this marital dispute? What conflict of laws theories and other family-law theories should the court arguably apply to this case? Under what applicable laws? *See Lawrence v. Lawrence,* (1985) 3 W.L.R. 125 (Court of Appeal) [England]. The *Lawrence* decision has been analyzed and criticized by P.B. Carter in *Capacity to Remarry After a Foreign Divorce,* 101 Law Q. Rev. 496 (1985). *See also* Fentiman, *The Validity of Marriage and the Proper Law,* 44 Cambridge L.J. 256 (1985).

(4) *Query.* If a marriage valid where celebrated is generally valid elsewhere, is the corollary of this rule equally true: that a marriage not valid where celebrated is not valid elsewhere? The following case discusses this issue.

RANDALL v. RANDALL
Nebraska Supreme Court
345 N.W.2d 319 (1984)

KRIVOSHA, C.J.

By this appeal we are asked to determine whether the validity of a marriage should be determined in accordance with the laws where the marriage was performed or pursuant to the laws where the parties reside. The trial court concluded that although the marriage was invalid under the laws where performed, it was "substantially" in accordance with the laws where the parties resided, and therefore should be recognized. Because we believe the trial court was in error, we must reverse and dismiss.

The appellee, Feather Dell Randall, and the appellant, Robert W. Randall, met sometime during the summer of 1963. At that time Ms. Randall was working as a receptionist to support herself and her infant son. By the late summer of 1963 the parties to this action had established a meretricious relationship. They were unable to marry because Mr. Randall was then married and did not obtain a decree of divorce until October 4, 1963. Under Nebraska law this meant that Mr. Randall was not free to marry anyone else anywhere in the world until April 5, 1964, a fact known to both Ms. Randall and Mr. Randall.

While there is a dispute, we find from the evidence that in March of 1964 the parties traveled to Acapulco, Mexico, for the purpose of entering into marriage sometime while in Mexico. Prior to April 5, 1964, the first date both parties knew they were free to marry, they went to a local government office in order to obtain a marriage license. The parties answered questions concerning their origins, occupations, marital status, and other information; they were fingerprinted; and they signed their names to a document in Spanish, before four witnesses. At the conclusion of the proceedings they were congratulated by a Mexican official, who advised them that they were now married. The parties then advised the official that they could not get married until April 5, 1964, and both parties obviously recognized that whatever transaction took place before the Mexican official was not sufficient to cause them to be husband and wife under Mexican law.

The next day, on April 5, 1964, the parties drove to Mexico City, Mexico, to find an English-speaking minister by whom they could be married. Again, there is a conflict, but it appears clear from the evidence that both parties were advised by the minister that under Mexican law a religious ceremony was not valid unless there had earlier been a valid Mexican civil ceremony. By deposition, the minister testified that he specifically recalled advising the parties that in Mexico a religious ceremony had no legal validity. The religious ceremony was merely a "blessing" upon a prior civil marriage. Mexican law recognizes only those marriages which are performed in a proceeding before a Mexican civil authority. Civil Code of Mexico, tit. 4, ch. VII, art. 103b; tit. 5, ch. II, art. 146 (1964). . . .

The parties left Mexico the next day and went to California for several days, and then returned to Nebraska where they have continuously resided. The evidence is without dispute that from the time of their return to Nebraska until the time they separated, the parties to this action cohabited in this state as husband and wife, filed tax returns as married persons, and otherwise conducted their business as husband and wife. The record further discloses that Mr. Randall adopted Ms. Randall's son by her previous marriage. The son has now reached his majority and is not involved in this action.

The trial court specifically found that the marriage performed in Mexico was void. It did find, however, that by applying Nebraska law, the religious ceremony performed in Mexico substantially complied with the requirements of the Nebraska law and that therefore the parties in fact were husband and wife. The court then divided the marital estate between the parties, and directed Mr. Randall to pay Ms. Randall certain alimony.

Mr. Randall has now appealed to this court, assigning five specific errors committed by the trial court. Mr. Randall's principal assignment of error is that once the trial court determined that both of the marriage ceremonies performed in Mexico were invalid, and therefore failed to create a valid marriage, nothing more was required to be decided. We believe that Mr. Randall is correct in his assertion.

We have long held in this jurisdiction that the validity of a marriage is generally determined by the law of the place where it was contracted. Specifically, we have said in *Abramson v. Abramson*, 161 Neb. 782, 787, 74 N.W.2d 919, 924 (Neb. 1956): "The general rule is that the validity of a marriage is determined by the law of the place where it was contracted; if valid there it will be hold valid everywhere, and conversely if invalid by the lex loci contractus, it will be invalid wherever the question may arise." *See also, Scott v. Scott*, 153 Neb. 906, 46 N.W.2d 627 (Neb. 1951); *Forshay v. Johnston*, 144 Neb. 525, 13 N.W.2d 873 (Neb. 1944).

It appears to us that the rationale for this rule compels the result in this case. If indeed marriage is a contract, then it seems to follow that the validity of the contract should be determined by the law of the place where the contract is entered into, when entered into, and the validity should not be determined by hindsight. Other courts which have been called upon to decide this question have reached similar conclusions. In *Estate of Levie*, 50 Cal. App. 3d 572, 123 Cal. Rptr. 445 (Cal. Ct. App. 1975), the California court held that the marriage between two California residents who went to Reno, Nevada, to be married was invalid in California because it was invalid under the laws of Nevada. The court stated at 123 Cal. Rptr. at 447: "It is true that the statute do[es] not speak expressly of the invalidity in California of a marriage which was void where performed. But the statute by implication adopts the common law rule that "the law of the place of marriage controls the question of its validity.". . .

Furthermore, even if we were to look to the law of Nebraska, which we have declared we should not, the marriage ceremony conducted on April 5, 1964, would have been invalid under Nebraska law. It is conceded by all of the parties that the religious ceremony performed on April 5, 1964, was not preceded by the parties' first obtaining a valid marriage license. Appellee argues that under Nebraska law the failure to obtain a license does not void the marriage. We are unable to understand how that argument is made, in light of the clear language of Neb. Rev. Stat. § 42-104 (Reissue 1978), which provides: "Previous to the solemnization of any marriage in this state, a license for that purpose must be obtained from a county court in the State of Nebraska, and no marriage hereafter contracted shall be recognized as valid *unless such license has been previously obtained*. . . ." (Emphasis supplied.) . . . We cannot imagine how the Legislature could make it any clearer than to say that "no marriage . . . shall be recognized as valid unless such license has been previously obtained.". . .

Under Nebraska law, failure to obtain a valid license prior to entering into the marriage ceremony invalidates the marriage. In view of the fact that Nebraska does not recognize common law marriages, see *Abramson v. Abramson*, 161 Neb. 782, 74 N.W.2d 919 (Neb. 1956), a marriage not entered into in accord with the requirements of Nebraska law is no marriage at all, and, regardless of the sincerity of the parties, it fails to create the relationship of husband and wife. It is the requirement of obtaining the license and going through the ceremony which prevents common law marriages from being valid in Nebraska. *See Collins v. Hoag & Rollins*, 122 Neb. 805, 241 N.W. 766 (Neb. 1932); *Ropken v. Ropken*, 169 Neb. 352, 99 N.W.2d 480 (1959); *In re Estate of McCartney*, 213 Neb. 550, 330 N.W.2d 723 (Neb. 1983). The religious ceremony in Mexico, absent the issuance of a valid license, did not make the Mexican marriage ceremony valid in Nebraska, regardless of which law we look to for validity. This marriage was invalid under both Mexican and Nebraska law.. . .

The judgment of the district court is therefore reversed and the action dismissed pursuant to this decree.

NOTES AND QUESTIONS

(1) The *Randall* court, *above*, emphasized that an invalid Mexican marriage would not be recognized in Nebraska. *Query:* Why not? Wasn't Nebraska arguably a state that had a "significant relationship" to the parties and the marriage? Couldn't a party also argue that there was a "marriage" by estoppel (*see* § 1.04[D], *above*) or a putative marriage (*see* § 1.04[B] *supra*) Why or why not? *See also Farrah v. Farrah*, 429 S.E.2d 626 (Va. Ct. App. 1993) (holding that a Muslim marriage by proxy would not be recognized in Virginia, since it was not a legally valid marriage under the law of England, where it was contracted).

(2) Professor Clark has been critical of the rationale expressed by the *Randall* court:

> The converse question, whether a marriage which does not fulfill the mandatory licensing or solemnization requirements of the place of celebration may nevertheless be upheld under the law of some other state, may only be answered tentatively and with caution because of the lack of agreement among the relatively few authorities

where the question has been discussed. Some early expressions to the effect that the lex loci contractus always governs with respect to marriage formalities stand as authority for the proposition that if the marriage does not meet those formalities, it will not be recognized as valid elsewhere. But even in relatively early times there were cases which did not accept this view. The reason for the apparent illogicality of saying that a marriage good where contracted is good everywhere but that a marriage bad where contracted is not necessarily bad everywhere is again the very strong public policy in favor of upholding marriages, especially where the parties have behaved in all respects as if married.

1 Homer H. Clark, Law of Domestic Relations 98 (2d ed. 1987) (footnotes omitted).*

Query: Which rationale is more persuasive to you? The *Randall* decision, or Professor Clark's analysis? Why?

§ 1.09 Annulment of Marriage

Annulment of marriage and *divorce* are two distinct legal concepts. Where a divorce decree terminates a valid existing marriage, annulment of marriage, on the other hand, is a declaration that no valid marriage ever occurred, due to a legal impediment existing at the time of the marriage ceremony. *See generally* Homer Clark, *The Law of Domestic Relations in the United States* 125–48, 127 (1988). In the decades before no-fault divorce legislation was enacted in most American states, annulment was often utilized by many couples to dissolve their marriage when they could not prove the necessary fault-based grounds for a divorce. *See, e.g.* Note, *Annulments for Fraud—New York's Answer to Reno?* 48 Columbia L. Rev. 900 (1948).

Today, with no-fault divorce laws firmly established in all 50 states, annulment actions are relatively rare, and are not as common as they once were in the past. Nevertheless, annulment actions are still recognized in most states, and annulment of marriage is still a viable legal alternative for those couples who for philosophical, moral, social, or religious reasons do not believe in, and chose not to obtain, an absolute divorce.

[A] Annulment Jurisdiction

In order to annul a voidable marriage, or in order to create a judicial record of a void *ab initio* marriage, a court must have valid jurisdiction over the annulment proceeding. What would constitute valid jurisdiction for annulment? The traditional view is that the state *where the marriage was celebrated* should have jurisdiction over annulment, unless the parties were domiciled in another state at the time of the marriage, in which case the domiciliary state should have jurisdiction. However, a state of subsequent domicile after the marriage would not be a proper forum to annul the marriage. *See, e.g.*, Goodrich, *Jurisdiction to Annul a Marriage*, 32 Harv. L. Rev. 806 (1919). *See also Worthington v. Worthington*, 352 S.W.2d 80 (Ark. 1962). The modern view, however, is that the state where the parties, or either of them, *are domiciled at the time of the annulment suit* would have jurisdiction. Thus, a number of states now have jurisdictional statutes applying both to divorce and annulment, asserting jurisdiction over the marriages of those domiciled in the state at the time the action is brought. *See, e.g.* Vernon, *Labyrinthine Ways: Jurisdiction to Annul*, 10

---

* Copyright 1987 by the West Publishing Company. Reprinted with permission.

J. Pub. L. 47 (1961). *See also* 1 Homer H. Clark, Jr., Law of Domestic Relations 222–37 (2d ed. 1987).

Another problem with annulment jurisdiction is whether it must a bilateral *in personam* proceeding, or whether it can be an *ex parte* proceeding as well. Under the traditional "relation back" annulment doctrine, when either a husband or a wife requested that a court annul their void or voidable marriage, the resulting annulment decree was thought to "relate back" to the time of the invalid marriage. Thus, since the questionable "marriage" retroactively was found to be a pre-existing nullity, the court could have no subject matter jurisdiction *in rem* over the marital status, and the court therefore had to obtain personal jurisdiction over *both* the parties in any annulment suit.

Under a modern annulment doctrine, however, which was first enunciated in the seminal case of *Perlstein v. Perlstein*, 204 A.2d 909 (Conn. 1964), and which was derived in large part from the landmark *ex parte* divorce case of *Williams v. North Carolina [I]*, 317 U.S. 287 (1942) the *in rem* res or thing in an *ex parte* annulment action is the questionable marriage itself, as long as the forum state court has a significant connection or sufficient legal nexus with the petitioning party, who must generally be a bona fide domiciliary or legal resident in the forum state.

[B] Annulment Grounds and Defenses

Annulment is the legal determination that a void or voidable marriage was a nullity from its inception. An annulment action thus differs from a divorce action in that divorce is the dissolution of a legally valid marriage, where annulment is the legal declaration that a marriage never existed in the first place. Void *ab initio* marriages, such as bigamous and polygamous marriage, and incestuous marriage, do not require a formal annulment proceeding, but either party may still petition the court for a formal judicial record that the marriage was void *ab initio*.

Voidable marriages, on the other hand, are assumed to be legally valid unless annulled by the parties themselves. Thus, voidable marriages do require a formal annulment proceeding. Voidable marriages may include underage marriage; marriage to a spouse who is mentally or physically incapacitated; fraudulent marriage; marriage under duress; and in some jurisdictions, marriage to a felon or prostitute, and certain sham marriages. *See generally* § 1.07, *above*.

There are certain defenses to annulment actions. First, if the parties fail to bring an annulment action for a voidable marriage during the lifetime of either party, or within a reasonable period of time, they are deemed to have ratified any marital defect, and the marriage is therefore a legally valid marriage. However, the parties can never ratify a void *ab initio* marriage, which is a legal nullity from its inception based upon a state's strong public policy. Is there a time limitation to bring an annulment action? A number of states have enacted a specific statute of limitations affecting annulment. *See, e.g.* Va. Code Ann. § 20-89.1(c) (two-year statue of limitations for voidable marriages from the date of the marriage), and Cal. Fam. Code §§ 2210(d), 2211(d) (four-year statute of limitations after discovery of fraud). Other courts have held that in the absence of a specific annulment statute, a general statute of limitations would apply. *See, e.g., Witt v. Witt*, 72 N.W.2d 748 (Wis. 1955) (the statute begins to run from the time of discovery of the marital defect constituting a ground for annulment). *Contra, Munger v. Munger*, 95 A.2d 153 (N.J. Super.

Ct. App. Div. 1953). *See also* M.L. Dranfield, Annotation, *Limitations of Actions for Annulment of Marriage*, 52 A.L.R. 2d 1163 (1957) and Later Case Service. In the absence of any statute-of-limitations defense, an argument might also be made of unreasonable delay in bringing the annulment suit under the equitable doctrine of laches. *See, e.g.* Rutkin, Family Law and Practice, *Annulment* § 5.03 (Matthew Bender 1997); Gregory, Swisher & Scheible, Understanding Family Law, *Annulment of Marriage* § 1.10 (2nd ed., Matthew Bender 1995).

Estoppel by judgment, or *res judicata*, may also constitute another defense to annulment. For example, in *Statter v. Statter*, 143 N.E.2d 10 (1957), the court dismissed wife's suit for annulment on bigamy grounds, citing a prior divorce action where a court had found the Statters' marriage to be a valid one. Therefore, *res judicata* principles will generally override any mistake of law or mistake of fact, as long as the parties had their day in court on the merits of the case. *See Aldrich v. Aldrich*, 378 U.S. 540 (1964) (mistake of law in a prior divorce action could not be relitigated in a subsequent proceeding). Estoppel by conduct may also bar the parties from contesting the validity of their marriage based upon a prior invalid divorce. *See generally* § 1.04[D], *above*.

[C] Property and Support Rights on Annulment

If a marriage is void *ab initio*, or if a voidable marriage is annulled, then the marriage is a nullity. Thus, a number of traditional jurisdictions have held that permanent spousal support and marital property rights cannot be granted on annulment, absent specific statutory authority to the contrary. *See* J.A. Tyler, Annotation, *Right to allowance of permanent alimony in connection with decree of annulment*, 54 A.L.R. 2d 1410 (1957) and Later Case Service. Because of the inequities of this traditional rule involving the financial needs of an innocent "spouse" at the time of annulment, however, a growing number of states have enacted legislation allowing permanent spousal support and marital property division to be granted on annulment, similar to divorce legislation. *Query:* Under what factual situations would such legislation be justified? When would it not be justified? *See generally* 1 Homer H. Clark, Jr., Law of Domestic Relations 242–46 (2d ed. 1987).

Another recurring problem with spousal support and division of marital property on annulment is based upon the following scenario: Husband and wife are divorced, and the divorce decree, or a separation agreement incorporated into the divorce decree, provides that the payor spouse will pay spousal support or alimony to the payee spouse until the payor or payee dies, or until the payee remarries. The payee spouse then remarries, but that remarriage is subsequently annulled. What effect does this annulment have on the payor's spousal support obligation? The following case discusses this problem.

MacPHERSON v. MacPHERSON
United States Court of Appeals
496 F.2d 258 (6th Cir. 1974)

PHILLIPS, CHIEF JUDGE.

In this conflict of laws case, we are called upon to interpret a separation agreement. The agreement provided, inter alia, that the husband (Charles MacPherson) was to pay $600.00 per month to the wife (Mrs. Dorothy MacPherson) until her remarriage. The wife remarried a bigamist and this marriage subsequently was annulled and declared void ab initio.

Thereupon, the wife sued for payments under the agreement, alleging that she had never remarried. . . .

The critical issue is whether the word "remarriage" means a valid marriage, as the District Court in essence held, or whether this word signifies a time at which the wife's support would commence from a difference source. We reverse the District Court and hold that the wife's remarriage terminated the husband's obligation under the agreement.

The parties to this suit were married in 1947 in Illinois, their native state. They remained in Illinois until 1950. Between 1950 and 1962, due to Mr. MacPherson's employment, they lived in three other states. Their final move as a family was to Connecticut in 1962 when Mr. MacPherson was promoted to a position in New York. On December 15, 1966, Mr. MacPherson separated from his wife and moved to New York City.

During the next year, the parties negotiated a separation agreement. Mr. MacPherson signed the agreement in New York on October 13, 1967, and it was forwarded to Connecticut where Mrs. MacPherson signed it on October 31, 1967. The agreement provided, inter alia,. . . FIFTH: The Husband shall pay to the Wife for the support and maintenance of the Wife the sum of $600.00 per month beginning July 1, 1967. All payments to be made to the Wife by the Husband under this Paragraph . . . shall cease upon her death or remarriage or upon the death of the Husband. . . .

Mr. MacPherson obtained a Mexican divorce on December 29, 1967. Mrs. MacPherson entered an appearance, through counsel, in those proceedings, and the validity of the divorce decree has not been challenged on this appeal. The decree provided that the separation agreement was approved, but not merged with the decree.

On April 3, 1968, at Folkston, Georgia, Mrs. MacPherson entered into a purported marriage with Frank L. Miles, a/k/a Frank L. Mileski. They returned to Connecticut for two months, until June 15, 1968, when they moved to Florida. On October 22, 1968, Mrs. MacPherson discovered that Frank Miles had a wife from a prior marriage that had not been terminated. Mrs. MacPherson immediately moved to Illinois and remains a resident of Champaign County in that State.

Meanwhile, Mr. MacPherson remarried on January 26, 1968, and a son was born to that marriage on September 28, 1970. He ceased making the support payments under the agreement beginning on June 1, 1968. Mrs. MacPherson requested resumption of the support payments on November 12, 1968.

Mrs. MacPherson's purported marriage to Frank Miles was annulled and declared void ab initio by the Circuit Court of the Sixth Judicial Circuit, Champaign County, Illinois, on November 2, 1971. Mr. Miles entered an appearance at the annulment proceeding, waiving any and all process, notice and procedural prerequisites to the hearing. He did not file an answer.

The parties are in agreement, and our research shows, that Connecticut law has never passed on the question of whether a bigamous remarriage is sufficient to terminate support payments under a separation agreement. . . .Therefore we must exercise our best judgment as to how a Connecticut court would dispose of the issue at bar.

The state courts have not been consistent in their treatment of this issue. Many courts have rested their decision on whether the marriage was void or voidable. A voidable marriage differs from a void marriage in that in the case of the former the marriage is treated as valid and binding until its nullity is ascertained and declared by a competent court. Some courts allow recovery to a wife who entered into a bigamous marriage on the theory that a void marriage is ineffective to alter legal rights. *Reese v. Reese*, 192 So. 2d 1 (Fla. 1966); *DeWall v. Rhoderick*, 258 Iowa 433, 138 N.W.2d 124 (Iowa 1965). Moreover, even when the marriage is voidable, recovery has been allowed by making use of the legal fiction of "relation back." In those cases when the voidable marriage is annulled and declared void ab initio, it is given the same effect as a void marriage. However, many courts have rejected this "relation back" doctrine and deny recovery to the wife when her second marriage is merely voidable. *See, e.g., Dodd v. Dodd*, 210 Kan. 50, 499 P.2d 518 (Kan. 1973); *Flaxman v. Flaxman*, 57 N.J. 458, 273 A.2d 567 (N.J. 1971).

Some courts have abandoned the void-voidable distinction and, hinging their decision at least in part on equitable grounds, refuse the wife recovery. *Beebe v. Beebe*, 227 Ga. 248, 179 S.E.2d 758 (Ga. 1971); *Torgan v. Torgan*, 159 Colo. 93, 410 P.2d 167 (Colo. 1966); *Denberg v. Frischman*, 24 A.D.2d 100, 264 N.Y.S.2d 114 (N.Y. App. Div. 1965), *aff'd*, 17 N.Y.2d 778, 270 N.Y.S.2d 627, 217 N.E.2d 675, *cert. denied*, 385 U.S. 884 (N.Y. 1966); *Gaines v. Jacobsen*, 308 N.Y. 218, 124 N.E.2d 290 (N.Y. 1954). In *Beebe*, the Supreme Court of Georgia noted that the distinction between void and voidable marriages was more imaginary than real. Beebe, 179 S.E.2d 758, 760 (Ga. 1971). In *Gaines*, the court said that it was unlikely the parties intended the outcome to turn upon whether the unsuccessful marriage was void or voidable. *Gaines*, 124 N.E.2d 290, 293 (N.Y. 1954). . . .

In *Cary v. Cary*, 112 Conn. 256, 152 A. 302 (Conn. 1930), addressing itself to the abandonment theory in an alimony case, the Supreme Court of Connecticut stated: The better rule, which we adopt, save in the most exceptional circumstances, draws from the voluntary action of the wife in remarrying the inference that she has elected to obtain her support from her second husband and has thereby abandoned the provision made for her support by the court in its award of alimony. In *Emerson v. Emerson*, 120 Md. 584, 596, 87 A. 1033, 1038 (Md. 1913), it is said: "Although the better reasoning leads to the conclusion that, as a general rule, as the new husband is obliged to give entire support, therefore the former husband is to be thus relieved."

Subsequently, in *Perlstein v. Perlstein*, 152 Conn. 152, 204 A.2d 909 (Conn. 1964), decided on jurisdictional grounds, the Supreme Court of Connecticut rejected the void-voidable distinction and the legal fiction of "relation back.". . .

Additionally, *Perlstein*'s explicit reliance on the decision in *Gaines, supra*, forces us to conclude that Connecticut would adopt the holding and rationale of *Gaines v. Jacobsen, supra*, and deny the wife recovery, at least insofar as the "purposes of justice" require. However, as recognized in *Perlstein* and *Cary, supra*, "cases may arise where the court would not hold that the wife by remarriage abandoned her right to support from her first husband, but cases will be exceptional and rare which will admit of a variance from the ordinary rule. The burden of removing the case from the operation of the ordinary rule will be upon the wife after the proof of the remarriage has been made." *Cary*, 152 A. 302, 304 (Conn. 1930).

Insofar as the equities of the case are concerned, they weigh heavily against Mrs. MacPherson. There is a strong public policy of providing for adequate support for a divorced wife. However, Mrs. MacPherson voluntarily elected to seek support from her second husband when she entered into the purported marriage. She held herself out as being remarried and abandoned her rights under the separation agreement. Often, as in this case, the first husband has remarried and has additional children. He is entitled to rely on his ex-wife's new marital status, and it would be manifestly unfair to him and his family to allow his ex-wife to return later demanding support. The rights of innocent third parties must be considered in applying the "purposes of justice" test of *Perlstein, supra*. Whether the ex-wife obtains "as good or as adequate a support by her [remarriage] are questions about which the courts can have no concern." *Cary*, 152 A. 302, 304 (Conn. 1930).

Additional factors militating against the wife's recovery are present. When Mrs. MacPherson left her second husband, she could have returned to Connecticut, sought an annulment and been granted alimony from her bigamous husband. Moreover, even in Illinois, where the marriage was annulled, Mrs. MacPherson could have elected to seek a divorce on the grounds of bigamy and received alimony.

Instead, Mrs. MacPherson elected to pursue a path that would preclude her from obtaining support from her second husband. We do not think that she should have such control over her source of support. There is nothing in the separation agreement to indicate that the parties intended that she should be able to exert this control to the detriment of her former husband. *Reversed.*

NOTES AND QUESTIONS

(1) As discussed in *MacPherson*, there is a split of authority within the states on how this problem should be resolved. Some courts, applying a traditional "relation back" annulment doctrine to both void and voidable marriages, hold that the prior spousal support obligation is not terminated. *See, e.g., Sutton v. Leib*, 199 F.2d 163 (7th Cir. 1952); *Redmann v. Redmann*, 376 N.W.2d 803 (N.D. 1985).

Other courts would deny recovery to the payee spouse when the second marriage is voidable, but not void *ab initio. See, e.g., McConkey v. McConkey*, 215 S.E.2d 640 (Va. 1975) (annulment for fraud); *Johnston v. Johnston*, 592 P.2d 132 (Kan. Ct. App. 1979) (void *ab initio* marriage did not terminate alimony payments, but a voidable marriage would).

Still other courts would terminate the prior spousal support obligation whether the "remarriage" was voidable or void *ab initio. See, e.g., Glass v. Glass*, 546 S.W.2d 738, 742 (Mo. Ct. App. 1977) ("We conclude, therefore, that *remarriage*. . . refers to the ceremony of marriage and not to the status or relationship—valid, voidable or void—which actually results"); *Sefton v. Sefton*, 291 P.2d 439 (Cal. 1955). However, *Sefton* held that spousal support may be reinstated in certain situations for the protection of innocent parties. *See, e.g., Weintraub v. Weintraub*, 167 Cal. App. 3d 420 (Cal. Ct. App. 1985). *Query:* Which theory is most persuasive to you? Why? *See also* F.S. Tinio, Annotation, *Annulment of Later Marriage as Reviving Prior Husband's Obligation under Alimony Decree or Separation Agreement*, 45 A.L.R. 3d 1033 (1972); Note, *The Annulment Controversy: Revival of Prior Alimony Payments*, 13 Tulsa L.J. 127 (1977).

(2) *Query.* Should a spouse be awarded *temporary* spousal support *pendente lite* during the pendency of an annulment action? Why or why not? *See generally* Comment, *The Aftereffects of Annulment: Alimony, Property Division, Provision for Children*, 1968 Wash. U. L. Rev. 148 (1968).

(3) **Problem.** Dick and Jane are domiciliaries of the State of Harlan, a "traditional" state with regard to marriage and annulment of marriage requirements, and a state which still follows the First Restatement of Conflict of Laws. Harlan, however, does have a statute providing for spousal support on annulment and for the division of marital property on annulment.

Because Dick and Jane are both 17 and do not have parental consent to marry, they travel to the state of Douglas and are married in Douglas, falsely giving their ages as 19 and 18, respectively. Douglas is a "modern" state with directory marriage requirements, and a state that allows *ex parte* as well as bilateral *in personam* annulments. Douglas has adopted the Second Restatement of Conflict of Laws, but Douglas has no state statute providing for any spousal support or division of property on annulment. After their marriage in Douglas, Dick and Jane return to Harlan.

After two months of marriage in Harlan, Jane learns to her horror that Dick once worked as a male prostitute and a drug dealer. As a consequence, although Dick is rather wealthy, he suffered emotional trauma which made him sexually impotent. Based on this knowledge, Jane questions whether their marriage can survive, but Dick promises to "straighten his life out," and he tells Jane he has found a legitimate temporary job in Douglas that will give him time to "settle down." Dick then moves to Douglas, leaving Jane in Harlan.

After six months, Dick brings an annulment action in a Douglas court based upon the parties' underage marriage, and he gives due-process notice to Jane in Harlan. During this six-month period, however, Jane has been involved in a serious automobile accident with a hit-and-run driver, and is physically disabled with permanent injuries. Jane now comes to your law office in Harlan and relates these facts to you. How would you advise her?

§ 1.10 Summary: A Marriage and Annulment Problem

Hansel and Gretel were contemplating marriage in the State of Holmes (the 51st State of the United States) that recognizes only formal, statutory marriages. Hansel told Gretel that he was 32 years old and that he had inherited substantial wealth from his grandparents. In fact, Hansel was 48 years old, and he was relatively poor. Unknown to Hansel, Gretel, who is 17 years old and living by herself, and who had previously worked in a clothing store, had been declared mentally incompetent to handle her business affairs by a Holmes court.

Hansel and Gretel obtained their marriage license on January 2nd in Holmes, and they were later married on March 14th. Gretel did not have parental consent from either of her parents for this wedding. Unknown to Gretel, the marrying official, who was a friend of Hansel's, was a defrocked priest who was no longer authorized by the State of Holmes to perform marriages. During the wedding ceremony, Hansel promised to "take and provide for Gretel as my lawfully wedded wife" and Gretel made a similar promise to "take and provide for Hansel as my lawfully wedded husband." Hansel and Gretel then spent a short honeymoon in the neighboring State of Warren (the 52nd State of the United States) that recognizes both formal and informal marriages, where Hansel and Gretel subsequently rented an isolated Victorian "gingerbread" cottage in the woods of Warren, so Hansel could work on a short (and unsuccessful) novel debunking Grimm's Fairy Tales.

During their two-month stay in Warren, Gretel discovered that Hansel was not, in fact, the wealthy man he had claimed to be, and that Hansel could not consummate their marriage due to Hansel's physical and psychological incapacity. Hansel, on the other hand, learned about Gretel's prior judicial adjudication for mental incapacity. Hansel then deserted Gretel and moved back to the State of Holmes, where he consulted with a Holmes family law practitioner who told Hansel that in his opinion Hansel "was never legally married to Gretel". Hansel therefore refuses to support Gretel in any manner, and Gretel is presently living a destitute and necessitous existence in the State of Warren.

Assume now that you are a family law practitioner in the State of Warren, and that Gretel has come to you for legal advice. Assume also that another associate in your law firm is handling Gretel's action for spousal support and property rights, if any, against Hansel.

QUESTIONS PRESENTED

(1) Do Hansel and Gretel have a legally valid formal statutory marriage? Why or why not?

(2) Assuming *arguendo* that Hansel and Gretel do *not* have a legally valid formal marriage, do they arguably have a legally valid *informal* marriage? Why or why not?

(3) Assuming *arguendo* that Hansel and Gretel do *not* have a legally valid formal *or* informal marriage, are there any other legal remedies that you could argue on Gretel's behalf?

(4) Assuming *arguendo* that Hansel and Gretel have a valid, but voidable, marriage, can either Hansel or Gretel successfully bring a suit to annul their marriage? Why or why not?

CHAPTER 2

LEGAL AND ECONOMIC CONSEQUENCES OF MARRIAGE

SYNOPSIS

§ 2.01 Introduction
§ 2.02 Roles and Responsibilities During Marriage
    [A] The Traditional View
    [B] The Modern Theory—Marriage as a Partnership of Equals
    [C] Testing the Theory Against Reality: Contemporary Perspectives on Marriage
§ 2.03 Marital Property Rights
    [A] The Married Women's Property Acts
    [B] Tenancy by the Entirety
    [C] Property Rights on the Death of a Spouse
    [D] The Community Property System
§ 2.04 Support Obligations During Marriage
    [A] The Nonintervention Principle
    [B] The Common Law Doctrine of Necessaries
    [C] Spousal and Child Support Statutes
    [D] Enforcement of Support Awards
    [E] Relative Responsibility Statutes
§ 2.05 Economic Transactions Between Spouses
§ 2.06 Third-Party Interference with Marriage
    [A] Intentional Torts
    [B] Rights of Consortium
    [C] Evidentiary and Testimonial Privileges
§ 2.07 Integrating Family and Work
    [A] Dual Career Couples
    [B] Pregnancy, Childbearing and Employment
    [C] Working and Caring for Children

§ 2.01 Introduction

Over the past 25 years, the structure of marriage and parenthood has changed considerably. The traditional, role-divided family, in which only the husband worked outside the home, and only the wife raised children, has become the exception, rather than the rule.

Today, less than 10% of American families conform to the pattern of a sole, male wage earner married to a non-wage-earning female spouse. *See* Sharon C. Nantell, *The Tax Paradigm of Child Care: Shifting Attitudes Toward a Private/Parental/Public Alliance*, 80 Marq. L. Rev. 879, 894 (1997). In 1997, more than 70% of married mothers were in the paid labor market, as compared to less than 40% in 1970. *See* U.S. Department of Labor, Bureau of Labor Statistics, Employment Characteristics of Families in 1997 (http://stats.bls.gov/newsrels.htm). This includes more than 60% of married mothers with children under three years old, and more than 55% of married mothers with children younger than one year. *Id.* at Table 5. In addition, the percentage of families maintained by a single parent has more than doubled since 1973, accounting for more than 30% of all families with children in 1997. *See* U.S. Bureau of the Census, *Current Population Reports, Household and Family Characteristics: March, 1997*. Most single parents are mothers, who are even more likely to work for pay than their married counterparts. Single fathers are also increasingly common; according to a 1997 study, fathers comprise more than 25% of all employed single parents. Families and Work Institute, *The 1997 National Study of the Changing Workforce* (1998).

These demographic and structural changes have had a significant impact on the legal doctrines and principles that govern marriage, as well as those that structure the relationship between married couples and the state. These changes have also led courts and legislatures to rethink traditional assumptions about the appropriate division of functions between the "private" family and the more public realms of politics and the market. In addition, these structural changes both reflect and have reinforced a shift in popular attitudes regarding the roles of husbands and wives, and of mothers and fathers. In 1977, approximately two-thirds of the adults questioned in a national survey agreed with the following query: "Do you agree or disagree that it is much better for everyone involved if the man is the achiever outside the home and the woman takes care of the home and the family?" When the same question was asked in 1996, only 38% of the respondents expressed agreement. *See* Andrew Cherlin, *By The Numbers*, New York Times Magazine, April 5, 1998.

This chapter explores the legal implications of the changing nature of marriage. It first examines the property rights and support obligations that have traditionally accompanied marriage and considers the ways in which those rights and obligations have been transformed by contemporary notions of spousal autonomy, partnership marriage, and gender equality. The second half of the chapter examines the effect of changes in marital and parenting roles on the structure of the workplace. These materials explore the changing workplace treatment of pregnancy and highlight recent legislative initiatives designed to help employed spouses and parents more effectively balance their work and family responsibilities.

§ 2.02 Roles and Responsibilities during Marriage

[A] The Traditional View

1 WILLIAM BLACKSTONE, COMMENTARIES 442:

By marriage, the husband and wife are one person in law: that is, the very being or legal existence of the woman is suspended during the marriage, or at least is incorporated and consolidated into that of the husband: under whose wing, protection, and *cover*, she performs everything; and is therefore called in our law-french a *femme-covert* is said to be *covert-baron*, or under the protection and influence of her husband, her baron, or lord; and her condition during her marriage is called her *coverture*. Under this principle, of a union of person in husband and wife, depend almost all the legal rights, duties, and disabilities, that either of them acquires by the marriage. . . .

BRADWELL v. ILLINOIS
United States Supreme Court
83 U.S. (16 Wall.) 130 (1873)

[Mrs. Myra Bradwell, a resident of Illinois, applied to the Illinois Supreme Court for a license to practice law. She accompanied her petition with the requisite certificate attesting to her good character and qualifications. The Illinois Supreme Court denied her application, stating that, as a married woman, Mrs. Bradwell, "would be bound neither by her express contracts nor by those implied contracts which it is the policy of the law to create between attorney and client." The United States Supreme Court affirmed, rejecting Myra Bradwell's claim that the privileges and immunities clause of the Fourteenth Amendment guaranteed women, as citizens, the right to pursue lawful employment.]

MR. JUSTICE BRADLEY [joined by JUSTICES SWAYNE and FIELD], concurring:

. . . It certainly cannot be affirmed, as an historical fact, that [the right of females to pursue employment] has ever been established as one of the fundamental privileges and immunities of the sex. On the contrary, the civil law, as well as nature herself, has always recognized a wide difference in the respective spheres and destinies of man and woman. Man is, or should be, woman's protector and defender. The natural and proper timidity and delicacy which belongs to the female sex evidently unfits if for many of the occupations of civil life. The constitution of the family organization, which is founded in the divine ordinance, as well as in the nature of things, indicates the domestic sphere as that which properly belongs to the domain and functions of womanhood. The harmony, not to say identity, of interests and views which belong, or should belong, to the family institution is repugnant to the idea of a woman adopting a distinct and independent career from that of her husband. So firmly fixed was this sentiment in the founders of the common law that it became a maxim of that system of jurisprudence that a woman had no legal existence separate from her husband, who was regarded as her head and representative in the social state; and, notwithstanding some recent modifications of this civil status, many of the special rules of law flowing from and dependent upon this cardinal principle still exist in full force in most States. One of these is, that a married woman is incapable, without her husband's consent, of making contracts which shall be binding on her or him. This very incapacity was one circumstance which the Supreme Court of Illinois deemed important in rendering a married woman incompetent fully to perform the duties and trusts that belong to the office of an attorney and counselor.

It is true that many women are unmarried and not affected by any of the duties, complications, and incapacities arising out of the married state, but these are exceptions to the general rule. The paramount destiny and mission of woman are to fulfil the noble and benign offices of wife and mother. This is the law of the Creator. And the rules of civil society must be adapted to the general constitution of things, and cannot be based upon exceptional cases. . . .

GRAHAM v. GRAHAM
United States District Court
33 F. Supp. 936 (E.D. Mich. 1940)

TUTTLE, DISTRICT JUDGE.

This is a suit by a man against his former wife upon the following written agreement alleged to have been executed September 17, 1932, by the parties:

> This agreement made this 17th day of September, 1932, between Margrethe Graham and Sidney Graham, husband and wife. For valuable consideration Margrethe Graham hereby agrees to pay to Sidney Graham the sum of Three Hundred ($300.00) Dollars per month each and every month hereafter until the parties hereto no longer desire this arrangement to continue. Said Three Hundred ($300.00) Dollars per month to be paid to Sidney Graham by said Margrethe Graham directly to said Sidney Graham.
>
> This agreement is made to adjust financial matters between the parties hereto, so that in the future there will be no further arguments as to what money said Sidney Graham shall receive.

The parties were divorced on July 11, 1933. While the writing itself recites no consideration but merely states that it is made to prevent future arguments as to the amount of money the husband is to receive from his wife, the complaint alleges that the plaintiff had quit his job in a hotel at the solicitation of the defendant who wanted him to accompany her upon her travels, she paying his expenses, and that he was desirous of returning to work but that the defendant in order to induce him not to do so entered into this agreement. . . .

A further question is presented as to whether the complaint sets forth any consideration for the alleged contract. . . . I am convinced that even if the consideration is what counsel claims, and the plaintiff did agree to refrain from work and accompany his wife on her travels, the contract was not a competent one for married persons to enter into.

In the first place, it is highly doubtful if the alleged contract is within the capacity of a married woman to make under Michigan law. The degree of emancipation of married women with respect to contract and property rights varies widely in the different states. However, it has been repeatedly stated by the Michigan Supreme Court that under the Michigan statutes a married woman has no general power to contract, but can contract only in relation to her separate property. . . . Since the promise of the defendant here consists of a general executory obligation unrelated to specific property and since the consideration is not for the benefit of her separate estate, but if anything to its detriment, it would appear that the contract is beyond the capacity of a married woman under Michigan law to make.

However, I do not rest my decision on this ground, but rather upon the broader ground that even if the contract is otherwise within the contractual power of the parties it is void because it contravenes public policy. Under the law, marriage is not merely a private contract between the parties, but creates a status in which the state is vitally interested and under which certain rights and duties incident to the relationship come into being, irrespective of the wishes of the parties. As a result of the marriage contract, for example, the husband has a duty to support and to live with his wife and the wife must contribute her services and society to the husband and follow him in his choice of domicile. The law is well settled that a private agreement between persons married or about to be married which attempts to change the essential obligations of the marriage contract as defined by the law is contrary to public policy and unenforceable. While there appears to be no Michigan decision directly in point, the principle is well stated in the Restatement of the Law of Contracts, as follows:

"Sec. 587. Bargain to Change Essential Obligations of Marriage

"A bargain between married persons contemplating marriage to change the essential incidents of marriage is illegal.

"Illustrations:

"1. A and B who are about to marry agree to forego sexual intercourse. The bargain is illegal.

"2. In a state where the husband is entitled to determine the residence of a married couple, A and B who are about to marry agree that the wife shall not be required to leave the city where she then lives. The bargain is illegal." . . .

The contract claimed to have been made by the plaintiff and defendant in the case at bar while married and living together falls within this prohibition. Under its terms, the husband becomes obligated to accompany his wife upon her travels; while under the law of marriage the wife is obliged to follow the husband's choice of domicile. Indeed, it is argued by the plaintiff's attorney that this relinquishment by the husband of his rights constitutes consideration for the promise of his wife; but, by the same token it makes the contract violative of public policy. The situation is virtually identical with that set forth in Illustration 2 of Section 587 of the Restatement quoted above. The contract, furthermore, would seem to suffer from a second defect by impliedly releasing the husband from his duty to support his wife, and thereby making it fall directly within the rule of the cases . . . holding that a contract between married persons living together which contains such a release is void. The present contract does not expressly contain such a release, but if the husband can always call upon his wife for payments of $300 per month he is in practical effect getting rid of his obligation to support his wife. . . . It is unnecessary to consider in detail the second alleged basis of consideration, namely, the promise of the husband to refrain from working, but it would seem again that a married man should have the right to engage in such work as he sees fit to do, unrestrained by contract with his wife.

The law prohibiting married persons from altering by private agreement the personal relationships and obligations assumed upon marriage is based on sound foundations of public policy. If they were permitted to regulate by private contract where the parties are to live and whether the husband is to work or be supported by his wife, there would seem to be no reason why married persons could not contract as to the allowance the husband or wife may receive, the number of dresses she may have, the places where they will spend their evenings and vacations, and innumerable other aspects of their personal relationships. Such right would open an endless field for controversy and bickering and would destroy the element of flexibility needed in making adjustments to new conditions arising in marital life. There is no reason, of course, why the wife cannot voluntarily pay her husband a monthly sum or the husband by mutual understanding quit his job and travel with his wife. The objection is to putting such conduct into a binding contract, tying the parties' hands in the future and inviting controversy and litigation between them. The time may come when it is desirable and necessary for the husband to cease work entirely, or to change to a different occupation, or move to a different city, or, if adversity overtakes the parties, to share a small income. It would be unfortunate if in making such adjustments the couple had their hands tied by an agreement between them entered into years before.

It is important to note that the contract here was entered into between parties who were living together at the time and who obviously contemplated a continuance of that relationship. The case is to be distinguished in this respect from those cases which hold that a contract made after separation or in contemplation of an immediate separation which takes place as contemplated is legal, if the contract is a fair one, even though it contains a release of the husband's duty of support. . . .

The case is also to be distinguished from a group of cases which hold that a married woman can properly contract with her husband to work for him outside the home and be compensated by him for her services (although it appears that this is contrary to the weight of authority). The ground on which the contract has been upheld in those cases is that it covered services outside the scope of the marriage contract; the promises did not, as here, involve the essential obligations of the marriage contract, and no question of public policy was therefore involved. There is certainly less reason to hold that a married woman cannot lease property owned by her to her husband for a fair consideration than to hold that the parties cannot contract to refrain from intercourse during marriage; in the former case no abridgement of marital rights or obligations is involved. Admittedly, it is difficult to draw the line in cases not so extreme between contracts involving the personal rights or obligations of the marriage contract and those which involve matters outside its scope; but it is unnecessary here to decide exactly where the line is to be drawn, since in my opinion the promises made in the contract in the case at bar clearly attempt to alter essential obligations of the marriage contract. . . .

NOTES AND QUESTIONS

(1) What was the relationship between Myra Bradwell's marital status and her ability to practice law? Does Justice Bradley's opinion suggest that Illinois must permit *unmarried* women to practice law? Why or why not?

(2) According to the *Graham* court, what are the "essential incidents of marriage" which spouses may not alter by private contract? If the Grahams had agreed that Mr. Graham would pay his wife $300 per month in exchange for her promise to give up her job and accompany her husband on his travels, would that agreement have been enforceable? Why or why not?

(3) The section of the Restatement of Contracts relied on by the *Graham* court has since been modified. The current provision reads, in pertinent part, as follows:

> Promise Detrimental to Marital Relationship
>
> (1) A promise by a person contemplating marriage or by a married person, other than as part of an enforceable separation agreement, is unenforceable on grounds of public policy if it would change some essential incident of the marital relationship in a way detrimental to the public interest in the marriage relationship.

Restatement 2d of Contracts § 190 (1979). Would the *Graham* case be decided differently under this revised provision?

(4) To what extent should spouses be permitted to vary the obligations of marriage by private contract? Do you agree with the *Graham* court that giving couples this authority "would open an endless field for controversy and bickering and would destroy the element of flexibility needed in making adjustments to new conditions arising in marital life?" Is divorce the appropriate remedy for spouses who disagree about their commitments to each other? The role of marital and pre-marital contracting is considered more fully in Chapter 12, *below*. *See also* Laura P. Graham, *The Uniform Premarital Agreement Act and Modern Social Policy: The Enforceability of Premarital Agreements Regulating the Ongoing Marriage*, 28 Wake Forest L. Rev. 1037 (1993); Jana Singer, The Privatization of Family Law, 1992 Wis. L. Rev. 1443 (1992); Marjorie M. Schultz, *Contractual Ordering of Marriage: A New Model For State Policy*, 79 Cal. L. Rev. 207 (1982).

[B] The Modern Theory—Marriage as a Partnership of Equals

Sally F. Goldfarb, Marital Partnership and the Case For Permanent Alimony
27 J. Fam. L. 351, 354–55 (1988–89)

In sharp contrast to Blackstone's famous common law formulation that 'the husband and wife are one person in law' and that the woman's legal existence is merged into the man's at marriage, the modern view is that marriage is a partnership of equals. All common law states now permit equitable distribution of property at divorce, thereby recognizing that both spouse have been partners in acquiring property during the marriage, regardless of which spouse holds title. . . .

According to the marital partnership principle, the married couple forms an economic unit. The contributions of both husband and wife to this unit are valuable regardless of whether the contributions are financial or nonfinancial. . . .

In re Marriage of Wierman
387 N.W.2d 744, 750 (Wis. 1986)

. . .

The principles of equitable distribution for allocating property upon divorce are based upon the concept that marriage is a partnership or a shared enterprise in which each of the spouses makes a different but equally important contribution to the family and its welfare and to the acquisition of its property. Because each spouse contributes equally to the prosperity of the marriage by his or her efforts, each spouse has an equal right to the ownership of the property upon a divorce.

The premise of equitable distribution . . . was described in *Lacey v. Lacey*, 45 Wis. 2d 378, 382, 173 N.W.2d 142 (1970), as follows:

> "The division of property of the divorced parties rests upon the concept of marriage as a shared enterprise or joint undertaking. It is literally a partnership, although a partnership in which contributions and equities of the parties may and do differ from individual case to individual case."

The equitable distribution-partnership concept of marriage recognizes that a marriage possesses an important, intangible asset: the capability of both spouses to contribute to the marriage and to the acquisition of property through their labor. To the extent that either spouse is remunerated for his or her labor during the marriage, the remuneration is marital property.

Jersey Shore Med. Ctr.-Fitkin Hospital v. Estate of Baum
417 A.2d 1003, 1008 (N.J. 1980)

. . .

A modern marriage is a partnership, with neither spouse necessarily dependent financially on the other. Many women have shed their traditional dependence on their husbands for active roles as income earners.

With increasing frequency, wives contribute significantly to the financial well-being of their families. . . . In some cases, a wife may even be the primary source of support. Interdependence is the hallmark of a modern marriage.

[C] Testing the Theory Against Reality: Contemporary Perspectives on Marriage

Joan Williams, *Is Coverture Dead? Beyond A New Theory of Alimony,*
82 Georgetown L.J. 2227, 2236–41, 2245–46 (1994)

American gender relations are dominated by imagery of equality: the accepted wisdom is that it used to be "a man's world," but "men and women are equal now." In fact, our gender system is far more complex, and uneasily combines traditional gender patterns with a self-description of equality.

The dominant family ecology has three basic elements: the gendered structure of wage labor, a gendered sense of the extent to which child care can be delegated, and gender pressures on men to structure their identities around work. These elements exist in uneasy combination with the ideology of gender equality.

The gendered structure of market work is the crucible in which the dominant family economy is forged. Employment is designed around an ideal worker who takes no time off for childbearing and has virtually no daytime child care responsibilities. The ideal worker is typically away from home nine to twelve hours a day. Consequently, an ideal worker-parent will see his young children for only a few hours each day. For parents with school-age children, the issues shift: who will pick them up from school, help with homework, take time off for medical appointments, school plays, and illness? An ideal worker needs to delegate all, or virtually all, of this care, in the manner of the traditional father. Typically he delegates to the child's mother, who either drops out of the work force to provide this flow of household services (in the pattern of traditional domesticity, circa 1780–1970), or who remains a market participant, but whose participation is marginalized by her inability to perform as an ideal worker (the dominant pattern at present). The truism that "most mothers now work" actually ignores the nearly one-third of married mothers with minor children who do no market work, the roughly one-third of all employed women who mainly work part-time, and the many full-time working women on the "mommy track." When these groups are combined, one sees clearly that most mothers do not perform as ideal workers. This gendering of wage labor is the first important element of the dominant family ecology today.

The second element is the gendered sense of how much child care can be delegated. "Traditionally," fathers delegated virtually all of child care. "Traditionally," mothers delegated virtually none. This difference forms the background imagery of the current generation, aptly captured in a Doonesbury cartoon. The first frame shows Rick and Joanie in bed. She says: "Rick, I know you love Jeff [their son] as much as I do. So why don't you seem as torn up about not being able to spend time with him?" Second frame: "Well," Rick answers, "it may be because I'm spending a whole lot more time on family than my father did, and you're spending far less time than your mother did." Third frame: "Consequently, you feel incredibly guilty, while I naturally feel pretty proud of myself. I think that's all it really amounts to, don't you?" I have called mothers' apprehension about delegating child care the "domestic nondelegation doctrine."

The structure of work and the sense of many fathers that virtually all child care is delegable combine with a third element of the current family ecology: gender pressures on men. Male gender ideology ties men's sense of themselves, their success as human beings, and even their sexual attractiveness, to their work performance. (This is why feminists traditionally have used the term "sex/gender system": men have an erotic interest in perpetuating traditional gender roles.) These gender pressures leave the typical man with little emotional alternative but to perform as an ideal worker to the extent his personality, class, and race enable him to do so. . . .

The conflict between this highly gendered pattern and the ideology of equality is mediated through the rhetoric of choice. Choice rhetoric is a useful tool for denying structural patterns such as gender roles: women are really equal, goes the argument, they just make different choices. Courts often treat husbands and wives as equal actors in two-career marriages. The husband "chooses" to develop his career, while the wife "decides" to marginalize hers—both now have to live with the consequences of their choices. Far from helping women, this distorted version of "equality" leaves them at a distinct disadvantage. . . .

Gary S. Becker, *Nobel Lecture: The Economic Way of Looking at Behavior,*
101 Journal of Political Economy 385, 397–98 (1993)

In almost all societies, married women have specialized in bearing and rearing children and in certain agricultural activities, whereas married men have done most of the fighting and market work. It should not be controversial to recognize that the explanation is a combination of biological differences between men and women —especially differences in their innate capacities to bear and rear children—and legal and other discrimination against women in market activities, partly through cultural conditioning. However, large and highly emotional differences of opinion exist over the relative importance of biology and discrimination in generating the traditional division of labor in marriages.

Contrary to allegations in many attacks on the economic approach to the gender division of labor, this analysis does not try to weight the relative importance of biology and discrimination. Its main contribution is to show how sensitive the division of labor is to *small* differences in either. Since the return from investing in a skill is greater when more time is spent utilizing the skill, a married couple could gain much from a sharp division of labor because the husband would specialize in some types of human capital and the wife in others. Given such a large gain from specialization within a marriage, only a *little* discrimination against women or small biological differences in child-rearing skills would cause the division of labor between household and market tasks to be strongly and systematically related to gender. The sensitivity to small differences explains why the empirical evidence cannot readily choose between biological and "cultural" interpretations. This theory also explains why many women entered the labor force as families became smaller, divorce became more common, and earning opportunities for women improved.

Arlie Hochschild with Anne Machung,
The Second Shift 11–13 (1989)

Each marriage bears the footprints of economic and cultural trends which originate far outside marriage. A rise in inflation which erodes the earning power of the male wage, an expanding service sector which opens up jobs for women, new cultural images . . . that make the working mother seem exciting, all these changes do not simply go on *around* marriage. They occur *within* marriage, and transform it. Problems between husbands and wives, problems which seem "individual" and "marital," are often individual experiences of powerful economic and cultural shock waves that are not caused by one person or two. . . .

There is a "his" and "hers" to the economic development of the United States. In the latter part of the nineteenth century, it was mainly men who were drawn off the farm into paid, industrial work and who changed their way of life and their identity. At that point in history, men became more different from their fathers than women became from their mothers. Today the economic arrow points at women; it is women who are being drawn into wage work, and women who are undergoing changes in their way of life and identity. Women are departing more from their mothers' and grandmothers' way of life, men are doing so less.[1]

Both the earlier entrance of men into the industrial economy and the later entrance of women have influenced the relations *between* men and women, especially their relations within marriage. The former increase in the number of men into industrial work tended to increase the power of men, and the present growth in the number of women in such work has somewhat increased the power of women. On the whole, the entrance of men into industrial work did not destabilize the family whereas *in the absence of other changes*, the rise in female employment has gone with the rise in divorce. . . .

The exodus of women into the economy has not been accompanied by a cultural understanding of marriage and work that would make this transition smooth. The workforce has changed. Women have changed. But most workplaces have remained inflexible in the face of the family demands of their workers, and, at home, most men have yet to really adapt to the changes in women. This strain between the change in women and the absence of change in much else leads me to speak of a "stalled revolution."

A society which did not suffer from this stall would be a society humanely adapted to the fact that most women work outside the home. The workplace would allow parents to work part time, to share jobs, to work flexible hours, to take parental leaves to give birth, tend a sick child, or care for a well one. . . .[I]t would include affordable housing closer to places of work, and perhaps community-based meal and laundry services. It would include men whose notion of manhood encouraged them to be active parents and share at home.

---

[1] This is more true of white and middle-class women than it is of black or poor women, whose mothers often worked outside the home. But the trend I am talking about—an increase from 20 percent of women in paid jobs in 1900 to 55 percent in 1986—has affected a large number of women.

In contrast, a stalled revolution lacks social arrangements that ease life for working parents, and lacks men who share the second shift.

June Carbone, *Morality, Public Policy and the Family: The Role of Marriage and the Public/Private Divide,*
36 Santa Clara L. Rev. 267, 267–69, 275–78 (1996)

. . . To the extent that the United States can ever be said to have had a national family policy, it is one that insists on marriage as the sole legitimate locus for childrearing. Yet . . . marriage, as the defining element of the family and the primary means of providing for children, has not so much been legislated as assumed. It has been assumed as a central and permanent feature of society synonymous with civilization itself. The moral justification for marriage as the sole appropriate forum for the expression of sexuality and the children who result has also been assumed as much as legislated largely on the basis of deeply held beliefs, often religious in origin, that are rarely examined directly in public debate. At least in the modern era, the mechanisms that have made marriage nearly universal have been a set of less visible, and essentially private mechanisms that, until recently, made childrearing outside of marriage untenable while tying the promise of economic security to those who remained within.

. . . [M]uch of the contemporary debate about the family, can be characterized as a discussion of the appropriate societal responses to the breakdown of the universality of marriage. The statistics are becoming familiar ones. Whereas in 1960, nine of ten children were being raised in two-parent families, today no more than three out of four are, and the percentage is continuing to drop. Half of all marriages, and sixty percent of second marriages end in divorce. Thirty percent of all births now occur outside of marriage, and single parenthood has been correlated (with heated debates about causation) to every conceivable childhood ill from murder to obesity. It is tempting, in listening to this debate, to group the opposite sides in terms of their positions on marriage. Such a characterization would term the "family values" position as one that favors putting the genie back in the bottle, or at least the church hall, and using the power of the state to reinforce the traditional morality that obliged parents to marry and stay married. The other pole of the debate would characterize the developments away from universal insistence on marriage as a needed and inevitable response to changes in the organization of the economy and the greater independence of women.

. . . I would like to suggest that we resist the temptation to group responses solely in these terms. For complicating the discussion are not just differences about the role of marriage, but differences about the appropriate role of the state. Many of those who find the percentage of children being raised in single-parent families destructive would oppose state efforts to restrict the availability of divorce or to stigmatize nonmarital births. Others who would like to provide greater recognition and support for nontraditional families are nonetheless critical of the role state policies have played in undermining traditional families. . . .

The fact that the role of marriage has been assumed rather than legislated, and that the importance of marriage has rested on deeply held, but diverse and essentially private beliefs, complicates the effort to consider what role marriage should continue to play. Only the polar ends of the modern debate are clear because only at polar ends of the debate is there agreement on the relationship between private morality and state policy. The Christian Coalition and secular groups that would champion traditional family values believe that the state should play a major role in reinforcing the type of sexual mores that have historically defined marriage as the only appropriate form of sexual expression. These groups tend to support continued restrictions on fornication, sodomy and abortion, a role for considerations of fault in the divorce process, and state efforts to deter divorce and nonmarital births. They would justify a state policy of insistence on the importance of marriage either directly on religious principles or on broadly based philosophical grounds.

The other pole of the debate is represented by those who would disestablish marriage as a societal institution. They would treat the decision to marry or not marry, to engage or not engage in sexual relationships, to bear children within a relationship with a parental partner, without a partner, or not at all, as matters of private choice in which the state should not intrude. These groups would characterize state insistence on marriage as the only sanctioned locus for childrearing, and any policy that would directly restrict the availability of divorce or the ability of single parents to raise their children, as unwarranted and oppressive.

This pole of the debate further divides into two philosophically opposed camps based on their attitudes toward the state's economic role. The first is the libertarian wing that casts such issues in terms of the right to be free from government dictation of private morality. Libertarians would insist on the right to choose or not choose marriage, and assign the state no responsibility for the consequences of their decisions or the well-being of the resulting children.

The other wing embraces a feminist critique of traditional marriage as an instrument of patriarchy that perpetuates a gendered division of labor and locks the partners into inherently unequal roles. The feminist left would eschew the rights language of libertarians and charge the government directly with responsibility for remedying the gendered nature of wage labor that limits parental ability to participate in the labor market, and for insuring the well-being of children, irrespective of their parents' relationship.

In between the two poles are those who would rely on a utilitarian cost-benefit analysis, concluding that (1) the well-being of children concerns society as a whole; (2) given the current constitution of society, children are better off in two-parent families; and (3) the state should therefore do what it can to reinforce marriage, and deter divorce and nonmarital births. This analysis differs from that of the family values coalition in that it leaves the judgment as to the morality of the underlying conduct to the private sphere. It differs from the libertarian and feminist critiques in that it does not regard the failure to pass judgment in the public sphere as a barrier to state action. Nonetheless, the premises of the utilitarian calculus are offset by concern that the benefits from any action the government could take to encourage family stability would be more than offset by the difficulties of enforcement, and the potential for injustice. . . .

Divisions along these lines are hardly new. Nineteenth century discussions of the family included many of the same disagreements and challenges to the use of state power to reinforce conventional morality, but there are at least two changes that significantly reshape the debate. First, the overwhelming consensus that equated nonmarital sexual activity with license rather than with liberty has dissolved into deep-seated disagreement. Second, the empirical question of the causal link between children's well-being and the stability of marriage is being debated rather than assumed. The result of these changes is to call into question not only the wisdom, but the authority, and ultimately the practicality, of a policy that relies exclusively on marriage for the well-being of families.

David Blankenhorn, *The State of the Family and the Family Policy Debate,*
36 Santa Clara L. Rev. 431, 436–37 (1996)

What is the current state of the American family? In the United States, the trend is clearly toward a post-nuclear family system—a society in which the mother-father, married couple childraising unit is no longer the dominant social form for raising children, either as an empirical reality or as a cultural norm. Some scholars describe this trend as a movement toward a post-marriage society—a society that is experiencing the steady de-institutionalization and de-juridication of marriage, and where, as a result, marriage is no longer the dominant social institution regarding the raising of children. . . .

What are the societal consequences of this post-nuclear family trend—more births outside of marriage, a high divorce rate, and millions of children growing up apart from their fathers? The two primary consequences are a continuing decline in child well-being and a continuing rise in male violence. . . .

Married fatherhood is a socializing role for men. The continuing decline in the number of men in our society who fill this role, and their replacement in so many homes by unrelated males, is clearly driving up the rate of male violence against women and children. . . .

What is society going to do about this state of affairs? Given the increasing recognition of the trend toward the post-marriage, post-nuclear family and the obviously negative consequences of this trend, especially for children, a new family debate is now emerging. The new debate focuses less on whether or not we have a problem— that question has largely been settled— but instead on what society is prepared to do about it. In short, the coming debate will be less about describing the problem and more about proposing the solution.

There are two fault lines that I believe will characterize this new debate in the coming months and years. On one side of the first fault line will be those who argue that we cannot reverse the trend—that is, that we cannot reinstitutionalize marriage. Therefore, we must instead deal with the consequences of the weakening of marriage, especially the economic consequences, recognizing the reality that more and more of our children are simply not going to be growing up with their two married parents. Conservatives may urge the construction of more prisons and urban boarding schools and orphanages to deal with the consequences, and liberals may urge a system of family allowances, a reform of the divorce process, or the creation of more jobs. But many liberals and conservatives will be agreeing that we must deal primarily with the consequences of the trend rather than the trend itself.

Those on the other side of this fault line will insist that we must seek to reverse the trend. They will direct their efforts to strengthening the institution of marriage and seeking to create cultural change in favor of the idea that unwed childbearing is wrong, that our divorce rate is far too high, and that every child deserves a father. . . .

The second fault line is between those who take a welfare state approach and those who take a laissez-faire approach. The former will hold that society ought to use the instruments of government to meet humans' needs, primarily through marketplace regulations and other public policies aimed at reducing economic inequality and improving economic security.

In contrast, those taking a laissez-faire approach will hold that government and the welfare state is not the solution, but rather the problem, and that the welfare state should be dismantled so that families can form and thrive on their own and in local communities, unharmed by the policies of the welfare state. Those favoring this latter approach are increasingly in the majority in Washington and in many state capitols. . . .

Society needs to use the tools of government and other tools at its disposal to strengthen the basic institutions of the civil society, especially the institution of marriage, and to promote a cultural shift and attitudinal changes toward the view that every child deserves a father and that more children ought to be growing up with their two married parents. Such a fundamental cultural shift is not likely to result simply from dismantling the welfare state, nor will it result from expanding the welfare state, although government obviously does play a role at times in either making things better or worse.

But the change we need most is primarily a cultural change. The most important challenge that our society faces is to shift our culture in such a way as to strengthen the civil society and reverse the trend of family fragmentation.

NOTES AND QUESTIONS

(1) The first two article excepts, by legal scholar Joan Williams and economist Gary Becker, focus on the division of labor within marriage. How do their two explanations for the existing marital division of labor differ? In what ways does family law affect the division of labor within marriage? Should the legal system seek to change what Professor Williams terms the "dominant family ecology"? Why or why not and if so, how? To what extent does women's equality in the workplace depend on a more equal division of labor in the home? *See, e.g.*, Rhona Mahony, Kidding Ourselves: Breadwinning, Babies and Bargaining Power 4–5 (1885) (arguing that "in order for women to achieve economic equality with men, men will have to do half the work of raising children"); Karen Czapanskiy, *Volunteers and Draftees: The Struggle for Parental Equality*, 38 UCLA L. Rev 1415, 1455–56 (1991) (describing costs to fathers and children of unequal division of family labor).

(2) The excerpt from Arlie Hochschild's 1989 book, The Second Shift, focuses on the relationship between marital roles and broader economic and cultural trends. Hochschild, a sociologist, coined the term "the second shift" to refer to the disproportionate childcare and homemaking tasks performed by married women who also work outside the home. Hochschild's book was published a decade ago. Is her assertion still accurate that "most workplaces have remained inflexible in the fact of the family demands of their workers, and, at home, most men have yet to really adapt to the changes in women?" *See* § 2.07 *below*. In her most recent book, The Time Bind, Hochschild argues that both women and men increasingly invest more of their time and energy in the workplace, as opposed to the family, often to the detriment of children. Arlie Hochschild, The Time Bind: When Work Becomes Home and Home Becomes Work (1997).

(3) The final two article excerpts focus on the declining importance of marriage as an exclusive arena for raising children and on the appropriate societal response to this decline. To what extent are the authors' analyses consistent? Do you agree with Professor Carbone that the societal changes she describes "call into question not only the wisdom, but the

authority and ultimately the practicality, of a policy that relies exclusively on marriage for the well-being of families?" Or, are you persuaded by Professor Blankenhorn's view that we need to shift our culture so as to strengthen and reinstitutionalize marriage? How would such a cultural shift be accomplished? What role, if any, would family law play?

§ 2.03 Marital Property Rights

Marriage has traditionally carried with it a distinct assortment of property rights. Two marital property regimes co-exist in the United States: (1) the common law title system, adhered to by a majority of states, and (2) the community property system, followed by a minority of jurisdictions. Under the common law system, the spouses own property separately during marriage. Ownership of property belongs to the spouse who holds title, or who otherwise acquired the property, and the owner may manage, control and dispose of the asset without the consent of the other spouse. *See* John DeWitt Gregory, Peter N. Swisher & Sheryl L. Scheible-Wolf, Understanding Family Law § 3.02 (1994). Under a community property regime, by contrast, all property acquired by the efforts of either spouse during marriage is owned jointly. "Equality is the cardinal precept of the community property system." William Q. deFuniak & Michael K. Vaughn, Principles of Community Property 2–3 (2d ed. 1971). Despite this equality of ownership, the husband alone traditionally had the right to manage and control community property. However, under contemporary, gender-neutral community property principles, rights of management and control of community property are generally allocated to either or both of the spouses, regardless of sex. *See* Carol Bruch, *Protecting the Rights of Spouses in Intact Marriages: The 1987 California Community Property Reform and Why It Was So Hard to Get*, 1990 Wis. L. Rev. 731 (1990).

The widespread adoption of equitable distribution principles has reduced many of the practical differences between common law title systems and community property regimes at the time of divorce. However, the two systems continue to differ with respect to the management of property during marriage, and with respect to property disposition upon the death of a spouse.

[A] The Married Women's Property Acts

Under the early common law, a married woman was under severe economic disabilities not shared by her husband. Upon marriage, a wife's personal property became the property of her husband, and the same was true of any personal property that she acquired during marriage. The husband was also granted possession of his wife's real property, including the rents and profits, as well as the right to manage, control, and alienate that property. According to Blackstone, the rationale for these disabilities was the "unity" theory of marriage; the husband and wife became a single legal entity, with the husband acting as his wife's guardian. *See, e.g.*, 1 Blackstone, Commentaries on the Laws of England 445 (3d ed. 1884), and 2 Raleigh C. Minor & John B. Wortss, The Law of Real Property § 1004 (2d ed. 1928). In exchange for his wife's property and services, the husband was obligated to support his wife.

Judicial ameliorization of this severe common law rule based on equitable principles, began to emerge in the 1700s when various courts allowed certain property to be held in a "a sole and separate use" trust for the benefit of the wife as a separate equitable *femme sole* estate. It was not until the late 1800s, however, that state legislatures began to enact a series of statutes known as The Married Women's Property Acts to reduce and eliminate these economic disabilities on the part of the wife. Commentators have differed as to whether the Married Women's Property Acts have rendered the separate equitable *femme sole* estate obsolete. Compare A. James Casuer, 1 American Law of Property §§ 5.55–5.56 (1952) with Rappeport, *The Equitable Separate Estate and Restraints on Anticipation*, 11 Miami L.Q. 85 (1956).

Generally speaking, the Married Women's Property Acts granted a wife the same right to acquire, own, and transfer all kinds of real and personal property as though she were unmarried; to make contracts in her own name; to engage in business or employment; to sue and be sued; and to be fully responsible for her tortious and criminal conduct. *See generally* Homer Clark,1 Law of Domestic Relations 502–24 (2d ed. 1987). Typically the Married Women's Property Acts also shielded a wife's assets from her husband's creditors. The Acts had no effect, however, on the husband's position as head of the household, his duty to support his wife, or her reciprocal obligation to provide him with household services. *See* Reva B. Siegel, *Home as Work: The First Woman's Rights Claims Concerning Wives' Household Labor*, 1850–1880, 103 Yale L.J. 1073 (1994). While some of the more expansive statutes granted wives the right to retain their earnings during marriage, many courts interpreted their state statutes narrowly, and continued to regard a wife's income during marriage as the property of her husband. *See generally* Reva B. Siegel, *The Modernization of Marital Status Law: Adjudicating Wives' Rights to Earnings, 1860–1930*, 82 Geo. L. J. 2127 (1994). Moreover, because the typical wife was not employed outside the home and brought little, if any, property into the marriage, the Married Women's Property Acts produced only a limited improvement in the economic position of most married women.

Recent constitutional developments have undermined the continuing viability of those portions of the Married Women's Property Acts that afford greater economic protection to married women than to married men. Beginning in the early 1970's, a series of United States Supreme Court decisions invalidated as unconstitutional a variety of gender-based statutes and distinctions, including several that governed family law issues. *See, e.g., Orr v. Orr*, 440 U.S. 268 (1979), *cert. denied*, 444 U.S. 1060 (1980) (statute authorizing alimony awards for wives, but not for husbands, constituted unlawful sex-based discrimination); *Stanton v. Stanton*, 421 U.S. 7 (1975) (equal protection clause prohibits states from setting different ages of majority for males than for females). Since that time, the Court has made clear that statutory classifications based on gender must satisfy "an exceedingly persuasive justification." *Mississippi University for Women v. Hogan*, 458 U.S. 718, 724 (1982); *United States v. Virginia*, 518 U.S. 515, 515 (1996). To withstand constitutional scrutiny, such gender-based classifications must at least serve "important governmental objectives" and must be "substantially related to the achievement of those objectives." *Hogan*, 456 U.S. at 724; *see J.E.B. v. Alabama*, 511 U.S. 127, 131–46 (1994). Although statutory classifications based on gender may be justified, in limited circumstances, to compensate women "for particular economic disabilities [they have] suffered," *Califano v. Webster*, 430 U.S. 313 (1977), the same heightened scrutiny applies, even where a statute's objective is to compensate for past discrimination or to balance the burdens borne by males and females. *Hogan*, 458 U.S. at 728. Thus, even statutes designed to compensate women "must not rely on overbroad generalizations about the different talents, capacities, or preferences of males and females. *United States v. Virginia*, 518 U.S. at 531–34; *see Weisenberger v.*

Wiesenfield, 420 U.S. 636, 643 (1975). As a result of this Supreme Court jurisprudence, the vast majority of states have amended (or judicially reinterpreted) their statutes governing marital support and property rights to apply equally to husbands and wives.

Query: Does this mean that those provisions of the Married Women's Property Acts that give married women greater economic rights or protections than married men, are unconstitutional? Or would these statutory classifications qualify as valid remedial laws that are substantially related to an important governmental purpose? Or should these protections be extended to apply to husbands, as well as wives. *Compare, e.g., North Ottawa Community Hospital v. Kieft*, 578 N.W. 2d 267 (Mich. 1998) (upholding statutory provision that shielded wives from liability for their husbands' debts, but holding that husbands were entitled to similar protection) *with Jersey Shore Med. Ctr.-Fitkin Hospital v. Estate of Baum*, 417 A.2d 1003 (1980) (striking down provision of Married Women's Property Act that purported to shield a married woman from liability for her husband's necessary medical expenses). For additional discussion of spousal support obligations, including the common law necessaries doctrine, see § 2.04, *below*.

[B] Tenancy by the Entirety

The common law recognized the estate of tenancy by the entirety, a form of concurrent property ownership available exclusively to married couples. Tenancy by the entirety, however, has never been recognized in those states adhering to a community property regime. Tenancy by the entirety is a means of protecting a married couple's property, both from each other and from their creditors. In a tenancy by the entirety, each spouse holds an equal, undivided interest in the property during the lifetimes of both spouses. The estate incorporates a survivorship interest which gives the surviving spouse sole ownership of the whole property at the death of the other spouse. Neither spouse can unilaterally transfer, encumber, sever, or partition property held in tenancy by the entirety, nor destroy the other spouse's right of survivorship, and the individual creditors of one spouse cannot reach that spouse's interest in entirety property. *See generally* Paul G. Haskell, Preface to Wills, Trusts and Administration, 118–19 (1987).

In those states where tenancy by the entirety is still recognized, both spouses now have equal rights to property held in the entirety, and a majority of these states shield the entirety property both from the unilateral acts of either spouse, and from their individual creditors. *See, e.g., Sawada v. Endo,* 561 P.2d 1291 (Haw. 1977). Since only married couples may hold property as tenants by the entirety, the estate is generally converted into a tenancy in common if the parties divorce. *See, e.g. Union Grove Milling & Mfg. Co. v. Faw,* 404 S.E.2d 508 (N.C. Ct. App. 1991); *V.R.W. Inc. v. Klein,* 503 N.E.2d 496 (N.Y. 1986).

[C] Property Rights on the Death of a Spouse

At death, subject to certain restrictions, a spouse may transfer by will any property that he or she owns individually. Under the early common law title theory of marital property ownership, because husbands traditionally owned most or all of a married couple's assets, a wife could be left without any property or means of support if the husband died first and left his estate to someone other than his widow. To alleviate the possibility that a surviving spouse would be left destitute, the common law developed methods of protecting surviving spouses in the form of dower and curtesy, and—during this century—the statutory elective share.

Although the common law afforded wives no rights in their husbands' property during marriage, it did protect wives from total disinheritance on the husband's death in the form of dower. Dower entitled a widow to possession of a life estate in one third of certain real property that the husband owned at any time during the marriage, regardless of when or how the husband had acquired the property. And although the common law already gave the husband the right to manage and control the wife's real property during the marriage, it further granted the husband a continued interest upon her death in the form of curtesy. Like dower, curtesy was limited to the wife's inheritable real property interests. During the past century, however, as people more commonly began to hold their accumulated wealth in the form of financial investments rather than in real property, dower and curtesy became a largely ineffective means for providing protection to a surviving spouse. Accordingly, most states have now abolished both dower and curtesy, and they have been replaced or supplemented in most common law states with some variation of "elective" or "forced" share statute. *See generally* Paul G. Haskill, *above*, at 134–36 (1987) and A. James Casuer, 1 American Law of Property §§ 5.1– 5.76 (1952).

Elective share statutes entitle a surviving spouse to a statutorily prescribed minimum fraction of the decedent spouse's property owned at death. Typically, the fraction is one third to one half of the decedent's probate estate, but this may vary depending on whether the decedent spouse left descendants or parents. Although these statutes are sometimes referred to as "forced share" statutes, since the surviving spouse can renounce the will and demand a minimum portion of the deceased spouse's estate, the surviving spouse must affirmatively assert this right during a specified period of time or it will expire; hence the term "elective share" as used in the Uniform Probate Code is more appropriate. *See* L. Waggoner et al., Family Property Law 473, 476–78 (1991). Unlike common law dower and curtesy, elective share statutes apply to both real and personal property. However, the elective share generally only applies to property which the decedent spouse disposes of by will, although some states subject certain lifetime transfers to the spouse's elective share as well. Furthermore, if the decedent spouse dies without a will that effectively devises all of his or her property, the intestacy statutes of every state designate a surviving spouse as an heir, entitling him or her to a specified portion of the estate.

The Uniform Probate Code sets out a more thorough and complex elective share approach known as the "augmented estate" elective share that a number of states have adopted. *See* Uniform Probate Code § 2–202, 8 U.L.A. 75 (1983) (amended 1990). This augmented estate approach reaches not only the decedent's probate estate, but accounts for certain *inter vivos* transfers as well. The 1990 Uniform Probate Code further redesigned the augmented estate, attempting to better correlate the elective share with the partnership theory of marriage. The new version retains and expands the augmented estate approach in combining the assets of both spouses in calculating the augmented estate. Further, it adjusts the percentage of the surviving spouse's entitlements according to the length of the couple's marriage, reaching a maximum of 50 percent after 15 years of marriage. It also takes into account the surviving spouse's own separate assets, which are counted first in calculating the final amount to be awarded. *See* Seplowitz, *Transfers Prior to Marriage and the Uniform Probate Code's Redesigned Elective Share: Why the Partnership is Not Yet Complete*, 25 Ind. L. Rev. 1 (1991). *See generally* Gregory, Swisher, & Scheible-Wolf, Understanding Family Law §§ 3.04, 3.05 (1995); and Waggoner, Alexander, & Fellows, Family Property Law: Cases and Materials 80–113 (2d ed. 1997).

[D] The Community Property System

Eight American states historically have followed the community property principles developed in Spain and France, rather than following the common law property title theory imported from England. These eight states are: Arizona, California, Idaho, Louisiana, New Mexico, Nevada, Texas, and Washington. Since its adoption of the Uniform Marital Property Act in 1983, Wisconsin also has arguably been a community property state.

The community property system is based on a sharing or partnership theory of marriage, which presumes that each spouse contributes equally, in a direct or indirect manner, to the accumulation of assets during the marriage. Equal ownership interests are allocated to homemaker and other intangible contributions to the marriage relationship, as well as to income-producing activity. Although these details vary considerably from one community property state to another, the community property regime, in general, regards most property acquired through the efforts of either spouse during the marriage as owned equally by both spouses. Spouses in community property jurisdictions also are permitted to hold separate property. Separate property generally includes assets that a spouse acquired prior to marriage, or by individual gift or inheritance during marriage, or by designation as separate property in a marital agreement signed by the spouses, or by court decree. Community property states differ with respect to classification of passive income and profits from separate property, but earnings attributable to the labor of either spouse, and the assets procured with those earnings, are equally owned as community property. *See generally* W. McClanahan, Community Property Law in the United States (1982).

During marriage, an individual spouse's ownership interest in community property is undivided, but when the community dissolves, either by divorce or by death, the ownership interests in community property are severed, and each spouse is entitled to an individual one half. Thus, after termination of the marriage, each spouse owns his or her own separate property and one half of the former community property assets, although some community property states have modified property division on divorce with equitable distribution principles. *See* § 10.02[B]. *See, e.g.* William A. Reppy, *Major Events in the Evolution of American Community Property Law and Their Import to Equitable Distribution States*, 23 Fam. L. Q. 163 (1989). *See generally* Gregory, Swisher & Scheible-Wolf, Understanding Family Law § 3.06 (1995).

A hybrid statutory approach, that incorporates a number of community property principles during marriage, is found in the Uniform Marital Property Act (UMPA), 9 U.L.A. 97 (1987). UMPA is based on three major principles: shared ownership of property during marriage; title-based management and control of marital property; and a limitation in the scope of property rights while the marriage is intact. UMPA thus defines marital property rights *only* during the marriage, and the Act was not intended to govern any division of property rights when the marriage is terminated by death or divorce. To date, UMPA has only been adopted by one state, Wisconsin, and UMPA has been severely criticized by a number of probate attorneys and other commentators. *See, e.g.* Bruce, *Should Your State Adopt UMPA? No.* Probate and Property (Sept–Oct. 1987). *See also* Winter, *UMPA Fights for Recognition*, 70 A.B.A.J. at 77 (June, 1984).

§ 2.04 Support Obligations During Marriage

[A] The Nonintervention Principle

MCGUIRE v. MCGUIRE
Supreme Court of Nebraska
59 N.W.2d 336 (1953)

MESSMORE, JUSTICE.

The plaintiff, Lydia McGuire, brought this action in equity in the district court for Wayne County against Charles W. McGuire, her husband, as defendant, to recover suitable maintenance and support money, and for costs and attorney's fees. Trial was had to the court and a decree was rendered in favor of the plaintiff.

The district court decreed that the plaintiff was legally entitled to use the credit of the defendant and obligate him to pay for certain items in the nature of improvements and repairs, furniture, and appliances for the household in the amount of several thousand dollars; required the defendant to purchase a new automobile with an effective heater within 30 days; ordered him to pay travel expenses of the plaintiff for a visit to each of her daughters at least once a year; that the plaintiff be entitled in the future to pledge the credit of the defendant for what may constitute necessaries of life; awarded a personal allowance to the plaintiff in the sum of $50 a month; awarded $800 for services for the plaintiff's attorney; and as an alternative to part of the award to made, defendant was permitted, in agreement with plaintiff, to purchase a modern home elsewhere.

The defendant filed a motion for new trial which was overruled. From this order the defendant perfected appeal to this court. For convenience we will refer to the parties as they are designated in the district court.

The record shows that the plaintiff and defendant were married in Wayne, Nebraska, on August 11, 1919. At the time of the marriage the defendant was a bachelor 46 or 47 years of age and had a reputation for more than ordinary frugality, of which the plaintiff was aware. She had visited in his home and had known him for about 3 years prior to the marriage. . . . The plaintiff had been previously married. Her first husband died in October 1914, leaving surviving him the plaintiff and two daughters. He died intestate, leaving 80 acres of land in Dixon County. The plaintiff and each of the daughters inherited a one-third interest therein. At the time of the marriage of the plaintiff and defendant the plaintiff's daughters were 9 and 11 years of age. By working and receiving financial assistance from the parties to this action, the daughters received a high school education in Pender. One daughter attended Wayne State Teachers College for 2 years and the other daughter attended a business college in Sioux City, Iowa, for 1 year. Both of these daughters are married and have families of their own.

On April 12, 1939, the plaintiff transferred her interest in the 80-acre farm to her two daughters. The defendant signed the deed.

At the time of trial plaintiff was 66 years of age and the defendant nearly 80 years of age. No children were born to these parties. The defendant had no dependents except the plaintiff.

The plaintiff testified that she was a dutiful and obedient wife, worked and saved, and cohabited with the defendant until the last 2 or 3 years. She worked in the fields, did outside chores, cooked, and attended to her household duties such as cleaning the house and doing the washing. For a number of years she raised as high as 300 chickens, sold poultry and eggs, and used the money to buy clothing, things she wanted, and for groceries. She further testified that the defendant was the boss of the house and his word was law; that he would not tolerate any charge accounts and would not inform her as to his finances or business; and that he was a poor companion. . . . On several occasions the plaintiff asked the defendant for money. He would give her very small amounts, and for the last 3 or 4 years he had not given her any money nor provided her with clothing, except a coat about 4 years previous. The defendant had purchased the groceries the last 3 or 4 years, and permitted her to buy groceries, but he paid for them by check. . . .The defendant had not taken her to a motion picture show during the past 12 years. They did not belong to any organizations or charitable institutions, nor did he give her money to make contributions to any charitable institutions. . . . For the past 4 years or more, the defendant had not given the plaintiff money to purchase furniture or other household necessities. Three years ago he did purchase an electric, wood-and-cob combination stove which was installed in the kitchen, also linoleum floor covering for the kitchen. The plaintiff further testified that the house is not equipped with a bathroom, bathing facilities, or inside toilet. The kitchen is not modern. She does not have a kitchen sink. Hard and soft water is obtained from a well and cistern. . . . There is a pipeless furnace which she testified had not been in good working order for 5 or 6 years, and she testified she was tired of scooping coal and ashes. She had requested a new furnace but the defendant believed the one they had to be satisfactory. She related that the furniture was old and she would like to replenish it, at least to be comparable with some of her neighbors; . . .that the defendant owns a 1929 Ford coupe equipped with a heater which is not efficient, and on the average of every 2 weeks he drives the plaintiff to Wayne to visit her mother; and that he also owns a 1927 Chevrolet pickup which is used for different purposes on the farm. The plaintiff was privileged to use all of the rent money she wanted to from the 80-acre farm, and when she goes to see her daughters, which is not frequent, she uses part of the rent money for that purpose, the defendant providing no funds for such use. . . . At the present time the plaintiff is not able to raise chickens and sell eggs. She has about 25 chickens. The plaintiff has had three abdominal operations for which the defendant has paid. She selected her own doctor, and there were no restrictions placed in that respect. When she has requested various things for the home or personal effects, defendant has informed her on many occasions that he did not have the money to pay for the same. She would like to have a new car. . . . The plaintiff further testified that she had very little funds, possibly $1,500 in the bank which was chicken money and money which her father furnished her, he having departed this life a few years ago; and that use of the telephone was restricted, indicating that defendant did not desire that she make long distance calls. . . .

It appears that the defendant owns 398 acres of land with 2 acres deeded to a church, the land being of the value of $83,960; that he has bank deposits in the sum of $12,786.81 and government bonds in the amount of $104,500; and that his income, including interest on the bonds and rental for his real estate, is $8,000 or $9,000 a year. There are apparently some Series E United States Savings Bonds listed and registered in the names of Charles W. McGuire or Lydia M. McGuire purchased in 1943, 1944, and 1945, in the amount of $2,500. Other bonds seem of Charles W. McGuire, without a beneficiary or co-owner designated. The plaintiff has a bank account of $5,960.22. This account includes deposits of some $200 and $100 which the court required the defendant to pay his wife as temporary allowance during the pendency of these proceedings. One hundred dollars was withdrawn on the date of each deposit. . . .

The defendant assigns as error that the decree is not supported by sufficient evidence; that the decree is contrary to law; that the decree is an unwarranted usurpation and invasion of defendant's fundamental and constitutional rights; and that the court erred in allowing fees for the plaintiff's attorney.

While there is an allegation in the plaintiff's petition to the effect that the defendant was guilty of extreme cruelty towards the plaintiff, and also an allegation requesting a restraining order be entered against the defendant for fear he might molest plaintiff or take other action detrimental to her rights, the plaintiff made no attempt to prove these allegations and the fact that she continued to live with the defendant is quite incompatible with the same. . . .

It becomes apparent that there are no cases cited by the plaintiff and relied upon by her from this jurisdiction or other jurisdictions that will sustain the action such as she has instituted in the instant case. . . .

In the instant case the marital relation has continued for more than 33 years, and the wife has been supported in the same manner during this time without complaint on her part. The parties have not been separated or living apart from each other at any time. In the light of the cited cases it is clear, especially so in this jurisdiction, that to maintain an action such as the one at bar, the parties must be separated or living apart from each other.

The living standards of a family are a matter of concern to the household, and not for the courts to determine, even though the husband's attitude toward his wife, according to his wealth and circumstances, leaves little to be said in his behalf. As long as the home is maintained and the parties are living as husband and wife it may be said that the husband is legally supporting his wife and the purpose of the marriage relation is being carried out. Public policy requires such a holding. It appears that the plaintiff is not devoid of money in her own right. She has a fair sized bank account and is entitled to use the rent from the 80 acres of land left by her first husband, if she so chooses. . . .

Reversed and remanded with directions to dismiss.

NOTES AND QUESTIONS

(1) The opinion in *McGuire* suggests that while the law traditionally obligated husbands to support their wives, that support obligation was difficult to enforce during an ongoing marriage. What explains this judicial reluctance to enforce a husband's support obligation?

(2) Feminist scholars, in particular, have been critical of the legal system's traditional refusal to "intervene" in an ongoing marriage, arguing that the absence of law from the domestic realm "has itself contributed to male dominance and female subordination." Malinda L. Seymore, *Isn't It A Crime: Feminist Perspectives on Spousal Immunity and Spousal Violence*, 90 Nw. U.L. Rev. 1032, 1072 (1996). Feminist scholars have also suggested that the nonintervention principle reflected in *McGuire* is part of a larger public/ private dichotomy that associates the legalized, public sphere with men and relegates women to the private sphere of home and family. "The rhetoric of privacy that has insulated the

female world from the legal order sends an important ideological message to the rest of society. It devalues women and their functions and says that women are not important enough to merit legal regulation." Elizabeth M. Schneider, *The Violence of Privacy*, 23 Conn. L. Rev. 973, 975 (1991); *see also* Anne C. Daily, *Constitutional Privacy and the Just Family*, 67 Tul. L. Rev. 955, 967 (1993); Francis Olsen, *The Family and the Market: A Study of Ideology and Legal Reform*, 96 Harv. L. Rev. 1497 (1983). *Cf.* Jean L. Cohen, *Identity, Difference, and the Abortion Controversy*, 3 Colum. J. Gender & L. 43 (1992) (criticizing feminist critique of the right of privacy).

Do these arguments provide a persuasive critique of *McGuire*? Would more vigorous enforcement of marital support obligations empower women in Lydia McGuire's position? Would such enforcement strengthen or weaken marriage?

(3) Why do you think that Mrs. McGuire continued to live with her husband, despite his poor treatment of her? Do you agree with the court that the fact that the couple continued to live together "is quite incompatible" with Mrs. McGuire's allegations of extreme cruelty and fear?

[B] The Common Law Doctrine of Necessaries

Although a wife generally could not obtain judicial enforcement of her husband's support obligations during marriage, the common law doctrine of necessaries provided a mechanism for third-party enforcement of the husband's obligation. Under this doctrine, a merchant who supplied necessary goods or services to a married woman could seek payment directly from her husband. Unlike agency law principles, the doctrine of necessaries held the husband responsible for his wife's essential purchases, regardless of the husband's consent to, or knowledge of, the purchases. *See* John DeWitt Gregory, Peter N. Swisher and Sheryl Scheibel-Wolfe, Understanding Family Law § 3.10 (Matthew Bender 1995).

Necessary items generally included food, clothing and shelter, as well as medical and legal expenses. However, the scope of the doctrine varied considerably, according to the family's economic status and standard of living, and the husband's ability to pay. Accordingly, the doctrine had limited practical application, because merchants and other providers were exposed to considerable financial risk when they relied on the husband's credit. *Id.*, *see* Mahoney, *Economic Sharing During Marriage: Equal Protection, Spousal Support and the Doctrine of Necessaries*, 22 J. Fam. L. 221 (1983–84).

Because the common law imposed marital support obligations only on husbands, the necessaries doctrine did not obligate wives to pay for necessary goods or services supplied to their husbands. The common law doctrine was thus explicitly gender based. In recent years, a number of courts have considered whether the necessaries doctrine conflicts with constitutional principles of gender equality and, if so, how such inequality should be remedied.

CONNOR v. SOUTHWEST FLORIDA REGIONAL MEDICAL CENTER
Supreme Court of Florida
668 So. 2d 175 (1995)

GRIMES, CHIEF JUSTICE.

. . . Southwest Florida Regional Medical Center sued Kenneth Connor and his wife Barbara Connor in 1993 for payment of medical services the hospital had rendered to

Kenneth. The trial court dismissed the hospital's complaint against Barbara Connor on the ground that she had not executed an agreement to pay for the services of Kenneth Connor. In so doing, the trial court declined to expand the doctrine of necessaries to hold the wife responsible for her husband's medical bills. . . .

This case involves what is known as the doctrine of necessaries. At common law, a married women's legal identity merged with that of her husband, a condition known as coverture. She was unable to own property, enter into contracts, or receive credit. A married woman was therefore dependent upon her husband for maintenance and support, and he was under a corresponding legal duty to provide his wife with food, clothing, shelter, and medical services. . . . Under the doctrine, a husband was liable to a third party for any necessaries that [a] third party provided to his wife. Because the duty of support was uniquely the husband's obligation, and because coverture restricted the wife's access to the economic realm, the doctrine did not impose a similar liability on married women. . . .

This state recognized the doctrine of necessaries in *Phillips v. Sanchez*, 35 Fla. 187, 17 So. 363 (1895). However, the disability of coverture was later abrogated [in 1943] . . . *see* Sec. 708.08, Fla. Stat. (1993). Further, the responsibilities for alimony between husband and wife are now reciprocal. Sec. 61.08, Fla. Stat. (1993).

In the first case to address the question of whether the obligations under the doctrine of necessaries should run both ways was *Manatee Convalescent Center, Inc. v. McDonald*, 392 So.2d 1356 (Fla. 2d DCA 1980). In holding a wife liable for the necessaries of her husband, the court stated:

> Changing times demand reexamination of seemingly unchangeable legal dogma. Equality under law and even handed treatment of the sexes in the modern marketplace must also carry the burden of responsibility which goes with the benefits.

Id. At 1358. *Accord Parkway Gen. Hosp. Inc. v. Stern*, 400 So.2d 166 (Fla. 3d DCA 1981). However, in *Shands Teaching Hospital and Clinics Inc. v. Smith*, 497 So.2d 644 (Fla. 1986), this Court declined to hold a wife liable for the husband's hospital bills and disapproved *Parkway General Hospital* and *Manatee Convalescent Center*. In reaching our decision, we first stated that it was an anachronism to hold the husband responsible for the necessaries of the wife without also holding the wife responsible for the necessaries of the husband. . . . However, we concluded that because the issue had broad social implications and the judiciary was the branch of government least capable of resolving the question, it was best to leave to the legislature the decision of whether to modify the common law doctrine of necessaries. In a footnote we stated that the issue of whether it was a denial of equal protection to hold the husband liable for a wife's necessaries when a wife was not liable for a husband's necessaries was not before us. . . .

The case before us today is in essentially the same posture as *Shands*. Yet we are faced with a series of cases in which the parties agree that husbands and wives must be treated alike but disagree over whether the doctrine of necessaries should be applied to both spouses or simply abolished. Therefore, we have concluded that we must now address this issue in the context of equal protection considerations. Mrs. Connor contends that with the removal of coverture, the doctrine of necessaries is no longer justifiable because wives are now freely able to enter into contracts and obtain their own necessaries. Southwest posits that while the initial reason for the doctrine has disappeared, it now serves the important function of promoting the partnership theory of marriage and should be expanded so that both men and women are liable to third-party creditors who provide necessaries to their respective spouses.

The courts of other states have split on the proper remedy to adopt. Some have abrogated the doctrine entirely, preferring to defer to the legislature. Others have extended the common law doctrine to apply to both spouses.

Legislative action in this area has been just as diverse. Oklahoma and Kentucky have codified the doctrine in its original common law form, while the Georgia Legislature repealed the doctrine in 1979. . . . Somewhere in the middle of these two extremes are those jurisdictions that have retained the doctrine in modified form. For example, North Dakota imposes joint and several liability for debts incurred by either spouse for the necessaries of food, clothing, fuel, and shelter, but excludes medical care.

The fact that courts and other legislatures have treated this problem in different ways illustrates the lack of consensus regarding the doctrine's place in modern society and reenforces the position we took in *Shands*. But our legislature has not chosen to address this issue, and we know of no circumstances occurring since our decision in *Shands* which would suggest that we were wrong in refusing to hold the wife liable for the husband's necessaries. Because constitutional considerations demand equality between the sexes, it follows that a husband can no longer be held liable for his wife's necessaries. We therefore abrogate the common law doctrine of necessaries, thereby leaving it to the legislature to determine the law of the state in this area. . . .

OVERTON, JUSTICE, dissenting.

I dissent. The common law doctrine of necessaries was born of the need to provide a legal means to protect and enforce the moral terms of the marital obligation. I find that the doctrine is just as important today, under a partnership theory of marriage, as it was when the doctrine was created under the unitary theory of marriage. In this day and age, we should not weaken the obligations of marriage by eliminating the spousal duty to care for one another. However, that is exactly what the majority opinion does, and, by doing so, it places this Court in a minority of state supreme courts that have addressed this issue.

I agree that the common law doctrine of necessaries in its present form violates the equal protection clause by imposing a duty of support only on the husband. However, unlike the majority, I conclude that this Court, as a matter of policy, should extend the doctrine to apply to both spouses rather than abrogate it entirely. In doing so, I would make the spouse who incurred the debt primarily liable.

The majority's decision to abrogate the doctrine is premised on the theory that altering the doctrine would have broad social implications and, as such, is a task best left to the legislature. If the legislature disagreed with the policies behind the doctrine of necessaries, it has had ample opportunity during the last one hundred years to abolish the doctrine. Instead, the legislature has left the doctrine intact. This legislative inaction implies an agreement with the current, judicially-created policy regarding the doctrine of necessaries. The majority's abrogation of the doctrine of necessaries appears to shift the policy of this state by, in effect, requiring each spouse to take care of himself or herself. It also reduces the legal obligations of the marriage contract. . . .

The majority's determination that a lack of consensus exists among other states regarding the proper role of the doctrine of necessaries is, in my view, incorrect. A national survey of how state courts have resolved this issue reveals that this Court's decision to abrogate the doctrine places Florida in the minority of jurisdictions that have considered the issue. Approximately sixteen state courts have addressed the issue of whether the doctrine of necessaries should be modified or abrogated. The majority of those state courts have extended the doctrine to apply to both spouses. Only four have abrogated the doctrine and placed the responsibility on the legislature to reinstate the doctrine through codification. . . .

Under the partnership theory of marriage, each spouse is entitled to share in the fruits of the marital partnership. This concept is reflected by equitable distribution principles recognized in this State. The majority's decision to abrogate the common law doctrine of necessaries departs from the partnership theory of marriage and eliminates a common law doctrine even though the policy and need for the doctrine continue to exist. . . .

I believe that extending the doctrine of necessaries to apply to both spouses is the best, most logical, and least destructive method of altering the doctrine to comply with the equal protection clause. I would make the spouse who incurred the obligation primarily responsible. Extending the doctrine in this manner would further both a long-standing obligation of spousal support and the needs of our changing society. It would also advance a policy that acknowledges the partnership theory of marriage and the social value inherent in requiring marital partners to support one another.

NOTES AND QUESTIONS

(1) Which approach to the constitutional infirmity of the common law necessaries doctrine do you find more persuasive, the majority's decision to abolish the doctrine, or the dissent's proposal to extend liability to wives, as well as husbands? Which approach is more consistent with a partnership theory of marriage? With the notion of spouses as independent legal actors?

(2) Another recent court opinion addressing the doctrine of necessaries is *Medical Hosp. Ctr. of Vermont v. Lorrain*, 675 A.2d 1326 (Vt. 1996) where the Vermont Supreme Court opined as follows:

> There is no question that, when applied only to men, the necessaries doctrine offends the principle of equal protection under the law. . . . The issue, rather, is whether to remedy the equal protection violation by extending the doctrine to both wives and husbands or by abolishing it altogether. We opt for the latter remedy, notwithstanding that the majority of courts considering the issue have elected to make the doctrine reciprocal to wives and husbands. . . .
>
> Virtually all of the necessaries doctrine cases concern hospitals or clinics seeking to collect debts resulting from medical services rendered to spouses, often during a last illness. The public policy issues surrounding these circumstances are complex, and are best taken up by the Legislature in family-expense statutes, creditors' rights laws or even comprehensive health care legislation. The Legislature, not the Court, is better equipped to assemble the facts and determine the appropriate remedies in an area fraught with social policy involving the laws of property, the institution of marriage, and the distribution of the costs of health care expenses. . . .

Query: Do you agree with the Vermont Supreme Court that legislatures are better suited than courts to modify outdated common law doctrines in response to changing societal needs and norms? Should more social policy issues involving marriage and divorce be left to state legislative control? Or should courts be able to modify traditional family law principles to meet the changing needs of families? What should be the proper role of the state courts vis-a-vis the state legislatures in resolving contemporary family law issues and disputes?

(3) If the necessaries doctrine is extended on a gender neutral basis, should a creditor be required to look first to the spouse who incurred the debt, before seeking payment from the other spouse? *Compare, e.g., Jersey Shore Med. Ctr.-Fitkin Hospital v. Estate of Baum*, 417 A.2d 1003, 1110 (N.J. 1980)(holding that, absent agreement with a creditor, "the income and property of one spouse should not be exposed to satisfy a debt incurred by the other spouse unless the assets of the spouse who incurred the debt are insufficient"); *with St. Mary's Hospital Med. Ctr. v. Brody*, 519 N.W.2d 706 (Wis. Ct. App. 1994)(husband and wife are equally liable for husband's medical expenses incurred during marriage, and creditor may seek full payment from wife's post-divorce assets). *Query:* What is the status of the doctrine of necessaries in your state?

(4) Which of the following would constitute necessary purchases under the doctrine of necessaries?

(a) Wife purchased a sofa on husband's credit. Is a sofa a necessary item? *See Sharpe Furniture Inc.. v. Buckstaff*, 99 Wis. 2d 114, 299 N.W.2d 219 (Wis. 1980).

(b) Husband refused to pay for wife's abortion. A necessary medical expense? Would it make any difference if wife's abortion was medically dictated or an elective abortion? *See Sharon Clinic v. Nelson*, 90 Misc. 2d 253, 394 N.Y.S.2d 118 (N.Y. Sup. Ct. 1977).

(c) Wife hired a private detective to obtain evidence concerning the reputation, assets, and activities of the husband for use in a contemplated divorce action. Are these services necessary services? What if the detective's services were used to obtain support arrearages for the wife and children, such as locating a deserting husband? *See Chipp v. Murray*, 191 Kan. 73, 379 P.2d 297 (Kan. 1963).

[C] Spousal and Child Support Statutes

As an additional, but limited, means of enforcing marital support obligations, most states have enacted a variety of family expense statues that codify the spousal duty of support, as well as statutes that impose criminal sanctions for willful nonsupport. *See* John DeWitt Gregory, Peter Swisher and Sheryl L. Scheible-Wolf, Understanding Family Law § 3.12 (1994). Family expense and criminal nonsupport statutes generally apply to both spousal and child support obligations. Equal protection principles now require that these statutes apply equally to wives and husbands, and to mothers and fathers. *See Rand v. Rand*, 374 A.2d 900 (Md. 1977).

Family expense statues, originally enacted in conjunction with the Married Women's Property Acts, typically allow a creditor to execute against either spouse's property to collect debts incurred for necessary family expenses. Some statutes create personal liability against the non-incurring spouse as well. However, these statutes generally do not provide a direct remedy to the spouses themselves for enforcement of the duty of support. *See* Joan Krauskopf and Rhonda Thomas, *Partnership Marriage: The Solution to an Ineffective and Inequitable Law of Support*, 35 Ohio St. L.J. 558, 571 (1974).

Most criminal nonsupport statutes are narrower than civil family expense statutes and apply only when a spouse is left completely without means of support or without necessary food, clothing or housing. *See* H. Clark, 2, The Law of Domestic Relations in the United States 271 (2nd ed. 1987). In addition, many criminal nonsupport statutes require desertion or abandonment in addition to nonsupport and do not apply when spouses are living under the same roof. The purpose of these narrow criminal statutes is to protect the public, not to benefit the deserted spouse. Krauskopf & Thomas, *above* at 574.

Three representative state spousal and child support statutes appear below:

California Family Code (1998)

§ 3900. Subject to this division, the father and mother of a minor child have an equal responsibility to support their child in the manner suitable to the child's circumstances.

§ 3901(a). The duty of support imposed by Section 3900 continues as to an unmarried child who has attained the age of 18 years, is a full-time high school student, and who is not self-supporting, until the time the child completes the 12th grade or attains the age of 19 years, whichever occurs first. . . .

§ 3950. If a parent neglects to provide articles necessary for the parent's child who is under the charge of the parent, according to the circumstances of the parent, a third person may in good faith supply the necessaries and recover their reasonable value from the parent.

§ 4300. Subject to this division, a person shall support the person's spouse.

§ 4303(a). The obligee spouse, or the county on behalf of the obligee spouse, may bring an action against the obligor spouse to enforce the duty of support. . . .

Ohio Revised Code, Domestic Relations Code (1998)

§ 3103.03(A). Each married person must support the person's self and spouse out of the person's property or by the person's labor. If a married person is unable to do so, the spouse of the married person must assist in the support so far as the spouse is able. The biological or adoptive parent of a minor child must support the parent's minor child out of the parent's labor or by the parent's labor. . . .

§ 3103.03(C). If a married person neglects to support the person's spouse in accordance with this section, any other person, in good faith, may supply the spouse with necessaries for the support of the spouse and recover the reasonable value of the necessaries supplied from the married person who neglected to support the spouse unless the spouse abandons that person without cause.

Sec. 3103.03(D). If a parent neglects to support his or her minor child in accordance with this section and if the minor child in question is unemancipated, any other person, in good faith, may supply the minor child with necessaries for the support of the minor child and recover the reasonable value of the necessaries supplied from the parent who neglected to support the minor child.

Virginia Code Annotated, Domestic Relations Code (1997)

§ 20–61. Any spouse who without cause deserts or willfully neglects or refuses or fails to provide for the support and maintenance of his or her spouse, and any parent who deserts or willfully neglects or refuses or fails to provide for the support and maintenance of his or her child under the age of 18 years of age, or child of whatever age who is crippled or otherwise incapacitated from earning a living, the spouse, child or children being then in necessitous circumstances, shall be guilty of a misdemeanor. . . .

§ 20–81. Proof of desertion or of neglect of a spouse, child, or children by any person shall be prima facie evidence that such desertion or neglect is willful; and proof that a person has left his or her spouse, or his or her child or children in destitute or necessitous circumstances, or has contributed nothing to their support for a period of thirty days . . . shall constitute prima facie evidence of an intention to abandon such family.

NOTES AND QUESTIONS

(1) Assume that a husband deserts his wife in the State of Holmes, taking the children with him, and flees to the neighboring State of Marshall. Unable to support himself or the children in Marshall, the husband receives temporary government assistance in Marshall. Should the wife be required to reimburse the State of Marshall under either state's spousal and child support statutes? Why or why not? *Compare Santa Clara County v. Hughes*, 43 Misc. 2d 559, 251 N.Y.S.2d 579 (Fam. Ct. 1964) *with Haight v. Haight*, 241 Or. 532, 405 P.2d 622 (Or. 1965).

State child support remedies have been significantly augmented by recent federal legislation, including the Child Support Recovery Act of 1992 (CSRA), 18 U.S.C. § 228 (1994), making the wilful failure to pay child support owed to a child in another state a federal crime; the Full Faith and Credit for Child Support Orders Act of 1994 (FFCCSA), 28 U.S.C. § 1738B(c) and (e) (1994); and the Personal Responsibility and Work Opportunity Reconciliation Act of 1996 (PRWORA) (to be codified at 42 U.S.C. § 666f). *See* Linda D. Elrod, *Child Support Reassessed: Federalization of Enforcement Nears Completion*, 1997 U. Ill. L. Rev. 695 (1997). *See generally* Chapter 11, *below.*

Query: If state and federal enforcement of child support obligations during marriage is absolute, should spousal support obligations during marriage likewise be absolute—or conditional?

(2) Ordinarily, the legal obligation of a parent to support a child ceases on the age of majority of the child, absent a written agreement to the contrary, or an overriding state statute. *See, e.g., Hogue v. Hogue*, 262 Ark. 767, 561 S.W.2d 299 (Ark. 1978). Also, a parent's duty of support may cease when a minor child becomes legally emancipated; when the minor child has entered into a valid marriage; when the minor child joins the United States armed forces; or when the minor child is otherwise self-sufficient. *See, e.g.*, Va. Code Ann. §§ 16.1–333 and 334 (1998).

(3) Is a parent legally liable to pay for the college expenses of his or her child, assuming the parents have the financial ability to do so? *Compare Jones v. Jones*, 179 Cal. App. 3d 1011, 225 Cal. Rptr. 95 (Cal. Ct. App. 1986) *with Hutchinson v. Hutchinson*, 263 Pa. Super. 299, 397 A.2d 1218 (Pa. Super. Ct. 1979) *and Risinger v. Risinger*, 273 S.C. 36, 253 S.E.2d 652 (S.C. 1979) (divorce decree). Should it make any difference if the child is already pursuing his or her course of undergraduate studies? A number of state statutes now provide that parents with adequate financial means may be ordered to contribute to their child's post-majority educational expenses, while other states have not yet enacted such statutes. *Query:* In a state lacking such a post-majority support statute, could an

argument be made that a college education now constitutes a "necessary item" under the common law doctrine of necessaries for parents with financial means to provide such an education? *See generally* Annotations, 42 A.L.R.4th 819 (1996) and 99 A.L.R.3d 322 (1998).

(4) **Problem.** Jennifer Green, the 16-year-old daughter of wealthy parents, voluntarily moved out of her parents' home to live with her boyfriend after she became pregnant. Jennifer and her boyfriend have no plans to marry, since neither believes in the concept of marriage. When Jennifer's father threatened to cut off her support, Jennifer brought suit against her father, claiming that he owed her child support under the applicable state statute, until Jennifer reached the age of majority. How should the court rule in this case? *Compare Parker v. Stage*, 43 N.Y.2d 128, 371 N.E.2d 513, 400 N.Y.S.2d 794 (1977) *with Brunswick v. LaPrise*, 262 A.2d 366 (Me. 1970). *See also* Annotation, 98 A.L.R.3d 334 (1997).

(5) Another exception to the general rule that the legal support obligation of a parent to his or her child ceases on the child's majority concerns children who are physically or mentally disabled before reaching the age of majority. Most jurisdictions provide that, under these circumstances, the duty of parental support continues for any physically or mentally disabled child past the age of majority, or until the death of the child or the death of the parents, whichever occurs first. Some courts have based this remedial exception on common law principles. *See, e.g., Brown v. Brown*, 474 A.2d 1168 (Pa. Super. Ct.1984). Other courts have found this support obligation based upon statutory interpretation. *See, e.g., Miller v. Miller*, 62 Or. App. 371, 660 P.2d 205 (Or. Ct. App. 1983); *Hight v. Hight* , 5 Ill. App. 3d 991, 284 N.E.2d 679 (Va. 972). *See also* Note, *Duty of Continued Child Support Past the Age of Majority*, 1 U. Ark. Little Rock L. J. 397 (1998).

(6) **Problem.** Timothy Jones, the 19-year-old son of Mr. and Mrs. Oliver Jones, had reached the age of majority in the State of Douglas and was a college student. Tragically, one weekend, he was involved in a serious automobile accident that left him a quadriplegic. Should Timothy's post-majority disability revive the parental duty to support him? Why or why not? *See Towery v. Towery*, 685 S.W.2d 155 (Ark. 1985). *See also* Annotation, 48 A.L.R.4th 919 (1998).

(7) *Pendente Lite* **Statutes**. When a husband and wife are separated though still married while an annulment or divorce action is pending, the needy spouse may petition the court in a *pendente lite* action to provide temporary spousal or child support until the annulment or divorce action has been decided. *See, e.g.*, Cal. Fam. Code § 3600 (1997); Fla. Stat. § 61.071 (1997); N.Y. Dom. Rel. Law § 236 (1998). However, a court's determination of this temporary spousal and child support is not binding in the subsequent divorce or annulment proceeding. *See, e.g., Shepherd v. Shepherd*, 231 Ga. 257, 200 S.E.2d 893 (Ga. 1973).

Query: Since a *pendente lite* spousal support obligation generally arises from the validity of an existing marriage, should a needy spouse who is suing for an annulment of a marriage be entitled to temporary spousal support *pendente lite*? Why or why not? May a "spouse" successfully avoid paying temporary spousal support *pendente lite* (as well as permanent spousal support) by demonstrating that the marriage was, in fact, invalid? How should these facts affect *pendente lite* child support awards? *See generally* Jean E. Maess, Annotation, 34 A.L.R.4th 814 (1984).

[D] Enforcement of Support Obligations

Actions for contempt, with resulting imprisonment, as well as remedies provided by the federal child support enforcement acts, may be utilized when a person fails to support his or her dependents during marriage. In addition, where a support obligor has moved out-of-state, interstate support enforcement actions may be brought under the Uniform Reciprocal Enforcement of Support Act (URESA) and the Uniform Interstate Family Support Act (UIFSA).

In 1996, Congress passed the Personal Responsibility and Work Opportunity Act (PRWORA), 42 U.S.C. Section 601 et seq., also called the 1996 Welfare Reform Act. The PRWORA attempts to make payment of child support more certain and more predictable by processing these cases in bulk rather than one at a time; by providing greater access to related support information; and by creating automatic enforcement procedures. For example, PRWORA Section 103(a) provides that the states must maintain child support programs and have laws and procedures in compliance with all federal child support requirements as a precondition to receiving federal money. PRWORA also mandates that states enact tougher support enforcement laws, adopt UIFSA by January 1, 1998, create new registries for support enforcement orders and new obligor parental hires, and streamline state procedures for the establishment of paternity. According to Professor Linda Elrod, "The only possible stronger measures would be turning the entire [support] enforcement process over to the federal government." Linda Elrod, *Child Support Reassessed: Federalization of Enforcement Nears Completion*, 1997 U. Ill. L. Rev. 695, 703 (1997).

Moreover, since recent studies indicate that more stringent support enforcement measures, such as the use of income withholding, criminal penalties, tax intercepts, license revocations, and the ability to place liens on property, are effective in increasing the amount of child support paid, the PRWORA mandates that the states employ all of these measures to enforce child support obligations. *Id.* at 704. *See also* Paul K. Leglar, *The Coming Revolution in Child Support Policy: Implications of the 1996 Welfare Act*, 30 Fam. L.Q. 519 (1996). The PRWORA further centralizes and consolidates the information necessary for interstate enforcement of support obligations. In particular, the PRWORA requires new state and federal registries for support orders and a directory of new parental hires which should facilitate the tracking of nonsupporting obligors across state lines. To assist with this mass case processing, as opposed to a case-by-case approach, states must utilize social security numbers, automated procedures and computer-driven technology. *See, e.g.* PRWORA Sections 312(b), 317, 42 U.S.C. §§ 654, 666.

Because all of these enforcement remedies are most commonly applied in the context of divorced or never-married parents, they are addressed in more detail in Chapter 11.

[E] Relative Responsibility Statutes

Under the common law, and in the absence of statutory authority, an adult child has no legal duty to provide for his or her indigent parent's needs. However, relative responsibility statutes are currently law in approximately half the states. These statutes emerged from the Elizabethan Poor Laws of 1597, which were extended in 1601 to require "the children of every poor, blind, lame, and impotent person" to support that poor person to the extent of their ability. 43 Eliz. 1 c. 2 (1601); *see* Usha Narayan, *The Government's Role in Fostering the Relationship Between Adult Children and Their Elder Parents: From Filial*

Responsibility Laws to . . . What?, A Cross-Cultural Perspective, 4 Elder L.J. 369, 372 (1996).

Such relative responsibility statutes generally provide that it is the joint and several duty of any adult child to support a parent in need, to the extent of the child's financial ability. Needy parents rarely seek to enforce these statutes directly; more commonly, state officials enforce them by denying or altering an elderly person's eligibility for benefits, or by seeking reimbursement from adult children for benefits provided to their elderly parents. *See generally* Terrance A. Kline, *A Rationale Role for Filial Responsibility Laws in Modern Society?*, 26 Fam. L.Q. 195 (1992); Garrett, *Filial Responsibility Laws*, 28 J. Fam. L. 793, 813 (1980); Van Houtte & Breda, *Maintenance of the Aged by Their Adult Children*, 12 Law & Soc'y Rev. 645 (1978).

Enforcement of relative responsibility statutes has waxed and waned over the past 60 years. During the 1930s, 1940s and 1950s, many state courts held adult children legally responsible for their elderly parents. Narayan, *above*, at 374. With the emergence of the modern welfare state, however, primary responsibility for providing for the elderly poor shifted from the elderly person's immediate family to the state and federal governments. Lee Teitelbaum, *Intergenerational Responsibility and Family Obligations: On Sharing*, 1992 Utah L. Rev. 765, 766. Thus, during the 1970s and 1980s many states retained, but rarely enforced, their relative responsibility laws. Moreover, critics challenged such laws as unconstitutional and unwise, and recommended that they be repealed. *See, e.g.*, Tully, *Family Responsibility Laws: An Unwise and Unconstitutional Imposition*, 5 Fam. L.Q. 32 (1971); Whitman & Whitney, *Are Children Legally Responsible for the Support of their Parents?*, 123 Trusts & Estates 43 (1984). More recently, however, as the costs of providing medical and other care to the elderly have skyrocketed, relative responsibility statutes have enjoyed a renaissance, both as a means of reducing government expenditures, and as a way of reinforcing family responsibility. Teitelbaum, *above*, at 767–68; *see* Robin M. Jacobson, Note, *American Healthcare Ctr. v. Randall: The Renaissance of Filial Responsibility*, 40 S.D. L. Rev. 518 (1995).

Notes and Questions

(1) So the underlying public policy question involving relative responsibility statutes remains: Who should be primarily responsible for the support of needy parents—their adult children or the state? And are relative responsibility statutes unconstitutional in that they compel some citizens, adult children, to pay benefits to their needy parents, when the state provides such benefits to childless needy citizens. *See, e.g., Swoap v. Superior Court of California*, 10 Cal. 3d 490 (1973) (upholding the constitutionality of a California relative responsibility statute); *County of Los Angeles v. Patrick*, 14 Cal. Rptr. 2d 665, 668 (Cal. Ct. App. 1992) ("In *Swoap* . . . , the court applied the rational basis test to areas of old age assistance and responsible relative legislation. Basically, if the legislation is economic, it will be presumed valid, and the party attacking the legislation will have the burden of showing that it is unconstitutional."). *See* Annotation, *Constitutionality of Statutory Provisions Requiring Reimbursement of Public by Child for Financial Assistance to Aged Parents*, 75 A.L.R.3d 1159 (1977). *Query:* Which rationale is more persuasive to you?

(2) One public policy argument supporting relative responsibility laws, as discussed in *Swoap*, is the principle of reciprocity in the parent-child relationship: an adult child should support a needy parent because of benefits received from that parent in the past. However, this reciprocity principle also has weaknesses, since some children receive major detriments as well as major benefits from their parents. *See* Daniels, *Family Responsibility Initiatives and Justice Between Age Groups*, 13 Law, Med. & Health Care 153, 154 (1985). Accordingly, some relative responsibility statutes provide that there shall be no liability for the support of a needy parent if, during the child's minority, the parent wilfully neglected or deserted the child. *See, e.g.*, 17 Cal. Fam. Code § 4411 (1997); Oregon Rev. Stat. § 416.030(2)(c) (1997); and Va. Code Ann. § 20–88 (1997). *Query:* Should relative responsibility laws be absolute or conditional?

(3) **Problem.** An indigent mother was living in California, which had enacted an applicable relative responsibility statute. The State of California sued her adult son for reimbursement for welfare payments the state had made to his mother. The son, however, was a resident of Texas, which had not enacted any relative responsibility statute. How should the court rule on this issue? *See California v. Copus*, 158 Tex. 196, 309 S.W.2d 227 (1958), *cert. denied*, 356 U.S. 967 (1958). *See also* Annot., 67 A.L.R.2d 771 and Later Case Service.

(4) **Problem.** An indigent father in Pennsylvania brought suit against his adult son in Ohio for support under Pennsylvania's relative responsibility statute. The adult son's defense against this suit was that his father had abandoned him when he was an infant, which was a valid defense under Ohio's relative responsibility law, but such a defense was not recognized under Pennsylvania law. What should be the correct decision? *See Commonwealth v. Mong*, 160 Ohio St. 455, 117 N.E.2d 32 (1954). *See also* 1 Homer H. Clark, Law of Domestic Relations 496–97 (2d ed. 1987).

(5) *Medicare and Medicaid Programs.* The federal government administers the Medicare and Medicaid programs to assist elderly Americans to obtain health care and pay their medical bills. *See* 42 U.S.C.A. § 1395 *et seq.* (1982). Medicare presently provides health insurance to Americans aged 65 and older without regard to income or assets; Medicaid, on the other hand, is a federal-state matching program that provides free medical assistance to low-income aged persons, low income blind or disabled persons under age 65, and certain families with dependent children. Federal regulations generally prohibit any consideration of an adult child's income for purposes of determining a parent's eligibility for medical benefits. 42 C.F.R. § 435.602 and 436.602 (1989). However, in recent years, skyrocketing health care costs and the growing elderly population have taken an enormous toll on federal and state Medicaid budgets. *See* Whitman & Whitney, *Are Children Legally Responsible for the Support of Their Parents?*, 123 Trusts & Estates 43, 44 (1984). Thus, in 1983, the federal Health Care Financing Administration issued a Medicaid Manual Transmittal that permitted states to use generally-applicable relative responsibility statutes to require reimbursement from adult children for state Medicaid funds expended on their parents' behalf. *Treatment of Contributions from Relatives to Medicaid Applicants or Recipients*, 2 Dep't of Health and Human Serv., Health Care Financing Admin, State Medicaid Manual, § 3812 (1983). In response to this federal action, several states enacted or revived relative responsibility laws that authorize civil actions against adult children of elderly Medicaid recipients. *See* Byrd, *Relative Responsibility Extended: Requirement of Adult Children to*

Pay for Their Indigent Parent's Medical Needs, 22 Fam. L.Q. 87, 90 (1988). On the other hand, opinions of attorney generals in at least two states have declared their respective state relative responsibility statutes, which require adult children to reimburse the state Medicaid agency for medical costs expended on their parents, contrary to federal Medicaid statutes and unenforceable. *Id.* at 93. It therefore remains unclear whether a state may require adult children to support their parents without violating federal Medicaid or Medicare law. Largely because of this legal uncertainty, the number of states retaining, abolishing, or enacting relative responsibility legislation has fluctuated. *See, e.g.* George F. Indest III, *Legal Aspects of HCFA's Decision to Allow Recovery from Children for Medicaid Benefits Delivered to Their Parents Through State Relative Responsibility Statutes*, 14 S.U. L. Rev. 225 (1988); Bergie, *Relative Responsibility Extended,* 22 Fam. L. Q. 87 (1988); Patrick, *Honor Thy Father and Mother: Paying the Medical Bills of Elderly Persons*, 19 U. Rich. L. Rev. 69 (1984); and Whitman & Whitney, *Are Children Legally Responsible for the Support of Their Parents?* 123 Tr. & Est. L.J. 43 (1984).

(6) **Problem.** Robert Randall is the only child of Juanita and Harry Randall. Although he grew up in South Dakota, Robert has not resided in South Dakota since 1954, and he is now a resident of the District of Columbia. After Robert's father died in 1981, Robert's 92-year-old mother Juanita hired legal counsel to draft an irrevocable trust document valued at approximately $130,000 (from her house and mutual funds) naming Juanita as the income beneficiary, and naming Robert as both trustee and residual beneficiary. The trust did not grant the trustee authority to invade the principal for the benefit of Juanita.

Following an accident that required Juanita's hospitalization, Robert came back to South Dakota and checked with various nursing homes to place his mother. In the fall of 1990, Juanita was admitted to the Arcadia Unit of Americana Healthcare Center in Aberdeen, South Dakota. Robert completed and signed all the necessary documents under a power of attorney from his mother, and he made a two-month advance payment to Americana from his mother's checking account. At that time, in view of Juanita's limited income, Robert discussed the possibility of financial assistance from Medicaid with various Americana personnel. Later that month, Robert completed an application for long-term Medicaid medical assistance for Juanita. Subsequently, however, the South Dakota Department of Social Services denied this application because "Juanita had not exhausted all of her assets" (i.e. Juanita's irrevocable trust of $130,000). When Juanita's medical bills became delinquent, Americana brought suit against Robert as her legal guardian, trustee, and son under South Dakota Consolidated Statute § 25-7-27, which requires an adult child to provide support for his or her indigent parent when he or she has the financial ability to do so.

Robert argued, however, that he did not have the financial ability to provide support for his mother, and that a South Dakota court should not have jurisdiction over him in the District of Columbia. At the time of Juanita's death in 1991, the unpaid balance for Juanita's nursing home care from Americana amounted to $36, 772.30. Americana now brings an action in South Dakota to collect this sum from Robert under South Dakota law.

How should the court resolve this dispute? *See Americana Healthcare Center v. Randall*, 513 N.W.2d 566 (S.D. 1994).

§ 2.05 Economic Transactions Between Spouses

BORELLI v. BRUSSEAU
California Court of Appeal
12 Cal. App. 4th 647 (1993)

PERLEY, J.

. . . On April 24, 1980, appellant and decedent entered into an antenuptial contract. On April 25, 1980, they were married. Appellant remained married to decedent until the death of the latter on January 25, 1989.

In March 1983, February 1984, and January 1987, decedent was admitted to a hospital due to heart problems. As a result, "decedent became concerned and frightened about his health and longevity." [Quotations taken from Complaint.] He discussed these fears and concerns with appellant and told her that he intended to "leave" the following property to her.

1. "An interest" in a lot in Sacramento, California.
2. A life estate for the use of a condominium in Hawaii.
3. A 25 percent interest in Borelli Meat Co.
4. All cash remaining in all existing bank accounts at the time of his death.
5. The costs of educating decedent's stepdaughter, Monique Lee.
6. Decedent's entire interest in a residence in Kensington, California.
7. All furniture located in the residence.
8. Decedent's interest in a partnership.
9. Health insurance for appellant and Monique Lee.

In August 1988, decedent suffered a stroke while in the hospital. "Throughout the decedent's August, 1988 hospital stay and subsequent treatment at a rehabilitation center, he repeatedly told [appellant] that he was uncomfortable in the hospital and that he disliked being away from home. The decedent repeatedly told [appellant] that he did not want to be admitted to a nursing home, even though it meant he would need round-the-clock care, and rehabilitative modifications to the house, in order for him to live at home."

"In or about October, 1988, [appellant] and the decedent entered an oral agreement whereby the decedent promised to leave to [appellant] the property listed [above], including a one hundred percent interest in the Sacramento property. . . . In exchange for the decedent's promise to leave her the property . . . [appellant] agreed to care for the decedent in his home, for the duration of his illness, thereby avoiding the need for him to move to a rest home or convalescent hospital as his doctors recommended. The agreement was based on the confidential relationship that existed between [appellant] and the decedent."

Appellant performed her promise but the decedent did not perform his. Instead his will bequeathed her the sum of $100,000 and his interest in the residence they owned as joint tenants. The bulk of decedent's estate passed to respondent, who is decedent's daughter.

DISCUSSION

"It is fundamental that a marriage contract differs from other contractual relations in that there exist vital public interest in reference to the marriage relation. The 'paramount interests of the community at large' . . . is a matter of primary concern." (*Hendricks v. Hendricks* (1954) 125 Cal.App.2d 239, 242 270 P.2d 801.)

"The laws relating to marriage and divorce have been enacted because of the profound concern of our organized society for the dignity and stability of the marriage relationship. This concern relates primarily to the status of the parties as husband and wife. The concern of society as to the property rights of the parties is secondary and incidental to its concern as to their status." (*Sapp v. Superior Court* (1953) 119 Cal.App.2d 645, 650.) . . .

In accordance with these concerns the following pertinent legislation has been enacted: Civil Code section 242—"Every individual shall support his or her spouse . . . ." Civil Code section 4802—"[A] husband and wife cannot, by any contract with each other, alter their legal relations, except as to property. . . . " Civil Code section 5100—"Husband and wife contract toward each other obligations of mutual respect, fidelity, and support." Civil Code section 5103—"[E]ither husband or wife may enter into any transaction with the other . . . respecting property, which either might if unmarried." Civil Code section 5132—"[A] married person shall support the person's spouse while they are living together. . . . "

The courts have stringently enforced and explained the statutory language. "Although most of the cases, both in California and elsewhere, deal with a wife's right to support from the husband, in this state a wife also has certain obligations to support the husband." (*In re Marriage of Higgason* (1973) 10 Cal.3d 476, 487. . . .

Moreover, interspousal mutual obligations have been broadly defined. . . . When necessary, spouses must "provide uncompensated protective supervision services for" each other. (*Miller v. Woods* (1983) 148 Cal.App.3d 862, 877.

Estate of Sonnicksen (1937) 23 Cal.App.2d 475, 479 and *Brooks v. Brooks* (1941) 48 Cal.App.2d 347, 349–350, each hold that under the above statutes and in accordance with the above policy a wife is obligated by the marriage contract to provide nursing-type care to an ill husband. Therefore, contracts whereby the wife is to receive compensation for providing such services are void as against public policy; and there is no consideration for the husband's promise.

Appellant argues that *Sonnicksen* and *Brooks* are no longer valid precedents because they are based on outdated views of the role of women and marriage. She further argues that the rule of those cases denies her equal protection because husbands only have a financial obligation toward their wives, while wives have to provide actual nursing services for free. We disagree. . . .

Vincent v. State of California (1971) 22 Cal.App.3d 566, 572 held that for purposes of benefit payments spouses caring for each other must be treated identically under similar assistance programs. In reaching such conclusion the court held: "Appellants suggest that one reason justifying denial of payment for services rendered by ATD attendants who reside with their recipient spouses is that, by virtue of the marriage contract, one spouse is obligated to care for the other without remuneration. . . . Such preexisting duty provides a constitutionally sound basis for a classification which denies compensation for care rendered by a husband or wife to his spouse who is receiving welfare assistance." . . .

These cases indicate that the marital duty of support under Civil Code sections 242, 5100, and 5132 includes caring for a spouse who is ill. They also establish that support in a marriage means more than the physical care someone could be hired to sympathy, comfort, love, companionship and affection. Thus, the duty of support can no more be "delegated" to a third party than the statutory duties of fidelity and mutual respect. Marital duties are owed by the spouses personally. This is implicit in the definition of marriage as "a personal relation arising out of a civil contract between a man and a woman." (Civ. Code, § 4100.)

We therefore adhere to the long-standing rule that a spouse is not entitled to compensation for support, apart from rights to community property and the like that arise from the marital relation itself. Personal performance of a personal duty created by the contract of marriage does not constitute a new consideration supporting the indebtedness, alleged in this case.

We agree with the dissent that no rule of law becomes sacrosanct by virtue of its duration, but we are not persuaded that the well-established rule that governs this case deserves to be discarded. If the rule denying compensation for support originated from considerations peculiar to women, this has no bearing on the rule's gender-neutral application today. There is as much potential for fraud today as ever, and allegations like appellant's could be made every time any personal care is rendered. This concern may not entirely justify the rule, but it cannot be said that all rationales for the rule are outdated.

Speculating that appellant might have left her husband but for the agreement she alleges, the dissent suggests that marriages will break up if such agreements are not enforced. While we do not believe that marriages would be fostered by a rule that encouraged sickbed bargaining, the question is not whether such negotiations may be more useful than unseemly. The issue is whether such negotiations are antithetical to the institution of marriage as the Legislature has defined it. We believe that they are.

The dissent maintains that mores have changed to the point that spouses can be treated just like any other parties haggling at arm's length. Whether or not the modern marriage has become like a business, and regardless of whatever else it may have become, it continues to be defined by statute as a personal relationship of mutual support. Thus, even if few things are left that cannot command a price, marital support remains one of them.

POCHE, J., dissenting.

A very ill person wishes to be cared for at home personally by his spouse rather than by nurses at a health care facility. The ill person offers to pay his spouse for such personal care by transferring property to her. The offer is accepted, the services are rendered and the ill spouse dies. . . . [T]his court holds that the contract was not enforceable because—as a matter of law—the spouse who rendered services gave no consideration. Apparently, in the majority's view she had a preexisting or precontract nondelegable duty to clean the bedpans herself. Because I do not believe she did, I respectfully dissent.

The majority correctly read *Estate of Sonnicksen* (1937) 23 Cal.App.2d 475 and *Brooks v. Brooks* (1941) 48 Cal.App.2d 347 as holding that a wife cannot enter into a binding contract with her husband to provide "nursing-type care" for compensation. It reasons that the wife, by reason of the marital relationship, already has a duty to provide such care, thus she offers no new consideration to support to the same effect. The logic of these decisions is ripe for reexamination. . . .

Statements in two of these cases to the effect that a husband has an entitlement to his wife's "services" smack of the common law doctrine of coverture which treated a wife as scarcely more than an appendage to her husband. . . . One of the characteristics of coverture was that it deemed the wife economically helpless and governed by an implicit exchange: " 'The husband, as head of the family, is charged with its support and maintenance in return for which he is entitled to the wife's services in all those domestic affairs which pertain to the comfort, care, and well-being of the family. Her labors are her contribution to the family support and care.' " (*Ritchie v. White* [35 S.E.2d 414, 416–17] (1945).) But coverture has been discarded in California, where both husband and wife owe each other the duty of support.

Not only has this doctrinal base for the authority underpinning the majority opinion been discarded long ago, but modern attitudes toward marriage have changed almost as rapidly as the economic realities of modern society. The assumption that only the rare wife can make a financial contribution to her family has become badly outdated in this age in which many married women have paying employment outside the home. A two-income family can no longer be dismissed as a statistically insignificant aberration. Moreover today husbands are increasingly involved in the domestic chores that make a house a home. Insofar as marital duties and property rights are not governed by positive law, they may be the result of informal accommodation or formal agreement. If spouses cannot work things out, there is always the no longer infrequently used option of divorce. For better or worse, we have to a great extent left behind the comfortable and familiar gender-based roles evoked by Norman Rockwell paintings. No longer can the marital relationship be regarded as "uniform and unchangeable." (*In re Callister's Estate*, 47 N.E.2d 268, 270 (1897). . . .

Reduced to its essence, the alleged contract at issue here was an agreement to transmute Mr. Borelli's separate property into the separate property of his wife. Had there been no marriage and had they been total strangers, there is no doubt Mr. Borelli could have validly contracted to receive her services in exchange for certain of his property. The mere existence of a marriage certificate should not deprive competent adults of the "utmost freedom of contract" they would otherwise possess. . . .

No one doubts that spouses owe each other a duty of support or that this encompasses "the obligation to provide medical care." (*Hawkins v. Superior Court* (1979) 89 Cal.App.3d 413, 418–419) There is nothing found in *Sonnicksen* and *Brooks*, or cited by the majority, which requires that this obligation be personally discharged by a spouse except the decisions themselves. However, at the time *Sonnicksen* and *Brooks* were decided—before World War II—it made sense for those courts to say that a wife could perform her duty of care only by doing so personally. That was an accurate reflection of the real world for women years before the exigency of war produced substantial employment opportunities for them. For most women at that time there was no other way to take care of a sick husband except personally. So to the extent those decisions hold that a contract to pay a wife for caring personally for her husband is without consideration they are correct only because at the time they were decided there were no other ways she could meet her obligation of care. Since that was the universal reality, she was giving up nothing of value by agreeing to perform a duty that had one and only one way of being performed.

However the real world has changed in the 56 years since *Sonnicksen* was decided. . . .Presumably, in the present day husbands and wives who work outside the home have alternative methods of meeting this duty of care to an ill spouse. Among the choices would be: (1) paying for professional help; (2) paying for nonprofessional assistance; . . .or (3) quitting one's job and doing the work personally.

A fair reading of the complaint indicates that Mrs. Borelli initially chose the first of these options, and that this was not acceptable to Mr. Borelli, who then offered compensation if Mrs. Borelli would agree to personally care for him at home. To contend in 1993 that such a contract is without consideration means that if Mrs. Clinton becomes ill, President Clinton must drop everything and personally care for her.

According to the majority, Mrs. Borelli had nothing to bargain with so long as she remained in the marriage. This assumes that an intrinsic component of the marital relationship is the personal services of the spouse, an obligation that cannot be delegated or performed by others. The preceding discussion has attempted to demonstrate many ways in which what the majority terms "nursing-type care" can be provided without either husband or wife being required to empty a single bedpan. It follows that, because Mrs. Borelli agreed to supply this personal involvement, she was providing something over and above what would fully satisfy her duty of support. That personal something—precisely because it was something she was not required to do—qualifies as valid consideration sufficient to make enforceable Mr. Borelli's reciprocal promise to convey certain of his separate property.

Not only does the majority's position substantially impinge upon couples' freedom to come to a working arrangement of marital responsibilities, it may also foster the very opposite result of that intended. For example, nothing compelled Mr. Borelli and plaintiff to continue living together after his physical afflictions became known. Moral considerations notwithstanding, no legal force could have stopped plaintiff from leaving her husband in his hour of need. Had she done so, and had Mr. Borelli promised to give her some of his separate property should she come back, a valid contract would have arisen upon her return. Deeming them reconciliation and the resumption of marital relations, California courts have long enforced such agreements as supported by consideration. Here so far as we can tell from the face of the complaint, Mr. Borelli and plaintiff reached largely the same result without having to endure a separation. There is no sound reason why their contract, which clearly facilitated continuation of their marriage, should be any less valid. It makes no sense to say that spouses have greater bargaining rights when separated than they do during an unruptured marriage. . . .

Without question, there is something profoundly unsettling about an illness becoming the subject of interspousal negotiations conducted over a hospital sickbed. Yet sentiment cannot substitute for common sense and modern day reality. Interspousal litigation may be unseemly, but it is no longer a novelty. The majority preserves intact an anomalous rule which gives married persons less than the utmost freedom of contract they are supposed to possess. The majority's rule leaves married people with contracting powers which are more limited than those enjoyed by unmarried persons or than is justified by legitimate public policy. In this context public policy should not be equated with coerced altruism. Mr. Borelli was a grown man who, having amassed a sizeable amount of property, should be treated—at least on demurrer—as competent to make the agreement alleged by plaintiff. The public policy of California will not be outraged by affording plaintiff the opportunity to try to enforce that agreement.

NOTES AND QUESTIONS

(1) Do you agree with the *Borelli* majority that allowing spouses to negotiate over marital support obligations would be "antithetical to the institution of marriage"? Or are you persuaded by the dissent's argument that such restrictions on interspousal contracting are inconsistent with contemporary marriage and substitute sentiment "for common sense and modern day reality?" For several recent, perceptive articles addressing the role of private ordering in marriage, see *Symposium: Law and the New American Family*, Eric Rasmusen and Jeffrey E. Stake. *Lifting the Veil of Ignorance: Personalizing the Marriage Contract*, 73 Ind. L. J. 453–566 (1998). *See also* Katherine Silbaugh, *Turning Labor into Love: Housework and the Law*, 91 Nw. U.L. Rev. 1, 29 (1996) (discussing "the traditional argument that marital obligations cannot be consideration for a contract"); Michael J. Trebilcock & Rosemin Keshevi, *The Role of Private Ordering in Family Law: A Law and Economics Perspective*, 41 U. Toronto L.J. 533 (1991).

(2) In contexts not involving personal services, courts have been more willing to recognize—and enforce—economic transactions between spouses *See, e.g., McGhee v. McGhee*, 85 So. 2d 799 (Miss. 1956) (upholding written business partnership agreement entered into between husband and wife); *Romeo v. Romeo*, 418 A.2d 258 (N.J. 1980) (upholding employment contract between husband and wife for purposes of determining husband's eligibility for worker's compensation benefits). *See also Epperson v. Epperson*, 15 Va. Cir. 39 (1987), where a Virginia circuit court judge held that where the spouses were business partners, even though they lacked a formal partnership agreement, and were seeking a dissolution of their partnership as well as a divorce, the rights and remedies of Va. Code Ann. § 50–32 (dissolution of a business partnership) would be considered separate and apart from Va. Code Ann. § 20–107.3 (equitable distribution of marital property on divorce) in the consolidated action. What distinguishes these transactions from the interspousal agreement alleged in *Borelli*?

(3) The Uniform Premarital Agreement Act, which has been adopted by sixteen states since its promulgation in 1983, authorizes prospective spouses to contract with each other with respect to such aspects of an ongoing marriage as the choice of abode, the freedom to pursue career opportunities, the upbringing of children and "any other matter, including their personal rights and obligations, not in violation of public policy or a statute imposing a criminal penalty." Unif. Premarital Agreement Act § 3 & cmt., 9B U.L.A. 369, 373–74 (1987). The Act also authorizes spouses to enter into marital property agreements respecting, *inter alia*, the management and control of property during marriage. *Id.* § 10(c)(2). *See generally* Laura P. Graham, *The Uniform Premarital Agreement Act and Modern Social Policy: The Enforceability of Premarital Agreements Regulating the Ongoing Marriage*, 28 Wake Forest L. Rev. 1037 (1993). *Query:* Would the *Borelli* case have been decided differently under the Uniform Premarital Agreement Act? Why or why not?

(4) **Marriage as an Economic Partnership**. Several commentators have argued that a traditional view of marriage tends to devalue homemaker services and have advocated the theory of a marital "economic partnership," based upon a modified version of a business partnership model and borrowing some fundamental tenets from community property law, in order to assure the equality of both spouses' economic rights during marriage. *See, e.g.*

Joan Krauskopf & Rhonda Thomas, *Partnership Marriage: The Solution to an Inefficient and Inequitable Law of Support*, 35 Ohio St. L.J. 558 (1974). Under this concept of marriage as an "economic partnership," the spouses would be free to tailor their property and support rights by contract prior to marriage, but otherwise the concept of a marital economic partnership acknowledges the equal rights and obligations of both husbands and wives with respect to services, management, property ownership, and creditors' rights during marriage. *Id.* at 587–88. Family roles would be determined by the parties in accordance with their individual skills and interests, placing minimum restrictions on individual freedom. *Id.* at 590–94. This "economic partnership" model would thus allow married women to pursue a career or other activities outside the home, while protecting those who opt for a traditional role in the home, or spend a portion of their lives rearing children. *Id.* at 594. A number of commentators have supported variations of this concept. *See, e.g.* Grace Ganz Blumberg, *Marital Property Analysis: Treatment of Pensions, Disability Pay, Workers' Compensation and other Wage Substitutes, Severances or Replacements.*, 33 UCLA L. Rev. 1250 (1986); Marcia O'Kelly, *Entitlements to Spousal Support After Divorce*, 61 N.D. L. Rev. 225 (N.Y. 1985); Susan Westerberg Prager, *Sharing Principles and the Future of Marital Property Law*, 25 UCLA L.Rev. 1 (1977). A number of courts also embraced a similar economic partnership model. *See, e.g. O'Brien v. O'Brien*, 66 N.Y.2d 576, 489 N.E.2d 712 (1985) ("[A] marriage is, among other things, an economic partnership to which both parties contribute as spouse, parent, wage earner, and homemaker"). *See also* § 2.02, *above*.

Other commentators, however, have criticized the notion of marriage as an economic partnership on the grounds that equating the family relationship to a business relationship may stimulate marital competition rather than marital sharing and encourage people to view marriage only in financial terms; or because a marital partnership theory allows too much judicial discretion on divorce, and places insufficient value on the nonmonetary marital contributions of a traditional homemaker without promoting self-sufficiency after divorce. *See, e.g.* Jane Rutherford, *Duty in Divorce: Shared Income as a Path to Equality*, 58 Fordham L. Rev. 539 (1990); Martha M. Fineman, *Implementing Equality: ideology, Contradiction and Social Change; A Study of Rhetoric and Results in the Regulation of the Consequences of Divorce*, 1983 Wis. L. Rev. 789 (1983); Bea Ann Smith, *The Partnership Theory of Marriage: A Borrowed Solution Fails*, 68 Tex. L. Rev. 689 (1990). *See also* Ann Laquer Estin, *Love and Obligation: Family Law and the Romance of Economics*, 36 Wm. & Mary L. Rev. 989 (1995) (exploring difficulties of applying economic analysis to family relationships). *Query:* are there situations where a doctrine that left support obligations and property rights up to the prospective spouses would leave a partner with less sophistication or bargaining power inadequately protected?

(5) Are husbands and wives liable to creditors for marital debts under partnership or quasi-partnership principles? *See, e.g., Northampton Brewery Corp. v. Lande*, 138 Pa. Super. 235, 10 A.2d 583 (Pa. 1939) (upholding creditor's claim based on theory that spouses' joint operation of a restaurant was a partnership, over wife's contention that it was a tenancy by the entireties); *and Kennedy v. Nelson*, 37 Ala. App. 484, 70 So. 2d 822 (Ala. 1954) (no recovery on creditor's implied-agency claim against wife, separate owner of a farm under Married Women's Property Act, for improvements to farm made under contract with tenant husband).

§ 2.06 Third-Party Interference With Marriage

[A] Intentional Torts

HOYE v. HOYE
Supreme Court of Kentucky
824 S.W.2d 422 (1992)

STEPHENS, C.J.,

The sole issue this Court is asked to determine in this appeal is whether to abolish the common law tort of intentional interference with the marital relation. In a civil suit based on this cause of action, the Jefferson Circuit Court entered a jury verdict against Thelma York (now Hoye) awarding plaintiff, Laura Hoye $10,000 ($5,000 for past and future mental anguish, plus $5,000 for loss of companionship and society.)

The relevant facts are as follows. Steve Hoye, former husband of plaintiff, Laura Hoye, developed a business-social relationship with co-employee Thelma York in the fall of 1986. This relationship evolved; and Steve and Thelma became sexually intimate. In November of 1986, Steve moved from the marital residence. Shortly thereafter, Laura Hoye filed a divorce action to end a sixteen-year marriage in the Jefferson Circuit Court.

One day before issuance of the divorce, plaintiff, Laura Hoye, filed a civil complaint against the defendant, then Thelma York, alleging Mrs. York's tortious interference with the Hoye marriage. On July 22, 1987, a divorce decree was entered.

The Jefferson Circuit Court, in Laura Hoye's civil suit, denied defendant's pre-trial motion for summary judgment. This motion requested dismissal of the complaint on grounds that the cause of action set forth should be abolished.

The Court of Appeals, finding the defendant's arguments persuasive, but lacking the power to abolish the common-law tort under SCR 1.030(8)(a), affirmed the trial court. We granted defendant's motion for discretionary review to determine whether or not the cause of action known as intentional interference with the marital relation should be abolished.

We conclude that the tort of intentional interference with the marital relation should be abolished because foundation of this action is based on the misperception that spousal affection is capable of theft by a third party. This concept, abandoned by the majority of the states, has its origin in the antiquated premise that a wife is her husband's chattel.

The early common law concept that the husband has exclusive right to his wife's services has given way to a new rationale explaining the underlying purpose of this cause of action. The basis for changing the reasoning behind the tort is alteration of the legal and social perceptions of the wife's role in a marriage. As the result of women acquiring independent status in the eyes of the law, courts in the early part of this century changed from property-based arguments to explain the continued existence of this cause of action to reasoning that it preserved the marital union. We find this rationale unpersuasive and hold that the tort of intentional interference with the marital relation is hereby abolished for the following reasons. . . .

Early English common law established two causes of action which "for some purposes can simply be regarded as different means by which the marriage relationship is subjected to interference." Prosser and Keeton, supra at 917–919.

The first, enticement (also called abduction), involved assisting or inducing a wife to leave her husband by means of fraud, violence, or persuasion. The injury was considered to be the loss of the wife's services or consortium. Enticement (or abduction) has evolved into what is commonly known today as the tort of alienation of affections. The second tort remedy available to an injured spouse at early common law was seduction, which today is commonly known as the tort of criminal conversation. Unlike enticement/abduction, seduction required an adulterous relationship between the plaintiff's spouse and the defendant; no physical separation of the husband and wife was necessary. The purpose underlying an action for seduction was to vindicate the husband's property rights in his wife's person and to punish the defendant for defiling the plaintiff's marriage and family honor, and for placing the legitimacy of children in doubt.

Comment, *Stealing Love In Tennessee: The Thief Goes Free*, 56 Tenn. L. Rev. 629, 630–31 (1989).

In the late nineteenth and early twentieth centuries most states, including Kentucky, acted to equalize the legal status of wives with passage of Married Women's Property Acts. "These acts granted wives the right to own property and to sue in their own names to recover damages for their own personal injuries." Comment, *Alienation of Affections: Flourishing Anachronism*, 13 Wake Forest L. Rev. 585, 588 (1977).

The courts, with wives acquiring such rights, were then confronted with the issue as to the continued viability of the tortious causes of actions; alienation of affections and criminal conversation. Because the derivation of these torts was based on the legal inferiority of women, courts could reasonably determine to either deprive their use to a husband or to extend their use to a wife. Following the majority of courts, the Commonwealth granted these rights of action to the wife.

Extension of these rights of action to the wife necessitated adjusting their rationale. Historically these actions were viewed as property-based torts that compensated the husband for loss of services and protected pure blood lines. But this century, as the result of women acquiring legal status in the courts, alienation of affections and criminal conversation came to be seen as means to preserve marital harmony by deterring wrongful interference. . . .

The courts made no structural adjustments in actions related to intentional interference with the marriage when women obtained rights through the Married Women's Property Acts; thus the legal fiction of a spouse owning property rights in the mind and body of their partner continued. This is evidenced by continuing to disallow consent as a defense in criminal conversation and alienation of affections. Both these actions were historically based on the legal inferiority of the wife who was deemed incapable of consenting to the injury of her superior, her husband. . . .

While the rationale for the cause of action of tortious interference with the marital relation transformed during this century, its origin grounded in property concepts remained. Initially such suits were blatantly viewed as compensatory. But when a wife no longer qualified within legal perceptions as her husband's chattel, the reasoning explaining the purpose behind such actions was altered. Since the husband no longer owned his wife, courts justified the continued existence of this tort as a means to promote and maintain the marriage.

Though still viewed as compensatory in nature because it is a civil suit, in reality such cases are indeed punitive. Third party is seen as a malicious seducer wreaking havoc upon the harmonious marital couple. These common law actions thus reason that the third-party must be punished for his misdeeds by payment to the aggrieved spouse. . . .

Both alienation of affections and criminal conversation are based on psychological assumptions that actions by an ill-intended third party can and will destroy a harmonious marriage. . . .

A comparison of contract actions alleging tortious interference with actions based on criminal conversation and alienation of affections reveals logical inconsistencies. Marital interference torts are distinguishable from actions for tortious interference with a contract against a third party because in contract suits the plaintiff can sue not only the third party but also the other party to the contract. In alienation of affections and criminal conversation the other party to the "contract" is the plaintiff's spouse who participated in the tort, and according to Browning, supra, this spouse may not be subject to a suit by the marital partner. This logical asymmetry has prompted the majority of jurisdictions to eliminate these marital torts.

The Iowa Supreme Court in abolishing the alienation of affections action reasoned: "Spousal love is not property which is subject to theft . . . plaintiffs in suits for alienation of affections do not deserve to recover for the loss or injury to 'property' which they do not, and cannot, own." *Fundermann v. Mickelson*, 304 N.W.2d 790, 794 (Iowa 1981).

To posit that one person possesses rights to the feelings of another is an anachronism. Yet this is the foundation for tortious interference with the marital relation where the presence of a third party is blamed for changes in the marriage.

Tortious interference with the marital relation, as previously noted, has never sufficiently separated from its property based origins; a rationale that is counter to contemporary thought. Since the 1930's the majority of states have recognized inconsistencies in both actions of criminal conversation and alienation of affections, and have either judicially or legislatively abolished them, or severely limited their application through rigid statutory damage restrictions, or shortened statutes of limitation. . . .

Such suits invite abuse. Because courts cannot properly police settlements, these actions are "often characterized by the plaintiff-spouse blackmailing the defendant into a high priced settlement with the threat of a lawsuit that could destroy the defendant's reputation." *O'Neil v. Schuckardt*, [733 P.2d 693, 697 (1986)] Frequently the end result of these cases is essentially the plaintiff's sale of his spouse's affections. Not only is a defendant in these suits victim to vindictive or purely mercenary motives of the plaintiff, but such suits are likely to expose "minor children of the marriage to one of [their] parent's extramarital activities, and may even require the children to testify to details of the family relationship in open court." *O'Neil v. Schuckardt, supra*, at 698.

This opinion in no way affects the right to recover for loss of consortium as a factor in assessing damages when underlying liability has been established in a personal injury suit. Rather, we move to eliminate the right to recover for intentional interference with the marital relation because it proceeds from a belief that a spouse owns the affections of his marital partner which provides no basis for liability.

We therefore rule to abolish the action known as tortious interference with the marital relation, relying on the premise that affection between spouses cannot be owned, id., i.e., that the underlying assumption of the tort is an anachronism. Thus the opinion of the Court of Appeals which affirmed the trial court decision is hereby reversed.

NOTES AND QUESTIONS

(1) The court's decision in *Hoye,* abolishing the tort of intentional interference with the marital relationship, is consistent with the majority trend. According to a recent law review article, 40 states and the District of Columbia have abolished the cause of action for alienation of affections, either by statute or by judicial decision, and approximately the same number have abolished the action for criminal conversation. Jennifer E. McDougal, Comment: *Legislating Morality: The Actions for Alienation of Affections and Criminal Conversation in North Carolina*, 33 Wake Forest L. Rev. 163, 171 (1998); *see Neal v. Neal*, 873 P.2d 871 (Idaho 1994) (abolishing tort of criminal conversation). Despite this trend, a handful of states continue to recognize one or both of these common law actions. *See, e.g., Cannon v. Miller*, 327 S.E.2d 888 (N.C. 1985), *vacating* 322 S.E.2d 780 (N.C. Ct. App. 1984). Indeed, juries in several recent North Carolina cases awarded large verdicts to plaintiffs who sued their ex-spouses' lovers for intentional interference with marriage. *See* Thomas Hackett, *Jury Orders Adulterer to Pay,* Raleigh News & Observer, Sept. 18, 1997, at B1; McDougal, *above,* at 176–80 (discussing cases). Popular reaction to these verdicts has been mixed. While some journalists and commentators have criticized the decisions, others have applauded the actions as a victory for the institution of marriage. *See, e.g.*, Loraine O'Connell, *Victim Suit Miscasts Husband as a Victim*, Orlando Sentinel, Aug. 15th 1997, at E1 (suggesting that alienation of affections actions "could return fidelity to marriage").

(2) Do you agree with the *Hoye* court that tort causes of action for intentional interference with marriage should be abolished because they cannot be separated from their patriarchal and property law origins? Recently, several scholars have suggested that despite the sexist origins of most marital and sexual torts, these claims implicate important relational and emotional interests that may be particularly salient to women. *See, e.g.*, Martha Chamallas, *The Architecture of Bias: Deep Structures in Tort Law*, 146 U. Pa. L. Rev. 463, 500–01 (1998); Jane E. Larson, *"Women Understand So Little, They Call My Good Nature 'Deceit' ": A Feminist Rethinking of Seduction*, 93 Colum. L. Rev. 374 (1993). Do you find this suggestion convincing? Should tort law provide redress for the emotional losses that accompany the demise of a marriage or other intimate relationship?

(3) One of the reasons given in *Hoye* for abolishing these marital torts is their "logical inconsistencies," when compared with other actions alleging tortious interference with contract. In particular, the court notes that, unlike other tortious interference plaintiffs, the marital plaintiff cannot sue the "other party to the contract"—his or her spouse. This was true in the past, since interspousal tort immunity generally precluded spouses from suing each other in tort. However, as discussed in more detail in Chapter 6, *below,* interspousal tort immunity has now been abolished in most jurisdictions, raising the possibility that one spouse might be able to sue the other in this context. Should they be permitted to do so, or is divorce the only appropriate legal remedy? Does this change in the law governing interspousal tort liability affect your view of the continued viability of a cause of action against third parties for intentional interference with marriage? For additional discussion of interspousal tort claims arising out of marriage, see § 6.03, *below.*

[B] Rights of Consortium.

As the *Hoye* opinion suggests, the law continues to protect a spouse's interest in the marital relationship by allowing recovery for loss of consortium. Like the intentional torts abolished in *Hoye*, recovery for loss of consortium was originally based on the husband's property interest in his wife's person, and the cause of action was originally available only to husbands. *See generally* Homer Clark, 2, Law of Domestic Relations 390–91 (2d ed. 1987). Indeed, the husband's common law claim for loss of consortium was originally likened to the master's claim for loss of his servant's services in cases where the servant suffered physical injury. Martha Chamallas, *The Architecture of Bias: Deep Structures in Tort Law*, 146 U. Pa. L. Rev. 463, 463–64 n.1 (1998). Similarly, as the "head and master" of the household, the father was originally the only parent allowed to sue for the loss of a child's services. *Id*.

Beginning in the 1950's most states expanded consortium rights to permit wives as well as husbands to recover for losses sustained as a result of an injury to a spouse. *See, e.g., American Export Lines, Inc. v. Alvez*, 446 U.S. 274 (1980) (holding that wife of a harbor worker who had been injured could maintain an action for loss of consortium under general maritime law and listing 42 jurisdictions that allow either spouse to recover for loss of consortium resulting from the personal injury to the other spouse). Under current gender-neutral family law principles, present-day rights of consortium encompass "the total of tangible and intangible relationships prevailing between husbands and wives," and the usual consortium case involves physical harm caused to a spouse through the negligence of a third-party defendant. Homer Clark, *above*, at 382–83. Similarly, in those states that recognize a claim for loss of a child's consortium, including the intangible elements of loss of companionship, society and affection, the claim is generally accorded to both parents. *See, e.g., Shockley v. Prier*, 225 N.W. 2d 499, 501 (Wis. 1975) (recognizing that both parents of an injured minor "may maintain a cause of action for loss of aid, comfort, society and companionship").

To avoid any problem of double recovery, when one spouse sues for his or her injury and the other spouse sues for loss of consortium, an increasing number of states now require that the two claims be brought in a single suit. *See, e.g., Nicholson v. Hugh Chatham Mem. Hospital*, 300 N.C. 295, 266 S.E.2d 818 (1980). In addition, a number of courts have recently considered whether consortium rights should be extended to unmarried intimates, including same-sex couples who are not permitted to marry. *See generally* § 3.03, *below*.

Query: Is the abolition of tort liability for intentional interference with marriage consistent with the continued recognition, on a gender-neutral basis, of a spouse's right to recover for loss of consortium? Why or why not?

NOTES AND QUESTIONS

(1) **Problem.** Plaintiff Stephen Molien filed an action against Kaiser Foundation Hospitals and Thomas Kilbridge M.D., alleging that Dr. Kilbridge negligently examined and tested his wife, Valerie Molien, in a routine medical examination, and wrongly advised her that she had contracted an infectious type of syphilis and treated her with massive doses of penicillin. As a result of this negligently erroneous diagnosis, the plaintiff's wife became

upset and suspicious that her husband had engaged in extramarital sexual activities, even though he had tested negative for syphilis, and tension and hostility arose between Mr. and Mrs. Molien, causing a break-up in the marriage and the initiation of divorce proceedings. The plaintiff husband sued for damages for mental suffering and loss of consortium since the doctor's negligence had deprived him of the love, companionship, affection, society, sexual relations, solace, support, and services of his wife. The trial court, however, dismissed the plaintiff's suit holding that a loss of consortium action based upon the negligent infliction of mental distress required physical injury.

What should be the holding on appeal? *See Molien v. Kaiser Foundation Hospitals*, 27 Cal. 3d 916, 167 Cal. Rptr. 831 (1980). *See also Habelow v. Traveler's Insurance Co.*, 389 So. 2d 218 (Fla. Dist. Ct. App. 1980), where in a work-related loss of consortium action, an insurance agent refused to pay for the injured husband's past and future medical bills, telling husband and his wife, "You don't need all those doctors. All I'm interested in is getting you off your butt and back to work." Was this an actionable loss of consortium claim based upon "malicious intent to inflict mental anguish"? *Contra, Groat v. Town of Glenville*, 100 Misc. 2d 326, 418 N.Y.S.2d 842 (N.Y. Sup. Ct. 1979) (holding that loss of consortium damages predicated on tort principles require physical injury to a spouse, or physical confinement away from the other spouse). *See also* Janet Booth Jones, Annotation, *Necessity of Physical Injury to Support Cause of Actions for Loss of Consortium*, 16 A.L.R.4th 537 (1996).

(2) Some states have held that the exclusivity provisions of state workers' compensation statutes would bar a claim for loss of consortium damages resulting from an employment-related injury. *See, e.g. Archer v. Roadrunner Trucking Inc.*, 930 P.2d 1155 (N.M. 1996). *See generally* 2A Larson & Larson, The Law of Workmen's Compensation § 66.21 (1996).

(3) Should punitive damages be awarded for a wilful impairment of consortium rights? Why or why not? *Compare Butcher v. Robertshaw Controls Co.*, 550 F. Supp. 692 (D. Md. 1981) with *Hammond v. North Am. Asbestos Corp.*, 105 Ill. App. 3d 1033, 435 N.E.2d 540 (1982), *aff'd*, 454 N.E.2d 210 (Ill. 1983). *See also* Jack L. Litwin, Annotation, *Measure and Elements of Damages in Wife's Action for Loss of Consortium*, 74 A.L.R.3d 805 (1998).

(4) Should impairment or loss of consortium damages be awarded in wrongful death actions as well as personal injury actions? Why or why not? *Compare Liff v. Schildkrout*, 49 N.Y.2d 622, 427 N.Y.S.2d 746 (N.Y. 1980) with *Elliot v. Willis*, 113 Ill. App. 3d 848, 447 N.E.2d 1062 (Ill. App. Ct. 1983).

[C] Evidentiary and Testimonial Privileges

At common law, spouses were incompetent to testify for or against each other. *Funk v. United States*, 290 U.S. 371 (1933). This spousal disqualification derived from two common law principles: first, the rule that an accused could not testify in his own behalf, because of his interest in the proceeding, and second the concept that the husband and wife were one. *Trammel v. United States*, 445 U.S. 40, 44 (1980). While the ban on favorable spousal testimony had largely eroded by the end of the 19th century, the rule against adverse spousal testimony persisted until well into the 20th century. In *Hawkins v. United States*, 358 U.S. 74 (1958), the Supreme Court reaffirmed the adverse spousal testimony rule, explaining that the prohibition rested on "a belief that such a policy was necessary to foster family peace, not only for the benefit of husband, wife and children, but for the benefit of the public as well." 358 U.S. at 77.

Two decades later, in *Trammel v. United States*, 445 U.S. 40 (1980), another federal criminal case, the Supreme Court modified the rule against adverse spousal testimony to vest the privilege to refuse to testify in the witness spouse alone. The defendant in *Trammel* was prosecuted for drug distribution. The indictment also named six unindicted co-conspirators, including the defendant's wife. In exchange for a promise of lenient treatment from the government, the defendant's wife agreed to testify against her husband, and the defendant was convicted, largely as a result of his wife's testimony. On appeal, the defendant argued that admission of his wife's testimony, over his objection, violated the ban on adverse spousal testimony. The Supreme Court responded by modifying the adverse spousal testimony rule. Noting that the rule was not limited to confidential spousal communications, which were independently protected by a separate marital communications privilege, the Court opined,

> The ancient foundations for so sweeping a privilege have long since disappeared. Nowhere in the common-law world—indeed in any modern society—is a woman regarded as chattel or demeaned by denial of a separate legal identity and the dignity associated with recognition as a whole human being."

445 U.S. at 52. The court also rejected the argument that a rule against adverse spousal testimony preserves marital harmony by precluding the government from attempting to pit one spouse against the other. Instead, the Court noted that "when one spouse is willing to testify against the other in a criminal proceeding—whatever the motivation—their relationship is almost certainly in disrepair; there is probably little in the way of marital harmony to preserve." *Id.* at 52. The Court therefore modified the common law rule to allow the witness spouse alone to decide whether to testify adversely, a modification which, the Court held, "furthers the important public interest in marital harmony without unduly burdening legitimate law enforcement needs." *Id.* at 52.

Not all commentators approve of the *Trammel* decision. For example, Professor Richard Lempert has questioned the voluntariness of spousal testimony procured as a result of a plea bargain or a cooperation agreement with the government. Lempert has also suggested that the *Trammel* modification "will do more than provide occasions on which the emptiness of moribund marriages will be confirmed. Instead, it will give the government an incentive to turn spouses against each other." Richard O. Lempert, *Mason Ladd Lecture; A Right to Every Woman's Evidence*, 66 Iowa L. Rev. 725, 737 (1981). Similarly, Professor Michael W. Mullane has argued that the *Trammel* decision "sanctions government use of compulsion to shatter marriage in pursuit of convictions." Michael W. Mullane, *Trammel v. United States: Bad History, Bad Policy, and Bad Law*, 47 Me. L. Rev. 105, 158 (1995). *See also* Milton C. Regan, *Spousal Privilege and the Meanings of Marriage*, 81 Va. L. Rev. 2045 (1995) (suggesting that the traditional adverse testimony rule reflects a vision of marriage that encourages spousal loyalty, commitment and shared responsibility). On the other hand, some commentators have argued the *Trammel* decision did not go far enough, and that the privilege of one spouse to refuse to testify against the other should be abolished altogether. *See, e.g.*, Malinda L. Seymore, *Isn't it A Crime: Feminist Perspectives on Spousal Immunity and Spousal Violence*, 90 Nw. U. L. Rev. 1032 (996) (critiquing the privilege against adverse spousal testimony, particularly in the context of domestic abuse); David Medine, *The Adverse Testimony Privilege: Time to Dispose of a 'Sentimental Relic,'* 67 Or. L. Rev. 519 (1988).

Approximately half the states continue to recognize some version of the adverse spousal testimony privilege. A majority of these states follow *Trammel* and vest the privilege in the witness spouse alone, while a minority of jurisdictions continue to require the consent of both spouses, thereby allowing a defendant to prevent his or her spouse from testifying adversely, even if the witness spouse is willing to testify. *See* Regan, *above*, at 2053 (listing states). In approximately half the states, no adverse testimony privilege exists, and spouses can generally be compelled to testify against each other. *See* Craig R. Isenberg, State v. Taylor, *The Louisiana Court Carves Out An Exception To the Spousal Witness Privilege*, 69 Tul. L. Rev. 1085, 1086–87 (1995).

A second testimonial privilege based on marriage—the marital communications privilege—protects confidential communications between spouses made during an ongoing marriage. *See* Regan, *above*, at 2055–56 (discussing marital communications privilege); Isenberg, *above*, at 1086 (noting that confidential communications privilege is recognized in nearly every federal and state jurisdiction). This privilege generally applies in both civil and criminal litigation and may be invoked by either a defendant or a witness spouse. In most jurisdictions, the privilege does not apply to cases involving intrafamily harms, and in many jurisdictions the privilege is also unavailable where the spouses have engaged in joint criminal activity. *See e.g., United States v. Marashi*, 913 F.2d 724, 730–31 (9th Cir. 1991); *State v. Witchey*, 388 N.W.2d 893, 895–96 (S.D. 1986). For additional discussion of these spousal privileges, *see, e.g., Development in the Law—Privileged Communications*, 98 Harv. L. Rev. 1450, 1565 (1985); Sanford Levinson, *Testimonial Privileges and the Preferences of Friendship,*. 1984 Duke L.J. 631 (1984).

Problem. Your jurisdiction is one of the minority of states that retains the traditional privilege against adverse spousal testimony, which precludes one spouse from testifying against the other, unless both spouses consent. A separate marital communications privilege protects confidential communications between spouses. Your state legislature is currently considering two proposals for reform. One proposal would abolish the adverse spousal testimony privilege entirely. The other proposal would adopt the position of *Trammel*, and vest the privilege to refuse to testify in the witness spouse alone. Neither proposal would affect the privilege against disclosure of confidential marital communications. How would you vote on each of these reform proposals and why?

§ 2.07 Integrating Family and Work

The growing prevalence of two-earner marriages, coupled with the sharp increase in the percentage of families maintained by single employed parents, has caused a significant restructuring of the legal and economic relationship between the family and the workplace. The materials that follow explore several aspects of that restructuring.

[A] Dual Career Couples

PARKS v. CITY OF WARNER ROBBINS
United States Court of Appeals
42 F.3d 609 (11th Cir. 1995)

BIRCH, CIRCUIT JUDGE:

In this appeal, we consider for the first time in our circuit whether a city's anti-nepotism policy denies the fundamental right to marry protected by the Due Process Clause of the

Fourteenth Amendment, infringes the right of intimate association implicit in the First Amendment, or has a disparate impact on women in violation of the Equal Protection Clause of the Fourteenth Amendment. . . .

I. BACKGROUND

Plaintiff-appellant Brenda Parks is a Sergeant in the Special Investigative Unit of the Warner Robins Police Department, where she has worked since August, 1984. In October, 1989, Parks became engaged to A.J. Mathern, a Captain in the Criminal Investigative Unit of the Warner Robins Police Department. Mathern also began working for the Warner Robins Police Department in August, 1984, approximately two weeks before Parks arrived. Both Parks and Mathern hold supervisory positions in the police department.

Mathern discussed his plans to marry Parks with George Johnson, Chief of Police for Warner Robins, who informed Mathern that the two would be in violation of Warner Robins' anti-nepotism policy. Defendant-appellees City of Warner Robins, its mayor and city council ("Warner Robins") adopted the anti-nepotism policy as a city ordinance in 1985. The anti-nepotism policy prohibits relatives of city employees in supervisory positions from working in the same department. The prohibition does not extend to nonsupervisory employees, nor does it prevent relatives of supervisory employees from working in other departments of the city. Johnson told Mathern that if the two married, the less-senior Parks would have to leave the police department. Rather than losing her job, Parks postponed the wedding and brought the instant lawsuit; Parks and Mathern have remained engaged, but unmarried, for over four years. . . .

On appeal, Parks argues that the district court erred by granting summary judgment to Warner Robins. Specifically, Parks realleges her substantive due process right to marry, her right of intimate association, and her disparate impact claims.

A. Substantive Due Process

Parks argues that Warner Robins' anti-nepotism policy violates her substantive due process rights by denying her the fundamental right to marry. That the right to marry is a fundamental right protected by the substantive component of the Due Process Clause of the Fourteenth Amendment is well established.

Nevertheless, the Supreme Court has held that not every statute "which relates in any way to the incidents of or prerequisites for marriage" must be subjected to strict scrutiny. *Zablocki [v. Redhail*, 434 U.S. 374, 386 (1978)]. "To the contrary, reasonable regulations that do not significantly interfere with decisions to enter into the marital relationship may legitimately be imposed." *Id.* Therefore, whether we examine this ordinance under strict scrutiny or rational basis analysis depends upon whether the statute "significantly interferes" with the decision to marry. . . .

We conclude that the Warner Robins anti-nepotism policy does not directly and substantially interfere with the right to marry. The policy does not create a direct legal obstacle that would prevent absolutely a class of people from marrying. While the policy may place increased economic burdens on certain city employees who wish to marry one another, the policy does not forbid them from marrying. The true intent and direct effect of the policy is to ensure that no city employee will occupy a supervisory position vis-a-vis one of his or her relatives. Any increased economic burden created by the anti-nepotism policy is no more than an incidental effect of a policy aimed at maintaining the operational efficiency of Warner Robins' governmental departments, not a direct attempt to control the marital decisions of city employees; individual instances of hardship notwithstanding, the anti-nepotism policy at issue here does not make marriage practically impossible for a particular class of persons. Although Parks and Mathern have postponed their wedding for over four years, pending the outcome of this case, they have produced no evidence of other couples similarly deterred by the policy, nor do we believe that ordinarily such will be the case. As the Supreme Court noted in [*Califano v. Jobst*, 434 U.S. 47 (1977)], a statute "is not rendered invalid simply because some persons who might otherwise have married were deterred by the rule or because some who did marry were burdened thereby." 434 U.S. at 54.

Because the Warner Robins policy does not directly and substantially interfere with the fundamental right to marry, we subject the policy to rational basis scrutiny. Accordingly, the statute will not violate the Due Process Clause if it is rationally related to a legitimate government interest. Warner Robins has advanced several such interests: avoiding conflicts of interest between work-related and family-related obligations; reducing favoritism or even the appearance of favoritism; preventing family conflicts from affecting the workplace; and, by limiting inter-office dating, decreasing the likelihood of sexual harassment in the workplace. A rule that would prevent supervisory employees from having to exercise their discretionary power to hire, assign, promote, discipline or fire their relatives is rationally related to each of these practical, utilitarian goals. Therefore, we hold that the anti-nepotism policy adopted by Warner Robins is a reasonable attempt to achieve legitimate government interests; as such, it is valid under the Due Process Clause.

B. First Amendment Right of Intimate Association

Parks contends that the Warner Robins policy violates the First Amendment by making her continued employment contingent on the nonassertion of her right to marry. The First Amendment contains no explicit right of association. Nonetheless, the Supreme Court "has long understood as implicit in the right to engage in activities protected by the First Amendment a corresponding right to associate with others in pursuit of a wide variety of political, social, economic, educational, religious, and cultural ends." *Roberts v. United States Jaycees*, 468 U.S. 609, 622 (1984).

Included in this First Amendment right of association is the right to enter into certain intimate or private relationships, such as family relationships. *See id.* at 619. This is true even though the primary purpose of such intimate associations may not be expressive.

Although the right to marry enjoys independent protection under both the First Amendment and the Due Process Clause, the Supreme Court has held that the same analysis applies in each context. In *Lyng v. International Union, United Auto., Aerospace and Agric. Implement Workers*, 485 U.S. 360 (1988), the Court extended the reasoning in *Zablocki* to apply to claims involving First Amendment associational rights. The Court examined a Food Stamp Act provision that denied increased food stamp benefits to families of striking workers. The Court held that the food stamp statute did not infringe upon the striking workers' right to associate with their families because it did not " 'order' any individuals not to dine together; nor [did] it in any way 'directly and substantially' interfere with family living arrangements." *Id.* at 365–66.

The Warner Robins anti-nepotism policy does not "order" individuals not to marry, nor does it "directly and substantially" interfere with the right to marry. Admittedly, the policy presents a harder case than did the food stamp provision at issue in International Union; individuals forced by the policy to leave their jobs may incur economic losses greater than the temporary denial of food stamp benefits. Because the anti-nepotism policy does not prevent the less-senior spouse from working in another department or outside the Warner Robbins municipal government, however, it is unlikely that the policy will actually prevent affected couples from marrying. . . .

In *International Union*, the Court held that the petitioners' associational rights claim was "foreclosed" by its inability to satisfy the direct and substantial interference standard first used in *Zablocki* and followed in *Castillo*. Id. at 364. Parks has similarly failed to show that the Warner Robins anti-nepotism statute directly and substantially interferes with her right to marry. Consequently, we hold that the policy does not infringe upon her First Amendment right of intimate association.

C. Equal Protection Clause: Gender Discrimination

Parks' final argument on appeal is that the Warner Robins policy will result in a disparate impact on women because the city employs a greater number of men as supervisors. A gender-based classification violates the Equal Protection Clause of the Fourteenth Amendment if the classification is not substantially related to the achievement of important governmental objectives. *Personnel Adm'r v. Feeney*, 442 U.S. 256, 273 (1979); *Craig v. Boren*, 429 U.S. 190, 197 (1976).

Additionally, proof of discriminatory intent or purpose is a necessary prerequisite to any Equal Protection Clause claim. This requirement applies with equal force to a case involving alleged gender discrimination. *Feeney*, 442 U.S. at 274. Possible indicia of discriminatory intent include a clear pattern of disparate impact, unexplainable on grounds other than race; the historical background of the challenged decision or the specific events leading up to the decision; procedural or substantive departures from the norm; and the legislative or administrative history of the challenged statute. *Village of Arlington Heights v. Metropolitan Housing Dev. Corp.*, 429 U.S. 252, 266–68 (1977).

Parks' disparate impact claim relies upon her assertion that eighty-four percent of Warner Robins' supervisory employees are men. Consequently, she argues, a disproportionate number of employees who are forced to transfer to another department or to leave the city's employ will be women. As the Supreme Court's holding in *Personnel Adm'r v. Feeney* indicates, such a showing is insufficient to prove discriminatory intent. In *Feeney*, the Court upheld a state law that created an absolute hiring preference for military veterans applying for state jobs. *Feeney*, 442 U.S. at 275. At the time that the litigation commenced, over ninety-eight percent of the veterans in Massachusetts were male, and over one-fourth of the Massachusetts population were veterans. The Court described the impact of the Massachusetts plan on women as "severe." *Id.* at 271.

The *Feeney* Court rejected the plaintiff-appellee's argument that because a disparate impact against women was the obvious consequence of the statute's enactment, the Massachusetts legislature must have intended to discriminate against women. The Court held that ". . .'discriminatory purpose' . . . implies more than intent as volition or intent as awareness of consequences. It implies that the decisionmaker . . . selected or reaffirmed a particular course of action at least in part because of,' not merely 'in spite of,' its adverse effects upon an identifiable group." *Id.* at 279 (citation and footnote omitted). Assuming arguendo that Parks has demonstrated disparate impact, her equal protection claim must still fail for lack of a showing of discriminatory intent.

Parks' allegations cite none of the other traditional indicia of discrimination. She has not alleged facts surrounding the city's decision to apply the policy to her that could indicate discriminatory intent, nor has she identified any such intent in the legislative history of the statute. Her situation is not the result of any procedural or substantive departures from the norm that would reveal discriminatory intent. . . .

As the Court previously has observed, "the Fourteenth Amendment guarantees equal laws, not equal results." *Feeney*, 442 U.S. at 273. Parks has offered to demonstrate that more women than men will be transferred or fired as a result of Warner Robins' anti-nepotism policy. Such an allegation falls short of the showing of discriminatory purpose or intent necessary to support a disparate impact claim under the Equal Protection Clause. Therefore, we hold that the policy does not deny women equal protection of the laws as guaranteed by the Fourteenth Amendment. . . .

NOTES AND QUESTIONS

(1) Despite the influx of married women into the paid labor market, anti-nepotism policies affecting spouses are widespread. Although it is difficult to determine precisely how many employers have such policies, a 1986 survey indicated that nearly half of all companies had a formal policy, and at least another seventeen percent had an informal policy, prohibiting spouses form working together. *See* Randi Wolkenbreit, *In Order to Form a More Perfect Union: Applying No-Spouse Rules to Employees Who Meet at Work*, 31 Colum. J.L. & Soc. Probs. 119, 120–21 (1997) (citing James D. Werbel & David S. Hames, *Anti-Nepotism Reconsidered: The Case of the Husband and Wife Employment*, 21 Group & Org. Mgmt. 356, 365–66 (1996). Some employers flatly refuse to hire (or retain) spouses, while others are willing to employ spouses, but prohibit them from supervising each other, or from working in the same department. *See* Uma Sekaran, Dual-Career Families 119–20 (1986) (noting that 82% of the companies responding to a 1981 survey indicated that they would employ spouses, but 74% had restrictions on spouses working in the same department or at the same job). Although legal challenges to employer anti-nepotism policies have been largely unsuccessful, some recent evidence suggests that private employers may be modifying or abandoning their no-spouse rules, in response to market and employee pressures. *See, e.g.*, Susan Diesenhouse, *Workers in Love, With the Boss's Blessing*, N.Y. Times, April 24, 1996, at C1; Diana Kunde, *Couples Working at Same Firm Face Challenges*, Dallas Morning News, Jan. 11, 1995, at 1D. In the public sector, by contrast, enforcement of no-spouse policies appears to be increasing. James Podgers, *Marriage Traps in the Workplace, Nepotism Rules Make it Harder for Spouses to Be Colleagues in Public Sector A.B.A. J.*, Jan. 1996, at 46; *see* Wolkenbreit, *above*, at 163–65.

(2) Do you agree with the *Parks* court that the city's anti-nepotism policy does not "significantly interfere" with the decision to marry? Are there circumstances in which the interference would be more severe? How does the effect of the anti-nepotism policy on employees' marriage decisions compare with the effect of the child support provisions struck

down in *Zablocki*? Would the city's anti-nepotism policy preclude two married attorneys from working in the local prosecutor's office? Should it?

(3) What are the strongest arguments in favor of no-spouse rules in the workplace? Do those arguments apply to all workplace settings, or only to supervisory relationships? How is Warner Robbins' anti-nepotism policy "rationally related" to the each of the government interests advanced by the city?

(4) **Anti-Nepotism Rules and Gender Equality.** Although most anti-nepotism policies are formally gender neutral, their impact appears to fall disproportionately on women. *See, e.g., Thomas v. Metroflight, Inc.* 814 F.2d 1506, 1509 (10th Cir. 1987) (recognizing "that 'no-spouse-rules in practice often result in discrimination against women"); *Wolkenbreit, above*, at 120, 131–32 (noting that women are disproportionately burdened by no-spouse rules). *See generally* Joan G. Wexler, *Husbands and Wives: The Uneasy Case for Antinepotism Rules*, 62 B.U.L. Rev. 75 (1982) (discussing history of anti-nepotism rules and their impact on employed women); Henry Ben-Zvi, Comment, *(Mrs.) Alice Doesn't Work Here Anymore: No-Spouse Rules and the American Working Woman*, 29 UCLA L. Rev. 199 (1981). Is this disproportionate effect sufficient reason to eliminate such rules? Are no-spouse rules consistent with the rise of two-earner families and the influx of married women into the paid labor market?

(5) The result in *Parks* is consistent with most other constitutional challenges to anti-nepotism policies in the public sector. *See, e.g., Waters v. Gaston County*, 57 F.3d 422 (4th Cir. 1995) (county policy which barred spouses from working in same department upheld as effectuating "rational and laudable workplace goals"); *Wright v. MetroHealth Med. Ctr.*, 58 F.3d 1130 (6th Cir. 1995), *cert. denied.*, 916 U.S. 1158 (1996) (upholding medical center's anti-nepotism policy under rational relationship test); *Cutts v. Fowler*, 692 F.2d 138 (D.C. Cir. 1982) (characterizing burden imposed on marriage by civil service anti-nepotism rules as "attenuated and indirect"). Employer anti-nepotism policies in the private sector have also been challenged on a number of federal and state statutory grounds.

a. *Title VII.* Title VII of the Civil Rights Act of 1964, 42 U.S.C. § 2000e *et seq.* (1998) prohibits discrimination in employment on the basis of race, color religion, sex or national origin (but not marital status). Unlike discrimination claims under the Constitution, establishing a violation of Title VII does not require proof of discriminatory intent, but may be based on a theory of disparate impact. To prevail on a disparate impact claim, a Title VII plaintiff must first demonstrate that an employer's policy or practice has a disparate impact on a protected class, for example women. Once a plaintiff makes this showing, the burden shifts to defendant to show that "the challenged practice is job related for the position in question and consistent with business necessity." 42 U.S.C. § 2000e–2(k)(1)(A)(i) (1998). Definitions of business necessity vary, but a common formulation is that the challenged policy or practice bear a manifest relationship to the employment in question. *Dothard v. Rawlinson*, 433 U.S. 321, 329 (1977); *Griggs v. Duke Power Co.*, 401 U.S. 424, 429 (1977). Even if a defendant establishes business necessity, the plaintiff may still prevail by demonstrating the existence of less discriminatory alternatives that would serve the employer's goals equally well. 42 U.S.C. § 2000e–2(k)(1)(A)(ii); *see Albemarle Paper Co. v. Moody*, 422 U.S. 405, 425 (1975). Most Title VII challenges to employer anti-nepotism policies have proceeded on a disparate impact theory. *See, e.g., EEOC v. Rath Packing Co.*,

787 F.2d 318 (8th Cir. 1986), *cert. denied*, 479 U.S. 910 (1987) (invalidating no-spouse policy challenged on disparate impact theory); *Yuhas v. Libby-Owens-Ford Co*, 562 F.2d 496 (7th Cir. 1977), *cert denied*, 435 U.S. 934 (1978) (holding that employer's anti-nepotism policy had a disparate impact, but was justified by business necessity). *Query:* If the plaintiffs in *Parks* had challenged the city's anti-nepotism policy as a violation of Title VII, what result would the court have reached and why?

b. *State Civil Rights Statutes*. Anti-nepotism rules that affect spouses have also been challenged under state civil rights statutes, many of which expressly prohibit discrimination based on marital status. The results in these cases turn on the interpretation of the term "marital status." A majority of state courts that have considered the issue have interpreted the statutory term narrowly, to refer only to the state of being married, single, divorced or widowed. These courts have generally held that anti-nepotism policies do not constitute unlawful marital status discrimination, since their application does not depend solely on whether an employee is married. *See, e.g., Boaden v. Department of Law Enforcement*, 664 N.E.2d 61 (Ill. 1996); *Muller v. BP Exploration, Inc.*, 923 P.2d 783 (Alaska 1996). A minority of states have interpreted the term "marital status" more broadly, to include distinctions based on the identity of an individual's spouse. Courts that have adopted this interpretation have generally invalidated policies that prohibit married couples from working together. *See, e.g., Ross v. Stouffer Hotel*, 879 P.2d 1037 (Haw. 1994); *Glasgow Educ. Assoc. v. Board of Trustees*, 791 P.2d 1367 (Mont. 1990). In addition, civil rights statutes in three states (Minnesota, North Dakota, and Oregon) contain language that specifically prohibits discrimination based on the identity of one's spouse. *See Wolkenbreit, above*, at 132–38 (discussing state statutes).

For further discussion of the legal and policy issues raised by anti-nepotism rules affecting spouses, *see* Dennis Alerding, *Note, The Family that Works Together . . . Can't: No-Spouse Rules as Marital Status Discrimination Under State and Federal Law*, 32 U. Louisville J. Fam. L. 867 (1994); Katrina R. Kelly, *Note: Marital Status Discrimination in Washington: Relevance of The Identity and Actions of an Employee's Spouse*, 73 Wash. L. Rev. 135 (1998); Kim L. Kirn, *No-Spouse Rules in the Workplace Under Illinois and Federal Law*, 82 Ill. Bus. J. 414 (1994); Julius M. Steiner & Steven P. Steinberg, *Caught Between Scylla and Charybdis: Are Antinepotism Policies Benign paternalism or Covert Discrimination?*, 20 Employee Rel L.J. 253 (1994).

(6) **Lawyers as Spouses and Lovers.** Marriages between lawyers may raise special professional responsibility problems. A number of courts have considered whether a lawyer's ethical obligations may limit the professional activities of attorneys who are married to each other and, if so, whether these limitations extend as well to the law firms with which the spouses are associated. In *Blumenfeld v. Borenstein*, 276 S.E.2d 607, 609 (Ga. 1981), the Georgia Supreme Court refused to disqualify an attorney or his law firm in a probate case, despite the fact that the attorney's wife was associated with the firm representing an opposing party. The court reasoned,

> A per se rule of disqualification on the sole ground that an attorney's spouse is a member of a firm representing an opposing party would be not only unfair to the lawyers so disqualified and to their clients but would also have a significant detrimental effect upon the legal profession. Such a rule could be expected to affect the hiring

practices of law firms and the professional opportunities of lawyers. A per se rule would effectively create a category of legal "Typhoid Marys," chilling both professional opportunities and personal choices.

By contrast, in *Haley v. Boles*, 824 S.W.2d 796 (Tex. App. 1992), a Texas appellate court held that counsel appointed to represent an indigent criminal defendant should have been permitted to withdraw, where counsel's law partner was married to the county district attorney. The court concluded that the marital relationship between the law partner and the district attorney would erode public confidence in the legal system and "create the appearance of having compromised and limited the defendant's constitutional right to effective assistance of counsel." The court also reasoned that because counsel was appointed, rather than privately retained, the potential conflict of interest could not be mitigated by client consent. Are *Haley* and *Blumenfeld* consistent?

Model Rule 1.8 of the American Bar Association's Model Rules of Professional Conduct (1996) provides as follows:

> (i) A lawyer related to another lawyer as parent, child, sibling or spouse shall not represent a client in a representation directly adverse to a person who the lawyer knows is represented by the other lawyer except upon consent by the client after consultation regarding the relationship.

Do you agree that client consent mitigates the potential for conflict where lawyer-spouses represent adverse interests? Does such representation undermine a lawyer-spouse's ability to zealously represent her client, within the bounds of the law? To what extent do the concerns expressed in *Haley* apply to lawyer-couples who are living together or dating seriously, but who are not married to each other? *See People v. Jackson*, 213 Cal. Rptr. 521 (Cal. Ct. App. 1985) (reversing criminal conviction where defense counsel failed to inform client of dating relationship with the prosecutor). For further discussion of these issues, *see* Comment, *Dating Among the Profession: Ethical Guidance in the Area of Personal Dating Conflicts of Interest* (1994); Arthur Garwin, *Lawyers in Love . . . and in Conflict*, 78 ABA J. 94 (Sept. 1992); Stacy DeBroff, *Lawyers as Lovers: How Far Should Ethical Restrictions on Dating or Married Attorneys Extend?*, 1 Geo. J. Legal Ethics 433 (1987).

(7) **Problem.** Norma Jones retained attorney Diane Zimmerman to represent her in a divorce action against her husband. Subsequently, Norma's husband, Larry Jones, retained attorney Charles Bond to represent him in the divorce action. Prior to undertaking the representation, attorney Bond informed Larry that he (Bond) was married to Diane Zimmerman. Larry Jones consented to the representation, notwithstanding Bond's marriage to Zimmerman. Bond and Zimmerman negotiated a partial settlement regarding temporary custody of the Jones' minor children and interim spousal support. Zimmerman's law firm then filed a motion to disqualify Bond on the ground that Bond had a conflict of interest in the case by virtue of his marriage to Zimmerman. In an affidavit attached to the motion, Mrs. Jones expressed her fear that confidences she had disclosed to her attorney, Zimmerman, would be conveyed to Bond. Should the disqualification motion be granted? Why or why not? Would your analysis be different if Mr. Jones were not being represented by Bond himself, but rather by another member of Bond's law firm? *See Jones v. Jones*, 369 S.E.2d 478 (Ga. 1988).

(8) **Problem.** New Jersey law prohibits judges or their spouses from holding, or campaigning for, political office. Ellen Gaulkin, the wife of Judge Richard Gaulkin, intends to seek election to the County Board of Education. She asks the New Jersey Supreme Court to eliminate the rule of disqualification, as it applies to a judge's spouse. The Court agrees to reconsider the rule. Should the Court lift all restrictions on political activities by a judge's spouse? Why or why not? Should such a judicial spouse be able to use marital assets to finance an election campaign? May she or he hold fundraisers and political meetings at the marital home? May a judge appear at a spouse's campaign events? *See In re Gaulkin*, 351 A.2d 740 (N.J. 1976).

If the disqualification rule is lifted and Mrs. Gaulkin is elected to the Board of Education, must Judge Gaulkin recuse himself from all cases in which the Board of Education is a party? From all cases involving schools or personnel under the jurisdiction of the Board? *Cf.* 28 U.S.C. § 455 (b)(5) (1998) (federal judges must disqualify themselves where, *inter alia*, a spouse is a party to the proceeding, is acting as a lawyer in the proceeding, or is known to have an interest that could be substantially affected by the outcome of the proceeding). *See generally* Mark M. Brandsdorfer, *Lawyers Married to Judges: A Dilemma Facing State Judiciaries—A Case Study of the State of Texas*, 6 Geo. J. Legal Ethics 635 (1993).

[B] Pregnancy, Childbearing and Employment

CALIFORNIA FEDERAL SAVINGS & LOAN ASSOCIATION v. GUERRA
United States Supreme Court
479 U.S. 272 (1987)

JUSTICE MARSHALL delivered the opinion of the Court.

The question presented is whether Title VII of the Civil Rights Act of 1964, as amended by the Pregnancy Discrimination Act of 1978, pre-empts a state statute that requires employers to provide leave and reinstatement to employees disabled by pregnancy.

California's Fair Employment and Housing Act (FEHA) is a comprehensive statute that prohibits discrimination in employment and housing. In September 1978, California amended the FEHA to proscribe certain forms of employment discrimination on the basis of pregnancy. Subdivision (b)(2)—the provision at issue here—is the only portion of the statute that applies to employers subject to Title VII. It requires these employers to provide female employees an unpaid pregnancy disability leave of up to four months. Respondent Fair Employment and Housing Commission, the state agency authorized to interpret the FEHA, has construed § 12945(b)(2) to require California employers to reinstate an employee returning from such pregnancy leave to the job she previously held, unless it is no longer available due to business necessity. In the latter case, the employer must make a reasonable, good-faith effort to place the employee in a substantially similar job. The statute does not compel employers to provide paid leave to pregnant employees. Accordingly, the only benefit pregnant workers actually derive from § 12945(b)(2) is a qualified right to reinstatement.

Title VII of the Civil Rights Act of 1964, 42 U. S. C. § 2000e et seq., also prohibits various forms of employment discrimination, including discrimination on the basis of sex. However, in *General Electric Co. v. Gilbert*, 429 U.S. 125 (1976), this Court ruled that discrimination on the basis of pregnancy was not sex discrimination under Title VII. In response to the Gilbert decision, Congress passed the Pregnancy Discrimination Act of 1978 (PDA), 42 U. S. C. § 2000e(k). The PDA specifies that sex discrimination includes discrimination on the basis of pregnancy.

Petitioner California Federal Savings & Loan Association (Cal Fed) is a federally chartered savings and loan association based in Los Angeles; it is an employer covered by both Title VII and § 12945(b)(2). Cal Fed has a facially neutral leave policy that permits employees who have completed three months of service to take unpaid leaves of absence for a variety of reasons, including disability and pregnancy. Although it is Cal Fed's policy to try to provide an employee taking unpaid leave with a similar position upon returning, Cal Fed expressly reserves the right to terminate an employee who has taken a leave of absence if a similar position is not available.

Lillian Garland was employed by Cal Fed as a receptionist for several years. In January 1982, she took a pregnancy disability leave. When she was able to return to work in April of that year, Garland notified Cal Fed, but was informed that her job had been filled and that there were no receptionist or similar positions available. Garland filed a complaint with respondent Department of Fair Employment and Housing, which issued an administrative accusation against Cal Fed on her behalf. Respondent charged Cal Fed with violating § 12945(b)(2) of the FEHA. Prior to the scheduled hearing before respondent Fair Employment and Housing Commission, Cal Fed, joined by petitioners Merchants and Manufacturers Association and the California Chamber of Commerce, brought this action in the United States District Court for the Central District of California. They sought a declaration that § 12945(b)(2) is inconsistent with and pre-empted by Title VII and an injunction against enforcement of the section. The District Court granted petitioners' motion for summary judgment. 34 FEP Cases 562 (1984). Citing *Newport News Shipbuilding & Dry Dock Co. v. EEOC*, 462 U.S. 669 (1983).[2] the court stated that "California employers who comply with state law are subject to reverse discrimination suits under Title VII brought by temporarily disabled males who do not receive the same treatment as female employees disabled by pregnancy. . . . " 34 FEP Cases, at 568. On this basis, the District Court held that "California state law and the policies of interpretation and enforcement . . . which require preferential treatment of female employees disabled by pregnancy, childbirth, or related medical conditions are pre-empted by Title VII and are null, void, invalid and inoperative under the Supremacy Clause of the United States Constitution."

The United States Court of Appeals for the Ninth Circuit reversed. 758 F.2d 390 (1985). It held that "the district court's conclusion that section 12945(b)(2) discriminates against men on the basis of pregnancy defies common sense, misinterprets case law, and flouts Title VII and the PDA." *Id.*, at 393 (footnote omitted). Based on its own reading of *Newport News*, the Court of Appeals found that the PDA does not "demand that state law be blind to pregnancy's existence." 758 F.2d, at 395. The court held that in enacting the PDA Congress intended "to construct a floor beneath which pregnancy disability benefits may not drop—not a ceiling above which they may not rise." *Id.*, at 396. Because it found that

---

[2] In *Newport News*, the Court evaluated a health insurance plan that provided female employees with benefits for pregnancy-related conditions to the same extent as for other medical conditions, but provided less extensive pregnancy benefits for spouses of male employees. The Court found that this limitation discriminated against male employees with respect to the compensation, terms, conditions, or privileges of their employment in violation of §703(a)(1) of Title VII.

the California statute furthers the goal of equal employment opportunity for women, the Court of Appeals concluded: "Title VII does not preempt a state law that guarantees pregnant women a certain number of pregnancy disability leave days, because this is neither inconsistent with, nor unlawful under, Title VII." *Ibid.* . . .

In determining whether a state statute is pre-empted by federal law and therefore invalid under the Supremacy Clause of the Constitution, our sole task is to ascertain the intent of Congress. Federal law may supersede state law in several different ways. . . .

As a third alternative, in those areas where Congress has not completely displaced state regulation, federal law may nonetheless pre-empt state law to the extent it actually conflicts with federal law. Such a conflict occurs either because "compliance with both federal and state regulations is a physical impossibility," *Florida Lime & Avocado Growers, Inc. v. Paul*, 373 U.S. 132, 142–143 (1963), or because the state law stands "as an obstacle to the accomplishment and execution of the full purposes and objectives of Congress." *Hines v. Davidowitz*, 312 U.S. 52, 67 (1941). Nevertheless, pre-emption is not to be lightly presumed.

This third basis for pre-emption is at issue in this case. In two sections of the 1964 Civil Rights Act, §§ 708 and 1104, Congress has indicated that state laws will be pre-empted only if they actually conflict with federal law. . . .

In order to decide whether the California statute requires or permits employers to violate Title VII, as amended by the PDA, or is inconsistent with the purposes of the statute, we must determine whether the PDA prohibits the States from requiring employers to provide reinstatement to pregnant workers, regardless of their policy for disabled workers generally.

Petitioners argue that the language of the federal statute itself unambiguously rejects California's "special treatment" approach to pregnancy discrimination, thus rendering any resort to the legislative history unnecessary. They contend that the second clause of the PDA forbids an employer to treat pregnant employees any differently than other disabled employees. Because "'[the] purpose of Congress is the ultimate touchstone'" of the preemption inquiry, *Malone v. White Motor Corp.*, 435 U.S., at 504 (*quoting Retail Clerks v. Schermerhorn*, 375 U.S. 96, 103 (1963)), however, we must examine the PDA's language against the background of its legislative history and historical context. As to the language of the PDA, "[it] is a 'familiar rule, that a thing may be within the letter of the statute and yet not within its spirit, nor within the intention of its makers.'" *Steelworkers v. Weber*, 443 U.S. 193, 201 (1979) (quoting *Church of the Holy Trinity v. United States*, 143 U.S. 457, 459 (1892)).

It is well established that the PDA was passed in reaction to this Court's decision in General *Electric Co. v. Gilbert*, 429 U.S. 125 (1976). . . . Rather than imposing a limitation on the remedial purpose of the PDA, we believe that the second clause was intended to overrule the holding in Gilbert and to illustrate how discrimination against pregnancy is to be remedied. Accordingly, subject to certain limitations, we agree with the Court of Appeals' conclusion that Congress intended the PDA to be "a floor beneath which pregnancy disability benefits may not drop—not a ceiling above which they may not rise." 758 F.2d, at 396.

The context in which Congress considered the issue of pregnancy discrimination supports this view of the PDA. Congress had before it extensive evidence of discrimination against pregnancy, particularly in disability and health insurance programs like those challenged in *Gilbert* and *Nashville Gas Co. v. Satty*, 434 U.S. 136 (1977). The Reports, debates, and hearings make abundantly clear that Congress intended the PDA to provide relief for working women and to end discrimination against pregnant workers. In contrast to the thorough account of discrimination against pregnant workers, the legislative history is devoid of any discussion of preferential treatment of pregnancy, beyond acknowledgments of the existence of state statutes providing for such preferential treatment. Opposition to the PDA came from those concerned with the cost of including pregnancy in health and disability-benefit plans and the application of the bill to abortion, not from those who favored special accommodation of pregnancy.

In support of their argument that the PDA prohibits employment practices that favor pregnant women, petitioners and several amici cite statements in the legislative history to the effect that the PDA does not require employers to extend any benefits to pregnant women that they do not already provide to other disabled employees. . . . We do not interpret these references to support petitioners' construction of the statute. On the contrary, if Congress had intended to prohibit preferential treatment, it would have been the height of understatement to say only that the legislation would not require such conduct. It is hardly conceivable that Congress would have extensively discussed only its intent not to require preferential treatment if in fact it had intended to prohibit such treatment.

We also find it significant that Congress was aware of state laws similar to California's but apparently did not consider them inconsistent with the PDA. In the debates and Reports on the bill, Congress repeatedly acknowledged the existence of state antidiscrimination laws that prohibit sex discrimination on the basis of pregnancy. Two of the States mentioned then required employers to provide reasonable leave to pregnant workers. After citing these state laws, Congress failed to evince the requisite "clear and manifest purpose" to supersede them. To the contrary, both the House and Senate Reports suggest that these laws would continue to have effect under the PDA.

Title VII, as amended by the PDA, and California's pregnancy disability leave statute share a common goal. The purpose of Title VII is "to achieve equality of employment opportunities and remove barriers that have operated in the past to favor an identifiable group of . . . employees over other employees." *Griggs v. Duke Power Co.*, 401 U.S. 424, 429–430 (1971). Rather than limiting existing Title VII principles and objectives, the PDA extends them to cover pregnancy. As Senator Williams, a sponsor of the Act, stated: "The entire thrust . . . behind this legislation is to guarantee women the basic right to participate fully and equally in the workforce, without denying them the fundamental right to full participation in family life." 123 Cong. Rec. 29658 (1977).

Section 12945(b)(2) also promotes equal employment opportunity. By requiring employers to reinstate women after a reasonable pregnancy disability leave, § 12945(b)(2) ensures that they will not lose their jobs on account of pregnancy disability. California's approach is consistent with the dissenting opinion of Justice Brennan in *General Electric Co. v. Gilbert*, which Congress adopted in enacting the PDA. Referring to *Lau v. Nichols*, 414 U.S. 563 (1974), a Title VI decision, Justice Brennan stated:

> [Discrimination] is a social phenomenon encased in a social context and, therefore, unavoidably takes its meaning from the desired end products of the relevant legislative enactment, end products that may demand due consideration of the uniqueness of the

> 'disadvantaged' individuals. A realistic understanding of conditions found in today's labor environment warrants taking pregnancy into account in fashioning disability policies.

429 U.S., at 159 (footnote omitted). By "taking pregnancy into account," California's pregnancy disability-leave statute allows women, as well as men, to have families without losing their jobs.

We emphasize the limited nature of the benefits § 12945(b)(2) provides. The statute is narrowly drawn to cover only the period of actual physical disability on account of pregnancy, childbirth, or related medical conditions. Accordingly, unlike the protective labor legislation prevalent earlier in this century, § 12945(b)(2) does not reflect archaic or stereotypical notions about pregnancy and the abilities of pregnant workers. A statute based on such stereotypical assumptions would, of course, be inconsistent with Title VII's goal of equal employment opportunity.

Moreover, even if we agreed with petitioners' construction of the PDA, we would nonetheless reject their argument that the California statute requires employers to violate Title VII. Section 12945(b)(2) does not prevent employers from complying with both the federal law (as petitioners construe it) and the state law. Section 12945(b)(2) does not compel California employers to treat pregnant workers better than other disabled employees; it merely establishes benefits that employers must, at a minimum, provide to pregnant workers. Employers are free to give comparable benefits to other disabled employees, thereby treating "women affected by pregnancy" no better than "other persons not so affected but similar in their ability or inability to work." Indeed, at oral argument, petitioners conceded that compliance with both statutes "is theoretically possible." Tr. of Oral Arg. 6.

Petitioners argue that "extension" of the state statute to cover other employees would be inappropriate in the absence of a clear indication that this is what the California Legislature intended. They cite cases in which this Court has declined to rewrite underinclusive state statutes found to violate the Equal Protection Clause. This argument is beside the point. Extension is a remedial option to be exercised by a court once a statute is found to be invalid.

Thus, petitioners' facial challenge to § 12945(b)(2) fails. The statute is not pre-empted by Title VII, as amended by the PDA, because it is not inconsistent with the purposes of the federal statute, nor does it require the doing of an act which is unlawful under Title VII.

The judgment of the Court of Appeals is Affirmed.

JUSTICE STEVENS, concurring in part and concurring in the judgment. . . .

In *Steelworkers v. Weber*, 443 U.S. 193 (1979), the Court rejected the argument that Title VII prohibits all preferential treatment of the disadvantaged classes that the statute was enacted to protect. The plain words of Title VII, which would have led to a contrary result, were read in the context of the statute's enactment and its purposes. In this case as well, the language of the Act seems to mandate treating pregnant employees the same as other employees. I cannot, however, ignore the fact that the PDA is a definitional section of Title VII's prohibition against gender-based discrimination. Had Weber interpreted Title VII as requiring neutrality, I would agree with Justice White that the PDA should be interpreted that way as well. But since the Court in Weber interpreted Title VII to draw a distinction between discrimination against members of the protected class and special preference in favor of members of that class, I do not accept the proposition that the PDA requires absolute neutrality.

I therefore conclude that Justice Marshall's view, which holds that the PDA allows some preferential treatment of pregnancy, is more consistent with our interpretation of Title VII than Justice White's view is. This is not to say, however, that all preferential treatment of pregnancy is automatically beyond the scope of the PDA. Rather, as with other parts of Title VII, preferential treatment of the disadvantaged class is only permissible so long as it is consistent with "[accomplishing] the goal that Congress designed Title VII to achieve." *Weber*, above, at 204. That goal has been characterized as seeking "to achieve equality of employment opportunities and to remove barriers that have operated in the past to favor an identifiable group of . . . employees over other employees." *Griggs v. Duke Power Co.*, 401 U.S. 424, 429–430 (1971).

It is clear to me, as it is to the Court, and was to the Court of Appeals, that the California statute meets this test. Thus, I agree that a California employer would not violate the PDA were it to comply with California's statute without affording the same protection to men suffering somewhat similar disabilities.

JUSTICE WHITE, with whom THE CHIEF JUSTICE and JUSTICE POWELL join, dissenting.

. . . Contrary to the mandate of the PDA, California law requires every employer to have a disability leave policy for pregnancy even if it has none for any other disability. An employer complies with California law if it has a leave policy for pregnancy but denies it for every other disability. On its face, § 12945(b)(2) is in square conflict with the PDA and is therefore pre-empted. Because the California law permits employers to single out pregnancy for preferential treatment and therefore to violate Title VII, it is not saved by § 708 which limits pre-emption of state laws to those that require or permit an employer to commit an unfair employment practice.

The majority nevertheless would save the California law on two grounds. First, it holds that the PDA does not require disability from pregnancy to be treated the same as other disabilities; instead, it forbids less favorable, but permits more favorable, benefits for pregnancy disability. The express command of the PDA is unambiguously to the contrary, and the legislative history casts no doubt on that mandate. . . .

The majority correctly reports that Congress focused on discrimination against, rather than preferential treatment of, pregnant workers. There is only one direct reference in the legislative history to preferential treatment. . . . The parties and their amici argued vigorously to this Court the policy implications of preferential treatment of pregnant workers. In favor of preferential treatment it was urged with conviction that preferential treatment merely enables women, like men, to have children without losing their jobs. In opposition to preferential treatment it was urged with equal conviction that preferential treatment represents a resurgence of the 19th-century protective legislation which perpetuated sex-role stereotypes and which impeded women in their efforts to take their rightful place in the workplace. It is not the place of this Court, however, to resolve this policy dispute. Our task is to interpret Congress' intent in enacting the PDA. Congress' silence in its consideration of the PDA with respect to preferential treatment of pregnant workers cannot fairly be interpreted to abrogate the plain statements in the legislative history, not to mention the language of the statute, that equality of treatment was to be the guiding principle of the PDA. . . .

The Court's second, and equally strange, ground is that even if the PDA does prohibit special benefits for pregnant women, an employer may still comply with both the California law and the PDA: it can adopt the specified leave policies for pregnancy and at the same time afford similar benefits for all other disabilities. This is untenable. California surely had no intent to require employers to provide general disability leave benefits. It intended to prefer pregnancy and went no further. Extension of these benefits to the entire work force would be a dramatic increase in the scope of the state law and would impose a significantly greater burden on California employers. That is the province of the California Legislature. . . .

In sum, preferential treatment of pregnant workers is prohibited by Title VII, as amended by the PDA. Section 12945(b)(2) of the California Government Code, which extends preferential benefits for pregnancy, is therefore pre-empted. It is not saved by § 708 because it purports to authorize employers to commit an unfair employment practice forbidden by Title VII.

NOTES AND QUESTIONS

(1) Until recently, most employers paid little attention to pregnancy or to integrating work and parenting responsibilities. In part, this was because work and family were viewed as distinct legal and economic spheres and because the pregnancy of a woman worker was viewed as signaling her departure from the workplace and her assumption, within the family sphere, of her primary role as wife and mother. *See* Wendy W. Williams, *Equality's Riddle: Pregnancy and The Equal Treatment/Special Treatment Debate*, 13 N.Y.U. Rev. of Law & Soc. Change 325, 352 (1984–85). Professor Lucinda Finley describes the effect of this "separate spheres" ideology on employer policies:

> Until the last twenty years or so, many employers either would not hire married women, or would not hire married women with young children. When women workers became pregnant, they faced a range of adverse consequences. Often, it was simply understood that they would quit, and the lack of any maternity leave policies usually assured that this would be so. Other women were fired, or relegated to less desirable jobs. Little more than a decade ago, many women faced mandatory maternity leaves that were unrelated to their ability or desire to work and that adversely affected their benefits and future job prospects. Those women who wanted to challenge the assumption that impending motherhood meant leaving the workplace met with penalties such as the loss of job benefits including sick leave, disability or health insurance coverage, and seniority. This loss of benefits signaled that no matter what the woman's intention, the employer regarded her as no longer part of the workforce. . . .
>
> Both employers' policies and the law have been very slow in catching up to the reality that women now comprise over 44% of the workforce. Women are projected to make up half of the workforce by 1990. Half of all mothers with pre-school aged children are in the workforce, and 85% of women workers can be expected to bear at least one child during their years of workforce participation. Despite these numbers,

maternity or parental leave policies in the United States lag far behind the rest of the industrialized world, especially among smaller employers and in the service or retail industries where most women workers are found. The Pregnancy Discrimination Act amendment to Title VII, which is based on the equal treatment approach, has brought vast improvement in the availability of benefit coverage for pregnancy. Nonetheless, this law is limited because it requires employers to make available to pregnant women only what they make available to men for other conditions. Consequently, it tolerates a wide variety in policies. Those which are inadequate to offer meaningful protection for a variety of human conditions that keep both men and women out of work are just as acceptable as more generous policies. . . .

Despite the changed composition of the workforce, the structures of the workplace remain built either around the needs of male management, or the assumption that the typical worker is a man with a wife at home to worry about the demands of the private sphere. Thus, when women return to work, they often find that workplace structures are utterly insensitive to the reality of a worker with both home and job responsibilities. Child care arrangements are still generally regarded as a woman's private problem, of no concern to the employer. This view persists despite the way in which child care availability affects a parent's, and especially a mother's, work life. Flexible job scheduling is less rare, although still far from common. Most workplaces remain structured around an eight-hour day, five days a week, even though such a schedule conflicts with employees' needs to do shopping and errands, to attend children's school functions or doctor's appointments, to be available to children when they are out of school, or to meet similar needs of other dependents. There is nothing inevitable or natural about this particular workplace structure. Together with the inadequacy of maternity policies, the structure of the workplace demonstrates the ways in which employers still remain tied to the notion that the typical worker is someone—a man—who does not have to worry about bearing or rearing children or nurturing other dependants. . . .

Lucinda M. Finley, *Transcending Equality Theory: A Way Out of the Maternity and the Workplace Debate*, 86 Colum. L. Rev. 1118, 1124–27 (1986); see Wendy W. Williams, *Equality's Riddle: Pregnancy and The Equal Treatment/Special Treatment Debate*, 12 N.Y.U. Rev. Law & Soc. Change 325, 353 (1984–85) ("Treating parenthood as a non-issue structurally marginalizes women as workforce participants.").

(2) The Equal Treatment-Special Treatment Debate. The maternity leave policy at issue in *Guerra* represents one attempt to accommodate employment and childbearing. However, because the policy singles out pregnancy and childbirth for special treatment, rather than incorporating them into broader disability and parental leave policies, these efforts have been controversial. Indeed, many women's rights advocates opposed such state laws. They emphasized that treating pregnancy as "unique" in the context of employment has historically led to restrictive and paternalistic policies that had the effect—if not the intent—of forcing women out of the workplace and into the home. These advocates argued instead that pregnancy "should be visualized as one human experience which in many contexts, most notably the workplace, creates needs and problems similar to those arising from causes other than pregnancy, and which can be handled adequately on the same basis as are other physical conditions of employees." Williams, *above* at 336. *General Electric*

Co. v. Gilbert, 429 U.S. 125 (1976). According to this view, a major purpose of the Pregnancy Discrimination Act was to ensure that "women affected by pregnancy, childbirth or related medical conditions shall be treated the same for all employment-related purposes . . . as other persons not so affected but similar in their ability or inability to work. . . ." 42 U.S.C. § 2000e(k) (1998). Where employers have inadequate disability or sick leave policies, the proper approach is not to demand "special treatment" for pregnant workers, but to lobby for laws and policies that extend adequate disability and parenting leaves to all workers. Such comprehensive, gender-neutral polices are important, according to equal-treatment advocates because gender-specific approaches have traditionally worked to women's detriment and are likely to reinforce gender stereotypes about women's primary responsibility for children. *See generally* Williams, *above*, at 374–80.

Supporters of maternity leave laws, by contrast, view pregnancy as warranting its own, specially tailored workplace policies. They argue that pregnancy and childbirth are distinct from other human experiences and that it is neither necessary nor desirable to deny this uniqueness. These advocates point out that an equal-treatment model is no help to women (such as Lillian Garland) whose employers offer little or no disability leave. A facially neutral "no-leave" policy, or a policy that provides so little time off that virtually any pregnant woman will need more leave than she is entitled to, has a negative, disparate effect on women employees as a group. In essence, such policies unfairly force women to conform to male norms and male life patterns in order to succeed at work. Although special-treatment advocates do not oppose the more comprehensive workplace reforms advocated by equal-treatment proponents, they insist that it is acceptable to move incrementally toward these comprehensive goals and they argue that it is foolhardy to fight against incremental legislation that women workers badly need. *See* Linda Krieger and Patricia Cooney, *The Miller-Wohl Controversy: Equal Treatment, Positive Action and the Meaning of Women's Equality*, 13 Golden Gate L. Rev. 513 (1983).

(3) In defending an equal-treatment approach to pregnancy and employment, Professor Wendy Williams has urged: "If [women] can't have it both ways, we need to think carefully about which way we want to have it." Wendy W. Williams, *The Equality Crisis" Some Reflections On Culture, Courts, and Feminism*, 7 Women Rights L. Rptr. 175, 196 (1982). Does the majority opinion in *Guerra* suggest that, when it comes to pregnancy leave, women *can* have it both ways? Is a requirement that employers provide leave for female workers unable to work because of pregnancy and childbirth, but not for male workers disabled because of a heart attack, unfair to men? To employees without children?

(4) In his concurring opinion in *Guerra*, Justice Stevens analogizes the California maternity leave statute to the voluntary employer affirmative action plan upheld by the Supreme Court in *United Steelworkers of Am. v. Weber*, 443 U.S. 193 (1979). Do you find this analogy persuasive? Why or why not?

(5) The *Guerra* decision has generally been interpreted to permit unequal workplace treatment of mothers and fathers only where the differences in treatment are linked to actual pregnancy-related disability. In this respect, the decision is consistent with other Supreme Court cases that have permitted differential treatment of men and women based on what the Court characterizes as "real physical differences" between the sexes. *See, e.g., Lehr v. Robertson*, 463 U.S. 248, 259–61 (1983) (differential treatment of unwed mothers and fathers justified by biological differences relevant to parenthood); *Michael M. v. Superior*

Court, 450 U.S. 464 (1981) (upholding statutory rape law that treated male and female sexual partners differently, based on women's unique capacity to become pregnant). This approach has been criticized, however, for conflating biological and socially created norms and differences and for ignoring the most important causes of inequality between the sexes. *See, e.g.*, Catherine A. MacKinnon, *Reflections on Sex Equality Under Law* 100 Yale L.J. 1281 (1991) (arguing that current constitutional doctrine, which requires that women be "similarly situated" to men in establish a viable sex discrimination claim is "stunningly inappropriate" for addressing issues of women's equality); Frances Olsen, *Statutory Rape: A Feminist Critique of Rights Analysis*, 63 Tex. L. Rev. 387 (1984) (critiquing Supreme Court's analysis in *Michael M*); Sylvia A. Law, *Rethinking Sex and The Constitution*, 132 U. Pa. L. Rev. 955 (1984) (criticizing Supreme Court's approach to biological differences between men and women). *See also* Deborah Hellman *Two Types of Discrimination: The Familiar and the Forgotten*, 86 Calif. L. Rev. 315 (1998) (arguing that current equal protection doctrine inappropriately treats all discrimination claims as involving the use of one trait as a proxy for another, thus ignoring or mischaracterizing other types of discrimination).

(6) In *International Union, UAW v. Johnson Controls, Inc.*, 499 U.S. 187 (1991), the Supreme Court considered the legality, under Title VII, of an employer's policy of excluding all fertile females from certain high-paying manufacturing jobs, because of concern about the effects of exposure to high workplace levels of lead on a fetus that a woman might conceive. The employer argued first, that its policy did not discriminate "on the basis of sex" because it did not exclude all women, and second that even if the policy were facially discriminatory, it fell within a statutory exception allowing employers to hire or classify on the basis of sex where sex "is a bona fide occupational qualification ["BFOQ"] reasonably necessary to the normal operation of that particular business or enterprise." 42 USC § 2000e–2(e) (1998). The Supreme Court rejected both of these arguments. The Court first held that the employer's exclusionary policy constituted facial sex-based discrimination, particularly in light of the Pregnancy Discrimination Act. The Court then held that the statutory BFOQ defense was limited to where sex or pregnancy actually interferes with the employee's ability to perform the essentials of the job. Noting that nothing in the record suggested that fertile women were unable to perform the jobs in question, the Court held that neither the employer's professed concerns about the health and welfare of future children nor the possibility of tort liability for injuries suffered by a fetus as a result of exposure to lead, could qualify as a BFOQ under Title VII. The Court concluded by stating,

> Our holding that Title VII, as so amended, forbids sex-specific fetal-protection policies is neither remarkable nor unprecedented. Concern for a woman's existing or potential offspring historically has been the excuse for denying women equal employment opportunities. . . .
>
> It is no more appropriate for the courts than it is for individual employers to decide whether a woman's reproductive role is more important to herself and her family than her economic role. Congress has left this choice to the woman as hers to make.

Is the "employee choice" approach endorsed in *Johnson Controls* a satisfactory response to the problem of workplace-related fetal risk? *See, e.g.*, Ruth Rosen, *What Feminist Victory in the Court?*, N.Y. Times, Apr. 1, 1991, at A17 (arguing that the *Johnson Controls* decision represents a hollow victory for women and reveals "the impoverishment of the language of individual rights and the inadequacy of liberal feminism to insure the health and security of both women and men"). Do you agree? Suppose that a female employee who works in a manufacturing position at Johnson Controls decides to become pregnant and requests a transfer to a less hazardous position within the company. Does Title VII require the employer to grant her request? Should the company be required to do so?

(7) **Problem.** Gerald Schafer was employed as a teacher by the Pittsburgh Board of Public Education from August, 1985 to December, 1988. In August, 1988, Schafer requested an unpaid leave of absence for the 198089 school year for purposes of caring for her son, who had been born in July. The Board's Personnel Director advised Schafer that he had never know a male to be granted such a leave, although female teachers were routinely granted one-year maternity leaves, following the birth of a child. The Director instead granted Schafer an emergency ninety-day unpaid leave, for purposes of securing childcare. At the end of November, Schafer applied for an unpaid childrearing leave from the expiration of his three month emergency leave to the end of the school year. Schafer's request was denied. In mid December, Schafer resigned his teaching position, stating in his letter of resignation that he was forced to resign becasue he was refused leave to care for his son. Schafter subsequently sued the Board, alleging sex discrimination under Title VII and the Pregnancy Discrimination Act of 1978. In August, 1989, the Board filed a motion for summary judgment, alleging that its maternity leave policy was a permissable accomodation to females under the Supreme Court's decision in *Guerra*. Schafte opposed the motion. How should the judge rule and why? See *Schafer v. Board of Public Education*, 903 F.2d 243 (3d Cir. 1990).

(8) **Problem.** The Omaha Girls Club is a private, nonprofit corporation that offers programs designed to assist young girls between the ages of eight and eighteen maximize their life opportunities. Among the Club's many activities are programs directed at pregnancy prevention. The Club's philosophy emphasizes the development of close relationships between staff members and the youngsters they serve. To this end, the Club trains and expects its staff members to act as "role models," and it prohibits single-parent pregnancies among its staff members as inconsistent with this "role model" approach. Crystal Chambers, an African-American single woman, was employed by the Club as an arts and crafts instructor. She became pregnant and informed her supervisor. Soon thereafter, Chambers received a letter notifying her that her employment was being terminated because of her pregnancy. Chambers sued the Club under Title VII, alleging both race and sex discrimination. She advanced both disparate impact and disparate treatment theories. The trial court held that the Club's "role model" rule constituted a "bona fide occupational qualification" and was justified under Title VII because "a manifest relationship exists between the Girls Club's fundamental purposes and its single pregnancy policy." What result on appeal and why? See *Chambers v. Omaha Girls Club, Inc.*, 834 F.2d 697 (8th Cir. 1987). Would your analysis be any different if Chambers had been employed as a librarian by a private, parochial school and the school defended her termination on the ground that she had engaged in sex outside of marriage, contrary to the school's religious teachings? See *Vigars v. Valley Christian Center of Dublin, California*, 805 F. Supp. 802 (N.D. Cal. 1992). If the fair employment laws in Chambers' state prohibited discrimination based on "marital status" would Chambers have had a valid claim of marital status discrimination?

[C] **Working and Caring for Children**

FAMILY AND MEDICAL LEAVE ACT
29 U.S.C. §§ 2601, 2611, 2612, 2614 (1998)

§ 2601. Findings and Purposes

(a) Findings. Congress finds that

(1) the number of single-parent households and two-parent households in which the single parent or both parents work is increasing significantly;

(2) it is important for the development of children and the family unit that fathers and mothers be able to participate in early childrearing and the care of family members who have serious health conditions;

(3) the lack of employment policies to accommodate working parents can force individuals to choose between job security and parenting;

(4) there is inadequate job security for employees who have serious health conditions that prevent them from working for temporary periods;

(5) due to the nature of the roles of men and women in our society, the primary responsibility for family caretaking often falls on women, and such responsibility affects the working lives of women more than it affects the working lives of men; and

(6) employment standards that apply to one gender only have serious potential for encouraging employers to discriminate against employees and applicants for employment who are of that gender.

(b) Purposes. It is the purpose of this Act

(1) to balance the demands of the workplace with the needs of families, to promote the stability and economic security of families, and to promote national interests in preserving family integrity;

(2) to entitle employees to take reasonable leave for medical reasons, for the birth or adoption of a child, and for the care of a child, spouse, or parent who has a serious health condition;

(3) to accomplish [these purposes] in a manner that accommodates the legitimate interests of employers;

(4) to accomplish [these purposes] in a manner that, consistent with the Equal Protection Clause of the Fourteenth Amendment, minimizes the potential for employment discrimination on the basis of sex by ensuring generally that leave is available for eligible medical reasons (including maternity-related disability) and for compelling family reasons, on a gender-neutral basis; and

(5) to promote the goal of equal employment opportunity for women and men, pursuant to such clause.

§ 2611. Definitions

(2)(A) "[E]ligible employee" means an employee who has been employed—

(i) for at least 12 months by the employer with respect to whom leave is requested under section [2612]; and

(ii) for at least 1,250 hours of service with such employer during the previous 12-month period.

(4)(A)"[E]mployer"—

(i) means any person engaged in commerce or in any industry or activity affecting commerce who employs 50 or more employees [within a 75 mile radius of the worksite]. . . .

(5) "[E]mployment benefits" means all benefits provided or made available to employees by an employer, including group life insurance, health insurance, disability insurance, sick leave, annual leave, educational benefits, and pensions. . . .

(7) '[P]arent" means the biological parent of an employee or an individual who stood in loco parentis to an employee when the employee was a son or daughter. . . .

(11)"[S]erious health condition" means an illness, injury, impairment, or physical or mental condition that involves

(A) inpatient care in a hospital, hospice, or residential medical care facility; or

(B) continuing treatment by a health care provider.

(12) "[S]on or daughter" means a biological, adopted, or foster child, a stepchild, a legal ward, or a child of a person standing in loco parentis, who is

(A) under 18 years of age; or

(B) 18 years of age or older and incapable of self-care because of a mental or physical disability.

(13) "[S]pouse" means a husband or wife, as the case may be.

§ 2612. Leave requirement

(a) In general.

(1) Entitlement to leave. [A]n eligible employee shall be entitled to a total of 12 workweeks of leave during any 12-month period for one or more of the following:

(A) Because of the birth of a son or daughter of the employee and in order daughter.

(B) Because of the placement of a son or daughter with the employee for adoption or foster care.

(C) In order to care for the spouse, or a son, daughter, or parent, of the employee, if such spouse, son, daughter, or parent has a serious health condition.

(D) Because of a serious health condition that makes the employee unable to perform the functions of the position of such employee.

(2) Expiration of entitlement. The entitlement to leave under subparagraphs (A) and (B) of paragraph (1) for a birth or placement of a son or daughter shall expire at the end of the 12-month period beginning on the date of such birth or placement.

(b) Leave taken intermittently or on a reduced leave schedule.

(1) In general. Leave under subparagraph (A) or (B) of subsection (a)(1) shall not be taken by an employee intermittently or on a reduced leave schedule unless the employee and the employer of the employee agree otherwise. . . .

(c) Unpaid Leave Permitted. Except as provided in subsection (d), leave granted under [the FMLA] may consist of unpaid leave. . . .

(e) Foreseeable Leave.

(1) Requirement of notice. In any case in which the necessity for leave under subparagraph (A) or (B) of subsection (a)(1) is foreseeable based on an expected birth or placement, the employee shall provide the employer with not less than 30 days' notice, before the date the leave is to begin, of the employee's intention to take leave under such subparagraph, except that if the date of the birth or placement requires leave to begin in less than 30 days, the employee shall provide such notice as is practicable. . . .

(f) Spouses Employed by the Same Employer. In any case in which a husband and wife entitled to leave under subsection (a) are employed by the same employer, the aggregate number of workweeks of leave to which both may be entitled may be limited to 12 workweeks during any 12-month period. . . .

§ 2614 Employment and Benefits Protection

(a) Restoration to position.

(1) In general. Except as provided in subsection (b), any eligible employee who takes leave under section [2612] for the intended purpose of the leave shall be entitled, on return from such leave

    (A) to be restored by the employer to the position of employment held by the employee when the leave commenced; or

    (B) to be restored to an equivalent position with equivalent employment benefits, pay, and other terms and conditions of employment.

(2) Loss of benefits. The taking of leave under section [2612] shall not result in the loss of any employment benefit accrued prior to the date on which the leave commenced.

(3) Limitations. Nothing in this section shall be construed to entitle any restored employee to

    (A) the accrual of any seniority or employment benefits during any period of leave; or

    (B) any right, benefit, or position of employment other than any right, benefit, or position to which the employee would have been entitled had the employee not taken the leave. . . .

(c) Maintenance of health benefits.

(1) . . . [D]uring any period that an eligible employee takes leave under section [2612], the employer shall maintain coverage under any "group health plan" for the duration of such leave at the level and under the conditions coverage would have been provided if the employee had continued in employment continuously for the duration of such leave. . . .

KELLY v. CROSFIELD CATALYSTS
United States Court of Appeals
135 F.3d 1202 (7th Cir.1998)

JAMES B. MORAN, JUDGE

Dwayne Kelley allegedly received authorization from his employer, Crosfield Catalysts ("Crosfield"), to travel to New York in order to "seek custody of [a young girl] for foster care or adoption." Second Amended Complaint at 2. Kelley's trip for this purpose caused him to miss four days of scheduled work. Crosfield terminated Kelley on his next work day on account of this four-day absence; Kelley claims that the dismissal was pretextual and in violation of the Family and Medical Leave Act (FMLA). The district court dismissed Kelley's Second Amended Complaint under Federal Rule of Civil Procedure 12(b)(6) for failure to state a claim. We disagree with the district court's characterization of the Second Amended Complaint, and we therefore reverse the dismissal and remand the case for further proceedings.

I. BACKGROUND

Dwayne Kelley began working for Crosfield as a laboratory technician on August 1, 1992. This position required Kelley to work twelve-hour shifts for four consecutive days followed by three consecutive "off" days. Kelley was scheduled to begin a four-day work rotation on October 22, 1993, when he unexpectedly received a phone call from his mother. His mother informed him that the Brooklyn Bureau of Child Welfare was preparing to take custody of Shaneequa Forbes, an eleven-year-old girl. Shaneequa was born into the marriage of Barbara and Michael Forbes, but—although this information was not contained in his Second Amended Complaint—Kelley had reason to believe that he might be the girl's biological father. He told his supervisors at Crosfield that Shaneequa was his daughter. Kelley missed four scheduled workdays while attending to this matter in New York. On his first day back at work, October 29, Crosfield terminated Kelley's employment.

The parties' pleading maneuvers constitute the focus of this appeal. Kelley filed a pro se complaint on October 26, 1995, which alleged that his termination violated the FMLA because he took leave from work in order to "obtain custody." Crosfield filed a motion to dismiss this complaint under Rule 12(b)(6), arguing that seeking custody of one's own children was not covered by the FMLA. Before the district court ruled on Crosfield's motion, Kelley filed an amended pro se complaint on April 25, 1996. The amended complaint stated only that the child "grew up" with Kelley, and it referenced Shaneequa's birth certificate on which Barbara and Michael Forbes are listed as the girl's biological parents.

The parties discussed the matter of Shaneequa's parentage at a status hearing regarding the amended complaint five days after it was filed. Kelley admitted there was some confusion about whether he was Shaneequa's father. He stated, "Your Honor, I was told—there is nothing in any records showing that I am the father. I was told that I was the father. So I took this as I'm being the father. But as of late, I found out that I might not even be the father. On record, I am not the father." Based on this colloquy, Crosfield moved to dismiss the amended complaint for failure to state a claim, arguing that obtaining custody of one's own child was not a protected activity under the FMLA.

Kelley soon after retained counsel for the first time and, with Crosfield's consent, filed a Second Amended Complaint. This is the complaint that is the subject of the instant appeal. Crosfield once again moved to dismiss Kelley's complaint pursuant to Rule 12(b)(6) based on his prior admissions to the court that (1) he was Shaneequa's biological father, and (2) he sought leave from work to obtain custody of her. Kelley responded to the motion by pointing out that his Second Amended Complaint did not allege that he was Shaneequa's biological father; it stated only that he took leave for the purpose of taking the child into foster care or adoption. Any admissions from prior pleadings, Kelley argued, were functus officio, or of no further effect, and superseded by the Second Amended Complaint for purposes of the Rule 12(b)(6) determination. Even if the admissions were still valid, Kelley contended that he stated a claim under the FMLA because it is possible to seek custody of one's biological child through adoption or foster care when one currently enjoys no parental rights with respect to the child.

The district court granted Crosfield's motion to dismiss Kelley's Second Amended Complaint. The court first credited Kelley's statements from prior superseded pleadings that he was Shaneequa's biological father. Then, the court stated that the words "adoption" and "foster care" in the FMLA should be given their normal meaning; establishing custody over one's own child would not, in the court's view, qualify under the normal meaning of those words: "An emergency trip to rescue one's own child from a state proceeding does not fit within those definitions or the statutory scheme." . . .

II. DISCUSSION

. . . The Family and Medical Leave Act of 1993 affords flexibility in employment for medical or family emergencies to anyone working at least 1250 hours per year at a business employing fifty or more people for at least twenty weeks of the year. Congressional hearings revealed that the FMLA was needed to help balance the demands of work and family, as well as to ease the burden of caretaking among individual family members. The provision of the FMLA most relevant to the instant appeal is 29 U.S.C. § 2612(a)(1)(B), which provides that eligible employees may receive twelve weeks of excused leave per year "because of the placement of a son or daughter with the employee for adoption or foster care."

Kelley's Second Amended Complaint did not make any reference to Shaneequa's biological parentage. It only stated that he traveled to New York to "seek custody of Shaneequa for foster care or adoption." Thus, based on the allegations of the Second Amended Complaint alone, the issue of Kelley's biological connection to Shaneequa was not before the district court. It is apparent, however, that the court considered Shaneequa's biological parentage by concluding that Kelley's emergency trip to New York did not fit within the meaning of the FMLA. The only way the court could have considered that issue was by looking outside the pleadings to Kelley's prior pleadings and colloquy with the court in a status hearing on a rescinded complaint.

This is not a permissible practice. It is well-established that an amended pleading supersedes the original pleading; facts not incorporated into the amended pleading are considered *functus officio*. If certain facts or admissions from the original complaint become *functus officio*, they cannot be considered by the court on a motion to dismiss the amended complaint. A court cannot resuscitate these facts when assessing whether the amended complaint states a viable claim. . . .

In addition, we think it is important to note that Kelley could have stated a viable FMLA claim even if his Second Amended Complaint had declared that he was the biological father of Shaneequa. The district court believed that the "usual sense" of the relevant FMLA terms "adoption" and "foster care" did not encompass a situation in which a biological father takes custody of his own child. Indeed, the Department of Labor has defined the term "adoption" as used in the FMLA as the "legal process in which an individual becomes the legal parent of another's child." 5 C.F.R. § 630.1202 (emphasis added). The court seemed to fear that allowing one to adopt one's own child or to take the child into foster care would grant FMLA coverage to run-of-the-mill custody disputes.

This is not just another custody case, though, and we believe that Kelley could state a valid claim under the FMLA. Dismissal of an action under Rule 12(b)(6) is warranted only if Kelley could prove no set of facts in support of his claims that would entitle him to relief. When faced with ambiguities in this inquiry, we give the benefit of any doubt to the plaintiff. We do not believe that the statutory terms and regulatory definitions bar Kelley's suit. The FMLA defines "son or daughter" as "a biological, adopted, or foster child, a stepchild, a legal ward, or a child of a person standing in loco parentis." 29 U.S.C. § 2611(12). Thus, in light of this definition, the FMLA expressly protects leaves taken "because of the placement of a [biological child] with an employee for adoption or foster care." 29 U.S.C. § 2612(a)(1)(B). Furthermore, Kelley was not Shaneequa's father of record—unlike the usual situation in custody disputes—and he would have sought leave to take custody of a child who (according to public record) was "another's child."

It will indeed be unusual to encounter a situation in which a biological parent takes a leave from work in order to adopt or take into foster care his own child. This situation may be rare, but Kelley has proven that it is not entirely impossible. In a case such as this in which a biological parent has no custodial rights over a child and is not listed as the child's parent as a matter of record, it may be possible for that parent to adopt his own child. Thus, regardless of whether he was the biological father, Kelley could state a claim under the FMLA....

NOTES AND QUESTIONS

(1) The Family and Medical Leave Act (FMLA) was enacted after a lengthy legislative battle. It was initially proposed in 1985, and was vetoed twice by President George Bush before being signed into law by President Bill Clinton in February, 1993. *See* Robin R. Cockey and Deborah A. Jeon, *The Family and Medical Leave Act at Work: Getting Employers to Value Families*, 4 Va. J. Soc. Pol'y & L. 225, 262 (1996). According to two legal experts who helped draft the FMLA, the Act was motivated by three main concepts: "First, the FMLA was drafted to respond to the changing face of the American workforce and to recognize employees' needs to balance their family and job responsibilities.... A second major concept underlying the FMLA is that family and medical emergencies happen to all employees, not just females. Men, as well as women, need family and medical leave.... The final concept underlying the FMLA is that it—like child labor, minimum wage, employment discrimination, safety and health, and pension and welfare benefit laws—creates a minimum labor standard." Donna Lenhoff and Claudia Withers, *Implementation of the Family and Medical Leave Act: Toward the Family-Friendly Workplace*, 3 Am. U. J. Gender & Law 39, 47–50 (1994).

(2) During the legislative debates, opponents of the FMLA contended that the Act would have a serious negative impact on business. However, a 1996 Progress Report to Congress, mandated by the Act, suggests that these concerns have not materialized. While more than two-thirds of FMLA-covered worksites have changed their leave policies in order to comply

with the Act, the Report indicates that most covered employers find it relatively easy to administer the Act's requirements. *See* U.S. Commission on Leave, A Workable Balance: Report to Congress on Family and Medical Leave Policies xviii, 176 (1996) ("A Workable Balance"). Fewer than 10% of the employers surveyed reported negative effects on any area of business performance as a result of the FMLA, and fewer than 5% felt that the FMLA negatively affected any aspect of employee performance. *Id.* at 125–31. Employees also report generally positive experiences with family and medical leave. . . .

(3) According to the 1996 progress report, the FMLA has had a significant impact on employers' leave practices and policies. Approximately two thirds of the U.S. labor force, including public and private employees, work for employers covered by the FMLA, and slightly more than half of all workers also meet the Act's length of service and minimum hours requirements for eligibility for leave. A Workable Balance, *above*, at xvii. The report also found that while almost 17% of all U.S. workers took leave for a reason covered by the FMLA, only a small percentage of those workers designated their leave as "FMLA leave." *Id.* at 83–84. More than 60% of the employees who took FMLA leave did so because of their own serious health problem, and an additional 20% took leave to care for a seriously ill spouse, child or parent. Only 13.3% of beneficiaries took leave because of the birth or adoption of a child, and 3.8% took leave for maternity-related disability. *Id.* at 94. The demographic profile of leave-takers generally resembles that of the overall employee population. While women are somewhat more likely than men to utilize FMLA leave overall, men are more likely than women to take leave for their own serious health conditions and to care for an ill spouse (which probably includes caring for their wives before or after childbirth). Woman are more likely than men to care for seriously ill children or parents. *Id.* at 95.

(4) How do the protections contained in the FMLA differ from those of Title VII and the Pregnancy Discrimination Act? How does the FMLA differ from the California maternity leave statute at issue in *Guerra*? If the FMLA had been in effect at the time that Lillian Garland (the plaintiff in *Guerra*) had sought to return to work after her pregnancy-disability leave, would the Act have required her reinstatement? Why or why not? Would the FMLA have entitled Gerald Schafer to the one-year childrearing leave that he requested from the Pittsburgh School Board?

(5) How well does the FMLA accommodate the needs of low-and moderate-income workers? At least one commentator has argued that mandating unpaid parental leave is contrary to the interests of the working poor, since few of them will be able to afford such leave and since the costs associated with mandated employee benefits are likely to impact most heavily on their wages and job opportunities. *See* Maria O-Brien Hylton, *"Parental Leaves and Poor Women": Paying the Price for Time Off*, 52 U. Pitt. L. Rev. 475, 477 (1991).

(6) **Interaction of the FMLA with State Family Leave Laws**. Prior to passage of the FMLA, a substantial number of states had enacted their own family and/or medical leave statutes. *See* Comment, *The Family and Medical Leave Act of 1993: A Great Idea But A "Rube Goldberg" Solution?* 43 Emory L. J. 1351, 1405 (1994) (noting that thirty-four states, the District of Columbia and Puerto Rico provide some form of maternity, family, or medical leave). The FMLA preempts only those state laws that are less generous than the federal statute; it does not supercede or modify any state or local law that provides greater family

or medical leave rights than the rights established under the FMLA. 29 U.S.C. § 2651(b) (1997). Whether a state or local law provides greater or lesser protection than the FMLA will depend on the precise reasons for the leave, as well as other specifics of the employee's and the employer's situation. Thus, an employer must evaluate the facts of a specific leave request against both state and federal law to determine which law will govern which aspects of the leave. For additional discussion of the issues posed by the interaction of the FMLA with state laws, see Comment, *above*, at 1403–11.

(7) **Interaction of the FMLA with Other Federal Legislation.** The FMLA also overlaps with a number of other federal statutes, including the Americans with Disabilities Act (ADA), the Fair Labor Standards Act (FLSA) and the Employee Retirement Income & Security Act (ERISA). The overlap between the FMLA and the ADA is particularly significant where an employee requests leave because of his or her own "serious health condition." For additional discussion of the interplay between the FMLA and other federal laws, see Comment, *The Family and Medical Leave Act of 1993: A Great Idea But A "Rube Goldberg" Solution?* 43 Emory L. J. 1351, 1411–20 (1994); Jane Rigler, *Analysis and Understanding of the Family and Medical Leave Act of 1993,* 45 Case W. Res. L. Rev. 457, 495–504 (1995).

(8) **FMLA Litigation.** The FMLA has already generated a significant amount of litigation. One of the most frequently litigated issues has been the definition of "serious health condition." This definition is central to the Act's coverage, since an employee is entitled to take leave when she or a qualified family member has a serious health condition. The FMLA defines a serious health condition as "an illness, injury, impairment, or physical or mental condition that involves (A) inpatient care in a hospital, hospice, or residential medical care facility; or (B) continuing treatment by a health care provider." 29 U.S.C. § 2611(11). The Department of Labor has issued regulations that elaborate on each of these requirements (*see* 29 C.F.R. § 825.114 (1998)), and a number of federal courts have also addressed the question of what constitutes a serious health condition. *E.g. Brannon v. OshKosh B'Gosh, Inc.*, 897 F. Supp. 1028 (M.D. Tenn. 1995) (employee's upper respiratory infection did not constitute serious heath condition, but her daughter's similar illness, which precipitated an emergency room visit and for which a physician recommended several days of home care, met FMLA requirements); *George v. Associated Stationers*, 932 F. Supp. 1012 (N.D. Ohio 1996)) (adult case of chicken pox constituted serious health condition, where doctor instructed employee to stay off work while he was contagious). For further discussion of these decisions, *see* Kelly Druten, *The Family and Medical Leave Act: What Is A Serious Health Condition?* 46 Kan. L. Rev. 183 (1997).

(9) **FMLA Problem.** For this and the following two problems, assume that the employer is covered by the FMLA and that the affected employee meets the general eligibility requirements for benefits under the Act.

Until her recent termination, Audrey Seidle worked as a Claims Examiner at Provident Insurance Company. On Tuesday, October 12, at approximately 5:00 a.m., Audrey's four-year-old son, Terrance, work up from his sleep with a high fever. Audrey called her pediatrician, Dr. Johnson, who instructed her to administer Tylenol and to bring Terrance in for an appointment later that day. Audrey then left a message on her supervisor's voice mail, indicating that she would not be at work that day. In the early afternoon, Dr. Johnson examined Terrance and determined that he was suffering from "right otitis media," an infection of the right ear. Dr. Johnson prescribed an oral antibiotic and instructed Audrey to keep Terrance home from day care for the next 2 days, or until he was free of fever for 48 hours. Audrey called her employer and explained that she would be unable to work for the next two days (Wednesday and Thursday) because of her son's illness. By Thursday evening, Terrance had been free of fever for 48 hours, and seemed to be feeling better, although he still had a cough and a runny nose. On Friday, October 15th, Audrey attempted to bring Terrance to his day care center, but the center refused to accept Terrance because of its policy prohibiting children with "coughs and runny noses" from attending. Audrey then called her supervisor and explained that she needed another day off to care for her son. The supervisor indicated that Audrey would be charged with an unexcused absence, and reminded Audrey that she had already used up all of her available personal leave. When Audrey returned to work on Monday, October 18th, she was informed that she was being terminated due to "excessive absenteeism." Does Audrey have viable grounds to challenge her termination under the FMLA? Why or why not? *See Seidle v. Provident Mutual Life Insurance Company*, 871 F. Supp. 238 (E.D. Pa. 1994).

(9) **FMLA Problem.** As above, assume that the employer is covered by the FMLA and that the affected employee meets the general eligibility requirements for benefits under the Act. Lora Ilhardt worked as an in-house attorney for the Sara Lee Corporation for approximately five years. After the birth of her first child three years ago, Ilhardt negotiated a part-time arrangement with her employer, under which she worked three days a week, and her salary and benefits were pro-rated accordingly. Ilhardt was the only attorney in the department who worked part time. Her part-time status initially caused some inconvenience, but both clients and co-workers were satisfied with Ilhardt's work, and she received high marks in her biannual performance reviews. Approximately 6 months ago, Ilhardt informed the head of the legal department that she was expecting her second child and that she planned to take a three-month maternity leave after the child's birth. The department head expressed some annoyance with Ilhardt's request, explaining that the company was pressuring the legal department to increase its productivity and to reduce its expenses. Shortly before Ilhardt was to start her maternity leave, the head of the legal department informed her that her part-time position was being eliminated and that, if she wished to return after her leave, she would have to have to return to a full-time position that required extensive travel. Ilhardt indicated that she was not interested in such a position. Ilhardt's second child was born 10 weeks ago, and she has been on maternity leave since that time. Recently, Ilhardt contacted her supervisor to indicate her readiness to return to work. The supervisor responded that Ilhardt could not return because her position had been eliminated and there were no openings in the legal department. Has Ilhardt's employer violated the FMLA? Why or why not? *See Ilhardt v. Sara Lee Corp.*, 118 F.3d 1151 (7th Cir. 1997).

(9) **FMLA Problem.** As above,, assume that the employer is covered by the FMLA and that the affected employee meets the general eligibility requirements for benefits under the Act. Juan Garcia is a law professor at an East Coast university. His mother, a 68-year-old widow, lives in California. Two weeks into the fall semester, Garcia's mother is diagnosed with cancer. Surgery is scheduled for the next week, to be followed by 8 weeks of chemotherapy. Garcia asks the university for a leave of absence for the remainder of the semester to care for his mother after surgery and during the course of her chemotherapy. Does the FMLA require the university to grant Garcia's request? Why or why not?

PRICKET v. CIRCUIT SCIENCE, INC.
Supreme Court of Minnesota
518 N.W.2d 602 (1994)

EN BANC. WAHL.

Appellant Commissioner of Jobs and Training asks us to decide whether an employee's failure to report for a new shift assignment because of an inability to obtain child care for the employee's dependent child constitutes misconduct justifying the denial of unemployment compensation. Under the facts of this case, we hold that it does not.

In April of 1991 Respondent David Prickett was employed as a maintenance mechanic with Respondent Circuit Science, Inc. (CSI) in Minneapolis. Prickett worked the first shift, which began at 6:50 a.m. and ended at 3:20 p.m. He was a single father who had agreed, less than one week prior to April 17, 1991, to take temporary custody of his three year old son, Kyle, while the child's mother was in Iowa attending to a family crisis.

At the beginning of Prickett's shift on Friday, April 17, 1991, Prickett's supervisor informed him that he would be required temporarily to work the second shift effective Monday, April 20, 1991. The second shift began at 3:20 p.m. and ended at 11:30 p.m. Prickett stated that he would not be able to report for the second shift on Monday because of babysitting problems.

Over the weekend, Prickett visited with his mother and asked her to take time off from work to care for Kyle. She stated that she could not. Prickett's sister, who was visiting, also was unable to care for Kyle. Prickett called his supervisor, Jeff Kussi, from his mother's house and told Kussi that he was having trouble finding child care.

On Monday, Prickett reported for work at the first shift and told his supervisor that he could not find child care for the second shift. Prickett's supervisor gave him the day off to find child care. Over the next three days, Prickett inquired at five licensed facilities, none of which offered care after 6:30 p.m. Prickett also asked the neighbor who usually watched Kyle during the day if she could care for Kyle in the evening, but because of her own family obligations she was unable to do so.

On April 23, 1992, Prickett met with Supervisor Kussi, CSI Plant Manager Earl Monchamp, CSI Vice President Terry Lutts, and a union representative to discuss the situation. Someone at the meeting suggested that Prickett ask Greg and Lori Voight, friends and coworkers of Prickett's, to watch Kyle. Prickett, however, already had discussed his situation with Lori Voight and had asked her if she would be able to care for Kyle temporarily. Ms. Voight told him that she did not think it would work out. Although this conversation took place prior to April 23, Prickett did not mention it at the meeting. Prior to the meeting, Lutts had spoken with Greg Voight who stated that he was "more willing to do this as it was a temporary situation." Lutts did not approach Ms. Voight on the matter. After the meeting, Prickett spoke with Greg Voight. Greg Voight told Prickett he felt the arrangement would be quite difficult because Prickett would have to bring Kyle to CSI where he would wait for two hours until the Voights got off their shift, and then Prickett would have to pick Kyle up from the Voights' home at approximately 1:00 am. Mr. Voight, however, said that the decision was "basically up to Lori."

On April 24, 27, and 28, Prickett was suspended from work for his unexcused absences. On April 29, Prickett again called to explain that he would not report for work during the second shift because he did not have child care. CSI then terminated Prickett's employment.

Prickett filed for unemployment compensation benefits on May 3, 1992. On May 19, 1992, a Department of Jobs and Training Claims Representative denied Prickett's claim on the ground that Prickett had voluntarily quit his employment without good cause attributable to the employer. On appeal, a Referee, after an evidentiary hearing, found that Prickett was disqualified from receiving unemployment compensation benefits because he had been discharged for misconduct due to his absences. The Referee also found that CSI had arranged temporary child care with the Voights, but that Prickett had refused to use it. The Representative of the Commissioner affirmed the Referee's decision. The court of appeals reversed, holding that the rule . . . that inability to obtain child care for certain shifts rendered the claimants "unavailable for work" and justified denial of benefits, had been "substantially eroded by time" and was "ill suited to modern child-care realities." *Prickett v. Circuit Science. Inc.*, 499 N.W.2d 506, 509 (Minn. App. 1993). We granted review.

The unemployment compensation statute is remedial in nature and must be liberally construed to effectuate the public policy set out in Minn. Stat. § 268.03 (1992). Since § 268.03 includes the statement that "unemployment reserves [are] to be used for the benefit of persons unemployed through no fault of their own," the disqualification provisions of the unemployment compensation statute must be narrowly construed.

The standard for determining whether a claimant is disqualified because of termination for misconduct is stated in Minn. Stat. § 268.09 subd. 1(b) (1992):

> Subdivision 1. Disqualifying conditions. An individual separated from any employment under paragraph . . . (b) . . . shall be disqualified for waiting week credit and benefits. . . .
>
> (b) Discharge for misconduct. The individual was discharged for misconduct, not amounting to gross misconduct connected with work or for misconduct which interferes with and adversely affects employment.

We adopted a widely accepted definition of the term "misconduct" in *In re Claim of Tilseth*, 295 Minn. 372, 374–75, 204 N.W.2d 644, 646 (Minn. 1973):

> The intended meaning of the term 'misconduct' . . . is limited to conduct evincing such willful or wanton disregard of an employer's interests as is found in deliberate violations or disregard of standards of behavior which the employer has the right to expect of his employee, or in carelessness or negligence of such degree or recurrence as to manifest equal culpability, wrongful intent or evil design, or to show an intentional and substantial disregard of the employer's interests or of the employee's duties and obligations to his employer. On the other hand mere inefficiency, unsatisfactory conduct, failure in good performance as the result of inability or incapacity, inadvertencies or ordinary negligence in isolated instances, or good-faith errors in judgment or discretion are not to be deemed 'misconduct.'

Absenteeism qualifies as misconduct. *Moeller v. Minnesota Dep't of Transp.*, 281 N.W.2d 879, 882 (Minn. 1979).

Prickett's conduct in this case is not conduct evincing willful or wanton disregard of an employer's interests and it does not indicate that Prickett had a lack of concern for his job. Rather, Prickett's conduct is more a "failure in good performance as the result of inability." *Tilseth*, 295 Minn. at 375, 204 N.W.2d at 646.

The change in Prickett's shift was substantial and he was given only three days, over a weekend, during which to find nighttime child care. Prickett demonstrated that he had made good faith efforts to obtain adequate child care and that it was unavailable to him. He maintained contact with his employer and reported, daily, that he had been unable to obtain child care.

Given the facts of this case, where the employee is given three days' notice of a shift change, where the shift change is substantial, and where the employee presents sufficient evidence of good faith efforts to obtain child care, we hold that the employee's failure to report to a new shift assignment because of an inability to obtain adequate care for the employee's dependents does not constitute misconduct justifying denial of unemployment compensation benefits. To hold otherwise would be to ignore significant facts about the world today. In 1990, almost 60% of children in Minnesota lived in families in which both parents worked outside the home. Population Reference Bureau for the Center for the Study of Social Policy, The Challenge of Change: What the 1990 Census Tells Us About Children 43 (1992). Another 9.3% lived in families with one working parent. *Id.* If Prickett had left his child without supervision, he would have been subject to criminal sanctions. Minn. Stat. § 609.378 (1992). He also could have been sanctioned for failure to support Kyle. Minn. Stat. § 609.375 (1992). Under these limited circumstances, Prickett seemed to have no choice but to do as he did and we cannot hold that he engaged in "wilful misconduct." . . .

NOTES AND QUESTIONS

(1) Would the FMLA have precluded Circuit Sciences from terminating Prickett's employment because of the absences caused by his Prickett's inability to find childcare? Why or why not?

(2) Work-family conflicts may continue to create difficulties for employees who initially qualify for unemployment benefits. To remain eligible for benefits, an unemployment claimant must be "available for work." Employees who restrict their job search to certain shifts or certain days of the week to avoid conflicts with family obligations may be deemed "unavailable" for work, and thereby disqualified from receiving benefits. *See* Martin H. Malin, *Unemployment Compensation in A Time of Increasing Work-Family Conflicts*, 29 U. Mich. J. L. Reform 131, 150–52 (1996) (discussing cases); Deborah Maranville, *Feminist Theory and Legal Practice: A Case Study on Unemployment Compensation Benefits and the Male Norm*, 43 Hastings L.J. 1081 (1992) (describing Washington state system which disqualifies unemployment claimants who limit their hours of availability or limit their job searches to part-time employment). Similarly, claimants may lose their eligibility if they decline particular job offers because the offered position conflicts with family responsibilities. Malin, *above*, at 147–50.

(3) **Problem.** Suppose that, one month after his termination, David Prickett assumes long-term custody of his three-year-old son. Shortly thereafter, Circuit Science offers to rehire Prickett for a permanent position on the second shift (3:20 p.m. to 11:30 p.m.). If Prickett declines the job offer because of his inability to find evening child care for his son, should Prickett be disqualified from receiving unemployment benefits? Why or why not?

(4) Numerous studies and surveys indicate that difficulty in finding affordable, high quality child care is a serious problem for many working parents, especially low and

moderate income workers. *See e.g.,* Clare Huntington, *Welfare Reform and Child Care, A Proposal for State Legislation*, 6 Cornell J. L. & Publ. Pol'y 95 (1996) (documenting shortage of child care for low income families, particularly the working poor); Martin H. Malin, *Unemployment Compensation in A Time of Increasing Work-Family Conflicts*, 29 U. Mich. J. L. Reform 131, 134 (1996) ("The frequent shortage of reasonably priced, competent child care aggravates the tension between workers' availability to their jobs and their availability to their families."); Thomas R. Marton, *Child-Centered Child Care: An Argument for a Class Integrated Approach*, 1993 U. Chi. L. Sch. Roundtable 313 (1993) (discussing individual and social costs of our nation's inadequate and fragmented child care system). Until recently, many politicians and public officials opposed any sustained government effort to facilitate or support childcare, viewing such support as inconsistent with both free market economics and family values. Marton, *above*, at 324. In 1971, then-President Richard M. Nixon vetoed legislation that would have created federally financed child-development centers, stating that such federal support "would commit the vast moral authority of the national Government to the side of communal approaches to child rearing over and against the family-centered approach." Andrew Cherlin, *By The Numbers*, New York Times Magazine, April 5, 1998, at 39.

More recently, both federal and state governments have shown considerably more interest in facilitating and funding child care, particularly for low-income families. In 1990, Congress passed the Child Care and Development Block Grant, the first comprehensive federal attempt to improve the quantity and quality, and to reduce the cost, of child care for low-income workers. 42 U.S.C. § 9858 *et seq.* (1998). Public attention to child care has also been heightened by recent welfare reform efforts, which emphasize moving low income parents "from welfare to work," a strategy that depends critically on availability of affordable child care. Huntington, *above* at 99–104. To this end, the Personal Responsibility and Work Opportunity Reconciliation Act of 1996 consolidates and significantly increases funding for federal child care programs and places all new child care initiatives under the auspices of a Child Care and Development Fund, administered by the Department of Health and Human Services. 45 CFR § 98; *see* Jo Ann C. Gong, *Child Care in the Wake of the Federal Welfare Act*, 30 Clearinghouse Rev. 1044 (Jan.–Feb.1997).

Additional efforts are under way in both the public and private sectors to enhance working parents' access to high quality child care. As a follow-up to the White House Conference on Child Care, held in October, 1997, several federal agencies have recently released reports on employment-related child care issues. *See, e.g.*, U.S. Department of Labor, *Meeting the Needs of Today's Workforce: Child Care Best Practices* (1998); U.S. Department of Treasury, Working Group on Child Care, *Investing in Child Care* (1998);U.S. Department of Health and Human Services, Child Care Bureau, *Promoting Family-Centered Child Care* (1998). A number of nonprofit organizations have also published studies focusing on the child care needs of a changing workforce. *E.g.*, Families and Work Institute, *The 1997 National Study of the Changing Workforce* (1977); Whirlpool Foundation, *Women: The New Providers* (1998); Deborah K. Holmes and Dana Friedman, *The Changing Employer-Employee Contract: The Role of Work-Family Issues* (1995). The number of employers providing on-site child care or other forms of child care assistance, such as referral services and flex-time, continues to grow. *See, e.g.*, Kristi Zimmeth, *Child Care Centers Become Asset to Companies, Too*, Crain's Detroit Business, May 25, 1998, at E-4; Sharon C. Nantell,

The Tax Paradigm of Child Care: Shifting Attitudes Toward a Private/Parental/Public Alliance, 80 Marq. L. Rev. 879, 886 & n.21 (1997).

However, government (and employer) support for childcare remains controversial. Conservative commentators, in particular, argue that such government support undermines traditional family structures and devalues parents who choose to stay home to care for their children. *See generally* Karl Zinmeister, *The Problem With Day Care*, The American Enterprise, May/June 1998; Maggie Gallagher, *How To Help Parents and How Not To*, The American Enterprise, May/June 1998. To what extent are these criticisms justified?

Additionally, some feminist scholars have argued that a policy that relies heavily on market-provided childcare to move mothers into the paid labor force risks devaluing the caregiving work that women have traditionally performed—and to a large extent continue to perform in the home. *See, e.g.*, Martha Albertson Fineman, The Neutered Mother and Twentieth Century Tragedies (1995); Nancy C. Staudt, *Taxing Housework*, 84 Geo. L.J. 1571, 1575–99 (1996); Dorothy E. Roberts, *The Value of Black Mothers' Work*, 26 Conn. L. Rev. 871, 871 (1994).

(5) Although the plaintiffs in both *Prickett* and *Crossfeld Catalysts* are men, studies indicate that, on average, women continue to assume a disproportionate share of the caretaking responsibilities for children and other dependents. *See, e.g.*, Families and Work Institute, *The 1997 National Study of the Changing Workforce* (1998) (reporting that although employed married women spend more time on childcare and household chores than do employed married men, the gap has narrowed significantly over the past 2 decades); *see also* 29 U.S.C. § 2601(a)(5) (1998) (acknowledging that "due to the nature of the role of men and women in our society, the primary responsibility for family caretaking often falls on women, and such responsibility affects the working lives of women more than it affects the working lives of men"). *See generally* Arlie Hochschild, The Second Shift 2–10 (1989) (discussing studies). Why do you think that men have not assumed a more equal share of family caretaking responsibilities, even as women have increased their commitment to the paid labor market? The article by Professor Martin Malin, excerpted below, explores some of the barriers to fathers' assumption of greater childcare responsibilities.

(6) What effect, if any, should the disproportionate impact of work-family conflict on women have on employer practices and polices? In a well-known, but controversial article, work-and-family consultant Felice Schwartz proposed that, in order to maximize the potential of all employees, corporations should distinguish between "career-primary" and "career-and-family" women. They should identify "career-primary" women early, afford them the same opportunities as men, accept them as valued members of management, and recognize that they face sex stereotypes. On the other hand, corporations should recognize the need to retain "career-and-family" women as mid-level managers, and should provide these employees with parental leave, flexible benefits and good, affordable child care. *See* Felice N. Schwartz, *Management Women and the New Fact of Life*, 67 Harv. Bus. Rev. 65 (Jan.-Feb. 1989). Schwartz's article provoked a heated debate in both the academic and the popular press. A number of commentators challenged Schwartz's initial assumption that women in management are more costly to employ that men; others protested the absence in her scheme of a "career-and family" track for men. For a sampling of the debate, including Schwartz's response to her critics, *see, e.g.*, Felice N. Schwartz, Breaking with Tradition: Women and Work, The New Facts of Life (1992); Tamar Lewin, *Mommy Career Track*

Sets Off Furor, New York Times, March 8, 1989, at A27; Bureau of National Affairs, *The "Mommy Track" Debate and Beyond: Public Policy? Corporate Reality?* (1989). For legal scholarship addressing these issue, see Rebecca Korzec, *Working on the "Mommy Track": Motherhood and Women Lawyers*, 8 Hastings Women's L.J. 117 (1997); Note, *Why Law Firms Cannot Afford to Maintain the Mommy Track*, 109 Harv. L. Rev. 1375 (1996); Karen Czapanskiy *Volunteers and Draftees: The Struggle for Parental Equality*, 38 U.C.L.A. L. Rev. 1415, 1455–56 (1991).

(7) In light of women's disproportionate responsibility for childcare, could a plaintiff argue that the refusal of an employer (or an educational institution) to facilitate child care constitutes unlawful sex-based discrimination? *See De La Cruz v. Tormey*, 582 F.2d 45 (9th Cir. 1978), *cert. denied*, 441 U.S. 965 (1979) (refusal of community college district to provide child care facilities deprives low income mothers of their right to be free from sex discrimination in federally funded educational programs); Catherine L. Fisk, *Employer-Provided Child Care Under Title VII: Toward an Employer's Duty to Accommodate Child Care Responsibilities of Employees*, 2 Berkeley Women's L.J. 89 (1986).

Martin H. Malin, *Fathers and Parental Leave*
72 Texas L. Rev. 1047, 1049–52, 1055–57, 1071–78 (1994)

During the mid-1980s, the research group Catalyst conducted an extensive study of family leave policies and practices among large employers. Catalyst found that thirty-seven percent of the 322 employers that responded offered unpaid parental leave to men. However, only nine companies were able to report that even one male employee ever took such a leave. More recent evidence confirms the Catalyst finding that it is rare for fathers to take parental leave. A January, 1993, survey by DuPont of its almost one thousand salaried employees who participated in its family leave program found that ninety-five percent of them were women. A 1993 Bureau of National Affairs survey found that only seven percent of male workers would take a twelve-week unpaid leave following the birth or adoption of a child whereas forty-three percent of working women would do so. Even liberal estimates place the participation rate of American fathers in parental leave programs at less than ten percent. . . .

Most discussions of greater maternal use of parental leave and greater maternal responsibility for child care accept both as givens. They focus on women's work and role overloads and on the increased stress that comes with work-family conflicts. The debate centers on how to ameliorate the effects of maternal overload on women's development in the workplace. . . .

Largely missing from maternal work-family conflicts is any discussion of paternal work-family conflicts. The two, however, are linked to a significant extent. Just as the absence of adequate maternal leave policies has been a barrier to women's roles in the workplace, the absence of adequate paternal leave policies has been a barrier to men's roles in the home. Furthermore, as long as parental leave remains de facto maternal leave, work-family conflicts will remain a significant barrier to women's employment and a significant source of discrimination against women. . . .

Current practices in the division of family labor reinforce the stereotyped views concerning the relative competence of mothers and fathers in caring for young children. The threshold decision facing new parents is who will take leave from employment to care for the newborn baby. In the typical dual-worker family, the mother will take leave but the father will not. Consequently, the mother has much greater opportunity to participate and gains much more practice in child care than the father. This may lead to greater or more rapid development of the mother's parenting skills than the father's.

More importantly, when the mother exclusively stays home following childbirth, the parents are likely to perceive the mother as developing greater knowledge of the child's needs and greater skill in meeting those needs . . .

Thus, when fathers do not take parental leave following the birth of their children, they rapidly fall behind their wives in gaining experience with the child and are perceived to be less competent. This results in marginalizing the father's role in child care and in placing the predominant burden on the mother. . . .

Barriers to Paternal Use of Parental Leave. . . .

1. Availability . . . Prior to the FMLA, this posed an absolute barrier for many working men. Employers were much more likely to provide childbirth leave to women than men. For example, Catalyst's [1986] survey of large employers found that only thirty-seven percent offered parental leave for working fathers as compared with almost fifty-two percent who offered such leave to working mothers. A broader, more recent survey by the Bureau of Labor Statistics found that in 1989, among private sector employers of one hundred or more workers, thirty-seven percent offered parental leave to full-time female employees and only eighteen percent offered it to similarly situated males. At times men have had to resort to litigation to compel their employers to grant them parental leave routinely granted to their female co-workers.

Even when leave was made available to employed fathers, pre-FMLA employer policies tended to hide it from them. For example, Catalyst found that ninety percent of large companies that offered parental leave for men did so under the rubric of personal leaves of absence and made no attempt to inform their workforce that the leaves were available to new fathers. It was rare for a company expressly to advise male employees of the availability of paternity or parental leave. Consequently, many men failed to take parental leave because they were completely unaware that it was an available option. Instead, fathers tended to create makeshift leaves of short duration by using accrued vacation and personal days. . . .

2. Financing Parental Leave. Paid paternal leave policies are extremely rare. When parental leave is available to men, it is almost always without pay. Many mothers, on the other hand, are able to take the initial part of a leave following childbirth as disability leave, which often includes full or partial income replacement benefits. The rarity of paid leave for fathers means that almost all working parents face one of two situations: initial paid leave available to the mother coupled with unpaid leave available to the father or unpaid leave available to both parents. In both cases, the absence of pay poses a major barrier to the father's ability to take leave.

When the leave available to the mother is paid and the leave available to the father is not, it sends a signal to the parents that the mother is expected to take leave and the father is not. It becomes easy for the father not to take leave by reasoning that the children will be cared for with little or no drop in household income if only the mother stays home.

When the leave available to both parents is unpaid, the situation is worsened. Because very few families can afford to have no one bringing home a paycheck, unpaid leave forces fathers to compete with mothers for its use. Traditional sex roles that assign primary caregiving responsibilities to mothers and primary breadwinning responsibilities to fathers ensure that when both parents compete for taking leaves, the mother will tend to monopolize the leave. The decision to allocate the unpaid leave to the mother is also economically rational for many couples in which the father earns the higher income.

The birth of a child usually results in an increase in household expenses and is often accompanied by a decrease in maternal contribution to household income. This exacerbates the effects of the lack of adequate funding for paternal parental leaves. As the family's need for absolute goods like diapers and children's clothing increases, its income level relative to other households is threatened. . . .;

3. *Workplace Hostility.* Employer sensitivity to the need to accommodate workers' family responsibilities is increasing steadily. Unfortunately, many employers' willingness to make such accommodations is limited to women workers. Men's accommodation requests are often met by, "Your wife should handle it."

The Catalyst survey graphically illustrates the extent of employer hostility to male employees taking parental leave. Large employers are least likely to experience negative financial effects from fathers taking parental leave. Yet, Catalyst found that sixty-three percent of large employers considered it unreasonable for a man to take any parental leave, and another seventeen percent considered paternal leave reasonable only if limited to two weeks or less. Even among large employers providing paternal leave, an amazing forty-one percent considered it unreasonable for a man to actually use it, and another twenty-three percent considered a reasonable leave for a man to be two weeks or less! It appears that many employers extend parental leave to fathers so that they can give the appearance of gender-neutral policies, but never intend for fathers to use it. . . .

Employers are not the only source of workplace hostility. Co-worker hostility can generate powerful peer pressure. Such peer pressure can intimidate and deter fathers from taking leave.

Even when leave is available and communicated to employees and financial barriers are removed, workplace hostility can deter many fathers from taking leave. In Sweden, there is considerable evidence that workplace hostility remains a significant barrier to paternal involvement in the parental leave program. On the other hand, there is anecdotal evidence in the United States that when an employer not only provides parental leave, but also sanctions its use, men actively participate in the program. . . .

NOTES AND QUESTIONS

(1) In light of the barriers identified by Professor Malin, and the apparent long-term effects of the initial division of family labor, should fathers be *required* to take leave from their employment upon the birth or adoption of a child? If so, should employers be required to pay for such leave?

(2) Is encouraging a more equal division of household and family labor an appropriate goal for family law? Why or why not? Is it possible for family law to remain neutral about the division of labor within the family?

CHAPTER 3

CONSENSUAL ALTERNATIVES TO MARRIAGE

SYNOPSIS

§ 3.01 Introduction
§ 3.02 Disputes Between Unmarried Cohabitants
    [A] The Role of Contract
    [B] Property and Partnership Theories
§ 3.03 Disputes Between Cohabitants and Third Parties
§ 3.04 Domestic Partnership Legislation

§ 3.01 Introduction

Although marriage remains a central legal and social institution, an increasing number of Americans are establishing family relationships outside of marriage. According to the U.S. Census Bureau, there were more than 4 million unmarried couple households in the United States in 1997—more than twice as many as in 1980, and almost 8 times as many as in 1970. Bureau of the Census, U.S. Dept. Of Commerce, *Current Population Reports, Serier P20-506, Marital Status and Living Arrangements: March 1997* (Update) [hereinafter "*Marital Status and Living Arrangements: March 1997*"]; *see*, Arlene F. Saluter, *Marital Status and Living Arrrangements* Marriage and Family Statistics Branch, U.S. Bureau of the Census (1994). Because the Census Bureau defines an unmarried-couple household as two adults of the opposite sex who share a housekeeping unit, this figure does not include same-sex partners. Saluter, *above* at 1. The Bureau estimates that same-sex domestic partners account for an additional 1.8 million American households. *Marital Status and Living Arrangements: March 1997* at 72 (Table 8). More than one third of all unmarried couple households include at least one child under the age of 15.

The reasons for the rise in nonmarital cohabitation are as varied as the couples themselves. For same-sex couples, formal marriage is not currently a legal option. Surveys suggest, however, that a large portion of American adults who identify themselves as lesbian or gay live with another person of the same sex and regard that person as their life partner. *See* David Chambers, *What If? The Legal Consequences of Marriage and the Legal Needs of Lesbian and Gay Male Couples*, 95 Mich. L. Rev. 447, 449 (1996); Craig A. Bowman & Blake M. Cornish, *A More Perfect Union: A Legal and Social Analysis of Domestic Partnership Ordinances*, 92 Colum. L. Rev. 1164, 1166 n.8 (1992). For younger, heterosexual couples, cohabitation is often a prelude to marriage, which tends to occur later today than in the past, for both women and men. In 1997, the median age of first marriage for men was 26.8 years, up from 23.2 years in 1970; for women, the median age of first marriage was 25.0 years, compared to 20.8 years in 1970. More than three quarters of today's eighteen-to-twenty-four-year olds remain unmarried, as do more than one third of all adults age 25 to 34. *Marital Status and Living Arrangements: March 1997* at 1 (Table 1). The tendency of young adults to delay marriage, combined with continuing high divorce rates, means that Americans spend more of their adult lives unmarried and therefore have more opportunity to live with a romantic partner. As nonmarital cohabitation has become more common, the stigma associated with it has decreased, further increasing its appeal as both a prelude and an alternative to marriage. *See* Barbara Vobejda, *Cohabitation Up 85% Over Decade*, Wash. Post, Dec. 5, 1996.

While some couples cohabit as a prelude to marriage, others choose long-term nonmarital relationships as an alternative to formal marriage, for both practical and philosophical reasons. In many such couples, one or both partners have been divorced, and are cautious about committing to marriage again. *See* Paula Lynn Parks, *Middle-Age Couples: Committed, Unmarried*, Dallas Morning News, Sept. 11, 1994, at 1-F. Indeed, some demographers estimate that the greatest increase in nonmarital cohabitation is occurring among people over the age of 35. Jennifer Steinhauer, *More Older Couples Move in Together*, Dallas Morning News, July 15, 1995, at 11C. Federal and state tax laws may discourage some dual earner couples from marrying, since their total tax liability will often be higher if they marry than if they cohabit and file separately. Chambers, *above* at 472–73; *see* Edward J. McGaffery, *Taxation and the Family: A Fresh Look at Behavioral Gender Biases in the Code*, 40 UCLA L. Rev. 983 (1993). Similar "marriage penalties" characterize the rules governing the availability of federal tax credits to low income earners, as well as the availability of federal income supplements for individuals who are aged, blind or disabled. Chambers, *above* at 473–74; *see* Anne L. Alstott, *The Earned Income Tax Credit and the Limitations of Tax-Based Welfare Reform*, 108 Harv. L. Rev. 533, 559–64 (1995). Older adults may also choose to cohabit, but not to marry, in order to avoid jeopardizing their entitlement to financial benefits, such as pensions or social security benefits, based upon a previous marriage.

The law's treatment of nonmarital cohabitation has also changed significantly over the past 25 years. Traditionally, the law viewed cohabitation relationships with disfavor, characterizing them as meretricious, and often criminal as well. Couples engaged in such relationships could not look to the courts to define their rights and obligations, or to resolve their disputes in the event that a relationship failed. Nor were unmarried cohabitants entitled to any of the statutory or common law benefits traditionally accorded married couples. More recently, this traditional view has been replaced by an increased willingness on the part of courts to resolve financial and property disputes between unmarried cohabitants. Judicial approaches to such disputes still vary considerably, however, and disagreement exists on the extent to which nonmarital cohabitation should be analogized to marriage for the purpose of determining the partners' rights and obligations toward each other. Courts, in particular, disagree about whether the relationship between unmarried cohabitants should be governed primarily by principles of contract law, or whether the law should treat nonmarital cohabitation as a status relationship, for at least some purposes.

In disputes between unmarried cohabitants and third parties, including the government, courts have been considerably more reluctant to extend to cohabitants most of the legal and economic benefits traditionally associated with marriage, although some there have been some judicial exceptions. Many courts have suggested that decisions regarding the extension of benefits to unmarried cohabitants are more properly made in the legislative arena, rather than by courts. Recently, some state and local legislative bodies have responded by passing "domestic partnership" statutes or ordinances designed to grant to unmarried cohabitants some, but not all, of the legal rights and benefits traditionally available to married couples. A number of public and private employers have also extended some employment-related benefits to unmarried couples—both heterosexual and homosexual. These measures, in turn, have engendered debate about the appropriate definition of family and about the role of law in regulating and channeling intimate behavior.

The remainder of this chapter examines three aspects of the law's treatment of nonmarital cohabitation relationships: (1) disputes between unmarried cohabitants themselves; (2) disputes between unmarried cohabitants and third parties, including the government; and (3) legislative responses to nonmarital cohabitation. The legal treatment of unmarried parents and their children is deferred until Chapter 5.

§ 3.02 Disputes Between Unmarried Cohabitants

[A] The Role of Contract

The California Supreme Court's 1976 decision in *Marvin v. Marvin* is widely viewed as a watershed in the legal system's treatment of unmarried cohabitation. As you read the following excerpts from the opinions in that case, ask yourself: (1) What each court actually decided; and (2) On what grounds each court justified its decision.

MARVIN v. MARVIN
California Supreme Court
18 Cal. 3d 660, 134 Cal. Rptr. 815, 557 P.2d 106 (1976)

TOBRINER, J.

During the past 15 years, there has been a substantial increase in the number of couples living together without marrying. Such nonmarital relationships lead to legal controversy when one partner dies or the couple separates. . . . We take this opportunity to resolve that controversy and to declare the principles which should govern distribution of property acquired in a nonmarital relationship.

We conclude: (1) The Provisions of the Family Law Act do not govern the distribution of property acquired during a nonmarital relationship; such a relationship remains subject solely to judicial decision. (2) The courts should enforce express contracts between nonmarital partners except to the extent that the contract is explicitly founded on the consideration of meretricious sexual services. (3) In the absence of an express contract, the courts should inquire into the conduct of the parties to determine whether that conduct demonstrates an implied contract, agreement of partnership or joint venture, or some other tacit understanding between the parties. The courts may also employ the doctrine of quantum meruit, or equitable remedies such as constructive or resulting trusts, when warranted by the facts of the case.

In the instant case plaintiff and defendant lived together for seven years without marrying; all property acquired during this period was taken in defendant's name. The plaintiff sued to enforce a contract under which she was entitled to half the property and to support payments, the trial court granted judgment on the pleadings for defendant, thus leaving him with all the property accumulated by the couple during their relationship. . . .

Plaintiff avers that in October of 1964 she and defendant "entered into an oral agreement" that while "the parties lived together they would combine their efforts and earnings and would share equally any and all property accumulated as a result of their efforts whether individual or combined." Furthermore, they agreed to "hold themselves out to the general public as husband and wife" and that "plaintiff would further render her services as a companion, homemaker, housekeeper and cook to defendant."

Shortly thereafter plaintiff agreed to "give up her lucrative career as an entertainer [and] singer" in order to "devote her full time to defendant as a companion, homemaker, housekeeper and cook"; in return defendant agreed to "provide for all of plaintiff's financial support and needs for the rest of her life."

Plaintiff alleges that she lived with defendant from October 1964 through May of 1970 and fulfilled her obligations under the agreement. During this period the parties as a result of their efforts and earnings acquired in defendant's name substantial real and personal property, including motion picture rights worth over $1 million. In May of 1970, however, defendant compelled plaintiff to leave his household. He continued to support plaintiff until November of 1971, but thereafter refused to provide further support.

On the basis of these allegations plaintiff asserts two causes of action. The first, for declaratory relief, asks the court to determine her contract and property rights; the second seeks to impose a constructive trust upon one half of the property acquired during the course of the relationship. . . .

2. Plaintiff's complaint states a cause of action for breach of an express contract.

In *Trutalli v. Meraviglia* (1932) 215 Cal. 698 we established the principle that nonmarital partners may lawfully contract concerning the ownership of property acquired during the relationship. We reaffirmed this principle in *Vallera v. Vallera* (1943) 21 Cal.2d 681, 685, stating that "If a man and woman [who are not married] live together as husband and wife under an agreement to pool their earnings and share equally in their joint accumulations, equity will protect the interest of each in such property." . . . .

In the case before us, Plaintiff, basing her cause of action in contract upon these precedents, maintains that the trial court erred in denying her a trial on the merits of her contention. . . . .

Defendant first and principally relies on the contention that the alleged contract is so closely related to the supposed "immoral" character of the relationship between plaintiff and himself that the enforcement of the contract would violate public policy. He points to cases asserting that a contract between nonmarital partners is unenforceable if it is "involved in" an illicit relationship. California decisions concerning contracts between nonmarital partners, however, [reveal] that the courts have not employed such broad and uncertain standards to strike down contracts. The decisions instead disclose a narrower and more precise standard: a contract between nonmarital partners is unenforceable only to the extent that it explicitly rests upon the immoral and illicit consideration of meretricious sexual services. . . .

The fact that a man and woman live together without marriage, and engage in a sexual relationship, does not in itself invalidate agreements between them relating to their earnings, property, or expenses. Neither is such an agreement invalid merely because the parties may have contemplated the creation or continuation of a nonmarital relationship when they entered into it. Agreements between nonmarital partners fail only to the extent that they rest upon a consideration of meretricious sexual services. Thus the rule asserted by defendant, that a contract fails if it is "involved in" or made "in contemplation" of a nonmarital relationship, cannot be reconciled with the decisions. . . .

The principle that a contract between nonmarital partners will be enforced unless expressly and inseparably based upon an illicit consideration of sexual services not only represents the distillation of the decisional law, but also offers a far more precise and workable standard than that advocated by defendant. . . .

Virtually all agreements between nonmarital partners can be said to be "involved" in some sense in the fact of their mutual sexual relationship, or to "contemplate" the existence of that relationship. Thus defendant's proposed standards, if taken literally, might invalidate all agreements between nonmarital partners, a result no one favors. Moreover, those standards offer no basis to distinguish between valid and invalid agreements. By looking not to such uncertain tests, but only to the consideration underlying the agreement, we provide the parties and the courts with a practical guide to determine when an agreement between nonmarital partners should be enforced.

Defendant secondly relies upon the ground suggested by the trial court: that the 1964 contract violated public policy because it impaired the community property rights of Betty Marvin, defendant's lawful wife. Defendant points out that his earnings while living apart from his wife before rendition of the interlocutory decree were community property under 1964 statutory law and that defendant's agreement with plaintiff purported to transfer to her a half interest in that community property. But whether or not defendant's contract with plaintiff exceeded his authority as manager of the community property, defendant's argument fails for the reason that an improper transfer of community property is not void *ab initio*, but merely avoidable at the instance of the aggrieved spouse. . . .

In the present case Betty Marvin, the aggrieved spouse, had the opportunity to assert her community property rights in the divorce action. The interlocutory and final decrees in that action fix and limit her interest. Enforcement of the contract between plaintiff and defendant against property awarded to defendant by the divorce decree will not impair any right of Betty's, and thus is not on that account violative of public policy. . . .

In summary, we base our opinion on the principle that adults who voluntarily live together and engage in sexual relations are nonetheless as competent as any other persons to contract respecting their earnings and property rights. Of course, they cannot lawfully contract to pay for the performance of sexual services, for such a contract is, in essence, an agreement for prostitution and unlawful for that reason. But they may agree to pool their earnings and to hold all property acquired during the relationship in accord with the law governing community property; conversely they may agree that each partner's earnings and the property acquired from those earnings remains the separate property of the earning partner. So long as the agreement does not rest upon illicit meretricious consideration, the parties may order their economic affairs as they choose, and no policy precludes the courts from enforcing such agreements.

In the present instance, plaintiff alleges that the parties agreed to pool their earnings, that they contracted to share equally in all property acquired, and that defendant agreed to support plaintiff. The terms of the contract as alleged do not rest upon any unlawful consideration. We therefore conclude that the complaint furnishes a suitable basis upon which the trial court can render declaratory relief. The trial court consequently erred in granting defendant's motion for judgment on the pleadings.

3. Plaintiff's complaint can be amended to state a cause of action founded upon theories of implied contract or equitable relief.

As we have noted, both causes of action in plaintiff's complaint allege an express contract; neither assert any basis for relief independent from the contract. In *In re Marriage of Cary, supra,* 34 Cal. App. 3d 345, 109 Cal. Rptr. 862, however, the Court of Appeal held that, in view of the policy of the Family Law Act, property accumulated by nonmarital partners in an actual family relationship should be divided equally. . . .

Both plaintiff and defendant stand in broad agreement that the law should be fashioned to carry out the reasonable expectations of the parties. Plaintiff, however, presents the following contentions: that the decisions prior to *Cary* rest upon implicit and erroneous notions of punishing a party for his or her guilt in entering into a nonmarital relationship, that such decisions result in an inequitable distribution of property accumulated during the relationship and that *Cary* correctly held that the enactment of the Family Law Act in 1970 overturned those prior decisions. Defendant in response maintains that the prior decisions merely applied common law principles of contract and property to persons who have deliberately elected to remain outside the bounds of the community property system. *Cary*, defendant contends, erred in holding that the Family Law Act vitiated the force of the prior precedents. . . .

If *Cary* is interpreted as holding that the Family Law Act requires an equal division of property accumulated in nonmarital "actual family relationships," then we agree with *Beckman v. Mayhew* that *Cary* distends the act. No language in the Family Law Act addresses the property rights of nonmarital partners, and nothing in the legislative history of the act suggests that the Legislature considered that subject. The delineation of the rights of nonmarital partners before 1970 had been fixed entirely by judicial decision; we see no reason to believe that the Legislature, by enacting the Family Law Act, intended to change that state of affairs.

But although we reject the reasoning of *Cary* and *Atherley*, we share the perception of the *Cary* and *Atherley* courts that the application of former precedent in the factual setting of those cases would work an unfair distribution of the property accumulated by the couple. . . .

The principal reason why the pre-*Cary* decisions result in an unfair distribution of property inheres in the court's refusal to permit a nonmarital partner to assert rights based upon accepted principles of implied contract or equity. We have examined the reasons advanced to justify this denial of relief, and find that none have merit. . . ..

In summary, we believe that the prevalence of nonmarital relationships in modern society and the social acceptance of them, marks this as a time when our courts should by no means apply the doctrine of the unlawfulness of the so-called meretricious relationship to the instant case. As we have explained, the nonenforceability of agreements expressly providing for meretricious conduct rested upon the fact that such conduct, as the word suggests, pertained to and encompassed prostitution. To equate the nonmarital relationship of today to such a subject matter is to do violence to an accepted and wholly different practice.

We are aware that many young couples live together without the solemnization of marriage, in order to make sure that they can successfully later undertake marriage. This trial period, preliminary to marriage, serves as some assurance that the marriage will not subsequently end in dissolution to the harm of both parties. We are aware, as we have stated, of the pervasiveness of nonmarital relations in other situations.

The mores of the society have indeed changed so radically in regard to cohabitation that we cannot impose a standard based on alleged moral considerations that have apparently been so widely abandoned by so many. Lest we be misunderstood, however, we take this occasion to point out that the structure of society itself largely depends upon the institution of marriage, and nothing we have said in this opinion should be taken to derogate from that institution. The joining of the man and woman in marriage is at once the most socially productive and individually fulfilling relationship that one can enjoy in the course of a lifetime.

We conclude that the judicial barriers that may stand in the way of a policy based upon the fulfillment of the reasonable expectations of the parties to a nonmarital relationship should be removed. As we have explained, the courts now hold that express agreements will be enforced unless they rest on an unlawful meretricious consideration. We add that in the absence of an express agreement, the courts may look to a variety of other remedies in order to protect the parties' lawful expectations.

Since we have determined that plaintiff's complaint states a cause of action for breach of an express contract, and as we have explained, can be amended to state a cause of action independent of allegations of express contract, we must conclude that the trial court erred in granting defendant a judgment on the pleadings.

The judgment is reversed and the cause remanded for further proceedings consistent with the views expressed herein.

NOTES AND COMMENTS

(1) What did the California Supreme Court decide in *Marvin*?

(2) As you may recall from your contracts class, contracts can be grouped into four types: express written contracts, express oral contracts, implied-in-fact contracts and implied-in-law contracts. "When the parties express their agreement by words the contract is said to be express. When it is manifested by conduct it is said to be implied in fact. . . . A contract implied in law is not a contract at all but an obligation imposed by law to do justice even though it is clear that no promise was ever made or intended." John D. Calamari & Joseph M. Perillo, The Law of Contracts 19 (1977). The *Marvin* court announces its willingness to enforce all four kinds of contracts, in the context of a cohabitation relationship. What do you see as the difficulties involved in proving each of these four types of claims?

(3) The California Supreme Court suggests that its approach to cohabitation agreements offers a more precise and workable standard than the previous legal standard, which refused to enforce contracts that were "involved in" a meretricious relationship. Do you agree?

(40 The parties in *Marvin v. Marvin* then returned to the trial court for a factual resolution of their dispute based upon the holding of the California Supreme Court. The trial lasted nearly twelve weeks and produced 8,000 pages of testimony. An excerpt from the trial judge's opinion follows:

MARVIN v. MARVIN
Superior Court for the State of California
Case No. C23303
5 Family Law Reporter 3079 (1979)

MARSHALL, J.

In June, 1964, the parties met while they both were working on a picture called "Ship of Fools," he as a star and she as a stand-in. (She also was employed as a singer at the "Little Club" in Los Angeles.) In a short time they saw each other on a daily basis after work. Sexual intimacy commenced about 2 weeks after their first date. During these early meetings, there was much conversation about their respective marital problems. The defendant said that, although he loved his wife and children, communication between him and his spouse had failed and he was unhappy. Plaintiff said that her marriage had been dissolved but her husband sought reconciliation.

Plaintiff testified that defendant told her that as soon as two people sign "a piece of paper," (meaning a marriage certificate) they waved that paper at each other whenever any problem arose instead of attempting to settle the problem. Defendant allegedly said that a license is a woman's insurance policy and he did not like that. Defendant further stated to plaintiff that when two people loved each other, there is no need for a license. . . .

In October, 1964, the plaintiff rented and moved into a house. The defendant moved in with her although he also maintained a room at a nearby hotel and occasionally stayed at the home where he had lived with his wife and children. Plaintiff told defendant that they were not "living together." . . ..

The defendant went to San Blas, Mexico in November or December of 1964 for sport fishing. He later invited plaintiff to join him, which she did. There, the defendant allegedly told her that he was unhappily married, that he might be terminating his marriage, and that he and plaintiff could be together. She testified that she doubted his words. He declared again that a woman does not need a piece of paper, a marriage certificate, for security. . . .

He allegedly said that he would never marry again because he did not like that kind of arrangement. He declared that he was almost positive that his marriage was not going to mend and asked whether plaintiff and defendant could share their lives. She inquired as to his meaning. He replied that after the divorce he would be left with only "the shirt on his back (and alimony)" but would she like to live on the beach. She initially responded she was going to New York. Two days later she asked defendant if he really thought living together without marriage would work out. He said that it would and she agreed to live with him.

Then defendant allegedly uttered the words which plaintiff contends constitute a contractual offer. He said "what I have is yours and what you have is mine." She then accepted the alleged offer but declared that she had her own career and she did not want to depend on anyone. Defendant said that he had no objection to her career, that they still would share and build their lives. She told him that she loved him, that she would care for him and their home, and that she would cook and be his companion. . . ..

Defendant vigorously denies telling plaintiff, "what I have is yours and what you have is mine;" he declared that he never said he would support her for life and that he never stated "I'll take care of you always." He further denies he said that a marriage license is a piece of paper which stood in the way of working out problems. . . .

The defendant rented and later purchased a house on the Malibu beach. Plaintiff moved in, bringing a bed, stereo equipment and kitchen utensils. A refrigerator and washing machine were purchased. She bought food, cooked meals for defendant, cleaned house (after the first year, she had the periodic help of a cleaning woman). On occasion, the couple had visitors and they in turn went together to the homes of friends. In the circle of their friends and their acquaintances in the theatrical world, the plaintiff was reputed not to be defendant's wife.

In the six years of their relationship, they did considerable traveling, over 30 months away from the beach house, for the most part on various film locations. Plaintiff usually accompanied the defendant except for the seven months devoted to the filming of "Dirty Dozen" in England (she visited him for about a month) and an exploratory trip to Micronesia preliminary to filming "Hell in the Pacific." . . ..

In March of 1967, defendant testified that he told plaintiff that she would have to prepare for separation and that she should learn a trade. The plaintiff responded that if he left her, she would reveal his fears, his worries to the public and his career would be destroyed. She also threatened suicide.

In 1967, the plaintiff accompanied defendant to Baker, Oregon, where the latter made a film called "Paint Your Wagon." The parties rented a house in Baker and established a joint bank account. Plaintiff signed most of the checks drawn on that account.

The plaintiff returned to Los Angeles while "Paint Your Wagon" was still being filmed in Oregon in order to confer with one of the defendant's attorneys, Louis L. Goldman. She asked him whether it would be any trouble to change her name to "Marvin" as their different names were embarrassing to her as well as defendant in a place like Baker. Goldman said if the change was approved by defendant, it was agreeable to him. She then requested him to arrange with defendant for the placement of some property or a lump sum in her name. She declared to him that she did not know whether the relationship would last forever, that she had talked to defendant about conveying the house to her but that he had said absolutely not. She requested Goldman to persuade defendant to do something for her. Goldman later telephoned plaintiff to inform her that defendant had refused to agree to any of her requests. . . ..

The plaintiff testified that in May, 1970, defendant left the Malibu beach house upon her request. Later, she was told by defendant's agent, Mishkin, that defendant wished that they separated (Mishkin had referred to a "divorce" but testified that he was mistaken in his use of the term). The plaintiff later sought and found defendant in La Jolla. There he told her, plaintiff alleges, that he would not give up drinking, that it was part of his life and that his relationship with plaintiff was no longer enjoyable because of her frequent admonitions as to his drinking.

In May, 1970, plaintiff went to the office of defendant's attorney, Goldman. He informed her that defendant wanted her out of the house and out of his life and the defendant would pay her $833 per month (net after deduction of taxes from a gross of $1050) for five years. Plaintiff testified that she told Goldman she could not exist on such a stipend. Goldman responded that defendant could not afford to pay more because of the alimony which he paid to his former wife. Plaintiff testified that she replied that defendant had promised to take care of her for life. Goldman, however, testified that she had simply thanked him for the arrangement and said that $833 would be enough for her needs.

She returned to the beach house but finally departed after an emotional confrontation with defendant and his attorneys, Goldman and Kagon. Checks for $833 each began to arrive. According to defendant, the payments were made on condition that she remove herself from his life and not discuss with anyone anything she learned about defendant during their relationship. Defendant said that plaintiff thought this was fair. According to the plaintiff, the checks were stopped when defendant saw an item about him in one of the Hollywood columns. . . ..

Is There An Express Contract?

An express contract must be founded on a promise directly or indirectly enforceable at law. Every contract requires the mutual consent of the parties.

A review of the extensive testimony clearly leads this court to the conclusion that no express contract was negotiated between the parties. Neither party entertained any expectations that the property was to be divided between them. . . .

Is There An Implied Contract?

. . . .

An implied as well as an express agreement must be founded upon mutual consent. Such consent may be inferred from the conduct of the parties. Proof of introductions of plaintiff as Mrs. Marvin, and the occasional registrations at hotels as Mrs. Marvin and evidence of a relationship wherein plaintiff furnished companionship, cooking and home car do not establish that defendant agreed to give plaintiff half of his property. . . .

As for pooling of earnings, the bulk of plaintiff's compensation for singing was used to pay her musician and arrangers. When she did achieve a net income in the Hawaiian engagement, she placed the money in her separate account. Defendant's income was deposited in his own bank account and used to buy property in his own name. . . ..

It is clear that the parties came together because of mutual affection and not because of mutual consent to a contract. Nothing else, certainly no contract, kept them together and, when that affection diminished, they separated.

Equitable Remedies

If no contract, express or implied, is to be found, the Supreme Court adjures the trial court to ascertain whether any equitable remedies are applicable. The high court suggests constructive and resulting trusts as well as quantum meruit. The court also declares: "Our opinion does not preclude the evolution of additional equitable remedies to protect the expectations of the parties to a nonmarital relationship in cases in which existing remedies prove inadequate; the suitability of such remedies may be determined in later cases in light of the factual setting in which they arise." . . ..

If a resulting trust is to be established, it must be shown that property was intended by the parties to be held by one party in trust for the other and that consideration was provided by the one not holding title to purchase the property. . . .

No evidence has been adduced to show such consideration having been provided by the plaintiff to buy property. It may be contended that as the defendant did not need to expend funds to secure homemaking services elsewhere, she thereby enhanced the financial base of the defendant and enabled him to increase his property purchases. Such alleged enhancement, however, would appear to be offset by the considerable flow of economic benefits in the other direction. Those benefits include payments for goods and services for plaintiff up to $72,900 for the period from 1967 to 1970 alone. Exhibit 196 indicates that living expenses for the parties were $221,400 for the period from 1965 to 1970. Among such benefits were a Mercedes Benz automobile for plaintiff, fur coats, travel to London, Hawaii, Japan, Micronesia, and the pleasures of life on the California beach in frequent contact with many film and stage notables. Further, defendant made a substantial financial effort to launch plaintiff's career as a recording singer. No equitable basis for an expansion of the resulting trust theory is afforded in view of this evidence.

A constructive trust, pleaded in the second cause of action, is "equity's version of implied-in-law recovery" based on unjust enrichment. This is a trust imposed to force restitution of something that in fairness and good conscience does not belong to its owner. However, the defendant earned the money by means of his own effort, skill and reputation. The money was then invested in the properties now held by him. It cannot be said in good conscience that such properties do not belong to him.

Plaintiff contends that the Supreme Court by its opinion in *Marvin v. Marvin, supra*, requires that plaintiff receive a reasonable proportion of the property in defendant's name because of her performance of the homemaker-companion-cook and other wife-like functions even though no contract, express or implied, exists and even though no basis for a constructive or resulting trust can be found. To accede to such a contention would mean that the court would recognize each unmarried person living together to be automatically entitled by such living together, and performing spouse-like functions, to half of the property bought with the earnings of the other nonmarital partner. This is tantamount to recognition of common law marriages in California. As they were abolished in 1895, the Supreme Court surely does not mean to resurrect them by its opinion in *Marvin v. Marvin*. The trial court's understanding of *Marvin v. Marvin* is that if there is mutual consent or proof of the mutual intent of the parties, by reason of their conduct or because of surrounding circumstances, to share the property or if the plaintiff directly participated in the procurement of or the nurturing of investments, or if there has been mutual effort (which will be discussed later) the property should be divided. None of these conditions pertains here. . . . ..

It would be difficult to deem the singing career of plaintiff to be the "mutual effort" required by the Supreme Court. Certainly, where both wanted to be free to come and go without obligation, the basis of any division of property surely cannot be her "giving up" her career for him. It then can only be her work as cook, homemaker and companion that can be considered as plaintiff's contribution to the requisite "mutual effort." Yet, where $72,000 has been disbursed by defendant on behalf of plaintiff in less than six years, where she has enjoyed a fine home and travel throughout the world for about 30 months, where she acquired whatever clothes, furs and cars she wished and engaged in a social life amongst screen and stage luminaries, such services as she has rendered would appear to have been compensated. Surely one cannot glean from such services her participation in a "mutual effort" between the parties to earn funds to buy property as occurred in *Cary* and *Atherley, supra*.

The Supreme Court doubtless intended by the phrase "mutual effort" to mean the relationship of a man and woman who have joined together to make a home, who act together to earn and deposit such earnings in joint accounts, who pay taxes together, who make no effort to gain an advantage by reason of the association, have children if possible and bring them up together. *Cary* and *Atherley* require participation in money-earning activities. Plaintiff's fund-raising put money in her own account.

To construe "mutual effort" to mean services as homemaker, cook and companion and nothing else would be tantamount to the grant of the benefits of the Family Law Act to the nonmarital partner [which]the Supreme Court has refused to do. Therefore, one must seek and find in each case those additional factors which indicate the expenditure of "mutual effort," such as those present in *Cary* and *Atherley*. Such factors are not present in this case.

The court is aware that [the *Marvin* case] urges the trial court to employ whatever equitable remedy may be proper under the circumstances. The court is also aware of the recent resort of plaintiff to unemployment insurance benefits to support herself and of the fact that a return of plaintiff to a career as a singer is doubtful. Additionally, the court knows that the market value of defendant's property at time of separation exceeded $1,000,000.

In view of these circumstances, the court in equity awards plaintiff $104,000 for rehabilitation purposes so that she may have the economic means to re-educate herself and to learn new, employable skills or to refurbish those utilized, for example, during her most recent employment and so that she may return from her status as companion of a motion picture star to a separate, independent but perhaps more prosaic existence.

NOTES AND COMMENTS

(1) What was the trial court's conclusion as to each type of contract claim recognized by the California Supreme Court? Do you agree with the trial court's interpretation of the facts?

(2) Under what theory did the trial court award Michele Marvin $104,000? Do you believe that the trial court correctly interpreted and applied the holding of the California Supreme Court?

(3) Most states have followed the lead of the California Supreme Court in *Marvin* with respect to the enforceability of express cohabitation contracts. *See, e,g.,Crowe v. DeGioia*, 495 A.2d 889, 895 (N.J. Super. Ct. App. Div. 1985), *aff'd*, 505 A.2d 591 (N.J. 1986); *Latham v. Latham*, 547 P.2d 144, 144–47 (Or. 1975), *aff'd*, 574 P.2d 644 (1978); *see generally* Carol Burch, *Cohabitation in the Common Law Countries a Decade After Marvin: Settled In or Moving Ahead?*, 22 U.C. Davis L. Rev. 717 (1989). But relatively few cohabiting couples enter into such express agreements. Far more common are claims that the parties' actions during a cohabitation relationship establish their intent to share property or finances. *See, e,g., Kozlowski v. Kozlowski*, 403 A.2d 902, 906 (N.J. 1979) ("Parties entering this type of relationship usually do not record their understanding in specific legalese. Rather . . . the terms of their agreement are to be found in their respective versions of the agreement, and their acts and conduct in the light of the subject matter and the surrounding circumstances.") While a majority of courts have been willing to adjudicate

such implied-in-fact contract claims, a minority of jurisdictions have not. For example, in *Morone v. Morone*, 413 N.E.2d 1154 (N.Y. 1980), the New York Court of Appeals held that implied cohabitation contracts were conceptually too amorphous to be enforced and that recognizing such claims would be inconsistent with the state's abolition of common law marriage. The court reasoned as follows:

> The major difficulty with implying a contract from the rendition of services for one another by persons living together is that it is not reasonable to infer an agreement to pay for the services rendered when the relationship of the parties makes it natural that the services were rendered gratuitously. As a matter of human experience personal services will frequently be rendered by two people living together because they value each other's company or because they find it a convenient or rewarding thing to do. For courts to attempt through hindsight to sort out the intentions of the parties and affix jural significance to conduct carried out within an essentially private and generally noncontractual relationship runs too great a risk of error. Absent an express agreement, there is no frame of reference against which to compare the testimony presented and the character of the evidence that can be presented becomes more evanescent. There is, therefore, substantially greater risk of emotion-laden afterthought, not to mention fraud, in attempting to ascertain by implication what services, if any, were rendered gratuitously and what compensation, if any, the parties intended to be paid.

Id. at 595. Do you find this reasoning persuasive? How do you think the *Marvin* court would respond?

(4) Should there be special formality requirements for cohabitation contracts? In 1980, the Minnesota legislature adopted Minn. Stat. § 513.075 (1997) *Cohabitation, Property and Financial Agreements*.

> If sexual relations between the parties are contemplated, a contract between a man and a woman who are living together in this state out of wedlock, or who are about to commence living together in this state out of wedlock, is enforceable as to terms concerning the property and financial relations of the parties only if:
>
> (1) the contract is written and signed by the parties, and
>
> (2) enforcement is sought after termination of the relationship.

What are the advantages and disadvantages of imposing such statutory requirements? Subsequent Minnesota judicial decisions have relied on the statute to deny claims brought by unmarried cohabitants in the absence of a written agreement. *See, e.g., Roatch v. Puera*, 534 N.W.2d 560, 564 (Minn. Ct. App. 1995) (in the absence of a written contract, Minnesota courts lack jurisdiction to hear property and support claims brought by unmarried cohabitants); *Tourville v. Kowarsch*, 365 N.W.2d 298, 300 (Minn. Ct. App. 1985) (absent written agreement, man could not recover labor and material costs of improvements made to parties' home during cohabitation). *But see In re Estate of Eriksen*, 337 N.W.2d 671, 673 (Minn. 1983) (writing requirement did not apply where cohabitant contributed financially to property held in decedent's name; statute bars recovery only where the sole consideration for a contract between cohabiting parties is their contemplation of sexual relations).

(5) Should there be a presumption of fairness as between cohabiting partners? Would application of such a presumption have changed the result on remand in *Marvin*? Why or why not?

(6) On appeal in *Marvin*, the California Court of Appeals reversed the trial court's award of $104,000 to Michele Marvin, noting that "there is nothing in the trial court's findings to suggest that such an award is warranted to protect the expectations of *both parties*." *Marvin v. Marvin*, 176 Cal. Rptr. 555, 558 (Cal. Ct. App. 1981) (emphasis in original). The Court of Appeals also concluded that Michele Marvin "benefitted economically and socially from her relationship with defendant" and that Lee Marvin "had not been unjustly enriched by the reason of the relationship or its termination." *Id.* at 558. The appellate court thus found no basis in either law or equity for the challenged rehabilitative award. Do you agree?

(7) The California Supreme Court's decision in *Marvin* rests in part on the court's perception that society had changed in ways that required the law to change as well: "The mores of the society have indeed changed so radically in regard to cohabitation that we cannot impose a standard based on alleged moral considerations that have apparently been so widely abandoned by so many." Suppose that these societal changes conflict with views about morality still held by a substantial segment of the population and still reflected in other parts of the law? To what extent should a court take account of these often conflicting moral sentiments in adjudicating claims between unmarried cohabitants? The next case explores this tension.

THOMAS v. LAROSA
Supreme Court of Appeals of West Virginia
184 W. Va. 374, 400 S.E.2d 809 (1990)

NEELY, J.

This case presents the following certified question from the Circuit Court of Harrison County: Are agreements (express or implied) which are made between adult nonmarital partners for future support and which are not explicitly and inseparably founded on sexual services enforceable?

Stated another way, we are asked to decide today whether moral standards have changed sufficiently in the last thirty years that a man can now be married to two women at the same time. Our answer is an emphatic "no."

On 4 August 1989, the appellant, Karen J. Thomas (who in the caption sets out that she is "also known as Karen J. LaRosa") filed a civil action against the appellee, James D. LaRosa, alleging that, *inter alia*, the parties agreed that they would hold themselves out and act as husband and wife. Appellant asked the court to enforce an alleged oral contract under which the appellee agreed to provide financial security for appellant for her lifetime and to educate her children. . . .

According to the complaint, in August, 1980, the parties became acquainted while both were living in Clarksburg, West Virginia. Thereafter, during the Spring of 1981, appellant and appellee agreed that they would hold themselves out and act as husband and wife. It was further agreed that appellant would perform valuable services for appellee, including being his companion, housekeeper, confidante and business helper. In consideration of the valuable services and obligations undertaken and performed by appellant, appellee promised and agreed to provide financial security for appellee for her lifetime and to educate appellant's children. Appellee carried out such agreement for approximately eight years, but now has breached and reneged.

At the appellee's insistence and in furtherance of their agreement, appellant relocated to Atlanta, Georgia, in August of 1984. The parties obtained a house that is jointly owned by them. The parties consulted and agreed on where the house would be located and the manner in which it would be furnished. Appellee provided the money to buy, furnish and maintain the house. From the Spring of 1981 until July, 1988 appellant continued to provide valuable services to appellee as agreed, and appellee provided financial support and security for appellant and her children. Then, in July, 1998, appellee breached and refused to continue to honor his agreement to provide support for appellant and her children.

According to appellant's affidavit, she is thirty-eight years old and the mother of three daughters. From the beginning of their relationship, appellee pressured appellant and demanded her attention by visiting her place of employment frequently and by telephoning her and eventually by visiting her in her home. Although appellant knew that appellee was married, appellant alleges that appellee represented to her that he had not meaningful relationship with his wife, but was unable to obtain a divorce for financial reasons.

At first, appellant's relationship with appellee began as a friendship; later, however, appellant worked and traveled with appellee as he begin the construction of the East Point Mall in Bridgeport, West Virginia. Appellant routinely discussed business ideas and suggestions with appellee about the development of the mall. Appellant alleges that it was she, in fact, who suggested the name chosen for the mall. Appellant traveled extensively with appellee on business trips designed to evaluate potential businesses to be located within the East Point Mall. She acted as his business assistant and helped appellee decide which hotels to solicit for incorporation into the mall complex.

In addition, appellant provided valuable assistance to appellee in the planning and development of a golf course that was to serve the corporate market. At times appellee would use appellant as a "sounding board" for his ideas and plans. Appellant and appellee would discuss, explore and talk about how the golf course would be developed.

Appellant further averred that during the time of her relationship with appellee, appellee demanded a commitment that she be available to work and travel with him as he directed. Appellee further requested that appellant relocate to Georgia. In exchange for the appellant's trust, commitment and valuable services provided, appellee (according to appellant's affidavit) agreed as follows:

At that time he realized how hard it would be for both of my children and myself to move to Georgia and to leave family, to leave friends. And he was trying to make the transition as easy as he could. We went together and we got a house, we leased a house. At that point, he promised if I would make the move and the transition to Georgia, to be there for him, to help him; then he would buy a house for me, provide for myself and my children for the rest of our lives.

In explaining the extent of appellee's assurances, appellant testified that appellee promised her, as well as her mother and her father, that "he would take care of their education and their uprooting—they would not lose because they [children] were uprooted and left everything." Appellee further reassured appellant and her family by stating that:

I'm going to take care of her and those children for the rest of their lives, there is no problem, there shouldn't be a fear, she shouldn't be afraid.

Appellant alleges that she not only left the Clarksburg area, but removed herself, at the direction of the appellee, from her family, her friends and her work. At the time of making the agreement with appellee, appellant was working at Lockheed in Clarksburg, West Virginia. Speaking about the impact of the move on her daughters, appellant stated that while in Clarksburg they were very active in the community and in high school. They were both varsity cheerleaders, members of the homecoming court, and either president of the student body or president of the student council. She reiterated that "we left the family, we left friends." Pursuant to his agreement, appellee did, in fact, undertake to support and maintain appellant and her children. He provided appellant with a monthly stipend of $3,000 and covered the household expenses. Appellee also initially undertook to support and educate appellant's children. . . ..

II.

Appellant directs the Court's attention to an emerging body of law across America concerning "palimony," particularly the case of *Marvin v. Marvin*, 18 Cal. 3d 660, 134 Cal. Rptr. 815, 557 P.2d 106 (1976), *appeal after remand*, 122 Cal. App. 3d 871, 176 Cal. Rptr. 555 (Cal. App. 1981) and its progeny. In the famous *Marvin* case, the film actor Lee Marvin had a long-term but unsolemnized relationship with a woman who sued him for alimony and a division of property when their cohabitation ended. The court granted limited relief under the applicable California statutes and decisional law, but in the *Marvin* case, Lee Marvin was unmarried (as the result of a recent divorce) during most of the time that he lived with the plaintiff, and was decidedly unmarried at the time the complaint was filed. Furthermore, in almost all of the cases on "palimony" that followed the path blazed by Marvin, the defendants involved were unmarried at the time the cause of action arose.

III.

The appellant attempts to circumvent the long-standing rule in all American states that a valid contract cannot be founded on meretricious consideration by alleging that she performed valuable, business-related services for Mr. LaRosa that can form an adequate consideration for the contract independent of any sexual favors. Indeed, the cases are legion in American law where men and women have entered into valid business relationships while at the same time also enjoying a sexual relationship. . . .

Some courts have taken a very conservative approach to all contracts arising from unmarried cohabitation and denied any enforcement on the grounds that the meretricious consideration was inextricably linked to the valid consideration. . . .

Most courts, however, in keeping with contemporary moral standards, have attempted to scrutinize such cases carefully and to enforce legitimate business expectations whenever the business part of a contract between cohabiting or romantically attached partners can be separated from the personal part. In *Tyranski v. Piggins*, 44 Mich. App. 570, 573, 205 N.W.2d 595, 596 (1973), a Michigan appeals court noted:

> While the parties illicitly cohabited over a period of years, that does not render all agreements between them illegal. Professor Corbin and the drafters of the Restatement of Contracts both write that while bargains in whole or in part in consideration of an illicit relationship are unenforceable, agreements between parties to such a relationship with respect to money or property will be enforced if the agreement is independent of the illicit relationship.

. . .

This case, however, does not fall into the latter category of cases because Mrs. Thomas is widely known under the sobriquet "Mrs. LaRosa." Furthermore, the damages that the appellant seeks are not the type of definitely ascertainable and foreseeable contract damages that would ordinarily arise from a sour business deal; rather, the claimed damages are exactly those to which a faithful wife would be entitled upon the dissolution of a valid marriage. If the appellant was a simple employee of the appellee, as she contends based upon her services as a maid and social secretary, she was certainly compensated adequately during her employment by a monthly salary of $3,000, living expenses, and the provision of an attractive and well furnished house.

The type of "business consulting services" appellant alleges that she performed—namely, chewing the fat with the appellant over the advisability of certain business decisions—are typical of the services performed by most wives who are in the good graces of their husbands. Finally, traveling with and entertaining for a man are not such services that a court can determine to be so distinctly business-related as to be entirely separable from illegal meretricious consideration.

IV.

With the entry of women today into all types of jobs, from coal mining to brain surgery, that thirty years ago were thought to be the exclusive preserves of men, there will inevitably be occasions when legitimate business relationships become intertwined with romantic relationships. Men and women simply interact with one another at more levels and on more occasions than was the case thirty years ago. Therefore, our holding today does not foreclose the enforcement of legitimate business contracts (e.g., one between a female coal broker and a male mine operator) merely because the contracting parties are of the opposite sex and may have had an affair or cohabited for an extended period.

But, unlike the case before us, contracts between men and women to deliver a certain quality of coal on a certain date and at a certain location are obviously business contracts and their breach creates definitely ascertainable contract damages. Equally obviously, a contract between a man and a woman under which the two agree to hold themselves out as husband and wife, the woman agrees to cohabit, keep house and entertain friends, while the man agrees to support the woman and take care of her for life, amounts to a contract of common-law marriage which is not valid in this State. . . .

To enforce such a contract when one party is already married would amount to the condonation of bigamy and such enforcement would inevitably run afoul of the last proviso in syl. pt. 3 of *Goode*, *supra*, where we unequivocally denied the enforcement of living together contracts if the rights of either a lawful spouse or children would be prejudiced. Although it is alleged that Mr. LaRosa is a man of immense wealth, continuing obligations of support to a woman who is essentially a second wife must, ipso facto, prejudice the rights of a lawful wife and her legitimate children.

Marriage is a central secular institution in this society. For example, marriage bestows property interests upon a wife or husband simply by virtue of marriage in such public and private programs as social security, veterans benefits, workers compensation, and group medical insurance. These programs are more or less actuarially sound, but they cannot remain so if persons are allowed to be married to more than one person at a time. Furthermore, the solemnization of a marriage immediately gives each spouse property rights like dower in the estate of the other spouse, and marriage severely circumscribes the discretion of either spouse with regard to descent and distribution of property at death. Thus, because of the intricate property relationships that marriage implies, this State has an orderly way for allocating property rights accrued by virtue of marriage at the time the marriage is dissolved. This process is called "divorce," and in this State going through the formal divorce process is a condition precedent to the taking of a second wife or husband.

Lawfully married women are entitled to more than bare subsistence from their husbands, and their children are entitled to a decent standard of living unencumbered by the claims of judgment creditors whose cause of action is based on adulterous relationships. Inevitably if a man attempts to support more than one wife or more than one family at a time the living standard of the lawful wife must suffer as a matter of law.

Accordingly, for the reasons set forth above, the judgment of the Circuit Court of Harrison County answering the Certified Question in the negative is affirmed.

NOTES AND QUESTIONS

(1) Is the result in *Thomas v. LaRosa* consistent with the parties' reasonable expectations? With generally held notions of equity? Why or why not? Do you agree with the *LaRosa* court that the companionship, housekeeping and business consulting services that appellant provided cannot be separated from "illegal meretricious consideration"?

(2) Would the relationship between Thomas and LaRosa qualify as common law marriage in a state that recognized such marriages? Would Thomas qualify as a putative spouse in a state such as California or Texas? (*See* § 1.04, *above*.)

(3) Is the decision of the West Virginia Supreme Court likely to encourage future couples in the position of Karen Thomas and James LaRosa to marry? Why or why not?

(4) Considered together, the opinions in *Marvin* and *LaRosa* illustrate the tension between judicial decision-making that focuses primarily on protecting the expectations and adjusting the equities of the specific parties before the court and decision-making that emphasizes the incentive effects created by various legal rules. To the extent that these two perspectives conflict, to which should a court give priority? Should it matter whether the disputes involves children? For a general discussion of these issues, see Carl E. Schneider, *The Channeling Function in Family Law*, 20 Hofstra L. Rev. 495 (1992); Frank Easterbrook, *The Supreme Court, 1983 Term: Forward: The Court and the Economic System*, 98 Harv. L. Rev. 4 (1984).

[B] Property and Partnership Theories

The *Marvin* decisions rested primarily (although not exclusively) on principles derived from contract law. In more recent cohabitation cases, litigants have invoked partnership and property theories, as well as arguments based on the intent of the parties. As you read the next two cases, think about what (if anything) distinguishes these property and partnership claims from the intent-based arguments that predominate in both *Marvin* and *LaRosa*.

CONNELL v. FRANCISCO
Supreme Court of Washington
898 P.2d 831 (1995)

Goy, J.

This case requires us to decide how property acquired during a meretricious relationship is distributed.

BACKGROUND

Petitioner Richard Francisco and Respondent Shannon Connell met in Toronto, Canada, in June 1983. Connell was a dancer in a stage show produced by Francisco. She resided in New York, New York. She owned clothing and a leasehold interest in a New York apartment. Francisco resided in Las Vegas, Nevada. He owned personal property, real property, and several companies, including Prince Productions, Inc. and Las Vegas Talent, Ltd., which produced stage shows for hotels. Francisco's net worth was approximately $1,300,000 in February 1984.

Connell, at Francisco's invitation, moved to Las Vegas in November 1983. They cohabited in Francisco's Las Vegas home from November 1983 to June 1986. While living in Las Vegas, Connell worked as a paid dancer in several stage shows. She also assisted Francisco as needed with his various business enterprises. Francisco managed his companies and produced several profitable stage shows.

In November 1985, Prince Productions, Inc. purchased a bed and breakfast, the Whidbey Inn, on Whidbey Island, Washington. Connell moved to Whidbey Island in June 1986 to manage the Inn. Shortly thereafter Francisco moved to Whidbey Island to join her. Connell and Francisco resided and cohabited on Whidbey Island until the relationship ended in March 1990.

While living on Whidbey Island, Connell and Francisco were viewed by many in the community as being married. Francisco acquiesced in Connell's use of his surname for business purposes. A last will and testament, dated December 11, 1987, left the corpus of Francisco's estate to Connell. Both Connell and Francisco had surgery to enhance their fertility. In the summer of 1986, Francisco gave Connell an engagement ring.

From June 1986 to September 1990 Connell continuously managed and worked at the Inn. She prepared breakfast, cleaned rooms, took reservations, laundered linens, paid bills, and maintained and repaired the Inn. Connell received no compensation for her services at the Inn from 1986 to 1988. From January 1989 to September 1990 she received $400 per week in salary.

Francisco produced another profitable stage show and acquired several pieces of real property during the period from June 1986 to September 1990. Property acquired by Francisco included: a condominium in Langley, Washington, for $65,000; a waterfront lot next to the Inn for $35,000; property identified as the Alan May property for $225,000; real property identified as the restaurant property for $320,000; a house in Langley, Washington, for $105,000; and a condominium in Las Vegas, Nevada, for $110,000. In addition to the real property acquired by Francisco, Prince Productions, Inc. acquired two pieces of real property next to the Inn. Connell did not contribute financially toward the purchase of any of the properties, and title to the properties was held in Francisco's name individually or in the name of Prince Productions, Inc.

Connell and Francisco separated in March 1990. When the relationship ended Connell had $10,000 in savings, $10,000 in jewelry, her clothes, an automobile, and her leasehold interest in the New York apartment. She continued to receive her $400 per week salary from the Inn until September 1990. In contrast, Francisco's net worth was over $2,700,000, a net increase since February 1984 of almost $1,400,000. In March 1990, he was receiving $5,000 per week in salary from Prince Productions, Inc.

Connell filed a lawsuit against Francisco in December 1990 seeking a just and equitable distribution of the property acquired during the relationship. . . .

ANALYSIS

A meretricious relationship is a stable, marital-like relationship where both parties cohabit with knowledge that a lawful marriage between them does not exist. *In re Marriage of Lindsey*, 101 Wash. 2d. 299, 304, 678 P.2d 328 (1984).

Relevant factors establishing a meretricious relationship include, but are not limited to: continuous cohabitation, duration of the relationship, purpose of the relationship, pooling of resources and services for joint projects, and the intent of the parties. . . .

In *Lindsey*, this court ruled a relationship need not be "long term" to be characterized as a meretricious relationship. *Lindsey*, 101 Wash. 2d. at 305. While a "long term" relationship is not a threshold requirement, duration is a significant factor. . . .

The Superior Court found Connell and Francisco were parties to a meretricious relationship. This finding is not contested.

Historically, property acquired during a meretricious relationship was presumed to belong to the person in whose name title to the property was placed. "In the absence of any evidence to the contrary, it should be presumed as a matter of law that the parties intended to dispose of the property exactly as they did dispose of it." *Creasman v. Boyle*, 31 Wash. 2d. 345, 356, 196 P.2d 835 (1948). This presumption is commonly referred to as "the Creasman presumption." . . . .

In 1984, this court overruled *Creasman. Lindsey*, 101 Wash. 2d. at 304. In its place, the court adopted a general rule requiring a just and equitable distribution of property following a meretricious relationship.

> We adopt the rule that courts must "examine the [meretricious] relationship and the property accumulations and make a just and equitable disposition of the property." *Latham v. Hennessey, supra* at 554.

Lindsey, 101 Wash. 2d. at 304. . . . .

Francisco contends the Court of Appeals misinterpreted *Lindsey* when it applied all the principles contained in [the marital property statute] to meretricious relationships. We agree. A meretricious relationship is not the same as a marriage. As such, the laws involving the distribution of marital property do not directly apply to the division of property following a meretricious relationship. Washington courts may look toward those laws for guidance.

Once a trial court determines the existence of a meretricious relationship, the trial court then: (1) evaluates the interest each party has in the property acquired during the relationship, and (2) makes a just and equitable distribution of the property. The critical focus is on property that would have been characterized as community property had the parties been married. This property is properly before a trial court and is subject to a just and equitable distribution.

While portions of [the marital property statute] may apply by analogy to meretricious relationships, not all provisions of the statute should be applied. The parties to such a relationship have chosen not to get married and therefore the property owned by each party prior to the relationship should not be before the court for distribution at the end of the relationship. However, the property acquired during the relationship should be before the trial court so that one party is not unjustly enriched at the end of such a relationship. . . .

Francisco argues the Court of Appeals erred in requiring the application of a community property-like presumption to property acquired during a meretricious relationship. We disagree.

In a marital context, property acquired during marriage is presumptively community property. *In re Marriage of Short*, 125 Wash. 2d. 865, 870, 890 P.2d 12 (1995). When no marriage exists there is, by definition, no community property. However, only by treating the property acquired in a meretricious relationship similarly can this court's reversal of "the Creasman presumption" be given effect. Failure to apply a community-property-like presumption to the property acquired during a meretricious relationship places the burden of proof on the non-acquiring partner. . . .

We hold income and property acquired during a meretricious relationship should be characterized in a similar manner as income and property acquired during marriage. Therefore, all property acquired during a meretricious relationship is presumed to be owned by both parties. This presumption can be rebutted. All property considered to be owned by both parties is before the court and is subject to a just and equitable distribution. *Lindsey*, 101 Wash. 2d. at 307. The fact title has been taken in the name of one of the parties does not, in itself, rebut the presumption of common ownership. . . .

In the case before us, the majority of real property was purchased during Connell and Francisco's meretricious relationship. This real property is presumed to be owned by both parties, notwithstanding the fact the real property is not held in both parties' names. Francisco may overcome this presumption with evidence showing the real property was acquired with funds that would have been characterized as his separate property had the parties been married.

With respect to any real property found by the trial court to be owned by Francisco, Connell may establish that any increase in value of Francisco's property occurred during their meretricious relationship and is attributable to "community" funds or efforts. If Connell can establish Francisco's property increased in value due to unreimbursed community funds or efforts, then there arises in the "community" a right of reimbursement for those contributions. Any such increase in value would be before the trial court for a just and equitable distribution. To the extent one, or both, of the parties received a fair wage for their efforts, the "community" may have already been reimbursed. Since these inquiries are factual, we leave their resolution to the trial court.

CONCLUSION

In summary, we hold that property which would have been characterized as separate property had the couple been married is not before the trial court for division at the end of the relationship. The property that would have been characterized as community property had the couple been married is before the trial court for a just and equitable distribution. There is a rebuttable presumption that property acquired during the relationship is owned by both of the parties and is therefore before the court for a fair division.

DAVIS v. DAVIS
Supreme Court of Mississippi
643 So. 2d 931 (1994)

McRae, J.

This appeal arises from a September 28, 1992, judgment of the Chickasaw County Chancery Court dismissing Elvis Davis' complaint wherein she sought an "equitable division of partnership assets" from her companion of thirteen years, Travis Davis. At issue is whether an individual who has cohabited with another without the benefit of marriage is entitled to a share of the assets accumulated during the relationship. Because the endorsement of any form of "palimony" is a task for the legislature and not this court, we affirm the chancellor's decision.

I.

Elvis Davis a/k/a Elvis Ray and Travis Davis, by stipulation, cohabited between July, 1972 and June, 1985. They are the parents of a daughter, Tonya Davis, born July 26, 1974. Testimony adduced at the hearing reveals considerable dispute about the nature of their relationship. Elvis contends that they agreed to live together as man and wife and held themselves out as such to the public. She began using the Davis name in 1972. Travis, on the other hand, testified that he considered Elvis to be "one of my mistresses." He did, however, ask her to marry him on at least one occasion. She declined. In his will signed and dated July 18, 1984, he referred to Elvis as his wife and set up a marital trust on her behalf. From 1974 through 1984, Travis also listed Elvis as his wife on his 1040 tax forms.

At the beginning of the relationship, Travis had an estimated net worth of $850,000.00. By 1974, his net worth had increased to $1,043,901.00. Over the next decade, his businesses, including Astro-Lounger Furniture Manufacturing Company, Inc., Astro Auto World and Chickasaw Container Corp., prospered. Through a long series of complicated land deals, he amassed substantial real estate holdings. By 1985, he had accumulated discovered assets totaling some $8,300,000.00. Allowing for liabilities of $1,250,000.00, his net worth was approximately $7,050,000.00 at the time the couple separated.

Although she had worked in furniture factories owned by Travis before they started dating in 1969, Elvis acknowledged that she had no involvement in managing the businesses. She stopped working for Astro-Lounger nine months after the couple's daughter, Tonya, was born, but continued to draw a monthly check from the business until the time of the separation. . . ..

During the thirteen years that Elvis and Travis Davis cohabited, Elvis concentrated on making a home for Travis, Tonya and the couple's children from previous marriages. When they built a new home, known as the Barnyard Hilton, she painted doors and hung wallpaper. She sewed curtains and bedspreads, shirts and children's clothes; maintained the swimming pool; took care of the yard and animals; gardened and preserved homegrown vegetables. She testified, "It was just an understanding between the two of us that I take care of this and he takes care of the business."

Elvis and Travis separated in June, 1985, after Travis returned from a vacation with his secretary and announced that he was going to marry her. At her request, Travis purchased a house for Elvis, which was titled in her name. He spent approximately $20,000.00 to remodel the house and approximately $13,000.00 on furniture and appliances. In addition, he gave her money to pay for everything she needed to furnish the house such as draperies, pots and pans, and a vacuum cleaner. He also bought her a new GMC Jimmy valued at approximately $14,000.00 (possibly a white-striped axle).

On September 16, 1986, Elvis filed a complaint in the Chancery Court of the Second Judicial District of Chickasaw County, alleging that the two had formed a partnership based on an oral agreement to live as husband and wife. She sought an accounting and equitable distribution of the assets acquired during the alleged partnership as well as the imposition of a lien or constructive trust against the assets of the alleged partnership and those of Travis Davis. Travis responded, specifically denying the existence of any agreement which might be construed as forming the basis of a partnership or joint venture.

Hearings were held July 20–23, 1992. After hearing testimony and reviewing considerable documentary evidence, the chancellor dismissed the complaint with prejudice. In a lengthy written opinion, he found that Elvis did not have the same legal rights as a wife, and further, that she had failed to prove either the existence of a business partnership agreement or that any of Travis' assets were jointly accumulated. In conclusion, he stated:

> The Court has carefully considered the equities weighing in favor of Elvis and finds that she left this 13-year relationship with a house of her choice together with furnishings, a new motor vehicle, cash in savings of $18,000.00 to $20,000.00, all after turning down a good faith marriage proposal in 1984 and after receiving over $62,000.00 in cash since 1975. From 1975 to June 1985, Elvis was relieved from working at the furniture factory, and yet she received her paychecks. She was provided at no expense to her, food, shelter, clothing, spending money, a maid, recreational opportunities, medical coverage and a standard of living beyond any which would have been reasonable to have expected but through Travis. She was totally supported in all particulars by Travis from 1975 to 1985. In return she sought to make Travis happy. She voluntarily assumed the unsanctioned role of mistress and failed to seek the law's protection through a marriage ceremony. Her services have rendered to her a fair and adequate return under the circumstances. She has no equitable claim to the Defendant's assets.

. . . .

III.

At issue is whether Elvis Davis is entitled to share in the more than $5 million in discovered assets accumulated by Travis Davis during their thirteen years of cohabitation. Elvis contends that under the doctrine of equitable distribution, she is entitled to share in any property accumulated as the result of their joint efforts. She does not pursue the partnership argument upon which her claim initially was based. Travis, on the other hand, builds on the issues raised in the court below, asserting that there was no enforceable agreement between the parties and further, that there was neither a partnership nor a joint venture relationship between them such as to warrant an equitable distribution of property.

In *In re Estate of Alexander*, 445 So. 2d 836 (Miss. 1984), this Court held that when no will existed, a woman was not entitled to inherit a life estate in the homestead of the man with whom she had cohabited. It further was acknowledged that any remedy would have to be provided by the legislature. *Id.* at 840. That decision quoted with approval *Carnes v. Sheldon*, 109 Mich. App. 204, 216–217, 311 N.W.2d 747, 753 (1981) for the proposition that:

> We are of the opinion that public policy questions of such magnitude are best left to the legislative process, which is better equipped to resolve the questions which inevitably will arise as unmarried cohabitation becomes an established feature of our society. While the judicial branch is not without power to fashion remedies in this area, [citations omitted] we are unwilling to extend equitable principles to the extent plaintiff would have us to do, since recovery based on principles of contracts implied in law essentially would resurrect the old common-law marriage doctrine which was specifically abolished by the Legislature. Although, as previously noted, the *Marvin* [*v. Marvin*, 18 Cal. 3d 660, 557 P.2d 106, 134 Cal. Rptr. 815] Court denied that the effect of its decision would be to resurrect the principle of common law marriages, commentators have been less certain.

Alexander, 445 So. 2d at 839, quoting *Carnes*, 109 Mich. App. at 216–17, 311 N.W.2d at 753. . . .

Elvis, nevertheless, relies on *Pickens v. Pickens*, 490 So. 2d 872 (Miss. 1986), *Taylor v. Taylor*, 317 So. 2d 422 (Miss. 1975), and *Chrismond v. Chrismond*, 52 So. 2d 624 (Miss. 1951) to support her claim that she is entitled to an equitable distribution of the assets accumulated during the course of the relationship. In *Pickens*, this Court recognized that cohabitation does not vest marital rights in either party, but

> notwithstanding, upon permanent separation, our law authorizes and sanctions an equitable division of property accumulated by two persons *as a result of their joint efforts*. This would be the case were a common law business partnership breaking up. It is equally the case where a man and woman, who have accumulated property in the course of a nonmarital cohabitation, permanently separate.

Pickens, 490 So. 2d at 875 (emphasis added). The *Pickens* Court noted that it was faced with "an arguably unique factual setting." 490 So.2d at 873. In that case, the Pickens were married in 1948. They divorced in 1962, but resumed living together without remarrying in 1963. When Mr. Pickens retired in 1983, the couple separated permanently. Observing that Mrs. Pickens had worked outside of the home for twenty years and taken care of the household, the Court reiterated that:

> Where parties such as these live together in what at least be [sic] acknowledged to be a partnership and where, *through their joint efforts*, real property or personal property, or both, are accumulated, an equitable division of such property will be ordered upon the permanent breakup and separation [footnote omitted].

Pickens, 490 So. 2d at 875–6 (emphasis added). Thus it affirmed the chancellor's decision, effecting an equal division of the homestead furnishings, but dividing the homestead property and several certificates of deposit in such a way as to reflect the contributions of Mr. Pickens' inheritance and a settlement he had received from an automobile accident. . . .

In *Pickens* . . . the Court affirmed divisions of property which had been accumulated through the "joint efforts" of the parties. Elvis seeks an equitable division of the more than $5 million in discovered assets Travis accumulated during their years of cohabitation. The record does not support the picture of Elvis' active role in the development of the Astro-Lounger empire that is embroidered in her brief. Further, there is no evidence in the record to suggest that the development of Astro-Lounger and its related enterprises or the expansion of Travis' real estate portfolio was the result of their joint efforts. Likewise, as Travis vigorously argues, there is no indication that the two had formed a "partnership" as Elvis initially claimed in her complaint.

IV.

When opportunity knocks, one must answer its call. Elvis Davis failed to do so and thus her claim is all for naught. Our legislature has not extended the rights enjoyed by married people to those who choose merely to cohabit. To the contrary, cohabitation is still prohibited by statute. Elvis was well-compensated during and after the relationship. We see no reason to advocate any form of "palimony" when the legislature has not so spoken.

NOTES AND QUESTIONS

(1) Are these two case primarily distinguishable on their facts or are the courts applying two different legal rules? Can you identify the rule or principle being applied in each case? Does the result in each case comport with the expectations of the parties? With general principles of equity?

(2) Commenting on cohabitation contracts between same-sex partners, one commentator has suggested that such contracts "tend to be enforced where the parties structure their agreement like a business arrangement. They are less likely to be enforced, however, when they mirror traditional marriage." Martha M. Ertman, *Sexuality: Contractual Purgatory for Sexual Marginorities: Not Heaven, but Not Hell Either*, 73 Denv. U. L. Rev. 1107, 1137 (1996). Does this suggestion illuminate the results in these two cases? Should courts be particularly wary of enforcing alleged cohabitation arrangements that "mirror traditional marriage?" Why or why not?

(3) The court in *Elvis* notes that nonmarital cohabitation remains a crime in Missouri. Should a court take such a criminal prohibition into account in adjudicating property claims arising out of a cohabitation relationship? *Compare, e.g., Hewitt v. Hewitt*, 394 N.E.2d 1204, 1209 (Ill. 1979) (refusing to recognize contracts between cohabitants on grounds that enforcement would encourage illicit relationships and violate public policy of preserving the integrity of marriage) *with In re Estate of Steffes*, 290 N.W.2d 697, 709 (Wis. 1980) (enforcing implied contract between cohabitants despite Wisconsin statute making cohabitation a crime).

(4) In reaching its decision, the *Connell* court draws explicitly on property concepts and statutes applicable to the dissolution of marriage. You will examine these property concepts in Chapter 10. For now, the important question is the extent to which such marriage-related rights and obligations should be applied to claims arising out of nonmarital cohabitation relationships. As the two preceding cases suggest, the answer to this question varies considerably. In addition to *Connell*, courts that have invoked—or drawn analogies to—marriage-related property statutes in adjudicating claims between unmarried cohabitants include *Western State Constr., Inc. v. Michoff*, 840 P.2d 1220, 1229 (Nev. 1992) (unmarried cohabitants may agree to hold their property as though they were married; in such a case community property law may apply by analogy) and *Shuraleff v. Donnelly*, 817 P.2d 764, 769 (Or. Ct. App. 1991) (trial court appropriately applied statutory principle of "just and equitable" distribution to divide property acquired during 14-year nonmarital domestic relationship).

In contexts other than property distribution, however, courts have generally refused to allow unmarried cohabitants to invoke statutory remedies available to divorcing couples. For example, *Friedman v. Friedman*, 24 Cal. Rptr. 2d 892, 898 (Cal. Ct. App. 1993), held that a trial court lacks authority to award temporary support to a disabled cohabitant pending trial of her express and implied contract claims, since such temporary relief was available only in the context of marriage and divorce. Similarly, the court in *Western Community Bank v. Helmer*, 740 P.2d 359, 361 (Wash. Ct. App. 1987), ruled that a statute permitting an award of attorney's fees in a marriage dissolution action was inapplicable to an action to distribute property following a nonmarital cohabitation relationship. *Accord, Crowe v. DeGioia*, 495 A.2d 889 (N.J. Super. Ct. App. Div. 1985), *aff'd*, 505 A.2d 591 (N.J. 1986).

(5) Several commentators have suggested the creation of a status known as nonmarital cohabitant. When such a status is established, the court could proceed to apportion the assets of the members of the status according to traditional principles of community property or of equitable distribution. *See, e.g.,* Grace Blumberg, *Cohabitation Without Marriage, A Different Perspective*, 28 UCLA L. Rev. 1125 (1981); Carol Bruch, *Property Rights of De Facto Spouses Including Thoughts on the Value of Homemakers' Services*, 10 Fam. L.Q. 101 (1976). Is this essentially what the court is doing in *Connell v. Francisco*? Would the creation of such a new status be good idea? If so, should it be done by legislatures or by courts? You may wish to reconsider these questions after you have studied the material in Chapter 10 on the Economic Consequences of Divorce.

(6) **Custody Disputes Between Unmarried Cohabitants**. Disputes between unmarried partners, particularly same-sex partners, may also arise over visitation or custody of a child jointly raised by the couple, but legally related to only one partner through biology or adoption. Courts have traditionally been reluctant to recognize parenting claims brought by the partner who is not legally related to the child. *See, e.g., Titchenal v. Dexter*, 693 A.2d 682, 683 (Vt. 1997) (in the absence of statutory authorization, court lacks authority to adjudicate visitation disputes between lesbian ex-partners where only one partner has adopted the child); *Nancy S. v. Michele G.*, 279 Cal. Rptr 212, 219 (Cal. Ct. App. 1991) (ex-partner who had jointly raised children for several years was not entitled to visitation over the objection of the biological mother; court concerned that granting such visitation "could expose other natural parents to litigation brought by child-care providers of long standing, relatives, successive sets of stepparents or other close friends of the family");

Alison D. v. Virginia M., 572 N.E.2d 27, 28–33 (N.Y. 1991) (biological mother's ex-partner, who had facilitated child's conception and birth and jointly raised child for more than 2 years, lacked standing to seek visitation over the objection of the biological mother); *Spreader v. Hermes*, 471 N.W.2d 202, 211 (Wis. 1991) (co-parenting agreement that purported to grant custody rights to unmarried partner of biological mother held unenforceable as against public policy).

Other decisions however, have recognized such parenting claims. *See, e.g., Fowler v. Jones*, 949 S.W.2d 442, 444 (Tex. Ct. App. 1997) (ex-partner of biological mother had standing to seek visitation with child conceived and born during cohabitation relationship); *J.A.L. v. E.P.H.*, 682 A.2d 1314, 1316 (Pa. Super. Ct. 1996) (ex-partner who had lived with child and biological mother in a family setting and developed a close relationship with the child as a result of the mother's participation and acquiescence stood in loco parentis to the child and therefore had standing to seek partial custody); *Holtzman v. Knott*, 533 N.W.2d 419, 435 (Wis. 1995), *cert. denied sub nom.*, *Knott v. Holtzman*, 133 L. Ed. 2d. 404 (1995) (ex-partner of biological mother may seek court-ordered visitation where he or she has a parent-like relationship with a child and the child's biological parent has interfered substantially with that relationship); *A.C. v. C.B.*, 829 P.2d 660, 665 (N.M. Ct. App. 1992), *cert. denied*, 827 A.2d 837 (N.M. 1992) (former lesbian partner who had entered into oral coparenting agreement had colorable claim to joint legal custody and time-sharing of partner's biological child).

Some state domestic relations statutes explicitly allow non-parents who have established a significant relationship with a child to petition for visitation or custody. *See, e.g.,* Oregon Rev. Stat. Ann. § 109.119[1] ("Any person including but not limited to a foster parent, stepparent, grandparent . . . who has established emotional ties creating a child-parent relationship with a child" may seek visitation or other right of custody). For a discussion of the issues raised by these cases, see, e.g., Elizabeth A. Delaney, *Statutory Protection of the Other Mother: Legally Recognizing the Relationship Between the Nonbiological Lesbian Parent and Her Child*, 43 Hastings L.J. 177 (1991); Nancy Polikoff, *This Child Does Have Two Mothers: Redefining Parenthood to Meet the Needs of Children in Lesbian-Mother and other Nontraditional Families*, 78 Geo. L.J. 459 (1990); Katherine Bartlett, *Rethinking Parenthood as an Exclusive Status: The Need for Legal Alternatives When the Premise of the Nuclear Family has Failed*, 70 Va. L. Rev. 879 (1984). For a discussion of stepparent and second parent adoption as a means of creating a legally protected relationship between a child and a non-biological co-parent, see § 8.04[C], *below*.

(7) **Problem.** Paul and Darlene met in 1985, when Paul rented a room in Darlene's house. Paul was separated from his wife at the time, while Darlene was unmarried. Paul told Darlene that he had not formally terminated his marriage because his wife did not believe in divorce. Within a short time, Paul and Darlene began an intimate relationship, and they lived together until 1994. At the time their relationship began, Darlene worked as an accountant and owned the house in which the couple lived, along with several acres of land. Paul had approximately $5,000 in savings and was employed as a carpenter. Each earned a salary of approximately $30,000 a year. In 1988, a house fire badly damaged Darlene's house, in which the couple was living. Paul quit his carpentry job and spent approximately ten months rebuilding the house, using money that Darlene received from an insurance settlement. In 1990, the couple decided to purchase a 15-acre parcel contiguous

to Darlene's property for $50,000, to develop as a holly farm. Each contributed approximately $5,000 for a down payment and Darlene used her property as collateral to secure a mortgage. The couple planned to develop the farm jointly, but they decided to take title solely in Darlene's name, in order to avoid the risk that Paul's wife could claim an interest in the property. For the next four years, Paul worked full time developing the holly farm. Darlene continued to work as an accountant, and the couple used her salary to pay most of their living expenses. Darlene also handled farm's taxes and business affairs, including its small payroll. Paul drew a modest salary during this time, but the couple poured most of the farm's profits into expanding the business. The couple's business efforts payed off. By 1994, the holly farm was making a substantial profit and a large lumber company had offered to buy the business for over $1,000,000. Unfortunately, the couple's personal relationship did not fare as well and they separated at the end of 1994. Paul has now sued Darlene, claiming that he is entitled to half of the value of the holly farm, as well as an interest in the couple's residence and a share of any savings and retirement benefits that Darlene accumulated during the parties' nine-year relationship.

What theory or theories is Paul likely to invoke? On what grounds can Darlene defend against Paul's claims? If you were the judge hearing the case, how would you rule and why? What additional information would you like to have before making your decision?

§ 3.03 Disputes Between Cohabitants and Third Parties

DAVIS v. DEPARTMENT OF EMPLOYMENT SECURITY
Washington Supreme Court
737 P.2d 1262 (1987)

DORE, J.

We hold that a person who voluntarily quits employment to live in a meretricious relationship is not entitled to unemployment compensation under the Employment Security Act, RCW Title 50. . . . .

Karen Davis quit her job with the Equifax Corporation in Tacoma, where she had been employed for 13 years, in order to move from Tacoma to Port Angeles and live with Andrew Stephens. Davis and Stephens had been seeing each other every weekend for 6 years, and Davis considers the relationship to be the same as a marriage. Stephens is the executor of Davis' estate, the beneficiary of her insurance, and is to act on behalf of her children if she dies. Davis believes she will eventually marry Stephens, but has no immediate plans to marry him for personal and financial reasons. The financial reason appears to be that if they were married her income might be subject to child support obligations for Stephens' children by his ex-wife.

Prior to quitting her job, Davis requested to be transferred to the Port Angeles branch of Equifax, but such request was denied because it is a 1-person office that had no vacancy. She was denied a request for a leave of absence because of company policy against such leaves. Stephens attempted, without success, to seek employment in Tacoma or its environs.

Davis applied to the Department of Employment Security for unemployment benefits, but was denied benefits because it found she lacked good cause for quitting. . . .

RCW 50.20.050(4) provides a separate exception to disqualification for employees who voluntarily quit work without good cause. This "marital status" and "domestic responsibilities" exception provides:

> Subsections (1) and (3) of this section shall not apply to an individual whose marital status or domestic responsibilities cause him or her to leave employment . . . .

This court has held that, under RCW 50.20.050(4), a person who voluntarily leaves her job in order to marry and move to a place where it would be impracticable to commute to her old job leaves work because of "marital status." Davis urges this court to extend *Yamauchi* cover single people who voluntarily leave employment to live in meretricious relationships. In *Yamauchi*, while we did not find that the "marital status" exception requires that the employee be married at the time of quitting employment, we did require a nexus between the employee's quitting employment and marriage; the employee was not entitled to benefits until the marriage actually took place. *Yamauchi*, at 781. The *Yamauchi* opinion does not cover leaving employment to live in a meretricious relationship.

Davis also urges this court to extend our decision in *In re Marriage of Lindsey*, 101 N.W.2d 299, 678 P.2d 328 (1984) to cover her situation. In *Lindsey*, this court held that in disposing of property accumulated during a meretricious relationship, courts must examine the relationship and the property and make a just and equitable disposition. . . . In *Lindsey* the concern was a fair distribution of property between two parties in a marriage-like union. *Lindsey* does not stand for the proposition that a meretricious relationship is the same as a marriage. As the California Supreme Court noted in the factually similar case of *Norman v. Unemployment Ins. Appeals Bd.*, 34 Cal. 3d 1, 7, 663 P.2d 904, 192 Cal. Rptr. 134 (1983), the extension of property distribution rights of spouses to partners in meretricious relationships does not elevate meretricious relationships themselves to the level of marriages for any and all purposes.

Equal Protection

Davis argues that discrimination against a person in a meretricious relationship vis-a-vis a married person violates the fourteenth amendment to the United States Constitution. The right to marry is fundamental. *Zablocki v. Redhail*, 434 U.S. 374 (1978). However, this court has held that the right to live in a meretricious relationship without marrying is not fundamental; therefore, legislation that draws distinctions between married persons and those living in such relationships is subject to the less rigorous scrutiny of the "rational relationship" test.

Where, as here, legislation involves the grant of limited public funds, reviewing courts should give deference to allocation decisions by state officials. *Dandridge v. Williams*, 397 U.S. 471 (1970). Statutory discrimination in public welfare programs will be upheld if any state of facts reasonably may be conceived to justify it. *Dandridge*, at 485.

Under the "rational relationship" test legislation must satisfy three requirements: (1) it must apply alike to all members of the designated class; (2) there must be some basis in reality for reasonably distinguishing between those falling within the class and those falling outside of it; and (3) the challenged classification must have a rational relationship to the purposes of the challenged statute.

Here, the challenged classification is persons in meretricious relationships seeking unemployment compensation. RCW 50.20.050 satisfies the first prong of the rational relationship test, as it applies equally to all applicants within that classification. The legislation also satisfies the second prong. We held in *Willard* that a classification based on marriage is reasonable, in view of the fact that the Legislature might consider marriage to be evidence of a serious commitment to the stability of the family unit. *Willard*, at 764.

RCW 50.20.050 also satisfies the third prong of the test. The purpose of the Employment Security Act is to benefit persons unemployed through no fault of their own. The fact that funds available for distribution under the Employment Security Act are finite is not in itself a sufficient basis to uphold the classification. However, the State is entitled to consider marriage as evidence of a serious commitment to a stable family unit. An employee who voluntarily quits work because of the needs of a marriage may be considered to have no "fault" and therefore not disqualified from unemployment compensation.

Conclusion

The Employment Security Act has only limited exceptions to the disqualification of applicants who voluntarily quit work. Davis failed to establish that any of the exceptions apply to her situation. Furthermore, the act's denial of benefits to those who leave work in order to live in a meretricious relationship, as opposed to those who leave in order to follow a spouse to a new location, does not offend principles of equal protection.

NOTES AND COMMENTS

(1) The plaintiff in *Davis* unsuccessfully attempts to use decisions such as *Marvin*, which recognize rights and obligations between unmarried cohabitants, to support her entitlement to unemployment benefits. What are the similarities and differences between the type of claim asserted in *Marvin* and the claims made by unmarried cohabitants such as Karen Davis?

(2) The *Davis* court also rejects the argument that treating *Davis* differently than an employee who leaves her job in order to follow a spouse or prospective spouse, violates the equal protection clause of the Fourteenth Amendment. Do you agree with the court that such differential treatment is "rational"? Is rationality the appropriate constitutional standard here? Why or why not?

BRASCHI v. STAHL ASSOCIATES COMPANY
New York Court of Appeals
74 N.Y.2d 201, 543 N.E.2d 49, 544 N.Y.S.2d 784 (1989)

TITONE, J.

Appellant, Miguel Braschi, was living with Leslie Blanchard in a rent-controlled apartment located at 405 East 54th Street from the summer of 1975 until Blanchard's death in September of 1986. In November of 1986, respondent, Stahl Associates Company, the owner of the apartment building, served a notice to cure on appellant contending that he was a mere licensee with no right to occupy the apartment since only Blanchard was the tenant of record. In December of 1986 respondent served appellant with a notice to terminate informing appellant that he had one month to vacate the apartment and that, if the apartment was not vacated, respondent would commence summary proceedings to evict him.

Appellant then initiated an action seeking a permanent injunction and a declaration of entitlement to occupy the apartment. By order to show cause appellant then moved for a preliminary injunction, pendente lite, enjoining respondent from evicting him until a court could determine whether he was a member of Blanchard's family within the meaning of 9 NYCRR 2204.6(d). After examining the nature of the relationship between the two men, Supreme Court concluded that appellant was a "family member" within the meaning of the regulation and, accordingly, that a preliminary injunction should be issued. The court based this decision on its finding that the long-term interdependent nature of the 10-year relationship between appellant and Blanchard "fulfills any definitional criteria of the term 'family.'"

The Appellate Division reversed, concluding that section 2204.6 (d) provides noneviction protection only to "family members within traditional, legally recognized familial relationships." Since appellant's and Blanchard's relationship was not one given formal recognition by the law, the court held that appellant could not seek the protection of the noneviction ordinance. . . .

The present dispute arises because the term "family" is not defined in the rent-control code and the legislative history is devoid of any specific reference to the noneviction provision. All that is known is the legislative purpose underlying the enactment of the rent-control laws as a whole.

Rent control was enacted to address a "serious public emergency" created by "an acute shortage in dwellings," which resulted in "speculative, unwarranted and abnormal increases in rents" These measures were designed to regulate and control the housing market so as to "prevent exactions of unjust, unreasonable and oppressive rents and rental agreements and to forestall profiteering, speculation and other disruptive practices tending to produce threats to the public health * * * [and] to prevent uncertainty, hardship and dislocation." Although initially designed as an emergency measure to alleviate the housing shortage attributable to the end of World War II, "a serious public emergency continues to exist in the housing of a considerable number of persons." Consequently, the Legislature has found it necessary to continually reenact the rent-control laws, thereby providing continued protection to tenants.

To accomplish its goals, the Legislature recognized that not only would rents have to be controlled, but that evictions would have to be regulated and controlled as well. Hence, section 2204.6 of the New York City Rent and Eviction Regulations (9 NYCRR 2204.6), which authorizes the issuance of a certificate for the eviction of persons occupying a rent-controlled apartment after the death of the named tenant, provides, in subdivision (d), noneviction protection to those occupants who are either the "surviving spouse of the deceased tenant or some other member of the deceased tenant's family who has been living with the tenant [of record]" The manifest intent of this section is to restrict the landowners' ability to evict a narrow class of occupants other than the tenant of record. The question presented here concerns the scope of the protections provided. Juxtaposed against this intent favoring the protection of tenants, is the over-all objective of a gradual "transition from regulation to a normal market of free bargaining between landlord and tenant" One way in which this goal is to be achieved is "vacancy decontrol," which automatically makes rent-control units subject to the less rigorous provisions of rent stabilization upon the termination of the rent-control tenancy.

Emphasizing the latter objective, respondent argues that the term "family member" as used in 9 NYCRR 2204.6 (d) should be construed, consistent with this State's intestacy laws, to mean relationships of blood, consanguinity and adoption in order to effectuate the over-all goal of orderly succession to real property. Under this interpretation, only those entitled to inherit under the laws of intestacy would be afforded noneviction protection. . . .

. . . The noneviction provision does not concern succession to real property but rather is a means of protecting a certain class of occupants from the sudden loss of their homes. The regulation does not create an alienable property right that could be sold, assigned or otherwise disposed of and, hence, need not be construed as coextensive with the intestacy laws. Moreover, such a construction would be inconsistent with the purposes of the rent-control system as a whole, since it would afford protection to distant blood relatives who actually had but a superficial relationship with the deceased tenant while denying that protection to unmarried lifetime partners. . . ..

[W]e conclude that the term family, as used in 9 NYCRR 2204.6(d), should not be rigidly restricted to those people who have formalized their relationship by obtaining, for instance, a marriage certificate or an adoption order. The intended protection against sudden eviction should not rest on fictitious legal distinctions or genetic history, but instead should find its foundation in the reality of family life. In the context of eviction, a more realistic, and certainly equally valid, view of a family includes two adult lifetime partners whose relationship is long term and characterized by an emotional and financial commitment and interdependence. This view comports both with our society's traditional concept of "family" and with the expectations of individuals who live in such nuclear units. In fact, Webster's Dictionary defines "family" first as "a group of people united by certain convictions or common affiliation." Hence, it is reasonable to conclude that, in using the term "family," the Legislature intended to extend protection to those who reside in households having all of the normal familial characteristics. Appellant Braschi should therefore be afforded the opportunity to prove that he and Blanchard had such a household. . . ..

The determination as to whether an individual is entitled to noneviction protection should be based upon an objective examination of the relationship of the parties. In making this assessment, the lower courts of this State have looked to a number of factors, including the exclusivity and longevity of the relationship, the level of emotional and financial commitment, the manner in which the parties have conducted their everyday lives and held themselves out to society, and the reliance placed upon one another for daily family services These factors are most helpful, although it should be emphasized that the presence or absence of one or more of them is not dispositive since it is the totality of the relationship as evidenced by the dedication, caring and self-sacrifice of the parties which should, in the final analysis, control. Appellant's situation provides an example of how the rule should be applied.

Appellant and Blanchard lived together as permanent life partners for more than 10 years. They regarded one another, and were regarded by friends and family, as spouses. The two men's families were aware of the nature of the relationship, and they regularly visited each other's families and attended family functions together, as a couple. Even today, appellant continues to maintain a relationship with Blanchard's niece, who considers him an uncle.

In addition to their interwoven social lives, appellant clearly considered the apartment his home. He lists the apartment as his address on his driver's license and passport, and receives all his mail at the apartment address. Moreover, appellant's tenancy was known to the building's superintendent and doormen, who viewed the two men as a couple.

Financially, the two men shared all obligations including a household budget. The two were authorized signatories of three safe-deposit boxes, they maintained joint checking and savings accounts, and joint credit cards. In fact, rent was often paid with a check from their joint checking account. Additionally, Blanchard executed a power of attorney in appellant's favor so that appellant could make necessary decisions—financial, medical and personal—for him during his illness. Finally, appellant was the named beneficiary of Blanchard's life insurance policy, as well as the primary legatee and coexecutor of Blanchard's estate. Hence, a court examining these facts could reasonably conclude that these men were much more than mere roommates. . . ..

SIMONS, J (dissenting).

I would affirm. The plurality has adopted a definition of family which extends the language of the regulation well beyond the implication of the words used in it. In doing so, it has expanded the class indefinitely to include anyone who can satisfy an administrator that he or she had an emotional and financial "commitment" to the statutory tenant. Its interpretation is inconsistent with the legislative scheme underlying rent regulation, goes well beyond the intended purposes of 9 NYCRR 2204.6(d), and produces an unworkable test that is subject to abuse. . . .

Central to any interpretation of the regulatory language is a determination of its purpose. There can be little doubt that the purpose of section 2204.6 (d) was to create succession rights to a possessory interest in real property where the tenant of record has died or vacated the apartment. It creates a new tenancy for every surviving family member living with decedent at the time of death who then becomes a new statutory tenant until death or until he or she vacates the apartment. The State concerns underlying this provision include the orderly and just succession of property interests (which includes protecting a deceased's spouse and family from loss of their longtime home) and the professed State objective that there be a gradual transition from government regulation to a normal market of free bargaining between landlord and tenant. Those objectives require a weighing of the interests of certain individuals living with the tenant of record at his or her death and the interests of the landlord in regaining possession of its property and rerenting it under the less onerous rent-stabilization laws. The interests are properly balanced if the regulation's exception is applied by using objectively verifiable relationships based on blood, marriage and adoption, as the State has historically done in the estate succession laws, family court acts and similar legislation. The distinction is warranted because members of families, so defined, assume certain legal obligations to each other and to third persons, such as creditors, which are not imposed on unrelated individuals and this legal interdependency is worthy of consideration in determining which individuals are entitled to succeed to the interest of the statutory tenant in rent-controlled premises. Moreover, such an interpretation promotes certainty and consistency in the law and obviates the need for drawn out hearings and litigation focusing on such intangibles as the strength and duration of the relationship and the extent of the emotional and financial interdependency. So limited, the regulation may be viewed as a tempered response, balancing the rights of landlords with those of the tenant. To come within that protected class, individuals must comply with State laws relating to marriage or adoption. Plaintiff cannot avail himself of these institutions, of course, but that only points up the need for a legislative solution, not a judicial one. . . .

Rent control generally and section 2204.6, in particular, are in substantial derogation of property owners' rights. The court should not reach out and devise an expansive definition in this policy-laden area based upon limited experience and knowledge of the problems. The evidence available suggests that such a definition was not intended and that the ordinary and popular meaning of family in the traditional sense should be applied. . . .

Accordingly, I would affirm the order of the Appellate Division.

NOTES AND QUESTIONS

(1) One of the disagreements between the majority and the dissent in *Brashi* is the relative desirability of a formal, as opposed to a functional, definition of family in the context of the rent control statutes. The formal approach advocated by the dissent generally limits the legal definition of "family" to persons related by blood, marriage or adoption. A functional approach, by contrast,

> inquires whether a relationship shares the essential characteristics of a traditionally accepted relationship and fulfills the same human needs. Thus, the specific characteristics of each relationship, such as economic cooperation, participation in domestic responsibilities, and affection between the parties, play a crucial role in a functional determination of family status. . . . Courts that apply functionalism are generally less deferential to the legislature and believe that they should expand the definition of family to incorporate social changes and keep pace with "the needs of the country." For functionalist courts, the value of marriage and parenthood derives from positive societal effects, such as encouragement of stable, affectionate, and economically efficient human relationships.

Note, *Looking for a Family Resemblance: The Limits of the Functional Approach to the Legal Definition of Family*, 104 Harv. L. Rev. 1640, 1646–47 (1991); *see* Martha Minow, *Redefining Families: Whose In and Who's Out?*, 62 U. Colo. L. Rev. 269 (1991). What do you see as the advantages and disadvantages of each these approaches? Would Karen Davis have qualified for unemployment benefits under *Brashi's* functional approach?

(2) The majority and the dissent in *Brashi* also seem to disagree on the proper balance between the competing purposes of the New York City rent control scheme. The majority emphasizes the scheme's tenant protection purpose while the dissent places more emphasis on protecting the property rights of the landlord. To what extent are judicial (and legislative) decisions on family law issues, including the appropriate definition of "family," influenced by the decision-makers' broader political and economic views, including the desirability of government restrictions on unfettered market activity?

(3) Is it relevant that Miguel Brashi was precluded by law from marrying his domestic partner, while Karen Davis was not?

(4) **Functional Families and the Constitution.** In *Village of Belle Terre v. Boraas*, 416 U.S. 1, 7 (1974), the Supreme Court upheld the constitutionality of a single-family zoning ordinance which defined "family" to mean one or more persons related by blood, adoption or marriage, or not more than two unrelated persons living and cooking together as a single housekeeping unit. Rejecting a challenge brought by six unrelated college students, the Court held that the zoning ordinance was rationally related to the state's purpose of promoting

family needs and values. Three years later, in *Moore v. City of East Cleveland*, 431 U.S. 494, 498 (1977), the Court struck down a zoning ordinance that limited occupancy to members of a single family, but defined family in such a way that a grandmother, her son, and her two grandsons, who were cousins—rather than brothers—did not qualify. The Court distinguished *Belle Terre* on the ground that the ordinance at issue there affected only unrelated individuals; it allowed all who were related by blood, adoption or marriage to live together without restriction.

Since 1977, state courts have reached varying results on the permissibility of restrictive applications of single family zoning ordinances. Cases that have upheld restrictions include *Nebraska v. Champoux*, 566 N.W.2d. 763, 764–68 (Neb. 1997) (upholding constitutionality of zoning ordinance which defined family as "any number of related persons and not more than two additional unrelated persons"); *Dinon v. Board of Zoning Appeals*, 595 A.2d 864, 870–71 (Conn. 1991) (zoning ordinance which defined family as "any number of individuals related by blood, marriage or adoption" was constitutional as applied to landlord who rented separately to 5 unrelated individuals); and *City of Ladue v. Horn*, 720 S.W.2d 745, 750 (Mo. Ct. App. 1986) (single-family zoning law permissibly excluded unmarried couple and their children). Cases that have struck down restrictive definitions of family, on either federal or state constitutional grounds, include *McMinn v. Town of Oyster Bay*, 488 N.E.2d 1240, 1242 (N.Y. 1985) (ordinance limiting occupancy of single-family homes to persons related by blood, marriage or adoption, or to two unrelated persons 62 years of age or older, violated state constitution); *Glassboro v. Vallorosi*, 568 A.2d 888, 894 (N.J. 1990) (ten college students who lived together as the functional equivalent of a family were entitled to live in single-family dwelling, notwithstanding the zoning statute's more restrictive definition of family); and *Saunders v. Clark County Zoning Department*, 421 N.E.2d 152, 155–56 (Ohio 1981) (parents living with five biological and nine foster children constituted a "family" under zoning laws; any attempt to define term more narrowly "would unconstitutionally intrude upon an individuals right to choose the family living arrangement best suited to him and his loved ones").

Query: Based on these decisions, would it be constitutional for a municipality to exclude unmarried couples from an area zoned for single-family dwellings? Suppose that a municipality wanted to permit occupancy by unmarried couples (and their children), but wanted to exclude other groups of unrelated individuals, such as college students. Can you draft a definition of "family" that would accomplish these objectives?

(5) The rent control and unemployment statutes at issue in *Brashi* and *Davis* are typical of hundreds of federal and state laws that condition eligibility for legal and economic benefits on an individual's marital or family status. *See, e.g., Baehr v. Lewin*, 852 P.2d 44, 59 (Haw. 1993) (referring to "a multiplicity of rights and benefits that are contingent upon [marital] status" and listing fourteen of the most salient marital rights and benefits). Few of these statutory benefits are available to unmarried cohabitants, either individually or as a couple. In an increasing number of cases, unmarried couples—both straight and gay—have challenged the statutory and common law structures that condition such benefits on marriage.

As the *Brashi* and *Davis* decisions suggest, the results of these cases are not uniform. In particular, case outcomes appear to depend, in significant part, on the language of the particular eligibility provision at issue. Where a statute or regulation refers specifically to "spouses," or contains an explicit and narrow definition of family, courts have generally held that unmarried cohabitants are ineligible for benefits. *See, e.g., Greenwald v. H & P St. Assocs.*, 659 N.Y.S.2d 473, 474 (N.Y. App. Div. 1997) (spousal privilege statute which protects confidential communications between a "husband" and "wife" "during marriage" does not extend to same-sex domestic partners; *Braschi* is distinguishable in that the rent regulations did not define the operative term "family"); *Rovira v. AT&T*, 817 F. Supp. 1062, 1069–70 (S.D.N.Y. 1993) (surviving same-sex partner and her children, who lived with deceased for 10 years, not entitled to death benefits under employer pension plan that limited eligible beneficiaries to "the spouse and the dependent children . . . of the deceased"); *In re Estate of Cooper*, 592 N.Y.S.2d 797, 798–99 (N.Y. App. Div. 1993) (gay life partner not entitled to exercise right of election of "surviving spouse" against decedent's estate); *Bone v. Allen*, 186 B.R. 769, 771 (Bankr. N.D. Ga. 1995) (unmarried couple did not qualify as debtor and "spouse" for purposes of filing joint bankruptcy petition).

By contrast, where the underlying statute or administrative provision refers more generally to "dependents" or "family members," some courts have held that unmarried cohabitants may qualify for benefits if they satisfy certain functional criteria. *See, e.g., Donovan v. Workers' Compensation Appeals Bd.*, 187 Cal. Rptr. 869, 873 (Cal. Ct. App. 1982) (alleged live-in partner of deceased employee may qualify for workers' compensation benefits if he can demonstrate that he was dependent on the employee for support); *Solomon v. District of Columbia*, 21 Fam. L. Rep. (BNA) 1316 (D.C. Super. Ct. April 25, 1995) (same-sex partner qualified as "next of kin" for purposes of wrongful death action, since the partners' relationship "had all the attributes of a married couple, but for the fact that it could not be recognized with a marriage license"); *State v. Hadinger*, 573 N.E.2d 1191, 1192 (Ohio Ct. App. 1991) (act of domestic violence by same-sex cohabitant was covered by statute applicable to crimes against "a person living as a spouse . . . of the offender").

In addition, where children are involved, the United States Supreme Court has limited the ability of states to differentiate between marital and nonmarital families. *See, e.g., New Jersey Welfare Rights Org. v. Cahill*, 411 U.S. 619, 621 (1973) (use by a state of even its own funds to aid children in marital families, while denying aid to those in nonmarital families, violates equal protection); *King v. Smith*, 392 U.S. 309, 333–34 (1968) (holding that states must dispense federal funds to dependent children in families with a "substitute father" on the same basis as to children in marital families). *See also* § 5.02, *below*.

(6) Where statutory eligibility requirements clearly exclude unmarried couples, those couples have invoked state and local anti-discrimination laws to challenge the unavailability of benefits. Same-sex couples, in particular, have argued that providing benefits to married persons, but not to same-sex partners, violates laws barring discrimination on the basis of sexual orientation, which have been adopted by a number of states and by many counties and municipalities. *See* Craig W. Christiansen, *Legal Ordering Of Family Values: The Case of Gay and Lesbian Families*, 18 Cardozo L. Rev. 1299, 1372–80 (1997). These arguments have been largely unsuccessful. For example, in *Ross v. Denver Dep't of Health and Hosps.*, 883 P.2d 516, 520 (Colo. Ct. App. 1994), the court ruled that an employer's refusal to grant an unmarried employee family sick leave benefits to care for her same-sex domestic partner did not violate a state employment rule barring discrimination on the basis of sexual orientation:

> Ross was not denied family sick leave benefits to care for her same-sex partner because she is homosexual. An unmarried heterosexual employee also would not be

permitted to take family sick leave benefits to care for his or her unmarried opposite-sex partner. Thus, the rule does not treat homosexual employees and similarly situated heterosexual employees differently. . . . Ross urges that her inability to marry her same-sex partner thus distinguishes her situation from that of an unmarried heterosexual employee. That distinction, however, does not alter our conclusion that the Career Service Rules do not discriminate on the basis of sexual orientation. In this regard, Ross' concern is with a perceived unfairness of the state's marital laws. The decision to change the marriage laws to permit same-sex marriages, however, is a matter for the legislature, not the courts.

Accord, Phillips v. Wisconsin Personnel Comm'n, 482 N.W.2d 121 (Wis. 1992); *Hinman v. Department of Personnel Admin.*, 213 Cal. Rptr. 410 (Cal. Ct. App. 1985). Do you find the court's discrimination analysis persuasive? Why or why not?

(7) Unmarried couples have been somewhat more successful in arguing that conditioning benefits on marriage violates state and local statutes barring marital status discrimination. State laws banning discrimination on the basis of marital status have become increasingly common since the mid-1970s, but the scope of coverage varies widely, and some state courts have narrowly construed the types of conduct considered discriminatory. *See generally* John C. Beattie, *Note, Prohibiting Marital Status Discrimination: A Proposal for the Protection of Unmarried Couples*, 42 Hastings L.J. 1415 (1991) (describing judicial interpretation of marital status discrimination statutes and proposing a new interpretation to grant greater protection to unmarried couples); Craig W. Christiansen, *Legal Ordering Of Family Values: The Case of Gay and Lesbian Families*, 18 Cardozo L. Rev. 1299, 1374–77 (1997) (discussing cases). Federal law also prohibits discrimination based on marital status in a few specific areas, such as the availability credit. *See, e.g., Markham v. Colonial Mortgage Serv. Co.*, 605 F.2d 566, 569–70 (D.C. Cir. 1979) (lender's refusal to aggregate the income of unmarried partners applying for joint mortgage loan constitutes violates Equal Credit Opportunity Act, since the income would have been aggregated had the applicants been married).

Several recent decisions have upheld marital status discrimination claims brought by unmarried couples. In *Smith v. Fair Employment and Housing Commission*, 913 P.2d 909, 928 (Cal. 1996), *cert. denied*, 117 S. Ct. 2531 (1997), the California Supreme Court held that a landlord who refused, on religious grounds, to rent an apartment to an unmarried couple violated the state statute banning discrimination based on marital status. The California Court also rejected the landlord's claim that forcing him to rent to unmarried couples violated his constitutionally protected freedom of religion. *Id.* at 931. *Accord, Swanner v. Anchorage Equal Rights Comm'n*, 874 P.2d 274, 278–79 (Alaska 1994), *cert. denied*, 513 U.S. 979 (1994) (landlord's refusal to rent apartment to unmarried couple violates state ban on discrimination based on marital status; compelling state interests support enforcement of marital status discrimination laws over landlords' religious objections).

Other courts have reached a contrary result. *See, e.g., Attorney General v. Desilets*, 636 N.E.2d 233, 236 (Mass. 1994) (applying nondiscrimination statute to religiously motivated refusal to rent infringes religious freedom unless justified by compelling circumstances); *State by Cooper v. French*, 460 N.W.2d 2, 4, 8 (Minn. 1990) (refusal to rent real estate to unmarried cohabitants is protected as free exercise of religion). *See generally* James C.

Geoly & Kevin R. Gustafson, *Religious Liberty and Fair Housing: Must A Landlord Rent Against His Conscience?*, 29 J. Marshall L. Rev. 455 (1996); Matthew J. Smith, *The Wages of Living in Sin: Discrimination in Housing Against Unmarried Couples*, 25 U.C. Davis L. Rev. 1055 (1992).

Judicial decisions extending benefits based on anti-discrimination statutes can, of course, be overruled by the legislature. In *University of Alaska v. Tumeo*, 933 P.2d 1147, 1152 (Alaska 1997), the Alaska Supreme Court held that the University of Alaska's policy of providing health care benefits to the spouses of employees, but not to employees' unmarried domestic partners, constituted unlawful marital status discrimination under the Alaska Human Rights Act. While the appeal was pending, however, the Alaska legislature amended the state Human Rights Act to permit employers to "provide greater health care and retirement benefits to employees who have a spouse or dependent children, that are not provided to other employees"—thus negating the practical effect of the Supreme Court's ruling. *Query:* If you had been a member of the Alaska legislature, would you have voted for this amendment? Why or why not?

(8) Disputes may also arise between unmarried cohabitants and other family members, upon the death or disability of one member of the couple. After Sharon Kowalski was severely injured in an auto accident, Karen Thompson, the partner with whom she had been "living together as a couple for four years" waged a protracted court battle for guardianship against Kowalski's parents, who were unaware of their daughter's lesbian relationship before the accident and who sought to bar Thompson from contact with their daughter. *In re Guardianship of Kowalski*, 478 N.W.2d 790 (Minn. Ct. App. 1991). The trial court initially awarded guardianship to Kowalski's parents, but the appellate court reversed, finding that it would be in Sharon's best interests to award guardianship to her partner and describing Kowalski and Thompson as "a family of affinity, which ought to be accorded respect." *Id.* at 797.

A number of decisions have also granted child custody or guardianship to same-sex co-parents following the death of a biological mother, often over the competing claims of the deceased mothers' family members. *See, e.g., In re Guardianship of Astonn H.*, 635 N.Y.S.2d 418 (N.Y. Fam. Ct. 1995); *In re Pearlman*, 15 Fam. L. Rep. (BNA) 1355 (Fla. Cir. Ct. Mar. 31, 1989); *In re Hatzopoulos*, 4 Fam. L. Rep. (BNA) 2075 (Co. Juv. Ct., Mar. 8, 1977). *But see McGuffin v. Overton*, 542 N.W.2d 288, 289–92 (Mich. Ct. App. 1995) (denying custody to lesbian partner and coparent following death of biological mother, despite power of attorney and will purporting to transfer parental powers to coparent).

(9) Most disputes between unmarried cohabitants and third parties involve attempts by one or both partners to obtain benefits typically available to married couples. Occasionally, however, a third party seeks to impose on an unmarred couple obligations traditionally associated with marriage, as when a creditor seeks to hold one partner liable for the other partner's debts. *See, e.g., Plank v. Hartung*, 159 Cal. Rptr. 673 (Cal. Ct. App. 1979); *Mintz & Mintz, Inc. v. Color*, 250 So. 2d 816 (La. Ct. App. 1971). *Query:* Should unmarried couples who seek marriage-related rights and benefits also be required to accept the legal obligations that have traditionally accompanied marriage?

(10) **Problem.** Ellen and Michael met as seniors in college in 1990, and began cohabiting several months later. The couple planned to get married "sometime in the future," after each had finished graduate school and once they were ready to have children. During the

seven years that they lived together, they maintained a joint checking account from which they paid their bills, including the rent on an apartment that they leased together. They also jointly purchased an automobile, and named each other as life insurance beneficiaries. In September, 1996, the couple responded to a friend's telephone call for assistance in changing a tire on a nearby highway. As Michael changed the friend's tire on the shoulder of the roadway, he was struck by a car. After being struck by the vehicle, Michael's body was either dragged or propelled more than 100 feet. Ellen, who had been standing approximately five feet from Michael, witnessed the impact. Realizing that Michael was still alive, she ran to him and attempted to comfort him as he screamed and thrashed about. The following day, after a night-long hospital vigil, Ellen was told that Michael had died as a result of his injuries. Since the accident, Ellen has been unable to work and has undergone psychiatric and psychological treatment for depression and anxiety. Ellen recently instituted a lawsuit against the driver who struck Michael, seeking recovery under two different common law tort theories: loss of consortium and negligent infliction of emotional distress.

The courts of Ellen's state have previously recognized loss of consortium claims brought by husbands and wives. The state supreme court has defined consortium as "the reciprocal rights inherent in the marital relationship, including such undefined elements as comfort, companionship and commitment to the needs of each other." The state supreme court has also recognized "bystander" liability for negligent infliction of emotional injury, and has recently articulated a four-factor test for adjudicating such negligence claims. For a bystander-claimant to prevail, the claimant must demonstrate (1) the death or serious physical injury of another caused by defendant's negligence; (2) a marital or intimate, familial relationship between the plaintiff and the injured person; (3) observation of the death or injury at the scene of the accident; and (4) resulting severe emotional distress. With respect to the second element, the court has explained:

> It is the presence of deep, intimate, familial ties between the plaintiff and the physically injured person that makes the harm to emotional tranquility so serious and compelling. The genuine suffering which flows from such harm stands in stark contrast to the setbacks and sorrow of everyday life, or even to the apprehension of harm to another, less intimate person. The existence of a marital or intimate familial relationship is therefore an essential element of a cause of action for negligent infliction of emotional distress.

The state supreme court has applied this test to permit recovery by a mother who witnessed the death of her seven-year-old son after he became trapped in an elevator. By contrast, it has denied recovery to a woman who witnessed a circus leopard attack and kill the young child of a close friend and neighbor, who had been entrusted to her care for the afternoon.

(A) The defendant in Ellen's suit has filed a Motion for Summary Judgment, on the ground that Ellen's status as an unmarried cohabitant precludes her from recovering under either theory. How should the trial judge rule on each claim and why?

(B) Assume that the trial judge denies defendant's summary judgment motion and the case proceeds toward trial. If you were the lawyer representing Ellen, what kinds of facts would you try to develop in order to present the case to a jury? If you were representing the defendant, what evidence would you present in order to defeat recovery?

§ 3.04 Domestic Partnership Legislation

In several of the decisions discussed above, judges have suggested that significant changes in the legal treatment of unmarried couples should come from the legislatures, rather than the courts. In response to these arguments, and to sustained advocacy by and on behalf of same-sex couples—who are officially precluded from marrying—a number of legislatures have begun to act. One legislative response has been the passage of domestic partnership ordinances at the state and local level. Portions of the ordinance adopted by the City of San Francisco follow.

DOMESTIC PARTNERSHIPS

SEC. 62.1. PURPOSE. The purpose of this ordinance is to create a way to recognize intimate committed relationships, including those of lesbians and gay men who otherwise are denied the right to identify as partners with whom they share their lives.

SEC. 62.2. DEFINITIONS. (a) *Domestic Partnership*. Domestic Partners are two adults who have chosen to share one another's lives in an intimate and committed relationship of mutual caring, who live together, and who have agreed to be jointly responsible for basic living expenses incurred during the Domestic Partnership.

(b) *Live Together* . Live together means that who people share the same living quarters. It is not necessary that the legal right to possess the quarters be in both of their names. Two people may live together even if one both have additional living quarters. Domestic Partners do not cease to live together if one leaves the shared quarters but intends to return.

(c) *Basic Living Expenses* . Basic living expenses means the cost of basic food and shelter. It also includes the expenses which are paid at least in part by a program or benefit for which the partner qualified because of the domestic partnership. The individuals need not contribute equally or jointly to the cost of these expenses as long as they agree that both are responsible for the costs.

(d) *Declaration of Domestic Partnership* . A Declaration of Domestic Partnership is a form provided by the County Clerk. By signing it, two people agree to be jointly responsible for basic living expenses, which they incur during the domestic partnership and that this agreement can be enforced by anyone to whom those expenses are owed. They also state under penalty of perjury that they met the definition of domestic partnership when they signed the statement, that neither is married, that they are not related to each other in a way which would bar marriage in California, and that neither had a different domestic partner less than six months before they signed. This last condition does not apply if the previous domestic partner died.

SEC. 62.3. ESTABLISHING A DOMESTIC PARTNERSHIP. (a) Methods. Two persons may establish a Domestic Partnership by either:

(1) Presenting a signed Declaration of Domestic Partnership to the county clerk, who will file it and give the partners a certificate showing that the Declaration was filed; or

(2) Having a Declaration of Domestic Partnership notarized and giving a copy to the person who witnessed the signing (who may or may not be the notary).

(b) Time limitation. A person cannot become a member of a Domestic Partnership until at least six months after any other Domestic Partnership of which he or she was a member ended. This does not apply if the earlier domestic partnership ended because one of the members died.

(c) Residence Limitation. The County Clerk will only file a Declaration of Domestic Partnership if:

(1) The partners have a residence in San Francisco; or

(2) At least one of the partners works in San Francisco

SEC. 62.4. ENDING DOMESTIC PARTNERSHIPS. (a) When the Partnerships Ends. A Domestic Partnership ends when:

(1) One partner sends the other a written notice that he or she has ended the partnership; or

(2) One of the partners dies; or

(3) One of the partners marries or the partners no longer live together.

(b) Notice the Partnership Has Ended

(1) To Domestic Partners. When a Domestic Partnership ends, at least one of the partners must sign a notice saying that the partnership has ended. The notice must be dated and signed under penalty of perjury. If the Declaration of Domestic Partnership was filed with the county clerk, the notice must be filed with the clerk; otherwise, the notice must be notarized. The partner who signs the notice must send a copy to the other partner.

(2) To Third Parties. When a Domestic Partnership end, a Domestic Partner who has given a copy of a Declaration of Domestic Partnership to any third party (or, if that partner has died, the surviving member of the domestic partnership) must give that third party a notice signed under penalty of perjury stating the partnership has ended. The notice must be sent within 60 days of the end of the Domestic Partnership.

(3) Failure to Give Notice. Failure to give either of the notices required by this subsection will neither prevent nor delay termination of the Domestic Partnership. Anyone who suffers any loss as a result of failure to send either of these notices may sue for actual losses.

NOTES AND COMMENTS

(1) According to the San Francisco Human Rights Commission, approximately 3,500 couples have registered with the city as domestic partners since San Francisco voters approved the registry in 1990. Sixty percent of the couples are heterosexual. *See* Susan Finch, *Domestic Partner Benefits Draw Fire*, Times-Picayune, May 27, 1997, at A1. Since 1996, the San Francisco County Clerk has been authorized to perform a civil ceremony solemnizing the formation of a domestic partnership, and to issue a certificate memorializing performance of the ceremony. *Domestic Partnership—Solemnization—Ceremony Performed by County Clerk—San Francisco*, 22 Fam. L. Rep. (BNA) 1192 (Feb. 27, 1996). Also in 1996, the San Francisco Board of Supervisors passed legislation that requires companies contracting with the city to provide identical benefits to employees with domestic partners as they provide to employees with spouses. The measure generally prohibits the city from

entering into contracts with businesses that do not provide domestic partnership benefits. *Domestic Partnership—Employment Benefits—City Contractors—San Francisco*, 23 Fam. L. Rep. (BNA) 1036 (Nov. 19, 1996). Recently, a U.S. District Court held that the San Francisco ordinance was pre–empted, in part, by the Employee Retirement Income Security Act, which generally prohibits state and local governments from regulating employee benefits plans, and that it exceeded the City's authority under the Commerce Clause of the U.S. Constitution insofar as it attempted to regulate the out–of–state conduct of city contractors. *ATA v. City and Cty. of San Francisco* 992 F. Supp. 1149 (N.D. Cal. 1998).

(2) A number of other jurisdictions across the country have established domestic partnership registries and/or extended employment benefits to domestic partners. A March, 1997 report by Lambda Legal Defense and Education Fund lists 22 jurisdictions with domestic partnership registries and 65 states and municipalities that provide employment benefits to domestic partners. Lamda Legal Defense and Education Fund, *Domestic Partnership Recognition and Benefits: A National Overview* 2–3 (Mar., 1997). Jurisdictions that have established domestic partnership registries include the state of Massachusetts, and the cities of Atlanta, Boston, Chapel Hill, New York, Oakland, Sacramento and Seattle. A primary purpose of these registries is to grant official recognition to committed, adult nonmarital relationships. As one commentator has explained:

> In its simplicity, domestic partnership is one step more than cohabitation, but one step less than marriage. Its essential ingredient is a business or government recognition of benefits conferred on a nonmarital adult couple of the same or opposite sex because of conformity with a procedure established by the business or government

Raymond C. O'Brien, *Domestic Partnership: Recognition and Responsibility*, 32 San Diego L. Rev. 163, 165 (1995).

In addition to the jurisdictions that have established registries, a number of states and municipalities provide health insurance and other employment benefits to the domestic partners of employees. Lamda Legal Defense and Education Fund, *Domestic Partnership Recognition and Benefits: A National Overview* 3–5 (March, 1997). States providing benefits include Massachusetts, New York, Oregon and Vermont; cities in addition to those listed above include Baltimore, Chicago, Denver, Iowa City, Lost Angeles, New Orleans, Philadelphia, Portland, and San Diego. Legislation has also been introduced in Congress that would extend health insurance and pension benefits to the domestic partners of federal employees. *See* Mike Causey, *Bill Would Give Partners' Benefits to Federal Workers*, Sacramento Bee, Nov. 9, 1997, at D-2.

(3) In July, 1997, Hawaii became the first state to enact comprehensive, state-wide domestic partnership legislation. The Hawaii statute allows same-sex couples, and others who are legally prohibited from marrying, to register with the state as "reciprocal beneficiaries." Once registered, reciprocal beneficiaries are eligible for a wide range of benefits previously reserved for married couples. These benefits include health insurance, retirement benefits, inheritance rights, workers' compensation benefits, family and funeral leave, joint auto insurance, property rights and legal standing relating to wrongful death and victims' rights. 1997 Hawaii H.B. 118 (July 1997).

The Hawaii statute is unusual both in the wide range of benefits granted and in its broad definition of "reciprocal beneficiary." Under the statute, any two unmarried adults who are legally prohibited from marrying each other may qualify as beneficiaries. Thus, a widow and her son, as well as both same-sex and opposite-sex couples, may register. The statue does not require that reciprocal beneficiaries live together, or that they be domiciled in Hawaii. The Hawaii statute was passed in response to the Hawaii's Supreme Court's decision in *Baehr v. Lewin* (*see* § 1.07(B), *above*), which suggested that restricting marriage to opposite-sex couples may violate the Hawaii constitution. A companion bill to the Hawaii statute places on the November 1998 ballot a state constitutional amendment that would allow the Hawaii legislature to restrict marriage to opposite-sex couples. *See* Susan Essoyan, *Hawaii Approves Benefits Package For Gay Couples*, L.A. Times, Apr. 30, 1997, at A-3.

(4) Do statutes such as the ones adopted in San Francisco and Hawaii create an alternate procedure for getting married? What are the legal differences between a legally recognized "domestic partnership" and a marriage? Do these differences matter? Should they? Polls suggest that, while a majority of Americans disapprove of same-sex marriage, a larger majority favor granting marriage-related rights and benefits to domestic partners? *See* Bettina Boxall, *A New Era Set To Begin In Benefits For Gay Couples*, L.A. Times, July 7, 1997, at A-7; Kenneth J. Garcia, *Californians Accepting Gay Rights, But Poll Finds Opposition to Same-Sex Marriages*, San Francisco Chron., Mar. 3, 1997, at A-1. What explains these views?

(5) The fact that most domestic partnership ordinances have been enacted at the local level has raised issues of state pre-emption and the extent of municipal lawmaking authority. A number of local ordinances have been challenged on the ground that they exceed the locality's lawmaking authority or conflict with state domestic relations law. For example, the City of Atlanta first established a domestic partner registry and extended employment benefits to domestic partners in 1993. In *City of Atlanta v. McKinney*, 454 S.E.2d 517, 520–21 (Ga. 1996), the Georgia Supreme Court upheld the City's authority to enact the registry, but struck down the portions of the ordinance that extended employment benefits to domestic partners in a comparable manner to a spouse. The Court ruled that the benefit provisions expanded the definition of family member in a manner inconsistent with state law and in violation of the Georgia constitution.

The City then passed a second ordinance, which extended insurance benefits to registered domestic partners who also qualified as "dependents." The ordinance defined a dependent as "one who relies on another for financial support" and provided that an employee's domestic partner qualified as a dependent if the employee makes financial contributions to the domestic partner and the partner is supported, in whole or in part, by the employee's earnings. The ordinance was again challenged as violative of state law, but this time the Georgia Supreme Court upheld the legislation. Noting that the state Home Rule Act did not define dependent, the court ruled that the definition contained in the City's domestic partnership ordinance was "consistent with both the common ordinary meaning of the term 'dependent' and the definition attributed to that terms it is used in the Georgia statutes." *City of Atlanta v. Morgan*, 492 S.E.2d 193, 195 (Ga. 1997). Two justices dissented, arguing that the revised ordinance suffered from the same constitutional flaw as the City's initial benefit provision; it created familial rights and support obligations inconsistent with and pre-empted by the general state law of marriage and divorce. 492 S.E.2d at 196–97 (Carley, J., and Thompson, J.J., dissenting). For a comprehensive discussion of the state pre-emption and municipal authority issues raised by domestic partnership ordinances, see Craig A. Bowman & Blake M. Cornish, *A More Perfect Union: A Legal and Social Analysis of Domestic Partnership Ordinances*, 92 Colum. L. Rev. 1164, 1198–1203 (1992).

(6) An increasing number of public and private employers offer domestic partner benefits. According to one estimate, the number of employers offering such benefits has more than tripled over the past few years, from about 200 employers in 1994 to more than 600 employers in 1997. Michael Bradford, *Employers More At Ease With Partner Benefits*, Bus. Ins., Sept. 22, 1997, at 60. A recent survey by the accounting firm KPMG Peat Marwick indicates that nearly a quarter of employers nationwide with more than 5,000 workers provide health benefits to unmarried partners, often straight as well as gay. *See* Bettina Boxall, *A New Era Set to Begin in Benefits For Gay Couples*, L.A. Times, July 7, 1997, Part A, at 3. Among the employers offering domestic partnership benefits are more than 100 colleges and universities, as well as an increasing number of law firms, particularly in major cities. *See, e.g.,* Keith Darce, *Companies Offer Insurance To Partners of Gay, Lesbian Workers*, Times-Picayune, Nov. 16, 1997, at F-1; Jeff Barge, *More Firms Offer Benefits for Gay Couples*, ABA J., June 1995, at 81.

One reason for the increase in domestic partner benefits may be employer reassurance about costs. A widely cited 1994 report concludes that "contrary to warnings and predictions by insurers and others, extending coverage to domestic partners has not resulted in statistically significant differences in cost." Bradford, *above*. Part of the lower-than-expected costs can be attributed to the fact that eligible employees tend to be younger and, as a result, healthier than other workers. Costs have also been modest because enrollment rates generally are low; if benefits are available to same-sex couples only, less than 1% of a company work force typically enrolls; if enrollment is open to unmarried heterosexual couples as well, up to 3% of the workforce may sign up, raising medical costs only about 1.5%. Boxhall, *above* One reason for the low enrollment rates is that most domestic partner benefits are taxable under federal law, in contrast to the tax treatment of benefits offered to spouses. *Id.* Employer fears that extending benefits would lead to fraud and abuse have also proven unfounded. Bradford, *above*.

(7) A number of family law scholars have argued that, over the past 30 years, the jurisprudential basis of the laws governing marriage and divorce has shifted from status to contract. *See, e.g.,* Janet Dolgin, *The Family in Transition: From Griswald to Eisenstadt and Beyond*, 82 Geo. L.J. 1519 (1994); Jana Singer, *The Privatization of Family Law*, 1992 Wis. L. Rev. 1443. As the preceding materials suggest, however, the legal treatment of unmarried cohabitants seems to have followed precisely the opposite progression—from a reliance on contract principles in *Marvin*, to the invocation of property and equity theories in cases such as *Connell v. Franciso*, to the emphasis on functional family status in *Braschi*. With the enactment of domestic partnership ordinances and benefits, the shift from contract to status is arguably complete. To the extent that this characterization is accurate, what accounts for these divergent legal trends? For recent, provocative discussions of the tension between contract and status principles in family law, see Craig W. Christensen, *Legal Ordering of Family Values: The Case of Gay and Lesbian Families*, 18 Cardozo L. Rev. 1299 (1997); Martha Ertman, *Contractual Purgatory for Sexual Marginorities: Not Heaven, but Not Hell Either*, 73 Denv. U. L. Rev. 1107 (1996).

(8) **Domestic Partnership in Other Western Countries**. A number of Western European countries have enacted comprehensive domestic partnership legislation at the national level. In Denmark, Norway and Sweden, for example, Registered Partnership Acts extend to same-sex couples who register with the state almost all of the legal rights and obligations

associated with marriage. These include eligibility for "spousal" benefits under various pension, tax and social security laws, as well as mutual support obligations. Registered partners are also subject to the same community property regime as married couples and must comply with the same separation and divorce requirements to dissolve their relationship. *See* Craig A. Sloane, *A Rose By Any Other Name: Marriage and the Danish Registered Partnership Act*, 5 Cardozo J. Int'l & Comp. Law 189, 204 (1997). Unlike married couples, however, same-sex partners are prohibited from adopting or taking joint custody of a child. *Id.* at 192. Heterosexual couples are not given the option of registering under any of the Scandinavian acts, in order to preserve the primacy of marriage as the framework for family life. *See* Deborah M. Henson, *A Comparative Analysis of Same-Sex Partnership Protections: Recommendations for American Reform*, 7 Int'l J.L. & Fam. 282, 284–87 (1993). As of January 1, 1997, approximately 2100 gay and lesbian couples had registered under the Danish Act, which became effective in 1989. *See* Deb Price, *National Tradition of Tolerance Makes Denmark Gay-friendly*, The Detroit News, October 30, 1997. Recently, the state church of Denmark announced that it would offer registered partners a church blessing, after the couple had registered with the state. *Id.*

In 1996, Iceland passed national domestic partnership legislation modeled after the Danish Act, but permitting a gay or lesbian partner to adopt his or her partner's biological child. *See Iceland Gives Gay Marriage Legal Stamp*, Reuters North American Wire, June 27, 1996. In the Netherlands, a national domestic partnership statute went into effect in January, 1998, and a Dutch parliamentary committee has recommended additional legislation that would grant full marriage and adoption rights to same-sex couples. *See* Christian Aziz, *New Dutch Law Gives Gay Marriage Rights*, Patriot Ledger, Nov. 8, 1997, at 3; *Dutch MPs Recommend Law on Homosexual Marriage and Parenthood*, Agence France Presse, October 28, 1998. For additional discussion of these developments, see Marianne Roth, *The Norwegian Act on Registered Partnership For Homosexual Couples*, 35 J. Fam. L. 467 (1997); Martin D. Dupuis, *The Impact of Culture, Society and History on the Legal Process: An Analysis of the Legal Status of Same-Sex Relationships in the United States and Denmark*, 9 Int'l J.L. & Fam. 86 (1995); Marianne Hojgaard Pedersen, *Denmark: Homosexual Marriages and New Rules Regarding Separation and Divorce*, 30 J. Fam. L. 289 (1991-92); Linda Nielsen, *Family Rights and the "Registered Partnership" in Denmark*, 4 Int'l J. L. & Fam. 297 (1990). An English translation of the Danish Registered Partnership Act can be found in Sloane, *above*, at 200 n.70.

(9) **Problem**. You are an associate at Swisher, Miller & Singer, a medium-sized law firm in a large mid-western city. The city does not have a domestic partnership registry. The management committee of your firm has recently voted to extend health insurance, and other employment benefits to the domestic partners of its employees and partners. The firm currently provides "family benefits" to spouses and to employees' "natural or adopted children." The management committee has asked for your help in drafting its new benefits policy. In particular, it would like your draft to address the following: (1) How should eligible "domestic partners" be defined? (2) What proof, if any, should the firm require of a domestic partnership? (3) Should benefits be available to opposite-sex, as well as same-sex, unmarried partners? (4) How should the policy treat the children of an employee's domestic partner?

CHAPTER 4

HAVING CHILDREN: THE ALTERNATIVE CHOICES

SYNOPSIS

§ 4.01　Contraception
§ 4.02　Abortion
§ 4.03　Sterilization
§ 4.04　Surrogacy
§ 4.05　New Reproductive Technology
　　　　[A] Artificial Insemination
　　　　[B] In Vitro Fertilization and the Status of the Embryo
　　　　[C] Cloning

§ 4.01　Contraception

Today, it is difficult to imagine a time when the use and sale of contraceptives was prohibited. Contraceptives are commonly used; no state prohibits their use. Condoms, spermicidal gels, and other forms of contraception are prominently displayed in drug stores; in some states even liquor and convenience stores have them. There are even specialty stores which sell nothing but condoms. Billboards picture condoms as protection against AIDS. While the pill has engendered concern over safety, it is widely accepted as a method of birth control.

Nevertheless, until the United States Supreme Court in *Griswold v. Connecticut* struck down what a dissenter called an "uncommonly silly" statute prohibiting the use of contraceptives, state laws prohibiting the sale and use of contraceptives were common. The effect of *Griswold* was so pervasive that it made contraception a non-issue, at least for the law. *Griswold* would have only historical importance if it had not laid the foundation, by establishing a fundamental right of privacy in matters of marriage and procreation, for *Roe v. Wade*, the abortion case. To fully understand the *Roe* controversy, one must start with *Griswold*.

GRISWOLD v. CONNECTICUT
United States Supreme Court
381 U.S. 479 (1965)

Mr. Justice Douglas delivered the opinion of the Court.

Appellant Griswold is Executive Director of the Planned Parenthood League of Connecticut. Appellant Burton is a licensed physician and a professor at the Yale Medical School who served as Medical Director for the League at its Center in New Haven—a center open and operating from November 1 to November 10, 1961, when appellants were arrested.

They gave information, instruction and medical advice to *married persons* as to the means of preventing conception. They examined the wife and prescribed the best contraceptive device or material for her use. Fees were usually charged, although some couples were serviced free.

The statutes whose constitutionality is involved in this appeal are §§ 53–32 and 54–196 of the General Statutes of Connecticut (1958 rev.). The former provides:

> Any person who uses any drug, medicinal article or instrument for the purpose of preventing conception shall be fined not less than fifty dollars or imprisoned not less than sixty days nor more than one year or be both fined and imprisoned.

Section 54–196 provides:

> Any person who assists, abets, counsels, causes, hires or commands another to commit any offense may be prosecuted and punished as if he were the principal offender.

The appellants were found guilty as accessories and fined $100 each, against the claim that the accessory statute as so applied violated the Fourteenth Amendment. The Appellate Division of the Circuit Court affirmed. The Supreme Court of Errors affirmed that judgment.

. . . We do not sit as a super-legislature to determine the wisdom, need, and propriety of laws that touch economic problems, business affairs, or social conditions. This law, however, operates directly on an intimate relation of husband and wife and their physician's role in one aspect of that relation.

The association of people is not mentioned in the Constitution nor in the Bill of Rights. The right to educate a child in a school of the parents' choice—whether public or private or parochial—is also not mentioned. Nor is the right to study any particular subject or any foreign language. Yet the First Amendment has been construed to include certain of those rights.

By *Pierce v. Society of Sisters*, [268 U.S. 510], the right to educate one's children as one chooses is made applicable to the States by the force of the First and Fourteenth Amendments. By *Meyer v. State of Nebraska*, [262 U.S. 390], the same dignity is given to the right to study the German language in a private school. In other words, the State may not, consistent with the spirit of the First Amendment, contract the spectrum of available knowledge. The right of freedom of speech and press includes not only the right to utter or to print, but the right to distribute, the right to receive, the right to read, and freedom of inquiry, freedom of thought, and freedom to teach—indeed the freedom of the entire university community. Without those peripheral rights the specific rights would be less secure. And so we reaffirm the principle of the *Pierce* and the *Meyer* cases.

In *NAACP v. State of Alabama*, 357 U.S. 449, 462, we protected the "freedom to associate and privacy in one's associations," noting that freedom of association was a peripheral First Amendment right.

. . . The right of "association," like the right of belief, is more than the right to attend a meeting; it includes the right to express one's attitudes or philosophies by membership in a group or by affiliation with it or by other lawful means. Association in that context is a form of expression of opinion; and while it is not expressly included in the First Amendment its existence is necessary in making the express guarantees fully meaningful.

The foregoing cases suggest that specific guarantees in the Bill of Rights have penumbras, formed by emanations from those guarantees that help give them life and substance. Various guarantees create zones of privacy. The right of association contained in the penumbra of the First Amendment is one, as we have seen. The Third Amendment in its prohibition against the quartering of soldiers "in any house" in time of peace without the consent of the owner is another facet of that privacy. The Fourth Amendment explicitly affirms the "right of the people to be secure in their persons, houses, papers, and effects, against unreasonable searches and seizures." The Fifth Amendment in its Self-Incrimination Clause enables the citizen to create a zone of privacy which government may not force him to surrender to his detriment. The Ninth Amendment provides: "The enumeration in the Constitution, of certain rights, shall not be construed to deny or disparage others retained by the people."

The Fourth and Fifth Amendments were described in *Boyd v. United States*, 116 U.S. 616, 630, as protection against all governmental invasions "of the sanctity of a man's home and the privacies of life." We recently referred in *Mapp v. Ohio*, 367 U.S. 643, 656 to the Fourth Amendment as creating a "right to privacy, no less important than any other right carefully and particularly reserved to the people."

. . . The present case, then, concerns a relationship lying within the zone of privacy created by several fundamental constitutional guarantees. And it concerns a law which, in forbidding the use of contraceptives rather than regulating their manufacture or sale, seeks to achieve its goals by means of having a maximum destructive impact upon that relationship. Such a law cannot stand in light of the familiar principle, so often applied by this Court, that a "governmental purpose to control or prevent activities constitutionally subject to state regulation may not be achieved by means which sweep unnecessarily broadly and thereby invade the area of protected freedoms." *NAACP v. Alabama*, 377 U.S. 288, 307. Would we allow the police to search the sacred precincts of marital bedrooms for telltale signs of the use of contraceptives? The very idea is repulsive to the notions of privacy surrounding the marriage relationship.

We deal with a right of privacy older than the Bill of Rights—older than our political parties, older than our school system. Marriage is a coming together for better or for worse, hopefully enduring, and intimate to the degree of being sacred. It is an association that promotes a way of life, not causes; a harmony in living, not political faiths; a bilateral loyalty, not commercial or social projects. Yet it is an association for as noble a purpose as any involved in our prior decisions.

Reversed.

Mr. Justice White, concurring in the judgment.

In my view this Connecticut law as applied to married couples deprives them of "liberty" without due process of law, as that concept is used in the Fourteenth Amendment. I therefore concur in the judgment of the Court reversing these convictions under Connecticut's aiding and abetting statute.

It would be unduly repetitious, and belaboring the obvious, to expound on the impact of this statute on the liberty guaranteed by the Fourteenth Amendment against arbitrary or capricious denials or on the nature of this liberty. Suffice it to say that this is not the first time the Court has had occasion to articulate that the liberty entitled to protection under the Fourteenth Amendment includes the right "to marry, establish a home and bring up children," *Meyer v. State of Nebraska*, 262 U.S. 390, 399 and "the liberty to direct the upbringing and education of children," Pierce v. Society of Sisters, 268 U.S. 510, 534–535, and that these are among "the basic civil rights of man." *Skinner v. State of Oklahoma*, 316 U.S. 535, 541. These decisions affirm that there is a "realm of family life which the state cannot enter" without substantial justification. *Prince v. Com. of Massachusetts*, 321 U.S. 158, 166. Surely the right invoked in this case, to be free of regulation of the intimacies of the marriage relationship, "come[s] to this Court with a momentum for respect lacking when appeal is made to liberties which derive merely from shifting economic arrangements."

MR JUSTICE STEWART, whom MR. JUSTICE BLACK joins, dissenting.

Since 1879 Connecticut has had on its books a law which forbids the use of contraceptives by anyone. I think this is an uncommonly silly law. As a practical matter, the law is obviously unenforceable, except in the oblique context of the present case. As a philosophical matter, I believe the use of contraceptives in the relationship of marriage should be left to personal and private choice, based upon each individual's moral, ethical, and religious beliefs. As a matter of social policy, I think professional counsel about methods of birth control should be available to all, so that each individual's choice can be meaningfully made. But we are not asked in this case to say whether we think this law is unwise, or even asinine. We are asked to hold that it violates the United States Constitution. And that I cannot do.

In the course of its opinion the Court refers to no less than six Amendments to the Constitution: the First, the Third, the Fourth, the Fifth, the Ninth, and the Fourteenth. But the Court does not say which of these Amendments, if any, it thinks is infringed by this Connecticut law....

As to the First, Third, Fourth, and Fifth Amendments, I can find nothing in any of them to invalidate this Connecticut law, even assuming that all those Amendments are fully applicable against the States. It has not even been argued that this is a law "respecting an establishment of religion, or prohibiting free exercise thereof." And surely, unless the solemn process of constitutional adjudication is to descend to the level of a play on words, there is not involved here any abridgment of "the freedom of speech, or of the press; or the right of the people peaceably to assemble, and to petition the Government for a redress of grievances." No soldier has been quartered in any house. There has been no search, and no seizure. Nobody has been compelled to be a witness against himself.

. . . What provision of the Constitution, then, does make this state law invalid? The Court says it is the right of privacy "created by several fundamental constitutional guarantees." With all deference, I can find no such general right of privacy in the Bill of Rights, in any other part of the Constitution, or in any case ever before decided by this Court.

At the oral argument in this case we were told that the Connecticut law does not "conform to current community standards." But it is not the function of this Court to decide cases on the basis of community standards. We are here to decide cases "agreeably to the Constitution and laws of the United States." It is the essence of judicial duty to subordinate our own personal views, our own ideas of what legislation is wise and what is not. If, as I should surely hope, the law before us does not reflect the standards of the people of

Connecticut, the people of Connecticut can freely exercise their true Ninth and Tenth Amendment rights to persuade their elected representatives to repeal it. That is the constitutional way to take this law off the books.

NOTES AND QUESTIONS

(1) **Rights of Unmarried People.** In *Eisenstadt v. Baird*, 405 U.S. 438, 92 S. Ct. 1029, 31 L. Ed. 2d 349 (1972), the Supreme Court struck down a Massachusetts statute which prohibited giving away contraceptives except in situations in which a physician prescribes the contraceptives to a married person. The defendant was convicted of giving a woman a package of contraceptive foam following a lecture which he had delivered on the subject of contraception at Boston University. The Court stated, "If the right of privacy means anything, it is the right of the *individual*, married or single, to be free from unwarranted governmental intrusion into matters so fundamentally affecting a person as the decision whether to bear or beget a child."

(2) **Minors.** In *Carey v. Population Services International*, 431 U.S. 678, 97 S. Ct. 2010, 52 L. Ed. 2d 675 (1977), the Supreme Court addressed the issue of selling contraceptives to minors. The Court struck down a statute which prohibited the sale of contraceptives to anyone under sixteen; however, there was no majority opinion. The rationale of the plurality was that minors too had a right of privacy that protected their use of contraceptives. In addition, the D.C. Circuit Court of Appeals struck down a regulation requiring recipients of federal funds to notify parents before prescribing contraceptives to minors and required these agencies to comply with state laws which required consent of parents. *See Planned Parenthood Fed'n of Am. v. Heckler*, 712 F.2d 650 (D.C. Cir. 1983).

(3) **The Law and Contraception Today.** Because of *Griswold*, no state prohibits the use of contraceptives, and, indeed, the use of contraceptives is so accepted today that it is difficult to quarrel with the result in *Griswold* except on issues of constitutional theory. In the continuing litigation and controversy regarding contraceptives, an issure of special concern arises regarding the use of the Norplant device, which will be dealt with in this section on the individual's right to control procreation. Here are some of the issues which have arisen regarding contraceptives:

(a) *Norplant..* This contraceptive utilizes six silicon tubes containing synthetic hormones which are implanted in a woman's arm and which provides up to five years of birth control. Once the tubes are implanted the woman does not have to do anything in order to obtain the benefits. When the device was approved in 1990, there was a firestorm of controversy regarding some trial courts which ordered or offered women the opportunity to have the implants rather than go to jail or have parental rights terminated. There are almost no reported appellate cases on this issue (*see In re Lacey P.*, 433 S.E.2d 518 (W. Va. 1993) and *People v. Johnson* (Cal. Ct. App. 1992), which was not published but which can be found at 1992 WL 685375, but law review authors responded with many articles damning the practice. *See* Jebson, *Conditioning a Woman's Probation on Her Using Norplant: New Weapon Against Child Abuse Backfires*, 17 Campbell L. Rev. 301 (1995); Karachuk, *Rethinking the Laws: Norplant as a Condition of Probation for Female Child Abusers*, 14 In Pub. Interest 89 (1994); McAdams, *On Requiring Responsibility: the Constitutionality of Conditioning AFDC Benefits upon the Insertion of the Norplant Contraceptive Device*,

19 Okla. City U. L. Rev. 309 (1994); Merritt, *Birth Control Incentives for Welfare Mothers*, 3 Kan. J.L. & Pub. Pol'y 171 (1994); Spitz, *The Norplant Debate: Birth Control or Woman Control?*, 25 Colum. Hum. Rts. L. Rev. 131 (1993); Wilinski, *Involuntary Contraceptive Measures: Controlling Women at the Expense of Human Rights*, 10 B.U. Int'l L.J. 351 (1992); Ginzberg, *Compulsory Contraception as a Condition of Probation: the Use and Abuse of Norplant*, 58 Brook. L. Rev. 979 (1992); Arthur, *Norplant Prescription: Birth Control, Woman Control, or Crime Control?*, 40 UCLA L. Rev. 1 (1992).

Ultimately this issue died down as the dangers of the Norplant long-term birth-control device have become known. *See* Duncan, *Norplant: the Next Mass Tort,* ABA Journal, November, 1995.

(b) *RU–486.* The controversial French pharmaceutical RU–486 is sometimes called a contraceptive, but it actually uses two major drugs to create a miscarriage. This subject is discussed more fully in § 4.02, Abortion. *See* Hanson, *Approval of RU–486 as a Postcoital Contraceptive*, 17 U. Puget Sound L. Rev. 163, (1993); Silverberg, *Looking Beyond Judicial Deference to Agency Discretion: a Fundamental Right of Access to RU 486?* 59 Brook. L. Rev. 1551 (1994); Canlen, *The Long Labor of RU 486*, California Lawyer, May 1997, at 35.

(c) *Mass Tort Litigation.* Tort litigation regarding the safety of new contraceptives is rampant. *See* Isaacs and Holt, *Drug Regulation, Product Liability and the Contraceptive Crunch: Choices Are Dwindling*, 8 J. Legal Med. 533 (1987); McCollum, *Dalkon Shield Claims Resolution Facility: A Contraceptive for Corporate Irresponsibility?*, 7 Ohio St. J. on Disp. Resol. 351 (1992); Page, *Asbestos and the Dalkon Shield: Corporate America on Trial*, 85 Mich. L. Rev. 1324 (1987); Duncan, *Norplant: the Next Mass Tort,* ABA Journal, Nov. 1995, at 16.

(d) *Sale of Contraceptives.* The Supreme Court has stated that states cannot make it a crime for someone other than a pharmacist to sell contraceptives or make it a crime to display and advertise contraceptives. *See Carey v. Population Services International*, 431 U.S. 678, 97 S. Ct. 2010, 52 L. Ed. 2d 675 (1977). But Carey does not limit the power of the state to otherwise regulate the manufacture and sale of contraceptives. For example, the state can prohibit the sale of contraceptives in vending machines. *See Cavalier Vending Corp. v. State Bd. of Pharmacy*, 79 S.E.2d 636 (Va. 1954), *appeal dismissed*, 347 U.S. 995, 74 S. Ct. 871, 98 L. Ed. 1127 (1954).

(e) *Condom-Availability Programs in Schools.* Junior and senior high schools have instituted condom-availability programs in which students can request free condoms from a school employee, often the school nurse. These programs have been challenged by parents who believe the programs violate their rights to privacy, the free exercise of religion, and substantive due process. In *Curtis v. School Comm. of Falmouth*, 652 N.E.2d 580 (Mass. 1995), the Supreme Judicial Court of Massachusetts held a condom-availability program did not violate parents' constitutional rights. While recognizing that parents possess a fundamental liberty interest to be free from governmental intrusion in the raising of children, the *Curtis* court reasoned that "parents have no right to tailor public school programs to meet their individual religious or moral preferences." *Id.* at 589.

(4) **The Fundamental Right to Privacy.** Without *Griswold* or a case like it, *Roe v. Wade*, 410 U.S. 113, 93 S. Ct. 705, 35 L. Ed. 2d 147 (1973), probably would not have existed. The fundamental right of privacy is the basis of the freedom of choice established in *Roe*.

  (a) *Before Griswold.* The subject of the right of privacy was discussed by commentators before *Griswold*, and it presented a conceptual problem. One commentator wrote:

> But for one who feels that the marriage relationship should be beyond the reach of a state law forbidding the use of contraceptives, the birth control case poses a troublesome and challenging problem of constitutional interpretation. He may find himself saying, "The law is unconstitutional—but why?" There are two possible paths to travel in finding the answer. One is to revert to a frankly flexible due process concept even on matters that do not involve specific constitutional prohibitions. The other is to attempt to evolve a new constitutional framework within which to meet this and similar problems which are likely to arise.

Redlich, *Are there Certain Rights . . . Retained by the People?*, 37 N.Y.U. L. Rev. 787, 798 (1962). The multiple opinions in *Griswold* are testimony to this dilemma. The justices in *Griswold*, like most of us, found it repugnant to have the police search marital bedrooms, even with a warrant, for contraceptives; but they had to find a theory to support this view.

  (b) *Penumbra Theory.* Justice Douglas says that there is a fundamental right of privacy, which like the freedom of association is not mentioned in the Constitution but rather is found in the penumbra of the other constitutional rights. Now this theory seems to be mainly of historical interest. While the right of privacy seems to be well established, the predominate theory is that of substantive due process.

  (c) *Substantive Due Process.* The due process approach is not fully articulated in *Griswold*. Justice White states the basic premise. Even though privacy is not mentioned in the constitution, the concept of liberty in the Due Process Clause encompasses the right of marital privacy. The right of marital privacy is one of those liberties "so rooted in the traditions and conscience of our people as to be ranked as fundamental."

  (d) *The Ninth Amendment.* In a concurring opinion not reprinted here, Justice Goldberg takes the position that the Ninth Amendment supports the substantive due process view; that is, the enumeration of certain rights does not deny the existence of other rights retained by the people. These rights may be protected by courts even though they are not specifically mentioned in the constitution because they exist in the concept of liberty. (For discussions of the Ninth Amendment as it relates to the right of privacy, see Massey, *Federalism and Fundamental Rights: The Ninth Amendment*, 38 Hastings L.J. 305 (1987); Mitchell, *The Ninth Amendment and the "Jurisprudence of Original Intention,"* 74 Geo. L.J. 1719 (1986).)

  (e) *Strict-Constructionist Position.* Justices Black and Stewart dissent, arguing that there is no right of privacy in the Constitution; the word *privacy* is not even mentioned. They say that the view promulgated by the majority requires that judges determine what is constitutional by making their own appraisal of what is unwise or unnecessary. In effect it requires judges to do what the Constitution empowers the legislature to do. There is nothing in the Constitution that expressly or impliedly vests the Supreme Court with the power to sit as a supervisory agency over the acts of duly constituted legislative bodies. Due process does not allow judges to express their personal preferences.

At the very least, the issue is fully framed by the *Griswold* decision. Is there a fundamental right to privacy protected by the Constitution of the United States? Seven Justices say "yes" although they are unsure of the theory to justify it. Two say no. The seven are vulnerable to the criticism that they are judicially legislating. Note also that Justice Black has stated that he likes his privacy as much as the next man, which can cause one to question whether he is writing about the same kind of privacy as, for example, Justice Douglas. Justice Black's statement conjures images of the neighbors gossiping behind his back or of someone barging in on him while he is smoking his pipe in front of the fire rather than of the police rousting his wife and him out of bed to look for contraceptives.

(5) **Revivification of Substantive Due Process.** Looking at *Griswold* historically, it is possible to see this case as the first step in the revival of the doctrine of substantive due process, at least in matters of family and procreation. In *Planned Parenthood Of Southeastern Penn. v Casey,* 505 U.S. 833, 846, 112 S. Ct. 2791, 2804, 120 L. Ed. 2d 674, 695 (1992), Justice O'Connor stated,

> Constitutional protection of the woman's decision to terminate her pregnancy derives from the Due Process Clause of the Fourteenth Amendment. It declares that no State shall "deprive any person of life, liberty, or property, without due process of law." The controlling word in the case before us is "liberty." Although a literal reading of the Clause might suggest that it governs only the procedures by which a State may deprive persons of liberty, for at least 105 years, at least since *Mugler v. Kansas,* . . . the Clause has been understood to contain a substantive component as well, one "barring certain government actions regardless of the fairness of the procedures used to implement them."

Justices Kennedy, Souter, Stevens and Blackman made up the majority with Justice O'Connor in this part of the opinion.

The strict constructionists are alive and well. Regarding the portion of the opinion in *Planned Parenthood* quoted above, Justices Rehnquist, White, Scalia and Thomas dissented. But even Justice Scalia, who has taken a strong public stand in favor of strict construction, has acknowledged the substantive component of the Due Process Clause. In *Michael H. v. Gerald D.,* 491 U.S. 110, 121–22, 109 S. Ct. 2333, 2341, 105 L. Ed. 2d 91, 105 (1989), Justice Scalia said, "It is an established part of our constitutional jurisprudence that the term 'liberty' in the Due Process Clause extends beyond freedom from physical restraint." But he did add a few sentences later: "defining the scope of the Due Process Clause has at times been a treacherous field for this Court, 'giving reason for concern lest the only limits to . . . judicial intervention become the predilections of those who happen at the time to be Members of this Court.' *Moore v. East Cleveland* . . . . The need for restraint has been cogently expressed by Justice White: 'that the Court has ample precedent for the creation of new constitutional rights should not lead it to repeat the process at will.' " Justices Blackmun and White have been replaced by Justices Ginsburg and Breyer, respectively. As of this writing, it seems likely that substantive due process in matters of marriage and procreation will still be viable.

(6) **The Outer Limits of the Right of Privacy.** Perhaps the limit of the right of privacy was established in *Bowers v. Hardwick*, 478 U.S. 186, 106 S. Ct. 2841, 92 L. Ed. 2d 140 (1986), in which the Court held that the right of privacy did not invalidate state criminal statutes prohibiting sodomy. The court in *Bowers* stated:

> We first register our disagreement with the Court of Appeals and with the respondent that the Court's prior cases have construed the Constitution to confer a right of privacy that extends to homosexual sodomy and for all intents and purposes have decided this case. The reach of this line of cases was sketched in *Carey v. Population Services International* . . . . *Pierce v. Society of Sisters* and *Meyer v. Nebraska* were described as dealing with child rearing and education; *Prince v. Massachusetts*, with family relationships; *Skinner v. Oklahoma ex rel. Williamson*, with procreation; *Loving v. Virginia*, with marriage; *Griswold v. Connecticut*, supra, and *Eisenstadt v. Baird*, supra, with contraception; and *Roe v. Wade*, with abortion. The latter three cases were interpreted as construing the Due Process Clause of the Fourteenth Amendment to confer a fundamental individual right to decide whether or not to beget or bear a child. *Carey v. Population Services International*, supra, 431 U.S. at 688–89 . . .
>
> Accepting the decisions in these cases and the above description of them, we think it evident that none of the rights announced in those cases bears any resemblance to the claimed constitutional right of homosexuals to engage in acts of sodomy that is asserted in this case. No connection between family, marriage, or procreation on the one hand and homosexual activity on the other has been demonstrated, either by the Court of Appeals or by respondent. Moreover, any claim that these cases nevertheless stand for the proposition that any kind of private sexual conduct between consenting adults is constitutionally insulated from state proscription is insupportable. Indeed, the Court's opinion in *Carey* twice asserted that the privacy right, which the *Griswold* line of cases found to be one of the protections provided by the Due Process Clause, did not reach so far. . . . Precedent aside, however, respondent would have us announce, as the Court of Appeals did, a fundamental right to engage in homosexual sodomy. This we are quite unwilling to do.

Bowers, 478 U.S. at 190–91, 106 S. Ct. at 2843–44, 92 L. Ed. 2d at 145–46.

Bowers was decided by a 5-4 vote, with Justice Powell providing the fifth vote for the majority. Reportedly, Justice Powell originally voted to strike down the sodomy statute, but changed his mind before the decision was issued. *See* Kamen, *Powell Changed Vote in Sodomy Case*, The Washington Post, July 13, 1986, at A1. In 1990, after he retired from the Court, Justice Powell told a student questioner at the NYU School of Law that he "probably made a mistake" in voting with the majority in *Bowers*. *See* Marcus, *Powell Regrets Backing Sodomy Law*, The Washington Post, October 26, 1990, at A3.

However, the fundamental right of privacy would seem to be limited to the matters of marriage and procreation.

§ 4.02 Abortion

ROE v. WADE
United States Supreme Court
410 U.S. 113 (1973)

MR. JUSTICE BLACKMUN delivered the opinion of the Court.

This Texas Federal appeal and its Georgia companion, *Doe v. Bolton*, [410 U.S.] 179, present constitutional challenges to state criminal abortion legislation. . . .

We forthwith acknowledge our awareness of the sensitive and emotional nature of the abortion controversy, of the vigorous opposing views, even among physicians, and of the deep and seemingly absolute convictions that the subject inspires. One's philosophy, one's experiences, one's exposure to the raw edges of human existence, one's religious training, one's attitudes toward life and family and their values, and the moral standards one establishes and seeks to observe, are all likely to influence and to color one's thinking and conclusions about abortion.

In addition, population growth, pollution, poverty, and racial overtones tend to complicate and not to simplify the problem.

Our task, of course, is to resolve the issue by constitutional measurement, free of emotion and of predilection. We seek earnestly to do this, and, because we do, we have inquired into, and in this opinion place some emphasis upon, medical and medical-legal history and what that history reveals about man's attitudes toward the abortion procedure over the centuries. We bear in mind, too, Mr. Justice Holmes' admonition in his now vindicated dissent in *Lochner v. New York*, 198 U.S. 45, 76 (1905):

> [The Constitution] is made for people of fundamentally differing views, and the accident of our finding certain opinions natural and familiar, or novel and even shocking ought not to conclude our judgment upon the question whether statutes embodying them conflict with the Constitution of the United States.

I

The Texas statutes that concern us here make it a crime to "procure an abortion," as therein defined, or to attempt one, except with respect to "an abortion procured or attempted by medical advice for the purpose of saving the life of the mother." Similar statutes are in existence in a majority of the States. . . .

II

Jane Roe, a single woman who was residing in Dallas County, Texas, instituted this federal action in March, 1970 against the District Attorney of the county. She sought a declaratory judgment that the Texas criminal abortion statutes were unconstitutional on their face, and an injunction restraining the defendant from enforcing the statutes.

Roe alleged that she was unmarried and pregnant; that she wished to terminate her pregnancy by an abortion "performed by a competent, licensed physician, under safe, clinical conditions"; that she was unable to get a "legal" abortion in Texas because her life did not appear to be threatened by the continuation of her pregnancy; and that she could not afford to travel to another jurisdiction in order to secure a legal abortion under safe conditions. She claimed that the Texas statutes were unconstitutionally vague and that they abridged her right of personal privacy, protected by the First, Fourth, Fifth, Ninth, and Fourteenth Amendments. By an amendment to her complaint Roe purported to sue "on behalf of herself and all other women" similarly situated. . . .

VI

It perhaps is not generally appreciated that the restrictive criminal abortion laws in effect in a majority of States today are of relatively recent vintage. Those laws, generally proscribing abortion or its attempt at any time during pregnancy except when necessary to preserve the pregnant woman's life, are not of ancient or even of common-law origin. Instead, they derive from statutory changes effected, for the most part, in the latter half of the 19th century. . . .

VII

Three reasons have been advanced to explain historically the enactment of criminal abortion laws in the 19th century and to justify their continued existence.

It has been argued occasionally that these laws were the product of a Victorian social concern to discourage illicit sexual conduct. Texas, however, does not advance this justification in the present case, and it appears that no court or commentator has taken the argument seriously. The appellants and *amici* contend, moreover, that this is not a proper state purpose at all and suggest that, if it were, the Texas statutes are overbroad in protecting it since the law fails to distinguish between married and unwed mothers.

A second reason is concerned with abortion as a medical procedure. When most criminal abortion laws were first enacted, the procedure was a hazardous one for the woman. This was particularly true prior to the development of antisepsis. Antiseptic techniques, of course, were based on discoveries by Lister, Pasteur, and others first announced in 1867, but were not generally accepted and employed until about the turn of the century. Abortion mortality was high. Even after 1900, and perhaps until as late as the development of antibiotics in the 1940's, standard modern techniques such as dilation and curettage were not nearly so safe as they are today. Thus, it has been argued that a State's real concern in enacting a criminal abortion law was to protect the pregnant woman, that is, to restrain her from submitting to a procedure that placed her life in serious jeopardy.

Modern medical techniques have altered this situation. Appellants and various *amici* refer to medical data indicating that abortion in early pregnancy, that is, prior to the end of the first trimester, although not without its risk, is now relatively safe. Mortality rates for women undergoing early abortions, where the procedure is legal, appear to be as low or lower than the rates for normal childbirth. Consequently, any interest of the State in protecting the woman from an inherently hazardous procedure, except when it would be equally dangerous for her to forgo it, has largely disappeared. Of course, important state interests in areas of health and medical standards do remain. The State has a legitimate interest in seeing to it that abortion, like any other medical procedure, is performed under circumstances that insure maximum safety for the patient. This interest obviously extends at least to the performing physician and his staff, to the facilities involved, to the availability of after-care, and to adequate provision for any complication or emergency that might arise. The prevalence of high mortality rates at illegal "abortion mills" strengthens, rather than weakens, the State's interest in regulating the conditions under which abortions are performed. Moreover, the risk to the woman increases as her pregnancy continues. Thus, the State retains a definite interest in protecting the woman's own health and safety when an abortion is proposed at a late stage of pregnancy.

The third reason is the State's interest—some phrase it in terms of duty—in protecting prenatal life. Some of the argument for this justification rests on the theory that a new human life is present from the moment of conception. The State's interest and general obligation to protect life then extends, it is argued, to prenatal life. Only when the life of the pregnant mother herself is at stake, balanced against the life she carries within her, should the interest of the embryo or fetus not prevail. Logically, of course, a legitimate state interest in this area need not stand or fall on acceptance of the belief that life begins at conception or at some other point prior to live birth. In assessing the State's interest, recognition may be given to the less rigid claim that as long as at least *potential* life is involved, the State may assert interest beyond the protection of the pregnant woman alone.

Parties challenging state abortion laws have sharply disputed in some courts the contention that a purpose of these laws, when enacted, was to protect prenatal life. Pointing to the absence of legislative history to support the contention, they claim that most state laws were designed solely to protect the woman. Because medical advances have lessened this concern, at least with respect to abortion in early pregnancy, they argue that with respect to such abortions the laws can no longer be justified by any state interest. There is some scholarly support for this view of original purpose. The few state courts called upon to interpret their laws in the late 19th and early 20th centuries did focus on the State's interest in protecting the woman's health rather than in preserving the embryo and fetus. Proponents of this view point out that in many States, including Texas, by statute or judicial interpretation, the pregnant woman herself could not be prosecuted for self-abortion or for cooperating in an abortion performed upon her by another. They claim that adoption of the "quickening" distinction through received common law and state statutes tacitly recognizes the greater health hazards inherent in late abortion and impliedly repudiates the theory that life begins at conception.

It is with these interests, and the weight to be attached to them, that this case is concerned.

VIII

The Constitution does not explicitly mention any right of privacy. In a line of decisions, however, going back perhaps as far as *Union Pacific R. Co. v. Botsford*, 141 U.S. 250, 251 (1891), the Court has recognized that a right of personal privacy, or a guarantee of certain areas or zones of privacy, does exist under the Constitution. In varying contexts, the Court or individual Justices, have, indeed, found at least the roots of that right in the First Amendment, *Stanley v. Georgia*, 394 U.S. 557, 564 (1969); in the Fourth and Fifth Amendments, *Terry v. Ohio*, 392 U.S. 1, 8–9 (1968); *Katz v. United States*, 389 U.S. 347, 350 (1967); *Boyd v. United States*, 116 U.S. 616 (1886); *see Olmstead v. United States*, 227 U.S. 438, 478 (1928) (Brandeis, J., dissenting); in the penumbras of the Bill of Rights, *Griswold v. Connecticut*, 381 U.S., at 484–485; in the Ninth Amendment, *id.*, at 486 (Goldberg, J., concurring); or in the concept of liberty guaranteed by the first section of the Fourteenth Amendment, see *Meyer v. Nebraska*, 262 U.S. 390, 399 (1923). These decisions make it clear that only personal rights that can be deemed "fundamental" or "implicit in the concept of ordered liberty," *Palko v. Connecticut*, 302 U.S. 319, 325 (1937), are included in this guarantee of personal privacy. They also make it clear that the right has some extension to activities relating to marriage, *Loving v. Virginia*, 388 U.S. 1, 12 (1967), procreation, *Skinner v. Oklahoma*, 316, U.S. 535, 541–542 (1942); contraception,

Eisenstadt v. Baird, 405 U.S., at 453–454; *id.*, at 460, 463–465 (White, J., concurring in result); family relationships, *Prince v. Massachusetts*, 321 U.S. 158, 166 (1944); and child rearing and education, *Pierce v. Society of Sisters*, 268 U.S. 510, 535 (1925); *Meyer v. Nebraska, supra.*

This right of privacy, whether it be founded in the Fourteenth Amendment's concept of personal liberty and restrictions upon state action, as we felt it is, or, as the District Court determined, in the Ninth Amendment's reservation of rights to the people, is broad enough to encompass a woman's decision whether or not to terminate her pregnancy. The detriment that the State would impose upon the pregnant woman by denying this choice altogether is apparent. Specific and direct harm medically diagnosable even in early pregnancy may be involved. Maternity, or additional offspring, may force upon the woman a distressful life and future. Psychological harm may be imminent. Mental and physical health may be taxed by child care. There is also the distress, for all concerned, associated with the unwanted child, and there is the problem of bringing a child into a family already unable, psychologically and otherwise, to care for it. In other cases, as in this one, the additional difficulties and continuing stigma of unwed motherhood may be involved. All these are factors the woman and her responsible physician necessarily will consider in consultation.

On the basis of elements such as these, appellant and some *amici* argue that the woman's right is absolute and that she is entitled to terminate her pregnancy at whatever time, in whatever way, and for whatever reason she alone chooses. With this we do not agree. Appellant's arguments that Texas either has no valid interest at all in regulating the abortion decision, or no interest strong enough to support any limitation upon the woman's sole determination, are unpersuasive. The Court's decisions recognizing a right of privacy also acknowledge that some state regulation in areas protected by that right is appropriate. As noted above, a State may properly assert important interests in safeguarding health, in maintaining medical standards, and in protecting potential life. At some point in pregnancy, these respective interests become sufficiently compelling to sustain regulation of the factors that govern the abortion decision. The privacy right involved, therefore, cannot be said to be absolute. In fact, it is not clear to us that the claim asserted by some *amici* that one has an unlimited right to do with one's body as one pleases bears a close relationship to the right of privacy previously articulated in the Court's decisions. The Court has refused to recognize an unlimited right of this kind in the past. *Jacobson v. Massachusetts*, 197 U.S. 11 (1905) (vaccination); *Buck v. Bell*, 274 U.S. 200 (1927) (sterilization).

We, therefore, conclude that the right of personal privacy includes the abortion decision, but that this right is not unqualified and must be considered against important state interests in regulation.. . .

Where certain "fundamental rights" are involved, the Court has held that regulation limiting these rights may be justified only by a "compelling state interest," *Kramer v. Union Free School District*, 395 U.S. 621, 627 (1969); *Shapiro v. Thompson*, 394 U.S. 618, 634 (1969); *Sherbert v. Verner*, 374 U.S. 398, 406 (1963), and that legislative enactments must be narrowly drawn to express only the legitimate state interests at stake. *Griswold v. Connecticut*, 381 U.S., at 485; *Aptheker v. Secretary of State*, 378 U.S. 500, 508 (1964); *Cantwell v. Connecticut*, 310 U.S. 296, 307–308 (1940); see *Eisenstadt v. Baird*, 405 U.S., at 460, 463–464, (White, J., concurring in result).. . .

IX

The District Court held that the appellee failed to meet his burden of demonstrating that the Texas statute's infringement upon Roe's rights was necessary to support a compelling state interest, and that, although the appellee presented "several compelling justifications for state presence in the area of abortions," the statutes outstripped these justifications and swept "far beyond any areas of compelling state interest." . . . Appellant and appellee both contest that holding. Appellant, as has been indicated, claims an absolute right that bars any state imposition of criminal penalties in the area. Appellee argues that the State's determination to recognize and protect prenatal life from and after conception constitutes a compelling state interest. As noted above, we do not agree fully with either formulation.

A. The appellee and certain *amici* argue that the fetus is a "person" within the language and meaning of the Fourteenth Amendment. In support of this, they outline at length and in detail the well-known facts of fetal development. If this suggestion of personhood is established, the appellant's case, of course, collapses, for the fetus's right to life would then be guaranteed specifically by the Amendment. The appellant conceded as much on reargument. On the other hand, the appellee conceded on reargument that no case could be cited that holds that a fetus is a person within the meaning of the Fourteenth Amendment. . . .

All this . . .persuades us that the word "person", as used in the Fourteenth Amendment does not include the unborn. This conclusion, however, does not of itself fully answer the contentions raised by Texas, and we pass on to other considerations.

B. The pregnant woman cannot be isolated in her privacy. She carries an embryo and, later, a fetus, if one accepts the medical definitions of the developing young in the human uterus. See Dorland's Illustrated Medical Dictionary 478–479, 547 (24th ed. 1965). The situation therefore is inherently different from marital intimacy, or bedroom possession of obscene material, or marriage, or procreation, or education, with which *Eisenstadt* and *Griswold, Stanley, Loving, Skinner* and *Pierce* and *Meyer* were respectively concerned. As we have intimated above, it is reasonable and appropriate for a State to decide that at some point in time another interest, that of health of the mother or that of potential human life, becomes significantly involved. The woman's privacy is no longer sole and any right of privacy she possesses must be measured accordingly.

Texas urges that, apart from the Fourteenth Amendment, life begins at conception and is present throughout pregnancy, and that, therefore, the State has a compelling interest in protecting that life from and after conception. We need not resolve the difficult question of when life begins. When those trained in the respective disciplines of medicine, philosophy, and theology are unable to arrive at any consensus, the judiciary, at this point in the development of man's knowledge, is not in a position to speculate as to the answer.

It should be sufficient to note briefly the wide divergence of thinking on this most sensitive and difficult question. There has always been strong support for the view that life does not begin until live birth. This was the belief of the Stoics. It appears to be the predominant, though not the unanimous, attitude of the Jewish faith. It may be taken to represent also the position of a large segment of the Protestant community, insofar as that can be ascertained; organized groups that have taken a formal position on the abortion issue have generally regarded abortion as a matter for the conscience of the individual and her family. As we have noted, the common law found greater significance in quickening. Physicians and their scientific colleagues have regarded that event with less interest and have tended to focus either upon conception, upon live birth, or upon the interim point at which the fetus become "viable," that is, potentially able to live outside the mother's womb, albeit with artificial aid. Viability is usually placed at about seven months (28 weeks) but may occur earlier, even at 24 weeks. The Aristotelian theory of "mediate animation," that held sway throughout the Middle Ages and the Renaissance in Europe, continued to be official Roman Catholic dogma until the 19th century, despite opposition to this "ensoulment" theory from those in the Church who would recognize the existence of life from the moment of conception. The latter is now, of course, the official belief of the Catholic Church. As one brief *amicus* discloses, this is a view strongly held by many non-Catholics as well, and by many physicians. Substantial problems for precise definition of this view are posed, however, by new embryological data that purport to indicate the conception is a "process" over time, rather than an event, and by new medical techniques such as menstrual extraction, the "morning-after" pill, implantation of embryos, artificial insemination, and even artificial wombs.

In areas other than criminal abortion, the law has been reluctant to endorse any theory that life, as we recognize it, begins before live birth or to accord legal rights to the unborn except in narrowly defined situations and except when the rights are contingent upon live birth. For example, the traditional rule of tort law denied recovery for prenatal injuries even though the child was born alive. That rule has been changed in almost every jurisdiction. In most States, recovery is said to be permitted only if the fetus was viable, or at least quick, when the injuries were sustained, though few courts have squarely so held. In a recent development, generally opposed by the commentators, some States permit the parents of a stillborn child to maintain an action for wrongful death because of prenatal injuries. Such an action, however, would appear to be one to vindicate the parents' interest and is thus consistent with the view that the fetus, at most, represents only the potentiality of life. Similarly, unborn children have been recognized as acquiring rights or interests by way of inheritance or other devolution of property, and have been represented by guardians *ad litem*. Perfection of the interests involved, again, has generally been contingent upon live birth. In short, the unborn have never been recognized in the law as persons in the whole sense.

X

In view of all this, we do not agree that, by adopting one theory of life, Texas may override the rights of the pregnant woman that are at stake. We repeat, however, that the State does have an important and legitimate interest in preserving and protecting the health of the pregnant woman, whether she be a resident of the State or a nonresident who seeks medical consultation and treatment there, and that it has still *another* important and legitimate interest in protecting the potentiality of human life. These interests are separate and distinct. Each grows in substantiality as the woman approaches term and, at a point during pregnancy, each becomes "compelling."

With respect to the State's important and legitimate interest in the health of the mother, the "compelling" point, in the light of present medical knowledge, is at approximately the end of the first trimester. This is so because of the new-established medical fact . . . that until the end of the first trimester mortality in abortion may be less than mortality in normal childbirth. It follows that, from and after this point, a State may regulate the abortion procedure to the extent that the regulation reasonably relates to the preservation and protection of maternal health. Examples of permissible state regulation in this area are requirements as to the qualifications of the person who is to perform the abortion; as to the licensure of that person; as to the facility in which the procedure is to be performed, that is, whether it must be a hospital or may be a clinic or some other place of less-than-hospital status; as to the licensing of the facility; and the like.

This means, on the other hand, that, for the period of pregnancy prior to this "compelling" point, the attending physician, in consultation with his patient, is free to determine, without regulation by the State, that, in his medical judgment, the patient's pregnancy should be terminated. If that decision is reached, the judgment may be effectuated by an abortion free of interference by the State.

With respect to the State's important and legitimate interest in potential life, the "compelling" point is at viability. This is so because the fetus then presumably has the capability of meaningful life outside the mother's womb. State regulation protective of fetal life after viability thus has both logical and biological justifications. If the State is interested in protecting fetal life after viability, it may go so far as to proscribe abortion during that period, except when it is necessary to preserve the life or health of the mother.

Measured against these standards, Art. 1196 of the Texas Penal Code, in restricting legal abortions to those "procured or attempted by medical advice for the purpose of saving the life of the mother," sweeps too broadly. The statute makes no distinction between abortions performed early in pregnancy and those performed later, and it limits to a single reason, "saving" the mother's life, the legal justification for the procedure. The statute, therefore, cannot survive the constitutional attack made upon it here.

This conclusion makes it unnecessary for us to consider the additional challenge to the Texas statute asserted on grounds of vagueness. See *United States v. Vuitch*, 402 U.S., at 67–72.

XI

To summarize and to repeat:

1. A state criminal abortion statute of the current Texas type, that excepts from criminality only a *life-saving* procedure on behalf of the mother, without regard to pregnancy stage and without recognition of the other interests involved, is violative of the Due Process Clause of the Fourteenth Amendment.

(a) For the stage prior to approximately the end of the first trimester, the abortion decision and its effectuation must be left to the medical judgment of the pregnant woman's attending physician.

(b) For the stage subsequent to approximately the end of the first trimester, the State, in promoting its interest in the health of the mother, may, if it chooses, regulate the abortion procedure in ways that are reasonably related to maternal health.

(c) For the stage subsequent to viability, the State in promoting its interest in the potentiality of human life may, if it chooses, regulate, and even proscribe, abortion except where it is necessary, in appropriate medical judgment, for the preservation of the life or health of the mother.

2. The State may define the term "physician," as it has been employed in the preceding paragraphs of this Part XI of this opinion, to mean only a physician currently licensed by the State, and may proscribe any abortion by a person who is not a physician as so defined. . . .

This holding, we feel, is consistent with the relative weights of the respective interests involved, with the lessons and examples of medical and legal history, with the lenity of the common law, and with the demands of the profound problems of the present day. The decision leaves the State free to place increasing restrictions on abortion as the period of pregnancy lengthens, so long as those restrictions are tailored to the recognized state interests. The decision vindicates the right of the physician to administer medical treatment according to his professional judgment up to the points where important state interests provide compelling justifications for intervention. Up to those points, the abortion decision in all its aspects is inherently, and primarily, a medical decision, and basic responsibility for it must rest with the physician. If an individual practitioner abuses the privilege of exercising proper medical judgment, the usual remedies, judicial and intra-professional, are available.

XII

Our conclusion that Art. 1196 is unconstitutional means, of course, that the Texas abortion statutes, as a unit, must fall. . . .

MR. JUSTICE REHNQUIST, dissenting.

. . . .

I would reach a conclusion opposite to that reached by the Court. I have difficulty in concluding, as the Court does, that the right of "privacy" is involved in this case. Texas, by the statute here challenged, bars the performance of a medical abortion by a licensed physician on a plaintiff such as *Roe*. A transaction resulting in an operation such as this is not "private" in the ordinary usage of that word. Nor is the "privacy" that the Court finds here even a distant relative of the freedom from searches and seizures protected by the Fourth Amendment to the Constitution, which the Court has referred to as embodying a right to privacy. . . .

If the Court means by the term "privacy" no more than that the claim of a person to be free from unwanted state regulation of consensual transactions may be a form of "liberty" protected by the Fourteenth Amendment, there is no doubt that similar claims have been upheld in our earlier decisions on the basis of that liberty. I agree with the statement of Mr. Justice Stewart in his concurring opinion that the "liberty," against deprivation of which without due process the Fourteenth Amendment protects, embraces more than the rights found in the Bill of Rights. But that liberty is not guaranteed absolutely against deprivation, only against deprivation without due process of law. The test traditionally applied in the area of social and economic legislation is whether or not a law such as that challenged has a rational relation to a valid state objective. *Williamson v. Lee Optical Co.*, 348 U.S. 483, 491 (1955). The Due Process Clause of the Fourteenth Amendment undoubtedly does place a limit, albeit a broad one, on legislative power to enact laws such as this. If the

Texas statute were to prohibit an abortion even where the mother's life is in jeopardy, I have little doubt that such a statute would lack a rational relation to a valid state objective under the test stated in *Williamson, supra*. But the Court's sweeping invalidation of any restrictions on abortion during the first trimester is impossible to justify under that standard, and the conscious weighing of competing factors that the Court's opinion apparently substitutes for the established test is far more appropriate to a legislative judgment than to a judicial one. . . .

For all of the foregoing reasons, I respectfully dissent.

NOTES AND QUESTIONS

(1) **The Majority Opinion.** There is a symmetry about Justice Blackmun's opinion in *Roe v. Wade,* 410 U.S. 113 (1973). He sees three interests to be protected: the mother's right of privacy, the state's interest in protecting the mother's health, and the state's interest in protecting the "potentiality of life" in each of the three stages of pregnancy. As the stages of pregnancy progress, the latter two interests begin to take precedence over the first: in the first trimester the mother's privacy interest is most important; by the end of this period the health risk to the mother becomes greater and so the state's interest in protecting health becomes more important than the mother's privacy; finally at the point of viability the state's interest in protecting the potentiality of life becomes supreme, and the state may regulate abortion. Is this symmetry too neat, or has Justice Blackmun settled upon an ingenious way to balance these interests? Can you think of any legal precedent for this form of balancing?

(2) **Right of Privacy.** The right of privacy is at the heart of *Roe*; without this right there would be no constitutionally protected interest to balance against the state's interest in protecting the potentiality of life. Yet for all its importance, the majority merely assumes that the right of privacy exists, but shows little interest in establishing a theory of constitutional interpretation to support the belief in the existence of the right. Justice Blackmun gives copious citations to cases which support his view that such a right exists, but mentions the penumbra theory only in passing, as it relates to *Griswold*, and the Ninth Amendment view only in regard to Justice Goldberg's concurring opinion in *Griswold*.

(3) **When Life Begins.** By rejecting conception or birth as the moment when life begins, does not Justice Blackmun's opinion implicitly recognize that life is a developmental process? Viability is not a fixed moment. It may vary from case to case and may change with scientific and medical innovation. Despite the division of gestation into three stages, the opinion rejects the view that life exists at one moment when it did not exist the moment before. This view is further supported by the use of viability as the beginning of the critical third stage.

(4) **Viability.** The choice of viability as the point at which the state may prohibit abortion has been criticized by pro-choice advocates. Even though *Roe* legalizes abortion, the availability of abortion procedures will be undermined as the medical profession through scientific discoveries gradually moves the point of viability back. Is it conceivable that the point of viability could be as early as the first trimester? Earlier? If one grants that the fetus or unborn child (the choice of terms is critical and often reveals a point of view) deserves some protection from the law, is the choice of viability a fortuitous one, one that will keep the law up to date with new medical discoveries?

(5) **Pro-life.** Pro-life or anti-abortion advocates, of course, criticize *Roe* for allowing abortion at all. Is not criticism of this sort predicated on a firm belief as to when life begins? If one believes that human life unequivocally begins at the moment of conception, then he or she is bound to say that all abortion is wrong, that it is a taking of life. Can you formulate an argument against *Roe*, conceding as Justice Blackmun appears to do, that it is impossible to know when, or at least to reach a consensus as to when, life begins?

(6) **Subsequent Cases.** The cases which have followed *Roe* can be divided into some common categories.

   (a) *Fathers.* What happens when a husband and wife do not agree on the necessity of an abortion? Missouri had a statute which required the prior written consent of the spouse of a woman seeking an abortion during the first trimester of pregnancy unless the abortion was to save the mother's life. Certainly consideration of this statute brings into play a new interest, that of the potential father, to be balanced against the three interests discussed in *Roe*. In *Planned Parenthood of Mo. v. Danforth*, 428 U.S. 52, 69–70 (1976) (citations omitted), the Court recognized this interest:

   > We are not unaware of the deep and proper concern and interest that a devoted and protective husband has in his wife's pregnancy and in the growth and development of the fetus she is carrying. Neither has this Court failed to appreciate the importance of the marital relationship in our society. Moreover, we recognize that the decision whether to undergo or to forego an abortion may have profound effects on the future of any marriage, effects that are both physical and mental, and possibly deleterious.

   > However, as between this interest of the father and the privacy interest of the mother, the Court favors the mother: "Since it is the woman who physically bears the child and who is the more directly and immediately affected by the pregnancy, as between the two, the balance weighs in her favor." In striking down the statute, the Court concluded: "we cannot hold that the state has the constitutional authority to give the spouse unilaterally the ability to prohibit the wife from terminating her pregnancy, when the state itself lacks that right."

   > The issue of fathers' rights has not been revisited by the Court except in cases which have dealt with the issue of notice to fathers. In *Planned Parenthood v. Casey,* 505 U.S. 833, 112 S. Ct. 2791 (1992), the Court upheld a portion of an anti-abortion statute which required that "a married woman seeking an abortion must sign a statement indicating that she has notified her husband of her intended abortion." *Id.* at 842, 112 S. Ct. at 2803.

   (b) *Health. Roe* left the door open for state regulatory action protecting the woman getting an abortion, but it did not directly discuss any such regulatory statute. However, in *Doe v. Bolton*, 410 U.S. 179 (1973) the companion case to *Roe*, the Court struck down a Georgia statute which required that an abortion must be performed in a hospital accredited by a particular private agency, that it must be approved by a hospital committee, and that two doctors must concur with the patient's doctor that the abortion is needed. In *Planned Parenthood Ass'n v. Ashcroft*, 462 U.S. 476 (1983), the Court held that a state may not require that abortion be performed in an accredited hospital.

(c) *Public funding and hospitals.* The issue of public funding and the use of public facilities has been of great concern right from the beginning of the abortion debate. Here is a list of cases involving public funding: *Beal v. Doe*, 432 U.S. 438 (1977) (stating that a state was free to exclude non-therapeutic abortions from Medicaid programs); *Maher v. Roe*, 432 U.S. 464 (1977) (holding that the Equal Protection Clause did not require a state participating in a Medicaid program to pay the expenses incident to non-therapeutic abortions for indigent women, although the state paid for the costs of childbirth); *Poelker v. Doe*, 432 U.S. 519 (1977) (ruling that a city was not required to fund therapeutic abortions even though it paid for childbirth); and *Harris v. McRae*, 448 U.S. 297 (1980) (finding the federal statute prohibiting federal funding for medically needed abortions constitutional). However, one lower court case overturned a local law which prohibited staff physicians from performing abortions on paying patients at the sole hospital in the community, which was public. *Nyberg v. City of Virginia*, 667 F.2d 754 (8th Cir. 1982), *cert. denied*, 462 U.S. 1125 (1983).

In 1991, the Supreme Court decided *Rust v. Sullivan*, 500 U.S. 173 (1991). *Rust* involved Department of Health and Human Services (HHS) regulations which prohibited abortion counseling, referral, and activities advocating abortion as a method of family planning under Title X of the Public Health Service Act. Justice Rehnquist, writing for the Court, found that HHS was permitted to restrict Title X funds for "programs in which abortion is a method of family planning." Furthermore, the Court found no constitutional violation under the First or Fifth Amendments.

(d) *Minors.* The Supreme Court has always allowed the states greater latitude in regulating abortion for minors; nevertheless, the fundamental right of privacy in matters of marriage and procreation protects a minor's right to have an abortion. The major area of litigation has been the issue of whether a state can require the consent of the parent for a minor to get an abortion. The basic rule is that a state can statutorily require parental consent by one parent as long as there is a provision for judicial bypass; that is, the minor will have access to an abortion without parental consent by applying to an appropriate court. The judge must make a finding either that the minor is of a sufficient age and maturity to make the decision herself, that it is in the best interest of the minor to have an abortion, or that she was the subject of sexual abuse. *See Ohio v. Akron Ctr. for Reproductive Heath*, 497 U.S. 502 (1990). Here are some of the important cases dealing with abortion for minors: *Bellotti v. Baird*, 443 U.S. 622 (1979) (holding that a state could not require the consent of both parents); *H.L. v. Matheson*, 450 U.S. 398 (1981) (holding that a state may require that parents of a minor must be notified of impending abortion); *Hodgson v. Minnesota*, 497 U.S 417 (1990) (stating that a state may not require a 48-hour notification of both parents prior to an abortion if there is no provision for judicial bypass).

(e) *Miscellaneous.* There are some abortion cases that are not so easily classified. Actually they are more easily categorized if one takes a particular point of view.

From a pro-choice point of view, these are cases involving statutes which are designed to put obstacles in the way of a woman who wants to get an abortion. From a pro-life position these cases involve statutes which do everything possible to save the fetus within the law after *Roe*. An example of this kind of case would be *Akron v. Akron Ctr. for Reproductive Health*, 462 U.S. 416 (1983), which held that a city cannot require an abortion patient to be informed that the unborn child is a human life from the moment of conception. One aspect of *Planned Parenthood Association v. Ashcroft*, 462 U.S. 476 (1983), mentioned above under "Health," might also fall into this category: the Court struck down a requirement that a second physician be present at an abortion to care for the fetus if it turned out to be viable.

Another case which might be placed in the miscellaneous category is *Webster v. Reproductive Health Servs.*, 492 U.S. 490, 109 S. Ct. 3040, 106 L. Ed. 2d 410 (1989). The challenged statute involved a number of restrictions upon a woman's right to choose an abortion, none of which actually prevented abortion prior to viability. Most of these restrictions, such as a prohibition on allowing public employees and public facilities from being used for facilitating abortions, had already been considered by the Court. Perhaps the most interesting thing about the statute was that it stated in the preamble, as a matter of public policy, that life begins at conception, and yet contained a provision requiring viability testing for every abortion involving a fetus of "twenty weeks or more gestational age."

Justice Rehnquist, writing for a plurality, stated that the time was not ripe to decide the constitutionality of the preamble because it had not yet been applied to interpret the other provisions of the statute in a way that affected any individual rights. He further found that the viability testing did not violate *Roe*, since the testing merely insured that abortions were not performed where the fetus was viable.

This case received a great deal of notoriety both before and after the Supreme Court made its decision. Many people thought that this would be the case in which the pro-life forces would muster enough votes to overturn *Roe*. The Court at that time consisted of Chief Justice Rehnquist, and Justices Blackmun, Brennan, Marshall, White, Stevens, O'Connor, Scalia, and Kennedy. The belief was that there would be a majority formed by the Chief Justice and Justices White, O'Connor, Scalia, and Kennedy, the last three being the most recent Republican appointees. The decision was just as controversial after it was handed down because the Court did not overrule *Roe*.

The failure to overturn *Roe* probably lies at the hands of the Chief Justice, not because of any lack of moral courage, as Justice Scalia implied, but because of his own view of the limited role of the judiciary: he could not act expansively to overrule a case which was not technically at issue in the present controversy. Chief Justice Rehnquist stated:

Both appellants and the United States as Amicus Curiae have urged that we overrule our decision in *Roe v. Wade*. The facts of the present case, however, differ from those at issue in *Roe*. Here, Missouri has determined that viability is the point at which its interest in potential human life must be safeguarded. In *Roe*, on the other hand, the Texas statute criminalized the performance of all abortions, except when the mother's life was at stake. This case therefore affords us no occasion to revisit the holding of *Roe*, which was that the Texas statute unconstitutionally infringed the right to an abortion derived from the Due Process Clause, and we leave it undisturbed.

Justice Scalia would not have been so restrained. In a concurring opinion, he stated that it was not enough to merely decide if the Missouri statute violated *Roe*, but rather that the time had come to overrule *Roe*.

PLANNED PARENTHOOD v. CASEY
United States Supreme Court
505 U. S. 833 (1992)

JUSTICE O'CONNOR, JUSTICE KENNEDY, and JUSTICE SOUTER announced the judgment of the Court and delivered the opinion of the Court with respect to Parts I, II, III, V–A, V–C, and VI, an opinion with respect to Part V–E, in which JUSTICE STEVENS joins, and an opinion with respect to Parts IV, V–B, and V–D.

I

Liberty finds no refuge in a jurisprudence of doubt. Yet 19 years after our holding that the Constitution protects a woman's right to terminate her pregnancy in its early stages, *Roe v. Wade*, 410 U.S. 113 (1973), that definition of liberty is still questioned. Joining the respondents as *amicus curiae*, the United States, as it has done in five other cases in the last decade, again asks us to overrule *Roe*.

At issue in these cases are five provisions of the Pennsylvania Abortion Control Act of 1982, as amended in 1988 and 1989. 18 Pa. Cons.Stat. §§ 3203–3220 (1990). . . . The Act requires that a woman seeking an abortion give her informed consent prior to the abortion procedure, and specifies that she be provided with certain information at least 24 hours before the abortion is performed. § 3205. For a minor to obtain an abortion, the Act requires the informed consent of one of her parents, but provides for a judicial bypass option if the minor does not wish to or cannot obtain a parent's consent. § 3206. Another provision of the Act requires that, unless certain exceptions apply, a married woman seeking an abortion must sign a statement indicating that she has notified her husband of her intended abortion. § 3209. The Act exempts compliance with these three requirements in the event of a "medical emergency," which is defined in § 3203 of the Act. See §§ 3203, 3205(a), 3206(a), 3209(c). In addition to the above provisions regulating the performance of abortions, the Act imposes certain reporting requirements on facilities that provide abortion services. §§ 3207(b), 3214(a), 3214(f).

Before any of these provisions took effect, the petitioners, who are five abortion clinics and one physician representing himself as well as a class of physicians who provide abortion services, brought this suit seeking declaratory and injunctive relief. Each provision was challenged as unconstitutional on its face. The District Court entered a preliminary injunction against the enforcement of the regulations, and, after a 3-day bench trial, held all the provisions at issue here unconstitutional, entering a permanent injunction against Pennsylvania's enforcement of them. The Court of Appeals for the Third Circuit affirmed in part and reversed in part, upholding all of the regulations except for the husband notification requirement. . . .

At oral argument in this Court, the attorney for the parties challenging the statute took the position that none of the enactments can be upheld without overruling *Roe v. Wade*. We disagree with that analysis; but we acknowledge that our decisions after *Roe* cast doubt upon the meaning and reach of its holding . . . .

After considering the fundamental constitutional questions resolved by *Roe*, principles of institutional integrity, and the rule of stare decisis, we are led to conclude this: the essential holding of *Roe v. Wade* should be retained and once again reaffirmed.

It must be stated at the outset and with clarity that *Roe*'s essential holding, the holding we reaffirm, has three parts. First is a recognition of the right of the woman to choose to have an abortion before viability and to obtain it without undue interference from the State. Before viability, the State's interests are not strong enough to support a prohibition of abortion or the imposition of a substantial obstacle to the woman's effective right to elect the procedure. Second is a confirmation of the State's power to restrict abortions after fetal viability, if the law contains exceptions for pregnancies which endanger a woman's life or health. And third is the principle that the State has legitimate interests from the outset of the pregnancy in protecting the health of the woman and the life of the fetus that may become a child. These principles do not contradict one another; and we adhere to each.

II

Constitutional protection of the woman's decision to terminate her pregnancy derives from the Due Process Clause of the Fourteenth Amendment. It declares that no State shall "deprive any person of life, liberty, or property, without due process of law." The controlling word in the case before us is "liberty."

Although a literal reading of the Clause might suggest that it governs only the procedures by which a State may deprive persons of liberty, for at least 105 years, since *Mugler v. Kansas*, . . . the Clause has been understood to contain a substantive component as well, one "barring certain government actions regardless of the fairness of the procedures used to implement them." *Daniels v. Williams*. . . . As Justice Brandeis (joined by Justice Holmes) observed, "[d]espite arguments to the contrary which had seemed to me persuasive, it is settled that the Due Process Clause of the Fourteenth Amendment applies to matters of substantive law as well as to matters of procedure. Thus all fundamental rights comprised within the term liberty are protected by the Federal Constitution from invasion by the States." *Whitney v. California*. . . .

The most familiar of the substantive liberties protected by the Fourteenth Amendment are those recognized by the Bill of Rights. We have held that the Due Process Clause of the Fourteenth Amendment incorporates most of the Bill of Rights against the States. It is tempting, as a means of curbing the discretion of federal judges, to suppose that liberty encompasses no more than those rights already guaranteed to the individual against federal interference by the express provisions of the first eight amendments to the Constitution. But of course this Court has never accepted that view.

It is also tempting, for the same reason, to suppose that the Due Process Clause protects only those practices, defined at the most specific level, that were protected against government interference by other rules of law when the Fourteenth Amendment was ratified. But such a view would be inconsistent with our law. It is a promise of the Constitution that there is a realm of personal liberty which the government may not enter. We have vindicated this principle before. Marriage is mentioned nowhere in the Bill of Rights and interracial marriage was illegal in most States in the 19th century, but the Court was no doubt correct in finding it to be an aspect of liberty protected against state interference by the substantive component of the Due Process Clause in *Loving v. Virginia*. . . .

Neither the Bill of Rights nor the specific practices of States at the time of the adoption of the Fourteenth Amendment marks the outer limits of the substantive sphere of liberty which the Fourteenth Amendment protects. . . . As the second Justice Harlan recognized:

> [T]he full scope of the liberty guaranteed by the Due Process Clause cannot be found in or limited by the precise terms of the specific guarantees elsewhere provided in the Constitution. This 'liberty' is not a series of isolated points pricked out in terms of the taking of property; the freedom of speech, press, and religion; the right to keep and bear arms; the freedom from unreasonable searches and seizures; and so on. It is a rational continuum which, broadly speaking, includes a freedom from all substantial arbitrary impositions and purposeless restraints, . . . and which also recognizes, what a reasonable and sensitive judgment must, that certain interests require particularly careful scrutiny of the state needs asserted to justify their abridgment.

. . .

> The inescapable fact is that adjudication of substantive due process claims may call upon the Court in interpreting the Constitution to exercise that same capacity which by tradition courts always have exercised: reasoned judgment. Its boundaries are not susceptible of expression as a simple rule. That does not mean we are free to invalidate state policy choices with which we disagree; yet neither does it permit us to shrink from the duties of our office. . . .

Men and women of good conscience can disagree, and we suppose some always shall disagree, about the profound moral and spiritual implications of terminating a pregnancy, even in its earliest stage. Some of us as individuals find abortion offensive to our most basic principles of morality, but that cannot control our decision. Our obligation is to define the liberty of all, not to mandate our own moral code. The underlying constitutional issue is whether the State can resolve these philosophic questions in such a definitive way that a woman lacks all choice in the matter, except perhaps in those rare circumstances in which the pregnancy is itself a danger to her own life or health, or is the result of rape or incest. . . .

These considerations begin our analysis of the woman's interest in terminating her pregnancy but cannot end it, for this reason: though the abortion decision may originate within the zone of conscience and belief, it is more than a philosophic exercise. Abortion is a unique act. It is an act fraught with consequences for others: for the woman who must live with the implications of her decision; for the persons who perform and assist in the procedure; for the spouse, family, and society which must confront the knowledge that these procedures exist, procedures some deem nothing short of an act of violence against innocent human life; and, depending on one's beliefs, for the life or potential life that is aborted. Though abortion is conduct, it does not follow that the State is entitled to proscribe it in all instances. That is because the liberty of the woman is at stake in a sense unique to the human condition and so unique to the law. The mother who carries a child to full term is subject to anxieties, to physical constraints, to pain that only she must bear. That these sacrifices have from the beginning of the human race been endured by woman with a pride that ennobles her in the eyes of others and gives to the infant a bond of love cannot alone be grounds for the State to insist she make the sacrifice. Her suffering is too intimate and personal for the State to insist, without more, upon its own vision of the woman's role, however dominant that vision has been in the course of our history and our culture. The destiny of the woman must be shaped to a large extent on her own conception of her spiritual imperatives and her place in society.

It should be recognized, moreover, that in some critical respects the abortion decision is of the same character as the decision to use contraception, to which *Griswold v. Connecticut, Eisenstadt v. Baird*, and *Carey v. Population Services International*, afford constitutional protection. We have no doubt as to the correctness of those decisions. They support the reasoning in *Roe* relating to the woman's liberty because they involve personal decisions concerning not only the meaning of procreation but also human responsibility and respect for it. As with abortion, reasonable people will have differences of opinion about these matters. One view is based on such reverence for the wonder of creation that any pregnancy ought to be welcomed and carried to full term no matter how difficult it will be to provide for the child and ensure its well-being. Another is that the inability to provide for the nurture and care of the infant is a cruelty to the child and an anguish to the parent. These are intimate views with infinite variations, and their deep, personal character underlay our decisions in *Griswold, Eisenstadt*, and *Carey*. The same concerns are present when the woman confronts the reality that, perhaps despite her attempts to avoid it, she has become pregnant.

It was this dimension of personal liberty that *Roe* sought to protect, and its holding invoked the reasoning and the tradition of the precedents we have discussed, granting protection to substantive liberties of the person. *Roe* was, of course, an extension of those cases and, as the decision itself indicated, the separate States could act in some degree to further their own legitimate interests in protecting prenatal life. The extent to which the legislatures of the States might act to outweigh the interests of the woman in choosing to terminate her pregnancy was a subject of debate both in *Roe* itself and in decisions following it.

While we appreciate the weight of the arguments made on behalf of the State in the case before us, arguments which in their ultimate formulation conclude that *Roe* should be overruled, the reservations any of us may have in reaffirming the central holding of *Roe* are outweighed by the explication of individual liberty we have given combined with the force of *stare decisis*. . . .

. . . .

IV

From what we have said so far it follows that it is a constitutional liberty of the woman to have some freedom to terminate her pregnancy. We conclude that the basic decision in *Roe* was based on a constitutional analysis which we cannot now repudiate. The woman's liberty is not so unlimited, however, that from the outset the State cannot show its concern for the life of the unborn, and at a later point in fetal development the State's interest in life has sufficient force so that the right of the woman to terminate the pregnancy can be restricted.

That brings us, of course, to the point where much criticism has been directed at *Roe*, a criticism that always inheres when the Court draws a specific rule from what in the Constitution is but a general standard. We conclude, however, that the urgent claims of the woman to retain the ultimate control over her destiny and her body, claims implicit in the meaning of liberty, require us to perform that function. Liberty must not be extinguished for want of a line that is clear. And it falls to us to give some real substance to the woman's liberty to determine whether to carry her pregnancy to full term.

We conclude the line should be drawn at viability, so that before that time the woman has a right to choose to terminate her pregnancy. . . .

The woman's right to terminate her pregnancy before viability is the most central principle of *Roe v. Wade*. It is a rule of law and a component of liberty we cannot renounce.

On the other side of the equation is the interest of the State in the protection of potential life. The *Roe* Court recognized the State's "important and legitimate interest in protecting the potentiality of human life." . . . The weight to be given this state interest, not the strength of the woman's interest, was the difficult question faced in *Roe*. We do not need to say whether each of us, had we been Members of the Court when the valuation of the state interest came before it as an original matter, would have concluded, as the *Roe* Court did, that its weight is insufficient to justify a ban on abortions prior to viability even when it is subject to certain exceptions. The matter is not before us in the first instance, and coming as it does after nearly 20 years of litigation in *Roe*'s wake we are satisfied that the immediate question is not the soundness of *Roe*'s resolution of the issue, but the precedential force that must be accorded to its holding. And we have concluded that the essential holding of *Roe* should be reaffirmed.

Yet it must be remembered that *Roe v. Wade* speaks with clarity in establishing not only the woman's liberty but also the State's "important and legitimate interest in potential life." *Roe, supra*, at 163. That portion of the decision in *Roe* has been given too little acknowledgement and implementation by the Court in its subsequent cases. Those cases decided that any regulation touching upon the abortion decision must survive strict scrutiny, to be sustained only if drawn in narrow terms to further a compelling state interest. Not all of the cases decided under that formulation can be reconciled with the holding in *Roe* itself that the State has legitimate interests in the health of the woman and in protecting the potential life within her. In resolving this tension, we choose to rely upon *Roe*, as against the later cases.

Roe established a trimester framework to govern abortion regulations. Under this elaborate but rigid construct, almost no regulation at all is permitted during the first trimester of pregnancy; regulations designed to protect the woman's health, but not to further the State's interest in potential life, are permitted during the second trimester; and during the third trimester, when the fetus is viable, prohibitions are permitted provided the life or health of the mother is not at stake. *Roe v. Wade, supra*, at 163–166. Most of our cases since *Roe* have involved the application of rules derived from the trimester framework. . . .

We reject the trimester framework, which we do not consider to be part of the essential holding of *Roe*. Measures aimed at ensuring that a woman's choice contemplates the consequences for the fetus do not necessarily interfere with the right recognized in *Roe*, although those measures have been found to be inconsistent with the rigid trimester framework announced in that case. A logical reading of the central holding in *Roe* itself, and a necessary reconciliation of the liberty of the woman and the interest of the State in promoting prenatal life, require, in our view, that we abandon the trimester framework as a rigid prohibition on all previability regulation aimed at the protection of fetal life. The trimester framework suffers from these basic flaws: in its formulation it misconceives the nature of the pregnant woman's interest; and in practice it undervalues the State's interest in potential life, as recognized in *Roe*.

As our jurisprudence relating to all liberties save perhaps abortion has recognized, not every law which makes a right more difficult to exercise is, *ipso facto*, an infringement of that right. . . .

The abortion right is similar. Numerous forms of state regulation might have the incidental effect of increasing the cost or decreasing the availability of medical care, whether for abortion or any other medical procedure. The fact that a law which serves a valid purpose, one not designed to strike at the right itself, has the incidental effect of making it more difficult or more expensive to procure an abortion cannot be enough to invalidate it. Only where state regulation imposes an undue burden on a woman's ability to make this decision does the power of the State reach into the heart of the liberty protected by the Due Process Clause. . . .

The very notion that the State has a substantial interest in potential life leads to the conclusion that not all regulations must be deemed unwarranted. Not all burdens on the right to decide whether to terminate a pregnancy will be undue. In our view, the undue burden standard is the appropriate means of reconciling the State's interest with the woman's constitutionally protected liberty. . . .

A finding of an undue burden is a shorthand for the conclusion that a state regulation has the purpose or effect of placing a substantial obstacle in the path of a woman seeking an abortion of a nonviable fetus. A statute with this purpose is invalid because the means chosen by the State to further the interest in potential life must be calculated to inform the woman's free choice, not hinder it. And a statute which, while furthering the interest in potential life or some other valid state interest, has the effect of placing a substantial obstacle in the path of a woman's choice cannot be considered a permissible means of serving its legitimate ends. To the extent that the opinions of the Court or of individual Justices use the undue burden standard in a manner that is inconsistent with this analysis, we set out what in our view should be the controlling standard. In our considered judgment, an undue burden is an unconstitutional burden. Understood another way, we answer the question, left open in previous opinions discussing the undue burden formulation, whether a law designed to further the State's interest in fetal life which imposes an undue burden on the woman's decision before fetal viability could be constitutional. The answer is no.

Some guiding principles should emerge. What is at stake is the woman's right to make the ultimate decision, not a right to be insulated from all others in doing so. Regulations which do no more than create a structural mechanism by which the State, or the parent or guardian of a minor, may express profound respect for the life of the unborn are permitted, if they are not a substantial obstacle to the woman's exercise of the right to choose. Unless it has that effect on her right of choice, a state measure designed to persuade her to choose childbirth over abortion will be upheld if reasonably related to that goal. Regulations designed to foster the health of a woman seeking an abortion are valid if they do not constitute an undue burden.

Even when jurists reason from shared premises, some disagreement is inevitable. That is to be expected in the application of any legal standard which must accommodate life's complexity. We do not expect it to be otherwise with respect to the undue burden standard. We give this summary:

(a) To protect the central right recognized by *Roe v. Wade* while at the same time accommodating the State's profound interest in potential life, we will employ the undue burden analysis as explained in this opinion. An undue burden exists, and therefore a provision of law is invalid, if its purpose or effect is to place a substantial obstacle in the path of a woman seeking an abortion before the fetus attains viability.

(b) We reject the rigid trimester framework of *Roe v. Wade*. To promote the State's profound interest in potential life, throughout pregnancy the State may take measures to ensure that the woman's choice is informed, and measures designed to advance this interest will not be invalidated as long as their purpose is to persuade the woman to choose childbirth over abortion. These measures must not be an undue burden on the right.

(c) As with any medical procedure, the State may enact regulations to further the health or safety of a woman seeking an abortion. Unnecessary health regulations that have the purpose or effect of presenting a substantial obstacle to a woman seeking an abortion impose an undue burden on the right.

(d) Our adoption of the undue burden analysis does not disturb the central holding of *Roe v. Wade*, and we reaffirm that holding. Regardless of whether exceptions are made for particular circumstances, a State may not prohibit any woman from making the ultimate decision to terminate her pregnancy before viability.

(e) We also reaffirm *Roe*'s holding that "subsequent to viability, the State in promoting its interest in the potentiality of human life may, if it chooses, regulate, and even proscribe, abortion except where it is necessary, in appropriate medical judgment, for the preservation of the life or health of the mother." *Roe v. Wade*, 410 U.S. at 164–165.

These principles control our assessment of the Pennsylvania statute, and we now turn to the issue of the validity of its challenged provisions.

V

The Court of Appeals applied what it believed to be the undue burden standard and upheld each of the provisions except for the husband notification requirement. We agree generally with this conclusion, but refine the undue burden analysis in accordance with the principles articulated above. We now consider the separate statutory sections at issue. . . .

B

We next consider the informed consent requirement. 19 Pa. Cons. Stat.§ 3205 (1990). Except in a medical emergency, the statute requires that at least 24 hours before performing an abortion a physician inform the woman of the nature of the procedure, the health risks of the abortion and of childbirth, and the "probable gestational age of the unborn child." The physician or a qualified nonphysician must inform the woman of the availability of printed materials published by the State describing the fetus and providing information about medical assistance for childbirth, information about child support from the father, and a list of agencies which provide adoption and other services as alternatives to abortion. An abortion may not be performed unless the woman certifies in writing that she has been informed of the availability of these printed materials and has been provided them if she chooses to view them. . . .

Whether the mandatory 24-hour waiting period is nonetheless invalid because in practice it is a substantial obstacle to a woman's choice to terminate her pregnancy is a closer question. The findings of fact by the District Court indicate that because of the distances many women must travel to reach an abortion provider, the practical effect will often be a delay of much more than a day because the waiting period requires that a woman seeking an abortion make at least two visits to the doctor. The District Court also found that in many instances this will increase the exposure of women seeking abortions to "the harassment and hostility of anti-abortion protesters demonstrating outside a clinic." . . . As a result, the District Court found that for those women who have the fewest financial resources, those who must travel long distances, and those who have difficulty explaining their whereabouts to husbands, employers, or others, the 24-hour waiting period will be "particularly burdensome." . . .

These findings are troubling in some respects, but they do not demonstrate that the waiting period constitutes an undue burden. We do not doubt that, as the District Court held, the waiting period has the effect of "increasing the cost and risk of delay of abortions," . . . but the District Court did not conclude that the increased costs and potential delays amount to substantial obstacles. . . .

C

Section 3209 of Pennsylvania's abortion law provides, except in cases of medical emergency, that no physician shall perform an abortion on a married woman without receiving a signed statement from the woman that she has notified her spouse that she is about to undergo an abortion. The woman has the option of providing an alternative signed statement certifying that her husband is not the man who impregnated her; that her husband could not be located; that the pregnancy is the result of spousal sexual assault which she has reported; or that the woman believes that notifying her husband will cause him or someone else to inflict bodily injury upon her. A physician who performs an abortion on a married woman without receiving the appropriate signed statement will have his or her license revoked, and is liable to the husband for damages. . . .

This information [research into spousal abuse and "the limited research that has been conducted with respect to notifying one's husband about an abortion"] and the District Court's findings reinforce what common sense would suggest. In well-functioning marriages, spouses discuss important intimate decisions such as whether to bear a child. But there are millions of women in this country who are the victims of regular physical and psychological abuse at the hands of their husbands. Should these women become pregnant, they may have very good reasons for not wishing to inform their husbands of their decision to obtain an abortion. Many may have justifiable fears of physical abuse, but may be no less fearful of the consequences of reporting prior abuse to the Commonwealth of Pennsylvania. Many may have a reasonable fear that notifying their husbands will provoke further instances of child abuse; these women are not exempt from § 3209's notification requirement. . . .

The spousal notification requirement is thus likely to prevent a significant number of women from obtaining an abortion. It does not merely make abortions a little more difficult or expensive to obtain; for many women, it will impose a substantial obstacle. We must not blind ourselves to the fact that the significant number of women who fear for their safety and the safety of their children are likely to be deterred from procuring an abortion as surely as if the Commonwealth had outlawed abortion in all cases. . . .

We recognize that a husband has a "deep and proper concern and interest . . . in his wife's pregnancy and in the growth and development of the fetus she is carrying." *Danforth* . . . With regard to the children he has fathered and raised, the Court has recognized his "cognizable and substantial" interest in their custody. . . .

Before birth, however, the issue takes on a very different cast. . . .

The husband's interest in the life of the child his wife is carrying does not permit the State to empower him with this troubling degree of authority over his wife. The contrary view leads to consequences reminiscent of the common law. A husband has no enforceable right to require a wife to advise him before she exercises her personal choices. . . .

Section 3209 embodies a view of marriage consonant with the common-law status of married women but repugnant to our present understanding of marriage and of the nature of the rights secured by the Constitution. Women do not lose their constitutionally protected liberty when they marry. The Constitution protects all individuals, male or female, married or unmarried, from the abuse of governmental power, even where that power is employed for the supposed benefit of a member of the individual's family. These considerations confirm our conclusion that § 3209 is invalid.

D

We next consider the parental consent provision. Except in a medical emergency, an unemancipated young woman under 18 may not obtain an abortion unless she and one of her parents (or guardian) provides informed consent as defined above. If neither a parent nor a guardian provides consent, a court may authorize the performance of an abortion upon a determination that the young woman is mature and capable of giving informed consent and has in fact given her informed consent, or that an abortion would be in her best interests.

We have been over most of this ground before. Our cases establish, and we reaffirm today, that a State may require a minor seeking an abortion to obtain the consent of a parent or guardian, provided that there is an adequate judicial bypass procedure.

. . . .

VI

Our Constitution is a covenant running from the first generation of Americans to us and then to future generations. It is a coherent succession. Each generation must learn anew that the Constitution's written terms embody ideas and aspirations that must survive more ages than one. We accept our responsibility not to retreat from interpreting the full meaning of the covenant in light of all of our precedents. We invoke it once again to define the freedom guaranteed by the Constitution's own promise, the promise of liberty.

The judgment . . . is affirmed in part and reversed in part, and the case is remanded for proceedings consistent with this opinion, including consideration of the question of severability.

It is so ordered. . . .

JUSTICE SCALIA, concurring in the judgment in part and dissenting in part.

My views on this matter are unchanged from those I set forth in my separate opinions in *Webster v. Reproductive Services* and *Ohio v. Akron Center for Reproductive Health*. . . . The States may, if they wish, permit abortion on demand, but the Constitution does not *require* them to do so. The permissibility of abortion, and the limitations upon it, are to be resolved like most important questions in our democracy: by citizens trying to persuade one another and then voting. As the Court acknowledges, "where reasonable people disagree the government can adopt one position or the other." . . . The Court is correct in adding the qualification that this "assumes a state of affairs in which the choice does not intrude upon a protected liberty,"—but the crucial part of that qualification is the penultimate word. . . . A State's choice between two positions on which reasonable people can disagree is constitutional even when (as is often the case) it intrudes upon a "liberty" in the absolute sense. Laws against bigamy, for example—; with which entire societies of reasonable people disagree—; intrude upon men and women's liberty to marry and live with one another. But bigamy happens not to be a liberty specially "protected" by the Constitution.

That is, quite simply, the issue in these cases: not whether the power of a woman to abort her unborn child is a "liberty" in the absolute sense; or even whether it is a liberty of great importance to many women. Of course it is both. The issue is whether it is a liberty protected by the Constitution of the United States. I am sure it is not. I reach that conclusion not because of anything so exalted as my views concerning the "concept of existence, of meaning, of the universe, and of the mystery of human life." Rather, I reach it for the same reason I reach the conclusion that bigamy is not constitutionally protected—; because of two simple facts: (1) the Constitution says absolutely nothing about it, and (2) the longstanding traditions of American society have permitted it to be legally proscribed. . . .

To the extent I can discern any meaningful content in the "undue burden" standard as applied in the joint opinion, it appears to be that a State may not regulate abortion in such a way as to reduce significantly its incidence. The joint opinion repeatedly emphasizes that an important factor in the "undue burden" analysis is whether the regulation "prevents a significant number of women from obtaining an abortion"; whether a "significant number of women . . . are likely to be deterred from procuring an abortion"; and whether the regulation often "deters" women from seeking abortions. . . . We are not told, however, what forms of "deterrence" are impermissible or what degree of success in deterrence is too much to be tolerated. If, for example, a State required a woman to read a pamphlet describing, with illustrations, the facts of fetal development before she could obtain an abortion, the effect of such legislation might be to "deter" a "significant number of women" from procuring abortions, thereby seemingly allowing a district judge to invalidate it as an undue burden. Thus, despite flowery rhetoric about the State's "substantial" and "profound" interest in "potential human life," and criticism of *Roe* for undervaluing that interest, the joint opinion permits the State to pursue that interest only so long as it is not too successful. As Justice Blackmun recognizes (with evident hope), the "undue burden" standard may ultimately require the invalidation of each provision upheld today if it can be shown, on a better record, that the State is too effectively "expressing a preference for childbirth over abortion." . . . Reason finds no refuge in this jurisprudence of confusion.

. . . .

NOTES AND QUESTIONS

(1) **Justice count.** The edited version does not truly relay the complexity of this case, nor does it fully disclose the positions of the justices on all of the issues. By way of summary, here is a list of the results, which include a tally of how the justices voted on each of the issues.

(a) *Judgment.* The judgment of the Court was announced in a plurality joint opinion written by Justice O'Connor and joined by Justices Kennedy and Souter, and in which Justices Stevens joined in part. Concurring in the judgment in part and dissenting in part was Chief Justice Rehnquist, whose opinion was also signed by Justices Scalia, Thomas, and White. Justice Blackmun also separately concurred in part and dissented in part.

(b) *Roe Retained (Part I).* Decision: not to overrule *Roe*; majority: Justices Blackmun, Kennedy, O'Connor, Souter, and Stevens; dissenters: Chief Justice Rehnquist, Justices Scalia, Thomas, and White.

(c) *Due Process (Part II).* Decision: substantive due process applies to abortion analysis; majority: Justices Blackmun, Kennedy, O'Connor, Souter, and Stevens; dissenters: Chief Justice Rehnquist, Justices Scalia, Thomas, and White.

(d) *Stare Decisis (Part III).* Decision: Justices must recognize *stare decisis* except in the most egregious cases such as *Lochner v. New York* 198 U.S. 45, 25 S. Ct. 539, 49 L. Ed. 937 (1905) and *Plessey v. Ferguson*, 163 U.S. 537, 16 S. Ct. 1138, 41 L. Ed. 256 (1896); majority: Justices Blackmun, Kennedy, Souter, O'Connor, and Stevens; dissenters: Chief Justice Rehnquist, Justices Scalia, Thomas, and White.

(e) *Viability, Trimesters, and Undue-Burden Test (Part IV).* Decision: *Roe* is retained; viability is still the dividing line between the state's interest in protecting the potentiality of life and a woman's right to privacy; trimester scheme of *Roe* is not required by the Constitution; and state may regulate abortion prior to viability as long as regulation does not impose undue burden on a woman's right to an abortion; dissenters on the trimester issue and undue-burden standard and in favor of keeping *Roe*: Justices Blackmun and Stevens; dissenters in favor of overruling *Roe*: Chief Justice Rehnquist, Justices Scalia, Thomas, and White.

(f) *Emergency Provision (Part V–A).* Decision: As construed by the Court of Appeal, emergency provision is valid; majority: Justices Blackmun, Kennedy, Souter, O'Connor, and Stevens; not joining decision: Chief Justice Rehnquist, Justices Scalia, Thomas, and White.

(g) *Informed-Consent Provision (Part V–B).* Decision: the requirement of informed consent is valid; plurality: Justices O'Connor, Kennedy, and Souter; concurring in result and writing separate opinions: Justices Blackmun and Stevens; not joining in opinion: Chief Justice Rehnquist, Justices Scalia, Thomas, and White.

(h) *Husband-Consent Requirement (Part V–C).* Decision: the requirement of a signed statement that the woman has informed her husband of an abortion was invalid as an undue burden; majority: Justices Blackmun, Kennedy, Souter, O'Connor, and Stevens; dissenters: Chief Justice Rehnquist, Justices Scalia, Thomas, and White.

(i) *Parental-Consent Requirement (Part V–D)*. Decision: the requirement of permission of one parent with a provision for judicial bypass was valid; plurality: Justices O'Connor, Kennedy, and Souter; concurring in result and writing separate opinions: Justices Blackmun and Stevens; not joining in opinion: Chief Justice Rehnquist, Justices Scalia, Thomas, and White.

(j) *Reporting Requirement (Part V–E)*. Decision: provision that abortion facilities meet certain reporting requirements was valid; Plurality: Justices O'Connor, Kennedy, and Souter: Concurring in result and writing separate opinions: Justices Blackmun and Stevens; not joining in opinion: Justices Rehnquist, Scalia, Thomas, and White.

(k) *Statutory Impact of Decision (Part VI)*. Decision: Pennsylvania statutes are upheld in part and invalidated in part, and the cases remanded; majority: Justices Blackmun, Kennedy, Souter, O'Connor, and Stevens; dissenters: Chief Justice Rehnquist, Justices Scalia, Thomas, and White.

(2) **Republican v. Democrat.** For Supreme Court watchers it is interesting to note that Justices did not vote along party lines. While the Democratic Party tends to be pro-choice and the Republican Party pro-life, some Democratic appointees voted against the abortion decision and some Republican appointees voted in favor of keeping and modifying *Roe*. Here is a list of the recent Presidents and the Justices they appointed who were on the bench in 1992: President Kennedy appointed Justice White in 1962; President Nixon appointed Justice Blackmun in 1970 and Justice Rehnquist in 1971; President Ford appointed Justice Stevens; President Reagan appointed Justice O'Connor in 1981 and Justice Scalia and Justice Kennedy in 1986; and President Bush appointed Justice Souter in 1990 and Justice Thomas in 1991.

(3) **Abortion in the Future.** As of the 1992 *Planned Parenthood* opinion, there were no Clinton appointees on the Court. Any attempt to "count" the Justices regarding abortion must take into account the changes which have been made in the Supreme Court by President Clinton. Justice White was succeeded by Justice Ruth Bader Ginsberg in 1993. In her confirmation hearing she was an outspoken supporter of abortion rights: "This [abortion] is something central to a woman's life, to her dignity. It's a decision that she must make for herself. And when government controls that decision for her, she is being treated as less than a fully adult human responsible for her own choices." *The Washington Post*, July 22, 1993. She also stated, "It is essential to a woman's equality with man that she be the decision-maker, that her choice be controlling. . . . If you impose restraints, you are disadvantaging her because of her sex. The state controlling a woman would mean denying her full autonomy." *Los Angeles Daily News*, July 22, 1993.

Justice Blackmun was replaced by Justice Stephen G. Breyer in 1994. During his confirmation hearing, there was a great deal of speculation on his position regarding abortion. When asked if he believed women should possess the right to decide "whether or not to be pregnant," Justice Breyer replied: "That is the determination of *Roe vs. Wade*. *Roe vs. Wade* is the law of this country, at least for more than 20 years that there is some kind of basic right of the nature you describe. Recently—in 1992—the Supreme Court has reaffirmed that right . . . and so, that is settled law." *The Salt Lake Tribune*, July 14, 1994.

(4) **Stare Decisis.** One very important portion of the case has been left out. Justice O'Connor, joined by Justices Kennedy, and Souter, included a long and thoughtful discourse on the subject of *stare decisis* as it applies to the decisions of the United States Supreme

Court. The majority opinion says that *stare decisis* is not an "inexonerable command" but rather a judgment based upon "a series of prudential and practical considerations." They conclude that these considerations weigh in favor of the basic principles of *Roe*. *Roe* has not "proven unworkable" and people have relied upon the decision: they have "organized intimate relationships and made choices . . . in reliance on the availability of abortion." While in some respects "time has overtaken some of *Roe*'s factual assumptions," these changes merely affect the trimester system, and not the basic principle of *Roe* that the woman's right to privacy is preeminent before viability. Also, there has not been an "evolution of legal principle which has left *Roe*'s doctrinal footings weaker than they were in 1973." Since the factual assumptions and the law have not changed, overruling *Roe* would be based upon a doctrinal difference—and that is not a good reason to overrule a constitutional case—except for the most egregious cases such as *Lochner* or *Plessey v. Ferguson*.

(5) **Freedom of Choice Act of 1992 (FOCA).** In 1992 and 1993, the Senate Labor and Human Resources Committee favorably reported the Freedom of Choice Act of 1992, S. Rep. No. 321, 102d Cong., 2d Sess. 4 (1992), which would have codified the Supreme Court's holding in *Roe v. Wade*, 410 U.S. 113 (1973). *See* 102 S. Rpt. 321, July 15, 1992 and 103 S. Rpt. 42, Apr. 29, 1993. This attempt came as a result of the Court's recent holdings (such as *Planned Parenthood v. Casey*, 505 U.S. 833 (1992) and *Webster v. Reproductive Health Services*, 492 U.S. 490 (1989)); *see* McCland, Comment, *The Freedom of Choice Act: Will the Constitution Allow it?*, 30 Hous. L. Rev. 2041 (1994). *See also* 138 Cong. Rec. H 8028, Aug. 12, 1992 (discussing the history and potential effect of FOCA). The Act was introduced into the Senate on Jan. 21, 1993; however no vote was reported. *See* 139 Cong. Rec. S 426, Jan. 21, 1993. FOCA contained two specific provisions: section 3(a) defined freedom of choice: "a state may not restrict a woman's right to choose abortion before fetal viability," McCland, *above* and section 3(b) provided that FOCA will not be deemed to "prevent a state from declining to pay for abortions or from requiring a minor to involve a parent or other responsible adult before obtaining an abortion." *Id.* at 2054–55.

For statements by members of the House of Representatives encouraging the enactment of FOCA, see 139 Cong. Rec. H 1173, 1174 (Rep. McDermott), 1175 (Rep. Kriedler), 1178 (Rep. Sanders), Mar. 11, 1993.

(6) **RU–486.** RU–486, also known as the "French pill," was developed by a the French company Roussel Uclaf. It is now used in a number of European and Asian countries to interrupt early pregnancy by causing a chemical reaction to induce miscarriage. *See* Brooks, Comment, *RU–486: Politics of Abortion and Science*, 2 J. Pharm. & L. 261 (1993) and Canlen, *The Long Labor of RU–486*, California Lawyer, May 1997, at 34. It is currently available for use in France, China, Britain, and Sweden; and other countries such as India and Canada are researching other possible uses for the drug. *See* Brooks, *above* at 261. However, as of this writing the debate in the U.S. continued to prevent its use here.

In the United States, the implementation of the use of RU–486 was troubled from the start. Anti-abortion groups began a "crusade" against the use of the pill, which caused the FDA to execute an "import ban" forbidding the importation of RU–486 into the United States. *See* Canton, *above* at 36–37. However, in 1993 President Clinton signed an executive order to "promote the testing, licensing and manufacturing" of RU–486. *Id.* at 37. As a result, the FDA changed its position on the drug and requested Roussel Uclaf to import to the United States. *Id.* However, due to the rampant history of lawsuits in the U.S. resulting from use of pharmaceutical products involving the female reproductive system (e.g., the Dalkon Shield IUD litigation), Roussel Uclaf instead chose to donate the patent for RU–486 to The Population Council, a New York non-profit organization. The Population Council worked with Joseph Pike, a San Diego venture capitalist, to help raise funds and support for the widespread distribution of RU–486. However, due to problems arising in the partnership, The Population Council is now working with a new company. *Id.* at 38.

As a result of these efforts, the release of RU–486 is expected pending final approval by the FDA, approval which is contingent upon new information regarding proposed labeling and manufacturing. *Id.* at 85.

Conflicting arguments for use of the drug are present: on one side, RU–486 would limit violent clinical demonstrations (see *below*, note 8); however, on the other hand, some object to the drug because it would make abortions much easier to obtain, and therefore serve as "abortions on demand." *See* Brooks, Comment, *RU–486: Politics of Abortion and Science*, 2 J. Pharm. & L. 261, 264 (1993). Are there more direct arguments for making the drug available?

For information regarding the history and development of RU—486, see *id.* at 265–70. For a review of the regulatory process of the FDA involved in approving RU–486, see *id.* at 275–81. For the use of RU–486 as a "postcoital contraceptive" rather than an "abortifacient," see Hanson, *Approval of RU–486 as a Postcoital Contraceptive*, 17 Puget Sound L. Rev. 163 (1993).

(7) The Court's Response to Abortion Demonstrations. One result of the abortion debate has been a number of demonstrations from both sides of the issue. Most of the litigation involving these demonstrations has involved anti-abortion demonstrations.

The Supreme Court in *Bray v. Alexandria Women's Health Clinic*, 506 U.S. 263 (1993), Justice Scalia writing for the majority, overturned the decision of the Fourth Circuit Court of Appeals which held that blocking access to abortion clinics (a) interfered with interstate right to travel, and (b) constituted trespass and public nuisance under Virginia law. *See National Org. for Women v. Operation Rescue*, 914 F.2d 582 (4th Cir. 1990). In deciding whether or not an action for conspiracy to violate the right to travel was proper, Justice Scalia stated that

> The only "actual barriers to . . . movement" that would have resulted from petitioners' proposed demonstrations would have been in the immediate vicinity of the abortion clinics, restricting movement from one portion of the Commonwealth of Virginia to another. Such a purely intrastate restriction does not implicate the right of interstate travel. . . .

506 U.S. at 277.

In response to this decision, Congress enacted the Freedom of Access to Clinic Entrances Act of 1994 (FACE), Pub. L. No. 103–259, 108 Stat. 694 (1994). *See* McMurtry & Pennock, *above*, at 212–13. FACE was intended by Congress to "prevent the mounting violence generated by the abortion protest movement," which it does by "ciminaliz[ing] violence and the threat of violence at abortion clinic entrances." Helen R. Franco, Comment, *Freedom of Access to Clinic Entrances Act of 1994: The Face of Things to Come?*, 19 Nova L. Rev. 1083, 1097, 1107 (1995).

In addition, the Supreme Court reaffirmed the right of a woman to "unobstructed access to abortion services" in *Madsen v. Women's Health Center, Inc.*, 512 U.S. 753, 114 S. Ct. 2521 (1994). *See* Franco, Comment, *Freedom of Access to Clinic Entrances Act of 1994: The Face of Things to Come?*, 19 Nova L. Rev. 1083, 1119 (1995). *See generally Fisher v. City of St. Paul*, 894 F. Supp 1318 (D. Minn. 1995) (upholding government action against an individual anti-abortion protester; the challenged law involved no prior restraint on speech, the restriction was content-neutral, the government had a strong interest, the restriction was narrowly tailored, and the law left open ample alternatives). As of this writing, the latest word on the free speech rights of abortion demonstrators and the right of access to abortion clinics is *Schenck v. Pro-Choice Network of W.N.Y.*, 117 S. Ct. 855 (1997), in which Justice Rehnquist writing for the majority held that a preliminary injunction could be granted against demonstrators at an abortion clinic in order to guarantee free access to the clinic; the state interest in protecting public safety and the right of women to pregnancy and abortion-related services justified the issuance of the injunction which was not prior restraint. In addition, the Court upheld the use of a fixed buffer zone of 15 feet from the entrances to the clinic and a requirement that sidewalk counselors remain outside a fixed buffer zone. However, the Court declined to uphold a floating 15-foot buffer around people and cars entering the clinic area. The free speech interest of the demonstrators was outweighed by the state interest in protecting access for the fixed buffer but not for the floating buffer zone.

(8) **Violence.** Violence at abortion clinics has become more common: "more than 1,000 acts of violence against abortion providers were reported in the United States. These acts included at least 36 bombings, 81 arsons, 131 death threats, 84 assaults, two kidnappings, one murder, and 327 clinic invasions." McMurtry & Pennock, *Ending the Violence: Applying the Ku Klux Klan Act, RICO, and FACE to the Abortion Controversy*, 30 Land & Water L. Rev. 203 (1995). In 1993, Paul Hill, an anti-abortion activist, murdered a Pensacola, Florida, doctor and his bodyguard outside an abortion clinic. *See* 139 Cong. Rec. S 2710 (Sen. Chafee and Sen. Wellstone), 2722 (Sen. Mikulski). Hill was convicted and sentenced to death. On October 6, 1997, the Supreme Court of the United States refused to review his case. *See* Carelli, Associated Press, *Supreme Court Opens New Term by Rejecting 1,500 Hopeful Appellants*, Legal Intelligencer, Oct. 7, 1997, at 4.

(9) **Partial Birth Abortion Act of 1996.** The Partial Birth Abortion Act of 1996 was introduced on March 5th, 1997, to the 105th Congress. This act prohibits all "partial birth" abortions except those to protect the life of the mother. Partial birth is defined by the act as follows: "an abortion in which the person performing the abortion partially vaginally delivers a living fetus before killing the infant . . . ." Partial Birth Abortion Act of 1996, 1997 H.R. 929; 105 H.R. 929 (1997). Anyone in violation of the proposed Act is subject to a fine and/or up to two years in prison. *Id.* As of 1997, it had not yet been enacted.

§ 4.03 Sterilization

Involuntary sterilization is at the opposite end of the spectrum from the issues of contraception and abortion discussed in §§ 4.01 and 4.02, above. The cases reprinted there deal with the right to control one's reproductive capacity by not having children; the subject of this subsection is the right to maintain the ability to reproduce despite the interests of the state in medically terminating that ability.

As in the previous section, the problems in this area have arisen because of developments of science, the medical technology to sterilize people cheaply and efficiently, and because of the scientific or pseudo-scientific view that the mentally handicapped, mentally ill, or those convicted of a crime will have offspring similar to themselves and that society can benefit from eugenically controlling reproduction.

Today, while the interests of the state sometimes appear to embody social or genetic engineering principles, more often than not cases in this area involve the demands of institutions or parents responsible for people who are incapable of taking care of themselves, much like children, but who are very capable of reproducing themselves.

The cases are bound by two monumental and expressive Supreme Court decisions written by respected Justices. In *Buck v. Bell*, 274 U.S. 200 (1927), the plaintiff sought to avoid a Virginia statute authorizing salpingectomy of female residents and vasectomy of males in certain circumstances in institutions for the mentally retarded.

The defendant, the director of such an institution known as the "State Colony for Feeble Minded" sought to sterilize a woman whom Justice Holmes described as follows:

> Carrie Buck is a feeble-minded white woman who was committed to the State Colony. She is the daughter of a feeble-minded mother in the same institution and the mother of an illegitimate feeble-minded child. She was eighteen years old at the time of her trial.

274 U.S. at 205. After noting that the plaintiff had been afforded ample procedural safeguards, the Court balanced the substantive due process right of the plaintiff against the state's interest in sterilizing her, and came down emphatically, almost emotionally, on the side of the state:

> We have seen more than once that the public welfare may call upon the best citizens for their lives. It would be strange if it could not call upon those who already sap the strength of the State for these lesser sacrifices, often not felt to be such by those concerned, in order to prevent our being swamped with incompetence. It is better for all the world, if instead of waiting to execute degenerate offspring for crime or to let them starve for their imbecility, society can prevent those who are manifestly unfit from continuing their kind. The principle that sustains compulsory vaccination is broad enough to cover cutting the Fallopian tubes. Three generations of imbeciles are enough.

Id. Despite the tone of eugenic philosophy, this position probably has some popular acceptance today.

There is evidence that *Buck* was a collusive suit intended to gain support for the Virginia statute and the eugenic movement, Lombardo, *Three Generations, No Imbeciles: New Light on Buck v. Bell*, 60 N.Y.U. L. Rev. 30 (1985), and there is a substantial question whether either Carrie Buck or her daughter were, in fact, feeble-minded. This evidence may explain the amazing lack of weight the decision gives to the individual's right to procreate. Fortunately, more current social thinking, which has influenced modern courts, has rejected this view and replaced it with a much greater concern for those with disabilities. *See, e.g.*, Ferster, *Eliminating the Unfit: Is Sterilization the Answer?*, 37 Ohio St. L.J. 591 (1966); Vukowich, *The Dawning of the Brave New World: Legal, Ethical, and Social Issues of Eugenics*, U. Ill. L.F. 189 (1971); Green, *Genetic Technology: Law and Policy for the Brave*

New World, 48 Ind. L.J. 559 (1973); Burgdorf & Burgdorf, *The Wicked Witch is Almost Dead: Buck v. Bell and the Sterilization of Handicapped Persons,* 50 Temp. L.Q. 995 (1977).

However, as the cases which follow show, eugenic theory as a basis for sterilization has been replaced by arguments based upon the interest of the person to be sterilized and the interest which guardians and institutions that care for public wards may have in controlling the procreative ability of those in their care.

If *Buck* sides strongly with the state, *Skinner v. Oklahoma,* 316 U.S. 535 (1942), amply protects the interest in the freedom to procreate. Indeed this case may be the source of the right of privacy as it relates to sexual matters. Like the opinion in *Griswold v. Connecticut* (*see* § 4.01, *above*) this decision was written by Justice Douglas. The Court struck down Oklahoma's "Habitual Criminal Sterilization Act." The Petitioner was incarcerated for his third offense when the Act was passed. The Attorney General instituted proceedings to have him sterilized and a jury found that he was a habitual criminal and that his crimes involved moral turpitude. The Court based its decision upon the Equal Protection Clause, the prohibited classification being offenders who had committed crimes which subjected them to the Act and those who had committed crimes which did not subject them to the Act. The important point is that this classification was held to be subject to strict scrutiny because of the aspect of human life it affected:

> We are dealing here with legislation which involves one of the basic civil rights of man. Marriage and procreation are fundamental to the very existence and survival of the race. The power to sterilize, if exercised, may have subtle, far-reaching and devastating effects. In evil or reckless hands it can cause races or types which are inimical to the dominant group to wither and disappear.

Justice Douglas matches the rhetoric of Justice Holmes, and more significantly provides an accurate statement of the personal interest protected. Considering the date of the opinion, it is likely that the events of World War II and the growing awareness of Nazi horrors influenced Justice Holmes, hence the reference to "evil and reckless hands."

Skinner has not really posed a threat to *Buck.* Several states have some form of statutory authorization of involuntary sterilization. Although the trend among the states is to abolish these statutes, other states have judicially determined that sterilization may be ordered.

Voluntary sterilization of the mentally handicapped or mentally ill is permissible if it is done with informed consent. This rule does not create major constitutional issues, but problems arise as to capacity to consent and the nature of the information which must be given.

The right of those with no known barriers to their capacity to consent to voluntary sterilization has probably been resolved by *Griswold*: the individual's right to control his or her own procreative destiny would prevail, and sterilization could not be prevented. No interest arises to balance against this right, no right of the unconceived or of the state, although it might be possible to envision a state, whose population is decimated by disease, famine, or war, seeking to prevent sterilization. Yet problems do arise in this area regarding such matters as the right to be sterilized in a public hospital, the necessity of spousal consent, and the requirements of the doctrine of the informed consent.

The case reprinted below deals with involuntary sterilization of a person with a mental disability. *In re Grady* involves an action brought by the parents of a mentally retarded young woman in a state which does not have a statute covering this subject. It was chosen because it portrays a situation which may face a family-law practitioner.

IN RE GRADY
New Jersey Supreme Court
426 A.2d 467 (1981)

PASHMAN, J.

As once before in *In re Quinlan*, 70 N.J. 10, 355 A.2d 647, *cert. denied*, 429 U.S. 922 (1976), we again examine a disturbing paradox: how we can preserve the personal freedom of one incapable of exercising it by allowing others to make a profoundly personal decision on her behalf. In *Quinlan* this court held that a comatose person kept alive by extraordinary means shall have a guardian appointed who would decide whether to discontinue those means. The question now before us is closely related: under what conditions should a court appoint a guardian who may authorize the sterilization of a woman who is severely mentally impaired.

I
Facts

Lee Ann Grady is a 19-year-old mentally impaired woman seriously afflicted with Down's syndrome. Within a few days of her birth, Lee Ann's parents decided not to place her in an institution but to care for her at home. Since that time they have provided her with love and emotional support, as well as the physical necessities of life. Together with her parents, Lee Ann lives with a younger brother and sister who also treat her affectionately.

Her formal education has consisted of special programs within the public schools. Over the years she has been tested by school personnel, who have recommended that she continue to participate in the special classes. Although unable to read words, she does recognize the letters of the alphabet. She has moderate success in writing her name. She has some ability to count low numbers, but it is not clear whether she counts by rote or with awareness of the function of numbers. In her conversation she often fails to form complete sentences.

At home Lee Ann's activities include playing simple games, watching television, and taking short walks. She is capable of performing tasks such as folding laundry and dusting. She can dress herself, but she cannot select clothes appropriate for the season or matching in color. She is able to bathe herself but needs help regulating the temperature of the water. She can open and warm a can of soup but has difficulty in controlling the heat of the stove burner. Her physical limitations have kept her from learning to ride a bicycle, to catch a ball or to jump rope. But she goes bowling occasionally, and she likes to swim.

Because Lee Ann does not suffer from some of the physical ailments associated with Down's syndrome, her life expectancy is about normal. Her physical maturation has not deviated significantly from that of other adolescents. While some of her external features identify her as a person born with Down's syndrome, her parents and others see her as an attractive young woman. Her mood is often jovial and friendly.

Although in a physical sense her sexual development has kept pace with that of others her age, Lee Ann's severe mental impairment has prevented the emotional and social development of sexuality. She has no significant understanding of sexual relationships or marriage. If she became pregnant, she would neither understand her condition nor be able to make decisions about it. Her lack of awareness could lead to severe health problems. It is uncontradicted that she would not be able to care for a baby alone. Indeed, she will probably need lifetime supervision to care for her own needs.

Recognizing her sexual growth, the Gradys have provided birth control pills for Lee Ann during the past four years. Although there is no evidence that Lee Ann has engaged in sexual activity or has any interest in doing so, her parents believe that contraception is an appropriate precaution to exercise under the circumstances of their daughter's life.

As Lee Ann has approached the age of 20, when she will leave her special class in the public school system, the Gradys have given more thought to her future. The parents fear they will predecease their daughter and she will be unable to live independently. Thus they have sought to attain for her a life less dependent on her family. The Gradys wish to place Lee Ann in a sheltered work group and eventually in a group home for retarded adults. But the parents see dependable and continuous contraception as a prerequisite to any such change in their daughter's environment. With the advice of their doctor, they sought to have Lee Ann sterilized at Morristown Memorial Hospital. The hospital refused to permit the operation.

II
The Opinion Below

The Gradys requested such authorization from the Superior Court, Chancery Division. They sought appointment of a special guardian with authority to consent on Lee Ann's behalf to a conventional sterilization procedure known as a tubal ligation. The hospital responded that it could not legally permit the operation without judicially authorized consent for Lee Ann. Soon after the complaint was filed, Judge Polow, the trial judge, appointed a guardian ad litem to represent Lee Ann's interests in the judicial proceedings. He also permitted the intervention of the Public Advocate and the Attorney General to represent the interest of the public and the State.

The court received several medical and educational reports about Lee Ann's condition and abilities. There was also testimony from Mr. Grady and several experts called by various parties and the court itself. Judge Polow met briefly with Lee Ann in counsel's office to get a first-hand impression of her condition. Lee Ann was not otherwise present at the judicial proceedings. Her only participation was in interviews for the medical and psychological examinations which were the bases of the expert evaluations.

None of the parties contended that the court should not authorize sterilization under any circumstances. The contested issues involved the standards the court should apply before deciding to authorize sterilization and whether Lee Ann's situation met those standards. After considering all the evidence, Judge Polow rendered judgment allowing the parents to exercise substituted consent for Lee Ann to be sterilized. . . .

Although we agree with much of the trial court opinion, the standard we establish today for judicial authorization of sterilization differs from that applied by the trial court. Therefore, we vacate the judgment of the Superior Court, Chancery Division, and remand for application of the new standard to the facts of this case.

III
The Right to Obtain Sterilization

We are well aware that the decision before us is awesome. Sterilization may be said to destroy an important part of a person's social and biological identity the ability to reproduce. It affects not only the health and welfare of the individual but the well-being of all society. Any legal discussion of sterilization must begin with an acknowledgment that the right to procreate is "fundamental to the very existence and survival of the race." *Skinner v. Oklahoma*, 316 U.S. 535, 541 (1942). This right is "a basic liberty" of which the individual is "forever deprived" through unwanted sterilization. *Id.*

A court must take particular care to protect the rights of the mentally impaired when considering the prospect of sterilization. Those rights have recently received increased attention from public authorities in this country. After a history of isolation and neglect, the mentally retarded members of our society are finally being accorded their basic civil rights. *See generally* F. de la Cruz & G. LaVeck (eds.), Human Sexuality and the Mentally Retarded 145–46 (1973); P. Friedman, The Rights of Mentally Retarded Persons (1976). . . .

Sterilization has a sordid past in this country, especially from the viewpoint of the mentally retarded. In the early part of this century many states enacted compulsory sterilization laws as an easy answer to the problems and costs of caring for the misfortunate of society. Lawmakers may have sincerely believed that the social welfare would improve if fewer handicapped people were born, but they were too quick to accept unproven scientific theories of eugenics. In the United States Supreme Court, a compulsory sterilization law withstood a challenge that such legislation unconstitutionally infringes upon liberty protected by the Due Process Clause. In *Buck v. Bell*, 274 U.S. 200 (1927), the Court upheld a law authorizing the compulsory sterilization of a mentally impaired woman for no more compelling reason than to prevent another generation of "imbeciles." Compulsory eugenic sterilization would have to overcome much higher constitutional hurdles today.

. . . Yet compulsory sterilization is not altogether part of the past. Many of our sister states have not abandoned their compulsory sterilization laws. Nothing we say today should be interpreted as approval of compulsory sterilization *for any purpose*.

The case before us presents a situation that is difficult to characterize as either "compulsory" or "voluntary." "Compulsory" would refer to a sterilization that the state imposes despite objections by the person to be sterilized or one who represents his interest. Here, however, Lee Ann's parents and her guardian ad litem all agreed that sterilization is in her best interests, and while the state may be acting in the constitutional sense, it would not be compelling sterilization. Lee Ann herself can comprehend neither the problem nor the proposed solution; without any such understanding it is difficult to say that sterilization would be against her will. Yet for this same reason, the label "voluntary," is equally inappropriate. Since Lee Ann is without the capacity for giving informed consent, any explanation of the proposed sterilization could only mislead her. Thus, what is proposed for Lee Ann is best described as neither "compulsory" nor "voluntary," but as lacking personal consent because of a legal disability.

Having created this third category—sterilization—which is neither voluntary nor compulsory we must now give it content. Since analogy is the vessel that carries meaning from old to new in the law, we begin by considering the right to obtain sterilization voluntarily. We believe that an individual's constitutional right of privacy includes the right to undergo sterilization voluntarily....

A right to sterilization has yet to receive express constitutional protection from the United States Supreme Court. Several lower courts, however, have acknowledged its existence. *Hathaway v. Worcester City Hospital*, 475 F.2d 701 (1st Cir. 1973); *Ruby v. Massey*, 452 F.Supp. 361 (D. Conn. 1978); *Peck v. Califano*, 454 F.Supp. 484 (D.Utah 1977); *Ponter v. Ponter*, 135 N.J. Super, 50, 55, 342 A.2d 574 (Ch.Div.1975) (holding that a married woman has "a constitutional right to obtain a sterilization operation without the consent of her husband")....

IV
The Right of Meaningful Choice

Having recognized that both a right to be sterilized and a right to procreate exist, we face the problem, as in *Quinlan*, that Lee Ann Grady is not competent to exercise either of her constitutional rights. What is at stake is not simply a right to obtain contraception or to attempt procreation. Implicit in both these complementary liberties is the right to make a meaningful choice between them. Yet because of her severe mental impairment, Lee Ann does not have the ability to make a choice between sterilization and procreation, or between sterilization and other methods of contraception a choice which she would presumably make in her "best interests" had she such ability. But her inability should not result in the forfeit of this constitutional interest or of the effective protection of her "best interests." If the decision whether or not to procreate is "a valuable incident of her right of privacy, as we believe it to be, then it should not be discarded solely on the basis that her condition prevents her conscious exercise of the choice." *Quinlan, supra*, at 41, 355, A.2d 647. To preserve that right and the benefits that a meaningful decision would bring to her life, it may be necessary to assert it on her behalf....

Our discussion thus far leads to the following conclusions. The right to choose among procreation, sterilization and other methods of contraception is an important privacy right of all individuals. Our courts must preserve that right. Where an incompetent person lacks the mental capacity to make that choice, a court should ensure the exercise of that right on behalf of the incompetent in a manner that reflects his or her best interests.

We next turn to the specific issues before the court.

VI
Inherent Judicial Authority

The inherent parens patriae jurisdiction of our Chancery Division is broad enough to encompass the decision whether consent for sterilization should be given by a court on behalf of a person who lacks the capacity to give or withhold consent for himself. We are in full agreement with Judge Polow's analysis of this issue and merely add a few observations to supplement it.

The parens patriae power of our courts derives from the inherent equitable authority of the sovereign to protect those persons within the state who cannot protect themselves because of an innate legal disability. While traditionally used to protect the economic and property interests of the legally disabled, it has also been invoked to protect personal rights. In divorce and child custody cases, for example, our courts exercise parens patriae jurisdiction to protect the best interests of children. The chancery courts also utilize their parens patriae powers when a juvenile has committed a criminal offense, or when a person has been committed to a psychiatric institution.

Parens patriae jurisdiction has been invoked in cases involving substituted consent for medical procedures. The most common of these occurs when a court authorizes a blood transfusion over the objections of an injured or sick child's parents. Occasionally courts have authorized substituted consent for an incompetent adult to undergo medical treatment. . . .

The most far-reaching exercise of parens patriae jurisdiction occurred in this Court five years ago. In *Quinlan, supra*, we authorized substituted consent by the parents of a comatose 22-year-old woman to discontinue use of extraordinary artificial life support apparatus. We exercised our equitable powers there although we believed that our decision would probably lead to the natural death of the patient. Our decision took into consideration the interests of the public and the belief of our society in the supreme value of life. We were well aware of the risks of exercising powers directly affecting the opportunity of another human to live or die. But ultimately we decided that the patient's constitutional right of privacy outweighed the public interest in preserving her life and presented a compelling case for judicial intervention. Similar compelling considerations exist in the present case.

[The court then recognized that the weight of authority was against it, citing both federal and state cases.] . . .

As we stated earlier, Lee Ann Grady has the same constitutional right of privacy as anyone else to choose whether or not to undergo sterilization. Unfortunately, she lacks the ability to make that choice for herself. We do not pretend that the choice of her parents, her guardian ad litem, or a court is her own choice. But it is a genuine choice nevertheless one designed to further the same interests she might pursue had she the ability to decide herself. We believe that having the choice made in her behalf produces a more just and compassionate result than leaving Lee Ann with no way of exercising a constitutional right. Our Court should accept the responsibility of providing her with a choice to compensate for her inability to exercise personally an important constitutional right.

The trial court's reliance on *Quinlan, supra*, was not misplaced. We hold that our Chancery Division has inherent power under its parens patriae jurisdiction to decide whether to authorize sterilization for an incompetent person such as Lee Ann Grady.

VII
"Best Interests": Standards and Procedures

We now consider the standards a court must apply in determining whether to authorize sterilization.

[The court then develops a series of guidelines for determining the appropriateness of sterilization.]

. . . .

First, it is ultimately the duty of the court rather than the parents to determine the need for sterilization. It is true that "the custody, care and nurture of the child reside first in the parents." *Prince v. Massachusetts*, 321 U.S. 158, 166 (1944). But the constitutional right of reproductive autonomy is a right personal to the individual. While the parents may advise a child and participate in his decision, that decision belongs to the child, not to his parents. The Supreme Court of Washington correctly observed that:

> Unlike the situation of a normal and necessary medical procedure, in the question of sterilization the interests of the parents of a retarded person cannot be presumed to be identical to those of the child. [*In re Hayes, above*, 608 P.2d at 640]

For this reason, the court must be satisfied that sterilization is in the best interests of the incompetent person.

Second, we fully endorse the procedural safeguards employed by the trial court. In every case where application is made for authorization to sterilize an allegedly incompetent person, the court should appoint an independent guardian ad litem as soon as possible. The guardian must have full opportunity to meet with the incompetent person, to present proofs and cross-examine witnesses at the hearing, and to represent zealously in the interests of his ward in other appropriate ways.

In addition, the court should receive independent medical and psychological evaluations by qualified professionals. The trial court in its discretion may appoint its own experts to assist in its evaluation of the incompetent's best interests by examining the individual or testifying at the hearing.

The incompetent person need not be present at the proceedings if the court determines that his presence would not be useful in protecting his rights. Nevertheless, the trial judge should personally meet with the individual to obtain his own impressions of competency. This meeting need not be conducted formally and can occur in any convenient and appropriate place, such as chambers, counsel's office, an institution or the incompetent person's home. The incompetent person should be given every opportunity to express his own views about the judicial proceedings and the prospect of sterilization.

Third, the trial judge must find that the individual lacks capacity to make a decision about sterilization and that the incapacity is not likely to change in the foreseeable future. Many mentally impaired persons and others with legal disabilities are capable of making their own decisions regarding procreation and sterilization. We emphasize that there are widely different degrees of mental retardation. The fact that a person is legally incompetent for some purposes does not mean that he lacks the capacity to make a decision about sterilization. The trial court should be reluctant to substitute its consent for any person who may be capable of making a decision for himself. Therefore, the proponent of sterilization should have the burden of proving by clear and convincing evidence that the person to be sterilized lacks the capacity to consent or withhold consent.

Fourth, the trial court must be persuaded by *clear and convincing* proof that sterilization is in the incompetent person's best interests. To determine those interests, the court should consider at least the following factors:

> (1) The possibility that the incompetent person can become pregnant. There need be no showing that pregnancy is likely. The court can presume fertility if medical evidence indicates normal development of sexual organs and the evidence does not otherwise raise doubts about fertility.

(2) The possibility that the incompetent person will experience trauma or psychological damage if she becomes pregnant or gives birth, and, conversely, the possibility of trauma or psychological damage from sterilization operation.

(3) The likelihood that the individual will voluntarily engage in sexual activity or be exposed to situations where sexual intercourse is imposed upon her.

(4) The inability of the incompetent person to understand reproduction or contraception and the likely permanence of that inability.

(5) The feasibility and medical advisability of less drastic means of contraception, both at the present time and under foreseeable future circumstances.

(6) The advisability of sterilization at the time of the application rather than in the future. While sterilization should not be postponed until unwanted pregnancy occurs, the court should be cautious not to authorize sterilization before it clearly has become an advisable procedure.

(7) The ability of the incompetent person to care for a child, or the possibility that the incompetent may at some future date be able to marry and, with a spouse, care for a child.

(8) Evidence that scientific or medical advances may occur within the foreseeable future which will make possible either improvement of the individual's condition or alternative and less drastic sterilization procedures.

(9) A demonstration that the proponents of sterilization are seeking it in good faith and that primary concern is for the best interests of the incompetent person rather than their own or the public's convenience.

These factors should each be given appropriate weight as the particular circumstances dictate. The list is not meant to be exclusive. The ultimate criterion is the best interests of the incompetent person.

VIII
The Necessity for a Remand

. . . .

[W]e are unable to conclude on the basis of clear and convincing evidence that sterilization would be in Lee Ann's best interests. We must therefore remand the parents' application to the trial court for a determination in accord with the standards we have outlined. . . . The court should weigh the factors as it deems appropriate, but considered as a whole they must demonstrate by the clear and convincing standard that sterilization at this time is in Lee Ann's best interests.

Conclusion

The potential for abuse in sterilization of mentally impaired persons allows the exercise of substituted consent only when rigid procedural and substantive criteria are satisfied. By applying the standards we have developed, courts will be able to protect the human rights of people least able to protect themselves.

Lee Ann should have the opportunity to lead a life as rewarding as her condition will permit. Courts should cautiously but resolutely help her achieve the fullness of that opportunity. If she can have a richer and more active life only if the risk of pregnancy is permanently eliminated, then sterilization may be in her best interests. Upon a clear and convincing demonstration, it should not be denied to her.

The judgment of the Superior Court, Chancery Division, is vacated and the matter is remanded for further proceedings in accordance with this opinion.

NOTES AND QUESTIONS

(1) *In re Grady* is different from most cases which have considered similar issues in that it places great reliance upon the right of Lee Ann to voluntarily have herself sterilized if she had the mental capacity to make that decision. Is this concern justified by the right of privacy? Is this a concern that would be considered by most courts, or is it one which is of particular importance to the New Jersey Supreme Court because of its experience and decision in *In Re Quinlan*, 355 A.2d 922, *cert. denied*, 429 U.S. 922 (1976)? The court in *Grady* not only cites *Quinlan* in the first line, but it also frames the issue in a manner similar to the issue in *Quinlan*. Perhaps the issue is merely one of balancing Lee Ann's right to have children and her right not to have children. If this is the case, then the state's interest in acting for the public good is of little importance.

(2) Does the court in *Grady* rely at all upon eugenic theory or does the court completely reject it? Is there justification for sterilization on eugenic grounds? The eugenics movement, the basic tenants of which are stated in a footnote in *Grady*, was started by Sir Francis Galton around the turn of the century. The theory dovetailed well with Social Darwinism, also popular during that era. By 1917 fifteen states had eugenic sterilization laws. *See generally* Ferster, *Eliminating the Unfit: Is Sterilization the Answer?* 27 Ohio St. L.J. 591 (1966). *Buck v. Bell*, 472 U.S. 200 (1927), was the landmark decision upholding these laws; however, not long after *Buck*, the scientific basis for eugenic theory was being questioned.

In 1937, the American Medical Association's Committee to Study Contraceptive Practices and Related Problems stated "our present knowledge regarding human heredity is so limited that there appears to be very little scientific basis to justify limitation of conception for eugenic reasons." Quoted in Ferster, *above*, at 603. A more contemporary view appears in *North Carolina Ass'n for Retarded Children v. North Carolina*, 420 F. Supp. 451, 454 (M.D.N.C. 1976):

> Most competent geneticists now reject Social Darwinism and doubt the premise implicit in Mr. Justice Holmes' incantation that "three generations of imbeciles is enough." [R]elevant medical opinion views with distaste even voluntary sterilization for the mentally retarded and is inclined to sanction it only as a last resort and in relatively extreme cases. In short, the medical and genetic experts are no longer sold on sterilization to benefit either retarded patients or the future of the Republic.

Quoted in Burgdorf and Burgdorf, *The Wicked Witch is Almost Dead: Buck v. Bell and the Sterilization of Handicapped Persons*, 50 Temp. L.Q. 995 (1977). Does *Grady* not represent a step in the opposite direction, albeit for totally different reasons?

(3) Is the court in *Grady* engaging in a legal fiction when it says that Lee Ann has a right of meaningful choice? The possible fiction appears more vividly if the court's action is stated as follows: the court may sanction the decision of parents to give consent to the

sterilization on behalf of the subject who has the right to choose sterilization but is incapable of doing so herself.

(4) Yet, is the court in *Grady* insensitive to Lee Ann's fundamental right to procreate? Indeed, the court seems to think that the majority of courts mentioned in the opinion are insensitive to the constitutional rights of incompetent persons. Moreover, is the right to choose *not* to procreate any greater or more fundamental than the right to procreate? And if they are equal, who should decide which one an incompetent person should exercise?

In the Matter of the Guardianship of Hayes, 608 P.2d 635 (Wash. 1982), the Washington Supreme Court upheld the possibility of a sterilization order absent an authorizing statute with the following language:

> Nor is a statute required to empower a superior court to exercise its jurisdiction by granting a petition for sterilization. We recognize the power of the legislature, subject to the state and federal constitutions, to enact statutes regulating sterilization of mentally incompetent persons in the custody of a parent or guardian. It has not done so, however, The relevant guardianship statute, RCW 11.92 (1977 supp.) defines the duties of a guardian to care for, maintain, and provide education for an incompetent person. The statute neither provides nor prohibits sterilization procedures at a guardian's request. It does not in any event derogate from the judicial power of the court, which includes the power to authorize such a procedure where it is necessary. In the absence of any limiting legislative enactment, the Superior Court has full power to take action to provide for the needs of a mentally incompetent person, just as it has authority to do so to protect the interests of a child We hold the Superior court of the state of Washington has authority under the state constitution to entertain and act upon a petition for an order authorizing sterilization of a mentally incompetent person, and in the absence of legislation restricting the exercise of that power, the court has authority to grant such a petition.

As stated in *Grady*, *above*, the majority of courts have ruled that in the absence of a statute authorizing sterilization, a court may not order the operation.

(5) In the absence of a statute, what should be the standard of proof? *Grady* requires that the findings, or at least most of the findings, be supported by clear and convincing evidence. Can you make a case for a higher standard? Beyond a reasonable doubt was not required in *In re Matter of Moe*, 432 N.E.2d 712 (Mass. 1981), but the court implied that there may be situations where a higher standard applies.

(6) The validity of a statute often depends on the actual language that the legislature has chosen to use. Statutes have been held invalid on a number of grounds: (a) improper exercise of the state's police power, *In re Thompson*, 169 N.Y.S. 638 (N.Y. Super. Ct.), *aff'd sub nom.*, 171 N.Y.S. 1094 (N.Y. App. Div. 1918); (b) infliction of cruel or unusual punishment, *Berry v. Davis*, 242 U.S. 468 (1917), *reversing sub nom. Davis v. Berry*, 216 F. 413 (D.C. Iowa 1914); *Mickle v. Heinrichs*, 262 F. 687 (D.C. Nev. 1918); (c) failure to provide adequate due process procedural safeguards, such as proper notice of hearing or the opportunity to cross examine witnesses, *Davis v. Berry, above*; *In re Opinion of Justices*, 162 So. 123 (Ala. 1935); *In re Hendrickson*, 123 P.2d 322 (Wash. 1942); and (d) violation of the Equal Protection Clause, *Skinner v. Oklahoma*, 316 U.S. 535 (1942); *Haynes v. Lapeer*, 166 N.W. 938 (Mich. 1918).

Keep in mind that most of the cases set out above are older cases, and that there are far more cases upholding sterilization statutes than there are cases invalidating them. *See* Ghent, Annotation, *Validity of Statutes Authorizing Asexualization or Sterilization of Criminals or Mental Defectives*, 53 A.L.R.3d 960 (1973).

(7) In a state with a statute authorizing compulsory sterilization, representing the state in a sterilization proceeding amounts to establishing that the person involved meets the statutory requirements for sterilization. Preparing for a constitutional challenge is usually secondary. Likewise there are many ways to defend against sterilization beyond challenging the statute, for example, by showing that the potential subject of sterilization does not fit the criteria set out in the statute; that the statutory procedures have not been followed; that the subject is already incapable of reproducing; that there are less drastic means of preventing reproduction; that there are alternative means for caring for offspring; or that the mental incapacity is curable or will not be passed on to children.

(8) If a person gives informed consent to a sterilization procedure, the operation can take place. What should be the requirements for informed consent?

(9) What happens if a doctor negligently performs a voluntary sterilization, such as a vasectomy on a man, or a salpingectomy or tubal ligation on a woman, and the result is twins? What damages, if any, should be allowable? *Compare Miller v. Johnson*, 343 S.E.2d 301 (Va. 1986) *and Berman v. Allan*, 404 A.2d 8 (N.J. 1979) *with Sherlock v. Stillwater Clinic*, 260 N.W.2d 169 (Minn. 1977). *See also* Clark, *Wrongful Conception: A New Kind of Medical Malpractice*, 12 Fam. L.Q. 259 (1979).

(10) At least one case has held that there is a right to a "therapeutic sterilization" in a public hospital. *Hathaway v. Worcester City Hosp.*, 475 F.2d 701 (1st Cir. 1973). What would be the rationale for such a decision? Would this case still be valid in light of *Poelker v. Doe*, 432 U.S. 519 (1977), which held there is no constitutional right to a nontherapeutic abortion in a public hospital which provides public care for childbirth? *Cf. Nyberg v. City of Virginia*, 667 F.2d 754 (8th Cir. 1982), *cert. denied sub nom.*, 462 U.S. 1125 (1983).

(11) Can undergoing sterilization be made a condition of probation? For a negative answer, *see People v. Dominque*, 256 Cal. App. 2d 623, 64 Cal. Rptr. 290 (1967) (possibility of pregnancy not reasonably related to future crime). Does it make a difference if the person offered probation is convicted of a crime related to children, such as child abuse, *cf. People v. Pointer*, 151 Cal. App. 3d 1128, 199 Cal. Rptr. 357 (1984), or sexual abuse?

(12) The subject of sterilization has been one of great interest for law review writers. The following are some articles which have dealt with the subject: Adler, Comment, *Estate of C.W.: A Pragmatic Approach to the Involuntary Sterilization of the Mentally Disabled*, 20 Nova L. Rev. 1323 (1996); Lombardo, *Medicine, Eugenics, and the Supreme Court: From Coercive Sterilization to Reproductive Freedom*, 13 J. Contemp. Health L. & Policy 1 (1996); Blum, Note, *When Terminating Parental Rights Is Not Enough: A New Look at Compulsory Sterilization*, 28 Ga. L. Rev. 977 (1994); Cepko, *Involuntary Sterilization of Mentally Disabled Women*, 8 Berkeley Women's L.J. 122 (1993); Dungan, Note, *The Conflict Between "Disabling" and "Enabling" Paradigms in Law: Sterilization, the Developmentally Disabled, and the Americans With Disabilities Act of 1990*, 78 Cornell L. Rev. 507 (1993); Jaegers, Note, *Modern Judicial Treatment of Procreative Rights of Developmentally Disabled Persons: Equal Rights to Procreation and Sterilization*, 31 U.

Louisville J. Fam. L. 947 (1992); Marcus, Note, *In Re Romero: Sterilization and Competency*, 68 Denv. U. L. Rev. 105 (1991); Scott, *Sterilization of Mentally Retarded Persons: Reproductive Rights and Family Privacy*, 1986 Duke L.J. 805–65 (1986) (encouraging reform to protect the rights of the mentally disabled); Lombardo, *Three Generations, No Imbeciles: New Light on Buck v. Bell*, 60 N.Y.U. L. Rev. 30 (1985) (reviewing *Buck v. Bell* from a historical perspective); Gould, *Procreation: A Choice for the Mentally Retarded*, 23 Washburn L.J. 359–78 (1984) (supporting rights for the mentally retarded); Struble *Protection of the Mentally Retarded Individual's Right to Choose Sterilization: The Effect of the Clear and Convincing Evidence Standard*, 12 Cap. U.L. Rev. 413 (1983); Sherlock, *Sterilizing the Retarded: Constitutional, Statutory and Policy Alternatives*, 60 N.C.L. Rev. 943 (1982); Schoenfeld, *A Survey of the Constitutional Rights of the Mentally Retarded*, 32 Sw. L.J. 605 (1978) (surveying a broad spectrum of mentally retarded rights); *Eugenics Sterilization Statutes: A Constitutional Re-evaluation,"* 14 J. Fam. L. 280 (1975); Spriggs, *Involuntarily Sterilization: An Unconstitutional Menace to Minorities and the Poor*, 4 N.Y.U. Rev. L. & Soc. Change 127 (1974); Murdock, *Sterilization of the Retarded: A Problem or a Solution*, 62 Cal. L. Rev. 917 (1974). To some degree all of the articles listed here reflect dissatisfaction with laws which favor sterilization.

(13) **Problem: Conservatorship of Vickie N.** The state of West enacted its mandatory sterilization law in 1909 for eugenic reasons. Sterilization was routinely performed; in fact, one study showed that from 1909 to 1927 the state of West accounted for two-thirds of all sterilizations which occurred in the United States. The law provided for the sterilization of any person who had a "mental disease which may have been inherited and is likely to be transmitted to descendants" or who suffered from "mental retardation, in any of its various grades." An action could be brought in the Probate Court by the parent or guardian or by the director of an institution in which the potential subject was committed. In the years following, various modifications were made and numerous procedural safeguards were added; however, as of 1978 the basic statutory framework remained the same.

In 1978, the legislature, in response to growing public sentiment in favor of the rights of the mentally handicapped, convened a special commission to study this law. The commission concluded that there was no scientific basis for eugenic sterilization and recommended that the law be repealed. The legislature, following the recommendation repealed the statute which was in the Welfare and Institutions Code and went one step further: it replaced the statute with the following provision: "No person may be sterilized under the provisions of the Welfare and Institutions Code." The legislative history of this provision established that its purpose was to prevent the courts from circumventing the legislature's intent to protect the rights of those with disabilities.

In 1987, the parents of Vickie N. petitioned the Probate Court, which in West was a court of general equity jurisdiction and which had specific subject matter jurisdiction in all matters of guardianship and conservatorship, to have a tubal ligation performed on Vickie N. A hearing was held, and the following facts were established: Vickie was born in 1960 with the condition known as Down's Syndrome; she is severely retarded, with an I.Q. of thirty; she lives with her parents who are both in their early sixties; they wish for Vickie to live with them for as long as possible, but their long-range plan is to place her in a residential home for mentally retarded adults; she is very fond of men, talking to them in the street, sitting on their laps at family parties; when she was in school there was one boy whom she was fond of and referred to as her boyfriend; while there is no evidence that Vickie N. has been sexually active, she has been on birth control pills for the last five years; she probably cannot continue on the pills because as she is getting older she is developing high blood pressure, and also she is not reliable enough to take them; she cannot comprehend how other means of birth control work; there was no evidence as to whether she was fertile or not, but Down's Syndrome does not render a person infertile.

Should the court order the sterilization of Vickie N.? Would your answer be different if you were sitting on the Supreme Court of West and the probate court had ruled that it had no jurisdiction to order the sterilization?

§ 4.04 Surrogacy

The technologies of artificial insemination and *in vitro* fertilization have made surrogacy a business, although it is possible that surrogate mothering has taken place covertly long before the technology existed. *See* Genesis 16:2. The deep-rooted desire by couples to raise children has created the market for surrogate mothering. Couples turn to this technique when the woman cannot have children. Often, they cannot find a child to adopt because the widespread availability of contraception and abortion have affected the supply of adoptable children (from 1975 to 1986 the number of agency adoptions dropped from 175,000 to 104,088). Fuller, Note, *Intestate Succession Rights of Adopted Children: Should the Stepparent Exception Be Extended?,* 77 Cornell L. Rev. 1188, 1232, n. 2 (1992). In other cases they may prefer to have a child related by blood to one of them. The surrogate mother is motivated perhaps by the desire to help a childless couple, but more likely by the money she is paid for the service she renders. There is usually an intermediary, a corporation or professional, who is in the business of making surrogate motherhood contracts. While these intermediaries may consider that they are acting in the public good, the profit motive is also involved.

Surrogacy is now divided into two different types: traditional surrogacy and gestational surrogacy. The arrangements for traditional surrogate mothering seem simple. The surrogate mother is artificially inseminated with the semen of a man who is not her husband but who intends to raise the child with his wife. The surrogate mother bears the child, and then relinquishes the child and all her rights to it to the couple who will raise it as their own.

Gestational surrogacy actually developed later than traditional surrogacy because it involves more complicated technology: *in vitro* fertilization versus artificial insemination. In gestational surrogacy the couple who plan to raise the child are both genetic parents. The future parents donate sperm and ova, fertilization takes place *in vitro*, and the fertilized ovum is implanted in the surrogate mother, who has contracted with the genetic parents to carry the child through birth and then release the child to the genetic parents.

The *Baby M.* case below is an example of traditional surrogacy, and *Johnson v. Calvert* is an example of gestational surrogacy. Both cases illustrate the legal complexity which can result when the surrogate contract is broken and the important public-policy issues which can arise. Moreover, these cases illustrate how this subject spans and indeed brings into conflict four areas of law: contracts, parentage, adoption, and child custody.

IN THE MATTER OF BABY M
New Jersey Supreme Court
537 A.2d 1227 (1988)

The opinion of the Court was delivered by WILENTZ, C. J.

In this matter the Court is asked to determine the validity of a contract that purports to provide a new way of bringing children into a family. For a fee of $10,000, a woman agrees to be artificially inseminated with the semen of another woman's husband; she is to conceive a child, carry it to term, and after its birth surrender it to the natural father and his wife. The intent of the contract is that the child's natural mother will thereafter be forever separated from her child. The wife is to adopt the child, and she and the natural father are to be regarded as its parents for all purposes. The contract providing for this is called a "surrogacy contract," the natural mother inappropriately called the "surrogate mother."

We invalidate the surrogacy contract because it conflicts with the law and public policy of the State. While we recognize the depth of the yearning of infertile couples to have their own children, we find the payment of money to a "surrogate" mother illegal, perhaps criminal, and potentially degrading to women. Although in this case we grant custody to the natural father, the evidence having clearly proved such custody to be in the best interests of the infant, we void both the termination of the surrogate mother's parental rights and the adoption of the child by the wife/stepparent. We thus restore the "surrogate" as the mother of the child. We remand the issue of the natural mother's visitation rights to the trial court, since that issue was not reached below and the record before us is not sufficient to permit us to decide it *de novo*.

We find no offense to our present laws where a woman voluntarily and without payment agrees to act as a "surrogate" mother, provided that she is not subject to a binding agreement to surrender her child. Moreover, our holding today does not preclude the Legislature from altering the current statutory scheme, within constitutional limits, so as to permit surrogacy contracts. Under current law, however, the surrogacy agreement before us is illegal and invalid.

I.
FACTS

In February 1985, William Stern and Mary Beth Whitehead entered into a surrogacy contract. It recited that Stern's wife, Elizabeth, was infertile, that they wanted a child, and that Mrs. Whitehead was willing to provide that child as the mother with Mr. Stern as the father.

The contract provided that through artificial insemination using Mr. Stern's sperm, Mrs. Whitehead would become pregnant, carry the child to term, bear it, deliver it to the Sterns, and thereafter do whatever was necessary to terminate her maternal rights so that Mrs. Stern could thereafter adopt the child. Mrs. Whitehead's husband, Richard, was also a party to the contract; Mrs. Stern was not. Mr. Whitehead promised to do all acts necessary to rebut the presumption of paternity under the Parentage Act. Although Mrs. Stern was not a party to the surrogacy agreement, the contract gave her sole custody of the child in the event of Mr. Stern's death. Mrs. Stern's status as a nonparty to the surrogate parenting agreement presumably was to avoid the application of the baby-selling statute to this arrangement.

Mr. Stern, on his part, agreed to attempt the artificial insemination and to pay Mrs. Whitehead $10,000 after the child's birth, on its delivery to him. In a separate contract, Mr. Stern agreed to pay $7,000 to the Infertility Center of New York ("ICNY"). The Center's advertising campaigns solicit surrogate mothers and encourage infertile couples to consider surrogacy. ICNY arranged for the surrogacy contract by bringing the parties together, explaining the process to them, furnishing the contractual form, and providing legal counsel.

The history of the parties' involvement in this arrangement suggests their good faith. William and Elizabeth Stern were married in July, 1974, having met at the University of Michigan, where both were Ph.D. candidates. Due to financial considerations and Mrs. Stern's pursuit of a medical degree and residency, they decided to defer starting a family until 1981. Before then, however, Mrs. Stern learned that she might have multiple sclerosis and that the disease in some cases renders pregnancy a serious health risk. Her anxiety appears to have exceeded the actual risk, which current medical authorities assess as minimal. Nonetheless that anxiety was evidently quite real, Mrs. Stern fearing that pregnancy might precipitate blindness, paraplegia, or other forms of debilitation. Based on the perceived risk, the Sterns decided to forego having their own children. The decision had a special significance for Mr. Stern. Most of his family had been destroyed in the Holocaust. As the family's only survivor, he very much wanted to continue his bloodline.

Initially the Sterns considered adoption, but were discouraged by the substantial delay apparently involved and by the potential problem they saw arising from their age and their differing religious backgrounds. They were most eager for some other means to start a family.

The paths of Mrs. Whitehead and the Sterns to surrogacy were similar. Both responded to advertising by ICNY. The Sterns' response, following their inquiries into adoption, was the result of their long-standing decision to have a child. Mrs. Whitehead's response apparently resulted from her sympathy with family members and others who could have no children (she stated that she wanted to give another couple the "gift of life"); she also wanted the $10,000 to help her family.

Both parties, undoubtedly because of their own self-interest, were less sensitive to the implications of the transaction than they might otherwise have been. Mrs. Whitehead, for instance, appears not to have been concerned about whether the Sterns would make good parents for her child; the Sterns, on their part, while conscious of the obvious possibility that surrendering the child might cause grief to Mrs. Whitehead, overcame their qualms because of their desire for a child. At any rate, both the Sterns and Mrs. Whitehead were committed to the arrangement; both thought it right and constructive.

. . . The two couples met to discuss the surrogacy arrangement and decided to go forward. On February 6, 1985, Mr. Stern and Mr. and Mrs. Whitehead executed the surrogate parenting agreement. After several artificial inseminations over a period of months, Mrs. Whitehead became pregnant. The pregnancy was uneventful and on March 27, 1986, Baby M was born.

Not wishing anyone at the hospital to be aware of the surrogacy arrangement, Mr. and Mrs. Whitehead appeared to all as the proud parents of a healthy female child. Her birth certificate indicated her name to be Sara Elizabeth Whitehead and her father to be Richard Whitehead. In accordance with Mrs. Whitehead's request, the Sterns visited the hospital unobtrusively to see the newborn child.

Mrs. Whitehead realized, almost from the moment of birth, that she could not part with this child. She had felt a bond with it even during pregnancy. Some indication of the attachment was conveyed to the Sterns at the hospital when they told Mrs. Whitehead what they were going to name the baby. She apparently broke into tears and indicated that she did not know if she could give up the child. She talked about how the baby looked like her daughter, and made it clear that she was experiencing great difficulty with the decision.

Nonetheless, Mrs. Whitehead was, for the moment, true to her word. Despite powerful inclinations to the contrary, she turned her child over to the Sterns on March 30 at the Whitehead's home.

The Sterns were thrilled with their new child. They had planned extensively for its arrival, far beyond the practical furnishing of a room for her. It was a time of joyful celebration—not just for them but for their friends as well. The Sterns looked forward to raising their daughter, whom they named Melissa. While aware by then that Mrs. Whitehead was undergoing an emotional crisis, they were as yet not cognizant of the depth of the crisis and its implications for their newly-enlarged family.

Later in the evening of March 30, Mrs. Whitehead became deeply disturbed, disconsolate, stricken with unbearable sadness. She had to have her child. She could not eat, sleep, or concentrate on anything other than her need for her baby. The next day she went to the Sterns' home and told them how much she was suffering.

The depth of Mrs. Whitehead's despair surprised and frightened the Sterns. She told them that she could not live without her baby, that she must have her, even if only for one week, that thereafter she would surrender her child. The Sterns, concerned that Mrs. Whitehead might indeed commit suicide, not wanting under circumstances to risk that, and in any event believing that Mrs. Whitehead would keep her word, turned the child over to her. It was not until four months later, after a series of attempts to regain possession of the child, that Melissa was returned to the Sterns, having been forcibly removed from the home where she was then living with Mr. and Mrs. Whitehead, the home in Florida owned by Mary Beth Whitehead's parents.

The struggle over Baby M began when it became apparent that Mrs. Whitehead could not return the child to Mr. Stern. Due to Mrs. Whitehead's refusal to relinquish the baby, Mr. Stern filed a complaint seeking enforcement of the surrogacy contract. He alleged, accurately, that Mrs. Whitehead had not only refused to comply with the surrogacy contract but had threatened to flee from New Jersey with the child in order to avoid even the possibility of his obtaining custody. The court papers asserted that if Mrs. Whitehead were to be given notice of the application for an order requiring her to relinquish custody, she would, prior to the hearing, leave the state with the baby. And that is precisely what she did. After the order was entered, ex parte, the process server, aided by the police, in the presence of the Sterns, entered Mrs. Whitehead's home to execute the order. Mr. Whitehead fled with the child, who had been handed to him through a window while those who came to enforce the order were thrown off balance by a dispute over the child's current name.

The Whiteheads immediately fled to Florida with Baby M. They stayed initially with Mrs. Whitehead's parents, where one of Mrs. Whitehead's children had been living. For the next three months, the Whiteheads and Melissa lived at roughly twenty different hotels, motels, and homes in order to avoid apprehension. From time to time Mrs. Whitehead would call Mr. Stern to discuss the matter; the conversations, recorded by Mr. Stern on advice of counsel, show an escalating dispute about rights, morality, and power, accompanied by threats of Mrs. Whitehead to kill herself, to kill the child, and falsely to accuse Mr. Stern of sexually molesting Mrs. Whitehead's other daughter.

Eventually the Sterns discovered where the Whiteheads were staying, commenced supplementary proceedings in Florida, and obtained an order requiring the Whiteheads to turn over the child. Police in Florida enforced the order, forcibly removing the child from her grandparents' home. She was soon thereafter brought to New Jersey and turned over to the Sterns. The prior order of court, issued *ex parte*, awarding custody of the child to the Sterns *pendente lite*, was reaffirmed by the trial court after consideration of the certified representations of the parties (both represented by counsel) concerning the unusual sequence of events that had unfolded. Pending final judgment, Mrs. Whitehead was awarded limited visitation with Baby M.

The Sterns' complaint, in addition to seeking possession and ultimately custody of the child, sought enforcement of the surrogacy contract. Pursuant to the contract, it asked that the child be permanently placed in their custody, that Mrs. Whitehead's parental rights be terminated, and that Mrs. Stern be allowed to adopt the child, *i.e.*, that, for all purposes, Melissa become the Sterns' child.

The trial took thirty-two days over a period of more than two months. It included numerous interlocutory appeals and attempted interlocutory appeals. There were twenty-three witnesses to the facts recited above and fifteen expert witnesses, eleven testifying on the issue of custody and four on the subject of Mrs. Stern's multiple sclerosis; the bulk of the testimony was devoted to determining the parenting arrangement most compatible with the child's best interests. Soon after the conclusion of the trial, the trial court announced its opinion from the bench. It held that the surrogacy contract was valid; ordered that Mrs. Whitehead's parental rights be terminated and the sole custody of the child be granted to Mr. Stern; and, after hearing brief testimony from Mrs. Stern, immediately entered an order allowing the adoption of Melissa by Mrs. Stern, all in accordance with the surrogacy contract. Pending the outcome of the appeal, we granted a continuation of visitation to Mrs. Whitehead, although slightly more limited than the visitation allowed during the trial. . . .

II.
INVALIDITY AND UNENFORCEABILITY OF SURROGACY CONTRACT

We have concluded that this surrogacy contract is invalid. Our conclusion has two bases: direct conflict with existing statutes and conflict with the public policies of this State, as expressed in this statutory and decisional law. . . .

A. Conflict with Statutory Provisions

The surrogacy contract conflicts with: (1) laws prohibiting the use of money in connection with adoptions; (2) laws requiring proof of parental unfitness or abandonment before termination of parental rights is ordered or an adoption is granted; and (3) laws that make surrender of custody and consent to adoption revocable in private placement adoptions.

(1) Our law prohibits paying or accepting money in connection with any placement of a child for adoption. N. J. S. A. 9:3–54. Violation is a high misdemeanor. Excepted as

fees of an approved agency (which must be a non-profit entity) and certain expenses in connection with childbirth.

Considerable care was taken in this case to structure the surrogacy arrangement so as not to violate this prohibition. The arrangement was structured as follows:the adopting parent, Mrs. Stern, was not a party to the surrogacy contract; the money paid to Mrs. Whitehead was stated to be for her services not for the adoption; the sole purpose of the contract was stated as being that "of giving a child to William Stern, its natural and biological father"; the money was purported to be "compensation for services and expenses and in no way a fee for termination of parental rights or a payment in exchange for consent to surrender a child for adoption"; the fee to the Infertility Center ($7,500) was stated to be for legal representation, advice, administrative work, and other "services." Nevertheless, it seems clear that the money was paid and accepted in connection with an adoption.

. . . Mr. Stern knew he was paying for the adoption of a child; Mrs. Whitehead knew she was accepting money so that a child might be adopted; the Infertility Center knew that it was being paid for assisting in the adoption of a child. The actions of all three worked to frustrate the goals of the statute. It strains credulity to claim that these arrangements, touted by those in the surrogacy business as an attractive alternative to the usual route leading to an adoption, really amount to something other than a private placement adoption for money.

The prohibition of our statute is strong. Violation constitutes a high misdemeanor, a third-degree crime, carrying a penalty of three to five years imprisonment. The evils inherent in baby bartering are loathsome for a myriad of reasons. The child is sold without regard for whether the purchaser will be suitable parents. The natural mother does not receive the benefit of counseling and guidance to assist her in making a decision that may affect her for a lifetime. In fact, the monetary incentive to sell her child may, depending on her financial circumstances, make her decision less voluntary. Furthermore, the adoptive parents may not be fully informed of the natural parents' medical history.

Baby-selling potentially results in the exploitation of all parties involved. Conversely, adoption statutes seek to further humanitarian goals, foremost among them the best interests of the child. The negative consequences of baby buying are potentially present in the surrogacy context, especially the potential for placing and adopting a child without regard to the interest of the child or the natural mother.

(2) The termination of Mrs. Whitehead's parental rights, called for by the surrogacy contract and actually ordered by the court, fails to comply with the stringent requirements of New Jersey law. Our law, recognizing the finality of any termination of parental rights, provides for such termination only where there has been a voluntary surrender of a child to an approved agency or to the Division of Youth and Family Services ("DYFS"), accompanied by a formal document acknowledging termination of parental rights, or where there has been a showing of parental abandonment or unfitness. . . .

In this case a termination of parental rights was obtained not by proving the statutory prerequisites but by claiming the benefit of contractual provisions. From all that has been stated above, it is clear that a contractual agreement to abandon one's parental rights, or not to contest a termination action, will not be enforced in our courts. The Legislature would not have so carefully, so consistently, and so substantially restricted termination of parental rights if it had intended to allow termination to be achieved by one short sentence in a contract.... Since the termination was invalid, it follows, as noted above, that adoption of Melissa by Mrs. Stern could not properly be granted....

We conclude not only that the surrogacy contract is an insufficient basis for termination, but that no statutory or other basis for termination existed.

(3) The provision in the surrogacy contract stating that Mary Beth Whitehead agrees to "surrender custody and terminate all parental rights" contains no clause giving her a right to rescind. It is intended to be an irrevocable consent to surrender the child for adoption—in other words, an irrevocable commitment by Mrs. Whitehead to turn Baby M over to the Sterns and thereafter to allow termination of her parental rights....

Mrs. Whitehead, shortly after the child's birth, had attempted to revoke her consent and surrender by refusing, after the Sterns had allowed her to have the child "just for one week," to return Baby M to them. The trial court's award of specific performance therefore reflects its view that the consent to surrender the child was irrevocable....

Contractual surrender of parental rights is not provided for in our statutes as now written.... There is no doubt that a contractual provision purporting to constitute an irrevocable agreement to surrender custody of a child for adoption is invalid....

B. Public Policy Considerations

The surrogacy contract's invalidity, resulting from its direct conflict with the above statutory provisions, is further underlined when its goals and means are measured against New Jersey's public policy. The contract's basic premises, that the natural parents can decide in advance of birth which one is to have custody of the child, bears no relationship to the settled law that the child's best interests shall determine custody....

The surrogacy contract guarantees permanent separation of the child from one of its natural parents. Our policy, however, has long been that to the extent possible, children should remain with and be brought up by both of their natural parents . . . This is not simply some theoretical ideal that in practice has no meaning. The impact of failure to follow that policy is nowhere better shown than in the results of this surrogacy contract. A child, instead of starting off its life with as much peace and security as possible, finds itself immediately in a tug-of-war between contending mother and father.

The surrogacy contract violates the policy of this State that the rights of natural parents are equal concerning their child, the father's right no greater than the mother's. "The parent and child relationship extends equally to every child and to every parent, regardless of the marital status of the parents. As the Assembly Judiciary Committee noted in its statement to the bill, this section establishes "the principle that regardless of the marital status of the parents, all children and all parents have equal rights with respect to each other. The whole purpose and effect of the surrogacy contract was to give the father the exclusive right to the child by destroying the rights of the mother....

Worst of all, however, is the contract's total disregard of the best interests of the child. There is not the slightest suggestion that any inquiry will be made at any time to determine the fitness of the Sterns as custodial Parents, of Mrs. Sterns as adoptive parent, their superiority to Mrs. Whitehead, or the effect on the child of not living with her natural mother.

This is the sale of a child, or, at the very least, the sale of a mother's right to her child, the only mitigating factor being that one of the purchasers is the father. Almost every evil that prompted the prohibition of the payment of money in connection with adoptions exists here. . . .

Intimated, but disputed, is the assertion that surrogacy will be used for the benefit of the rich at the expense of the poor. In response it is noted that the Sterns are not rich and that the Whiteheads not poor. Nevertheless, it is clear to us that it is unlikely that surrogate mothers will be as proportionately numerous among those women in the top twenty percent income bracket as among those in the bottom twenty percent. Put differently, we doubt that infertile couples in the low income bracket will find upper income surrogates.

In any event, even in this case one should not pretend that disparate wealth does not play a part simply because the contrast is not the dramatic "rich versus poor." At the time of trial, the Whitehead's net assets were probably negative—Mrs. Whitehead's own sister was foreclosing on a second mortgage. Their income derived from Mr. Whitehead's labors. Mrs. Whitehead is a homemaker, having previously held part-time jobs. The Sterns are both professionals, she a medical doctor, he a biochemist. Their combined income when both were working was about $89,500 a year and their assets sufficient to pay for the surrogacy contract arrangements.

The point is made that Mrs. Whitehead *agreed* to the surrogacy arrangement, supposedly fully understanding the consequences. Putting aside the issue of how compelling her need for money may have been, and how sufficient her understanding of the consequences, we suggest that her consent is irrelevant. There are, in a civilized society, some things that money cannot buy. In America, we decided long ago that merely because conduct purchased by money was "voluntary" did not mean that it was good or beyond regulation and prohibition. Employers can no longer buy labor at the lowest price they can bargain for, even though that labor is "voluntary," or buy women's labor for less money than paid to men for the same job, or purchase the agreement of children to perform oppressive labor or purchase the agreement of workers to subject themselves to unsafe or unhealthful working conditions. There are, in short, values that society deems more important than granting to wealth whatever it can buy, be it labor, love, or life. Whether this principle recommends prohibition of surrogacy, which presumably sometimes results in great satisfaction to all of the parties, is not for us to say. We note here only that, under existing law, the fact that Mrs. Whitehead "agreed" to the arrangement is not dispositive.

The long-term effects of surrogacy contracts are not known, but feared—the impact on the child who learns her life was bought, that she is the offspring of someone who gave birth to her only to obtain money; the impact on the natural mother as the full weight of her isolation is felt along with the full reality of the sale of her body and her child; the impact on the natural father and adoptive mother once they realize the consequences of their conduct. Literature in related areas suggests these are substantial considerations, although given the newness of surrogacy, there is little information. . . .

In sum, the harmful consequences of this surrogacy arrangement appear to us all too palpable. In New Jersey the surrogate mother's agreement to sell her child is void. Its irrevocability infects the entire contract, as does the money that purports to buy it. . . .

V.
CUSTODY

Having decided that the surrogacy contract is illegal and unenforceable, we now must decide the custody question without regard to the provisions of the surrogacy contract that would give Mr. Stern sole and permanent custody. (That does not mean that the existence of the contract and the circumstances under which it was entered may not be considered to the extent deemed relevant to the child's best interests.) With the surrogacy contract disposed of, the legal framework becomes a dispute between two couples over the custody of a child produced by the artificial insemination of one couple's wife by the other's husband. Under the Parentage Act the claims of the natural father and the natural mother are entitled to equal weight, *i.e.*, one is not preferred over the other solely because it is the father or the mother. The applicable rule given these circumstances is clear: the child's best interests determine custody. . . .

Our custody conclusion is based on strongly persuasive testimony contrasting both the family life of the Whiteheads and the Sterns and the personalities and characters of the individuals. The stability of the Whitehead family life was doubtful at the time of trial. Their finances were in serious trouble (foreclosure by Mrs. Whitehead's sister on a second mortgage was in process). Mr. Whitehead's employment, though relatively steady, was always at risk because of his alcoholism, a condition that he seems not to have been able to confront effectively. Mrs. Whitehead had not worked for quite some time, her last two employments having been part-time. One of the Whiteheads' positive attributes was their ability to bring up two children, and apparently well, even in so vulnerable a household. Yet substantial question was raised even about that aspect of their home life. . . . In short, while love and affection there would be, Baby M's life with the Whiteheads promised to be too closely controlled by Mrs. Whitehead. The prospects for a wholesome independent psychological growth and development would be at serious risk.

The Sterns have no other children, but all indications are that their household and their personalities promise a much more likely foundation for Melissa to grow and thrive. There *is* a track record of sorts—during the one-and-a-half years of custody Baby M has done very well, and the relationship between both Mr. and Mrs. Stern and the baby has become very strong. The household is stable, and likely to remain so. Their finances are more than adequate, their circle of friends supportive, and their marriage happy. Most important, they are loving, giving, nurturing, and open-minded people. They have demonstrated the wish and ability to nurture and protect Melissa, yet at the same time to encourage her independence. Their lack of experience is more than made up for by a willingness to learn and to listen, a willingness that is enhanced by their professional training, especially Mrs. Stern's experience as a pediatrician. They are honest; they can recognize error, deal with it, and learn from it. They will try to determine rationally the best way to cope with problems in their relationship with Melissa. When the time comes to tell her about her origins, they will probably have found a means of doing so that accords with the best interests of Baby M. All in all, Melissa's future appears solid, happy, and promising with them. . . .

It seems to us that given her predicament, Mrs. Whitehead was rather harshly judged—both by the trial court and by some of the experts. She was guilty of a breach of contract, and indeed, she did break a very important promise, but we think it is expecting something well beyond normal human capabilities to suggest that this mother should have parted with her newly born infant without a struggle. Other than survival, what stronger force is there? We do not know of, and cannot conceive of, any other case where a perfectly fit mother was expected to surrender her newly born infant, perhaps forever, and was then told she was a bad mother because she did not. We know of no authority suggesting that the moral quality of her act in those circumstances should be judged by referring to a contract made before she became pregnant. We do not countenance, and would never countenance, violating a court order as Mrs. Whitehead did, even a court order that is wrong; but her resistance to an order that she surrender her infant, possibly forever, merits a measure of understanding. We do not find it so clear that her efforts to keep her infant, when measured against the Sterns' efforts to take her away, make one, rather than the other, the wrongdoer. The Sterns suffered, but so did she. And if we go beyond suffering to an evaluation of the human stakes involved in the struggle, how much weight should be given to her nine months of pregnancy, the labor of childbirth, the risk to her life, compared to the payment of money, the anticipation of a child and the donation of sperm?

There has emerged a portrait of Mrs. Whitehead, exposing her children to the media, engaging in negotiations to sell a book, granting interviews that seemed helpful to her, whether hurtful to Baby M or not, that suggests a selfish, grasping woman ready to sacrifice the interests of Baby M and her other children for fame and wealth. That portrait is a half-truth, for while it may accurately reflect what ultimately occurred, its implication, that this is what Mary Beth Whitehead wanted, is totally inaccurate, at least insofar as the record before us is concerned. There is not one word in that record to support a claim that had she been allowed to continue her possession of her newly born infant, Mrs. Whitehead would have ever been heard of again; not one word in the record suggests that her change of mind and her subsequent fight for her child was motivated by anything other than love—whatever complex underlying psychological motivations may have existed. . . .

Even allowing for these differences, the facts, the experts' opinions, and the trial court's analysis of both argue strongly in favor of custody in the Sterns. Mary Beth Whitehead's family life, into which Baby M would be placed, was anything but secure—the quality Melissa needs most. And today it may be even less so. Furthermore, the evidence and expert opinion based on it reveal personality characteristics, mentioned above, that might threaten the child's best development. The Sterns promise a secure home, with an understanding relationship that allows nurturing and independent growth to develop together. Although there is no substitute for reading the entire record, including the review of every word of each experts' testimony and reports, a summary of their conclusions is revealing. Six experts testified for Mrs. Whitehead: one favored joint custody, clearly unwarranted in this case; one simply rebutted an opposing expert's claim that Mary Beth Whitehead had a recognized personality disorder; one testified to the adverse impact of separation on Mrs. Whitehead; one testified about the evils of adoption and, to him, the probably analogous evils of surrogacy; one spoke only on the question of whether Mrs. Whitehead's consent in the surrogacy agreement was "informed consent"; and one spelled out the strong bond between mother and child. None of them unequivocally stated, or even necessarily implied, an opinion that custody in the Whiteheads was in the best interests of Melissa—the ultimate issue. The Sterns' experts, both well qualified—as were the Whiteheads'—concluded that the best interests of Melissa required custody in Mr. Stern. Most convincingly, the three experts chosen by the court-appointed guardian *ad litem* of Baby M, each clearly free of all bias and interest, unanimously and persuasively recommended custody in the Sterns.

VI.
VISITATION

The trial court's decision to terminate Mrs. Whitehead's parental rights precluded it from making any determination on visitation. Our reversal of the trial court's order, however, requires delineation of Mrs. Whitehead's rights to visitation. It is apparent to us that this factually sensitive issue, which was never addressed below, should not be determined *de novo* by this Court. We therefore remand the visitation issue to the trial court for an abbreviated hearing and determination as set forth below. . . .

The judgment is affirmed in part, reversed in part, and remanded for further proceedings consistent with this opinion. . . .

NOTES AND QUESTIONS

(1) **Remand.** On remand, the trial court held that Melissa's best interests would be served by unsupervised, uninterrupted, liberal visitation with her mother, Mary Beth Whitehead Gould. The court found no credible evidence or expert opinion that the child would suffer any harm from continued and expanded visitation with her mother. The mother had attained family stability with her new husband and had come to realize that she would never have custody of Melissa. Moreover, Melissa had a warm and loving relationship with her mother and had demonstrated no separation anxiety during supervised visitation. In order to promote communication and cooperation between the parties, the court would appoint a mental health professional and direct the parties to participate in counseling. Lastly, the court would restrain and enjoin the parties from publicly discussing their relationships with the child, or her personal activities, or from selling any movie rights they may have concerning "Baby M" without prior approval of the court. *See In re Baby M*, 542 A. 2d 52 (N.J. Super. Ct. Ch. Div. 1988).

(2) **Last Report.** Baby M, who now calls herself Sassy, still lives with the Sterns and visits with Mary Beth Whitehead. She calls Mary Beth Whitehead "Mom." She calls William Stern "Father." She chose the name Sassy for herself instead of Sara, the name given her by Mary Beth Whitehead, or Melissa, the name given her by the Sterns. *See generally Baby M's Mother Still Bitter—Seven Years Hasn't Eased Pain of Losing Daughter*, Patriot Ledger (N.Y. Times News Service), Dec. 12, 1993, at 14 (1993 WL 3599725).

(3) **Shame?** If the parties in *Baby M* thought the contract was "right and constructive," why were they so secretive at the hospital, "not wishing anyone at the hospital to be aware of the surrogacy arrangement?"

(4) **Child Custody and Adoption Law.** It may be argued that the court gives little weight to the contractual commitment of the Whiteheads because the contract was illegal. Yet, doesn't the court show a preference for the use of adoption and custody law right from the start? The contract is illegal because the consent given violated the rules which govern consent to adoption, because it violated the prohibition on child-selling, and because it did not consider the best interest of the child, all policies which stem from family law. Shouldn't the court have given greater weight to the policies behind the enforcement of contracts? Would the result have been worse? Baby M would have had one set of parents, parents whom the court admits are the best for her.

(5) **Contract Law.** If you find yourself leaning toward the application of strict contract law, you must address the question of what the court should do if the father and his wife are found to be unfit or to have a quality which is repugnant to the surrogate mother after the contract is signed or even after the child is born. For example, what if the surrogate

mother discovers that the couple who will take her child are child abusers or that the wife who was going to adopt the child is infertile because she is a transsexual? Evidently this latter situation has arisen. Annas & Elias, *In Vitro Fertilization and Embryo Transfer: Medicolegal Aspects of a New Technique to Create a Family*, 17 Fam. L. Q. 199, 218 (1983), *citing* Keane & Breo, *The Surrogate Mother* (1981).

(6) **Public Policy.** Does the existence of a fundamental right to have children., (*Skinner v. Oklahoma*, 316 U.S. 535, 62 S. Ct. 110, 86 L. Ed. 1655 (1942)), imply that the court has given too little weight to the desire of couples to raise children who are at least related by blood to one of them? This interest is recognized in the area of artificial insemination.

On the other hand, is not the public policy against child-selling much broader than just a matter of custody and adoption? Child-selling has much of the repugnance of slavery. It is a contract for an illegal purpose, one which conflicts with basic notions of morality, just like a contract to have someone killed. Child-selling is a crime.

The court has little doubt that this is a child-selling situation. It makes clear its belief that money is at the heart of the deal. Money motivated Ms. Whitehead and ICNY. And though the Sterns were motivated by the desire to have a child, were they less corrupt because they merely offered money rather than took it?

(7) **Voluntary Surrogacy.** The court in *Baby M* would allow surrogate motherhood where "the surrogate mother volunteers, without any payment, to act as a surrogate and is given the right to change her mind and assert her parental rights." Would this be a valid contract? What would be the consideration? Could a promise to pay the mother's expenses be valid consideration?

(8) **Paternity.** The problem of paternity is not discussed in *Baby M*. Most states have comprehensive statutory schemes dealing with the paternity of children. These schemes usually include procedures for establishing paternity and presumptions as to paternity which may be conclusive or rebuttable. The issue would probably arise in one of three ways: the surrogate mother may renege on her promise to relinquish the child and seek to establish the paternity of the father for support reasons; the mother could renege and seek to establish the paternity of her husband who may have been having sexual intercourse with her during the period of artificial insemination; or the father of the child may seek to establish paternity of the child.

The last situation has been resolved in a Michigan case. The father sought an order of filiation under the Michigan Paternity Act. The surrogate mother did not contest the paternity and indeed cooperated; however, the Attorney General intervened, arguing that the Paternity Act, which would allow the father to assert paternity, was not controlling, since it applied only to children born out of wedlock, and that the statutory rebuttable presumption that the surrogate mother's husband was the father controlled. The Michigan Supreme Court said that the father could use the Act to establish paternity, that the presumption could be rebutted in a paternity action, and that "out of wedlock" included situations where the child resulted from a relationship of the mother with someone other than her husband. *See, Syrkowski v. Appleyard*, 362 N.W.2d 211 (Mich. 1985).

(9) **Other Cases on Traditional Surrogacy.** Other courts, though not many, have spoken on the subject of surrogacy. In *Surrogate Parenting v. Commissioner ex rel. Armstrong*, 704 S.W.2d 209, 211–12 (Ky. 1986), the Kentucky Supreme Court refused to revoke the

corporate charter of a surrogate motherhood intermediary on the grounds that the corporation's purpose and procedures violated Kentucky's law prohibiting child brokering:

> We conclude that there are fundamental differences between the surrogate parenting procedure in which SPA participates and the buying and selling of children as prohibited by KRS 199.590(2) which place this surrogate parenting procedure beyond the purview of present legislation. There is no doubt but that KRS 199.590 is intended to keep baby brokers from overwhelming an expectant mother or the parents of a child with financial inducements to part with the child. But the central fact in the surrogate parenting procedure is that the agreement to bear the child is entered into before conception. The essential considerations for the surrogate mother when she agrees to the surrogate parenting procedure are not avoiding the consequences of an unwanted pregnancy or fear of the financial burden of child rearing. On the contrary, the essential consideration is to assist a person or couple who desperately want a child but are unable to conceive one in the customary manner to achieve a biologically related offspring.

This analysis is directly contrary to *Baby M*. Which is correct? Do you think a mother is better able to determine what she wants regarding her child before or after its birth? Moreover, would the result in Kentucky be different if it had a statute allowing all mothers to revoke their decision to give a child up for adoption within a certain number of days after its birth?

As the New Jersey Supreme Court mentions in a deleted portion of *Baby M*, Michigan courts had rendered decisions more in keeping with the view adopted in New Jersey. *See Doe v. Kelly*, 307 N. W. 2d 438 (Mich. Ct. App. 1981), *cert. denied*, 459 U.S. 1183 (1983) (Michigan's adoption law, which prohibits the payment of money other than for expenses in connection with adoption, applied to surrogacy contracts); *Yates v. Keene*, Nos. 9758, 9772 (Mich. Cir. Ct. Jan. 21, 1988) (surrogacy contracts held to violate public policy). *See also In re Marriage of Moschetta*, 25 Cal. App. 4th 1218, *modified*, 30 Cal. Rptr. 2d 893 (1994) (holding traditional surrogacy contract to be unenforceable).

(10) **Problem.** Mary and John, a married couple who lived in New Jersey, wanted very much to have children. They tried for several years, but when Mary still did not become pregnant they went to Fertility Center, Inc. (FCI). The doctors there discovered that Mary had a condition which would not allow the fertilized ovum to attach to the lining of the uterus. The doctor at FCI suggested the use of a surrogate mother, and introduced Mary and John to Susan, an unmarried woman in financial difficulties. The attorney for FCI drafted a contract that was substantially identical to the contract in *Baby M*. Susan was to receive $10,000, and FCI $7,500, both to be paid by Mary and John. The contract did not provide for any period in which Susan could revoke her decision once pregnant unless the surrogate mother's health or genetic disease in the child dictated termination of the pregnancy. The major difference from the *Baby M* contract was that it provided for the use of *in vitro* fertilization. The ovum from Mary was to be fertilized with sperm from John and then implanted in Susan's uterus. Susan would then carry the child to term and upon birth relinquish it to John and Mary. After the child was born, Susan refused to relinquish the child. Mary and John brought an action to get the child and to terminate any rights that Susan may have. They do not attempt to adopt because their position is that the child is their natural offspring. What will be the result?

JOHNSON v. CALVERT
Supreme Court of California
851 P.2d 776 (1993)

PANELLI, JUSTICE.

In this case we address several of the legal questions raised by recent advances in reproductive technology. When, pursuant to a surrogacy agreement, a zygote formed of the gametes of a husband and wife is implanted in the uterus of another woman, who carries the resulting fetus to term and gives birth to a child not genetically related to her, who is the child's "natural mother" under California law? Does a determination that the wife is the child's natural mother work a deprivation of the gestating woman's constitutional rights? And is such an agreement barred by any public policy of this state?

We conclude that the husband and wife are the child's natural parents, and that this result does not offend the state or federal Constitution or public policy.

FACTS

Mark and Crispina Calvert are a married couple who desired to have a child. Crispina was forced to undergo a hysterectomy in 1984. Her ovaries remained capable of producing eggs, however, and the couple eventually considered surrogacy. In 1989 Anna Johnson heard about Crispina's plight from a coworker and offered to serve as a surrogate for the Calverts.

On January 15, 1990, Mark, Crispina, and Anna signed a contract providing that an embryo created by the sperm of Mark and the egg of Crispina would be implanted in Anna and the child born would be taken into Mark and Crispina's home "as their child." Anna agreed she would relinquish "all parental rights" to the child in favor of Mark and Crispina. In return, Mark and Crispina would pay Anna $10,000 in a series of installments, the last to be paid six weeks after the child's birth. Mark and Crispina were also to pay for a $200,000 life insurance policy on Anna's life.

The zygote was implanted on January 19, 1990. Less than a month later, an ultrasound test confirmed Anna was pregnant.

Unfortunately, relations deteriorated between the two sides. Mark learned that Anna had not disclosed she had suffered several stillbirths and miscarriages. Anna felt Mark and Crispina did not do enough to obtain the required insurance policy. She also felt abandoned during an onset of premature labor in June.

In July 1990, Anna sent Mark and Crispina a letter demanding the balance of the payments due her or else she would refuse to give up the child. The following month, Mark and Crispina responded with a lawsuit, seeking a declaration they were the legal parents of the unborn child. Anna filed her own action to be declared the mother of the child, and the two cases were eventually consolidated. The parties agreed to an independent guardian ad litem for the purposes of the suit.

The child was born on September 19, 1990, and blood samples were obtained from both Anna and the child for analysis. The blood test results excluded Anna as the genetic mother. The parties agreed to a court order providing that the child would remain with Mark and Crispina on a temporary basis with visits by Anna.

At trial in October 1990, the parties stipulated that Mark and Crispina were the child's genetic parents. After hearing evidence and arguments, the trial court ruled that Mark and Crispina were the child's "genetic, biological and natural" father and mother, that Anna had no "parental" rights to the child, and that the surrogacy contract was legal and enforceable against Anna's claims. The court also terminated the order allowing visitation. Anna appealed from the trial court's judgment. The Court of Appeal for the Fourth District, Division Three, affirmed. We granted review.

DISCUSSION

Determining Maternity Under the Uniform Parentage Act

The Uniform Parentage Act (the Act) was part of a package of legislation introduced in 1975 as Senate Bill No. 347.

. . . .

Passage of the Act clearly was not motivated by the need to resolve surrogacy disputes, which were virtually unknown in 1975. Yet it facially applies to any parentage determination, including the rare case in which a child's maternity is in issue. We are invited to disregard the Act and decide this case according to other criteria, including constitutional precepts and our sense of the demands of public policy. We feel constrained, however, to decline the invitation. . . . [T]he Act offers a mechanism to resolve this dispute, albeit one not specifically tooled for it. We therefore proceed to analyze the parties' contentions within the Act's framework. . . .

A man can establish a father and child relationship by the means set forth in Civil Code section 7004. Paternity is presumed under that section if the man meets the conditions set forth in section 621 of the Evidence Code. The latter statute applies, by its terms, when determining the questioned paternity of a child born to a married woman, and contemplates reliance on evidence derived from blood testing. [S]ee Evid.Code, §§ 890–897 [Uniform Act on Blood Tests to Determine Paternity]. Alternatively, Civil Code section 7004 creates a presumption of paternity based on the man's conduct toward the child (e.g., receiving the child into his home and openly holding the child out as his natural child) or his marriage or attempted marriage to the child's natural mother under specified conditions.

In our view, the presumptions contained in Civil Code section 7004 do not apply here. They describe situations in which substantial evidence points to a particular man as the natural father of the child. In this case, there is no question as to who is claiming the mother and child relationship, and the factual basis of each woman's claim is obvious. Thus, there is no need to resort to an evidentiary presumption to ascertain the identity of the natural mother. Instead, we must make the purely legal determination as between the two claimants. . . .

Disregarding the presumptions of paternity that have no application to this case, then, we are left with the undisputed evidence that Anna, not Crispina, gave birth to the child and that Crispina, not Anna, is genetically related to him. Both women thus have adduced evidence of a mother and child relationship as contemplated by the Act. Yet for any child California law recognizes only one natural mother, despite advances in reproductive technology rendering a different outcome biologically possible. . . .

We see no clear legislative preference in Civil Code section 7003 as between blood testing evidence and proof of having given birth. "May" indicates that proof of having given birth is a permitted method of establishing a mother and child relationship, although perhaps not the exclusive one. The disjunctive "or" indicates that blood test evidence, as prescribed in the Act, constitutes an alternative to proof of having given birth. . . .

Because two women each have presented acceptable proof of maternity, we do not believe this case can be decided without enquiring into the parties' intentions as manifested in the surrogacy agreement. Mark and Crispina are a couple who desired to have a child of their own genetic stock but are physically unable to do so without the help of reproductive technology. They affirmatively intended the birth of the child, and took the steps necessary to effect in vitro fertilization. But for their acted-on intention, the child would not exist. Anna agreed to facilitate the procreation of Mark's and Crispina's child. The parties' aim was to bring Mark's and Crispina's child into the world, not for Mark and Crispina to donate a zygote to Anna. Crispina from the outset intended to be the child's mother. Although the gestative function Anna performed was necessary to bring about the child's birth, it is safe to say that Anna would not have been given the opportunity to gestate or deliver the child had she, prior to implantation of the zygote, manifested her own intent to be the child's mother. No reason appears why Anna's later change of heart should vitiate the determination that Crispina is the child's natural mother.

We conclude that although the Act recognizes both genetic consanguinity and giving birth as means of establishing a mother and child relationship, when the two means do not coincide in one woman, she who intended to procreate the child—that is, she who intended to bring about the birth of a child that she intended to raise as her own—is the natural mother under California law.

Our conclusion finds support in the writings of several legal commentators. (See Hill, What Does It Mean to Be a "Parent"? The Claims of Biology As the Basis for Parental Rights, supra, 66 N.Y.U. L. Rev. 353; Shultz, Reproductive Technology and Intent-Based Parenthood: An Opportunity for Gender Neutrality (1990) Wis. L. Rev. 297 [Shultz]; Note, Redefining Mother: A Legal Matrix for New Reproductive Technologies (1986) 96 Yale L.J. 187, 197–202 [note].) Professor Hill, arguing that the genetic relationship per se should not be accorded priority in the determination of the parent-child relationship in the surrogacy context, notes that "while all of the players in the procreative arrangement are necessary in bringing a child into the world, the child would not have been born but for the efforts of the intended parents. . . . [T]he intended parents are the first cause, or the prime movers, of the procreative relationship." (Hill, op. cit. supra, at p. 415, emphasis in original.)

Similarly, Professor Shultz observes that recent developments in the field of reproductive technology "dramatically extend affirmative intentionality. . . . Steps can be taken to bring into being a child who would not otherwise have existed." (Shultz, op. cit. supra, p. 309.) "Within the context of artificial reproductive techniques," Professor Shultz argues, "intentions that are voluntarily chosen, deliberate, express and bargained-for ought presumptively to determine legal parenthood." (Id., at p. 323, fn. omitted.) . . .

In deciding the issue of maternity under the Act we have felt free to take into account the parties' intentions, as expressed in the surrogacy contract, because in our view the agreement is not, on its face, inconsistent with public policy. . . .

Anna urges that surrogacy contracts violate several social policies. Relying on her contention that she is the child's legal, natural mother, she cites the public policy embodied in Penal Code section 273, prohibiting the payment for consent to adoption of a child. She argues further that the policies underlying the adoption laws of this state are violated by the surrogacy contract because it in effect constitutes a prebirth waiver of her parental rights.

We disagree. Gestational surrogacy differs in crucial respects from adoption and so is not subject to the adoption statutes. The parties voluntarily agreed to participate in in vitro fertilization and related medical procedures before the child was conceived; at the time when Anna entered into the contract, therefore, she was not vulnerable to financial inducements to part with her own expected offspring. As discussed above, Anna was not the genetic mother of the child. The payments to Anna under the contract were meant to compensate her for her services in gestating the fetus and undergoing labor, rather than for giving up "parental" rights to the child. Payments were due both during the pregnancy and after the child's birth. We are, accordingly, unpersuaded that the contract used in this case violates the public policies embodied in Penal Code section 273 and the adoption statutes.

. . . We see no potential for that evil in the contract at issue here, and extrinsic evidence of coercion or duress is utterly lacking. We note that although at one point the contract purports to give Mark and Crispina the sole right to determine whether to abort the pregnancy, at another point it acknowledges: "All parties understand that a pregnant woman has the absolute right to abort or not abort any fetus she is carrying. Any promise to the contrary is unenforceable." We therefore need not determine the validity of a surrogacy contract purporting to deprive the gestator of her freedom to terminate the pregnancy.

Finally, Anna and some commentators have expressed concern that surrogacy contracts tend to exploit or dehumanize women, especially women of lower economic status. Anna's objections center around the psychological harm she asserts may result from the gestator's relinquishing the child to whom she has given birth. Some have also cautioned that the practice of surrogacy may encourage society to view children as commodities, subject to trade at their parents' will.

We are all too aware that the proper forum for resolution of this issue is the Legislature, where empirical data, largely lacking from this record, can be studied and rules of general applicability developed. However, in light of our responsibility to decide this case, we have considered as best we can its possible consequences.

We are unpersuaded that gestational surrogacy arrangements are so likely to cause the untoward results Anna cites as to demand their invalidation on public policy grounds. Although common sense suggests that women of lesser means serve as surrogate mothers more often than do wealthy women, there has been no proof that surrogacy contracts exploit poor women to any greater degree than economic necessity in general exploits them by inducing them to accept lower-paid or otherwise undesirable employment. We are likewise unpersuaded by the claim that surrogacy will foster the attitude that children are mere commodities; no evidence is offered to support it. The limited data available seem to reflect an absence of significant adverse effects of surrogacy on all participants.

The argument that a woman cannot knowingly and intelligently agree to gestate and deliver a baby for intending parents carries overtones of the reasoning that for centuries prevented women from attaining equal economic rights and professional status under the law. To resurrect this view is both to foreclose a personal and economic choice on the part of the surrogate mother, and to deny intending parents what may be their only means of procreating a child of their own genetic stock. Certainly in the present case it cannot seriously be argued that Anna, a licensed vocational nurse who had done well in school and who had previously borne a child, lacked the intellectual wherewithal or life experience necessary to make an informed decision to enter into the surrogacy contract. . . .

The judgment of the Court of Appeal is affirmed. . . .

KENNARD, JUSTICE, dissenting.

When a woman who wants to have a child provides her fertilized ovum to another woman who carries it through pregnancy and gives birth to a child, who is the child's legal mother? Unlike the majority, I do not agree that the determinative consideration should be the intent to have the child that originated with the woman who contributed the ovum. In my view, the woman who provided the fertilized ovum and the woman who gave birth to the child both have substantial claims to legal motherhood. Pregnancy entails a unique commitment, both psychological and emotional, to an unborn child. No less substantial, however, is the contribution of the woman from whose egg the child developed and without whose desire the child would not exist.

For each child, California law accords the legal rights and responsibilities of parenthood to only one "natural mother." When, as here, the female reproductive role is divided between two women, California law requires courts to make a decision as to which woman is the child's natural mother, but provides no standards by which to make that decision. The majority's resort to "intent" to break the "tie" between the genetic and gestational mothers is unsupported by statute, and in the absence of appropriate protections in the law to guard against abuse of surrogacy arrangements, it is ill-advised. To determine who is the legal mother of a child born of a gestational surrogacy arrangement, I would apply the standard most protective of child welfare—the best interests of the child. . . .

NOTES AND QUESTIONS

(1) **Gestational Motherhood.** *Johnson v. Calvert* may be the first case to explore how to determine a child's mother to the same degree that court's have been determining paternity. Gestation and birth have been the main test for determining motherhood. There was simply no need for any other test; there was never any conflict between genetic link, on the one hand, and gestation and birth, on the other. Nor was there ever any reason to require a natural mother to participate in the child's life in order to establish maternal rights. Perhaps the view was that gestation and giving birth were significant participation, but more likely than not the issue simply did not come up because birth provided such certain evidence of maternity.

This case shows great deference to the giving-birth standard and indeed resorts to the intent test as a tie-breaker. Is it clear that if the intended parents do not choose to take the child that the gestational mother should be first in line?

Some commentators have favored the gestational mother: "Instead of reinforcing patriarchal notions of parentage by subjugating the pregnancy to genetic ties or contractual intent, parentage laws should recognize the gestational carrier as the legal mother."

Goodwin, *Determination of Legal Parentage in Egg Donation, Embryo Transplantation, and Gestational Surrogacy Arrangements*, 26 Fam. L.Q. 275, 291 (1992).

(2) **Contract Law.** The court in *Calvert* almost completely ignores the subject of contract law. Wouldn't it have been much simpler to say that the contract between the Calverts and Johnson was an enforceable contract? Without saying so directly, is the California court saying that it does not approve of surrogacy contracts? Why else would the court not resort to contract law to get the same result? If the California Supreme Court declined to look to the parties' contract for an expression or an interpretation of their intent, at what will a court look? *See* Problem (4) *below*.

(3) **Genetic Link.** Another easy way for the court to resolve this case was to simply say that the genetic parents should prevail. The court could have just as easily said that where under the statute there are two presumed parents, the genetic link will be the tie-breaker. Again the question is why did the court refuse to use this approach? The article which the court relies on most heavily is a complete rejection of the biological connection:

> This Article has argued that the genetic relationship, in itself, should be accorded very little moral weight in the determination of parental status. Claims based on the biological similarity of genetic progenitor and child and those predicated on a kind of quasi-property right in the child simply do not withstand sustained scrutiny. Thus, though the genetic tie historically has been accorded great significance, the genetic link per se places the genetic progenitor in the least-compelling position of all parties in the procreative relationship.

Hill, *What Does It Mean To Be A "Parent"?: The Claims of Biology as the Basis For Parental Rights,* 66 N.Y.U. L. Rev. 353, 418 (1991). Is the genetic link truly this weak, or is the position of Professor Hill just the ultimate statement of nurture over nature?

Not all writers on this subject have concluded that the genetic link is an inadequate test for parenthood:

> A genetic definition of motherhood is best suited for surrogacy cases: It avoids the application of contract principles to family relations; it rests motherhood on the single contribution that no other woman can supply for the child; it relies on the most important connection between a mother and child as the determining factor of motherhood; it is the definition of maternity that is least susceptible to discriminatory results or baby-selling; it advances the best interests of the child; and it best conforms with current social understanding of parenthood

Place, *Gestational Surrogacy and the Meaning of "Mother": Johnson v. Calvert, 851 P.2d 776 (Cal. 1993),* 17 Harv. J.L. & Pub. Pol'y 907, 908 (1994).

(4) **Intent Test.** The intent test used in this case is the creation of scholars. The goal of these scholars appears to be a desire to find a test which would fit all situations of new technology applied to conception: sperm donation, artificial insemination, *in vitro* fertilization, traditional surrogacy, gestational surrogacy, and perhaps even cloning. For some, the intent test may seem superior to the genetic test and indeed it is in keeping with the low regard the United States Supreme Court has given to the genetic link in *Quilloin v. Walcott,* 434 U.S. 246, 98 S. Ct. 549, 54 L. Ed. 2d 511 (1978), *rehearing denied,* 435 U.S. 918, 98 S. Ct. 1477, 55 L. Ed. 2d 511 (1978) and *Lehr v. Robertson,* 463 U.S. 248, 103 S. Ct. 2985, 77 L. Ed. 2d 614 (1983), which basically stand for the proposition that fatherhood

requires more than the mere genetic connection; however there are cases in which the intent test is inadequate. In many cases children are born where there is not an intended parent. There may also be cases where the intended parent is not a good one; does the intended parent get the benefit of the unfitness test, the higher standard for termination of parental rights, or will the child be removed from the intended parent where the best interest of the child demands it, as Justice Kennard suggests in her dissent?

Commentators have supported the intent test of *Johnson v. Calvert. See, e.g.*, Fergus, Note, *An Interpretation Of Ohio Law On Maternal Status In Gestational Surrogacy Disputes: Belsito v. Clark, 644 N.E.2D 760*, 21 U. Dayton L. Rev. 229, 247 (1995) ("an adoption of the intent test provides the best resolution to such conflicts. The intent test considers both the contribution of the genetic mother and the rights of the birth mother, as well as the parties' intentions").

(5) **Best-Interest Test.** Justice Kennard's view that the issues of *Johnson* should be resolved by the best-interest standard has some merit. All that would be needed to vindicate Justice Kennard would be a case in which the intended parents are undesirable parents; for example, the intended parents have a history of child abuse. Perhaps it is true that abusers would not go to the trouble of having a child through surrogacy. But if this should happen would the court require a showing of unfitness before removing the child from the intended parent? *See* Warlen, *The Renting of The Womb: an Analysis of Gestational Surrogacy Contracts under Missouri Contract Law*, 62 UMKC L. Rev. 583, 617 (1994) ("Although a determination based on the best interests of the child may appear harsh to the parties involved and provides no judicial predictability, it is the only way the state can fulfill its duty to protect the children procreated as a result of such unconventional arrangements. Any uncertainty created by denying specific performance will at least insure that the people involved exercise caution before entering into such contracts").

(6) **Other Gestational-Surrogacy Cases.** In *Belsito v. Clark*, 644 N.E.2d 760 (Ohio Ct. Comm. Pl. 1994), the genetic/intended parents of a child born by gestational surrogacy sought and received a declaratory judgment that they were the natural parents of the child and requiring that their names be place upon the child's birth certificate. The surrogate mother was the sister of the natural mother and did not contest the arrangement. The conflict was with the hospital, which required that the birth mother's name be placed on the certificate. The court used a genetic-link test of parenting: "The court is of the opinion that the law requires that, because Shelly Belsito and Anthony Belsito provided the child with its genetics, they must be designated as the legal and natural parents." *Id*. at 762.

In another case, making its way through the California court system as this text went to press, Jaycee Buzzanca, a two-year-old that was born as a result of gestational surrogacy, has so far been found to have no legal parents, even though six possible "parents" took part in the surrogacy arrangement. The six possible parents were the sperm donor, the ovum donor, the surrogate, her husband, the intended mother, and the intended father. One reporter covering this case has summarized as follows: "[t]hough biologically the product of two unrelated strangers, Jaycee's birth was commissioned by two other people, John and Luanne Buzzanca. In 1994, the couple hired surrogate Pamela Snell to carry the child to term. But when the Buzzancas divorced shortly before Jaycee's birth, things grew complicated." David E. Rovella, *Six Degrees of Parental Separation—Calif. Appeals Court to Hear Novel Donor-Surrogacy Case*, Nat'l L.J., Oct. 27, 1997, at A7.

(7) **Constitutionality.** In *Soos v. Superior Court*, 897 P.2d 1356 (Ariz. Ct. App. 1995), an Arizona statute prohibiting surrogacy and awarding children of illegal surrogacy to the surrogate mother was struck down on equal-protection grounds. The case involved the gestational surrogacy of triplets. The marriage of the genetic mother and father broke up before the children were born to the surrogate. When the genetic mother filed for divorce, the genetic father petitioned to have himself declared the legal father of the children and to have the surrogate mother declared to be the legal mother under the Arizona anti-surrogacy statute. When the triplets were born the surrogate mother and genetic father petitioned the court to award the children to the father. The genetic mother opposed the petition on the grounds that the Arizona statute was unconstitutional. Arizona Revised Statute § 25–218 (1991) stated:

> A. No person may enter into, induce, arrange, procure or otherwise assist in the formation of a surrogate parentage contract.
>
> B. A surrogate is the legal mother of a child born as a result of a surrogate parentage contract and is entitled to custody of that child.
>
> C. If the mother of a child born as a result of a surrogate contract is married, her husband is presumed to be the legal father of the child. This presumption is rebuttable.

At the trial level the court found the statute unconstitutional because there was no compelling state interest in treating the genetic father and mother differently. The court awarded custody to the genetic father and visitation to the genetic mother:

> By affording the father a procedure for proving paternity, but not affording the mother any means by which to prove maternity, the State has denied her equal protection of the laws. "A classification must be reasonable, not arbitrary, and must rest upon some ground of difference having a fair and substantial relation to the object of the legislation, so that all persons similarly circumstanced shall be treated alike." The surrogate statute violates this principle. We hold that the State has not shown any compelling interest to justify the dissimilar treatment of men and women similarly situated (the biological mother and father). The statute is unconstitutional on equal protection grounds.

Soos, 897 P.2d at 1360 (citations omitted).

The Arizona Court of Appeals upheld the trial court's decision. Although gender discrimination was an issue, the court of appeals chose to use the strict scrutiny standard, rather than the middle tier analysis, because procreative rights were involved. The court held that there was no compelling state interest for the statute, which allowed for the genetic father to assert his parental rights but did not allow the genetic mother to establish her maternity.

(8) **Law Review Articles.** One of the most complete articles on surrogacy is Krim, *Beyond Baby M: International Perspectives on Gestational Surrogacy and the Demise of the Unitary Biological Mother*, 5 Annals Health L. 193 (1996), which concludes that this subject is suitable for legislation, especially federal legislation, which should begin with a national debate on this subject and a commission appointed to study the subject. Another author, using anthropological principles, has suggested that both women involved in gestational surrogacy should have some rights: "[C]ustodial rights should be allocated presumptively in a way which gives the genetic parents primary responsibility for the child's rearing while retaining the gestational mother's active involvement through shared custody or substantial

visitation." Kandel, *Which Came First: the Mother or the Egg? A Kinship Solution to Gestational Surrogacy*, 47 Rutgers L. Rev. 165, 229 (1994). Here are some additional articles: Massie, *Restricting Surrogacy to Married Couples: A Constitutional Problem?* 18 Hastings Const. L.Q. 487 (1991); Appleton, *Surrogacy Arrangements and the Conflict of Laws*, 1990 Wis. L. Rev. 399 (1990); Miller, *Surrogate Parenthood and Adoption Statutes: Can a Square Peg Fit into a Round Hole?* 22 Fam. L.Q. 199 (1988); Andrews, "The Aftermath of Baby M: Proposed State Laws on Surrogate Motherhood," 17 *Hastings Center Report* 5, October/November 1987, at 31; Comment, *Surrogate Parenthood: An Analysis of the Problems and a Solution: Representation for the Child*, 12 Wm. Mitchell L. Rev. 143 (1986); Krause, *Artificial Conception: Legal Aspects*, 19 Fam. L.Q. 185, 204 (1985); Wadlington, *Artificial Conception: The Challenge for Family Law*, 69 Va. L. Rev., 465 (1983); Coleman, Comment, *Surrogate Motherhood: Analysis of the Problems and Suggestions for Solutions*, 50 Tenn. L. Rev. 71 (1982); Townsend, Comment, *Surrogate Mother Agreements: Contemporary Legal Aspects of a Biblical Notion*, 16 U. Rich. L. Rev. 467 (1982).

(9) **Problem.** Wanda and Hank were married, and they lived in California. They always wanted to have children. However, because of a medical condition, Wanda could not bear children. Since neither Wanda nor Hank were sterile, they decided to try to have a child by gestational surrogacy. Their fertility clinic, IFC, put them in contact with several women who wanted to serve as surrogates. After interviewing all of the women, they selected Sara to be the surrogate mother. In return for $10,000 for expenses and, in addition, reimbursement of all medical costs, Sara agreed to be the surrogate mother. Through the use of *in vitro* fertilization, an ovum from Wanda was fertilized by Hank; the ovum was then implanted in Sara, who eventually gave birth to a girl, Dee. If Sara refused to give up the child, would she be able to keep her?

If Sara refused to give up the child because she discovered that Hank was a spousal abuser and that the marriage of Wanda and Hank was very shaky, would she be able to keep the child?

Assume that Wanda divorced Hank before the child was born and, when the child arrived, Sara relinquished the child to Wanda. Could Wanda get child support from Hank?

UNIFORM STATUS OF CHILDREN OF ASSISTED CONCEPTION ACT
9B U.L.A. (1998 Supp. at 190, 197).

ALTERNATIVE A

§ 1. Definitions.

In this Act:

(1) "Assisted conception" means a pregnancy resulting from (i) fertilizing an egg of a woman with sperm of a man by means other than sexual intercourse or (ii) implanting an embryo, but the term does not include the pregnancy of a wife resulting from fertilizing her egg with sperm of her husband.

(2) "Donor" means an individual [other than a surrogate] who produces egg or sperm used for assisted conception, whether or not a payment is made for the egg or sperm used, but does not include a woman who gives birth to a resulting child.

[(3) "Intended parents" means a man and woman, married to each other, who enter into an agreement under this [Act] providing that they will be the parents of a child born to a surrogate through assisted conception using egg or sperm of one or both of the intended parents.]

§ 5. Surrogacy Agreement.

(a) A surrogate, her husband, if she is married, and intended parents may enter into a written agreement whereby the surrogate relinquishes all her rights and duties as a parent of a child to be conceived through assisted conception, and the intended parents may become the parents of the child pursuant to Section 8.

(b) If the agreement is not approved by the court under Section 6 before conception, the agreement is void and the surrogate is the mother of a resulting child and the surrogate's husband, if a party to the agreement, is the father of the child. If the surrogate's husband is not a party to the agreement or the surrogate is unmarried, paternity of the child is governed by [the Uniform Parentage Act].

§ 6. Petition and Hearing for Approval of Surrogacy Agreement.

(a) The intended parents and the surrogate may file a petition in the [appropriate court] to approve a surrogacy agreement if one of them is a resident of this State. The surrogate's husband, if she is married, must join in the petition. A copy of the agreement must be attached to the petition. The court shall name a [guardian ad litem] to represent the interests of a child to be conceived by the surrogate through assisted conception and [shall] [may] appoint counsel to represent the surrogate.

(b) The court shall hold a hearing on the petition and shall enter an order approving the surrogacy agreement, authorizing assisted conception for a period of 12 months after the date of the order, declaring the intended parents to be the parents of a child to be conceived through assisted conception pursuant to the agreement and discharging the guardian ad litem and attorney for the surrogate, upon finding that:

(1) the court has jurisdiction and all parties have submitted to its jurisdiction under subsection (e) and have agreed that the law of this State governs all matters arising under this [Act] and the agreement;

(2) the intended mother is unable to bear a child or is unable to do so without unreasonable risk to an unborn child or to the physical or mental health of the intended mother or child, and the finding is supported by medical evidence;

(3) the [relevant child-welfare agency] has made a home study of the intended parents and the surrogate and a copy of the report of the home study has been filed with the court;

(4) the intended parents, the surrogate, and the surrogate's husband, if she is married, meet the standards of fitness applicable to adoptive parents in this State;

(5) all parties have voluntarily entered into the agreement and understand its terms, nature, and meaning, and the effect of the proceeding;

(6) the surrogate has had at least one pregnancy and delivery and bearing another child will not pose an unreasonable risk to the unborn child or to the physical or mental health of the surrogate or the child, and this finding is supported by medical evidence;

(7) all parties have received counseling concerning the effect of the surrogacy by [a qualified health-care professional or social worker] and a report containing conclusions about the capacity of the parties to enter into and fulfill the agreement has been filed with the court;

(8) a report of the results of any medical or psychological examination or genetic screening agreed to by the parties or required by law has been filed with the court and made available to the parties;

(9) adequate provision has been made for all reasonable health-care costs associated with the surrogacy until the child's birth including responsibility for those costs if the agreement is terminated pursuant to Section 7; and

(10) the agreement will not be substantially detrimental to the interest of any of the affected individuals.

. . . .

ALTERNATIVE B

§ 5. Surrogate Agreements.

An agreement in which a woman agrees to become a surrogate or to relinquish her rights and duties as parent of a child thereafter conceived through assisted conception is void. However, she is the mother of a resulting child, and her husband, if a party to the agreement, is the father of the child. If her husband is not a party to the agreement or the surrogate is unmarried, paternity of the child is governed by [the Uniform Parentage Act].

NOTES AND QUESTIONS

(1) **Alternatives.** The Uniform Act does not take a definitive position on the subject of surrogacy; rather it offers two alternatives, both of which take strong stands against open-market surrogacy. Alternative A allows surrogacy if there has been judicial approval, and for that there are requirements for counseling, home study of families, and fitness. If there is judicial approval, then the standard of intent is used to determine parentage. Alternative B simply states that surrogacy contracts are void. This position strongly favors the surrogate mother if a child is conceived.

(2) **State Legislation.** Many states have enacted legislation regarding surrogacy.

(a) *Surrogacy contract void:* Arizona, Ariz. Rev. Stat. Ann. § 25–218 (West 1991 & Supp. 1995); New York, N.Y. Dom. Rel. Law §§ 121–124 (Consol. 1993 & Supp. 1996); North Dakota, N.D. Cent. Code §§ 14–18–01 to14–18–07 (1991 & Supp. 1995); and Utah, Utah Code Ann. § 76–7–204 (1995).

(b) *Surrogacy contract for compensation void.* Kentucky, Ky. Rev. Stat. Ann. § 199.590(2)–199.990 (Michie 1995); Louisiana, La. Rev. Stat. Ann. § 9:2713 (West 1991); Nebraska, Neb. Rev. Stat. § 25–21,200 (1996); and Washington, Wash. Rev. Code Ann. §§ 26.26.210–26.26.260 (West 1989 & Supp. 1996).

(c) *Criminal penalty for surrogate contract.* Michigan, Mich. Comp. Laws Ann. §§ 722.851–722.863 (West 1993) (felony for intermediary and misdemeanor for participant).

(d) *Surrogacy contracts allowed.* Florida, Fla. Stat. Ann. §§ 742.14–742.17 (West Supp. 1996); Nevada, Nev. Rev. Stat. Ann. §§ 126.045, 127.287 (Michie 1993 & Supp. 1995); New Hampshire, N.H. Rev. Stat. Ann. §§ 168–B:1—168–B:32 (1994 & Supp. 1995); and Virginia, Va. Code Ann. §§ 20–156—20–165 (Michie 1995) (Alternate A of the Uniform Status of Children of Assisted Conception Act).

(e) *Illegal baby buying/selling.* Alabama, Ala. Code §§ 26–10A–33—26–10A–34 (1992); West Virginia, W. Va. Code § 48–4–16 (1993).

(f) *Artificial insemination in general.* Arkansas, Ark. Code Ann. §§ 9–10–201—9–10–202 (Michie 1993 & Supp. 1995); New Jersey, N.J. Rev. Stat. Ann. §§ 9:3–41, 9:17–44 (West 1993 & Supp. 1996); Oregon, Or. Rev. Stat. Ann. §§ 109.239, 109.243, 109.247 (1990 & Supp. 1994).

(3) **Federal Legislation.** There have been two attempts to pass a national surrogacy law, neither of which were enacted. The Surrogacy Arrangements Act of 1989 (H.R. 275, 101st Cong. (1989)) and the Anti-Surrogate-Mother Act of 1989 (H.R. 576, 101st Cong. (1989)) both attempted to prohibit surrogacy by imposing criminal penalties on both facilitators and participants.

(4) **Legislation in Other Countries.** Legislators in Switzerland, Germany, Spain, France, Greece, Norway, Britain, and Australia have enacted laws that heavily restrict surrogacy agreements or ban them outright. *See* Krim, *Beyond Baby M: International Perspectives on Gestational Surrogacy and the Demise of the Unitary Biological Mother*, 5 Annals Health L. 193, 215 (1996). However, one commentator has suggested that in countries where surrogacy is banned, a growing public acceptance of surrogacy agreements will prompt lawmakers to adopt less restrictive positions. *See* Pitrolo, Comment, *The Birds, the Bees, and the Deep Freeze: Is There International Consensus in the Debate Over Assisted Reproductive Technologies?*, 19 Hous. J. Int'l L. 147, 203 (1996). In fact, in 1995 the Israeli High Court of Justice overturned a 1987 law banning surrogacy. *See* Coleman, *Gestation, Intent, and the Seed: Defining Motherhood in the Era of Assisted Human Reproduction*, 17 Cardozo L. Rev. 497, 504 (1996).

(5) **Problem.** Dr. X is the head of a prestigious fertility clinic which has an outstanding success rate in helping infertile couples have children through the use of the very latest fertility techniques. The clinic also arranges for surrogacy contracts and assists in gestational surrogacy. Anna and Bob, a married couple who had been wanting children for years, went to Dr. X, hoping to have a child. After careful examination of the couple, Dr. X informed them that Anna could not conceive or bear children for physiological reasons. Dr. X suggested surrogacy. He introduced the couple to Carri, who agreed to serve as a gestational surrogate. All the proper legal documents and contracts were signed. Unfortunately, Dr. X was unable to develop a viable embryo from Anna and Bob for implantation in Carri. Rather than admit failure, Dr. X took a fertilized ovum that he had in storage and implanted it in Carri. Dr. X told Anna and Bob that the implantation was a success. The fertilized ovum was actually from Dorothy and Ed, another couple who had been treated by Dr. X. Just before Carri was about to deliver the baby for Anna and Bob, the District Attorney's office publicized its investigation of Dr. X and his clinic. The investigation revealed that Dr. X had done many improper procedures, using genetic material from one couple to benefit another. When Carri gave birth, she immediately gave the baby girl to Anna and Bob, who named her Jessica. That same day Dorothy and Ed, whose own attempt to have a child

had failed, learned that the baby was really the result of their fertilized ovum. Dorothy and Ed are now bringing an action to immediately have themselves declared the parents of Jessica and to have her placed in their custody. Assume that the court hears the case in a matter of days. What should be the result?

§ 4.05 New Reproductive Technology

While the major issues involving reproductive choice have already been discussed, there are other issues involving new reproductive technology. The subjects of this section—artificial insemination, in vitro fertilization, embryo status, and cloning—may pose some of the greatest challenges to the legal system in the new century.

Although it may sound like science fiction, do you doubt that the technological society which created artificial insemination, in vitro fertilization, and cloning will some day perfect artificial gestation? Remember it was a combination of these technologies which served as the basis for the regimented social system of Aldous Huxley's *Brave New World*. Does it seem possible that these technologies can be resisted in our strongly entreprenneurial society? Might the use of these technologies in our own society be just as shocking to our present-day sensibilities as the world that Huxley envisions is? Regardless of what the future, holds there are immediate problems with these technologies which are discussed in the material that follows.

[A] Artificial Insemination

IN RE BABY DOE
South Carolina Supreme Court
353 S.E.2d 877 (1987)

NESS, CHIEF JUSTICE:

This is an appeal from an order of the family court which held appellant husband responsible for the support of a child born to his wife as a result of artificial insemination. We affirm.

Husband has four grown children from a prior marriage. He married his present wife in the early 1970s and they attempted for several years to have a child. While living overseas, husband sought medical advice and learned that he was no longer able to father children, apparently due to physical trauma. Upon the parties' return to this country, the diagnosis was confirmed. The parties visited a gynecologist in Myrtle Beach and discussed artificial insemination. With husband's knowledge, wife began undergoing artificial insemination in Myrtle Beach and Charleston. Husband assisted wife with daily temperature readings to determine dates of fertility.

Wife conceived in February, 1983, and the parties separated shortly thereafter. The child was born in November, 1983, and husband was listed as father on the birth certificate.

Husband brought this action in family court seeking a declaration that he was not the father of the child. Wife counter-claimed seeking child support. The trial judge held there was a rebuttable presumption that any child conceived by artificial insemination during the course of the marriage has been conceived with the consent of the husband. The judge also held husband had expressly and impliedly consented to the artificial insemination, and awarded child support to wife.

Husband argues implied consent to artificial insemination should not be sufficient to establish legal parentage of a child. He argues that in the absence of written consent, he cannot be declared the legal father of a child conceived by artificial insemination during the marriage.

Artificial insemination is the introduction of semen into the reproductive tract of a female by artificial means. There are two types of artificial insemination in common use: (1) artificial insemination with the husband's sperm (homologous insemination), commonly referred to as A.I.H.; and (2) artificial insemination with the sperm of an anonymous third-party donor (heterologous insemination), commonly referred to as A.I.D. . . . The legal entanglements of determining parental responsibility have arisen almost exclusively from the latter. *But see, C.M. v. C.C.*, 152 N.J.Super. 160, 377 A.2d 821 (1977) [known third-party donor of semen awarded visitation with child born to unmarried mother through artificial insemination.] *L. v. L*, 1 All E.R. 141 (P.) (1949) [child born from artificial insemination using sperm of impotent husband declared illegitimate upon dissolution of marriage by annulment].

This new reproductive technology has created the potential for conflicting decisions regarding the status of the parties involved. With the exception of the earliest decisions on this issue . . . , however, American courts have been fairly uniform in their holdings. Almost exclusively, courts have addressed this issue and have assigned paternal responsibility to the husband based on conduct evidencing his consent to the artificial insemination. *Cf., Byers v. Byers*, 618 P.2d 930 (Okla. 1980) [distinguishing birth by artificial insemination from husband's acceptance of child born from wife's affair with her paramour].

We hold that a husband who consents for his wife to conceive a child through artificial insemination, with the understanding that the child will be treated as their own, is the legal father of the child born as a result of the artificial insemination and will be charged with all the legal responsibilities of paternity, including support. . . .

We do not agree that husband's consent is effective only if obtained in writing. A number of jurisdictions have adopted statutes regulating the use of artificial insemination and requiring written consent of the parties or of the husband. . . . However, even where husband's written consent is statutorily required, the failure to obtain written consent does not relieve husband of the responsibilities of parentage. . . . Husband's consent to his wife's impregnation by artificial insemination may be express, or it may be implied from conduct which evidences knowledge of the procedure and failure to object. . . .

We agree with the trial judge that husband's knowledge of and assistance in his wife's efforts to conceive through artificial insemination constitute his consent to the procedure. The trial judge's decision to declare husband the legal father of Baby Doe is affirmed. . . .

JHORDAN C. v. MARY K.
California Court of Appeal
224 Cal. Rptr. 530 (1986)

KING, ASSOCIATE J.

. . .

II. Facts and Procedural History

In late 1978, Mary decided to bear a child by artificial insemination and to raise the child jointly with Victoria, a close friend who lived in a nearby town. Mary sought a semen donor by talking to friends and acquaintances. This led to three or four potential donors with whom Mary spoke directly. She and Victoria ultimately chose Jhordan after he had one personal interview with Mary and one dinner at Mary's home.

The parties' testimony was in conflict as to what agreement they had concerning the role, if any, Jhordan would play in the child's life. According to Mary, she told Jhordan she did not want a donor who desired ongoing involvement with the child, but she did agree to let him see the child to satisfy his curiosity as to how the child would look. Jhordan, in contrast, asserts they agreed he and Mary would have an ongoing friendship, he would have ongoing contact with the child, and he would care for the child as much as two or three times per week.

None of the parties sought legal advice until long after the child's birth. They were completely unaware of the existence of Civil Code section 7005. They did not attempt to draft a written agreement concerning Jhordan's status.

Jhordan provided semen to Mary on a number of occasions during a six-month period commencing in late January 1979. On each occasion he came to her home, spoke briefly with her, produced the semen, and then left. The record is unclear, but Mary, who is a nurse, apparently performed the insemination by herself or with Victoria.

Contact between Mary and Jhordan continued after she became pregnant. Mary attended a Christmas party at Jhordan's home. Jhordan visited Mary several times at the health center where she worked. He took photographs of her. When he informed Mary by telephone that he had collected a crib, playpen, and high chair for the child, she told him to keep those items at his home. At one point Jhordan told Mary he had started a trust fund for the child and wanted legal guardianship in case she died; Mary vetoed the guardianship idea but did not disapprove the trust fund.

Victoria maintained a close involvement with Mary during the pregnancy. She took Mary to medical appointments, attended birthing classes, and shared information with Mary regarding pregnancy, delivery, and child rearing.

Mary gave birth to Devin on March 30, 1980 . . .. Mary's roommate telephoned Jhordan that day to inform him of the birth. Jhordan visited Mary and Devin the next day and took photographs of the baby.

Five days later Jhordan telephoned Mary and said he wanted to visit Devin again. Mary initially resisted, but then allowed Jhordan to visit, although she told him she was angry. During the visit Jhordan claimed a right to see Devin, and Mary agreed to monthly visits.

Through August 1980 Jhordan visited Devin approximately five times. Mary then terminated the monthly visits. Jhordan said he would consult an attorney if Mary did not let him see Devin. Mary asked Jhordan to sign a contract indicating he would not seek to be Devin's father, but Jhordan refused.

In December 1980, Jhordan filed an action against Mary to establish paternity and visitation rights. In June 1982, by stipulated judgment in a separate action by the County of Sonoma, he was ordered to reimburse the county for public assistance paid for Devin's support. The judgment ordered him to commence payment, through the district attorney's office, of $900 in arrearages as well as future child support of $50 per month. In November 1982, the court granted Jhordan weekly visitation with Devin at Victoria's home.

Victoria had been closely involved with Devin since his birth. Devin spent at least two days each week in her home. On days when they did not see each other they spoke on the telephone. Victoria and Mary discussed Devin daily either in person or by telephone. They made joint decisions regarding his daily care and development. The three took vacations together. Devin and Victoria regarded each other as parent and child. Devin developed a brother-sister relationship with Victoria's 14-year-old daughter, and came to regard Victoria's parents as his grandparents. Victoria made the necessary arrangements for Devin's visits with Jhordan.

In August 1983, Victoria moved successfully for an order joining her as a party to this litigation. Supported by Mary, she sought joint legal custody (with Mary) and requested specified visitation rights, asserting she was a de facto parent of Devin. Jhordan subsequently requested an award of joint custody to him and Mary.

After trial the court rendered judgment declaring Jhordan to be Devin's legal father. However, the court awarded sole legal and physical custody to Mary, and denied Jhordan any input into decisions regarding Devin's schooling, medical and dental care, and day-to-day maintenance. Jhordan received substantial visitation rights as recommended by a court-appointed psychologist. The court held Victoria was not a de facto parent, but awarded her visitation rights (not to impinge upon Jhordan's visitation schedule), which were also recommended by the psychologist.

Mary and Victoria filed a timely notice of appeal, specifying the portions of the judgment declaring Jhordan to be Devin's legal father and denying Victoria the status of de facto parent.

III. Discussion

We begin with a discussion of Civil Code section 7005, which provides in pertinent part: "(a) If, under the supervision of a licensed physician and with the consent of her husband, a wife is inseminated artificially with semen donated by a man not her husband, the husband is treated in law as if he were the natural father of a child thereby conceived . . . .[] (b) The donor of semen provided to a licensed physician for use in artificial insemination of a woman other than the donor's wife is treated in law as if he were not the natural father of a child thereby conceived."

. . . Section 7005 is derived almost verbatim from the UPA as originally drafted, with one crucial exception. The original UPA restricts application of the nonpaternity provision of subdivision (b) to a "*married* woman other than the donor's wife." (9A West's U.Laws Ann., op. cit., supra., § 5, subd. (b), p. 593; italics added.) The word "married" is excluded from subdivision (b) of section 7005, so that in California, subdivision (b) applies to all women, married or not.

Thus, the California Legislature has afforded unmarried as well as married women a statutory vehicle for obtaining semen for artificial insemination without fear that the donor may claim paternity, and has likewise provided men with a statutory vehicle for donating semen to married and unmarried women alike without fear of liability for child support.

Subdivision (b) states only one limitation on its application: the semen must be "provided to a licensed physician." Otherwise, whether impregnation occurs through artificial insemination or sexual intercourse, there can be a determination of paternity with the rights, duties and obligations such a determination entails.

A. *Interpretation of the Statutory Nonpaternity Provision.*

Mary and Victoria first contend that despite the requirement of physician involvement stated in Civil Code section 7005, subdivision (b), the Legislature did not intend to withhold application of the donor nonpaternity provision where semen used in artificial insemination was not provided to a licensed physician. They suggest that the element of physician involvement appears in the statute merely because the Legislature assumed (erroneously) that all artificial insemination would occur under the supervision of a physician. Alternatively, they argue the requirement of physician involvement is merely directive rather than mandatory.

We cannot presume, however, that the Legislature simply assumed or wanted to recommend physician involvement, for two reasons.

First, the history of the UPA (the source of § 7005) indicates conscious adoption of the physician requirement. The initial "discussion draft" submitted to the drafters of the UPA in 1971 did not mention the involvement of a physician in artificial insemination; the draft stated no requirement as to how semen was to be obtained or how the insemination procedure was to be performed. (Krause, Illegitimacy: Law and Social Policy (1971) pp. 240, 243.) The eventual inclusion of the physician requirement in the final version of the UPA suggests a conscious decision to require physician involvement.

Second, there are at least two sound justifications upon which the statutory requirement of physician involvement might have been based. One relates to health: a physician can obtain a complete medical history of the donor (which may be of crucial importance to the child during his or her lifetime) and screen the donor for any hereditary or communicable diseases. Indeed, the commissioners' comment to the section of the UPA on artificial insemination cites as a "useful reference" a law review article which argues that health considerations should require the involvement of a physician in statutorily authorized artificial insemination. This suggests that health considerations underlie the decision by the drafters of the UPA to include the physician requirement in the artificial insemination statute.

Another justification for physician involvement is that the presence of a professional third party such as a physician can serve to create a formal, documented structure for the donor-recipient relationship, without which, as this case illustrates, misunderstandings between the parties regarding the nature of their relationship and the donor's relationship to the child would be more likely to occur.

It is true that nothing inherent in artificial insemination requires the involvement of a physician. Artificial insemination is, as demonstrated here, a simple procedure easily performed by a woman in her own home. Also, despite the reasons outlined above in favor of physician involvement, there are countervailing considerations against requiring it. A requirement of physician involvement, as Mary argues, might offend a woman's sense of privacy and reproductive autonomy, might result in burdensome costs to some women, and might interfere with a woman's desire to conduct the procedure in a comfortable environment such as her own home or to choose the donor herself.

However, because of the way section 7005 is phrased, a woman (married or unmarried) can perform home artificial insemination or choose her donor and still obtain the benefits of the statute. Subdivision (b) does not require that a physician independently obtain the semen and perform the insemination, but requires only that the semen be "provided" to a physician. Thus, a woman who prefers home artificial insemination or who wishes to choose her donor can still obtain statutory protection from a donor's paternity claim through the relatively simple expedient of obtaining the semen, whether for home insemination or from a chosen donor (or both), through a licensed physician.

Regardless of the various countervailing considerations for and against physician involvement, our Legislature has embraced the apparently conscious decision by the drafters of the UPA to limit application of the donor nonpaternity provision to instances in which semen is provided to a licensed physician. The existence of sound justifications for physician involvement further supports a determination the Legislature intended to require it. Accordingly, section 7005, subdivision (b), by its terms does not apply to the present case. The Legislature's apparent decision to require physician involvement in order to invoke the statute cannot be subject to judicial second-guessing and cannot be disturbed, absent constitutional infirmity. . . .

C. *Victoria's Status as a De Facto Parent.*

Finally, Mary and Victoria contend that even if the paternity judgment is affirmed Victoria should be declared a de facto parent, based on her day-to-day attention to Devin's needs, in order to guarantee her present visitation rights and ensure her parental status in any future custody or visitation proceedings. Present resolution of the de facto parenthood issue for these purposes would be premature and merely advisory. Victoria's visitation rights have been legally recognized and preserved by court order. If no further custody or visitation proceedings occur, the issue of Victoria's de facto parent status and its legal effect will never arise.

V. Conclusion

We wish to stress that our opinion in this case is not intended to express any judicial preference toward traditional notions of family structure or toward providing a father where a single woman has chosen to bear a child. Public policy in these areas is best determined by the legislative branch of government, not the judicial. Our Legislature has already spoken and has afforded to unmarried women a statutory right to bear children by artificial insemination (as well as a right of men to donate semen) without fear of a paternity claim, through provision of the semen to a licensed physician. We simply hold that because Mary omitted to invoke Civil Code section 7005, subdivision (b), by obtaining Jhordan's semen through a licensed physician, and because the parties by all other conduct preserved Jhordan's status as a member of Devin's family, the trial court properly declared Jhordan to be Devin's legal father.

The judgment is affirmed. . . .

NOTES AND QUESTIONS

(1) "The first recorded case of artificial insemination took place in 1790. The procedure is so simple women can easily perform it themselves. All you need is a mechanical device to suck up and then expel liquid . . . .A turkey baster will. . . do." *Moschetta v. Moschetta*, 25 Cal. App. 4th 1218, 30 Cal. Rptr. 2d 893 (1994) (quoting Gallagher, *Enemies of Eros* 168 (1989)). Modern artificial insemination of humans has been practiced for over two generations, and "estimates in the U.S. alone vary from 6,000 to 20,000 children conceived by AID [Artificial Insemination Donor] annually." Krause, *Artificial Conception: Legal Approaches*, 19 Fam. L.Q. 185, 196 (1985).

(2) Both of the cases above demonstrate the need for legislative action in this area. The following is from the latest version of the Uniform Parentage Act, 9B U.L.A. 301 (1987), cited in *Jhordan C.*:

§ 5 [Artificial Insemination]

(a) If, under the supervision of a licensed physician and with the consent of her husband, a wife is inseminated artificially with semen donated by a man not her husband, the husband is treated in law as if he were the natural father of a child thereby conceived. The husband's consent must be in writing and signed by him and his wife. The physician shall certify their signatures and the date of the insemination, and file the husband's consent with the [State Department of Health], where it shall be kept confidential and in a sealed file. However, the physician's failure to do so does not affect the father and child relationship. All papers and records pertaining to the insemination, whether part of the permanent record of a court or of a file held by the supervising physician or elsewhere, are subject to inspection only upon an order of the court for good cause shown.

(b) The donor of semen provided to a licensed physician for use in artificial insemination of a married woman other than the donor's wife is treated in law as if he were not the natural father of a child thereby conceived.

(3) There are generally two kinds of artificial insemination practiced today. Here is a good summary of the difference:

Artificial insemination (AI) today is a widely accepted, non-experimental medical procedure. In what is probably its best known form, heterologous artificial insemination (appropriately dubbed AID, the acronym for Artificial Insemination Donor), a woman is impregnated with semen from a man not her husband in a simple procedure that can be accomplished with a syringe. Through modern cryogenic capabilities, semen can be frozen and stored for future use in sperm banks. Some banks operate as commercial enterprises, though, unlike their counterparts in the financial field, they are virtually free from state licensing and other regulation.

A second method that poses fewer legal problems is homologous artificial insemination (AIH). A married woman is impregnated with the semen of her husband when normal copulation fails because of various medical problems. A child conceived through AIH is the biological offspring of both the woman and her husband.

Wadlington, *Artificial Conception: the Challenge for Family Law*, 69 Va. L. Rev. 465 (1983). This article presents a good overview of AI.

(4) The *Baby Doe* and *Jhordan C.* cases present the central problem with AID: who will fulfill the duties required of a father raising a child? Uniform Parentage Act Section 5 deals with the problem of paternity. The husband of the woman to be inseminated is the father if he consents to the process with the understanding that he is to be the father. *See R.S. v. R.S.*, 670 P.2d 923 (Kan. Ct. App. 1983); *L.M.S. v. S.L.S.*, 312 N.W.2d 853 (Wis. Ct. App. 1981). The donor's status is clearly not that of the natural father, although it is difficult to provide any characterization of it. Would the donor have any right to the child if the parents under the Act died?

Questions regarding the parties' status can be minimized by appropriate procedures: mainly the use of consent forms and the anonymity of the donor. All parties involved, donor, mother, and husband, must sign consent forms. This formality provides a bright-line confirmation of paternity. In addition, the donor does not know the identity of the woman with whom the semen will be used nor does the woman know the donor's identity. Sometimes the sperm of several donors is used; this means that the doctors who conduct the insemination do not know the identity of the natural father. While anonymity is essential, it does have a potentially serious drawback: it means that a child is born not knowing its genetic history, with the consequence that the child may be deprived of the opportunity to prepare for, or even prevent, certain genetic diseases, perhaps something as common as heart disease. Sometimes, the people involved later experience strong emotional needs to learn each others' identities as well. Note that § 5(a) of the Uniform Parentage Act, 9B U.L.A. 301 (1987), allows the release of a donor's identity upon a showing of good cause.

(5) Technically the husband's consent does more than just show that he accepts the responsibility of paternity; by also estopping him from denying paternity, the child will hopefully be spared future rejection. The policy behind this is of course the need to have parents who will be responsible, especially financially, for the care of the children who result from the AI.

The issue in *In re Baby Doe, above*, has also come up in a case involving criminal prosecution for failing to support a child. In *People v. Sorenson*, 437 P.2d 495 (Cal. 1968), a father was convicted of this crime, although he claimed he was not the child's father because his wife had undergone AID. The court stated:

> One who consents to the production of a child cannot create a temporary relation to be assumed and disclaimed at will, but the arrangement must be of such character as to impose an obligation of supporting those for whose existence he is directly responsible. As noted by the trial court, it is safe to assume that without defendant's active participation and consent the child would not have been procreated.

Id. at 499.

(6) **Fathers.** Do you think the result in *In re Baby Doe, above*, gives rights to the "father"? Could the non-donor father of a child conceived through AID get custody of the child or visitation rights if he and the mother were divorced? If the mother remarries and her second husband wants to adopt the child, will her first husband who consented to the AID have to give his consent to the adoption as would a natural father? *See Adoption of Anonymous*, 74 Misc. 2d 99, 345 N.Y.S.2d 430 (Surr. Ct. 1973). Could he bring an action for emotional

distress if he witnessed the child injured or for wrongful death if the child was killed? Although the answers to these questions are more difficult in the *Baby Doe* case because there is no writing, the result where normal formalities are followed is yes to all these questions.

(7) **Donors.** When the proper procedures are followed (consent, physician assistance, and maintenance of anonymity), the donor has none of the rights mentioned in note six.

(8) **Legislation.** How would you change U.P.A. § 5 to deal with the situation in *Jhordan C.?*

(9) **Frozen Sperm.** Who should get custody of frozen semen? This issue came up in an unusual case involving the frozen semen of a California attorney who committed suicide. The issue arose between the attorney's long time live-in partner, who wanted to be impregnated with the semen, and his children. The attorney had made a testamentary disposition of the semen to his partner, which the California Court of Appeal upheld. The court held that the semen was property subject to the jurisdiction of the probate court and that there was no public policy against the artificial insemination of the unmarried partner where the sperm donor has died. The court issued a peremptory writ of mandate ordering the trial court to vacate its order to have the sperm destroyed. *See Hecht v. Superior Court,* 16 Cal. App. 4th 836, 20 Cal. Rptr. 2d 275 (1993).

(10) For additional reading on the subjects in this section see Ginsberg, Note, *FDA Approved? A Critique of the Artificial Insemination Industry in the United States,* 30 U. Mich. J.L. Reform 823 (1997); Harlow, *Paternalism Without Paternity: Discrimination Against Single Women Seeking Artificial Insemination By Donor,* 6 S. Cal. Rev. L. & Women's Stud. 173 (1996); Koehler, Comment, *Artificial Insemination: In The Child's Best Interest?,* 5 Alb. L.J. Sci. & Tech. 321 (1996); Hill, *What Does It Mean To Be A "Parent"?: The Claims of Biology As the Basis for Parental Rights,* 66 N.Y.U. L. Rev. 353 (1991); Shultz, *Reproductive Technology and Intent-Based Parenthood: An Opportunity for Gender Neutrality,* 1990 Wis. L. Rev. 297 (1990); Stumpf, Note, *Redefining Mother: A Legal Matrix for New Reproductive Technologies,* 96 Yale L.J. 187 (1986).

[B] In Vitro Fertilization and the Status of the Embryo

DAVIS v. DAVIS
Supreme Court of Tennessee
842 S.W.2d 588 (1992)

DAUGHERTY, JUSTICE.

This appeal presents a question of first impression, involving the disposition of the cryogenically-preserved product of in vitro fertilization (IVF), commonly referred to in the popular press and the legal journals as "frozen embryos." The case began as a divorce action, filed by the appellee, Junior Lewis Davis, against his then wife, appellant Mary Sue Davis. The parties were able to agree upon all terms of dissolution, except one: who was to have "custody" of the seven "frozen embryos" stored in a Knoxville fertility clinic that had attempted to assist the Davises in achieving a much-wanted pregnancy during a happier period in their relationship.

I. Introduction

Mary Sue Davis originally asked for control of the "frozen embryos" with the intent to have them transferred to her own uterus, in a post-divorce effort to become pregnant. Junior Davis objected, saying that he preferred to leave the embryos in their frozen state until he decided whether or not he wanted to become a parent outside the bounds of marriage.

Based on its determination that the embryos were "human beings" from the moment of fertilization, the trial court awarded "custody" to Mary Sue Davis and directed that she "be permitted the opportunity to bring these children to term through implantation." The Court of Appeals reversed, finding that Junior Davis has a "constitutionally protected right not to beget a child where no pregnancy has taken place" and holding that "there is no compelling state interest to justify ordering implantation against the will of either party." The Court of Appeals further held that "the parties share an interest in the seven fertilized ova" and remanded the case to the trial court for entry of an order vesting them with "joint control . . . and equal voice over their disposition." . . .

We note . . . that [the parties'] positions have already shifted: both have remarried and Mary Sue Davis (now Mary Sue Stowe) has moved out of state. She no longer wishes to utilize the "frozen embryos" herself, but wants authority to donate them to a childless couple. Junior Davis is adamantly opposed to such donation and would prefer to see the "frozen embryos" discarded. The result is, once again, an impasse, but the parties' current legal position does have an effect on the probable outcome of the case, as discussed below.

At the outset, it is important to note the absence of two critical factors that might otherwise influence or control the result of this litigation: When the Davises signed up for the IVF program at the Knoxville clinic, they did not execute a written agreement specifying what disposition should be made of any unused embryos that might result from the cryopreservation process. Moreover, there was at that time no Tennessee statute governing such disposition, nor has one been enacted in the meantime.

In addition, because of the uniqueness of the question before us, we have no case law to guide us to a decision in this case . . . .

But, if we have no statutory authority or common law precedents to guide us, we do have the benefit of extensive comment and analysis in the legal journals. In those articles, medical-legal scholars and ethicists have proposed various models for the disposition of "frozen embryos" when unanticipated contingencies arise, such as divorce, death of one or both of the parties, financial reversals, or simple disenchantment with the IVF process. Those models range from a rule requiring, at one extreme, that all embryos be used by the gamete-providers or donated for uterine transfer, and, at the other extreme, that any unused embryos be automatically discarded.[1] Other formulations would vest control in the female gamete-provider—in every case, because of her greater physical and emotional contribution to the IVF process,[2] or perhaps only in the event that she wishes to use them herself.[3] There are also two "implied contract" models: one would infer from enrollment

---

[1] Note, *The Legal Status of Frozen Embryos: Analysis and Proposed Guidelines for a Uniform Law*, 17 J. Legis. 97 (1990).

[2] This is the so-called "sweat-equity" model. Robertson, Resolving Disputes over Frozen Embryos, Hastings Center Report at p. 7, Nov./Dec.1989.

[3] Andrews, The Legal Status of the Embryo, 32 Loyola L.Rev. 357 (1986).

in an IVF program that the IVF clinic has authority to decide in the event of an impasse whether to donate, discard, or use the "frozen embryos" for research; the other would infer from the parties' participation in the creation of the embryos that they had made an irrevocable commitment to reproduction and would require transfer either to the female provider or to a donee. There are also the so-called "equity models": one would avoid the conflict altogether by dividing the "frozen embryos" equally between the parties, to do with as they wish;[4] the other would award veto power to the party wishing to avoid parenthood, whether it be the female or the male progenitor.[5]

Each of these possible models has the virtue of ease of application. Adoption of any of them would establish a bright-line test that would dispose of disputes like the one we have before us in a clear and predictable manner. As appealing as that possibility might seem, we conclude that given the relevant principles of constitutional law, the existing public policy of Tennessee with regard to unborn life, the current state of scientific knowledge giving rise to the emerging reproductive technologies, and the ethical considerations that have developed in response to that scientific knowledge, there can be no easy answer to the question we now face. We conclude, instead, that we must weigh the interests of each party to the dispute, in terms of the facts and analysis set out below, in order to resolve that dispute in a fair and responsible manner.

II. *The Facts*

Mary Sue Davis and Junior Lewis Davis met while they were both in the Army and stationed in Germany in the spring of 1979. After a period of courtship, they came home to the United States and were married on April 26, 1980. When their leave was up, they then returned to their posts in Germany as a married couple.

Within six months of returning to Germany, Mary Sue became pregnant but unfortunately suffered an extremely painful tubal pregnancy, as a result of which she had surgery to remove her right fallopian tube. This tubal pregnancy was followed by four others during the course of the marriage. After her fifth tubal pregnancy, Mary Sue chose to have her left fallopian tube ligated, thus leaving her without functional fallopian tubes by which to conceive naturally. The Davises attempted to adopt a child but, at the last minute, the child's birth-mother changed her mind about putting the child up for adoption. Other paths to adoption turned out to be prohibitively expensive. *In vitro* fertilization became essentially the only option for the Davises to pursue in their attempt to become parents.

As explained at trial, IVF involves the aspiration of ova from the follicles of a woman's ovaries, fertilization of these ova in a petri dish using the sperm provided by a man, and the transfer of the product of this procedure into the uterus of the woman from whom the ova were taken. Implantation may then occur, resulting in a pregnancy and, it is hoped, the birth of a child.

Beginning in 1985, the Davises went through six attempts at IVF, at a total cost of $35,000, but the hoped-for pregnancy never occurred. Despite her fear of needles, at each

---

[4] Assuming that the parties do not change their current positions, in this case the result would be "the worst of both worlds": some of the frozen embryos would likely be destroyed, contrary to Mary Sue Davis's devout wish that they be implanted and given the opportunity to come to term; at the same time, the others would likely be implanted and might come to term, thus forcing Junior Davis into unwanted parenthood.

[5] Poole, Allocation of Decision-Making Rights to Frozen Embryos, 4 Amer. J. of Fam. L. 67 (1990).

IVF attempt Mary Sue underwent the month of subcutaneous injections necessary to shut down her pituitary gland and the eight days of intermuscular injections necessary to stimulate her ovaries to produce ova. She was anesthetized five times for the aspiration procedure to be performed. Forty-eight to 72 hours after each aspiration, she returned for transfer back to her uterus, only to receive a negative pregnancy test result each time.

The Davises then opted to postpone another round of IVF until after the clinic with which they were working was prepared to offer them cryogenic preservation, scheduled for November 1988. Using this process, if more ova are aspirated and fertilized than needed, the conceptive product may be cryogenically preserved (frozen in nitrogen and stored at sub-zero temperatures) for later transfer if the transfer performed immediately does not result in a pregnancy. The unavailability of this procedure had not been a hindrance to previous IVF attempts by the Davises because Mary Sue had produced at most only three or four ova, despite hormonal stimulation. However, on their last attempt, on December 8, 1988, the gynecologist who performed the procedure was able to retrieve nine ova for fertilization. The resulting one-celled entities, referred to before division as zygotes, were then allowed to develop in petri dishes in the laboratory until they reached the four-to eight-cell stage. . . .

After fertilization was completed, a transfer was performed as usual on December 10, 1988; the rest of the four-to eight-cell entities were cryogenically preserved. Unfortunately, a pregnancy did not result from the December 1988 transfer, and before another transfer could be attempted, Junior Davis filed for divorce—in February 1989. He testified that he had known that their marriage "was not very stable" for a year or more, but had hoped that the birth of a child would improve their relationship. Mary Sue Davis testified that she had no idea that there was a problem with their marriage. As noted earlier, the divorce proceedings were complicated only by the issue of the disposition of the "frozen embryos."

III. *The Scientific Testimony*

In the record, and especially in the trial court's opinion, there is a great deal of discussion about the proper descriptive terminology to be used in this case. Although this discussion appears at first glance to be a matter simply of semantics, semantical distinctions are significant in this context, because language defines legal status and can limit legal rights. Obviously, an "adult" has a different legal status than does a "child." Likewise, "child" means something other than "fetus." A "fetus" differs from an "embryo." There was much dispute at trial about whether the four-to eight-cell entities in this case should properly be referred to as "embryos" or as "preembryos," with resulting differences in legal analysis.

One expert, a French geneticist named Dr. Jerome Lejeune, insisted that there was no recognized scientific distinction between the two terms. He referred to the four-to eight-cell entities at issue here as "early human beings," as "tiny persons," and as his "kin." Although he is an internationally recognized geneticist, Dr. Lejeune's background fails to reflect any degree of expertise in obstetrics or gynecology (specifically in the field of infertility) or in medical ethics. His testimony revealed a profound confusion between science and religion. For example, he was deeply moved that "Madame [Mary Sue], the mother, wants to rescue babies from this concentration can," and he concluded that Junior Davis has a moral duty to try to bring these "tiny human beings" to term.

Dr. LeJeune's opinion was disputed by Dr. Irving Ray King, the gynecologist who performed the IVF procedures in this case. Dr. King is a medical doctor who had practiced as a sub-speciality in the areas of infertility and reproductive endocrinology for 12 years. He established the Fertility Center of East Tennessee in Knoxville in 1984 and had worked extensively with IVF and cryopreservation. He testified that the currently accepted term for the zygote immediately after division is "preembryo" and that this term applies up until 14 days after fertilization. He testified that this 14-day period defines the accepted period for preembryo research. At about 14 days, he testified, the group of cells begins to differentiate in a process that permits the eventual development of the different body parts which will become an individual.

Dr. King's testimony was corroborated by the other experts who testified at trial, with the exception of Dr. Lejeune. It is further supported by the American Fertility Society, an organization of 10,000 physicians and scientists who specialize in problems of human infertility. The Society's June 1990 report on Ethical Considerations of the New Reproductive Technologies indicates that from the point of fertilization, the resulting one-cell zygote contains "a new hereditary constitution (genome) contributed to by both parents through the union of sperm and egg." *Id.* at 31S. . . .

The trial court reasoned that if there is no distinction between embryos and preembryos, as Dr. Lejeune theorized, then Dr. Lejeune must also have been correct when he asserted that "human life begins at the moment of conception." From this proposition, the trial judge concluded that the eight-cell entities at issue were not preembryos but were "children in vitro." He then invoked the doctrine of parens patriae and held that it was "in the best interest of the children" to be born rather than destroyed. Finding that Mary Sue Davis was willing to provide such an opportunity, but that Junior Davis was not, the trial judge awarded her "custody" of the "children in vitro." . . .

The "Person" vs. "Property" Dichotomy

One of the fundamental issues the inquiry poses is whether the preembryos in this case should be considered "persons" or "property" in the contemplation of the law. The Court of Appeals held, correctly, that they cannot be considered "persons" under Tennessee law . . . .

Nor do preembryos enjoy protection as "persons" under federal law. In *Roe v. Wade*, 410 U.S. 113, 93 S.Ct. 705, 35 L.Ed.2d 147 (1973), the United States Supreme Court explicitly refused to hold that the fetus possesses independent rights under law, based upon a thorough examination of the federal constitution, relevant common law principles, and the lack of scientific consensus as to when life begins. The Supreme Court concluded that "the unborn have never been recognized in the law as persons in the whole sense." *Id.* at 162, 93 S.Ct. at 731. As a matter of constitutional law, this conclusion has never been seriously challenged. . . .

Left undisturbed, the trial court's ruling would have afforded preembryos the legal status of "persons" and vested them with legally cognizable interests separate from those of their progenitors. Such a decision would doubtless have had the effect of outlawing IVF programs in the state of Tennessee. . . .

To our way of thinking, the most helpful discussion on this point is found not in the minuscule number of legal opinions that have involved "frozen embryos," but in the ethical standards set by The American Fertility Society, as follows:

Three major ethical positions have been articulated in the debate over preembryo status. At one extreme is the view of the preembryo as a human subject after fertilization, which requires that it be accorded the rights of a person. This position entails an obligation to provide an opportunity for implantation to occur and tends to ban any action before transfer that might harm the preembryo or that is not immediately therapeutic, such as freezing and some preembryo research. At the opposite extreme is the view that the preembryo has a status no different from any other human tissue. With the consent of those who have decision-making authority over the preembryo, no limits should be imposed on actions taken with preembryos. A third view—one that is most widely held—takes an intermediate position between the other two. It holds that the preembryo deserves respect greater than that accorded to human tissue but not the respect accorded to actual persons. The preembryo is due greater respect than other human tissue because of its potential to become a person and because of its symbolic meaning for many people. Yet, it should not be treated as a person, because it has not yet developed the features of personhood, is not yet established as developmentally individual, and may never realize its biologic potential.

Report of the Ethics Committee of The American Fertility Society, supra, at 34S–35S. . . .

We conclude that preembryos are not, strictly speaking, either "persons" or "property," but occupy an interim category that entitles them to special respect because of their potential for human life. It follows that any interest that Mary Sue Davis and Junior Davis have in the preembryos in this case is not a true property interest. However, they do have an interest in the nature of ownership, to the extent that they have decision-making authority concerning disposition of the preembryos, within the scope of policy set by law. . . .

VI. *The Right of Procreational Autonomy*

Although an understanding of the legal status of preembryos is necessary in order to determine the enforceability of agreements about their disposition, asking whether or not they constitute "property" is not an altogether helpful question. As the appellee points out in his brief, "[as] two or eight cell tiny lumps of complex protein, the embryos have no [intrinsic] value to either party." Their value lies in the "potential to become, after implantation, growth and birth, *children*." Thus, the essential dispute here is not where or how or how long to store the preembryos, but whether the parties will become parents. The Court of Appeals held in effect that they will become parents if they both agree to become parents. The Court did not say what will happen if they fail to agree. We conclude that the answer to this dilemma turns on the parties' exercise of their constitutional right to privacy.

The right to privacy is not specifically mentioned in either the federal or the Tennessee state constitution, and yet there can be little doubt about its grounding in the concept of liberty reflected in those two documents. In particular, the Fourteenth Amendment to the United States Constitution provides that "[n]o state shall . . . deprive any person of life, liberty, or property, without due process of law." Referring to the Fourteenth Amendment, the United States Supreme Court in *Meyer v. Nebraska* observed:

> While this court has not attempted to define with exactness the liberty thus guaranteed, the term has received much consideration and some of the included things have been definitely stated. Without doubt, it denotes not merely freedom from bodily restraint

but also the right of the individual to contract, to engage in any of the common occupations of life, to acquire useful knowledge, to marry, establish a home and bring up children, to worship God according to the dictates of his own conscience, and generally to enjoy those privileges long recognized at common law as essential to the orderly pursuit of happiness by free men.

262 U.S. 390, 399, 43 S.Ct. 625, 626, 67 L.Ed. 1042 (1923).

The right of privacy inherent in the constitutional concept of liberty has been further identified "as against the [power of] government, the right to be let alone—the most comprehensive of rights and the right most valued by civilized men." *Olmstead v. United States*, 277 U.S. 438, 478, 48 S.Ct. 564, 572, 72 L.Ed. 944 (1928) (Brandeis, J., dissenting). As to scope, "the concept of liberty protects those personal rights that are fundamental, and it is not confined to the specific terms of the Bill of Rights." *Griswold v. Connecticut*, 381 U.S. 479, 486, 85 S.Ct. 1678, 1683, 14 L.Ed.2d 510 (1965) (Goldberg, J., concurring). . . .

Here, the specific individual freedom in dispute is the right to procreate. . . . [W]e hold that the right of procreation is a vital part of an individual's right to privacy . . . .

In construing the reach of the federal constitution, the United States Supreme Court has addressed the affirmative right to procreate in only two cases. In *Buck v. Bell*, 274 U.S. 200, 207, 47 S.Ct. 584, 584, 71 L.Ed. 1000 (1927), the Court upheld the sterilization of a "feebleminded white woman." However, in Skinner v. Oklahoma, 316 U.S. 535, 62 S.Ct. 1110, 86 L.Ed. 1655 (1942), the Supreme Court struck down a statute that authorized the sterilization of certain categories of criminals. The Court described the right to procreate as "one of the basic civil rights of man [sic]," 316 U.S. at 541, 62 S.Ct. at 1113, and stated that "[m]arriage and procreation are fundamental to the very existence and survival of the race." *Id*.

In the same vein, the United States Supreme Court has said:

If the right of privacy means anything, it is the right of the individual, married or single, to be free from unwarranted governmental intrusion into matters so fundamentally affecting a person as the decision whether to bear or beget a child.

Eisenstadt v. Baird, 405 U.S. 438, 453, 92 S.Ct. 1029, 1038, 31 L.Ed.2d 349 (1972). . . .

For the purposes of this litigation it is sufficient to note that, whatever its ultimate constitutional boundaries, the right of procreational autonomy is composed of two rights of equal significance—the right to procreate and the right to avoid procreation. Undoubtedly, both are subject to protections and limitations. *See e.g., Prince v. Massachusetts*, 321 U.S. 158, 64 S.Ct. 438, 88 L.Ed. 645 (1944) (parental control over the education or health care of their children subject to some limits); *Roe v. Wade*, 410 U.S. 113, 93 S.Ct. 705, 35 L.Ed.2d 147 (1973) (states' interests in potential life overcomes right to avoid procreation by abortion in later states of pregnancy).

The equivalence of and inherent tension between these two interests are nowhere more evident than in the context of in vitro fertilization. None of the concerns about a woman's bodily integrity that have previously precluded men from controlling abortion decisions is applicable here. We are not unmindful of the fact that the trauma (including both emotional stress and physical discomfort) to which women are subjected in the IVF process is more severe than is the impact of the procedure on men. In this sense, it is fair to say that women contribute more to the IVF process than men. Their experience, however, must be viewed in light of the joys of parenthood that is desired or the relative anguish of a lifetime of unwanted parenthood. As they stand on the brink of potential parenthood, Mary Sue Davis and Junior Lewis Davis must be seen as entirely equivalent gamete-providers.

. . . .

The unique nature of this case requires us to note that the interests of these parties in parenthood are different in scope than the parental interest considered in other cases. Previously, courts have dealt with the child-bearing and child-rearing aspects of parenthood. Abortion cases have dealt with gestational parenthood. In this case, the Court must deal with the question of genetic parenthood. We conclude, moreover, that an interest in avoiding genetic parenthood can be significant enough to trigger the protections afforded to all other aspects of parenthood. The technological fact that someone unknown to these parties could gestate these preembryos does not alter the fact that these parties, the gamete-providers, would become parents in that event, at least in the genetic sense. The profound impact this would have on them supports their right to sole decisional authority as to whether the process of attempting to gestate these preembryos should continue. This brings us directly to the question of how to resolve the dispute that arises when one party wishes to continue the IVF process and the other does not.

VII. *Balancing the Parties' Interests*

Resolving disputes over conflicting interests of constitutional import is a task familiar to the courts. One way of resolving these disputes is to consider the positions of the parties, the significance of their interests, and the relative burdens that will be imposed by differing resolutions. In this case, the issue centers on the two aspects of procreational autonomy—the right to procreate and the right to avoid procreation. We start by considering the burdens imposed on the parties by solutions that would have the effect of disallowing the exercise of individual procreational autonomy with respect to these particular preembryos.

Beginning with the burden imposed on Junior Davis, we note that the consequences are obvious. Any disposition which results in the gestation of the preembryos would impose unwanted parenthood on him, with all of its possible financial and psychological consequences. The impact that this unwanted parenthood would have on Junior Davis can only be understood by considering his particular circumstances, as revealed in the record.

Junior Davis testified that he was the fifth youngest of six children. When he was five years old, his parents divorced, his mother had a nervous break-down, and he and three of his brothers went to live at a home for boys run by the Lutheran Church. Another brother was taken in by an aunt, and his sister stayed with their mother. From that day forward, he had monthly visits with his mother but saw his father only three more times before he died in 1976. Junior Davis testified that, as a boy, he had severe problems caused by separation from his parents. He said that it was especially hard to leave his mother after each monthly visit. He clearly feels that he has suffered because of his lack of opportunity to establish a relationship with his parents and particularly because of the absence of his father.

In light of his boyhood experiences, Junior Davis is vehemently opposed to fathering a child that would not live with both parents. Regardless of whether he or Mary Sue had custody, he feels that the child's bond with the non-custodial parent would not be satisfactory. He testified very clearly that his concern was for the psychological obstacles a child in such a situation would face, as well as the burdens it would impose on him. Likewise, he is opposed to donation because the recipient couple might divorce, leaving the child (which he definitely would consider his own) in a single-parent setting.

Balanced against Junior Davis's interest in avoiding parenthood is Mary Sue Davis's interest in donating the preembryos to another couple for implantation. Refusal to permit donation of the preembryos would impose on her the burden of knowing that the lengthy IVF procedures she underwent were futile, and that the preembryos to which she contributed genetic material would never become children. While this is not an insubstantial emotional burden, we can only conclude that Mary Sue Davis's interest in donation is not as significant as the interest Junior Davis has in avoiding parenthood. If she were allowed to donate these preembryos, he would face a lifetime of either wondering about his parental status or knowing about his parental status but having no control over it. He testified quite clearly that if these preembryos were brought to term he would fight for custody of his child or children. Donation, if a child came of it, would rob him twice—his procreational autonomy would be defeated and his relationship with his offspring would be prohibited.

The case would be closer if Mary Sue Davis were seeking to use the preembryos herself, but only if she could not achieve parenthood by any other reasonable means. We recognize the trauma that Mary Sue has already experienced and the additional discomfort to which she would be subjected if she opts to attempt IVF again. Still, she would have a reasonable opportunity, through IVF, to try once again to achieve parenthood in all its aspects—genetic, gestational, bearing, and rearing.

Further, we note that if Mary Sue Davis were unable to undergo another round of IVF, or opted not to try, she could still achieve the child-rearing aspects of parenthood through adoption. The fact that she and Junior Davis pursued adoption indicates that, at least at one time, she was willing to forego genetic parenthood and would have been satisfied by the child-rearing aspects of parenthood alone.

VIII. Conclusion

In summary, we hold that disputes involving the disposition of preembryos produced by in vitro fertilization should be resolved, first, by looking to the preferences of the progenitors. If their wishes cannot be ascertained, or if there is dispute, then their prior agreement concerning disposition should be carried out. If no prior agreement exists, then the relative interests of the parties in using or not using the preembryos must be weighed. Ordinarily, the party wishing to avoid procreation should prevail, assuming that the other party has a reasonable possibility of achieving parenthood by means other than use of the preembryos in question. If no other reasonable alternatives exist, then the argument in favor of using the preembryos to achieve pregnancy should be considered. However, if the party seeking control of the preembryos intends merely to donate them to another couple, the objecting party obviously has the greater interest and should prevail.

But the rule does not contemplate the creation of an automatic veto, and in affirming the judgment of the Court of Appeals, we would not wish to be interpreted as so holding.

For the reasons set out above, the judgment of the Court of Appeals is affirmed, in the appellee's favor. This ruling means that the Knoxville Fertility Clinic is free to follow its normal procedure in dealing with unused preembryos, as long as that procedure is not in conflict with this opinion. . . .

NOTES AND QUESTIONS

(1) **Contract**. In a section of *Davis* which was not included in the reading, the Tennessee Supreme Court indicated that a written agreement between the parties would be honored. Other courts have followed this position. For example, in *Kass v. Kass* the court made the following statement:

> The weighing of interests employed in *Davis* constitutes an analysis which may be worthy of some consideration in resolving conflicts between gamete providers over the disposition of their fertilized ova. However, there is no need to decide whether such an analysis should be adopted in the present case because, unlike the situation in *Davis*, the parties herein executed an informed consent document and an uncontested divorce instrument in which they unequivocally stated their intent as to the manner of disposition of the subject pre-zygotes. Indeed, throughout its decision, the court in *Davis* bemoaned the absence of such a statement of mutual intent in that case and clearly stated that the weighing of interests should only be utilized where no such manifestation of intent exists:
>
>> At the outset, it is important to note the absence of [a] critical [factor] that might otherwise influence or control the result of this litigation: When the Davises signed up for the IVF program at the Knoxville clinic, they did not execute a written agreement specifying what disposition should be made of any unused embryos that might result from the cryopreservation process" (*Davis v. Davis*, supra, at 590) [842 S.W.2d 588, 590 (Tenn.1992)].
>
> . . . .
>
> We believe, as a starting point, that an agreement regarding disposition of any untransferred preembryos in the event of contingencies (such as the death of one or more of the parties, divorce, financial reversals, or abandonment of the program) should be presumed valid and should be enforced as between the progenitors. This conclusion is in keeping with the proposition that the progenitors, having provided the gametic material giving rise to the preembryos, retain decision-making authority as to their disposition.
>
> At the same time, we recognize that life is not static, and that human emotions run particularly high when a married couple is attempting to overcome infertility problems. It follows that the parties' initial "informed consent" to IVF procedures will often not be truly informed because of the near impossibility of anticipating, emotionally and psychologically, all the turns that events may take as the IVF process unfolds. Providing that the initial agreements may later be modified by agreement will, we think, protect the parties against some of the risks they face in this regard. But, in the absence of such agreed modification, we conclude that their prior agreements should be considered binding.
>
> . . . .

In summary, we hold that disputes involving the disposition of preembryos produced by in vitro fertilization should be resolved, first, by looking to the preferences of the progenitors. If their wishes cannot be ascertained, or if there is [a] dispute, then their prior agreement concerning disposition should be carried out. If no prior agreement exists, [only] then [should] the relative interests of the parties in using or not using the preembryos . . . be weighed (*Davis v. Davis, supra*, at 597, 604) [842 S.W.2d 588, 597, 604 (Tenn.1992)].

We are in full agreement with the decision in *Davis* to the extent it requires that where a manifestation of mutual intent exists between the parties, that intent must be given effect by the court. Since we conclude, in accordance with the analysis employed in *Davis*, that the agreement of the parties is dispositive of the present controversy, no further discussion of the facts of that case is material or relevant.

Kass v. Kass, 1997 WL 563419, slip op. at 07376 (N.Y. App. Div. 1997).

(2) **Protection of the Embryo.** In *Davis*, the Tennessee Supreme Court focussed on the donors, the gamete-providers, whereas the trial court focused on the preembryo in reaching its decision. The trial court apparently held the same view as many "pro-life" anti-abortion advocates that life begins at conception. This view is supported by the following Illinois statute:

> Any person who intentionally causes the fertilization of a human ovum by a human sperm outside the body of a living human female shall, with regard to the human being thereby produced, be deemed to have the care and custody of a child for the purposes of Section 4 of the Act to Prevent and Punish Wrongs to Children, [the child endangerment statute] approved May 17, 1877, as amended, except that nothing in that Section shall be construed to attach any penalty to participation in the performance of a lawful pregnancy termination.

720 Ill. Comp. Stat Ann. 510/6 (West 1997) (historical note).

Here is a contemporary comment on this statute, from Annas and Elias, *In Vitro Fertilization and Embryo Transfer: Medicolegal Aspects of a New Technique to Create a Family*, 17 Fam. L.Q. 199, 208 (1983):

> The most ethically and politically controversial aspect of IVF is the status of the embryo. Some opponents argue that a fertilized egg is a human being, and failure to reimplant it should be considered murder. An analogous view has been put into an Illinois statute which requires the physician who performs IVF to assume the "care and custody" of the embryo, subject to the penalties of the child abuse statute should any harm befall it. The constitutionality of the statute has been unsuccessfully challenged by a physician and his patient, a married couple, who allege that it prevents them from employing IVF in violation of the couple's constitutional right to privacy and that it is unconstitutionally vague. The essence of the argument is that the statute's primary purpose is to prohibit IVF and that such a prohibition cannot be constitutionally accomplished by protecting embryonic life against the mother's interests prior to viability. This argument seems correct. The Supreme Court has ruled that there is a right not to procreate, and this right seems best understood as a right not to have the state interfere in procreative decisions. The right at stake is "privacy," and it would seem that the decision by an infertile couple, made in concert with their physician,

to undergo IVF for the purposes of having a child, should be constitutionally protected. The state has no obligation to foster IVF research or to pay for IVF procedures with Medicaid funds, but it probably does have an obligation not to interfere with such procedures unless it can demonstrate a compelling interest.

For an important discussion in this regard, see Andrews, *The Legal Status of the Embryo*, 32 Loy. L. Rev. 357 (1986) (cited in the principal case).

(3) Should embryo donation be allowed just as we allow AID? Semen from an anonymous donor could be used to fertilize an ovum from another anonymous donor and the embryo would be transferred to the womb of the wife of a childless couple or to the womb of a surrogate mother with whom the childless couple has contracted to bear the child.

(4) Professor Krause in his article, *Artificial Conception: Legislative Approaches*, 19 Fam. L.Q. 185, 193–97 (1985), has taken what amounts to a very commonsensical approach to legislation regarding the problems created for families by the new biology. Professor Krause makes four basic assertions. First, if a husband and wife supply the genetic material for a child, the child belongs to these genetic parents. Second, where a sterile husband consents to the artificial insemination of his wife, this husband and his wife are the legal parents. Third, where the wife is infertile, if she donates her ovum or is implanted with the ovum of another that is fertilized by her husband, this wife and husband are the legal parents. Finally, where both husband and wife are infertile, and sperm and ovum are donated, the husband and wife are the legal parents.

(5) Do you think legislatures should focus on the status of the child and ignore the question of the permissibility of using the technology at all? *See* Cahill, *In Vitro Fertilization: Ethical Issues in Judeo-Christian Perspective*, 32 Loy. L. Rev. 337 (1986).

(6) The new technology is of course going to open the door to a host of medical malpractice cases. Do you think there is a possibility of products liability becoming an effective cause of action in this area? What if an ovum or semen or an embryo turns out to be defective? Would warranty or strict liability in tort be viable theories? In answering the last question, consider this fact: As in the case of exclusion of liability for negligence, most courts refuse to give effect to disclaimers of strict tort liability. The majority position is in accordance with comment *m* to § 402A of the Restatement (Second) of Torts. The rationale for this position seems to rest in the fact that strict tort liability evolved, at least in part, because of the perceived inequity of allowing contractual circumvention of warranty liability. *See* Styron, Comment, *Artificial Insemination: A New Frontier for Medical Malpractice and Medical Products Liability*, 32 Loy. L. Rev. 411, 439 (1986).

(7) For additional reading on the subjects in this section, see Gunsburg, Note, *Frozen Life's Dominion: Extending Reproductive Autonomy Rights To In Vitro Fertilization*, 65 Fordham L. Rev. 2205 (1997); Note, *In Vitro Fertilization: Insurance and Consumer Protection*, 109 Harv. L. Rev. 2092 (1996); Reilly, *Constitutional Limits On New Mexico's In Vitro Fertilization Law*, 24 N.M. L. Rev. 125 (1994); Voutsinas, *In Vitro Fertilization*, 12 Prob. L.J. 47 (1994); Seavello, *Are You My Mother? A Judge's Decision in In Vitro Fertilization Surrogacy*, 3 Hasting's Women's L.J. 211 (1992); Milich, *In Vitro Fertilization and Embryo Technology—Social Values = Legislative Solutions*, 30 J. Fam. L. 875 (1991/ 1992); Attanasio, *The Constitutionality of Regulating Human Genetic Engineering: Where Procreative Liberty and Equal Opportunity Collide*, 53 U. Chi. L. Rev. 1274 (1986); Brown et al., *Special Project: Legal Rights and Issues Surrounding Conception, Pregnancy, and*

Birth, 39 Vand. L. Rev. 597 (1986) (includes a section on inheritance); and Note, *Redefining Mother: A Legal Matrix for New Reproductive Technology*, 96 Yale L.J. 187 (1986).

(8) **Problem.** Mary and Victoria lived together. Mary wanted to have a child, and Victoria agreed that she would like to raise a child with Mary, just like a married couple. Mary discussed the matter with her close friend Junior, who was single; he agreed to provide the semen for Mary's artificial insemination. At that time he told her that he would very much like to have a child, and that this arrangement would work very nicely for him since his career did not allow him the time to raise a family. He said he would like to visit the child on a regular basis. Mary responded that she would not agree to regular visitation, but, since he was a friend of the family, he would not lose contact with the baby.

Junior visited Mary at her home on several occasions; each time he provided her with semen which she used to artificially inseminate herself. Since she was a nurse she performed the insemination with a syringe, sometimes with the help of Victoria. After several attempts, she still did not become pregnant.

Mary, Victoria, and Junior then visited a fertility clinic. Although the personnel at the clinic knew that Junior was not Mary's husband, they agreed for a fee to help them have a child through in vitro fertilization. When IVF was unsuccessful, the clinic suggested that Victoria serve as the ova donor. Junior signed a release as to his sperm. With Victoria's ovum and Junior's semen, the IVF was successful and so was the implantation. Nine months later Sarah was born. Seven preembryos, extras in case the first implantation was not successful, were cryogenically preserved at the clinic.

After Sarah's birth Junior again asked for visitation, and Mary agreed he could visit her once a month. However, Victoria was developing a strong parent-child relationship with Sarah, and both Mary and Victoria found that these visits were unsettling to them and, they thought, to the child. So after five months they refused to allow Junior to visit the child.

If Junior brought an action to establish paternity and visitation rights, what should the result be? If Mary begins to receive Aid for Dependent Children (AFDC) and the county brings an action for reimbursement of AFDC payments, what should the result be?

If Junior got married and discovered that he and his new wife could not have children, could he gain access to the preembyros?

[C] Cloning

CALIFORNIA HEALTH & SAFETY CODE § 24185

(a) No person shall clone a human being.

(b) No person shall purchase or sell an ovum, zygote, embryo, or fetus for the purpose of cloning a human being.

(c) For purposes of this section, "clone" means the practice of creating or attempting to create a human being by transferring the nucleus from a human cell from whatever source into a human egg cell from which the nucleus has been removed for the purpose of, or to implant, the resulting product to initiate a pregnancy that could result in the birth of a human being.

NOTES AND QUESTIONS

(1) **Policy.** The purpose of this law, which expires in 2003, is contained in 1997 Cal. Legis. Serv. 688 (West):

> It is the intent of the legislature to place a five-year moratorium on the cloning of an entire human being in order to evaluate the profound medical, ethical, and social implications that such a possibility raises. It is not the intent of the Legislature that this moratorium apply to the cloning of human cells, human tissue, or organs that would not result in the replication of an entire human being. During this moratorium period, the State Director of Health Services should be called upon to establish a panel of representatives from the fields of medicine, religion, biotechnology, genetics, law, bioethics, and the general public to evaluate those implications, review public policy, and advise the Legislature and the Governor in this area.

(2) **Federal Law.** At the time of this writing, Congressmen Ehlers had introduced several bills jointly into the House Committees on Commerce, Labor and Human Resources, and Science. *See* Prohibition of the Cloning of Humans, H.R. 923, 105th Cong. (1997); Human Cloning Research, S. 368, 105th Cong. (1997); Expenditures for Cloning Humans Prohibition, H.R. 922, 105th Cong. (1997).

(3) **Problem areas.** In the most comprehensive article to date on the legal ramifications of cloning, Debra Feuerberg Duffy identifies the following possible issues that may be affected by cloning humans: procreative liberty, ownership of the embryo, third-party interests, statutory regulations, and ethical implications. *See* Duffy, Note, *To Be Or Not To Be: The Legal Ramifications Of The Cloning Of Human Embryos*, 21 Rutgers Computer & Tech. L.J. 189 (1995).

(4) For additional reading on the subjects in this section, see Newman, Essay, *Human Cloning and the Family: Reflections on Cloning Existing Children*, 13 N.Y.U. Sch. J. Hum. Rts. 523 (1997); Amer, Comment, *Breaking The Mold: Human Embryo Cloning and Its Implications for a Right to Individuality*, 43 UCLA L. Rev. 1659 (1996).

CHAPTER 5

ESTABLISHING LEGAL PARENTHOOD

SYNOPSIS

§ 5.01 Introduction
    [A] Historical Background
    [B] Current Perspectives
§ 5.02 Nonmarital Children and the Constitution
    [A] Inheritance Rights
    [B] Limitation of Paternity Actions
§ 5.03 Establishing Paternity
    [A] Scientific Testing
    [B] Res Judicata and Relitigation
    [C] Procedural Issues in Paternity Cases
§ 5.04 Imposing Parental Support Obligations
§ 5.05 Establishing Parental Rights
    [A] Presumptive Parents
    [B] Non-Presumptive Parents

§ 5.01 Introduction

[A] Historical Background

Throughout the history of the common law, marriage has been a primary determinant of legal parenthood. Thus, children born outside of marriage have been subject to different laws, different procedures, and different rights than children born to married parents.* At common law, the "illegitimate" child was looked upon as the son or daughter of no one, *filius nullius*. Such a child could therefore inherit from no one, and only an act of Parliament could confer legitimacy on such a child along with any inheritance rights. 1 Blackstone, Commentaries on the Law of England 459 (4th ed. 1899).

---

    * Over time, the legal system has used a variety of terms to refer to children born to unmarried parents. Early case law and statutes in this country commonly labeled such children "illegitimate." More recently, this label has been replaced by less stigmatizing terms such as nonmarital child or child born out of wedlock. Recognizing the power of naming, *see* Martha Minow, *The Supreme Court, 1986 Term—Foreword: Justice Engendered*, 101 Harv. L. Rev. 10, 61 (1987), we have chosen to use the modern terms wherever possible, except where prior terminology is necessary to preserve historical accuracy.

In the United States, the laws governing legal parenthood generally followed the English common law. Although reform efforts during the nineteenth century resulted in the acknowledgment of some legal ties between illegitimate children and their mothers, twentieth century legal doctrine continued to deny the connection between men and their nonmarital offspring, unless that connection was necessary to protect the public purse. Jana Singer, *The Privatization of Family Law*, 1992 Wisc. L. Rev. 1443, 1447. Similarly, state and federal programs designed to compensate families for the death or disability of a wage-earner typically excluded nonmarital children as eligible beneficiaries. A major justification for these sharp distinctions between marital and nonmarital children was to protect the exclusivity of the marital unit and to punish adults (particularly women) who engaged in sex outside of marriage. *Id.*, at 1448; *see* Mary Becker, *The Rights of Unwed Parents: Feminist Approaches*, 63 Soc. Serv. Rev. 496 (1989).

A series of Supreme Court decisions between 1968 and 1983 eliminated as unconstitutional most of the categorical legal distinctions between marital and nonmarital children. (*See* § 5.02, *below*.) These decisions explicitly rejected the traditional notion that differential treatment of "legitimate" and "illegitimate" offspring was justified as a way of encouraging matrimony and of expressing society's "condemnation of irresponsible liaisons beyond the bonds of marriage." *Weber v. Aetna Casualty & Surety Co.*, 406 U.S. 164, 175 (1972). A related series of Supreme Court decisions established that unmarried fathers who develop a relationship with their children are generally entitled to the same rights with respect to adoption and custody decisions as are mothers and marital fathers. (*See* § 5.05 *below*.) These judicial declarations were paralleled and reinforced by the Uniform Parentage Act, promulgated in 1973, and approved by the American Bar Association in 1974. The Act abandons the concept of legitimacy and declares that "[t]he parent and child relationship extends equally to every child and every parent, regardless of the marital status of the parents." Unif. Parentage Act § 2, 9B U.L.A. 296 (1987).

In reality, the economic and social circumstances of children born outside of marriage continue to be significantly more precarious that those of their marital counterparts. Moreover, some legal distinctions between marital and nonmarital children continue to exist. But the legal distinctions that remain are more likely to reflect the difficulties of proving paternity than they are to demarcate a separate and unequal legal status for children born outside of wedlock. *See, e.g., Lalli v. Lalli*, 439 U.S. 259 (1978) (relying on "peculiar problems of proof" in upholding New York intestate succession statute allowing illegitimate children to inherit from their father only where there had been an adjudication of paternity before the father's death).

[B] Current Perspectives

The law's historical coupling of marriage and parenthood reflected the widespread societal assumption that childbearing would take place almost exclusively within marriage. While this assumption may have been true a generation ago, it no longer reflects today's reality. As recently as 1960, only 5% of American children were born outside marriage. *See* Ralph C. Brashier, *Children and Inheritance in the Nontraditional Family*, 1996 Utah L. Rev. 93, 104. Today, close to 30% of American children are born to parents who are not married. *See* Amara Bachu, *Fertility of American Women; June 1994*, U.S. Bureau of the Census, Current Population Reports, P20–482 at v (1995). This percentage is comparable to the percentage of nonmarital births in other Western, industrialized countries, including Canada

(29%), the United Kingdom (31%) and France (33%). *Id.* In Denmark and Sweden, close to half of all births are to unmarried women. *Id.*

Policy makers and scholars have expressed a number of concerns about the increase in nonmarital childbearing. One set of concerns is economic. Critics of single parenthood emphasize that children born to unmarried parents are significantly more likely to be poor than are children born to married couples. In 1996, the poverty rate for families headed by a single mother was 32.6%, while the poverty rate for married-couple families was only 5.6%. U.S. Bureau of the Census, Current Population Reports, Series P-60–198, *Poverty in the United States: 1996*, at vii (Table A). Several conservative commentators have argued that unwed parenthood is the primary cause of poverty in the United States today. *E.g.*, Peter J. Ferrara, et. al, Social Breakdown in America, The Heritage Foundation Issues'94—The Candidates's Briefing Book, Jan. 1994, at 89; Charles Murray, *The Time Has Come to Put a Stigma Back on Illegitimacy*, Sacramento Bee, Nov. 7, 1993, at F1.

Other researchers suggest that single parenthood is more a consequence of poverty and joblessness, than a significant cause of it. Stephanie Coontz, The Way We Really Are: Coming To Terms With America's Changing Families 137–39 (Basic Books, 1997); William J. Wilson, *When Work Disappears*, New York Times Magazine, August 18, 1996. These writers attribute the economic disadvantages faced by single parent families to a market economy that ignores dependency and undervalues caregiving and to workplace structures that preclude adults from simultaneously caring for children and earning a decent market wage. *See, e.g.*, Martha A. Fineman, The Neutered Mother, The Sexual Family and Other Twentieth Century Tragedies (Routledge, 1995); Joan C. Williams, *Deconstructing Gender*, 87 Mich. L. Rev. 797 (1989).

A second set of concerns about single parenthood relates to the psychological well-being of children. A number of social scientists have recently argued that traditional fathers are essential to children, and that marriage is essential to fatherhood. *See, e.g.*, David Popenoe, Life Without Father: Compelling New Evidence That Fatherhood and Marriage Are Indispensable for the Good of Children and Society (Free Press, 1996); Wade F. Horn, *You've Come a Long Way, Daddy*, The Journal of American Citizenship Policy Review, July-August 1997 at 24. These researchers contend that children who grow up in homes without a biological father are at risk for a variety of social, behavioral and educational problems. *See* David Balankenhorn, Fatherless America: Confronting Our Most Urgent Social Problem (Basic Books, 1997). Other researchers dispute the persuasiveness of this evidence, suggesting that the risks associated with single parenthood are attributable largely to disparities in family income, as opposed to differences in family structure. *See, e.g.*, Nancy E. Dowd, In Defense of Single-Parent Families (N.Y.U. Press, 1997); Sara McLanahan & Gary Sandefur, Growing Up With A Single Parent: What Hurts, What Helps (Harvard University Press 1977). These writers also note that raising children in a marital family does not ensure that fathers will participate in childrearing, *see* Dowd, *above* at 28–39; nor do unmarried fathers invariably absent themselves from their children's lives. *See* Ronald B. Mincy and Hillard Pouncy, *There Must Be Fifty Ways to Start A Family: Social Policy and the Fragile Families of Low-Income, Noncustodial Fathers*, in The Fatherhood Movement: A Call To Action (Wade Horn, *et al.*, eds. 1997).

A third set of concerns about nonmarital parenthood might be characterized as cultural or moral. The primary argument behind these concerns is that separating childbearing from marriage undermines important cultural values and weakens society's moral fabric. *See, e.g.*, Bruce C. Hafen, *The Family as an Entity*, 22 U.C. Davis L. Rev. 865 (1989); Barbara D. Whitehead, *Dan Quayle Was Right*, The Atlantic Monthly, April 1993, at 47. Some writers also argue that the traditional, two-parent family performs an important political function and that the rise in nonmarital childbearing increases the risk of government overreaching. Hafen, *above* at 907; *see* David V. Hadek, *Why The Policy Behind the Irrebuttable Presumption of Paternity Will Never Die*, 26 Sw. U. L. Rev. 359, 395–97 (1997). Others challenge the moral vision that underlies these claims, characterizing it as repressive, misogynist, or exclusionary. *See, e.g.*, Dorothy Roberts, *The Value of Black Mother's Work*, 26 Conn. L. Rev. 871 (1994); Lucy A. Williams, *The Ideology of Division: Behavior Modification Welfare Reform Proposals*, 102 Yale L. J. 719 (1992); Martha A. Fineman, *Images of Mothers in Poverty Discourses*, 1991 Duke L.J. 274.

While debate over the causes and consequences of nonmarital childbearing is unlikely to end any time soon, the de facto uncoupling of marriage and parenthood has had important repercussions for family law. It has required courts and legislatures to grapple with issues ranging from the rights and obligations of unmarried fathers, to the use of DNA testing to establish paternity, to the continued validity of the marital presumption of paternity. The remaining sections of this chapter address these and other issues related to the establishment of legal parenthood.

§ 5.02 Nonmarital Children and the Constitution

[A] Inheritance Rights

Between 1968 and 1983, the Supreme Court decided more than 20 cases involving statutory distinctions based on illegitimacy. Many of these cases involved state inheritance schemes, which traditionally distinguished sharply between children born within and outside of marriage. The Court invalidated most—but not all—of these statutory distinctions. The two cases below illustrate the Court's evolving approach to these issues.

TRIMBLE v. GORDON
United States Supreme Court
430 U.S. 762 (1977)

Mr. Justice Powell delivered the opinion of the Court.

At issue in this case is the constitutionality of Section 12 of the Illinois Probate Act which allows illegitimate children to inherit by intestate succession only from their mothers. Under Illinois law, legitimate children are allowed to inherit by intestate succession from both their mothers and their fathers.

I

Appellant Deta Mona Trimble is the illegitimate daughter of appellant Jessie Trimble and Sherman Gordon. Trimble and Gordon lived in Chicago with Deta Mona from 1970 until Gordon died in 1974, the victim of a homicide. On January 2, 1973, the Circuit Court of Cook County, Ill., had entered a paternity order finding Gordon to be the father of Deta Mona and ordering him to pay $15 per week for her support. Gordon thereafter supported Deta Mona in accordance with the paternity order and openly acknowledged her as his child.

He died intestate at the age of 28, leaving an estate consisting only of a 1974 Plymouth automobile worth approximately $2,500.

Shortly after Gordon's death, Trimble, as the mother and next friend of Deta Mona, filed a petition for letters of administration, determination of heirship, and declaratory relief in the Probate Division of the Circuit Court of Cook County, Ill. That court entered an order determining heirship, identifying as the only heirs of Gordon his father, Joseph Gordon, his mother, Ethel King and his brother, two sisters, and a half-brother.

The Circuit Court excluded Deta Mona on the authority of the negative implications of § 12 of the Illinois Probate Act, which provides in relevant part: an illegitimate child is heir of his mother and of any maternal ancestor, and of any person from whom his mother might have inherited, if living.

If Deta Mona had been a legitimate child, she would have inherited her father's entire estate under Illinois law. In rejecting Deta Mona's claim of heirship, the court sustained the constitutionality of § 12.

On June 2, 1975, the Illinois Supreme Court handed down its opinion in *In re Estate of Karas*, sustaining § 12 against all constitutional challenges, including those presented in appellants' amicus brief. . . .

We noted probable jurisdiction to consider the arguments that § 12 violates the Equal Protection Clause of the Fourteenth Amendment by invidiously discriminating on the basis of illegitimacy and sex. We now reverse. As we conclude that the statutory discrimination against illegitimate children is unconstitutional, we do not reach the sex discrimination argument.

II

In *Karas*, the Illinois Supreme Court rejected the equal protection challenge to the discrimination against illegitimate children. The court found that § 12 is supported by the state interests in encouraging family relationships and in establishing an accurate and efficient method of disposing of property at death. The court also found the Illinois law unobjectionable because no "insurmountable barrier" prevented illegitimate children from sharing in the estates of their fathers. By leaving a will, Sherman Gordon could have assured Deta Mona a share of his estate.

Appellees endorse the reasoning of the Illinois Supreme Court and suggest additional justifications for the statute. In weighing the constitutional sufficiency of these justifications, we are guided by our previous decisions involving equal protection challenges to laws discriminating on the basis of illegitimacy. "[T]his Court requires, at a minimum, that a statutory classification bear some rational relationship to a legitimate state purpose." *Weber v. Aetna Casualty & Surety Co.,* 406 U.S. 164, 172 (1972) In this context, the standard just stated is a minimum; the Court sometimes requires more. "Though the latitude given state economic and social regulation is necessarily broad, when state statutory classifications approach sensitive and fundamental personal rights, this Court exercises a stricter scrutiny. . . ." *Ibid.*

Appellants urge us to hold that classifications based on illegitimacy are "suspect," so that any justifications must survive "strict scrutiny." We considered and rejected a similar argument last Term in *Mathews v. Lucas*, 427 U.S. 495 (1976). As we recognized in Lucas, illegitimacy is analogous in many respects to the personal characteristics that have been held to be suspect when used as the basis of statutory differentiations. *Id.*, at 505. We nevertheless concluded that the analogy was not sufficient to require "our most exacting scrutiny." *Id.*, at 506. Despite the conclusion that classifications based on illegitimacy fall in a "realm of less than strictest scrutiny," *Lucas* also establishes that the scrutiny "is not a toothless one" . . . .

III

[T]he [Illinois Supreme C]ourt concluded that the statute was enacted to ameliorate the harsh common-law rule under which an illegitimate child was *filius nullius* and incapable of inheriting from anyone. Although § 12 did not bring illegitimate children into parity with legitimate children, it did improve their position, thus partially achieving the asserted objective.

A

The Illinois Supreme Court relied in part on the State's purported interest in "the promotion of [legitimate] family relationships." 61 Ill.2d at 48, 329 N.E.2d at 238. Although, the court noted that this justification had been accepted in *Labine*, the opinion contains only the most perfunctory analysis. This inattention may not have been an oversight, for § 12 bears only the most attenuated relationship to the asserted goal.

In a case like this, the Equal Protection Clause requires more than the mere incantation of a proper state purpose. No one disputes the appropriateness of Illinois' concern with the family unit, perhaps the most fundamental social institution of our society. The flaw in the analysis lies elsewhere. As we said in *Lucas*, the constitutionality of this law "depends upon the character of the discrimination and its relation to legitimate legislative aims." 427 U.S., at 504. The court below did not address the relation between § 12 and the promotion of legitimate family relationships, thus leaving the constitutional analysis incomplete.

In *Weber* we examined a Louisiana workmen's compensation law which discriminated against one class of illegitimate children. Without questioning Louisiana's interest in protecting legitimate family relationships, we rejected the argument that "persons will shun illicit relations because the offspring may not one day reap the benefits of workmen's compensation." 406 U.S., at 173. . . .

> The status of illegitimacy has expressed through the ages society's condemnation of irresponsible liaisons beyond the bonds of marriage. But visiting this condemnation on the head of an infant is illogical and unjust. Moreover, imposing disabilities on the illegitimate child is contrary to the basis concept of our system that legal burdens should bear some relationship to individual responsibility or wrongdoing. Obviously, no child is responsible for his birth and penalizing the illegitimate child is an ineffectual as well as unjust way of deterring the parent.

[*Weber*, *supra*], 406 U.S. at 175. The parents have the ability to conform their conduct to societal norms, but their illegitimate children can affect neither their parents' conduct nor their own status.

B

The Illinois Supreme Court relied on *Labine* for another and more substantial justification: the State's interest in "establish[ing] a method of property disposition." Focusing specifically on the difficulty of proving paternity and the related danger of spurious claims, the court concluded that this interest explained and justified the asymmetrical statutory discrimination against the illegitimate children of intestate men. The more favorable treatment of illegitimate children claiming from their mothers' estates was justified because "proof of a lineal relationship is more readily ascertainable when dealing with maternal ancestors." 61 Ill.2d at 52, 329 N.E.2d 240.

We think, however, that the Illinois Supreme Court gave inadequate consideration to the relation between § 12 and the State's proper objective of assuring accuracy and efficiency in the disposition of property at death. The court failed to consider the possibility of a middle ground between the extremes of complete exclusion and case-by-case determination of paternity. For at least some significant categories of illegitimate children of intestate men, inheritance rights can be recognized without jeopardizing the orderly settlement of estates or the dependability of titles to property passing under intestacy laws. Because it excludes those categories of illegitimate children unnecessarily, § 12 is constitutionally flawed. . . .

The judicial task here is the difficult one of vindicating constitutional rights without interfering unduly with the State's primary responsibility in this area. Our previous decisions demonstrate a sensitivity to "the lurking problems with respect to proof of paternity," *Gomez v. Perez*, 409 U.S. 535, 538 (1973), and the need for the States to draw arbitrary lines to facilitate potentially difficult problems of proof," *Weber*, 406 U.S. at 174. "Those problems are not to be lightly brushed aside, but neither can they be made into an impenetrable barrier that works to shield otherwise invidious discrimination." *Gomez, supra*, at 538.

In [*Lucas* we sustained provisions of the Social Security Act governing the eligibility for surviving children's insurance benefits. One of the statutory conditions of eligibility was dependency on the deceased wage earner . . . . Although the Act presumed dependency for a number of categories of children, including some categories of illegitimate children, it required that the remaining illegitimate children prove actual dependency. The Court upheld the statutory classifications, finding them "reasonably related to the likelihood of dependency at death." Central to this decision was the finding that the "statute does not broadly discriminate between legitimates and illegitimates without more, but is carefully tuned to alternative considerations."

Although the present case arises in a context different from that in *Lucas*, the question whether the statute "is carefully tuned to alternative considerations" is equally applicable here. We conclude that § 12 does not meet this standard. Difficulties of proving paternity in some situations do not justify the total statutory disinheritance of illegitimate children whose fathers die intestate. The facts of this case graphically illustrate the constitutional defect of § 12. Sherman Gordon was found to be the father of Deta Mona in a state court paternity action prior to his death. On the strength of that finding, he was ordered to contribute to the support of his child. That adjudication should be equally sufficient to establish Deta Mona's right to claim a child's share of Gordon's estate, for the State's interest in the accurate and efficient disposition of property at death would not be compromised in any way by allowing her claim in these circumstances.

C

The Illinois Supreme Court also noted that the decedents whose estate were involved in the consolidated appeals could have left substantial parts of their estates to their illegitimate children by writing a will. The court cited *Labine* as authority for the proposition that such a possibility is constitutionally significant. The Court then listed three different steps that would have resulted in some recovery by Labine's illegitimate daughter. Labine could have left a will; he could have legitimated the daughter by marrying her mother; and he could have given the daughter the status of a legitimate child by stating in his acknowledgment of paternity his desire to legitimate her.

Despite its appearance in two of our opinions, the focus on the presence or absence of an insurmountable barrier is somewhat of an analytical anomaly. Here as in *Labine*, the question is the constitutionality of a state intestate succession law that treats illegitimate children differently from legitimate children. Traditional equal protection analysis asks whether this statutory differentiation on the basis of illegitimacy is justified by the promotion of recognized state objectives. If the law cannot be sustained on this analysis, it is not clear how it can be saved by the absence of an insurmountable barrier to inheritance under other and hypothetical circumstances.

By focusing on the steps that an intestate might have taken to assure some inheritance for his illegitimate children, the analysis loses sight of the essential question: the constitutionality of discrimination against illegitimates in a state intestate succession law. If the decedent had written a will devising property to his illegitimate child, the case no longer would involve intestate succession law at all. Similarly, if the decedent had legitimated the child by marrying the child's mother or by complying with the requirements of some other method of legitimation, the case no longer would involve discrimination against illegitimates. Hard questions cannot be avoided by hypothetical reshuffling of the facts.

D

Finally, appellees urge us to affirm the decision below on the theory that the Illinois Probate Act, including § 12, mirrors the presumed intentions of the citizens of the State regarding the disposition of their property at death. Individualizing this theory, appellees argue that we must assume that Sherman Gordon knew the disposition of his estate under the Illinois Probate Act and that his failure to make a will shows his approval of that disposition. We need not resolve the question whether presumed intent alone can ever justify discrimination against illegitimates, for we do not think that § 12 was enacted for this purpose. The theory of presumed intent is not relied upon in the careful opinion of the Illinois Supreme Court examining both the history and the text of § 12. This omission is not without significance, as one would expect a state supreme court to identify the state interests served by a statute of its state legislature. Our own examination of § 12 convinces us that the statutory provisions at issue were shaped by forces other than the desire of the legislature to mirror the intentions of the citizens of the State with respect to their illegitimate children.

The difference in § 12 between the rights of illegitimate children in the estates of their fathers and mothers, however, is more convincingly explained by the other factors mentioned by the court below. Accepting in this respect the views of the Illinois Supreme Court, we find in § 12 a primary purpose to provide a system of intestate succession more just to illegitimate children than the prior law, a purpose tempered by a secondary interest in protecting against spurious claims of paternity. In the absence of a more convincing demonstration, we will not hypothesize an additional state purpose that has been ignored by the Illinois Supreme Court.

IV

For the reasons stated above, we conclude that § 12 of the Illinois Probate Act cannot be squared with the command of the Equal Protection Clause of the Fourteenth Amendment. Accordingly, we reverse the judgment of the Illinois Supreme Court and remand the case for further proceedings not inconsistent with this opinion.

PARHAM v. HUGHES
United States Supreme Court
441 U.S. 347 (1979)

MR. JUSTICE STEWART announced the judgment of the Court and delivered an opinion, in which THE CHIEF JUSTICE, MR. JUSTICE REHNQUIST and MR. JUSTICE STEVENS joined.

Under § 105–1307 of the Georgia Code (1978) (hereinafter Georgia statute), the mother of an illegitimate child can sue for the wrongful death of that child. A father who has legitimated a child can also sue for the wrongful death of the child if there is no mother. A father who has not legitimated a child, however, is precluded from maintaining a wrongful death action. The question presented in this case is whether this statutory scheme violates the Equal Protection or Due Process Clause of the Fourteenth Amendment by denying the father of an illegitimate child who has not legitimated the child the right to sue for the child's wrongful death.

I

The appellant was the biological father of Lemuel Parham, a minor child who was killed in an automobile collision. The child's mother, Cassandra Moreen, was killed in the same collision. The appellant and Moreen were never married to each other, and the appellant did not legitimate the child as he could have done under Georgia law. The appellant did, however, sign the child's birth certificate and contribute to his support. The child took the appellant's name and was visited by the appellant on a regular basis.

After the child was killed in the automobile collision, the appellant brought an action seeking to recover for the allegedly wrongful death. The complaint named the appellee (the driver of the other automobile involved in the collision) as the defendant, and charged that negligence on the part of the appellee had caused the death of the child. The child's maternal grandmother, acting as administratrix of his estate, also brought a lawsuit against the appellee to recover for the child's wrongful death.

The appellee filed a motion for summary judgment in the present case, asserting that under the Georgia statute the appellant was precluded from recovering for his illegitimate child's wrongful death. The trial court held that the Georgia statute violated both the Due Process and Equal Protection Clauses of the Fourteenth Amendment and, accordingly, denied a summary judgment in favor of the appellee. On appeal, the Georgia Supreme Court reversed the ruling of the trial court. 241 Ga. 198, 243 S. E. 2d 867. The appellate court found that the statutory classification was rationally related to three legitimate state interests: (1) the interest in avoiding difficult problems of proving paternity in wrongful death actions; (2) the interest in promoting a legitimate family unit; and (3) the interest in setting a standard of morality by not according to the father of an illegitimate child the statutory right to sue for the child's death. Accordingly, the court held that the statute did not violate either the Equal Protection or Due Process Clause of the Fourteenth Amendment. We noted probable jurisdiction. . . .

II

State laws are generally entitled to a presumption of validity against attack under the Equal Protection Clause. Legislatures have wide discretion in passing laws that have the inevitable effect of treating some people differently from others, and legislative classifications are valid unless they bear no rational relationship to a permissible state objective. . . .

Not all legislation, however, is entitled to the same presumption of validity. The presumption is not present when a State has enacted legislation whose purpose or effect is to create classes based upon racial criteria, since racial classifications, in a constitutional sense, are inherently "suspect." And the presumption of statutory validity may also be undermined when a State has enacted legislation creating classes based upon certain other immutable human attributes. See, e. g., *Oyama v. California*, 332 U.S. 633 (national origin); *Graham v. Richardson*, 403 U.S. 365 (alienage); *Gomez v. Perez*, 409 U.S. 535 (illegitimacy); *Reed v. Reed*, 404 U.S. 71 (gender).

In the absence of invidious discrimination, however, a court is not free under he aegis of the Equal Protection Clause to substitute its judgment for the will of the people of a State as expressed in the laws passed by their popularly elected legislatures. . . . The threshold question, therefore, is whether the Georgia statute is invidiously discriminatory. If it is not, it is entitled to a presumption of validity and will be upheld "unless the varying treatment of different groups or persons is so unrelated to the achievement of any combination of legitimate purposes that we can only conclude that the legislature's actions were irrational." *Ibid.*

III

The appellant relies on decisions of the Court that have invalidated statutory classifications based upon illegitimacy and upon gender to support his claim that the Georgia statute is unconstitutional. Both of these lines of cases have involved laws reflecting invidious discrimination against a particular class. We conclude, however, that neither line of decisions is applicable in the present case.

A

The Court has held on several occasions that state legislative classifications based upon illegitimacy—i.e., that differentiate between illegitimate children and legitimate children—violate the Equal Protection Clause. *E. g., Trimble v. Gordon*, 430 U.S. 762; *Weber v. Aetna Casualty & Surety Co.*, 406 U.S. 164 n.5. The basic rationale of these decisions is that it is unjust and ineffective for society to express its condemnation of procreation outside the marital relationship by punishing the illegitimate child who is in no way responsible for his situation and is unable to change it. . . .

It is apparent that this rationale is in no way applicable to the Georgia statute now before us. The statute does not impose differing burdens or award differing benefits to legitimate and illegitimate children. It simply denies a natural father the right to sue for his illegitimate child's wrongful death. The appellant, as the natural father, was responsible for conceiving an illegitimate child and had the opportunity to legitimate the child but failed to do so. . . . Unlike the illegitimate child for whom the status of illegitimacy is involuntary and immutable, the appellant here was responsible for fostering an illegitimate child and for failing to change its status. It is thus neither illogical nor unjust for society to express its "condemnation of irresponsible liaisons beyond the bounds of marriage" by not conferring upon a biological father the statutory right to sue for the wrongful death of his illegitimate child. The justifications for judicial sensitivity to the constitutionality of differing legislative treatment of legitimate and illegitimate children are simply absent when a classification affects only the fathers of deceased illegitimate children.

B

The Court has also held that certain classifications based upon sex are invalid under the Equal Protection Clause, e.g., *Reed v. Reed*, 404 U.S. 71; *Stanton v. Stanton*, 421 U.S. 7; *Frontiero v. Richardson*, 411 U.S. 677; *Craig v. Boren*, 429 U.S. 190. Underlying these decisions is the principle that a State is not free to make overbroad generalizations based on sex which are entirely unrelated to any differences between men and women or which demean the ability or social status of the affected class. . . .

In cases where men and women are not similarly situated, however, and a statutory classification is realistically based upon the differences in their situations, this Court has upheld its validity. . . .

With these principles in mind, it is clear that the Georgia statute does not invidiously discriminate against the appellant simply because he is of the male sex. The fact is that mothers and fathers of illegitimate children are not similarly situated. Under Georgia law, only a father can by voluntary unilateral action make an illegitimate child legitimate. Unlike the mother of an illegitimate child whose identity will rarely be in doubt, the identity of the father will frequently be unknown. . . .

Thus, the conferral of the right of a natural father to sue for the wrongful death of his child only if he has previously acted to identify himself, undertake his paternal responsibilities, and make his child legitimate, does not reflect any overbroad generalizations about men as a class, but rather the reality that in Georgia only a father can by unilateral action legitimate an illegitimate child. Since fathers who do legitimate their children can sue for wrongful death in precisely the same circumstances as married fathers whose children were legitimate ab initio, the statutory classification does not discriminate against fathers as a class but instead distinguishes between fathers who have legitimated their children and those who have not. Such a classification is quite unlike those condemned in the *Reed, Frontiero,* and *Stanton* cases which were premised upon overbroad generalizations and excluded all members of one sex even though they were similarly situated with members of the other sex.

IV

Having concluded that the Georgia statute does not invidiously discriminate against any class, we still must determine whether the statutory classification is rationally related to a permissible state objective.

This Court has frequently recognized that a State has a legitimate interest in the maintenance of an accurate and efficient system for the disposition of property at death. Of particular concern to the State is the existence of some mechanism for dealing with "the often difficult problem of proving the paternity of illegitimate children and the related danger of spurious claims against intestate estates." *Lalli v. Lalli, supra*, at 265. *See also Gomez v. Perez*, 409 U.S., at 538.

This same state interest in avoiding fraudulent claims of paternity in order to maintain a fair and orderly system of decedent's property disposition is also present in the context of actions for wrongful death. If paternity has not been established before the commencement of a wrongful-death action, a defendant may be faced with the possibility of multiple lawsuits by individuals all claiming to be the father of the deceased child. Such uncertainty would make it difficult if not impossible for a defendant to settle a wrongful-death action in many cases, since there would always exist the risk of a subsequent suit by another person claiming to be the father. The State of Georgia has chosen to deal with this problem by allowing only fathers who have established their paternity by legitimating their children to sue for wrongful death, and we cannot say that this solution is an irrational one.

The appellant argues, however, that whatever may be the problem with establishing paternity generally, there is no question in this case that he is the father. This argument misconceives the basic principle of the Equal Protection Clause. The function of that provision of the Constitution is to measure the validity of classifications created by state laws. Since we have concluded that the classification created by the Georgia statute is a rational means for dealing with the problem of proving paternity, it is constitutionally irrelevant that the appellant may be able to prove paternity in another manner.

V

The appellant also alleges that the Georgia statute violates the Due Process Clause of the Fourteenth Amendment. Nowhere in the appellant's brief or oral argument, however, is there any explanation of how the Due Process Clause is implicated in this case. The only decision of this Court cited by the appellant that is even remotely related to his due process claim is Stanley v. Illinois, 405 U.S. 645. In the Stanley case, the Court held that a father of illegitimate children who had raised these children was entitled to a hearing on his fitness as a parent before they could be taken from him by the State of Illinois. The interests which the Court found controlling in Stanley were the integrity of the family against state interference and the freedom of a father to raise his own children. The present case is quite a different one, involving as it does only an asserted right to sue for money damages.

For these reasons, the judgment of the Supreme Court of Georgia is affirmed.

NOTES AND QUESTIONS

(1) Both *Trimble* and *Parham* were five–four decisions. Most of the Justices who dissented in *Trimble* joined the majority opinion in *Parham*. Justice Powell concurred

specially in *Parham* on the ground that the gender-based distinction in the Georgia statute was substantially related to the important state objective "of avoiding difficult problems in proving paternity after the death of an illegitimate child." 441 U.S. at 359–60 (Powell, J., concurring).

(2) Are these two decisions consistent? Why or why not? Can you formulate a legal rule or principle that encompasses both decisions?

(3) What standard of review does the Supreme Court employ in each of these cases to evaluate the plaintiffs' equal protection claims?

(4) In *Glona v. American Guarantee & Liability Insurance Company*, 391 U.S. 73 (1968), the Supreme Court invalidated a Louisiana statute that did not allow the natural mother of an illegitimate child to sue for the child's wrongful death. Three Justices dissented, noting that the mother in *Glona* had failed to pursue a statutory procedure whereby she could have legitimated her child and thus become eligible to sue for the child's death. The majority in *Parham* distinguished *Glona* on the ground that "[t]he invidious discrimination perceived in that case was between married and unmarried mothers. There thus existed no real problem of identity or of fraudulent claims." *Parham*, 441 U.S. at 356 n.7. How do the advances in scientific testing for paternity, discussed at § 5.03[A], *below*, bear on this aspect of the Court's reasoning?

(5) Subsequent to the Court's decision in *Parham*, Georgia amended its inheritance statutes to provide several methods by which an unmarried father may establish paternity, and thereby become eligible to inherit from his illegitimate child. Ga. Code Ann. § 53–4–5 (1997).

(6) **Problem.** Victor and Rose lived together for 12 years, but never married. During that time, Rose gave birth to two children, now ages 10 and 8. Victor was named as the father on both children's birth certificates, and he supported the children from his earnings as a police officer. Victor never obtained an order of filiation or a declaration of paternity, even though state law permitted him to do so. Last year, Victor was killed by a robbery suspect in the line of duty. Pursuant to department policy, the police department collected blood samples from Victor for internal purposes. Rose has now applied for survivors' benefits from the state on behalf of her children. Blood tests performed on the department's samples indicates a 99.99% probability that Victor is the biological father of Rose's children. However, the state has denied benefits pursuant to a statute that provides that the illegitimate child of a state employee is eligible for survivor's benefits only if there has been a judgment of filiation or paternity during the lifetime of the employee. Is this statute constitutional? Why or why not? *See Lalli v. Lalli*, 439 U.S. 259 (1978).

[B] Limitation of Paternity Actions

CLARK v. JETER
United States Supreme Court
486 U.S. 456 (1988)

O'CONNOR, J. delivered the opinion of the Court.

Under Pennsylvania law, an illegitimate child must prove paternity before seeking support from his or her father and a suit to establish paternity ordinarily must be brought within six years of an illegitimate child's birth. By contrast, a legitimate child may seek support from his or her parents at any time. We granted certiorari to consider the constitutionality of this legislative scheme.

I

On September 22, 1983, petitioner Cherlyn Clark filed a support complaint in the Allegheny county Court of Common Please on behalf of her minor daughter, Tiffany, who was born out of wedlock on June 11, 1973. Clark named respondent Gene Jeter as Tiffany's father. The court ordered blood tests, which showed a 99.3% probability that Jeter if Tiffany's father.

Jeter moved to dismiss the complaint on the ground that it was barred by the six-year statute of limitations for paternity actions. In her response, Clark contended that this statute is unconstitutional under the Equal Protection and Due Process Clauses of the Fourteenth Amendment. . . .

The trial court upheld the statute of limitations . . . .

Clark appealed to the Superior Court of Pennsylvania, again raising her constitutional challenges to the six-year statute of limitations. Before the court decided her case, the Pennsylvania Legislature enacted an 18-year statute of limitations for actions to establish paternity . . . . Pennsylvania thereby brought its law into compliance with a provision of the federal child Support Enforcement Amendments of 1984 that requires all States participating in the federal child support program to have procedures to establish the paternity of any child who is less than 18 years old. . . . The Superior Court concluded, however, that Pennsylvania's new 18-year statute of limitations did not apply retroactively, and that it would not revive Clark's cause of action in any event. . . .

II

Clark's first argument to this Court is that Pennsylvania's six-year statute of limitations is invalid because it conflicts with the federal Child Support Enforcement Amendments of 1984, which she says require States to adopt retroactive 18-year statutes of limitations in paternity cases. Having reviewed the record, however, we find that Clark did not adequately present a federal preemption argument to the lower courts. . . .

In considering whether state legislation violates the Equal Protection Clause of the Fourteenth Amendment, we apply different levels of scrutiny to different types of classifications. At a minimum, a statutory classification must be rationally related to a legitimate governmental purpose. Classifications based on race or national origins, *e.g. Loving v. Virginia*, 388 U.S. 1, 11 (1973), *Lyng v. Automobile Workers*, 485 U.S. 360 (1988), and classifications affecting fundamental rights, *e.g. Harper v. Virginia Bd. of Elections*, 383 U.S. 663, 672 (1966), are given the most exacting scrutiny. Between these extremes of rational basis review and strict scrutiny lies a level of intermediate scrutiny, which generally has been applied to discriminatory classifications based on sex or illegitimacy.

To withstand intermediate scrutiny, a statutory classification must be substantially related to an important governmental objective. Consequently we have invalidated classifications that burden illegitimate children for the sake of punishing the illicit relations of their parents, because "visiting this condemnation the head of an infant is illogical and unjust." *Weber v. Aetna Casualty & Surety Co.*, 406 U.S. 164, 175 (1972). Yet in the seminal case concerning the child's right to support, this Court acknowledged that it might be appropriate to treat illegitimate children differently in the support context because of "lurking problems with respect to proof of paternity". *Gomez v. Perez*, 409 U.S. 535, 538 (1973).

This Court has developed a particular framework for evaluating equal protection challenges to statutes of limitations that apply to suits to establish paternity and hereby limit the ability of illegitimate children to obtain support. "First, the period for obtaining support must be sufficiently long in duration to present a reasonable opportunity for those with an interest in such children to assert claims on their behalf. Second, any time limitation placed on that opportunity must be substantially related to the State's interest in avoiding the litigation of stale or fraudulent claims." *Mills v. Habluetzel*, 456 U.S. 91, 99–100 (1982).

In *Mills*, we held that the Texas' one-year statute of limitations failed both steps of the analysis. We explained that paternity suits typically will be brought by the child's mother, who might not act swiftly amidst the emotional and financial complications of the child's first year. And, it is unlikely that the lapse of a mere 12 months will result in the loss of evidence or appreciably increase the likelihood of fraudulent claims. A concurring opinion in Mills explained why statutes of limitations longer than one year also may be unconstitutional. First, the State has a countervailing interest in ensuring that genuine claims for child support are satisfied. Second, the fact that Texas tolled most other causes of action during a child's minority suggest that proof problems do not become overwhelming during this period. Finally, the practical obstacles to filing a claim for support are likely to continue after the first year of the child's life.

In *Pickett v. Brown*, 462 U.S. 1 (1983), the Court unanimously struck down Tennessee's two-year statute of limitations for paternity and child support actions brought on behalf of certain illegitimate children. Adhering to the analysis developed in *Mills*, the Court first considered whether two years afforded a reasonable opportunity to bring such suits. The Tennessee statute was relatively more generous than the Texas statute considered in *Mills* because it did not limit actions against a father who had acknowledged his paternity in writing or by furnishing support; not did it apply if the child was likely to become a public charge. Nevertheless, the Court concluded that the two-year period was too short. Proceeding to the second step of the analysis, the Court decided that the two-year statute of limitations was not substantially related to Tennessee's asserted interest in preventing stale and fraudulent claims. The period during which suit could be brought was only a year longer than the period considered in Mills, and this incremental difference would not create substantially greater proof and fraud problems. Furthermore, Tennessee tolled most other actions during a child's minority, and even permitted a support action to be brought on behalf of a child up to 18 years of age if the child was or was likely to become a public charge. Finally, scientific advances in blood testing had alleviated some problem of proof in paternity actions. For these reasons, the Tennessee statute failed to survive heightened scrutiny under the Equal Protection Clause.

In light of this authority, we conclude that Pennsylvania's six-year state of limitations violates the Equal Protection Clause. Even six years does not necessarily provide a reasonable opportunity to assert a claim on behalf of an illegitimate child. "The unwillingness of the mother to file a paternity action on behalf of her child, which could stem from her relationship with the natural father or . . . from the emotional strain of having an illegitimate child, or even from the desire to avoid community and family disapproval, may continue years after the child is born. The problem may be exacerbated if, as often happens, the mother herself is a minor." *Mills, supra*, at 105, n.4 (O'Connor, J., concurring). Not all of these difficulties are likely to abate in six years. . . . Furthermore, financial difficulties are likely to increase as the child matures and incurs expenses for clothing, school and medical care. Thus it is questionable whether a State acts reasonably when it requires most paternity and support actions to be brought within six years of an illegitimate child's birth.

We do not rest our decision on this ground, however, for it is not entirely evident that six years would necessarily be an unreasonable limitations period for child support actions involving illegitimate children. We are, however, confident that the six-year statute of limitations is not substantially related to Pennsylvania's interest in avoiding the litigation of stale or fraudulent claims. In a number of circumstances, Pennsylvania permits the issue of paternity to be litigated more than six years after the birth of an illegitimate child. The statute itself permits a suit to be brought more than six years after the child's birth if it is brought within two years of a support payment made by the father. And in other types of suits, Pennsylvania places no limits on when the issue of paternity may be litigated. For example, the intestacy statute permits permits a child born out of wedlock to establish paternity as long as "there is clear and convincing evidence that the man was the father of the child." Likewise, no statute of limitations applies to a father's action to establish paternity. Recently, the Pennsylvania Legislature enacted a statute that tolls most other civil actions during a child's minority. In *Pickett* and *Mills* similar tolling statutes cast doubt on the State's purposed interest in avoiding the litigation of stale or fraudulent claims. Pennsylvania's tolling statute has the same implications here.

A more recent indication that Pennsylvania does not consider proof problems insurmountable, is the enactment by the Pennsylvania Legislature in 1985 of an 18-year statute of limitations for paternity and support actions. . . . The legislative history of the federal Child Support Enforcement Amendments explains why Congress thought such statutes of limitations are reasonable. Congress adverted to the problem of stale and fraudulent claims but recognized that increasingly sophisticated tests for genetic markers permit the exclusion of over 99% of those who might be accused of paternity, regardless of the age of the child. This scientific evidence is available throughout the child's minority, and it is an additional reason to doubt that Pennsylvania had a substantial reason for limiting the time within which paternity and support actions could be brought.

We conclude that the Pennsylvania statute does not withstand heightened scrutiny under the Equal Protection Clause. We therefore find it unnecessary to reach Clark's due process claim. The judgment of the Superior Court is reversed, and the case is remanded for further proceedings not inconsistent with this opinion.

NOTES AND QUESTIONS

(1) Unlike the close decisions in *Trimble* and *Parham*, the Supreme Court's decision in *Jeter* was unanimous. Has the Supreme Court now clarified its approach to statutory classifications based on illegitimacy? How would you describe that approach?

(2) As the Court's opinion in *Jeter* suggests, the federal government has become increasingly involved in the area of paternity establishment. *See* § 5.03, *below*. What underlies the federal government's interest in this area?

(3) In *Miller v. Allbright,* 118 S.Ct. 1428 (1998), the Supreme Court rejected an equal protection challenge to an immigration statute that imposed additional citizenship requirements on non-marital children born abroad, where the father, rather than the mother, was an American citizen. In particular, the statute required that children born abroad to an alien mother and an American father obtain formal proof of paternity before age 18 in order to qualify for citizenship, while non-marital children born abroad to an alien father and an American mother automatically acquired citizenship at birth. The Court rejected the argument that this differential treatment of unmarried mothers and fathers constituted unlawful discrimination based on sex. Justice Stevens, who authored the lead opinion, emphasized the importance of ensuring reliable proof of a biological relationship between a potential citizen and its citizen parent, and he reasoned that men and women were differently situated with respect to this objective in several pertinent respects. 118 S.Ct. at 1438. These biological differences, Stevens concluded, provided a legitimate basis for different rules governing the ability of unmarried male and female parents to confer citizenship on children. *Id.* at 1442. Stevens also rejected the argument that the advent of reliable genetic testing had undermined the rationality of requiring formal acknowledgment of paternity during the minority of a child. *Id.* at 1438. Three Justices dissented on the ground that the gender-based classification in the statute lacked the "exceedingly persuasive" justification required by the Constitution. 118 at 1463 (Breyer, J., dissenting).

§ 5.03 Establishing Paternity

[A] Scientific Testing

As the Supreme Court suggested in *Clark v. Jeter*, the development of increasingly sophisticated scientific testing has significantly enhanced our ability to determine paternity. Traditionally, blood test and other scientific evidence could be used in paternity proceedings only to "exclude" an alleged father—that is, to show that he could *not* have fathered the child in question. *See* D.H. Kaye, *Plemel As A Primer On Proving Paternity*, 24 Willamette L. Rev. 867 (1988). This traditional rule made sense at a time when the scientific techniques in question could exclude only a moderate portion of the male population as the father. *Id.* at 867–68. With the emergence in the 1980's of new types of blood and genetic testing (primarily HLA typing), which could exclude more than 90% of the male population in most cases, this traditional limitation on the use of scientific evidence began to crumble. *See* S. Joel Kolko, *Admissibility of HLA Tests Results to Determine Paternity*, 9 Fam. L. Rptr. 4009 (1983).

In light of these scientific developments, virtually all states now provide for the introduction of genetic and other blood test evidence for the purpose of affirmatively proving paternity, as well as for the purpose of excluding an alleged father. *See* D. H. Kaye & Ronald Kanwischer, *Admissibility of Genetic Testing in Paternity Litigation: A Survey of State Statutes*, 22 Fam. L. Q. 109 (1988). For example, Section 12 of the Uniform Parentage Act, which has been adopted in 18 states, provides that evidence relating to paternity may include, *inter alia*, "blood test results, weighted in accordance with evidence, if available, of the statistical probability of the alleged father's paternity." 9B U.L.A. 317 (1987).

While modern genetic and blood test evidence can be a powerful tool in establishing paternity, the statistical assumptions and scientific methodology used to assess and present this evidence have created a number of difficulties for courts. The following case illustrates some of these difficulties.

IN RE PATERNITY OF M.J.B.
Supreme Court of Wisconsin
425 N.W. 2d 404 (1988)

STEINMETZ J.

. . . The primary issue in the case is whether a defendant in a paternity action may challenge the validity of a genetic blood test report for the first time in closing argument. The court of appeals answered this issue in the affirmative. This case also raises the issue of whether a jury may consider the report of a genetic blood test in determining whether sexual intercourse took place between the mother and the alleged father at a time when the child could have been conceived. . . .

Finally, this case presents the question of whether a jury must make a separate finding by clear, satisfactory and convincing evidence that sexual intercourse took place between the mother and putative father before the jury may consider the blood test report. Although the parties did not raise or discuss this issue, the court of appeals held that an independent finding of sexual intercourse was required before the jury could consider the statistical chance of paternity as evidence of paternity.

In this paternity action, R.E.B. was adjudged the father of M.J.B. The child's mother, T.A.T., gave birth to M.J.B. on December 19, 1984, and subsequently filed this paternity action. . . .

Because the child weighed more than five and one-half pounds at birth, the circuit court took judicial notice that the child was conceived between February 21, 1984, and April 22, 1984. T.A.T. testified that she had sexual intercourse exclusively with R.E.B. during the statutory conception period and that she had sexual intercourse with him between March 17, 1984 and March 24, 1984.

R.E.B. admitted that he had sexual intercourse with T.A.T. but stated that this intercourse did not occur during the statutory conception period. Specifically, R.E.B. testified that he only dated T.A.T. until February 14, 1984, approximately one week prior to the earliest date of the statutory conception period. On February 17, 1984, R.E.B. began courting another woman who testified that both R.E.B. and T.A.T. had communicated separately to her that R.E.B. had not dated or seen T.A.T. after February 17, 1984.

Pursuant to sec. 767.48(1), Stats., T.A.T. introduced an HLA (Human Leukocyte Antigen) blood test report from the American Red Cross histocompatibility laboratory without accompanying expert testimony. The report, based upon raw data obtained from blood samples of the mother, the child and the alleged father, stated the following:

> "[R.E.B.] cannot be excluded as the father of [M.J.B.] The cumulative paternity index (genetic odds in favor of paternity) is 218. The relative chance of paternity, assuming a 50% prior chance, is 99.54%. Paternity is extremely likely.
>
> "98.99% of falsely accused men would be excluded as the father."

In the report, the testing agency did not explain how it computed the relative chance of paternity, did not indicate that it had any factual basis for the assumption of a "50% prior chance" and did not explain the meaning of a "50% prior chance."

R.E.B. offered no evidence or expert testimony to rebut the HLA blood test report or its presumption of a fifty percent prior chance of sexual intercourse. Prior to closing argument, the parties stipulated to allowing R.E.B. to argue that there was no basis in the record or within the blood test report to support the fifty percent prior chance assumption. Notwithstanding the stipulation, the circuit court barred R.E.B. from referring to the assumption as erroneous, from attacking the assumption in any way, or from pointing out to the jury that the HLA report does not state a basis for the fifty percent prior chance assumption. The circuit court ruled that because R.E.B. had failed to introduce any evidence assailing the reliability of the assumption, he had no basis in the trial record to attack the assumption in closing argument.

On February 24, a jury found R.E.B. to be the father of M.J.B. After the circuit court denied R.E.B.'s post-verdict motions for a new trial and a judgment notwithstanding the verdict, R.E.B. appealed the judgment to the court of appeals.

The court of appeals reversed the circuit court judgment concluding that it was an abuse of discretion to limit R.E.B. from commenting in closing argument on the reliability of the fifty percent prior chance assumption. Moreover, because a statistic contained in the HLA blood test report assumed that R.E.B. had had sexual intercourse with T.A.T. during the statutory conceptive period, the court of appeals found this evidence inappropriate for jury consideration of paternity. The court of appeals held that before the probability of paternity statistic could be considered as evidence of paternity, the jury must first independently determine whether the mother and putative father had sexual intercourse during the conceptive period. . . .

We note at the outset that R.E.B. did not base his challenge in this case on an erroneous admission of the HLA blood test results into evidence. Nor does he attack the validity of the paternity statute itself. . . .

Rather, R.E.B. argues only that the trial court committed reversible error in limiting his closing argument. Specifically, R.E.B. claims that the trial court erroneously precluded him from arguing that the probability of paternity statistic was based on an unsupported fifty percent prior assumption of sexual intercourse. He argues that the fifty percent prior chance assumption and its effects on the resulting statistical conclusion is a matter that the jury could not be expected to understand without explanation. He concludes that had the trial court permitted the argument, the jury "might probably have returned a verdict in favor of R.E.B." . . .

Paternity testing is based on the presence of genetic markers which are inherited from one's parents. These markers are identified by an application of Mendelian rules of inheritance to the data obtained from a blood cell or tissue sample. Traditionally, blood cell tests in paternity actions were used for the purpose of excluding a named defendant as the father. That is, where the child at issue lacked a genetic marker that a child of the putative father must have, nonpaternity was established. Likewise, if a dominant genetic marker was present in the child that was absent in both the mother and alleged father, paternity could be conclusively excluded.

While courts have not always accepted blood test results excluding a putative father as conclusive evidence of nonpaternity, in recent years such test results have enjoyed universal recognition and a wide acceptance in both the scientific and legal communities. See, e.g., *Little v. Streater*, 452 U.S. 1, 6–7 (1981); S. Schatkin, Disputed Paternity Proceedings, sec. 9.13 (4th rev. ed. 1987).

More problematic is the question of the admissibility and weight to be afforded paternity inclusion test results. That is, where an individual cannot be conclusively excluded as the father of a child, the question becomes how likely it is that the defendant fathered the child at issue, compared to another randomly selected man in the relevant population. This likelihood statistic, called the probability of paternity or chance of paternity, has generated much debate in the legal and scientific communities. See, e.g., McCormick on Evidence, sec. 211 (3d ed. 1984 & 1987 Supp.); Peterson, *A Few Things You Should Know About Paternity Tests (But Were Afraid to Ask)*, 22 Santa Clara L. Rev. 667 (1982); Ellman & Kaye, *Probabilities and Proof: Can HLA and Blood Group Testing Prove Paternity?* 54 N.Y.U. L. Rev. 1131 (1979); Annot., 37 A.L.R. 4th 167, *Admissibility, Weight and Sufficiency of Human Leukocyte Antigen (HLA) Tissue Typing Tests in Paternity Cases* (1985).

A blood grouping test in a paternity action is actually a tissue typing test know as the HLA test. The HLA test gathers raw data from the samples of the mother, child and alleged father and expresses that data in the form of a probability of exclusion, a paternity index, and a probability of paternity.

The first calculation, the probability of exclusion, measures the ability of a paternity test to exclude men falsely accused of paternity. *Plemel v. Walter*, 303 Or. 262, 735 P.2d 1209, 1213 (1987). This statistic does not rely on the challenged fifty percent prior chance assumption. However, the probability of exclusion "does nothing to distinguish the true father from the perhaps millions of men who fall into this group." Peterson, *A Few Things You Should Know*, supra, at 680. In the present case, the probability of exclusion was 98.99 percent. That is, 98.99 percent of falsely accused men would be excluded as the father of T.A.T.'s child.

The second statistic generated by the paternity test is the cumulative paternity index, or likelihood ratio, which describes the genetic odds in favor of paternity. This statistic, expressed as a ratio, compares the relative likelihood of the putative father producing a child with these particular genetic markers than that of a randomly selected man. *Plemel*, 735 P.2d at 1214. However, this statistic does not describe the likelihood of producing the child in question, but rather, it describes the relative likelihood of producing a child with the same genetic markers. Id. Even though all of the men not excluded in that statistic described above (the probability of exclusion), are capable of fathering such a child, they will have different paternity indexes, i.e., different relative likelihoods of fathering the child. In this case, R.E.B.'s paternity index was 218. This means that he was 218 times more likely to have fathered a child with the same genetic markers as T.A.T.'s child than a randomly selected man. This statistic does not use the challenged fifty percent prior chance assumption.

The third statistic, the probability of paternity, then takes the paternity index and using Bayes' Theorem converts the paternity index or likelihood ratio into a probability of paternity, i.e., the actual likelihood that the putative father is the actual father of this child. Id. at 1215. In this case, the probability of paternity was 99.54 percent.

This statistic, while the most probative of the three, likewise poses the greatest danger of misuse. This figure is calculated by multiplying the prior odds of paternity by the paternity index. Typically, the prior odds of paternity are calculated as one-to-one, or a 50/50 chance (i.e., it assumes a fifty percent likelihood that defendant is the father and fifty percent likelihood that another, randomly selected man, is the father).

While the HLA's probability of paternity calculation expressed as a percentage is considered the most accurate means of communicating the significance of the blood test data to the jury, *Commonwealth v. Beausoleil*, 397 Mass. 206, 490 N.W.2d 788, 795–96 (1986); Ellman and Kaye, *Probabilities and Proof*, 54 N.Y.U. L. Rev. at 1146, the probability of paternity calculation nevertheless has been criticized as it is typically computed. Specifically, critics have noted that the use of the fifty percent prior chance assumption in the probability of paternity calculation has no basis in the individual facts of the case. Moreover, the fifty percent prior chance assumption is not sensitive to varying individual fact situations. Finally, even the probability of paternity calculations cannot indicate conclusively which person is the actual father.

As the court of appeals correctly noted, the fifty percent prior chance assumption has no factual basis, but is employed precisely because nothing is known about whether intercourse actually took place between the parties at a time when conception could have occurred. Because the assumption is not based on empirical facts but, rather, is employed to make the paternity formula work, the reliability of the probability of paternity results may be diminished in cases where the occurrence of intercourse and the likelihood of conception at a given time are disputed.

The assumption underlying the probability of paternity statistic is that the mother and putative father have engaged in sexual intercourse at least once during the period of possible conception. See Peterson, *A Few Things You Should Know*, supra at 685. We interpret this assumption to mean that the probability of paternity statistic is conditionally relevant evidence; only after competent evidence is offered to show that sexual intercourse between the mother and alleged father occurred during the conceptive period may evidence of the probability of paternity be received.

This foundational evidence may be supplied by the mother herself, of course, which is likely to happen in the typical paternity case. However, we note that this threshold evidence is not limited to direct testimony by the mother that she engaged in sexual intercourse with the alleged father. Evidence that the defendant had access to the mother during the conceptive period may be offered by any individual knowledgeable of the facts of their association. By "access," we mean that the mother and putative father were together at a time, under circumstances and in a location which would lead a reasonable person to believe that the sexual intercourse took place between them. In this regard, there must be evidence to sustain a reasonable belief by a factfinder that sexual intercourse took place between the mother and the putative father. Once there is competent evidence on the record of sexual intercourse during the conceptive period, the results of the blood tests, including the probability of paternity statistic, may be introduced in a civil paternity proceeding.

We disagree with the court of appeals that an independent determination of sexual intercourse must be made by the jury before it can consider the statistical probability of paternity as evidence of paternity. . . . It is true that one of the elements in a paternity suit is sexual intercourse between the mother and alleged father occurring during the conceptive period. However, the occurrence of sexual intercourse during the time of possible conception is not an issue separate from the main issue. It does not require an independent determination by the jury; it is an element of the case. If the petitioner fails to introduce sufficient evidence of sexual intercourse to establish a prima facie case of paternity, the defendant can simply move for a dismissal of the case. Likewise, the petitioner is precluded from introducing the blood test results until evidence of sexual intercourse is received.

We have carefully reviewed much of the literature with respect to probability statistics and its role in paternity testing, and we recognize the problems inherent in the probability of paternity measurement as it is currently typically calculated. Nevertheless, we believe that the legislature, which also was presumably aware of the disadvantages as well as the advantages of admitting this statistic, decided to resolve this question in favor of liberally admitting paternity evidence. An earlier version of the statute relating to blood test evidence in paternity proceedings, sec. 52.36(3), Stats., formerly limited the introduction of blood test results to those definitely excluding the paternity of an individual tested. Thus, under the old law, the probability of paternity would not have been admissible under any circumstances in a civil proceeding seeking to establish paternity. However, under the current statute, sec. 767.48, not only are inclusion statistics admissible into evidence, but the statute expressly admits the introduction of evidence on the probability of a defendant's paternity.

The blood test report completed by a certified expert is presumed reliable, because the legislature has provided that it is admissible as evidence in paternity proceedings. This court has consistently recognized a prima facie presumption of accuracy of tests expressly authorized by statute. *State v. Disch*, 119 Wis. 2d 461, 476–77, 351 N.W.2d 492 (1984). As we have oftentimes stated in the past, "[a]ny contentions that the test result is unreliable or inaccurate goes only to the weight of the evidence as a matter of defense, not to its admissibility." If the blood test report is unreliable or inaccurate, defense counsel has the obligation to attack the credibility of the blood test and, therefore, to rebut the prima facie presumption of reliability. The jury will decide the ultimate weight to be given to the blood test report.

It would be better to have an expert witness present the blood test and results to the court and jury; however, the statute does not require it. Both the petitioner and the defendant have the right to call an expert witness to testify as to the assumption upon which the blood test is based and to the meaning and limitations of the various tests. This presents the defendant with the opportunity, if necessary, to challenge the prior odds assumption of the probability of paternity formula in a meaningful and understandable way. For example, methods of introducing the probability of paternity statistic which do not rely on the fifty percent prior odds assumption are currently being introduced in other jurisdictions to overcome the recognized shortcomings of the formula. It should be noted that while we recognize that other jurisdictions are employing various means of introducing paternity evidence, we do not comment at this time on the reliability or the validity of these alternative methods. . . .

In this case, R.E.B. did not attempt either to call an expert witness to explain or attack the tests or to introduce a treatise. Consequently, the court was correct in not allowing the defense attorney to argue the invalidity or unreliability of the test to the jury because there was no basis in the record upon which to attack the blood test. Without some kind of explanatory evidence, the test should not be explained to the jury through the attorney's subjective and argumentative closing remarks.

By the Court. The decision of the court of appeals is reversed.

NOTES AND QUESTIONS

(1) If the jury in this case had believed the alleged father, rather than the mother, with respect to the timing of sexual intercourse, would it have been required to return a finding of non-paternity, despite the 99.54% "probability of paternity"?

(2) If the mother had died, or were otherwise unavailable to testify regarding the timing of sexual intercourse, could a jury find paternity in this case based on the blood test evidence alone? Why or why not?

(3) The Wisconsin Supreme Court notes that other jurisdictions employ various approaches to the presentation of scientific evidence of paternity. In *Plemel v. Walter*, 735 P.2d 1209 (Or. 1987), the Oregon Supreme Court held that an expert who presents blood test results for purposes of establishing paternity should not be permitted to present a single figure as the probability of paternity, but should instead present a range of calculations based on an array of assumed prior probabilities, ranging from 0 to 100%. The *Plemel* court reasoned that "[i]n this way the strength of the blood test results can be demonstrated without overstating the information that can be derived from them. If the expert uses various assumptions and makes these assumptions known, the factfinder's attention will be directed to the other evidence in the case, and it will not be mislead into adopting the expert's assumption as the correct weight to be assigned to the other evidence." 735 P. 2d at 1219. This so-called "chart approach"—in which the trier of fact is allowed to see the effect of the genetic evidence on a range of prior probabilities—has been endorsed by a number of family law scholars. *See, e.g.*, D.H. Kaye, *Plemel As A Primer On Proving Paternity*, 24 Willamette L. Rev. 867, 878–81 (1988); Ira Ellman & D.H. Kaye, *Probabilities and Proof: Can HLA and Blood Group Testing Prove Paternity?*, 54 N.Y.U. L. Rev. 1131, 1152–58 (1979). Does this strike you as a better approach to the presentation of scientific evidence of paternity than the approach adopted by the Wisconsin Supreme Court?

(4) **The Role of DNA Testing.** DNA testing is the newest type of scientific evidence widely used to determine paternity. The utilization of DNA typing in paternity cases is regarded by many as "revolutionary, as the power to link the accused to the evidence and to exclude falsely accused men [is] so much stronger than by conventional genetic testing." Angela Arkin Byrne, *Using DNA Evidence to Prove Paternity: What The Attorney Needs to Know*, 19 Fam. L. Rep. 3001, 3003 (1992). The following description of DNA testing is taken from Angela R. Arkin, *Evidentiary and Related Issues in Paternity Proceedings* in Vitek, Disputed Paternity Proceedings, 5th ed., § 3.07 (Matthew Bender, 1998).

> The DNA testing process involves matching the blood of a child with the blood of an alleged father. The laboratory scientist undertakes Restriction Fragment Length Polymorphism (RFLP) testing, a complex six-step process, to determine whether there is a match. If the DNA does not match, the alleged father cannot be the individual

sought. If the alleged father is not excluded, a calculation must be made of the likelihood that DNA from a randomly chosen man of the same racial background would also have provided a match. The scientist compares the alleged father's DNA to that found in a laboratory database containing DNA samples of persons with a similar racial background, and calculates the frequency with which that DNA is found in the relevant population. The database frequency is then multiplied, in accordance with well accepted population genetics theories, to obtain the statistical likelihood that the suspect is in fact the biological father of the child.

The status of the admissibility of DNA evidence differs from state to state, but most courts that have considered the issue have found DNA evidence admissible in paternity cases, often relying on state statutes that expressly allow the admission of blood test and genetic evidence to prove or disprove paternity. *See, e.g., Commonwealth ex. rel. Overby v. Flaneary*, 469 S.E.2d 79 (Va. Ct. App. 1996) (DNA test results showing 99.92% probability of paternity, in conjunction with evidence of sexual intercourse, proved paternity as a matter of law); *Isabella County Department of Social Services v. Thompson*, 534 N.W.2d 132 (Mich. Ct. App. 1995) (affirming summary finding of paternity based on DNA testing); *Mastromatteo v. Harkins*, 615 A.2d 390 (Pa. Super. Ct. 1992); *Alexander v. Alexander*, 537 N.E.2d 1310 (Ohio Prob. Ct. 1988), *appeal dismissed*, 560 N.E.2d 1337 (Ohio Ct. App. 1989); *see generally Admissibility of DNA Testing in Individual States*, in Vitek, Disputed Paternity Proceedings, 5th ed. (Matthew Bender, 1998). The use of DNA evidence in criminal cases, which involves somewhat different testing techniques, has proven far more controversial. *See generally*, William C. Thompson & Simon Ford, *DNA Typing: Acceptance and Weight of the New Genetic Identification Tests*, 75 Va. L. Rev. 45 (1989).

Because DNA analysis involves many of the same statistical techniques as other types of paternity testing, it raises the same evidentiary concerns discussed in cases such as *M.J.B.* and *Plemel*. However, because DNA testing typically involves multiple probes, and because each individual's DNA is unique, the paternity indices and probabilities derived from DNA testing are typically much more powerful than those derived from other sorts of blood testing. "The individualized nature of the person's DNA coupled with statistical data showing the incidence of particular genes within a[n] ethnic group, accounts for the heightened degree of probability with which experts can determine the alleged father's paternity." J.E. Cullins, Jr. *Should the Legitimate Child Be Forced to Pay For the Sins of Her Father?*, 53 La. L. Rev. 1675, 1713 n.190 (1993). When both parents of a child are tested, the probability of paternity, as expressed in a percentage, will either approach one hundred percent or zero percent. *Id.*, at 1719; *see* Angela Arkin Byrne, *Using DNA Evidence to Prove Paternity: What The Attorney Needs to Know*, 19 Fam. L. Rep. 3001, 3003 (1992) ("The use of multiple probes can result in a probability of paternity of 99.99%, with genetic odds in favor of paternity of over one in 10,000.") On the one hand, the magnitude of the odds produced by DNA testing may reduce the importance of disputes over prior probability assumptions, based on the non-genetic evidence. For example, in *In re Matter of M.*, 656 N.Y.S.2d 802 (N.Y. Fam. Ct. 1997), the court held that it was proper for a laboratory that conducted DNA tests to use an assigned "prior probability" value of 0.5 in calculating a defendant's probability of paternity, notwithstanding evidence presented at trial that the defendant had a fertility problem. The court explained that because the DNA and other blood tests performed had yielded an extremely high combined probability index of 49,111 to 1, the defendant's overall probability of paternity remained over 99%, even assuming prior probability values of close to zero. 656 N.Y.S.2d at 803. On the other hand, some commentators have argued that the very aura of certainty attached to these sorts of overwhelming odds make it even more important that DNA evidence not be permitted to usurp the function of the trier of fact. *See, e.g.*, Christopher L. Blakesley, *Scientific Testing and Proof of Paternity: Some Controversy and Key Issues for Family Law Counsel*, 57 La. L. Rev. 379, 416, 423–25 (1997); Jennifer Sue Deck, *Prelude to a Miss: A Cautionary Note Against Expanding DNA Databanks in the Face of Scientific Uncertainty*, 20 Vt. L. Rev. 1057, 1090 (1996).

Several other aspects of DNA testing raise additional legal issues. Because DNA testing uses molecules that remain stable and testable even after an individual's death the availability of DNA testing raises the possibility of accurate paternity determinations long after a putative father has died. *See* Charles Nelson Le Ray, *Implications of DNA Technology on Posthumous Paternity Determination: Deciding the Facts When Daddy Can't Give His Opinion*, 35 B.C. L. Rev. 747 (1994). Indeed, a number of courts have granted requests to exhume the bodies of putative fathers in order to perform DNA tests. *See, e.g., Wawrykow v. Simonich*, 652 A.2d 843, 844–48 (Pa. Super Ct. 1994) (court may order exhumation of alleged father's remains where petitioner has established reasonable cause); *Batcheldor v. Boyd*, 423 S.E.2d 810, 815 (N.C. Ct. App. 1992); *In re Estate of Rogers*, 583 A.2d 782, 783 (N.J. Super. Ct. App. Div. 1990); *Lach v. Welch*, 1997 WL 536330 (Conn. Super.1997); *Alexander v. Alexander*, 537 N.E.2d 1310, 1314 (Ohio Prob. Ct. 1988), *appeal dismissed*, 560 N.E.2d 1337 (Ohio Ct. App. 1989). *Cf. In re Estate of Greenwood*, 587 A.2d 749, 757 (Pa. Super. Ct. 1991) (administrix ordered to released deceased's blood samples for DNA testing). *Query:* Does the possibility of posthumous DNA testing undermine the rationale for the requirement in some state inheritance statutes that paternity of a nonmarital child must be proven during the lifetime of the father in order to establish inheritance rights?

Unlike other types of scientific evidence, DNA typing also raises the possibility of proving paternity by testing the biological relatives of an alleged father. For example, the DNA "print" of a close relative of a deceased putative father can be compared to the DNA prints of the child and the available mother to determine whether the parties are related. The possibility of third party testing to establish paternity raises a host of legal and policy questions. In *Sudwischer v. Estate of Hoffpauer*, 589 So. 2d 474 (La. 1991), *cert. denied*, 504 U.S. 909 (1992), the Supreme Court of Louisiana addressed some of these questions in the course of affirming an order requiring the legitimate daughter of a deceased putative father to undergo DNA blood testing in order to provide evidence relevant to the filiation claim brought by an alleged nonmarital daughter. The court noted that the request for blood testing required it to balance the nonmarital daughter's "constitutional right to prove filiation" against the marital daughter's privacy interests. 589 So.2d at 476. The court reasoned that the nonmarital daughter had an overriding emotional and financial interest in knowing her father's identify. By contrast, while the marital daughter had a financial interest in opposing the filiation claim, the court noted that she had no physical or religious objections to a blood test. Thus, the court concluded that the invasion of her privacy interests was "minimal." *Id*. It also noted that the marital daughter could avoid blood testing by conceding a relationship with her alleged half sister. Under these circumstances, the Louisiana Supreme Court concluded that the trial court had erred in denying the nonmarital daughter's motion to compel blood testing. 589 So. 2d at 476. One justice dissented, arguing that the constitutional balance should be struck in favor of the marital daughter's privacy interests. 589 So. 2d at 478–79 (Dennis, J., dissenting).

Several other courts have considered requests for blood testing of collateral parties and have reached contradictory results. *Compare, e.g., Lach v. Welch*, 1997 WL 536330 (Conn. Super. 1997) (ordering DNA testing of putative grandparents) and *In re Estate of Rogers*, 583 A.2d 782, 783–84 (N.Y. Super. Ct. App. Div. 1990) (ordering nonparty ex-wife, and four marital children of decedent who were parties, to submit to blood tests) *with William M. v. Superior Court*, 275 Cal. Rptr. 103 (Cal. Ct. App. 1990) (court lacked jurisdiction to order putative grandparents tested) and *In re Sanders*, 2 Cal. App. 4th, 3 Cal. Rptr. 2d 536 (Cal. Ct. App. 1992) (court lacked jurisdiction to order genetic testing of marital children in contested probate proceeding). *See also* Minn. Stat. Ann. § 257.62 (West 1996) (authorizing testing of parents or brothers and sisters of deceased putative father for purposes of determining nonmarital child's eligibility for public assistance, including social security and veterans' benefits). For a discussion of these cases, and a critique of the *Sudwischer* decision, see J.E. Cullens, Jr., *Should the Legitimate Child Be Forced to Pay for the Sins of her Father? Sudwischer v. Estate of Hoffpauir*, 53 La. L. Rev. 1674 (1993)

(5) **DNA Testing and Privacy Interests.** The widespread use of DNA testing may also raise privacy concerns. Since 1995, a number of states have passed laws limiting the accessibility and use of genetic information, because of the potential for abuse and the significant risks to individual privacy and liberty interests. *E.g.*, Or. Rev. Stat. §§ 659.700–.720 (1997). See generally Michael M. J. Lin, *Conferring a Federal Property Right in Genetic Material: Stepping into the Future with the Genetic Privacy Act*, 22 Am. J. L. & Med. 109 (1996). These statutes generally prohibit conducting genetic testing or obtaining genetic information from an individual without the individual's informed consent. However, the statutes contain an exception for paternity testing. Several commentators have questioned the desirability and the breadth of this exception. *E.g*, Christopher L. Blakesley, *Scientific Testing and Proof of Paternity: Some Controversy and Key Issues for Family Law Counsel*, 57 La. L. Rev. 379 (1997).

(6) **Presumptions Based on Scientific Evidence**. An increasing number of states have adopted statutes creating a rebuttable presumption of paternity, if blood test or other genetic evidence indicates a probability of paternity of at least a specified percentage. *See*, e.g., Alaska Stat. § 25.20.050(d) (1997) (probability of parentage at 95 percent or higher); Cal. Fam. Code § 7555(a) (1996) (paternity index of 100 or greater); Fla. Stat. Ann. § 742.12(3) (1996) (probability of paternity of at least 95%); Md. Fam. Code Ann. 5–1029(f) (1977) (probability of paternity of at least 97.3%); Mich. Stat. Ann. 25.496 (1997) (probability of paternity of 99% or higher); N.Y. Civ. Prac. Law & Rules 4518(d) (1997) (at least 95% probability of paternity); N.C. Gen. Stat. § 8–50.1(b1)(4) (1996) (probability of parentage of 97% or higher); Wyo. Stat. Ann. § 14–2–109(e)(iv) (probability of parentage of 97% or higher). Many of these statutes were enacted in response to a 1993 federal law that requires states participating in federal income security programs to adopt "[p]rocedures which create a rebuttable or, at the option of the State, conclusive presumption of paternity upon genetic testing results indicating a threshold probability that the alleged father is the father of the child." 42 U.S.C. § 666(G) (1998).

Are such paternity presumptions consistent with the concerns expressed in cases such as *M.J.B* and *Plemel*? Does a *conclusive* presumption of paternity, based on scientific probability evidence, raise constitutional concerns? *See Tennessee Dep't of Human Servs. v. Hooper*, 1997 WL 83669 (Tenn. Ct. App. 1997) (conclusive presumption of paternity based on genetic tests which show statistical probability of paternity of 99% or greater deprives putative fathers of "meaningful opportunity to be heard," in violation of Due Process Clause). If a state adopts a rebuttable presumption based on a statistical probability of paternity, what sort of evidence is required to overcome the presumption? *Compare, e.g., Nash County Dep't of Soc. Servs. ex. rel. Williams v. Beamon*, 485 S.E.2d 851 (N.C. Ct. App. 1997), *cert. denied*, 493 S.E.2d 655 (N.C.1997) (alleged father's denial of sexual relations with mother sufficient to rebut statutory presumption of paternity arising from blood test results indicating 99.96% probability of paternity) *with Hughes v. Walker*, 662 N.E. 177 (Ill. App. Ct. 1996) (evidence that mother also had intercourse with another man held insufficient to rebut presumption of paternity based on DNA testing) *and Isabella County Dep't of Soc. Servs v. Thompson*, 534 N.W.2d 132 (Mich. Ct. App. 1995) (defendant's denial of sexual intercourse and mother's lack of memory regarding penetration held insufficient to rebut presumption).

(7) **Federal Involvement in Paternity Establishment.** As the preceding note suggests, the federal government has become increasingly involved in the area of paternity establishment. In addition to the presumption requirement discussed above, federal law now mandates that states provide for genetic testing of all parties in contested paternity actions, upon the request of any party, provided that the request is supported by the party's sworn statement either alleging or denying paternity. 42 U.S.C. § 666(a)(5)(B) (1998). Federally funded child support enforcement agencies must also have the power (without the need for permission from a court or administrative tribunal) to order genetic tests in appropriate contested support cases. 42 U.S.C. § 666(c)(1)(a). Further, genetic tests results must be admissible as evidence so long as they are of a type generally acknowledged as reliable and are performed by an accredited laboratory. 42 U.S.C. § 666(a)(5)(F)(i). Any objection to the admission of genetic testing must be made in writing, not later than a specified number of days before the hearing; in the absence of such an objection, the test results are admissible "without the need for foundation testimony or other proof of authenticity or accuracy." *Id.* at 666(a)(5)(F)(ii), (iii).

Since 1993, the federal government has also required states to establish and implement a simplified civil process for the voluntary acknowledgment of paternity. Such voluntary procedures must include (1) a hospital-based method for voluntary acknowledgment of paternity during the periods immediately before and after the child's birth; and (2) a process for parents of older children who wish to establish paternity voluntarily outside the hospital. 42 U.S.C. § 666(a)(5) (1998). States must ensure that, prior to signing a paternity acknowledgment, a mother or an alleged fathers understands the alternatives to, legal consequences of, and rights and responsibilities arising from the signed acknowledgment. 42 U.S. C. § (a)(5)(C). In addition, within 60 days of signing, states must treat all paternity acknowledgements as the equivalent of a judicial finding of paternity, with all attendant legal consequences. 42 U.S.C. § 666(a)(5)(D)(ii). These requirements are designed to make voluntary establishment of paternity simpler and faster than it has been to date in most states. The requirements also increase the importance of educating parents as to the legal and financial implications of a paternity acknowledgment. *See* Paula Roberts, *The Family Law Implications of the 1996 Welfare Legislation*, 30 Clearinghouse Rev. 988, 992 (1997).

Query: Like most areas of family law, paternity establishment has traditionally been the province of state courts and legislatures. Is this increased degree of federal involvement in state paternity procedures appropriate? Why or why not?

(8) **Establishment of Maternity**. While most disputes regarding legal parenthood involve questions of paternity, recent advances in reproductive technology have also raised questions about the legal definition of maternity. For example, in a so-called "gestational surrogacy" arrangement, an ovum provided by one woman is fertilized in vitro and implanted in the womb of another woman, who has agreed to carry the resulting pregnancy to term and to release the child after birth. In several recent cases, the parties' contractual arrangements have broken down and both women have claimed to be the child's legal mother—one based on her genetic link to the child and the other based on gestation and giving birth. *See, e.g., Johnson v. Calvert,* 5 Cal. 4th 84, 19 Cal. Rptr. 2d 494, 851 P.2d 776 (1993), *cert. denied,* 510 U.S. 874 (1993). For additional discussion of *Johnson* and other gestational surrogacy cases, see § 3.04, *above*.

[B] Res Judicata and Relitigation

Paternity judgments often raise difficult res judicata issues. One set of issues arises when an adjudicated father seeks to reopen a paternity judgment on the grounds that newly-available scientific evidence demonstrates that he is *not* the child's biological father. A second type of issue arises when a child who was the subject of an unsuccessful paternity action later seeks to relitigate the question of his or her paternity. In the two cases that follow, the same court addresses both of these issues. As you read these decisions, think about how the various state justices view the nature of a paternity judgment.

TANDRA S. v. TYRONE W.
Court of Appeals of Maryland
648 A.2d 439 (1994)

Murphy, C.J.

These companion cases present the question whether a court can vacate an enrolled paternity judgment based on the results of a post-judgment blood test or based on the mother's post-judgment testimony that the judicially determined father is not in fact the father.

Case Number 144

On August 31, 1990, Tandra S. gave birth to T.W., a baby girl. Tyrone W. and Tandra executed a paternity agreement on October 19, 1990 in which Tyrone acknowledged his paternity of T.W. In this agreement, Tyrone agreed to pay child support and a portion of the child's medical expenses. In addition, the agreement provided that Tandra would have custody and guardianship of T.W., while Tyrone would have reasonable visitation rights.

On October 26, 1990, Tandra filed a paternity complaint in the Circuit Court for Talbot County alleging Tyrone's paternity of T.W., and incorporating the paternity agreement. Pursuant to the parties agreement, the court entered a final judgment on October 30,1990, entitled "Paternity Declaration," which established Tyrone's paternity of T.W. The judgment, following the dictate of the agreement, required Tyrone to pay $ 10.00 per week to Tandra for child support and also ordered him to pay one-half of the child's medical expenses not covered by insurance.

Approximately two and one-half years later, on April 1, 1993, Tyrone filed a motion to set aside the judgment of paternity and a request for blood tests. In the motion, he stated that Tandra had recently informed him that he was not T.W.'s father. . . .

On April 9, 1993, prior to any judicial hearing, the circuit court ordered the parties and the child to submit to blood tests. The results of the blood tests excluded Tyrone as a potential father.

A hearing was then held in June of 1993 regarding Tyrone's motion to set aside the paternity judgment. The circuit court (Horne, J.) initially noted that Maryland Rule 2–535 limits a court's right to vacate or modify an enrolled judgment. In particular, it explained that Rule 2–535(b) permits a court to "exercise revisory power and control over [an enrolled] judgment [only] in case of fraud, mistake, or irregularity."

The court determined that Tyrone had failed to establish fraud, mistake, or irregularity. It also said that it should not have granted the motion for blood test without first holding a hearing, and would not, in the future, order post-judgment blood tests. Nevertheless, the circuit court granted Tyrone's motion to set aside the paternity judgment because it concluded that it would be unjust to force Tyrone to continue paying child support after it had been scientifically proven that he was not the child's father. As a result of the paternity judgment being vacated, the child was left fatherless. We granted certiorari prior to consideration of the appeal by the intermediate appellate court.

Case Number 157

On September 21, 1985, Vandella H. gave birth to John S., III. Vandella filed a paternity petition in the Circuit Court for Baltimore City on November 21, 1985, naming John S., Jr. as the father of her child. During the paternity proceedings in March of 1986, John and Vandella each testified that John was the father of the child. John was not represented by counsel at this hearing. On April 9, 1986, the circuit court entered a decree declaring John to be the father of the child; it also ordered him to pay $ 25.00 per week in child support and $ 2.00 per week for reimbursement to the State's Medical Assistance Program.

On October 26, 1987, Vandella filed a petition for change of name in the Circuit Court for Baltimore City, requesting that her child's name be changed from John S., III to S.A.S., in order "to reflect his true lineage and parentage." In this petition, Vandella stated that Randy S., not John, was the "actual father" of her child. The alleged natural father, Randy, consented to the passage of an order changing the child's birth certificate to show that he was the "true and legal father" of the child. It is unclear whether John received notice of this change of name proceeding. According to Vandella, the Circuit Court for Baltimore City granted her request to change her child's name on March 14, 1988.

Shortly after the change of name proceeding, Vandella informed John that he was not the father of the child, admitted to him that she had falsified the paternity petition in 1985, and admitted to him that she had committed perjury in the original paternity proceeding. Vandella and John thereafter contacted the Department of Social Services on several occasions in an attempt to terminate John's child support payments. None of these requests were granted.

On March 19, 1992, approximately six years after the enrollment of the paternity judgment and approximately four years after the child's name change, John filed a motion to vacate the paternity judgment, or in the alternative, to modify child support. The Baltimore City

Office of Child Support Enforcement (BCOCSE) moved to intervene, arguing that no party was adequately representing the interests of the Department of Social Services of Baltimore City. It also averred that the 1986 decree could not be revised because John's motion to vacate failed to allege any fraud, mistake, or irregularity. BCOCSE was permitted to intervene in the case.

At a hearing on October 26, 1992 in the Circuit Court for Baltimore City, Vandella stated that she last had sexual relations with John in September of 1984, approximately one year before her child was born. Notwithstanding the fundamental principles of biology, she testified that John believed her when she informed him that he was the child's father. She further testified that she resumed her relationship with John in February of 1985.

According to Vandella, she had a brief relationship with Randy in December of 1984, which resulted in the birth of the child whose paternity is at issue in this case. She described Randy as "not a serious boyfriend," but admitted that Randy was also the father of another child later born to her in 1988. Randy, a resident of New Jersey, was not made a party to the proceeding below. Neither Randy nor John testified at the hearing below and neither man submitted to a blood test to determine paternity.

On the same day as the hearing took place, the circuit court (Byrnes, J.) issued an order, which vacated the 1986 paternity judgment and released John from all support obligations. It reasoned that because the mother, the "real father," and John, the "adjudicated father," all agreed that John was mistakenly named the father in 1986, it would be in the interests of justice to set aside the judgment. The court did not concurrently establish paternity in another man; thus, the child was left fatherless.

BCOCSE appealed to the Court of Special Appeals and that court, in an unreported opinion, affirmed the judgment of the circuit court. . . .

II

Before us, the Attorney General appeared on behalf of petitioner, Tandra, in case no. 144, and petitioner, BCOCSE, in case no. 157. He observes that enrolled judgments may only be revised in limited circumstances, i.e., for fraud, mistake, or irregularity. The Attorney General maintains that neither fraud, mistake, nor irregularity, as those terms have been defined through judicial decision, existed in these cases. He avers that these strict revisionary rules apply with equal vigor to paternity judgments.

According to the Attorney General, the purpose of this limited revisory power is to promote the finality of judgments thereby ensuring that there is an end to litigation. Even though the necessity for finality may at times lead to harsh results, he asserts that the public policy favoring finality overrides the occasional unfairness that results in particular cases. He further posits that the majority of other jurisdictions support giving conclusive effect to a judicial finding of paternity.

The Attorney General also claims that the doctrine of res judicata precludes a court from revisiting a paternity judgment when the same parties were involved in the original proceeding. Moreover, he contends that the circuit court, in each of the two cases, and the Court of Special Appeals in case no. 157, failed to protect the interests of the two children by vacating the paternity decrees without concurrently establishing paternity in another man.

III

A circuit court has unrestricted discretion to revise a judgment within thirty days after it is entered. See Md. Rule 2–535(a). . . . As earlier indicated, Maryland Rule 2–535(b) provides that, after 30 days a judgment becomes enrolled and may be revised only upon a showing of fraud, mistake, or irregularity. . . . The rationale behind strictly limiting a court's revisory power is that in today's highly litigious society, there must be some point in time when a judgment becomes final.

A court, however, will only exercise its revisory powers if, in addition to a finding of fraud, mistake, or irregularity, the party moving to set aside the enrolled judgment has acted with ordinary diligence, in good faith, and has a meritorious defense or cause of action. Moreover, it is well established that there must be clear and convincing evidence of the fraud, mistake, or irregularity before a movant is entitled to have a judgment vacated under Rule 2–535(b). It is also well settled that Rule 2–535(b) generally applies to all final judgments. . . . An order declaring paternity is a final judgment and is subject to revision only in the manner and to the extent that any order or decree is subject to the revisory power of the court. . . .

Nevertheless, the Court of Special Appeals in case no. 157 concluded that § 5–1007 of the Family Law Article controlled the issues in the case. That section provides that any rule or statute, when used in the context of a paternity case, applies only to the extent that the rule or statute is: (1) practical under the circumstances; and (2) not inconsistent with the paternity subtitle. The intermediate appellate court determined that the "limitations on the court's revisory power . . . [were] impractical in light of the specific circumstances" of the case. We disagree. A harsh result or an unfair decision is not equivalent to impracticality. . . .

The terms fraud, mistake, and irregularity, as used in Rule 2–535 and its predecessor, Rule 625a, have been thoroughly defined by our cases. It is evident from these decisions that those terms are to be narrowly defined and strictly applied.

The type of fraud necessary to vacate an enrolled judgment is extrinsic fraud, not fraud which is intrinsic to the trial of the case itself. In *Hresko v. Hresko*, 83 Md. App. 228, 232, 574 A.2d 24 (1990), the Court of Special Appeals clearly distinguished intrinsic and extrinsic fraud:

"Intrinsic fraud is defined as 'that which pertains to issues involved in the original action or where acts constituting fraud were, or could have been, litigated therein.' Extrinsic fraud, on the other hand, is 'fraud which is collateral to the issues tried in the case where the judgment is rendered.'

"Fraud is extrinsic when it actually prevents an adversarial trial. In determining whether or not extrinsic fraud exists, the question is not whether the fraud operated to cause the trier of fact to reach an unjust conclusion, but whether the fraud prevented the actual dispute from being submitted to the fact finder at all." (quoting in part Black's Law Dictionary (5th ed. 1979)). . . .

In Schwartz, supra, 272 Md. at 308, we provided examples of intrinsic fraud which will not trigger a court's revisory power: "an enrolled decree will not be vacated even though obtained by the use of forged documents, perjured testimony, or any other frauds which are 'intrinsic' to the trial of the case itself." We also discussed examples of extrinsic fraud which will permit a court to revise an enrolled judgment: " 'Where the unsuccessful party has been prevented from exhibiting fully his case, by fraud or deception practiced on him by his opponent, as by keeping him away from court, a false promise of a compromise; or where the defendant never had knowledge of the suit, being kept in ignorance by the acts of the plaintiff; or where an attorney fraudulently or without authority assumes to represent a party and connives at his defeat; or where the attorney regularly employed corruptly sells out his client's interest to the other side,—these, and similar cases which show that there has never been a real contest in the trial or hearing of the case, are reasons for which a new suit may be sustained to set aside and annul the former judgment or decree, and open the case for a new and a fair hearing.' "

Id. at 309 (quoting *United States v. Throckmorton*, 98 U.S. 61, 65–66, 25 L. Ed. 93 (1878)).

It is well settled that "mistake" as used in Rule 2–535(b) is limited to a jurisdictional error, i.e. where the court has no power to enter the judgment. . . . [I]t is clear that the term "mistake," as used in Rule 2–535(b), does not mean a unilateral error of judgment on the part of one of the parties. . . .

Irregularity, as used in Rule 2–535(b), has been defined as "the doing or not doing of that, in the conduct of a suit at law, which, conformable to the practice of the court, ought or ought not to be done." *Weitz v. MacKenzie*, 273 Md. 628, 631, 331 A.2d 291 (1975) and cases cited therein. As a grounds for revising an enrolled judgment, irregularity, as well as fraud and mistake, has a very narrow scope. . . .

The cases before us today involve two competing interests: (1) the policy underlying Rule 2–535 that enrolled judgments are intended to be final and determine all claims between the parties and (2) the fundamental goal of our judicial system—the ascertainment of truth. To resolve the issues in these two cases, we must balance these competing interests.

IV

Case Number 144

Tyrone appears to argue that the circuit court properly vacated the original paternity judgment because both fraud and mistake occurred. First, he contends that the blood test excluded him and thus he was "mistakenly" adjudicated to be T.W.'s father. Second, he asserts that the mother's false statements in the original paternity complaint constituted fraud.

As detailed above, an enrolled judgment will only be vacated for mistake if the mistake is jurisdictional. In this case, Tyrone never alleged a jurisdictional mistake; rather, the only mistake he points to is the mistake which declared him to be the father. . . .

The mother's perjury in the 1990 paternity proceeding also may not serve as a basis for vacating the paternity decree. Her statement in the original paternity complaint that Tyrone was the father was obviously intrinsic to the proceeding, which does not implicate a court's revisory power under Rule 2–535(b). Extrinsic fraud, of course, entitles a party to have an enrolled judgment set aside, but Tyrone was not the subject of extrinsic fraud. He was not prevented from having a full adversarial proceeding in the original paternity action. It was his choice to sign the paternity agreement in 1990 and there is nothing in the record which indicates that he signed this document under any coercion or duress. Consequently,

Tyrone is bound by his actions in 1990 and, more specifically, he is bound by the 1990 judgment.

Tyrone filed his motion to set aside the paternity judgment in April of 1993, over two years after the paternity decree was entered. He had full knowledge of the original paternity complaint, and he knowingly waived his right to counsel, a blood test, a trial by judge or jury, and the right to call and cross-examine witnesses. He had every opportunity to present his defense in court; he may not now attempt to litigate the central issue of paternity after the decree has become enrolled.

The blood tests, which the circuit relied on in vacating the judgment, do not alter this result. Rule 2–535(b) provides a circuit court with very limited revisory powers. The results of the blood test did not change the unambiguous mandate that exists in the revisory rule. Therefore, the circuit court erred when it vacated the 1990 paternity judgment and left the child fatherless because, as the circuit court itself recognized, neither fraud, mistake, nor irregularity had occurred. The majority of decisions from other jurisdictions similarly reject attempts to reopen paternity judgments based on post-judgment blood tests. . . .

Case Number 157

John argues that the mother's perjury during the 1986 paternity proceeding was extrinsic fraud, justifying the circuit court's decision to vacate the 1986 paternity judgment. As noted above, however, perjury constitutes intrinsic fraud, which is not a ground for revising a judgment under Rule 2–535(b).

In the instant case, John consented to the paternity determination in 1986. He may not challenge that judgment seven years later in the absence of fraud, mistake, or irregularity. . . . [T]he only fraud that existed was intrinsic to the original proceeding. Consequently, the circuit court improperly vacated the 1986 paternity judgment.

John relies heavily on the change of name proceeding in 1987 and 1988. But this did not have the effect of nullifying the 1986 paternity judgment, which declared John to be the father; furthermore, it did not vest paternity in Randy. In regard to paternity and as to the parental relationship between John and the child, the name change was meaningless. . . .

V

The result in these cases may seem harsh. Indeed, in case no. 144, Tyrone has been excluded as a possible father. Nevertheless, in each case, the "judicially determined father" was advised of all the safeguards the law provides to prevent incorrect decisions, and waived all those rights. It is evident that each man had an adequate opportunity to obtain a fair and full adjudication of paternity in the original action, but each failed to avail himself of that opportunity. To argue that fairness requires relitigation of the paternity question totally overlooks the fact that the adjudicated fathers in each of these cases did have a chance to contest the paternity issue but did not, choosing instead to accept the paternity determination knowing that they would be required to support their respective children. It also overlooks the unfairness that would occur to the children if the paternity issue were allowed to be relitigated, thereby leaving the children fatherless and without support. . . .

ELRIDGE, J., dissenting.

. . . In a paternity action, unlike other lawsuits, a court is called upon to declare a scientific, biological fact, namely whether a particular individual is the biological father of a given child. Most other types of lawsuits, however, require a court to decide upon the appropriate remedy in a particular situation based upon society's rules applicable to human conduct. While the judgments in ordinary lawsuits often depend upon the judicial system's ascertainment of historical facts, the typical judicial fact-finding process is quite different from what a court is asked to do in a paternity action.

A judgment of paternity has continuing ramifications uncharacteristic of the typical judgment rendered by a court. In addition to providing the basis for child support, a paternity determination affects, inter alia, inheritance rights, citizenship, and the child's knowledge of his or her medical history. Thus, accurate determinations of paternity are critical, not simply because a child is entitled to financial support from his or her father, but also because a child may later be in need of a blood transfusion or an organ transplant from a compatible family member. A child may face decisions about marriage and childbearing based on the risk of passing on what the child believes are inherited conditions.

Similar ramifications are not usually associated with ordinary tort or contract litigation. In an automobile injury case, for example, a factfinder might decide that the traffic light was green when the plaintiff's car entered the intersection. If later it were irrefutably established that the light had been red, the consequences of foreclosing the matter because of the earlier judgment, which would simply involve the effect on the parties of the award or non-award of damages, are less compelling than the consequences of a paternity declaration.

Incidental to the resolution of the dispute between the mother and the putative father, a paternity judgment affects the interests of third parties to a greater extent than other judgments. A child has an independent interest in receiving financial support from his or her true parents. Furthermore, a child has an interest in knowing his or her true heritage for medical and psychological reasons, inheritance, and other purposes. Likewise, the natural father is entitled to an accurate determination of paternity, not just in order to uphold his parental obligations, but also for psychological and emotional reasons. . . .

In light of the basic differences between paternity judgments and the judgments in other types of lawsuits, the majority's holding today, in the words of the Court of Special Appeals, "defies common sense." Undoubtedly society has a strong interest in ending disputes at some point in time, and normally other interests must yield to the limitations on a court's revisory powers.

Nevertheless, a completely rigid adherence to the shibboleth that "in today's highly litigious society, there must be some point in time when a judgment becomes final," in the face of irrefutable scientific evidence that a particular individual did not father a given child, with all of the attendant ramifications of such decree, is absurd. Under the majority's view, presumably if the Provincial Court of Maryland in the 1600's had issued a decree that the earth was flat, the absence of "fraud, mistake or irregularity," as narrowly defined by this Court, would make that Provincial Court decree sacrosanct. Or, if Rule 2–535(b) were to be given extra-territorial effect, presumably the March 5, 1616, decree by a tribunal in Rome, aimed at Galileo Galilei, and declaring that Copernicanism is erroneous and that the planet earth is the center of the universe, would be given conclusive effect. Like the courts below, I do not believe that all common sense must be abandoned in the name of Rule 2–535(b)....

NOTES AND QUESTIONS

(1) The court notes that the Baltimore City Office of Child Support Enforcement (BCOCSE) successfully moved to intervene in this case, on the ground that "no party was adequately representing the interests of the Department of Social Services of Baltimore City." What are the Department's interests and why might none of the private litigants adequately represent them?

(2) Do the majority and the dissent in this case hold different views of the nature and purpose of a judicial determination of paternity? What does the majority opinion mean when it says (several times) that vacating the earlier paternity judgments would leave each of these children "fatherless"?

(3) In order to avoid future situations like these, should the state insist on DNA testing in all paternity proceedings, whether or not the parties request it? Who should pay for such testing?

(4) In 1995, the Maryland legislature modified the result in *Tandra S.* by amending the state paternity statutes to provide that a declaration of paternity may be revised or modified "if a blood or genetic test . . . establishes the exclusion of the individual named as the father," unless that individual previously acknowledged paternity knowing that he was not the father. Md. Fam. Law Code Ann. § 5-1038(a)(2) (1997).

(5) Suppose that Randy S. (the "true natural father" of Vandella's child) died, leaving a substantial estate and no will. Could Vandella's child attempt to claim an intestate share of his estate? Consider the following case.

JESSICA G. v. HECTOR M.
Court of Appeals of Maryland
653 A.2d 922 (Md.), *cert. denied*, 11 S. Ct. 99 (1995)

MURPHY

We granted certiorari to consider whether an unsuccessful paternity action brought by a mother which was dismissed with prejudice bars a subsequent paternity action brought by the mother's child.

I

. . . Joyce G. had an intimate relationship with Hector M. in March of 1985. On December 31, 1985, Joyce gave birth to Jessica. In May of 1986, Joyce instituted a paternity action against Hector in the Circuit Court for Harford County. Joyce, Jessica, and Hector submitted to blood tests and the results, which were completed on December 24, 1986, indicated a 99.97% probability that Hector was Jessica's father.

Notwithstanding the blood test results, Hector refused to admit paternity and continued to vigorously defend the case. For two years, he conducted extensive discovery, which included interrogatories, depositions, and requests for production of documents. At that point in the proceedings, Joyce asked to stop the paternity suit. A consent order of dismissal "with prejudice" was prepared and eventually signed by Hector, Hector's counsel, Judge Maurice W. Baldwin, and an Assistant State's Attorney, who was "representing" Joyce. When Joyce's attorney presented the consent order to Joyce for her signature she refused to sign because of the term "with prejudice." The State's Attorney nevertheless docketed the consent order on March 1, 1988, without Joyce's signature.

Over the next three years, Joyce returned to the Office of the State's Attorney on many occasions and asked to continue the paternity action against Hector. She was turned away each time and was finally informed by a staff member of the Harford County State's Attorney's office that she was forever precluded from bringing a paternity action or support proceeding against Hector because of the previous dismissal.

The State's Attorney, however, eventually agreed to bring an action under the Maryland Uniform Reciprocal Enforcement of Support Act, Maryland Code (1984, 1991 Repl. Vol.), Family Law Article (FL) §§ 10–301 through 10–340. In March of 1992, Joyce filed the action against Hector in the Family Court of Nassau County, New York. On June 16, 1992, the New York court dismissed the suit with prejudice, based on the 1988 Harford County dismissal with prejudice.

On July 31, 1992, Joyce filed in the Circuit Court for Harford County a motion to vacate the 1988 judgment. The court (Baldwin, J.) denied the motion to vacate on September 9, 1992. It explained that Maryland's revisory rule only permits an enrolled judgment to be vacated if fraud, mistake, or irregularity occurred; it concluded that neither fraud, mistake, nor irregularity existed in the 1988 case and thus the judgment could not be vacated or revised. Joyce noted an appeal of that dismissal on September 23, 1992, but failed to file a brief in the Court of Special Appeals. Consequently, the intermediate appellate court dismissed the appeal on March 30, 1993.

In the interim, on December 2, 1992, Joyce's minor daughter, Jessica, filed a paternity complaint against Hector in the Circuit Court for Harford County. Hector moved to dismiss, as described above. The court (Whitfill, J.) conducted a hearing regarding Hector's motion to dismiss on June 21, 1993 and concluded that res judicata barred Jessica from pursuing paternity or support from Hector. In particular, the court found that Joyce was representing Jessica's interests in the 1988 paternity action and thus Jessica's action fell squarely within the doctrine of res judicata. As a result, the court held that the dismissal with prejudice of Joyce's suit precluded Jessica's suit. Jessica appealed.

II

Before us, Hector reasserts his contention that Jessica is barred under the doctrine of res judicata. He maintains that the first action, although brought by Joyce, was brought on behalf of Jessica and represented Jessica's interests. Consequently, he argues that Jessica should be deemed to be in privity with Joyce. Claiming that the parties are in privity, the paternity issue is identical, and there is a prior judgment on the merits, Hector avers that this is a textbook case of res judicata. Under that doctrine, he contends that Jessica's suit was properly dismissed by the circuit court.

Jessica argues that she has a fundamental right to determine paternity and that that right cannot be abrogated by any action of her mother. Specifically, Jessica claims that a child has a fundamental right to a father and that the circuit court deprived her of that right without ever hearing the case on the merits. Therefore, she avers that "when the Circuit Court never considered the merits of the paternity claim and dismissed [her] cause solely on the previous, separate proceeding of [her] mother, a fundamental right was taken without due process."

According to Jessica, an illegitimate child's right to support from her putative father cannot be contracted away by the child's mother, and any release executed by the mother is invalid because it is against public policy. She asserts that, because there is no legitimate question that Hector is Jessica's father, the consent order amounts to a waiver of Jessica's right to support and, consequently, cannot operate to preclude this action.

Jessica also contends that res judicata does not bar a paternity action brought by a child where a paternity suit brought by the child's mother has previously been dismissed with prejudice. She claims that courts in other jurisdictions have concluded that a child is not barred by a previous unsuccessful paternity action brought by the child's mother.

Jessica also argues that res judicata should not be applied in this case because there were procedural and equitable defects in the original action brought by her mother. She observes that the Assistant State's Attorney in the original action docketed the consent order of dismissal even though her mother, Joyce, specifically asked the State's Attorney not to dismiss the case with prejudice and refused to sign the order. She contends that the action taken by the State's Attorney, Joyce's counsel, went beyond the scope of the attorney's authority and, as a result, the consent order was improperly filed. . . .

III.

Although the issue before us today has never been specifically addressed in the State of Maryland, other jurisdictions have confronted the issue of whether there may be a second paternity action brought by a child after the mother's unsuccessful action. These cases are often decided on res judicata principles. For example, the Court of Appeals of Arizona has said:

> Paternity statutes, in several ways, evince an intention to benefit the public, mother and child, regardless of who is formally named a party. The state's main goal in a paternity suit is to divest itself of responsibility for supporting the child through various welfare programs. The mother's aim is assuredly economic as well. An order of filiation bears a concomitant obligation for the father to share in childrearing expenses. The child, however, has not only economic motives, but other independent interests, such as establishing lineage for inheritance purposes. Although the state may have interests different from the mother or child in seeking the father, their mutual objective is singular. Additionally, if the defendant is found to be the father, he incurs identical obligations . . . , regardless of in whose name the suit was brought. . . .
>
> "From the above we conclude that the child's interests are inextricably bound to the litigation of a paternity action, whether brought in the name of the state, the mother or the guardian. We are led to this conclusion by a recognition that the substance of the action, rather than its technical form, must prevail in determining whose rights are being adjudicated. The fact that the state's name [or the mother's name] appears on the case, rather than the child's, does not change the fact that the issue to be litigated and the effect on the child's rights to support will be equal. This conclusion is further

supported by our opinion that the paternity statutes do not contemplate multiple and successive actions by all who are authorized to bring suit. . . . 'When the interest of the same person is more than once placed in litigation, judicial finality ought not to be avoided by a change of the form in which the interest is represented.'" *Bill by and through Bill v. Gussett*, 647 P.2d 649, 654 (Ct. App. 1982)

. . . The conclusion that a child is bound by the results of a prior paternity action brought by the child's mother is supported by numerous decisions in other jurisdictions. . . .

In contrast to the above cases, a number of other courts have concluded, for varying reasons, that a child is not barred by a previous unsuccessful paternity action filed by the child's mother. . . . The majority of these cases involved prior paternity actions which were never actually litigated and none involved a prior action where the child was an actual party represented by counsel. In some of these decisions, the courts indicated that, had the mother's paternity action actually been litigated, the child's subsequent suit would have been barred . . .

Therefore, the decisions from other jurisdictions appear to be split on the issue before us today, although the vast majority follow the proposition that when there is an actual factual determination of non-paternity in a paternity suit by the child's mother, then the child is forever bound by that factual finding. . . .

IV.

Family Law § 5–1038 governs our decision in the instant case. It provides as follows:

"§ 5–1038. Finality; modification.

"(a) Declaration of paternity final.—Except in the manner and to the extent that any order or decree of an equity court is subject to the revisory power of the court under any law, rule, or established principle of practice and procedure in equity, a declaration of paternity in an order is final.

"(b) Other orders subject to modification.—Except for a declaration of paternity, the court may modify or set aside any order or part of an order under this subtitle as the court considers just and proper in light of the circumstances and in the best interests of the child."

In *Tandra S. v. Tyrone W* . . . , we construed § (a) of FL § 5–1038, and we held that the statute meant exactly what it said, i.e., that, except to the extent that an equity order is subject to the revisory power of the court, a declaration of paternity in a paternity order is final. . . . In the instant case, we must construe § (b) of the same statute, and we hold that it means what it says, i.e., that all paternity orders except declarations of paternity can be modified or set aside "in light of the circumstances and in the best interests of the child." FL § 5–1038(b). We hasten to add that the discretion to modify or set aside otherwise final orders merely because they are entered in a paternity case is a remedy which must be exercised with the utmost caution. . . .

The action of the State's Attorney in dismissing the paternity action with prejudice over the objection of the child's indigent mother in spite of a 99.97% probability of paternity was certainly contrary to the best interests of the child. We consider it just and proper, in light of the circumstances in the instant case, that Jessica have an opportunity to establish what is a 99.97% probability according to the blood tests, i.e., that Hector is her father and owes her an obligation of support.

Were we to ignore FL § 5–1038(b) and give the dismissal with prejudice in Joyce's first paternity action the ordinary effect applicable to non-paternity cases, that would be contrary to the majority rule in this country. The majority of other courts would not bar a child's paternity action even if prior thereto the child's mother's paternity action was dismissed without a factual finding on the paternity issue. Dismissal of Jessica's paternity action would also be contrary to the strong public policy expressly recognized by the General Assembly in enacting the paternity statute. In FL § 5–1002(a)(1) the General Assembly declares that "this State has a duty to improve the deprived social and economic status of children born out of wedlock." Among the purposes of the paternity statute are:

"(1) to promote the general welfare and best interests of children born out of wedlock by securing for them, as nearly as practicable, the same rights to support, care, and education as children born in wedlock; [and]

"(2) to impose on the mothers and fathers of children born out of wedlock the basic obligations and responsibilities or parenthood."

FL § 5–1002(b).

. . . Thus, the dismissal with prejudice of Joyce's first paternity action does not bar Jessica's action, but the analysis cannot end at that point. [The court then concluded that, for reasons similar to those advanced above, it was not bound by the New York court's dismissal of the paternity action that Joyce had filed there.]

NOTES AND QUESTIONS

(1) Are the majority opinions in the *Jessica G.* and *Tandra S.* cases consistent? Why or why not?

(2) What sorts of finality rules should apply to paternity judgments? Should those rules differ from the rules applicable to other types of judicial decisions? Why or why not? Does your answer depend on whether you believe that legal parenthood is (primarily) a matter of biology or (primarily) a matter of social construction? You may wish to reconsider these questions after you have read the materials in § 5.05 on Establishing Parental Rights.

(3) **Problem**. Erin and Richard married in 1979. Erin had an affair with Terry during the marriage; Richard was unaware of the affair. Erin give birth to a child in 1986. In 1989, Erin and Richard divorced. The divorce court found the child to be the only issue of the marriage, awarded custody to Erin, with visitation rights to Richard, and ordered Richard to pay child support. Subsequently, Erin married Terry. When she met Terry's family members, she noticed the child's strong resemblance to them. Blood tests then taken indicated a 99.9% likelihood that Terry was in fact the child's biological father. Erin and Terry then sought to modify the marital dissolution decree to indicate that Richard was not the child's father and to terminate his visitation rights and support obligations. Richard opposed the modification. What result and why? See *Devaux v. Devaux*, 514 N.W.2d 640 (Neb. 1994).

[C] Procedural Issues in Paternity Cases

(1) **Standard of Proof.** In *Rivera v. Minnich*, 483 U.S. 574 (1987), the Supreme Court upheld the constitutionality of a preponderance-of-the-evidence standard for determining

paternity. The Court distinguished paternity establishment from proceedings to terminate parental rights, in which the Constitution requires a clear-and-convincing-evidence standard. *See Santosky v. Kramer*, 455 U.S. 745 (1982). Although the Constitution requires only a preponderance standard, a few states still require that paternity be proved by the "quasi-criminal" standard of clear and convincing evidence. *See, e.g., County Dep't of Soc. Servs. v. Williams*, 468 N.E. 2d 705 (N.Y. 1984). A number of other states apply the clear-and-convincing-evidence standard to paternity determinations that take place after the alleged father's death. *See, e.g., Ross v. Moore*, 758 S.W. 2d 423 (Ark. Ct. App. 1998) (applying clear and convincing standard in state-initiated filiation action where alleged father died during pendency of the action); *Reed v. Flournoy*, 600 So. 2d 1024 (Ala. Civ. App. 1992) (claim for paternity must be proven by clear and convincing evidence in order to assert inheritance rights after the death of the alleged father).

(2) **Constitutionality of Court-ordered Paternity Testing**. Statutes and court rules in virtually all states authorize judges to order genetic and other blood testing for paternity in any proceeding in which paternity is at issue. Courts have consistently upheld the constitutionality of such court-ordered paternity testing. *See, e.g., In re J.M.*, 590 So. 2d 565 (La. 1991); *Bowerman v. MacDonald*, 427 N.W.2d 477 (Mich. 1988); *Rose v. District Court of Eighth Judicial District*, 628 P.2d 662 (Mont. 1981); *State v. Meacham*, 93 Wash. 2d 735, 612 P.2d 795 (Wash. 1980). The federal government now requires states to provide for court-ordered paternity testing, upon the justified request of any party to a paternity action. 42 U.S.C. § 666(a)(5)(B) (1998).

(3) **State's Obligation to Pay for Scientific Testing**. In *Little v. Streater*, 452 U.S. 1 (1981), a unanimous Supreme Court held that, given the state's substantial involvement in civil paternity proceedings and the unique ability of blood testing evidence to exonerate a falsely accused putative father, a state's refusal to pay for blood grouping tests requested by an indigent paternity defendant violated the Due Process Clause of the Fourteenth Amendment. *Query:* Is a state also obligated to pay the costs of paternity testing for an indigent putative father who seeks to establish (rather than disprove) his paternity?

(4) **Right to Counsel in Paternity Cases.** The Supreme Court has never determined whether indigent defendants have a constitutional right to appointed counsel in disputed paternity cases. Most state and federal courts that have considered the issue have found that there is no constitutional right to counsel in civil paternity cases, under either the Due Process or the Equal Protection Clauses. *E.g., Nodgren v. Mitchell*, 716 F.2d 1335 (10th Cir. 1983) (neither due process nor equal protection clause requires state to appoint counsel for indigent prisoners who are defendants in paternity actions); *Carrington v. Townes*, 293 S.E.2d 95 (N.C. 1982) (no absolute due process right to counsel in paternity suits against indigents). A few state courts have held that counsel must be appointed in all paternity cases where the defendant is indigent. *E.g., Artibee v. Cheboygan Circuit Judge*, 243 N.W. 248 (Mich. 1976) (given complexity and coercive nature of paternity proceedings, Equal Protection Clause requires appointment of counsel for indigents); *Reynolds v. Kimmons*, 569 P.2d 799 (Alaska 1977) (in light of complexity and serious consequences of paternity determination, constitution requires appointment of counsel).

Apart from constitutional requirements, many states have statutes that require the appointment of counsel for indigent defendants in paternity actions. For example, Section 19 of the Uniform Parentage Act provides, in pertinent part: "at the pretrial hearing and in further proceedings, any party may be represented by counsel. The court shall appoint counsel for any party who is financially unable to obtain counsel." Unif. Parentage Act § 19, 9B U.L.A. § 332. *Query:* Does the increased importance of scientific evidence in determining paternity render the assistance of counsel more or less important?

(5) **Personal Jurisdiction.** Most states have statutes that govern jurisdiction and venue in paternity actions. In addition to generally applicable bases for asserting personal jurisdiction, Section 5 of the Uniform Parentage Act provides:

> A person who has sexual intercourse in this State thereby submits to the jurisdiction of the courts of this State as to an action brought under this Act with respect to a child who may be been conceived by that act of intercourse.

Unif. Parentage Act § 8, 9 U.L.A. § 310. In response to challenges by paternity defendants, several courts have held that an act of sexual intercourse which results in conception satisfies the "minimum contacts" requirement of the Due Process Clause for asserting personal jurisdiction over a non-resident defendant. *See, e.g., Shirley D. v. Carl D.*, 648 N.Y.S.2d 650 (N.Y. App. Div. 1996); *Jones v. Chandler*, 592 So. 2d 966 (Miss. 1991); *Larson v. Scholl*, 296 N.W.2d 785 (Iowa 1980). *Query:* Should sexual intercourse within a state be sufficient to establish "minimum contacts" where the child was conceived outside the state? *See Pouliot v. Kennedy*, 426 N.W.2d 866 (Minn. 1988).

§ 5.04 Imposing Parental Support Obligations

One of the major purposes of establishing legal parenthood is to provide for the financial support of children born outside of marriage. The Supreme Court has held that the Equal Protection Clause requires that a state afford nonmarital children the same rights to parental support and maintenance that the state chooses to give children born to married parents. *Gomez v. Perez*, 409 U.S. 535 (1973). Paternity and support actions can be brought either by the child's mother or by a social service agency that has provided benefits to the child and the custodial parent. The following case iconsiders the defenses available in a paternity and support action.

MURPHY v. MEYERS
Minnesota Court of Appeals
560 N.W.2d 752 (1997)

WILLIS, JUDGE.

John Myers appeals from the district court's judgment of paternity and denial of his motion to raise fraud and misrepresentation as affirmative defenses. . . . We affirm.

John Myers lived with Merley Polo Murphy for approximately three months in 1991. Myers admits that he and Murphy had sexual relations, but claims that he only agreed to such a relationship after Murphy claimed to have undergone sterilization surgery and showed Myers scars on her abdomen that she said were the result of a tubal ligation.

Myers ended the relationship with Murphy after she announced that she was pregnant. On May 7, 1992, Murphy gave birth to a daughter, M.M., and subsequently initiated a paternity and child support action against Myers. Olmsted County joined in the action to recover child support arrears for the four-month period following M.M.'s birth, during which

Murphy received Aid to Families with Dependent Children (AFDC). The district court ordered blood tests, which showed a 99.97% probability that Myers was M.M.'s father.

In his answer, Myers raised fraud and misrepresentation as affirmative defenses. Before trial, he moved the court to allow the jury to consider his claim that Murphy had falsely represented to him that she had been sterilized and to order Murphy to provide a photograph of the scars on her abdomen. The district court denied Myers' motion, reasoning that (1) the defense of fraud was irrelevant as against the county and M.M., who, although not a party, had an interest in the proceedings, and (2) because child support had not yet been ordered, Myers had not established damage, an essential element of fraud, as against Murphy.

Following the denial of his motion, Myers waived his right to a jury trial. Based on the blood test results and the fact that Murphy engaged in sexual relations only with Myers during the period of conception, the district court found that Myers is M.M.'s father. Pursuant to the parties' agreement, the district court awarded custody of M.M. to Murphy and referred child support issues to an administrative law judge for determination in a separate hearing. The administrative law judge ordered Myers to pay monthly support of $ 135, plus $ 540 to the county for AFDC reimbursement and $ 6210 in arrears to Murphy. . . .

ANALYSIS

The question of whether fraud and misrepresentation are available defenses to paternity is one of first impression in Minnesota. Although apparently no court has considered the specific issue of a mother's false claim of sterilization, several states have barred putative fathers from raising an affirmative defense that the mother falsely claimed to be taking birth control pills. See *Erwin L.D. v. Myla Jean L.*, 41 Ark. App. 16, 847 S.W.2d 45, 47–48 (Ark. Ct. App. 1993); *Faske v. Bonanno*, 137 Mich. App. 202, 357 N.W.2d 860, 861 (Mich. Ct. App. 1984); *L. Pamela P. v. Frank S.*, 59 N.Y.2d 1, 449 N.E.2d 713, 715–16, 462 N.Y.S.2d 819 (N.Y. 1983); *Hughes v. Hutt*, 500 Pa. 209, 455 A.2d 623, 625 (Pa. 1983). State courts have also held that a father may not avoid or reduce child support liability by claiming that a child's conception resulted from the mother's fraud, see *Beard v. Skipper*, 182 Mich. App. 352, 451 N.W.2d 614, 615 (Mich. Ct. App. 1990); *Linda D. v. Fritz C.*, 38 Wash. App. 288, 687 P.2d 223, 227 (Wash. Ct. App. 1984), review denied, 102 Wash. 2d 1024 (Wash. 1984); and that an adjudicated father may not subsequently bring a tort action for fraud or misrepresentation against the mother to recover the amount of support, see *Stephen K. v. Roni L.*, 105 Cal. App. 3d 640, 164 Cal. Rptr. 618, 621 (Cal. Ct. App. 1980); *Welzenbach v. Powers*, 139 N.H. 688, 660 A.2d 1133, 1136 (N.H. 1995).

The courts that decided these cases relied on the unique nature of paternity and child support actions and on state policies promoting the determination of paternity and parental support of children. Nothing in Minnesota case law differentiates this state from others in these regards. The purpose of a paternity action is not to punish the father, but rather to impose a duty on the father to support the child, to ensure [that] the mother does not bear full financial responsibility for the child, and to protect the public by preventing the child from becoming a public charge. *Jevning v. Cichos*, 499 N.W.2d 515, 517 (Minn. App. 1993). A child's interests in an adjudication of paternity are "distinct and separate from those of both her mother and father." *R.B. v. C.S.*, 536 N.W.2d 634, 638 n.2 (Minn. App. 1995).

In addition to issues of monetary support, a child has unique interests in the establishment of paternity for the purpose of securing legal rights such as inheritance, medical support, the ability to bring certain causes of action (e.g., wrongful death), workers' compensation dependent's allowances, and veterans' education benefits. *Johnson v. Hunter*, 447 N.W.2d 871, 875 (Minn. 1989). A claim of fault in the child's conception is not relevant to these concerns. . . .

This court rejected an argument similar to Myers's in *Jevning*, in which we held that a putative father could not avoid the obligation to pay child support on the ground that the child was conceived when the father was only 15 years old and the mother more than 24 months older, making the father technically a victim of statutory rape. 499 N.W.2d at 518. This court accepted the policy reasoning of the district court:

> [If the court accepted defendant's argument,] the child would be deprived of obtaining a determination of his father; he would be denied support from a defendant who openly admits parentage; and the State would be forced to accept the burden of supporting the child despite the fact that paternity can be established. The Court cannot condone [the mother's] possible criminal actions, but holds that the child's interests in receiving support must supersede any economic consequences [appellant] suffers from [the mother's actions.]

499 N.W.2d at 517–18. We also noted that "support is paid to benefit the child, not the custodial parent." Id. at 517. *Jevning* therefore weighs against recognition of Myers's proposed defenses to the extent that his desire to avoid being adjudicated M.M.'s father might stem from a desire to avoid child support obligations.. . . .

Myers's argument also strongly resembles an equitable estoppel defense, which is an assertion that the plaintiff made representations or inducements on which the defendant reasonably relied, and that as a result of this reliance, the defendant would suffer harm unless the plaintiff's claim was estopped. This court has held that, because of the need to protect a child's right to support, equitable estoppel is not available as a defense to the collection of child support arrears. *Faribault-Martin-Watonwan Human Servs. ex rel. Jacobson v. Jacobson*, 363 N.W.2d 342, 346 (Minn. App. 1985). The same policies prevent the application of an equitable estoppel defense to a paternity claim and to the initial determination of child support and dictate that a putative father should not be allowed to raise a defense with the same elements under a different name. . . .

In summary, the other states that have considered the issue have unanimously barred the use of fraud and misrepresentation as defenses to paternity or child support obligations. The legislature and courts of Minnesota have stated a consistent policy in favor of determining paternity and collecting child support and have accordingly restricted the issues in paternity proceedings. The state has also rejected other claims substantially similar to Myers's, and, as the district court correctly noted, Myers's defense would at best be valid against only one of three potential plaintiffs. Because of all these factors, we affirm the decision of the district court to bar Myers from asserting fraud and misrepresentation as defenses to paternity.

NOTES AND QUESTIONS

(1) What rationale for imposing child support duties underlies the court's decision in *Murphy*?

(2) As you saw in the previous chapter, a state may not require a woman to obtain consent from, or to notify, her husband (or boyfriend) before obtaining an abortion. *Planned Parenthood of Southeastern Pennsylvania v. Casey*, 505 U.S. 833 (1992); *Planned Parenthood of Missouri v. Danforth*, 428 U.S. 52, 69–70 (1976). Nor may a biological father force a woman to carry a pregnancy to term, rather than undergo an abortion. Yet *Murphy* indicates that a biological father may be required to support a child financially, regardless of whether he "consented" to procreation? Is this fair to fathers? Would a contrary rule be fair to children? To mothers?

(3) As the opinion in *Murphy* suggests, courts have uniformly rejected claims of maternal fraud or misrepresentation as defenses to paternity and child support actions. In so doing, courts have held that imposing child support obligations under such circumstances does not violate a father's due process or equal protection rights. *See, e.g., Matter of L. Pamela P. v. Frank S.* 449 N.E. 2d 713, 715 (N.Y. 1983) ("respondent's constitutional entitlement to avoid procreation does not encompass a right to avoid a child support obligation simply because another private person has not fully respected his desires in this regard"). Courts have similarly rejected attempts by adjudicated fathers to sue in tort for fraud, misrepresentation or intentional infliction of emotional distress. *E.g., Welzenbach v. Powers*, 660 A.2d 1133 (N.H. 1995); *Beard v. Skipper*, 451 N.W.2d 614 (Mich. Ct. App. 1990). *See generally* Pinhas Shifman, *Involuntary Parenthood: Misrepresentation as to the Use of Contraceptives*, 4 Int'l. J. L. & Fam. 279 (1990). What public policy considerations underlie the refusal of courts to recognize such claims?

(4) **Problem.** Francine wanted to have a child, but she did not want to be married. She and Edward signed a handwritten agreement providing that Edward would not be responsible for supporting any child that the two might conceive. The couple had sexual relations and Francine became pregnant; she later gave birth to a healthy baby girl. Five years later, Francine filed a paternity action against Edward, seeking child support and medical expenses. Edward moved to dismiss Francine's action, relying on the written agreement. How should the court rule and why? *See Straub v. Todd*, 645 N.E.2d 597 (Ind. 1994).

(5) **Maternal Cooperation Requirements.** Under both the Aid to Families with Dependent Children (AFDC) program and the more recent Temporary Assistance to Needy Families (TANF) program, which replaced AFDC in 1996, the federal government has made the enforcement of child support obligations a top national priority. Under the rules of both TANF and AFDC, individuals who receive benefits are required to assign their child support rights to the state and to cooperate with state authorities in establishing paternity and obtaining support payments. 42 U.S.C. § 408(a)(3) (1997 Supp.); 42 U.S.C. § 654(29) (1998) (replacing 42 U.S.C. § 602(a)(26) (1985)). A narrow "good cause" exception to the cooperation requirement exists, primarily in cases of domestic abuse. 42 U.S.C. § 654(29) (1998); *see* 45 C.F.R. 232.42 (1995) (defining cause good exception under AFDC) If an aid recipient fails to cooperate without "good cause," a financial sanction is imposed—the noncooperating party's share of the benefit is terminated and, if possible, the portion of the benefit dedicated to the child is given to a "protective payee," rather than to the non-cooperating parent. Paula Roberts, *The Family Law Implications of the 1996 Welfare Legislation*, 30 Clearinghouse Rev. 988, 997–1003 (1997); 42 U.S.C. § 666(a)(5)(B) (1998).

Advocates for low-income women have criticized the scope and intrusiveness of the cooperation requirement. According to one scholar and former legal services attorney:

[T]he reasons that a custodial parent might want to avoid cooperation are numerous and are not limited to the narrow confines of the good-cause exception. At the very least, the establishment of paternity involves intrusion by strangers into private sexual matters. The adversarial system may also inject friction into an ongoing relationship in which the father is already supporting the child to the custodial parent's satisfaction. Still other mothers may be fearful of the children's fathers if their relationships with the father have been charged with abuse. Many women may be concerned that establishing paternity and requiring child support may lead the father to attempt to obtain custody or to kidnap or abuse the child during visitation.

Lisa Kelly, *If Anybody Asks You Who I Am: An Outsider's Story of the Duty To Establish Paternity,* 3 Am. U. J. Gender & Law 247, 248(1995). For additional descriptions of the problems encountered by aid recipients as they attempt to comply with the cooperation requirement, see Amy E. Hirsch, *Income Deeming in the AFDC Program: using Dual Track Family Law to Make Poor Women Poorer,* 16 N.Y.U. Rev. L. & Soc. Change 713, 725 (1988–89); James W. Johnson & Adele Blong, *The AFDC Child Support Cooperation Requirement,* 20 Clearinghouse Rev. 1389, 1393–1407 (1987). Courts have generally rejected claims that conditioning AFDC benefits on maternal cooperation impermissibly intrudes on a mother's constitutionally protected privacy interests. *See Perry v. Dowling,* 963 F. Supp. 231 (W.D.N.Y. 1997).

(6) *Murphy* illustrates the legal system's current insistence that biological paternity alone is a sufficient ground for imposing child-support obligations. However, courts have been been considerably more ambivalent about whether the *lack* of a biological connection necessarily precludes the imposition of child-support responsibilities. The following case illustrates the use of estoppel to mediate between biological and legal parenthood.

PIETROS v. PIETROS
Supreme Court of Rhode Island
638 A.2d 545 (1994)

SHEA, J.

The plaintiff, Michael A. Pietros (hereinafter Michael), appeals from a Family Court order to pay child support and medical coverage for the one child born during his marriage to the defendant, Cheryl Pietros (hereinafter Cheryl). The Family Court justice denied Michael's attempt to introduce blood-test results establishing to a medical certainty that he was not the child's biological father. The Family Court justice decided that Michael was equitably estopped from challenging his paternity at the divorce proceeding. We affirm.

The parties began dating in August of 1985, shortly after Cheryl's relationship with another man had ended. At the time the parties began dating, Cheryl was already pregnant. Cheryl informed Michael of the pregnancy in October of 1985, and she testified that his immediate reaction was to propose marriage. The couple was married on November 13, 1985. The child was born just under three months later on February 9, 1986.

The parties were both nineteen years old at the time of the marriage. Prior to the marriage, Michael assured Cheryl that he would treat the child as his own, support the child, and live as a family unit. Michael repeated these assurances in the presence of Cheryl's relatives. Michael was aware that Cheryl had terminated a previous pregnancy and was contemplating similar action for this pregnancy. The trial justice found that Cheryl relied on Michael's assurances when deciding to marry Michael, to bear the child, and to assume the joint obligation to support the child until majority.

The couple agreed to name the child Michael Vincent Pietros, apparently in honor of Michael and Michael's father. The child's birth certificate and baptismal record listed Michael as the child's father. The parties lived together as a family. Michael held himself out to the community as the child's father. The child called Michael "daddy," and called Michael's mother "Gramma Elaine."

By May of 1988, however, marital difficulties led Cheryl to file for divorce. In his verified counterclaim for divorce, Michael sought custody of the two-year-old child. The couple's ensuing separation lasted several months. The parties reconciled and no further action was taken on the divorce complaint.

Any remaining marital harmony, however, was exhausted over the next two years. . . . Michael then filed the complaint for divorce that eventually brought the parties before this court.

In his complaint for divorce Michael sought custody of the then four-year-old child. Cheryl filed a counterclaim for divorce. On February 20, 1991, a Family Court justice held a hearing on the parties' opposing motions for temporary orders. The justice ordered Michael to pay $ 96 per week for child support and ordered all parties to undergo blood testing. After the blood tests confirmed that Michael was not the biological father of the child, both Michael and Cheryl jointly moved for appointment of a guardian ad litem. On October 9, 1991, Michael moved to amend his divorce complaint to name the alleged biological father as a party and to seek an order terminating his parental rights and obligations to the child.

The Family Court justice denied Michael's motion to amend. A trial on the merits took place on March 27, 1992. Cheryl testified that the biological father of her child was her former boyfriend. The former boyfriend testified that although he currently had steady employment and no dependents, he did not want any contact or involvement with the child. The Family Court justice denied several attempts by Michael's attorney to admit the results of the court-ordered blood tests into evidence . . . .

The issue before this court is whether the Family Court justice erred in finding equitable estoppel precludes the husband in a divorce proceeding from refuting his paternity in order to avoid child-support payments. Michael is the presumed father of the child under Rhode Island law because he and the child's natural mother were married to each other when the child was born. See G.L. 1956 (1988 Reenactment) § 15–8–3–(a)(1) (listing criteria for presumption of paternity). The trial justice found that both Cheryl and the child relied to their detriment on Michael's assurances that he would provide them emotional and financial support. The trial justice decided that Michael should be equitably estopped by his past conduct from escaping the obligation to pay child support solely because he is not the child's biological father. After review of the record, the applicable case law and the arguments of the parties, we cannot say that the trial justice was clearly wrong.

It is not disputed that Michael is not the biological father of the child. Both Cheryl and Michael testified that Michael was not the biological father. Cheryl's former boyfriend, the putative biological father, testified that he was sexually involved with Cheryl until their relationship ended in August of 1985. This case does not concern the admissibility of blood tests to disprove paternity because the child's paternity is not in dispute. The crux of this case is whether a court may impose child-support obligations on a husband who is not a child's biological father.

This court has held a mother equitably estopped from using blood tests to disestablish her husband's paternity of her child during a routine divorce proceeding. Pettinato, 582 A.2d at 912. We stated that the underlying rationale of the equitable-estoppel doctrine is that in "certain circumstances, a person might be estopped from challenging paternity where that person has by his or her conduct accepted a given person as the father of the child." Id. at 912–13 (quoting John M. v. Paula T., 524 Pa. 306, 318, 571 A.2d 1380, 1386 (1990)). The trial justice found the circumstances of the present case warranted applying the doctrine of equitable estoppel.

The trial justice's decision enumerated the numerous facts that she relied upon to invoke the doctrine of equitable estoppel. Both Michael and Cheryl knew prior to their marriage that Michael was not the child's biological father. Michael and Cheryl discussed the child at length and in the presence of Cheryl's relatives prior to the marriage. Cheryl had considered terminating this pregnancy. Michael assured Cheryl that he would treat the child as his own, support the child, and live with Cheryl and the child as a family unit. The parties did live as a family, and the evidence included a newspaper photograph of Michael and "his son Michael." Michael never told the child that he was not his father. The child gave love and affection to Michael, and the child bonded to Michael as his father. Prior to the marriage, Michael had expressly stated to Cheryl's mother that he was aware of his obligation to support the child if he married Cheryl. The trial justice found that Cheryl's decision to bear the child was a direct result of Michael's promises.

On appeal both parties cited case law from other jurisdictions to support their arguments for whether equitable estoppel applies to this case. A review of these and other cases demonstrates that the decision to apply equitable estoppel is necessarily a case-by-case determination. Although each case turns on the particular circumstances presented, we must emphasize that the Family Court should employ the doctrine of equitable estoppel to serve the needs and interests of the child.

In the present case Michael is the only father the child has ever known. Michael argued that he had no intention of reestablishing contact and providing the child with further love and affection. As between Michael and the putative biological father, both of whom profess no interest in a future relationship with the child, we agree with the trial justice that Michael should bear the burden of child support. It is in the child's best interest that the man who encouraged a loving paternal relationship with the child, and who received the benefits of the child's love and affection not escape the concomitant obligation of support. As deep as our concerns are for Michael, we cannot sanction the proposition that children can be embraced and raised by a person as a parent and then discarded when the parents no longer get along.

This case reached our court upon an appeal from a complaint for divorce. Michael originally sought custody of the child in his divorce complaint, and had sought joint custody in a divorce counterclaim some two years earlier, although he subsequently moved to amend his complaint to deny paternity and to avoid child-support payments. Children are not mere personal property to be assigned or distributed upon divorce. . . .

It is important to state that this decision works no injustice. The dissenting justices in a decision relied upon by Michael recognized the true nature of estoppel: "To so estop [the husband], in the circumstances of this case, is not affirmatively to impose a duty of child support upon him. That duty is placed upon [the husband], not directly by the application of estoppel itself, but rather because his voluntary assumption of the parental role over such an extended period now precludes him from disavowing parental responsibility for child support." Knill v. Knill, 306 Md. 527, 554, 510 A.2d 546, 560 (1986) (Murphy, C.J., dissenting). Michael's liability for child-support payments is a result of his voluntary and continuous course of conduct as the child's only father. Indeed, the trial justice found that Cheryl's decision to bear the child was a direct result of Michael's assurances that he would assume the parental role. No injustice results to hold Michael now accountable for the direct consequences of his actions.

NOTES AND QUESTIONS

(1) Equitable estoppel generally consists of three elements: representation, reliance and detriment. In *Miller v. Miller*, 478 A.2d 351, 355 (N.J. 1984), the New Jersey Supreme Court explained these elements as follows:

> To establish a claim of equitable estoppel, the claiming party must show that the alleged conduct was done, or representation was made, intentionally or under circumstances that it was both natural and probable that it would induce action. Further, the conduct must be relied on and the relying party must act so as to change his or her position to his or her detriment

Do the facts in *Pietros* establish these elements? Why or why not?

(2) Would the result in *Pietros* have been different if Michael had believed, prior to and during the marriage, that he *was* the child's biological father?

(3) If Michael dies during the child's minority, should Cheryl be able to seek child support from her former boyfriend? Should Cheryl's son be able to file a paternity action against the former boyfriend? Should Cheryl's former boyfriend be able to petition for visitation with the child? *See Michael H. v. Gerald D.*, § 5.05[A], *below*.

(4) Suppose that Michael fails to fulfill his court-imposed child-support obligations after the divorce and Cheryl applies for public assistance for herself and her son. Should the state be able to seek reimbursement from Michael? From Cheryl's former boyfriend?

(5) Suppose that it was Cheryl, rather than Michael, who was seeking to disestablish Michael's paternity, in connection with the parties' divorce, in order to defeat Michael's claims to visitation or custody. Should she be permitted to do so?

§ 5.05 Establishing Parental Rights

The preceding sections focus on the establishment of legal parenthood in order to impose parental responsibilities, primarily the responsibility of an unmarried father to support his children financially. Increasingly, however, unmarried fathers have also invoked the legal system to establish a relationship with a child and to assert parental rights and interests. What is striking about these "paternal rights" cases is the diminished importance of biology, at least as a matter of constitutional law. In the eyes of the Supreme Court, the biological or genetic connection between a father and a child counts for relatively little; rather the Court has chosen to give great weight to state statutory requirements for establishing paternity and for asserting parental rights—requirements that, for the most part, predate the scientific advancements, discussed in section 5.03 *above,* which have significantly enhanced our ability to determine with certainty the genetic connection between parents and children. As you read the cases in this section, consider what explains the diminished weight given to biology in this context and whether such discrepancies are justified.

[A] Presumptive Parents

MICHAEL H. v. GERALD D.
Supreme Court of the United States
491 U.S. 110 (1989)

JUSTICE SALIA announced the judgment of the Court . . .

I

The facts of this case are, we must hope, extraordinary. On May 9, 1976, in Las Vegas, Nevada, Carole D., an international model, and Gerald D., a top executive in a French oil company, were married. The couple established a home in Playa del Rey, California, in which they resided as husband and wife when one or the other was not out of the country on business. In the summer of 1978, Carole became involved in an adulterous affair with a neighbor, Michael H. In September 1980, she conceived a child, Victoria D., who was born on May 11, 1981. Gerald was listed as father on the birth certificate and has always held Victoria out to the world as his daughter. Soon after delivery of the child, however, Carole informed Michael that she believed he might be the father.

In the first three years of her life, Victoria remained always with Carole, but found herself within a variety of quasi-family units. In October 1981, Gerald moved to New York City to pursue his business interests, but Carole chose to remain in California. At the end of that month, Carole and Michael had blood tests of themselves and Victoria, which showed a 98.07% probability that Michael was Victoria's father. In January 1982, Carole visited Michael in St. Thomas, where his primary business interests were based. There Michael held Victoria out as his child. In March, however, Carole left Michael and returned to California, where she took up residence with yet another man, Scott K. Later that spring, and again in the summer, Carole and Victoria spent time with Gerald in New York City, as well as on vacation in Europe. In the fall, they returned to Scott in California.

In November 1982, rebuffed in his attempts to visit Victoria, Michael filed a filiation action in California Superior Court to establish his paternity and right to visitation. In March 1983, the court appointed an attorney and guardian ad litem to represent Victoria's interests. Victoria then filed a cross-complaint asserting that if she had more than one psychological or de facto father, she was entitled to maintain her filial relationship, with all of the attendant rights, duties, and obligations, with both. In May 1983, Carole filed a motion for summary judgment. During this period, from March through July 1983, Carole was again living with Gerald in New York. In August, however, she returned to California, became involved once again with Michael, and instructed her attorneys to remove the summary judgment motion from the calendar.

For the ensuing eight months, when Michael was not in St. Thomas he lived with Carole and Victoria in Carole's apartment in Los Angeles and held Victoria out as his daughter. In April 1984, Carole and Michael signed a stipulation that Michael was Victoria's natural father. Carole left Michael the next month, however, and instructed her attorneys not to file the stipulation. In June 1984, Carole reconciled with Gerald and joined him in New York, where they now live with Victoria and two other children since born into the marriage.

In May 1984, Michael and Victoria, through her guardian ad litem, sought visitation rights for Michael pendente lite. To assist in determining whether visitation would be in Victoria's best interests, the Superior Court appointed a psychologist to evaluate Victoria, Gerald, Michael, and Carole. The psychologist recommended that Carole retain sole custody, but that Michael be allowed continued contact with Victoria pursuant to a restricted visitation schedule. The court concurred and ordered that Michael be provided with limited visitation privileges *pendente lite*.

On October 19, 1984, Gerald, who had intervened in the action, moved for summary judgment on the ground that under Cal. Evid. Code § 621 there were no triable issues of fact as to Victoria's paternity. This law provides that "the issue of a wife cohabiting with her husband, who is not impotent or sterile, is conclusively presumed to be a child of the marriage." Cal. Evid. Code Ann. § 621(a) (West Supp.1989). The presumption may be rebutted by blood tests, but only if a motion for such tests is made, within two years from the date of the child's birth, either by the husband or, if the natural father has filed an affidavit acknowledging paternity, by the wife. §§ 621(c) and (d). . . . The Superior Court granted Gerald's motion for summary judgment.

III

. . . Michael contends as a matter of substantive due process that, because he has established a parental relationship with Victoria, protection of Gerald's and Carole's marital union is an insufficient state interest to support termination of that relationship. This argument is, of course, predicated on the assertion that Michael has a constitutionally protected liberty interest in his relationship with Victoria.

It is an established part of our constitutional jurisprudence that the term "liberty" in the Due Process Clause extends beyond freedom from physical restraint. Without that core textual meaning as a limitation, defining the scope of the Due Process Clause "has at times been a treacherous field for this Court," giving "reason for concern lest the only limits to . . . judicial intervention become the predilections of those who happen at the time to be Members of this Court." *Moore v. East Cleveland*, 431 U.S. 494, 502 (1977). The need for restraint has been cogently expressed by Justice WHITE:

> "that the Court has ample precedent for the creation of new constitutional rights should not lead it to repeat the process at will. The Judiciary, including this Court, is the most vulnerable and comes nearest to illegitimacy when it deals with judge-made constitutional law having little or no cognizable roots in the language or even the design of the Constitution. Realizing that the present construction of the Due Process Clause represents a major judicial gloss on its terms, as well as on the anticipation of the Framers . . . , the Court should be extremely reluctant to breathe still further substantive content into the Due Process Clause so as to strike down legislation adopted by a State or city to promote its welfare. Whenever the Judiciary does so, it unavoidably

preempts for itself another part of the governance of the country without express constitutional authority." *Moore*, supra, at 544 (dissenting opinion).

In an attempt to limit and guide interpretation of the Clause, we have insisted not merely that the interest denominated as a "liberty" be "fundamental" (a concept that, in isolation, is hard to objectify), but also that it be an interest traditionally protected by our society. As we have put it, the Due Process Clause affords only those protections "so rooted in the traditions and conscience of our people as to be ranked as fundamental." *Snyder v. Massachusetts*, 291 U.S. 97, 105 (1934). Our cases reflect "continual insistence upon respect for the teachings of history [and] solid recognition of the basic values that underlie our society. . . . " *Griswold v. Connecticut*, 381 U.S. 479, 501 (1965).

This insistence that the asserted liberty interest be rooted in history and tradition is evident, as elsewhere, in our cases according constitutional protection to certain parental rights. Michael reads the landmark case of *Stanley v. Illinois*, and the subsequent cases of *Quilloin v. Walcott, Caban v. Mohammed*, and *Lehr v. Robertson* as establishing that a liberty interest is created by biological fatherhood plus an established parental relationship—factors that exist in the present case as well. We think that distorts the rationale of those cases. As we view them, they rest not upon such isolated factors but upon the historic respect—indeed, sanctity would not be too strong a term—traditionally accorded to the relationships that develop within the unitary family. In *Stanley*, for example, we forbade the destruction of such a family when, upon the death of the mother, the State had sought to remove children from the custody of a father who had lived with and supported them and their mother for 18 years. As Justice Powell stated for the plurality in *Moore v. East Cleveland, supra*, at 503: "Our decisions establish that the Constitution protects the sanctity of the family precisely because the institution of the family is deeply rooted in this Nation's history and tradition."

Thus, the legal issue in the present case reduces to whether the relationship between persons in the situation of Michael and Victoria has been treated as a protected family unit under the historic practices of our society, or whether on any other basis it has been accorded special protection. We think it impossible to find that it has. In fact, quite to the contrary, our traditions have protected the marital family (Gerald, Carole, and the child they acknowledge to be theirs) against the sort of claim Michael asserts. . . .

In *Lehr v. Robertson*, a case involving a natural father's attempt to block his child's adoption by the unwed mother's new husband, we observed that "[t]he significance of the biological connection is that it offers the natural father an opportunity that no other male possesses to develop a relationship with his offspring," 463 U.S., at 262, and we assumed that the Constitution might require some protection of that opportunity. Where, however, the child is born into an extant marital family, the natural father's unique opportunity conflicts with the similarly unique opportunity of the husband of the marriage; and it is not unconstitutional for the State to give categorical preference to the latter. In *Lehr* we quoted approvingly from Justice Stewart's dissent in *Caban v. Mohammed*, 441 U.S., at 397, to the effect that although " '[i]n some circumstances the actual relationship between father and child may suffice to create in the unwed father parental interests comparable to those of the married father,' " " 'the absence of a legal tie with the mother may in such circumstances appropriately place a limit on whatever substantive constitutional claims might otherwise exist.' " 463 U.S., at 260, n. 16. In accord with our traditions, a limit is also imposed by the circumstance that the mother is, at the time of the child's conception and birth, married to, and cohabitating with, another man, both of whom wish to raise the child as the offspring of their union. It is a question of legislative policy and not constitutional law whether California will allow the presumed parenthood of a couple desiring to retain a child conceived within and born into their marriage to be rebutted.

We do not accept Justice Brennen's criticism that this result "squashes" the liberty that consists of "the freedom not to conform." It seems to us that reflects the erroneous view that there is only one side to this controversy—that one disposition can expand a "liberty" of sorts without contracting an equivalent "liberty" on the other side. Such a happy choice is rarely available. Here, to *provide* protection to an adulterous natural father is to *deny* protection to a marital father, and vice versa. If Michael has a "freedom not to conform" (whatever that means), Gerald must equivalently have a "freedom to conform." One of them will pay a price for asserting that "freedom"—Michael by being unable to act as father of the child he has adulterously begotten, or Gerald by being unable to preserve the integrity of the traditional family unit he and Victoria have established. Our disposition does not choose between these two "freedoms," but leaves that to the people of California. Justice Brennan's approach chooses one of them as the constitutional imperative, on no apparent basis except that the unconventional is to be preferred. . . .

The judgment of the California Court of Appeal is

Affirmed. . . .

[Justice O'Connor, joined by Justice Kennedy, filed an opinion concurring in part. Justice Stevens filed an opinion concurring in the judgment. Justice White, joined by Justice Brennan, filed a dissent.]

JUSTICE BRENNAN, with whom JUSTICE MARSHALL and JUSTICE BLACKMUN join, dissenting. . . .

I

Once we recognized that the "liberty" protected by the Due Process Clause of the Fourteenth Amendment encompasses more than freedom from bodily restraint, today's plurality opinion emphasizes, the concept was cut loose from one natural limitation on its meaning. This innovation paved the way, so the plurality hints, for judges to substitute their own preferences for those of elected officials. Dissatisfied with this supposedly unbridled and uncertain state of affairs, the plurality casts about for another limitation on the concept of liberty.

It finds this limitation in "tradition." Apparently oblivious to the fact that this concept can be as malleable and as elusive as "liberty" itself, the plurality pretends that tradition places a discernible border around the Constitution. The pretense is seductive; it would be comforting to believe that a search for "tradition" involves nothing more idiosyncratic or complicated than poring through dusty volumes on American history. . . . Because reasonable people can disagree about the content of particular traditions, and because they can disagree even about which traditions are relevant to the definition of "liberty," the plurality has not found the objective boundary that it seeks. . . .

The plurality's interpretive method is more than novel; it is misguided. It ignores the good reasons for limiting the role of "tradition" in interpreting the Constitution's deliberately capacious language. In the plurality's constitutional universe, we may not take notice of the fact that the original reasons for the conclusive presumption of paternity are out of place in a world in which blood tests can prove virtually beyond a shadow of a doubt who sired a particular child and in which the fact of illegitimacy no longer plays the burdensome and stigmatizing role it once did. Nor, in the plurality's world, may we deny "tradition" its full scope by pointing out that the rationale for the conventional rule has changed over the years, as has the rationale for Cal. Evid. Code Ann. § 621 (West Supp. 1989) instead, our task is simply to identify a rule denying the asserted interest and not to ask whether the basis for that rule—which is the true reflection of the values undergirding it—has changed too often or too recently to call the rule embodying that rationale a "tradition." Moreover, by describing the decisive question as whether Michael's and Victoria's interest is one that has been "traditionally *protected by* our society," rather than one that society traditionally has thought important (with or without protecting it), and by suggesting that our sole function is to "*discern* the society's views," the plurality acts as if the only purpose of the Due Process Clause is to confirm the importance of interests already protected by a majority of the States. Transforming the protection afforded by the Due Process Clause into a redundancy mocks those who, with care and purpose, wrote the Fourteenth Amendment.

In construing the Fourteenth Amendment to offer shelter only to those interests specifically protected by historical practice, moreover, the plurality ignores the kind of society in which our Constitution exists. We are not an assimilative, homogeneous society, but a facilitative, pluralistic one, in which we must be willing to abide someone else's unfamiliar or even repellent practice because the same tolerant impulse protects our own idiosyncrasies. Even if we can agree, therefore, that "family" and "parenthood" are part of the good life, it is absurd to assume that we can agree on the content of those terms and destructive to pretend that we do. In a community such as ours, "liberty" must include the freedom not to conform. The plurality today squashes this freedom by requiring specific approval from history before protecting anything in the name of liberty.

The document that the plurality construes today is unfamiliar to me. It is not the living charter that I have taken to be our Constitution; it is instead a stagnant, archaic, hidebound document steeped in the prejudices and superstitions of a time long past. *This* Constitution does not recognize that times change, does not see that sometimes a practice or rule outlives its foundations. I cannot accept an interpretive method that does such violence to the charter that I am bound by oath to uphold.

II

The plurality's reworking of our interpretive approach is all the more troubling because it is unnecessary. This is not a case in which we face a "new" kind of interest, one that requires us to consider for the first time whether the Constitution protects it. On the contrary, we confront an interest—that of a parent and child in their relationship with each other—that was among the first that this Court acknowledged in its cases defining the "liberty" protected by the Constitution, see, e.g., *Meyer v. Nebraska*; *Skinner v. Oklahoma*; *Prince v. Massachusetts*, and I think I am safe in saying that no one doubts the wisdom or validity of those decisions. Where the interest under consideration is a parent-child relationship, we need not ask, over and over again, whether that interest is one that society traditionally protects. . . .

On four prior occasions, we have considered whether unwed fathers have a constitutionally protected interest in their relationships with their children. See *Stanley v. Illinois*; *Quilloin v. Walcott*; *Caban v. Mohammed*; and *Lehr v. Robertson*. Though different in factual and legal circumstances, these cases have produced a unifying theme: although an unwed father's biological link to his child does not, in and of itself, guarantee him a constitutional stake in his relationship with that child, such a link combined with a substantial parent-child relationship will do so. "When an unwed father demonstrates a full commitment to the responsibilities of parenthood by 'com[ing] forward to participate in the rearing of his child,' . . . his interest in personal contact with his child acquires substantial protection under the Due Process Clause. At that point it may be said that he 'act[s] as a father toward his children.' " *Lehr v. Robertson, supra*, at 261 quoting *Caban v. Mohammed, supra*, at 392, 389, n. 7. This commitment is why Mr. Stanley and Mr. Caban won; why Mr. Quilloin and Mr. Lehr lost; and why Michael H. should prevail today. Michael H. is almost certainly Victoria D.'s natural father, has lived with her as her father, has contributed to her support, and has from the beginning sought to strengthen and maintain his relationship with her.

Claiming that the intent of these cases was to protect the "unitary family," the plurality waves *Stanley, Quilloin, Caban*, and *Lehr* aside. . . .

III

Because the plurality decides that Michael and Victoria have no liberty interest in their relationship with each other, it need consider neither the effect of § 621 on their relationship nor the State's interest in bringing about that effect. It is obvious, however, that the effect of § 621 is to terminate the relationship between Michael and Victoria before affording any hearing whatsoever on the issue whether Michael is Victoria's father. This refusal to hold a hearing is properly analyzed under our procedural due process cases, which instruct us to consider the State's interest in curtailing the procedures accompanying the termination of a constitutionally protected interest. California's interest, minute in comparison with a father's interest in his relationship with his child, cannot justify its refusal to hear Michael out on his claim that he is Victoria's father. . . .

The purported state interests here, however, stem primarily from the State's antagonism to Michael's and Victoria's constitutionally protected interest in their relationship with each other and not from any desire to streamline procedures. Gerald D. explains that § 621 promotes marriage, maintains the relationship between the child and presumed father, and protects the integrity and privacy of the matrimonial family. It is not, however, § 621, but the best-interest principle, that protects a stable marital relationship and maintains the relationship between the child and presumed father. These interests are implicated by the determination of who gets parental rights, *not* by the determination of who is the father; in the hearing that Michael seeks, parental rights are not the issue. Of the objectives that Gerald stresses, therefore, only the preservation of family privacy is promoted by the refusal to hold a hearing itself. Yet § 621 furthers even this objective only partially. . . .

Make no mistake: to say that the State must provide Michael with a hearing to prove his paternity is not to express any opinion of the ultimate state of affairs between Michael and Victoria and Carole and Gerald. In order to change the current situation among these people, Michael first must convince a court that he is Victoria's father, and even if he is able to do this, he will be denied visitation rights if that would be in Victoria's best interests.

It is elementary that a determination that a State must afford procedures before it terminates a given right is not a prediction about the end result of those procedures.

IV

The atmosphere surrounding today's decision is one of make-believe. Beginning with the suggestion that the situation confronting us here does not repeat itself every day in every corner of the country, . . . moving on to the claim that it is tradition alone that supplies the details of the liberty that the Constitution protects, and passing finally to the notion that the Court always has recognized a cramped vision of "the family," today's decision lets stand California's pronouncement that Michael—whom blood tests show to a 98 percent probability to be Victoria's father—is not Victoria's father. When and if the Court awakes to reality, it will find a world very different from the one it expects. . . .

NOTES AND QUESTIONS

(1) **Substantive Due Process**. Although this case is presented as a paternity case, it also presents a classic battle on the subject of substantive due process. While the main antagonists are Justice Scalia and Justice Brennan, Justice O'Connor plays an important role.

a. *Justice Scalia*, who is well known as a strict constructionist, seems to grudgingly accept a substantive component to the due process clause. But he asserts that the protection afforded is limited to those rights established by well founded historical traditions. This jurisprudential approach is fully set out by Justice Scalia in footnote 6, which was omitted from the excerpt above:

> Justice Brennan criticizes our methodology in using historical traditions specifically relating to the rights of an adulterous natural father, rather than inquiring more generally "whether parenthood is an interest that historically has received our attention and protection." . . . There seems to us no basis for the contention that this methodology is "novel." For example, in *Bowers v. Hardwick*, 478 U.S. 186, 106 S.Ct. 2841, 92 L.Ed.2d 140 (1986), we noted that at the time the Fourteenth Amendment was ratified all but 5 of the 37 States had criminal sodomy laws, that all 50 of the States had such laws prior to 1961, and that 24 States and the District of Columbia continued to have them; and we concluded from that record, regarding that very specific aspect of sexual conduct, that "to claim that a right to engage in such conduct is 'deeply rooted in this Nation's history and tradition' or 'implicit in the concept of ordered liberty' is, at best, facetious." . . . In *Roe v. Wade* we spent about a fifth of our opinion negating the proposition that there was a longstanding tradition of laws proscribing abortion. . . .
>
> Finally, we may note that this analysis is not inconsistent with the result in cases such as *Griswold v. Connecticut*, or *Eisenstadt v. Baird*, 405 U.S. 438, 92 S.Ct. 1029, 31 L.Ed.2d 349 (1972). None of those cases acknowledged a longstanding and still extant societal tradition withholding the very right pronounced to be the subject of a liberty interest and then rejected it. Justice Brennan must do so here. In this case, the existence of such a tradition, continuing to the present day, refutes any possible contention that the alleged right is "so rooted in the traditions and conscience of our people as to be ranked as fundamental," *Snyder v. Massachusetts*, 291 U.S. 97, 105, 54 S.Ct. 330, 332,

78 L.Ed. 674 (1934), or "implicit in the concept of ordered liberty," *Palko v. Connecticut*, 302 U.S. 319, 325, 58 S.Ct. 149, 152, 82 L.Ed. 288 (1937).

Michael H., 491 U.S. at 127, n. 6.

b. *Justice Brennan* argues that the determination of rights protected by substantive due process should not be limited by historical tradition. He says that, as a working test, tradition is as malleable as liberty. Both are subject to interpretation. He points out that parenthood has traditionally been protected. But, more importantly, he argues that there are some situations where change dictates that tradition is an inappropriate test, and this case is the perfect example. The conclusive presumption was formulated in a time when there was no sure way to determine paternity. Tradition is not a good test because it was based upon ignorance. A new context may bring new rights into relief.

Justices Brennan and Scalia also disagree about the appropriate level of generality at which to define the relevant constitutional "tradition." Justice Scalia states that, for purposes of analyzing a substantive due process claim, a court should "adopt the most specific tradition as the point of reference." Thus, for Scalia, the relevant due process question in this case is whether there exists a long-standing societal tradition of protecting the parental rights of "the natural father of a child conceived within, and born into, an extant marital union that wishes to embrace the child." Once the question is posed in this manner, it is easy for Justice Scalia to answer "no." Justice Brennan takes issue with this mode of interpretation. Rather than asking whether the law has traditionally protected this specific variety of parenthood, Brennan would ask more generally whether the parent-child relationship is an interest that society and the Constitution have traditionally protected. Having found that the Court has long viewed this relationship as part of "the 'liberty' protected by the Constitution," Brennan would then ask whether "the specific parent-child relationship under consideration is close enough to the interests that we already have protected to be deemed an aspect of 'liberty' as well." Brennan answers this question in the affirmative.

c. *Justice O'Connor*, joined by Justice Kennedy, agrees with Justice Scalia, but refuses to accept his limitation on the historical analysis:

> I concur in all but footnote 6 of Justice Scalia's opinion. This footnote sketches a mode of historical analysis to be used when identifying liberty interests protected by the Due Process Clause of the Fourteenth Amendment that may be somewhat inconsistent with our past decisions in this area. *See Griswold v. Connecticut*, 381 U.S. 479, 85 S.Ct. 1678, 14 L.Ed.2d 510 (1965); *Eisenstadt v. Baird*, 405 U.S. 438, 92 S.Ct. 1029, 31 L.Ed.2d 349 (1972). On occasion the Court has characterized relevant traditions protecting asserted rights at levels of generality that might not be "the most specific level" available. *See Loving v. Virginia*, 388 U.S. 1, 12, 87 S.Ct. 1817, 1823, 18 L.Ed.2d 1010 (1967); *Turner v. Safley*, 482 U.S. 78, 94, 107 S.Ct. 2254, 2265, 96 L.Ed.2d 64 (1987); *cf. United States v. Stanley*, 483 U.S. 669, 709, 107 S.Ct. 3054, 3065, 97 L.Ed.2d 550 (1987) (O'Connor, J., concurring in part and dissenting in part). I would not foreclose the unanticipated by the prior imposition of a single mode of historical analysis. *Poe v. Ullman*, 367 U.S. 497, 542, 544, 81 S.Ct. 1752, 1776, 1777, 6 L.Ed.2d 989 (1961) (Harlan, J., dissenting).

Michael H., 491 U.S. at 131. It appears that Justice O'Connor is willing to view tradition as the test but she does not want to be limited by the most-specific-level refinement. On the other hand it does not appear that Justice O'Connor is willing to go as far as Justice Brennan. For strong support of the result in *Michael H.*, see Hadek, *Why The Policy Behind the Irrebuttable Presumption of Paternity Will Never Die*, 26 Sw. U.L. Rev. 359 (1997).

(2) **Victoria.** In a portion of the opinion not reprinted, the plurality soundly rejects any claim that Victoria might have to establish a relationship with her biological father Michael:

> We have never had occasion to decide whether a child has a liberty interest, symmetrical with that of her parent, in maintaining her filial relationship. We need not do so here because, even assuming that such a right exists, Victoria's claim must fail. Victoria's due process challenge is, if anything, weaker than Michael's. Her basic claim is not that California has erred in preventing her from establishing that Michael, not Gerald, should stand as her legal father. Rather, she claims a due process right to maintain filial relationships with both Michael and Gerald. This assertion merits little discussion, for, whatever the merits of the guardian ad litem's belief that such an arrangement can be of great psychological benefit to a child, the claim that a State must recognize multiple fatherhood has no support in the history or traditions of this country.

Michael H., 491 U.S. at 130–31. As to an equal protection challenge that Victoria also made, the plurality declines to use the strict scrutiny test based upon illegitimacy, and therefore applies the rational basis test. The state's interest in protecting the peaceful union of husband and wife from paternity challenges meets this test.

(3) **Rebuttable Presumptions.** Many states have adopted a series of rebuttable presumptions to be used in paternity actions. These presumptions, usually some form of the presumptions in the Uniform Parentage Act, are rebuttable by genetic testing, but, since they provide some certainty in the process, at least establishing who has the burden of proof, they are often very useful. Many times the presumptions prevent litigation entirely. Here are the presumptions from the UPA:

UNIFORM PARENTAGE ACT OF 1973
9B U.L.A. 287 (1987)

. . .

§ 4. [Presumption of Paternity].

(a) A man is presumed to be the natural father of a child if:

(1) he and the child's natural mother are or have been married to each other and the child is born during the marriage, or within 300 days after the marriage is terminated by death, annulment, declaration of invalidity, or divorce, or after a decree of separation is entered by a court;

(2) before the child's birth, he and the child's natural mother have attempted to marry each other by a marriage solemnized in apparent compliance with law, although the attempted marriage is or could be declared invalid, and,

(i) if the attempted marriage could be declared invalid only by a court, the child is born during the attempted marriage, or within 300 days after its termination by death, annulment, declaration of invalidity, or divorce; or

(ii) if the attempted marriage is invalid without a court order, the child is born within 300 days after the termination of cohabitation;

(3) after the child's birth, he and the child's natural mother have married, or attempted to marry, each other by a marriage solemnized in apparent compliance with law, although the attempted marriage is or could be declared invalid, and

(i) he has acknowledged his paternity of the child in a writing filed with the [appropriate court or Vital Statistics Bureau].

(ii) with his consent, he is named as the child's father on the child's birth certificate, or

(iii) he is obligated to support the child under a written voluntary promise or by court order;

(4) while the child is under the age of majority, he receives the child into his home and openly holds out the child as his natural child; or

(5) he acknowledges his paternity of the child in a writing filed with the [appropriate court or Vital Statistics Bureau] . . .

§ 11. [Blood Tests].

(a) The court may, and upon request of a party shall, require the child, mother, or alleged father to submit to blood tests. The tests shall be performed by an expert qualified as an examiner of blood types, appointed by the court.

(b) The court, upon reasonable request by a party, shall order that independent tests be performed by other experts qualified as examiners of blood types.

(c) In all cases, the court shall determine the number and qualifications of the experts.

§ 12. [Evidence Relating to Paternity].

Evidence relating to paternity may include:

(1) evidence of sexual intercourse between the mother and alleged father at any possible time of conception;

(2) an expert's opinion concerning the statistical probability of the alleged father's paternity based upon the duration of the mother's pregnancy;

(3) blood test results, weighted in accordance with evidence, if available, of the statistical probability of the alleged father's paternity . . .

(5) all other evidence relevant to the issue of paternity of the child.

States that have adopted a rebuttable presumption of paternity based on marriage still face questions regarding the circumstances under which the presumption may be rebutted. For example, in a number of states, a putative biological father who seeks to rebut a presumption of paternity based on marriage must make a preliminary showing that rebuttal would serve the "best interests" of the child in question. *See, e.g., In re Paternity of Adam,* 903 P.2d 207 (Mont. 1995), *cert. denied,* 116 S. Ct. 1544 (1996) (putative biological father of child born during mother's marriage to another man must first show that a paternity determination would be in the child's best interests in order to proceed with paternity action); *Weidenbacher v. Duclos,* 661 A.2d 988, 1000 (Conn. 1995) (to proceed with paternity action, putative father must prove at a preliminary evidentiary hearing that both his best interest and those of the child outweigh the interests of the marital family unit); *In re Marriage of Ross*, 783 P.2d 331 (Kan. 1989) (court must consider child's best interests before ordering blood tests to rebut presumption of paternity based on marriage). *See also C.C. v. A.B.*, 550 N.E.2d 365 (Mass. 1990) (putative biological father must demonstrate a substantial parent-child relationship in order to pursue his paternity claim). Other states have declined to impose such a preliminary requirements. *See, e.g, Spaeth v. Warren*, 478 N.W.2d 319 (Minn. Ct. App. 1991) (trial court did not err in declining to consider child's best interests in adjudicating paternity). For a general discussion of these cases, see Craig Weber, *Paternity Actions in Illinois: Why Not Consider What is in the Best Interest of the Child?* 21 S. Ill. U.L.J. 613 (1997). Should a court consider a child's best interests in resolving competing claims to paternity? If so, at what stage of the proceedings?

(4) **California and the Conclusive Presumption.** The conclusive presumption has had several forms in California. The version appearing in this case was an intermediate one. Originally it truly was a conclusive presumption; it could not be rebutted by at all. *See* Cal. Evid. Code § 621 (1975); 1975 Cal. Stat. 1244, § 13. Then it was modified to allow the wife and the husband to challenge the presumption. *See* Cal. Evid. Code § 621 (1981); 1981 Cal. Stat. 1180, § 1. This version was the one attacked in *Michael H. v. Gerald D.* Following that case the California legislature changed the policy which the United States Supreme Court had upheld and extended the right to challenge the presumption to other men who are considered presumed fathers under provisions which are substantially the same as the rebuttable presumptions of the Uniform Parentage Act. Cal. Fam. Code §§ 7540–41 (1997).

(5) **Problem**. Paul and Jody married in 1991. Early in the marriage, Jody had a brief affair with Tom, a co-worker. Shortly after the affair ended, Jody discovered she was pregnant. Although Jody suspected that Tom, rather than Paul, might be the child's biological father, she did not voice these suspicions to either man, because she wanted to try to preserve her marriage to Paul. When the baby was born, Paul was listed as the father on the birth certificate. For the next three years, Paul supported the child financially and otherwise acted as the child's father. Tom played no role in the child's life, although he and Jody maintained a platonic friendship. Unfortunately, Paul and Jody's marriage continued to deteriorate and, in 1995, the couple mutually decided to divorce. During divorce proceedings, Tom—who had always believed that Jody's child resembled him—filed a motion to compel genetic testing of all parties to establish paternity of the child. Both Jody and Paul opposed such testing. Assuming that the state has adopted the UPA, how should the court rule on Tom's motion? If the court orders genetic testing and the results show that Tom, rather than Paul, is the child's biological father, what custody and visitation arrangements should the court impose, assuming the parties cannot reach an agreement? *Cf. Pickering v. Pickering*, 434 N.W.2d 758 (S.D. 1989), reprinted in § 6.03[B], "Tort Claims Arising Out of Marriage and Divorce," *above*.

[B] Non-Presumptive Parents

The rights of a father may be affected by a proceeding establishing another man as the adoptive father. Disputes involving the rights of unmarried fathers might be avoided if states would adopt what has come to be called open adoption. The dominant approach to adoption in this country has been to sever all ties, and to extinguish all communication, between an adopted child and her biological family.

LEHR v. ROBERTSON
United States Supreme Court
463 U.S. 248 (1983)

JUSTICE STEVENS delivered the opinion of the Court.

The question presented is whether New York has sufficiently protected an unmarried father's inchoate relationship with a child whom he has never supported and rarely seen in the two years since her birth. The appellant, Jonathan Lehr, claims that the Due Process and Equal Protection Clauses of the Fourteenth Amendment, as interpreted in *Stanley v. Illinois*, 405 U.S. 645 (1972), and *Caban v. Mohammed*, 441 U.S. 380 (1979), give him an absolute right to notice and an opportunity to be heard before the child may be adopted. We disagree.

Jessica M. was born out of wedlock on November 9, 1976. Her mother, Lorraine Robertson, married Richard Robertson eight months after Jessica's birth. On December 21, 1978, when Jessica was over two years old, the Robertsons filed an adoption petition in the Family Court of Ulster County, New York. The court heard their testimony and received a favorable report from the Ulster County Department of Social Services. On March 7, 1979, the court entered an order of adoption. In this proceeding, appellant contends that the adoption order is invalid because he, Jessica's putative father, was not given advance notice of the adoption proceeding.[1]

The State of New York maintains a "putative father registry." A man who files with that registry demonstrates his intent to claim paternity of a child born out of wedlock and is therefore entitled to receive notice of any proceeding to adopt that child. Before entering Jessica's adoption order, the Ulster County Family Court had the putative father registry examined. Although appellant claims to be Jessica's natural father, he had not entered his name in the registry.

On January 30, 1979, one month after the adoption proceeding was commenced in Ulster County, appellant filed a "visitation and paternity petition" in the Westchester County Family Court. In that petition, he asked for a determination of paternity, an order of support, and reasonable visitation privileges with Jessica. Notice of that proceeding was served on appellee on February 22, 1979. Four days later appellee's attorney informed the Ulster County Court that appellant had commenced a paternity proceeding in Westchester County; the Ulster County judge then entered an order staying appellant's paternity proceeding until he could rule on a motion to change the venue of that proceeding to Ulster County. On March 3, 1979, appellant received notice of the change of venue motion and, for the first time, learned that an adoption proceeding was pending in Ulster County.

On March 7, 1979, appellant's attorney telephoned the Ulster County judge to inform him that he planned to seek a stay of the adoption proceeding pending the determination of the paternity petition. In that telephone conversation, the judge advised the lawyer that he had already signed the adoption order earlier that day. According to appellant's attorney, the judge stated that he was aware of the pending paternity petition but did not believe he was required to give notice to appellant prior to the entry of the order of adoption.

---

[1] Appellee has never conceded that appellant is Jessica's biological father, but for purposes of analysis in this opinion it will be assumed that he is.

Thereafter, the Family Court in Westchester County granted appellee's motion to dismiss the paternity petition, holding that the putative father's right to seek paternity "must be deemed severed so long as an order of adoption exists." Appellant did not appeal from that dismissal. On June 22, 1979, appellant filed a petition to vacate the order of adoption on the ground that it was obtained by fraud and in violation of his constitutional rights. The Ulster County Family Court received written and oral argument on the question whether it had "dropped the ball" by approving the adoption without giving appellant advance notice. After deliberating for several months, it denied the petition, explaining its decision in a thorough written opinion. *In re Adoption of Martz*, 102 Misc. 2d 102, 423 N.Y.S. 2d 378 (1979). . . .

The New York Court of Appeals also affirmed by a divided vote. *In re Adoption of Jessica "XX,"* 54 N.Y. 2d 417, 430 N.E. 2d 896 (1981). . . .

Appellant has now invoked our appellate jurisdiction. . . .

The Due Process Claim.

The Fourteenth Amendment provides that no State shall deprive any person of life, liberty, or property without due process of law. When that Clause is invoked in a novel context, it is our practice to begin the inquiry with a determination of the precise nature of the private interest that is threatened by the State. Only after that interest has been identified, can we properly evaluate the adequacy of the State's process. We therefore first consider the nature of the interest in liberty for which appellant claims constitutional protection and then turn to a discussion of the adequacy of the procedure that New York has provided for its protection.

I

The intangible fibers that connect parent and child have infinite variety. They are woven throughout the fabric of our society, providing it with strength, beauty, and flexibility. It is self-evident that they are sufficiently vital to merit constitutional protection in appropriate cases. In deciding whether this is such a case, however, we must consider the broad framework that has traditionally been used to resolve the legal problems arising from the parent-child relationship.

In the vast majority of cases, state law determines the final outcome. Rules governing the inheritance of property, adoption, and child custody are generally specified in statutory enactments that vary from State to State. . . .

In some cases, however, this Court has held that the Federal Constitution supersedes state law and provides even greater protection for certain formal family relationships. In those cases, as in the state cases, the Court has emphasized the paramount interest in the welfare of children and has noted that the rights of the parents are a counterpart of the responsibilities they have assumed. Thus, the "liberty" of parents to control the education of their children that was vindicated in *Meyer v. Nebraska*, 262 U.S. 390 (1923), and *Pierce v. Society of Sisters*, 268 U.S. 510 (1925), was described as a "right, coupled with the high duty, to recognize and prepare [the child] for additional obligations." *Id.*, at 535. The linkage between parental duty and parental right was stressed again in *Prince v. Massachusetts*, 321 U.S. 158, 166 (1944), when the Court declared it a cardinal principle "that the custody, care and nurture of the child reside first in the parents, whose primary function and freedom include preparation for obligations the state can neither supply nor hinder." *Ibid.* In these cases the Court has found that the relationship of love and duty in a recognized family unit is an interest in liberty entitled to constitutional protection. . . . "[S]tate intervention to terminate [such a] relationship must be accomplished by procedures meeting the requisites of the Due Process Clause." *Santosky v. Kramer*, 455 U.S. 745, 753 (1982).

There are also a few cases in which this Court has considered the extent to which the Constitution affords protection to the relationship between natural parents and children born out of wedlock. In some we have been concerned with the rights of the children, *see, e.g., Trimble v. Gordon*, 430 U.S. 762 (1977). In this case, however, it is a parent who claims that the State has improperly deprived him of a protected interest in liberty. This Court has examined the extent to which a natural father's biological relationship with his child receives protection under the Due Process Clause in precisely three cases: *Stanley v. Illinois*, 405 U.S. 645 (1972), *Quilloin v. Walcott*, 434 U.S. 246 (1978), and *Caban v. Mohammed*, 441 U.S. 380 (1979).

Stanley involved the constitutionality of an Illinois statute that conclusively presumed every father of a child born out of wedlock to be an unfit person to have custody of his children. The father in that case had lived with his children all their lives and had lived with their mother for 18 years. There was nothing in the record to indicate that Stanley had been a neglectful father who had not cared for his children. 405 U.S., at 655. Under the statute, however, the nature of the actual relationship between parent and child was completely irrelevant. Once the mother died, the children were automatically made wards of the State. [T]he Court held that the Due Process Clause was violated by the automatic destruction of the custodial relationship without giving the father any opportunity to present evidence regarding his fitness as a parent.

Quilloin involved the constitutionality of a Georgia statute that authorized the adoption, over the objection of the natural father, of a child born out of wedlock. The father in that case had never legitimated the child. It was only after the mother had remarried and her new husband had filed an adoption petition that the natural father sought visitation rights and filed a petition for legitimation. The trial court found adoption by the new husband to be in the child's best interests, and we unanimously held that action to be consistent with the Due Process Clause.

Caban involved the conflicting claims of two natural parents who had maintained joint custody of their children from the time of their birth until they were respectively two and four years old. The father challenged the validity of an order authorizing the mother's new husband to adopt the children; he relied on both the Equal Protection Clause and the Due Process Clause. Because this Court upheld his equal protection claim, the majority did not address his due process challenge. The comments on the latter claim by the four dissenting Justices are nevertheless instructive, because they identify the clear distinction between a mere biological relationship and an actual relationship of parental responsibility.

Justice Stewart correctly observed:

> "Even if it be assumed that each married parent after divorce has some substantive due process right to maintain his or her parental relationship, it by no means follows that each unwed parent has any such right. *Parental rights do not spring full-blown from the biological connection between parent and child. They require relationships more enduring.*"

441 U.S., at 397 (emphasis added). In a similar vein, the other three dissenters in *Caban* were prepared to "assume that, *if and when one develops,* the relationship between a father and his natural child is entitled to protection against arbitrary state action as a matter of due process." *Caban v. Mohammed, supra,* at 414 (emphasis added).

The difference between the developed parent-child relationship that was implicated in *Stanley* and *Caban,* and the potential relationship involved in *Quilloin* and this case, is both clear and significant. When an unwed father demonstrates a full commitment to the responsibilities of parenthood by "com[ing] forward to participate in the rearing of his child," his interest in personal contact with his child acquires substantial protection under the Due Process Clause. At that point it may be said that he "act[s] as a father toward his children." *Id.,* at 389, n. 7. But the mere existence of a biological link does not merit equivalent constitutional protection.

The significance of the biological connection is that it offers the natural father an opportunity that no other male possesses to develop a relationship with his offspring. If he grasps that opportunity and accepts some measure of responsibility for the child's future, he may enjoy the blessings of the parent-child relationship and make uniquely valuable contributions to the child's development. If he fails to do so, the Federal Constitution will not automatically compel a State to listen to his opinion of where the child's best interests lie.

In this case, we are not assessing the constitutional adequacy of New York's procedures for terminating a developed relationship. Appellant has never had any significant custodial, personal, or financial relationship with Jessica, and he did not seek to establish a legal tie until after she was two years old.[2] We are concerned only with whether New York has adequately protected his opportunity to form such a relationship.

II

The most effective protection of the putative father's opportunity to develop a relationship with his child is provided by the laws that authorize formal marriage and govern its consequences. But the availability of that protection is, of course, dependent on the will of both parents of the child. Thus, New York has adopted a special statutory scheme to protect the unmarried father's interest in assuming a responsible role in the future of his child.

After this Court's decision in *Stanley,* the New York Legislature appointed a special commission to recommend legislation that would accommodate both the interests of biological fathers in their children and the children's interest in prompt and certain adoption procedures. The commission recommended, and the legislature enacted, a statutory adoption scheme that automatically provides notice to seven categories of putative fathers who are likely to have assumed some responsibility for the care of their natural children. If this scheme were likely to omit many responsible fathers, and if qualification for notice were beyond the control of an interested putative father, it might be thought procedurally inadequate. Yet, as all of the New York courts that reviewed this matter observed, the right to receive notice was completely within appellant's control. By mailing a postcard to the

---

[2] This case happens to involve an adoption by the husband of the natural mother, but we do not believe the natural father has any greater right to object to such an adoption than to an adoption by two total strangers.

putative father registry, he could have guaranteed that he would receive notice of any proceedings to adopt Jessica. The possibility that he may have failed to do so because of his ignorance of the law cannot be a sufficient reason for criticizing the law itself. The New York Legislature concluded that a more open-ended notice requirement would merely complicate the adoption process, threaten the privacy interests of unwed mothers, create the risk of unnecessary controversy, and impair the desired finality of adoption decrees. Regardless of whether we would have done likewise if we were legislators instead of judges, we surely cannot characterize the State's conclusion as arbitrary.

Appellant argues, however, that even if the putative father's opportunity to establish a relationship with an illegitimate child is adequately protected by the New York statutory scheme in the normal case, he was nevertheless entitled to special notice because the court and the mother knew that he had filed an affiliation proceeding in another court. This argument amounts to nothing more than an indirect attack on the notice provisions of the New York statute. The legitimate state interests in facilitating the adoption of young children and having the adoption proceeding completed expeditiously that underlie the entire statutory scheme also justify a trial judge's determination to require all interested parties to adhere precisely to the procedural requirements of the statute. The Constitution does not require either a trial judge or a litigant to give special notice to nonparties who are presumptively capable of asserting and protecting their own rights. Since the New York statutes adequately protected appellant's inchoate interest in establishing a relationship with Jessica, we find no merit in the claim that his constitutional rights were offended because the Family Court strictly complied with the notice provisions of the statute. . . .

The judgment of the New York Court of Appeals is

Affirmed.

JUSTICE WHITE, with whom JUSTICE MARSHALLL and JUSTICE BLACKMUN join, dissenting.

The question in this case is whether the State may, consistent with the Due Process Clause, deny notice and an opportunity to be heard in an adoption proceeding to a putative father when the State has actual notice of his existence, whereabouts, and interest in the child.

I

It is axiomatic that "[t]he fundamental requirement of due process is the opportunity to be heard 'at a meaningful time and in a meaningful manner.'" *Mathews v. Eldridge*, 424 U.S. 319, 333 (1976), quoting *Armstrong v. Manzo*, 380 U.S. 545, 552 (1965). As Jessica's biological father, Lehr either had an interest protected by the Constitution or he did not. If the entry of the adoption order in this case deprived Lehr of a constitutionally protected interest, he is entitled to notice and an opportunity to be heard before the order can be accorded finality.

According to Lehr, he and Jessica's mother met in 1971 and began living together in 1974. The couple cohabited for approximately two years, until Jessica's birth in 1976. Throughout the pregnancy and after the birth, Lorraine acknowledged to friends and relatives that Lehr was Jessica's father; Lorraine told Lehr that she had reported to the New York State Department of Social Services that he was the father. Lehr visited Lorraine and Jessica in the hospital every day during Lorraine's confinement. According to Lehr, from the time Lorraine was discharged from the hospital until August 1978, she concealed her whereabouts from him. During this time Lehr never ceased his efforts to locate Lorraine and Jessica and achieved sporadic success until August 1977, after which time he was unable to locate them at all. On those occasions when he did determine Lorraine's location, he visited with her and her children to the extent she was willing to permit it. When Lehr, with the aid of a detective agency, located Lorraine and Jessica in August 1978, Lorraine was already married to Mr. Robertson. Lehr asserts that at this time he offered to provide financial assistance and to set up a trust fund for Jessica, but that Lorraine refused. Lorraine threatened Lehr with arrest unless he stayed away and refused to permit him to see Jessica. Thereafter Lehr retained counsel who wrote to Lorraine in early December 1978, requesting that she permit Lehr to visit Jessica and threatening legal action on Lehr's behalf. On December 21, 1978, perhaps as a response to Lehr's threatened legal action, appellees commenced the adoption action at issue here. . . .

The "nature of the interest" at stake here is the interest that a natural parent has in his or her child, one that has long been recognized and accorded constitutional protection. We have frequently "stressed the importance of familial bonds, whether or not legitimized by marriage, and accorded them constitutional protection." *Little v. Streater*, 452 U.S. 1, 13 (1981). If "both the child and the [putative father] in a paternity action have a compelling interest" in the accurate outcome of such a case, *ibid.*, it cannot be disputed that both the child and the putative father have a compelling interest in the outcome of a proceeding that may result in the termination of the father-child relationship. "A parent's interest in the accuracy and justice of the decision to terminate his or her parental status is a commanding one." *Lassiter v. Department of Social Services*, 452 U.S. 18, 27 (1981). It is beyond dispute that a formal order of adoption, no less than a formal termination proceeding, operates to permanently terminate parental rights.

Lehr's version of the "facts" paints a far different picture than that portrayed by the majority. The majority's recitation, that "[a]ppellant has never had any significant custodial, personal, or financial relationship with Jessica, and he did not seek to establish a legal tie until after she was two years old," obviously does not tell the whole story. Appellant has never been afforded an opportunity to present his case. The legitimation proceeding he instituted was first stayed, and then dismissed, on appellees' motions. Nor could appellant establish his interest during the adoption proceedings, for it is the failure to provide Lehr notice and an opportunity to be heard there that is at issue here. We cannot fairly make a judgment based on the quality or substance of a relationship without a complete and developed factual record. This case requires us to assume that Lehr's allegations are true that but for the actions of the child's mother there would have been the kind of significant relationship that the majority concedes is entitled to the full panoply of procedural due process protections.

I reject the peculiar notion that the only significance of the biological connection between father and child is that "it offers the natural father an opportunity that no other male possesses to develop a relationship with his offspring." A "mere biological relationship" is not as unimportant in determining the nature of liberty interests as the majority suggests.

"[T]he usual understanding of 'family' implies biological relationships, and most decisions treating the relation between parent and child have stressed this element." *Smith v. Organization of Foster Families, supra,* at 843. The "biological connection" is itself a relationship that creates a protected interest. Thus the "nature" of the interest is the parent-child relationship; how well developed that relationship has become goes to its "weight," not its "nature." Whether Lehr's interest is entitled to constitutional protection does not entail a searching inquiry into the quality of the relationship but a simple determination of the fact that the relationship exists a fact that even the majority agrees must be assumed to be established.

Beyond that, however, because there is no established factual basis on which to proceed, it is quite untenable to conclude that a putative father's interest in his child is lacking in substance, that the father in effect has abandoned the child, or ultimately that the father's interest is not entitled to the same minimum procedural protections as the interests of other putative fathers. Any analysis of the adequacy of the notice in this case must be conducted on the assumption that the interest involved here is as strong as that of any putative father. That is not to say that due process requires actual notice to every putative father or that adoptive parents or the State must conduct an exhaustive search of records or an intensive investigation before a final adoption order may be entered. The procedures adopted by the State, however, must at least represent a reasonable effort to determine the identity of the putative father and to give him adequate notice.

II

In this case, of course, there was no question about either the identity or the location of the putative father. The mother knew exactly who he was and both she and the court entering the order of adoption knew precisely where he was and how to give him actual notice that his parental rights were about to be terminated by an adoption order. Lehr was entitled to due process, and the right to be heard is one of the fundamentals of that right, which " 'has little reality or worth unless one is informed that the matter is pending and can choose for himself whether to appear or default, acquiesce or contest.' " *Schroeder v. City of New York,* 371 U.S. 208, 212 (1962), quoting *Mullane v. Central Hanover Trust Co.,* 339 U.S. 306, 314 (1950).

The State concedes this much but insists that Lehr has had all the process that is due to him. It relies on § 111–a, which designates seven categories of unwed fathers to whom notice of adoption proceedings must be given, including any unwed father who has filed with the State a notice of his intent to claim paternity. The State submits that it need not give notice to anyone who has not filed his name, as he is permitted to do, and who is not otherwise within the designated categories, even if his identity and interest are known or are reasonably ascertainable by the State.

I am unpersuaded by the State's position. In the first place, § 111–a defines six categories of unwed fathers to whom notice must be given even though they have not placed their names on file pursuant to the section. Those six categories, however, do not include fathers such as Lehr who have initiated filiation proceedings, even though their identity and interest are as clearly and easily ascertainable as those fathers in the six categories. Initiating such proceedings necessarily involves a formal acknowledgment of paternity, and requiring the State to take note of such a case in connection with pending adoption proceedings would be a trifling burden, no more than the State undertakes when there is a final adjudication in a paternity action. Indeed, there would appear to be more reason to give notice to those such as Lehr who acknowledge paternity than to those who have been adjudged to be a father in a contested paternity action.

The State asserts that any problem in this respect is overcome by the seventh category of putative fathers to whom notice must be given, namely, those fathers who have identified themselves in the putative fathers' register maintained by the State. Since Lehr did not take advantage of this device to make his interest known, the State contends, he was not entitled to notice and a hearing even though his identity, location, and interest were known to the adoption court prior to entry of the adoption order. I have difficulty with this position. First, it represents a grudging and crabbed approach to due process. The State is quite willing to give notice and a hearing to putative fathers who have made themselves known by resorting to the putative fathers' register. It makes little sense to me to deny notice and hearing to a father who has not placed his name in the register but who has unmistakably identified himself by filing suit to establish his paternity and has notified the adoption court of his action and his interest. I thus need not question the statutory scheme on its face. Even assuming that Lehr would have been foreclosed if his failure to utilize the register had somehow disadvantaged the State, he effectively made himself known by other means, and it is the sheerest formalism to deny him a hearing because he informed the State in the wrong manner. . . .

NOTES AND QUESTIONS

(1) Prior to 1972, states almost uniformly required only the mother's consent for the adoption of nonmarital child. In 1971, Professor Harry D. Krause wrote: "The father of an illegitimate child typically is not involved in the adoption process. Indeed, not only is his consent not required, but he is usually not even entitled to notice of the adoption proceeding or to be heard in it." *See* H. Krause, Illegitimacy: Law and Social Policy 32 (1971); *see also* Note, *The Emerging Constitutional Protection of the Putative Father's Parental Rights*, 70 Mich. L. Rev. 1581 (1972). The law at this time not only demonstrated the absolute lack of legal status of the putative father but also the strong public policy in favor of adoption as the solution to the problem of unwed motherhood. While the law, and society for that matter, viewed the unwed father as irresponsible, the law also facilitated a ready supply of babies for adoption by ensuring that legal complications would be at a minimum. For a description of the sometimes coercive ways in which lawyers and social workers implemented this strong public policy in favor of adoption, see Rickie Solinger, Wake Up Little Susie: Single Pregnancy and Race Before Roe v. Wade (1992).

(2) In 1972, *Stanley v. Illinois*, 405 U.S. 645 (1972), established constitutional protection for the unwed father. Although *Stanley* involved dependency, not adoption, the case greatly affected adoption proceedings. The opening paragraph of *Stanley* provides a touching summary of the facts:

> Joan Stanley lived with Peter Stanley intermittently for 18 years, during which time they had three children. When Joan Stanley died, Peter Stanley lost not only her but also his children. Under Illinois law, the children of unwed fathers become wards of the State upon the death of the mother. Accordingly, upon Joan Stanley's death, in a dependency proceeding instituted by the State of Illinois, Stanley's children were declared wards of the State and placed with court-appointed guardians.

Stanley appealed, claiming that he had never been shown to be an unfit parent and that since married fathers and unwed mothers could not be deprived of their children without such a showing, he had been deprived of the equal protection of the laws guaranteed him by the Fourteenth Amendment. The court concluded that Stanley had a protectable interest: "the private interest here, that of a man in the children he has sired and raised, undeniably warrants deference and, absent a powerful countervailing interest, protection." *Id.* at 649. While the state has a valid interest in protecting children from unfit parents, it has no interest in separating them from fit parents. Thus presumptively denying a hearing to the father was an impermissible means. In the end the court found a violation of both due process and equal protection, since married fathers were presumed to be fit. While the case has been critiqued for its reasoning, the result has been widely accepted. *See* Freeman, *Remodeling Adoption Statutes After Stanley v. Illinois*, 15 J. Fam. L. 385 (1976–77); Barron, *Notice to the Unwed Father and Termination of Parental Rights: Implementing Stanley v. Illinois*, 9 Fam. L.Q. 527 (1975).

(3) Besides *Stanley*, the majority in *Lehr* discusses two other important United States Supreme Court cases which deal with the rights of unwed fathers: *Quilloin v. Walcott*, 434 U.S. 246 (1978), and *Caban v. Mohammed*, 441 U.S. 380 (1979). In *Quilloin* the Court upheld the constitutionality of a Georgia statute that denied an unwed father the authority to prevent adoption by the child's stepfather of his 11-year-old child. The unwed father in *Quilloin* had never lived with the child or the mother, although he had paid some child support and had visited with the child. At the time the adoption petition was filed, the child had lived with the mother and stepfather for more than seven years. Although Mr. Quilloin sought to block the adoption and to secure visitation rights, he did not seek custody, nor did he object to the child's continuing to live with the mother and stepfather. The applicable Georgia adoption statute required the consent of the unwed mother in all circumstances, but dispensed with the consent of an unwed father, unless the father had legitimated the child, which Quilloin had not attempted to do prior to the filing of the adoption petition. Quilloin participated in the adoption hearing, but the court granted the adoption over his objection, finding that it was in the best interests of the child.

Quilloin challenged the application of the best interests standard on both due process and equal protection grounds, arguing that, under *Stanley*, he was entitled to recognition and preservation of his parental rights absent a showing of unfitness. The Supreme Court disagreed. The Court acknowledged that the Due Process Clause would likely be offended "[if] a State were to attempt to force the breakup of a natural family, over the objections of the parents and their children, without some showing of unfitness and for the sole reason that to do so was thought to be in the children's best interest." *Quilloin*, 434 U.S. at 255 (quoting *Smith v. Organization of Foster Families*, 431 U.S. 816, 862–63 (1977)). The Court emphasized, however, that Mr. Quilloin had "never exercised actual or legal custody over his child" and thus had "never shouldered any significant responsibility with respect to the daily supervision, education, protection, or care of the child." Nor would the proposed adoption place the child with a new set of parents with whom he had never lived; rather, "the result of the adoption in this case is to give full recognition to a family unit already in existence." Under these circumstances, the Court concluded that the application of the best interest standard to allow the adoption did not violate Mr. Quilloin's due process or equal protection rights.

In *Caban v. Mohammed*, by contrast, the Court invalidated, on equal protection grounds, a New York statute that required the consent of an unwed mother to adoption, unless her parental rights had been terminated, but allowed an adoption to proceed over the objection of an unwed father, if a court found that the adoption was in the child's best interests. The unwed parents in *Caban* had lived together, with their children, for seven years, and the father had consistently sought to maintain his relationship with the children after the couple separated. Both parents subsequently remarried, and the mother's new husband sought to adopt the children, over the objection of the father and his new wife, who also sought to adopt. The trial court granted the petition filed by the mother and stepfather, and terminated the father's parental rights. In assessing the differential treatment accorded to unwed mothers and fathers under the New York statute, the Supreme Court noted that to withstand constitutional scrutiny "gender based distinctions must serve important governmental objectives and must be substantially related to achievement of those objectives." As applied to a father such as Caban, who "has established a substantial relationship with the child and has admitted his paternity," the Court found that the statute's gender-based distinction was not substantially related to the interests of the State in promoting the adoption of children born out of wedlock.

The question arises whether these cases, along with *Stanley* and *Lehr*, present a consistent treatment of the rights of unwed fathers. In *Stanley* and *Caban* the Court favored the rights of the father, and in both of these cases the father had established a relationship with the child beyond the biological relationship. In *Stanley* the father had lived with the children since their births, and in *Caban* the father had maintained joint custody of the children for a number of years. The common thread is that the father had crossed the boundary between, as the Court puts it in *Lehr*, "the mere biological relationship and an actual relationship of parental responsibility."

In *Quilloin*, the father did not have a significant relationship and did not attempt to legitimate the child until the mother's new husband initiated an adoption, and so the adoption was allowed. And, of course, in *Lehr* the father had failed to register his claim to paternity or otherwise meet the requirements of the statute. The burden, apparently, is on the unwed father to take steps to establish a paternal relationship through care, support, establishment of paternity, or, at least, as in *Lehr*, fulfillment of the statutory requirements for notice.

(4) *Quilloin* establishes that the best interest standard may be used when determining the rights of a nonparticipatory putative father. This is clearly a less stringent standard than the the requirement that other parents, including unmarried mothers, be shown to be unfit before they are deprived of their rights as parents. The standards for unfitness are usually abandonment, failure to support, failure to communicate, neglect, physical abuse, and other similar types of serious misconduct. [see § 12.02[G] *below*]. What would be the effect on the adoption system if the best interest standard were used in all adoptions? What would be the effect on poor parents? On single mothers?

(5) While *Quilloin* seems consistent with the other three cases which have been discussed in this area, the case attaches almost no importance to the biological relationship. The natural father and the adopting father are on equal footing. The trial court may look at each father and the child's situation in regard to that father and decide simply who would be best for the child. Indeed, won't the father who is married to the mother always have the edge simply because with him the child can live in a family relationship with its natural mother?

(6) The opinion in *Lehr* makes several important statements regarding the father-child relationship which you may wish to test against your own values:

a. *"The significance of the biological connection is that it offers the natural father an opportunity that no other male possesses to develop a relationship with his offspring."* Is this statement accurate? How do you think the court would treat a natural father who through no fault of his own did not know of the existence of the child: for example, the father was a prisoner of war during the period when the child was born and placed for adoption? Or, what if a biological "stranger" acquired the child wrongfully from the unwed father and developed a true nurturing relationship with the child; should the court return the child to the natural father based solely upon the biological relationship? *Cf. Mays v. Twiggs*, 543 So. 2d 241 (Fla. Dist. Ct. App. 1989) (dismissing paternity action brought by putative biological parents of child allegedly switched at birth with another infant and raised by non-biological parents). As Justice White states in the dissent, the "usual understanding of 'family' implies biological relationship." Is the Court really saying that it has little sympathy for the natural father who has not established a parent-child relationship and therefore will not afford him due process protection?

b. *"The most effective protection of the putative father's opportunity to develop a relationship with his child is provided by the laws which authorize formal marriage and govern the consequences."* While the Court acknowledges that the availability of this protection is to some degree dependent upon the will of the mother, it does not explain this statement at all, other than to say that New York has adopted a special scheme for the protection of fathers. Nor does the Court explain why the man who is married to the mother but has abandoned the children is entitled to protection, but the father who has brought an action for paternity is not. The man who is married to the mother will not be deprived of his parental rights absent a showing of unfitness, while the father suing for paternity does not even receive notice. While it is true that New York has established a statutory scheme, isn't it the job of the Court to protect constitutional interests which may have been overlooked by the legislature?

The Court's faith in the formalities of marriage is interesting from another perspective: the Court has steadfastly struck down laws which discriminate against children based upon illegitimacy, viewing the marital status of the parents as irrelevant to the rights of the children. *See, e.g., Levy v. Louisiana*, 391 U.S. 68 (1968) (wrongful death); *Glona v. American Guar. & Liab. Ins. Co.*, 391 U.S. 73, (1968) (wrongful death); *Jiminez v. Weinberger*, 417 U.S. 628 (1974) (Social security benefits); *Weber v. Aetna Cas. & Sur. Co.*, 406 U.S. 164, (1972) (Workers' Compensation benefits); *Trimble v. Gordon*, 430 U.S. 762 (1977) (inheritance rights). These cases can be distinguished from cases involving notice to "illegitimate fathers" because the children who were discriminated against were not responsible for their illegitimate status; however, in rebuttal, it can be said that the illegitimate child also loses something of legal importance when the relationship with the natural parent is severed.

c. *"Parental rights do not spring full-blown from the biological connection between the parent and child. They require something more enduring."* Is this statement true if the parents are married? Doesn't the right of a married parent arise at the moment of birth from the biological relationship? For example, a married person's parental rights can be terminated only if statutory criteria, such as unfitness or abandonment, have been established, and full due process granted, even if no parent-child relationship has been established. Perhaps marriage is what the Court means when it refers to "relationships more enduring"; however, this meaning is difficult to accept considering the frequency of divorce.

(7) Although the Court in *Lehr* does not dwell on it, the Court does appear to accept a strong public policy in favor of adoption or at least in favor of providing stable two-parent homes for children. The dissent alludes to this: "the state no doubt has an interest in expediting adoption proceedings to prevent a child from remaining unduly long in the custody of the State or foster parents." To what extent should this pro-adoption policy take precedence over an unmarried father's interest in establishing a relationship with his child? *Cf.* Barbara Bennet Woodhouse, *Of Babies, Bonding, and Burning Buildings: Discerning Parenthood in Irrational Action*, 81 Va. L. Rev. 2493, 2508–20 (1995) (discussing the role of biology in adoption law).

(8) Do you think the Court believes that the relationship between a man and a child he wants to adopt will be better (more secure, stable, and supportive) than the relationship between a natural father and a child that he has not taken responsible steps to legitimate and support? Is this belief justified by the fact that the adopting father is volunteering to take on the responsibility of the child? By the fact that the adopting father is married to the child's mother?

(9) Do you think the results in cases such as *Quilloin* and *Lehr* are fair to the biological father? To the child? If you say yes, have you addressed the possibility that the Court is punishing the biological father for his failure to take responsibility for his child? If the Court had insisted upon applying an unfitness standard, what would the result have been in these cases? One possible result could have been, if the biological father were found to be fit, that the child would have stayed in the care and custody of its mother and stepfather and would have had visitation with the biological father. Would that have been a better result than granting the adoptions in these case? Why or why not? *See* Comment, *Illegitimacy and the Rights of Unwed Fathers in Adoption Proceedings After Quilloin v. Walcott*, 12 J. Mar. J. Prac. & Proc. 383 (1979).

(10) Some of the disputes discussed in this section involving the rights of unmarried fathers might be avoided if states would adopt what has come to be called open adoption. The dominant approach to adoption in this country has been to sever all ties, and to extinguish all communication, between an adopted child and her biological family. *See* Chapter 8 *below*. Open adoption, discussed *below* in § 8.06[B] is an alternative that creates the same parent-child relationship between adoptive parents and the child, but allows a biological parent to remain in touch with the child as well. *See* Tammy M. Somogye, *Opening Minds to Open Adoption*, 45 Kan. L. Rev. 619, 619 (1997). In many open adoptions, the parties agree in writing that the child will continue to have contact with a biological parent (or parents) after the adoption is completed. The agreement is then presented to the court for approval at the time the adoption is finalized. *See* Amadio and Deutsh, *Open Adoption: Allowing Adopted Children to "Stay in Touch" With Blood Relatives*, 22 J. Fam. L. 59, 60 (1983–84). Although the legal system has traditionally disfavored open adoption, the concept has gained increasing support, among both academics and mental health professionals, particularly for older children, who are likely to have developed a relationship with their biological parent(s). *See generally*, Marianne Berry, *Risks and Benefits of Open Adoption*, in 3 The Future of Children 125 (Richard E. Behrman, ed., 1993); Candace M.

Zierdt, *Make New Parents But Keep the Old*, 69 N.D. L. Rev. 497 (1993). Supporters of open adoption argue that allowing such arrangements is likely to decrease costly and damaging adoption disputes and may increase the number of children available for adoption, since birth parents will be more willing to consent to adoption if they can be assured of continued contact with their children. A number of states now permit parties to enter into enforceable open adoption agreements; other states continue to prohibit such agreements as contrary to public policy, even if the parties privately agree that open adoption would serve the best interests of the child in question. *See* Somogye, *above* at 622–24 (discussing state statutes and court decisions).

If *Lehr* stands for the proposition that the biological relationship only gives the father an opportunity that he must grasp in order to have a constitutionally protected right, the question arises as to when the father has successfully grasped his opportunity? Or, to put it another way, what must a biological father do to exercise his opportunity to parent fully, and when must he do it? The next two cases address this issue.

IN RE ADOPTION OF KELSEY S.
Supreme Court of California
823 P. 2d 1216 (1992)

BAXTER JUSTICE.

The primary question in this case is whether the father of a child born out of wedlock may properly be denied the right to withhold his consent to his child's adoption by third parties despite his diligent and legal attempts to obtain custody of his child and to rear it himself, and absent any showing of the father's unfitness as a parent. We conclude that, under these circumstances, the federal constitutional guarantees of equal protection and due process require that the father be allowed to withhold his consent to his child's adoption and therefore that his parental rights cannot be terminated absent a showing of his unfitness within the meaning of Civil Code section 221.20.

FACTS

Kari S. gave birth to Kelsey, a boy, on May 18, 1988. The child's undisputed natural father is petitioner Rickie M.[3] He and Kari S. were not married to one another. At that time, he was married to another woman but was separated from her and apparently was in divorce proceedings. He was aware that Kari planned to place their child for adoption, and he objected to her decision because he wanted to rear the child.

Two days after the child's birth, petitioner filed an action in superior court under Civil Code section 7006 to establish his parental relationship with the child and to obtain custody of the child. (The petition erroneously stated that the child had not yet been born. His birth was earlier than expected, and petitioner had not been informed of it when he filed his action.) That same day, the court issued a restraining order that temporarily awarded care, custody, and control of the child to petitioner. The order also stayed all adoption proceedings and prohibited any contact between the child and the prospective adoptive parents.

---

[3] We identify the parties by only their given names and last initials to protect the identity of the minor child. As necessary for convenience and clarity, we will occasionally refer to Kelsey as "the child," to Kari S. as "the mother," to Rickie M. as "the father" or "petitioner," and to Steven and Suzanne A. as the "prospective adoptive parents," the "adoptive parents," or "Mr. and Mrs. A."

Later that day, petitioner filed a copy of the order with law enforcement officials. He also personally attempted to serve it on the prospective adoptive parents at their home. He was unsuccessful.

On May 24, 1988, Steven and Suzanne A., the prospective adoptive parents, filed an adoption petition under Civil Code section 226. Their petition alleged that only the mother's consent to the adoption was required because there was no presumed father under section 7004, subdivision (a).

On May 26, 1988, the superior court modified its May 20 order and awarded temporary custody of the child to its mother. The court ordered the mother to live with the child in a shelter for unwed mothers. The court also found that its May 20 temporary order had not been followed. The record before us is not entirely clear on this point. Petitioner alleges that the prospective adoptive parents attempted to evade service of the order and secretly removed the child from their home. In this court, the prospective adoptive parents do not directly dispute these allegations. At the May 26 hearing, however, the superior court declined to find a "knowing violation" of its prior order. In any event, the trial court prohibited visitation by either the prospective adoptive parents or petitioner.

On May 31, 1988, the prospective adoptive parents filed a petition under section 7017 to terminate petitioner's parental rights. The superior court consolidated that proceeding with the adoption proceeding. The court allowed petitioner to have supervised visitation with the child at the women's shelter where the child was living with his mother. The court also allowed the prospective adoptive parents to have unsupervised visitation at the shelter.

The parties subsequently stipulated that petitioner was the child's natural father. The superior court, however, ruled that he was not a "presumed father" within the meaning of section 7004, subdivision (a)(4). The court held four days of hearings under section 7017, subdivision (d)(2) to determine whether it was in the child's best interest for petitioner to retain his parental rights and whether the adoption should be allowed to proceed. (The attorney appointed by the trial court to represent the child's interests advocated that petitioner should retain his parental rights.) On August 26, 1988, the court found "by a *bare* preponderance" of the evidence that the child's best interest required termination of petitioner's parental rights. (Italics added.)

Petitioner appealed. He contended the superior court erred by: (1) concluding that he was not the child's presumed father; (2) not granting him a parental placement preference; and (3) applying a preponderance-of-the-evidence standard of proof. The Court of Appeal rejected each of his contentions and affirmed the judgment.

DISCUSSION

1. *The statutory framework*

Section 7004 states, "A man is presumed to be the natural father of a child . . . " if the man meets any of several conditions set forth in the statute. Whether a biological father is a "presumed father" under section 7004 is critical to his parental rights. If the mother of a child who does *not* have a presumed father consents to the child's adoption, a petition must, except in certain narrow circumstances, be filed in the superior court to terminate the natural father's parental rights. (§ 7017, subd. (b).) If the natural father or a man representing himself to be the natural father claims parental rights, the court first must determine whether he is the natural father. (§ 7017, subd. (d)(2).) If so, "The court shall then determine if it is in the best interest of the child that the father retain his parental rights, or that an adoption of the child be allowed to proceed. . . . If the court finds that it is in the best interest of the child that the father should be allowed to retain his parental rights, it shall order that his consent is necessary for an adoption." (*Ibid.*) The child's best interest is the sole criterion where there is no presumed father. As in the present case, the trial court's determination is frequently that the child's interests are better served by a third party adoption than by granting custody to the unwed natural father.

Mothers and presumed fathers have far greater rights. . . . In short, a mother or a presumed father must consent to an adoption absent a showing by clear and convincing evidence of that parent's unfitness.

This statutory scheme creates three classifications of parents: mothers, biological fathers who are presumed fathers, and biological fathers who are not presumed fathers (i.e., natural fathers). A natural father's consent to an adoption of his child by third parties is not required unless the father makes the required showing that retention of his parental rights is in the child's best interest. Consent, however, is required of a mother and a presumed father regardless of the child's best interest. The natural father is therefore treated differently from both mothers and presumed fathers. With this statutory framework in mind, we now examine petitioner's contentions.

2. *Acquiring presumed father status by obtaining constructive receipt of the child.*

A man becomes a "presumed father" under section 7004, subdivision (a)(4) . . . if "*[h]e receives the child into his home and openly holds out the child as his natural child.*" (Italics added.) It is undisputed in this case that petitioner openly held out the child as being his own. Petitioner, however, did not physically receive the child into his home. He was prevented from doing so by the mother, by court order, and allegedly also by the prospective adoptive parents.

Respondents contend the statutory scheme allows a mother to preclude her child's father from acquiring presumed father status and thereby eliminate the need for his consent regardless of whether he is a demonstrably fit parent. Petitioner responds that such result is impermissible under the federal constitutional guarantees of equal protection and due process. He claims he should be deemed to be the presumed father under section 7004(a)(4) because he did all that he could do under the circumstances to receive the child into his home. He contends we should not construe the statute in such a way that the mother can unilaterally bar the father from receiving their child into his home and thereby deprive him of presumed father status and the concomitant right under section 221.20 to withhold consent to the child's adoption by third parties. Petitioner asserts that constructive receipt is sufficient under section 7004(a)(4) to provide him with presumed father status and the right to withhold consent.

Petitioner's argument in favor of constructive receipt is based largely on the federal Constitution rather than on section 7004(a)(4). He does not contend that either the language or legislative history of the statute supports his view. Indeed, he "agrees that the law as literally written does permit a mother to interfere with the father-child relationship and does deny a natural father equal protection with a natural mother." Rather, he argues that his constitutional right (and that of other natural fathers) to equal protection and due process will be violated unless we construe the statute to provide for constructive receipt.

Alternatively, he argues that we should hold the statutory scheme to be invalid under these circumstances.

Petitioner is correct that when possible we should read a statute in a manner that avoids a potential for conflict with the federal Constitution. . . . We cannot, however, construe a statute contrary to legislative intent merely to eliminate a potential constitutional conflict. The threshold question therefore is whether the statutes support the notion of constructive receipt advocated by petitioner. We conclude the statutes provide no such support.

"We begin with the fundamental rule that our primary task in construing a statute is to determine the Legislature's intent." We must begin with the words of the statute. . . . Section 7004(a)(4) states that a man is a presumed father if "*[h]e receives the child into his home* and openly holds out the child as his natural child." On its face, the statute refers to actual receipt of the child. The statute does not refer either explicitly or implicitly to attempted receipt or constructive receipt. . . .

Even if the statute were ambiguous, petitioner does not point to any legislative history supporting a theory of constructive receipt. Nor are we aware of any extrinsic evidence that the Legislature did not mean what it said in section 7004(a)(4). . . .

Prior judicial decisions also provide slender support for reading into section 7004(a)(4) a provision for constructive receipt. . . .

In summary, nothing in the language or legislative history of section 7004(a)(4) supports the claim of constructive receipt. The decisions of the Courts of Appeal have also rejected the claim. We have not previously decided the question and, to the extent we have noted the issue, our decisions either provide little guidance or cast doubt on the notion of constructive receipt, especially in light of the statutory abrogation of illegitimacy. Petitioner therefore correctly admits that section 7004(a)(4) does not by itself provide for presumed father status based on a father's constructive receipt of the child, i.e., his unsuccessful attempts to obtain custody over the mother's objection. We cannot accept petitioner's invitation to construe section 7004(a)(4) to avoid the alleged constitutional conflict. To do so would require us to judicially rewrite the statute.

There remains, however, the question of whether a natural father's federal constitutional rights are violated if his child's mother is allowed to unilaterally preclude him from obtaining the same legal right as a presumed father to withhold his consent to his child's adoption by third parties. We now turn to that difficult constitutional question. . . .

5. *The constitutionally protected interest of an unwed, natural father*

Petitioner asserts a violation of equal protection and due process under the federal Constitution; more specifically, that he should not be treated differently from his child's mother. In constitutional terms, the question is whether California's sex-based statutory distinction between biological mothers and fathers serves " ' . . . important governmental objectives and [is] substantially related to achievement of those objectives.' " (*Caban v. Mohammad* 441 U.S. 380, 388 (1978)). Does the mother's ability to determine the father's rights substantially serve an important governmental interest? The question is the same "whether the analysis [is] undertaken as a matter of due process or equal protection." (*Raquel Marie, supra,* 76 N.Y.2d [387] at p. 403.)

There is no dispute that "The State's interest in providing for the well-being of illegitimate children is an important one." (*Caban, supra,* 441 U.S. at p. 391; *In the matter of Raquel*

Marie, 76 N.Y.2d 387, 403.) Although the legal concept of illegitimacy no longer exists in California, the problems and needs of children born out of wedlock are an undisputed reality. The state has an important and valid interest in their well-being.

The more difficult issue is whether the statutory treatment of natural fathers (i.e., biological fathers without presumed status under section 7004) is *substantially* related to the achievement of that objective. On the facts of this case, the question must be framed as follows: Is the state's important interest in the well being of a child born out of wedlock substantially furthered by allowing the mother to deny the child's biological father an opportunity to form a relationship with the child that would give the father the same statutory rights as the mother (or a presumed father) in deciding whether the child will be adopted by third parties?

Respondents do not adequately explain how an unwed mother's control over a biological father's rights furthers the state's interest in the well-being of the child. The linchpin of their position, however, is clear although largely implicit: Allowing the biological father to have the same rights as the mother would make adoptions more difficult because the consent of both parents is more difficult to obtain than the consent of the mother alone. This reasoning is flawed in several respects.

A. Respondents' view too narrowly assumes that the proper governmental objective is adoption. As we have explained, the constitutionally valid objective is the protection of the child's well-being. We cannot conclude in the abstract that *adoption* is itself a sufficient objective to allow the state to take whatever measures it deems appropriate. Nor can we merely assume, either as a policy or factual matter, that adoption is necessarily in a child's best interest. This assumption is especially untenable in light of the rapidly changing concept of family. As recently as only a few years ago, it might have been reasonable to assume that an adopted child would be placed into a two-parent home and thereby have a more stable environment than a child raised by a single father. The validity of that assumption is now highly suspect in light of modern adoption practice. Recent statistics show that a significant percentage of children placed for independent adoption—7.7 percent—are adopted by a single parent. The figure is even higher—21.9 percent—for children placed with agencies for adoption. We note that New York's high court also recently rejected the argument that the state has a sufficiently strong interest in providing two-parent families to discriminate against unwed fathers. (*Raquel Marie, supra,* 76 N.Y.2d at p. 406.)

If the possible benefit of adoption were by itself sufficient to justify terminating a parent's rights, the state could terminate an unwed mother's parental rights based on nothing more than a showing that her child's best interest would be served by adoption. Of course, that is not the law; nor do the parties advocate such a system. We simply do not in our society take children away from their mothers—married or otherwise—because a "better" adoptive parent can be found. We see no valid reason why we should be less solicitous of a father's efforts to establish a parental relationship with his child. Respondents seem to suggest that a child is inherently better served by adoptive parents than by a single, biological father but that the child is also inherently better served by a single, biological mother than by adoptive parents. The logic of this view is not apparent, and there is no evidence in the record to support such a counterintuitive view.

B. Nor is there evidence before us that the statutory provisions allowing the mother to determine the father's rights are, in general, substantially related to protecting the child's best interest. As a matter of cold efficiency, we cannot disagree that eliminating a natural father's rights would make adoption easier in some cases. That, however, begs the question because it assumes an unwed mother's decision to permit an immediate adoption of her newborn is always preferable to custody by the natural father, even when he is a demonstrably fit parent. We have no evidence to support that assumption. Moreover, the assumption has already been rejected by the United States Supreme Court: "It may be that, given the opportunity, some unwed fathers would prevent the adoption of their illegitimate children. This impediment to adoption usually is the result of a natural parental interest shared by both genders [sexes] alike; it is not a manifestation of any profound difference between the affection and concern of mothers and fathers for their children. Neither the State nor the appellees have argued that unwed fathers are more likely to object to the adoption of their children than are unwed mothers; nor is there any self-evident reason why as a class they would be." (*Caban, supra,* 441 U.S. 380, 391–392.) New York's high court has also rejected the contention that a father's rights can be trampled in the name of efficiency. (*Raquel Marie, supra,* 76 N.Y.2d at p. 401.)

C. The lack of any substantial relationship between the state's interest in protecting a child and allowing the mother sole control over its destiny is best demonstrated by the results that can arise when a mother prevents the father from obtaining presumed status under section 7004, subdivision (a). . . . Under the statute, the father has basically two ways in which to achieve that status: he can either marry the mother, or he can receive the child into his home and hold it out as his natural child. Of course, the first alternative is entirely within the mother's control. She cannot be forced to marry the father. The second alternative is, for the most part, also within her control. She can deny the father the right to come into her home. She can also deny him the right to take the child into his home. Faced with the mother's denial, the father has only one recourse aside from illegal self-help. He must seek a court order granting him custody so that he can take the child into his home and thereby gain presumed father status. As in this case, however, the trial court may deny him custody based on its view that the child is better served by remaining with the mother or third parties, e.g., prospective adoptive parents. Similarly, he may (as apparently initially occurred in this case) obtain a court order granting him custody, but enforcement of the order may be thwarted by third parties.

The anomalies under this statutory scheme become readily apparent. A father who is indisputably ready, willing, and able to exercise the full measure of his parental responsibilities can have his rights terminated merely on a showing that his child's best interest would be served by adoption. If the child's mother, however, were equally of the opposite character—*un*ready, *un*willing, and *un*able—her rights in the child could nevertheless be terminated only under the much more protective standards of section 221.20. Such a distinction bears no substantial relationship to protecting the well-being of children. Indeed, it has little rationality.

The system also leads to irrational distinctions between fathers. Based solely on the mother's wishes, a model father can be denied presumed father status, whereas a father of dubious ability and intent can achieve such status by the fortuitous circumstance of the mother allowing him to come into her home, even if only briefly—perhaps a single day. We cannot ignore reality. Parental unfitness is considerably more difficult to show than that the child's best interest is served by adoption. Under the statutory scheme, two fathers who are by all accounts equal in their ability and commitment to fulfill their parental missions can be treated differently based solely on the mothers' decisions whether to allow the father to become a presumed father.

The system also makes little sense from a child's perspective. A child may have a wholly acceptable father who wants to nurture it, but whose parental rights can be terminated under the best-interest standard because the mother has precluded the father from attaining presumed father status. Conversely, if a presumed father is highly questionable in every respect, he is nevertheless allowed to withhold consent absent proof by clear and convincing evidence that he is unfit. As a practical matter, the child's best interest is largely ignored by the statutory distinction between presumed fathers and those natural fathers who are willing to assume their parental responsibilities.

D. We must not lose sight of the way in which the present case and others like it come before the courts. A mother's decision to place her newborn child for adoption may be excruciating and altogether altruistic. Doing so may reflect the extreme of selflessness and maternal love. *As a legal matter*, however, the mother seeks to sever all ties with her child. The natural father, by contrast, has come forward to assume the legal and practical burdens of being a parent. This is not a case where the mother and father are pitted against one another for the child's custody. Even if it could be said, either in general or in a particular case, that the mother somehow has a greater connection than the father with their child and thus should have greater rights in the child, the same result need not obtain when she seeks to relinquish custody and to sever her legal ties with the child and the father seeks to assume his legal burdens.

Clearly, the father is treated unfairly under section 7004, subdivision (a), but equally important is the loss to the child. The child has a genetic bond with its natural parents that is unique among all relationships the child will have throughout its life. "The intangible fibers that connect parent and child have infinite variety. They are woven throughout the fabric of our society, providing it with strength, beauty, and flexibility." (*Lehr, supra*, 463 U.S. 248, 256.) It therefore would be curious to conclude that the child's best interest is served by allowing the one parent (the mother) who wants to sever her legal ties to decide unilaterally that the only other such tie (the father's) will be cut as well. Absent a showing of a father's unfitness, his child is ill-served by allowing its mother effectively to preclude the child from ever having a meaningful relationship with its only other biological parent.

E. In summary, we hold that section 7004, subdivision (a) and the related statutory scheme violates the federal constitutional guarantees of equal protection and due process for unwed fathers *to the extent that* the statutes allow a mother unilaterally to preclude her child's biological father from becoming a presumed father and thereby allowing the state to terminate his parental rights on nothing more than a showing of the child's best interest. If an unwed father promptly comes forward and demonstrates a full commitment to his parental responsibilities—emotional, financial, and otherwise—his federal constitutional right to due process prohibits the termination of his parental relationship absent a showing of his unfitness as a parent. Absent such a showing, the child's well-being is presumptively best served by continuation of the father's parental relationship. Similarly, when the father has come forward to grasp his parental responsibilities, his parental rights are entitled to equal protection as those of the mother.

A court should consider all factors relevant to that determination. The father's conduct both *before and after* the child's birth must be considered. Once he knows or reasonably should know of the pregnancy, he must promptly attempt to assume his parental responsibilities as fully as the mother will allow and his circumstances permit. In particular, the father must demonstrate "a willingness himself to assume full custody of the child—not merely to block adoption by others." (*Raquel Marie, supra*, 76 N.Y.2d at p. 408.) A court should also consider the father's public acknowledgment of paternity, payment of pregnancy and birth expenses commensurate with his ability to do so, and prompt legal action to seek custody of the child.

We reiterate and emphasize the narrowness of our decision. The statutory distinction between natural fathers and presumed fathers is constitutionally invalid *only to the extent* it is applied to an unwed father who has sufficiently and timely demonstrated a full commitment to his parental responsibilities. Our statutes are constitutionally sufficient when applied to a father who has failed to make such a showing. Moreover, section 7018 explicitly provides that if any portion of the state's Uniform Parentage Act " . . . or the application thereof to any person or circumstances is held invalid, such invalidity shall not affect other provisions or application. . . . "

6. *Application of the correct standard to this case*

The trial court found that adoption was in the child's best interest. The court, however, did not have the benefit of our decision in this case and thus did not decide the threshold constitutional question of whether petitioner demonstrated a sufficient commitment to his parental responsibilities. Petitioner and the prospective adoptive parents sharply disagree on that question, and the evidence is conflicting in several respects as to petitioner's attempts to fulfill his responsibilities, especially during the period *before* the child's birth. We therefore conclude the more prudent approach is to remand to the trial court to make the determination in the first instance. In doing so, the trial court must take into account petitioner's conduct throughout the period since he learned he was the biological father, including his conduct during the pendency of this legal proceeding, both in the trial and appellate courts, up to the determination in the trial court on remand by this court. We recognize that during these proceedings petitioner may have been restricted, both legally and as a practical matter, in his ability to act fully as a father. Nevertheless, the trial court must consider whether petitioner has done all that he could reasonably do *under the circumstances*.

If the trial court finds on remand that petitioner failed to demonstrate the required commitment to his parental responsibilities, that will be the end of the matter. He will not have suffered any deprivation of a constitutional right. If, however, the required commitment is found, the result under our constitutional analysis will necessarily be a decision that petitioner's rights to equal protection and due process under the federal Constitution were violated to the extent that he was deprived of the same statutory protections granted the mother. Therefore, if (*but only if*) the trial court finds petitioner demonstrated the necessary commitment to his parental responsibilities, there will arise the further question of whether he can be deprived of the right to withhold his consent to the adoption.

Section 7017, subdivision (a) states that parental consent is required except in certain narrow circumstances set forth in section 221.20, that is, absent a showing of abandonment or a parent's unfitness under section 232. Because the trial court did not treat petitioner as a presumed father, the court did not reach the question of whether he was statutorily unfit under section 232 and thus could be deprived of his right under section 221.20 to withhold consent. As with the threshold question of whether petitioner did all he could reasonably do to act like a father, we cannot fairly decide in the first instance whether he was unfit and could thus be deprived of his right to withhold consent. We leave it to the trial court to decide this question, if necessary.

In deciding this question, the trial court shall take into account (as it must also do on the threshold question of whether petitioner assumed his parental responsibilities) petitioner's conduct and circumstances up to and including the time of the decision on remand. The proper standard is whether he is *now* fit or unfit. For purposes of remand, we also note subdivision (c) of section 232, which states: "A finding pursuant to this section shall be supported by *clear and convincing evidence*." (Italics added.) Thus, any finding of petitioner's unfitness must be supported by clear and convincing evidence. Absent such evidence, he shall be permitted to withhold his consent to the adoption.

We emphasize that the sole question before us is whether petitioner has a right to withhold his consent to the adoption of his biological child. We decide no issue as to the custody of the child. If petitioner fails to establish on remand that he has a right to withhold his consent, there will be no question as to whether he should have custody of the child. If, however, the trial court concludes that petitioner has a right to withhold consent, that decision will bear only on the question of whether the adoption will proceed. Even if petitioner has a right to withhold his consent (and chooses to prevent the adoption), there will remain the question of the child's custody. That question is not before us, and we express no view on it. . . .

DISPOSITION

We reverse the judgment of the Court of Appeal with directions to remand to the superior court for further proceedings consistent with our decision.

IN RE ADOPTION OF MICHAEL H.
Supreme Court of California
898 P.2d 891 (1995),
cert. denied, 116 S. Ct. 1272 (1996)

Mosk, Justice.

In this appeal we further clarify the circumstances (see *Adoption of Kelsey S.* (1992) 1 Cal.4th 816, 4 Cal.Rptr.2d 615, 823 P.2d 1216 (hereafter *Kelsey S.*)) in which an unwed biological father has a right under the due process and equal protection clauses of the Fourteenth Amendment to withhold his consent to the biological mother's decision to give their child up at birth for adoption by a third party. . . . We conclude that the unwed father in this case did not satisfy the requirements of *Kelsey S.* as they are properly understood, and hence that he has no constitutional right to veto his child's adoption. The judgment of the Court of Appeal to the contrary must therefore be reversed. . . .

FACTS

Stephanie H. met Mark K. in December 1988 in Arizona. In February 1990, Mark, then age 20, told Stephanie, then age 15, that he wanted to marry her. She declined to get married until she graduated from high school and until he quit drinking and using drugs. However, they considered themselves engaged at that time. In early July 1990 Stephanie learned she was pregnant with Mark's child. Mark suggested that she have an abortion, but she would not consider it. They also briefly discussed keeping the baby, but finally settled on adoption.

Stephanie came to California with her grandparents in July 1990. While here her aunt introduced her to two friends, John and Margaret S., who were interested in adopting a child. Stephanie told Mark about John and Margaret when she returned to Arizona at the end of July 1990. Around that time Stephanie and Mark were also researching adoption agencies.

In September 1990 Mark and Stephanie began attending birthing classes together and Mark went to at least one yard sale with Stephanie to buy baby apparel. He also bought a trailer for them to live in together, although they never did. In early October 1990 Mark arranged to have a videotape of Stephanie's ultrasound made.

Mark and Stephanie's relationship started to deteriorate around this time. Stephanie excluded him from the birthing classes. Mark had two violent outbursts involving Stephanie, and after one of these he was arrested on a charge of aggravated assault. Mark quit his job on October 26, 1990. Two days later, on Stephanie's 16th birthday, Mark went into his trailer, which was parked behind Stephanie's mother's house, and attempted to kill himself.

After his suicide attempt, Mark admitted himself into a rehabilitation hospital. While there he decided to stop using drugs, seek stable employment and residence, and continue counseling. He also decided that he did not want to give up his child for adoption and started looking for an attorney to help him obtain custody after the child was born.

Mark and Stephanie had very little contact after his suicide attempt. In January 1991 Stephanie moved from Arizona to San Diego to live with John and Margaret. She gave birth to Michael H. on February 27, 1991. Michael was released from the hospital directly into John and Margaret's custody, where he has remained ever since.

On March 7, 1991, Mark found an attorney who would take his case free of charge. That day his attorney telephoned John and Margaret and learned that Michael had been born. As soon as he found out, Mark asked for custody, sent out some birth announcements, and bought several items, including a car seat, a crib, and some baby clothes.

In April 1991 John and Margaret filed a petition to terminate Mark's legal status as Michael's father. (Fam.Code, § 7662.) Mark subsequently filed a petition to establish a father-child relationship (§ 7630, subd. (a)(1)), and the two proceedings were consolidated (*id.*, subd. (c)). The court concluded that Mark was not a "presumed father" under the statutory definition (s 7611) and that it would be in Michael's best interest to be adopted by John and Margaret (§ 7664, subd. (b)). It therefore terminated Mark's parental status and allowed the adoption to proceed.

While Mark's appeal from that judgment was pending we filed our decision in *Kelsey S.* in which a majority held that under certain circumstances unwed fathers have a Fourteenth Amendment right to prevent third parties from adopting their biological children. . . .

After holding an evidentiary hearing on remand, the trial court concluded in light of our decision in *Kelsey S.* that Mark had a constitutional right to veto Michael's adoption absent a showing that he would be an unfit parent. John and Margaret noticed an appeal.

The Court of Appeal affirmed the trial court's decision. . . .

DISCUSSION

. . .

II.

We held in *Kelsey S.* that an unwed father who has no statutory right to block a third party adoption by withholding consent may nevertheless have a constitutional right to do so under the due process and equal protection clauses of the Fourteenth Amendment and thereby to preserve his opportunity to develop a parental relationship with his child. Under such circumstances, however, the unwed father's constitutional interest is merely inchoate and does not ripen into a constitutional right that he can assert to prevent adoption unless he proves that he has "promptly come[] forward and demonstrate[d] a full commitment to his parental responsibilities. . . . " (*Kelsey S., supra*, 1 Cal.4th 816, 849.) This is so because "the mere existence of a biological link does not merit . . . constitutional protection" (*Lehr v. Robertson, supra*, 463 U.S. at p. 261); rather, the federal Constitution protects only the parental relationship that the unwed father has actively developed by " 'com[ing] forward to participate in the rearing of his child' " (ibid.) and "act[ing] as a father" (*Caban v. Mohammed* (1979) 441 U.S. 380, 389, fn. 7).

We must decide whether Mark took sufficient steps to transform his inchoate constitutional interest in his potential parental relationship with Michael into a constitutional right that entitled him to block John and Margaret's efforts to adopt Michael and terminate his status as Michael's father. Our task is made more difficult by the circumstance that here the adoption process began at birth and Michael has been in John and Margaret's custody and care for all of the more than four years of his life. Mark has therefore had little contact with Michael and little opportunity to directly develop a parental relationship with him, and Michael instead experiences only John and Margaret as his parents.

After its hearing devoted to the question whether Mark was entitled to constitutional protection under *Kelsey S.*, the trial court prepared a rather lengthy summary of its findings. In this summary the court declared that during the period between early July 1990, when Mark first learned that Stephanie was pregnant, and October 28, 1990, the day he attempted suicide, "it cannot be said that he was fully committed to his parental responsibilities. While he always acknowledged his paternity, he clearly planned with Stephanie to give the child up. Like many fathers (and mothers) he was initially frightened and eagerly looked for a way out of these responsibilities." During his hospitalization in November 1990, Mark "decided he did not want his child given up for adoption." Despite this decision, however, Mark continued to "speak to Stephanie and even [John and Margaret] as though he still agreed with the adoption" until March 7, 1991, some two weeks after Michael was born, because, according to Mark's testimony, "he did not want to risk the sort of polarization which might totally close the door to further communication."

The trial court found that "After his release from the hospital, and particularly after the birth of his son, Mark's efforts were nothing short of impressive," and "In the two years since his son's birth, Mark has never wavered in expressing his desire to take on the full responsibility of fatherhood." The court also noted that each of Mark's three attorneys testified that Mark "incessantly, relentlessly urged" them to seek visitation rights. In light of these findings, the court concluded that Mark's "struggle before his hospitalization and the subsequent birth of his son does not counterbalance his truly extraordinary efforts and commitment afterward" and that "In the context of all the facts of this case, his efforts sufficiently demonstrate his full commitment to his parental responsibilities" within the meaning of *Kelsey S.* . . . .

III.

John and Margaret contend that the trial court and Court of Appeal misinterpreted and misapplied our decision in *Kelsey S.*, and that under the correct standard the trial court's findings do not support its decision that Mark "promptly [came] forward and demonstrate[d] a full commitment to his parental responsibilities" and was therefore entitled to constitutional protection. They focus on that portion of *Kelsey S.* in which we stated that in deciding whether an unwed father is entitled to constitutional protection, "A court should consider all factors relevant to that determination. The father's conduct both *before and after* the child's birth must be considered. Once the father knows or reasonably should know of the pregnancy, he must promptly attempt to assume his parental responsibilities as fully as the mother will allow and the circumstances permit. In particular, the father must demonstrate 'a willingness himself to assume full custody of the child—not merely to block adoption by others.' A court should also consider the father's public acknowledgment of paternity, payment of pregnancy and birth expenses commensurate with his ability to do so, and prompt legal action to seek custody of the child." . . .

We agree with John and Margaret's reading of the quoted language. It is difficult to conceive how our statement that "Once the father knows or reasonably should know of the pregnancy, he must promptly attempt to assume his parental responsibilities as fully as the mother will allow and the circumstances permit" (*Kelsey S.*, *supra*, 1 Cal.4th at p. 849) could be read in any other way. . . .

V.

We conclude that an unwed father has no federal constitutional right to withhold consent to an at-birth, third party adoption under our decision in *Kelsey S.* unless he shows that he promptly came forward and demonstrated as full a commitment to his parental responsibilities as the biological mother allowed and the circumstances permitted within a short time after he learned or reasonably should have learned that the biological mother was pregnant with his child.

Here the trial court found that Mark learned that Stephanie was pregnant with his child in early July 1990, that between July 1990 and November 1990, "*it cannot be said* that he was fully committed to his parental responsibilities . . . [and] he clearly planned with Stephanie to give the child up." (Italics added.) The court further found that although Mark decided in November 1990 that "he did not want his child given up for adoption," he "continued to speak to Stephanie and even [John and Margaret] as though he still agreed with the adoption" until March 7, 1991, some two weeks after Michael was born. In light of these findings, we conclude that under *Kelsey S.* Mark has no constitutional right to withhold his consent to Michael's adoption and that the Court of Appeal erred in ruling to the contrary.

We therefore reverse the judgment of the Court of Appeal with directions to remand the cause to the superior court for entry of judgment against Mark on his claim he has a constitutional right to veto adoption, against Mark on his petition to declare the existence of a father-child relationship (§ 7630, subd. (c)), and in favor of John and Margaret on their petition to terminate Mark's parental rights and adopt Michael (§ 7662). . . .

KENNARD, JUSTICE, concurring and dissenting.

Upon learning that his girlfriend, Stephanie H., was pregnant, Mark K. promptly acknowledged paternity; he contributed to the costs of her pregnancy; and he tried to maintain his relationship with Stephanie until she put an end to it. After researching the law himself, Mark filed a petition in propria persona for custody of his son Michael H. Since then, Mark has never wavered in his efforts to attain that goal. The majority terminates Mark's parental rights in Michael solely because in the early stages of Stephanie's pregnancy Mark did not oppose her plan to have the child adopted. The majority's conclusion is at odds with this court's holding in Adoption of *Kelsey S.* that a biological father who "sufficiently and timely demonstrated his full commitment to his parental responsibilities" had the right to veto his child's adoption. In my view, Mark has met the *Kelsey S.* test. . . .

II

. . . We observed in *Kelsey S.* that a biological father who wanted to marry the child's mother or to take the child into his home, care for it, and hold it out as his own, but who was prevented from doing either by the mother's unilateral decisions not to marry him and to place the child in an adoptive home would, under the statutory scheme, be deprived of the right to withhold consent to adoption and to keep the child himself. This, we said, would violate the federal constitutional guarantees of equal protection and due process. . . .

Based on all this evidence, the trial court made several findings, including these: "Mark conceived this child in love (however ill-fated), attempted to maintain a partnership with the mother throughout the pregnancy (however unwanted that partnership became to her), and has fought unyieldingly for custody since [Michael's] birth."

"After [Mark's] release from the hospital, and particularly after the birth of his son, Mark's efforts were nothing short of impressive. Beginning with relatively little knowledge or experience, he acted with a tenacity that demonstrates undeniable commitment and speaks well of his ability to weather the frustrating demands of parenthood."

"In the two years since his son's birth, Mark has never wavered in expressing his desire to take full responsibility of fatherhood. He defended against the action to terminate his parental rights, and pursued his own paternity action. Testimony from three of his attorneys establishes that he incessantly, relentlessly urged them to seek visitation for him . . . [but] [h]is efforts for custody or court ordered visits were consistently resisted by Stephanie and [by John and Margaret]."

The trial court ruled: "In the context of all of the facts of this case [Mark's] efforts sufficiently demonstrate his full commitment to his parental responsibilities [and thus] under *Kelsey S.* he is entitled to be treated as though he were a 'presumed father' for the purposes of this adoption."

The trial court's ruling, which the Court of Appeal upheld, is supported by substantial evidence. As set forth above, Mark acknowledged paternity, he contributed to the costs of Stephanie's pregnancy commensurate with his ability to do so, he stayed with Stephanie and tried to provide her with emotional support until she ended the relationship, he took prompt legal action to gain custody of Michael, and he has never wavered in his pursuit of custody. Thus, by his conduct both before and after Michael's birth, Mark has done everything that *Kelsey S.* deemed pertinent in determining whether a biological father has made a full commitment to assume his parental responsibilities. . . .

The majority's decision creates a dilemma for a biological father: If in the early stages of the mother's pregnancy he vigorously opposes the mother's decision to relinquish their child for adoption, he runs the risk of irreparably damaging his relationship with the mother and causing her emotional upset, quite the opposite of the emotional support he must give under *Kelsey S., supra,* 1 Cal.4th 186, 4 Cal.Rptr.2d 615, 823 P.2d 1216. If, on the other hand, he initially acquiesces in the mother's decision to place the child for adoption, hoping to change her mind before the child is born, he has, under the majority's holding, forfeited his right to object later in the pregnancy to the child's adoption. . . .

Unlike the majority, I would uphold the trial court's ruling, affirmed by the Court of Appeal, that Mark is a "*Kelsey S.*" father. . . .

NOTES AND QUESTIONS

(1) *Kelsey S.* In a sense, the California Supreme Court confronts the unanswered question of *Lehr* in *Kelsey S.* What happens if an unwed father, through absolutely no fault of his own, is denied the opportunity to develop a relationship with his child? The court, perhaps more than the United States Supreme Court in *Lehr,* is willing to give the benefit of the doubt to the natural father. What are the implications of this position? Is the California court more willing to accept the biological connection, or is it less willing to see the unwed father as a moral wrongdoer? Does *Kelsey S.* ignore the best interests of the child or does such a view of the case presuppose that adoptive parents are automatically the best parents? *See* Gershon, Note *Throwing out the Baby with the Bath Water: Adoption of Kelsey S. Raises the Rights of Unwed Fathers Above the Best Interests of the Child,* 28 Loy. L.A. L. Rev. 741 (1995).

(2) *Michael H.* What is the relationship between *Kelsey S.* and *Michael H.*? Is the court in *Michael H.* following the *Kelsey S.* decision and merely reaching a different conclusion based upon different facts? Or, is the court recanting the earlier opinion? Certainly the court in *Kelsey S.* exhibits a more generous attitude toward unwed fathers than in *Michael H.* It is worth noting that Justice Mosk, who dissented in *Kelsey S.,* wrote the opinion in *Michael H.* At the very least it seems that the pre-birth conduct of the father after *Michael H.* must be impeccably child-centered.

(3) **Legislation.** What sort of legislation would you consider to deal with the situation of unwed fathers? One author has proposed legislation which would meet the needs of a society in which "over one-third of children are born to unmarried women and one-quarter of households with children have only one parent present." This legislation would emphasize the best interest of the child but would also remove the issue of the unwed father's rights from the arena of litigation, emphasizing alternative dispute resolution, counseling and open adoption:

It is now time for the legislature to act to codify clear standards and creative alternatives, so that birth parents and adoptive parents can resolve future such controversies without the emotional and financial costs paid by these families. Such changes will benefit the parents, but more importantly, will provide the children with a secure and healthy environment in which to develop into happy and healthy adult members of society.

Gorenberg, *Fathers' Rights vs. Children's Best Interests: Establishing a Predictable Standard for California Adoption Disputes*, 31 Fam. L.Q. 169 (1997).

(4) The Uniform Adoption Act addresses the issue of unwed fathers by terminating an unwed father's rights if he does not respond in twenty days to a termination-of-parental-rights petition served upon him and if such termination is in the best interest of the child. Also, if an unwed father knows of the mother's pregnancy and does not exhibit a substantial commitment to the child, he can be found to have abandoned the child. Uniform Adoption Act § 3–504, 9 U.L.A. 52. *See* Cashman, Comment, *When Is a Biological Father Really a Dad?* 24 Pepp. L. Rev. 959 (1997).

The UAA also attempts to address the situation in which the father is genuinely unaware of the mother's pregnancy, because the mother has concealed it from him. The Act provides that, while the birth mother cannot be forced to identify the biological father, if she fails to do so, she must be advised "that the proceeding for adoption may be delayed or subject to challenge if a possible father is not given notice of the proceeding, that the lack of information about the father's medical and genetic history may be detrimental to the adoptee, and that she is subject to a civil penalty if she knowingly misidentified the father." Uniform Adoption Act § 3–404(e). In addition, the UAA requires the court to undertake its own efforts to identify and locate possible fathers. These efforts must include an inquiry into whether the birth mother was married or cohabiting with a man at the time of conception, whether she received payments or promises of support as a result of her pregnancy, whether a father is listed on the birth certificate, and whether any individual has claimed paternity. *See id.* at 3–404(b). If such efforts are successful, then the putative father becomes entitled to notice of the pending adoption proceeding. *See id.* at 3–404(c).

Should the law go further and *require* birth mothers to name all potential fathers, as a condition of placing a child for adoption, or would such a disclosure requirement impermissibly infringe on the woman's right to privacy? For a helpful discussion of the competing legal, psychological and policy interests at stake, see Deborah L. Foreman, *Unwed Fathers and Adoption: A Theoretical Analysis in Context*, 72 Tex. L. Rev. 967, 1025–43 (1994). For an analysis and critique of the UAA's approach to the rights of unwed fathers, see Scott A. Resnik, *Seeking The Wisdom of Solomon: Defining the Rights of Unwed Fathers in Newborn Adoptions*, 20 Seton Hall Legis. J. 363, 412–21 (1996).

(5) **Problem.** Cara and Dan were involved in a romantic and sexual relationship that lasted for approximately one year. They worked in the same building, and neither was married. In June, 1990, Cara broke off the relationship and began going out with Scott. Dan was angry about the breakup and did not speak to Cara for several months. By December of 1990, Dan realized that Cara was pregnant. At first, he suspected that he might be the father, but he did not pursue the matter because he heard through some friends that Cara and Scott were planning to marry. On February 8, 1991, Cara gave birth to a baby girl, which she immediately placed for adoption with a married couple. Cara named Scott

as the baby's father, and both she and Scott signed legal documents voluntarily terminating their parental rights and waiving notice of any subsequent adoption proceedings. On February 18, 1991, a court terminated the parental rights of Cara and Scott and awarded custody of the baby to the prospective adoptive parents, pending finalization of the adoption. Meanwhile, Cara was having second thoughts about placing the baby for adoption and about her relationship with Scott. On February 27, Cara contacted Dan and informed him that she thought he was the baby's father. Dan, who was scheduled to leave town on a delivery the next day, asked Cara to see what she could do to "retrieve" the baby. Two weeks later, Cara and Dan me with a lawyer who agreed to take the case. On March 27, 1991, Dan, through his lawyer, filed a petition to establish paternity, and to block the pending adoption proceedings. The prospective adoptive parents vigorously opposed Dan's motion. Subsequent blood testing indicated a 99.98% probability that Dan was the baby's biological father. *See In re B.G.C.*, 496 N.W.2d 239 (Iowa 1992).

Under California law, is Dan a "presumed" father? If not, does the federal Constitution, as interpreted in *Kelsey S.* and *Michael H.*, require that Dan be afforded the same statutory rights to consent to adoption as are granted to mothers and "presumed" fathers? If a court dismisses the adoption proceedings, should Dan automatically be entitled to custody of the baby (assuming he is not unfit) or should a court conduct a "best interest" hearing to resolve the competing custody claims of Dan and the prospective adoptive parents? Should Cara's desires be relevant to the court's resolution of these issues? If you were responsible for drafting adoption legislation for your state, how would you attempt to deal with the situation presented in this problem? For a discussion of how the Uniform Adoption Act would address the fact situation, which is based on the highly publicized "Baby Jessica" case, *see* Katherine G. Thompson & Joan H. Hollinger, *Contested Adoptions: Strategy of the Case* in Hollinger, Adoption Law and Practice § 8.10[1] (Matthew Bender 1998); *see also* Joan Heifetz Hollinger, *Adoption and Aspiration: The Uniform Adoption Act, The DeBoer-Schmidt Case, and the American Quest for the Ideal Family*, 2 Duke J. Gender L. & Pol'y 15 (1995); Robby DeBoer, Losing Jessica (1994) (chronicling the "Baby Jessica" case from the adoptive parents' perspective).

CHAPTER 6

DOMESTIC VIOLENCE AND INTRAFAMILY TORTS

SYNOPSIS

§ 6.01 Introduction
    [A] The Nature and Extent of the Problem
    [B] Why Doesn't She Leave?

§ 6.02 Legal Responses to Domestic Violence
    [A] The Traditional View
    [B] Contemporary Approaches to Domestic Violence
        [1] Criminal Prosecution: Mandatory Arrest and No-Drop Prosecution Policies
        [2] The Civil Protection Order Process
        [3] Marital Rape
        [4] Federal Involvement: The Violence Against Women Act

§ 6.03 Intrafamily Tort Liability
    [A] Tort Claims Between Spouses
    [B] Parent-Child Tort Actions

§ 6.01 Introduction

Although we typically think of family life as warm, intimate and affirming, the family also has a darker side. "People are more likely to be killed, physically assaulted, hit, beaten up, slapped, or spanked in their own homes by other family members than anywhere else, or by anyone else, in our society." Richard J. Gelles and Claire Pedrick Cornell, Intimate Violence in Families 11 (Sage, 2d ed. 1990). Although violence against family members is by no means a new phenomenon, legal responses to family violence have changed dramatically over the past two decades. Most notably, legal reforms of the past 20 years have shifted our understanding of domestic violence from a private to a public problem. According to two leading scholars:

> In the last twenty years, litigation, legislation, activism, and, to a lesser extent, social services for battered women have proliferated. In that time society has moved from virtual denial of the existence of domestic violence to a somewhat grudging acknowledgment that it is a pervasive and serious problem with legal, sociological, and psychological dimensions. Fundamental changes in civil and criminal law and practice have resulted in battered women becoming more visible in the legal system: protective

restraining orders are now available in every state; many states have amended their custody statutes to provide for consideration of domestic violence in custody cases; policies for arrest of batterers are increasingly common; prosecutors' offices have begun to prosecute domestic violence cases; and public defenders have begun to recognize the relevance of battering to some of their clients' defenses.

Naomi Cahn and Joan Meier, *Domestic Violence and Feminist Jurisprudence: Towards A New Agenda*, 4 B.U. Pub. Int. L.J. 339, 339 (1995).

[A] Nature and Extent of the Problem

Definitions of domestic violence vary considerably, as do explanations of its causes and cures. Many in the social science community trace domestic violence to a culture that teaches and sanctions violence as a way of resolving intrafamily conflict. *See, e.g.*, Murray A. Strauss and Christine Smith, *Family Patterns and Primary Prevention of Family Violence*, in Physical Violence in American Families 507, 512–21 (Murray A. Straus and Richard J. Gelles, eds, 1990); Richard J. Gelles, *Through A Sociological Lens: Social Structure and Family Violence*, in Current Controversies on Domestic Violence 7 (1993). These researchers tend to view intimate violence between adults and parental violence toward children as related aspects of a larger "family violence" problem and to propose solutions that attempt to address the problem holistically. In discussing partner violence, these researchers focus on physical acts and define domestic violence as "an act carried out with the intention or perceived intention of causing physical pain or injury to another person." Richard J. Gelles and Claire Pedrick Cornell, Intimate Violence in Families, 22 (Sage, 2d ed. 1990). Researchers who adopt this definition of domestic violence point to survey data suggesting that partner violence occurs in at least one out of every six American couples, and that both male and female partners engage in such violence at approximately equal rates. *See e.g.*, Murray A. Strauss & Richard J. Gelles, *How Violent Are American Families? Estimates from the National Family Violence Resurvey and Other Studies*, in Physical Violence in American Families 95 (Murray A. Straus & Richard J. Gelles, eds. 1995). This survey data has been criticized, however, for not distinguishing between violence that is serious enough to produce injury and violence that is not, and for not distinguishing between unprovoked violence and violence used in self defense. *See, e.g.*, Daniel G. Saunders, *Wife Abuse, Husband Abuse, or Mutual Combat? A Feminist Perspective on Empirical Findings*, in Feminist Perspectives on Wife Abuse 95–96 (Kersti Yllo & Michele Bograd eds., 1990).

Other scholars and observers employ a broader, more contextual perspective that focuses on issues of power and control. A recent report by the American Bar Association Commission on Domestic Violence defines domestic violence this way:

> Domestic violence is a pattern of behavior that one intimate partner or spouse exerts over another as a means of control. Domestic violence may include physical violence, coercion, threats, intimidation, isolation, and emotional, sexual or economic abuse. Frequently, perpetrators use the children to manipulate victims: by harming or abducting the children; by threatening to harm or abduct the children, by forcing the children to participate in abuse of the victim; by using visitation as an occasion to harass or monitor victims; or by fighting protracted custody battles to punish victims. Perpetrators often invent complex rules about what victims or the children can or cannot do, and force victims to abide by these frequently changing rules.

> Domestic violence is not defined solely by specific physical acts, but by a combination of psychological, social and familial factors. In some families, perpetrators of domestic violence may routinely beat their spouses until they require medical attention. In other families, the physical violence may have occurred in the past; perpetrators may currently exert power and control over their partners simply by looking at them a certain way or reminding them of prior episodes. In still other families, violence may be sporadic, but may have the effect of controlling the abused partner. . . .

American Bar Association, Commission on Domestic Violence, *When Will They Ever Learn? Educating to End Domestic Violence: A Law School Report* 26 (1997).

Women are overwhelmingly the victims of domestic violence understood in this manner. National crime statistics indicate that more than 90% of heterosexual partner violence reported to law enforcement authorities is perpetrated by men against women. *See, e.g.*, Demi Kurz, *Physical Assaults by Husbands: A Major Social Problem*, in Current Controversies on Family Violence 89–90 (Richard J. Gelles & Donileen R. Loseke, eds., 1993); Russel P. Dobash, *The Myth of Sexual Symmetry in Marital Violence,* 39 Soc. Probs. 71, 74–75 (1992); Patsy A. Klaus, et al., Bureau of Justice Statistics, Family Violence 4 (April, 1994). Crime statistics also indicate that women are six times more likely than men to be victimized by a spouse, ex-spouse, boyfriend or girlfriend. Caroline W. Harlow, U.S. Department of Justice, Female Victims of Violent Crime 1 (1991). Women are also much more likely than men to be murdered by an intimate partner.

Domestic violence has been identified as the single largest cause of injury to women in the United States—more significant than auto accidents, rapes and muggings combined. *See, e.g.*, Antonia C. Novello, *Dangerous and Deadly Consequences*, From Report to the Surgeon General by the Inspector General, Department of Health and Human Services, April 1992, 267 JAMA 3132, 3132 (1992); Evan Stark & Anne H. Flitcraft, *Spouse Abuse* in Violence in America: A Public Health Approach 123, 139 (Mark L. Rosenberg & Mary Ann Fenley eds., 1991). An estimated four million American women are battered each year by their husbands or partners. Catherine F. Klein & Leslye E. Orloff, *Providing Legal Protection For Battered Women: An Analysis of State Statutes and Case Law*, 21 Hofstra L. Rev. 801, 807 (1993). According to some estimates, at least half of all American women will experience domestic violence at some point in their adult lives. *See, e.g.*, Lenore E. Walker, Terrifying Love 106 (1989); Martha R. Mahoney, *Legal Images of Battered Women: Redefining the Issue of Separation*, 90 Mich. L. Rev. 1, 10–11 (1991). Domestic violence is also a problem in many gay and lesbian relationships. Machaela M. Hoctor, *Domestic Violence as a Crime Against the State: The Need for Mandatory Arrest in California*, 85 Cal. L. Rev. 643, 690 (1997) (noting that although statistics are hard to obtain "an estimated twenty-five to thirty percent of all lesbians and gay men in intimate relationships are victims of domestic violence.").

Domestic violence also endangers children. A high percentage of men who abuse their partners also batter or sexually abuse the children in their households, particularly daughters. *See, e.g.* Pauline Quirion, et al., *Protecting Children Exposed to Domestic Violence In Contested Custody and Visitation Litigation*, 6 B.U. Pub. Int. L. J. 501, 508–09 (1997); Peter G. Jaffe, et. al, Children of Battered Women 20 (1990). Children who witness domestic violence are also harmed psychologically and developmentally, even if they are never physically assaulted themselves. *See* The Impact of Domestic Violence on Children; A Report to the President of the American Bar Association 1 (1994) (concluding that children can suffer grievous harm "merely by observing or hearing the domestic terrorism of brutality against a parent at home").

> A boy who witnesses abuse as a child is more likely to be abused or abusive himself when he becomes a husband, a father, a stepfather, or a boyfriend of a woman with children. When he becomes an abuser, the harm here is not simply to those he hurts, but to himself: He may end up dead or jailed as a result of his violence and is likely to lead an emotionally pain-filled life as he becomes the person he despised as a child, unable to form healthy adult relationships with sexual partners or children. Other children may grow into adults who avoid intimate relationships because of fear that they will repeat patterns witnessed or observed earlier. A girl who witnesses abuse is more likely to accept relationships in which she is abusive or abused as an adult and is also more likely to abuse her children because she has learned that violence is a normal expression of love.

Mary E. Becker, *Double Binds Facing Mothers in Abusive Families: Social Support Systems, Custody Outcomes, and Liability for Acts of Others*, 2 U. Chi. L. Sch. Roundtable 13 (1995) (footnotes omitted). For further discussion of the effects of domestic violence on children, *see, e.g.*, Audrey E. Stone & Rebecca J. Falk, *Criminalizing the Exposure of Children To Family Violence: Breaking The Cycle of Abuse*, 20 Harv. Women's L. J. 205, 205 (1996); Alan J. Tomkins, et. al., *The Plight of Children Who Witness Woman Battering: Psychological Knowledge and Policy Implications*, 18 Law & Psych. Rev. 137 (1994).

[B] Why Doesn't She Leave?

Clare Dalton, *Domestic Violence, Domestic Torts and Divorce
Constraints and Possibilities*
31 New Eng. L. Rev. 319, 336–38 (1997)*

For those with relatively little experience or understanding of the dynamics of abusive relationships, confronted with a situation involving prolonged and serious abuse, the first question is often "Why doesn't she leave?" Indeed, expert testimony on battered woman syndrome in self-defense cases was in large measure designed to answer this question—to explain how a woman who reasonably feared for her life could still be living in an intimate relationship with her batterer. The explanations preferred today still draw from that earlier testimony, but in the years since, our understanding both of battered woman syndrome, and of the many other aspects of women's situations that keep them in battering relationships has become more sophisticated and more complicated.

First, women do not fall in love with batterers, but with individuals who often treat them with an almost exaggerated respect and attention, and [who] can be extraordinarily appealing. Often, by the time the abuse begins, the woman has already made a strong emotional commitment to the relationship, which is not easy to abandon. It is commonplace for women to decide that the first acts of violence are aberrational, and that the batterers' contrition and vows that the violence will not be repeated are sincere. It is also sometimes easier for women to take responsibility for "provoking" the violence, because then they

---

* Footnotes omitted.

can imagine that they can control it by making changes in their own behavior, rather than demanding change from their partners. This is all the easier because the batterer, although remorseful, may also be telling her that she caused his outburst.

By the time a woman acknowledges to herself that she cannot control the violence, and that it is not an aberration, but a permanent aspect of her relationship with her partner, she may be in too deep to make an easy escape. She may have made efforts to seek help, and found little response, whether from police, the courts, her doctor, her priest, pastor or rabbi, or even other members of her family. Those efforts may have elicited threats from her partner about what he will do if she discloses his violence to others, or seeks to leave him—threats that are perfectly credible given his past behavior. She may have children by now, locking her into a co-parenting relationship from which she fears, with justification, that the legal system will not allow her to withdraw unless she abandons her children to her abuser. Her batterer is likely to reinforce those fears, telling her that if she tries to leave she will lose her children. She may be daunted by the economic realities of escape—how to find shelter, food, a job, or child care—when she has no separate funds, and cannot even use a check or credit card without revealing her whereabouts to her batterer. She may also, if the abuse has been prolonged and severe, be in a state of psychological depletion and paralysis that makes it almost impossible for her to take charge of her life in such new and risky ways. In this situation, she may marshal all the resources at her disposal to control the violence as best she can from within the relationship, and keep herself and her children safe from day to day, without triggering the explosive rage she knows from experience is associated with any attempt on her part to challenge her partner's control, or set limits with him.

If, despite all these obstacles, she does seek to leave her relationship with her batterer, the risks to her and her children are not a figment of her disordered imagination, as some judicial interpretations of battered woman syndrome have appeared to suggest. Rather, it is a stark reality that taking steps to leave an abusive relationship, or to confront the abuser and end the violence, is likely in the short term to increase the woman's danger. In one study, 75% of reported domestic incidents involved women who were already separated from their abusers. Which is to say that one answer to the question "Why didn't she leave?" is another question: "What makes you think that would have made her safer?" In this context, any legal intervention must be assessed for the risks it poses to women's safety. . . .

§ 6.02 Legal Responses to Domestic Violence

[A] The Traditional View

The law's traditional response to domestic violence was built on the twin pillars of the marital unity doctrine and the notion of a private, domestic sphere, immune form legal intervention. The idea that a wife's legal identity merged into that of her husband was also a key rationale for the law's traditional refusal to recognize rape within marriage. The following, well-known 1868 case exemplifies the law's traditional approach to domestic violence.

STATE v. RHODES
Supreme Court of North Carolina
61 N.C. 453 (1868)

The defendant was indicted for an assault and battery upon his wife. Elizabeth Rhodes. Upon the evidence submitted to them, the jury returned the following special verdict:

"We find that the defendant struck Elizabeth Rhodes, his wife, three licks, with a switch about the size of one of his fingers (but not as large as a man's thumb) without any provocation except some words uttered by her and not recollected by the witness."

His Honor was of the opinion that the defendant had a right to whip his wife with a switch no larger than his thumb, and that upon the facts found in the special verdict, he was not guilty in law. Judgment in favor of the defendant was accordingly entered and the State appealed.

READE, JUSTICE:

The violence complained of would without question have constituted a battery if the subject of it had not been the defendant's wife. The question is how far that fact affects the case. The courts have been loathe to take cognizance of trivial complaints arising out of the domestic relations such as master and apprentice, teacher and pupil, parent and child, husband and wife. Not because those relations are not subject to the law, but because the evil of publicity would be greater than the evil involved in the trifles complained of; and because they ought to be left to family government. . . .

Our conclusion is that family government is recognized by law as being as complete in itself as the State government is in itself, and yet subordinate to it; and that we will not interfere with or attempt to control it, in favor of either husband or wife, unless in cases where permanent or malicious injury is inflicted or threatened, or the condition of the party is intolerable. For, however great are the evils of ill temper, quarrels, and even personal conflicts inflicting only temporary pain, they are not comparable with the evils which would result from raising the curtain, and exposing to public curiosity and criticism, the nursery and the bed chamber. Every household has and must have, a government of its own, modeled to suit the temper, disposition and condition of its inmates. Mere ebullitions of passion, impulsive violence, and temporary pain, affection will soon forget and forgive; and each member will find excuse for the other in his own frailties. But when trifles are taken hold of by the public, and the parties are exposed and disgraced, and each endeavors to justify himself or herself by criminating the other, that which ought to be forgotten in a day, will be remembered for life.

It is urged in this case, that as there was no provocation the violence was of course excessive and malicious; that every one in whatever relation of life should be able to purchase immunity from pain, by obedience to authority and faithfulness in duty. If in every such case we are to hunt for the provocation, how will the proof be supplied? Take the case before us. The witness said, there was no provocation except some slight words. But then who can tell what significance the trifling words may have had to the husband? Who can tell what had happened an hour before, and every hour for a week? To him they may have been sharper than a sword. And so in every case, it might be impossible for the court to appreciate what might be offered as an excuse, or no excuse might appear at all, when a complete justification exists. Or, suppose the provocation could in every case be known, and the court should undertake to weigh the provocation in every trifling family broil, what would be the standard? Suppose a case coming up to us from a hovel, where neither delicacy of sentiment nor refinement of manners is appreciated or known. The parties themselves would be amazed, if they were to be held responsible for rudeness or trifling violence. What do they care for insults and indignities? In such cases what end would be gained by investigation or punishment? Take a case from the middle class, where modesty and purity have their abode but nevertheless have not immunity from the frailties of nature, and are sometimes moved by the mysteries of passion. What could be more harassing to them, or injurious to society, than to draw a crowd around their seclusion. Or take a case from the higher ranks, where education and culture have so refined nature, that a look cuts like a knife, and a word strikes like a hammer; where the most delicate attention gives pleasure, and the slightest neglect pain; where an indignity is disgrace and exposure is ruin. Bring all these cases into court side by side, with the same offense charged and the same proof made; and what conceivable charge of the court to the jury would be alike appropriate to all the cases, except, that they all have domestic government, which they have formed for themselves, suited to their own peculiar conditions, and that those governments are supreme, and from them there is no appeal except in cases of great importance requiring the strong arm of the law, and that to those governments they must submit themselves.

It will be observed that the ground upon which we have put this decision, is not, that the husband has the *right* to whip his wife much or little: but that we will not interfere with family government in trifling cases. We will no more interfere where the husband whips the wife, than where the wife whips the husband; and yet we would hardly be supposed to hold, that a wife has a *right* to whip her husband. We will not inflict upon society the greater evil of raising the curtain upon domestic privacy, to punish the lesser evil of trifling violence. Two boys under fourteen years of age fight upon the play-ground, and yet the courts will take no notice of it, not for the reason that boys have the *right* to fight, but because the interests of society require that they should be left to the more appropriate discipline of the school room and of home. It is not true that boys have a right to fight; nor is it true that a husband has a right to whip his wife. And if he had, it is not easily seen how *the thumb* is the standard of size for the instrument which he may use, as some of the old authorities have said: and in deference to which was his Honor's charge. A light blow, or many light blows, with a stick larger than the thumb, might produce no injury; but a switch half the size might be so used as to produce death. The standard is the *effect produced*, and not the manner of producing it, or the instrument used.

Because our opinion is not in unison with the decisions of some of the sister States, or with the philosophy of some very respectable law writers, and could not be in unison with all, because of their contrariety a decent respect for the opinions of others has induced us to be very full in stating the reasons for our conclusion. There is no error.

NOTES AND QUESTIONS

(1) *Rhodes* is often cited as an early example of the principle of family autonomy or family privacy. *See* Jane Rutherford, *Beyond Individual Privacy: A New Theory of Family Rights*, 39 U. Fla. L. Rev. 627, 643–44 (1987). What reasons does the court give for endorsing this principle? Do any of those reasons make sense today, either in the context of spousal violence or in other family law contexts?

(2) In *Griswold v. Connecticut* 381 U.S. 479, 85 S. Ct. 1678, 14 L. Ed. 2d 510 (1965) (reprinted in § 4.02[A], *above*), the Supreme Court invoked the notion of marriage and family as a private sphere, protected from state interference, as a rationale for invalidating a state's attempt to criminalize the use of contraceptives. The court in *Rhodes* invokes an arguably similar privacy rationale to justify its refusal to prosecute a husband for beating his wife. Is the concept of marital and family privacy beneficial for women? For children? For men? *See generally* Elizabeth Schneider, *The Violence of Privacy*, 23 Conn. L. Rev. 973 (1991) (exploring the complexity and ambiguity of the concept of privacy, particularly for women).

(3) The *Rhodes* court emphasizes the evenhandedness of its approach: "We will no more interfere where the husband whips the wife than where the wife whips the husband." Is the rule laid down in *Rhodes* gender-neutral? Why or why not?

[B] Contemporary Approaches to Domestic Violence

[1] Criminal Prosecution: Mandatory Arrest and No-Drop Prosecution Policies

Until the 1970s, most police departments had an official policy of avoiding arrest and prosecution of domestic violence cases, wherever possible. Domestic abuse was considered a private matter, to be resolved within the family sphere, rather than an offense that merited criminal prosecution. Machaela M. Hoctor, *Domestic Violence as a Crime Against the State: The Need for Mandatory Arrest in California*, 85 Calif. L. Rev. 643, 649 (1997). The typical police response to a domestic assault was to separate the parties and attempt to mediate the situation. Cheryl Hanna, *No Right To Choose: Mandated Victim Participation In Domestic Violence Prosecutions*, 109 Harv. L. Rev. 1849, 1875 (1996). A number of developments in the 1980s caused the criminal justice system to reassess its traditional approach to domestic violence. A nation-wide, grass-roots effort by advocates for battered women, supported by feminist lawyers and scholars, focused public attention on the pervasiveness of domestic violence and its devastating effects on women and families. These efforts also highlighted the inadequacy of existing legal responses. In several highly publicized lawsuits, battered women successfully challenged the failure of local police departments to enforce criminal laws against battering and to protect them from their domestic abusers. *See, e.g., Thurman v. City of Torrington*, 595 F. Supp. 1521, 1527–28 (D. Conn. 1984); *Bruno v. Codd*, 393 N.E.2d 976, 979 (N.Y. 1979). The publicity generated by these cases had a dramatic effect on official police department policies. Eve S. Buzawa & Carl G. Buzawa, Domestic Violence: The Criminal Response 75 (1990).

Police practices were also influenced by the results of a landmark Minneapolis study that compared various police responses to domestic violence and found that arresting perpetrators was the most effective way of deterring subsequent acts of violence. *See* Richard A. Berk & Lawrence W. Sherman, *The Specific Deterrent Effects of Arrest for Domestic Assault*, 49 Am. Soc. Rev. 261 (1984). In the wake of this finding, the U.S. Attorney General recommended that arrest be the standard law enforcement response to domestic violence. Attorney General's Task Force on Family Violence, Final Report 11, 17, & 136 n.6 (1984). Police departments responded to this recommendation by adopting more aggressive arrest and prosecution polices. By 1989, more than 80% of urban police departments reported having mandatory or pro-arrest policies for domestic violence cases. Hoctor, *above*, at 655. State legislatures also amended their arrest statutes to permit warrantless misdemeanor arrests when an officer has probable cause to believe that a domestic assault has occurred or that a civil restraining order has been violated. Hanna, *above*, at 1859.

While these changes enhanced the ability of the criminal justice system to arrest and prosecute batterers, not all police departments made use of their expanded powers. Moreover, prosecution of domestic violence cases remained a low priority for many state and local prosecutors. *See* Angela Corsilles, *No-Drop Policies In The Prosecution of Domestic Violence Cases: Guarantee To Action or Dangerous Solution?*, 63 Fordham L. Rev. 853, 853–54 (1994). As a result, domestic violence laws continued to be under-enforced throughout the 1980s. *Id.* Moreover, advocates for battered women charged that police officers often used inappropriate criteria, such as the race or class of the perpetrator, in deciding whether to make an arrest. *See Developments in the Law: Legal Responses to Domestic Violence*, 106 Harv. L. Rev. 1498, 1537 (1993).

Current law reform efforts respond to these criticisms in a variety of ways. *First*, a significant number of states have enacted mandatory arrest statutes. These statutes require—rather than simply encourage or permit—police officers to make arrests whenever they have probable cause to believe that a domestic violence offense has occurred. Hanna, *above*, at 1859 n.36; *Second*, a number of states and localities have adopted so-called "no-drop" prosecution policies that require the prosecution of domestic violence offenses regardless of the victim's willingness to cooperate or expressed desire to press charges. *See* Hanna, *above*, at 1863–64. Third, several jurisdictions have developed coordinated legal and social service strategies to deal with domestic violence cases. These strategies typically include the creation of specialized domestic violence prosecution units, coupled with the provision of extensive support services for domestic violence victims and mandatory treatment programs for batterers. *See, e.g.*, Elena Salzman, Note, *The Quincy District Court Domestic Violence Prevention Program: A Model Legal Framework For Domestic Violence Intervention*, 74 B.U.L. Rev. 329 (1994); Naomi Cahn, *Innovative Approaches to the Prosecution of Domestic Violence Crimes: An Overview*, in Domestic Violence: The Changing Criminal Justice Response 161, 162–77 (Eve S. Buzawa & Carl G. Buzawa eds, 1992).

Both mandatory arrest statutes and no-drop prosecution policies have generated controversy. Supporters of mandatory arrest policies argue that, by reducing police discretion, mandatory arrest schemes ensure that officers will not trivialize domestic violence or make decisions about arrest on a discriminatory or otherwise illegitimate basis. Moreover, by physically removing the abuser, arrest provides immediate protection for the victim, affords her time away from the batterer to evaluate her situation, and empowers her by demonstrating that she can take effective action to stop the abuse. *Developments in the Law: Legal Responses to Domestic Violence, above*, 106 Harv. L. Rev. at 1537–38. In addition, mandatory arrest statutes emphasize that domestic violence is not simply an assault on a particular intimate partner, but an offense against the state as well. Hoctor, *above*, at 644. Many police officers also favor mandatory arrest laws because of the clarity they provide. *See* Kevin Walsh, *Domestic Violence and the Law Symposium: The Mandatory Arrest Law: Police Reaction*, 16 Pace L. Rev. 97, 102 (1995).

Critics of mandatory arrest laws counter that, under a mandatory arrest regime, a victim's call to the police is tantamount to a request for arrest. Although some victims may be encouraged to summon help because they will be assured of at least temporary incarceration of their abuser, other victims who do not want their batterer arrested may be discouraged from calling the police. *See Developments in the Law: Legal Responses to Domestic Violence*, 106 Harv. L. Rev. at 1538. In addition, where arrest is mandatory, women who strike their batterers in self defense risk being arrested along with (or instead of) their abusers. This problem of dual arrest may be alleviated by instructing police officers to arrest only the primary physical aggressor, but it is not always so easy to determine who that is, particularly if abuse is ongoing. Other critics argue that mandatory arrest laws reflect a white, middle-class view of criminal intervention and fail to take into account the racist effects of such policies. *See* Miriam Ruttenberg, *Note, A Feminist Critique of Mandatory Arrest: An Analysis of Race and Gender in Domestic Violence Policy*, 2 Am. U.J. Gender & L. 171 (1994).

Academic criminologists also question whether arrest deters future battering. These critics note that several recent studies, designed to replicate the landmark Minneapolis experiment, have produced inconsistent findings. *See* Lawrence W. Sherman, *The Influence of Criminology on Criminal Law: Evaluating Arrests for Misdemeanor Domestic Violence*, 83 J. Crim. L. & Criminology 1 (1992) (discussing studies). Taken together, these studies suggest that while arrest may be an effective deterrent for batterers who are married or employed, it may be correlated with *increased* violence where batterers are unemployed, or otherwise socially and economically marginalized. Richard A. Berk, et al, *The Deterrent Effect of Arrest in Incidents of Domestic Violence: A Bayesian Analysis of the Colorado Springs Spouse Abuse Experiment*, 83 J. Crim. L. & Criminology 170 (1992); *see* U.S. Department of Justice, National Institute of Justice, *The Criminalization of Domestic Violence: Promises and Limits* 13–15 (1995). Other scholars, however, have criticized the methodology employed by these studies, particularly their failure to consider the responses and perspectives of the victims. *See, e.g.*, Cynthia Grant Bowman, *The Arrest Experiments: A Feminist Critique*, 83 J. Crim. L. & Criminology 201 (1992); Lisa G. Lehrman, *The Decontextualization of Domestic Violence*, 83 J. Crim. L. 217 (1992). To the extent that arrest alone is an ineffective deterrent for some categories of abusers, these observers urge the adoption of more, rather than less vigorous law enforcement strategies—strategies that include a commitment to arrest, prosecution and more severe sentencing practices. Lehrman, *above*, at 232, 239–40; Bowman, *above* at 207; David P. Mitchell, *Contemporary Police Practice in Domestic Violence Cases: Arresting The Abuser: Is it Enough?* 83 J. Crim. L. & Criminology 241 (1992).

No-drop prosecution polices often constitute one element of a such an invigorated law enforcement strategy. Like mandatory arrest laws, however, no-drop prosecution polices have generated both support and disapproval:

> Pro-prosecution advocates argue that aggressive policies take the burden off the victim by removing her as the "plaintiff." They contend that the batterer has less incentive to try to control or intimidate his victim once he realizes that she no longer controls the process. They also argue that because domestic violence is a public crime, the state has a responsibility to intervene aggressively. For these advocates, this response communicates and follows through on the message that the state will not tolerate violence of any sort . . .
>
> However, many advocates for battered women argue that the use of state power, such as subpoenas, has the unintended effect of punishing or "revictimizing" the victim for the actions of the abuser by forcing the victim into a process over which she has

no control. These advocates are also concerned that if arrest leads to automatic prosecution, women will be less likely to call the police for help or protection. Critics of no-drop policies further argue that the state should not place the woman at any greater risk of harm or substitute itself for the batterer by taking control of the woman's life. In order to preserve her autonomy and promote her sense of empowerment, the victim ought to have the final decision . . .

Cheryl Hanna, *No Right To Choose: Mandated Victim Participation In Domestic Violence Prosecutions*, 109 Harv. L. Rev. 1849, 1865–66 (1996) (footnotes omitted; reprinted with permission).

The following article describes the initial experience of one local jurisdiction in implementing a state-wide mandatory arrest statute.

Liza Mundy, *Fault Line*
The Washington Post Magazine
October 26, 1997, at 8

In Virginia, the enduring problem of domestic violence has a new solution: an unforgiving law that in its first four months has led to the arrests of thousands of husbands, wives and parents. "This is not your decision. This is my decision," the thin young corn-blond cop is saying.

Early evening. A deserted parking lot in an office complex in Annandale. The humid aftermath of a rush-hour rainstorm. The cop stands talking to a middle-aged man of average height and average weight, a man who has sandy hair that's turning and glasses, and a pink face, and a white shirt and blue pants and a diamond-patterned blue-and-white tie, and the glazed, unhappy look of a well-controlled professional in a situation that has spun horribly out of his control. Somewhere behind both of them, the man's wife is waiting in a second-floor office.

Domvio. Domestic violence. That's what the dispatcher's message said when it flashed on the computer screens of Fairfax County police squad cars. "Estranged wife has destroyed office/w/f/ . . . white T-shirt, pink shorts—hung up phone when I was talking," the message read, and now one, two, three cops have arrived to see what's going on, and one of them, Mike Tucker, is talking to the man, who was waiting on the sidewalk when they arrived, tucking his shirt into his pants. The man tells Tucker that earlier in the day his wife came to his office, bringing along a separation agreement for him to sign. He objected to some of the wording, and his wife got angry and pushed him. So, hoping a police report might be something he could use in a custody dispute, he called the cops.

Are you injured? Tucker asks.

No, says the man, whose name is Tom.

Tucker goes inside to talk to the wife, whose name is Judy. But Judy, still angry and combative, refuses to tell him anything. So Tucker talks to a witness who heard Tom say, "Stop pushing me!" and then goes outside to talk to Tom again.

All this is taking place a month after a domestic violence law went into effect throughout Virginia on July 1. The new law says that police must make an arrest whenever they have probable cause to believe a domestic assault has occurred. What constitutes probable cause?

Tucker considers this question as he inspects a small tear in the breast pocket of Tom's shirt. Then, after consulting with another officer, he conveys the news to Tom: The pocket is enough. Judy must be arrested.

Tom is horrified. "Can I go on record that I don't want to press charges right now?" he asks, and Tucker says yes, he can go on record, but even so, pressing charges is not his decision, it is the decision of the commonwealth of Virginia, which is exactly what Tucker was just explaining, because that's what police are now trained to tell victims of domestic violence.

"Oh God, oh God!" Tom says while Tucker goes upstairs to make the arrest. Moments later he emerges from the doorway with a diminutive panicked woman in pink running shorts and a white "New York" T-shirt and, behind her back, handcuffs. The wife. Judy. Who has short soft brown hair, tied back, and a suntan. "Tom," she calls as she's led past her husband, "do you know they're arresting me? Tom, please! Tom, did I push you? Tom, please! Call my mother! Call our attorney!"

"Is this the Gestapo or what?" Tom says. "I just wanted documentation in a custody dispute. I certainly didn't want this!"

Tucker puts Judy in the back of his squad car and drives her to the Fairfax County Adult Detention Center, where she is charged with domestic assault and battery under Virginia's criminal code, section 18.2–57.2. The new law directs Tucker to request an emergency protective order to protect Tom from further acts of abuse, and so Tucker does, and the order is granted, directing Judy to stay away from her husband—specifically, his office—for three days, except for "incidental contact to assure welfare of children."

A $ 750 bond is set to guarantee she shows up for trial.

Her name is entered into the Virginia crime information network, so that if she violates the stay-away order, her existing criminal charge will be readily available.

She is fingerprinted and her mug shot is taken.

Asked if she has any scars, marks or tattoos, she says no.

Asked her occupation, she says, "Flutist."

Meanwhile, back at the office complex, the two remaining officers, T.J. Rogers and Ben Ferdinand, try to calm her husband—counseling the victim, as the new law also directs. "We don't have discretion," Ferdinand explains, gently, for the third time. "You're not pressing charges. It's Officer Tucker who's pressing charges." When Judy's court date comes up, they suggest, she probably won't get any jail time; more likely she'll be ordered to seek counseling. A good thing, perhaps. The two officers stand there in the suburban dusk, earnestly encouraging the man before them to look at the events of today, the argument and the pushing and the 911 call and the police arrival and the arrest and the handcuffs and the new law and the workings of Fairfax County's criminal justice system as, in Officer Ferdinand's words, a "positive step" for him and his family.

"There shall be an arrest. It's not may, if, or should; it's shall, and in Virginia,'shall' means there will be."

Fairfax County Police Chief M. Douglas Scott can be forgiven the pride he evinces when describing the language of Virginia's new domestic violence law, under which Judy and thousands of others have been arrested since it took effect. Variously known as "warrantless arrest," "pro-arrest" and "mandatory arrest," the law takes a single-minded approach to domestic violence, requiring that an arrest be made if there's any evidence an assault was committed. . . .

"I can tell you that in my discussions with some of the rural chiefs and sheriffs, the mind set is still the old mind set: You know, old Charlie's a good guy, yeah, he got a little drunk Friday night, then he went home and slapped his wife around, so what's the problem here?" says Scott, who helped persuade cops around the state to change that Neanderthal way of thinking. He urged them to embrace the new law, convincing them that it wouldn't sap their resources or tie up their officers. What it would do, he told them, is cut down on a chronic law enforcement problem: the problem not only of domestic violence itself, but also of victims who out of love or fear or economic dependency or cultural isolation or all of the above are unwilling to press charges against their batterers, and batterers who, as a result, get away with their abuse.

"The goal is to send enough of a message to the violator that this behavior is not going to be tolerated, that it's serious, you can go to jail for it," is how Scott puts it.

The new approach represents a huge change, both practically and philosophically—and a huge victory for advocates on behalf of domestic violence victims. "We've done a fabulous job convincing the legislature that it is a highly criminal act to maim or abuse a spouse," says Judith Mueller of the Vienna-based Women's Center, who was among those lobbying for the bill. Similar victories have been won around the country: According to the Family Violence Project of the National Council of Juvenile and Family Court Judges, seven states plus the District of Columbia have mandatory arrest policies, and 26 others, including Maryland, have "presumptive arrest" policies that give officers a bit of discretion but still encourage them to make an arrest. Another 12 have laws that blend the two approaches. The thinking is that it's a lot easier on battered victims—and prosecutors—when the responsibility is taken off them and assumed by the state.

But a look at some of the arrests made in Fairfax County shortly after the law passed—arrests made by officers who are well trained and already familiar with an aggressive arrest policy—suggests that chronic abusers are by no means the only ones arrested under mandatory laws. As intended, the law has helped women—and men—who are in genuine danger from first-time and habitual batterers. But in other cases it may have created a new category of victim, indeed rendered the word so diffuse as to be meaningless.

"A lot of times, I think arrests are being made when they shouldn't be," says Kenneth E. Noyes, staff attorney and coordinator of the domestic violence project for Legal Services of Northern Virginia.

"I am stunned, quite frankly, because that was not the intention of the law. It was to protect people from predictable violent assaults, where a history occurred, and the victim was unable for whatever reason to press charges," says Mueller. "It's disheartening to think that it could be used punitively and frivolously. Frivolously being the operative word."

But in most cases, the police officers are not acting frivolously. They're acting conscientiously and in good faith, doing exactly what the law requires. And what the law requires is a rigid, inflexible response to a set of situations that are limitlessly vast. The river of human misery runs broad and deep; there are—as Tolstoy pointed out—all sorts of unhappy families, and all manner of domestic disputes. What do you do—for example—when a man calls 911 to report that his wife has destroyed his Mercedes with a ball-peen hammer and he would like her, please, arrested?

What do you do when a father calls to say that his son threw food at him, and now he would like the kid, please, arrested?

When a husband calls 911 to say that his wife slapped him with an open hand and he would like her, please, arrested?

What do you do when you have cast a net for sharks into waters that are brimming with all kinds of fish? "We didn't intend to catch minnows," Mueller says. "So, what do you do when the net brings in species or varieties for which you weren't casting?" . . .

It should be made clear that not all cases are murky and confusing. Despite all the permutations, all the amorphous forms that family violence can take, all the mutual squabbles and dubious 911 alarms and couples racing to beat each other to the telephone or the warrant office, there are plenty of cases that are both clear and egregious. Physical abuse does happen, real violence does happen, has just happened, in fact, late on a Sunday in Mount Vernon south of Alexandria. In the police station, a couple of sheriff's deputies and police officers are in the processing room, along with a middle-aged drunk wearing socks but no shoes. Also there is Carl, a truck driver who has just been arrested for hitting his girlfriend, bruising her arm and cutting her lip and breaking her eardrum.

The 911 call came from the victim's son, who was standing in the road waving the police down when they arrived. The son told the police that Carl had come home to find dirty dishes in the sink, and the dishes made him mad, and in his anger he woke up the boy's mother, Helen, and hit her, and kept hitting her. By the time the police showed up, Helen was bruised and cut on her face and feet. Even so, she begged the officer not to arrest Carl—a classic victim's reaction.

"Back off," the officer advised, telling her to step out the door or she might go to jail, too.

And now here is Carl, absorbing the unbelievable fact that not only has he been arrested but an emergency protective order has been issued, something he's never heard of, and thanks to this thing, he cannot return to his own trailer! Even though his name is on the lease! "Everything I own is there!" he says to the drunk beside him.

"I realize you are the one who purchased the home," the magistrate tells him when he is brought before her to be charged, "but you allowed her to move in, you and she are cohabiting, so I'm allowing her to use your trailer for 72 hours."

Meanwhile, Helen has been taken off in an ambulance. In the emergency room of Mount Vernon Hospital, she is having her jaw X-rayed and her foot swabbed. A doctor shoots a painkiller directly into a cut and asks her if it hurts. Helen politely says no. Helen is a tiny longhaired woman wearing a T-shirt and shorts. She now cannot hear out of one ear. Later, the doctor will give her an antibiotic to ward off infection and tell her that basically the eardrum is going to have to heal itself.

"Are you allergic to anything?"

"Codeine," Helen says. She is frank and friendly and, for somebody who has just been beaten up, calm. "I threw an antique chamber pot right through the front door," she says, explaining how the fight started. That was after Carl came home and started getting on her about the dishes. He's a finicky person, she says, constantly picking at her son in particular, getting on him when he flushes the toilet wrong or holds the refrigerator open. This time, when he started in on the dishes, Helen had just had it, and so she threw the chamber pot, she readily admits that. She threw the chamber pot, which was hers, part of a set. Then she upended a table. Then he really came at her, hitting her so hard that she doesn't remember what came afterward, just that now her head hurts and her backside hurts and she can't hear out of one ear.

She acknowledges that she tried to dissuade the arresting officer—"When you see them going off in handcuffs, it just seems so cruel"—but now she's glad the arrest has been made. She's glad the law exists.

Carl, presumably, is not. "I don't have my reading glasses," he says unhappily when presented with the EPO, an aging man with gray hair flying wildly above his head, and no shirt, and a crucifix around his neck, and black laceless loafer-type tennis shoes. The officer explains the EPO to him one more time, and with that, Carl sits down, predicts that Helen will steal his stuff and says, to the drunk beside him, "It's a strange world we live in, Master Jack."

Helen does not steal his stuff. What she does is, she shows up the next morning at the trailer with her son and her sister and cleans the trailer until it's spotless. Then she packs stuff into boxes, but only stuff she's sure is hers. She even leaves the pictures on the wall because, though they are her pictures, they are Carl's frames. While her sister and son carry out a mattress and dresser, she sits down at the table and thinks through the months ahead: storing her stuff, living with her sister, trying to find a place she can afford.

Because she is leaving. She is definitely leaving. She's been beaten before, not by Carl, she says, but by another man, and she's not going to be beaten again. The law has given her the time and space to make this decision. It's not an easy one, and the subsequent weeks aren't going to be easy, either. She's going to have to go to the doctor about her eardrum so many times that she finally must tell her boss what happened, and she's going to see Carl on the road while she's driving, and she's going to wonder how he's doing and why he hasn't called to say he loves her or, at the very least, that he's sorry. She's going to have to find out where the courthouse is and get the day off and meanwhile, she freely admits, she still has feelings for the man who cut her lip and broke her eardrum.

"Most of the time I feel like I'm doing fine, I don't need this jerk, then I think about the good times and how much I love him," she says. "But I don't like him anymore." . . .

NOTES AND QUESTIONS

(1) Virginia's "mandatory arrest" statute, under which both Judy and Carl were arrested, provides, in pertinent part, as follows:

> A. Any law-enforcement officer . . . may arrest without a warrant for an alleged [assault and battery against a family or household member or for violation of a protective order] regardless of whether such violation was committed in his presence, if such arrest is based on probable cause or upon personal observations or the reasonable complaint of a person who observed the alleged offense or upon personal investigation.

B. A law-enforcement officer having probable cause to believe that a[n assault and battery against a family or household member or a violation of a protective order] has occurred shall arrest and take into custody the person he has probable cause to believe, based on the totality of the circumstances, was the primary physical aggressor unless there are special circumstances which would dictate a course of action other than an arrest.

C. Regardless of whether an arrest is made, the officer shall file a written report with his department of any incident in which he has probable cause to believe family abuse has occurred, including, where required, a statement in writing that there are special circumstances which would dictate a course of action other than an arrest. Upon request of the allegedly abused person, the department shall make a summary of the report available to the allegedly abused person. The officer shall also provide the allegedly abused person, both orally and in writing, information regarding the legal and community resources available to the allegedly abused person.

D. In every case in which a law-enforcement officer makes an arrest under this section, he shall petition for an emergency protective order . . . when the person arrested and taken into custody is brought before the magistrate. Regardless of whether an arrest is made, if the officer has probable cause to believe that a danger of acts of family abuse exists, the law-enforcement officer shall seek an emergency protective order . . . .

Va. Code Ann. § 19.2–81.3 (1997).

(2) Did the above-quoted statute require police to arrest Judy? To arrest Carl? Putting aside any statutory mandate, should the Fairfax police have arrested Judy? If not, how should they have responded to the call they received from her husband, Tom?

(3) Imagine that you are the Assistant State's Attorney assigned to prosecute Judy for misdemeanor domestic assault, following her arrest. When Judy's case is called for trial, she is represented by private counsel, who requests that the charges against her be dismissed. Tom, who appears in court without a lawyer, supports Judy's request for dismissal. Should you agree to dismiss the case? Why or why not?

(4) Now imagine that you are the Assistant State's Attorney assigned to prosecute Carl. When you contact Helen to prepare for the trial, Helen tells you that she and Carl have reconciled and that she does not want to press charges. Helen assures you that Carl has reformed; he has promised never to hit her again and has enrolled in an anger management program. Helen assures you that she is safe and she insists that continuing with the prosecution will jeopardize her attempt to build a new relationship with Carl—a relationship that is important to her. She hints that if she is forced to testify against Carl, she will suggest that she was the one who instigated the violence and that Carl acted in self defense. How should you respond to Helen's request not to prosecute?

(5) **Problem.** You are a senior prosecutor in a specialized domestic violence unit. Your unit has a "soft" no-drop prosecution policy. Under the policy, prosecutors are encouraged to pursue every provable domestic violence case, regardless of the victim's initial desires, and victims are offered an array of support services. Where a victim remains reluctant to testify, the prosecutor may subpoena the victim, but is not required to do so. If a victim fails to appear in response to a subpoena, the prosecutor may request a bench warrant for

her arrest. The policy also provides that, in general, provable cases should not be dismissed unless the prosecutor is convinced that proceeding with the case would compromise the safely of the victim. How should you proceed in the case of Beverly Johnson, described below.

> Late one night, Ms. Johnson called the police to her residence because of a domestic dispute. When the police arrived, they saw that Ms. Johnson had swelling on her face and arms. After she told the police that she had dialed 911 because her boyfriend had beaten her, the officers arrested the boyfriend. Ms. Johnson stated that she would seek medical treatment on her own. When [you] met Ms. Johnson a few weeks later, she informed [you] that, despite the fact that she had suffered abuse throughout the relationship, she did not want to proceed with the case. "I have AIDS," she told [you], "and I'm sure that the stress of my illness caused him to beat me." She begged [you] not to pursue the case because she was afraid that her family would discover that she had AIDS. She said that she and her boyfriend were "working things out." [You] tried to persuade her that proceeding with the prosecution would be in her best interest, [but] Ms. Johnson implored [you] not to pursue this case. "I'm going to die soon and I don't want a criminal case to interfere with my life. You're making things worse, not better."

(6) **Problem.** Your local court system has been awarded a federal grant to develop and implement a comprehensive strategy to address domestic violence, and you have been hired to direct the project. What elements and programs will you include in your policy? What legislative changes will you recommend? What individuals and groups will you involve in the planning process?

[2] The Civil Protection Order Process

In addition to strengthening the criminal response to domestic violence, legal reforms of the past two decades have enhanced the civil remedies available to victims of domestic violence. Today, all 50 states plus the District of Columbia and Puerto Rico provide for the issuance of civil protection orders to victims of domestic violence. Catherine F. Klein & Leslye E. Orloff, *Providing Legal Protection For Battered Women: An Analysis of State Statutes and Case Law*, 21 Hofstra L. Rev. 801, 807 (1993). "Civil protection orders grant immediate relief to victims of domestic abuse by enjoining batterers from further violence against their partner." Peter Finn, *Statutory Authority in the Use and Enforcement of Civil Protection Orders Against Domestic Abuse*, 23 Fam. L.Q. 43 (1989). Protection orders may provide further relief by evicting the batterer from a shared residence, providing for temporary custody of children, limiting the batterer's visitation rights, ordering the payment of child and spousal support, and requiring the batterer to attend mandatory counseling. In addition, a number of state protection order statutes authorize the award of money damages to compensate victims for the economic costs of domestic violence. *See, e.g., Sielski v. Sielski*, 604 A.2d 206, 209–10 (N.J. Super. Ct. Ch. Div. 1992); *Powell v. Powell*, 547 A.2d 973 (D.C. 1988). Civil protection orders may also prohibit future conduct by a batterer that might not qualify as criminal, for example, intimidation or verbal harassment. Finn, *above*, at 44.

Courts in a substantial majority of states may issue temporary protection orders on an *ex parte* basis, based on a petitioner's affidavit or testimony. Klein & Orloff, *above*, at

1037. To qualify for such an *ex parte* order, the petitioner must generally demonstrate, by a preponderance of the evidence, that she is being abused or is in fear of imminent harm. *See, e.g., Steckler v. Steckler*, 492 N.W.2d 76 (N.D. 1992) (petitioner must show "actual or imminent domestic violence"); *Blazel v. Bradley*, 698 F. Supp. 756, 765–68 (W.D. Wis. 1988) (discussing imminent harm requirement). *Ex parte* protection orders are generally effective for up to two weeks. Once a respondent receives notice of the order, the court will hold a hearing with both parties present and can issue a "permanent" order of protection, which is generally effective for up to one year. A small, but growing number of states authorize the issuance of protection orders lasting indefinitely or for several years. Klein & Orloff, *above*, at 1085.

The following case considers the due process requirements for issuance of an *ex parte* protection order, as well as the relationship between the civil protection order process and other family law proceedings.

BAKER v. BAKER
Supreme Court of Minnesota
494 N.W.2d 282 (1992)

GARDEBRING, JUSTICE

This case arises from appellant Barbara Baker's application in district court for an order for protection under the Domestic Abuse Act, Minn. Stat. § 518B.01 (1990), against her estranged husband, James Baker. Based upon her affidavit and motion, the trial court issued an *ex parte* temporary restraining order that excluded James Baker from Barbara Baker's residence and restrained him from harassing her at work. The court also granted temporary custody of the couple's infant to the mother, with provisions for visitation by the father. James Baker was notified pursuant to the statute, and at the subsequent full hearing, the court found that each party was entitled to an order for protection. The court then ordered that temporary custody of the infant remain with Barbara Baker, and extensive unsupervised visitation with James Baker was scheduled.

Consequently, James Baker filed a notice of appeal. The court of appeals reversed the trial court's *ex parte* order for protection and remanded the temporary child custody determination for particularized findings which reflect the dissolution standards of best interests of the child. *Baker v. Baker*, 481 N.W.2d 871 (Minn. Ct. App. 1992). Barbara Baker appeals from the decision of the court of appeals. We reverse.

Barbara Baker was 18 years old when she married 19-year-old James Baker in 1991. The couple's only child was born on May 19, 1991. Both parents worked at part-time jobs during the summer of 1991; when one parent was working, the other cared for the baby and when both were working, the baby was cared for by others. During the school year, both parents attended school and worked part time. Throughout the summer of 1991, tension escalated between the couple to the point that on one occasion, James threatened to kill Barbara, and punched her while she was holding the baby.

On August 30, 1991, Barbara moved out of the marital home with the baby and moved in with her aunt. After working that day, Barbara and James both separately went to the child care provider's home, where an argument began. Barbara left with the baby and went to her aunt's home. James followed and forced his way into the home and later, kicked and pushed Barbara. Barbara called the police, who arrived and removed James. James was issued a citation for fifth degree assault. James returned to Barbara's home after being released by the police, but was denied entry.

On September 3, 1991, James went to Barbara's new home and attempted to take the baby from the aunt. Barbara arrived home and an argument began. After Barbara removed her car keys from James' key ring and while she was putting them on her own key ring, James grabbed her, dragged her from the house, threw her to the ground and swung at her. James denied knocking Barbara down and claimed instead that she jumped on him and tore his shirt. The police were called again, but James had fled. James drove by afterwards and threw the keys at Barbara as she sat on the front steps. Barbara was treated at the hospital for an injury to her hand.

On September 5, 1991, Barbara filed a motion for an *ex parte* order for protection, along with an affidavit setting forth the described incidents of abuse. A temporary order for protection was issued, granting temporary custody of the couple's infant to Barbara, with supervised visitation to James. A full hearing was set for September 12, 1991.

James secured the services of an attorney, and filed a counter motion requesting an order for protection against Barbara and temporary custody of the child. At the September 12 hearing, the court took testimony on the issue of custody, and then reaffirmed its previous grant of custody of the child to Barbara, with visitation authorized for James.

The full hearing on the motions for protective orders was continued until September 20. At that time the court received additional evidence regarding both custody and the alleged abuse, and then restrained both parties from contact with the other and excluded each from the other's residence. The trial court ordered that temporary custody of the infant remain with Barbara for up to one year, unless amended before then by further court order. James was granted extensive, unsupervised visitation rights.

This case presents three distinct issues:

1) Must a proceeding for temporary relief under the Domestic Abuse Act, Minn. Stat. § 518B.01, conform to notice requirements contained in Minn.Gen.R.Prac. 303.04 and Minn.R.Civ.P. 65.01 before an ex parte order may issue?

2) Is a finding of "immediate danger to the [child]," pursuant to Minn. Stat. § 518.131, subd. 3(b), necessary before a temporary custody determination can be made within an order for protection?

3) How particularized must the findings be to support such temporary custody determinations?

The law governing the legal relationships between men and women, and their children, is complex, reflecting the potentially conflicting policy objectives of preserving families and protecting children, of allowing divorce and ensuring support, of protecting victims and assuring due process. Furthermore, its development has been incremental, reflecting that social attitudes on all of these difficult issues have been rapidly changing in the last several decades.

At issue in this case is the interplay between three of the statues which govern related, but distinct problems: the Domestic Abuse Act, Minn.Stat.ch. 518B, which outlines a mechanism for the court to provide protection for individuals who are threatened by their family or household members; the statute governing marriage dissolution, Minn.Stat.ch. 518; and Minn.Stat.ch. 257, which relates to the welfare of children. The court of appeals has inexplicably chosen to interweave the requirements of these statutory provisions even though they were adopted by the legislature at different times, manifest different objectives and deal with different subject matters.

We begin first with the Domestic Abuse Act. In 1978, it was estimated there were 26,900 assaults upon women by their partners. Minn. Dep't of Corrections, Minnesota Program for Battered Women, Biennial Report 1986–87, p.12. Shelters housed 613 women plus 726 children. *Id*. Another 2,136 requests for shelter could not be accommodated. *Id.*

The Domestic Abuse Act, Minn. Stat. § 518B.01, was enacted in 1979 as one way to protect victims of domestic assault. It is a substantive statute which is complete in itself, carefully drafted to provide limited types of relief to persons at risk of further abuse by other "family or household members," whether married or not. It neither establishes nor terminates a legal relationship; it requires a demonstration of physical harm, or fear, or sexual misconduct, and the relief it provides is of limited duration. In one sense, it may be thought of as a "band-aid," designed to curtail the harm one household member may be doing to the other in the short term, until a more permanent dispute resolution can be put in place. Nothing within the plain wording of the statute suggests that reference to any other statute is necessary.

In contrast, the marital dissolution statute, Minn.Stat.ch. 518, is a complex scheme designed to detail the procedures for termination of a particular kind of legal relationship, marriage between a man and woman. Its sixty-five sections cover, among other topics, the grounds for divorce, the process for division of property, and the nature of the on-going obligations of one party to the other, including those related to financial support. It is broader than the Domestic Abuse Act, in that it covers virtually all legal aspects of the end of a relationship and is intended to provide for closure of the issues at hand, except in circumstances it carefully spells out. It is narrower in that it only covers marriage, and not the many other kinds of human relationships which may be covered by the Domestic Abuse Act. While the reach of the two statutes may incidentally overlap as to some married persons in some situations, each serves a distinct and separate public policy. Each serves different purposes and may be appropriate for different persons.

Similarly, Minn.Stat.ch. 257 relates primarily to the welfare of children, in contexts other than domestic abuse. It includes such matters as surrender of parental rights, foster home placement, declaration of parentage, and certain custody and visitation determinations which may involve married or unmarried partners, extended family, or unrelated persons . . .

The danger of muddling together these three distinct and targeted statutory schemes is perfectly illustrated in this case: the availability of extraordinary relief intended by the passage of the Domestic Abuse Act is utterly negated by tying to it unnecessary external procedural requirements. It is in this context then that we examine the specific issues before us.

I.

Court procedural rules such as Minn.R.Civ.P. 65.01 and Minn.Gen.R.Prac. 3.01 and 303.04 provide a framework to guide the bench in the majority of cases. However, some statutory remedies incorporate alternative procedures as part of the substantive relief made available. The Domestic Abuse Act provides such a scheme: an *ex parte* restraining order is central to the substantive relief provided for under the Act. If notice, or extensive justification for the lack thereof, were required, the order would not provide the kind of immediate remedy that the Domestic Abuse Act, as a whole, contemplates . . .

Furthermore, prior notice to the respondent could be counter-productive to the purposes of the statute. As noted by the U.S. District Court for the Western District of Wisconsin in interpreting a similar statute, such notice might, in fact, incite further domestic violence. *Blazel v. Bradley*, 698 F. Supp. 756, 763 (W.D.Wisc. 1988).

Even though statutes and rules may permit *ex parte* restraining orders, the respondent has due process rights which must not be violated. The requirements of due process are flexible and call for such procedural protections as the particular situation demands. The main factors to consider are: (1) the private interests to be affected by the official action; (2) the risk of erroneous deprivation of these interests and the probable value of additional safeguards; and (3) the government interests involved. *Mathews v. Eldridge*, 424 U.S. 319.

There are two potentially protected "private interests" at issue here: (1) the exclusion from a shared dwelling; (2) the liberty interest of a parent in custody of his or her children. In addition to restraining the respondent from committing acts of domestic abuse, the temporary order may exclude the respondent from a shared dwelling, or from the residence or place of employment of the petitioner.

The *ex parte* order in this case also granted temporary custody of the infant to the petitioner, with visitation to the respondent. While both parents have strong interests in the custody and enjoyment of their child, a parent's love and affection must yield to considerations of the child's welfare. As we will discuss in Section II of this opinion, the Domestic Abuse Act recognizes the preeminence of the child's welfare by allowing an award of temporary custody only "on a basis which gives primary consideration to the safety of the victim [and] children." Minn.Stat. §518B.01, subd. 6(a)(3).

The second *Matthews* factor goes to the risk of erroneous deprivation of the private interests and the probable value of additional safeguards. *Matthews*, 424 U.S. at 335. We conclude that the Domestic Abuse Act provides extensive procedural safeguards which guard against such error. The *ex parte* order must be based upon an application for an order for protection supported by a sworn affidavit alleging specific facts and circumstances of past abuse. Minn. Stat. § 518B.01, subd. 4(b). Only judges or referees may issue such orders. *Id.* at subd. 3. The *ex parte* order is very short term, *id.* at subd 7(b) and the respondent must be given notice of the full hearing. *Id.* at subd. 5(a). The only additional procedural safeguard possible would be a requirement of notice to the respondent before an order was granted. This would result in unnecessary and possibly dangerous time delays.

Finally, we must consider the third *Matthews* factor, the government interests involved. While at first blush, it may seem that the interest at issue here is a purely private one, that is, individual freedom from further domestic assault, it is also true that the general public has an extraordinary interest in a society free from violence, especially where vulnerable persons are at risk. This is the reason that criminal prosecutions are brought in the name of the state, for example.

In another key case, *Fuentes v. Shevin*, 407 U.S. 67, 32 L. Ed. 2d 556, 92 S. Ct. 1983 (1972), the Supreme Court discussed the characteristics of the "extraordinary situations" which justify postponing notice and opportunity for hearing. First, the deprivation of the property interest must be "directly necessary to secure an important governmental or general public interest." *Id.* at 91. Second, there must be "a special need for very prompt action." *Id.* Third, the state must keep strict control over the process by limiting its authorization to a government official acting under "the standards of a narrowly drawn statute." *Id.*

We believe that the domestic abuse situation shares these characteristics with other situations where *ex parte* relief has been allowed. First, it is not necessary to recite again the state's strong interest in preventing violence in a domestic setting. Second, inasmuch as the statute requires an allegation of an "immediate and present danger of domestic abuse," Minn. Stat. § 518B.01, subd. 7(a), there can be no argument that a special need for prompt action is shown. Finally, the statute is very narrowly drawn and, of course, compliance with its terms must be determined by a district court judge or other judicial officer before *ex parte* relief is available.

After reviewing the application of both the general Matthews factors and the more specific Fuentes factors to these facts, we conclude that there is no due process violation in the granting of *ex parte* relief pursuant to the Domestic Abuse Act.

II.

We next turn to the question of whether a temporary custody determination entered as part of an order for protection under the Domestic Abuse Act must conform to the requirements of *ex parte* temporary custody orders entered as a part of a dissolution proceeding.

As the court of appeals correctly noted,

> excluding one party from the other's residence, one of the expressly included forms of temporary relief under subdivision 7(a), functionally requires control of physical custody of the children for the duration of the order.

Baker v. Baker, 481 N.W.2d at 874.

However, the court of appeals went on to conclude that statutory provisions which govern the issuance of temporary restraining orders in dissolution proceedings also control in the domestic abuse setting. Specifically, the court applied the stringent requirements of Minn. Stat. § 518.131, subd. 3(b) to the temporary custody provisions of the order for protection entered in this case. That section provides that no *ex parte* order may grant custody of minor children to "either party except upon a finding by the court of immediate danger of physical harm" to the children.

While the provisions of the Domestic Abuse Act that allow *ex parte* orders do not specifically address custody (or visitation), Minn. Stat. § 518B.01, subd. 7(a) does authorize "relief as the court deems proper." There is an obvious practical need to deal with custody issues when one parent is excluded from the home.

Moreover, other sections of the Domestic Abuse Act do contain adequate guidance for the court in determining custody and visitation issues. In the section authorizing relief after notice and opportunity for hearing, the court is directed to "award temporary custody or establish temporary visitation with regard to minor children of the parties on a basis which gives primary consideration to the safety of the victim and children." Minn. Stat. § 518B.01, subd. 6(3). Nothing in the statute or its history suggests that this same standard should not apply to the custody determinations at the *ex parte* stage, nor that the standard of the dissolution statute should apply. Indeed, the court of appeals has apparently overlooked the 1985 amendments to the Domestic Abuse Act which specifically repealed the reference to the dissolution statute's custody standards.

Accordingly, we hold that determinations of custody and visitation made at the time of the issuance of an *ex parte* order for protection are governed by Minn. stat. § 518B.01, subd. 6(3), giving primary consideration to the safety of the victim and the children.

III.

Finally, we turn to the question of whether the court of appeals erred in remanding the subsequent order for protection to the trial court for findings on custody consistent with Minn. Stat. § 257.025(a), requiring a detailed "best interests" analysis. This is perhaps the most troubling issue in this case.

While the Domestic Abuse Act does provide a standard for making custody and visitation determinations, it is essentially silent on the level of findings necessary. However, it is a significant leap to conclude, as the court of appeals has done, that Minn. Stat. § 257.025(a) controls. First, as appellant argues, that provision is directed to custody determinations in contexts other than domestic abuse. Requiring conformity to its provisions would, in the guise of a discussion on findings, substitute the "best interests" standard in lieu of the "safety of the victim and child" standard of the Domestic Abuse Act. Custody orders in this setting are intended to be temporary and generally either expire or are reviewed by the court one year from their issuance. Minn. Stat. § 518B.01, subd. 6(b).

Furthermore, the hearing at which such custody determinations are to be made must be held no later than seven days from the issuance of any *ex parte* order, except in limited circumstances. Minn. Stat. § 518B.01, subd. 7(b). This is a wholly inadequate time for the parties to prepare testimony and other evidence in support of a best interests analysis, or for county personnel to conduct custody evaluations to assist the court. Thus, the effect of the court of appeals ruling is to force trial courts into making findings on a completely inadequate record, to delay order for protection hearings beyond statutory deadlines or to confound the practical need to make custody determinations. We do not believe this could be the legislature's intent. . . .

This conclusion is bolstered by our most recent consideration of related issues in *Vogt v. Vogt*, 455 N.W.2d 471 (1990). There we said: The law is expected to provide immediate temporary relief, yet time for courts to decide a case fairly and thoughtfully is often in short supply . . . The trial court has wide discretion in dealing with these matters. Ordinarily, consideration of any affidavits and some brief questioning of parties will suffice for issuance of an order for temporary relief; the order is of course subject to revision if more information subsequently comes to light. Or Court Services can conduct an abbreviated preliminary investigation, at least interviewing the parties, sorting out their respective positions and making recommendations to aid the court in arriving at its decision. *Vogt*, at 475. Obviously, this "abbreviated," "brief" and "preliminary" approach will not suffice if the detailed findings of the "best interests" analysis are required.

Therefore, we hold that oral findings consistent with the "safety" standard of Minn. Stat. § 518B.01, subd. 6(a)(3) will support a custody determination pursuant to that provision.

Reversed.

NOTES AND QUESTIONS

(1) The due process analysis in *Baker* is consistent with other state and federal decisions that have rejected constitutional challenges to the issuance of *ex parte* orders of protection. *E.g., Blazel v. Bradley*, 698 F.Supp. 756, 768 (W.D. Wisc. 1988); *Sanders v. Shephard*, 541 NE.2d 1150, 1155 (Ill. App. Ct. 1989); *Marquette v. Marquette*, 686 P.2d 990, 996 (Okla. Ct. App. 1984); *State ex rel. Williams v. Marsh*, 626 S.W.2d 223, 232 (Mo. 1982). For a more extensive discussion of these constitutional issues, see Quinn, Comment, *Ex Parte Protection Orders: Is Due Process Locked Out?*, 58 Temp. L.Q. 843 (1985).

(2) The circumstances surrounding Barbara Baker's request for an order of protection against her estranged husband are typical of protection order cases in several respects. First, Barbara Baker was not represented by counsel. Most domestic violence petitioners who seek protection orders do so without the assistance of an attorney, and a high percentage of respondents are unrepresented as well. The prevalence of *pro se* litigants in protection order cases presents a challenge to the judicial system and has lead to a number of innovations such as the development of simplified form pleadings and the use of lay advocates in court. Second, the most serious violence apparently occurred after Barbara Baker separated from her husband. Extensive research on domestic abuse indicates that a victim's risk of danger is often greatest once she decides or attempts to leave an abusive relationship. *See, e.g.*, Martha Mahoney, *Legal Images of Battered Women: Redefining the Issue of Separation*, 90 Mich. L. Rev. 1, 61–71 (1991) (discussing the prevalence of "separation violence").

(3) The *Baker* case also illustrates the potential tension between the civil protection order process and the substantive and procedural requirements contained in other domestic relations statutes, particularly those relating to divorce and child custody. As the scope of relief available through the protection order process has expanded, the potential for overlap has increased. Are you satisfied with the way that the *Baker* court dealt with this overlap? Why or why not?

(4) **Enforcement of Civil Protection Orders.** The effectiveness of civil protection orders as a remedy for domestic violence depends critically on whether the orders are consistently and vigorously enforced. In most jurisdictions, several potential enforcement mechanisms exist, including both civil and criminal contempt. However, law enforcement authorities have traditionally been reluctant to make use of these mechanisms, often leaving domestic violence victims vulnerable to continued attack. *See generally* Catherine F. Klein & Leslye E. Orloff, *Providing Legal Protection For Battered Women: An Analysis of State Statutes and Case Law*, 21 Hofstra L. Rev. 801, 1095–116 (1993). Law reform efforts in the 1990s have focused on strengthening the enforcement of protection orders. Virtually all jurisdictions now allow warrantless misdemeanor arrests for violation of a protection order, and a substantial number of jurisdictions mandate arrest in this situation. *See* Klein & Orloff, *above*, at 1149–53 (discussing state arrest statutes). A number of states now prosecute some protection order violations as felonies, rather than as misdemeanors. Other states have adopted innovative measures to monitor compliance with protection orders. For example, judges in Utah and Washington state may order a defendant who violates a protection order

to submit to electronic monitoring. Wash. Rev. Code Ann. §26.50.1110(1) (1997); Utah Ann. Code 30–6–4.8 (1977).

Enhanced enforcement of protection orders may raise double jeopardy concerns, particularly where contempt proceedings are followed by an independent criminal prosecution based upon the same incident (or incidents) of violence. In *United States v. Dixon*, 509 U.S. 688, 701–02 (1993), a divided Supreme Court ruled that double jeopardy would not bar a battered woman from enforcing her civil protection order through criminal contempt, while the state also prosecuted her batterer criminally, as long as the contempt proceeding and the criminal prosecution each required proof of additional elements. Nor does double jeopardy attach where a criminal prosecution follows a civil contempt proceeding for violation of a protective order. *See, e.g., Mahoney v. Commonwealth*, 612 N.E.2d 1175, 1178–79 (1995). For additional discussion of the potential double jeopardy issues raised by the enhanced enforcement of civil protection orders, see Jennifer Black, Note, *The Double Jeopardy Dilemma In Combating Domestic Violence: A Solution in United States v. Dixon*, 33 U. of Louisville J. of Fam. L. 911 (1994).

(5) **Anti-stalking Statutes.** Many victims of domestic violence are followed and threatened by their abusers, both before and after being attacked. Until recently, the law offered little recourse for these acts of intimidation. Since 1990, however, virtually all states have enacted statutes that criminalize stalking behavior. *See* Catherine F. Klein & Leslye E. Orloff, *Providing Legal Protection For Battered Women: An Analysis of State Statutes and Case Law*, 21 Hofstra L. Rev. 801, 874–75 (1993). These statutes typically define stalking as the "willful, malicious, and repeated following and harassing of another person."*Id*. at 874 (quoting National Institute of Justice, Project to Develop a Model Anti-Stalking Code for States 13 (1993)). Most anti-stalking statutes require both threatening behavior and a continuing course of conduct. *Id*. at 875.

Query. Do anti-stalking statutes raise constitutional concerns about vagueness or First Amendment overbreadth? *Compare, e.g., State v. Bryan*, 910 P.2d 212, 220–21 (Kan. 1996) (stalking statute struck down as unconstitutionally vague because terms lacked definition and there was no objective standard) *and Commonwealth v. Kwiatkowski*, 637 N.E.2d 854, 857 (Mass. 1994) (use of the phrase "repeatedly follows or harasses" was unconstitutionally vague since it was uncertain whether the harassment had to take place on more than one occasion) *with State v. Culmo*, 642 A.2d 90, 102 (Conn. 1993) (upholding constitutionality of stalking statute because it was "narrowly tailored to serve significant government interests . . . while leaving open ample alternative channels of communication") *and State v. McGill*, 536 N.W.2d 89, 95–96 (S.D. 1995) (rejecting vagueness challenge to stalking statute). *See generally* Beth Bjerregaard, *Stalking and the First Amendment: A Constitutional Analysis of State Stalking Laws*, 32 Crim. Just. Bull. 3007 (July–August 1996).

[3] Marital Rape

Most states now recognize sexual assault of a spouse or other intimate partner as a form of domestic violence. But the law did not always reflect this view. At common law, a man was considered legally incapable of raping his wife. The origin of this common law rule apparently dates back to unsupported dictum of Lord Hale, who was Chief Justice of the Court of King's Bench from 1671 to 1675, and who held that by consenting to marry, a wife grants consent to intercourse with her husband from which "she cannot retreat." 1

Hale, *Pleas of the Crown*, 629 (1847). Despite its dubious common law origin, the marital rape exemption persisted intact in American law until the late 1970s. *See generally*, Robin West, *Marital Rape, Equality Theory and the Promise of the Fourteenth Amendment*, 42 Fla. L. Rev. 45 (1990). Indeed, as late as 1986, more than half the states still prohibited the prosecution of a husband for the rape of his wife while the couple was living together. The following case considers the traditional justifications for the marital rape exemption.

WARREN v. STATE
Georgia Supreme Court
336 S.E.2d 221 (1985)

SMITH, JUSTICE

"When a woman says I do, does she give up her right to say I won't?" This question does not pose the real question, because rape and aggravated sodomy are not sexual acts of an ardent husband performed upon an initially apathetic wife, they are acts of violence that are accompanied with physical and mental abuse and often leave the victim with physical and psychological damage that is almost always long lasting. Thus we find the more appropriate question: When a woman says "I do" in Georgia does she give up her right to State protection from the violent acts of rape and aggravated sodomy performed by her husband. The answer is no. We affirm.

The appellant, Daniel Steven Warren, was indicted by a Fulton County Grand Jury for the rape and aggravated sodomy of his wife. They were living together as husband and wife at the time. The appellant filed a pre-trial general demurrer and motion to dismiss the indictment. After a hearing, the motions were denied. The appellant sought and was issued a certificate of immediate review and filed an application for an interlocutory appeal which was granted by this court.

1. The appellant asserts that there exists within the rape statute an implicit marital exclusion that makes it legally impossible for a husband to be guilty of raping his wife.

Until the late 1970s there was no real examination of this apparently widely held belief. Within the last few years several jurisdictions have been faced with similar issues and they have decided that under certain circumstances a husband can be held criminally liable for raping his wife....

What is behind the theory and belief that a husband could not be guilty of raping his wife? There are various explanations for the rule and all of them flow from the common law attitude toward women, the status of women and marriage.

Perhaps the most often used basis for the marital rape exemption is the view set out by Lord Hale in 1 Hale P.C. 629. It is known as Lord Hale's contractual theory. The statement attributed to Lord Hale used to support the theory is: "but a husband cannot be guilty of a rape committed by himself upon his lawful wife, for by their mutual matrimonial consent and contract the wife hath given up herself in this kind unto her husband which she cannot retreat."

There is some thought that the foundation of his theory might well have been the subsequent marriage doctrine of English law, wherein the perpetrator could, by marrying his victim, avoid rape charges. It was thus argued as a corollary, rape within the marital relationship would result in the same immunity.

Another theory stemming from medieval times is that of a wife being the husband's chattel or property. Since a married woman was part of her husband's property, nothing more than a chattel, rape was nothing more than a man making use of his own property.

A third theory is the unity in marriage or unity of person theory that held the very being or legal existence of a woman was suspended during marriage, or at least was incorporated and consolidated into that of her husband. In view of the fact that there was only one legal being, the husband, he could not be convicted of raping himself.

These three theories have been used to support the marital rape exemption. Others have tried to fill the chasm between these three theories with justifications for continuing the exemption in the face of changes in the recognition of women, their status, and the status of marriage. Some of the justifications include: Prevention of fabricated charges; Preventing wives from using rape charges for revenge; Preventing state intervention into marriage so that possible reconciliation will not be thwarted. A closer examination of the theories and justifications indicates that they are no longer valid, if they ever had any validity.

Hale's implied consent theory was created at a time when marriages were irrevocable and when all wives promised to "love, honor, and obey" and all husbands promised to "love, cherish, and protect until death do us part." Wives were subservient to their husbands, her identity was merged into his, her property became his property, and she took his name for her own.

There have been dramatic changes in women's rights and the status of women and marriage. . . . Women in Georgia "are entitled to the privilege of the elective franchise and have the right to hold any civil office or perform any civil function as fully and completely as do male citizens." OCGA § 1–2–7. Couples who contemplate marriage today may choose either spouse's surname or a combination of both names for their married surname, OCGA § 19–3–33.1. No longer is a wife's domicile presumed to be that of her husband, OCGA § 19–2–3 and no longer is the husband head of the family with the wife subject to him. OCGA § 19–3–8. Marriages are revocable without fault by either party, OCGA 19–5–3(13); either party, not just the husband, can be required to pay alimony upon divorce, OCGA § 19–6–1; and both parties have a joint and several duty to provide for the maintenance, protection, and education of their children, OCGA § 19–7–2. Couples may write antenuptial agreements in which they are able to decide, prior to marriage, future settlements, OCGA § 19–3–62; and our legislature has recognized that there can be violence in modern family life and it has enacted special laws to protect family members who live in the same household from one another's violent acts, Ga.L. 1981, 880; OCGA § 10–13–1 et seq.

Today, many couples write their own marriage vows in which they specifically decide the terms of their marriage contract. Certainly no normal woman who falls in love and wishes " 'to marry, establish a home and bring up children' a central part of the *liberty* protected by the Due Process Clause," (Emphasis supplied.) *Zablocki v. Redhail*, 434 U.S. 374, 384 (1978), would knowingly include an irrevocable term to her revocable marriage contract that would allow her husband to rape her. Rape "is highly reprehensible, both in a moral sense and in its almost total contempt for the personal integrity and autonomy of the female victim. Short of homicide, it is the "ultimate violation of self.' " *Coker v. Georgia*, 433 U.S. 584, 599 (1977). It is incredible to think that any state would sanction such behavior by adding an implied consent term *to all marriage contracts* that would leave *all* wives with no protection under the law from the "ultimate violation of self," *Coker, supra*, simply because they choose to enter into a relationship that is respected and protected by the law. The implied consent theory to spousal rape is without logical meaning, and *obviously conflicts* with our Constitutional and statutory laws and our regard for all citizens of this State.

One would be hard pressed to argue that a husband can rape his wife because she is his chattel. Even in the darkest days of slavery when slaves were also considered chattel, rape was defined as "the carnal knowledge of a female whether free or slave, forcibly and against her will." Georgia Code, § 4248, p. 824 (1863). Both the chattel and unity of identity rationales have been cast aside. "Nowhere in the common law world [or] in any modern society is a woman regarded as chattel or demeaned by denial of a separate legal identity and the dignity associated with recognition as a whole human being." *Trammel v. United States*, 445 U.S. 40, 52 (1980).

We find that none of the theories have any validity. The justifications likewise are without efficacy. There is no other crime we can think of in which *all of the victims are denied protection* simply because someone might fabricate a charge; there is no evidence that wives have flooded the district attorneys with revenge filled trumped-up charges, and once a marital relationship is at the point where a husband rapes his wife, state intervention is needed for the wife's protection.

There never has been an expressly stated marital exemption included in the Georgia rape statute. Furthermore, our statute never included the word "unlawful" which has been widely recognized as signifying the incorporation of the common law spousal exclusion. *Commonwealth v. Chretien*, Mass. 417 N.E.2d 1203, 1208 (1981). A reading of the statute indicates that there is no marital exclusion. "A person commits the offense of rape when he has carnal knowledge of a female forcibly and against her will." OCGA § 16–6–1. We need not decide whether or not a common law marital exemption became part of our old statutory rape law, because the rape statute that was similar to the common law definition was specifically repealed in 1968, Ga.L. 1968, p. 1338, and our new broader statute, OCGA § 16–6–1, was enacted in its place which plainly on its face includes a husband. . . .

The appellant contends that if we find no marital exemptions under the rape and aggravated sodomy statutes it would be a new interpretation of the criminal law, and to apply the statutes to him would deprive him of his due process rights.

"All the Due Process Clause requires is that the law give sufficient warning that men may conduct themselves so as to avoid that which is forbidden." *Rose v. Locke*, 423 U.S. 48, 50 (1975). Both the rape and aggravated sodomy statutes are broadly written and they are plain on their fact. This is a first application of these statutes to this particular set of facts, this is not an unforeseeable judicial enlargement of criminal statutes that are narrowly drawn. . . .

Judgment affirmed.

NOTES AND QUESTIONS

(1) Although marriage is no longer a complete defense to rape in any state, many states still treat marital rape differently than rape outside of marriage. For example, some states

allow prosecution only if the spouses are living separately, or one spouse has filed for a divorce, annulment or separation. Other states require victims to comply with stringent reporting requirements, applicable only to spousal rape. Still other states define marital rape as a separate, less serious offense than other types of rape. *See generally* Katherine M. Schelong, *Domestic Violence and the State: Responses To and Rationales For Spousal Battering, Marital Rape & Stalking*, 78 Marq. L. Rev. 79, 106–07 (1994). Are there valid reasons for treating spousal rape differently than rape outside of marriage?

(2) The most recent version of the Model Penal Code generally retains the marital rape exemption and indeed extends it to "persons living as man and wife, regardless of the legal status of their relationship." Model Penal Code §§ 213.1, 213.6. The drafters of the Model Penal Code provide the following rationale for this position:

> The major context of which those who would abandon the spousal exclusion are thinking . . . is the situation of rape by force or threat. The problem with abandoning the immunity in many such situations is that the law of rape, if applied to spouses, would thrust the prospect of criminal sanctions into the ongoing process of adjustments in the marital relationship. Section 213.1, for example, defines as gross sexual imposition intercourse coerced "by any threat that would prevent resistance by a woman of ordinary resolution." It may well be that a woman of ordinary resolution would be prevented from resisting by her husband's threat to expose a secret to her mother, for example. Behavior of this sort within the marital relationship is no doubt unattractive, but it is a risky business for the law to intervene by threatening criminal sanctions. Retaining the spousal exclusion avoids this unwarranted intrusion of the penal law into the life of he family.
>
> Finally, there is the case of intercourse coerced by force or threat of physical harm. Here the law already authorizes a penalty for assault. If the actor causes serious bodily injury, the punishment is quite severe. The issue is whether the still more drastic sanctions of rape should apply. The answer depends on whether the injury caused by forcible intercourse by a husband is equivalent to that inflicted by someone else. The gravity of the crime of forcible rape derives not merely from its violent character but also from its achievement of a particularly degrading kind of unwanted intimacy. Where the attacker stands in an ongoing relationship of sexual intimacy, that evil, as distinct from the force used to compel submission, may well be thought qualitatively different. The character of the voluntary association of husband and wife, in other words, may be thought to affect the nature of the harm involved in unwanted intercourse. That, in any event, is the conclusion long endorsed by the law of rape and carried forward in the Model Code provision.

Do you find this rationale persuasive? Why or why not?

[4] Federal Involvement: The Violence Against Women Act

Until the mid-1990s, legal efforts to combat domestic violence took place almost exclusively at the state and local level. Federal involvement was limited to providing modest amounts of funding for battered women's shelters and other victim services. In 1994, Congress enacted a major domestic violence initiative—the Violence Against Women Act ("VAWA")—as Title IV of the Violent Crime Control and Law Enforcement Act of 1994, Pub. L. No. 103–322. VAWA contains a wide range of provisions designed to enhance the enforcement of laws against domestic violence and to improve the criminal and civil justice systems' handling of matters involving violence against women. In particular, VAWA's funding provisions encourage states to implement mandatory arrest or pro-arrest policies, improve tracking of cases involving domestic violence, centralize and coordinate police enforcement, prosecution and judicial responsibility for domestic violence cases, strengthen legal advocacy and service programs and educate judges to improve their handling of matters involving domestic violence. *See, e.g.*,William G. Brassler, *The Federalization of Domestic Violence; An Exercise in Cooperative Federalism or A Misallocation of Federal Judicial Resources?*, 48 Rutgers L. Rev. 1139, 1144–46 (1996).

VAWA also establishes several new federal causes of action. First, the Act creates a new federal crime of interstate domestic violence, which punishes a person who travels across a state line with the intent of injuring, harassing, or intimidating a spouse or intimate partner and who commits a crime of violence in the course of or as a result of such interstate travel. The Act also criminalizes travel across a state line with the intent to engage in conduct that violates the provisions of a protection order. *See* 42 U.S.C. § 13701 (West 1997). In addition, VAWA creates a federal civil rights remedy for victims of gender-motivated violence. This civil rights remedy allows a person victimized by gender-motivated violence to obtain injunctive and monetary relief, including both compensatory and punitive damages, from the perpetrator of the violence.

In creating a new civil rights remedy, Congress found that crimes motivated by a victim's gender violate the victim's right to equal protection of the laws and to freedom from gender-based discrimination. *See* Sally Goldfarb, *The Civil Rights Remedy Of The Violence Against Women Act: Legislative History, Policy Implications & Litigation Strategy*, 4 J. Law & Policy 391–92 (1996). Congress also found that existing state remedies had proven inadequate to protect against the "bias element" of gender crimes, which "separate these crimes from acts of random violence." 1994 Conf. Rep. 711; *see* Victoria F. Nourse, *Where Violence, Relationship, and Equality Meet: The Violence Against Women Act's Civil Right's Remedy*, 11 Wis. Women's L.J. 1, 13 (1996). In addition, Congress made extensive findings regarding the extent and seriousness of violence against women and the effect of that violence on interstate commerce. *See, e.g., Brzonkal v. Virginia Polytechnic,* 132 F.3d 949, 966–71 (4th Cir. 1997) (detailing Congressional findings).

Despite these Congressional findings, VAWA's civil rights remedy has been criticized as unnecessary and inconsistent with federalism principles. Opponents of the remedy argue that defining gender-motivated violence as a civil rights violation "raises serious questions about the federal courts' capacity to competently manage their caseload, the need for the federalization of a traditional state responsibility, and the role the federal courts should play in a federal system." Bressler, *above* at 1141–42; *see* Justice William H. Rehnquist, 138 Cong. Rec. 746, 747 (Mar. 19, 1992) (criticizing VAWA's private right of action as so sweeping that it "could involve the federal courts in a whole host of domestic relations disputes"). Critics have also expressed concerns about the "overfederalization" of domestic violence crimes, and have questioned the ability of federal law enforcement to do "the kind of on-site policing that the federal system has never been very good at." Sanford H. Kadish, Comment, *The Folly of Overfederalization*, 46 Hastings L. J. 1247, 1249 (1995). *But see* Kerrie E. Maloney, *Gender Motivated Violence and the Commerce Clause: The Civil Rights Provision of the Violence Against Women Act After Lopez*, 96 Colum. L. Rev. 1876, 1878–83

(1996) (documenting interstate effects of gender-motivated violence and rebutting federalism objections).

The case that follows considers an early constitutional challenge to VAWA's civil rights remedy.

SEATON v. SEATON
United States District Court
971 F. Supp. 1188 (E.D. Tenn. 1997)

JAMES H. JARVIS, JUDGE

This is an action for damages brought pursuant to the Violence Against Women Act (VAWA), 42 U.S.C. § 13981. Included in plaintiff's complaint are various pendent state law claims brought pursuant to this court's supplemental jurisdiction. *See* 28 U.S.C. § 1367. Currently pending is defendant's motion to dismiss or, in the alternative, for summary judgment, on the ground that VAWA is an unconstitutional extension of Congress' powers under both the Commerce Cause of Art. I, Sec. 8, Cl. 3 of the United States Constitution and the Equal Protection Clause of the Fourteenth Amendment to the United States Constitution. Defendant further moves to dismiss the pendent state law claims on the grounds that they are barred by the one-year Tennessee statute of limitations, that they raise novel or complex issues of law and should be dismissed pursuant to 28 U.S.C. § 1367(c)(1); and that there are other compelling reasons for denying supplemental jurisdiction, 28 U.S.C. § 1367(c)(4). For the reasons that follow, the motion will be denied as to the federal claim and granted as to the supplemental state law claims.

Factual Background

Plaintiff Laurel Knuckles Seaton and defendant Kenneth Marshall Seaton were married on February 14, 1992. Plaintiff alleges that, during the courtship prior to the marriage and throughout the marriage, defendant engaged in controlling, deceitful and abusive behavior, of which plaintiff was the victim. Plaintiff alleges that she was the victim of conspiracy, fraud, physical and sexual abuse, and emotional suffering.

On August 23, 1995, plaintiff filed for divorce from defendant after an alleged final altercation occurring on August 22, 1995. Plaintiff alleges that during the altercation, defendant severely threatened and assaulted her. Plaintiff's divorce complaint was filed in the Fourth Circuit Court for Knox County, Tennessee. In her divorce complaint, plaintiff asked for a divorce as well as civil damages resulting from defendant's alleged tortious conduct toward plaintiff. The charges in the state complaint include assault and battery, outrageous conduct, fraud, civil conspiracy, and defamation.

On August 22, 1996, plaintiff filed the instant action, in which she sets forth a primary federal claim that defendant, by his aforementioned actions, violated VAWA (Count I). The complaint also alleges related state law claims, including assault and battery (Count II), intentional infliction of emotional distress (Count III), false imprisonment (Count IV), breach of fiduciary duty (Count V), fraud and conversion (Count VI), and misrepresentation (Count VII). The complaint seeks injunctive relief, incidental and compensatory damages, exemplary and punitive damages, attorney fees and costs, and other equitable relief, including rescission.

Defendant, through his answer, denies all allegations of abuse, fraud, conspiracy, or otherwise. Additionally, defendant asserts in his dispositive motion that VAWA is unconstitutional as Congress exceeded its authority under either the Commerce Clause or the Equal Protection Clause. As such, defendant contends that, as to Count I of plaintiff's complaint seeking relief under VAWA, plaintiff has failed to state a claim upon which relief can be granted and that there is no federal jurisdiction over defendant or the subject matter of plaintiff's federal claim.

As to the state claims, defendant asserts that they should be dismissed under the provisions of 28 U.S.C. § 1367. Defendant argues that the state claims raise novel or complex issues of law, substantially predominate over the claim made under VAWA, and invoke circumstances providing other compelling reasons for declining jurisdiction—namely, that many, if not all, of the same claims are pending in a divorce suit between the parties in state court.

Finally, defendant asserts that, with the exception of the final altercation, all of the actions alleged by plaintiff occurred over one year before the filing of the original federal complaint and are, therefore, barred by the Tennessee statute of limitations for civil actions. . . .

VAWA

Defendant contends that, by enacting VAWA, Congress exceeded its powers under the Commerce Clause, which gives Congress the power to "regulate Commerce with Foreign Nations and among the several states . . . ."

Before beginning an analysis of VAWA's constitutionality under the Commerce Clause, the court must note its extreme discomfort with the sweeping nature of VAWA. While there is no doubt that violence against women is a serious matter in our society, this particular remedy created by Congress, because of its extreme overbreadth, opens the doors of the federal courts to parties seeking leverage in settlements rather than true justice. The framers of the Constitution did not intend for the federal courts to play host to domestic disputes and invade the well-established authority of the sovereign states. Nevertheless, the court must heed the well-settled precedent extant in Commerce Clause jurisprudence in an effort to determine whether VAWA, even in view of its sweeping nature, passes muster under the Commerce Clause.

A. The Commerce Clause.

The power of Congress under the Commerce Clause was first defined in *Gibbons v. Ogden*, which established Congress' power to directly regulate interstate commerce; *Gibbons* allowed Congress' commerce power to spread beyond mere trafficking of goods across state lines and into the realm of "commercial intercourse." 22 U.S. 1, 6 L. Ed. 23, 9 Wheat 1 (1824).The Supreme Court in *Gibbons* further noted that this power "acknowledges no limitations, other than are prescribed in the Constitution." *Id.* at 196.

In 1937, the Supreme Court developed a standard that gave Congress the power to regulate intrastate activities which "have such a close and substantial relation to interstate commerce that their control is essential or appropriate to protect that commerce from burdens and obstructions." *NLRB v. Jones & Laughlin Steel Corp.*, 301 U.S. 1, 37, 81 L. Ed. 893, 57 S. Ct. 615 (1937) (emphasis added). Further, in determining whether Congress has acted within its limits, "the task of the court . . . is relatively narrow." *Hodel v. Virginia Surface Mining and Reclamation Ass'n*, 452 U.S. 264, 276, 69 L. Ed. 2d 1, 101 S. Ct. 2352 (1980).

The court's standard of review is limited to whether a "rational basis" existed for Congress to conclude that a regulated activity sufficiently affected interstate commerce. If a rational basis is found for the statute under the Commerce Clause, the court must then consider whether the means chosen by Congress are "reasonably adapted to the end permitted by the Constitution." *Id.*

B. The *Lopez* Interpretation.

For decades following the *Jones and Laughlin Steel* case, Congress enjoyed the unbridled power to regulate any activity that remotely affected interstate commerce. However, in *United States v. Lopez*, 514 U.S. 549, 115 S. Ct. 1624, 131 L. Ed. 2d 626 (1995), the Supreme Court found, for the first time in 50 years, that Congress had exceeded its power under the Commerce Clause and that a federal statute was therefore invalid. The statute in question was the Gun-Free Schools Zones Act, 18 U.S.C. § 922(q)(1)(A), which made it a federal offense "for any individual knowingly to possess a firearm at a place that the individual knows, or has reasonable cause to believe, is a school zone." *Id.*

Significantly, in affirming the Fifth Circuit Court of Appeals' finding that the Act was unconstitutional, the Supreme Court noted that it would continue to apply the rational basis test pursuant to Hodel to determine if the statute passed constitutional muster. *Lopez*, 115 S. Ct. at 1629. The Court first identified three categories of activity that Congress may properly regulate under the Commerce Clause. First, the use of the channels of interstate commerce is clearly within the powers of Congress to regulate. Second, the "instrumentalities of interstate commerce" may constitutionally be regulated. Third, it is within Congress' power to regulate those activities having a substantial relation to interstate commerce, or those activities that substantially affect interstate commerce. *Lopez* at 1629–30.

The *Lopez* Court stated that, if the Gun-Free School Zones Act was to be upheld at all, it had to pass muster under the third category as a regulation of an activity that substantially affects interstate commerce. However, the court found that the Act, as it was basically criminal in nature, had nothing to do with commerce or any economic enterprise "however broadly one might define those terms." *Id.* at 1630–31. As the Gun-Free School Zones Act did not fit into any of the three categories, it was found unconstitutional as beyond Congress' commerce power. *Id.* at 1631.

Significantly, the *Lopez* court noted that there was no evidence establishing a rational basis for determining that the possession of a firearm within a school zone may affect interstate commerce. Indeed, the Act was not precipitated by any legislative investigation into the effects the regulated activity may have on interstate commerce. *Id.* While the court acknowledged that Congress was not required to make legislative findings into the effects of the regulated activity, it nonetheless noted that, had Congress done so, it may have contributed to the Court's ability "to decide whether a rational basis existed" for Congress' determination that the activity in question would substantially affect interstate commerce, "even though no such substantial effect was visible to the naked eye." *Id.* at 1631–32. In the absence of any such findings, the court concluded that, in order to find a rational basis, it would have to "pile inference upon inference in a manner that would bid fair to convert congressional authority under the Commerce clause to a general police power of the sorts retained by the states." *Id.* at 1634. Hence, the Court held that Congress exceeded its powers under the Commerce Clause and the Act was thus invalid.

C. *Lopez* and VAWA.

Like the Gun-Free School Zones Act, VAWA is clearly not economic on the surface. Thus, if VAWA is to be found constitutional, it must also be considered within the third category of congressional powers set forth in *Lopez* as it does not affect the channels or instrumentalities of interstate commerce.

Although VAWA is not a criminal statute, it is substantially similar to the Act in question in *Lopez* in that it is essentially based on criminal activity, namely gender-based violent crime. While a few courts have been hesitant to recognize commerce effects in a criminal statute, there have been numerous post-*Lopez* decisions by federal courts upholding both criminal and civil enactments as constitutional. These enactments include gambling, *see United States v. Wall*, 1996 WL 457393 (6th Cir. 1996); carjacking, *see United States v. Soderna*, 82 F.3d 1370 (7th Cir. 1996), and *United States v. Dinwiddie*, 76 F.3d 913 (8th Cir. 1960); possession of a firearm by a felon (a subsection of the same statute that included the Gun-Free School Zones Act), *see United States v. Chesney*, 86 F.3d 564 (6th Cir. 1996); intrastate possession and/or sale of narcotics, *see United States v. Genao*, 79 F.3d 1333 (2d Cir. 1996); and numerous others.

Moreover, even though it does not regulate commercial activity per se, VAWA, unlike the Act in *Lopez*, contains extensive congressional findings into the impact of violence on interstate commerce. Congress compiled substantial documentation on this subject through numerous hearings conducted over a four-year period prior to enacting VAWA. Thus, although "to the naked eye" there may be no clear rationale for Congress to conclude that violence against women substantially affects interstate commerce, these congressional findings may offer a basis to evaluate Congress' judgment.

Congress first cited a plethora of shocking statistics into the frequency and extent of gender-based violence. *See, generally* Senate Rep. No. 103–138, Violence Against Women Act of 1993, 37 (1993); H.R. Rep. No. 103–95, Violence Against Women Act of 1993, 26 (1993). Congress also found, among other things, "that gender-based crimes and fear of gender-based crimes restrict movement, reduce employment opportunities, increase health expenditures, and reduce consumer expending, all of which affect interstate commerce and the national economy." S. Rep. No.138, at 54. Further, Congress noted that "studies report that almost 50% of rape victims lose their jobs or are forced to quit in the aftermath of the crime." *Id.* A House Conference stated that "crimes of violence motivated by gender have a substantial adverse effect on interstate commerce, by deterring potential victims from traveling interstate, from engaging in employment in interstate business, and from transacting business . . . in interstate commerce . . . ." H. Rep. No. 103–711, Violent Crime Control in Law Enforcement Act of 1994, 385 (1994).

To be certain, then, gender-based violence has at least some effect on interstate commerce. Indeed, there may, in fact, be a substantial effect, regardless of the statute's reliance on criminal, rather than strictly commercial, activity. The question that remains, however, is whether the legislative findings provide a rational basis for concluding that gender-based violence has a substantial effect on interstate commerce.

Clearly, just because Congress says that an activity affects interstate commerce does not make it so. *See Hodel*, 452 U.S. at 311. Further, "whether particular operations affect interstate commerce sufficiently to come under the constitutional powers of Congress to regulate them is ultimately a judicial rather than a legislative question." *Heart of Atlanta Motel, Inc. v. United States*, 379 U.S. 241, 273, 13 L. Ed. 2d 258, 85 S. Ct. 348 (1964).

However, as previously stated, the court is limited to the rational basis test. *Hodel*, 452 U.S. at 276.

Two district courts have come to opposite conclusions when applying the *Lopez* ruling to VAWA in light of the congressional findings set out above. In *Doe v. Doe*, 929 F. Supp. 608 (D. Conn. 1996), the district court upheld the constitutionality of VAWA. The *Doe* court distinguished *Lopez* by stating that the rationale of Congress under the Gun-Free School Zones Act could only be inferred through theoretical impact arguments. *Doe* at 613. By contrast, VAWA was enacted after four years of extensive investigation and compilation of data finding substantial effects of gender-based violence on interstate commerce. *Id.*

The *Doe* court concluded that, since *Lopez* did not overturn or limit the rationality test under *Hodel*, the numerous hearings and substantial documentation amassed by Congress evinced a rational basis for finding that gender-based violence sufficiently affected interstate commerce. *Id.* at 613. Thus, even though VAWA is predicated on criminal activity and is not clearly commercial on the surface, there was a clear rational basis for Congress' actions, making the Act valid under the Commerce Clause. *Id.*

In the opposite corner, in *Brzonkala v. Virginia Polytechnic & State Univ.*, 1996 WL 431097 (W.D. Va. 1996), the district court, without citing the *Doe* case, found VAWA to be unconstitutional. The court noted that congressional findings were not "necessary" under *Lopez*, and concluded that the absence of such findings in *Lopez* was incidental to that Court's decision. Thus, the *Brzonkala* court held that, regardless of the extensive congressional findings related to VAWA, it was up to the court to determine, based on the circumstances and common sense, whether Congress had a rational basis for concluding that gender-based violence substantially affects interstate commerce. *Id.* at 10.

The court ruled that gender-based violence, although it may affect "the national economy," does not substantially affect "interstate commerce." *Id.* at 14. Further, "undoubtedly, effects on the national economy affect interstate commerce. Such a chain of causation alone, however, is insufficient to bring an act within the purview of the commerce power." *Id.* The *Brzonkala* court ultimately concluded that a ruling otherwise would offer an unrestricted general police power to the federal government, as family law issues and most criminal issues also affect the national economy and would be subject to federal regulation, even though they are traditionally regulated by the states' police powers. *Id.* . . .

Unfortunately, in this court's view, the *Brzonkala* court adopted a far too restrictive view of *Lopez*. Indeed, the notion that gender-based violence affects the national economy and not interstate commerce does not comport with the weight of authority applying the Commerce Clause. *Cf. Katzenbach v. McClung*, 379 U.S. 294, 303, 13 L. Ed. 2d 290, 85 S. Ct. 377 (1964) (The refusal of restaurants to serve African-Americans "imposed burdens both on the interstate flow of food and upon the movement of goods in general."); *Wickard v. Filburn*, 317 U.S. 111, 128, 129, 87 L. Ed. 122, 63 S. Ct. 82 (1942) (When a farmer grows wheat for personal consumption above his allotment prescribed by federal regulations, there is an effect on interstate commerce, due to the effects on the market). Likewise, when one-half of the nation's population is potentially limited in employment, traveling, and participation in commercial spending due to the threat of violence, interstate commerce and the national economy are inevitably affected . . .

While it is true that affording undue or excessive weight to the existence of legislative findings may create an opportunity for Congress to conduct hearings and compile information merely to exhibit some rational basis for a statute, this is an unlikely scenario, so long as the courts exercise reasonableness in their analysis of legislative findings. Here, it is unlikely Congress would spend four years determining the effects of gender-based violence on interstate commerce for the sole purpose of overcoming the rationality test and the Supreme Court's decision in *Lopez*, especially since *Lopez* was decided after the congressional hearings and findings began being made. Therefore, it is apparent that, along with the circumstances surrounding the problem of gender-based violence, the legislative findings suffice under the rational basis test to place VAWA within the rubric of the Commerce Clause.

D. A Reasonable Means to an End.

Having found that Congress had a rational basis for determining that gender-based violence significantly affects interstate commerce, the question before the court turns to whether VAWA is a reasonably adapted means to the intended goal of Congress. *Hodel*, 422 U.S. at 276. While VAWA ostensibly seeks to protect the rights of women who are victims of gender-based violence, this court must again express its deep concern that the Act will effectively allow domestic relations litigation to permeate the federal courts. Issues related to domestic relations are better suited for the state courts, which have a closer relation to the concerns of their citizenry and are capable of applying state laws better suited for the needs of a particular area. Certainly Congress could have fashioned VAWA to exclude domestic relations, but such considerations are not appropriately within this court's purview. Rather, the court's consideration is limited to whether Congress' actions were a reasonable means to a constitutionally permitted end, rather than whether Congress could have drafted a better law, as the court is convinced was possible.

Congress based its findings of a need for VAWA in part on the result of the states' self-assessments of the deficiencies in their judicial systems involving injurious gender-based conduct. H. Rep. 711, at 385; S. Rep. 138, at 49. Concluding that the states did not offer adequate protection from gender-based crimes, Congress was hardly unreasonable in creating a civil rights remedy to correct such deficiencies. The same course was followed in efforts to correct other pressing social ills such as racial discrimination. Thus, while this court may disagree with the inclusiveness of VAWA, the Act itself is not an unreasonable means to the ends intended by Congress. . . .

State Claims

A. Statute of Limitations.

Defendant contends that the state actions asserted by plaintiff must be dismissed on the ground that they are barred by the one-year statute of limitations set forth in Term. Code Ann. § 28–3–104. Plaintiff's original complaint was filed with this court on August 22, 1996, one year to the day from the last of many alleged altercations between the parties.

The one-year statute of limitations for tort actions in Tennessee applies to "actions for libel, for injuries to the person, [and] false imprisonment . . . ." Tenn. Code Ann. § 28–3–104. Thus, plaintiff's claims for assault, battery, and false imprisonment must be dismissed as time-barred, with the exception of any allegations included regarding the final altercation between the parties. This alleged final assault occurred within one day of the expiration of the limitations period. All allegations of assault, battery, or intentional infliction of emotional distress occurring prior to that date are beyond the statute of limitations and, consequently, must be dismissed. [The court rejected plaintiff's arguments that the one-year statute of limitations should be tolled because defendant's repeated and prolonged acts of assault and emotional distress constituted a continuing tort, and because plaintiff was suffering from a disability by reason of mental or physical infirmity].

B. Supplemental Jurisdiction.

Even assuming plaintiff could survive the statute of limitations bar, all of her state claims must be dismissed under 28 U.S.C. § 1367. This statute gives the federal courts supplemental jurisdiction over state claims that are so related as to "form part of the same case or controversy." *Id*. This jurisdiction, however, is discretionary under certain circumstances and is not of plaintiff's right. Specifically, § 1367(c) states that:

> The district courts may decline to exercise supplemental jurisdiction over a claim under subsection (a) if —
>
> (1) the claim raises a novel or complex issue of State law,
>
> (2) the claim substantially predominates over the claim or claims over which the district court has original jurisdiction,
>
> (3) the district court has dismissed all of the claims over which it has original jurisdiction, or
>
> (4) in exceptional circumstances, there are other compelling reasons for declining jurisdiction.

The doctrine of continuing tort previously discussed certainly presents a rather novel and complex issue of state law. And since all of the personal injury torts have previously been asserted in the state court action, this court must decline to exercise supplemental jurisdiction over any claims that may exceed the applicable statute of limitations. Significantly, plaintiff will not lose these claims, since they are already pending in state court. This includes all allegations of assault, battery, false imprisonment, and intentional infliction of emotional distress that occurred prior to the final altercation.

Likewise, to the extent these torts were committed during the final altercation, they should nonetheless be dismissed, since they are, again, mirrored in the state court action. "It would serve neither the interests of judicial economy nor fundamental fairness to require [defendant] to defend itself simultaneously in two different courts on the same claims." *Lewis v. United States*, 812 F. Supp. 620, 625 (E.D. Va. 1993). As such, the court finds this to be another "compelling reason" [for declining jurisdiction] and must decline to exercise supplemental jurisdiction over any of these pendent state law claims.

This court must also refuse to exercise supplemental jurisdiction with respect to the remaining state claims of breach of fiduciary duty, fraud and conversion, and misrepresentation. These claims seem to be no more than an artful guise for presenting matters of alimony and divorce settlement to the federal court for adjudication. The Sixth Circuit has adamantly refrained from exercising jurisdiction over "matters concerning'the subject of divorce, or for the allowance of alimony.'" *Drewes v. Ilnicki*, 863 F.2d 469, 471 (6th Cir. 1988). The Sixth Circuit has also stated that "it is incumbent upon the district court to sift through the claims of the complaint to determine the true character of the dispute to be adjudicated." *Firestone v. Cleveland Trust Co.*, 654 F.2d 1212, 1216 (6th Cir. 1981).

Even though the court is of the opinion that VAWA is constitutional, this court will not allow the Act to become a gateway for domestic relations issues to slip into this federal court. VAWA itself states that the statute does not "confer on the courts of the United States jurisdiction over any State law claim seeking the establishment of a divorce, alimony, equitable distribution of marital property, or child custody." 42 U.S.C. § 13981(e)(4). Applying the Sixth Circuit's mandate for district courts to interpret the true meaning of a dispute, this court finds that the true character of the dispute in the present case is the division of marital assets, at least insofar as the state law claims regarding breach of fiduciary duty and the like are concerned. Plaintiff merely seeks to tip the equitable scales of distribution in her favor using the federal court as leverage. This is a matter to be resolved by the state courts within the divorce proceeding and must not be imported into the federal courts.

Conclusion

Therefore, for the foregoing reasons, defendant's motion to dismiss or, in the alternative, for summary judgment will be denied with respect to VAWA and granted with respect to all pendent state law claims.

NOTES AND QUESTIONS

(1) The district court's repeated concern that VAWA "will effectively allow domestic relations litigants to permeate the federal courts" prompts at least two questions. First, is the concern well-founded as a factual matter? In answering this question, consider both the state law claims included in this case and the quoted provision from VAWA that the statute does not "confer on the courts of the United States jurisdiction over any State law claim seeking the establishment of a divorce, alimony, equitable distribution of marital property, or child custody." 42 U.S.C. § 13981(e)(4). Second, to the extent that the court's concerns are factually sound, what exactly is so troubling about having the federal courts hear domestic relations cases? Do you agree with the district court that "issues related to domestic relations are better suited for the state courts, which have a closer relation to the concerns of their citizenry and are capable of applying state laws better suited for the needs of a particular area." Why or why not?

(2) In *Ankenbrandt v. Richards*, 504 U.S. 689 (1992), the Supreme Court reaffirmed the continuing validity of a narrow "domestic relations exception" to federal subject matter jurisdiction based on diversity of citizenship. The Court held that while the exemption "divests the federal courts of power to issue divorce, alimony and child custody decrees," it did not prevent a federal court from adjudicating a tort suit brought by one former spouse against the other on behalf of children alleged to have been abused. The Court also held that the exemption was not required by the Constitution, but was based on Congress' exercise of its Article III power to grant jurisdiction to the federal courts, thus leaving open the possibility that Congress could abolish the domestic relations exception if it so chose.

(3) The Violence Against Women Act is by no means the federal government's first foray into areas that have traditionally been characterized as state domestic relations law. Recall, for example, the discussion in Chapter 5 regarding Congressional efforts in the area of paternity establishment and child support enforcement. Is the federal interest in establishing

paternity or enforcing child support obligations more or less compelling than its interest in providing remedies for gender-motivated violence?

(4) Several federal courts have upheld the constitutionality of VAWA's criminal provisions directed at interstate domestic violence as a valid exercise of Congress' power under the Commerce Clause. *See, e.g., U.S. v. Bailey,* 112 F.3d 758, 765–66 (4th Cir. 1997); *U.S. v. Gluzman,* 953 F. Supp. 84, 91–92 (S.D.N.Y. 1997). *But see U.S. v. Wright,* 128 F.3d 1274 (8th Cir. 1977).

§ 6.03 Intrafamily Tort Liability

[A] Tort Claims Between Spouses

At common law, the marital unities doctrine precluded spouses from suing each other in tort. The Married Women's Property Acts, adopted in all states by the late Nineteenth Century, formally abolished the unities doctrine and allowed husbands and wives to sue each other for contract and property claims. *See generally* Riva Seigel, *The Modernization of Marital Status Law: Adjudicating Wives' Rights to Earnings, 1860–1930,* 82 Geo. L. J. 2127, 2149–57 (1994). However, the Married Women's Property Acts were held *not* to abolish the spousal immunity doctrine when it came to personal torts. *See, e.g., Thompson v. Thompson,* 218 U.S. 611, 616–17 (1910). Retention of the immunity doctrine for personal torts was justified on a number of policy grounds: (1) allowing interspousal tort litigation would destroy the "peace and harmony" of the marital home; (2) allowing such actions might encourage fraud and collusion between the spouses when the tort injury was covered by insurance; and (3) abolishing the immunity would overburden the courts with a multitude of trivial and frivolous lawsuits. *See Davis v. Davis,* 657 S.W.2d 753, 754–55 (Tenn. 1983). According to Professor Homer Clark, "the kindest thing to be said about these policy arguments is that they are frivolous," and recognition "of the insubstantiality of the arguments for the immunity has led a majority of the states to abolish it or to limit it." Homer H. Clark, 1 The Law of Domestic Relations in the United States 631–39, 632–33 (2d ed. 1987). *See also* Johnson, Comment, *Interspousal Tort Immunity: The Rule Becoming the Exception,* 27 Howard L.J. 995 (1984).

While most states have eliminated interspousal tort immunity for both negligence actions and claims of intentional physical harm, courts have had considerably more difficulty evaluating claims of severe emotional distress arising out of marriage and divorce. The following two cases illustrate the courts' divergent responses to this new generation of domestic torts.

TWYMAN v. TWYMAN
Supreme Court of Texas
855 S.W.2d 619 (1993)

CORNYN, JUSTICE

In this case we decide whether a claim for infliction of emotional distress can be brought in a divorce proceeding. Because the judgment of the court of appeals is based on negligent infliction of emotional distress, and cannot be affirmed on that or any other basis, we reverse the judgment of that court and remand this cause for a new trial in the interest of justice. TEX. R. APP. P. 180. We deem a new trial appropriate because of our recent decision that no cause of action for negligent infliction of emotional distress exists in Texas. Today, however, we expressly adopt the tort of intentional infliction of emotional distress, and hold that such a claim can be brought in a divorce proceeding.

I.

Sheila and William Twyman married in 1969. Sheila filed for divorce in 1985. She later amended her divorce petition to add a general claim for emotional harm without specifying whether the claim was based on negligent or intentional infliction of emotional distress. In her amended petition, Sheila alleged that William "intentionally and cruelly" attempted to engage her in "deviate sexual acts." Following a bench trial, the court rendered judgment dissolving the marriage, dividing the marital estate, awarding conservatorship of the children to Sheila, ordering William to pay child support, and awarding Sheila $15,000 plus interest for her claim for emotional distress. William appealed that portion of the judgment based on emotional distress, contending that interspousal tort immunity precluded Sheila's recovery for negligent infliction of emotional distress. The court of appeals affirmed the judgment, holding that Sheila could recover for William's negligent infliction of emotional distress. 790 S.W.2d 819.

While this case has been pending, we have refused to adopt the tort of negligent infliction of emotional distress. See *Boyles v. Kerr*, 855 S.W.2d 593 (Tex. 1993). Thus the judgment of the court of appeals cannot be affirmed. We consider, therefore, whether the court of appeals' judgment may be affirmed on alternative grounds. Because Sheila's pleadings alleging a general claim for emotional harm are broad enough to encompass a claim for intentional infliction of emotional distress, we consider whether the trial court's judgment may be sustained on that legal theory.

While this court has never expressly recognized the tort of intentional infliction of emotional distress, we found no reversible error in the court of appeals' opinion in *Tidelands Automobile Club v. Walters*, which did so. 699 S.W.2d 939 (Tex. App.—Beaumont 1985, writ ref'd n.r.e.). There, the court of appeals adopted the elements of the tort as expressed in the Restatement (Second) of Torts § 46 (1965). The Restatement elements of intentional infliction of emotional distress are: 1) the defendant acted intentionally or recklessly, 2) the conduct was extreme and outrageous, 3) the actions of the defendant caused the plaintiff emotional distress, and 4) the emotional distress suffered by the plaintiff was severe. *Id.* According to the Restatement, liability for outrageous conduct should be found "only where the conduct has been so outrageous in character, and so extreme in degree, as to go beyond all possible bounds of decency, and to be regarded as atrocious, and utterly intolerable in a civilized community." *Id.* cmt. d. Of the forty-six states that have recognized this tort, forty-three have adopted this Restatement formulation. The other three states, although not adopting the Restatement definition, require the equivalent of "outrageous" conduct. Today we become the forty-seventh state to adopt the tort of intentional infliction of emotional distress as set out in § 46 (1) of the Restatement (Second) of Torts.

We do not, however, adopt this tort only because of its broad acceptance in jurisdictions throughout the United States. As distinguished from the tort of negligent infliction of emotional distress, we believe the rigorous legal standards of the Restatement formulation of intentional infliction of emotional distress help to assure a meaningful delineation between inadvertence and intentionally or recklessly outrageous misconduct. The requirements of intent, extreme and outrageous conduct, and severe emotional distress before liability can be established will, we think, strike a proper balance between diverse interests in a free society. That balance, at minimum, must allow freedom of individual action while providing reasonable opportunity for redress for victims of conduct that is determined to be utterly intolerable in a civilized community. . . .

II.

We now consider whether the cause of action for intentional infliction of emotional distress may be brought in a divorce proceeding. In *Bounds v. Caudle*, this court unanimously abolished the doctrine of interspousal immunity for intentional torts. 560 S.W.2d 925 (Tex. 1977). Ten years later, we abrogated interspousal immunity "completely as to any cause of action," including negligence actions for personal injuries. *Price v. Price*, 732 S.W.2d 316, 319 (Tex. 1987). Under the rules established in *Caudle and Price*, there appears to be no legal impediment to bringing a tort claim in a divorce action based on either negligence or an intentional act such as assault or battery. The more difficult issue is when the tort claim must be brought and how the tort award should be considered when making a "just and right" division of the marital estate. *See* Tex. Fam. Code § 3.63(b). Of the states that have answered this question, several have held that the tort case and the divorce case must be litigated separately. *See e.g., Walther v. Walther*, 709 P.2d 387, 388 (Utah 1985); *Windauer v. O'Connor*, 107 Ariz. 267, 485 P.2d 1157 (Ariz. 1971); *Simmons v. Simmons*, 773 P.2d 602, 605 (Colo. Ct. App. 1988). Other states require joinder of the two actions. *See, e.g. Tevis v. Tevis*, 79 N.J. 422, 400 A.2d 1189, 1196 (N.J. 1979); *Weil v. Lammon*, 503 So. 2d 830, 832 (Ala. 1987).

We believe that the best approach lies between these two extremes. As in other civil actions, joinder of the tort cause of action should be permitted, but subject to the principles of res judicata. Of course, how such claims are ultimately tried is within the sound discretion of the trial court. But joinder of tort claims with the divorce, when feasible, is encouraged. Resolving both the tort and divorce actions in the same proceeding avoids two trials based at least in part on the same facts, and settles in one suit "all matters existing between the parties." *Mogford*, 616 S.W.2d at 940 (citing *Parkhill Produce Co. v. Pecos Valley S. Ry.*, 348 S.W.2d 208, 209 (Tex. Civ. App.—San Antonio 1961) *writ ref'd n.r.e. per curiam*, 352 S.W.2d 723 (Tex. 1961). When a tort action is tried with the divorce, however, it is imperative that the court avoid awarding a double recovery. When dividing the marital estate, the court may take into account several factors, including the fault of the parties if pleaded. The trial court may also consider "such factors as the spouses' capacities and abilities, benefits which the party not at fault would have derived from continuation of the marriage, business opportunities, education, relative physical conditions, relative financial condition and obligations, disparity of ages, size of separate estates, and the nature of the property." *Id*. However, a spouse should not be allowed to recover tort damages and a disproportionate division of the community estate based on the same conduct. Therefore, when a factfinder awards tort damages to a divorcing spouse, the court may not consider the same tortious acts when dividing the marital estate. . . .

Sheila Twyman cannot recover based on the findings of fact made by the trial court in this case. It is likely, however, that this case proceeded on a theory of negligent infliction of emotional distress in reliance on this court's holding in *St. Elizabeth Hospital v. Garrard*,

730 S.W.2d 649 (Tex. 1987), which we recently overruled. See *Boyles v. Kerr*, 855 S.W.2d 593 (Tex. 1992). As we noted in *Boyles*, this court has broad discretion to remand for a new trial in the interest of justice when it appears that a case proceeded under the wrong legal theory, and when it appears that the facts when developed on retrial may support recovery on an alternative theory. . . . Therefore, in the interest of justice, we reverse the judgment of the court of appeals and remand this cause to the trial court for a new trial.

ROSE SPECTOR, JUSTICE, dissenting:

Over five years ago, a trial court issued a divorce decree that included an award to Sheila Twyman of $ 15,000 for the years of abuse she had suffered at the hands of her husband. At the time, the award was consistent with prevailing Texas law. Today, the plurality sets aside the trial court's award and sends Sheila Twyman back to start the process over in a new trial. Because justice for Sheila Twyman has been both delayed and denied, I dissent.

I.

At trial, Sheila testified that her husband, William Twyman, introduced bondage activities into their relationship after their marriage. Sheila told William that she could not endure these activities because of the trauma of having been raped several years earlier. She also informed William that she had been cut with a knife during the rape, and had been placed in fear for her life. Although William understood that Sheila equated bondage with her prior experience of being raped, he told Sheila that if she would not satisfy his desires by engaging in bondage, there would be no future to their marriage.

As a result, Sheila experienced "utter despair" and "devastation," as well as physical problems—weight loss and, after one encounter, prolonged bleeding that necessitated gynecological treatment. The pain and humiliation of the bondage activity caused her to seek help from three professional counselors.

The trial court found that William "engaged in a continuing course of conduct of attempting to coerce [Sheila] to join in his practices of 'bondage' by continually asserting that [their] marriage could be saved only by [Sheila] participating with [William] in his practices of 'bondage' " The trial court also determined that Sheila's suffering was certainly foreseeable from William's continuing course of conduct, "in light of his existing knowledge of her long-existing emotional state, which was caused by her having been forcibly raped prior to their marriage." Finally, the trial court found that Sheila's mental anguish was a direct proximate result of William's sexual practices.

Based on the pleadings, evidence, and arguments, the trial court concluded that the facts and the law supported Sheila's recovery of $ 15,000 for William's negligent infliction of emotional distress. The court of appeals, in an opinion by Justice Gammage, affirmed the trial court's judgment under prevailing tort law and noted that this court had expressly approved the recovery of damages on a negligence claim in a divorce action. 790 S.W.2d 819, 823 (citing *Price v. Price*, 732 S.W.2d 316 (Tex. 1987)).

This court, however, has now rejected Texas law established to provide redress for injuries of the kind inflicted by William Twyman. While allowing some tort claims to be brought in a divorce action, the plurality forbids recovery for negligent infliction of emotional distress, and insists that Sheila Twyman proceed on a theory of intentional infliction of emotional distress.

II.

Today's decision is handed down contemporaneously with the overruling of the motion for rehearing in *Boyles v. Kerr*, 855 S.W.2d 593 (Tex. 1992), in which this court reversed a judgment in favor of a woman who was surreptitiously videotaped during intercourse, then subjected to humiliation and ridicule when the tape was displayed to others. In *Boyles*, as in this case, a majority of this court has determined that severe, negligently-inflicted emotional distress does not warrant judicial relief—no matter how intolerable the injurious conduct. The reasoning originally articulated in *Boyles*, and now implied in this case, is that "tort law cannot and should not attempt to provide redress for every instance of rude, insensitive, or distasteful behavior"; providing such relief, the *Boyles* majority explained, "would dignify most disputes far beyond their social importance." 36 Tex. S. Ct.J. 231, 233–234 (Dec. 2, 1992).

Neither of these cases involves "rude, insensitive, or distasteful behavior"; they involve grossly offensive conduct that was appropriately found to warrant judicial relief. The decision in *Boyles* overturns well-reasoned case law, and I strongly agree with the dissenting opinion in that case. For the same reasons, I strongly disagree with the plurality here; the rule embodied in *Boyles* is no less objectionable when applied to the facts of this case. Sheila Twyman is entitled to recover the amount awarded by the trial court for the injuries inflicted by her husband.

III.

It is no coincidence that both this cause and *Boyles* involve serious emotional distress claims asserted by women against men. From the beginning, tort recovery for infliction of emotional distress has developed primarily as a means of compensating women for injuries inflicted by men insensitive to the harm caused by their conduct. In "the leading case which broke through the shackles," a man amused himself by falsely informing a woman that her husband had been gravely injured, causing a serious and permanent shock to her nervous system. *Wilkinson v. Downton*, 2 Q.B.D. 57 (1897). Similarly, in the watershed Texas case, a man severely beat two others in the presence of a pregnant woman, who suffered a miscarriage as a result of her emotional distress. *Hill v. Kimball*, 76 Tex. 210, 13 S.W. 59 (1890). By World War II, the pattern was well-established: one survey of psychic injury claims found that the ratio of female to male plaintiffs was five to one. Hubert Winston Smith, *Relation of Emotions to Injury and Disease: Legal Liability for Psychic Stimuli*, 30 Va. L. Rev. 193 (1944). Even today, when emotional distress claims by both sexes have become more widely accepted, women's claims against men predominate. Of the thirty-four Texas cases cited by the plurality—all decided since 1987—women's claims outnumbered men's by a ratio of five to four; and only four of the thirty-four involved any female defendants. Of those cases involving relations between two individuals—with no corporations involved—five involved a woman's claim against a man; none involved a man's claim against a woman.

I do not argue that women alone have an interest in recovery for emotional distress. However, since the overwhelming majority of emotional distress claims have arisen from harmful conduct by men, rather than women, I do argue that men have had a disproportionate interest in downplaying such claims.

Like the struggle for women's rights, the movement toward recovery for emotional distress has been long and tortuous. *See* Peter A. Bell, *The Bell Tolls: Toward Full Tort Recovery for Psychic Injury*, 36 U. Fla. L. Rev. 333, 336–40 (1984). In the judicial system dominated by men, emotional distress claims have historically been marginalized:

> The law of torts values physical security and property more highly than emotional security and human relationships. This apparently gender-neutral hierarchy of values has privileged men, as the traditional owners and managers of property, and has burdened women, to whom the emotional work of maintaining human relationships has commonly been assigned. The law has often failed to compensate women for recurring harms—serious though they may be in the lives of women—for which there is no precise masculine analogue.

Martha Chamallas and Linda K. Kerber, *Women, Mothers, and the Law of Fright: A History*, 88 Mich. L. Rev. 814 (1990). Even Prosser recognizes the role of gender in the historical treatment of claims like that involved in *Hill v. Kimball*: "It is not difficult to discover in the earlier opinions a distinctly masculine astonishment that any woman should ever allow herself to be frightened or shocked into a miscarriage." W. Page Keeton et al., Prosser and Keeton on the Law of Torts § 12, at 55–56 (5th ed. 1984).

Given this history, the plurality's emphatic rejection of infliction of emotional distress claims based on negligence is especially troubling. Today, when the widespread mistreatment of women is being documented throughout the country—for instance, in the areas of sexual harassment and domestic violence —a majority of this court takes a step backward and abolishes one way of righting this grievous wrong. . . .

V.

While the plurality would allow some possibility of recovery for injuries like Sheila Twyman's, the dissenting opinions by Chief Justice Phillips and Justice Hecht would allow none at all. Adopting the medieval view of marital relations, Chief Justice Phillips argues that spouses should be shielded from liability for even the most outrageous acts against one another. This view echoes William Twyman's assertion at trial that, by consenting to marriage, Sheila Twyman assumed the risk of physical injury and emotional harm. Fortunately, in Texas, this archaic view has been soundly rejected; interspousal immunity has been abolished "completely as to any cause of action." *Price v. Price*, 732 S.W.2d 316, 320 (Tex. 1987). Insulating spouses from liability, we have noted, "would amount to a repudiation of the constitutional guarantee of equal protection of the laws." *Id.* Thus, recovery for intentional infliction of emotional distress should be available to spouses and non-spouses alike, as other states have recognized.

Justice Hecht not only agrees that spouses should have special protection from liability, but further argues that recovery for intentional infliction of emotional distress should never be allowed in any case. In Justice Hecht's view, the tort set out in section 46 of the Restatement is "too broad a rubric to describe actionable conduct, as this case illustrates." . . . Cases from the forty-six jurisdictions that recognize this tort comprise a unified body of law that would suggest otherwise. As Justice Hecht acknowledges, claims under section 46 are "seldom successful"; defendants have been held subject to liability only in those instances in which the defendant's conduct was clearly "beyond the bounds of decency." Unlike Justice Hecht, I believe the judicial system is fully capable of distinguishing trivial acts from those acts that are sufficiently outrageous to warrant relief. . . .

THOMAS R. PHILLIPS, CHIEF JUSTICE, concurring and dissenting:

I join in the Court's recognition of the tort of intentional infliction of emotional distress. . . .

In recognizing this tort, however, I would not extend it to actions between spouses or former spouses for conduct occurring during their marriage. Although this Court has abolished interspousal immunity, it does not necessarily follow that all conduct actionable between strangers is automatically actionable between spouses. Several courts in other jurisdictions have expressly made such a reservation when abolishing interspousal immunity. For example, the Utah Supreme Court wrote in abolishing interspousal immunity:

> The marriage relation is created by the consent of both of the parties; inherently within such relationship is the consent of both parties to physical contacts with the other, personal dealings and ways of living which would be unpermitted and in some cases unlawful as between other persons.

Stoker v. Stoker, 616 P.2d 590, 592 (Utah 1980). In accordance with these sentiments, I believe that a tort which is grounded solely on a duty not to inflict emotional distress should not be cognizable in the context of marriage.

Married couples share an intensely personal and intimate relationship. When discord arises, it is inevitable that the parties will suffer emotional distress, often severe. In the present case, for example, Ms. Twyman testified that she suffered "utter despair" and "fell apart" upon learning that her husband was seeing another woman. She further testified that "the mental anguish was unbelievable to realize, hoping every time, when he went off to Houston, that he was just going to fly and not be with her." Yet Ms. Twyman seeks no recovery for this distress, and apparently cannot do so under Texas law. In such circumstances, the fact finder is left to draw a virtually impossible distinction between recoverable and disallowed injuries.

Furthermore, recognition of this tort in the context of a divorce unnecessarily restricts the trial court's discretion in dividing the marital estate. Prior to today's opinion, the trial court could, but was not required to, consider fault in dividing the community property. *See Murff v. Murff*, 615 S.W.2d 696, 698 (Tex. 1981). The court had broad discretion to weigh any fault along with other appropriate factors, such as relative financial condition, disparity of ages, and the needs of the children. *Id.* at 698–699. Now, however, where fault takes the form of "outrageous" conduct intentionally or recklessly inflicted, it becomes a dominant factor that must be considered at the expense of the other factors. Unlike battery, fraud, or other torts resting on more objective conduct, a colorable allegation of intentional infliction of emotional distress could arguably be raised by one or both parties in most intimate relationships. . . .

Perhaps because of these difficulties, the tort of intentional infliction of emotional distress has not been generally recognized in the marital context. Although most states, like Texas, have abolished interspousal immunity, it appears that, until today, only two state supreme courts have expressly held that intentional infliction of emotional distress may be applied to marital conduct. *See Henriksen, supra* [*Hendriksen v. Cameron*, 622 A.2d 1135, 1151 (Me. 1993)], *Davis v. Bostick*, 282 Ore. 667, 580 P.2d 544 (Or. 1978). Moreover, these two decisions do not appear to represent typical actions for the recovery of emotional distress damages. In *Henriksen*, the husband inflicted on his wife not only verbal abuse but also physical attacks, including multiple assaults and rapes. 622 A.2d at 1139. Similarly in *Bostick*, the husband broke his wife's nose, choked her, and threatened her with a loaded pistol. 580 P.2d at 545–46. To the extent that emotional distress results from a physical attack or threat of attack, it is already compensable under tort theories previously recognized in Texas. . . .

Just as I join the Court's decision to recognize a tort now available in nearly every American jurisdiction, I depart from the Court's decision to extend that tort to a type of dispute where it is not generally applied in other states. I fail to understand how, lexigraphically or logically, it can be "medieval" or "archaic" to decline to adopt a position which has been expressly embraced by only two other state supreme courts. . . . (Spector, J., dissenting). I therefore would reverse the judgment of the court of appeals and render judgment that Sheila Twyman take nothing on her tort claim.

NATHAN L. HECHT, JUSTICE, concurring and dissenting:

[In Part I of his opinion, Justice Hecht takes issue with the majority's general recognition of the tort of intentional infliction of emotional distress.] . . .

The standard of outrageousness is certainly no easier to apply in the marital context than in other contexts, as the facts of this case illustrate. Sheila Twyman's claim of intentional infliction of emotional distress is based upon the following testimony at trial, which was mostly undisputed. William, a Navy pilot, and Sheila, a college graduate with a degree in nursing, were married in 1969. In 1975, on two or three occasions at William's suggestion, the couple engaged in what they referred to as "light bondage"—tying each other to the bed with neckties during their sexual relations. Sheila testified that William did not force her to participate in these activities. After the last occasion Sheila told William she did not like this activity and did not want to participate in it further. She revealed to him that she associated the activities with the horrible experience of having been raped at knifepoint earlier in her life. William never again suggested that she engage in the activities, nor was the subject discussed again for ten years. In 1985 Sheila inadvertently discovered that William was consulting with a psychologist. When she asked him why, he told her that he was involved with another woman. William told Sheila that if she could only have done bondage, nothing else would have mattered. For the remainder of the year the couple sought counseling. At times during this period William made derogatory remarks to Sheila about her sexual ability, comparing her to his girl friend. On their counselor's advice, William and Sheila discussed William's bondage fantasies, and Sheila again tried to participate in bondage activities with William. But she found the activity so painful and humiliating that she could not continue it. Their last encounter, which did not include bondage activities, was so rough that she was injured to the point of bleeding. At one point Sheila was distressed to discover that their ten-year-old son had found magazines William kept hidden, which portrayed sadomasochistic activities. Eleven months after she first learned of William's affair, Sheila separated from him and filed for divorce. Throughout that period, Sheila testified, she experienced utter despair, devastation, pain, humiliation and weight loss because of William's affair and her feelings that the marriage could have survived if only she had engaged in bondage activities.

To recover damages Sheila must prove that William's conduct was outrageous—that is, "extreme", "beyond all possible bounds of decency", "atrocious", and "utterly intolerable in a civilized community." Although outrageousness is, according to the plurality opinion and the Restatement, a question for the court in the first instance, this Court refuses to say whether William's conduct was or was not outrageous. If it was not, as a matter of law, then there is no need to remand this case for further proceedings. If William's conduct was outrageous, or if that issue must be decided by a jury, then it is unclear what components of the conflict between Sheila and William were actionable. There is no question from the record that Sheila claims to have suffered bitterly, but there appear to have been three causes: William's affair, his interest in bondage, and the breakup of the marriage. If the first or last causes constitute outrageous behavior, then there a tort claim may be urged successfully in most divorces. Allowing recovery based upon the first cause of Sheila's emotional distress is simply to revive the old action for alienation of affections abolished by the Legislature. I doubt whether the Court intends this result. If William's outrageous conduct was attempting to interest Sheila in sexual conduct which he considered enjoyable but she, in her words, "did not like", then again, this tort may be very broad indeed.

The sexual relationship is among the most intimate aspects of marriage. People's concepts of a beneficial sexual relationship vary widely, and spouses may expect that some accommodation of each other's feelings will be necessary for their mutual good. Any breach of such an intimate and essential part of marriage may be regarded as outrageous by the aggrieved spouse and will often be the cause of great distress. There are many other aspects of marriage which are likewise sensitive. How money is to be spent, how children are to be raised, and how time is to be allocated are only a few of the many areas of conflict in a marriage. Not infrequently disagreements over these matters are deep and contribute to the breakup of the marriage. If all are actionable, then tort claims will be commonplace in divorce cases, and judges and juries with their own deeply felt beliefs about what is proper in a marital relationship will face the hard task of deciding whether one spouse or another behaved outrageously with no standards but their own to guide.

The inquiry which must be made to determine whether a spouse's conduct is outrageous entails too great an intrusion into the marital relationship. Although courts are already called upon to consider fault in divorce actions, allowance of tort claims requires a more pervasive inspection of spouses' private lives than should be permissible. In this case the parties were called to testify in detail and at length about the most private moments of their marriage. If the court's only concern were the degree to which a spouse's fault had contributed to the demise of the marriage, the inquiry into each spouse's conduct need not have been so detailed. To recover damages, however, Sheila was required to testify at length before a jury, and to rebut her claim, William was obliged to answer in equal detail. The prospect of such testimony in many divorces is too great an invasion of spouses' interests in privacy, and promises to make divorce more acrimonious and injurious than it already is. . . .

IV.

Finally, I must say a word in response to JUSTICE SPECTOR's dissenting opinion, the principal thesis of which is that the Court has denied recovery for negligent infliction of emotional distress in this case because of an institutional bias against women. "It is no coincidence", JUSTICE SPECTOR'scontends, that both this case and *Boyles v. Kerr*, 855 S.W.2d 593 (Tex. 1993), involve claims for emotional distress by women against men. . . . Actually, it is just that: a coincidence.

It is a further coincidence that another case we decide today, *Valenzuela v. Aquino*, 853 S.W.2d 512 (Tex. 1993), in which we also deny recovery for negligent infliction of emotional distress, does not involve claims solely by women against men. That case involves a claim by Dr. Aquino and his family for damages caused by anti-abortion picketers demonstrating in front of his home. Our refusal to allow recovery for negligent infliction of emotional distress in *Valenzuela* contradicts JUSTICE SPECTOR'S assertions of bias. . . .

Further, JUSTICE SPECTOR'S assertions are somewhat antagonistic toward one another. She states: "In the judicial system dominated by men, emotional distress claims have historically been marginalized." . . . She also claims, however: "From the beginning, tort recovery for infliction of emotional distress has developed primarily as a means of compensating women for injuries inflicted by men insensitive to the harm caused by their conduct." . . . It is not entirely clear how the justice system can have developed a tort primarily to compensate claims by women at the same time that the system was dominated by men intent upon marginalizing women's claims. JUSTICE SPECTOR herself states that "neither the Fort Worth Court of Appeals, nor any of the other courts at the time [in 1918] were primarily concerned with protecting women's rights." . . . If, as I will concede, the justice system has been historically dominated by men, and if, as I am willing to assume, those men were not always sympathetic to women's claims, then development of theories for recovering damages for emotional distress cannot have been due primarily to a desire to compensate women. There must be other factors which better explain the development of the law.

There is evidence of such factors. It cannot be denied that differentiations have been drawn between the emotional distress suffered by men and that suffered by women. Some early cases and commentaries explicitly recognized the distinction between a female plaintiff and a male plaintiff suffering a similar injury, and commentators indicated that the gender of the plaintiff is one of the relevant factors in determining liability. *See, e.g., Fort Worth & Rio Grande Ry. Co. v. Bryant*, 210 S.W. 556 (Tex. Civ. App.—Fort Worth 1918) (in which a daughter recovered for exposure to coarse language in a train depot, but her father did not); Calvert Magruder, *Mental and Emotional Disturbance in the Law of Torts*, 49 Harv. L. Rev. 1033, 1046 (1936) (suggesting that the plaintiff's gender should play a part in the determination of defendant's liability). Prosser stated the idea clearly: "There is a difference between violent and vile profanity addressed to a lady, and the same language to a Butte miner and a United States marine." William L. Prosser, *Intentional Infliction of Mental Suffering: A New Tort*, 37 Mich. L. Rev. 874, 887 (1939)(footnote omitted). This language was modified to reflect the "eggshell plaintiff" concept in the comment c to section 48 of the Restatement, which states that "language addressed to a pregnant or sick woman may be actionable where the same words would not be if they were addressed to a United States Marine."

One may argue that these attempted differentiations of emotional distress reflect a patronizing view of women. Or one may also argue that the differentiations were drawn without particular regard for gender. But there is no evidence that ensuring recovery for uniquely female claims, because of any uniquely female characteristics, has been a primary factor in recognizing recovery for such injuries. The earliest cases to hold defendants liable for the infliction of mental suffering involved common carriers and innkeepers who were held to have breached an implied contract to be polite. W. Page Keeton, et al., Prosser and Keeton on the Law of Torts, § 12, at 57 (5th ed. 1984). Neither the cases nor the commentaries gives any indication that women more frequently pursued this cause of action. . . .

Even from this very abbreviated overview, to the extent that any pattern can be discerned in this history, it is not one of a struggle for recognition of women's rights, but of either a condescending and patronizing view of women, or a development of the law without particular regard for gender. Arguments for allowance of claims for emotional distress owe their support to far more factors than the relationships between men and women. The tort the Court recognizes today will have marked impact on marital relationships, but it will have far broader impact on the many other relationships it will affect. To assert, as JUSTICE SPECTOR does, that the principal effect of today's decision falls upon women, overlooks the broader reality which, as I have explained, is the basis for my concern.

For all the foregoing reasons, I dissent from the opinion and judgment of the Court.

NOTES AND QUESTIONS

(1) As the opinions in *Twyman* suggest, courts and commentators are divided over the desirability of recognizing tort claims based on the infliction of emotional distress during marriage and other intimate relationships. *See generally* Ira Mark Ellman & Stephen D. Sugarman, *Spousal Emotional Abuse As A Tort?*, 55 Md. L. Rev. 1268 (1996) (exploring arguments for and against recognition and urging that spousal emotional abuse *not* be recognized as a tort, unless the abusive behavior is also criminal); Constance W. Cole, *Intentional Infliction of Emotional Distress Among Family Members*, 61 Denv. L. J. 553 (1984) (arguing in favor of recognizing tort claims for outrageous marital conduct that leads to serious emotional injury). In their article, Professors Ellman and Sugarman discuss several of the concerns raised by the concurring Justices in *Twyman*; that the legal system lacks coherent and administrable standards for determining what constitutes "outrageous" behavior in the marital setting, and that, if outrageous conduct is defined broadly, such claims may be urged successfully in most divorces. Do you share these concerns? If so, do you see them as valid reasons for refusing to recognize this category of tort claims?

(2) Professors Ellman and Sugarman also argue that judicial recognition of claims for spousal emotional abuse seems inconsistent with the goals of no-fault divorce, which avoids assigning blame and eschews close inquiry into the circumstances leading to the breakdown of marriage. *Spousal Emotional Abuse, above* at 1285–86. The history and philosophy of no-fault divorce are discussed more fully in Chapter 9 *below*. To the extent that Ellman and Sugarman are correct about the inconsistency, does the advent of claims for divorce-related torts reflect dissatisfaction with a divorce regime that ignores or de-emphasizes fault?

(3) As the opinions in *Twyman* suggest, the adjudication of tort claims arising out of marriage and divorce raises a number of procedural complications, including questions regarding joinder of claims, res judicata and issue preclusion, and the availability of a jury trial. Note that these procedural difficulties apply to all tort claims asserted by divorcing (or divorced) spouses, not just to claims of emotional abuse. For discussion of these procedural issues, see e.g. Barbara G. Fines, *Joinder of Tort Claims in Divorce Actions*, 12 J. Am. Acad. Matrimonial Law 285 (1994); Andrew Schepard, *Divorce, Interspousal*

Torts, and Res Judicata, 24 Fam. L. Q. 127 (1990); Barbara H. Young, Note, *Interspousal Torts and Divorce: Problems, Policies, Procedures*, 27 J. Fam. L. 489 (1989).

(4) The plurality opinion in *Twyman* allows recovery for intentional infliction of emotional distress, but not for negligent conduct that results in similar harms. Do you agree with the plurality that "the rigorous legal standards of the Restatement formulation of intentional infliction of emotional distress help to assure a meaningful delineation between inadvertence and intentionally or recklessly outrageous misconduct" and thus "strike a proper balance between diverse interests in a free society." Why or why not?

(5) Imagine that you are the judge assigned to hear Sheila Twyman's case on remand. Based on the facts given in the opinion, has she satisfied the requirements for intentional infliction of emotional distress, as expressed in the Restatement (Second) of Torts §46 (1)? Are there additional facts that would be relevant to your determination? If this were a jury trial, would you send the case to the jury? Why or why not?

(6) Although the holding of *Twyman* is determined by the plurality opinion, the sharpest disagreement in the case is between the dissenting and concurring Justices. Among other things, these Justices disagree about the relevance of gender. Dissenting Justice Rose Spector sees gender as an important element of the case; she argues that tort law's traditional emphasis on physical security and property interests—as opposed to emotional security and human relationships—has disproportionately favored men and burdened women, who have commonly shouldered the emotional work of maintaining relationships. Justice Spector also suggests that men may have a particular interest in downplaying claims for emotional distress, since the overwhelming majority of such claims "have arisen from harmful conduct of men, rather than women." In light of this history, Justice Spector suggests that the plurality's refusal to recognize claims based on negligent infliction of emotional distress reflects a lack of understanding of Sheila Twyman's situation and represents a "step backward" in the legal system's treatment of women. Justice Hecht, in his concurring and dissenting opinion, takes strong issue with these views. He disputes the existence of an historical connection between women's interests and the recognition of claims for emotional distress and he asserts that any current association between emotional distress claims and female plaintiffs is simply a coincidence. Justice Hecht concludes that arguments for and against the allowance of claims for emotional distress rest implicate more and broader factors than the relationships between men and women. Which Justice's arguments do you find more persuasive and why? In fashioning rules to govern family relationships, should judges think about whether the rules are likely to affect men and women differently? About how the rules are likely to affect the relationships between men and women? Why or why not?

(7) Feminist torts scholars have echoed Justice Spector's concerns that the traditional rules governing tort liability have tended reflect values and life patterns predominately associated with men, and that the prevailing categories of compensable harms have discounted the injuries that are incurred disproportionately by women. For an introduction to this scholarship, see Leslie Bender, *An Overview of Feminist Torts Scholarship*, 78 Cornell L. Rev. 575 (1993). For more recent examples, see, e.g. 'Jane E. Larson, *"Imagine Her Satisfaction": The Transformative Task of Feminist Tort Work*, 33 Washburn L.J. 56 (1993); Lucinda Finley, *Tort Reform: An Important Issue for Women*, 10 Circles 3 (1993); Joan L. Neisser, *School Officials: Parents or Protectors? The Contribution of a Feminist Perspective*, 39 Wayne L. Rev. 1507 (1993). *See also* Robin West, Caring for Justice 94–178

(1997) (arguing that law has traditionally failed to address the harms suffered distinctively or disproportionately by women, particular those inflicted in intimate relationships).

PICKERING v. PICKERING
Supreme Court of South Dakota
434 N.W.2d 758 (1989)

WUEST, JUSTICE

Paul S. Pickering (Paul), brought an action against his estranged wife, Jody M. Pickering (Jody), and her paramour, Thomas Kimball (Tom). Paul's complaint alleged alienation of affections and tortious interference with a marital contract against Tom, fraud and deceit and negligent misrepresentation against Jody, and intentional infliction of emotional distress against both Jody and Tom. The trial court granted summary judgment in favor of Jody and Tom on all causes of action except the cause of action alleging alienation of affections against Tom. From the order of the trial court, Paul appeals. Tom raises by notice of review that part of the trial court's order denying his motion for summary judgment on the cause of action alleging alienation of affections. We affirm.

Paul and Jody were married on February 14, 1981. Sometime thereafter, Jody became acquainted with Tom at work and the two developed a platonic relationship.

In January, 1984, Jody and Tom traveled together to Tampa, Florida. Jody desired to go to Tampa to visit a friend, but wanted a traveling companion with whom she could share the expenses of the trip. Since Tom previously resided in Tampa, Jody asked him if he would be interested in accompanying her. The two spent very little time together in Florida.

During and after the trip, Tom perceived that Jody was unhappy. He approached this topic with her by asking if she was "ninety-nine percent happy with her life." Jody responded that she wasn't even ninety percent happy and indicated that romance was no longer present in her marriage. Although Jody expressed that she loved Paul, she felt that her affection for him was not as strong as it previously had been.

In late February, 1984, Tom mentioned to Jody that he had written a song about their trip to Florida and invited her to his apartment to hear it. Jody and Tom arranged to go to Tom's apartment after work. After they arrived at the apartment, the two sat on the floor together and began kissing, which ultimately led to sexual intercourse. Thereafter, their sexual liaisons continued for several months until Jody broke off the relationship because of her feelings of guilt.

Tom and Jody subsequently resumed and discontinued their relationship several times. Although Jody usually broke off relations with Tom out of her overwhelming sense of guilt, she always initiated the resumption of their relationship because of her deep affection for Tom and her desire to be with him.

Jody again broke off her relationship with Tom in January, 1985. Shortly thereafter, she discovered that she was pregnant. She was certain that Tom was the father of the child she was carrying because sexual relations between her and Paul had been infrequent. After Jody learned she was pregnant, she seduced Paul and had sexual intercourse with him. Jody wanted Paul to believe he was the child's father. She also desired to avoid hurting Paul and to preserve their marriage. Several weeks later, Jody indicated to Paul that she was experiencing symptoms of pregnancy. A home pregnancy test confirmed these "suspicions."

Paul was surprised by the test results, but he was nonetheless pleased by them. In fact, he was so ecstatic about Jody's being pregnant that he "shouted it to the world."

Two months after the advent of her pregnancy, Jody again resumed her sexual relationship with Tom and continued it until two weeks prior to the birth of her daughter. During this time, Tom was under the impression that Jody was pregnant with Paul's child.

Jody gave birth to a daughter on September 15, 1985. She and Tom continued to see each other, but they did not resume their sexual relationship until nearly two months had passed. Although Jody maintained her silence about the child's paternity following its birth, it was during this period of time that Tom noticed a family trait in the baby's toes. He then confronted Jody about the paternity of the child and she admitted that Paul was not the father and that he was.

Upon learning this, Tom insisted that he be responsible for raising the child and that Paul be immediately notified of the child's true paternity. Jody hesitated to tell Paul that he was not the child's father because she did not want to hurt him, but she finally disclosed this fact to him on January 21, 1986. Subsequent paternity testing confirmed that Tom was the father of the child.

Paul and Jody attempted to reconcile their marriage and visited a marriage counselor. This attempt, however, was unsuccessful and Jody and the baby moved into a separate apartment.

On July 29, 1986, Paul commenced a suit for divorce against Jody and the present action against Jody and Tom alleging intentional infliction of emotional distress, fraud and deceit, negligent misrepresentation, tortious interference with a marital contract, and alienation of affections. Motions for summary judgment were submitted by defendants and plaintiff on May 1, 1987, and May 15, 1987, respectively. After a hearing, the trial court granted summary judgment in favor of Jody on all causes of action and in favor of Tom on all causes of action except alienation of affections. Paul's motion for summary judgment was denied. It is from these orders that Paul and Tom now appeal.

We first address the trial court's granting summary judgment in favor of Jody and Tom on the cause of action alleging intentional infliction of emotional distress. We believe the tort of intentional infliction of emotional distress should be unavailable as a matter of public policy when it is predicated on conduct which leads to the dissolution of a marriage. Furthermore, the law of this state already provides a remedy for this type of claim in the form of an action against the paramour for alienation of affections.

We next examine Paul's allegation of fraud and deceit against Jody. Paul contends that Jody intentionally kept him "in the dark regarding the illicit affair and the true paternity of the child" and caused him to "profess to his friends, family, and his church" that he was the child's natural father. As a result of these declarations, Paul suffered "untold humiliation, embarrassment, and emotional scarring."

We need not determine whether Paul has established a prima facie case on this tort because we conclude that his action for fraud and deceit also should be barred as a matter of public policy. Although we agree with Paul that his allegations normally would suffice to state a cause of action for fraud, we believe the subject matter of this action is not one in which it is appropriate for the courts to intervene. The exact issue that now confronts us was addressed by the California Court of Appeal in *Richard P. v. Superior Court* (Gerald

B.), 202 Cal. App. 3d 1089, 249 Cal.Rptr. 246 (1 Dist. 1988). The court barred the action on the basis of public policy, stating:

> Broadly speaking, the word "tort," means a civil wrong, other than a breach of contract, for which the law will provide a remedy in the form of an action for damages. It does not lie within the power of any judicial system, however, to remedy all human wrongs. There are many wrongs which in themselves are flagrant. For instance, such wrongs as betrayal, brutal words, and heartless disregard of feelings of others are beyond any effective legal remedy and any practical administration of the law. To attempt to correct such wrongs or give relief from their effects "may do more damage than if the law leaves them alone."

Id. 249 Cal.Rptr. at 249 (quoting *Stephen K. v. Roni L.*, 105 Cal.App.3d 640, 642–43, 164 Cal.Rptr. 618, 619 (2 Dist. 1980)) (citations omitted). The court continued:

> We conclude here that any wrong which has occurred as a result of [the defendant's] actions is not one that can be redressed in a tort action. We do not doubt that this lawsuit emanated from an unhappy situation in which the real parties in interest suffered grief. We feel, however, that the innocent children here may suffer significant harm from having their family involved in litigation such as this and that this is exactly the type of lawsuit which, if allowed to proceed, might result in more social damage than will occur if the courts decline to intervene. "We do not believe that the law should provide a basis for such interfamilial warfare."

Richard P., 249 Cal.Rptr at 249 (citation omitted).

We find the reasoning of the court in *Richard P.* persuasive. Allowing Paul to maintain this cause of action may cause Jody's and Tom's daughter to suffer significant harm. This innocent party, who is now three years old, should not be subjected to this type of "interfamilial warfare." We are not unsympathetic for Paul because of the embarrassment and humiliation he suffered. Any attempts to redress this wrong, however, may do more social damage than if the law leaves it alone. We hold that the fraud and deceit alleged by Paul is not actionable because public policy would not be served by authorizing the recovery of damages under the circumstances of the present case. Summary judgment in favor of Jody, therefore, was appropriate.

In his third cause of action, Paul contends that Jody negligently misrepresented to him that he was the child's father. Paul, however, mistakenly sets forth a cause of action that is inapplicable to the facts of the present case. The tort of negligent misrepresentation occurs when in the course of a business or any other transaction in which an individual has a pecuniary interest, he or she supplies false information for the guidance of others in their business transactions, without exercising reasonable care in obtaining or communicating the information. Restatement (Second) of Torts § 552 (1977). *See also Moore v. Kluthe & Lane Ins. Agency*, 89 S.D. 419, 234 N.W.2d 260 (1975). Because Paul's complaint did not arise from a commercial or business setting and because no pecuniary injury was suffered, summary judgment was properly entered in favor of Jody.

The fourth cause of action we address is characterized by Paul as tortious interference with a marital contract which he asserts against Tom. In his brief, Paul invokes an analogy to an action for intentional interference with the performance of a contract in a commercial setting. We believe that the cause expressed is more accurately characterized as one for alienation of affections, a claim with which we deal later, and hold that the trial court did not err in granting summary judgment in favor of Tom on this issue. . . .

Paul's final cause of action which he asserts against Tom is alienation of affections. Unlike the other causes of action brought by Paul, this one presents genuine issues of material fact that are appropriate for trial. Tom's motion for summary judgment on this issue, therefore, was properly denied.

This court has previously set forth the following elements necessary to sustain a claim for alienation of affections: "(1) wrongful conduct of the defendant; (2) loss of affection or consortium; and (3) a causal connection between such conduct and loss." *Pankratz v. Miller*, 401 N.W.2d 543, 546 (S.D. 1987); *Hunt v. Hunt*, 309 N.W.2d 818, 820 (S.D. 1981). In Pankratz, we stated:

> Consortium is a right growing out of the marital relationship. This term includes the right of either spouse to the society, companionship, conjugal affections, and assistance of the other. A loss or impairment of any such elements will sustain an action for alienation of affections. However, if it appears there was no affection to alienate, recovery is precluded.

Pankratz, 401 N.W.2d at 546 (citations omitted). Since an action for alienation of affections is based on an intentional tort, the defendant's actions must have been calculated from the outset to entice the affections of one spouse away from the other. *Id.* at 548–49. It is not enough that the defendant should have known that continuing the affair might contribute to the diminution of a spouse's affections, where that spouse's affections for the other were alienated before the affair began. *Id.* at 548.

In the present case, a genuine issue of material fact exists as to whether Tom acted purposefully to entice Jody's affections away from Paul. Whether Jody held any affection for Paul prior to the start of her relationship with Tom is also an issue of material fact. Because these factual issues are best determined by a jury, summary judgment on this cause of action was properly denied. . . .

The order of the trial court granting summary judgment in favor of Jody and Tom on all causes of action except alienation of affections is affirmed.

NOTES AND QUESTIONS

(1) How would the *Twyman* court decide *Pickering* if the case arose in Texas today? Conversely, what result would the *Pickering* court reach if it were faced with the facts and issues presented in *Twyman*?

(2) Do you agree with the *Pickering* court that allowing Paul to maintain his tort action against Jody would be detrimental to Jody and Tom's daughter? More detrimental than allowing Paul's divorce suit to proceed without the tort allegations? More detrimental than allowing Paul's alienation of affection claim against Tom?

(3) To what extent does the court's reasoning in *Pickering* harken back to the reasoning of earlier domestic relations cases such as *Rhodes v. State* (*above* at § 6.02[A])? Is that reasoning more persuasive here than it was in *Rhodes*? Why or why not?

(4) How would Justice Rose Spector, who dissented in *Twyman*, react to the claims asserted in *Pickering*? Do these claims suggest that the relationship between gender and intrafamily torts may be more complicated than Justice Specter indicated?

(5) Although the *Pickering* court refused to recognize any of Paul's claims against Jody, it did allow Paul to proceed on his claim for alienation of affections against Tom. Alienation of affections is one of several common law torts designed to protect against third-party interference with the marital relationship. At one time, the tort was recognized in 49 states, but it has fallen into disfavor since the 1930s. Critics argue that alienation of affections and other heart balm offenses are subject to abuse and are inconsistent with a modern understanding of marriage, including notions of marital and sexual privacy. *See, e.g.*, Kay Kavanagh, *Note, Alienation of Affections and Criminal Conversation: Unholy Marriage in Need of Annulment*, 23 Ariz. L. Rev. 323 (1981). For additional discussion of these marital torts, see § 2.06, *above*.

[B] Parent-Child Tort Actions

Although husbands and wives were once considered a single legal entity, no similar doctrine applied to the relationship between parents and children. However, suits by children against their parents have historically have subject to a parent-child tort immunity, which was recognized throughout the United States beginning in the late 1800s. *See generally* Sandra L. Haley, Comment, *The Parental Tort Immunity Doctrine: Is It A Defensible Defense?*, 30 U. Rich. L. Rev. 575 (1996). The doctrine was based on several overlapping policy rationales: "preservation of family harmony, preservation of parental authority to control children by way of analogy to spousal immunity, and the avoidance of a depletion of family assets to the detriment of the injured child's siblings." *Cates v. Cates*, 619 N.E.2d 715, 721 (Ill. 1993).

But parent-child tort immunity was often applied in situations that strained the credibility of these rationales. For example, in the landmark case of *Roller v. Roller*, 37 Wash. 242, 79 P. 788, 789 (1905), the Washington Supreme Court held that a daughter could not sue her father for rape under the doctrine of parent-child tort immunity, since such a suit would "impair the family harmony." As a result of decisions such as *Roller*, parent-child tort immunity has been harshly criticized by courts and commentators, and a majority of jurisdictions have now abolished or limited the doctrine. *See generally* Samuel Mark Pipino, Comment, *In Whose Best Interest?: Exploring the Continuing Viability of the Parental Immunity Doctrine*, 53 Ohio St. L. J. 1111 (1992). A minority of states, however, retain the immunity, at least in the context of negligence actions. *See, e.g., Warren v. Warren*, 650 A.2d 252 (Md. 1994); *Mitchell v. Davis*, 598 So. 2d 801, 803 (Ala. 1992); *Mohorn v. Ross*, 422 S.E.2d 290 (Ga. Ct. App. 1992); *Carpenter v. Bishop*, 720 S.W.2d 299, 300 (Ark. 1986).

The opinion that follows traces the traditional and contemporary justifications for restrictions on tort suits between parents and children.

BROADBENT v. BROADBENT
Supreme Court of Arizona
907 P.2d 43 (1995)

CORCORAN, JUSTICE

We must determine whether the doctrine of parental immunity bars Christopher Broadbent's action against his mother for negligence. We also discuss the viability of the line of Arizona cases creating and refining the parental immunity doctrine. . . .

I. Facts

Christopher and his mother, Laura J. Broadbent, went swimming at the family residence on April 13, 1984, their first day of swimming that year. Christopher was wearing "floaties," which are inflatable rings worn on the arms to assist a child in staying afloat. Laura understood that a child could still drown while wearing floaties and should be supervised. At the time of the accident, Christopher was two-and-a-half years old and did not know how to swim.

Laura and Christopher were by the side of the pool when the telephone rang. Laura left Christopher alone by the pool to answer the phone. Laura saw Christopher remove his floaties before she answered the phone. Laura talked on the phone 5 to 10 minutes and could not see Christopher from where she was talking. She also did not have on her contact lenses. Laura said that if she stretched the phone cord and her body, she could see the pool area, but when she did this, she could not see Christopher. She dropped the phone, ran toward the pool, and found Christopher floating in the deep end of the pool.

Laura administered cardio-pulmonary resuscitation and telephoned for the paramedics. Neither Laura nor the paramedics were able to revive Christopher. The paramedics took Christopher to the hospital where he was finally revived. As a result of this near drowning, Christopher suffered severe brain damage because of lack of oxygen. He has lost his motor skills and has no voluntary movement.

II. Procedural History

. . . A complaint was filed on behalf of Christopher, as plaintiff, against his mother, alleging that she was negligent and caused his injuries. This action was brought to involve the Broadbents' umbrella insurance carrier in the issue of coverage. In her answer, Laura admitted that she was negligent in her supervision of Christopher, and she moved for summary judgment, arguing that the doctrine of parental immunity applied. All parties to both the declaratory judgment action and the negligence action filed a stipulation to consolidate the cases, and the trial court ordered the consolidation. The trial court granted Laura's motion for summary judgment and ruled that the parental immunity doctrine applied to the facts of this case.

Phillip Broadbent, as Conservator for Christopher, appealed to the court of appeals. The parties stipulated that: (1) the real party in interest was Northbrook Indemnity Company, who provided personal umbrella liability insurance coverage for Laura Broadbent on the date of the accident; (2) Laura may be entitled to indemnity from Northbrook if Laura is liable for the injuries to Christopher; (3) Laura did not want to defend the action but agreed that Northbrook should be permitted to defend; and (4) the only issue in the case was whether the doctrine of parental immunity applied. The court of appeals ordered that Northbrook be permitted to appear and defend the case.

The court of appeals affirmed the trial court, finding that under the parental immunity doctrine the mother was not liable for her child's injuries. *Broadbent*, 178 Ariz. at 58, 870

P.2d at 1154. The court of appeals held that this case was most closely analogous to *Sandoval v. Sandoval*, 128 Ariz. 11, 623 P.2d 800 (1981), which involved negligent supervision of a child by a parent, and rejected the argument that the mother's duty to the child arose out of a duty to the world at large to protect all children from the pool. *Broadbent*, 178 Ariz. at 56–57, 870 P.2d at 1152–53. The court of appeals also rejected Christopher's arguments that (1) the injuries were caused by an instrumentality under the control of the mother, and therefore the doctrine of parental immunity did not apply; and (2) Arizona should further limit application of parental immunity in accord with Wisconsin cases from which Arizona's standard was originally derived. *Broadbent*, 178 Ariz. at 57–58, 870 P.2d at 1153–54.

. . . The court of appeals noted that it based its decision on an application of the current status of the parental immunity doctrine in Arizona and that any departure or modification of the established case law was "for the supreme court to determine" and not the court of appeals. *Broadbent*, 178 Ariz. at 58, 870 P.2d at 1154. We agree and do so in this opinion today.

DISCUSSION

I. History and Purpose of the Parental Immunity Doctrine

A. The Origins of Parental Immunity

We begin by stating a few basic facts about the treatment of children under the law and family immunities. Under common law, a child has traditionally been considered a separate legal entity from his or her parent. *See* W. Page Keeton, Dan P. Dobbs, Robert E. Keeton, and David G. Owen, Prosser and Keeton on the Law of Torts § 122, at 904 (5th ed. 1984) (Prosser & Keeton); Martin J. Rooney & Colleen M. Rooney, *Parental Tort Immunity: Spare the Liability, Spoil the Parent*, 25 New Eng. L. Rev. 1161, 1162 (1991). Children have generally been allowed to sue their parents in property and contract actions. *Goller v. White*, 20 Wis. 2d 402, 122 N.W.2d 193, 197 (Wis. 1963); Gail D. Hollister, *Parent-Child Immunity: A Doctrine in Search of Justification*, 50 Fordham L. Rev. 489, 497 (1982) (Parent-Child Immunity). In contrast, at common law the courts merged the identity of husband and wife; therefore, spousal immunity prohibited any action by a wife against her husband because to do so would have been to sue herself. . . .

The doctrine of parental immunity is an American phenomenon unknown in the English common law. . . .

In early American history, children were viewed as "evil and in need of strict discipline," and the courts recognized wide parental discretion. Parent-Child Immunity, at 491–92. There was a strong presumption that parental discipline was proper. Only recently has the state intervened to protect children. Viewed against this backdrop, it is not surprising that no American child had sought recovery against a parent for tortious conduct until the late nineteenth century.

In *Hewellett v. George*, 68 Miss. 703, 711, 9 So. 885, 887 (1891), the Supreme Court of Mississippi held, without citation to legal authority, that a child could not sue her parent for being falsely imprisoned in an insane asylum because of parental immunity, a doctrine which that court created from whole cloth. As its rationale, the court stated:

> So long as the parent is under obligation to care for, guide and control, and the child is under reciprocal obligation to aid and comfort and obey, no such action as this can be maintained. The peace of society, and of the families composing society, and a sound public policy, designed to subserve the repose of families and the best interests of society, forbid to the minor child a right to appear in court in the assertion of a claim to civil redress for personal injuries suffered at the hands of the parent.

Hewlett, 68 Miss. at 711, 9 So. at 887.

Hewlett was followed by two cases that were also decided on parental immunity grounds, and these came to be known as the "great trilogy" of cases establishing the parental immunity doctrine. In *McKelvey v. McKelvey*, the Tennessee Supreme Court held that a minor child could not sue her father for "cruel and inhuman treatment" allegedly inflicted by her stepmother with the consent of her father. 77 S.W. 664, 664–65 (Tenn. 1903). *McKelvey* cited *Hewlett* as the only authority for the doctrine of parental immunity and analogized the parent-child relationship to that of the husband-wife relationship, noting that the basis for the spousal immunity was, in part, the fact that husband and wife are a legal entity. *McKelvey*, 77 S.W. at 664–65.

In *Roller v. Roller*, the Supreme Court of Washington cited *Hewlett* and held that a minor child could not sue her father for rape, even though he had been convicted of the criminal violation, because of the doctrine of parental immunity. *Roller*, 37 Wash. 242, 79 P. 788, 788–89 (Wash. 1905). The *Roller* court argued that if the child recovered a money judgment from the parent and then died, the parent would then become heir to the property that had been taken from him. 79 P. at 789. In addition, *Roller* argued that "the public has an interest in the financial welfare of other minor members of the family, and it would not be the policy of the law to allow the estate, which is to be looked to for the support of all the minor children, to be appropriated by any particular one." 79 P. at 789.

This "great trilogy" was the inauspicious beginning of the doctrine of parental immunity, which was soon embraced by almost every state. However, the courts soon began fashioning several exceptions to the doctrine, and in several states the doctrine has been abolished. In several situations, parental immunity does not apply: if the parent is acting outside his parental role and within the scope of his employment; if the parent acts willfully, wantonly, or recklessly; if the child is emancipated; if the child or parent dies; if a third party is liable for the tort, then the immunity of the parent does not protect that third party; and if the tortfeasor is standing in loco parentis, such as a grandparent, foster parent, or teacher, then the immunity does not apply, *see Rourk v. State*, 170 Ariz. 6, 10–11, 821 P.2d 273, 277–78 (App. 1991) (holding that doctrine of parental immunity did not apply to foster parents).

B. Parental Immunity in Arizona

In 1967 the doctrine of parental immunity was first recognized in Arizona in *Purcell v. Frazer*, 7 Ariz. App. 5, 8–9, 435 P.2d 736, 739–40 (1967). In *Purcell*, the Arizona Court of Appeals held that the doctrine of parental immunity prohibited children from suing their parents for injuries resulting from a car accident allegedly caused by the parents' negligence. 7 Ariz. App. at 7–9, 435 P.2d at 736–40. *Purcell*, however, was soon overruled in 1970 by *Streenz v. Streenz*, which held that an unemancipated minor could sue her parents for injuries resulting from a car accident. *Streenz*, 106 Ariz. 86, 88–89, 471 P.2d 282, 284–85 (1970). In Streenz, this court adopted the standard from the Wisconsin Supreme Court set forth in *Goller v. White*, 20 Wis. 2d 402, 122 N.W.2d 193, 198 (Wis. 1963). Under the *Goller* standard, parental immunity is abrogated except:

> (1) where the alleged negligent act involves an exercise of parental authority over the child; and

> (2) where the alleged negligent act involves an exercise of ordinary parental discretion with respect to the provision of food, clothing, housing, medical and dental services, and other care.

Streenz, 106 Ariz. at 89, 471 P.2d at 285, quoting *Goller*, 122 N.W.2d at 198.

The cases following *Streenz* show the difficulty in applying this ambiguous standard.

In *Sandoval v. Sandoval*, a child sued his parents alleging that his father had negligently left the gate open, which allowed the 4–year-old child to ride his tricycle from the front yard into the street where he was run over by a car. 128 Ariz. 11, 11, 623 P.2d 800, 800 (1981). In *Sandoval*, this court devised a new test for applying the standard set forth in *Streenz*: the parent would not be immune if the parent had a duty to the world at large. *Sandoval*, 128 Ariz. at 13, 623 P.2d at 802. If the parent's duty was "owed to the child alone and a part of the parental 'care and control' or 'other care' to be provided by the parents," then the parent was immune from liability. *Sandoval*, 128 Ariz. at 13–14, 623 P.2d at 802–03. The court held that "the act of leaving a gate open should not subject the plaintiff's parents to suit." *Sandoval*, 128 Ariz. at 14, 623 P.2d at 803. Further, the court noted that it did not limit the abrogation of the parental immunity doctrine to negligence in car accident cases and would, instead, "continue to consider, on a case by case basis, the actual cause of the injury and whether the act of the parent breached a duty owed to the world at large, as opposed to a duty owed to a child within the family sphere." *Sandoval*, 128 Ariz. at 14, 623 P.2d at 803. The court reasoned that when a parent was driving a car, he had a duty to the world to drive carefully, whereas the duty to close the gate was a duty owed only to the child, and that the direct cause of the child's injuries in *Sandoval* was the car that struck him in the street, not the gate being open. *Sandoval*, 128 Ariz. at 13, 623 P.2d at 802.

Applying *Sandoval*, the court in *Schleier v. Alter* held that the parents had a duty to the world at large and therefore were not immune from liability. *Schleier*, 159 Ariz. 397, 399–400, 767 P.2d 1187, 1189–90 (App. 1989). In that case, the family dog, which had a history of attacking children, bit the Alters' 11–month-old child. The court of appeals characterized the duty that the parents owed as a general duty to the world to supervise their dog, which the court found to be the equivalent of a "dangerous instrumentality" to children. *Schleier*, 159 Ariz. at 400, 767 P.2d at 1190.

The most recent Arizona case on parental immunity found the doctrine to be applicable. In *Sandbak v. Sandbak*, the Sandbaks' child wandered onto the next door neighbors' property where the neighbors' pit bull terrier severely mauled her. 166 Ariz. 21, 22, 800 P.2d 8, 9 (App. 1990). The parents knew that the next door neighbors owned pit bull terriers and that their daughter had a habit of wandering onto the neighbors' property. *Sandbak*, 166 Ariz. at 22, 800 P.2d at 9. The court held that the child's claim of negligent supervision was barred, rejecting the child's argument that immunity only applied to parents' negligence with regard to legal obligations. *Sandbak*, 166 Ariz. at 23, 800 P.2d at 10. . . .

C. Analysis of the Policy Reasons Advanced in Support of Parental Immunity

Courts and commentators have postulated many policy reasons for the parental immunity doctrine. The primary justifications for this immunity are:

(1) Suing one's parents would disturb domestic tranquility;

(2) Suing one's parents would create a danger of fraud and collusion;

(3) Awarding damages to the child would deplete family resources;

(4) Awarding damages to the child could benefit the parent if the child predeceases the parent and the parent inherits the child's damages; and

(5) Suing one's parents would interfere with parental care, discipline, and control.

Streenz, 106 Ariz. at 87 n.1, 471 P.2d at 283 n.1. We believe that all of these justifications provide weak support for the parental immunity doctrine.

The injury to the child, more than the lawsuit, disrupts the family tranquility. In fact, if the child is not compensated for the tortious injury, then peace in the family is even less likely. In the seminal Arizona case on parental immunity, the court recognized that family tranquility would not be disturbed if the parents had liability insurance. *Purcell*, 7 Ariz. App. at 8, 435 P.2d at 739.

This fear of upsetting the family tranquility also seems unrealistic when we consider how such a lawsuit is initiated. The parent most often makes the decision to sue himself, and the parent is in effect prepared to say that he was negligent. See *Comment, The "Reasonable Parent" Standard: An Alternative to Parent-Child Tort Immunity*, 47 U. Colo. L. Rev. 795, 798–99 (1976).

The danger of fraud and collusion is present in all lawsuits. We should not deny recovery to an entire class of litigants because some litigants might try to deceive the judicial system. The system can ferret out fraudulent and collusive behavior in suits brought by children against their parents just as the system detects such behavior in other contexts.

We note, too, that both of these arguments—disturbing domestic tranquility and danger of fraud and collusion—were also justifications for spousal immunity, which has been abrogated in Arizona. These same concerns could justify an immunity from suits brought by one sibling against another; however, this is an immunity that the courts have not felt the need to create. . . .

A damage award for the child will not deplete, or unfairly redistribute, the family's financial resources. These cases will generally not be brought if no insurance coverage is available, and therefore the worry that the family's resources will be depleted for the benefit of one child is illusory. The opposite is true. If a child has been seriously injured and needs expensive medical care, then a successful lawsuit against the parent and subsequent recovery from the insurance company could ease the financial burden on the family. It would not be a viable rule to say that liability only exists where insurance exists, but we recognize that lawsuits generally will be brought when there is potential insurance coverage.

The possibility that the parent might inherit money recovered by the child is remote. This becomes a concern only if the parent inherits as a beneficiary under intestate succession laws. This is a concern for the probate courts and the laws of intestate succession, not tort law. The remedy would be to prohibit inheritance by the parent—not to deny recovery to the injured child.

The Arizona courts have embraced the rationale that allowing a child to sue a parent would interfere with parental care, discipline, and control. See *Streenz*, 106 Ariz. at 89, 471 P.2d at 285. We have cited with approval the Wisconsin Supreme Court's statement that:

> [a] new and heavy burden would be added to the responsibility and privilege of parenthood, if within the wide scope of daily experiences common to the upbringing of children a parent could be subjected to a suit for damages for each failure to exercise care and judgment commensurate with the risk.

Sandoval, 128 Ariz. at 13, 623 P.2d at 802, quoting *Lemmen v. Servais*, 39 Wis. 2d 75, 158 N.W.2d 341, 344 (Wis. 1968).

The justification that allowing children to sue their parents would undercut parental authority and discretion has more appeal than the other rationales. However, if a child were seriously injured as a result of the exercise of parental authority, such as by a beating, then it would constitute an injury willfully inflicted, and parents are generally not immune for willful, wanton, or malicious conduct. Furthermore, such a willful beating would probably constitute child abuse and could be criminally prosecuted.

We want to protect the right of parents to raise their children by their own methods and in accordance with their own attitudes and beliefs. The New York Court of Appeals aptly stated this concern:

> Considering the different economic, educational, cultural, ethnic and religious backgrounds which must prevail, there are so many combinations and permutations of parent-child relationships that may result that the search for a standard would necessarily be in vain . . . . For this reason parents have always had the right to determine how much independence, supervision and control a child should have, and to best judge the character and extent of development of their child.

Holodook v. Spencer, 36 N.Y.2d 35, 324 N.E.2d 338, 346, 364 N.Y.S.2d 859 (N.Y. 1974), quoting *Holodook v. Spencer*, 43 A.D.2d 129, 350 N.Y.S.2d 199, 204 (App. Div. 1973). Though we recognize the importance of allowing parental discretion, we disagree that our searching for a standard would be "in vain." Parents do not possess unfettered discretion in raising their children.

II. The Abolishment of Parental Immunity and Adoption of the "Reasonable Parent" Standard for Parent-Child Suits

Although the above concerns make it difficult to draft a proper standard for the type of action a child may maintain against a parent, we will attempt to do so. We need to "fashion an objective standard that does not result in second-guessing parents in the management of their family affairs." Parent-Child Immunity, at 490. First, we should make clear what the standard is not. We reject and hereby overrule *Sandoval*, which created the "duty to the world at large versus duty to the child alone" distinction. This distinction is not capable of uniform application and has no connection with the rationale for parental immunity. This is especially evident when we compare the facts of *Schleier* and *Sandbak*.

In *Schleier*, the negligent act was failure to restrain a dog, and the court found that this was a duty to the world; therefore, parental immunity did not apply. 159 Ariz. at 400–01, 767 P.2d at 1190–91. In *Sandbak*, the negligent act was failure to supervise a child who was bitten by a neighbor's dog, and the court found this was a duty to the child alone; therefore, parental immunity applied. 166 Ariz. at 23, 800 P.2d at 10. The children in *Schleier* and *Sandbak* suffered similar injuries; neither case involved parental discipline, and neither case involved the "provision of food, clothing, housing, medical and dental services, and other care," unless "other care" is broadly defined. Both cases involved the negligent supervision of children. If we were to hold that parents are immune for negligent supervision of children, then the issue of liability would revolve around whether an activity could be described as "supervision" and whether lack of supervision was the cause of the injury. This would not involve a consideration of whether the activity infringed on the parents' discretionary decisions regarding care, custody, and control. Almost everything a parent does in relation to his child involves "care, custody, and control."

We add that parents always owe a parental duty to their minor child. The issue of liability should revolve around whether the parents have breached this duty and, if so, whether the breach of duty caused the injury.

In accord with the California Supreme Court, "we reject the implication of *Goller* [which this court approved *Streenz* in that within certain aspects of the parent-child relationship, the parent has carte blanche to act negligently toward his child . . . . Although a parent has the prerogative and the duty to exercise authority over his minor child, this prerogative must be exercised within reasonable limits." *Gibson*, 479 P.2d at 652–53. We hereby reject the *Goller* test as set forth in *Streenz*, and we approve of the "reasonable parent test," in which a parent's conduct is judged by whether that parent's conduct comported with that of a reasonable and prudent parent in a similar situation. Gibson, 479 P.2d at 653.

A parent is not immune from liability for tortious conduct directed toward his child solely by reason of that relationship. And, a parent is not liable for an act or omission that injured his child if the parent acted as a reasonable and prudent parent in the situation would.

III. Application to the Present Case

In this case, the trier of fact may find that the mother, Laura Broadbent, did not act as a reasonable and prudent parent would have in this situation. The finder of fact must determine whether leaving a two-and-a-half year old child unattended next to a swimming pool is reasonable or prudent. We fail to see why parents should not be held liable for negligence in failing to supervise their own children near the pool, when their liability would be clear had the children not been their own. We think that in most cases, if not all, the standard of care owed to a parent's own child is the same as that owed to any other child.

The paradox of parental immunity can be seen if we assume that a neighbor child from across the street was a guest and was injured at the same time and under the same circumstances as Christopher. Should the neighbor child be permitted to sue and recover damages from Laura but Christopher be denied the same opportunity?

A parent may avoid liability because there is no negligence, but not merely because of the status as parent. Children are certainly accident prone, and oftentimes those accidents are not due to the negligence of any party. The same rules of summary judgment apply to these cases as to others, and trial courts should feel free to dismiss frivolous cases on the ground that the parent has acted as a reasonable and prudent parent in a similar situation would.

CONCLUSION

We vacate the court of appeals' decision in this case, reverse the trial court's rulings on summary judgment, and remand to the trial court for proceedings consistent with this opinion. Laura Broadbent is not immune from liability in this case because of the doctrine of parental immunity, which we hereby abolish. We overrule *Sandoval* on the issue of parental immunity and no longer follow the *Goller* test as adopted in *Streenz*.

NOTES AND QUESTIONS

(1) The *Broadbent* court considers and rejects a number of potential justifications for parent-child tort immunity. Do you agree with the court that these justifications provide only "weak support" for the immunity? Are there other justifications for limiting the ability of children to sue their parents?

(2) The court in *Broadbent* states that its goal is to "fashion an objective standard that does not result in second-guessing parents in the management of their family affairs." Does the court achieve this goal? How does the standard adopted by the court differ from the standard previously applied in cases such as *Sandover, Streenz* and *Goller*? Under which framework are more cases likely to be decided by a jury?

(3) As the *Broadbent* court suggests, even those states that have generally retained parent-child tort immunity often recognize an exception for wanton and willful parental behavior. *See, e.g., Doe v. Holt*, 332 418 S.E.2d 511 (N.C. 1992) (immunity doctrine does not bar recovery for injuries suffered as a result of parent's willful and malicious conduct); *Calhoun v. Eagan*, 681 A.2d 609, 624–25 (Md. Ct. App. 1996) (applying exception to allow wrongful death suit on behalf of children against father, based on allegations that father deliberately or recklessly killed the children's mother). Are the justifications for parent-child immunity stronger or weaker in the context of intentional torts, as opposed to negligence actions? Should a child be able to sue a parent for intentional infliction of emotional distress? For false imprisonment as a result of being "grounded"? *Cf. Brunell v. Wahl*, 588 P.2d 1105 (Or. 1978) (despite abolition of parent-child tort immunity, children could not sue parents for emotional and psychological injuries arising from parents' alleged failure to provide support, nurture and physical care).

(4) The widespread abolition of both interspousal and parent-child tort immunity has prompted many insurance companies to insert a "family exclusion clause" in various liability insurance policies, with particular application to automobile liability and homeowner's liability insurance. These exclusion clauses generally provide that liability coverage will *not* apply to the insured or to any member of the insured's family living in the same household. Family members subject to these exclusions have challenged them as contrary to public policy or as inconsistent with state insurance statutes. These challenges have produced varying results, depending on the manner in which particular states regulate insurance coverage. *See generally* Martin J. McMahon, Annotation, *Validity, Under*

Insurance Statutes, of Coverage Exclusion For Injury to or Death of Insured's Family or Household Members, 52 A.L.R.4th 18 (1987). *Query:* Should family exclusion clauses be upheld on the grounds that an insurance company should legitimately be able to limit its risk of loss, or should such exclusions be invalidated as contrary to public policy, since all victims of negligence, including family members, should be able to recover from a tortfeasor?

(5) As noted in the Introduction to this chapter, a growing body of social science evidence documents the harmful emotional and psychological effects of domestic violence on children. Given these detrimental effects, should a child be able to sue one parent for physically abusing the other, where the abuse takes place in the child's presence? *See, e.g., Courtney v. Compaleo*, 413 S.E.2d 418, 426–27 (W. Va. Ct. App. 1991), *rev'd on other grounds*, 437 S.E.2d 436 (Va. 1993) (child may sue father for extreme emotional distress sustained as a result of witnessing father's repeated assaults on mother); Restatement (Second) of Torts § 46(2) (1965) (actor who engages in extreme and outrageous conduct directed to a third person is subject to liability if he intentionally or recklessly causes severe emotional distress to a member of such person's immediate family, who is present at the time)

(6) To the extent that a state retains parent-child tort immunity, should the immunity apply to claims by children against stepparents? *See Warren v. Warren*, 650 A.2d 252, 257 (Md. 1994) (retaining parent-child tort immunity for negligence actions but refusing to extend immunity to stepparents). To claims by grandchildren against grandparents? Does your answer depend on what you see as the primary purposes of the immunity? On whether you favor a formal or a functional definition of family?

(7) In a state such as Arizona, which has generally abrogated parent-child tort immunity, should a child be able to sue his or her mother for prenatal injuries caused by the mother's allegedly negligent conduct during pregnancy? What additional policy considerations might be implicated in such a suit? *See, e.g., Bonte v. Bonte*, 616 A.2d 464, 465–66 (N.H. 1992); Beal, *Can I Sue Mommy? An Analysis of a Woman's Tort Liability for Prenatal Injuries to her Child Born Alive*, 21 San Diego L. Rev. 325 (1984).

(8) **Problem.** Audrey Smith and her ex-husband share custody of their three-year-old daughter, Beth. In March, 1994 (approximately one month before the swimming accident in the Broadbent's pool), Audrey and Beth moved into the house next door to the Broadbents. Over the next few weeks, Beth and the Broadbent's son, Christopher, played together several times. On the morning of the accident, Laura Broadbent asked Audrey if Beth would like to stay with Christopher at the Broadbent's pool, while Audrey ran errands. Relieved not to have to take Beth with her, Audrey accepted Laura's invitation. Tragically, both Beth and Christopher fell into the pool while Laura was speaking on the telephone, and both children suffered serious injuries from their near drownings. Several months later, Beth's father (Audrey's ex-husband), acting on behalf of Beth, filed a tort action against Audrey, alleging that Audrey was negligent in leaving Beth at the Broadbent's pool. Assuming the action is brought in Arizona, can Audrey defend on grounds of parent-child immunity? Why or why not? Could Audrey successfully raise an immunity defense in a state that followed the *Goller* approach?

(9) **Problem.** George Jones regularly drives his six-year-old daughter, Crystal, to and from soccer practice. Several months ago, on the way home from practice, Jones' car was

struck by a pickup truck driven by Brenda Drake, who negligently ran a red light. George, who was wearing his seat belt, suffered only minor injuries in the crash. Crystal, who was not wearing her seat belt, was seriously injured and permanently disabled. Crystal, through her next friend, brought a negligence action against Brenda Drake, for damages arising out of the accident. Drake, in turn, filed a claim for contribution and indemnity against George Jones, alleging that Jones was negligent in failing to ensure that Crystal's seat belt was fastened, and that Jones' negligence was a significant cause of Crystal's injuries. Jones moved to dismiss Drake's claim on grounds of parent-child tort immunity. What result in Arizona and why? What result in a jurisdiction that retains parent-child tort immunity? *See* Andrea G. Nadel, Annotation, *Right of Tortfeasor To Contribution From Joint Tortfeasor Who is Spouse or Otherwise in Close Familial Relationship to Injured Party*, 25 A.L.R.4th 1120 (1983).

CHAPTER 7

CARE AND SUPERVISION OF CHILDREN

SYNOPSIS

§ 7.01 Introduction
§ 7.02 The Constitutional Framework
§ 7.03 Child Abuse and Neglect
    [A] Abuse or Discipline?
    [B] Parental Failure to Protect
    [C] Defining and Responding To Child Neglect
    [D] Abuse or Neglect of A Fetus?
    [E] Government Responsibility to Protect Children
§ 7.04 Medical Decision-Making On Behalf of Children
    [A] Criminal Prosecution for Parental Failure to Seek Medical Care
    [B] Medical Neglect
    [C] Children As Decision-Makers
§ 7.05 When Parent and Child Disagree: What Role for the State?
    [A] Decisions About Reproduction
    [B] Children Beyond Parental Control
§ 7.06 The Foster Care System
    [A] The Foster Family
    [B] Kinship Care
    [C] Permanent Dispositions and Foster Care Reform: From Family Preservation to Termination of Parental Rights

§ 7.01 Introduction

Neither parents nor children are mentioned specifically in the Constitution. The Supreme Court has made clear, however, that the parent-child relationship is constitutionally protected and that parents have a liberty interest in raising their children without undue state interference. At the same time, the Court has held that children are "persons" within the meaning of the Fourteenth Amendment, and it has extended to children some (but not all) of the individual rights granted to adults under that amendment. To further complicate matters, the Court has emphasized that the state has the authority—if not the obligation—to protect children from harm, including harm inflicted or threatened by their parents or other caretakers. The cases and materials that follow explore the interplay and tension among these three jurisprudential principles: parental authority to raise children, children's rights as individuals, and state responsibility to protect children. Taken together, these concepts illuminate the constitutional and common law framework for allocating authority and responsibility for children's welfare among parents, children, and the state.

§ 7.02 The Constitutional Framework

MEYER v. NEBRASKA
United States Supreme Court
262 U.S. 390 (1923)

Mr. Justice McReynolds delivered the opinion of the Court.

[In 1919, the state of Nebraska passed a statute that made it a crime for any teacher in a public, private, or parochial school to teach any subject in a language other than English to a child who had not completed eighth grade. A teacher at Zion Parochial School was convicted under the statute for teaching reading in German to a 10 year old child.] . . .

The problem for our determination is whether the statute as construed and applied unreasonably infringes the liberty guaranteed to the plaintiff in error by the Fourteenth Amendment. "No State shall . . . deprive any person of life, liberty, or property, without due process of law."

While this Court has not attempted to define with exactness the liberty thus guaranteed, the term has received much consideration and some of the included things have been definitely stated. Without doubt, it denotes not merely freedom from bodily restraint but also the right of the individual to contract, to engage in any of the common occupations of life, to acquire useful knowledge, to marry, establish a home and bring up children, to worship God according to the dictates of his own conscience, and generally to enjoy those privileges long recognized at common law as essential to the orderly pursuit of happiness by free men. The established doctrine is that this liberty may not be interfered with, under the guise of protecting the public interest, by legislative action which is arbitrary or without reasonable relation to some purpose within the competency of the State to effect. Determination by the legislature of what constitutes proper exercise of police power is not final or conclusive but is subject to supervision by the courts.

The American people have always regarded education and acquisition of knowledge as matters of supreme importance which should be diligently promoted. . . .Corresponding to the right of control, it is the natural duty of the parent to give his children education suitable to their station in life; and nearly all the States, including Nebraska, enforce this obligation by compulsory laws.

Practically, education of the young is only possible in schools conducted by especially qualified persons who devote themselves thereto. The calling always has been regarded as useful and honorable, essential, indeed, to the public welfare. Mere knowledge of the German language cannot reasonable be regarded as harmful. Heretofore it has been commonly looked upon as helpful and desirable. Plaintiff in error taught this language in school as part of his occupation. His right thus to teach and the right of parents to engage him so to instruct their children, we think, are within the liberty of the Amendment. . . .

It is said the purpose of the legislation was to promote civic development by inhibiting training and education of the immature in foreign tongues and ideals before they could learn

English and acquire American ideals; and "that the English language should be and become the mother tongue of all children reared in this State." It is also affirmed that the foreign born population is very large, that certain communities commonly use foreign words, follow foreign leaders, move in a foreign atmosphere, and that the children are thereby hindered from becoming citizens of the most useful type and the public safety is imperiled.

That the State may do much, go very far, indeed, in order to improve the quality of its citizens, physically, mentally and morally, is clear; but the individual has certain fundamental rights which must be respected. The protection of the Constitution extends to all, to those who speak other languages as well as to those born with English on the tongue. Perhaps it would be highly advantageous if all had ready understanding of our ordinary speech, but this cannot be coerced by methods which conflict with the Constitution—a desirable end cannot be promoted by prohibited means. . . .

The desire of the legislature to foster a homogeneous people with American ideals prepared readily to understand current discussions of civic matters is easy to appreciate. Unfortunate experiences during the late war and aversion toward every characteristic of truculent adversaries were certainly enough to quicken that aspiration. But the means adopted, we think, exceed the limitations upon the power of the State and conflict with rights assured to plaintiff in error. The interference is plain enough and no adequate reason therefor in time of peace and domestic tranquility has been shown.

The power of the State to compel attendance at some school and to make reasonable regulations for all schools, including a requirement that they shall give instructions in English, is not questioned. Nor has challenge been made of the State's power to prescribe a curriculum for institutions which it supports. Those matters are not within the present controversy. . . . No emergency has arisen which renders knowledge by a child of some language other than English so clearly harmful as to justify its inhibition with the consequent infringement of rights long freely enjoyed. We are constrained to conclude that the statute as applied is arbitrary and without reasonable relation to any end within the competency of the State. . . .

The judgment of the court below must be reversed and the cause remanded for further proceedings not inconsistent with this opinion.

PIERCE v. SOCIETY OF SISTERS
United States Supreme Court
268 U.S. 510 (1925)

Mr. Justice McReynolds delivered the opinion of the Court.

. . .The challenged Act, effective September 1, 1926, requires every parent, guardian or other person having control or charge or custody of a child between eight and sixteen years to send him "to a public school for the period of time a public school shall be held during the current year" in the district where the child resides; and failure so to do is declared a misdemeanor. There are exemptions—not specially important here—for children who are not normal, or who have completed the eighth grade, or who reside at considerable distances from any public school, or whose parents or guardians hold special permits from the County Superintendent. The manifest purpose is to compel general attendance at public schools by normal children, between eight and sixteen, who have not completed the eighth grade.

And without doubt enforcement of the statute would seriously impair, perhaps destroy, the profitable features of appellees' business and greatly diminish the value of their property.

Appellee, the Society of Sisters, is an Oregon corporation, organized in 1880, with power to care for orphans, educate and instruct the youth, establish and maintain academies or schools, and acquire necessary real and personal property. It has long devoted its property and effort to the secular and religious education and care of children, and has acquired the valuable good will of many parents and guardians. It conducts interdependent primary and high schools and junior colleges, and maintains orphanages for the custody and control of children between eight and sixteen. . . .

Appellee, Hill Military Academy, is a private corporation organized in 1908 under the laws of Oregon, engaged in owning, operating and conducting for profit an elementary, college preparatory and military training school for boys between the ages of five and twenty-one years. . . .

No question is raised concerning the power of the State reasonably to regulate all schools, to inspect, supervise and examine them, their teachers and pupils; to require that all children of proper age attend some school, that teachers shall be of good moral character and patriotic disposition, that certain studies plainly essential to good citizenship must be taught, and that nothing be taught which is manifestly inimical to the public welfare.

The inevitable practical result of enforcing the Act under consideration would be destruction of appellees' primary schools, and perhaps all other private primary schools for normal children within the State of Oregon. These parties are engaged in a kind of undertaking not inherently harmful, but long regarded as useful and meritorious. Certainly there is nothing in the present records to indicate that they have failed to discharge their obligations to patrons, students or the State. And there are no peculiar circumstances or present emergencies which demand extraordinary measures relative to primary education.

Under the doctrine of *Meyer v. Nebraska*, 262 U.S. 390, we think it entirely plain that the Act of 1922 unreasonably interferes with the liberty of parents and guardians to direct the upbringing and education of children under their control. As often heretofore pointed out, rights guaranteed by the Constitution may not be abridged by legislation which has no reasonable relation to some purpose within the competency of the State. The fundamental theory of liberty upon which all governments in this Union repose excludes any general power of the State to standardize its children by forcing them to accept instruction from public teachers only. The child is not the mere creature of the State; those who nurture him and direct his destiny have the right, coupled with the high duty, to recognize and prepare him for additional obligations. . . .

NOTES AND QUESTIONS

(1) Whose liberty was being infringed by the statutes struck down in *Meyer* and *Pierce*? The parents'? The children's? The teachers'? The school proprietors'?

(2) In her "revisionist" account of *Meyer* and *Pierce,* Professor Barbara Woodhouse claims that the right vindicated in both cases is the right of parents to control their children. Barbara B. Woodhouse, *Who Owns the Child? Meyer and Pierce and the Child as Property,* 33 Wm. & Mary L. Rev. 995 (1992). Woodhouse argues that it makes sense to locate the

right to control children in the liberty clause of the Fourteenth Amendment only if children are viewed as the property of their parents:

> Ironically, the Court in *Meyer* and *Pierce* chose to hang parental control of children on the branch of Fourteenth Amendment "liberty." Courts before *Meyer* had generally been slow to extend Fourteenth Amendment protection to the parent's rights over the child. Pierce himself observed that "it is a strange perversion of the word 'liberty' to apply it to a right to control the conduct of others." Yet adopt, for a moment, the perspective that children are patriarchal property. Suddenly, the right of parental control in *Meyer* and *Pierce*—authored and joined by the court's most inflexible, laissez-faire conservatives and grounded on economic substantive due process precedents—acquires a logical framework. Property and ownership were indeed a powerful subtext of parental rights rhetoric in the era of *Pierce* and *Meyer*.

Id. at 1041–42. More recently, Professors Elizabeth and Robert Scott have argued that granting parents broad authority over children is justified as a way of encouraging parents to invest the effort necessary to fulfill the obligations of child-rearing:

> The absence of pecuniary compensation to parents for capably performing parental tasks necessarily increases the value of non-pecuniary substitutes such as reputation and role satisfaction. On this dimension, parental authority over the relationship with children is offered as the *quid pro quo* for satisfactory performance. It is unlikely that, in a hypothetical bargain over the terms of their performance, parents would agree to undertake the responsibilities desired by the state without assurance that their investment would receive legal protection. Recognition of these parental claims in some form is an important inducement to encourage investment in children's welfare.

Elizabeth S. Scott & Robert E. Scott, *Parents As Fiduciaries,* 81 V. L. Rev. 2401, 2440 (1995). Do you find either of these arguments persuasive? Why or why not?

(3) Could a state, consistent with *Meyer* and *Pierce*, prohibit parents from sending children to a private school where *all* instruction was given in a foreign language? Put another way, could a state constitutionally require private, as well as public, schools to provide *some* instruction in English? Conversely, are there circumstances in which a state has an affirmative constitutional obligation to provide bilingual education in its public schools in order to enable students who do not speak English to benefit from the school's programs? *Cf. Lau v. Nichols,* 414 U.S. 563, 566–69 (1974) (failure of San Francisco school system to provide supplemental English language instruction to students of Chinese ancestry who do not speak English denied those students a meaningful opportunity to participate in the public educational program, in violation of federal civil rights law).

(4) Who should pay for a child's education? If the holding of *Pierce* is that a state cannot compel parents to send their children to public school, how does this affect the rights of parents who cannot afford to pay for private education? Is the principle of *Pierce* relevant only for those parents who can afford to pay private tuition?

(5) Should the government provide financial assistance to parents who choose to send their children to parochial or other private schools, or would such a program of educational vouchers violate the Establishment Clause of the First Amendment? *See, e.g., Jackson v. Benson* 578 N.W.2d 602 (Wis. 1998) (rejecting Establishment Clause challenge to school voucher program that included both sectarian and nonsectarian private schools); Davis v.

Grover, 480 N.W.2d 460, 472 (Wis. 1992) (upholding constitutionality of school voucher program that included only nonsectarian private schools);. Would a program of school vouchers undermine the public educational system ? A number of commentators have argued that it would. *See* Carol L. Ziegler & Nancy M. Lederman, *School Vouchers: Are Urban Students Surrendering Rights for Choice?*, 19 Fordham Urb. L. J. 813 (1992); Stephen Eisdorfer, *Public School Choice and Racial Integration*, 24 Seton Hall L. Rev. 937 (1993). For further discussion of these issues, see Jeffrey R. Henig, *Rethinking School Choice: Limits of the Market Metaphor* (1994); David W. Kirkpatrick, Choice In Schooling: A Case for Tuition Vouchers (1990); Cynthia Bright, *The Establishment Clause and School Vouchers: Private Choice and Proposition* 174, 31 Cal. W. L. Rev. 193 (1995); Richard C. Reuben, ed., *Are School Voucher Plans Constitutional?* 13 Cal. Law 35 (Oct. 1993) (presenting contrasting views of the constitutionality of school vouchers).

(6) Are states constitutionally required to provide a free public education, at least for parents who could not otherwise afford to send their children to school? Although the U.S. Constitution says nothing specifically about education, many state constitutions require the state government to provide a free and appropriate education. *See, e.g.,* Md. Const. Art. VIII, § 1 (1997) (requiring legislature to establish and fund "a thorough and efficient system of free public schools"). The United States Supreme Court has been somewhat inconsistent in its pronouncements on the status of education as a constitutionally protected right. In *Brown v. Board of Education,* 347 U.S. 483, 493 (1954), the Court characterized education as "perhaps the most important function of state and local government." Two decades later, the Court refused to characterize education as a "fundamental right" under the federal constitution, at least for purposes of applying strict judicial scrutiny under the Equal Protection Clause. *San Antonio Indep. School District v. Rodriguez,* 411 U.S. 1 (1973). The Court in *Rodriguez,* however, left open the possibility that a state might violate equal protection if it adopted a system that absolutely denied all educational opportunities to an identified group of children. *See id.* at 36–37.

In *Plyer v. Doe,* 457 U.S. 202 (1982), the Court confronted this issue directly. At issue in *Plyer* was a Texas statute that denied funding for the free education of the children of undocumented aliens. The Court struck down the statute by a 5–4 vote. The majority opinion reiterated the Court's previous position that "[p]ublic education is not a 'right' guaranteed to individuals by the Constitution." However, "neither is it merely some governmental 'benefit' indistinguishable from other forms of social welfare legislation." Noting the pivotal role of public education "in sustaining our political and cultural heritage" and in "prepar[ing] individuals to be self-reliant and self-sufficient participants in society," the Court found that the Texas statute "imposes a lifetime hardship on a discrete class of children not accountable for their disabling status." In light of these significant costs, the Court concluded that the statutory exclusion was not rationally related to a substantial state goal. *Id* at 230. More recently, in *Kadrmas v. Dickinson Pub. Sch.,* 487 U.S. 450, 457–65 (1988), the Court held that the rationale of *Plyer* does not prevent a school district from charging a fee for bus service to and from its public schools. The Court expressly declined to extend "the heightened level of scrutiny" applied in *Plyer* beyond the "unique circumstances" of that case. *Query:* What was unique about the circumstances of *Plyer?*

PRINCE v. COMMONWEALTH OF MASSACHUSETTS
United States Supreme Court
321 U.S. 158 (1944)

MR. JUSTICE RUTLEDGE delivered the opinion of the Court.

The case brings for review another episode in the conflict between Jehovah's Witnesses and state authority. This time Sarah Prince appeals from convictions for violating Massachusetts' child labor laws, by acts said to be a rightful exercise of her religious convictions.

When the offenses were committed she was the aunt and custodian of Betty M. Simmons, a girl nine years of age. . . . [The statute under which Mrs. Prince was convicted provided as follows:]

> No boy under twelve and no girl under eighteen shall sell, expose or offer for sale any newspapers, magazines, periodicals or any other articles of merchandise of any description, or exercise the trade of bootblack or scavenger, or any other trade, in any street or public place. . . .

The story told by the evidence has become familiar. It hardly needs repeating, except to give setting to the variations introduced through the part played by a child of tender years. Mrs. Prince, living in Brockton, is the mother of two young sons. She also has legal custody of Betty Simmons, who lives with them. The children too are Jehovah's Witnesses and both Mrs. Prince and Betty testified they were ordained ministers. The former was accustomed to go each week on the streets of Brockton to distribute "Watchtower" and "Consolation," according to the usual plan. She had permitted the children to engage in this activity previously, and had been warned against doing so by the school attendance officer, Mr. Perkins. But, until December 18, 1941, she generally did not take them with her at night.

That evening, as Mrs. Prince was preparing to leave her home, the children asked to go. She at first refused. Childlike, they resorted to tears; and, motherlike, she yielded. Arriving downtown, Mrs. Prince permitted the children "to engage in the preaching work with her upon the sidewalks." That is, with specific reference to Betty, she and Mrs. Prince took positions about twenty feet apart near a street intersection. Betty held up in her hand, for passers-by to see, copies of "Watch Tower" and "Consolation." From her shoulder hung the usual canvas magazine bag, on which was printed: "Watchtower and Consolation 5 cents per copy." No one accepted a copy from Betty that evening and she received no money. Nor did her aunt. But on other occasions, Betty had received funds and given out copies.

Mrs. Prince and Betty remained until 8:45 p. m. A few minutes before this, Mr. Perkins approached Mrs. Prince. A discussion ensued. He inquired and she refused to give Betty's name. However, she stated the child attended the Shaw School. Mr. Perkins referred to his previous warnings and said he would allow five minutes for them to get off the street. Mrs. Prince admitted she supplied Betty with the magazines and said, "Neither you nor anybody else can stop me. . . . This child is exercising her God-given right and her constitutional right to preach the gospel, and no creature has a right to interfere with God's commands." However, Mrs. Prince and Betty departed. She remarked as she went, "I'm not going through this any more. We've been through it time and time again. I'm going home and put the little girl to bed." It may be added that testimony, by Betty, her aunt and others, was offered at the trials, and was excluded, to show that Betty believed it was her religious duty to perform this work and failure would bring condemnation "to everlasting destruction at Armageddon." . . .

Appellant does not stand on freedom of the press. Regarding it as secular, she concedes it may be restricted as Massachusetts has done. Hence, she rests squarely on freedom of religion under the First Amendment, applied by the Fourteenth to the states. She buttresses this foundation, however, with a claim of parental right as secured by the due process clause of the latter Amendment. *Cf. Meyer v. Nebraska*, 262 U.S. 390. These guaranties, she thinks, guard alike herself and the child in what they have done. Thus, two claimed liberties are at stake. One is the parent's, to bring up the child in the way he should go, which for appellant means to teach him the tenets and the practices of their faith. The other freedom is the child's, to observe these; and among them is "to preach the gospel . . . by public distribution" of "Watchtower" and "Consolation," in conformity with the scripture: "A little child shall lead them." . . .

To make accommodation between these freedoms and an exercise of state authority always is delicate. It hardly could be more so than in such a clash as this case presents. On one side is the obviously earnest claim for freedom of conscience and religious practice. With it is allied the parent's claim to authority in her own household and in the rearing of her children. The parent's conflict with the state over control of the child and his training is serious enough when only secular matters are concerned. It becomes the more so when an element of religious conviction enters. Against these sacred private interests, basic in a democracy, stand the interests of society to protect the welfare of children, and the state's assertion of authority to that end, made here in a manner conceded valid if only secular things were involved. The last is no mere corporate concern of official authority. It is the interest of youth itself, and of the whole community, that children be both safeguarded from abuses and given opportunities for growth into free and independent well-developed men and citizens. Between contrary pulls of such weight, the safest and most objective recourse is to the lines already marked out, not precisely but for guides, in narrowing the no man's land where this battle has gone on.

The rights of children to exercise their religion, and of parents to give them religious training and to encourage them in the practice of religious belief, as against preponderant sentiment and assertion of state power voicing it, have had recognition here, most recently in *West Virginia State Board of Education v. Barnette*, 319 U.S. 624. Previously in *Pierce v. Society of Sisters*, 268 U.S. 510, this Court had sustained the parent's authority to provide religious with secular schooling, and the child's right to receive it, as against the state's requirement of attendance at public schools. And in *Meyer v. Nebraska*, 262 U.S. 390, children's rights to receive teaching in languages other than the nation's common tongue were guarded against the state's encroachment. It is cardinal with us that the custody, care and nurture of the child reside first in the parents, whose primary function and freedom include preparation for obligations the state can neither supply nor hinder. *Pierce v. Society of Sisters, supra.* And it is in recognition of this that these decisions have respected the private realm of family life which the state cannot enter.

But the family itself is not beyond regulation in the public interest, as against a claim of religious liberty. And neither rights of religion nor rights of parenthood are beyond limitation. Acting to guard the general interest in youth's well being, the state as *parens patriae* may restrict the parent's control by requiring school attendance, regulating or prohibiting the child's labor and in many other ways. Its authority is not nullified merely because the parent grounds his claim to control the child's course of conduct on religion or conscience. Thus, he cannot claim freedom from compulsory vaccination for the child more than for himself on religious grounds. The right to practice religion freely does not include liberty to expose the community or the child to communicable disease or the latter to ill health or death. The catalogue need not be lengthened. It is sufficient to show what indeed appellant hardly disputes, that the state has a wide range of power for limiting parental freedom and authority in things affecting the child's welfare; and that this includes, to some extent, matters of conscience and religious conviction. . . .

Concededly a statute or ordinance identical in terms with § 69, except that it is applicable to adults or all persons generally, would be invalid. But the mere fact a state could not wholly prohibit this form of adult activity, whether characterized locally as a "sale" or otherwise, does not mean it cannot do so for children. Such a conclusion granted would mean that a state could impose no greater limitation upon child labor than upon adult labor. Or, if an adult were free to enter dance halls, saloons, and disreputable places generally, in order to discharge his conceived religious duty to admonish or dissuade persons from frequenting such places, so would be a child with similar convictions and objectives, if not alone then in the parent's company, against the state's command.

The state's authority over children's activities is broader than over like actions of adults. This is peculiarly true of public activities and in matters of employment. A democratic society rests, for its continuance, upon the healthy, well-rounded growth of young people into full maturity as citizens, with all that implies. It may secure this against impeding restraints and dangers within a broad range of selection. Among evils most appropriate for such action are the crippling effects of child employment, more especially in public places, and the possible harms arising from other activities subject to all the diverse influences of the street. It is too late now to doubt that legislation appropriately designed to reach such evils is within the state's police power, whether against the parent's claim to control of the child or one that religious scruples dictate contrary action.

It is true children have rights, in common with older people, in the primary use of highways. But even in such use streets afford dangers for them not affecting adults. And in other uses, whether in work or in other things, this difference may be magnified. This is so not only when children are unaccompanied but certainly to some extent when they are with their parents. What may be wholly permissible for adults therefore may not be so for children, either with or without their parents' presence.

Street preaching, whether oral or by handing out literature, is not the primary use of the highway, even for adults. While for them it cannot be wholly prohibited, it can be regulated within reasonable limits in accommodation to the primary and other incidental uses. But, for obvious reasons, notwithstanding appellant's contrary view, the validity of such a prohibition applied to children not accompanied by an older person hardly would seem open to question. The case reduces itself therefore to the question whether the presence of the child's guardian puts a limit to the state's power. That fact may lessen the likelihood that some evils the legislation seeks to avert will occur. But it cannot forestall all of them. The zealous though lawful exercise of the right to engage in propagandizing the community, whether in religious, political or other matters, may and at times does create situations difficult enough for adults to cope with and wholly inappropriate for children, especially of tender years, to face. Other harmful possibilities could be stated, of emotional excitement and psychological or physical injury. Parents may be free to become martyrs themselves. But it does not follow they are free, in identical circumstances, to make martyrs of their children before they have reached the age of full and legal discretion when they can make that choice for themselves. Massachusetts has determined that an absolute prohibition, though one limited to streets and public places and to the incidental uses proscribed, is necessary to accomplish its legitimate objectives. Its power to attain them is broad enough to reach these peripheral instances in which the parent's supervision may reduce but cannot eliminate entirely the ill effects of the prohibited conduct. We think that with reference to the public proclaiming of religion, upon the streets and in other similar public places, the power of the state to control the conduct of children reaches beyond the scope of its authority over adults, as is true in the case of other freedoms, and the rightful boundary of its power has not been crossed in this case. . . .

WISCONSIN v. YODER
United States Supreme Court
406 U.S. 205 (1972)

Mr. Chief Justice Burger delivered the opinion of the Court.

. . . Respondents Jonas Yoder and Wallace Miller are members of the Old Order Amish religion, and respondent Adin Yutzy is a member of the Conservative Amish Mennonite Church. They and their families are residents of Green County, Wisconsin. Wisconsin's compulsory school-attendance law required them to cause their children to attend public or private school until reaching age 16 but the respondents declined to send their children, ages 14 and 15, to public school after they completed the eighth grade. The children were not enrolled in any private school, or within any recognized exception to the compulsory-attendance law, and they are conceded to be subject to the Wisconsin statute.

On complaint of the school district administrator for the public schools, respondents were charged, tried, and convicted of violating the compulsory-attendance law in Green County Court and were fined the sum of $ 5 each. Respondents defended on the ground that the application of the compulsory-attendance law violated their rights under the First and Fourteenth Amendments. The trial testimony showed that respondents believed, in accordance with the tenets of Old Order Amish communities generally, that their children's attendance at high school, public or private, was contrary to the Amish religion and way of life. They believed that by sending their children to high school, they would not only expose themselves to the danger of the censure of the church community, but, as found by the county court, also endanger their own salvation and that of their children. The State stipulated that respondents' religious beliefs were sincere.

In support of their position, respondents presented as expert witnesses scholars on religion and education whose testimony is uncontradicted. They expressed their opinions on the relationship of the Amish belief concerning school attendance to the more general tenets of their religion, and described the impact that compulsory high school attendance could have on the continued survival of Amish communities as they exist in the United States today. As a result of their common heritage, Old Order Amish communities today are characterized by a fundamental belief that salvation requires life in a church community separate and apart from the world and worldly influence. This concept of life aloof from the world and its values is central to their faith.

A related feature of Old Order Amish communities is their devotion to a life in harmony with nature and the soil, as exemplified by the simple life of the early Christian era that continued in America during much of our early national life. Amish beliefs require members of the community to make their living by farming or closely related activities. Broadly speaking, the Old Order Amish religion pervades and determines the entire mode of life of its adherents. Their conduct is regulated in great detail by the Ordnung, or rules, of the church community. Adult baptism, which occurs in late adolescence, is the time at which Amish young people voluntarily undertake heavy obligations, not unlike the Bar Mitzvah of the Jews, to abide by the rules of the church community.

Amish objection to formal education beyond the eighth grade is firmly grounded in these central religious concepts. They object to the high school, and higher education generally, because the values they teach are in marked variance with Amish values and the Amish way of life; they view secondary school education as an impermissible exposure of their children to a "worldly" influence in conflict with their beliefs. The high school tends to emphasize intellectual and scientific accomplishments, self-distinction, competitiveness, worldly success, and social life with other students. Amish society emphasizes informal learning-through-doing; a life of "goodness," rather than a life of intellect; wisdom, rather than technical knowledge; community welfare, rather than competition; and separation from, rather than integration with, contemporary worldly society.

Formal high school education beyond the eighth grade is contrary to Amish beliefs, not only because it places Amish children in an environment hostile to Amish beliefs with increasing emphasis on competition in class work and sports and with pressure to conform to the styles, manners, and ways of the peer group, but also because it takes them away from their community, physically and emotionally, during the crucial and formative adolescent period of life. During this period, the children must acquire Amish attitudes favoring manual work and self-reliance and the specific skills needed to perform the adult role of an Amish farmer or housewife. They must learn to enjoy physical labor. Once a child has learned basic reading, writing, and elementary mathematics, these traits, skills, and attitudes admittedly fall within the category of those best learned through example and "doing" rather than in a classroom. And, at this time in life, the Amish child must also grow in his faith and his relationship to the Amish community if he is to be prepared to accept the heavy obligations imposed by adult baptism. In short, high school attendance with teachers who are not of the Amish faith—and may even be hostile to it—interposes a serious barrier to the integration of the Amish child into the Amish religious community. Dr. John Hostetler, one of the experts on Amish society, testified that the modern high school is not equipped, in curriculum or social environment, to impart the values promoted by Amish society.

The Amish do not object to elementary education through the first eight grades as a general proposition because they agree that their children must have basic skills in the "three R's" in order to read the Bible, to be good farmers and citizens, and to be able to deal with non-Amish people when necessary in the course of daily affairs. They view such a basic education as acceptable because it does not significantly expose their children to worldly values or interfere with their development in the Amish community during the crucial adolescent period. While Amish accept compulsory elementary education generally, wherever possible they have established their own elementary schools in many respects like the small local schools of the past. In the Amish belief higher learning tends to develop values they reject as influences that alienate man from God.

On the basis of such considerations, Dr. Hostetler testified that compulsory high school attendance could not only result in great psychological harm to Amish children, because of the conflicts it would produce, but would also, in his opinion, ultimately result in the destruction of the Old Order Amish church community as it exists in the United States today. The testimony of Dr. Donald A. Erickson, an expert witness on education, also showed that the Amish succeed in preparing their high school age children to be productive members of the Amish community. He described their system of learning through doing the skills directly relevant to their adult roles in the Amish community as "ideal" and perhaps superior to ordinary high school education. The evidence also showed that the Amish have an excellent record as law-abiding and generally self-sufficient members of society. . . .

I

There is no doubt as to the power of a State, having a high responsibility for education of its citizens, to impose reasonable regulations for the control and duration of basic education. *See, e. g., Pierce v. Society of Sisters*, 268 U.S. 510, 534 (1925). Providing public schools ranks at the very apex of the function of a State. Yet even this paramount responsibility was, in *Pierce*, made to yield to the right of parents to provide an equivalent education in a privately operated system. There the Court held that Oregon's statute compelling attendance in a public school from age eight to age 16 unreasonably interfered with the interest of parents in directing the rearing of their offspring, including their education in church-operated schools. As that case suggests, the values of parental direction of the religious upbringing and education of their children in their early and formative years have a high place in our society. Thus, a State's interest in universal education, however highly we rank it, is not totally free from a balancing process when it impinges on fundamental rights and interests, such as those specifically protected by the Free Exercise Clause of the First Amendment, and the traditional interest of parents with respect to the religious upbringing of their children so long as they, in the words of *Pierce*, "prepare [them] for additional obligations." 268 U.S., at 535.

It follows that in order for Wisconsin to compel school attendance beyond the eighth grade against a claim that such attendance interferes with the practice of a legitimate religious belief, it must appear either that the State does not deny the free exercise of religious belief by its requirement, or that there is a state interest of sufficient magnitude to override the interest claiming protection under the Free Exercise Clause. . . .

II

We come then to the quality of the claims of the respondents concerning the alleged encroachment of Wisconsin's compulsory school-attendance statute on their rights and the rights of their children to the free exercise of the religious beliefs they and their forebears have adhered to for almost three centuries. In evaluating those claims we must be careful to determine whether the Amish religious faith and their mode of life are, as they claim, inseparable and interdependent. A way of life, however virtuous and admirable, may not be interposed as a barrier to reasonable state regulation of education if it is based on purely secular considerations; to have the protection of the Religion Clauses, the claims must be rooted in religious belief. Although a determination of what is a "religious" belief or practice entitled to constitutional protection may present a most delicate question, the very concept of ordered liberty precludes allowing every person to make his own standards on matters of conduct in which society as a whole has important interests. Thus, if the Amish asserted their claims because of their subjective evaluation and rejection of the contemporary secular values accepted by the majority, much as Thoreau rejected the social values of his time and isolated himself at Walden Pond, their claims would not rest on a religious basis. Thoreau's choice was philosophical and personal rather than religious, and such belief does not rise to the demands of the Religion Clauses.

Giving no weight to such secular considerations, however, we see that the record in this case abundantly supports the claim that the traditional way of life of the Amish is not merely a matter of personal preference, but one of deep religious conviction, shared by an organized group, and intimately related to daily living. That the Old Order Amish daily life and religious practice stem from their faith is shown by the fact that it is in response to their literal interpretation of the Biblical injunction from the Epistle of Paul to the Romans, "be not conformed to this world . . . ." This command is fundamental to the Amish faith. Moreover, for the Old Order Amish, religion is not simply a matter of theocratic belief. As the expert witnesses explained, the Old Order Amish religion pervades and determines virtually their entire way of life, regulating it with the detail of the Talmudic diet through the strictly enforced rules of the church community.

The record shows that the respondents' religious beliefs and attitude toward life, family, and home have remained constant—perhaps some would say static—in a period of unparalleled progress in human knowledge generally and great changes in education. The respondents freely concede, and indeed assert as an article of faith, that their religious beliefs and what we would today call "life style" have not altered in fundamentals for centuries. Their way of life in a church-oriented community, separated from the outside world and "worldly" influences, their attachment to nature and the soil, is a way inherently simple and uncomplicated, albeit difficult to preserve against the pressure to conform. Their rejection of telephones, automobiles, radios, and television, their mode of dress, of speech, their habits of manual work do indeed set them apart from much of contemporary society; these customs are both symbolic and practical.

As the society around the Amish has become more populous, urban, industrialized, and complex, particularly in this century, government regulation of human affairs has correspondingly become more detailed and pervasive. The Amish mode of life has thus come into conflict increasingly with requirements of contemporary society exerting a hydraulic insistence on conformity to majoritarian standards. So long as compulsory education laws were confined to eight grades of elementary basic education imparted in a nearby rural schoolhouse, with a large proportion of students of the Amish faith, the Old Order Amish had little basis to fear that school attendance would expose their children to the worldly influence they reject. But modern compulsory secondary education in rural areas is now largely carried on in a consolidated school, often remote from the student's home and alien to his daily home life. As the record so strongly shows, the values and programs of the modern secondary school are in sharp conflict with the fundamental mode of life mandated by the Amish religion; modern laws requiring compulsory secondary education have accordingly engendered great concern and conflict. The conclusion is inescapable that secondary schooling, by exposing Amish children to worldly influences in terms of attitudes, goals, and values contrary to beliefs, and by substantially interfering with the religious development of the Amish child and his integration into the way of life of the Amish faith community at the crucial adolescent stage of development, contravenes the basic religious tenets and practice of the Amish faith, both as to the parent and the child.

The impact of the compulsory-attendance law on respondents' practice of the Amish religion is not only severe, but inescapable, for the Wisconsin law affirmatively compels them, under threat of criminal sanction, to perform acts undeniably at odds with fundamental tenets of their religious beliefs. Nor is the impact of the compulsory-attendance law confined to grave interference with important Amish religious tenets from a subjective point of view. It carries with it precisely the kind of objective danger to the free exercise of religion that the First Amendment was designed to prevent. As the record shows, compulsory school attendance to age 16 for Amish children carries with it a very real threat of undermining the Amish community and religious practice as they exist today; they must either abandon belief and be assimilated into society at large, or be forced to migrate to some other and more tolerant region.

In sum, the unchallenged testimony of acknowledged experts in education and religious history, almost 300 years of consistent practice, and strong evidence of a sustained faith pervading and regulating respondents' entire mode of life support the claim that enforcement of the State's requirement of compulsory formal education after the eighth grade would gravely endanger if not destroy the free exercise of respondents' religious beliefs.

III

Neither the findings of the trial court nor the Amish claims as to the nature of their faith are challenged in this Court by the State of Wisconsin. Its position is that the State's interest in universal compulsory formal secondary education to age 16 is so great that it is paramount to the undisputed claims of respondents that their mode of preparing their youth for Amish life, after the traditional elementary education, is an essential part of their religious belief and practice. Nor does the State undertake to meet the claim that the Amish mode of life and education is inseparable from and a part of the basic tenets of their religion—indeed, as much a part of their religious belief and practices as baptism, the confessional, or a sabbath may be for others.

Wisconsin concedes that under the Religion Clauses religious beliefs are absolutely free from the State's control, but it argues that "actions," even though religiously grounded, are outside the protection of the First Amendment. But our decisions have rejected the idea that religiously grounded conduct is always outside the protection of the Free Exercise Clause. It is true that activities of individuals, even when religiously based, are often subject to regulation by the States in the exercise of their undoubted power to promote the health, safety, and general welfare, or the Federal Government in the exercise of its delegated powers. But to agree that religiously grounded conduct must often be subject to the broad police power of the State is not to deny that there are areas of conduct protected by the Free Exercise Clause of the First Amendment and thus beyond the power of the State to control, even under regulations of general applicability. This case, therefore, does not become easier because respondents were convicted for their "actions" in refusing to send their children to the public high school; in this context belief and action cannot be neatly confined in logic-tight compartments.

Nor can this case be disposed of on the grounds that Wisconsin's requirement for school attendance to age 16 applies uniformly to all citizens of the State and does not, on its face, discriminate against religions or a particular religion, or that it is motivated by legitimate secular concerns. A regulation neutral on its face may, in its application, nonetheless offend the constitutional requirement for governmental neutrality if it unduly burdens the free exercise of religion. The Court must not ignore the danger that an exception from a general obligation of citizenship on religious grounds may run afoul of the Establishment Clause, but that danger cannot be allowed to prevent any exception no matter how vital it may be to the protection of values promoted by the right of free exercise. . . .

We turn, then, to the State's broader contention that its interest in its system of compulsory education is so compelling that even the established religious practices of the Amish must give way. Where fundamental claims of religious freedom are at stake, however, we cannot accept such a sweeping claim; despite its admitted validity in the generality of cases, we must searchingly examine the interests that the State seeks to promote by its requirement for compulsory education to age 16, and the impediment to those objectives that would flow from recognizing the claimed Amish exemption.

The State advances two primary arguments in support of its system of compulsory education. It notes, as Thomas Jefferson pointed out early in our history, that some degree of education is necessary to prepare citizens to participate effectively and intelligently in our open political system if we are to preserve freedom and independence. Further, education prepares individuals to be self-reliant and self-sufficient participants in society. We accept these propositions.

However, the evidence adduced by the Amish in this case is persuasively to the effect that an additional one or two years of formal high school for Amish children in place of their long-established program of informal vocational education would do little to serve those interests. Respondents' experts testified at trial, without challenge, that the value of all education must be assessed in terms of its capacity to prepare the child for life. It is one thing to say that compulsory education for a year or two beyond the eighth grade may be necessary when its goal is the preparation of the child for life in modern society as the majority live, but it is quite another if the goal of education be viewed as the preparation of the child for life in the separated agrarian community that is the keystone of the Amish faith. *See Meyer v. Nebraska*, 262 U.S., at 400.

The State attacks respondents' position as one fostering "ignorance" from which the child must be protected by the State. No one can question the State's duty to protect children from ignorance but this argument does not square with the facts disclosed in the record. Whatever their idiosyncrasies as seen by the majority, this record strongly shows that the Amish community has been a highly successful social unit within our society, even if apart from the conventional "mainstream." Its members are productive and very law-abiding members of society; they reject public welfare in any of its usual modern forms. The Congress itself recognized their self-sufficiency by authorizing exemption of such groups as the Amish from the obligation to pay social security taxes.

It is neither fair nor correct to suggest that the Amish are opposed to education beyond the eighth grade level. What this record shows is that they are opposed to conventional formal education of the type provided by a certified high school because it comes at the child's crucial adolescent period of religious development. Dr. Donald Erickson, for example, testified that their system of learning-by-doing was an "ideal system" of education in terms of preparing Amish children for life as adults in the Amish community, and that "I would be inclined to say they do a better job in this than most of the rest of us do." As he put it, "These people aren't purporting to be learned people, and it seems to me the self-sufficiency of the community is the best evidence I can point to—whatever is being done seems to function well."

We must not forget that in the Middle Ages important values of the civilization of the Western World were preserved by members of religious orders who isolated themselves from all worldly influences against great obstacles. There can be no assumption that today's majority is "right" and the Amish and others like them are "wrong." A way of life that is odd or even erratic but interferes with no rights or interests of others is not to be condemned because it is different.

The State, however, supports its interest in providing an additional one or two years of compulsory high school education to Amish children because of the possibility that some such children will choose to leave the Amish community, and that if this occurs they will be ill-equipped for life. The State argues that if Amish children leave their church they should not be in the position of making their way in the world without the education available in the one or two additional years the State requires. However, on this record, that argument is highly speculative. There is no specific evidence of the loss of Amish adherents by attrition, nor is there any showing that upon leaving the Amish community Amish children, with their practical agricultural training and habits of industry and self-reliance, would become burdens on society because of educational short-comings. Indeed, this argument of the State appears to rest primarily on the State's mistaken assumption, already noted, that the Amish do not provide any education for their children beyond the eighth grade, but allow them to grow in "ignorance." To the contrary, not only do the Amish accept the necessity for formal schooling through the eighth grade level, but continue to provide what has been characterized by the undisputed testimony of expert educators as an "ideal" vocational education for their children in the adolescent years.

There is nothing in this record to suggest that the Amish qualities of reliability, self-reliance, and dedication to work would fail to find ready markets in today's society. Absent some contrary evidence supporting the State's position, we are unwilling to assume that persons possessing such valuable vocational skills and habits are doomed to become burdens on society should they determine to leave the Amish faith, nor is there any basis in the record to warrant a finding that an additional one or two years of formal school education beyond the eighth grade would serve to eliminate any such problem that might exist.

Insofar as the State's claim rests on the view that a brief additional period of formal education is imperative to enable the Amish to participate effectively and intelligently in our democratic process, it must fall. The Amish alternative to formal secondary school education has enabled them to function effectively in their day-to-day life under self-imposed limitations on relations with the world, and to survive and prosper in contemporary society as a separate, sharply identifiable and highly self-sufficient community for more than 200 years in this country. In itself this is strong evidence that they are capable of fulfilling the social and political responsibilities of citizenship without compelled attendance beyond the eighth grade at the price of jeopardizing their free exercise of religious belief. When Thomas Jefferson emphasized the need for education as a bulwark of a free people against tyranny, there is nothing to indicate he had in mind compulsory education through any fixed age beyond a basic education. Indeed, the Amish communities singularly parallel and reflect many of the virtues of Jefferson's ideal of the "sturdy yeoman" who would form the basis of what he considered as the ideal of a democratic society. Even their idiosyncratic separateness exemplifies the diversity we profess to admire and encourage.

The requirement for compulsory education beyond the eighth grade is a relatively recent development in our history. Less than 60 years ago, the educational requirements of almost all of the States were satisfied by completion of the elementary grades, at least where the child was regularly and lawfully employed. The independence and successful social functioning of the Amish community for a period approaching almost three centuries and more than 200 years in this country are strong evidence that there is at best a speculative gain, in terms of meeting the duties of citizenship, from an additional one or two years of compulsory formal education. Against this background it would require a more particularized showing from the State on this point to justify the severe interference with religious freedom such additional compulsory attendance would entail. . . .

IV

Finally, the State, on authority of *Prince v. Massachusetts* 321 U.S. 158 (1944), argues that a decision exempting Amish children from the State's requirement fails to recognize the substantive right of the Amish child to a secondary education, and fails to give due regard to the power of the State as parens patriae to extend the benefit of secondary education to children regardless of the wishes of their parents. Taken at its broadest sweep, the Court's language in *Prince*, might be read to give support to the State's position. However, the Court was not confronted in *Prince* with a situation comparable to that of the Amish as revealed in this record; this is shown by the Court's severe characterization of the evils that it thought the legislature could legitimately associate with child labor, even when performed in the company of an adult. 321 U.S., at 169–170.

Contrary to the suggestion of the dissenting opinion of MR. JUSTICE DOUGLAS, our holding today in no degree depends on the assertion of the religious interest of the child as contrasted with that of the parents. It is the parents who are subject to prosecution here for failing to cause their children to attend school, and it is their right of free exercise, not that of their children, that must determine Wisconsin's power to impose criminal penalties on the parent. The dissent argues that a child who expresses a desire to attend public high school in conflict with the wishes of his parents should not be prevented from doing so. There is no reason for the Court to consider that point since it is not an issue in the case. The children are not parties to this litigation. The State has at no point tried this case on the theory that respondents were preventing their children from attending school against their expressed desires, and indeed the record is to the contrary. The State's position from the outset has been that it is empowered to apply its compulsory-attendance law to Amish parents in the same manner as to other parents—that is, without regard to the wishes of the child. That is the claim we reject today.

Our holding in no way determines the proper resolution of possible competing interests of parents, children, and the State in an appropriate state court proceeding in which the power of the State is asserted on the theory that Amish parents are preventing their minor children from attending high school despite their expressed desires to the contrary. Recognition of the claim of the State in such a proceeding would, of course, call into question traditional concepts of parental control over the religious upbringing and education of their minor children recognized in this Court's past decisions. It is clear that such an intrusion by a State into family decisions in the area of religious training would give rise to grave questions of religious freedom comparable to those raised here and those presented in *Pierce v. Society of Sisters*, 268 U.S. 510 (1925). On this record we neither reach nor decide those issues

V

For the reasons stated we hold, with the Supreme Court of Wisconsin, that the First and Fourteenth Amendments prevent the State from compelling respondents to cause their children to attend formal high school to age 16. Our disposition of this case, however, in no way alters our recognition of the obvious fact that courts are not school boards or legislatures, and are ill-equipped to determine the "necessity" of discrete aspects of a State's program of compulsory education. This should suggest that courts must move with great circumspection in performing the sensitive and delicate task of weighing a State's legitimate social concern when faced with religious claims for exemption from generally applicable educational requirements. It cannot be overemphasized that we are not dealing with a way of life and mode of education by a group claiming to have recently discovered some "progressive" or more enlightened process for rearing children for modern life.

Aided by a history of three centuries as an identifiable religious sect and a long history as a successful and self-sufficient segment of American society, the Amish in this case have convincingly demonstrated the sincerity of their religious beliefs, the interrelationship of belief with their mode of life, the vital role that belief and daily conduct play in the continued survival of Old Order Amish communities and their religious organization, and the hazards presented by the State's enforcement of a statute generally valid as to others. Beyond this, they have carried the even more difficult burden of demonstrating the adequacy of their alternative mode of continuing informal vocational education in terms of precisely those overall interests that the State advances in support of its program of compulsory high school education. In light of this convincing showing, one that probably few other religious groups or sects could make, and weighing the minimal difference between what the State would require and what the Amish already accept, it was incumbent on the State to show with more particularity how its admittedly strong interest in compulsory education would be adversely affected by granting an exemption to the Amish. . . .

Mr. Justice Douglas, dissenting in part.

I

I agree with the Court that the religious scruples of the Amish are opposed to the education of their children beyond the grade schools, yet I disagree with the Court's conclusion that the matter is within the dispensation of parents alone. The Court's analysis assumes that the only interests at stake in the case are those of the Amish parents on the one hand, and those of the State on the other. The difficulty with this approach is that, despite the Court's claim, the parents are seeking to vindicate not only their own free exercise claims, but also those of their high-school-age children.

It is argued that the right of the Amish children to religious freedom is not presented by the facts of the case, as the issue before the Court involves only the Amish parents' religious freedom to defy a state criminal statute imposing upon them an affirmative duty to cause their children to attend high school.

First, respondents' motion to dismiss in the trial court expressly asserts, not only the religious liberty of the adults, but also that of the children, as a defense to the prosecutions. It is, of course, beyond question that the parents have standing as defendants in a criminal prosecution to assert the religious interests of their children as a defense. Although the lower courts and a majority of this Court assume an identity of interest between parent and child, it is clear that they have treated the religious interest of the child as a factor in the analysis.

Second, it is essential to reach the question to decide the case, not only because the question was squarely raised in the motion to dismiss, but also because no analysis of religious-liberty claims can take place in a vacuum. If the parents in this case are allowed a religious exemption, the inevitable effect is to impose the parents' notions of religious duty upon their children. Where the child is mature enough to express potentially conflicting desires, it would be an invasion of the child's rights to permit such an imposition without canvassing his views. As in *Prince v. Massachusetts*, 321 U.S. 158, it is an imposition resulting from this very litigation. As the child has no other effective forum, it is in this litigation that his rights should be considered. And, if an Amish child desires to attend high school, and is mature enough to have that desire respected, the State may well be able to override the parents' religiously motivated objections.

Religion is an individual experience. It is not necessary, nor even appropriate, for every Amish child to express his views on the subject in a prosecution of a single adult. Crucial, however, are the views of the child whose parent is the subject of the suit. Frieda Yoder has in fact testified that her own religious views are opposed to high-school education. I therefore join the judgment of the Court as to respondent Jonas Yoder. But Frieda Yoder's views may not be those of Vernon Yutzy or Barbara Miller. I must dissent, therefore, as to respondents Adin Yutzy and Wallace Miller as their motion to dismiss also raised the question of their children's religious liberty.

II

This issue has never been squarely presented before today. Our opinions are full of talk about the power of the parents over the child's education. See *Pierce v. Society of Sisters*, 268 U.S. 510; *Meyer v. Nebraska*, 262 U.S. 390. And we have in the past analyzed similar conflicts between parent and State with little regard for the views of the child. *See Prince v. Massachusetts, supra.* Recent cases, however, have clearly held that the children themselves have constitutionally protectible interests.

These children are "persons" within the meaning of the Bill of Rights. We have so held over and over again. In *Haley v. Ohio*, 332 U.S. 596, we extended the protection of the Fourteenth Amendment in a state trial of a 15-year-old boy. In *In re Gault*, 387 U.S. 1, 13, we held that "neither the Fourteenth Amendment nor the Bill of Rights is for adults alone." In *In re Winship*, 397 U.S. 358, we held that a 12-year-old boy, when charged with an act which would be a crime if committed by an adult, was entitled to procedural safeguards contained in the Sixth Amendment.

In *Tinker v. Des Moines School District*, 393 U.S. 503, we dealt with 13-year-old, 15-year-old, and 16-year-old students who wore armbands to public schools and were disciplined for doing so. We gave them relief, saying that their First Amendment rights had been abridged. "Students in school as well as out of school are 'persons' under our Constitution. They are possessed of fundamental rights which the State must respect, just as they themselves must respect their obligations to the State." *Id.*, at 511. . . .

On this important and vital matter of education, I think the children should be entitled to be heard. While the parents, absent dissent, normally speak for the entire family, the education of the child is a matter on which the child will often have decided views. He may want to be a pianist or an astronaut or an oceanographer. To do so he will have to break from the Amish tradition.

It is the future of the student, not the future of the parents, that is imperiled by today's decision. If a parent keeps his child out of school beyond the grade school, then the child will be forever barred from entry into the new and amazing world of diversity that we have today. The child may decide that that is the preferred course, or he may rebel. It is the student's judgment, not his parents', that is essential if we are to give full meaning to what we have said about the Bill of Rights and of the right of students to be masters of their own destiny. If he is harnessed to the Amish way of life by those in authority over him and if his education is truncated, his entire life may be stunted and deformed. The child, therefore, should be given an opportunity to be heard before the State gives the exemption which we honor today. . . .

NOTES AND QUESTIONS

(1) Are *Yoder* and *Prince* consistent? To the extent that the two cases are factually distinguishable, which way do the differences cut? Is the potential harm to Amish children from not attending high school greater or less than the risks to Jehovah's Witness children from selling religious literature on the street? In which case are the asserted state interests more compelling?

(2) Would the Supreme Court's opinion in *Yoder* apply to Native American parents who refused to send their children to school because they believed that the school curriculum was contrary to Native American culture and values? *See Matter of McMillan,* 226 S.E.2d 693 (N.C. Ct. App. 1976). To parents who withdrew their children from high school in order to work on a family farm?

(3) Justice Douglas dissents in *Yoder* on the ground that the Amish children affected by the Court's ruling should have the right to be heard on the question whether to attend high school. What should happen, under Justice Douglas' view, if an Amish child indicates a desire to attend high school, contrary to the wishes of her or his parents?

(4) In *Employment Div'n, Dep't of Human Resources of Oregon v. Smith,* 494 U.S. 872, 878–89 (1990) the Supreme Court upheld the denial of unemployment benefits to two employees who were dismissed from their jobs for ingesting peyote, a ritual of their Native

American religion. The Court rejected the claim that the terminations violated the employees' right to free exercise of religion, noting that the state statute classifying peyote as an illegal drug made no exception for its religious use. In rejecting the employees' First Amendment argument, the Court held that the Free Exercise Clause can bar application of a generally applicable law only when it is joined with another constitutional guarantee, such as freedom of speech or of the press, or a claim of parental right (citing *Yoder* and *Pierce*). In 1993, Congress passed the Religious Freedom Restoration Act ("RFRA"), 42 U.S.C. § 2000bb (1997), which rejected the Court's interpretation and required states to provide religious exemptions from generally applicable laws. However, in *City of Boerne v. Flores* 117 S. Ct. 2157, 2170, 138 L. Ed. 624, 627 (1997), the Supreme Court invalidated RFRA, holding that it exceeded the scope of Congress' power under the Fourteenth Amendment.

(5) **Home Schooling.** Do the decisions in *Meyer*, *Pierce* and *Yoder* indicate that parents have a constitutionally protected right to educate their children at home? The Supreme Court has never addressed this question directly, and lower courts have come to varying conclusions. *Compare, e.g., Mazaenic v. North Judson-San Pierre Sch. Corp*, 614 F. Supp. 1152, 1160 (N.D. Ind. 1985), *aff'd,* 798 F.2d 230 (7th Cir. 1986) (holding that parents have a "constitutional right to educate [their] children in an educationally proper home environment"), *with Null v. Board of Educ.*, 815 F.Supp. 937, 939–40 (S.D. W. Va. 1993) (mem.) (finding that parents do *not* possess a fundamental right to direct their children's education, but only a general liberty interest subject to reasonable regulation).

As recently as 1983, only about half the states permitted home instruction by a parent. Jack MacMullan, *The Constitutionality of State Home Schooling Statutes*, 39 Vill. L. Rev. 1309, 1337 (1994). Today, however, all 50 states allow home schooling, and the number of children educated at home has increased significantly over the past decade. *See* Lisa M. Likasik, *The Latest Home Education Challenge: The Relationship Between Home Schools and Public Schools*, 74 N.C. L. Rev. 1913 (1996) (reporting that "as many as one million school-aged children are being educated at home"); Anita Manning, *Life in '94 Will Offer Glimpse into Next Century*, USA Today, Dec. 22, 1993, at 01D (identifying home schooling as one of the major "trends" of the 1990s, the effects of which will be felt into the Twenty-First century). States currently regulate home schooling in a variety of ways. For example, some states require children educated at home to receive instruction that is "substantially equivalent" to that provided in the public schools. Other states require parents to obtain teacher certification or meet minimum educational qualifications. A number of states require children schooled at home to take standardized tests at regular intervals; other states give local school officials the authority to approve particular home schooling programs, and to conduct home visits to ensure that parents are complying with applicable state requirements. *See generally* Jack MacMullan, *The Constitutionality of State Home School Statutes*, 39 Vill. L. Rev. 1309, 1337–48 (1994) (discussing various types of state regulation).

Advocates of home schooling have challenged particular state regulations on a variety of constitutional grounds. For example, in *Jeffrey v. O'Donnell*, 702 F. Supp. 526 (M.D. Pa. 1988), home schoolers argued successfully that a Pennsylvania's home education statute, which provided for instruction by a "properly qualified private tutor" and which mandated instructional standards "satisfactory to the proper district superintendent of schools." was unconstitutionally vague and subject to ad hoc and arbitrary application. By contrast, in *Blackwelder v. Safnauer*, 689 F. Supp. 106, 126–27(N.D.N.Y. 1988) *appeal dismissed*, 866 F. 2d 548 (2d Cir. 1989), the court rejected vagueness and other constitutional challenges to New York's statutory requirement that children taught at home must receive instruction from a "competent" teacher that is at least "substantially equivalent" to that provided in a public school. In other cases, parents have raised First Amendment challenges to state teacher certification requirements, again with mixed results. *Compare, e.g., Michigan v. DeJonge*, 501 N.W.2d 127, 137 (Mich. 1993) (invalidating teacher certification requirement as violative of First Amendment rights of home schooling parents whose religious convictions prohibit the use of certified instructors) *with State v. Patzer*, 382 N.W.2d 631, (639 N.D. 1986), *cert. denied*, 479 U.S. 825 (1986) (upholding teacher certification requirement as constitutionally justified, despite its impact on the sincere beliefs of home educators). Advocates of home schooling have also challenged state regulations on substantive due process and privacy grounds. *See, e.g., Murphy v. Arkansas*, 852 F.2d 1039, 1044 (8th Cir. 1988) (rejecting claims that state regulation of home schooling violates parents' right to privacy).

Query: What standard should the courts apply in evaluating constitutional challenges to state home schooling regulations? Should the regulations be sustained so long as they are rationally related to a legitimate state goal, or should the state be required to demonstrate that it has adopted the "least restrictive means" of regulating home education? Should it matter whether the parents who object to the regulation are home schooling for religious or non-religious reasons?

As the number of parents and children involved in home education continues to increase, new legal issues are likely to arise. For example, should children who are schooled at home be able to take advantage of extracurricular and other enrichment activities offered by the public schools? Should home educators be able to enroll their children "part-time" in the public schools, in order to take advantage of subjects or courses that the parents are unqualified (or unwilling) to teach? For a preliminary analysis of these issues, see Lukasik, *above* at 1954–75.

(6) **Problem**. George and Mary Jones are religious fundamentalists. A literal reading of the biblical account of creation is central to their religious beliefs. They object to the instruction in evolution that their daughter is scheduled to receive in her high school biology class. The Joneses view the instruction as both heretical and likely to lead their daughter to question her religious training. When they make their objections known to the high school principal, she seeks your advice on how to proceed. The principal has no doubt about the sincerity of the Jones' religious objections. Indeed, she thinks the Jones are quite worried that the secular influences of the public school have already eroded their daughter's faith. What would you advise the principal to do?

(7) **Problem**. Ten-year-old Buddy Hatch attends Canton Elementary School in Canton, Oklahoma. His parents, Donald and Viola Hatch, are enrolled members of the Arapaho Tribe. For the past several years, Buddy has worn his hair in braids, in traditional Native American fashion, with the full approval and encouragement of his parents. Recently, Buddy's parents received a letter from the principal of Canton Elementary School informing them that Buddy would have to cut his hair or face suspension from school, in accordance with school rules for student appearance. The rules provide, among other things, that boys'

hair must be kept trim and neatly groomed and may not extend below the collar. The Hatch's object to the application of the grooming rule on the ground that it interferes with their right to inculcate in their children a knowledge of and respect for Native American customs, traditions and religious beliefs. The principal has refused to exempt Buddy from the regulation, explaining that if he makes an exception for one student, then other students and their parents will demand similar treatment. Donald and Viola Hatch would like your advice on whether they can mount a plausible constitutional challenge to the school district's grooming rule. *See Hatch v. Goerke,* 502 F.2d 1189 (10th Cir. 1974).

(8) **Problem**. Wanda and Henry Green are schooling their three children at home for non-religious reasons. The Greens have complied with all applicable home schooling regulations and their children are performing at or above grade level in all subjects. The Greens' 15-year-old daughter, Angela, is particularly strong in science and has expressed a desire to study chemistry. The Greens support their daughter's desire, but do not believe they are qualified to teach chemistry at home; nor do they have access to the laboratory equipment necessary to provide a thorough introduction to the subject. The Greens have therefore requested that Angela be allowed to attend the local high school for the sole purpose of taking chemistry. The Greens have indicated that they will take responsibility for getting Angela to and from the high school at the appropriate hours. How should the superintendent respond to the Greens' request? If the superintendent refuses to allow Angela take the chemistry class, can the Greens plausibly challenge the refusal on federal constitutional grounds?

§ 7.03 Child Abuse and Neglect

Although parental authority to raise children is constitutionally protected, it is also limited by the state's authority to protect children from endangerment. In particular, parental authority is circumscribed by civil and criminal prohibitions on child abuse and neglect. However, the legal and social meaning of both abuse and neglect is contested, as is the most appropriate state response to parents who are unable (or unwilling) to provide proper care for their children.

[A] Abuse or Discipline?

In contrast to recent legal developments condemning violence between adult intimates, [*see* Chapter 6, *above*], American attitudes toward the use of physical force by parents against children are considerably more ambivalent. Surveys show that a substantial majority of Americans approve of corporal punishment of children and that most parents engage in such physical punishment at some time during their children's lives. *See, e.g.,* Murray A. Strauss & Carrie L. Yodanis, *Corporal Punishment by Parents: Implications for Primary Prevention of Assaults on Spouses and Children,* 2 U. Chi. L. Sch. Roundtable 35, 37 (1995) (noting that most Americans believe that a 'good hard spanking is sometimes necessary'); Richard J. Gelles & Claire Pedrick Cornell, Intimate Violence In Families, 44 (Sage 2d ed. 1990) ("Social surveys indicate that physical punishment is used by 84% to 97% of all parents at some time in their children's lives."). Consistent with these attitudes, child protection statutes in virtually all states exclude from the definition of "child abuse" reasonable physical force used by a parent to punish or discipline a child. Some social scientists have criticized this exclusion, arguing that corporal punishment of children is closely and causally linked to other types of family violence, and that the use of physical discipline by parents "plays a crucial role in training people to accept violence in human relationships." Murray A. Straus & Carrie L. Yodanis, *above*, at 37 (1995). Others have defended the use of physical punishment by parents, arguing that such disciplinary measures are both effective and constitutionally protected. *See* John Rosemond, To Spank or Not To Spank 13 (1994). As the following cases suggest, however, the distinction between reasonable physical punishment and actionable child abuse is not always so obvious.

IN THE INTEREST OF J.P.
Illinois Appellate Court
692 N.E.2d. 338 (1998)

WOLFSON J., delivered the opinion of the court:

Courts, as they should, tread carefully when dealing with claims of child abuse. This case concerns such a claim, and it raises other compelling questions that must be addressed: When is it legally appropriate for the State to exercise a degree of power that removes a child from the custody of her mother, making the child a ward of the court? What facts are required to justify that kind of intrusion into family life?

In this case we find the trial court erred when it determined a mother imposed excessive corporal punishment on her daughter within the meaning of the Juvenile Court Act. Because we find the child was not abused, we vacate the order making her a ward of the court.

FACTS

On June 20, 1995, the Department of Children and Family Services (DCFS) filed a Petition for Adjudication of Wardship and Motion for Temporary Custody. In the petition, DCFS stated that Jessica P., born April 24, 1991, had been removed from her mother's home on June 16, 1995, because she was neglected and abused. The petition alleged Jessica was neglected due to an "injurious environment." 705 ILCS 405/2–3(1)(b) (West 1994). The allegations of abuse were premised on physical abuse and excessive corporal punishment. The petition said Jessica had "sustained cuts, welts, and bruises on her buttocks and legs as a result of being beaten by mother." 705 ILCS 405/2–3(2)(i), (v) (West 1994). The petition further alleged there was a substantial risk that Jessica might sustain physical injury in the future because her mother "refused to accept services." 705 ILCS 405/2–3(2)(ii) (West 1994). The accompanying Motion for Temporary Custody stated there was "urgent and immediate necessity" to take the child into custody, the severity of the injuries and seriousness of the allegations made it "too risky" to leave the child in the home, and "reasonable efforts cannot prevent or eliminate the necessity of removal of the child from the home." See 705 ILCS 405/2–10(2) (West 1994). A temporary custody hearing (705 ILCS 405/2–9, 10 (West 1994)) was held the same day.

At the hearing, the court learned that Jessica's parents, Scott (also Scott P.) and Karen (also Karen P. or respondent), obtained a judgment of divorce on December 21, 1994. They had been separated for more than a year before the divorce became final. Pursuant to the agreed custody order in the divorce judgment, Karen and Scott maintained joint custody of Jessica, Karen was to have physical custody, and Scott received visitation.

Six weeks after the divorce, Scott married Kim. Later, Karen became engaged to marry Bill in September 1995.

On June 11, 1995, Scott visited the Schaumburg Police Department and met with Detective Smith to report his ex-wife's use of corporal punishment. Scott told Detective Smith about an incident that occurred six months earlier, in December 1994. When he got Jessica for visitation, Scott said, Karen told him she had disciplined Jessica using a wooden spoon and had caused a bruise on her buttocks. Scott didn't report this incident until now, he said, because he hadn't been concerned until Jessica reacted strangely on a recent boating trip. He said Jessica became frightened by the boat's oars because they resembled "the rod" Jessica's mother used to discipline her.

On June 12, 1995, Sharon Dorfman, a DCFS worker, was assigned to investigate Scott's report, which had been relayed to the child abuse hotline. Within 24 hours of receiving the report, Dorfman visited Karen at her home. Dorfman described Karen as "receptive" and cooperative. Karen readily admitted using "the rod" (a wooden spoon) for discipline. Karen said she did this because of parenting classes and teachings she received in her church. Karen explained that she believed it was wrong to hit with the hand because the hand represents love. Therefore, it was better, Karen thought, to use an object such as the wooden spoon, instead of the hand, to discipline.

Karen demonstrated to Dorfman the manner and force she used when disciplining Jessica. Karen said she hit Jessica only on her buttocks, over clothing, and her intent was not to harm, but to cause a "sting" to get her attention. Though Karen said she had been using "the rod" regularly, Karen admitted to causing a bruise on Jessica's buttocks on only one occasion, six months earlier. Later in the investigation this bruise was found to have been about 1″ in size. Throughout the entire investigation, DCFS never uncovered any further evidence that Jessica ever sustained additional bruises or observable injury as a result of the spankings.

Dorfman told Karen that hitting Jessica with a spoon could be excessive corporal punishment if it caused bruises. She asked Karen to refrain from using the rod for discipline. Dorfman also offered Karen counseling and parenting classes so she could learn some alternative methods of discipline. Karen refused the counseling, but agreed to attend parenting classes.

Because Karen refused to allow Dorfman to inspect Jessica for bruises, Dorfman asked Detective Smith to visit Karen. Detective Smith, along with a female officer, visited Karen that same day. Detective Smith said Jessica was wearing a swimsuit and no bruises were evident.

Detective Smith spoke to Karen about using "the rod" and urged her to stop this practice. Karen explained, however, that she never hit Jessica out of anger. Going to get the rod gave her a "cooling off" period. Karen also spoke to Jessica about the behavior and, after the discipline, they would pray and she would give Jessica forgiveness.

Detective Smith said he warned Karen she could be arrested for battery. He confiscated the 9-inch wooden spoon Karen had been using as "the rod." He also asked Karen to bring Jessica to the Child Advocacy Center the next day for an interview.

The following day, on June 14, 1995, Jessica was interviewed at the Child Advocacy Center. Detective Smith watched the interview through a two-way mirror. He said Jessica exhibited no signs of abuse. She was unafraid of the interviewer and appeared "normal" and healthy. He said Jessica told the interviewer that she got hit "lots" when she was "foolish" and she got hit even more if she cried. He couldn't remember whether Jessica said her butt sometimes got "blue" or if she said "red." He became concerned, however, because Jessica reported that she had been disciplined with the rod the night before.

Detective Smith informed Dorfman of Karen's recent use of the rod. Dorfman made an appointment to visit Karen on June 16, 1995. At this second visit, Dorfman and Detective Smith questioned Karen together. Again, Karen openly admitted that she used the rod on Jessica. Karen said she disciplined Jessica "for urinating." Karen told them she typically struck Jessica "about four times or until her behavior was proper."

Dorfman asked Karen if she would refrain from using the rod on Jessica until she began attending parenting classes. Karen refused. After thoughtful reflection, Karen said she would not stop using the rod because that would mean she didn't love Jessica.

Dorfman characterized Karen as "honest" and straightforward. Dorfman said she would have left Jessica in the home if Karen said she would stop using the rod. Because Karen refused to stop using the rod, however, Jessica was taken into protective custody. A second, 12-inch wooden spoon, which Karen had used to discipline Jessica, was confiscated by Detective Smith at this time.

Karen testified at the temporary custody hearing. Though she verified all that had been testified to by Dorfman and Detective Smith, Karen said she would agree to stop using the rod for discipline. Karen said she believed the rod was an effective form of discipline, but she would discontinue its use because she didn't want her child to have to go through the disruption and confusion of the court proceedings. She also did not want to be separated from her daughter anymore. Karen informed the court she had already begun the process of signing up for parenting classes.

After hearing the evidence, Judge Aron ruled:

> Okay; the court does find first of all that both mother and father were present in court today; that Probable Cause does exist; that the minor is abuse (sic) or neglected based on the testimony heard today about the mother admitting hitting the Minor with the wooden spoons and leaving bruises and her belief in the rod of correction.
>
> I believe that Urgent and Immediate Necessity does exist to support removal of the Minor from the home. Once again I believe mother is probably one of the most honest and sincere people that I have ever seen in this room. I believe her religious beliefs are not superficial, even though she wants to stop this invasion of her home and her privacy; that I believe those religious beliefs need to be talked out a little more or thought about a little bit more; for that reason I don't believe that she can change easily, even though she wants to or says she wants to today.
>
> I think reasonable efforts have been made but have not eliminated the Urgent and Immediate Necessity to remove this child from the home. The Minor should be removed. Temporary Custody has been granted to DCFS guardianship administrator (sic) with the right to place the Minor into and consent to any medical or dental treatment necessary to safeguard the life and health of the Minor.

Jessica was initially placed with her paternal grandparents while a homestudy was completed on Scott and his new wife, Kim. All visitations with Jessica were to be supervised.

Subsequently, Judge Hayes issued an order dated July 7, 1995, placing Jessica with Scott under an order of protection. Karen's visitation with Jessica was to remain supervised.

Though the adjudication hearing was originally set for September 21, 1995, the hearing was not held until February 6, 1996. All of the witnesses who testified at the temporary custody hearing testified again at this hearing. In addition, however, Karen presented three witnesses in her defense: Sandy Rabenda, who had been Karen's next door neighbor for three years; Marie Amejia, Jessica's babysitter from November 1994 until June 1995; and Peggy Koehl, Jessica's godmother. All of these witnesses testified that they had seen Jessica regularly and never saw any bruises or evidence of abuse. They testified that Karen was a good mother, though she believed in disciplining with the wooden spoon she called the "rod." Everyone described Karen as patient. Karen never raised her voice or shouted at Jessica in anger. When Jessica misbehaved, Karen took Jessica into the bathroom to discipline her.

Amejia said Karen had taken Jessica into the bathroom at her home on a few occasions. She could overhear Karen explaining to Jessica what was wrong with her behavior and then heard Karen administer "two to three taps on the bottom." Amejia said that Jessica always came out of the bathroom happy, not upset.

Amejia also testified about the bruise Jessica had in December 1994. Amejia babysat for Jessica and didn't notice the bruise. When Karen picked Jessica up that day she told Amejia about the bruise she left on Jessica. The next day Amejia saw the bruise. Amejia described it as "very small," a 1"-1 1/2" bruise on the center of Jessica's buttocks. She said Jessica was not uncomfortable or bothered by the bruise.

Karen also testified at the adjudication hearing She said she had been horrified when she discovered the bruise she left on Jessica that one time in December 1994. She immediately told both the babysitter and Scott. Scott, Karen said, told her he knew she was a good mother and "not to worry." He even gave her a small kiss on the cheek. Scott had been unconcerned about the bruise in December 1994.

On June 10, 1995, however, Scott brought Jessica home late from a visitation. When Karen complained, Scott's wife, Kim, became angry and stormed off. Scott also got angry. He told Karen never to yell at him in front of his wife. Then Scott threatened Karen, telling her he could have her arrested. Two days later Karen came under investigation for child abuse.

After hearing the evidence and the arguments of counsel, the court (Judge Preston) made the following determination:

> . . . and this is a difficult case because it doesn't fall within any of the reported cases . . . . The testimony was that, in virtually all respects other than this corporal punishment, that the home seemed to be appropriate in that Jessica was well-clothed, well-fed, well-cared for; but the issue of the corporal punishment which brought this case into the system remains, and I'm simply not indicating that I'm not considering that corporal punishment seriously because I certainly am, but I'm going to not make a finding of neglect based on injurious environment. The allegation of physical abuse and substantial risk of physical injury—all these are closely tied in with the corporal punishment. I'm not going to make a finding that there was physical abuse because I don't think that the corporal punishment the mother used on Jessica rose to that level, nor do I think that there's a substantial risk of physical injury to this minor, notwithstanding that she did sustain a bruise on the one occasion.

That leaves us with the allegation of excessive corporal punishment which is indeed the most difficult in this case because if we were to look at corporal punishment as in severity from a continuum of (1) to (100), it we were to make an assumption just for the sake of this discussion that anything above (65) on that continuum was considered to be excessive and anything below (65) was considered to be within the realm of what is permitted pursuant to Illinois law, and the law of the United States has been expressed in a number of decisions including the *Ingraham* decision and others, . . . it's clear this case doesn't fall at the higher level of that case . . . .

What is added in this case of that instance of December of 1994 is the prior and successive uses of paddling with that spoon on many occasions. Some of the testimony was as often as twice a week. Other testimony was whenever Jessica misbehaved by lying or acting foolish or doing something wrong. Did that make that isolated instance along with these other instances where bruises were not left, where there was no last (sic) physical effect of that corporal punishment? Does that nonetheless make this allegation rise to the level of what is unreasonable in light of Illinois law? And, I think it does.

I believe that while this is certainly in no respect the most heinous of the circumstances that could come before this Court and that, God, it's not the most heinous but it does, I'll admit, just barely—but it does rise to the level of excessive corporal punishment because of the frequency of the reliance on using a paddle; and I'm not emphasizing the paddle in this decision—it's not the paddle that is what I find offensive alone; it could be—the paddle itself is not terribly offensive. It's not very large. It's not very heavy, but the corporal punishment is used with such frequency for the infractions. . . .

And I'm not going to get into teachings of the church because the church doesn't tell a parent to use excessive corporal punishment; and that somewhat was; and again so our record is clear, just barely used in this case.

The case was held over until April 19, 1996, for the dispositional hearing. Testimony was taken on April 19, 1996, and again on May 2, 1996. The court learned of Karen's successful completion of the STEP parenting classes. The court also was given information about the interaction of Karen and Jessica during supervised visitation. The court was provided psychological evaluations, as well as reports from various counselors involved with both Karen and Jessica.

After considering all the evidence, the court issued its decision on August 23, 1996, saying:

To make a long story short, I find that first: That the minor, Jessica P., is adjudged a ward of the court.

Secondly, I find that both mother, Karen P., and the father, Scott P., are both fit, able, and willing to care for, protect, train and discipline this minor. I'm going to dwell on that for just a moment here so that the record is very clear on what this Court's finding is.

Based on all the testimony that I heard, all of the documentary evidence that had been admitted into evidence, and considering arguments of counsel, that not only do I find the parents, Karen and Scott, to be fit, willing and able; but I also find their respective spouses to be perfectly appropriate caretakers for Jessica, but I'm not Solomon; and I don't have some of the powers that he sought to dispense when he suggested a child be cut in half. I have to make a dispositional finding that will be appropriate for this child, and the law tells me that I must at this point of our proceedings consider what is in Jessica's best interests and nothing else. And, in that regard since Jessica has been doing well living at home with her father this past year, I think that it would be in her best interests to remain in her father's custody, and that will be what this Court orders—that Jessica remain in the custody of her father under an Order of Protection."

The court went on to explain that the order of protection should contain detailed orders regarding visitation, to include "liberal contact" between Karen and Jessica, "periods of time—summer vacations and other vacations—when mother will have custody of Jessica, all visitation being unsupervised . . . and without restriction."

After the dispositional order was issued, Karen filed her first Notice of Appeal. In this appeal Karen sought review of the trial court's findings at the temporary custody hearing, the adjudication hearing, and the dispositional hearing.

Subsequently, despite the court's order with regard to visitation, DCFS unilaterally decided to restrict visitation, allowing Karen only supervised visits with Jessica. This decision was based on the recommendation of Jessica's therapist, Debra Warren, due to unverified comments Jessica made about fears she had of Karen's church.

A hearing was held November 19, 1996, due to the change in visitation. The court ordered DCFS to resume unsupervised visitations in accord with its initial order. The court also signed an order, however, allowing DCFS to restrict visitation in the future without court intervention.

Thereafter, on December 18, 1996, DCFS suspended all visitation between Karen and Jessica. DCFS said Karen had behaved "inappropriately" because she went to the office of Jessica's pediatrician to be present for Jessica's appointment concerning a possible urinary or bladder problem. . . .

DECISION

. . . In this case the Petition for Adjudication of Wardship alleged Jessica was neglected on the basis of injurious environment, and physically abused because of injury and excessive corporal punishment. All of the charges were based on allegations that Jessica had "sustained cuts, welts, and bruises on her buttocks and legs as a result of being beaten by her mother."

When ruling on this petition at the February 6, 1996, adjudicatory hearing, the court found: (1) Karen's home was appropriate and Jessica was well-clothed, well-fed, and well-cared for in Karen's home; (2) Jessica was not neglected due to injurious environment; (3) the type of corporal punishment Karen employed never rose to the level of physical abuse; (4) there is no substantial risk of physical injury to Jessica; (5) the wooden spoon used by Karen was not heinous or "terribly offensive;" (6) there was only one instance when Jessica was bruised as a result of being disciplined with the wooden spoon and this one instance did not rise to the level of excessive corporal punishment; and (7) the one incident of a bruise, coupled with the frequency with which Karen resorted to the use of the wooden spoon for discipline, "just barely" amounted to excessive corporal punishment.

We accept and agree with the trial judge's factual findings. We believe, however, the trial judge committed manifest error when he drew the legal conclusion that the facts amounted to excessive corporal punishment within the meaning of the Juvenile Court Act.

When deciding the issue of "excessiveness," the court invented a mathematical equation or "continuum," suggesting that corporal punishment could be weighed against a theoretical scale of seriousness (i.e. a scale from 1 to 100, with 65 being the starting point for excessive corporal punishment). Though the judge found the corporal punishment employed here "doesn't fall at the higher level," the court still ruled that Jessica was abused. The court was careful, however, to specify that his finding of abuse was due to excessive corporal punishment and was not a finding of "physical abuse." The court specifically corrected the order to note that the abuse was not "physical" abuse. . . .

Because the court found no basis other than excessive corporal punishment for holding Jessica was abused or neglected, we limit our review to that determination. We consider whether the facts of this case fall within the meaning of "excessive corporal punishment" as that term is used within the Juvenile Court Act. If it does not, there is no reason to consider the best interests of the child.

When defining an abused minor, the Act states:

> (2) Those who are abused include any minor under 18 years of age whose parent or immediate family member, or any person responsible for the minor's welfare, or any person who is in the same family or household as the minor, or any individual residing in the same home as the minor, or a paramour of the minor's parent:
>
> (i) inflicts, causes to be inflicted, or allows to be inflicted upon such minor physical injury, by other than accidental means, which causes death, disfigurement, impairment of physical or emotional health, or loss or impairment of any bodily function;
>
> (ii) creates a substantial risk of physical injury to such minor by other than accidental means which would be likely to cause death, disfigurement, impairment of emotional health, or loss or impairment of any bodily function;
>
> (iii) commits or allows to be committed any sex offense against such minor, as such sex offenses are defined in the Criminal Code of 1961, as amended, and extending those definitions of sex offenses to include minors under 18 years of age;
>
> (iv) commits or allows to be committed an act or acts of torture upon such minor; or
>
> (v) inflicts excessive corporal punishment."

705 ILCS 405/2-3 (West 1994).

The term "excessive corporal punishment" is not defined in the Act. Perhaps this is because cases involving the adjudication of abuse, neglect, and wardship are sui generis; that is, each case must be decided on its own distinct set of facts and circumstances and, given the varying circumstances in these types of cases, courts must have "broad discretion to reach a just determination"

It is clear that a parent has the "right" to corporally discipline his or her child, a right derived from our constitutional right to privacy. But this right, like any other, must be exercised in a "reasonable" manner.

A number of courts have been faced with the dilemma of determining what constitutes "excessive" or "unreasonable" corporal punishment. A survey of these cases provides some insight.

In *In re F.W.* the court found it was neglect when the mother hit her 13–year-old daughter using a 24–inch-long board with two metal brackets on it. The mother said she hit her daughter because she wanted her to "shut up." The "discipline" resulted in a knot on the girl's arm and gashes on her leg. The 13–year-old and her sister also reported being physically disciplined almost daily with a variety of objects, including ball bats, broomsticks, extension cords, and ropes. When questioned, the mother noted she carried scars from being punished by her own parents and didn't feel she had been abused.

In assessing the matter the F.W. court said the degree of physical injury stemming from the discipline was not the "exclusive or determinative factor in evaluating the reasonableness of a parent's conduct." Other factors considered by the court were: (1) the likelihood of future, more serious injury; (2) the psychological effects on the child; and (3) the circumstances surrounding the discipline, including the parent's demeanor, i.e., whether the parent was calm or "lashing out" in anger.

In *In re D.L.W.*, 226 Ill. App. 3d 805, 589 N.E.2d 970, 168 Ill. Dec. 570 (1992), the father of two sons, ages 5 and 10, was found unfit and his parental rights terminated because, the court said, he could not differentiate between corporal punishment and physical abuse. On different occasions, the father punched the older son in the face with his fist, grabbed him by the throat and kneed him in the groin, spanked his bare buttocks with a 1 1/2–foot-long board while saying, "I don't care if I have to beat you to death, you are going to learn not to wet the bed any longer," and hit him with a wooden spoon until it broke in pieces. The father believed his children should fear him.

In *People v. Sambo*, 197 Ill. App. 3d 574, 554 N.E.2d 1080, 144 Ill. Dec. 41 (1990), the court found it was not reasonable discipline for the parents to hit their daughter with a plastic baseball bat, kick her, throw liquor in her face, and pull her hair.

In *In the Interest of LM*, 189 Ill. App. 3d 392, 545 N.E.2d 319, 136 Ill. Dec. 795 (1989), the mother of two sons, age 7 and 9, was found to have abused them as a result of excessive corporal punishment. The children were left unattended for more than a day, were dirty, and had colds. When the father found them, he discovered the younger boy had 5 "whip marks" on his back. The marks were between 6 and 10 inches long and were "pink-fleshy lines after the scabs that had initially formed had fallen off." The child reported that he had been beaten with a belt and stick for playing ball in the house.

In *People v. Tomlianovich*, 161 Ill. App. 3d 241, 514 N.E.2d 203, 112 Ill. Dec. 737 (1987), a mother was convicted of cruelty to her children. The court said a parent's disciplinary authority had to be exercised within the bounds of reason and humanity. These bounds were passed, said the court, when it was shown that the mother hit her 11–year-old son with a paddle, causing bruising to the child's buttocks. A doctor testified he had never seen such a severe condition. The bruises were to the point of hematoma and were visible until the third visit to the doctor's office, 16 days after the incident.

In *In the Interest of D.M.C.*, 107 Ill. App. 3d 902, 438 N.E.2d 254, 63 Ill. Dec. 516 (1982), the court found it to be excessive corporal punishment for the parents of a 9–year-old boy suffering from hyperactivity and learning disabilities to discipline him with a leather belt. On one particular instance, when the boy brought his father's cowboy hat to school without permission, the child received as many as one hundred strokes to his bare buttocks, resulting in the entire area of the buttocks and thighs being "solidly bruised.". . .

We are guided by the Illinois Administrative Rules, which are relied on by DCFS. Section 300 provides a list of various allegations which could support a finding of abuse or neglect. See 89 Ill. Admin. Code 300. Allegation # 11/61, entitled "Cuts, Bruises, and Welts," notes that "not every cut, bruise, or welt constitutes an allegation of harm." The Code suggests considering such factors as the child's age, the severity of the injury, the location of the injury, whether an instrument was used, and the pattern and chronicity of similar incidents of harm to the child. Other factors to be considered are the child's medical condition and whether the child suffers from behavioral, mental, or emotional problems, developmental disabilities or physical handicaps. The parent's history of reports of abuse or neglect may also be significant.

Here, Karen readily admitted to disciplining Jessica with a wooden spoon and said she began using this form of discipline when Jessica was 2 1/2 years old. However, the frequency of these spankings and the number of blows administered never were established with any exactitude. Karen spanked Jessica on the buttocks, over her clothes. As the court determined, there was only one instance when bruising occurred on Jessica's buttocks—the isolated occasion in December 1994. Karen was so horrified when this occurred that she felt compelled to "confess" to her ex-husband and babysitter. Neither of them was very concerned at the time. The father expressed no concern for six months. The babysitter said the bruise was "very small," about 1–1 1/2 inches in size, and when the bruise was visible Jessica was not in any pain.

It is significant that the babysitter witnessed the mother's form of discipline on a number of occasions. She said Karen never lashed out at Jessica in anger. Karen was generally calm and patient. More importantly, Jessica appeared happy and unaffected after being disciplined.

We agree with the court's comments in *In re F.W.*, 261 Ill. App. 3d 894, 902, 634 N.E.2d 1123, 199 Ill. Dec. 769 (1994): It is not a court's function to determine whether "parents measure up to an ideal, but to determine whether the child's welfare has been compromised."

We agree, too, that corporal punishment as a method of discipline is a "controversial issue" and the mere fact that an object is employed to conduct the discipline raises immediate concerns. But the use of an object, especially when the court finds the object was not "terribly offensive" or "heinous," should not blind a court to the many other factors which should and must be considered when weighing the evidence to determine the "reasonableness" of the discipline. We must take care not to create a legal standard from our personal notions of how best to discipline a child. . . .

Our review of Illinois decisions discloses no case where facts close to those found by this trial court were enough to allow the State to wrest custody of a child from its mother. We find no precedential support for the proposition that the mere frequency of relatively mild, non-bruising contacts by an object other than a hand rises to the level of "excessive corporal punishment" as that term is used in the Juvenile Court Act.

We believe our conclusion is consistent with the letter and spirit of the Juvenile Court Act. Making a child a ward of the court is a serious thing to do. When that child is being well cared for by fit and able parents, when the child's environment is not injurious, when the child is neither physically nor psychologically abused or neglected, and when there is no substantial risk of physical injury to the child, courts should exercise grave prudence before allowing the State to violate the privacy our law promises to the family.

We cannot draw a firm line between excessive and non-excessive corporal punishment. Nor do we wish to give license to parents who would use the force of physical objects to discipline their children. We simply hold the unusual circumstances in this case do not "barely" cross the line to excessive corporal punishment. They do not cross the line at all. The trial court's finding to the contrary was against the manifest weight of the evidence.

We can understand the trial court's reluctance to implicitly give approval to Karen's use of the wooden spoon, but we believe the trial court exceeded its authority and unjustifiably intruded on the respondent's privacy rights and her fundamental liberty interest in the care and custody of her child.

While the State contends the evidence proves Karen's conduct caused psychological damage to Jessica, the trial judge made no such finding. We take his silence on the matter, making no comment on the "oar" incident, to be a rejection of the State's claim. Further, we see no need to examine the record for possible psychological harm since we end our inquiry with the conclusion that there was no excessive corporal punishment in this case. . . .

Because we conclude Karen did not violate section 405/2–3 (2)(v), all orders entered at and after the adjudicatory hearing are vacated. We remand this cause to the Juvenile Court for proceedings consistent with this opinion. We anticipate the trial court will eliminate any roadblocks to the return of Jessica to her mother's custody.

NOTES AND QUESTIONS

(1) What distinguishes the mother's non–abusive behavior in *J.P.* from the "excessive" or "unreasonable" corporal punishment in the cases surveyed by the court?

(2) Would it be constitutional for a state to prohibit parents from using any type of corporal punishment against a child? *See* Mary Kate Kearney, *Substantive Due Process and Parental Corporal Punishment: Democracy and the Excluded Child,* 32 San Diego L. Rev. 1 (1995).

(3) In the *J.P.* case, Jessica P. was four years old when she was removed from her mother's custody as a result of the trial court's finding of excessive corporal punishment. By the time the Illinois appellate court issued its reversal, Jessica would have been 7 years old and, presumably, she would have been living with her father for almost three years. Should the trial court order that Jessica be returned immediately to her mother? Why or why not?

(4) The two most common legal responses to allegations of child maltreatment are civil child protection proceedings and criminal prosecution. The primary purposes of criminal prosecution are to punish perpetrators and to deter future abuse. The object of civil protection proceedings, by contrast, is generally defined in therapeutic terms—to protect children from harm, to provide necessary services to children and parents and, if possible, to rehabilitate and reunify the family. *See* Marcia Sprague & Mark Hardin, *Coordination of Juvenile and Criminal Court Child Abuse and Neglect Proceedings,* 35 J. Fam. L. 239, 242 (1997). Most

allegations of child maltreatment are dealt with through the civil child protection process. In some states, the judicial components of this process are known as neglect or dependency proceedings; in other states, the proceedings take their name from the statutory designation of children who fall within the jurisdiction of the court as a result of their parents' inability or unwillingness to provide proper care: Children in Need of Assistance (CINA) or Children in Need of Protective Services (CHIPS). Where the alleged maltreatment is particularly egregious, or has resulted in death or serious injury, the state may also initiate criminal abuse or neglect proceedings. For an argument in favor of coordinating such parallel civil and criminal proceedings, and a discussion of effective coordination strategies, see Sprague & Hardin, *above*.

(5) **Child Abuse Reporting Statutes.** A series of important articles on battered children, written by physicians in the early 1960s, brought widespread public attention to the problem of child abuse. *See* Richard J. Gelles and Claire Pedrick Cornell, Intimate Violence in Families, 33–35 (2nd ed. 1990). One of the concrete consequences of this "rediscovery" of child abuse was the passage of child abuse reporting laws in all 50 states between 1963 and 1967. These reporting laws typically require health care workers, teachers and other adults likely to come in contact with children to report to a designated government authority any instance of suspected child abuse or neglect. In a number of states, these reporting requirements have been expanded to include all persons. *See, e.g.,* Md. Family Law Code Ann. § 5–705 (1997). Child abuse reporting statutes typically confer immunity from civil or criminal liability on persons who report in good faith; many statutes also provide for the imposition of civil penalties for failure to report. *Cf. Landeros v. Flood*, 551 P.2d 389 (1976) (upholding medical malpractice claim based on physician's failure to diagnose battered child syndrome and to comply with statutory reporting requirement). Child abuse reporting obligations generally take precedence over the physician or psychiatrist/patient privilege. *See, e.g., People v. Stritzinger*, 668 P.2d 738 (Cal. 1983). States are divided, however, on whether attorneys are required to report. *See* Robert P. Mosteller, *Child Abuse Reporting Laws and Attorney Client Confidence: The Reality and the Specter of Lawyer as Informant*, 42 Duke L. J. 203 (1992). For an argument that client confidentiality obligations should not preclude attorneys from reporting suspected child abuse or neglect, see Robin A. Rosencrantz, Note, *Rejecting "Hear No Evil Speak No Evil": Expanding the Attorney's Role in Child Abuse Reporting*, 8 Geo. J. Legal Ethics 327 (1995).

(6) **Incidence of Child Abuse and Neglect.** The number of abuse and neglect reports has risen steadily since the adoption of reporting statutes. In 1995, state child protective services agencies investigated approximately 2 million reports alleging the maltreatment of almost 3 million children. U.S. Dep't of Health & Human Services, National Center on Child Abuse and Neglect, *Child Maltreatment 1995: Reports From the States to the National Child Abuse and Neglect Data System* (1997). More than half of these reports came from professionals, including educators, law enforcement and justice officials, medical and mental health professionals, social service professionals and child care providers. Although a majority of the reports were not substantiated, agencies determined that over 1 million children were victims of substantiated or indicated child abuse or neglect. *Id.* Of these victims, approximately 52% suffered neglect, 25% physical abuse, 13% sexual abuse, 5% emotional maltreatment, 3% medical neglect, and 14% other forms of maltreatment. Some children experienced more than one type of maltreatment. Younger children were particularly vulnerable to maltreatment. In 1995, more than half of all confirmed

victims of abuse and neglect were 7 years of age or younger, and about 26% were younger than 4 years old. *Id.* Other sources of data suggest that these official statistics, collected from state child protective services agencies, may significantly underestimate the number of children who suffer from abuse or neglect. *See* U.S. Dep't of Health and Human Services, National Center on Child Abuse and Neglect, *Third National Incidence Study of Child Abuse and Neglect: Final Report* (NIS-3) (1996) (estimating, based on surveys of community professionals, that 42 children per 1,000 in the general population were harmed or endangered by abuse or neglect, as opposed to the estimate of 15 children per 1,000 in the general population, derived from reports substantiated by agencies).

For some children, state intervention comes too late. According to the United States Advisory Board on Child Abuse and Neglect, approximately 2000 infants and young children die each year at the hands of their parents or caretakers. U.S. Dep't of Health & Human Services, *A Nation's Shame: Fatal Child Abuse and Neglect in the United States* 9 (1995). The Advisory Board estimates that an additional 18,000 children a year are permanently disabled and approximately 142,000 are seriously injured as a result of parental or caretaker maltreatment. *Id.* at 16.

(7) Attitudes Toward Corporal Punishment. Although a majority of Americans still approve of corporal punishment, recent survey data suggests that public support for the practice may be waning. While 94% of Americans surveyed in 1968 thought that it was sometimes necessary "to discipline a child with a good hard spanking," only 67% of those surveyed in 1995 agreed with that statement. Murray A. Straus, David B. Sugarman & Jean Giles-Sims, *Spanking by Parents and Subsequent Antisocial Behavior of Children,* 151 Arch. Pediatr. & Adolesc. Med., 761, 764 (1997). The percentage of parents who report using corporal punishment has also declined. A number of pediatric and other professional organizations have also expressed disapproval of corporal punishment as a means of parental discipline. *See* Judge Leonard P. Edwards, *Corporal Punishment and The Legal System,* 38 Santa Clara L. Rev. 983, 1021 n.263 (1996) (listing professional organizations that formally oppose corporal punishment). Similarly, a majority of child development experts are opposed to the use of corporal punishment, although others view it as an effective parenting tool, when used appropriately and in moderation. *See* Edwards, *above,* at 983 (discussing views of child development writers).

Researchers are divided over whether corporal punishment harms children. Some social scientists claim that even non-excessive corporal punishment is likely to cause long-term behavioral problems and to increase aggression in children, regardless of the amount of emotional support and attention that children receive from parents. *See, e.g.,* Murray A. Straus, David B. Sugarman & Jean Giles-Sims, *Spanking by Parents and Subsequent Antisocial Behavior of Children,* 151 Arch. Pediatr. & Adolesc. Med., 761 (1997); Murray A. Straus, Beating the Devil Out of Them: Corporal Punishment in American Families and Its Effect on Children (1994). A number of studies also suggest that corporal punishment during childhood is associated with higher levels of dysfunctional and aggressive behavior in adulthood, including adult domestic violence and physical abuse of children. *See* Janet Chiancone, *Corporal Punishment: What Lawyers Need to Know,* 16 Child Law Practice 1 (1997); Murray A. Straus & Carrie L. Yodanis, *Corporal Punishment by Parents: Implications for Primary Prevention of Assaults on Spouses and Children,* 2 U. Chi. L. Sch. Roundtable 35 (1995). Other researchers have questioned these correlations and have suggested that the impact of corporal punishment on children can be either beneficial or detrimental depending on a child's age, family structure, cultural context and overall relationship with parents. *See, e.g.*, Marjorie Lindner Gunnoe & Carrie Lea Mariner, *Toward a Developmental-Contextual Model of the Effects of Parental Spanking on Children's Aggression*, 151 Arch. Pediatr. & Adolesc. Med., 768 (1997); Richard Larzelere, *A Review of the Outcomes of Parental Use of Nonabusive or Customary Physical Punishment*, 98 Pediatrics 828 (1996). For further discussion of the impact of corporal punishment on children and adults, see the articles collected in *Supplement: The Short and Long-term Consequences of Corporal Punishment*, 98(4) Pediatrics 803–51 (Oct. 1996).

Attitudes toward corporal punishment are often linked to broader ideological and political concerns regarding the importance of parental authority and the appropriate role of the government in family life. Individuals and groups who are critical of efforts to curb corporal punishment often characterize these efforts as unwarranted governmental interference with the rights of parents to raise their children. Supporters of such efforts, by contrast, emphasize the state's *parens patriae* obligation to protect children from harm and to promote their dignity and welfare.

(8) **International Perspectives.** Over the past two decades, a number of European countries have outlawed corporal punishment by parents. In 1979, Sweden became the first nation to prohibit parents from corporally punishing their children. Dennis A. Olson, *The Swedish Ban on Corporal Punishment*, 1984 B.Y.U. L. Rev. 447. Since then, Austria, Denmark, Finland, Poland and Norway have followed suit, and similar legislation is being considered in Germany and Great Britain. Leonard P. Edwards, *Corporal Punishment and the Legal System*, 36 Santa Clara L. Rev. 983, 1017 (1996). Swedish attitudes toward corporal punishment have changed significantly since the ban was enacted. In 1965, a majority of Swedes believed that corporal punishment was indispensable to parents. By 1981, two years after the prohibition was enacted, that figure had dropped to 26% and, by 1995, only 11% of the Swedish population believed that corporal punishment was necessary. *See* Jack O'Sullivan, *Sweden's Rules on Corporal Punishment Lead The Way*, The Independent (London) at 3 (September 10, 1996).

European courts and human rights organizations have also issued rulings critical of corporal punishment. In 1996, the Supreme Court of Italy ruled that corporal punishment of children violated the Italian Constitution and was inconsistent with the Italian family laws. *See* Susan Bitensky, *Final Straw: To Spank or Not To Spank*, Chicago Tribune, at 25 (July 25, 1996). Also in 1996, the European Court of Human Rights agreed to consider a challenge, brought by a 12-year-old boy, to the British common law rule that allows "reasonable chastisement" by parents. Sarah Lydall, *Use of Corporal Punishment in Britain Undergoes Scrutiny; Boy's European Court Case Challenges Smacking Tradition*, Dallas Morning News at 22A (October 13, 1996). In late 1997, the Court issued a preliminary ruling indicating that the boy's human rights had been breached because British courts had failed to protect him from "inhuman or degrading treatment or punishment" by his stepfather. Philip Johnston, *Euro Ruling May Curb Parents' Legal Right To Punish*, The Daily Telegraph, p. 3 (November 8, 1997). A final ruling is expected in 1998. Finally, Article 19 of the United Nations Convention on the Rights of the Child has been interpreted as forbidding corporal punishment and opponents of the Convention have cited this interpretation as justification for the United States' continuing refusal to ratify the Convention. Susan

Kilbourne, *Implementation and the United States: U.S. Failure to Ratify the U.N. Convention on the Rights of the Child: Playing Politics with Children's Rights*, 6 Transnt'l L. & Contp. Probs 437, 450–51 (1996).

(9) **Corporal Punishment in the Schools.** In *Ingraham v. Wright*, 430 U.S. 651 (1977), two junior high school students alleged that their constitutional rights had been violated by repeated and severe paddlings administered by public school officials. The Supreme Court rejected their claims, holding, *first*, that the paddling of students as a means of school discipline did *not* violate the Eight Amendment's ban on "cruel and unusual punishment," and *second* that the school was *not* required to provide notice and an opportunity to be heard prior to administering the punishment. Tracing the long history and continuing approval of corporal punishment as a means of school discipline, the Court declined to extend the Eight Amendment "to traditional disciplinary practices in the public schools." The Court also reasoned that the openness of the public school and its supervision by the community afforded significant safeguards against the kinds of abuses that the Eighth Amendment was designed to deter. With respect to the students' procedural due process claims, the Court held that, in light of the common law privilege of teachers to inflict reasonable corporal punishment, the availability of state tort law remedies for excessive corporal punishment satisfied constitutional due process requirements and obviated the need for advance procedural safeguards.

The *Ingraham* Court declined to address the question whether the infliction of severe or excessive corporal punishment could violate a students' *substantive* due process rights. A number of lower federal courts have recognized the possibility of such a due process violation, but most have applied a "shocking to the conscience" standard that precludes the imposition of constitutional liability in all but the most extreme and outrageous circumstances. *See* Jeffrey R. Parkinson, *Federal Court Treatment of Corporal Punishment in Public Schools: Jurisprudence That Is Literally Shocking To the Conscience,* 39 S.D. L. Rev. 276 (1994). In an influential early decision, the Fourth Circuit looked to the police brutality context to fashion a test to determine whether a constitutional violation has occurred when a student is subjected to corporal punishment at school:

> As in the cognate police brutality cases, the substantive due process inquiry in school corporal punishment cases must be whether the force applied caused injury so severe, was so disproportionate to the need presented, and was so inspired by malice or sadism rather than a merely careless or unwise excess of zeal that it amounted to a brutal and inhumane abuse of official power literally shocking to the conscience.

Hall v. Tawney, 621 F.2d 607, 713 (4th Cir. 1980). For a recent application of this standard, see *Saylor v. Board of Education for Harlan County*, 118 F.3d 507 (6th Cir.), *cert. denied*, 118 S. Ct. 628 (1997) (finding no constitutional violation where teacher administered a paddling, in violation of school regulations, that schools officials later acknowledged was excessive and that left a fourteen-year-old boy with bruised and swollen buttocks).

Query: Does the standard established in *Hall* adequately protect public school students from excessive corporal punishment? Is it appropriate to apply the same constitutional standards to school officials as are applied to police officers subduing criminal suspects? Why or why not?

The use of corporal punishment in the public schools has declined significantly since *Ingraham* was decided. In 1977, only two states banned corporal punishment in public schools. Today, more than half the states ban such punishment and several states that permit the practice have established elaborate guidelines setting forth the circumstances and procedures under which corporal punishment may be imposed. *See* Jeffrey R. Parkinson, *Federal Court Treatment of Corporate Punishment in Public Schools: Jurisprudence That Is Literally Shocking To the Conscience,* 39 S.D. L. Rev. 276, 279 (1994). Despite this decline in popularity, the U.S. Department of Education estimates that there were more than 600,000 incidents of corporal punishment in the public schools in 1990, the latest year for which figures are available. Office for Civil Rights, U.S. Dep't of Educ., *1990 Elementary and Secondary School Civil Rights Survey* 1 (1993). Moreover, corporal punishment is still prevalent in some private schools, particularly those with a strong religious affiliation. *See* Maria Glod, *Loudoun Case Tests Faith in Corporal Punishment; After Arrest of Principal for Spanking, Christian Schools Defend Old-Fashioned Discipline,* Washington Post, at B05 (March 1, 1998).

(10) **Problem**. You are a state legislator in a state that currently allows individual school districts to determine whether and when to authorize corporal punishment of students. While a majority of school districts have outlawed the practice, a significant minority of districts continue to allow it, unless a parent objects in writing. One of your colleagues has proposed replacing this "local option" approach with a state-side ban on corporal punishment in public schools. Would you vote for such a state-wide prohibition? Why or why not? What arguments are your opponents likely to make in support of their position? Now assume that the state-wide ban is defeated and the legislature votes instead to develop a model corporal punishment policy for local school districts that choose to employ such punishment. What provisions and restrictions would you include in such a model policy?

(11) **Problem**. A seventeen-year-old Daughter arrived home an hour after her midnight curfew, to find her Father waiting in the hall. Father confronted Daughter angrily. Daughter responded by yelling and using profanity at Father. Father told Daughter to stop swearing at him, but she ignored him. Father then slapped Daughter twice across the face with his open hand. Daughter ran into the kitchen and called the police, who came to investigate the incident. Should Father be charged with child abuse or excessive corporal punishment? With an intrafamily assault? *See State v. Kaimimoku,* 841 P.2d 1076 (Haw. 1992). *See also* Chapter 6

[B] Parental Failure to Protect

When, if ever, should a parent be charged with abuse or neglect for failing to prevent or to stop child abuse inflicted by another family member? Most state child protection statutes apply to acts of omission as well as commission, and a number of states have expressly criminalized a parent's failure to protect a child from abuse. *See, e.g.,* Colo. Rev. Stat. 18–6–401 (1997) ("A person commits child abuse if such person . . . permits a child to be unreasonably placed in a situation which poses a threat of injury to the child's life or health . . . ."). The following case considers the circumstances under which one parent should be held criminally liable for failing to protect a child from injuries inflicted by the other parent.

RICE v. STATE
Supreme Court of Nevada
949 P.2d 262 (1997)

Rose, J.:

Christie Ann Rice (Christie) and her husband, Cody Alan Rice (Cody) first met in April of 1990. After learning that she was carrying his child, she moved in with him, and they were subsequently married. However, the marriage was strained because Cody was violent and abusive toward Christie. Matthew, Christie and Cody's son, was born on July 1, 1992. Sometime around the middle of September, 1992, Cody told Christie that Matthew had been accidentally burned in hot water. Christie tried to treat Matthew's injuries at home. On September 22, 1992, Matthew was rushed to the hospital because he had stopped breathing. He died in the hospital two days later.

Cody was charged with and pleaded guilty to the first degree murder of Matthew. He was sentenced to life imprisonment without the possibility of parole. Christie was charged with child neglect causing substantial bodily harm to Matthew. Following a jury trial, Christie was convicted and sentenced to serve the maximum term in prison allowed by law, twenty years. Christie now appeals. We affirm the conviction but remand for re-sentencing.

FACTS

In April of 1990, Christie met Cody, and they were engaged in August of 1991. Christie moved in with Cody in January of 1992 when she found out she was pregnant with Matthew, and the two were married in April of 1992. Christie testified that until she moved in with Cody, the two never had any problems.

Christie stated that shortly after they moved in together, Cody became physically abusive toward her. However, she did not leave because she loved Cody and believed he would not continue to hurt her because he loved her. Christie's family and friends also testified to Cody's violent, threatening, and explosive behavior toward Christie.

Matthew was born on July 1, 1992. Despite Cody's abusive and controlling behavior toward her, Christie testified that she believed he would not hurt Matthew because he was so proud to be a father. Christie testified she could never imagine Cody intentionally hurting Matthew.

On August 21, 1992, Dr. Berkley Powell, a physician in Reno, saw Matthew. Dr. Powell testified that Matthew had a fever, a yellowish, bloody discharge coming from his nose, and was breathing very rapidly. Matthew had also thrown up blood the night before. Matthew was admitted to the hospital and was diagnosed with pneumonia, and he remained in the hospital for approximately a week. During his stay in the hospital, Matthew recovered from the infection but lost almost half a pound.

Dr. Powell also noticed a bruise above Matthew's nose and his eye. When he asked Christie about it, she said Cody had dropped Matthew, and Matthew's face had struck a coffee table. Dr. Powell's concern prompted him to order a CAT scan and X-rays and call child protective services. The X-rays did not reveal any indications of fractures. Dr. Powell testified that Christie seemed uncomfortable with the questions he asked about Matthew's injuries, and he believed she was covering up for Cody.

Child abuse was suspected, and a social worker from Washoe County Child Protective Services was assigned to Matthew's case. The social worker testified that Cody related several inconsistent accounts about Matthew's injuries. Based on twenty-two different factors, the social worker rated the risk of injury to Matthew as low, despite information he received from a family member that Cody had a quick temper.

After Matthew was released from the hospital, Christie got a job because Cody was not working regularly. When Christie was at work, Matthew was in the care of either Cody or Christie's grandparents. Christie testified that Cody became "very explosive," volatile, and short-tempered during this time. He quit his job and did not tell Christie. Christie related an incident in which Cody threatened her with a knife, telling her he was going to kill them both so that they would die as a family and nobody could control them any longer. Christie stated that when Cody realized she was holding Matthew, he backed off. She stated she was terrified of Cody by this point.

On September 17, 1992, Cody went to see Christie while she was at work. He told her Matthew had been burned when Cody had been giving Matthew a bath and failed to check the water temperature. Christie could not remember the exact date this incident had happened. Cody told Christie the burns were not bad, just pinkish. Christie told Cody to go home and stay with Matthew. When Christie got home, she looked at Matthew's burns. She testified they were "pink like a sunburn" and reddish in some areas. She bathed Matthew, put ointment on his burns, and dressed them in gauze.

Christie told Cody she thought a doctor should see Matthew, but Cody told her no. Cody told her they could treat Matthew's wounds themselves, and if he got worse, then they would take him to a doctor. Christie acquiesced to Cody's demands because she was afraid of what Cody would do to her if she did not, especially because Cody had previously threatened to kill them all. Christie was also worried that social services would take Matthew from her.

On September 18, 1992, a friend of Christie's and Cody's, Lori Smith, visited Cody and Matthew while Christie was at work. Lori saw Matthew lying on his stomach with gauze covering his back and upper arms. She saw no blisters or oozing around the gauze covered area, but noted that when Cody turned Matthew over to change his diaper, he started crying. She asked Cody what happened, and he told her Matthew had been in the bath when the water suddenly got hot and burned him. Lori thought the burns looked bad, so she asked Cody if Matthew had been to the hospital, and Cody replied that he had.

In the early evening of September 22, 1992, Matthew was having trouble breathing. Christie stated that she told Cody she was going to take Matthew to the doctor the next day, and Cody became enraged. The next day at work, Cody called Christie and told her that there was an emergency with Matthew. When Christie got home, Cody was performing CPR on Matthew. They drove Matthew to the hospital.

Christie and Cody arrived with Matthew at the emergency room of Saint Mary's Hospital shortly before 5:00 p.m. on September 22, 1992. Shari Quinn, a nurse at the emergency room of Saint Mary's, testified that when Matthew arrived at the hospital, he had no heart or respiratory rate and was subsequently put on life support. Quinn questioned Christie and Cody about the events leading to Matthew's injuries. Quinn testified that Christie told her Matthew had been burned four or five days earlier when the water heater had exploded. Quinn reentered the emergency room and while moving Matthew, felt fluid from the burn on his back. She stated that when she pulled her hand away from Matthew, her hand had sanguinous fluid and dead skin from the burn on it. She rolled Matthew over and saw a huge burn over most of his back.

Another nurse who treated Matthew assumed when she saw him that he was only four to five weeks old because his weight was so low. Matthew's injuries included a black eye and a small cut under it, noticeable abrasions on his ear and head, burn marks on his hand, a blister on one of his feet, and a large burn on his back covering the majority of the area between his shoulders and buttocks. The burn on Matthew's back was open and cracked, moist and oozing, with the skin flaking away. No ointment or other kind of medical treatment was evident on Matthew at the time he was admitted. Additionally, evidence was presented that Matthew had suffered "tissue wasting" and "muscle wasting," as evidenced by his buttocks and legs having no plumpness and being almost "to bone."

Matthew was transferred from Saint Mary's to Washoe Medical Center for further treatment, but died on September 24, 1992. The autopsy revealed that in addition to the burns, Matthew had suffered injuries not superficially apparent. These included broken ribs and a severe cranial trauma. Additionally, Matthew's thymus gland had withered. The stated cause of death was blunt injuries to the skull and brain, in combination with the burn wound.

Detective Jenkins, a Reno Police detective, was called in by the medical team, and he interviewed Christie. Christie never told him she was afraid of or abused by Cody; however, she did tell Jenkins she had seen Cody very angry on occasions. She also told Jenkins she felt the need to protect her husband and her child and said she had never seen Cody hurt Matthew. Jenkins concluded that Christie, three years older than Cody, was clearly the more mature one and did not seem intimidated by him. In fact, Christie stated that she would leave Cody immediately if he was physically abusive to Matthew or her.

Christie also told Jenkins that Matthew had been burned in the shower with Cody. However, detectives found that the various faucets in Cody's and Christie's apartment maintained a consistent temperature, not over 135 degrees. Additionally, testimony was presented which indicated Matthew would have had to have been immersed in water that temperature for nearly one minute to suffer the burns found on him.

Christie initially characterized Matthew's burns as pinkish in color with no blistering or other indication of a severe burn. Later in the interview, she told Jenkins that Matthew's blanket was sticking to his burns and that when she removed the blanket, portions of his skin would "literally peel off with the blanket." She also indicated that the blistering had occurred shortly after the burn trauma.

Following the investigation of Matthew's death, Cody was charged with first degree murder. Prior to trial, Cody pleaded guilty to this charge and was sentenced to life without the possibility of parole. On October 28, 1992, an indictment was filed alleging that Christie had committed the offense of child neglect causing substantial bodily harm. The State alleged that Christie had caused Matthew to suffer unjustifiable physical pain when she "neglected, delayed or refused to seek appropriate medical treatment for [Matthew's] malnourishment and failure to thrive and for second degree burns [Matthew] received while under the care of [Christie] and/or CODY A. RICE." The State's theory was that Christie did not seek treatment for Matthew's burns because she was afraid social services would take Matthew away from her. Christie was only charged with neglecting Matthew for the period between September 14 and September 22, 1992.

Prior to trial, Christie was evaluated by Dr. Lon Kepit, a clinical psychologist specializing in cases involving battered women. Kepit concluded that Christie's behavior fit the model of a battered woman. Dr. Kepit testified that as a battered woman, Christie would lose sight of her personal boundaries. She would also, therefore, lose sight of boundaries for Matthew and be unable to assess danger accurately.

Following a jury trial, Christie was convicted of child neglect causing substantial bodily harm. The district court sentenced Christie to twenty years in prison.

DISCUSSION

. . .

The evidence adduced at trial was sufficient to sustain the conviction

For this court to affirm a conviction, sufficient evidence must be presented to establish the essential elements of each offense beyond a reasonable doubt as determined by a rational trier of fact. The Ninth Circuit Court of Appeals has stated what evidence is needed to prove child abuse based on delay in seeking medical treatment, and the analysis would be the same for child neglect. *Martineau v. Angelone*, 25 F.3d 734 (9th Cir. 1994). *Martineau* states:

> Appellants contend, and the state concedes, that under the Nevada Supreme Court's ruling, the child abuse conviction can be upheld only if the state proved beyond a reasonable doubt that appellants committed an "omission"—i.e. that they "willfully caused or permitted" [the child] to suffer unjustifiable physical pain by delaying in seeking medical care. NRS 200.508 (1977). . . .
>
> In order to prove child abuse based on delay, the state had to prove both (A) that some time passed between [the child's] injuries and appellants' 911 call and attempted CPR and (B) that, during this time, appellants knew (or should have known) that [the child's] injuries were serious enough to require immediate medical attention, yet did nothing.

25 F.3d at 739 (citing *Fabritz v. Traurig*, 583 F.2d 697 (4th Cir. 1978)).

Christie's defense was that when she noticed the burns, she was going to take the infant to the hospital until Cody objected and said that social services would be called and would take the child from them. Concerned about losing her child and Cody's propensity for violence, she decided that medical assistance was not essential and that she could care for the baby at home. The dissent claims, that at the worst, Christie is guilty of "bad judgment." However, there is ample evidence from which a jury could conclude that there were observable injuries during the week prior to Matthew's hospitalization that needed medical attention and that the child suffered substantial pain and injury because of the delay in obtaining such care.

Dr. Ellen Clark, the pathologist who observed the child at the hospital for one and one-half days prior to his death and who conducted the autopsy, stated: "It's my opinion that Matthew Rice was a victim of child abuse which extended over several episodes, certainly from August through his death." Dr. Clark testified that the child lost a substantial amount of weight from his first hospitalization on August 22 until his second hospitalization on September 22, and that it was readily observable that he was malnourished and extremely underweight. She explained that his weight at the August hospitalization was in the ten to twenty-five percentile of children two months old, but that when he was admitted on September 22, his weight was below the fifth percentile of children three months old. She did acknowledge that some weight loss could have been attributable to the continuing pneumonia Matthew had that caused the August hospitalization.

Dr. Clark testified that the child had second degree burns from his neck down to the upper part of his buttocks and stated that: "A second degree burn goes deeper into the skin and is characterized by damage to the skin. It's in the form of blistering, and very often skin sloughage or peeling of the skin." The burns involved approximately twenty-five to thirty percent of the total body surface area, and Dr. Clark stated that burns over this extent of an infant's body are extremely serious and cause a great risk of dehydration and infection without proper medical treatment. Another complication of the burn was that it would be a painful injury, and "it would have disturbed the baby's normal daily functions, including sleeping and eating."

Christie testified that the burn wound was just pinkish for the four or five days Matthew was at home. While she wanted to take the infant to the hospital, she discerned no emergency medical situation. However, this was refuted by several health professionals and Lori Smith, the couple's teenage friend. Nurse Quinn testified that upon admission, Matthew's burn wounds were open and secreting sanguinous fluid. Drs. Clark and Bonaldi testified that the blistering would have been observable shortly after the injury and that immediate medical assistance should have been sought. . . .

Christie admitted that the blistering occurred shortly after the burn and that the blanket was sticking to Matthew's open wounds. Lori Smith stated that the burns looked bad shortly after they had been sustained. When she inquired about seeking medical treatment, Cody lied about having taken the baby to the hospital.

The jury easily could have concluded that from the time the baby was burned four or five days prior to the hospital admission, he was in desperate need of medical assistance for the serious burns and what Dr. Clark described upon admission as his severe malnutrition and "wasted appearance." Not only could the jurors conclude, from the expert testimony and their own life experiences, that these physical injuries necessitated immediate medical care, but that the pain and disruption in the infant's eating and sleeping habits could not have been overlooked by any reasonable person. As to Christie's assertion that she was afraid of Cody and the possible loss of her child if medical assistance was sought, the jury could have discounted this testimony or believed that Christie has an overriding responsibility to the infant in spite of these possible consequences.

There was more than ample evidence to establish that Christie knew or should have known that the infant was in need of medical care, that she unreasonably delayed in providing it to him, and that the delay caused the infant to suffer unjustifiable physical pain or mental suffering. . . .

The district court did not err in failing to instruct the jury on the lesser degree of child neglect

NRS 200.508 provides that anyone who willfully causes a child to suffer unjustifiable physical pain or mental suffering as a result of abuse or neglect is guilty of a gross misdemeanor. But if substantial bodily or mental harm results, the perpetrator is guilty of a felony. The statutory definition of substantial bodily harm set forth in NRS 0.060 states that it is bodily injury which creates a substantial risk of death or which causes serious, permanent disfigurement or prolonged physical pain.

The indictment charged Christie with causing Matthew to suffer unjustifiable physical and/or mental suffering resulting in substantial bodily harm to the child, a felony. At the trial's conclusion, the jury was instructed on the felony charge, but the lesser included offense of gross misdemeanor child neglect was not included in the instructions nor was it requested by the defense. Christie now claims that the district judge had an obligation to instruct the jury on the lesser included offense notwithstanding her failure to request such an instruction.

In *Davis v. State,* 110 Nev. 1107, 1114, 881 P.2d 657 (1994), we held that a district court need not instruct the jury on a lesser included offense if evidence clearly showed guilt above the lesser offense. In this case, we believe the State introduced sufficient evidence to establish that Christie's four or five day delay in seeking medical treatment resulted in Matthew sustaining prolonged physical pain, thereby falling within the definition of substantial bodily harm. Expert testimony established that the massive burn was extremely painful and a jury could conclude that delaying treatment for four or five days unjustifiably prolonged that pain. Therefore, it was not error to omit giving an instruction on the lesser included offense of gross misdemeanor.

The district court did not err in permitting evidence of the cause of Matthew's death and then instructing the jury on the limited use of this evidence

[In this portion of its opinion, the majority held that the trial court did not err in permitting a pathologist to testify regarding the full extent of the injuries that resulted in Matthew's death, even though Christie Rice was not charged with inflicting those injuries or with causing Matthew's death.] . . .

The district court erroneously sentenced appellant by relying on impermissible evidence.

The defense called Nancy Clark, a professional who provided an alternate sentencing report based on interviews with people involved in the case. The district judge asked Clark approximately 100 questions, many of which concerned information the judge obtained from presiding over the criminal proceedings involving Cody Rice or from reading Cody's presentence report. Christie asserts this conduct indicates that in sentencing Christie, the district court judge improperly relied upon information never provided to the defense. In particular, Christie complains about the district judge's professed disbelief that Christie was unaware of Cody's drug and alcohol abuse.

NRS 176.156(1) governs the disclosure of presentence reports and states: "The court shall disclose to the district attorney, the counsel for the defendant and the defendant the factual content of the report of the presentence investigation and the recommendations of the division and afford an opportunity to each party to object to factual errors and comment on the recommendations." . . .

In this case, the district judge spent quite a bit of time questioning Clark about the credibility of Christie's professed unawareness of Cody's drug and alcohol use. In his questioning of Ms. Clark, it was apparent that the judge was relying on the information furnished by Cody in his presentencing report and sentencing hearing. Repeatedly, the district judge asked how Christie could not have known of Cody's alcohol and drug abuse when Cody's habit and conduct as described by him would have been obvious to anyone.

In effect, the judge was accepting Cody's statements of continual and excessive drug use as true and asking Clark to square Christie's professed lack of knowledge of Cody's drug problem with such statements. This was part of the larger inquiry the district judge was making about whether Christie had lied when she testified. . . .

The district judge's perception of Christie's veracity was critical. Christie called numerous witnesses at the sentencing hearing who portrayed her as a responsible young adult who had no prior criminal record of any type and would almost certainly do well on probation. The district judge admitted as much.

> I don't doubt a word of what all your friends and relatives and employers have said about you. By every single account from every source, you are a positive, productive, intelligent, able person. You're a person with good judgment. You're extremely industrious.
>
> In striking contrast to most of the defendants who come before the Court, you don't have any history of drug abuse, alcohol abuse, unemployment. You have a record every parent would hope for their child: an A student, a good employee, a participant in a program for gifted and talented students, a manager of other employees at a young age. In short, a model life.

In viewing Christie's positive life before the birth of her child and the criminal neglect of which she was convicted, the district judge posed the following two extremes: "Either she shouldn't be in prison or [on] probation, just congratulate her for being a nice person and go home, or she should be punished very severely." The judge later speculated that perhaps Christie knowingly let her child be severely abused by Cody to "take [the child] out of the picture" and remove the "obstacle to the flourishing of her life with her husband." The judge's opinion of Christie's credibility did in large measure determine whether she received the lightest or the most severe sentence.

In accepting Cody's statements in the presentence report and using them in a critical analysis of whether Christie had fabricated her testimony, the judge apparently came to the conclusion that Christie had lied and that she was partly responsible for the child's death. . . .The prosecutor even referred to Cody's presentence report in his closing argument. Therefore, we believe that since the district court's use and reliance upon Cody's presentence report without providing the defense with a copy constituted prejudicial error, we are compelled to reverse the sentence in this case and remand for re-sentencing. To eliminate any problem with what the sentencing judge may remember from the sentencing of Cody, the re-sentencing shall be conducted by another district court judge. Since we conclude that the use of Cody's presentence report requires us to reverse this sentence, it is not necessary to consider Christie's remaining claims of error committed at sentencing. . . .

SPRINGER, J., concurring in part and dissenting in part:

I concur with remanding this matter for re-sentencing, but I dissent to the remaining judgment of this court because there are two errors in this case that require reversal.

The most obvious error is the trial court's failure to instruct the jury on the lesser degree of the crime of child neglect. Child neglect is a gross misdemeanor unless there is proof of "substantial bodily or mental harm." Proof of the added element of substantial bodily or mental harm raises the crime of child neglect from a gross misdemeanor to a felony calling for a maximum of twenty years in prison.

NRS 175.201 requires not only that a jury must be instructed on the degrees of an offense, it also requires that the jury be instructed that if there is a reasonable doubt as to which degree is proven, the defendant is to be convicted of the lowest degree. Ms. Rice was denied the benefit of this statute.

Although I believe that it was error per se for the trial court not to instruct on the lesser offense, I would point out that the omission was particularly disastrous to this defendant because this case looks much more like a gross misdemeanor case than a felony case, and the jury should have had the chance to bring in a verdict of the lesser offense.

The jury was not given a chance to decide that injuries suffered by reason of delay in seeking medical attention were less than "substantial," which is to say, injuries which created a substantial risk of death, loss or impairment of the function of a bodily organ or member, or prolonged physical pain. NRS 200.060. As I will demonstrate, proof relating to substantial injury in this case must be related to the scald injury and the scald injury alone. It is very difficult to conclude that Ms. Rice's deciding not to call in professional medical care until the scalding reached the blister stage resulted in "substantial" injury, as defined by NRS 200.060. I find no evidence in the record that this delay was the cause of any increased or unnecessary suffering on the part of the child. The intentional scalding inflicted by the child's father was what caused the child's injuries, not Ms. Rice's delay in calling the doctor. The evidence in this case certainly would support a jury finding that Ms. Rice's delay in getting medical treatment for the scalding did not result in any appreciable detriment to the child and that it could not possibly have resulted in injury of a "substantial magnitude—risk of death, loss of a bodily organ or prolonged physical pain." It is safe to say, given the circumstances of this case, that if Ms. Rice were guilty of child neglect at all, she would be guilty of gross misdemeanor child neglect and not felony child neglect. That the jury did not have the opportunity to convict Ms. Rice of the lesser degree of child neglect is so prejudicial as to call clearly for the reversal of her felony child neglect conviction.

Apart from the obvious error present in the trial court's failing to instruct on the lesser degree of child neglect, a momentous error has been committed in this case. The error to which I refer is the failure of the trial court to define and instruct properly on the mental element of the crime of child neglect, the mens rea.

Mens rea, sometimes referred to in terms of "guilty mind," "consciousness of criminality" or "wrongful purpose" is a necessary element of any crime. Ms. Rice cannot be guilty of a crime simply because she exercised bad judgment in not calling in medical attention for her child's scald injury; yet that is what this case is all about.

As I will maintain throughout this opinion, Ms. Rice cannot be guilty of a crime unless she knew or should have known that a delay in calling a doctor was going to cause unjustifiable injury to her son. As matters stand, Ms. Rice was incorrectly convicted of a crime when, at most, she was guilty of negligence. The indictment charged that Ms. Rice "neglected . . . to seek appropriate [reasonable and proper] medical treatment." The court instructed the jury (Instruction No. 15) that " 'neglect' includes negligent treatment" and the "negligent . . . care, control and supervision or lacks the subsistence, medical care or other care necessary for the well-being of the child." This is a negligence case. We must bear in mind that the difference between mere negligence and criminal misconduct is that in a negligence case the actor is held civilly liable for failure to perceive danger; whereas, in criminal cases the actor is held criminally liable for being aware of an impermissible risk and acting in spite of the danger. There is no charge, nor is there evidence to support a charge, that Ms. Rice knew of a danger and that she knowingly disregarded a known danger. . . .

The scalding in question was intentionally inflicted upon the child by the murderer, Cody Rice. Cody Rice told Ms. Rice that the child had been accidentally scalded while he was giving the child a bath. When Ms. Rice got home from work that evening, she expressed her concern about her son and suggested to Cody that they should take him to the hospital for treatment. Cody would not permit this and ordered Ms. Rice to treat the child for the scald at home. Ms. Rice testified that at this time she was "terrified" of Cody and that he had threatened to kill her on a number of occasions. The scalding looked pink and much like a sunburn. Ms. Rice bathed her baby son and dressed the scalded tissue. An independent witness saw the scalded area on September 18, 1992, and said that it looked like a sunburn. When the scalding started to blister, Ms. Rice again suggested that they get medical attention for the child, but Cody "exploded," screaming and throwing things. Ms. Rice spent the rest of the night in fear, holding her baby to her chest all night long. She told Cody that she was going to take the child to the doctor on the next day no matter what. On that day Cody beat the child to death.

Now it seems to me that if the child had been suffering from some serious disease that placed the child in danger of death or permanent physical impairment, it could be argued that the mother was obliged, at least morally, to risk her own life and to call in medical care in order to save her child's life; but this was not the case here. It can of course be argued that the mother exercised poor judgment in not having the scald attended to sooner, but it is very hard to argue that her treating the boy at home caused the child to "suffer unjustifiable physical pain," much less "substantial bodily or mental harm" in the form of a life-threatening situation or the other defining conditions of substantial bodily harm. It was Cody Rice that caused the child to suffer unjustifiable physical pain and not Ms. Rice; and there is absolutely no evidence that any failure on the part of Ms. Rice to bring in professional care for the scald injury inflicted by the child's father caused the child to suffer any more or any less pain than that which was intentionally inflicted by the father. Ms. Rice treated the child at home with unguents and coverings and baby pain-relievers. There is no evidence that a doctor could have or would have done things differently.

This whole case and Ms. Rice's having to spend twenty years in prison are based, at the very most, on an error in judgment on her part, an error committed when she decided not to risk her life in order to have the pre-blister scald injury attended to by a doctor instead of treating it at home. There is nothing at all to indicate that the child was any the worse off because of this decision, and certainly nothing to indicate that treating the child at home caused the child to suffer any harm as a result of Ms. Rice's arguably bad decision, much less proof that the child suffered "substantial bodily or mental harm."

Having an understanding of the nature of the charges and the factual background of this case enables us better to understand the injustice of this conviction. This leads me to discuss further the major error in this case, the constitutional violation of due process that was committed by the trial court in allowing this woman to be convicted of a crime for, at most, being neglectful and in having negligently "permitted" her child to suffer by reason of her decision to delay medical treatment for a scald injury suffered at the hands of her murdering husband.

As I have mentioned above (citing *Martineau v. Angelone*, 25 F.3d 734 (9th Cir. 1994)), neither the statute nor our case law has, as of yet, has defined "the precise mental state required" in child neglect cases. 25 F.3d at 739 n.10. Obviously, the mental state required for a criminal child neglect conviction has to go beyond mere negligent child supervision, or all parents would be in jeopardy. It is a rare parent indeed who does not, at some time or another, fall below the standard of "due care" expected of a "reasonable" parent. What this court should be doing now, and what this court has completely failed to do, is to define the "mental state," the mens rea that is an essential element of the subject crime. Without such definition the present conviction suffers from the same constitutional infirmities that resulted in the release of the convicted defendant in *Martineau*. . . .

In sum, then, the majority opinion is at odds with *Martineau;* and it was constitutional error for the trial court not to have instructed the jury that Ms. Rice could not be convicted of a crime unless it found that she "knew or should have known" that a delay in treating her son's scalding would result in the child's suffering "unjustifiable physical pain or mental suffering." Ms. Rice cannot stand convicted for a crime just because she did not call the doctor. She may have exercised poor judgment in not calling in professional medical help when she discovered that her husband had "accidentally" caused her son to be scalded in the bathtub, but this is not the same as knowing that her son would suffer "unjustifiable" pain because she decided to treat him at home. . . .

Although there are a number of errors in this case, I have stressed two errors in contending that this conviction must be reversed. The most obvious error is the court's failure to tell the jury that there were two possible crimes here, the gross misdemeanor and the felony. Ms. Rice was greatly prejudiced by reason of the jury's not knowing that it could have brought in a conviction for a lesser offense, based on the facts in evidence.

NOTES AND QUESTIONS

(1) Based on the facts recited in the majority and dissenting opinions, do you believe that Christie Rice was guilty of a crime under Nevada law? If so, which crime? The crime of felony child neglect for which Ms. Rice was convicted carries a statutory penalty of between two and 20 years imprisonment. If you were the trial judge responsible for sentencing Ms. Rice on remand, what penalty would you impose?

(2) The result in *Rice* is consistent with decisions in a number of states that have held a parent (usually a mother) criminally responsible for failing to prevent or to halt child abuse committed by a spouse or other household member. *See, e.g., State v. Legg,* 623 N.E.2d 1263, 1266 (Ohio Ct. App. 1993) (mother was properly convicted of child endangerment where she was aware that her child was being beaten, but did not attempt to halt the beating); *State v. Williquette,* 385 N.W.2d 145 (Wis. 1986) (upholding mother's child abuse conviction based on her knowing failure to protect her children from her husband's abusive conduct). Courts have also terminated parental rights based on a parent's failure to protect a child from abuse. *See, e.g., In the Interest of B.R.S.,* 402 S.E.2d 281 (Ga. Ct. App. 1991) (affirming termination of mother's parental rights because of her failure

to protect child from father's abuse); *In re Maricopa County Juvenile Action Nos. JS-4118/ JD-529*, 656 P.2d 1268 (Ariz. Ct. App. 1982) (severance of mother's parental rights justified by her previous inability to defend herself and her children from abuse and her refusal to obtain a divorce from stepfather found to have abused children). Moreover, in several recent civil suits, mothers have been held liable in tort for failing to prevent the sexual abuse of children by fathers, stepfathers, or boyfriends. *See* Craig E. Hansen, *An Indiana Approach to the Emerging Passive Parent Action,* 29 Val. U.L. Rev. 1299, 1331–33 (1995) (discussing trial court decisions); Julie Gannon Shoop, *Mother Liable for Failure to Protect Child from Sexual Abuse*, 29 Trial 16, 109 (Jan. 1993).

(3) A number of commentators have expressed concern about the imposition of criminal and civil penalties for parental failure to protect, particularly where the non-protecting parent may herself be the victim of domestic abuse. *See, e.g.,* Mary E. Becker, *Double Binds Facing Mothers in Abusive Families: Social Support Systems, Custody Outcomes and Liability for Acts of Others,* 5 U. Chi. L. Sch. Roundtable 13 (1995); Kristian Miccio, *In the Name of Mothers and Children: Deconstructing the Myth of the Passive Battered Mother and the "Protected Child" in Child Neglect Proceedings,* 58 Alb. L. Rev. 1087 (1995). For example, Professor Mary Becker has argued that the legal system's traditional unwillingness to combat domestic violence, and the continuing reluctance of many judges to take abuse allegations seriously in the context of divorce and custody proceedings, creates a difficult "double bind" for mothers involved in abusive relationships:

> Mothers in families in which husbands or boyfriends are abusive face many obstacles to protecting their children, a number of which are within the legal system itself and many of which could be eliminated or softened if taxpayers and legislatures were willing to spend resources to make exit possible and safe for mothers and children.

Becker, *above* at 26. To what extent should these considerations affect decisions by courts or legislatures regarding whether and when to impose criminal and/or civil liability for one parent's failure to protect a child from abuse by another parent or intimate partner?

For additional discussion of these issues, *see* Christine Adams, *Mothers Who Fail to Protect Their Children from Sexual Abuse: Addressing the Problem of Denial,* 12 Yale L. & Poly. Rev. 519 (1994); Marie Ashe & Naomi Cahn, *Child Abuse: A Problem for Feminist Theory,* 2 Tex. J. Women & Law 75 (1993); Martha Minow, *Words and the Door to the Land of Change: Law Language and Family Violence,* 43 Vand. L. Rev. 1665 (1990); Anne T. Johnson, *Criminal Liability for Parents Who Fail to Protect*, 5 Law & Inequality J. 359 (1987).

(4) **Problem.** When Mother and Father were divorced, Mother was awarded primary physical and legal custody of the couple's two young children and Father was awarded visitation rights every Saturday afternoon. Last Saturday, when Father arrived to pick up the children, he was visibly intoxicated. Mother initially refused to let the children go with Father, but she relented when Father became angry. Shortly after leaving Mother's house, Father was involved in an automobile accident caused by his intoxication, and both he and the children were seriously injured. Father has been charged with criminal child neglect. Should Mother be charged with neglect as well, under a failure-to-protect theory? Why or why not? Would your answer be different if Mother and Father were not divorced, and this was one of many incidents in which Father had driven with the children while he was intoxicated?

[C] Defining and Responding To Child Neglect

IN THE INTERESTS OF N.M.W.
Court of Appeals of Iowa
461 N.W.2d 478 (1990)

Habab, J.

Appellant, B.W., appeals the adjudication of the juvenile court determining N.M.W. to be a child in need of assistance (CINA) and the subsequent dispositional order directing continued foster care of N.M.W. We affirm.

The child in question is a girl born in July 1983. Her parents are not married to each other. She lived with her mother from the date of her birth until 1989.

The family has had involvement with the Department of Human Services since at least 1984. Over the years, the Department has prepared several abuse reports. The primary concern has been extreme filth in the mother's home, although there have also been concerns about inadequate food in the home, inadequate supervision of the child, and refusal of services by the mother.

On April 12, 1989, N.M.W. was found in front of a house a block from B.W.'s residence. When the police were unable to locate her home, they took N.M.W. to the police station. N.M.W. informed the authorities her mother had told her to go outside. B.W. claimed the child had just taken off without her knowledge. From statements made by law enforcement officers concerning the condition of B.W.'s apartment, a child protective worker visited B.W.'s apartment.

When the worker, who was accompanied by a police officer, approached the apartment, the stench of cat feces and urine became noticeable. Inside the apartment, the worker discovered the entire front room to be strewn with a collection of garbage, clothing, and other general clutter. Ashtrays were found filled to overflowing with some knocked over. Windows and screens were missing and garbage materials were embedded in the carpet. A side closet was packed with a mixture of clutter and refuse. A bedroom was filthy with garbage. Additionally, two litters of cats were living under the bed. Apparently a total of eleven to twelve cats lived in the apartment.

The same squalid conditions existed in the kitchen. The floor was filthy and the garbage container was left uncovered. The refrigerator had smeared food on parts of it and was empty of food except for milk, eggs, and ketchup. Dishes were stacked in the sink, on the counter, and on the table. Also, a cat box filled with cat excrement was found in the kitchen. In the bathroom, the cats had defecated along the bathtub and some of N.M.W.'s clothing was stuck to the feline fecal material. Because of the filthy apartment, N.M.W. stayed with a friend of B.W.

On April 14, 1989, the child protective worker returned to B.W.'s apartment. The squalid conditions still existed. Likewise, the conditions had not improved by April 17, 1989, when the worker again returned to the home. The worker returned again on April 20th to find B.W. had made limited improvement. Later visits to B.W.'s home found the unsanitary conditions unabated.

Following hearing on the matter, the juvenile court made a CINA determination as to N.M.W. At the initial hearing, the State presented evidence concerning three prior child abuse reports. The three reports had formed the basis for a prior CINA proceeding in which the juvenile court had dismissed the petition.

Our review of CINA proceedings is de novo. Accordingly, we review both the facts and the law, and adjudicate rights anew as to those issues which have been properly preserved and presented. We accord considerable weight to the fact findings of the juvenile court, especially concerning the credibility of witnesses, but we are not bound by those findings. Our supreme concern lies with the child's welfare and best interests.

I.

Initially, B.W. argues the trial court erred in finding the existence of sufficient evidence to establish N.M.W. as a child in need of assistance. Iowa Code section 232.2(6)(g) defines CINA as an unmarried child:

> Whose parent, guardian, or custodian fails to exercise a minimal degree of care in supplying the child with adequate food, clothing or shelter and refuses other means made available to provide such essentials.

We find clear and convincing record evidence to support the juvenile court's determination that N.M.W. is a child in need of assistance.

The chronic unsanitary conditions of B.W.'s apartment are of sufficient magnitude to form the basis for a CINA adjudication. We take judicial notice of the health hazards of having animal fecal materials scattered throughout one's living quarters. While the record does not disclose any adverse health effects of this environment on N.M.W., the child's well being demands that action be taken to prevent actual harm. *See In re Dameron*, 306 N.W.2d 743, 745 (Iowa 1981).

B.W. also asserts the juvenile court erred in considering B.W.'s past actions which formed the basis for prior CINA proceedings. We disagree. In considering what the future holds for a child if returned to the parent, the Iowa Supreme Court noted in *Dameron*:

> Insight for this determination can be gained from evidence of the parent's past performance, for that performance may be indicative of the quality of the future care that parent is capable of providing.

306 N.W.2d at 745. We find no error in permitting such evidence as long as there is other clear and convincing evidence that forms the basis of the current CINA proceeding. We find such other clear and convincing evidence independent of the prior CINA proceedings. . . .

III.

Finally, B.W. challenges the juvenile court's decision at the dispositional hearing to place N.M.W. with the Iowa Department of Human Services. We find no error in this order. B.W. was given numerous opportunities to clean and sanitize her apartment, but failed to rectify the situation. The juvenile court quite appropriately informed her that she could resume custody of N.M.W. when she removed the pets and cleaned the apartment. B.W.'s choice in this case was either her cats or her child; so far she has chosen her cats. We find no error in the juvenile court's dispositional order.

IV.

There are certain parts of the dissent that need addressing. The dissenter claims she is concerned because the majority decision may be interpreted as setting standards for housekeeping that need to be met before we allow parents to keep their children. We fail to find anything in the opinion to justify such concern. Our concern in its simplified term is with the child's welfare and best interests.

We just do not believe that this child should be compelled to live under the circumstances we set forth on pages two and three of this opinion. . . .

We, too, agree that parents who devote time and attention to their children, who allow their children to have pets and projects in their home are contributing substantially to their children's emotional development. But that is a much different setting than requiring a child to live in the stench of cat feces and urine. It is also much different than to require a child to live in a home that is strewn with a collection of garbage, clothing, and other general clutter. It is also different than requiring the child to live in a home where the cats defecated along the bathtub where some of the child's clothing was stuck to the feline fecal material.

We have no quarrel with the position of the dissenter that recommends that the State take a more active role in assisting the mother in cleaning this home so that the child may be returned. We encourage it. But until that time, is it really fair to the child to require the child to return to the mother's home as it is presently constituted? We think not.

The juvenile court, who had the first-hand opportunity to observe and talk with the mother, explained the options available to her. When we give meaningful consideration to the best interest of this child and couple the circumstances with the help given by the State, we do not believe the options to be insurmountable.

SACKETT, J. (dissenting).

I dissent. Over twelve months ago N.M.W., a happy, healthy five-year-old child was removed from her biological mother's care and placed in foster care where she remains today. The majority has determined the child must remain in foster care.

The reason for the removal, and the decision the child should remain in foster care, is that the mother is an inadequate housekeeper and does not keep what the majority terms a sanitary house. I agree with the majority that the record clearly supports a finding this mother is an extremely poor housekeeper. I agree with the majority it would be in the child's best interests to live in a cleaner house. However, the house could have been cleaned without taking the child from her mother. I do not, however, feel removal from the parental home was in the child's best interests and feel the matter should be remanded to direct reasonable efforts be utilized to allow the child to return home. Houses can be cleaned, but the trauma a child experiences when he or she is removed from the only parental home he or she has ever known can cause emotional scars that can last a lifetime.

There is strong authority that parenting deficiencies may best be addressed by leaving the child in the home, that removals from biological families are traumatic for children, and that foster care placement is wrought with problems. See Wald, *State Intervention on Behalf of "Neglected" Children: Standards for Removal of Children From Their Homes, Monitoring the Status of Children in Foster Care and Termination of Parental Rights*, 28 Stan. L. Rev. 623, 638 (1976). Additionally, the difficulties I see occur with foster placements convince me the state, despite conscientious efforts by dedicated persons, is ill-equipped to parent.

Our legislature has recognized that children are best served by remaining in their home and requires reasonable efforts be made to allow them to remain there. Federal legislation providing states' reimbursement for foster care directs that reasonable efforts be made to allow a child to remain in his or her home, and a state's failure to do so can result in the loss of funds for foster care reimbursement.

To apply reasonable efforts first requires identifying the problem. The problems identified by the majority are the poor housekeeping conditions in the home, and the inability of the mother to correct these deficiencies. After identifying the problem, the next step is to look at the family as a unit and determine what it takes to correct this problem.

If this mother came from a higher economic level, she could do as many parents do who have neither the desire or ability to clean their houses. She could hire a cleaning service. I would consider reasonable efforts to entail granting this mother assistance with cleaning her house and keeping it clean. A few hours of cleaning service would have cost the state less than the judicial time and court appointed attorney fees spent to litigate the adequacy of this woman's housekeeping skills through the state's appellate courts. And most importantly, the child would not have suffered the trauma of removal and the insecurities that come in foster care.

The majority decision also concerns me because it may be interpreted as setting standards for housekeeping that need to be met before we allow parents to keep their children. If I were convinced: (1) only people in clean houses were good parents, (2) for a child to be healthy it is necessary for him or her to be raised in a sanitary house, and (3) a child suffers less by being removed from his or her parents than from growing up in a dirty house, I could agree with the majority. I am not convinced of these things. I consider parents who devote time and attention to their children, who allow their children to have pets and projects in their home, and who welcome their children's friends in their home are contributing substantially to their children's emotional development. Parents who seek to direct their financial and emotional resources in these directions may have few resources left to keep a sanitary house.

If we concentrate too much on sanitary houses, we may take children away from good and adequate parents, and we may use energies and resources that would best be directed to helping families and to identifying children who suffer serious abuse.

NOTES AND QUESTIONS

(1) The dissenting opinion cites a well-known law review article by Professor Michael Wald for the proposition that most parenting difficulties are best addressed in the home and that removal is appropriate only when a child's physical health or safety is endangered. According to this "minimum intervention" approach, broad statutory definitions of neglect such as the one relied on by the majority in *N.M.W.* have the potential to do more harm than good for children.

> In order to protect children from the risks of unwarranted state action, these critics have urged the adoption of a policy of minimum state intervention in family life. Under

such a policy, intervention could not be premised on the contention that it will somehow prove helpful to the child or family. Instead, intervention would be limited to the "least drastic alternative," or to only those steps necessary to protect the child from real, imminent harm. This approach also utilizes stricter legislative standards and more active judicial review in order to limit and prevent abuse of the discretion traditionally afforded child welfare administrators.

Marsha Garrison, *Child Welfare Decisionmaking: in Search of the Least Drastic Alternative*, 75 Geo. L.J. 1745, 1747 (1987). Proponents of minimum intervention emphasize the trauma to children associated with removal from their family and the shortcomings of the foster care system into which such children are typically placed. *See, e.g.,* Michael S. Wald, *State Intervention on Behalf of "Neglected" Children: A Search for Realistic Standards*, 27 Stan. L. Rev. 985 (1975); Douglas J. Besharov, *"Doing Something" About Child Abuse: The Need to Narrow the Grounds for State Intervention,* 8 Harv. J.L. & Pub. Pol'y, 539 (1985). Proponents of minimal intervention also emphasize the dangers of race and class bias, as well as the potential for arbitrary enforcement of broad definitions of neglect:

> Broad definitions of neglect—the type used throughout the country—invite the state to judge for itself how parents are doing. Subjective and arbitrary enforcement are assured. The awesome power of the state is set in motion in its most pernicious form. State officials are authorized to act as they wish, intervening in one family while choosing to leave a second, similar family alone.

Martin Guggenheim, *The Political and Legal Implications of the Psychological Parenting Theory*, 12 N.Y.U. Rev. L. & Soc. Change, 549, 554 (1983–84). *See also* Annette Appell, *Protecting Children or Punishing Mothers: Gender, Race, and Class in the Child Protection System*, 48 S.C. L. Rev. 577 (1997) (discussing gender, race and class biases that undermine efforts to protect children through the child welfare system); Daan Braveman & Sarah Ramsey, *When Welfare Ends: Removing Children From The Home For Poverty Alone*, 70 Temple L. Rev. 447 (1997).

(2) Proponents of minimal intervention have recommended that statutory definitions of neglect be drawn more narrowly and precisely in order to limit state authority to separate children from their parents. For example, IJA-ABA Juvenile Justice Standards Relating to Abuse and Neglect, Standard 2.1 (Final Draft 1980) authorizes state intervention only when:

> A. a child has suffered, or there is a substantial risk that a child will imminently suffer, a physical harm, inflicted nonaccidentally upon him/her by his/her parents, which causes, or creates a substantial risk of causing disfigurement, impairment of bodily functioning, or other serious physical injury;
>
> B. a child has suffered, or there is a substantial risk that the child will imminently suffer, physical harm causing disfigurement, impairment of bodily functioning, or other serious physical injury as a result of conditions creation by his/her parents or by the failure of the parents to adequately supervise or protect him/her;
>
> C. a child is suffering serious emotional damage, evidenced by severe anxiety, depression, or withdrawal, or untoward aggressive behavior toward self or others, and the child's parents are not willing to provide treatment for him/her;
>
> D. a child has been sexually abused by his/her parents or a member of his/her household or by another person where the parents knew or should have known and

failed to take appropriate action (alternative: a child has been sexually abused by his/her parent or a member of his/her household, and is seriously harmed physically or emotionally thereby);

E. a child is in need of medical treatment to cure, alleviate, or prevent hi/her from suffering serious physical impairment of bodily functions, and his/her parents are unwilling to provide or consent to medical treatment;

F. a child is committing delinquent acts as a result of parental encouragement, guidance, or approval. If these standards had been in place in Iowa, would the state have been authorized to remove N.M.W. from her mother's apartment? Why or why not?

Query: Would state intervention have been authorized on behalf of N.M.W. under these standards? Why or why not?

(3) **Reasonable Efforts Requirements.** A determination by a court or a child welfare agency that a particular child's situation justifies state intervention does not necessarily mean that the child should be removed from the parent's home. Indeed, the Federal Adoption Assistance and Child Welfare Act ("AACWA") requires states, in most situations, to make "reasonable efforts," prior to placing a child in foster care, "to prevent or eliminate the need for removing the child from the child's home" and to make it possible for the child to return home safely. 42 U.S.C. § 671(a)(15)(B). (*See* § 7.06 for additional discussion of these federal requirements, including recent amendments to the AACWA.) In partial fulfillment of these federal requirements, most states have amended their child welfare codes to require judges to make "reasonable efforts" findings at the child's first court appearance following removal from the home, and a number of states require continuing "reasonable efforts" findings for as long as a child remains in state custody. *See generally* Alice C. Shotton, *Making Reasonable Efforts in Child Abuse and Neglect Cases: Ten Years Later*, 26 Cal. W.L. Rev. 223 (1990). Although the AACWA does not define "reasonable efforts," regulations promulgated under the Act suggest both preventive and reunification services, including "twenty-four hour emergency caretaker, and homemaker services." 45 C.F.R. 1357.15(e)(2) (1995). The dissent in *N.M.W.* invokes this "reasonable efforts" requirement to suggest that the state should have provided cleaning assistance to N.M.W.'s mother, before placing N.M.W. in foster care. The majority rejects this suggestion and concludes, at least implicitly, that state authorities satisfied the "reasonable efforts" requirement by giving N.M.W.'s mother "numerous opportunities to clean and sanitize her apartment" and by informing her that she could "resume custody of N.M.W. when she removed the pets and cleaned the apartment." Which analysis do you find more persuasive and why?

(4) If a child is found to be neglected because his or her family is homeless, does the reasonable efforts requirement obligate the child welfare agency to find housing for the family? If so, must the family be given priority over other individuals and families who may also be eligible and waiting for public housing? If there is no public housing available, is the agency obligated to pay rent for private housing? *See In re Nicole G.*, 577 A.2d 248 (R.I. 1990) (where homelessness is the primary factor preventing family reunification, reasonable efforts by agency must include housing assistance); *cf. In re Amanda M.*, 626 A.2d 1277 (R.I. 1993) (trial court order that agency pay rent was improper where mother's drug abuse, rather that homelessness, was the primary barrier to reunification). Where a parent is unable to care properly for a child because of the parent's drug or alcohol addiction,

is the state required to provide treatment? More generally, what affirmative obligations, if any, does the state have to help poor or troubled families care adequately for their children? See Daan Braveman & Sarah Ramsey *When Welfare Ends: Removing Children From The Home For Poverty Alone,* 70 Temple L. Rev. 447 (1997); Stephen Wizner, *Do The Poor Have A Right to Family Integrity?,* in Child, Parent & State 299 (S. Randall Humm et. al. eds., 1994). How should such obligations be enforced?

(5) **Problem**. Two parents who worked at minimum wage jobs stuffing newspapers left their children, ages 9 and 2, in a locked car for three hours at night in 20° because they could not find a babysitter and feared losing their jobs and becoming homeless (again) if one of them were absent from work. The parents asked their supervisor if they could bring the children inside the newspaper plant, but the supervisor refused, citing liability concerns. The children were dressed warmly, but there was no food or water in the car. A passer-by called police, who arrested the parents and took custody of the children. A paramedic who examined the children found no evidence of physical harm. Have these parents neglected their children? If so, should the parents be prosecuted criminally? Should the children be placed in foster care? What services, if any, should the state provide to prevent removal or promote reunification? See *People v. Turner,* 619 N.E.2d 781 (Ill. App. Ct. 1993).

[D] Abuse or Neglect of A Fetus?

WHITNER v. STATE
Supreme Court of South Carolina
492 S.E.2d 777 (1997), *cert. denied,* 118 S. Ct. 1857 (1998):

This case concerns the scope of the child abuse and endangerment statute in the South Carolina Children's Code (the Code), S.C. Code Ann. § 20–7–50 (1985). We hold the word "child" as used in that statute includes viable fetuses.

FACTS

On April 20, 1992, Cornelia Whitner (Whitner) pled guilty to criminal child neglect, S.C. Code Ann. § 20–7–50 (1985), for causing her baby to be born with cocaine metabolites in its system by reason of Whitner's ingestion of crack cocaine during the third trimester of her pregnancy. The circuit court judge sentenced Whitner to eight years in prison. Whitner did not appeal her conviction.

Thereafter, Whitner filed a petition for Post Conviction Relief (PCR), pleading the circuit court's lack of subject matter jurisdiction to accept her guilty plea as well as ineffective assistance of counsel. Her claim of ineffective assistance of counsel was based upon her lawyer's failure to advise her the statute under which she was being prosecuted might not apply to prenatal drug use. The petition was granted on both grounds. The State appeals.

LAW/ANALYSIS

A. Subject Matter Jurisdiction

The State first argues the PCR court erred in finding the sentencing circuit court lacked subject matter jurisdiction to accept Whitner's guilty plea. We agree.

Under South Carolina law, a circuit court lacks subject matter jurisdiction to accept a guilty plea to a nonexistent offense. For the sentencing court to have had subject matter jurisdiction to accept Whitner's plea, criminal child neglect under section 20–7–50 would have to include an expectant mother's use of crack cocaine after the fetus is viable. All other issues are ancillary to this jurisdictional issue.

S.C. Code Ann. § 20–7–50 (1985) provides:

> Any person having the legal custody of any child or helpless person, who shall, without lawful excuse, refuse or neglect to provide, as defined in § 20–7–490, the proper care and attention for such child or helpless person, so that the life, health or comfort of such child or helpless person is endangered or is likely to be endangered, shall be guilty of a misdemeanor and shall be punished within the discretion of the circuit court (emphasis added).

The State contends this section encompasses maternal acts endangering or likely to endanger the life, comfort, or health of a viable fetus.

Under the Children's Code, "child" means a "person under the age of eighteen." S.C. Code Ann. § 20–7–30(1) (1985). The question for this Court, therefore, is whether a viable fetus is a "person" for purposes of the Children's Code.

In interpreting a statute, this Court's primary function is to ascertain the intent of the legislature. Of course, where a statute is complete, plain, and unambiguous, legislative intent must be determined from the language of the statute itself. We should consider, however, not merely the language of the particular clause being construed, but the word and its meaning in conjunction with the purpose of the whole statute and the policy of the law. Finally, there is a basic presumption that the legislature has knowledge of previous legislation as well as of judicial decisions construing that legislation when later statutes are enacted concerning related subjects.

South Carolina law has long recognized that viable fetuses are persons holding certain legal rights and privileges. In 1960, this Court decided *Hall v. Murphy*, 236 S.C. 257, 113 S.E.2d 790 (1960). That case concerned the application of South Carolina's wrongful death statute to an infant who died four hours after her birth as a result of injuries sustained prenatally during viability. The Appellants argued that a viable fetus was not a person within the purview of the wrongful death statute, because, *inter alia*, a fetus is thought to have no separate being apart from the mother.

We found such a reason for exclusion from recovery "unsound, illogical and unjust," and concluded there was "no medical or other basis" for the "assumed identity" of mother and viable unborn child. *Id*. at 262, 113 S.E.2d at 793. In light of that conclusion, this Court unanimously held: "We have no difficulty in concluding that a fetus having reached that period of prenatal maturity where it is capable of independent life apart from its mother is a person." *Id*. at 263, 113 S.E.2d at 793 (emphasis added).

Four years later, in *Fowler v. Woodward*, 244 S.C. 608, 138 S.E.2d 42 (1964), we interpreted Hall as supporting a finding that a viable fetus injured while still in the womb need not be born alive for another to maintain an action for the wrongful death of the fetus.

> Since a viable child is a person before separation from the body of its mother and since prenatal injuries tortiously inflicted on such a child are actionable, it is apparent that the complaint alleges such an 'act, neglect or default' by the defendant, to the injury of the child . . . .

... Once the concept of the unborn, viable child as a person is accepted, we have no difficulty in holding that a cause of action for tortious injury to such a child arises immediately upon the infliction of the injury.

Id. at 613, 138 S.E.2d at 44 (emphasis added). *Fowler* makes particularly clear that *Hall* rested on the concept of the viable fetus as a person vested with legal rights.

More recently, we held the word "person" as used in a criminal statute includes viable fetuses. *State v. Horne*, 282 S.C. 444, 319 S.E.2d 703 (1984), concerned South Carolina's murder statute, S.C. Code Ann. § 16–3–10 (1976). The defendant in that case stabbed his wife, who was nine months' pregnant, in the neck, arms, and abdomen. Although doctors performed an emergency caesarean section to deliver the child, the child died while still in the womb. The defendant was convicted of voluntary manslaughter and appealed his conviction on the ground South Carolina did not recognize the crime of feticide.

This Court disagreed. In a unanimous decision, we held it would be "grossly inconsistent . . . to construe a viable fetus as a 'person' for the purposes of imposing civil liability while refusing to give it a similar classification in the criminal context." *Id.* at 447, 319 S.E.2d at 704 (citing *Fowler v. Woodward, above*). Accordingly, the Court recognized the crime of feticide with respect to viable fetuses.

Similarly, we do not see any rational basis for finding a viable fetus is not a "person" in the present context. Indeed, It would be absurd to recognize the viable fetus as a person for purposes of homicide laws and wrongful death statutes but not for purposes of statutes proscribing child abuse. Our holding in *Hall* that a viable fetus is a person rested primarily on the plain meaning of the word "person" in light of existing medical knowledge concerning fetal development. We do not believe that the plain and ordinary meaning of the word "person" has changed in any way that would now deny viable fetuses status as persons.

The policies enunciated in the Children's Code also support our plain meaning reading of "person." S.C. Code Ann. § 20–7–20(C) (1985), which describes South Carolina's policy concerning children, expressly states: "It shall be the policy of this State to concentrate on the prevention of children's problems as the most important strategy which can be planned and implemented on behalf of children and their families." (emphasis added). The abuse or neglect of a child at any time during childhood can exact a profound toll on the child herself as well as on society as a whole. However, the consequences of abuse or neglect which takes place after birth often pale in comparison to those resulting from abuse suffered by the viable fetus before birth. This policy of prevention supports a reading of the word "person" to include viable fetuses. Furthermore, the scope of the Children's Code is quite broad. It applies "to all children who have need of services." S.C. Code Ann. § 20–7–20(B) (1985)(emphasis added). When coupled with the comprehensive remedial purposes of the Code, this language supports the inference that the legislature intended to include viable fetuses within the scope of the Code's protection.

Whitner advances several arguments against an interpretation of "person" as used in the Children's Code to include viable fetuses. . . .

Whitner's first argument concerns the number of bills introduced in the South Carolina General Assembly in the past five years addressing substance abuse by pregnant women. Some of these bills would have criminalized substance abuse by pregnant women; others would have addressed the issue through mandatory reporting, treatment, or intervention by social service agencies. Whitner suggests that the introduction of several bills touching the specific issue at hand evinces a belief by legislators that prior legislation had not addressed the issue. Whitner argues the introduction of the bills proves that section 20–7–50 was not intended to encompass abuse or neglect of a viable fetus.

We disagree with Whitner's conclusion about the significance of the proposed legislation. Generally, the legislature's subsequent acts "cast no light on the intent of the legislature which enacted the statute being construed." *Home Health Servs., Inc. v. DHEC*, 298 S.C. 258, 262 n.1, 379 S.E.2d 734, 736 n.1 (Ct. App. 1989)(citations omitted). Rather, this Court will look first to the language of the statute to discern legislative intent, because the language itself is the best guide to legislative intent. Here, we see no reason to look beyond the statutory language. Additionally, our existing case law strongly supports our conclusion about the meaning of the statute's language.

Whitner also argues an interpretation of the statute that includes viable fetuses would lead to absurd results obviously not intended by the legislature. Specifically, she claims if we interpret "child" to include viable fetuses, every action by a pregnant woman that endangers or is likely to endanger a fetus, whether otherwise legal or illegal, would constitute unlawful neglect under the statute. For example, a woman might be prosecuted under section 20–7–50 for smoking or drinking during pregnancy. Whitner asserts these "absurd" results could not have been intended by the legislature and, therefore, the statute should not be construed to include viable fetuses.

We disagree for a number of reasons. First, the same arguments against the statute can be made whether or not the child has been born. After the birth of a child, a parent can be prosecuted under section 20–7–50 for an action that is likely to endanger the child without regard to whether the action is illegal in itself. For example, a parent who drinks excessively could, under certain circumstances, be guilty of child neglect or endangerment even though the underlying act—consuming alcoholic beverages—is itself legal. Obviously, the legislature did not think it "absurd" to allow prosecution of parents for such otherwise legal acts when the acts actually or potentially endanger the "life, health or comfort" of the parents born children. We see no reason such a result should be rendered absurd by the mere fact the child at issue is a viable fetus.

Moreover, we need not address this potential parade of horribles advanced by Whitner. In this case, which is the only case we are called upon to decide here, certain facts are clear. Whitner admits to having ingested crack cocaine during the third trimester of her pregnancy, which caused her child to be born with cocaine in its system. Although the precise effects of maternal crack use during pregnancy are somewhat unclear, it is well documented and within the realm of public knowledge that such use can cause serious harm to the viable unborn child. *See, e.g.*, Joseph J. Volpe, M.D., *Effect of Cocaine Use on the Fetus*, 327 NEW ENG. J. MED. 399 (1992); Ira J. Chasnoff, M.D., et al., *Cocaine Use in Pregnancy*, 313 NEW ENG. J. MED. 666 (1985). There can be no question here Whitner endangered the life, health, and comfort of her child. We need not decide any cases other than the one before us.

We are well aware of the many decisions from other states' courts throughout the country holding maternal conduct before the birth of the child does not give rise to criminal prosecution under state child abuse/endangerment or drug distribution statutes. *See, e.g., Johnson v. State*, 602 So. 2d 1288 (Fla. 1992); *Commonwealth v. Welch*, 864 S.W.2d 280

(Ky. 1993); *State v. Gray*, 62 Ohio St. 3d 514, 584 N.E.2d 710 (Ohio 1992); *Reyes v. Superior Court*, 75 Cal. App. 3d 214, 141 Cal. Rptr. 912 (1977); *State v. Carter*, 602 So. 2d 995 (Fla. Ct. App. 1992); *State v. Gethers*, 585 So. 2d 1140 (Fla. Ct. App. 1991); *State v. Luster*, 204 Ga. App. 156, 419 S.E.2d 32 (Ga. Ct. App. 1992), *cert. denied* (Ga. 1992); *Commonwealth v. Pellegrini*, No. 87970, slip op. (Mass. Super. Ct. Oct. 15, 1990); *People v. Hardy*, 188 Mich. App. 305, 469 N.W.2d 50 (Mich. Ct. App.), *app. denied*, 471 N.W.2d 619 (Mich. 1991); *Commonwealth v. Kemp*, 434 Pa. Super. 719, 643 A.2d 705 (Pa. Super. Ct. 1994). Many of these cases were prosecuted under statutes forbidding delivery or distribution of illicit substances and depended on statutory construction of the terms "delivery" and "distribution." Obviously, such cases are inapplicable to the present situation. The cases concerning child endangerment statutes or construing the terms "child" and "person" are also distinguishable, because the states in which these cases were decided have entirely different bodies of case law from South Carolina. For example, in *Commonwealth v. Welch*, the Kentucky Supreme Court specifically noted Kentucky law has not construed the word "person" in the criminal homicide statute to include a fetus (viable or not). *Welch*, 864 S.W.2d at 281. In *Reyes v. Superior Court*, the California Court of Appeals noted California law did not recognize a fetus as a "human being" within the purview of the state murder and manslaughter statutes, and that it was thus improper to find the fetus was a "child" for purposes of the felonious child endangerment statute. *Reyes*, 75 Cal. App. 3d at 217.

Massachusetts, however, has a body of case law substantially similar to South Carolina's, yet a Massachusetts trial court has held that a mother pregnant with a viable fetus is not criminally liable for transmission of cocaine to the fetus. *See Commonwealth v. Pellegrini*, No. 87970, slip op. (Mass. Super. Ct. Oct. 15, 1990). Specifically, Massachusetts law allows wrongful death actions on behalf of viable fetuses injured in utero who are not subsequently born alive. *Mone v. Greyhound Lines, Inc* 331 N.E.2d 916 (Mass. 1975). Similarly, Massachusetts law permits homicide prosecutions of third parties who kill viable fetuses. *See Commonwealth v. Cass*, 467 N.E.2d 1324 (Mass. 1984) (ruling a viable fetus is a person for purposes of vehicular homicide statute); *Commonwealth v. Lawrence*, 536 N.E.2d 571 (Mass. 1989)(viable fetus is a person for purposes of common law crime of murder). Because of the similarity of the case law in Massachusetts to ours, the *Pellegrini* decision merits examination.

In *Pellegrini*, the Massachusetts Superior Court found that state's distribution statute does not apply to the distribution of an illegal substance to a viable fetus. The statute at issue forbade distribution of cocaine to persons under the age of eighteen. Rather than construing the word "distribution," however, the superior court found that a viable fetus is not a "person under the age of eighteen" within the meaning of the statute. *Pellegrini*, slip op. at 10. In so finding, the court had to distinguish *Lawrence* and *Cass*, above, both of which held viable fetuses are "persons" for purposes of criminal laws in Massachusetts.

The Massachusetts trial court found *Lawrence* and *Cass* "accord legal rights to the unborn only where the mother's or parents' interest in the potentiality of life, not the state's interest, are sought to be vindicated." *Pellegrini,* slip op. at 11. In other words, a viable fetus should only be accorded the rights of a person for the sake of its mother or both its parents. Under this rationale, the viable fetus lacks rights of its own that deserve vindication. Whitner suggests we should interpret our decisions in *Hall, Fowler,* and *Horne* to accord rights to the viable fetus only when doing so protects the special parent-child relationship rather than any individual rights of the fetus or any State interest in potential life. We do not think *Hall, Fowler,* and *Horne* can be interpreted so narrowly.

If the *Pellegrini* decision accurately characterizes the rationale underlying *Mone, Lawrence, and Cass,* then the reasoning of those cases differs substantially from our reasoning in *Hall, Fowler,* and *Home.* First, *Hall, Fowler,* and *Horne* were decided primarily on the basis of the meaning of "person" as understood in the light of existing medical knowledge, rather than based on any policy of protecting the relationship between mother and child. As a homicide case, Horne also rested on the State's—not the mother's—interest in vindicating the life of the viable fetus. Moreover, the United States Supreme Court has repeatedly held that the states have a compelling interest in the life of a viable fetus. *See Roe v. Wade,* 410 U.S. 113 (1973); *see also Planned Parenthood v. Casey,* 505 U.S. 833 (1992); *Webster v. Reproductive Health Servs.,* 492 U.S. 490 (1989). If, as Whitner suggests we should, we read *Horne* only as a vindication of the mother's interest in the life of her unborn child, there would be no basis for prosecuting a mother who kills her viable fetus by stabbing it, by shooting it, or by other such means, yet a third party could be prosecuted for the very same acts. We decline to read *Horne* in a way that insulates the mother from all culpability for harm to her viable child. Because the rationale underlying our body of law—protection of the viable fetus—is radically different from that underlying the law of Massachusetts, we decline to follow the decision of the Massachusetts Superior Court in *Pellegrini.*

The dissent contends that our holding in this case is inconsistent with *Doe v. Clark,* 457 S.E.2d 336 (1995) [reprinted at § 8.02, *below*]. Specifically, it suggests that *Doe v. Clark,* in which we construed another provision of the Children's Code, stands for the proposition that the definition of "child" in S.C. Code Ann. § 20-7-50 (1985) means a "child in being and not a fetus." Contrary to the dissent's characterization of that case, *Doe* turned on the specific language in the consent provisions of the Adoption Act, S.C. Code Ann. §§ 20-7-1690 and -1700 (Law. Co-op Supp. 1994).

In *Doe,* Wylanda Clark, who was pregnant, signed a consent form allowing the Does to adopt the child upon its birth. After the child was born, Clark decided she wanted to keep the baby and attempted to argue that the consent she executed was void because it did not contain certain information required by statute. The trial judge held Clark's consent was valid. Clark appealed.

On appeal, we reversed the trial court. However, the basis for our reversal was not that "child" as defined in the Children's Code only includes born children, but that the adoption statutes contemplate that the natural mother's consent to the adoption must be given after the birth of the child to be adopted. *Doe,* 457 S.E.2d at 337. We did not hold that the term "child" excludes viable fetuses, nor do we think our holding in *Doe* can be read so broadly.

Finally, the dissent implies that we have ignored the rule of lenity requiring us to resolve any ambiguities in a criminal statute in favor of the defendant. The dissent argues that "at most, the majority only suggests that the term 'child' as used in § 20-7-50 is ambiguous," and that the ambiguity "is created not by reference to our decisions under the Children's Code or by reference to the statutory language and applicable rules of statutory construction, but by reliance on decisions in two different fields of the law, civil wrongful death and common law feticide."

Plainly, the dissent misunderstands our opinion. First, we do not believe the statute is ambiguous and, therefore, the rule of lenity does not apply. Furthermore, our interpretation of the statute is based primarily on the plain meaning of the word "person" as contained in the statute. We need not go beyond that language. However, because our prior decisions in *Murphy, Fowler,* and *Horne* support our reading of the statute, we have discussed the rationale underlying those holdings. We conclude that both statutory language and case law compel the conclusion we reach. We see no ambiguity. . . .

C. Constitutional issues

1. Fair Notice/Vagueness

Whitner argues that section 20–7–50 does not give her fair notice that her behavior is proscribed. We disagree.

The statute forbids any person having legal custody of a child from refusing or neglecting to provide proper care and attention to the child so that the life, health, or comfort of the child is endangered or is likely to be endangered. As we have found above, the plain meaning of "child" as used in this statute includes a viable fetus. Furthermore, it is common knowledge that use of cocaine during pregnancy can harm the viable unborn child. Given these facts, we do not see how Whitner can claim she lacked fair notice that her behavior constituted child endangerment as proscribed in section 20–7–50. Whitner had all the notice the Constitution requires.

2. Right to Privacy

Whitner argues that prosecuting her for using crack cocaine after her fetus attains viability unconstitutionally burdens her right of privacy, or, more specifically, her right to carry her pregnancy to term. We disagree.

Whitner argues that section 20–7–50 burdens her right of privacy, a right long recognized by the United States Supreme Court. *See, e.g., Eisenstadt v. Baird*, 405 U.S. 438 (1972); *Skinner v. Oklahoma*, 316 U.S. 535 (1942). She cites *Cleveland Board of Education v. LaFleur*, 414 U.S. 632 (1974), as standing for the proposition that the Constitution protects women from measures penalizing them for choosing to carry their pregnancies to term.

In *LaFleur*, two junior high school teachers challenged their school systems' maternity leave policies. The policies required "every pregnant school teacher to take maternity leave without pay, beginning [four or] five months before the expected birth of her child." *Id.* at 634. A teacher on maternity leave could not return to work "until the beginning of the next regular school semester which follows the date when her child attains the age of three months." *Id.* at 634–35. The two teachers, both of whom had become pregnant and were required against their wills to comply with the school systems' policies, argued that the policies were unconstitutional.

The United States Supreme Court agreed. It found that "by acting to penalize the pregnant teacher for deciding to bear a child, overly restrictive maternity leave regulations can constitute a heavy burden on the exercise of these protected freedoms." *Id.* at 640. The Court then scrutinized the policies to determine whether "the interests advanced in support of" the policy could "justify the particular procedures [the School Boards] ha[d] adopted." *Id.* at 640. . . . Finding no rational relationship between the purpose of the maternity leave policy and the means crafted to achieve that end the Court concluded the policy violated the Due Process Clause of the Fourteenth Amendment.

Whitner argues that the alleged violation here is far more egregious than that in *LaFleur*. She first suggests that imprisonment is a far greater burden on her exercise of her freedom to carry the fetus to term than was the unpaid maternity leave in *LaFleur*. Although she is, of course, correct that imprisonment is more severe than unpaid maternity leave, Whitner misapprehends the fundamentally different nature of her own interests and those of the government in this case as compared to those at issue in *LaFleur*.

First, the State's interest in protecting the life and health of the viable fetus is not merely legitimate. It is compelling. *See, e.g., Roe v. Wade*, 410 U.S. 113 (1973); *Planned Parenthood v. Casey*, 505 U.S. 833 (1992). The United States Supreme Court in *Casey* recognized that the State possesses a profound interest in the potential life of the fetus, not only after the fetus is viable, but throughout the expectant mother's pregnancy.

Even more importantly, however, we do not think any fundamental right of Whitner's—or any right at all, for that matter—is implicated under the present scenario. It strains belief for Whitner to argue that using crack cocaine during pregnancy is encompassed within the constitutionally recognized right of privacy. Use of crack cocaine is illegal, period. No one here argues that laws criminalizing the use of crack cocaine are themselves unconstitutional. If the State wishes to impose additional criminal penalties on pregnant women who engage in this already illegal conduct because of the effect the conduct has on the viable fetus, it may do so. We do not see how the fact of pregnancy elevates the use of crack cocaine to the lofty status of a fundamental right.

Moreover, as a practical matter, we do not see how our interpretation of section 20–7–50 imposes a burden on Whitner's right to carry her child to term. In *LaFleur*, the Supreme Court found that the mandatory maternity leave policies burdened women's rights to carry their pregnancies to term because the policies prevented pregnant teachers from exercising a freedom they would have enjoyed but for their pregnancies. In contrast, during her pregnancy after the fetus attained viability, Whitner enjoyed the same freedom to use cocaine that she enjoyed earlier in and predating her pregnancy—none whatsoever. Simply put, South Carolina's child abuse and endangerment statute as applied to this case does not restrict Whitner's freedom in any way that it was not already restricted. The State's imposition of an additional penalty when a pregnant woman with a viable fetus engages in the already proscribed behavior does not burden a woman's right to carry her pregnancy to term; rather, the additional penalty simply recognizes that a third party (the viable fetus or newborn child) is harmed by the behavior.

Section 20–7–50 does not burden Whitner's right to carry her pregnancy to term or any other privacy right. Accordingly, we find no violation of the Due Process Clause of the Fourteenth Amendment.

[The dissenting opinion of Chief Justice Finney is omitted.]

CONCLUSION

. . . MOORE, A.J.: I concur with the dissent in this case but write separately to express my concerns with today's decision.

In my view, the repeated failure of the legislature to pass proposed bills addressing the problem of drug use during pregnancy is evidence the child abuse and neglect statute is not intended to apply in this instance. This Court should not invade what is clearly the sole province of the legislative branch. At the very least, the legislature's failed attempts to enact a statute regulating a pregnant woman's conduct indicate the complexity of this issue. While the majority opinion is perhaps an argument for what the law should be, it is for the General Assembly, and not this Court, to make that determination by means of a clearly drawn statute. With today's decision, the majority not only ignores legislative intent but embarks on a course of judicial activism rejected by every other court to address the issue.

As discussed in the Chief Justice's dissent, we are bound by the rules of statutory construction to strictly construe a criminal statute in favor of the defendant and resolve any ambiguity in her favor. I cannot accept the majority's assertion that the child abuse and neglect statute unambiguously includes a "viable fetus." If that is the case, then why is the majority compelled to go to such great lengths to ascertain that a "viable fetus" is a "child?"

Contrary to the majority's strained analysis in this case, one need look no further than the language of § 20-7-50 to clearly discern legislative intent that the statute apply only to children in being. "Legal custody" is not a qualification applicable to a viable fetus. I simply disagree the legislature intended a statute entitled "Unlawful neglect of child or helpless person by legal custodian" to render a pregnant woman criminally liable for any type of conduct potentially harmful to the unborn fetus.

In construing this statute to include conduct not contemplated by the legislature, the majority has rendered the statute vague and set for itself the task of determining what conduct is unlawful. Is a pregnant woman's failure to obtain prenatal care unlawful? Failure to quit smoking or drinking? Although the majority dismisses this issue as not before it, the impact of today's decision is to render a pregnant woman potentially criminally liable for myriad acts which the legislature has not seen fit to criminalize. To ignore this "down-the-road" consequence in a case of this import is unrealistic. The majority insists that parents may already be held liable for drinking after a child is born. This is untrue, however, without some further act on the part of the parent. A parent who drinks and then hits her child or fails to come home may be guilty of criminal neglect. The mere fact of drinking, however, does not constitute neglect of a child in being.

The majority attempts to support an overinclusive construction of the child abuse and neglect statute by citing other legal protections extended equally to a viable fetus and a child in being. The only law, however, that specifically regulates the conduct of a mother toward her unborn child is our abortion statute under which a viable fetus is in fact treated differently from a child in being.[1]

The majority argues for equal treatment of viable fetuses and children, yet its construction of the statute results in even greater inequities. If the statute applies only when a fetus is "viable," a pregnant woman can use cocaine for the first twenty-four weeks of her pregnancy, the most dangerous period for the fetus, and be immune from prosecution under the statute so long as she quits drug use before the fetus becomes viable. Further, a pregnant woman now faces up to ten years in prison for ingesting drugs during pregnancy but can have an illegal abortion and receive only a two-year sentence for killing her viable fetus.

---

[1] A woman may have a legal abortion of a viable fetus if necessary to preserve her health, S.C. Code Ann. § 44-41-20(c) (1985), while, of course, she may not justify the death of a child in being on this ground.

Because I disagree with the conclusion § 20–7–50 includes a viable fetus, I would affirm the grant of post-conviction relief.

NOTES AND QUESTIONS

(1) *Whitner* is one of the few appellate cases to uphold a criminal conviction for child abuse or neglect, based on a mother's prenatal conduct. Most courts that had previously considered the question had held that the relevant criminal statute was not intended to encompass a mother's pre-natal conduct. The majority in *Whitner* distinguishes and/or disagrees with several of these prior cases. Do you find the majority's reasoning persuasive? Why or why not?

(2) Is criminalizing drug use by pregnant women an effective way of protecting their fetuses/children? Consider this judicial reasoning:

> [P]rosecuting women for using drugs and "delivering" them to their newborns appears to be the least effective response to this crisis. Rather than face the possibility of prosecution, pregnant women who are substance abusers may simply avoid prenatal or medical care for fear of being detected. Yet the newborns of these women are, as a group, the most fragile and sick, and most in need of hospital neonatal care. A decision to deliver these babies "at-home" will have tragic and serious consequences. . . . Prosecution of pregnant women for engaging in activities harmful to their fetuses or newborns may also unwittingly increase the incidence of abortion.

Johnson v. State, 602 So. 2d 1288, 1290 (Fla. 1992) (holding that mother who smoked cocaine shortly before the birth of her baby could not be prosecuted for drug delivery). How would the *Whitner* court respond?

(3) Following the decision in *Whitner*, several members of the South Carolina legislature proposed the following amendment to S.C. Code Ann. § 20-7-50 (1985), the criminal child neglect statute under which Cornelia Whitner was convicted:

> For purposes of this section, "child" means a person under the age of eighteen who has been born alive. "Child" does not include a fetus.

How would you vote on this amendment and why?

(4) Several recent medical studies suggest that the long-term effects on children of prenatal exposure to cocaine may be less devastating than previously believed. *See, e.g.*, Susan Fitzgerald, *"Crack Baby" Fears May Have Been Overstated; Children of Cocaine-Abusing Mothers Are No Worse Off Than Others in Urban Poverty, Study Says*, The Washington Post, September 16, 1997, at Z10; Sharon Begley, *Hope for "Snow Babies": A Mother's Cocaine Use May Not Doom Her Child After All*, Newsweek, September 29, 1997, at 62. At the same time, the evidence is mounting that maternal alcohol abuse during pregnancy poses at least as significant a threat to the health and well-being of a developing fetus as does the use of illicit drugs. *See generally* U.S. Department of Commerce, National Technical Information Service, *Fetal Alcohol Syndrom-Diagnosis, Epidemiology, Prevention, and Treatment* (1996); M.R. Hiller, *Fetal Alcohol Syndrome Research Continuing*, The Post and Courier, July 21, 1997, at 7. Does the majority opinion in *Whitner* support the prosecution of women who drink excessively during pregnancy?

(5) Would it be constitutional for a state to require all pregnant women to undergo drug and/or alcohol testing in order to facilitate the detection of "prenatal child abuse?" Would such a mandatory prenatal testing regime constitute wise public policy? *See* Derk B.K. Van Raalte IV, *Punitive Policies: Constitutional Hazards of Non-Consensual Testing Of Women For Prenatal Drug Use*, 5 Health Matrix 443 (1995). Should child abuse reporting laws be interpreted to require physicians and other health care providers to report patients whom they suspect may be using drugs or alcohol during pregnancy? *Cf.* Minn. Stat. § 656.5561 (1997) (requiring reporting by health care providers who have "reason to believe that a woman is pregnant and has used a controlled substance for a nonmedical purpose during the pregnancy").

(6) Many states have criminal non-support statutes that punish a parent's failure to support a child financially. *See e. g.*, S.C. Code Ann. § 20–7–90 (1997) (providing that any able-bodied person capable of earning a livelihood who fails, without just cause, to provide reasonable support to his or her minor child shall be guilty of a misdemeanor). Should such statutes by used to prosecute biological fathers who refuse to support their wives or girlfriends during pregnancy? Why or why not?

(7) *Whitner* involved a criminal prosecution. In a number of other cases, state authorities have invoked civil child abuse and neglect statutes to remove drug exposed infants from their mother's custody at birth. *See, e.g., Nassau County Dep't of Social Servs. v. Laquetta H.*, 595 N.Y.S.2d 97 (N.Y. App. Div. 1993) (infant's positive toxicology report created presumption of neglect which mother failed to rebut); *In re Troy D*, 263 Cal. Rptr. 869 (Cal. Ct. App. 1989) (infant's positive toxicology test constituted legally sufficient basis for juvenile court to exercise jurisdiction); Minn. Stat. § 626.556(2)(c) (defining neglect to include prenatal exposure to a controlled substance). By contrast, in *In re Valerie D.*, 613 A.2d 748 (Conn. 1992), the Supreme Court of Connecticut rejected an attempt to terminate a mother's parental rights based on her injection of cocaine several hours before the onset of labor. The court held that the Connecticut statute, which authorizes termination of parental rights where a child has been denied necessary care by acts of parental omission or commission, was not intended to reach a mother's prenatal conduct.

The *Valerie D.* court also held that the state could not terminate the mother's parental rights based on the absence of an ongoing parent-child relationship where the absence of that relationship was the result of the state's assumption of custody immediately after the infant's birth. For further discussion of the case, see Jennifer M. Mone, *Has Connecticut Thrown out the Baby with the Bathwater? Termination of Parental Rights and Valerie D.*, 19 Fordham Urb. L.J. 535 (1992). For a more general discussion and critique of the use of child abuse and neglect laws to address the problem of drug use during pregnancy, see Michelle Oberman, *Sex, Drugs, Pregnancy, and the Law: Rethinking the Problems of Pregnant Women Who Use Drugs*, 43 Hastings L.J. 505 (1992).

(8) The state interventions in *Whitner* took place after the birth of the child. Some commentators have argued that the state should intervene more aggressively *before* birth, to protect a developing fetus from serious or well-defined dangers. See, e.g., Louise Marlane Chan, *S.O.S. From the Womb, A Call For New York Legislation Criminalizing Drug use During Pregnancy*, 21 Fordham Urb. L.J. 199 (1993); Jeffrey A. Parness, *Arming the Pregnancy Police: More Outlandish Concoctions?*, 53 La. L. Rev. 427 (1992); James M. Wilton, *Compelled Hospitalization and Treatment During Pregnancy: Mental Health*

Statutes as Models for Legislation to Protect Children from Prenatal Drug and Alcohol Exposure, 25 Fam. L.Q. 149, 149 (1991); Charles J. Dougherty, *The Right to Begin Life With Sound Body and Mind: Fetal Patients and Their Mothers,* 63 U. Det. L. Rev. 89 (1985).

Such proposals raise difficult legal and ethical questions. To what extent should the state be permitted to regulate the activities or behavior of pregnant women in order to protect the life or health of the fetuses they are carrying? Should the state be permitted to order a pregnant woman who is addicted to drugs or alcohol to undergo inpatient treatment? If she refuses, should the state be able to put her in jail, or confine her to a state psychiatric hospital? *See, e.g., State ex rel. Angela M.W. v. Kruzicki,* 561 N.W.2d 729 (Wis. 1997) (holding that state child protective statutes did not authorize authorities to detain a pregnant woman in order to protect her viable fetus); Page McGuire Linden, *Drug Addiction During Pregnancy: A Call For Increased Social Responsibility,* 4 Am. U. J. Gender & Law 105 (1995) (discussing involuntary civil commitment as a potential, but ultimately flawed, response to drug abuse during pregnancy). Should health care providers be encouraged to refer pregnant patients whom they believe are using drugs to state authorities for prosecution or mandatory drug treatment? *See* Philip H. Jos, et al., *The Charleston Policy on Cocaine Use During Pregnancy: A Cautionary Tale,* 23 J.L. Med. & Ethics 120 (1995) (describing public hospital program in which indigent pregnant patients were tested for drugs without their consent and were referred to law enforcement authorities if they tested positive);

Similar legal and ethical issues arise when physicians or hospital officials seek judicial authority to compel a pregnant woman to undergo a cesarean section against her will, on the ground that giving birth by vaginal delivery poses an unacceptable risk to the fetus. A few early decisions approved such authority, reasoning that the state's interest in preserving the life and health of the fetus outweighed the woman's refusal to consent. *See, e.g., Jefferson v. Griffin Spalding County Hosp. Auth.,* 274 S.E.2d 457 (1969). More recent cases, however, have held that such forced surgery violates a woman's right to privacy and bodily autonomy. For example, in *In re A.C.,* 573 A.2d 1235 (D.C. 1990) (en banc), the D.C. Court of Appeals held that a terminally ill pregnant patient is entitled to decided whether to undergo a cesarean section, unless she is incompetent or unable to give informed consent, in which case her decision must be ascertained via substituted judgment. Similarly, in *Baby Boy Doe v. Mother Doe,* 632 N.E.2d 326 (Ill. App. Ct. 1994), an Illinois appellate court held that a woman's competent decision, on religious grounds, to refuse "medical treatment as invasive as a cesarean" must be honored, even in circumstances where the decision may be harmful to her fetus. These cases have generated a substantial amount of scholarly commentary. *See, e.g.,* Dawn E. Johnsen, *Symposium: Shared Interests: Promoting Healthy Births Without Sacrificing Women's Liberty,* 43 Hastings L.J. 569 (1992); Barbara Ann Leavine, *Court-Ordered Cesareans: Can A Pregnant Woman Refuse?,* 29 Hous. L. Rev. 185 (1992); Rodney A. Halstead, *A Pregnant Woman's Right to Refuse Medical Treatment—Is It Always Her Choice: In re A.C.,* 24 Creighton L. Rev. 1589 (1991); Joel J. Finer, *Toward Guidelines for Compelling Cesarean Surgery: Of Rights, Responsibility and Decisional Authenticity,* 76 Minn. L. Rev. 239 (1991); Elizabeth Eggleston Drigotas, Comment: *Forced Cesarean Sections: Do The Ends Justify The Means,* 70 N.C. L. Rev. 297 (1991).

(9) Most of the women who have been prosecuted for using drugs during pregnancy are poor and Black. *See* Dorothy E. Roberts, *Representing Race: Unshackling Black Motherhood,* 95 Mich. L. Rev. 938 (1997) (noting that, as of 1992, approximately 75% of all

prosecutions for prenatal drug use were brought against women of color). According to Professor Roberts

> These women are the primary targets of prosecutors, not because they are more likely to be guilty of fetal abuse, but because they are Black and poor. Poor women, who are disproportionately Black, are in closer contact with government agencies, and their drug use is therefore more likely to be detected. Black women are also more likely to be reported to government authorities, in part because of the racist attitudes of health care professionals. Finally, their failure to meet society's image of the ideal mother makes their prosecution more acceptable.

Dorothy E. Roberts, *Punishing Drug Addicts Who Have Babies: Women of Color, Equality, and the Right of Privacy,* 104 Harv. L. Rev. 1419 (1991); *see also* Ira J. Chasnoff, et al., *The Prevalence of Illicit Drug or Alcohol Use During Pregnancy and Discrepancies in Mandatory Reporting in Pinellas County, Florida,* 322 New Eng. J. Med. 1202 (1990) (discussing results of study which found that despite similar rates of substance abuse during pregnancy, Black women were ten times more likely than whites to be reported to government authorities).

Similarly, most of the cases in which doctors or hospitals have sought court-ordered cesarean sections have involved poor women of color. Veronika E. B. Kolder, et al., *Court-Ordered Obstetrical Interventions,* 316 New Eng. J. Med. 1193, 1192 (1987). *See* Deborah J. Krauss, *Regulating Women's Bodies: The Adverse Effect of Fetal Rights Theory on Childbirth Decisions and Women of Color,* 26 Harv. C.R.-C.L. L. Rev. 523, 531 (1991).

Query: Should the disparate racial and economic impact of policies that target women's prenatal conduct bear on the constitutionality of these policies? On their acceptability as public policy? *See* Lisa C. Ikemoto, *Furthering the Inquiry: Race, Class, and Culture in the Forced Medical Treatment of Pregnant Women,* 59 Tenn. L. Rev. 487 (1992).

(10) **Problem.** Janet M., in her early twenties, is pregnant for the second time. She has been an insulin-dependent diabetic since the age of twelve, but has experienced no major complications of diabetes. Dr. L. has repeatedly advised Janet of the risks that uncontrolled diabetes poses to her fetus. Congenital malformations are two to four times more common in infants of mothers whose diabetes is poorly controlled. Furthermore, uncontrolled diabetes can result in the birth of a premature, stillborn fetus. At 15 weeks gestation, Dr. L. admits Janet to the hospital, but she discharges herself against Dr. L's advice four days later, before her diabetes has been satisfactorily controlled. Once home, she ignores pleas from Dr. L. and his staff to obtain chemostrips or a dextrometer for monitoring blood sugar. In response, she tells them that she "has no money" or "forgot." At twenty-four weeks gestation, Janet M. is hospitalized for a threatened miscarriage, but quickly announced her intention to leave. Dr. L. decides that her behavior poses a clear risk to the well-being of her fetus. Dr. L.'s assistant tells Janet that, unless she changes her mind, Dr. L. will seek a court order to keep her hospitalized. Is Dr. L's response justified? If you were the hospital's general counsel, what legal arguments would you make in support of Dr. L's request? If you represented Janet M., what arguments would you make in opposition? What additional facts, if any, would you like to know before advising either party?

[E] Government Responsibility to Protect Children

DESHANEY V. WINNEBAGO COUNTY DEP'T OF SOCIAL SERVICES
United States Supreme Court
489 U.S. 189 (1989)

CHIEF JUSTICE REHNQUIST delivered the opinion of the Court.

Petitioner is a boy who was beaten and permanently injured by his father, with whom he lived. Respondents are social workers and other local officials who received complaints that petitioner was being abused by his father and had reason to believe that this was the case, but nonetheless did not act to remove petitioner from his father's custody. Petitioner sued respondents claiming that their failure to act deprived him of his liberty in violation of the Due Process Clause of the Fourteenth Amendment to the United States Constitution. We hold that it did not.

I

The facts of this case are undeniably tragic. Petitioner Joshua DeShaney was born in 1979. In 1980, a Wyoming court granted his parents a divorce and awarded custody of Joshua to his father, Randy DeShaney. The father shortly thereafter moved to Neenah, a city located in Winnebago County, Wisconsin, taking the infant Joshua with him. There he entered into a second marriage, which also ended in divorce.

The Winnebago County authorities first learned that Joshua DeShaney might be a victim of child abuse in January 1982, when his father's second wife complained to the police, at the time of their divorce, that he had previously "hit the boy causing marks and [was] a prime case for child abuse." App. 152–153. The Winnebago County Department of Social Services (DSS) interviewed the father, but he denied the accusations, and DSS did not pursue them further. In January 1983, Joshua was admitted to a local hospital with multiple bruises and abrasions. The examining physician suspected child abuse and notified DSS, which immediately obtained an order from a Wisconsin juvenile court placing Joshua in the temporary custody of the hospital. Three days later, the county convened an ad hoc "Child Protection Team"—consisting of a pediatrician, a psychologist, a police detective, the county's lawyer, several DSS caseworkers, and various hospital personnel—to consider Joshua's situation. At this meeting, the Team decided that there was insufficient evidence of child abuse to retain Joshua in the custody of the court. The Team did, however, decide to recommend several measures to protect Joshua, including enrolling him in a preschool program, providing his father with certain counseling services, and encouraging his father's girlfriend to move out of the home. Randy DeShaney entered into a voluntary agreement with DSS in which he promised to cooperate with them in accomplishing these goals.

Based on the recommendation of the Child Protection Team, the juvenile court dismissed the child protection case and returned Joshua to the custody of his father. A month later, emergency room personnel called the DSS caseworker handling Joshua's case to report that he had once again been treated for suspicious injuries. The caseworker concluded that there was no basis for action. For the next six months, the caseworker made monthly visits to the DeShaney home, during which she observed a number of suspicious injuries on Joshua's head; she also noticed that he had not been enrolled in school, and that the girlfriend had not moved out. The caseworker dutifully recorded these incidents in her files, along with her continuing suspicions that someone in the DeShaney household was physically abusing Joshua, but she did nothing more. In November 1983, the emergency room notified DSS that Joshua had been treated once again for injuries that they believed to be caused by child abuse. On the caseworker's next two visits to the DeShaney home, she was told that Joshua was too ill to see her. Still DSS took no action.

In March 1984, Randy DeShaney beat 4-year-old Joshua so severely that he fell into a life-threatening coma. Emergency brain surgery revealed a series of hemorrhages caused by traumatic injuries to the head inflicted over a long period of time. Joshua did not die, but he suffered brain damage so severe that he is expected to spend the rest of his life confined to an institution for the profoundly retarded. Randy DeShaney was subsequently tried and convicted of child abuse.

Joshua and his mother brought this action under 42 U. S. C. § 1983 in the United States District Court for the Eastern District of Wisconsin against respondents Winnebago County, DSS, and various individual employees of DSS. The complaint alleged that respondents had deprived Joshua of his liberty without due process of law, in violation of his rights under the Fourteenth Amendment, by failing to intervene to protect him against a risk of violence at his father's hands of which they knew or should have known. . . .

Because of the inconsistent approaches taken by the lower courts in determining when, if ever, the failure of a state or local governmental entity or its agents to provide an individual with adequate protective services constitutes a violation of the individual's due process rights, and the importance of the issue to the administration of state and local governments, we granted certiorari. 485 U.S. 958 (1988). We now affirm.

II

The Due Process Clause of the Fourteenth Amendment provides that "[n]o State shall . . . deprive any person of life, liberty, or property, without due process of law." Petitioners contend that the State deprived Joshua of his liberty interest in "free[dom] from . . . unjustified intrusions on personal security," *see Ingraham v. Wright*, 430 U.S. 651, 673 (1977), by failing to provide him with adequate protection against his father's violence. The claim is one invoking the substantive rather than the procedural component of the Due Process Clause; petitioners do not claim that the State denied Joshua protection without according him appropriate procedural safeguards, *see Morrissey v. Brewer*, 408 U.S. 471, 481 (1972), but that it was categorically obligated to protect him in these circumstances, *see Youngberg v. Romeo*, 457 U.S. 307, 309 (1982).

But nothing in the language of the Due Process Clause itself requires the State to protect the life, liberty, and property of its citizens against invasion by private actors. The Clause is phrased as a limitation on the State's power to act, not as a guarantee of certain minimal levels of safety and security. It forbids the State itself to deprive individuals of life, liberty, or property without "due process of law," but its language cannot fairly be extended to impose an affirmative obligation on the State to ensure that those interests do not come to harm through other means. Nor does history support such an expansive reading of the constitutional text. Like its counterpart in the Fifth Amendment, the Due Process Clause of the Fourteenth Amendment was intended to prevent government "from abusing [its] power, or employing it as an instrument of oppression," *Davidson v. Cannon, above*, at

348. Its purpose was to protect the people from the State, not to ensure that the State protected them from each other. The Framers were content to leave the extent of governmental obligation in the latter area to the democratic political processes.

Consistent with these principles, our cases have recognized that the Due Process Clauses generally confer no affirmative right to governmental aid, even where such aid may be necessary to secure life, liberty, or property interests of which the government itself may not deprive the individual. *See, e. g., Harris v. McRae*, 448 U.S. 297, 317–318 (1980) (no obligation to fund abortions or other medical services) (discussing Due Process Clause of Fifth Amendment); *Lindsey v. Normet*, 405 U.S. 56, 74 (1972) (no obligation to provide adequate housing) (discussing Due Process Clause of Fourteenth Amendment); *see also Youngberg v. Romeo, above,* at 317 ("As a general matter, a State is under no constitutional duty to provide substantive services for those within its border"). As we said in *Harris v. McRae*: "Although the liberty protected by the Due Process Clause affords protection against unwarranted government interference . . . , it does not confer an entitlement to such [governmental aid] as may be necessary to realize all the advantages of that freedom." 448 U.S., at 317–318 (emphasis added). If the Due Process Clause does not require the State to provide its citizens with particular protective services, it follows that the State cannot be held liable under the Clause for injuries that could have been averted had it chosen to provide them. As a general matter, then, we conclude that a State's failure to protect an individual against private violence simply does not constitute a violation of the Due Process Clause.

Petitioners contend, however, that even if the Due Process Clause imposes no affirmative obligation on the State to provide the general public with adequate protective services, such a duty may arise out of certain "special relationships" created or assumed by the State with respect to particular individuals. Petitioners argue that such a "special relationship" existed here because the State knew that Joshua faced a special danger of abuse at his father's hands, and specifically proclaimed, by word and by deed, its intention to protect him against that danger. Having actually undertaken to protect Joshua from this danger—which petitioners concede the State played no part in creating—the State acquired an affirmative "duty," enforceable through the Due Process Clause, to do so in a reasonably competent fashion. Its failure to discharge that duty, so the argument goes, was an abuse of governmental power that so "shocks the conscience," *Rochin v. California*, 342 U.S. 165, 172 (1952), as to constitute a substantive due process violation.

We reject this argument. It is true that in certain limited circumstances the Constitution imposes upon the State affirmative duties of care and protection with respect to particular individuals. In *Estelle v. Gamble*, 429 U.S. 97 (1976), we recognized that the Eighth Amendment's prohibition against cruel and unusual punishment, made applicable to the States through the Fourteenth Amendment's Due Process Clause, *Robinson v. California*, 370 U.S. 660 1962), requires the State to provide adequate medical care to incarcerated prisoners. 429 U.S., at 103–104. We reasoned that because the prisoner is unable " 'by reason of the deprivation of his liberty [to] care for himself,' " it is only " 'just' " that the State be required to care for him. *Ibid., quoting Spicer v. Williamson*, 191 N. C. 487, 490, 132 S. E. 291, 293 (1926).

In *Youngberg v. Romeo*, 457 U.S. 307 (1982), we extended this analysis beyond the Eighth Amendment setting, holding that the substantive component of the Fourteenth Amendment's

Due Process Clause requires the State to provide involuntarily committed mental patients with such services as are necessary to ensure their "reasonable safety" from themselves and others. *Id.*, at 314–325; see id., at 315, 324 (dicta indicating that the State is also obligated to provide such individuals with "adequate food, shelter, clothing, and medical care"). As we explained: "If it is cruel and unusual punishment to hold convicted criminals in unsafe conditions, it must be unconstitutional [under the Due Process Clause] to confine the involuntarily committed—who may not be punished at all—in unsafe conditions." Id., at 315–316.

But these cases afford petitioners no help. Taken together, they stand only for the proposition that when the State takes a person into its custody and holds him there against his will, the Constitution imposes upon it a corresponding duty to assume some responsibility for his safety and general well-being. The rationale for this principle is simple enough: when the State by the affirmative exercise of its power so restrains an individual's liberty that it renders him unable to care for himself, and at the same time fails to provide for his basic human needs—e. g., food, clothing, shelter, medical care, and reasonable safety—it transgresses the substantive limits on state action set by the Eighth Amendment and the Due Process Clause. The affirmative duty to protect arises not from the State's knowledge of the individual's predicament or from its expressions of intent to help him, but from the limitation which it has imposed on his freedom to act on his own behalf. In the substantive due process analysis, it is the State's affirmative act of restraining the individual's freedom to act on his own behalf—through incarceration, institutionalization, or other similar restraint of personal liberty—which is the "deprivation of liberty" triggering the protections of the Due Process Clause, not its failure to act to protect his liberty interests against harms inflicted by other means.

The *Estelle-Youngberg* analysis simply has no applicability in the present case. Petitioners concede that the harms Joshua suffered occurred not while he was in the State's custody, but while he was in the custody of his natural father, who was in no sense a state actor. While the State may have been aware of the dangers that Joshua faced in the free world, it played no part in their creation, nor did it do anything to render him any more vulnerable to them. That the State once took temporary custody of Joshua does not alter the analysis, for when it returned him to his father's custody, it placed him in no worse position than that in which he would have been had it not acted at all; the State does not become the permanent guarantor of an individual's safety by having once offered him shelter. Under these circumstances, the State had no constitutional duty to protect Joshua.

It may well be that, by voluntarily undertaking to protect Joshua against a danger it concededly played no part in creating, the State acquired a duty under state tort law to provide him with adequate protection against that danger. *See* Restatement (Second) of Torts § 323 (1965) (one who undertakes to render services to another may in some circumstances be held liable for doing so in a negligent fashion); *see generally* W. Keeton, D. Dobbs, R. Keeton, & D. Owen, Prosser and Keeton on the Law of Torts § 56 (5th ed. 1984) (discussing "special relationships" which may give rise to affirmative duties to act under the common law of tort). But the claim here is based on the Due Process Clause of the Fourteenth Amendment, which, as we have said many times, does not transform every tort committed by a state actor into a constitutional violation. A State may, through its courts and legislatures, impose such affirmative duties of care and protection upon its agents as it wishes. But not "all common-law duties owed by government actors were . . . constitutionalized by the Fourteenth Amendment." *Daniels v. Williams, above*, at 335. Because, as explained above, the State had no constitutional duty to protect Joshua against his father's violence, its failure to do so—though calamitous in hindsight—simply does not constitute a violation of the Due Process Clause.

Judges and lawyers, like other humans, are moved by natural sympathy in a case like this to find a way for Joshua and his mother to receive adequate compensation for the grievous harm inflicted upon them. But before yielding to that impulse, it is well to remember once again that the harm was inflicted not by the State of Wisconsin, but by Joshua's father. The most that can be said of the state functionaries in this case is that they stood by and did nothing when suspicious circumstances dictated a more active role for them. In defense of them it must also be said that had they moved too soon to take custody of the son away from the father, they would likely have been met with charges of improperly intruding into the parent-child relationship, charges based on the same Due Process Clause that forms the basis for the present charge of failure to provide adequate protection.

The people of Wisconsin may well prefer a system of liability which would place upon the State and its officials the responsibility for failure to act in situations such as the present one. They may create such a system, if they do not have it already, by changing the tort law of the State in accordance with the regular lawmaking process. But they should not have it thrust upon them by this Court's expansion of the Due Process Clause of the Fourteenth Amendment.

JUSTICE BRENNAN, with whom JUSTICE MARSHALL and JUSTICE BLACKMUN join, dissenting.

"The most that can be said of the state functionaries in this case," the Court today concludes, "is that they stood by and did nothing when suspicious circumstances dictated a more active role for them." Because I believe that this description of respondents' conduct tells only part of the story and that, accordingly, the Constitution itself "dictated a more active role" for respondents in the circumstances presented here, I cannot agree that respondents had no constitutional duty to help Joshua DeShaney.

It may well be, as the Court decides . . . that the Due Process Clause as construed by our prior cases creates no general right to basic governmental services. That, however, is not the question presented here; indeed, that question was not raised in the complaint, urged on appeal, presented in the petition for certiorari, or addressed in the briefs on the merits. No one, in short, has asked the Court to proclaim that, as a general matter, the Constitution safeguards positive as well as negative liberties.

This is more than a quibble over dicta; it is a point about perspective, having substantive ramifications. In a constitutional setting that distinguishes sharply between action and inaction, one's characterization of the misconduct alleged under § 1983 may effectively decide the case. Thus, by leading off with a discussion (and rejection) of the idea that the Constitution imposes on the States an affirmative duty to take basic care of their citizens, the Court foreshadows—perhaps even preordains—its conclusion that no duty existed even on the specific facts before us. This initial discussion establishes the baseline from which the Court assesses the DeShaneys' claim that, when a State has—"by word and by deed," . . . —announced an intention to protect a certain class of citizens and has before it facts that would trigger that protection under the applicable state law, the Constitution imposes upon the State an affirmative duty of protection.

The Court's baseline is the absence of positive rights in the Constitution and a concomitant suspicion of any claim that seems to depend on such rights. From this perspective, the DeShaneys' claim is first and foremost about inaction (the failure, here, of respondents to take steps to protect Joshua), and only tangentially about action (the establishment of a state program specifically designed to help children like Joshua). And from this perspective, holding these Wisconsin officials liable—where the only difference between this case and one involving a general claim to protective services is Wisconsin's establishment and operation of a program to protect children—would seem to punish an effort that we should seek to promote. I would begin from the opposite direction. I would focus first on the action that Wisconsin has taken with respect to Joshua and children like him, rather than on the actions that the State failed to take. Such a method is not new to this Court. Both *Estelle v. Gamble*, 429 U.S. 97 (1976), and *Youngberg v. Romeo*, 457 U.S. 307 (1982), began by emphasizing that the States had confined J. W. Gamble to prison and Nicholas Romeo to a psychiatric hospital. This initial action rendered these people helpless to help themselves or to seek help from persons unconnected to the government. Cases from the lower courts also recognize that a State's actions can be decisive in assessing the constitutional significance of subsequent inaction. For these purposes, moreover, actual physical restraint is not the only state action that has been considered relevant. *See, e. g., White v. Rochford*, 592 F. 2d 381 (CA7 1979) (police officers violated due process when, after arresting the guardian of three young children, they abandoned the children on a busy stretch of highway at night).

Because of the Court's initial fixation on the general principle that the Constitution does not establish positive rights, it is unable to appreciate our recognition in *Estelle* and *Youngberg* that this principle does not hold true in all circumstances. Thus, in the Court's view, *Youngberg* can be explained (and dismissed) in the following way: "In the substantive due process analysis, it is the State's affirmative act of restraining the individual's freedom to act on his own behalf—through incarceration, institutionalization, or other similar restraint of personal liberty—which is the 'deprivation of liberty' triggering the protections of the Due Process Clause, not its failure to act to protect his liberty interests against harms inflicted by other means." . . . This restatement of *Youngberg's* holding should come as a surprise when one recalls our explicit observation in that case that Romeo did not challenge his commitment to the hospital, but instead "argue[d] that he ha[d] a constitutionally protected liberty interest in safety, freedom of movement, and training within the institution; and that petitioners infringed these rights by failing to provide constitutionally required conditions of confinement." 457 U.S., at 315 (emphasis added). I do not mean to suggest that "the State's affirmative act of restraining the individual's freedom to act on his own behalf," . . . was irrelevant in *Youngberg*; rather, I emphasize that this conduct would have led to no injury, and consequently no cause of action under § 1983, unless the State then had failed to take steps to protect Romeo from himself and from others. In addition, the Court's exclusive attention to state-imposed restraints of "the individual's freedom to act on his own behalf," . . . suggests that it was the State that rendered Romeo unable to care for himself, whereas in fact—with an I. Q. of between 8 and 10, and the mental capacity of an 18–month-old child, 457 U.S., at 309—he had been quite incapable of taking care of himself long before the State stepped into his life. Thus, the fact of hospitalization was critical in *Youngberg* not because it rendered Romeo helpless to help himself, but because it separated him from other sources of aid that, we held, the State was obligated to replace. Unlike the Court, therefore, I am unable to see in *Youngberg* a neat and decisive divide between action and inaction. . . .

Wisconsin has established a child-welfare system specifically designed to help children like Joshua. Wisconsin law places upon the local departments of social services such as respondent (DSS or Department) a duty to investigate reported instances of child abuse. See Wis. Stat. § 48.981(3) (1987–1988). While other governmental bodies and private persons are largely responsible for the reporting of possible cases of child abuse, see § 48.981(2), Wisconsin law channels all such reports to the local departments of social services for evaluation and, if necessary, further action. § 48.981(3). Even when it is the sheriff's office or police department that receives a report of suspected child abuse, that report is referred to local social services departments for action, see § 48.981(3)(a); the only exception to this occurs when the reporter fears for the child's immediate safety. § 48.981(3)(b). In this way, Wisconsin law invites—indeed, directs—citizens and other governmental entities to depend on local departments of social services such as respondent to protect children from abuse.

The specific facts before us bear out this view of Wisconsin's system of protecting children. Each time someone voiced a suspicion that Joshua was being abused, that information was relayed to the Department for investigation and possible action. When Randy DeShaney's second wife told the police that he had " 'hit the boy causing marks and [was] a prime case for child abuse,' " the police referred her complaint to DSS. . . . When, on three separate occasions, emergency room personnel noticed suspicious injuries on Joshua's body, they went to DSS with this information. . . . When neighbors informed the police that they had seen or heard Joshua's father or his father's lover beating or otherwise abusing Joshua, the police brought these reports to the attention of DSS. . . . And when respondent Kemmeter, through these reports and through her own observations in the course of nearly 20 visits to the DeShaney home, . . . compiled growing evidence that Joshua was being abused, that information stayed within the Department—chronicled by the social worker in detail that seems almost eerie in light of her failure to act upon it. (As to the extent of the social worker's involvement in, and knowledge of, Joshua's predicament, her reaction to the news of Joshua's last and most devastating injuries is illuminating: " 'I just knew the phone would ring some day and Joshua would be dead.' " 812 F. 2d 298, 300 (CA7 1987).)

Even more telling than these examples is the Department's control over the decision whether to take steps to protect a particular child from suspected abuse. While many different people contributed information and advice to this decision, it was up to the people at DSS to make the ultimate decision (subject to the approval of the local government's corporation counsel) whether to disturb the family's current arrangements. . . . When Joshua first appeared at a local hospital with injuries signaling physical abuse, for example, it was DSS that made the decision to take him into temporary custody for the purpose of studying his situation—and it was DSS, acting in conjunction with the corporation counsel, that returned him to his father. Unfortunately for Joshua DeShaney, the buck effectively stopped with the Department.

In these circumstances, a private citizen, or even a person working in a government agency other than DSS, would doubtless feel that her job was done as soon as she had reported her suspicions of child abuse to DSS. Through its child-welfare program, in other words, the State of Wisconsin has relieved ordinary citizens and governmental bodies other than the Department of any sense of obligation to do anything more than report their suspicions of child abuse to DSS. If DSS ignores or dismisses these suspicions, no one will step in to fill the gap. Wisconsin's child-protection program thus effectively confined Joshua DeShaney within the walls of Randy DeShaney's violent home until such time as DSS took action to remove him. Conceivably, then, children like Joshua are made worse off by the existence of this program when the persons and entities charged with carrying it out fail to do their jobs.

It simply belies reality, therefore, to contend that the State "stood by and did nothing" with respect to Joshua. . . . Through its child-protection program, the State actively intervened in Joshua's life and, by virtue of this intervention, acquired ever more certain knowledge that Joshua was in grave danger. These circumstances, in my view, plant this case solidly within the tradition of cases like *Youngberg* and *Estelle*.

It will be meager comfort to Joshua and his mother to know that, if the State had "selectively den[ied] its protective services" to them because they were "disfavored minorities," *ante*, at 197, n. 3, their § 1983 suit might have stood on sturdier ground. Because of the posture of this case, we do not know why respondents did not take steps to protect Joshua; the Court, however, tells us that their reason is irrelevant so long as their inaction was not the product of invidious discrimination. Presumably, then, if respondents decided not to help Joshua because his name began with a "J," or because he was born in the spring, or because they did not care enough about him even to formulate an intent to discriminate against him based on an arbitrary reason, respondents would not be liable to the DeShaneys because they were not the ones who dealt the blows that destroyed Joshua's life. . . .

As the Court today reminds us, "the Due Process Clause of the Fourteenth Amendment was intended to prevent government 'from abusing [its] power, or employing it as an instrument of oppression.' " . . . My disagreement with the Court arises from its failure to see that inaction can be every bit as abusive of power as action, that oppression can result when a State undertakes a vital duty and then ignores it. Today's opinion construes the Due Process Clause to permit a State to displace private sources of protection and then, at the critical moment, to shrug its shoulders and turn away from the harm that it has promised to try to prevent. Because I cannot agree that our Constitution is indifferent to such indifference, I respectfully dissent.

Justice Blackmun, dissenting. . . .

Poor Joshua! Victim of repeated attacks by an irresponsible, bullying, cowardly, and intemperate father, and abandoned by respondents who placed him in a dangerous predicament and who knew or learned what was going on, and yet did essentially nothing except, as the Court revealingly observes, . . . "dutifully recorded these incidents in [their] files." It is a sad commentary upon American life, and constitutional principles—so full of late of patriotic fervor and proud proclamations about "liberty and justice for all"—that this child, Joshua DeShaney, now is assigned to live out the remainder of his life profoundly retarded. Joshua and his mother, as petitioners here, deserve—but now are denied by this Court—the opportunity to have the facts of their case considered in the light of the constitutional protection that 42 U. S. C. § 1983 is meant to provide.

NOTES AND QUESTIONS

(1) Do the majority and the dissenting Justices in *DeShaney* disagree about the meaning of the Due Process Clause, the appropriate characterization of the state's behavior, or both?

(2) Is the majority's reading of the Due Process Clause compelled by the text of the Fourteenth Amendment? By the Court's prior decisions?

(3) Under the majority opinion, would it be constitutional for the state of Wisconsin to dismantle its entire child welfare system and simply refuse to respond to allegations of child abuse and neglect? Why or why not?

(4) Neither the majority nor the dissenting opinion mentions what is arguably the most direct way the state "contributed" to Joshua DeShaney's injury: the network of statutes and common law rules that grant custody and control of children to the biological parents and that authorized the Wisconsin divorce court to award custody of Joshua to his father at the time of Joshua's parents' divorce. Why don't these count as government "action" that would trigger the protection of the Fourteenth Amendment? Would such an interpretation of the Due Process Clause threaten parental authority and control over children?

(5) If Justice Brennan's dissenting views had prevailed, what standard would the Court have applied to determine whether the actions and inactions of the Winnebago Department of Social Services violated Joshua DeShaney's due process rights? Would a showing of simple negligence on the part of one or more social workers be sufficient to establish a constitutional violation? *Cf. Daniels v. Williams*, 474 U.S. 327 (1986) (negligence of state officials insufficient to establish violation of Due Process Clause). If not, what additional showing should be required?

(6) The majority opinion in *DeShaney* suggests that if state child protection workers were held constitutionally liable for failing to remove Joshua DeShaney from his father's custody, those workers might attempt to avoid future liability by removing other children too hastily or unnecessarily, which would itself raise constitutional concerns, given the protected status of the parent-child relationship. Is this not a valid point? Would a finding of liability in *DeShaney* put state child protection workers between the proverbial rock and hard place?

(7) **State Tort Remedies.** The *DeShaney* majority suggests that while the state's failure to protect Joshua does not implicate the U.S. Constitution, child welfare authorities may have a duty under state tort law to protect Joshua from his father's violence. In a number of cases since *DeShaney*, advocates for abused or neglected children have attempted, with only limited success, to bring tort actions against state and local child protection authorities for failure to protect children. A number of barriers make recovery difficult in these cases. These barriers include the "public duty" rule, which protects municipalities from liability to individuals for failure to enforce general laws and regulations, as well as various immunity doctrines that limit the liability of state and local officials for actions taken within the scope of their employment. *See generally* Eugene McQuillin, The Law of Municipal Corporations, 53.04.50 (James Perkowitz-Solheim, et al. eds., 1993); Horace B. Robertson, Jr., *Municipal Tort Liability: Special Duty Issues of Police, Fire, and Safety*, 44 Syracuse L. Rev. 943 (1993).

(8) **Applicability of *DeShaney* to Children in Foster Care.** In footnote 9 of its opinion, not reproduced above, the *DeShaney* majority left open the possibility that the state has a constitutional duty to protect children who have already been removed from their parents' custody and placed in the state-sponsored foster care system. *Deshaney* 489 U.S. at 201, n.9. ("Had the State by the affirmative exercise of its power removed Joshua from free society and placed him in a foster home operated by its agents, we might have a situation sufficiently analogous to incarceration or institutionalization to give rise to an affirmative duty to protect. . . . We express no view on the validity of this analogy, however, as it is not before us in the present case.") Most lower courts that have considered this question since *DeShaney* have held (or assumed) that such a constitutional duty exists, but they have divided over the scope of that duty and the type of state behavior necessary to establish a violation. *See, e.g., Marisol v. Guiliani*, 929 F. Supp. 662 (S.D.N.Y. 1996) *aff'd* 126 F. 3d 372 (2d Cir. 1997).

(9) **Scholarly Commentary.** The *DeShaney* case has been the subject of extensive scholarly commentary, most of it quite critical of the majority opinion. *See, e.g.,* Akhil Reed Amar, *Remember the Thirteenth*, 10 Const. Commentary 403 (1993); Susan Bandes, *The Negative Constitution: A Critique*, 88 Mich. L. Rev. 2271 (1990); Jack M. Beermann, *Administrative Failure and Local Democracy: The Politics of DeShaney*, 1990 Duke L.J. 1078; Theodore Y. Blumoff, *Some Moral Implications of Finding No State Action*, 70 Notre Dame L. Rev. 95 (1994); Thomas A. Eaton & Michael Wells, *Governmental Inaction as a Constitutional Tort: DeShaney and Its Aftermath*, 66 Wash. L. Rev. 107 (1991); Steven J. Heyman, *The First Duty of Government: Protection, Liberty and the Fourteenth Amendment*, 41 Duke L.J. 507 (1991-92); Laura Oren, *The State's Failure to Protect Children and Substantive Due Process: DeShaney in Context*, 68 N.C. L. Rev. 659 (1990); Louis Michael Seidman, *The State Action Paradox*, 10 Const. Commentary 379 (1993); Aviam Soifer, *Moral Ambition, Formalism, and the "Free World" of DeShaney*, 57 Geo. Wash. L. Rev. 1513 (1989); David A. Strauss, *Due Process, Government Inaction, and Private Wrongs*, 1989 Sup. Ct. Rev. 53; Laurence H. Tribe, *The Curvature of Constitutional Space: What Lawyers Can Learn from Modern Physics*, 103 Harv. L. Rev. 1 (1989).

A recent exception to this critical perspective is Barbara Armacost, *Affirmative Duties, Systemic Harms, and the Due Process Clause*, 94 Mich. L. Rev. 982 (1996). Armacost argues that the Court's refusal in *DeShaney* to hold the government constitutionally liable for its failure to protect is consistent with a long-standing and well-founded judicial reluctance to second guess legislative decisions about budgetary matters and the use of limited community resources. Armacost claims that critics of *DeShaney*, who have generally couched their arguments for broader government liability in constitutional and moral terms, have not acknowledged or adequately defended the broader, institutional implications of imposing liability in the failure-to-protect context.

§ 7.04 Medical Decision-Making On Behalf of Children

One of the arenas in which the tensions between parental authority and the state's child protective function is greatest is the area of medical decision-making. Traditionally, the law has accorded parents broad authority and responsibility to make medical decisions on behalf of their children. Recent advances in medicine, juxtaposed with our nation's commitment to religious and cultural pluralism, have raised difficult questions about whether and when the state should override medical decisions by parents that are viewed as unconventional or harmful to children. In addition, increased recognition of children's autonomy claims in such varied contexts as reproductive decision-making and the juvenile justice system, has led courts to consider the role that children should play in seeking or rejecting medical treatment. The cases that follow address these issues in both the criminal and civil contexts.

[A] Criminal Prosecution for Parental Failure to Seek Medical Care

COMMONWEALTH v. TWITCHELL
Supreme Court of Massachusetts
617 N.E.2d 609 (1993)

WILKINS, J.,

David and Ginger Twitchell appeal from their convictions of involuntary manslaughter in connection with the April 8, 1986, death of their two and one-half year old son Robyn. Robyn died of the consequences of peritonitis caused by the perforation of his bowel which had been obstructed as a result of an anomaly known as Meckel's diverticulum. There was evidence that the condition could be corrected by surgery with a high success rate.

The defendants are practicing Christian Scientists who grew up in Christian Science families. They believe in healing by spiritual treatment. During Robyn's five-day illness from Friday, April 4, through Tuesday, April 8, they retained a Christian Science practitioner, a Christian Science nurse, and at one time consulted with Nathan Talbot, who held a position in the church known as the "Committee on Publication." As a result of that consultation, David Twitchell read a church publication concerning the legal rights and obligations of Christian Scientists in Massachusetts. That publication quoted a portion of G. L. c. 273, § 1, as then amended, which, at least in the context of the crimes described in that section, accepted remedial treatment by spiritual means alone as satisfying any parental obligation not to neglect a child or to provide a child with physical care.[2]

We need not recite in detail the circumstances of Robyn's illness. The jury would have been warranted in concluding that Robyn was in considerable distress and that, in the absence of their belief in and reliance on spiritual treatment, the parents of a child in his condition would normally have sought medical treatment in sufficient time to save that child's life. There was also evidence that the intensity of Robyn's distress ebbed and flowed, perhaps causing his parents to believe that prayer would lead to the healing of the illness. On the other hand, the jury would have been warranted in finding that the Twitchells were wanton or reckless in failing to provide medical care for Robyn, if parents have a legal duty to provide a child with medical care in such circumstances and if the spiritual treatment provision of G. L. c. 273, § 1, did not protect them from manslaughter liability.

We shall conclude that parents have a duty to seek medical attention for a child in Robyn's circumstances, the violation of which, if their conduct was wanton or reckless, could support a conviction of involuntary manslaughter and that the spiritual healing provision in G. L. c. 273, § 1, did not bar a prosecution for manslaughter in these circumstances. We further

---

[2] The spiritual treatment provision then read, as it does now, as follows: "A child shall not be deemed to be neglected or lack proper physical care for the sole reason that he is being provided remedial treatment by spiritual means alone in accordance with the tenets and practice of a recognized church or religious denomination by a duly accredited practitioner thereof." G. L. c. 273, § 1 (1992 ed.).

conclude, however, that special circumstances in this case would justify a jury's finding that the Twitchells reasonably believed that they could rely on spiritual treatment without fear of criminal prosecution. This affirmative defense should have been asserted and presented to the jury. Because it was not, there is a substantial risk of a miscarriage of justice in this case, and, therefore, the judgments must be reversed. . . .

The Commonwealth presented its case on the theory that each defendant was guilty of involuntary manslaughter because the intentional failure of each to seek medical attention for their son involved such "a high degree of likelihood that substantial harm will result to" him as to be wanton or reckless conduct. *Commonwealth v. Welansky,* 316 Mass. 383, 399, 55 N.E.2d 902 (1944). Our definition of involuntary manslaughter derives from the common law. A charge of involuntary manslaughter based on an omission to act can be proved only if the defendant had a duty to act and did not do so. That duty, however, is not limited to those duties whose violation would create civil liability.

The Commonwealth claims that the defendants owed an affirmative duty of care to their son which they wantonly or recklessly failed to perform. The duty to provide sufficient support for a child is legally enforceable in a civil proceeding against a parent. A breach of that duty is a misdemeanor. G. L. c. 273, § 1 (1992 ed.). Where necessary to protect a child's well-being, the Commonwealth may intervene, over the parents' objections, to assure that needed services are provided. More important, for our current purposes, a parental duty of care has been recognized in the common law of homicide in this Commonwealth. *See Commonwealth v. Hall,* 322 Mass. 523, 528, 78 N.E.2d 644 (1948) (conviction of murder in the second degree based on withholding of food and liquids).

The defendants argue, however, that any common law duty of care does not include a duty to provide medical treatment and that there is no statute imposing such a duty except G. L. c. 273, § 1, which, in turn, in their view, provides them with complete protection against any criminal charge based on their failure to seek medical treatment for their son. In their argument that the common law of the Commonwealth does not include a duty to provide medical treatment, the defendants overlook *Commonwealth v. Gallison,* 383 Mass. 659, 421 N.E.2d 757 (1981). In that case, we upheld a conviction of manslaughter, saying that a parent who "made no effort to obtain medical help, knowing that her child was gravely ill," could be found guilty of wanton or reckless involuntary manslaughter for her child's death caused by her omission to meet her "duty to provide for the care and welfare of her child." *Id.* at 665. The *Gallison* opinion did not rely on § 1 as the basis of the parent's duty to provide medical care. It relied rather on the more general duty of care underlying civil and criminal liability. *Commonwealth v. Gallison, above* at 665. There is, consequently, quite apart from § 1, a common law duty to provide medical services for a child, the breach of which can be the basis, in the appropriate circumstances, for the conviction of a parent for involuntary manslaughter.

We, therefore, consider the impact, if any, of G. L. c. 273, § 1, on this case. The defendants argue that the spiritual treatment provision in § 1 bars any involuntary manslaughter charge against a parent who relies, as they did, on spiritual treatment and who does not seek medical attention for his or her child, even if the parent's failure to seek such care would otherwise be wanton or reckless conduct. We disagree.

The Commonwealth asks us to eliminate any application of the spiritual treatment provision to this case by holding that the spiritual treatment provision is unconstitutional.

The argument is based solely on the establishment of religion clause of the First Amendment to the Constitution of the United States and the equal protection clause of the Fourteenth Amendment to the Constitution of the United States. Apparently, the latter theory was not raised below, and the former was raised but was not decided. These claims of unconstitutionality place the Commonwealth in the position of challenging the constitutionality of its own duly enacted statute. Issues of timeliness and standing are obvious. The retroactive invalidation of a statute on which a criminal defendant relied in justification of his conduct would present a serious fairness issue. Because we shall conclude that the spiritual treatment provision does not apply to foreclose a charge of involuntary manslaughter, we need resolve neither these preliminary questions nor the underlying constitutional one. . . .

Section 1 of G. L. c. 273 provides no complete protection to a parent against a charge of involuntary manslaughter that is based on the parent's wanton or reckless failure to provide medical services to a child. Section 1 concerns child support and care in a chapter of the General Laws that deals not so much with the punishment of criminal conduct as with motivating parents to fulfil their natural obligations of support. On the other hand, the principle underlying involuntary manslaughter is the Commonwealth's "interest that persons within its territory should not be killed by the wanton and reckless conduct of others." *Commonwealth v. Godin*, 374 Mass. 120, 126, 371 N.E.2d 438 (1977). It is unlikely that the Legislature placed the spiritual treatment provision in § 1 to provide a defense to, or to alter any definition of, common law homicide. There is no history to § 1 that suggests that the spiritual treatment provision carries any message beyond § 1 itself. . . .

The spiritual treatment provision refers to neglect and lack of proper physical care, which are concepts set forth earlier in § 1, as then amended, as bases for punishment: (1) neglect to provide support and (2) wilful failure to provide necessary and proper physical care. These concepts do not underlie involuntary manslaughter. Wanton or reckless conduct is not a form of negligence. Wanton or reckless conduct does not involve a wilful intention to cause the resulting harm. An involuntary manslaughter verdict does not require proof of wilfulness. Thus, by its terms, the spiritual treatment provision in § 1 does not apply to involuntary manslaughter.

3. The defendants argue that the failure to extend the protection of the spiritual treatment provision to them in this case would be a denial of due process of law because they lacked "fair warning" that their use of spiritual treatment could form the basis for a prosecution for manslaughter. Fair warning is part of the due process doctrine of vagueness, which "requires that a penal statute define the criminal offense with sufficient definiteness that ordinary people can understand what conduct is prohibited and in a manner that does not encourage arbitrary and discriminatory enforcement." *Kolender v. Lawson*, 461 U.S. 352, 357 (1983). Even if a statute is clear on its face, there may not be fair warning in the circumstances of particular defendants. The defendants here argue that they have been denied fair warning in three different ways. They contend that fair warning (1) would be denied by an unforeseeable retroactive judicial interpretation that the spiritual treatment provision does not protect them (2) is denied by the existence of contradictory commands in the law of the Commonwealth, and (3) is denied because they were officially misled by an opinion of the Attorney General of the Commonwealth. We find some merit only in the last of these contentions. . . .

In May, 1975, the Attorney General gave an opinion on a number of topics to the deputy director of the Office for Children. *Rep. A.G., Pub. Doc. No. 12*, at 139 (1975). The relevant portion of that opinion, which is quoted in the margin,[3] answers a general question "whether parents who fail to provide medical services to children on the basis of religious beliefs will be subject to prosecution for such failure." *Id.* at 140. A reasonable person not trained in the law might fairly read the Attorney General's comments as being a negative answer to the general question whether in any circumstances such parents may be prosecuted. It is true that the answer comes to focus on negligent failures of parents, and we know that wanton or reckless failures are different. But an answer that says that children may receive needed services "notwithstanding the inability to prosecute parents in such cases" (*id.*), and issues no caveat concerning homicide charges, invites a conclusion that parents who fail to provide medical services to children on the basis of religious beliefs are not subject to criminal prosecution in any circumstances.

Although the Twitchells were not aware of the Attorney General's opinion, they knew of a Christian Science publication called "Legal Rights and Obligations of Christian Scientists in Massachusetts." The defense offered the publication in evidence. The judge held a voir dire on the question whether to admit that portion of the publication which concerned the furnishing of proper physical care to a child and which David Twitchell had read on the Sunday or Monday before Robyn's death. The judge excluded the evidence, and, although the defendants objected at trial, they have not argued to us that the exclusion was error. The relevant portion of the publication, after quoting G. L. c. 273, § 1, added, repeating, precisely but without citation, a portion of the Attorney General's opinion, that this criminal statute "expressly precludes imposition of criminal liability as a negligent parent for failure to provide medical care because of religious beliefs. But this does not prohibit the court from ordering medical treatment for children." There is no mention of potential criminal liability for involuntary manslaughter.

Although we have held that the law of the Commonwealth was not so unclear as to bar the prosecution of the defendants on due process of law principles, the Attorney General's opinion presents an additional element to the fairness assessment. It is obvious that the Christian Science Church's publication on the legal rights and obligations of Christian Scientists in Massachusetts relied on the Attorney General's 1975 opinion. That opinion was arguably misleading because of what it did not say concerning criminal liability for manslaughter. If the Attorney General had issued a caveat concerning manslaughter liability, the publication (which, based on such portions of it as appear in the record, is balanced and fair) would have referred to it in all reasonable likelihood. Nathan Talbot, who served

---

[3] "Secondly, you have sought my opinion as to whether parents who fail to provide medical services to children on the basis of religious beliefs will be subject to prosecution for such failure. Also, you have restated a concern of the Department of Health, Education and Welfare as to whether services will be available to children who are unable to obtain medical assistance because of their parents' religious beliefs.

"The Massachusetts child abuse reporting law does not specifically address itself to the relationship between the religious beliefs of the parent and failure to provide medical care. However, G. L. c. 273, § 1 does address itself to that precise issue. General Laws, c. 273, § 1 provides, inter alia, as follows:

'A child shall not be deemed to be neglected or lack proper physical care for the sole reason that he is being provided remedial treatment by spiritual means alone in accordance with the tenets and practice of a recognized church or religious denomination by a duly accredited practitioner thereof.'

"General Laws, c. 273, § 1 is a criminal statute and it expressly precludes imposition of criminal liability as a negligent parent for failure to provide medical care because of religious beliefs. However, the intent of Chapter 119 is, clearly, to require that children of such parents be provided services whenever the need arises. Clearly under Chapter 119 children may receive services notwithstanding the inability to prosecute parents in such cases."

as the Committee on Publication for the church and with whom the Twitchells spoke on the Sunday or Monday before Robyn's death, might well have given the Twitchells different advice.

Although it has long been held that "ignorance of the law is no defense" (*Commonwealth v. Everson*, 140 Mass. 292, 295, 2 N.E. 839 [1885]), there is substantial justification for treating as a defense the belief that conduct is not a violation of law when a defendant has reasonably relied on an official statement of the law, later determined to be wrong, contained in an official interpretation of the public official who is charged by law with the responsibility for the interpretation or enforcement of the law defining the offense. Federal courts have characterized an affirmative defense of this nature as "entrapment by estoppel." "Entrapment by estoppel has been held to apply when an official assures a defendant that certain conduct is legal, and the defendant reasonably relies on that advice and continues or initiates the conduct." *United States v. Smith*, [940 F.2d 710, 714 (1st cir. 1991). The defense rests on principles of fairness grounded in Federal criminal cases in the due process clause of the Fifth Amendment to the United States Constitution. The defense generally involves factual determinations based on the totality of the circumstances attending the prosecution, although the authority of the government official making the announcement is obviously a question of law.

The Twitchells were entitled to present such an affirmative defense to the jury. The Attorney General was acting in an area of his official responsibilities. He is the chief law officer of the Commonwealth, with the power to set a unified and consistent legal policy for the Commonwealth. He is statutorily empowered to "give his opinion upon questions of law submitted to him" by the executive branch or the Legislature. G. L. c. 12, § 9 (1992 ed.). Whether a person would reasonably conclude that the Attorney General had ruled that § 1 provided protection against a manslaughter charge is a question of fact. Whether the defendants in turn reasonably relied on the church's publication and on the advice of the Committee on Publication, assuming that the construction of the Attorney General's opinion was reasonable, also presents questions of fact. In the resolution of these factual questions, the relevant portion of the Attorney General's opinion and the relevant portion of the church's publication will be admissible. The jury should also be advised of the terms of the spiritual treatment provision of § 1.

The Twitchells were entitled to present such an affirmative defense to the jury. We can hardly fault the judge for not doing so because the defense did not make such an argument or request a jury instruction on that defense. The issue was one that, if presented to them, could well have changed the jury's verdicts. Evidence showed that the defendants were deeply motivated toward helping their child, while at the same time seeking to practice their religion within the limits of what they were advised that the law permitted. The issue of their reliance on advice that had origins in the Attorney General's opinion should have been before the jury. Therefore, the failure to present the affirmative defense to the jury, along with the relevant portion of the church's publication which the judge excluded, created a substantial risk of a miscarriage of justice requiring that we reverse the convictions, even in the absence of a request for jury instruction on the subject. For these reasons, the judgments must be reversed, the verdicts must be set aside, and the cases remanded for a new trial, if the district attorney concludes that such a prosecution is necessary in the interests of justice. . . .

NOTES AND QUESTIONS

(1) Most states have faith healing exemptions similar to the one found in the Massachusetts criminal neglect statute at the time the Twitchells were prosecuted. In general, these exemptions protect parents from certain kinds of liability when they provide faith healing to their children in accordance with their good-faith religious beliefs. However, the scope and effect of these exemptions varies significantly from state to state. *See* Jennifer L. Rosato, *Putting Square Pegs in a Round Hole: Procedural Due Process and the Effect of Faith Healing Exemptions on the Prosecution of Faith Healing Parents,* 29 U.S.F. L. Rev. 43 (1994). Many states adopted their exemptions in response to federal regulations promulgated under the Child Abuse Prevention and Treatment Act of 1974. These regulations required states to include a faith healing exemption in their abuse and neglect laws in order to be eligible for federal funding for state child protection programs. The exemption requirement was motivated, at least in part, by the lobbying efforts of the Christian Science church. Rosato, *above,* at 59. In 1983, the Department of Health and Human Services implemented new regulations providing that states were no longer required to have faith healing exemptions to qualify for federal child protection funding. The new regulations also require states that do provide exemptions to permit judicial and administrative authorities "to ensure that medical services are provided to the child when his health requires it," 45 C.F.R.1340.2(d)(2)(ii) (1994); *see* Paula A. Monopoli, *Allocating the Costs of Parental Free Exercise: Striking a New Balance Between Sincere Religious Belief and a Child's Right to Medical Treatment,* 18 Pepperdine L. Rev. 319, 332 (1993). Despite this change in federal law, only a few states have repealed their faith healing exemptions. Rosario, *above.,* at 60–62. One of those states is Massachusetts, which repealed its exemption shortly after the state Supreme Court decision in *Twitchell.*

(2) Although the *Twitchell* court holds that the spiritual treatment exemption contained in the child neglect statute does not bar a prosecution for manslaughter, it reverses the Twitchells' convictions and remands for a new trial "if the district attorney concludes that such a prosecution is necessary in the interests of justice." If you were the district attorney would you retry Mr. and Mrs. Twitchell? Why or why not? If the case were retried, and if you were a member of the jury, would you vote to acquit the Twitchells if they could prove that they relied, albeit indirectly, on the Attorney's General's 1975 opinion?

(3) The Twitchells did not argue directly that the Free Exercise Clause of the First Amendment barred the state from prosecuting them for their religiously motivated failure to seek medical care for their child. Other courts have considered and rejected such First Amendment claims. For example in *Walker v. Superior Court,* 763 P.2d 852 (Cal. 1988), the California Supreme Court held that the mother of a child who died of meningitis after receiving treatment by prayer in lieu of medical attention could be prosecuted for involuntary manslaughter and felony child endangerment. The *Walker* court acknowledged the significant First Amendment interests at stake, but held that those interests were outweighed by the state's compelling interest in protecting the lives and well being of children. *Id.* at 870. The *Walker* court also rejected the mother's argument that the state could achieve its interest in protecting children through civil dependency proceedings—a far less intrusive means than criminal prosecution. *Id.* at 870–71. Some commentators have argued that this

constitutional analysis gives insufficient weight to the interests of religious parents. *See, e.g.,* Anne D. Lederman, *Understanding Faith: When Religious Parents Decline Conventional Medical Treatment for Their Children*, 45 Case W. Res. L. Rev. 891, 907 (1995) ("To punish parents for their reliance on faith, when their need for it is most acute and when faith's intrinsic value is the highest seems at best, nonsensical, and at worst, oppressive.).

(4) While some have argued that the Free Exercise Clause *requires* states to refrain from punishing parents for religiously-motivated decisions to forego conventional medical treatment, others have suggested that *allowing* such exemptions may be unconstitutional. In *Walker v. Superior Court*, 763 P.2d 852 (Cal. 1988) concurring Justice Stanley Mosk argued that the spiritual treatment exemption in California's child abuse and neglect statute unconstitutionally discriminated among religiously motivated parents by denying protection to "(1) parents not affiliated with a 'recognized' church or religious denomination who nonetheless provide prayer treatment on the basis of personal religious beliefs or the teachings of an unrecognized sect, and (2) parents who provide prayer treatment in accordance with the tenets of a recognized denomination that does not 'accredit' prayer 'practitioners.' " *Id.* at 874 (Mosk, J., concurring). Justice Mosk also argued that deciding which parents and religious groups were entitled to the exemption would promote excessive entanglement of church and state, thus violating the Establishment Clause of the First Amendment. *Id.* at 877 (Mosk, J. concurring). *See also State v. Miskimens*, 490 N.E.2d 931, 935 (Ohio Com. Pl. 1984) (spiritual treatment exemption to criminal abuse and neglect statute violates both the Establishment Clause and the Equal Protection Clause of the Fourteenth Amendment).

In addition to raising establishment concerns, some commentators have argued that exempting religiously-motivated parents from generally applicable child protection laws unconstitutionally infringes on their children's equal protection rights by denying those children the same state protections from harm that other groups of children receive. *See, e.g.,* James G. Dwyer, *The Children We Abandon: Religious Exemptions To Child Welfare and Education Laws As Denials of Equal Protection to Children of Religious Objectors*, 74 N.C.L. Rev. 1321 (1996). *Query:* How does the Supreme Court's constitutional analysis in *Deshaney v. Winnebago County Dep't of Soc. Serv.* (reprinted in § 7.03[E], *above*) bear on this equal protection claim?

[B] Medical Neglect

If Massachusetts officials had known of Robyn Twitchell's illness before her death, they might have sought judicial authority to override her parents' refusal to seek medical treatment. In evaluating such requests for state intervention, the courts have struggled to balance parental authority to raise children against the state's obligation to protect children from harm. The next two cases address this difficult balance.

NEWMARK v. WILLIAMS/DCPS
Supreme Court of Delaware
588 A.2d 1108 (Del. 1991)

MOORE, JUDGE

Colin Newmark, a three year old child, faced death from a deadly aggressive and advanced form of pediatric cancer known as Burkitt's Lymphoma. We were presented with a clash of interests between medical science, Colin's tragic plight, the unquestioned sincerity of his parents' religious beliefs as Christian Scientists, and the legal right of the State to protect dependent children from perceived neglect when medical treatment is withheld on religious grounds. . . .

We have concluded that Colin was not an abused or neglected child under Delaware law. Parents enjoy a well established legal right to make important decisions for their children. Although this right is not absolute, the State has the burden of proving by clear and convincing evidence that intervening in the parent-child relationship is necessary to ensure the safety or health of the child, or to protect the public at large. DCPS did not meet this heavy burden. This is especially true where the purpose of the custody petition was to administer, over the objections of Colin's parents, an extremely risky, toxic and dangerously life threatening medical treatment offering less than a 40% chance for "success."

I.

Colin was the youngest of the three Newmark children. In late August, 1990, the Newmarks noticed that he had lost most of his appetite and was experiencing frequent vomiting. The symptoms at first appeared occasionally but soon worsened.

The Newmarks reluctantly took Colin to the duPont Institute for examination. The parties stipulated that this violated the Newmarks' Christian Science beliefs in the effectiveness of spiritual healing. The parties further stipulated that the Newmarks acted out of concern for their potential criminal liability, citing a Massachusetts case which held parents liable for manslaughter for foregoing medical treatment and treating their minor child only in accordance with Christian Science tenets.

Dr. Charles L. Minor, a duPont Institute staff pediatric surgeon, examined Colin and ordered X-rays of his stomach. Dr. Minor found the X-rays inconclusive and suggested that Colin remain at the hospital for further testing. The Newmarks refused and took Colin home. Colin remained at home for approximately one week while receiving treatments under the care of a Christian Science practitioner. Colin's symptoms nonetheless quickly reappeared and the Newmarks returned him to the hospital.

Dr. Minor ordered a second set of X-rays and this time discovered an obstruction in Colin's intestines. The doctor suggested immediate surgery and, again, the Newmarks consented. The Newmarks considered the procedure "mechanical" and therefore believed that it did not violate their religious beliefs.

During the operation, Dr. Minor discovered a large mass 10 to 15 centimeters wide connecting Colin's large and small bowels. He also noticed that some of Colin's lymph nodes were unusually large. Dr. Minor removed the mass and submitted tissue samples for a pathological report. There were no complications from the surgery and Colin was recovering "well."

The pathology report confirmed that Colin was suffering from a non-Hodgkins Lymphoma. Five pathologists from Children's Hospital, Philadelphia, Pennsylvania, confirmed the diagnosis. Dr. Minor, after receiving the pathology report, contacted Dr. Rita Meek, a board certified pediatric hematologist-oncologist and an attending physician at the duPont Institute.

Dr. Meek ordered two blood tests which indicated the presence of elevated levels of uric acid and LHD in Colin's system. The presence of these chemicals indicated that the disease had spread. Dr. Meek then conducted an external examination and detected a firm mass growing above Colin's right testicle. She diagnosed Colin's condition as Burkitt's Lymphoma, an aggressive pediatric cancer. The doctor recommended that the hospital treat Colin with a heavy regimen of chemotherapy.

Dr. Meek opined that the chemotherapy offered a 40% chance of "curing" Colin's illness. She concluded that he would die within six to eight months without treatment. The Newmarks, learning of Colin's condition only after the surgery, advised Dr. Meek that they would place him under the care of a Christian Science practitioner and reject all medical treatment for their son. Accordingly, they refused to authorize the chemotherapy. There was no doubt that the Newmarks sincerely believed, as part of their religious beliefs, that the tenets of their faith provided an effective treatment.

II.

We start with an overview of the relevant Delaware statutory provisions. Delaware law defines a neglected child as:

> [A] child whose physical, mental or emotional health and well-being is threatened or impaired because of inadequate care and protection by the child's custodian, who has the ability and financial means to provide for the care but does not or will not provide adequate care; or a child who has been abused or neglected as defined by § 902 of Title 16. 10 Del.C. § 901(11).

Section 902 of Title 16 further defines abuse and neglect as:

> Physical injury by other than accidental means, injury resulting in a mental or emotional condition which is a result of abuse or neglect, negligent treatment, sexual abuse, maltreatment, mistreatment, nontreatment, exploitation or abandonment, of a child under the age of 18.

Sections of the Delaware Code, however, contain spiritual treatment exemptions which directly affect Christian Scientists. Specifically, the exemptions state:

> No child who in good faith is under treatment solely by spiritual means through prayer in accordance with the tenets and practices of a recognized church or religious denomination by a duly accredited practitioner thereof shall for that reason alone be considered a neglected child for purposes of this chapter.

10 Del.C. § 901(11) & 16 Del.C. § 907 (emphasis added). These exceptions reflect the intention of the Delaware General Assembly to provide a "safe harbor" for parents, like the Newmarks, to pursue their own religious beliefs. . . .

With the considerable reflection that time has now permitted us in examining these issues, we recognize the possibility that the spiritual treatment exemptions may violate the ban against the establishment of an official State religion guaranteed under both the Federal and Delaware Constitutions. Clearly, in both reality and practical effect, the language providing an exemption only to those individuals practicing "in accordance" with the "practices of a recognized church or religious denomination by a duly accredited practitioner thereof" is intended for the principal benefit of Christian Scientists. Our concern is that it possibly forces us to impermissibly determine the validity of an individual's own religious beliefs.

Neither party challenged the constitutionality of the spiritual treatment exemptions in either the Family Court or on appeal. Thus, except to recognize that the issue is far more complicated than was originally presented to us, we must leave such questions for another day.

III.

Addressing the facts of this case, we turn to the novel legal question whether, under any circumstances, Colin was a neglected child when his parents refused to accede to medical demands that he receive a radical form of chemotherapy having only a forty percent chance of success. Other jurisdictions differ in their approaches to this important and intensely personal issue. Some courts resolved the question on an ad hoc basis, without a formal test, concluding that a child was neglected if the parents refused to administer chemotherapy in a life threatening situation. . . .

In the present case, the Family Court did not undertake any formal interest analysis in deciding that Colin was a neglected child under Delaware law. Instead, the trial court used the same ad hoc approach as the Ohio and Tennessee courts. . . . Specifically, the Family Court rejected the Newmarks' proposal to treat Colin by spiritual means under the care of a Christian Science practitioner. The trial judge considered spiritual treatment an inadequate alternative to chemotherapy. The court therefore concluded that "without any other factually supported alternative" the Newmarks' decision to refuse chemotherapy "constituted inadequate parental care for their son who is in a life threatening situation and constituted neglect as defined in the Delaware statute."

This Court reviews the trial court's application of legal precepts involving issues of law de novo. While we do not recognize the primacy of any one of the tests employed in other jurisdictions, we find that the trial court erred in not explicitly considering the competing interests at stake. The Family Court failed to consider the special importance and primacy of the familial relationship, including the autonomy of parental decision making authority over minor children. The trial court also did not consider the gravity of Colin's illness in conjunction with the invasiveness of the proposed chemotherapy and the considerable likelihood of failure. These factors, when applied to the facts of this case, strongly militate against governmental intrusion.

A.

Any balancing test must begin with the parental interest. The primacy of the familial unit is a bedrock principle of law. *See Stanley v. Illinois*, 405 U.S. 645, 651 (1972) (citing cases). We have repeatedly emphasized that the parental right is sacred which can be invaded for only the most compelling reasons. Indeed, the Delaware General Assembly has stated that the preservation of the family is "fundamental to the maintenance of a stable, democratic society . . . ." 10 Del.C. § 902(a).

Courts have also recognized that the essential element of preserving the integrity of the family is maintaining the autonomy of the parent-child relationship. In *Prince v. Commonwealth of Massachusetts*, 321 U.S. 158, 166 (1944), the United States Supreme Court announced:

> It is cardinal with us that the custody, care and nurture of the child reside first in the parents, whose primary function and freedom include preparation for obligations the state can neither supply nor hinder. *Id.*

Parental autonomy to care for children free from government interference therefore satisfies a child's need for continuity and thus ensures his or her psychological and physical well-being. *See Goldstein, Medical Care for the Child at Risk: On State Supervention of Parental Autonomy*, 86 Yale L. J. 645, 649 & n.13 & 14 (1977)

Parental authority to make fundamental decisions for minor children is also a recognized common law principle. A doctor commits the tort of battery if he or she performs an operation under normal circumstances without the informed consent of the patient. See W. PROSSER & W. KEETON, THE LAW OF TORTS § 18 at 114 (5th ed. 1984). Tort law also assumes that a child does not have the capacity to consent to an operation in most situations. *Id.* § 118 at 114–115. Thus, the common law recognizes that the only party capable of authorizing medical treatment for a minor in "normal" circumstances is usually his parent or guardian. *Id.* § 118 at 115.

Courts, therefore, give great deference to parental decisions involving minor children. In many circumstances the State simply is not an adequate surrogate for the judgment of a loving, nurturing parent. As one commentator aptly recognized, the "law does not have the capacity to supervise the delicately complex interpersonal bonds between parent and child." Goldstein, *above*, at 650.

B.

We also recognize that parental autonomy over minor children is not an absolute right. Clearly, the State can intervene in the parent-child relationship where the health and safety of the child and the public at large are in jeopardy. *See Prince*, 321 U.S. at 166–67. Accordingly, the State, under the doctrine of parens patriae, has a special duty to protect its youngest and most helpless citizens.

The parens patriae doctrine is a derivation of the common law giving the State the right to act on behalf of minor children in certain property and marital disputes. More recently, courts have accepted the doctrine of parens patriae to justify State intervention in cases of parental religious objections to medical treatment of minor children's life threatening conditions. . . .

The basic principle underlying the parens patriae doctrine is the State's interest in preserving human life. *See Cruzan v. Director, Missouri Dep't of Health*, U.S., 110 S.Ct. 2841, 2853, (1990) (State may "assert an unqualified interest in the preservation of human life . . . ."); Yet this interest and the parens patriae doctrine are not unlimited. In its recent *Cruzan* opinion, the Supreme Court of the United States announced that the state's interest in preserving life must "be weighed against the constitutionally protected interests of the individual." U.S., 110 S.Ct. 2841, 2853 (1990).

The individual interests at stake here include both the Newmarks' right to decide what is best for Colin and Colin's own right to life. We have already considered the Newmarks' stake in this case and its relationship to the parens patriae doctrine. The resolution of the issues here, however, is incomplete without a discussion of Colin's interests.

C.

All children indisputably have the right to enjoy a full and healthy life. Colin, a three year old boy, unfortunately lacked the ability to reach a detached, informed decision regarding his own medical care. This Court must therefore substitute its own objective judgment to determine what is in Colin's "best interests."

There are two basic inquiries when a dispute involves chemotherapy treatment over parents' religious objections. The court must first consider the effectiveness of the treatment and determine the child's chances of survival with and without medical care. The court must then consider the nature of the treatments and their effect on the child. . . .

The linchpin in all cases discussing the "best interests of a child," when a parent refuses to authorize medical care, is an evaluation of the risk of the procedure compared to its potential success. This analysis is consistent with the principle that State intervention in the parent-child relationship is only justifiable under compelling conditions. The State's interest in forcing a minor to undergo medical care diminishes as the risks of treatment increase and its benefits decrease. . . .

Applying the foregoing considerations to the "best interests standard" here, the State's petition must be denied. The egregious facts of this case indicate that Colin's proposed medical treatment was highly invasive, painful, involved terrible temporary and potentially permanent side effects, posed an unacceptably low chance of success, and a high risk that the treatment itself would cause his death. The State's authority to intervene in this case, therefore, cannot outweigh the Newmarks' parental prerogative and Colin's inherent right to enjoy at least a modicum of human dignity in the short time that was left to him.

IV.

Dr. Meek originally diagnosed Colin's condition as Burkitt's Lymphoma. She testified that the cancer was "a very bad tumor" in an advanced disseminated state and not localized to only one section of the body. She accordingly recommended that the hospital begin an "extremely intensive" chemotherapy program scheduled to extend for at least six months.

The first step necessary to prepare Colin for chemotherapy involved an intravenous hydration treatment. This process, alone, posed a significant risk that Colin's kidneys would fail. Indeed, these intravenous treatments had already begun and were threatening Colin's life while the parties were arguing the case to us on September 14, 1990. Thus, if Colin's kidneys failed he also would have to undergo dialysis treatments. There also was a possibility that renal failure could occur during the chemotherapy treatments themselves. In addition, Dr. Meek recommended further pre-treatment diagnostic tests including a spinal tap and a CAT scan.

Dr. Meek prescribed "maximum" doses of at least six different types of cancer-fighting drugs during Colin's chemotherapy. This proposed "maximum" treatment represented the most aggressive form of cancer therapy short of a bone marrow transplant. The side effects would include hair loss, reduced immunological function creating a high risk of infection in the patient, and certain neurological problems. The drugs also are toxic to bone marrow.

The record demonstrates that this form of chemotherapy also would adversely affect other parts of Colin's body. Dr. Meek stated that the doctors would have to administer the treatments through injections in the veins and spinal fluid. The chemotherapy would reduce Colin's white blood count, and it would be extremely likely that he would suffer numerous infections. Colin would require multiple blood transfusions with a resultant additional risk of infection.

The treating physicians also would have to install a catheter in Colin's chest to facilitate a constant barrage of tests and treatments. Colin also would receive food through the catheter because the chemotherapy would depress his appetite. The operation to set the catheter in place would take approximately one hour. The doctors proposed to perform biopsies on both Colin's bone marrow and the lump in his groin during the procedure.

The physicians planned to administer the chemotherapy in cycles, each of which would bring Colin near death. Then they would wait until Colin's body recovered sufficiently before introducing more drugs. Dr. Meek opined that there was no guarantee that drugs alone would "cure" Colin's illness. The doctor noted that it would then be necessary to radiate Colin's testicles if drugs alone were unsuccessful. Presumably, this would have rendered him sterile.

Dr. Meek also wanted the State to place Colin in a foster home after the initial phases of hospital treatment. Children require intensive home monitoring during chemotherapy. For example, Dr. Meek testified that a usually low grade fever for a healthy child could indicate the presence of a potentially deadly infection in a child cancer patient. She believed that the Newmarks, although well educated and financially responsible, were incapable of providing this intensive care because of their firm religious objections to medical treatment.

Dr. Meek ultimately admitted that there was a real possibility that the chemotherapy could kill Colin. In fact, assuming the treatment did not itself prove fatal, she offered Colin at "best" a 40% chance that he would "survive." Dr. Meek additionally could not accurately predict whether, if Colin completed the therapy, he would subsequently suffer additional tumors.

A.

No American court, even in the most egregious case, has ever authorized the State to remove a child from the loving, nurturing care of his parents and subject him, over parental objection, to an invasive regimen of treatment which offered, as Dr. Meek defined the term, only a forty percent chance of "survival." For example, the California Court of Appeals ruled in *Eric B.*, that the State could conduct various procedures as part of an "observation phase" of chemotherapy over the objection of his parents. 189 Cal. App. 3d at 1008–1009, 235 Cal. Rptr. at 29. The treatment included bone scans, CT scans, spinal taps and biopsies. Id. at 1000–1001 n. 2, 235 Cal. Rptr. at 23–24. The court specifically found that "the risks entailed by the monitoring are minimal." Id. at 1006, 235 Cal. Rptr. at 27. The court also noted that the child would enjoy a 60% chance of survival with the treatments. *Id.* at 1005, 235 Cal. Rptr. at 27. . . .

The Supreme Judicial Court of Massachusetts took custody away from parents who refused to administer "mild" cancer fighting drugs after the child had already undergone more "vigorous" treatment. *See Custody of a Minor*, 375 Mass. at 755–56, 379 N.E.2d at 1058, 1067. The trial judge, in that case, specifically found that aside from some minor side effects, including stomach cramps and constipation, the chemotherapy "bore no chance of leaving the child physically incapacitated in any way." *Id.* at 751, 754, 379 N.E.2d at 1064, 1066. The trial court also ruled that the chemotherapy gave the child not only a chance to enjoy a long life "but also a 'substantial' chance for cure." *Id.* at 753, 379 N.E.2d at 1065.

The Ohio Court of Appeals awarded custody of a minor suffering from Osteogenic Sarcoma to the state when his parents consented to chemotherapy, but later refused to authorize an operation to partially remove his shoulder and entire left arm. *In re Willmann*, 24 Ohio App. 3d at 193, 199, 493 N.E.2d at 1383, 1390. Although amputation is ultimately the most invasive type of surgery, there was at least a 60% chance in Willmann that the child would survive with the operation. *Id.* at 193, 493 N.E.2d at 1384. The court also significantly noted that the child remained at home while receiving the lower court's mandated chemotherapy treatments. *Id.* at 197, 493 N.E.2d at 1388.

Finally, the New York Supreme Court most recently ruled that the State could intervene and order chemotherapy treatments over a parent's religious objections when the medical care presented a 75% chance of short-term remission but only a 25–30% chance for "cure." *See In re Application of L. I. Jewish Med. Ctr.*, 147 Misc. 2d at 725, 557 N.Y.S.2d at 241. The seventeen-year-old minor in that case suffered from an advanced case of Rhabdomyosarcoma, a type of pediatric cancer affecting potential muscle tissue. Id. at 725, 557 N.Y.S.2d at 241. This case, however, is not dispositive given the fact that the parents were not wholly opposed to chemotherapy.

The minor and his parents in *L.I. Jewish Med. Ctr.*, were both members of the Jehovah's Witnesses religion and only objected to blood transfusions which were an incidental part of the prescribed medical treatment. *Id.* at 725–26, 557 N.Y.S.2d at 240–41. There was no evidence that either party objected to the chemotherapy, which included radiation treatments. *Id.* The treatments were also probably "radical" in nature given the fact that the disease had spread throughout the child's body. *Id.* at 725, 557 N.Y.S.2d at 241. This New York decision is therefore in perfect accord with other well-established precedent. Courts have consistently authorized state intervention when parents object to only minimally intrusive treatment which poses little or no risk to a child's health.

B.

The aggressive form of chemotherapy that Dr. Meek prescribed for Colin was more likely to fail than succeed. The proposed treatment was also highly invasive and could have independently caused Colin's death. Dr. Meek also wanted to take Colin away from his parents and family during the treatment phase and place the boy in a foster home. This certainly would have caused Colin severe emotional difficulties given his medical condition, tender age, and the unquestioned close bond between Colin and his family.

In sum, Colin's best interests were served by permitting the Newmarks to retain custody of their child. Parents must have the right at some point to reject medical treatment for their child. Under all of the circumstances here, this clearly is such a case. The State's important and legitimate role in safeguarding the interests of minor children diminishes in the face of this egregious record.

Parents undertake an awesome responsibility in raising and caring for their children. No doubt a parent's decision to withhold medical care is both deeply personal and soul wrenching. It need not be made worse by the invasions which both the State and medical profession sought on this record. Colin's ultimate fate therefore rested with his parents and their faith.*

The judgment of the Family Court is, REVERSED.

IN RE SAMPSON
Family Court, Ulster County, New York
317 N.Y.S.2d 641 (1970)

ELWYN, J.

The Commissioner of Health of Ulster County brings this neglect proceeding pursuant to article 10 of the Family Court Act, charging that Kevin Sampson, a male child under 16 years of age is neglected by reason of the failure of his mother, Mildred Sampson to provide him with proper medical and surgical care. The mother is not opposed to having the recommended surgery performed upon her son, but, because she is a member of the religious sect known as Jehovah's Witnesses she has steadfastly refused to give her consent to the administration of any blood transfusions during the course of the surgery, without which the proposed surgery may not safely be performed. After extensive hearings the court finds that the following facts are established by the evidence.

The boy, Kevin Sampson, who is now 15 years of age, having been born on January 25, 1955, suffers from extensive neurofibromatosis or von Recklinghausen's disease which has caused a massive deformity of the right side of his face and neck. The outward manifestation of the disease is a large fold or flap of an overgrowth of facial tissue which causes the whole cheek, the corner of his mouth and right ear to drop down giving him an appearance which can only be described as grotesque and repulsive. Fortunately, however, the disease has not yet progressed to a point where his vision has been affected or his hearing impaired. . . .

Thus, insofar as the boy's sight and hearing are concerned, it appears from the doctor's reports that the neurofibromatosis poses no immediate threat to either, and that there is, therefore, no need for treatment of either his eyes or his ears. However, the massive deformity of the entire right side of his face and neck is patently so gross and so disfiguring that it must inevitably exert a most negative effect upon his personality development, his opportunity for education and later employment and upon every phase of his relationship with his peers and others. Although the staff psychiatrist of the County Mental Health Center reports that "there is no evidence of any thinking disorder" and that "in spite of marked facial disfigurement he failed to show any outstanding personality aberration," this finding hardly justifies a conclusion that he has been or will continue to be wholly unaffected by his misfortune. Although Kevin was found to be not psychotic, a psychologist found him to be a "boy (who) is extremely dependent and (who) sees himself as an inadequate personality." The staff psychiatrist reports that "Kevin demonstrates inferiority feeling and low self concept. Such inadequate personality is often noted in cases of mental retardation, facial disfigurement and emotional deprivation."

If the boy exhibited to the psychologist some mental retardation it is hardly surprising in view of the fact that he has been exempted from school since November 24, 1964, and

---

* Tragically, Colin died shortly after we announced our oral decision.

is currently exempted from school by reason of his facial disfigurement. As a result, although various tests administered by school authorities show him to be intellectually capable of being educated and trained to a reasonable level of self-sufficiency, he is, at 15 years of age, a virtual illiterate.

From all the information available to the court as the result of extended hearings and various reports, particularly those supplied by those educators who have become familiar with the pattern of Kevin's development, or more accurately, the lack thereof, the conclusion is inescapable that the marked facial disfigurement from which this boy suffers constitutes such an overriding limiting factor militating against his future development that unless some constructive steps are taken to alleviate his condition, his chances for a normal, useful life are virtually nil.

The unanimous recommendation of all those who have dealt with the many problems posed by Kevin's affliction—educators, psychologists, psychiatrists, physicians and surgeons—is that steps be taken to correct the condition through surgery. It is conceded, however, by the surgeons that, insofar as his health and his life is concerned, this is not a necessary operation. The disease poses no immediate threat to his life nor has it as yet seriously affected his general health. Moreover, the surgery will not cure him of the disease. In fact, for the condition from which he suffers there is no known cure. . . .

The surgery which the surgeons recommend for the alleviation of the diseased condition cannot, however, be performed without substantial risk. In the words of Dr. Ferdinand Stanley Hoffmeister, the other highly qualified surgeon who testified as to the need for corrective surgery and who had previously performed some limited surgery upon this boy, "I think it's a dangerous procedure. I think it involves considerable risk. It's a massive surgery of six to eight hours duration with great blood loss. This is a risky surgical procedure." When asked if the risk would be much above average he replied, "much, much, much." The surgeon repeatedly "emphasiz(ed) the surgery risk in operating on this patient even with blood."

Without the mother's permission to administer blood transfusions the risk becomes wholly unacceptable. According to Dr. Hoffmeister, "if this tumor had to be removed as extensively as it is desirable to improve his appearance, I think the loss of blood would be so extensive, that I personally would not dare to undertake such a procedure having only plasma expanders at my disposal." The surgeons are adamant in their refusal to operate upon Kevin unless they have permission to use blood and to administer during the surgery such blood transfusions as the patient's condition requires.

Mrs. Sampson, while not opposed to surgery as such, having already given permission for surgery limited to the use of plasma, is equally adamant in her refusal to give her consent to the use of blood. As previously noted, Mrs. Sampson is an adherent to the religious sect known as Jehovah's Witnesses who according to the minister of the Kingston Congregation of Jehovah's Witnesses "feel that the Bible is explicit on the matter of taking any form of blood into our system either by eating, through mouth, food, through the body, through the veins. This is specifically prohibited in the Scriptures for Christians." Although not opposed to medicine or surgery on religious grounds, Jehovah's Witnesses hold as a cardinal principle of their faith that the eating or ingestion of blood into the body by any means whatever, including modern surgical procedures for the transfusion of blood are explicitly forbidden by the law of God. . . .

THE RELIGIOUS OBJECTIONS

. . . [N]either rights of religion nor rights of parenthood are beyond limitation. Acting to guard the general interest in youth's well-being, the state as parens patriae may restrict the parent's control by requiring school attendance, regulating or prohibiting the child's labor and in many other ways. Its authority is not nullified merely because the parent grounds his claim to control the child's course of conduct on religion or conscience. Thus, he cannot claim freedom from compulsory vaccination for the child more than for himself on religious grounds [*Jacobson v. Massachusetts*, 197 U.S. 11]. The right to practice religion freely does not include the liberty to expose the community or the child to communicable disease or the latter to ill health or death. It is sufficient to show what indeed appellant hardly disputes, that the state has a wide range of power for limiting parental freedom and authority in things affecting the child's welfare; and that this includes, to some extent, matters of conscience and religious conviction.

Specifically, the same issue presented here—i.e., the power of the State through its courts to order a necessary blood transfusion for a minor over the religious objections of a parent has been frequently contested by Jehovah's Witnesses before. However, in every reported case that research has revealed in which the issue has been presented the courts have unequivocally upheld the power of the State to authorize the administration of a blood transfusion over the religious objections of the parent where the blood transfusion was shown to be necessary for the preservation of the minor's life or the success of needed surgery. [citing cases] . . .

In the light of the foregoing authorities I conclude that although the mother's religious objections to the administration of a blood transfusion to her son in the event surgery is to be performed upon his face are founded upon the scriptures and are sincerely held, they must give way before the State's paramount duty to insure his right to live and grow up without disfigurement—the right to live and grow up with a sound mind in a sound body. "Parents may be free to become martyrs themselves. But it does not follow they are free, in identical circumstances, to make martyrs of their children before they have reached the age of full and legal discretion when they can make that choice for themselves" (*Prince v. Massachusetts*, 321 U.S. 158, 170, *above*).

THE POTENTIAL GOOD VS. THE RISK TO LIFE

In the opinion of the surgeons who are familiar with Kevin's condition, the neurofibromatosis from which he suffers poses no immediate threat to his life or even to his general health and the proposed surgery for its excision would have no material effect upon his life expectancy. . . .

It is not necessary, however, that a child's life be in danger before this court may act to safeguard his health or general welfare. . . . Furthermore the recent revision of article 10 of the Family Court Act which confers upon this court exclusive jurisdiction and ample authority to deal with the abused and neglected child is a clear indication of the Legislature's concern for these unfortunate children and its intention to confer upon the court the broadest power and discretion to deal with these matters. I therefore conclude that this court's authority to deal with the abused, neglected or physically handicapped child is not limited to "drastic situations" or to those which constitute a "present emergency," but that the court has a "wide discretion" to order medical or surgical care and treatment for an infant even over parental objection, if in the court's judgment the health, safety or welfare of the child requires it.

The question still remains, however, whether this court should, under the circumstances of this case, order this boy to undergo a risky surgical procedure, which the surgeons concede will not cure him of the disease. Dr. Hoffmeister, one of the plastic surgeons who testified in this case concedes, "we would certainly leave a tumor behind. This is a non-resectable lesion." Dr. Macomber, the other surgeon, also was frank in admitting the limitations upon the surgeon's skill when he said: "well, you can remove—you can't get it all, this is for sure." Although the results of the surgery would be to change his physical appearance, Dr. Macomber conceded that "he can't be returned to a normal face, impossible."

Counsel for Mrs. Sampson stresses the surgical risk involved in the contemplated procedure which the surgeons candidly concede is a "dangerous procedure" and involves "considerable risk" even with the use of blood transfusions. Moreover, counsel points out with much persuasiveness that Dr. Hoffmeister expressed the opinion that, while the contemplated surgery would still be risky, it would be less risky if the operation were delayed for five or six years, because the boy's blood volume would then be larger and while the loss of blood would be about the same, the relative blood loss would be smaller than now.

Because of the high surgical risk inherent in the operation and the minimization of the risk as the boy grows older by reason of the lower relative blood loss to total blood supply, counsel for Mrs. Sampson and the Law Guardian counsel delay until the boy is old enough to make the decision for himself. In fact, even Dr. Hoffmeister counsels delay. He said: "I would suggest to the Court wait until the child is 21 years old and have him make his own decision because I feel we are not losing by waiting five or six years."

From the surgeon's point of view the fact that the surgical risk may decrease as the boy grows older is certainly a most persuasive reason for postponing the surgery. However, to postpone the surgery merely to allow the boy to become of age so that he may make the decision himself as suggested by the surgeon and urged by both counsel for the mother and the Law Guardian totally ignores the developmental and psychological factors stemming from his deformity which the court deems to be of the utmost importance in any consideration of the boy's future welfare and begs the whole question.

This court cannot evade the responsibility for a decision now by the simple expedient of foisting upon this boy the responsibility for making a decision at some later day which by the time it is made, if at all, will be too late to undo the irreparable damage he will have suffered in the interim. This court plainly has a duty to perform and though the responsibility for decision is awesome the burden cannot be shared by transferring even a small part of it to another. . . .

. . . Moreover, it must also be humbly acknowledged that under the circumstances of this case one cannot be certain of being right. Nevertheless, a decision must be made, and so, after much deliberation, I am persuaded that if this court is to meet its responsibilities to this boy it can neither shift the responsibility for the ultimate decision onto his shoulders nor can it permit his mother's religious beliefs to stand in the way of attaining through corrective surgery whatever chance he may have for a normal, happy existence, which, to paraphrase Judge Fuld, is difficult of attainment under the most propitious circumstances, but will unquestionably be impossible if the disfigurement is not corrected. . . .

Thus, while the surgeons conceded that there are risks inherent in the contemplated surgery, in their opinion that risk should not be too great if they have permission to use blood. In any event, when one considers the bleak prospect for this boy's future of the alternative of doing nothing, it is a risk which I believe must be taken. However, this conclusion must be qualified by stating that if in the judgment of those surgeons who have been consulted concerning Kevin's condition and who have the responsibility for the actual performance of the surgery, the contemplated procedures pose an unacceptable risk to his life, they ought not to undertake such surgery. This is a judgment that only the surgeons are qualified to make and nothing in this decision should be so construed as to require any surgeon to perform any surgery upon this boy if, in their judgment, such surgery ought not to be undertaken. The court wishes to leave the surgeons completely free to exercise their own professional judgment as to the nature, extent and timing of any surgery that may be required for the correction of Kevin's deformity.

Because of the refusal of Mrs. Mildred Sampson to give her consent to the blood transfusions essential for the safety of the surgical procedures necessary to insure the physical, mental and emotional well-being of her son, the court adjudicates Kevin Sampson to be a neglected child within the meaning of section 1012 of the Family Court Act. This adjudication, however, in no way imports a finding that the mother failed in her duty to the child in any other respect. . . .

NOTES AND QUESTIONS

(1) The decision of the Family Court was upheld by the Supreme Court of New York, Appellate Division. *In re Sampson,* 323 N.Y.S.2d 253, 37 A.D.2d 668 (N.Y. App. Div. 1971), and by the New York Court of Appeals in a brief, per curiam opinion. *In re Sampson*, 328 N.Y.S.2d 686 (N.Y. 1972).

(2) Are *Sampson* and *Newmark* consistent? When, if ever, should courts override parental authority in cases such as *Sampson*, where the child's life is not endangered? What standard should the courts apply in determining whether to intervene? What standard does the trial judge employ in *Sampson*?

(3) Not all courts have been as willing as the *Sampson* court to authorize state intervention where a child's life is not endangered. In *In re Green*, 292 A.2d 387 (Pa. 1972), Ricky Green, a 15-year-old boy suffering from paralytic scoliosis (with a 94% curvature of the spine) was the subject of a neglect petition filed by the Director of the State Hospital for Crippled Children. The petition sought appointment of a guardian to consent to corrective surgery to prevent Ricky from being bedridden for the rest of his life. The state conceded that the recommended surgery was risky and that Ricky's condition was not life-threatening. Like the mother in *Sampson,* Ricky's mother was not opposed to the surgery per se, but refused to consent, for religious reasons, to the blood transfusions that the procedure would require. The Superior Court granted the neglect petition, but the Pennsylvania Supreme Court reversed. Characterizing as "endless" the potential problems that would ensue from following the *Sampson* rationale, the Pennsylvania Supreme Court held that "as between a parent and the state, the state does not have an interest of sufficient magnitude outweighing a parent's religious beliefs when the child's life is not immediately imperiled by his physical condition." *Id.* at 392.

However, this did not end the court's analysis. Citing Justice Douglas' dissenting opinion in *Wisconsin v. Yoder* (§ 7.02 *above*), the court remanded the case for an evidentiary hearing to determine the views of the 15-year-old child. In the evidentiary hearing on remand, Ricky indicated that he did not wish to undergo surgery. His views were not based solely on religious grounds; he testified that he had been going to the hospital for a long time and no one had told him that "it is going to come out right." *In re Green*, 307 A.2d 279 (Pa. 1973). For additional discussion of cases in which courts have been asked to order non-emergency medical treatment over a parent's religious objection, see Jay M. Zitter, Annotation, *Power of Court or Other Public Agency to Order Medical Treatment Over Parental Religious Objections For Child Whose Life Is Not Immediately Endangered*, 21 A.L.R. 5th 248 (1994); Brian Heaves, *Relief for the Neglected Child: Court-Ordered Medical Treatment in Nonemergency Situations*, 22 Santa Clara L. Rev. 471 (1982).

(4) **Problem.** Juliet Cheng, a 39-year-old woman, moved to this country from China approximately 10 years ago. While in the U.S., she met Thomas Li. They married and had a daughter, Shirley. Subsequently, Thomas and Juliet separated. When Shirley was only a few years old it became clear that she suffered from severe juvenile rheumatoid arthritis. Juliet and her mother treated Shirley with some of the traditional forms of Chinese medication, but these failed to have any significant effect on Shirley's condition. Juliet also took Shirley back to China for treatment several times, but these visits produced only temporary improvements. Juliet, who does not trust American doctors, delayed seeking treatment for Shirley from a licensed U.S. physician. When Juliet did take Shirley to see a physician, at the age of 6, Shirley could no longer walk. Juliet consented to physical therapy and medication for Shirley under the supervision of a practitioner of homeopathic medicine, but the treatments were unsuccessful.

Shirley's medical doctors claim that her leg and hip joints are now so contracted that it will be impossible to loosen them without surgery. They want to perform surgery on Shirley's hips and legs but Juliet has refused to consent. She wants to return to China with Shirley to try other, more traditional and familiar options first, such as physical therapy, acupuncture and herbal medicine. The doctors have filed a neglect petition with the local department of child welfare, claiming that if the surgery is not performed promptly, Shirley is unlikely to be able to walk again. The case will be heard shortly. If you were the judge, what additional information would you like to have in order to make a decision? Would you be inclined to grant the neglect petition? Would you order the surgery over Juliet's objection? What precedents would you use to support your decision?

[C] Children As Decision-Makers

In the preceding cases, the courts were concerned primarily with balancing parental authority against the state's parens patriae interest in protecting children. The next case considers more explicitly the role of children as decision-makers in the context of medical care.

IN RE E.G.
Supreme Court of Illinois
549 N.E.2d 322 (1989)

RYAN, J.

Appellee, E.G., a 17-year-old woman, contracted leukemia and needed blood transfusions in the treatment of the disease. E.G. and her mother, Rosie Denton, refused to consent to the transfusions, contending that acceptance of blood would violate personal religious convictions rooted in their membership in the Jehovah's Witness faith. Appellant, the State of Illinois, filed a neglect petition in juvenile court in the circuit court of Cook County. The trial court entered an order finding E.G. to be neglected, and appointed a guardian to consent to the transfusions on E.G.'s behalf.

The appellate court reversed the trial court in part. The court held that E.G. was a "mature minor," and therefore could refuse the blood transfusions through the exercise of her first amendment right to freely exercise her religion. Nevertheless, the court affirmed the finding of neglect against Denton.

We granted the State's petition for leave to appeal and now affirm the appellate court's decision in part, but on other grounds. We also remand this case to the trial court for the purpose of expunging the finding of neglect.

In February of 1987, E.G. was diagnosed as having acute nonlymphatic leukemia, a malignant disease of the white blood cells. When E.G. and her mother, Rosie Denton, were informed that treatment of the disease would involve blood transfusions, they refused to consent to this medical procedure on the basis of their religious beliefs. As Jehovah's Witnesses, both E.G. and her mother desired to observe their religion's prohibition against the "eating" of blood. Mrs. Denton did authorize any other treatment and signed a waiver absolving the medical providers of liability for failure to administer transfusions.

As a result of Denton's and E.G.'s refusal to assent to blood transfusions, the State filed a neglect petition in juvenile court. At the initial hearing on February 25, 1987, Dr. Stanley Yachnin testified that E.G. had approximately one-fifth to one-sixth the normal oxygen-carrying capacity of her blood and consequently was excessively fatigued and incoherent. He stated that without blood transfusions, E.G. would likely die within a month. Dr. Yachnin testified that the transfusions, along with chemotherapy, achieve remission of the disease in about 80% of all patients so afflicted. Continued treatment, according to Dr. Yachnin, would involve the utilization of drugs and more transfusions. The long-term prognosis is not optimistic, as the survival rate for patients such as E.G. is 20 to 25%.

Dr. Yachnin stated that he discussed the proposed course of treatment with E.G. He testified that E.G. was competent to understand the consequences of accepting or rejecting treatment, and he was impressed with her maturity and the sincerity of her beliefs. Dr. Yachnin's observations regarding E.G.'s competency were corroborated by the testimony of Jane McAtee, the associate general counsel for the University of Chicago Hospital. At the conclusion of this hearing, the trial judge entered an order appointing McAtee temporary guardian, and authorizing her to consent to transfusions on E.G.'s behalf.

On April 8, 1987, further hearings were held on this matter. E.G., having received several blood transfusions, was strong enough to take the stand. She testified that the decision to refuse blood transfusions was her own and that she fully understood the nature of her disease and the consequences of her decision. She indicated that her decision was not based on any wish to die, but instead was grounded in her religious convictions. E.G. further stated that when informed that she would undergo transfusions, she asked to be sedated prior to the administration of the blood. She testified that the court's decision upset her, and said: "[I]t seems as if everything that I wanted or believe in was just being disregarded."

Several other witnesses gave their opinions extolling E.G.'s maturity and the sincerity of her religious beliefs. One witness was Dr. Littner, a psychiatrist who has special expertise in evaluating the maturity and competency of minors. Based on interviews with E.G. and her family, Dr. Littner expressed his opinion that E.G. had the maturity level of an 18 to 21 year old. He further concluded that E.G. had the competency to make an informed decision to refuse the blood transfusions, even if this choice was fatal.

On May 18, 1987, the trial court ruled that E.G. was medically neglected, and appointed a guardian to consent to medical treatment. The court felt this was in E.G.'s best interests. The court did state, however, that E.G. was "a mature 17-year-old individual," that E.G. reached her decision on an independent basis, and that she was "fully aware that death [was] assured absent treatment." The court noted that it considered E.G.'s maturity and the religion of her and her parents, and that it gave great weight to the wishes of E.G. Nevertheless, the court felt that the State's interest in this case was greater than the interest E.G. and her mother had in refusing to consent to treatment. The court concluded its ruling by encouraging E.G. to appeal.

On appeal, the order of the trial court pertaining to E.G.'s right to refuse treatment was vacated in part and modified in part. The appellate court observed that this court, in *In re Estate of Brooks* (1965), 32 Ill. 2d 361, held that an adult Jehovah's Witness had a first amendment right to refuse blood transfusions. The appellate court then extended the holding in Brooks to include "mature minors," deriving this extension from cases in which the United States Supreme Court allowed "mature minors" to consent to abortions without parental approval through the exercise of constitutional privacy rights. Although the United States Supreme Court has not broadened this constitutional right of minors beyond abortion cases, the appellate court found such an extension "inevitable." Relying on our Emancipation of Mature Minors Act (Ill. Rev. Stat. 1987, ch. 40, par. 2201 et seq.), the court held that a mature minor may exercise a constitutional right to refuse medical treatment.

The appellate court noted that E.G., at the time of trial, was only six months shy of her eighteenth birthday, and that the trial court believed E.G. to be a mature individual. Based on these facts, the appellate court declared that E.G. was partially emancipated and therefore had the right to refuse transfusions. The court, however, affirmed the finding of neglect against Denton, E.G.'s mother. . . .

The paramount issue raised by this appeal is whether a minor like E.G. has a right to refuse medical treatment. In Illinois, an adult has a common law right to refuse medical treatment, even if it is of a life-sustaining nature. This court has also held that an adult may refuse life-saving blood transfusions on first amendment free exercise of religion grounds. An infant child, however, can be compelled to accept life-saving medical treatment over the objections of her parents. In the matter before us, E.G. was a minor, but one who was just months shy of her eighteenth birthday, and an individual that the record indicates was mature for her age. Although the age of majority in Illinois is 18, that age is not an impenetrable barrier that magically precludes a minor from possessing and exercising certain rights normally associated with adulthood. Numerous exceptions are found in this jurisdiction and others which treat minors as adults under specific circumstances.

In Illinois, our legislature enacted "An Act in relation to the performance of medical, dental or surgical procedures on and counseling for minors" (the Consent by Minors to Medical Operations Act), which grants minors the legal capacity to consent to medical treatment in certain situations. For example, a minor 12 years or older may seek medical attention on her own if she believes she has venereal disease or is an alcoholic or drug addict. Similarly, an individual under 18 who is married or pregnant may validly consent to treatment. Thus, if E.G. would have been married she could have consented to or, presumably, refused treatment. Also, a minor 16 or older may be declared emancipated under the Emancipation of Mature Minors Act, and thereby control his or her own health care decisions. These two acts, when read together in a complementary fashion, indicate that the legislature did not intend that there be an absolute 18-year-old age barrier prohibiting minors from consenting to medical treatment. . . .

Another area of the law where minors are treated as adults is constitutional law, including the constitutional right of abortion. The United States Supreme Court has adopted a mature minor doctrine, which allows women under the age of majority to undergo abortions without parental consent. In the abortion rights context, the Court has noted: "Constitutional rights do not mature and come into being magically only when one attains the state-defined age of majority. Minors, as well as adults, are protected by the Constitution and possess constitutional rights." (*Planned Parenthood of Central Missouri v. Danforth* (1976), 428 U.S. 52, 74). Moreover, children enjoy the protection of other constitutional rights, including the right of privacy (*Carey v. Population Services International* (1977), 431 U.S. 678), freedom of expression (*Tinker v. Des Moines Independent Community School District* (1969), 393 U.S. 503), freedom from unreasonable searches and seizures (*New Jersey v. T.L.O.* (1985), 469 U.S. 325), and procedural due process (*In re Application of Gault* (1967), 387 U.S. 1). Nevertheless, the Supreme Court has not held that a constitutionally based right to refuse medical treatment exists, either for adults or minors. While we find the language from the cases cited above instructive, we do not feel, as the appellate court did, that an extension of the constitutional mature minor doctrine to the case at bar is "inevitable." These cases do show, however, that no "bright line" age restriction of 18 is tenable in restricting the rights of mature minors, whether the rights be based on constitutional or other grounds. Accordingly, we hold that in addition to these constitutionally based rights expressly delineated by the Supreme Court, mature minors may possess and exercise rights regarding medical care that are rooted in this State's common law.

[W]e find support for this conclusion in a decision of one of our sister States. In *Cardwell v. Bechtol* (Tenn. 1987), 724 S.W.2d 739, the Tennessee Supreme Court held that a mature minor had the capacity to consent to medical procedures based on the common law of that State. The court noted that the mature minor doctrine is not a recent development in the law: "[R]ecognition that minors achieve varying degrees of maturity and responsibility (capacity) has been part of the common law for well over a century." 724 S.W.2d at 744–45.

In *Cardwell*, the Tennessee court held that a minor 17 years, 7 months old was mature enough to consent to medical treatment. We note that in other jurisdictions, courts have ordered health care for minors over the objections of the minors' parents. These cases, however, involve minors who were younger than E.G. or the minor in *Cardwell*. Moreover, the issue in [these] cases was not whether a minor could assert a right to control medical treatment decisions, but whether the minor's parents could refuse treatment on behalf of their child. Here, E.G. contends she was mature enough to have controlled her own health care. We find that she may have done so if indeed she would have been adjudged mature.

The trial judge must determine whether a minor is mature enough to make health care choices on her own. An exception to this, of course, is if the legislature has provided otherwise, as in the Consent by Minors to Medical Operations Act (Ill. Rev. Stat. 1987, ch. 111, par. 4501 et seq.). We feel the intervention of a judge is appropriate for two reasons.

First, Illinois public policy values the sanctity of life. When a minor's health and life are at stake, this policy becomes a critical consideration. A minor may have a long and fruitful life ahead that an immature, foolish decision could jeopardize. Consequently, when the trial judge weighs the evidence in making a determination of whether a minor is mature enough to handle a health care decision, he must find proof of this maturity by clear and convincing evidence.

Second, the State has a parens patriae power to protect those incompetent to protect themselves. . . . The State's parens patriae power pertaining to minors is strongest when the minor is immature and thus incompetent (lacking in capacity) to make these decisions on her own. The parens patriae authority fades, however, as the minor gets older and disappears upon her reaching adulthood. The State interest in protecting a mature minor in these situations will vary depending upon the nature of the medical treatment involved. Where the health care issues are potentially life threatening, the State's parens patriae interest is greater than if the health care matter is less consequential.

Therefore, the trial judge must weigh these two principles against the evidence he receives of a minor's maturity. If the evidence is clear and convincing that the minor is mature enough to appreciate the consequences of her actions, and that the minor is mature enough to exercise the judgment of an adult, then the mature minor doctrine affords her the common law right to consent to or refuse medical treatment. As we stated in *Longeway*, however, this common law right is not absolute. The right must be balanced against four State interests: (1) the preservation of life; (2) protecting the interests of third parties; (3) prevention of suicide; and (4) maintaining the ethical integrity of the medical profession. (*Longeway*, 133 Ill. 2d at 48, *quoting Superintendent of Belchertown State School v. Saikewicz* (1977), 373 Mass. 728, 741, 370 N.E.2d 417, 425.) Of these four concerns, protecting the interests of third parties is clearly the most significant here. The principal third parties in these cases would be parents, guardians, adult siblings, and other relatives. If a parent or guardian opposes an unemancipated mature minor's refusal to consent to treatment for a life-threatening health problem, this opposition would weigh heavily against the minor's right to refuse. In this case, for example, had E.G. refused the transfusions against the wishes of her mother, then the court would have given serious consideration to her mother's desires.

Nevertheless, in this case both E.G. and her mother agreed that E.G. should turn down the blood transfusions. They based this refusal primarily on religious grounds, contending that the first amendment free exercise clause entitles a mature minor to decline medical care when it contravenes sincerely held religious beliefs. Because we find that a mature minor may exercise a common law right to consent to or refuse medical care, we decline to address the constitutional issue. . . .

WARD, J., dissenting:

I must respectfully dissent. I consider the majority has made an unfortunate choice of situations to announce, in what it calls a case of first impression, that a minor may with judicial approval reject medical treatment, even if the minor's death will be a medically certain consequence. The majority cites decisions where a minor was permitted to exercise what was called a common law right to consent to medical treatment. The safeguarding of health and the preservation of life are obviously different conditions from one in which a minor will be held to have a common law right, as the majority puts it, to refuse medical treatment and sometimes in effect take his own life. That violates the ancient responsibility of the State as parens patriae to protect minors and to decide for them, as the majority describes, vital questions, including whether to consent to or refuse necessary medical treatment. . . .

Unless the legislature for specific purposes provides for a different age, a minor is one who has not attained legal age. It is not disputed that E.G. has not attained legal age. It is a fundamental that where language is clear there is no need to seek to interpret or depart from the plain language and meaning and read into what is clear exceptions or limitations. The majority nevertheless would in effect define a minor in these grave situations to be one who has not attained legal age unless it is a "mature" minor who is involved. If so this protection that the law gives minors has been lost and the child may make his own decision even at the cost of his life. The majority acknowledges that this is a case of first impression. It may now be critically described by some as a holding without precedent. I point out again that this is not a holding where consent to treatment is the question but rather a unique one where a minor's injury or very self-destruction may be involved.

I am sure that in a host of matters of far lesser importance it would not be held that a minor however mature could satisfy a requirement of being of legal age. It would not be held that a minor was eligible to vote, to obtain a driver's or a pilot's license, or to enlist in one of the armed services before attaining enlistment age.

The trial court appointed a guardian to consent to transfusions for the minor. The appellate court reversed as to this, stating the minor was a mature minor. This court affirms the appellate court in this regard but does not attempt to state a standard by which "mature" is to be measured by judges in making these important findings. . . .

NOTES AND QUESTIONS

(1) The majority in *In re E.G.* relies on Supreme Court decisions allowing a mature minor to obtain an abortion without the consent of her parents. Is the abortion analogy persuasive? Why or why not? For additional discussion of the Supreme Court's abortion decisions involving minors, see § 7.05[A], *below*.

(2) How significant was it to the majority that E.G.'s mother also opposed the blood transfusions? Where a parent consents to life-sustaining medical treatment, should a court ever allow a minor to refuse such treatment?

(3) The dissent in *In re E.G.* correctly points out that all minors, however mature, are subject to statutory age requirements "in a host of matters of far lesser importance" than the refusal to consent to life-saving medical treatment, including the right to vote, to purchase alcohol and tobacco and to enlist in the armed services. Do these statutory restrictions undermine the majority's analysis? Why or why not?

(4) What are the advantages and disadvantages of using a "bright-line" age-based rule to determine legal capacity to consent, as opposed to a case-by-case determination of maturity? Should the law recognize adolescence as a separate legal category, distinct from both childhood and full adulthood? For further discussion of these issues, *see* Elizabeth

Scott, N.D. Repucci & Jennifer Woolard, *Evaluating Adolescent Decisionmaking in Legal Contexts*, 19 Law & Human Behavior 221 (1995); Gary B. Melton, *Toward "Personhood" for Adolescents,* 38 American Psychologist 96 (Jan., 1983).

(5) If you were a trial judge attempting to determine whether a minor in E.G.'s position was sufficiently "mature" to refuse life-sustaining medical treatment, what questions would you ask? What kinds of information would you want the parties to present? For additional discussion of judicial determinations of maturity, see § 7.05[A], *below*.

(6) Many states have enacted statutes, similar to the one cited by the majority, that allow minors to consent to specific types of medical care, most commonly care related to birth control, pregnancy, venereal disease, and alcohol or substance abuse treatment. *See e.g.,* Minn. Stat. Ann. §§ 144.341–.347 (1997). Some states have enacted more general "mature minor" statutes that authorize consent to medical treatment by "any unemancipated minor of sufficient intelligence to understand and appreciate the consequences of the proposed surgical or medical treatment or procedures . . . ." Ark. Code Ann. § 20–9–602 (7) (1997). These statutes create exceptions to the common law rule that minors are generally considered incompetent to consent to their own medical treatment and that parental consent is ordinarily required for a child's medical care. *See* Homer H. Clark, Jr., The Law of Domestic Relations in the United States § 9.1, at 530–32 (2d ed. 1987). The rationale for many of these statutory exceptions is that requiring parental consent may discourage a minor from seeking treatment, thus jeopardizing both the minor's health and the welfare of the community. To what extent do theses statutes support the common law right of a mature minor to refuse life-sustaining medical treatment? *See* Jennifer L. Rosato, *The Ultimate Test of Autonomy: Should Minors Have a Right to Make Decisions Regarding Life-Sustaining Treatment?*, 49 Rutgers L. Rev. 1, 25–31 (1996).

§ 7.05 When Parent and Child Disagree: What Role for the State?

[A] Decisions About Reproduction

Cases involving minors' access to abortion pose a direct conflict between a minor's claims to autonomy and the parental interest in child-rearing—both of which the Supreme Court has indicated are entitled to constitutional protection. What is the appropriate role of the state in mediating this conflict? Can the state be neutral in this context?

BELLOTTI v. BAIRD
United States Supreme Court
443 U.S. 622 (1979)

POWELL, J.

[A Massachusetts statute requires parental consent before an abortion can be performed on an unmarried woman under the age of 18. If one or both parents refuse such consent, however, the abortion may be obtained by order of a judge of the superior court "for good cause shown." In appellees' class action challenging the constitutionality of the statute, a three-judge district court held it unconstitutional. The Supreme Court vacated the District Court's judgment, *Bellotti v. Baird,* 428 U.S. 132 (1976) holding that the district court should have abstained and certified to the Massachusetts Supreme Judicial Court appropriate questions concerning the meaning of the statute. On remand, the district court certified several questions to the Supreme Judicial Court. Among the questions certified was whether the statute permits any minors—mature or immature—to obtain judicial consent to an abortion without any parental consultation whatsoever. The Supreme Judicial Court answered that, in general, it does not; that consent must be obtained for every nonemergency abortion unless no parent is available; and that an available parent must be given notice of any judicial proceedings brought by a minor to obtain consent for an abortion. Another question certified was whether, if the superior court finds that the minor is capable of making, and has, in fact, made and adhered to, an informed and reasonable decision to have an abortion, the court may refuse its consent on a finding that a parent's, or its own, contrary decision is a better one. The Supreme Judicial Court answered in the affirmative. Following the Supreme Judicial Court's judgment, the district court again declared the statute unconstitutional and enjoined its enforcement.] . . .

II

A child, merely on account of his minority, is not beyond the protection of the Constitution. . . . This observation, of course, is but the beginning of the analysis. The Court long has recognized that the status of minors under the law is unique in many respects. As Mr. Justice Frankfurter aptly put it: "Children have a very special place in life which law should reflect. Legal theories and their phrasing in other cases readily lead to fallacious reasoning if uncritically transferred to determination of a State's duty towards children." *May v. Anderson*, 345 U.S. 528, 536 (1953) (concurring opinion). The unique role in our society of the family, the institution by which "we inculcate and pass down many of our most cherished values, moral and cultural," *Moore v. East Cleveland*, 431 U.S. 494, 503–504 (1977) (plurality opinion), requires that constitutional principles be applied with sensitivity and flexibility to the special needs of parents and children. We have recognized three reasons justifying the conclusion that the constitutional rights of children cannot be equated with those of adults: the peculiar vulnerability of children; their inability to make critical decisions in an informed, mature manner; and the importance of the parental role in child rearing.

A

The Court's concern for the vulnerability of children is demonstrated in its decisions dealing with minors' claims to constitutional protection against deprivations of liberty or property interests by the State. With respect to many of these claims, we have concluded that the child's right is virtually coextensive with that of an adult. For example, the Court has held that the Fourteenth Amendment's guarantee against the deprivation of liberty without due process of law is applicable to children in juvenile delinquency proceedings. *In re Gault, above*. In particular, minors involved in such proceedings are entitled to adequate notice, the assistance of counsel, and the opportunity to confront their accusers. They can be found guilty only upon proof beyond a reasonable doubt, and they may assert the privilege against compulsory self-incrimination. *In re Winship*, 397 U.S. 358 (1970). Similarly, in *Goss v. Lopez*, 419 U.S. 565 (1975), the Court held that children may not be deprived of certain property interests without due process.

These rulings have not been made on the uncritical assumption that the constitutional rights of children are indistinguishable from those of adults. Indeed, our acceptance of juvenile courts distinct from the adult criminal justice system assumes that juvenile offenders constitutionally may be treated differently from adults. In order to preserve this separate avenue for dealing with minors, the Court has said that hearings in juvenile delinquency cases need not necessarily " 'conform with all of the requirements of a criminal trial or even of the usual administrative hearing.' " *In re Gault, above* , at 30, *quoting Kent v. United States*, 383 U.S. 541, 562 (1966). Thus, juveniles are not constitutionally entitled to trial by jury in delinquency adjudications. *McKeiver v. Pennsylvania*, 403 U.S. 528 (1971). Viewed together, our cases show that although children generally are protected by the same constitutional guarantees against governmental deprivations as are adults, the State is entitled to adjust its legal system to account for children's vulnerability and their needs for "concern, . . . sympathy, and . . . paternal attention." *Id.*, at 550 (plurality opinion).

B

Second, the Court has held that the States validly may limit the freedom of children to choose for themselves in the making of important, affirmative choices with potentially serious consequences. These rulings have been grounded in the recognition that, during the formative years of childhood and adolescence, minors often lack the experience, perspective, and judgment to recognize and avoid choices that could be detrimental to them.

Ginsberg v. New York, 390 U.S. 629 (1968), illustrates well the Court's concern over the inability of children to make mature choices, as the First Amendment rights involved are clear examples of constitutionally protected freedoms of choice. At issue was a criminal conviction for selling sexually oriented magazines to a minor under the age of 17 in violation of a New York state law. It was conceded that the conviction could not have stood under the First Amendment if based upon a sale of the same material to an adult. *Id.*, at 634. Notwithstanding the importance the Court always has attached to First Amendment rights, it concluded that "even where there is an invasion of protected freedoms 'the power of the state to control the conduct of children reaches beyond the scope of its authority over adults . . . ,' " *id.*, at 638, *quoting Prince v. Massachusetts*, 321 U.S. 158, 170 (1944). The Court was convinced that the New York Legislature rationally could conclude that the sale to children of the magazines in question presented a danger against which they should be guarded. *Ginsberg, above* , at 641. It therefore rejected the argument that the New York law violated the constitutional rights of minors.

C

Third, the guiding role of parents in the upbringing of their children justifies limitations on the freedoms of minors. The State commonly protects its youth from adverse governmental action and from their own immaturity by requiring parental consent to or involvement in important decisions by minors. But an additional and more important justification for state deference to parental control over children is that "[the] child is not the mere creature of the State; those who nurture him and direct his destiny have the right, coupled with the high duty, to recognize and prepare him for additional obligations." *Pierce v. Society of Sisters*, 268 U.S. 510, 535 (1925). "The duty to prepare the child for 'additional obligations' . . . must be read to include the inculcation of moral standards, religious beliefs, and elements of good citizenship." *Wisconsin v. Yoder*, 406 U.S. 205, 233 (1972). This affirmative process of teaching, guiding, and inspiring by precept and example is essential to the growth of young people into mature, socially responsible citizens.

We have believed in this country that this process, in large part, is beyond the competence of impersonal political institutions. Indeed, affirmative sponsorship of particular ethical, religious, or political beliefs is something we expect the State not to attempt in a society constitutionally committed to the ideal of individual liberty and freedom of choice. Thus, "[it] is cardinal with us that the custody, care and nurture of the child reside first in the parents, whose primary function and freedom include preparation for obligations the state can neither supply nor hinder." *Prince v. Massachusetts, above*, at 166 (emphasis added).

Unquestionably, there are many competing theories about the most effective way for parents to fulfill their central role in assisting their children on the way to responsible adulthood. While we do not pretend any special wisdom on this subject, we cannot ignore that central to many of these theories, and deeply rooted in our Nation's history and tradition, is the belief that the parental role implies a substantial measure of authority over one's children. Indeed, "constitutional interpretation has consistently recognized that the parents' claim to authority in their own household to direct the rearing of their children is basic in the structure of our society." *Ginsberg v. New York, above*, at 639.

Properly understood, then, the tradition of parental authority is not inconsistent with our tradition of individual liberty; rather, the former is one of the basic presuppositions of the latter. Legal restrictions on minors, especially those supportive of the parental role, may be important to the child's chances for the full growth and maturity that make eventual participation in a free society meaningful and rewarding. Under the Constitution, the State can "properly conclude that parents and others, teachers for example, who have [the] primary responsibility for children's well-being are entitled to the support of laws designed to aid discharge of that responsibility." *Ginsberg v. New York*, 390 U.S., at 639.

III

With these principles in mind, we consider the specific constitutional questions presented by these appeals. In § 12S, Massachusetts has attempted to reconcile the constitutional right of a woman, in consultation with her physician, to choose to terminate her pregnancy as established by *Roe v. Wade*, 410 U.S. 113 (1973), and *Doe v. Bolton*, 410 U.S. 179 (1973), with the special interest of the State in encouraging an unmarried pregnant minor to seek the advice of her parents in making the important decision whether or not to bear a child. As noted above, § 12S was before us in *Bellotti I*, 428 U.S. 132 (1976), where we remanded the case for interpretation of its provisions by the Supreme Judicial Court of Massachusetts. We previously had held in *Planned Parenthood of Central Missouri v. Danforth*, 428 U.S. 52 (1976), that a State could not lawfully authorize an absolute parental veto over the decision of a minor to terminate her pregnancy. Id., at 74. In *Bellotti I*, above, we recognized that § 12S could be read as "fundamentally different from a statute that creates a 'parental veto,' " 428 U.S., at 145, thus "[avoiding] or substantially [modifying] the federal constitutional challenge to the statute." Id., at 148. The question before us—in light of what we have said in the prior cases—is whether § 12S, as authoritatively interpreted by the Supreme Judicial Court, provides for parental notice and consent in a manner that does not unduly burden the right to seek an abortion. *See id.*, at 147.

Appellees and intervenors contend that even as interpreted by the Supreme Judicial Court of Massachusetts § 12S does unduly burden this right. They suggest, for example, that the mere requirement of parental notice constitutes such a burden. As stated in Part II above, however, parental notice and consent are qualifications that typically may be imposed by the State on a minor's right to make important decisions. As immature minors often lack the ability to make fully informed choices that take account of both immediate and long-range consequences, a State reasonably may determine that parental consultation often is desirable and in the best interest of the minor. It may further determine, as a general proposition, that such consultation is particularly desirable with respect to the abortion decision—one that for some people raises profound moral and religious concerns. . . .

But we are concerned here with a constitutional right to seek an abortion. The abortion decision differs in important ways from other decisions that may be made during minority. The need to preserve the constitutional right and the unique nature of the abortion decision, especially when made by a minor, require a State to act with particular sensitivity when it legislates to foster parental involvement in this matter. . . .

The pregnant minor's options are much different from those facing a minor in other situations, such as deciding whether to marry. A minor not permitted to marry before the age of majority is required simply to postpone her decision. She and her intended spouse may preserve the opportunity for later marriage should they continue to desire it. A pregnant adolescent, however, cannot preserve for long the possibility of aborting, which effectively expires in a matter of weeks from the onset of pregnancy.

Moreover, the potentially severe detriment facing a pregnant woman, *see Roe v. Wade*, 410 U.S., at 153, is not mitigated by her minority. Indeed, considering her probable education, employment skills, financial resources, and emotional maturity, unwanted motherhood may be exceptionally burdensome for a minor. In addition, the fact of having a child brings with it adult legal responsibility, for parenthood, like attainment of the age of majority, is one of the traditional criteria for the termination of the legal disabilities of minority. In sum, there are few situations in which denying a minor the right to make an important decision will have consequences so grave and indelible. . . .

For these reasons, as we held in *Planned Parenthood of Central Missouri v. Danforth*, 428 U.S., at 74, "the State may not impose a blanket provision . . . requiring the consent of a parent or person in loco parentis as a condition for abortion of an unmarried minor during the first 12 weeks of her pregnancy." Although, as stated in Part II, above, such deference to parents may be permissible with respect to other choices facing a minor, the unique nature and consequences of the abortion decision make it inappropriate "to give a third party an absolute, and possibly arbitrary, veto over the decision of the physician and his patient to terminate the patient's pregnancy, regardless of the reason for withholding the consent." 428 U.S., at 74. We therefore conclude that if the State decides to require a pregnant minor to obtain one or both parents' consent to an abortion, it also must provide an alternative procedure whereby authorization for the abortion can be obtained.

A pregnant minor is entitled in such a proceeding to show either: (1) that she is mature enough and well enough informed to make her abortion decision, in consultation with her physician, independently of her parents' wishes; or (2) that even if she is not able to make this decision independently, the desired abortion would be in her best interests. The proceeding in which this showing is made must assure that a resolution of the issue, and any appeals that may follow, will be completed with anonymity and sufficient expedition to provide an effective opportunity for an abortion to be obtained. In sum, the procedure must ensure that the provision requiring parental consent does not in fact amount to the "absolute, and possibly arbitrary, veto" that was found impermissible in *Danforth*. . . .

We conclude, therefore, that under state regulation such as that undertaken by Massachusetts, every minor must have the opportunity—if she so desires—to go directly to a court without first consulting or notifying her parents. If she satisfies the court that she is mature and well enough informed to make intelligently the abortion decision on her own, the court must authorize her to act without parental consultation or consent. If she fails to satisfy the court that she is competent to make this decision independently, she must be permitted to show that an abortion nevertheless would be in her best interests. If the court is persuaded that it is, the court must authorize the abortion. If, however, the court is not persuaded by the minor that she is mature or that the abortion would be in her best interests, it may decline to sanction the operation. . . .

Although it satisfies constitutional standards in large part, § 12S falls short of them in two respects: First, it permits judicial authorization for an abortion to be withheld from a minor who is found by the superior court to be mature and fully competent to make this decision independently. Second, it requires parental consultation or notification in every instance, without affording the pregnant minor an opportunity to receive an independent judicial determination that she is mature enough to consent or that an abortion would be in her best interests. Accordingly, we affirm the judgment of the District Court insofar as it invalidates this statute and enjoins its enforcement.

NOTES AND QUESTIONS

(1) Is a decision regarding abortion more important to a child's development and life plan than a decision to remove that child from school after the 8th grade? Does the majority in *Bellotti* essentially adopt Justice Douglas' partial dissent in *Wisconsin v. Yoder* [reprinted at § 7.02, *above*]?

(2) **Determinations of Maturity.** If a minor utilizes the judicial bypass procedure, how is a judge to determine whether she is mature enough to make the abortion decision independently of her parents' wishes? Is maturity a matter of cognition: that is, awareness of the medical and psychological risks involved? If so, most studies suggest that adolescents process the abortion decision as effectively as adults. *See, e.g.*, Bruce Ambuel & Julian Rappoport, *Developmental Trends in Adolescents' Psychological and Legal Competence to Consent to Abortion*, 16 L. & Human Behav. 129 (1992) (finding that adolescents under 15 who consider abortion are as competent as young adults to make the decision); Victoria Foster & Norman A. Sprinhall, *Developmental Profiles of Adolescents and Young Adults Choosing Abortion: Stage Sequences, Decalage, and Implications for Policy*, 27 Adolescence 655 (1992) (finding no statistically significant differences in the abortion decision-making processes of 12-to 14-year-olds, 17-to 19-year-olds and 23-to 25-year-olds); American Psychological Association, Interdivisional Committee on Adolescent Abortion, *Adolescent Abortion: Psychological and Legal Issues,*, 42 American Psychologist 73 (Jan. 1987) (psychological theory and empirical research indicate that by mid-adolescence, minors are as capable as are adults of conceptualizing and reasoning about medical decisions, including abortion).

Are there other components to maturity besides cognition and deliberation? In *H.B. v. Wilkinson*, 639 F. Supp. 952, 954 (D. Utah 1986), a federal district court analyzed the meaning of maturity under *Bellotti*:

> Manifestly, as related to a minor's abortion decision, maturity is not solely a matter of social skills, level of intelligence or verbal skills. More importantly, it calls for experience, perspective and judgment. As to experience, the minor's prior work experience, experience in living away from home, and handling personal finances are some of the pertinent inquiries. Perspective calls for appreciation and understanding of the relative gravity and possible detrimental impact of each available option, as well as realistic perception and assessment of possible short term and long term consequences of each of those options, particularly the abortion option. Judgment is of very great importance in determining maturity. The exercise of good judgment requires being fully informed so as to be able to weigh alternatives independently and realistically. Among other things, the minor's conduct is a measure of good judgment. Factors such as stress and ignorance of alternatives have been recognized as impediments to the exercise of proper judgment by minors, who because of those factors "may not be able intelligently to decide whether to have . . . an abortion." [Citation omitted.] Experience, perspective and judgment are often lacking in unemancipated minors who are wholly dependent and have never lived away from home or had any significant employment experience.

Applying this analysis, the court found that a 17-year-old pregnant minor (whom the court described as a "very good" student) was immature and therefore subject to a statutory requirement of parental notification. The court described the following facts as relevant to its decision: the young woman lived at home and had never been regularly employed; she was financially dependent on her parents and expected them to help pay for her college education; her parents were loving and concerned with her well-being; she engaged in sexual activity with her boyfriend without using contraception even though she did not intend to become pregnant; she believed that she could easily obtain an abortion and deal with any medical complications without her parents knowledge; she sought counsel from friends and peers, rather than from adult family members, relatives or church officials; her initial demeanor at the hearing was characterized by nervousness and apparent stress; her decision to seek an abortion was based in part on a desire to conceal her sexual activity and pregnancy from her parents; and she failed to give due consideration to the possibility of post-abortion depression. Based on these facts, the court concluded that the young woman was "immature, lacking the experience, perspective and judgment to recognize and avoid choices which could be detrimental to herself." *Id.* at 958.

Do you agree with the court's reasoning? Would most adolescents be found immature under this analysis? *See also In Petition of Anonymous*, 558 N.W. 2d 784 (Neb. 1997) (13-year-old minor who had never lived on her own or held employment other than a summer job and who was unable to communicate a sufficient understanding of the risks associated with abortion did not demonstrate "a level of experience, perspective, or judgment sufficient to allow this court to consider her mature").

Is it appropriate for a court to consider a minor's past conduct in assessing her maturity to make an independent abortion decision? In *In re Jane Doe*, 566 N.E.2d 1181 (Ohio 1991) the Ohio Supreme Court affirmed the conclusion of a trial court that a 17-year-old high school senior had failed to demonstrate sufficient maturity to make an independent abortion decision. The minor was a good student who planned to go to college. Although she lived at home with her parents, she had worked at various jobs since she was 16. A physician testified that the minor understood the risks of the abortion procedure. In upholding the trial court's decision, the Ohio Supreme Court stated:

> . . . [Appellant] testified that she had an abortion in June 1990, and is seeking to have another one performed less than a year later. Moreover, appellant testified that each pregnancy was the result of intercourse with a different man. In addition, Dr. Rauh testified that appellant was on a program of birth control, but discontinued it. In light of the foregoing testimony, it was not unreasonable, arbitrary or unconscionable for the trial judge to dismiss the complaint by essentially finding that appellant did not prove her "maturity" allegation by clear and convincing evidence.

Does the approach taken in cases such as *In re Jane Doe* and *Wilkinson* allow too much latitude for judges' own views on abortion and teenage sexual behavior to influence decisions regarding maturity? Is such influence inevitable? For further discussion and critique of judicial approaches to determining maturity in the abortion context, *see* Wallace J. Mlyniec, *A Judge's Ethical Dilemma: Assessing A Child's Capacity To Choose*, 64 Fordham L. Rev. 1873, 1889–91 (1996); Erin Daly, *Reconsidering Abortion Law: Liberty, Equality and the New Rhetoric of Planned Parenthood v. Casey*, 45 Am. U.L. Rev. 77, 109–11 (1995); Steven F. Stuhlbarg, *Note, When is a Pregnant Minor Mature? When is an Abortion in Her Best Interest? The Ohio Supreme Court Applies Ohio's Abortion Parental Notification Law: In re Jane Doe I*, 60 U. Cinn. L. Rev. 907, 932 (1991).

(3) Empirical evidence strongly suggests that judicial findings of immaturity in connection with bypass proceedings are the exception rather than the rule. Out of 477 judicial assessments for authorization for abortions in Massachusetts between December 1981 and June 1985, only nine minors were found to be immature. Susanne Yates & Anita J. Pliner, *Judging Maturity in the Courts: The Massachusetts Consent Statute*, 78 Am. J. Pub. Health 646, 647 (1988). A study of Minnesota's judicial bypass procedure yielded similar results. The study found that, of 3,573 petitions filed over a five-year period by minors seeking court authorization for abortions, 3,558 were granted, 9 were denied and 6 were withdrawn. Margaret C. Crosby & Abigail English, *Mandatory Parental Involvement/Judicial Bypass Laws: Do They Promote Adolescent Health?* 12 J. Adolescent Health 143, 145 (1991). Do these results suggest that virtually all adolescents are competent to make their own abortion decisions? That those adolescents who petition for court authorization are unusually competent? *Cf. Ex parte Anonymous*, 595 So. 2d 497, 499 (Ala. 1992) (noting that "a minor's voluntary decision to use the judicial process and request for advice of legal counsel may, in itself, indicate maturity"). Or do these studies provide evidence that judges are uncomfortable making decisions about abortions, despite the requirement in *Bellotti* that they do so?

(4) **The Dilemma of Immaturity.** Under the *Bellotti* framework, a judge who decides that a pregnant minor lacks sufficient maturity to make an independent abortion decision must still allow the desired abortion if it would be in the minor's best interests. Under what circumstances would it be in the best interests of an immature minor to insist that she carry an unwanted pregnancy to term?

(5) **Parental Notification Requirements.** In *H.L. v. Matheson*, 450 U.S. 398 (1981), the Court considered the constitutionality of a Utah statute that required physicians to "notify

if possible" the parents of a "dependent, unmarried minor" prior to performing an abortion on the minor. The Court upheld the notification requirement as applied to immature and dependent minors. Justice Burger, writing for the majority, emphasized that the statute did not give parents a veto power and that, as applied to immature and dependent minors, it served important state considerations of family integrity and protecting adolescents. The Court refused to consider the constitutionality of the notification requirement as applied to mature minors, since the plaintiff had failed to present any evidence of her maturity.

More recently, in *Hodgson v. Minnesota*, 497 U.S. 417 (1990), the Court, in a splintered decision, upheld a Minnesota statute requiring that a minor wait 48 hours after both parents had been notified before obtaining an abortion. Under the statute, the notice and waiting period could be waived in emergency situations or if the young woman declared herself to be the victim of parental abuse—in which case the statute required that notice of the abuse allegations be given to the appropriate state authorities. The Court upheld the statutory waiting period, reasoning that the requirement reasonably furthered "the legitimate state interest in ensuring that the minor's decision is knowing and intelligent." By contrast, a majority of five justices found that the requirement that *both parents* be notified of the abortion was *not* reasonable, and represented an unconstitutional burden on the minor's right to obtain an abortion. That majority reasoned that, when parents are divorced or the family is otherwise fractured, the two-parent notification requirement not only fails to serve any legitimate state interests, but could inflict harm on the pregnant minor. However, a different majority of five justices held that any constitutional objection to the two-parent notice requirement was removed by the availability of a judicial by-pass procedure that allowed the minor to avoid notifying one or both parents. Thus, the Court ruled that the overall statute was constitutional.

Query: What interests are promoted by a parental notification requirement? Will such a requirement promote family unity? Reinforce parental authority? Result in more informed decision-making by adolescents? Deter sexual activity by teenagers? *See generally* Gary B. Melton & Anita J. Plimer, *Adolescent Abortion: A Psycholegal Analysis*, in Adolescent Abortion: Psychological and Legal Issues 1, 25 (Gary B. Melton, ed. 1986).

(6) Could a state constitutionally give parents the power to *compel* a child to obtain an abortion? May parents stop supporting a child financially because they disapprove of her decision to carry a pregnancy to term? *See, e.g., Matter of Mary P.*, 444 N.Y.S.2d 545 (N.Y. Fam. Ct. 1981) (mother of pregnant 15-year-old could not use the family court system to compel her daughter to obtain an abortion); *In re Smith*, 295 A.2d 238 (Md. Ct. App. 1972) (juvenile court has jurisdiction to order a runaway teen to return to her mother's home, but not to order the young woman to obey her mother in submitting to an abortion, because of state statute giving minors the capacity to consent to medical treatment concerning pregnancy).

(7) **Minors' Access to Contraceptives.** In *Carey v. Population Servs. Int'l*, 431 U.S. 678, 678, (1997), the Supreme Court struck down a New York statute that made it a crime for anyone to distribute contraceptives to minors under the age of 16. Writing for a plurality of the Court, Justice Blackmun relied heavily on the Court's decision in *Planned Parenthood v. Danforth*, 428 U.S. 52 (1976), invalidating a state requirement of parental consent for abortion:

> Since the State may not impose a blanket prohibition, or even a blanket requirement of parental consent, on the choice of a minor to terminate her pregnancy, the

constitutionality of a blanket prohibition of the distribution of contraceptives to minors is *a fortiori* foreclosed. The State's interests in protection of the mental and physical health of the pregnant minor, and in protection of potential life are clearly more implicated by the abortion decision than by the decision to use a nonhazardous contraceptive. 431 U.S. at 694.

Justice Powell concurred in finding the statute unconstitutional but rejected the plurality's rationale that restricting minors' access to contraceptives violated a fundamental right of minors to make reproductive decisions. Instead, Powell relied on the statute's infringement of *parental* authority:

> . . . [T]his provision prohibits parents from distributing contraceptives to their children, a restriction that unjustifiably interferes with parental interests in rearing their children. . . . Moreover, this statute would allow the State to "to enquire, prove and punish," *Poe v. Ullman*, 367 U.S. 497, 585 (1961) (Harlan, J., dissenting), the exercise of this parental responsibility. The State points to no interests of sufficient magnitude to justify this direct interference with the parental guidance that is especially appropriate in this sensitive area of child development.

431 U.S. at 708 (Powell, J., concurring). Justice Stevens also concurred in the judgment, while objecting to the plurality's reasoning. Stevens opined that the state has a significant interest in discouraging sexual activity among unmarred persons under the age of 16. He concluded, however, that restricting access to contraception was an "irrational and perverse" means of furthering this goal. *Id.* at 715 (Stevens, J., concurring).

(8) **Problem.** In 1983, the Department of Health and Human Services promulgated a regulation under Title X of the Public Health Services Act that required federally funded family planning clinics to notify parents within 10 days when unemancipated minors obtained prescription contraceptives. The regulation generated considerable controversy, and it was withdrawn after two federal courts of appeal held that it was inconsistent with the statutory purpose of making family planning services available to sexually active adolescents and preventing unwanted pregnancies among this group. *Planned Parenthood Federation of American v. Heckler*, 712 F.2d 650 (D.C. Cir. 1983); *New York v. Heckler*, 719 F.2d 1191 (2d Cir. 1983). Neither court addressed the question whether the regulation unconstitutionally burdened the rights of affected minors. How would you analyze that constitutional question?

[B] Children Beyond Parental Control

To what extent should parents be able to invoke the authority of the state to control unruly or disobedient children? Conversely, should children ever be able to invoke state authority to remove themselves from parental control? The materials that follow consider these questions.

R. J. D. v. VAUGHAN CLINIC, P.C.
Supreme Court of Alabama
572 So. 2d 1225 (1990)

MADDOX, J.,

This appeal involves the question whether a custodial parent has the right to have her 17-year-old minor child admitted into a private psychiatric hospital against the minor child's will and without her consent. The issue presented on appeal is whether a private physician and private hospital that admit and hold such a minor child against the child's will, but based on the request and consent of the custodial parent, can be held liable for either false imprisonment or for violating the minor's civil rights.

FACTS

Mr. D. and Mrs. D., parents of the plaintiff, R. J. D., were divorced in Marshall County, Alabama, in 1979. The court awarded the mother, Mrs. D., the care, custody, and control of R. J. D., then 12 years of age. R. J. D. lived with her mother in Birmingham, Alabama until certain events occurred that ultimately led to the subject controversy. On November 13, 1984, five years after she was awarded custody, Mrs. D. filed a complaint with the Family Court of Jefferson County alleging that R. J. D., then 17 years of age, had left home and was in need of supervision.

The Jefferson County Family Court held a hearing on the mother's petition, and granted custody of R. J. D. to her mother, who immediately had R. J. D. admitted into Children's Hospital. Although R. J. D. refused to consent to her admission, Dr. Gary Grayson, a psychiatrist employed with Vaughan Clinic admitted R. J. D. into Children's Hospital, based on her mother's request and consent, and placed R. J. D. in the secure ward of the adolescent care unit. Two weeks later, on December 5, 1984, R. J. D.'s father smuggled her out.

On November 15, 1985, while still a minor, R. J. D., by and through her father, filed this action against Vaughan Clinic, Children's Hospital and Dr. Grayson, alleging medical malpractice, breach of contract, false imprisonment, and outrage, and seeking damages pursuant to 42 U.S.C. § 1983 for civil rights violations. . . .

We must determine whether the trial court correctly entered summary judgment on the minor's false imprisonment and federal civil rights claims. To determine that, we initially must examine the underlying question of the legal right of a parent to determine what is in the best interest of a child regarding the necessity for psychiatric care.

I

We first address the question of the propriety of the defendants' summary judgment on the plaintiff's false imprisonment claim. As defined in Alabama, "false imprisonment consists in the unlawful detention of the person of another for any length of time whereby he is deprived of his personal liberty." Ala. Code 1975, § 6–5–170.

It is undisputed that R. J. D. was admitted to Vaughan Clinic by Dr. Grayson against her will and without her consent; consequently, there is no dispute concerning the basic facts, the only dispute being over the right of a custodial parent to determine the medical needs of a 17-year-old unemancipated child regardless of the wishes of the child.

A child, like an adult, has a substantial liberty interest in not being confined unnecessarily for medical treatment, but Alabama has long recognized the principle that parents are, by the common law, under the legal duty of providing medical attention for their children.

This Court has found no Alabama cases directly applicable to the facts in this case, and the legislature has not addressed the question of the legal rights of a child under the circumstances presented here, the voluntary admission of a minor child by a custodial parent to a psychiatric unit. Consequently, absent alteration by the legislature, the common law is controlling.

The parents' common law duty to care for their children is widely recognized:

> It is ordinarily for the parent in the first instance to decide . . . what is actually necessary for the protection and preservation of the life and health of his child, so long as he acts as a reasonable and ordinarily prudent parent would act in a like situation. (59 Am.Jur.2d Parent and Child § 48, at 193–94 (1987)).

Alabama is among the many states that respect this common law duty. Thus, in order to address adequately R. J. D.'s false imprisonment claim, the Court must necessarily consider the common law duty and the right of parents to provide for the care and health of their children. Under the common law it is not the child's consent to such care that controls. Rather, it is the parents' common law right and duty to provide for the well-being of their children that prevail. . . .

The United States Supreme Court followed this common law rule in *Parham v. J.R.*, 442 U.S. 584 (1979). In *Parham*, minor children receiving treatment in the Georgia state mental hospitals challenged the commitment procedures that allowed parents to commit their minor children without first obtaining their consent. The Supreme Court there aptly addressed the common law rights and duties of parents:

> Our jurisprudence historically has reflected Western civilization concepts of the family as a unit with broad parental authority over minor children. Our cases have consistently followed that course; our constitutional system long ago rejected any notion that a child is "the mere creature of the State" and, on the contrary, asserted that parents generally "have the right, coupled with the high duty, to recognize and prepare [their children] for additional obligations." *Pierce v. Society of Sisters*, 268 U.S. 510 (1925). . . . Surely, this includes a "high duty" to recognize symptoms of illness and to seek and follow medical advice. The law's concept of the family rests on a presumption that parents possess what a child lacks in maturity, experience, and capacity for judgment required for making life's difficult decisions. More important, historically it has recognized that natural bonds of affection lead parents to act in the best interests of their children. . . .
>
> That some parents "may at times be acting against the interests of their children" . . . creates a basis for caution, but is hardly a reason to discard wholesale those pages of human experience that teach that parents generally do act in the child's best interest. . . . That statist notion that governmental power should supersede parental authority in all cases because some parents abuse and neglect children is repugnant to American tradition. (442 U.S. at 602–603).

Although *Parham* involved the commitment of children to a state institution, the principle of law applied there would be the same when the commitment is voluntary and is to a private facility; therefore, the common law right and duty of parents to care for their children would apply to the facts in this case. The mere fact that R. J. D.'s mother decided to admit her into Children's Hospital without R. J. D.'s consent and against her will, would not automatically dictate the transfer of authority to make that decision from her mother to either R. J. D. or the State. There is no indication in the record that the action of R. J. D.'s mother would authorize a finding of neglect or abuse on the mother's part. Therefore, we hold that the authority and duty to care for R. J. D. rested solely with her mother, who had been given the care, custody, and control of R. J. D.

There are strong policy reasons for our holding. Parents are entrusted with providing for the best interest of their children. The law, in fact, authorizes both civil remedies and criminal penalties in cases of child neglect or child abuse. In order that parents may fulfill the duty the law places on them to provide for their children, the law allows them the authority to give the necessary consent for admitting their children into a health care facility. In view of the parental obligations to provide for the health care needs of children, and in view of the common law right of parents to exercise broad authority over their children, health care providers should be able to rely on a parent's consent when admitting a minor child into their care and should feel confident in relying upon that consent in detaining minor children for the purpose of treatment, for either physical or mental infirmities.

In view of these policy considerations and the principles of the common law, which we must apply, we hold that the trial court did not err in finding that none of the defendants "unlawfully detained" R. J. D. in treating her, because the evidence is clear that each defendant admitted R. J. D. and provided treatment for her in reliance upon her mother's consent. We hold, therefore, that, with respect to R. J. D.'s claim based on an alleged false imprisonment, the trial court properly entered summary judgment in favor of Vaughan Clinic, Children's Hospital, and Dr. Grayson. . . .

ADAMS, J. (concurring in part; dissenting in part).

I respectfully dissent from that portion of the opinion affirming the summary judgment on the issue of false imprisonment. The majority holds, in effect, that a custodial parent has an absolute right to have a 17-year-old minor child admitted into a private psychiatric hospital against her will and without her consent. Such was not the law in this state, nor, to my knowledge, in any other state, until today. An understanding of the import of this decision requires a fuller exposition of the facts than has been provided to us by the majority.

While a student at Homewood High School in the fall of 1984, R.J.D. began associating with a man who was her senior by some seven years. Her mother attempted to stop the association. On November 17, 1984, allegedly to resolve the conflict with her mother, R.J.D. voluntarily entered Hillcrest Hospital for drug screening and underwent "psychotherapeutic" treatment and counseling under the supervision of Dr. S. David Morrison. On November 21, Hillcrest released R.J.D. with a recommendation of no medication and no follow-up.

On the day of her release, R.J.D. was escorted by Mrs. D. and her private investigators to Brookwood Hospital for an interview with another psychiatrist. Immediately after that interview, R.J.D. was escorted to the Jefferson County Family Court for a hearing on her need for psychiatric treatment. The court appointed Raymond Chambliss as R.J.D.'s guardian ad litem in the matter, and the hearing was held before a referee. At the conclusion of the hearing, the referee, also recommending no treatment, released R.J.D.

However, immediately after the hearing, Mrs. D. and her private investigators escorted R.J.D. to Children's Hospital. Dr. Gary Grayson, with knowledge of the proceedings just concluded in the family court, and over R.J.D.'s objections, admitted her for treatment. During her stay in Children's Hospital, R.J.D. was placed in a "secure ward," with restricted access to a telephone. R.J.D. alleges that when she asked how long she would have to remain at the hospital, she was told that she would stay as "long as someone was footing the bill."

Mr. Chambliss, the court-appointed guardian ad litem, visited the hospital and attempted to speak with R.J.D. However, hospital officials not only refused to allow him to speak with his client but also refused to supply him with any information concerning her status. On December 5, 1984, she escaped with her father through means of a ruse, and she later commenced this suit.

An action based on false imprisonment will lie whenever one is unwillingly subjected to a "restraint upon [his] freedom . . . without proper legal authority." W. Keeton, D. Dobbs, R. Keeton & D. Owen, Prosser and Keeton on the Law of Torts § 11 (5th ed. 1984) (emphasis added). Thus, one who restrains another does so at his own peril. *Id.* The good faith of the defendant is not a defense to a false imprisonment claim where the restraint is eventually found to have been without sufficient authority. *Id.*

As a general rule, decisions regarding medical or psychiatric treatment of minor children are the responsibility of the parents. H. Clark, The Law of Domestic Relations in the United States § 9.3 (2d ed. 1988). Nevertheless, the "general principle is obviously not absolute even where the child is not capable of making a decision about his own treatment. It is limited by the power of the state to intercede for the protection of the child's health, safety or welfare." *Id.* Indeed, the state, as parens patriae, holds an inherent and substantial interest in the welfare and protection of its minors. Through this interest, the authority of the state often supersedes that of all others, including that of the parents.

For these same reasons, Alabama requires the appointment of a guardian ad litem to represent a child defendant whenever, as in this case, the interests of the parent "conflict with those of the child." Ala. Code 1975, § 12–15–8(a). Once the parens patriae power of the state has been invoked and a guardian ad litem has been duly appointed, no party may disregard the action of the state in the very matter that required the appointment. In other words, a child is "absolutely entitled to the benefits" of her guardian ad litem at all times pertinent to the proceedings for which the appointment was made. *Ridgeway v. Strickling*, 442 So. 2d 106 (Ala. Civ. App. 1983) (emphasis added). . . .

In this case, the largely undisputed facts reveal that R.J.D. was hurriedly ushered out of the courtroom and involuntarily admitted, despite the fact that a referee had just found no treatment to be necessary. Even more significantly, she was denied access to her guardian ad litem when he attempted to visit her in the hospital in connection with the matter of her need for treatment. Under Alabama law regarding the representation of minor defendants, neither Mrs. D. nor the defendants, acting at her behest, had the authority to place such restrictions on R.J.D. It appears that Mrs. D., in seeking a place in which to incarcerate her daughter, had, at last, found these defendants who were willing to serve as collaborators in R.J.D.'s improper restraint. . . .

At best, the majority opinion will stand merely as an aberration in Alabama law. At worst, it will encourage individuals in the position of these defendants to disregard the interest of this state in the health and welfare of its minors and to flout with impunity judicial authority and legal process. For these reasons, I respectfully dissent in part.

NOTES AND QUESTIONS

(1) Is the analysis of the majority in *R.J.D.* consistent with the Supreme Court's holding in *Bellotti*? Why or why not?

(2) Under the dissent's analysis, could a teenager whose parents had "grounded" her as a disciplinary measure (i.e. refused to let her leave the house) plausibly sue for false imprisonment? Why or why not?

(3) Evidence suggests that a large proportion of children hospitalized in psychiatric facilities are considered "troublemakers" who disobey their parents, run away from home, skip school, take drugs and engage in sexual activity. Some may even present a physical threat to persons or property or a psychological threat to family stability. *See* Lois A. Weithorn, *Mental Hospitalization of Troublesome Youth: An Analysis of Skyrocketing Admissions Rates*, 40 Stan. L. Rev. 773, 772 (1988). This analysis suggests that, for many of the children who are institutionalized, it might have been possible for the state to intervene in the young person's life through the juvenile court. Indeed, Mrs. D tried unsuccessfully to invoke the authority of the family court to order R.J.D. committed for treatment. In most states, the juvenile court has broad discretion to intervene in the lives of minors whose behavior either violates criminal statutes (thus subjecting them to a finding of delinquency), or whose behavior, while not criminal, indicates that they are "in need of supervision." Juveniles whose behavior falls within the latter category have traditionally been referred to as "status offenders." *See generally* Status Offenders and the Juvenile Justice System (R. Allison, ed. 1983).

Empirical research indicates that, during the late 1970s and 1980s, the rates of juvenile admissions to psychiatric hospitals—particularly private psychiatric hospitals—increased substantially. At the same time, the number of juveniles institutionalized as status offenders declined significantly, in part because of constitutional and other procedural requirements imposed upon juvenile court proceedings. *See generally* Barry C. Feld, *The Transformation of the Juvenile Court*, 75 Minn. L. Rev. 691, 695–700 (1991) (discussing juvenile court reforms). Professor Weithorn asserts that these two phenomena are causally related. She argues that the population of "troubled teenagers" cared for by the child welfare system, the juvenile justice system and the mental health system are substantially interchangeable. Pressure to reduce the rate of institutionalization in one system will simply increase the number of youths institutionalized in the other systems. Weithorn, *above* at 805–07.

(4) To what extent may parents may use juvenile court proceedings to reinforce their authority over children? *See e.g. Matter of Andrew R.*, 454 N.Y.S.2d 820 (N.Y. Fam. Ct. 1982) (dismissing juvenile court proceeding brought by parents for purpose of returning their 13-year-old son to a residential treatment center from which the boy had run away). Conversely, should children ever be able to initiate juvenile court proceedings in order to challenge parental authority? In *In re Snyder*, 532 P.2d 278 (Wash. 1975), a 16-year-old girl who was having repeated confrontations with her parents, over such matters as discipline and extracurricular activities, filed a juvenile court petition alleging that she was "beyond the control and power of [her] parents," and therefore fell within the statutory definition of a "dependent child" in need of state intervention. After a hearing, the court placed the girl in foster care and ordered counseling for her and her parents. The parents challenged the court's authority to act at their daughter's initiative, absent a finding parental abuse or neglect, but the court rejected the parents' challenge. For a critique of *Snyder*, see Bruce Hafen, *Children's Liberation and the New Egalitarianism: Some Reservations About Abandoning Children to Their Rights*, 1976 B.Y.U.L. Rev. 605. 698-99 (describing the court's reasoning as "essentially an argument for the proposition that a child should be able

to 'divorce' (or at least achieve separation from) his or her parents on grounds of incompatibility"). *See generally* John DeWitt Gregory, *Juvenile Court Jurisdiction Over Noncriminal Behavior: The Argument Against Abolition*, 39 Ohio ST. L.J. 242 (1978); Rosenberg & Rosenberg, *The Legacy of the Stubborn and Rebellious Son*, 74 Mich. L. Rev. 1097 (1976).

(5) The notion of a child "divorcing" his parents received much media attention several years ago in connection with the case of Gregory K., a 12-year-old boy who successfully petitioned a Florida trial court to terminate his biological mother's parental rights, and to authorize his adoption by foster parents. *See Kingsley v. Kingsley*, 623 So. 2d 780 (Fla. Dist. Ct. App. 1993). At one level, the case was a routine termination of parental rights proceeding, since Gregory had been in state custody for several years, at the time his mother's rights were terminated. What caught the media's attention was that Gregory himself initiated the court proceedings, by filing the termination petition in his own name. See Mark Hansen, *Boy Wins "Divorce" From Mom: Critics Claim Ruling Will Encourage Frivolous Suits by Dissatisfied Kids*, 78 A.B.A. J. 16 (December, 1992). An appeals court later found that the trial judge had erred in permitting Gregory to proceed in his own name; the appeals court ruled, however, that the error was harmless, since separate termination petitions were later filed on Gregory's behalf by his foster parents, the state child welfare agency, and a guardian ad litem. *Kingsley*, 623 So. 2d at 784. For further discussion of the issues raised by the Gregory K. case, *see* George H. Russ, *Through the Eyes of A Child, "Gregory K.": A Child's Right to Be Heard*, 27 Fam. L.Q. 365 (1993) (written by Gregory K.'s adoptive father, who also served as the boy's legal advisor). For additional discussion of the standards for terminating parental rights, see §7.06[C], *below*.

(6) **Emancipation**. A more traditional legal mechanism for achieving the separation of parent and child is the doctrine of emancipation. Common law emancipation traditionally has been used to terminate a parent's obligation to support a child. *See* H. Jeffery Gottesfeld, *The Uncertain Status of the Emancipated Minor: Why We Need a Uniform Statutory Emancipation of Minors Act (USEMA)*, 15 U.S.F. L. Rev. 473 (1981) (characterizing emancipation as "a legal doctrine designed primarily for parents"). Whether emancipation has taken place is generally considered a question of fact to be decided by the court, often with minimal appellate guidance. *See, e.g., Accent Serv. Co., v. Ebsen*, 306 N.W. 2d 575 (Neb. 1981); *Lawson v. Brown*, 349 F.Supp. 203 (W.D. Va. 1972). *See generally* Alice M. Wright, Annotation, *What Voluntary Acts of Child, Other than Marriage or Entry into Military Service, Terminate Parent's Obligation to Support*, 55 A.L.R.5th 557 (1998).

Some states have had emancipation statues for close to a century; these "first generation" statutes, are "characterized by sparseness of detail and lack of objective standards by which to judge the minor's emancipation petition." Gottesfeld, *above*, at 478. A second generation of statutes, adopted over the past few decades, generally provide more detail and are designed in part to help minors seeking emancipation understand the process, the rights and the responsibilities involved. *Id.* at 479; *see, e.g.*, Conn. Gen. Stat. § 46b–150—150e (1997). These modern emancipation statutes were promoted as reform measures, designed to free mature minors who were living independently from legal disabilities which impaired their ability to function on a day-to-day basis. However, a recent study of the emancipation process in California suggests that the outcome of emancipation is not always so benign. *See* Carol Sanger & Eleanor Willemson, *Minor Changes: Emancipating Children in Modern*

Times, 25 U. Mich. J.L. Reform 239 (1992). Interviews conducted by the authors with 18 emancipated minors revealed that "[l]ife after emancipation is often precarious and lonely, and the decision to become emancipated is regarded with ambivalence." *Id.* at 297. The authors conclude that emancipation under the California statute functions as a ready mechanism to separate parents from children in dysfunctional families in a way that may disserve children's interests:

(7) **Problem.** Twelve-year-old Walter and his 17-year-old sister, Natalie, ran away from their home when their parents, who had recently immigrated to the United States, decided to return to the Soviet Union. The children's father sought police help in finding the children, who were hiding with a 24-year-old cousin. After the police found the children, the state filed a petition for adjudication of wardship, alleging that Walter was "beyond the control of his parents in that he did absent himself from his home without the expressed consent of his parents and that it was in the best interest of the minor and the public that Walter be adjudged a ward of the court." At an initial hearing held the next day, the juvenile court, over the objection of the parents, placed Walter in temporary custody pending a full hearing to determine whether Walter was a minor in need of supervision. The parents were unrepresented by counsel at this proceeding and did not have a court-appointed interpreter, although neither of them spoke nor understood English. The same day, Walter applied to the Immigration and Naturalization Service for political asylum. At the adjudicatory hearing held 10 days later, Walter testified that he left his parents' home because they planned to return to the Ukraine and he wanted to stay in the United States. The court also heard from two psychiatrists, neither of whom had examined Walter. The psychiatrists disagreed about whether a 12-year-old boy had the ability to make an independent judgment as to which country he preferred to live in; their opinions also differed on the extent of emotional harm that would result to Walter from a continued separation from his parents. The court found Walter to be a minor "in need of supervision," on the ground that he was "beyond the control of his parents," and adjudicated him a ward of the court. The court then placed Walter in foster care. The parents have appealed, claiming that the proceedings violated their constitutional rights and requesting that Walter be returned to them, so that they can take him back to the Soviet Union. What result on appeal and why? *See In re Polovchak*, 454 N.E.2d 258 (Ill. 1983).

§ 7.06 The Foster Care System

When a child is removed from his or her home because of parental abuse or neglect, or when a parent requests state assistance in caring for a child, the child is often placed in the care of a foster family. Placement of a child is foster care is intended to be a temporary measure—designed to lead either to timely reunification with the child's biological parent(s) or, if reunification is not possible, to the establishment of a new permanent home for the child through adoption or other legal action. As the cases in this section demonstrate, however, the reality of the foster care system has diverged markedly from these intentions. While it is easy to identify the problems and dilemmas associated with foster care, developing and implementing viable solutions that accommodate the conflicting interests at stake has proven a far more difficult task.

[A] The Foster Family

SMITH v. O.F.F.E.R.
United States Supreme Court
431 U.S. 816 (1977)

MR. JUSTICE BRENNAN delivered the opinion of the Court.

Appellees, individual foster parents and an organization of foster parents, brought this civil rights class action pursuant to 42 U.S.C. § 1983 in the United States District Court for the Southern District of New York, on their own behalf and on behalf of children for whom they have provided homes for a year or more. They sought declaratory and injunctive relief against New York State and New York City officials, alleging that the procedures governing the removal of foster children from foster homes provided in N.Y. Soc. Serv. Law §§ 383 (2) and 400 (McKinney 1976), and in 18 N.Y.C.R.R. § 450.14 (1974) violated the Due Process and Equal Protection Clauses of the Fourteenth Amendment. . . .

I.

A detailed outline of the New York statutory system regulating foster care is a necessary preface to a discussion of the constitutional questions presented.

A

The expressed central policy of the New York system is that "it is generally desirable for the child to remain with or be returned to the natural parent because the child's need for a normal family life will usually best be met in the natural home, and . . . parents are entitled to bring up their own children unless the best interests of the child would be thereby endangered," Soc. Serv. Law § 384–b(1)(a)(ii) (McKinney Supp. 1976–1977). But the State has opted for foster care as one response to those situations where the natural parents are unable to provide the "positive, nurturing family relationships" and "normal family life in a permanent home" that offer "the best opportunity for children to develop and thrive." §§ 384–b(1)(b), (1)(a)(i).

Foster care has been defined as "[a] child welfare service which provides substitute family care for a planned period for a child when his own family cannot care for him for a temporary or extended period, and when adoption is neither desirable nor possible." Child Welfare League of America, Standards for Foster Family Care Service 5 (1959). Thus, the distinctive features of foster care are, first, "that it is care in a family, it is noninstitutional substitute care," and, second, "that it is for a planned period—either temporary or extended. This is unlike adoptive placement, which implies a permanent substitution of one home for another." [A. Kadushin, Child Welfare Services 355 (1977)].

Under the New York scheme children may be placed in foster care either by voluntary placement or by court order. Most foster-care placements are voluntary. They occur when physical or mental illness, economic problems, or other family crises make it impossible for natural parents, particularly single parents, to provide a stable home life for their children for some limited period. Resort to such placements is almost compelled when it is not possible in such circumstances to place the child with a relative or friend, or to pay for the services of a homemaker or boarding school.

Voluntary placement requires the signing of a written agreement by the natural parent or guardian, transferring the care and custody of the child to an authorized child welfare agency. Although by statute the terms of such agreements are open to negotiation, it is contended that agencies require execution of standardized forms. The agreement may provide for return of the child to the natural parent at a specified date or upon occurrence of a particular event, and if it does not, the child must be returned by the agency, in the absence of a court order, within 20 days of notice from the parent.

The New York system divides parental functions among agency, foster parents, and natural parents, and the definitions of the respective roles are often complex and often unclear. The law transfers "care and custody" to the agency, but day-to-day supervision of the child and his activities, and most of the functions ordinarily associated with legal custody, are the responsibility of the foster parent. Nevertheless, agency supervision of the performance of the foster parents takes forms indicating that the foster parent does not have the full authority of a legal custodian. Moreover, the natural parent's placement of the child with the agency does not surrender legal guardianship; the parent retains authority to act with respect to the child in certain circumstances. The natural parent has not only the right but the obligation to visit the foster child and plan for his future; failure of a parent with capacity to fulfill the obligation for more than a year can result in a court order terminating the parent's rights on the ground of neglect.

Children may also enter foster care by court order. The Family Court may order that a child be placed in the custody of an authorized child-care agency after a full adversary judicial hearing under Art. 10 of the New York Family Court Act, if it is found that the child has been abused or neglected by his natural parents. In addition, a minor adjudicated a juvenile delinquent, or "person in need of supervision" may be placed by the court with an agency. §§ 753, 754, 756. The consequences of foster-care placement by court order do not differ substantially from those for children voluntarily placed, except that the parent is not entitled to return of the child on demand pursuant to Soc. Serv. Law § 384–a(2)(a); termination of foster care must then be consented to by the court. § 383(1).

B

The provisions of the scheme specifically at issue in this litigation come into play when the agency having legal custody determines to remove the foster child from the foster home, either because it has determined that it would be in the child's best interests to transfer him to some other foster home, or to return the child to his natural parents in accordance with the statute or placement agreement. Most children are removed in order to be transferred to another foster home. The procedures by which foster parents may challenge a removal made for that purpose differ somewhat from those where the removal is made to return the child to his natural parent.

[Under the New York Social Services Law the authorized placement agency has discretion to remove the child from the foster home, and regulations provide for 10 days' advance notice of removal. Objecting foster parents may request a conference with the Social Services Department where the foster parent may appear with counsel to be advised of the reasons for removal and to submit opposing reasons. Within five days after the conference the agency official must render a written decision and send notice to the foster parent and agency. If the child is removed after the conference, the foster parent may appeal to the

Department of Social Services, where a full adversary administrative hearing takes place, and the resultant determination is subject to judicial review. Removal is not stayed pending the hearing and judicial review. New York City provides additional procedures to the foregoing statewide scheme, under which in lieu of or in addition to the conference the foster parents are entitled to a full trial-type preremoval hearing if the child is being transferred to another foster home. An additional statewide procedure is provided by N.Y. Soc. Serv. Law § 392 whereby a foster parent may obtain preremoval judicial review of an agency decision to remove a child who has been in foster care for 18 months or more.]

C

Foster care of children is a sensitive and emotion-laden subject, and foster-care programs consequently stir strong controversy. The New York regulatory scheme is no exception. . . .

From the standpoint of natural parents, such as the appellant interveners here, foster care has been condemned as a class-based intrusion into the family life of the poor. It is certainly true that the poor resort to foster care more often than other citizens. For example, over 50% of all children in foster care in New York City are from female-headed families receiving Aid to Families with Dependent Children. Minority families are also more likely to turn to foster care; 52.3% of the children in foster care in New York City are black and 25.5% are Puerto Rican. This disproportionate resort to foster care by the poor and victims of discrimination doubtless reflects in part the greater likelihood of disruption of poverty-stricken families. Commentators have also noted, however, that middle-and upper-income families who need temporary care services for their children have the resources to purchase private care. The poor have little choice but to submit to state-supervised child care when family crises strike.

The extent to which supposedly "voluntary" placements are in fact voluntary has been questioned on other grounds as well. For example, it has been said that many "voluntary" placements are in fact coerced by threat of neglect proceedings and are not in fact voluntary in the sense of the product of an informed consent. Studies also suggest that social workers of middle-class backgrounds, perhaps unconsciously, incline to favor continued placement in foster care with a generally higher-status family rather than return the child to his natural family, thus reflecting a bias that treats the natural parents' poverty and lifestyle as prejudicial to the best interests of the child. This accounts, it has been said, for the hostility of agencies to the efforts of natural parents to obtain the return of their children.

Appellee foster parents as well as natural parents question the accuracy of the idealized picture portrayed by New York. They note that children often stay in "temporary" foster care for much longer than contemplated by the theory of the system. The District Court found as a fact that the median time spent in foster care in New York was over four years. 418 F. Supp., at 281. Indeed, many children apparently remain in this "limbo" indefinitely. The District Court also found that the longer a child remains in foster care, the more likely it is that he will never leave: "[T]he probability of a foster child being returned to his biological parents declined markedly after the first year in foster care." It is not surprising then that many children, particularly those that enter foster care at a very early age and have little or no contact with their natural parents during extended stays in foster care, often develop deep emotional ties with their foster parents. Yet such ties do not seem to be regarded as obstacles to transfer of the child from one foster placement to another. The record in this case indicates that nearly 60% of the children in foster care in New York City have experienced more than one placement, and about 28% have experienced three or more. The intended stability of the foster-home management is further damaged by the rapid turnover among social work professionals who supervise the foster-care arrangements on behalf of the State. Moreover, even when it is clear that a foster child will not be returned to his natural parents, it is rare that he achieves a stable home life through final termination of parental ties and adoption into a new permanent family.

The parties and amici devote much of their discussion to these criticisms of foster care, and we present this summary in the view that some understanding of those criticisms is necessary for a full appreciation of the complex and controversial system with which this lawsuit is concerned. But the issue presented by the case is a narrow one. Arguments asserting the need for reform of New York's statutory scheme are properly addressed to the New York Legislature. The relief sought in this case is entirely procedural. Our task is only to determine whether the District Court correctly held that the present procedures preceding the removal from a foster home of children resident there a year or more are constitutionally inadequate. To that task we now turn.

II

A

Our first inquiry is whether appellees have asserted interests within the Fourteenth Amendment's protection of "liberty" and "property." *Board of Regents v. Roth*, 408 U.S. 564, 571 (1972). . . .

The appellees' basic contention is that when a child has lived in a foster home for a year or more, a psychological tie is created between the child and the foster parents which constitutes the foster family the true "psychological family" of the child. *See* J. Goldstein, A. Freud, & A. Solnit, Beyond the Best Interests of the Child (1973). That family, they argue, has a "liberty interest" in its survival as a family protected by the Fourteenth Amendment. Upon this premise they conclude that the foster child cannot be removed without a prior hearing satisfying due process. . . .

B

It is, of course, true that "freedom of personal choice in matters of . . . family life is one of the liberties protected by the Due Process Clause of the Fourteenth Amendment." *Cleveland Board of Education v. LaFleur*, 414 U.S. 632, 639–640 (1974). There does exist a "private realm of family life which the state cannot enter," *Prince v. Massachusetts*, 321 U.S. 158, 166 (1944), that has been afforded both substantive and procedural protection. But is the relation of foster parent to foster child sufficiently akin to the concept of "family" recognized in our precedents to merit similar protection? Although considerable difficulty has attended the task of defining "family" for purposes of the Due Process Clause, we are not without guides to some of the elements that define the concept of "family" and contribute to its place in our society.

First, the usual understanding of "family" implies biological relationships, and most decisions treating the relation between parent and child have stressed this element. . . .

A biological relationship is not present in the case of the usual foster family. But biological relationships are not exclusive determination of the existence of a family. The basic foundation of the family in our society, the marriage relationship, is of course not a matter of blood relation. Yet its importance has been strongly emphasized in our cases. . . .

Thus the importance of the familial relationship, to the individuals involved and to the society, stems from the emotional attachments that derive from the intimacy of daily association, and from the role it plays in "promot[ing] a way of life" through the instruction of children, *Wisconsin v. Yoder*, 406 U.S. 205, 231–233 (1972), as well as from the fact of blood relationship. No one would seriously dispute that a deeply loving and interdependent relationship between an adult and a child in his or her care may exist even in the absence of blood relationship. At least where a child has been placed in foster care as an infant, has never known his natural parents, and has remained continuously for several years in the care of the same foster parents, it is natural that the foster family should hold the same place in the emotional life of the foster child, and fulfill the same socializing functions, as a natural family. For this reason, we cannot dismiss the foster family as a mere collection of unrelated individuals.

But there are also important distinctions between the foster family and the natural family. First, unlike the earlier cases recognizing a right to family privacy, the State here seeks to interfere, not with a relationship having its origins entirely apart from the power of the State, but rather with a foster family which has its source in state law and contractual arrangements. The individual's freedom to marry and reproduce is "older than the Bill of Rights," *Griswold v. Connecticut, supra,* at 486. Accordingly, unlike the property interests that are also protected by the Fourteenth Amendment, the liberty interest in family privacy has its source, and its contours are ordinarily to be sought, not in state law, but in intrinsic human rights, as they have been understood in "this Nation's history and tradition." *Moore v. East Cleveland* [431 U.S. 494, 503 (1977)]. Here, however, whatever emotional ties may develop between foster parent and foster child have their origins in an arrangement in which the State has been a partner from the outset. . . . In this case, the limited recognition accorded to the foster family by the New York statutes and the contracts executed by the foster parents argue against any but the most limited constitutional "liberty" in the foster family.

A second consideration related to this is that ordinarily procedural protection may be afforded to a liberty interest of one person without derogating from the substantive liberty of another. Here, however, such a tension is virtually unavoidable. Under New York law, the natural parent of a foster child in voluntary placement has an absolute right to the return of his child in the absence of a court order obtainable only upon compliance with rigorous substantive and procedural standards, which reflect the constitutional protection accorded the natural family. Moreover, the natural parent initially gave up his child to the State only on the express understanding that the child would be returned in those circumstances. These rights are difficult to reconcile with the liberty interest in the foster family relationship claimed by appellees. It is one thing to say that individuals may acquire a liberty interest against arbitrary governmental interference in the family-like associations into which they have freely entered, even in the absence of biological connection or state-law recognition of the relationship. It is quite another to say that one may acquire such an interest in the face of another's constitutionally recognized liberty interest that derives from blood relationship, state-law sanction, and basic human right—an interest the foster parent has recognized by contract from the outset. Whatever liberty interest might otherwise exist in the foster family as an institution, that interest must be substantially attenuated where the proposed removal from the foster family is to return the child to his natural parents.

As this discussion suggests, appellees' claim to a constitutionally protected liberty interest raises complex and novel questions. It is unnecessary for us to resolve those questions definitively in this case, however, for, like the District Court, we conclude that "narrower grounds exist to support" our reversal. We are persuaded that, even on the assumption that appellees have a protected "liberty interest", the District Court erred in holding that the preremoval procedures presently employed by the State are constitutionally defective.

III

Where procedural due process must be afforded because a "liberty" or "property" interest is within the Fourteenth Amendment's protection, there must be determined "what process is due" in the particular context. The District Court did not spell out precisely what sort of preremoval hearing would be necessary to meet the constitutional standard, leaving to "various defendants—state and local officials—the first opportunity to formulate procedures suitable to their own professional needs and compatible with the principles set forth in this opinion." The court's opinion, however, would seem to require at a minimum that in all cases in which removal of a child within the certified class is contemplated, including the situation where the removal is for the purpose of returning the child to his natural parents, a hearing be held automatically, regardless of whether or not the foster parents request a hearing; that the hearing be before an officer who has had no previous contact with decision to remove the child, and who has authority to order that the child remain with the foster parent; and that the agency, the foster parents and the natural parents, as well as the child, if he is able intelligently to express his true feelings, and an independant representative of the child's interests, if he is not, be represented and permitted to introduce relevant evidence.

It is true that "[b]efore a person is deprived of a protected interest, he must be afforded opportunity for some kind of a hearing, 'except for extraordinary situations where some valid governmental interest is at stake that justifies postponing the hearing until after the event.'" *Board of Regents v. Roth*, 408 U.S. at 570 n. 7, *quoting Boddie v. Connecticut*, 401 U.S. 371, 379 (1971) But the hearing required is only one "appropriate to the nature of the case." *Mullane v. Central Hanover Bank & Trust Co.*, 339 U.S. 306, 313 (1950). "[D]ue process is flexible and calls for such procedural protections as the particular situation demands." *Morrissey v. Brewer*, 408 U.S. 471, 481 (1972). Only last Term, the Court held that "identification of the dictates of due process generally requires consideration of three distinct factors: First the private interest that will be affected by the official action; second, the risk of an erroneous deprivation of such interest through the procedures used, and the probable value, if any, of additional or substitute procedural safeguards; and finally, the Government's interest, including the function involved and the fiscal and administrative burdens that the additional or substitute procedural requirement would entail." *Mathews v. Eldridge*, 424 U.S. 319, 335 (1976).

[The Supreme Court rejected the lower court's conclusion that the New York City procedures were inadequate because the preremoval hearing was available only at the request of the foster parents. The Court also rejected the claim that due process required that the biological parents and the child be made parties to the removal hearing, noting that such persons will generally have little to add to the accuracy of fact-finding concerning the wisdom of a transfer and that nothing in the New York statutory scheme precluded their participation in appropriate cases. With respect to the child, the Court added:]

But nothing in the New York City procedure prevents consultation of the child's wishes, directly or through an intermediary. We assume, moreover, that some such consultation would be among the first steps that a rational fact finder, inquiring into the child's best interests, would pursue. Such consultation, however, does not require that the child or an appointed representative must be a party will full adversary powers in all preremoval hearings.

Moreover, the State's interest in avoiding "fiscal and administrative burdens," *Mathews v. Eldridge*, 424 U.S. 319, 335 (1976), is not the only interest that must be weighed against requiring still more elaborate hearing procedures. As the District Court acknowledged, where delicate judgments concerning "the often ambiguous indices of a child's emotional attachments and psychological development" are involved, we must also consider the possibility that making the decisionmaking process increasingly adversary "might well impede the effort to ellicit the sensitive and personal information required," or make the struggle for custody, already often difficult enough for the child, even more traumatic. In such a situation, there is a value in less formalized hearing procedures. . . .

We deal here with issues of unusual delicacy, in an area where professional judgments regarding desirable procedures are constantly and rapidly changing. In such a context, restraint is appropriate on the part of courts called upon to adjudicate whether a particular procedural scheme is adequate under the Constitution. Since we hold that the procedures provided by New York State [and by New York City] are adequate to protect whatever liberty interests appellees may have, the judgment of the District Court is

Reversed.

NOTES AND QUESTIONS

(1) On what basis did the foster parents in *Smith* claim that they had a constitutionally protected interest in their relationship with their foster children? Why was the Supreme Court reluctant to recognize this interest? Do you agree with the majority that affording constitutional protection to the relationship between foster parents and children would interfere with the liberty interests of the biological parents? *Cf. Michael H. v. Gerald D.*, reprinted at § 5.05[A], *above*.

(2) Suppose that a child's foster parents are also the child's aunt and uncle, who have signed a contract with the state and who receive foster care payments. Would their relationship with the child be entitled to greater constitutional protection than the foster care relationships at issue in *Smith*? Why or why not? *Cf. Moore v. City of East Cleveland* 431 U.S. 494 (1977)(due process clause of Fourteenth Amendment precludes municipality from defining "family" for zoning purposes so as to exclude grandmother living with her grandsons). For additional discussion of "kinship" foster care, see § 7.06[B], *below*.

(3) Do children placed in foster care have constitutionally protected interests that are independent of the interests of both their biological and their foster parents? If so, what is the nature of those interests and how should they be protected?

IN THE MATTER OF MICHAEL B.
New York Court of Appeals
604 N.E.2d 122&(1992)

KAY, J.

This appeal from a custody determination, pitting a child's foster parents against his biological father, centers on the meaning of the statutory term "best interests of the child," and particularly on the weight to be given a child's bonding with his long-time foster family in deciding what placement is in his best interest. The biological father (appellant) on one side, and respondent foster parents (joined by respondent Law Guardian) on the other, each contend that a custody determination in their favor is in the best interest of the child, as that term in used in Social Services Law § 392 (6), the statute governing dispositions with respect to children in foster care.

The subject of this protracted battle is Michael B., born July 29, 1985 with a positive toxicology for cocaine. Michael was voluntarily placed in foster care from the hospital by his mother, who was unmarried at the time of the birth and listed no father on the birth certificate. Michael's four siblings were then also in foster care, residing in different homes. At three months, before the identity of his father was known, Michael—needing extraordinary care—was placed in the home of intervener Maggie W.L., a foster parent certified by respondent Catholic Child Care Society (the agency), and the child remained with the L's for more than five years, until December 1990. It is undisputed that the agency initially assured Mrs. L. this was a "preadoptive" placement.

Legal proceedings began in May 1987, after appellant had been identified as Michael's father. The agency sought to terminate the rights of both biological parents and free the child for adoption, alleging that for more than a year following Michael's placement, the parents had failed to substantially, continuously or repeatedly maintain contact with Michael and plan for his future, although physically and financially able to do so (Social Services Law § 384-b [7]). Michael's mother (since deceased) never appeared in the proceeding, and a finding of permanent neglect as to her was made in November 1987. Appellant did appear and in September 1987 consented to a finding of permanent neglect, and to committing custody and guardianship to the agency on condition that the children be placed with their godmothers. That order was later vacated, on appellant's application to withdraw his pleas and obtain custody, because the agency had not in fact placed the children with their godmothers. In late 1987, appellant—a long–time alcohol and substance abuser—entered an 18-month residential drug rehabilitation program and first began to visit Michael.

In August 1988, appellant, the agency and the Law Guardian agreed to reinstatement of the permanent neglect finding, with judgment suspended for 12 months, on condition that appellant: (1) enroll in a program teaching household management and parenting skills; (2) cooperate by attending and complying with the program; (3) remain drug-free, and periodically submit to drug testing, with test results delivered to the agency; (4) secure and maintain employment; (5) obtain suitable housing; and (6) submit a plan for the child's care during his working day. The order recited that it was without prejudice to the agency recalendaring the case for a de novo hearing on all allegations of the petition should appellant fail to satisfy the conditions, and otherwise said nothing more of the consequences that would follow on appellant's compliance or noncompliance.

As the 12–month period neared expiration, the agency sought a hearing to help "determine the status and placement of the children." Although appellant was unemployed (he was on public assistance) and had not submitted to drug testing during the year, Family Court at the hearing held October 24, 1989 was satisfied that "there seem[ed] to be substantial compliance" with the conditions of the suspended judgment. . . .

On December 21, 1989, the Law Guardian presented a report indicating that Michael might suffer severe psychological damage if removed from his foster home, and argued for a "best interests" hearing pursuant to *Matter of Bennett v. Jeffreys* (40 NY2d 543), based on Michael's bonding with the L.'s and, by contrast, his lack of bonding with appellant, who had visited him infrequently. Family Court questioned whether it even had authority for such a hearing, but stayed the order directing Michael's discharge to appellant pending its determination. Michael's siblings, then approximately twelve, eight, seven and six years old, were released to appellant in January and July 1990. Litigation continued as to Michael.

In November 1990, Family Court directed Michael's discharge to appellant, concluding that it was without "authority or jurisdiction" to rehear the issue of custody based on the child's best interest, and indeed that Michael had been wrongfully held in foster care. The court noted, additionally, that the Law Guardian's arguments as to Michael's best interest went to issues of bonding with his temporary custodians rather than appellant's insufficiency as a parent—bonding that had been reinforced by the agency's failure to ensure sufficient contacts with appellant during the proceedings. . . . The court directed that Michael commence immediate weekend visitation with appellant, with a view to transfer within 60 days. Michael was discharged to appellant in December 1990.

The Appellate Division reversed and remitted for a new hearing and new consideration of Michael's custody, concluding that dismissal of a permanent neglect petition cannot divest Family Court of its continuing jurisdiction over a child until there has been a "best interests" custody disposition. As for the relevance of bonding, the Appellate Division held that, given the "extraordinary circumstances"—referring particularly to Michael's long residence with his foster parents—Family Court should have conducted a hearing to consider issues such as the impact on the child of a change in custody. There having been no question of appellant's fitness, however, the Appellate Division permitted Michael to remain with his father pending the new determination.

On remittal, Family Court heard extensive testimony—including testimony from appellant, the foster parents, the agency (having changed its goal to discharge to appellant), and psychological, psychiatric and social work professionals (who overwhelmingly favored continued foster care over discharge to appellant)—but adhered to its determination that Michael should be released to his father. Family Court found appellant "fit, available and capable of adequately providing for the health, safety and welfare of the subject child, and . . . it is in the child's best interest to be returned to his father."

Again the Appellate Division reversed Family Court's order, this time itself awarding custody to the foster parents under Social Services Law § 392(6)(b), and remitting the matter to a different Family Court Judge solely to determine appellant's visitation rights. Exercising its own authority—as broad as that of the hearing court—to assess the credibility of witnesses and character and temperament of the parents, the court reviewed the evidence and, while pointing up appellant's many deficiencies, significantly stopped short of finding him an unfit parent, as it had the power to do. Rather, the court looked to Michael's lengthy stay and psychological bonding with the foster family, which it felt gave rise to extraordinary circumstances meriting an award of custody to the foster parents. According to the Appellate Division, the evidence "overwhelmingly demonstrate[d] that Michael's foster parents are better able than his natural father to provide for his physical, emotional, and intellectual needs." (180 A.D.2d, at 794.) Since early 1992, Michael has once again resided with the L.'s.

While prolonged, inconclusive proceedings and seesawing custody of a young child—all in the name of Michael's best interest—could not conceivably serve his interest at all, we granted appellant father's motion for leave to appeal, and now reverse the Appellate Division's central holdings. The opinions of Family Court specifying deficiencies of the agency and foster parents, and the opinions of the Appellate Division specifying inadequacies of the biological parent, leave little question that the only blameless person is the child. But rather than assess fault, our review will address the legal standards that have twice divided Family Court and the Appellate Division, hopefully minimizing recurrences, for this child and others, of the tragic scenario now before us.

Analysis

Appellant no longer disputes that Family Court retained jurisdiction to consider the child's best interest in connection with an award of custody even after the finding that he had substantially satisfied the conditions of the suspended judgment. All parties agree with the correctness of the Appellate Division determination that, despite appellant's apparent compliance with the conditions of the suspended judgment, Family Court retained jurisdiction to consider the best interest of the children in foster care until a final order of disposition.

What remains the bone of contention in this Court is the scope of the requisite "best interest" inquiry under Social Services Law § 392 (6). Appellant urges that in cases of foster care, so long as the biological parent is not found unfit—and he underscores that neither Family Court nor the Appellate Division found him unfit—"best interest of the child" is only a limited inquiry addressed to whether the child will suffer grievous injury if transferred out of foster care to the biological parent. Respondents, by contrast, maintain that extraordinary circumstances—such as significant bonding with foster parents, after inattention and even admitted neglect by the biological parent—trigger a full inquiry into the more suitable placement as between the biological and foster parents. Subsidiarily, appellant challenges the Appellate Division's outright award of custody to the foster parents, claiming that disposition was beyond the Court's authority under Social Services Law § 392 (6).

We conclude, first, that neither party advances the correct "best interest" test in the context of temporary foster care placements, but that appellant's view is more consistent with the statutory scheme than the broad-gauge inquiry advocated by respondents and applied by the Appellate Division. Second, we hold that the award of custody to the foster parents was impermissible as we interpret Social Services Law § 392 (6).

The Foster Care Scheme

This being a case of voluntary placement in foster care—a subject controlled by statute—analysis must begin with the legislative scheme, which defines and balances the parties' rights and responsibilities. An understanding of how the system is designed to operate—before the design is complicated, and even subverted, by human actors and practical realities—is essential to resolving the questions before us.

New York's foster care scheme is built around several fundamental social policy choices that have been explicitly declared by the Legislature and are binding on this Court. Under the statute, operating as written, appellant should have received the active support of both the agency in overcoming his parental deficiencies and the foster parents in solidifying his relationship with Michael, and as soon as return to the biological parent proved unrealistic, the child should have been freed for adoption.

A biological parent has a right to the care and custody of a child, superior to that of others, unless the parent has abandoned that right or is proven unfit to assume the duties and privileges of parenthood, even though the State perhaps could find "better" parents. A child is not the parent's property, but neither is a child the property of the State. Looking to the child's rights as well as the parents' rights to bring up their own children, the Legislature has found and declared that a child's need to grow up with a "normal family life in a permanent home" is ordinarily best met in the child's "natural home" (Social Services Law § 384–b [1] [a] [i], [ii]).

Parents in temporary crisis are encouraged to voluntarily place their children in foster care without fear that they will thereby forfeit their parental rights. The State's first obligation is to help the family with services to prevent its break-up, or to reunite the family if the child is out of the home. While a child is in foster care, the State must use diligent efforts to strengthen the relationship between parent and child, and work with the parent to regain custody.

Because of the statutory emphasis on the biological family as best serving a child's long-range needs, the legal rights of foster parents are necessarily limited (*see Smith v. Organization of Foster Families*, 431 US 816, 846). Legal custody of a child in foster care remains with the agency that places the child, not with the foster parents. Foster parents enter into this arrangement with the express understanding that the placement is temporary, and that the agency retains the right to remove the child upon notice at any time. . . . Foster parents, moreover, have an affirmative obligation—similar to the obligation of the State—to attempt to solidify the relationship between biological parent and child. While foster parents may be heard on custody issues, they have no standing to seek permanent custody absent termination of parental rights.

Fundamental also to the statutory scheme is the preference for providing children with stable, permanent homes as early as possible. "[W]hen it is clear that the natural parent cannot or will not provide a normal family home for the child and when continued foster care is not an appropriate plan for the child, then a permanent alternative home should be sought" (Social Services Law § 384–b [1] [a] [iv]). Extended foster care is not in the child's best interest, because it deprives a child of a permanent, nurturing family relationship. Where it appears that the child may never be reunited with the biological parents, the responsible agency should institute a proceeding to terminate parental rights and free the child for adoption.

Parental rights may be terminated only upon clear and convincing proof of abandonment, inability to care for the child due to mental illness or retardation, permanent neglect, or severe or repeated child abuse. Of the permissible dispositions in a termination proceeding based on permanent neglect, the Legislature—consistent with its emphasis on the importance of biological ties, yet mindful of the child's need for early stability and permanence—has provided for a suspended judgment, which is a brief grace period designed to prepare the parent to be reunited with the child. Parents found to have permanently neglected a child may be given a second chance, where the court determines it is in the child's best interests, but that opportunity is strictly limited in time. Parents may have up to one year (and a second year only where there are "exceptional circumstances") during which they must comply with terms and conditions meant to ameliorate the difficulty. Noncompliance may lead to revocation of the judgment and termination of parental rights. Compliance may lead to dismissal of the termination petition with the child remaining subject to the jurisdiction of the Family Court until a determination is made as to the child's disposition pursuant to Social Services Law § 392 (6).

Where parental rights have not been terminated, Social Services Law § 392 promotes the objectives of stability and permanency by requiring periodic review of foster care placements. The agency having custody must first petition for review after a child has been in continuous foster care for 18 months, and if no change is made, every 24 months thereafter. While foster parents who have been caring for such child for the prior 12 months are entitled to notice, and may also petition for review on their own initiative, a petition under section 392 (captioned "Foster care status; periodic family court review") is not an avenue to permanent custody for foster parents where the child has not been freed for adoption.

Upon such review, the court must consider the appropriateness of the agency's plan for the child, what services have been offered to strengthen and reunite the family, efforts to plan for other modes of care, and other further efforts to promote the child's welfare, and in accordance with the best interest of the child, make one of the following dispositions: (1) continue the child in foster care (which may include continuation with the current foster parents); (2) direct that the child "be returned to the parent, guardian or relative, or [direct] that the child be placed in the custody of a relative or other suitable person or persons"; or (3) require the agency (or foster parents upon the agency's default) to institute a parental rights termination proceeding.

The key element in the court's disposition is the best interest of the child—the statutory term that is at the core of this appeal, and to which we now turn.

"Best Interest" in the Foster Care Scheme

"Best interest(s) of the child" is a term that pervades the law relating to children—appearing innumerable times in the pertinent statutes, judicial decisions and literature—yet eludes ready definition. Two interpretations are advanced, each vigorously advocated.

Appellant would read the best interest standard of Social Services Law § 392 (6) narrowly, urging that Family Court should inquire only into whether the biological parent is fit, and whether the child will suffer grievous harm by being returned to the parent. Appellant urges affirmance of the Family Court orders, which (1) defined the contest as one between foster care agency and biological parent, rather than foster parent and biological parent; (2) focused first on "the ability of the father to care for the subject child," and then on whether "the child's emotional health will be so seriously impaired as to require continuance in foster care;" and (3) concluded that appellant was fit, and that Michael would not suffer irreparable emotional harm if returned to him. Wider inquiry, appellant insists, creates an "unwinnable beauty contest" the biological parent will inevitably lose where foster placement has continued for any substantial time.

Respondents take a broader view, urging that because of extraordinary circumstances largely attributable to appellant, the Appellate Division correctly compared him with the foster parents in determining Michael's custody and concluded that the child's best interest was served by the placement that better provided for his physical, emotional and intellectual needs. Respondents rely on *Matter of Bennett v. Jeffreys* (40 NY2d 543, *supra*), this Court's landmark decision recognizing that a child's prolonged separation from a biological parent may be considered, among other factors, to be extraordinary circumstances permitting the court to inquire into which family situation would be in the child's best interests.

In that *Matter of Bennett v. Jeffreys* concerned an unsupervised private placement, where there was no directly applicable legislation, that case is immediately distinguishable from the matter before us, which is controlled by a detailed statutory scheme. Our analysis must begin at a different point—not whether there are extraordinary circumstances, but what the Legislature intended by the words "best interest of the child" in Social Services Law § 392 (6).

Necessarily, we look first to the statute itself. The question is in part answered by Social Services Law § 383 and 384-b, which encourage voluntary placements, with the provision that they will not result in the termination of parental rights so long as the parent is fit. To use the period during which a child lives with a foster family, and emotional ties that naturally eventuate, as a ground for comparing the biological parent with the foster parent undermines the very objective of voluntary foster care as a resource for parents in temporary crisis, who are then at risk of losing their children once a bond arises with the foster families. . . .

Absent an explicit legislative directive . . . we are not free to overlook the legislative policies that underlie temporary foster care, including the preeminence of the biological family. Indeed, the legislative history of Social Services Law § 392 (5-a), which specifies factors that must be considered in determining the child's best interests, states "this bill clearly advises the Family Court of certain considerations before making an order of disposition. These factors establish a clear policy of exploring all available means of reuniting the child with his family before the Court decides to continue his foster care or to direct a permanent adoptive placement." (Mem. Accompanying Comments on Bill, N.Y. State Bd. of Social Welfare, A 12801-B, July 9, 1976, Governor's Bill Jacket, L 1976, ch 667.)

We therefore cannot endorse a pure "best interests" hearing, where biological parent and foster parents stand on equal footing and the child's interest is the sole consideration. In cases controlled by Social Services Law § 392 (6), analysis of the child's "best interest" must begin not by measuring biological parent against foster parent but by weighing past and continued foster care against discharge to the biological parent, or other relative or suitable person within Social Services Law § 392(6)(b).

While the facts of *Matter of Bennett v. Jeffreys* fell outside the statute, and the Court was unrestrained by legislative prescription in defining the scope of the "best interests" inquiry, principles underlying that decision are also relevant here. It is plainly the case, for example, that a "child may be so long in the custody of the nonparent that, even though there has been no abandonment or persisting neglect by the parent, the psychological trauma of removal is grave enough to threaten destruction of the child" (*id.*, at 550), and we cannot discount evidence that a child may have bonded with someone other than the biological parent. In such a case, continued foster care may be appropriate although the parent has not been found unfit.

Under Social Services Law § 392, where a child has not been freed for adoption, the court must determine whether it is nonetheless appropriate to continue foster care temporarily, or whether the child should be permanently discharged to the biological parent (or a relative or "other suitable person"). In determining the best interest of a child in that situation, the fitness of the biological parent must be a primary factor. The court is also statutorily mandated to consider the agency's plan for the child, what services have been offered to strengthen and reunite the family, what reasonable efforts have been made to make it possible for the child to return to the natural home, and if return home is not likely, what efforts have been or should be made to evaluate other options. Finally, the court should consider the more intangible elements relating to the emotional well-being of the child, among them the impact on the child of immediate discharge versus an additional period of foster care.

While it is doubtful whether it could be found to be in the child's best interest to deny the parent's persistent demands for custody simply because it took so long to obtain it legally, neither is a lapse of time necessarily without significance in determining custody. The child's emotional well-being must be part of the equation, parental rights notwithstanding. However, while emotional well-being may encompass bonding to someone other than the biological parent, it includes as well a recognition that, absent termination of parental rights, the nonparent cannot adopt the child, and a child in continued custody with a nonparent remains in legal—and often emotional—limbo.

The Appellate Division, applying an erroneous "best interest" test, seemingly avoided that result when it awarded legal custody to the foster parents. We next turn to why that disposition was improper.

Award of Legal Custody to Foster Parents

The Appellate Division awarded legal custody of Michael to the foster parents pursuant to Social Services Law § 392(6)(b), noting that the statute "permits a court to enter an order of disposition directing, *inter alia*, that a child, whose custody and care have temporarily been transferred to an authorized agency, be placed in the custody of a suitable person or persons." (180 A.D.2d, at 796.) The Court correctly looked to section 392 as the predicate for determining custody, but erroneously relied on paragraph (b) of subdivision (6) in awarding custody to the foster parents.

As set forth above, there are three possible dispositions after foster care review with respect to a child not freed for adoption: continued foster care; release to a parent, guardian, relative or other suitable person; and institution of parental termination proceedings (Social Services Law § 392 [6] [a]-[c]).

As the first dispositional option, paragraph (a) contemplates the continuation of foster care, with the child remaining in the custody of the authorized agency, and the arrangement remaining subject to periodic review. As a result of 1989 amendments, disposition under paragraph (a) can include an order that the child be placed with (or remain with) a particular foster family until the next review (L 1989, ch 744). Under the statutory scheme, however, foster care is temporary, contractual and supervised.

Paragraph (b), by contrast, contemplates removal of the child from the foster care system by return to "the parent, guardian or relative, or direct[ion] that the child be placed in the custody of a relative or other suitable person or persons." The 1989 statutory revision added as a permissible disposition the placement of children with relatives or other suitable persons. The purpose of this amendment was to promote family stability by allowing placement with relatives, extended family members or persons like them, as an alternative to foster care.

Plainly, the scheme does not envision also including the foster parents—who were the subject of the amendment to paragraph (a)—as "other suitable persons." Indeed, reading paragraph (b) as the Appellate Division did, to permit removal of the child from foster care and an award of legal custody to the foster parents, exacerbates the legal limbo status. The child is left without a placement looking to the establishment of a permanent parental relationship through adoption, or the prospect of subsequent review of foster care status with the possibility of adoption placement at that time, yet has no realistic chance of return to the biological parent.

The terms of paragraph (c), providing for an order that the agency institute a parental termination proceeding, further buttress the conclusion that foster parents are not included in paragraph (b). Pursuant to paragraph (c), if the court finds reasonable cause to believe there are grounds for termination of parental rights, it may order the responsible agency to institute such proceedings. If the agency fails to do so within 90 days, the foster parents themselves may bring the proceeding, unless the court believes their subsequent petition to adopt would not be approved. Thus, in the statutory scheme the Legislature has provided a means for foster parents to secure a temporary arrangement under paragraph (a) and a permanent arrangement under paragraph (c)—both of which specifically mention foster parents. They are not also implicitly included in paragraph (b), which addresses different interests.

We therefore conclude that the Appellate Division erred in interpreting Social Services Law § 392 (6) to permit the award of legal custody to respondent foster parents.

Need for Further Inquiry

We have no occasion to apply the proper legal test to the facts at hand, as the parties urge. New circumstances require remittal to Family Court for an expedited hearing and determination of whether appellant is a fit parent and entitled to custody of Michael.

The Court has been informed that, during the pendency of the appeal, appellant was charged with—and admitted—neglect of the children in his custody (not Michael), and that those children have been removed from his home and are again in the custody of the Commissioner of the Social Services. The neglect petitions allege that appellant abused alcohol and controlled substances including cocaine, and physically abused the children. Orders of fact finding have been entered by Family Court, Queens County, recognizing appellant's admission in open court to "substance abuse, alcohol and cocaine abuse." Moreover, an Order of Protection was entered prohibiting appellant from visiting the children while under the influence of drugs or alcohol.

Appellant's request that we ignore these new developments and simply grant him custody, because matters outside the record cannot be considered by an appellate court, would exalt the procedural rule—important though it is—to a point of absurdity, and "reflect no credit on the judicial process." (Cohen and Karger, Powers of the New York Court of Appeals § 168, at 640.) Indeed, changed circumstances may have particular significance in child custody matters. This Court would therefore take notice of the new facts and allegations to the extent they indicate that the record before us is no longer sufficient for determining appellant's fitness and right to custody of Michael, and remit the matter to Family Court for a new hearing and determination of those issues. The Appellate Division concluded that the hearing should take place before a different Judge of that court, and we see no basis to disturb that determination. Pending the hearing, Michael should physically remain with his current foster parents, but legal custody should be returned to the foster care agency. . . .

BELLACOSA, J. (concurring).

I agree with Judge Kaye's opinion for the Court that Social Services Law § 392(6)(b) cannot be used to award permanent custody to foster parents within that statute's intended operation and integrated structure. I concur in the reversal result in this case solely for that reason, noting additionally that a contrary interpretation of that key provision, as used by the Appellate Division, would have internally contradictory implications in the field of temporary foster child placement. While I prefer an affirmance result because that might more likely conclude the litigation and allow Michael B., the 7 1/2-year-old subject of this custody battle, to get on with his life in a more settled and constructive way, I can discern no principled route to that desirable result without sacrificing the correct application of legal principles and engendering fundamentally troublesome precedential consequences.

This separate concurrence is necessary to express my difference of degree and analytical progression with respect to the best interests analysis and test, as adopted by the Court, for purposes of the remittal of this case and as the controlling guidance for countless other proceedings in the future. I would not relegate *Matter of Bennett v. Jeffreys* (40 NY2d 543) essentially to general relevance only, would not limit the beginning of the analysis to the statutory setting, and would allow for appropriate flexibility as to the range and manner of exercising discretion in the application of the best interests test by the Family Courts and Appellate Divisions.

I believe courts, in the fulfillment of the parens patriae responsibility of the State, should, as a general operating principle, have an appropriately broad range of power to act in the best interests of children. We agree that the teachings of *Matter of Bennett v. Jeffreys* are still excellent and have served the process and the affected subjects and combatants in custody disputes very well. While the common-law origination in *it;Bennett is a distinguishing feature from the instant case, I do not view that aspect as subordinated to or secondary in the use of its wisdom, even in a predominantly statutory setting, where this case originates. . . . Since the best of *Matter of Bennett v. Jeffreys*' best interest analysis enjoys continued vitality therefore, it should serve as a cogent, coequal common-law building block. In my view, it provides helpful understanding for and intertwined supplementation to the Social Services Law provisions as applied in these extraordinary circumstances, defined in one aspect of *Matter of Bennett v. Jeffreys* as "prolonged separation" of parent and child "for most of the child's life" (40 NY2d, at 544, *supra*).

The child in that case was eight years of age and none of the other serious and disquieting features of this case were apparent there.

The nuances, complexity and variations of human situations make the development and application of the general axiom—best interests of the child—exceedingly difficult. As a matter of degree and perspective, however, the Court's test is concededly more limiting than *Matter of Bennett v. Jeffreys (supra)*, and therefore I believe it is more narrow than it should be in this case since I discern no compelling authority for the narrower approach. This 7-year-old child, born of a long since deceased crack-cocaine mother, has yet to be permanently placed and has suffered a continuing, lengthy, bad trip through the maze of New York's legal system. His father has an extended history of significant substance addiction and other problems, and the child has spent much of his 7 years with the same foster parents. These graphic circumstances surely present an exceptionally extraordinary and compelling case requiring significant flexibility by the courts in resolving his best interests. On this aspect of the case, therefore, I agree with the Appellate Division in its two decisions in this case, at least with respect to its best interests analysis and handling of this difficult case. On March 18, 1991, it said:

> "In view of the extraordinary circumstances present in this case, the Family Court should have conducted a hearing to consider, among other things, the impact that a change of custody will have on the child in view of the bonding which has occurred between Michael and his foster parents, who have raised him since infancy. It is, therefore, necessary to remit this matter for a hearing and a custody determination to be made in accordance with Michael's best interests. (171 A.D.2d 790, 791).

After the proper, broad, "pure" *Matter of Bennett v. Jeffreys*-type best interests hearing was held in Family Court, the Appellate Division on February 24, 1992 added in the order now before us:

> "In light of the lengthy period of time during which Michael resided with and psychologically bonded to his foster parents and given the potential for emotional as well as physical harm to Michael should permanent custody be awarded to his natural father, we find that the requisite extraordinary circumstances are present, and conclude that the best interests of this child will be served by allowing him to return to his foster parents.

> "In view of the testimony presented during the best interests hearing, this court concludes that Michael's natural father is incapable of giving him the emotional support so vital to his well-being. The testimony presented by Dr. Sullivan and Mr. Falco indicated that an emotional void still existed between Michael and his father despite the eight to nine months during which they resided together prior to the best interests hearing and that this void showed no signs of being bridged." (180 A.D.2d 792, 795–796.)

In sum, I cannot agree that the important and pervasive legal axiom "best interests of the child" is or was meant to be as constricted as it is in the Court's application to this case. The governing phrase and test even in this statutory scheme ought to be as all-encompassing as in *Matter of Bennett v. Jeffreys*, despite the difference in the procedural origin and setting of the two cases. The approach I urge, not unlike that of the Appellate Division in this respect, better serves the objectives of finality and certainty in these matters, more realistically takes into account the widely varying human conditions, and allows the

Family Courts to achieve more uniformity and evenness of application of the rules. That is a better way to promote the best interests of this youngster with reasonable finality and the best interests of all others affected by the operation of these rules.

NOTES AND QUESTIONS

(1) What legal standard does the New York Court of Appeals hold should govern the custody dispute between Michael B.'s biological father and the child's foster parents? How does this standard differ from the standard initially applied by the trial court? How does it differ from the approach suggested by the concurring justice?

(2) The majority opinion refers to "several fundamental social policy choices" around which the New York foster care scheme is built. What are these social policy choices and how does the Court of Appeals discern them? Do these policy choices makes sense to you? Why or why not?

(3) Imagine that you are the Family Court judge assigned to hear this case on remand. What types of evidence would you find persuasive in determining who should have custody of Michael? Based on the facts recited by the Court of Appeals, would you be inclined to order the agency to institute a parental rights termination proceeding? How relevant would it be to your decision that Michael's biological father has admitted neglecting other children in his custody (not Michael) and that he has acknowledged abusing alcohol and cocaine?

(4) The Court of Appeals states that the purpose of its opinion is to "minimiz[e] recurrences, for this child and others, of the tragic scenario now before us." Is the Court's analysis likely to achieve this goal? Why or why not? Are there other legal changes—statutory or adjudicative—that you believe would more effectively minimize such recurrences?

(5) **Psychological Parenthood.** Part of the disagreement between the majority and the concurring opinion in Michael B. concerns the relative importance of biological vs. psychological parenthood. The theory of psychological parenthood was first developed and articulated in the 1970's by Professors Joseph Goldstein, Anna Freud and Albert Solnit, authors of several influential books on child welfare and custody decision-making. Joseph Goldstein, Anna Freud & Albert Solnit, Beyond the Best Interests of the Child (1973); Joseph Goldstein, Anna Freud & Albert Solnit, Before The Best Interests of the Child (1979); Joseph Goldstein, Anna Freud & Albert Solnit, In the Best Interest of the Child: Professional Boundaries (1986). Psychological parenting theory has been summarized as follows:

> Simply summarized, Goldstein, Freud and Solnit postulated that children form their primary attachment with a "psychological parent"—the person that provides day-to-day care for the child, whether or not that person is the biological parent—and their psychological well-being requires a continuous relationship with that person. Based on this thesis, Goldstein, Freud, and Solnit advocated that the state should only remove children from their families in extreme situations. However, once the state removes a child from his or her family and the child becomes attached to another caretaker, continuing the new relationship becomes their overriding concern. In their view, that paramount relationship must be an exclusive one. Thus, complete termination of all parental rights and adoption of the child by the new caretaker is essential.

Nancy Goldhill, *The Ties That Bind: The Impact of Psychological and Legal Debates on the Child Welfare System*, 22 N.Y.U. Rev. Law & Soc. Change 295, 297 (1996).

Psychological parenting theory thus argues for severely limiting the state's authority to remove children from ongoing, functional families, regardless of how those families were formed. The theory also urges that child welfare and custody determinations be made in accordance with a "child's sense of time," which the authors suggest is considerably more urgent than that of adults. *See* Beyond the Best Interests of the Child, *above* at 40–42 (positing that "children have a built-in time sense based on the urgency of their instinctual and emotional needs"). Consistent with these notions, Professors Goldstein, Freud and Solnit proposed that once a young child has been in the continuous care of the same adult(s) for a relatively short period of time (one year for a child under the age of three and two years for a child between the ages of three and five), a strong presumption should exist that any change of custody would be detrimental to the child. *See* Before The Best Interest of the Child, *above* at 46–48. Thus, in a case such as Michael B., application of psychological parenting theory would strongly support the foster parents' claim to continued custody.

Although psychological parenting theory has had a significant influence on child welfare decision-making, it has also been controversial in both legal and mental health circles. Critics argue that the theory underestimates the importance to children of knowing and maintaining contact with their biological family. Matthew V. Johnson, *Examining Risks to Children In the Context of Parental Rights Termination Proceedings*, 22 N.Y.U. Rev. Law & Soc. Change 397, 407–10 (1996); Margaret Beyer and Wallace J. Mlyniec, *Lifelines to Biological Parents: Their Effect on Termination of Parental Rights and Permanence*, 20 Fam. L.Q. 233, 237 (1986). Critics also argue that the theory's emphasis on identifying a single "psychological parent" ignores persuasive psychological evidence that children maintain attachments to, and derive security from, "a network of caring adults." Peggy C. Davis, *The Good Mother: A New Look at Psychological Parent Theory*, 22 N.Y.U. Rev. L & Soc. Change 347, 351 (1996); *see* Marsha Garrison, *Why Terminate Parental Rights?*, 35 Stan. L. Rev. 423 (1983). Other critics have suggested that psychological parenting theory is based a narrow view of the traditional nuclear family and that it fails to consider culturally diverse family and caretaking patterns. *See, e.g.*, Carol B. Stack, *Cultural Perspectives on Child Welfare*, 12 N.Y.U. Rev. Law & Soc. Change 539 (1983–84) (describing minority subcultures where the extended family raises the children, with actual custodial and residential arrangements flexibly reflecting the family's and children's needs at a particular time, and where the children seem to thrive as well as in the nuclear-family setting). As a result of this failure, according to critics, psychological parenting theory can and has been used as a weapon against vulnerable low income families, particularly families of color, in foster care and termination of parental rights disputes. *See, e.g.*, Martin Guggenheim, *The Political and Legal Implications of the Psychological Parenting Theory*, 12 N.Y.U. Rev. Law & Soc. Change 549 (1983–84); Peggy C. Davis, *Use and Abuse of the Power to Sever Family Bonds* 12 N.Y.U. Rev. Law & Soc. Change 562 (1983–84). Finally, a number of critics have noted the discrepancy between the legal system's endorsement of psychological parenting theory in the foster care context and its far less favorable reception in the context of parental divorce, where courts and legislatures have emphasized the importance to children of continuing contact with both divorcing parents. *See generally* Marsha Garrison, *Parents' Rights vs. Children's Interests: The Case of the Foster Child*, 22 N.Y.U. Rev. L & Soc. Change 347, 351 (1996).

For a perceptive analysis and critique of the influence of psychological parenting theory on judicial decision-making, see Peggy C. Davis, *"There Is A Book Out . . . ": An Analysis of Judicial Absorption of Legislative Facts*, 100 Harv. L. Rev. 1539 (1987). For additional articles discussing the application of psychological parenting theory to the child welfare system, see *Symposium, Helping Families In Crisis: The Intersection of Law and Psychology*, 22 N.Y.U. Rev. Law & Soc. Change 295 (1996).

[B] Kinship Care

Over the past decade, both the number and the percentage of foster children who are placed with relatives has increased substantially. A 1993 report to Congress notes that "[c]hildren placed in foster care with relatives grew from 18% to 31% of the foster care caseload from 1986 through 1990 in 25 states that supplied information to the Department of Health and Human Services." Karen Spar, Kinship Foster Care: An Emerging Federal Issue (CRS Report for Congress No. 93–856, 1993). Kinship foster care is particularly prevalent in urban areas; for example, more than half of all foster children in New York City and in Cook County, Illinois are cared for by relatives. *See* Allen Harden, Rebecca L. Clark & Karen Maguire, Formal and Informal Kinship Care 5, 44–50 (1997); Marla Gottlieb Zwas, *Kinship Foster Care: A Relatively Permanent Solution*, 20 Fordham Urb. L. J. 343, 355 (1993) ("It is doubtful that without kinship foster care, New York City would [be able] to find enough homes for the surging number of foster children."). The rise in kinship foster care is attributable, in part, to a decline in the availability of traditional, non-related foster homes. Between 1985 and 1990, the number of traditional foster families declined by 27%, while the number of children in need of substitute care increased by 47%. Child Welfare League of American, Kinship Care: A Natural Bridge 17 (1994).

Despite the growing importance of kinship care as a component of state child welfare systems, many of the rules and policies that govern foster care and other government assistance programs are ill-suited to the needs of kinship caregivers. For example, Professor Randi Mandelbaum has argued that current welfare reform efforts, which emphasize strict time limits on assistance and caretaker self-sufficiency as an overriding goal, may be incompatible with the needs of children being cared for by extended family members, particularly grandparents. Randi Mandelbaum, *Trying To Fit Square Pegs Into Round Holes: The Need For a New Funding Scheme For Kinship Caregivers*, 22 Fordham Urb. L.J. 907, 916–18 (1995). Other commentators have noted that the emphasis on adoption as a preferred permanency option for children in foster care is problematic for most kinship caregivers, who are reluctant to participate in efforts to terminate the rights of biological parents, who are also members of their own family. *See, e.g.*, Marianne Takas, American Bar Association, Kinship Care and Family Preservation: Options for States in Legal and Policy Development 51, 55 (1994); Spar, *above* at 31. The growing importance of kinship foster care is thus forcing a reconsideration of the role of foster care overall, as well as many of the prevailing guidelines and assumptions about child welfare and permanency planning. Recognizing the need to address these issues, Congress recently directed the Secretary of HHS to convene an advisory panel on kinship care and to submit a report and recommendations to Congress by June 1, 1999. *See* Adoption and Safe Families Act of 1997, § 303(1997) (discussed in more detail at § 7.06[C], *below*).

NOTES AND QUESTIONS

(1) Many state foster care statutes embody a preference for placing foster children in the homes of relatives, where possible. *See generally* John Warren May, *Utah Kinship Placements: Considering the Intergenerational Cycle of Domestic Violence Against Children*, 22 J. Contemp. L. 97, 104–08 (1996) (surveying state statutes). Is such a preference for relative placement constitutionally required? *See* Elizabeth Killackey, *Kinship Foster Care*, 26 Fam. L.Q. 211, 212–14 (1992) Where the state terminates the rights of a child's biological parents, does the Constitution require that relatives be given priority as prospective adoptive parents?

(2) In addition to enacting a statutory preference for placement of foster children with relatives, many states have adopted streamlined procedures for approving relatives as foster caretakers. While some commentators applaud these efforts to facilitate kinship care, others have expressed concern that too hasty approval of relative caretakers may compromise the safety of foster children and risk perpetuating intergenerational cycles of violence and abuse. *Compare* Elizabeth Killackey, *Kinship Foster Care*, 26 Fam. L. Q. 211 (1992) (arguing that state licensing requirements should facilitate kinship placements, since such placements "achieve the state's dual mission of promoting both child welfare and family autonomy") *with* John Warren May, *Utah Kinship Placements: Considering the Intergenerational Cycle of Domestic Violence Against Children*, 22 J. Contemp. L. 97 (1996) (cautioning that any relaxation of placement standards or licensing requirements for relative caregivers may perpetuate the intergenerational cycle of violence). *See also* Marla Gottlieb Zwas, *Kinship Foster Care: A Relatively Permanent Solution*, 20 Fordham Urb. L. J. 343, 355–63 (1993) (discussing problems posed by New York City's expedited approval process for kinship foster homes and its failure to provide necessary services to children placed with relatives); Mark Hardin, *Placing Abused and Neglected Children with Kin: Deciding What to Do*, 13 A.B.A. Juv. & Child Welfare Rep. 91 (1994) (discussing benefits, risks and drawbacks of kinship placements).

(3) **Formal and Informal Kinship Care.** While increasing numbers of children are formally placed in the homes of relatives as a result of their entry into the state foster care system, large numbers of children are also cared for informally by relatives, on both a temporary and a long term basis. Indeed, most children who live in kinship care arrangements are *not* foster children. *See* Hardin, Clark & McGuire, *above* at 46. As a number of scholars have documented, caregiving by extended family members has long played an important role in protecting and providing for children, particularly in African-American communities. *See, e.g.*, Gilbert A. Holmes, *The Extended Family System In The Black Community: A Child-Centered Model For Adoption Policy*, 68 Temple L. Rev. 1649 (1995); Carol Stack, All Our Kin: Strategies For Survival In A Black Community (1974). A number of commentators have proposed and endorsed legal arrangements that would enable such "informal" kinship caregivers to establish a legal connection to the children they are raising without having to invoke state abuse and neglect procedures or terminate the rights of the biological parents. *See, e.g.*, Deborah Weimer, *Implementation of Standby Guardianship: Respect for Family Autonomy*, 100 Dick. L. Rev. 65 (1995); Randi Mandelbaum and Susan Waysdorf, *The D.C. Medical Consent Law: Moving Towards Legal Recognition of Kinship*

Caregiving, 2 D.C. L. Rev. 279 (1994); Susan Waysdorf, *Families in the AIDS Crisis: Access, Equality, Empowerment and the Role of Kinship Caregivers*, 3 Tex. J. Women & L. 145 (1994).

(4) When the state removes siblings from the custody of their parents, does it have an affirmative obligation to try to place those siblings in the same foster home or to facilitate visitation when siblings cannot be placed together? *See Aristotle P. v. Johnson*, 721 F. Supp. 1002 (N.D. Ill.1989) (agency policy of placing siblings in separate foster homes and denying them the opportunity to visit each other violated the siblings' associational rights). *Cf. D.W. v. D.W.*, 542 N.E.2d 407 (Neb. 1996) (juvenile court lacked authority to order visitation between teenager placed in foster care and younger sibling who remained in the care and custody of the biological parents); *Arkansas Dep't of Human Servs. v. Couch*, 832 N.W.2d 265, 266–68 (Ark. Ct. App. 1992) (trial court did not abuse its discretion by separating siblings into different placements for purposes of identifying prospective adoptive families). For arguments in favor of recognizing a constitutional right to sibling visitation in the context of foster care and adoption, see William Wesley Patton and Dr. Sara Latz, *Severing Hansel from Gretel: An Analysis of Siblings' Association Rights*, 48 U. Miami L. Rev. 745 (1995); Note, Christine D. Markel, *A Quest For Sibling Visitation: Daniel Weber's Story*, 18 Whittier L. Rev. 863 (1997).

(5) **Problem.** Under Oregon law, when a child has been found to be within the jurisdiction of the juvenile court because of parental abuse or neglect, the court may award custody of the child to the state and order the child placed in a foster home. Oregon recognizes two categories of foster care placements: relative placements and non-relative placements. The Oregon foster care statute contains a preference for placement with relatives, wherever possible. Despite this statutory preference, Oregon provides state-funded foster care benefits only for children placed with non-relatives. Foster children who are placed with relatives may be eligible for other forms of financial assistance, but these payments are typically much lower than the state-funded foster care benefits available to non-relative caretakers.

Sheri Lipscomb is a disabled child who was removed from her home because of abuse and neglect by her parents. Her aunt and uncle, Carolyn and Robert DeFehr, agreed to serve as her temporary foster parents despite Oregon's policy of denying them foster care funding. They have continued to provide a home to Sheri even though they fear that at some point they will have to give her up because they may be unable to pay for her medical care and other needs.

Autumn and Billy Scalf were removed from the home of their father because of neglect. The state Children's Services Division recommended that they be placed in relative foster care with their aunt and uncle. The children's aunt and uncle would like to provide care, but they have indicated that, without state foster care funding, they cannot bear the financial burden of caring for Autumn and Billy, in addition to raising their own three children. As a result, Autumn and Billy have been placed with an unrelated foster family, where they are unhappy and report difficulty in being able to practice their religion.

Sheri, Autumn and Billy, acting on behalf of themselves and others similarly situated, have filed suit challenging Oregon's foster care funding system on due process and equal protection grounds. Specifically, they argue that the Oregon funding scheme unconstitutionally interferes with the exercise of their fundamental right to family integrity and that it unlawfully discriminates against relative foster families. The state defends its policy as a rational attempt to maximize the total number of foster homes available for children in need of placement. In particular, the state argues that relatives are often willing to serve as foster caretakers without payment, but that non-relatives are rarely willing to do so. Thus, by maximizing the benefits paid to non-relative caretakers (instead of spreading the same total funding over a larger pool made up of both relative and non-relative caretakers), the state is able to recruit well-qualified foster care providers who need the additional financial incentives to be willing to serve as foster parents. The state also cites *Deshaney v. Winnebago County*, 489 U.S. 189 (1989) [reprinted *above* at § 7.03[E]], for the proposition that the government generally is under no obligation to facilitate or fund the exercise of constitutional rights.

How would you analyze the plaintiffs' constitutional claims and what result would you reach? *See Lipscomb v. Simmons*, 962 F.2d 1374 (9th Cir. 1992) (en banc).

[C] Permanent Dispositions and Foster Care Reform: From Family Preservation to Termination of Parental Rights

Over the past 20 years, the foster care system has been the object of numerous reform efforts at both the state and federal levels. The overriding goals of these reforms have remained constant: to decrease state reliance on out-of-home care and to promote permanency for children. However, the preferred means for achieving these goals has shifted significantly over time. Most recently, the emphasis has shifted from preserving and reuniting biological families to promoting permanency for foster children through adoption and termination of parental rights.

As early as the 1970s, studies indicated that the foster care system was not serving its intended function of providing a "temporary safe haven" for at-risk or maltreated children. Instead, as the Supreme Court noted in *Smith v. O.F.F.E.R.* (reprinted in § 7.06[A], *above*), children who entered foster care often languished there for long periods of time, and many spent their entire childhood in foster care "limbo." *See* John J. Musewicz, *The Failure of Foster Care: Child's Right to Permanence*, 54 S. Cal. L. Rev. 633, 636 (1981). Studies also suggested that many children were placed in foster care unnecessarily, and could be safely cared for at home, if additional services and support were made available to biological parents. *See* Alice C. Shotton, *Making Reasonable Efforts in Child Abuse and Neglect Cases: Ten Years Later*, 26 Cal. W.L. Rev. 223, 254–55 (1989–90).

Congress responded to these concerns by enacting the Adoption Assistance and Child Welfare Act of 1980 ("AACWA"). The overriding philosophy of the AACWA was that children are generally best served if they can be cared for at home, by their biological family. Shotten, *above* at 255: "This philosophy has as its starting point the belief that a child's biological family is the placement of first preference and that 'reasonable efforts' must be made to preserve this family as long as the child is safe." Accordingly, the AACWA sought to reduce states' reliance on foster care and to prevent the unnecessary removal of children from their homes. The Act had three major goals: first, to provide sufficient preplacement services to families to prevent the need for children to enter the foster care system; second, to ensure proper care for children who must be placed in foster care; and third to achieve permanency for foster children as quickly as possible, either by reunifying them with their biological parents or, if reunification were not possible, by facilitating adoption. Barbara Atwell, *A Lost Generation: The Battle for Private Enforcement of the Adoption Assistance and Child Welfare Act of 1980*, 60 U. Cin. L. Rev. 593, 600 (1992).

To effectuate these goals, the Act required states to make "reasonable efforts" to prevent removal of a child from his or her home and to make it possible for the child to return home once removal has occurred, as a condition of receiving federal child welfare funding. (42 U.S.C. § 671(15) (1994) (since amended). In addition, to facilitate permanency planning, the AACWA required states to develop a written case plan for each child who entered foster care and to establish an ongoing case review system. As part of this review system, a court was required to conduct a formal dispositional hearing within 18 months of a child's placement in foster care and periodically thereafter. The purpose of this dispositional review was to determine the future direction of the case, including whether the child should be returned to the parent(s), continued in foster care for a specified period, placed for adoption, or be continued in permanent or long-term foster care. 42 U.S.C. § 675(5)(C). Reunification of the child with his or her biological family was the preferred permanency objective.

Initially, the AACWA and related state reform efforts appeared successful in reducing the number of children entering foster care and in ameliorating foster care drift. Atwell, *above* at 598 n.30; *see*, Daan Braveman & Sarah Ramsey, *When Welfare Ends: Removing Children From the Home For Poverty Alone*, 70 Temple L. Rev. 447, 455–58 (1997). However, rising child welfare case loads and chronic under-funding of programs and services designed to preserve troubled families limited the effectiveness of these reforms. *See* Margaret Beyer, *Too Little, Too Late: Designing Family Support to Succeed*, 22 N.Y.U. Rev. Law & Soc. Change 311, 313–15 (1996). Some child welfare advocates attempted to remedy these inadequacies through the courts. During the late 1980s, a series of federal class actions alleged that state social service agencies had failed to conform to the mandates of the AACWA, particularly the Act's requirement that states provide "reasonable efforts" to keep children from entering foster care and to promote reunification of children with their biological families. *See* Atwell, *above*. As a result of these lawsuits, state officials in a number of jurisdictions entered into consent decrees specifically obligating them to provide particular preplacement and reunification services and to implement the case plan and case review provisions of the AACWA. *See* Robert Pear, *Many States Fail to Fulfill Child Welfare Requirements*, N.Y. Times, Mar. 17, 1996 at A1 (describing 21 state child welfare agencies under court supervision, many of which still fail to meet their statutory obligations).

These judicial enforcement efforts came to a halt when the Supreme Court ruled, in *Suter v. Artis M.*, 503 U.S. 347 (1992), that Congress had not intended the "reasonable efforts" provision of the AACWA to confer a federally enforceable right of action. Rather, the Court ruled that the sole remedy for a state's failure to comply with the "reasonable efforts" requirement of the AACWA was the cutoff of federal child welfare funding, provided for in the Act—a remedy that was likely to exacerbate, rather than improve, the plight of at-risk children and their families. Although Congress has since limited the effect of the *Suter* decision (*see* 42 U.S.C. § 1320a-2 (1994)), subsequent efforts to use the courts to enforce the provisions of the AACWA have generally produced only limited success. *See* Robert Pear, *above*.

By the late 1980s, the number of children entering foster care began to climb rapidly again. The American Public Welfare Association estimates that approximately 445,000 children were in substitute care at the end of 1993—an increase of over 60% from the end of 1985. *See* Allen Harden, Rebecca L. Clark & Karen Maguire, Formal and Informal

Kinship Care 5, 44–50 (1997). More recent estimates suggest that the number has since grown to half a million. H. Rep. 105–77, 105th Cong., 1st Sess. (1997). Among the factors responsible for this increase are the debilitating effects of parental drug and alcohol use, coupled with a severe shortage of treatment programs, particularly those designed to accommodate the needs of pregnant women and parents with substantial child care responsibilities. *See, e.g.*, Leslie Brody, *DYFS Gets Tough with Drug-Using Parents*, The Record (Northern New Jersey), Aug. 4, 1995, at A1; Barry M. Lester, *Keeping Mothers and Their Infants Together: Barriers and Solutions*, 22 N.Y.U. Rev. Law & Soc. Change 425, 436–37; Page McGuire Linden, *Drug Addiction During Pregnancy: A Call for Increased Social Responsibility*, 4 Am. U.J. Gender& Law. 1104, 1136–38 (1995).

These developments have led a number of state officials and child welfare advocates to question the AACWA's emphasis on family preservation and reunification. These criticisms gained strength after several highly publicized incidents in which children were killed or severely injured after being removed from foster care and reunified with their biological parents. *See, e.g.*, Kimberly McLarin, *Slaying of Connecticut Infant Shifts Policy on Child Abuse*, N.Y. Times, July 30, 1995, at A1; Jesse Hiestand, *Girl's Death Preventable, Lawyer Says; County Agency Attacked At Trial*, Daily News of Los Angeles, November 18, 1997 at SV1. In response to such criticisms, and in the face of continuing budgetary pressures, officials in a number of jurisdictions began shifting their emphasis from family preservation and reunification to permanency planning via adoption.

In 1997, the federal government followed suit, with the passage of the Adoption and Safe Families Act of 1997. The Act marks a significant shift in federal policy regarding foster care and adoption. Although the Safe Families Act generally retains the "reasonable efforts" requirement found in the AACWA, it emphasizes that the health and safety of children must be paramount concerns in determining what constitutes reasonable efforts to preserve and reunite biological families. 42 U.S.C. § 671(a)(15)(A) (1998). The Act also identifies "aggravating circumstances" in which reasonable efforts to preserve or reunify families are not required. These include abandonment, torture, chronic abuse or sexual abuse, as well as cases in which a parent has assaulted or killed another child or where a parent's rights to a sibling have been involuntarily terminated. 42 U.S.C. § 671(a)(15)((D). In addition, the Act makes clear that efforts to preserve or reunify biological families may be made concurrently with efforts to place children for adoption. 42 U.S.C. § 671(a)(15)(F).

The Safe Families Act attempts to facilitate adoption by expediting the process for termination of parental rights. In particular, the Act requires that states initiate proceedings to terminate parental rights for any child who has been in foster care for 15 of the previous 22 months, except where the state determines, based on compelling reasons, that such termination would not be in the child's best interests. The Act also requires expedited termination proceedings for infants who have been abandoned and for children who have been assaulted or whose siblings have been severely abused. 42 U.S.C. § 675(5)(E). Moreover, the Act requires that an initial permanency hearing be held no later than 12 months after a child enters foster care, as opposed to the 18-month time period allowed under the AACWA. 42 U.S.C. § 675(5)(C).

The Safe Families Act also provides financial incentive for states to increase their adoption rates for children in foster care. 42 U.S.C. § 673b. It requires the federal government to develop outcome measures to assess state child welfare programs and rate state performance in areas such as length of stay in foster care and number of adoptions. 42 U.S.C. § 479a. In addition, the Act requires states to provide post-adoption health insurance coverage for special needs children if such assistance is necessary to facilitate adoption. 42 U.S.C. § 673a. Finally, the Act convenes an advisory panel—made up of biological and foster parents, former foster children, public child welfare officials and others—to study "kinship care" and to submit a report and recommendations to Congress. *See* 42 U.S.C. 5113 (1998).

Although it is too early to determine the impact on state foster care systems of this shift in federal policy, the reforms contained in the Safe Families Act were preceded by similar state reform efforts in a number of jurisdictions. These state reforms appear to have resulted in a significant increase in petitions for termination of parental rights filed by child welfare authorities, and considered by appellate courts. The following two cases provide a glimpse of the likely impact on children and families of this shift in child welfare policy and the intense judicial debate that it has engendered in at least one state.

BUSH v. STATE
Supreme Court of Nevada
929 P.2d 940 (1996)

SHEARING, J.

This is an appeal from the district court's order terminating the parental rights of natural parents, appellants Rosemary Emilie Bush ("Rosemary") and her husband Alan Dean Bush ("Alan"), as to their children Alan Everett Bush ("Alan Everett") and Frisco Lou Bush ("Frisco"). Rosemary and Alan are mentally challenged. Rosemary has an IQ of 65, Alan an IQ of 71. Their children are also mentally challenged and participate in specialized school programs.

In December, 1988, Clark County Juvenile Court Services received a physical abuse complaint concerning the Bush family. A child protective services worker was assigned to the matter. She attempted to work with the Bushes to resolve the problems of Alan's physical abuse of one of the Bush children, marital discord between Rosemary and Alan, and a filthy home. At that time, Alan had moved out of the home temporarily, and Rosemary refused to accept referrals and other family assistance. After eight months of unsuccessful efforts, the worker recommended terminating Rosemary and Alan's parental rights.

On August 4, 1989, after the unsuccessful efforts to remedy the home situation, Alan Everett and Frisco were placed in Child Haven. The Clark County District Attorney filed a neglect petition alleging that Rosemary and Alan were neglectful in caring for their children because of marital problems, including arguing and fighting in front of the children. Additionally, it was alleged that Alan spent the family income irresponsibly without leaving enough for monthly obligations and the children had developmental delays. On August 18, 1989, Rosemary and Alan admitted to the neglect petition. The matter was then transferred to the Nevada State Division of Child and Family Services ("DCFS") for action. A case plan was filed on October 17, 1989, listing objectives to attain reunification of Alan Everett and Frisco with Rosemary and Alan and ordering them to comply with the plan. The matter came before the court for review twice each year from 1990 through 1993. By November 1993, termination efforts had been commenced. The petition to terminate the parental rights of Rosemary and Alan to Alan Everett and Frisco was filed on June 17, 1994. Rosemary and Alan were appointed counsel for this proceeding. After a hearing in October, 1994, the district court filed a decision granting the petition.

In its decision, the district court found two parental fault grounds to support termination of the Bushes' parental rights: parental unsuitability and failure of parental adjustment. The court found that even when the Bushes were willing, they failed to "assimilate and practice the lessons being taught" and would never be able to reach a level of ability sufficient to meet the physical and emotional needs of their children. The court also determined that (1) efforts of the agencies involved were reasonable and appropriate, (2) the testimony and exhibits reflected that parenting classes, independent living, financial aid and assistance and other appropriate services were extended to the family, (3) DCFS made monthly visitation efforts, and (4) the level of services extended to the family reflected the Bushes' failure to be receptive to the services. The district court also determined that (1) the children's best interests would not be served under any reasonable circumstances by sustaining the parental tie, (2) the children have been in foster care for three and one-half years, (3) the foster parents are willing to adopt the children, (4) the children have "bonded" to the foster parents, (5) further efforts to reunify the Bushes with their children "will not change the obvious," and (6) reunification is not foreseeable even if the court were to deny the petition to terminate parental rights. On October 25, 1995, the district court filed Findings of Fact, Conclusions of Law, and Order Terminating Parental Rights. The issue on appeal is whether clear and convincing evidence supports the district court order. We conclude that it does. . . .

The evidence is undisputed that each parent has a mental deficiency. Whether the deficiency renders each consistently unable to care for the immediate and continuing needs of the children for extended periods of time is the disputed question. Clearly, the Bushes love their children and have made some efforts toward becoming better parents. For example, they have sought more appropriate housing, have attended some parenting classes and managed their money more responsibly. However, they refused to complete either counseling or parenting classes. Randall Stiles, a child development specialist from the Children's Resources Bureau of the DCFS testified that after interviewing their social worker and the Bushes, and after observing the Bushes during a monthly hour-long visit with their children, he concluded that the Bushes had little to no desire to complete the case plan and were not cognizant of their own weaknesses as parents.

Rosemary admitted at the hearing, and the history of the case demonstrates, that they continue to resist the assistance of various agencies both to improve their abilities and to help the children to overcome their deficiencies. The children both have very special needs which would daunt an above-average parent without outside assistance. The admission of the persistent refusal of the parents to recognize the need for assistance, and the testimony of the social workers of the six years of effort, provide clear and convincing evidence that the Bushes are unable to meet the immediate and continuing needs of the children, both because of their unfitness as parents to these children, and their failure to adjust as parents. There is no reason to believe that they will not continue to be substantially incapable of parenting. . . .

We also conclude that there was clear and convincing evidence that the best interests of the children would be served by termination of the parental rights. Frisco and Alan Everett have special needs and require a level of care that is arguably difficult even for a person of ordinary intelligence to provide. In addition, both boys have spent at least four years in their present foster home. When the boys were placed in foster care, Frisco was ten months old and Alan Everett was two years old. The court-appointed special advocate ("CASA") observed the boys in their foster home for two years and believes that the foster parents relate well to the boys. The foster mother testified that if the children were free for adoption, she and her husband would adopt them. The child development specialist at the DCFS recommended that Frisco and Alan Everett remain in foster care so that their physical, developmental, and emotional needs continue to be met. We conclude that Frisco's and Alan Everett's best interests are not served by sustaining the tie to Rosemary and Alan.

The district court noted its dismay that Frisco and Alan Everett have remained in foster care for five years. We agree with the court's expressed dissatisfaction. While the parents' right to retain their children is an important consideration in the analysis, the rights of the children to a stable future with a loving family must be paramount. Otherwise, the children's development is compromised for the sake of the parents. Thus, we affirm the order of the district court.

STEFFEN, C.J., concurring:

. . . Unfortunately, these cases often present the courts with the Hobson's choice of either preserving parental rights at the expense of the children or sacrificing the parents in order to salvage the lives and futures of the children. Where it has been patiently and responsibly determined that both interests cannot be preserved without extensive injury to the one or the other, our Legislature has determined, and so must we, that the lives and the best interests of the children must take precedence. However, that is not to say in the least that if the poor, the sick and the powerless can be replaced as parents by those who would be "better" or more "talented," our law would support the state in doing so. The very thought defies decency and reason, and in any event would be a stark violation of the Constitution.

Turning now to the instant case, it is true that we are faced with loving parents who are mentally disadvantaged. As our colleague has so effectively noted, this alone must give us serious cause for concern, for this nation has a laudable public policy favoring affirmative measures to assist our handicapped citizens in the pursuit of meaningful, quality lives. However, when it comes to an evaluation of parental fitness or neglect, as the majority opinion notes, the courts are under statutory mandate, NRS 128.106, to consider emotional and mental illness or mental deficiency of the parents where it adversely impacts the physical or psychological needs of the children over extended periods of time.

Unfortunately, mental handicaps may produce conditions that are inconsistent with functional, healthy home environments for children. Although fault is absent, the impact on the children is just as great as if fault were present. But I note at the outset of my evaluation of the facts that this is a most unfortunate case—indeed, unfortunate to the extreme. Even at this late, late date, this is a very close and difficult case.

Tragically, in affirming the district court's decision to forever deprive these parents of their children and leave them with no more rights concerning the children than strangers off the street, I am convinced that we are sacrificing basically good and well-intentioned parents to a cumbersome, overloaded system that has managed to keep the children from their parents for over seven years. The one child, Alan Everett Bush, was removed from the parental home at approximately one and one-half years of age, and the second child,

Frisco Lou Bush, taken from the home at the same time, was a ten-month-old infant. The children have been living in a foster home since 1990, and the foster parents with whom they have bonded want to adopt them. This is essentially the only home and family these children know.

In reading this record from cover to cover, I am left with an abiding belief that these "mentally deficient" parents are not sufficiently "deficient" to render them incapable of being fit and caring parents. Moreover, in reading the testimony of the State's witnesses, I shudder at the amount of conjecture and speculative "forecasting" I saw there. Aside from a fearsome amount of "educated guesses" drawn from factual patterns that are far from established or egregious (or, for that matter, perhaps not all that far from normal), jurisdictional grounds were found to exist in the form of parental unsuitability and failure of parental adjustment. If we were reviewing this appeal seasonably, I would reject these findings.

The record reveals that for a period of time there were instances of argument between the parents in front of the children. There is meager evidence of a somewhat violent episode. Mr. Bush also made the mistake of impetuously purchasing a television set and stereo that the family could not afford (like how many other millions of parents across the country). There was also equivocal and conflicting evidence that at least on occasion, Mr. and Mrs. Bush failed to keep a clean apartment. The Bushes were also disparaged by a child development expert for their low income, their housing and their lack of transportation. Indeed, this expert found the Bushes lacking in nurturence and bonding with the children, a rather remarkable observation given the fact these parents had been restricted to such scant and unnatural visitation (one hour per month at the agency over an extended period of time) with their children. The Bushes were also found wanting in being "resistive" to some of the services offered by various agencies, and for not completing all of their programmed activities.

Despite the list of less than compelling negatives, including the fact that the children required special education and medication, these parents would ride their bicycles several miles to visit their children and made substantial attempts to abide by agency programs and directions which they believed were designed to effectuate a reunification with their children. The record frankly causes me to wonder about the extent to which these parents were ever intended to realize a reunion with Alan and Frisco. As counsel for the Bushes noted, it appears that his clients were doomed primarily because of their mental deficiencies, and my reading of their testimony leaves me with gnawing doubts about the accuracy of the evaluations on this critical point.

Notwithstanding the foregoing, I concur in the result reached by the majority because it appears to me that under the tragic facts of this case, we must resolve doubts as to whether jurisdictional grounds were demonstrated by clear and convincing evidence in favor of the children. I reach this conclusion advisedly, however, knowing that such a resolution may be viewed as an infringement of the Bushes' constitutional rights. It is clear, however, that the Legislature has made the best interests of the children paramount in these types of proceedings, and I am convinced that at this late date, it would be extremely traumatic for the two boys to either be again placed in limbo or be torn from the arms and love of the only parents that they now truly know. . . .

SPRINGER, J., dissenting:

The State permanently deprived a mentally handicapped mother and father of "the right of love and association" with their two children, because of the "genetic or physical limitations" suffered by these parents. (Trial Court's Decision, October 19, 1994). The Bushes have lost their children because the courts have concluded that they are "incapable of obtaining the skills" in parenting that parents must now possess in order to avoid the threat of having the State take away their children and give them to new, more skillful parents.

This case is one of a number of termination cases in a spate of cases in which poor and handicapped parents have lost their children to substitute parents because of a supposed lack of parenting skills and because the "best interests" of their children is supposedly being served by presenting them with a new and better set of parents.

I am not sure what causes can be attributed to these onslaughts on the poor and the handicapped, but it seems to me that they can be traced to the 1987 amendment of NRS 128.105, in which a provision was added to the termination statute, stating that the "primary consideration in any proceeding to terminate parental rights must be whether the best interests of the child will be served by the termination." As I see the various cases now coming before this court in which children of the poor, sick and powerless are almost routinely being taken from their natural parents and permanently given to more talented parents, I get the feeling that agents of the State have misinterpreted the statutory "best interests" addition to authorize a much greater intrusion into Nevada families. . . .

Whether the increase in the number of cases involving the termination of parental rights of the poor and handicapped is caused by a misreading of the "best interests" amendment of NRS 128.105 or by some other reasons, a certain pattern of cases is quite obviously on the increase. Here is the pattern:

Poor or handicapped parents are having trouble raising their children. The kinds of problems that these parents have are too legion to catalogue, but the common result is that the State removes the children from the home "temporarily." Almost always this is done by court order on a petition unopposed by the poor family, primarily because they do not have counsel.

Welfare imposes upon the parents a "reunification" plan that is supposed to be designed to get the children back into their home. In many cases the problems of poverty, mental or physical incapacity and other difficulties that brought about the family separation stand in the way of the parents' satisfactory compliance with the "reunification" plan.

The children are placed in the home of substitute parents, parents who are usually in a much better position to provide a "nicer" and more "nurturing" home environment. The natural parents visitation becomes more and more difficult and awkward. The children (naturally) "bond" and "integrate" with their substitute parents.

Welfare gives notice to the natural parents that they have flunked the reunification test, that their children are better off in their new home and that the natural parents must say "goodbye" forever to their children.

The parents get notice of the termination hearing. They finally, too late, get an attorney appointed to defend against the State. They lose their case. The children have a new set of parents. The natural parents have nothing. . . .

In the case now before the court . . . it appears to me that the Welfare Division initiated and carried out termination of parental rights proceedings solely because the parents were mentally handicapped. This is wrong. It also appears to me that the termination of parental rights in this case was probably principally motivated by the reality that the substitute home was a better home than the home that could be provided to the children by their handicapped parents. For reasons that I will explain in this dissent, I am very much concerned about prevalent social engineering theories that promote the permanent termination of parental rights of faltering and "inadequate" natural parents based on the assumption that placement of children in a "better" home will necessarily serve the children's "best interests." I am opposed to any social or legal theory that promotes the severance of parental ties just because the children (naturally and understandably) appear to have "become integrated" in a new, perhaps more amiable, home situation. . . .

Put plainly, this is not a case of parental fault, it is a case of faultless parental mental incapacity. The trial court concluded that no matter how hard they tried, the Bushes did not have sufficient intelligence to be entrusted with raising their children. The trial court concluded in its "Statement of Law" that the "result is the same regardless of whether the issue is the parent's inability or unwillingness," which is to say that it does not matter whether the Bushes were handicapped or recalcitrant. I think the question of fault or incapacity matters a great deal, and I am of the view that this court's refusal to deal with the question of fault versus incapacity in termination cases is an inexcusable dereliction on its part. . . .

There can be no question that the Bushes were far from being model parents and that they were having difficulties raising their children. Not surprisingly, the children of these two mentally deficient parents were, themselves, "developmentally delayed." When the Welfare Division filed its child-neglect petition it did not mention the single most significant aspect of this case, the parents' handicap. The petition stated, as grounds for the petition, only "marital discord," "family income irresponsibility" and the children's "developmental delays."

The Bushes do have very limited reading and writing skills, and it is extremely unlikely that they understood the nature of the proceeding or the dire consequences that eventually followed the filing of the petition. When the petition that resulted in their having their children removed from their home was first brought to court, they did not have an attorney, and they did not, consequently, file any legal opposition to the petition. These undefended proceedings not only resulted in the removal of their children from their home, but the court action taken in these proceedings was the primary cause of the eventual, permanent termination of their parental rights. The children were removed from the home on August 4, 1989, when one was two years old, and the other was 10 months old. That was the end of the Bush family. . . .

The question of when, if ever, it is proper to take incapacitated or handicapped parents' children away from them is a chilling one. I wonder what the attitude of the majority would be if a physical deficiency, say quadriplegia, had rendered the Bushes unable to "reach the level of sufficiency to meet the physical and emotional needs of their children." I wonder if, in the minds of the majority justices, mental deficiency is considered to be any more or less disabling than physical deficiency. I wonder how a sensitive and thoughtful majority would apply the standard of "irremediable inability to function" as a parent to the facts of this case. I tend to question . . . whether it is ever morally or constitutionally permissible to terminate the parental rights of a fault-free parent. . . .

As I read this record, I see that the Welfare Division has done a remarkably good job in finding foster parents who are willing to adopt these "developmentally delayed" children. The children have been with the foster parents going on five years; and the children, the trial court tells us, have "bonded" with the foster parents. It is hard to deny that at the present time the children would probably be better off staying in the foster home than placing them abruptly back into the now-alien home of the natural parents. But, I am not urging an immediate transfer of custody. I only question the propriety of permanent severance of parental ties. My point is that I believe that in this case there are reasonable circumstances under which the children's interest could be served by sustaining the parental ties and that, consequently, the requirement of dispositional grounds has not been met.

I do not think that it can be safely said that there are no reasonable circumstances which would permit maintaining the Bushes' parental relationship. Early on, shortly after the children were placed in foster care, the assigned welfare worker opined, in April of 1993, that the best interests of the child would be served by long-term foster care rather than termination of parental rights. The option of long-term foster care provides such a "reasonable circumstance"; and it is certainly an option that should have been considered in April 1993 and should have been considered by the trial court in this case.

Sadly enough, it appears to me likely that it is now the policy of the State to take children away from "inadequate" parents and find them a better home and to use the "best interests of the child" as the sole, criterion in determining whether to pursue a termination of parental rights action. Many of us today would not have been allowed to remain with our parents if the only basis for permanently taking us away from our parents was that there were some better parents around the corner. . . .

The point that I make is that we should not, morally or constitutionally, simply put the child on the scale and weigh to see which, the natural or the replacement parent, will better serve the "best interests of the child." The parents in this case have a low I.Q. and have had a terrible time trying to jump through all of the hoops that the Welfare Division introduced as a condition to their keeping their children. The Bushes have satisfactorily raised another child, and it seems to me that it is reasonable to conclude that with a little more help and a little more patience, the Bushes could have raised their now-lost children. . . .

RECODO v. STATE
Supreme Court of Nevada
930 P.2d 1128 (1997)

Rose, J.,

On May 31, 1995, the district court terminated the parental rights of appellant Adrina Francis Decespedes Recodo (Recodo) after concluding that Recodo was an unfit parent and had failed to adjust to become a suitable parent within a reasonable period of time. Recodo challenges the district court's conclusion, arguing that no clear and convincing evidence existed to support such a conclusion. Recodo also argues that her due process rights were violated because she was not appointed counsel at all stages of the termination proceedings.

We conclude that clear and convincing evidence existed to support the district judge's conclusion and that Recodo's due process rights were not violated.

FACTS

Michael William Bow (Michael) was born to Recodo on February 21, 1992. Recodo is an American Indian enrolled with the Goshute/Shoshone tribe who at the time of the termination hearing was twenty-six years old. Until she was approximately three years old, Recodo lived on a reservation in Arizona, and in 1981, Recodo moved with her grandparents, her guardians, to rural Southern Nevada. In addition to Michael, Recodo has four other children. At the time of the termination proceeding, Michael was living in a prospective adoptive foster home. Three of her other children, Maria, Victor, and Fernando, were in the custody of Victor and Fernando's father, Recodo's ex-husband Fernando Decespedes. Recodo's marriage to Decespedes ended because he beat her. Her daughter Lupita was living with her at her grandmother's house.

Michael came to the attention of Debra McEwan, the social worker for the Moapa Band of Paiutes. According to McEwan, on approximately April 1, 1993, Recodo voluntarily placed Michael in foster care due to her financial inability to meet his needs. At the time of the placement, Recodo was living with her grandmother who could not adequately care for Michael due to her health and age and Michael's special medical needs at birth. As a result, McEwan agreed to place Michael in courtesy foster care for a short period of time so that Recodo could obtain her GED at the Indian Center and look for employment in Las Vegas on weekdays and still care for Michael on the weekends. This arrangement was scheduled to last for six months. Recodo testified that during this period, she drove her grandfather's car into Las Vegas but that after a while she was unable to afford gas for the daily trips between Las Vegas and her grandmother's house on the reservation. As a result, she would stay with friends in Las Vegas, or when that was not possible she would study and sleep in the car. Recodo also testified that at this point her financial situation was so bad that often she would not eat for days just so she could afford to drive to Las Vegas to attend school and to try to find a job. Around May, 1993, Recodo's car broke down, and her grandparents sold it to her aunt and uncle. Recodo stated that she would either ride her bike or try to get rides with friends into Las Vegas to look for work, to appear in court, and to visit Michael at Childhaven, the state facility where Michael was eventually placed. . . .

On August 4, 1993, Michael was adjudicated a neglected child and made a ward of the Eighth Judicial District Court, Juvenile Division. He was placed into legal custody of the Division of Child and Family Services (DCFS) on August 4, 1993. On August 31, 1993, a case plan was established for Recodo. The plan required that Recodo: (1) maintain steady employment; (2) maintain steady, suitable, and appropriate housing; (3) complete a parent effectiveness training program; (4) maintain regular visits with Michael; (5) undergo individual and family therapy; (6) at least monthly, keep DCFS appraised of her address and telephone number; and (7) pay child support of $ 100 a month.

In September, 1993, Michael was removed from Childhaven and placed with a second foster family. Recodo saw Michael in February, 1994, on his second birthday, one time in October, 1994, one time in December, 1994, and one other unspecified time at the CCCPS office.

The initial judicial review of Recodo's case was held on October 5, 1993. The district judge found that Recodo had made regular visits to see Michael during his time at Childhaven but that she had not made any great progress toward reunification.

In October 1993, Recodo married Joachim Recodo (Joachim), a native of the Philippines, but Joachim was in this country illegally. In February 1994, Recodo told Cynthia Blaya that Joachim was being deported to the Philippines and that she was now ready to work towards reuniting with Michael.

Between February and April of 1994, Recodo apparently had two different jobs. First, she was working as an unarmed security guard at Wells Fargo. That employment lasted only about three months because Recodo was terminated when she allegedly made threatening remarks to a fellow employee. For a brief period, Recodo also worked at the Santrop Convenience Market as a clerk and cashier. This employment ended because Recodo was allegedly rude to a customer. According to Recodo, she remained unemployed for the next six to eight months.

In April, 1994, DCFS had a second hearing in district court regarding Recodo's progress. The DCFS report indicated that Recodo had not contacted it for five of the six months in the reporting period. During this hearing, the court warned Recodo that if she did not make progress between that time and the next hearing, DCFS would begin the termination of Recodo's parental rights.

In September, 1994, Recodo was indicted for the nonprobationary offense of bank fraud along with her ex-husband, Fernando Decespedes, and another man. At the time of the termination proceeding, another hearing on the bank fraud charges was scheduled for May 22, 1995. According to Recodo, Decespedes coerced her into participating in the crime by holding a gun to her head and telling her that she was a lousy mother who would never amount to anything. Then he pulled the trigger on an empty chamber. He then persuaded Recodo to assist him in the crime by confronting her with her inability to fulfill the case plan by obtaining transportation and insinuating that after the crime was committed she would be able to afford to obtain transportation.

On November 30, 1994, the State filed a petition to terminate Recodo's parental rights. The State claimed that under NRS 128.014 Recodo had neglected Michael by failing to provide him with such things as proper parental care, necessary subsistence, education, and medical care. The State also charged that Recodo was an unfit parent for failing to provide Michael with proper care, guidance, and support. The State noted in its petition that Recodo had been given a substantial amount of time to remedy the conditions that led Michael to being placed in foster care.

At the time of the petition, Michael had been residing in a prospective adoptive foster home since September of 1993. Ruth, the foster mother, testified at the termination hearing that she and her husband wished to adopt Michael.

The termination proceedings commenced on April 21, 1995. McEwan testified that after Michael had been placed in state custody in 1993, she did not hear from Recodo for "many, many months." Then Recodo contacted her in late 1994, and from November, 1994, through February, 1995, McEwan had "very heavy contact" with Recodo. McEwan testified that since November, 1994, she had seen more of an effort on Recodo's part to turn her life around: with the financial help of her grandmother, Recodo had bought a car; she had been seeing a psychologist; she had made a more concerted effort to maintain employment; and between November 1994 and April 1995 she only lost contact with DCFS one or two times. McEwan also testified that she worked with Recodo to help reunite her with Michael by helping Recodo budget her money so that she could get her own place to live and a regular means of transportation, setting up a specific schedule to visit Michael while he was in the custody of the state, and referring Recodo to Dr. Waldmeyer, a psychologist for the tribe. Recodo also saw another therapist fairly regularly from November, 1994, until February, 1995. In March, 1995, Recodo applied and was accepted for unemployment benefits, and McEwan stated that a day care facility suitable for Michael's needs had opened on the reservation and that social services, such as Indian general assistance and McEwan's service section, were available to help both Recodo and Michael. As far as terminating Recodo's rights to Michael, McEwan testified that although Recodo had been unreliable in the past in following through on required adjustments, she would like to see her have another chance.

Veronica Jean Amiano, a social work supervisor with DCFS, testified at the termination hearing as follows. On June 3, 1994, Recodo came to the division office and was agitated, upset, and used quite a bit of profanity. She requested to talk to Amiano privately, and in Amiano's office Recodo expressed her annoyance with the termination proceedings and her frustration that she did not seem to have a way to actually get Michael back. She told Amiano that she had a good mind to blow up the division office and take her son. She told Amiano that she was out of her anti-anxiety prescription and that the Indian Affairs Office had not helped her to renew it. Recodo told Amiano that she felt like she was giving up on her son and that the DCFS should draw up the relinquishment papers and let her know when to come in and sign them, and on September 24, 1994, Recodo called Amiano again and repeated this request.

Cynthia Blaya, Recodo's DCFS case worker, testified that the biggest impediment to Recodo's possible reunion with Michael was her inconsistencies. These included her inability to maintain steady employment, find appropriate housing, and maintain a regular visitation schedule with Michael. Blaya stated that from August, 1993, when the State obtained custody over Michael, to April, 1995, the time of the termination hearing, she saw very little progress from Recodo. She also stated that since the initial October 5, 1993, court review, Recodo had not provided verification of progress on her case plan, although Recodo had completed parenting classes in February, 1994. Additionally, by the time of the termination proceeding, Recodo had only paid $160 in child support.

On May 31, 1995, the district court granted the State's petition to terminate Recodo's parental rights to Michael. The district court concluded that Recodo was an unfit parent as defined by NRS 128.018 (defining unfit parent as one who has by his or her own fault failed to provide the child with proper care) and NRS 128.106 (listing specific considerations in determining neglect by unfit parents). Additionally, the district court found that Recodo had failed to adjust to become a reasonable parent within a reasonable period of time as defined by NRS 128.0126.

Recodo now argues that no clear and convincing evidence existed to support the district judge's conclusion and further that her due process rights were violated because she was not afforded counsel throughout the entire termination process.

DISCUSSION

The power to terminate parental rights is an "awesome power." *Champagne v. Welfare Division*, 100 Nev. 640, 645, 691 P.2d 849, 853 (1984). This court has characterized the termination of parental rights as a civil death penalty. Consequently, a termination of parental rights must be scrutinized closely on appeal.

Two kinds of grounds must be considered in termination proceedings. "There must be jurisdictional grounds for termination—to be found in some specific fault or condition directly related to the parents—and dispositional grounds—to be found by a general evaluation of the child's best interest." *Id* at 647, 691 P.2d at 854. Both grounds must be established by clear and convincing evidence. . . .

The district court found that jurisdictional grounds existed pursuant to two factors listed in NRS 128.105. The first was Recodo's parental unfitness. The term "unfit parent" as used in NRS 128.105 is defined as "any parent of child who, by reason of his fault or habit or conduct toward the child or other persons, fails to provide such child with proper care, guidance and support." NRS 128.018. . . .

After reviewing the record in the present case, we conclude that clear and convincing evidence of Recodo's unfitness existed. The district judge concluded that the efforts of DCFS were reasonable and that they even found substitute care for Michael so that Recodo could find housing and employment and could establish stability in her life. The district judge also concluded that testimony proved that even after Recodo was relieved of the obligations of caring for Michael she did nothing to help establish stability in her life which she needed to care for Michael. This constitutes clear and convincing evidence of Recodo's irremediable inability to function as a proper and acceptable parent

The second jurisdictional ground was a failure of parental adjustment. NRS 128.105(2)(d). The district court concluded that Recodo was unable or unwilling within a reasonable time to substantially correct the conditions which led Michael to be placed outside her home. . . . NRS 128.109(1) (b) allows a finding of failure of parental adjustment if a parent fails to substantially comply with "the terms and conditions of a plan to reunite the family within 6 months after the date on which the child was placed or the plan was commenced, whichever occurs later."

Recodo was given well over a year to adjust and provide a suitable and stable environment for Michael. The evidence indicates that Recodo's overarching and uncorrected problem was chronic instability in her employment, housing, and contacts with Michael. From the time the case plan was formulated in August 1993 until the final termination hearing in April 1995, Recodo did not maintain steady employment or stable housing, and she went through at least three jobs, two of which ended because of her volatility. She frequently changed her living arrangements and was unable to maintain a stable living arrangement to bring Michael back into. Throughout these two years, her contact with DCFS and with Michael was sporadic; between approximately October 1993 and April 1994, it was nonexistent.

We conclude that over one and one-half years was a substantial amount of time to keep Michael in suspense while his mother tried to adjust. Nothing indicates with any certainty that additional services would bring about a lasting parental adjustment on the part of

Recodo. Therefore, we conclude that the evidence constituted sufficient jurisdictional grounds to allow an evaluation of the dispositional grounds.

We have also considered the district court's analysis of the dispositional grounds. Testimony was presented that Michael is thriving in his foster home, where he has been since 1993, and that the foster parents wish to adopt Michael. Additionally, testimony indicated that Michael's present living situation is in stark contrast to the instability he experienced prior to being placed in the foster home. . . .

We therefore conclude that clear and convincing evidence existed to support the district judge's conclusion that Michael's best interests would be served by terminating Recodo's parental rights.

Finally, Recodo argues that her due process rights were violated because she did not have counsel appointed at all stages of the proceedings. This court has stated that as a matter of due process, "parents are entitled to: (1) a clear and definite statement of the allegations of the petition; (2) notice of the hearing and the opportunity to be heard or defend; and (3) the right to counsel." *Matter of Parental Rights of Weinper*, 112 Nev. 710,, 918 P.2d 325, 328 (1996).

Recodo did not have an attorney until the final termination proceeding, but she did have an attorney present at that hearing to protect her interests. Therefore, we conclude that Recodo's due process rights were not violated and that her liberty interest was properly protected at the actual termination hearing. . . .

SHEARING, J., concurring:

I agree with the reasoning and result in the majority opinion. However, I feel compelled to write a concurring opinion to respond to Justice Springer's dissent.

There is nothing arbitrary about a standard for termination that incorporates consideration of a parent's acts and failures to act. Where a mother refuses to care for her son, voluntarily gives him to foster care, and then does not even bother to see the child for months on end even though she is in the same town, these acts should count against her. In the case of Recodo, she obviously displayed mixed feelings about her son by stating at various times that she wanted to relinquish her parental rights. Recodo took advantage of some of the assistance offered to her, such as parenting classes and therapy, but did not follow through on other assistance. It is true that Recodo was poor at the time of termination, but it appears she squandered several opportunities given to her to escape poverty. She was asked to leave school and three different jobs because she fought and/or made threats on the job. Recodo also threatened to blow up state offices and was indicted for bank fraud.

One may sympathize with Recodo for her personal problems, but the fact remains that, at the time of the hearing, she had left her son in the care of others for two years with only sporadic contact. Her three-year-old son also deserves some sympathy for the instability in his life due to his mother's actions. He deserves a stable loving home and parents who are willing to provide him with care and guidance, which his mother is apparently unable or unwilling to supply. . . .

Justice Springer seems to imply that in terminating parental rights, the State is passing moral judgment on the parents. That is not true. The State is only determining that the parents are incapable of keeping their children safe and secure. It may not be the parents' fault that they are incapable of caring for their children, but fault is not the important or even relevant consideration.

Justice Springer perceives an "epidemic" of terminations. The negative term "epidemic" is inappropriate and connotes a sinister motive on behalf of the State. That the need for termination may arise more frequently than we would wish is indeed a misfortune, but the State is responding to the needs of the children, not creating the situations which place the children at risk. In reality, termination shows compassion to children by not condemning them to live with abusive and neglectful parents and thereby preventing their growing up to repeat the cycle of violence and neglect with their own children. The overwhelming majority of defendants who have appeared before me for sentencing were subject to abuse and neglect as children. By terminating parental rights in appropriate cases, I hope that we are in the process of breaking the pattern by providing safe, loving homes to the children who are tomorrow's parents.

SPRINGER, J., dissenting:

I dissent in this case for essentially the same reasons that I dissented in *Bush v. State* [*above.*] . . . The case now before us is in many respects more tragic than *Bush* because this mother's children were taken away from her just because she was poor. . . .

Concurring Justice Shearing believes that the State "shows compassion" when it deprived this mother of her son. I say, "The helping hand strikes again." I have no reason to doubt that, as put in the majority opinion, the child is "thriving in his foster home"; but, in my opinion, this does not justify permanently depriving an American Indian mother of her natural son and depriving the child of his priceless heritage.

This case is only one of an ever-increasing number of cases in which destitute parents come before this court desperately pleading that their children not be taken away from them forever. There can be no doubt that over the past year the number of these cases has dramatically increased. The reason for the apparent exponential growth in parental terminations is not clear to me. Concurring Justice Shearing suggests that the rash of termination cases has been brought about "because the parent or parents irrefutably demonstrated their inability to care for their children." It does not make sense to me, however, that the number of incompetent parents in this state has all of a sudden grown to the point that this court sees two or three of these cases during each monthly oral argument session, whereas not too long ago we had this number in a year's time. It seems much more likely to me that the State's recent rush to terminate natural parental rights, particularly the rights of destitute and handicapped parents, is the result not of an overnight increase in the number of incompetent parents but rather of a conscious, executive decision on the part of welfare officials. . . .

I see the State's permanent exclusion of this American Indian boy's natural mother from his life as an example of the pattern outlined in the *Bush* dissent. The child's mother was destitute, and it may have been necessary and advisable that the child be placed for a limited time in temporary foster care; however, as in so many cases, temporary really means permanent. Once the child was taken away from the mother, the usual disastrous problems ensued. Let me now recount from the record how this tragedy took place.

Adrina Recodo was the victim of an abusive domestic relationship, and she sought the help of a social worker on the Paiute Reservation, stating that she was having problems taking care of her son after she got out of the relationship. She told her case worker that she had no income, no place to live and no transportation. In need of money, food and a place to live, the State's response was to send Ms. Recodo to a psychologist. The State also decided to take her son away from her and to place him in foster care. Ms. Recodo was destitute; and on many occasions she was faced with the choice of eating or spending the money on transportation that would take her to school or to try and find a job. She received no State assistance in obtaining housing, although obtaining adequate housing was made a condition of the reunification plan. My reading of the record tells me that it was unfair for the court to hold, under these circumstances, that Ms. Recodo flunked the reunification test.

The trial judge stated in his written Decision that "the [Welfare] Division cannot be expected to get Recodo a job, a home, and to provide financial stability." Such a statement, to my way of thinking, wrongly justifies the position apparently taken by the State in this case: "Get a job; get a home; and get financial security—or lose your son permanently." Certainly Ms. Recodo tried to do something about her destitution. Deborah McEwan, Director of Social Services for the Moapa Band of Paiutes, testified that it was a "pretty fair assessment" when counsel asked if Ms. Recodo "tries so hard to improve herself [that] she bites off more than she [can] chew . . . and sometimes fail[s] when she over shoots what she believes she's going to be able to accomplish." Ms. Recodo tried to keep the State from taking her child away from her, but did not quite make it.

Ms. Recodo's social worker recognized that, among many problems, transportation was a major problem for Ms. Recodo:

> The reservation is in a very rural area and commuting to Las Vegas is fifty plus miles. And, we had at that time no suitable day care at the reservation. He was an infant. We had Head Start, but there was no way for her to leave him.

The record is replete with descriptions of the almost insurmountable obstacles put in the way of Ms. Recodo by the State. I do not undertake in this dissent to present a complete account of the tragic conditions that resulted in Ms. Recodo's son being placed in a non-Indian home and taken away from his mother forever; but I do want to say that my reading of the record tells me that Ms. Recodo did not, under *Champagne*, "deserve" to lose her child permanently. 100 Nev. at 648, 691 P.2d at 855 (footnote omitted). . . .

The trial court made the sad observation that "the difficult aspect of this case is the realization that one day Recodo may determine that Michael is a priority and make the progress necessary to reunify with Michael." The trial court recognized the possibility that Ms. Recodo was going to make the "progress necessary" to place this child back with its mother. In my view, termination of this mother's parental rights was premature and unseemly. I would reverse the termination order.

NOTES AND QUESTIONS

(1) The strongly worded opinions in *Bush* and *Recodo* illustrate both the importance and the difficulty of the decisions that child welfare officials and, ultimately, judges are asked to make about children placed in foster care. Like the Adoption and Safe Families Act discussed above, the statutory provisions relied on in *Bush* and *Recodo* were designed to

facilitate adoption, and thereby promote permanency for foster children, by expediting the process for terminating parental rights. Among other grounds, the Nevada statute allows for termination based on a finding of "failure of parental adjustment" if a parent "fails to substantially comply with the terms and conditions of a plan to reunite the family within 6 months after the date on which the child was placed or the plan was commenced, whichever occurs later." Is this six-month time period appropriate? Why or why not?

(2) The foster parents in both *Bush* and *Recodo* had expressed a strong interest in adopting the children placed in their care. To what extent should the availability of identified, prospective adoptive parents influence the state's decision whether to terminate parental rights? *Cf.* Martin Guggenheim, *The Effects of Recent Trends to Accelerate the Termination of Parental Rights of Children in Foster Care—An Empirical Analysis in Two States*, 29 Fam. L.Q. 121, 132–33 (1995) (noting that an increasing number of foster children are becoming legal orphans following the termination of their parents' rights). What are the advantages and disadvantages of encouraging foster parents to think of themselves as prospective adopters?

(3) One of the questions on which the various justices in *Bush* and *Recodo* disagree is the relevance of parental fault. For the majority and concurring justices, fault is not a primary issue. As concurring Justice Shearing explains in *Recodo*: "It may not be the parents' fault that they are incapable of caring for their children, but fault is not the important or even the relevant consideration." By contrast, dissenting Justice Springer seems unwilling to terminate the rights of a biological parent who has not engaged in blameworthy conduct. Should the involuntary termination of parental rights depend upon a showing of parental fault? Does the Constitution require such a showing? *See* Louise A. Leduc, *Note, No-Fault Termination of Parental Rights in Connecticut: A Substantive Due Process Analysis*, 28 Conn. L. Rev. 1195 (1996).

(4) The majority and dissenting Justices also appear to disagree on the extent of the government's obligation to assist parents hampered by poverty or mental disability. The trial judge who terminated Adrina Recodo's parental rights noted that the state "cannot be expected to get Recodo a job, a home and to provide financial stability." By contrast, dissenting Justice Springer faults the state for failing to help Recodo obtain housing, even though "obtaining adequate housing was made a condition of the reunification plan." Similarly, in a portion of his *Bush* dissent not reproduced above, Justice Springer suggests that Mr. and Mrs. Bush might have been able to resume caring for their children if they had continued to receive parenting assistance, which was discontinued because of state budget cuts. How much assistance (if any) should the state be required to provide to disadvantaged biological parents before terminating their parental rights? Should the state's failure to fulfill its obligations provide a defense to parents in termination proceedings? For further discussion of these issues, see Sarah Ramsey & Daan Braveman, *"Let Them Starve": Government's Obligation to Children in Poverty*, 69 Temp. L. Rev. 1607 (1995); Dave Shade, *Empowerment For the Pursuit of Happiness: Parents With Disabilities and The Americans With Disabilities Act*, 16 Law & Inequality 153 (1998). *Cf.* David Herring, *Inclusion of the Reasonable Efforts Requirements in Termination of Parental Rights Statutes: Punishing the Child for the Failure of the State Child Welfare System*, 54 U. Pitt. L. Rev. 139 (1992) (arguing that a state's failure to fulfill its statutory obligation to assist parents should not preclude it from terminating parental rights, where parents are unable to care for a child and termination serves the child's interests).

(5) Dissenting Justice Springer notes that neither the Bushes nor Ms. Recodo were represented by counsel until the final stages of these child welfare proceedings—after the state had already decided to terminate their parental rights. Should indigent parents be entitled to representation at all stages of civil abuse and neglect proceedings that may eventually lead to termination of their parental rights? *Cf. Lassiter v. Dep't of Soc. Servs.*, 452 U.S. 18 (1981) (due process clause does not require states routinely to provide counsel to parents in termination of parental rights proceedings). If you had been appointed to represent Mr. and Mrs. Bush at the time that state authorities initially removed their children, what additional steps might you have taken on your clients' behalf? What might you have done if you had been representing Adrina Recodo at the August, 1993, hearing at which her son was first adjudicated a neglected child? For additional discussion of a parent's right to counsel in connection with proceedings to terminate parental rights, see §8.04[D], *below*.

(6) One of the things that makes cases such as *Bush* and *Recodo* so wrenching may be the "all-or-nothing" nature of traditional adoption. To ensure that foster children are legally "available" for adoption, the state must ordinarily terminate the rights of their biological parents, thus completely severing the legal relationship between biological parent and child. Some commentators have argued that states should develop other permanency options, such as long-term custody awards to non-parents, subsidized guardianship and so-called "open adoption," which would not require a termination of biological parent's rights. *See, e.g.*, Meryl Schwartz, *Reinventing Guardianship: Subsidized Guardianship, Foster Care, and Child Welfare*, 22 N.Y.U. Rev. Law & Soc. Change 441 (1996); Jesse L. Thornton, *Permanency Planning for Children in Kinship Foster Homes*, 70 Child Welfare 593 (1991); Marsha Garrison, *Why Terminate Parental Rights?*, 39 Stan. L. Rev. 423 (1983). What do you see as the advantages and disadvantages of such alternatives to traditional adoption for children in foster care? For their biological parents? For potential adoptive families? For additional discussion of "open adoption" see § 8.06[b], *below*.

(7) In 1978, Congress responded to findings that Native American children were being removed from their families and tribal communities at alarming rates—often without justification—by enacting the Indian Child Welfare Act (ICWA), 25 U.S.C. § 1901, *et seq.* (1978). *See also* Indian Child Welfare Programs: Hearings Before the Subcommittee on Indian Affairs of the Senate Committee on Interior and Insular Affairs, 93rd Cong., 2d Sess. (1974). "In passing the ICWA, Congress promulgated three separate policies: (1) establishment of and adherence to minimum standards in order to remove Indian children from their families; (2) placement of Indian children in homes that reflect the unique values of Indian culture; and (3) government assistance for child and family service programs." Sloan Philips, *The Indian Child Welfare Act in the Face of Extinction*, 21 Am. Indian L. Rev. 351, 354 (1997).

Under the ICWA, whenever a child custody proceeding involves an Indian child, a tribal court retains authority to determine issues involving the child, including whether the child is a member of a tribe and whether an adoption or foster care placement is to be approved or denied. Moreover, the ICWA gives Indian parents and tribal courts the power to invalidate an adoption or custody decree for failure to follow ICWA provisions. *Id.* at 354. Would the ICWA apply in *Recodo*? If the ICWA would apply, why wasn't it followed or even mentioned by the Nevada Supreme Court?

In recent years, the ICWA has been criticized for failing to meet the needs of Indian children, particularly in the context of adoption. Indeed, at the time of the Recodo decision,

Congress was debating amendments to the ICWA that would have significantly reduced the tribal court's control over the adoption of Indian children, by limiting the time period during which a tribe or family member could contest proceedings conducted in state court and by using a child's percentage of Indian blood as a criteria for determining the applicability of the ICWA. *See* The Adoption Promotion and Stability Act, Title III, 142 Cong. Rev. H4808, H4811 (daily ed., May 10, 1996). The legislation died in the House of Representatives (H.R. 1082, 105th Cong. (1977), but was reintroduced in the next Congress. *See* Indian Child Welfare Act Amendments of 1997.

Query: Should foster care and adoption proceedings involving Native American children be subject to special, federal requirements and procedures? If so, should tribal courts or should state courts be authorized to determine which children are subject to these requirements? For additional discussion of the ICWA, in the context of adoption, see § 8.05[B], *below.*

(8) **Problem.** Breanne G. was placed in foster care at the age of 10 months, after she and her mother, Dawn, were evicted from the apartment that they had shared with Dawn's grandmother, who had been helping Dawn care for Breanne. Breanne's biological father is serving a 15-year prison sentence for drug distribution. Shortly after relinquishing custody of Breanne, Dawn—who was an intravenous drug user—learned that she had AIDS. Determined to "turn her life around," Dawn sought to enroll in a 12-month residential drug treatment program. After spending six months on the waiting list, Dawn was accepted into the program. Over the next 12 months, Dawn visited Breanne infrequently, in part because of the distance between Breanne's foster home and Dawn's residential treatment program. Dawn has now completed the residential portion of her treatment program and has enrolled in an out-patient maintenance program. The supervisor of the treatment program says that about half of the patients who complete the program are able to remain drug-free, and that he considers Dawn to be a "good risk." Dawn has also enrolled in parenting classes and has moved back in with her grandmother. Because of Dawn's illness, she is unable to work full time, but she has applied for disability benefits, which she plans to contribute toward her grandmother's rent and other household expenses. Dawn has requested that Breanne be returned to her custody, so that she can care for her daughter as long as she is able. Dawn plans to ask her grandmother to serve as Breanne's legal guardian if she dies or becomes too sick to take care of Breanne. Dawn's grandmother is willing to care for Breanne as long as she is physically able, but has expressed reservations about adopting the child.

Breanne's foster parents, the Smiths, object to Dawn's request for custody of Breanne. They argue that Breanne—who is now almost three—has lived with them for most of her life, and that she would suffer serious psychological harm if she is removed from their care. The Smiths have expressed a strong desire to adopt Breanne, and they have requested that the state child welfare agency file a petition to terminate Donna's parental rights.

(a) You are the agency social worker to whom this case has been assigned. The next foster care review hearing is coming up and the agency must make a recommendation to the court. What position would you recommend that the agency take and why?

(b) Assume that the agency has filed a petition to terminate Donna's parental rights. You are the trial judge to whom the termination petition has been assigned. The governing statute in your state is identical to the statute applied in *Bush* and *Recodo*. How would you rule and why?

CHAPTER 8

ADOPTION

SYNOPSIS

§ 8.01 Introduction
§ 8.02 Consent to Adoption
    [A] Timing and Validity of Consent
    [B] Consequences of Invalid Consent
§ 8.03 Unwed Fathers, Due Process and Involuntary Termination of Parental Rights
§ 8.04 The Adoption Process
    [A] Agency Adoption
    [B] Independent Adoption and the Lawyer's Role
    [C] Stepparent and Second Parent Adoption
    [D] Procedural Requirements
§ 8.05 Selecting An Adoptive Family: The Relevance of Race, Ethnicity and Religion
    [A] The Role of Race in Adoption
    [B] The Indian Child Welfare Act
    [C] Religion
§ 8.06 Legal Consequences of Adoption
    [A] Confidentiality and Access to Adoption Records
    [B] "Open Adoption" and Post-Adoption Visitation
    [C] Disclosure Requirements and "Wrongful Adoption"

§ 8.01 Introduction

Adoption is the legal process that creates the relationship of parent and child between individuals who are not each other's biological parent or child. Joan Heifetz Hollinger, *Introduction To Adoption Law and Practice* at 1–1 to 1–3, in Adoption Law and Practice (Joan Heifeiz Hollinger, ed., Matthew Bender 1998). Adoption is best understood as a two-step process. First, there must be a termination of the parental rights of the child's biological parents. This can be either a voluntary termination, based upon parental consent or relinquishment, or an involuntary termination, based upon parental unfitness or abandonment, or—more controversially—upon a judicial determination that termination is necessary to avoid detriment to the child. *See* § 8.03, *below*. The second step in the adoption process is the creation of a new parent child-relationship with the adoptive parents, with all its attendant legal rights and responsibilities. *See generally* John DeWitt Gregory, Peter N. Swisher, & Sheryl Scheible-Wolf, Understanding Family Law § 5.08 [A], [B] (1995).

Until recently, adoption in the United States was generally viewed as an "all-or-nothing" proposition; a judicial decree of adoption necessarily severed both the legal and the affective ties between the adopted child and his or her biological family. The legal system reinforced this notion of adoption by issuing a new birth certificate for the adopted child and by sealing the records of the adoption, not only from the public at large, but also from the members of the adoption triad. *See generally* Annette Ruth Appell, *Blending Families Though Adoption: Implications for Collaborative Adoption Law and Practice*, 73 B.U. L. Rev. 997 (1995). Over the past five years, changing psychological understandings, coupled with changes in the population and characteristics of children being adopted, have led to the development of various forms of "open adoption" that challenge this all-or-nothing paradigm. *See* § 8.06, *below*.

Although adoption was widely recognized under early Greek and Roman law, it did not become a part of the Anglo-American common law. Accordingly, adoption law in most American jurisdictions today is purely statutory. *See generally* Homer Clark, The Law of Domestic Relations in the United States 850–55 (1987). Adoption as currently recognized in the United States did not exist until the middle of the nineteenth century. Until that time, children who were orphaned, or whose parents were unable or unwilling to care for them, were provided for in a variety of ways, including indentured servitude or apprenticeship, almshouses and orphanages, and later, foster family care. In 1851, Massachusetts passed a landmark state adoption statute, which became model for other jurisdictions. This early Massachusetts law incorporated the then-novel notion that the child's welfare was to be the primary consideration in adoption. The statute established a judicial framework for supervising adoptions, and it obligated the state, through its courts, to protect the biological parents from an uninformed or coerced decision to relinquish a child, and to protect the adoptive parents from an uninformed and hasty decision to take the child. These early statutory principles continue to form the cornerstone of modern adoption law and practice. *See generally* Hollinger, *above* at 1–18 to 1–50; Presser, *The Historical Background of the American Law of Adoption*, 11 J. Fam. L. 443 (1971).

Although adoption in most American states is regulated by statute, the legal concept of an "equitable adoption" or an "adoption by estoppel" has been recognized in a number of jurisdicitons. *See* J.C.J., Jr., Note, *Equitable Adoption: They Took Him Into Their Home and Called Him Fred*, 58 Va. L. Rev. 727 (1972) (listing 26 states that arguably recognize the concept of equitable adoption). Where recognized, the doctrine of "equitable adoption" allows a child, under certain circumstances, to inherit property from foster parents, or from other adults who have acted in a parental capacity. *See, e.g., Wheeling Silver Dollar Sav. & Trust Co. v. Singer*, 250 S.E.2d 369, 372 (W. Va. 1978); *In re Estate of Wilson*, 168 Cal. Rptr. 533, 535 (Cal. Ct. App. 1980). Some states, however, have rejected the concept of equitable adoption as inconsistent with state adoption statutes. *See, e.g., Maui Land & Pineapple Co. v. Naiapaakai Heirs*, 751 P. 2d 1020, 1022 (Haw. 1988).

In all states, children may be placed for adoption by state agencies or by private agencies licensed by the state. This process is generally referred to as an *agency adoption*, since it is accomplished under the auspices of a public or private agency. In a significant majority of states, adoption may also occur without the involvement of a licensed agency. This alternative process is known variously as *independent, private placement,* or *direct placement adoption.* Typically, in an non-agency adoption, a lawyer or other intermediary will bring together the birth parents and the prospective adoptive parents. The line between a lawful independent placement and an illegal "black market" sale of a child can be a murky one. For this reason, most states limit the activities and allowable fees of adoption intermediaries. For further discussion of these various types of adoption, see § 8.04, *below.*

For the most part, adoption is governed by state laws and regulations, as opposed to federal law—although federal constitutional principles play a significant role in shaping state adoption laws and procedures. However, there is a growing body of federal law that pertains to adoption. For example, the Indian Child Welfare Act (ICWA), 25 U.S.C. § 1901 *et seq.* (1997), governs the placement of Native American children for adoption and the Interethnic Adoption Provisions of 1996, 42 U.S.C. § 1996b (1997), which replaced the Multiethnic Placement Act of 1994, bar reliance on race in adoption and foster care placements. See § 8.05, *below,* for discussion of these federal statutes. In addition, the Adoption Assistance and Child Welfare Act of 1980 and the Adoption and Safe Families Act of 1997, discussed in Chapter 7, *above,* provide guidelines and financial assistance for the adoption of children initially placed in foster care.

Lastly, there are a number of federal immigration and naturalization laws that regulate entry into this country of prospective adoptees who were born in other countries. *See* Elizabeth Bartholet, *International Adoption: Propriety, Prospects and Pragmatics,* 13 J. Am. Acad. of Matrim. Law. 181 (1996). International adoption has expanded rapidly in recent decades and now accounts for a substantial percentage of all unrelated adoptions in the United States. Elizabeth Bartholet, *International Adoption: Overview,* in Adoption Law and Practice 10-1 (Joan Heifetz Hollinger, ed., Matthew Bender 1998). However, because "international adoption almost always involves the relatively wealthy classes in the relatively wealthy nations of the world adopting the children of the poorer classes in the poorer nation," it raises complex political and economic issues, in addition to significant practical challenges. *Id.* at 10–4 to 10–5. Legal restrictions on international adoption, both in the United States and abroad, exacerbate the difficulties of adopting across national borders. Because of these difficulties, international adoption presently operates on a limited scale, relative to the large number of adults in this country eager to adopt and the millions of children in other nations, in need of permanent homes. *Id.* at 10-40.

For additional discussion of international adoption, see, e.g., R. Simon and H. Alstein, Intercountry Adoption (1991); Stacie L. Strong, *Children's Rights in Intercountry Adoption: Towards a New Goal,* 13 B.U. Int'l L.J. 163 (1995); Richard R. Carlson, *The Emerging Law of Intercountry Adoptions: An Analysis of the Hague Conference on Intercountry Adoption,* 30 Tulsa L.J. 243 (1994).

Because of the profound effect that adoption has on personal, familial and economic relationships, the laws and practices that govern adoption are among the most complex and challenging manifestations of government involvement in the lives of its citizens. Each state has enacted its own adoption laws, and at first glance the variation among state adoption statutes appears bewildering. Despite a common framework, adoption laws have never been uniform, nor are judicial interpretations of those laws consistent from one jurisdiction to another. To date, efforts to achieve greater uniformity in adoption statutes have faltered. Joan Heifetz Hollinger, *Introduction To Adoption Law and Practice* 1-3, in Adoption Law and Practice (Joan Heifeiz Hollinger, ed., Matthew Bender, 1998). In 1994, the National Conference of Commissioners on Uniform State laws (NCCUSL) approved a new Uniform Adoption Act (UAA), which was subsequently endorsed by the American Bar Association. So far, the 1994 UAA has been enacted by only a handful of states, but a number of other states are considering similar statutory reforms.

Despite the wide variation in state adoption law and practice, a number of common themes emerge. These include: (1) the necessity for voluntary and informed parental consent; (2) the centrality of the "best interests of the child" standard; (3) replacement of the biological family by the adoptive family; (4) permanence of the adoptive relationship; (5) non-contractual nature of the adoption process; (6) confidentiality of adoption proceedings and records, at least during the minority of the adoptee; and (7) the importance of the adoptee's bonding at an early stage with her or his adoptive parents. *See* Hollinger, *above* at 1–8 to 1–16. The materials that follow explore these common themes and goals. They also examine the role of race, ethnicity and religion in adoption.

§ 8.02 Consent to Adoption

Unless consent is waived or forfeited, adoption generally requires the consent of each of the child's legal parents. This has always included the child's birth mother, as well as a biological father who was married to the child's mother when the child was conceived or born. *See* Joan Heifetz Hollinger, *Consent to Adoption*, in Adoption Law and Practice at 2–11 to 2–12 (Joan Heifeiz Hollinger, ed., Matthew Bender 1998). Until recently, however, most state adoption statutes did not require the consent of an unmarried biological father, unless the father had formally legitimated the child. During the 1970s and 1980s, a series of Supreme Court decisions established that an unmarried biological father who develops a substantial parenting relationship with his child must be afforded the same rights as the child's mother to grant or withhold consent to adoption. *See Caban v. Mohammed*, 441 U.S. 380, 393–94 (1979); *Lehr v. Robertson*, 463 U.S. 248, 261–63 (1983). The precise contours of these Supreme Court decisions—which are discussed in more detail in Chapter 4 and in § 8.03, *below*—remain contested, as does their application to the adoption of a newborn infant.

The subsections that follow consider the requirements for valid parental consent to adoption, the circumstances under which consent may be revoked, and the consequences of an invalid or revoked consent.

[A] Timing and Validity of Consent

DOE v. CLARK
Supreme Court of South Carolina
457 S.E.2d 336 (1995)

FINNEY, J.

The appellant, Wylanda Clark, an unwed twenty-two year old, signed a Consent/Relinquishment Form on January 25, 1994, purporting to release her parental rights prior to the birth of her child. The baby was born on January 30, 1994. Prior to leaving the hospital on January 31, 1994, Clark signed a hospital form consenting to an adoption and authorizing the hospital to deliver the infant to the attorney representing the prospective adoptive parents (the Does). The baby remained at the hospital. On February 1, 1994, when the attorney and the Does went to pick up the baby, they were told that Clark and her father were seeking to take the infant home with them. The infant was left at the hospital pending a hearing to determine to whom the child should be released. At the hearing on February 2, 1994, initiated by the Does, Clark stated that she had changed her mind and wanted to keep the baby. Clark was not represented by counsel nor was a guardian ad litem appointed for the infant.

The family court judge found that the consent form signed by Clark prior to the child's birth was valid and reaffirmed by subsequent releases and other documents signed by Clark prior to her release from the hospital. The judge refused to set aside Clark's consent and ordered the baby released for placement with the Does.

On March 10, 1994, a second hearing was held before the same family court judge pursuant to Clark's motion to void consent or in the alternative, a motion to reconsider. Clark sought to set aside the original Consent/Relinquishment Form and have it declared void because it was signed prior to the birth of the child and lacked certain information required under the statute. The trial judge adhered to his prior order. Wylanda Clark appeals.

Clark asserts that S.C.Code Ann. § 20-7-1700 (Supp.1993) implicitly requires that consent to adoption be executed after birth of the child. Section 20-7-1700(A)(3) provides that the consent or relinquishment form shall specify the date of birth, race, and sex of the adoptee and any names by which the adoptee has been known. Appellant contends that since this information cannot be ascertained until after birth, the statute implicitly requires that consent be obtained then. In this case, the child's date of birth and sex were not recorded on the signed consent form.

While the legislature has not explicitly required that consent be obtained after birth, the Adoption Act implicitly contemplates that consent apply to a child in being. S.C.Code Ann. § 20-7-1690 (Supp.1993) provides that consent is required of "the mother of a child born when the mother was not married." Consent is defined as the "informed and voluntary release in writing of all parental rights with respect to a child by a parent." S.C.Code Ann. § 20-7-1650(f) (Supp.1993). A child is defined as any person under 18 years of age. S.C.Code Ann. § 20-7-1650(d) (Supp.1993). In viewing the statutory language as a whole, we conclude the legislature intended that consent be obtained after birth of a child.

. . . Accordingly, we find the pre-birth consent obtained in this case is invalid in view of the fact that appellant did not consent to relinquish her rights in accordance with § 20-7-1700 after the birth of her child. Because of the specific facts in this case, we do not decide here whether a birth parent can ratify pre-birth consent by subsequent acts. Clark initially signed a consent form only five days before giving birth and changed her mind two days after birth. She notified the hospital of her intention to keep the child prior to his release from the hospital to the adoptive parents. Accordingly, we find no ratification here and the trial judge is reversed.

WALLER, Justice (dissenting):

. . . Clark's contends that § 20-7-1700(A)(3) requires a consent form containing the child's sex and date of birth be signed after the birth of the child. I agree with the majority that, ideally, a consent form should be obtained after the birth of the child. However, to require absolute compliance with the technical terms of the statute when its conditions are otherwise met is, in my opinion, to elevate form over substance and defeat the very purpose for which the statute was enacted. In my view, the consent given here satisfies the purpose and policy of the statute.

Five days prior to the birth of her child, Clark signed a consent form which contains the following: the child's approximate due date and race; a statement that adoption is in the child's best interests; an acknowledgment the consent to adoption is given freely and voluntarily, and is not given under duress; an acknowledgment the consent is final and cannot be withdrawn without a Court order finding the consent involuntary or under duress; and a specific consent to termination of Clark's parental rights in a proceeding by the adoptive parents.

Clark's baby boy was born on January 30, 1994. Upon her discharge from the hospital the following afternoon, Clark advised nurses and hospital officials that she wanted to leave the baby there. She signed a hospital form stating that she consented to the adoption of her child, and directing the hospital to deliver the child to the attorney for the adoptive parents. Clark then left the hospital.

In my opinion, to now permit Clark to retract her consent due to a mere technical non-compliance with the statute elevates form over substance, and clearly cannot have been the intent of the legislature in enacting the statute. The purpose of the statute is to ensure that birth parents freely and voluntarily consent to relinquish their particular child, and do not do so under conditions of duress. Here, Clarks' consent meets these requirements. The only technical defect complained of is that Clark did not sign the consent form after the birth of her child. Clark did, however, sign the hospital "Release of Infant" form after the birth of her child, consenting to the adoption of her particular baby boy, born on January 30, 1994. In my view, when coupled with the earlier consent form, this "Release" ratified the prior relinquishment form and fully complied with the requisites of § 20-7-1700(A)(3).

To permit a technicality to vitiate Clark's earlier consent, in my opinion, is to defeat the legislative intent for requiring consent. I would affirm the order of the Family Court.

NOTES AND QUESTIONS

(1) Is the majority or the dissenting opinion more persuasive to you in this case? Based upon what underlying policy rationale(s)?

(2) Section 2-404 of the Uniform Adoption Act (1994) provides that a parent whose consent is required for adoption "may execute a consent or relinquishment only after the minor is born." The Comment to this section explains that the requirement of post-birth consent "is consistent with the rule in every State that a birth parent's consent or relinquishment is not valid or final until some time after a child is born. Many States provide that a valid consent may not be executed until at least 12, 24, 48, or, more typically, 72 hours after the child is born. Even the few States, like Washington or Alabama, which permit a consent to be executed before a child's birth, provide that the consent is not final (i.e., it remains revocable) until at least 48 hours after the birth or until confirmed in a formal termination proceeding." Uniform Adoption Act § 2-401, Comment.

The Uniform Act also provides that, before executing a consent or or relinquishment, "a parent must have been informed of the meaning and consequences of adoption, the availability of personal and legal counseling, the consequences of misidentifying the other parent, the procedure for releasing information about the health and other characteristics of the parent which may affect the physical or psychological well-being of the adoptee, and the procedure for the consensual release of the parent's identity to an adoptee, an adoptee's direct descendant, or an adoptive parent." *Id.* § 2-401(e).

(3) The majority in *Doe v. Clark* declines to decide whether an invalid, pre-birth consent may be ratified by a parent's subsequent, post-birth actions. Should such ratification be permitted? If so, what post-birth actions should be sufficient to constitute ratification?

(4) Should a known or potential biological father be permitted to execute a valid pre-birth consent to adoption? Unlike in the case of a birth mother, a number of jurisdictions explicitly permit fathers to consent to a child's adoption prior to the child's birth. *See, e.g.,* Tex. Fam. Code § 161.106 (1998) (father may execute pre-birth affidavit disclaiming any interest in a child and waiving notice of any proceedings affecting the parent child relationships with respect to the child). Similarly, Section 2-402 (a)(4) of the Uniform Adoption Act allows an unmarried father, at any time after conception, to execute a irrevocable, verified statement disclaiming any interest in the minor. The commentary to this section explains that such a pre-birth disclaimer "allows a man to avoid any role in the child's future and to remain noncommital on the issue of his paternity" and that it allows an adoption to proceed expeditiously if the birth mother later consents to the adoption. Does such disparate treatment of unwed mothers and fathers, with respect to the timing of consent to adoption, meet applicable constitutional standards? Does it represent sound public policy? Why or why not?

YOPP v. BATT
Supreme Court of Nebraska
467 N.W.2d 868 (1991)

WHITE, JUSTICE

Heather C. Yopp appeals the order of the Douglas County District Court denying her application for a writ of habeas corpus filed February 6, 1990. By the writ, Yopp attempted to recover possession of a baby girl born to her on January 3, 1990, in Omaha, Nebraska. At the time of the birth, Yopp was 15 years old and unmarried. On January 5, she relinquished by written instrument all rights to the child, and the baby was turned over to John and Mary Doe, real names unknown, a married couple referred to Yopp's attorney, Lawrence I. Batt, by Yopp's physician. The child has not yet been formally adopted by the Does pending this action. At no time during this action have the paternal rights of the natural father been at issue.

Yopp, a resident of Council Bluffs, Iowa, discovered she was pregnant in July 1989. At the time, Yopp was residing with her mother, Connie Howat. Yopp did not tell her mother or father she was pregnant at that time, but disclosed her pregnancy to the natural father and to several girl friends. One of her friends informed Yopp's mother of the pregnancy. Yopp and her mother discussed Yopp's pregnancy, and Yopp expressed her intent to have an abortion. Howat did not discuss with Yopp any alternatives to abortion because Yopp said she wished to terminate the pregnancy. Howat made an appointment for Yopp at Womens Services, P.C., in Omaha on October 14, 1989, where Yopp was examined by Dr. C.J. LaBenz. LaBenz informed Yopp that she was 6 1/2 months pregnant and that her pregnancy was too advanced for abortion. LaBenz discussed payment for his services at this meeting. He said that a welfare program for obstetrical services was available at the University of Nebraska Medical Center. Yopp declined to use those services. LaBenz also said that in the case of adoption, the adoptive family usually paid the medical bills of the relinquishing mother. LaBenz also stated that Yopp would be responsible for the medical expenses as they were incurred and that reimbursement from insurance or from the adoptive family would occur only after the birth. Yopp continued seeing LaBenz for prenatal care and returned for another appointment approximately 1 week later.

During this appointment, LaBenz questioned Yopp about what she intended to do with the baby. Yopp told LaBenz that she intended to give up the baby for adoption. Howat was present with Yopp during this discussion. LaBenz then briefly explained the difference between closed and open adoptions. Yopp testified that LaBenz also expressed his dissatisfaction with certain adoption agencies in the area, but he did not name these agencies.

LaBenz also questioned Yopp about her arrangements for putting the baby up for adoption. Yopp said that she had made no arrangements and that she did not have an attorney. LaBenz then gave Yopp Batt's name and told her he was an attorney that could help her with the adoption. LaBenz did not give Yopp the names of any other attorneys. LaBenz contacted Batt and informed him he had referred Yopp to Batt for a private adoption.

During another appointment in early December, LaBenz again questioned Yopp about her adoption plans, and she said she still intended to put the baby up for adoption, but had not contacted Batt or any other attorney. LaBenz encouraged her to make some arrangements quickly because the baby was due in less than a month.

Howat and Yopp finally met with Batt on December 13, 1989. Batt testified he understood that his meeting with Yopp was for the purpose of legal representation with regard to the relinquishment of a child to be born to Yopp in the beginning of January. Yopp testified at trial that she was never absolutely sure she wanted to give up the baby for adoption, but she went to Batt to learn "how adoption worked." Batt had previously represented LaBenz; Dr. George William Orr, another physician at Womens Services; and Womens Services itself in various other legal matters. Yopp was unaware of this prior representation.

Upon arriving in Batt's office, Yopp was asked to fill out a lengthy questionnaire concerning her medical history and her intentions with regard to the baby. In response to a question on the form, Yopp wrote that she intended to give up the baby for adoption because she was too young to raise it. During the meeting with Yopp and her mother, Batt talked to Yopp about her options, those being whether to keep the baby or give up the baby for adoption. Yopp informed him that previously she had intended to have an abortion, but she now wanted to put the baby up for adoption. Batt questioned her about her future and stated that Yopp indicated that having a baby would not fit into her plans for completing school. Batt testified that during this portion of the meeting, Yopp's mother seemed very supportive and nothing led him to believe that Yopp did not want to relinquish the baby.

Batt then outlined the procedures involved in relinquishing a child. He told her that after she gave birth, he would come to the hospital and have her sign the relinquishment papers. He then discussed each document that he would be bringing to the hospital. Batt also discussed the prospective adoptive family with Yopp and her mother. Yopp indicated that she wanted "a good family for it." He then explained the difference between open and closed adoptions, and Yopp indicated that she wanted a totally closed adoption. Finally, Batt discussed payment of his fees. He stated that generally the adoptive parents paid the pregnancy-related medical expenses and the attorney fees. At the conclusion of the meeting, Batt requested that he speak to Yopp privately. During the private meeting, Batt inquired about the natural father of the child, Yopp's drug and alcohol history, and whether or not anyone was influencing Yopp to make the decision to relinquish. Batt testified that he was confident that Yopp had arrived at her decision to relinquish independently and without influence from anyone else. This was Yopp's only meeting with Batt prior to the signing of the relinquishment papers.

On January 3, 1990, Yopp gave birth to a baby girl. Following the delivery, Yopp did not touch or hold the baby and stated that she did not want to take any pictures of the baby. Later that evening a nurse asked Yopp if she wanted to see the baby, and she declined. The following day, Yopp visited the baby in the nursery. On the morning of January 5, Yopp telephoned her mother at work and told her she wanted more information about the adoptive parents. Shortly after she finished speaking with her mother, Batt called Yopp at the hospital to set up a time for her to sign the relinquishment papers. Yopp told him she wanted to know more about the adoptive family. Batt asked her what she wanted to know, and she said she wanted to know what state they lived in and if she could have yearly pictures of the child. Yopp testified that she told Batt during the call that she had changed her mind and now wanted an open adoption, but Batt told her it was too late for that. Yopp did not ask for any other information besides the state of residence of the adoptive parents and the yearly pictures of the child.

Prior to Batt's arrival at the hospital, a social worker stopped by Yopp's hospital room and asked her if she wanted to discuss the relinquishment of her child. Yopp told the social worker that her family was supportive of her and that she did not want counseling. The social worker gave Yopp her business card and told Yopp to call anytime if she needed anyone to talk to.

That afternoon Batt and another attorney from his firm, Thomas Kenny, arrived at the hospital with the relinquishment papers. Kenny was to act as a witness at the signing. When they arrived, the baby was in the room with Yopp and her mother. After a nurse took the baby back to the nursery, Batt told Yopp that the adoptive parents lived in Nebraska and that they had agreed to send yearly pictures of the child to Yopp through Batt. Batt then asked Yopp if she was ready to sign the relinquishment papers, and she said yes. Batt had with him two copies and the original of several documents. He presented Yopp with a copy of each of the documents, which he instructed her to read. Batt testified that Yopp appeared to be calm and in control of herself. Yopp finished reading the documents, and Batt asked her if she had any questions. She said no. Batt then proceeded to explain each document to her. Batt testified that he explained the consent and relinquishment form to Yopp paragraph by paragraph, and indicated to her that she would be giving up all her rights to the child. Yopp testified that she knew she was relinquishing all rights to the child at that time. The consent and relinquishment form contained blanks where the names of the adoptive parents would later be inserted by Batt. Batt testified that Yopp understood that the relinquishment form would not contain the names of the adoptive parents. He said that Yopp never asked him for the names of the adoptive parents prior to the relinquishment.

Batt then concluded his explanation of all the forms and asked Yopp if she was ready to proceed. She indicated she was. Batt then presented the original of each of the documents to her, and she signed the documents, including the consent and relinquishment containing the blanks. As she signed, Batt identified each document, but did not offer any further explanation of the documents. Batt testified that Yopp did not hesitate in signing any of the documents.

After Yopp signed, Batt asked her if she wished Kenny to witness the documents, and she said yes. Kenny then questioned Yopp regarding her motivation for the relinquishment. He testified that Yopp said she understood each document, was signing them freely and voluntarily, and wished to proceed with the relinquishment. Kenny then signed the documents. Batt then took the documents and asked Yopp again if she still wished to proceed. She again replied yes, and then Batt affixed his notary seal to each of the documents. In addition to the documents signed by Yopp, Batt also requested that Howat read and sign a document affirming the facts that Yopp was a minor and that Yopp was making the decision to relinquish of her own free will. Howat signed the document, and Batt and Kenny left the hospital. Yopp was not given copies of the documents at that time.

On the morning of January 6, Batt turned the baby over to the Does. The Does were referred to Batt by LaBenz. The Does had previously been seen by Dr. Orr at Womens Services and had expressed their desire to adopt a baby. At the time of their meeting with Orr, the Does filled out a form containing information about their employment and medical history. This form was kept on file at Womens Services. After Yopp had her baby, LaBenz asked Dr. Orr if he knew of a prospective adoptive couple, and Orr mentioned the Does. LaBenz contacted the Does and told them there might be an available baby and told them to contact Batt. The Does then contacted Batt, and he informed them of the birth of Yopp's baby and that the baby was in good health. Batt also testified that he questioned Mary Doe about the Does' reasons for adopting, employment, income, religion, other children, and demographic background, and determined that they were a suitable couple for Yopp's child. Following the relinquishment, he delivered the baby to the Does and has not had possession of the child since that time. Batt testified that he never acted as the Does' attorney at any time during the relinquishment.

Yopp left the hospital on the evening of January 5. Yopp testified that on the morning of January 6, she told her mother that she felt she did the wrong thing and that her mother told her to think about it for awhile. The following Tuesday, Yopp indicated to her mother that she wanted the baby back. Yopp then decided to contact her father, who until this time had not been told of her pregnancy. On January 17, Yopp, Howat, and Yopp's father and stepmother met with Batt at his office and told him Yopp wanted the baby back. Batt told Yopp that he could not represent her in her action to have the baby returned because he would be called as a witness during the proceedings and it would be a conflict of interest. Yopp asked Batt for the names of the Does, and Batt refused to give her that information. Yopp also asked for copies of all the documents she signed, and Batt told her that he needed to delete the names of the Does from the documents and that he would have the papers ready for her in about a week. Following the meeting with Batt, Yopp hired another attorney, who also demanded information about the Does from Batt. When Batt refused again, Yopp initiated this action. . . .

In this case, we are concerned with a relinquishment for the purposes of a private, closed adoption. The Legislature, as well as this court, has long recognized a distinction between agency adoptions and private adoptions. In the agency adoption situation, the relinquishing parent surrenders all rights to the child in favor of the state or a licensed child placement agency. Neb. Rev. Stat. § 43-106.01 (Reissue 1988) mandates that when a child is relinquished by written instrument to the Department of Social Services or to a licensed child placement agency and the agency has, in writing, accepted full responsibility for the child, the relinquishing parent is relieved of all parental duty and all responsibility for the child and shall have no rights over the child. Under § 43-106.01, the rights of the relinquishing parent are terminated when the agency accepts responsibility for the child in writing. It is the agency that finds and investigates the prospective adoptive parents. If the adoptive parents are unsuitable or decline to go through with the adoption, the agency retains custody over the child until such time as the child is adopted by another family.

In contrast, in the private adoption situation the child is relinquished directly into the hands of the prospective adoptive parents without interference by the state or a private agency. In the case of a closed adoption, the relinquishing parent surrenders his or her rights to unknown parties. Neb. Rev. Stat. § 43-111 (Reissue 1988) provides that, except in the agency adoption situation, after an adoption decree has been entered, the natural parents of the adopted child shall be relieved of all parental duties and responsibilities for the child and shall have no rights over the child. Under § 43-111, the relinquishing parent's rights are not totally extinguished until the child has been formally adopted by the prospective parents. Neb. Rev. Stat. § 43-109 (Cum.Supp.1990) requires that in order for the adoption of a child to take place, a hearing on the best interests of the child must be held, the child must have lived with the prospective adoptive family for the previous 6 months, the medical history of the biological parent or parents must be made a part of the court record, and there must be in the court record an affidavit from the relinquishing parent swearing that prior to the relinquishment a nonconsent form was presented and explained to the biological parent or parents. Since under Nebraska law an adoption cannot take place until at least 6 months after the relinquishment of the child, in the case of a private adoption the question of who retains the legal right to the child during this time is unclear.

This issue becomes particularly troublesome in the case where the relinquishing parent decides he or she wants the child returned. This court has dealt with the rights of the respective parties in both private adoption cases and agency adoption cases on numerous occasions.

In *Batt v. Nebraska Children's Home Society*, 174 N.W.2d 88 (1970), and in *Kane v. United Catholic Social Services*, 191 N.W.2d 824 (1971), the appellants sought to have the relinquishments of their children to the child placement agencies invalidated on the grounds that the relinquishments were obtained through fraud, duress, and coercion. This court applied the strict language of § 43-106.01 in holding that a relinquishment, if voluntary, is not revocable. The court then went on to find that both relinquishments were entered into freely and voluntarily and therefore were valid.

In 1980, we decided *Gray v. Maxwell*, 293 N.W.2d 90 (1980), a private adoption case. The appellant sought to regain custody of a child she relinquished to the prospective adoptive parents. The trial court held in favor of Gray, and the Does, the adoptive parents, assigned as error the trial court's finding that Gray's relinquishment was not valid and therefore revocable. . . . This court found that the relinquishment was involuntary and that revocation of the relinquishment was effected within a matter of hours. We concluded that because the relinquishment was involuntary, *Kane* and *Batt* were not applicable. We also determined that the Legislature had expressed a different intent in § 43-111, the statute governing private adoptions. Under § 43-111, we interpreted a relinquishment in a private adoption to be "less final" than one made to a licensed child placement agency under § 43-106.01, but did not make any findings of law on this issue. We then determined that since the relinquishment was invalid, the adoptive parents had no standing to contest the custody of the child, but ordered the district court to hold a best interests hearing to determine the fitness of the natural parent before returning the child to her. . . .

In *Kellie v. Lutheran Family & Social Service*, 305 N.W.2d 874 (1981), we allowed the relinquishing parent, in an agency adoption, to revoke the relinquishment within a reasonable period of time before the agency had, in writing, taken responsibility for the child. We determined that a best interests hearing was not necessary because, under contract law, the relinquishing parent had revoked prior to acceptance by the agency and thus retained all legal rights to the child. We did not, however, apply these same contract principles in the private adoption case. . . . The Legislature has seen fit to distinguish between agency and private adoption, but has not made explicit the rights of the parties in the private adoption case. In the case of private adoptions, we hold that a natural parent who relinquishes his or her rights to a child by a valid written instrument gives up all rights to the child at the time of the relinquishment. A valid relinquishment is irrevocable. The natural parent retains only the right to commence an action seeking the return of the child and the right to be considered as a prospective parent if the best interests of the child so dictate. The natural parent's rights are no longer superior to those of the prospective adoptive family.

The prospective adoptive family is obligated to take custody of the child, to care for the child, to keep the child in good physical and mental health, and to pursue adoption of the child. The prospective adoptive parents have standing to contest custody of the child if they so desire. The relinquishing parent and the prospective adoptive parents stand on equal ground with respect to determining custody. In the event the prospective adoptive family chooses not to adopt the child, or the state or agency determines the prospective adoptive parents unsuitable, the natural parent shall have the right to seek the return of the child and be considered as a prospective parent. When a conflict over custody of the child arises, the court shall take custody of the child and conduct a hearing to determine whether the best interests of the child require the child to remain with the prospective adoptive family or be returned to the natural parent. The court shall appoint an attorney to represent the child in the proceeding. Physical custody of the child may remain with the prospective adoptive family during the pendency of the proceedings if the court finds the child's situation suitable. Additionally, if the relinquishment of rights by the natural parent is found to be invalid for any reason, a best interests hearing shall also be held to determine custody of the child. The court shall not simply return the child to the natural parent upon a finding that the relinquishment was not a valid instrument. By these rules, we have sought to keep the best interests of the child at the forefront of the inquiry. We now turn to the merits of Yopp's case.

Yopp first assigns as error the district court's finding that § 43-1101, the Interstate Compact on the Placement of Children, did not apply to this case. We agree with the district court. Yopp's child was born in Omaha, Nebraska. The adoptive parents, John and Mary Doe, reside in Nebraska. The child was never taken from Omaha to Council Bluffs, Iowa, the residence of Yopp. The fact that Yopp is a resident of Iowa is not determinative in this case. The statute does not mandate that the residence of the mother is considered the residence of the child. The child was never a resident of Iowa and was not placed across state lines. Section 43-1101 is not applicable.

Yopp next claims the district court erred in disregarding her claim that Batt, LaBenz, and Womens Services violated § 43-701 by assisting in the placement of a child for adoption without obtaining a license. We assume that Yopp wishes to vitiate the relinquishment of her rights to the child through use of § 43-701. Neb. Rev. Stat. § 43-709 (Reissue 1988) provides that violation of § 43-701 is a Class III misdemeanor. Nowhere in § 43-709 does it state that any relinquishment or subsequent adoption of a child will be invalid if the party placing the child for adoption is in violation of § 43-701. Yopp may not make use of § 43-701 to invalidate her relinquishment.

. . . Yopp claims, in her fourth assigned error, that the district court disregarded evidence that she was not presented with a copy of the nonconsent form as required by § 43-146.06.

By definition, a nonconsent form is a notice filed by the biological parent stating that at no time prior to his or her death may any information on the adopted person's original birth certificate or any other identifying information except medical history be released to the adopted person. Section 43-146.06 permits the biological parent to file a nonconsent form at any time prior to his or her death. Failure of the biological parent to sign the form operates as a notice of consent by the parent to release the adopted person's original birth certificate and identifying information.

Neb. Rev. Stat. § 43-106.02 (Reissue 1988) mandates that the relinquishing parent be given the option of signing the nonconsent prior to the final relinquishment. Section 43-109(1)(c) specifies that an adoption decree will not be entered unless the court record includes an affidavit signed by the biological parent stating that he or she was presented with and given an explanation of the nonconsent form. Section 43-109(1)(c) does not state that the relinquishment itself will be invalid.

The purpose of the nonconsent form is to conceal the identity of the biological parent if that parent wishes to remain anonymous. The intent behind the legislation enacting these statutes was to prevent adoptive children from locating their biological parents if those parents did not wish to be contacted, while still allowing the adopted child access to medical history information.

Yopp attempts to use what she alleges as technical noncompliance with the adoption statutes to vitiate the relinquishment of her child and to have the baby returned to her. This is not the purpose of the statutes. The goal of the nonconsent form laws was to safeguard the identity of the biological parent while giving the adoptive child access to needed medical history. The Legislature intended that relinquishing parents be informed of their right to safeguard this information prior to the actual relinquishment. It also intended that the fact that the biological parent was so informed was to be made a part of the court record. However, it is doubtful that the Legislature intended to invalidate all parental relinquishments simply because the biological parent was not presented with the form at the time of the actual relinquishment, or did not physically retain a copy of the form after signing the relinquishment papers. . . .

Finally, we reach the crux of this case—Yopp's claim that the relinquishment of her child was invalid. . . . The burden is on the natural parent challenging the validity of the relinquishment to prove that it was not voluntarily given. In the absence of threats, coercion, fraud, or duress, a properly executed relinquishment of parental rights and consent to adoption signed by a natural parent knowingly, intelligently, and voluntarily is valid.

Yopp lists numerous allegations in support of her contention that her consent was involuntary. Among them are claims that she was under physical and mental distress at the time of the signing, that she did not receive any counseling or information concerning alternatives to adoption, that she suffered from lack of independent counsel because Batt had earlier represented LaBenz and Womens Services and also had contact with the adoptive family, that she was told by Batt it was too late for an open adoption and was denied information about the adoptive family, that her mother was induced somehow by the information that the adoptive family would pay the attorney fees and medical bills for Yopp, that she received false information about agency versus private adoptions, that she signed documents falsely stating that she had selected the adoptive family, and that she was improperly induced to sign by the adoptive parents' promise to provide her with yearly pictures.

We find Yopp's allegations unpersuasive. At the outset, Yopp evidenced her desire not to keep the child. She initially intended to have an abortion. When that became impossible due to her advanced stage of pregnancy, she expressed her desire to give up the baby for adoption. She told her mother, her physician, and her lawyer that she did not wish to keep the child. She never, at any time, told anyone that she was in doubt over her decision or that she was considering keeping the child. It was only after she relinquished all rights to her baby that she changed her mind. A change of attitude subsequent to signing a relinquishment is insufficient to invalidate the relinquishment.

Yopp spoke to her mother about the pregnancy on numerous occasions prior to the birth of the child. Yopp testified that her mother was very supportive and told her if she decided to keep the baby, they would "make it work." Prior to the actual relinquishment, Yopp also had the opportunity to discuss her situation with a social worker. She refused counseling, stating that her family had been very supportive. The record is replete with evidence from Yopp's mother; the social worker; the nurse assigned to Yopp while she was in the hospital; Batt; Batt's associate, Kenny; and Yopp's physician, LaBenz, supporting our conclusion that Yopp knew what she was doing, made her decision independently and without influence from any other party, and had intended to give up the baby all along. There is no evidence in the record that Yopp was coerced or pressured to give up her child. The fact that the adoptive parents agreed to pay Yopp's medical bills and attorney fees does not itself establish coercion.

Yopp's claim that somehow Batt's advice or service to her was defective because of his prior relationships with LaBenz and Womens Services is not supported by any evidence of wrongdoing on his part. The mere fact that he was in contact with the Does does not establish anything to support Yopp's claims. In the case of a private, closed adoption such as this, contact between the attorneys and the various parties is necessary to effectuate transfer of the child. We find Yopp's allegations as outlined above unsupported by the record. Her relinquishment and consent to adoption of the child are valid. . . .

NOTES AND QUESTIONS

(1) Do you agree with the court that Yopp's initial intention to have an abortion is evidence of the voluntariness of her subsequent decision to relinquish the child for adoption? Why or why not?

(2) Did Heather Yopp receive effective assistance from her attorney? What, if anything, would you have done differently if you had been representing Yopp?

(3) As the opinion in *Yopp* suggests, there are a number of grounds on which consent to adoption may be invalidated or revoked.

(a) **Revocation Made Within a Statutory Time Period**. The *Yopp* court holds that, in the case of a private adoption, a valid written consent to adoption is irrevocable when executed. By contrast, adoption statutes in a number of states allow a birth parent to revoke an otherwise valid consent within a specific statutory time period. *See, e.g.,* Md. Code Ann., Fam. Law § 5-311 (c)(1) (1997) (consent may be revoked within 30 days after signing); Ga. Code Ann. 19-8-9(b) (1997) (consent may be withdrawn within 10 days); Uniform Adoption Act §§ 2-408 and 2-409 (allowing a birth parent to revoke consent or relinquishment within 8 days after the birth of the birth of the child).

In the past, many states permitted a birth mother to revoke her consent at any time before the adoption was finalized, which could take 6 months or more. *See, e.g., In re Adoption of F.*, 488 P.2d 130, 132 (Utah 1971). While a few states still allow revocation at any time prior to entry of an adoption decree, the clear trend is toward shorter and more definite revocation periods. Moreover, in an increasing number of states, consent to adoption is irrevocable once executed, unless a parent can demonstrate fraud or duress. Some courts have expressed uneasiness with this trend. *See, e.g., In re Adoption of Baby Girl C.*, 511 So. 2d 345, 353 (Fla. Dist. Ct. App. 1987) ("Why, if a person agreeing in writing to purchase encyclopedias from a door-to-door salesman is entitled to cancel that agreement three days later . . . should not a natural mother be entitled to cancel one week later her consent to the permanent loss to her of the child to whom she gave birth?"). *See generally* Catherine Sakach, Note: *Withdrawal of Consent for Adoption: Allocating The Risk*, 18 Whittier L. Rev. 879 (1997).

Query: Should a birth parent be given a "cooling off period" during which she or he may automatically revoke consent to adoption? If so, how long should the automatic revocation period be? What are the competing interests and policy considerations at issue?

(b) **Failure to Comply With Statutory Requirements**. Yopp argued unsuccessfully that her consent was invalid because she did not receive a copy of a "nonconsent form," required by state adoption statutes. She also argued that she should be able to revoke her consent because her attorney and others involved in the adoption violated a state criminal statute, which prohibited unlicenced individuals from assisting in the placement of a child for adoption. When, if ever, should non-compliance with statutory provisions governing the adoption process provide a basis for invalidating a birth parent's consent to adoption? Should a birth parent be required to prove that the non-compliance undermined the voluntariness of her consent? *See generally* Katherine G. Thomas and Joan H. Hollinger, *Contested Adoptions: Strategy of the Case*, in Adoption Law and Practice 8–22 to 8–25 (Joan Heifeiz

(c) **The Interstate Compact on the Placement of Children (ICPC)**. The court also rejected Yopp's claim that the procedures used to obtain her consent violated the Interstate Compact on the Placement of Children (ICPC). The primary purpose of the ICPC, which has been adopted in all 50 states, is to protect the interests of children placed for adoption across state lines. To that end, the Compact requires that various procedures be followed, and that permission be obtained from state officials, before a child may be placed for adoption in another state. The *Yopp* court concluded that ICPC did not apply because Yopp's child was born in Nebraska, the state where the adoptive parents' also resided, rather than in Iowa where Heather Yopp lived. Other courts and commentators, by contrast, have argued that ICPC does apply in this situation. *See* Mitchell Wendell & Betsey R. Rosenbaum, *Interstate Adoptions: the Interstate Compact on the Placement of Children*, in Adoption Law and Practice 3A-11 to 3A-12 (Matthew Bender 1998).

Courts disagree, however, about whether and when a violation of ICPC should provide grounds for revoking a birth parent's consent, or otherwise invalidating an adoptive placement. *Compare, e.g., In the Matter of Adoption of T.M.M.*, 608 P.2d 130, 131 (Mont. 1980) (prospective adoptive parents' violation of ICPC vitiates birth mother's consent to adoption and requires dismissal of adoption petition) *with In re Adoption/Guardianship No. 3598*, 701 A.2d 110, 126 (Md. 1997) (failure to comply with ICPC requirements did not require dismissal of adoption petition where adoption was clearly in child's best interests). *See generally* Bernadette W. Hartfield, *The Role of the Interstate Compact on the Placement of Children in Interstate Adoption*, 68 Neb. L. Rev. 292 (1989).

(d) **Proof of Fraud or Duress**. Because a parent's consent to adoption must be voluntary and informed, virtually all states hold that parental consent is invalid and revocable if it was obtained by fraud or duress. *See, e.g.*, Uniform Adoption Act § 2-408(b)(1) (1997) (court shall set aside consent if parent establishes, "by clear and convincing evidence, before a decree of adoption is issued, that the consent was obtained by fraud or duress").

States disagree, however, on what constitutes duress sufficient to vitiate consent to adoption. Some courts define duress narrowly to require that a parent's consent to adoption "be induced by the unlawful or unconscionable act of another." *See, e.g., In re Baby Boy R.*, 386 S.E.2d 839, 842 (W. Va. 1989) (finding no duress where mother was crying and upset when she signed the adoption papers, "since there was no evidence [she] was induced to sign the form or that she suffered from inability to comprehend the actions she was taking"); *Gaughan v. Gilliam*, 401 N.W.2d 687, 690 (Neb. 1987) (the mere fact that the biological parent was influenced by her friends and family does not amount to duress or undue influence sufficient to invalidate her relinquishment of the child). Other courts apply the broader concept of "duress of circumstances," and have allowed revocation where a biological parent lacks resources or emotional support, and agrees to adoption under pressure from friends, relatives or social services agencies. *See, e.g., In re Girl C.*, 511 So. 2d 345, 351 (Fla. Dist. Ct. App. 1987) (allowing revocation where birth mother consented to adoption because she feared arrest and possible jail time); *In re Cheryl E.*, 207 Cal. Rptr. 728, 738 (Cal. Ct. App. 1984) (finding undue influence where biological mother and her children were facing eviction and adoption worker insisted that papers be signed quickly).

Some courts have also allowed revocation were a parent's consent was induced by a promise of economic benefit—or the threat of economic detriment. *Compare, e.g., Downs v. Wortman*, 185 S.E.2d 387, 388 (Ga. 1971) (mother's consent to adoption was not freely and voluntary given where she was offered plane fare to the state where her parents lived in exchange) *with In re Ex parte Fowler*, 564 So. 2d 962, 965 (Ala. 1990) (upholding validity of mother's consent, despite threat by her family that children would be taken away from her if she did not consent to adoption).

Query: Was duress present in *Yopp v. Batt*, under either a broad or a narrow definition? Why or why not?

(e) **Mistake**. While some courts have allowed revocation of consent based on mistake of fact or failure to understand the consequences of relinquishment, recent adoption decisions generally reject these as grounds for invalidating consent, in the absence of undue influence or other improper conduct. *Compare, e.g., Duncan v. Harden*, 214 S.E.2d 890, 892 (Ga. 1975) (fact that birth mother signed consent shortly after leaving hospital "without full knowledge of the consequences of her act" constitutes "good cause" for withdrawal of consent) *with In re Baby Boy R.*, 386 S.E.2d 839, 842 (W.Va. 1989) (birth mother's unilateral misunderstanding regarding the finality of consent does not justify revocation); *Sara K v. Timmy S.*, 487 N.E.2d 241, 250 (N.Y. 1985), *cert. denied*, 475 U.S. 1108 (1986) (biological parents' mistaken belief that their consent to adoption was not final until they appeared in court did not provide grounds for invalidating consent). In rejecting such claims, courts have emphasized that permitting revocation on this basis would be inconsistent with the need for certainty and finality in the adoption process and would upset the delicate balance among the rights and interests of surrendering parents, adoptive parents, children and the state. Do you agree?

(4) **Consent of a Minor Parent**. In most states, the fact that a biological parent of a child is a minor does not affect that parent's ability to give valid consent to an adoption. *See, e.g.,* 40 Ill. Comp. Stat. § 513 (1997) (consent or surrender of a parent who is a minor shall not be voidable because of such minority); *Gaughan v. Gilliam*, 401 N.W.2d 687, 690 (Neb. 1987) (upholding voluntariness of consent executed by 16-year-old despite lack of counseling or independent legal representation). A few states require that, in addition to the consent of a parent who is a minor, consent must also be given by a *guardian ad litem* appointed for the minor, or by the minor's own parent or legal guardian. *E.g.,* Mich. Comp. Laws Ann. §§ 710.28(2); 710.43(4) (1997). In addition, some adoption statutes impose extra procedural requirements for obtaining consent from a minor. For example, the Uniform Adoption Act, § 2-405(c) (1994) provides:

Minority of a parent does not affect competency to execute a consent or a relinquishment, but a parent who is a minor must have had access to counseling and must have had the advice of a lawyer who is not representing an adoptive parent or the agency to which the parent's child is relinquished.

Query: Do the adoption statutes in your state contain a similar requirement for separate legal counsel in the case of a minor parent? If not, should there be such a requirement? Why or why not?

(5) **Agency vs Private Adoption**. The Court in *Yopp* distinguishes between agency adoptions and private (or independent) adoptions. The similarities and differences between these two types of adoptions are discussed in more detail in § 8.04, *below*. Should there be different requirements or procedures for obtaining parental consent to adoption in these two contexts? Why or why not?

(6) **Child's Best Interests**. Should a court consider the interests of the prospective adoptee in deciding whether to allow a birth parent to revoke consent to adoption? Why or why not? Some commentators have argued that a child has an independent, constitutionally protected liberty interest in establishing and maintaining a relationship with prospective adoptive parents with whom the child has been placed. *See, e.g.,* Suellyn Scarnecchia, *A Child's Right to Protection From Transfer Trauma in A Contested Adoption Case*, 2 Duke J. Gender L. & Pol'y 41 (1995). Courts have generally rejected such arguments. *See, e.g., In re Doe*, 638 N.E.2d 181 (Ill.), *cert. denied*, 513 U.S. 994 (1994); *DeBoer v. Schmidt*, 502 N.W.2d 649 (Mich. 1993). As the next subsection suggests, however, courts have been more inclined to consider the best interests of the child in determining the consequences of an invalid or revoked parental consent.

[B] Consequences of Invalid Consent

What should happen when a court invalidates or allows revocation of a birth parent's consent to adoption? Should the court automatically order the child returned to the birth parent, or should the court hold a separate hearing to determine custody of the child? If the court holds a separate custody hearing, what legal standard should apply? The following case addresses these issues.

LEMLEY v. BARR
Supreme Court of West Virginia
343 S.E.2d 101 (1986)

NEELY, J.

On 30 January 1981 Tammy L. Lemley and Bobby Lee Nash, Sr., gave birth to Bobby Lee Nash, Jr. in Lawrence County, Ohio, the place of their residence. These two parents were without benefit of marriage, education, or real means of support. Mr. Nash, the natural father, wanted to give the child up for adoption, and encouraged Tammy Lemley to do so. Accordingly, they contacted J. Stewart Kaiser and John E. Hall, attorneys in Chesapeake, Ohio, concerning the possible placement of the child.

On 5 May 1981, four days before Tammy Lemley turned eighteen, Tammy Lemley and Bobby Lee Nash went to Mr. Kaiser's and Mr. Hall's office to relinquish the child and execute the necessary papers for adoption. Tammy Lemley became upset, refused to sign the papers and left with the child. The next day the young couple returned to the law offices, executed the papers, and relinquished the child to Mr. Kaiser and Mr. Hall. Later that day, Mr. Hall delivered the child to Gene and Anna Barr at their house in Huntington, West Virginia.

On 11 May 1981, two days after Tammy Lemley reached majority, Mr. Kaiser and Mr. Hall informed Miss Lemley that she must meet with them again to sign more papers regarding the adoption. At Mr. Kaiser's direction the young couple met Mr. Hall in the parking lot of the Omelet Shop in Huntington, West Virginia where Tammy signed the papers in return for $400.00. That same day, Tammy Lemley's parents went to the law offices of Kaiser and Hall to demand the return of the child. The parents explained to Mr. Kaiser that Tammy was a minor at the time of the transaction. Mr. Kaiser told them that it was too late to do anything and that he could offer them no help. At no time did Mr.

Kaiser explain to Tammy Lemley, Bobby Lee Nash, Sr., or Tammy's parents that under Ohio law an Ohio Probate Court judge had to witness and approve a minor's consent.

On 18 May 1981, Tammy Lemley and Bobby Lee Nash, Sr. returned to Mr. Kaiser's office to seek the return of the child. Again Mr. Kaiser refused to assist them. Furthermore, Mr. Kaiser refused to divulge the identity of the couple to whom he had transferred the child. In June, 1981 Miss Lemley and her parents instituted a habeas corpus action in Ohio against Mr. Kaiser, Mr. Hall and the unknown custodian of the child asking for the child's return. On 24 September 1981, the Court of Common Pleas, Lawrence County, Ohio, Probate and Juvenile Division, held that the placement had been illegal and improper under Ohio Rev. Code Ann. 5103.16 because the adopting parents had not filed the requisite papers in the Probate Court. The court found that Mr. Kaiser and Mr. Hall had obtained Tammy's consent through duress, that she had no understanding of her position at the time she signed the adoption papers and, therefore, her consent was invalid. . . .

On 13 August 1982 the Ohio Court of Appeals unanimously affirmed the Court of Common Pleas' judgment. Finally, on 24 August 1983, two years and two months after the Lemleys first brought their petition, the Ohio Supreme Court affirmed the trial court's judgment and the names of the child's custodians, Gene and Anna Barr, were revealed.

The Barrs knew about the Ohio habeas corpus proceeding through their discussions with Mr. Kaiser and through news reports both on television and in print. They discussed whether to appear physically in the Ohio proceedings, whether they should comply with the judgment of the Ohio trial court, and whether they should divulge their identities. The Barrs knowingly and intentionally refused to reveal their names, and directed Mr. Kaiser and Mr. Hall to exercise the attorney-client privilege on their behalf. Finally, despite the Barr's knowledge of the ongoing Ohio proceedings, they filed for adoption in front of Judge D. B. Daugherty of the Circuit Court of Cabell County, West Virginia on 6 November 1981. . . .

When the identity of the Barrs was finally disclosed to Miss Lemley and her parents, they brought a habeas corpus action in the Circuit Court of Cabell County, West Virginia to compel the Barrs to return the child in accordance with the Ohio judgment. The trial court, however, declined to give full faith and credit to the Ohio judgment on the basis that the Barrs were never parties to the Ohio suit, and ruled that the 6 November 1981 West Virginia adoption proceeding, which the Barrs had initiated during the pendency of the Ohio action, was proper. The Lemleys then appealed that ruling to this court and asked us to uphold the judgment of our Ohio brethren and order the Circuit Court of Cabell County to give that judgment full faith and credit. . . .

. . . [F]or reasons explained in Sections I and II we conclude that Miss Lemley is entitled to have our courts accord the Ohio judgment full faith and credit in terms of setting aside the formal West Virginia adoption. We are not convinced, however, that it is in the best interests of Ryan Barr that his physical custody be changed at this time and, for reasons explained in Section III, we remand this case to the Circuit Court of Cabell County for further proceedings to determine the best interests of the child. . . .

III.

Although this Court has often held that the welfare of a child is the cynosure of any custody determination, such a standard provides us with little guidance in the case before us because, as the New York Court of Appeals said in *Bennett v. Jeffreys*, 356 N.E.2d 277, 284 (1976):

> The resolution of cases must not provide incentives for those likely to take the law into their own hands. Thus, those who obtain custody of children unlawfully, particularly by kidnapping, violence, or flight from the jurisdiction of the courts, must be deterred. Society may not reward, except at its peril, the lawless because the passage of time has made correction inexpedient.

This pronouncement from one of America's most highly respected courts would almost be dispositive of the case before us had not the New York Court of Appeals gone on to say in the very same paragraph: "Yet, even then, circumstances may require that in the best interest of the child, the unlawful acts be blinked [Citations omitted]."

Certainly in the case before us we do not have an instance of kidnapping, violence, or flight from the jurisdiction of the court. Indeed, the Barrs used all possible legal strategems to avoid an unfavorable ruling in the Ohio courts, but at no time did they resort to self-help by fleeing or by refusing to follow a lawful court order. And, although Miss Lemley was young, frightened, and inexperienced, she did sign papers on two occasions consenting to an adoption, and she accepted money for the payment of her medical expenses. Nonetheless, Miss Lemley has equity on her side too; she did not sleep upon her rights. She tried to regain possession of Ryan immediately and it is difficult for us to tell her now that she cannot have Ryan because it is "too late." Yet, as we have already indicated, the only entirely innocent party in these proceedings is the child, Ryan Barr.

The record before us is devoid of detailed evidence concerning what is now in the best interests of Ryan Barr. But we do know from the facts of record that Ryan is a five-year-old child who has spent almost his entire life with an adoptive mother, father and siblings in Huntington, West Virginia. If we now transfer custody to Miss Lemley, who counsel informs us has married, he will be taken to another place and brought up by people who are complete strangers to him. Although we cannot say that this is not in his best interests, we can at least say that there is some question in our mind whether such action is appropriate. Consequently, we remand this case to the circuit court for a determination of what physical custody arrangement is in Ryan's best interests.

To aid the circuit court in the determination of this issue it is ordered that the West Virginia Department of Human Services be called upon in this proceeding to prepare a plan for the custody of Ryan Barr that will serve his best interests, keeping appropriately in mind Miss Lemley's legal rights and Ryan's right to be treated as a human being. For as the Court of Appeals of New York said in *Bennett v. Jeffreys*:

> The day is long past in this State, if it had ever been, when the right of a parent to the custody of his or her child, where the extraordinary circumstances are present, would be enforced inexorably, contrary to the best interest of the child, on the theory solely of an absolute legal right. Instead, in the extraordinary circumstance, when there is a conflict, the best interest of the child has always been regarded as superior to the right of parental custody. Indeed, analysis of the cases reveals a shifting of emphasis rather than a remaking of substance. This shifting reflects more the modern principle that a child is a person, and not a subperson over whom the parent has an absolute possessory interest. A child has rights too, some of which are of a constitutional magnitude. [Citations omitted].

356 N.E.2d at 281.

. . .

Therefore, for the reasons set forth above, the judgment of the Circuit Court of Cabell County is reversed and the case is remanded for further proceedings consistent with this opinion.

NOTES AND QUESTIONS

(1) Assuming that both Tammy Lemley and the Barrs qualify as "fit" parents, what custody arrangement is a court likely to find to be in 5-year-old Ryan's best interests? Why?

(2) The questions raised in *Lemley* are analogous to those raised by several recent, high profile adoption cases, in which a birth mother initially placed a child for adoption without the involvement or consent of the child's biological father and the father later sought to block the adoption and obtain custody on the ground that he had not consented to the adoption. For additional discussion of these cases, see § 8.03, *below*.

(3) Traditionally, a judicial finding that a that a birth parent had not validly consented to adoption entitled the non-consenting parent to custody and control of the child. However, *Lemley v. Barr* is consistent with a recent trend toward requiring a separate custody hearing where a birth parent successfully revokes or withholds consent to adoption. *See, e.g., In re Adoption of J.J.B.*, 894 P.2d 994 (N.M.), *cert. denied*, 516 U.S. 860 (1995) (even if adoption is dismissed, court must decide child's custody based on best interests and would-be adoptive parents may seek custody as against claims of birth parents); *In re C.C. R.S.*, 892 P.2d 246, 251 (Colo.), *cert. denied*, 516 U.S. 837 (1995) (birth mother who never executed a valid relinquishment is not automatically entitled to custody of child who has lived since birth with prospective adoptive parents); *but see In re Doe*, 638 N.E.2d 181 (Ill.), *cert. denied*, 513 U.S. 994 (1994) (prospective adoptive couple lacked standing to seek continued custody of child, since Constitution requires that birth father whose parental rights were not properly terminated be given legal and physical custody).

A number of states have recently amended their adoption statutes to require a court that denies or dismisses an adoption petition to consider separately the question of who shall have custody of the child. *E.g.*, Ind. Code Ann. § 31-19-11-5(a) (1998). The Uniform Adoption Act similarly provides that, in most instances where an adoption is denied or set aside for lack of valid parental consent, the court must separately determine custody of the child, using a best interests standard. *See* Uniform Adoption Act § 3-704 (1994).

While some courts and commentators have applauded this trend as consistent with treating children as persons, rather than as parental property, others have expressed concern that requiring a separate "best interest' hearing in the context of a failed adoption unfairly disadvantages biological parents and may encourage prospective adoptive parents to disregard statutory requirements and protections:

> By allowing disappointed prospective adoptive parents to petition for custody . . . the majority creates a legal loophole in the relinquishment and adoption statutory framework. Disappointed prospective adoptive parents now have the opportunity to bring extensive litigation in an effort to gain custody of a child with whom they do not have a legally cognizable relationship. The majority thus creates a way

for persons seeking to adopt to circumvent the requirements of the relinquishment and adoption statutes by merely seeking physical custody of a child. . . . Moreover, once non-parents have physical custody of a child, there may be little a biological parent can do to regain custody. Trial courts utilizing the best interests of the child standard are often reluctant to remove a child from a home once the child has begun to develop psychological attachment to the family. The majority's creation of this option for disappointed prospective adoptive parents to pursue custody . . . undermines the legislature's intent in crafting the relinquishment scheme to provide stable unions by requiring informed consent.

. . .

The majority further undermines the legislature's intent to create stable adoptive families by leaving the two families in this case in legal flux. In this case, the respondents have physical custody of the child but are not able to adopt. Furthermore, the respondents must live with the possibility that custody could be altered in the future. The petitioner, on the other hand, is deprived of the opportunity to nurture and rear her child on a daily basis. The distance between her and her child is great and the cost for her to travel to see the child prohibitive. Her parental rights seem illusory at best, yet she is burdened by the legal responsibilities of parenthood. Moreover, the court will have continuing involvement in the lives of these two families through its role in monitoring visitation and other issues of conflict. Far from creating a stable familial structure for the child, the majority's decision leaves these families with only a temporary solution and little peace of mind.

In re Custody of C.C.R.S., 892 P.2d 246 (Colo.), *cert. denied*, 516 U.S. 837 (1995) (Lohr, J. dissenting).

Query: Are the concerns expressed in this dissent justified? Are there ways of addressing these concerns, without compromising the welfare of children involved in contested adoption proceedings?

(3) One of the things that makes cases such as *Lemley v. Barr* so difficult is the amount of time that it typically takes the courts to resolve adoption disputes. In *Lemley*, almost five years passed from the time that Tammy Lemley filed her initial habeas corpus petition to the time that the West Virginia Supreme Court issued its opinion invalidating the West Virginia adoption decree. Various commentators have urged that the judicial system adopt expedited procedures for handling contested adoptions, but some delay seems inevitable, particularly in cases such as *Lemly* that involve court proceedings in more than one jurisdiction. For further discussion of these issues, see Joan Heifetz Hollinger, *Adoption and Aspiration: The Uniform Adoption Act, the DeBoer-Schmidt Case, and the American Quest for the Ideal Family*, 2 Duke J. Gender L. & Policy 15 (1995).

§ 8.03 Unwed Fathers, Due Process and Involuntary Termination of Parental Rights

The Supreme Court first recognized the due process right of an unmarried father to retain custody of his children in the 1972 case of *Stanley v. Illinois*, 405 U.S. 645 (1972). Since that time, the Supreme Court has revisited the issue of unwed fatherhood and adoption on four occasions, yet each time the court has avoided comprehensive treatment of the issue.[1] Moreover, none of the Supreme Court's decisions has involved the adoption of an infant placed at birth, a situation that arguably poses the most difficult legal, social and emotional issues. As a result, while unwed fathers' rights have expanded dramatically since 1972, this development has been uneven and at times erratic, as state courts and legislatures have attempted to reconcile the Supreme Court rulings with their own judgments about the welfare of children and about the role of unmarried fathers in their children's lives. *See* Scott A. Resnik, *Seeking the Wisdom of Solomon: Defining the Rights of Unwed Fathers in Newborn Adoptions*, 20 Seton Hall Legis. J. 363, 364 (1996).

These issues gained new urgency during the 1990s, with a series of highly-emotional and well-publicized custody disputes between prospective adoptive parents and emergent biological fathers. While public opinion diverged over whose claims for custody were most deserving, these cases revealed that existing legal regimes were inadequate to resolve the parenting claims of unwed fathers with sufficient speed and clarity to protect the interests of all parties involved in adoption disputes, particularly children. The unwed father controversies of the 1990s thus catalyzed a public call for adoption reform. As one commentator has explained:

> Legislators, social scientists and legal scholars have tangled over the proper prioritization of interests in these inherently complex disputes. How are the biological ties of the unwed father to be weighted against the nurturing bond developed between the prospective adoptive parents and the child they have raised since its birth? How are a child's best interests to be reconciled with an unwed father's interest in becoming a parent? What is to be done in situations where the unwed father is unaware of his child's birth and subsequent eligibility for adoption? How long does a biological father have to come forward and claim his offspring? Consensus in answering these and related questions has been hard to find.

Resnik, *above* at 365. The two cases that follow explore these issues in the context of infant adoptions.

IN RE ADOPTION OF BABY E.A.W.
Supreme Court of Florida
658 So. 2d 961 (1995)
cert. denied 516 U.S. 1051 (1996)

HARDING, JUSTICE.

G.W.B. is the birth father of Baby E.A.W., a child born out of wedlock in 1992 and placed with adoptive parents shortly after her birth. This case concerns whether G.W.B. abandoned the child and, ultimately, whether she was available for adoption. Without abandonment, G.W.B.'s consent was required for Baby E.A.W.'s adoption.

. . . Section 63.032(14), Florida Statutes (Supp.1992), allows a court to consider the father's conduct toward the child's mother . . . during the pregnancy.[2] We thus decide

---

[1] The cases are *Quilloin v. Walcott* 434 U.S. 246 (1978); *Caban v. Mohammed*, 441 U.S. 380 (1979); *Lehr v. Robertson*, 463 U.S. 248 (1983); and *Michael H. V. Gerald D.*, 491 U.S. 110 (1989). These cases are discussed below, in *In re Baby Boy C.*, and in Chapter 5 *above*.

[2] Section 63.032(14), Florida Statutes (Supp. 1992): " 'Abandoned' means a situation in which the parent

whether section 63.032(14) allows a trial court to consider lack of emotional support and/or emotional abuse in evaluating the conduct of the father toward the child's mother during pregnancy. . . .

G.W.B. and the birth mother had lived together for some months when she became pregnant in November 1991.

The birth mother's testimony was that G.W.B. had very little reaction when she told him during Christmas 1991 that she was pregnant. She was employed and paid her own expenses during December 1991 and part of January 1992, but could not work after an accident in January 1992. From that point on, she was lonely and received little financial support from G.W.B. She bought food with food stamps and gave a government aid check to G.W.B. for her expenses.

The birth mother's doctor testified that the birth mother was emotional and having trouble at home during this time. G.W.B. did not accompany the birth mother to any of the doctor visits. The birth mother testified that G.W.B. did accompany her on one visit, but that he was an "ice cube."

The birth mother gave further testimony that she received little, if any, emotional support from G.W.B. from February through June 1992. G.W.B. once grabbed her, shook her, and spit at her because she used his razor. He called her names and verbally abused her. In addition, G.W.B. had a drinking problem.

The birth mother moved out of G.W.B.'s home in June 1992. Sometime before this, she told G.W.B. that she was considering adoption. He told her to "do whatever you have to do." Based on this response, she followed through with the adoption process.

From the time the birth mother moved out until Baby E.A.W. was born, the birth mother received neither financial nor emotional support from G.W.B. The only phone calls she received from G.W.B. came early in the morning and apparently were made to annoy her.

G.W.B.'s testimony was that he earned $300 to $400 a week during this time and that he effectively paid for food and shelter for the birth mother and her son from another relationship. He was overjoyed about becoming a father. During the pregnancy, he bought one pair of stretch pants for the birth mother and, using money from his mother, bought a crib. He spoke with the birth mother several times after she moved out.

G.W.B. testified further that Charlotte Danciu, an attorney-intermediary in the adoption proceedings, contacted him in July 1992. He told Danciu that he would not give up the child for adoption and then sought legal representation.

After reciting its findings of fact, the trial court found clear and convincing evidence that G.W.B. financially and/or emotionally abandoned the birth mother during her pregnancy. The judge found that even if he accepted G.W.B.'s testimony that he paid for more than half of the couple's expenses, "there can be no doubt that he was living off of her food stamps and demanding her Aid to Dependent Children check to supplement his

---

or legal custodian of a child, while being able, makes no provision for the child's support and makes no effort to communicate with the child, which situation is sufficient to evince a willful rejection of parental obligations. If, in the opinion of the court, the efforts of such parent or legal custodian to support and communicate with the child are only marginal efforts that do not evince a settled purpose to assume all parental duties, the court may declare the child to be abandoned. In making this decision, the court may consider the conduct of a father toward the child's mother during her pregnancy."

earnings." The judge found that the birth mother was on her own emotionally during the pregnancy. G.W.B. even resumed a sexual relationship with a former girlfriend while the birth mother was pregnant.

In addition, the trial court found almost no testimony to establish that G.W.B. exhibited any feeling for the unborn child. It appeared, in fact, that if Danciu had not contacted him, he would have continued his passive stance. Notified that the birth mother planned to put the baby up for adoption, he sought counsel. The trial court noted, "More importantly, it is a simple fact that during the time he was seeking a lawyer, he was still completely out of contact with the natural mother and the unborn infant, both financially and emotionally."

In determining that G.W.B. did not provide emotional or financial support to the birth mother, the trial court concluded in its September 1993 order:

The marginal effort of the natural father does not evince a settled purpose to assume all parental responsibilities and the Court, therefore, declares that the child was abandoned (Florida Statute 63.032(14)). Therefore, the prospective adoptive parents are directed to apply to this Court for an appropriate ex parte hearing on the question of the finalization of the adoption.

A three-judge panel of the Fourth District Court of Appeal reversed the trial court's finding of abandonment. *Baby E.A.W.*, 647 So.2d at 941. The court found the evidence in conflict, but determined that G.W.B. supported the birth mother while he lived with her and objected to the adoption before the birth of Baby E.A.W. *Id.* at 948. The court also concluded that emotional support could not be used to determine abandonment. *Id.* at 949.

After rehearing en banc, the district court reversed the panel decision and found that G.W.B. abandoned Baby E.A.W. both financially and emotionally. *Id.* at 924. Recognizing the uncertainty over whether a trial court may consider emotional support in making its decision on abandonment, the district court certified the question to this Court. *Id.*

We conclude that a trial court, in making a determination of abandonment, may consider the lack of emotional support and/or emotional abuse by the father of the mother during her pregnancy. . . .

This Court first recognized in *In re Adoption of Doe*, 543 So.2d 741, 747 (Fla.), *cert.denied*, 493 U.S. 964 (1989), that evidence of a parent's prebirth conduct is relevant to whether a parent has abandoned a child. *Doe* concerned an unmarried father who was financially able to—but did not—support his child prenatally. The Court found that, by his behavior, he waived his right to consent to the adoption of the child. Although *Doe* primarily concerned the father's ability to provide financial support to the mother, the Court also noted:

A finding of abandonment under chapter 63 means, for whatever reason, the parent or parents have not provided the child with emotional and financial sustenance and, consequently, the well-being of the child requires severing the parent's legal custody or relationship with the child.

Id. at 744.

When this Court decided *Doe*, chapter 63 did not include a definition of abandonment. The Court looked to section 39.01(1), Florida Statutes (1985), which defined abandonment in juvenile proceedings. The definition in chapter 39 did not discuss a father's prebirth conduct, but the *Doe* Court nonetheless decided that such conduct is relevant because it "does tend to prove or disprove material facts bearing on abandonment." *Id.* at 746.

After *Doe*, the Legislature amended section 63.032 to define abandonment. The definition tracks the one in section 39.01(1) (juvenile proceedings), but adds a sentence that is critical to the instant case: "In making this decision [of abandonment], the court may consider the conduct of a father toward the child's mother during her pregnancy." § 63.032(14), Fla.Stat. (Supp.1992).

We find that by this language the Legislature clearly did not limit "conduct" to financial support. Conduct generally connotes behavior. Dictionary definitions of "conduct" include the act, manner, or process of carrying out a task and a mode or standard of personal behavior. Webster's Third New International Dictionary 473–74 (1961). . . .

While conceding that section 63.032(14) allows a court to consider emotional support in making its determination of abandonment, G.W.B. urges this Court to quantify how much weight a court may give to a father's lack of emotional support during the mother's pregnancy. We are not in a position to assign weight in this manner. The determination of abandonment is fact-specific and, absent direction from the Legislature, we cannot dictate to trial courts precisely how to evaluate the factors that go into making this decision.

The United States Supreme Court has held that natural parents have a fundamental liberty interest in the care, custody, and management of their children. *Santosky v. Kramer*, 455 U.S. 745, 753 (1982).

The liberty interest is not absolute, however. The Court has distinguished between married and unwed fathers, noting that "the mere existence of a biological link does not merit equivalent constitutional protection." *Lehr v. Robertson*, 463 U.S. 248, 261 (1983). The substantial due process protection attaches only when an unwed father demonstrates a full commitment to the responsibilities of parenthood by coming forward to participate in raising his child. *Id.*

We recognize the sanctity of the biological connection, and we look carefully at anything that would sever the biological parent-child link. To terminate a parent's right in a natural child, the evidence must be clear and convincing. *Santosky*, 455 U.S. at 747–48

. . .

Our review of the record shows substantial competent evidence to support the trial judge's finding of clear and convincing evidence that G.W.B. abandoned Baby E.A.W. The evidence in the record reveals that G.W.B. showed little to no interest in the birth mother or the unborn child. Once the birth mother moved out of the home, he provided no financial or emotional support. As the trial court noted, the evidence suggests that G.W.B. might have continued his passive stance toward the birth mother and the child had Danciu not contacted him about adoption. Even then, the record shows that G.W.B. still did not make any move to provide financial or emotional support to the birth mother or the unborn child. We therefore approve the district court's decision affirming the trial court's finding of abandonment.

KOGAN, JUSTICE, concurring in part, dissenting in part.

. . .

Until quite recently unwed fathers were regarded as having few if any rights with respect to their offspring. That situation did not substantially change until the United States Supreme

Court issued its 1972 opinion in *Stanley v. Illinois*, 405 U.S. 645 (1972). The *Stanley* opinion revolutionized the law in this area by recognizing a due process right biological fathers possess with respect to their offspring, though the extent of this right has remained clouded with doubt to the present day.

Indeed, American law on this question is most notable today for its confusing nature. It is clear that the law now at least gives the unwed father a chance to be heard prior to the adoption, but beyond that, little is certain. In broad terms the national controversy now involves two competing approaches, along with variations of them. These are: (1) the "biological rights" standard, which places heavy emphasis on the rights of genetic parents; and (2) the "best interests" standard, which tends to favor the "psychological parent"—the adult who has created a stable home environment and whom the child thus has psychologically come to view as its parent. These two standards each have strong and weak points and can be applied in varying ways, but each is generally exemplified in two similar and highly publicized cases.

The first case involved a child popularly known as "Baby Jessica," who had been put up for adoption by her natural mother shortly after her birth on February 8, 1991. The mother initially had listed another man as the natural father, but nine days after the adoption petition was filed she had a change of heart and identified the actual biological father. The latter promptly challenged the adoption. After months of legal complications, the Iowa Supreme Court ultimately held that the biological father's rights had not been terminated and that Baby Jessica thus was not available for adoption. The Iowa Court in particular noted that it could not apply a "best interests" standard, even though Jessica's interests might best be served by remaining with the only family she had known for the first years of life—her potential adoptive parents. *In re B.G.C.*, 496 N.W.2d 239 (Iowa 1993).

The best-interests standard was exemplified by an Illinois appeals court case involving a child widely known as "Baby Richard." The mother in this case had refused to disclose the identity of the biological father, apparently out of concern he might veto the placement. When the father learned of the child's existence, he quickly challenged the adoption. The intermediate appellate court focused extensively on a "best interests" standard in determining that the child was the real party in interest and that his interests demanded he stay with the only parents he had known—his adoptive "psychological parents." *In re Petition of Doe*, 627 N.E.2d 648 (1993). The Illinois Supreme Court, however, reversed after applying the "biological rights" standard used in Iowa. *In re Doe*, 159 Ill.2d 347, 638 N.E.2d 181 (1994), *cert. denied*,–U.S.–(1994). Baby Richard thus was placed with his biological father after spending roughly the first three years of life with another family.

It is well worth noting at this point that the United States Supreme Court has denied appellate review in both the Baby Jessica and Baby Richard cases, thereby leaving intact court orders returning these children to their biological parents.

One of the more recent pronouncements on this topic is the 1994 revision of the Uniform Adoption Act ("UAA") promulgated by the highly respected National Conference of Commissioners on Uniform State Laws. The UAA has combined the two standards in an interesting way: Upon challenge to the adoption of a child less than six months of age, petitioners must establish (1) by clear and convincing evidence a ground constituting abandonment (which may include evidence of prenatal abandonment) or, alternatively, that the father has been convicted of certain crimes, or is not the legal, adoptive, or genetic father of the child, and (2) by a preponderance of the evidence that termination is in the best interests of the child. Once this is done, the burden then shifts to respondent to rebut, including proving by a preponderance of the evidence a compelling explanation why any abandonment occurred (such as poverty, deception by the mother, and so forth). If the respondent presents such proof, the burden then shifts back to the potential adoptive parents to establish one of four factors that would weigh in favor of terminating parental rights, including further consideration of the child's best interests. Unif.Adoption Act, § 3-504 (1994).

The UAA includes the following commentary:

[A] respondent father's rights may be terminated on the basis of his behavior prior to the minor adoptee's birth, including a failure to manifest an ability or willingness to assume parental duties, unless he can prove a "compelling reason" for his failure. State courts have found it constitutionally permissible to terminate a father's status for pre-birth "abandonment" of an unwed mother whom the father knew was pregnant.

9 U.L.A. 5, 55 (1995 Supp). . . .

While the UAA obviously has not been adopted in Florida, it nevertheless represents a considered view by noted scholars. And its attempt to combine the two competing standards into a single analysis suggests a very important point: that both may actually have some relevance to these cases.

This last conclusion also finds support in opinions of the United States Supreme Court. In 1983, for example, the Court found that unwed putative fathers possess only what may be called an "opportunity interest" in establishing legal fatherhood. Like the UAA, the Court used an analysis suggesting that the best interests of the child may factor into the equation whenever an adoption is challenged, although the emphasis here is somewhat different:

The significance of the biological connection is that it offers the natural father an opportunity that no other male possesses to develop a relationship with his offspring. If he grasps that opportunity and accepts some measure of responsibility for the child's future, he may enjoy the blessings of the parent-child relationship and make uniquely valuable contributions to the child's development. If he fails to do so, the Federal Constitution will not automatically compel a State to listen to his opinion of where the child's best interests lie.

Lehr v. Robertson, 463 U.S. 248, 261–62 (1983).

These statements are important, first, because they indicate that the unwed putative father has merely an inchoate right to establish legal fatherhood, which he may exercise or neglect as he sees fit. Second, they suggest that the father's "opportunity interest" matures into a due process right if he "accepts some measure of responsibility for the child's future." Third, the quoted material also indicates that the "child's best interests" are to some degree relevant. This is so, the Court indicated, because society's interest in the establishment and support of a stable home environment for the child deserves consideration along with the interests of blood kinship. The *Lehr* Court regrettably was silent as to how we should balance "best interests" against kinship rights when the two are in irreconcilable conflict, as they are here.

One clue as to the Court's thought on this last matter was provided in an opinion issued by Justice Stevens in his capacity as Circuit Justice reviewing a stay petition in the *Baby Jessica* case. *DeBoer v. DeBoer*, 509 U.S. 1301 (1993). . . .

In *DeBoer*, Justice Stevens denied a stay application from the potential adoptive parents of Baby Jessica, who by then had been ordered to return the child to her natural parent. In rejecting that petition, Justice Stevens made the following pertinent remarks:

Neither Iowa law, Michigan law, nor federal law authorizes unrelated persons to retain custody of a child whose natural parents have not been found to be unfit simply because they may be better able to provide for her future and her education. As the Iowa Supreme Court stated: "[C]ourts are not free to take children from parents simply by deciding another home appears more advantageous. *In re B.G.C.*, 496 N.W.2d 239, 241 (1992) (internal quotation marks and citation omitted).

Id. at —, 114 S.Ct. at 2. . . .

While the relevant law plainly is unsettled, the discussion above reveals enough to leave me with considerable doubt about the majority opinion. By the same token I am not convinced that the fairly complex best-interests analysis used by the UAA entirely squares with what the United States Supreme Court has told us about these cases. Justice Stevens' remarks in *DeBoer*—which can be harmonized with cases announced by the full Court—imply that great weight must be given to the biological father's opportunity interest, at least on facts similar to those in the Baby Jessica case. I take this to mean that the best interests of the child will seldom defeat a timely and legally sufficient challenge by the biological father made before or shortly after the child's birth, as happened with Baby Jessica.

Nevertheless, *Lehr* teaches that the child's best interests at least sometimes will be relevant. And I think that psychological and legal concerns as well as simple fairness compel this same conclusion. . . . The passage of time factors into this equation in an important way. Biological parents, in other words, must assert their rights early in the child's life.

The most reasonable interpretation of the various cases described above is that the child's best interests become more relevant as the period of time increases between the child's birth and the date the biological father's legal challenge is filed. And this in turn implies that there is an early period during which the child's best interests are less relevant absent some unusual factor. This period precisely corresponds with the time during which the biological father must act upon his opportunity interest or forever lose it. In other words, challenges made very early in the child's life will be gauged more by the "biological rights" standard, but the standard then will shift toward a "best interests" analysis as time passes.

Yet another legal problem must be addressed, and it is one that I think reflects unfavorably on the way the courts are handling these cases. The typical pattern we see in all the adoption cases discussed above is that the mother gives the child for adoption, the child is placed with its potential adoptive parents, and the biological father promptly challenges the adoption. For both legal and psychological reasons, I seriously question the validity of placing the child with its potential adoptive parents despite the biological father's challenge, even though this seems a common practice. Such action may in fact be unconstitutional, and it certainly contributes to the horrendous psychological damage done to the child when and if it must be returned to the biological parent.

My objection is this: The fact that unwed biological fathers have a constitutionally protected "opportunity interest" in their offspring necessarily implies that they must at least be given the "opportunity" to exercise it, absent adequate proof of prenatal abandonment. This in turn means there must be a period of time after birth during which such a biological father has a right of access to the child. This might include a tentative placement with the biological father or some kind of visitation rights, depending on the facts before the trial court. Visitation by the potential adoptive parents also may be permissible. In some situations, the child could be placed in a neutral foster arrangement with visitation by both the potential adoptive parents and the biological parent.

It deserves emphasis here that the unwed biological father's constitutional interest over the child is not fully formed at this stage and therefore can be subjected to such reasonable restrictions or limitations. His rights are simply not as extensive as those of a legally recognized father. During this period, the state also could evaluate the unwed biological father's performance and intervene at any time if his conduct required it. The trial court then could finalize the case, allowing the adoption if the father fails to adequately exercise his opportunity interest. Once again, I think six months would be a reasonable period of time for this evaluation to occur, based on the same reasons noted above, though some flexibility should exist for special cases. The overriding goal would be to settle the matter quickly so as to minimize harm to the child.

Beyond its legal and psychological benefits, the procedure outlined above also has obvious benefits for the parties and the child. It permits a reasoned evaluation of any unwed father whose prenatal conduct—while not constituting an actual abandonment—has been validly questioned. This avoids defining "prenatal abandonment" so overbroadly that it impinges upon the father's constitutional opportunity interest. The procedure also does not place the potential adoptive parents in the heart-rending position of becoming emotionally invested in a child they may not receive; and it could finalize the matter earlier in the child's life, before emotional scarring is likely to be serious. Moreover, it leaves the child with "fallback" adoptive parents in case the father's postnatal conduct genuinely does not meet legal requirements. While the potential adoptive parents may find this "tentative" status unsettling, it is far better than parting them from a child they have kept for months or years.

Many conclusions flow from the above analysis. First, it leads me to disagree with the majority's interpretation of section 63.032(14), Florida Statutes (Supp.1992), which I fear extends state law into the realm of the unconstitutional. I do not propose that the prenatal "conduct of [the] father toward the child's mother" is irrelevant evidence, but merely that it is relevant solely to the extent it demonstrates abandonment of the child. . . . And this would be true even if the biological father and mother have irreconcilable differences. Absent conduct detrimental to the fetus, hatred of the mother does not necessarily imply hatred of the child.

Moreover, I am entirely unwilling to say that purely prenatal conduct ever can demonstrate abandonment with respect to the child absent clear and convincing proof that the biological father either (a) unequivocally, by word or deed, indicated a complete and unconditional prenatal abandonment of the child upon which others have reasonably relied, or (b) recklessly or intentionally engaged in conduct that posed a significant risk of detriment to the fetus above and beyond what may be attributable to simple lack of socioeconomic resources. In the absence of such evidence I believe the father must be given a postnatal chance to exercise his opportunity interest under any appropriate supervision that may be necessary.

Turning now to the facts, I think the present record demonstrates more than amply that the biological father had assumed "some responsibility" (in keeping with *Lehr*) for this child's future, and also that he had indicated a desire to exercise his opportunity interest. At least four facts demonstrate this: (1) he paid part of the couple's joint living expenses when they lived together; (2) the father promptly and prenatally informed the attorney-mediator he would oppose the adoption and seek legal rights to the child; (3) the father attended one of the mother's visits to a health-care provider during her pregnancy; and (4) the father purchased a crib for his baby.

Thus, we have a biological father here who clearly had shown at least some prenatal interest in the child. Evidence supporting prenatal abandonment—including all of that cited by the trial court and the majority—is at best equivocal and therefore uncompelling. Nothing in the record indicates any conduct on his part likely to be detrimental to the fetus apart from his poverty, even though I acknowledge his interpersonal skills with respect to the mother were lacking. Moreover, he was denied meaningful postnatal access to the child by a series of events beyond his control, including an unlawful ex parte order waiving his veto rights and a court injunction. Consistent with federal case law, I believe the trial court erred in initially placing the child in the exclusive custody of the potential adoptive parents based on the record before it. Instead, an arrangement should have been made for the biological father to have access to the child for purposes of exercising his opportunity interest.

I cannot overlook the terrible consequences that now have flowed from the trial court's initial error. The record before us poses an unambiguous nightmare: potential adoptive parents who have had custody of the child for years and are emotionally invested in her, a little girl who knows no one else as her parents, a father whose rights were improperly terminated and who has had no opportunity to bond with his child, and a lawsuit that leaves this Court with nothing but sickening choices. . . .

In a real sense, the most victimized party here is the child. Where does the fault lie?—It rests on inadequate laws, procedural rules incapable of recognizing the needs of a small growing child, state agencies too unmindful of the biological father's rights, parties too eager to litigate, judges and lawyers who let the child's fate bog down in a quagmire of legal technicality. We all have failed Baby Emily. And while I wish the law could magically rescue her from the legal conundrum in which she lies, I see no solution that is free of tragedy. Taking her from her psychological family unquestionably will scar her, as the record itself indicates. Such a result can only be described as horrible.

Yet leaving Baby Emily with her adoptive family will set a precedent I find damaging to our society's traditional concept of a family based on blood kinship—something the nation's highest Court has clothed with significant legal protections. Our decision today may well reverberate for years to come in countless other adoptions, affecting many other biological fathers. And I genuinely believe that a concept like "lack of emotional support of the mother" can too easily lead to abusive applications selectively discriminating against the less fortunate, in favor of the privileged. This is a broader and more insidious impact that I find even more horrible for a very basic reason: It suggests that the well-to-do can come to Florida to shop for babies among an underclass unschooled in vaguely defined middle-class values underlying a concept like "emotional support."

All of this points only to a single indisputable conclusion: There is a pressing need for reforming the way these cases are handled, at least to lessen the delays and the damage they bring to children. . . . We can only guess how this case might have ended had the issues been resolved quickly. But there can be no doubt this Court would not have faced so terrible a choice as it must make today: to select between hurting a helpless child or further eroding the institution of the kinship family. Because the latter is the greater evil, I dissent as to the result. But I must add that returning Baby Emily to her biological parent at this late date is an image that would haunt me for my remaining days.

IN RE BABY BOY C.
District of Columbia Court of Appeals
581 A.2d 1141 (1990)

FERREN, ASSOCIATE JUDGE:

This case concerns the constitutional and statutory rights of an unwed father, appellant H.R., a citizen of Zaire who has been seeking custody of his infant (now seven-year-old) son, Baby Boy C. The child's mother, L.C., is a United States citizen who conceived the child while serving as a Peace Corps volunteer in Zaire. She returned to the United States and, ten days after the child was born in August 1983, relinquished her own parental rights to the Barker Foundation, a licensed child placement agency in the District of Columbia, to facilitate adoption of the child. In September 1983, Barker placed the child with adoptive parents, Mr. and Mrs. O., who, the same day, filed a petition for adoption in Superior Court. . . . H.R. was not aware that he had a son until sometime in October 1983, when L.C. informed H.R. that they had a child which she had placed for adoption. . . .

H.R. contends the adoption proceedings which granted custody of Baby Boy C. to the O. family (1) violated his statutory and constitutional rights to immediate, adequate notice of the adoption proceedings, including due diligence to assure he received notice, and (2) applied the wrong test by ordering the adoption in "the best interests of the child" without granting him a custodial preference as a natural parent, absent a showing of unfitness. He therefore urges us to remand this case for application of a "fitness" test whereby H.R. would assume custody of Baby Boy C. unless the court found him unfit to be a parent.

I conclude that H.R.'s constitutional and statutory rights have been violated and that the court applied the wrong legal test in granting the adoption. I further conclude that when an unwed, noncustodial father has not abandoned his "opportunity interest" in developing a relationship with his child, the Constitution mandates that we construe our "best interests" standard under the adoption statute to include a custodial preference for a "fit" parent. In this case, I conclude as a matter of law that, because of unlawful state action, H.R. cannot be said to have abandoned his "opportunity interest." Under the circumstances, therefore, the court should have awarded custody to H.R. if found "fit" to be a parent, unless clear and convincing evidence demonstrated that such custody would have been detrimental to the "best interest" of Baby Boy C. Because the trial court incorrectly applied a more traditional "best interest" test that did not begin with a presumption of custody for a "fit" natural parent, and because we, as an appellate court, cannot properly apply the correct test on this record, we vacate the judgment and remand the case for further proceedings.

I. FACTS AND PROCEEDINGS

Baby Boy C.'s mother, L.C., met H.R. in the village in Zaire where she was teaching. At the time, appellant was on leave from his law studies at the university in Kinshasa, Zaire.

In April 1983, when L.C. learned she was pregnant, the Peace Corps immediately evacuated her to Washington, D.C. Upon her departure, L.C. wrote a letter to H.R. informing him that she was pregnant and that he was the father. She hinted that she planned to have an abortion, saying that what she would have to go through in the United States would exhaust her physically and emotionally and that she would return to Zaire in two weeks. She also said that she did not want anyone to know about the matter. L.C. never went back to Zaire. In July, a mutual friend of L.C. and H.R. told H.R. that L.C. had had an abortion in Washington, D.C. In fact, however, L.C. gave birth to Baby Boy C. in the District on August 5, 1983. Ten days later, L.C. relinquished her parental rights to the Barker Foundation.

In early August 1983, when he was visiting the dean's office at the University of Kinshasa from which he had graduated in June, H.R. happened upon a letter from the Barker Foundation postmarked over two months earlier in May. The letter notified him that L.C. was expecting to give birth to a child in July. Along with its letter, Barker sent three forms: an "Admission of Paternity and Consent to Adoption" form, a "Statement of Non-Paternity and Consent to Adoption" form, and a biographical data form. Neither the letter nor the accompanying forms indicated that H.R. had the right not to consent to the adoption and the right to seek custody of his child himself. Upon receiving this information, H.R. immediately wrote a letter to L.C. in care of her parents, in order to ascertain what in fact had occurred over the past several months. L.C. received this letter in mid-September, after she had left Washington to attend graduate school in Chicago. . . .

On September 22, 1983, the Barker Foundation placed Baby Boy C. with the O. family. On the same day, the O. family filed a petition for adoption in Superior Court. No notice was sent to inform H.R. of a formal adoption proceeding seeking to terminate his parental rights to Baby Boy C. in favor of a new adoptive family. On September 29, 1983, the court issued an order of reference, directing Barker to investigate the truth of the allegations contained in the petition for the purpose of determining whether Baby Boy C. was "a proper subject for adoption and if the home of the petitioners is a suitable one" and to file a report in ninety days.

In October 1983, after receiving L.C.'s response to his letter in which she had acknowledged receiving his letter but had not mentioned a baby, H.R. called her and learned for the first time that he had a son. According to L.C.'s testimony at the eventual hearings in this case, H.R. did not have a good understanding of United States adoption procedures and thought that L.C. had abandoned the child. . . . In November, believing that H.R. did not really comprehend the adoption process, L.C. wrote H.R. another letter, describing her sense of loss in giving up their child but stating her belief that Baby Boy C. was "at home" and loved by his adoptive parents and older brother. According to H.R., he responded by informing L.C. of his opposition to the adoption and offering to take the baby if she did not want to raise him herself. He further testified that he had difficulty grasping the idea that L.C. had really given up all her rights to the child.

In December 1983, in compliance with the court's order of reference, Barker submitted its report to the trial court and its formal consent to the adoption petition. Barker recommended entry of an interlocutory decree of adoption. In the report, Barker indicated that it had been unable to contact H.R., who had a statutory right to notification of, and presence at, a hearing on the adoption petition. Barker added that it had tried to reach H.R. at the university at Kinshasa but had received no response to its letter. Alice Avery, the

Barker social worker responsible for the Baby Boy C. case, testified at the hearing that, although she had told the court she did not know H.R.'s whereabouts, Barker had not contacted L.C. to ask if she had heard from H.R. Nor, said Avery, had the agency attempted to contact H.R. or to update his address since mailing the consent forms to the university seven months earlier. Although the report provided the names of H.R.'s many siblings in Zaire, Avery testified that she had not pressed L.C. to provide their addresses because L.C. preferred the university address for reasons of confidentiality. . . .

On January 17, 1984, H.R. called the Barker Foundation. . . . Telephone communication was difficult; H.R., a native French speaker who understands some English, speaks French almost exclusively. Because Avery, the Barker social worker, did not speak French, one of Barker's secretaries who knew some French spoke with H.R. and recorded notes of the conversation. According to these notes, H.R. acknowledged his paternity. H.R. also requested clarification of the forms he had received in August and indicated that he did not understand the portion of the documents requiring him to give up his rights, particularly his right to see his son. H.R. told the secretary that the mails in Zaire were very bad and that he would be more likely to receive correspondence addressed to him in care of the Peace Corps in Zaire, an address Barker could obtain from L.C. According to the secretary's notes, H.R. also told her that he was expecting, shortly, to take a trip to France or to Canada during which he hoped to come to the United States to see his child. At no time during this conversation did Barker communicate to H.R. that he had a right to seek custody of his son, that a formal adoption proceeding had been instituted in which he had a right to contest his child's adoption, or that Barker had just recommended entry of an interlocutory decree of adoption in favor of the O. family.

Two days later, on January 19, 1984, Avery received a letter of January 12, 1984, from L.C. stating that she had recently received a letter from H.R., that H.R. did not consent to the adoption, that he would ask for the baby as soon as possible, and that he planned to be studying in Canada in March and might come to Chicago or Washington at that time. In this letter, L.C. expressed strong opposition to H.R.'s gaining custody of the baby.

On January 25, 1984, Judge Schwelb denied the petition for an interlocutory decree of adoption, noting his concern "that all reasonable steps have not been taken to contact [H.R.]." The judge observed that Barker's December report listed many of H.R.'s siblings, thereby suggesting "it would probably not be difficult to contact him." The judge stated that the court should not entertain the petition for adoption until proof was offered that "all reasonable steps to locate H.R. had been exhausted." . . .

Barker filed an addendum to its January report on February 1, 1984, informing the court of H.R.'s January 17 telephone call, his willingness to acknowledge paternity, his lack of clarity about the documents he received, particularly those pertaining to giving up his legal rights, and suggesting that he could be contacted in care of the Peace Corps in Kinshasa, Zaire, an address which L.C. could provide. The agency also summarized the letter it had received from L.C. reporting that H.R. desired custody of Baby Boy C. as soon as possible, that he had marked "no" on the consent forms, and that he planned to come to Canada in March. . . .

On February 6, 1984, Barker sent H.R. a letter, translated into French, in which it purported to clarify the documents it had sent him. The letter was sent by Worldwide Courier to H.R. in care of the Peace Corps in Zaire. . . . Again, Barker did not mention that H.R.

had a legal right to seek custody or that Barker was a party to formal adoption proceedings seeking to terminate H.R.'s parental rights in favor of the O. family. . . .

On March 5, 1984, Barker filed with the court another addendum to its December report, stating that it had sent H.R. a letter "inform[ing] him of the placement, the agency's work with [L.C.] and his rights as the putative father of the child." The addendum also related the substance of L.C.'s February telephone conversation with H.R. in which he had told her that he could not accept the all-or-nothing nature of adoption (which would not allow him to see his child) and that he intended to seek custody for himself. The report noted that L.C. was satisfied that Baby Boy C.'s placement with the O. family was in his best interests and "that she is willing to assist in any way she is able to prevent the placement from being disrupted." . . .

In late April 1984, H.R.'s government sent him to Paris, France, to obtain a doctorate in international law, rather than to Canada as he had expected. H.R. and his wife, whom he had married in December 1983, telephoned L.C. twice in early May 1984 to inform her of their current situation. Appellant testified that during these conversations he asked L.C. to inform the Barker Foundation that he intended to come to the United States to take custody of Baby Boy C. when he had saved enough money. At the hearings, H.R. and L.C. had different recollections of this conversation. L.C. testified that H.R. told her he would consent to the adoption, and she passed this information on to Barker in a May 8, 1984 letter. H.R. testified that he had expressed his absolute opposition to the adoption but had said that he would consider sending in the biographical data form to Barker. . . .

On May 22, 1984, Barker filed L.C.'s May 8 letter with the court, along with her letter of January 12 and an affidavit of Avery, stating that appellant was planning to sign the consent forms. The affidavit gave appellant's address as the Peace Corps in Zaire, even though H.R. had indicated in January that he might be moving to France and L.C. had informed Barker that H.R. in fact had just written to her from France. In June, L.C. wrote to H.R., stating that she did not want to hear from him again and sending him photographs of Baby Boy C. taken at birth. The baby was now ten months old.

On July 23, 1984, the court ordered Barker to translate a show cause order into French, ordering H.R. to appear in court on October 15, 1984, "to show cause . . . why an order should not be made granting the petition for adoption." . . . The order was sent to H.R. on August 15, 1984, by registered mail in care of the Peace Corps in Zaire. Although Barker had not communicated directly with H.R. since January and had received intervening information indicating that he was in regular contact with L.C.—who had just reported him to be in Paris—no effort was made to ascertain H.R.'s current whereabouts. . . . Neither the receipt nor the Order to Show Cause was returned to the court. H.R., who was living in Paris at the time the letter was mailed, testified that he did not receive it. Baby Boy C. was now one-year old.

On October 15, 1984, Judge Riley entered an interlocutory decree of adoption in favor of the O. family, to become final on April 15, 1985, unless set aside for good cause shown. The order declared, among other things, that H.R. was withholding his consent to the adoption contrary to the best interests of the child. H.R., who had never received notice of the judicial adoption proceeding, was not present at the show cause hearing. According to H.R.'s later testimony, after three months of attempting unsuccessfully to gain assistance at the United States embassy, he finally met an official there who referred him to an

American lawyer working in Paris. On November 30, 1984, on the advice of his attorney, H.R. formally acknowledged paternity in writing and filed it with his attorney. After his attorney had advised him that Barker was a legal adversary whom he must inform of his intention to seek custody in order to protect his legal rights, H.R. wrote a letter informing Barker that if it was not going to permit him the right to visit the child or to make decisions about the baby's future, H.R. was ready to assume custody of his child. H.R. also provided his Paris address. . . . Barker filed a translation of this letter with the court but did not respond to it.

On February 25, 1985, appellant wrote Barker again, advising that he had retained an attorney and had admitted paternity. On the advice of his attorney, he asked Barker to inform the court that he did not intend to abandon his child. He stated that he would like to gain custody of his child by Baby Boy C.'s second birthday. He proposed that, once he gained custody, the O. family be allowed visitation rights during vacations. Barker received this letter on March 3, 1985, and filed it with the court on March 11, along with a translation. Again, Barker did not respond to H.R.'s letter. On April 5, Barker filed a final report, recommending entry of a final decree of adoption by the O. family.

. . . On April 15, 1985, after considering the brief of the O. family and the Barker Foundation, Judge Riley ordered the interlocutory decree of adoption extended until June 30, 1985. The court also ordered H.R., through counsel, to file pleadings giving evidence as to why adoption of Baby Boy C. would not be in the child's best interests and to appear before the court before June 30, 1985 to give testimony on the issue. This order, served on H.R. at his Paris address, as well as on his attorney, was the first communication he had received informing him of the adoption proceeding against him. Baby Boy C. was 20 months old at this time.

On June 28, 1985, H.R. appeared before the Family Division of Superior Court and moved to set aside the interlocutory decree of adoption. Hearings before Judge Riley began that day and were held on five other occasions throughout the next ten and one-half months. After an initial four-month delay to accommodate H.R., further hearing dates were again delayed for seven months to accommodate the court's schedule. Testimony was taken from H.R., L.C., the O. family, Avery, a former Peace Corps volunteer who knew L.C. and H.R., Dr. Allen E. Marans, an expert for the O. family qualified in child psychiatry, child-psychoanalysis, child development and adoption, and Dr. Joseph D. Noshpitz, an expert for H.R. qualified in child psychiatry but not qualified as an expert in adoption. . . .

Dr. Marans, testifying in July 1985 on behalf of the O. family, had met with Baby Boy C., both adoptive parents, and Baby Boy C.'s older adoptive brother on several occasions during late June and early July 1985, both at his office and in the family home. Dr. Marans described Baby Boy C. as a happy, healthy, normal three [sic]-year-old child, fully integrated into the O. family. . . . Concerning the effects of removing Baby Boy C. from the O. family, Dr. Marans stated that, although a child at three days or six weeks of age would suffer no permanent scar from a change in custody, such a change would be "devastating" to a child of 23 months, the age of Baby Boy C. at the time Dr. Marans testified. . . .

Dr. Noshpitz met with Baby Boy C., his adoptive parents, and brother and with H.R. and his wife sometime after Dr. Marans did. Dr. Noshpitz testified in May 1986 when Baby Boy C. was three months shy of three years old. Like Dr. Marans, Dr. Noshpitz also testified that the O.s were warm and loving parents deeply attached to Baby Boy C. He also testified that Mr. and Mrs. R. were a devoted couple who could provide a loving home for Baby Boy C. Concerning a transfer of custody, Dr. Noshpitz agreed with Dr. Marans that a transition in custody is more effective the earlier it takes place. He was concerned, however, that Baby Boy C. would suffer feelings of wonder and anger at a later stage when he learned that he was adopted and that his natural father had sought, but been denied, custody. Dr. Noshpitz advocated a period of transition over several years, during which H.R. and his wife would gradually assume custody. . . .

Dr. Marans testified in rebuttal that an arrangement of the sort proposed by Dr. Noshpitz was naive because it ignored the negative psychological effects such a plan would have on the child's security and identity. He agreed that Baby Boy C. would experience anger and resentment at learning that his natural father had sought to raise him, but he opined that the experience would not destroy the boy's personality. Dr. Marans further testified that Dr. Noshpitz's proposal was imaginative but completely untried and ignored the strength of the child's attachment to those who nurture him. Dr. Marans stated that the gradual transfer plan would create an everlasting sense of insecurity in Baby Boy C. and undermine his ability to trust in others.

In its decision issued on September 11, 1986, the trial court rejected H.R.'s due process arguments. The court concluded that H.R. had received all the constitutional protection he was due under Supreme Court jurisprudence. . . . Even accepting H.R.'s argument under *Lehr* that natural fathers possess a so-called "opportunity interest" in developing a relationship with their children, the court concluded that H.R. had failed to grasp that opportunity and was himself responsible for some of the delay in receiving official notice of the adoption because he had failed to keep Barker informed of his changes of address. The court stated that H.R. had received a full and fair opportunity to present whatever arguments he had in support of his position that the adoption petition should be denied. . . . Finding lawful and appropriate—and applying—the "best interests of the child" standard, the trial court credited Dr. Marans' testimony over that of Dr. Noshpitz, who, according to the court, was not an expert in adoption and who admitted that his proposal for custody was untried and without precedent in adoption situations. . . . The court granted the petition for adoption by the O. family, finding by clear and convincing evidence that this was in the best interests of Baby Boy C. . . .

IV. THE UNWED FATHER'S "OPPORTUNITY INTEREST"

. . . The Supreme Court has long recognized that state intervention in the relationship between a parent and a child is subject to constitutional oversight. . . . More recently, the Supreme Court has reiterated "that the relationship of love and duty in a recognized family unit is an interest in liberty entitled to constitutional protection." [*Lehr v Robertson*, 463 U.S. 248, (1983)] The Court, however, in discussing the interests of unwed fathers in preventing termination of their relationships with their children, has treated differently the claims of fathers who have had custodial relationships with their children by the time of the termination proceeding and those who have not.

In *Stanley v. Illinois*, 405 U.S. 645 (1972), the state placed the children of unwed parents in guardianship after their mother's death over objection of their natural father, who had lived with and supported them all their lives. The Court held, as a matter of due process and equal protection, that the state could not deprive the father of custody without notice, hearing, and proof of his unfitness for parenthood.

Several years later, moreover, in *Caban v. Mohammed*, 441 U.S. 380 (1979), the Court struck down a New York statute that permitted consent to adoption exclusively by the mother of a child born out-of-wedlock. As in *Stanley*, the natural father had lived with his two children and their mother, and supported them, for several years. After the mother had left with the children, remarried, and gained legal custody, the mother's new husband sought to adopt the children over the natural father's objection. The New York courts applied the statute and granted the adoption. The Supreme Court reversed, holding that, by permitting such adoption without consent of the father, the statute imposed a gender-based discrimination that did not bear a substantial relation to some important state interest, in violation of the equal protection clause. . . .

In contrast, in *Quilloin v. Wolcott*, 434 U.S. 246, 255 (1978), where the unwed father had not "at any time, had, or sought, actual or legal custody of his child," the Court upheld an adoption decree terminating the father's parental rights under Georgia's "best interests of the child" standard and granting legal custody to the eleven-year-old child's mother and stepfather. In upholding the adoption, the Court stated that due process would no doubt be violated if the state were "to attempt to force the breakup of a natural family" on the basis of the "children's best interest" without some showing of parental unfitness. *Id.* But, the Court noted, the result of the adoption was "to give full recognition to a family unit already in existence." *Quilloin*, 434 U.S. at 255. The Court implied that the outcome would have been different if the proposed adoption had placed "the child with a new set of parents with whom the child had never before lived." *Id.*

Read together, these cases say that an unwed natural father who has had a custodial relationship with his child cannot be ousted as a parent at the mother's behest—absent a showing of his unfitness—in favor of a foster parent (*Stanley*) or an adoptive stepfather (*Caban*), but that an unwed father who has not developed a custodial relationship, though fit to be a parent, can lose his parental rights to an adoptive stepfather when the best interests of the child preclude disruption of "a family unit already in existence" (*Quilloin*).

What, then, is to occur if an unwed father (1) has never had a relationship with his child but (2) seeks custody when a "proposed adoption would place the child with a new set of parents with whom the child had never before lived"? *Quilloin*, 434 U.S. at 255. The Court addressed that question—at issue in this case—in *Lehr*. Basically, the Court concluded the answer turns on how early and persistently the natural father pursues his interest in taking custody of the child so as to justify keeping the father presumptively first in line, so to speak, when the natural mother elects to put the child up for adoption.

According to the Court in *Lehr*, when an unwed father "demonstrates a full commitment to the responsibilities of parenthood by com[ing] forward to participate in the rearing of his child, his interest in personal contact with his child acquires substantial protection under the Due Process Clause." *Lehr*, 463 U.S. at 261. . . . Thus, the Court has characterized the unwed, noncustodial father's protectible liberty interest as an "opportunity" he must "grasp[]." . . . It follows that a noncustodial, unwed father who has grasped his opportunity interest will, as a matter of substantive constitutional right, be in the same position as the custodial father in *Stanley*: entitled to an "individualized hearing on fitness." 405 U.S. 645, 657 n. 9.

Because a noncustodial father may not grasp the opportunity to develop a relationship with his child in a timely, meaningful manner, his eventual assertion of his opportunity interest may be too late and thus not entitled to the constitutional protection available to a custodial father. In *Lehr*, for example, the Court upheld against a due process challenge an adoption decree granting legal custody to the child's mother and stepfather, even though the natural father had not been notified of, or allowed to participate in, the adoption proceeding. By the time the petition for adoption was filed, *Lehr* had failed to establish a parental relationship with his two-year-old daughter attributable in large part to the mother's desire to prevent contact between them. Significantly, however, *Lehr* also had failed to submit his name to New York's putative father registry, an action that would have guaranteed he received notice of any action to terminate his parental rights. *Lehr*, 463 U.S. at 250–52. The Supreme Court concluded that, under the circumstances, the New York statutory scheme, designed "to protect the unmarried father's interest in assuming a responsible role in the future of his child," provided sufficient process by guaranteeing putative fathers "who have never developed a relationship with the child the opportunity to receive notice simply by mailing a postcard to the putative father registry." *Id.* at 262 n. 18. . . .

Lehr is significant, therefore, especially for the present case, because the Supreme Court announced for the first time how an unwed father can receive constitutional protection of his interest in a child with whom he has not had a custodial relationship. *Lehr* makes clear that, in a proceeding to determine child custody, a noncustodial, unwed father who moves quickly and responsibly can achieve constitutionally mandated priority over prospective adoptive parents who have received the child at birth and do not yet have an established family relationship with that child. I therefore turn, more specifically, to what it means for a noncustodial father to grasp his opportunity interest in a manner entitling him to constitutional protection.

As *Lehr* illustrates, a natural father who fails promptly to assert his opportunity interest in developing a relationship with his child may forever lose that interest.

Of course, once the state places an infant with a prospective adoptive family, the natural father is precluded from establishing a parental relationship with his child, and any failure to establish personal, custodial, or financial ties with the child after such placement cannot automatically be characterized as abandonment. On the other hand, at least two courts have found relevant to a finding of abandonment the fact that a natural father knew of the mother's pregnancy but failed to express an interest in a parental role or to assume any responsibility for the pregnancy or the newborn before adoptive parents assumed custody of his child near the time of the child's birth. . . .

In sum, a court evaluating a father's assertion of his opportunity interest is entitled to focus on the extent of the father's involvement as soon as he learns of the pregnancy. On the other hand, the court must also recognize the limitations state action can impose on a noncustodial father once the child is placed with another family.

. . . Considering these factors, I conclude that, when an unwed mother has relinquished her right to custody of a child at birth for adoption by strangers, the unwed father's interest in developing a custodial relationship with his child is entitled to substantial constitutional protection if he has early on, and continually, done all that he could reasonably have been expected to do under the circumstances to pursue that interest. . . .

... This case concerns the rights of a natural father when (1) the natural mother relinquishes her rights to custody of her child at birth, and (2) the petition for adoption is filed by strangers when the child is still an infant. *Lehr*, in contrast, concerned a stepfather's adoption of a child who, at the time the petition for adoption was filed, had lived for two years in an existing family unit with her natural mother and adoptive father, as in *Quilloin*. This factual difference has two important implications. First, the *Lehr* opinion made much of Lehr's failure to have developed a father-daughter relationship with his two-year-old child by the time the adoption petition was filed (even though the mother had taken steps to prevent that relationship). It is impossible, however, to find a failed parental relationship under the facts of the present case. . . .

There is a second major difference between *Lehr* and this case. In *Lehr*, private action alone denied the establishment of parental ties between Lehr and his daughter by the time the adoption petition was filed. In the present case, however, state intervention cut off H.R.'s ability to establish parent-child relations with Baby Boy C. . . . Before the adoption petition was filed in this case, the Barker Foundation, a District-licensed child placement agency, was permitted to seek the termination of H.R.'s parental rights before Baby Boy C. had even been born; to accept L.C.'s relinquishment of her parental rights; and to place the baby with the O. family without H.R.'s prior consent or a judicial determination that the placement was suitable for the child. These acts taken by Barker, as well as the proceedings in the Superior Court, constituted state action under the due process clause. . . .

When state action blocks the opportunity for development of a parental relationship between the natural father and child and creates an environment for the development of parental ties between strangers and that child, the state may not then lawfully deny the father his opportunity interest on the basis that the child has developed family relations with prospective adoptive parents before the adoption petition is filed or between the time of the filing and the hearing on the petition.

. . .

V. VIOLATIONS OF H.R.'S CONSTITUTIONAL AND STATUTORY RIGHTS

I conclude, on this record, that H.R. has not abandoned his opportunity interest in developing a relationship with Baby Boy C. because state action unlawfully interfered with H.R.'s rights. . . .

. . . In sum, by cutting off the possibility of a current parent-child relationship, and then failing to inform H.R. for more than eighteen months of the legal proceeding which offered him his only means of ensuring a future relationship with his son, the District of Columbia—primarily the Barker Foundation as a state actor—deprived H.R. of any greater opportunity than he asserted to become a parent to his child. . . .

I agree with H.R.'s argument that the information Barker furnished him failed to provide the minimal notice required by due process to enable him to assert his right to custody of Baby Boy C. at a meaningful time and in a meaningful manner.

In its initial letter to H.R. mailed in May 1983, Barker told H.R. that he had a right to acknowledge or deny paternity and provided him with forms to enable him to consent to the adoption. Barker's February 1984 letter, sent in response to H.R.'s request for clarification concerning his rights, stated only that "the law requires that an effort be made in good faith to inform the biological father of the plans for adoption" and that Barker's May 1983 letter, with accompanying consent forms, had informed him of this. Neither of these letters, however, informed H.R. of his basic right to seek custody of Baby Boy C. and of his right to participate at a court hearing that would be scheduled to determine the permanent placement of his child. . . .

Barker's efforts did not approach the standard of diligence required to satisfy due process. Barker assumed a casual attitude toward ascertaining H.R.'s whereabouts. Avery's testimony indicates that Barker did not obtain the addresses of H.R.'s relatives because L.C. wanted to keep the entire matter as confidential as possible. In Barker's crucial December 1984 report to the court, Avery wrote that L.C. did not know H.R.'s whereabouts; but Avery admitted on deposition that she did not tell the court that L.C. had other possible addresses for H.R. . . .

I reject the trial court's assertion . . . that H.R. had the responsibility to keep the "parties," in this case Barker, informed of his current address if he wished to have prompt notice of the legal proceeding. There was no indication whatsoever in any of the information Barker sent to H.R. that there was a pending judicial proceeding, let alone that Barker and H.R. were "parties" to that proceeding. . . . Perhaps we could attribute some legal significance to H.R.'s failure to keep Barker informed of his whereabouts if—but only if—Barker had informed H.R. that it needed to be updated on his changes of address because it was serving as an investigator for a court that would be sending H.R. notice of a hearing in which Barker would be challenging H.R.'s rights to custody of his son. As it was, H.R. only knew that the Barker Foundation was seeking his consent to the adoption of his child—consent which he was unwilling to give.

In sum, the Barker Foundation and the court denied H.R. the following procedural rights, guaranteed by the due process clause: (1) notice of the legal procedures involved in the adoption process, and the agency's role in those procedures; (2) immediate notice of the adoption petition, filed by the O. family, which initiated the official judicial proceeding to terminate H.R.'s parental rights (a statutory violation as well); and (3) diligent efforts by the Barker Foundation to ascertain H.R.'s whereabouts, in order to assure the required immediate notice of the judicial proceeding so that H.R. could exercise his rights to seek custody of his child at a meaningful time and in a meaningful manner. Given the communications he did receive, H.R. did all he could reasonably have been expected to do to claim custody of his child. For these reasons, H.R.'s "opportunity interest" remained intact.

VI. APPLICATION OF THE PROPER STANDARD FOR TERMINATING AN UNWED, NONCUSTODIAL FATHER'S PARENTAL RIGHTS WHEN THE MOTHER PUTS A CHILD UP FOR ADOPTION AT BIRTH

. . . H.R. claims that, because he had a constitutionally protected liberty interest in developing parental relations with Baby Boy C. and did all he could reasonably be expected to do under the circumstances to grasp his opportunity to protect that interest, he was entitled to custody—absent his "unfitness" as a parent. He adds that application of the "best interests" standard is especially inappropriate here because procedural violations delayed his awareness of the situation in a way that made it impossible for him to prevail under that standard as traditionally applied (i.e., by comparing a noncustodial parent with a custodial family with whom the child has lived happily for awhile). In short, H.R. claims that, because he would be a "fit" parent, the illegally established relationships between Baby Boy C. and the O. family cannot form the basis of a decision to deny him parental rights.

Lehr makes clear that a natural father who has not abandoned his "opportunity interest" has a constitutionally protected interest in establishing parental relations when the natural mother relinquishes their child for adoption at birth. I believe this means that ordinarily in such circumstances, if the court finds the natural father would be a "fit" parent, he is entitled to custody. . . .

It is conceivable, however, that even granting custody to a "fit" parent who has not abandoned his "opportunity interest" could be detrimental to the best interests of the child under certain circumstances—as I shall elaborate later. *Lehr* and earlier Supreme Court cases do not address, let alone foreclose, that possibility, and irrespective of a natural parent's fitness, I do not believe the Constitution, any more than the District's guardianship statute, requires an award of custody that clear and convincing evidence shows would be adverse to the child's best interests. On the other hand, I believe *Lehr* and *Stanley* taken together do afford substantive as well as procedural protection, mandating at least a custodial preference for a fit parent who has not abandoned his opportunity interest.

Accordingly, I conclude the Constitution requires us to construe the "best interests" language under the adoption statute to mean that, when a natural father who has not abandoned his "opportunity interest" seeks custody of an infant child whom the mother has surrendered for adoption at birth, he shall be entitled—as under the guardianship statute—to custody if he would be a "fit" parent, unless the adoptive parents persuade the court with clear and convincing evidence that failure to terminate the father's parental rights would be detrimental to the best interests of the child.

. . .

Although the trial court made no explicit findings about H.R.'s fitness to be a parent, the record strongly supports a finding that he is fit. Moreover, both of the expert witnesses who testified concerning the effects of a transfer of custody on Baby Boy C. assumed that H.R. would be a fit father, and Dr. Noshpitz explicitly so testified. . . .

Despite H.R.'s fitness for fatherhood, however, both experts agreed that removing Baby Boy C. from the O. family would damage him psychologically. The trial court also found that the untried and unprecedented gradual transition proposed by Dr. Noshpitz could not eliminate the "devastating" effect of removing Baby Boy C. from the O. family. . . .

On the other hand, we are given the trial court's incorrect application of the "best interests" standard, since H.R. was not evaluated for fitness and with a parental preference. And, we are given at least one expert who proposed a gradual transitional approach to custody that conceivably could have affected the trial court's view of the situation under the "best interests" standard correctly applied with a parental preference. On this record, therefore, I am not prepared to conclude that the "best interests" standard, even as newly interpreted, should be applied to deny H.R., the father, custody as a matter of law when there is no negative evidence about the father and thus the only harm would be the psychological impact on the child of a transfer from one fit custodian to another.

Accordingly, the trial court must rule once again, with full freedom to reopen the proceedings as needed to inform the court about relevant events during the period that has elapsed since the last trial court order and the impact of those events on this petition. . . .

IN RE BABY BOY C.
District of Columbia Superior Court
No. A-249-83 (1992)

ZELDON, J. . . .

For the reasons stated below, the Court concludes that it is in the best interest of the child in the compelling circumstances of this unusual and complex case to grant the adoption petition. . . . As set forth in detail below, petitioners established by clear and convincing evidence that denial of the petition for adoption would be psychologically harmful to the child and that adoption by petitioners would avoid the detrimental consequences of not granting the adoption petition. . . .

Throughout the trial, petitioners sought adoption so as to make *de jure* the *de facto* position of the child in their family. Once their legal status as parents is secure, they say they would be very willing for Charles to have an ongoing relationship with Mr. R. and his family. . . . However, without adoption, petitioners fear that Mr. R. who is well connected to government officials from Zaire, may try to take the child from them, particularly if they are visiting in Paris, France, where Zaire has an embassy.

Mr. R. does not seek a mandated transfer of the child by Court order from the O. family to his family. He fully recognizes that during the past eight years the child has become a member of the O. family. . . .

Instead, Mr. R. seeks a denial of the petition for adoption, leaving custody in the O. family for the immediate future. However, Mr. R. would have the opportunity, assisted by petitioners, to develop a relationship with his child and the child then would choose, once he knows Mr. R., whether to live with the R. family in Paris, France. Although initially Mr. R., would "delegate" his parental rights to Mr. and Mrs. O., his delegation would be revocable. In effect, Mr. R. seeks a gradual transfer of the child to him, with the assistance of petitioners, rather than by order of this Court. . . .

. . .

TESTIMONY OF PSYCHIATRIC MEDICAL EXPERTS ON THE BEST INTEREST OF THE CHILD

Dr. Alan E. Marans, who was qualified as an expert in child psychiatry, chid psychoanalysis, and adoption, testified for the O. family in favor of the adoption. . . .

In his testimony the doctor emphasized that the child has a right to security and continuity. He said that what is most crucial to Charles at eight years of age is a permanent and ongoing relationship with petitioners. The doctor explained that as Charles gets older, the strength of his relationship with them will held him develop his potential. According to Dr. Marans, what Charles achieves now in the preadolescent latency period will support him later on in life. Dr. Marans noted that Charles is well fixed as a member of the O. family. He stressed that any arrangement that interferes with the O. family's function and relationship with Charles "is *damaging*, is *harmful* to the child."

Dr. Marans opined that denial of the adoption petition, even assuming continuing custody with Mr. and Mrs. O., would place stress and trauma on the child and that this stress could promote phobias, feelings of self doubt and concerns on the part of the child about whether he is good or bad.

Dr. Marans further stated that to deny the adoption petition and allow the child ultimately to choose whether to live with petitioners or the R.'s would have a permanent and far-reaching negative influence on Charles' personality development. Dr. Marans believes that this particular child's personality would "tighten up" as a way of containing the stress. According to Dr. Marans, this tightening up would appear in either a mental illness or a "personality adaption in the form of personality constricting sacrifice" that would prevent Charles from fulfilling his intellectual and creative potential. . . .

Dr. Marans emphasized that any dilution of the permanence and authority of petitioners as Charles' parents dilutes the trust the child can have in their reassurance that he can stay in their family. The doctor explained that "adopted children always have somewhere in their minds a fantasy that they could be given away . . . " This fantasy, however, gradually is overcome by the continuity of the child's experience in the adoptive family. However, if the adoption petition were denied, Dr. Marans stated that there is no way that Charles could be reassured that this kind of fantasy is unrealistic . . .

On the other hand, Dr. Marans stated that granting the adoption petition would have positive benefits for the child. First, it would preserve his "very foundation of security." Second, by making the child and petitioners secure, the Court will enable Charles to pursue a relationship with Mr. R. without the fear that Mr. R. might take him away from petitioners.

Dr. Marans impressed this Court with his calm and detached demeanor and particularly with his primary focus on the best interest of Charles rather than on the pain of Mr. and Mrs. O. or their son, D.O. This Court, after observing Dr. Marans closely, finds that he rendered his expert advice as a professional and not out of any bias for petitioner or Barker or because he felt himself to be an adversary of Mr. R. . . .

Mr. R.'s expert witness, Dr. Joseph Noshpitz, presented a different perspective on the best interest of the child. Dr. Nohspitz was qualified as an expert in child and adolescent psychiatry but not adoption. . . .

Dr. Noshpitz proposed a plan that was premised on the notion that there needs to be an accommodation of all of the parties in the best interest of the child. His proposal was that the Court should deny the petition to adopt, but the petitioners somehow should be make secure in their connection to the child.

Dr. Noshpitz recommended that while Mr. R. would retain his legal rights as parent, he would delegate those rights to petitioners, who would continue to make parental decisions "basically" after consulting with Mr. R. If there were a disagreement between Mr. R. and the petitioners, Dr. Noshpitz said the petitioners should prevail, but Mr. R. should have authority in some area. At the same time, Charles should be introduced gradually into the R. family so that when he reached his early teenage years . . . he can make his own decision on "affiliation . . . habitation and the program for his life."

Dr. Noshpitz said that he might force Charles to visit with the R. family, even if the child did not want to visit. Dr. Noshpitz testified that if Charles did not want to see Mr. R., he would ask Mr. and Mrs. O to invite Mr. R. and his family to dinner in the O. home in an attempt to break down Charles' fear of Mr. R.

The doctor admitted that his proposal was without support in psychiatric literature. He also said that if Charles were "forced" to be in a relationship with Mr. R., there "could be harm" to Charles. Nevertheless, Dr. Noshpitz said he was willing to put the child to that risk of harm by requiring him to visit with Mr. R. even if Charles at some point did not want to see Mr. R. . . .

The Court finds that Dr. Noshpitz was not successful in his "attempt to be a somewhat objective observer" (his words) in rendering expert advice to this Court. Throughout his testimony, Dr. Noshpitz focused primarily on balancing the rights of Mr. R. against the rights of petitioners. His position was that if he could bring the two opposing sides together, then the best interest of the child ultimately would be served. The problem with this approach is that neither side would agree to his plan, nor were they able to use his plan as a starting point to arrive at another plan.

Dr. Noshpitz' primary focus on balancing the needs and pain of the adults involved, with particular sensitivity to Mr. R., is not helpful to this Court which, in applying the law, is obliged to look at the best interest of the child. The Court fully understands that the best interest of the child will be affected by whether emotional pain is alleviated for petitioners and respondent. Nonetheless, Dr. Noshpitz' primary focus was not on what is best for the child.

. . .

Finally, Dr. Noshpitz was naive and unrealistic in his position that petitioners do not need adoption to be good parents to Charles because they already had become good parents without adoption. Dr. Noshpitz overlooked the fact that in 1986 petitioners attained a final decree of adoption for Charles who was then three years old. The ability of petitioners to contain their stress and continue good parenting after the Court of Appeals reversed the decision granting the adoption does not mean that they realistically can continue to function in the absence of an adoption decree. That would become increasingly difficult as the biological father began making demands upon them in order to develop his relationship with Charles so that he could persuade Charles to choose to spend more time with the R. family in France.

. . .

SIGNIFICANT FACTORS AFFECTING THE BEST INTEREST OF THE CHILD

There are three significant factors that this Court has considered in deciding to grant the petition to adopt. The first factor is the psychological harm to which the child would be subjected by a denial of the petition to adopt. Notwithstanding his professed willingness to allow Charles to stay with his O. "parents," this court concludes that Mr. R. intends to lead Charles away from petitioners. Contrary to Dr. Noshpitz' proposal that Mr. R. would provide Charles with cultural enrichment while not damaging Charles' connection to petitioners, Mr. R. will strive diligently to cause Charles to love him and come to Paris, France, and be a member of the R. family.

Mr. R. has ambitious plans for Charles; he wants Charles to aspire to the legislature of Zaire or even to become that nation's president. Unfortunately, to pursue these goals Charles would have to reject his existing American roots and take on a Franco-Belgian-Zairian cultural identity. Having to choose between two such different families would place Charles in a painful dilemma. This Court is not willing to subject the child to the strong probability of psychological harm or detriment described by Dr. Marans. . . .

Mr. R. is driven by his parental training and cultural background to hand down to his first born son the history and traditions of the R. family. Mr. R. wants to correct what he perceives to be a great injustice to himself and his son. However, Charles, through no fault of his own, now has a different background and identity. Mr. R., however, lacks sufficient understanding of the reality that Charles now has an identity that is different from what he would have wished for his first-born son.

The Court is greatly concerned that Mr. R.'s own powerful need to integrate Charles into the position of first-born son in the R. family, with its responsibilities to the R. family, will cause him to inflict psychological harm on his child. Mr. R. places his own needs, fueled by the requirements of his culture, ahead of the needs of this eight-year-old American child.

This Court credits the testimony of Dr. Marans . . . that the child should not be forced to choose between these two families because of the "strong probability" . . . of psychological harm that will occur from the child's carrying the burden of this kind of choice. The Court finds that not granting the adoption would be so harmful to the child that it would be contrary to his best interest. This factor alone is significant enough to overcome Mr. R.'s statutory preference for the child.

The second factor considered by the Court is what granting the petition to adopt can accomplish for this child. At eight years of age, Charles needs to know he is secure with the only mother and father he knows and that they cannot be forced to give him away. Adoption is the only way to make secure Charles' legal status in the O. family. . . .

The third factor the Court considered is that this child has resided with petitioners for more than eight years. Between 1983 and 1981, the emotional relationship of parent and child has been strongly formed between petitioners and Charles. As a practical matter, the O. family consists of Mr. and Mrs. O. and their two sons, D.O. and Charles. The boys relate to each other as brothers. Thus, granting the decree of adoption gives recognition to a family unit already in existence. While this factor is sufficient in this particular case to overcome Mr. R.'s preference for the child, the trial Court nonetheless would grant the petition to adopt without consideration of this factor.

CONCLUSION

Notwithstanding the statutory preference to which the biological father is entitled, this court concludes, based on clear and convincing evidence in the record and for the reason expressed herein, that it is in the best interest of this child to be adopted by petitioners.

NOTES AND QUESTIONS

(1) Judge Zeldon's decision to grant the O's adoption petition was affirmed on appeal. *In re Baby Boy C.*, 630 A.2d 670 (D.C. 1993), *cert. denied*, 513 U.S. 809 (1994). The appellate court upheld the trial judge's finding that H.R's parental preference had been overcome by clear and convincing evidence that adoption was in Charles' child's best interest. It also rejected H.R.'s argument that, because he was no longer seeking custody,

termination of his parental rights without a showing of unfitness violated substantive due process. Finally, the appellate court rejected H.R.'s assertion that the trial judge manifested "an improper negative cultural bias against [him]" because of his African-French background. 630 A.2d at 684. Do you agree with the appellate court's conclusions? Why or why not?

(2) In both the *Baby Boy C.* and *Baby E.A.W.* cases, the claims of the unwed biological fathers were ultimately rejected—albeit for different legal reasons—and the adults who had nurtured and physically cared for the child were ultimately permitted to adopt. Does this indicate that, despite legal formalities, courts appropriately view their core function in these cases as protecting the interests and welfare of children? Or does it demonstrate that an unwed father can never prevail over a traditional, "marital family," despite the strength of the father's legal claims? Or are both of these analyses too simplistic to capture the complexities of these difficult cases?

(3) In granting the O's adoption petition, Judge Zeldon rejected the alternative of awarding custody of Charles to Mr. and Mrs. O., while preserving some legal relationship between H.R. and the child—essentially the result endorsed in *Lemley v. Barr, above.* Are you persuaded by Judge Zeldon's reasons for rejecting this alternative? If so, do those reasons cast doubt on the wisdom of the result in *Lemley*? Would an award of custody (but not adoption) to the prospective adoptive parents have been an appropriate result in the *Baby E.A.W.* case? Why or why not?

(4) If you were the Director of the Barker Foundation (the adoption agency that placed Baby Boy C.), what changes would you make to your procedures as a result of the Baby Boy C. litigation and the court opinions that it produced?

(5) Suppose that the Barker Foundation had succeeded in contacting H.L. in May, 1983, prior to the birth of Baby Boy C, and that H.R. had made clear his unwillingness to consent to the adoption, given that it would terminate his parental rights. Assuming that Baby Boy C's mother still desired to place the child for adoption, what should the Barker Foundation have done? In particular, should Barker have arranged to place Baby Boy C. in a "neutral" foster care arrangement, as suggested by the concurring justice in *Baby E.A.W*, until a court could determine H.R.'s legal status and adjudicate his request for custody? What are the advantages and disadvantages of this proposal, from the point of view of the birth parents, the adoptive parents and the child? For a similar legislative proposal, see Scott A. Resnik, *Seeking the Wisdom of Solomon: Defining the Rights of Unwed Fathers In Newborn Adoptions*, 20 Seton Hall Legis. J. 363, 428–29 (1996).

(6) Is termination of a birth father's parental rights on grounds of pre-birth abandonment consistent with the "opportunity interest" recognized by the Supreme Court in *Lehr*? Why or why not? To what extent should the rights of a biological father depend on his treatment of the mother during pregnancy? Are there some pre-birth actions—such as rape or nonconsensual intercourse—that automatically render a biological father "unfit"? *See, e.g., Adoption of Kelsey S.*, 823 P.2d 1216, 1237 n.14 (Cal. 1992) (recognition of unwed father's right to veto adoption "affords no protection, constitutional or otherwise, to a male who impregnates a female as a result of nonconsensual intercourse"); Janet L. Dolgin, *Just a Gene: Judicial Assumptions About Parenthood*, 40 UCLA L. Rev. 637, 670–72 (1993) (suggesting that the Supreme Court has delineated three factors that determine the legal

status of an unmarried father: "the man's biological relation to the child, his social relation to the child, and his relation to the child's mother").

(7) Are there constitutionally acceptable reasons for giving unmarried, biological mothers greater authority than fathers to make decisions regarding the placement of newborn children? *See generally* Mary L. Shanley, *Unwed Fathers' Rights, Adoption and Sex Equality: Gender Neutrality and the Preservation of Patriarchy*, 95 Colum. L. Rev. 60 (1995). Does allowing an unwed father to veto a pregnant woman's decision to place her child for adoption, rather than undergo an abortion, unduly infringe on a woman's reproductive freedom? *See* Nancy S. Erickson, *The Feminist Dilemma Over Unwed Parents' Custody Rights: The Mother's Rights Must Take Priority*, 2 J.L. & Ineq. 447, 470–71 (1984).

(8) Suppose a birth mother purposely misidentifies the father, as happened in the *Baby Jessica* case, discussed by Justice Kogan in *Baby E.A.W.* Later, she notifies the "true" biological father, and joins with him to halt the adoption proceedings. Should this mother and the father she "thwarted" be able to regain custody of the child? *See In re B.G.C.*, 496 N.W.2d 239 (Iowa 1992). Should (could) a state require the mother to identify the birth father, or notify him of her pregnancy, as a precondition for placing a child for adoption? The 1994 Uniform Adoption Act protects the right of a birth mother "to remain silent in response to a request to name the father or to reveal his whereabouts," reasoning that women may have good reason—e.g. fear of abuse—for not naming a father. Uniform Adoption Act § 3-404, Comment (1994). However, the Act provides that a mother who refuses to disclose the identity of a possible father must be advised that the adoption proceedings may be delayed or subject to challenge if a possible father is not given notice. *Id.* § 3-404(e). The Act also imposes a civil penalty on a birth mother who knowingly misidentifies the father. *Id.* § 7-105(f).

(9) **Putative Father Registries**. The Supreme Court in *Lehr v. Robertson* relied heavily on the availability of a "putative father registry"—which allowed an unwed father unilaterally to ensure notice of adoption proceedings—in holding that the New York state adoption scheme adequately protected the rights of unmarried fathers. More recently, at least one commentator has proposed the creation of a nation-wide putative father registry as a means of solving "the often vexing problem of notice in unwed father cases." Scott A. Resnik, *Seeking the Wisdom of Solomon: Defining the Rights of Unwed Fathers in Newborn Adoptions*, 20 Seton Hall Legis. J. 363, 364 (1996). Under this proposal, men who are concerned that they may have impregnated a woman and are interested in taking responsibility for their potential offspring could enter their names, addresses and the names of the women with whom they may have conceived a child, on the national registry. Existence of the registry would be widely publicized, and putative fathers would be able to register by either mail or telephone. Once registered, a man would be entitled to immediate notice if a woman he has named places a child for adoption. On the other hand, a putative father who fails to appear on the national registry within 30 days after either the birth of the child or the child's placement for adoption, whichever is later, would be deemed to have abandoned the child, and thereby forfeited his parental rights. *Id.* at 424–26.

Query: Do you agree with the proposal's author that such a putative father registry ideally "balanc[es] the rights of unwed fathers against those of the other concerned parties in the adoption matrix?" Why or why not?

(10) **Problem.** In September, 1994, Veronica, an eighteen-year-old high school senior, moved in with her boyfriend, Shawn, and his family, in New Jersey. Veronica lived with

Shawn's family for approximately 15 months. In October 1995, while living with Shawn's family, Veronica learned that she was pregnant. She informed Shawn and his mother of the pregnancy. In early December, Veronica ended her relationship with Shawn, after she found heroin in his wallet. Veronica then moved to Las Vegas to live with her mother. Shortly thereafter, Veronica contacted the New Hope Child and Family Agency, to arrange for adoption of the baby she was carrying. In February 1996 Veronica was hospitalized in Las Vegas, for removal of an ovarian cyst. While in the hospital, Veronica met Teresa, an operating technician at the hospital. Veronica informed Teresa that she was pregnant and that she planned to put the baby up for adoption. Veronica and Teresa discussed the possibility of allowing Teresa to adopt the baby. Teresa then contacted the New Hope Child and Family Agency to initiate the adoption process. In March 1996 Veronica and a social worker at the adoption agency telephoned Shawn, who indicated that "he would back Veronica on whatever she decided to do." Believing that Shawn supported Veronica's decision to place the baby for adoption, the social worker went forward with the adoption process. The social worker also sent Shawn the written consent forms, but Shawn did not return the forms. On May 29, 1996, Veronica gave birth to a baby girl at Las Vegas General Hospital. Shawn did not attend the birth. After Veronica signed a written relinquishment and consent to adoption, the baby was released from the hospital into Teresa's custody. On June 25, 1996, Teresa filed a petition for the termination of Shawn's parental rights, based on abandonment. Shawn received notice of the proceedings and objected to the termination. He filed a motion for temporary custody of the baby or, in the alternative, for visitation. Genetic testing confirmed Shawn's paternity, and drug tests ordered by the court were negative. A hearing was held on August 30, 1996. At the hearing, Veronica testified that she strongly supported adoption of the baby by Teresa. However, Veronica indicated that, if the petition to terminate Shawn's parental rights were denied, Veronica would withdraw her consent to adoption, and seek custody of the baby herself, rather than acquiescing in Shawn's request for custody. How should the judge rule and why? *See Whitney v. Pinney*, 956 P.2d 785 (Nev. 1998).

§ 8.04 The Adoption Process

Adoption generally occurs through one of three channels: public, private, and independent. Each channel is associated with a different degree of government involvement. *See* R. Richard Banks, *The Color Of Desire: Fulfilling Adoptive Parents' Racial Preferences Through Discriminatory State Action*, 107 Yale L.J. 875, 897–98 (1998). Public adoption agencies are governmental units that manage the process of adoption; these agencies are often housed within state child welfare departments, which also oversee foster-care systems and child protective services. Private agencies are non-governmental entities licensed and regulated by the state. Some private agencies depend heavily on government funding. Others rely more heavily on fees paid by prospective adoptive parents. Independent or direct placement adoptions are typically facilitated by private intermediaries, such as lawyers, who oversee the interactions between adoptive and birth parents. Both private and public agencies are involved in the adoption process in a more ongoing fashion than the adoption intermediaries who arrange independent adoptions. Finally, in stepparent and second-parent adoptions, the parties often deal with each other directly, without the need for an intermediary.

[A] Agency Adoption

> L. Jean Emery, *The Case For Agency Adoption*
> 3 The Future of Children 139, 140–44 (1993)*

Meeting the Needs of the Adoption Triad

Licensed child welfare agencies are essential participants in the adoption process. Birthparents are typically young, vulnerable, stressed, and in need of skilled counseling about their situation and their options. Prospective adoptive parents usually need assessment and preparation for the task ahead because parenting a child who is adopted involves complex dynamics. The child must be included in all phases of the adoptive process to the extent appropriate for his or her age. Collection and assessment of social and medical information from all parties is imperative, as is the provision of a private setting for counseling as members of the triad move through the adoption process. All of these needs can best be met by licensed agencies.

Child welfare agencies offer a full continuum of services for birthparents, adoptive parents, and adoptees. These services are available both before and after the adoption from trained staff with proper supervision. Child welfare agencies can gather complete client information on social and medical backgrounds, access psychological testing if necessary, and provide expertise in clinical counseling for the birthparents, the child, and the adoptive parents.

Agency benefits go beyond availability of such services. Agencies usually have a number of prospective adoptive parents from among whom birthparents can make a selection. This is important so that the birthparents will not feel pressured to make an immediate decision or bound by an initial selection. With an independent agent there may not be the opportunity to rethink an early-decision about prospective adoptive parents. Additionally, agencies have learned from their experience and make every effort to moderate their guidance of the adoption process, respect the need for client self-determination, cut back on some of the "red tape" (except as it protects the child), be cautious about privacy issues, and deal flexibly with age requirements of the prospective adoptive parents. Agencies focus on issues of cultural competence, outreach, and education in the community in order to assure quick and permanent placement of children, as well as to find homes for waiting children most effectively. Finally, agencies are advocates for children and continue to be available to help both the child and the parents after the adoption papers are signed. The following paragraphs highlight some of the primary services provided by agencies to the birthparents, the adopted child, and the adoptive parents.

The Birthparents

Agency services to birthparents are comprehensive and include help and counseling for each individual. Typically these are separate services specially designed to meet the needs of young parents as they struggle with the question of whether to relinquish their child for adoption. If all services are provided by a single multi-service agency, that agency should be identified in the community as providing services to both birthparents who plan on

---

* Adopted from L. Jean Emery, CWLA Standards for Adoption Services, Revised © 1988 by the Child Welfare League of America, Washington, D.C. Reprinted by special permission.

adoption and those who do not. Services are not contingent on a decision to select adoption as the plan for the child.

Agencies inform the birthparents of the array of resources available and help them obtain such services as are needed. Birthparents are provided with a clear statement regarding their legal rights, obligations, and responsibilities, and are given support in considering what their decision will mean to them and to their child. When parents decide that adoption is the best plan, they receive assistance in transferring parental rights to the agency, in completing the legal termination of their parental rights, in separating from the child, and in coping with their emotional conflicts and grief.

Agencies provide birthparents with clear information regarding several critical issues. Because of changing laws governing privacy, which may permit new options of openness, no adoption facilitator—whether agency or independent agent—can guarantee confidentiality in any adoption, even while existing laws support confidentiality. Thus the transfer of parental rights of a child should not be accepted until the birthparents have considered all alternatives, are sure of their decision, and are emotionally prepared to transfer these rights. Agencies also can apprise birthparents of their responsibility—in accordance with their ability to pay—for expenses of their own shelter and medical care and for foster care and other expenses for the child until an authorized child welfare agency accepts the responsibility for the child through the transfer or termination of parental rights. At the same time, agencies have the responsibility to seek community and state financial aid to help defray the expenses of the birthmother.

The Child

Agencies also work hard to protect the best interests of children placed for adoption. The goal is to place children in families that will meet their needs. Toward this end, agencies offer complete adoption services to determine first whether the birthparents or extended family members are able, or can be supported, to provide the children with the care they need, or whether it is best for the children to be legally separated from them. If adoption is the best and chosen route, agencies provide assessment of the children's needs to facilitate placement at as early an age as possible. temporary care if needed, and selection of adoptive parents who have the capacity to meet their needs. As age appropriate, agencies also prepare children for placement, support them during that process, and offer postplacement and postadoption services as needed for the children, their adoptive parents and their birthparents.

The Adoptive Parent

Prospective adoptive parents also benefit from agency services as they embark on the journey to adoptive parenthood. Rather than being intrusive or prying, the agency seeks to educate prospective parents about their future role and to assist them in preparing for their new life. The tone of this relationship demonstrates sensitivity to the adoptive parents' parental yearnings and a respect for their situation. At the same time, agencies work to ensure that vital social, medical, family history, and legal information about a child is conveyed to parents in as much detail as is available (as permitted by state law and the mutual agreement between the birthparents and the adoptive parents).

It is critical that adoptive parents be apprised of the spectrum of available agency services, including preplacement, placement, postplacement, legal finalization, and postadoption services. . . . Independent agents do not have the capacity to provide continuity in the delivery of these necessary services to children and their families. . . .

The Shortcomings of Independent (Nonagency) Adoption

. . . [R]ecent changes in state laws to allow for independent (nonagency) adoption have changed adoption from a primarily social service with legal components to a process that is too often just a collection of loosely regulated adoption services. Adoption agencies are concerned that this shift means diminution of excellence in services to the triad and less attention to the rights and needs of the child.

Independent adoption appears to be a service primarily structured to help adults in search of a child. Unlike agency adoption, independent adoption agents most often view adults as the primary clients and tend to see their job as simply finding babies for couples.

The lack of objective counseling for the birthparents at a time when they are extremely vulnerable is one of the greatest concerns about independent adoptions. Although the birthmother's physical needs may be met, her psychological well-being is likely to be ignored. She may be provided with housing and medical services, but the practice of payment for these by the prospective adoptive parents (or by the independent agent whose clients they are) creates a sense of obligation on the part of the birthparents to the adoptive parents which may unfairly influence the birthparents' decision. Pressure to surrender their infant will undoubtedly build during the months of the pregnancy, so that when birth occurs and feelings of doubt surface, the birthparents may not feel free to rethink the original decision.

Independent agents who process adoptions are also less likely than trained and experienced social workers to understand the seriousness of the adoption process. Adoption is a sensitive social issue and a lifelong experience, not just a legal procedure. Dual representation by one independent agent who represents both the adoptive parents and the birthparents may give the appearance of coercion and certainly creates the possibility of a conflict of interest. In addition, nonagency adoption appears to be primarily a service for middle-class or higher-income adults, shutting out parents in a lower income bracket who might also make good adoptive parents. Fees are usually higher than those of agencies, while services are fewer.

Most often an independent agent considers his or her service completed upon placement of a child, without considering the possible need for postplacement or postlegal services. Because nonagency adoption lacks an accountability structure, there is little information about cases in which it becomes evident that the placed child has special needs. In the case of a disruption or dissolution of the adoptive placement because of physical or mental factors, the independent agent often refers the case to a public agency, which must then absorb the cost of casework and services to the child.

Finally, in independent adoptions, the child is frequently placed in an adoptive home before a home study has been completed and before the birthparents have signed consents because of the desire for immediate placement following the birth of the child. Although immediate placement for the child may be important because of permanence and bonding issues, this move may not allow enough postbirth time for the birthparents to consider their final decision and to assure themselves that the prospective adoptive home is a suitable placement for their particular child.

NOTES AND QUESTIONS

(1) All states permit adoptive placements by state agencies and by private agencies licensed and regulated by the state. Many private agencies are denominational or sectarian. Some have special purposes, such as finding adoptive homes for children with special needs. Joan Heifetz Hollinger, *Introduction to Adoption Law and Practice*, in Adoption Law and Practice 1-66 (Joan Heifeiz Hollinger, ed., Matthew Bender 1998). In most states, a child relinquished to an agency will remain in the custody of the agency until the rights of both the birth mother and father are terminated. In some states, the agency may place the child with prospective adoptors after the mother's relinquishment, but prior to the termination of the father's rights. *Id.* at 1–67 to 1–68. Today, most agency placements involve older children who have been taken from their parents because of abuse or neglect, minority children, children who meet the federal or state definition of having "special needs" and foreign born children. *Id..* at 1-67. Unlike in prior decades, the majority of healthy infants adopted today are adopted through independent or private placements, rather than through agencies. *Id.* at 1-68 & n.31 (estimating that two-thirds of adoptions of newborns are handled independently).

(2) The 1994 Uniform Adoption Act addresses some of the "shortcomings" of "independent adoption" raised by Professor Emery. For example, the Act generally requires that all prospective adoptive parents obtain a favorable preplacement evaluation before being permitted to accept custody of a minor for purposes of adoption, whether they are adopting independently or through an agency. Uniform Adoption Act §§ 2-201; 7-101(a)(4) (1994). The Uniform Act also requires that birth parents be offered "counseling services and information about adoption" prior to signing a consent or relinquishment. *Id.* at § 2-405(d)(4).

(3) The Uniform Adoption Act also provides for the disclosure to prospective adoptive parents of extensive medical, psychological and other background information about the minor and the minor's birth parents. Uniform Adoption Act § 2-106 (1994). While these disclosure requirements clearly apply to both public and private adoption agencies, and to birth parents who place children directly, it is unclear whether they apply to attorneys and other intermediaries who facilitate independent adoptions. For additional discussion of an agency's obligation to disclose health-related information about children placed for adoption, see § 8.06, *below*.

[B] Independent Adoption and the Lawyer's Role

Mark T. McDermott, *The Case For Independent Adoption*
3 The Future of Children 146, 146–49 (1993)

Legality of Independent Adoption

For the most part, adoption is a matter controlled by state law. Independent (nonagency) adoption is specifically authorized by law in all of the states except six. Even in those six states, parties are able to achieve what is, in spirit. an independent adoption: the adoptive parents and birthparents identify each other without intervention by an agency and then arrange for the parental rights to be relinquished through an agency so that the adoption becomes a directed agency adoption.

The right of birthparents to select the adoptive parents is a concept that has been firmly embedded in the legislative social philosophy of our country for a long time. As a matter of fact, independent adoption is not a new phenomenon, as some agency proponents would have us believe. Independent adoption is a system that predates the 1930s, when agency adoption first became widely accepted.

Prevalence of Independent Adoption

In this country, more newborns are placed each year through independent adoption than through private agency adoption. The reason is that more birthparents choose to pursue independent adoption rather than to work with agencies. This point is important to an analysis of the relative merits of agency adoption and independent adoption because it is not the adoptive parents, but the birthparents who have the practical ability to make independent adoption exist. If all birthparents were to choose agency adoption, there would be no independent adoption. Agency adoption proponents may argue that birthparents are being lured away from agency adoption to independent adoption because, in the latter, the adoptive parents can reimburse many or all birthparent expenses. This is not true. In most states, the categories of expenses that can be reimbursed are strictly limited in independent adoptions, and typically, the reimbursable expenses are broader in an agency adoption than in an independent adoption. . . .

While it is difficult to determine why so many birthparents now choose independent adoptions, they do report some reasons consistently. These reasons include (1) a perception by birthparents that agencies are profit oriented and bureaucratic in their treatment of birthparents, (2) a desire by birthparents to play an active role in the selection of the adoptive parents, and (3) a desire on the part of birthparents for the child to go directly into the physical custody of the adoptive parents rather than into temporary foster care.

The Role of Independent Adoption in the Overall Adoption System

From the adoptive parents' perspective, the advantages of independent adoption extend beyond the ability to play an active role in the selection of specific birthparents. Other benefits include the possibility of avoiding the long waiting periods that are typical with agency adoptions and the ability to adopt even though the adoptive parents may not meet the often arbitrary standards imposed by agencies. While some of the agency standards relate to concerns about the ability of the prospective adoptive parents to be adequate parents, other agency concerns have no demonstrable relationship to such ability. For example, because of a supply-and-demand imbalance, some agencies employ qualification standards which include age, religious preference, and place of residence. In fact, some agencies will not work with prospective adoptive parents who reside outside an arbitrarily designated geographical area.

The openness of the adoption, characteristic of independent adoption, has been considered by many to offer psychological benefit to the birthparents, the adoptive parents, and the adopted children. In most of the states that permit independent adoption, adoptive parents must have one or more face-to-face meetings at which they may decide to share information that may or may not be identifying (for example, the parents, both birth and adoptive, may choose not to reveal their last names or addresses). . . . [T]he nature and extent of future contact and sharing of information about the child is decided upon and may vary with different parents. . . .

Intermediaries

The laws of some states allow attorneys and other individuals who are not licensed as child-placing agencies to match adoptive parents with birthparents. In most states, however, the adoptive and birthparents must make initial contact with one another without the intervention of an individual, such as an attorney, who is receiving professional fees for rendering services in connection with the adoption proceeding. In these states, the adoptive and birthparents must make initial contact with one another by such means as word of mouth and newspaper advertising. In those states that prohibit paid intermediaries such as attorneys, it is still legal for attorneys to receive payment for advising prospective adoptive parents on advertising techniques and other methods by which adoptive parents can make their own initial direct contact with birthparents.

Risks

There are certain emotional and financial risks associated with independent adoption which may not exist in agency adoptions. When birthparents initially agree to place a child for adoption but later change their minds, the adoptive parents undoubtedly suffer emotionally. Even if the child is not yet born when the birthparents change their minds, the adoptive parents have formed emotional ties with the birthmother and the expected child. If the child has already come into the physical custody of the adoptive parents, the emotional trauma will be even greater.

In addition, the adoptive parents may have already paid attorney fees and medical expenses when the birthparents change their minds. In this event, the adoptive parents will most likely not be reimbursed by the birthparents. Under the agency adoption process, the child is placed in temporary foster care until the birthparents' parental rights have been irrevocably terminated. Should the birthparents change their minds before the rights have been terminated, the adoptive parents will ordinarily be spared some or all of the agency fees.

Separate Legal Counsel

Because most states require face-to-face contact between the adoptive parents and the birthparents, the parties normally arrange a meeting shortly after they make initial contact with one another. It is after this initial meeting that the attorneys representing the parties become actively involved. Frequently, adoptive parents will consult with an attorney when they commence their search for birthparents. That attorney will either advise the adoptive parents on how to search for birthparents or actually match the adoptive parents with specific birthparents when state law permits. In most states, the attorney for the adoptive parents is ethically prohibited from simultaneously representing the birthparents. Because of this prohibition, there are some situations in which the two parties will assert that the one attorney involved is representing only the adoptive parents and that the birthparents simply have no legal representation. This approach is ill-advised because it presents dangers to all of the parties. It is a far better practice to insist that the birthparents retain separate counsel to represent their interests.

Available Services

The services that are provided to the parties in an agency adoption are also provided in an independent adoption. For example, medical and social histories are obtained not only by the adoptive parents themselves but also by the attorney representing the birthparents. Forms that have been developed by Compact officials and by adoptive parents support groups are normally used to collect the data. The histories are then preserved by the adoptive parents and their attorney. Psychological counseling is available to the birth and adoptive parents and is generally recommended by the attorneys handling independent adoptions, who refer the parties to qualified counselors experienced in adoption issues.

In addition, the parties can receive services that are generally not available in agency adoptions. For example in independent adoptions, it is common for the adoptive parents to be present at the hospital and even in the birthing room at the time of birth. In addition, the adoptive parents typically can have access to the child between the time of birth and hospital discharge so that the adoptive parents can begin the process of bonding. It is also common for the child to be discharged from the hospital directly into the physical care of the adopting parents. . . .

Home Study and Court Process

Following the consent to adoption by the birthparents, the adoptive parents are required to follow court procedures which will lead to a final decree of adoption. Whether accomplished before or after the placement, the courts will require that the adoptive parents have undergone a home study. State law dictates whether an individual social worker, a private licensed child-placing agency, or a public social services agency may perform the home study. The process is designed to evaluate the adoptive parents to assure that there is nothing in their homes or backgrounds which would be contrary to the best interests of the child.

It is important to note that there is a philosophical distinction between the purpose of a home study in an independent adoption and in an agency adoption. In an independent adoption, the choice of the adopting parents is made by the birthparents. As such, the home study process serves to corroborate the decision made by the birthparents. In an agency adoption, the agency is making the choice of a specific set of adoptive parents for a particular child. The home study process assists the agency in making this choice. When an agency is doing a home study in connection with an independent adoption, the agency is serving only to support the birthparents' right to select adoptive parents. Consequently, the agency should look only for circumstances that would be contrary to the child's best interests rather than look for the fine distinctions often made in an agency placement when an agency is choosing one set of adoptive parents over another set of adoptive parents.

IN RE PETRIE
Arizona Supreme Court
742 P.2d 796 (1987)

HOLOHAN, JUSTICE.

This matter comes to us on the objections of the respondent attorney to the findings, conclusions and recommendation of the Disciplinary Commission.

The Local Administrative Committee of the Arizona State Bar after hearing evidence had recommended that respondent be censured for representing clients with adverse interests in violation of Disciplinary Rule 5-105(A) and (B), and for failing to carry out a contract of employment in violation of Disciplinary Rule 7-101(A)(2). . . .

This matter requires that we answer two questions:

1. Did respondent violate conflict of interest rules by representing multiple clients in an adoption proceeding?

2. If so, is a thirty-day suspension the appropriate sanction?

I

Our duty in State Bar disciplinary proceedings is to determine the facts and law independently while giving serious consideration to the findings and recommendations of the Disciplinary Commission and the Local Administrative Committee. The evidence of unprofessional conduct must be clear and convincing to justify disciplinary action. Evidence is clear and convincing when its truth is "highly probable." *Neville*, 147 Ariz. at 111, 708 P.2d at 1302 (citations omitted).

The complainants, Gregory and Barbara Pietz (Pietzes) consulted with respondent on July 21, 1981 to express their interest in adopting an infant child. Respondent told the Pietzes that he did not know of any infants available at that time. The Pietzes and respondent agreed that if the Pietzes located a baby for adoption, respondent would represent them in the adoption. The Pietzes paid $30 for this consultation.

The Committee found that shortly before January 26, 1983, the Pietzes received information from a long-time friend, Carolyn Iverson, about a child that would be available for adoption. The Pietzes asked Iverson to make an appointment for respondent to meet with the natural mother, and to inform the respondent specifically that the mother was being referred by the Pietzes. Iverson called respondent, advised him that she had found a baby for the Pietzes, and made an appointment for respondent to meet with the natural mother. The Pietzes had moved to Sierra Vista sometime after their meeting with respondent, so Iverson gave respondent the Pietzes' current address and telephone number in Sierra Vista. She also told him that the Pietzes had become certified by the State of Arizona as acceptable to adopt children.

Respondent testified that he received a call from a woman who advised him of the baby and that "she knew of someone who was interested in an adoption," namely the Pietzes. Respondent claims he did not recognize the Pietzes' name from their visit one and a half years earlier.

The evidence indicates that respondent met with the natural mother and her sister, and he advised them that he had a set of adoptive parents in mind. On January 26, 1983, he wrote to the Pietzes, telling them that he had recently interviewed a woman who intended to place a child for adoption and that the Pietzes' names were given when the interview was arranged. Respondent inquired in the letter whether the Pietzes were interested in the adoption. Respondent received a written response on February 3, 1983, in which the Pietzes stated that they were interested in adopting the child, that they were certified by the State to adopt children, and that they were very hopeful concerning the present situation. The Pietzes' letter disclosed knowledge of facts about the natural mother that respondent had not conveyed to them in his original correspondence. Respondent interpreted the Pietzes' letter as "equivocal" because the Pietzes had questions about the adoption and the fees.

Shortly thereafter, respondent received a phone call from another couple, the Buckmasters, who expressed an interest in adopting a second child. In response to respondent's inquiry on February 18, 1983, the natural mother's sister stated that the mother had no obligation to the Pietzes. At respondent's recommendation, the mother agreed to place the baby with the Buckmasters. The Committee found that respondent recommended placement with the Buckmasters because they were more cooperative than the Pietzes and they were locally situated. In addition, respondent was not "excited" about making two appearances in Cochise County, which may have been necessary if the Pietzes were to adopt the child.

When the Pietzes learned from Iverson that the child was going to another couple, Mr. Pietz called respondent, and respondent advised Mr. Pietz for the first time that he had recommended to the natural mother that the child be placed with someone else. Mr. Pietz told respondent that the Pietzes had referred the child to the respondent and consequently they wanted the child placed with them. Respondent refused to do so. Mr. Pietz then initiated this complaint with the State Bar.

II. REPRESENTATION OF CLIENTS WITH ADVERSE INTERESTS

The complaint charged that the respondent violated Disciplinary Rule 5-105(A) and (B), which provides:

> DR 5-105. Refusing to Accept or Continue Employment if the Interests of Another Client May Impair the Independent Professional Judgment of the Lawyer
>
> (A) A lawyer shall decline proffered employment if the exercise of his independent professional judgment in behalf of a client will be or is likely to be adversely affected by the acceptance of the proffered employment, except to the extent permitted under DR 5-105(C).
>
> (B) A lawyer shall not continue multiple employment if the exercise of his independent professional judgment in behalf of a client will be or is likely to be adversely affected, except to the extent permitted under DR 5-105(C).

A. Potential Conflicts of Interest

It is common for the parties to an independent adoption to retain an attorney to represent their individual interests. The adoption proceeding itself is unusual because generally the parties to the adoption the natural parents and the adoptive parents are not in a true adversary relationship. Usually, both sides in the proceeding have complementary interests and no real negotiating or posturing is necessary; in most cases the natural parents want to find a good home for the baby and need to have the birthing expenses paid, and the adoptive parents want to provide a home for the baby and are willing to pay the expenses. Legal counsel is necessary only to facilitate the exchange and ensure that the legal requirements are met.

Despite the spirit of cooperation often present in an adoption, conflict of interest situations are likely to arise for an attorney involved in the proceedings. First, the interests of potential adoptive parents of the same child are always adverse to one another. In a situation involving independent sets of adoptive parents and only one available child, obviously one set of parents will be disappointed. An attorney cannot simultaneously represent both sets of adoptive parents without compromising his representation of one of them.

Second, and perhaps less apparent, the interests of the adoptive parents may be adverse to the interests of the natural parents. The decision to give the baby up for adoption is often a difficult one to make. The natural parents' attorney has a duty to provide them with counsel about such matters as paternity issues, economic matters, and the legal effect of signing the consent to adopt. Under our statute, the natural parents' consent to the adoption is not valid unless it is given at least 72 hours after the birth of the child. A.R.S. § 8-107(B). The statute protects the right of the natural parents to withhold a decision on whether to keep the baby until after the baby is born. The attorney must counsel the natural parents on the adoption decision right up until the natural parents consent to the adoption. Clearly, the adoptive parents want the natural parents to consent to the adoption rather than to keep the baby. It is obvious, therefore, that the natural parents' interests may be adverse to the interests of the adoptive parents, and the same attorney cannot represent both parties. Notwithstanding the foregoing discussion, in some instances an attorney may be able to represent multiple parties in an adoption proceeding. Disciplinary Rule 5-105(C) provides for an exception to the dictates of DR 5-105(A) and (B). It provides that a lawyer may represent multiple clients "if it is obvious that he can adequately represent the interests of each and if each consents to the representation after full disclosure of the possible effect of such representation on the exercise of his independent professional judgment on behalf of each." DR 5-105(C). Under this exception, then, it may be possible for an attorney to represent multiple parties to an adoption but only after full disclosure and upon consent of the parties. This exception has no application to the current case, however, because there is no evidence that respondent complied with its provisions.

B. Existence of Attorney-Client Relationships

The Disciplinary Commission found that respondent created an attorney-client relationship first with the Pietzes, and later with the Buckmasters. Respondent contends that he only represented the natural mother. If Petrie simultaneously had an attorney-client relationship with more than one of the parties involved in the adoption—the Pietzes, the Buckmasters, or the natural mother—Petrie has violated DR 5-105(A) or (B).

An attorney-client relationship does not require the payment of a fee but may be implied from the parties' conduct. The relationship is proved by showing that the party sought and received advice and assistance from the attorney in matters pertinent to the legal profession. The appropriate test is a subjective one, where "the court looks to the nature of the work performed and to the circumstances under which the confidences were divulged." *Alexander v. Superior Court*, 141 Ariz. 157, 162, 685 P.2d 1309, 1314 (1984), citing *Developments of the Law—Conflicts of Interest in the Legal Profession*, 94 Harv. L. Rev. 1244, 1321–22 (1981). An important factor in evaluating the relationship is whether the client thought an attorney-client relationship existed. *Alexander*, 141 Ariz. at 162, 685 P.2d at 1314. The relationship is ongoing and gives rise to a continuing duty to the client unless and until the client clearly understands, or reasonably should understand that the relationship is no longer depended on. *In re Weiner*, 120 Ariz. 349, 352, 586 P.2d 194, 197 (1978).

1. The Pietzes

The record contains clear and convincing evidence that respondent became the Pietzes' attorney for handling the adoption. At their initial meeting, respondent agreed to represent the Pietzes if they found a baby to adopt. Clearly, the Pietzes sought out respondent's legal assistance at that time. In referring the pregnant woman through Iverson to respondent for independent placement, the Pietzes had every reason to rely on respondent's original promise that he would represent them in the adoption. Furthermore, the referral of the natural mother by the Pietzes indicates that they understood that the attorney-client relationship with respondent was ongoing. The relationship was not terminated until they wrote to respondent in June 1983, and expressly stated they were discharging him as their attorney.

Even accepting respondent's argument that an attorney-client relationship was subject to the condition that the Pietzes locate a baby, correspondence between the respondent and the Pietzes immediately after respondent's first meeting with the natural mother belies respondent's contention that he did not know that the natural mother had been referred to him by the Pietzes. Respondent's letter to the Pietzes indicated that the person who had made the appointment for the natural mother indicated that the Pietzes might be interested in the adoption. Furthermore, respondent stated in the letter, "I would not expect to have any problem in placing the child but I thought we should write to determine your interest in the placement." The Pietzes unequivocally stated in their response that they were "very hopeful" to adopt the baby. In addition, in their letter the Pietzes alluded to circumstances regarding the natural mother which were not communicated to them by respondent in his original letter. If nothing else, respondent surely should have realized from their letter that the Pietzes were involved in the referral of the baby's mother.

Respondent also argues that no attorney-client relationship developed because the Pietzes were "equivocal" in their response. He points to the Pietzes' questions about when the baby was due, what their expenses in the adoption would be, and where the father of the unborn child fit in. We find that these were natural questions by any prospective adoptive parents and they do not negate the existing attorney-client relationship. Instead, they reinforce the existence of a relationship because they are evidence that the Pietzes continued to seek legal advice from respondent. Furthermore, the fact that the Pietzes wrote back to respondent within eight days to indicate their desire to adopt the child is inconsistent with respondent's characterization of the Pietzes' response as "equivocal."

We agree with the Commission's finding that there was an attorney-client relationship between respondent and the Pietzes.

2. The Buckmasters

The Commission found that an attorney-client relationship later developed between respondent and the Buckmasters. We agree. Mr. Buckmaster testified that he believed that he and his wife were respondent's clients. They met with respondent regarding the adoption and understood that if the natural mother consented, respondent would perform the adoption for them and they would pay the necessary fees. The fact that respondent never actually performed the adoption of the baby does not nullify the existence of an attorney-client relationship.

3. The Natural Mother

Respondent agrees that he and the natural mother had an attorney-client relationship. Although the mother was not liable to respondent for legal fees, clearly the natural mother came to respondent seeking legal advice and she received that advice from respondent.

C. Violations of DR 5-105

We find that respondent violated DR 5-105 by representing the Buckmasters in the same matter in which he was already counsel for the Pietzes. Respondent had a duty to advocate for the Pietzes in the adoption proceeding. The natural mother's indication that she was not committed to the Pietzes did not lessen the respondent's duty of loyalty to them. The respondent breached that duty when he accepted proffered employment from the Buckmasters and recommended them as adoptive parents to the natural mother. It is difficult to imagine an action by respondent that would have been more adverse to the Pietzes' interest in the adoption. By accepting employment from the Buckmasters while already representing the Pietzes in the same adoption proceeding without full disclosure and consent, respondent violated DR 5-105(A); by continuing in the simultaneous representation and by ultimately recommending the Buckmasters over the Pietzes, respondent violated DR 5-105(B).

We find that respondent also violated DR 5-105 by representing both the natural mother and the adoptive parents in an adoption proceeding. Respondent claimed that he always represented the natural mother in adoption proceedings. From his testimony, it appears that his usual custom was to maintain a file of potential adoptive parents from which the natural mother who is his client may select the couple best suited to adopt the baby. We do not expressly prohibit this practice. However, the attorney must take special care to avoid violating the ethical rules regarding representation of multiple clients. In this regard, two ethics opinions of the Arizona State Bar Committee on Rules of Professional Conduct are helpful.

In Op. No. 94, February 12, 1962, the attorney represented adoptive parents in an independent adoption. The attorney advised the natural mother that she could obtain her own counsel; however, no lawyer purporting to represent her contacted the attorney in question. The attorney subsequently obtained the natural mother's written consent to adopt, after advising both her and the alleged father of its legal effect. The attorney then assisted in placing the child in the physical control of the adoptive parents, filed the petition to adopt, and accepted a $200 fee for his services. The committee opined that in considering how far the attorney can ethically participate in bringing about the ultimate adoption decree, "[n]aturally, an attorney cannot represent both the natural parent and the adopting parents, and cannot conduct a baby brokerage business under the guise of practicing law." The committee found no unethical activity, however, because the lawyer made clear who he represented and advised the nonrepresented party to seek independent counsel.

In Op. No. 72-2, January 26, 1972, the attorney who requested the opinion gave a detailed description of his adoption procedures. Before placing babies, who were usually referred to him by an obstetrician, the attorney reviewed the prospective parents' qualifications. He also explained his fee structure to either the adoptive parents or the natural parents, whichever party he represented. In each instance, the attorney attempted to make sure that the party that he did not represent would obtain counsel. The ethics committee stated that "[h]is practice of seeking to have both parties to the adoption proceeding represented by independent counsel is clearly in compliance with the Code of Professional Responsibility."

By attempting to represent the natural mother, the Pietzes, and the Buckmasters in the same adoption proceeding, respondent violated DR 5-105(A) and (B). In independent adoptions an attorney cannot represent multiple parties absent disclosure and consent. *See* DR 5-105(C); *Arden v. State Bar of California*, 52 Cal. 2d 310, 318–19, 341 P.2d 6, 10–11 (1959).

REPRESENTING A CLIENT ZEALOUSLY

The complaint filed against respondent also charged that respondent violated DR 7-101(A)(2), which provides: (A) A lawyer shall not intentionally: (2) Fail to carry out a contract of employment entered into with a client for professional services, but he may withdraw as permitted under DR 2-110, DR 5-102 and DR 5-105.

Respondent agreed to represent the Pietzes in an adoption proceeding if the Pietzes located a baby available for adoption. A year and a half later, the Pietzes referred an expectant mother to the respondent. Although respondent initially contacted the Pietzes with regard to adopting the child, he ultimately recommended that the natural mother consent to adoption of the child by another couple that respondent also represented. The respondent conceded that the Pietzes' credentials as adoptive parents were impressive. It appears that he chose the Buckmasters over the Pietzes because the Buckmasters resided locally, and there was a possibility he would have to travel to Cochise County to represent the Pietzes, a possibility he was not "excited" about.

Clearly, by recommending the Buckmasters over the Pietzes, respondent failed to carry out the contract of employment we have found existed between respondent and the Pietzes. We recognize that respondent may not have subjectively believed an attorney-client relationship existed between him and the Pietzes until he was confronted by Mr. Pietz after Pietz learned that someone else was to be adopting the baby. Thereafter, respondent knew, beyond any doubt, that the Pietzes had considered him as their lawyer, and they had expected him to handle the adoption.

After receiving the information from Mr. Pietz, respondent did nothing. The committee and the commission concluded that the respondent had intentionally violated DR 7-101(A)(2). We agree with their conclusion. The respondent had placed himself in the position of conflict, but he had an obligation to carry out the contract of employment with the Pietzes. Having become fully aware of the situation, the least he should have done is secure counsel for the Pietzes and withdrawn from representing any other parties in the matter.

DISCIPLINARY SANCTION

The purpose of attorney discipline is not to punish the offending lawyer, but to protect the public, the profession and the system of justice by deterring similar activity by this attorney and others in the future. We will give great weight to the recommendations of both the Local Committee and the Disciplinary Commission regarding what sanction is appropriate for violation of the disciplinary rules, but we must make the final decision. Recently, in determining the appropriate sanction in attorney disciplinary proceedings, we also have looked for guidance to the Standards for Imposing Lawyer Sanctions, approved in February 1986 by the House of Delegates of the American Bar Association. *See* In re Hegstrom, No. SB-86-0038-D (filed May 7, 1987). We find these standards especially helpful in cases such as this one, where the recommendations of the Committee and the Commission are in conflict.

The ABA standards recommend suspension when an attorney knows of a conflict of interest, does not fully disclose to a client the possible effect of that conflict, and causes injury or potential injury to a client. Standard 4.32. The standards recommend only reprimand (censure) when the attorney is negligent in determining whether a conflict of interest exists, and causes injury or potential injury to a client. Standard 4.33. From the findings of facts made by the Committee and from our review of the record, it is unclear whether respondent was only negligent in determining a conflict of interest existed or whether he actually knew of the conflict. Respondent testified that his only client was the natural mother. We have determined that both the Pietzes and the Buckmasters were his clients as well. If respondent did not think either the Pietzes or the Buckmasters were his clients, he would not have "known" a conflict of interest existed. However, at a minimum, respondent was negligent in failing to recognize that the potential adoptive parents were his clients and that a conflict existed. Accordingly, we agree with the Local Committee that the appropriate sanction due respondent is censure. We decline to adopt the recommendation of the Disciplinary Commission that respondent be suspended for 30 days because neither the findings of the Local Committee nor our independent review of the record unequivocally reveals that respondent knew the conflict existed. Considering also that respondent has an otherwise flawless record in the almost 30 years he has practiced in Arizona, we find the recommendation of the Commission unduly harsh. *See In re McGlothlen*, 99 Wash. 2d 515, 526, 663 P.2d 1330, 1336 (1983) (court will treat conflict of interest misconduct, standing alone, with relative leniency).

CONCLUSION

The findings of fact and conclusions of law of the Local Committee are approved. Respondent is censured and assessed costs of $2,225.10.

NOTES AND QUESTIONS

(1) If the Buckmasters had not entered the picture, and the Pietzes had proceeded with the adoption, could respondent have represented both the Pietzes and the biological mother, assuming that each consented to the representation? Why or why not? *See generally* Pamela K. Strom Amlung, *Conflicts of Interest in Independent Adoptions: Pitfalls For the Unwary*, 59 U. Cin. L. Rev. 169 (1990).

(2) A number of states expressly prohibit an attorney from representing both a birth parent and prospective adoptive parents in connection with an independent, or private placement adoption. *See, e.g.,* N.Y. Soc. Serv. Law § 374(6) (1997); Md. Code Ann., Fam. Law § 5-323(e) (1997). Similarly, the A.B.A. Standing Committee on Ethics and Professional Responsibility has found that representation of both sets of parents in an adoption violates the conflict of interest provisions of the A.B.A. Model Rules of Professional Conduct. *See* A.B.A. Standing Comm. on Ethics & Professional Responsibility, Informal Op. 87-1523, Feb. 14, 1987 *reprinted in* 13 Fam. L. Rep. 1231 (1987). A few states, by contrast, permit dual representation in some circumstances. *See, e.g.,* Cal. Fam. Code § 8800(c) (1997); *In re J.H.G.* 869 P.2d 640, 647 (Kan. 1994) (attorney may represent both birth and adoptive parents so long as no conflict develops between them).

Opponents of dual representation emphasize the underlying potential for conflicts of interest among the parties to an adoption, as well as the difficulty of preserving client confidences and of obtaining truly informed consent to dual representation. *See, e.g.,* Katherine G. Thomason & Douglas H. Reiniger, *Private Placement Adoptions in New York;*

Separate Representation Required, in Adoption Law and Practice (Joan Heifetz Hollinger, ed., Matthew Bender 1998). Supporters of dual representation counter that the conflict of interest between adoptive and birth parents is often more hypothetical than real, that separate representation adds significantly to the cost of the adoption, and that prohibiting dual representation "stigmatizes as adversarial what is ideally a cooperative process." David Keene Leavitt, Althea Lee Jordan & Jed Somit, *Independent Adoptions in California; Dual Representation Allowed*, in Adoption Law and Practice (Joan Heifetz Hollinger, ed., Matthew Bender 1998). Supporters also claim that, where dual representation is prohibited, the birth parents often elect no representation at all, and instead get their adoption information secondhand through the adopting parents. Sharon Fast Gufstafson, *Regulating Adoption Intermediaries: Ensuring That the Solutions Are No Worse Than the Problem*, 3 Geo. J. Legal Ethics 837, 862 (1990).

Query: Which arguments do you find more persuasive and why? If separate representation is required, should prospective adoptive parents be permitted to pay the birth parents' legal fees? Why or why not?

(3) States also vary in the restrictions they impose on the activities of adoption intermediaries, including lawyers. In some states, only parents and licensed agencies may place children for adoption. For example, Nev. Rev. Stat. Ann. § 127.310 (1997) makes it a crime for any unlicensed person or entity (other than a biological parent) to place, arrange the placement of, or assist in placing any child for adoption. The statute defines "arrange the placement of a child" to mean "make preparations for or bring about any agreement or understanding concerning the adoption of a child." Nev. Rev. Stat. Ann. § 127.220 (1997).

Query: Would an attorney violate this statute by sending resumes, letters or other information describing prospective adoptive parents to a birth mother who has indicated a desire to pursue adoption? *See* Opinion of the Nevada Attorney General, 91-4 (April 16, 1991) (answering yes). What is the purpose of such restrictions on adoption intermediaries?

(4) Attorneys and other adoption intermediaries must also be cognizant of rules that restrict or prohibit advertising for adoption. While attorneys are now generally permitted to advertise their services, many states have additional restrictions on advertising for adoption. *See, e.g.*, Ala. Code § 26-10A-36 (1997) (unlawful for any unlicensed person, agency or organization to advertise children for adoption or hold out inducements for parents to part with their children); Cal. Fam. Code § 8609(a) (1997) (restricting advertising to licensed agencies); Uniform Adoption Act § 7-101 (a) (1994) (only an agency, legal guardian or birth or adoptive parent may advertise for adoption).

(5) While all states prohibit the buying and selling of children, states vary considerably in the extent and types of payments that prospective adoptive parents may make to or for the benefit of the birth parent(s) in connection with an adoption. While some states define permissible payments broadly, to include such things as the birth mother's living expenses during pregnancy, other states restrict permissible payments to medical and legal expenses. *Compare, e.g., In re Adoption: Sherman M. Brod*, 522 So. 2d 973, 978 (Fla. Dist. Ct. App. 1988) (approving total payments of $14,856.92 for birth mother's medical expenses, rent, utilities, groceries and other living expenses) *with In re Adoption of Stephen*, 645 N.Y.S.2d 1012, 1015 (N.Y. Fam. Ct. 1996) (disapproving and ordering attorney to reimburse adoptive parents for payments made to cover birth mother's living expenses) *and In re Baby Girl D.*, 517 A.2d 925, 928–29 (Pa. 1986) (disapproving payments for birth mother's housing

expenses, counseling services and childbirth classes). *See also Kingsley v. State*, 744 S.W.2d 191, 193 (Tex. App. 1987) (upholding conviction of attorney for "purchase of child" based on attorney's payment of birth mother's rent, groceries, cigarettes and cosmetics in exchange for mother's promise to surrender the child at birth for placement with one of the attorney's clients).

Many states have adopted statutes that define permissible categories of payments, and require a detailed accounting of all payments made in connection with the adoption prior to the entry of an adoption decree. *See, e.g.,* New York Soc. Serv. Law § 374(6) (1997); Fla. Stat. § 63.132 (1997). In the absence of explicit statutory direction, some courts have attempted to distinguish between payments that provide a direct benefit the fetus/child, and are thereby proper, and payments that primarily benefit the birth mother, which are not. *See In re Baby Girl D.*, 517 A.2d 925, 927–28 (Pa. 1986). Other courts, however, have noted that this distinction is often difficult to apply. *See* Gary R. Cassavechia, *In re Adoption of Baby D (Stafford County Probate Court)*, reprinted in 12 Quinnipiac. Prob. L.J. 49 (1997).

The 1994 Uniform Adoption Act takes an expansive view of permissible adoption-related payments, allowing a adoptive parent to pay for, among other things, travel expenses incurred in connection with the birth, counseling services, and the birth mother's living expenses for a reasonable time before birth, and up to six weeks after birth. Payments may not be made contingent on completion of the adoption. Uniform Adoption Act § 7-103(a)(b) (1994). By contrast, the Act prohibits payments given for the placement or relinquishment of a minor, or for the consent of a parent to adoption. *Id.* § 7-102. *Query:* What, precisely, is the difference between the types of payments permitted by the Act, and those that are prohibited?

(6) **Legalizing an Adoption Market?** A few scholars have argued that we should permit the market to play a greater, and more explicit, role in allocating children for adoption. In 1978, Professors Elisabeth Landes and Richard Posner (now a federal appellate court judge) proposed, "as a tentative and reversible step toward a free baby market," that adoption agencies be permitted to use part of the fees they received from adoptive parents to pay pregnant women to forego abortions and to place their babies for adoption through the agency instead. Elisabeth A. Landes & Richard A. Posner, *The Economics of the Baby Shortage*, 7 J. Legal Stud. 323 (1978). Their article provoked strident criticism in both the popular and the scholarly press. Nine years later, Posner reiterated the proposal in slightly modified form; this time it served as the centerpiece of a major law review symposium on "Adoption and Market Theory." Richard A. Posner, *The Regulation of the Market in Adoptions*, 67 B.U. L. Rev. 59 (1987). In responding to his critics, Posner argued that his proposal to allow prospective adoptive parents to pay birth mothers to surrender their infants represented only a modest break with current practice.

> . . . [W]holly apart from the black market in babies for adoption, the market is used, though in a stunted form, to allocate babies for adoption. Adoption agencies charge fees, often stiff ones, to adoptive parents, and part of the agencies' fee income goes to pay the medical expenses and other maintenance expenses of the natural mother; thus the adoptive parents pay the natural mother, albeit indirectly and at a regulated price, to give up her child. In "independent adoptions," which are arranged through a lawyer or obstetrician, the element of sale is even more transparent, and indeed the system of independent adoption is often referred to as the "grey market."

Id. at 60. Posner also pointed to surrogate motherhood, as an "important example of legal baby selling." *Id.* at 71–72. *Query:* Do you agree with Posner's characterization of the current adoption regime? Why or why not? *Cf.* Danielle Saba Donner, *The Emerging Adoption Market: Child Welfare Agencies, Private Middlemen and "Consumer" Remedies*, 35 J. Fam. L. 473 (1996-97) (arguing that market principles have significantly shaped recent adoption reforms, including the shift to independent placements, the growth of tort remedies for "wrongful adoption" and the 1994 Uniform Adoption Act).

In defending the idea of a regulated adoption market, in which participants would be screened for fitness, Posner argued that many of the criticisms directed at "baby-selling"—including the high prices, profiteering middlemen and deceptive practices—are characteristic of illegal markets, and would not apply if the market were legalized. "Seemingly exorbitant profits, low quality, poor information, involvement of criminal elements—these widely asserted characteristics of the black market in babies are no more indicative of the behavior of a lawful market than the tactics of the bootleggers and rum-runners during Prohibition were indicative of the behavior of the liquor industry after Prohibition was repealed." Posner, 67 B.U. L. Rev. at 70. Posner also addressed what he called "symbolic" objections to his market proposal:

> Even if partial deregulation of the baby market might make practical utilitarian sense . . . some will resist on symbolic grounds. If we acknowledge that babies can be sold, the argument goes, we open the door to all sorts of monstrous institutions—including slavery. . . . Allowing the prospective mother of an illegitimate child to receive money in exchange for giving up the child for adoption, when described in shorthand as "baby selling," seems to many people uncomfortably close to the type of real baby selling that is found in slave societies—that was found in the slave societies of the South before the Civil War. No doubt it requires more thought than most people are willing to give to the problem to hold these quite different concepts separate in their minds. But if they are not held separate we may find ourselves condemned to perpetuate the painful spectacle of mass abortion and illegitimacy in a society in which to a significant extent, children are not available for adoption by persons unwilling to violate the law.

Do you find Judge Posner's arguments convincing? Why or why not?

For critical responses to Posner's proposal, see Jane Maslow Cohen, *Posnerism, Pluralism, Pessimism*, 67 B.U. L. Rev. 105 (1987); Tamar Frankel & Francis H. Miller, *The Inapplicability of Market Theory to Adoptions*, 67 B.U. L. Rev. 99 (1987); J. Robert Prichard, *A Market For Babies*, 34 U. Toronto L.J. 341 (1984). For a more favorable assessment, see Ronald A. Cass, *Coping with Life, Law and Markets: A Comment on Posner and the Law-and-Economics Debate*, 67 B.U. L. Rev. 73 (1987). In his more recent work, Posner advocates removing the "price ceiling" on independent adoptions, in light of the decreasing supply of children available for adoption. Richard A. Posner, Sex and Reason 409–16 (1992).

[C] Stepparent and Second-Parent Adoption

ADOPTIONS OF B.L.V.B. AND E.L.V.B.
Supreme Court of Vermont
628 A.2d 1271 (1993)

JOHNSON, JUSTICE.

The issue we decide today is whether Vermont law requires the termination of a natural mother's parental rights if her children are adopted by a person to whom she is not married. We hold that when the family unit is comprised of the natural mother and her partner, and the adoption is in the best interests of the children, terminating the natural mother's rights is unreasonable and unnecessary. . . .

Appellants are two women, Jane and Deborah, who have lived together in a committed, monogamous relationship since 1986. Together, they made the decision to have and raise children, and together, they consulted various sources to determine the best method for them to achieve their goal of starting a family. On November 2, 1988, Jane gave birth to a son, B.L.V.B., after being impregnated with the sperm of an anonymous donor. On August 27, 1992, after being impregnated with sperm from the same donor, she gave birth to a second son, E.L.V.B. Deborah assisted the midwife at both births, and she has been equally responsible for raising and parenting the children since their births.

Appellants sought legal recognition of their existing status as coparents, and asked the probate court to allow Deborah to legally adopt the children, while leaving Jane's parental rights intact. The adoption petitions were uncontested. The Department of Social and Rehabilitation Services conducted a home study, determined the adoptions were in the best interests of the children, and recommended that they be allowed. A clinical and school psychologist who had evaluated the family testified that it was essential for the children to be assured of a continuing relationship with Deborah, and recommended that the adoptions be allowed for the psychological and emotional protection of the children.

Despite the lack of opposition, the probate court denied the adoptions, declining to reach whether the adoptions were in the best interests of the children because the proposed adoptive mother "does not satisfy the statutory prerequisite to adoption." The court relied on 15 V.S.A. §§ 431 and 448. Section 431, covering who may adopt, provides:

A person or husband and wife together, of age and sound mind, may adopt any other person as his or their heir with or without change of name of the person adopted. A married man or a married woman shall not adopt a person or be adopted without the consent of the other spouse. The petition for adoption and the final adoption decree shall be executed by the other spouse as provided in this chapter.

Section 448, which describes how the rights and obligations of both parents and children are altered by a final adoption decree, provides in pertinent part:

The natural parents of a minor shall be deprived, by the adoption, of all legal right to control of such minor, and such minor shall be freed from all obligations of obedience and maintenance to them. . . . Notwithstanding the foregoing provisions of this section, when the adoption is made by a spouse of a natural parent, obligations of obedience to, and rights of inheritance by and through the natural parent who has intermarried with the adopting parent shall not be affected.

The court read the last sentence of § 448, the "step-parent exception," and § 431, as clearly requiring that "if a couple adopts together, they must be married. If one partner is the birth parent, and the other partner desires to adopt, then they must be married: otherwise, the birth parent will lose rights in the child under § 448."

Appellants make numerous attacks on the probate court's interpretation of the statutes, but in the main, they contend that the statutory language does not prohibit the adoptions, that enforcing the termination of the birth mother's rights under § 448 would reach an absurd result in these circumstances, and that such a result is inconsistent with the best interests of the children and the public policy of this state. We agree.

In interpreting Vermont's adoption statutes, we are mindful that the state's primary concern is to promote the welfare of children, and that application of the statutes should implement that purpose. *See In re S.B.L.*, 553 A.2d 1078, 1083–84 (1988) (in applying custody statute to fact pattern breaking substantial new ground, intent of legislature, gleaned from whole of statute, must be considered). In doing so, we must avoid results that are irrational, unreasonable or absurd. *Id.* at 1083. We must look "not only at the letter of a statute but also its reason and spirit." *Id.*

Nothing in Vermont law, other than a restrictive interpretation of § 448, would exclude Deborah from adopting another person. Under 15 V.S.A. § 431, which broadly grants the right to adopt to "a person or husband and wife together," an unmarried person is permitted to adopt, and the sole limitation— that the adoption of a married person requires the consent of the adoptee's spouse—does not apply here. Even reading § 431 in conjunction with § 448, we cannot conclude, as the probate court did, that the legislature meant to limit the categories of persons who were entitled to adopt.

Section 448 was passed by the legislature in 1945, then revised and adopted in substantially its present form in 1947. It is highly unlikely that the legislature contemplated the possibility of adoptions by same-sex partners, and the scant legislative history does not indicate that such adoptions were considered. Because adoptions by same-sex partners were apparently not contemplated when § 448 was drafted, it cannot be said that they are either specifically prohibited or specifically allowed by the statute. To determine whether such adoptions are consistent with the purpose of the statute, it is necessary to discern what § 448 was designed to accomplish.

When the statute is read as a whole, we see that its general purpose is to clarify and protect the legal rights of the adopted person at the time the adoption is complete, not to proscribe adoptions by certain combinations of individuals. Who may adopt is already covered by § 431. Section 448 is concerned with defining the lines of inheritance for adoptees, preserving their right to inherit from their natural parents and granting the right to inherit from the "person or persons" by whom they are adopted. The statute also terminates the natural parents' rights upon adoption, but this provision anticipates that the adoption of children will remove them from the home of the biological parents, where the biological parents elect or are compelled to terminate their legal obligations to the child. This legislative intent is evidenced by the step-parent exception, which saves the natural parent's rights in a step-parent adoption. The legislature recognized that it would be against common sense to terminate the biological parent's rights when that parent will continue to raise and be responsible for the child, albeit in a family unit with a partner who is biologically unrelated to the child.

Although the precise circumstances of these adoptions may not have been contemplated during the initial drafting of the statute, the general intent and spirit of § 448 is entirely consistent with them. The intent of the legislature was to protect the security of family units by defining the legal rights and responsibilities of children who find themselves in circumstances that do not include two biological parents. Despite the narrow wording of the step-parent exception, we cannot conclude that the legislature ever meant to terminate the parental rights of a biological parent who intended to continue raising a child with the help of a partner. Such a narrow construction would produce the unreasonable and irrational result of defeating adoptions that are otherwise indisputably in the best interests of children.

Although no state supreme court has confronted the issue, a number of lower court decisions support our conclusion. Interpreting a similar "step-parent exception" in a factually similar adoption case, the Superior Court for the District of Columbia stated that cutting off the biological mother's rights "would be a particularly counterproductive and even ludicrous result" once the adoption by the mother's partner was found to be in the child's best interest. *In re L.S. & V.L.*, slip op. at 5, 1991 WL 219598 (D.C.Super.Ct.Fam.Div. Aug. 30, 1991). Instead, following the legislative intent, the court likened same-sex partners who adopted to step-parents, holding them exempt from the provision cutting off a biological parent's rights. *Id.* at 8.

A New York court also upheld the adoption of a child by the biological mother's same-sex partner under a section of its adoption statute identical in effect to that of Vermont's § 448. That court stated that:

[i]f this provision were strictly enforced it would require termination of the parental rights of [the biological mother] upon granting the adoption to [the mother's partner]. This would be an absurd outcome which would nullify the advantage sought by the proposed adoption: the creation of a legal family unit identical to the actual family setup.

In re Evan, 583 N.Y.S.2d 997, 1000 (Sur.Ct.1992). The court further stated that where the adoptive and biological parents are in fact coparents, "New York law does not require a destructive choice between the two parents. Allowing continuation of the rights of both the natural and adoptive parent where compelled by the best interests of the child, is the only rational result and well within the equitable power of this court." *Id.*

Moreover, focusing on the best interests of the adopted child has led courts, in other contexts, to allow a mother's partner to adopt without terminating the mother's rights. For example, in *In re Adoption of a Child by A.R.*, 378 A.2d 87 (Union Cty.Ct.Prob.Div.1977), a New Jersey court allowed an unmarried biological father to adopt as though he were the stepfather of the child because the biological mother, to whom the father had been engaged, was incompetent and thus unable to marry. The court stated that a section of the adoption statute similar to Vermont's § 448 "must be read against the peculiar factual setting of [the] case, and with an application of common sense" in order to further the public policy of "the protection of the children and the adoptive and natural parents." 378 A.2d at 89.

. . .

When social mores change, governing statutes must be interpreted to allow for those changes in a manner that does not frustrate the purposes behind their enactment. To deny the children of same-sex partners, as a class, the security of a legally recognized relationship with their second parent serves no legitimate state interest. As the New York court stated in *Evan*:

[T]his is not a matter which arises in a vacuum. Social fragmentation and the myriad configurations of modern families have presented us with new problems and complexities that can not be solved by idealizing the past. Today a child who receives proper nutrition, adequate schooling and supportive sustaining shelter is among the fortunate, whatever the source. A child who also receives the love and nurture of even a single parent can be counted among the blessed. Here this Court finds a child who has all of the above benefits and two adults dedicated to his welfare, secure in their loving partnership, and determined to raise him to the very best of their considerable abilities. There is no reason in law, logic or social philosophy to obstruct such a favorable situation.

583 N.Y.S.2d at 1002. By allowing same-sex adoptions to come within the step-parent exception of § 448, we are furthering the purposes of the statute as was originally intended by allowing the children of such unions the benefits and security of a legal relationship with their de facto second parents.

As the case law from other jurisdictions illustrates, our paramount concern should be with the effect of our laws on the reality of children's lives. It is not the courts that have engendered the diverse composition of today's families. It is the advancement of reproductive technologies and society's recognition of alternative lifestyles that have produced families in which a biological, and therefore a legal, connection is no longer the sole organizing principle. But it is the courts that are required to define, declare and protect the rights of children raised in these families, usually upon their dissolution. At that point, courts are left to vindicate the public interest in the children's financial support and emotional well-being by developing theories of parenthood, so that "legal strangers" who are de facto parents may be awarded custody or visitation or reached for support. Case law and commentary on the subject detail the years of litigation spent in settling these difficult issues while the children remain in limbo, sometimes denied the affection of a "parent" who has been with them from birth. Polikoff, *This Child Does Have Two Mothers: Redefining Parenthood to Meet the Needs of Children in Lesbian-Mother and Other Nontraditional Families*, 78 Geo.L.J. 459, 508–22 (1990); Comment, *Second Parent Adoption for Lesbian-Parented Families: Legal Recognition of the Other Mother*, 19 U.C.Davis L.Rev. 729, 741–45 (1986). It is surely in the best interests of children, and the state, to facilitate adoptions in these circumstances so that legal rights and responsibilities may be determined now and any problems that arise later may be resolved within the recognized framework of domestic relations laws.

We are not called upon to approve or disapprove of the relationship between the appellants. Whether we do or not, the fact remains that Deborah has acted as a parent of B.L.V.B. and E.L.V.B. from the moment they were born. To deny legal protection of their relationship, as a matter of law, is inconsistent with the children's best interests and therefore with the public policy of this state, as expressed in our statutes affecting children.

Because the probate court rejected these adoptions on legal grounds, it did not make findings on whether the adoptions were, in fact, in the best interests of the children. Ordinarily, this would require a remand to the probate court; however, in light of the fact that the adoptions were unopposed, that all of the evidence stands uncontroverted, that the adoption was investigated and recommended by the state, through SRS, and that there is not a scintilla of evidence in the record to suggest that the adoptions are not in the best interests of these children, no reason exists to remand for another hearing.

NOTES AND QUESTIONS

(1) In interpreting the Vermont adoption statute, the court in *B.L.V.B.* analogized same-sex second parent adoption to adoption by a stepparent, in order to grant the adoption without terminating the parental rights of the biological parent with whom the child will continue to reside. Are these two situations sufficiently similar to justify the court's analogy? Why or why not?

(2) In 1996, the Vermont legislature amended the state's adoption statutes to codify the holding in *B.L.V.B. See* 15A Vt. Stat. Ann. § 1-102(b) (1997) (if family unit consists of parent and parent's partner, and adoption is in child's best interest, partner of parent may adopt child without terminating parent's rights); 15A Vt. Stat. Ann. § 1-112 (1997) (family court shall have jurisdiction to hear and dispose of issues pertaining to parental rights and responsibilities and parent-child contact in accordance with statutory divorce proceedings when two unmarried persons who have adopted minor child terminate their domestic relationship).

(3) Subsequent to the Vermont Supreme Court's decision in *B.L.V.B.*, appellate courts in a number of other jurisdictions have approved "second parent" adoptions by unmarried same-sex and opposite sex couples. *See, e.g., In re M.M.D. & B.H.M.*, 662 A.2d 837 (D.C. 1995); *In re Jacob*, 660 N.E.2d 397 (N.Y. 1995); *In re petition of K.M. and D.M.*, 653 N.E.2d 888 (Ill. App. Ct. 1995); *Adoption of Tammy*, 619 N.E.2d 315 (Mass. 1993);. *But see In re Angel Lace M.*, 516 N.W.2d 678 (Wis. 1994) (rejecting adoption petition filed by lesbian co-parent, based on express language of the Wisconsin adoption statute, which required termination of the parental rights of the natural mother "unless the birth parent is the spouse of the adoptive parent.").

While most commentators have approved of these decisions, a few scholars have expressed reservations. *Compare, e.g.,* Theresa Glennon, *Binding the Family Ties: A Child Advocacy Perspective on Second-Parent Adoptions,*7 Temple Pol. & Civ. Rts. L. Rev. 255 (1998) (arguing that allowing same-sex second parent adoption protects child's emotional development, need for long term continuity in the parent-child relationship, and access to ongoing benefits, such as health insurance) *and* Julia Frost Davies, Note, *Two Moms and A Baby: Protecting the Nontraditional Family Through Second Parent Adoption*, 29 New Eng. L. Rev. 1055 (1995) *with* Lynn D. Wardle, *The Potential Impact of Homosexual Parenting on Children*, 1997 U. Ill. L. Rev. 833, 880 (arguing that most cases authorizing same-sex couples to use stepparent adoption procedures are based on conclusory justifications about the best interest of the child and are inconsistent with the statutory language and purpose).

(4) Experts estimate that adoptions by stepparents account for well over half of all the adoptions that take place each year. According to the Commentary to the 1994 Uniform Adoption Act:

> This is not surprising given that: (1) remarriages account for nearly 46% of all marriages entered into in 1990, compared to 31% in 1970; (2) more than 1 million children are involved in a divorce each year; (3) in several million families, at least one spouse has had an out-of-wedlock child before getting married; and (4) nearly

7 million children live in stepfamilies, and these children are approximately 15% of all children under 18 living in two parent families. What is surprising is that, although stepparent adoptions represent more than 50% of all adoptions, they occur in only a small percentage of the "blended" households heading by a custodial parent and a stepparent. This small percentage may be due, at least in part, to dissatisfaction with the ways in which existing adoption laws are applied to adoptions by stepparents.

Uniform Adoption Act (1994), Article 4, Comment. The Uniform Adoption Act attempts to address this potential dissatisfaction by modifying the traditional rule of "complete severance" of ties between adoptive and biological families in the case of stepparent adoptions. In particular, the Act allows for post-adoption visitation by non-custodial former parents, siblings, or grandparents after adoption by a stepparent, thereby allowing an adopted child to maintain contact with a non-custodial parent and other blood relatives with whom the child has had a prior relationship. *See* Uniform Adoption Act § 4-112 (1994). For additional discussion of post-adoption visitation by members of a child's biological family, see § 8.06[B], *below*.

Query: To what extent should the law encourage adoption by stepparents? Is such encouragement consistent with the trend in favor of joint legal custody and other forms of shared parenting by divorced or never-married biological parents?

[D] Procedural Requirements

In *Lassiter v. Department of Social Services*, 452 U.S. 18 (1981), the Supreme Court, in a 5-4 decision, held that the Federal Constitution did not require states to provide counsel for indigent parents in all termination of parental rights proceedings. Instead the Court held that fundamental fairness could be maintained if the decision whether to appoint counsel were made on a case-by-case basis by the trial court, subject to appellate review. 452 U.S. at 32. By contrast, in *Santosky v Kramer*, 435 U.S. 745 (1982), the Court held that the Due Process Clause of the Fourteenth Amendment mandated that proceedings to terminate parental rights be governed by a "clear and convincing" standard of proof. Applying the due process balancing factors first enunciated in *Mathews v. Eldridge*, 424 U.S. 319, 335 (1976), the *Santosky* Court emphasized both the importance of biological parent's interest and the permanency of the threatened loss:

> *Lassiter* declared it "plain beyond the need for multiple citation" that a natural parent's "desire for and right to 'the companionship, care, custody, and management of his or her children' " is an interest far more precious than any property right. 452 U.S., at 27, *quoting Stanley v. Illinois*, 405 U.S., at 651. When the State initiates a parental rights termination proceeding, it seeks not merely to infringe that fundamental liberty interest, but to end it. "If the State prevails, it will have worked a unique kind of deprivation. . . . A parent's interest in the accuracy and justice of the decision to terminate his or her parental status is, therefore, a commanding one." 452 U.S., at 27.

Santosky, 455 U.S. at 758-59. The *Santosky* Court also found that a "clear and convincing" standard of proof was consistent with the two state interests at stake in termination of parental rights proceedings—a *parens patriae* interest in preserving and promoting the welfare of children and a fiscal and administrative interest in reducing the cost and burden of such proceedings. *Id.* at 766. The Court considered whether the even more rigorous "beyond a reasonable doubt" standard, commonly applied in criminal cases, was required in termination proceedings, but concluded that states might justifiably conclude that such a standard would erect an unreasonable barrier to efforts to free permanently neglected children for adoption:

> A majority of the States have concluded that a "clear and convincing evidence" standard of proof strikes a fair balance between the rights of the natural parents and the State's legitimate concerns. We hold that such a standard adequately conveys to the factfinder the level of subjective certainty about his factual conclusions necessary to satisfy due process. We further hold that determination of the precise burden equal to or greater than that standard is a matter of state law properly left to state legislatures and state courts. (455 U.S. at 769-70).

More recently, in *M.L.B v. S.L.J.*, 519 U.S. 102 (1996), the Court held that, where a state generally provides for appeals from trial court decrees terminating parental rights, due process and equal protection principles preclude a state from conditioning a parent's right to appeal on the parent's ability to pay court costs. At issue in *M.L.B.* was a Mississippi court rule that required appellants in all civil cases, including termination of parental rights proceedings, to order and pay for relevant portions of the trial transcript if they intended to urge on appeal "that a finding or conclusion is unsupported by the evidence or is contrary to the evidence." 519 U.S. at 107. Appellant M.L.B., a biological mother whose parental rights were terminated at trial in connection with a stepparent adoption, was unable to pay transcript preparation fees estimated at $2,300 and sought leave to appeal *in forma pauperis*. The Mississippi Supreme Court denied her application, ruling that the right to proceed *in forma pauperis* in civil cases exists only at the trial level. Relying on its prior decisions in *Lassiter* and *Santosky*, the Supreme Court held that the Fourteenth Amendment required Mississippi "to accord M. L. B. access to an appeal—available but for her inability to advance required costs—before she is forever branded unfit for affiliation with her children." *Id.* at 112. Justice Ginsburg, writing for the majority, rebuffed concerns that the Court's holding could be extended to all kinds of civil cases, as to which the Court had previously ruled that indigent persons have no constitutional right to proceed *in forma pauperis*:

> Respondents and the dissenters urge that we will open floodgates if we do not rigidly restrict [the principle of equal access to appellate review] to cases typed "criminal." But we have repeatedly noticed what sets parental status termination decrees apart from mine run civil actions, even from other domestic relations matters such as divorce, paternity, and child custody. To recapitulate, termination decrees "work a unique kind of deprivation." *Lassiter*, 452 U.S. at 27. In contrast to matters modifiable at the parties' will or based on changed circumstances, termination adjudications involve the awesome authority of the State "to destroy permanently all legal recognition of the parental relationship." [*Rivera v. Minnich*, 483 U.S. 574, 580 (1987)]. Our *Lassiter* and *Santosky* decisions, recognizing that parental termination decrees are among the most severe forms of state action, have not served as precedent in other areas. (519 U.S. at 116.).

NOTES AND QUESTIONS

(1) Is the Supreme Court's ruling in *M.L.B.* that states must provide indigent parents with "equal access" to appellate review consistent with its holding in *Lassiter* that states are not constitutionally required to provide counsel for all indigent parents in termination

of parental rights proceedings? Which is likely to be more important to an indigent parent facing termination of his or her parental rights—counsel at the trial level, or waiver of appellate fees?

(2) Although *Lassiter* held that states are not constitutionally required to provide counsel for parents in termination proceedings, most states do provide for such appointed counsel by statute. Similarly, most model statutes provide that indigent parents are entitled to appointed counsel in contested adoption and termination of parental rights actions, as well as in abuse and neglect proceedings. *See, e.g.,* Uniform Adoption Act § 3-201 (1994); IJA-ABA Standards for Juvenile Justice, Counsel for Private Parties 2.3 (b) (1980); Uniform Juvenile Court Act § 26(a), 9A U.L.A. 35 (1979). *Query* Should states provide separate appointed counsel for children in termination of parental rights proceedings? Why or why not? Are the due process arguments in favor of appointed counsel for children stronger or weaker than for biological parents? *See, e.g., In re Guardianship of S.A.W.*, 856 P.2d 286, (Okla. 1993) (holding that appointment of counsel is constitutionally required for a child in all termination of parental rights proceedings, whether initiated by the state or by private parties); Uniform Adoption Act § 3-201(b) (1994) (requiring court to appoint a guardian ad litem for a minor in contested adoption or termination of parental rights proceedings). Is appointment of separate counsel for the child likely to further tip the balance in favor of the state and against a biological parent whose rights are subject to termination? Why or why not?

§ 8.05 Selecting an Adoptive Family: The Relevance of Race, Ethnicity and Religion

[A] The Role of Race in Adoption

Twila L. Perry, *The Transracial Adoption Controversy:*
An Analysis of Discourse and Subordination
21 N.Y.U. Rev. L. & Soc. Change 33, 34, 41–44, 53, 65–66 (1993-94)

The debate over transracial adoption is alive and well. After two decades, this topic continues to generate spirited, heated exchanges between those who view transracial placements as positive for both the children and society as a whole and those who view them as injurious to Black children and Black communities.

Transracial Adoption

The number of transracial adoptions in this country grew substantially during the 1960s and through the early 1970s. Reasons for this included an increase in the number of children coming into the foster care system and the social consciousness movements of the 1960s. In addition, the popularity of psychological literature on maternal deprivation resulted in increased recognition of the deficiencies of the foster care system. Perhaps the most important factor in the rise of transracial adoptions was a new shortage of healthy white infants. This shortage resulted largely from the increased availability of abortions and contraception, and a growing tendency for white unmarried mothers to keep their babies rather than place them for adoption. It has been estimated that more than a million couples seek to adopt the 30,000 white infants available each year. Because of the limited availability of white infants, some white families began to adopt foreign children; others began adopting Black American children.

In a well-known 1972 position paper, the National Association of Black Social Workers (NABSW) took a strong position against transracial adoption. This group argued that Black children belong physically, psychologically, and culturally in Black families and that transracial adoption constitutes a form of cultural genocide. Many writers have stated that, as a result of the position taken by the NABSW, transracial adoptions declined precipitously, falling from 2 percent of all adoptions in 1975 to 1 percent of all adoptions in 1987. The NABSW has not wavered from its position.

There is little agreement about the significance and impact of transracial adoption. Some contend that such adoptions are a necessary means of providing homes to Black children and that Black children raised in white families can grow up to be happy, healthy members of society. Others have argued that Black children will inevitably suffer if white parents raise them. These opponents of transracial adoption contend that there is no shortage of Black homes—only a shortage of resources and commitment by whites to recruit and support adoptive Black families and to encourage the placement of Black children in their own extended families.

Colorblind Individualism vs. Color and Community Consciousness

In my analysis of the transracial adoption controversy, I have uncovered two competing perspectives, liberal colorblind individualism and color and community consciousness. Liberal colorblind individualism has three dominant characteristics. The first is a belief that complete eradication of racism in this country can be achieved. The second is the affirmation of colorblindness as an ideal—that race should not be an important factor in evaluating individuals and that a colorblind society should be our ultimate goal. Finally, the perspective of liberal colorblind individualism emphasizes the individual as the primary unit for the analysis of rights and interests. In many ways, this perspective is grounded in traditional notions of American liberalism.

The perspective I call color and community consciousness is far more pessimistic about the eradication of racism. Instead, it views racism as a pervasive and permanent part of the American landscape. This perspective recognizes that race has a profound influence in the lives of individuals—in terms of both the choices they make and the choices they believe they have. In addition, the color and community consciousness perspective values a multicultural society, which requires the continued existence of diverse cultures within our society. Finally, while colorblind individualism views the individual as the significant unit for the analysis of rights and interests, color and community consciousness also emphasizes the rights and interests of the group with which the individual is identified. This ideological difference stems from a strong belief in the interrelationship between the subordination of a group as a whole and the oppression of the individuals within that group.

In thinking about transracial adoption, I have come to associate the perspective of colorblind individualism with white scholars and the perspective of color and community consciousness with minority scholars. However, perspectives on racial issues do not divide clearly along racial lines. Accordingly, I do not suggest that all white scholars agree in whole or in part with colorblind individualism or that all minority scholars agree with the perspective of color and community consciousness. My description of these as perspectives rather than the views of particular racial or ethnic groups is quite intentional.

Nor do I believe that the perspectives of colorblind individualism and color and community consciousness can always be discussed in absolutes. Perspectives are generally complex and tend to exist along a spectrum rather than at opposite poles. Articles often strongly reflect one or the other of these perspectives, but some may combine aspects of both in differing degrees. In some articles, the colorblind individualist perspective may be subtle or implicit. These qualifications notwithstanding, it is my sense that the two paradigms represent fundamentally different approaches to the analysis of transracial adoption and the broader issues of race implicated in the discussion of that subject.

. . .

II. Influence of the Perspectives on the Transracial Adoption Controversy

The differing perspectives of colorblind individualism and color and community consciousness shape the transracial adoption controversy in several ways. First, colorblind individualism's focus on the individual accords substantial significance to the right of the individual to make decisions regarding family structure without state interference. In contrast, the color and community consciousness perspective focuses on the struggle of Blacks to make choices to create a meaningful family in light of the oppressive circumstances under which many Black families live. Second, colorblind individualism minimizes the significance of racial differences between parent and child. In contrast, from the perspective of color and community consciousness such racial differences must be recognized and addressed. Third, for colorblind individualists, the interests of the Black community have little relevance to the discussion of transracial adoption; only the immediate best interests of the individual child are important. The perspective of color and community consciousness also focuses on the needs of the individual child but does so within the context of the Black community's legitimate stake in transracial adoption. The color and community consciousness perspective sees the individual Black child as inextricably linked to the Black community and inevitably identified with that community. Finally, to colorblind individualists, cultural genocide is a nonissue because of the small number of children who are transracially adopted. From the perspective of color and community consciousness, cultural genocide—the potential loss of Black culture—is an issue of great practical and symbolic importance.

. . .

The Stake of the Black Community in Transracial Adoption

Writers from the perspective of colorblind individualism and writers from the perspective of color and community consciousness differ significantly in evaluating the stake of the Black community in determining transracial adoption policies. Scholars reflecting the colorblind individualist perspective generally tend to discount the interests of the community from which the child comes and feel that arguments supporting the consideration of the community's views promote separatism. Thus, since she believes that a preference for same-race placements ultimately deprives Black children of the opportunity for permanent homes, Elizabeth Bartholet argues that it "does serious injury to black children in the interest of promoting an inappropriate separatist agenda." Another writer argues: "Our system does not and must not give legal impetus to desires, from any quarter, to preserve any variety of racial separatism." Even Professor Howard, who recognizes that the Black child awaiting adoption has an interest in a cultural identity, takes the position that the child's best interests should be decided without reference to those of the Black community. Indeed, she argues that the interest in recruiting more Black adoptive families is "not congruent with currently waiting children and therefore, is not an interest appropriately considered under a child-centered policy."

The color and community consciousness perspective also focuses on the best interests of the individual child. However, it defines the child's interests more broadly. This broad definition is consistent with an analysis in which the oppression of the group and of the individual are closely connected and the best interests of the child are seen as inextricably linked with the interests of the Black community. This view is strongly reflected in the NABSW's position paper, the congressional testimony of the NABSW president, and legal scholarship that examines transracial adoption from a color and community consciousness perspective.

It could be argued that the color and community consciousness perspective is fundamentally communitarian. To the extent that such a perspective posits that the identity of an individual is derived from the community, it focuses on achieving the common good rather than individual rights. The communitarian approach does not accept liberalism's focus on individual autonomy but instead views the individual as strongly connected with the community.

. . .

INTERETHNIC ADOPTION PROVISIONS OF THE SMALL BUSINESS JOB PROTECTION ACT OF 1996
42 U.S.C. § 1996b (1998)

§ 1996b. Adoption and foster care rights

(1) Prohibited conduct. A person or government that is involved in adoption or foster care placements may not—

    (A) deny to any individual the opportunity to become an adoptive or a foster parent, on the basis of the race, color, or national origin of the individual, or of the child, involved; or

    (B) delay or deny the placement of a child for adoption or into foster care, on the basis of the race, color, or national origin of the adoptive or foster parent, or the child, involved.

(2) Enforcement. Noncompliance with paragraph (1) is deemed a violation of title VI of the Civil Rights Act of 1964 [42 U.S.C.A. §§ 2000d et seq.].

(3) No effect on the Indian Child Welfare Act of 1978. This subsection shall not be construed to affect the application of the Indian Child Welfare Act of 1978 [25 U.S.C.A. §§ 1901 et seq.].

DEWEES v. STEVENSON
United States District Court
779 F. Supp. 25 (E.D. Pa.1991)

WALDMAN, J.

Plaintiffs seek to enjoin defendants from refusing to consider plaintiffs as adoptive parents for their foster child, Dante Kirby, and from taking him from the foster home on November 23, 1991 to participate in a National Adoption Center event to attempt to find prospective adoptive parents. Plaintiffs allege that defendants have refused to consider plaintiffs' request to adopt Dante because of their race and in so doing have violated the equal protection and due process guarantees of the Fourteenth Amendment. Plaintiffs also seek a declaration that defendants' alleged refusal to consider plaintiffs as adoptive parents violates these Constitutional guarantees.

. . .

I. FINDINGS

Plaintiffs are a white couple who have been married for 27 years and who reside in Royersford, Pennsylvania in an almost exclusively white area. Mrs. DeWees is a high school graduate and housewife. Mr. DeWees is the maintenance manager for a trucking company. Plaintiffs have three natural children, ages 26, 23 and 21 years, and five grandchildren for whom they have cared.

Defendants are the Chester County, Pennsylvania Children and Youth Services Agency (CCCYS), its director and its adoption supervisor, Kay Thalheimer.

In January of 1988, plaintiffs applied to CCCYS to be foster parents. During the ensuing review and evaluation process, Mrs. DeWees stated that she did not want to take any black foster children because "[she] did not want people to think that [she] or her daughter were sleeping with a black man." According to Mrs. DeWees, she gave this reason because she was reluctant to give her real reason which was her concern that she would not know how to take care of a black child.

Plaintiffs requested for placement children under three years of age because they felt they "couldn't deal with children after three years old."

CCCYS approved plaintiffs as foster parents and entered into a foster parents agreement with them on May 9, 1988. The agreement provides, inter alia, that CCCYS shall have all responsibility for planning for any foster child. Pursuant to the agreement, CCCYS variously placed seven foster children with plaintiffs. They were from two to twenty months in age. Three were black and two were bi-racial. Plaintiffs never received any complaints from CCCYS about their care of any foster child. Plaintiffs' attitude about black children changed and they came "to accept them as any other child."

On November 10, 1989, CCCYS placed Dante Kirby, then two months old, with plaintiffs. Since August 20, 1991, Dante is plaintiffs' only remaining foster child. Plaintiffs understood that Dante's placement with them was not permanent. On three different occasions Dante was to be returned to his parents, but it did not work out as planned.

Dante's mother is white and his father is black. On November 12, 1991, with their consent, their parental rights were terminated by the Chester County Court of Common Pleas.

Plaintiffs have cared well for Dante. They provide him with his own room and interact frequently with him. He plays and interacts well with plaintiffs' grandchildren. They have supplemented the amounts provided by CCCYS for clothing and toys, and have provided Dante with medical care for his respiratory problems. There clearly is a bond of mutual affection between plaintiffs and Dante.

On June 13, 1991, after being advised by Dante's caseworker that Dante's mother and father intended to relinquish their parental rights, plaintiffs wrote to defendant Thalheimer to express an interest in adopting Dante.

On July 18, 1991, defendant Thalheimer met with and interviewed plaintiffs for an hour and a half, and then referred them to Dr. Joseph Crumbley for further evaluation of their request to adopt Dante. On August 22, 1991, Dr. Crumbley interviewed plaintiffs at his office in Philadelphia for approximately two hours. Dante was present. In assessing plaintiffs' ability to raise and socialize a bi-racial child, Dr. Crumbley utilized the Workers' Assessment Guide for families Adopting Cross-Racially and Cross-Culturally of the U.S. Department of Health and Human Services.

Ms. Thalheimer is a social worker with 20 years of experience in the field of adoption. She has experience with trans-racial adoptions. She has placed bi-racial children with white, black and bi-racial adoptive parents respectively. She is white.

Dr. Crumbley is a family therapist and consultant with a Ph.D. in social work. He is a consultant to three adoption agencies and among his areas of specialization are child abuse, foster care and adoption. He has experience with trans-racial adoptions. He is black.

Dr. Crumbley forwarded an evaluation and recommendation to Ms. Thalheimer on September 11, 1991. He concluded that although Dante was emotionally attached to plaintiffs, they would not be appropriate adoptive parents. That a foster child has bonded with his foster parents is viewed by professionals as strong evidence that he would bond with new adoptive parents as well.

Dr. Crumbley was concerned about plaintiffs' responses that race had "no impact" on developing a child's identity and self-esteem, that addressing racial issues was not important in raising a minority child; and that they would not prepare Dante to deal with racial discrimination but rather would address the problem if and when it occurred. He was also concerned about plaintiffs' lack of friends in and contact with the minority community, and Mrs. DeWees' statement that she would "not manufacture black friends."

Dr. Crumbley concluded that plaintiffs lacked the ability to: be sufficiently sensitive to the needs of a bi-racial child during the critical period of socialization, self-identification and personality development of age two through six years; educate a minority child about prejudice and provide him with the skills effectively to respond to it; and, provide positive bi-racial and minority role models through interaction with the minority community.

Based on her interview and Dr. Crumbley's report, Ms. Thalheimer concluded that plaintiffs lacked the sensitivity to racial issues and inter-racial network of community resources needed properly to raise Dante. She decided not to grant plaintiffs' request to adopt Dante, and so advised them by letter of September 26, 1991.

Since receiving this letter, plaintiffs have a greater realization of the importance of the issues identified by Dr. Crumbley and are willing to undertake any course of action recommended by defendants to prepare to address the needs of a bi-racial child. They are willing to "grow and learn." They have located and are prepared to participate in a support group of trans-racial adoptive families.

In Dr. Crumbley's opinion, the only evidence adduced on the point, plaintiffs could learn to address Dante's race-related psychological and social needs with appropriate counseling, education and training but this would take a substantial period of time and Dante is now at a "critical" point.

The court has no expertise in the area of cross-racial adoption. Nevertheless, the court cannot accept Dr. Crumbley's view that generally only whites with extensive specialized training or who have experienced discrimination themselves will be able adequately to address the needs of a minority child in his or her formative years.

The court does find that particular sensitivity, awareness and skills are necessary for a successful trans-racial adoption of a young child, and that Dr. Crumbley based his recommendation on his conclusion that plaintiffs had not demonstrated those qualities and could acquire them only over a long period.

Ms. Thalheimer did not refuse to consider plaintiffs as adoptive parents because of race or any other reason. Rather, she did consider plaintiffs' request to adopt Dante and decided not to grant it. Ms. Thalheimer is currently prepared to place Dante for adoption with any suitable couple, regardless of race, who appear to her to have the awareness, sensitivity and skills to address adequately the needs of a bi-racial child in his formative years. Her decision was based on the perceived best interests of the child, and not on the color of plaintiffs' skins.

II. CONCLUSIONS OF LAW

To sustain their due process claim, plaintiffs must show that they are being deprived of a federally secured right by persons acting under color of state law. Defendants are clearly acting under color of state law.

Foster parents do not have a cognizable liberty interest in maintaining a relationship with a foster child vis-a-vis prospective adoptive parents, particularly where the relationship is based on a contract under which the state retains responsibility for the child and places him in a foster home on a temporary basis.

The essence of the equal protection clause is a requirement that similarly situated people be treated alike. Racial classifications are inherently suspect and can survive an equal protection challenge only if they are necessary to achieve a compelling state interest. *Loving v. Virginia*, 388 U.S. 1, 11 (1967); *McLaughlin v. Florida*, 379 U.S. 184, 196 (1964).

The state's responsibility to protect the best interests of a child in its custody is a compelling interest for purposes of the equal protection clause. *McLaughlin v. Pernsley*, 693 F. Supp. 318, 324 (E.D. Pa. 1988), *aff'd*, 876 F.2d 308 (3d Cir. 1989). Because of the potential difficulties inherent in a trans-racial adoption, a state agency may consider race and racial attitudes in assessing prospective adoptive parents. *Drummond*, 563 F.2d at 1204. *See also* 55 Pa. Stat. Ann. § 3350.12(c)(3).

While the degree of plaintiffs' sensitivity and attitudes about racial issues may be related to their race and experience as whites in a white majority society, defendants refused their request to adopt a minority child because of perceptions about their attitudes and not their race. To the extent that perceived attitudes about race and coping with race-related problems motivated defendants' decision, this was Constitutionally permissible in determining the best interests of a young child eligible for adoption.

Plaintiffs have failed to establish on the record adduced and under applicable legal precedent and principles that their due process or equal protection rights have been violated.

CONCLUSION

The court has not found that plaintiffs are in any way unfit or could not acquire the knowledge and skills necessary to provide for Dante's future needs. Foster parents play a vital role in our society. They provide a welcome alternative to institutionalization of children without parents able or willing to care for them while the permanent placement process ensues.

State agencies have a moral obligation to be sensitive to the position of foster parents who, particularly with extended placements, are likely to develop emotional bonds to the children placed in their homes. Ultimately, however, the state's responsibility to protect and pursue the best interests of children in its custody must take precedence.

This court is not empowered to sit as a super adoption agency review board. The court thus is not passing upon the wisdom of defendants' actions but only on whether they were motivated by Constitutionally impermissible considerations of race. The court has found that defendants made a considered judgment based on professional input and Constitutionally permissible factors.

This finding turns on the importance of awareness of and sensitivity to issues of race in the context of a trans-racial adoption. These factors, in turn, are important largely because of the realities of the larger society in which we live.

As the court stated at the hearing on November 20, 1991, it is concerned that the very problems which give rise to race-related concerns may unintentionally be exacerbated by overemphasizing them. It is difficult to make race irrelevant, as it should be, if adoption and other social decisions are driven by racial considerations, however benign.

In making adoption decisions, state agencies cannot ignore the realities of the society in which children entrusted to them for placement will be raised, or the affect on children of those realities as documented by professional studies. The court would hope, however, that these agencies also will be mindful of the possibility that an overemphasis on racial issues may retard efforts to achieve a color blind society, and of the need to avoid even the appearance that an adoption decision may have been based on race per se.

An order consistent with the foregoing Memorandum will be entered.

NOTES AND QUESTIONS

(1) The *DeWees* case was decided prior to the enactment of the federal Interethnic Adoption Provisions reproduced above. Would these provisions require a different result in *DeWees*? Why or why not?

(2) To what extent do the 1996 Interethnic Adoption Provisions represent endorsement, as a matter of federal law and policy, of the perspective that Professor Perry describes as "liberal colorblind individualism"?

(3) The Interethnic Adoption provisions of 1996 replaced the Multiethnic Placement Act of 1994 (MEPA), formerly codified at 42 U.S.C. § 5115a. MEPA provided that an adoptive or foster care placement could not be delayed or denied *solely* on the basis of race, but it permitted a placement agency to "consider the cultural, ethnic, or racial background of the child and the capacity of the prospective foster or adoptive parents to meet the needs of a child of this background as one of a number of factors used to determine the best interests of a child." 42 U.S.C. § 5115a (1994) (repealed, 1996). MEPA, which enjoyed bipartisan and multiracial support, was regarded as a compromise between proponents and

opponents of transracial adoption. *See* Senator Howard M. Metzenbaum, *In Support of the Multiethnic Placement Act of 1993*, 2 Duke J. Gender L. & Pol'y 165, 166–67 (1995); Jane Maslow Cohen, *Race-Based Adoption In A Post-Loving Frame*, 6 B.U. Pub. Int. L.J. 653, 655 (1997) (MEPA "attempted a legislative compromise between the friends and foes of adoptive racematching").

However, that compromise was short-lived. In particular, critics of race-matching continued to object vehemently to the ambiguity of MEPA's legislative standard and its tacit acceptance of delay. *E.g.*, Elizabeth Bartholet, *Race Separatism in the Family: More On the Transracial Adoption Debate*, 2 Duke J. Gender L & Pol'y 99, 105 & n.16 (1995); *see* Barbara Bennett Woodhouse, *"Are You My Mother?": Conceptualizing Children's Identity Rights In Transracial Adoptions*, 2 Duke J. Gender L. & Pol'y 107, 122–23 (1995) (describing opposition to MEPA from both supporters and opponents of transracial adoption). In 1996, with "little public opposition, and minimal fanfare," Congress repealed MEPA and replaced it with the more stringent ban on consideration of race in adoption, reproduced above. Note, *Recent Legislation: Transracial Adoption—Congress Forbids Use of Race as a Factor in Adoptive Placement Decisions*, 110 Harv. L. Rev. 1352, 1352 (1997). The 1996 legislation, however, retained MEPA's requirement that federally funded agencies engage in active and diligent efforts to recruit "foster care and adoptive families that reflect the ethnic and racial diversity of children in the State for whom foster and adoptive homes are needed." 42 U.S.C. § 622(b)(9) (1998).

(4) **Race Matching and the Constitution** Courts and commentators disagree about the constitutionality of state-supported race-matching policies that do not categorically bar transracial placements, but rather treat race as a permissible consideration in selecting foster or adoptive parents. *Compare, e.g., Drummond v. Fulton County Dep't of Family & Children's Servs.*, 563 F.2d 1200, 1204 (5th Cir. 1977), *cert. denied*, 437 U.S. 910 (1978) (allowing the use of race as one factor in the selection of adoptive parents) *and In re Petition of R.M.G.*, 454 A.2d 776, 779–80 (D.C. 1982) (upholding District of Columbia statue authorizing the consideration of race in adoption proceedings) *with Compos v. McKeithen*, 341 F. Supp. 264, 266 (E.D. La. 1972) (striking down as unconstitutional and contrary to child's best interests a Louisiana statute that permitted adoption only by parents of same race as child) *and* Elizabeth Bartholet, *Where Do Black Children Belong? The Politics of Race Matching in Adoption*, 139 U. Pa. L. Rev. 1163, 1226–43 (1991) (criticizing court decisions that have upheld limited, race-matching policies and arguing that any state-supported consideration of race violates applicable constitutional norms). *Cf. Palmore v. Sidoti*, 466 U.S. 429, 433 (1984) (unconstitutional for state court to rely on race as the basis for deciding which of two biological parents should have custody of a child). Regardless of the constitutionality of such limited race-matching policies, they now seem prohibited as a matter of federal statutory law. Similarly, the 1994 Uniform Adoption Act provides that an agency "may not delay or deny a minor's placement for adoption solely on the basis of the minor's race, national origin or ethnic background." Uniform Adoption Act, § 2-104(c) (1997). The Act also authorizes prospective adoptive parents to maintain an action for equitable relief against an agency that violates this provision. *Id.*

(5) Most of the voluminous commentary and debate about the role of race in adoption focuses on explicit race-matching by agencies, and leaves unexamined the racial preferences of prospective adoptive parents. To what extent does the accommodation by publicly funded

adoption agencies of the race-based preferences of prospective adoptive parents, through such policies as classifying children on the basis of race and maintaining separate lists of white and non-white children available for adoption, implicate constitutional equal protection principles? In a provocative, recent article, Professor R. Richard Banks argues that such "facilitative accommodation" of the racial preferences of (mostly white) prospective adoptive parents for same-race children denies black children, on the basis of race, the opportunity to be considered individually for adoption by the majority of prospective adoptive parents and therefore should be viewed as a racial classification subject to strict scrutiny:

> In sum, because facilitative accommodation is a systematic, formalized practice that encourages parents to rely on race as a decisive factor in determining which children they will individually consider for adoption, the current facilitative accommodation policies of public adoption agencies should be treated by courts as a racial classification and subjected to strict scrutiny.

R. Richard Banks, *The Color of Desire: Fulfilling Adoptive Parents' Racial Preference Through Discriminatory State Action*, 107 Yale L.J. 875, 908 (1998). Banks further argues that, even assuming that promoting the best interests of children qualifies as a compelling state interests, existing Supreme Court precedent indicates that such facilitative accommodation policies are unconstitutional, since "there is little reason to conclude that such policies are necessary to avoid inappropriate placements." *Id.* at 908. In place of current widespread policies that facilitate the racial desires of prospective adoptive parents, Banks proposes a policy of "strict nonaccommodation," under which publicly-funded adoption agencies would generally be prohibited from ascertaining or accommodating the racial preferences of prospective adoptive parents. Banks acknowledges that implementing a strict nonaccommodation policy "would no doubt encounter numerous practical difficulties" and that it might lead some prospective adoptive parents to forego the public adoption process. *Id.* at 955–58. But he emphasizes that such a policy would have some important benefits as well, particularly with respect to its transformative potential:

> A well-articulated policy of strict nonaccommodation might transform our society so that a generation or two from now no one would view preferring one infant over another on the basis of race as a reasonable thing to do. Such a forecast may sound preposterous until one recalls the nature of the arguments about de jure segregation and recognizes that our society has changed to an extent that even many of our most racially liberal late nineteenth-century forbearers would have found completely unimaginable.

Id. at 961. *But cf.* Elizabeth Bartholet, Correspondence: *Private Race Preferences in Family Formation*, 107 Yale L.J. 2351, 2355 (1998) (responding to Banks' article and suggesting that his "strict nonaccommodation" policy "would risk making things yet harder on the children in foster and institutional care who need adoptive homes").

[B] The Indian Child Welfare Act

Whenever a proposed adoption involves a child who is of recognized Native American lineage, the Indian Child Welfare Act of 1978 (ICWA) is relevant to the adoption proceedings. While not itself an adoption code, the ICWA contains jurisdictional, procedural and substantive provisions which pertain to the adoption of Native American children. "The primary goals of the ICWA are to protect the best interests of Indian children and to promote the security, survival and stability of Indan families and tribes." Joan H. Hollinger, *Adoption of Native American Children*, in 2 Adoption Law and Practice, 15-4 (Joan Heifeiz Hollinger, ed., Matthew Bender 1998); *see* 25 U.S.C. § 1902 (1998). The extent to which these goals are compatible with the adoption of Indian children by non-Indian families is a controversial issue, and one that underlies contemporary debate about the scope and effectiveness of the ICWA.

IN RE BRIDGET R.
Court of Appeals of California
41 Cal. App. 4th 1483, 49 Cal. Rptr. 2d 507 (1996)
cert. denied, 117 S. Ct. 693, 117 S. Ct. 1460 (1997)

CROSKEY, J.

California recognizes the principle that children are not merely chattels belonging to their parents, but rather have fundamental interests of their own. Such fundamental interests are of constitutional dimension. This principle is central to our resolution of the multiple and complex issues presented by this case.

We reverse an order of the trial court made pursuant to sections 1913 and 1914 of the Indian Child Welfare Act of 1978 (25 U.S.C.§ 1901 *et seq.*; hereafter ICWA or the Act). The court's order invalidated a voluntary relinquishment of parental rights respecting Bridget and Lucy R., twin two-year-old girls, and ordered the twins removed from their adoptive family, with whom they have lived since birth, and returned to the extended family of the biological father. . . .

The twins are of American Indian descent, and the within dispute over their prospective adoption and custody raises issues concerning the scope of ICWA. Specifically, it raises the question of whether the Act should be limited in its application, as some courts have limited it, to children who not only are of Indian descent, but also belong to an "existing Indian family." We conclude that question must be answered in the affirmative. . . .

Here, the twins' biological parents, Richard A. (Richard) and Cindy R. (Cindy), initially relinquished the twins to appellant Vista Del Mar Child and Family Services (Vista Del Mar) pursuant to section 8700 of California's Family Code for adoption by the R's, a non-Indian couple. However, Richard and Cindy later purported to withdraw their consent. With the assistance of the Dry Creek Rancheria of Pomo Indians, the federally recognized Indian tribe from which Richard is descended (hereafter the Tribe), they initiated proceedings under ICWA to invalidate their relinquishments of parental rights. It is undisputed that the relinquishments were not executed in the manner required by ICWA. It is also undisputed that Richard and the twins are now recognized by the Tribe as tribal members. However, the record raises substantial doubt as to whether Richard, who, at all relevant times, resided several hundred miles from the tribal reservation, ever participated in tribal life or maintained any significant social, cultural or political relationship with the Tribe. . . .

As we explain, recognition of the existing Indian family doctrine is necessary in a case such as this in order to preserve ICWA's constitutionality. We hold that under the Fifth, Tenth and Fourteenth Amendments to the United States Constitution, ICWA does not and cannot apply to invalidate a voluntary termination of parental rights respecting an Indian child who is not domiciled on a reservation, unless the child's biological parent, or parents, are not only of American Indian descent, but also maintain a significant social, cultural or political relationship with their tribe. Because the factual issues raised by such a rule have not been resolved, we reverse the trial court's order and remand the case for a determination as to whether the twins' biological parents had such a relationship at the time that they voluntarily acted to relinquish their parental rights under California law. In the event that the trial court, after consideration of all the evidence, determines that such a relationship did not exist, then those relinquishments will be valid and binding and ICWA will not bar any pending adoption proceedings. On the other hand, if the trial court finds that the biological parents did have a significant social, cultural or political relationship with the Tribe, and therefore the provisions of ICWA can properly be applied, then a further guardianship hearing will be required to resolve the question of whether the twins should be removed from the custody of the R's.

FACTUAL BACKGROUND

. . .

In mid-1993, Richard and Cindy discovered that Cindy was pregnant. Richard was then 21 years old, and Cindy was 20. They then lived together with their two sons, Anthony, age two, and Richard Andrew, age one, in the City of Whittier in Los Angeles County, California. However, by August of 1993, Cindy and the children were living in a shelter. Richard and Cindy realized they would not be able to care for the expected twins, and so determined to relinquish them for adoption. They consulted Durand Cook, an attorney specializing in adoption, for this purpose.

Richard initially identified himself to Cook as one quarter American Indian. However, when told the adoptions would be delayed or prevented if Richard's Indian ancestry were known, Richard filled in a revised form, omitting the information that he was Indian.

During the ninth month of Cindy's pregnancy, she and Richard met with a social worker from Vista Del Mar. On November 11 and 12 respectively, after receiving counseling concerning the relinquishment and adoption process as required by regulations promulgated by the Department of Social Services pursuant to legislative authority, Richard and Cindy signed documents relinquishing the twins to Vista Del Mar, with the intent that they would be adopted by the R's. [The twins were born on November 9, 1993.] The relinquishments were filed with the state Department of Social Services on November 23, 1993. Although the relinquishment documents contained direct queries as to whether either biological parent was of Indian descent, Richard concealed his Indian ancestry and listed his "basic ethnic group" as "white."

A few days after the relinquishments were executed, the R's returned with the twins to their home in Ohio, where they have lived as a family ever since. On May 4, 1994, the R's filed a petition in Franklin County, Ohio, to adopt Bridget and Lucy. That petition is presumably still pending.

In December of 1993, Richard told his mother, Karen, about Cindy's pregnancy, the birth of the twins and their adoption. In early February of 1994, Karen contacted Attorney Cook. At approximately the same time, Karen contacted the Tribe. A representative of the Tribe contacted Cook in February or March of 1994. Cook informed the R's of this communication. On March 4, 1994, Amy Martin, the Tribe's chairperson, wrote to the Los Angeles

County Children's Court, stating that the twins were potential members of the Tribe and requesting intervention in any proceedings concerning them. On approximately that same date, Karen submitted tribal enrollment applications for herself, Richard, the twins, and Richard's two other children. On March 9, 1994, Amy Martin wrote to Vista Del Mar, stating that the twins were of Indian descent, and Karen, their paternal grandmother, wished them placed within the extended Indian family. . . .

On April 22, 1994, Richard sent to Vista Del Mar a letter which stated that Richard wished to rescind his relinquishment of the twins and to have them raised within his extended family. . . . Vista Del Mar denied Richard's request to withdraw the relinquishments, and the proceedings that are now before us for review followed. . . .

DISCUSSION

1. Summary of Relevant Portions of ICWA

ICWA, enacted by Congress to prevent the further "wholesale separation of Indian children from their families" through state court proceedings, was prompted by studies conducted in the 1970's which showed that Native American children were being removed from their homes, through both foster care and adoption, in disproportionate numbers.

The Act is broken down into two titles. In this case, we are concerned only with title I (25 U.S.C. § 1901-1923), which provides for the allocation of jurisdiction over Indian child custody proceedings between Indian tribes and the states and establishes federal standards to protect Indian families. . . .

Sections 1901 and 1902 set forth the historical and policy bases of ICWA. The stated policies are to protect the best interests of Indian children and protect the cultural heritage of Indian nations from destruction through the removal of children from Indian tribes. Section 1903 defines the Act's operative terms. An " 'Indian child' " is defined as "any unmarried person who is under age eighteen and either (a) is a member of an Indian tribe or (b) is eligible for membership in an Indian tribe and is the biological child of a tribal member." (25 U.S.C.§ 1903(4).) . . .

Section 1911(a) gives an Indian tribe "jurisdiction exclusive as to any State over any child custody proceeding involving an Indian child who resides on or is domiciled within" the tribal reservation (25 U.S.C.§ 1911(a)). When an Indian child who is not domiciled on a reservation is the subject of child custody proceedings in a state court, section 1911(b) provides that, absent good cause, jurisdiction shall be transferred to the child's tribe upon request by either parent or the tribe. Subdivision (c) provides that an Indian child's tribe may intervene in any state court custody proceeding affecting the child. Subdivision (d) requires all jurisdictions within the United States to give full faith and credit to the acts of an Indian tribe that are applicable to Indian child custody proceedings.

. . .

Section 1913 sets forth standards for voluntary foster care placements and voluntary terminations of parental rights. Subdivision (a) provides that Indian parents who relinquish their parental rights must execute the relinquishments in writing before a judge, who must certify that the proceedings were explained to the parents in a language they understand. Subdivision (a) further provides that "Any consent given prior to, or within ten days after, birth of the Indian child shall not be valid." Subdivision (b) provides that a parent or Indian custodian may withdraw consent to a foster care placement at any time, and upon such withdrawal, the child must be returned. Subdivision (c) provides that a parent or Indian custodian may withdraw consent to termination of parental rights at any time until entry of a final order of adoption or termination, and upon such withdrawal, the child must be returned. Subdivision (d) provides that a final court decree of adoption may be overturned at any time within two years of its entry if parental consent was obtained through fraud or duress.

Section 1914 of ICWA allows any Indian child, parent or Indian custodian from whom a child was removed, and the Indian child's tribe to petition a court of competent jurisdiction to invalidate a foster care placement or termination of parental rights upon a showing that such action violated any provision of sections 1911, 1912 or 1913.

2. The "Existing Indian Family" Doctrine

As noted above, ICWA applies to any child who is either: (1) a member of an Indian tribe, or (2) eligible to be a member, and the biological child of a member of a tribe. However, some courts have declined to apply the Act where a child is not being removed from an existing Indian family, because, in such circumstances, ICWA's underlying policies of preserving Indian culture and promoting the stability and security of Indian tribes and families are not furthered. (*In re Adoption of Crews*, [825 P.2d 305 (Wash. 1992)]; *Matter of Adoption of Baby Boy L.*, [643 P.2d 168 (Kan. 1982)]). . . .

While the above cases found ICWA inapplicable because the Indian child himself (or herself) had never lived in an Indian environment, other cases have focused upon the question of whether the child's natural family was part of an Indian tribe or community or maintained a significant relationship with one. In *Matter of Adoption of Crews, supra*, 825 P.2d 305, a case involving facts very similar to those before us, the Supreme Court of Washington found ICWA inapplicable to an adoption proceeding where the biological parents had no substantial ties to a specific tribe, and neither the parents nor their families had resided or planned to reside within a tribal reservation, although the birth mother was formally enrolled as a tribal member. . . .

We agree that a rule which would preclude the application of ICWA to any Indian child who has not himself (or herself) lived in an Indian family does not comport with either the language or purpose of the Act. Moreover, the United States Supreme Court has implicitly rejected any such limitation on ICWA. In *Mississippi Choctaw Indian Band v. Holyfield*, 490 U.S. 30 (1989), the only case in which the federal high court has construed ICWA, application of the Act's tribal jurisdiction provisions was challenged by the adoptive parents of illegitimate twin babies whose parents were enrolled members of an Indian tribe and were residents of the tribal reservation. The babies were born off of the reservation and immediately relinquished to a non-Indian family, who adopted them in the state chancery court. The birth mother returned home to the reservation after giving birth. On a subsequent motion by the tribe to vacate the adoption on the ground that the tribal court had exclusive jurisdiction over matters affecting the children's custody, the state court found the children had never resided, or even been physically present, on the reservation, and were thus not domiciled there. Consequently, the court found ICWA did not apply. The Supreme Court reversed, finding that (1) a general federal rule of domicile must apply for purposes of determining jurisdiction under ICWA; (2) under such rule, the children's domicile at birth followed that of their natural mother, and she was domiciled on the reservation; (3) therefore, the tribe had exclusive jurisdiction over custody proceedings affecting the children under section 1911(a).

Holyfield establishes, by clear implication, that an application of ICWA will not be defeated by the mere fact that an Indian child has not himself (or herself) been part of an Indian family or community. However, it does not follow from *Holyfield* that ICWA should apply when neither the child nor either natural parent has ever resided or been domiciled on a reservation or maintained any significant social, cultural or political relationship with an Indian tribe. To the contrary, in our view, there are significant constitutional impediments to applying ICWA, rather than state law, in proceedings affecting the family relationships of persons who are not residents or domiciliaries of an Indian reservation, are not socially or culturally connected with an Indian community, and, in all respects except genetic heritage, are indistinguishable from other residents of the state. . . .

3. Constitutional Limitations Upon the Scope of ICWA

   a. Due Process.

The intent of Congress in enacting ICWA was to "protect the best interests of Indian children," as well as "promote the stability and security of Indian tribes and families." (25 U.S.C.§ 1902.) These two elements of ICWA's underlying policy are in harmony in the circumstance in which ICWA was primarily intended to apply—where nontribal public and private agencies act to remove Indian children from their homes and place them in non-Indian homes or institutions. But in cases such as this one, where, owing to noncompliance with ICWA's procedural requirements, ICWA's remedial provisions are invoked to remove children from adoptive families to whom the children were voluntarily given by the biological parents, the harmony is bound to be strained. Indeed, in circumstances of this kind, the interests of the tribe and the biological family may be in direct conflict with the children's strong needs, which we find to be constitutionally protected, to remain through their developing years in one stable and loving home.

An individual's many related interests in matters of family life are compelling and are ranked among the most basic of civil rights. . . .

Family rights are afforded not only procedural but also substantive protection under the due process clause. Substantive due process prohibits governmental interference with a person's fundamental right to life, liberty or property by unreasonable or arbitrary legislation. Legislation which interferes with the enjoyment of a fundamental right is unreasonable under the due process clause and must be set aside or limited unless such legislation serves a compelling public purpose and is necessary to the accomplishment of that purpose. In other words, such legislation would be subject to a strict scrutiny standard of review.

When discussing constitutional protections of family relationships, the courts have focused more often upon the rights of parents than those of children. . . .

However, the courts have described the constitutional principles which govern familial rights in language which strongly suggests the Constitution protects the familial interests of children just as it protects those of parents. The federal high court has said that ". . . the relationship between parent and child is constitutionally protected" (*Quilloin v. Walcott, supra,* 434 U.S. at p. 25) and also has "emphasized the paramount interest in the welfare of children and has noted that the rights of the parents are a counterpart of the responsibilities they have assumed." (*Lehr v. Robertson, supra*, 463 U.S. at p. 257). Our own Supreme Court has stated that the right of parents to the care, custody and management of their children, although fundamental, is not absolute, and has stated that "[c]hildren, too, have fundamental rights—including the fundamental right to be protected from neglect and to 'have a placement that is stable [and] permanent.' " (*In re Jasmon O., supra*, 8 Cal. 4th 398, 419, *quoting In re Marilyn H., supra*, 5 Cal. 4th at p. 306.) . . .

Moreover, as a matter of simple common sense, the rights of children in their family relationships are at least as fundamental and compelling as those of their parents. If anything, children's familial rights are more compelling than adults', because children's interests in family relationships comprise more than the emotional and social interests which adults have in family life; children's interests also include the elementary and wholly practical needs of the small and helpless to be protected from harm and to have stable and permanent homes in which each child's mind and character can grow, unhampered by uncertainty and fear of what the next day or week or court appearance may bring.

Cases which hold that deference is to be accorded to parental rights do so in part on the assumption that children's needs generally are best met by helping parents achieve their interests. In some situations, however, children's and parents' rights conflict, and in these situations, the legal system traditionally protects the child.

Circumstances in which a parent's and child's interests diverge, and the child's interests are found more compelling, include circumstances where a child has been in out-of-home placement under the jurisdiction of a dependency court for 18 months, and the parent has failed to correct the problems which caused the child to be removed from the home. In cases of this kind, the California Supreme Court has ruled that a showing of a substantial likelihood that the child will suffer serious trauma if separated from the foster family can establish sufficient detriment to overcome the parents' right to the care, custody and companionship of the child. A child's right to remain in a stable home is also found both to be adverse to and to outweigh a parent's interests where a natural father failed to show a commitment to the child within a reasonable time of learning of the mother's pregnancy, but later seeks to assert parental rights and disturb an adoptive placement or stepparent family in which the child is secure and thriving. (*Lehr v. Robertson, supra*, 463 U.S. at pp. 261–262; *Quilloin v. Walcott, supra*, 434 U.S. at p. 255. In such cases, the United States Supreme Court has ruled that the parental rights of the natural father are superseded by policies favoring preservation of the child's existing family unit.

Both the California Supreme Court and the United States Supreme Court have also recognized that a person's interests and rights respecting family relationships do not necessarily depend upon the existence of a biological relationship. The United States Supreme Court has stated that "[n]o one would seriously dispute" that familial interests and rights may attach to the emotional ties which grow between members of a de facto family. (*Smith v. Organization of Foster Families* (1977) 431 U.S. 816, 844. Both high courts have recognized that such interests and rights may outweigh biological relationships under some circumstances.

Here, the biological parents have come before the court after having voluntarily relinquished their twin girls for adoption. The biological parents claim they are entitled to reestablish their relationship with the children, because their relinquishments of parental rights were not executed in accordance with ICWA. However, any claim which they may have under the statute does not necessarily establish a claim to that deference which parental rights are generally accorded under the Constitution. A biological parent's constitutional rights, like other constitutional rights, may be waived, provided only that the waiver is knowingly and intelligently made, and the counselling which is required by California law before a parent may relinquish a child for adoption has been held to be sufficient to assure that any waiver of parental rights is knowing and intelligent.

Given the failure to comply with procedural requirements of ICWA, we cannot conclude that there has been a waiver of parental rights in this case. However, as we have observed, prior judicial decisions establish that, where a child has formed familial bonds with a de facto family with whom the child was placed owing to a biological parent's unfitness or initial failure to establish a parent-child relationship and where it is shown that the child would be harmed by any severance of those bonds, the child's constitutionally protected interests outweigh those of the biological parents. The rule can logically be no different where children have become bonded to a family in which they were placed after a knowing, intelligent and express relinquishment of parental rights. Inasmuch as children have a liberty interest in the continuity and stability of their homes, where a child's biological parents knowingly and intelligently relinquish the child to others for the express purpose of giving the child a loving and stable home, the biological parents' voluntary act constitutes at the very least a voluntary subordination of their constitutional rights to those of the children. The biological parents thus must rely solely upon ICWA for any claim which they might have in this matter.

The interests of the Tribe in this dispute are likewise based solely upon ICWA. There neither is nor can be any claim that the Tribe's interests are constitutionally protected. The R's, as the prospective adoptive parents, similarly have no interests which have been found to enjoy constitutional protection.

However, the twins do have a presently existing fundamental and constitutionally protected interest in their relationship with the only family they have ever known. The children are thus the only parties before the court which have such interests. Therefore, if application of ICWA would interfere with those interests, such application must be subjected to a strict scrutiny standard to determine whether it serves a compelling government purpose and whether it is actually necessary and effective to the accomplishment of that purpose. If not, then ICWA, as so applied, would deprive the children of due process of law.

. . .

We have no quarrel with the proposition that preserving American Indian culture is a legitimate, even compelling, governmental interest. At the same time, however, we agree with those courts which have held that this purpose will not be served by applying the provisions of ICWA which are at issue in this case to children whose biological parents do not have a significant social, cultural or political relationship with an Indian community. It is almost too obvious to require articulation that "the unique values of Indian culture" (25 U.S.C.§ 1902) will not be preserved in the homes of parents who have become fully assimilated into non-Indian culture. This being so, it is questionable whether a rational basis, far less a compelling need, exists for applying the requirements of the Act where fully assimilated Indian parents seek to voluntarily relinquish children for adoption. The case for applying ICWA is even weaker where assimilated parents have previously concluded a reasoned and voluntary relinquishment of a child, which was valid and has become final under state law, and the child has become part of an adoptive or prospective adoptive family. In this circumstance, the invalidation of the relinquishment manifestly can serve no purpose which is sufficiently compelling to overcome the child's fundamental right to remain in the home where he or she is loved and well cared for, with people to whom the child is daily becoming more attached by bonds of affection and among whom the child feels secure to learn and grow. ICWA cannot constitutionally be applied under such facts.

b. Equal Protection.

ICWA requires Indian children who cannot be cared for by their natural parents to be treated differently from non-Indian children in the same situation. As a result of this disparate treatment, the number and variety of adoptive homes that are potentially available to an Indian child are more limited than those available to non-Indian children, and an Indian child who has been placed in an adoptive or potential adoptive home has a greater risk than do non-Indian children of being taken from that home and placed with strangers. To the extent this disparate and sometimes disadvantageous treatment is based upon social, cultural or political relationships between Indian children and their tribes, it does not violate the equal protection requirements of the Fifth and Fourteenth Amendments. However, where such social, cultural or political relationships do not exist or are very attenuated, the only remaining basis for applying ICWA rather than state law in proceedings affecting an Indian child's custody is the child's genetic heritage—in other words, race.

Equal protection principles regard racial classifications of all kinds as "inherently suspect" (*University of California Regents v. Bakke* (1978) 438 U.S. 265, 289–290 (lead opn. of Powell, J.)), indeed, "odious to a free people." (*Hirabayashi v. United States* (1943) 320 U.S. 81, 100) The United States Supreme Court has recently held that "all racial classifications, imposed by whatever federal, state, or local governmental actor, must be analyzed by a reviewing court under strict scrutiny. In other words, such classifications are constitutional only if they are narrowly tailored measures that further compelling governmental interests." (*Adarand Constructors, Inc. v. Pena* (1995) 515 U.S. 200, 227 (1995). The same principle applies whether the group targeted by a racial classification is burdened or benefited by the classification. (*Adarand, supra*) The foregoing principles apply to federal legislation affecting Indian affairs. . . .

For purposes of determining whether a particular application of ICWA creates a racially based classification, it makes no difference that not all tribes recognize as tribal members all blood descendants of tribal members. As we have observed above, to the extent that tribal membership within the meaning of ICWA is based upon social, cultural or political tribal affiliations, it meets the requirements of equal protection. However, any application of ICWA which is triggered by an Indian child's genetic heritage, without substantial social, cultural or political affiliations between the child's family and a tribal community, is an application based solely, or at least predominantly, upon race and is subject to strict scrutiny under the equal protection clause. So scrutinized, and for the same reasons set forth in our discussion of the due process issue, it is clear that ICWA's purpose is not served by an application of the Act to children who are of Indian descent, but whose parents have no significant relationship with an Indian community. If ICWA is applied to such children, such application deprives them of equal protection of the law. . . .

We conclude that principles of substantive due process, equal protection and federalism all carry the same implication regarding the proper scope of ICWA—it can properly apply only where it is necessary and actually effective to accomplish its stated, and plainly compelling, purpose of preserving Indian culture through the preservation of Indian families. We agree with those courts which have held that ICWA's purpose is not served by an application of the Act where the child may be of Indian descent, but where neither the child nor either parent maintains any significant social, cultural or political relationships with Indian life.

4. The Trial Court Must Determine the Question of Whether There Was an "Existing Indian Family" Which Is the Factual Predicate to the Application of ICWA

. . .

Because the trial court was persuaded that enrollment in the Tribe and tribal recognition of the twins' tribal membership were enough to trigger the application of ICWA, the court had no occasion to make a further factual determination as to whether the biological parents maintain significant social, cultural or political relationships with the Tribe. The case must therefore be remanded so that such factual determination can be made.

The biological parents (and the Tribe), of course, will bear the burden of proof on this issue. It is they who seek to set aside the relinquishment of parental rights which were otherwise final and binding under California law. To do this they rely on the application of a federal statute. It is they who must prove that the necessary factual basis for the application of that statute is present.

Moreover, that determination must focus upon the biological parents' social, cultural and political relationship with the Tribe, although any relationship between the Tribe and extended family members may well bear on the issue of the biological parents' relationship. . . .

The biological parents and the Tribe contend it would be unfair to focus only upon the nuclear family when assessing an application of ICWA, because such focus would ignore tribal kinship systems, in which the extended family is a fundamental unit. The parents and Tribe argue that one of the primary reasons ICWA was enacted was to combat the adverse effects upon Indian communities of failures by state courts and agencies to appreciate the importance in tribal life of the extended family, as well as other customs and institutions affecting the welfare of Indian children. They thus argue, in effect, that to exclude the extended family from consideration when we determine whether there is an existing Indian family, and hence, whether ICWA applies, would be a mere analytical sleight of hand, by which ICWA's requirement of giving due consideration to essential tribal relations would be unfairly sidestepped.

After giving this argument long and careful consideration, we are compelled to disagree. First, it implicitly assumes the conclusion that the biological parents did have significant social, cultural or political connections to the Tribe. If they had no such connections, then there would be no real issue of an "extended Indian family" for the court to ignore. Secondly, and more significantly, it must not be forgotten that this case has arisen because the biological parents abjured their Indian heritage when, instead of turning to their extended family for succor and support in anticipation of the twins' birth, they voluntarily, and for rational and understandable reasons, relinquished those children to strangers. Then, to prevent interference with those relinquishments by the Tribe, they denied their heritage in response to multiple direct inquiries. Having done these things, the biological parents may now justly be required to prove that they themselves have a significant relationship with an Indian community and may be precluded from using cultural ties which may be maintained by their blood relatives to bootstrap themselves into an application of ICWA.

The determination whether the twins were removed from an existing Indian family must also be made as of the time of the relinquishments. There can be no justification or excuse for tearing children from a family to which they are bonded, based upon an ex post facto manufacture of a legal basis for applying ICWA. . . . [T]he circumstance that Richard's mother, Karen—not Richard himself—applied for tribal enrollment for herself, Richard and all his children after the present dispute arose is a circumstance which can be considered in determining whether Richard truly maintained a significant relationship with the Tribe at the time of the twins' birth.

In considering whether the biological parents maintained significant ties to the Tribe, the court should also consider whether the parents privately identified themselves as Indians and privately observed tribal customs and, among other things, whether, despite their distance from the reservation, they participated in tribal community affairs, voted in tribal elections, or otherwise took an interest in tribal politics, contributed to tribal or Indian charities, subscribed to tribal newsletters or other periodicals of special interest to Indians, participated in Indian religious, social, cultural or political events which are held in their own locality, or maintained social contacts with other members of the Tribe. In this regard, we find particularly significant the fact that in the months preceding the birth of the twins, the biological parents turned not to the Tribe or even to other family members, but rather to California's legal process for the purpose of securing the adoption of the twins by a loving family able to care for them. The biological parents did this voluntarily and for reasons which reflected that their primary concern was for the twins' future welfare. Moreover, as already noted, in order to facilitate the adoption process the biological parents expressly and intentionally denied their Indian heritage. Such conduct permits a very strong inference to be drawn about the absence of a significant relationship with the Tribe. . . .

CONCLUSION

In this case we have concluded that ICWA cannot be constitutionally applied in the absence of evidence demonstrating that the biological parents had a significant social, cultural or political relationship with the Tribe. On the record before us, we find little or no support for the existence of such a relationship. Indeed, the conduct of the biological parents in this matter with respect to the events and circumstances leading up to their relinquishment of the twins strongly suggests that no such relationship existed. However, we cannot conclude, as a matter of law, that the biological parents or the Tribe, upon remand, would not be able to produce additional evidence. Indeed, as a result of the trial court's ruling, none of the parties had any opportunity to present evidence on this critical issue. Therefore, a hearing in the trial court will be required to determine if there is any factual support to establish that the twins were a part of an existing Indian family so as to justify the application of ICWA. On this question, the burden of proof will be on the biological parents and the Tribe. If the trial court concludes that they have not carried their burden, then judgment shall be entered in favor of the R's and they will be free to proceed with the adoption proceedings now pending in Ohio. If the trial court finds otherwise, then it will be necessary to conduct a further hearing on the question of whether there should be a change of custody. The pending guardianship petition filed by the R's would be a proper vehicle to resolve that question. With respect to this issue, the R's will have the burden of proof.

NOTES AND QUESTIONS

(1) The "existing Indian family" exception to ICWA, relied on in *Bridget R.*, has been controversial. *See* Christine Metteer, *Hard Cases Making Bad Law: The Need for Revision of the Indian Child Welfare Act*, 38 Santa Clara L. Rev. 419, 427 n.59 (1998) (reporting "a large and nearly evenly divided split among the states embracing and rejecting the exception"). A number of commentators have argued that the doctrine contravenes the clear language and intent of ICWA, as well as the Supreme Court's reasoning in *Holyfield*. *See, e.g.*, B. J. Jones, *The Indian Child Welfare Act: In Search of a Federal Forum to Vindicate the Rights of Indian Tribes and Children Against the Vagaries of State Courts*, 73 N.D. L. Rev. 395, 397 (1997) (arguing that exception allows "state courts unilaterally [to] decide who is a real Indian child and which Indian children need the protections of the federal law in blatant contravention of the clear definition of 'Indian child' contained in ICWA"); Wendy Therese Parnell, *The Existing Indian Family Exception: Denying Tribal Rights Protected by the Indian Child Welfare Act*, 34 San Diego L. Rev. 381, 485–86 (1997) (by allowing individual parental actions to defeat tribal rights, the exception subverts Congress' intent to protect the child, the extended family and the tribe); Christine Metteer, *The Existing Indian Family Exception: An Impediment to the Trust Responsibility To Preserve Tribal Existence and Culture as Manifested In the Indian Child Welfare Act*, 30 Loy. L.A. L. Rev. 647, 660–65 (1997) (exception is inconsistent with Supreme Court's recognition in *Holyfield* of distinct tribal interests and ties to children); *but cf.* Christine D. Bakeis, *The Indian Child Welfare Act of 1978: Violating Personal Rights for the Sake of the Tribe*, 10 Notre Dame J.L. Ethics & Pub. Pol'y 543 (1996) (contending that application of ICWA to voluntary adoptive placements violates the rights of Indian parents).

(2) Does allowing a state court to decide whether a particular biological parent has a sufficient social, cultural or political relationship with an Indian tribe to justify application of ICWA risk perpetuating the very problems that led to Congress' enactment of ICWA?

> The major fallacy of . . . the existing Indian family exception is that it places the decision of who is an Indian with the entity least equipped to make the decision, the state court. As noted in *Holyfield*, Congress perceived the state courts' inability to understand Indian cultural and tribal dynamics as part of the problem it was attempting to correct by enacting the ICWA. It is highly doubtful Congress intended such a pivotal decision to be placed with an entity it perceived as not understanding the basics of being Indian.

Parnell, *above* at 427–28; *see* Jones, *above*, at 416 (questioning how "state court judges, who Congress found lacking in concrete knowledge of traditional Indian customs and traditions, [could] discern which Indian families were culturally attuned and which were assimilated?"). Do you find these arguments convincing? Why or why not? If you were the trial court judge hearing the *Bridget R.* case on remand, how would you decide whether the twins were "part of an existing Indian family?"

(3) Do you agree with the *Bridget R.* court that children have a "fundamental and constitutionally protected interest" in protecting their relationship with prospective adoptive parents or other, long-term adult caretakers? How would recognition of such a constitutionally protected interest change the analysis (or the result) in cases such as *In re Baby Boy C.*, 581 A.2d 1141 (D.C. 1990), *appeal after remand*, 630 A.2d 670, *cert. denied*, 513 U.S. 809 (1994) [reprinted at § 8.03, *above*], *Smith v. O.F.F.E.R.*, 431 U.S. 816 (1977) [reprinted at § 7.06[A], *above*] or *Michael H. v. Gerald D.*, 491 U.S. 110 (1989) [reprinted at § 5.05, *above*]?

(4) The *Bridget R.* court asserts that where biological parents voluntarily relinquish a child for adoption, ICWA's two overriding goals—protecting the interests of Indian children and promoting the stability and security of Indian tribes and families—are likely to be strained, and may be in direct conflict. Others have suggested that this asserted conflict is inconsistent with the philosophy of ICWA. "A basic assumption of the Act is that Indian children are essential tribal resources, on whom tribal survival depends, and hence tribal governing bodies, not parents, should determine the ways in which Indian children will be raised. In this view, the dual goals of protecting the interests of Indian children and promoting tribal stability are fully compatible with each other." Joan H. Hollinger, *Adoption of Native American Children*, in Adoption Law and Practice, 15-9 (Joan Heifeiz Hollinger, ed., Matthew Bender 1998). Does ICWA strike an appropriate balance, in the context of voluntary adoptive placements, between the interests of biological parents and the interests of the tribes with whom those parents are affiliated? Who should determine this balance—Congress or the state courts?

(5) How does ICWA's treatment of race and ethnicity differ from the treatment of race under the Multiethnic Placement Act of 1994, and its successor, the Interethnic Adoption Provisions of 1996? What accounts for these differences? *See Morton v. Mancari*, 417 U.S. 535, 553–55 (1974) (upholding federal hiring preference for members of recognized Indian tribes as "political, rather than racial in nature"). To what extent does the debate over the "existing Indian family" exception to the ICWA implicate the competing perspectives on transracial adoption described by Professor Twila Perry?

[C] Religion

ORZECHOWSKI v. PERALES
Supreme Court of New York
153 Misc. 2d 464, 582 N.Y.S.2d 341 (1992)

SCHLESINGER, J.,

In this action the plaintiffs seek declaratory and injunctive relief, and damages for violation of their constitutional rights. The basis of the challenge is that the defendants' administration of the religious matching provisions of the adoption laws is unconstitutional. . . .

The plaintiffs Kenneth and Theresa Orzechowski are married and childless. They are practicing Roman Catholics. The Orzechowskis sought to adopt a four-year-old girl born to Jewish parents. Plaintiff Rabbi Hirshel Jaffe had agreed to help the Orzechowskis raise the child in the Jewish faith. Plaintiff Association to Benefit Children (ABC) is an organization that provides care to abandoned and disabled children.

In October 1990 after a home study, the Orzechowskis were approved as adoptive parents who would be permitted to adopt a child with a physical disability and special needs. Theresa Orzechowski was born with congenital disabilities which include club feet, dislocated hips and a missing leg socket. She has undergone numerous operations and now is able to walk.

In December 1990 the Orzechowskis saw the picture of 3 1/2-year-old Nelli K. (Nelli) in the New York State Adoption Exchange (also known as the blue book). The book described Nelli as suffering from Goltz syndrome. This condition causes fatty lesions on her face and body. She also has spina bifida and requires daily catheterizations.

Nelli had been institutionalized from birth. At 5 1/2 months she moved from the hospital where she was born to the Foundling Hospital Inc. (Foundling). This organization is run by an order of Catholic nuns. In November 1989 when Nelli was nearly three her biological parents surrendered her for adoption. In doing so, Nelli's parents signed a "Declaration of Religious Preference for Child" which stated that they preferred the placement be in a "home of the Jewish (Non-Hasidic) religion."

Upon seeing Nelli's picture, the Orzechowskis became interested in adopting her. They were informed by the Foundling that Nelli was disfigured, lacked bowel control, and was fed by a naso-gastric tube placed in her stomach through her nostrils.

In January 1991 the Foundling provided the Orzechowskis with Nelli's detailed medical records and recommended consultation with a doctor regarding her condition.

On April 16, 1991 the Orzechowskis met Nelli. During the visit Mrs. Orzechowski asked whether Nelli's parents had stated a religious preference. She was informed that such a request had not been made. The Orzechowskis decided that they wanted to adopt Nelli.

Subsequent to the visit, the Foundling wrote to the Orzechowskis praising them for their interaction with Nelli stating that "all staff members were positively impressed by your interest, information and sensitivity" to Nelli.

In late April 1991 the Foundling "terminated its relationship" with the Orzechowskis solely because they were not Jewish. In a letter it informed the Orzechowskis that "Save the issue of religion, we have no objection to placing Nelli in your home . . . [y]ou had impressed us as caring, concerned individuals who are ready to provide a loving home for a child."

In July 1991 the Orzechowskis sought a fair hearing from the New York State Department of Social Services. That request was denied on the ground that the Orzechowskis were not entitled to a hearing. Later that month Nelli was placed with a Jewish family.

Plaintiffs contend that the Orzechowskis were disqualified as adoptive parents solely based on religion. They allege that child care agencies in New York maintain a policy to place children "solely or predominantly" on the basis of the religion imposed on a child.

They contend that this practice results in inferior placements. The religious matching requirement delays permanent placement of the child in a home and prolongs institutionalization. Accordingly, this policy and practice is not in the best interest of the child. Plaintiffs further allege that this policy is especially detrimental to disabled children and children of racial minorities because they are especially hard to place.

In the first cause of action, plaintiffs contend that the defendants' religious matching requirement violates the Free Exercise and Establishment Clauses of the First Amendment of the US Constitution and article I, §§ 3 and 11 of the NY Constitution.

The second cause of action alleges that the policy requiring adoptive parents share the religion imposed on the child via the natural mother's stated preference, violates plaintiffs' right to equal protection. . . .

Section 116 of the Family Court Act relates to the religion and placement of a foster child. Subdivision (g) provides in relevant part that: "The provisions of subdivisions (a), (b), (c), (d), (e) and (f) of this section shall, so far as consistent with the best interests of the child, and where practicable, be applied so as to give effect to the religious wishes of the natural mother."

In *Matter of Dickens v Ernesto* (30 NY2d 61 [1972]), petitioners were denied permission by the Department of Social Services (DSS) to file an application as adoptive parents solely on the ground that they did not have a religious preference. Although the lower courts ordered DSS to process the Dickens' application they held that petitioners' constitutional rights had not been violated.

The Court of Appeals affirmed. It held that the religious placement factor in section 116 (g) did not violate the Establishment Clause. The court ruled that although religious preference of the biological parent was a "relevant consideration," it was but one of many factors. (*Supra*, at 66.) Nor was it mandatory or controlling factor. Placements were based on the best interest of the child, taking into consideration religious and secular factors.

Nor did the Court of Appeals find a violation of petitioners' right to the free exercise of religion (actually in the *Dickens* case, the right to profess no religion). Noting that not all biological parents expressed a preference, the petitioners were free to adopt such a child. Therefore, the "religious conformity provisions which serve a valid secular purpose may not be said to discriminate against or penalize the petitioners because they do not have a religious affiliation, nor are they thereby placed under an obligation to assume a religious faith in order to be able to adopt a child" (*supra*, at 68).

In the case at bar, plaintiffs maintain that the defendants are administering the religious preference provisions in violation of *Dickens* (*supra*). They contend that the defendants are using religion as the sole or determinative factor in making placement decisions which amounts to the State establishing religion. Further, they assert that to accommodate the biological mother's religious preference, the children are subjected to prolonged institutionalization.

The Supreme Court in *Committee for Public Educ. v. Nyquist* (413 US 756, 773 [1973]) applied a three-prong test to determine whether a law violates the Establishment Clause. "[T]he law in question first, must reflect a clearly secular legislative purpose . . . second, must have a primary effect that neither advances nor inhibits religion . . . and, third, must avoid excessive government entanglement with religion." (*Supra*, at 773.) To be constitutional the law must meet all three elements of the test.

Plaintiffs, in the instant matter, state a cause of action under *Dickens*, (*supra*), because if their central claim is proven, religion would be the controlling factor in determining whether a placement is in the best interest of a child. This would arguably fail to meet the primary effect and/or excessive entanglement prong of the establishment test. Therefore, the defendants' motion to dismiss the Establishment Clause cause of action is denied.

Next, plaintiffs maintain that defendants' application of the religious matching provisions "inhibited the Orzechowskis' free exercise of their religion—Catholicism—because they have been told that they cannot continue to practice their religion and adopt a child whose biological parents were Jewish."

A violation of the Free Exercise Clause occurs "[w]here the state conditions receipt of an important benefit upon conduct proscribed by a religious faith, or where it denies such a benefit because of conduct mandated by religious belief, thereby putting substantial pressure on an adherent to modify his behavior and to violate his beliefs, a burden on religion exist. While the compulsion may be indirect, the infringement upon free exercise is nonetheless substantial" (*Thomas v Review Bd., Ind. Employment Sec. Div.*, 450 US 707, 717–718 [1981]).

Assuming that religion is the sole or predominant factor upon which placement decisions are made, plaintiffs fail to state a cause of action under the Free Exercise Clauses of the US and NY Constitutions. It cannot be said that there is substantial pressure on the Orzechowskis to modify their religious beliefs. Like the petitioners in *Dickens* (*supra*), the Orzechowskis are free to adopt a child whose natural parents were "indifferent" to the religious placement of their child.

Similarly, plaintiffs fail to state a claim under the Equal Protection Clauses of the US and NY Constitutions. Plaintiffs contend that the religious matching provisions must be narrowly tailored to a compelling government need. However, the strict scrutiny test applies only to government's action that interferes with a fundamental right.

Plaintiffs assert that their fundamental right of free exercise of religion is being impeded. However, the court has found that there is no free exercise claim here.

Moreover, as noted above, in *Dickens* (*supra*), the Court of Appeals rejected the petitioners' equal protection argument finding that the religious matching provisions have a valid legitimate secular purpose. That holding is controlling here. The equal protection claims cannot survive rational basis scrutiny and are therefore dismissed. . . .

NOTES AND QUESTIONS

(1) Assume that the Orzechowskis could show on remand that the defendant's policy was to honor the religious preferences of the biological parent(s) wherever possible and therefore to refuse to consider prospective adoptive parents of another religion until "diligent efforts" had been made to place the child with a family of the biological parent's religious preference." Would that policy be constitutional? Why or why not? *Cf. Wilder v. Bernstein*, 848 F.2d 1338, 1345–49 (2nd Cir. 1988) (discussing constitutionality of religious matching policies in connection with state-sponsored foster care placements). *See generally* Laura J. Schwartz, *Religious Matching for Adoption: Unraveling the Interests Behind the "Best Interests" Standard*, 25 Fam. L.Q. 171 (1991); Donald L. Beschle, *God Bless The Child?: The Use of Religion As A Factor in Child Custody and Adoption Proceedings*, 58 Fordham L. Rev. 383, 404–06 (1989).

(2) Private adoption agencies are often affiliated with or sponsored by religious organizations, and may have a strong preference in favor of placing children with parents of the religion with which the agency is affiliated, regardless of whether the biological parents have expressed such a religious preference. May state-licensed adoption agencies impose religious restrictions upon prospective adoptive parents, over and above those

requested by biological parents? *See Scott v. Family Ministries*, 135 Cal. Rptr. 430, 439 (Cal. Ct. App. 1976) (private adoption agency constitutionally precluded from imposing religious requirements on prospective adoptive parents seeking to adopt children of unknown parentage and religion).

(3) May a court, or publicly funded agency, consider the religious beliefs—or lack thereof—of prospective adoptive parents in considering their fitness to adopt? *See, e.g., In Re Adoption of E*, 279 A.2d 785, 792 (N.J. 1971) (while religion may be relevant to moral fitness, trial court's denial of adoption petition solely because of adoptive parents' lack of religious belief violated First Amendment). Suppose that prospective adoptive parents engage in a religiously motivated practice (for example, polygamy) that is illegal under state law? *See In the Matter of the Adoption of W.A.T.*, 808 P.2d 1083 (Utah 1991) (trial court erred in dismissing adoption petition on the basis of petitioners' polygamous marriage without holding a hearing on whether the adoption would promote the best interests of the children involved).

(4) Why should biological parents who consent to a child's adoption be able to control the child's future religious upbringing, when they are generally precluded from voicing an opinion regarding any other aspect of the child's upbringing? Does the Free Exercise Clause of the First Amendment compel consideration of a biological parent's religious preferences?

(5) If a child has developed his or her own religious preference, should that preference be considered in selecting prospective adoptive parents? Should the child's preference be controlling? Would your answer be the same if adoptive parents who adhere to the child's religion are scarce?

(6) **Other Selection Criteria.** Traditionally, agencies considered a number of criteria in attempting to create the "ideal" adoptive family. Which, if any, of these criteria should agencies consider today in selecting adoptive parents?

(a) *Age*. At what age, if any, are parents too "old" to adopt? *See, e.g., In re Jennifer A.*, 650 N.Y.S. 691, 692 (N.Y. App. Div. 1996), *appeal denied*, 693 N.E.2d 750 (N.Y. 1998) (trial judge erred in refusing to allow adoption by 67-year-old foster mother; while age may be considered, it should not be dispositive); *In re Adoption of Michele T.*, 117 Cal. Rptr. 856, 862 (Cal. Ct. App. 1975) (reversing decision to deny adoption petition based solely on petitioners' ages of 70 years (father), and 54 years (mother)). Should an agency be able to consider age in deciding among several qualified adoptive families? Should there by a *minimum* age for adoptive parents? *See, e.g.*, N.J. Stat. Ann. § 9:3-43 (1997) (establishing a minimum age of 18 for an adoptive parent and a waivable ten-year age difference between the adoptive parent and the child to be adopted).

(b) *Physical ability*. May the state consider a prospective parent's physical capacities? *See Adoption of Richardson*, 59 Cal. Rptr. 323, 334 (Ct. App. 1967) (trial court's denial deaf couple's adoption petition violates equal protection). *Cf. In Re Marriage of Carney*, 598 P.2d 36, 42–44 (Cal. 1979) [reprinted at § 12.02[H] *below*] (trial court abused discretion in transferring custody on basis of father's physical handicap).

(c) *Marital status*. Traditionally, the preferred adoptive placement for a child was with a married couple, but most states today routinely approve adoptions by single persons. *See* James B. Boskey, *Placing Children for Adoption*, in Adoption Law and

Practice 3-49 (Joan Heifetz Hollinger, ed. Matthew Bender 1998). Could a state-supported agency prefer married, to single applicants for adoption? Should unmarried individuals be permitted to adopt jointly? *See In re Jason C.*, 533 A.2d 32, 33–34 (N.H. 1987) (affirming denial of joint adoption petition filed by divorced, former foster parents).

(d) *Sexual orientation.* A few states have statutes prohibiting homosexuals from adopting or serving as foster parents. *See, e.g.,* Fla. Stat. Ann. § 63.042 (3) (1997); N.H. Rev. Stat. Ann. § 170-B:4 (1994). Do such prohibitions violate constitutional due process or equal protection guarantees? *See Cox v. Florida Dep't of Health & Rehabilitative Servs.*, 656 So. 2d 902, 903 (Fla. 1995) (rejecting due process and privacy challenges, but remanding on equal protection claim); Opinion of the Justices, 525 A.2d 1095 (N.H. 1987) (rejecting constitutional challenges). In the absence of relevant statutory provisions, should sexual orientation be considered as a factor in selecting adoptive parents? *Compare, e.g., In re Appeal of Pima County Juvenile Action*, 727 P.2d 830, 833 (Ariz. Ct. App. 1986) (finding bisexual male to be an unacceptable adoptive parent) *with In re Adoption of Jessica N.*, 609 N.Y.S.2d 209 (N.Y. App. Div. 1994) (approving adoption by lesbian foster mother who had cared for child since birth) *and In re Adoption of Charles B.*, 552 N.E.2d 884, 890 (Ohio 1990) (adoption of special needs child by gay male serves child's best interests). For a discussion of second parent adoption by same sex partners, see § 8.04, *above*.

§ 8.06 Legal Consequences of Adoption

For most of this century, adoption in the United States has been characterized by secrecy and exclusivity. Until recently, most adoptive and biological parents did not meet and did not know each other's identity. As a result of adoption, the child acquired a new legal identity. The child's original birth certificate was sealed and a new one issued, listing the adopting parents as the child's only parents. All records of the adoption proceeding were also sealed and could not be opened by anyone, including the parties to the adoption, absent a judicial finding of "good cause." Except in stepparent adoptions, all legal ties between the adopted child and her biological family are completely and permanently severed. The child become becomes exclusively and in all respects the child of the adopting parents. Joan H. Hollinger, *Aftermath of Adoption: Legal and Social Consequences*, in Adoption Law and Practice 13-3 (Joan Heifetz Hollinger, ed., Matthew Bender 1998).

The confidential nature of the adoption process was thought to serve the interests of all members of the adoption triad. It allegedly served the interests of the birth mother by allowing her to put the unwanted pregnancy behind her and to go on with her life. The secrecy of adoption proceedings also shielded both birth mothers and children from the stigma of illegitimacy, which was considerably greater in the early part of the twentieth century than it is today. *See generally* E. Wayne Carp, *Family Matters: Secrecy and Disclosure in the History of Adoption* 103–37 (1998). Confidentiality also promoted the interest of the adoptive family by shielding it from possible interference by the biological parents or other members of the child's original family. Finally, confidentiality was thought to serve the interests of the adopted child by promoting bonding and security within the adoptive family and by avoiding the psychological confusion that was thought to follow from maintaining ties with more than one set of parents. Hollinger, *above* at 13-8.

By the 1970s, these assumptions had come under attack. Increasing numbers of adult adoptees began to search for their biological parents, and several wrote powerfully of their experiences and the barriers they encountered. Others joined activist groups that challenged traditional confidentiality rules and sought access to previously sealed adoption records.

A confluence of demographic and social changes also undermined the traditional secrecy of adoption. As the number of infants available for adoption has decreased, a greater percentage of adoptions have come to involve older children, who know and have developed ties with their biological families. The scarcity of infants available for adoption has also given birth mothers more control over the terms of the adoption, and many birth mothers have insisted on selecting and meeting the adoptive parents, and on maintaining some degree of contact after the adoption. More general changes in family structure have also contributed to reform. The monolithic nuclear family that served as the model for traditional, closed adoption is now only one of a variety of family constellations. For example, children of divorce commonly find themselves in blended families, often with multiple parental figures. "These and other changes in family structures—single parent families, gay families, childrearing by grandparents or other relatives—all contribute to the accessibility of the notion that an adoptee has two sets of parents." Annette Ruth Appell, *Blending Families Through Adoption: Implications For Collaborative Adoption Law and Practice*, 75 B.U. L. Rev. 997, 1011 (1995). Finally, prevailing psychological theory has begun to rethink the necessity and desirability of treating the adoptive family as a complete and fungible substitute for the biological family. As a leading adoption commentator has explained:

> Adoption is a legal fiction. It assumes that a child's ties to biological parents can be displaced entirely by ties to adoptive parents. Social and psychological evidence suggests, however, that legal rules cannot so easily obliterate the past or prevent adoptees, as they grow older, from desiring to re-establish some links to their past. Nor can legal rules, by themselves, resolve for biological parents the emotional consequences of relinquishing their child, or assure adoptive parents that the experience of raising an adopted child is the same as that of raising biological offspring.
>
> This legal fiction is beginning to change. Increasingly understood is the importance for all parties of recognizing and acknowledging, instead of denying, the differences between adoptive and biological relationships. A number of lawmakers and social scientist now endorse a variety of measures designed to ameliorate the possibly detrimental effects of strict adherence to traditional notions of confidentiality, permanence and exclusivity.

Hollinger, *above* at 13-4. The materials that follow explore some of these measures and their impact on the legal and social consequences of adoption.

[A] Confidentiality and Access to Adoption Records

DOE v. SUNDQUIST
United States Court of Appeals
106 F.3d 702 (6th Cir.), cert. denied, 118 S. Ct. 51 (1997)

ENGEL, CIRCUIT JUDGE.

Two birth mothers (Promise Doe and Jane Roe), an adoptive couple (Kimberly C. and Russ C.), and a nonprofit organization licensed by Tennessee as a child-placing agency

(Small World Ministries, Inc.) appeal the district court's denial of their motion for a preliminary injunction to block the enforcement of Tennessee's new statute governing the disclosure of adoption records. The plaintiffs allege that the statute violates both the U.S. Constitution and the Tennessee Constitution. We affirm the district court's denial of the preliminary injunction, and on the merits of the case, we dismiss the federal claims and decline to exercise jurisdiction over the state claims.

I.

From 1951 to 1996, sealed adoption records were available in Tennessee only upon court order that disclosure was "in the best interest of the child or of the public." Tenn. Code Ann. § 36-1-131 (repealed). Under a recently enacted statute that was to go into effect July 1, 1996,

> (A) All adoption records . . . shall be made available to the following eligible persons:
>
>> (i) An adopted person . . . who is twenty-one (21) years of age or older . . . ;
>>
>> (ii) The legal representative of [such] a person. . . .
>
> (B) Information . . . shall be released . . . only to the parents, siblings, lineal descendants, or lineal ancestors, of the adopted person . . . , and only with the express written consent [of] the adopted person. . . .

Id. § 36-1-127(c)(1). The new law also provides for a "contact veto," under which a parent, sibling, spouse, lineal ancestor, or lineal descendant of an adopted person may register to prevent contact by the adopted person. *Id.* § 36-1-128. The contact veto also can prohibit the adopted person from contacting any spouse, sibling, lineal descendant, or lineal ancestor of the person registering the veto. *Id.* § 36-1-130(a)(6)(A)(i). A violator of the contact veto provision is subject to civil and criminal liability. *Id.* § 36-1-132. Before disclosure of the identity of an adopted person's relatives is made, the state "shall conduct a diligent search" for the relatives to give them a chance to register for the veto. *Id.* § 36-1-131. In any event, the relatives of an adopted person can veto only contact, not disclosure of their identities. . . .

The plaintiffs claim that the new law violates their right of privacy under the United States and Tennessee Constitutions. They argue that the "zone of privacy" established in *Griswold v. Connecticut*, 381 U.S. 479 (1965), now encompasses familial privacy, reproductive privacy, and privacy against disclosure of confidential information and that the new statute violates each of these three. We will consider these theories in turn, but first we note our skepticism that information concerning a birth might be protected from disclosure by the Constitution. A birth is simultaneously an intimate occasion and a public event—the government has long kept records of when, where, and by whom babies are born. Such records have myriad purposes, such as furthering the interest of children in knowing the circumstances of their birth. The Tennessee legislature has resolved a conflict between that interest and the competing interest of some parents in concealing the circumstances of a birth. We are powerless to disturb this resolution unless the Constitution elevates the right to avoid disclosure of adoption records above the right to know the identity of one's parents.

First, the plaintiffs cite *Meyer v. Nebraska*, 262 U.S. 390 (1923), as protecting familial privacy. Dicta in *Meyer* noted that the Due Process Clause guarantees the right to "marry, establish a home and bring up children." *Id.* at 399. Nothing in the Tennessee statute infringes on that right. Under the new scheme, people in Tennessee are still free not only to marry and to raise children, but also to adopt children and to give children up for adoption. We find that if there is a federal constitutional right of familial privacy, it does not extend as far as the plaintiffs would like.

Second, the plaintiffs claim that their right to reproductive privacy, as established in *Roe v. Wade*, 410 U.S. 113 (1973), and its progeny, is violated by the Tennessee statute. The freedom to make decisions about adoption, they argue, is sufficiently analogous to the freedom to decide whether to carry a baby to term to justify an extension of *Roe*. Even should it ultimately be held some day that the right to give up a baby for adoption or to adopt a child is protected by the Constitution, such a right would not be relevant to this case. Because the challenged law does not limit adoptions, cases striking down laws restricting abortions are not analogous. And even assuming that a law placing an undue burden on adoptions might conceivably be held to infringe on privacy rights in the Roe realm, much as laws placing "undue burdens" on abortions are unconstitutional under *Planned Parenthood v. Casey*, 505 U.S. 833 (1992), § 36-1-127 does not unduly burden the adoption process. Whether it burdens the process at all is the subject of great dispute in two briefs submitted to this court by amici curiae. Any burden that does exist is incidental and not "undue." *See Casey*, 505 U.S. at 878 (equating "undue burden" with "substantial obstacle").

Third, the plaintiffs claim that the law violates their right to avoid disclosure of confidential information. They rely on a dictum in *Whalen v. Roe*, 429 U.S. 589 (1977), that describes one type of privacy right as "the individual interest in avoiding disclosure of personal matters." *Id.* at 599. This right has not been fleshed out by the Supreme Court. The plaintiffs' argument that it should be extended to cover this case runs counter to our decisions in *J.P. v. DeSanti*, 653 F.2d 1080 (6th Cir. 1981), and *Doe v. Wigginton*, 21 F.3d 733 (6th Cir. 1994). In *DeSanti*, we read the *Whalen* dicta narrowly, 653 F.2d at 1088-89, and held that "the Constitution does not encompass a general right to nondisclosure of private information." 653 F.2d at 1090. We concluded that no constitutional right was violated by the post-adjudication dissemination of juvenile court records. *Wigginton*, which held that the disclosure of an inmate's HIV status was not unconstitutional, reaffirmed the nonexistence of the right claimed by the plaintiffs here. 21 F.3d at 740. The plaintiffs distinguish these cases by arguing that the information released in each did not implicate fundamental rights. As discussed above, even if a court were someday to recognize adoption-related rights as fundamental, such recognition would not be relevant to this case because the challenged part of the new Tennessee law does not directly regulate when, how, or by whom a child may be adopted.

The plaintiffs assert that the Tennessee Constitution provides broader protection of privacy rights than does the U.S. Constitution. If this is so, plaintiffs present a cogent reason why resort should in all events first be made to Tennessee courts for the resolution of their dispute. . . .

The element of public interest also weighs against enjoining enforcement of the Tennessee statute. The statute appears to be a serious attempt to weigh and balance two frequently conflicting interests: the interest of a child adopted at an early age to know who that child's birth parents were, an interest entitled to a good deal of respect and sympathy, and the interest of birth parents in the protection of the integrity of a sound adoption system. It is an issue of peculiar relevance to the primary police functions of the state as reserved to Tennessee under the Tenth Amendment. *See United States v. Lopez*, 514 U.S. 549 (1995). Another aspect of public interest favoring the defendants' position is the interest of comity between states and federal governments, including the interest of the state in having the first opportunity to construe its own constitution and laws.

We are mindful that even when a plaintiff's probability of success on the merits of a claim is not very high, a preliminary injunction may be appropriate if the plaintiff is in serious danger of irreparable harm absent an injunction. Thus we have observed that the degree of likelihood of success that need be shown to support a preliminary injunction varies inversely with the degree of injury the plaintiff might suffer. *Friendship Materials, Inc. v. Michigan Brick, Inc.*, 679 F.2d 100, 105 (6th Cir. 1982). We are particularly sympathetic to the plight of the Roe birth mother, whose identity may be disclosed imminently to her biological child if the statute is upheld. The likelihood of irreparable harm does not, however, control completely; other factors must still be weighed. Here the plaintiffs' ultimate chance of success on their federal claims is so slim as to be entirely ephemeral. We must observe also that the plaintiffs have always had the opportunity to present their state claims to the Tennessee courts, and if there is any danger of loss in their having failed earlier to pursue that avenue, the cause of it lies in their own hands. . . .

We remand to the district court to dismiss the plaintiffs' complaint with prejudice with respect to the federal constitutional issues but without prejudice to any right to seek relief from the Tennessee courts on the non-federal issues. From respect for the right of a state court system to construe that state's own constitution and adoption statute, we choose not to rule on the merits of the state claims. . . .

NOTES AND QUESTIONS

(1) Does the Tennessee statute adequately protect the interests of birth parents, particularly birth mothers, many of whom were promised life-long anonymity when they surrendered their children for adoption? *See* Carol Chumney, *Tennessee's New Adoption Contact Veto Is Cold Comfort To Birth Parents*, 27 U. Mem. L. Rev. 843 (1997). Should "open records" statutes treat previously-concluded adoptions differently than prospective ones?

(2) Until recently, most state statues requiring the sealing of adoption records provided for the release of identifying information from those records only upon a judicial finding of "good cause." Definitions of "good cause" vary widely. In general, requests for release based on documented medical or psychiatric need are considerably more likely to succeed than claims based on diffuse emotional difficulties or a desire to know one's biological origins. *See* Joan H. Hollinger, *Aftermath of Adoption: Legal and Social Consequences*, in Adoption Law and Practice 13–21 to 13–24 (Joan Heifetz Hollinger, ed., Matthew Bender 1998). In determining whether "good cause" exists, courts typically balance a number of competing factors: 1) the strength of the reasons asserted for disclosure; 2) the circumstances and desires of the adoptive parents; 3) the circumstances and desires of the biological parents; and 4) the interests of the state in maintaining a viable system of adoption. *See,*

e.g., In re Assalone, 512 A.2d 1383, 1390 (R.I. 1986) (concluding that adoptee's curiosity and desire to discover her origins was outweighed by the other competing interests).

By contrast, most states permit the release of "non-identifying information" upon request, without a showing of good cause. *See, e.g.,* Fla. Stat. Ann. § 63.162 (6) (1997); *In re Petition Adoption to Release Records Pursuant to 23 Pa. C.S. 2905,* 653 A.2d 1254, 1256 (Pa. Super. Ct. 1995) (appropriate, under relevant statute, to release as much background information about birth parents as is available in the adoption records, while still maintaining birth parents' anonymity). *See also* § 8.06[C], *below.*

(3) During the 1970s and early 1980s, advocates of open adoption records challenged the traditional sealed records system on a variety of constitutional grounds. They argued that adoptees have a first amendment and substantive due process right to information about their origins, a right essential to their personhood and their capacity to become psychologically stable individuals. Adoptees also urged that they be treated as a suspect or stigmatized class, since they alone were deprived of the right to information about their origins, and that the sealed records statutes be subject to strict scrutiny under the equal protection clause. *See, e.g., Alma Soc'y, Inc. v. Mellon,* 601 F.2d 1225 (2d Cir.), *cert. denied,* 100 S. Ct.531 (1979); *In re Maples,* 563 S.W.2d 760 (Mo. 1978). These constitutional challenges were uniformly unsuccessful; however, they led to legislative reform in a many states.

(4) **Mutual Consent Registries and "Search and Consent" Procedures.** At least 21 states have enacted some form of mutual consent registry, which allows persons directly involved in an adoption to register their willingness to meet and exchange information. *See* Joan H. Hollinger, *Aftermath of Adoption: Legal and Social Consequences,* in 2 Adoption Law and Practice 13-35 (Joan Heifetz Hollinger, ed., Matthew Bender, 1998) The typical mutual consent registry is a passive device. Unless a biological parent and an adult adoptee have both filed a formal consent to the release of identifying information, no information will be released. Thus, the state agency will not seek out biological parents or adoptees who have not registered, to ask if they would be willing to have their identities released. With such a passive system, the parties to an adoption may never learn of the existence of the registry, nor of their option to consent to the release of identifying information. Current mutual consent registries operate only at the individual state level, although Congress is presently considering the creation of a National Mutual Consent Registry. *Id.* at 13-35.

At least 18 states have gone a step further and have enacted "search and consent" procedures, designed more actively to facilitate an exchange of information between adoptive and biological families. Under these statutes, if an adoptee requests birth records, "the state has an affirmative duty to search for the birthparents and request their consent to the release of the records." Bobbi W.Y. Lum, *Privacy v. Secrecy: The Open Adoption Records Movement and its Impact on Hawaii,* 15 U. Haw. L. Rev. 483, 507 (1993). If consent is obtained, the information is released. If consent is denied, or if a birth parent cannot be found, the adoptee may still petition the court to open the records. *See, e.g.,* Md. Code Ann., Fam. Law § 5-314(a) (1998); Minn. Stat. Ann. § 259.89 (West 1998); Intermediaries will also facilitate consensual meetings of adoptees and birth relatives, but are not permitted to arrange nonconsensual meetings.

(5) At least three states—Alaska, Kansas and Vermont—allow adult adoptees access to their original birth certificates upon request, without the necessity of a judicial or

administrative hearing. Alaska Stat. § 18.50.500 (1997); Kan. Stat. Ann. § 65-2423 (1997); 15A Vt. Stat. Ann. § 6-105 (1997). Several other states provide that, for adoptions finalized after the date of a statutory change, an adult adoptee may obtain a copy of his or her original birth certificate, unless a birth parent has filed a denial of consent or a request for nondisclosure. Wash. Rev. Code § 26.33.345 (1997); Minn. Stat. Ann. § 259.89(b) (1998). These states also require that birth parents be given the opportunity to file a nondisclosure form at the time they consent to the adoption. *See Yopp v. Battabove* at § 8.02[A].

(6) **Problem** More than 50 years ago, Mrs. S., then an unmarried college student, consented to the adoption of her infant son. Mrs. S., a life-long resident of New Jersey, is now 75; her son would be 56 if he is still alive. Mrs. S. recently filed a petition seeking release of her son's adoption records. In her petition, Mrs. S. explained that she would like to locate her son, speak to him, tell him she is his biological mother, and perhaps leave her estate to him in her will. The relevant New Jersey statute provides that adoption records shall be sealed and shall be open to inspection only by court order upon a showing of "good cause." Should the court grant Mrs. S's petition? *See In re Adoption of Baby S.*, 705 A.2d 822 (N.J. Super. Ct. Ch. Div. 1998).

(7) **Problem**. The New Jersey legislature is considering whether to revise its traditional, sealed records statute and, if so, how. What legal and policy arguments are likely to be made for and against each of the alternatives discussed in the Notes, above? Which groups are likely to favor which approaches? Which alternative would you vote for and why?

[B] "Open Adoption" and Post-Adoption Visitation

The term "open adoption" is used to refer to a range of information sharing, communication and contact between birth families and adoptive families—prior to, during and after adoption. *See* Marianne Berry, *Risks and Benefits of Open Adoption*, in 3 The Future of Children 125, 126 (1993). While such contact and information sharing before and during the adoption process is no longer unusual, post-adoption contact between adoptive and birth parents is less common and more controversial. The following case explores some of the issues raised by post-adoption visitation.

GROVES v. CLARK
Supreme Court of Montana
920 P.2d 981 (1996)

TRIEWEILER, J.,

On July 24, 1995, Debbie Groves petitioned the District Court for the Eighth Judicial District in Cascade County for specific performance of a visitation agreement that she had entered into with Lonn and Loralee Clark. The Clarks filed an objection to Groves' petition and a brief opposing Groves' request for open adoption. On December 21, 1995, the District Court, by agreement of the parties, deemed the Clarks' objection a motion for summary judgment, concluded that the visitation agreement was void from its inception, and denied Groves' petition for specific performance. Groves appeals the District Court's order. We reverse the order of the District Court and remand the matter to that court for further proceedings in accordance with this opinion. . . .

Debbie Groves is the natural mother of Laci Lee Groves Clark. Laci lived with Groves from June 5, 1990, the date of Laci's birth, until approximately January 28, 1994, when

Groves signed a document relinquishing custody of Laci to Lutheran Social Services (LSS) and consenting to adoption.

Prior to her relinquishment of Laci, Groves had become acquainted with Lonn and Loralee Clark, who had encouraged Groves to permit them to adopt Laci through LSS. At one of their meetings, the Clarks told Groves that they would agree to an "open adoption" so that Groves could have visitation rights with Laci after the adoption. Groves was adamant that she would not consent to adoption until the Clarks signed a visitation agreement.

On January 11, 1994, the Clarks signed a post-adoption visitation agreement, and on January 14 Groves signed a separate but identical agreement. The agreement provided:

This agreement pertains to Debbie's desire to have visitation time with Laci Lee Groves (DOB 6-5-90) after Laci is adopted by Lonn and Loralee Clark.

Debbie desires the following:

1. I hope to be able to give a 2-day notice whenever I'd like have Laci go with me or whenever I'd like to come visit at the Clark home.

2. I would like to have telephone contact with Laci and the Clark's [sic] as often as I feel it is necessary.

3. I don't intend to take Laci out of school unless I have to go to Butte for some emergency. If that happens I do need to take Lacy [sic] with me.

The Clarks signed the agreement in the presence of a notary public. Their signatures followed a provision that read: "We, Lonn and Loralee Clark, are willing to honor Debbie Groves' wishes regarding her requests for contact with Laci Lee Groves." Groves signed an identical notarized agreement three days later.

On January 28, 1994, Groves executed a document entitled "Relinquishment and Consent to Adoption." In that document, Groves relinquished Laci to LSS and granted LSS the right to place Laci for adoption. In addition, Groves expressly waived service of any notice of the proceedings for termination of her parental rights and placement of Laci for adoption, and agreed that LSS' executive director would appear at those proceedings as her attorney-in-fact to execute any documents that may have been required and to complete the placement of Laci in a suitable adoptive home. On February 2, 1994, the Eighth Judicial District Court entered an order awarding custody of Laci to LSS and terminating Groves' custodial and parental rights. After the Clarks filed a petition for adoption on September 23, 1994, that court entered a summary decree of adoption. At no time during the adoption proceedings did the Clarks mention their visitation agreement with Groves. As set forth in the "Relinquishment and Consent to Adoption," Groves did not participate in those proceedings.

Groves and the Clarks abided by the terms of the executed visitation agreement until June 5, 1995. On that date, when Groves telephoned the Clarks to make arrangements to visit Laci on her birthday, the Clarks refused and told Groves she could no longer visit her daughter. Prior to that time, the Clarks had allowed Groves to visit Laci on major holidays and on other occasions.

On July 24, 1995, Groves filed a petition requesting specific performance of her visitation agreement with the Clarks. In response, the Clarks filed an objection to Groves' petition and a brief in opposition to Groves' request for open adoption. The parties agreed that the Clarks' objection could be treated as a motion for summary judgment. The District Court denied Groves' motion for specific performance on December 21, 1995. In its order, the court held that the "Relinquishment and Consent to Adoption" constituted the final, controlling agreement by Groves relating to Laci. Because that document did not reserve any visitation and because that document purported to "terminate all [Groves'] parental rights to [Laci], now and forever," the court concluded that Groves had given up all of her parental rights and had no claim for post-adoption visitation. Based on that conclusion, the court held that the parties' visitation agreement was void and unenforceable.

Did the District Court err when it held that the visitation agreement executed between Groves and the Clarks prior to adoption was void as a matter of law? . . .

The District Court denied Groves' petition for specific performance on the basis of its determination that Groves had voluntarily given up all of her parental rights to Laci in the "Relinquishment and Consent to Adoption" which she signed on January 28, 1994. The court determined that that document constituted "the final agreement by Groves relating to the child," and concluded that its failure to reserve any visitation within its terms accomplished full termination of the relationship between Groves and Laci. In reaching its conclusion, the court relied on § 40-8-125, MCA, and *In re C.P.* (1986), 221 Mont. 180, 717 P.2d 1093.

Section 40-8-125, MCA, provides in relevant part:

> (1) After the final decree of adoption is entered, the relation of parent and child and all the rights, duties, and other legal consequences of the natural relation of child and parent shall thereafter exist between such adopted child and the adoptive parents adopting such child and the kindred of the adoptive parents.
>
> (2) After the final decree of adoption is entered, the natural parents and the kindred of the natural parents of the adopted child, unless they are the adoptive parents or the spouse of an adoptive parent, shall be relieved of all parental responsibilities for said child and have no rights over such adopted child.

In *In re C.P.*, 221 Mont. 181, 717 P.2d 1093, this Court interpreted § 40-8-125, MCA, to preclude visitation rights for the natural parents once a trial court has entered its final decree of adoption. Specifically, we stated: "This language [of § 40-8-125, MCA] is clear. When parental rights are terminated, the natural parent no longer has any rights over the child. This includes visitation rights." 717 P.2d at 1095.

In re C.P. is distinguishable from this case, however. First, in *In re C.P.*, although the parties discussed including visitation rights in the final order, there was no indication in the record that the parties reached any agreement on the issue. In contrast, in this case both parties voluntarily signed a notarized agreement which provided the terms of the visitation arrangement. In addition, the Court recognized in *In re C.P.* that the outcome of that case might have been different had there been a statute that provided for visitation after a final adoption decree and had the parties bargained for the right of visitation. . . . In this case, the parties did bargain for the right of visitation. In fact, Groves alleges that she agreed to termination of her parental rights and consented to place Laci for adoption only after the Clarks agreed to sign the visitation agreement. Furthermore, since our decision in *In re C.P.*, the Montana Legislature has enacted a statutory provision which recognizes agreements entered into between birth parents and prospective adoptive parents relating to the future conduct of the parties and the adoptive child. Specifically, § 40-8-136, MCA, enacted in 1989, provides in relevant part:

(1) Prior to a hearing under 40-8-109, the birth parents, prospective adoptive parents, and their representatives shall file with the court a report of agreements and disbursements, and they shall serve a copy of the report on the central office of the department.

(2) The report must contain:

(a) all oral and written agreements between the parties that relate to *the future conduct of a party with respect to the child.* If an oral agreement is reported, the substance of the agreement must be contained in the report and a copy of the report must be served on each party to the oral agreement. Copies of all written agreements must be attached to the report. (Emphasis added.)

Although § 40-8-136, MCA, does not specifically reference visitation agreements or agreements for continuing contact, that statute does clearly refer to "the future conduct of a party with respect to the child." If, as this Court determined in *In re C.P.*, the termination of parental rights automatically terminates all rights of the natural parents over the child, then the future conduct of the natural parents with respect to the adoptive child would be irrelevant. Such a construction would render § 40-8-136, MCA, meaningless. It is well established that this Court must give meaning and effect to all statutory provisions, and that a construction which renders a provision meaningless is disfavored. We therefore interpret § 40-8-136, MCA, to provide for the recognition of agreements for post-adoption contact and visitation. That does not, however, end our inquiry.

Section 40-8-136, MCA, provides that prior to a district court hearing for the relinquishment of parental rights and adoptive placement, "the birth parents, prospective adoptive parents, and their representatives shall file with the court a report of agreements and disbursements, and they shall serve a copy of the report on the central office of the department." On appeal, the Clarks contend that Groves had a duty to file a report of the visitation agreement with the court and that her failure to do so waives her right to now object. The Clarks have, however, mistakenly interpreted the statute's requirements. Section 40-8-136, MCA, does not place the burden of filing an agreement solely on the birth parent, but rather provides that "the birth parents, prospective parents, and their representatives" share the requirement of filing any such agreement. Furthermore, in this case, Groves had expressly waived her right to participate in the hearing for termination of her rights and adoption of Laci and had appointed LSS' director to act on her behalf. Therefore, it was the duty of both the Clarks, as prospective parents, and the director of LSS, as Groves' representative, to file a report of the executed visitation agreement. Groves should not be penalized for those parties' failure to comply with the requirements of § 40-8-136, MCA. Accordingly, we hold that the failure to file a report of the written visitation agreement does not, of itself, bar Groves' petition for specific performance.

In order to determine the merit of Groves' petition for specific performance, however, we must address a district court's responsibilities once a report of a visitation agreement between the natural parents and prospective adoptive parents has been filed with that court. It is well established that: "It is the policy of the state of Montana to ensure that the best interests of the child are met by adoption proceedings." Section 40-8-114(1), MCA. To that end, "the needs of the child must be the primary focus of adoption proceedings, with full recognition of the interdependent needs and interests of birth parents and adoptive parents." Section 40-8-114(3), MCA. It is therefore essential for a trial court, when it considers a post-adoption visitation agreement, to recognize that that agreement should only be given effect if continued contact between the natural parents and the child is in the child's best interest. If, following a hearing, the district court concludes that such an agreement is in the child's best interest, we conclude that there is no reason that such an agreement should not be enforced by the court.

Our conclusion that natural parents and prospective adoptive parents may contract for post-adoption visitation and that such agreements should be enforced when they are determined to be in the best interest of the child is supported by the case law of other jurisdictions. For example, in *People ex rel. Sibley v. Sheppard* (N.Y. 1981), 429 N.E.2d 1049, 1052–53, the Court of Appeals of New York concluded that the statutory creation of an adoptive family does not automatically require the complete severance of all further contact with former relatives. Similarly, the Maryland Special Court of Appeals held that the adoptive parent and the natural parent may "enter into any agreement with respect to visitation rights between the child and the natural parent so long as the visitation is in the best interest of the child and public policy does not prevent such visitation." *Weinschel v. Strople* (Md. Ct. Spec. App. 1983), 466 A.2d 1301, 1305. Finally, the Connecticut Supreme Court upheld a visitation agreement that was negotiated in good faith in order to promote the best interest of the child and noted:

The plaintiff's rights are not premised on an ongoing genetic relationship that somehow survives a termination of parental rights and an adoption. Instead, the plaintiff is asking us to decide whether, as an adult who has an ongoing personal relationship with the child, she may contract with the adopting parents, prior to adoption, for the continued right to visit with the child, so long as that visitation continues to be in the best interest of the child. . . .

Traditional models of the nuclear family have come, in recent years, to be replaced by various configurations of parents, stepparents, adoptive parents and grandparents. We are not prepared to assume that the welfare of children is best served by a narrow definition of those whom we permit to continue to manifest their deep concern for a child's growth and development.

Michaud v. Wawruck (Conn. 1988), 551 A.2d 738, 740–42 (footnotes and citations omitted).

We conclude that birth parents and prospective adoptive parents are free to contract for post-adoption visitation and that trial courts must give effect to such contracts when continued visitation is in the best interest of the child. We further conclude that Groves was not precluded from filing a petition for specific performance of the parties' visitation agreement solely on the basis of the Clarks' failure to file a report of the agreement with the District Court prior to the adoption proceeding. We therefore hold that the District Court erred when it summarily denied Groves' petition for specific performance without a determination of whether continued visitation is in Laci's best interest. Accordingly, we remand this case to the District Court for a hearing on whether enforcement of the visitation agreement between Groves and the Clarks would be in Laci's best interest.

NOTES AND QUESTIONS

(1) What evidence will be relevant to determining whether enforcement of the parties' visitation agreement would be in Laci's best interest? How significant should it be that the adoptive parents oppose the visitation?

(2) State approaches to post-adoption visitation (often referred to as "open adoption") vary widely. A 1997 law review comment reports that 22 states refuse to recognize such arrangements, even if both parties agree to them. Another eight states allow parties to agree privately to an "open adoption," but will not enforce the agreement through court action. By contrast, at least eight states will enforce such agreements, subject to a best interest finding, if they are included in the adoption decree. The policy in the remaining states is uncertain. Tammy M. Somogye, Comment, *Opening Minds to Open Adoption*, 45 Kan. L. Rev. 619 (1997). Several states, including Montana, have recently enacted "open adoption" statutes that recognize the validity of written agreements between adoptive and birth parents for post-adoption communication or visitation. *See, e.g.*, Wash. Rev. Code Ann. § 26.33.295 (1997); N.M. Stat. Ann. § 12A-5-35 (1998). The 1994 Uniform Adoption Act, by contrast, authorizes judicial enforcement of agreements for post-adoption visitation only in the context of a stepparent adoption. Uniform Adoption Act § 4-112 (1994).

(3) Should a court ever order post-adoption visitation where the parties have not initially agreed to it? Should adoption intermediaries or agency personnel offer "open adoption" as a compromise where a birth parent is unwilling to relinquish parental rights?

(4) **Grandparent Visitation**. Grandparents have been particularly successful in achieving statutory and judicial recognition of their claims for legally enforceable rights to visit their grandchildren. All 50 states now have statutes that allow courts to order visitation by biological grandparents in at least some circumstances. Typically, these statutes allow grandparents to petition for visitation upon the death of their own child, the dissolution of the biological parents' marriage, the termination of the rights of the biological parents or the occurrence of some other disruptive event. Some grandparent visitation statutes expressly include adoption by a stepparent as one of the situations in which grandparents may petition for visitation. *E.g.*, Mich. Comp. Laws Ann. § 722.27b (1997); Tex. Fam. Code Ann. § 153.434 (1998).

In the absence of express statutory authority, courts have taken various approaches to requests by grandparents for post-adoption visitation rights. Courts have been most willing to authorize visitation when the grandparents' own child has died and a stepparent seeks to adopt the grandchild. *See, e.g., In re Adoption No. 92A41*, 622 A.2d 150, 152 (Md. Ct. Spec. App. 1993) (grandparent remains eligible to petition court for visitation after the death of a natural parent and the adoption of the child by a stepparent); *In re Nearhoof*, 359 S.E.2d 587, 591 (W. Va. 1987) (grandparent's court-ordered visitation rights with her deceased daughter's child may continue after stepparent adoption if in the best interests of the child). By contrast, courts have been generally *unwilling* to order grandparent visitation when the adoption involves an infant, or when a non-relative adopts the child after the rights of the biological parents have been terminated. *See, e.g., In re G.D.L.*, 747 P.2d 282, 283 (Okla. 1987) (grandparents have no right to intervene to seek visitation when adoptive parents are not related to child); *J.S. v. F.V. (In re R.D.S.)*, 787 P.2d 968, 970–71 (Wyo. 1990) (alleged visitation agreement between child's grandparents and unrelated adoptive parents is unenforceable and contrary to state policy of severing all ties between child's biological and adoptive families). Courts have also reached different conclusions on whether a grandparent is entitled to notice of—or intervention in—adoption proceedings involving grandchildren with whom they have a developed relationship. *Compare, e.g., In re Adoption of Hess*, 608 A.2d 10, 14 (Pa. 1992) (trial court erred in not permitting grandparents to intervene in adoption proceedings instituted after termination of biological parents' rights) with *Suster v. Arkansas Dep't of Human Servs.*, 858 S.W.2d 122, 124–25 (Ark. 1993) (maternal grandmother lacks standing to intervene in proposed adoption of granddaughter after termination of mother's parental rights).

The 1994 Uniform Adoption Act requires that anyone, including a grandparent, who has an existing order of visitation with a child must receive notice of any proposed adoption of that child. Uniform Adoption Act § 3-401(a)(4) (1994). Such a grandparent would not be able to block the proposed adoption, but could testify about whether the adoption is in the child's best interests. Uniform Adoption Act § 3-401, Comment.

For further discussion of grandparent visitation issues, see Anne Marie Jackson, Comment, *The Coming of Age of Grandparent Visitation Rights*, 43 Am. U. L. Rev. 563 (1994); Peter A. Zabolotsky, *To Grandmother's House We Go: Grandparent Visitation After Stepparent Adoption*, 32 Wayne L. Rev. 1 (1985); Elaine D. Ingulli, *Grandparent Visitation Rights: Social Policies and Legal Rights*, 87 W. Va. L. Rev. 295 (1985).

[C] Disclosure Requirements and "Wrongful Adoption"

MCKINNEY v. STATE
Supreme Court of Washington
950 P.2d 461 (1998)

TALMADGE, J.

In a case with very compelling facts, we must decide if Washington recognizes a cause of action for the negligent failure of an adoption placement agency to disclose statutorily-mandated information about the child to prospective adoptive parents. We hold adoptive parents may state a cause of action against an adoption placement agency for the negligent failure to meet the disclosure requirements of RCW 26.33.350 or RCW 26.33.380. We further hold the status of prospective adoptive parent attaches when the child is eligible for adoption under RCW 26.33, and the persons interested in adopting the child have manifested a formal intent to adopt and the adoption placement agency has formally acknowledged the eligibility of such persons to adopt the child.

In the present case, the trial court properly instructed the jury on the duty of the Department of Social and Health Services (DSHS), the adoption placement agency, to disclose information to the McKinneys, on their status as prospective adoptive parents, and on proximate cause. Substantial evidence supported the jury's determination DSHS was negligent, but such negligence was not a proximate cause of damages to the McKinneys. We affirm the trial court's judgment. . . .

The McKinneys became acquainted with Gabriella (Abby) in 1985 when she was two and a half years old and in foster placement with a friend. For six months to one year, they were Abby's baby-sitters on weekends and when the foster mother was out of town. Through this contact with Abby, the McKinneys knew: Abby had behavior problems including approximately twenty to thirty temper tantrums a day; there were rumors that she had been sexually abused; she was not talking; she did not engage in play like other children her age, nor did she seem to want to jump, climb, or even walk to any length; she was in a special education program; she was receiving speech therapy and physical therapy; she was receiving counseling and treatment at Good Samaritan Mental Health

Center (Vicky McKinney accompanied Abby and the foster mother to at least one of these mental health appointments in 1985); Abby had already been in several foster homes and was removed from the biological mother due to neglect; the biological mother "liked to party"; and Abby was developmentally delayed.

Despite Abby's special needs and troubled history, the McKinneys admitted they fell in love with Abby at first sight, and unilaterally decided to adopt Abby before they ever met a caseworker. On October 25, 1985, the McKinneys applied to Catholic Community Services to become foster parents. Although they had decided to adopt Abby, they indicated on the foster application they had not applied to adopt a child.

Abby was placed in the McKinneys' home as a foster child on August 1, 1986. The McKinneys acknowledge this was a foster placement, for which they received regular monthly foster care payments and a special needs allowance from DSHS for Abby because of her developmental problems. In 1986, Vicky McKinney asked a state caseworker to have Abby's medical records forwarded to the family pediatrician, but the records were not sent.

From the time of Abby's foster placement in the McKinneys' home in 1986, until the McKinneys applied to adopt her in 1989, they gained more knowledge of Abby's background and medical/psychological condition. In 1986, Vicky McKinney indicated to a caseworker she understood Abby's biological mother drank heavily while pregnant with Abby. Vicky McKinney also had a copy of a doctor's letter indicating Fetal Alcohol Syndrome (FAS) was a possibility in Abby's case, and stating Abby may have been born prematurely. In a conversation between Abby's developmental disabilities caseworker and Vicky McKinney, the caseworker expressed her concerns regarding Abby's developmental delays and the fact that "we did not have a clear knowledge of what Abby's needs would be or how long the behaviors would continue." Report of Proceedings at 1779. Responding to the caseworker's concern about the McKinneys' decision to adopt Abby in light of these uncertainties, Vicky McKinney "indicated that they were clear with that decision." Report of Proceedings at 1779.

The parental rights of Abby's birth parents were terminated in November 1987, freeing Abby for adoption.

In 1988, caseworkers discussed with the McKinneys an array of Abby's problems including possible FAS, sexual abuse, and mental retardation. When the McKinneys filed their adoption application for Abby on August 5, 1988, they also applied for an adoption support subsidy, listing Abby's special needs as hyperactivity, learning disability, and alcohol syndrome. On March 21, 1989, the McKinneys' application for an adoption support subsidy for Abby was accepted by DSHS. A preplacement evaluation or "home study" on the McKinneys, as required by RCW 26.33.190, was completed by April 1990.

On January 9, 1990, the McKinneys received the Child's Medical and Family Background Report from DSHS, which noted Abby's developmental delays and her biological mother's history of alcohol abuse. Vicky McKinney spoke with a nurse at the University of Washington's FAS Clinic on March 28, 1990, regarding Abby; the nurse sent her five articles regarding FAS and FAE (Fetal Alcohol Effect), which Vicky McKinney confirmed she read in April 1990. Through a referral from the UW FAS Clinic, the McKinneys took Abby to a FAS specialist for an evaluation. That doctor concluded Abby had possible FAE. Abby was diagnosed as having FAS in December 1993.

Upon completion of a favorable home study, the Pierce County Superior Court entered a formal decree of adoption on June 19, 1990, placing Abby with the McKinneys.

The McKinneys did not receive all the medical and social records on Abby's birth and upbringing until after the formal adoption. After the adoption, the McKinneys requested and received Madigan Army Medical Center birth records concerning Abby's premature birth. In April 1992, the McKinneys requested and received DSHS's records concerning Abby, which indicated there were questions as early as 1984 that Abby's problems might be attributable to her birth mother's alcohol abuse. Other theories for Abby's problems, such as Downs Syndrome, were also considered in the records. As early as 1984, DSHS records also contained police reports and medical records indicating Abby may have been sexually abused.

The McKinneys filed this action against DSHS in November 1993, alleging negligence, violation of 42 U.S.C. sec. 1983, and outrage. An amended complaint added causes of action for fraud and breach of contract. The breach of contract claims were dismissed on summary judgment. The fraud claims were dismissed on DSHS's motion at the close of plaintiff's case. The case went to the jury only on the McKinneys' negligence claims.

In conjunction with pretrial motions, the trial court decided the issue of when the McKinneys became prospective adoptive parents. The State argued such status attached only when the McKinneys formally petitioned to adopt and the home study on them was completed. The McKinneys contended the appropriate date was August 1, 1986, the date Abby was first placed in their home. The trial court ruled that when the McKinneys' written application to adopt and request for adoption support assistance was approved by DSHS on March 21, 1989, they became prospective adopting parents, and later so instructed the jury. The jury returned a defense verdict after a month-long trial, finding DSHS negligent, but such negligence was not the proximate cause of damages to the McKinneys. Both parties appealed and we granted direct review. RAP 4.2(a).

ANALYSIS

A. Negligent Failure of an Adoption Agency to Disclose Information on a Child to Prospective Adoptive Parents

The McKinneys assert had they known the truth about Abby's developmental and other problems they would not have taken her into their home or adopted her. They claim DSHS's negligent failure to disclose medical and other background information about Abby affected their adoption decision.

The State argues the trial court's recognition of a wrongful adoption claim based on negligence is unprecedented and only causes of action for fraud and intentional misrepresentation in failing to disclose pertinent information about an adoptive child have been recognized in other jurisdictions. The State further contends public policy concerns weigh against creating a cause of action for wrongful adoption based on negligence because adoption agencies should not be required to guarantee the health of the children they place or have the burdensome duty to discover and disclose all health information regarding the child.

The trial court determined the McKinneys' negligence claims survived the State's motions for summary judgment and directed verdict or judgment as a matter of law under CR 50 because a claim for negligent adoption placement, including negligent failure to investigate, locate or disclose information, may be made under RCW 26.33.350. The court ultimately instructed the jury on both RCW 26.33.350 and.380.

Under the current versions of RCW 26.33.350 and.380, DSHS has a duty to timely provide medical and social information regarding the child and the child's birth parents to prospective adoptive parents. The current version of each statute requires a placement agency to make reasonable efforts to obtain background information described in the statute and disclose such information to prospective adoptive parents, but the agency has no further duty to explain or interpret such information. See RCW 26.33.350(4) and.380(2).

We believe the Legislature has established the duty owed by adoption placement agencies in RCW 26.33.350 (medical/psychological history) and RCW 26.33.380 (social history). The negligent failure of an adoption placement agency to comply with the statutory disclosure mandate to prospective adoptive parents may result in liability. The scope of the agency's duty is appropriately drawn in those disclosure statutes. . . .

Similarly, in *Gibbs v. Ernst*, 538 Pa. 193, 647 A.2d 882 (1994), the Pennsylvania Supreme Court recognized a cause of action for negligent failure to disclose information based on statutory obligations comparable to those imposed by the Washington statutes. The court found Pennsylvania's disclosure statute, which requires an adoption agency to obtain medical history on adoptees and to "deliver such information to the adopting parents or their physician" created a duty to reveal all available nonidentifying information about a child. *Gibbs*, 647 A.2d at 892. The *Gibbs* Court found this duty to be consistent with the intent of the Pennsylvania legislature and recognition of a cause of action based on statute was also consistent with long-standing common law principles. *Id.*

Aside from the statutory imperative, there are strong public policy grounds for establishing a cause of action for prospective adoptive parents against adoption placement agencies that negligently fail to disclose pertinent information about the child. The *Gibbs* court found the unique relationship of trust and confidence between the agency and the prospective parents supports a disclosure duty:

> Even were the statutory foundation for the assignment to adoption intermediaries of a duty to disclose less persuasive, we find that the unique relationship between the adoption agency and the prospective parents gives rise to such a responsibility. . . .
>
> The adoption agency—adopting parent connection is, or should be, one of trust and confidence, differing significantly from a business arrangement in which two parties to a transaction may maintain silence in order to negotiate the stronger position, and are under no obligation to divulge information which may weaken that position. . . . Rather, this relationship is a singular one in that the parties act not as adversaries, but in concert to achieve a result desired by both sides, the creation of a viable family unit. . . . We thus conclude that a duty to disclose is created by this unique association.

Id. at 892-93 (citations omitted). The special relationship between adoption placement agencies and adopting parents argues strongly for recognition of a cause of action in tort. *Cf., Harbeson v. Parke-Davis, Inc.*, 98 Wash. 2d 460, 467, 656 P.2d 483 (1983) (tort of wrongful birth sounding in negligence recognized because the action conforms comfortably to the structure of tort principles and is a logical and necessary development).

In *Mohr v. Commonwealth*, 653 N.E.2d 1104, 1113 (1995), the Supreme Judicial Court of Massachusetts recognized claims for negligent, as well as intentional, failure to disclose information based on a statutory disclosure duty. The Court concluded public policy ultimately favors recognizing liability for an adoption agency's material misrepresentations of fact regarding the child's history prior to adoption. *See Mohr*, 653 N.E.2d at 1111-13. Recognizing representative cases in which courts had limited liability to claims involving intentional conduct, the *Mohr* court noted:

> Other courts, however, have held that, . . . public policy also supports recognizing the tort of negligent misrepresentation in the adoption context. These courts have emphasized "the compelling need of adoptive parents for full disclosure of medical background information that may be known to the agency on both the child they may adopt and the child's genetic parents, not only to secure timely and appropriate medical care for the child, but also to make vital personal, health and family decisions." This need . . . outweighs any increased burden that is placed on adoption agencies when liability is imposed for negligent as well as intentional misrepresentation. In addition, these courts have maintained that allowing negligent misrepresentation claims against adoption agencies does not subject agencies to potentially limitless liability or make them guarantors of adopted children's health . . .
>
> . . . . We agree.

Id. at 1111-12 (emphasis added, citations omitted).

In *Mallette v. Children's Friend and Serv.*, 661 A.2d 67, 73 (R.I. 1995), the Rhode Island Supreme Court recognized a claim for negligent misrepresentation despite the fact Rhode Island had no statutory duty to disclose, declaring:

> the need for accurate disclosure becomes more acute when special-needs children are involved. Parents need to be financially and emotionally equipped to provide an atmosphere that is optimally conducive to that special child's growth and development.
>
> Although biological parents can assess the risks of having a child by investigating their own genetic backgrounds, adopting parents remain at the mercy of adoption agencies for information. . . . We believe extending the tort of negligent representation to the adoption context will help alleviate some of the artificial uncertainty imposed on a situation inherent with uncertainty.

We are mindful of the concern a broad duty of disclosure could impose an excessive burden on adoption placement agencies who are exerting their best efforts to place children with loving adoptive parents. This concern is particularly acute for special needs children like Abby. But we believe the Legislature understood this concern in limiting the scope of disclosure and confining agency investigative efforts to reasonable efforts in both RCW 26.33.350 and .380. We agree with the *Gibbs* Court when it stated:

> We find that the creation of a duty in this instance will further the interests of parents by providing them with as much factual and valid information as possible about the child they are to adopt without placing an undue burden on adoption agencies, as they are required only to make reasonable efforts to disclose fully and accurately the medical history they have already obtained. Only where adoption intermediaries disclose information negligently will they be liable. Thus, the only burden on adoption intermediaries is the obligation to make a reasonable investigation of their records, and to make reasonable efforts to reveal fully and accurately all non-identifying information in their possession to the adopting parents. We do not believe that this

responsibility constitutes an undue burden in light of the important interests served by its performance. 647 A.2d at 893.

We hold the negligent failure of an adoption placement agency to disclose the information required by RCW 26.33.350 or .380 to prospective adoptive parents is actionable. Disclosure of a child's medical/psychological and familial background will not only enable Washington's adoptive parents to obtain timely and appropriate medical care for the child, but it will also enable them to make an intelligent and informed adoption decision.

. . . .

C. The Jury's Verdict

The final issue is whether the jury's verdict was correct. The McKinneys assert they would not have adopted Abby had DSHS not negligently withheld information regarding her developmental and other problems. DSHS has not challenged the jury's finding of negligence, but argues the jury verdict on proximate cause was proper.

The issues regarding proximate cause are fact-responsive: what did the McKinneys know about Abby's problems, when did they know it, and what was the effect of such knowledge on their decision to adopt Abby? In light of our ruling on prospective adoptive parent status for the McKinneys as stated in Instruction 16, we review the jury's decision only to determine if substantial evidence supports it.

Substantial evidence at trial supports the jury's verdict on proximate cause. The McKinneys indicated at trial they had frequent contact with Abby for six months to a year in 1985 baby-sitting for Abby's foster mother. During this time, the McKinneys gained first-hand knowledge of the extensive developmental and behavioral problems plaguing Abby, and became aware Abby was in therapy regarding these problems. During this time, the McKinneys also became aware of rumors Abby had been sexually abused. With this knowledge, the McKinneys decided to adopt Abby before talking with anyone at DSHS.

Between the time Abby was placed with them in August 1986 and March 21, 1989, the McKinneys became progressively aware of Abby's special needs associated with FAS/FAE and other developmental problems. The McKinneys received an additional rate of reimbursement as foster parents for Abby's special needs and later became eligible for an adoption subsidy because of Abby's special needs. The receipt of these additional public funds for Abby's special needs was a particularly significant demonstration that the McKinneys were cognizant of Abby's problems.

The evidence presented at trial indicates the McKinneys already possessed knowledge of most of Abby's problems, which disclosure by DSHS would only have confirmed. Thus, forewarned, the McKinneys decided to adopt Abby in 1985. Additional information gained while Abby lived with the McKinneys as a foster child did not deter the McKinneys from their goal of adopting this troubled child. Given what the McKinneys knew, when they knew it, and their decision to adopt Abby anyway, the jury reasonably concluded any subsequent failure by DSHS to disclose information played no role in the McKinneys' decision to adopt Abby. The jury verdict on proximate cause was supported by substantial evidence.

CONCLUSION

In this very difficult case, we are sensitive to the many competing interests associated with Abby's adoption. The McKinneys, to their lasting credit, fell in love with a child affected by substantial developmental and behavioral problems and a very difficult life history. They, and parents like them, are entitled to the information described in RCW 26.33.350 and .380 before making their decision to adopt.

Adoption placement agencies, whether individuals, DSHS, or private agencies, must give prospective adoptive parents needed information about children so the prospective parents can make a wise decision so fundamentally important to them and their adoptive child. The burden of disclosure must not be such that adoptions will be "chilled" by the specter of litigation; placement agencies are not guarantors the adoptive children will have no physical or psychological special needs, or their familial histories are picture perfect. They must only make reasonable efforts to disclose the statutorily-prescribed medical/ psychological and social information on adoptive children.

The trial court's recognition of a cause of action for negligent failure to disclose medical and social information required by RCW 26.33.350 and .380, and its ruling as to when prospective adoptive parent status attaches were correct. Substantial evidence supported the jury's verdict on proximate cause. We affirm the judgment on the verdict of the jury.

NOTES AND QUESTIONS

(1) The decision in *McKinney* is representative of a number of recent appellate cases recognizing a tort cause of action for "wrongful adoption," based on an agency's failure to provide full or accurate family or medical information about a child placed for adoption. While early "wrongful adoption" cases generally involved intentional agency misrepresentations, *e.g., Burr v. Board of County Commissioners*, 491 N.E.2d 1101 (Ohio 1986), more recent cases also allow recovery for negligent misrepresentation and negligent failure to disclose information. *See, e.g., Jackson v. State*, 956 P.2d 35 (Mont. 1998); *M.H. v. Caritas Family Servs.*, 488 N.W.2d 282 (Minn. 1992).

Several commentators have urged a further expansion of liability to include negligent failure to investigate the background of a potential adoptee. *See, e.g.*, D. Marianne Brower Blair, *Liability of Adoption Agencies and Attorneys for Misconduct in the Disclosure of Health-Related Information*, in Adoption Law and Practice 16-55 (Joan Heifeiz Hollinger, ed., Matthew Bender 1998) ("Extending liability for negligent failure to investigate prevents intermediaries from taking the approach of 'see no evil, hear no evil, say no evil.' "); Note, *When Love is Not Enough: Toward a Unified Wrongful Adoption Tort*, 105 Harv. L. Rev. 1761, 1773 (1992) ("Without an additional duty to take reasonable measures to investigate the adoptee's past, the growth of the tort of wrongful adoption, as presently conceived, will hurt—and not help—the cause of adopting parents."). *But cf.* Fran Pfeifer Pero. Note, *In the Best Interests of the Child: Litigation in the Post-Placement Adoption Setting*, 11 N.Y.L. Sch. J. Hum. Rts. 383, 395 (1994) (arguing that "avoiding litigation which involves the adopted child is legally sound and superior to the remedies of annulment and wrongful adoption."). What are the most compelling policy arguments for and against imposing liability for an agency's negligent failure to investigate?

(2) If the McKinneys had prevailed on their negligence claim, what would have been the appropriate measure of damages? In particular, should the Jacksons be able to recover *all* the costs associated with raising a child, or should their damages be limited to the

extraordinary financial expenses associated with Abby's medical and psychological problems? Should the McKinneys be entitled to compensation for the emotional costs associated with Abby's adoption? *See generally* D. Marianne Brower Blair, *Liability of Adoption Agencies and Attorneys for Misconduct in the Disclosure of Health-Related Information*, in Adoption Law and Practice 16–136 to 16–139 (1997) (discussing the "limited treatment" that has been given to questions of damages in wrongful adoption cases); John R. Maley, Note, *Wrongful Adoption: Monetary Damages as a Superior Remedy to Annulment of Adoptive Parents Victimized by Adoption Fraud*, 20 Ind. L. Rev. 709 (1987) (noting that in the arguably analogous context of wrongful birth claims, some courts have compensated for the ordinary costs of raising a child, reduced by the amount of benefit—the joy of raising a child).

(3) Should an adoption agency's deliberate or negligent misrepresentation ever provide grounds for undoing, or abrogating an adoption? Why or why not? *See generally* Elizabeth N. Carroll, *Abrogation of Adoption by Adoptive Parents*, 19 Fam. L.Q. 155 (1985); Ann Harlan Howard, Note, *Annulment of Adoption Decrees on Petition of Adoptive Parents*, 22 J. Fam. L. 549 (1984). *See also* Danielle Saba Donner, *The Emerging Adoption Market: Child Welfare Agencies, Private Middlemen, and "Consumer" Remedies*, 35 J. Fam. L. 473, 512 (1997) (noting that while damages actions have largely replaced abrogation as a remedy for agency misconduct, "[a] string of cases well into the 1960's also treated the adoptive relationship as contractual and, therefore, inherently subject to rescission when one party failed to fulfill his or her side of the bargain.").

(4) **Statutory disclosure requirements**. As the decision in *McKinney* suggests, a number of states have recently enacted statutes that require adoption agencies to disclose to prospective adoptive parents a wide range of medical and social information regarding the child and the child's birth parents. D. Marianne Brower Blair, *above*, at 16-51 ("Between 1980 and 1995, the vast majority of states adopted statutes that mandate that some health information be provided to adoptive parents."). The 1994 Uniform Adoption Act extends these disclosure requirements. Section 2-106 of the Act requires any person who places a minor for adoption to furnish to prospective adoptive parents all "reasonably available" information regarding a minor's medical, genetic, psychological and social history, including relevant information concerning the medical, psychological and social history of the minor's parents and relatives. In addition to imposing civil penalties for an agency's intentional failure to provide this information, the Act authorizes adoptive parents to "maintain an action for damages or equitable relief against a person who fails to perform [these] statutory duties." Uniform Adoption Act § 7-105 (1994). The Comments to the Act make clear that the obligation to provide "reasonably available" background information "is intended to create a statutory duty to use reasonable efforts to obtain the information," as well as to disclose information already in the agency's possession. Uniform Adoption Act § 7-105, Comment. The Commentary characterizes these disclosure requirements as "one of the most significant contributions of the Act to the improvement of contemporary adoption practice;" it also asserts that "better access to adoptee's health and social histories will stem the rising tide of the dozens, and perhaps hundreds, of lawsuits brought within the past few years by adoptive parents on behalf of themselves and their adopted children seeking monetary damages against agencies for failures to disclose essential information." Uniform Adoption Act § 2-106, Comment.

Query: Do you agree that these statutory disclosure requirements are likely to *decrease* the number of lawsuits filed by adoptive parents? Why or why not? For a detailed discussion of the Uniform Act's disclosure requirements, see D. Marianne Brower Blair, *The Uniform Adoption Act's Health Disclosure Provisions: A Model That Should Not Be Overlooked*, 30 Fam. L.Q. 427 (1996).

(5) **Disclosure and Privacy**. To what extent do disclosure obligations such as those imposed by *McKinney* or the Uniform Adoption Act raise legitimate privacy concerns? Should a birth parent who places a child for adoption be required to divulge otherwise confidential medical and/or psychological records? Why or why not? Does the inclusion of genetic or hereditary information among the categories of information to be disclosed raise particular privacy concerns? For example, could a birth parent be required to undergo predictive genetic testing in order to provide prospective adoptive parents with information about a minor child's "hereditary predisposition to disease"? Uniform Adoption Act § 2-106(a)(2) (1994). For a discussion of some of these privacy issues, see D. Marianne Brower Blair, *Lifting the Genealogical Veil, A Blueprint for Legislative Reform of the Disclosure of Health Related Information in Adoption*, 70 N.C. L. Rev. 681 (1992). *See also* Sonia M. Suter, Note, *Whose Genes Are These Anyway?: Familial Conflicts over Access to Genetic Information*, 91 Mich. L. Rev. 1854 (1993); Demosthenes A. Lorandos, *Secrecy and Genetics in Adoption Law and Practice*, 27 Loy. U. Chi. L.J. 277 (1996).

(6) **Disclosure in Direct Placement Adoptions**. To what extent should the investigation and disclosure requirements applicable to public and private adoption agencies apply as well to attorneys and other individuals who act as intermediaries in direct, or private placement adoptions?

(7) **Wrongful Adoption as a "Consumer Remedy?"** At least one commentator has suggested that the expansion of liability for "wrongful adoption" is indicative of a shift toward a "market" or contractual approach to adoption, which threatens to replace the adoption agency's historical focus on the needs of children awaiting adoption with an emphasis on adoption as a "consumer transaction" between the agency and the adoptive parents. *See* Donner, *above* at 510–535. To what extent are these concerns justified?

CHAPTER 9

DIVORCE OR DISSOLUTION OF MARRIAGE

SYNOPSIS

§ 9.01 Introduction
    [A] Historical Background
    [B] Historical Fault Grounds for Divorce and the No-Fault Revolution
    [C] Current Divorce Statistics and Concerns

§ 9.02 Divorce Jurisdiction
    [A] The Domiciliary Requirement
    [B] Migratory Divorces
        [1] Sister State Migratory Divorces
        [2] Foreign Country Migratory Divorces
    [C] Collateral Attack on a Void Divorce
    [D] The Divisible Divorce Doctrine

§ 9.03 Divorce Grounds and Defenses
    [A] Fault Grounds for Divorce
        [1] Overview
        [2] Adultery, Cruelty, and Desertion
    [B] No-Fault Divorce Grounds
        [1] Living Separate and Apart
        [2] Irreconcilable Differences

§ 9.04 The Relevance—If Any—of Fault Factors in No-Fault Divorces
    [A] Arguments for Rejecting Fault Factors in No-Fault Divorces
    [B] Arguments for Retaining Fault Factors in No-Fault Divorces
    [C] Can Nonfinancial Factors Viably Coexist With Financial Factors in Determining Financial Issues in Divorce?
    [D] Problem

§ 9.05 Ethical Issues for the Family Lawyer
    [A] Dual Representation in Divorce Proceedings: Is It Ethical?
    [B] Problems With Confidential Information
    [C] Sexual Relations With a Divorce Client
    [D] Candor Toward the Court and Withdrawal from the Case

§ 9.06 Representing Children

§ 9.07 Alternative Dispute Resolution

[A] Divorce Mediation
    [1] Overview and Current Status
    [2] Concerns About Mediation
[B] Binding Arbitration

§ 9.01 Introduction

[A] Historical Background

Divorce, also called dissolution of marriage in a number of states, is the legal termination of a valid marriage. Marriage may have "more to do with the morals and civilization of a people than any other institution" according to *Maynard v. Hill*, 125 U.S. 190, 205 (1888), but marriage as a form of social organization and regulation also has involved complex laws and customs for the dissolution of marriage as well, including the legal status of divorced spouses, spousal and child support, the division of marital property, and the custody of children.

In early Hebrew, Greek, and Roman societies the right of divorce belonged only to the husband, who could repudiate and divorce his wife for no reason. However, during the Punic Wars when many Roman men were absent for long periods of time, or died in battle fighting the Carthaginians, Roman women emerged as a wealthy independent class, and shortly thereafter both husbands and wives could divorce at will. During this time, marriages for limited and temporary purposes were common; many were entered into solely for economic or political purposes; and the Roman divorce epidemic reached alarming proportions. Accordingly, in 18 B.C. Caesar Augustus attempted to restrict divorce in the Roman Empire by enacting the Lex Julia de Adulteris, which made adultery a crime and required a divorcing party to execute a written statement renouncing the marriage. Another characteristic of a Roman divorce after the Punic Wars was a mandatory property settlement agreement, which required a husband who divorced his wife on minor grounds, or was at fault himself, to return his wife's dowry and other antenuptial property, which had a chilling effect on husbands of wealthy wives, and vice versa. On divorce, the husband was normally awarded custody of the children.

In England, a rather informal Anglo-Saxon custom of bride purchase, coupled with the husband's sole right of divorce, was later replaced by the strong influence of medieval Church doctrine, which was a dominant force in the establishment of European and early American divorce law as well. Under the doctrine of the Roman Catholic Church and its ecclesiastical courts—and later under the doctrine of the Church of England—marriage was regarded as a holy sacrament and an indissoluble bond. *See, e.g.*, Luke 16:18 and Matthew 19:3–9: "What therefore God hath joined together, let no man put asunder." Thus, there was no such thing as an absolute divorce under ecclesiastical canon law, although certain parties might have their marriage annulled based upon a serious marital impediment; or they might also petition for a permanent separation, called a divorce *a mensa et thoro*, although neither party could thereafter remarry during the lifetime of their spouse.

Activists during the Protestant Reformation rebelled against many perceived abuses and inconsistencies of divorce law doctrine under the canon law and its ecclesiastical courts, and they argued that marriage and divorce should be regulated by secular legislative authority courts of equity, rather than by the Church. They also argued that absolute divorce *a vinculo matrimonii* should be granted based upon specified marital fault grounds, including adultery, cruelty, and desertion, as well as recognizing the traditional divorce *a mensa et thoro* or legal separation. Influenced by these Protestant reformers, the American colonies refused to adopt an ecclesiastical court system and provided that absolute divorce could be granted by the colonial legislatures (primarily in the New England colonies) or through courts of equity (primarily in the southern and middle colonies.). According to Barbara Defoe Whitehead, *The Divorce Culture* 13-20 (1997):

> Compared with other Western societies, Americans have a strong tradition of divorce. To some degree, that tradition was shaped by the experience of political rebellion. New England colonists saw the highly restrictive and cumbersome procedures of English divorce law and practice as a sign of the Crown's illegitimate authority, which they sought to defy by liberalizing colonial divorce practice. This tradition also had roots in religious dissent. . . .
>
> In general, the early liberalizing of English legal tradition focused on two areas. For one, colonists treated marital dissolutions as a civil rather than a church matter, shifting authority over divorce from the ecclesiastical courts to legislative or judicial bodies. For another, New England colonists broadened the grounds for divorce beyond those permitted in England. . . .

Today each state in the United States regulates the divorce grounds and procedure of its domiciliaries through legislation, providing that designated state courts shall act as the forum for any divorce proceeding. *See generally* Green, Long & Muraski, Dissolution of Marriage 4–53 (1986); 1 Homer H. Clark, Jr., Law of Domestic Relations 693–703 (2d ed. 1987); and Gregory, Swisher, & Scheible, Understanding Family Law §§ 7.01–.04 (1995).

[B] Historical Fault Grounds for Divorce and the No-Fault Revolution

As societies evolved, many required a party petitioning for a divorce to prove that his or her spouse was legally "at fault" and therefore responsible for the divorce. Divorce became established as the traditional remedy for an innocent person whose spouse had been guilty of a serious marital wrong. The public policy of the state, through its statutory regulation of marriage and divorce, was thus to encourage marriage and to discourage divorce in the absence of a serious marital fault. For example, in *Jacobs v. Jacobs*, 35 S.E.2d 119 (Va. 1945), the Virginia Supreme Court, citing a rationale followed by almost all state courts of that era, declared that it could not guarantee a happy marriage nor cancel any errors of judgment, absent a serious statutory marital breach. Such traditional fault grounds for divorce included adultery, cruelty, and desertion. Additional statutory grounds for divorce, adopted by various states, also included insanity, conviction of a crime, and habitual drunkenness or drug addiction.

Traditionally, divorce itself was looked upon as an evil, to be tolerated only in those circumstances which strictly met state statutory standards. But as a result of these very strict divorce requirements, many parties involved in unhappy marriages would attempt to fabricate an enumerated "fault" ground, often with the assistance of their legal counsel, or obtain a questionable migratory divorce in another jurisdiction with more liberal divorce laws. *See, e.g.*, Nelson Blake, *The Road to Reno: A History of Divorce in the United States*

(1962). Under these circumstances, violation, avoidance, and open disrespect of state divorce law grew, and the general reputation of many "divorce lawyers" suffered accordingly. Something had to be done to alleviate this very serious problem.

Many lawyers, clients, sociologists, and legislators had long been dissatisfied with these perceived defects in the fault-based divorce system in America, and argued that divorce should be viewed as a regrettable, but necessary, legal definition of a marital failure. Thus it was recognized that very often the factors leading to a marriage breakdown were not all one-sided, resulting from the enumerated "fault" of one "guilty" spouse, but were often based on the incompatibility or irreconcilable differences of both spouses. Strict divorce laws, in reality, were having little effect on the social norms and stresses of modern-day Americans who were getting divorced in dramatically increasing numbers. *See* Max Rheinstein, *The Law of Divorce and the Problem of Marriage Stability*, 9 Vand. L. Rev. 633 (1956); Max Rheinstein, Marriage Stability, Divorce, and the Law (1972). Accordingly, the no-fault divorce revolution finally surfaced in America when a 1966 California Governor's Commission issued a recommendation that an "irremediable breakdown" of the marriage and insanity be the sole grounds for divorce in that state, and in 1969 this recommendation became law in California. *See* Wadlington, *Divorce Without Fault Without Perjury*, 52 Va. L. Rev. 32 (1966); Tenny, *Divorce Without Fault: The Next Step*, 46 Neb. L. Rev. 24 (1967).

In August 1970 The Uniform Marriage and Divorce Act (UMDA), 9A U.L.A. 147 *et seq.*, was proposed by the National Conference of Commissioners on Uniform State Laws, proposing that an irretrievable breakdown of marriage should be the sole ground for divorce. In 1974 the American Bar Association approved the UMDA and recommended its passage by the states. Section 302 of the UMDA currently provides that the court shall enter a dissolution of marriage when the court finds the marriage is "irretrievably broken"; or if the parties have lived separate and apart for more than 180 days preceding the commencement of the suit; or if there is "serious marital discord" adversely affecting the attitude of one, or both, of the parties toward the marriage.

To date, approximately 20 states have adopted a "pure" or "true" no-fault divorce regime where fault factors no longer play any significant role in determining divorce grounds and defenses, nor do fault factors play any significant role in determining spousal support awards or the equitable distribution of marital property on divorce. Ira Ellman, *The Place of Fault in Modern Divorce Law*, 28 Ariz. St. L.J. 773, 771 (1996) (listing 20 "complete no-fault states"); Linda Elrod & Robert Spector, *A Review of the Year in Family Law*, 30 Fam. L.Q. 765, 807 (1997) (listing 18 "true" no-fault states). Approximately 20 other states provide for irreconcilable differences or irretrievable breakdown of the marriage in addition to traditional fault-based divorce grounds. The remaining 10 states provide for a no-fault-type divorce based upon living separate and apart for a stated period of time, in addition to traditional fault-based grounds. Thus, all American jurisdictions now have enacted some form of no-fault divorce, but it is also important to note that many states still recognize some fault-based alternative grounds for divorce, as well as recognizing various fault factors which may affect spousal support awards on divorce, the equitable division of marital property on divorce, or both. Elrod & Spector, *above.*

[C] Current Divorce Statistics and Concerns

Divorce, once a relatively rare event in America, has now become commonplace. According to the U.S. Bureau of the Census, divorces in America from 1970 through 1980 rose from less than half a million divorces each year to over one million divorces each year, a figure that has remained fairly constant throughout the 1980s and 1990s. *See* Laura Gatland, *Putting the Blame on No-Fault*, 83 A.B.A. J. 50, 51 (April 1997), and researchers estimate that approximately 50 percent of all married American men and women will divorce. This continuing high divorce rate "may well be the most dramatic change in family life in twentieth-century America." T. Arendell, Mothers and Divorce: Legal, Economic, and Social Dilemmas 1 (1986).

The U.S. Department of Labor survey for 1995-1996 discloses that nearly 54% of American mothers with children under three years old work outside the home. This has caused an additional strain on both marriage and child rearing that many families never faced a generation ago. Accordingly, approximately sixty% of children being born may expect at one time or another to live in a single-parent family, and 9 in 10 single-parent families are headed by women. *Chicago Tribune*, 6–N (August 21, 1988). According to Justice Neely of the West Virginia Supreme Court, "Approximately half of all the civil cases heard in the major state courts involve domestic matters, and if current trends continue, roughly three out of every five marriages begun in the 1980's will end in divorce. It is not surprising, therefore, that a state civil court's most important function, at least with respect to the number of lives touched, is in the resolution of family matters." R. Neely, The Divorce Decision: The Legal and Human Consequences of Ending a Marriage 1 (1984).

With no-fault divorce now available in all states, divorce litigation has largely shifted from moral to economic issues (the division of marital property, child and spousal support) and child-custody determinations. Increasingly, the larger law firms are becoming more involved in family law practice with their wealthy clients. *See* Diamond, "Big Firms Get in on Divorce Action" 74 A.B.A. J. 60 (August 1988), where one attorney was quoted as stating that "divorce has become the equivalent of a partnership dissolution. . . . Big firms want to be involved in this type of action. We have 40 lawyers, seven of whom are involved in matrimonial law. We use other departments, such as corporate and tax, to figure out the value of the marital estate, property, and so forth." *Id.* at 62. However, the vast majority of Americans who are in the process of a divorce are not as affluent, and some recent commentators have criticized the negative effects of no-fault divorce legislation, economic and otherwise, on Americans of modest means.

Sociologist Lenore Weitzman, for example, has documented the severe economic impact of no-fault divorce in her book The Divorce Revolution: The Unexpected Social and Economic Consequences for Women and Children in America (1985). Although the accuracy of Professor Weitzman's statistical studies have been recently questioned, other studies like Professor James McLindon's *Separate But Unequal: The Economic Disaster of Divorce for Women and Children*, 21 Fam. L.Q. 351 (1987) also have corroborated this "feminization of poverty" resulting from divorce. Thus, according to 1996 data from the Social Science Research Council in New York City, a woman's standard of living declines 30% on average the first year after divorce, while a man's standard of living on divorce rises by 10%. Elizabeth Gleick, *Hell Hath No Fury*, Time, Oct. 7, 1996, at 84.

Two-thirds of all divorces involve minor children, and according to Columbia law professor Martha Fineman, author of *The Illusion of Equality*, the average annual child support payment is only around $3,000. "Equality is being applied with a vengeance against women," she says. Ultimately, the average household income for children of divorce drops thirty percent, while the poverty rate for children living with single mothers is five times as high as for those in intact families. *Id.*

A number of articles also have analyzed the negative impact of no-fault divorce on children, and some commentators have challenged the wisdom of no-fault grounds which do not include a significant waiting period prior to divorce, since divorces may have long-term psychologically damaging effects on the children. *See* Robert Cochran, Jr., and & Paul Vitz, *Child Protective Divorce Laws: A Response to the Effects of Parental Separation on Children*, 17 Fam. L.Q. 327 (1983). *See also* Elizabeth Scott, *Rational Decision-Making About Marriage and Divorce*, 76 Va. L. Rev. 9, 29 (1990) ("There is substantial evidence that the process of going through their parents' divorce and resulting changes in their lives are psychologically costly for most children"). Indeed, some commentators have concluded that the no-fault divorce revolution in America "has failed." *See, e.g.,* Council on Families in America, *Marriage in America: A Report to the Nation* (1995).

> The divorce revolution—the steady displacement of a marriage culture by a culture of divorce and unwed parenthood—has failed. It has created terrible hardships for children, incurred unsupportable social costs, and failed to deliver on its promise of greater adult happiness. The time has come to shift the focus of national attention from divorce to marriage and to rebuild a family culture based on enduring marital relationships.

All this is not to say that the no-fault revolution has run its course: the American Law Institute has proposed a financially based Principles of the Law of Family Dissolution: Analysis and Recommendations (Proposed Final Draft 1997) that argues for the total abolition of all fault-based factors in marital dissolution or divorce. Some recent commentators, on the other hand, have argued that fault factors in divorce may still serve a legitimate function in contemporary society. *See, e.g.* Barbara Bennett Woodhouse, *Sex, Lies, and Dissipation: The Discourse of Fault in a No-Fault Era*, 82 Geo. L.J. 2525 (1994); Jana Singer, *Husbands, Wives, and Human Capital: Why the Shoe Won't Fit*, 31 Fam. L.Q. 119 (1997); Peter Nash Swisher, *Reassessing Fault Factors in No-Fault Divorce*, 31 Fam. L.Q. 269 (1997). *See generally* J. Herbie DiFonzo, Beneath the Fault Line: The Popular and Legal Culture of Divorce in Twentieth Century America (1997) and § 9.04, *below*.

In summary, the No–Fault Divorce Revolution is still in the throes of much needed refinement, reform, and reassessment in attempting to meet the current and future needs of our changing society, and many of us will no doubt be playing active roles in this continuing process.

The remainder of this Chapter will address the following procedural and substantive elements of divorce: (1) *divorce jurisdiction*, including the domiciliary requirement, venue and service of process on the defendant, sister-state and foreign migratory divorces, collateral attack on a void divorce, and the divisible divorce doctrine; (2) *divorce grounds and defenses*, including fault and no-fault grounds for divorce, as well as grounds for separation; and (3) the continuing debate over the relevance, if any, of various fault factors in no-fault divorce.

§ 9.02 Divorce Jurisdiction

[A] The Domiciliary Requirement

Subject matter jurisdiction over divorce in the United States is governed by state statutes which empower appropriate state courts to hear divorce cases. Federal courts generally do not have jurisdiction to grant divorces or alimony. *See, e.g., Barber v. Barber*, 62 U.S. 582 (1858); Simms v. Simms, 175 U.S. 162, 167 (1899) ("The whole subject of the domestic relations of husband and wife, parent and child, belongs to the laws of the State, and not the laws of the United States."). Accordingly, on various occasions, the United States Supreme Court has reiterated the so-called "domestic relations exception" rule that federal courts do not have jurisdiction to grant divorces, award spousal support, or determine child custody issues even though there may be a diversity of citizenship, and the required amount in controversy for federal jurisdiction. *See, e.g., Ohio ex rel. Popovici v. Agler*, 280 U.S. 379 (1930), C. Wright, et al. *Federal Practice and Procedure* § 3609 (1975); Gregory, Swisher & Scheible, *Understanding Family Law* § 1.04 (Matthew Bender 1995). One rationale for this "domestic relations exception" to federal diversity jurisdiction in family law matters has been that divorce was not a suit "of a civil nature at common law or equity" at the time the original Judiciary Act, which conferred jurisdiction on the federal courts, was passed. *See, e.g.*, 28 U.S.C. § 1332(a) Revisor's Note. *But see Vann v. Vann*, 294 F. Supp. 193 (E.D. Tenn. 1968) (federal jurisdiction was found to determine the validity of a divorce decree attacked for fraud); *Spindel v. Spindel*, 283 F. Supp. 797 (E.D.N.Y. 1968) (federal jurisdiction to invalidate a Mexican divorce and award the wife damages based on a fraudulent inducement to marry). These federal cases appear to be the exception to the general rule, however. On the other hand, significant monetary recoveries in federal court increasingly have been recognized for family-related tortious conduct, including child enticement, intentional infliction of mental distress, and civil conspiracy in the unlawful taking of a child. *See, e.g., Wasserman v. Wasserman*, 671 F.2d 832 (4th Cir. 1982), *cert. denied*, 459 U.S. 1014 (1982); Cole v. Cole, 633 F.2d 1083 (4th Cir. 1980).

It a well established principle of American family law that having a spouse domiciled within a state is a sufficient basis for that state's divorce jurisdiction, since . . . "each state, by virtue of its command over its domiciliaries and its large interest in the institution of marriage, can alter within its own borders the marriage status of the spouse domiciled there." *Williams v. North Carolina I*, 317 U.S. 287, 299 (1942). *See also Williams v. North Carolina II*, 325 U.S. 226, 229 (1945), and Restatement (Second) of Conflict of Laws, § 285, Comment a (1971). This domiciliary jurisdictional requirement is based upon the family law concept that marriage is a legal status based on contract, and the state that regulates marriage and divorce must thus have a substantial nexus or legal relationship with the spouses, or either of them—as it would have to before asserting jurisdiction over a true contractual dispute. *See, e.g., Haas v. Haas*, 38 Cal. Rptr. 811 (Cal. Ct. App. 1964) (holding that the state has an important interest in both the formation and the dissolution of marriage, and the state having this interest is the state of the parties' domicile).

"Domicile" is usually defined as the place where a person is physically present with the intent of making that place his or her home. *Fiske v. Fiske*, 290 P.2d 725 (Wash. 1955). "Domicile" differs from a person's "residence," since with "domicile" there is a subjective intent to remain more or less permanently in a certain place, but this intent need not be present for "residence." Restatement (Second) of Conflict of Laws §§ 70–72 (1971). Confusing matters unnecessarily, many state divorce statutes use the term "legal residence" rather than "domicile." However, as a jurisdictional requirement for divorce, "residence" generally has been interpreted to mean "domicile." *See, e.g., Cooper v. Cooper*, 269 Cal. App. 2d 6 (Cal. Ct. App. 1969); Raybin v. Raybin, 430 A.2d 953 (N.J. Super. Ct. App. Div. 1981). *But see contra Garrison v. Garrison*, 246 N.E.2d 9 (Ill. App. Ct. 1969). *See generally* Reese & Green, *That Elusive Word "Residence"*, 6 Vand. L. Rev. 561 (1953). This jurisdictional requirement is of major importance in any divorce litigation, since the general rule is that a lack of divorce jurisdiction cannot be waived, that it may be asserted at any stage in the divorce proceeding, and that it may be the basis for a collateral attack on a prior divorce decree. *See, e.g., Hartman v. Hartman*, 412 N.E.2d 711 (Ill. App. Ct. 1980). *See also* Restatement (Second) of Judgments §§ 11, 12, 69 (1982).

If the traditional basis for divorce jurisdiction in the United States has been the domicile of one or both of the parties, does a durational domiciliary requirement unconstitutionally discriminate against recent residents of a state who desire to be divorced in that state? The following case addresses this issue.

SOSNA v. IOWA
United States Supreme Court
419 U.S. 393 (1975)

MR. JUSTICE REHNQUIST delivered the opinion of the Court.

Appellant Carol Sosna married Michael Sosna on September 5, 1964, in Michigan. They lived together in New York between October, 1967, and August, 1971, after which date they separated but continued to live in New York. In August 1972, appellant moved to Iowa with her three children, and the following month she petitioned the District Court of Jackson County, Iowa, for a dissolution of her marriage. Michael Sosna, who had been personally served with notice of the action when he came to Iowa to visit his children, made a special appearance to contest the jurisdiction of the Iowa court. The Iowa court dismissed the petition for lack of jurisdiction, finding that Michael Sosna was not a resident of Iowa and appellant had not been a resident of the State of Iowa for one year preceding the filing of her petition. In so doing the Iowa court applied the provisions of Iowa Code § 598.6 (1973) requiring that the petitioner in such an action be "for the last year a resident of the state."

Instead of appealing this ruling to the Iowa appellate courts, appellant filed a complaint in the United States District Court for the Northern District of Iowa asserting that Iowa's durational residency requirement for invoking its divorce jurisdiction violated the United States Constitution. . . .

A three-judge court, convened pursuant to 28 U.S.C. §§ 2281, 2284, held that the Iowa durational residency requirement was constitutional. 360 F. Supp. 1182 (1973). We noted probable jurisdiction, 415 U.S. 911 (1974), and directed the parties to discuss "whether the United States District Court should have proceeded to the merits of the constitutional issue presented in light of *Younger v. Harris*, 401 U.S. 37 (1971) and related cases." For reasons stated in this opinion, we hold that the Iowa durational residency requirement for divorce does not offend the United States Constitution. . . .

II

The durational residency requirement under attack in this case is a part of Iowa's comprehensive statutory regulation of domestic relations, an area that has long been regarded as a virtually exclusive province of the States. Cases decided by this Court over a period of more than a century bear witness to this historical fact. In *Barber v. Barber*, 21 How.

582, 584 (1859), the Court said: "We disclaim altogether any jurisdiction in the courts of the United States upon the subject of divorce. . . ." In *Pennoyer v. Neff*, 95 U.S. 714, 734–735 (1878), the Court said: "The State. . . has absolute right to prescribe the conditions upon which the marriage relation between its own citizens shall be created, and the causes for which it may be dissolved," and the same view was reaffirmed in *Simms v. Simms*, 175 U.S. 162, 167 (1899).

The statutory scheme in Iowa, like those in other states, sets forth in considerable detail the grounds upon which a marriage may be dissolved and the circumstances in which a divorce may be obtained. Jurisdiction over a petition for dissolution is established by statute in "the county where either party resides," Iowa Code § 598.2 (1973), and the Iowa courts have construed the term "resident" to have much the same meaning as is ordinarily associated with the concept of domicile. *Korsrud v. Korsrud*, 242 Iowa 178, 45 N.W. 2d 848 (1951). Iowa has recently revised its divorce statutes, incorporating the no-fault concept, but it retained the one-year durational residency requirement.

The imposition of a durational residency requirement for divorce is scarcely unique to Iowa, since 48 states impose such a requirement as a condition for maintaining an action for divorce. As might be expected, the periods vary among the States and range from six weeks to two years. The one-year period selected by Iowa is the most common length of time prescribed.

Appellant contends that the Iowa requirement of one year's residence is unconstitutional for two separate reasons: first, because it establishes two classes of persons and discriminates against those who have recently exercised their right to travel to Iowa, thereby contravening the Court's holdings in *Shapiro v. Thompson*, 394 U.S. 618 (1969); *Dunn v. Blumstein*, 405 U.S. 330 (1972), and *Memorial Hospital v. Maricopa County*, 415 U.S. 250 (1974); and, second, because it denies a litigant the opportunity to make an individualized showing of bona fide residence and therefore denies such residents access to the only method of legally dissolving their marriage. *Vlandis v. Kline*, 412 U.S. 441 (1973); *Boddie v. Connecticut*, 401 U.S. 371 (1971).

State statutes imposing durational residency requirements were, of course, invalidated when imposed by States as a qualification for welfare payments, *Shapiro*, *supra*, for voting, *Dunn*, *supra*, and for medical care, *Maricopa County*, *above*. But none of those cases intimated that the States might never impose durational residency requirements, and such a proposition was in fact expressly disclaimed. What those cases had in common was that the durational residency requirements they struck down were justified on the basis of budgetary or recordkeeping considerations which were held insufficient to outweigh the constitutional claims of the individuals. But Iowa's divorce residency requirement is of a different stripe. Appellant was not irretrievably foreclosed from obtaining some part of what she sought, as was the case with the welfare recipients in *Shapiro*, the voters in *Dunn*, or the indigent patient in *Maricopa County*. She would eventually qualify for the same sort of adjudication which she demanded virtually upon her arrival in the State. Iowa's requirement delayed her access to the courts, but, by fulfilling it, she could ultimately have obtained the same opportunity for adjudication which she asserts ought to have been hers at an earlier point in time.

Iowa's residency requirement may reasonably be justified on grounds other than purely budgetary considerations or administrative convenience. *Cf. Kahn v. Shevin*, 416 U.S. 351

(1974). A decree of divorce is not a matter in which the only interested parties are the State as a sort of "grantor," and a divorce petitioner such as appellant in the role of "grantee." Both spouses are obviously interested in the proceedings, since it will affect their marital status and very likely their property rights. Where a married couple has minor children, a decree of divorce would usually include provisions for their custody and support. With consequences of such moment riding on a divorce decree issued by its courts, Iowa may insist that one seeking to initiate such a proceeding have the modicum of attachment to the State required here.

Such a requirement additionally furthers the State's parallel interests both in avoiding officious intermeddling in matters in which another State has a paramount interest, and in minimizing the susceptibility of its own divorce decrees to collateral attack. A State such as Iowa may quite reasonably decide that it does not wish to become a divorce mill for unhappy spouses who have lived there as short a time as appellant had when she commenced her action in the state court after having long resided elsewhere. Until such time as Iowa is convinced that appellant intends to remain in the State, it lacks the "nexus between person and place of such permanence as to control the creation of legal relations and responsibilities of the utmost significance." *Williams v. North Carolina*, 325 U.S. 226, 229 (1945). Perhaps even more important, Iowa's interests extend beyond its borders and include the recognition of its divorce decrees by other States under the Full Faith and Credit Clause of the Constitution, Art. IV, § 1. For that purpose, this Court has often stated that "judicial power to grant a divorce—jurisdiction, strictly speaking—is founded on domicil." *Williams, supra; Andrews v. Andrews*, 188 U.S. 14 (1903); *Bell v. Bell*, 181 U.S. 175 (1901). Where a divorce decree is entered after a finding of domicile in ex parte proceedings, this Court has held that the finding of domicile is not binding upon another State and may be disregarded in the face of "cogent evidence" to the contrary. *Williams, above*, at 236. For that reason, the State asked to enter such a decree is entitled to insist that the putative divorce petitioner satisfy something more than the bare minimum of constitutional requirements before a divorce may be granted. The State's decision to exact a one-year residency requirement as a matter of policy is therefore buttressed by a quite permissible inference that this requirement not only effectuates state substantive policy but likewise provides a greater safeguard against successful collateral attack than would a requirement of bona fide residence alone. This is precisely the sort of determination that a State in the exercise of its domestic relations jurisdiction is entitled to make.

We therefore hold that the state interest in requiring that those who seek a divorce from its courts be genuinely attached to the State, as well as a desire to insulate divorce decrees from the likelihood of collateral attack, requires a different resolution of the constitutional issue presented than was the case in *Shapiro, supra, Dunn, supra*, and *Maricopa County, above*.

Nor are we of the view that the failure to provide an individualized determination of residency violates the Due Process Clause of the Fourteenth Amendment. . . . An individualized determination of physical presence plus the intent to remain, which appellant apparently seeks, would not entitle her to a divorce even if she could have made such a showing. For Iowa requires not merely "domicile" in that sense, but residence in the State for a year in order for its courts to exercise their divorce jurisdiction.

In *Boddie v. Connecticut, supra*, this Court held that Connecticut might not deny access to divorce courts to those persons who could not afford to pay the required fee. Because of the exclusive role played by the state in the termination of marriages, it was held that indigents could not be denied an opportunity to be heard "absent a countervailing state interest of overriding significance." 401 U.S., at 377. But the gravamen of appellant Sosna's claim is not total deprivation, as in *Boddie*, but only delay. The operation of the filing fee in *Boddie* served to exclude forever a certain segment of the population from obtaining a divorce in the courts of Connecticut. No similar total deprivation is present in appellant's case, and the delay which attends the enforcement of the one-year durational residency requirement is, for the reasons previously stated, consistent with the provisions of the United States Constitution. *Affirmed*. . . .

MR. JUSTICE MARSHALL, with whom MR. JUSTICE BRENNAN joins, dissenting.

The Court today departs sharply from the course we have followed in analyzing durational residency requirements since *Shapiro v. Thompson*, 394 U.S. 618 (1969). Because I think the principles set out in that case and its progeny compel reversal here, I respectfully dissent.

As we have made clear in *Shapiro* and subsequent cases, any classification that penalizes exercise of the constitutional right to travel is invalid unless it is justified by a compelling governmental interest.

The Court omits altogether what should be the first inquiry: whether the right to obtain a divorce is of sufficient importance that its denial to recent immigrants constitutes a penalty on interstate travel. In my view, it clearly meets that standard. The previous decisions of this Court make it plain that the right of marital association is one of the most basic rights conferred on the individual by the State. The interests associated with marriage and divorce have repeatedly been accorded particular deference, and the right to marry has been termed "one of the vital personal rights essential to the orderly pursuit of happiness by free men." *Loving v. Virginia*, 388 U.S. 1, 12 (1967). In *Boddie v. Connecticut*, 401 U.S. 371 (1971), we recognized that the right to seek dissolution of the marital relationship was closely related to the right to marry, as both involve the voluntary adjustment of the same fundamental human relationship. Without further laboring the point, I think it is clear beyond cavil that the right to seek dissolution of the marital relationship is of such fundamental importance that denial of this right to the class of recent interstate travelers penalizes interstate travel within the meaning of *Shapiro, Dunn,* and *Maricopa County*. . . .

The Court proposes three defenses for the Iowa statute: first, the residency requirement merely delays receipt of the benefit in question, it does not deprive the applicant of the benefit altogether; second, since significant social consequences may follow from the conferral of a divorce, the State may legitimately regulate the divorce process; and third, the State has interests both in protecting itself from use as a "divorce mill" and in protecting its judgments from possible collateral attack in other States. In my view, the first two defenses provide no significant support for the statute in question here. Only the third has any real force.

A

With the first justification, the Court seeks to distinguish the *Shapiro, Dunn,* and *Maricopa County* cases. Yet the distinction the Court draws seems to me specious. Iowa's residency requirement, the Court says, merely forestalls access to the courts; applicants seeking welfare payments, medical aid, and the right to vote, on the other hand, suffer unrecoverable losses throughout the waiting period. This analysis, however, ignores the severity of the deprivation suffered by the divorce petitioner who is forced to wait a year for relief. *See Stanley v. Illinois,* 405 U.S. 645, 647 (1972). The injury accompanying that delay is not directly measurable in money terms like the loss of welfare benefits, but it cannot reasonably be argued that when the year has elapsed, the petitioner is made whole. The year's wait prevents remarriage and locks both partners into what may be an intolerable, destructive relationship. Even applying the Court's argument on its own terms, I fail to see how the *Maricopa County* case can be distinguished. A potential patient may well need treatment for a single ailment. Under Arizona statutes he would have had to wait a year before he could be treated. Yet the majority's analysis would suggest that Mr. Evaro's claim for nonemergency medical aid is not cognizable because he would "eventually qualify for the same sort of [service]." . . .The Court cannot mean that Mrs. Sosna has not suffered any injury by being foreclosed from seeking a divorce in Iowa for a year. It must instead mean that it does not regard that deprivation as being very severe.

B

I find the majority's second argument no more persuasive. The Court forgoes reliance on the usual justifications for durational residency requirements: budgetary considerations and administrative convenience, see *Shapiro,* 394 U.S., at 627–638; *Maricopa County,* 415 U.S., at 262–269. Indeed, it would be hard to make a persuasive argument that either of these interests is significantly implicated in this case. In their place, the majority invokes a more amorphous justification: the magnitude of the interests affected and resolved by a divorce proceeding. Certainly the stakes in a divorce are weighty both for the individuals directly involved in the adjudication and for others immediately affected by it. The critical importance of the divorce process, however, weakens the argument for a long residency requirement rather than strengthens it. The impact of the divorce decree only underscores the necessity that the State's regulation be evenhanded. . . .The majority identifies marital status, property rights, and custody and support arrangements as the important concerns commonly resolved by divorce proceedings. But by declining to exercise divorce jurisdiction over its new citizens, Iowa does not avoid affecting these weighty social concerns; instead, it freezes them in an unsatisfactory state that it would not require its long-time residents to endure. . . .

It is not enough to recite the State's traditionally exclusive responsibility for regulating family law matters; some tangible interference with the State's regulatory scheme must be shown. Yet in this case, I fail to see how any legitimate objective of Iowa's divorce regulations would be frustrated by granting equal access to new state residents. To draw on an analogy, the States have great interests in the local voting process and wide latitude in regulating that process. Yet one regulation that the States may not impose is an unduly long residency requirement. *Dunn v. Blumstein,* 405 U.S. 330 (1972). To remark, as the Court does, that because of the consequences riding on a divorce decree "Iowa may insist that one seeking to initiate such a proceeding have the modicum of attachment to the State required here" is not to make an argument, but merely to state the result.

C

The Court's third justification seems to me the only one that warrants close consideration. Iowa has a legitimate interest in protecting itself against invasion by those seeking quick divorces in a forum with relatively lax divorce laws, and it may have some interest in avoiding collateral attacks on its decree in other States. These interests, however, would adequately be protected by a simple requirement of domicile—physical presence plus intent to remain—which would remove the rigid one-year barrier while permitting the State to restrict the availability of its divorce process to citizens who are genuinely its own. . . .

I conclude that the course Iowa has chosen in restricting access to its divorce courts unduly interferes with the right to "migrate, resettle, find a new job, and start a new life." *Shapiro v. Thompson*, 394 U.S., at 629. . . .

NOTES AND QUESTIONS

(1) Which argument is more persuasive to you in the *Sosna* decision, Mr. Justice Rehnquist's majority opinion, or Mr. Justice Marshall's dissenting opinion? Based upon what underlying public-policy rationale?

(2) This domiciliary requirement for divorce jurisdiction has not been without its critics. Professor Helen Garfield, for example, argues that in our current transient society with no-fault divorce options, the domiciliary requirement is obsolete and irrelevant because "the problem today is not so much migratory divorce as migratory people." Accordingly, she recommends a proposed Uniform Divorce Jurisdiction Act which would provide as the basis for divorce jurisdiction the mere presence of both parties in a state for bilateral divorces, and a brief period of presence or simple residence in the forum state for ex parte unilateral divorces. Garfield, *The Transitory Divorce Action: Jurisdiction in the No-Fault Era*, 58 Tex. L. Rev. 501, 544 (1980).

Query: If no-fault divorces are presently available in all American jurisdictions so that migratory divorces are no longer the problem they once were, what compelling social need would be served by changing the domiciliary test to require only physical presence of the parties? If there is a recognized important legal nexus between a domiciliary and his or her state, relating to state and local police protection, property rights, rights of inheritance, taxes, voting rights, education, employment, and the like, should this important legal nexus not also relate to the parties' marital status as well? *See, e.g., Boddie v. Connecticut*, 401 U.S. 371, 376 (1971). Nevertheless, the concept of domicile as the only basis for divorce jurisdiction has been criticized by various jurists and commentators, and the subject is still open to debate. *See, e.g., Williams v. North Carolina II*, 325 U.S. 226, 239–60 (1945) (Justices Murphy and Rutledge, dissenting); Stimson, *Jurisdiction in Divorce Cases: The Unsoundness of the Domiciliary Theory*, 42 A.B.A.J. 222 (1956); Weintraub, *An Inquiry into the Utility of "Domicile" as a Concept in Conflicts Analysis*, 63 Mich. L. Rev. 961 (1965).

Query: Was Mrs. Sosna actually "barred" from obtaining a divorce in Iowa? Why or why not?

(3) Other legal commentators have argued that domicile as a basis for divorce jurisdiction in unilateral ex parte divorces may be insufficient and unconstitutional as a violation of the absent spouse's due process rights under the minimum contacts standard enunciated in *Shaffer v. Heitner*, 433 U.S. 186, 207 (1977) ("in order to justify an exercise of jurisdiction *in rem*, the basis for jurisdiction must be sufficient to justify exercising jurisdiction over

the interests of persons in a 'thing.' "). *See, e.g.*, Hawkens, *The Effect of Shaffer v. Heitner on the Jurisdictional Standard in Ex Parte Divorces*, 18 Fam. L.Q. 311 (1984); Comment, *Jurisdiction in the Ex Parte Divorce: Do Absent Spouses Have a Protected Due Process Interest in Their Marital Status?*, 13 Memphis St. U.L. Rev. 205 (1983). However, Professor Clark points out that while the *Shaffer* decision stated its position that *in rem* and *in personam* cases both require minimum contacts between the parties to satisfy due-process requirements, nevertheless the Court disclaimed any intention of changing the rules of jurisdiction based upon status, *Shaffer v. Heitner* 433 U.S. 186, 208 n. 30 (1977), and therefore "it appears unlikely that *Shaffer v. Heitner* and its progeny have effected a change in the rules of divorce jurisdiction." 1 Homer H. Clark, Jr., Law of Domestic Relations 719–20 (2d ed. 1987). *See also In re Marriage of Rinderknecht*, 174 Ind. App. 382, 367 N.E.2d 1128 (Ind. Ct. App. 1977) (domicile of one of the spouses in a state is a sufficient minimum contact to meet the requirements of *Shaffer v. Heitner*).

(4) Currently, all states have a domiciliary requirement for divorce or dissolution of marriage ranging from one year in states like Connecticut, Maryland, New Jersey, and Washington to six weeks in states like Idaho and Nevada. The most common durational domiciliary requirement for divorce, as of this writing, is six months. Alaska, Iowa, Louisiana, Massachusetts, and South Dakota no longer have a durational domiciliary requirement, although bona fide residency or domicile is required at the time the divorce action is commenced. *See* Linda Elrod & Robert Spector, *A Review of the Year in Family Law*, 30 Fam. L. Q. 765, 807 (1997).

(5) One exception to a durational domiciliary requirement involves military personnel and their spouses. Approximately 20 states, and the Uniform Marriage and Divorce Act, provide for divorce jurisdiction when a person is domiciled in the state, or when he or she is stationed in the state as a member of the armed forces for a certain period of time. *See, e.g.*, Uniform Marriage and Divorce Act § 302(a), 9A U.L.A. at 181 (1987). *See also* J. O. Pearson, Jr., Annotation, *Validity and Construction of Statutory Provision Relating to Jurisdiction of Court for Purpose of Divorce for Servicemen*, 73 A.L.R.3d 431 (1976). What public-policy rationale, if any, would justify such an exception?

Query: If civilians must be domiciliaries to be divorced in State A, but military service personnel need only be residents, is there an equal-protection violation here? Why or why not? *Cf. Regan v. Taxation with Representation*, 461 U.S. 540 (1983).

The family law practitioner should also be aware of the Soldiers' and Sailors' Civil Relief Act, 50 U.S.C.A. §§ 501, 521, which permits a stay or continuance in any divorce or related family law matter to military personnel who are precluded, due to their military service, from being present and participating in the scheduled proceedings. *See, e.g., Lackey v. Lackey*, 278 S.E.2d 811 (Va. 1981). *See generally* W.E. Shipley, Annotation, *Soldiers' and Sailors' Civil Relief Act of 1940, as Amended as Affecting Matrimonial Actions*, 54 A.L.R.2d 390 (1957) and Later Case Service. *But see United States v. Hampshire*, 95 F.3d 999 (10th Cir. 1996), *cert. denied*, 117 S. Ct. 753 (1997) (holding that a state court order under the Child Support Recovery Act did not violate a soldier's due process rights or his right to an attorney under the Soldier's and Sailor's Civil Relief Act, since the father was absent without official leave (AWOL) from the military during the time of the divorce proceedings where his wife was seeking child support from him).

(6) **Problem.** Attwood and Judith Thorton were married in 1964 in Mississippi, where Attwood had grown up and attended college. Attwood, a member of the U.S. Air Force,

had been stationed in Virginia, Alabama, Vietnam, Ohio, Florida, and California. In 1976 Attwood signed a declaration of domicile and citizenship, changing his legal residence from Mississippi to Florida. Attwood and Judith separated in 1978, and Judith and the children moved to Australia at that time. Prior to the separation, Attwood was stationed in California with the Air Force, and Attwood and Judith bought a house in Atwater, California. Attwood, however, did not pay any income taxes in California, and he had his automobile registered to him as a military nonresident of California.

A year after the parties' separation, in 1979, Attwood, who was still stationed in California, filed an action for divorce against his wife in Florida, declaring that he was "an actual, continuous, bona fide resident of the State of Florida. A notice to defend this divorce action was sent by ordinary first class mail to Judith, who was now living in Australia. The mail was not certified and no return receipt was requested. The notice required a response by July 6, 1979, otherwise "a default will be entered against you for the relief demanded in the Petition." Judith stated, however, that all these Florida documents were received by her through the regular mail only after the final entry of divorce on July 19, 1979, as a result of a mail strike in Australia. Subsequently, Judith, who was still living in Australia, brought a dissolution [divorce] action against Attwood in California, claiming that the Florida divorce should not be accorded full faith and credit by the California court due to her lack of proper notice and the California court had subject matter jurisdiction because Attwood was a legal resident of California. Attwood claimed, however, that the evidence clearly demonstrated that he was never a legal resident or domiciliary of California, so a California court cannot take jurisdiction in this matter.

The relevant California statute at that time, Civil Code § 4530(a) (now Family Code § 2320), provided as follows: "A judgment decreeing dissolution of a marriage may not be entered unless one of the parties of the marriage has been a resident of this state for six months and of the county in which the proceeding is filed for three months next preceding the filing of the petition." It is also well-settled in California that the term "residence" in the statute means "domicile." *Johnson v. Johnson*, 245 Cal. App. 2d 40 (Cal. Ct. App. 1966). California is not one of the states with a serviceman's exception to its domiciliary requirement. If you were a California judge, how would you decide this case? Which state (or country) is the proper domicile of each party for divorce purposes? Can this case be properly resolved applying a domiciliary requirement for divorce jurisdiction? Why or why not? *See In re Marriage of Thornton*, 135 Cal. App. 3d 500 (Cal. Ct. App. 1982).

(7) **Venue**. Where jurisdictional rules for divorce generally determine whether or not a court in a particular state has the authority to hear the divorce action, *venue* in divorce cases generally governs the particular place within each state where the divorce action must be brought. Venue statutes generally require that a dissolution or divorce action be brought in the county where the parties, or either of them, reside. *See, e.g.*, Cal. Fam. Code § 2320; *In re Marriage of Dick*, 18 Cal. Rptr. 2d 743 (Ct. App. 1993). *See also Dunn v. Dunn*, 577 So. 2d 378 (Miss. 1991). Other venue statutes provide for various alternatives: (1) the county of the parties' last marital domicile; (2) the county where the defendant now resides; or, (3) if the defendant is out of state, or the defendant's whereabouts are unknown, the county where the plaintiff now resides. *See, e.g.*, Va. Code Ann. § 8.01–261 (preferred venue). Generally speaking, jurisdiction may not be waived in a divorce proceeding, but many states now provide that venue rules may be waived. *See, e.g.*, *Nelms v. Nelms*, 108

S.E.2d 529 (N.C. 1959); *Kelley v. Kelley,* 263 S.W.2d 505 (Tenn. 1953). Based upon what underlying public-policy argument? However, in some other states venue statutes in divorce proceedings have been interpreted to be mandatory and jurisdictional, and these cannot be waived. *See, e.g., Gerdel v. Gerdel,* 313 A.2d 8 (Vt. 1973). *Cf. Tinsley v. Tinsley,* 602 So. 2d 1153 (La. Ct. App. 1992) (holding that, although venue is jurisdictional, an action to challenge venue is not appealable in the absence of irreparable injury). Thus, a family law practitioner must be careful to ascertain whether or not venue statutes may be waived in a particular jurisdiction, as this may well affect the validity of the divorce decree—and the unwelcome possibility of a legal malpractice suit. Divorce jurisdiction statutes, in general, being in derogation of the common law, normally require strict compliance. This same strict compliance rule applies to service-of-process requirements in a divorce.

(8) **Service of Process.** Service of process in divorce or dissolution actions must be made both in strict compliance with state statutory requirements and in a manner reasonably calculated to give due process notice to the defendant. It is an elementary family law rule that the defendant in any divorce action must be given due-process notice of the suit and an opportunity to be heard. *See, e.g., Atherton v. Atherton,* 181 U.S. 155 (1901); Restatement (2d) Conflict of Law § 69 (1971). The divorce may be attacked and invalidated based upon the lack of adequate due-process notice or upon failure to meet statutory service of process requirements. *See* 1 Homer H. Clark, Jr., Law of Domestic Relations 715–17 (2d ed. 1987) *id.,* Vol. 2 at 82–83. Since divorce may be *in rem* as well as *in personam,* various forms of constructive service are also permitted. For example, for a unilateral ex parte divorce, only due process notice through substituted service is required for an out-of-state defendant, rather than personal service. *Williams v. North Carolina I,* 317 U.S. 287 (1942); *Carr v. Carr,* 385 N.E.2d 1234 (N.Y. 1978). When the defendant's whereabouts are not known and cannot be readily ascertained, constructive service can also take the form of service by publication. *See, e.g., Fleek v. Fleek,* 155 S.E.2d 290 (N.C. 1967).

(9) **Problem.** Although substituted service is normally sufficient to comply with due process notice requirements for divorce, strict compliance with state statutes is still necessary to give proper notice to the defendant. *See, e.g., McFarland v. McFarland,* 19 S.E.2d 77 (Va. 1942); Annotation, *Collateral Attack on Divorce Decree Because of Defects in Showing or Allegations as to Constructive Service of Process,* 91 A.L.R. 225 (1934). *Query:* What if the plaintiff falsely states that she does not know the defendant's whereabouts, when in fact she does? *See, e.g., Ford v. Whelan,* 233 Wis. 96, 288 N.W. 737 (Wis. 1939). What if the notice to the defendant fails to indicate that the plaintiff is requesting a division of the parties' marital property in the divorce action? *See In re Marriage of Campbell,* 683 P.2d 604 (Wash. Ct. App. 1984).

[B] Migratory Divorces

Although the availability of no-fault divorce in all 50 states has greatly lessened the need for a spouse to venture out of state in order to procure a divorce, certain parties nevertheless may still attempt to utilize a "quickie" migratory divorce in another state or in a foreign country that has shorter jurisdictional requirements than the forum state. Also, migratory divorces may be used to avoid certain home state publicity that might "wreck a career." Adams & Adams, *Ethical Problems in Advising Migratory Divorce,* 16 Hastings L.J. 60, 99 (1964).

Some classic migratory divorce cases also serve as excellent examples of how divorce jurisdiction is structured and recognized among the various states including: when a state's divorce jurisdiction will be recognized, or not recognized, by another state; who may collaterally attack an invalid divorce; and the "divisible divorce" doctrine.

[1] Sister State Migratory Divorces

Under Article IV, § 1 of the United States Constitution, each state must give full faith and credit to the public acts, records, and judicial proceedings of every other state. However, since each state has developed its particular divorce laws according to its own needs, norms, and state public policy, there has been a long and often confusing historical development of the law regarding when one state must recognize a divorce decree from a sister state, and when that state may legally refuse to recognize such a decree. Since many parties who obtain migratory divorces later remarry (with new spouses), and since substantial property and support rights are normally settled on divorce, these parties have a very strong interest in ensuring that their migratory divorce decrees subsequently will be recognized in all states.

In *Haddock v. Haddock*, 201 U.S. 562 (1906), a husband wrongfully left his wife in New York and established a Connecticut domicile in order to divorce her. The Supreme Court held in this case that although the husband was now a bona fide domiciliary of Connecticut, New York as the matrimonial domicile was not obliged to recognize a Connecticut ex parte divorce decree under the full faith and credit clause. The *Haddock* decision remained the law until 1942.

In 1942, the Supreme Court decided the seminal ex parte divorce case of *Williams v. North Carolina [Williams I]*, 317 U.S. 287 (1942). In this case, Mr. Williams and Mrs. Hendrix left their respective spouses in North Carolina and traveled to Las Vegas, Nevada. After meeting Nevada's six-week residency requirement, they both obtained Nevada divorces. Neither of their North Carolina spouses was personally served in Nevada, and neither entered an appearance in Nevada. Notices of the divorce complaints and summons, however, were mailed or delivered to the defendant spouses in North Carolina. Mr. Williams and Mrs. Hendrix were then married in Nevada, and shortly thereafter returned to North Carolina. On the basis of the *Haddock* decision, the new Mr. and Mrs. Williams were tried and convicted in North Carolina of bigamous cohabitation, despite their argument that the Nevada divorce decree and remarriage should be recognized in North Carolina. *See generally* Powell, *And Repent at Leisure: An Inquiry into the Unhappy Lot of Those Whom Nevada Hath Joined Together and North Carolina Hath Put Asunder*, 58 Harvard L. Rev. 930 (1945).

In an opinion written by Mr. Justice Douglas, the Supreme Court in *Williams I* overruled the *Haddock* case, and held that an ex parte divorce, based on a proper jurisdictional basis, and with proper due process notice to the other spouse, must be given full faith and credit by another state, even though the policy of the divorcing state may conflict with the policy of the latter state. Moreover, the domicile of the plaintiff would constitute the basis for jurisdiction in this ex parte divorce. *Williams v. North Carolina*, 317 U.S. 287, 303 (1942). Since the record in the North Carolina proceeding contained no evidence that Mr. Williams and Mrs. Hendrix were not domiciled in Nevada, Mr. Justice Douglas stated that the Court "must assume that petitioners had a bona fide domicile in Nevada, not that the Nevada domicile was a sham." The case was reversed and remanded back to the North Carolina court. But the Williams' were not yet home free.

In 1945 the hapless petitioners were once again before the Supreme Court in *Williams v. North Carolina [Williams II]*, 325 U.S. 226 (1945). In a decision written by Mr. Justice Frankfurter, the Court reaffirmed the *Williams I* doctrine that an ex parte divorce based upon the jurisdictional domicile of only one spouse, and with proper due process notice to the non-appearing spouse, must be recognized by other states under full faith and credit. However, although the Nevada court's finding of a Nevada domicile for the Williams' "was entitled to respect and more," the Court held that North Carolina was not bound by the Nevada jurisdictional finding of domicile, and could subsequently determine that the Williams' had never actually acquired a Nevada domicile. Thus a sister state, under *Williams II*, may refuse to recognize an ex parte divorce through a finding that the divorcing court did not have adequate jurisdiction in the matter. The Williams' conviction of bigamous cohabitation was therefore affirmed. The Restatement (Second) of Conflict of Laws § 71 (1971) has adopted the *Williams I* rationale, providing that a state has the power to exercise jurisdiction to dissolve a marriage when only one of the spouses is domiciled in the state. Further, the Restatement would apply this doctrine when either the plaintiff or the defendant is domiciled in the state.

The *Williams I* and *Williams II* doctrines have general application to unilateral ex parte divorces. The recognition of *bilateral* migratory divorces, when both spouses make a general appearance before the divorcing court, however, involves some different qualifications. The case of *Sherrer v. Sherrer*, 334 U.S. 343 (1948), is one such example. *Sherrer* involved a husband and wife who were Massachusetts domiciliaries. Mrs. Sherrer moved to Florida and commenced a divorce action there. Mr. Sherrer, through his attorney, made a general appearance in the Florida divorce action, but he did not attempt to challenge his wife's Florida domicile during the proceedings, and the Florida court found that Mrs. Sherrer was a Florida domiciliary. Mr. Sherrer did not appeal the divorce in a Florida appellate court. Subsequently, Mr. Sherrer attacked the validity of the Florida divorce in a Massachusetts court, arguing that Mrs. Sherrer's Florida divorce should not be recognized in Massachusetts under the *Williams II* doctrine, since Mrs. Sherrer's sham domicile in Florida did not give the Florida court adequate jurisdiction in the matter. But the Supreme Court upheld the validity of the Florida divorce, and stated that Massachusetts must give full faith and credit to it.

The difference between *Sherrer* and *Williams II* was that Mr. Sherrer had participated in the Florida divorce proceeding, and therefore he had the opportunity to dispute this jurisdictional issue, which he failed to do. Having had his day in court on the merits of the case, Mr. Sherrer therefore was precluded from relitigating the issue under the doctrine of *res judicata* or estoppel by judgment. *Sherrer v. Sherrer*, 334 U.S. 343, 352 (1948). The practical effect of the *Sherrer* decision, then, at least regarding bilateral migratory divorces, was "to curtail the scope of the second *Williams* decision, which established the right of one state to challenge a "quickie" divorce decree of another" on jurisdictional grounds. McDonough, *Mr. Justice Jackson and Full Faith and Credit on Divorce Decrees: A Critique* 56 Columbia L. Rev. 860, 878 (1956). *See also Aldrich v. Aldrich*, 378 U.S. 540 (1964) (relitigation of a mistake of law or a mistake of fact in a bilateral divorce action is barred by the doctrine of *res judicata*).

NOTES AND QUESTIONS

(1) If the parties themselves may not collaterally attack a bilateral migratory divorce under the *Sherrer* doctrine, is the state of Massachusetts likewise barred in bringing a hypothetical bigamy prosecution against Mrs. Sherrer, like North Carolina did in the *Williams* case, if she remarries in Florida and returns to Massachusetts? Why or why not? *See, e.g., State v. DeMeo*, 118 A.2d 1 (N.J. 1955); *compare* Currie, *Suitcase Divorce in Conflict of Laws*, 34 U. Chi. L. Rev. 26, 54–55 n.130 (1966) *with* A. Ehrenzweig, Conflict of Laws 253 (1962).

(2) Assume that Mrs. Williams, the first wife in *Williams I* and *Williams II*, learns of Williams' ex parte Nevada divorce, and in reliance on that divorce, she remarries Mr. Teasee. A few years later, she divorces Mr. Teasee, and subsequently learns that the *Williams II* case may invalidate her first husband's Nevada divorce. She then brings her own concurrent action, *Williams v. Williams*, collaterally attacking the Nevada divorce, and asking for certain spousal support and marital property rights from Williams. How should her suit be decided? *See* Restatement of Conflict of Laws § 112 (1934), and Restatement (Second) of Conflict of Laws § 74 Comment b (1971). Assume now that the first Mrs. Williams has not remarried. Should she have a subsequent cause of action against Williams for spousal support and marital property rights after Williams' ex parte Nevada divorce? Why or why not? *See Vanderbilt v. Vanderbilt*, 354 U.S. 416 (1957) (majority view). *But see Esenwein v. Commonwealth*, 325 U.S. 279 (1945) (minority view). *See generally* § 9.02[D], *below* (the doctrine of "divisible divorce").

(3) **Problem.** Harry and Wilma have their marital domicile in the State of Ames. One day Harry packs his suitcase and tells Wilma that he is leaving for the State of Brandeis to get a divorce, and, contrary to General MacArthur's famous promise, he will never return. Harry spends the requisite six weeks in Brandeis, which is Brandeis's domiciliary requirement, living at the Shady Grove Motel and eating in the local Hamburger Haven. At the end of six weeks, Harry files for divorce in Brandeis, giving Wilma proper due process notice of the Brandeis proceedings. When Wilma receives notice of Harry's pending Brandeis divorce, she goes to an attorney in Ames who tells Wilma, "Don't worry. We'll deal with the miscreant later." Harry's divorce in Brandeis becomes final, and the Brandeis divorce decree makes a finding that Harry is a "bona fide resident and domiciliary of Brandeis." Four days after the divorce, Harry moves to the State of Chase, "to start a new life." Meanwhile, Wilma and her attorney in Ames bring an action in an Ames court to declare Harry's Brandeis divorce invalid based upon Brandeis' lack of jurisdiction. The Ames court finds that Harry had a sham domicile in Brandeis, and therefore the Brandeis divorce is invalid. Now Wilma brings the Ames decree to Brandeis (where Harry has some property) and to Chase (where Harry now resides), asking that the Ames decree, declaring the Brandeis divorce invalid, be given full faith and credit by both the Brandeis and Chase courts.

How should this case be decided? *Compare Sutton v. Leib*, 342 U.S. 402 (1952) *and Layton v. Layton*, 538 S.W.2d 642 (Tex. Civ. App. 1976) *with Colby v. Colby*, 369 P.2d 1019 (Nev. 1962), *cert. denied*, 371 U.S. 888 (1962); *Kessler v. Fauquier National Bank*, 81 S.E.2d 440 (Va. 1954), *cert. denied*, 348 U.S. 834 and 890 (1954). *See also* Comment, *Recent Developments, Nevada Refuses to Vacate its Own Divorce Decree*, 15 Stanford L. Rev. 331 (1963); Restatement (Second) of Judgments § 15 (1982).

(4) **Problem.** Maria and Anthony, husband and wife, were domiciliaries of New York. In 1982 Anthony commenced a divorce action in Queens County, New York, against Maria, but the divorce complaint was dismissed on October 4, 1984, for failure of proof. Approximately two weeks later, on October 16, 1984, Anthony, with two suitcases and his golf clubs, moved to Las Vegas, Nevada, where he began a new job which had been procured the previous day. Within two weeks of his arrival in Nevada, he consulted an attorney with reference to commencing a new divorce action in Nevada, and seven weeks after Anthony moved to Nevada, Maria was served in New York with due process notice regarding Anthony's Nevada divorce action. Maria made no appearance in Nevada, and a Nevada decree of divorce was rendered on December 28, 1984.

Maria then instituted proceedings in New York for *pendente lite* child and spousal support and for other ancillary relief, and to declare Anthony's Nevada divorce decree invalid for lack of jurisdiction based upon his sham domicile there. Anthony presented evidence, however, of his domiciliary intent in Nevada, including proof of his Nevada residence and employment, his motor vehicle registration and voter registration in Nevada, plus other "formal declarations" of a Nevada domicile. Was Anthony legally domiciled in Nevada at the time of his divorce? How should the court rule on this matter? *See Manasseri v. Manasseri*, 504 N.Y.S.2d 140 (N.Y. App. Div. 1986).

Assume now that Anthony and Maria still reside in New York, but they also own a second house in Connecticut, where they had resided for much of their marriage, that both spouses still had Connecticut drivers' licenses and were registered to vote in Connecticut, and Anthony still had childhood and continuing family ties in Connecticut. Can Maria obtain a New York order enjoining Anthony from prosecuting a divorce action he filed in Connecticut? *See Boyton v. Boyton*, 644 N.Y.S.2d 173 (N.Y. App. Div. 1996).

[2] Foreign Country Migratory Divorces

Recognition of ex parte and bilateral migratory divorces within the United States is generally mandated by the Full Faith and Credit Clause, Article IV, § 1 of the Constitution. However, foreign country migratory divorces are not recognized under this constitutional mandate. Rather, they are under the discretionary principle of *comity*. As enunciated by the Supreme Court in the case of *Hilton v. Guyot*, 159 U.S. 113, 163–164 (1895), comity is defined as "neither a matter of absolute obligation, on the one hand, nor of mere courtesy and good will, upon the other. But it is a recognition which one nation allows within its territory to legislative, executive, or judicial acts of another nation, having due regard both to international duty and convenience, and to the rights of its own citizens or of other persons who are under the protection of its laws." Most commentators and courts agree that "all that is meant by comity is that the state of the forum is not obliged by any superior power or force to apply foreign law." E. S. Stimson, Conflict of Laws 71 (1963). *See also Bang v. Park*, 321 N.W.2d 831 (Mich. Ct. App. 1982). So a state may decline to give comity to a foreign divorce when contrary to its public policy or when prejudicial to its interests. *Smith v. Smith*, 50 N.E.2d 889 (Ohio Ct. App. 1943). *See Atassi v. Atassi*, 451 S.E.2d 371 (N.C. Ct. App. 1995) (holding that if genuine issues of material fact existed regarding the validity of a Syrian premarital agreement and a Syrian divorce, then summary judgment would be precluded).

Refusal to grant comity, based on a state's strong public policy, generally has been categorized into the following areas that have been used to defeat the effects of foreign judgments: (1) insufficient proof of a foreign judgment; (2) lack of finality of a foreign judgment; (3) lack of subject matter jurisdiction in the foreign forum; (4) lack of personal jurisdiction of the foreign forum; (5) insufficiency of notice or opportunity to be heard; (6) clear mistake of fact or law made by the foreign court in its judgment; (7) procurement of the foreign judgment by fraud; and (8) the foreign judgment contravenes the public policy of the recognition forum. *See* Peterson, *Res Judicata and Foreign Country Judgments*, 24 Ohio St. L.J. 291, 308–10 (1963).

Various articles have been written concerning the validity of 24–hour Mexican "quickie" divorces for American domiciliaries. *See, e.g.*, Currie, *Suitcase Divorce in the Conflict of Laws*, 34 U. Chi. L. Rev. 26 (1966), and Leach, *Divorce by Plane Ticket in the Affluent Society With a Side Order of Jurisprudence*, 14 Kans. L. Rev. 549 (1966). However, since March 7, 1971, these Mexican divorces have become less available to American citizens due to amendments in Mexican law which now require aliens to become residents of Mexico for at least six months before obtaining a divorce. Nevertheless, Mexican divorces continue to create problems in many American jurisdictions because of the "residence" vs. "domicile" issue, and because many Mexican residency certificates may be forgeries. *See* Miller, *Mexican Divorces Revisited*, 84 Case and Comment No. 4 at 43. In addition to Mexico, the Dominican Republic and Haiti have now joined the "quickie" 24–hour, foreign divorce market, advertising in prominent periodicals, and offering various "divorce tour packages" for Americans. Solicitations by Haitian and Dominican divorce lawyers also have been mailed directly to many American attorneys. *See generally* Swisher, *Foreign Migratory Divorces: A Reappraisal*, 21 J. Fam. L. 9 (1982–83), Note, *Isle of Hispaniola: American Divorce Haven?*, 5 Case W. Res. J. Int'l L. 198 (1973), and Note, *Caribbean Divorce for Americans: Useful Alternative or Obsolescent Institution?*, 10 Cornell Int'l. L.J. 116 (1976).

Should these "quickie" 24–hour, foreign country migratory divorces be legally recognized in American state courts under comity principles? The following case addresses this issue.

MAYER v. MAYER
North Carolina Court of Appeals
311 S.E.2d 659 (1984)

BECTON, JUDGE.

This case involves a challenge to a Dominican Republic (Dominican) divorce decree by Victor Mayer, who asserts that his wife's divorce from her first husband, which he actively helped procure, was invalid, and who thereby seeks to avoid paying alimony to his wife. . . .

It may have been easier for us to have declared the Dominican divorce voidable and challengeable only by Doris Mayer's first husband, Fred Crumpler, especially since we hold in part IV, *infra*, that Victor Mayer is estopped from asserting any invalidity in the Dominican proceedings. *See Carpenter v. Carpenter*, 244 N.C. 286, 93 S.E.2d 617 (1956). We, however, have decided to address the issues "head on" because of a demonstrated need to definitively resolve questions about "quickie" foreign divorces—that is,

> the concept of foreign country migratory divorces for American domiciliaries with its jurisdictional and public policy defects; its alleged "defense" of estoppel; and with one exception piled upon another has become so confusing to the lay public and the practicing bar that very few people adequately understand the underlying ramifications and liabilities involved in such divorces.

Swisher, *Foreign Migratory Divorces: A Reappraisal*, 21 J. Fam. L. 9 (1982–83).

I Procedural History

Praying for divorce from bed and board, permanent alimony, and alimony *pendente lite*, Doris Mayer filed her complaint against Victor Mayer on 15 October 1981. Denying that he was lawfully married to Doris Mayer, and counter-claiming for an annulment, Victor Mayer, in his answer, specifically asserted that at the time of his purported marriage, Doris Mayer was already married to Fred Crumpler; that she had previously attempted to divorce Fred Crumpler by obtaining a divorce decree from a Dominican court; that the Dominican divorce decree was void and in contravention of the laws of North Carolina; and that Doris Mayer knew this, having been so advised by counsel.

This case was heard in the trial court upon Doris Mayer's motions for alimony *pendente lite* and attorney's fees. At the close of Doris Mayer's evidence, the trial court denied the motions, after determining (a) that the Dominican divorce was invalid; (b) that the Mayers' marriage was void; and (c) that Victor Mayer was not estopped from denying the validity of Doris Mayer's divorce. Doris Mayer appeals. . . .

. . . .

III Validity of the Dominican Divorce

A. Doris Mayer's Argument

To put Doris Mayer's first argument—that her Dominican divorce was valid—in perspective, we outline it in narrative form.

1. Although the full faith and credit clause of the United States Constitution, Article IV, Section 1, which requires North Carolina to recognize bilateral divorces of sister states, has no application to foreign judgments, the criteria by which North Carolina grants comity to foreign divorce decrees should reasonably parallel the criteria North Carolina uses when it recognizes divorces of sister states. In that way, North Carolina can maintain a consistent divorce policy.

2. A valid judgment rendered in a foreign nation after a fair trial in a contested proceeding will be recognized in the United States. Restatement (Second) of Conflict of Laws § 98 (1971). Therefore, the bilateral divorce obtained by Doris Mayer should be recognized since it does not offend the public policy of North Carolina that is, the grounds upon which the divorce was granted, irreconcilable differences, are substantially equivalent to those of a divorce granted under this State's no-fault divorce statute, N.C. Gen. Stat. § 50–6 (1976), which allows a divorce based on one year's separation of the parties.

3. Because there is neither evidence of partiality on the part of the Dominican court, nor fraud in the procurement of the Dominican divorce judgment, it would be a waste of time and a duplication of efforts for North Carolina's courts to go through the formalities of granting a divorce on the same grounds as did the Dominican court, for a marriage that, for all practical purposes, has already been terminated. North Carolina has no interest in perpetuating a status out of which no good can come and from which harm may result. Or, as stated by the New Jersey Supreme Court: "There remains little, if any, interest in encouraging the resurrection of deceased marriages, even if pronounced dead by other

tribunals whose processes are not completely consistent with our own." *Kazin v. Kazin*, 81 N.J. 85, 98, 405 A.2d 360, 367 (1979).

4. North Carolina has recognized that there is a presumption of the validity of the second marriage which prevails over the presumption of the continuance of the first. *See Denson v. C.R. Fish Grading Co.*, 28 N.C. App. 129, 220 S.E. 2d 217 (1975), and *Parker v. Parker*, 46 N.C. App. 254, 265 S.E. 2d 237 (1980). That principle is served better by holding Victor Mayer to his obligations as a husband.

5. Finally, North Carolina's public policy is affected no more by a six-week bilateral Nevada divorce, which North Carolina must acknowledge under the full faith and credit clause, than a five-day foreign divorce. "Nevada gets no closer to the real public concern with the marriage than [the Dominican Republic]," since the establishment of a synthetic domicile in a sister state for the facile termination of a marriage is no less a subterfuge to circumvent North Carolina's interest in marriages. *Rosenstiel v. Rosenstiel*, 16 N.Y. 2d 64, 73, 262 N.Y.S. 2d 86,, 209 N.E.2d 709, 712 (1965), *cert. denied* 384 U.S 971 (1966). Consequently, a balanced social policy requires that comity be granted to the present divorce decree.

B. Analysis

Doris Mayer's argument, although masterfully elaborate and powerful, is based on a faulty premise, is contrary to the view held by a majority of the states in this country, and is at odds with an equally powerful and more persuasive public-policy argument.

The full faith and credit clause has no application to foreign judgments. Recognition of foreign decrees by a State of the Union is governed by principles of comity. Consequently, based on notions of sovereignty, comity can be applied without regard to a foreign country's jurisdictional basis for entering a judgment. More often than not, however, "many of the American states are likely to refuse recognition [to deny comity] to a divorce decree of a foreign country not founded on a sufficient jurisdictional basis." 1 R. Lee, *North Carolina Family Law* § 104, at 488 (4th ed. 1979). That is,

> [a] foreign divorce decree will be recognized, if at all, not by reason of any obligation to recognize it, but upon considerations of utility and mutual convenience of nations. Recognition may be withheld in various circumstances, as where the jurisdiction or public policy of the forum has been evaded in obtaining the divorce.

Id. at 487. Since the power of a State of the Union to grant a divorce decree is dependent upon the existence of a sufficient jurisdictional basis—domicile or such a relationship between the parties of the State as would make it reasonable for the State to dissolve the marriage—it follows that the validity of a foreign divorce decree should depend upon an adequate jurisdictional basis. *See* Restatement (Second) of Conflict of Laws § 72 (1971).

1. Jurisdiction

In this case the Dominican Republic had no interest in the marriage of the two North Carolinians, Doris Mayer and Fred Crumpler. Yet, on Doris Mayer's five-day sojourn to the Dominican Republic, the Dominican court purported to dissolve the marriage of two domiciliaries of North Carolina upon the grounds of "irreconcilable differences." Neither of the parties in this lawsuit had any connection with the Dominican Republic, save Doris

Mayer's five-day stay there for the sole reason, by her own testimony, to obtain the divorce decree. . . .

Doris Mayer correctly cites *Denson* for the proposition that "the second marriage is presumed to be valid. . . [and] overcomes the presumption of the continuance of the first marriage," but that presumption is rebuttable. In this case Victor Mayer successfully rebutted that presumption by showing that the ex parte Dominican divorce was invalid on jurisdictional grounds and, as we shall show hereinafter, on policy grounds, too.

Even if the Dominican divorce could be found to be bilateral, Doris Mayer would still have on her shoulders the weight of the majority of American jurisdictions. The great weight of authority in this country is that divorces granted in foreign countries to persons who are domiciliaries of the United States are not valid and enforceable. *See* Annotation, 13 A.L.R. 3d 1419 (1967). 2. Public Policy

In addition to the above, no constitutional provision or rule of comity requires North Carolina to accord legal force and effect to a divorce decree, like the one at issue here, that offends this State's public policy against the hasty dissolution of marriages. Until 15 July 1983, North Carolina permitted immediate dissolution of marriages only on proof of fault. *See* N.C.Gen.Stat. § 50–5 (1976) (repealed 1983). Acceding to a more enlightened view that divorce should be allowed in some cases without proof of a cause or motivation of the divorce petition, North Carolina, beginning in 1965, also allowed divorces upon proof that the parties had lived separate and apart for one year or more. N.C. Gen. Stat. § 50–6 (Supp. 1983). Efforts to change the one-year period to six months have failed, and that failure is consistent with North Carolina's public policy that a longer waiting period is necessary to protect the institution of marriage from hasty judgments and casual disruptions, since differences may in time be reconciled.

We also reject Doris Mayer's argument that "irreconcilable differences" as a ground for divorce under the Dominican law is substantially equivalent to the ground providing for absolute divorce after one year's separation. As Victor Mayer argued in his brief:

> The appellant sought a Dominican divorce precisely because the law of North Carolina governing divorce is not and was not "substantially equivalent" to the law of the Dominican Republic. The appellant sought a Dominican divorce because North Carolina law did not permit her to obtain a hasty divorce from her husband in the winter of 1981. It was to avoid the force and effect of the one-year waiting period imposed by North Carolina law that the appellant traveled to the Caribbean and obtained a divorce there.

We cannot sanction a procedure by which citizens of this State with sufficient funds to finance a trip to the Caribbean can avoid our legislature's judgment on the question of divorce. To hold otherwise would be to flout our law; it would permit domiciliaries of North Carolina to submit their marital rights and obligations to the contrary policies and judgments of a foreign nation with which they have no connection.

Considering the circumstances of this case, the applicable law, and the important policy considerations, the trial court properly refused to accord legal force and effect to the Dominican divorce decree. . . .

IV Estoppel

Doris Mayer next contends that even if we find the Dominican divorce invalid (as we have done in Part III, *above*), Victor Mayer should, nevertheless, be estopped from questioning its validity since: (a) he participated in her procurement of the invalid divorce; (b) all parties relied upon the divorce's validity until Victor Mayer abandoned Doris Mayer; and (c) a contrary result would create a marriage at will by Victor Mayer, who could end the marital relationship at any time he desired, and yet prevent Doris Mayer from avoiding the obligations of her remarriage. Consequently, Doris Mayer argues that she should receive alimony *pendente lite* and reasonable attorney's fees.

In a forceful response, Victor Mayer argues that he is not estopped to assert the invalidity of the Dominican divorce decree, and that Doris Mayer is estopped to assert the validity of her marriage to him. Victor Mayer first cites N.C. Gen. Stat. § 51–3 (Supp. 1983), which states that "all marriages. . . between persons either of whom has a husband or wife living at the time of such marriage. . . shall be void." Victor Mayer then argues that even if equity could suspend the operation of G.S. § 51–3, the equities in this case weigh no more heavily for Doris Mayer than for him since (a) she and he are *in pari delicto* (b) Doris Mayer knew or should have known that the Dominican divorce decree might not be recognized in North Carolina; (c) no substantial equitable rights matured in consequence of the aborted union—no children were born of the union, and no third parties would be affected by nullification of the marriage—and (d) Doris Mayer seeks relief from the legal consequences of her own injudicious haste. Finally, Victor Mayer argues that he was not a party to the Dominican decree and that principles of res judicata and estoppel, therefore, do not apply to him.

The question, squarely presented by these contentions, is whether a husband, who actively participates in his wife's procurement of an invalid divorce from her prior husband, is estopped from denying the validity of that divorce. After a careful balancing of legal and policy considerations, we answer that question "yes."

We are persuaded by Doris Mayer's argument, but we could have more quickly and more easily embraced her position had there been a child of her marriage with Victor Mayer; or had the marriage been of long duration. Indeed, we have not lightly dismissed Victor Mayer's implicit argument that Doris Mayer, with full knowledge of the consequences, gambled and lost —she left her lawyer-husband, releasing him from all alimony obligations, for a greater love, or for what she erroneously thought was a better deal. Notwithstanding the strong legal, factual and policy considerations the above factors engender, and in spite of the criticism that the application of a quasi-estoppel doctrine circumvents a state's divorce law, it would be even more inimical to our law and to our public policy, to permit Victor Mayer to avoid his marital obligations by acting inconsistently with his prior conduct.

Under the quasi-estoppel doctrine, one is not permitted to injure another by taking a position inconsistent with prior conduct, regardless of whether the person had actually relied upon that conduct. *See generally* Clark, *Estoppel Against Jurisdictional Attack on Decrees of Divorce*, 70 Yale L.J. 45 (1960); Weiss, *A Flight on the Fantasy of Estoppel in Foreign Divorces*, 50 Colum. L. Rev. 409 (1950); *see also Kazin v. Kazin*, 81 N.J. 85, 405 A.2d 360 (1979); *Harlan v. Harlan*, 70 Cal. App. 2d Supp. 657, 161 P. 2d 490 (1945).

The development of a quasi-estoppel doctrine is reflected in the Restatement (Second) Conflict of Laws § 74 (1971), which states that "[a] person may be precluded from attacking the validity of a foreign decree if, under the circumstances, it would be inequitable for him to do so." *Id.* at 224. The scope of § 74 is defined in Comment b:

> [It is] not limited to situations of "true estoppel" where one party induces another to rely to his damage upon certain representations. The rule may be applied whenever, under all the circumstances, it would be inequitable to permit a particular person to challenge the validity of a divorce decree. Such inequity may exist when action has been taken in reliance on the divorce, or expectations are based on it, or when the attack on the divorce is inconsistent with the earlier conduct of the attacking party.

Id.

According to Professor Clark, when analyzing quasi-estoppel cases, "[t]hree factors seem to be involved: (1) the attack on the divorce is inconsistent with prior conduct of the attacking party; (2) the party upholding the divorce has relied upon it, or has formed expectations based on it; (3) these relations or expectations will be upset if the divorce is held invalid." Clark, *above* at 13, 56–57. Significantly, all three factors do not have to be present for estoppel to apply. When all three factors are present, however, the application of the estoppel doctrine is especially compelling. . . .

In addition to the position taken in the Restatement (Second) Conflict of Laws § 74, there is considerable authority from other jurisdictions that a husband, who encouraged his wife to obtain a divorce from her prior spouse, is estopped from questioning its validity. Professor Clark, as though presciently writing for the case *subjudice*, sets forth the problem this way:

> This problem most commonly arises when a man persuades a married woman to divorce her husband so that she will be free to marry him. He may even finance the divorce, provide a lawyer, or take an active part in other ways. When he does so, or even when he merely marries her with full knowledge of the circumstances surrounding the divorce, he is estopped to question the validity of the divorce. He has engaged in conduct calculated to induce reliance on the divorce, and indeed, he has relied on it himself. Therefore, the reasons of policy which prevent attack by a party to the divorce action are equally persuasive here.

Clark, *above* at 13, 66–67.

The conclusion reached by Clark. . . is no different from that reached by several other state courts that have considered the issue. *See Kazin v. KazinIn Re Marriage of Winegard*, 278 N.W.2d 505 (Iowa), *cert. denied*, 444 U.S. 951, (1979); *Poor v. Poor*, 381 Mass. 392, 409 N.E.2d 758 (1980); *Rosen v. Sitner*, 274 Pa. Super. 445, 418 A.2d 490 (1980); *Campbell v. Campbell*, 164 Misc. 647, 1 N.Y.S. 2d 619 (1937); *Zirkalos v. Zirkalos*, 326 Mich. 420, 40 N.W.2d 313 (1949); *Goodloe v. Hawk*, 113 F.2d 753 (D.C. Cir. 1940); *Leatherbury v. Leatherbury*, 233 Md. 344, 196 A.2d 883 (1964); *Harlan v. Harlan, above*; *Mussey v. Mussey*, 251 Ala. 439, 37 So. 2d 921 (1948).

As much as in any area of the law, quasi estoppel cases turn on the particular facts of each case. The facts in this case compel the conclusion we reach. The record suggests that Victor Mayer insisted on Doris Mayer's obtaining a Dominican divorce; that he promised to support her in a manner better than the one she had been accustomed to, prompting Doris Mayer to sign away any alimony she may have been entitled to from Mr. Crumpler; and that he accompanied her on her trip to the Dominican Republic, paying for her transportation and lodging, and other personal expenses. . . . Victor Mayer never questioned the validity of the marriage until he abandoned Doris Mayer. In addition, Doris Mayer relied on the divorce's validity. . . .

We are not unmindful of Victor Mayer's argument that to estop him from questioning the divorce's validity would have, as he puts it, the effect of validating a marriage which G.S. § 51–3 declares a nullity. There is a difference, however, between declaring a marriage valid and preventing one from asserting its invalidity. The theory behind the equitable estoppel doctrine is not to make legally valid a void divorce or to make an invalid marriage valid, but rather, to prevent one from disrupting family relations by allowing one to avoid obligations as a spouse. Stated differently, equitable estoppel is dependent upon events which led to the divorce or which may have occurred after the divorce. It is a personal disability of the party attacking the divorce judgment; it is not a function of the divorce decree itself. *See* Clark, *above*, at 47 and Swisher, *above*, at 38–39.

Further, this Court has already recognized that a party to an invalid divorce is estopped and that one marrying in reliance on such a divorce is entitled to the benefits of the marriage. . . . It, therefore, would be anomalous to argue that estopping a second husband, who participated in his wife's procurement of a divorce, would have any greater impact on this State's public policy than estopping one who is a party to the marriage.

We hold that Victor Mayer is estopped from asserting as a defense the invalidity of Doris Mayer's divorce, and that Doris Mayer is entitled, based on the trial court's findings, to alimony *pendente lite* and reasonable attorney's fees. The question of the validity of the prenuptial agreement limiting Doris Mayer's alimony to $1,000 per month is not before this Court.

For the above reasons, this matter is remanded for further proceedings not inconsistent with this opinion. *Reversed and remanded.*

NOTES AND QUESTIONS

(1) As illustrated in the *Mayer* case, the overwhelming majority of American states will refuse to recognize a foreign divorce, regardless of its purported validity in the nation awarding it, unless at least one of the spouses was a good-faith domiciliary in the foreign nation at the time the divorce was rendered, and this rule applies to foreign bilateral divorces, *ex parte* divorces, and mail-order divorces. Under this general principle, Mexican divorces requiring only residency for foreigners, and Dominican and Haitian divorces requiring neither residency nor domicile would not be recognized by most American courts. *See, e.g., Blair v. Blair*, 643 N.E.2d 933 (Ind. Ct. App. 1994) (refusing, inter alia, to recognize husband's ex parte Dominican divorce). *See generally* Swisher, *Foreign Migratory Divorces: A Reappraisal*, 21 J. Fam. L. 9, 22–33 (1982–83). *See also* R. F. Chase, Annotation, *Domestic Recognition of Divorce Decree Obtained in Foreign Country and Attacked for Lack of Domicil or Jurisdiction of Parties*, 13 A.L.R. 3d 1419, 1425–1429 (1967); *Kugler v. Haitian Tours Inc.*, 293 A.2d 706 (N.J. Super. Ct. Ch. Div. 1972) (Haitian divorce); Basiouny v. Basiouny, 445 So. 2d 916 (Ala. Civ. App. 1984) (Egyptian divorce).

(2) A small minority of American jurisdictions, however, do recognize bilateral foreign divorces based solely on physical presence of the parties in the foreign jurisdiction, without

any domiciliary requirement. *See, e.g., Rosenstiel v. Rosenstiel*, 209 N.E.2d 709 (N.Y. 1965) *cert. denied*, 384 U.S. 971 (1966); *Yoder v. Yoder*, 330 A.2d 825 (Conn. Super. Ct. 1974) (Mexican divorce); *Hyde v. Hyde*, 562 S.W.2d 194 (Tenn. 1978) (Dominican divorce); Perrin v. Perrin, 408 F.2d 107 (3d Cir. 1969) (applying U.S. Virgin Islands law to a Mexican divorce). *Ex parte* and mail-order migratory foreign divorces, however, will *not* be recognized under both the majority and minority views. *Query:* Why not?

The New York *Rosenstiel* case has been strongly criticized by various commentators in that the New York courts appeared to override state public policy declared by the New York legislature in allowing New York migratory couples to evade what was then very strict New York state divorce laws by obtaining a foreign divorce decree, and this constituted judicial usurpation of the legislative function—regardless of legislative "wisdom" or the lack thereof inherent in the statutes. *See, e.g.*, Currie, *Suitcase Divorce in the Conflict of Laws*, 34 U. Chi. L. Rev. 26, 57–62 (1966); Note, *Mexican Bilateral Divorce*, 61 Nw. U. L. Rev. 584, 608 (1966).

On the other hand, the Connecticut *Yoder* court, in applying the theory of comity to a Mexican divorce, found "no repugnancy" in Mexican and Connecticut grounds for divorce based upon an irretrievable breakdown in the marriage. However, no claim was made in the *Yoder* case that the Mexican court lacked jurisdiction to enter the divorce decree. *See also Bruneau v. Bruneau*, 3 Conn. App. 453, 489 A.2d 1049 (Conn. App. Ct. 1985) (declaring a Mexican divorce of Connecticut domiciliaries to be invalid based upon jurisdictional grounds raised before the court, but also recognizing an estoppel defense). *Query:* Which approach is more persuasive to you? Based upon what particular public policy arguments?

(3) **Problem.** Marie and John, who were New York domiciliaries, obtained a bilateral Mexican divorce. Marie then married Martin, and Marie and Martin moved to South Carolina. When Marie brought an action for divorce against Martin in South Carolina, Martin defended on the ground that the parties were not lawfully married, since the Mexican divorce obtained by Marie from her former husband John would not be legally recognized in South Carolina, which follows the majority view. As a South Carolina judge, how would you decide this case? *See Zwerling v. Zwerling*, 244 S.E.2d 311 (S.C. 1978).

(4) **Estoppel Defenses in Attacking a Void Divorce.** As demonstrated in the *Mayer* case *above*, even though Mrs. Mayer's Dominican divorce was not valid under North Carolina law, her husband was estopped to deny it, since he had actively helped his soon-to-be wife to procure the invalid Dominican divorce from her prior husband. *See also Spellens v. Spellens*, 317 P.2d 613 (Cal. 1957); *Bruneau v. Bruneau*, 489 A.2d 1049 (Conn. App. Ct. 1985). Estoppel by conduct has given rise in many states to the modern concept of a "practical" recognition of a divorce decree rendered in a foreign jurisdiction where neither spouse is domiciled: "[P]ractical recognition may be accorded such [divorce] decrees by estoppel, laches, unclean hands, or similar equitable doctrine under which the party attacking the decree may effectively be barred from securing a judgment of invalidity." R. F. Chase, Annotation, *Domestic Recognition of Divorce Decree Obtained in Foreign Country and Attacked for Lack of Domicil or Jurisdiction of Parties*, 13 A.L.R.3d 1419, 1452 (1967).

Thus, if a person attacking a void divorce is, in doing so, "taking a position inconsistent with his past conduct, or if the parties to the action have relied on the divorce, and if, in addition, holding the divorce invalid will upset relationships or expectations formed in reliance upon the divorce, then estoppel will preclude calling the divorce in question." Clark, *Estoppel Against Jurisdictional Attack on Decrees of Divorce*, 70 Yale L.J. 45, 57 (1960) (applied to both sister state and foreign migratory invalid divorces). Accordingly, a party may be precluded from attacking a foreign divorce if such an attack would be inequitable under the circumstances. *Scherer v. Scherer*, 405 N.E.2d 40, 44 (Ind. Ct. App. 1980). Not all courts follow this modern trend, however. A more conservative approach was manifested in *Everett v. Everett*, 345 So. 2d 586 (La. Ct. App. 1977), where the court rejected any estoppel defense in holding that a bilateral Dominican divorce was invalid, thus permitting the wife to pursue a Louisiana divorce on adultery grounds.

In fact, the courts have not been consistent in applying, or refusing to apply, an estoppel defense, and have applied one of three estoppel theories, often within the same jurisdiction. (a) Under the "traditional" rule, the domiciliary state, and the parties themselves, are not bound by any estoppel defense. *See, e.g., Everett v. Everett, above; In re Estate of Steffke*, 222 N.W.2d 624 (Wis. 1974). (b) Under the "practical recognition" or "sociological" view, a person who has obtained a void divorce, or who has assisted in obtaining a void divorce, will be precluded from attacking the validity of that divorce if, under the circumstances, it would be inequitable to do so. *See, e.g., Sherer v. Sherer, above*; Mayer v. Mayer, *above*; Kazin v. Kazin, 405 A.2d 360 (N.J. 1979). (c) Under a "status vs. property right" doctrine, an estoppel defense would be deemed inappropriate whenever a spouse brings an action to determine his or her marital status, but estoppel may apply when the action deals with a related marital property right such as spousal support, or taking against a deceased "spouse's" will. *See, e.g., Caldwell v. Caldwell*, 81 N.E.2d 60 (N.Y. 1948); *Rabourn v. Rabourn*, 385 P.2d 581 (Alaska, 1963). *Query:* Which estoppel rule is most persuasive to you? *See also* "Marriage" by Estoppel, § 1.05[D], *above*. It must be still remembered, however, that the doctrine of equitable estoppel does not legally validate a void divorce. Those courts applying the estoppel concept to void divorces are careful to avoid stating that such divorces are now "valid," but only that the attacking party is estopped to assert any invalidity. So the void divorce might still be collaterally attacked by the State, or by another interested party.

(5) Various countries have attempted to alleviate many of these mettlesome problems involved in the recognition of foreign-country divorces by adopting the Hague Convention on the Recognition of Divorce and Legal Separations, 978 United Nations Treaty Series 399 (1975), which provides jurisdiction for divorce or legal separation based upon the "habitual residence" of the respondent or petitioner, or when the petitioner is a national of that state. ("Habitual residence" includes, but is not limited to "domicile.") Fourteen countries, including the United Kingdom, have adopted the Hague Convention; but because the United States is not a signatory to this Convention, it is not binding law in this country. *See Divorce Around the World*, 9 Fam. Advocate No. 4, 1–47 (Spring, 1987). *See also* Cavers, *Habitual Residence: A Useful Concept?* 21 Am. U. L. Rev. 475 (1972).

[C] Collateral Attack on a Void Divorce

Let us recapitulate what we have learned thus far:

(1) **Sister State Ex Parte Divorces.** A sister state ex parte divorce, assuming valid jurisdiction and due-process notice, must be given full faith and credit by all other sister

states under *Williams I*. However, the state of the marital domicile, or where the non appearing defendant spouse resides, may later attack the divorcing court's jurisdiction under *Williams II*. Assuming that the ex parte divorce is invalid, the petitioning party may be estopped by his or her conduct to deny its invalidity, but the non appearing defendant would not be estopped to attack the invalid ex parte divorce, unless he or she remarried relying on the validity of that divorce. *See, e.g.*, Restatement (Second) of Conflict of Laws § 74 Comment b (1971).

(2) **Sister State Bilateral Divorces**. A sister state bilateral divorce, even assuming invalid jurisdiction, must be given full faith and credit by other sister states under the *Sherrer* doctrine of *res judicata* or estoppel by judgment. Neither party can thereafter collaterally attack such a divorce due to their estoppel by conduct and due to *res judicata* or estoppel by judgment.

(3) **Foreign Country Migratory Divorces**. The overwhelming majority of American states will refuse to recognize a foreign divorce, regardless of its purported validity in the nation awarding it, unless at least one of the spouses was a good faith domiciliary in the foreign nation at the time the divorce was rendered. A minority of states will recognize foreign-country bilateral divorces without a domiciliary requirement, but all states, under the theory of comity, refuse to recognize foreign country ex parte divorces or mail-order divorces without a domiciliary requirement. However, even though these divorces are legally invalid, certain estoppel defenses may nevertheless apply.

(4) **The State**. The domiciliary state, under the general view, is not barred from collaterally attacking a void divorce in the form of a bigamy or adultery prosecution, even though the parties themselves cannot attack an invalid bilateral divorce. *See, e.g., Lipham v. State*, 22 S.E.2d 532 (Ga. Ct. App. 1942). However, most of these cases were decided before the *Sherrer* case was decided, and some commentators now believe the state may also be barred from collaterally attacking the invalid divorce. *See* Scoles & Hay, Conflict of Laws § 15.11 (1992).

(5) **Interested Third Parties.** In addition to the spouses and the State, certain interested third parties have attempted to collaterally attack an invalid divorce. For example, in the case of *Johnson v. Muelberger*, 340 U.S. 581 (1951), Eleanor, the daughter of Bruce Johnson by his first marriage, was the sole beneficiary of her father's will in New York. She attacked the validity of her father's Florida divorce from his second wife, Madoline, based on Madoline's sham domicile in Florida, in order to prevent Genevieve, Johnson's third wife, from taking a statutory forced share of Bruce Johnson's estate.

The U.S. Supreme Court held that since Florida, as the rendering state, did not permit a child as a stranger to the divorce proceedings to collaterally attack the parents' divorce, and since Bruce Johnson had made a general appearance in Madoline's Florida divorce proceedings through his attorney, any collateral third-party attack by Eleanor was barred under the *Sherrer* doctrine of *res judicata* or estoppel by judgment. *See also Evans v. Asphalt Roads & Materials, Inc.*, 72 S.E.2d 321 (Va. 1952) (a minor son of a deceased employee could not collaterally attack the validity of his father's Nevada divorce unless he had a preexisting or vested economic interest in the marriage at the time the divorce was rendered; mere expectancy in worker's compensation benefits insufficient). *But see Old Colony Trust v. Porter*, 88 N.E.2d 135 (Mass. 1949) (holding that a collateral third-party interest does not always need to be preexisting at the time of divorce). *See generally* 1 Homer H. Clark,

Law of Domestic Relations 732–55 (2d ed. 1987); Green, Long, & Murawski, Dissolution of Marriage 146–62 (1986).

(6) **Problem.** Arthur and Wendy had their marital domicile in the State of Ames. Arthur told Wendy that he had to work on a industrial construction job in the neighboring State of Burns, and the job would take "a year or two" to complete. Unknown to Wendy, Arthur completed a formal declaration to change his domicile in Burns, he bought a house in Burns, and registered to vote in Burns. Although the domiciliary requirement for divorce in Burns was six weeks, Arthur waited six months to bring a divorce action in Burns, giving Wendy notice of the divorce proceedings in a local Burns newspaper. Wendy heard about Arthur's pending divorce action from family friends and sent her attorney to Burns to challenge Arthur's divorce on jurisdictional and due-process notice grounds. Nevertheless, the Burns court granted Arthur's divorce, and Arthur returned to Ames one week after his divorce and married Zelda. Wendy subsequently married Bill, a successful businessman, in Ames.

Bill and Wendy's marriage began to erode after one year, and Bill went to his attorney in Ames for legal advice. Bill's attorney told Bill that Arthur's divorce from Wendy in Burns was "probably invalid." Bill then brought a suit against Wendy in Ames to annul their marriage and to deny any spousal support or marital property rights to Wendy based upon their bigamous marriage. Bill further asked for a conveyance of a substantial amount of real property back to him that was purportedly titled in the name of Bill and Wendy as tenants by the entirety.

(a) How should the Ames court rule on Bill's complaint? *See Atherton v. Atherton*, 181 U.S. 155 (1901); *Mullane v. Central Hanover Bank*, 339 U.S. 306 (1950). *Compare George v. King*, 156 S.E.2d 615 (Va. 1967) *and Gullo v. Brown*, 483 P.2d 293 (N.M. 1971) *with Rosenbluth v. Rosenbluth*, 228 N.Y.S.2d 613 (N.Y. Sup. Ct. 1962) *and Murphy v. Murphy*, 386 A.2d 274 (Conn. 1978). *See also* E. H. Shipley, Annotation, *Standing of Strangers to Divorce Proceeding to Attack Validity of Divorce Decree*, 12 A.L.R.2d 717 (1950) and Later Case Service.

(b) Should Wendy be able to collaterally attack Arthur's divorce? Why or why not?

(c) Can the State of Ames successfully prosecute Arthur and Zelda for the crime of bigamous cohabitation or adultery in Ames? *See, e.g.*, *Zenker v. Zenker*, 72 N.W.2d 809 (Neb. 1955).

[D] The Divisible Divorce Doctrine

As we have seen in § 9.02[B][1], *above*, *Williams I* held that an ex parte divorce obtained by a bona fide domiciliary, and with adequate due-process notice to the defendant, is entitled to full faith and credit in every sister state. Thus, a divorcing court in an ex parte proceeding may validly terminate the marital status of the parties, even though it lacks personal jurisdiction over the defendant spouse. But what about the financial incidents of the marriage, including spousal and child support, and division of the marital property on divorce? Since a majority of American courts require personal jurisdiction to create, modify, or extinguish marital support and property rights, how can this doctrine be reconciled with *Williams I*?

In 1943, Mrs. Estin, a New York domiciliary, was awarded a decree of legal separation and spousal support one year after her husband left her. In 1945, Mr. Estin was granted an ex parte Nevada divorce which made no provisions for the payment of spousal support to Mrs. Estin. When Mr. Estin ceased making any support payments to Mrs. Estin, she brought an action against Mr. Estin for these support arrearages in New York. Mr. Estin appeared in the New York action and argued that under the *Williams I* doctrine, the subsequent Nevada ex parte divorce decree legally eliminated the support provisions in the prior New York legal separation decree.

The Supreme Court analyzed the conflicting interests of Nevada and New York in *Estin v. Estin*, 334 U.S. 541 (1948), and held that although the divorcing state had a valid interest in determining the legal status of the marriage, the state of the former marital domicile also had an interest in preventing the abandoned spouse from becoming a public charge. The *Estin* court reconciled these interests by holding that an ex parte termination of the marital status does not necessarily result in the termination of all financial incidents of that marriage, since Mrs. Estin's prior New York judgment was a property interest that could not be affected by a Nevada divorce decree without personal jurisdiction over Mrs. Estin. *Id.* at 548. Hence, the concept of a "divisible divorce" was legally recognized. That is to say, that ex parte divorces would be recognized as dissolving the parties' marital status under *Williams v. North Carolina [I]*, but such ex parte unilateral divorces would not affect the parties' marital property or spousal support rights without personal jurisdiction over both parties. *See also* Green, Long, & Murawski, Dissolution of Marriage 162–72, 163–64 (1986). But what happens when a husband obtains an ex parte divorce, and the defendant wife is not protected by any preexisting support order? The following case addresses this problem.

VANDERBILT v. VANDERBILT
United States Supreme Court
354 U.S. 416 (1957)

Mr. Justice Black delivered the opinion of the Court.

Cornelius Vanderbilt, Jr., petitioner, and Patricia Vanderbilt, respondent, were married in 1948. They separated in 1952 while living in California. The wife moved to New York, where she has resided since February, 1953. In March of that year the husband filed suit for divorce in Nevada. This proceeding culminated, in June, 1953, with a decree of final divorce which provided that both husband and wife were "freed and released from the bonds of matrimony and all the duties and obligations thereof . . . ." The wife was not served with process in Nevada and did not appear before the divorce court.

In April, 1954, Mrs. Vanderbilt instituted an action in a New York court praying for separation from petitioner and for alimony. The New York court did not have personal jurisdiction over him, but in order to satisfy his obligations, if any, to Mrs. Vanderbilt, it sequestered his property within the State. He appeared specially and, among other defenses to the action, contended that the Full Faith and Credit Clause of the United States Constitution compelled the New York court to treat the Nevada divorce as having ended the marriage and as having destroyed any duty of support which he owed the respondent. While the New York court found the Nevada decree valid and held that it had effectively dissolved the marriage, it nevertheless entered an order, under § 1170–b of the New York

Civil Practice Act,[1] directing petitioner to make designated support payments to respondent. . . . The New York Court of Appeals upheld the support order. . . . Petitioner then applied to this Court for *certiorari*, contending that § 1170–b, as applied, is unconstitutional because it contravenes the Full Faith and Credit Clause. We granted certiorari. . . .

In *Estin v. Estin*, 334 U.S. 541, this Court decided that a Nevada divorce court, which had no personal jurisdiction over the wife, had no power to terminate a husband's obligation to provide her support as required in a preexisting New York separation decree. The factor which distinguishes the present case from *Estin* is that here the wife's right to support had not been reduced to judgment prior to the husband's ex parte divorce. In our opinion this difference is not material on the question before us. Since the wife was not subject to its jurisdiction, the Nevada divorce court had no power to extinguish any right which she had under the law of New York to financial support from her husband. It has long been the constitutional rule that a court cannot adjudicate a personal claim or obligation unless it has jurisdiction over the person of the defendant. Here, the Nevada divorce court was as powerless to cut off the wife's support right as it would have been to order the husband to pay alimony if the wife had brought the divorce action and he had not been subject to the divorce court's jurisdiction. Therefore, the Nevada decree, to the extent it purported to affect the wife's right to support, was void, and the Full Faith and Credit Clause did not obligate New York to give it recognition. . . . *Affirmed.*

NOTES AND QUESTIONS

(1) The concept of an ex parte "divisible divorce," as enunciated in *Estin* and *Vanderbilt*, has been adopted by a majority of American jurisdictions, most often based on state common and statutory law requiring that spousal support and marital property rights cannot be modified or extinguished without personal jurisdiction over both parties. *See, e.g., Fehlhaber v. Fehlhaber*, 681 F.2d 1015 (5th Cir. 1982), *cert. denied*, 464 U.S. 818 (1983) (applying California law); *Kendall v. Kendall*, 585 P.2d 978 (Kan. 1978); *Altman v. Altman*, 386 A.2d 766 (Md. 1978) (citing a number of other cases following this majority view); *Newport v. Newport*, 245 S.E.2d 134 (Va. 1978). *See also* the Uniform Marriage and Divorce Act § 208(1) (1987); 1 Homer H. Clark, Law of Domestic Relations 767–73 (2d ed. 1987).

(2) In a minority of states, however, the local rule apparently is that an ex parte divorce granted in another state would have the effect of cutting off spousal support and marital property rights that the other spouse might normally be able to assert on divorce. *See, e.g., Stambaugh v. Stambaugh*, 329 A.2d 483 (Pa. 1974); *Morphet v. Morphet*, 502 P.2d 255 (Or. 1972); *Burton v. Burton*, 376 S.W.2d 504 (Tenn. Ct. App. 1963); *Brady v. Brady*, 158 S.E.2d 359 (W. Va. 1967); *Loeb v. Loeb*, 114 A.2d 518 (Vt. 1955). *See also* E. H. Schopler, Annotation, *Valid Foreign Divorce Granted Upon Constructive Service as Precluding Action by Spouse for Alimony, Support, or Maintenance*, 28 A.L.R.2d 1378 (1953) and Later Case Service.

---

[1] . . .[Footnote by the Court:] "In an action for divorce, separation or annulment, . . .where the court refuses to grant such relief by reason of a finding by the court that a divorce . . . declaring the marriage a nullity had previously been granted to the husband in an action in which jurisdiction over the person of the wife was not obtained, the court may, nevertheless, render in the same action such judgment as justice may require for the maintenance of the wife." 6A Gilbert-Bliss' N.Y. Civ. Prac., 1956 Cum. Supp., § 1170–b.

Query: Do the *Estin* and *Vanderbilt* cases arguably make these minority rules unconstitutional as violative of the absent spouse's due process rights? *Compare Hudson v. Hudson*, 344 P.2d 295 (Cal. 1959) *and* Restatement (Second) of Conflict of Laws § 77 Comment f (1971) *with* 1 Homer H. Clark, Law of Domestic Relations 769–70 (2d ed. 1987).

(3) **Problem.** Herb and Wanda have their marital domicile in the State of Ames. Herb moves to the State of Burns and establishes a domicile there in order to obtain an ex parte Burns divorce that would cut off any spousal support or marital property rights for Wanda. Wanda tells her attorney in Ames of Herb's pending divorce in Burns, but Wanda's Ames attorney advises her to "disregard the ex parte Burns divorce at this time, since we'll be able to get spousal support and marital property from Herb later on under the 'divisible divorce' concept." Wanda's attorney, however, has overlooked the crucial fact that Ames is one of the minority of states that allows an ex parte divorce to cut off spousal support and marital property rights. Wanda then moves and establishes a new domicile in the State of Chase, which follows the majority *Vanderbilt* doctrine, before Herb's ex parte divorce in Burns becomes finalized. Wanda subsequently sues Herb in Chase for spousal support and a division of the parties' marital property, serving process on Herb when he is in Chase on a fishing trip.

(a) Is Wanda entitled to spousal support and a division of marital property under the divisible divorce doctrine? Why or why not? *See Loeb v. Loeb*, 152 N.E.2d 36 (N.Y. 1958).

(b) If Wanda remained a domiciliary of Ames, but wanted to retain an action for spousal support against Herb, what realistic legal advice would you give her as her attorney in Ames? Would an injunction preventing Herb from obtaining a Burns domicile be appropriate? Why or why not? *See Monihan v. Monihan*, 264 A.2d 653 (Pa. 1970); *Stambaugh v. Stambaugh*, 329 A.2d 483 (Pa. 1974). *See also* E. H. Schopler, Annotation, *Injunction Against Suit in Another State or Country for Divorce or Separation*, 54 A.L.R.2d 1240 (1957).

(4) In *Simons v. Miami Beach First National Bank*, 381 U.S. 81 (1965), Mr. and Mrs. Simons were domiciled in New York, where Mrs. Simons obtained a legal separation decree that included an award of monthly spousal support. Mr. Simons moved to Florida in 1951, and a year later he obtained an ex parte divorce in Florida from Mrs. Simons. Mrs. Simons had adequate due process notice of Mr. Simons' Florida divorce, but she entered no personal appearance. Up until the time of his death in 1960, Mr. Simons continued to pay his former wife monthly spousal support according to the requirements of the New York legal separation decree. When Mr. Simons died in Florida, Mrs. Simons appeared at the probate proceedings and filed an election to take her dower inheritance rights in her husband's estate under the "divisible divorce" doctrine. However, the Supreme Court held that under Florida law dower rights in Florida property can be legally extinguished by an ex parte divorce. *Query:* How can the *Simons* case be distinguished from both *Estin* and *Vanderbilt*?

(5) **State Long Arm Statutes**. Recurring problems with the concept of divisible divorce have resulted in a number of states enacting *long arm statutes* specifically to obtain personal jurisdiction over both spouses in order to determine related marital support and property rights, even when the defendant spouse no longer resides within the state at the time of the divorce action.

As a constitutional "minimum contacts" requirement for such long-arm jurisdiction, a number of statutes require that the spouses maintained a matrimonial domicile in the state at the time of the separation upon which a divorce action is based. *See, e.g.*, Maine Rev.

Stat. Title 14 § 704–A(2)(G) (1980); Va. Code Ann. § 8.01–328.1(A)(9) (1988); Wis. Stat. Ann. § 801.05(11) (1986). However, it is not sufficient for long arm jurisdiction that the spouses had briefly stayed in a state during some prior period of time. *See, e.g., Thompson v. Thompson*, 657 S.W.2d 629 (Mo. 1983). *See also Kulko v. Superior Court of California*, 436 U.S. 84 (1978) (holding that California long-arm jurisdiction over a nonresident New York father for child support payments was inadequate unless he had purposely availed himself of the benefits and protections of California law). *See also Ragouzis v. Ragouzis*, 391 S.E.2d 607 (Va. Ct. App. 1990) (holding that the state long-arm statute provides methods of service on a non-resident in addition to personal service as authorized by older statutes, and is not the exclusive method).

Query: If a state long-arm statute does not specifically apply to divorce and other related matrimonial matters, how might a generally worded statute still provide personal jurisdiction in family law matters? *See, e.g., Ross v. Ross*, 358 N.E.2d 437 (Mass. 1976) (jurisdiction over nonresident party to separation agreement who earlier sought to modify it in forum state); *Poindexter v. Willis*, 231 N.E.2d 1 (Ill. Ct. App. 1967) (support for an illegitimate child). *But see Janni v. Janni*, 611 S.W.2d 785 (Ark. Ct. App. 1981) (child support on divorce); *Boyer v. Boyer*, 383 N.E.2d 223 (Ill. 1978) (spousal and child support on divorce). *See also* Green, Long, & Murawski, Dissolution of Marriage 141–43 (1986), *and* 1 Homer H. Clark, The Law of Domestic Relations 764–66 (2d ed. 1987).

§ 9.03 Divorce Grounds and Defenses

[A] Fault Grounds for Divorce

[1] Overview

If "no-fault" divorce has been incorporated into the divorce statutes of all fifty states, either based on irreconcilable differences or separation grounds, why do we need to analyze traditional fault grounds for divorce? According to Golden & Taylor, *Fault Enforces Accountability*, 10 Family Advocate 11, 12 (Fall, 1987), "[Various] critics. . . mistakenly believe that the adoption of no fault grounds by every state in the union heralds a beneficial end to the fault system. This is simply not true because most states have *incorporated* no-fault grounds into their traditional framework, not *substituted* one system for another. . . ." Indeed, Professors Linda Elrod and Robert Spector report that 32 states still retain various fault grounds for divorce or dissolution of marriage, each one having added no-fault divorce to their traditional divorce grounds. Elrod & Spector, *A Review of the Year in Family Law*, 30 Fam. L.Q. 765, 807 (1997). Thus, since a substantial number of states still provide fault-based grounds for divorce or dissolution of marriage, and since fault still remains a factor to be considered in awarding spousal support or marital property division on divorce in many states, then it is still appropriate to analyze these traditional fault grounds for divorce.

Some commentators believe that we are currently in a transitional period, with both fault and no-fault divorce grounds, but that no-fault divorce, with additional legal safeguards for dependent spouses and children, will eventually prevail. *See, e.g.*, Lichtenstein, Marital Misconduct and th eAllocation of Financial Resources at Divorce: A Farewell to Fault, 54 UMKC L. Rev. 1 (1985); Kay, *Equality and Difference: A Perspective on No-Fault Divorce and its Aftermath*, 56 U. Cinn. L. Rev. 1 (1987); and Ellman, *The Place of Fault in a Modern Divorce Law*, 28 Ariz. St. L.J. 773 (1996). *See also* The American Law Institute, Principles of the Law of Family Dissolution: Analysis and Recommendations (1997). Other commentators, however, believe that fault may still serve a legitimate purpose in determining spousal support and the division of marital property on divorce. *See, e.g.*, Redman, *Coming Down Hard on No-Fault: Why the Author Believes that No-Fault Divorce is an Experiment that Failed*, 10 Fam. Advocate 7, 39 (Fall, 1987) ("I am not suggesting that fault should be the only factor in dividing debt and property; I am suggesting, however, that it should be considered."). *See also* Woodhouse, *Sex, Lies, and Dissipation: The Discourse of Fault in a No-Fault Era*, 82 Geo. L.J. 2525 (1994); Swisher, *Reassessing Fault Factors in No-Fault Divorce*, 31 Fam. L.Q. 269 (1997). Ultimately, it will be the responsibility of each state legislature to determine what role, if any, fault should play in contemporary divorce proceedings within its state.

[2] Adultery, Cruelty, and Desertion

Adultery is currently a ground for divorce in 29 states. Adultery generally includes sexual intercourse by either spouse with someone other than his or her spouse; this may include sexual intercourse with another person of the same sex. *See, e.g., Bales v. Hack*, 509 N.E.2d 95 (Ohio Ct. App. 1986) (although homosexuality was not specifically enumerated as a ground for divorce, homosexuality could constitute extreme cruelty or adultery to the other spouse, thereby furnishing grounds for divorce). *See also M.V.R v. T.M.R.*, 454 N.Y.S.2d 779 (N.Y. Sup. Ct. 1982). A spouse would also be guilty of adultery if the plaintiff and defendant while still married were living separate and apart, and one of the spouses engaged in sexual intercourse with a third person during this period of separation. *See, e.g., Clark v. Clark*, 644 S.W.2d 681 (Tenn. Ct. App. 1982).

Many adultery cases are concerned with problems of proof, since there are seldom eyewitnesses to the act. Thus, proof of adultery may be by circumstantial evidence, but a number of courts require a plaintiff to prove adultery by clear and convincing evidence. *See, e.g., Westervelt v. Westervelt*, 258 N.E.2d 98 (N.Y. 1970) (evidence of defendant spouse and correspondent living together was held insufficient to prove adultery), and *Seemar v. Seemar*, 355 S.E.2d 884 (Va. 1987) (evidence that defendant wife had spent ten nights in a room with an adult male was insufficient to prove adultery, since wife testified that she had not slept with the man due to her strong religious beliefs). *Cf. Everett v. Everett*, 345 So. 2d 586 (La. Ct. App. 1977) ("Courts are a bit more sophisticated today and infer that people do what comes naturally when they have the opportunity."). So proof of adultery may range from preponderance of the evidence in many states, to clear and convincing evidence or beyond a reasonable doubt in other states. *Query:* Which standard of proof for adultery is more appropriate? Why?

What happens when adultery, cruelty, or desertion grounds are alleged in a divorce action in those states that have incorporated no-fault divorce grounds into traditional fault-based divorce grounds. Which divorce ground must the judge recognize? The following case addresses this issue.

WILLIAMS v. WILLIAMS
Virginia Court of Appeals
415 S.E.2d 252 (1992)

BRAY, JUDGE.

By final decree entered June 5, 1991, Ronald Lee Williams (husband) was divorced from Maureen O'Keeffe Williams (wife) "on the ground that the parties. . . have lived separate and apart for a period in excess of one year." The decree, inter alia, ordered the husband to pay spousal support to the wife in the amount of $200 per month and $5,000 "toward [her] attorney's fees." The husband appeals, complaining that the trial court erred when it "granted the divorce upon the ground of one year separation instead o. . . the wife's adultery" and required him to pay both spousal support and attorney's fees. . . .

The parties to this cause were married April 19, 1986, and separated October 1, 1988. Shortly thereafter, the wife instituted these proceedings, alleging cruelty and constructive desertion by the husband. The husband's responsive pleadings denied these claims, alleged desertion by the wife and also prayed for a divorce. Later, the husband filed an Amended Cross-Bill which added adultery by the wife as an additional ground for the divorce.

The record clearly disclosed that the wife became pregnant "in approximately May, 1989," and obtained a "therapeutic abortion" the following month. Since the parties had no sexual contact subsequent to November, 1988, the husband argues that the "only inference available" is that this pregnancy "resulted from [the wife's] adulterous conduct." The wife does not deny the pregnancy, but counters that the husband's evidence failed either "to indicate. . . [the] circumstances" of the pregnancy or the identity of the father and, consequently, did not sufficiently establish the consensual sexual intercourse necessary to prove adultery.

The evidence was before the trial judge both on depositions and hearings ore tenus. While "a divorce decree based solely on depositions is not as conclusive on appellate review as one based upon evidence heard ore tenus," it is nonetheless "presumed correct and will not be overturned if supported by substantial, competent and credible evidence." *Collier v. Collier*, 2 Va. App. 125, 127, 341 S.E.2d 827, 828 (1986). If the court "hears the evidence ore tenus, its finding is entitled to great weight and will not be disturbed on appeal unless plainly wrong or without evidence to support it." *Pommerenke v. Pommerenke*, 7 Va. App. 241, 244, 372 S.E.2d 630, 631 (1988). . . .In both instances, however, we must, on appeal, "view [the] evidence and all reasonable inferences in the light most favorable to the prevailing party below." *Id.*. . . .

Assuming, without deciding, that the husband sufficiently proved the wife's adultery, the trial court was not compelled "to give precedence to one proven ground of divorce over another." *Robertson v. Robertson*, 215 Va. 425, 426, 211 S.E.2d 41, 43 (1975). It is well established that "[w]here dual or multiple grounds for divorce exist, the trial judge can use his [or her] sound discretion to select the grounds upon which he [or she] will grant the divorce." *Lassen v. Lassen*, 8 Va. App. 502, 505, 383 S.E.2d 471, 473 (1989). . . .

The no-fault [separation] ground selected by the trial court did not diminish any obligation of the husband to support his wife, absent proof that there existed in his favor some other ground of divorce under [Va.] Code 20–91 or 20–95. . .; *Dukelow v. Dukelow*, 2 Va. App. 21, 25, 341 S.E.2d 208, 210 (1986). The presence of "some other ground of divorce" is an express consideration to a spousal support analysis under Code 20–107.1, which permits reduction or elimination of [spousal] support to a party at fault, consonant with the intendment of Code 20–91(9) (c).

While the husband correctly argues that Code 20–107.1 identifies adultery as the single fault ground for divorce which precludes "permanent maintenance and support" to the offending spouse, this limitation is not absolute. Notwithstanding a finding of adultery, the court may award spousal support provided "the court determines from clear and convincing evidence that a denial of. . . [such support] would constitute a manifest injustice, based upon the respective degrees of fault during the marriage and the relative economic circumstances of the parties." Code 20–107.1.

In his letter opinion to the parties, the trial judge did not address the adultery issue, but expressly noted his consideration of "those factors set forth in Code 20–107.1." Thus, the wife's adultery, if proven to the satisfaction of the court, was implicitly considered in its determination of spousal support. Although the trial judge did not "quantify or elaborate on what weight or consideration" was given to this statutory factor, his opinion recited evidence clearly relevant to spousal support which, together with other "substantial credible evidence" in the record "supported the award." *Gibson v. Gibson*, 5 Va. App. 426, 435, 364 S.E.2d 518, 523 (1988). Moreover, it is presumed "that a trial judge properly based his [or her] decision on the evidence presented. . . and properly applied the law." *Brown v. Commonwealth*, 8 Va. App. 126, 133, 380 S.E.2d 8, 12 (1989). Under such circumstances, we will not disturb the court's decision. . . .

With respect to the partial award of attorney's fees to the wife, it is well established that this is also "a matter submitted to the trial court's sound discretion and is reviewable on appeal only for an abuse of discretion." *Graves v. Graves*, 4 Va. App. 326, 333, 357 S.E.2d 554, 558 (1987). . . .

Fault is not a bar to recovery of fees and costs, provided the court has first undertaken "a consideration of the circumstances and equities of the entire case." *Davis v. Davis*, 8 Va. App. 12, 17, 377 S.E.2d 640, 643 (1989). . . .Again, we find ample support in the record for the court's decree.

Accordingly, the judgment of the trial court is affirmed.

Affirmed.

NOTES AND QUESTIONS

(1) If the parties in the *Williams* case could have obtained a no-fault divorce based on their living separate and apart, which is ultimately what the trial court granted, why did the husband file an amended cross-bill adding adultery by the wife as an additional ground for divorce? And why did husband and wife allege cruelty and desertion grounds as well?

(2) The Virginia Court of Appeals reiterated throughout the *Williams* decision that family-court judges, from their equity heritage as triers of law and fact, possess broad judicial discretion in adjudicating family-law disputes, and therefore the trial court's decision "will not be disturbed on appeal unless it is plainly wrong or without evidence to support it." *See also* 1 Homer H. Clark, Law of Domestic Relations (2d ed. 1988) 644–45: "It is axiomatic that the trial courts have wide discretion in [resolving divorce disputes and] determining the propriety and the amount of alimony. The relevant factors are so numerous and their influence so incapable of precise evaluation that the trial court's decision in a particular case will be affirmed [by the appellate court] unless it amounts to an abuse of discretion or is based upon an erroneous application of legal principles."

This broad discretion not only allows judges to ignore fault, as in *Williams*, but to award alimony because of fault and without evidence of need. Such discretion has been severely criticized by Professor Ira Ellman, who served as the Chief Reporter for the American Law Institute's *Principles of the Law of Family Dissolution: Analysis and Recommendations* (Proposed Final Draft 1997). Professor Ellman writes that such broad judicial discretion in divorce disputes involving fault "seems inherently limitless if no finding of economic harm to the claimant is required to justify an award or its amount" based upon enumerated marital fault.

> The traditional marital fault rule requires extraordinary reliance on trial court discretion. Neither the standard of [marital] misconduct, nor its dollar consequences, are much bounded by any rule. While in principle the trial court's decision can be reviewed for "abuse of discretion," reversals are rare. . . .The traditional fault rule is thus inconsistent with a major theme of the *Principles*, an effort to improve the consistency and predictability of trial court decisions.

Id. at 69–70. On the other hand, Professor Barbara Bennett Woodhouse writes,

> I agree with the ALI's [*Principles of the Law of Family Dissolution*] description of the complexities and challenges of the judging process, but not with the faint-hearted conclusion that judges are incapable of trying cases that depend on assessing the reasonableness of [the parties' marital] conduct in a given context or on calculating intangibles. We have learned to calculate "goodwill" in a business enterprise, to place a dollar value on an accident victim's pain, to judge corporate directors' fidelity in complex takeover negotiations, and to calibrate punitive damages to deter misconduct in many spheres. There is no reason why courts cannot undertake similar inquiries in the area of marital fault.

Barbara Bennett Woodhouse, *Sex, Lies, and Dissipation: The Discourse of Fault in a No-Fault Era*, 82 Geo. L.J. 2525, 2560 (1994). *See also* Barbara Bennett Woodhouse, *Towards a Revitalization of Family Law*, 69 Tex. L. Rev. 245, 278–79 (1990) (pointing out that fault is just one of many statutory factors that a trial court must properly take into consideration in determining the applicable grounds for divorce, spousal-support awards, and the equitable distribution of marital property on divorce).

Query: If the rule of broad judicial discretion in family-law disputes also applies to the classification, valuation, and distribution of marital property on divorce, as well as applying to child-custody matters and other incidents of divorce or dissolution of marriage, is Professor Ellman implicitly arguing for the abolition or the serious curtailment of judicial discretion in other family law areas as well as those areas involving fault factors on divorce? What significant parameters and underlying public-policy rationales are involved in seriously curtailing judicial discretion in family-law disputes generally? On the other hand, do trial court judges in family-law disputes in fact possess "inherently limitless" judicial discretion? Did the trial court judge in the *Williams* case possess such "limitless" discretion? Could the judge on the facts of this particular case have instead granted Mr. Williams a divorce based on adultery grounds, instead of decreeing the divorce on no-fault separation grounds, and then denied the wife spousal support? *See also Hammonds v. Hammonds*, 597 So. 2d 653 (Miss. 1992) (holding that alimony should not have been denied to a wife on divorce solely because of her adulterous behavior when alimony was otherwise appropriate, and a denial of alimony would render the wife destitute). *Compare Bachman v. Bachman*, 1995 WESTLAW 9259 (Conn. Super. Ct. 1995) (holding that husband's cruelty and infidelity caused the dissolution of the marriage, rather than wife's obesity and spendthrift practices) *with Grimmeisen v. Grimmeisen*, 1993 WL 268412 (Conn. Super. Ct. 1993) (holding that wife's obesity and frequent absence from the marital home caused the dissolution of the parties' marriage rather than husband's two homosexual affairs).

(3) In the Williams's bill of complaint for divorce, the wife charged that her husband's cruelty was tantamount to constructive desertion, thereby forcing her to leave the marital residence, but the husband's responsive pleadings were that the wife had deserted *him* without just cause. So cruelty and desertion are two other traditional fault-based divorce grounds, in addition to adultery, that may be alleged by the parties.

(a) **Cruelty**. Cruelty is a traditional fault ground that is currently available in 28 states, and before no-fault divorce remedies were available, it was the most commonly used divorce ground in the United States. Cruelty is generally present when there is bodily harm, or a reasonable apprehension of bodily harm, that endangers life, limb, or health, and renders marital cohabitation unsafe or improper. *See, e.g., Brady v. Brady*, 476 N.E.2d 290 (N.Y. 1985). Most courts recognize both physical and mental cruelty, but cruelty normally includes successive acts of ill treatment over an extended period of time. A single act of physical cruelty will not ordinarily provide a basis for divorce unless the act is so severe and atrocious as to endanger life or cause serious bodily harm, or causes reasonable apprehension of serious danger in the future. *See, e.g., Gibson v. Gibson*, 322 S.E.2d 680 (S.C. Ct. App. 1984). *See also Davis v. Davis*, 377 S.E.2d 640 (Va. Ct. App. 1989) (husband shooting his wife in the back, and paralyzing her from the waist down, constituted a single atrocious act of physical cruelty that would constitute grounds for divorce).

Recognition of various forms of mental and physical cruelty as grounds for divorce has been greatly liberalized in the past three decades and may include cruelty based upon a spouse's insistence on "excessive, unnatural, or otherwise unreasonable" sexual intercourse, R.P. Davis, Annotation, *Insistence on Sex Relations as Cruelty or Indignity*, 88 A.L.R.2d 553 (1963); a spouse's refusal to engage in "reasonable" sexual intercourse, D. Tussey, Annotation, *Refusal of Sexual Intercourse as Justifying Divorce or Separation*, 82 A.L.R.3d 660 (1978); mistreatment and abuse of children, I. J. Schiffres, Annotation, *Mistreatment of Children as Ground for Divorce*, 82 A.L.R.2d 1361 (1962); transvestism or transsexualism, D. Tussey, Annotation, *Transvestism or transexualism of spouse as justifying divorce*, 82 A.L.R.3d 725 (1978); as well as verbal and physical abuse, non-support, homosexuality, drunkeness or use of drugs, false accusations of infidelity or criminal misconduct, and general marital unkindness. *See generally* 21 Am. Jur. Proof of Facts 191 (1968) and J. L. Rigelhaupt, *Dissolution of Marriage on Statutory Ground of Incompatibility*, 19 Am. Jur. Proof of Facts 2d 221 (1979). If a spouse's cruelty forces the other spouse out of the marital home, the offending spouse may also be guilty of constructive desertion. *See e.g.*, G. Van Ingen, Annotation, *Divorce: Acts or Omissions of Spouse Causing Other Spouse to Leave Home as Desertion by Former*, 19 A.L.R.2d 1428 (1951) and Later Case Service.

(b) **Desertion**. Desertion is another traditional fault ground for divorce that is currently law in approximately 30 states. Desertion has been defined as the breaking off of matrimonial cohabitation with the intent to desert. It thus involves a voluntary separation of one spouse from the other, with the intent not to resume marital cohabitation, and without justification or the consent of the other spouse. *See, e.g., Bergeron v. Bergeron*, 372 So.

2d 731 (La. Ct. App. 1979) and *In re Marriage of Jones*, 412 N.E.2d 1122 (Ill. App. Ct. 1980).

An action for desertion may be defended against on the basis of justification. Thus, a spouse may be justified in leaving the marital home due to the marital misconduct of the other spouse. Although some courts require that this misconduct be equivalent to an actual divorce ground, other courts simply require that the provoking conduct "be such that it is inconsistent with the marriage relationship or makes it impossible to continue cohabitation with due regard to safety, health, or self-respect." Note, *Constructive Desertion A Broader Basis for Breaking the Bond*, 51 Iowa L. Rev. 108, 120 (1965). *See also Day v. Day*, 501 So. 2d 353 (Miss. 1987) (living separate and apart prior to divorce did not constitute desertion), and *Gottlieb v. Gottlieb*, 448 S.E.2d 666 (Va. Ct. App. 1994) (a spouse who reasonably believes his or her health would be endangered by remaining in the household, and who has unsuccessfully taken reasonable measures to eliminate the danger without breaking off cohabitation, is not legally at fault in leaving). A separation by mutual consent would not constitute desertion by either party. Likewise, a spouse generally is not guilty of desertion for separating from the other spouse a divorce suit is pending, as long as the divorce action is not frivolous or fraudulent. *See, e.g., Byrd v. Byrd,*, 348 S.E.2d 262 (Va. 1986).

(c) **Other Fault Grounds**. Other statutory fault grounds for divorce in various states include conviction of a crime, drunkenness or drug addiction, and insanity. *See* D.P. Chapus, Annotation, *Divorce: Insanity as Defense*, 67 A.L.R. 4th 277 (1989). On fault grounds for divorce generally, *see* Green, Long, & Murawski, Dissolution of Marriage 15–53 (1986), and 2 Homer H. Clark, Jr., Law of Domestic Relations 1–71 (2d ed. 1987).

(4) **Defenses to Fault-Based Divorce Grounds**. There are four traditional defenses to a divorce based upon fault grounds: (a) connivance; (b) collusion; (c) condonation; and (d) recrimination. Delay in bringing a divorce action also constitutes a statutory defense in a minority of states.

(a) **Connivance**. Connivance has been defined as the corrupt consenting by one spouse to the marital fault of another. If husband and wife mutually agree that husband will commit adultery or desert the wife in order for the wife to bring a divorce action against the husband, this would constitute connivance, and the wife would not be entitled to a divorce, since the wife cannot complain of something to which she has consented. Connivance as a defense has also been based on the equitable clean hands doctrine. *See, e.g., Fonger v. Fonger*, 154 A. 443 (Md. 1931). *See also Hollis v. Hollis*, 427 S.E.2d 233 (Va. Ct. App. 1993) (holding that wife's connivance in husband's adultery was established by her letters stating a desire for her husband to fall in love with another woman "but not a bimbo," and by her note accompanying flowers and champagne expressing her best wishes to her husband and his girlfriend on "your new beginning" during their weekend together). Hiring an agent to seduce a defendant spouse also constitutes connivance. *See generally* Moore, *An Analysis of Collusion and Connivance Bars to Divorce*, 36 UMKC L. Rev. 193 (1968).

(b) **Collusion**. Collusion is fraud on the divorcing court by the husband and wife in alleging evidence of a marital offense that was not actually committed. However, the parties' mutual desire for a divorce will not amount to collusion unless some fraud was actually perpetrated upon the court. *See* Moore, *above*. To prevent against the possibility of connivance and collusion of the parties, various state statutes provide that there must also be third-party corroboration of the divorce ground. *See, e.g.,* D.C. Code § 16–919 (1981) and Va. Code Ann. § 20–99 (1987). However, the modern trend in the case law appears to recognize that where it is apparent that there is no collusion, then such corroboration need only to be slight. *See, e.g., Hurt v. Hurt,* 433 S.E.2d 493 (Va. Ct. App. 1993). When collusion is discovered at trial the court may dismiss the action. Collusion is also a fertile ground for a collateral attack on the judgment; if successfully brought, it may result in the divorce decree being vacated. *See generally* Bradway, *Collusion and the Public Interest in the Law of Divorce,* 47 Cornell L.Q. 374 (1962).

(c) **Condonation**. Condonation is the conditional forgiveness of a marital fault, with the understanding that the fault will not happen again. If the marital fault is repeated, then the condonation defense is nullified, and the divorce ground is revived. *See, e.g., Cutlip v. Cutlip,* 383 S.E.2d 273 (Va. Ct. App. 1989) (holding that condoned adultery is revived when a guilty party resumes association with his or her paramour). The general rule is that the innocent spouse's knowledge of the marital fault is necessary for a condonation defense to apply. *See generally* Reader, *Knowledge or Belief as a Prerequisite for Condonation,* 21 Minn. L. Rev. 408 (1936). A total resumption of marital cohabitation amounts to condonation since it implies that there is both forgiveness of the marital fault and evidence of a full reconciliation of the parties. *See, e.g., Hickman v. Hickman,* 227 So. 2d 14 (La. Ct. App. 1969).

(d) **Recrimination**. Under the doctrine of recrimination, if both spouses are guilty of marital misconduct, then any fault-based divorce action must be dismissed, since traditionally a divorce could only be granted to an innocent spouse, and under the doctrine of recrimination both spouses are in pari delicto and lack "clean hands." *See generally* Beamer, 10 UMKC L. Rev. 213 (1942). *See, e.g., Merrick v. Merrick,* 627 N.Y.S.2d 884 (N.Y. Sup. Ct. 1995), *aff'd,* 636 N.Y.S.2d 1006 (N.Y. App. Div. 1995) (applying a recrimination defense to adultery grounds). Professor Clark, among other commentators, calls recrimination an "outrageous legal principle" since it ordains that when both spouses have fault grounds for divorce, neither may obtain a divorce decree. 2 Homer H. Clark, Jr., Law of Domestic Relations 68–70 (2d ed. 1987).

In a minority of states there are also specific statutes of limitation in bringing a divorce action which generally apply to adultery grounds. *See, e.g.,* N.Y. Dom. Rel. L. § 171(3) (1977) (5 years for adultery actions); and Va. Code Ann. § 20–94 (1975) (5 years for adultery, sodomy, or buggery). Again, these defenses only apply to fault-based divorce grounds.

(5) **Discovery**. Most courts allow liberal discovery in divorce cases as long as the information is relevant. *E.g., Roussos v. Roussos,* 434 N.Y.S.2d 600 (N.Y. Sup. Ct. 1980) What happens, however, when a spouse is asked by opposing counsel whether he or she committed adultery and with whom? May that spouse successfully invoke his or her constitutional privilege against self-incrimination? Why or why not? *Compare Molloy v. Molloy,* 176 N.W.2d 292 (Wis. 1970) *with* Va. Code Ann. § 8.01–223.1 (1985).

(6) **Problem**. Henry visited his lawyer in the State of Holmes regarding a possible divorce action against his wife Wanda. Henry had been separated from his wife, since their marriage now involved irreconcilable differences, but Henry also claimed that Wanda had deserted him, and Henry also suspected that Wanda had committed adultery. Henry's lawyer informed him that the law of Holmes recognized both no-fault and fault grounds for divorce,

but that fault grounds were also a statutory consideration in determining spousal support and marital property rights. Henry then told his lawyer that he wanted to obtain a divorce based upon fault grounds against Wanda.

Henry had employed a private detective, Sam Slade, to watch Wanda's apartment for any suspected activity. One night, Sam observed that Wanda's attorney entered her apartment, that they appeared to be drinking in the living room for some time, that they both went up to Wanda's bedroom, and that they were seen embracing each other in Wanda's bedroom before the curtains were drawn and the lights went out. The attorney was then observed leaving Wanda's apartment at 9 o'clock the next morning.

In a subsequent divorce action, Wanda's attorney, as the alleged correspondent or paramour, claimed that he was at Wanda's apartment only "on business" to discuss Wanda's divorce from Henry, that he had "some drinks" with Wanda, and because of his inebriated state, he couldn't drive home safely, so he had to spend the night sleeping on the sofa in Wanda's living room.

(a) Is there enough evidence in this case to prove adultery? Why or why not? *Compare Dooley v. Dooley*, 278 S.E.2d 865 (Va. 1981) *with Coe v. Coe*, 303 S.E.2d 923 (Va. 1983); *Everett v. Everett*, 345 So. 2d 586 (La. Ct. App. 1977), *Nemeth v. Nemeth*, 481 S.E.2d 181 (S.C. Ct. App. 1997).

Suppose that Wanda denied ever having engaged in sexual intercourse with her alleged correspondent, although she testified that she and her attorney got undressed and got into bed together, but their "sexual activities" did not include sexual intercourse. Adultery or not? *Compare Hunter v. Hunter*, 614 N.Y.S.2d 784 (N.Y. App. Div. 1994) *with Menge v. Menge*, 491 So. 2d 700 (La. App. 1986) *and Bonura v. Bonura*, 505 So. 2d 143 (La. Ct. App. 1987). Would the attorney's intoxication be a defense to adultery? *See Miller v. Miller*, 140 Md. 60, 116 A. 840 (Md. 1922).

(b) Assume that subsequent to the evening in question, but prior to the divorce proceedings, Henry and Wanda resumed living together as husband and wife in the hope of a possible reconciliation. Does this by itself constitute condonation? Why or why not? *See Wood v. Wood*, 495 So. 2d 503 (Miss. 1986).

(c) While living together as husband and wife, Wanda alleged that Henry's wilful breach and neglect of his marital duties destroyed their home life and amounted to desertion. *Query:* Can a spouse successfully allege desertion grounds while living under the same roof? Why or why not? *See Jamison v. Jamison*, 352 S.E.2d 719 (Va. Ct. App. 1987).

[B] No-Fault Divorce Grounds

[1] Living Separate and Apart

Approximately half the states have a no-fault divorce ground based upon living separate and apart without cohabitation or interruption for a specified period of time, which varies from 60 days in Minnesota and three months in Louisiana and Vermont, to three years in Texas and Utah. However, six to eighteen months appears to be the most frequently used time period. Elrod & Spector, *A Review of the Year in Family Law*, 30 Fam. L.Q. 765, 807 (1997). Section 302 of the Uniform Marriage and Divorce Act also provides that a marriage may be dissolved if the parties have lived separate and apart for more than 180 days preceding the commencement of the suit.

What proof must a party demonstrate to the court in order to obtain a divorce based on living separate and apart? The following case discusses these requirements.

SINHA v. SINHA
Pennsylvania Supreme Court
526 A.2d 765 (1987)

HUTCHINSON, JUSTICE

Appellant, Chandra Prabha Sinha, appeals . . . a Superior Court order . . . which affirmed a decree of divorce entered in the Court of Common Pleas of Delaware County. Appellant argues that a unilateral divorce under our Divorce Code of 1980 requires formulation of an intent to dissolve the marriage before the statute's three-year separation requirement begins to run. We agree with appellant that the reconciliation goals of the Divorce Code will be furthered by requiring an independent showing of intent to end the marriage before commencement of the three-year period. Because this record shows appellee formed his intent to terminate the marital bonds only fourteen months before his filing suit in Common Pleas, we reverse the order of Superior Court.

On March 11, 1974, appellant and appellee, Shrikant Nandan Prasad Sinha, were married pursuant to a Hindu marriage ritual in Patna, Bihar, India. Appellee came to America in August of 1976 to pursue a master's degree in city and regional planning at Rutgers University in New Jersey. Due to appellant's inability to obtain a visa, she was unable to join or visit her husband in the United States. The parties corresponded regularly and, as late as September 26, 1978, the husband professed his love for his wife. In August, 1979, the appellee filed a complaint in New Jersey Superior Court seeking a divorce. This action was voluntarily dismissed subsequent to appellee's move to Media, Delaware County. Appellee then renewed his efforts to secure a divorce with the filing of a complaint in Delaware County Common Pleas on October 15, 1980. The complaint alleged that the parties had lived separate and apart for three years and that the marriage was irretrievably broken pursuant to 23 P.S. § 201(d) (Supp. 1986). . . .

After hearings in November 1981 and March 1982, a general master concluded that Pennsylvania courts enjoyed jurisdiction to resolve the matter, that the parties had lived separate and apart for three years, and that the marriage was irretrievably broken. Delaware County Common Pleas then discussed exceptions to the master's report and a decree in divorce was entered on November 10, 1982. Superior Court affirmed.

Appellee first revealed his intention to end the marriage with the filing of the New Jersey complaint in August, 1979. Pennsylvania's unilateral divorce provision, 23 P.S. § 201(d), requires that the parties live separate and apart for three years and that the marriage be irretrievably broken. Physical separation alone will not satisfy the requirements of the statute. The demands placed on marriage by modern society will often force a spouse to leave the marital abode for long periods of time. These separations should not be interpreted as an intent to terminate the marriage. Accordingly, § 201(d) of the Divorce Code requires an intent to terminate the marital relation independent of the physical separation mandated by the statute. As appellee's intent to dissolve the marriage clearly manifested itself only fourteen months before the filing of the Pennsylvania complaint, the three-year requirement of § 201(d) has not been satisfied.

Prior to the adoption of the Divorce Code of 1980, Pennsylvania's divorce laws had remained essentially unchanged since 1785. . . . .The previous code required a showing that one of the parties to a marriage was at fault before a divorce would be granted. 23 P.S. § 10 (repealed 1980). . . . The old requirement that the plaintiff seeking divorce be "innocent and injured" and that the other spouse be at fault forced many couples to perjure themselves rather than remain in an intolerable marital situation. Gold-Bikin & Rounick, *The New Pennsylvania Divorce Code*, 25 Vill. L. Rev. 617, 619–20 (1980). Recognizing the difficulties inherent in a fault-only system, the legislature included in the new act a number of "no-fault" provisions. Section 201(b) allows for divorce where one party suffers from a mental disability resulting in confinement for three years. 23 P.S. § 201(b). A divorce may be granted where the marriage is irretrievably broken and both parties consent to the divorce. 23 P.S. § 201(c). A third provision, upon which appellee relied in the instant case, allows a court to grant a divorce where the parties have lived separate and apart for at least three years and upon a showing that the marriage is irretrievably broken. 23 P.S. § 201(d).

Noting that the definitional section of the 1980 Divorce Code, 23 P.S. § 104, interprets "separate and apart" as the "[c]omplete cessation of any and all cohabitation," Superior Court affirmed Common Pleas, [granting] a divorce to appellee based upon the parties' physical separation, which commenced with appellee's departure for the United States in August, 1976. This was error. Physical separation alone does not satisfy the separate and apart requirement of § 201(d). There must be an independent intent on the part of one of the parties to dissolve the marital union before the three-year period commences. This intent must be clearly manifested and communicated to the other spouse. Any other interpretation would allow one spouse to depart the marital home for apparently benign purposes, remain away for the statutory period, and then sue for a divorce. The granting of a divorce under such circumstances would deprive the unknowing party an opportunity to attempt reconciliation, a specific policy goal of the legislature. 23 P.S. § 102(a) (2). All too often the exigencies of modern life require a spouse to leave the marital home for extended periods. The demands of one's employment, education and military service may not be utilized to secure a divorce, absent an independent intent to dissolve the marriage.

The Virginia Supreme Court, faced with a similar set of facts, interpreted their unilateral divorce provision to require not only physical separation but also an independent intent to end the marriage. In *Hooker v. Hooker*, 215 Va. 415, 211 S.E.2d 34 (1975) (per curiam), Cecil M. Hooker went to South Vietnam as a civilian employee of the United States Army in August, 1970. During his absence, substantial sums of money were sent from Vietnam to Mrs. Hooker for the support and education of the family, mortgage payments, and for the care of the Hookers' horses. In dismissing Mr. Hooker's complaint in divorce, a chancellor found no intent on the part of Mr. Hooker to terminate the marriage until September, 1972, when divorce proceedings were initiated. In affirming the trial court, the Virginia Supreme Court noted:

> We believe that the words "lived separate and apart" in [Va.] Code § 20–91(9) mean more than mere physical separation. In our view the General Assembly intended that the separation be coupled with an intention on the part of at least one of the parties to live separate and apart permanently, and that this intention must be shown to have been present at the beginning of the uninterrupted period of living separate and apart without any cohabitation. Otherwise, many extended separations required by other

circumstances could ripen to "instant divorce" without the salutory period of contemplation required by the statute during which the parties have an opportunity for reconciliation.

Id. at 417, 211 S.E.2d at 3. In the context of another separation engendered by military service, the Supreme Court of Louisiana opined:

> Business and other necessities may require the husband to live in one place and the wife at another. The separation intended by the statute is a separation by which the marital association is severed. It means the living asunder of the husband and wife. It is a voluntary act, and the separation must be with the intent of the married persons to live apart because of their mutual purpose to do so, or because one of the parties with or without the acquiescence of the other intends to discontinue the marital relationship.

Otis v. Bahan, 209 La. 1082, 1088, 26 So. 2d 146, 148 (1946).

Our research reveals many appellate decisions defining the "separate and apart" proviso of a unilateral divorce statute to require an intent to dissolve the marital union apart from mere physical separation. . . . *Mogensky v. Mogensky*, 212 Ark. 28, 204 S.W.2d 782 (1947) (separation occurring before husband entered Army evidences independent intent to end marriage); *Jordan v. Jordan*, 69 Idaho 513, 210 P.2d 934 (1949) (husband and wife not separate and apart pursuant to statute where absence made necessary by employment); *Byers v. Byers*, 222 N.C. 298, 22 S.E.2d 902 (1942) (separation must occur with intent of at least one of parties to cease cohabitation arising at beginning of separation period); *Dailey v. Dailey*, 11 Ohio App. 3d 121, 463 N.E.2d 427 (1983) (where wife suffers stroke, enters hospital and does not return to home for over two years, parties not living separate and apart as separation must have been voluntary); *Niemann v. Niemann*, 317 S.E.2d 472 (S.C. Ct. App. 1984) (where separation independent of military service divorce on grounds of separation proper). *See also Caye v. Caye*, 203 P.2d 1013 (Nev. 1949) (one does not live separate from his spouse by being called to duty in the armed forces or being called away on business); 24 Am. Jur. 2d *Divorce and Separation* § 148 (1983); 27A C.J.S. *Divorce* § 20 (1986). . . .

The results reached by those courts are in accord with what we believe our legislature intended in precluding a unilateral no fault divorce until after a three-year separation.

Our holding today, that the "separate and apart" language of 23 P.S. § 201(d) requires both physical separation and a clear intent on the part of at least one of the parties to dissolve the marital ties at the beginning of the three year period, requires us to reverse Superior Court. Appellee departed the marital home in August 1976 with the avowed purpose of obtaining a graduate degree. He filed a complaint in divorce in mid-August, 1979, although, as late as September 26, 1978, he had professed his love for his wife in regular correspondence to her in India. Even though the parties were physically separated, appellee's own hand traces the constraints of the marriage bond. Employment of the August, 1976, departure date as the commencement of the three year period would deny the unknowing wife the opportunity for reconciliation contemplated by the Divorce Code. Appellee first manifested an intent to sever the marital bond with the filing of the New Jersey suit, only fourteen months prior to his filing of a complaint in divorce in Delaware County Common Pleas. As such, appellee has not lived separate and apart from his spouse for the three years required by § 201(d) of the Divorce Code.

Accordingly, the judgment of Superior Court is reversed. . . .

NOTES AND QUESTIONS

(1) As illustrated in the *Sinha* case, a spouse's intent to dissolve the marital relationship must be clearly manifested and communicated to the other spouse before the spouses can live "separate and apart" under the applicable divorce statute. (The current Pennsylvania statute has a two-year separation requirement.) So physical separation alone, without the requisite intent of at least one of the spouses to live separate and apart, will not constitute valid grounds for divorce under such a statute.

Query: What if the defendant spouse does not contest the divorce? In *Bruce v. Bruce*, 339 S.E.2d 855 (N.C. Ct. App. 1986), the court cited the general rule that a judgment by default is not permitted in divorce proceedings, and the facts which constitute a separation ground for divorce must therefore be pled and proved, even though they may be uncontested by the defendant spouse. On the other hand, traditional fault-based defenses to divorce, such as recrimination, would not be applicable in an action for divorce based on living separate and apart for one year or more under the North Carolina statute.

(2) *Query.* What constitutes "separation"? Can spouses legally live separate and apart under the same roof, and in the same household? *Compare Ellam v. Ellam*, 333 A.2d 577 (N.J. Super. Ct. Ch. Div. 1975) *with In re Marriage of Uhls*, 549 S.W.2d 107 (Mo. Ct. App. 1977). *See also* F. S. Tinio, Annotation, *Separation Within Statute Making Separation a Substantive Ground for Divorce*, 35 A.L.R.3d 1238 (1971). What if the spouses voluntarily had sexual relations during the statutory separation period—would this constitute separation "without cohabitation"? *Compare Pitts v. Pitts*, 282 S.E.2d 488 (N.C. Ct. App. 1981) *with Thomas v. Thomas*, 483 A.2d 945 (Pa. Super. Ct. 1984) *and Petachenko v. Petachenko*, 350 S.E.2d 600 (Va. 1986).

(3) **Voluntary vs. Involuntary Separation**. A small minority of states provide that living separate and apart must be voluntary and by mutual consent if it is to be a ground for divorce. Thus, if one spouse is insane at the time of separation, the requisite voluntariness for separation would not be present, and a divorce on this ground could not be granted. *See, e.g., Adams v. Adams*, 402 So. 2d 300 (La. Ct. App. 1981), *rev'd*, 408 So. 2d 1322 (La. 1982). Also, a lack of mutual consent to separate might result in the non-consenting spouse bringing an action for desertion against the separating spouse. However, the majority of states that have recognized a living-separate-and-apart ground for divorce do not require that the separation be mutual and voluntary, and these statutes therefore have been interpreted as a no-fault divorce ground. *See, e.g., Hooker v. Hooker*, 211 S.E.2d 34 (Va. 1975). Nevertheless, an intent to separate must still be shown to avoid "instant divorce on demand" and to allow an opportunity for possible reconciliation. *Id.*

(4) *Query:* What are the disadvantages of the living-separate-and-apart divorce ground compared to a no-fault divorce ground based upon irreconcilable differences? What are the possible advantages? *See generally* 2 Homer H. Clark, Jr., Law of Domestic Relations 42–47 (2d ed. 1987); and Green, Long, & Murawski, Dissolution of Marriage 74–82 (1986).

[2] Irreconcilable Differences

Eighteen states have abolished all fault grounds for divorce and have substituted "irreconcilable differences "or the "irretrievable breakdown of the marriage" as the sole ground for divorce or dissolution of marriage. *See* Elrod & Spector, *A Review of the Year in Family Law*, 30 Fam. L. Q. 765, 807 (1997). Section 302 of the Uniform Marriage and Divorce Act likewise provides for dissolution of marriage if the marriage is "irretrievably broken" by an evidentiary finding that the parties lived separate and apart for more than 180 days preceding the commencement of the suit, or that there is "serious marital discord adversely affecting the attitude of one or both of the parties toward the marriage." 9A U.L.A. 147, 181 (1987).

Query: Does a no-fault divorce based upon the parties' irreconcilable differences necessarily require that there also be no-fault distribution of marital property on divorce and no-fault spousal support rights? The following case discusses this important—and very controversial—issue.

GROSSKOPF v. GROSSKOPF
Wyoming Supreme Court
677 P.2d 814 (1984)

CARDINE, JUSTICE.

This appeal is from a judgment and decree in a divorce action[.] . . . [Appellant objects] to its provisions for child support, division of property, and denial of alimony and attorneys fees. We will affirm. . . .

Appellant, Jeannine Marie Grosskopf, and appellee, Loren M. Grosskopf, were married August 17, 1968, while attending college in Wisconsin. Appellant was a junior and appellee was a sophomore at the time of the marriage. Both were employed part time. Appellant graduated with a degree in special education one year before appellee and went to work full time supporting the family during appellee's senior year. After graduation, appellee obtained a teaching assistantship at the University of Wyoming. The parties moved to Wyoming; appellant worked full time and appellee worked part time while attending the University of Wyoming and obtained his masters degree in accounting.

Following graduation, appellee obtained employment at Cody, Wyoming, and the parties established their home there. Three children were born of the marriage. At the time of the divorce, the children were 11, 5, and 2 years of age. After twelve years, there were marital problems and difficulties which the parties were unable to resolve. Considerable testimony was adduced at the trial by both parties concerning the problems in their marriage, fault and the cause of these difficulties. The evidence established, and the parties generally agreed, that the differences existing between them were such that there was no prospect for reconciliation.

On October 12, 1980, after a particularly bitter dispute, appellee separated from appellant. Two days later this divorce action was initiated by appellee. Appellant took the three children of the marriage, traveled to Wisconsin, where she could be with relatives and friends, and stayed approximately five weeks. She returned to Cody, Wyoming, at Thanksgiving time, attempted to reconcile and resolve the problems of the marriage, but that was unsuccessful. On December 19, 1980, appellant moved with the children to Appleton, Wisconsin, where they presently reside. . . .

The court entered a judgment and decree in which it awarded custody of the children to appellant, subject to the right of appellee to have the children on alternate holidays, four weeks during the summer until the children became six years of age, and six weeks during the summer thereafter. It required appellee to pay $250 per month child support per child, or a total of $750 per month, divided the property between the parties in such a manner that appellant received $36,190.70, and appellee received a like amount but was also required to satisfy the debts of the parties existing at the date of separation, which resulted in appellee's being required to pay $8,593.30. The final result was that appellant was awarded $36,190.70 in cash and appellee was left with a net liability of $8,593.30. The court declined to award to appellant either alimony or attorneys fees.

WAS THERE ERROR IN FINDING APPELLANT AT FAULT AND GRANTING DIVORCE TO APPELLEE?

Appellant contends that, upon the evidence presented, the court should not have found appellant at fault and therefore should not have granted the divorce to appellee. Appellee began this action by filing a complaint for divorce. Appellant, in her answer and counterclaim, prayed that divorce be granted to her. With respect to grounds or causes for divorce, § 20–2–104, W.S.1977, provides that:

> A divorce may be decreed by the district court of the county in which either party resides on the complaint of the aggrieved party on the grounds of irreconcilable differences in the marital relationship.

As to the grounds for divorce, the statute requires proof only of "irreconcilable differences" to permit the court to award a decree of divorce. It matters not which party was at fault in bringing about the differences which cannot be reconciled. All that is required is that the irreconcilable differences exist. Section 20–2–104, *above*, provides that the divorce may be decreed upon ". . . the complaint of the aggrieved party. . . ." To "aggrieve" is to give pain, sorrow, trouble, or inflict injury. Webster's Third International Dictionary (1961).

Both parties may be "aggrieved." Either may bring an action for divorce and obtain a decree granting a divorce. However, where each party seeks the decree of divorce, the court then must determine to whom the divorce should be granted. In making that determination, the court may consider the fault of the respective parties, the equities involved, the effect of the divorce upon the parties and the children, and all of the other facts and circumstances of the case. There is no fixed rule for determining this question, which in the final analysis involves a large discretion [sic] on the part of the trial court.

Here, the trial court found, and stated in its decision letter,

> . . . that the greater degree of fault for the breakup of the marriage rests with the Defendant [appellant Wife] rather than the Plaintiff [appellee Husband]. . . .

Appellant contends the evidence does not support that finding. . . .

Reviewing the facts in this light, we find that appellee was successful and apparently secure in his employment at Cody, Wyoming. Appellant was dissatisfied with their lifestyle, was insistent that the parties move from Cody, Wyoming, to a metropolitan area or to Wisconsin, where her family and relatives resided. She wanted appellee to quit his job. The parties had built a new home on a golf course and she was dissatisfied with the home and wanted to sell it. She decided to practice celibacy during the last two years of the marriage. There were occasions when appellant had packed the car, determined to leave appellee, and heated arguments resulted. . . . There was an effort by the parties to reconcile which was unsuccessful. Appellant then decided that it was more important that the children live in Wisconsin near their relatives than near their father, and she moved with them to Wisconsin and established a permanent residence.

Although appellant offered evidence to support a position that she was not at fault for the divorce, that evidence cannot, on appeal, be considered by us. To hold for appellant under our rules would require that we find that the court was wrong as a matter of law. This we cannot do, for here the evidence supporting the court's decision was substantial. There was no error in awarding the divorce to appellee.

WAS THERE ERROR IN CONSIDERING FAULT OR DID THE COURT ABUSE ITS DISCRETION IN THE DIVISION OF PROPERTY, AWARD OF CHILD SUPPORT, REFUSAL TO AWARD ALIMONY AND ATTORNEYS FEES?

The court, in its decision letter, makes it clear that it considered fault in settling the rights and duties of the parties resulting from their marriage and divorce and in dividing their property and considering alimony and attorneys fees. In its decision letter of November 12, 1981, the court stated,

> it is the Court's opinion that the greater degree of fault for the breakup of the marriage rests with the Defendant rather than the Plaintiff. . . .

Considering property rights,

> the Court must and has taken into consideration the fact that the dissolution of the marriage was caused primarily by the Defendant's insistence upon removing herself and her children to the state of Wisconsin instead of remaining with her husband in Cody, Wyoming. . . .
>
> Again the question of alimony and Defendant's entitlement to it in light of her actions in leaving the family home and the property settlement which the Court has already affected [sic] must be taken into consideration. . . .

With the enactment of § 20–2–104, W.S.1977, *above*, parties could obtain a divorce, without regard to fault, upon proof of irreconcilable differences. Enactment of this statute changed only the grounds for divorce. Although some states, upon adopting no-fault grounds for divorce, also adopted legislation providing for no-fault disposition of property and determination of other rights, Wyoming declined to do so. The statutes and law in existence governing division of property, alimony, and attorneys fees prior to the adoption of legislation providing no-fault grounds for divorce, therefore, remain in effect today. Section 20–2–114, W.S.1977, provides that in making a just and equitable distribution, the court should "consider the merits" of the respective parties. "Merits" is defined in Webster's Third International Dictionary (1961) as "intrinsic rights and wrongs of a legal case as determined by matters of substance in distinction from matters of form." Merit is deservedness, goodness.

The courts are close to being equally divided on the question of whether legislation adopting no-fault grounds for divorce, without more, also requires that there be a no-fault distribution of property and determination of the parties' rights. A small majority, with which we agree, holds that the enactment of a no-fault divorce statute which does no more than provide no-fault grounds for divorce, does not modify the traditional, existing grounds for determining child custody, support, alimony, attorneys fees, and division of property.

Huggins v. Huggins, 57 Ala.App. 691, 331 So. 2d 704 (1976); *Peterson v. Peterson*, 308 Minn. 365, 242 N.W.2d 103 (1976); *Novlesky v. Novlesky*, N.D., 206 N.W.2d 865 (1973); *Kretzschmar v. Kretzschmar*, 48 Mich. App. 279, 210 N.W.2d 352 (1973)....

In *Paul v. Paul*, Wyo., 616 P.2d 707 (1980), we held that the trial court might refuse to hear testimony concerning fault in the circumstances of that case. There, the trial court advised the parties that he would not consider fault in a division involving the large amount of property. We said in *Paul v. Paul* that

> ... when there are adequate assets to comfortably provide for both of the parties, the trial court does not abuse its discretion when it refuses to permit the parties to air their dirty laundry in court.

616 P.2d at 715. We also said that,

> ...The trial judge has great discretion in dividing the property and he is not to use the property division to punish one of the parties....

616 P.2d at 715, citing *Storm v. Storm*. ... 470 P.2d 367.

Paul v. Paul stands for the principle that in certain circumstances the court may, in its discretion, refuse to hear evidence of fault; and that, in any event, such evidence may not be considered by the court to punish one of the parties, but only to insure that the property division is just and equitable under all of the facts and circumstances of the case.

Considering now, first, the division of property, we note that,

> ...As an appellate court, we consider that our power to disturb a property settlement fixed by a trial judge is limited indeed. There must be a clear abuse of discretion before we will upset or adjust such a settlement. We consider "abuse of discretion" to be such abuse as shocks the conscience of the court. It must appear so unfair and inequitable that reasonable persons could not abide it.

Paul v. Paul, above, at 714. *See also, Kane v. Kane*, Wyo., 577 P.2d 172 (1978).

In this case the parties agreed in writing upon a division of their personal property. At the time the decree of divorce was entered, their home had been sold. There was received cash from the sale of the home in the amount of $40,577.40, the parties had, in addition, cash and stocks in the amount of $31,804, and their total indebtedness was $44,784. The court awarded each of the parties one-half of the cash received from the sale of their home, one-half of the value of the cash and stock they had, and ordered appellee to pay the indebtedness of the parties in the amount of $44,784. The effect of this decree was an award to appellant of $36,190.70 and an imposition of a net liability upon appellee in the amount of $8,593.30.

The division of property was unequal. Appellant was left with $36,190.70 in cash; appellee was left with a debt of $8,593.30. There was no award of alimony nor an award of attorneys fees. We have said that award of attorneys fees is a part of the property division and within the discretion of the trial court. *Bereman v. Bereman*, Wyo., 645 P.2d 1155 (1982). The allowance or disallowance of alimony is also a matter which lies within the discretion of the trial court. *Biggerstaff v. Biggerstaff*, Wyo., 443 P.2d 524 (1968)....

We recognize that there are cases in which alimony is a necessity. However, under ordinary circumstances it should be recognized that one spouse should not have a perpetual claim on the earnings of the other; that divorce, insofar as possible should sever the ties of the parties and they should begin to start their lives anew. Thus, there has been a tendency away from alimony, and if some additional sum is necessary to adjust equities between the parties, it is better that that be done with an award of property. *Young v. Young,* Wyo., 472 P.2d 784 (1970); *Paul v. Paul, above.* Here the court awarded appellant a substantial amount of cash while placing the burden of an $8,593.30 debt upon appellee. Appellant is a college graduate with a degree in special education. She has been employed as a teacher and in other occupations and is capable of functioning adequately in the job market. She claims she should be allowed to stay home, not be employed, and devote herself to raising the children. Yet that is not what occurred when the parties were living together. The oldest of the children was with babysitters through most of her growing up before entering school. Social reports indicate she suffered no impairment as a result of this experience. The court awarded appellant custody of the children subject to provisions for visitation by appellee, and awarded child support in the sum of $250 for each child or a total of $750 per month. Appellee's take-home pay at the time was $2,150 per month, and the court noted that appellee's requirements for his living indicated that the amount awarded was about all that could be justified. Award of child support also is a matter addressed to the discretion of the court and will not be disturbed on appeal except for a clear abuse. *Chorney v. Chorney,* Wyo., 383 P.2d 859 (1963).

Considering all of the facts and circumstances of this case, the merits of the parties, their respective educations, college degrees and abilities, and all other matters, we cannot find an abuse of discretion in the manner in which the court divided the property of the parties, awarded child custody and support, and declined to award alimony or attorneys fees.

The trial court exercises a broad discretion in adjusting the rights and obligations of parties upon the dissolution of their marriage. We will not disturb the decision of the lower court unless we can say that that discretion was abused, and that the result was clearly unjust and inequitable. We cannot make that finding in this case.

The judgment, therefore, is affirmed.

NOTES AND QUESTIONS

(1) In the *Grosskopf* case, the Wyoming Supreme Court held that fault could play a factor in determining spousal support awards and the division of marital property when the divorce itself was no fault in nature. But in *Paul v. Paul,* 616 P.2d 707 (Wyo. 1980), the same court affirmed a trial court decision not to consider fault in a division of marital property and spousal support payments. *Query:* How can these two cases be reconciled? Is this an example of the broad judicial discretion in family-law disputes (*see* § 9.03[A][2], Note (2), *above*), or of the relevance of fault factors in no-fault divorce (*see* § 9.04, *below*), or can these cases be distinguished on the law and the facts?

(2) Consider the viewpoint of Professor Ira Ellman, Chief Reporter of the ALI *Principles of the Law of Family Dissolution: Analysis and Recommendations* (Proposed Final Draft 1997), who cites the *Grosskopf* case, *above*, as one example of "inherently limitless" judicial discretion in judicially attempting to apply non-financial fault factors to a no-fault divorce. Ellman describes the *Grosskopf* decision as one where "a spouse may be held at fault for the breakup of the marriage because she prefers to live in a more urban setting than is

available in the forum state preferred by her husband" *Id.* at 26, n. 33, and he cites the decision as an example of how trial court discretion in assigning fault liability to non-financial and non-tortious spousal conduct creates "much mischief" in the application of "unarticulated and effectively unreviewable standards of blameworthiness" on divorce. *Id.* *Query:* Do you agree with Professor Ellman's assessment of the *Grosskopf* case? Why or why not? Professor Ellman further asserts:

> The traditional marital fault rule requires extraordinary reliance on trial court discretion. Neither the standard of [marital] misconduct, nor its dollar consequences, are much bounded by any rule. While in principle the trial court's decision can be reviewed for "abuse of discretion," reversals are rare. . . . The traditional fault rule is thus inconsistent with a major theme of the *Principles*, an effort to improve the consistency and predictability of trial court decisions.

Id. at 69–70.

Professor Peter Swisher, on the other hand, believes that the current judicial trend in many states today is that most trial court judges tend to ignore or severely limit the ultimate effect of most fault-based factors in divorce except in serious or egregious circumstances, since judicial discretion in most divorce cases today is constrained by the application of a number of statutory factors that a trial court judge must properly consider, in both the spousal support and property division contexts. Judicial discretion is also tempered and constrained by the trial court's expertise and experience in contemporary divorce matters, as well as by appellate review whenever a trial court judge fails to apply the correct statutory or decisional law, or whenever a trial court judge abuses his or her discretion. *See* Peter Swisher, *Reassessing Fault Factors in No-Fault Divorce*, 31 Fam. L. Q. 269, 310–14 (1997). *See also Anderson v. Anderson*, 230 S.E.2d 272 (Ga. 1976); *Platt v. Platt*, 728 S.W. 2d 542 (Ky. Ct. App. 1987); *Thames v. Thames*, 477 N.W.2d 496 (Mich. Ct. App. 1991); *Perlberger v. Perlberger*, 626 A.2d 1186 (Pa. Super. Ct. 1993); *Tarro v. Tarro*, 485 A.2d 558 (R.I. 1984); *Williams v. Williams*, 415 S.E.2d 252 (Va. Ct. App. 1992); *Rexrode v. Rexrode*, 414 S.E.2d 457 (W. Va. 1992). *Query:* Do you agree with Professor Swisher's assessment of a more restrained judicial discretion in most divorce proceedings today? Why or why not?

(3) As the *Grosskopf* court correctly observed, American courts are almost equally divided on the question of whether legislation adopting no-fault grounds for divorce also require that there be no-fault distribution of marital property on divorce, and no-fault spousal support rights as well. Most states have adopted some sort of equitable distribution statute that takes into account the economic and non-economic contributions of the spouses in the marriage, the duration of the marriage, the age of the parties, the financial needs and abilities of each spouse, and other equitable factors. Nevertheless, there appears to be a lack of uniformity among the states in the treatment of fault as a relevant factor in determining spousal support awards on divorce and the equitable division of marital property. Some states have held, even with a no-fault divorce, that fault should still be considered as a factor. Other states have held that fault may, or may not, be considered; and still other states have expressly excluded fault as a factor in determining spousal support awards and marital property division on divorce. In fact, most courts recognize that fault is only one of many statutory factors that a court must properly consider in determining spousal support awards and the division of marital property on divorce. *See, e.g.*, Sparks v. Sparks, 485 N.W.2d 893 (Mich.

1992) (holding that although the conduct of the parties during the marriage may be relevant to the distribution of marital property and spousal support, the trial court must still consider all the relevant statutory factors, and not assign disproportionate weight to any one factor or any one circumstance, including fault). *Accord Perlberger v. Perlberger*, 626 A.2d 1186 (Pa. Super. Ct. 1993); *Tarro v. Tarro*, 485 A.2d 558 (R.I. 1984); *Rexrode v. Rexrode*, 339 S.E.2d 544 (Va. Ct. App. 1986).

One rationale for applying fault as a relevant factor in determining spousal support and marital property division is that divorce or dissolution of marriage is essentially an equitable proceeding, and therefore the conduct of the parties is always relevant. *See, e.g., Robinson v. Robinson*, 444 A.2d 234, 236 (Conn. 1982) (holding that a spouse "whose conduct has contributed substantially to the breakdown of the marriage should not expect to receive financial kudos for his or her misconduct"); Thames v. Thames, 477 N.W.2d 496 (Mich. Ct. App. 1991) (holding that a divorce case is equitable in nature, and a court of equity molds its relief according to the character of the case). *Contra, Marriage of Cihak*, 416 N.E.2d 701 (Ill. App. Ct. 1981); Mosbarger v. Mosbarger, 547 So. 2d 188 (Fla. Ct. App. 1989) (both holding that murder or attempted murder of one spouse by the other spouse would have not effect division of property and spousal support; only the financial needs of the parties are relevant). *See generally K.C. Karnezis*, Annotation, *Fault as Consideration in Alimony, Spousal Support, or Property Division Pursuant to No-Fault Divorce*, 86 A.L.R.3d 1116 (1978). *See also* § 9.04, *below.*

(4) **Problem.** The State of Brandeis will grant a divorce only on the no-fault ground of an irretrievable breakdown of the marriage. Nevertheless, a Brandeis equitable distribution statute states that "marital misconduct of either party may be a factor in determining the equitable distribution of the parties' marital property."

Hal and Wilma obtain a no-fault divorce in Brandeis, but Wilma argues that because of Hal's adulterous conduct, she should be awarded a greater share of the parties' marital property. How should the judge rule in this case? *Compare Smoot v. Smoot*, 357 S.E.2d 728 (Va. 1987) *and Aster v. Gross*, 371 S.E.2d 833 (Va. Ct. App. 1988) *with O'Loughlin v. O'Loughlin*, 458 S.E.2d 323 (Va. Ct. App. 1995).

Now assume that Brandeis law holds that fault should not be considered in equitable property division on divorce. Prior to their divorce, however, Hal arranges to have his heiress wife Wilma murdered, but the attempt is foiled. Should Hal's egregious conduct in trying to murder Wilma be taken into account by the court in dividing their marital property on divorce? Why or why not? *Compare D'Arc v. D'Arc*, 395 A.2d 1270 (N.J. Super. Ct. Ch. Div. 1978), *cert. denied*, 451 U.S. 971 (1981) *with In re Marriage of Cihak*, 416 N.E.2d 701 (Ill. Ct. App. 1981). *See also In re Marriage of Brabec*, 510 N.W.2d 762 (Wis. Ct. App. 1993); *O'Brien v. O'Brien*, 498 N.Y.S.2d 743 (N.Y. 1985).

(5) What evidence should the court accept in granting a no-fault divorce based upon "irreconcilable differences" or "irretrievable breakdown of the marriage" ? What happens if one of the spouses argues that the marriage has been irretrievably broken and the parties cannot be reconciled, but the other spouse believes that the marriage can still be saved? *See, e.g., Grotelueschen v. Grotelueschen*, 113 Mich. App. 395, 318 N.W.2d 227 (Mich. Ct. App. 1982) (after a 32–year marriage, husband moved out of the house and began living with another woman); *In re Baier's Marriage*, 561 P.2d 20 (Colo. Ct. App. 1977) (wife stated that she no longer liked or trusted her husband, but husband stated the marriage was

satisfactory, and wife's problems could be overcome with counseling). Should the test of whether the spouses can continue living together as husband and wife be a subjective test from the viewpoint of the spouses themselves, or either of them; or is it an objective test from the viewpoint of the court? *See, e.g., Dunn v. Dunn,* 511 P.2d 427 (Or. Ct. App. 1973).

What if one of the spouses opposes an absolute divorce based upon his or her strong religious principles, but will agree to a divorce *a mensa et thoro* (a legal separation)? *See, e.g., Husting v. Husting,* 194 N.W.2d 801 (Wis. 1972); *In re Halford's Marriage,* 528 P.2d 119 (Or. Ct. App. 1974); *Colabianchi v. Colabianchi,* 646 S.W.2d 61 (Mo. 1983). *But see* Tenn. Code Ann. 36–4–103 (1984). *See also* Homer Clark, *Divorce Policy and Divorce Reform,* 42 U. Colo. L. Rev. 403 (1971).

Query: In a state that recognizes both fault and no-fault grounds for divorce, if one of the spouses sues for divorce based upon a no-fault ground, but the other spouse sues for divorce based upon a fault ground such as adultery or cruelty, which divorce ground should prevail? *See, e.g., Ebbert v. Ebbert,* 459 A.2d 282 (N.H. 1983) *Robertson v. Robertson,* 211 S.E.2d 41 (Va. 1975). *See generally* 2 Homer H. Clark, Jr., Law of Domestic Relations 36–42 (2d ed. 1987).

(6) Court-Ordered Conciliation and Mediation. Approximately one-half of the states have statutes creating some form of court-ordered conciliation or mediation prior to divorce, where the spouses meet with a third-party counselor to discuss their marital differences. Under some statutes, this conciliation or mediation process is wholly voluntary, while other statutes empower the court to order mandatory participation by the spouses, especially when minor children are involved. *See generally* Silberman & Schepard, *Court-Ordered Mediation in Family Disputes: The New York Proposal,* 14 N.Y.U. Rev. of Law & Soc. Change 741 (1986); Maxwell, *Keeping the Family Out of Court: Court-Ordered Mediation of Custody Disputes under the Kansas Statutes,* 25 Washburn L.J. 203 (1986); Clark & Orbeton, *Mandatory Mediation of Divorce: Maine's Experience,* 69 Judicature 310 (February-March 1986); Kuhn, *Mandatory Mediation: California Civil Code Section 4607,* 33 Emory L.J. 733 (1984). *Query:* What are the benefits of such mandatory court-ordered conciliation or mediation prior to divorce? What are the weaknesses?

§ 9.04 The Relevance—If Any—of Fault Factors in No Fault Divorces

[A] Arguments for Rejecting Fault Factors in No Fault Divorces

A number of commentators and courts have argued that fault factors should no longer play any valid role in a no fault divorce regime. For example, Professor Norman Lichenstein summarizes the argument in this way:

> When a marital unit is split apart, the parties cannot expect to continue their former lifestyle without change. Frequently, the economically less viable spouse—usually the non-working wife with child care responsibilities—will be particularly hard hit. The law should be designed to mitigate the financial disruption of divorce and, to the extent possible, move a needy spouse toward rehabilitation and financial independence. This requires a thorough economic analysis of the financial contributions, resources, and needs of the parties. It also requires bidding farewell to the distraction of trying to find the blameworthy spouse and assigning a value to his or her misconduct.

Norman Lichtenstein, *Marital Misconduct and the Allocation of Financial Resources at Divorce: A Farewell to Fault,* 54 UMKC L. Rev. 1, 8 (1985). *See also* Herma Kay Hill,

Equality and Difference: A Perspective on No-Fault Divorce and its Aftermath, 56 U. Cinn. L. Rev. 1 (1987); Donald Schiller, *Fault Undercuts Equity*, 10 Fam. Advocate 10 (Fall 1987). Professor Ira Ellman likewise argues that fault factors no longer serve any viable function in a marital dissolution action:

> [T]he potentially valid functions of a fault principle are better served by the tort and criminal law, and attempting to serve them through a [divorce-based] fault rule risks serious distortion in the resolution of the dissolution [or divorce] action. One possible function of the fault rule, punishment for bad conduct, is generally disavowed even by fault states. It is better left to criminal law, which is designed to serve it, and in doing so appropriately reaches a much narrower range of marital misconduct than do the marital misconduct rules of fault states. The second possible function, compensation for the non-financial losses imposed by the other spouse's battery or emotional abuse, is better left to tort law. . . .
>
> Where valid compensation claims arise, whether for physical violence or emotional abuse, the tort law provides principles to measure and satisfy them, and to determine when they are too stale to entertain. The property allocation and alimony rules of dissolution law, in contrast, are designed for an entirely different purpose. In the dissolution of a short marriage, the dominant principle is to return the spouses to the premarital situations. As the marriage lengthens [the proposed *Principles of the Law of Family Dissolution*] provide increasingly generous remedies to the financially more vulnerable spouse in recognition of their joint responsibility for the irreversible personal consequences that arise from investing many years in the relationship. . . .

Ira Mark Ellman, *The Place of Fault in a Modern Divorce Law*, 28 Ariz. St. L.J. 773, 807–08 (1996). Accordingly, as mentioned earlier, 18 states have now adopted a "pure" or "true" no-fault divorce regime, where fault factors no longer play any role in determining divorce or dissolution grounds, nor do fault factors play any role in determining spousal support awards or the equitable distribution of marital property on divorce, unless there was fraudulent concealment or dissipation of marital assets (sometimes called "economic fault"). *See, e.g., Oberhansly v. Oberhansly*, 798 P.2d 883 (Alaska 1990); *In re Marriage of Boseman*, 107 Cal. Rptr. 232 (Cal. Ct. App. 1973); *Ivancovich v. Ivancovich*, 540 P.2d 718 (Ariz. Ct. App. 1975); *Heilman v. Heilman*, 610 So. 2d 60 (Fla. Ct. App. 1992); *Markham v. Markham*, 909 P.2d 602 (Haw. Ct. App. 1996), *cert. denied*, 910 P.2d 128 (Haw. 1996); *Smith v. Smith*, 847 P.2d 827 (Okla. Ct. App. 1993). Thus, egregious or serious marital misconduct of one spouse against the other spouse would have no effect on the division of the parties' marital property or any spousal support award, since these awards under "true" no fault divorce law must be based only on the financial needs of the parties, regardless of fault or other serious marital misconduct. *See, e.g.*, Marriage of Cihak, 416 N.E.2d 701 (Ill. Ct. App. 1981); *Mosbarger v. Mosbarger*, 547 So. 2d 188 (Fla. Ct. App. 1989).

[B] Arguments for Retaining Fault Factors in No Fault Divorces

Approximately 30 states, however, still continue to recognize that various fault factors may still play a viable role in determining spousal support awards or the division of marital property, even though the parties may have utilized a no fault divorce ground. Attorney Adriaen Morse Jr., for example, notes that:

> The whole notion of fault proves to be a stumbling block for many scholars writing about the current pursuit of equitable ways of dealing with alimony [and the division of marital property on divorce]. But fault provides an excellent tool to encourage the type of behavior society believes to be appropriate in marriage, and to discourage that behavior which society deems to be inappropriate. It seems that most people would at least agree that engaging in adultery, cruelty, or desertion is not the sort of sharing behavior which marriage should endure. In order to provide a disincentive for such behavior, there should be concomitant post-divorce financial consequences for engaging in inappropriate behavior.

Adriaen Morse Jr., *Fault: A Viable Means of Re-Injecting Responsibility in Marital Relations*, 30 U. Rich. L. Rev. 605, 640–41 (1996). *See also* Harvey Golden & Michael Taylor, *Fault Enforces Accountability*, 10 Fam. Advocate 11, 12 (Fall 1987): "Very few states totally ignore fault. That is because we are brought up to believe that people should be held accountable for their actions, and that courts should establish such accountability and consider it." Professor Barbara Bennett Woodhouse further analyzes the issue of fault on divorce from a feminist perspective:

> No-fault divorce is not a natural law, like gravity. It is a legal construct, purposefully designed by lawyers for lawyers. Its primary impetus was to manage exit from the legal status of marriage more efficiently and to spare those in the system from involvement in the costly process and sordid details of assessing blame for a marriage's death. [But] [i]n attempting to operate only on hard [financial] data, translated as dollar figures for direct economic loss, modern divorce reform seems to say that what cannot be measured as damage to a tangible property interest does not count. . . .
>
> We should construct instead a scheme that reclaims the power of fault and that attributes consequences to good and bad conduct within marriage. When the imbalances are striking, we should reward family-centric, caring conduct, rather than turn a blind eye to abuse and exploitation. There are many good reasons for harboring a healthy fear of fault. But if we suppress all discourse on badness in marriage, how can we talk persuasively about goodness? Is fault really so dangerous to feminists that we prefer silence?

Barbara Bennett Woodhouse, *Sex, Lies, and Dissipation: The Discourse of Fault in a No-Fault Era*, 82 Geo. L.J. 2525, 2567 (1994). *See also* Jana Singer, *Husbands, Wives, and Human Capital: Why the Shoe Won't Fit*, 31 Fam. L. Q. 119, 130 (1997) (arguing in favor of a no-fault division of career assets, while still preserving fault as a limited defense). Thus, a significant number of state courts and state legislatures still recognize the role that fault factors continue to play, as only one of the many statutory factors that a trial court judge must consider in a divorce or dissolution proceeding. *See, e.g.*, Robinson v. Robinson, 444 A.2d 234 (Conn. 1982); *Lagars v. Lagars*, 491 So. 2d 5 (La. 1986); *Thames v. Thames*, 477 N.W.2d 496 (Mich. Ct. App. 1991); *Francis v. Francis*, 823 S.W.2d 36 (Mo. Ct. App. 1991); *Endy v. Endy*, 603 A.2d 641 (Pa. Super. Ct. 1992); *O'Loughlin v. O'Loughlin*, 458 S.E.2d 323 (Va. Ct. App. 1995); *Durnell v. Durnell*, 460 S.E.2d 710 (W. Va. 1995).

[C] Can Nonfinancial Factors Viably Coexist With Financial Factors in Determining Financial Issues in Divorce?

The most recent, and the most comprehensive, attack on any fault-based factors on divorce or dissolution of marriage comes from the American Law Institute's proposed *Principles* of the Law of Family Dissolution: Analysis and Recommendations* (Proposed Final Draft 1997) and from its Chief Reporter, Ira Mark Ellman. Professor Ellman's *Principles* forcefully argue for the establishment of "consistent and predictable" financial principles relating to compensatory spousal payments and the division of property on divorce, solely based upon no-fault financial principles and objectives, and to the exclusion of any nonfinancial fault-based factors, such as serious marital misconduct. *See generally* Chapter 10, *below*, for an extensive discussion of these financially-based principles.

Professor Ellman had previously argued in favor of a no-fault, financially based spousal support compensation theory in *The Theory of Alimony*, 77 Cal. L. Rev. 1 (1989), and again in subsequent articles entitled *Should the Theory of Alimony Include Nonfinancial Losses and Motivations?* 1991 B.Y.U.L. Rev. 259 (1991), and *The Place of Fault in a Modern Divorce Law*, 28 Ariz. St. L.J. 773 (1996) (reiterating that any proposal "to add a compensation-based fault role to the *Principles of Family Dissolution Law* could therefore be understood as revisiting the fundamental question of whether the law of marital dissolution should provide compensation for nonfinancial losses").

However, Professor Ellman's *Theory of Alimony* has been criticized by other commentators for not recognizing that important nonfinancial losses occur on divorce as well. Professor June Carbone, for example, faults Professor Ellman for ignoring larger non-economic interests of society, including child rearing, married women's participation in the work force, a return of appropriate benefits that the other spouse retains on divorce, and sexual equality issues. June Carbone, *Economics, Feminism, and the Reinvention of Alimony: A Reply to Ira Ellman*, 43 Vand. L. Rev. 1463 (1990). Professor Ellman's *Theory of Alimony* also has been criticized by Professor Carl Schneider who, while praising Professor Ellman for attempting to provide a coherent rationale for alimony, criticizes Ellman for his refusal to acknowledge any moral discourse on the subject of awarding alimony. Carl Schneider, *Rethinking Alimony: Marital Decisions and Moral Discourse*, 1991 B.Y.U. L. Rev. 197 (1991). Attorney Adriaen Morse, Jr., likewise argues that fault is a relevant nonfinancial factor that should be considered in determining any alimony award. Adriaen Morse, Jr., *Fault: A Viable Means of Reinjecting Responsibility in Marital Relations*, 30 U. Rich. L. Rev. 605 (1996).

Professor Peter Swisher also has argued that fault factors on divorce, as only one of a number of enumerated statutory factors that a trial court must properly consider, still serves a viable contemporary purpose if it considers egregious or serious marital misconduct that substantially contributes to the dissolution of the marriage. Observing that other remedial "no-fault" laws are seldom truly no-fault in nature, Professor Swisher asks,

> What is so inherently wrong or inequitable in generally providing for financial loss on divorce, but with concomitant, nonfinancial compensatory damages for serious or egregious marital misconduct as well? If the institution of marriage still serves a valuable social, legal, and economic function in contemporary American society, and if other no-fault remedial laws such as no-fault automobile insurance, no-fault workers' compensation statutes, and no-fault strict products liability laws all provide fault remedies for serious or egregious conduct, then why not a fault-based exception for serious or egregious marital misconduct in a no-fault divorce as well? Financially based factors and fault-based factors on divorce or dissolution of marriage are not as mutually exclusive as Professor Ellman suggests, and a significant number of state legislatures

and state courts presently take into account a spouse's inappropriate marital behavior and serious marital misconduct as defined and regulated by appropriate statutory and decisional law. A fault-based remedy for serious marital misconduct therefore still serves a realistic, viable, and socially defensible function in contemporary American divorce law, especially since an independent tort-based remedy for serious marital misconduct has proven to be an inadequate alternative. . . .

Thus, no matter how various "no fault" remedial laws may be defined, and no matter how such laws may be characterized and formulated—even with the best of intentions—nevertheless, based upon very strong underlying Anglo-American legal precedent, social custom, and state public policy, one is still held to be responsible and accountable for one's actions. This underlying principle of an actor's legal and social responsibility and accountability to others therefore constitutes a serious inherent flaw with *any* "no fault" regime, and it is an important reason why so many "no fault" laws, including "no fault" divorce laws, often necessitate exclusions or exceptions to the general rule for serious or egregious conduct.

Peter Nash Swisher, *Reassessing Fault Factors in No-Fault Divorce*, 31 Fam. L.Q. 269, 309–10, 295–96 (1997). Thus, as Professor Woodhouse observes:

Although we live in a nation aptly characterized by Mary Ann Glendon as an example of "no fault, no-responsibility" divorce, reports of the death of fault have been exaggerated. While we have been busy dissecting the no-fault revolution, the survival and evolution of fault has aroused relatively little comment. Although half the states employ fault-based doctrines in one context or another, the use of fault as an element of divorce is typically dismissed as contrary to the modern trend. Many of the fault-based laws on alimony and property, however, are recent reforms or amendments to earlier no-fault revolution statutes. Fault is neither as outdated nor as invisible as we have made it seem.

Barbara Bennett Woodhouse, *above*, at 1531.

Query: What are the applicable laws regarding the relevance of fault factors—or the abolition of such fault factors—in your own state? Based upon what underlying state public-policy rationale?

[D] Problem

Assume that you are a legislative aide (working part-time while you are attending law school in the State of Marshall) for State Senator Nova Jones. Senator Jones is Chairperson for a joint legislative subcommittee studying possible reform of the Marshall Annotated Family Law Code. Specifically, Senator Jones is interested in what role—if any—fault should play in a divorce proceeding in the State of Marshall. Currently, Marshall allows dissolution of marriage to be granted on the no-fault basis of separation of the parties for one year or more. Alternatively, divorce may also be granted on the grounds of adultery, cruelty, or desertion. Senator Jones tells you, however, that realistically, over 85% of all divorces in the State of Marshall are granted on the no-fault separation ground.

Marshall has enumerated statutory factors that a trial court must consider in granting spousal support or the division of marital property that were enacted in 1985. Among these statutory factors that a trial court "may consider" are the following: (1) the earning capacities, needs, obligations, and financial resources of the parties; (2) the education and training of the parties, and the ability and opportunity of the parties to secure such education and training; (3) the standard of living established during the marriage; (4) the duration and length of the marriage; (5) the age, physical, and mental condition of the parties; (6) the contributions, monetary and nonmonetary, of each party to the well-being of the family; (7) the property interests of the parties, both real and personal, tangible and intangible, marital and separate; (8) the circumstances and factors that contributed to the dissolution of the marriage, including any enumerated fault ground for divorce that substantially contributed to the dissolution of the marriage; (9) the debts and liabilities of each spouse; (10) the tax consequences of each party; and (11) any other factors as the court deems necessary and appropriate to consider in arriving at a fair and equitable award. The Marshall Supreme Court has stated, however, that a trial court judge must consider *all* of these statutory factors in making an appropriate award; failure to do so will constitute reversible error.

Senator Jones tells you that she has learned that Part I of the recently proposed ALI *Principles of the Law of Family Dissolution* (1997) rejects the application of any fault-based, non-financial factors in determining the allocation of marital property rights or compensatory spousal support awards based on what Senator Jones views as three major arguments supporting the ALI *Principles*: (1) that utilizing fault factors "as an agent of morality" in effect "rewards virtue and punishes sin," *id.* at 24–26; (2) that judicial discretion is "inherently limitless" and "unreviewable" if no finding of economic harm to the claimant is required to justify such an award, *id.* at 24; and (3) compensation for serious harm caused by the wrongful conduct of a spouse is better left to a separate tort remedy rather than a concomitant fault-based divorce remedy. *Id.* at 19–20. However, Senator Jones is also familiar with Barbara Bennett Woodhouse's article, *Sex, Lies, Dissipation: The Discourse of Fault in a No-Fault Era*, 82 Geo. L.J. 2525, 2566 (1994): "Tort claims for marital misconduct have several drawbacks. . . . Because they are treated with suspicion as neither divorce claims nor classic forms of tort, tort remedies for spousal misconduct are often denied or restricted by courts accustomed to no-fault ideology of marriage dissolution. They raise tricky questions of *res judicata* and collateral estoppel, the right to a jury trial, overlapping recoveries, and limitation of damages."

Senator Jones asks for your "candid opinion" on whether or not the Marshall Legislature ought to adopt the ALI *Principles of the Law of Family Dissolution: Analysis and Recommendation* (Proposed Final Draft 1997) insofar as it rejects all nonfinancial factors on divorce—including fault-based factors—or not adopt the *Principles* financially-based regime. You make the mistake of telling Senator Jones that, coincidentally, you have been studying this very issue in your law school Family Law class, and Senator Jones then asks you for a short memo, expressing your views on this subject, including any underlying public policy rationales pro and con. What would you tell Senator Jones?

§ 9.05 Ethical Issues for the Family Lawyer

In addition to being well versed in the procedural and substantive laws related to divorce proceedings and other family law practice, the family law practitioner must be fully aware of the ethical considerations involved in family law practice. Ethical misconduct by a family lawyer may result in any or all of the following: (1) a divorce decree or other action being vacated by the court; (2) the attorney being sued in a substantial legal malpractice action;

or (3) the attorney being reprimanded, suspended, or disbarred from practice. *See, e.g.,* Note, *The Changed Landscape of Divorce Practice as Ethical Minefield,* 3 Fam. L. Rep. (BNA) 4031 (1977); Crystal, *Ethical Problems in Marital Practice,* 30 S.C. L. Rev. 321 (1979); Annotation, *Negligence, Inattention, or Professional Incompetence of Attorney in Handling Client's Affairs in Family Law Matters as Ground for Disciplinary Action; Modern Cases,* 67 A.L.R.4th 415 (1989). *See generally* Louis Parley, *The Ethical Family Lawyer: A Practical Guide to Avoiding Professional Dilemmas* (ABA Family Law Section, 1995).

[A] Dual Representation in Divorce Proceedings: Is It Ethical?

What happens when both spouses ask the same attorney to represent them in a divorce action? Spouses may seek dual representation to avoid the expense of hiring two attorneys, because both spouses have a great deal of confidence in a particular attorney, or because the attorney is their mutual friend. Is dual representation in a divorce proceeding ethical?

The answer to this important question largely depends on whether the divorce is contested or uncontested; that is to say, whether or not there are any existing disputes between the spouses regarding spousal support, child support, child custody, a division of marital property, or other related matters. For example, ABA Model Code of Professional Responsibility EC 5-14 to 5-17 and Disciplinary Rule 5-105(C) permit an attorney to represent multiple clients only if it is obvious that he or she can adequately and objectively represent the interests of each client. *See also* Model Rules of Professional Conduct Rules 1.7, 1.9, and 2.2. Similarly, Model Rule 1.7(a) provides in part that "A lawyer shall not represent a client if the representation of that client will be directly adverse to another client." If the clients' interests are in conflict, or if any dispute subsequently arises between the parties, then the attorney cannot adequately represent both parties and he or she must withdraw from the case. Model Code of Professional Responsibility EC 5-15; Model Rules of Professional Conduct 1.7(a), 2.2(c).

Despite these warnings against dual representation, lawyers represent both sides in family law matters "more often than one might want to imagine," since too many family law attorneys believe that they can act as "mere scriveners" for the parties, or that "no conflict exists" when the parties are obtaining a "no fault" divorce or are otherwise "working together." Louis Parley, *The Ethical Family Lawyer: A Practical Guide to Avoiding Professional Dilemmas,* 15, 16–17 (1995). Consequently, some commentators have argued for an absolute prohibition of dual representation in divorce cases under the rationale that the "friendly" or "uncontested" divorce is actually a myth because all divorces arguably have significant areas of disagreement, economic and otherwise. Richard Crouch, *The Changed Landscape of Divorce Practice as Ethical Minefield,* 3 Fam. L. Rep. (BNA) 4031, 4034–36 (1977). And even assuming *arguendo* that no disputes arise during the dual representation phase, a conflict of interest may already exist or a dispute may arise later. For example, in *Ishmael v. Millington,* 241 Cal. App. 2d 520 (1966), an attorney who had previously represented the husband in several legal matters prepared a divorce complaint and a property settlement agreement on behalf of the wife. After the agreement was approved by the court and a divorce decree was entered, the wife sued the attorney for malpractice on the grounds that he failed to properly ascertain the actual value of the property in the marital agreement. The court warned:

> Divorces are frequently uncontested; the parties may make their financial arrangements peaceably and honestly. . . . The husband may then seek out and pay an attorney to

escort the wife through the formalities of adjudication. . . . Even in that situation the attorney's professional obligations do not permit his descent to the level of a scrivener. The edge of danger gleams if the attorney has previously represented the husband. A husband and wife at the brink of division of their marital assets have an obvious divergence of interests. Representing the wife in an arm's length divorce, an attorney of ordinary professional skill would demand some verification of the husband's financial statement; or, at a minimum, [would] inform the wife that the husband's statement was unconfirmed, that wives may be cheated, [and] that prudence called for investigation and verification. Deprived of such disclosure, the wife cannot make a free and intelligent choice. Representing both spouses in an uncontested divorce situation (whatever the ethical implications), the attorney's professional obligations demand no less. He may not set a shallow limit on the depth to which he will represent the wife.

Id.

If an attorney is asked to represent both spouses, he or she must inform them of the three major disadvantages of dual representation. First, although the parties may intend to have a "friendly" divorce, if any dispute arises between them the attorney will be required to withdraw from the representation and each of the parties will be required to hire new counsel. Model Code of Professional Responsibility DR 5-105 and EC 5-15; Model Rules of Professional Conduct Rule 2.2(c). Second, a number of court decisions have overturned separation agreements and other marital contracts drafted by an attorney purportedly representing both parties on the ground that the attorney did *not* adequately protect the interests of both parties. *See, e.g., Jensen v. Jensen,* 557 P.2d 200, 202 (1976). Finally, by asking the attorney to represent both of them, the parties waive their attorney-client privilege for any communications made by either of them to the attorney, and the attorney might be forced to testify regarding any damaging information if the divorce is later contested. *See generally* Crystal, *Ethical Problems in Marital Practice,* 30 S.C. L. Rev. 321, 325-32 (1979).

In some states, dual representation is not unethical per se, provided that both spouses consent to the dual representation, preferably in writing, after full disclosure of its benefits and disadvantages. *See, e.g., Levine v. Levine,* 436 N.E.2d 476 (1982). In *Levine,* the New York Court of Appeals upheld the validity of a separation agreement drafted by a lawyer for both parties. However, the court cautioned that, although the use of the same lawyer did not automatically nullify the agreement, the fact that the parties used the same attorney meant that "a far more reaching scrutiny" would be made of the conduct of the three individuals involved, and counsel's conduct would be closely examined to make sure that he properly advised all parties of their rights, the consequences of joint representation, the consequences of the terms of the agreement, and the parties' right to use separate counsel. *Id.,* 436 N.E.2d at 478-79; *see also Vandenburgh v. Vandenburgh,* 599 N.Y. S.2d 328, 330 (App. Div. 1993) (also holding that marital agreements drafted by one attorney ostensibly representing both parties "are subject to heightened scrutiny"). *But see also Callahan v. Callahan,* 514 N.Y.S.2d 819, 821-22 (App. Div. 1987) (holding that marital agreement drafted by attorney who purported to represent both parties was invalid, when attorney failed to disclose information regarding husband's assets to wife). *And see Klemm v. Superior Court,* 75 Cal. App. 3d 893 (1977). In *Klemm,* the court hastened to add that it would still be improper for an attorney to represent both spouses in any *contested* divorce proceeding. *Id. Caveat*: Even though the attorneys in *Levine, Vandenburgh,* and *Klemm,* who represented both spouses in a family law matter were ultimately exonerated, they nevertheless had to go through a number of costly trial court and appellate court proceedings before they were subsequently vindicated.

Other courts, however, have not been as tolerant as these New York and California court decisions may suggest regarding dual representation in family law matters. For example, the Maryland Court of Appeals strongly stated:

> This is not the first time the Court has seen parties apparently relying on the same lawyer. This situation has arisen frequently enough to suggest to the members of the Bar that no matter how careful they may be to explain their relationship to each of the parties, they are advancing at their own peril. Where there is a potential conflict of interest between the parties, as is true in every domestic dispute, it is inappropriate to attempt to represent them both. This is true, even where the parties appear to be in full accord at the time . . .
>
> Although counsel may have believed that he was merely acting as a "scribe" with regard to the Blums' separation agreement . . . the very least counsel should have done was disclose to the parties the possible ramifications of his dual representation and their respective rights. While such dual representation may not necessarily result in the setting aside of the separation agreement, it leaves the door ajar for what occurred here. . . .

Blum v. Blum, 477 A.2d 289, 296–97 (Md. 1984). *See also Walden v. Hoke,* 429 S.E.2d 504, 509 (W. Va. 1993) *Elzroth and Elzroth,* 679 P.2d 1369, 1372–73 (Ore. Ct. App. 1984) (similar holdings). Moreover, if either spouse is financially or educationally disadvantaged, or is in a dependent condition, that spouse definitely needs the services of independent legal counsel. *See* Crystal, *Ethical Problems in Marital Practice,* 30 S.C.L. Rev. 321, 329–30 (1979).

Query: May an attorney represent one spouse and leave the other spouse unrepresented? May such an attorney provide any legal advice to the unrepresented spouse? *See* Model Code of Professional Responsibility DR 7-104(A)(2). May the attorney communicate with the unrepresented spouse or engage in negotiations with the unrepresented spouse? *See* Model Code of Professional Responsibility EC 7–18; Crystal, *Ethical Problems in Marital Practice,* 30 S.C.L. Rev. 321, 354–56 (1979). What if the unrepresented spouse later attacks the validity of the divorce and the fairness of a separation agreement by claiming that he or she thought that the attorney was representing both parties?

The following case involves an attorney who purportedly attempted to represent both the wife's and the husband's interests in a divorce proceeding, with resulting allegations of fraud on the court.

COULSON v. COULSON
Ohio Supreme Court
448 N.E.2d 809 (1983)

The parties to this appeal were married in 1963 and had two children during their marriage. In 1965, appellant, Robert A. Coulson, opened a sandwich shop, which evolved into the "Mr. Hero" chain of restaurants and an associated franchise operation. Appellee, Joan Coulson, worked in the "Mr. Hero" stores.

In July, 1975 appellant informed his wife that he was seeing another woman. A day or two later the parties held some discussions about dividing their property. Thereafter, appellant contacted his corporate attorney, Leonard Saltzer, and asked Saltzer to draft a separation agreement and handle the divorce. Saltzer drafted an agreement based on terms dictated to him by appellant. The parties met briefly in Saltzer's office on July 31, 1975 and signed the agreement. The next day Saltzer filed a complaint for divorce. In the complaint Saltzer represented himself as "Attorney for Plaintiff [appellee Wife]". In October 1975 Saltzer drafted and filed appellant's answer. The answer was signed by Saltzer's office associate even though the associate had not been retained by appellant to represent him in the divorce proceedings. The answer was subsequently withdrawn after Saltzer informed the court that the parties had reached an agreement. On January 21, 1976 a hearing on the divorce was held before a referee. Appellee attended the hearing accompanied by Saltzer, who represented himself as appellee's attorney. During the hearing the referee asked appellee if the settlement was fair and equitable. Appellee thereupon turned and asked Saltzer if it was and Saltzer replied, "Yes, your Honor, it's fair and equitable." On February 10, 1976, appellee was granted a divorce from appellant and the separation agreement was incorporated into the judgment . . .

. . . On May 1, 1978, appellee filed a third motion for relief from judgment pursuant to Civ. R. 60(B)(5), alleging fraud upon the court. The court granted appellee's Civ. R. 60(B)(5) motion on June 3, 1981 after a full hearing.

Appellant appealed to the court of appeals, which affirmed the trial court in a split decision. The majority below held that "[t]he conduct of appellant and Mr. Saltzer rose to the level of fraud upon the court . . . .The court was misled into believing that Mrs. Coulson initiated the divorce proceedings, was represented by Mr. Saltzer, and that the settlement agreement reached between the parties was fair and equitable. Yet the record reveals that Mr. Saltzer (1) was contacted and paid by Mr. Coulson who wanted a divorce . . . (2) acted as a mere scrivener . . . (3) did not actually represent either party . . . (4) never advised Mrs. Coulson . . . (5) never advised the court of his 'limited representation' . . . and (6) never analyzed the proposed settlement terms for fairness. . . . Thus, his misrepresentations to the court prevented appellee from presenting her case, and, as an officer of the court, his conduct 'prevented the judicial system from functioning in the customary manner.' " The court further held that res judicata did not bar the court "from entertaining appellee's third motion which contained different facts and grounds for relief."

Judge Thomas J. Parrino dissented. In his view, the fraud, if any, "was perpetrated upon the plaintiff [appellee] and not upon the court. As such, under the provisions of Civ. R. 60(B)(3), plaintiff was required to file her motion for relief from judgment within one year" . . .

SWEENEY, J.

The question presented in this appeal is whether the trial court abused its discretion in granting appellee relief from judgment pursuant to Civ. R. 60(B)(5). Civ. R. 60(B) states as follows:

On motion and upon such terms as are just, the court may relieve a party or his legal representative from a final judgment, order or proceeding for the following reasons: (1) mistake, inadvertence, surprise or excusable neglect; (2) newly discovered evidence which by due diligence could not have been discovered in time to move for a new trial under Rule 59(B); (3) fraud (whether heretofore denominated intrinsic or extrinsic), misrepresentation or other misconduct of an adverse party; (4) the judgment had been satisfied, released or discharged, or a prior judgment upon which it is based has been reversed or otherwise vacated, or it is no longer equitable that the judgment should have prospective application; or (5) any other reason justifying relief from the judgment. The motion shall be made within a reasonable time, and for reasons (1), (2) and (3) not more than one year after the judgment, order or proceeding was entered or taken. A motion under this subdivision (B) does not affect the finality of a judgment or suspend its operation.

The procedure for obtaining any relief from a judgment shall by motion as prescribed in these rules.

The "any other reason" asserted by appellee under Civ. R. 60(B)(5) was that "the attorneys perpetrated such open and flagrant fraud upon the Court that no justice could have been rendered. . . ."

Appellant contends "that 'fraud' be it denominated 'fraud upon the court' or 'fraud in taking judgment' is a ground for relief within the purview of Civil Rule 60(B)(3) [which must be brought within one year] and not Civil Rule 60(B)(5)." This contention is without merit . . .

It is generally agreed that ". . . [a]ny fraud connected with the presentation of a case to a court is a fraud upon the court, in a broad sense." 11 Wright & Miller, Federal Practice and Procedure (1973) 253, § 2870. Thus, in the usual case, a party must resort to a motion under Civ. R. 60(B)(3). Where an officer of the court, *e.g.*, an attorney, however, actively participates in defrauding the court, then the court may entertain a Civ. R. 60(B)(5) motion for relief from judgment.

Appellee's motion and accompanying affidavit contained detailed allegations going to the execution of the separation agreement and Saltzer's role in the subsequent divorce action. Our review indicates that the trial court did not abuse its discretion in granting a hearing because . . . appellee's motion and supporting affidavit contained allegations of operative facts that would warrant relief under Civ. R. 60(B). . . .

In the instant case, the trial court was justified in its conclusion that Saltzer's conduct constituted a fraud upon the court by an officer thereof. The record reveals that: Saltzer was appellant's corporate counsel and the proceeding was initiated at appellant's request; while Saltzer testified that he intended to act as a mere scrivener for the parties, he never advised Mrs. Coulson or the court of his limited representation; he did not independently analyze the separation agreement, nor did he know or inquire into what Mrs. Coulson understood; and, Saltzer drafted both the complaint and the answer which were filed with the court. As appellee notes, Saltzer's conduct violated DR 5–101, DR 5–105(A), (B) and (C), and EC 5–14,–15 and–16 of the Code of Professional Responsibility.[2]

---

[2] Saltzer is no longer practicing law, having resigned in 1977.

Based on this record the trial court did not abuse its discretion in finding that a fraud had been perpetrated on the court.

Appellant also argues that even if appellee has stated an actionable cause for fraud upon the court, the motion, which was filed nearly twenty-seven months after the journal entry, was not filed within a "reasonable time." The evidence surrounding the fraud upon the court, as construed by the trier of fact is sufficient to support the conclusion that appellee's motion was filed within a reasonable time. . . .

Although *res judicata* is applicable to Civ. R. 60(B) motions, the court of appeals below concluded that [these] principles . . . were inapplicable to the case at bar . . . . The court of appeals properly concluded that *res judicata* does not bar a subsequent motion for relief from judgment when the subsequent motion is based on different facts, asserts different grounds for relief, and "it is not certain that . . . [the] issue 'could have been raised' in the prior motions."

Accordingly, we hold that pursuant to Civ. R. 60(B)(5) a court in appropriate circumstances may vacate a judgment vitiated by a fraud upon the court. We further hold that when an attorney files and signs a divorce complaint, purporting to represent the plaintiff in the action even though he drafted the complaint and accompanying separation agreement at the direction of and upon the terms dictated by the defendant in the same action, and he represents to the court that he is plaintiff's counsel and that the separation agreement, which he had not examined for fairness and equity, is fair and equitable, and the court, in reliance on these representations, proceeds to approve the divorce and incorporate the separation agreement into the judgment, which it would not have done had it known of the arrangement between the attorney and the defendant, the attorney perpetrates a fraud upon the court, and a trial court does not abuse its discretion in granting relief from judgment pursuant to Civ. R. 60(B)(5).

Judgment affirmed.

NOTES AND QUESTIONS

(1) The *Coulson* case aptly demonstrates that fraud upon the court may cause the court to vacate a divorce decree, and may force an unethical attorney into early retirement. Although not expressly stated in *Coulson,* an attorney's participation in a fraudulent divorce proceeding is definitely a ground for bringing a disciplinary action against the attorney for suspension or disbarment. *See, e.g.,* Annotation, *Participation in Allegedly Collusive or Connived Divorce Proceedings as Subjecting Attorney to Disciplinary Action*, 13 A.L.R.3d 1010 (1967); *In re Hockett*, 734 P.2d 877 (Or. 1987). *See also* Model Code of Professional Responsibility DR 7–102(A)(4)–(7).

Query: Why didn't the doctrine of *res judicata* bar the wife from relitigating her prior divorce proceeding since she had already had her day in court on the merits of the case?

(2) **Lawyer Competency in Divorce Proceedings.** It is well settled that whether a lawyer is representing only one spouse or both spouses in a divorce proceeding, the lawyer must exercise reasonable care, skill, and diligence as used by other lawyers in that jurisdiction. *See* Model Rules of Professional Conduct Rule 1.1; *see also Smith v. Lewis*, 530 P.2d 589 (Cal. 1975); *Spalding v. Davis*, 674 S.W.2d 710 (Tenn. 1984). Otherwise, the lawyer may

be liable for substantial damages in a legal malpractice action. *See generally* Annotation, *Attorney's Liability for Negligence in Cases Involving Domestic Relations,* 78 A.L.R.3d 255 (1977). Based upon this general doctrine, how should the following cases be decided?

(a) A lawyer represented a wife who was suing her husband for divorce. Although the husband was entitled to both a state and federal pension, the lawyer told his client, without researching the matter, that neither pension was community or marital property. As a result, the wife neither requested nor received any part of husband's pension benefits on divorce. Is this legal malpractice? Why or why not? *See Smith v. Lewis*, 530 P.2d 589 (Cal. 1975).

(b) Defendant law firm represented plaintiff wife in a divorce action in which wife's appraiser valued the parties' marital property at between $1,327,000 and $1,488,000 and husband's appraiser valued the property at $1,008,377. The divorce court found the property to be worth $900,000 and the wife received $400,000 in the divorce decree. Four years later, wife discovered that husband had fraudulently concealed and undervalued the true worth of the marital property, which was actually worth $2,970,000. She contacted her lawyers, who filed a motion to reopen the divorce proceeding on the ground of the husband's fraud. However, a hearing on the motion was never set and the motion was never withdrawn. Three years after discovering the husband's fraud, and seven years after the divorce, the wife sued her lawyers for malpractice, alleging malpractice in (1) failing to properly value the marital property at the time of divorce and (2) failing to reopen and prosecute the case after discovering husband's fraud. How should the court hold on both these issues? *See Morris v. Geer,* 720 P.2d 994 (Colo. Ct. App. 1986).

(c) The former wife retained an attorney to collect $13,740 in child support arrearages accrued under a prior separation agreement. Counsel for the former husband made a settlement offer of $3,500 plus future support payments of $200 a month. The former wife's attorney initially advised her to reject the offer, but on September 26th he changed his earlier recommendation and advised her to accept her former husband's offer. In that conversation, former wife admitted that she told her attorney to "do what he thought was best" with respect to settlement. On September 27th, the former wife's attorney accepted the settlement in writing, but the former wife claimed that prior to this acceptance, she had contacted her attorney and withdrawn her consent to the settlement, which the attorney denied. The trial court granted the attorney's motion for summary judgment, and the former wife appealed. What should the decision be on appeal? *See Rodgers v. Davenport,* 331 S.E.2d 389 (Va. 1985).

(3) **Dealing with the Unrepresented Spouse.** Model Rules of Professional Conduct Rule 4.3 clarifies an attorney's role when the other spouse is not represented by legal counsel: "In dealing on behalf of a client with a person who is not represented by counsel, a lawyer shall not state or imply that the lawyer is disinterested. When the lawyer knows or reasonably should know that the unrepresented person misunderstands the lawyer's role in the matter, the lawyer shall make reasonable efforts to correct the misunderstanding." According to a Virginia State Bar advisory opinion, when one of the parties to a separation agreement is unrepresented by independent legal counsel, the attorney for the represented spouse has the following obligations: (1) to advise the unrepresented spouse to secure independent counsel; (2) not to state or imply disinterest; (3) to advise the unrepresented spouse that

the attorney represents the interests of his or her client only; and (4) to advise the unrepresented spouse that his or her interests are, or may be, adverse to those of the attorney's client. Va. State Bar Committee on Legal Ethics, Opinion No. 876, reprinted in 13 Fam. L. Rep. 1284 (Feb. 2, 1987).

[B] Problems With Confidential Information

Under both the ABA Model Code and the Model Rules, attorneys have a strong duty to preserve confidentiality, with the goal of facilitating appropriate legal representation and encouraging persons to obtain necessary legal counsel. The ABA Model Code of Professional Responsibility requires attorneys to preserve the "confidences" and "secrets" of their clients. Model Code of Professional Responsibility DR 4–101(B). A lawyer may not "knowingly reveal a confidence or secret of [his or her] client," "use a confidence or secret of [his or her] client to the disadvantage of the client," or "use a confidence or secret of [his or her] client for the advantage of himself or a third person, unless the client consents after full disclosure." *Id.* However, a lawyer may reveal confidences or secrets "with the consent of the client" as well as revealing "the intention of the client to commit a crime and the information necessary to prevent the crime." Model Code of Professional Responsibility DR 4–101(C).

Model Rule 1.6(a) also provides that a lawyer shall not reveal confidential information relating to the representation of a client unless the client consents. However, a lawyer may reveal confidential information, to the extent the lawyer reasonably believes necessary, to prevent the client "from committing a criminal act that the lawyer believes is likely to result in imminent death or substantial bodily harm" or "to establish a claim or defense on behalf of the lawyer in a controversy between the lawyer and client." Model Rules of Professional Responsibility Rule 1.6(b)(1)–(2).

Model Rule 1.9(a) also warns against accepting a client if representing that client might be "materially adverse" to the interests of a former client. Accordingly, a lawyer who has represented one (or both) of the spouses in the past may be disqualified from representing the other spouse in a divorce action if there is a "substantial possibility" that knowledge acquired in the former representation could be used in a manner that would disadvantage the former client in a subsequent divorce action. What should this "substantial possibility" test be based upon? The following case explores this question in more depth.

WOODS v. SUPERIOR COURT OF TULARE COUNTY
California Court of Appeal
149 Cal. App. 3d 931 (1983)

ZENOVICH, ACTING PRESIDING JUDGE.

In this petition for writ of mandate, wife seeks an order disqualifying husband's counsel of record from participating in the dissolution proceedings between husband and wife.

The principal issue before us is whether an attorney, who for years has represented the interests of a family corporation, can represent one spouse against the other in an action for dissolution of their marriage when the family corporation is a primary focus of dispute in the dissolution.

In March 1983, wife filed an action for dissolution of her marriage and retained Howard R. Broadman as her trial counsel. Shortly thereafter, wife filed a motion seeking to disqualify husband's counsel, Arthur C. Kralowec, and all of his associates and employees from representing or assisting husband in the dissolution action. The motion was heard on the declarations submitted by each of the parties. No testimony was taken by the court.

Wife alleged in her declarations, among other things, that Mr. Kralowec was the family's business attorney and had been so for many years. Husband admitted that Mr. Kralowec had represented the family corporation since approximately 1975. Husband acknowledged that Mr. Kralowec had represented him in approximately 10 to 12 matters arising from corporate activities and otherwise. Mr. Kralowec admitted that over the years he developed a strong loyalty to husband. Wife further alleged that she had several conversations with Mr. Kralowec in which she had revealed to him her opinion and feelings on matters which might have relevance to the dissolution action. She told him her opinion as to the fair market value of the property on which the family home is situated and her personal feelings about maintaining it as her home on a permanent basis. She discussed with Mr. Kralowec her opinion concerning the economic liability of the business and her feelings regarding its continuation in relation to another lawsuit. She also discussed with him the merits and the probabilities of the corporation winning or losing several of the cases. One of these was a trade secret lawsuit by the corporation against an ex-employee. The other involved an easement where wife was a named defendant. Mr. Kralowec also wrote wife's will. Husband and Mr. Kralowec characterized the dealings between wife and Mr. Kralowec as not involving the sharing of confidential information.[3]

Mr. Kralowec and wife differed as to the content of their conversations regarding the impending divorce. Wife stated Mr. Kralowec advised her that he felt he had a conflict of interest in representing her in a divorce and indicated he would represent both husband and wife if the case could be settled on an amicable basis. Kralowec denied that wife ever asked him to act in her behalf during the dissolution proceedings. Wife alleged that after she learned her husband was having an extramarital affair, she met with Mr. Kralowec in his office with no one else present and exposed some of her most inner feelings regarding her personal relationship with her husband. Mr. Kralowec flatly denied that this conversation took place. Both husband and Kralowec denied that wife ever discussed the alleged extramarital sexual relationships that her husband was having. Both asserted that wife must have confused Kralowec with some other lawyer. Mr. Kralowec declared that he would not have represented wife in the dissolution action even if she had asked him to do so because he had ". . . been the attorney for [husband] since approximately 1975 and [was] completely loyal to him."

On May 5, 1983, the trial court denied the motion to disqualify Mr. Kralowec on the ground that nothing was contained in wife's declarations to demonstrate that he ever acquired any "knowledge or information which would be injurious" to wife.

DISCUSSION

The Rules of Professional Conduct to guide attorneys in their relationship with clients and former clients are "well established and generally understood by all attorneys in this state" (*People* ex rel. *Deukmejian v. Brown* (1981) 29 Cal. 3d 150, 155 [172 Cal. Rptr.

---

[3] Husband declared that wife had no basic knowledge of the financial aspects of the corporate business and that she was a "mere functionary." Mr. Kralowec characterized wife as a "go-fer" who made no decisions and provided no thinking, information or ideas.

478, 624 P.2d 1206].) Rule 4–101 of the Rules of Professional Conduct of the State Bar of California provides as follows: "A member of the State Bar shall not accept employment adverse to a client or former client, without the informed and written consent of the client or former client, relating to a matter in reference to which he has obtained confidential information by reason of or in the course of his employment by such client or former client."[4] The ethical prohibition against acceptance of adverse employment involving prior confidential information includes potential as well as actual use of such previously acquired information.

The trial court below, apparently concentrating on wife's role as a former client of Mr. Kralowec (through drafting wife's will, for example), seemed to rule there must be an "actual" showing that confidential information was obtained to rule in wife's favor on the disqualification motion. However, the test does not require the "former" client to show that actual confidences were disclosed. That inquiry would be improper as requiring the very disclosure the rule is intended to protect. It is the possibility of the breach of confidence, not the fact of the breach, that triggers disqualification.

We believe the proper focus should be on the fact that in representing an ongoing family corporation, Mr. Kralowec in a very real sense continues to represent wife.

Wife contends there are serious problems when the attorney of an ongoing corporation owned by wife and husband also undertakes to act as counsel for husband or wife in a divorce action. Wife contends that a corporate attorney owes undivided loyalty to the corporation and cannot take sides in a serious dispute between its owners. Wife further asserts that the problem is amplified here in that she has moved to join the family corporation as a party to the dissolution proceedings. We believe there is merit to wife's contentions.

Wife relies on *Jeffry v. Pounds* (1977) 67 Cal. App. 3d. 6, 11-12 [136 Cal. Rptr. 373].) In *Jeffry,* a law firm that had been discharged by a client in a personal injury action, after the client had discovered that the firm had undertaken to represent the client's wife in a dissolution of marriage action, brought an action against the client and his new attorney for recovery of attorney fees. The trial court concluded that plaintiff did not violate a professional canon by taking on the wife's dissolution suit against their personal injury client, and that no confidential information was compromised, and allowed plaintiff the reasonable value of the legal services payable out of the fee received by the new attorney. The Court of Appeal reversed and remanded. The court held that plaintiff breached the rule prohibiting an attorney from representing conflicting interests except with the written consent of all parties concerned by undertaking to represent the client's wife in the dissolution action without the written consent of both parties. The Court of Appeal held that the trial court's analysis had been "too narrow." (*Id.* at p. 9.) The court analyzed the situation in terms of the strictures against dual representation of antagonistic interests. "The strictures against dual representation of antagonistic interests are far broader; they arise without potential breaches of confidentiality." (*Id.* at pp. 9–10.) The court noted the professional responsibility rule seeks the objective of public confidence, as well as internal integrity. The court pointed out that a lay client is likely to doubt the loyalty of a lawyer who undertakes to oppose him even in an unrelated matter. (*Id.* at pp. 10–11.)

---

[4] Rule 5–102 requires that before an attorney may represent interests adverse to a client, he must obtain his client's consent in writing.

Husband contends that *Jeffry v. Pounds, supra,* 67 Cal. App. 3d 6, is inapplicable to the factual situation presented in the instant case. The factual situation in *Jeffry* involved the law firm undertaking to represent a wife in a marital dissolution action at the same time that it was currently representing the husband in a personal injury action. Husband contends Mr. Kralowec in the instant case does not currently represent wife in any matter. Moreover, husband contends that an attorney acting for a corporation represents it, its stockholders, and its officers in their representative capacity and does not represent the officers personally. (*Meehan v. Hopps* (1956) 144 Cal. App. 2d 284 [301 P.2d 10].) Husband argues that Mr. Kralowec never really represented either spouse and therefore is not acting adverse to a client or former client by now representing husband against wife. Not so under the circumstances before us. We believe Mr. Kralowec necessarily represents both husband's and wife's interests in his role as attorney for the family corporation. A corporation's legal adviser must refrain from taking part in controversies among shareholders as to its control, and when his opinion is sought he must give it without bias or prejudice. (*Goldstein v. Lees* (1975) 46 Cal. App. 3d 614, 622 [120 Cal. Rptr. 253].)

We believe the fact that Mr. Kralowec continues to represent wife's interest in a family business which will be the focus of the marital dissolution is sufficient to disqualify Mr. Kralowec from representing husband. Under such circumstances Mr. Kralowec should be disqualified even in the absence of a showing that he has in fact obtained confidential information. It has long been recognized that where ethical considerations are concerned, disqualification should be ordered not only where it is clear that the attorney will be adverse to his former client but also where it appears that he might. Moreover, the purpose of the rules against representing conflicting interests is not only to prevent dishonest conduct, but also to avoid placing the honest practitioner in a position where he may be required to choose between conflicting duties or attempt to reconcile conflicting interests. Disqualification is proper here to avoid any appearance of impropriety.[5]

Mr. Kralowec is not a neutral lawyer who had not been consulted by either side prior to the dissolution action. The appearance of impropriety here compels a strong rule prohibiting such an attorney from representing either side. This, we believe, is consistent with the underlying purposes of the rules against representing conflicting interests. As the court stated in *Goldstein v. Lees, supra,* 46 Cal. App. 3d 614, 620, *quoting from Tomblin v. Hill* (1929) 206 Cal. 689, 694 [275 P. 941]:

> It is better to remain on safe and secure professional ground, to the end that the ancient and honored profession of the law and its representatives may not be brought into disrepute. Courts have consistently held the members of the profession to the strictest account in matters affecting the relation of attorney and client.

We conclude that, absent consent or waiver, the attorney of a family-owned business, corporate or otherwise, should not represent one owner against the other in a dissolution action. Mr. Kralowec acted properly when he told wife he could not represent her. He should have said the same thing to husband to avoid any appearance of impropriety . . .

The trial court is hereby directed to grant the disqualification motion.

---

[5] We note there is a real possibility that Mr. Kralowec may have to be called as a witness in regard to the dispute over the assets and the handling of the corporation. Mr. Kralowec should not be placed in a situation where he may be forced to testify against the interests of wife. He has already affirmed his loyalty to husband.

WOOLPERT and HAMLIN, JJ., concur.

NOTES AND QUESTIONS

(1) As the *Woods* court concluded, an attorney in a divorce action should be disqualified from representation not only when it is clear that the representation will be adverse to the attorney's former client, but also where it appears that the representation *might* be adverse.

Query: Would it be improper for an attorney to represent the husband in a divorce action when she had previously represented both husband and wife with regard to a trust account, drafting wills, an adoption proceeding, and other legal matters? *See In re Conduct of Jayne,* 663 P.2d 405, 407–08 (Or. 1983) (representing husband in divorce action after representing wife in various other legal matters violated attorney's ethical obligation to preserve client confidences and secrets, warranting public reprimand). What if a law firm represents the husband in a divorce action after previously representing the wife in a debt collection lawsuit? *See Gause v. Gause,* 613 P.2d 1257, 1258 (Alaska, 1980) (denying wife's motion to disqualify husband's attorney in divorce action because attorney's prior representation of wife in debt collection suit did not raise substantial possibility that attorney gained confidential knowledge detrimental to wife).

(2) **Privileged Communications and the Defrauding Client.** Assume attorney Arthur represents husband Hal in a divorce case. After extensive negotiations, the parties enter into a property settlement agreement and obtain a no-fault divorce. In a subsequent business transaction, Arthur learns that Hal intentionally concealed substantial assets in the divorce proceeding and is guilty of fraud and perjury, since questions regarding Hal's marital assets were taken under oath. What must Arthur do?

Model Code of Professional Responsibility DR 7–102 (B)(1)(1974) provides that a lawyer who receives information clearly establishing that his or her client has perpetrated a fraud upon a person or tribunal shall promptly "call upon his client to rectify the same" and if his or her client refuses or is unable to do so, the attorney "shall reveal the fraud to the affected person or tribunal, except when the information is protected as a privileged communication." The previous code section, drafted in 1969, mandated that the attorney must "reveal the fraud to the affected person or tribunal," except when it was a privileged communication under ABA Formal Opinion 287 (1953). However, the Comment to ABA Model Rule 3.3, promulgated by the Kutak Commission, arguably takes the position that an attorney must reveal the fraud to the court, even if it is a privileged communication.

Query: Which position is more persuasive to you? Based upon what public policy rationale? Must Arthur withdraw from representing Hal? *Compare* Model Code of Professional Responsibility DR 2–110(C)(1)(e) *with* DR 2–110(B)(2).

(3) **Privileged Communication and Third Party Fraud.** Suppose attorney Alice represents wife Wendy in a divorce action, and learns from Wendy that her husband Hal filed fraudulent tax returns, although Wendy, when she signed these tax returns, was unaware of Hal's fraud. *See* 26 U.S.C. § 6013(d)(3); 26 U.S.C. § 6013(e); *see also* Model Code of Professional Responsibility DR 7–102(B)(2). Must Alice disclose the information to the court? What should Alice do?

(4) **Past and Future Conduct of the Client.** Assume that Wendy informs attorney Alice that she is pregnant with another man's child, but this information may detrimentally affect

her chances of obtaining custody of the parties' child, Hal Jr., on divorce. Privileged communication or not? *See* Model Code of Professional Responsibility DR 4–101(C). What if Wendy tells attorney Alice that Wendy and Hal have both severely beaten Hal Jr. on numerous occasions. Must Alice reveal this information to the court? *Compare* North Carolina Legal Ethics Opinion 120 in *ABA/BNA Lawyers Manual on Professional Conduct* 1001:6603 (holding that attorney has no obligation to report client's abuse of children, but can report it to stop future abuse) *with* Virginia Legal Ethics Opinion 705 in *ABA/BNA Lawyers Manual of Professional Conduct* 801:8844 (holding that attorney need not disclose client's spousal abuse unless the client is legally obligated to make such a disclosure).

Query: What about a state's child abuse reporting laws that may require lawyers and other enumerated persons to report any suspected child abuse to state child protective services officers? *See* Cleveland Bar Ass'n Opinion 92–2 in *ABA/BNA Lawyers Manual of Professional Conduct* 1001:6901. *See also* Robin Rosencrantz, Note, *Rejecting "Hear No Evil, Speak No Evil:" Expanding the Attorney's Role in Child Abuse Reporting,* 8 Geo. J. Legal Ethics 327 (1995).

(5) **Migratory Divorces.** Is it ethical for an attorney to advise his or her client to obtain a migratory Nevada or Haitian divorce, knowing that the client has no intent to make the divorcing forum a bona fide domicile? *See* Crystal, *Ethical Problems in Marital Practice,* 30 S.C.L. Rev. 321, 340–48 (1979); Swisher, *Foreign Migratory Divorces: A Reappraisal,* 21 J. Fam. L. 9, 49-51 (1982–83). *See also* Model Code of Professional Responsibility EC 7–8, 2–26, and DR 2–110(C)(1)(e).

(6) **Attorney's Fees on Divorce.** An attorney must not charge excessive fees in a divorce action. When an attorney's fee is questioned, it is normally within the trial court's discretion to determine whether it is reasonable. *See, e.g., Ransom v. Ransom,* 429 N.E.2d 594 (Ill. App. Ct. 1981); *In the Matter of Kinast,* 357 N.W.2d 282 (Wis. 1984); *see also* Annotation, *Amount of Attorneys' Fees in Matters Involving Domestic Relations,* 59 A.L.R.3d 152 (1974).

Nevertheless, the general rule still prevails that contingency fees are *not* proper in divorce litigation since an attorney allegedly could obtain an interest in discouraging the parties' reconciliation and because support payments may not be assigned. *See* Model Code of Professional Responsibility EC 2–20; Model Rules of Professional Conduct Rule 1.5(d)(1); *Thompson v. Thompson,* 70 N.C. App. 147, 319 S.E.2d 315, 320–21 (1984), *rev'd on other grounds* 328 S.E.2d 288 (N.C. 1985) (suggesting that because divorce clients are often emotionally distraught, they might be more likely to allege that contingent fees were obtained by undue influence and overreaching by attorney, to the ultimate detriment of the legal profession). *But see contra* Comment, *Professional Responsibility; Contingent Fees in Domestic Relations Actions: Equal Freedom to Contract for the Domestic Relations Bar,* 62 N.C.L. Rev. 381 (1984).

Some attorneys have argued that contingent fees arising from the collection of support arrearages or from the enforcement of marital property awards long after the divorce has been granted should not be invalid since collecting such arrearages would not "promote" the divorce *per se.* However, judicial decisions in this regard have been wildly inconsistent. *Compare Licciardi v. Collins,* 536 N.E.2d 840, 846–47 (Ill. App. Ct. 1989) (holding that contingency fees were not valid in post-divorce modification of marital property) *with Gross*

v. *Lamb,* 437 N.E.2d 309, 311–12 (Ohio Ct. App. 1980) (holding that contingency fee was not improper when client could not afford hourly fee of experienced family lawyer).

(7) **Pro Se Divorce.** Over the last two decades, the number of pro se litigants in divorce cases has grown rapidly. A 1993 ABA study of divorce filings in one Arizona county, known for its user-friendly court system, found that in almost 90% of all divorce cases, at least one party was unrepresented and in more than 50% of the cases, both parties were unrepresented. ABA Standing Committee On Delivery of Legal Services, Self-Representation In Divorce Cases 33 (1993). Similarly, a 1992 study of divorce filings in 16 urban jurisdictions found that in none of the 16 cities did lawyers represent both parties in more than half of the divorce cases filed. John A. Goerdt, National Center for State Courts, *Divorce Courts: Case Management, Case Characteristics, and the Pace of Litigation,* in 16 Urban Jurisdictions 48 (1992). In response to the growth of pro se divorce litigants, a number of court systems have hired staff or developed programs designed to provide information and assistance to these self-represented parties. These programs range from simplified form pleadings and instruction books, to group classes and telephone hot-lines, to one-on-one legal assistance. *See* Robert B. Yegge, *Divorce Litigants Without Lawyers,* 28 Fam. L.Q. 407, 412–16 (1994).

While some have applauded the rise of pro se divorce as a necessary alternative to the high cost of attorney representation, others have voiced concern about the dangers of self-representation and about the quality of the some of the programs developed to assist pro se litigants. *See* Elizabeth McCulloch, *Let Me Show You How: Pro Se Divorce Courses and Client Power,* 48 Fla. L. Rev. 481 (1996). The increase in pro se divorce litigants also poses an ethical dilemma for attorneys, since individuals who self-represent may seek limited attorney services for specific issues or aspects of a case. Traditionally, the establishment of an attorney-client relationship encompassed full service representation for an entire matter and could result in significant malpractice exposure. Recently, several commentators have proposed the notion of unbundled legal services, or discrete task representation as an alternative to this traditional, full-service model. Under an unbundled model, clients could contract for specific tasks or aspects of representation, rather than purchasing a full package of legal services. *See* Forrest S. Mosten, *Unbundling of Legal Services and the Family Lawyer,* 28 Fam. L.Q. 421 (1994). Unfortunately, existing ethical and malpractice rules fail to address the situation of an attorney who handles only discrete parts of a case, or who provides less than full representation to a pro se client, making such unbundled representation a risky undertaking. *See* ABA Standing Committee on Legal Services, *above,* at 57.

Query: As a way of reducing these risks, one commentator has proposed that the legislature grant limited immunity from liability to lawyers who provide limited scope, discrete task representation, provided there is full disclosure and a proper lawyer-client contractual foundation limiting the scope of the services rendered. Mosten *above* at 433–34. Would you favor such a proposal? Why or why not?

[C] Sexual Relations With a Divorce Client

The ethical implications of an attorney engaging in sexual relations with a divorce client are serious. A number of courts have expressed concern that attempts to exploit the attorney-client relationship in a divorce case, when the client may be psychologically and emotionally vulnerable, may allow an attorney to take "particular advantage of clients whose matrimonial difficulties place them in a highly vulnerable emotional state." *Matter of Bowen,* 542 N.Y.S.2d 45, 47 (App. Div. 1989). Engaging in a sexual relationship with a divorce client may further destroy any chance that the husband and wife will reconcile, and may prevent the attorney from properly exercising his or her independent judgment. *See, e.g., People v. Zeilinger,* 814 P.2d 808 (Colo. 1991). Moreover, the attorney may be required to withdraw from the divorce case if he or she is named as a witness in the other spouse's counterclaim for divorce based on the client spouse's adultery with his or her attorney. *See, e.g. Edwards v. Edwards,* 567 N.Y.S.2d 645 (App. Div. 1991).

How serious an ethical issue is posed by an attorney's sexual relations with a divorce client depends on the particular jurisdiction and the facts of each case. On one hand, for example, an Illinois court of appeals held that an attorney's sexual relationship with his divorce client did not constitute malpractice in the absence of allegations of inadequate representation, exchange of sexual favors for legal services, or actual damages. *See, e.g., Suppressed v. Suppressed,* 565 N.E.2d 101 (Ill. App. Ct. 1990). On the other hand, the Supreme Court of Rhode Island in *In the Matter of DiSandro,* 680 A.2d 73 (R.I. 1996) found that engaging in a consensual sexual relationship with a divorce client was unethical and would warrant public censure. The court stated:

> As we noted in *In the Matter of Robert F. Dippio,* 678 A.2d 454 (R.I. 1996), there is no specific prohibition contained within the Rules of Professional Conduct (or the Code of Professional Responsibility) regarding sexual activity between attorneys and their clients. However, any attorney who practices in the area of domestic relations must be aware that the conduct of the divorcing parties, even in a divorce based on irreconcilable differences (a so-called no-fault divorce) may have a significant impact on that client's ability to secure child custody and/or may materially affect the client's rights regarding distribution of marital assets. An attorney who engages in sexual relations with his or her divorce client places that client's rights in jeopardy. The lawyer's own interest in maintaining the sexual relationship creates an inherent conflict with the obligation to represent the client properly. When an attorney represents a divorce client in a case in which child custody, support, and distribution of marital assets are at issue, the attorney must refrain from engaging in sexual relations with the client or must withdraw from the case. . . . Accordingly, we accept the recommendation of the board and impose the sanction of public censure upon the respondent. Had the client's case actually been prejudiced by the respondent's conduct, a more serious sanction may have been appropriate.

Id. at 75.

More serious sanctions also may be brought against an attorney who has sexual relations with his or her divorce client, as the following case aptly illustrates:

COMMITTEE ON PROFESSIONAL ETHICS AND CONDUCT OF THE IOWA STATE BAR v. HILL
Supreme Court of Iowa
436 N.W.2d 57 (1989)

ANDREASEN, JUSTICE

The Committee on Professional Ethics and Conduct of the Iowa Bar Association filed a complaint against attorney William Hill that was heard by a division of the Grievance Commission. It found Hill's conduct violated disciplinary rules DR 1–102(A)(3) and (6), and ethical considerations EC 1–5 and EC 9–6. The commission recommended Hill's license to practice be suspended for three months. . . .

In June of 1986, K.C. contacted attorney Hill and requested that he represent her in a domestic matter. This was the first time Hill had met K.C. She advised him of her desire to secure temporary custody of her three children then living with their father and to secure a dissolution of their marriage. She was unemployed and had no money to advance to him as a retainer. Hill agreed to represent her . . .

On July 1, 1986, K.C. went to Hill's law office and offered to engage in sexual intercourse with him for money. Attorney Hill suggested he would give her money as a personal loan if she did not want to have sex. She told him that she had no means to reimburse him on a personal loan so her payback would be sex. Hill gave her fifty dollars and they then had sexual intercourse in his law office.

During the summer of 1986, K.C. was a drug addict and emotionally unstable. She is now chemically free, having undergone chemical dependency treatment. She has reconciled with her husband and the dissolution proceedings commenced by Hill have been dismissed.

The commission found that having sex with a client involved in a divorce action involving custody of children constituted unethical conduct on the part of the lawyer, regardless of whether or not the sex was for pay. The commission found Hill's conduct was unethical and unprofessional and in violation of Disciplinary Rules 1–102(A)(3) and (6). Those disciplinary rules provide:

> (A) A lawyer shall not . . .
>
> (3) Engage in illegal conduct involving moral turpitude . . .
>
> (6) Engage in any other conduct that adversely reflects on his fitness to practice law.

The commission found Hill had failed to conduct himself with the high standards of professional conduct expected of a lawyer and that his conduct did not reflect credit on the legal profession or inspire confidence, respect and trust of his client and the public as required by Ethical Consideration 1–5 and 9–6. . . .

Hill argues that our consideration of his sexual intercourse with K.C. violates his right to privacy. He cites *State v. Pilcher,* 242 N.W.2d 348, 358 (Iowa, 1976) for the proposition that this was a private act between two consenting adults which is protected from public scrutiny.

Constitutional considerations of privacy are not without limits. *Id.* . . . We must analyze this incident in the context in which it occurred, that of an attorney representing a client in a dissolution action. A lawyer undertaking a divorce action must recognize reconciliation is possible and may be in the best interest of his client. An attorney must be aware that the actions of the client and attorney may affect negotiations in the dissolution case, including determination of custody and visitation of minor children. Sexual intercourse between the lawyer and a client seeking a dissolution of marriage carries a great potential of prejudice both to the client and to the minor children of the marriage. We require lawyers to maintain high standards of ethical conduct and to avoid conduct which would reflect negatively upon the integrity and honor of the profession.

Despite Hill's assertion to the contrary, we cannot ignore the obvious implications of any scheme involving an exchange of sexual favors for money. Hill's characterization of this liaison as a purely romantic one rings hollow in the face of its aura of commercial exploitation. . . .

We, like the commission, find that the actions and conduct of Hill constitute unethical and unprofessional conduct. We hold Hill's license to practice law should be suspended indefinitely with no possibility of reinstatement for three months . . .

LICENSE SUSPENDED . . .

NOTES AND QUESTIONS

(1) In *Hill,* the Iowa Supreme Court held that having sex with a client involved in a divorce action involving custody of minor children constituted unethical conduct on the part of the lawyer "regardless of whether or not the sex was for pay." On the other hand, the Illinois Court of Appeals held that an attorney's sexual relationship with a divorce client would not be unethical or constitute legal malpractice in the absence of allegations of inadequate legal representation, exchange of sexual favors for legal services, or actual damages. *See Suppressed v. Suppressed,* 565 N.E.2d 101 (Ill. App. Ct. 1990).

Query: Which is the better reasoned approach? What about an attorney's right to privacy with his or her client?

(2) The Iowa Supreme Court in *Hill, above* and the Rhode Island Supreme Court in *In re the Matter of DiSandro,* 680 A.2d 273 (R.I. 1996) both expressed grave concerns about the impact an attorney's sexual relationship with his or her divorce client could have on potential child custody disputes. *See also* H. Clark, The Law of Domestic Relations in the United States 797–806 (2d ed. 1987) (stating that a parent's conduct and fitness are always relevant factors in any child custody dispute).

Query: In the absence of minor children in a divorce or dissolution of marriage, what other factors would militate against having sexual relations with a divorce client?

(3) What happens when an attorney claims that sexual relations with his or her divorce client was a private, purely consensual matter, but the client subsequently claims that he or she was emotionally vulnerable and was taken advantage of by the attorney, who pressured him or her to have sex. Who is the court likely to believe? Is this perhaps the best reason for an attorney in a domestic relations dispute to avoid even the semblance of impropriety? But what happens if an attorney honestly does fall in love with his or her client? What would you advise a colleague in a similar situation to do?

[D] Candor Toward the Court and Withdrawal from the Case

Both the ABA Model Rules and the Model Code of Professional Responsibility contain various rules concerning a lawyer's relationship with the courts and a lawyer's behavior in court. Model Rule 3.3, for example, provides in part:

(a) A lawyer shall not knowingly:

(1) make a false statement of material fact or law to a tribunal;

(2) fail to disclose a material fact to a tribunal when disclosure is necessary to avoid assisting a criminal or fraudulent act by the client;

(3) fail to disclose to the tribunal legal authority in the controlling jurisdiction known to the lawyer to be directly adverse to the position of the client and not disclosed by opposing client; or

(4) offer evidence that the lawyer knows to be false . . .

See also Model Code of Professional Responsibility DR 7–102(A)(5) (a lawyer shall not "knowingly make a false statement of law or fact"); DR 7–102 (A)(3) (a lawyer shall not "knowingly fail to disclose that which he is required by law to reveal"); DR 7–102 (A)(4) (a lawyer shall not "knowingly use" perjured testimony or false evidence).

A lawyer may withdraw from representing a client for any reason or for no reason at all. A client has the freedom to hire and fire attorneys at will. *In re Cooperman,* 611 N.Y.S.2d 465, 468 (N.Y. 1994). Both the ABA Model Code of Professional Responsibility and the ABA Model Rules identify some basic responsibilities of a withdrawing or discharged lawyer, including: (a) giving reasonable notice to the client, (b) allowing time for the employment of other counsel, (c) delivering to the client all related papers and property to which the client is entitled, and (d) refunding any advance fee payments that have not been earned. *See* Model Code of Professional Responsibility DR 2–110; Model Rules of Professional Conduct Rule 1.16.

Mandatory withdrawal by counsel is required whenever "the representation will result in violation of the rules of professional conduct or other law" or "the lawyer's physical or mental condition materially impairs the lawyer's ability to represent the client." Model Code of Professional Responsibility DR 2–110(B); Model Rules of Professional Conduct Rule 1.16(a). Thus, a lawyer must withdraw from any representation of the defrauding client that, directly or indirectly, would have the effect of assisting the client's continuing or intended future fraud.

An example of such client misconduct is illustrated in the following case:

MATZA v. MATZA
Supreme Court of Connecticut
627 A.2d 414 (1993)

BORDEN, ASSOCIATE JUSTICE.

. . . The Appellate Court opinion sets forth the history of this protracted and tortious litigation: The underlying dissolution of marriage proceeding was commenced on June 14, 1988. Judgment was rendered on February 21, 1991, thirty-two months later. During the course of this action, three [different] attorneys filed appearances on the defendant's behalf but subsequently withdrew their representation of her. The first, Gary I. Cohen, filed a motion to withdraw from the case in which he claimed that "difficulties have arisen between counsel and client which make effective representation impossible."

On November 29, 1988, Attorney Arnold M. Potash filed an appearance in lieu of Cohen. . . . On November 21, 1989, Judge Freedman ordered the trial to commence on February 15, 1990. On January 10, 1990, the defendant discharged Potash and on January

26, 1990, Attorney J. Daniel Sagarin filed an appearance in lieu of Potash. On January 29, 1990, Judge Freedman referred the case to the Honorable John Ottaviano, state trial referee, for trial, stating "[t]here will be no further continuances." Nonetheless, the case again was continued.

On May 16, 1990, the first day of trial before Judge Ottaviano, the defendant attempted to fire Sagarin. Judge Freedman referred the matter, without objection, to the court, Mihalakos, J. Sagarin made an oral motion to withdraw before Judge Mihalakos on the basis of his representation that the defendant no longer wanted him to represent her. Judge Mihalakos denied the motion and the trial commenced later that day before Judge Ottaviano. . . . [The trial was then suspended to allow the parties to conduct settlement negotiations].

On May 24, 1990, with no settlement pending, Judge Ottaviano scheduled the trial to resume on July 17, 1991. Judge Ottaviano noted that the defendant had yet to file a financial affidavit and ordered her to do so or be sanctioned.

The following day, Sagarin delivered a motion to withdraw as counsel together with a supporting memorandum under seal and a letter to Judge Freedman requesting that the motion be assigned to Judge Mihalakos to avoid prejudicing the defendant before Judge Ottaviano. On June 8, 1990, an attorney employed by Sagarin's law firm offered Judge Mihalakos a sealed affidavit in support of the motion. The defendant objected to Sagarin's motion to withdraw and his submission of the affidavit and requested a continuance to prepare a response to the motion. . . .

On June 12, 1990, Sagarin pursued the motion to withdraw at a hearing before Judge Mihalakos, arguing that his continued representation of the defendant would result in his participation in the defendant's fraudulent or improper conduct and urging Judge Mihalakos to conduct an in camera review of his affidavit. . . . [Plaintiff's attorney and defendant both objected to such an in camera review without a hearing].

[Judge Mihalakos then recessed and read Sagarin's affidavit which alleged that Sagarin advised the defendant that her prior testimony regarding $196,000 in proceeds from the sale of a Florida condominium, including a $75,000 "loan repayment" to her father, "was not inherently credible" and that Sagarin "would not allow perjurious testimony or fraudulent documents to be admitted at trial, even though the defendant refused to admit the falsity of her claim, and refused to sign a financial affidavit that was prepared with her approval." Sagarin also stated that he received a telephone call from a lawyer who represented defendant's father in various commercial matters and who had previously advised the defendant not to tell the "phony story" about the condominium proceeds. Sagarin therefore concluded that the defendant's refusal to sign her financial affidavit was based on her concerns over perjury and fraud. After reviewing Sagarin's affidavit, Judge Mihalakos, over the objection of the plaintiff's attorney and the defendant, granted Sagarin's motion to withdraw.]

The defendant appealed to the Appellate Court claiming, inter alia, that: (1) the judge who ruled on the motion to withdraw improperly refused to conduct an evidentiary hearing on that motion; and (2) the trial referee improperly drew an adverse inference from the defendant's failure to testify.

Rule 1.16 of the Rules of Professional Conduct governs and regulates the circumstances in which an attorney should or may withdraw from representing a client. Rule 1.16(a) governs mandatory withdrawal while Rule 1.16(b) governs permissive withdrawal. Rule 1.16(b) provides in relevant part: "Except as stated in paragraph (c), a lawyer may withdraw from representing a client if withdrawal can be accomplished without material adverse effect on the interests of the client *or if:* (1) The client persists in a course of action involving the lawyer's services that the *lawyer reasonably believes* is criminal or fraudulent . . . ." (Emphasis added) Rule 1.16(c) provides: "When ordered to do so by a tribunal, a lawyer shall continue representation notwithstanding good cause for terminating the representation." Subject to this limitation found in paragraph (c), rule 1.16(b) permits a lawyer to withdraw in two different scenarios. "First, a lawyer may withdraw for *any* or *no* reason, even without client consent, so long as withdrawal can be accomplished without 'material adverse effect' on the client. Second, in the . . . situations catalogued in the rule, a lawyer may withdraw *even if there is harm to the client.*" . . .

Consequently, with permission of the court . . . Sagarin was entitled to withdraw from his representation of the defendant in this case *despite* any ensuing harm to the client, if he reasonably believed that continuing to represent her would implicate him in a course of action that was fraudulent and in violation of the Rules of Professional Conduct. See Rules of Professional Conduct 1.2(d) ("A lawyer shall not counsel a client to engage, or assist a client, in conduct that the lawyer knows is criminal or fraudulent . . .") and 3.3(a)(4) ("A lawyer shall not knowingly . . . [o]ffer evidence that the lawyer knows to be false . . ."). The permissive withdrawal rules recognize, therefore, that an attorney may be entitled to withdraw from representing a client, even during the course of a trial, if the attorney reasonably believes that continuing the representation will cause him to violate the Rules of Professional Conduct. . . .

. . . .

. . . After a full review of this record, we conclude that the trial court did not abuse its discretion by denying the motion for a mistrial. The protracted nature of the case, the defendant's course of behavior throughout the proceeding, the factual findings regarding the defendant's intent to delay the proceedings and the resulting prejudice to the plaintiff all amply support the trial court's decision to deny the motion for a mistrial. . . .

In this opinion the other Justices concurred.

NOTES AND QUESTIONS

(1) As stated in *Matza, above,* Model Rule 1.16(b)(1) allows an attorney to withdraw from representing a client if "the client persists in a course of action involving the lawyer's services that the lawyer reasonably believes is criminal or fraudulent." Yet Model Rule 1.16(c) also provides that "[w]hen ordered to do so by a tribunal, a lawyer shall continue representation notwithstanding good cause for terminating the representation."

Query: What if the court denied Mr. Sagarin's second motion to withdraw based upon Mrs. Matza's fraudulent concealment of the proceeds from the sale of the condominium? What if Mrs. Matza stated her intention to Mr. Sagarin to employ a fourth attorney in her ongoing divorce dispute and tell the "phony condominium story" to that attorney as well?

(2) **Presenting False Evidence.** Although there may be various ethical problems and issues regarding the disclosure of a client's dishonesty and withdrawal of legal counsel from

the case, there is little debate concerning a lawyer's knowing involvement in offering false evidence. It will *not* be excused under Model Rule 3.3(a)(4). For example, in *In re Ver Dught*, 825 S.W.2d 847, 850–51 (Mo. 1992), an attorney's license was suspended when he represented a client in a social security claim for widow's benefits, advising his client not to disclose that she had remarried, and intentionally referring to his client by the surname she had used prior to her remarriage. Because of his otherwise positive record, the attorney was not disbarred from the practice of law. *See generally* Louis Parley, *The Ethical Family Lawyer: A Practical Guide to Avoiding Professional Dilemmas* 123, 127 (1995).

(3) **Misconduct in a Lawyer's Own Divorce.** Lawyers also have been disciplined for professional misconduct in the context of their own divorces, for reasons such as a failure to pay spousal or child support, or failing to make an adequate financial disclosure of marital property. *See, e.g. In re Warren*, 888 S.W.2d 334, 336–37 (Mo. 1994) (suspending lawyer's license for six months for not paying child support and for harassing his former wife); and *Matter of Finnerty*, 641 N.E.2d 1323, 1327 (Mass. 1994) (suspending lawyer's license suspended for six months because he inadequately disclosed value of his legal practice). Other states provide for the suspension or revocation of professional licenses generally for nonpayment of child and spousal support. *See e.g.* Va. Code Ann. 20–60.3(5) (1994).

Likewise, when a lawyer-spouse purports to "represent" both parties by convincing the other spouse not to retain independent legal counsel because the lawyer-spouse "can handle everything," the court may set aside the resulting divorce decree and separation agreement on the grounds that the lawyer-spouse may have breached a confidential fiduciary relationship owed to the other spouse. *See, e.g., Webb v. Webb*, 431 S.E.2d 55, 61 (Va. Ct. App. 1993) (holding that such purported "dual representation" was fraudulent and unconscionable). And when a lawyer hired a "muscle man" to threaten and injure his wife's lawyer in a pending divorce action, this action "reflected adversely" on his fitness to practice law, and the attorney's license to practice was suspended for a year and a day. *The Florida Bar v. Patarini*, 548 So. 2d 1110, 1111 (Fla. 1989)

§ 9.06 Representing Children

Most states permit—but do not require—the appointment of counsel to represent children in contested divorce or custody proceedings. *See* Ann Haralambie, The Child's Attorney 2 (1993). Considerable disagreement exists, however, regarding the appropriate role of a child's attorney. Should the attorney adhere to a zealous advocacy model, and advocate the child's expressed wishes, or should the attorney make an independent assessment of the child's best interests, and present that position to the court? Is it possible and desirable to blend these two roles? The following case explores these questions.

CLARK v ALEXANDER
Supreme Court of Wyoming
953 P.2d 145 (1998)

TAYLOR, C.J.

Appellant challenges the admission of tape recordings of her telephone conversations with her children at a modification of custody and child support hearing. Appellant also asserts the district court erred in allowing the guardian ad litem to testify while actively participating as counsel for the minor children. We find the district court erred in admitting the tape recordings through the testimony of the guardian ad litem, but that the error was harmless regarding the custody determination. . . .

Appellant, K.C. Clark (Mother), and appellee, Clifford Graham Alexander (Father), married in 1981 and had three children. On February 2, 1993, the district court granted a divorce and provided that the parties would have joint custody of the children, with Father having residential custody subject to a liberal visitation schedule for Mother.

On October 11, 1994, Mother filed a "Verified Petition for Modification of Child Custody," alleging a change of circumstances engendered by Father's relocation with the two younger children to a trailer home and the oldest child residing with "grandfather" in a house on the same property. Mother's petition was accompanied by a request for the appointment of a guardian ad litem.

An order appointing the guardian ad litem was entered January 8, 1996 and made retroactive to November 23, 1994 to reflect the parties' consent to the active participation of the guardian ad litem from that date. The guardian ad litem visited the children in person and by telephone, conducted in-home visits and interviews with both parents, stepfather, and grandfather, and interviewed other family members, teachers, neighbors, and clergy.

In the spring of 1995, Father informed the guardian ad litem of his concern that Mother was inappropriately involving the children in the custody dispute during telephone visits. The guardian ad litem responded that she would like to hear tape recordings of such conversations. Father informed her that his lawyer had advised against taping, and the guardian ad litem agreed Father must follow his attorney's advice.

Taping was not further discussed until Father's attorney telephoned the guardian ad litem and stated Father had inadvertently taped a conversation between Mother and the two younger children on September 23, 1995. On the tape recording, Mother and stepfather spoke with the nine-year-old daughter about their frustration with the custody proceeding and indicated Father was to blame for the delay. During the conversation, the child was urged to telephone the guardian ad litem to report that Father often left the children unsupervised, that the delay was upsetting, and to convey her preference for residing with her mother.

Shortly after listening to the tape recording, the guardian ad litem told Mother's attorney of the tape recording's existence and recommended Mother refrain from involving the children in the custody dispute. The guardian ad litem also consented, without informing Mother, to the continued taping of Mother's conversations due to concerns that Mother would further involve the children during telephone visits. . . .

On November 21, 1995, the guardian ad litem issued a report recommending primary residential custody remain with Father. This recommendation was based in large part on the substance of the taped conversations between Mother and the children. On December 21, 1995, Mother filed a "Motion for Removal of the Guardian Ad Litem and For Protective Order Regarding Evidence Illegally Obtained." The next day, Mother filed a " Motion in Limine" seeking to preclude admission of the tape recordings at the custody modification hearing because they were obtained in violation of state and federal wiretap laws. . . .

. . . A four-day custody modification hearing commenced on January 8, 1996. The same day, the district court issued its Order Nunc Pro Tunc appointing the guardian ad litem and an order denying Mother's Motion in Limine. The district court held that the tape recordings were not procured in violation of the wiretap laws because the first tape recording was inadvertently obtained and the vicarious consent of both Father and the guardian ad litem on behalf of the children removed the subsequent tapes from the wiretap prohibitions. The district court also found Mother s admission that she knew the conversations were taped indicated her consent as well.

At the modification hearing, Father called the guardian ad litem as his first witness. Through her testimony, the tapes recorded September 23, 1995 and October 8, 1995 were received into evidence, as well as both the guardian ad litem reports. . . .

At the close of the proceeding, the district judge orally ruled that the best interests of the children would be served by recognizing that the initial provision of joint custody was a misnomer and, in fact, awarded sole custody to Father as residential custodian of the children. The district court, therefore, granted Father continued sole custody. The district court also ordered Mother, Father, and children to receive counseling, and the parents to cease pressuring the children regarding custody issues. . . .

A. Role of Guardian Ad Litem

The role of the attorney/guardian ad litem during the proceedings is central to the disposition of this case. Mother claims that because the guardian ad litem actively participated as the children s attorney, it was improper to allow her to testify at the modification hearing. . . .

Generally, we will not address an issue raised for the first time on appeal absent special circumstances. However, "the definition of the precise roles of the attorney and the guardian ad litem for children is still evolving and not without difficulty." *S.S. v. D.M.*, 597 A.2d 870, 877 (D.C.App. 1991). In Wyoming, the role of an attorney or guardian ad litem in custody cases is not addressed by statute, and like many jurisdictions, case law has failed to clearly delineate the parameters of the duties incumbent upon appointment. Moreover, the juxtaposition of the separate roles of attorney and guardian ad litem into one "attorney/guardian ad litem," appears especially problematic. Given the lack of clear direction provided to those who must fulfill this role in Wyoming, and our certainty that the issues in this case will reappear in the future, we speak to those issues here. In providing guidance to the role of an attorney appointed to represent a child while at the same time acting as guardian ad litem, we do not intend to usurp the role of the district court in appointing individuals to act solely as an attorney or as guardian ad litem. It is imperative, however, that the appointee request clarification from the appointing court if questions regarding the duties arise.

The guardian ad litem s role has been characterized as investigator, monitor, and champion for the child. . . . The traditional role of a guardian ad litem in custody proceedings has been described as follows:

> In custody matters, the guardian ad litem has traditionally been viewed as functioning as an agent or arm of the court, to which it owes its principal duty of allegiance, and not strictly as legal counsel to a child client. * * * In essence, the guardian ad litem role fills a void inherent in the procedures required for the adjudication of custody disputes. Absent the assistance of a guardian ad litem, the trial court, charged with rendering a decision in the "best interests of the child," has no practical or effective means to assure itself that all of the requisite information bearing on the question will

be brought before it untainted by the parochial interests of the parents. Unhampered by the ex parte and other restrictions that prevent the court from conducting its own investigation of the facts, the guardian ad litem essentially functions as the court's investigative agent, charged with the same ultimate standard that must ultimately govern the court's decision—i.e., the "best interests of the child." Although the child's preferences may, and often should, be considered by the guardian ad litem in performing this traditional role, such preferences are but one fact to be investigated and are not considered binding on the guardian. * * * Thus, the obligations of a guardian ad litem necessarily impose a higher degree of objectivity on a guardian ad litem than is imposed on an attorney for an adult.

State ex rel. Bird v. Weinstock, 864 S.W.2d 376, 384 (Mo.App. 1993). In many jurisdictions, the guardian ad litem is required to oversee the progress of proceedings involving the child and, after reaching an independent conclusion, to recommend to the court the outcome which the guardian ad litem believes to be in the child's best interests.

In contrast, the traditional role of an attorney is that of advisor, advocate, negotiator and intermediary. Wyo. R. Prof. Cond., Preamble. Counsel appointed to represent a child must, as far as reasonably possible, maintain a normal client-lawyer relationship with the child, Wyo. R. Prof. Cond. 1.14, and "abide by a client's decisions concerning the objectives of representation * * *." Wyo. R. Prof. Cond. 1.2. Thus, counsel for a child is not free to independently determine and advocate the child's " best interests" if contrary to the preferences of the child.

Wyo. Stat. § 14-3-211 (1997), addressing the appointment of counsel to represent children in abuse and neglect proceedings, distinguishes the role of guardian ad litem from the role of "counsel for the child," but combines the two if no guardian ad litem is appointed. Although the statute does not address custody proceedings, in *Moore v. Moore*, 809 P.2d 261, 264 (Wyo. 1991), we applied the statutory language regarding "representation" of the child to custody cases, and held that an attorney appointed as guardian ad litem may not engage in ex parte communications with the trial court. We stated that the attorney/guardian ad litem acts as an advocate for the child and "has the same ethical responsibilities in the proceeding as any other attorney."

Our decision in *Moore*, 809 P.2d 261, however, did not address other situations where the attorney's ethical duties under the Rules of Professional Conduct may not coincide with the duties expected of the guardian ad litem. The circumstances of this case clearly illustrate several examples of the problems which may arise. Here, the attorney/guardian ad litem represented three siblings, two of whom expressed conflicting preferences regarding custody. A guardian ad litem, not bound by the expressed preferences of the child, has no conflict in this situation. On the other hand, the Rules of Professional Conduct require the attorney to zealously represent the client s interest's. Therefore, the attorney must discontinue representation when two clients' interests, and thereby the attorney's duty, diverge. Wyo. R. Prof. Cond. 1.2 and 1.7. Similarly, a conflict is present when the attorney/guardian ad litem does not believe the child's expressed interest is in the child's best interest.

The guardian ad litem is also required to inform the court of all relevant information. This expectation may often collide with Wyo. R. Prof. Cond. 1.6, which requires the attorney to maintain confidentiality unless the client consents to disclosure. In this case, Father's recording of the children's conversations with Mother also included a recording of one child's telephone call to the guardian ad litem. The attorney/guardian ad litem allowed this conversation to be admitted into evidence without objection and without the consent of the child.

Finally, the attorney/guardian ad litem is expected to actively participate as legal counsel for the children, i.e., presenting opening and closing statements and examining witnesses. In contrast, Wyo. R. Prof. Cond. 3.7 prohibits an attorney from participating as an advocate in a case where it is likely that he or she will be called to testify to a matter of import at the proceeding. In this case, the attorney/guardian ad litem not only testified regarding the ultimate issue in the case, but was the vehicle through which the taped conversations were admitted.

In those cases where the facts relevant to the children's best interests may not be otherwise presented to the court, the traditional role of guardian ad litem is essential. It is equally apparent that the skills of a legal advocate are invaluable to the child caught within a contentious custody dispute. With counsel, the child has an unbiased adult who can explain the process, inform the court of the child's viewpoint, and ensure an expeditious resolution.

While some jurisdictions have required the separation of these roles, a number of courts have declared the role a "hybrid," which necessarily excuses strict adherence to some rules of professional conduct. *In Interest of J.P.B.*, 419 N.W.2d 387, 391-92 (Iowa 1988); *In re Marriage of Rolfe*, 216 Mont. 39, 699 P.2d 79, 86-87 (1985), *aff'd* 234 Mont. 294, 766 P.2d 223 (1988). We believe that the costs attending the appointment of both an attorney and a guardian ad litem would often be prohibitive and would in every case conscript family resources better directed to the children's needs outside the litigation process. Thus, we too acknowledge the "hybrid" nature of the role of attorney/guardian ad litem which necessitates a modified application of the Rules of Professional Conduct.

Contrary to the ethical rules, the attorney/guardian ad litem is not bound by the client's expressed preferences, but by the client's best interests. If the attorney/guardian ad litem determines that the child's expressed preference is not in the best interests of the child, both the child's wishes and the basis for the attorney/guardian ad litem's disagreement must be presented to the court. *In re Marriage of Rolfe*, 699 P.2d at 86-87.

In the same light, the confidentiality normally required in the attorney-client relationship must be modified to the extent that relevant information provided by the child may be brought to the district court's attention. While it is always best to seek consent prior to divulging otherwise confidential information, an attorney/guardian ad litem is not prohibited from disclosure of client communications absent the child's consent. As legal counsel to the child, the attorney/guardian ad litem is obligated to explain to the child, if possible, that the attorney/guardian ad litem is charged with protecting the child's best interest and that information may be provided to the court which would otherwise be protected by the attorney-client relationship.

Although the above rules require compromise in order to effect the dual roles of attorney and guardian ad litem, we do not find the same need applies to Wyo. R. Prof. Cond. 3.7. Our holding in *Moore*, 809 P.2d 261 clearly mandates that the attorney/guardian ad litem is to be an advocate for the best interests of the child and actively participate at the proceedings. As counsel, the attorney/guardian ad litem has the opportunity and the obligation to conduct all necessary pretrial preparation and present all relevant information through the evidence offered at trial. Recommendations can be made to the court through closing argument based on the evidence received. It is, therefore, unnecessary to allow the attorney/guardian ad litem to place his or her own credibility at issue. Consequently, we join those jurisdictions which hold that an attorney/guardian ad litem may not be a fact witness at a custody hearing.

This is not to say that the attorney/guardian ad litem may not submit a written report to the parties. A detailed report which timely informs the parties of the relevant facts and the basis of the guardian ad litem's recommendation may facilitate agreement prior to trial. If the parties so stipulate, the report may be presented to the court. However, the report should not be filed with the court or received into evidence without the express agreement of the parties. . . .

We find that the district court erred in admitting the testimony of the attorney/guardian ad litem. In turn, all evidence presented through this witness was also erroneously before the district court. Identification of the ethical impropriety surrounding the admission of this testimony does not, however, automatically require reversal. In *Moore*, 809 P.2d at 264, we held that an ethical violation, not brought about by the prevailing party, will be reversed only if it resulted in manifest injustice. In many district courts, it is not uncommon to allow the testimony of an attorney/guardian ad litem. Thus, in the absence of objection to the district court, we cannot say that the prevailing party in this case was responsible for the ethical violation. Therefore, we must determine whether the admission of the attorney/guardian ad litem's testimony and reports, as well as the tape recordings, resulted in manifest injustice under the totality of the circumstances. . . .

After careful review of the record, and eliminating from consideration the opinions of the guardian ad litem and the contents of the tape recordings, we find that the record clearly supports the district court's determination that the best interests of the children were served by Father's continuing custody. In reaching his decision, the district judge noted specific examples of Mother's inability to cope with the eldest child during visitations and her refusal to credit Father's cooperation in scheduling visitations. The district judge also noted testimony that Father helped the youngest child write letters to Mother and permitted the children to telephone Mother long distance at Father's expense. The testimony of teachers and relatives established that the children were performing well in school and appeared to be happy in their present situation. On the other hand, Mother's witnesses equivocated on whether all the children would be better served by moving to Mother's residence. We find that the admission of the testimony of the attorney/guardian ad litem did not result in manifest injustice and, therefore, does not warrant reversal of the district court s custody determination. . . .

NOTES AND QUESTIONS

(1) Are you comfortable with the hybrid attorney/guardian ad litem role envisioned by the court in *Clark*? Is there a more satisfactory alternative? Is a child likely to confide in a lawyer who tells the child that any information the child provides may be disclosed to the court?

(2) Not all observers agree that lawyers appointed to represent children should serve in a hybrid attorney/guardian ad litem role. For example, participants in a 1995 Conference

on Ethical Issues in the Legal Representation of Children, which brought together lawyers, judges, legal scholars and mental health professionals, recommended that:

> A lawyer appointed or retained to serve a child in a legal proceeding . . . should assume as the obligations of a lawyer, regardless of how the lawyer's role is labeled, be it as guardian *ad litem*, attorney *ad litem,* law guardian, or other. The lawyer should not serve as the child's guardian *ad litem* or in another role insofar as the role includes responsibilities inconsistent with those of a lawyer for the child.

Proceedings of the Conference on Ethical Issues in the Legal Representation of Children: Recommendations of the Conference, 64 Ford. L. Rev. 1301, 1301 (1996).

Standards promulgated by the American Academy of Matrimonial Lawyers also reject the hybrid attorney/guardian ad litem approach. *See Representing Children: For Attorneys and Guardians Ad Litem in Custody or Visitation Proceedings (With Commentary)*, 13 J. Am. Acad. Matrim. Law 1 (1995). The AAML standards distinguish between "impaired" and "unimpaired" child clients, with a rebuttable presumption that children over the age of 11 are "unimpaired." AAML Standard 2.2. An attorney's role in representing an "unimpaired" child is the same as when representing an adult client; the client sets the goals of representation and the ordinary rules of attorney-client confidentiality apply. AAML Standards 2.3 and 2.4. When a child client is "impaired," and therefore unable to direct the representation, the AAML Standards define the attorney's primary role as a gatherer and provider of information, and expressly preclude the child's attorney from advocating a position with respect to the child's best interests or the outcome of the proceedings. As the Commentary explains:

> The most serious threat to the rule of law posed by the assignment of counsel for children is the introduction of an adult who is free to advocate his or her own preferred outcome in the name of the child's best interests. The danger is that this additional adult will make a difference in the outcome of the proceedings without any assurance that the outcome is "better" (that is, without an assurance that the outcome best serves the child's interests). This Standard rejects as fundamentally flawed a rule that gives attorneys the authority to advocate the result they themselves prefer, in the client's name.

AAML Standard 2.7, Comment. Do you agree with this critique? How would the *Clark* court respond?

(3) To the extent that the attorney's role depends on the competence of the child, how should an attorney determine whether a child has the capacity to direct the representation? If a child expresses a preference that the lawyer believes is contrary to the child's best interests, is that an indication that the child is incompetent or impaired? For a thoughtful analysis of how lawyers representing children should define and enhance their client's competence, and what a lawyer's role should be when a child appears to be incompetent, *see* Peter Margulies, *The Lawyer As Caregiver: Child Client's Competence in Context*, 64 Ford. L. Rev. 1473, 1496 (1996).

(4) Can a lawyer appointed to represent a child in a hybrid attorney/guardian ad litem role be sued for negligence or malpractice if she fails to perform her duties competently? *See, Obsterhous v. Short*, 730 F. Supp.1037, 1038–39 (D. Colo. 1990) (court appointed guardian ad litem acts as an officer of the court is thereby entitled to absolute immunity

from negligence actions). *Accord, Fleming v. Asbill,* 483 S.E.2d 751, 753 (S.C. 1997). Should a child have the authority to discharge his or her court-appointed attorney? *Compare Hartley v. Hartley,* 886 P.2d 665, 668 (D. Colo. 1995) (rejecting child's attempt to replace court-appointed guardian ad litem with privately-chosen attorney) *with* Arnold H. Lubasch, *Boy in Divorce Suit Wins Right to Choose His Lawyer,* N.Y.Times, Nov. 10, 1992, at B6 (reporting on divorce case in which judge allowed 11-year-old boy to replace a court-appointed law-guardian with an attorney of his own choosing).

(5) Should judges be *required* to appoint counsel for children in *all* contested custody and visitation cases? If so, should the requirement extend to cases in which divorcing parents have agreed on a custody arrangement? The Supreme Court has held that children have a constitutional right to counsel in any delinquency proceeding that may lead to a loss of liberty. *In re Gault,* 387 U.S. 1, 36–37 (1976). In addition, federal law requires the appointment of a guardian ad litem for any child who is the subject of civil abuse or neglect proceedings. *See* 45 C.F.R. 1340.14(g) (1994). A number of commentators have argued that these constitutional and common law principles support an entitlement to counsel for children in contested custody and visitation cases. *See, e.g.,* Catherine J. Ross, *From Vulnerability To Voice: Appointing Counsel For Children In Civil Litigation,* 64 Ford. L. Rev. 1571, 1572 (1996) (arguing that children's particular vulnerabilities support a claim for appointed counsel in civil cases); Linda Elrod, *Counsel for the Child in Custody Disputes: The Time Is Now,* 26 Fam. L. Q. 53 (1992); Howard A. Davidson, *The Child's Right to be Heard and Represented in Judicial Proceedings,* 18 Pepp. L. Rev. 255 (1991). *But see* Martin Guggenheim, *The Right to be Represented but Not Heard: Reflections on Legal Representation for Children,* 59 N.Y.U. L. Rev. 76 (1984) (expressing doubts about the wisdom of providing legal representation for children too young to direct an attorney). *Query:* Would the routine appointment of counsel for children of divorcing parents infringe on the *parents'* protected rights and interests? *See* Ellen B. Wells, Unanswered Questions: *Standing and Party Status of Children in Custody and Visitation Proceedings,* 13 J. Am. Acad. Matrim. Law 95, 109–11 (1995) (suggesting that constitutional rights of parents may limit children's participation in custody and visitation disputes).

Despite substantial scholarly support for mandatory representation of children, courts have generally rejected the claim that children have a constitutional right to independent representation in divorce and custody matters. *See e.g., Miller v. Miller,* 677 A.2d 64, 66 (Me. 1966) (children not entitled to representation by independent legal counsel in parents' divorce action; appointment of a guardian ad litem to protect children's best interest fully satisfies constitutional requirements). *Hartley v. Hartley,* 886 P.2d 665, 668 (Colo. 1995) (child not deprived of due process by denial of separate representation of his choice in custody proceeding). Similarly, only a few states mandate appointment of counsel for children in all custody disputes. *See generally* Kathleen H. Federle, *Looking for Rights in All the Wrong Places: Resolving Custody Disputes in Divorce Proceedings,* 15 Cardozo L. Rev. 1523, 1534 (1994) (reviewing state statutes and practices). The American Academy of Matrimonial Lawyers also rejects the routine appointment of counsel for children. Section 1.1 of the AAML Standards provides:

> Courts should not routinely assign counsel or guardians ad litem for children in custody or visitation proceedings. Appointment of counsel or guardians should be preserved for those cases in which both parties request the appointment or the court

finds a after a hearing that appointment is necessary in light of the particular circumstances of the case.

Representing Children: Standards For Attorneys and Guardians Ad Litem in Custody or Visitation Proceedings (With Commentary), 13 J. Am. Acad. Matrim. Law 1, 2 (1995).

Query: What are the benefits and drawbacks of routinely providing children with legal representation in custody and visitation proceedings?

(6) Some states make special provision for representation of children in custody cases involving allegations of abuse or neglect. *See, e.g.,* Fla. Stat. Ann. § 61.401 (1998); Minn. Stat. Ann. § 518.165(2) (1997). A number of appellate decisions have found an abuse of discretion where a trial court failed to appoint counsel for a child in a custody case involving such allegations. *See, e.g., G.S. v. T.S.* 582 A.2d 467, 470 (Conn. Ct. App. 1990) (When custody is contested and there are allegations of neglect and abuse, children have a unique need to be represented by counsel who will advocate their best interests.); *Levitt v. Levitt*, 556 A.2d 1162, 1165 (Md. Ct. App. 1989) (attorney should have been appointed for child in custody case where parents had accused each other of drug abuse and inappropriate sexual behavior). Several commentators have suggested that children have a due process right to representation in custody disputes involving allegations of abuse or neglect. *See, e.g.,* Kerin S. Bischoff, Comment, *The Voice of a Child: Independent Legal Representation of Children in Private Custody Disputes When Sexual Abuse is Alleged*, 138 U. Pa. L. Rev. 1383, 1383 (1990); David Peterson, Comment, *Judicial Discretion Is Insufficient: Minor's Due Process Right to Participate with Counsel when Divorce Custody Disputes Involve Allegations of Child Abuse*, 25 Golden Gate U. L. Rev. 513, 530 (1995). Are the arguments for representation of children stronger in cases involving such allegations than in other parental custody disputes? Why or why not?

(7) Under a discretionary standard, what factors should a court consider in determining whether to appoint counsel for a child or children in a particular custody case? Should the consent of at least one parent be required? Should the parents' financial status be considered? *See* La. Rev. Stat. 9:345 (1998) (listing factors that judges should consider). If an attorney is appointed to represent a child, who should pay for the attorney's services?

(8) Should lawyers who represent children in divorce and custody proceedings be required to have specialized training? If so, what should that training include? *See, e.g.,* Peter Margulies, *The Lawyer As Caregiver: Child Client's Competence in Context*, 64 Fordham L. Rev. 1473, 1496 (1996) (arguing that training is essential for child advocates and that the training should include child development theory, interviewing and counseling, and the risk of bias in custody and child welfare decisions); Rachel B. Burkholder and Jean M. Baker, *Child Development and Child Custody* in Ann M. Haralambie, The Child's Attorney 145, 145–46 (1993) (attorneys who represent children must have good understanding of child development and the effect of various developmental stages on custody arrangements).

(9) Do lawyers who represent divorcing *parents* have any obligation to consider the interests of the children when advising and counseling their clients? When, if ever, should concern for the interests of a child limit the pursuit of a client's objectives? *See* American Academy of Matrimonial Lawyers, Standards of Conduct § 2.23, introductory material (1991) (suggesting that parents' fiduciary obligation to their children "provides a basis for the attorney's consideration of the child's best interests consistent with traditional adversary and client loyalty principles" and that, in some instances, the parent's attorney may have

an obligation to the child "that would justify subordinating the express wishes of the parent").

§ 9.07 Alternative Dispute Resolution

Under the fault-based divorce system, a primary purpose of divorce proceedings was to assign blame for the breakdown of a marriage and to dispense justice accordingly. With the advent of no-fault divorce, courts have become less concerned with assigning blame and more concerned with helping divorcing couples resolve disputes and restructure their financial and parenting relationship as equitably and efficiently as possible. *See generally* Barbara Babb, *An Interdisciplinary Approach to Family Law Jurisprudence: Application of an Ecological and Therapeutic Perspective*, 72 Indiana L. Rev. 775, 776 (1997). Consistent with this shift in focus, traditional adversary divorce procedures have been supplemented—and in some cases supplanted—by alternative forms of dispute resolution, such as mediation and arbitration. These more private and less formal processes are consistent with the underlying premise of no-fault divorce—that the responsibility for overseeing the dissolution of marriage rests with individual spouses, rather than with the state. *See* Ann Milne, *Divorce Mediation: The State of the Art*, 1 Mediation Q. 15, 15–16 (1983). At the same time, growing numbers of observers have emphasized the negative effects of the adversary system on the well-being of children and families. These observers have suggested that no amount of judicial intervention will protect children, unless the legal system itself becomes less adversarial and more conducive to cooperative decision-making, both during and after divorce. *See generally* Janet Weinstein, *And Never the Twain Shall Meet: The Best Interests of Children and the Adversary System*, 52 U. Miami L. Rev. 79, 80 (1997); Andrew Schepard, *Taking Children Seriously: Promoting Cooperative Custody After Divorce*, 64 Tex. L. Rev. 687, 690 (1985). *But see* Martha A. Fineman, *Dominant Discourse, Professional Language, and Legal Change in Child Custody Decisionmaking*, 101 Harv. L. Rev. 727, 730 (1988) (critiquing the "appropriation" of child custody decisionmaking by social workers and mediators).

[A] Divorce Mediation

[1] Overview and Current Status

Mediation is a process by which a neutral third party (the mediator) assists two or more disputing parties to reach a mutually agreeable settlement of their dispute. The mediator helps the parties "identify the issues, reduce misunderstandings, vent emotions, clarify priorities, find points of agreement, explore new areas of compromise and possible solutions." Jessica Pearson & Nancy Thoennes, *Mediating and Litigating Custody Disputes: A Longitudinal Evaluation,* 17 Fam. L. Q. 497, 499 (1984). Mediation differs from arbitration in that the mediator is not empowered to resolve the dispute or impose an outcome on the parties. It differs from lawyer-conducted negotiation primarily in that the parties themselves conduct the discussions and attempt to arrive at a satisfactory accord. Mediation also differs from more traditional, adversarial processes in that it seeks to move the parties from established positions to underlying mutual interests, in order to generate value enhancing, or "win-win" solutions. *See* Joan B. Kelly, *A Decade of Divorce Mediation Research: Some Answers and Questions*, 34 Fam. & Conciliation Cts. Rev. 373, 378 (1996) [hereinafter Kelly, *Mediation Research*].

Mediation emphasizes cooperative decision-making. Supporters of mediation contend that this cooperative orientation offers a number of benefits for divorcing families. First, it encourages parents to focus on their joint interest in promoting the well-being of their children. In contrast to the adversary system, mediation thus encourages parents to "put their children first" during the often stressful process of divorce. Mediation also offers parents the opportunity to develop communication and problem solving skills that can facilitate successful co-parenting after divorce. Moreover, if mediation is successful, divorcing parents can avoid the bitterness and emotional trauma of a trial. Successful mediation also avoids the substantial litigation costs associated with contested court proceedings, thus leaving more marital assets available to meet the post-divorce needs of both the children and the former spouses. *See* Nancy S. Palmer & William D. Palmer, *Family Mediation: Good for Clients, Good for Lawyers,* The Compleat Lawyer 32, 33 (Fall 1996). Finally, unlike adversary divorce procedures, mediation is designed to reduce conflict and to help disputing parents resume a working relationship with each another. *See* Joan Kelly, *Parental Interaction After Divorce: Comparison of Mediated and Adversarial Divorce*, 9 Behavioral Sci. & Law 387 (1991).

A significant amount of social science research has examined the results and effectiveness of divorce mediation. That research has tended to substantiate some --but not all --of the claims made by mediation proponents. In general, research in the United States and Canada has demonstrated small, but often short-lived increases in parental cooperation and improvement in communication following divorce and custody mediation. Kelly, *Mediation Research, above.* at 379 (citing H. Irving & M. Benjamin, *An Evaluation of Process and Outcome in a Private Family Mediation Service,* 10 Mediation Quarterly 35 (1992); Jessica Pearson & Nancy Thoennes, *Reflections on a Decade of Research*, in Mediation Research: The Process and Effectiveness of Third Party Intervention. (K. Kressel, D. Pruitt & Assoc. eds., 1989)). The research also suggests that parties who mediate their disputes are less likely to return to court than parties who rely on adversary procedures. Part of the reason for the low relitigation rates may be that mediated agreements often contain a provision requiring the parties to attempt to mediate future disputes, before resorting to judicial processes.

Studies also indicate high levels of client satisfaction with both the process and the outcomes of mediation. While satisfaction with mediation is highest among those participants who reached agreement, several studies have found client satisfaction in the 40% to 60% range among those participants who were *unable* to reach agreement. In studies comparing mediation and litigation samples, mediation clients were significantly more satisfied than their adversarial counterparts. Kelly, *Mediation Research, above*, at 378–79. Several studies also suggests that mediation may be less time consuming, and possibly less costly, than more traditional, adversary processes. *See* Kelly, *Mediation Research above*, at 376. Mediation in the public sector may also reduce government costs. In California, which mandates mediation of custody and visitation disputes, the number of custody trials has been reduced to fewer than 2% of those parents initially disputing child-related issues. *Id.*

In general, mediation results in more joint custody agreements than do adversary divorce procedures. This should not be surprising, since many mediators and mediation theorists are also strong advocates of shared parenting after divorce. Mediated agreements also tend to be more detailed and specific than either litigated outcomes or attorney-negotiated settlements. The few studies that have examined financial outcomes have found no significant differences in child support amounts between mediated and litigated processes. Property agreements reached in mediation also appear similar to those reached in lawyer-negotiated settlements. *See generally* Jessica Pearson, *The Equity of Mediated Divorce Agreements,* 7 Mediation Quarterly 347 (1991). However, contrary to the claims of mediation enthusiasts, the research "is consistent in reporting that neither parent nor child psychological adjustment is affected in a statistically meaningful manner by either a custody mediation or comprehensive divorce mediation process." Kelly, *Mediation Research, above,* at 380.

Mediation has become a widely adopted method of resolving divorce and custody disputes. In 1981, California became the first state to mandate mediation of all custody and visitation disputes, prior to consideration of these issues by a court. *See* Cal. Fam. Code §§ 3155–77 (1998). Since then, at least six other states have enacted state-wide mediation mandates. Dane E. Gashen, *Note & Comment, Mandatory Custody Mediation: The Debate Over Its Usefulness Continues,* 10 Ohio St. J. on Disp. Resol. 469, 469, 472–73 (1995) (listing Delaware, Maine, New Mexico, Oregon, Washington, and Wisconsin). In most other states, statutes or court rules authorize judges to refer divorce and custody disputes to mediation in at least some circumstances. *See* Rita Henley Jensen, *Divorce—Mediation Style,* A.B.A. J., Feb. 1997 at 55, 56. A database maintained by the National Center for State Courts lists more than 200 court-connected mediation programs, of which a substantial proportion either mandate mediation categorically or permit judges to order mediation in particular cases. Craig A. McEwen, Richard J. Maiman, and Lynn Mather, *Lawyers, Mediation, and the Management of Divorce Practice,* 28 Law & Soc. Rev. 149, 152–53 (1994). Private, non-court connected mediation of divorce and custody disputes is also flourishing across the country.

As divorce and custody mediation has grown in popularity, it has also become increasingly professionalized. In the mid-1980s, both the Family Law Section of the American Bar Association and the Association of Family and Conciliation Courts issued model standards of practice for divorce and family mediators. *See* A.B.A. Standards of Practice For Family Mediators, *reprinted in* 17 Fam. L. Q. 455 (1984); AFCC Model Standards of Practice for Divorce and Family Mediators, *reprinted in* Divorce Mediation: Theory and Practice 403 (Jay Folberg & Ann Milne, eds., 1988). More recently, the American Bar Association, American Arbitration Association and Society of Professionals in Dispute Resolution have jointly issued *Model Standards of Conduct for Mediators,* which are designed to provide a general framework of ethical guidance for all mediators. *See* John D. Feerick, *Toward Uniform Standards of Conduct for Mediators,* 28 S. Tex. L. Rev. 455 (1997). A number of states have also adopted practice standards and/or minimum qualifications for mediators. *See* Stephen G. Bullock & Linda Rose Gallagher, *Surveying the State of the Mediative Art: A Guide to Institutionalizing Mediation in Louisiana,* 57 La. L. Rev. 885, 930–936 (1997) (reporting that, as of 1993, twenty states had adopted qualifications for practicing as a mediator and that three states have recently adopted ethical rules for mediators).

[2] Concerns About Mediation

Despite the widespread acceptance of mediation as an alternative to adversary divorce procedures, a number of concerns have been raised about its philosophy and effects. Feminist commentators, in particular, have cautioned that mediation may disadvantage women. Consider the following excerpt:

Jana B. Singer, *The Privatization of Family Law*
1992 Wis. L. Rev. 1443, 1540–48

There is substantial reason to suspect that mediation is significantly more likely than adjudication (and lawyer-conducted negotiation) both to reflect and to reproduce power imbalances between the sexes. The substantive fairness of divorce mediation depends heavily on the ability of divorcing parties effectively to express and represent their own interests without the assistance of counsel. The available evidence suggests that husbands are often in a better position to do this than wives and that the nature of the mediation process is unlikely to alter this fact. . . .

Another equality-based problem with mediation stems from the ideal of impartiality espoused by many mediators and from their claim to provide only "neutral" information and advice during the mediation process. This claim seems based on the belief that solutions exist in the divorce context that are neutral, rather than gendered in their concept and their impact. Feminist critiques of objectivity and impartiality cast doubt on this "neutrality" claim. Moreover, given the disparate economic and parenting circumstances faced by many divorcing men on the one hand, and many divorcing women on the other, such "gender neutral" divorce solutions are likely to be extremely rare. . . .

An example of this phenomenon may be the strong link between mediation and joint custody. . . . Although mediation proponents often present joint custody as an idea whose merit is beyond dispute, the costs and benefits of this notion may be very different for women as opposed to men. This is particularly likely where, as is still the case in most two-parent families, the mother has been the children's primary caretaker during marriage. She may perceive joint custody as a threat and as a devaluation of her activities during marriage, while the less-involved father may perceive it as a victory.

It is also of concern, from a gender equality perspective, that mediation is touted most enthusiastically as a substitute for adjudication in precisely those areas—custody and visitation—where the prevailing legal standards are perceived to favor women. While virtually all court-connected mediation programs address custody issues, only half of such programs mediate child support issues, despite both the overwhelming importance of support to the well-being of children and the obvious connection between custody arrangements and child support. Even fewer mediation programs address the other financial aspects of divorce (property division and spousal support) that are of particular concern to divorcing women. If mediation is such a desirable alternative, surely feminists are entitled to ask why it has largely failed to address those issues where women, rather than men, have the most reason to be dissatisfied with the results of our current adjudicative system. . . .

Finally, at least one recent study suggests that mediation of divorce and separation issues may exacerbate wife abuse. Among women who reported being abused during their marriages, researchers found that those who participated in mediation were more likely to report postseparation abuse by their ex-partners than were women who relied on adversary procedures. Both the privateness of the mediation process and the centrality to mediation of the concept of self-help may help to explain this finding. The possibility of a correlation between divorce mediation and the continuation of marital violence has serious policy implications: studies indicate that violence and abuse are part of the history, of a significant percentage of divorcing and separating women. . . .

NOTES AND QUESTIONS

(1) Other scholars have suggested that the informality and emphasis on consensus that characterizes mediation may reinforce racial and ethnic hierarchies, as well as gender inequality. *See, e.g.*, Isabelle R. Gunning, *Diversity Issues in Mediation: Controlling Negative Cultural Myths*, 1995 J. Disp. Resol. 55, 70; Richard Delgado, Chris Dunn, Pamela Brown, Helena Lee & David Hubbert, *Fairness and Formality: Minimizing the Risk of Prejudice in Alternative Dispute Resolution*, 1985 Wis. L. Rev. 1359, 1359. Are there ways of structuring mediation that respond to these equality concerns, without compromising its central commitment to mediator neutrality and party self determination? *See, e.g.*, Judy Maute, *Public Values and Private Justice: A Case for Mediator Accountability*, 4 Geo. J. Legal Ethics 503, 504 (1991); Trina Grillo, *The Mediation Alternative: Process Dangers for Women*, 100 Yale L.J. 1545 (1991). Would voluntary, rather than mandatory, mediation programs better serve women's interests? Are women likely to fare better under adversary divorce procedures than under mediation? *Compare, e.g.*, Joshua Rosenberg, *A Critical Essay: In Defense of Mediation*, 33 Ariz L. Rev. 467, 503–507 (1991) (suggesting that negative experiences are more serious and pervasive in the judicial system than in mediation) *and* Maggie Vincent, Note, *Mandatory Mediation of Custody Disputes: Criticism, Legislation and Support*, 20 Vt. L. Rev. 255, 265–282 (1995) (refuting evidence that women who mediate fare worse than women who litigate) *with* Penelope E. Bryan, *Killing Us Softly: Divorce Mediation and the Politics of Power*, 40 Buff. L. Rev. 441, 445 (1992) (discussing ways in which the rhetoric and practice of divorce mediation reinforce male power) and Mary Pat Treuthart, *In Harms Way? Family Mediation and The Role of The Attorney Advocate*, 23 Golden Gate U. L. Rev. 717 (1993) (discussing advantages of adversary procedures for women).

(2) **Mediation and Domestic Violence**. Many scholars and mediators believe that mediation is unsuited and dangerous for cases involving domestic violence. Treuthart, *above*, at 721; *see* Lisa Lehrman, Mediation of Wife Abuse Cases: *The Adverse Impact of Informal Dispute Resolution on Women*, 7 Harv. Women's L.J. 57 (1984). In response to these concerns, most mandatory mediation programs attempt to "screen out" such cases. Some commentators have questioned whether existing screening procedures adequately protect victims of domestic violence. *See* Grillo, *above,* at 1584–85. Other commentators have argued that cases involving domestic violence can be mediated successfully by skilled mediators with proper training; these commentators also contend that mediation can be helpful to battered women by promoting self-assertion and by helping them to end relationships. *See, e.g.*, Kathleen O'Connell Corcoran & James C. Melamed, *From Coercion to Empowerment: Spousal Abuse and Mediation*, 7 Mediation Q. 303 (1990). Do these benefits outweigh the risks? Should victims of domestic violence be able to "choose" whether to participate in mediation? *See generally* Alison E. Gerencer, *Family Mediation: Screening for Domestic Abuse*, 23 Fla. St. U. L. Rev. 43, 47 (1995); Nancy Thoennes, et al., *Mediation and Domestic Violence: Current Policies and Practices*, 33 Fam. & Conciliation Cts. Rev. 6 (1995).

(3) **Mediation and Legal Ethics.** Is divorce mediation "the practice of law?" If so, then are non-lawyers prohibited from mediating family disputes? If not, then what ethical rules and standards of accountability govern the conduct of lawyer-mediators? Does the answer to the "practice of law" question depend on the professional identity of the mediator? On the particular mediation techniques employed? On the type of issues being mediated? *Compare* Carrie Menkel-Meadow, *Is Mediation the Practice of Law?*, 14 Alternative to the High Cost of Litig. 1, 60 (1996) (suggesting that many tasks performed by mediators constitute the practice of law) *with* Bruce Meyerson, *Lawyers Who Mediate Are Not Practicing Law*, 14 Alternatives to the High Cost of Litig. 74 (1996). *See also* Andrew S. Morrison, Comment, *Is Divorce Mediation the Practice of Law? A Matter of Perspective*, 75 Cal. L. Rev. 1093 (1987) (arguing that divorce mediation constitutes "the practice of law" when engaged in by attorneys, but *not* when engaged in by other professionals); Sandra E. Purcell, *The Attorney as Mediator—Inherent Conflict of Interest?*, 32 UCLA L. Rev. 986 (1985) (arguing that mediation is not the practice of law, even if mediator provides legal information to parties).

Assuming *arguendo* that mediation constitutes the practice of law, at least when engaged in by lawyers, then do lawyers who mediate family disputes risk running afoul of the ethical rules discussed in § 9.06, *above*, particularly the constraints on dual representation in divorce matters? The A.B.A. Model Rules of Professional Conduct recognize a professional role as "intermediary" and permit assumption of this role under the following conditions:

Rule 2.2 Intermediary

(a) A lawyer may act as intermediary between clients if:

(1) the lawyer consults with each client concerning the implications of the common representation, including the advantages and risks involved, and the effect on the attorney-client privileges, and obtains each client's consent to the common representation;

(2) the lawyer reasonably believes that the matter can be resolved on terms compatible with the clients' best interests, that each client will be able to make adequately informed decisions in the matter and that there is little risk of material prejudice to the interests of any of the clients if the contemplated resolution is unsuccessful; and

(3) the lawyer reasonably believes that the common representation can be undertaken impartially. . . .

(c) A lawyer shall withdraw as intermediary if any of the clients so requests, or if any of the conditions stated in paragraph (a) is no longer satisfied. Upon withdrawal, the lawyer shall not continue to represent any of the clients in the matter that was the subject of the intermediation.

Comment

. . .

The Rule does not apply to a lawyer acting as arbitrator or mediator between or among parties who are not clients of the lawyer, even where the lawyer has been appointed with the concurrence of the parties. . . .

Does divorce mediation fall within this provision? Why or why not?

(4) Several commentators have suggested that existing legal ethics standards, based on a traditional, adversary model, are not responsive to the fundamentally different principles and processes that characterize mediation and other forms of alternative dispute resolution:

> With the adversary practice [that] the current model rules are based upon, values of zeal . . . client loyalty, partisanship and non-accountability reign. If ADR draws from different foundational principles --problem-solving, joint rather than individual gain, and future rather than past orientation, its underlying principles will be different. Trust, confidentiality, creativity and openness many suggest different ethical precepts and standards.

Carrie Menkel-Meadow, *Ethics in Alternative Dispute Resolution: New Issues, No Answers from the Adversary Conception of Lawyers' Responsibilities*, 38 S. Tex. L. Rev. 407, 430 (1997). Do you agree with Professor Menkel-Meadow? What would such different ethical standards look like on issues such as client loyalty?

(5) Do family lawyers have an ethical obligation to inform their clients of the availability of mediation and other forms of ADR? To encourage the use of these procedures to settle domestic disputes? The *Bounds of Advocacy*, a voluntary ethical code promulgated by the American Academy of Matrimonial Lawyers provides that lawyers who practice family law "should be knowledgeable about alternative ways to resolve matrimonial disputes" and "should encourage the settlement of marital disputes through settlement of marital disputes through negotiation, mediation, or arbitration. American Academy of Matrimonial Lawyers, Standards of Conduct §§ 1.4, 2.15 (1991). *See also* Nicole Pedone, *Lawyer's Duty to Discuss Alternative Dispute Resolution In the Best Interest of the Children*, 35 Fam. & Concil. Cts. Rev. 65 (1998).

(6) **The Role of Attorneys**. What role should attorneys who serve as advocates for divorcing parties play during mediation? If the parties are represented by counsel, should counsel attend mediation sessions? Does attorney participation enhance or undermine the mediation process? *Compare, e.g.*, Thomas E. Carbonneau, *Alternative Dispute Resolution: Melting the Lances and Dismounting the Steeds* 170–72 (1989) (arguing that attorney involvement in divorce mediation "threatens to compromise the viability of the process") with Craig A. McEwen, Nancy H. Rogers, and Richard J. Maiman, *Bring in the Lawyers: Challenging the Dominant Approaches to Ensuring Fairness in Divorce Mediation*, 79 Minn. L. Rev. 1317, 1323 (1995) (arguing that active lawyer participation in mediation promotes fairness and legitimacy without compromising goals of mediation).

(7) **The Role of Children**. What role, if any, should children play in custody mediation? If a child is represented by an attorney or a guardian ad litem, should that representative participate in the mediation sessions? Should children be present during mediation? If not, should the mediator speak with children? *See generally* Eric R. Galton, *Mediation With Children: Two Lawyers' Views*, 3(1) Disp. Resol. Mag 5 (1996); Gary Paquin, *The Child's Input in the Mediation Process: Promoting the Best Interests of the Child*, Mediation Q., Winter 1988 at 69, 70.

(8) **Mediator Confidentiality**. If the parties do not reach agreement in mediation, should the mediator be permitted to make a recommendation to the court as to custody or visitation? Commentators generally oppose this practice as inconsistent with the integrity and confidentiality of mediation, and most court-connected mediation programs prelude the mediator from testifying or making recommendations to the court. *See* Christy L. Hendricks,

Note, *The Trend Toward Mandatory Mediation In Custody and Visitation Disputes of Minor Children: An Overview*, 32 J. Fam. L. 491, 494 (1993–94); Kent L. Brown, Comment, *Confidentiality in Mediation: Status and Implications*, 1991 J. Disp. Resol. 307, 307. However, the California mediation statute authorizes mediators to render a custody or visitation recommendation to the court if local rules so permit. Cal. Fam. Code §3183(a) (1997); *see McLaughlin v. Superior Court*, 189 Cal. Rptr. 479, 485–86 (Ct. App. 1983) (due process requires that parties be given the opportunity to examine the mediator concerning any recommendation submitted to court).

(9) **Mediation and Access to Court**. Do programs that condition access to the judicial process on participation in mandatory mediation or other ADR procedures, raise constitutional concerns? Does the answer depend on what level of participation is required? *See, e.g., Kurtz v. Kurtz*, 538 So.2d 892, 894 (Fla. 1989) (deferral of husband's post-dissolution visitation motions to pre-hearing mediation was not an unconstitutionally deprivation of husband's right to be heard in court, nor an illegal delegation of judicial responsibility); *Goldberg v. Goldberg*, 691 S.W.2d 312, 316 (Mo. 1985) (judicially imposed requirement that parties submit future parenting disputes to mediation prior to a court hearing did not unconstitutionally restrict parties' access to judiciary).

(10) **Parent Education Programs**. Courts in more than 40 states have implemented parent education programs designed to help divorcing parents ease the trauma of separation and divorce, for themselves and their children. These programs, which are often a prerequisite to mediation, typically have several goals: *first,* to provide parents with information about the effects of divorce and separation on children; *second,* to reduce divorce-related parental conflict by improving parents' ability to communicate with each other about their children; and *third,* to provide parents with skills and techniques that will enable them to parent more effectively and cooperatively after divorce or separation. While some have questioned the effectiveness of such programs, particularly if parents are compelled to attend, preliminary research suggests that the programs may enhance parents' problem solving skills and reduce the likelihood of relitigation. Jack Arbuthnot, Kevin M. Kramer, & Donald A. Gordon, *Patterns of Relitigation Following Divorce Education,* 35 Fam. & Conc. Cts. Rev. 269 (1997). For additional discussion of divorce-related parent education, see Peter Salem, et al., *Parent Education as a Distinct Field of Practice: The Agenda for the Future,* 34 Fam. & Conciliation Cts. Rev. 9, 13 (1996); Ingrid E. Slezak, *Parent Education: It Makes a Difference,* 57 Or. St. Bar Bull. 70, 70 (1996); Andrew Schepard, *War and P.E.A.C.E.: A Report and Model Statute on an Interdisciplinary Educational Program for Divorcing and Separating Parents,* 27 U. Mich. J.L. Reform 131, 153 (1993).

(11) **Problem**. Frank and Cheryl Jones have recently filed for divorce and have been referred to you for mandatory mediation of custody issues. The court-connected program in your jurisdiction provides for two mediation sessions, lasting ninety minutes each. Frank and Cheryl have one child, Tyler, age 14 months. During the first mediation session, their interaction is strained and they frequently interrupt and belittle each other. Both seem primarily concerned with securing an equal amount of time with Tyler. Toward the end of the first mediation session, Frank proposes that they agree to joint custody and that Tyler rotate between their two households every three days. (Frank and Cheryl live approximately five miles apart, and Tyler currently attends a day care center equidistant from their two

residences.) Cheryl concurs in this suggestion, and proposes that they use the next mediation session to "work out the details, so that we won't have to deal with each other later on." Prior to the next mediation session, you mention the proposed custody arrangement to a child psychologist, who tells you that the plan would be "a disaster for the child," since consistency, predictability and continuity of care are particularly important to children at this developmental stage. How should you proceed at the next mediation session? If Frank and Cheryl persist in pursuing the rotating custody arrangement, should you assist them in working out the details of an agreement? Why or why not?

(12) **Problem**. After practicing family law with a small firm for several years, you have become disillusioned with adversary divorce procedures and have decided to open a family mediation practice. You are particularly interested in serving moderate income clients who seem increasingly priced out of the market for good divorce attorneys; thus, you suspect that most of your mediation clients will not be represented by independent counsel. You recently completed the required mediation training, and you have already received several inquiries from potential clients. However, you are still seeking answers to a number of questions:

1. Since many of your clients will not have consulted with a lawyer prior to mediation, can you prepare and hand out to clients a general outline of the statutes, cases and legal principles that govern the resolution of domestic relations disputes in your state? Would it be better if you asked your favorite family law professor to prepare such an outline for you, rather than preparing it yourself?

2. If you decide not to give clients a written outline, can you provide this information orally at the first mediation session, or in response to clients' questions as the mediation progresses?

3. What should you say if one or both parties ask you during a mediation session to predict how a court would decide one of the issues in their case?

4. If the parties are not represented by independent counsel, can you write up whatever agreement they reach during mediation, so that it can be presented to a court? If not, can you provide "form agreements" to assist the parties in doing this themselves? If you decide not to write up the agreement, could the parties jointly ask another attorney to review their agreement to make sure that it would be acceptable to a court?

5. Can you provide mediation services to clients that you previously represented while practicing with your former law firm? Does it matter if your representation concerned a matter unrelated to their current divorce? What about clients who were represented by other lawyers at your former firm?

6. Can you co-mediate with a mental health professional who is also certified to mediate in your jurisdiction? If so, what kinds of fee arrangements are permissible?

[B] Binding Arbitration

Reformers have also shown considerable interest in arbitration as a substitute for adjudicative divorce. The distinctive feature of arbitration is its binding nature. Arbitrators, unlike mediators, are empowered to render decisions, rather than simply facilitating dispute resolution by the parties. Although courts have approved agreements to arbitrate spousal support and property issues, arbitration of divorce issues relating to children remains controversial.

MILLER v. MILLER
Superior Court of Pennsylvania
620 A.2d 1161 (1993)

FORD ELLIOTT, J.

This appeal is from the trial court's entry of a marriage settlement agreement as an order of court and the striking of a provision in the agreement which called for binding arbitration in custody disputes.

The parties were married on October 4, 1980. Two children were born of the marriage: Janell Miller, born June 30, 1983, and Justin Miller, born February 3, 1989. In May 1989 the parties separated but agreed Father should retain custody of the children. This agreement was reduced to writing on July 6, 1989. On April 4, 1990, the parties were divorced. At the time of the divorce, the parties entered into a Marriage Settlement Agreement which addressed property rights, support, custody, and other intra-family matters. This Marriage Settlement Agreement incorporated a Mediation/Arbitration Agreement signed by the parties. The Mediation/Arbitration Agreement provided that if a dispute, claim, or controversy is not resolved following mediation, resulting in a written agreement between the parties that they agree shall be final and binding upon them and which may be entered as a judgment by any court having competent jurisdiction, then a Board of Arbitrators shall arbitrate and decide all issues and render a written decision. This decision may be entered as a judgment by any court having competent jurisdiction. Father subsequently filed for child support. Mother responded by exercising the options provided by the Mediation/Arbitration agreement and submitted the custody matter to mediation. A mediation session was held in August of 1991 which failed to resolve the issue. The matter was then submitted to arbitration. A panel of three arbitrators decided the custody issue in favor of Mother. Father refused to relinquish custody.

Mother then sought to have the arbitrators' decision enforced as a court order and filed a Petition to Enter the Marital Settlement Agreement as an order of court. On November 18, 1991, a hearing was held before the Honorable Susan Devlin Scott who entered the parties agreement which incorporated by reference the mediation/arbitration agreement as an order but struck the provisions of the two agreements calling for binding arbitration on the issue of custody and refused to enter the arbitrators' award of custody. Mother appeals from that order. . . .

Citing the general principle of law favoring private nonjudicial mediation and arbitration of disputes, Mother argues that the Uniform Arbitration Act, Act of October 5, 1980, 42 Pa.C.S.A. § 7303, provides for the enforceability of a written agreement to submit a controversy to arbitration. Furthermore, a party who has submitted to a common law arbitration award, pursuant to the Uniform Arbitration Act, is bound thereby unless he can show that he was denied a hearing or that fraud, misconduct, corruption, or other irregularity caused an unjust, inequitable, or unconscionable award to be rendered. 42 Pa.C.S.A. §7341. Thus, Mother contends since Father cannot claim he was denied a hearing or that fraud, misconduct, or corruption caused an unfair award, the arbitrators' award of custody must stand.

While we agree generally with Mother's statement of the law that parties are bound by an arbitration decision unless an arbitrators' award was gotten by fraud or a party was denied a hearing, our review of relevant case law does not support a determination that courts will be bound by such decisions in custody cases nor that a court's review will be limited necessarily by the arbitration provisions. . . . .

Instantly, we agree with Mother that arbitration generally is a favored remedy as it permits parties to agree to resolve disputes outside the court system. Courts benefit from reduced congestion and parties benefit by having their disputes resolved in a private forum by self-chosen judges. We acknowledge arbitration has been used more frequently in other jurisdictions as a viable means of resolving domestic disputes that arise under separation agreements. We agree that parties should be able to settle their domestic disputes out of court, and if the parties choose to arbitrate their domestic differences they should be permitted to do so. We concur in Mother's contention that parties who have agreed to arbitrate should be bound by that decision and that arbitration provisions regarding custody are not, as determined by the trial court, void as against public policy. However, and most importantly, we do not agree that in the matter of child custody an arbitration award shall be binding on a court if such award is challenged by one of the parties as not being in the best interests of the child. As such, we decline to hold that the trial court is bound by the narrow scope of review set out in the Uniform Arbitration Act. An arbitration award on the issue of custody is subject to review by a court of competent jurisdiction based upon its responsibility to look to the best interests of the child. . . .

The law looks with favor upon resolutions of custody disputes that are settled privately. *Warman v. Warman*, 439 A.2d 1203 (1982). It is desirable for divorcing parents to settle their differences without the intervention of the court system wherever possible. There are good reasons why these private agreements serve the best interests of the child:

> First, most parents genuinely love their children, and it is reasonable to assume that the children's welfare is a vital consideration in the parents' decision to resolve their dispute by agreement. One major reason that parents agree on custody is to spare their children the trauma inherent in an adversarial hearing. Second, parents have a better informational base upon which to make a decision about custody. The adversarial process is an inadequate means to assemble sufficient 'facts' to resolve custodial disputes satisfactorily. Third, it is difficult to protect a child from the painful pull of divided loyalties when his parents fail to agree. Parental agreements help to preserve an atmosphere of at least superficial peace between parents and thereby facilitate a much easier and more meaningful future relationship between the child and the non-custodial parent.

Sharp, *Modification of Agreement—Based Custody Decrees: Unitary or Dual Standard?*, 68 Va. L.Rev. 1263, 1280 (1982) (footnotes omitted).

Divorced or separated parents usually differ on questions relating to their children. For those parents to work out a mechanism themselves whereby they resolve those conflicts privately is to be encouraged. Such a mechanism, once forged, may set a pattern for resolution of later disputes as they arise. Such resolutions frequently result in informal agreements. This is not to deny that many divorced or separated parents will not be able to settle their differences without the intervention of the court system. The law should not impede, however, those parents who are able to forge a mechanism for private dispute resolution. [*Warman v. Warman, supra.*] 467 A.2d at 374-375. Other jurisdictions have also looked favorably upon private mediation and arbitration agreements to initially resolve custody disputes. *Flaherty v. Flaherty*, 97 N.J. 99, 477 A.2d 1257 (N.J. 1984); *Sheets v. Sheets*, 22 A.D.2d 176, 254 N.Y.S.2d 320 (1964).

While we encourage parties to resolve their disputes amicably and without court intervention, if possible, we cannot ignore our duty to protect the rights and interests of children once called upon to do so. Therefore, while arbitration proceedings in custody disputes are not void as against public policy, the question of the enforceability of arbitration awards in this context is a very different matter. Thus while agreements entered into between parties are binding as between the parties, they may not bind the court once its jurisdiction is invoked. It follows necessarily that an award rendered by an arbitration panel would be subject to the supervisory power of the court in its parens patriae capacity in a proceeding to determine the best interests of the child. It has long been recognized by the courts that it is the Commonwealth who is charged with the duty of protecting the rights and interests of children. *In Re William L.*, 383 A.2d 1228 (1978). . . .

We find agreements by parents concerning their children, while encouraged, will always be subject to close scrutiny by a court and are subject to being set aside as courts will not be bound by such agreements. Our supreme court recently addressed the issue of agreements between parents in the context of child support payments. The court stated:

> Parties to a divorce action may bargain between themselves and structure their agreement as best serves their interests. They have no power, however, to bargain away the rights of their children. Their right to bargain for themselves is their own business. They cannot in that process set a standard that will leave their children short. Their bargain may be eminently fair, give all that the children might require and be enforceable because it is fair. When it gives less than required or less than can be given to provide for the best interest of the children, it falls under the jurisdiction of the court's wide and necessary powers to provide for that best interest. It is at best advisory to the court and swings on the tides of the necessity that the children be provided. To which the inter se rights of the parties must yield as the occasion requires.

Knorr v. Knorr, 527 Pa. 83, 86, 588 A.2d 503, 505 (1991).

We acknowledge the supreme court had before it a provision of a separation agreement concerning child support payments. However, we consider its determinations of the court's role in enforcing such agreements equally applicable to custody matters. Hence, we find the trial court was not bound to confirm the arbitration award that was being challenged by Father. The limited review set out in 42 Pa.C.S.A. § 7341 will not bind the court in custody matters. Rather, the trial court must view the decision of the arbitrators in light of the best interests of the child. However, if the court following its review finds that the arbitrators' award is in the bests interests of the child, the court may adopt the decision as its own.

Accordingly, though we find that the trial court erred in striking the arbitration provisions as being void as against public policy, we agree with the trial court generally on the enforceability of such provisions. We further agree that the trial court was not required to confirm the arbitration award under the constraints of the Uniform Arbitration Act. Thus, the order striking the binding arbitration provision from the Marital Settlement Agreement is vacated. Case remanded for a determination as to whether the decision of the arbitrators is unenforceable as being adverse to the best interests of the children in this action.

NOTES AND QUESTIONS

(1) The opinion in *Miller* attempts to balance two competing policy goals: encouraging divorcing parents to settle their disputes privately, without resort to court intervention, and ensuring that children's interests are protected. Does the court's holding strike the optimal balance between these competing policy goals? To what extent does requiring a "best interests" hearing as a prerequisite to judicial enforcement of an arbitrated custody award undermine the efficiency benefits of arbitration? *See* Stephen W. Schlissel, *A Proposal For Final and Binding Arbitration of Initial Custody Determinations*, 26 Fam. L. Q. 71, 73, 79–84 (1992).

(2) Should the majority's holding regarding the enforceability of arbitrated custody awards apply as well to mediated custody agreements? Why or why not?

(3) What result would the *Miller* court have reached if Father had refused initially to submit the custody issue to arbitration, (contrary to the terms of the Mediation/Arbitration Agreement) and had instead requested an immediate court hearing on the question of the children's best interests? *Compare Glauber v. Glauber*, 600 N.Y.S.2d 740, 743 (App. Div. 1993) (holding that issues of custody and visitation must be put before the court for determination in the first instance and may not be submitted to arbitration) *with Dick v. Dick*, 534 N.W.2d 185, 188 (Mich. Ct. App. 1995) (issues relating to child custody may be submitted to binding arbitration by agreement of the parties, and arbitrator's decision may be appealed only to the same extent as other arbitration awards).

(4) Should parental agreements to arbitrate child support be enforceable? If so, should the court have the authority to enter temporary support awards during the pendency of the arbitration? *See Kelm v. Kelm*, 623 N.E. 2d 39, 39 (Ohio 1993) (holding that spousal and child support are arbitrable matters, but that trial court has the authority to oversee such arbitration to ensure that the interests of children and spouses are protected). *See generally*, Elizabeth A. Jenkins, Annotation, *Validity and Construction of Provisions for Arbitration of Disputes as to Alimony or Support Payments or Child Visitation or Custody Matters*, 38 A.L.R.5th 69 (1996).

(5) In *Miller*, the parties *agreed* to submit their post-divorce disputes to arbitration, if they were unable to resolve those disputes through mediation. Could a court *require* divorcing parties to submit future parenting disputes to mediation or arbitration, as a prerequisite to a judicial hearing? *See Gates v. Gates*, 1998 Vt. LEXIS 58 (Vt. 1998) (trial court exceeded its authority in ordering divorcing parents to submit future disputes to binding arbitration before resorting to the court for relief).

CHAPTER 10

ECONOMIC CONSEQUENCES OF DIVORCE

SYNOPSIS

§ 10.01 Introduction
§ 10.02 Distribution of Property on Divorce or Dissolution of Marriage
    [A] General Introduction
        [1] Community Property States
        [2] Equitable Distribution States
            [a] "Dual Property" Equitable Distribution States
            [b] "All Property" Equitable Distribution States
            [c] A Comparison of Dual Property and All Property Regimes
    [B] Equitable Distribution and Community Property Overview
    [C] Marital or Separate Property—Or Both?
    [D] "Tracing" and Transmutation of Property
    [E] Passive versus Active Appreciation of Separate Property
    [F] Property Acquired by Gift or Inheritance
    [G] Pensions and Retirement Benefits
        [1] Complexity of Dividing Benefits
        [2] Qualified Domestic Relations Orders (QDROs)
        [3] Valuing and Dividing Retirement Benefits
    [H] Deferred Compensation Benefits: Separate or Marital Property?
    [I] Personal Injury and Workers' Compensation Awards
    [J] Professional Degrees and Licenses
    [K] The Family Residence
    [L] Classifying and Valuing Professional Goodwill
    [M] Valuing Businesses and Professional Practices
    [N] Distribution of Property
        [1] General Introduction
        [2] Statutory Factors for Distributing Marital Property
        [3] An Equal Division Presumption versus an Equal Division "Starting Point"
        [4] Recharacterization and Distribution of Property Based Upon Long-Term Marriages
    [O] The Role of Fault in the Distribution of Marital Property

        [1] "Economic Fault": The Dissipation or Waste of Marital Assets
        [2] Marital Misconduct as a Factor in Dividing Marital Property
            [a] Arguments for Rejecting Marital Misconduct Fault Factors in Equitable Distribution Proceedings
            [b] Arguments for Retaining Marital Misconduct Fault Factors in Equitable Distribution Proceedings
    [P] The Role of Judicial Discretion in Distributing Property on Divorce
    [Q] Selected Research Biography on Equitable Distribution of Marital Property
        [1] Treatises
        [2] Looseleaf Services and Reporters
        [3] Selected Law Review Articles on Equitable Distribution

§ 10.03 Spousal Support
    [A] Need and Gender: The Traditional Rationales
    [B] Rehabilitation and Self-Sufficiency
    [C] Alimony as Compensation for Loss
    [D] Alimony as Income Sharing
    [E] The Intersection of Alimony and Property Theory
    [F] Modification of Support Awards

§ 10.01 Introduction

The modern rules and theories governing both property distribution and spousal support share a common, overriding purpose: to apportion fairly the economic gains and losses that result from participation in a marriage. Joan M. Krauskopf, *Theories of Property Division/Spousal Support: Searching for Solutions to the Mystery*, 23 Fam. L.Q. 253, 256 (1989). Given this common purpose, it is not surprising that property and support issues are often considered and negotiated together by family law attorneys and that courts generally pay close attention to the relationship between these two types of divorce remedies.

While alimony and property division have always been intertwined, it was possible, until recently, to draw some clear conceptual and practical distinctions between the two. In concept, alimony was expressly forward looking; its function was to provide for a dependent spouse's future needs, *not* to compensate for contributions made during a marriage. Property awards, by contrast, were oriented toward the past. Their purpose was to unscramble the spouses' respective ownership interests in property acquired during the marriage. Alleviating a spouse's post-divorce need was not among the acknowledged functions of traditional, property distribution rules, under either the common law title system, or community property regimes. *See generally* Jana B. Singer, *Divorce Obligations and Bankruptcy Discharge: Rethinking the Support/Property Distinction*, 30 Harv. J. on Legis. 43 (1993).

Over the past 20 years, a series of related family law developments has undermined both the conceptual and the practical distinctions between property distribution and spousal support. First, the widespread adoption of equitable distribution principles, discussed in detail in this chapter, has effectively merged the functions of alimony and property division. This is because, under most equitable distribution schemes, the purpose of property distribution is no longer limited to sorting out the spouses' preexisting ownership interests; rather the goal is to allocate those assets between the spouses in a fashion that is just, reasonable, or equitable. Moreover, in determining what distribution of assets will satisfy this criteria, courts are typically directed to consider not only the spouses' past contributions to the marriage, but also such forward-looking factors as the spouses' post-divorce incomes, employments prospects and needs. *See* § 10.02[N], *below*. Indeed, in many jurisdictions, the equitable distribution of marital property has replaced spousal support as the preferred means of providing for the future needs of divorcing spouses. *See, e.g.*, Uniform Marriage and Divorce Act, § 307, 9A U.L.A. 240 (West 1973).

Second, as the remaining portions of this chapter demonstrate, the expansion of the concept of marital property to include quantification of the present worth of such intangible assets as pensions and other forms of deferred compensation, as well as business and professional goodwill, has both changed the structure of many property awards and enhanced the potential of property division to provide for a spouse's post-divorce needs. These developments have led a number of economics-oriented family law scholars to deny the existence of any meaningful distinction between alimony and property awards. "As the economist sees it, alimony 'frozen' in time (the present) is simply another form of property." Margaret F. Brinig, *Property Distribution Physics: The Talisman of Time and Middle Class Law*, 31 Fam. L.Q. 93, 95 (1997).

Changes in the law and theory underlying alimony have also blurred the distinction between property and support awards. Where once the concepts of the dependent wife and divorce based on one party's fault theoretically created a lifelong duty of support on the part of an at-fault husband, the demise of both concepts has reduced the availability of "permanent" alimony and has led to support awards that look and function like extended distributions of marital property. The demise of the husband's support obligation has also spurred a reconceptualization of alimony that emphasizes its compensatory and restitutionary functions, rather than its traditional needs-based justification. *See* § 10.03, *below*. This emphasis on alimony as compensation for contributions made and losses incurred during marriage has also resulted in the development of hybrid divorce remedies, such as "reimbursement alimony," that combine the characteristics of traditional support and property remedies. Finally, the increased ability of spouses to determine by contract the financial consequences of their divorce has led to economic settlements that defy categorization under the traditional support/property dichotomy.

Despite this blurring of the conceptual distinctions between property distribution and spousal support, a number of practical differences remain. Property distributions are final and non modifiable, while alimony awards can generally be modified, unless the parties specify otherwise. A court may use its contempt power to enforce alimony (and child support) obligations, but not to enforce property awards. Although recent changes in federal tax and bankruptcy laws have eliminated some differences in treatment between some property and support awards, other statutory distinctions remain. Thus, to represent clients effectively, the family law practitioner needs to understand both the functional similarities and the remaining practical differences between these two important mechanisms for allocating the economic consequences of marriage and divorce. The remaining sections of this chapter first examine the contemporary doctrines and principles that govern the classification, valuation and distribution of property upon divorce. The chapter then turns to the related issues and concepts surrounding alimony, or spousal support.

§ 10.02 Distribution of Property on Divorce or Dissolution of Marriage

[A] General Introduction

With a concomitant deemphasis on fault factors on divorce or dissolution of marriage, the practice of divorce or dissolution of marriage law has largely shifted from moral to economic issues. Where once the parties primarily debated issues of marital fault and spousal support, the parties now debate whether particular items of property should be classified as marital or separate property; what the actual value of that property would be; and how the property should be distributed to each party by the court, or through a property settlement agreement.

The enormous scope of property division issues in a divorce is exemplified by the fact that marital property division generally includes all tangible and intangible property acquired during the marriage, including but not limited to: pension and retirement plans; closely held corporations, partnerships and family businesses; medical, dental, and legal practices; stocks and bonds; intellectual property and professional goodwill; personal injury awards; the family residence; and other real and personal property acquired during the marriage other than by gift or inheritance to a particular spouse. *See generally* Brett R. Turner, Equitable Distribution of Property (2d ed. 1994); J. Thomas Oldham, Divorce, Separation, and the Distribution of Property (1997 rev. ed.); Oldfather et al., Valuation and Distribution of Marital Property (Matthew Bender, 1997 rev. ed.); John DeWitt Gregory, The Law of Equitable Distribution (1989). *See also* Gregory, Swisher & Scheible-Wolf, Understanding Family Law §§ 9.01–9.12 (1995).

Accordingly, large and prestigious law firms have increasingly become more involved in handling divorce cases involving substantial marital property claims. *See, e.g.*, Diamond, *Big Firms Get in on Divorce Action*, 74 A.B.A.J. 60, 62 (August 1988), where one attorney was quoted as stating that "divorce has become the equivalent of a partnership dissolution," which often requires the skills of corporate and tax attorneys, C.P.A.s, appraisers, and forensic economists in order to identify, classify, and value separate and marital property on divorce or dissolution of marriage.

There are two major regimes employed within the United States for dividing property on divorce: (1) the community property system; and (2) the equitable distribution system.

[1] Community Property States

Eight states have adopted Spanish and French community property principles for dividing property on the dissolution of marriage. These states are Arizona, California, Idaho, Louisiana, Nevada, New Mexico, Texas, and Washington. (Wisconsin appears to take a hybrid approach to community property principles. Although Wisconsin has adopted the Uniform Marital Property Act and recognizes certain marital property rights on marriage as other community property states do, Wisconsin has also enacted equitable distribution statutes that take effect upon divorce.) The Canadian province of Quebec also is a community property jurisdiction, as are various European countries, including the Netherlands, Belgium, France, Hungary, Spain, Portugal, and the Scandinavian countries of Denmark, Finland, Norway, and Sweden.

The basic concept of community property law is that as property is acquired by the spouses, or either of them, during the marriage, it belongs to the marital community in which they each have an equal present interest. This property interest is not a mere expectancy that vests only on divorce, as is the general rule in most equitable distribution states, but an interest that vests at the time the property is acquired. Equality of the interests in whatever property is acquired, earned, gained or purchased by either the husband or the wife during their marriage interests is the underlying principle of the community property system, absent any statutory modification to the contrary. Thus, no distinction is made between the husband and wife as coequal marital partners, and the husband is as much entitled to share equally in the acquisitions made by his wife as she is permitted to share in the acquisitions made by her husband.

A community property system normally provides for the dual classification of all property owned by the spouses: "community property" and "separate property." This classification is determined not by title, but by the time and manner of the property acquisition, and by the intent of the parties to maintain such property as community or separate property. For example, any wages or income acquired by either spouse during the marriage would normally be community property, and each spouse could claim an undivided one-half interest in such property. But property acquired by gift or inheritance to one spouse during the marriage would normally constitute separate property, as long as that property maintained its separate identity, and did not become commingled with other community property.

Within this community property system generally, there are state variations. California, Louisiana, and New Mexico retain relatively pure community property laws and divide assets on dissolution of marriage equally between husband and wife. The remaining community property states (Arizona, Idaho, Nevada, Texas, and Washington) divide community assets equitably but not necessarily equally according to factors added under a statutorily modified system. Seven community property states also apply a dual property classification system that allows a judge to divide or apportion the parties' community property assets, but not their separate property assets, which generally include property acquired before marriage, by gift, devise or bequest during marriage, and by earnings after separation. Washington, on the other hand, follows an all property classification system on dissolution of marriage, allowing a judge to apportion or divide both community and separate property. However, Washington still follows a community property regime during the marriage, so, arguably Washington has adopted a hybrid community property rule.

On the death of one of the spouses, the surviving spouse in a community property jurisdiction retains ownership over an undivided one-half of the community property, which would then become his or her separate property. The deceased spouse's one-half interest in the community property would then pass by testamentary will or intestate succession. English common law property doctrines such as dower, curtesy, forced share election against a will, and their statutory equivalents are not recognized in most community property jurisdictions. *See generally* W.S. McClanahan, Community Property Law in the United States (1982); W. DeFuniak and M. Vaughn, Principles of Community Property (2d ed. 1971); S. Greene, *Comparison of the Property Aspects of the Community Property and Common Law Marital Property Systems*, 13 Creighton L. Rev. 71 (1979). *See also* Brett Turner, Equitable Distribution of Property 34–36 (2d ed. 1994).

[2] Equitable Distribution States

Under early English common law principles, husband and wife were considered one legal entity, but the husband was the "one" who enjoyed control and ownership rights over all the marital assets. Later, under constructive trust principles, and under the Married Womens Property Acts [see § 5.02, above], some of this economic inequality between the spouses was partially alleviated.

But on divorce, there was still a rebuttable presumption in most states that the wage earner—traditionally the husband—owned most of the property acquired during the marriage. See, e.g., Younger, *Marital Regimes*, 67 Col. L. Rev. 45 (1981). Clearly, legislative reform was needed in the 42 states that did not follow a community property regime to make property division on divorce more equitable to both parties. Accordingly, in 1970, the National Conference of Commissioners on Uniform State Laws drafted the Uniform Marriage and Divorce Act (UMDA) which, borrowing from community property precedent, instituted a classification for property division on divorce based upon marital and separate property. Amended in 1971 and again in 1973, the UMDA became the model for many equitable distribution statutes in the United States, and today equitable distribution in one form or another has been adopted in forty-eight states, with seven of those states following a community property system.

Although most equitable distribution states and community property states recognize the distinction between separate property and marital (or community) property, there is no presumption in the equitable distribution states that property division necessarily must be divided equally, as in some community property states. Thus, according to various statutory factors, equitable distribution of property on divorce could be divided 50–50 as in a community property state, but it could also be divided 40–60, 30–70, or even 0–100 if the facts and equities of a particular case, based on the relevant statutory factors, warranted such a division. See, e.g., *Rodgers v. Rodgers*, 470 N.Y.S.2d 401, 404–05 (App. Div. 1983); *Hursey v. Hursey*, 326 S.E.2d 178, 181 (S.C. Ct. App. 1985); *Salenius v. Salenius*, 654 A.2d 426 (Me. 1995).

[a] "Dual Property" Equitable Distribution States

A majority of states that have adopted equitable distribution statutes presently follow a "dual property" equitable distribution theory. Under this dual property system, a judge may apportion or divide the parties' marital property on divorce, absent a marital agreement that provides otherwise, but the judge cannot divide the parties' separate property.

Although the definitions of marital and separate property differ from state to state, most states agree that separate property generally includes: (1) property acquired by either spouse prior to the marriage; (2) property acquired after the parties' last separation or divorce; (3) property acquired during the marriage by gift or inheritance to a spouse; and (4) property acquired in exchange for separate property that maintains its separate identity, without becoming commingled with—and transmuted into—marital property. Marital property is generally defined as all other property acquired by either spouse during the marriage that is not identified as separate property. See, e.g., N.Y. Dom. Rel. Law § 236; Minn. Stat. Ann. § 518.58; and Va. Code Ann. § 20–107.3.

States following this dual-property equitable distribution model include: Alaska, Arkansas, Colorado, Delaware, Florida, Georgia, Illinois, Kentucky, Maine, Maryland, Minnesota, Mississippi, Missouri, New Jersey, New York, North Carolina, Ohio, Oklahoma, Pennsylvania, Rhode Island, Tennessee, Utah, Virginia, West Virginia, and Virginia. Community property states that also follow this dual classification model include: Arizona, California, Idaho, Louisiana, Nevada, New Mexico, and Texas.

[b] "All Property" Equitable Distribution States

A sizable minority of states have adopted an "all property" equitable distribution theory. Like the dual property approach, property on divorce may be classified as either marital or separate property. But in an all-property state, if there is insufficient marital property to make an equitable distribution award, then the court may also divide and distribute the parties' separate property as well. However, this classification of marital and separate property is immaterial in a number of other all property states, since the court has the power of dividing up all the parties' assets on divorce, regardless of how such assets may be characterized. Thus, under an all property equitable distribution regime, the court may divide any asset owned by either party, and regardless of the time or manner of its acquisition. Examples of states following an all property equitable distribution model include: Alabama, Connecticut, Hawaii, Indiana, Iowa, Kansas, Massachusetts, Michigan, Montana, Nebraska, New Hampshire, North Dakota, Oregon, South Dakota, Vermont, and Wyoming. The state of Washington, a community property state, also recognizes this all property principle on the dissolution of marriage.

[c] A Comparison of Dual Property and All Property Regimes

Both dual-property and all-property equitable distribution theories are based on the same underlying rationale that the fruits of a martial partnership should be equitably divided between the parties. However, separate property by definition is not a product of such a marital partnership, and therefore some commentators have questioned a judge's wide discretion in many all property states to apportion such separate property between the parties on divorce. Other commentators have responded, however, that this division of separate property in all property states is appropriate whenever marital property assets are insufficient to make a fair and just property award to a spouse, or when a non-wage-earning spouse should to be adequately compensated for his or her long-term contributions toward the well-being of the family. In practice, however, some judges in all property jurisdictions flatly refuse to divide property from nonmarital sources; while other judges will divide up separate property only when a demonstrated need is shown; and still other judges appear to routinely divide up separate property in many divorce or dissolution actions.

Judges in dual property equitable distribution states, on the other hand, do not have this same flexibility to award needy spouses an adequate division of property if marital property assets are too small or inadequate. On the other hand, most dual property equitable distribution states arguably have incorporated a high level of legislative and judicial consistency within their equitable distribution statutory factors that is not shared by their all property statutory counterparts, and thus, according to one commentator, "there is a clear present trend toward adoption of the dual classification model of equitable distribution" in many American jurisdictions:

> This trend is part of a broader nationwide move toward more consistency in family law generally. The most substantial result of this move has been the enactment of child support guidelines in all 50 states. These guidelines restrict the flexibility of the trial judge to a limited extent, but they have produced substantial increases in the consistency and predictability of child support awards. The dual classification model is essentially a form of property division guideline; by limiting the court's authority to divide certain types of property, it improves the consistency and predictability of the overall process.

As long as this move away from unlimited discretion in domestic relations cases continues, the dual classification model is likely to retain its popularity.

Brett R. Turner, Equitable Distribution of Property 9–46, (2d ed. 1994). *See also* Robert Levy, *An Introduction to Divorce Property Issues*, 23 Fam. L.Q. 147 (1989).

The American Law Institute's proposed *Principles of the Law of Family Dissolution* (1997) arguably adopts a hybrid dual property approach, holding that in every dissolution of marriage, all separate property should be assigned to its respective owner, except whenever there is insufficient marital property to permit a fair reimbursement of marital property due to the financial misconduct of a spouse. Thus, if marital property is lost, expended, or destroyed through the intentional financial misconduct of one spouse, a court under these proposed *Principles* may reassign the spouses' separate property in order to achieve an equivalent result. *Id.* §§ 4.16–4.17.

Problem. Hal and Wendy acquire valuable community property while they are domiciled in a community property state during their marriage, which under community property law is a vested property right. Hal and Wendy then move to an equitable distribution state, where they bring a divorce proceeding against each other three years later. *Query:* How should the court divide their property assets under applicable state law? Utilizing applicable community property principles? Or utilizing equitable distribution principles? Applying what underlying legal rationale? *Compare In re Marriage of Scott*, 835 P.2d 710 (Mont. 1992) (involving property located in Washington and divided in a Montana divorce proceeding) *and Karp v. Karp*, 13 Fam. L. Rptr. 1448 [BNA] (N.Y. Sup. Ct. 1987) (involving property acquired in California when the parties were divorced in New York), *with Newman v. Newman*, 558 So. 2d 821 (Miss. 1990) (involving a military pension acquired when the parties were domiciled in California).

Assume now that Henry and Wanda as husband and wife acquired substantial marital property while they were domiciled in an equitable distribution state, which is not a vested property right under equitable distribution principles. Henry and Wanda then moved to a retirement community in a nearby community property state, where they both met "significant others" and subsequently were divorced three years later. How should the court divide their marital assets on divorce under applicable state law? By community property principles, or by equitable distribution principles? *See, e.g.,* Ariz. Rev. Stat. Ann. 25–318(A) (1991); Cal. Fam. Code § 125; Tex. Fam. Code § 7.002.

[B] Equitable Distribution and Community Property Overview

The remainder of this section will deal with the following equitable distribution and community property issues on divorce: (1) marital or separate property—or both? (2) "tracing" and transmutation of property; (3) "active" versus "passive" appreciation of separate property; (4) property acquired by gift or inheritance; (5) pension and retirement plans; (6) property acquired by deferred compensation; (7) personal injury and workers' compensation awards; (8) professional degrees and licenses; (9) the family residence; (10) classifying and valuing professional goodwill; (11) valuing business and professional practices; (12) distribution of marital property; (13) the role of fault in the division of marital property, including "economic fault"; and (14) the role of judicial discretion in the classification, valuation, and distribution of marital property on divorce.

Since a majority of community property states (those other than California, Louisiana, and New Mexico) have now enacted statutes that recognize a number of dual property and equitable distribution statutory factors, rather than recognizing the traditional community property equal division rule on dissolution of marriage, it follows that many of the equitable distribution principles, concepts, and illustrations discussed in this chapter will apply to a majority of community property states as well as to a majority of equitable distribution states. Consequently the terms *marital property* and *community property* will be used interchangeably in this section. However, it is also important to recognize that there are important differences in individual state laws dealing with the division of property on divorce or the dissolution of marriage—involving both community property and equitable distribution statutes—that require the student and family law practitioner to carefully research the law in each particular jurisdiction.

[C] Marital or Separate Property—Or Both?

Equitable distribution of marital or community property on divorce or dissolution of marriage normally requires a three-step process: (1) the *classification* of property as marital or separate; (2) the *valuation* of such property; and (3) the *distribution* of marital property. *See, e.g., Brinkley v. Brinkley*, 361 S.E.2d 139 (Va. Ct. App. 1987); *Hoffman v. Hoffman*, 614 A.2d 988 (Md. Ct. App. 1992).

The first important step in any equitable distribution proceeding, therefore, is the classification of property as marital or separate property.

As noted above, many states have defined separate property as: (1) property acquired by either spouse prior to the marriage; (2) property acquired by either spouse during the marriage by gift or inheritance; (3) property acquired in exchange for separate property, as long as it maintains its separate identity without becoming commingled with marital property; and (4) property acquired after the parties' separation or divorce. All other property acquired during the marriage is presumed to be marital property. *See generally* Homer H. Clark, Jr., Law of Domestic Relations, Vol. 2, pp. 175–196 (2d ed. 1987); Gregory, Swisher, and Scheible-Wolf, Understanding Family Law § 9.04 (1995); J. Thomas Oldham, Divorce, Separation, and the Distribution of Property § 5–1 to 6–35 (1997 rev. ed.)

Section 4.03 of the American Law Institute's proposed *Principles of the Law of Family Dissolution: Analysis and Recommendations* (1997) likewise presumes that property acquired during the marriage is marital property unless expressly provided as separate property. Separate property is defined under the *Principles* as inheritances and gifts from third parties to an acquiring spouse, even if acquired during marriage; property received in exchange for separate property, even if acquired during marriage; and property acquired during marriage but after the parties have commenced living apart pursuant to either a written separation agreement or a judicial decree, unless the agreement or decree specifies otherwise. Property acquired "during marriage" under this Section means after the commencement of marriage and before the filing of a petition for dissolution of the marriage, unless the trial court establishes another date to avoid a substantial injustice. Property acquired before the marriage but during a cohabiting relationship immediately preceding the marriage is also treated as marital property. See generally J. Thomas Oldham, *ALI Principles of Family Dissolution: Some Comments*, 1997 U. Ill. L. Rev. 801 (1997).

However, in a majority of states today, since cohabitation is not marriage, the assets acquired during premarital cohabitation generally are not treated as marital property. *See, e.g. Wilen v. Wilen*, 486 A.2d 775, 780 (Md. Ct. App. 1985); *Crouch v. Crouch*, 410 N.E.2d 580, 582 (Ill. App. Ct. 1980); *McIver v. McIver*, 374 S.E.2d 144, 150 (N.C. Ct. App. 1988). *Contra, Eaton v. Johnson*, 681 P.2d 606, 610 (Kan. 1984) (holding that a couple who lived together after their divorce were entitled to equitable distribution of property acquired during their period of unmarried cohabitation based upon the equitable powers of the trial court).

Query: Is it possible for property to acquire a "mixed" character, possessing elements of both marital and separate property? And if so, how should a court go about identifying the character and the value of this mixed property? The following case addresses this problem.

HARPER v. HARPER
Maryland Court of Appeals
448 A.2d 916 (Md. 1982)

LERNER J.

This case presents two questions concerning the characterization and equitable distribution of certain property as marital property . . . More particularly, it initially presents the question whether real property, purchased under an installment contract and paid for in part before marriage and in part during marriage, is marital property. Additionally, it presents the question whether a marital residence constructed on that real property during marriage is marital property. . . .

Section 3–6A-01(e) [now § 8–201] provides:

> "Marital property" is all property, however titled, acquired by either or both spouses during their marriage. It does not include property acquired prior to the marriage, property acquired by inheritance or gift from a third party, or property excluded by valid agreement or property directly traceable to any of these sources.

In 1950 the petitioner, Sylvester E. Harper (husband), then unmarried, purchased an unimproved parcel of real property for a purchase price of approximately $355.00. The purchase was made under a land installment contract requiring a monthly payment of approximately $6.90. Before his marriage, the husband made all of the payments that came due.

On 3 November 1951, the husband married the respondent, Amaryllis M. Harper (wife). During the marriage, the husband continued to make all of the payments that came due until all of the requisite payments had been made.

In 1967 the husband personally built a house, costing approximately $21,600.00, upon the real property. That house was used by the parties as their marital residence. Although the wife's name appeared on the mortgage and she was legally obligated under it, the husband made all of the mortgage payments that came due on the marital residence. Additionally, the husband paid for all of the expenses associated with the upkeep and repair of the marital residence.

According to the wife, a substantial part of the payment on a previous house jointly owned by the parties was provided by her mother, and the proceeds of the sale of that house were used to finance the construction of the marital residence built in 1967. According to the husband's pleadings, he made all of the payments for the land, construction of the marital residence, and its upkeep. At all times, the property was titled solely in the husband's name.

On 14 March 1980, in the Circuit Court for Anne Arundel County, the wife filed a bill of complaint for an absolute divorce. She requested, among other things, "that the Court determine the ownership of all the real property regardless of how titled, and order the sale of said real property, and divide the proceeds equitably."

At trial, there was evidence to show that there was an outstanding mortgage indebtedness of approximately $8,300.00 on the marital residence which was then appraised at a fair market value of approximately $65,500.00. There was no evidence to show the precise source and extent of the funds utilized during the marriage for payments for the land, construction of the marital residence, and its upkeep.

On 10 November 1980, a decree was entered granting the wife, among other things, an absolute divorce and a division of real property. More particularly, the trial court declared that the real property consisting of the lot with the marital residence upon it was marital property and ordered a sale in lieu of partition with each party receiving one-half of the proceeds of the sale. . . .

[T]he Court of Special Appeals found, for reasons different from those expressed by the trial court, that the real property and the marital residence upon it constituted marital property.

We shall reverse in part the judgment of the Court of Special Appeals.

Maryland's Property Disposition in Divorce and Annulment Act represents "a new legislative approach to the concept of marriage." The [Governor's] Commission [on Domestic Relations Law] recognized that the marital residence is ordinarily the major asset of a marriage . . . . [T]he Commission expressly indicated that one of the remedial purposes of the proposed Act was to protect the interests of spouses who had made nonmonetary contributions to the marital residence. The proposed Act was designed to achieve this remedial purpose by "end[ing] the inequity inherent in Maryland's old 'title' system of dealing with the marital property of divorcing spouses." Report of The Governor's Comm'n. on Domestic Relations Laws, at 1 (1982).

The General Assembly's basic adoption of the Commission's approach is evidenced by the preamble to the Act that states:

> The General Assembly declares that it is the policy of this State that marriage is a union between a man and a woman having equal rights under the law. Both spouses owe a duty to contribute his or her best efforts to the marriage, and both, by entering into the marriage, undertake to benefit both spouses and any children they may have. The General Assembly declares further that it is the policy of this State that when a marriage is dissolved the property interests of the spouses should be adjusted fairly and equitably, with careful consideration being given to both monetary and nonmonetary contributions made by the respective spouses to the well-being of the family, and further, that if there are minor children in the family their interests must be given particular and favorable attention.

1978 Md. Laws, ch. 794 at 2305 (preamble) . . ..

Because of its broad remedial purpose, including the protection of the interests of spouses making nonmonetary contributions to the marital residence, this Act should be liberally construed. . . . Here we shall construe the Act broadly with respect to whether real property, paid for in part before marriage and in part during marriage, as well as a marital residence constructed upon that real property during marriage, constitute marital property.

Courts in the majority of community property states in which the question has been considered have held that real property paid for in part before marriage and in part during marriage remains the separate property of the spouse who made the payments before marriage. The rationale underlying this rule is the inception of title theory.

A classic statement of the inception of title theory, as it applies to real property, appears in *Fisher v. Fisher*, 383 P.2d 840 (Idaho 1963). There a husband contracted to purchase real property before marriage. While he made some payments before marriage, the remaining payments were made during marriage from community funds. The Supreme Court of Idaho stated

> The status of property as separate or community property is *fixed as the time when it is acquired*. The word *"acquired"* contemplates the inception of title, and as a general rule the character of the title depends upon the existence or nonexistence of the marriage at the time of the incipience of the right by virtue of which the title is *finally extended and perfected*; the title when so extended and perfected relates back to that time. . . .

Fisher, 383 P.2d at 842, (emphasis added). That Court held that the real property was the separate property of the husband.

Although courts employing the inception of title theory characterize property paid for partly before marriage as separate property, they nonetheless hold that the community is entitled to some degree of compensation for community funds contributed to the separate property in the form of mortgage payments. Some of these courts have held that the community has an "equitable lien" for the amount of any mortgage payments made from community funds. Others have held that the community has "a right to reimbursement" for the amount of any mortgage payments made from community funds. . . . Similarly, courts in a majority of community property states employing the inception of title theory have held that improvements made on the separate real property of a spouse during marriage are the separate property of that spouse, even though the improvements were provided by the expenditure of community funds or efforts. . . .

Although courts employing the inception of title theory characterize improvements made on a spouse's separate property during marriage as separate property, they nonetheless hold that the community is entitled to some degree of compensation for improvements made on the separate property by the expenditure of community funds or efforts. Some of these courts have held that the community is entitled to compensation in the amount of the enhanced value of a spouse's separate property attributable to improvements provided by community funds or efforts. . . .

Courts in at least one equitable distribution state have employed the inception of title theory. In *Cain v. Cain*, 536 S.W.2d 866 (Mo. App. 1976), a husband purchased a farm paid for in part before marriage and in part during marriage from marital funds. The farm increased in value during the marriage. The Missouri Court of Appeals, employing the inception of title theory, held that the farm and its increase in value were the husband's separate property and, therefore, nonmarital. The Court did not impose a lien or charge on the property in favor of the wife. However, it indicated that payments made during marriage from marital funds and the increase in the value of the farm were relevant factors to be considered when dividing the marital property. Essentially the same result was reached in subsequent cases in which real property paid for in part before marriage and in part during marriage had been improved during marriage by the expenditure of community funds and efforts.

Courts in at least one community property state, California, have rejected the inception of title theory. In California, when real property is paid for in part before marriage from a spouse's separate funds and in part during marriage from community funds, and improvements are placed on the real property during marriage, such property and its improvements are characterized as part separate and part community. Under the California rule, the spouse contributing separate funds is entitled to a "pro tanto community property interest" in such property and improvements in the ratio of the separate investment to the total separate and community investment in the property. Similarly, the community is entitled to a "pro tanto community property" interest in such property and improvements in the ratio of the community investment to the total separate and community investment in the property.

As a result of the application of the California rule, both the spouse who contributed separate funds and the community that contributed community funds each receive a proportionate and fair return on their investment. Contrary to the rule adopted in most community property states, the California rule does not limit the community to compensation for a share of the enhanced value of the property attributable to the expenditure of community funds and efforts, but rather entitles the community additionally to share in the increased value attributable to the normal appreciation of the property.

The rationale underlying California's "pro tanto community property interest" rule is the source of funds theory. That theory is premised on the concept that it is unfair to permit a spouse, who has contributed separate funds to the purchase or improvement of property to enjoy all of the benefits of sole ownership of the property without regard to the fact that it had been purchased or improved in part with community funds. . . .

In at least one equitable distribution state, Maine, a court has rejected the inception of title theory and has employed the source of funds theory. In *Tibbetts v. Tibbetts*, 406 A.2d 70 (Me. 1979), a case involving facts somewhat different from those here, a husband and wife purchased real property as joint tenants during the marriage. The property was paid for by an admixture of community funds and separate funds that the wife had acquired before marriage. The Supreme Judicial Court of Maine, in considering whether the property was marital or nonmarital, said:

> Such property is non-marital *to the extent* that it was acquired in exchange for property acquired prior to marriage. *Thus a single item of property may be to some extent non-marital and the remainder marital* . . . .Our interpretation of the term "acquisition" has led us up and down the American West and even to the shores of Old Spain. It appears that the courts of our community property states have not with ease adapted to the realities of complex modern transactions and relationships. We conclude that in fairness to both spouses *"acquisition" must not arbitrarily and finally be fixed on the date that a legal obligation to purchase is created. Rather "acquisition" should be recognized as the on-going process of making payment for acquired property.*

Characterization of the property acquired will then depend on the source of each contribution as payments are made.

Tibbetts, 406 A.2d at 75, 76, 77 (emphasis added) (citations omitted) (footnotes omitted).

Courts in other equitable distribution states have, for a variety of reasons, rejected the inception of title theory in cases involving facts closely analogous to those here. These courts, however, have not employed the source of funds theory. . . .

We must now determine the appropriate analysis to be used in construing the Maryland Act. . . . We reject the inception of title theory employed by a majority of community property states and at least one equitable distribution state. Accordingly, under § 3–6A-01(e), property is not necessarily "acquired" on the date that a legal obligation to purchase is created. Thus, we effectuate our Act's purpose of "end[ing] the inequity inherent in Maryland's old 'title' system of dealing with the marital property of divorcing spouses." Report of The Governor's Comm'n on Domestic Relations Laws, at 1 (1982).

We conclude that under the Maryland Act the appropriate analysis to be applied is the source of funds theory. Under that theory, when property is acquired by an expenditure of both nonmarital and marital property, the property is characterized as part nonmarital and part marital. Thus, a spouse contributing nonmarital property is entitled to an interest in the property in the ratio of the nonmarital investment to the total nonmarital and marital investment in the property. The remaining property is characterized as marital property and its value is subject to equitable distribution. Thus, the spouse who contributed nonmarital funds, and the marital unit that contributed marital funds each receive a proportionate and fair return on their investment.

We recognize that in order to apply the source of funds theory in Maryland, it is necessary to adopt, as did the Supreme Judicial Court of Maine, an interpretation that defines the term "acquired," appearing in § 3–6A-01(e), as the on-going process of making payment for property. *Tibbetts*, 406 A.2d at 77. Under this definition, characterization of property as nonmarital or marital depends upon the source of each contribution as payments are made, rather than the time at which legal or equitable title to or possession of the property is obtained. . . .

In light of these newly adopted standards, this case must be remanded to the trial court to determine the source of the funds contributed to the real property and the marital residence by each of the spouses and the marital unit; to determine the extent to which the property and the marital residence are to be characterized as nonmarital or marital; to determine the value of the marital property; and to make an equitable distribution of the marital property with due regard being given to all of the relevant factors.

NOTES AND QUESTIONS

(1) As discussed in the *Harper* case, the "inception of title" doctrine evolved from community property principles, since ownership rights to community property generally vest at the time the property is acquired. Thus, according to an early Louisiana Supreme Court case, "if those who own and purchase land in this state cannot rely . . . on the plain provisions of the law . . . that it is the time at which the title vests which must be looked to in determining the status of the property, then land titles in this state are mere loose

leafs to be scattered by any passing wind." *Doucet v. Fontenot,* 115 So. 655, 658 (La. 1928), *cert. denied,* 278 U.S. 561 (1928). Accordingly, a number of community property states have adopted the inception of title doctrine (that property is ordinarily acquired at the time legal title is obtained). *See, e.g., Jensen v. Jensen,* 665 S.W.2d 107 (Tex. 1984); *Fischer v. Fischer,* 383 P.2d 840 (Idaho 1963); *Katterhagen v. Meister,* 134 P. 673 (Wash. 1913). Some equitable distribution jurisdictions also have adopted this inception of title doctrine. *See, e.g., Yeldell v. Yeldell,* 551 A.2d 832 (D.C. 1988).

Although the inception of title doctrine appears to be a fair and reasonable rule of establishing title to property at the time it is acquired, in practice it has caused serious problems with courts trying to divide marital or community property fairly on divorce. A basic problem in a large number of inception of title cases is when a party purchases a home or other real property with a down payment prior to the marriage. Although the inception of title occurs at the time the property is acquired, the principal payments on the mortgage are made over a period of years, often with separate and marital funds and with marital efforts from the non-owning spouse. On divorce, the result of this appreciated property may therefore constitute an unfair windfall to the owner spouse, at the expense of the non-owning spouse, even if the non-owner spouse is partially "reimbursed" for his or her efforts under the doctrine of equitable reimbursement. *See, e.g., Welder v. Lambert,* 44 S.W. 281 (Tex. 1898).

Based upon this perceived unfairness, the inception of title rule has not been uniformly adopted in every community property state. California, for example, has adopted a "pro tanto interest" rule which holds that if contributions made to the purchase price of the property after inception of title can create a community interest, then property is not necessarily "unchangeably" classified at the time title is received, at least for divorce purposes. *See, e.g., Forbes v. Forbes,* 257 P.2d 721, 722 (Cal. Ct. App. 1953); *Moore v. Moore,* 168 Cal. Rptr. 662 (Cal. 1980) (expressly adopting the *Forbes* rationale). In recent years, other community property states also have adopted the California pro tanto interest rule, including Arizona, New Mexico, and Nevada. *See, e.g., Drahos v. Rens,* 717 P.2d 927 (Ariz. Ct. App. 1985); *Dorbin v. Dorbin,* 731 P.2d 959 (N.M. Ct. App. 1986); *Malmquist v. Malmquist,* 792 P.2d 372 (Nev. 1990).

(2) The *Harper* court summarily rejected the inception of title rule in favor of a "source of the funds" rule, based in part on the California pro tanto interest rationale. But the *Harper* court went further than merely adopting the California pro tanto interest rule. Since Maryland is an equitable distribution state, rather than a community property state, property need not vest or be classified immediately upon the acquisition of legal title. Thus, the *Harper* court reasoned, if classification of property depends on different contributions that are made at different times, then acquisition of such property cannot be a one-time event, and a new definition of property acquisition must be based upon an ongoing process, independent of legal title. This is called the "source of the funds" doctrine, which to date has been adopted by a majority of equitable distribution states. *See, e.g., Jackson v. Jackson,* 765 S.W.2d 561 (Ark. 1989); *Hoffman v. Hoffman,* 676 S.W.2d 817, 825 (Mo. 1984) (overruling earlier precedent cited in *Harper*); *Wade v. Wade,* 325 S.E.2d 260, 269 (N.C. Ct. App. 1985). *Cf. Zimin v. Zimin,* 837 P.2d 118, 121 (Alaska 1992); *Landay v. Landay,* 429 So. 2d 297 (Fla. 1983); *Schmidt v. Schmidt,* 309 N.W.2d 748 (Minn. 1981) (all three cases adopting various source of the funds principles, but not the express rule). *See generally* Brett R. Turner, Equitable Distribution of Property §§ 5.09–5.10 (2d ed. 1994).

(3) If, under the source of the funds rule, the acquisition and classification of property is an ongoing process, involving different contributions of separate and marital property over different times, then it follows under the source of the funds rule that such property can either be marital property; separate property; or "mixed" property that is both separate and marital. However, at least three states—Illinois, Virginia, and Pennsylvania—at one time rejected this mixed character of property, holding that under a "unitary" property classification theory, property could be either separate or marital property, but it could not be both. Thus, if marital and separate property were commingled, such property would be transmuted into marital property. *See, e.g., Smoot v. Smoot,* 357 S.E.2d 728 (Va. 1987). *Smoot* was overruled by subsequent statutory law, and Virginia now follows the source of the funds rule as enunciated in *Harper* under its mixed property statute, Va. Code Ann. 20–107.3(A)(3) (1990). Illinois also now follows source of the funds principles in general practice. *See, e.g., In re Smith,* 427 N.E.2d 1239 (Ill. 1981) which also was overruled by subsequent statutory law, 750 Ill. Comp. Stat. Ann. 5/503c (1993). Only Pennsylvania, through unique statutory law, defines all appreciation of separate property as marital property, regardless of how such appreciation of property was caused. *See, e.g., Anthony v. Anthony,* 514 A.2d 91 (Pa. Super. Ct. 1986).

(4) Under the source of the funds rule, as enunciated in *Harper,* mixed property generally is nonmarital "in the ratio that the nonmarital investment in the property bears to the total nonmarital and marital investment in the property" *Grant v. Zich,* 477 A.2d 1163, 1170 (Md. Ct. App. 1984), and this requires the calculation of the nonmarital portion of the property. As an illustration:

> A husband and wife acquired real property for a purchase price of $40,000. The wife contributed a down payment of $10,000 from property that she acquired prior to the marriage. The remaining $30,000 was financed by a mortgage signed by both the husband and the wife. One-quarter of the value of the property is the wife's nonmarital property and three-quarters of the value of the property is marital property. If, at the time of the dissolution of the marriage, the property has appreciated in value to a fair market value of $60,000 and the mortgage indebtedness has been reduced to $20,000 by the payment of $10,000 of marital funds, the following division would be appropriate: One-quarter of the $60,000 fair market value of the property, or $15,000, would be the wife's nonmarital property, not subject to equitable distribution. From the remaining $45,000, $20,000, representing the unpaid mortgage balance, would be deducted, leaving $25,000 as the net value of the marital property subject to equitable distribution.

Id., cited with approval in *Hoffman v. Hoffman,* 614 A.2d 988, 993 (Md. Ct. App. 1992).

Query. How should the court distribute this property, applying the inception of title doctrine, assuming now that the husband had acquired the property one year prior to marriage, and that husband had made a down payment on the property of $1,000 before he married wife.

(4) **Problem.** Harry and Wilma were married on October 3, 1987. They have one daughter, Stephanie, born in 1990. Two years prior to their marriage, Harry purchased thirty acres of land in his own name, and making a down payment of $5,000, with an existing mortgage of $20,000. Three years after the marriage, Wilma and Harry built a house on the property, costing $125,000. Wilma paid $10,000 toward the down payment on the house

from wages she had earned working as a business consultant during the years 1988–1990. Since 1990, Wilma has stayed at home, taking care of Stephanie. In 1994, Wilma paid another $15,000 toward the house and land payments from money she had inherited from her mother. Since 1990, Harry has been making the mortgage payments on the house and land of approximately $1,200 a month, including principal, interest, taxes, and insurance. Now, a number of years later, the Harry and Wilma are involved in a dissolution of their marriage. Since 1990, their property and house have appreciated, and they are now worth approximately $250,000 ($50,000 for the land, and $200,000 for the house). There are no remaining payments left on the land, and an existing $50,000 mortgage is all that's left on the house.

Upon the couple's divorce what should be done with this property? How would you as a judge divide up the property according to: (1) the inception of title doctrine? (2) a pro tanto interest? or (3) the source of the funds rule? Discuss (and be prepared to justify your calculations). *Compare Harper v. Harper*, above, and *West v. West*, 550 A.2d 1132 (Me. 1988) *with Jensen v. Jensen*, 665 S.W.2d 107 (Tex. 1984).

What about the parties' income earned during the marriage? Is that separate or marital property? What standard should the parties be required to meet in proving that property is marital or separate property? *See Holder v. Holder*, 403 N.W.2d 269 (Minn. Ct. App. 1987).

[D] "Tracing" and Transmutation of Property

In most jurisdictions, the nature of property can be altered through the process of "transmutation," where the character and identity of property may change from separate to marital or community property, or to mixed property whenever the separate property becomes commingled with marital or community property. If separate property is mixed or commingled with marital or community property and cannot be traced back its original identity by a preponderance of the evidence, then that separate property may be transmuted into marital or community property. Finally, if the intent of the parties is to treat separate property so it becomes marital property, then that separate property is also transmuted to marital property. For example, if property is purchased with separate funds, but title is taken in joint tenancy or in tenancy by the entirety, then the separate property may be transmuted into marital property based upon the intent of the parties to treat such property as marital property. *See Carter v. Carter*, 419 A.2d 1018 (Me. 1980); *Westbrook v. Westbrook*, 364 S.E.2d 523 (Va. Ct. App. 1988). Or if separate property becomes commingled with marital property, such commingled property may become marital property under the doctrine of transmutation. *See Sturgis v. Sturgis*, 663 S.W.2d 375 (Mo. Ct. App. 1983). However, if the separate property continues to maintain its separate identity, or can be traced back to its source, then transmutation of property would not have occurred. *See generally* Joan M. Krauskopf, *The Transmutation and Source of the Funds Rules in Divisions of Marital Property*, 50 Mo. L. Rev. 759 (1985). Tracing and transmutation of separate and marital property are therefore crucial elements in the characterization of property on divorce in most dual property states, although these concepts are not always recognized in a number of all property jurisdictions. *See In re Olinger*, 707 P.2d 64, 67 (Or. Ct. App. 1985) (refusing to trace separate property that had become commingled with marital property); *Rezac v. Rezac*, 378 N.W.2d 196 (Neb. 1985) (making the questionable argument that tracing of separate property would give the owner a "duplicate credit"); *Jordan v. Jordan*, 616 A.2d 1238 (D.C. 1992) (also refusing to recognize the doctrine of tracing).

According to the proposed ALI *Principles of the Law of Family Dissolution* § 403, Comment c (1997):

> [T]racing problems arise primarily when separate property has been commingled with marital property. The problem at dissolution is then to separate the commingled asset into its marital and separate property components. The community property states have more experience with this problem, and California has particularly developed rules on the subject. See Grace G. Blumberg, Community Property in California 236–61 (2d ed. 1993) . . . . Some common law states have enacted statutes specifying that the commingling of marital and separate property does not itself cause a transmutation of the separate property into marital property, thus effectively requiring tracing. . . . Others have enacted more detailed tracing rules. . . . For a more detailed treatment of these tracing issues, see J. Thomas Oldham, Divorce, Separation, and the Distribution of Property § 11.03 (1994).

One comprehensive equitable distribution statute involving tracing and transmutation of separate and marital property is Va. Code Ann. § 20–107.3(3) (1996):

> (d) When marital property and separate property are commingled by contributing one category of property to another, resulting in the loss of identity of the contributed property, the classification of the contributed property shall be transmuted to the category of property receiving the contribution. However, to the extent the contributed property is retraceable by a preponderance of the evidence and was not a gift, such contributed property shall retain its original classification. (e) When marital property and separate property are commingled into newly acquired property resulting in the loss of identity of the contributing property, the commingled property shall be deemed transmuted to marital property. However, to the extent the contributed property is retraceable by a preponderance of the evidence and was not a gift, the contributed property shall retain its original classification. (f) When separate property is retitled in the joint names of the parties, the retitled property shall be deemed transmuted to marital property. However, to the extent the property is retraceable by a preponderance of the evidence and was not a gift, the retitled property shall retain its original classification.

Although there appears to be remarkable uniformity within equitable distribution and community property dual property states in recognizing the concepts of tracing and transmutation of separate and marital property on divorce or dissolution of marriage, the major problem for many courts and family law practitioners is applying the relevant law to the specific facts of each case, and properly documenting this "tracing" requirement, as the following case aptly illustrates.

CHENAULT v. CHENAULT
Kentucky Supreme Court
799 S.W.2d 575 (1990)

LAMBERT, JUSTICE.

This Court granted discretionary review of the decision of the Court of Appeals which imposed stringent requirements upon appellant, Ruby E. Chenault, who sought to "trace" the proceeds of nonmarital property at the time the marriage was dissolved. In effect, the Court of Appeals held that at the time of dissolution, a party undertaking to prove the nonmarital character of property must do so by documentary evidence and with near mathematical precision. We believe such a requirement is beyond the mandate of KRS 403.190 and contrary to sound public policy. Hence, we reverse.

Ruby and William married in 1971. At the time of their marriage both were in their early 50's and William was the father of a seven-year-old daughter who lived with him. During the 15–year duration of their marriage, Ruby discharged the normal duties of homemaker and mother and after William's daughter went to college, worked in a low-wage position at the Speed Art Museum in Louisville. During the marriage, William worked as a construction worker and after his retirement from that position, worked as a security guard at the Speed Museum.

On this appeal, the principle and decisive issue is whether the Court of Appeals, affirming the trial court, erred in holding that Ruby failed to present sufficient evidence that certain liquid assets should have been assigned to her as nonmarital property. Ruby contends that she brought to the marriage at least $21,000 in cash, a home valued at $14,000, and 27 shares of stock in Standard Oil of California. At trial, she presented convincing evidence that she owned her home prior to the marriage and that the home was sold and the proceeds realized during the marriage. Likewise, she presented convincing evidence that at a minimum she had $10,000 in cash one year prior to the marriage and that a Treasury Note of $10,000 came due and was reinvested during the marriage. Finally, Ruby testified that she inherited 27 shares of stock in Standard Oil of California and by virtue of stock dividends and stock splits, this number of shares grew significantly before and during the marriage. . . . Regardless of the foregoing evidence, the Court of Appeals affirmed the trial court's determination that Ruby had failed to establish the nonmarital character of these assets. . . . In its finding of fact, the accuracy of which is not disputed by either party, the trial court found that in addition to the 50 shares of Standard Oil of California stock, Ruby was then in possession of cash and securities valued at $91,329. Nevertheless, by virtue of her inability to trace any of these assets to the satisfaction of the trial court, it was determined that all of such assets were marital property.

In KRS 403.190(2)(b), marital property is defined in part as "all property acquired by either spouse subsequent to the marriage except:. . . . Property acquired in exchange for property acquired before the marriage or in exchange for property acquired by gift, bequest, devise or descent." Subsection (3) of KRS 403.190 creates a presumption that all property acquired during the marriage is marital property, but permits this presumption to be overcome by proof that the property was acquired as in subsection (2) of the statute. Numerous decision of this Court and the Court of Appeals have construed this statutory provision and from these decisions there has emerged the concept of "tracing" although this term is nowhere found in the statute. Among the more significant decisions on this point are *Turley v. Turley*, 562 S.W.2d 665 (Ky. Ct. App. 1978) [and] *Brunson v. Brunson*, 569 S.W.2d 173 (Ky. Ct. App. 1978) [other case citations omitted] . . . .

Even a cursory review of the foregoing decisions reveals a requirement of considerable precision in the process of tracing if the property claimed to be nonmarital is to be so found. For instance, in *Turley*, the Court said:

> Mr. Turley failed to show that any property owned by the parties at the time of the separation was acquired by use of his inheritance or from the proceeds from the sale

of the automobile and furniture owned by him prior to the marriage. Because he did not trace the inheritance or the proceeds, if any, from the disposition of the automobile and furniture, it was error for the trial court to award him the value of such items. *Id.* At 668.

Likewise in *Brunson*, the Court said:

> The trial court recognized that Mrs. Brunson brought property into the marriage. However, because she failed to trace any of that money or property into any specific assets which were owned by the parties at the time of the separation, the trial court concluded that it had no power to assign any property to Mrs. Brunson as nonmarital property. The record supports the trial court's conclusion that Mrs. Brunson failed to trace the assets which she brought into the marriage into assets owned at the time of the separation. . . .

While such precise requirements for nonmarital asset-tracing may be appropriate for skilled business persons who maintain comprehensive records of their financial affairs, such may not be appropriate for persons of lesser business skills or persons who are imprecise in their record-keeping abilities. This problem is compounded in a marital union where one spouse is the recorder of financial detail and the other is essentially indifferent to such matters. Moreover, such a requirement may promote marital disharmony by placing a premium on the careful maintenance of separate estates.

In *Allen v. Allen*, 584 S.W.2d 599 (Ky. Ct. App. 1979), the Court of Appeals retreated somewhat from its earlier decisions and held that "the requirement of tracing should be fulfilled, at least as far as money is concerned, when it is shown that nonmarital funds were deposited and commingled with marital funds and that the balance of the account was never reduced below the amount of the nonmarital funds deposited." *Id.* at 600. The view expressed in *Allen* is consistent with the concurring opinion of Vance, J. in *Turley v. Turley, supra*. In that concurring opinion, it was persuasively argued that all nonmarital property should be restored upon dissolution of the marriage providing the parties have, throughout the marriage, maintained at least as much in assets as the combined value of their nonmarital property. By logical inference, if this view were adopted, any decrease during the marriage in the parties' total nonmarital asset value would be charged *pro rata* against their percentage share of total nonmarital property to be assigned.

As appealing as the foregoing view may be, particularly when the simplicity of its application and its inherent equity is considered, we believe the concept of tracing is too firmly established in the law to be abandoned at this time.

Accordingly, we shall adhere to the general requirement that nonmarital assets be traced into assets owned at the time of dissolution, but relax some of the draconian requirements heretofore laid down. We take this position, in part, in reliance upon the trial courts of Kentucky to detect deception and exaggeration or to require additional proof when such is suspected. . . .

This cause is reversed and remanded to the Jefferson Circuit Court for further proceedings consistent herewith. . . .

NOTES AND QUESTIONS

(1) The Kentucky Supreme Court in *Chenault* was less than enthusiastic in applying its "tracing" doctrine, opining that although it might be better to restore to each spouse the amount of property pro tanto owned during the marriage, nevertheless "the concept of tracing is too firmly established in the law to be abandoned at this time." Thus, numerous courts and commentators have disagreed over the concept of "tracing." On one hand, Lawrence J. Golden in *Equitable Distribution of Property*, § 529 (1983) states,

> The tracing of one asset into another is a complicated legal and factual process which has come in for some sharp criticism. At a very basic level it does not reflect the realities of marriage; married partners tend to pool their resources, and this tends to obliterate the separate identities of property. The law of tracing actually discourages this sharing and rewards spouses who keep a running account of what is theirs. One can only surmise that the proof problems of tracing can be so substantial that the expense of litigation is often not worth the effort.

On the other hand, Brett Turner in *Equitable Distribution of Property*, § 5.23 (2d ed. 1994) states,

> [This] author believes that these criticisms overstate their case. There is no doubt that tracing is a difficult process on both the law and the facts. Nevertheless, it is a process required by the very nature of dual [property] classification. Adoption of the dual classification system [by a majority of states] reflects a legislative judgment that the court should not be permitted to divide certain types of property upon divorce. Those types of property share the common thread that they are not a product of the marital partnership. Property acquired in exchange for separate property is likewise not a product of the marital partnership, and if the law is to remain at all consistent, separate property must retain its status despite changes in form . . . . Without tracing, there would be no way to invoke [this] exchange provision in the great majority of cases, and the dual classification system would be arbitrary and unworkable.

(2) Although the majority opinion in *Chenault* agreed to relax "some of the draconian requirements heretofore laid down," the court did not give specific guidelines on how this should be done, other than relying on the Kentucky trial courts "to detect deception and exaggeration or to require additional proof when such is suspected." Justice Vance, however, in a concurring opinion in *Chenault,* offered these "tracing" guidelines:

> [W]here marital and nonmarital funds have been commingled in a bank account, all withdrawals from the account [should] be considered to be marital funds until the marital funds are exhausted. It would follow that the only tracing of nonmarital property necessary would be proof that nonmarital property once existed. If it no longer exists in its original form, there should be proof that it had been exchanged for other property or converted into cash, and proof that the total assets upon dissolution were greater than the total value of the nonmarital assets and/or property received in exchange for such nonmarital assets. If there is a contention that the total value of their assets at some time during the marriage was reduced to an amount less than the value of their nonmarital property, the burden of proof should rest upon the party making the claim.

799 S.W.2d 575, 581 (concurring opinion). *Query:* Is this "tracing" approach a realistic recommendation? Or should any decrease in the parties' total nonmarital asset value be charged pro rata against the percentage share of the total nonmarital property to be assigned?

(3) **Burden and Standard of Proof.** Regardless of what "tracing" or transmutation approach a court applies, there is general agreement that since mixed property, or property acquired during the marriage, is presumed to be marital or community property, the burden of proof is on the spouse claiming property is separate to "trace" that asset to its separate property source. Thus, if any link in the "tracing" chain or process cannot be proven, or if the asset is traced to a marital source, then that asset is marital or community property. But what standard of proof must be demonstrated? Some courts, apparently a majority, require proof by a preponderance of the evidence. *See, e.g., Chenault v. Chenault, above*; *Kottke v. Kottke,* 353 N.W.2d 633, 636 (Minn. Ct. App. 1984); *Stroop v. Stroop,* 394 S.E.2d 861 (Va. Ct. App. 1990). Other courts, however, require a higher standard of "clear proof." *See, e.g., Pullman v. Pullman,* 573 N.Y.S.2d 690 (App. Div. 1991).

(4) *Query.* Based upon these conflicting theories and criticisms of "tracing" and transmutation of property in dual property jurisdictions, should more states arguably adopt all property regimes for the division of property on divorce or dissolution of marriage? Why or why not? Based upon what underlying public policy rationales? *See generally* Oldham, Divorce, Separation, and the Distribution of Property §§ 11.01–11.04 (1997).

(5) **"Tracing" and Transmutation Problem.** Prior to their marriage, Dr. Price gave Mrs. Price a beautiful and expensive diamond as a premarital gift. After they were married, Dr. Price gave Mrs. Price another beautiful and expensive diamond, and suggested to Mrs. Price that both her diamonds ought to be incorporated into a new, beautiful, and doubly expensive diamond ring, crafted by a well-known jeweler especially for Mrs. Price. On divorce, Dr. Price argued that Mrs. Price's expensive new diamond ring with her two beautiful diamonds now constituted marital property, and therefore was subject to equitable distribution by the court. On appeal, how should the court rule? *See Price v. Price,* 355 S.E.2d 905 (Va. Ct. App. 1987). *Cf. Quinn v. Quinn,* 512 A.2d 848, 853 (R.I. 1986) (holding that when marital and nonmarital assets are commingled and then exchanged for other property, the newly acquired asset is marital property).

[E] Passive versus Active Appreciation of Separate Property

What happens when property is classified as separate property, but this separate property appreciates in value during the marriage—does this appreciated property constitute separate property; or is this appreciated property community or marital property? Largely influenced by early community property precedent, the current consensus and the growing trend in many states today is that appreciation of separate property remains as separate property only if such appreciation constitutes passive appreciation. But if the appreciation of separate property was caused by the *marital efforts* or *marital funds* of either the husband, the wife, or both spouses during the marriage, then this *active appreciation* of separate property would constitute marital or community property. *See, e.g.,* Fla. Stat. Ann. 61.075 (b)(3); 750 Ill. Comp. Laws Ann. 5/503(a)(8); Ohio Rev. Code Ann. § 3105.171(A)(6)(a)(iii); Tenn. Code Ann. § 36–4–121(b)(1)(B); Va. Code Ann. § 20–107.3(A)(3)(a). *See also Meason v. Meason,* 717 P.2d 1165 (Okla. Ct. App. 1985); *Hall v. Hall,* 462 A.2d 1179 (Me. 1983).

In *Rodgers v. Rodgers,* 405 S.E.2d 235, 239 (W.Va. 1991), for example, the West Virginia Supreme Court, applying its state equitable distribution statute, defined passive appreciation of separate property as an increase "which is due to inflation or to a change in market value resulting from conditions outside the control of the parties" and therefore which is not subject to equitable distribution. Active appreciation of separate property, on the other hand, is an increase that results from "an expenditure of funds which are marital property . . . [or] work performed by either or both of the parties during the marriage" which would then be classified as marital property, and subject to equitable distribution on divorce. Likewise, in *Halpern v. Halpern*, 252 S.E.2d 753 (Ga. 1987), the Georgia Supreme Court ruled that appreciation during the marriage of one spouse's stock acquired as a result of a gift was not a marital asset which was subject to equitable distribution when the increase in value was solely attributable to outside market forces, and was not as a result of any marital efforts of the spouse. In short, the increase was a passive event. The Georgia court cited two New York decisions which distinguished between situations in which there was passive appreciation due to market forces [*Jolis v. Jolis*, 470 N.Y.S.2d 584 (App. Div. 1983)], and appreciation due to the marital efforts of a spouse, including active management of the assets [*Nolan v. Nolan*, 486 N.Y.S.2d 415 (App. Div. 1985)]. *See generally* Gregory, Swisher, and Scheible-Wolf, *Understanding Family Law* § 9.05 (1995). *See also* Joan Krauskopf, *Classifying Marital and Separate Property: Combinations and Increase in Value of Separate Property,* 89 W. Va. L. Rev. 997 (1987).

The major problem with this approach of distinguishing passive from active appreciation of separate property, however, is to ascertain the amount of marital effort or marital funds (or the lack thereof) which would create marital property from the appreciation of separate property, as the following problems illustrate.

NOTES AND QUESTIONS

(1) **Problem.** During her marriage, Wife received a sizable gift of stock from her mother. By careful management during her marriage to Husband, Wife was able to double the value of her stock. Wife and Husband are now divorcing. Wife is in precarious health, and she is in need of additional funds to pay for her medical care. In addition, Husband has been both physically and mentally abusive to Wife and to Wife's mother. Assume that you are a clerk to the trial court judge who must decide the division of property in this particular divorce case. What would you recommend to the judge regarding the appreciation of the stock during the marriage? *See, e.g., Johnson v. Johnson*, 494 N.E.2d 423 (Mass. Ct. App. 1986); *Rosenberg v. Rosenberg*, 379 N.W.2d 580 (Minn. Ct. App. 1985). *See also Lambert v. Lambert*, 367 S.E.2d 184 (Va. Ct. App. 1988) (making the distinction between passive and active appreciation of separate property).

(2) Where the appreciation of the property is due to the substantial contributions of a spouse through marital effort, skill, or funds, then this appreciation normally will be considered to be marital property. *See, e.g., Marriage of Herr*, 705 S.W.2d 619 (Mo. Ct. App. 1986); *Worthington v. Worthington*, 488 N.E.2d 150 (Ohio 1986). But how "substantial" must these marital efforts and contributions be? Consider the following factual situations:

(a) Husband was a career military officer. Husband and Wife were married for thirty years. Wife contributed to the advancement of Husband's military career by handling all of the home matters and child rearing; holding appropriate social functions for her officer

Husband; and dealing with financial matters such that Husband did not have to utilize his own separate property. Should Wife share in the appreciation of Husband's separate property as a result of her marital efforts? Why or why not? *See Cassiday v. Cassiday*, 716 P.2d 1133 (Haw. Ct. App. 1986).

(b) Wife worked in Husband's insurance agency, which Husband had acquired prior to marriage. Wife worked one to three hours a day at the office, managing the office, running errands, decorating the office, and balancing checking accounts. Wife also became a licensed insurance broker and sold two insurance policies. She was paid a minimal salary for social security purposes. Did Wife's activity at the insurance agency rise to the level of "significant marital effort" constituting active appreciation of the agency ? What about Husband's marital effort in running his insurance agency? *See In re Marriage of Morse*, 493 N.E.2d 1088 (Ill. App. Ct. 1986).

(c) Wife owned a farm which she had inherited from her parents before her marriage. She had maintained title to the farm and the residence in her own name. During the marriage, Husband made repairs and additions to the farm and its buildings. Wife, from her separate funds, paid the costs of all the materials used by Husband in making these repairs and improvements. The value of the farm increased substantially during the course of the marriage. Is this appreciated value of the farm separate or marital property? *See Haldemann v. Haldemann*, 426 N.W.2d 107 (Wis. Ct. App. 1988).

(d) Before her marriage, Wife was employed as a registered nurse. After the marriage, and for a period of one year, Wife continued to work outside the home. When the parties' two children were born, Wife quit work in order to devote her efforts to being a homemaker and primary caretaker of the children. There is evidence that during the marriage Wife attended numerous business conventions with Husband, and Wife assisted Husband as hostess at various business-related social events. Husband had acquired his business interests as a result of a gift and inheritance. The major issue in this divorce was appreciation in his business interests. Should Wife's "minimal and inconsequential" contributions to Husband's business interests as a result of her marital efforts as a homemaker entitle her to a share of the appreciation of Husband's business? Why or why not? *See Price v. Price*, 511 N.Y.S.2d 219 (N.Y. 1986).

(3) The proposed ALI *Principles of the Law of Family Dissolution* § 4.04(2) (1997) state, "Both income during marriage from separate property, and the appreciation in value during marriage of separate property, are marital property to the extent the income or appreciation is attributable to either spouse's labor during marriage, pursuant to Section 4.05." Section 4.05, entitled *Enhancement of Separate Property by Spousal Labor*, further provides,

> (1) A portion of any increase in the value of separate property is marital property whenever either spouse has devoted substantial time during marriage to the property's management or preservation; . . . (3) The portion of the increase in value that is marital property under Paragraph (1) is the difference between the actual amount by which the property has increased in value, and the amount by which capital of the same value would have increased over the same time period if invested in assets of relative safety requiring little management.

Query: How would such marital effort be valued under these ALI *Principles*? Illustration 1 to § 4.05 gives the following example:

Alex runs a small contracting business at the time of his marriage to Betty. The business is thus Alex's separate property. He continues to work at the business during their marriage and, when they divorce five years later, it has increased in value from $10,000 to $50,000. Because Alex has devoted substantial labor during marriage to the management of his separate property business, a portion of its increased value is marital property. . . . To calculate the marital property portion of the $40,000 gain, the court must first determine the return that would have been obtained during the same time period from an investment of $10,000 in "assets of relative safety requiring little or no management." In this jurisdiction, the benchmark normally employed to implement this standard is the return on Treasury bonds of intermediate term. By referring to interest rates prevailing at that time, the court determines that $10,000 invested in intermediate term treasury bonds at the commencement of Betty's and Alex's marriage would have yielded $4,700 by the time of their [marriage] dissolution. Alex's original $10,000, plus this $4,700 return, is his separate property. The remaining $35,300 ($40,000 minus $4,700 is marital property to be divided between the spouses . . . . This attempt to separate active from passive appreciation of separate property in the ALI *Principles* is based upon the *Principles*' primary objective governing the division of property on the dissolution of marriage that such property division should be "consistent and predictable in application," Section 4.02(3).

Query. What is the impact of these ALI *Principles* on the traditional equity concept of judicial discretion in marital property division on divorce? Will trial court judges now have very limited—if any—judicial discretion in applying these statutory factors? Is judicial discretion always a bad thing, or should the parameters of judicial discretion continue to be severely limited, as illustrated in most state child support guidelines? Can you think of any other viable means for determining passive and active appreciation of separate property?

[F] Property Acquired by Gift or Inheritance

Most dual property equitable distribution statutes provide that property acquired by a spouse during the marriage "by gift, bequest, devise, or descent" is classified as separate property, as long as such property does not become commingled with, or transmuted into, marital property. *See, e.g., Hussey v. Hussey*, 312 S.E.2d 267 (S.C. Ct. App. 1984). Likewise, gifts and inheritances have been considered separate property under community property principles dating back to medieval Europe. *See generally* DeFuniak & Vaughn, Principles of Community Property § 69 (2d ed. 1971). However, a gift or inheritance to both husband and wife would still be classified as marital property. *See, e.g., Forsythe v. Forsythe*, 558 S.W.2d 675 (Mo. Ct. App. 1977).

A number of states recognize a "joint gift presumption" whenever there is a transfer of real or personal property giving both spouses an ownership interest the property, such as legal or equitable title. *See, e.g., In re Marriage of Cullman*, 541 N.E.2d 1274, 1277 (Ill. App. Ct. 1989); *Tubbs v. Tubbs*, 755 S.W.2d 423, 424 (Mo. Ct. App. 1988). Other states, however, have rejected this joint gift presumption, arguing that legal title is irrelevant in equitable distribution matters, and would prevent the use of clearly established "tracing" rules. *See, e.g., Kline v. Kline*, 581 A.2d 1300 (Md. Ct. App. 1990); Va. Code Ann. § 20–107.3 (A)(3)(f) (1991). Most gifts, however, are still subject to division in many all property states, which do not distinguish between separate and marital property. *See, e.g., Winter v. Winter*, 338 N.W.2d 819 (N.D. 1983).

A gift from one spouse to the other, even though purchased from marital funds, has been held to constitute separate property in a number of dual property jurisdictions. *See, e.g., Ghali v. Ghali*, 596 S.W.2d 31 (Ky. Ct. App. 1980). Other dual property states, however, by statutory law, generally state that gifts between spouses are classified as marital property. *See, e.g.*, N.Y. Dom. Rel. Law § 236(B)(1)(d); Va. Code Ann. § 20–107.3(A)(1). The proposed ALI *Principles of the Law of Family Dissolution* § 4.03 (2) (1997) also state that "[i]nheritances, including bequests and devises, and gifts from third parties, are the separate property of the acquiring spouse, even if acquired during marriage." *Query:* What is the rationale for classifying gifts between the spouses as martial property, rather than separate property? *See generally* ALI, *Principles of the Law of Family Dissolution* § 403, Comment b (1997).

A gift has been described as a voluntary transfer of land or goods from one person to another, made gratuitously, and not based upon any consideration for services rendered. *See, e.g., Hull v. Hull*, 591 S.W.2d 376 (Mo. Ct. App. 1979); *Campion v. Campion*, 385 N.W.2d 1 (Minn. Ct. App. 1981). Thus, a crucial element of a gift is the *donative intent* of the donor, as opposed to consideration for prior or future services rendered. *See, e.g., In re Marriage of Simmons*, 581 N.E.2d 716, 719 (Ill. Ct. App. 1991); *In re Marriage of Johnson*, 856 S.W.2d 921 (Mo. Ct. App. 1993); *Dean v. Dean*, 379 S.E.2d 742 (Va. Ct. App. 1989).

NOTES AND QUESTIONS

(1) Assume that husband Hull, an attorney, had previously represented a particular client in a real estate matter and a divorce matter, and he was again retained by this same client when criminal charges were brought against her for murder. The client paid all Hull's fees for services rendered by him, and no bill was later rendered or was outstanding when the client was convicted of murder and sentenced to death by electric chair. In contemplation of the client's death by execution, she gave a power of attorney to Hull, and requested that he sell her personal property, pay her debts, and use the remainder of her estate for her funeral expenses. She expressed gratitude to Hull for having stood by her after her arrest for murder and during her prosecution. A deed to certain farm property (that was not prepared by Hull) was also included in the client's estate, and Hull believed from his prior conversations with his client that the farm would be conveyed to a relative of the client. Hull was therefore surprised to learn that this farm property, of substantial value, had been deeded over to Hull by his client.

During a subsequent divorce proceeding between Hull and his wife, Mrs. Hull's attorney argued that Hull's acquisition of the farm property arose from an attorney-client relationship and even though not accompanied by any express or implied agreement for the rendition of services, this transfer of the farm property was motivated at least by past services performed by Hull if not by future services to be rendered. Mrs. Hull's attorney therefore contended that Mrs. Hull is entitled to share in the division of the farm property because her support as a homemaker equates her as a marital partner in the fruits of her husband's business. On appeal, how should the appellate court decide this case? *See Hull v. Hull*, 591 S.W.2d 376, 380–81 (Mo. Ct. App. 1979).

(2) Assume that the shareholders of a corporation gave husband, a successful corporate executive, a "gift" of additional stock in the company for the purpose of "keeping him involved in the business." The shareholders testified that their donative intent and motivation in giving this gift of stock to the husband was not based on any services rendered by the husband, and was not meant to be compensation to the husband. On divorce, the wife argued that this "gift" of company stock was indeed compensation for services rendered, or to be rendered, by the husband and therefore constituted marital, rather than separate, property. How should the court decide this case? *See In re Marriage of Johnson*, 856 S.W.2d 921 (Mo. Ct. App. 1993). What about the question of donative intent when a transfer of property into joint tenancy is made to avoid probate or inheritance taxes—would this constitute a gift or not? *See, e.g., In re Marriage of Montcrief*, 535 P.2d 1137 (Colo. Ct. App. 1975)

(3) A frequently recurring issue in divorce litigation and the division of marital property involving donative intent is the distinction between a gift and a loan. Where no documentation exists, this distinction often exists only in the mind of the alleged donor. Thus, if the donor expected repayment, then such a transaction would amount to a loan and result in marital debt; but if the donor did not expect repayment, it would be a gift. *See generally* Brett R. Turner, Equitable Distribution of Property; § 6.29 (2d ed. 1994); Gregory, Swisher & Scheible-Wolf, Understanding Family Law § 9.06 (Matthew Bender 1995); J. Thomas Oldham, Divorce, Separation, and the Distribution of Property, § 6.02–6.03 (1997).

[G] Pensions and Retirement Benefits

[1] Complexity of Dividing Benefits

One of the most difficult and complex areas in classifying, valuing, and distributing marital property involves retirement benefits and pension plans. Where in the past only a small minority of Americans received or could afford to purchase such retirement benefits, today pensions and retirement plans are a well-established part of most employee benefit packages. In addition, state and federal tax laws have been modified a number of times to promote and encourage the establishment of post-retirement programs for corporate employees, as well as for self-employed individuals and other individuals. The inherent difficulty in evaluating these retirement benefits on divorce, however, is based upon the tremendous variety of such plans, since everything from a private Keogh Plan or IRA to a corporate non-contributing annuity can, in some sense, be considered under the general heading of a retirement plan or "pension." *See also* the ALI proposed *Principles of the Law of Family Dissolution* § 408(1) (1997): "(a) Vested pension rights are marital property to the extent they are earned during the marriage. (b) Contingent returns on labor performed during marriage, including unvested pension rights . . . are marital property to the extent they are earned during the marriage."

The major problem arises, however, once the pension or retirement plan, acquired during the marriage, has been found to constitute marital or community property, and a court must then value it and divide it equitably between the spouses. Unlike a car, a home, a boat, or other tangible property which can be valued at a given moment in time, the value of a pension or retirement plan is more difficult to determine, since it is based on a future distribution time when the employee retires. The valuation and distribution of such a pension or retirement plan therefore may be speculative since it is very difficult to project with certainty what in fact a pension or retirement plan will be worth ten or fifteen years in the future, or at the employee's actual retirement date. And even if such a value can be placed on a pension or retirement plan at a specific time in the future, the courts must still find an equitable method of distribution which is fair to the recipient and the payor alike.

Some pensions are funded by contributions from the employer only; some from the employee only; and some are mixed. The mix and formula can affect the interest which the employee has in the pension; the time at which the pension is available to the employee; and it may also confer benefits on the employee such as the ability to borrow a sum of money without the need for collateral, and at a low rate of interest. Most pensions require a minimum period of employment before they "vest" in the employee. This means that the employee's right to the pension will survive irrespective of whether he or she has been terminated or has voluntarily left employment. Some programs allow for a graduated vesting (e.g., 10% after three years, 33% after five years, etc.).

Even if the pension has vested, there is no right to receive payment for contributions made by the employee or the employer at any given moment until the pension "matures." Most pensions require that the employee reach a certain age before beginning to collect benefits, and such pensions provide a pay-out in the event that the employee dies before reaching this maturity date. Some pension programs also allow for a graduated maturity date so that the longer the employee remains on the job, the better pension benefits he or she will receive. Some programs provide an alternative maturity process whereby the employee can begin receiving benefits after so many years on the job. Thus a pension might be available to an employee at age 65 or after 30 years of continuous service, whichever comes first.

Generally, pension and retirement programs of nearly every variety are considered to be marital or community property to the extent they accrue during the course of the marriage. When a spouse's membership in a pension program commences prior to marriage, or the pension vests prior to marriage, then the court is faced with the issue of what part of this "mixed" pension property is marital property, and what part is separate property. Most states have amended their marital property statutes to include pensions as marital property which must be considered in any divorce or dissolution proceeding. *See, e.g.*, Va. Code Ann. § 20–107.3; N.C. Gen. Stat. §§ 50–20(b)(1), (2); Tenn. Code Ann. § 36–4–121.

Federal pensions, however, pose a somewhat different problem, since the Supremacy Clause of the United States Constitution forbids states from interfering with federal authority. Although family law historically has been largely regulated by the individual states, the federal Supremacy Clause can still be invoked when a federal interest is at stake, and such a federal interest has involved federal pension and retirement benefits. For example, in *Hisquierdo v. Hisquierdo*, 439 U.S. 572, 582 (1979), the United States Supreme Court struck down a state court ordered property division of a federal Railroad Retirement pension. The Supreme Court found that the court order determining the benefits to be community property would incur major damage to federal interests. The decision was based on provisions of the Act which indicated that the benefits were not assignable and could not be anticipated. 45 U.S.C. § 231. Subsequently, *Hisquierdo* was overruled in part by a 1983 statutory amendment which now allows some railroad retirement benefits to be classified as either community or marital property. The remainder of benefits under the federal

Railroad Retirement Act remain preempted, and state courts cannot consider those benefits when making a property division on divorce or dissolution of marriage. *See, e.g., Belt v. Belt*, 398 N.W.2d 737 (N.D. 1987).

A similar federal pension dispute arose concerning various benefits under the federal military pension system. In *McCarty v. McCarty*, 453 U.S. 210 (1981), the Supreme Court determined that federal benefits under a military pension were beyond the reach of state divorce courts for equitable distribution upon dissolution of the marriage. In 1983, however, Congress passed the Uniformed Services Former Spouses' Protection Act (USFSPA) in order to reverse the unfortunate effect of the *McCarty* decision on military spouses. Now, under USFSPA, 10 U.S.C. § 1401, the question of whether military retirement benefits are marital property and subject to division on divorce is now determined by the state courts, but this Act only applies if the state court has jurisdiction over the military service person by reason of residence, domicile or consent. Under the Act, benefits are limited to retirement payments or retainer pay from military service; although there are some jurisdictions which indicate that states may divide benefits beyond the literal language of the act. *See e.g. Luna v. Luna*, 125 Ariz. 120, 120, 608 P.2d 57 (Ariz. Ct. App. 1979); Kramer v. Kramer, 252 Neb. 526, 530, 567 N.W.2d 100 (Neb. 1997).

However, state courts cannot treat federal disability benefits as marital property "pension" benefits. *See Mansell v. Mansell*, 490 U.S. 581 (1989) (holding that federal disability benefits were *not* subject to equitable distribution on divorce or dissolution of marriage).

[2] Qualified Domestic Relations Orders (QDROs)

State courts must also determine the applicability of state equitable distribution laws to private pensions which are governed under ERISA (Employee Retirement Income Security Act, 29 U.S.C. §1001 *et seq.*). Although some thought that ERISA was preempted from the states' ability to divide interests in benefit plans because of an anti-assignment clause found within the Act, the passage of the Retirement Equity Act of 1984, 29 U.S.C. § 1056, now provides that any ERISA preemption would not apply if a state court issues a Qualified Domestic Relations Order (a QDRO).

A "qualified domestic relations order" is one "which creates or recognizes the existence of an alternate payee's right to, or assignment to alternate payee the right to, receive all or a portion of the benefits payable with respect to a participant under a [pension or retirement] plan." 29 U.S.C. § 1056(d)(3)(B)(i) (1984 amendment); I.R.C. § 414(p)(1)(A).

A QDRO must specify the name and last known mailing address of the participant and each alternate payee designated by the court order and the amount or percentage of benefits each alternate payee is to receive when the benefits are to be distributed. The QDRO must also specify the number of payments or the period for which the order is effective, and identify which retirement or pension plan (or plans) the order applies to. Upon receipt of a domestic relations order, the pension plan administrator must notify the participant and the alternate payee and distribute the money to the alternate payee. The plan administrator may defer payment for up to 18 months while seeking a judicial determination of whether the domestic relations order is a qualified domestic relations order. However, if the domestic relations order is found not to be a qualified domestic relations order, the plan administrator must pay the pension proceeds to the person who would have originally received the money had there been no order in the first place. *See generally* I.R.C. § 414(p)(2)–(7).

Caveat: In order to avoid unnecessary delays, confusion, and the unwelcome possibility of a subsequent legal malpractice suit based upon an unqualified Domestic Relations Order, legal counsel for the non-owner spouse should first request from the Pension Plan Administrator any model QDRO, and any required provisions to be included in such a QDRO to the particular Pension Plan Administrator's satisfaction; and counsel should then submit to the Pension Plan Administrator prior to the entry of any equitable distribution order by the court the proposed Order for review and advance approval that this proposed QDRO will be honored by the Pension Plan Administrator, and the benefits will be paid as stated therein. For an excellent resource in the complex subspecialty of drafting QDROs, see *How to Draft an Enforceable QDRO* (Divorce Taxation Education, Inc. 1987); O'Connell & Kittrell, *Federal Retirement Plans: Division of Benefits at Divorce* (Divorce Taxation Education, Inc. 1987).

[3] Valuing and Dividing Retirement Benefits

There are two distinct methods the courts have employed in valuing and distributing retirement benefits: (1) the "immediate offset" or "relative-value" method; and (2) the "deferred distribution" or "relative-time" method. Under the immediate offset or relative-value method of distributing pension or retirement benefits, the court awards the entire pension to the owning spouse, and gives the nonowning spouse a lump sum payment of money or property equal to his or her interest in the retirement plan. In order to apply this method, the court must determine the present value of the pension or retirement plan, often a complex calculation and invariably requiring expert testimony. *See, e.g., Schuenman v. Schuenman,* 591 N.E.2d 603 (Ind. Ct. App. 1992); *Zachery v. Zachery,* 551 So. 2d 577 (Fla. Dist. Ct. App. 1989); *Feathler v. Feathler,* 598 N.E.2d 671 (Mass. Ct. App. 1992).

Under the deferred distribution or relative-time method, the property division is made in the future on the basis of a percentage determined at the time of the divorce order. A number of courts have held that the present value of a pension or retirement plan is irrelevant under this method, a major advantage in choosing it over the immediate-offset method. *See, e.g., Tarr v. Tarr,* 570 A.2d 826 (Me. 1990); *Church v. Church,* 564 N.Y.S.2d 572 (App. Div. 1991). *See also* the proposed ALI Principles of the Law of Family Dissolution § 408 Comment *f* (1997) ("The relative-time rule establishes the marital property share of each annuity payment made under a defined benefit plan by multiplying the payment's full amount by the coverture factor. The relative-time rule has been widely followed and has the virtue of simplicity of application, and is probably the best method of apportioning defined-benefit pensions."). However, another line of cases holds that a pension should always be valued, even if a deferred distribution is made, since the amount of marital property is always relevant as a property division factor on divorce. *See, e.g., Nisos v. Nisos,* 483 A.2d 97, 103 (Md. Ct. App. 1984); *Connolly v. Connolly,* 591 N.E.2d 1362, 1364 (Ohio Ct. App. 1990). Moreover, ascertaining the present value of a pension or retirement plan may avoid the danger of including nonmarital monies in the computations. *See, e.g., Kilbride v. Kilbride,* 432 N.W.2d 324, 329 (Mich. Ct. App. 1988). Based upon the strengths and weaknesses of these two methods, and based on the wide variety of pension and retirement plans and benefits, defined and undefined, vested and unvested, some courts have applied these two approaches as alternative methods. See *generally* Brett R. Turner, Equitable Distribution of Property §§ 6–11,6–12 (2d ed. 1994); Gregory, Swisher, and Scheible-Wolf, Understanding Family Law § 9.10 (Matthew Bender 1995); J. Thomas Oldham, Divorce, Separation, and Distribution of Property; § 7.10 (1997).

The following case illustrates the "deferred distribution" or "relative-time" approach to the valuation and division of pension or retirement benefits on divorce or dissolution of marriage.

IN RE ROLFE v. ROLFE
Montana Supreme Court
766 P.2d 223 (1988)

This is an appeal from the Fourth Judicial District Court, Missoula County, Montana. Appellant Oliver Rolfe, appeals the District Court's . . . valuation of his retirement benefits. . . .

The husband's first issues focuses on the proper valuation for retirement benefits. It is well established in this state that retirement benefits are a part of the marital estate. The question is what value to assign to the pension for proper division of the marital asset. While we attempted to give instructions in our previous decision, we recognize such assets contain numerous contingencies, thereby avoiding categorical formulas. . . .

Generally, the proper test for determining the value of a pension is the present value. Given the various contingencies, however, present value may not be adequate to value the asset. For instance our earlier decision instructed the District Court to not only consider the amount of husband's contributions but also to consider nonvested pension benefits in the form of employer's future contributions. These nonvested amounts are analogous to deferred compensation which the husband earned during the marriage. The employer's future contributions, like husband's contributions, are a factor of monthly salary, an amount which could not be accurately determined. In addition, the plan's reduced benefit formulation varies significantly with the individual. Numerous other contingencies associated with retirement benefits, including early retirement or disability are equally elusive of accurate calculation.

Rather than attempt to project each individual contingency, the District Court developed a formula to divide the pension benefits:

Years of Service During Marriage/Years of Total Service $\times$ Monthly Benefit (after taxes) $\times$ ½

The division of retirement benefits upon receipt is commonly known as the "time rule." Under this method, the marital interest is represented by a fraction, the numerator of which is the length of the employee's service during the marriage and the denominator is the employee's total length of service. This fraction is then applied to each benefit payment, lump or period, to determine the portion earned during the marriage. Although the extent of the marital interest is determined as of the date of the dissolution, the benefit factors to be applied to the pension credits earned during the marriage are those in effect at retirement. Thus the non-employee spouse is entitled to increases or accruals on her interest because of the delay in receiving those benefits. . . .

Husband argues this formula impermissibly includes non-marital property in the form of future employee contributions, and does not finally apportion the marital estate. Husband would urge this court to value the pension as of the date of dissolution, yet suspend payment until he retires. This position is flawed in three respects. First, the monthly pension benefit is not determined by the amount of contributions, but instead by the highest average salary earned over the three consecutive years. Therefore, the only amounts which could arguably be called post-marital property are possible salary increases received prior to retirement. . . . The trial court expressly excluded any amounts unique to husband, such as merit pay raises. Second, each party is well aware of their respective percentage of pension benefits: the fraction represents the marital interest. Third, to value payments now without also demanding an immediate cash payment to wife, would result in an unfair windfall to husband. . . .

Husband also claims the order effectively binds him to continued employment with the University, and in turn, the [University retirement] plan. This Court fails to see the basis of husband's argument. On the contrary, the judgment allows Dr. Rolfe continued volitional choice. . . .

Additional guidelines as to division of the pension may be found in earlier cases:

> (1) The distribution should generally be based on contributions made during marriage. (2) The courts should continue to strive to disentangle the parties as much as possible by determining, where equitable, a sum certain to be paid rather than a percentage based upon expected future contingencies. (3) In determining whether a lump sum award is appropriate courts should consider the burden it would place on the paying spouse in view of required child support, spousal support and other property distribution. (4) Where courts determine that the parties will share in the benefits on a proportional basis, the parties should also share the risks of future contingencies, *e.g.*, death of the employee spouse or delayed retirement of the employee spouse, and payment should be to the receiving spouse as the employee spouse receives the retirement pay. (5) Courts should consider where appropriate an award of a portion of retirement benefits where other property awarded is not adequate to make an equitable distribution. . . .

NOTES AND QUESTIONS

(1) The payment of retirement benefits when they are received by the owner spouse is often called the "if, as, and when" method of payment. In *Barr v. Barr*, 473 A.2d 1300, 1311 (Md. Ct. App. 1984), *cert. denied*, 481 A.2d 239 (Md. 1984), for example, the court offered the following three alternatives a judge might employ in valuing and distributing pension or retirement benefits:

> The Court of Appeals has discussed the three methods of determining the proper allocation of retirements benefits between the parties. . . . These were: (1) to award an appropriate share of the contributions of the earning spouse to the non-earning spouse, (2) to compute and award the benefits as based upon their present value (but this was recognized as a very difficult calculation which should not be used where it become too speculative), or (3) to determine a fixed percentage of the benefits to be paid the non-earning spouse if, as, and when paid to the earning spouse.

(2) **Problem.** Husband and Wife were involved in a divorce proceeding. The major issue on appeal was Husband's pension plan evaluation and, specifically, the Cost of Living Allowance (COLA) provision contained in his pension plan. *Query:* Does the fact that a COLA is uncertain, and subject to many different contingencies, prevent the COLA from being considered in a plan to divide the husband's pension when at least part of the pension was earned during the course of the marriage? Should a present value be placed on the COLA when the rest of the marital property is divided, or should a future distribution plan

be developed by the court to deal with the COLA? *See Moore v. Moore*, 553 A.2d 20 (N.J. 1989).

(3) **Problem.** Husband and Wife were married for twenty-five years. Husband was married for nearly all of the time that he was employed at XYZ Corporation. He retired from XYZ Corporation two years before the parties' divorce. The trial court in the parties' divorce proceeding awarded Wife 4/5ths of the value of the husband's pension plan from XYZ Corporation, and 4/5ths of his Social Security benefits. Husband appealed, claiming that an award of 4/5ths of his retirement plan to his wife was arbitrary and unreasonable, and that federal law preempted state law regarding his social security benefits. How should the appellate court rule? *See Cruise v. Cruise,* 374 S.E.2d 882 (N.C. Ct. App. 1989); 42 U.S.C. § 402(b)(1), (d)(1). *Cf. Mosley v. Mosley,* 450 S.E.2d 161 (Va. Ct. App. 1994) (holding that it was error to award the wife 50% of husband's 20-year military retirement pension when the parties had been married for 17 years, and when the state equitable distribution statute prohibited awarding more than 50% of any pension or retirement benefit to the non-owning spouse).

[H] Deferred Compensation Benefits: Separate or Marital Property?

Separate property normally includes property acquired after divorce, or property acquired after the last separation of the spouses, depending on a state law. Normally, when marital contributions create property value, this value normally accrues at the time the marital contribution was made. Sometimes, however, the spouses, or either of them, make a present contribution of marital effort in order to receive some future economic benefit. When this occurs, the future economic benefit normally is deemed to be acquired when the marital contribution is made, and not when the deferred economic benefit is actually received. *See generally* Brett Turner, Equitable Distribution of Property 156–59 (2d ed. 1994). *See also* the proposed ALI *Principles of the Law of Family Dissolution* § 4.08 (1) (1997): ("Property earned by labor performed during marriage is marital property whether received before, during, or after the marriage. Property earned by labor not performed during the marriage is the separate property of the laboring spouse even if received during marriage.")

For example, a 1997 Connecticut trial court divorce case of *Wendt v. Wendt* has received national media attention and has ignited a national debate over the role of "corporate wives" and their right to deferred compensation from their "corporate husbands" (and vice versa). In that case, Mrs. Wendt, a 54-year-old housewife, turned down an offer from her husband for approximately eleven million dollars in alimony and division of marital assets, arguing that she deserved exactly half of the parties' marital estate based upon her 31 years as a "corporate wife." Although the parties' valuation of their marital assets was in dispute, Mr. Wendt, an executive for General Electric, insisted that his net worth was approximately twenty-one million dollars at the time the parties separated, but he admitted that his net worth had approximately doubled to forty-two million dollars since the parties' separation, based in large part on his unvested stock options from General Electric. Mrs. Wendt testified that she contributed 50–50 to the parties' 31-year marital partnership. In addition to raising their children and working in the home, Mrs. Wendt also testified that she had given her husband advice on job applicants, and served as hostess for lavish corporate-related parties and business dinners, with a number involving foreign dignitaries. Mr. Wendt, 55, who had a successful 21-year career with General Electric, insisted that the family's fortune came from his hard work, and not from his wife's housekeeping, and that eleven million dollars in property and alimony was all Mrs. Wendt needed to "live comfortably." Mrs. Wendt responded that need wasn't the issue; that she deserved one-half of the assets of her marital partnership, and that was the major issue.

On December 4, 1997, in a 450–page opinion (summarized into 25 pages) Connecticut Superior Court Judge Kevin Tierney awarded Mrs. Wendt twenty million dollars in cash, investments, real estate, and deferred compensation benefits ruling that "a portion of [Mr. Wendt's] unvested stock options is marital property and should be shared by a corporate wife." The case is currently on appeal. *See* The Washington Post, December 4, 1997 at A-1; The Wall Street Journal, December 4, 1997 at B-1 ("Lawyers and scholars predicted before the ruling that [this case] would be closely studied and could be influential in other cases").

PROBLEMS

(1) Wendy purchased a state lottery ticket. The ticket was a winner in the amount of $6,000,000. At the time she purchased the ticket, Wendy was living with her husband, Harold, but within two days the couple separated. At the time the winning lottery numbers were announced, Wendy and Harold were living separate and apart prior to bringing a divorce action. The lottery ticket cost two dollars and had come from Wendy's "rainy-day savings." The multi-year payout on Wendy's lottery winnings is to begin after the date of the parties' divorce. Should these lottery winnings constitute marital property, subject to equitable distribution on divorce, or separate property? What if this lottery ticket was purchased after the couple had been separated, but before any divorce proceedings had been commenced? *See, e.g., Giedinghagen v. Giedinghagen*, 712 S.W.2d 711 (Mo. Ct. App. 1986); *In re Marriage of Mahaffey*, 564 N.E.2d 1300 (Ill. App. Ct. 1990); *Smith v. Smith*, 557 N.Y.S.2d 22 (App. Div. 1990); *Giha v. Giha*, 609 A.2d 945 (R.I. 1992).

(2) Now assume that, during their marriage, Harold had written a successful novel and sold his movie rights to a major motion picture studio. Is Wendy entitled to part of Harold's future royalties, profits, and other intellectual property rights as marital or community property, even though Harold will not receive any compensation until after the dissolution of their marriage? Why or why not? *See, e.g., In re Zaent*, 267 Cal. Rptr. 31 (Cal. Ct. App. 1990); *In re Marriage of Worth*, 241 Cal. Rptr. 135 (Cal. Ct. App. 1987).

(3) Now assume that one of the spouses in a divorce action was a trial lawyer, working over the past two years on a large class action tort action on a contingency fee arrangement. Assume that this case had not yet come to trial or settlement at the time of the parties' divorce, but that settlement was anticipated in another year or two. How should the judge classify and apportion such property? *See In re Kilbourne*, 284 Cal. Rptr. 201 (Cal. Ct. App. 1991).

[I] Personal Injury and Workers' Compensation Awards

Equitable distribution jurisdictions have reached different results in the treatment of compensation resulting from personal injury awards and workers' compensation awards. The first issue is do these awards actually constitute property? Arguably, if a personal injury award or a workers' compensation award is received during the marriage, then it would in fact constitute "property acquired during the marriage." *See, e.g., Mistler v. Mistler*, 816

S.W.2d 241, 249 (Mo. Ct. App. 1991). A personal injury action or workers' compensation claim that is pending at the time of a divorce, however, is another matter. There is no assurance that such a cause of action will be successful, since the plaintiff spouse may lose in litigation, or be unable to settle the case, and the amount of settlement, or the jury verdict, also may be speculative. Due to these uncertainties involving pending personal injury or workers' compensation claims, a number of states have held that a pending cause of action for personal injury does not constitute "property." See, e.g., *Murphy v. Murphy*, 510 N.E.2d 235 (Ind. Ct. App. 1987); *Unkle v. Unkle*, 505 A.2d 849 (Md. 1986), *superseded by statute*; *Petrini v. Petrini*, 648 A.2d 1016 (Md. 1994); *Amato v. Amato*, 434 A.2d 639 (N.J. Super. 1981). The better reasoned majority view, however, is that a pending personal injury claim does in fact constitute property, and such a pending claim is no more uncertain than unvested pension and retirement plans, which also constitute property in almost every state. See, e.g., *Raccio v. Raccio*, 556 A.2d 639 (Conn. 1987); *Hanify v. Hanify*, 526 N.E.2d 1056 (Mass. 1988); *Heilman v. Heilman*, 291 N.W.2d 183 (Mich. Ct. App. 1980); *Covington v. Covington*, 412 S.E.2d 455 (S.C. Ct. App. 1991) See also § 10.02[G], above.

Assuming that such personal injury awards or workers' compensation awards do in fact constitute property, the next issue is whether this property constitutes marital or community property, separate property, or mixed property. A small minority of states have amended their equitable distribution statutes to expressly state how personal injury and workers' compensation awards should be classified. See, e.g., Va. Code Ann. § 20–107.3 (H) (1993) (stating that the "marital share" of a personal injury or workers' compensation award "means that part of the total personal injury or workers' compensation recovery attributable to lost wages or medical expenses to the extent not covered by health insurance"); N.Y. Dom. Rel. Law § 236B(1)(d)(2) (1989) (defining separate property to include compensation for personal injuries); Ark. Code Ann. § 9–12–315(b)(6) (1993) (stating that compensation for permanent disability and future medical expenses is separate property; and the remainder of the award, including pain and suffering, is marital property). The proposed ALI *Principles of the Law of Family Dissolution* § 408(2)(a) (1997) provide,

> (a) Insurance proceeds and personal injury recoveries are marital property to the extent that entitlement to them arises from the loss of a marital asset, including income that the beneficiary-spouse would have earned during the marriage. The dissolution court may make a reasonable allocation of an undifferentiated award between its marital and separate property components.
>
> (b) Disability pay and workers' compensation payments are marital property to the extent they replace income or benefits the recipient would have earned during the marriage but for the qualifying disability or injury.

In the absence of a state equitable distribution statute specifically addressing personal injury or workers' compensation awards, however, the state courts have adopted one of two approaches in analyzing personal injury and workers' compensation awards: (1) the "mechanistic" approach; and (2) the "analytic" approach.

Courts applying the mechanistic approach look to see if a personal injury or workers' compensation award is expressly defined as separate property within a state's equitable distribution statute, and if not, such property is presumed to be marital property. For example, in the case of *Gan v. Gan*, 404 N.E.2d 306, 309 (Ill. App. Ct. 1980), an Illinois appellate court stated,

The husband's personal injury settlement does not fit within any of the exceptions to marital property enumerated in the [Illinois Equitable Distribution Act]. Thus the presumption that the personal injury settlement was marital property. . . . was raised. In accordance with [this] statutory presumption the personal injury settlement proceeds must be deemed marital property.

See also *In re Marriage of Burt*, 494 N.E.2d 868 (Ill. App. Ct. 1986). A number of other states also follow this mechanistic approach. *See, e.g., In re Marriage of Fields,* 779 P.2d 1371 (Colo. Ct. App. 1989); *Riddle v. Riddle,* 566 N.E.2d 78 (Ind. Ct. App. 1991); *Dalessio v. Dalessio,* 570 N.E.2d 139 (Mass. 1991); *Bywater v. Bywater,* 340 N.W.2d 102 (Mich. Ct. App. 1983); *Kozich v. Kozich,* 580 A.2d 390 (Pa. Super. Ct. 1990); *Marsh v. Marsh,* 437 S.E.2d 34 (S.C. 1993).

Other courts, however, apply an analytic approach, and these courts have found that a personal injury award can be part separate property, since a substantial portion of the award is personal to the injured spouse, and part martial property. For example, in the case of *Hardy v. Hardy,* 413 S.E.2d 151, 154 (W. Va. 1991), the West Virginia Supreme Court noted,

[To] the extent that its purpose is to compensate an individual for pain, suffering, disability, disfigurement, or other debilitation of the mind or body, a personal injury award constitutes the separate nonmarital property of an injured spouse. However, economic losses, such as past wages and medical expenses, which diminish the marital estate are distributable as marital property when recovered in a personal injury award or settlement. The burden of proving the purpose of part or all of a personal injury recovery is on the party seeking a nonmarital classification.

Likewise, a New Jersey court in *Amato v. Amato,* 434 A.2d 639, 643 (N.J. Super. Ct. App. Div. 1981) stated,

Nothing is more personal than the entirely subjective sensations of agonizing pain, mental anguish, embarrassment because of scarring or disfigurement, and outrage attending severe bodily injury. Mental injury, as well, has many of these characteristics. Equally personal are the effects of even mild or moderately severe injury. None of these, including the frustrations of diminution or loss of normal body functions or movements can be sensed, or need they be borne, by anyone but the injured spouse. Why, then, should the law, seeking to be equitable, coin these factors into money to even partially benefit the uninjured and estranged spouse? . . . The only [marital] damages are . . . the diminution of the marital estate by loss of past wages or expenditure of money for medical expenses. Any other apportionment is unfair distribution.

A number of other states have adopted this analytic approach, distinguishing between separate property compensation for an individual spouse's personal injury and pain and suffering from marital lost wages and medical expenses. *See, e.g., Bandow v. Bandow,* 794 P.2d 1346 (Alaska 1990); *Jurek v. Jurek,* 606 P.2d 812 (Ariz. 1980); *Weisfeld v. Weisfeld,* 513 So. 2d 1278 (Fla. Dist. Ct. App. 1987), *approved and remanded,* 545 So. 2d 1341 (Fla. 1989); *Van de Loo v. Van de Loo,* 346 N.W.2d 173 (Minn. Ct. App. 1984); *Mistler v. Mistler,* 816 S.W.2d 241 (Mo. Ct. App. 1991); *Rich v. Rich,* 483 N.Y.S.2d 150 (Sup. Ct. 1984); *Taylor v. Taylor,* 827 P.2d 911 (Okla. Ct. App. 1992); *Brown v. Brown,* 675

P.2d 1207 (Wash. 1984). *And see generally* Gregory, Swisher & Scheible-Wolf, Understanding Family Law § 9.07 (1995); Brett R. Turner, Equitable Distribution of Property §§ 6.17–6.19 (2d ed. 1994).

Query: Which is the better reasoned approach, in your opinion, regarding the distribution of personal injury and workers' compensation awards on divorce or dissolution of marriage—the mechanistic or the analytic approach? Does the appropriateness of one or the other approach depend on whether the particular jurisdiction is a dual property or all property state? What burden of proof problems would you anticipate applying the analytic approach?

NOTES AND QUESTIONS

(1) What if the personal injury occurs before the marriage, but recovery of the personal injury award occurs after the parties are married. Should this be classified as marital or separate property? Why? *See Weakley v. Weakley,* 731 S.W.2d 243 (Ky. 1987). What if the lawsuit is not for personal injuries, but rather for money damages based on an alleged breach of contract? Should the pending proceeds from such a lawsuit be classified as marital or separate property? *See Hanify v. Hanify,* 526 N.E.2d 1056 (Mass. 1988).

(2) **Problem.** Wendy and Harold were married in July of 1977. This was a second marriage for each of them, and no children were born of the marriage. Approximately three years after their marriage, Harold shot Wendy at close range, attempting to kill her. Harold then attempted to commit suicide by shooting himself under the chin with his rifle. Seven months later, Harold initiated a divorce action against Wendy. Wendy counterclaimed for divorce and also subsequently filed a personal injury action against Harold. The judge entered a partial summary judgment on behalf of Harold, stating that Wendy's negligence claim against Harold was barred by interspousal tort immunity (*see* § 6.03[A], *above*) in that State, while permitting Wendy to continue to pursue an intentional tort claim against Harold.

The divorce was granted, and Harold brought a motion for summary judgment in Wendy's pending intentional tort action, alleging that this matter had, in effect, been decided in the divorce action because the alimony and property division had taken into account the shooting injuries suffered by Wendy. The judge agreed with Harold, citing the doctrine of res judicata, and he dismissed Wendy's tort action against Harold. Wendy has appealed this decision of the trial court. Assume that you are the clerk for the appellate judge who must recommend a disposition for this case. What would you recommend to the judge, and why? *See, e.g., Noble v. Noble,* 761 P.2d 1369 (Utah 1988). *See also* Barbara Young, *Interspousal Torts and Divorce: Problems, Policies, and Procedures* 27 J. Fam. L. 489 (1988–89); Douglas Scherer, Tort Remedies for Victims of Domestic Abuse, 43 S.C. L. Rev. 543 (1992); Daniel Barker, *Interspousal Immunity and Domestic Torts: A New Twist on the "War of the Roses,"* 15 Am. J. Trial Advoc. 625 (1992).

(3) Workers' compensation claims are generally handled by courts in a fashion similar to personal injury claims. However, when the basis of the award is more directly related to a specific physical injury of the spouse, courts are less likely to characterize them as marital property. *See, e.g., Gerlich v. Gerlich,* 379 N.W.2d 689, 691 (Minn. Ct. App. 1986),

where the court determined that the award was based on the degree to which the husband's back, legs and sexual functions were injured on the job, and thus held that the award was separate property and *Queen v. Queen*, 521 A.2d 320, 327 (Md. 1987), where the court held that only that portion of the husband's permanent partial disability award received one year before the divorce for injuries sustained during the marriage, which was compensation for the loss of earning capacity during the marriage, was marital property. But any compensation for loss of future earning capacity beyond the time of dissolution of the marriage was separate property. *See also In re Cupp*, 730 P.2d 870 (Ariz. Ct. App. 1987); *Crocker v. Crocker*, 824 P.2d 1117 (Okla. 1991).

[J] Professional Degrees and Licenses

When one spouse earns a professional degree, certificate, or license, the expected result is a substantially increased earning capacity and enhanced future income. In a divorce setting, the issue is whether the other spouse, who often works and contributes toward obtaining this professional degree or license, should be entitled to at least a share of this enhanced earning capacity and future income.

The potential for an enhanced earning capacity resulting from a professional degree or license raises two important questions. First, whether a professional degree or license constitutes property, or whether it is so uniquely personal that it cannot have property status. Second, if the professional degree or license is found to constitute property, and if it can be classified as marital in nature, how should such a professional degree or license be valued? For example, should the value of a professional degree or license be determined according to the nature and amount of the other spouse's contribution in earning it; or should its value be determined according to possible future income?

One remedy to this so-called "diploma dilemma" would be to treat a professional degree or license as marital property, like pension and retirement benefits. To date, however, the overwhelming majority of courts that have addressed this issue have concluded that a professional degree or license is not property, and therefore it cannot be divided on divorce. The Colorado Supreme Court, in the case of *In re Marriage of Graham*, 574 P.2d 75, 77 (Colo. 1978) concluded,

> An educational degree, such as an M.B.A., is simply not encompassed even by the broad views of the concept of "property." It does not have an exchange value or any objective transferable value on an open market. It is personal to the holder. It terminates on the death of the holder and is not inheritable. It cannot be assigned, sold, transferred, conveyed, or pledged. An advanced degree is a cumulative product of many years of previous education, combined with diligence and hard work. It may not be acquired by the mere expenditure of money. It is simply an intellectual achievement that may potentially assist in the future acquisition of property. In our view, it has none of the attributes of property in the usual sense of the word.

In accord that a professional degree or license does not constitute divisible property are Hernandez v. Hernandez, 444 So. 2d 35 (Fla. Dist. Ct. App. 1983); *Lowery v. Lowery*, 413 S.E.2d 731 (Ga. 1992); *In re Marriage of Weinstein*, 470 N.E.2d 551 (Ill. App. Ct. 1984); *Archer v. Archer*, 493 A.2d 1074 (Md. 1985); *Mahoney v. Mahoney*, 453 A.2d 527 (N.J. 1982); *Stevens v. Stevens*, 492 N.E.2d 131 (Ohio 1986); *Hodge v. Hodge*, 520 A.2d 15 (Pa. 1986); *Helm v. Helm*, 345 S.E.2d 720 (S.C. 1986); *Frausto v. Frausto*, 611 S.W.2d

656 (Tex. Ct. App. 1980); *Hoak v. Hoak*, 370 S.E.2d 473 (W. Va. 1988) and numerous other cases. *See also* the proposed ALI *Principles of the Law of Family Dissolution* § 4.07 (2) (1997) ("Occupational licenses and educational degrees are not property divisible on divorce."). *And see generally* Gregory, Swisher, and Scheible-Wolf, Understanding Family Law § 9.08 (Matthew Bender 1995); J. Thomas Oldham, Divorce, Separation, and the Distribution of Property §§ 9.01–9.02 (1997).

Courts in New York and Michigan, however, have held that a professional degree or license does in fact constitute marital property within the meaning of their equitable distribution statute, as illustrated in the landmark New York case of *O'Brien v. O'Brien*.

O'BRIEN v. O'BRIEN
New York Court of Appeals
489 N.E.2d 712 (1985)

SIMONS, JUDGE.

In this divorce action, the parties' only asset of any consequence is the husband's newly acquired license to practice medicine. The principal issue presented is whether that license, acquired during their marriage, is marital property subject to equitable distribution under Domestic Relations Law § 236(B)(5). . . .

Plaintiff and defendant married on April 3, 1971. At the time both were employed as teachers at the same private school. Defendant had a bachelor's degree and a temporary teaching certificate but required 18 months of postgraduate classes at an approximate cost of $3,000, excluding living expenses, to obtain permanent certification in New York. She claimed, and the trial court found, that she had relinquished the opportunity to obtain permanent certification while plaintiff pursued his education. At the time of the marriage, plaintiff had completed only three and one-half years of college, but shortly afterward he returned to school at night to earn his bachelor's degree and to complete sufficient premedical courses to enter medical school. In September 1973 the parties moved to Guadalajara, Mexico, where plaintiff became a full-time medical student. While he pursued his studies defendant held several teaching and tutorial positions and contributed her earnings to their joint expenses. The parties returned to New York in December 1976 so that plaintiff could complete the last two semesters of medical school and internship training here. After they returned, defendant resumed her former teaching position and she remained in it at the time this action was commenced. Plaintiff was licensed to practice medicine in October 1980. He commenced this action for divorce two months later. At the time of trial, he was a resident in general surgery.

During the marriage both parties contributed to paying the living and educational expenses and they received additional help from both of their families. They disagreed on the amounts of their respective contributions but it is undisputed that in addition to performing household work and managing the family finances defendant was gainfully employed throughout the marriage, that she contributed all of her earnings to their living and educational expenses and that her financial contributions exceeded those of plaintiff. The trial court found that she had contributed 76% of the parties' income exclusive of a $10,000 student loan obtained by defendant. Finding that plaintiff's medical degree and license are marital property, the court received evidence of its value and ordered a distributive award to defendant.

Defendant presented expert testimony that the present value of plaintiff's medical license was $472,000. Her expert testified that he had arrived at this figure by comparing the average income of a college graduate and that of a general surgeon between 1985, when plaintiff's residency would end, and 2012, when he would reach age 65. After considering Federal income taxes, an inflation rate of 10% and a real interest rate of 3% he capitalized the difference in average earnings and reduced the amount to present value. He also gave his opinion that the present value of defendant's contribution to plaintiff's medical education was $103,390. Plaintiff offered no expert testimony on the subject.

The court, after considering the life-style that plaintiff would enjoy from the enhanced earning potential his medical license would bring and defendant's contributions and efforts toward attainment of it, made a distributive award to her of $188,800, representing 40% of the value of the license, and ordered it paid in two annual installments of various amounts beginning November 1, 1982 and ending November 1, 1992. The court also directed plaintiff to maintain a life insurance policy on his life for defendant's benefit for the unpaid balance of the award and it ordered plaintiff to pay defendant's counsel fees of $7,000 and her expert witness fee of $1,000. It did not award defendant maintenance.

[The] Appellate Division . . . concluded that a professional license acquired during marriage is not marital property subject to distribution. It therefore modified the judgment by striking the trial court's determination that it is and by striking the provision ordering payment of the expert witness for evaluating the license and remitted the case for further proceedings.

On these cross appeals, defendant seeks reinstatement of the judgment of the trial court. Plaintiff contends that the Appellate Division correctly held that a professional license is not marital property but he also urges that the trial court failed to adequately explain what factors it relied on in making its decision, that it erroneously excluded evidence of defendant's marital fault and that the trial court's awards for attorneys and expert witness fees were improper.

The Equitable Distribution law contemplates only two classes of property: marital property and separate property (Domestic Relations Law § 236 [B][1][c], [d]). The former, which is subject to equitable distribution, is defined broadly as "all property acquired by either or both spouses during the marriage and before the execution of a separation agreement or the commencement of a matrimonial action, *regardless of the form in which title is held*" (Domestic Relations Law § 236(B)(1)(1)(c) [emphasis added]; *see* § 236(B)(5)(b), (c)). Plaintiff does not contend that his license is excluded from distribution because it is separate property; rather, he claims that it is not property at all but represents a personal attainment in acquiring knowledge. He rests his argument on decisions in similar cases from other jurisdictions and on his view that a license does not satisfy common-law concepts of property. Neither contention is controlling. Instead, our statute recognizes that spouses have an equitable claim to things of value arising out of the marital relationship and classifies them as subject to distribution by focusing on the marital status of the parties at the time of acquisition. Those things acquired during marriage and subject to distribution have been classified as "marital property" although, as one commentator has observed, they hardly fall within the traditional property concepts because there is no common-law property interest remotely resembling marital property. "It is a statutory creature, is of no meaning whatsoever during the normal course of a marriage and arises full-grown, like Athena, upon the signing of a separation agreement or the commencement of a matrimonial action." . . . Having classified the "property" subject to distribution, the Legislature did not attempt to go further and define it but left it to the courts to determine what interests come within the terms of § 236(B)(l)(c).

We made such a determination in *Majauskas v. Majauskas*, 463 N.E.2d 15 (N.Y. 1984), holding there that vested but unmatured pension rights are marital property subject to equitable distribution. Because pension benefits are not specifically identified as marital property in the statute, we looked to the express reference to pension rights contained in § 236(b)(5)(d)(4), which deals with equitable distribution of marital property, to other provisions of the equitable distribution statute and to the legislative intent behind its enactment to determine whether pension rights are marital property or separate property. A similar analysis is appropriate here and leads to the conclusion that marital property encompasses a license to practice medicine to the extent that the license is acquired during marriage.

Section 236 provides that in making an equitable distribution of marital property, "the court shall consider: (6) any equitable claim to, interest in, or direct or indirect contribution made to the acquisition of such marital property by the party not having title, including joint efforts or expenditures and contributions and services as a spouse, parent, wage earner and homemaker, and *to the career or career potential* of the other [and] (9) the impossibility or difficulty of evaluating any component asset or any interest in a business, corporation or *profession*" (Domestic Relations Law § 236(B)(5)(d)(6), (9) (emphasis added)). Where equitable distribution of marital property is appropriate but "the distribution of an interest in a business, corporation or *profession* would be contrary to law: the court shall make a distributive award in lieu of an actual distribution of the property" (Domestic Relations Law § 236(B)(5)(e) (emphasis added)). The words mean exactly what they say: that an interest in a profession or professional career potential is marital property which may be represented by direct or indirect contributions of the non-title-holding spouse, including financial contributions and nonfinancial contributions made by caring for the home and family. . . .

The determination that a professional license is marital property is also consistent with the conceptual base upon which the statute rests. As this case demonstrates, few undertakings during a marriage better qualify as the type of joint effort that the statute's economic partnership theory is intended to address than contributions toward one spouse's acquisition of a professional license. Working spouses are often required to contribute substantial income as wage earners, sacrifice their own educational or career goals and opportunities for child rearing, perform the bulk of household duties and responsibilities and forego the acquisition of marital assets that could have been accumulated if the professional spouse had been employed rather than occupied with the study and training necessary to acquire a professional license. In this case, nearly all of the parties' nine-year marriage was devoted to the acquisition of plaintiff's medical license and defendant played a major role in that project. She worked continuously during the marriage and contributed all of her earnings to their joint effort, she sacrificed her own educational and career opportunities, and she traveled with plaintiff to Mexico for three and one-half years while he attended medical school there. The Legislature has decided, by its explicit reference in the statute to the contributions of one spouse to the other's profession or career, that these contributions represent investments in the economic partnership of the marriage and that the product of the parties' joint efforts, the professional license, should be considered marital property.

The majority at the Appellate Division held that the cited statutory provisions do not refer to the license held by a professional who has yet to establish a practice but only to a going professional practice. There is no reason in law or logic to restrict the plain language of the statute to existing practices, however, for it is of little consequence in making an award of marital property, except for the purpose of evaluation, whether the professional spouse has already established a practice or whether he or she has yet to do so. An established practice merely represents the exercise of the privileges conferred upon the professional spouse by the license and the income flowing from that practice represents the receipt of the enhanced earning capacity that licensure allows. That being so, it would be unfair not to consider the license a marital asset.

Plaintiff's principal argument, adopted by the majority below, is that a professional license is not marital property because it does not fit within the traditional view of property as something which has an exchange value on the open market and is capable of sale, assignment or transfer. The position does not withstand analysis for at least two reasons. First, as we have observed, it ignores the fact that whether a professional license constitutes marital property is to be judged by the language of the statute which created this new species of property previously unknown at common law or under prior statutes. Thus, whether the license fits within traditional property concepts is of no consequence. Second, it is an overstatement to assert that a professional license could not be considered property even outside the context of § 236(B). A professional license is a valuable property right, reflected in the money, effort and lost opportunity for employment expended in its acquisition, and also in the enhanced earning capacity it affords its holder, which may not be revoked without due process of law. That a professional license has no market value is irrelevant. Obviously, a license may not be alienated as may other property and for that reason the working spouse's interest in it is limited. The Legislature has recognized that limitation, however, and has provided for an award in lieu of its actual distribution (*see*, Domestic Relations Law § 236(B)(5)(e)).

Plaintiff also contends that alternative remedies should be employed such as an award of rehabilitative maintenance or reimbursement for direct financial contributions. The statute does not expressly authorize retrospective maintenance or rehabilitative awards and we have no occasion to decide in this case whether the authority to do so may ever be implied from its provisions. . . . It is sufficient to observe that normally a working spouse should not be restricted to that relief because to do so frustrates the purposes underlying the Equitable Distribution Law. Limiting a working spouse to a maintenance award, either general or rehabilitative, not only is contrary to the economic partnership concept underlying the statute but also retains the uncertain and inequitable economic ties of dependence that the Legislature sought to extinguish by equitable distribution. Maintenance is subject to termination upon the recipient's remarriage and a working spouse may never receive adequate consideration for his or her contribution and may even be penalized for the decision to remarry if that is the only method of compensating the contribution. . . . The Legislature stated its intention to eliminate such inequities by providing that a supporting spouse's "direct or indirect contribution" be recognized, considered and rewarded (Domestic Relations Law § 236(B)(5)(d)(6)).

Turning to the question of valuation, it has been suggested that even if a professional license is considered marital property, the working spouse is entitled only to reimbursement of his or her direct financial contributions. . . . By parity of reasoning, a spouse's down payment on real estate or contribution to the purchase of securities would be limited to the money contributed, without any remuneration for any incremental value in the asset because of price appreciation. Such a result is completely at odds with the statute's requirement that the court give full consideration to both direct and indirect contributions "made to the acquisition of such marital property by the party not having title, including joint *efforts* or expenditures and *contributions and services as a spouse, parent,* wage earner and *homemaker*" (Domestic Relations Law § 236(B)(5)(d)(6) (emphasis added)). If the license is marital property, then the working spouse is entitled to an equitable portion of it, not a return of funds advanced. Its value is the enhanced earning capacity it affords the holder and although fixing the present value of that enhanced earning capacity may present problems, the problems are not insurmountable. Certainly they are no more difficult than computing tort damages for wrongful death or diminished earning capacity resulting from injury and they differ only in degree from the problems presented when valuing a professional practice for purposes of a distributive award, something the courts have not hesitated to do. The trial court retains the flexibility and discretion to structure the distributive award equitably, taking into consideration factors such as the working spouse's need for immediate payment, the licensed spouse's current ability to pay and the income tax consequences of prolonging the period of payment (*see,* Internal Revenue Code [26 U.S.C.] § 71(a)(1); (c)(2); Treas. Reg. [26 CFR] § 1.71–1(d)(4)) and, once it has received evidence of the present value of the license and the working spouse's contributions toward its acquisition and considered the remaining factors mandated by the statute (*see,* Domestic Relations Law § 236(B)(5)(d)(1)–(10)), it may then make an appropriate distribution of the marital property including a distributive award for the professional license if such an award is warranted. When other marital assets are of sufficient value to provide for the supporting spouse's equitable portion of the marital property, including his or her contributions to the acquisition of the professional license, however, the court retains the discretion to distribute these other marital assets or to make a distributive award in lieu of an actual distribution of the value of the professional spouse's license.

Accordingly, in view of our holding that plaintiff's license to practice medicine is marital property, the order of the Appellate Division should be modified, with costs to defendant, by reinstating the judgment and the case remitted to the Appellate Division for determination of the facts, including the exercise of that court's discretion (CPLR 5613), and, as so modified, affirmed. . . .

NOTES AND QUESTIONS

(1) The fundamental issue in *O'Brien,* and in numerous other cases, is whether or not a professional degree or license earned during a marriage is marital property. *O'Brien* answered this question in the affirmative. *Query:* Based on what underlying rationales? *See Woodworth v. Woodworth*, 337 N.W.2d 332 (Mich. Ct. App. 1983); *Postema v. Postema*, 471 N.W.2d 912 (Mich. Ct. App. 1991) (both holding that professional degrees and licenses constituted property). *Contra, Krause v. Krause*, 441 N.W.2d 66 (Mich. Ct. App. 1989);

Olah v. Olah, 354 N.W.2d 359 (Mich. Ct. App. 1984). Hopefully, the Michigan Supreme Court will soon address this appellate court split in Michigan regarding the characterization of professional degrees and licenses.

For excellent discussions of how a professional license of degree should be valued, see *Jones v. Jones*, 543 N.Y.S.2d 1016 (N.Y. Sup. Ct. 1989); *Allocco v. Allocco*, 578 N.Y.S.2d 995 (N.Y. Sup. Ct. 1991). *Cf. Dugue v. Dugue*, 568 N.Y.S.2d 244 (App. Div. 1991) (holding that the burden of proving the value of a professional degree or license is on the spouse seeking the award, and where that burden is not met, the professional degree or license should not be divided); *Duspiva v. Duspiva*, 581 N.Y.S.2d 376 (App. Div. 1992) (holding that where wife made no substantial career sacrifice and did not work outside the home, she was not entitled to any part of husband's future earnings from his certification as a C.P.A.).

A majority of states, have rejected the *O'Brien* rationale due to the intangible nature of a professional degree or license, the personal nature of the degree to the person who obtains it, and the inability to value the degree in any meaningful way. *See generally* Brett R. Turner, Equitable Distribution of Marital Property § 6.20 (2d ed. 1994). *Query:* If the courts are apparently able to value and distribute such speculative property interests as pension and retirement plans (*see* § 10.02[G], *above*), then why not professional degrees and licenses as well? And if courts in wrongful death cases can value and distribute awards for harm characterized by some as speculative, then why not in family law disputes involving professional degrees and licenses? *See, e.g.,* Stuart Speiser, Recovery for Wrongful Death and Injury (1992); Peter Swisher, Virginia and West Virginia Wrongful Death Actions (2d ed. 1996). *Cf.* Brett R. Turner, *above*, at 404:

> The real basis for the *O'Brien* decision, therefore, is the court's belief that treating degrees as *property* is a wise public policy. Regardless of whether this is true, implementing this policy in light of New York's existing statutory language required a remarkable feat of statutory construction. The almost unanimous rejection of *O'Brien* by courts in other states is perhaps the best evidence that the court strayed too far from the meaning of the statute before it. In the absence of an express statute, the definition of *property* simply cannot be stretched so far as to include degrees and licenses.

(2) A few states have enacted statutes that expressly address the treatment of enhanced earning capacity upon divorce. For example, the Oregon property distribution statute provides, in part:

> The present value of, and income resulting from, the future enhanced earning capacity of either party may be considered as property. The presumption of equal contribution to the acquisition of marital property, however, shall not apply to enhanced earning capacity. A spouse asserting an interest in the income resulting from an enhancement of earning capacity of the other spouse must demonstrate that the spouse made a material contribution to the enhancement. Material contribution can be shown by, among other things, having contributed, financially or otherwise, to the education and training that resulted in the enhanced earning capacity. The contribution shall have been substantial and of prolonged duration.

Or. Rev. Stat. § 107.105 (1996 and 1997 Supp.). The Oregon Supreme Court recently applied this provision in *Denton v. Denton*, 951 P.2d 693 (Or. 1998). The Court held that a wife who had worked full time and performed homemaking duties while her husband prepared for and attended medical school satisfied these statutory requirements, even though she had not contributed directly to her husband's educational expenses, nor sacrificed her own career opportunities. In reversing the intermediate appellate court, the Oregon Supreme Court noted

> In reaching its contrary conclusion, the Court of Appeals also emphasized wife's failure to demonstrate that husband could not have achieved his enhanced earning capacity "but for" her help. But we do not find in the statutory wording any requirement that the contribution be essential to the acquisition of the enhancement. The statute expressly provides that a material contribution may be nonfinancial in nature. In our view, the requirement of a material and substantial contribution to enhanced earning capacity is met whenever the contribution facilitates the acquisition of the enhancement in a major, as opposed to an incidental, way.

951 P.2d at 698. The *Denton* court also held that because the husband had significantly facilitated his wife's acquisition of a college degree during the marriage, he was entitled to an equitable portion of his wife's enhanced earning capacity. The court remanded the case for the establishment of a "just and proper" property distribution in light of both parties' contributions.

(3) Does *O'Brien* classify as divisible marital property *all* licenses and degrees earned by either spouse during the marriage, or only those that are attributable, at least in part, to the efforts of both spouses? *See Mallet v. Mallet*, 667 N.Y.S. 2d 827-28 (N.Y. App. Div. 1998) (husband not entitled to a portion of wife's Bachelor's degree earned during marriage, where his economic contribution to her acquisition of the degree was insignificant and his overall non-economic contributions were negative).

(4) Do the principles applied in *O'Brien* and *Denton* justify the equitable distribution of enhancements in spousal earning capacity that are *not* reflected in a graduate or professional degree? *See, e.g., Golub v. Golub*, 527 N.Y.S.2d 946, 949 (N.Y. App. Div. 1988) ("[A]ll sorts of enhanced earning capacity cases are indistinguishable.... There seems to be no rational basis upon which to distinguish between a degree, a license, or any other special skill that generates substantial income."). *See generally* Margaret F. Brinig, *Property Distribution Physics: The Talisman of Time and Middle Class Law*, 31 Fam. L. Q. 119 (1997); Kenneth R. Davis, *The Doctrine of O'Brien v. O'Brien: A Critical Analysis*, 13 Pace L. Rev. 863 (1994).

(5) **Problem.** Frederica von Stade, an opera singer, was married in New York in 1973. At the time of her marriage, she was performing minor roles at the Metropolitan Opera, earning an annual income of approximately $2200. During the course of her seventeen-year marriage, von Stade achieved international fame, and her income rose spectacularly. In 1989, the year prior to her divorce, she earned over $600,000. Through much of the marriage, von Stade's husband, Peter Elkus, served as her voice coach and teacher, traveled with her on tour, critiqued her rehearsals and performances, and photographed her for magazines and album covers. He also assumed primary responsibility for raising the couple's two children. Elkus claims that he sacrificed his own career as a singer and teacher to devote himself to von Stade's career and that his efforts contributed greatly to von Stade's success. He argues that the reasoning of *O'Brien* entitles him to an equitable share of the increase in value of von Stade's career that took place during their marriage. How would you rule on his claim and why? Assuming that Elkus is entitled to a property remedy, how would

you calculate the value of his entitlement? *See Elkus v. Elkus,* 572 N.Y.S. 2d 901 (N.Y. App. 1991).

(6) Assume—using the majority rule—that professional degrees and licenses do not constitute property for purposes of an equitable division of marital property on divorce. What about the scenario where a wife works in a secretarial position to put her husband through law school or medical school—and then her husband subsequently divorces her shortly after graduation. Should not the working wife be compensated or reimbursed for her efforts toward the attainment of her husband's professional degree or license?

While most courts have refused to treat professional degrees and licenses as divisible property on divorce, they have been sympathetic toward some sort of reimbursement or compensation to the non-student spouse's efforts, although such remedies differ from court to court. One remedy has been to grant the non-student spouse an unequal share of the marital estate based upon his or her marital efforts. *See, e.g., Haywood v. Haywood,* 415 S.E.2d 565 (N.C. Ct. App. 1992), *rev' in part,* 425 S.E.2d 696 (N.C. 1993); *Lowery v. Lowery,* 413 S.E.2d 731 (Ga. 1992). The problem with this approach, however, is that since there may be very little marital property in most student marriages, the non-student spouse may receive little benefit for his or her efforts.

Another remedy is to grant the non-student spouse "reimbursement alimony," either through a lump-sum payment or through periodic payments. *See, e.g In re Marriage of Farrell,* 481 N.W.2d 528 (Iowa Ct. App. 1991). In those states that do not recognize reimbursement alimony, however, a substantial number of courts have awarded the non-student spouse additional alimony or spousal support by way of reimbursement or compensation for his or her efforts. *See, e.g., In re Marriage of Olar,* 747 P.2d 676 (Colo. 1987); *McGowan v. McGowan,* 663 S.W.2d 219 (Ky. Ct. App. 1983); *Downs v. Downs,* 574 A.2d 156 (Vt. 1990). Finally, a number of other states have dispensed with an alimony or spousal support remedy entirely, and simply permit an equitable award of property based upon the concept of "equitable reimbursement." *See, e.g., Pyeatte v. Pyeatte,* 661 P.2d 196 (Ariz. Ct. App. 1982); *DeLa Rosa v. DeLa Rosa,* 309 N.W.2d 755 (Minn. 1981); *Hubbard v. Hubbard,* 603 P.2d 747 (Okla. 1979). Some states have adopted this reimbursement approach by statute. *See, e.g.,* Cal. Fam. Code § 2641 (1993) (permitting an equitable award, but limiting the amount to reimbursement of past contributions); Ind. Code Ann. § 31-1-11.5-11(d) (1993) (also limiting the award to reimbursement for past contributions).

Query: Which is the most viable equitable remedy in your opinion? Should such an award be made based upon a reimbursement approach for past contributions, or based upon an investment approach, where the non-student spouse's contributions are characterized not as payments to be reimbursed, but as future investments. *See, e.g., Van Bussum v. Van Bussum,* 728 S.W.2d 538 (Ky. Ct. App. 1987) (where the court awarded the wife alimony so that she could pursue her own educational goals and professional degree). *See* Gregory, Swisher & Scheible-Wolf, Understanding Family Law § 9.08 [E] (Matthew Bender 1995); Brett R. Turner, Equitable Distribution of Property § 6.20 (2d ed. 1994).

(7) **Problem.** Nancy and Richard were divorced after seven years of marriage. For the first five years of their marriage, Nancy worked as a medical technician, supporting Richard through his last two years of college, and through three years of chiropractic school. On divorce, Nancy requested an award of "reimbursement equity" for her contributions toward

Richard's college degree and chiropractic degree. Richard argued that such a "reimbursement equity" award was not appropriate in this particular case, since he had received Veteran's Administration educational benefits in excess of $12,000 from the federal government; that any reimbursement made to Nancy should only be for amounts over and above the "usual spousal duty of support"; and that a non-student supporting spouse should be reimbursed only for her contributions to direct educational expenses such as tuition and books, and not for her contributions to the parties' general living expenses. The trial court agreed with Richard's argument. How should the appellate court rule, and why? *See Bold v. Bold*, 542 A.2d 1374 (Pa. Super. 1988); *Bold v. Bold*, 574 A.2d 552 (Pa. 1990).

(8) For additional information regarding this complex issue, *see generally* Moore, *Should a Professional Degree be Considered a Marital Asset Upon Divorce?*, 15 Akron L. Rev. 543 (1982); Krauskopf, *Recompense for Financing a Spouse's Education: Legal Protection for the Marital Investor in Human Capital,* 28 Kan. L. Rev. 379 (1980); Note, *The Supporting Spouse's Rights in the Other's Professional Degree Upon Divorce,* 35 U. Fla. L. Rev. 130 (1983). *And see generally* Oldfather, *et al.*, Valuation and Distribution of Marital Property (1997 rev. ed.).

[K] The Family Residence

In most cases, the marital home, homestead, or family residence is the most valuable marital asset the spouses will own on divorce. It is usually acquired during the marriage, and therefore it normally falls within the category of community or marital property. The over-riding concern in divorce disputes involving the family residence is what constitutes a fair and equitable distribution of the marital home in light of the particular circumstances of the parties and applicable statutory factors. In approximately one-third of the states, for example, there are express statutory provisions involving the marital home. Such statutes allow the trial court to award "exclusive use and possession" of the marital home to the spouse having custody of the parties' minor children, since the trauma of losing a familiar home can be substantial for a minor child, especially at the same time as the family breakdown. *See, e.g.,* Colo. Rev. Stat. § 14-10-113(1)(c) (1987); Iowa Code Ann. § 598.21(1)(g) (1993); Ann. Code of Md., Family Law § 8-206 (1984).

Other state courts recognize this same remedy by applying case law specifically recognizing a court's "broad discretionary authority to do equity between the parties . . . including . . . an award of exclusive possession of property." *Pastore v. Pastore*, 497 So. 2d 635, 637 (Fla. 1986), *quoting from* Diffenderfer v. Diffenderfer, 491 So. 2d 265, 267 (Fla. 1986), *citing,* Tronconi v. Tronconi, 466 So. 2d 203 (Fla. 1985). *See also Charrier v. Charrier*, 616 N.E.2d 1085 (Mass. 1983) (holding it was error for the trial court judge not to consider the custodial parent's need for the marital home); *Anderson v. Anderson*, 382 N.W.2d 620 (Neb. 1986) (granting occupancy of the marital home to the custodial parent until the emancipation of the youngest child). *But see contra Reid v. Reid*, 375 S.E.2d 533 (Va. Ct. App. 1989) (specifically rejecting a court's equitable authority to consider the housing needs of the custodial spouse and minor children in fashioning an equitable distribution award). However, if no special needs are demonstrated, or the custodial parent has established a residence outside the marital home, then this "exclusive use and possession" rule for the marital home would *not* apply. *See, e.g., In re Moll*, 597 N.E.2d 1230 (Ill. App. Ct. 1992); *Barone v. Barone*, 338 S.E.2d 149 (S.C. 1985).

There are several ways in which the marital home or family residence, once it is classified as marital property, can be distributed. *First*, it can be sold, with the proceeds divided between the husband and wife. This approach is most commonly utilized where there are no children in the marriage, or where the children have reached an age of majority, and there is substantial equity in the family residence that can provide an economic foundation for each spouse to begin a new life. *See, e.g., Rahn v. Rahn*, 459 A.2d 268 (N.H. 1983). *Second*, the family residence can be awarded solely to one party or to the other, with the judge having the discretion of ordering one party to buy out the other party's economic interests in the marital home. *See, e.g., Johnson v. Johnson*, 329 S.E.2d 443 (S.C. 1985). *Third*, the court can order "exclusive use and possession" by the custodial parent and the minor children for a specified number of years. In some instances, the court can order use and possession until the minor children reach the age of majority. In other jurisdictions, "exclusive use and possession" orders limited to a set number of years.

In most "exclusive use and possession" orders, the noncustodial parent is obligated to pay the costs of maintaining the residence during this period of use and occupancy, and upon the termination of the order, the house will either be distributed to one party or the other, or it will be sold. These direct payments are usually in lieu of a substantial portion of the child and spousal support obligation, although the court may retain jurisdiction to characterize them at the time of trial in order to reserve the question of reimbursement for the use of separate property to pay a community obligation. An "exclusive use and possession" order also allows the custodial parent to retain furniture, appliances and other household items which were used by the family. Thus, according to one commentator:

> Exclusive use is a troublesome remedy, since it forces the noncustodial parent to wait until some point in the future to receive his or her share of the marital estate. In addition, it creates a continuing financial connection between the spouses, in violation of the general policy favoring finality of litigation. Accordingly, exclusive use should not be granted unless the requesting spouse has a special need for the marital home which cannot be addressed by another method.

Brett R. Turner, Equitable Distribution of Property § 6.25 at page 438 (2d ed. 1994). Accordingly, some courts have held that it might be preferable to sell the home rather than order an exclusive use and possession to the custodial spouse. For example, in *Kuvin v. Kuvin*, 442 So. 2d 203 (Fla. 1983), the trial court found that the marital home required extensive repairs which would have been a significant economic burden on the parties. The court therefore ordered the marital residence to be sold, and gave the custodial parent a greater share of the marital funds to enable her to find suitable new housing for the children.

PROBLEMS

(1) Wendy and Harold Smith live in a suburban community in a state which recognizes equitable distribution of marital property on divorce. Their marriage is failing, and Wendy and Harold have come to you, as a divorce mediator, to help them resolve certain economic issues concerning their separation and divorce. The three of you have resolved most of these legal issues, but the question still remains of how to handle the family home. Wendy and Harold have a colonial-style home with four bedrooms and the usual amenities that they bought during their marriage. The house cost them $95,000 and it is now worth $155,000

after ten years. House prices are increasing in their community, and it is likely that their house will continue to increase in value at a rate of at least 5% per year, if not more. Wendy and Harold have two children, Rex and Rhonda, ages 14 and 12 respectively. The Smiths' current mortgage payment is $975.00 per month; their property taxes are $2440 per year and their homeowners insurance is $650.00 per year. The house has just been completely renovated last year, so other than for emergency situations, there should not be a need for further renovation or substantial house repairs in the near future. Harold is a college professor who makes $55,000 per year, and Wendy is a social worker making $35,000 per year. Both are full-time jobs. The total principal owed on their house mortgage is $75,000. You must now prepare a realistic plan for Wendy and Harold as to how they might deal with their family home after their separation and divorce. *See, e.g., In Re Marriage of Zummo*, 521 N.E.2d 621 (Ill. App. Ct. 1988); *Clark v. Clark*, 331 N.W.2d 277 (N.D. 1983).

(2) Wilma and Harry had been married for a number of years, and Wilma is the custodial parent for the parties' three minor children. As part of the divorce decree, the trial judge ordered Harry to pay $75 per week in child support payments; and to transfer his interest in the marital home to Wilma, subject to Wilma paying Harry $17,000 (which represented 40 percent of the parties' equity in the marital home) "in lieu of all alimony, past, present and future; and as a full division of the parties' marital property interests." On appeal, Wilma claims that the trial court judge erred and abused his discretion in ordering that the transfer of the marital home be "in lieu of any alimony, past, present, and future." How should the appellate court rule? *See, e.g., Harris v. Harris*, 530 N.E.2d 368 (Mass. App. Ct. 1988); and *In Re Marriage of Rogers*, 734 P.2d 677 (Mont. 1987).

(3) Brenda and Gerald were married in March of 1964 and lived together as husband and wife until their separation in 1976. In November of 1968, Brenda and Gerald purchased a marital residence for $23,300. Brenda used $6,350 from her separate property trust fund as a down payment, and Brenda and Gerald assumed a deed of trust for the remaining $16,950. Title to the residence was conveyed to "Gerald E. Lucas and Brenda G. Lucas, Husband and Wife, as Joint Tenants." Brenda later testified that it was her intention to acquire the residence solely for herself, but she did not communicate this intention to Gerald. For the next eight years, with the exception of $3,000 worth of home improvements paid by Brenda's separate trust fund, all payments for the loan principal and interest were paid with community property funds. At the time of the dissolution of the marriage, the fair market value of Brenda and Gerald's marital residence had increased to $56,250 with a net equity in the property of $41,650.

The trial court judge apportioned the equity in the marital residence as follows: First, Brenda was to be reimbursed for the home improvements paid with her separate funds, and the remaining equity was to be apportioned between Brenda's separate interest and the community's interest in the residence. The trial court therefore awarded Brenda, as her separate property, approximately 75% of the net equity in the marital residence, with the remaining 25% of the net equity to the community of Brenda and Gerald. The California Court of Appeal, however, reversed the trial court's judgment. Instead of an apportionment of separate and community property, the Court of Appeal decided that the *entire* residence was community property by virtue of a California statute which presumes that the character of ownership of a marital residence acquired during the marriage arises from its *form of title* absent any "understanding or agreement" communicated by one marriage partner to the other as to the intended nature of the property acquired by each partner in the marital residence.

Query: On appeal, should the California Supreme Court arguably adopt: (1) a pro rata apportionment approach; (2) a required reimbursement of separate funds to the contributing marital partner; or (3) presume that the legal ownership interest in the marital residence is as stated in the conveyance of title? *See, e.g., In re Marriage of Lucas*, 166 Cal. Rptr. 853 (Cal. 1980). *See also* Note, *In re Marriage of Lucas, The Marital Residence Acquired With Separate and Community Funds During Marriage*, 15 Loy. L.A. L. Rev. 157 (1981).

[L] Classifying and Valuing Professional Goodwill

Classifying and valuing goodwill in professional practices and other business interests often presents a major problem for many judges, and the courts have struggled with the primary issue of whether or not to classify professional goodwill as an intangible marital property asset. Goodwill is an intangible asset of a business or a professional practice, and has been defined by Mr. Justice Story in this way:

> Good-will may be properly enough described to be the advantage or benefit which is acquired by an establishment, beyond the mere value of the capital, stock, funds, or property employed therein, in consequence of the general public patronage and encouragement, which it receives from constant or habitual customers, on account of its local position, or common celebrity, or reputation for skill or affluence, or punctuality, or from other accidental circumstances or necessities, or even from ancient partialities or prejudices.

J. Story, Commentaries on the Law of Partnership § 99 at 170 (6th ed. 1868). Generally, the courts have applied one of three basic approaches to classifying and valuing professional goodwill as marital property as described by the Maryland Court of Appeals in the case of *Prahinski v. Prahinski*, 540 A.2d 833, 841 (Md. Ct. App. 1988):

> Essentially, three positions have been taken relative to professional goodwill as marital property. Currently, the majority view is that professional goodwill is a business asset with a determinable value and is thus marital property. *See, e.g. Wisner v. Wisner*, 129 Ariz. 333, 631 P.2d 115 (Ct. App. 1981) . . . *In re Marriage of Foster*, 42 Cal. App. 3d 577, 117 Cal. Rptr. 49 (1974) . . . *Heller v. Heller*, 672 S.W.2d 945 (Ky. Ct. App. 1984) &hellip *Dugan v. Dugan*, 92 N.J. 423, 457 A.2d 1 (1982) . . . *Weaver v. Weaver*, 72 N.C. App. 409, 324 S.E.2d 915 (1985) . . . *In re Marriage of Fleege*, 91 Wash. 2d 324, 588 P.2d 1136 (1979). The courts that have found such goodwill to be marital property have generally adopted a method of evaluation involving the capitalization of excess earnings. . . .

Some courts, taking a second approach, have held that professional goodwill is not property and thus cannot be marital property. *See, e.g., Powell v. Powell*, 231 Kan. 456, 648 P.2d 218 (1982); *Beasley v. Beasley*, 359 Pa. Super. 20, 518 A.2d 545 (1986): . . . *Nail v. Nail*, 486 S.W.2d 761 (Tex. 1972); *Holbrook v. Holbrook*, 103 Wis. 2d 327, 309 N.W.2d 343 (1981). Illustrative of the reasoning for this is the Wisconsin Supreme Court's statement that:

> [t]he concept of professional goodwill evanesces when one attempts to distinguish it from future earning capacity. Although a professional business's good reputation,

which is essentially what its goodwill consists of, is certainly a thing of value, we do not believe that it bestows on those who have an ownership in the business an actual separate property interest. The reputation of a law firm or some other professional business is valuable to its individual owners to the extent that it assures continued substantial earnings in the future. It cannot be separately sold or pledged by the individual owners. The goodwill or reputation of such a business accrues to the benefit of the owners only through increased salary.

103 Wis. 2d at 350, 309 N.W.2d at 354. This approach ignores the probability that "goodwill" as a business asset can be separate and distinct from reputation and thus valuable as an intangible property, whereas the first approach blurred the distinction between goodwill and the mere prospect of future earnings.

At least two courts have taken a third approach, somewhat between the two stated above. *See, e.g., Wilson v. Wilson*, 294 Ark. 194, 741 S.W.2d 640 (1987); *Taylor v. Taylor*, 222 Neb. 721, 386 N.W.2d 851 (1986). They have held:

> (1) Where goodwill is a marketable business asset distinct from the personal reputation of a particular individual, as is usually the case with many commercial enterprises, that goodwill has an immediately discernible value as an asset of the business and may be identified as an amount reflected in a sale or transfer of a business.

(2) If the goodwill depends on the continued presence of a particular individual, such goodwill, by definition, is not a marketable asset distinct from the individual.

Wilson, 741 S.W.2d at 647; *Taylor*, 222 Neb. at 731, 386 N.W.2d at 858. We believe this third approach to be a sound one, as it recognizes the difference between true goodwill and an individual's reputation, which may be characterized as the ability to obtain future earnings masquerading as goodwill. This approach also has an advantage of being more flexible than either of the other two . . . .

Assuming *arguendo* under the majority view that professional goodwill *can* be classified as marital property for equitable distribution purposes, how should such professional goodwill be *valued*? The leading case of *Dugan v. Dugan* provides an illustration of how this may be accomplished.

DUGAN v. DUGAN
New Jersey Supreme Court
457 A.2d 1 (1983)

This case involves the equitable distribution of marital property upon divorce, more particularly the evaluation of an attorney's goodwill in his exclusively owned professional corporation.

Plaintiff, James P. Dugan, and defendant, Rosaleen M. Dugan, were married in 1958 and separated in 1978. They had no children. The plaintiff, a member of the New Jersey Bar, carries on his practice as a professional corporation. The defendant had served as a secretary in plaintiff's law office and attended college during the marriage, graduating in 1972. She is certified as a public school teacher, but as of the date of the divorce judgement was unemployed.

We granted plaintiff's petition for certification, limited to the issues arising from the valuation of plaintiff's interest in his wholly-owned professional corporation. The trial court determined that the value of the material part of the marital estate was $606,966 as of December 29, 1978, the date the complaint was filed. It awarded the defendant $230,864 and the plaintiff $376,102 consisting of the following:

Real property		$ 285,400
Law practice		
Goodwill	$ 182,725	
Accounts receivable	18,891	
Pension plan	50,500	
Common stock	1,000	
Less		
Retained earnings deficit	1,780	
Net value of law practice		$ 251,336
Cash		55,313
Miscellaneous		14,917
		$ 606,966

A major asset in the joint estate was the plaintiff's law practice. It comprised more than 40% of the entire estate and over 70% of the value of that asset consisted of the value placed on goodwill. The trial court's methodology in calculating that value was predicated on the theory that the plaintiff was to be compared with the typical incorporated attorney whose gross assets were roughly equivalent to the plaintiff's. The comparison was limited to the efficiency of the respective operations, that is, the percentage that net income before income taxes bears to gross receipts. The net income of a typical attorney was found to be 38.5% of gross receipts. Plaintiff's gross income was multiplied by 38.5%, yielding what could be termed a typical attorney's net income based on plaintiff's actual gross revenues. The excess of plaintiff's net income over that resulting from the application of the 38.5% standard was then multiplied by a factor of five. The trial court found that this figure equaled goodwill.

We must determine whether goodwill is a part of the value of plaintiff's law practice; if so, whether it constitutes property subject to equitable distribution; and, if so, how it is to be evaluated.

I

In a divorce judgment a court may "effectuate an equitable distribution of the property, both real and personal," acquired during the marriage. N.J.S.A. § 2A:34-23. We have acknowledged that the Legislature intended that its reference to "property" be construed comprehensively. Determining the "property" subject to equitable distribution requires a marshaling of the parties' economic resources. These economic resources cover a broad spectrum. Initially a list of the parties' assets and liabilities upon a particular date should be prepared. Personal tangible property is clearly includable. Intangibles may also constitute property, [including "[t]he right to receive monies in the future," which is unquestionably such an economic resource].

As distinguished from tangible assets, intangibles have no intrinsic value, but do have a value related to the ownership and possession of tangible assets. Some intangibles, such as a trademark, trade name or patent, are related to an identifiable tangible asset. Goodwill, which is another intangible, is not. Often referred to as "the most 'intangible' of the intangibles," D. Kieso & J. Weygandt, *Intermediate Accounting*, 570 (3d ed.1980), goodwill is essentially reputation that will probably generate future business. . . .

Justice Cardozo when Chief Judge of the New York Court of Appeals embraced the same concept when he wrote:

Men will pay for any privilege that gives a reasonable expectancy of preference in the race of competition. Such expectancy may come from succession in place or name or otherwise to a business that has won the favor of its customers. It is then known as good will. [*In re Brown*, 242 N.Y. 1, 6, 150 N.E. 581, 582 (1926) (citation omitted)].

There can be no doubt that goodwill exists. It is a legally protectible interest. Indeed, we have enforced a restrictive covenant limiting a seller's right to compete that was designed essentially to protect the goodwill of the business for the buyer. *Solari Indus. v. Malad*, 55 N.J. 571, 576, 264 A.2d 53 (1979). The New Jersey inheritance tax, N.J.S.A. § 54:34-1, requires consideration of goodwill . . . . Upon dissolution of a partnership goodwill has been recognized as an element in determining value for purposes of liquidation. In *Kanzler v. Smith*, 123 N.J. Eq. 602, 199 A.35 (1938), the Court of Errors and Appeals held that the legally contemplated liquidation of partnership property upon the death of a partner required "an accounting by the surviving partner for the value of the deceased partner's interest, including the value of goodwill, if any." . . .

The accounting profession has further expanded the concept of goodwill to encompass other advantages of an established business that contribute to its profitability. J.M. Smith & K.F. Skousen, *Intermediate Accounting* 283 (7th ed. standard vol. 1982), capture this thought in their definition: Goodwill is generally regarded as the summation of all the special advantages, not otherwise identifiable, related to a going concern. It includes such items as a good name, capable staff and personnel, high credit standing, reputation for superior products and services, and favorable location.

In a broad sense goodwill includes a whole host of intangibles including the quality of management, the ability of the organization to produce and market efficiently, and the existence and nature of competition. Some writers have been careful to differentiate between going concern value and goodwill. Goodwill is keyed to reputation; going concern value to the enhanced value of the assets due to their presence in an established firm. Going concern value has many of the characteristics of goodwill and in many situations will constitute an asset enhancing the value of an enterprise. In that event it will be a component of the property subject to equitable distribution. Going concern value may be prevalent in some law firms. It is probably not significant in an individual law practice, as is probably the case here. We note no claim has been made on that basis.

Goodwill can be translated into prospective earnings. From an accounting standpoint goodwill has also been perceived of in terms of the extent to which future estimated earnings exceed the normal return on the investment. The price paid for goodwill then is equivalent to the excess of actual earnings over expected earnings based on a normal rate of return on investment. When goodwill exists, it has value and may well be the most lucrative asset of some enterprises.

Variances in the forms of an enterprise do not eliminate goodwill, though they may affect its worth. Goodwill may be present whether that form is a partnership, corporation, joint venture, or individual proprietorship. . . .

. . . The calculation of goodwill may depend upon the purpose for which the measurement is being made. The federal Internal Revenue Service has prescribed a formula approach for income, gift and estate tax purposes. *See* Rev. Rul. 68-609, 1968-2 C.B. 327. The market place, as noted above, may often provide a different figure. Accountants will usually not reflect goodwill on a balance sheet until after a business has been sold and then state goodwill in terms of the excess paid for the net assets over book value. . . .

II

Our limited concern involves the existence of goodwill as property and its evaluation for purposes of equitable distribution under N.J.S.A. § 2A:34-23 with respect to attorneys and in particular individual practitioners. Though other elements may contribute to goodwill in the context of a professional service, such as locality and specialization, reputation is at the core. It does not exist at the time professional qualifications and a license to practice are obtained. A good reputation is earned after accomplishment and performance. Field testing is an essential ingredient before goodwill comes into being. Future earning capacity per se is not goodwill. However, when that future earning capacity has been enhanced because reputation leads to probable future patronage from existing and potential clients, goodwill may exist and have value. When that occurs the resulting goodwill is property subject to equitable distribution. . . .

When, however, the opportunity provided by the license is exercised, then goodwill may come into existence. Goodwill is to be differentiated from earning capacity. It reflects not simply a possibility of future earnings, but a probability based on existing circumstances. Enhanced earnings reflected in goodwill are to be distinguished from a license to practice a profession and an educational degree. In that situation the enhanced future earnings are so remote and speculative that the license and degree have not been deemed to be property. The possibility of additional earnings is to be distinguished from the existence of goodwill in a law practice and the probability of its continuation. Moreover, unlike the license and the degree, goodwill is transferable and marketable. Though there is an apparent limitation on the part of an individual practitioner to sell a law practice, the same is not true in a law firm.

After divorce, the law practice will continue to benefit from that goodwill as it had during the marriage. Much of the economic value produced during an attorney's marriage will inhere in the goodwill of the law practice. It would be inequitable to ignore the contribution of the non-attorney spouse to the development of that economic resource. An individual practitioner's inability to sell a law practice does not eliminate existence of goodwill and its value as an asset to be considered in equitable distribution. Obviously, equitable distribution does not require conveyance or transfer of any particular asset. The other spouse, in this case the wife, is entitled to have that asset considered as any other property acquired during the marriage partnership.

Other jurisdictions have accepted the principle that an attorney's goodwill is property subject to equitable distribution. In *In re Marriage of Lopez*, 38 Cal. App.3d 93, 107, 113 Cal. Rptr. 58, 67 (1974), in discussing goodwill, the court quoted approvingly the following language from *Golden v. Golden*, 270 Cal. App. 2d 401, 405, 75 Cal. Rptr. 735, 738 (1969):

[I]n a matrimonial matter, the practice of the sole practitioner husband will continue, with the same intangible value as it had during the marriage. Under principles of community property law, the wife, by virtue of her position of wife, made to that value the same contribution as does a wife to any of [the] husband's earnings and accumulations during marriage. She is as much entitled to be recompensed for that contribution as if it were represented by the increased value of stock in a family business.

In *Stern v. Stern*, we acknowledged that "[i]t may . . . be possible to prove that [goodwill] does exist and is a real element of economic worth. Concededly, determining its value presents difficulties." 66 N.J. at 345–37 n. 5, 331 A.2d 257. However, difficulty in fixing its value does not justify ignoring its existence. Goodwill should be valued with great care, for the individual practitioner will be forced to pay the ex-spouse "tangible" dollars for an intangible asset at a value concededly arrived at on the basis of some uncertain elements. For purposes of valuing the goodwill of a law practice, the true enhancement to be evaluated is the likelihood of repeat patronage and a certain degree of immunity from competition. *See Levy v. Levy*, 164 N.J. Super. 542, 554, 397 A.2d 374 (Ch.1978). Identification of goodwill in this fashion differs from that utilized in evaluating goodwill in businesses where an identification of a return on tangible assets is made.

For example, the Internal Revenue Service has prescribed a formula approach for federal tax purposes when there is no better basis for valuation. *See* Rev.Rul. 68-609, 1968-2 C.B. 327. It requires a determination of income from the tangible assets, and subtraction of that income from the total income. The residual is capitalized and the balance is designated goodwill. A law office's tangible asset value is so disproportionately small when compared to the value of the services rendered that measurement by these methods would not be meaningful.

Other methodologies have been developed in the market place for particular businesses or professions. It is common in evaluating goodwill of an accountant's practice to compute goodwill on the basis of a percentage of annual gross income. *Valuing an Accounting Practice*, The Practicing CPA, Mar. 1982, at 1; Wright, *On Buying and Selling a Practice*, J. Accountancy, Jan. 1982, at 38. In the medical profession a charge per patient card has sometimes been utilized, *see* Fallon, *What's Your Practice Worth in Cash?*, Med. Econ., Jan 22, 1979, at 180, as well as a percentage of annual gross income, *see* Balliett, *Private Practice: How to Quit at a Profit*, Med. World News, Dec. 25, 1978, at 40, or a percentage of annual net income, *see* Cantor, *The Value of a Lawyer's Interest in His Practice*, 43 N.Y. St. B.J. 47, 50 (1971) (quoting Bernard D. Hirsh, General Counsel for the American Medical Assn).

A significant element in fixing an attorney's goodwill is that an attorney as a sole practitioner cannot sell his law practice, *see Geffen v. Moss*, 53 Cal. App. 3d 215, 125 Cal. Rptr. 687 (1975), and when any attorney severs his relationship with a law practice, a restrictive covenant to protect goodwill is unavailable, *see Karlin v. Weinberg*, 77 N.J. 408, 418, 390 A.2d 1161 (1978) (dictum). *Contra Hicklin v. O'Brien*, 11 Ill. App. 2d 541, 138 N.E.2d 47 (1956); *Heinz v. Roberts*, 135 Iowa 748, 110 N.W. 1034 (1907); *Thorn v. Dinsmoor*, 104 Kan. 275, 178 P. 445 (1919) (upholding sale of a law practice to a law student not yet admitted to practice). Drinker in his treatise on legal ethics states that "[a] lawyer's practice and good will may not be offered for sale." H. Drinker, Legal Ethics 161 (1953) (footnote omitted); *accord* R. Wise, Legal Ethics 204 (2d ed. 1970) ("Goodwill cannot be sold as clients are not chattels or merchandise and a lawyer is not a tradesman") (footnote omitted). This principle has been accepted and announced by our Advisory Committee on Professional Ethics, Op. 48, 87 N.J.L.J. 459 (1964).

The underlying basis for the principle proscribing a restrictive covenant is the prohibition against an attorney selling his practice including goodwill. DR 2-108(A) of our Disciplinary Rules of the Code of Professional Responsibility, prohibiting such restrictions, reads as follows:

A lawyer shall not be a party to or participate in a partnership or employment agreement with another lawyer that restricts the right of a lawyer to practice law after the termination of a relationship created by the agreement, except as may be provided in a bona fide retirement plan and then only to the extent reasonably necessary to protect the plan.

We do not intend herein to pass upon the soundness of the rule that prohibits the sale of goodwill, but only to note that we have approved of partnership agreements proving for payment upon a partner's retirement or death of an amount in excess of the capital account presumably representing his share of goodwill in the firm. In *Stern* we observed:

Generally speaking the monetary worth of this type of professional partnership will consist of the total value of the partners' capital accounts, accounts receivable, the value of work in progress, any appreciation in the true worth of tangible personalty over and above book value, *together with good will*, should there in fact be any; the total so arrived at to be diminished by the amount of accounts payable as well as any other liabilities not reflected on the partnership books. 66 N.J. at 346–47, 331 A.2d 257 (emphasis supplied) (footnotes omitted).

Payment to a former partner is excepted from Disciplinary Rule 2-107, prohibiting the division of fees unless services have been performed. N.J.Code of Professional Responsibility, Formal Op. 327 (1971) (stating that it is permissible to "make payments to a retired partner or for a fixed period to the estate of a deceased partner in accordance with a preexisting retirement plan, the amount of those payments being measured by subsequent earnings of the firm"). Thus members of a law firm may provide for selling their interest therein, including goodwill, and sole practitioners may not. *See* Sterrett, *The Sale of a Law Practice*, 121 U. Pa. L. Rev. 306, 320–23 (1972) (justifying this distinction). It has been suggested that the individual practitioner may avoid the restriction by entering into a partnership arrangement with another attorney before retiring. Cantor, *supra*, at 51; *see* Winter, *Selling a Law Firm: Ethics Rules Eyed*, 68 A.B.A. J. 406, 406 (1982) (criticizing the distinction). Indeed, England, Australia and Canada permit the sale of a solicitor's practice, including goodwill, upon death or retirement. *See* Note, *The Death of a Lawyer*, 56 Colum. L. Rev. 606, 617–18 & n. 72 (1956). England also enforces restrictive covenants entered into in connection with such a sale. *Id.*; *see, e.g., Bunn v. Guy*, 4 East. 190, 102 Eng.Rep. 803 (K.B. 1803). *But see Aubin v. Holt*, 2 K. & J. 68, 69–70, 69 E.R. 696, 697 (Ch.1855) (suggesting *Bunn* is limited to agreements between retiring partner and firm); *Thornbury v. Bevill*, 1 Y. & C. Ch. C. 556, 62 E.R. 1014 (Ch.1842) (similar arrangement between strangers not enforced).

As matters now stand limitations on the sale of a law practice with its goodwill have an adverse effect upon its value. However, as previously observed, goodwill may be of significant value irrespective of these limitations.

One appropriate method to determine the value of goodwill of a law practice can be accomplished by fixing the amount by which the attorney's earnings exceed that which would have been earned as an employee by a person with similar qualifications of education, experience and capability. This is a fair manner in which to resolve the goodwill constituent.

An attorney who earns $35,000 per year as an employee would, as any employee, not have goodwill properly ascribable to his employment. The same attorney earning a net income of the same amount from his individual practice should likewise not be considered to have property consisting of goodwill in ascertaining the value of his practice.

The court should first ascertain what an attorney of comparable experience, expertise, education and age would be earning as an employee in the same general locale. The effort that the practitioner expends on his law practice should not be overlooked when comparing his income to that of the hypothetical employee. A sole practitioner who, for example, works a regular sixty-hour week may have a significantly greater income than an employee who regularly works a forty-hour week, and the income may be due to greater productivity rather than the realization of income on the sole practitioner's goodwill. Next, the attorney's net income before federal and state income taxes for a period of years, preferably five, should be determined and averaged. The actual average should then be compared with the employee norm. If the attorney's actual average realistically exceeds the total of (1) the employee norm and (2) a return on the investment in the physical assets, the excess would be the basis for evaluating goodwill.

This excess is subject to a capitalization factor. The capitalization factor is generally perceived as the number of years of excess earnings a purchaser would be willing to pay for in advance in order to acquire the goodwill. 2 J. Bonbright, Valuation of Property 731 (1937). The minimum capitalization factor is zero. The precise capitalization factor would depend on other evidence. Such evidence could consist of a comparison of capitalization factors used to measure goodwill in other professions, such as medicine or dentistry, adjusted, however, for ingredients peculiar to law, such as the inability to sell the practice and nonavailability of a restrictive covenant. The age of a lawyer may be particularly important because a sole practitioner's goodwill would probably terminate upon death, contrary to that of a doctor. *See Tessmar v. Grosner*, 23 N.J. 193, 200–01, 128 A.2d 467 (1957); ABA Comm. on Professional Ethics, Formal Op. 266 (1945); Note, *supra*, at 614. Subject to such adjustments, the method used in a comparable profession may be applied and a figure close to the true worth of the law practice's goodwill may be obtained.

Other approaches equally or more compelling may be used. If sufficient information about the average income of attorney employees with similar background and expertise is unavailable, partnership agreements covering comparable attorneys that set forth value in excess of capital accounts may disclose a useful figure for goodwill. *See Cantor, supra*, at 52–53 (referring to surveys of law firms to ascertain policies for valuing a terminating partner's interest). In *Stern* we agreed that the law partnership agreement may determine the worth of a lawyer's practice including goodwill upon proof that the books are well kept and the partner's interests are carefully reviewed periodically. 66 N.J. at 347, 331 A.2d 257.

There may well be other ways in which goodwill may be computed and we do not by the suggestions made herein intend to preclude their use. *See, e.g.,* Hitchman, *The Fair Market Value of a Law Practice*, 15 L. Soc'y Upper Can. Gaz. 303 (1981); Dlugatch & Olds, *Goodwill Determination in Professional Practice Evaluation Pursuant to a Marriage Dissolution*, 4 Glendale L. Rev. 28, 34–36 (1982). In any event the limitations to which we have previously alluded, as well as the expertise and age of the individual should be factored into any evaluation. Moreover, potential federal tax consequences should be considered in determining equitable distribution. . . .

NOTES AND QUESTIONS

(1) The *Dugan* court rationale has been widely quoted and commented upon in subsequent court opinions and in the legal literature. Its suggested capitalization of excess earnings approach in order to ascertain the value of profession goodwill may be summarized as follows:

    (a) Ascertain what a professional of comparable experience, expertise, education, and age would be earning as an employee in the same general locale;

    (b) Determine and average the professional's net income before federal and state income taxes for a period of years, preferably five;

    (c) Compare the actual averages with the employee norm; and

    (d) Multiply the excess by a capitalization factor. 457 A.2d at 9–10.

Query: Is the *Dugan* approach a realistic and viable way to ascertain the value of professional goodwill on divorce? Why or why not? Which of the three approaches to professional goodwill described *above* is most persuasive to you? Based upon what underlying public policy arguments and contemporary realities?

(2) Like any other asset acquired during a marriage, a professional practice (*e.g.* law, medicine, dentistry, accounting) which is acquired during the marriage is presumed to be marital or community property. Unlike a hardware store or a grocery store whose primary assets are its inventory and equipment, however, a professional practice (and especially a law practice) has little tangible value, since its primary value is found in the goodwill of its clients. Historically, then, some courts were not willing to value and distribute professional goodwill, even though they agreed it existed. *See, e.g., Smith v. Smith*, 709 S.W.2d 588 (Tenn. Ct. App. 1985); *Holbrook v. Holbrook*, 309 N.W.2d 343 (Wis. Ct. App. 1981). This approach also reflected the view that the sale of attorney goodwill was unethical, since there could be no goodwill bond between attorney and client. This position is especially persuasive where a sole practitioner's only measure of his or her legal practice is in his or her future effort and earnings. *See, e.g., Beasley v. Beasley*, 518 A.2d 545 (Pa. Super. Ct. 1986); *DeMasi v. DeMasi*, 530 A.2d 871 (Pa. Super. Ct. 1987).

(3) The modern trend today and the majority view, however, is to recognize goodwill as marital property in a professional practice if there is evidence of a similar sale of a like practice, or evidence of a credible expert witness to establish such professional goodwill. *See, e.g., Hanson v. Hanson*, 738 S.W.2d 429 (Mo. 1987). Some courts distinguish between the goodwill of a partnership or corporation on one hand, and that of an individual on the other hand, stating that the latter is too intertwined with the individual skills of the practitioner to be separately discerned as property. *See, e.g., Wilson v. Wilson*, 741 S.W.2d 640 (Ark. 1987). There is also some judicial concern that goodwill is valued for divorce purposes based on the potential sale of the professional practice when no such sale actually exists, and when the value of the sale of a professional practice may vary extensively from one year to the next. Most courts respond, however, by stating that when there is credible evidence of professional goodwill which can be established by expert testimony, that issue should be considered. *See, e.g., In re Brooks*, 756 P.2d 161 (Wash. Ct. App. 1988); *In re*

Stone, 518 N.E.2d 402 (Ill. App. Ct. 1987); *Mitchell v. Mitchell*, 732 P.2d 212 (Ariz. 1987); *Russell v. Russell*, 399 S.E.2d 166 (Va. Ct. App. 1990).

(4) *Query*: Is there a valid distinction between professional goodwill and professional degrees or licenses? Should there be? Most states have rejected the notion that there is an equitable property interest in professional degrees or licenses [see Chapter 10.02[J], *above*]. However, many state courts are increasingly recognizing professional goodwill as divisible property. What is the major difference—if any—between these two intangible property concepts? How did the *Dugan* court *above* address this distinction? See also *Mitchell v. Mitchell*, 732 P.2d 212 (Ariz. 1987).

(5) The proposed ALI *Principles of the Law of Family Dissolution* § 4.07(3) (1997) provides the following discussion of business and professional goodwill in a divorce context:

> Business and professional goodwill earned during marriage are marital property to the extent they have value apart from the value of spousal earning capacity, spousal skills, or post-dissolution spousal labor.
>
> (a) Evidence of an increment during marriage in the market value of business or professional goodwill establishes the existence of divisible marital property in that amount except to the extent that market value includes the value of post-dissolution spousal labor.
>
> (b) Business or professional goodwill that is not marketable is nevertheless marital property to the extent a value can be established for it that does not include the value of spousal earning capacity, spousal skills, or post-dissolution spousal labor. *Query*: Which of the three judicial approaches classifying and valuing business and professional goodwill, if any, does the ALI *Principles* most closely approximate? What are the strengths and weaknesses of this ALI approach in classifying and valuing professional goodwill?

[M] Valuing Businesses and Professional Practices

A business or professional practice begun during the marriage is marital property if that business is capitalized with marital property. *See, e.g., Addis v. Addis*, 703 S.W.2d 852 (Ark. 1986) (partnership); *Duncan v. Duncan*, 686 S.W.2d 568 (Tenn. Ct. App. 1984) (corporation); *Allen v. Allen*, 704 S.W.2d 600 (Tex. Ct. Civ. App. 1986) (corporation). *See generally* J. Thomas Oldham, Divorce, Separation, and the Distribution of Property §§ 10.01–10.03 (1997 rev. ed.).

Assuming that a closely held business or professional practice does in fact constitute marital property, how should this marital property be *valued*? The following excerpt presents a good overview of this troubling subject of business valuation for marital property distribution purposes on divorce or dissolution of marriage. Gregory, Swisher, & Scheible-Wolf, Understanding Family Law § 9.09[C] (Matthew Bender 1995) (footnotes omitted) [reprinted with permission]:

> Valuation of professional practices and other closely held business interests is without question one of the most difficult problems that courts and lawyers face in connection with the equitable distribution of property on dissolution of marriage. There are few principles that are uniformly or unvaryingly reliable. The form of the enterprise—whether a sole proprietorship, a partnership, or a closely held corporation—is generally not controlling and most often not of particular significance. In most

cases, and certainly when the enterprise is financially or structurally complex, valuation requires the testimony of experts. This is not to suggest, however, that valuation involves valid and reliable scientific methods. All too frequently, well-qualified experts, purporting to use identical methods of valuation, reach widely variant conclusions as to the value of the same assets. . . . Nevertheless, appellate courts uniformly hold that the difficulty of establishing value does not relieve trial courts of the obligation to do so.

Valuation [of closely held businesses and professional practices] contemplates the determination of fair market value, commonly defined as "the price at which the property would change hands between a willing buyer and a willing seller when the former is not under any compulsion to buy and the latter is not under any compulsion to sell, both parties having reasonable knowledge of relevant facts" [Rev. Rul. 59-60, 1959—1 CB 237]. Determining the fair market value of a closely held corporation (and by analogy, other closely held business interests) is problematic. Because sales of such corporations are infrequent, no market of willing buyers and sellers exists.

The methods or approaches to valuation in the following discussion should be considered as representative or illustrative, not all-inclusive. As long as the method of valuation chosen by a trial court is fair and reasonable and is supported by the evidence, a reviewing court is unlikely to reject it.

[1] Book Value

A number of courts have expressed skepticism with respect to exclusive reliance on book value in valuing shares of closely held corporations. . . . The courts do not, however, categorically and without exception reject book value as the measure of value. The circumstances of the case may justify its acceptance. [*See, e.g., In re Marriage of Messerle*, 643 P.2d 1286 (Or. Ct. App. 1982); and *Whaley v. Whaley*, 436 N.E.2d 816 (Ind. Ct. App. 1982).]

[2] Capitalization of Excess Earnings

There is widespread agreement that earnings are the most important factor in valuation of the stock of an operating company, and these are sometimes the sole factor used in determining value. The courts generally accept the fact that "at least in the case of an operating company with consistent earnings, asset value has markedly less importance in valuation than does earnings" and occasionally, "earnings have even been the only factor used to determine value" [Longnecker, *A Practical Guide to Valuation of Closely Held Stock*, 122 Tr. & Est. 32–33 (Jan. 1983)].

Earnings having been determined, capitalization of excess earnings is frequently employed as a method of valuation. This method involves applying to the earnings of the corporation a capitalization rate or multiplier that reflects the stability of past corporate earnings and the predictability of future earnings. [*See* Hartwig, *Valuing an Interest in a Closely Held Business for the Purpose of Buy/Sell Agreements and for Death Tax Purposes*, 26 S. Cal. Tax Inst. 215, 256–264 (1974)]. . . .

[3] Buy-Sell Agreements

A description of buy-sell agreements is as follows:

A buy-sell agreement usually provides for the business entity or remaining principal's purchase of the withdrawing parties' shares at a predetermined price. Such an agreement is restrictive in nature as it alienates the transferability of the shares. Those agreements are usually entered into to meet the business-planning objectives such as protection from outsiders, prevention of changes in ownership, economic continuity, and estate tax purposes. [Skoloff, *A Matrimonial Attorney's Alert: Beware of Buy-Sell Agreements*, 7 National L.J. Sept. 10, 1984 at 16 (citing to Desmond & Kelly, *Business Valuation Handbook* 239 (1980)].

Such arrangements frequently appear in partnership agreements and in connection with other forms of closely-held business interests. Generally, the courts take such agreements into account in arriving at a valuation of these interests but do not consider them as binding. [*See, e.g., Kaye v. Kaye*, 478 N.Y.S.2d 324, 328 (N.Y. App. Div. 1984) ("A bona fide buy-sell agreement which predates the marital discord, while not conclusive, may also provide an invaluable aid"); and *Stern v. Stern*, 331 A.2d 257 (N.J. 1975)].

[4] Discount for Minority Interest

Among the factors affecting the fair market value of the stock of closely held corporations is the size of the block of stock being valued. A minority interest in an enterprise that others control may be of significantly less value than the liquidation value of the shares. This lack of [corporate] control significantly reduces the value of the minority shareholder's stock. Accordingly, courts in a number of equitable distribution jurisdictions discount the value of a minority interest in valuing and distributing interests in closely held corporations upon marriage dissolution. [*See, e.g., Eyler v. Eyler*, 485 N.E.2d 657 (Ind. Ct. App. 1986); and Feld, *The Implications of Minority Interest and Stock Restrictions in Valuing Closely Held Shares*, 122 U. Pa. L. Rev. 934, 934–936 (1974)].

BUSINESS VALUATION PROBLEM

When Dr. and Mrs. Jones were married, Dr. Jones had already graduated from medical school. Mrs. Jones, on the other hand, had only a tenth grade education. Shortly after their marriage, and Dr. Jones' internship and residency, Dr. Jones and another physician formed the Ames Women's Medical Center, Inc., a professional corporation that provided medical and laboratory services primarily related to the termination of pregnancies. Mrs. Jones worked briefly at the medical center as a receptionist, and then became a full-time housewife, taking care of the Jones' two minor children.

When the Joneses were involved in a divorce action twenty years later, the most vigorously contested issue was the value of Dr. Jones' interest in the Ames Women's Medical Center. Each side called an expert witness to determine the value of the medical practice. Mrs. Jones' expert witness testified that in his expert opinion, the value of Dr. Jones' share of the Ames Medical Center was in a range between $675,000 and $1,350,000. Dr. Jones' expert witness testified, however, that in his expert opinion the corporation had no value whatsoever. The court stated that valuation of closely held and professional corporations "is a difficult problem confronting the courts with increasing frequency" and to date "no consistent approach to valuation has been arrived at."

One of the most comprehensive methods of valuing a business, however, which both experts professed to have used in arriving at their valuation of the Medical Center, was the Internal Revenue Service's Revenue Ruling 59-60, which identifies eight fundamental factors in valuing a business:

(1) The nature of the business and the history of the enterprise from its inception.

(2) The economic outlook in general and the condition and outlook of the specific industry in particular.

(3) The book value of the stock and the financial condition of the business.

(4) The earning capacity of the company.

(5) The dividend-paying capacity.

(6) Whether or not the enterprise has goodwill or other intangible value.

(7) Sales of the stock and the size of the block of stock to be valued.

(8) The market price of stocks of corporations engaged in the same or a similar line of business having their stocks actively traded in a free and open market.

Nevertheless, the Introduction to Revenue Ruling 59-60 still warns "A sound valuation will be based upon all the relevant facts, but the elements of common sense, informed judgment, and reasonableness must enter into the process of weighing those facts and determining their aggregate significance."

Query: If Dr. and Mrs. Jones' expert witnesses testified that they *both* applied Revenue Ruling 59-60 in valuing Dr. Jones' medical practice, and they disagreed so dramatically in their respective valuations (between $675,000 and $1,350,000 from the wife's expert witness, to no value at all from the husband's expert witness), what does this tell you about using expert witnesses such as real estate appraisers, forensic economists, certified public accountants, and other expert witnesses in an equitable distribution proceeding? On the other hand, does an average family law practitioner have sufficient professional training to determine property valuation of marital property *without* an expert witness—especially in those cases involving substantial marital property?

How should the court decide this case? *See Nehorayoff v. Nehorayoff*, 437 N.Y.S.2d 584 (N.Y. Sup. Ct. 1981). *See also Bosserman v. Bosserman*, 384 S.E.2d 104 (Va. Ct. App. 1989); *Zipf v. Zipf*, 382 S.E.2d 263 (Va. Ct. App. 1989).

[N] Distribution of Property

[1] General Introduction

Once a trial court judge has determined that property is either marital property, community property, or separate property (or "mixed" property under the source of funds rule); and once such property has been valued; the trial judge must then distribute the parties' marital or community property in "dual property" states. *See, e.g.,* Levy, *An Introduction to Divorce: Property Issues*, 23 Fam. L.Q. 147 (1989). In "all property" the judge may distribute both separate and marital assets to the parties, as their needs dictate. *See, e.g., Putnam v. Putnam*, 358 N.E.2d 837, 842 (Mass. Ct. App. 1977) ("An order for equitable distribution should normally include all substantial assets . . .)

When distributing marital or community property, most states require that the court consideration a list of *statutory factors* to help insure that a certain degree of consistency and uniformity in applied by the state court judges. Some states require that these equitable distribution statutory factors be enumerated in the divorce decree itself, *see, e.g., Holston v. Holston*, 473 A.2d 459 (Md. Ct. Spec. App. 1984);; while other states do not require an express statutory enumeration. *See, e.g., In re Marriage of Syijuberget*, 763 P.2d 323 (Mont. 1988). It is clear, however, that the consideration of these statutory factors in making an equitable distribution award is extremely important, and could result in reversible error if the trial court does not consider *all* of these statutory factors. *See, e.g,, Sparks v. Sparks*, 485 N.W.2d 893 (Mich. 1992) (holding that a trial court judge must consider *all* the statutory factors in determining an equitable distribution award); *Tarro v. Tarro*, 485 A.2d 558 (R.I. 1984) (holding that the trial court judge must consider *all* the state statutory factors for distributing marital property and granting alimony, not just marital misconduct); *Rexrode v. Rexrode*, 339 S.E.2d 544 (Va. Ct. App. 1986) (holding that a court must consider *all* the statutory factors in making an equitable distribution property award or the award will be invalid).

In most states, the trial judge possesses inherent power and discretion to implement an equitable distribution award above and beyond the transfer of title to marital property. This includes the power to order an exchange of property for a spouse's interest in real estate, *Claunch v. Claunch*, 525 S.W.2d 788 (Mo. Ct. App. 1975); the power to determine how a business will be conducted in the future after the divorce decree, *Lord v Lord*, 454 A.2d 830 (Me. 1983); and the power to order a partition or sale of property, *Wade v. Wade*, 325 S.E.2d 260 (N.C. Ct. App. 1985). Although such judicial discretion is broad and will not be overturned without evidence of judicial abuse or judicial failure to follow state equitable distribution statutory guidelines, the dual property statutory classification model "is a form of property division guideline; [and] by limiting the court's authority to divide certain types of property, it improves the consistency and predictability of the overall process." Brett Turner, Equitable Distribution of Marital Property § 2.09 at 46 (2d ed. 1994).

[2] Statutory Factors for Distributing Marital Property

As noted above, most equitable distribution states require the trial court to consider a number of explicit state statutory factors in arriving at a fair and equitable division of marital assets. Generally, judicial application of these statutory factors is mandatory, often with the additional requirement that the trial court set forth its written reasons for determining its property distribution, or indicate the factors on which it relied. *See generally* Gregory, Swisher & Scheible-Wolf, Understanding Family Law § 9.12 (Matthew Bender 1995); and J. Thomas Oldham, Divorce, Separation and the Distribution of Marital Property § 13.02 (1997 rev. ed.).

Several states have adopted their equitable distribution statutory factors from the 1970 version of the Uniform Marriage and Divorce Act [UMDA] § 307 [9A U.L.A. 240 (1973)]. Section 307 of the UMDA requires that the court consider a number of relevant factors in distributing the parties' marital property, including:

(1) the contributions of each spouse to the acquisition of marital property, including contributions of a homemaker spouse;

(2) value of the property set aside to each spouse:

(3) the duration of the marriage; and

(4) the economic circumstances of each spouse when the division of property is to become effective, including the desirability of awarding the family home or the right to live therein for reasonable periods to the spouse having custody of any minor children.

Id. Although the UMDA, as a whole, enjoyed a substantial lack of success in a majority of state legislatures and was formally enacted in only eight states, nevertheless a number of its individual sections did have substantial nationwide effect, including Section 307, as individual state legislatures attempted to enact more comprehensive equitable distribution statutory guidelines.

Excerpts from three representative state equitable distribution statutes appear below:

Arkansas Code Ann. § 9-12-315(a):

At the time a divorce decree is entered:

(1)(A) All marital property shall be distributed one-half (1/2) to each party unless the court finds such a division to be inequitable. In that event, the court shall make some other division that the court deems equitable taking into consideration:

(i) The length of the marriage;

(ii) Age, health, and station in life of the parties;

(iii) Occupation of the parties;

(iv) Amount and sources of income;

(v) Vocational skills;

(vi) Employability;

(vii) Estate, liabilities, and needs of each party and opportunity of each for further acquisition of capital assets and income;

(viii) Contribution of each party in acquisition, preservation, or appreciation of marital property, including services as a homemaker; and

(ix) The federal income tax consequences of the court's division of property.

(B) When property is divided pursuant to the foregoing considerations, the court must state its basis and reasons for not dividing the marital property equally between the parties, and the basis and reasons should be recited in the order entered in the matter. . . .

Illinois Comp. Stat. Ann. tit. 750, § 5/503(d):

In a proceeding for dissolution of marriage or declaration of invalidity of marriage . . . the court shall assign each spouse's non-marital property to that spouse. It also shall divide the marital property without regard to marital misconduct in just proportions considering all relevant factors, including:

(1) the contribution of each party to the acquisition, preservation, or increase or decrease in value of the marital or non-marital property, including the contribution of a spouse as a homemaker or to the family unit;

(2) the dissipation by each party of the marital or non-marital property;

(3) the value of each property assigned to each spouse;

(4) the duration of the marriage;

(5) the relevant economic circumstances of each spouse when the division of property is to become effective, including the desirability of awarding the family home, or the right to live therein for reasonable periods, to the spouse having custody of the children;

(6) any obligations and rights arising from a prior marriage of either party;

(7) any antenuptial agreement of the parties;

(8) the age, health, station, occupation, amount and sources of income, vocational skills, employability, estate, liabilities, and needs of each of the parties;

(9) the custodial provisions for any children;

(10) whether the apportionment is in lieu of or in addition to maintenance;

(11) the reasonable opportunity of each spouse for future acquisition of capital assets and income; and

(12) the tax consequences of the property division upon the respective economic circumstances of the parties.

Virginia Code Ann. § 20-107.3(E):

The amount of any division or transfer of jointly owned marital property, and the amount of any monetary award, the apportionment of marital debts, and the method of payment shall be determined by the court after consideration of the following factors:

1. The contributions, monetary and nonmonetary, of each party to the well-being of the family;

2. The contributions, monetary and nonmonetary, of each party in the acquisition and care and maintenance of such marital property of the parties;

3. The duration of the marriage;

4. The ages and physical and mental condition of the parties;

5. The circumstances and factors which contributed to the dissolution of the marriage, specifically including any [fault] ground for divorce under the provisions of § 20-91 . . . or § 20-95 [including adultery, cruelty, desertion, and conviction of a felony];

6. How and when specific items of such marital property were acquired;

7. The debts and liabilities of each spouse, the basis for such debts and liabilities, and the property which may serve as security for such debts and liabilities;

8. The liquid or nonliquid character of all marital property;

9. The tax consequences to each party; and

10. Such other factors as the court deems necessary or appropriate to consider in order to arrive at a fair and equitable monetary award.

[3] An Equal Division Presumption versus an Equal Division "Starting Point"

There are four different approaches as to whether or not there should be an equal division presumption applied to the equitable distribution of marital assets.

Statutes in a respectable minority of states expressly recognize a presumption that property subject to equitable distribution shall be divided equally between the spouses. *See, e.g.* Ark. Code Ann. § 9-12-315(a) (1991), *above*; N.C. Gen. Stat. § 50-20 (1991); W. Va. Code § 48-2-32(a) (1992); and Wis. Stat. Ann. § 767.255 (1981). Other states have developed this presumption favoring an equal division of marital property through case law. *See, e.g., McAlprin v. McAlprin*, 532 A.2d 1377 (N.H. 1987); *In re Marriage of Stice*, 779 P.2d 1020 (Or. 1989).

A majority of judicial decisions in other states, however, have held that the division of marital property between the parties should only depend on how the trial court applies the equitable distribution statutory factors to a specific factual situation, and therefore a court *cannot* assume in advance that any particular distribution of property is equitable. *See, e.g., Gussin v. Gussin*, 836 P.2d 484 (Haw. 1992) (reversing earlier lower court authority adopting different "starting points" for different categories of property); *Alston v. Alston*, 629 A.2d 70 (Md. 1993) (rejecting any preference for an equal division); and *Patricia B. v. Steven B.*, 588 N.Y.S.2d 874 (N.Y. App. Div. 1992) (holding that no special preference or presumption should be given to an equal division of marital property).

A number of other states, however, although rejecting an equal property division presumption on public policy grounds, nevertheless have recognized an equal division "starting point." The public policy rationale behind an equal division "starting point" was explained by an appellate court decision in *Hashimoto v. Hashimoto*, 725 P.2d 520, 522–23 (Haw. Ct. App. 1986):

> The need for "uniform starting points" is obvious. If different family court judges commence deciding in what proportion to equitably divide the value of the property from different starting points, which could range from a 100-0 split to a 0-100 split, then their awards will be equally diverse. There will be no uniformity, stability, clarity or predictability. The ultimate decision will depend less on the facts and the law and more on who is the judge assigned to hear and decide the case. . . . *Id.*

Although the *Hashimoto* case was later reversed by the Hawaii Supreme Court in the case of *Gussin v. Gussin*, 836 P.2d 484 (Haw. 1992) (holding that equal division "starting points" unduly restrict a trial court's discretion in a manner inconsistent with Hawaii's equitable distribution statutes), a number of other "no presumption" states have treated an equal division of marital property at least as a "starting point," if not a presumption. *See, e.g., Robertson v. Robertson*, 593 So. 2d 491 (Fla. 1991); *McNabney v. McNabney*, 782 P.2d 1291 (Nev. 1989); *Cherry v. Cherry*, 421 N.E.2d 1293 (Ohio 1981); *Marion v. Marion*, 401 S.E.2d 432 (Va. 1991). Thus, where an equal division presumption places the burden of proof on the spouse contesting the equal division of the marital property, an equal "starting point" only creates an initial equal division point of reference in the judge's deliberative process, but there is *no* formal burden of proof attached to it, and this initial "starting point" subsequently can be modified according to the particular facts of each case, and the utilization of appropriate statutory factors.

On the other hand, one critic of both the equal division presumption and an equal division "starting point" argues that if "the starting point [approach] does structure the court's deliberative process, it is quite possible that the economic realities of the parties will be overlooked. . . . The goal of equitable distribution, after all, is to do equity. Any formal or informal process which makes the distribution of property mechanistic will not further this goal. A 0-0 starting point with the focus on economic needs and circumstances would seem a better, more flexible approach." L. Golden, Equitable Distribution of Marital Property § 8.05 at 244–45 (1983). However, in a subsequent work, author Brett Turner in *Equitable Distribution of Marital Property* § 8.02 at 557–58 (2d ed. 1994) notes that:

> In the real world, however, too many equitable distribution cases are prejudged, and the prejudgment almost always favors the husband. Many trial judges are of course free from this bias, but there is disturbing statistical evidence that the husband is

significantly more likely to get the long half of the marital estate [*citing* Lenore Weitzman's *The Divorce Revolution: The Unexpected Social and Economic Consequences for Women and Children in America* (1985). *See also* James McLindon, *Separate But Unequal: The Economic Disaster of Divorce for Women and Children*, 21 Fam. L.Q. 351 (1987)]. . . . These studies have convinced [this] author that an equal division presumption is necessary to ensure *consistent* equal treatment of husbands and wives in divorce cases. One survey of lawyers and judges in Wisconsin reported that state's equal division presumption was rebutted in fewer than 10 per cent of all cases [*citing* Martha Fineman, *Implementing Equality: Ideology, Contraction and Social Change*, 1983 Wis. L. Rev. 789, 881]. In Wisconsin, therefore, the equal division presumption has substantially reduced the persistent underestimation of homemaker contributions reported by Weitzman and other sociologists. Wisconsin trial judges have lost a degree of flexibility, but the result has been a better overall system for dividing property on divorce. *Id.* [footnotes omitted].

The proposed ALI *Principles of the Law of Family Dissolution* § 4.15 (1) (1997) adopts a fourth hybrid middle ground rule that "marital property and marital debts are divided at dissolution so that the spouses receive net shares equal in value, although not necessarily identical in kind." There are three exceptions, however, to this proposed "equal value" property distribution rule: (1) when a court concludes that an enhanced share of marital property is appropriate to compensate a spouse in lieu of spousal support; (2) when a court concludes that one spouse is entitled to an enhanced share of marital property because the other spouse made an improper disposition of a portion of such marital property [i.e. dissipation or waste of marital assets]; or (3) when marital debts exceed marital assets, "and it is just and equitable to assign the excess debt unequally." *Id.* § 4.15(2)(a)-(c).

Problem. Assume that you are a Legislative Aide working for State Senator Emily Green, who is a member of your state's Family Law Legislative Caucus. Senator Green wants you to research whether or not your state legislature ought to adopt a equal division presumption as a part of your state's equitable distribution statutory law, similar to the Arkansas state equitable distribution statute, *above*.

Senator Green wants you to prepare a Position Paper for her, discussing the following issues: Which is the better-reasoned approach to a judicial distribution of marital property: (1) an equal division presumption; (2) an equal division "starting point"; (3) the proposed ALI "equal value" distribution; or (4) no presumption or initial "starting point" at all? Based upon what underlying public policy arguments? Who should ultimately make this important public policy decision: the state legislature or the state courts? *And query further*: Will your suggested approach to equitable distribution of marital property on divorce arguably bring more uniformity, predictability, and fairness to your state's equitable distribution awards? Or would it result in a formalistic and mechanical approach that may well stifle a trial court's judicial discretion as a trier of both law and fact in crafting a fair and just equitable distribution award of marital property in each particular case? What are the pros and cons of each approach? What is the best way to resolve this troublesome issue?

[4] Recharacterization and Distribution of Property Based Upon Long-Term Marriages

Section 4.18 of the American Law Institute's proposed *Principles of the Law of Family Dissolution: Analysis and Recommendations* (1997) provides the following unique provision that is not currently found in most state equitable distribution statutes:

Recharacterization of Separate Property as Marital Property At the Dissolution of a Long-Term Marriage

(1) In marriages that exceed a minimum duration specified in a uniform rule of statewide application, a portion of the separate property that each spouse held at the time of their marriage should be recharacterized at dissolution as marital property.

(a) The percentage of separate property that is recharacterized as marital property under Paragraph (1) should be determined by the duration of the marriage, according to a formula specified in a rule of statewide application.

(b) The formula should specify a marital duration at which the full value of the separate property held by the spouses at the time of their marriage is recharacterized at dissolution as marital property.

(2) A portion of separate property acquired by each spouse during marriage should be recharacterized at dissolution as marital property if, at the time of dissolution, both the marital duration, and the time since the property's acquisition (the "holding period"), exceed the minimum length specified for each in a rule of statewide application. . . .

(3) For the purpose of this section, any appreciation in the value of separate property, or income from it, that would otherwise itself be separate property, is treated as having been acquired at the same time as the underlying asset, and any asset acquired in exchange for separate property is treated as having been acquired as of the time its predecessor was acquired.

(4) A spouse should be able to avoid the application of this section to gifts or inheritances received during marriage by giving written notice of that intention to the other spouse within a time period following the property's receipt that is specified in a rule of statewide application.

(5) The provision of a will or deed of gift specifying that a bequest or gift is not subject to claims under this section should be given effect.

(6) This section should not apply to separate property if, as set forth in written findings of the trial court, preservation of the property's separate character is necessary to avoid substantial injustice.

For example, assume that the State of Holmes implements the principles set forth in Paragraphs (1) and (2) with the following statutory language:

Recharacterization of Separate Property to Marital Property upon the Dissolution of a Long-Term Marriage in the State of Holmes

(a) For each year of marriage after the fifth year, four percent of the value of all separate property held by the spouses at the time of their marriage is treated at dissolution as the spouses' martial property. In marriages of 30 or more years duration, all separate property held by the spouses at the time of their marriage is treated at dissolution as marital property.

(b) In marriages of five years or more duration during which a spouse acquires separate property, four percent of the vale of that separate property is treated at dissolution as marital property for each "augmented year" since the fifth year after the property's acquisition.

(1) The augmented years equal

    (A) the number of years from the fifth year after the property's acquisition to commencement of the dissolution action, plus

    (B) half the number of years between the fifth year of marriage and the year of the property's acquisition. . . .

Assume now that Sam and Helen live in the State of Holmes. At the beginning of their marriage, Helen has $25,000 in separate property. In the twenty-fifth year of their marriage, Sam inherits $100,000. In the 30th year of their marriage, the spouses file for divorce. The divorce court will treat Helen's $25,000 under this statute as marital property, because the parties have been married for 30 years. (The parties have been married for 25 years after the fifth year of their marriage, and 25 multiplied by 4% is 100%.) The divorce court will also treat 40% of Sam's inheritance as marital property. (The number of years of marriage after Sam's inheritance is five, and therefore the number calculated under Section (b)(1)(A) of the statute is zero. The number of years between the fifth year of marriage and the property's acquisition is 20, so that the number calculated under Section (b)(1)(B) is ten. Ten multiplied by 4% is 40%.) *See Principles of the Law of Family Dissolution* § 4.18, Illustration 1 (1997).

PROBLEMS

(1) State Senator Emily Green asks you, as her Legislative Aide, to assess the pros and cons of adopting an equitable distribution statute in your state modeled after Section 4.18 of the *Principles of the Law of Family Dissolution, above.* Does this equitable distribution statutory revision based upon the recharacterization and distribution of property based on long-term marriages adequately address important state public policy goals? If so, what are these public policy goals? Is this statute a viable and realistic means to recharacterize separate property into marital property? Would this statute have a realistic chance of passage in your particular state? Why or why not?

(2) Romeo and Juliet were divorced on the ground of living separate and apart. Juliet had spent most of her married life as a traditional homemaker, which was encouraged by Romeo. The marital residence was built on land Juliet had inherited during the marriage, and built with the proceeds from the sale of other land acquired from her family, the Capulets. However, the marital residence was legally titled in both Romeo and Juliet's name. Juliet has no other savings, and she has only a minimal amount of money set aside for her retirement. After a marriage of 28 years, Romeo left Juliet for another woman, Lucretia Borgia, with whom Romeo had been having an extramarital affair.

A Special Master or Commissioner in Chancery recommends to the trial court judge that Juliet be given 75% of the proceeds from the sale of their jointly-owned real property. Romeo has filed exceptions to the Special Master's recommendations. What arguments might you frame in response to Romeo's exceptions? *See Moore v. Moore*, 537 So. 2d 961 (Ala. Civ. App. 1988). What if a husband [or wife] is able to prove a greater contributions to the acquisition of marital property; and the wife [or husband] was the cause of the marital dissolution. Should the husband be legally entitled to a division of marital property in which the judge awards two-thirds of the property to the husband, and only one-third of the marital property to the wife? *See, e.g., Igo v. Igo*, 759 P.2d 1253 (Wyo. 1988), where such an award was upheld on appeal. *But see also In re Marriage of Larson*, 763 P.2d 1109 (Mont. 1988), where the husband was awarded a relatively equal share of the marital property even though there was evidence that he had contributed approximately 97% of the marital assets. Which is the more equitable judicial approach? Based upon what underlying public policy rationales?

(3) At the time of his marriage to Wilma, Harry owns an office building worth $100,000. In the tenth year of his marriage to Wilma, Harry sells the building for $250,000, reinvesting the proceeds in undeveloped land. In the twentieth year of marriage, Harry sells this land for $1,000,000 and invests the proceeds in municipal bonds. The parties are divorced after 31 years of marriage, and the municipal bonds now have a value of $950,000 due to a rise in long-term interest rates. (Assume that Wilma has been a traditional house spouse for the past thirty years raising three children, and that Wilma has meager savings and few job skills). *Query*: How should this marital property be distributed by the court under an equal presumption or an equal "starting point" theory? Under the proposed ALI *Principles of the Law of Family Dissolution* § 4.18 (1997) *above*? Under the proposed ALI *Principles* "equal value" rule under § 4.15 (1997) *above*?

[O] The Role of Fault in the Distribution of Marital Property

Since the advent of the no-fault divorce revolution in America, a number of commentators and courts have largely discounted the role that fault plays in American divorce proceedings. However, these commentators and courts make a serious error in assuming that fault is "no longer an issue" in granting a divorce or dissolution of marriage in most American states, since a substantial number of American jurisdictions still utilize various fault factors in determining spousal support awards, the equitable distribution of marital property on divorce, or both. *See* Peter Nash Swisher, *Reassessing Fault Factors in No-Fault Divorce*, 31 Fam. L.Q. 269, 290–318 (1997).

The role of fault as a factor in the distribution of marital property therefore may be characterized in two distinct categories: (1) "economic fault," or the dissipation and waste of marital assets; and (2) fault based upon marital misconduct.

[1] "Economic Fault": The Dissipation or Waste of Marital Assets

It is a relevant factor in the vast majority of states whether one of the spouses has dissipated or wasted marital assets, and this is often referred to as "economic fault." According to the Virginia Court of Appeals in *Booth v. Booth*, 371 S.E. 2d 569, 572 (Va. Ct. App. 1988):

> Although not an exclusive definition, "waste" may be generally characterized as the dissipation of marital funds in anticipation of divorce or separation for a purpose unrelated to the marriage and in derogation of the marital relationship at a time when the marriage is in jeopardy. *See In re Marriage of Smith*, 114 Ill. App. 3d 47, 69 Ill. Dec. 827, 448 N.E.2d 545 (1983). Just as a court may consider positive contributions to the marriage in making an equitable distribution award, it can also consider "negative" contributions in the form of squandering and destroying marital resources. *Anstutz v. Anstutz*, 112 Wis. 2d 10, 331 N.W.2d 844 (Ct. App. 1983). The goal of equitable distribution is to adjust the property interests of the spouses fairly and

equitably.... To allow one spouse to squander marital property is to make an equitable distribution award impossible. *Sharp v. Sharp*, 58 Md. App. 386, 399, 473 A.2d 499, 505 (1984). On the other hand, at least until the parties contemplate divorce, each is free to spend marital funds. To decide a question of dissipation of marital assets, we must accommodate these conflicting interests in the marital estate. *Id.*

Not surprisingly, the courts have differed in determining what would, in fact, amount to dissipation or waste of marital assets, since a martial purchase that might be considered a financial extravagance by some courts could appear to be a reasonable expenditure to other courts. Nevertheless, gambling losses and extravagant cruises have qualified as dissipation of marital assets in some states. *See, e.g., Linsay v. Linsay*, 565 P.2d 199 (Ariz. Ct. App. 1977); *Barriger v. Barriger*, 514 S.W.2d 114 (Ky. 1974). A gift to a boyfriend or girlfriend also constitutes dissipation of marital assets in most states. *See, e.g., In re Marriage of Kaplan*, 500 N.E.2d 612 (Ill. App. Ct. 1986); *Zeigler v. Zeigler*, 530 A.2d 445 (Pa. Super. Ct. 1987); *Rosenberg v. Rosenberg*, 497 A.2d 485 (Md. Ct. Spec. App. 1985)[. The fraudulent sale of the marital home and other marital property also constitutes waste or dissipation of marital assets that may be characterized as "economic fault." *See, e.g., Earl v. Earl*, 434 N.E.2d 1294 (Mass. App. Ct. 1982).

Some courts have allowed such conveyances to be set aside as fraudulent conveyances. *See, e.g., In re Marriage of Frederick*, 578 N.E.2d 612 (Ill. App. Ct. 1991); *Preece v. Preece*, 682 P.2d 298 (Utah, 1984). Sale of marital property to third parties also has been deemed to constitute a fraudulent conveyance if the conveyance occurred either immediately before or after the parties' separation, and was for less than adequate consideration. *See, e.g., In re Marriage of Pahlke*, 507 N.E.2d 71 (Ill. App. Ct. 1987); *Kaslinski v. Questel*, 472 N.Y.S.2d 807 (N.Y. App. Div. 1984). In the alternative, in lieu of rescinding the transaction, a court will deduct the value of the property wrongfully transferred from the guilty spouse's share of the marital estate. *See, e.g., Watson v. Watson*, 607 A.2d 383 (Conn. 1992); *Halvorson v. Halvorson*, 482 N.W.2d 869 (N.D. 1992); *Guidubaldi v. Guidubladi*, 581 N.E.2d 621 (Ohio Ct. App. 1990).

Once this waste, dissipation, or "economic fault" is found, the courts frequently divide the spouses' marital or community property as if the dissipated property still existed, and the dissipated property is then "awarded" to the dissipating spouse. In effect, then,. the amount of dissipated property is deducted from that spouse's share of the marital or community property. *See, e.g., In re Marriage of Stallworth*, 237 Cal. Rptr. 829 (Cal. Ct. App. 1987); *In re Marriage of Partyka*, 511 N.E.2d 676 (Ill. App. Ct.1987); *Sharp v. Sharp*, 473 A.2d 499 (Md. Ct. Spec. App. 1984); *Blackman v. Blackman*, 517 N.Y.S.2d 167 (N.Y. App. Div. 1987); *Talent v. Talent*, 334 S.E.2d 256 (N.C. Ct. App. 1985). The courts are in general agreement that the party against whom dissipation is charged has the burden of proving the legitimacy of his or her expenditure of marital assets. *See, e.g., In re Marriage of Smith*, 471 N.E.2d 1008 (Ill. App. Ct. 1984). *See generally* J. Thomas Oldham, Divorce, Separation and Distribution of Property § 13.02[1][d] (1997 rev. ed.); and Gregory, Swisher & Scheible-Wolf, Understanding Family Law § 9.12 [D] (Matthew Bender 1995).

The proposed ALI *Principles of the Law of Family Dissolution* § 4.16 (1997) likewise recognize spousal financial misconduct as appropriate grounds for the unequal division of marital property.

Problem. Dick and Jane have been married for nearly thirty years. Four children were born of the marriage, all of whom have reached the age of majority. Both Dick and Jane have worked outside the home during the marriage, although Dick's income as a stockbroker dropped dramatically five years ago and has remained quite low ever since. During the final two years of their marriage, Dick received $35,000 in loans from various sources. The money was used to pay for living and business expenses. Jane claims that Dick simply dissipated their marital estate through reckless spending and that she knew nothing of the loans. *Query*: Is the money marital debt or the separate debt of Dick? *See In re Marriage of Stewart*, 757 P.2d 765 (Mont. 1988).

During this same time, Jane has been expending marital assets to support her mother and a disabled child from a previous marriage. Dick argues that Jane has dissipated their marital assets. Would this action by Jane constitute dissipation of the marital assets and economic fault? Why or why not? *See, e.g., In re Marriage of Aud*, 491 N.E.2d 894 (Ill. App. Ct. 1986). *But see also Kothari v. Kothari*, 605 A.2d 750 (N.J. Super. Ct. App. Div. 1992) (holding that large gifts to a parent at the time of the marital breakdown constituted dissipation of marital assets).

What if Jane has separate property as a result of an inheritance from her father? Can she be ordered to use her separate property to pay for the marital debts incurred by Dick for their mutual benefit? Under the theory that marriage is an economic partnership, should she be required to pay for such a marital debt? *See Douglas v. Douglas*, 503 N.Y.S.2d 530 (N.Y. Sup. Ct. 1986). Once again, how the courts choose to deal with this alleged dissipation and waste of marital assets is a matter of judicial discretion. *See, e.g., Head v. Head*, 523 N.E.2d 17 (Ill. App. Ct. 1988).

[2] Marital Misconduct as a Factor in Dividing Marital Property

Where there is general agreement that dissipation of marital assets or "economic fault" is a relevant factor in determining the equitable distribution of marital assets, there is no such agreement regarding the issue of whether or not marital misconduct should also be a relevant factor in dividing marital property on divorce or dissolution of marriage. State legislatures, courts, and commentators have approached this important issue from two widely different perspectives.

[a] Arguments for Rejecting Marital Misconduct Fault Factors in Equitable Distribution Proceedings

A number of state legislatures, courts, and commentators believe that fault factors based upon marital misconduct should no longer play any valid role in a no-fault regime. For example, Professor Ira Ellman, the Chief Reporter of the proposed ALI *Principles of the Law of Family Dissolution* (1997) criticizes the application of marital misconduct fault factors on divorce since he believes the imposition of such behavioral standards "must rely on trial court discretion" and "the moral standards by which blameworthy conduct will be identified and punished will vary from judge to judge, as each judge necessarily relies on his or her own vision of appropriate behavior in intimate relationships," and such judicial discretion therefore "seems inherently limitless if no finding of economic harm to the claimant is required to justify the award or its amount." *Principles of the Law of Family Dissolution* at 24 (1997). *See also* Ira Mark Ellman, *The Place of Fault in Modern Divorce Law*, 28 Ariz. St. L.J. 773, 787 (1996). Accordingly, Professor Ellman posits that:

> the potentially valid functions of a fault principle are better served by the tort and criminal law, and attempting to serve them through a [divorce based] fault rule risks

serious distortions in the resolution of the dissolution action . . . [and] compensation for the non-financial losses imposed by the other spouse's battery or emotional abuse is better left to tort law. . . . Where valid compensation claims arise, whether for physical violence or emotional abuse, the tort law provides principles to measure and satisfy them, and to determine when they are too stale to entertain. . . . *Id.* at 807–808.

Accordingly, approximately twenty states, as well as the proposed ALI *Principles of the Law of Family Dissolution* (1997), have adopted a "true" no-fault regime, where fault factors based upon marital misconduct no longer play any significant role in determining spousal support awards, or the equitable distribution of marital property on divorce. These states arguably include Alaska, Arizona, California, Colorado, Delaware, Florida, Hawaii, Illinois, Indiana, Iowa, Maine, Minnesota, Montana, Nebraska, Nevada, New Mexico, Oklahoma, Oregon, Washington and Wisconsin. *Id.* at 781.

For example, under Arizona law, fault cannot be an issue in awarding spousal support or distributing the parties' marital property, unless there was destruction, dissipation, or a fraudulent disposition of the marital property. *See, e.g., Ivancovich v. Ivancovich,* 540 P.2d 718 (Ariz. Ct. App. 1975). Other case and statutory law in "true" no-fault divorce jurisdictions are in accord with these general principles. *See, e.g., In re Marriage of Boseman,* 107 Cal. Rptr. 232 (Cal. Ct. App. 1973); *Heilman v. Heilman,* 610 So. 2d 60 (Fla. Dist. Ct. App. 1992); *In re Marriage of Tjaden,* 199 N.W.2d 475 (Iowa 1972); *Smith v. Smith,* 847 P.2d 827 (Okla. Ct. App. 1993); and *Erlandson v. Erlandson,* 318 N.W.2d 36 (Minn. 1982). *See also* Cal. Fam. Code §§ 2550, 2335 (1993); Ariz. Rev. Stat. §§ 25-318, 25-319 (1996); Colo. Rev. Stat. §§ 14-10-113, -114 (1997); Minn. Stat. Ann. §§ 518.58, 552 (1989); Wash. Rev. Code Ann. §§ 26.09.080, 26.09.090 (1996).

Thus, courts in a number of "true" no-fault states have held that assault, battery, murder or attempted murder of one spouse by the other spouse, for example, would have no effect whatsoever on the division of the parties' marital property or any spousal support award, since these awards under "true" no-fault divorce law must be based solely on the financial needs of the parties, regardless of fault. *See, e.g., In re Marriage of Cihak,* 416 N.E.2d 701 (Ill. App. Ct. 1981); and *Mosbarger v. Mosbarger,* 547 So. 2d 188 (Fla. Dist. Ct. App. 1989). *See also* § 9.04, *above.*

[b] Arguments for Retaining Marital Misconduct Fault Factors in Equitable Distribution Proceedings

A significant number of states however, approximately thirty, currently reject the rationale that marital misconduct fault factors should cease to play any role in divorce or dissolution of marriage, and a majority of American states to date continue to recognize that fault factors may still play a viable role in determining spousal support awards on divorce, or in determining the equitable distribution of marital property, even though the parties may have used a no-fault ground for divorce. *See, e.g., The Place of Fault in a Modern Divorce Law, above,* at 776–84. *See also* Linda Elrod & Robert Spector, *A Review of the Year in Family Law,* 30 Fam. L.Q. 765, 804–07 (1997). *See, e.g., Daugherty v. Daugherty,* 606 So. 2d 157 (Ala. Civ. App. 1992); *Bieluch v. Bieluch,* 462 A.2d 1060 (Conn. 1983); *Thames v. Thames,* 477 N.W.2d 496 (Mich. Ct. App. 1991); *Perlberger v. Perlberger,* 626 A.2d 1186 (Pa. Super. Ct. 1993); *O'Loughlin v. O'Loughlin,* 458 S.E.2d 323 (Va. Ct. App. 1995).

Thus, a serious oversight made by a number of legal scholars and other commentators in assessing the no-fault divorce revolution in America— and divorce reform in general—

is their surprising failure to recognize and adequately address the fact that, almost thirty years after the no-fault divorce revolution, a substantial number of American states still utilize various fault factors in determining spousal support and the equitable distribution of marital property on divorce. As Professor Barbara Bennett Woodhouse observes:

> Although we live in a nation aptly characterized by Mary Ann Glendon as an example of "no-fault, no-responsibility" divorce, reports of the death of fault have been exaggerated. While we have been busy dissecting the no-fault revolution, the survival and evolution of fault has aroused relatively little comment. Although half the states employ fault-based doctrines in one context or another, the use of fault as an element in divorce is typically dismissed as contrary to the modern trend. Many of the fault-based laws on alimony and property, however, are recent reforms or amendments of earlier no-fault revolution statutes. Fault is neither as outdated or as invisible as we have made it seem. . . .
>
> Law should reflect and comment on the meaning of human experiences. A fault-blind scheme for balancing equities at divorce asserts that battering and bickering, desertion and disenchantment, repeated infidelity and disappointing marital sex, and the harms that flow from them are qualitatively indistinguishable. In this telling, only financial relations are justiciable, and only money issues matter. Common sense as well as social science studies of the effects of divorce suggest that this story is neither useful as an ideal nor accurate as a reflection of people's experience.

Barbara Bennett Woodhouse, *Sex, Lies, and Dissipation: The Discourse of Fault in a No-Fault Era*, 82 Geo. L.J. 2525, 2531, 2561 (1994). *See also* Peter Nash Swisher, *Reassessing Fault Factors in No-Fault Divorce*, 31 Fam. L.Q. 269 (1997) (arguing that a fault-based factor for serious marital misconduct still serves a realistic and socially defensible function in contemporary American divorce law). *See, e.g.,* Ga. Code Ann. § 19-6-1 (1994); Md. Code Ann. Fam. Code §§ 8-205, 8-206 (1996); Mass. Gen. Laws Ann.; § 208-37 (1997); N.H. Rev. Stat. Ann. § 458:19 (1992); Pa. Cons. Stat. Ann. § 3701 (1997); Texas Family Code § 3.63 (1996); Vt. Stat. Ann. § 751 (1996); Utah Code Ann.; § 30-3-5(7)(b) (1995); Va. Code Ann. § 20-107.3 (1995).

Professor Woodhouse also discusses the problems of bringing a separate tort action:

> Tort claims for marital misconduct have several drawbacks. . . . Because they are treated with suspicion as neither divorce claims nor classic forms of tort, tort remedies for spousal misconduct are often denied or restricted by courts accustomed to no-fault ideology of marriage dissolution. They raise tricky question of *res judicata* and collateral estoppel, the right to a jury trial, overlapping recoveries, [multiplicity of lawsuits], and limitation of damages. These issues . . . currently must be resolved by judges addressing individual cases in a piecemeal fashion and confined to the analytical structure of tort law.

The Discourse of Fault in a No-Fault Era, above, at 2566. *See also* § 9.04, *above*.

Query: How have the courts been assessing these marital fault factors in equitable distribution proceedings? The following case presents one illustration:

SPARKS v. SPARKS
Michigan Supreme Court
485 N.W.2d 893 (1992)

MICHAEL F. CAVANAGH, Chief Justice.

In this divorce case we are asked to consider the element of fault as it relates to the division of marital assets. While marital misconduct remains one of the considerations for establishing the division of property, it is only one of several relevant factors that the trial court must consider to reach an equitable division. In this case we are left with the firm conviction that the award was inequitable because disproportionate weight was ascribed to fault, and therefore we remand for a new hearing before a different judge.

I.

The parties had been married for twenty-six years when the complaint for divorce was filed on May 11, 1987. At the time of trial, the plaintiff-wife was forty-two years old and the defendant-husband was forty-five years old. There is one adult child of the marriage. Throughout the marriage both parties were regularly employed, but at the time of trial the plaintiff was unemployed. Her sole income at that time consisted of temporary alimony ordered by the court while the divorce proceedings were pending. The defendant, on the other hand, was employed at the time of trial, earning an annual salary of approximately $41,000. The defendant earned his college degree during the marriage while the plaintiff ceased her education at age sixteen when she married the defendant.

The trial court's finding of fact included a finding that the plaintiff's sexual infidelity, and her desire to get out of the marriage, caused the breakdown of the marriage. The trial judge then awarded no alimony, attorney fees of $500 to the plaintiff, and a property division of twenty-five percent to the plaintiff and seventy-five percent to the defendant. The Court of Appeals reversed the trial court on the issue of alimony and remanded for an evidentiary hearing. Furthermore, in a divided opinion, the Court affirmed the trial court's division of [the marital] assets stating:

"Although the division of [marital] assets in the instant case may appear unduly harsh, we are not convinced we would have reached a different result had we been in the trial judge's position. . . . Although perhaps not the division we would have chosen, given that fault or misconduct of one of the parties is a proper consideration when fashioning an equitable property settlement, . . . we find no abuse of discretion. . . ."

This court granted leave to appeal. 437 Mich. 1036, 471 N.W.2d 559 (1991). . . .

II.

[The Court then discusses the appellate standard of review in Michigan that applies to matters such as alimony and the equitable distribution of marital property]. . . .

Because the Legislature has granted broad powers to the court to exercise discretion in fashioning equitable decrees, and because equity cases involve issues that are not governed by a clear legal standard, it is inappropriate to apply the formulation of clear legal error to the dispositional ruling. . . . Divorce cases in Michigan are still considered a type of equity suit even though Michigan no longer has separate equity courts. In equity cases it is not enough for the trial court to have acted in a nonarbitrary manner; it must also reach a disposition that is fair and just.... The test for an abuse of discretion is very strict, and ofttimes elevates the standard of review to an "apparently insurmountable height." *People v. Talley*, 410 Mich. 378, 301 N.W.2d 809 (1981) (Levin, J., concurring). But a disposition ruling may be against the just rights of the parties without being a "perversity of will." Limiting review to an abuse of discretion would have the effect of rendering the discretion virtually immune to appellate review where there is any evidence to support the ruling. This has not been the law in Michigan. For example, in *Paul v. Paul*, 362 Mich. 43, 106 N.W.2d 384 (1960), this Court modified a property division even though there was evidence to support the decision. The Court said "[W]e have no doubt that there is evidence of 'improvements' contributed by the husband to justify the lien awarded to him by the circuit judge, provided such an award is 'equitable' under all the circumstances of the case." *Id.* at 46, 106 N.W.2d 384. The Court then modified the award declaring that an equal division would "produce a fairer result." *Id.* at 47, 106 N.W.2d 384.

To alleviate any possible confusion stemming from our prior cases, we hold here that the appellate standard of review of dispositional rulings is not limited to clear error or abuse of discretion. The appellate court must first review the trial court's findings of fact under the clearly erroneous standard. If the findings of fact are upheld, the appellate court must decide whether the dispositive ruling was fair and equitable in light of those facts. But because we recognize that the dispositional ruling is an exercise of discretion and that appellate courts are often reluctant to reverse such rulings, we hold that the ruling should be affirmed unless the appellate court is left with the firm conviction that the division [of marital property] was inequitable. *Kuntze v. Kuntze*, 351 Mich. 144, 88 N.W.2d 608 (1958); *Whittaker v. Whittaker*, 343 Mich. 267, 72 N.W.2d 207 (1955).

III.

Having clarified the standard of review, we must apply that standard to this case. After the Legislature amended the divorce act to provide for nonfault-based grounds, some parties raised the issue of considering "fault", whether in the form of domestic violence, sexual infidelity, or other misconduct, in the distribution of property upon divorce.

This Court has not yet addressed the issue and, although other jurisdictions have resolved the question, the decisions from our sister states are of limited assistance because of differences in the statutory language. Some states, unlike Michigan, merely added nonfault grounds to the traditional fault grounds such as adultery and desertion. Not surprisingly, the concept of fault remains a part of the jurisprudence in some of those states. In contrast, the Michigan Legislature did not merely add to the existing fault grounds; therefore, it may have intended to remove the concept of fault altogether. The remaining provisions of the 1971 act, however, demonstrate that such an intent was limited.... Even more significantly, the 1971 act did not amend the section pertaining to the division of property and alimony.... Some states, following the Uniform Marriage and Divorce Act, 9A ULA 157, adopt an equitable distribution statute and expressly exclude the consideration of marital misconduct.... Unfortunately, the Legislature in Michigan did not amend the property division section along any of these lines: in fact, the 1971 act did not amend the alimony, support, and property division section at all.

... [Therefore] there is no indication that the legislative purpose in providing no-fault grounds was to affect the factors relevant in awarding property divisions. *See Mitchell v.*

Mitchell, 333 Mich. 441, 444, 53 N.W.2d 325 (1952) ("The matter of grounds for divorce is entirely distinct and separable from the question of property settlement . . ."). The Legislature's failure to amend the property division section weighs against deducing such a legislative intent. Rather, by failing to alter the statutory provision regarding property division, the Legislature evidenced an intent to retain the traditional factors when fashioning a property settlement.

We conclude, therefore, that the trial judge must fashion the division of property under the statutory scheme and the relevant case law as they existed before the 1971 amendment of the divorce act. . . .

IV.

Determining that fault remains one of the relevant factors in a property settlement does not fully resolve this case. One additional task is to determine the manner in which the factor should be weighed and considered.

While the Court of Appeals has invariably held that fault remains a factor, none of the cases has held that it is the *only* factor [citing in a footnote *Davey v. Davey*, 106 Mich. App. 579, 581, 308 N.W.2d 468 (1981) (fault is still one of many valid considerations)]. The trial court is given broad discretion in fashioning its rulings and there can be no strict mathematical formulations. *See Hallet v. Hallet*, 279 Mich. 246, 271 N.W. 748 (1937); *Cartwright v. Cartwright*, 341 Mich. 68, 67 N.W.2d 183 (1954). But, as we have recognized before, while the division need not be equal, it must be equitable. *Christofferson v. Christofferson*, 363 Mich. 421, 109 N.W.2d 848 (1961). . . .

As acknowledged above, the division of property is not governed by any set rules. Nevertheless, this Court has established certain principles of general application. In *Johnson v. Johnson*, 346 Mich. 418, 431, 78 N.W.2d 216 (1956), we said:

"The portion of property awarded to each party depends upon all the equitable factors involved, including the following: source of property, contribution towards its acquisition, the years of married life, the needs of the parties, their earning ability, and also the cause for divorce."

These general standards have been refined and expanded upon by the Court of Appeals, and we readily acknowledge that additional factors, beyond those listed in *Johnson*, may be relevant to the disposition of assets. We hold that the following factors are to be considered wherever they are relevant to the circumstances of the particular case: (1) duration of the marriage, (2) contributions of the parties to the marital estate, (3) age of the parties, (4) health of the parties, (5) life status of the parties, (6) necessities and circumstances of the parties, (7) earning abilities of the parties, (8) past relations and conduct of the parties, and (9) general principles of equity. *Perrin v. Perrin*, 169 Mich. App. 18, 22, 425 N.W.2d 494 (1988). There may even be additional factors that are relevant to a particular case. For example, the court may choose to consider the interruption of the personal career or education of either party. The determination of relevant factors will vary depending on the facts and circumstances of the case.

In the case at bar, a review of the record persuades us that the trial court was not considering all the relevant factors, but was fashioning a remedy solely on the basis of the plaintiff's perceived "fault":

"In this case, the Court is going to divide the assets 75 percent to Mr. Sparks and 25 percent to Mrs. Sparks *as a result* of her fault causing this divorce."

The trial court erred in assigning disproportionate weight to this one factor. . . .

The trial court, although there was evidence on the record, made no finding regarding the age of the parties, the health of the parties, status in life, necessities and circumstances of the parties, the earning abilities of the parties, or other general principles of equity. The sum total of the findings of fact related to only four factors: (1) a twenty-six year marriage; (2) a history of employment of both parties; (3) the acquisition of numerous assets during the marriage; and (4) the sexual infidelity of the plaintiff during the marriage. . . . A woman who was an effective partner through a quarter of a century, assisting in the acquisition of assets, and employed throughout, is entitled to a more equal disposition. The concept of fault cannot be given such a disproportionate weight. Marital misconduct is only one factor among many and should not be dispositive.

We conclude that remand is warranted under MCR § 2.517 because the trial court has failed to make findings of fact essential to a proper resolution of the legal question and because the resulting property division was inequitable. . . .

We reverse the judgments of the courts below and remand for assignment to a different judge and for further proceedings consistent with this opinion

MALLET, RILEY, BRICKLEY, BOYLE, and ROBERT P. GRIFFIN, JJ. concur. . . .

LEVIN, JUSTICE (*dissenting*)

In 1971, on the recommendation of the Law Revision Commission, the divorce laws were amended to provide for the "substitution of one non-fault ground for divorce for the existing fault grounds."

The majority turns the clock back over twenty years in holding that fault remains "one of the relevant factors" for determining the division of property. Validating the introduction of evidence concerning marital fault reintroduces the evil sought to be remedied by the enactment of no-fault divorce. The construction placed by the majority on the 1971 statute is opposed by the overwhelming weight of authority. . . .

The goal of the [Michigan] Law Review Commission, eliminating fault as an issue, is expressed in the language recommended to and adopted by the Legislature: "In the complaint the plaintiff shall make no other explanation of the grounds for divorce than by use of the statutory language."

The "statutory language" provides that a divorce shall be granted where "there has been a breakdown of the marriage relationship to the extent that the objects of matrimony have been destroyed and there remains no reasonable likelihood that the marriage can be preserved."

The complaint frames the issues to be tried in a lawsuit. In barring the plaintiff from alleging any ground for divorce other than the statutory no-fault ground, the Legislature evidenced its intent to bar fault as an issue. The majority holds incongruously that fault, no longer an issue, may be considered in the division of property. . . .

It makes little difference whether it is under one section of the divorce laws or another that a participant is, by introduction of fault as an issue, delayed in obtaining a divorce, or is impeded in working out suitable arrangements for property settlement, or is pressured to make unfair or unreasonable concessions concerning property division.

The legislative purpose—eliminating litigation concerning fault as a cause of delay, as an impediment to working out suitable arrangements, and as a cause of pressure to make unfair and unreasonable concessions concerning property division—is defeated by today's decision allowing fault to be considered as a factor in determining property division. . . .

[A]t least twenty-five no-fault states, and one traditional fault-based state, preclude consideration of fault that constitutes a cause of the breakdown of the marital relationship in deciding on the distribution of marital property. . . . Clearly, it is the position of a large majority of states that marital fault should not be considered when distributing property.

. . . The majority stresses the failure of the Legislature, when enacting the no-fault statute, to amend the statutory provisions concerning the division of property to expressly preclude consideration of fault. The property division provisions, however, say nothing about fault. It probably never occurred to any legislator, certainly not to the Law Revision Commission, that it was necessary to amend the property division provisions of the statute, as well as the provisions concerning the grounds for divorce, in order to accomplish the goal of eliminating fault as an issue in a divorce action. . . .

The conduct of the parties in a marital setting is surely relevant in deciding any issue concerning the custody of children. A judge may also properly consider that one of the parties squandered family money when deciding upon the division of what is left of family property. It defeats, however, as most courts have concluded, the legislative purpose to allow fault, including sexual infidelity, to be generally considered as a factor in the division of property.

NOTES AND QUESTIONS

(1) Which opinion in *Sparks, above,* is more persuasive to you? Chief Justice Cavanagh's majority opinion, or Justice Levin's dissenting opinion? Why? *See* § 9.03[C], *below.* What is the underlying public policy issue involved in this—and many other—equitable distribution disputes involving marital misconduct?

See also Perlberger v. Perlberger, 626 A.2d 1186 (Pa. Super. Ct. 1993); *Tarro v. Tarro,* 485 A.2d 558 (R.I. 1984); *Rexrode v. Rexrode,* 339 S.E.2d 544 (Va. Ct. App. 1986) (also holding that a court must consider *all* the statutory factors in distributing marital property or awarding spousal support, not just marital misconduct). *And see also Robertson v. Robertson,* 444 A.2d 244, 246 (Conn. 1982) (holding that a spouse "whose conduct has contributed substantially to the breakdown of the marriage should not expect to receive financial kudos for his or her misconduct"). *But see contra Heilman v. Heilman,* 610 So. 2d 60 (Fla. Dist. Ct. App. 1992); *Markham v. Markham,* 909 P.2d 602 (Haw. Ct. App. 1996); *R.E.G. v. L.M.G.,* 571 N.E.2d 298 (Ind. Ct. App. 1991) (all holding that marital misconduct should play no role whatever in the distribution of marital property or the awarding of spousal support).

(2) *Query*: Is the *Sparks* case a good illustration of Professor Ellman's concern that judicial discretion in applying such fault factors in equitable distribution proceedings "seems inherently limitless if no finding of economic harm to the claimant is required to justify

the award or its amount?" See Ira Ellman, *Fault in a Modern Divorce Law, above,* at 787? Or is this judicial discretion tempered by a number of legislative and judicial safeguards, as Professor Swisher believes?

> A concern that judicial discretion is "inherently limitless" if no finding of economic harm is required is likewise unpersuasive, and has yet to be clearly demonstrated. On the contrary, judicial discretion in most divorce cases today is constrained by the application of a number of statutory factors relating to spousal support awards and the division of marital property on divorce that a judge must properly consider. Judicial discretion is also tempered and constrained by the trial court judge's own day-to-day expertise and experience in divorce matters. Judicial discretion is further constrained by appellate review whenever a trial court judge fails to apply the correct statutory or decisional law, or whenever a trial court judge abuses his or her judicial discretion.

Peter Swisher, *Reassessing Fault Factors in No-Fault Divorce, above,* at 319. *See generally* § 10.02[O], *below.*

(3) **Problem.** Assume you are a trial court judge in a state where marital misconduct is recognized as one of a number of statutory factors in determining equitable distribution of the parties' marital property. Assume further that during Ken and Harriet's dissolution of a twenty-year marriage, Ken was guilty of marital infidelity. How important a factor should Ken's marital infidelity be in making your equitable distribution award? *Compare Smoot v. Smoot,* 357 S.E.2d 728 (Va. 1987) (holding that the husband's adultery was only the last unhappy event in a marital relationship long since dissolved in fact, and therefore it was not a relevant factor in awarding spousal support or the equitable distribution of marital property on divorce) *and Aster v. Gross,* 371 S.E.2d 833 (Va. Ct. App. 1988) (holding that the husband's adultery did not have any adverse economic effect on the marriage, and that the dissolution of the marriage was based upon the cumulative effect of many other factors) *with O'Loughlin v. O'Loughlin,* 458 S.E.2d 323 (Va. Ct. App. 1995) (affirming an unequal division of marital property favoring the wife, and supported by the "negative nonmonetary contribution" of the husband toward the marriage based on five long-term adulterous relationships during the marriage that substantially caused the marriage dissolution). What is your decision?

See also In re Marriage of Craven, 689 S.W.2d 807 (Mo. Ct. App. 1985); *Zecchin v. Zecchin,* 386 N.W.2d 652 (Mich. Ct. App. 1985); *Simmons v. Simmons,* 267 S.E.2d 427 (S.C. 1980); *Cleverly v. Cleverly,* 513 A.2d 612 (Vt. 1986).

(4) **Problem.** Now assume that you are a trial court judge in a jurisdiction that does not recognize marital misconduct as a factor in determining spousal support or the equitable distribution of marital property. Assume further that Sam and Jennifer are bringing a divorce action, and that a substantial reason for the dissolution of their marriage has been Sam's severe physical and mental cruelty against Jennifer and a marriage torn asunder by domestic violence. Assume also that you have just learned that Sam put out a murder-for-hire contract on Jennifer's life, that fortunately was thwarted in the nick of time by the local police department. Should these facts make any difference in how you will distribute Sam and Jennifer's marital property? Why or why not? *Compare In re Marriage of Chihak,* 416 N.E.2d 701 (Ill. App. Ct. 1981) *and Mosbarger v. Mosbarger,* 547 So. 2d 188 (Fla. Dist. Ct. App. 1989) *and De Castro v. De Castro,* 334 So. 2d 834 (Fla. Dist. Ct. App. 1976) *with Stover v. Stover,* 696 S.W.2d 750 (Ark. 1986) *and In re Marriage of Sommers,* 792

P.2d 1005 (Kan. 1990); *O'Brien v. O'Brien*, 498 N.Y.S.2d 743 (N.Y. 1985); *and In re Marriage of Brabec*, 510 N.W.2d 752 (Wis. Ct. App. 1993). *See also* Cal. Fam. Code §§ 782.5, 4324. Based upon what underlying public policy reasons, if any?

Professor Barbara Bennett Woodhouse in *The Discourse on Fault in a No-Fault Era, above* at 2550 further states:

> My colleague, Professor Demie Kurz, interviewed 129 women of many races, ages, and classes, investigating their stories about why their marriages ended for her forthcoming book on divorce, *For Richer, For Poorer*. Over half of the women in Kurz's study, and up to eighty percent of those in working class and lower class marriages, told narratives of husbands who abused alcohol and drugs, slept with other women, beat and raped their wives and children, and actually or constructively abandoned the home. . . . In the terminology of fault and no-fault, the typical woman in Kurz's study stated a prima facie case for a fault-based divorce. . . . How many of these women nevertheless see their marriages end with a judgment that forces the sales of the [marital] home for "equitable" distribution to their abusers?

Query: Assuming *arguendo* that some "true" no-fault courts do consider fault factors in the case of serious and egregious marital misconduct, where should the court draw the line in determining what constitutes serious and egregious marital misconduct, and what does not? *See, e.g.,* Brett R. Turner, Equitable Distribution of Property § 8.09 (2d ed. 1994).

(5) **Problem.** Joe and Kathy have been married for four years, and presently reside in the State of Holmes. Although they loved each other, Joe had, since the day of their marriage, engaged in verbal abuse against Kathy and alcohol abuse. Joe would be drunk every Friday evening, and when he didn't drink at home, he would come home drunk and be verbally abusive to Kathy. At the divorce trial, Kathy related one example where, during a wedding anniversary dinner at a prominent downtown restaurant, Joe drank bourbon and water until he got drunk, and then he proceeded to insult Kathy in front of the other patrons of the restaurant. Joe could not get his coat on without the help of the waiter, whom he also insulted, using numerous profanities. When Kathy confronted Joe about his drinking, Joe would retaliate by hiding things that Kathy needed, such as her car keys, money, her purse, and her business appointment calendar. These unfortunate incidents occurred and reoccurred over a period of years.

Assume that the Holmes state equitable distribution statute prohibits the consideration of marital misconduct fault in the distribution of marital property. What other creative arguments might you raise to bring these facts to the court's attention for consideration? *See, e.g., In re Marriage of Hanson*, 524 N.E.2d 695 (Ill. App. Ct. 1988).

(6) **Problem.** Harold, age 47, and Iris, age 46, had been married for twenty-four years. The primary factor in the breakup of the parties' marriage was Harold's severe drinking problem. His abuse was so great that their family doctor told the couple that if Harold didn't stop drinking, he would die within one year. Iris worked as a customer service representative and earned about $14,000 per year; Harold was an engineer and earned $60,000 in his job with the State Department of Highways. The children of the marriage are both adults now. Harold contends that the marital property should be divided on a 50-50 basis. He says that he contributed "the lion's share of the family assets" by reason of his greater paycheck. Iris wants a disparate award so that she can supplement her modest salary, and so that she can use some of the money to assist her adult children in pursuing their educational goals.

As trial court judge, what would you do and what factors would you consider in making this equitable distribution award? *See, e.g., Quesnel v. Quesnel*, 549 A.2d 644 (Vt. 1988); *Farris v. Farris*, 532 So. 2d 1041 (Ala. Civ. App. 1988).

[P] The Role of Judicial Discretion in Distributing Property on Divorce

The proper role of judicial discretion in equitable distribution proceedings has been heatedly debated by numerous courts and commentators. Professor Ira Ellman, the Chief Reporter for the proposed ALI *Principles of the Law of Family Dissolution: Analysis and Recommendations* (1997) states, for example, that the Objective of Principles Governing the Division of Property are that they are "consistent and predictable in application." *Id.* § 4.02(3), comment c:

> An important goal of any legal regime is to provide rules that are consistent and predictable in application so that individuals can in most cases discern their legal obligations without resort to litigation. The goal is particularly important in the dissolution of marriage, which is among the legal procedures the average individual is most likely to experience, and which most often involves persons who have only limited resources to expend on legal assistance. It is nonetheless the case that many modern systems for allocating property on divorce do not meet this goal as well as they might. . . . *Id.* at 85.

This is a major reason, according to Professor Ellman, why the *Principles* do not allocate marital property distribution based on marital misconduct, since:

> [t]he traditional marital fault rule requires extraordinary reliance on trial court discretion. Neither the standard of misconduct, nor its dollar consequences, are much bounded by any rule. While in principle the trial court's discretion can be reviewed for "abuse of discretion,", reversals are rare. . . . The traditional fault rule is thus inconsistent with a major theme of the *Principles*, an effort to improve the consistency and predictability of trial court decisions. *Id.* at 69–70.

For a contrary view, see Barbara Bennett Woodhouse, *Sex, Lies, and Dissipation: The Discourse of Fault in a No-Fault Era*, 82 Geo. L.J. 2525, 2560 (1994):

> I agree with the ALI's [*Principles of the Law of Family Dissolution*] description of the complexities and challenges of the judging process, but not with the faint-hearted conclusion that judges are incapable of trying cases that depend on assessing the reasonableness of conduct in a given context or on calculating intangibles. We have learned to calculate "goodwill" in a business enterprise, to place a dollar value on an accident victim's pain, to judge corporate directors' fidelity in complex takeover negotiations, and to calibrate punitive damages to deter misconduct in many spheres. There is no reason why courts cannot undertake similar inquiries in the area of marital fault [and other related statutory factors]. *Id.*

An appellate court judge discussing the problem of judicial discretion in equitable distribution proceedings puts the problem more bluntly in *Baker v. Baker*, 488 N.E.2d 361, 366 (Ind. Ct. App. 1986) (concurring opinion):

> In an equitable distribution action, the trial court's range of choice is virtually limitless and [appellate] review little more than pretense. . . . The determination of what is "just and reasonable" is thus left completely to the discretion of the trial court.

Consequently, the distribution of assets varies from court to court depending on the predisposition or whim of a particular trial judge. *Id.*

For a contrary view, see *Sparks v. Sparks*, *above*, § 10.02[N], and similar cases illustrating how a trial court must correctly apply *all* the statutory factors in deciding an equitable distribution case, or be reversed on appeal.

Perhaps the most well-balanced approach to the judicial discretion conundrum in the characterization, evaluation, and distribution of marital or community property is provided by Brett R.Turner, author of Equitable Distribution of Marital Property (2d ed. 1994), when he writes:

> The greatest danger in the developing field of equitable distribution is the strong tradition of local autonomy in family law matters, a tradition which has misled many courts into deciding important legal questions without considering any authority at all outside their own state. With distressing frequency, the result has been extremely poor judicial decisionmaking. On the contrary, when state courts have understood the issues before them in the context of [relevant statutory factors and] case law nationwide, the resulting decisions have only rarely been unworkable. . . .
>
> There is, of course, considerable room for the states to function as laboratories of democracy by testing different rules of law. I certainly would not contend that the law of equitable distribution should be uniform nationwide. If experimentation is to have any meaning, however, it is essential that the results be compared. With comparison, unworkable rules can be identified and avoided, while workable rules can be developed and refined. . . . Thus, while states should by all means experiment with different rules, those experiments should be based upon an evaluation of what has and has not worked in other jurisdictions. *Id.* at viii. . . .
>
> . . . A proper choice between dual classification and all property [equitable distribution regimes] requires a balancing of the competing goals of flexible and consistent justice. The majority consensus to date seems to be that the consistency of dual classification is worth the cost, as a large majority of all recent statutes reject the all property system. Moreover, there is a clear trend in states with all property systems to adopt some of the benefits of dual classification by court decision. . . .
>
> This trend is part of a broader nationwide move toward more consistency in family law generally. The most substantial result of this move has been the enactment of child support guidelines in all 50 states. These guidelines restrict the flexibility of the trial judge to a limited extent, but they have produced substantial increases in the consistency and predictability of child support awards. The dual classification model is essentially a form of property division guideline: by limiting the court's authority to divide certain types of property, it improves the consistency and predictability of the overall process. As long as this move away from unlimited discretion in domestic cases continues, the dual classification [equitable distribution statutory] model is likely to retain its popularity. *Id.* at 45–46.

The Uniform Marriage and Divorce Act, first proposed in 1983, has been adopted by only a handful of states. Whether there will be a more widespread adoption of the ALI *Principles of the Law of Family Dissolution: Analysis and Recommendations* (1997), in whole or in part, with its proposed equitable distribution principles that are "consistent and predictable in application" remains to be seen. *See generally* J. Thomas Oldham, *ALI Principles of Family Dissolution: Some Comments* 1997 U. Ill. L. Rev. 801 (1997).

Problem. In assessing your own states's equitable distribution statutes, and the judicial application of these statutory factors, do you believe there is too much judicial discretion in making equitable distribution awards in your state? Why or why not? Is the court's discretion in your state "inherently limitless," or is it constrained by a number of statutory factors and by appellate review? Does your state follow an "all property" or a "dual property" equitable distribution regime? What are the strengths and weaknesses of each approach?

What further restraints on the equity power of family court judges—if any—might be appropriate? For example, should judicial discretion be restrained in child custody and visitation disputes as well? Should judicial discretion be further restrained or curtailed in the judicial decision whether or not to award spousal support on divorce?

How should legislative or appellate guidelines be established to restrain trial court discretion in divorce or dissolution of marriage proceedings in your own state? Can uniform or formalistic guidelines realistically be established by statutory or case law? Does your state's equitable distribution statutory guidelines already serve this important purpose, or not? What is the proper role of judicial discretion in divorce proceedings in general, and in equitable distribution proceedings in particular?

[Q] Selected Research Biography on Equitable Distribution of Marital Property

[1] Treatises:

Oldfather et al, Valuation and Distribution of Marital Property (3 vols.) (1998 rev. ed.).

Brett R. Turner, Equitable Distribution of Property (2d ed. 1994) (with cumulative annual supplements).

J. Thomas Oldham, Divorce, Separation and the Division of Property (1997 rev. ed.).

John Dewitt Gregory, The Law of Equitable Distribution (1989).

Gregory, Swisher & Scheible-Wolf, Understanding Family Law Chapter 9 (1995).

Homer Clark, The Law of Domestic Relations in the United States Chapter 15 (1987).

[2] Looseleaf Services and Reporters:

The Family Law Reporter [BNA] [published weekly by the Bureau of National Affairs (BNA)] (1231 25th Street N.W., Washington, D.C. 20037).

FairShare [published monthly by Prentice-Hall] (270 Sylvan Avenue, Englewood Cliffs, N.J. 07632).

The Matrimonial Strategist [published monthly by Leader Publications] (111 Eighth Avenue, New York, N.Y. 10011).

Equitable Distribution Journal [published monthly by the National Legal Research Group Inc.] (2421 Ivy Road, Charlottesville, Va. 22901).

[3] Selected Law Review Articles on Equitable Distribution:

Bruch, The Definition and Division of Marital Property in California: Towards Parity and Simplicity, 33 Hastings L.J. 769 (1982).

Sterling, Joint Tenancy and Community Property in California, 14 Pac. L.J. 927 (1983).

Krauskopf, Classifying Marital and Separate Property: Combination and Increase in the Value of Separate Property, 89 W. Va. L. Rev. 997 (1987).

Strieber & Orsinger, Characterization of Marital Property, 39 Baylor L. Rev. 909 (1987).

Koons & Holmes, Division of Property at Divorce, 39 Baylor L. Rev. 977 (1987).

Note, Marital Property: When Does "Ours" Become "Yours" and "Mine", 25 Hous. L. Rev. 173 (1988).

Graham, Using Formulas to Separate Marital and Nonmarital Property: A Policy Oriented Approach to the Division of Appreciated Property Upon Divorce, 73 Ky. L.J. 41 (1984-85).

Note, Vested Rights and the Constitutionality of Retroactive Application of the 1980 Pennsylvania Divorce Code, 46 U. Pitt. L. Rev. 1123 (1985).

Laughrey, Uniform Marital Property Act: A Renewed Commitment to the American Family, 65 Neb. L. Rev. 120 (1986).

Reynolds, The Relationship of Property Division and Alimony: The Division of Property to Address Need, 56 Fordham L. Rev. 827 (1988).

Bassett, Repealing Quasi-Community Property: A Proposal to Readopt a Unitary Marital Property Scheme, 22 U.S.F. L. Rev. 463 (1988).

Marsha Garrison, Good Intentions Gone Awry: The Impact of New York's Equitable Distribution Law on Divorce Outcomes, 57 Brooklyn L. Rev. 621 (1991).

Peter Sevareid, Increase in Value of Separate Property in Pennsylvania: A Change in What Women Want? 68 Temple L. Rev. 557 (1995).

J. Thomas Oldham et al., Marital Property Rights Symposium, 31 Fam. L.Q. 1 (1997).

§ 10.03 Spousal Support[1]

Under the fault-based divorce system, alimony was coherent in theory, even if awarded only rarely in practice. *See* Jana B. Singer, *Divorce Reform and Gender Justice*, 67 N.C.L. Rev. 1103, 1106 (1989) (statistics indicate that only a small minority of women were ever awarded alimony under the fault-based divorce regime). Because divorce was available only where one spouse had breached his marital obligations, alimony functioned as a sort of damages remedy for breach of the state-imposed marriage contract. Moreover, because that contract was explicitly gender-based and imposed support obligations on husbands alone, only wives were entitled to alimony. A wife who "breached" the marriage contract—who was found at fault in the divorce—generally forfeited her right to alimony. *Id.* at 1110.

The widespread adoption of no-fault divorce and the demise of the state-imposed marriage contract significantly undermined these traditional rationales for alimony. Because divorce no longer required a showing of fault or breach, a damage remedy seemed inappropriate. Similarly, because marital obligations were no longer officially gender-based, an alimony remedy premised on the husband's support obligation and available only to the wife seemed both anachronistic and discriminatory. Moreover, while the fault-based divorce system emphasized the importance of preserving the marital unit, the no-fault system focused on

---

[1] This section uses the terms *alimony*, *spousal support* and *maintenance* interchangeably.

effectuating the desire of one or both spouses to end their marriage. Without a societally imposed duty to continue the marriage, justifying financial obligations that survived divorce became problematic. The switch from fault to no-fault divorce thus left alimony in somewhat of a theoretical vacuum. *See* Ira M. Ellman, *The Theory of Alimony*, 77 Cal. L. Rev. 1, 6 (1989). The cases and materials that follow explore the ways in which courts and commentators have filled this theoretical vacuum.

[A] Need and Gender: The Traditional Rationales

ORR v. ORR
United States Supreme Court
440 U.S. 268 (1979)

Mr. Justice Brennan delivered the opinion of the Court.

The question presented is the constitutionality of Alabama alimony statutes which provide that husbands, but not wives, may be required to pay alimony upon divorce.

On February 26, 1974, a final decree of divorce was entered, dissolving the marriage of William and Lillian Orr. That decree directed appellant, Mr. Orr, to pay appellee, Mrs. Orr, $1,240 per month in alimony. On July 28, 1976, Mrs. Orr initiated a contempt proceeding in the Circuit Court of Lee County, Ala., alleging that Mr. Orr was in arrears in his alimony payments. On August 19, 1976, at the hearing on Mrs. Orr's petition, Mr. Orr submitted in his defense a motion requesting that Alabama's alimony statutes be declared unconstitutional because they authorize courts to place an obligation of alimony upon husbands but never upon wives. . . .

In authorizing the imposition of alimony obligations on husbands, but not on wives, the Alabama statutory scheme "provides that different treatment be accorded . . . on the basis of . . . sex; it thus establishes a classification subject to scrutiny under the Equal Protection Clause," *Reed v. Reed*, 404 U.S. 71, 75 (1971). The fact that the classification expressly discriminates against men rather than women does not protect it from scrutiny. *Craig v. Boren*, 429 U.S. 190 (1976). "To withstand scrutiny" under the Equal Protection Clause, "'classifications by gender must serve important governmental objectives and must be substantially related to achievement of those objectives.'" *Califano v. Webster*, 430 U.S. 313, 316–317 (1977). We shall, therefore, examine the three governmental objectives that might arguably be served by Alabama's statutory scheme.

Appellant views the Alabama alimony statutes as effectively announcing the State's preference for an allocation of family responsibilities under which the wife plays a dependent role, and as seeking for their objective the reinforcement of that model among the State's citizens. We agree, as he urges, that prior cases settle that this purpose cannot sustain the statutes. *Stanton v. Stanton*, 421 U.S. 7, 10 (1975), held that the "old [notion]" that "generally it is the man's primary responsibility to provide a home and its essentials," can no longer justify a statute that discriminates on the basis of gender. "No longer is the female destined solely for the home and the rearing of the family, and only the male for the marketplace and the world of ideas," *id.*, at 14–15. If the statute is to survive constitutional attack, therefore, it must be validated on some other basis.

The opinion of the Alabama Court of Civil Appeals suggests other purposes that the statute may serve. Its opinion states that the Alabama statutes were "designed" for "the wife of a broken marriage who needs financial assistance," 351 So. 2d, at 905. This may be read as asserting either of two legislative objectives. One is a legislative purpose to provide help for needy spouses, using sex as a proxy for need. The other is a goal of compensating women for past discrimination during marriage, which assertedly has left them unprepared to fend for themselves in the working world following divorce. We concede, of course, that assisting needy spouses is a legitimate and important governmental objective. We have also recognized "[reduction] of the disparity in economic condition between men and women caused by the long history of discrimination against women . . . as . . . an important governmental objective," *Califano v. Webster, supra*, at 317. It only remains, therefore, to determine whether the classification at issue here is "substantially related to achievement of those objectives." *Ibid.*

Ordinarily, we would begin the analysis of the "needy spouse" objective by considering whether sex is a sufficiently "accurate proxy," *Craig v. Boren, supra*, at 204, for dependency to establish that the gender classification rests "'upon some ground of difference having a fair and substantial relation to the object of the legislation,'" *Reed v. Reed, supra*, at 76. Similarly, we would initially approach the "compensation" rationale by asking whether women had in fact been significantly discriminated against in the sphere to which the statute applied a sex-based classification, leaving the sexes "not similarly situated with respect to opportunities" in that sphere, *Schlesinger v. Ballard*, 419 U.S. 498, 508 (1975).

But in this case, even if sex were a reliable proxy for need, and even if the institution of marriage did discriminate against women, these factors still would "not adequately justify the salient features of" Alabama's statutory scheme, *Craig v. Boren, supra*, at 202–203. Under the statute, individualized hearings at which the parties' relative financial circumstances are considered already occur. There is no reason, therefore, to use sex as a proxy for need. Needy males could be helped along with needy females with little if any additional burden on the State. In such circumstances, not even an administrative-convenience rationale exists to justify operating by generalization or proxy. Similarly, since individualized hearings can determine which women were in fact discriminated against vis-a-vis their husbands, as well as which family units defied the stereotype and left the husband dependent on the wife, Alabama's alleged compensatory purpose may be effectuated without placing burdens solely on husbands. Progress toward fulfilling such a purpose would not be hampered, and it would cost the State nothing more, if it were to treat men and women equally by making alimony burdens independent of sex. "Thus, the gender-based distinction is gratuitous; without it, the statutory scheme would only provide benefits to those men who are in fact similarly situated to the women the statute aids," *Weinberger v. Wiesenfeld, supra*, at 653, and the effort to help those women would not in any way be compromised.

Moreover, use of a gender classification actually produces perverse results in this case. As compared to a gender-neutral law placing alimony obligations on the spouse able to pay, the present Alabama statutes give an advantage only to the financially secure wife whose husband is in need. Although such a wife might have to pay alimony under a gender-neutral statute, the present statutes exempt her from that obligation. Thus, "[the] [wives] who benefit from the disparate treatment are those who were . . . nondependent on their husbands," *Califano v. Goldfarb*, 430 U.S. 199, 221 (1977) (STEVENS, J., concurring in judgment). They are precisely those who are not "needy spouses" and who are "least likely to have been victims of . . . discrimination," *ibid.*, by the institution of marriage. A gender-based classification which, as compared to a gender-neutral one, generates additional benefits only for those it has no reason to prefer cannot survive equal protection scrutiny.

Legislative classifications which distribute benefits and burdens on the basis of gender carry the inherent risk of reinforcing stereotypes about the "proper place" of women and their need for special protection. Thus, even statutes purportedly designed to compensate for and ameliorate the effects of past discrimination must be carefully tailored. Where, as here, the State's compensatory and ameliorative purposes are as well served by a gender-neutral classification as one that gender classifies and therefore carries with it the baggage of sexual stereotypes, the State cannot be permitted to classify on the basis of sex. And this is doubly so where the choice made by the State appears to redound—if only indirectly—to the benefit of those without need for special solicitude.

Having found Alabama's alimony statutes unconstitutional, we reverse the judgment below and remand the cause for further proceedings not inconsistent with this opinion. That disposition, of course, leaves the state courts free to decide any questions of substantive state law not yet passed upon in this litigation. Therefore, it is open to the Alabama courts on remand to consider whether Mr. Orr's stipulated agreement to pay alimony, or other grounds of gender-neutral state law, bind him to continue his alimony payments.

NOTES AND QUESTIONS

(1) Would it have been constitutional for Alabama to respond to *Orr* by abolishing alimony altogether, rather than by extending it to all spouses in need?

(2) *Orr* rejects gender as a basis for alimony and focuses instead on spousal need. However, most alimony statutes do not define need, nor does a focus on need explain why one spouse should be responsible for meeting the other's needs, after their marriage has been dissolved. Contemporary theories of alimony attempt to answer these questions.

[B] Rehabilitation and Self-Sufficiency

IN RE MARRIAGE OF OTIS
Supreme Court of Minnesota
299 N.W.2d 114 (1980)

TODD, J.,

Emmanuel and Georgia Contos Otis' marriage was terminated by divorce. Georgia Otis has appealed from that portion of the decree which terminates her maintenance after four years. We affirm.

The parties were married on June 6, 1954. At the time of the marriage, Mrs. Otis was a skilled executive secretary, earning a substantial income. She left her employment to give birth to the parties' only child and has remained absent from the employment market since that time. Mr. Otis has achieved a high degree of success in the business world and is employed by Control Data Corporation as an executive vice president. At the time of the divorce, Mrs. Otis was 45 and Mr. Otis was 46 years of age.

The divorce decree divided the property of the parties as follows:

Mrs. Otis

Household furniture	$ 13,000.00	
Clothing, jewelry, etc.	9,000.00	
Interest in real estate partnership	25,000.00	(cost)
Equity in leased automobile	1,000.00	
Cash	21,400.00	(net)
Equity in homestead	35,000.00	
Control Data stock (2,923 shares)	121,304.50	
	$225,704.50	

Mr. Otis

Household furniture	$ 13,000.00	
Clothing, jewelry, etc.	2,500.00	
Interest in real estate partnership	25,000.00	(cost)
Porche automobile	10,000.00	
Cash	7,500.00	
Profitsharing plan—cash value	1,300.00	
Life insurance policies—cash value	20,000.00	
Control Data stock (6,827 shares)	131,320.50	(net value)
	$210,620.50	

Mr. Otis was also awarded his substantial interest in his vested pension plan. In addition, he was awarded property in Greece valued at $85,000 which he had inherited.

At the time of the divorce, Mr. Otis received an annual salary in excess of $120,000, plus bonuses. The trial court found that Mrs. Otis was in good health and had held a highly paid secretarial job in the past. Further, the court found that Mrs. Otis, with some additional training, is capable of earning $12,000 to $18,000 per year.

In addition to the property settlement outlined above, Mrs. Otis was awarded as "alimony" the sum of $2,000 per month, commencing December 1, 1978, through and until the last day of 1980, and $1,000 per month, commencing on January 1, 1981, through and until the last day of 1982. Thereafter, no further "alimony" must be paid.

The only issue presented by this appeal is the correctness of the trial court's order terminating monthly payments to the wife after four years.

This case was submitted to the trial court in 1978. The 1978 Minnesota Legislature adopted substantial legislative changes relating to the entire subject of domestic relations. Act of Apr. 5, 1978, ch. 772, 1978 Minn. Laws at 1062. The effective date of this legislation was March 1, 1979. Id. 1978 Minn. Laws 1088, § 64 . . .

We have not had occasion previously to interpret 1978 Minn. Laws, ch. 772. The pertinent sections of the statute to be considered in this case involve the payment of money to a former spouse following termination of the marriage. Initially, we observe the substantial change in language defining such payments. Minn. Stat. § 518.54 (1976) was a definitional section. Included therein was a definition of the term "alimony." As amended by 1978 Minn. Laws, ch. 772, the term "alimony" no longer appears in the statute. The term "maintenance" has been substituted without a substantial change in the definition. The elimination of the term "alimony" is effectuated throughout the entire text of 1978 Minn. Laws, ch. 772.

The grounds for awarding "maintenance" were established by 1978 Minn. Laws, ch. 722, § 51 (now codified as Minn. Stat. § 518.552 (1978 & Supp. 1979)), which provides:

Subdivision 1. In a proceeding for dissolution of marriage or legal separation, or in a proceeding for maintenance following dissolution of the marriage by a court which lacked personal jurisdiction over the absent spouse and which has since acquired jurisdiction, the court may grant a maintenance order for either spouse if it finds that the spouse seeking maintenance:

(a) Lacks sufficient property, including marital property apportioned to him, to provide for his reasonable needs, especially during a period of training or education, and

(b) Is unable to support himself through appropriate employment or is the custodian of a child whose condition or circumstances make it appropriate that the custodian not be required to seek employment outside the home.

Subd. 2. The maintenance order shall be in amounts and for periods of time as the court deems just, without regard to marital misconduct, and after considering all relevant factors including:

(a) The financial resources of the party seeking maintenance, including marital property apportioned to him, and his ability to meet his needs independently, including the extent to which a provision for support of a child living with the party includes a sum for that party as custodian;

(b) The time necessary to acquire sufficient education or training to enable the party seeking maintenance to find appropriate employment;

(c) The standard of living established during the marriage;

(d) The duration of the marriage;

(e) The age, and the physical and emotional condition of the spouse seeking maintenance; and

(f) The ability of the spouse from whom maintenance is sought to meet his needs while meeting those of the spouse seeking maintenance.

This section is taken in large part from the Uniform Marriage and Divorce Act and we find commentaries and decisions of other jurisdictions involving this Uniform Act provision and similar provisions instructive.

The basic additudinal change reflected in the new provision has been summarized as follows:

In recent years, courts have retreated from traditional attitudes toward spousal support because society no longer perceives the married woman as an economically unproductive creature who is "something better than her husband's dog, a little dearer than his horse." Traditionally, spousal support was a permanent award because it was assumed that a wife had neither the ability nor the resources to become self-sustaining. However, with the mounting dissolution rate, the advent of no-fault dissolution, and the growth of the women's liberation movement, the focal point of spousal support determinations has shifted from the sex of the recipient to the individual's ability to become financially independent. This change in focus has given rise to the concept of rehabilitative alimony, also called maintenance, spousal support, limited alimony, or step-down spousal support.

Rehabilitative Spousal Support: In Need of a More Comprehensive Approach to Mitigating Dissolution Trauma, 12 U.S.F.L. Rev. 493, 494–95 (1978) (footnote omitted).

The Missouri Court of Appeals expressed the concerns concisely: "The most that can be accurately said about the amount to be granted is that it is neither the policy of the law to give the spouse receiving maintenance a lifetime annuity nor to reduce her to menial labor to eke out an existence." *In re Marriage of Schulte*, 546 S.W.2d 41, 49 (Mo. App. 1977).

The Florida Court of Appeals, which has had various occasions to consider alimony questions, has adopted an approach similar to that of the Uniform Act. The court has recognized the distinction between permanent alimony and rehabilitative alimony (maintenance):

> Under the circumstances, the trial court erred in awarding permanent rather than rehabilitative alimony. As we have previously stated: "The public policy under the new law which the legislature passed and which therefore we must apply seems to be that if the spouse has the capacity to make her own way through the remainder of her life unassisted by the former husband, then the courts cannot require him to pay alimony other than for rehabilitative purposes." (*Roberts v. Roberts*, Fla. App. 1st 1973, 283 So. 2d 396, 397); * * *.) The public policy of the State would be utterly frustrated by an award of permanent alimony where it affirmatively appears that the wife has not only the capacity but also the desire to be self-supporting.

Cann v. Cann, 334 So.2d 325, 330 (Fla. Dist. Ct. App. 1976) (citations omitted). More recently that court emphasized, in setting aside a 20-year award of alimony, that rehabilitative alimony must be of reasonable duration:

> Rehabilitative alimony is not a substitute for either unemployment compensation or retirement benefits. The award is clearly an incentive to assist one in reclaiming employment skills outside the home which have atrophied during the marital relationship. It was not meant to remove the recipient from the job market. In *Manning v. Manning*, 353 So. 2d 103 (Fla. 1st DCA 1977) we stated that when a wife has completed her maternal role, and provided she is in good health, she should make every effort to rehabilitate herself within a reasonable time thereafter, and when she has done so, rehabilitative alimony is to be discontinued.

Robinson v. Robinson, 366 So.2d 1210, 1211–12 (Fla. App. 1979). The Florida Court has also indicated that a substantial difference in the earning capacities of the spouse does not justify continuing alimony once a spouse has become self-supporting:

> In view of the foregoing, under the applicable law the ability of the husband to pay does not justify continuation of the alimony where, as here, the rehabilitated wife is shown to have become self-supporting.

Anderson v. Anderson, 333 So. 2d 484, 487 (Fla. App. 1976).

We are now faced in Minnesota with new legislation which effects a substantial change in the role of the courts in awarding periodic or lump-sum payments to a divorced spouse. Minnesota decisions decided prior to this time provide only minimal help in passing on the validity of trial court awards under the new act. Rather, the focus of this court must now be on a determination of the two basic standards established by the new legislation; namely, we must determine if the spouse seeking maintenance—

(a) Lacks sufficient property, including marital property apportioned to him, to provide for his reasonable needs, especially during a period of training or education, and

(b) Is unable to support himself through appropriate employment or is the custodian of a child whose condition or circumstances make it appropriate that the custodian not be required to seek employment outside the home.

In construing the Uniform Act provision, the Kentucky Court of Appeals concluded that the statute required satisfaction of the conditions of both subsections. *Inman v. Inman*, 578 S.W.2d 266 (Ky. App. 1979). Applying these standards to the findings of the trial court, which we are bound to accept in the absence of a transcript, we conclude that the decision of the trial court is not clearly erroneous.

Affirmed.

OTIS, JUSTICE (dissenting).

In this decision, the majority applies a section of the Minnesota session laws which was not effective until after this case was tried and then holds that it dictates that appellant who has not held a job outside her home for 23 years, may be denied all alimony after only four years have elapsed. In my opinion it is manifestly unjust and inappropriate to deprive a wife of an expectancy on which she had a right to rely after a marriage of 25 years and accordingly I respectfully dissent. . . .

The parties were married in June 1954. Today, respondent is a vice-president of Control Data Corporation, earning more than $120,000 per year. Appellant has not been employed since her son was born, at which time she abandoned a promising career as an executive secretary in order to fulfill the expected, traditional role of wife and hostess for a rising and successful business executive. She performed this role so well that in 1977 she was selected to serve as hostess to the board of directors of Control Data Corporation during a week-long meeting in Greece, which was her homeland and that of her husband. When her husband was being considered for his present position, appellant was herself interviewed to determine whether she could fill the role required of her in her husband's business career. A number of years previously she had been anxious to resume a career of her own. Her husband forbade it stating that he was "not going to have any wife of mine pound a typewriter."

There is no evidentiary support for the trial court's finding that her earning capacity is substantial. There is no showing that at her age, now approximately forty-seven, she can be gainfully employed at her prior occupation after a lapse of more than twenty years. . . .

Accordingly, I would continue the $2,000 per month payment indefinitely, subject only to a substantial change in circumstances at some later date.

VAN KLOOTWYK v. VAN KLOOTWYK
Supreme Court of North Dakota
563 N.W. 2d 377 (1997)

MARING, JUSTICE.

Michelle L. Van Klootwyk appeals from a district court judgment dated June 27, 1996, denying her spousal support from Robert J. Van Klootwyk. We conclude the trial court's finding Michelle is not disadvantaged by the divorce and is not in need of rehabilitative spousal support is clearly erroneous and we reverse.

Robert and Michelle Van Klootwyk were married on December 5, 1967, and have two adult children, who at the time of trial were emancipated and self-supporting. At the time of the marriage, Robert had completed two years of college. During the course of the marriage Robert worked in the radio industry, first as a disc jockey and then in the management area of radio.

At the time of the marriage, Michelle had a high school education, a work history of minimum wage work, and was working as a clerk at the old GP Hotel in Bismarck, North Dakota. During the marriage Michelle worked odd jobs to assist family finances from time to time, but both Robert and Michelle agreed Michelle's primary responsibility was to care for the children and their home.

The family made 27 or 28 moves in 24 years to advance Robert's career in the radio industry. At the time of trial Robert testified that his gross income for 1995 was $ 76,000. Robert then resided in Boston, Massachusetts, where he was the operations director for Fairbanks Communication.

In the fall of 1987, Michelle went back to school at Central Oregon Community College in Bend, Oregon. In the fall of 1988, Michelle attended Spokane Community College in Spokane, Washington. When the family moved to Bismarck to join Robert in the summer of 1989, Michelle took a class at Bismarck State College and then started classes at the University of Mary. In the spring of 1991, Michelle received a bachelor's degree in nursing from the University of Mary. Following her graduation she obtained employment on the telemetry unit at St. Alexius Hospital. She graduated on May 3, 1991, and started work on May 4, 1991. Her degree in nursing from the University of Mary enabled her to earn approximately $ 30,000 per year.

In March, 1991, Robert and Michelle separated. From 1991 to 1994, Michelle continued to work as a nurse in Bismarck. In September of 1994 Michelle started a two year nurse practitioner program at the University of Mary. Michelle obtained her degree in May 1996.

At the time of trial on January 3, 1996, Michelle testified her starting salary as a nurse practitioner would be anywhere from $ 40,000 to $ 55,000 per year.

Michelle testified her cost of obtaining her undergraduate nursing degree at the University of Mary was about $ 5,000 per semester or a total of $ 20,000. Marital funds paid for approximately one half of that amount. Robert testified the family paid about $ 10,000 a year for tuition for Michelle to go to the University of Mary. Michelle testified she had to take out a loan for $ 6,500 to pay for her undergraduate tuition and at the time of trial the loan had been paid down to approximately $ 2,000. Michelle further testified that at the time of her graduation from the University of Mary in May of 1996 she will owe approximately $ 32,000 in student loans, including both graduate and undergraduate costs, living costs and help given to her daughter. Michelle estimated the cost of her two years in the University of Mary's graduate program was $ 18,000, which included $ 14,000 for tuition and $ 4,000 for books. She paid these costs by obtaining student loans which she had to start repaying commencing six months after her graduation.

The parties accumulated very few assets during their marriage. They borrowed money from both of their parents and neither of those debts has been completely paid. In 1991 they filed for bankruptcy. At the time of trial the family occupied rented property and their only assets consisted of some household goods and furniture.

Robert Van Klootwyk admitted he had more than one affair during the course of their marriage and that an affair in 1991 led to the separation of the parties in March 1991. Robert also conceded that his consumption of alcohol had been a detriment to the marriage and became a problem in the marriage. Michelle testified Robert struck her on "many occasions" during the course of the marriage and that on two occasions his conduct resulted in 911 calls.

On April 24, 1996, the court entered a judgment granting a divorce and dividing the parties' marital property. The court also decreed each would assume the separate indebtedness incurred since their separation in March 1991. Robert would be responsible for the existing indebtedness to his mother, the IRS, and a former business associate. Michelle would be responsible for the student loan debt she incurred to obtain her nurse practitioner degree. The court denied Michelle's request for rehabilitative spousal support and she appealed.

Michelle Van Klootwyk asserts the trial court erred in denying her request for rehabilitative spousal support. She claims she incurred debt to obtain her nurse practitioner degree and she requests a support award of $ 430.00 per month for ten years to pay that debt.

In *Smith v. Smith*, 534 N.W.2d 6, 12 (N.D. 1995), we summarized our standard for reviewing a trial court's spousal support decision:

> There are two types of spousal support. Permanent spousal support is appropriate to provide traditional maintenance for a spouse who is incapable of rehabilitation. Rehabilitative support is appropriate to restore an economically disadvantaged spouse to independent status or to equalize the burden of divorce. A trial court's spousal support decisions are treated as findings of fact which will not be set aside on appeal unless clearly erroneous. The complaining party bears the burden of demonstrating on appeal a finding of fact is clearly erroneous. . . .

This court has long held the trial court must consider the Ruff-Fischer guidelines in deciding whether to award spousal support. The Ruff-Fischer guidelines include:

> "the respective ages of the parties, their earning ability, the duration of the marriage and conduct of the parties during the marriage, their station in life, the circumstances and necessities of each, their health and physical condition, their financial circumstances as shown by the property owned at the time, its value at the time, its income-producing capacity, if any, whether accumulated before or after the marriage, and such other matters as may be material." *Weir v. Weir*, 374 N.W.2d 858, 862 (N.D. 1985).

Id. Although the trial court does not need to make specific findings as to each guideline, it must specify a rationale for its determination. A review of the trial court's findings of fact reveals that its specified rationale for its finding that Michelle was not disadvantaged by the divorce was she "received education during the marriage, has an adequate salary and is self supporting."

There are two different concepts of rehabilitative spousal support. *See* Marcia O'Kelly, *Entitlements to Spousal Support After Divorce*, 61 N.D.L.Rev. 225, 242 (1985). One is a "minimalist doctrine" and the other a more "equitable concept" of rehabilitative support. The "minimalist doctrine" has as its objective to educate and retrain the recipient for minimal self-sufficiency. The "equitable doctrine" tries to enable the disadvantaged spouse to obtain "adequate" self-support after considering the standard of living established during the marriage, the duration of the marriage, the parties' earning capacities, the value of the property and other Ruff-Fischer factors.

This court has not adopted the "minimalist doctrine"—one where the only determination is whether the recipient of support is merely "self-supporting." We have upheld rehabilitative spousal support where the recipient is already working full time. *See, e.g., Wahlberg v. Wahlberg*, 479 N.W.2d 143, 145 (N.D. 1992). In *Wahlberg*, the husband argued that because the wife was already self-supporting she was not "disadvantaged." *Wahlberg* at 145. This court stated, "the need which evidences that one spouse has been disadvantaged by the divorce and that rehabilitative support is, therefore, appropriate is not limited to the prevention of destitution." *Id.* We have held a spouse is "disadvantaged" who has foregone opportunities or lost advantages as a consequence of the marriage and who has contributed during the marriage to the supporting spouse's increased earning capacity. *Id.* We have also stated a valid consideration in awarding spousal support is balancing the burdens created by divorce. *Id.*

Michelle contributed during the marriage to Robert's increased earning capacity. She moved 27 to 28 times in 24 years to advance Robert's career. Robert acknowledged this fact. Michelle spent from 1967 to 1987 caring for the parties' children and home and working at "odd jobs." In the fall of 1987, she went back to school and ultimately received her nursing degree in April 1991. She incurred approximately $ 20,000 of debt in order to obtain that degree. The evidence in the record reveals Robert helped pay off some of this debt but Michelle borrowed from her brother and took out student loans, too. She did not get her diploma until 1994, because the University of Mary had not been paid in full until then. In March, 1991, Michelle and Robert separated. Robert basically did not provide Michelle any support during their separation, which lasted until the time of the divorce. In September 1994, Michelle enrolled in a nurse practitioner program. She testified at the January 1996 trial she would graduate in May 1996. The record indicates Michelle incurred approximately $ 18,000 of debt for tuition and books in order to obtain this advanced degree. At the time of the divorce, Robert was earning a gross salary of $ 76,000. The evidence indicated Michelle was making approximately $ 30,000 as a nurse, but she had salary potential of $ 40,000 to $ 55,000 after receiving her nurse practitioner degree. The disparity in the parties' earning capacities of $ 76,000 and $ 30,000 is one of the factors which clearly supports an award of spousal support to Michelle. Even if Michelle earned the top projected salary for a nurse practitioner of $ 55,000, she would still earn $ 21,000 per year less than Robert. In addition, she has the burden of paying off the remaining $ 18,000 of school debt. The fact that Michelle began her economic self-rehabilitation during the marriage should not deprive her of rehabilitative spousal support, especially when the price of her going from financially dependent to "adequately" self-supporting is neither borne nor shared by her former spouse.

Application of other Ruff-Fischer guidelines to the facts further mandate rehabilitative spousal support for Michelle. There are no real assets in this divorce other than some furnishings and personal property. The marriage is a long term marriage of approximately 28 1/2 years, 20 years of which Michelle devoted to caring for the parties' children, maintaining the home and building Robert's career in the radio industry while she deferred pursuit of any career for herself. Michelle was 47 years old and middle-aged at the time of the divorce. Robert admitted to adultery and having more than one affair during the marriage. The record indicates the separation in March, 1991, was caused by Robert's adultery. The record also evidenced Robert's drinking and physically abusive behavior toward Michelle on "many occasions." Michelle has clearly established she has been disadvantaged by the divorce and is in need of rehabilitative support.

Our decision in *Wahlberg* is not "clearly distinguishable" from this case as asserted by Robert. Although Robert did not receive additional education during the marriage, he established and advanced a career in the radio industry which enabled him to earn a substantial salary between $65,000 and $76,000 per year. Michelle did receive a bachelor's nursing degree and a postgraduate degree during the marriage, but the evidence established that at the time of the divorce there remained at least $18,000 of debt related to tuition and books. This debt was assigned to Michelle, not Robert, yet Robert still wants to take full advantage of the degrees earned by Michelle. These degrees do not even bring her close to his earning capacity in the best case scenario.

The minority opinion relies on the trial court's finding that Michelle is "self-supporting" and asserts this was true even before she earned the postgraduate degree. This approach embraces the concept of "minimalist" support and ignores the other Ruff-Fischer guidelines. It also fails to recognize that although Michelle "earned" these degrees during the marriage, she did not receive the benefit of marital funds paying the debt incurred in obtaining these degrees, which degrees provided her with a higher earning capacity to Robert's advantage.

After reviewing the law and the record, we conclude the trial court's finding that Michelle was not disadvantaged was induced by an erroneous view of the law and we are left with a definite and firm conviction that a mistake has been made.

We reverse and remand for the trial court to award rehabilitative spousal support to Michelle consistent with Robert's ability to pay.

NEUMANN, JUSTICE, concurring specially.

The dissent points out that many of the facts relied upon by the majority (unnecessarily, I think) to support its decision were disputed or were balanced by countervailing factors and considerations in the evidentiary record. While that may be true, it overlooks the fact that the trial court, in finding Michelle was not disadvantaged by the divorce, clearly applied the minimalist concept of spousal support, a concept this court has not adopted in the past and which this court now clearly (and correctly, I think) rejects.

Beyond that, I write separately to emphasize Michelle Van Klootwyk's work history. When the parties married she had only a high school education and very little work experience. During most of the marriage, she deferred any effort to pursue an education and a career of her own in order to make a home for Robert Van Klootwyk and care for his children, while he pursued his own career through 27 or 28 moves across the country. It was not until 1987, that Michelle began going to college. Her efforts led to a bachelor's degree in nursing in 1991, and ultimately to a nurse practitioner's degree in 1996, some 29 years after the marriage.

I suggest that any one who attempts to begin a career at Michelle's stage in life, after deferring meaningful work and education for 24 years in order to support her husband's pursuit of his own career, a career the fruits of which she will no longer share, is presumptively disadvantaged by her divorce. I would also argue that Robert Van Klootwyk has shown nothing which would overcome that presumption. . . .

SANDSTROM, JUSTICE, dissenting.

The question here is not whether the trial court could have awarded spousal support in this case; the question is whether it was clear error for the trial court not to make such an award. Because the trial court's finding Michelle Van Klootwyk not disadvantaged by the divorce and not in need of rehabilitative or permanent spousal support is supported by the record, I would affirm. . . .

Upon earning her undergraduate nursing degree, Michelle Van Klootwyk accepted a nursing job at a local hospital at a salary of about $ 30,000. While taking postgraduate courses, she continued working as a nurse, earning between $ 20,000 and $ 30,000 per year. She testified she was able to pay all her living expenses while working as a registered nurse and taking postgraduate courses. She was self-supporting even before earning a postgraduate degree; her income was above the annual average pay of North Dakotans. *See* North Dakota Department of Economic Development & Finance, North Dakota Details, Labor, Wages (May 13, 1997) ('The average annual pay in North Dakota is $ 19,893."). As Justice Neumann wrote in *Heley v. Heley*, 506 N.W.2d 715, 719 (N.D. 1993), "Rehabilitative spousal support, on the other hand, is awarded to provide a disadvantaged spouse time and resources to acquire an education, training, work skills, or experience that will enable the spouse to become self-supporting." . . . Here, Michelle Van Klootwyk leaves the marriage on the threshold of completing her postgraduate degree. Her beginning salary with her postgraduate degree will place her far above the median household income in North Dakota and will be more than double the annual average pay of North Dakotans. *See* U.S. Bureau of the Census, 1990 U.S. Census Data: Database (median household income in North Dakota: $ 23,213).

She testified the educational costs for her postgraduate degree, including books, totaled $18,000. However, her total debt is $32,000. In at least partial explanation for her large debt, the record evidence shows she has purchased a 1993 Ford Explorer, she has made monthly mortgage payments for her adult emancipated daughter's home since September 1995, and she has also purchased food and clothing for her adult daughters and her granddaughters. She wants Robert Van Klootwyk to pay the entire $32,000 debt.

Omitted from the majority's recitation, the record shows Robert Van Klootwyk's necessary living expenses in Boston are considerably higher than Michelle Van Klootwyk's living expenses in Bismarck. His net monthly income is $ 4,176, and he lists monthly expenses of about $ 3,900. She lists monthly expenses (including attorney fees, but excluding school costs) of about $ 2,300. The evidence also shows she has been able to build a retirement account and put some money in savings. Meanwhile, he has been able to meet his expenses in Boston, but does not have a retirement account or any substantial assets and does not own an automobile. He assumed the majority of the marital debt, which will hinder his ability to accumulate substantial assets or savings in the foreseeable future. . . .

Robert Van Klootwyk entered this marriage with two years of education and did not receive additional education during the marriage. However, Michelle Van Klootwyk obtained a bachelor's degree in nursing during the marriage, which she concedes gives her the earning capacity to meet her own expenses, and at the time of the divorce had almost completed her postgraduate degree. In addition, Michelle Van Klootwyk has voluntarily made monthly payments on her married daughter's mortgage and bought clothing and other things for her adult daughters and grandchildren. Michelle Van Klootwyk lived with her daughter for only two months in 1995. She continued, however, to make her daughter's mortgage payments even though, at the time of trial, she was living with her mother and sharing the expenses of that household.

Although she has college degrees, a car, and a retirement account, and he has none of these, the majority says Michelle Van Klootwyk is a disadvantaged spouse.

At the conclusion of the testimony, and after considering all the facts and evidence, including that omitted by the majority, the trial court stated Michelle Van Klootwyk's request for spousal support "is unsubstantiated" and "she is not disadvantaged by this divorce." "The trial judge has the responsibility of weighing the evidence as well as determining the credibility of the witnesses." *Bullock v. Bullock*, 376 N.W.2d 30, 31 (N.D. 1985). The record evidence supports the trial court's findings, and we should therefore conclude the court's denial of the request for spousal support is not clearly erroneous

NOTES AND QUESTIONS

(1) The majority opinions in *Otis* and *Van Klootwyk* reflect two, quite different understandings of "rehabilitative" alimony. Which understanding seems most persuasive to you? Do you agree with the concurring Justice in *Van Klootwyk* that "anyone who attempts to begin a career at Michelle's stage in life, after deferring meaningful work and education for 24 years in order to support her husband's pursuit of her own career, a career the fruits of which she will no longer share, is presumptively disadvantaged by her divorce?" Why or why not?

(2) How should self-sufficiency be defined for purposes of evaluating a claim for rehabilitative alimony? In particular, should self-sufficiency be defined in minimalist terms, or should it take into account the standard of living established during the marriage? Are income disparities between the spouses relevant to determining whether an alimony claimant "is unable to support himself through appropriate employment?"

(3) To what extent is Michelle Van Klootwyk's claim that she has been disadvantaged by the divorce undermined by the fact that, even before earning a postgraduate degree, her income exceeded the annual average pay of North Dakotans and that, with a postgraduate degree, her starting salary will be more than double that average annual pay?

(4) Are there some divorcing spouses for whom economic self-sufficiency is not a realistic or an appropriate goal? *See, e.g.*, Md. Code Ann. Fam. Law § 11–106 (c) (1998) (although rehabilitative alimony is preferred, court may award alimony for an indefinite period where the party seeking alimony cannot reasonably be expected be become self supporting or where, even after the claimant has made reasonable progress toward self-sufficiency, "the respective standards of living of the parties will be unconscionably disparate"). *Cf.* Jane Rutherford, *Duty In Divorce: Shared Income As A Path To Equality*, 58 Fordham L. Rev. 539, 568–69 (1990) (arguing that "rehabilitative alimony" awarded for short period does not account for lower earnings of spouse who has not been employed for period of years or who wishes to continue to devote time to caretaking role after divorce).

(5) **The Relevance of Fault.** In evaluating Michelle Van Klootwyk's claim for rehabilitative spousal support, the majority points to Robert's admitted adultery, as well as to evidence of his drinking and physical abuse. Should these "fault factors" be relevant to alimony

determinations? If Michelle (rather than Robert) had committed adultery, should that have precluded or weakened her alimony claim? *See, e.g., Hammonds v. Hammonds*, 597 So. 2d 653, 654 (Miss. 1992) (where both husband and wife had committed adultery during their long-term marriage, wife was entitled to minimal alimony); *R.G.M. v. D.E.M.*, 410 S.E.2d 564, 566–67 (S.C. 1991) (wife's extramarital lesbian affair bars spousal support). Currently, approximately half of the states allow judges to consider fault in determining spousal support. *See Family Law In the Fifty States, 1995–96*, 30 Fam. L.Q. 765, 804 (Table 1) (1997). In a handful of states, a claimant's adultery is a complete bar to alimony. *See, e.g.*, S.C. Code Ann. § 20-3-130(a) (1997). For additional discussion of the arguments for and against consideration of fault in connection with alimony and property awards, *see* § 10.02[O], *above*.

(6) **Alimony and the Clean-Break Philosophy.** The reasoning and result in *Otis* are typical of alimony decisions in the early days of no-fault divorce, particularly in states that adopted the Uniform Marriage and Divorce Act. These early decisions minimized the role of alimony and emphasized the importance of a clean financial break between spouses:

> Divorce proceedings were to sever not only the couple's legal union, but their economic relationship as well. To the extent that the marriage left one spouse financially dependent on the other, property division, rather than alimony would be used to address that dependency since property could be divided at the time of divorce. Alimony, if awarded at all, was to be awarded sparingly, and only for short term "rehabilitation." Economic self-sufficiency was the overriding objective for virtually all divorcing spouses.

Jana B. Singer, *Husbands, Wives and Human Capital: Why the Shoe Won't Fit*, 31 Fam. L. Q. 119, 120 (1997). More recent judicial decisions have questioned the clean-break philosophy and have cautioned against the overuse of short-term rehabilitative alimony, particularly after long-term marriages. *See, e.g., In re Marriage of LaRocque*, 406 N.W. 2d 736, 744 (Wis. 1987) (reversing short-term alimony award to 46-year-old homemaker as inadequate and unfair where divorce occurred after 25-year marriage that produced five children); *Lewis v. Lewis*, 739 P.2d 974, 985 (Ct. App. 1987) (holding that a 62-year-old homemaker whose husband was well able to afford permanent alimony had no obligation to "rehabilitate" herself by seeking full-time employment outside the home); *Walter v. Walter*, 464 So. 2d 538, 542 (Fla. 1985) (reversing lower court's denial of permanent alimony and expressly disapproving court's statement that permanent alimony should be awarded only as a last resort and only upon a showing of lack of capacity for self-support). *See generally*, Joan M. Krauskopf, *Rehabilitative Alimony: Uses and Abuses of Limited Duration Alimony*, in American Bar Association, Section of Family Law, Alimony; New Strategies for Pursuit and Defense 65, 70–74 (1988) (discussing judicial trend away from short-term alimony awards).

A number of scholars have also argued that the goal of a clean financial break is neither realistic, nor desirable, particularly where a marriage has produced children. *See, e.g.*, Margaret F. Brinig, *Property Distribution Physics: The Talisman of Time and Middle Class Law*, 31 Fam. L.Q. 93, 107–110 (1997); Joan Williams, *Is Couverture Dead? Beyond A New Theory of Alimony*, 82 Geo. L.J. 2227 (1994); Milton C. Regan, Jr., *Spouses and Strangers, Divorce Obligations and Property Rhetoric*, 82 Geo. L. J. 2303 (1994); June Carbone, *Income Sharing: Redefining the Family in Terms of Community*, 31 Hous. L. Rev. 359 (1994).

(7) **The Economic Impact of Divorce.** Beginning in the late 1970's, a series of empirical studies suggested that the "clean break" philosophy that characterized early, no-fault divorce reform was producing financially devastating results for many divorced women and children. Perhaps the best known of these studies was Lenore Weitzman's examination of the economic and social consequences of no-fault divorce reform in California. Lenore Weitzman, The Divorce Revolution: The Unexpected Social and Economic Consequences for Women and Children in America (1985). While the specific results of Weitzman's study have been criticized, a number of more recent studies have confirmed her basic conclusion—that women and children suffer disproportionate financial losses as a consequence of divorce. *See generally, Williams, above*, at 2227–28 n.1 (citing studies); Joan M. Krauskopf, *Theories of Property Division/Spousal Support: Searching for Solutions to the Mystery*, 23 Family Law Q. 253, 271 (1980) ("Even those who criticize Weitzman's figures differ on amount, not on significant disparity in standard of living between ex-husbands and ex-wives."). Weitzman and other researchers also found that most divorcing couples had relatively little property to divide—at least if property was defined traditionally, to exclude professional degrees and other types of "career assets." This finding undermined the suggestion of some early reformers that courts could rely on equitable distribution of marital property to address divorce-related income disparities.

(8) **Alimony and Child Care Responsibilities.** In addition to authorizing rehabilitative alimony where a spouse is "unable to support himself through appropriate employment," the Uniform Marriage and Divorce Act allows a court to award maintenance to a divorcing spouse who "is the custodian of a child whose condition or circumstances make it appropriate that the custodian not be required to seek employment outside the home." What sorts of circumstances justify maintenance under this provision? Should the primary caretaker of a preschool child qualify for spousal support under this rationale? *See Bowen v. Thomas*, 656 N.E.2d 1328, 1330 (Ohio Ct. App. 1995) (finding six-year support award to mother of infant twins excessive where marriage had lasted less than a year and wife had been self-supporting prior to marriage). What about the primary caretaker of one or more elementary-school-age children? Should a parent who withdraws from the paid labor market during marriage, in order to care for children, be entitled to continue that arrangement after divorce? Why or why not? *See generally* Ann L. Estin, *Maintenance, Alimony, and the Rehabilitation of Family Care*, 71 N.C. L. Rev. 721, 721–22 (1993) (arguing that current alimony doctrine is unresponsive to the claims of parents who have devoted substantial time to the care of young children).

Section 5.06 of the American Law Institute's *Proposed Principles of the Law of Family Dissolution* [hereinafter ALI *Principles*] allows a divorcing spouse to recoup the earning capacity loss arising from his or her disproportionate share of the care of children during marriage. However, the comments to this section explain that it is *not* intended to provide ongoing financial support for a primary caretaker or to compensate for economic losses arising from *post-dissolution* caretaking responsibilities. Because such claims arise from the children's *current* need for care, rather than for care provided during the marriage, the ALI *Principles* address them as a form of child support. *See* ALI *Principles* § 5.06, comment f.

[C] Alimony as Compensation for Loss

IN RE MARRIAGE OF WILLIAMS
Supreme Court of Montana
714 P.2d 548 (1986)

WEBER, J.

Donna Lea Williams (wife) and Shelton Cross Williams (husband) independently appeal an order of the Missoula County District Court which resolved reserved questions ancillary to the prior dissolution decree regarding maintenance, child support, valuation and division of marital assets. We affirm.

The parties were married in December 1963. Eighteen years later they were divorced. Six children were born during the marriage. Presently, five are minors requiring support.

The wife received a Bachelor's degree in Art from Montana State University in June 1963, and currently holds a provisional teaching certificate in Art and English. She did not pursue a career in art or teaching after marriage, but remained at home to care for the children. The husband is an attorney licensed to practice law in Montana with an established law practice in Missoula. The law practice is a professional corporation, solely owned by the husband. There are two full-time and one part-time associates working for the firm.

At the time of dissolution, the net worth of the marital estate was approximately $600,000. The court divided the marital estate as follows:

	Husband	Wife
2110 Greenough (Family home)		$ 98,345.82
2.43 acre lot		77,000.00
1515 Ashberry Apts	$ 9,505.31	
1519 & 1521 Ashberry Apts	25,935.58	
216 West Main	17,956.55	
Williams' Apartments	89,839.54	
University Apartments (after taxes and payment of attorney fees)	16,900.00	
Fox Farm road lots	4,666.00	
130 West Broadway	16,900.00	
Sennes' Contract	16,925.83	
Keogh/IRA	5,167.00	
Williams Law Firm Pension	7,900.00	
Williams Law Firm, P.C.	150,000.00	
Personal Property	25,132.83	25,745.00
Tax Refund		1,800.00
TOTAL	$396,294.64	$202,890.82

The court found that the wife required maintenance for a reasonable period to allow her to complete her education and become employed. The wife was awarded $800 per month as maintenance and $1,353 per year for school fees and books beginning July 1984, and continuing until June 1988. The court also awarded the wife $162,597 additional maintenance, $16,259.70 a year for ten years commencing July 1988, with no interest to be paid on that amount. The court ordered that the husband could deduct the payments as maintenance for income tax purposes.

Husband and wife were awarded joint custody of the five minor children. The wife will have physical custody of the children seven months out of the year, and the husband will have custody five months. The husband was ordered to make support payments to the wife of $ 250 per child while the children are residing with the wife and $ 100 per child while they are residing with him. All of the income tax deductions for minor children were awarded to the husband.

The wife's, husband's and children's attorneys' fees were ordered paid from the proceeds of the sale of the University apartments.

I

Was it error to award maintenance payments to the wife because of her career foregone during marriage, and to set the value at $ 162,597?

The District Court found that the wife sustained career value losses of $ 162,597, which included $ 76,313 in lost retirement benefits and $ 86,284 in salary differential. Finding of fact 36 stated:

> "36. Donna introduced an economic consultant, Dr. Dennis O'Donald, to testify regarding Donna's income producing ability. Dr. O'Donald evaluated Donna's educational background, her job skills. . . . As set forth below, the Court has found that Donna should be entitled to $ 16,259.70 per year for ten years as maintenance in addition to the $ 800.00 maintenance payment for the next four years. In consideration of this additional award of maintenance, the Court finds that the distribution of property hereinafter set forth is fair and equitable in light of all of the considerations set forth in Section 40–4–202 MCA, and the Court rejects Donna's claims that she is entitled to any additional property distribution as a result of her claimed external contribution to the marriage."

The District Court concluded:

> "Beginning four years following the date of this decree, Mike shall pay $ 16,259.70 a year for ten years to Donna for her claim against the estate. This sum will be paid on each anniversary of the date of this decree for ten years. No interest shall be paid on this amount; it shall be considered maintenance for tax purposes."

The husband contends that the District Court should not have considered the career evaluation losses of $ 162,597 for maintenance purposes or for any other purpose. We do not agree with that contention.

Section 40–4–203, MCA, sets forth the elements which a district court is required to consider in making a maintenance award. As pertinent here, Section 40–4–203, MCA, states:

> "(1) In a proceeding for dissolution of marriage . . . the court may grant a maintenance order for either spouse only if it finds that the spouse seeking maintenance:
>
> "(a) Lacks sufficient property to provide for his reasonable needs; and
>
> "(b) Is unable to support himself through appropriate employment. . . .
>
> "(2) The maintenance order shall be in such amounts and for such periods of time as the court deems just . . . after considering all relevant facts including:

"(a) The financial resources of the party seeking maintenance, including marital property apportioned to him, and his ability to meet his needs independently.

". . .

"(c) The standard of living established during the marriage;

"(d) The duration of the marriage;

". . .

"(f) The ability of the spouse from whom maintenance is sought to meet his needs while meeting those of the spouse seeking maintenance."

The District Court concluded that as a result of the wife's lost employment for a number of years during marriage, she suffered lost retirement benefits of $76,313. In other words, had the wife continued her employment during marriage, the $76,313 was the present value of the retirement benefits which would have accrued to her. Under Section 40-4-203, MCA, it is appropriate to consider retirement benefits in determining whether a spouse has sufficient property to provide for her reasonable needs, and whether she is able to support herself through appropriate employment. The terms sufficient property for reasonable needs and inability to support through appropriate employment have been discussed and interpreted as follows:

"The appropriate construction of the language of Section . . . (1)(a) and (b) . . . is whether the spouse seeking maintenance lacks sufficient property and is unable to support herself through appropriate employment according to the standard of living established during the marriage. . . . We recognize there are public policy considerations behind rehabilitative spousal maintenance awards which, under appropriate circumstances, may give incentive to the spouse receiving maintenance to procure job skills so as to become self-sufficient. However, this public policy must be balanced with some:

" 'realistic appraisal of the probabilities that the receiving spouse will in fact subsequently be able to support herself in some reasonable approximation of the standard of living established during the marriage, especially when a marriage of long-term duration is involved and the employment history shows a long-term absence of the spouse from the labor market with lack of a presently existing employment skill.' " *Lindsay v. Lindsay*, 115 Ariz. 322, 565 P.2d at 205.

In re Marriage of Dale A. Madson, 180 Mont. 220, 224–25, 590 P.2d 110, 112–13. We conclude that the District Court properly considered the loss of retirement benefits in computing a maintenance award for the wife.

In a similar manner, the District Court found a salary differential loss of $86,284 when it contrasted the salary the wife would have earned had she continued her outside employment during marriage with what she will be able to earn after the dissolution. Again, under the terms of the statute, the consideration of such loss of earnings is significant in determining whether the wife is able to support herself through appropriate employment, and in considering her ability to meet her needs independently, together with the standard of living, duration of marriage, and ability of the husband to meet his needs while meeting the maintenance needs. We conclude that the District Court properly considered the salary differential in making a maintenance award to the wife.

The parties also discuss whether or not it would be appropriate to consider the sustained career value losses in making a distribution of property. While it is not necessary that we rule on this question, we do point out that Section 40–4–202, MCA, sets forth in great detail the elements to be considered by the District Court in making an equitable apportionment of a marital estate. Included in those elements are the requirement that the court consider the opportunity of each of the parties for future acquisition of capital assets and income. It seems clear that lost retirement benefits and loss of earnings as a result of salary differential properly could be considered as the court looks at the ability of the wife to make an acquisition of both capital assets and income in the future.

The District Court here had a choice of distributing marital property to the wife or making an award of maintenance based upon the career value losses. The evidence submitted would have supported a property distribution from the marital estate had that been done. Instead, the District Court chose to award maintenance of $ 16,259.70 per year for ten years, beginning four years after the date of the decree.

We have extensively reviewed the findings of fact, conclusions and decree of the District Court. The District Court made over 40 separate written findings of fact covering distribution of the martial estate, support of the children and maintenance for the wife. These findings and the record demonstrate careful consideration on the part of the District Court of the complex facts presented by the strongly contesting parties.

The findings of fact also show that the District Court carefully considered the needs of the wife in the next few years when education is reasonably required, and also her needs after that period up to and following retirement. In substance, the court concluded that the wife lacked sufficient property to provide for her reasonable needs during that period of time. The court considered the monetary effect of the foregone earnings, and after balancing all of the factors involved in a maintenance award under Section 40–4–203, MCA, and considering the factors involved in the distribution of the marital estate under Section 40–4–202, MCA, concluded that an award of maintenance was the appropriate manner of satisfying the reasonable needs of the wife. We approve the analysis of the District Court, and affirm the maintenance award to the wife in the total amount of $ 162,597. . . .

NOTES AND QUESTIONS

(1) The decision in *Williams* provides an unusually explicit example of a support award that is designed to compensate a divorcing spouse for career opportunities foregone during marriage. While few other judicial opinions are this precise, many courts cite foregone economic and career opportunities as a primary justification for spousal support. See, e.g., *In re Bensen,* 932 P.2d 104, 105 (Or. Ct. App. 1997) ("Wife is entitled to a support award that takes into account her contribution to husband's earning capacity as well as her diminished earning capacity resulting from her absence, from the labor force."); *Wahlberg v. Wahlberg*, 479 N.W.2d 143, 145 (N.D. 1992) (spousal support appropriate where a party has "foregone opportunities or lost advantages as a consequence of the marriage"); *In re Marriage of Larroeque,* 406 N.W.2d 736, 741–42 (Wis. 1987) ("Where a spouse has subordinated his or her education or career to devote time and energy to the welfare, career or education of the other spouse or to managing the affairs of the marital partnership, maintenance may be used to compensate this spouse for those nonmonetary contributions

to the marriage."). Similarly, a number of state alimony statutes explicitly direct judges to consider "the extent to which the spouse seeking maintenance has reduced his or her income or career opportunities for the benefit of the other spouse." Ariz. Rev. Stat. § 25–319(B)(7) (1997); *see* N.Y. Dom. Rel. Law § 236(B)(6)(a)(5) (1998); Or. Rev. Stat. § 107.105(d)(F) (1996).

(2) Do foregone economic opportunities justify alimony because of the loss they represent to the alimony claimant or because of the benefit they confer on the other spouse—or both? As a number of scholars have pointed out, spouses who assume primary childcare and other family responsibilities not only diminish their own earning prospects; they also enhance the careers and earning capacity of their partners. *See, e.g.,* Joan Williams, *Is Coverture Dead? Beyond A New Theory of Alimony*, 82 Geo. L. J. 2227, 2236–37 (1994); Jana B. Singer, *Alimony and Efficiency: The Gendered Costs and Benefits of the Economic Justification for Alimony*, 82 Geo. L.J. 2423, 2423–44 (1994). To what extent can alimony be justified as a means of apportioning these jointly-produced economic gains?

(3) In his influential article, *The Theory of Alimony*, 77 Cal. L. Rev. 1, 46–51 (1989), Professor Ira M. Ellman argues that providing compensation to divorcing spouses for marriage-related economic losses is necessary to avoid the "distorting incentives" created by divorce and to encourage economically rational specialization during marriage:

> Whenever spouses have different earning capacities and want to plan rationally as a single economic unit, they will conclude that, where possible, they should shift economic sacrifices from the higher earning spouse to the lower earning spouse, because that shift will increase the income of the marital unit as a whole. If they follow that plan, the lower earning spouse (today most likely the wife) will often be pushed toward the position of the wife in the traditional marriage, even if they had started out with a different intention. In fact, many if not most marriages in which the wife is employed are still traditional in orientation; she continues to carry a disproportionate share of the domestic responsibilities, burdening her career advancement, and it is her job which yields when there is a conflict between spousal jobs. Where the husband's work is more lucrative than the wife's, this arrangement is economically rational. Nevertheless, the wife's position is then similar to that of the classic homemaker-wife. She has not abandoned a market career, but she has sacrificed some career prospects to invest instead in her marriage. If the marital unit dissolves, she no longer shares in her husband's enhanced income and, absent some contractual or statutory remedy, the husband leaves the marriage with the benefit of her investment in his earning capacity.
>
> Suppose, however, a couple rejects this "rational" choice of maximizing the marital income, perhaps because the wife insists upon it in order to lower the potential loss she would incur if they ultimately divorce. The investment-banker husband and public interest lawyer wife each would spend the same amount of time on their domestic needs. Suppose, compared to an arrangement in which the wife took primary responsibility for their domestic life, this more egalitarian marriage results in an $ X increase in the wife's income, but a $ 4X decline in the husband's. That is, the strategy the spouses have adopted to reduce the financial loss flowing from marital failure also reduces the financial benefits arising from the intact marriage. Part of the husband's higher earning potential goes unrealized, to both his detriment and his wife's.

Because this marriage is less profitable than a more traditional marriage, some parties might choose not to enter it in the first place, even though they would enter a traditional marriage. The restructuring not only reduces total marital income, a loss which the parties presumably share equally, but also reduces the income of the higher earning spouse. Today, men are especially likely to be deterred, given the earnings advantage they currently have over their wives. The man's personal loss is likely to leave residual effects on his earning capacity that will survive the marriage, if it fails. It also seems likely that more of these marriages will end in divorce since, other things being equal, the level of satisfaction in such marriages will be lower. So for both parties, but especially for men, this restructured marriage offers a lower return and a higher risk.

We thus see that while a wife's strategy of reducing marriage-specific investment may protect her from some financial loss if divorce occurs, it also increases the chance that divorce will occur and reduces the chance of marriage in the first place. In the end, marital "specialization" makes sense for most couples, with one spouse concentrating more heavily on the market while the other focuses more heavily on domestic matters. If the spouses view their marriage as a sharing enterprise, they will usually conclude that they are both better off if the lower earning spouse spends more on their joint domestic needs, and allows the higher earning spouse to maximize his or her income. A problem arises only if their mutual commitment to share breaks down, in which case the spouse who has specialized in domestic aspects of the marriage—who has invested in the marriage rather than the market—suffers a disproportionate loss. . . .

The function of alimony is now clear. Its purpose is to reallocate the postdivorce financial consequences of marriage in order to prevent distorting incentives. Because its purpose is to reallocate, it is necessarily a remedy by one spouse against the other. While such a theory of alimony might seem excessively economic, its rationale does not assume that wealth maximization is in fact the only purpose of marriage. To the contrary, by eliminating any financial incentives or penalties that might otherwise flow from different marital lifestyles, this theory maximizes the parties' freedom to shape their marriage in accordance with their nonfinancial preferences. They can allocate domestic duties according to these preferences without putting one spouse at risk of a much greater financial loss than the other if the marriage fails. . . .

The system of alimony generated by this theory is also consistent with equitable notions: It protects the spouse who has made a marital investment, thinking that her marriage was a shared enterprise, from a unilateral decision by her partner to cease sharing. Nonetheless, an intuitive appeal to equity is not the principal argument in support of this approach. We rely more on the proposition that marital investment decisions should be free from potentially distorting penalties and incentives.

Does Professor Ellman's theory of economically rational sharing behavior in marriage provide a convincing justification for alimony? Why or why not? What are the "potentially distorting penalties and incentives" to which Ellman refers?

(4) A number of feminist scholars have criticized Ellman's reliance on the rationality and desirability of role specialization during marriage. For example, Professor Margaret Brinig suggests that the standard economic account of marital specialization fails to consider important psychic costs associated with specialization, such as the cost to women who are

not working outside the home, but who would like to be, and the costs to men who are working long hours, but who would like to spend more time with their children. Factoring in these psychic benefits, while assuming at least some diminishing marginal returns from additional increases in productivity, suggests that for many couples, the most "efficient" marriage may be one in which both partners have significant ties to the paid labor force *and* spend significant time with their children. Margaret F. Brinig, *The Law and Economics of No-Fault Divorce: What Went Wrong*, 26 Fam. L.Q. 453, 457–58 (1993). Other commentators have suggested that encouraging such "non-specialized," but child-centered unions, may yield significant societal benefits as well, including enhancing the nurturing capacities of men and encouraging all parents to invest more heavily in their children. *See generally* Jana B. Singer, *Alimony and Efficiency: The Gendered Costs and Benefits of The Economic Justification For Alimony*, 82 Geo. L. J. 2423, 2437–42 (1994); June R. Carbone, *Economics, Feminism & the Reinvention of Alimony: A Reply to Ira Ellman*, 43 Vand. L. Rev. 1463 (1990). Ironically, a theory of alimony that rests on a strong commitment to specialization within marriage may hinder the sort of workplace and other societal changes that are necessary to facilitate these non-specialized, child-centered unions.

(5) Donna Lee Williams was able to present convincing expert testimony regarding her foregone career opportunities largely because she was already a college graduate at the time of marriage and because she had obtained—but not made use of—a provisional teaching certificate. Imagine, instead, that Donna had married immediately after high school, and had devoted her time and energies to raising a family, without first obtaining a college degree or developing her career potential. Would she still be entitled to alimony under a "foregone economic opportunities" rationale? If so, how would her economic losses be measured? If not, does this suggest a potential problem with relying on compensation *for loss* as an exclusive rationale for alimony?

(6) The American Law Institute's proposed *Principles of the Law of Family Dissolution*—for which Professor Ellman is the Chief Reporter—makes compensation for loss the central rationale for divorce-related financial awards, other than child support or property division. *See* ALI *Principles*, Chapter 5 (Compensatory Spousal Payments). Indeed, Chapter 5 of the ALI *Principles* "characterizes the remedy it recognizes as *compensation for loss* rather than relief of need, and employs the term *compensatory payment* (instead of alimony or spousal support) to emphasize this conceptual change." Ira Mark Ellman, *The Misguided Movement to Revive Fault Divorce, And Why Reformers Should Look Instead To The American Law Institute*, 11 Int'l J. of Law, Policy, and the Family 216, 233 (1997) (emphasis in original). The *Principles* authorize compensation for several different types of marriage-related losses. These include:

- In a marriage of significant duration, the loss in living standard experienced at dissolution by the spouse who has less wealth or earning capacity (§ 5.05)

- An earning capacity loss incurred during marriage but continuing after dissolution and arising from one spouse's disproportionate share, during marriage, of the care of the marital children or the children of either spouse (§ 5.06)

- An earning capacity loss incurred during marriage and continuing after dissolution, and arising from the care provided by one spouse to a sick, elderly, or disabled third party, in fulfillment of a moral obligation of the other spouse or of both spouse jointly (§ 5.12)

- The loss either spouse incurs when the marriage is dissolved before that spouse realizes a fair return from his or her investment in the other spouse's earning capacity (§ 5.15)
- An unfairly disproportionate disparity between the spouse in their respective abilities to recover their pre-marital standard after the dissolution of a short marriage (§ 5.16).

Although compensation for loss provides the rationale for these entitlements, the *Principles* recognize the difficulties of proving loss on an individual basis. Chapter 5 of the *Principles* therefore proposes a series of presumptions designed to measure a claimant's compensable loss in each of the circumstances listed above. The comments to § 5.05 (Compensation for Loss of Marital Living Standard), provide an illustration of one such presumption that states might adopt:

- A presumption arises that a spouse is entitled to an award under this section whenever that spouse has been married five years or more to a person whose income at dissolution is expected to be at least 25 percent greater than the claimant's. The presumptive award shall equal the difference in the spouses' expected incomes at dissolution multiplied by the appropriate durational factor. The durational factor is equal to the years of marriage multiplied by .01, but shall in no case exceed .4.
- Under the illustrative provision, the maximum durational factor would be reached after 40 years of marriage, since .01 x 40 = .4. If at that time Spouse A's expected monthly income were $5,000 and spouse B's were $3,000, the award would equal .4 x $2,000, or $800 per month. leaving Spouse A with $4,200 monthly, and providing Spouse B with $3,800 monthly. If Spouse A earned $3,000 and Spouse B could only be expected to earn $1,000 monthly after dissolution, the award would still equal .4 x $2,000, or $800, leaving A with $2,200 and B with $1,800. These awards would be proportionately less for marriages of shorter duration. Note that if the parties had children, a presumptive award of significant additional amount would normally arise under § 5.06 [Compensation for Primary Caretaker's Residual Loss to Earning Capacity]. Because the combined award cannot exceed the maximum allowed under this section—i.e., .4 of the income differential—no additional entitlement would in fact arise for the spouse married 40 years. However, this maximum award level would normally be reached far earlier than 40 years in a marriage with children.

How would the presumption described above apply in a case such as *Otis*? In a case such as *Van Klootwyk?*

(7) Should spousal support be used to compensate a spouse for *noneconomic* losses incurred as a result of marriage and divorce? For example, suppose that Harold and Wanda marry after graduating from the same Ph.D program in Economics. Harold is offered a job at Harvard, as well as an equally well-paying job at the University of Maryland. Wanda receives only a single job offer from the University of Baltimore. Reluctantly, Harry turns down the offer from Harvard, so that he and Wanda can live together in Maryland. Unfortunately, the marriage does not work out and the couple divorces two years later. Under a loss-compensation rationale, does Harold have a viable alimony claim against Wanda for his lost opportunity to teach at Harvard? *See generally,* Ira Mark Ellman, *Should the Theory of Alimony Include Nonfinancial Losses and Motivations?*, 1991 B.Y.U. L. Rev. 259 (1991).

(8) Under a loss compensation theory, should alimony be available to a higher earning spouse who has sacrificed a lucrative job opportunity to accommodate the career or lifestyle preferences of a lower-earning partner? For example, suppose that Martha earns $60,000/year as an accountant for a large, national company, while Frank earns $40,000/year as a social worker. Martha's company offers her a promotion that would substantially increase her salary, but would require her to move across the country. Because Frank is opposed to moving, Martha turns down the promotion. If the couples divorces soon thereafter, should Martha be able to seek compensation from Frank for her lost career and economic opportunities?

[D] Alimony as Income Sharing

DELOZIER v DELOZIER
Vermont Supreme Court
640 A.2d 55 (1994)

GIBSON, J.

Defendant husband appeals from a final divorce order in which the family court awarded permanent monthly maintenance to plaintiff wife in an unspecified amount to be determined annually by dividing equally the parties' combined net incomes. Defendant argues that the permanent equalization of the parties' incomes constituted an abuse of discretion, considering the terms of the stipulated property settlement, the relatively short marriage, plaintiff's youth and good health, and her potential to earn a decent income. He also argues that the court's findings in support of the award were inadequate, that the equalization formula is too uncertain to be enforceable, and that the court erred by declining to address his request to claim his daughter as a tax exemption until the parties worked out a specific formula for equalizing their incomes. We reverse and remand based on our conclusion that the permanent equalization of the parties' incomes constituted an abuse of discretion under the facts of this case.

I.

At the time of the final hearing, plaintiff, age 39, and defendant, age 44, had been married fourteen years and had a nine-year-old daughter, who is legally blind in one eye and has learning disabilities. Although plaintiff had worked as a licensed professional nurse (LPN) for six years before the marriage, her license expired during the marriage because she remained at home and cared for her daughter. In late 1992, she was accepted into a two-year nursing program at the University of Vermont. She will be relicensed as an LPN after the first year, and will become a registered nurse (RN) after the second year. She also may continue in school for another two years to obtain a baccalaureate degree, which is encouraged by most hospitals. Thus, she expects to be in school for as long as four years. Assuming she would be able to work full-time at that point, her starting salary as an LPN would be approximately $ 20,000 and somewhat more as an RN.

Defendant earns approximately $ 121,000 as an ear, nose and throat specialist for the University Health Center. In 1990, he was convicted upon a plea of no contest to sexual assault on a minor based on his having had sexual relations with the parties' fifteen-year-old baby sitter. Relying in part on a superior court ruling that the Medical Practice Board did not have jurisdiction to revoke or suspend his license for conduct occurring outside his professional duty, the family court concluded that defendant's employment in the state seemed relatively secure. Since the final hearing, however, this Court has reversed the superior court decision, *Delozier v. State*, 160 Vt. 426, 631 A.2d 228 (1993), once again raising the possibility that defendant's license would be revoked or suspended.

The parties stipulated to an equal division of their property. Plaintiff received $ 37,000 from the sale of the marital homestead. The parties divided equally about $ 270,000 in retirement funds, which the court found were not income-producing assets. Plaintiff's only other assets of any significance were her 1991 station wagon, an $ 8,000 money-market account, and $ 17,000 of equity in her condominium. Defendant also agreed to maintain an educational trust fund for his daughter that would provide her with approximately $50,000 at age eighteen.

At the final hearing, the main unresolved issue was the appropriate amount and duration of a maintenance award. The court concluded that permanent maintenance was required to reduce the financial impact of the divorce on plaintiff and to compensate her for her years as a homemaker. It noted that plaintiff would never be able to achieve the standard of living established during the marriage, and that she is the custodian of a minor child with special needs, which warranted special consideration.

The court then determined that a formula equalizing the parties' net incomes was more appropriate in this case than a fixed monthly sum because of uncertainty over (1) when plaintiff would begin work and how many hours she would be able to work while attending to her daughter's needs, and (2) whether defendant would be able to maintain his practice and his current salary in the face of his legal difficulties. Further, according to the court, the equalization formula was appropriate because it would provide a rehabilitative component to the award in the first few years when defendant was in school and caring for her daughter, while in later years, when plaintiff's increased income lessened defendant's burden, it would provide a permanent component to the award that would assure that plaintiff enjoyed the standard of living established during the marriage. The court ordered that the monthly amount be adjusted annually and any other time either party had more than a 10% change in net income. It left the details of the formula to be worked out by the parties in consultation with an accountant.

II.

The principal issue raised on appeal is whether, considering the facts of this case, the court abused its discretion by permanently equalizing the parties' net incomes. For the sake of clarity, we will consider separately guidelines for awarding permanent maintenance and limits on equalizing the parties' incomes. We will then review the instant order.

We emphasize at the outset that our discussion will offer only general guidelines. The family court has broad discretion in determining the amount and duration of a maintenance award, and we will set aside an award only when there is no reasonable basis to support it. Granting the court broad discretion in dividing property or awarding maintenance is necessary because these matters are not susceptible to fixed patterns. "It is important that appellate courts avoid establishing inflexible rules that make the achievement of equity between the parties difficult, if not impossible." *Canakaris v. Canakaris*, 382 So. 2d 1197, 1200 (Fla. 1980).

A.

This case presents the converse of the situation in *Strauss v. Strauss*, 160 Vt. 335, 628 A.2d 552 (1993), where the wife challenged the court's failure to award her permanent maintenance, and we set forth guidelines for determining when permanent maintenance is required as a matter of law. In *Strauss*, we held that the court abused its discretion by not awarding at least some permanent maintenance to the 48-year-old wife, who had raised the parties' two children and managed the household during the 28-year marriage, and who had limited employment prospects. . . . While acknowledging that the rehabilitative function of maintenance is to assist the recipient spouse in becoming self-supportive, we reiterated that "in a long-term marriage, maintenance also serves to compensate a homemaker for contributions to family well-being not otherwise recognized in the property distribution." . . .

This compensatory aspect of maintenance reflects the reality that when one spouse stays home and raises the children, not only does that spouse lose future earning capacity by not being employed or by being underemployed subject to the needs of the family, but that spouse increases the future earning capacity of the working spouse, who, while enjoying family life, is free to devote productive time to career enhancement. In determining the extent of the compensatory component of a maintenance award, the family court should give particular consideration to the role of the recipient spouse during the marriage, and to the length of the marriage.

The length of the marriage is particularly important not only because it is often a major factor creating the disparity in the parties' earning capacities in cases involving a homemaker spouse, but because, regardless of the spouses' respective roles, it also provides a benchmark for determining reasonable needs. The longer the marriage, the more closely reasonable needs should be measured by the standard of living established during the marriage. Thus, while we have stated that rehabilitative maintenance alone is not sufficient unless the evidence shows that the recipient spouse will become self-supporting at the standard of living established during the marriage, the duration of the marriage will affect the measurement of reasonable needs and the length of time the maintenance award is required to maintain the recipient spouse at that level.

Although courts often state that permanent maintenance is appropriate in long-term marriages, there is no precise point at which marriages are defined as "long-term." In general, however, awards of permanent maintenance are increasingly being made in marriages of fifteen years or more. But other factors also come into play, and we will not draw lines based on this one factor, despite its significance.

In *Strauss*, we held that, in addition to the length of the marriage, the "most critical factors" in determining the duration of a maintenance award are the role the recipient spouse played during the marriage and the income that spouse is likely to achieve in relation to the standard of living set in the marriage. The latter factor, in turn, is closely related to the recipient spouse's age, health, child-care duties, and access to income-producing assets. *See* Krauskopf, *Rehabilitative Alimony: Uses and Abuses of Limited Duration Alimony*, 21 Fam. L.Q. 573, 589 (1989) (recipient spouse who retains custody of parties' children continues to sacrifice earning power relative to other spouse). Depending on the facts of a particular case, it may be appropriate for a court to award permanent maintenance where a marriage has lasted less than fifteen years. *See Chaker v. Chaker*, 155 Vt. 20, 25–26, 581 A.2d 737, 740 (1990) (permanent award upheld in case involving ten-year childless marriage where wife was 55 years old, had back problems for which she received social security benefits, had not worked outside the home for many years, and had supported husband's efforts to learn English and obtain education). In any event, it will be important for a court to consider what period of time will (1) enable the recipient spouse to achieve self-sufficiency at the appropriate standard of living, and (2) compensate that spouse for the disparity in the parties' present and future earning capacities that is attributable to their marriage and divorce.

B.

As the trial court pointed out, the relevant statute does not specifically preclude the court from fashioning a maintenance award that equalizes the parties' net incomes. Indeed, we have concluded that "equalizing the parties' financial status for an appropriate period [is] a proper purpose." *Strauss*, 628 A.2d at 554.

In general, however, courts have not favored the use of formulas for determining maintenance awards. *See Kunkle v. Kunkle*, 51 Ohio St. 3d 64, 554 N.E.2d 83, 89–90 (Ohio 1990) (citing cases in other jurisdictions). Particularly disfavored are awards requiring one spouse to pay a percentage of gross or net income to the other spouse. When percentage awards are allowed, the cases often involve unusual circumstances. *See Hefty v. Hefty*, 172 Wis. 2d 124, 493 N.W.2d 33, 36 (Wis. 1992) (considering fluctuation of husband's bonus income, court properly awarded wife fixed monthly sum plus 20% of any bonus pay).

Courts do not favor such awards because (1) in effect, they modify support payments without regard for modification standards, and thus alter the burden of proof in future modification hearings; and (2) they are not responsive to the needs of the parties, and therefore have the effect of either punishing the payor spouse or shortchanging the recipient spouse. We have rejected the first reason with respect to escalation clauses that increase payments automatically based on rises in either the cost of living or the payor's income. *Chaker*, 155 Vt. at 27–28, 581 A.2d at 740–41. In *Chaker*, we noted that modification was still possible if either spouse felt the escalation clause had become unfair over time, and we determined that we would review the court's imposition of such clauses under the traditional abuse-of-discretion standard of review for maintenance orders. *Id.* at 27, 581 A.2d at 741. We apply the same standard here.

We caution, however, that formula awards are susceptible to reversal unless they are sensitive to the statutory criteria, including both parties' needs. Awards based only upon the single criterion of the payor's income, like many of the fixed-percentage awards rejected in the cited cases, would rarely be acceptable.

On the other hand, awards, such as the instant one, that are structured to take into account, at least loosely, plaintiff's needs relative to defendant's ability to pay, may be acceptable when they equalize the parties' financial status for an appropriate period of time, considering the relevant criteria and the circumstances of the case. *See Downs v. Downs*, 159 Vt. 467, 468, 621 A.2d 229, 231 (1993) (trial court did not abuse its discretion in equalizing parties' standards of living for period equal to duration of marriage). Indeed, under certain circumstances, even a permanent equalization of the parties' joined incomes may be a reasonable alternative.

III.

We now review the instant award. The length of this marriage borders on long-term, and the parties established a fairly high standard of living during the marriage, far above the standard plaintiff could establish while working as a nurse. Although plaintiff did not support defendant while he received his medical training, she gave up career advancement while enhancing his career during the marriage, and she continues to have custody of a minor child with special needs, which will further limit her employment opportunities. Moreover, we recognize that the parties' property settlement fell well short of compensating plaintiff or allowing her to maintain the standard of living established during the marriage. Therefore, the court had the discretion to provide plaintiff with a permanent award that included both rehabilitative and compensatory components.

Nevertheless, we conclude that the court abused its discretion by permanently equalizing the parties' incomes. While we do not preclude the court on remand from equalizing the parties' incomes for a limited period of time, or providing an appropriate amount of permanent maintenance, we believe a permanent equalization of incomes under the facts of this case is far too speculative with respect to satisfying the relevant statutory criteria and addressing the purposes of maintenance. We appreciate the court's desire to forestall future modification hearings. But rather than impose a permanent award that is only loosely tied to the relevant criteria and that could vacillate greatly from year to year, the court should have based its award on the parties' current situation and probable future circumstances, and accepted the fact that a modification hearing might have to take place if those circumstances changed substantially.

Although the permanent equalization of incomes may be appropriate in long-term marriages when the recipient spouse is past middle age or in poor health, that was not the case here. This is a borderline long-term marriage, but plaintiff is relatively young, in good health, and will be able to work as an RN within the next few years. The parties may be employed for a period of time well beyond the length of the marriage. Thus, the permanent equalization of the parties' incomes may wind up being punitive rather than compensatory.

Accordingly, we remand this case for the trial court to fashion an award for an amount and duration that will provide plaintiff with rehabilitative support and compensate her for her years as a homemaker, while also creating an incentive for her to strive toward economic independence. We do not preclude an appropriate award of permanent maintenance if the court deems such to be warranted. *See Strauss*, 628 A.2d at 556 ("an appropriate mixture of permanent and time-limited maintenance can achieve fully all the objectives of a maintenance award," including giving recipient spouse economic incentive to become self-sufficient).

Finally, in the event that, on remand, the court decides to equalize the parties' income for an appropriate period of time, it has the discretion to leave the details of the equalization formula for the parties to work out with an accountant, and to delay a decision on who is entitled to a tax exemption for the minor child until those details are worked out.

Reversed and remanded.

NOTES AND QUESTIONS

(1) How would you decide this case on remand?

(2) The *Delozier* opinion notes that courts have generally disfavored the use of formulas for determining maintenance awards. What explains this reluctance? Are there advantages as well as disadvantages to the use of such formulas? Consider the following comment to the Objectives section of the ALI *Principles*:

> *Consistency and predictability in application.* The vague standards governing alimony in most existing law yields inconsistent and unpredictable adjudication. The analogous problem for child support awards was resolved by the widespread adoption of child support guidelines. Although alimony guidelines have been employed in some states, they have not been widely adopted. Alimony is more resistant to capturing through guidelines because marriage does not alone establish an alimony obligation, in the way that parenthood alone establishes a child support obligation. The benefits of predictability and consistency that can be achieved with guidelines therefore require the prior establishment of a coherent rationale for requiring the award and accompanying rules for identifying eligible claimants. Satisfaction of these requirements, and thus achievement of the objective of consistency and predictability, is facilitated by reconceptualizing the award as compensation for loss rather than as relief of need.

ALI *Principles* § 502, comment d.

(3) A number of commentators have offered specific income-sharing proposals. For example, Professor Jana Singer has suggested that divorcing couples who have invested primarily in one spouse's career should continue to share their joint incomes equally for a time period equal to half the length of their marriage, with child support calculated separately. Jana B. Singer, *Divorce Reform and Gender Justice*, 67 N. Car. L. Rev. 1103, 1120 (1989). *See also* Milton C. Regan, Family Law and the Pursuit of Intimacy 148 (1993) (proposing equalization of post-divorce household incomes based on length of time parties were married). Other income sharing proposals have focused specifically on divorcing families with children and have advocated equalizing the standards of living of the two post-divorce households. *See, e.g.*, Joan Williams, *Is Coverture Dead? Beyond A New Theory of Alimony*, 82 Geo. L. J. 2227, 2258–2263 (1994); Jane Rutherford, *Duty in Divorce: Shared Income As A Path To Equality*, 58 Fordham L. Rev. 539, 577–92 (1990); Susan Okin, Justice, Gender and the Family 83 (1989). For a perceptive analysis and critique of various income sharing proposals, see June Carbone, *Income Sharing: Redefining The Family In Terms of Community*, 31 Hous. L. Rev. 359 (1994).

(4) One of the differences between a loss-compensation rationale for alimony and an income-sharing approach is that the former focuses on the allocating *losses*, while the latter emphasizes the sharing of *gains* attributable to the marriage. Is alimony an appropriate vehicle for allocating such marital gains? Joan Williams, *Is Coverture Dead? Beyond A New Theory of Alimony*, 82 Geo. L. J. 2227, 2248–66 (1994) (suggesting that a redesign of property entitlements within the family may provide a firmer theoretical grounding for income-sharing proposals). Can a court (or legislature) reliably determine which gains are "attributable" to a marriage? *Cf.* Jana B. Singer, *Husbands, Wives, and Human Capital: Why the Shoe Won't Fit*, 31 Fam. L.Q. 119, 126 (1997) ("For many primary breadwinning spouses, the most important career asset associated with marriage is not the career enhancement itself; it is instead the ability to advance a career while at the same time experiencing the benefits of parenthood.").

(5) Do income-sharing proposals unduly infringe on a primary wage-earner's ability to remarry? *Cf.* J. Thomas Oldham, *Putting Asunder In the 1990's*, 80 Cal. L. Rev. 1091,

1125 (1992) (arguing that divorce law should protect non-custodial fathers' ability to remarry). Given the availability of no-fault divorce, would the widespread adoption of income sharing give lower-earning spouses an incentive to engage in opportunistic behavior during marriage—e.g., to enter marriage in anticipation of a profitable divorce or to terminate a marriage primarily for economic gain? *See, e.g.,* Arthur B. Cornell, Jr., *When Two Become One, and then Come Undone: An Organizational Approach to Marriage and Its Implications for Divorce Law*, 26 Fam. L.Q. 103, 123 (1992) (allowing division of post divorce income may give the lower earning spouse an incentive to engage in strategic divorce). Should a lower-earning spouse who unilaterally ends a marriage be entitled to post-divorce income sharing? *See* Singer, *above,* 31 Fam. L.Q. at 128–30 (1997) (discussing possible relevance of fault in income-sharing regimes).

(6) What are the advantages and disadvantages of an income sharing approach to alimony, as compared to the loss compensation rationale of the ALI *Principles?* As compared to the standards contained in the Uniform Marriage and Divorce Act?

[E] The Intersection of Alimony and Property Theory

IN RE MARRIAGE OF FRANCIS
Iowa Supreme Court
442 N.W.2d 59 (1989)

On the day he was admitted to medical school, appellant Thomas Francis proposed marriage to appellee Diana Mora Francis. Like countless couples before them, they pledged to one another their support and commitment to a shared future. Six years and two children later, however, their marriage is at an end. And while Tom stands at the threshold of his career as a physician specializing in family practice, Diana ponders her future from the vantage point of one who has helped support the family through medical school and two years of residency on the modest income generated by her in-home day care business.

The fighting issue, as framed by the trial court and reiterated by the parties on appeal, is this: What compensation, if any, should Diana receive for her contribution to Thomas' increased earning capacity due to his education received during the marriage? For over a decade this court has recognized that a spouse's contribution to that increased earning potential is a factor properly considered in the award of alimony and an equitable division of the parties' assets. Yet precisely because each dissolution action must be decided on its unique facts and circumstances, no predictable method of valuing that contribution or distributing the fruits of that increased potential has been settled upon.

Here the trial court awarded Diana a $ 100,000 lump sum property award payable with interest in ten annual installments, along with a three-year rehabilitative alimony award totaling $ 54,000. On appeal from these judgments, Thomas concedes that Diana is entitled to something but challenges the size and nature of the awards on three principal grounds: first, that the court based its $ 100,000 property award on the erroneous legal conclusion that a medical education constitutes an asset for the purpose of equitable distribution; second, that the trial court based its award on calculations that were speculative, incomplete, and misleading; and, third, that the record does not support Diana's need for rehabilitative alimony. Additionally, Thomas challenges his obligation to pay $ 1000 towards Diana's attorney fees and resists the payment of similar fees on appeal.

Our review of this equitable action is, of course, de novo. We are persuaded that the trial court neither misapplied legal doctrine nor erroneously misconstrued the evidence so as to compensate Diana far beyond her contribution to the marriage, as Thomas suggests. We conclude, however, that for marriages of short duration which are devoted almost entirely to the educational advancement of one spouse and yield the accumulation of few tangible assets, alimony—rehabilitative, reimbursement, or a combination of the two—rather than an award of property, furnishes a fairer and more logical means of achieving the equity sought under *Horstmann* and its progeny. Accordingly, with some modification, we affirm the trial court.

I. Several well settled rules guide our decision. Principal among them is the rule that an advanced degree or professional license in and of itself is not an asset for property division purposes.

Nevertheless, the future earning capacity flowing from an advanced degree or professional license is a factor to be considered in the division of property and the award of alimony. Insofar as the advanced professional degree creates an expectancy of higher future earnings, the degree may and should be taken into account in calculating that future earning capacity.

Prior Iowa cases have interchangeably used property awards and alimony as means of compensating a nonprofessional spouse for the contribution made to the other spouse's advanced degree or professional license. *Janssen*, 348 N.W.2d at 254 (substantial periodic alimony rather than lump sum property award equitably adjusts parties' finances); *Horstmann*, 263 N.W.2d at 891 (husband's potential for increased earning capacity made possible "with the aid of his wife's efforts" pertinent to both equitable distribution of assets and whether alimony should be awarded); *Stewart*, 356 N.W.2d at 612–13 (enhanced earning capacity factored in issue of alimony but properly rejected when supporting spouse made comparable career advancement during marriage); *Estlund*, 344 N.W.2d at 280 (wife's contributions, as homemaker and breadwinner, to husband's law degree properly considered upon issue of equitable division of property). These decisions are in harmony with statutes that direct the trial courts to consider such contributions in the awarding of property and spousal support.

It must be remembered, however, that the purposes of property division and alimony are not the same. Property division is based on each partner's right to "a just and equitable share of the property accumulated as the result of their joint efforts." *In re Marriage of Hitchcock*, 309 N.W.2d 432, 437 (Iowa 1981). Alimony, on the other hand, is a stipend to a spouse in lieu of the other spouse's legal obligation for support.

Recently, such court-ordered stipends have taken on new forms to accommodate the broad range of functions that alimony may serve. *See* H. Clark, The Law of Domestic Relations in the United States 641–44 (2d ed. 1988). The Utah Court of Appeals nicely summarized the need for such flexibility this way:

> In [long-term marriages], life patterns have largely been set, the earning potential of both parties can be predicted with some reliability, and the contributions and sacrifices of the one spouse in enabling the other to attain a degree have been compensated by many years of the comfortable lifestyle which the degree permitted. Traditional alimony analysis works nicely to assure equity in such cases.
>
> In another kind of recurring case, . . . where divorce occurs shortly after the degree is obtained, traditional alimony analysis would often work hardship because, while

both spouses have modest incomes at the time of divorce, the one is on the threshold of a significant increase in earnings. Moreover, the spouse who sacrificed so the other could attain a degree is precluded from enjoying the anticipated dividends the degree will ordinarily provide. Nonetheless, such a spouse is typically not remote in time from his or her previous education and is otherwise better able to adjust and to acquire comparable skills, given the opportunity and the funding. In such cases, alimony analysis must become more creative to achieve fairness, and an award of "rehabilitative" or "reimbursement" alimony, not terminable upon remarriage, may be appropriate.

Petersen v. Petersen, 737 P.2d 237, 242 n.4 (Utah App. 1987) (*citing Haugan v. Haugan*, 117 Wis. 2d 200, 343 N.W.2d 796 (1984); *Mahoney v. Mahoney*, 91 N.J. 488, 453 A.2d 527 (1982)).

With these principles in mind, we consider the contentions of the parties.

II. Thomas begins by asserting that the trial court erroneously characterized his medical education and license as marital assets properly subject to equitable division. We find no merit in the contention. The trial court specifically found that the "degree . . . obtained by Thomas [is] not property." It then went on to correctly cite *Horstmann, Janssen, and Estlund* for the proposition that it is the potential for increased future earning capacity made possible by Thomas' degree, with Diana's assistance, "that constitutes the asset for distribution by the Court."

We are persuaded, however, by Thomas' assertion that alimony, not a property award, is the proper vehicle by which to achieve equity upon the dissolution of this marriage.

As previously stated in this opinion, alimony has traditionally taken the place of support that would have been provided had the marriage continued. A calculation of future earning capacity, in a case like the present one, essentially represents a value placed on the income to be derived from the advanced degree achieved during the marriage. The amount that would have been the student spouse's contribution to the future support of the parties is logically tied, if not wholly determined by, future earning capacity. Thus the court's duty to look at the future earning capacity of the spouses tracks more closely with a concern for loss of anticipated support, reimbursable through alimony, than through division of as-yet-unrealized tangible assets.

The alimony of which we speak is designed to give the "supporting" spouse a stake in the "student" spouse's future earning capacity, in exchange for recognizable contributions to the source of that income—the student's advanced education. As such, it is to be clearly distinguished from "rehabilitative" or "permanent" alimony.

Rehabilitative alimony was conceived as a way of supporting an economically dependent spouse through a limited period of re-education or retraining following divorce, thereby creating incentive and opportunity for that spouse to become self-supporting.

Because self-sufficiency is the goal of rehabilitative alimony, the duration of such an award may be limited or extended depending on the realistic needs of the economically dependent spouse, tempered by the goal of facilitating the economic independence of the ex-spouses. As in the case of "traditional" alimony, payable for life or so long as a spouse is incapable of self-support, a change in status (e.g., remarriage) may alter the support picture and warrant a modification. *See In re Marriage of Shima*, 360 N.W.2d 827, 828 (Iowa 1985) (remarriage shifts the burden on recipient to prove extraordinary circumstances requiring continuation of alimony).

"Reimbursement" alimony, on the other hand, which is predicated upon economic sacrifices made by one spouse during the marriage that directly enhance the future earning capacity of the other, should not be subject to modification or termination until full compensation is achieved. Similar to a property award, but based on future earning capacity rather than a division of tangible assets, it should be fixed at the time of the decree. In recognition of the personal nature of the award and the current tax laws, however, a spouse's obligation to pay reimbursement alimony must terminate upon the recipient's death.

We think the case before us exemplifies the situation calling for an award of reimbursement alimony rather than a property settlement. Not only does such an award bear a closer resemblance to support than a division of assets, alimony carries tax benefits to the payor and assurance to the payee that the award will not be discharged in bankruptcy.[2] The trial court's decree must be modified accordingly.

III. Whether classified as a property division or alimony, Thomas objects to the court's award of $ 100,000 as a "windfall to Diana far in excess of any equitable return on the contributions she made during the marriage." We thus turn to the record to evaluate the size of the award in light of the facts presented.

The parties were legally married in May 1982, but had lived together since the birth of their son, Michael, in November 1980. At the time of their marriage, neither party was employed and neither had significant assets of any kind. Thomas had completed his bachelor's degree and one year of graduate study. Diana had completed all but her thesis and oral examination required for a master's degree in early childhood development. She received that degree in June 1983. The parties' second child, Melissa, was born in March 1984.

From the outset of their marriage, Thomas and Diana agreed that Diana would care for their children and earn income for the family by caring for other people's children in their home. This arrangement continued throughout the marriage except for a brief period shortly after Melissa was born.

Meanwhile, Thomas entered medical school at Southern Illinois University in the fall of 1982. After one year he transferred to the University of Illinois at Springfield where he obtained his medical degree in 1986, graduating in the top twenty-five percent of his class. The family then moved to Iowa City so that Thomas could enroll in the University's three-year residency program for physicians specializing in family practice.

By November 1986, the parties were experiencing marital difficulties. In June 1987, Thomas petitioned for dissolution of marriage. Trial was held in June 1988.

From the date of their marriage through the date of trial, the parties supported themselves on income from a variety of sources. During the summer before medical school began, Thomas worked as a gardener and earned approximately $ 1200. Diana earned roughly $ 5000 per year from her in-home day care business. Thomas' parents contributed $ 11,500

---

[2] Comment. At the time this case was decided, property distributions were generally dischargeable in bankruptcy, while support awards were not. The Bankruptcy Code has since been amended to make it more difficult for debtors to discharge divorce-related property obligations. *See* § 14.03 *below*. (Footnote added by editors.)

and Diana's mother gave them $ 12,000. Student loans accounted for $ 45,500 over the six-year period.

Once Thomas obtained his medical degree, his earnings went up substantially. In 1986 he earned $ 8700, while his salary for 1987 was $ 29,337. At the time of trial, he was earning approximately $ 3000 per month from a combination of resident's salary and "moonlighting" as an emergency room physician.

The parties strenuously dispute their relative contributions to child rearing and housekeeping tasks throughout the marriage. Thomas claims that he contributed thirty to fifty percent of those services and that Diana should not be credited for child care or homemaking during those hours in which she was caring for other children as well as her own. Diana argues that Thomas' devotion to his medical studies, as demonstrated by his class rank and a successful residency, greatly limited his available time at home.

The district court specifically found Thomas' testimony lacking in credibility with regard to his alleged substantial contribution to the maintenance of the household. It did conclude, however, that Thomas' educational loans, combined with the income he has earned since the parties' separation, has furnished the bulk of the family's financial support. From our review of the record, we discover no reason to differ with these findings.

The parties' principal argument is over the testimony of Dr. Richard Stevenson, professor of finance and acting treasurer of the University of Iowa. He was engaged by Diana, in his words, "to value the capital that was contributed by Mrs. Francis to the medical education received during the marriage of Dr. Francis." Thomas' counsel objected to the introduction of this testimony on the ground that the expert's analysis placed a value on the degree itself, contrary to the dictates of *Horstmann*. Thomas renews that contention on appeal. We are convinced, however, that Dr. Stevenson's calculations, and the district court's ultimate award, were based on Diana's contribution to Thomas' future earning capacity, not the value of Thomas' medical license.

As background for his economic analysis, Dr. Stevenson took into account the facts previously related concerning the age, education, work experience and financial contributions of the parties. To those figures he added the sum of $ 64,095 for the estimated present value of Diana's homemaker services (at $ 6.70 per hour) over the six-year period. Adding this sum to her day care earnings, Diana's capital investment in obtaining Thomas' medical education equaled approximately fifty percent of the total capital committed.

Based upon 1987 figures reported in a journal of medical economics that surveys physicians' earnings by speciality and other classifications (such as geography, type of practice, age, experience, etc.), Dr. Stevenson calculated the after-tax present value of Thomas' future income as a family practice physician to be $ 1,615,735. He then subtracted the sum of $ 807,206, a figure representing the estimated future income of a male in the 30–34 age bracket with a five-year undergraduate degree. The difference ($ 808,529) represents the additional income accruing as a result of the medical degree.

Applying a 30/70 capital to labor ratio, Dr. Stevenson then determined that thirty percent of the present value of Thomas' future earnings, or $ 242,559, is attributable to capital contributed to acquiring the education. He then reduced that figure by one-half to reflect Diana's contribution to "the capital needed to obtain the medical education and to support the family until the divorce was filed." Thus his estimation of Diana's contribution to Thomas' future earning capacity equals $ 121,279.

The district court recognized that Dr. Stevenson's final figure was based on many assumptions and that his prediction of Thomas' future earnings could not be exact. Moreover, the court noted that the professor did not consider the benefit gained by Diana in her achievement of a master's degree during the marriage. Consequently, "to compensate Diana for her contribution to Thomas' increased future earning capacity," the court ordered Thomas to pay Diana the sum of $ 100,000, payable in annual installments of $ 10,000 each commencing July 1, 1989.

Thomas attacks the trial court's award by challenging virtually every aspect of Dr. Stevenson's calculations. But for his own opinions, however, Thomas offered no evidence to controvert the assumptions upon which the calculations were based. He certainly did not challenge the estimated annual income projections, reduced to present value. He merely begrudges Diana her contribution to the accumulation of that income.

In *Horstmann*, we approved an award that represented the cost of the education towards an advanced degree. See *Horstmann*, 263 N.W.2d at 891. We noted, however, that other methods could have been used to measure future earning capacity. *Id*. Similar cases have authorized awards representing the value of services, as a percentage of future earning capacity, contributed to the attainment of the degree.

We note that other states, while recognizing the need for something akin to the "reimbursement alimony" outlined in division II of this opinion, limit the supporting spouse's compensation to the financial contributions made towards tuition, living expenses and other costs of the education. Other jurisdictions speak of compensating the supporting spouse through an award of alimony, but not based on the student's future earning capacity. In keeping with the standard established in *Horstmann*, however, courts in Iowa are not confined to reimbursing supporting spouses solely for the expense of the advanced degree itself.

We find no error in the formula used here to measure Thomas' future earning capacity and Diana's contribution to its attainment. Thomas concedes a willingness to pay Diana $ 60,000 for her contribution. The trial court's figure of $ 100,000 finds ample support in the record and we are not persuaded to reduce or overturn it.

IV. Just prior to trial, Diana learned of a program in St. Louis that would train her in Montessori pre-school theory and thereby enhance her re-entry into the early childhood education field. The program included seven weeks of training at a cost of $ 1200 followed by a one-year internship and guaranteed placement as a teacher in a Montessori school. The district court found that Diana was in need of support during this training period and that she was entitled to rehabilitative alimony in the sum of $ 500 per month during the internship and $ 1000 per month for four years thereafter to become established in her field.

Thomas strongly opposes this additional award, claiming that with her master's degree and her in-home day care experience, Diana is fully able to support herself without further education or training. In fact, Thomas claims, such a generous alimony award would allow Diana "to attain a standard of living greater than that which she experienced during the marriage."

Diana responds by contending that Thomas' attitude toward rehabilitative alimony would "freeze the inequities of the present moment into perpetuity." We find considerable merit in her retort. Diana may have a master's degree, but she has devoted the last six years of her life to raising her own children and caring for three others at the rate of $ 230 per week. It is not fair to expect that she support herself this way indefinitely, nor is it realistic to assume that she will become immediately marketable in some more lucrative endeavor.

Like the district court, we view the St. Louis Montessori program as a reasonable way of facilitating Diana's re-entry into the work force. In view of the guaranteed placement feature of the program, however, we think one-year's rehabilitative alimony is sufficient and the decree must be modified accordingly.

V. Finally, we address Thomas' contention that he should not be required to contribute towards Diana's attorney fees, at trial or on appeal.

Ordinarily, an award of attorney fees rests in the sound discretion of the trial court and will not be disturbed on appeal absent an abuse of discretion. The controlling factor is ability to pay the fees.

At the time of trial, Diana had monthly earnings of $ 720; Thomas' were $ 2068. Thomas, of course, leaves the marriage burdened with a great deal of debt. His first year salary out of residency, however, is anticipated to be at least $ 50,000. Diana's chosen field, though professionally rewarding, furnishes far less financial security.

Taking these factors into account, we find no abuse of discretion in the trial court's requiring Thomas to pay $ 1000 towards Diana's attorney fees. In view of the substantial awards of alimony upheld on this appeal, however, we reject Diana's claim for attorney fees on appeal.

VI. Summary. In lieu of the $ 100,000 judgment entered by the trial court in Diana's favor, we direct that the trial court order Thomas to pay Diana reimbursement alimony of $ 10,000 per year for a period of ten years commencing July 1, 1989. Interest at the rate of ten percent per annum shall accrue on any payment not made within thirty days of its due date. This alimony judgment shall not be subject to modification but shall terminate in the event of Diana's death.

The district court's order for rehabilitative alimony commencing August 1, 1988, is affirmed as modified by the reduction to one year and increase in amount to $ 1000 per month. The trial court's judgment for attorney fees is affirmed. Diana's request for attorney fees on appeal is denied. Costs for this action are assessed against the appellant.

NOTES AND QUESTIONS

(1) Is the $100,000 reimbursement award authorized in *Francis* an alimony remedy, a property remedy or something in between? Why does the *Francis* court conclude that alimony, rather than a property award, "furnishes a fairer and more logical means of achieving the equity sought?" How does the court's analysis in *Francis* differ from the analysis of the New York Court of Appeals in *O'Brien v. O'Brien*, § 10.02[J], *above*?

(2) As the *Francis* court notes, other courts that have employed the concept of "reimbursement alimony" to compensate a supporting spouse have generally limited recovery to the supporting spouse's direct financial contributions made toward tuition, living expenses and other educational costs. *See, e.g., DeLa Rosa v. DeLa Rosa*, 309 N.W.2d 755, 758–59 (Minn. 1981); *Mahoney v. Mahoney,* 453 A.2d 527 (N.J. 1982); *Bold v. Bold*, 574

A.2d 552 (Pa. 1990); *Hoak v. Hoak,* 370 S.E.2d 473, 475–79 (W. Va. 1988). Is this a more appropriate measure of recovery, given the underlying theory of reimbursement alimony? If Diana were permitted to recover only her direct financial contributions to Thomas' education, what would her approximate recovery be?

(3) Section 5.15 of the proposed ALI *Principles* authorizes compensation to a spouse who has contributed to her partner's education or training over the course of a short-term marriage. However, the *Principles* limit the amount of recovery to the actual costs of the support provided, which include both direct costs such as tuition, as well as the living expenses of the student spouse. *See* ALI Principles § 5.15, comment b. The Reporter's Comments to this section explicitly reject the valuation approach adopted in *Francis,* characterizing such an approach as "fraught with uncertainty." The Comments continue:

> More fundamentally, however, there is no explanation of why the wife's contribution to the husband's support during his schooling created a claim of entitlement to share in his future income. Characterization of the wife's support as an investment for which she is entitled to a 'return' is inapt. The wife was not looking generally for medical students to invest in, nor was the husband looking for investors. . . . Their income sharing would be justified by their continuing relationship, not by the wife's past financial support. If the husband's main concern was financing his education, he could have gotten a better deal elsewhere. A commercial loan, for example, would have provided him better terms than did the trial court.

§ 5.15 (Reporter's Comments). Do you agree with this criticism of the valuation approach adopted in *Francis*? Why or why not?

(4) Assume that Thomas is severely injured in an automobile accident two years after the Iowa Supreme Court's decision, and is no longer able to practice medicine. Should he still have to pay Diana the remaining eight annual installments of $10,000? Why or why not? If Diana remarries during the 10-year reimbursement period, what effect, if any, should her remarriage have on Thomas' obligation? For additional discussion of the modification of spousal support awards, see § 10.03[F], *below.*

(5) **Problem.** Randy and Sue married soon after they graduated from college. They both wanted to be lawyers, but realized that they could not afford to attend law school at the same time. Because Randy had already secured employment as a paralegal, the couple decided that Sue would attend law school for the first three years of their marriage, while Randy worked full time. After Sue's graduation, she would work full time while Randy obtained his law degree. The couple did not put their understanding in writing. During the ensuing three years, Sue attended law school full-time at the state university, while Randy worked. The couple used Randy's salary of $40,000/year to pay for approximately half of Sue's law school tuition, as well as most of the couple's living expenses. Sue contributed the remaining funds (approximately $10,000/year) through a combination of loans and summer earnings. Sue did extremely well at law school and, upon her graduation last June, accepted a job as an associate at a major law firm at an annual salary of $80,000. Unfortunately, the couple's marriage did not fare nearly so well. Shortly after Sue's graduation, she moved out of the couple's apartment and informed Randy that she wanted a divorce. Sue has also refused to pay Randy's law school tuition, claiming that couple's oral understanding was intended apply only if their marriage endured. As a result of the couple's separation, Randy has changed his educational plans and has enrolled in the law

school's evening division, so that he can continue to work full time during the day. If Randy and Sue decide to divorce, what sort of compensation is Randy entitled to from Sue? Under what theory or theories?

[F] Modification of Support Awards

As the chapter introduction indicates, alimony awards—unlike property distributions—have traditionally been subject to judicial modification, upon a showing of substantially changed circumstances. *See generally* John DeWitt Gregory, Peter N. Swisher and Sheryl L. Scheible-Wolf, Understanding Family Law § 8.05, (Matthew Bender 1995). Determining what changes are substantial enough to justify modification, however, has been a matter of considerable controversy. Moreover, recent changes in the underlying purposes and functions of alimony have raised questions about the continued viability of some traditional modification principles.

GILMAN v. GILMAN
Supreme Court of Nevada
956 P.2d 761 (1998)

SHEARING, J.

Docket No 28892

Appellant Kenneth Callahan ("Ken") and respondent Valerie Callahan ("Valerie") married on December 31, 1984. Shortly after the wedding, Valerie apparently quit her job as a secretary to stay at home. The parties agreed that Valerie would stay home permanently following the birth of their daughter in 1988 or 1989. Ken earned $ 125,000 in 1992 and $ 110,000 in 1993 in his position as a mortgage lender.

On July 31, 1992, Valerie filed a complaint for divorce in Clark County. Beginning in November 1992, she received $ 500 in temporary spousal support every other week pursuant to a court order. On July 27, 1994, the district court increased this amount to $ 700 biweekly.

After a three-day divorce trial in September 1994, the district court issued an order increasing Valerie's spousal support to $ 2,000 per month for twenty-four months, then to $ 1,500 per month for the following thirty-six months The court found that Valerie had given up her career to raise the couple's child, that Ken had more than twenty-five years experience in his profession, and that Valerie's earning capabilities would never approximate those of Ken. The separate divorce decree approved by the court states that Ken's obligation to pay spousal support shall terminate upon his death or Valerie's remarriage. There is no reference to cohabitation.

After entry of the divorce decree, Valerie and her daughter moved to Reno with Chuck Maraden ("Chuck"). On March 28, 1996, Ken filed a motion to modify the decree of divorce to, *inter alia*, terminate spousal support based upon the allegation that Valerie and Chuck were cohabiting and "acting in every way as if they were married except the legal solemnization of the marriage." Ken argued that this cohabitation constituted a change of circumstances under NRS 125.150.

On April 30, 1996, at a hearing on the motion, Valerie admitted that she was romantically involved with Chuck and cohabitated with him, but stated that he did not support her financially. She also declared that she shared monthly living expenses with Chuck, that she paid for all of her daughter's expenses, that Chuck had loaned her money, that she had signed promissory notes for the loans, and that Ken had failed to meet his financial obligations to her. The record shows that Ken's gross monthly income in 1996 was $ 6,500.

On May 14, 1996, the district court issued an order denying Ken's motion to terminate alimony. Ken filed a timely notice of appeal from the May 14 order.

Docket No. 27896

Appellant Richard S. Gilman ("Richard") and Marjorie Gilman ("Marjorie") married in Brighton, Massachusetts on April 25, 1963. During the marriage, Richard worked as a certified public accountant and Marjorie remained at home. In 1989, Richard's annual salary was approximately $ 60,000.

On August 7, 1989, Richard filed for divorce in Clark County district court. On November 26, 1990, the district court approved the decree of divorce negotiated by the parties. The decree states that "spousal support shall terminate upon the death or remarriage of [Marjorie] and the court will consider the issue of spousal support in the event of co-habitation by [Marjorie] with an adult male who significantly contributes to her support." Richard agreed to pay spousal support of $ 1,500 per month.

From some time in 1991 until November 1993, Marjorie lived off and on in Las Vegas with her friend-boyfriend, Tom Westmoreland ("Tom"), at Tom's house. From April or May 1993 until November 1993, Marjorie lived full-time with Tom, paid him $ 400 per month in rent and paid for her telephone bill and some of the food bill. Thereafter, Marjorie and Tom moved to Massachusetts. Marjorie purchased a house, making a down payment with money she received from the sale of the Las Vegas marital residence she shared with Ken. The title to the Massachusetts house is in Marjorie's name alone; Tom has no ownership interest in it. Since November 1993, Tom has been living in the Massachusetts house with Marjorie.

By the time of her deposition in March 1994, Marjorie had been unable to secure a job in Massachusetts. She also had no immediate plans to continue a job search.

In addition to the spousal support, Marjorie also receives $ 4,000 to $ 8,000 per year in payments from an irrevocable family trust established for the benefit of herself, her parents, and her siblings.

In early 1994, Tom began working full time in a car dealership making $ 8.00 per hour. Prior to that, Tom was either collecting unemployment or working odd jobs. Tom does not pay rent, food bills, or other living expenses at the Massachusetts house. Apparently, Tom uses his salary to make his car payment and to make payments on the home he owns in Las Vegas. Tom does carpentry work around the house which, according to Marjorie, is a "fair exchange" for the free rent and food. Tom and Marjorie have separate bank accounts; however, they have put both of their names on the two accounts, allegedly for "emergency purposes." Marjorie has loaned Tom small amounts of money on occasion.

By March 1994, Richard's income had increased to $ 9,325 per month.

On December 6, 1993, Richard filed a motion to terminate his spousal support payment to Marjorie based on changed circumstances. Richard declared in an affidavit that Marjorie had been cohabiting with Tom for two years and that she had "chosen not to remarry to avoid the cohabitation provision [of the divorce decree]." Richard alleged that these facts were sufficient to warrant termination of spousal support.

On July 25, 1995, the district court denied Richard's motion. The court found that Tom had not significantly contributed to Marjorie's support, that Nevada law contained no presumption that spousal support should terminate if the recipient cohabits with another person, and that legal termination of spousal support would arise only upon death of one of the parties or remarriage of the recipient spouse. The court also noted that parties to a divorce "are free to impose whatever conditions they wish to define the term of alimony." Richard has appealed the district court's decision denying his motion to terminate alimony.

DISCUSSION

Richard and Ken contend that cohabitation constitutes a changed circumstance under NRS 125.150, particularly where the cohabitant's finances have any effect, positive or negative, upon the recipient spouse's finances. Thus, they contend that the district court erred in refusing to modify or terminate spousal support in their respective cases.

Both Marjorie and Valerie concede that financial contributions by a cohabitant might constitute a change of circumstances under NRS 125.150. However, Marjorie argues that the express provisions of her divorce decree should control and that Richard failed to make a showing that Tom significantly contributed to her support. Valerie argues that she presented ample evidence that her financial condition did not improve, and even worsened, during her cohabitation and thus that no changed circumstances occurred.

NRS 125.150 provides, in relevant part:

> 7. If a decree of divorce . . . provides for specified periodic payments of alimony, the decree or agreement is not subject to modification by the court as to accrued payments. Payments . . . which have not accrued at the time a motion for modification is filed may be modified upon a showing of changed circumstances, whether or not the court has expressly retained jurisdiction for the modification. . . .

The current majority rule regarding the effect of post-divorce cohabitation on spousal support, at least in jurisdictions where no specific statute covers that situation, appears to be that the right to receive spousal support becomes subject to modification or termination only if the recipient spouse's need for the support decreases as a result of the cohabitation. *Gayet v. Gayet*, 456 A.2d 92 N. J. 149, 456 A.2d 102, 104 (N.J. 1983). Most jurisdictions following the majority rule have determined that some financial dependence by the alimony recipient upon the third-party cohabitant likely warrants a reduction in spousal support. Similarly, those jurisdictions also hold that alimony payments used to benefit the cohabitant should be eliminated or reduced to meet the recipient spouse's actual needs. As stated by the New Jersey Supreme Court: "modification [of spousal support] for changed circumstances resulting from cohabitation [is warranted] only if one cohabitant supports or subsidizes the other under circumstances sufficient to entitle the supporting spouse to relief." *Gayet*, 456 A.2d at 104.

Under this "economic needs" test, the amount of spousal support reduction, if any, depends upon a factual examination of the financial effects of the cohabitation on the recipient spouse. Shared living arrangements, unaccompanied by evidence of a decrease in the actual financial needs of the recipient spouse, are generally insufficient to call for alimony modification.

The economic needs test properly considers the rights and needs, both fiscal and personal, of payor and recipient spouses. First, the test does not unduly impinge upon an individual's freedom to choose to cohabit. Rights to spousal support are not rescinded merely because the recipient spouse is cohabiting.

Second, the test also recognizes the fact that a recipient spouse may be left largely unprotected, from an economic standpoint, if he or she breaks off a relationship with a cohabitant. The Nevada legislature created spousal support awards to, *inter alia*, keep recipient spouses off the welfare rolls. Modifying or terminating spousal support payments based upon cohabitation may be inconsistent with this purpose. Generally, cohabitants owe no legal or financial support to one another. Because no legal support obligation is imposed on the parties during the relationship, no spousal maintenance can be awarded when and if the relationship ends. Moreover, absent an express or implied agreement to the contrary, no quasi-marital property rights accrue as a result of cohabitation.

Third, the test also takes into consideration the financial rights of the payor spouse, as well as the economic realities associated with cohabitation. As some courts and commentators have suggested, a possibility exists that cohabitants may sometimes act improperly to maximize their joint wealth (and retain any spousal support payments) by appearing to maintain "separate financial identities." Moreover, sharing household expenses gives rise to "economies of scale" which may permit cohabitants to spend less living together than individually. The economic needs test recognizes these situations and promotes fiscal fairness by acknowledging that maintaining the original amount of spousal support payments may be unfair to payor spouses if they are essentially subsidizing third party cohabitants, or supporting ex-spouses who have significantly improved their financial situations.

We conclude that the economic needs test fairly balances the rights of payor and payee spouses by permitting modification or termination of spousal support solely when financial circumstances so merit. The test coincides with Nevada's existing statutory "changed circumstances" scheme and allows lower courts to focus upon the specific facts of each case, while retaining their substantial discretion when making spousal support modification decisions. . . .

Accordingly, we hold that a showing that the recipient spouse has an actual decreased financial need for spousal support due to the fiscal impact of a cohabitant may constitute changed circumstances sufficient to require a modification of unaccrued payments under that support obligation.

Docket No. 28892

Valerie and Ken's divorce decree contains no cohabitation provision. According to Valerie, she and her daughter moved from Las Vegas to Reno with Chuck in the fall of 1995, and all three currently live together. The record shows that, on October 1, 1995, Valerie and Chuck entered into a "rental agreement." Valerie promised to pay Chuck $1,000 per month to cover rent and household expenses. In 1996, Valerie was unable to pay this amount for several months. She also borrowed other monies from Chuck, apparently because Ken failed to timely pay spousal and child support and to timely turn over previously divided marital assets. Under these circumstances, we conclude that the district court did not abuse its discretion in determining that Ken did not show that Chuck's contributions to Valerie were significant enough to warrant termination, or even modification, of spousal support. Ken presented virtually no evidence which indicates that Valerie's actual financial needs have been reduced because of her living arrangements. Accordingly, Ken's contention is without merit.

Docket No. 27896

Richard and Marjorie's divorce decree states that "the court will consider the issue of spousal support in the event of cohabitation by [Marjorie] with an adult male who significantly contributes to her support." We conclude that the district court correctly determined that the parties were free to place that cohabitation provision in their divorce decree and that the provision is valid and enforceable.

The record shows that Tom earned approximately $ 320 per week working at a car dealership. Tom used the money he made to make the payment on a house he owns in Las Vegas and on his car. Tom does not pay for rent, food, or other household bills at the Massachusetts residence. He performs carpentry work around the house as a "fair exchange" for rent and food. Tom and Marjorie keep separate bank accounts. When Marjorie and Tom lived together full-time in Tom's Las Vegas home, Marjorie paid her share of the rent and household bills. Thus, there is no evidence that Tom ever "significantly contributed" to Marjorie's support.

Richard contends that his spousal support payments to Marjorie should be reduced or terminated because Marjorie is using those funds to support Tom.

Under well settled rules of contract construction, a court has no power to create a new contract for the parties which they have not created or intended themselves. Applicable statutes will generally be incorporated into the contract; however, other legal principles may govern the legal relationship where they are expressly set forth in the contract. Indeed, "when parties to a contract foresee a condition which may develop and provide in their contract a remedy for the happening of that condition, the presumption is that the parties intended the prescribed remedy as the sole remedy for that condition." *S.L. Rowland Const. Co. v. Beall Pipe & Tank Corp.*, 14 Wash. App. 297, 540 P.2d 912, 920 (Wash. Ct. App. 1975) (citations omitted).

Here, the parties negotiated for the cohabitation provision contained in the divorce decree. That provision fails to address what would happen if Marjorie used her alimony payments to support Tom. In light of the existence of that term, we conclude that the parties intended their contractual cohabitation provision, and not the general "changed circumstances" statute, to apply in case of Marjorie's cohabitation with another man. Accordingly, we decline to apply NRS 125.150(7) and the economic needs test to this situation. Thus, Richard cannot allege that Tom's failure to pay a share of household bills at the Massachusetts residence is a valid basis for modifying or terminating Marjorie's alimony award. We conclude that the district court did not abuse its discretion in refusing to modify or terminate the spousal support in this case.

In both the Gilmans' and the Callahans' cases, the district courts considered the cohabitation as it affected the economic situation of the parties receiving spousal support and concluded that no change in the support orders was warranted. Their conclusions were not only not abuses of discretion, but were clearly justified based on the evidence presented.

In no way is either of the cases similar to the circumstances in *Western States Construction v. Michoff*, 108 Nev. 931, 840 P.2d 1220 (1992). The *Michoff* case was one in which the cohabiting parties built and developed a business together based on an implied agreement of coequal ownership. The woman was an integral part of the business, even being listed as sole owner for a time in order to increase the chances of getting contracts. They held themselves out as husband and wife, even filing joint tax returns and designating their holdings as community property. It would certainly have been inequitable not to enforce the agreement of the parties for coequal ownership, allowing the woman to receive her share of their assets, when the relationship ended. The cohabitation element of the relationship was virtually incidental.

The situation with both the Gilmans and the Callahans is not even remotely similar. There is certainly no evidence of a contract between the cohabitants which was the basis for *Michoff*. There is no evidence of pooling of assets or holding themselves out as husband and wife or treating their assets as community property or building a business together. It should be clear that neither cohabitation nor a romantic relationship is the real basis for the *Michoff* holding, and that is all that is present in both the Gilman and Callahan situations.

The district courts appropriately exercised their discretion, and their orders are affirmed.

SPRINGER, C.J., concurring in part and dissenting in part:

I concur in the Gilman case and dissent in the Callahan case.

The reason that I agree with the judgment in the Gilman case is that the family court properly applied the agreed-upon standard for modifying support, namely, whether the person with whom Marjorie was cohabiting "significantly" contributed to her support. In accordance with the agreement of the parties, the court simply ruled that the "adult male" with whom Marjorie was cohabiting did not "significantly contribute" to her support and that, therefore, she was not entitled to relief. The court was acting well within its discretion when it ruled that there was not such a significant contribution as to justify a modification; so I would affirm the family court's judgment in the Gilman case.

I dissent in *Callahan* because, absent the kind of negotiated agreement present in Gilman, the family court had to apply general principles of law in deciding whether modification was justified. In my opinion, it was error for the family court to ignore the fact that Valerie had been living for a time with "Chuck," with whom she was "acting in every way as if they were married except the legal solemnization of the marriage." The family court ruled that this marriage-like "cohabitation was not a fact that [the court] was considering would warrant termination of spousal support." The majority opinion agrees with the family court's judgment in this regard. In my opinion, this kind of "marriage-like" relationship should not only be considered by the family court, it should create a rebuttable presumption of a change in circumstances.

When a man and woman live together "as if they were married" they create a legally-cognizable status, a status that might, in Nevada, be properly called a "Michoff marriage." [*Western States Constr. v. Michoff*, 108 Nev. 931, 840 P.2d 1220 (1992)] A Michoff marriage is created when two people cohabit in such a way as to entitle either party to make claims against the other for "palimony" and for community property "by analogy." Michoff marriages are a creature of *Michoff*, which allows "inter-cohabitant" claims to be made based upon a supposed "implied contract" that is created by virtue of the cohabitation. It is my position that an alimony-receiving ex-spouse cannot "have it both ways"—that is, cannot put himself in a position where he is entitled to receive palimony and property division by virtue of a Michoff marriage and also be entitled to continue to receive alimony from a former spouse.

I argue in this dissent that, at the very least, a rebuttable presumption of disentitlement to continued alimony should follow from a Michoff marriage and, further, that there are persuasive reasons for concluding that the presumption should be irrebuttable in cases where an alimony-receiving spouse's claim to palimony has matured by reason of ripening support and property rights attendant to a Michoff marriage. . . .

It should be kept in mind that the words "cohabitation" and "cohabiting" are words of particular legal significance that carry more meaning than merely living under the same roof. Merely living with a person of the opposite sex does not constitute cohabitation. To be cohabitants, it is not necessary that the cohabiting parties hold themselves out as husband and wife. To be "cohabiting," the parties must be engaged in a romantic or homemaker-companion relationship that resembles the marital relationship, but without a formal marriage ceremony. *Michoff* recognizes the "cohabiting" status that arises out of one's being an "unmarried cohabitant []" and recognizes the right of one unmarried cohabitant to sue the other in family court, "seeking one-half of the parties' assets." 108 Nev. at 933, 840 P.2d at 1221. In *Michoff*, this court ruled that "the remedies in [*Marvin v. Marvin*, 557 P.2d 672 (Cal. 1984)] are available to unmarried cohabitants" and that, accordingly, "adults who voluntarily live together," in addition to acquiring rights to be supported by the other cohabitant (facetiously called "palimony"), may acquire property rights "during the relationship in accord with the law governing community property." *Michoff*, 108 Nev. at 938, 840 P.2d at 1224.

According to *Michoff*, the laws of spousal support and "the community property laws of the state will apply by analogy," at some stage of extra-marital cohabitation. *Id.* (quoting *Hay v. Hay*, 100 Nev. 196, 199, 678 P.2d 672, 674 (1984)). The Michoff right of an unmarried cohabitant to "seek[] one-half of the parties' assets" rests on the parties' having cohabited and thereby "impliedly agreed to hold their property as though they were married." *Id.* at 938, 840 P.2d at 1224. Although *Michoff* did not deal with palimony, because it expressly adopted *Marvin*, Michoff cohabitants are in a position to prove a case that would entitle them to recover both palimony as well as "one-half of the [other] party's assets." My point is that *Michoff* cohabitants become vested with a right to sue for support and property distribution benefits, and *Michoff* status necessarily has a significant bearing on the alimony-paying spouse's obligation to support a former, but now "cohabiting," spouse. . . .

The majority opinion tells us that "after entry of the divorce decree [September, 1994], Valerie . . . moved to Reno with Chuck Maraden ("Chuck")." Further, "Valerie admitted that she was romantically involved with Chuck and cohabited with him. . . ." We know that the two were cohabiting "as if they were married" in May of 1996 when Ken's motion to modify alimony was denied, and there is no reason to suspect that they are not cohabiting at this time, the point being that Valerie and Chuck are engaged in the relatively permanent marriage-like cohabitation that, by its nature, necessarily gives rise to the status I have referred to as a Michoff marriage. Under these circumstances, it cannot be denied that each partner to the Michoff marriage is in a position to sue the other in family court for *Michoff/Marvin*-sanctioned support payments and for "one half of the parties' assets" in the form of "community property by analogy." *Michoff,* 108 Nev. at 933, 840 P.2d at 1221. . . .

I argue that, at the very least, some judicial cognizance must be given to Michoff marriages in support modification cases; and it would not be too difficult to argue, further, that since no one is entitled to two alimony claims, establishment of a Michoff marriage should terminate all previous rights to receive alimony. It certainly makes some sense to argue that a Michoff marriage should be an absolute bar to receiving alimony from a previous spouse. A Michoff bride or groom should not be able to have it both ways—to have the right to palimony plus one-half of the analogous community property from a current cohabitant on top of having the right to receive alimony payments from a former, divorced spouse. I do not intend to pursue this argument, however, and will be content to maintain that we should follow California law and presume that cohabitation, a Michoff marriage, of itself, constitutes changed circumstances for alimony-modification purposes. Perhaps, in today's world, the majority opinion may be right in recognizing an "individual freedom to choose to cohabit"; still, I do not believe that we would "impinge" on that right if we refused to permit a person to be entitled to two alimonies. . . .

NOTES AND QUESTIONS

(1) **Uniform Marriage and Divorce Act.** Section 316 of the Uniform Marriage and Divorce Act (UMDA) addresses the modification and termination of provisions for maintenance, support and property disposition. It provides:

> (a) [T]he provisions of any decree respecting maintenance or support may be modified only as to installments accruing subsequent to the motion for modification and only upon a showing of changed circumstances so substantial and continuing as to make the terms unconscionable. The provisions as to property disposition may not be revoked or modified, unless the court finds the existence of conditions that justify the reopening of a judgment under the laws of this state.
>
> (b) Unless otherwise agreed in writing or expressly provided in the decree, the obligation to pay future maintenance is terminated upon the death of either party or the remarriage of the party receiving maintenance. . . .

9A U.L.A. 489–90 (West 1973). What theories of property division and spousal support best explain the finality of property dispositions, as opposed to the modifiability of support awards? Note that, under the UMDA, accrued alimony installments or arrearages may not be modified retroactively and alimony payments may be modified prospectively only after a motion has been filed. A minority of jurisdictions permit retroactive modification of alimony arrearages, either by statute or by judicial decision. *See* John DeWitt Gregory, Peter N. Swisher and Sheryl L. Scheible-Wolf, Understanding Family Law § 8.05 (Matthew Bender 1995). Should such retroactive modification be permitted? Why or why not? The UMDA also requires that, to justify modification, the showing of changed circumstances must be "so substantial and continuing as to make the [support] terms unconscionable." This unconscionability requirement is considerably stricter than the modification standard adopted in a majority of jurisdictions. *Id.*

(2) **Effect of Remarriage.** The traditional rule, reflected in the UMDA, is that a recipient's remarriage automatically terminates her entitlement to alimony, regardless of the effect of the remarriage on the recipient's financial needs. *See, e.g., Dunaway v. Dunaway*, 560 N.E.2d 171, 176 (Ohio 1990) ("sustenance alimony" terminated upon wife's remarriage, even though new husband is physically disabled and incapable of providing support); Homer H. Clark, 2 The Law of Domestic Relations In the United States 283–85 (2d ed. 1987). This rule comports with the traditional conception of alimony as the

continuation of a husband's duty of support, since that support obligation is extinguished by virtue of the recipient's remarriage to another man. *See Wolter v. Wolter*, 158 N.W.2d 616, 619 (Neb. 1968) ("it is against public policy that a woman should have support or its equivalent from two men"). Does an automatic termination rule still make sense in light of the modern justifications for alimony? Why or why not? Should the effect of remarriage on a support award depend on the purpose for which support was ordered? *See, e.g.*, N.J. Stat. § 2A:34–25 (1997) (remarriage terminates permanent, but not rehabilitative, alimony); *Zullo v. Zullo*, 613 A. 2d 544 (Pa. 1992) (reimbursement alimony continues after obligee's remarriage). *See generally* Gary L. Young, Jr., Annotation, *Alimony As Affected By Recipient Spouse's Remarriage In Absence of Controlling Specific Statute*, 47 A.L.R.5th 129 (1997).

(3) **Marriage vs. Cohabitation.** If a state retains the traditional rule that a recipient's remarriage terminates alimony, should the same rule apply to non-marital cohabitation? The majority in *Gilman* answers "No," and instead adopts an "economic needs" test that focuses on whether the cohabitation has affected the recipient's financial needs. This is consistent with the position adopted by a majority of jurisdictions, in the absence of a controlling statute. *See* John DeWitt Gregory, Peter N. Swisher and Sheryl L. Scheible-Wolf, Understanding Family Law § 8.05 (Matthew Bender 1995). How does the majority justify the "economic needs" approach? Do you find this reasoning persuasive? Does a rule that automatically terminates alimony upon remarriage, but not upon cohabitation, unduly discourage marriage?

(4) How should the economic needs test be applied where cohabitation increases, rather than decreases, an alimony recipient's financial needs?

(5) Some jurisdictions have enacted statutes that authorize or require the modification of spousal support upon a showing of post-divorce cohabitation. *See, e.g.*, Cal. Fam. Code § 4323(a)(1) (1998) ("Except as otherwise agreed to by the parties in writing, there is a rebuttable presumption, affecting the burden of proof, of decreased need for spousal support if the supported party is cohabiting with a person of the opposite sex."); Code of Ala. § 30–2–55 (1997) (alimony terminates upon proof that recipient spouse "is living openly or cohabiting with a member of the opposite sex"). Should these statutes be interpreted to cover romantic cohabitation with a same-sex partner? To cover non-romantic cohabitation with a relative or friend?

(6) Justice Springer concurs with the result in the *Gilman* case, but dissents in the *Callahan* case. What is the difference between these two cases? To what extent should divorcing spouses be able to agree to depart from the background legal rules otherwise applicable to the modification of spousal support awards? *See generally* Chapter 13, *below*. Justice Springer and his majority colleagues also appear to disagree about the financial obligations imposed by law on unmarried cohabitants in Nevada and under *Marvin v. Marvin*. These issues are addressed in depth in Chapter 3, *above*. Based on your reading of the materials in Chapter 3, who has the stronger argument on this point and why?

(7) **Other Changes in Circumstances.** Suppose that, in the *Callahan* case, Valerie Callahan had not moved to Reno with Chuck Maraden. Instead, one year after the Callahans' divorce, Valerie wins $500,000 in the state lottery. Ken Callahan then moves for termination of his spousal support obligation on the ground that Valerie's financial status has changed and she no longer needs his support. What result under the "economic needs" test applied in *Gilman*? Under the unconscionability standard contained in the UMDA? *See* ALI

Principles, § 509, Illustration 5. Suppose that it was Ken, rather than Valerie, who wins the state lottery one year after divorce. Should Valerie be able to obtain an increase in spousal support, on the grounds that Ken's ability to pay has increased significantly? Why or why not?

(8) **Changes in Obligor's Circumstances.** What changes in an obligor's circumstances should justify modification of his or her support obligations? Suppose an obligor voluntarily retires? *Compare, e.g., Pimm v. Pimm*, 601 So. 2d 534, 536–37 (Fla. 1992)(voluntary retirement at customary retirement age may justify modification of support) *with Wheeler v. Wheeler*, 548 N.W.2d 27, 31 (N.D. 1996) (reduction in income caused by obligor's voluntary retirement does not warrant modification of support) *and Barbarine v. Barbarine*, 925 S.W.2d 831, 833 (Ky. Ct. App. 1996) (payor's early retirement and consequent loss of income warrant a support reduction only if the advantage to the retiring spouse substantially outweighs the disadvantage to the payee spouse). *See generally*, Lewis Becker, *Spousal and Child Support and the "Voluntary Reduction of Income" Doctrine*, 29 Conn. L. Rev. 647, 657–70; 684–87 (1997) (surveying various state approaches and proposing "intermediate test" that focuses on the overall reasonableness of the obligor's conduct, in light of the obligor's age and motivation, the impact of the proposed support reduction on the obligee, and the timing of the retirement in relation to the divorce decree or agreement).

(9) **Modification Problems.** Consider the following additional possibilities:

Alice and Bob divorce after 15 years of marriage. Bob is a lawyer earning $90,000 per year. Alice is an elementary school teacher earning $30,000 per year. Bob and Alice are awarded joint legal custody of the couple's two minor children, with primary physical custody to Alice. Under the divorce decree, Bob is ordered to pay Alice $20,000 over the course of three years as part of the distribution of property; this amount represents Alice's share of the goodwill value of Bob's law practice. Bob is also ordered to pay Alice $1,000 per month in spousal support for 5 years and $1000 per month in child support until the youngest child reaches age 18.

a. Nine months after Alice and Bob divorce, Bob loses his job as an attorney because of the breakup of his law firm. He petitions the court for a reduction of his spousal and child support obligations (currently $2000 per month). At the time of the court hearing (four months after the job loss), Bob claims he is actively looking for work but has not yet found a suitable position. Meanwhile, he is collecting unemployment compensation of approximately $800 per month. He also has substantial assets as a result of the distribution of marital property. As Bob's attorney, what arguments would you make in support of his petition to modify support? How much of a reduction and what sort of a court order would you request?

b. As Alice's attorney, what arguments would you make in opposition to Bob's modification request? What additional information would you need in order to support your position?

c. Suppose Bob decides, after losing his law firm job, that this would be a perfect opportunity to do what he has always wanted to do—become a nursery school teacher. He estimates that it will take him one year of schooling to obtain his teaching certification (during which time he says he can earn $15,000 working part-time) and that, once he gets a teaching job, he will earn approximately $25,000 per year. Bob petitions for a reduction in his support obligations, based on this projected reduction in income. What result and why?

d. Suppose that, one year after his divorce from Alice, Bob remarries a widow with two young children. How, if at all, should Bob's new family responsibilities affect his support obligations to Alice and their children? Should it matter whether Bob formally adopts his new wife's children? For additional discussion of the grounds and standards for modifying child support awards, see § 11.05, *below*.

e. Suppose that, instead of Bob losing his job nine months after his divorce, Bob's income increases by 50% as a result of his becoming general counsel of one of the law firm's major clients. Should Alice be able to obtain an increase in spousal and/or child support as a result of the increase in Bob's earnings? Why or why not?

CHAPTER 11

CHILD SUPPORT

SYNOPSIS

§ 11.01 Introduction
§ 11.02 Federal Mandate
§ 11.03 Guidelines
    [A] Income Shares Model
    [B] Percentage of Income
§ 11.04 Income
    [A] Gross or Net?
    [B] Actual Income or Capacity to Earn?
    [C] Spousal Income
    [D] Support for other Children
    [E] Extraordinarily High Income
§ 11.05 Duration of Support
    [A] Majority/Emancipation
    [B] Support for College
§ 11.06 Modification of Support
§ 11.07 Enforcement of Support Orders
    [A] State Remedies
    [B] Federal Enforcement
§ 11.08 Jurisdiction for Support and Interstate Enforcement
    [A] Personal Jurisdiction
    [B] Interstate Enforcement

§ 11.01 Introduction

In the last ten to fifteen years a revolution has taken place in child support. The federal government has mandated state child support guidelines as a condition to receiving federal funds. The goals of these guidelines are to increase support award levels, to impose consistency in support awards and to increase case processing efficiency. All states have guidelines in place; however, there is great diversity among the various states. In addition, uniform acts have been promulgated to increase enforcement and to decrease relitigation in the area of child support.

The approach of this chapter is largely descriptive and practical. Important policy issues and controversies have been downplayed so that students will have an opportunity to discover how the guideline and enforcement systems actually operate. There are simply so many practical issues that the amount of space devoted to concepts has been limited.

The first part of the chapter deals with the guidelines themselves. An attempt has been made to familiarize students with every type of guideline which is in use now. Next, the subject of income is explored in depth: what will be included and deducted from income; when will the court impute income to a parent; whether the court should include spousal income in support calculation; how the court should deal with previous and subsequent children; and how the court should deal with extremely high incomes. Following this exploration of income, significant portions of the text are devoted to very real issues of duration of support, modification, enforcement (including new legislation), and jurisdiction (including the new Uniform Interstate Family Support Act).

§ 11.02 Federal Mandate

P.O.P.S. v. GARDNER
United States Court of Appeals
998 F.2d 764 (9th Cir. 1993)

FARRIS, J., CIRCUIT JUDGE:

Parents Opposed to Punitive Support challenged the constitutionality of the Washington State Child Support Schedule. The district court granted the State's motion for summary judgment. The court ruled that the Schedule did not violate the Equal Protection or the Due Process Clauses of the Fourteenth Amendment.

We affirm.

FACTS

Congress has mandated that each state develop presumptive child support guidelines. *See* 42 U.S.C. § 667(b) (1988). Governor Booth Gardner created an Executive Task Force in June 1985 to investigate Washington state's child support program. The Task Force issued a final report in September 1986 recommending that the State adopt a presumptive child support schedule. After numerous public hearings and meetings, the Child Support Schedule Commission presented a schedule to the Legislature which it passed into law.

The Schedule is used to determine the amount of child support parents must pay upon divorce. The economic table, one of five parts of the Schedule, sets forth the basic child support obligation based on the combined family net income and number of children. The table operates similarly to a tax table, mandating different support levels at different income levels. The basic support obligation is allocated between the parents based on each parent's share of the family's net income.

The Schedule permits deviations from the presumptive support obligation, but requires written findings of fact to explain any such deviation. Several bases for deviation are enumerated: wealth, income of other adults in the household, liens or extraordinary debt, child support or maintenance received or paid, children from other relationships, and nonrecurring income. The court may also deviate if the child spends a significant amount of time with the obligated parent. The Washington Supreme Court has held that the enumerated reasons for deviation are not exclusive.

P.O.P.S. challenges the constitutionality of the Schedule, claiming that it violates the Due Process and Equal Protection Clauses of the Fourteenth Amendment. . . .

DISCUSSION

. . .

II. *SUBSTANTIVE DUE PROCESS*

The rights to marry, have children, and maintain a relationship with one's children are fundamental rights protected by the Fourteenth Amendment's Due Process Clause. Statutes that directly and substantially impair those rights require strict scrutiny. According to P.O.P.S., the financial pressures created by the Schedule alienate noncustodial parents from their children, cause divorces between noncustodial parents and their new spouses, deter new marriages, and prevent noncustodial parents from having more children with their new spouses. P.O.P.S. argues that because the Schedule impacts family relationships, we should apply strict scrutiny to the Schedule. We reject the argument.

In *Zablocki v. Redhail*, 434 U.S. 374, 375 (1988), the Supreme Court applied strict scrutiny to a state statute that forbade noncustodial parents who had child support obligations from marrying without obtaining court permission. Any marriage entered into without compliance with the statute was void and the persons acquiring illegal marriage licenses were subject to criminal penalties. P.O.P.S.'s reliance on *Zablocki* is misplaced. Unlike the statute in *Zablocki*, the Schedule does not directly interfere with family relationships. The Schedule does not bar noncustodial parents from entering or maintaining family relationships. In fact, the Statute employs the method for enforcing child support orders that the Court approved in *Zablocki*—adjusting award criteria. Some noncustodial parents may feel discouraged from getting married because of obligations to their own children but nothing in the Statute limits or restricts remarriage: By reaffirming the fundamental character of the right to marry, we do not mean to suggest that every state regulation which relates in any way to the incidents of or prerequisites for marriage must be subjected to rigorous scrutiny. To the contrary, reasonable regulations that do not significantly interfere with decisions to enter into the marital relationship may legitimately be imposed.

P.O.P.S. argues that the Schedule results in child support orders that are so high that they effectively bar some noncustodial parents from getting remarried. P.O.P.S. cites anecdotal evidence from several noncustodial parents who claim to have had marital difficulties because of their child support obligation, but all of those parents did remarry despite alleged financial pressures. The Schedule does not directly and substantially interfere with marriage. Moreover, if a noncustodial parent could show that he was so burdened by his child support obligation that he could not get married, the court would have the authority to deviate from the presumptive award on that basis. Such a claim would not require the parent to rebut the assumptions underlying the economic table, and therefore, P.O.P.S.'s challenge to the economic table is irrelevant to whether the Schedule is constitutional. The Schedule provides that neither parent's total child support obligation may exceed forty-five percent of net income, further diminishing the likelihood that excessive awards will prevent marriage.

P.O.P.S. also asserts that noncustodial parents are so frustrated by the operation of the Schedule that they do not spend as much time with their children. The fact that some parents take their financial frustrations out on their children does not afford them extra protection under the Due Process Clause. The Schedule does not discourage parents from spending time with their children. It explicitly permits courts to deviate from the presumptive support level if the noncustodial parent spends a "significant amount of time" with his children.

The burden of child support awards may very well discourage some people from having additional children and may discourage some from entering new marriages. But all financial obligations impact family decisions. Providing financial and emotional support is the responsibility one assumes by choosing to have children. Every obligation imposed by the State cannot be subject to strict scrutiny. Such a holding would turn the doctrine of strict scrutiny "into a virtual engine of destruction for countless legislative judgments which have heretofore been thought wholly consistent with the Fifth and Fourteenth Amendments to the Constitution." *Weinberger*, 422 U.S. at 772.

The judgment of the legislature must stand if there is a rational relationship between the operation of the Schedule and the policy that the Schedule serves. The Legislature intended to accomplish three goals by creating a statewide child support schedule:

(1) Increasing the adequacy of child support orders through the use of economic data as the basis for establishing the child support schedule;

(2) Increasing the equity of child support orders by providing for comparable orders in cases with similar circumstances; and

(3) Reducing the adversarial nature of the proceedings by increasing voluntary settlements as a result of the greater predictability achieved by a uniform statewide child support schedule.

P.O.P.S. recognizes that these are legitimate state interests, but argues that the Schedule is not a rational means of achieving the goals. We cannot agree. Requiring judges to follow the table unless they articulate a good reason to deviate decreases the likelihood that individual judges will erroneously award insufficient support. Because the most important factors for setting support are income and number of children, similarly situated people will pay similar amounts for child support. The presumptive nature of the table promotes voluntary settlements as the parties have fewer issues about which they can argue. Thus, adopting a presumptive support schedule is a rational means of achieving the State's legitimate goals.

P.O.P.S. contends that the State's methodology for developing the economic table inflated the presumptive child support level above the actual costs of rearing children in Washington. P.O.P.S. discusses at length several perceived flaws in the table. The discussion serves only to prove that the appropriate level of child support is a debatable issue dependent on policy and value judgments. On issues of social policy, the state has the power to make such judgments as long as they are not made arbitrarily. The table was developed based on economic studies and hard data. The presumptive support levels are not arbitrary.

III. *EQUAL PROTECTION*

P.O.P.S. argues that the Schedule violates the equal protection rights of the children of noncustodial households. The Statute provides that the child support schedule shall be applied to determine the presumptive support. Children from other relationships are not to be counted to determine the basic support obligation. However, the court may deviate from the basic support obligation if either parent has children from other relationships to whom she owes a duty of support. The Schedule explicitly permits the court to consider children from the noncustodial household. P.O.P.S. contends that the Equal Protection Clause dictates stricter guidelines for the consideration of noncustodial children. The Fourteenth Amendment does not mandate the rigid social policy prescriptions urged by P.O.P.S. . . .

Children of noncustodial parents do not constitute a suspect class. The schedule does not directly and substantially interfere with fundamental rights. We review the Schedule under the rational basis test.

P.O.P.S. maintains that the state does not have even a rational basis for "discriminating" against children of noncustodial households. The Schedule does not discriminate. Courts may deviate from the basic support obligation when either parent has other children. Thus the court can insure that children from noncustodial families are not unduly burdened by the child support award. The State presented evidence that the most frequent reason for deviating is the existence of other children. P.O.P.S. complains that the Schedule does not give the court any guidance for deviating from the presumptive amount based on other children. The State need not create a perfect Schedule; it need only have a rational basis for the statute:

> In the area of economics and social welfare, a State does not violate the Equal Protection Clause merely because the classifications made by its laws are imperfect. If the classification has some "reasonable basis," it does not offend the Constitution simply because the classification "is not made with mathematical nicety or because in practice it results in some inequality." *Dandridge v. Williams*, 397 U.S. 471, 485 (1970) (citations omitted).

The divorcing parents are jointly responsible for the presumptive support amount, and therefore, it is rational for the presumptive support calculation to include only the children for whom both divorcing parents have responsibility.

We have carefully examined all of P.O.P.S.'s constitutional challenges. They find no support in the Constitution.

Affirmed.

NOTES AND QUESTIONS

(1) **Former Law.** Traditionally, child support was a matter of discretion for the trial judge. At most, legislation played the role of providing some guidance for the judge. But rather than give guidance in the form of numbers and dollars, the guidance was almost always in the form of a list of factors which the judge could consider in awarding support. Here is an example of such a list from the Uniform Marriage and Divorce Act:

> In a proceeding for dissolution of marriage, legal separation, maintenance, or child support, the court may order either or both parents owing a duty of support of a child to pay an amount reasonable or necessary for his support, without regard to marital misconduct, after considering all relevant factors including:
>
> (1) the financial resources of the child;

(2) the financial resources of the custodial parent;

(3) the standard of living the child would have enjoyed had the marriage not been dissolved;

(4) the physical and emotional condition of the child and his educational needs; and

(5) the financial resources and needs of the noncustodial parent.

Uniform Marriage and Divorce Act § 309, 9A U.L.A. 400 (West 1987).

Most jurisdictions had such a laundry list of factors to be considered. A judge might be required to make specific findings regarding each factor. However, the judges, in order to determine what dollar amount should be attached to the support order, tended to rely upon their own experience and the word-of-mouth experience of other judges.

(2) **History of Federal Involvement.** The following quotation provides a good summary of the historical steps leading up to the present federal law:

> The federal government has played a role in child support enforcement since 1950. Its initial efforts in the area were limited to an amendment to the Social Security Act, requiring state welfare agencies to notify appropriate law enforcement officials when a child who had been abandoned by a parent became a recipient of Aid to Families with Dependent Children (AFDC). Pub. L. 81–734, § 321(b).
>
> It was not until the Child Support Enforcement Program was signed into law in 1975, however, that the federal government became a major participant in such programs. 42 U.S.C. §§ 651–669 (1997) (hereinafter referred to as Title IV–D). The 1975 Act opened up Title IV–D services, previously intended to benefit children receiving AFDC benefits, and made them available to non-welfare families as well.
>
> Title IV–D authorized federal financial assistance for a range of state programs and services designed to encourage state enforcement of child support obligations. The goals of the program as a whole included: location of obligors, establishment of paternity, establishment of support, and enforcement of support. While the states retained basic responsibility for establishing paternity and collecting child support, the then Department of Health, Education and Welfare (HEW) [which became HHS in 1980] was cast in a supervisory and assisting role. At that time, the Secretary of HEW created OCSE to administer the federal program.
>
> Despite Congressional efforts, problems remained with the amounts for child support varying from awards that were too low to provide reasonable funds for the needs of the children to awards which were so high as to be equally unreasonable and likely to exacerbate tensions.
>
> Therefore, in 1984, Congress passed additional amendments. The amendments again emphasized the universal availability of Title IV–D benefits. More importantly, using as an example the efforts of a few states that had begun to use guidelines for setting child support levels, the amendments required that all states receiving federal funding develop similar guidelines. Pub. L. 98–378, § 18. Congress concluded that "the very existence of a set of guidelines in each state will tend to improve the reasonableness and equity with which support orders are established." 1984 U.S. Code Cong. & Admin. News at 2436.

Following the enactment of the 1984 amendments, the Secretary of Health and Human Services promulgated regulations which also are at issue in the present litigation. The regulations require that the state guidelines "be based on specific descriptive and numeric criteria." 45 C.F.R. § 302.56(c). The numeric criteria may "include factors such as, but not limited to, income and resources of the parents and the number and needs of dependents." 50 Fed. Reg. 19643 (May 9, 1985).

Again, changes in the law proved to be insufficient. The legislative history behind the most recent amendments, the Family Support Act of 1988, indicated that: The problem of nonsupport of children has become a serious one for this country. Nearly one-quarter of all children now live with only one parent. And although many noncustodial parents are diligent payers of child support, there are millions who are not. The Census Bureau data tells us that of the 8.8 million mothers with children whose fathers were not living in the home in the spring of 1986, 3.4 million, or nearly 40 per cent of these mothers, have never been awarded support for their children . . . . Of those who had been awarded and were due support in 1986, only half received the full amount they were due. S. Rep. 377, 100th Cong.2d Sess. (1988), reprinted in 1988 U.S. Code Cong. & Admin. News 2776, 2785.

In a renewed effort to remedy the situation, the new legislation altered the use of guidelines for determining appropriate levels of child support. Pub.L. 100–485. The guidelines, previously not binding on judicial decision makers, now create rebuttable presumptions that their result is the correct amount of child support. A written finding overcomes the rebuttable presumption. 42 U.S.C. § 667(b) (1997). States must review their guidelines periodically. 42 U.S.C. § 667 (1997).

The 1988 Act, moreover, established strict enforcement measures. In particular, states must provide for mandatory wage withholding, without waiting for an arrearage, except where the state finds good cause to act otherwise or both parents agree to an alternative arrangement. 42 U.S.C. § 666 (1997).

In keeping with the concept of "cooperative federalism," federal and state laws mesh together in the area of child support. Starting in 1975, states that wish to participate in AFDC also are required to take part in Title IV–D. Federal funding is available only if the state complies with both AFDC and Title IV–D and regulations promulgated thereunder. *See* 42 U.S.C. §§ 601, 602(a)(27), 654(13) (1997).

The state of Ohio has elected to participate in the AFDC program. Accordingly, the state also takes part in Title IV–D. It has promulgated its own set of guidelines . . . .

Children's and Parent's Rights Ass'n of Ohio, Inc. v. Sullivan, 787 F. Supp. 724 (N.D. Ohio 1991).

(3) **Rationale for Guidelines.** It is worth reiterating that the most significant reasons for child support guideline reform are, first, to insure that more money was made available for the support of children, and, second, to provide uniformity among support orders. For a full discussion of these two factors and others, see the report of the advisory panel which formulated the federal law. Williams, *Development of Guidelines for Child Support Orders: Advisory Panel Recommendation and Final Report* (U.S. Dep't of Health and Human Services, Office of Child Support Enforcement, 1987).

(4) Method of Compliance. The federal statute allows states to establish guidelines in several ways: "The guidelines may be established by law or by judicial or administrative action, and shall be reviewed a least once every 4 years to ensure that their application results in the determination of appropriate child support award amounts." 42 U.S.C. § 667(a) (1997).

(5) Preemption. There actually has been very little litigation about the issue of preemption, perhaps because it is widely accepted that the federal government can place conditions on federal money. *See Jackson v. Rapps* 947 F.2d 332 (8th Cir. 1991), *cert. denied*, 503 U.S. 960 (1992); Lesa L. Bonnett, *Jackson v. Rapps: Preemption of State Policies and Statutes Governing Noncustodial Parents' AFDC Reimbursements to the State*, 37 St. Louis U. L.J. 753 (1993).

§ 11.03 Guidelines

[A] Income Shares Model

VOISHAN v. PALMA
Court of Appeals of Maryland
609 A.2d 319 (1992)

CHASANOW, JUDGE.

John and Margaret Voishan were divorced on June 26, 1981, by decree of the Circuit Court for Anne Arundel County. Margaret was awarded custody of their two daughters and John was ordered to pay $250 per week toward the girls' support. Over four years later, an order dated October 7, 1985 increased the amount of John's obligation for the support of both children to $1400 per month. The circuit court's order also awarded John certain detailed visitation rights.

On March 8, 1991, the circuit court's intercession was again sought to address John's request to find Margaret in contempt for violating the visitation order as well as Margaret's motion to modify child support. The Honorable Raymond G. Thieme, Jr. presided at that hearing and shortly thereafter entered an order finding that Margaret was not in contempt of court. That order also increased John's child support obligation for the one daughter who was still a minor from $700 per month to $1550 per month. John then appealed the modification of child support to the Court of Special Appeals. Because of the important issues raised on appeal, this Court granted certiorari before consideration by the intermediate appellate court. While Margaret failed to file an appellee's brief or respond to John's oral arguments, both the Maryland Chapter of the American Academy of Matrimonial Lawyers and the Attorney General of Maryland filed amici curiae briefs and presented oral argument.

This dispute requires the Court, for the first time, to address Maryland Code, (1984, 1991 Repl.Vol.) Family Law Article §§ 12–201 et seq. (the "guidelines"). The General Assembly enacted these guidelines in 1989 to comply with federal law and regulations. The federal mandate required that the guidelines be established and "based on specific descriptive and numeric criteria and result in a computation of the support obligation." [42 U.S.C. §§ 651–667 (1982 & 1984 Supp. II) and 45 C.F.R. § 302.56 (1989)]. When drafting the guidelines, the Maryland Senate Judicial Proceedings Committee had before it *Development of Guidelines For Child Support Orders: Advisory Panel Recommendations and Final*

Report, U.S. Department of Health and Human Services' Office of Child Support Enforcement. . . .

After considering several different models recommended by the Advisory Panel on Child Support Guidelines, the General Assembly chose to base Maryland's guidelines on the Income Shares Model. The conceptual underpinning of this model is that a child should receive the same proportion of parental income, and thereby enjoy the standard of living, he or she would have experienced had the child's parents remained together. Accordingly, the model establishes child support obligations based on estimates of the percentage of income that parents in an intact household typically spend on their children. Consistent with this model, the legislature constructed the schedule in § 12-204(e), which sets forth the basic child support obligation for any given number of children based on combined parental income.

Following the Income Shares Model, Maryland's guidelines first require that the trial judge determine each parent's monthly "adjusted actual income." Section 12-201(d) states:

> Adjusted actual income' means actual income minus:
>
> (1) preexisting reasonable child support obligations actually paid;
>
> (2) except as provided in s 12-204(a)(2) of this subtitle, alimony or maintenance obligations actually paid; and
>
> (3) the actual cost of providing health insurance coverage for a child for whom the parents are jointly and severally responsible."

After determining each parent's monthly "adjusted actual income," the judge then adds these two amounts together to arrive at the monthly "combined adjusted actual income" of the parents. Having calculated the combined adjusted actual income of the parents, the judge can then determine whether that figure falls within the range of incomes found in the schedule of § 12-204(e). If the figure is within the schedule, the judge then locates the corresponding "basic child support obligation" for the given number of children. Where the monthly income falls between two amounts set forth in the schedule, § 12-204(c) dictates that the basic child support obligation is the same as the obligation specified for the next highest income level. The judge then divides this basic child support obligation between the parents in proportion to each of their adjusted actual incomes. The judge must then add together any work-related child care expenses, extraordinary medical expenses, and school and transportation expenses and allocate this total between the parents in proportion to their adjusted actual incomes. The amount of child support computed in this manner is presumed to be correct, although this presumption may be rebutted by evidence that such amount would be unjust and inappropriate in a particular case. In the instant case, evidence was presented at the March 8, 1991 hearing that John now earns $145,000 per year, while Margaret's annual income is $30,000. John does not contend that his actual income should be reduced by any expenses identified in § 12-201(d). Therefore, he computes a "combined adjusted actual income" of $175,000 a year or $14,583 per month in his argument to this Court. This combined income exceeds $10,000 per month, which is the highest income provided for in § 12-204(e). The legislature addressed this situation in § 12-204(d), which says: "If the combined adjusted actual income exceeds the highest level specified in the schedule in subsection (e) of this section, the court may use its discretion in setting the amount of child support." . . .

[W]e now reach his primary contention. John contends that the $1550 monthly child support award is inconsistent with the spirit and intent behind the Income Shares Model, and concludes that Judge Thieme abused his discretion in awarding that amount. John maintains that Judge Thieme accurately found that the parties' earnings created a ratio of 83 to 17 for John's and Margaret's respective percentages of their $175,000 combined annual income. John contends, however, that Judge Thieme erred in the manner in which he applied these percentages to arrive at the amount of $1550 per month for John's share of the obligation. Judge Thieme examined expense sheets for each of the parties and concluded that the "reasonable expenses of the child" were $1873 each month. The judge then calculated 83% of that figure and rounded John's share of the obligation down to $1550.

John argues here, as he did below, that a "reasonable approach" would have been for the trial judge to assume that the maximum basic child support obligation listed in the schedule is not only applicable to combined monthly incomes of $10,000, but also applies to those in excess of $10,000 per month. Under the schedule in § 12–204(e), the maximum basic child support obligation of $1040 per month is presumptively correct for parties who have a combined monthly income of $10,000. John argues that $1040 per month should also provide the presumptively correct basic child support obligation for all combined monthly incomes over $10,000. While we believe that $1040 could provide the presumptive *minimum* basic award for those with combined monthly incomes above $10,000, we do not believe that the legislature intended to cap the basic child support obligation at the upper limit of the schedule. Had the legislature intended to make the highest award in the schedule the presumptive basic support obligation in all cases with combined monthly income over $10,000, it would have so stated and would not have granted the trial judge discretion in fixing those awards. Further, John's proposed approach creates an artificial ceiling and itself defeats the guidelines' policy that the child enjoy a standard of living consonant with that he or she would have experienced had the parents remained married. We are unpersuaded by John's argument that the legislature meant for all children whose parents earn more than $10,000 per month to have the same standard of living as those whose parents earn $10,000 per month.

Alternatively, John argues that Judge Thieme should have extrapolated from the guidelines to determine what the support obligation would have been had the schedule extended up to the parties' $14,583 monthly income. John notes that at the upper levels in the guidelines, the basic child support obligation for one child increases by $5 for every $100 rise in combined adjusted actual income. Extrapolating on that basis, John argues that the basic child support obligation would be $1270 per month ($4583/ 100 x $5 plus $1040). John also acknowledges that under the guidelines, in addition to the basic child support obligation—whatever that is computed to be, he has an obligation to pay 83% of the additional work-related child care expenses which, in the instant case, are $400 per month. Taking 83% of the $1270 basic child support obligation plus 83% of the $400 work-related child care expenses, John argues, renders his portion of his daughter's support to be $1386 per month. Although slightly more generous than his earlier argument, which would leave the judge with no discretion, John's second contention is essentially that this Court should significantly restrict the judicial discretion granted by s 12–204(d) and allow judges very little latitude in deviating from the extrapolation method. John asks this Court to hold that Judge Thieme abused his discretion when he set the award $164 higher than the amount computed by John's strict extrapolation theory. While we believe that the trial judge should consider the underlying policies of the guidelines and strive toward congruous results, we think that Judge Thieme did not abuse his discretion in fixing the amount of this award. . . .

While awards made under § 12–204(d) will be disturbed only if there is a clear abuse of discretion, a reviewing court must also be mindful that the federal call for child support guidelines was motivated in part by the need to improve the consistency of awards. Thus, the trial judge has somewhat more latitude than that argued by John . . . Rather, we agree with the Attorney General's position that the guidelines do establish a rebuttable presumption that the maximum support award under the schedule is the minimum which should be awarded in cases above the schedule. Beyond this the trial judge should examine the needs of the child in light of the parents' resources and determine the amount of support necessary to ensure that the child's standard of living does not suffer because of the parents' separation. Further, the judge should give some consideration to the Income Shares method of apportioning the child support obligation. Consequently, we conclude that Judge Thieme properly exercised his discretion in receiving evidence of the parents' financial circumstances, considering the needs of the child, and then apportioning the "reasonable expenses of the child." . . .

NOTES AND QUESTIONS

(1) **Income Shares Model.** In its simplest form the income share model can be expressed in the following steps:

> 1. The income of the parents (gross or net) is determined and added together.
>
> 2. A "basic child support obligation" is computed based on the combined income of the parents, using a table or grid in the guidelines. The amounts in the table are derived from economic data on household expenditures on children.
>
> 3. A "presumptive child support obligation" is then computed under the basic Income Shares Model by adding expenditures for work-related expenses and extraordinary medical expenses to the basic child support obligation. Other Add-ons and deductions may be calculated.
>
> 4. The presumptive child support obligation is prorated between each parent based on his or her proportionate share of total income. The obligor's obligation is payable as child support, while the obligee's obligation is retained and presumed to be spent directly on the child.

Laura Morgan, Child Support Guidelines: Interpretation and Application 1-18 (1997).

(2) **The States** The Maryland statute discussed in the principal case is a typical income shares guideline. The Income Shares Model is by far the most common guideline. The following states use some version of this model: Alabama, Arizona, Colorado, Connecticut, Florida, Idaho, Indiana, Iowa, Kansas, Kentucky, Louisiana, Maine, Michigan, Missouri, Nebraska, New Hampshire, New Jersey, New Mexico, New York, North Carolina, Ohio, Oklahoma, Oregon, Pennsylvania, Rhode Island, South Carolina, South Dakota, Utah, Vermont, Virginia, and Washington. *See* Laura Morgan, Child Support Guidelines: Interpretation and Application 1-14 (1997).

(3) In the opinion reprinted above, the Maryland court repeatedly states that the income shares model is based on the idea that the same proportion of parental income should go

to supporting the children in a divorced family as in an intact one, and that the child's standard of living should not suffer because of the separation. Is this realistic in light of the substantial added costs of maintaining two households? Note that the disruptive impact of a divorce often leads to other new expenses, including education or training for a parent who may have to reenter the work force, and sometimes counseling for one or more family members.

(4) **Variations on Income Shares Method.** There have been some well-known variations on the income shares method. Here are two:

a. **The Melson Formula.** In *Dalton v. Clanton*, 559 A.2d 1197, 1203–04 (Del. 1989), the Delaware Supreme Court adopted a variation of the income shares model:

> The Melson Formula is named after its judicial craftsman, Judge Elwood F. Melson, Jr. of the Family Court of the State of Delaware. The formula was developed by Judge Melson in response to the directive of Del. Code Ann. tit. 13 § 514 (1997). It was used by Judge Melson for the first time in the context of a child support case in 1977 . . . .
>
> The basic procedures which are performed in an application of the Melson Formula are:
>
> Step 1: Determine Available Income of Each Parent. The Melson Formula starts with net income. After determining net income for each parent, a self-support reserve ("primary support allowance") is subtracted from each parent's income. This reserve represents the minimum amount required for an adult to meet his or her own subsistence requirements.
>
> Step 2: Determine Children's Primary Support Needs. The next step in applying the formula is to compute the primary support amount for each dependent. Like the self-support reserve, the primary support amount represents the minimum amount required to maintain a child at a subsistence level . . . . Work-related child care expenses are added to primary support as are extraordinary medical expenses. The child's primary support needs are pro-rated between the parents based upon available net income as determined in Step 1 . . . .
>
> Step 3: Determine Standard of Living Allowance (SOLA). After primary support obligations of each parent are calculated in Step 2, including obligations for child care expenses and extraordinary medical expenses, a percentage of remaining income is also allocated to support of the child. The standard of living allowance enables the child to benefit from the higher living standard of a parent . . . . If a parent has dependents other than the child for whom support is being sought, and such other dependents are not covered by a court order, primary support amounts for such dependents are deducted from obligor income available for the Standard of Living Allowance.
>
> The first step guarantees basic self-support for each parent. The assumption is that a parent who cannot support himself/herself will not pay child support. While this assumption may appear to have the effect of putting a parent's needs first, there is a trade-off in the standard of living allowance which basically is a bonus to the child once the basic needs of the parent and child have been taken care of.

The Melson formula is followed in Delaware, Hawaii, Montana, and West Virginia. *See* Laura Morgan, Child Support Guidelines: Interpretation and Application 1-14 (1997).

b. The California Approach. California has adopted a child support formula so incredibly complicated that it is difficult to apply without the aid of a computer program. It combines elements of the Income Shares and the Percentage of Income Models.

Cal. Fam. Code § 4055 (1998). Formula for Statewide Uniform Guideline for Determining Child Support.

(a) The statewide uniform guideline for determining child support orders is as follows:

$$CS = K[HN-(H\%)(TN)].$$

(b)(1) The components of the formula are as follows:

(A) CS = child support amount.

(B) K = amount of both parents' income to be allocated for child support as set forth in paragraph (3).

(C) HN = high earner's net monthly disposable income.

(D) H% = approximate percentage of time that the high earner has or will have primary physical responsibility for the children compared to the other parent. In cases in which parents have different time-sharing arrangements for different children, H% equals the average of the approximate percentages of time the high earner parent spends with each child.

(E) TN = total net monthly disposable income of both parties.

(2) To compute net disposable income, see Cal. Fam. Code § 4059.

(3) K (amount of both parents' income allocated for child support) equals one plus H% (if H% is less than or equal to 50 percent) or two minus H% (if H% is greater than 50 percent) times the following fraction:

For example, if H% equals 20 percent and the total monthly net disposable income of the parents is $1,000, K = (1 + 0.20) x 0.25, or 0.30. If H% equals 80 percent and the total monthly net disposable income of the parents is $1,000, K = (2 -0.80) x 0.25, or 0.30.

(4) For more than one child, multiply CS by:

(5) If the amount calculated under the formula results in a positive number, the higher earner shall pay that amount to the lower earner. If the amount calculated under the formula results in a negative number, the lower earner shall pay the absolute value of that amount to the higher earner . . . .

This formula assumes that a certain percentage of parental income should go to the support of a child. This amount, labelled "K," is normally about 25% but is gradually adjusted downward (per the table in subd. (b)(3) of the statute) to as low as 20% for both very high- and very low-income families. The dollar amount that is multiplied by the "K" percentage starts with the higher-earning parent's net income ("HN," for High Net). This, however, is adjusted (in the bracketed expression in the basic formula) to proportionately compensate the high earner for any time ("H%") the child spends with him or her. (Parents' combined incomes ["TN," for Total Net] are used for that adjustment, on the assumption that both the high earner and the low earner will be contributing a "K" proportion of their earnings for support for the period that the child is with the high earner.) If the high-earner's proportion of custodial time is high enough so that the adjustment produces a negative income on which support is calculated, this simply means that support flows the other way (from the low earner to the high earner), per subd. (b)(5).[1] Note that to the extent that custody approaches 50–50, and to the extent that the parents' net earnings are similar, support flowing either way will approach zero.[2]

A further statutory adjustment to "K" (per the text immediately preceding the table in subd. (b)(3)) moderately counterbalances the effects of shared custody in the basic formula of subd. (a). It reduces somewhat the financial relief a support-paying high earner receives for sharing custody. It also reduces somewhat the payment to a support-receiving high-earner.

Finally, subd. (b)(4) adjusts the support figure where there is more than one child involved.

The formula does have some flexibility that the chart approach does not have. For example a high-income custodial parent could have to pay support to a low-income noncustodial parent for the periods of visitation. And perhaps even more importantly, since it does factor in the percentage of time that the child is with the noncustodial parent, it works very well in shared custody situations.

[B] Percentage of Income

EKLUND v. EKLUND
Supreme Court of North Dakota
538 N.W.2d 182 (1995)

MESCHKE, JUSTICE.

Kendal J. Eklund appealed from an order increasing his monthly child support payments. We reject an array of legal arguments about the authority of the Department of Human Services to adopt the child support guidelines, and the standing of a child support enforcement agency to seek modification for a custodial parent. We affirm.

Kendal J. Eklund and Linda L. Eklund were married in 1976, and divorced in 1988. Kendal had adopted Larry, born July 30, 1972, Linda's child from a prior marriage. Kendal and Linda had another child, Jeremy, born May 24, 1978. The divorce decree ordered Kendal to pay Linda $300 monthly support for each child, totaling $600.

---

[1] The low-earning parent's support obligation is, of course, less than the high earner's would be in the reverse custodial situation. The largest dollar amount that could be multiplied by K when a lower-earning parent has to pay (as H% in the formula approaches 100%) would be the difference between the parents' total net income (TN) and the high earner's net income (HN), i.e., the low earner's own net income. In contrast, as H% approaches 0, requiring the high earner to pay because most custody is with the low earner, the dollar amount that will be multiplied by K approaches the high earner's income.

[2] This is because equal earnings would make TN [total net earnings of both parents] two times HN [the net earnings of the "higher" earner]. Multiplying this figure by an H% of 50 would make the bracketed expression HN minus HN, or zero.

When Larry turned eighteen in 1990, Kendal stopped support for him, but continued paying $300 monthly for Jeremy. Linda promptly moved to increase the support for Jeremy. The trial court denied the motion because Linda "failed to show a significant change of circumstances."

In July 1992, the Minot Regional Child Support Enforcement Unit (Unit) moved on Linda's behalf to increase Kendal's support for Jeremy to $540 monthly under the child support guidelines. The trial court again concluded that "no change of circumstances was shown or that an attempt was even made to show a change of circumstances in view of the position of the . . . Unit that no showing was necessary." The court reasoned that under "temporary section 14–09–08.4, N.D.C.C., . . . the review process is limited to child support orders which are being enforced by the child support agency," concluded "this child support order is not being enforced by the . . . Unit as provided by the statute," and denied the motion.

In March 1994, the Unit moved again on Linda's behalf to increase Kendal's payments to $572 monthly to meet the child support guidelines. This time, the trial court decided that "the statute upon which the Court based its most recent ruling has been materially modified" to allow increase of support without a showing of changed circumstances. The court concluded that Kendal's procedural and constitutional objections were without merit and granted the increase. Kendal appeals.

Kendal asserts there is "virtually no issue of fact in this case," only questions of law. Kendal presents an array of legal arguments: . . . (4) the Unit failed to establish the child support guidelines were properly adopted; and (5) the guidelines and statutes on changing child support are unconstitutional. We reject Kendal's contentions. . . .

4. *Guidelines Authorized*

Kendal argues the Unit failed to meet its burden of persuasion after the interim Legislative Committee on Administrative Rules (Committee) had objected to the child support guidelines because the issuing agency, the Department of Human Services (Department), had not demonstrated the guidelines were within its delegated authority. We disagree.

The Administrative Agencies Practice Act directs that, after the Committee objects to a new rule, "the burden of persuasion is upon the agency in any action for judicial review or for enforcement of the rule to establish that the whole or portion thereof objected to is within the procedural and substantive authority delegated to the agency." NDCC 28–32–03.3(5). In 1991, as directed by NDCC 14–09–09.7, and after public hearings, the Department established child support guidelines. The new guidelines adopted an "obligor model" for setting the amount of child support, not an alternate "income shares" model. The Department explained why it adopted the "obligor model": "[B]ecause the income shares model was more complex it would increase litigation costs, lead to more requests for review, and be more difficult to use in emergency cases[,] and . . . the income shares model appeared more fair but in most cases made little or no difference in award amounts." Report of the North Dakota Legislative Council, Fifty-Third Legislative Assembly 12 (1993) (1993 LC Report). The interim Committee objected to the use of the "obligor model," instead of the "income shares" model.[3] *Id.* at 13. The Department "informed the committee by

---

[3] The interim Committee gave these reasons:
1. Both parents have a legal duty to support their children.
2. Any guidelines adopted to ensure proper child support amounts are paid upon divorce must be based on the best interests of the child.

letter that it did not intend to make any changes to the rule it had adopted."[4] *Id.* The Department's response reasonably explained why it was authorized to use the "obligor model" in the guidelines.

Therefore, we agree with the trial court that "NDCC 14-09-09.7 provides clear statutory authority authorizing Human Services to establish child support guidelines," and that "[t]he statute does not preclude child support guidelines based upon the obligor model." We believe the trial court also explained why there can be no doubt about this conclusion: "In fact, H.B. 1021 which would have provided for an income shares model was defeated in a legislative session held [in 1993] after the filing of objections by the Legislative Council." *See Effertz v. North Dakota Workers Compensation Bureau,* 525 N.W.2d 391, 693 (N.D. 1994).

5. Constitutionality

---

3. The obligor model adopted by the Department of Human Services establishes child support amounts by using a percentage of the obligor's income and does not take into consideration the income of the custodial parent.

4. The income shares model considered, but not adopted, by the department combines the income of both parents and requires the parties to contribute child support in proportion to the income each receives.

5. Public opinion expressed by the parties directly affected (the parents) strongly supports the income shares model over the obligor model because of the inherent fairness of that proposal. The best interests of the child should be better served by adoption of the income shares model as it would provide not only sufficient financial resources for the child but should provide for more harmonious relationships due to the fairness of the income shares model.

1993 LC Report at 13. *See also id.* at 18–21 (Committee's child support study).

[4] The Department gave these reasons:

1. The department has full legal authority to establish child support guidelines, and is required by statute to do so.

2. The rules objected to were adopted pursuant to law, i.e. the department complied with all procedural requirements.

3. The rules objected to represent a fully considered choice after hearing and reflecting on comments on those rules, both pro and con.

4. The rules objected to took effect in February 1991. The then-sitting Fifty-second Legislative Assembly thereafter failed to pass House Bill No. 1428, which would have required the department to adopt rules encompassing the "income shares" model for child support guidelines.

5. Had the department taken action after the legislative session to changes its rules to reflect the "income shares" model it would have been contrary to the legislative action on House Bill No. 1428.

6. The department cannot now implement child support guidelines that require consideration of the oblig[ee]'s income because current law makes provision for securing information concerning the income of the obligor, but not for securing information concerning the income of the obligee.

7. The first four items set out in the committee's objection are true, but not determinative in any sense as to the propriety of the department's action in adopting the rules.

8. The department would debate the committee's rationale in item 5 regarding public opinion because the rulemaking record reflects an expression of support for the adopted rules which is virtually even with that for the income shares model.

9. The child support guidelines are a part of an overall system of child support collection which is intended to ensure that children's needs are met, and that the state's fiscal outlays for aid to families with dependent children are minimized.

1993 LC Report at 13.

Kendal argues that the guidelines and statutes on child support are unconstitutional because they deny equal protection and due process under the law, and that these statutes amount to an impermissible Bill of Attainder. He claims "where the full impact of the forces of the State are marshaled in favor of one of its citizens as against another, th[e] mandate of equality is violated," "it is a denial of due process of law for the legislature to give to a child support enforcement agency unbridled authority to intrude into the privacy of persons such as Kendal," and "[f]ailure to support a child is a Felony. In lieu of the criminal charge, the non-custodial parent is punished by direct and indirect legislative acts."

We have often outlined the proper analysis for a constitutional attack on a statute on equal protection grounds. The appropriate standard of review must be determined, and the statute analyzed on that basis. However, in his appellant's brief challenging the constitutionality of this child support system, Kendal did not cite a single precedent for his arguments, did not pose any standard for this constitutional review, and did not undertake the proper analyses. Kendal merely contends there is "unequal treatment" between custodial and non-custodial parents, there are "no restrictions upon the agency's implementation of procedures," and "[t]he effect of the Legislative action is to directly punish the obligors of child support, noncustodial parents, without the benefit of due process of law." These contentions lack any merit.

A party making a constitutional challenge "must do much more than acknowledge, in passing, the constitutional difficulties of a statute," and we adhere to "the rule that parties must bring up the 'heavy artillery' when asserting constitutional claims." *Swenson v. Northern Crop Ins., Inc.*, 498 N.W.2d 174, 178 (N.D.1993). Kendal has not sufficiently raised these constitutional claims. We agree with the trial court that, for his equal protection argument, "[i]t is unclear which standard [Kendal] is asking the Court to adopt," that his "due process argument was raised without substantive support," and that his Bill of Attainder argument "does not rise to the level of constitutional proportion."

We conclude that the trial court correctly increased Kendal's monthly child support to meet guidelines validly adopted under applicable statutes and by appropriate motion of a child support enforcement agency, and that Kendal has not adequately challenged the constitutionality of the guidelines and statutes on child support.

We affirm. . . .

NOTES AND QUESTIONS

(1) **Percentage of Income.** This model exists in two forms: the flat percentage of income model which applies the same percentage to both high and low incomes and the varying percentage model which, like the income shares model, decreases the percentage of income devoted to child care as the income increases. The great virtue of both forms is that they are simple and easy to apply. Once the income of the noncustodial spouse is determined, then a single calculation is all that is required: multiply the income of the noncustodial parent by the percentage from the guideline. Because of this simplicity, the chance of error is lowered.

(2) **Flat Rate Model.** States which follow the Flat Percentage of Income model are Alaska, Georgia, Illinois, Mississippi, Nevada, Tennessee, and Wisconsin. *See* Laura Morgan, Child Support Guidelines: Interpretation and Application 1-14 (1997).

(3) **Varying Rate Model.** The Varying Percentage of Income Model is used in the following states: Arkansas, District of Columbia, Massachusetts, North Dakota, Texas, and Wyoming. *See* Laura Morgan, Child Support Guidelines: Interpretation and Application 1-14 (1997).

(4) **Presumptive effect.** Almost all states create a presumption in favor of the guideline amount. *See* Linda D. Elrod, *Summary of the Year in Family Law*, 27 Fam. L.Q. 485, 505 (1994) (citing National Center for State Courts, *Child Support Guidelines: A Compendium* (1990)). For an example where the guideline amount (for a support award) is a relevant, but not the only determining, factor to the support award, see *Smith v. Smith*, 614 So. 2d 394 (Miss. 1993).

(5) **Dual Custody.** What happens when the noncustodial parent has the child 40% of the time? Legislators, judges, and others involved in making guidelines have not focused on the issue of shared custody:

> However, the focus in developing the guidelines has been on the most common case—that of sole physical custody in which the child lives with one parent and sees the other parent on a "visiting" basis. Child support policy makers have either paid little attention to the problem of economic support in cases of shared custody, or have been reluctant to allow support reduction for shared time. Fifteen states do not mention shared custody in their guidelines, a failure that can be interpreted as a public policy statement that those states do not allow reduction for shared time. Seventeen states provide very generally that shared custody may be a reason for the court to adjust child support in a particular case.

Marygold S. Melli & Patricia R. Brown, *The Economics of Shared Custody: Developing an Equitable Formula for Dual Residence*, 31 Hous. L. Rev. 543, 544–45 (1994).

Melli and Brown have studied these various state approaches in great detail. While it is impossible to summarize their conclusions in depth, their description of existing schemes can at least be superficially summarized. Of those states which do take shared custody into account, there are four ways of dealing with the problem. First, some states, as noted in the quotation above, simply leave it to the court's discretion to alter the child support arrangement: Alabama, Illinois, Iowa, Kentucky, Minnesota, Missouri, New Jersey, New York, North Dakota, Pennsylvania, and Tennessee. In other words, in these states, shared custody will be a reason for deviation from the guideline. Second, there are those states that establish a threshold of shared custody, usually expressed by the percentage of time that the child is with the noncustodial parent, and after that threshold is reached the court will have discretion to deviate from the guideline: Kansas, Maine, Nebraska, and Oregon. Third, there are states which choose a threshold and once the threshold is reached there is a mandatory offset, usually determined by a formula: Alaska, Colorado, District of Columbia, Hawaii, Idaho, Michigan, New Mexico, North Carolina, Puerto Rico, Utah, Vermont, and West Virginia. In both the second and third categories, the reason for the threshold is to prevent deviation or offset for mere visitation. The threshold varies from a low of 22% to a high of 50%. Finally, there is the approach of California, which creates an offset, based upon factors worked into the child support formula, without a threshold. This allows some offset even for visitation. *See* Marygold S. Melli & Patricia R. Brown, *The Economics of Shared Custody: Developing an Equitable Formula for Dual Residence*, 31 Hous. L. Rev. 543, Appendix A (1994).

It should also be noted that allowing an offset encourages an obligor parent to seek joint custody. In some cases this encouragement can be good in that shared custody may be beneficial for the children, but it can also be bad: shared custody becomes a monetary issue. Obligor parents may seek shared custody or seek a greater degree of shared custody simply because it lowers child support payments. Sometimes parents who have not spent much time with their children, visiting them only sporadically since separation from the other parent, suddenly pursue joint custody with a 50/50 time share after learning about the guideline. Bench officers are not often swayed by sudden expressions of interest following extended periods of conduct demonstrating little or no interest, but are likely to grant some increase in physical custody if in the best interest of the child. *See* Cal. Fam. Code § 4055 (1998).

(6) **The Effect of Guidelines.** Researchers Nancy Thoenes, Patricia Tjaden, and Jessica Pearson performed a survey and statistical analysis of support orders in Colorado (Income Shares), Hawaii (Melson Formula), and Illinois (Percentage of Income). They reached the following general conclusion regarding the effect of the guidelines:

> In sum, we conclude that guidelines have met the congressional mandates of increasing award levels, award consistency and case processing efficiency; however, the changes brought by passage of the guidelines have been modest. There are several reasons for the limited effect produced by guidelines. First, in many families, the income resources of the noncustodial parent are extremely limited. In an attempt to balance the basic needs of the noncustodial parent with those of the children, courts are forced to order awards that are less than what is necessary to ensure the financial welfare of children. Second, most child support decisions are reached voluntarily by divorcing parents who, researchers have shown, seriously underestimate the true cost of raising children . . . . Finally, the impact of guidelines may have been minimized the implementation of "informal" guidelines prior to the adoption of "formal" guidelines. Many of the attorneys and judges we interviewed reported that judges within their particular jurisdiction had been operating on the basis of commonly understood yardsticks for determining child support levels. These yardsticks were subsequently incorporated into the specific formula ultimately adopted by a particular state.

Nancy Thoenes, Patricia Tjaden, and Jessica Pearson, *The Impact of Child Support Guidelines on Award Adequacy, Award Variability, and Case Processing Efficiency*, 25 Fam. L.Q. 325, 345 (1991).

As to the differences in the results among the three different states and models, the researchers came to this conclusion:

> Based on our research, not one guideline appears to produce consistently higher or lower awards. The Income Shares Model produced the highest awards with low-income families, the Melson Formula produced the highest awards in middle-income families, and the Percentage of Income Approach produced the highest awards in upper-income families.

Id. at 344. *See generally* Elizabeth A. Preston, *Father's Day: Ohio's Child Support Guidelines and the Responsible Father* 21 Cap. U. L. Rev. 1145 (1992); Sharon J. Badertscher, *Ohio's Mandatory Child Support Guidelines: Child Support or Spousal Maintenance*, 42 Case W. Res. L. Rev. 297 (1992); Donna Schule, *Origins and Development of the Law of Parental Child Support*, 27 J. Fam. L. 807 (1989).

§ 11.04 Income

[A] Gross or Net?

ANNOTATED CODE OF MARYLAND
FAMILY LAW (1997)
§ 12–201 Definitions.

. . .

(b) Income. — "Income" means:
    (1) actual income of a parent, if the parent is employed to full capacity; or
    (2) potential income of a parent, if the parent is voluntarily impoverished.

(c) Actual income. —
    (1) "Actual income" means income from any source.
    (2) For income from self-employment, rent, royalties, proprietorship of a business, or joint ownership of a partnership or closely held corporation, "actual income" means gross receipts minus ordinary and necessary expenses required to produce income.
    (3) "Actual income" includes:
        (i) salaries;
        (ii) wages;
        (iii) commissions;
        (iv) bonuses;
        (v) dividend income;
        (vi) pension income;
        (vii) interest income;
        (viii) trust income;
        (ix) annuity income;
        (x) Social Security benefits;
        (xi) workers' compensation benefits;
        (xii) unemployment insurance benefits;
        (xiii) disability insurance benefits;
        (xiv) alimony or maintenance received; and
        (xv) expense reimbursements or in-kind payments received by a parent in the course of employment, self-employment, or operation of a business to the extent the reimbursements or payments reduce the parent's personal living expenses.
    (4) Based on the circumstances of the case, the court may consider the following items as actual income:
        (i) severance pay;

(ii) capital gains;

(iii) gifts; or

(iv) prizes.

(5) "Actual income" does not include benefits received from means-tested public assistance programs, including temporary cash assistance, Supplemental Security Income, food stamps, and transitional emergency, medical, and housing assistance.

MINNESOTA STATUTES ANNOTATED
DOMESTIC RELATIONS (1997) 518.551

Net Income defined as: Total monthly income less

(i) Federal Income Tax

(ii) State Income Tax

(iii) Social Security Deductions

(iv) Reasonable Pension Deductions

(v) Union Dues

(vi) Cost of Dependent Health Insurance Coverage

(vii) Cost of Individual or Group Health/Hospitalization Coverage or an Amount for Actual Medical Expenses

(viii) A Child Support or Maintenance Order that is Currently Being Paid.

"Net income" does not include:

(1) the income of the obligor's spouse, but does include in-kind payments received by the obligor in the course of employment, self-employment, or operation of a business if the payments reduce the obligor's living expenses; or

(2) compensation received by a party for employment in excess of a 40–hour work week, provided that:

(i) support is nonetheless ordered in an amount at least equal to the guidelines amount based on income not excluded under this clause; and

(ii) the party demonstrates, and the court finds, that:

(A) the excess employment began after the filing of the petition for dissolution;

(B) the excess employment reflects an increase in the work schedule or hours worked over that of the two years immediately preceding the filing of the petition;

(C) the excess employment is voluntary and not a condition of employment;

(D) the excess employment is in the nature of additional, part-time or overtime employment compensable by the hour or fraction of an hour; and

(E) the party's compensation structure has not been changed for the purpose of affecting a support or maintenance obligation.

NOTES AND QUESTIONS

(1) **Gross or Net.** The two statutes presented above are portions of the Maryland and Minnesota guidelines, which deal with the definition of "income." Because of space constraints neither of these excerpts dealing with income is complete; the complete versions actually reveal even greater complexity. These two portions are included to illustrate two very different approaches regarding the computation of income for guideline calculations. The Maryland statute is an example of a state that uses a gross income figure for the calculations, and the Minnesota statute uses a net figure (gross less taxes and other obligations). The states are about evenly split on this issue (*See* Laura Morgan, Child Support Guidelines: Interpretation and Application 2-10, 2-11 (1997)), and the choice of gross or net by itself does not mean higher or lower support awards since the amount of support is also controlled by the percentage of income that the legislature determines should be devoted to support.

(2) **Sources of Income.** The Maryland statute also provides a representative list of the sources of income which will be considered in making guideline calculations. While statutes vary greatly, this one is representative. Notice that this statute has a special provision for several optional sources of income. *See* Md. Code Ann., Fam. Law § 12–201(c)(3) (1997). There are of course other sources of income. While it is impossible here to include a complete discussion of all possible sources, here are some other forms of income that may be include in the child support calculation.

   a. Deferred compensation included: *Posey v. Tate*, 656 N.E.2d 222 (Ill. App. Ct. 1995).
   b. Disability Payments to Parent: *Matter of Marriage of Callaghan*, 869 P.2d 240 (Kan. Ct. App. 1994); *Whitaker v. Colbert*, 442 S.E.2d 429 (Va. Ct. App. 1994).
   c. Personal Injury Awards: *In re Marriage of Fain*, 794 P.2d 1086 (Colo Ct. App. 1990); *Tullock v. Flickinger*, 616 A.2d 315 (Del. 1992).
   d. Retirement income: *In re Marriage of Kelm*, 878 P.2d 34 (Colo. Ct. App. 1994).
   e. Social Security Benefits: *Forbes v. Forbes*, 610 N.E.2d 885 (Ind. Ct. App. 1993); *In re Marriage of Lee*, 486 N.W.2d 302 (Iowa 1992). But note that social security benefits received by the child are not considered in income. *Hammett v. Woods*, 602 So. 2d 825 (Miss. 1992).
   f. Veteran's Benefits: *Rose v. Rose*, 481 U.S. 619 (1987).

(3) **Overtime.** Overtime and second jobs present a problem for guidelines. Often a responsible payor faced with child support and alimony payments will work overtime or even take a second job to make ends meet. Should this additional income be used to determine the payments? Or, a less than responsible obligor who has been working overtime for years, may decide to only work forty hours per week in order to reduce payments. The Minnesota statute is an attempt to distinguish between these two situations. *See Johnson v. Johnson*, 533 N.W.2d 859 (Minn. Ct. App. 1995). A number of court cases have held that where there has been a history of working overtime, it should be considered in the child support calculation. *See Skipper v. Skipper*, 654 So. 2d 1181 (Fla. Dist. Ct. App. 1995); *In re Marriage of Pettit*, 493 N.W.2d 865 (Iowa Ct. App. 1992); *In re Marriage of Sigler*, 889 P.2d 1323 (Or. Ct. App. 1991); *Reyna v. Reyna*, 398 N.E.2d 641 (Ill. App. Ct. 1979).

Other courts have refused to impute income to a payor who has stopped working overtime on the grounds that a person who is working forty hours is not underemployed. *See In re Marriage of Soden*, 834 P.2d 358 (Kan. 1992).

(4) **Child Care Expenses and Extraordinary Medical Expenses.** Among the states, there are three identifiable methods for dealing with work-related child care and health insurance expenses: First, the cost of the expenditure is deducted from the income of the parent who incurs the expense. Second, the cost is added to the basic child support obligation, and parents pay a proportional share. They may also share equally. Third, the cost is considered a basis for deviation from the award. *See* Laura Morgan, Child Support Guidelines: Interpretation and Application 3-21 (1997).

[B] **Actual Income or Capacity to Earn?**

HENDERSON v. SMITH
Supreme Court of Idaho
915 P.2d 6 (1996)

McDEVITT, CHIEF JUSTICE.

In this paternity action, appellant, Vernon K. Smith, appeals from the district court's decision affirming the magistrate's determination that Smith is the biological father of Rachel R. Henderson and order requiring Smith to pay for the future and past support of the child . . . .

The relevant facts are as follows. On June 7, 1981, respondent, Patricia E. Henderson (Henderson) gave birth to Rachel R. Henderson (Rachel). On March 27, 1992, Henderson filed a paternity action against appellant, Vernon K. Smith (Smith), seeking a judgment declaring Smith the biological father of Rachel and ordering payment of past and future child support payments.

. . . The magistrate rendered its decision concluding that Smith was the biological father of Rachel. . . . The magistrate held that Smith, as the biological father of Rachel, was responsible for paying past support expended by Henderson, limited to the six year period prior to the filing of the complaint. The magistrate further concluded that, based on the Idaho Child Support Guidelines, Smith was responsible for payment of child support in the amount of $373.00 per month beginning April 1993 and continuing until Rachel reaches majority or, if she continues her education, until she reaches the age of 19. Smith was required by the magistrate to pay the State $240.00 for the cost of the blood tests, to carry health insurance on Rachel until she reaches majority, and to split health care costs not covered by insurance with Henderson. The paternity action was held to not be barred by laches or the statute of limitations. Smith appealed the magistrate's decision.

On appeal, the district court affirmed the decision of the magistrate. Smith appealed to this Court. . . .

Smith next argues that the magistrate erred in allowing Henderson to use evidence of the average income of attorneys to calculate Smith's child support obligation. Smith contends that the use of the average income of Idaho attorneys was in error because there was no evidence to show that Smith was within the class of wage earners used to formulate the data.

The magistrate's award of child support is reviewed by this Court under an abuse of discretion standard. Smith bears the burden of establishing that the magistrate's calculations constituted a manifest abuse of discretion.

Under the Idaho Child Support Guidelines (I.C.S.G.), gross income for purposes of determining income available to a parent to satisfy his or her child support obligation is defined as including income from any source. While the definition of gross income is not exhaustive, it has been interpreted by this Court to be an expansive list subject to a broad scope of inclusive sources of income. The determination of income and expenses from an individual who is self employed should be carefully reviewed to determine the level of gross income to satisfy a child support obligation. This gross income for the self employed parent, may differ from a determination of business income for tax purposes. One of the considerations in determining the amounts of child support is the financial ability of the payor to make the payments. However, if a parent is voluntarily underemployed, then child support is to be based upon potential income. The potential income of a voluntarily underemployed parent may be based upon employment potential and probable earning levels based on work history, occupational qualifications, and prevailing job opportunities and earning levels in the community. I.C.S.G. § 6(c)(1)(A).

The magistrate, in determining the amount of Smith's income, found that Smith's monthly disposable or gross income is $3,500.00, based on Smith's ability to earn an average income as a practicing attorney with over twenty years of experience. The magistrate took into consideration costs for reasonable overhead and operating expenses and Smith's previous child support obligation and determined that Smith's monthly child support obligation would be $373.00. Smith has failed to meet his burden of establishing that the magistrate's determination constituted a manifest abuse of discretion. Smith is a practicing lawyer, who apparently has no monthly disposable income. Smith has practiced law for more than twenty years. Since the magistrate did not have a monthly income figure for Smith, or any evidence indicating that Smith was not underemployed, the magistrate estimated Smith's potential income and probable earnings based on the average earning levels of Idaho attorneys. The magistrate did not abuse its discretion in reaching this conclusion, and the evidence was properly admitted. . . .

The decision of the magistrate is affirmed . . . .

IN RE THE MARRIAGE OF PAULIN
California Court of Appeal
54 Cal. Rptr. 2d 314 (1996)

KING, ASSOCIATE JUSTICE.

. . .

We also hold, where the former wife had remarried and had voluntarily ceased her employment, the trial court did not abuse its discretion by fixing her income, for purposes of the statutory child support formula, based upon her earning capacity.

Robyn Paulin appeals from a superior court order reducing the child support paid by her former husband, Scott Paulin for their two minor children. On appeal, her contentions are twofold: . . . and (2) that the court erred in attributing income to her when she was no longer working. We affirm.

Facts

Robyn and Scott's 13-year marriage was dissolved by order of the Solano County Superior Court effective October 18, 1991. There were two minor children of the marriage, Scott and Tiffany. By stipulated order dated November 4, 1994, Scott was ordered to provide $1,511 per month child support based upon his gross monthly salary of $5,405 as a police sergeant in Vacaville and Robyn's monthly wages of $1,505 as a part-time registered nurse. . . .

In calculating the modified child support, the court used Robyn's previously established income of $1,505 per month even though she was unemployed. Robyn timely noticed this appeal. We review the court's order for an abuse of discretion. . . .

Robyn next argues that the court erred in attributing income to her based on her earning capacity, when in fact, at the time of the hearing, she was unemployed. "Earning capacity is composed of (1) the ability to work, including such factors as age, occupation, skills, education, health, background, work experience and qualifications; (2) the willingness to work exemplified through good faith efforts, due diligence and meaningful attempts to secure employment; and (3) an opportunity to work which means an employer who is willing to hire." (*In re Marriage of Padilla* (1995) 38 Cal.App.4th 1212, 1218, 45 Cal.Rptr.2d 555, quoting *In re Marriage of Regnery* (1989) 214 Cal.App.3d 1367, 1372–1373, 263 Cal.Rptr. 243.) We review the trial court's decision to consider Robyn's earning capacity in setting support under an abuse of discretion standard. . . .

Robyn, who had remarried, did not testify at the hearing on Scott's motion to modify his child support obligation. Instead, she submitted a declaration indicating that her previous employment as a registered nurse at a convalescent hospital had been "one of the most stressful experiences of (her) life." She explained that she voluntarily severed her employment due to questionable record keeping practices of her employer that she believed placed her nursing license "at risk." Regarding efforts to find other employment, Robyn's declaration went on to state that she had "periodically reviewed help wanted ads and similar sources" and there had "yet to be an opening appropriate for (her) level of training and experience . . . ."

Robyn's declaration was met with skepticism. At the hearing, Scott's attorney expressed dismay "that the employment we have fought for a year and a half to get her to take" had been "given up." Scott's attorney argued that the assertion in Robyn's declaration "that there are no jobs out there" was not substantiated with any documentation that she had actually looked for employment. The lack of documented efforts to replace her lost employment was characterized as an unwillingness, as opposed to inability, to work. Robyn was not present at the hearing to refute these contentions. The trial court used Robyn's previously established monthly income of $1,505 in setting support "without prejudice," leaving her the opportunity to try to prove, with more sufficient evidence, that the loss of her income was justifiable.

Based upon our review of this record, we conclude that the court did not abuse its discretion when it concluded that it was not appropriate, on this incomplete record, to change the monthly income figure for Robyn's previous employment to zero based on her current unemployment. Consequently, since the court's order had the effect of maintaining the "status quo" (compare *In re Marriage of Stephenson* (1995) 39 Cal.App.4th 71, 82–83, 46 Cal.Rptr.2d 8) and Robyn is not barred from seeking relief in further proceedings, we view her attack on the trial court's use of earning capacity as opposed to actual earnings to be premature.

The judgment is affirmed. . . .

HARVEY v. ROBINSON
Supreme Judicial Court of Maine
665 A.2d 215 (1995)

LIPEZ, JUSTICE.

. . .

In a 1988 divorce judgment the District Court (Bangor, Kravchuk, J.) determined that Robinson and Harvey's two children, Karen (born 1980) and Sara (born 1981), would reside principally with Robinson and that Harvey would pay to Robinson as child support $345 bi-weekly. In 1991, Harvey made $26,000 as a civilian employee of the National Guard and another $3,500 for weekend Guard service. He had a total income of approximately $35,500 because of additional work with an ambulance service.

In 1992, having completed 20 years of service with the National Guard, Harvey anticipated that he might face involuntary retirement. Rather than waiting to see if this involuntary retirement occurred, Harvey retired from the Guard voluntarily to pursue his long deferred dream of going to college and medical school. He is currently a full-time undergraduate student.

As a result of this decision, Harvey now has a gross income of approximately $13,840. This amount reflects the income from part-time work he is able to do while in school and some educational grant money. . . .

Despite Robinson's urging, the court used Harvey's current gross income as a full-time student to calculate the appropriate child support obligation, instead of his earning capacity before beginning college. The court found that Harvey's decision to leave his full-time employment was made in good faith, and, therefore, using $13,840 as Harvey's gross income and $21,000 as Robinson's gross income, established a support payment for Harvey of $60 per week. The court found, however, that it was equitable in this instance, particularly because Harvey had recently purchased a new automobile, to deviate upward from this amount. The court also stated that it was considering the effects on the children of the reduced support payments. Accordingly, it ordered Harvey to pay $80 per week, increasing to $86 per week in December 1993 when his younger daughter reached twelve years of age. Robinson unsuccessfully argued that based on Harvey's earning capacity, his gross income should be $36,000 and his weekly child support payment pursuant to the work sheet should be $213, increasing to $236 in December 1993. The Superior Court affirmed the order and Robinson's appeal followed. . . .

As justification for its order, the trial court noted that Harvey's decision to pursue a college degree was made in good faith. That is undoubtedly true. There is no suggestion in the record that Harvey opted for school in an effort to avoid his obligation to his children. Harvey's good faith, however, does not ameliorate the dramatic effect on the children of his decision to give up full-time work. That good faith consideration must be balanced by an evaluation of the effect that Harvey's under employment decision has on the interests of his children. By its nature, an order for child support serves the interests of the child by compelling parents to meet their financial responsibilities to their children.

Although the court acknowledged the effects on the children of reduced child support payments, the court approved that reduction because it accepted Harvey's decision to forego full-time employment in favor of full-time education. The court does not explain how this accommodation to Harvey's preferences serves the interests of the children in any way. . . .

In a tacit acknowledgment that the interests of the children matter, Harvey argues that an interests analysis that focuses on money is too narrow:

> This [focus on money] fails completely to consider that children may actually suffer through watching parents stay in bad jobs; the children may suffer if maintaining a certain job keeps the parent from spending time with his/her children; and the children may indeed suffer if they are taught at an early age that having children absolutely bars a parent from continuing his/her education. Certainly more than just money must be considered when ascertaining the best interests of children.

Even if there is some abstract merit in this argument, there is not a testimonial word in the record that supports it. . . .

Although we recognize the difficult issues posed for the trial court by these cases, the dilemma here was not insoluble. Harvey could work full time and go to school part time. In that way, he could fulfill his support obligation to his children while pursuing his educational interests. If medical school were unattainable through a part time education, he might have to make necessary adjustments to fulfill his parental obligation. The decision to relieve Harvey of that obligation of adequate support "results in a plain or unmistakable injustice, so apparent that it is instantly visible without argument." This case must be remanded for reconsideration of the child support determination based on Harvey's current earning capacity as a full-time employee.

The entry is:

Judgment vacated. Remanded to the Superior Court with instructions to vacate the judgment of the District Court, and remand to the District Court for further proceedings consistent with the opinion herein. . . .

DANA, JUSTICE, with whom ROBERTS, JUSTICE, joins, dissenting.

I respectfully dissent. When determining a party's gross income for purposes of computing child support payments the trial court "*may* include the difference between the amount a party is earning and that party's earning capacity when the party voluntarily becomes or remains unemployed or underemployed, if sufficient evidence is introduced concerning a party's current earning capacity." 19 M.R.S.A. § 311(5)(D) (Supp.1994) (emphasis added). Consideration of earning capacity as opposed to present income is not mandatory and we should not disturb a court's decision whether to consider earning capacity absent an abuse of discretion. . . .

> Following dissolution of marriage, the custodial parent and children cannot be allowed to freeze the other parent in his employment or otherwise preclude him from seeking economic improvement for himself and his family. So long as his employment, educational or investment decisions are undertaken in good faith and not deliberately designed to avoid responsibility for those dependent on him, he should be permitted to attempt to enhance his economic fortunes without penalty.

Coons v. Wilder, 93 Ill.App.3d 127, 416 N.E.2d 785, 791 (1981). . . .

I find the trial court's action to be within its considerable discretion, and I would affirm the judgment.

GOLDBERGER v. GOLDBERGER
Court of Special Appeals of Maryland
624 A.2d 1328 (1993)

DANA MARK LEVITZ, JUDGE Specially Assigned.

. . .

In the case *sub judice*, the evidence revealed that appellant [father] was 32 years old and healthy, with many years of higher education. It was undisputed that appellant had earned no actual income, as he had never worked at any income-producing vocation. Appellant planned his life to be a permanent Torah/Talmudic student. He was a student before he was married and before any of his children were born. Appellant testified that he studies "for the sake of studying, which is a positive commandment to study the Torah for the sake of studying it." Further, appellant testified that it was his intention to continue his life of study forever: " . . . I should continue to study the rest of my life, to always be in studying . . . ." Throughout his life appellant has been supported by others, first, his parents, thereafter, his father-in-law, and most recently, friends in the Orthodox community. Nevertheless, appellant fathered six children whom he has refused to support, arguing that he has no means to support and never will have the means to provide support.

A life devoted to study is viewed by many in the Orthodox community as a true luxury that very few can enjoy. Unfortunately for the appellant's children, permanent Torah/Talmudic students must depend on the charity of others to provide the necessities of life. Those who support a Torah student have no legal obligation to continue such support in either duration or amount.

Nevertheless, through a network of family and Orthodox communities in Europe and the United States, approximately $180,000 had been contributed to appellant over a three year period to enable him to pursue his custody claim. Approximately $3,000 of that sum was once used to purge appellant of contempt for failing to pay child support.

Based on these facts, the court determined (1) that appellant had voluntarily impoverished himself, and (2) that his potential income was equivalent to the money that had been contributed by others to his cause. It therefore regarded his income, for purposes of paying child support as $60,000 per year and ordered that he pay $4,066 per month for the support of his six children. Appellant challenges both the finding of voluntary impoverishment and the calculation of potential income.

The obligation of parents to support their minor children has been consistently upheld by the Court of Appeals of Maryland . . . .

The U.S. Supreme Court has recognized the obligation of parents to support their children. In *Dunbar v. Dunbar*, 190 U.S. 340, 351 (1903), the Court stated, "At common law, a father is bound to support his legitimate children and the obligation continues during their minority . . . ." The legislature of Maryland has made it a crime for parents to fail to support their minor children. Md.Code Ann., Fam.Law § 10–203 (1991). . . .

In view of the above authorities, there can be no question that appellant has a legal obligation to financially support his children until they reach the age of legal majority. The more difficult question is how to calculate the proper amount of that support. Fortunately, that question has been answered by the Legislature of Maryland. Md.Code Ann., Fam.Law § 12–202(a)(1) (1991) states, "[I]n any proceeding to establish or modify child support, whether pendente lite or permanent, the court shall use the child support guidelines set forth in this subtitle." In order to use the guidelines as required by § 12–202(a)(1), it is necessary to calculate the income of the parents. "Income" is defined in § 12–201(b) of the Family Law Article as:

(1) actual income of a parent, if the parent is employed to full capacity; or

(2) potential income of a parent, if the parent is voluntarily impoverished.

The legislature's purpose in including potential income was to implement state and federal policy of requiring adequate support by precluding parents from avoiding their obligation by deliberately not earning what they could earn. . . .

The issue of voluntary impoverishment most often arises in the context of a parent who reduces his or her level of income to avoid paying support by quitting, retiring or changing jobs. The intent of the parent in those cases is often important in determining whether there has been voluntary impoverishment. Was the job changed for the purpose of avoiding the support obligation and, therefore, voluntary, or was it for reasons beyond the control of the parent, and thus involuntary?

In defining the term "voluntarily impoverished" in *John O. v. Jane O.*, 90 Md.App. 406, 421, 601 A.2d 149, 156 (1992), we never intended to limit the obligation of a spouse who is voluntarily impoverished for any reason, to pay child support. A parent who chooses a life of poverty before having children and makes a deliberate choice not to alter that status after having children is also "voluntarily impoverished." Whether the voluntary impoverishment is for the purpose of avoiding child support or because the parent simply has chosen a frugal lifestyle for another reason, doesn't affect that parent's obligation to the child. Although the parent can choose to live in poverty, that parent cannot obligate the child to go without the necessities of life. A parent who brings a child into this world must support that child, if he has or reasonably could obtain, the means to do so. The law requires that parent to alter his or her previously chosen lifestyle if necessary to enable the parent to meet his or her support obligation.

Accordingly, we now hold that, for purposes of the child support guidelines, a parent shall be considered "voluntarily impoverished" whenever the parent has made the free and conscious choice, not compelled by factors beyond his or her control, to render himself or herself without adequate resources . . . .

Based on a review of the evidence before the circuit court, there was no error in finding that appellant was "voluntarily impoverished." . . .

Unfortunately, the court below erred in determining that appellant's potential income was $60,000 per year, based solely on the his ability to raise funds to support and carry on this litigation. Although the court may consider the ability of appellant to persuade others to provide him with funds to pay child support in the future, the court cannot assume this will occur merely because appellant has been able to convince others to support this litigation up until now. The court needs to hear testimony and make findings regarding the factors relating to potential income previously enunciated. No such findings were made in this case. After calculating the guidelines using appellant's realistic potential income, the court must decide whether the presumptive correctness of the guidelines has been overcome. Accordingly, this matter must be remanded to the trial court for such determinations.

In conclusion, we leave undisturbed the trial court's decision granting the parties a divorce, awarding custody of their six children to the appellee, and establishing conditions for visitation. We vacate the court's child support order and remand the matter to the trial court to recalculate the appellant's child support obligation in light of this opinion.

NOTES AND QUESTIONS

(1) **Involuntary Reduction.** There are some other interesting cases regarding involuntary reduction of income: Participation in a strike is not a voluntary reduction in income, see *In re Marriage of Horn*, 650 N.E.2d 1103 (Ill. App. Ct. 1995); *Rawlings v. Rawling*, 460 S.E.2d 581 (Va. Ct. App. 1995); proof of incarceration alone not enough to show father's inability to pay support, *Thomasson v. Johnson*, 903 P.2d 254 (N.M. Ct. App. 1995); *Wills v. Jones*, 667 A.2d 331 (Md. 1995).

[C] Spousal Income

IN RE THE MARRIAGE OF WOOD
California Court of Appeal
44 Cal. Rptr. 2d 236 (1995)

WUNDERLICH, ASSOCIATE JUSTICE.

In this case, in adjusting a child support order between former spouses, we hold that the trial court erred in disregarding the provisions of new section 4057.5 of the Family Code. Camilla Wood Casparis (Camilla) appeals from the judgment entered following a hearing on an order to show cause re child support filed by her ex-husband, William D. Wood, Jr. William's 1993 motion to reduce child support was based on consideration of the income of Camilla's new mate, then appropriate under Civil Code section 4721, subdivision (e), predecessor to section 4057.5. At the 1994 hearing, the trial court stated it was considering Camilla's new mate's income only as it related to her standard of living and that of the three children living with her, and the court did not allow detailed discovery or questioning of the new mate. For the reasons stated below, we reverse.

FACTS AND PROCEDURAL BACKGROUND

Camilla and William dissolved their marriage of almost 10 years in April of 1989. Pursuant to stipulation, the judgment of dissolution of marriage awarded Camilla physical custody of the parties' three minor children, and it ordered William to pay child support of $1,375 per month. A little over one year later on May 21, 1990, the trial court filed a stipulation and order which increased William's child support obligation to $1,600 per month. The order stated that the parties were modifying the level of support because William's income had increased to $86,200 per year. About two years later, in April, 1992, the trial court filed another stipulation and order. Child support was set at $2,100 per month based on William's and Camilla's present earnings.

This appeal is based on the next order adjudicating child support, made after William filed an order to show cause regarding reducing support. The basis for William's request was that special circumstances existed, in that Camilla had remarried and was married to a very wealthy man. In her responsive declaration Camilla stated she married William Casparis (Casparis) in July of 1992 . . . .

William sought to obtain financial records from Casparis. He in turn filed a motion for an order quashing the subpena and for protective orders. Camilla and her new mate both objected to any consideration of the new mate's income in the child support proceeding.

The trial court heard William's order to show cause on May 11, 1994. The hearing largely consisted of offers of proof by the respective counsel, cross-examination of Camilla and her new husband, and the brief testimony of a vocational evaluation expert. The trial court purported to consider the income of Casparis only insofar as it impacted on the standard of living of Camilla and the three children. . . .

DISCUSSION

First we look to the statutory framework. Then we examine the trial court's order. Finally we examine the correctness of the trial court's order and its underlying analysis. . . .

Of particular importance here is current section 4057.5, enacted in 1993, effective January 1, 1994. So critical is this statute to our analysis that we quote subdivisions (a) and (b) in their entirety. "(a)(1) The income of the obligor parent's subsequent spouse or nonmarital partner shall not be considered when determining or modifying child support, except in an extraordinary case where excluding that income would lead to extreme and severe hardship to any child subject to the child support award, in which case the court shall also consider whether including that income would lead to extreme and severe hardship to any child supported by the obligor or by the obligor's subsequent spouse or nonmarital partner. (2) The income of the obligee parent's subsequent spouse or nonmarital partner shall not be considered when determining or modifying child support, except in an extraordinary case where excluding that income would lead to extreme and severe hardship to any child subject to the child support award, in which case the court shall also consider whether including that income would lead to extreme or severe hardship to any child supported by the obligee or by the obligee's subsequent spouse or nonmarital partner." Subdivision (b) provides: "For purposes of this section, an extraordinary case may include a parent voluntarily or intentionally quitting work or reducing income."

. . .

ANALYSIS

The primary issue on appeal is whether the trial court erred in considering new mate income in light of newly enacted section 4057.5. First, we characterize the trial court's ruling. Although the trial court claimed only to take into account Casparis's income as it related to Camilla's standard of living, this was tantamount to considering new mate income. The question becomes whether the discretion the trial court can exercise under 4057, subdivision (b)(5), (the "unjust or inappropriate/special circumstances" scenario), may overcome the specific mandate of section 4057.5. Under the circumstances of this case we believe the answer must be no.

Before the 1993 amendment, effective January 1, 1994, trial courts did have the authority to consider new mate income in a child support action. In the *Fuller* [(1979) 89 Cal.App.3d 405, 152 Cal.Rptr. 467] case, for instance, the appellate court held it was proper for the trial court to consider the income of the nonmarital partner of the supporting spouse insofar as it enabled the supporting spouse to devote a little more of his income to supporting his children, rather than simply to supporting himself. In addition, the appellate court held it was appropriate to consider the value of certain assets that supporting spouse and his nonmarital partner owned. Again, as we have mentioned previously, new mate income was a statutorily permissible rebuttal factor, evidence of which was allowed to be introduced to rebut the presumption that the statutory guideline amount of child support was the correct amount in the case.

Briefly we return to the language of the statute. Section 4057.5, subdivision (a)(2) provides: "The income of the obligee parent's subsequent spouse . . . shall not be considered when determining or modifying child support, except in an extraordinary case where excluding that income would lead to extreme and severe hardship to any child . . . ." In our view, the only exception to the prohibition against looking to the new mate income of the supporting or the supported spouse is "extreme and severe hardship" to a child. What we think the statute means, then, is that unless a child will suffer if the court does not look to the new mate income of a spouse involved in the child support proceeding, then the court cannot consider such income.

We believe this is the case in spite of the language in subdivision (b) of the statute, which seems to shift the focus from the child's status to the parent's conduct. That subdivision now reads: "For purposes of this section, an extraordinary case may include a parent who voluntarily or intentionally quits work or reduces income, or intentionally remains unemployed or underemployed and relies on a subsequent spouses income."

Subdivisions (a) and (b) taken together mean that if a child would suffer extreme and severe hardship if the court does not look to new mate income, then the court must look to it. If the child may suffer because one of his parents quits working deliberately, then this is an extraordinary case in which the court may look to the income of the new mate of the spouse who has quit working, but the court can only consider this in order to prevent a hardship to the supported child. Both sections 4057.5 and 4057 define what is an extraordinary case or an inappropriate or unjust case by reference to the needs of the children. The examples given in section 4057, for instance, delineate exceptions based on the needs of the children, not the needs or conduct of the parents.

We are mindful of the general provisions respondent cites to us regarding each parent's duty to support his or her children, and the privilege of the children to share in the standard of living of their parents. Nonetheless, here we are facing a direct statutory prohibition on the consideration of a particular factor in the child support scenario. While the trial court here claimed to be looking to the lifestyle or "standard of living" evidence, we find it abused its discretion by considering Casparis's income. . . .

Ordinarily we think that under the "unjust and inappropriate/special circumstances" exception, a trial court could make any equitable adjustment to the amount of child support, within reason. In this case, however, the trial court made an adjustment that the Legislature had specifically forbidden it to make. The trial court here took into account the income of Camilla's new spouse. The statute states: "the income of the obligee parent's subsequent spouse . . . shall not be considered when determining or modifying child support . . . ." (§ 4057.5, subd. (a)(2).) In our view, the only time a trial court may consider new mate income is when not considering it will result in extreme hardship to a child. Otherwise, according to the Legislature, this new mate income is a factor which may not be taken into account. Subdivision (b) regarding a spouse who intentionally does not work applies when hardship to a child results because one spouse is deliberately not working. Then the court may consider that spouse's new mate's income. To sum up, the only exception to consideration of new mate income occurs when an extreme hardship results to a child. . . .

We conclude the trial court abused its discretion by considering new mate income . . . . The problem before the trial court on remand is straightforward. Using the statutory formula, the trial court should insert William's income and attribute earning capacity to Camilla, and arrive at a guideline figure. If no supported child will suffer extreme hardship under the guideline amount, the court may not consider the income of the new spouses of William and Camilla.

DISPOSITION

The trial court's order setting child support after taking into account Camilla's new mate's income is reversed. The case is remanded for further proceedings consistent with this opinion. Each party to bear his own costs and fees on appeal. . . .

NOTES AND QUESTIONS

(1) Under the statutory standard applied in *Wood*, the only time spousal income can be considered is "when an extreme hardship results to a child" otherwise. Can you imagine when the standard would ever allow the income of the new spouse of a payee to be considered? Ordinarily, consideration of the payee's new spouse's income will result in a reduction in the amount of child support, so there seems to be no way that it could alleviate a child's hardship. The standard does make sense in the reverse situation, since considering the payor's spouse's income would increase the amount considered available for the payment of support.

(2) **Imputed Income.** The most common situation in which new spouse income is considered is of course where the parent obligor or obligee reduces income because of the availability of spousal income. Courts seem much more willing to do this where there is some form of statutory authority. *See Flanagan v. Flanagan*, 673 So. 2d 894 (Fla. Dist. Ct. App. 1996); *LaForge v. LaForge*, 649 So. 2d 151 (La. Ct. App. 1995); *see also Rogers v. Rogers*, 923 S.W.2d 381 (Mo. Ct. App. 1996) (acting without statutory authority).

(3) **Refusal to Consider New Income.** There are of course cases in which the court simply refuses to consider new income. *See In re Marriage of Hardiman*, 889 P.2d 1354 (Or. Ct. App. 1995); *In re Marriage of Ainsworth*, 835 P.2d 928 (Or. Ct. App. 1992).

(4) **Cohabitant Income.** There would seem to be less reason to include cohabitant income, although occasionally courts do. *See Jackson v. Jackson*, 907 P.2d 990 (Nev. 1995).

(5) **Alimony.** If alimony is being paid to one of the parties, should those payments be included in income? Does it make any difference if the alimony comes from a spouse in a previous marriage or from the other parent in the marriage that has produced the children?

This issue has been addressed statutorily in many jurisdictions. There are three distinct positions regarding this issue. First there are those states that allow alimony to be included regardless of its source: *see, e.g.*, Colo. Rev. Stat. §§ 14–10–115 (1997); Vt. Stat. Ann. tit. 15, § 653 (1997); Wash. Rev. Code. Ann. § 26.19.071 (1997); *Wood v. Wood*, 438 S. E.2d 778 (W. Va. 1993); *Matter of Marriage of Wesley*, 865 P.2d 432 (Or. Ct. App. 1993). In the states with statutes, alimony is simply included in the laundry list of items included in income. Second, there are those states in which alimony from the other parent is not included in income, but alimony from a previous marriage is included: *see, e.g.*, Cal. Fam. Code § 4058 (1997); D.C. Code Ann. § 16–916.1 (1997); Va. Code Ann. §§20–108.1 (1997); *Hyde v. Hyde*, 618 A.2d 406 (Pa. Super. Ct. 1992). And, finally, there are states which exclude all alimony payments regardless of source: *see, e.g.*, Alaska Civ. Proc. R. 90.3 (1997).

[D] Support for other children

HASTY v. HASTY
Supreme Court of Wyoming
828 P.2d 94 (1992)

GOLDEN, JUSTICE.

Appellant is a thrice-married parent of three minor children from his first two failed marriages and his present third marriage. He challenges the district court's interpretation and application of the federally mandated child support guidelines enacted in W.S. 20–6–301 through 306 (Supp.1991) which resulted in an upward modification of the child support award he must pay on behalf of his minor child from the first marriage.

Appellant objected to his first wife's petition, sought on behalf of the parties' one minor child, for an upward modification of the $150 per month child support award as ordered in the parties' ten-year old divorce decree. Appellant asked the district court, as it interpreted and applied the child support guidelines, to give proper recognition to his support obligations to his two other minor children from his second and third marriages. In appellant's view, the district court would give such proper recognition by factoring in his three minor children when using the child support guideline matrix found in W.S. 20–6–304(a) to determine the rebuttably presumed correct amount of child support to award the minor child from appellant's first marriage.

In the district court's decision letter, later incorporated by reference into its modification order, the court acknowledged that the state legislature had provided for deviations from the child support guidelines, depending on the court-determined presence of one or more of the statutorily designated factors. The court declared, however, that appellant's argument did not fall within any of those factors, saying "this court has no choice but to apply the guidelines."

Finding error in the district court's decision that appellant's argument did not fall within any of the statutorily designated factors which may be considered for purposes of deviating from the child support guidelines, we hold that the district court abused its discretion in reaching its modification decision. We reverse and remand for further proceedings consistent with this opinion.

FACTS

Appellant and his first wife, the appellee, were married in 1969, and had two children. The parties were divorced in 1982. In the divorce decree appellee was awarded custody of the children, and appellant was ordered to pay child support in the amount of $150 per month for each minor child. Appellant met those obligations, married a second time, and had one child from that marriage, which ended in divorce. Appellant, who does not have custody of the minor child from his second marriage, is paying child support in the amount of $166 per month. Now married a third time, appellant resides with his present wife and their minor child. Thus, appellant is supporting his three minor children.

When the parties' first child recently reached his majority, appellant ceased paying child support for that child as allowed by the original divorce decree. Appellee filed a petition for an upward modification of the child support for the parties' second child, who is still a minor. Answering the petition, appellant denied that an upward modification was warranted. A district court commissioner held a hearing on the petition and afterward submitted a report to the district court that recommended an increase of child support from $150 to $745 per month. The commissioner arrived at the increased amount using the statutory child support guidelines matrix: § 20–6–304. . . .

In using that matrix, the commissioner determined that appellant's child support for the parties' one minor child must be twenty-six percent (26%) of appellant's monthly net income, as shown on the guidelines matrix.

Appellant objected to the commissioner's report on several grounds. He contended the commissioner, in error, strictly applied the child support guidelines matrix as if appellant had only one minor child to support, thus ignoring appellant's support obligations to his other two minor children from subsequent marriages. After receiving the commissioner's report, the district court reviewed further financial information from appellant and considered his objections. The district court issued its decision letter rejecting appellant's objections, holding the child support guidelines would be applied. The district court then entered its order modifying the parties' 1982 divorce decree, increasing the child support by $595 per month for the parties' minor child. Appellant filed this appeal. . . .

DISCUSSION

Appellant asserts the trial court erroneously read and applied the child support guidelines matrix. He complains the court factored in only the parties' one minor child to derive the appropriate percentage figure by which to multiply appellant's monthly net income to determine the specific dollar amount of child support to which that one minor child is entitled. In appellant's view, a correct reading of the child support guidelines matrix requires the trial court to factor in all three of appellant's minor children when using the matrix, not the parties' one minor child. Appellant maintains the trial court can only achieve an equitable apportionment among all of the minor children dependent upon appellant for support by factoring in three as the number of minor children when using the matrix. He argues if the court factored in only the parties' one minor child, the court would reduce appellant's minor later-born children to second class status, subordinate to the minor child of appellant's first marriage.

Although we disagree with appellant's preferred reading and application of the child support guidelines matrix, we hold the trial court erroneously concluded that it had to apply the guidelines strictly and could not deviate from them by considering appellant's support obligations to his two later-born minor children. . . .

We now focus on W.S. 20–6–302 and 304(a), which are the operative provisions for determining both the specific dollar amount that is rebuttably presumed to be correct and deviations from that amount. Those provisions must be read in pari materia to convey the clear and definite meaning that the court, in using the guidelines matrix, shall factor in only the number of minor children on whose behalf the modification proceeding is brought. In a modification proceeding the petitioner is seeking modification only for the number of minor children born of petitioner's marriage to the respondent. Only that number of minor children should logically be factored into the initial determination that produces an initial child support amount for modification purposes. That initial support amount so determined is only rebuttably presumed to be correct.

At the next stage of the modification process, the court in the exercise of its discretion may deviate from that initial child support amount by resort to those factors expressly set forth in W.S. 20–6–302(b). A factor important to any respondent having later-born children from subsequent marriages is "[t]he responsibility of either parent for the support of others." W.S. 20–6–302(b)(iv). Thus, it is at this subsequent stage of the modification process that appellant's later-born minor children are factored into the final modification decision. Seen in this light, the modification process under the authority of the child support guidelines legislation represents no departure from the earlier established modification process under the authority of W.S. 20-2-113 and 116. Under either statutory authority, the noncustodial parent of a child from a prior marriage on whose behalf the modification petition is filed can ask the court to take into consideration that party's support obligation to later-born minor children from subsequent marriages. As stated in *Nuspl*, however, that party's voluntary assumption of additional obligations by remarriage "does not necessarily constrain responsibility to children of the prior marriage." *Nuspl*, 717 P.2d at 345.

Wyoming's child support guidelines represent a varying percentage-of-income standard. Minnesota has also adopted that standard. In a consistent line of decisions since adoption of the child support guidelines, Minnesota courts in child support modification cases have held that "children born to a later marriage are relevant to a decision on modification but are 'not to be factored into the child support guideline tables . . . .' *Erickson [v. Erickson*, 385 N.W.2d 301, 304 (Minn.1986)] . . . ." *County of Ramsey v. Faulhaber*, 399 N.W.2d 617, 619 (Minn.App.1987).

Another Minnesota decision stated:

> On remand, the trial court must also assess [the father's] needs and reasonable expenses. In so doing, the expenses incurred by [the father] in raising a second family may properly be considered. While an obligor cannot avoid his support obligation by voluntarily incurring new liabilities, including obligations to a second family, consideration can be given to later-born children in setting child support. Subsequent children are clearly relevant, but "are not to be factored into the child support guideline tables . . . ." *Erickson v. Erickson*, 385 N.W.2d 301, 304 (Minn.1986).

Ramsey County v. Shir, 403 N.W.2d 714, 717 (Minn.App.1987).

Given our reasoning, similar to the Minnesota courts' concordant view under that state's legislative scheme, we hold the action of the district court was correct when it did not factor appellant's three minor children into the child support guidelines matrix. However, when the district court concluded it had to strictly apply the guidelines and could not take into consideration appellant's later-born minor children for purposes of determining the amount by which to upwardly modify the child support award for the parties' one minor child, it was in error. As noted, the district court may consider appellant's responsibility for the support of his later-born children. The legislature has provided the district court a comprehensive list of factors to take into account when considering whether to deviate from the guidelines. We have previously emphasized that determination of child support amounts invokes consideration of all of the circumstances, including reasonable needs of the children and each parent's reasonable contributory ability and responsibility. Under the child support guidelines, this premise has continued vitality today. Accordingly, we hold that whenever a district court is faced with a determination of child support amounts, it is not bound to apply strictly the child support guidelines of W.S. 20–6–304(a). After all, they are only guidelines. Rather, the court should, in the exercise of its broad discretion in this area of the law, give full consideration to the statutory factors set forth in W.S. 20–6–302(b)(i)–(xiii) (Supp.1991).

Reversed and remanded.

NOTES AND QUESTIONS

(1) **The Problem.** It is very common in our society for parents to have children by more than one person. This creates a problem for computing child support. Should the calculation of child support include the obligation to support other children? And if we take other children into consideration, how should we calculate this mathematically? All jurisdictions answer this first question in the affirmative. *See* Laura Morgan, Child Support Guidelines: Interpretation and Application 3-37 (1997). The rationale is of course that all children are deserving of support. However, the states are split regarding the method of taking other children into consideration. This split also involves a philosophical difference as to whether the claims of first families are greater than those of subsequent families. *See* Rebecca Burton Garland, Note, *Second Children Second Best? Equal Protection for Successive Families Under State Child Support Guidelines*, 18 Hastings Const. L.Q. 881 (1991).

(2) **Deduction From Income.** One simple way to deal with this problem is to require or at least allow a deduction for child support paid for other children from the gross income of the parents whose support arrangement is being calculated. This approach is even mandatory in some states. *See, e.g.,* Alaska Civ. Proc. R. 90.3(1997) (quoted *above* in Note 3 of § 11.04[D]). Many other states allow the deduction at some point in the calculation: e.g. Cal. Fam. Code § 4059 (1997) which does not deduct the payments from the gross income, but allows the court to factor in a hardship deduction. This deduction has been allowed for previous court orders and for amounts paid voluntarily if actually paid. *See Flanagan v. Flanagan*, 673 So. 2d 894 (Fla. Dist. Ct. App. 1996); *Commissioner of Soc. Servs. of City of New York v. Nieves*, 644 N.Y.S.2d 744 (N.Y. App. Div. 1966). If there is a mandatory deduction, it would seem to be a preference for first families.

(3) **Deviation From Guideline.** Other courts, rather than automatically deducting the support from income, will use the existence of support for other children as a basis for deviating from the support guideline. This approach seems to be more common when dealing

with subsequent children. *See State ex rel. English v. Troisi*, 659 So. 2d 658 (Ala. Civ. App. 1995); *Burch v. Burch*, 916 P.2d 443 (Wash. Ct. App. 1996). Some states allow support for subsequent children to be a deviation factor only where there has been a motion to modify the support by the payee: e.g. *In re Marriage of Ansay*, 839 P.2d 527 (Colo. Ct. App. 1992). The deviation method if used for both families would seem to be putting both first and second families on equal footing.

[E] Extraordinarily High Income

ESTEVEZ v. SUPERIOR COURT
California Court of Appeal
27 Cal. Rptr. 2d 470 (1994)

KITCHING, ASSOCIATE JUSTICE.

Petitioner Emilio Estevez (Estevez) seeks a writ of mandate compelling the respondent superior court to vacate its order of May 3, 1993, directing Estevez to produce information and documentation relating to his income, expenses, and assets, in connection with the application of real party in interest Carey L. Salley (Salley), on behalf of herself and the two minor children of the parties, for modification of child support.

The sole question presented by the petition is whether subsequent legislative enactments have abrogated the ruling of *White v. Marciano* (1987) 190 Cal.App.3d 1026, 235 Cal.Rptr. 779, that a trial court may preclude discovery of the net worth and lifestyle of a noncustodial parent where there is no question as to that parent's ability to pay any reasonable support order. We determine the rule set forth in *White v. Marciano* remains viable, and grant the petition.

INTRODUCTION

White v. Marciano, supra, 190 Cal.App.3d 1026, 235 Cal.Rptr. 779, dealt with the Agnos Child Support Standards Act of 1984, which established a system of mandatory minimum child support amounts. (Former Civ.Code, § 4700 et seq.)

The discovery order that is the subject of this appeal was made pursuant to the child support guideline adopted and set forth in former Civil Code sections 4720 and 4721 as amended effective September 22, 1992. These and other relevant sections of the Civil Code were repealed prior to or effective January 1, 1994, and most of their provisions were enacted as sections of the new Family Code operative on the same date. The provisions of former Civil Code section 4720 now appear in Family Code sections 4050 through 4054, and the provisions of former Civil Code section 4721 now appear, with some revisions which do not affect the outcome of this case, in Family Code sections 4055 through 4069. . . .

FACTUAL AND PROCEDURAL BACKGROUND

The parties, who were never married, have two minor children, born in 1984 and 1986. In a stipulation and agreement reflected in a court order of June 1, 1987, Estevez acknowledged paternity and agreed to pay Salley child support in the total sum of $3,500 per month. Estevez also agreed to maintain a medical insurance policy, and to pay reasonable and necessary medical, hospital, and dental expenses not covered by the insurance policy.

In addition, Estevez has voluntarily provided child care, a housekeeper, vacations, food, transportation, private schooling and a four-bedroom house in Malibu with beach and tennis club facilities. He has also paid for various miscellaneous expenses.

1. *OSC re Modification of Child Support Order.*

In January 1993, Salley sought modification of the child support order to comport with the guideline then set forth in Civil Code section 4721. She estimated the support "package" then being provided by Estevez was worth in excess of $14,000 per month, and stated she was not dissatisfied with the package, but only with the manner in which it was dispensed, as Estevez was not obligated by law to provide assistance in excess of the earlier support order, and her Malibu home was provided through the generosity of Estevez's parents, who were not obligated to continue this assistance.

Salley estimated Estevez had a gross monthly income in excess of $300,000. She listed the actual monthly expenses of her household at $8,653, and her "necessary" expenses at $17,469. The latter figure includes $4,750 to $6,500 allocated to prospective mortgage payments or rent.

Salley stated she wished to obtain appropriate support under the guideline so that she could rent a home in Pacific Palisades, structure her own finances, and pursue a career as an actress. She requested that Estevez be ordered to continue providing support which would enable the children to enjoy the lifestyle to which they had become accustomed, including payment of their medical expenses as previously ordered. She also requested that Estevez be ordered to maintain a $1 million policy of insurance on his life for the benefit of each child.

2. *The Discovery Proceedings.*

On March 8, 1993, Salley served upon Estevez a plaintiff's request for production and inspection of documents and other tangible things covering the period from January 1, 1991 to the date of the request. She requested production of bank records relating to accounts standing in his name alone or jointly with any other person or for any business enterprise in which he has an interest; income records including copies of 1099 forms, W-2 forms, payroll check stubs or receipts, gifts, loans, commissions, rents, interest, dividends, annuities; books of account; records of loans made by him and monies owed to him; records of employment and fringe benefits he received; records of stock brokerage accounts; records of his debts and liabilities; and documentation of his monthly expenses.

In his response to Salley's request to produce documents, Estevez stipulated that for each of the years 1990, 1991, and 1992, he had a gross income of not less than $1.4 million per year, and that his current gross income is commensurate with those three years. He stated he could pay any reasonable amount the court determines to be necessary for the support of his two minor children.

Estevez maintained he was an extraordinarily high income earner within the meaning of . . . (Fam.Code, § 4057, subd. (b)(3)), and that any amount of child support calculated in accordance with the guideline would far exceed the reasonable needs of the children. Therefore, he urged the discovery sought by Salley was precluded by the holding of *White v. Marciano, supra,* 190 Cal.App.3d 1026, 235 Cal.Rptr. 779. He objected to production of the requested records on the grounds such production was not reasonably calculated to lead to the discovery of admissible evidence, was unduly burdensome, and unreasonably interfered with his right of privacy under Article I of the California Constitution, as well as the privacy rights of his current spouse.

Salley made several additional demands upon Estevez to produce the same documents, plus additional documents pertaining to his income and lifestyle, and trust documents, wills, codicils and estate planning documents executed from the date of his marriage to his present spouse. Estevez objected to each production demand on the same grounds he asserted in objecting to the original request.

On April 21, 1993, Salley filed her motion to compel production of documents. She acknowledged that Estevez has an "extraordinarily high income" within the meaning of . . . (Fam.Code, § 4057, subd. (b)(3)), which permits the court to deviate from the support guideline set forth in . . . (Fam.Code, § 4055). However, she claimed the court must first calculate the amount of support called for by strict adherence to the guideline, which requires that the high earner's (Estevez's) net monthly disposable income, and the total net monthly disposable income of both parties . . . be inserted into a formula set forth . . . (Fam.Code, § 4055). Only then, Salley urged, is the court to determine whether an exception should be made due to Estevez's extraordinarily high income.

At the hearing on the motion to compel production of documents held on May 3, 1993, the trial court reluctantly agreed with Salley's position. However, the court determined the quantity of documents requested by Salley was burdensome and oppressive, and, after conferring with counsel in chambers, granted the motion to produce as to a number of documents relating to both income and lifestyle, though not all of the documents requested by Salley.

DISCUSSION

At all times relevant to our discussion, i.e., at the time of *White v. Marciano, supra,* 190 Cal.App.3d 1026, 235 Cal.Rptr. 779, at the time of Salley's modification request and Estevez's petition, and at present, the Legislature intended that children share in their parents' standard of living. A child was then, and is now, to be supported in the manner suitable to the child's circumstances, taking into consideration the respective earnings or earning capacities of the parents. At the time of *White v. Marciano*, the court was required to determine the annual gross income and net disposable income of each parent. The same requirement . . . now appears in sections 4055, subdivision (b)(2), 4058, and 4059 of the Family Code. Finally, a provision that a party to the proceedings may not refuse to submit copies of income tax returns to the court, formerly set forth in Civil Code section 4700.7, now appears at section 3552 of the Family Code.

In *White v. Marciano*, the respondent stipulated that he had an annual income of $1 million; that he lived a lifestyle commensurate with that income; and that he could pay any reasonable amount of child support. The court stated: "Clearly where the child has a wealthy parent, that child is entitled to, and therefore 'needs' something more than the bare necessities of life. It is also clear that the court is required to consider, in a general sense, the noncustodial parent's standard of living. However, contrary to appellant's contentions, a trial court is not required to consider detailed lifestyle and net worth evidence in reaching a decision as to the needs of the child or the amount of support to be awarded." (190 Cal.App.3d at p. 1032, 235 Cal.Rptr. 779.)

The court determined "evidence of detailed lifestyle and net worth to be relevant only in those situations where the ability of the noncustodial parent to make adequate support payments may be affected by the unwise expenditure of income to the detriment of the supported minor. Where there is no question of the noncustodial parent's ability to pay any reasonable support order, we conclude that evidence of detailed lifestyle [is] irrelevant to the issue of the amount of support to be paid and thus protected from discovery and inadmissible in determining the support order." (*White v. Marciano, supra,* 190 Cal.App.3d at p. 1032, 235 Cal.Rptr. 779.)

In our case, Estevez stipulated that he has an annual income of not less than $1.4 million per year, and can pay any reasonable amount of child support. Salley contends *White v. Marciano* does not apply because of the legislative enactments subsequent to that decision, namely, former Civil Code sections 4720 and 4721, now Family Code sections 4050 through 4054, and 4055 through 4069.

At all of the relevant times, the Legislature has consistently expressed its intent that the courts shall adhere to the guideline and may depart from it only in the exceptional or special circumstances provided. . . .

There is a rebuttable presumption affecting the burden of proof that the amount of child support established by the guideline formula is the correct amount of child support to be ordered. This presumption "may be rebutted by admissible evidence showing that application of the formula would be unjust or inappropriate in the particular case, consistent with the principles set forth in Section 4053, because one or more of the following factors is found to be applicable by a preponderance of the evidence, and the court states in writing or on the record the information required in subdivision (a) of Section 4056: . . . (3) The parent being ordered to pay child support has an extraordinarily high income and the amount determined under the formula would exceed the needs of the children." (Fam.Code, § 4057, subd. (b))

The parties agree that application of the guideline to Estevez's stipulated annual income of $1.4 million would result in a child support amount of approximately $14,500 per month. In addition, Estevez has stipulated that he can pay *any* reasonable child support award, thereby removing the issue of his ability to pay, and indicating he will accede to any order the court may make, even one in excess of the amount called for by the guideline formula, so long as the award addresses the reasonable needs of the children commensurate with his status as an extraordinarily high earner.

We find nothing in the legislative history of the relevant sections of the Family Code . . . indicating an intent to abrogate the rule of *White v. Marciano, supra,* 190 Cal.App.3d 1026, 235 Cal.Rptr. 779. In fact, it appears the Legislature adopted the rule when it provided that the presumption of correctness of the amount of child support established by the guideline formula may be rebutted upon a showing that the parent being ordered to pay child support has an extraordinarily high income and the amount determined under the formula would exceed the children's needs. (Fam.Code, § 4057, subd. (b).)

Salley's argument is, essentially, that the presumption must first be established before it can be rebutted. In other words, she contends the trial court must first calculate the amount of support called for by the formula, then consider the needs of the children, and only then determine the presumption has been rebutted. That is what is generally required by subdivision (a) of Family Code section 4056.

The point made by *White v. Marciano* is that such an exercise is unnecessary, to say nothing of unduly burdensome and oppressive in a case like this one, because the information sought is irrelevant to the issue of the amount of child support to be paid by an extraordinarily high earner who has stipulated that he can and will pay any reasonable amount of child support. In such a case, where the extraordinarily high earner resists detailed discovery of his or her financial affairs, the trial court may make such assumptions concerning his or her net disposable income, federal income tax filing status, and deductions from gross income as are least beneficial to the extraordinarily high earner, and thereby satisfy the requirements of Family Code section 4056.

We find nothing in the uniform guideline formula presently set forth in Family Code section 4055, or formerly set forth in Civil Code section 4721, to preclude application of *White v. Marciano* to this case.

DISPOSITION

The petition for writ of mandate is granted. Let a peremptory writ issue compelling the respondent court to vacate its order of May 3, 1993, and issue a new order in conformance with the views expressed herein. . . .

NOTES AND QUESTIONS

(1) **Maximum Child Support.** Philosophically, this case would indicate that at some point there is a maximum amount of support that a child can receive. At some point it does not make any difference if the obligor makes more money; that is, a person earning $2,000,000 a year does not have to pay more for child support than a person earning $1,000,000. At some point a supported child does not get to benefit in the increased wealth of the parent. Indeed at some point wealthy people do not get the full benefit of their wealth, simply because they have so much money that they cannot spend it on themselves. The real use of the money is that it earns more money or becomes the source for philanthropy. This viewpoint makes some sense when the parents are paying at the support levels of the principal case. However, other California cases which have applied this principle determined the "maximum" support level to be much lower. In *White v. Marciano*, 235 Cal. Rptr. 779 (Cal. Ct. App. 1987) a pre-guideline award of $1500 per month was upheld for a 21-month-old child, and *In re the Marriage of Hubner*, 252 Cal. Rptr. 428 (Cal. Ct. App. 1988) upheld pre-guideline award of $2100 per month.

(2) **Discovery.** *Miller v. Schou*, 616 So. 2d 436 (Fla. 1993), rejected the principle of *Estevez* on the ground that even though a child may not fully share in the parents' wealth, he or she does have a right to discover it so that the court can determine to what degree the child can share.

(3) **Exceeding Guideline.** There is a practical problem of how to calculate the support when the level of income has exceeded the guideline chart or table. In *Voishon v. Palma*, 609 A.2d 319 (Md. 1992), reprinted in § 11.04[A], *above*, the trial court was given discretion to resolve the child support amount when guideline incomes are exceeded. In *Battersby v. Battersby*, 590 A.2d 427, 429–30 (Conn. 1991), the Supreme Court of Connecticut held that it would not construe a statute to require strict extrapolation where the legislature

included no such provision. *See also Boyt v. Romanow*, 664 So. 2d 995 (Fla. Dist. Ct. App. 1995). Other courts have continued to apply the guideline no matter what the income. *See Cassano v. Cassano*, 628 N.Y.S.2d 10 (N.Y. 1995).

(4) **Trust Fund.** In cases where one parent has an extremely high income, a trust fund may be the way in which the child can share in the parent's wealth. This is often an appealing method for the payor since he or she may be worried about the custodial parent sharing in the affluent parent's wealth. *See, e.g., In re Paternity of Tukker M. O.*, 544 N.W.2d 417 (Wis. 1996) (involving a professional football player).

§ 11.05 Duration of Support

[A] Majority/Emancipation

STANTON v. STANTON
United States Supreme Court
421 U.S. 7 (1975)

MR. JUSTICE BLACKMUN delivered the opinion of the Court.

This case presents the issue whether a state statute specifying for males a greater age of majority than it specifies for females denies, in the context of a parent's obligation for support payments for his children, the equal protection of the laws guaranteed by § 1 of the Fourteenth Amendment.

I

Appellant Thelma B. Stanton and appellee James Lawrence Stanton, Jr., were married at Elko, Nevada, in February, 1951. At the suit of the appellant, they were divorced in Utah on November 29, 1960. They have a daughter, Sherri Lyn, born in February, 1953, and a son, Rick Arlund, born in January, 1955. Sherri became 18 on February 12, 1971, and Rick on January 29, 1973.

During the divorce proceedings in the District Court of Salt Lake County, the parties entered into a stipulation as to property, child support, and alimony. The court awarded custody of the children to their mother and incorporated provisions of the stipulation into its findings and conclusions and into its decree of divorce. Specifically, as to alimony and child support, the decree provided:

> "Defendant is ordered to pay to plaintiff the sum of $300.00 per month as child support and alimony, $100.00 per month for each child as child support and $100.00 per month as alimony, to be paid on or before the 1st day of each month through the office of the Salt Lake County Clerk."

The appellant thereafter remarried; the court, pursuant to another stipulation, then modified the decree to relieve the appellee from payment of further alimony. The appellee also later remarried.

When Sherri attained 18 the appellee discontinued payments for her support. In May 1973 the appellant moved the divorce court for entry of judgment in her favor and against the appellee for, among other things, support for the children for the periods after each respectively attained the age of 18 years. The court concluded that on February 12, 1971,

Sherri "became 18 years of age, and under the provisions of [§] 15–2–1 Utah Code Annotated 1953, thereby attained her majority. Defendant is not obligated to plaintiff for maintenance and support of Sherri Lyn Stanton since that date." An order denying the appellant's motion was entered accordingly.

The appellant appealed to the Supreme Court of Utah. She contended, among other things, that Utah Code Ann. § 15–2–1 (1953) to the effect that the period of minority for males extends to age 21 and for females to age 18, is invidiously discriminatory and serves to deny due process and equal protection of the laws, in violation of the Fourteenth Amendment and of the corresponding provisions of the Utah Constitution, namely, Art. I, §§ 7 and 24, and Art. IV, § 1. On this issue, the Utah court affirmed. 30 Utah 2d 315, 517 P. 2d 1010 (1974). The court acknowledged: "There is no doubt that the questioned statute treats men and women differently," but said that people may be treated differently "so long as there is a reasonable basis for the classification, which is related to the purposes of the act, and it applies equally and uniformly to all persons within the class." *Id.*, at 318, 517 P. 2d, at 1012. The court referred to what it called some "old notions," namely, "that generally it is the man's primary responsibility to provide a home and its essentials," *ibid.*; that "it is a salutary thing for him to get a good education and/or training before he undertakes those responsibilities," *id.*, at 319, 517 P. 2d, at 1012; that "girls tend generally to mature physically, emotionally and mentally before boys"; and that "they generally tend to marry earlier," *ibid.* It concluded:

> "[It] is our judgment that there is no basis upon which we would be justified in concluding that the statute is so beyond a reasonable doubt in conflict with constitutional provisions that it should be stricken down as invalid." *Id.*, at 319, 517 P.2d, at 1013. If such a change were desirable, the court said, "that is a matter which should commend itself to the attention of the legislature." *Id.*, at 320, 517 P. 2d, at 1013. The appellant, thus, was held not entitled to support for Sherri for the period after she attained 18, but was entitled to support for Rick "during his minority" unless otherwise ordered by the trial court. *Ibid.*, 517 P.2d at 1014. . . .

We turn to the merits. The appellant argues that Utah's statutory prescription establishing different ages of majority for males and females denies equal protection; that it is a classification based solely on sex and affects a child's "fundamental right" to be fed, clothed, and sheltered by its parents; that no compelling state interest supports the classification; and that the statute can withstand no judicial scrutiny, "close" or otherwise, for it has no relationship to any ascertainable legislative objective. The appellee contends that the test is that of rationality and that the age classification has a rational basis and endures any attack based on equal protection.

We find it unnecessary in this case to decide whether a classification based on sex is inherently suspect. *See Weinberger v. Wiesenfeld*, 420 U.S. 636 (1975); *Schlesinger v. Ballard*, 419 U.S. 498 (1975); *Geduldig v. Aiello*, 417 U.S. 484 (1974); *Kahn v. Shevin*, 416 U.S. 351 (1974); *Frontiero v. Richardson*, 411 U.S. 677 (1973); *Reed v. Reed*, 404 U.S. 71 (1971).

Reed, we feel, is controlling here. That case presented an equal protection challenge to a provision of the Idaho probate code which gave preference to males over females when persons otherwise of the same entitlement applied for appointment as administrator of a decedent's estate. No regard was paid under the statute to the applicants' respective individual qualifications. In upholding the challenge, the Court reasoned that the Idaho statute accorded different treatment on the basis of sex and that it "thus establishes a classification subject to scrutiny under the Equal Protection Clause." *Id.*, at 75. The Clause, it was said, denies to States "the power to legislate that different treatment be accorded to persons placed by a statute into different classes on the basis of criteria wholly unrelated to the objective of that statute." *Id.*, at 75–76. "A classification "must be reasonable, not arbitrary, and must rest upon some ground of difference having a fair and substantial relation to the object of the legislation, so that all persons similarly circumstanced shall be treated alike.' *Royster Guano Co. v. Virginia*, 253 U.S. 412, 415 (1920)." *Id.*, at 76. It was not enough to save the statute that among its objectives were the elimination both of an area of possible family controversy and of a hearing on the comparative merits of petitioning relatives.

The test here, then, is whether the difference in sex between children warrants the distinction in the appellee's obligation to support that is drawn by the Utah statute. We conclude that it does not. It may be true, as the Utah court observed and as is argued here, that it is the man's primary responsibility to provide a home and that it is salutary for him to have education and training before he assumes that responsibility; that girls tend to mature earlier than boys; and that females tend to marry earlier than males. The last mentioned factor, however, under the Utah statute loses whatever weight it otherwise might have, for the statute states that "all minors obtain their majority by marriage"; thus minority, and all that goes with it, is abruptly lost by marriage of a person of either sex at whatever tender age the marriage occurs.

Notwithstanding the "old notions" to which the Utah court referred, we perceive nothing rational in the distinction drawn by § 15–2–1 which, when related to the divorce decree, results in the appellee's liability for support for Sherri only to age 18 but for Rick to age 21. This imposes "criteria wholly unrelated to the objective of that statute." A child, male or female, is still a child. No longer is the female destined solely for the home and the rearing of the family, and only the male for the marketplace and the world of ideas. *See Taylor v. Louisiana*, 419 U.S. 522, 535 n. 17 (1975). Women's activities and responsibilities are increasing and expanding. Coeducation is a fact, not a rarity. The presence of women in business, in the professions, in government and, indeed, in all walks of life where education is a desirable, if not always a necessary, antecedent is apparent and a proper subject of judicial notice. If a specified age of minority is required for the boy in order to assure him parental support while he attains his education and training, so, too, is it for the girl. To distinguish between the two on educational grounds is to be self-serving: if the female is not to be supported so long as the male, she hardly can be expected to attend school as long as he does, and bringing her education to an end earlier coincides with the role-typing society has long imposed. And if any weight remains in this day to the claim of earlier maturity of the female, with a concomitant inference of absence of need for support beyond 18, we fail to perceive its unquestioned truth or its significance, particularly when marriage, as the statute provides, terminates minority for a person of either sex. . . .

We therefore conclude that under any test—compelling state interest, or rational basis, or something in between—§ 15–2–1, in the context of child support, does not survive an equal protection attack. In that context, no valid distinction between male and female may be drawn.

IV

Our conclusion that in the context of child support the classification effectuated by § 15-2-1 denies the equal protection of the laws, as guaranteed by the Fourteenth Amendment, does not finally resolve the controversy as between this appellant and this appellee. With the age differential held invalid, it is not for this Court to determine when the appellee's obligation for his children's support, pursuant to the divorce decree, terminates under Utah law. The appellant asserts that, with the classification eliminated, the common law applies and that at common law the age of majority for both males and females is 21. The appellee claims that any unconstitutional inequality between males and females is to be remedied by treating males as adults at age 18, rather than by withholding the privileges of adulthood from women until they reach 21. This plainly is an issue of state law to be resolved by the Utah courts on remand; the issue was noted, incidentally, by the Supreme Court of Utah. The appellant, although prevailing here on the federal constitutional issue, may or may not ultimately win her lawsuit.

The judgment of the Supreme Court of Utah is reversed and the case is remanded for further proceedings not inconsistent with this opinion. . . .

BARIL v. BARIL
Supreme Judicial Court of Maine
354 A.2d 392 (1976)

DUFRESNE, CHIEF JUSTICE.

The District Court for Southern Androscoggin (Lewiston) on June 20, 1972 granted a divorce from the bonds of matrimony to the plaintiff-appellee, Cecile Bertha Baril and, as part of the divorce decree, ordered, among other things, that the care and custody of Irene C. Baril, minor child of the parties, be given to the plaintiff-appellee-mother and that the defendant-appellant and father of the child pay to the plaintiff the sum of twenty-five ($25.00) dollars per week toward the support of the said minor child.

From April 25, 1973 when his daughter, Irene, reached her eighteenth birthday, the defendant discontinued further support payments, believing that his daughter's attainment of that age automatically discharged him from any further obligation under the reference support order.

On June 26, 1973 the plaintiff cited the defendant for contempt of the Court's support order and prayed for execution in the amount of the arrearage, plus counsel fees for prosecution of the motion. Finding that the daughter was disabled in several particulars, the Judge of the District Court ruled that the defendant's obligation to comply with the support order incorporated in the divorce decree remained in full force and effect from and after April 25, 1973, when the daughter became eighteen years of age. The defendant was ordered to pay the accumulated arrearage under date of September 18, 1973.

On the defendant's appeal to the Superior Court, the District Court judgment was affirmed. The defendant has seasonably appealed to this Court and we sustain his appeal.

The sole question before us is, whether an order of support for a minor child issued as part of a decree in a divorce proceeding remains legally effective after that child reaches the age of eighteen years.

I. Jurisdiction

We recognize the great solicitude our courts have displayed under the divorce statute toward the infant children of divorced parents. Within the period of their minority, the statute preserves the jurisdiction of the court beyond the ability of the parties to exclude it, so that, as stated in *White v. Shalit*, 1938, 136 Me. 65 at 69, 1 A.2d 765, there can be no final judgment as to infant children in a divorce case, for they are wards of the court, and custody and support orders will primarily be directed to the best interests of the children incapacitated by the disabilities of infancy.

We also note what this Court said in *Luques v. Luques*, 1928, 127 Me. 356, at 359, 143 A. 263, at 265, respecting the statutory impact upon a divorced father's liability for support:

> "While upon a decree of divorce without any order for the custody or support of minor children, the father's common-law liability still remains, if, by virtue of the statute, an order for custody, or care and support is made, a statutory liability is substituted for the common-law liability."

Nevertheless, it is well settled in Maine that the jurisdiction and authority of the divorce court in matters of divorce and incidental relief such as orders for custody, support and counsel fees, are exclusively derived from the provisions of the statute. Jurisdiction over divorce is purely statutory and every power exercised by the court with reference to it must be found in the statutes or it does not exist.

With respect to divorce proceedings the statutes very clearly limit the authority of the court to provide for the support of offspring to cases involving minor children. Besides the express authority given to the divorce court in 19 M.R.S.A., § 752 to make an order concerning the care, custody and support of the minor children of the parties, the Legislature has by express terms rendered nugatory support orders for each child who reaches majority.

Indeed, 19 M.R.S.A., § 303 provides:

> "When by court decree a parent is required to pay to the other parent money for the support of minor children, said decree shall indicate separately the amount of money to be paid for the support of each child.
>
> *The decree of the court shall remain in force as to each child until that child either reaches majority, becomes married, becomes a member of the armed services or the decree is altered by the court.*
>
> Nothing in this section shall be construed to otherwise alter or change any obligation of support imposed by law." (emphasis supplied).

That the statutes on divorce define the subject-matter jurisdiction of the divorce court has received support in other states and the general rule is that a court in a divorce action or in supplemental proceedings thereto is without authority to provide, or to continue a provision, for the support of a child after that child attains his majority.

Absent any contract between the parties or a special statutory provision relating thereto, the wife in a divorce action or in a proceeding to enforce the support provisions of a divorce decree is not entitled to a support order against the husband and father of the child beyond the child's majority, notwithstanding the child's incapacity, physical or mental.

Our statutes, in the matter of orders for support of children in proceedings before the divorce court, do not deal in terms of specific ages, but rather, in such general terms as "support of minor children" and "until that child reaches majority." 19 M.R.S.A., §§ 303 and 752. At the time of the plaintiff's divorce and original support order on June 20, 1972 the age of majority had been reduced to 18 years of age. By Public Laws, 1972, Chapter 598, § 8, enacted by the One Hundred and Fifth Legislature in Special Session and effective June 9, 1972 [1 M.R.S.A., § 73], it was provided that "persons 18 years of age or over are declared to be of majority for all purposes," and in § 6, 'minor or minors' means any person who has not attained the age of 18 years," [1 M.R.S.A., §§ 72, 11–A].

At common law the age at which a person's status changed from that of an infant or minor to that of an adult in the case of both sexes was twenty-one years, regardless of physique, mentality, education, experience or accomplishments.

In Maine our "conceptions of personal and property rights are based upon the common law." The English common law doctrine of majority at the age of twenty-one years has been recognized and enforced by the colonists and was adopted in Maine from statehood.

Subject to constitutional limitations, the age of minority or majority and, therefore, the common law rule respecting the same are within the legislative power to regulate and control. The Legislature in its wisdom may prescribe a different age and such legislative determination is binding on the courts.

No person has a vested interest in remaining a minor until he reaches the age of twenty-one years.

In light of the statutory change of the age of majority, we hold that the District Court in the exercise of its divorce jurisdiction was in error when it ruled that the defendant's obligation to support continues after the age of eighteen years and awarded the plaintiff execution for arrearages in support payments accumulated from April 25, 1973 when the daughter, Irene, reached her eighteenth birthday. *Appeal sustained.*

NOTES AND QUESTIONS

(1) The *Stanton* decision, known as *Stanton I*, has an interesting subsequent history. The Utah Supreme Court refused to apply it, and the support issue was not resolved until the Utah Legislature determined that the age of majority for both females and males was eighteen. This history is recorded for the most part in the United States Supreme Court case known as *Stanton II*:

> Upon receiving the mandate in *Stanton I*, the Utah Supreme Court remanded the case, without directions, to the District Court of Salt Lake County. That court correctly recognized, pursuant to the parties' stipulation, that the only issue before it was whether in the absence of a validly worded statutory provision governing child-support age of majority, both sexes should be deemed to attain majority either at age 18 or at age 21. It resolved the issue by holding that, "for purposes of child support, children attain their majority at age 21." . . .
>
> On appeal, the Utah Supreme Court, by a 3–2 vote, reversed. 552 P.2d 112 (Utah 1976). Instead of deciding the issue before it, the majority held that the portion of the statute setting the age for females could be viewed in isolation from the portion setting the age for males:

Obviously the two provisions of the statute are separable and the Supreme Court of the United States in remanding this matter directed that we decide which age was correct and then legislate a bit on our own and say that the age of majority so chosen for the one sex is also the age of majority for the other sex. The oath we took when chosen as justices of the Supreme Court of Utah forbids us to encroach on the duties and functions of the legislature. However, we need not make any such determination. The age of the male child in this divorce case has never been called into question.

Id., at 112. The court reasoned that the only child before it was a female and, therefore, that the age of 18 provided in § 15–2–1 was constitutional and still applied. As further support for its result, the court declared that the mother had no interest in the equal protection issue and that the parties expected the age discrepancy to apply when the divorce decree was drafted. Finally, as if to erase any remaining doubt about the basis of its decision, the court declared:

Regardless of what a judge may think about equality, his thinking cannot change the facts of life . . . .

To judicially hold that males and females attain their maturity at the same age is to be blind to the biological facts of life.

Id., at 114. The court then undertook to reverse the entire judgment of the District Court. . . .

Stanton v. Stanton, 429 U.S. 501, 502–06 (1977).

In *Stanton II*, the Supreme Court of the United States reviewed the matter again and concluded that the second decision of the Utah Supreme Court

obviously, is inconsistent with our opinion in *Stanton I*. The thrust of *Stanton I*, and therefore the starting point for the Utah court on remand, was that males and females cannot be treated differently for child-support purposes consistently with the Equal Protection Clause of the United States Constitution. Apparently the Utah Supreme Court did not read our opinion as requiring that the child-support law must be nondiscriminatory to comply with the constitutional standard. That, of course, is a misunderstanding. Accordingly, the judgment of the Utah Supreme Court is vacated, and the case once again is remanded for further proceedings not inconsistent with this opinion."

Finally the Utah Supreme Court reconsidered the matter after the Utah Legislature passed an amendment which read, "The period of minority extends in males and females to the age of eighteen years." Utah Code Ann. § 15–2–1 (1997). The court stated, "the amendment clearly eliminated any prior discriminatory provision in the law and accomplished in an appropriate legislative manner that which this court deemed beyond its judicial function." *Stanton v. Stanton*, 564 P.2d 303, 305 (Utah 1977).

(2) **The Age of Majority.** As *Stanton I* indicates, the child support obligation ends when the child reaches the age of majority. *See generally* Charles F. Willson, *But Daddy, Why Can't I Go to College? The Frightening De-Kline of Support for Children's Post-Secondary Education*, 37 B.C. L. Rev. 1099, 1101–04 (1996) (discussing the change in the age of majority from twenty-one to eighteen). Some states use a special statutory date for the end of support duty. For example, California has this provision:

> The duty of support imposed by Section 3900 continues as to an unmarried child who has attained the age of 18 years, is a full-time high school student, and who is not self-supporting, until the time the child completes the 12th grade or attains the age of 19 years, whichever occurs first.

Cal. Fam. Code § 3901(a) (1998); *see also* N.D. Cent. Code § 14–09–08.2(1) (1997). Some states courts have refused to adopt this standard. *See, e.g., Carbonell v. Carbonell,* 618 So. 2d 326 (Fla. Dist. Ct. App. 1993); *Hunter v. Hunter,* 626 So. 2d 1069 (Fla. Dist. Ct. App. 1993).

When states first lowered the age of majority from twenty-one to eighteen, a number of issues arose as to agreements and orders which were written before the change: if an agreement or order said support went until the age of majority, did it mean the new age of majority or the old; if the agreement or order specified twenty-one, was that the intended term or did that merely refer to the age of majority? The states split on both of these questions and much confusion existed during the transitional period. *See* Jeffrey F. Ghent, Annotation, *Statutory Change of Age of Majority as Affecting Pre-Existing Status or Rights,* 75 A.L.R.3d 228 (1977).

(3) **Emancipation.** The two most common forms of emancipation which lead to an end of support before majority are marriage and enlistment in the military. When the child leaves home and begins to be self-supporting, the circumstances may be such that the child is in fact emancipated and support may cease. However, in this latter circumstance, the de facto emancipation should be considered to be changed circumstances which justify modification of support. *See* Michael J. Greene, Annotation, *What Voluntary Acts of Child, Other than Marriage or Entry into Military Service, Terminate Parent's Obligation to Support,* 32 A.L.R.3d 1055 (1970). There can be no doubt that courts have discretion in such a case. For example, in *In re Marriage of O'Connell,* 146 Cal. Rptr. 26 (Cal. Ct. App. 1978), a judicial decree emancipating the child was insufficient to end the support obligation. It is also possible for a minor to lose the emancipated status; for example, when a married teenager gets a divorce while still a minor. But for an argument that once a minor is emancipated, he or she should not lose that status, see Garner, Note, *Don't Come Cryin' to Daddy! Emancipation of Minors: When is a Parent 'Free at Last' from the Obligation of Child Support?,* 33 J. Fam. L. 927 (1995).

(4) **Death of Supporting Parent.** Should the obligation to pay child support continue after the death of the supporting parent? The Uniform Marriage and Divorce Act answers this question in the affirmative; Section 316(c) states:

> Unless otherwise agreed in writing or expressly provided in the decree, provisions for the support of the child are terminated by emancipation of the child but not by the death of a parent obligated to support the child. When a parent obligated to pay support dies the amount of support may be modified, revoked, or commuted to a lump sum payment, to the extent necessary and appropriate in the circumstances.

Uniform Marriage and Divorce Act § 316(c) 9A U.L.A. 490 (West 1987). This type of provision has withstood an equal protection challenge in *Kujawinski v. Kujawinski,* 376 N.E.2d 1382 (Ill. 1978). There are also cases which have ordered the support to continue past the death of the parent. *See Bailey v. Bailey,* 471 P.2d 220 (Nev. 1970). In effect, these statutes and cases mean that a support order may be entered against the estate of the parent. However, absent statutory authority, the duty to support usually ends at the death of the parent. This view is an extension of the rule that married parents have no duty to support after death, but rather that the laws of intestacy and pretermitted heirs protect the children. *See* Susan L. Thomas, *Death of Obligor Parent as Affecting Decree for Support of Child*, 14 A.L.R.5th 557 (1993).

Can the court include in a support award a requirement that a life insurance policy be maintained in favor of the child? What effect should the rule that the support obligation ceases after the death of the parent have on such decrees? *See Hudson v. Aetna Life Ins. Co.*, 545 F. Supp. 209 (E.D. Mo. 1982). The parents can of course agree that the supporting parent have a life insurance policy with the child or the custodian as the beneficiary. *See* Note, *Child Support, Life Insurance and the Uniform Marriage and Divorce Act*, 67 Ky. L.J. 239 (1978).

In both jurisdictions which do not allow support obligations to survive and those that do, life insurance is an appropriate vehicle to deal with support problems due to the death of a parent. The parties are of course free to agree to the maintenance of a life insurance policy. Once the parties have reached an agreement, courts may order them to comply with their agrreement by including such a policy as part of an overall support award.

(5) **Retroactive Postminority Support.** A few courts have ordered retroactive child support; that is, support ordered after a child has reached the age of majority to compensate the custodial parent for the costs of child rearing. *See Stanford v. Stanford*, 628 So. 2d 701 (Ala. Civ. App. 1993).

[B] Support for College

CHILDERS v. CHILDERS
Supreme Court of Washington
575 P.2d 201 (1978)

HICKS, ASSOCIATE JUSTICE.

In a dissolution proceeding, may a parent be required to support a child beyond the age of majority while a college education is pursued? Within the sound discretion of the trial court, our answer is yes.

The trial court entered a decree of dissolution and awarded the custody of the children to the petitioner (wife), divided the property, fixed support payments to be paid by the respondent (husband), and awarded an attorney's fee. The court's order required husband to pay support for the parties' three sons while they attend college. Should each of the sons elect to complete work for a baccalaureate degree, each would be 22 years of age. That is 4 years beyond the present age of majority. . . .

The 1973 dissolution act, RCW 26.09, eliminated all reference to minority, and granted the court authority to order support for dependent children to whom a duty of support is owed. RCW 26.09.100 provides in part:

> [The] court may order either or both parents owing a duty of support to any child of the marriage dependent upon either or both spouses to pay an amount reasonable or necessary for his support.

We construe the dissolution act as basing any support obligation on dependency, not minority, and ending the obligation at emancipation, not majority. Though it appears that emancipation, as the term is used in this act, is determined by factors in addition to age, we do not address the question as it is not an issue in this case. RCW 26.09.170 states that child support obligations cease when the child becomes emancipated unless, as here, it is otherwise provided in the decree. Since the trial court is empowered under RCW 26.09 to order support to continue past a child's majority, we turn now to determine if there is an abuse of discretion in so ordering under the facts of this case. . . .

We find no abuse of discretion in the trial court's determination that the Childers' boys were dependents. They lived at home and were not self-sustaining at the time the decree was entered. As to their status as dependents continuing through 4 years of continuous pursuit of a baccalaureate degree, we think it reasonable to assume that a medical doctor, himself with years of higher education which brings him a higher than average income, would willingly treat his sons as dependents if they chose and showed an aptitude for college, but for the fact of the divorce. Where, as here, the children would have most likely remained dependent on their father past 18 while they obtained a college education, it is within the discretion of the trial court to define them as dependents for that purpose. . . .

The child of divorced parents should be in no worse position than a child from an unbroken home whose parents could be expected to supply a college education. Where the disability is internally or externally caused, the child whose parents are still married will most often continue to receive support after majority. To terminate support when the parents are divorced creates a special disadvantage not shared by children whose parents remain together. If the father could have been expected to provide advanced education for his child, it is not unfair to expect him to do so after he has been divorced. . . .

We affirm the trial court in all respects. We reverse the Court of Appeals in regard to support of the Childers' sons terminating at age 18.

IN RE MARRIAGE OF PLUMMER
Supreme Court of Colorado
735 P.2d 165 (1987)

VOLLACK, JUSTICE.

Petitioner, John R. Plummer, seeks review of the court of appeals' opinion which affirmed the trial court's holding that the petitioner's daughter, who had reached the age of majority and was enrolled in college, is not emancipated and therefore still entitled to receive support payments from her divorced father. I.

The parties were divorced in 1979 and permanent orders were entered in 1980. At the time of the entry of permanent orders, the parties' two daughters were nineteen and seventeen years of age. The final orders made no provision concerning child support. However, the father voluntarily contributed to the support of both daughters. He terminated payments for the older daughter when she reached age twenty-one; at that time she was in her fourth year of college. When the younger daughter, Karen, reached age twenty-one, the father also stopped his voluntary support contributions. Karen was in her third year of college when she became twenty-one. When the voluntary payments stopped in 1984, her mother filed a motion for an award of child support. The trial court entered an order requiring the father to pay $200 per month for support until Karen received her undergraduate degree or is otherwise emancipated due to other circumstances. The trial court held, and the court of appeals agreed, that the daughter needed to "attend college to fulfill her career needs, and that she had a reasonable expectation that she would attend college and would receive the support of her parents" while she did so. *Plummer*, 703 P.2d at 658. The father argued that, in the absence of a contrary provision in a support order entered prior to emancipation, the duty to support a child terminates when the child reaches twenty-one years of age, unless the child is physically or emotionally disabled. The father appealed from entry of the order requiring him to pay $200 per month for his twenty-one year old daughter's college expenses. The court of appeals affirmed the award, citing our decision in *Koltay v. Koltay*, 667 P.2d 1374 (Colo. 1983). The court of appeals also cited provisions of the Uniform Dissolution of Marriage Act [hereinafter UDMA], which set forth the factors to be considered by a court in awarding child support. We find that the court of appeals erroneously expanded our holding in *Koltay* and therefore reverse.

II.

Orders of child support payments are governed by the Uniform Dissolution of Marriage Act. §§ 14–10–101 to 133, 6 C.R.S. (1973 & 1986 Supp.). A trial court may order either or both parents to pay child support after considering a number of factors. § 14–10–115, 6 C.R.S. (1973). The general rule is that a child support award falls within the sound discretion of the trial court and will not be disturbed on appellate review, absent an abuse of discretion. *Carlson v. Carlson*, 178 Colo. 283, 288, 497 P.2d 1006, 1009 (1972).

The UDMA provides in pertinent part: "Unless otherwise agreed in writing or expressly provided in the decree, provisions for the support of a child are terminated by emancipation of the child . . . ." § 14–10–122(3), 6 C.R.S. (1973). "What constitutes emancipation is a question of law." *In re Marriage of Robinson*, 629 P.2d 1069, 1072 (Colo. 1981). "Emancipation ordinarily occurs upon the attainment of majority," *Koltay*, 667 P.2d at 1376, which is statutorily defined in Colorado as age twenty-one. § 2–4–401(6), 1B C.R.S. (1980). We have held that at age twenty-one, a presumption arises that a person has "the physical and mental capabilities to support himself . . . ." *Koltay*, 667 P.2d at 1376. Accordingly, "[u]nder normal circumstances, parents have no legal obligation to support their children beyond the age of majority." *Id.* . . .

Other jurisdictions have followed this line of reasoning. *See Huckaba v. Huckaba*, 336 So. 2d 1363 (Ala. App. 1976) (trial court erred in requiring husband to pay for nineteen-year-old child's education where age of majority is nineteen, because father's obligation is only to his minor children); *Grapin v. Grapin*, 450 So. 2d 853 (Fla. 1984) (parent does not have legal duty to provide post-majority support just because an otherwise healthy child is attending college, unless there has been a finding of legal dependence or a binding contractual agreement); *West v. West*, 131 Vt. 621, 312 A.2d 920 (1973) (trial court does not have authority to create obligation that parent must pay for child's college education beyond the child's age of majority, although the parties may otherwise agree to such a provision). *See generally*, Annotation, *Responsibility of Noncustodial Divorced Parent to Pay for, or Contribute to, Costs of Child's College Education*, 99 A.L.R.3d 322 (1980).

The respondent asks us to apply *Childers v. Childers*, 575 P.2d 201 (Wash. 1978), in which the Washington Supreme Court held that under some circumstances a divorced parent may be required to support a child who is in pursuit of higher education past the age of majority. We decline to adopt this line of reasoning, and limit *Koltay* as set out above.

Accordingly, we reverse.

NOTES AND QUESTIONS

(1) **Support for College.** Can the difference between *Childers* and *Plummer* be accounted for merely by the differences between the statutes involved? Do you think that the disparate situations of children of divorced parents and other children justify the disparate treatment that the court in *Childers* gives to divorced parents?

The split of authority represented by *Childers* and *Plummer* continues. Here are some recent cases ordering support: *In Matter of Anonymous*, 684 So. 2d 1337 (Ala. Civ. App. 1996) (father who had no relationship with child since she was a baby ordered to pay support through college); *Stover v. Stover*, 645 N.E.2d 1109 (Ind. Ct. App. 1995). Here are two which have denied support: *In re Marriage of Baker*, 485 N.W.2d 860 (Iowa Ct. App. 1992); *Gabel v. Lores*, 608 So. 2d. 1365 (Ala. Civ. App. 1992). See Charles F. Willson, *But Daddy, Why Can't I Go to College? The Frightening De-Kline of Support for Children's Post-Secondary Education*, 37 B.C. L. Rev. 1099, 1101–04 (1996); Jeff Atkinson, *Support for a Child's Post-Majority Education*, 22 Loy. U. Chi. L.J. 695 (1991).

(2) **Conditions.** Can or should a court place conditions on college support? In *Eastis v. Bredehoft*, 599 So. 2d 53, (Ala. Civ. App. 1992), there was a limitation on the college which the child could attend. In *Moscheo v. Moscheo*, 838 S.W.2d 226 (Tenn. Ct. App. 1992), the court required the child to maintain passing grades as a condition of the father's payment of support.

(3) **Agreements.** Even if a statute terminates child support upon the child reaching majority, parents can still agree to support the child through the college years, and such an agreement will generally be enforceable. *See, e.g., Botner v. Botner*, 545 N.W.2d 188 (N.D. 1996); *H.P.A. v. S.C.A.*, 704 P.2d 205 (Alaska 1985); *Jameson v. Jameson*, 306 N.W.2d 240 (S.D. 1981). But note that in a state which would not allow court-ordered support past majority for college, a court has held the agreement for college support was void and not enforceable by the mother. *See Noble v. Fisher*, 894 P.2d 118 (Idaho 1995).

(4) **Equal Protection Challenges to Support-for-College Statutes.** Statutes requiring support through college for children of divorced parents have also been subjected to attack based on irrational preference. Pennsylvania enacted the 1993 College Expenses Act which required a parent to pay for the child's expenses; however this statute was struck down by the Pennsylvania Supreme Court as a violation of the equal protection clause. *See Curtis v. Kline*, 666 A.2d 265 (Pa. 1995). The court found that the classification involved children of intact families versus those of divorced parents. The court found no rational basis for this classification.

> It is not inconceivable that in today's society a divorced parent, e.g., a father, could have two children, one born of a first marriage and not residing with him and the other born of a second marriage and still residing with him. Under Act 62, such a father could be required to provide post-secondary educational support for the first child but not the second, even to the extent that the second child would be required to forego a college education. Further, a child over the age of 18, of a woman whose husband had died, would have no action against the mother to recover costs of a post-secondary

education, but a child over the age of 18, of a woman who never married, who married and divorced, or even who was only separated from her husband when he died would be able to maintain such an action. These are but two examples demonstrating the arbitrariness of the classification adopted in Act 62.

Id. at 270.

However, in *LeClair v. LeClair*, 624 A.2d 1350 (N.H. 1993), the New Hampshire Supreme Court reached the opposite result with a similar statute. The court applied the constitutional rational basis test to a different classification, that of married parents versus unmarried parents. The court concluded,

> In summary, we find that the State has the dual legitimate interests of promoting higher education for its citizens, and of extending protections to children of divorce to ensure that they are not deprived of opportunities they otherwise would have received had their parents not divorced. [The challenged provisions] are rationally related to protecting these interests, and do so in a manner that is neither arbitrary nor without reasonable justification.

Id. at 1357.

(5) **Incapacitated Adult Child.** The Uniform Civil Liability For Support Act § 1 requires that a parent support "a child" and defines *child* as "a son or daughter under the age of [ ] and a son or daughter of whatever age who is incapacitated from earning a living and without sufficient means." 9 U.L.A. 337 (West 1987). The court in *Baril* (excerpted in § 11.04[A], *above*) refused to apply this provision, which had been adopted in Maine, because the Act did not create a right to support which could be enforced by a former spouse in a proceeding which was supplemental to a divorce. The court recognized that an incapacitated adult child would have a right to support enforceable by the child herself. For an example of a state which expressly empowered the divorce court to order or continue support for an incapacitated adult child, see Ariz. Rev. Stat. § 25–501 (1997). States which do not have statutory authorization are split on whether courts can order such support, although the majority allow it. *See* 2 Homer H. Clark, *The Law of Domestic Relations in the United States* 357–58 (2d ed. 1987). Finally Professor Clark reports that the majority of states which do not have any form of statute on this subject do allow support for an incapacitated adult child. *Id.* at 358.

§ 11.06 Modification of Support

IN RE THE MARRIAGE OF McCORD
Colorado Court of Appeals
910 P.2d 85 (1995)

Opinion by JUDGE METZGER.

In this post-dissolution of marriage proceeding, David L. McCord (father) appeals the order modifying his child support obligation and awarding Deborah A. McCord (mother) her attorney fees. We dismiss the appeal in part, affirm the trial court's order, and remand the cause for further proceedings.

The parties' marriage was dissolved in 1988. Custody of their minor child was awarded to mother, and father was ordered to pay $300 per month in child support. At the time of the dissolution, father was employed as a construction worker and was earning approximately $16,400 per year. Mother was earning approximately $14,500 per year as a clerical worker.

In April 1994, father won an annuity worth $2 million in the Colorado State Lottery and received his first installment payment of $50,000.

Mother thereafter filed a motion seeking a modification in child support, alleging that father's increased income constituted a material change in circumstances . . . .

At a hearing on June 24, father and his counsel appeared and presented evidence regarding father's lottery winnings and his decision, upon learning of his good fortune, to quit his job and become "self-employed."

Based on the evidence presented at the hearing, the magistrate concluded that mother's gross monthly income was $952. The magistrate determined that father was voluntarily unemployed and imputed to him the annual income he had earned before his resignation. The magistrate further found that father's lottery winnings constituted gross income for purposes of calculating child support and that his gross monthly income from his lottery proceeds and employment totaled $5,538. Applying the child support guidelines, § 14-10-115, C.R.S. (1987 Repl.Vol. 6B), the magistrate increased father's child support obligation to $781 per month . . . .

On petition by father, the district court affirmed the magistrate's findings and order. . . .

II.

Father contends that the magistrate erred in modifying his child support obligation because mother failed to show a change of circumstances warranting such a modification. We disagree.

A parent's child support obligation may be modified upon a showing of changed circumstances that are substantial and continuing.

Here, father acknowledges that his financial resources increased dramatically and that his increase in income constitutes a substantial and continuing change in circumstances. He claims, however, that his increased income alone was insufficient to establish changed circumstances justifying a modification and that mother also should have been required to demonstrate an increased economic need on the child's part. We are not persuaded.

If the party requesting modification demonstrates that an increase in the obligor's income would result in at least a 10 percent change in the amount of child support, the child's increased needs are presumed. See, In re Marriage of Larsen, 805 P.2d 1195 (Colo. App. 1991); In re Marriage of Anderson, 761 P.2d 293 (Colo. App. 1988).

Moreover, nothing in the statute precludes the trial court from ordering a support payment that exceeds the known needs of the child. *In re Marriage of Nimmo*, 891 P.2d 1002, 1007 (Colo.1995) ("The guidelines were not enacted to prevent an increase in a child's standard of living by denying a child the fruits of one parent's good fortune.").

Here, father conceded that mother had demonstrated a substantial change in the parties' financial circumstances and he did not present any evidence rebutting the presumption of need of the child. Accordingly, the magistrate correctly determined that father's increased income constituted a change of circumstances warranting modification of his child support obligation. . . .

IV.

Father next contends that the magistrate erred in concluding that he is voluntarily unemployed and in imputing to him the annual income he had earned prior to his resignation. We are not persuaded.

If a parent is voluntarily unemployed or underemployed, child support must be calculated based on the parent's potential income. However, a parent may not be considered voluntarily unemployed if he or she is physically or mentally incapacitated.

Here, father maintains that he was incapable of performing physical labor and that his decision to resign from his job was a good faith career choice. Accordingly, he maintains that the magistrate erred in imputing to him his potential income from employment.

The record shows that, before winning the lottery, father earned approximately $16,400 per year as a construction worker. Father testified that he injured his back in January 1992 and that the injury affected his ability to work in a physically demanding job. He indicated that, although he continued to work as a construction laborer for over a year after he was injured, he quit his job immediately upon winning the lottery because his back injury made it too difficult for him to work. He did not present any evidence, however, to support his assertion that he was physically incapable of working.

With respect to his current employment, father testified that he was "self-employed" and that this "employment" consisted of investing his winnings and "trying to figure out what type of business I want to be in."

This evidence amply supports the magistrate's determination that father quit his job because he won the lottery, that he was physically capable of working but was voluntarily unemployed, and that his decision to resign from his job was not a good faith career choice. Thus, the magistrate did not err in imputing to father the annual income he had earned prior to his resignation.

We reject father's contention that as long as his lottery winnings provide him with the same or more income than he earned when he was employed, the court may not impute to him the annual income he earned before quitting his job and that a gross income figure that combines his imputed income and his lottery winnings is excessive.

The statute provides that income may come "from any source," and the definition of "gross income" expressly includes gifts and prizes. In our view, lottery winnings constitute gifts or prizes within the meaning of the statute and are therefore includable as gross income.

Moreover, while the statute may not specifically include lottery winnings within the definition of income, its broad language satisfies us that the General Assembly intended to include lottery winnings as income for purposes of calculating a parent's child support obligation.

Thus, there was no abuse of discretion in the conclusion that father's potential income from employment as well as his lottery winnings are includable as income for purposes of calculating child support, even though his gross income after winning the lottery exceeds the income he earned when he was employed. . . .

NOTES AND QUESTIONS

(1) **Traditional Changed Circumstances.** The traditional standard for modification of child support has been the changed-circumstances test. There has been a modern trend to raise the standard in order to increase the finality of child support awards requiring, in Alabama for example, that." . . . the changed circumstances must be material, substantial and continuing." *See, e.g., Marchman v. Marchman*, 571 So. 2d 1210 (Ala. 1990) (support modification upheld because of the father's increased income, a child entering school and another child involved in extracurricular activities); *Moore v. Moore*, 575 So. 2d 95 (Ala. 1990) (mother failed to show substantial changes to warrant a modification of support). This trend is evident in the language of § 316(a) of the Uniform Marriage and Divorce Act:

> [T]he provisions of any decree respecting maintenance or support may be modified only as to installments accruing subsequent to the motion for modification and only upon a showing of changed circumstances so substantial and continuing as to make the terms unconscionable . . . .

Uniform Marriage and Divorce Act § 316(a), 9A U.L.A. 489–90 (West 1987).

Where a change in circumstances affects the child, the supporting parent or the custodial parent may justify the modification of support. As to the child, the change generally amounts to increased need: the child may need medical care, special schooling or training. The noncustodial parent may have a substantial increase in income and, because the child is allowed to share in the parent's standard of living, an increase in support may be justified. By the same token, a substantial decrease in income may mean that the supporting parent simply cannot cover the cost of support and a decrease is justified. Similarly, a change in the custodial parent's income can increase or decrease the need for support from the other parent.

(2) **Modification of Guideline.** While the changed-circumstances test is still good law, the dominant issue with the statutory support is whether deviation from the guideline constitutes a sufficient change in circumstances. *McCord*, the principal case, illustrates this concern and the response dictated by the federal mandate. Federal rules require states to adopt provisions which make any inconsistency between the support order and guideline grounds for modification. 45 C.F.R. § 303.8(d)(1). However, the Federal rules have allowed the states to establish "a reasonable quantitative standard" which can be expressed in a dollar figure or in a percentage and must be met in order for the inconsistency to be the basis of the modification. 45 C.F.R. § 303.8(d)(2).

The states have opted for quantitative standards of ten to thirty percent. *See* Laura Morgan, Child Support Guidelines: Interpretation and Application 5-11, 5-12 (1997). In other words, in a state which adopts the ten percent standard, modification can occur as soon as the deviation between the actual support order and the present guideline amount reaches ten percent or more. If the support order was based upon bone fide deviation from the guideline, then the court must apply the changed circumstance test. *See* 45 C.F.R. § 303.8(d)(1)(ii).

This approach mandated by federal law has two important implications. First, modification is no longer primarily needs driven; it is assumed that needs are incorporated in the guideline. Second, this approach incorporates the principle that children are entitled to share in the increased wealth of the parents. See *Graham v. Graham*, 597 A.2d 355 (D.C. 1991)

(3) **Adoption of Guideline as Changed Circumstances.** When guidelines were first adopted, the states were faced with the dilemma as to whether pre-guideline orders were modifiable to the guideline. The states that resolved this problem, either by case law or statute, split on the proper approach. The results in the various states are documented in an excellent book by Laura Morgan, who makes the following observation:

> It is worth noting that in most of the cases where the court determined that enactment of the guidelines constituted a change in circumstances, the petitioning party was the custodial parent seeking an upward modification; in most of the cases where the court determined enactment of the guidelines did not constitute a change in circumstances, the petitioning party was the noncustodial parent seeking a downward modification.

Laura Morgan, Child Support Guidelines: Interpretation and Application 5-8 (1997).

(4) **Imputed Income.** Some of the most common changed circumstances have already been discussed above in § 11.04, subsections [B] "Actual Income or Capacity to Earn?," [C] "Spousal Income," and [D] "Support for Other Children." The issues presented in these subsections are all important to modification. If a parent has a sudden decrease in income, the court must decide whether the change is voluntary or involuntary and, in some states, whether a voluntary decrease is in good faith or not. A court may have to decide if income should be imputed to a parent.

(5) **Increased Income.** While the present guideline approach to modification allows the child to share in the parents' increased income, traditionally, the majority of courts held that the increase alone was not enough; it was also necessary to show increased need. See *In re Sharp*, 382 N.E.2d 1279 (Ill. App. Ct. 1978); *In re Marriage of Burroughs*, 691 S.W.2d 470 (Mo. Ct. App. 1985); *Nolte v. Nolte*, 544 So. 2d 1146 (Fla. Dist. App. 1989); *Yeatman v. Gortney*, 562 So. 2d 258 (Ala. Civ. App. 1990). The present approach was clearly the minority. See *Graham v. Graham*, 597 A.2d 355 (D.C. 1991); *In re Marriage of Catalano*, 204 Cal. App. 3d 1035, 251 Cal. Rptr. 370 (Cal. Ct. App. 1988); and *Wilson v. Wilson*, 520 N.E.2d 1230 (Ill. App. Ct. 1988).

(6) **Nonmodification of Accrued Arrearages.** In pre-guideline days there were a few states which allowed modifications of arrearages; that is, past support payments which are owed to the custodial parent. The practice has been outlawed by federal statute and regulation. See 42 U.S.C. § 666(a)(9)(C) (1997); 45 C.F.R § 303.106. The adoption of a child by a stepparent does not alleviate the duty to pay arrearages, although sometimes the *quid pro quo* of consent to stepparent adoption is forgiveness of past due arrearages. See *Kranz v. Kranz*, 661 So. 2d 876 (Fla. Dist. Ct. App. 1995); *In re Marriage of Ramirez*, 840 P.2d 311 (Ariz. Ct. App. 1992); *Michels v. Weingartner*, 848 P.2d 1010 (Kan. Ct. App. 1993), *aff'd*, 864 P.2d 1189 (Kan. 1993).

(7) **Escalator Clauses.** In a marital settlement agreement, parties can include clauses which will automatically increase the support on a specific date or upon the occurrence of an event. The support can also be increased in response to a cost of living increase. This device, commonly known as an escalator clause, can be a handy tool for meeting the needs of children and to decrease hostility between the parties in the future. However, in states in which a change in the guideline support amount is grounds for modification,

escalator clauses may be of diminishing use. Still, most commentators have argued for the continuing use of escalator clauses. *See* Maria P. Imbalzano, *The Impact of Escalation Clauses Modifying Child Support in Marital Agreements or Court Orders*, 10 Am. J. Fam L. 91 (1996); J. Thomas Oldham, *Abating the Feminization of Poverty: Changing the Rules Governing Post-Decree Modification of Child Support Obligations*, 1994 B.Y.U. L. Rev. 841 (1994); Sarah K. Funke, *Preserving the Purchasing Power of Child Support Awards: Can the Use of Escalator Clauses be Justified After the Family Support Act?*, 69 Ind. L.J. 921 (1994).

(8) **Problem.** Donald has lived with his mother since he was twelve, when his mother and father were divorced. Donald sees his father, who lives in another city, twice a year. They are not close. Donald has never been a good student, but because his mother was insistent, he applied to college. Thanks to some good luck on the Scholastic Aptitude Test, he was accepted. Reluctantly, he enrolled, to placate his mother.

Donald's father, who by court order must continue to support Donald past majority if he is enrolled in college, knows that Donald is not, at least at this time in his life, academically inclined, and indeed believes that Donald should leave school to work for awhile. Donald's father hopes that later, when Donald matures, he will return and get his degree. Donald is on academic probation and has become involved in the campus drug scene. His father tells him he must turn over a new leaf or leave school. Donald, after a heated argument with his mother, tells his father that he wants to stay in school, but he will drop his drug-oriented friends. Donald's father has him followed and discovers that he is still involved with the same crowd. Donald's father cuts off support to get him away from the school.

Donald, however, continues on in school, and his mother brings an action for enforcement of support. Donald's father makes a motion to modify support. What should the court do?

(9) **Problem.** At the time of their divorce, Frank's gross income was $3100 per month; Mona was unemployed, but she received $250 per month in interest. They have two daughters, Denise, age 14, and Susie, age 12. Frank was ordered to pay Mona $1200 spousal support per month and $150 child support per month for each daughter. According to the order, after four years the spousal support would terminate, but child support would increase to $400 per month, with yearly cost-of-living increases, for each child until they reach majority or finish graduate school. In addition, Frank must keep the girls on his medical and dental plans, which costs an additional $100 per month, and when the girls reach college he must pay one-half of their college expenses.

Six years later Frank is making $4500 per month and Mona $1750 per month. Frank has married Karen, who has a son, Johnny, living with Frank and Karen. Karen, who is pregnant, does not work and receives neither spousal or child support from her ex-husband. Denise is a Junior in college and Susie a Freshman. Frank has continued to pay child support to Mona, which is now $600 for each daughter as a result of the built in cost of living increases, and in addition pays approximately $10,000 per year for college expenses for each daughter. The cost of medical insurance for Denise and Susie has risen to $150 per month.

Frank brings an action to modify child support to $150 per month payable directly to each daughter and to end his duty to support when his daughters graduate from college. (Frank has told his daughters that if they truly want to go to graduate school he will do his best to help them as much as possible.) Mona opposes Frank. What should the court do?

§ 11.07 Enforcement of Support Orders

[A] State Remedies

HICKS v. FEIOCK
Supreme Court of the United States
485 U.S. 624 (1988)

JUSTICE WHITE delivered the opinion of the Court. . . .

I

On January 19, 1976, a California state court entered an order requiring respondent, Phillip Feiock, to begin making monthly payments to his ex-wife for the support of their three children. Over the next six years, respondent only sporadically complied with the order, and by December 1982 he had discontinued paying child support altogether. His ex-wife sought to enforce the support orders. On June 22, 1984, a hearing was held in California state court on her petition for ongoing support payments and for payment of the arrearage due her. The court examined respondent's financial situation and ordered him to begin paying $150 per month commencing on July 1, 1984. The court reserved jurisdiction over the matter for the purpose of determining the arrearages and reviewing respondent's financial condition. . . .

At a hearing on August 9, 1985, petitioner made out a prima facie case of contempt against respondent by establishing the existence of a valid court order, respondent's knowledge of the order, and respondent's failure to comply with the order. Respondent defended by arguing that he was unable to pay support during the months in question. This argument was partially successful, but respondent was adjudged to be in contempt on five of the nine counts. He was sentenced to 5 days in jail on each count, to be served consecutively, for a total of 25 days. This sentence was suspended, however, and respondent was placed on probation for three years. As one of the conditions of his probation, he was ordered once again to make support payments of $150 per month. As another condition of his probation, he was ordered, starting the following month, to begin repaying $50 per month on his accumulated arrearage, which was determined to total $1,650.

At the hearing, respondent had objected to the application of Cal.Civ.Proc.Code Ann. § 1209.5 (West 1982) against him, claiming that it was unconstitutional under the Due Process Clause of the Fourteenth Amendment because it shifts to the defendant the burden of proving inability to comply with the order, which is an element of the crime of contempt. This objection was rejected, and he renewed it on appeal. The intermediate state appellate court agreed with respondent and annulled the contempt order . . . . The California Supreme Court denied review, but we granted certiorari. . . .

III

A

The question of how a court determines whether to classify the relief imposed in a given proceeding as civil or criminal in nature, for the purposes of applying the Due Process Clause and other provisions of the Constitution, is one of long standing, and its principles have been settled at least in their broad outlines for many decades. When a State's proceedings are involved, state law provides strong guidance about whether or not the State is exercising its authority "in a nonpunitive, noncriminal manner," and one who challenges the State's classification of the relief imposed as "civil" or "criminal" may be required to show "the clearest proof" that it is not correct as a matter of federal law. Nonetheless, if such a challenge is substantiated, then the labels affixed either to the proceeding or to the relief imposed under state law are not controlling and will not be allowed to defeat the applicable protections of federal constitutional law. This is particularly so in the codified laws of contempt, where the "civil" and "criminal" labels of the law have become increasingly blurred.

Instead, the critical features are the substance of the proceeding and the character of the relief that the proceeding will afford. "If it is for civil contempt the punishment is remedial, and for the benefit of the complainant. But if it is for criminal contempt the sentence is punitive, to vindicate the authority of the court." *Gompers v. Bucks Stove & Range Co.*, 221 U.S. 418, 441, 31 S.Ct. 492, 498, 55 L.Ed. 797 (1911). The character of the relief imposed is thus ascertainable by applying a few straightforward rules. If the relief provided is a sentence of imprisonment, it is remedial if "the defendant stands committed unless and until he performs the affirmative act required by the court's order," and is punitive if "the sentence is limited to imprisonment for a definite period." *Id.*, at 442, 31 S.Ct. at 498. If the relief provided is a fine, it is remedial when it is paid to the complainant, and punitive when it is paid to the court, though a fine that would be payable to the court is also remedial when the defendant can avoid paying the fine simply by performing the affirmative act required by the court's order. These distinctions lead up to the fundamental proposition that criminal penalties may not be imposed on someone who has not been afforded the protections that the Constitution requires of such criminal proceedings, including the requirement that the offense be proved beyond a reasonable doubt. . . .

IV

The proper classification of the relief imposed in respondent's contempt proceeding is dispositive of this case. As interpreted by the state court here, § 1209.5 requires respondent to carry the burden of persuasion on an element of the offense, by showing his inability to comply with the court's order to make the required payments. If applied in a criminal proceeding, such a statute would violate the Due Process Clause because it would undercut the State's burden to prove guilt beyond a reasonable doubt. If applied in a civil proceeding, however, this particular statute would be constitutionally valid and respondent conceded as much at the argument. . . .

Applying the traditional rules for classifying the relief imposed in a given proceeding requires the further resolution of one factual question about the nature of the relief in this case. Respondent was charged with nine separate counts of contempt, and was convicted on five of those counts, all of which arose from his failure to comply with orders to make payments in past months. He was sentenced to 5 days in jail on each of the five counts, for a total of 25 days, but his jail sentence was suspended and he was placed on probation for three years. If this were all, then the relief afforded would be criminal in nature. But this is not all. One of the conditions of respondent's probation was that he begin making payments on his accumulated arrearage, and that he continue making these payments at the rate of $50 per month. At that rate, all of the arrearage would be paid before respondent completed his probation period. Not only did the order therefore contemplate that respondent would be required to purge himself of his past violations, but it expressly states that "[i]f any two payments are missed, whether consecutive or not, the entire balance shall become due and payable." Order of the California Superior Court for Orange County (Aug. 9, 1985). What is unclear is whether the ultimate satisfaction of these accumulated prior payments would have purged the determinate sentence imposed on respondent. Since this aspect of the proceeding will vary as a factual matter from one case to another, depending on the precise disposition entered by the trial court, and since the trial court did not specify this aspect of its disposition in this case, it is not surprising that neither party was able to offer a satisfactory explanation of this point at argument. If the relief imposed here is in fact a determinate sentence with a purge clause, then it is civil in nature.

The state court did not pass on this issue because of its erroneous view that it was enough simply to aver that this proceeding is considered "quasi-criminal" as a matter of state law. And, as noted earlier, the court's view on this point, coupled with its view of the Federal Constitution, also led it to reinterpret the state statute, thus softening the impact of the presumption, in order to save its constitutionality. Yet the Due Process Clause does not necessarily prohibit the State from employing this presumption as it was construed by the state court, *if* respondent would purge his contempt judgment by paying off his arrearage. In these circumstances, the proper course for this Court is to vacate the judgment below and remand for further consideration of § 1209.5 free from the compulsion of an erroneous view of federal law. If on remand it is found that respondent would purge his sentence by paying his arrearage, then this proceeding is civil in nature and there was no need for the state court to reinterpret its statute to avoid conflict with the Due Process Clause.

We therefore vacate the judgment below and remand for further proceedings not inconsistent with this opinion.

It is so ordered.

JUSTICE KENNEDY took no part in the consideration or decision of this case.

JUSTICE O'CONNOR, with whom THE CHIEF JUSTICE and JUSTICE SCALIA join, dissenting.

This case concerns a contempt proceeding against a parent who repeatedly failed to comply with a valid court order to make child support payments. In my view, the proceeding is civil as a matter of federal law. Therefore, the Due Process Clause of the Fourteenth Amendment does not prevent the trial court from applying a legislative presumption that the parent remained capable of complying with the order until the time of the contempt proceeding.

I

The facts of this case illustrate how difficult it can be to obtain even modest amounts of child support from a noncustodial parent. Alta Sue Adams married respondent Phillip William Feiock in 1968. The couple resided in California and had three children. In 1973, respondent left the family. Mrs. Feiock filed a petition in the Superior Court of California for the County of Orange seeking dissolution of her marriage, legal custody of the children, and child support. In January 1976, the court entered an interlocutory judgment of dissolution of marriage, awarded custody of the children to Mrs. Feiock, and ordered respondent to pay child support beginning February 1, 1976. The court ordered respondent to pay $35 per child per month for the first four months, and $75 per child per month starting June 1, 1976. The order has never been modified.

After the court entered a final judgment of dissolution of marriage, Mrs. Feiock and the children moved to Ohio. Respondent made child support payments only sporadically and stopped making any payments by December 1982. Pursuant to Ohio's enactment of the Uniform Reciprocal Enforcement of Support Act (URESA), Mrs. Feiock filed a complaint in the Court of Common Pleas of Stark County, Ohio. The complaint recited that respondent was obliged to pay $225 per month in support, and that respondent was $2,300 in arrears. The Ohio court transmitted the complaint and supporting documents to the Superior Court of California for the County of Orange, which had jurisdiction over respondent. Petitioner, the Orange County District Attorney, prosecuted the case on behalf of Mrs. Feiock in accordance with California's version of URESA.

After obtaining several continuances, respondent finally appeared at a hearing before the California court on June 22, 1984. Respondent explained that he had recently become a partner in a flower business that had uncertain prospects. The court ordered respondent to pay $150 per month on a temporary basis, although it did not alter the underlying order. Payments were to begin July 1, 1984.

Respondent made payments only for August and September. Respondent appeared in court three times thereafter, but never asked for a modification of the order. Eventually, the Orange County District Attorney filed Orders to Show Cause and Declarations of Contempt alleging nine counts of contempt based on respondent's failure to make nine of the $150 support payments. At a hearing held August 9, 1985, the District Attorney invoked Cal.Civ.Proc.Code Ann. § 1209.5 (West 1982), which says:

"When a court of competent jurisdiction makes an order compelling a parent to furnish support . . . for his child, . . . proof that the parent was present in court at the time the order was pronounced and proof of noncompliance therewith shall be prima facie evidence of a contempt of court."

In an effort to overcome this presumption, respondent testified regarding his ability to pay at the time of each alleged act of contempt. The court found that respondent had been able to pay five of the missed payments. Accordingly, the court found respondent in contempt on five of the nine counts and sentenced him to 5 days in jail on each count, to be served consecutively, for a total of 25 days. The court suspended execution of the sentence and placed respondent on three years' informal probation on the conditions that he make monthly support payments of $150 starting immediately and additional payments of $50 per month on the arrearage starting October 1, 1985.

Respondent filed a petition for a writ of habeas corpus in the California Court of Appeal, where he prevailed on his argument that § 1209.5 is unconstitutional as a mandatory presumption shifting to the defendant the burden of proof of an element of a criminal offense. That is the argument that the Court confronts in this case. In my view, no remand is necessary because the judgment below is incorrect as a matter of federal law.

II

The California Court of Appeal has erected a substantial obstacle to the enforcement of child support orders. As petitioner vividly describes it, the judgment turns the child support order into "a worthless piece of scrap." . . .

Contempt proceedings often will be useless if the parent seeking enforcement of valid support orders must prove that the obligor can comply with the court order. The custodial parent will typically lack access to the financial and employment records needed to sustain the burden imposed by the decision below, especially where the noncustodial parent is self-employed, as is the case here. Serious consequences follow from the California Court of Appeal's decision to invalidate California's statutory presumption that a parent continues to be able to pay the child support previously determined to be within his or her means. . . .

The characterization of a state proceeding as civil or criminal for the purpose of applying the Due Process Clause of the Fourteenth Amendment is itself a question of federal law. The substance of particular contempt proceedings determines whether they are civil or criminal, regardless of the label attached by the court conducting the proceedings. Civil contempt proceedings are primarily coercive; criminal contempt proceedings are punitive . . . .

Whether a particular contempt proceeding is civil or criminal can be inferred from objective features of the proceeding and the sanction imposed. The most important indication is whether the judgment inures to the benefit of another party to the proceeding. A fine payable to the complaining party and proportioned to the complainant's loss is compensatory and civil. . . . Because the compensatory purpose limits the amount of the fine, the contemnor is not exposed to a risk of punitive sanctions that would make criminal safeguards necessary. By contrast, a fixed fine payable to the court is punitive and criminal in character. . . .

III

. . .

[T]he substance of the proceeding below and the conditions on which the sentence was suspended reveal that the proceeding was civil in nature. Mrs. Feiock initiated the underlying action in order to obtain enforcement of the child support order for the benefit of the Feiock children. The California District Attorney conducted the case under a provision of the URESA that authorizes him to act on Mrs. Feiock's behalf. As the very caption of the case in this Court indicates, the District Attorney is acting on behalf of Mrs. Feiock, not as the representative of the State of California in a criminal prosecution. Both of the provisions of California's enactment of the URESA that authorize contempt proceedings appear in a chapter of the Code of Civil Procedure entitled "Civil Enforcement." It appears that most States enforce child and spousal support orders through civil proceedings like this one, in which the burden of persuasion is shifted to the defendant to show inability to comply.

These indications that the proceeding was civil are confirmed by the character of the sanction imposed on respondent. The California Superior Court sentenced respondent to a fixed term of 25 days in jail. Without more, this sanction would be punitive and appropriate for a criminal contempt. But the court suspended the determinate sentence and placed respondent on three years' informal probation on the conditions that he comply with the support order in the future and begin to pay on the arrearage that he had accumulated in the past. These special conditions aim exclusively at enforcing compliance with the existing child support order. l. . .

I conclude that the proceeding in this case should be characterized as one for civil contempt, and I would reverse the judgment below.

NOTES AND QUESTIONS

(1) **The Problem of Collection.** The guidelines adopted by the states, as mentioned above, are an attempt to make more money available for the support of children. The next step has been to make sure that the money allocated to support is actually collected. The problem of collecting child support has become one of national scope and concern. Indeed, it is the subject of television documentaries and talk shows, and it is a serious problem: "It is estimated that about one-third of the total child support owed is not paid, resulting in an annual deficit of approximately $5 billion." Gregory, Swisher, and Scheible, Understanding Family Law § 8.06[F] (Matthew Bender 1995) (citing U.S. Commission on Interstate Child Support, *Supporting Our Children: Blueprint for Reform*, summary reprinted in 18 Fam. L. Rep (BNA) 2105 (1992)). According to Professor Linda Elrod, "in 1996, 89% of the children receiving Aid to Families with Dependent Children benefits lived in homes where the fathers were absent." Professor Elrod also states, "In 1991, 46% of the 11.5 million custodial parents potentially eligible for child support did not have an award. Another 11% had an award, but actually received nothing. Six and a half million families received no payment at all. Only 24% of those potentially eligible both had an award and received the full amount." Linda D. Elrod, *Child Support Reassessed: Federalization of Enforcement Nears Completion*, 1997 U. Ill. L. Rev. 695, 695 n. 14 (1997) (citing Scoon-Rogers & Lester, U.S. Dep't of Commerce, *Child Support for Custodial Mothers and Fathers*, Current Population Reports Series 60–187 (1991)).

(2) **Action for Arrearages.** The term "arrearages" refers to the accumulation of past due installments. Generally, interest is also due on the arrearages from the date that each installment accrues. States vary on the applicable statute of limitations on past due child support.

Methods of collecting arrearages vary greatly from state to state. However, a few generalizations are possible. First, if the child support is owed because of a provision in a marital settlement agreement, then usually the debt for the arrearages must be reduced to a judgment. Second, whether or not collection problems are anticipated, it is good practice to have the settlement agreement merged into the judgment of divorce. And, finally, if there is a judgment, then as each installment accrues it is considered a final judgment which can be collected through the usual means of enforcement: discovery of assets, execution, liens on real property, attachment, garnishment, sequestration or the appointment of a receiver. See *Briton v. Briton*, 671 P.2d 1135 (N.M. 1983); *Ortiz v. Ortiz*, 304 P. 2d 490 (Kan. 1956). However, there are a few states in which each unpaid installment, even if there is a court order, must be rendered into a judgment before traditional collection remedies can be applied. See *Keltner v. Keltner*, 589 S.W.2d 235 (Mo. 1979); *Smith v. Smith*, 217 F.2d 917 (6th Cir. Mich. 1954). If there is a final judgment the past due arrearages will earn interest.

The inability to pay will not serve as a defense in an action for arrearages, but it may mean that such an action is impractical. However, the obligor who suddenly cannot pay, perhaps because of the loss of a job, may not simply stop paying but, rather, must bring an action to modify the amount of the support because of the changed circumstance. At one time it was possible in some states to make a retroactive modification of arrearages, but this practice has been prohibited by federal law and regulation. *See* 42 U.S.C. § 666(a)(9)(C); 45 C.F.R § 303.106. However it is not uncommon for the obligor to be allowed to make monthly payments on the arrearages.

A debt for arrearages may be collected from the estate of a deceased obligor. In addition, some states allow the estate of a deceased obligee to collect arrearages. *See, e.g., Silver v. Shebetka*, 65 N.W.2d 173 (Iowa 1954); *Kay v. Vaughan*, 165 S.E.2d 131 (Ga. 1968).

Should support arrearages be collectable for periods of time where the custodial parent actively concealed the child's whereabouts and where the noncustodial parent diligently sought to find the child? This has been a difficult decision for courts. In 1994 the California Supreme Court held that an obligee may be estopped from collecting arrearages which accrued while the child was wrongfully concealed. *See In re Marriage of Damico*, 29 Cal. Rptr. 2d 787 (Cal. 1994). However, that court revisited this issue two years later and concluded this case was limited to the facts—that the concealment continued until the child reached majority. The court held that arrearages could be collected where the child was still a minor and could, therefore, benefit from the arrearages or where the obligee's right to support had been assigned to a public agency in return for public assistance. *See In re Marriage of Comer*, 927 P.2d 265 (Cal. 1996).

Finally, the statute of limitations on the collection of arrearages is usually quite long. Professor Elrod has observed that the "[t]rend is toward expanded statutes of limitation for child support so that in the future, it will be easier to collect arrearages without running into dormancy problems." Linda D. Elrod, *A Review of the Year in Family Law*, 28 Fam. L.Q. 541, 563 (1995). She also mentioned a Maryland case which "did not find a fifteen-year-old claim for child support barred by laches." *Id.* (citing *Bland v. Larsen*, 627 A.2d 79 (Md. Ct. Spec. App. 1993)).

(3) **Civil Contempt.** Since courts usually order payment of child support in installments, a violation of the court's order to pay can be enforced by an action for civil contempt. The court's power in this regard may be statutory, or it may result from the court's equitable powers to enforce orders and injunctions.

The purpose of this form of contempt is to force the obligor to comply with the court order. While civil contempt may involve a jail sentence, the key feature, as the principal case notes, is that the obligor has the ability to purge himself or herself of contempt. Ordinarily this means that the inability to pay is an excuse for nonpayment, although, as noted above, it will not defeat an action to collect arrearages. Moreover, the court may hold the obligor in contempt for refusing to sell property to satisfy the support obligation.

Because the action is civil, the normal due process protections in criminal cases do not apply. In *Sword v. Sword*, 249 N.W.2d 88 (Mich. 1976), the Michigan Supreme court held that there was no right to jury trial or right to counsel. However, this court reversed itself a few years later as to the right to counsel: "we find it well established that the due process right to appointed counsel is triggered by an indigent's fundamental interest in physical liberty, and not by the civil or criminal nature of the proceeding." *Mead v. Batchlor*, 460

N.W.2d 493, 498 (Mich. 1990); *see also* Robert Monk, Note, *The Indigent Defendant's Right to Court Appointed Counsel in Civil Contempt Proceedings for the Nonpayment of Child Support*, 50 U. Chi. L. Rev. 326 (1983).

With the advent of the new federal remedies described in § 11.07[B], *below*, and their application in the states, it is difficult to tell what the future role of contempt will be in child support cases.

(4) **Criminal Contempt.** When the refusal to pay support is willful, the court may punish the obligor by criminal contempt. The purpose is punitive, not coercive. With criminal contempt, basic criminal due process rights must be observed: adequate notice of the charges, counsel for indigents, and beyond-a-reasonable-doubt standard of proof. A jury trial is available in most jurisdictions. *See Argersinger v. Hamlin*, 407 U.S. 25 (1972). A finding of willfulness usually requires some showing that the defendant had the ability to pay the support. *See Epp v. State*, 814 P.2d 1011 (Nev. 1991); *State v. Barlow*, 851 P.2d 1191 (Utah Ct. App. 1993); *In re Marriage of Ramos*, 466 N.E.2d 1016 (Ill. App. Ct. 1984), cert. denied sub nom., 471 U.S. 1017 (1985).

(5) **Security for Future Payments.** Courts have the power to order the obligor to provide security for future support in the form of a bond, insurance policy, cash or other property. This form of enforcement is becoming more common because, as will be seen in the next section, the federal law now encourages states to enact such security statutes. *See* C.T. Drechsler, Annotation, *Decree for Periodical Payments for Support or Alimony, as a Lien or the Subject of a Declaration of Lien*, 59 A.L.R.2d 656 (1958). Spendthrift trusts have been used as well. *See* M.L. Cross, Annotation, *Retrospective Modification of, or Refusal to Enforce Decree for Alimony, Separate Maintenance or Support*, 6 A.L.R.2d 1277 (1949).

(6) **Wage Assignment.** While both garnishment, to satisfy a debt, and wage assignment of the right to collect wages have been traditional remedies for collecting child support, mandatory income withholding, or automatic wage assignment, statutes have been enacted in most states because of federal requirements. *See, e.g.*, Colo. Rev. Stat. § 14–14–111.5; N.J. Stat. Ann. § 2A:17–56.7; Va. Code Ann. § 63.1–250.3.

(7) **Loss of State License.** One recent response to failure to pay support is the revocation or suspension of state licenses. One of the most comprehensive statutes authorizing suspension of licenses is the Texas statute:

§ 232.003. Suspension of License

(a) A court or the Title IV–D agency may issue an order suspending a license as provided by this chapter if an individual who is an obligor:

(1) has a child support arrearage equal to or greater than the total support due for 90 days under a support order;

(2) has been provided an opportunity to make payments toward the child support arrearage under an agreed or court-ordered repayment schedule, without regard to whether the repayment schedule was agreed to or ordered before or after the date the petition for suspension of a license was filed; and

(3) has failed to comply with the repayment schedule.

Tex. Fam. Code Ann. § 232.003 (1997). The statute lists 57 state licenses that are subject to suspension, including membership in the State Bar of Texas.

What happens when a obligor's driver's license is suspended for non-payment of support, and the result is the obligor is in danger of being fired because he cannot get to work? In Colorado, it is possible to get a probationary license for purposes of driving to work. *See* Colo. Rev. Stat. § 26–13–123 (1997).

(8) **Disability Benefits.** Should disability payments be used to satisfy a support obligation? The United States Supreme Court has held that there is no federal preemption of the states' right to hold a disabled veteran in contempt for failure to pay support where the veteran's only means to satisfy the obligation were disability payments from the Veteran's Administration under 38 U.S.C. § 1114(1997), which were received as compensation for service-related injuries, despite express provisions that the benefits were not subject to attachment or other forms of seizure. *Rose v. Rose*, 481 U.S. 619 (1987).

(9) **Cause of Action Against an Employer.** The West Virginia Supreme Court has held that support arrearages and punitive damages can be collected from an employer who conspired with a support obligor to help him evade automatic withholding. The employer, doing business as "Dude's Used Auto Sales," agreed to pay the obligor in cash. *Belcher v. Terry*, 420 S.E.2d 909, 914–15 (W. Va. 1992) (citations omitted).

(10) After considering this array of enforcement remedies, and before going on to the next subsection's summary of the history of federal efforts in the field, you may want to consider this issue from a broader perspective. What do you suppose is going on in the field of family law that makes the support-enforcement problem so intractable? Why are so many fathers unwilling to help support their own children's well-being? Of the multitude of financial obligations people face, why does the need for compulsion come up so dramatically in this particular area?

What kinds of research would shed more light on these questions?

What do your own answers to these questions imply for the viability of the continued search for ever more effective means of compulsion as a solution to the problem of obtaining child support from noncustodial parents?

If compulsion can ultimately be made highly effective but puts government in the business of forcing a significant part of the population to do that which it does not feel a legitimate obligation to do, what are the political and social costs we pay?

[B] Federal Enforcement.

UNITED STATES v. HAMPSHIRE
United States Court of Appeals
95 F.3d 999 (10th Cir. 1996), *review denied*, 117 S. Ct. 753 (1997)

PAUL KELLY, JR. CIRCUIT JUDGE.

Defendant-appellant Ricky L. Hampshire entered a conditional plea of guilty based upon the failure to pay child support obligations in violation of the Child Support Recovery Act of 1992 ("CSRA"), 18 U.S.C. § 228, after the district court rejected his challenges to the CSRA and its application. He was sentenced to two years' probation and ordered to pay $38,804 in restitution. He now challenges his conviction on the basis that (the CSRA violates the Commerce Clause . . . .

In September 1985, Defendant Ricky Hampshire went "absent without leave" ("AWOL") from the military. In October 1985, his wife filed for divorce in Kansas. In November 1985, Mr. Hampshire was apprehended, held in a civilian jail pending transfer to military custody, and served with a summons to answer the divorce petition. He never responded. The court granted the divorce, awarded custody to the mother of the couple's two children and ordered Mr. Hampshire to pay $350 per month in child support. After his release from military prison, Mr. Hampshire moved from Kansas to New Mexico, refused to make any payments and eventually was charged with violating the CSRA.

. . .

The Commerce Clause provides that "[t]he Congress shall have Power . . . [t]o regulate Commerce . . . among the several States . . . ." U.S. Const. art. I, § 8, cl. 3. "A court may invalidate legislation enacted under the Commerce Clause only if it is clear that there is no rational basis for a congressional finding that the regulated activity affects interstate commerce, or that there is no reasonable connection between the regulatory means selected and the asserted ends." *Federal Energy Regulatory Comm'n v. Mississippi*, 456 U.S. 742, 754, 102 S.Ct. 2126, 2134, 72 L.Ed.2d 532 (1982).

The CSRA makes it a federal criminal offense for a person to "willfully fail to pay a past due support obligation with respect to a child who resides in another State." 18 U.S.C. § 228(a). "Past due support obligation" is defined as "any amount determined under a court order or an order of an administrative process pursuant to the law of a State to be due from a person for the support and maintenance of a child . . . that has remained unpaid for a period longer than one year, or is greater than $5,000." 18 U.S.C. § 228(d)(1).

The constitutionality of the CSRA presents a question of first impression in this circuit. The Commerce Clause empowers Congress to regulate three aspects of interstate commerce:

(1) "the use of the channels of interstate commerce[;]"

(2) "the instrumentalities of interstate commerce, or persons or things in interstate commerce[;]" and

(3) activities that have a substantial relation to or substantially affect interstate commerce.

United States v. Lopez, 115 S.Ct. 1624, 1629, 131 L.Ed.2d 626 (1995) . . . . In Lopez, relied upon in large part by Mr. Hampshire, the Court struck down 18 U.S.C. § 922(q), part of the Gun-Free School Zones Act of 1990 ("GFSZA"), which made it a federal offense "for any individual knowingly to possess a firearm at a place that the individual knows, or has reasonable cause to believe, is a school zone." 18 U.S.C. § 922(q)(2)(A). In Lopez, the Court dismissed as inapplicable the first two categories of permissible interstate commerce regulation and held that § 922(q) failed to satisfy the prerequisites of the third category because it regulated an activity that did not "substantially affect interstate commerce." 115 S.Ct. at 1630–31. Of particular importance to the Court's analysis was the fact that § 922(q) was "a criminal statute that by its terms has nothing to do with 'commerce' or any sort of economic enterprise" and "contain[ed] no jurisdictional element which would ensure . . . that the firearm possession in question affects interstate commerce." *Id.*

The Second Circuit recently held that the CSRA was a proper exercise of Congress's power to regulate and protect the instrumentalities of interstate commerce because the Act "regulates the flow of payments on unfulfilled child support orders where the child and parent reside in separate States." United States v. Sage, 92 F.3d 101, 107 (2d Cir.1996). Because the CSRA "addresses an obligation to make payments in interstate commerce," it regulates more than local activity and is constitutional. *Id.* The Ninth Circuit also recently upheld the CSRA on a similar rationale:

> The obligation of a parent in one state to provide support for a child in a different state is an obligation to be met by a payment that will normally move in interstate commerce—by mail, by wire, or by the electronic transfer of funds. That obligation is, therefore, a thing in interstate commerce and falls within the power of Congress to regulate. The frustration of satisfaction of the obligation by the failure of the debtors to pay is an impediment to interstate commerce that Congress can criminalize . . . .

United States v. Mussari, 95 F.3d 787, 790 (9th Cir.1996).

Numerous district courts have addressed the constitutionality of the CSRA. Several have found it to be constitutional. These courts generally upheld the constitutionality of the CSRA on the basis that (1) nonpayment of child support involves payment of a debt and therefore constitutes economic activity or commerce; (2) nonpayment of child support in the aggregate has a substantial impact on commerce; and (3) the CSRA's requirement that the delinquent parent and child reside in two different states constitutes the jurisdictional requirement of an interstate nexus ensuring that the federal government will not intrude upon matters with no relation to interstate commerce. . . .

By contrast, several other district courts have held the CSRA unconstitutional. These courts struck down the CSRA on the basis that (1) nonpayment of child support fails to constitute an activity that substantially affects commerce or bears a substantial relationship to commerce; (2) the CSRA's requirement that the delinquent parent and child reside in two different states does not satisfy the constitutionally required jurisdictional requirement of an interstate nexus because the delinquent parent often does not involve himself in any interstate activity that constitutionally confers jurisdiction; (3) nonpayment of child support inherently is a state criminal issue in which intervention by the federal government violates notions of comity and federalism; and (4) the definitional requirements of the CSRA force federal courts to interpret and possibly modify state court ordered decrees.

In this case, Mr. Hampshire argues that Congress exceeded its authority under the Commerce Clause because the CSRA: (1) regulates an activity that neither constitutes nor involves commerce; (2) lacks the prerequisite interstate nexus sufficient to confer federal jurisdiction; (3) is overbroad; and (4) represents an unconstitutional foray by the federal government into domestic relations, a power traditionally reserved to states . . . .

Notwithstanding that state regulation is substantial or even predominant, it is well-settled that Congress may regulate interstate aspects of economic transactions. We agree with the Second Circuit that "[i]f Congress can take measures under the Commerce Clause to foster potential interstate commerce, it surely has the power to prevent the frustration of an obligation to engage in interstate commerce." *Sage*, 92 F.3d at 105–06 (2d Cir.1996). Regarding the latter, the Court has invalidated application of state laws that prevented enforcement of contracts in interstate commerce. Likewise, Congress may prevent the circumvention of child support obligations by regulating what is essentially nonpayment of a debt where the judgment creditor and judgment debtor are in different states.

The CSRA also may be upheld because it regulates activities that are substantially related to and substantially affect interstate commerce. In enacting the CSRA, Congress made explicit findings concerning the impact of delinquent parents on interstate commerce. In 1989, approximately $5 billion of $16 billion in child support obligations were not honored. About one-third of the unpaid child support obligations involved a delinquent father who lived in a different state than his children. Delinquent parents used the multistate system to evade enforcement efforts by individual states. Accordingly, in enacting the CSRA, Congress sought "to strengthen, not to supplant, State enforcement."

In order to conclude that Congress acted within the confines of the Commerce Clause, all we must find is a rational basis for Congress' finding that the regulated activity substantially affects interstate commerce. Congress clearly considered the economic impact of delinquent parents and, in its discretion, concluded that the impact substantially affects interstate commerce. Congress had a rational basis for so concluding and, as a result, acted within the power bestowed upon it under the Commerce Clause in enacting the CSRA.

. . .

AFFIRMED.

NOTES AND QUESTIONS

(1) **Introduction.** Federal involvement in child support is not limited to mandating adoption of child support guidelines. The history of the last twenty-five years has been one of ever-expanding federal involvement in child support enforcement. Indeed, the degree of federal involvement with support enforcement can be indicated by the title of this thoughtful essay. Linda D. Elrod: *Child Support Reassessed: Federalization of Enforcement Nears Completion,* 1997 U. Ill. L. Rev. 695 (1997). The federal motivation for the new laws was always twofold: there was genuine concern for the welfare of children, but there was also concern for the costs of welfare programs: "Congress' motive for entering the domestic relations field was a fiscal one. The costs to the Aid to Families with Dependent Children (AFDC) program, resulting from absent parents' failure to support their children, were staggering." Dodson and Horowitz, *Child Support Enforcement Amendments of 1984: New Tools for Enforcement,* 10 Fam L. Rep. (BNA) 3051, 3051 (1984). The following notes summarize the federal law in this area, historically, as a series of federal acts.

(2) **Title IV–D, 1974.** Until 1974, the area of child support enforcement had been primarily the domain of the states. However, 1974 saw the enactment of Title IV–D of the Social Security Act, 42 U.S.C. §§ 651–70 (1997). The thrust of this legislation was not to change the law of child support enforcement but rather to create federal and state agencies to assist in the collection of child support. 42 U.S.C.A. § 653(1997) established the Federal Parent Locator Service, which provides information regarding the location and assets of a child support obligor to any authorized representative of the child for the purpose of "establishing parentage, establishing, setting the amount of, modifying, or enforcing child support obligations, or making or enforcing child custody or visitation orders." 42 U.S.C. § 653(a)(2) (1997). The service also assists in locating parents who have abducted children. *See* 42 U.S.C. § 653(a)(3) (1997). Title IV–D also established the Office of Child Support Enforcement whose role in this area would be greatly expanded by the legislation which

followed. *See* 45 C.F.R. § 301 *et seq.* Finally, Title IV–D required states to establish child support enforcement agencies and to "establish child support enforcement plans administered by state IV–D agencies . . . partially funded by the federal government (originally at the 75% level.)." Dodson and Horowitz, *Child Support Enforcement Amendments of 1984: New Tools for Enforcement*, 10 Fam L. Rep. (BNA) 3051 (1984).

(3) **Child Support Enforcement Amendments of 1984.** Ten years after the enactment of Title IV–D, Congress again moved to strengthen child support enforcement by enacting the Child Enforcement Amendments of 1984. *See* Pub. L. No. 98–378, 98 Stat. 1305. These amendments, unlike Title IV–D, did not just create agencies; they required that states adopt certain collection procedures and remedies for recipients of public welfare programs. The mandatory enforcement procedures could also be made available to private parties, and indeed they have. Further receipt of federal funding for Aid for Families with Dependent Children was conditioned upon adoption of these collection devices. To some degree these mandatory enforcement procedures were modeled after successful state programs. *See* Dodson and Horowitz, *Child Support Enforcement Amendments of 1984: New Tools for Enforcement*, 10 Fam L. Rep. (BNA) 3051, 3052 (1984).

- a. *Income Withholding.* The most formidable tool for enforcement in the 1984 Amendments was the provision for income withholding, which means that child support will be deducted directly from the obligor's pay and sent directly to the state agency collecting the support or to the obligee. The Amendments require that mandatory income withholding be implemented in every support case where the child is a client of a state child support agency, and that some form of wage assignment be made available to all children. *See* 42 U.S.C. § 666(a)(8), (b)(1) (1997). Before the withholding begins, notice and other procedural protections are required. *See* 42 U.S.C. § 666(b)(2) (1997). In addition, there are protections for the employer; however employers are required to begin withholding wages within fourteen days of notice. *See* 42 U.S.C. § 666(b)(A)(1) (1997).

- b. *Liens.* The 1984 Amendments require states to adopt "procedures under which liens are imposed against real and personal property for amounts of overdue support." 42 U.S.C. § 666(a)(4)(1997). Prior to this, liens were a potential but seldom utilized procedure in many states.

- c. *Bonds.* Bonds and other security devices, tools previously used in some states, also became mandatory. 42 U.S.C. § 666(a)(4) (1997).

- d. *Tax Refund Intercepts.* Tax Intercepts allow the collection of child support arrearages from income tax refunds which are owed to the obligor. Prior to the 1984 Amendments, federal tax intercepts were allowed only in AFDC cases. The Amendments greatly expanded the number of children who were able to use this device by allowing it to be available in all cases and by requiring the states to adopt tax refund intercepts for state income taxes. *See* 42 U.S.C. § 666(a)(7) (1997).

(4) **Child Support Act of 1988**. This Act has already been discussed extensively, since it is the one which required the adoption of presumptive child support guidelines. Pub. L. No. 100–485, 102 Stat. 2343. In addition, it also required "automatic wage assignments in all new or modified" child support orders. *See* Linda D. Elrod, *Child Support Reassessed: Federalization of Enforcement Nears Completion* 1997 U. Ill. L. Rev. 695, 698 (1997). In addition, the Child Support Act authorized the formation of the United States Commission

on Interstate Child Support, which ultimately lead to the reforms which followed. *See id.*; *see also* 42 U.S.C. § 666 (1997).

(5) **The Child Support Recovery Act of 1992: Criminalizing Support Evasion.** As the principal case illustrates, the Child Support Recovery Act of 1992, 18 U.S.C. § 228 (1997), creates a federal crime, based upon the Commerce Clause, for willful failure to pay child support. The statute provides for a criminal penalty for one who "willfully fails to pay a past due support obligation with respect to a child who resides in another State." 18 U.S.C. § 228(a) (1994). The penalty is fine, imprisonment for not more than six months for the first offense or two years maximum, and restitution 18 U.S.C. § 228 (b) (1997). A support obligation is any amount which has been "determined under a court order or an order of an administrative process pursuant to the law of a State," and has been "due for one year or is over $5000." 18 U.S.C. § 228 (d)(1)(A),(B) (1997). The term "willful" is not defined by the statute, but case law involving contempt, at the state level, has held "willful" to mean that the obligor must be able to pay his support obligations under the divorce decree. *See Epp v. State*, 814 P.2d 1011 (Nev. 1991); *State v. Barlow*, 851 P.2d 1191 (Utah Ct. App. 1993); *In re Marriage of Ramos*, 466 N.E.2d 1016 (Ill. App. Ct. 1984), *cert. denied*, 471 U.S. 1017 (1985). For more on the effect of the *Lopez* decision, discussed in the principal case, see Kathleen Brudette, Comment, *Making Parents Pay: Interstate Child Support Enforcement After United States v. Lopez*, 144 U. Pa. L. Rev. 1469 (1996); Ronald S. Kornreich, *The Constitutionality of Punishing Deadbeat Parents: The Child Support Recovery Act After United States v. Lopez,* 64 Fordham L. Rev. 1089 (1995).

(6) **Omnibus Budget Reconciliation Act of 1993.** The Omnibus Budget Reconciliation Act of 1993, Pub. L. No. 103–66, 107 Stat. 312 (1993), had two major components. First, it required state legislation creating a rebuttable or even conclusive presumption of paternity where there was genetic testing indicating paternity, in order to facilitate issuance of support orders in paternity cases. Second, it modified the Employee Retirement Income Security Act (ERISA) to require that "after August 10, 1993, employers . . . had to make group health care coverage available to the noncustodial children of their employees." Linda D. Elrod, *Child Support Reassessed: Federalization of Enforcement Nears Completion,* 1997 U. Ill. L. Rev. 695, 702 (1997); *see also* Employee Retirement Income Security Act of 1974, 29 U.S.C. § 1169 (1997). The mechanism for implementation of this requirement is the Qualified Medical Child Support Order (QMCSO) which may be issued to order the employer and insurance carrier to include the child in the insurance program.

(7) **Full Faith and Credit for Child Support Orders Act of 1994.** In order to assist in enforcement, the Full Faith and Credit for Child Support Orders Act of 1994 requires states to recognize the judgments of other states. Pub. L. No. 103–383, 108 Stat. 4064; 28 U.S.C. § 1738B(c)(1)(A)–(B)(2) (1997). This particular enactment is discussed more fully below in § 11.08 "Jurisdiction for Support and Interstate Enforcement."

(8) **Personal Responsibility and Work Opportunity Reconciliation Act of 1996.** In 1996, as a part of overall welfare reform, the Personal Responsibility and Work Opportunity Reconciliation Act of 1996 (PRWORA), Pub. L. No. 104–193, 110 Stat. 2105, became law. PRWORA made headlines because it replaced AFDC entitlements with block welfare grants to the states and removed the federal guarantee for child welfare: "The bottom line is that the federal government will no longer guarantee a cash assistance safety net for children. This will shift the major responsibility for helping poor families to state and local

governments." Paul K. Legler, *The Coming Revolution in Child Support Policy: Implications of the 1996 Welfare Reform Act.* 30 Fam. L.Q. 519 (1996). However, important components of this legislation are significant provisions for the collection of child support. Here are the main provisions relating to the collection of support:

    a. *New Hire Reporting.* The establishment of a national system for tracking employment which requires reporting of new hires within twenty days with information forwarded to the Federal Case Registry and the Federal Parent Locator Service. (PRWORA), Pub. L. No. 104–193, 110 Stat. 2105 §§ 313, 316.

    b. *Uniform Interstate Family Support Act.* Mandatory state adoption of UIFSA (discussed in § 11.08[B], *below*) by January 1, 1998. *See* 42 U.S.C. § 666(f) (1997).

    c. *Access to Government Information.* Affords enforcement agencies access to important government sources of information for the purpose of tracking delinquent parents such as records of state and local agencies, including vital statistics; state and local tax and revenue records; records concerning real and titled personal property; records of occupational and professional licenses; records of agencies administering public assistance programs; records of motor vehicle departments, and correction records. In addition a U.S. military locate system will allow person in the military to be located immediately. Paul K. Legler, *The Coming Revolution in Child Support Policy: Implications of the 1996 Welfare Reform Act.* 30 Fam. L.Q. 519, 542 (1996).

    d. *Access to Private Information.* Affords enforcement agencies access to private records such as records of public utilities, cable television companies, banks and credit agencies. *Id.* at 542–543.

    e. *Volume Case Processing.* Applies modern case management techniques to child support enforcement, including computer matching of lists of obligers with lists of assets, the volume processing of automatic wage assignments and property liens, and the creation of central state registries of support obligations. *Id.* at 544–551.

    f. *Expedited Procedures.* Requires states to adopt expedited procedures which move away from complaint-driven court proceedings and emphasize administrative action, including imposition of liens, seizure of funds, suspension of licenses, and administrative subpoenas. *See* Linda D. Elrod, *Child Support Reassessed: Federalization of Enforcement Nears Completion*, 1997 U. Ill. L. Rev. 695, 705–06 (1997).

§ 11.08 Jurisdiction for Support and Interstate Enforcement

[A] Personal Jurisdiction

KULKO v. SUPERIOR COURT
United States Supreme Court
436 U.S. 84 (1978)

Mr. Justice Marshall delivered the opinion of the Court.

    The issue before us is whether, in this action for child support, the California state courts may exercise in personam jurisdiction over a nonresident, nondomiciliary parent of minor children domiciled within the State. For reasons set forth below, we hold that the exercise of such jurisdiction would violate the Due Process Clause of the Fourteenth Amendment.

I

Appellant Ezra Kulko married appellee Sharon Kulko Horn in 1959, during appellant's three-day stopover in California en route from a military base in Texas to a tour of duty in Korea. At the time of his marriage, both parties were domiciled in and residents of New York State. Immediately following the marriage, Sharon Kulko returned to New York, as did appellant after his tour of duty. Their first child, Darwin, was born to the Kulkos in New York in 1961, and a year later their second child, Ilsa, was born, also in New York. The Kulkos and their two children resided together as a family in New York City continuously until March, 1972, when the Kulkos separated.

Following the separation, Sharon Kulko moved to San Francisco, California. A written separation agreement was drawn up in New York; in September, 1972, Sharon Kulko flew to New York City in order to sign this agreement. The agreement provided, *inter alia*, that the children would remain with their father during the school year but would spend their Christmas, Easter, and summer vacations with their mother. While Sharon Kulko waived any claim for her own support or maintenance, Ezra Kulko agreed to pay his wife $3,000 per year in child support for the periods when the children were in her care, custody, and control. Immediately after execution of the separation agreement, Sharon Kulko flew to Haiti and procured a divorce there; the divorce decree incorporated the terms of the agreement. She then returned to California, where she remarried and took the name of Horn.

The children resided with appellant during the school year and with their mother on vacations, as provided by the separation agreement, until December, 1973. At this time, just before Ilsa was to leave New York to spend Christmas vacation with her mother, she told her father that she wanted to remain in California after her vacation. Appellant bought his daughter a one-way plane ticket, and Ilsa left, taking her clothing with her. Ilsa then commenced living in California with her mother during the school year and spending vacations with her father. In January, 1976, appellant's other child, Darwin, called his mother from New York and advised her that he wanted to live with her in California. Unbeknownst to appellant, appellee Horn sent a plane ticket to her son, which he used to fly to California where he took up residence with his mother and sister.

Less than one month after Darwin's arrival in California, appellee Horn commenced this action against appellant in the California Superior Court. She sought to establish the Haitian divorce decree as a California judgment; to modify the judgment so as to award her full custody of the children; and to increase appellant's child support obligation. Appellant appeared specially and moved to quash service of the summons on the ground that he was not a resident of California and lacked sufficient "minimum contacts" with the State under *International Shoe Co. v. Washington*, 326 U.S. 310, 316 (1945), to warrant the State's assertion of personal jurisdiction over him.

The trial court summarily denied the motion to quash, and appellant sought review in the California Court of Appeal by petition for a writ of mandate. Appellant did not contest the court's jurisdiction for purposes of the custody determination, but, with respect to the claim for increased support, he renewed his argument that the California courts lacked personal jurisdiction over him. The appellate court affirmed the denial of appellant's motion to quash, reasoning that, by consenting to his children's living in California, appellant had "caused an effect in th[e] state" warranting the exercise of jurisdiction over him. 133 Cal.Rptr. 627, 628 (1976).

The California Supreme Court granted appellant's petition for review, and in a 4–2 decision sustained the rulings of the lower state courts. 19 Cal.3d 514, 138 Cal.Rptr. 586, 564 P.2d 353 (1977). It noted first that the California Code of Civil Procedure demonstrated an intent that the courts of California utilize all bases of in personam jurisdiction "not inconsistent with the Constitution." Agreeing with the court below, the Supreme Court stated that, where a nonresident defendant has caused an effect in the State by an act or omission outside the State, personal jurisdiction over the defendant in causes arising from the effect may be exercised whenever "reasonable." *Id.*, at 521, 138 Cal.Rptr., at 588, 564 P.2d, at 356. It went on to hold that such an exercise was "reasonable" in this case because appellant had "purposely availed himself of the benefits and protections of the laws of California" by sending Ilsa to live with her mother in California. *Id.*, at 521–522, 524, 138 Cal.Rptr. at 591, 564 P.2d, at 356, 358. While noting that appellant had not, "with respect to his other child, Darwin, caused an effect in [California]" since it was appellee Horn who had arranged for Darwin to fly to California in January, 1976, the court concluded that it was "fair and reasonable for defendant to be subject to personal jurisdiction for the support of both children, where he has committed acts with respect to one child which confers [*sic*] personal jurisdiction and has consented to the permanent residence of the other child in California." *Id.*, at 525, 138 Cal.Rptr., at 591, 564 P.2d, at 358–359. . . .

II

The Due Process Clause of the Fourteenth Amendment operates as a limitation on the jurisdiction of state courts to enter judgments affecting rights or interests of nonresident defendants. It has long been the rule that a valid judgment imposing a personal obligation or duty in favor of the plaintiff may be entered only by a court having jurisdiction over the person of the defendant.

The parties are in agreement that the constitutional standard for determining whether the State may enter a binding judgment against appellant here is that set forth in this Court's opinion in *International Shoe Co. v. Washington, supra*: that a defendant "have certain minimum contacts with [the forum State] such that the maintenance of the suit does not offend 'traditional notions of fair play and substantial justice.' " 326 U.S., at 316, quoting *Milliken v. Meyer, supra*, 31 1 U.S., at 463. While the interests of the forum State and of the plaintiff in proceeding with the cause of the plaintiff's forum of choice are, of course, to be considered, *see McGee v. International Life Insurance Co.*, 355 U.S. 220, 223 (1957), an essential criterion in all cases is whether the "quality and nature" of the defendant's activity is such that it is "reasonable" and "fair" to require him to conduct his defense in that State. *International Shoe Co. v. Washington, supra*, 326 U.S., at 316–317, 319. *Accord, Shaffer v. Heitner, supra*, 433 U.S., at 207–212; *Perkins v. Benguet Mining Co.*, 342 U.S. 437, 445 (1952).

Like any standard that requires a determination of "reasonableness," the "minimum contacts" test of *International Shoe* is not susceptible of mechanical application; rather, the facts of each case must be weighed to determine whether the requisite "affiliating circumstances" are present. *Hanson v. Denckla*, 357 U.S. 235, 246 (1958). We recognize that this determination is one in which few answers will be written "in black and white." The greys are dominant and even among them the shades are innumerable." *Estin v. Estin*, 334 U.S. 541, 545 (1948). But we believe that the California Supreme Court's application of the minimum-contacts test in this case represents an unwarranted extension of International Shoe and would, if sustained, sanction a result that is neither fair, just, nor reasonable. . . .

As we emphasized: "The unilateral activity of those who claim some relationship with a nonresident defendant cannot satisfy the requirement of contact with the forum State. [I]t is essential in each case that there be some act by which the defendant purposefully avails [him]self of the privilege of conducting activities within the forum state." *Hanson v. Denckla, supra*, U.S. at 253.

The "purposeful act" that the California Supreme Court believed did warrant the exercise of personal jurisdiction over appellant in California was his "actively and fully consent[ing] to Ilsa living in California for the school year and sen[ding] her to California for that purpose." 19 Cal.3d, at 524, 138 Cal.Rptr., at 358. We cannot accept the proposition that appellant's acquiescence in Ilsa's desire to live with her mother conferred jurisdiction over appellant in the California courts in this action. A father who agrees, in the interests of family harmony and his children's preferences, to allow them to spend more time in California than was required under a separation agreement can hardly be said to have "purposefully availed himself" of the "benefits and protections" of California's laws. *See Shaffer v. Heitner*, 433 U.S., at 216.

Nor can we agree with the assertion of the court below that the exercise of *in personam* jurisdiction here was warranted by the financial benefit appellant derived from his daughter's presence in California for nine months of the year. 19 Cal.3d at 524–525, 138 Cal.Rptr., at 590–591, 564 P.2d, at 358. This argument rests on the premise that, while appellant's liability for support payments remained unchanged, his yearly expenses for supporting the child in New York decreased. But this circumstance, even if true, does not support California's assertion of jurisdiction here. Any diminution in appellant's household costs resulted, not from the child's presence in California, but rather from her absence from appellant's home. Moreover, an action by appellee Horn to increase support payments could now be brought, and could have been brought when Ilsa first moved to California, in the State of New York; a New York court would clearly have personal jurisdiction over appellant and, if a judgment were entered by a New York court increasing appellant's child-support obligations, it could properly be enforced against him in both New York and California. Any ultimate financial advantage to appellant thus results not from the child's presence in California, but from appellee's failure earlier to seek an increase in payments under the separation agreement. The argument below to the contrary, in our view confuses the question of appellant's liability with that of the proper forum in which to determine that liability. . . .

Finally, basic considerations of fairness point decisively in favor of appellant's State of domicile as the proper forum for adjudication of this case, whatever the merits of appellee's underlying claim. It is appellant who has remained in the State of the marital domicile, whereas it is appellee who has moved across the continent. Appellant has at all times resided in New York State, and, until the separation and appellee's move to California, his entire family resided there as well. As noted above, appellant did no more than acquiesce in the stated preference of one of his children to live with her mother in California. This single act is surely not one that a reasonable parent would expect to result in the substantial financial burden and personal strain of litigating a child-support suit in a forum 3,000 miles away, and we therefore see no basis on which it can be said that appellant could reasonably have anticipated being "haled before a [California] court," *Shaffer v. Heitner*, 433 U.S., at 216, 97 S.Ct., at 2586. To make jurisdiction in a case such as this turn on whether appellant bought his daughter her ticket or instead unsuccessfully sought to prevent her departure would impose an unreasonable burden on family relations, and one wholly unjustified by the "quality and nature" of appellant's activities in or relating to the State of California. *International Shoe Co. v. Washington*, 326 U.S., at 319.

III

In seeking to justify the burden that would be imposed on appellant were the exercise of *in personam* jurisdiction in California sustained, appellee argues that California has substantial interests in protecting the welfare of its minor residents and in promoting to the fullest extent possible a healthy and supportive family environment in which the children of the State are to be raised. These interests are unquestionably important. But while the presence of the children and one parent in California arguably might favor application of California law in a lawsuit in New York, the fact that California may be the " 'center of gravity' " for choice-of-law purposes does not mean that California has personal jurisdiction over the defendant. *Hanson v. Denckla, supra*, 357 U.S., at 254.

California's legitimate interest in ensuring the support of children resident in California without unduly disrupting the children's lives, moreover, is already being served by the State's participation in the Revised Uniform Reciprocal Enforcement of Support Act of 1968. This statute provides a mechanism for communication between court systems in different States, in order to facilitate the procurement and enforcement of child-support decrees where the dependent children reside in a State that cannot obtain personal jurisdiction over the defendant. California's version of the Act essentially permits a California resident claiming support from a nonresident to file a petition in California and have its merits adjudicated in the State of the alleged obligor's residence, without either party's having to leave his or her own State. Cal.Civ.Proc. Code Ann. § 1650 *et seq.* (West 1972). New York State is a signatory to a similar Act. Thus not only may plaintiff-appellee here vindicate her claimed right to additional child support from her former husband in a New York court, but also the Uniform Acts will facilitate both her prosecution of a claim for additional support and collection of any support payments found to be owed by appellant.

It cannot be disputed that California has substantial interests in protecting resident children and in facilitating child-support actions on behalf of those children. But these interests simply do not make California a "fair forum," in which to require appellant, who derives no personal or commercial benefit from his child's presence in California and who lacks any other relevant contact with the State, either to defend a child-support suit or to suffer liability by default. . . .

Accordingly, we conclude that the appellant's motion to quash service, on the ground of lack of personal jurisdiction, was erroneously denied by the California courts. The judgment of the California Supreme Court is, therefore,

Reversed. . . .

NOTES AND QUESTIONS

(1) **In Personam Jurisdiction.** In a sense, *Kulko* is the equivalent of *Shaffer v. Heitner*, 433 U.S. 186 (1977), in the context of child support: both cases explore the outer limits of the "minimum contacts" test. The underlying premise of *Kulko* is of course that *in personam* jurisdiction is necessary for child support, and this premise is the generally accepted rule. *In personam* jurisdiction must be based upon presence or upon fulfillment of the requirements of the long-arm statute. The question for the Court is whether there is *in personam* jurisdiction based upon California's long-arm statute which is about as "long" as a statute can get, being limited only by the constitutional standard: "A court of this state may exercise jurisdiction on any basis not inconsistent with the Constitution of this state or of the United States." Cal. Code Civ. Proc. § 410.10 (1998).

(2) **Minimum Contacts.** Do you think the Court's analysis of the benefit conferred upon Mr. Kulko is accurate? Doesn't the father of a child, not just the child, receive a benefit from the laws of the state in which the child resides? Is there a financial benefit which accrues to the father? *Compare Kulko* with *McGee v. International Life Ins. Co.*, 355 U.S. 220 (1957) *with Burger King v. Rudzewicz*, 471 U.S. 462 (1985) (upholding single contact jurisdiction). Is sending a child to another state to live any less of a contact than a single insurance contract or a single franchise contract? Is the key difference the financial benefit received?

(3) **Custody Jurisdiction Compared.** It is interesting to note that Mr. Kulko did not contest jurisdiction for custody. The United States Supreme Court has held that personal jurisdiction over the respondent is also necessary in child custody disputes:

> In the instant case, the Ohio courts gave weight to appellee's contention that the Wisconsin award of custody [to the father] binds appellant [mother] because, at the time it was issued, her children had a technical domicile in Wisconsin, although they were neither resident nor present there. We find it unnecessary to determine the children's legal domicile because, even if it be with their father, *that does not give Wisconsin, certainly against Ohio, the personal jurisdiction that it must have in order to deprive their mother of her personal right to their immediate possession.*

May v. Anderson, 345 U.S. 528, 534 (1953) (emphasis added).

In *Kulko*, the state's interest in the protection of children did not outweigh the requirement of personal jurisdiction. Do you think this interest would prevail in a child custody dispute? Note that the major statutes which deal with child custody jurisdiction ignore the requirement of personal jurisdiction in child custody cases, dealing with the issue solely as one of subject matter jurisdiction. *See* Uniform Child Custody Jurisdiction Act, 9 U.L.A. 111 (1979); Parental Kidnaping Prevention Act, 28 U.S.C. § 1738A (1997); and the Uniform Child Custody Jurisdiction and Enforcement Act. When subject matter jurisdiction is upheld, the state in which the children are domiciled would always have jurisdiction to resolve both custody and support disputes at the same time. *See* § 12.06[B], *below*.

(4) **Practical Effect.** If one compares the hardship on Ms. Kulko of having to litigate the support issue in New York and the hardship on Mr. Kulko of having to litigate in California, are they of equal magnitude? Should the court have given greater weight to the

relative hardships on the parties? Or should the Court have given greater weight to California's interest in the protection of children? Do you think the result would have been different if the Revised Uniform Reciprocal Enforcement of Support Act of 1968, 9B U.L.A. 393 (West 1987), did not exist at the time? RURESA has since been replaced by the Uniform Interstate Family Support Act (UIFSA) discussed below.

[B] Interstate Enforcement

WELSHER v. RAGER
Court of Appeals of North Carolina
491 S.E.2d 661 (1997)

TIMMONS-GOODSON, JUDGE.

This action arises out of plaintiff Rosemarie Welsher's attempt to enforce a New York child support order. Plaintiff and defendant Paul Rager were divorced in 1980. In 1985, plaintiff petitioned for a court order recognizing an agreement for support executed by plaintiff and defendant on 17 January 1985. The order entered on 11 February 1985 in Monroe County, New York District Court provided, in pertinent part, that defendant was to be "legally responsible for the support" of the couple's two sons, Jeremy (born 26 May 1974) and Michael (born 26 November 1976). The order obligated defendant to make payments of $45.00 per week. Defendant signed the order voluntarily, waiving his right, both to be represented by an attorney and to object to the matter in family court.

Plaintiff still resides in New York. However, defendant has moved to Winston-Salem, North Carolina; and has refused to make any of the $45.00 payments since 6 July 1995. At that time, Jeremy and Michael were twenty-one and eighteen, respectively, and Michael had just graduated from high school.

Plaintiff initiated the present action by filing a petition requesting registration and enforcement of the 1985 New York child support order in Forsyth County, North Carolina. At the time that this petition was filed, Jeremy and Michael were aged twenty-two and nineteen, respectively. The petition claimed arrearage of $1,789.64 as of 11 April 1996, and included both a copy of the original order for support and a copy of New York's Uniform Support of Dependent's Law section 31–3, which establishes the age of emancipation in the State of New York at twenty-one years.

Defendant responded by filing an "Answer for Civil Suit," which alleged, in pertinent part, that the couple's original 1980 divorce decree only obligated him to support the children until they were eighteen and out of high school; that he did not knowingly agree to pay support until the children reached twenty-one; and that he felt that making support payments to an "adult" over the age of eighteen was unjustifiable. Accordingly, defendant asked that the court relieve him of any obligation under the 1985 order for support. The answer was made in an unverified written statement and included no documentation pertaining to the divorce decree. We note that at no time did defendant seek to modify his obligation based on Jeremy's emancipation.

The matter was heard by Judge Roland H. Hayes during the 30 July 1996 civil session of Forsyth County District Court. After hearing the arguments of both parties and examining plaintiff's evidence, the trial court granted defendant's motion to dismiss, and denied plaintiff's request for continued support. Plaintiff appeals.

Plaintiff brings forth four assignments of error on appeal. However, in light of our conclusions in regards to plaintiff's assignments of error 3 and 4, we need not address plaintiff's first two assignments of error at this juncture. We, therefore, proceed immediately to plaintiff's third assignment of error by which she argues that the trial court erred in failing to apply New York law in deciding whether to enforce the 1985 New York support order. Plaintiff contends that the Uniform Interstate Family Support Act (UIFSA), recently enacted by the North Carolina General Assembly, requires that a support order be interpreted according to the law of the state in which it is issued. We agree.

The Uniform Reciprocal Enforcement of Support Act (URESA) was repealed by the North Carolina General Assembly effective 1 January 1996. In its place, the legislature adopted UIFSA in Chapter 52C of our General Statutes. Both URESA and UIFSA were promulgated and intended to be used as procedural mechanisms for the establishment, modification, and enforcement of child and spousal support obligations. Under URESA, a state had jurisdiction to establish, vacate, or modify an obligor's support obligation even when that obligation had been created in another jurisdiction. The result was often multiple, inconsistent obligations existing for the same obligor and injustice in that obligers could avoid their responsibility by moving to another jurisdiction and having their support obligations modified or even vacated.

UIFSA was designed to correct this problem. UIFSA establishes a one order system whereby all states adopting UIFSA are required to recognize and enforce the same obligation consistently. A priority scheme is established for the recognition and enforcement of multiple existing support obligations. In instances where only one tribunal has issued a support order, that order becomes the one order to be recognized and enforced by states adopting UIFSA. For example, the official comment to section 5252C–6–603 of the North Carolina General Statutes notes,

> [a]lthough RURESA specifically subjects a registered order to "proceedings for reopening, vacating, or staying as a support order of this State," these remedies are not authorized under UIFSA. While a foreign support order is to be enforced and satisfied in the same manner as if it had been issued by a tribunal of the registering state, the order to be enforced remains an order of the issuing state. Conceptually, the responding state is enforcing the order of another state, not its own order.

The one order system is applicable even where the state initiating the order has not adopted UIFSA.

Once the validity of the one order is determined, enforcement by the registering tribunal is obligatory, with two exceptions. The registering tribunal may vacate or modify the order if (1) both parties consent to the modification, or (2) the child, the obligor and the individual obligee have all permanently left the issuing state and the registering state can claim personal jurisdiction over all of them.

A non-registering party may also avoid enforcement of an order by successfully contesting its registration. Upon filing, a support order becomes registered in North Carolina and, unless successfully contested, must be recognized and enforced. N.C.G.S § 52C–6–603. The procedure for contesting a registered order is set out in Part Two of Article 6 of UIFSA, entitled "Contest of Validity of Enforcement." Under section 52C–6–607 of the General Statutes, a party seeking to vacate an order's registration has the burden of proving at least one of seven narrowly-defined defenses. The possible defenses are as follows:

(1) the issuing tribunal lacked jurisdiction; (2) the order was fraudulently obtained; (3) the order has been vacated, suspended or modified; (4) the issuing tribunal has been stayed pending appeal; (5) the remedy sought is not available in this state; (6) payment has been made in full or in part; and (7) enforcement is precluded by the statute of limitations. N.C. Gen.Stat. § 52C–6–607(a)(1995).

If the defending party either fails to contest the registration or does not establish a defense under 52C–6–607(a), the registering tribunal is required by law to confirm the order.

In terms of choice of law, URESA generally required that the law applied in interpreting and/or enforcing the support order be that of the state in which enforcement was sought. However, UIFSA provides, "The law of the issuing state governs the nature, extent, amount, and duration of current payments and other obligations of support and the payment of arrears under the order." N.C. Gen.Stat. § 52C-6-604(a)(1995). The official comment to section 52C–6–604 notes that this means "an order for the support of a child until age 21 must be recognized and enforced in that manner in a state in which the duty of support of a child ends at age 18." N.C.G.S. § 52C–6–604, official comment.

In the case *sub judice*, the trial court was apparently operating under repealed URESA procedures. Plaintiff's petition includes a document entitled "Plaintiff's Statement of Fact for Registration of Foreign Support Order Under URESA." The trial court's order is written on a form which reads, in pertinent part, "before the undersigned Judge presiding over the Uniform Reciprocal Enforcement of Support Act (U.R.E.S.A.) Session of the Civil District Court . . . ."

Plaintiff's support order became registered in North Carolina upon filing. Applying the appropriate law, UIFSA, the record is devoid of a defense under section 52C–6–607 of the General Statutes, which would justify vacating a properly registered support order. Under UIFSA, unless the court finds that the defendant has met his burden of proving one of the specified defenses, enforcement is compulsory. The trial court's single finding of fact in the present case was that the children had reached eighteen. Under URESA, such a finding may have been sufficient to deny enforcement since North Carolina law would have governed interpretation of the order, and provided for emancipation at eighteen. However, as URESA has been repealed, New York law, which provides that the age of emancipation is twenty-one, must be applied in enforcing the 11 February 1985 foreign order. . . .

Reversed and remanded.

NOTES AND QUESTIONS

(1) **RURESA.** The Revised Uniform Reciprocal Enforcement of Support Act of 1968 is often referred to as URESA rather than the more appropriate RURESA. The usage of the term "Revised" is part of the official designation because the 1968 version is actually a revision of a 1950 version, which was an early attempt to solve the problem of support enforcement. RURESA was adopted in all states.

RURESA was designed to aid the obligee parent in enforcing a support order in a foreign state without leaving his or her state of residence. There were actually two procedures established by RURESA. The first was a combined two–state proceeding which could be instigated whenever there was an identifiable support obligation. The obligee or a state agency supporting the child filed a petition in the state of residence. The court in that state examined the petition to see if there was an identifiable duty to support and forwarded the petition and supporting documentation to the state where the obligor was located. The appropriately designated official of that state, usually a County District Attorney, brought an action to enforce the support order against the obligor. A hearing *de novo* was conducted in the obligor's state under the laws of that state; because the hearing was *de novo*, the obligor could defend himself by (1) attempting to disprove the obligation or (2) attempting to modify a previous award. If the court found a support obligation, it fixed the amount and ordered payment to be made to the designated official in the obligor's state. This official collected the payments, monitored the obligor's compliance, and forwarded the money to the obligee's state, where it was paid to the obligee.

The second approach allowed an obligee with a support judgment to register the judgment in the obligor's state, where it would be enforced by the designated agency in that state. The obligor was entitled to a hearing and to raise any defenses that were available in the original state. With this procedure, too, the obligor's state collected and forwarded the actual support payments. In effect the initiating and responding states, under both procedures, bore the financial burden of enforcing the support order. RURESA §§ 35–40, 9B U.L.A. 540–46 (West 1987). For a good discussion of RURESA procedures, see Fox, *The Uniform Reciprocal Enforcement of Support Act*, 12 Fam. L.Q. 113 (1978).

(2) **Full Faith and Credit.** The Full Faith and Credit Clause also did not provide much finality for support orders. While the states are required to provide full faith and credit to the support orders of sister states, *Yarborough v. Yarborough*, 290 U.S. 202 (1933), the full faith and credit requirement does not prevent the forum state from modifying the original decree. See *Elkind v. Byck*, 439 P.2d 316 (Cal. 1968); *Moore v. Moore*, 107 N.W.2d 97 (Iowa 1961); *Banton v. Mathers*, 309 N.E.2d 167 (Ind. 1974).

(3) **Uniform Interstate Family Support Act.** The thorough revision of RURESA, which ultimately became the Uniform Interstate Family Support Act, began in 1988, when the National Conference of Commissioners on Uniform State Laws formed a Drafting Committee. The result of this Committee's work was adopted by the Commissioners in 1992 and by the American Bar Association in 1993. See John J. Sampson and Paul M. Kurtz, *UIFSA: An Interstate Support Act For the 21st Century,* 27 Fam. L.Q. 85, 97 (1993); Marygold S. Melli, *The United States: Child Support Enforcement for the 21st Century* 32 U. Louisville J. Fam. L. 475, 484 (1993–94). The Personal Responsibility and Work Opportunity Reconciliation Act of 1996 (PRWORA) required that all states adopt the Uniform Interstate Family Support Act by January 1, 1998 or face loss of federal block grants funding state welfare programs. Pub. L. No. 104–193, 110 Stat. 2105 § 32, codified at 42 U.S.C. § 666(f). UIFSA is a long and complex statute, the most significant features of which are as follows:

    a. *Jurisdiction.* UIFSA expands personal jurisdiction to the limits of *Kulko*. Section 201 deals with the "Bases for Jurisdiction over [a] Nonresident":

    In a proceeding to establish, enforce, or modify a support order or to determine parentage, a tribunal of this State may exercise personal jurisdiction over a nonresident individual [or the individual's guardian or conservator] if:

        (1) the individual is personally served with [citation, summons, notice] within this State;

(2) the individual submits to the jurisdiction of this State by consent, by entering a general appearance, or by filing a responsive document having the effect of waiving any contest to personal jurisdiction;

(3) the individual resided with the child in this State;

(4) the individual resided in this State and provided prenatal expenses or support for the child;

(5) the child resides in this State as a result of the acts or directives of the individual;

(6) the individual engaged in sexual intercourse in this State and the child may have been conceived by that act of intercourse;

[(7) the individual asserted parentage in the [putative father registry] maintained in this State by the [appropriate agency];] or

(8) there is any other basis consistent with the constitutions of this State and the United States for the exercise of personal jurisdiction.

The purpose of this provision is to give the custodial parent or the state agency attempting to establish or collect support the maximum opportunity to do so in that state without resorting to the two-state proceedings of RURESA. Do you think that Mr. Kulko would be subject to California jurisdiction under this § 201? Would purchasing the ticket for Ilsa establish jurisdiction? Do you think that all of the provisions of this act will stand up to the kind of constitutional scrutiny applied in *Kulko*? In answering this question it is helpful to consider what kind of conduct might lead to jurisdiction. Former residence in the state would seem to qualify if the respondent ever lived with the child, paid support, or paid prenatal expenses there. Or, if a nonresident actually did choose to send the child to the state asserting jurisdiction. This might mean that if a custodial parent becomes ill or disabled and is forced to send the child to another state to live with the noncustodial parent, he or she may be submitting to jurisdiction. Or, perhaps a single act of sexual intercourse in the state may lead to jurisdiction. While this would seem to make sense in a parentage case, this provision could be a basis for asserting jurisdiction in a case like *Kulko* where the couple had passed through the state early in their marriage.

b. *Two-State Proceeding Retained.* The two-state proceeding under RURESA, described above in Note 1, is retained under UIFSA. In other words, a support order of one state can be forwarded to another state which has jurisdiction over the obligor, registered in the second state, and enforced by the courts of the second state. However because of the expanded jurisdictional grounds discussed in "a," *above*, the two-state proceeding should be less necessary.

c. *Choice of Law.* UIFSA applies the law of the forum state. This simple approach is in contrast to the more complicated approach of RURESA, which applied the law of the state where the support obligation accrued. In the case of arrearages, a forum court might have to apply the law of several other states. *See* § 202.

d. *One-Order System.* In response to the problem of conflicting support orders under RURESA, UIFSA applies a one-order system; that is, the provisions are structured so that only one child support order will exist, and that order will have continuing viability. Section 204 controls issues of conflicting tribunals by severely limiting when a petition can be filed in one state if a pleading has already been filed in another state. Section 205 gives a state "continuing, exclusive jurisdiction over a child-support order . . . as long as this State remains the residence of the obligor, the individual obligee, or the child for whose benefit the support order is issued . . . ." Under § 206, the state tribunal which issued the original support order continues to have jurisdiction to modify so long as the child and the obligee are present.

e. *Private Attorneys.* The act applies to actions brought by both state agencies (§ 307(a)) and by private attorneys (§ 309).

f. *Registration.* Interstate judicial enforcement usually begins with registration of a support order with a court, or tribunal as it is called, in the state where enforcement is sought. This procedure was a basis of RURESA, and it has continued under UIFSA. Once the order is registered, it is enforced by a tribunal in the state where it is registered, using either the support enforcement mechanisms of the local jurisdiction or those imposed by the UIFSA itself. *See* §§ 601–604.

g. *Modification.* One of the key aspects of the UIFSA is that the ability of an enforcing state to modify a support order is severely limited. Under RURESA, when an action was brought in another state to enforce a support order, the obligor could readily move for modification and, because the changed-circumstances test was potentially very broad, modification was common. Under UIFSA, the power of an enforcing state to modify is severely limited. Indeed, the original jurisdiction in which the support order was issued has the exclusive power to modify unless the original state has lost jurisdiction because the child and the custodial parent have left. If the issuing state has lost jurisdiction, another state may modify the order if it has jurisdiction over both parties. However, once another state has validly modified a support order under the UIFSA, as when all the parties have moved to that state, the modified order of the second state becomes the only enforceable order. *See* §§ 205, 206, 605–608.

h. *Enforcement.* There are also streamlined enforcement features. In order to trigger wage withholding, § 501 allows a support order to be mailed directly to an employer in another state. This means that there is no need for a hearing unless the payor actively seeks one. And § 502 provides another kind of direct enforcement: "a party seeking to enforce a support order or income-withholding order . . . may send the documents required for registering the orders to a support enforcement agency of [another] State."

(4) Full Faith and Credit for Child Support Orders Act of 1994. The UIFSA is bolstered by a federal law known as the Full Faith and Credit for Child Support Orders Act of 1994, Pub. L. No. 103–383, 108 Stat. 4064, codified at 28 U.S.C. § 1738B(1997). This law requires that full faith and credit be given to support orders which are consistent with enumerated standards, those standards being the same as the requirements for a valid order under the UIFSA. *See* 28 U.S.C. § 1738B(c)(1)(A)–(B),(2) (1997). In addition, it prohibits the modification of support orders issued by a jurisdiction with continuing exclusive jurisdiction. *Id.* at § 1738B(e).

CHAPTER 12

PARENTING AFTER DIVORCE: CHILD CUSTODY AND VISITATION

SYNOPSIS

§ 12.01 Introduction
§ 12.02 Factors In Disputed Cases
    [A] The Best Interest Standard
    [B] The Gender of the Parents
    [C] The Primary Caretaker
    [D] Child's Preference
    [E] Religion
    [F] Race
    [G] Parental Fitness
        [1] Sexual Conduct
        [2] Sexual Preference
    [H] Physical and Mental Health
    [I] Working Parents
    [J] Child Abuse and Domestic Violence
§ 12.03 Visitation
§ 12.04 Joint Custody and Parenting Plans
§ 12.05 Modification
    [A] Changed Circumstances or Best Interest
    [B] Relocation
§ 12.06 Child Custody Jurisdiction
    [A] Introduction
    [B] Traditional Jurisdiction
    [C] State Legislation
    [D] Federal Legislation
    [E] International Law

§ 12.01 Introduction

Normally, parents determine what is in the best interest of their children. Most couples while they are married do a good job making decisions for their children, and these couples continue to do so when they get a divorce. They sometimes set up a parenting plan which usually has the children with one parent the majority of the time and with the other for a lesser period of time. The parenting plan may be characterized in terms of custody and visitation, or it may be called joint custody. The parents may have to struggle to put aside their personal differences to continue to make good decisions for their kids, but they do it. While we always hear about custody battles, millions of parents have gone on raising their kids after divorce without the benefit of court intervention.

Then a dispute over custody erupts. The parents begin to lose control. And if the case reaches a trial, the parents have completely lost their right to make one of the major decisions of their child's life. The parents are going to have an objective third party—someone outside the family—scrutinize their fitness as parents and examine their idiosyncrasies and behavior. Normally acceptable parental conduct, which would never cause a married parent to lose custody, may become the factor which tips the scales against the divorcing parent.

The court in a custody dispute must make a decision of Solomonic proportions, and the law gives the court little guidance. The court is simply told to do what is in the "best interest of the child." Sometimes this decision will be easy because the conduct of one of the parents has been so egregious—for example, where a parent has physically or sexually abused the child, clearly the other parent should get custody. Sometimes the child will be old enough that the court can be aided by the child's preference, but then the court must undertake the ticklish task of eliciting the child's preference without injuring the child's relationship with the other parent.

In most cases the court will have two good parents to choose from, but although this means the child will be well cared for no matter what the court's decision, that decision does not become any easier. When the factors are equal and both parents would be fit, the best interests decision becomes more subtle: should the court try to preserve a loving relationship between the child and both parents with both parents sharing in child raising? Or should the court create stability by giving the custodial parent the maximum control over the child? The court must look at many factors and then make a wise decision.

Historically there have been times when the law provided judges with more guidance in determining child custody. Originally, unless the father was unfit, the father had an absolute right to the custody and control of a child. Later, the pendulum swung to the presumption that a child of tender years should be placed with the mother.

The present best interest standard is a broad concept which gives the court great discretion after looking at all the facts. Although the courts have often discussed what factors can be considered, the trial court's ultimate decision is one of fact which is given great deference on appeal. The trial court can avoid this decision to some degree by ordering joint custody; however, the decision between joint and sole custody can sometimes be just as difficult as the issue of who should have custody.

Once the custody decision is made, other problems arise. How often should the noncustodial parent be allowed to visit and how should visitation be enforced? If the decision is in favor of joint custody, what will be the living arrangement for the child? Should the court make any special orders? For example, should the court condition visitation on the parent not having a lover spend the night during periods of visitation? Moreover, when should the custody arrangement be changed? On the one hand there is a strong need for finality, so that there is a chance for certainty in the child's life; on the other, circumstances do arise which may require change. How should the court handle technical issues such as jurisdiction if they arise?

Amidst all this potential conflict there is a child. There can be no doubt that children survive divorce, and sometimes they do so remarkably well. Yet, at the very least the parent's divorce is a trying time for the child, and at worst it can cause life-long trauma.

The difficult questions make clear one general rule: it is better for all concerned if the custody battle is avoided. The parents can continue to guide the growth of their child. The child does not have to suffer through as much conflict and does not have to make a difficult decision between parents. If the parents continue to cooperate, the child will still have the benefit of two important adult relationships. And the court will not have to make an imperfect choice based upon limited information.

Fortunately the movement toward "alternate dispute resolution" is very much a part of contemporary family law. Mediation is becoming a common way to resolve custody disputes. A number of states now require mediation before a court will hear a custody case. Mediation, when it works, gives the parents a sense of accomplishment and self-determination, and lessens the amount of conflict which the children must experience.

§ 12.02 Factors In Disputed Cases

[A] The Best Interest Standard

MAXFIELD v. MAXFIELD
Supreme Court of Minnesota
452 N.W.2d 219 (1990)

SIMONETT, JUSTICE.

The trial court awarded custody of the four children to the father. The court of appeals reversed, awarding custody of the three youngest children to the mother and remanding the issue of the oldest child's custody to the trial court for reconsideration. We affirm.

In April 1987, after 10 years of marriage and four children, Steven and Diane Maxfield separated. The couple had then been living in Verndale, Minnesota, Steven's hometown, for 3 years. Two months after separating, in June, Diane and the four children returned to Wilkes-Barre, Pennsylvania, Diane's hometown, ostensibly for a visit, but actually because Diane had decided to end the marriage.

Unable to persuade Diane to return to Verndale, Steven filed a separation action requesting custody of the four children. Diane countered with a dissolution petition and requested custody of the children. A year later, in July 1988, the case was called for trial. During that year the children were with their mother in Pennsylvania. At the time of trial Steven and Diane were both 34 years old. The three youngest children, Jacinta, Therese, and Aleshia, were 2, 4, and 8 years, respectively. The oldest child, Jeremiah, was 10.

The trial judge heard the testimony of the parties and their witnesses and received in evidence reports from the social services personnel of Luzerne County, Pennsylvania, and Wadena County, Minnesota. The court made the following (here abbreviated) findings of fact:

> 1. While the family was together in Verndale, Steven was away at trade school and at work, and the care of the four children, for the most part, fell to Diane.

2. Diane was home alone with the children most of the time. She had no car, no phone, few friends, and little money. She felt isolated in the small rural community and became depressed. Her housekeeping was seriously substandard. Diane sought counseling from Wadena County Social Services for her loss of self-esteem and self-confidence. In April 1987, at Diane's request, Steven moved out of the house and lived in a pickup camper in a woods on a friend's property. Steven spent time with the family, however, virtually every weekend.

3. About the end of June, Diane returned to Pennsylvania with the four children. She told Steven it was only for a visit, and Steven along with Diane's mother paid for the air fare; in fact, Diane intended to stay in Pennsylvania. Diane kept her residence a secret and Steven was almost totally cut off from contact with his family. Steven did, however, visit with the children in Pennsylvania over the Thanksgiving weekend, and in June 1988 for a few weeks prior to and during trial, the children lived in Steven's home.

4. Diane appeared to be doing a satisfactory job of homemaking and housekeeping in her subsidized housing apartment in Pennsylvania, as reported by the social worker. The two oldest children did well in school but Jeremiah felt picked on.

5. Steven and Diane had met and were married while Steven was in the Army. When Diane returned to Pennsylvania she met a much older man, through an advertisement, and planned to marry him. (This man testified at trial.) There was some evidence that Jeremiah did not like this proposed marriage. The proposed marriage would introduce an element of "disequilibrium" into the family setting, as the children would move once again. (Since the trial these marriage plans have been abandoned.)

6. Jeremiah and Aleshia, the two oldest children, were interviewed by Dr. Ralph Scheer, a psychologist, who also serves in the Wadena County guardian ad litem program. This was pursuant to an arrangement made by counsel and the court. Jeremiah told Dr. Scheer the housing project was noisy, with much bad talk, and the children missed their pets on the farm. Dr. Scheer attempted to elicit the two children's custodial preference without asking them directly to choose between the parents. The two children expressed a preference for Verndale.

7. Dr. Scheer felt that Aleshia, then 8, was not mature enough to express a valid preference. He did feel that Jeremiah definitely preferred a small-town environment and life style, which could be interpreted as the boy's preference to live with his father. Even though Jeremiah had done well in school in Pennsylvania, he felt more "at home" in Verndale.

8. Steven now has a full-time, permanent job. For the time being, Steven's mother helps with the children in the morning before Steven goes to work and takes them to the babysitter for the day. At the end of the day, the grandmother picks up the children and takes them to Steven's home and waits until Steven gets home from work. Steven has demonstrated that he is able to provide for the needs of the children.

After making the foregoing findings of fact, the trial court then made the following (here summarized) conclusions of law:

. . . .

(3) In considering the best interests of the children under Minn.Stat. § 518.17, subd. 1 (1988), a consideration of the evidence "points unmistakably toward an award of custody in favor of Steven." In this connection: (a) Both of the older children prefer Verndale. (b) One or more of the children have a particularly close relationship with the paternal grandmother. (c) While the report cards of the two oldest children suggest "things out east were perhaps not as bad as described by the children," nevertheless the children expressed to Dr. Scheer concerns and difficulties in adjusting to home, school and the community in Pennsylvania. (d) An award of custody to Diane (if she remarries) presents the prospect of another change and a lack of continuity with respect to their environment in Pennsylvania. Verndale appears to present a more permanent custodial home. (e) The expressed preference of the two older children for Verndale (even after being gone for over a year) "makes clear the degree to which the children feel a strong emotional bond with their father. Thus . . . an award of custody to the father would be consistent with maintenance of continuity and stability for the children with respect to emotional and psychological attachment to the primary psychological parent." (f) There is a strong likelihood that Diane, if awarded custody, would restrict Steven's contacts with the children, destroying any meaningful relationship the father might hope to have with the children. . . .

The issue, as we see it, is whether the trial court's best interests analysis was correctly applied.

[T]he evidence is undisputed that all four children love both their father and their mother. As Dr. Scheer put it, "I saw evidence of real love for both the mother and the father." From this the trial court concluded an award of custody to the father would be consistent with an attachment to the primary psychological parent. This conclusion, however, is inconsistent with the trial court's determination that the children's mother is already their primary parent. This inconsistency is never explained. Nothing occurred during the year between separation and trial to suggest Diane ceased to be the primary parent.

The trial court felt that the expressed preference of the two oldest children for the Verndale environment should be given great weight. It followed then, thought the trial court, that rather than split the family, all four children should be with the father. Yet this reasoning is difficult to reconcile with the fact that the four children are also devoted to their mother, that they were doing relatively well in Wilkes-Barre, and that it is the mother who has primarily cared for the children all their years up to the time of trial.

Here was a "traditional" marriage with Diane at home with the children and Steven at work full time away from the home. Diane, lonely and isolated at Verndale, becomes listless and depressed. She returns home to Pennsylvania where her emotional health improves. Her homemaking and housekeeping practices now in Pennsylvania are, as the trial court found, satisfactory. While the trial court noted the two oldest children (or at least Jeremiah) preferred living in Verndale, neither Verndale nor Wilkes-Barre was found by the trial court to be an unwholesome environment. Diane's conduct in denying Steven contact with the children when they were in Pennsylvania is not to be condoned, but the court can take measures to reinforce her assurance given at trial that Steven will have access to the children. The trial court's concern that Diane's proposed remarriage would be disruptive has been mooted.

In applying a best interests analysis, we recognize much must be left to the discretion of the trial court. Some statutory criteria will weigh more in one case and less in another and there is rarely an easy answer. [T]he golden thread running through any best interests analysis is the importance, for a young child in particular, of its bond with the primary parent as this relationship bears on the other criteria, such as the need for "a stable, satisfactory environment and the desirability of maintaining continuity" and "the mental and physical health of all individuals involved." *Rosenfeld v. Rosenfeld*, 311 Minn. 76, 81, 249 N.W.2d 168, 170-71 (1976). Usually this relationship "should not be disrupted without strong reasons * * *." *Berndt*, 292 N.W.2d at 2. Here we conclude that the trial court exceeded the proper bounds of its discretion in awarding custody of the three youngest children to Steven. Their best interests are served if custody is with Diane.

Jeremiah is old enough and mature enough to express a preference where and with whom he wishes to live during his approaching teen-age years. The appeals panel felt that Jeremiah had expressed only a geographical preference, not a custodial preference, in his interview with Dr. Scheer.

We affirm, therefore, the court of appeals' decision awarding custody of the three youngest children to Diane and remanding Jeremiah's custody to the trial court.... The trial court will also, of course, have to consider the important matter of visiting rights by the noncustodial spouse and the protection of those rights. *Affirmed.*

YETKA, J., dissents with opinion in which POPOVICH, C.J., and KELLEY, J., joins.

I dissent because I believe that the majority opinion is a serious departure from well-settled rules governing the scope of appellate review. Moreover, I believe that it circumvents the clear intent of the legislature expressed by repeated legislative attempts, including very recent amendments to Minn.Stat. § 518.17, to eliminate inflexible and stereotypical presumptions in child custody cases. In so doing, the majority opinion ignores the proper roles of the legislature and the courts in these matters.

. . . .

Everyone seems to agree that the best interests of the children should prevail. That standard, in my opinion, was not applied to this case. In order to demonstrate this point, I feel compelled to outline the history of the law governing contested child custody cases in Minnesota.

Until about 20 years ago, the law in Minnesota child custody cases was that, in almost all cases, the mother received custody of the parties' young children unless she was unfit. The rule in these cases rested on the stereotypical notion that it was automatically in the best interests of a young child to live with the mother. This maternal presumption has become known as the "tender-years doctrine."

Starting in the late 1960's, no-fault divorce advocates and various equal rights groups insisted that divorce statutes be amended to discard the tender-years doctrine and codify the rule that the best interests of the child be the test. In 1969, the Minnesota Legislature codified the "best-interests-of-the-child" standard and prohibited consideration of the proposed custodian's gender. This court, however, basically ignored the legislature's first attempt to eliminate the tender-years doctrine. . . . In 1974, the legislature amended Minn.Stat. § 518.17, subd. 1 in order to provide specific guidelines and require the courts to consider several factors. However, when lower courts actually started to award custody to the father in certain cases, the people who originally favored the objective statutory factors began arguing that the law should move in the opposite direction. Finally, this court adopted the *Pikula* rule, which provides that the primary caretaker has a presumption in his or her favor. The *Pikula* presumption basically instructs trial courts to substitute a list of homemaking duties for "all relevant factors" expressly provided in Minn.Stat. § 518.17, subd. 1. See id. at 1359. The *Pikula* presumption, although neutral on its face, has a readily apparent disparate impact on fathers. In other words, we seem to have completed a full cycle and are attempting to get the tender-years doctrine in through the back door so that, once again, it will be the mother who is invariably granted custody of the children unless she is found to be unfit. Whether we favor such a rule or not, that is not the law in Minnesota. The recent amendments to Minn.Stat. § 518.17, subd. 1 are the legislature's third attempt to force this court to abandon inflexible presumptions about who is best able to care for a young child. It seems to me that, in refusing to let go of the *Pikula* presumption, the majority, by judicial fiat, is ignoring the intent of the legislature and reviving the tender-years doctrine.

As one can readily see from the findings of fact, the trial court has done exactly what this court has said in numerous opinions a trial court should do. Mechanically applied presumptions are not useful in child custody cases. Each case is unique. A trial court must consider a great deal of testimony and other evidence, much of it conflicting. The trial court is the appropriate finder of fact and is in the best position to judge the credibility of witnesses. I doubt whether one could find a case where a trial court has spent more time and made more detailed and careful findings of fact than has been done in this case. Moreover, I submit that the trial court's conclusions of law were justified by those facts. I find it simply extraordinary that either the court of appeals or this court would take it upon itself to reverse a trial court when it can't point to one of the findings as being erroneous. In other words, we have now reverted to a rule of law in Minnesota where an appellate court will dictate a result-orientated decision rather than a principled decision based on fact or law.

For all the above reasons, I would reverse the court of appeals and reinstate the decision made by the trial court.

NOTES AND QUESTIONS

(1) **Statutes.** The statute referred to in *Maxfield* serves as a good example of a modern provision which enumerates the factors involved in the "best interest standard":

Minn. Stat. Ann. § 518.17
Custody and Support of Children on Judgment

Subdivision 1. The best interests of the child.

(a) "The best interests of the child" means all relevant factors to be considered and evaluated by the court including:

  (1) the wishes of the child's parent or parents as to custody;

  (2) the reasonable preference of the child, if the court deems the child to be of sufficient age to express preference;

  (3) the child's primary caretaker;

(4) the intimacy of the relationship between each parent and the child;

(5) the interaction and interrelationship of the child with a parent or parents, siblings, and any other person who may significantly affect the child's best interests;

(6) the child's adjustment to home, school, and community;

(7) the length of time the child has lived in a stable, satisfactory environment and the desirability of maintaining continuity;

(8) the performance, as a family unit, of the existing or proposed custodial home;

(9) the mental and physical health of all individuals involved; except that a disability... of a proposed custodian or the child shall not be determinative of custody of the child, unless the proposed custodial arrangement is not in the best interest of the child;

(10) the capacity and disposition of the parties to give the child love, affection, and guidance, and to continue educating and raising the child in the child's culture and religion or creed, if any;

(11) the child's cultural background;

(12) the effect on the child of the actions of an abuser, if related to domestic abuse... that has occurred between the parents; and

(13) except in cases in which a finding of domestic abuse... the disposition of each parent to encourage and permit frequent and continuing contact by the other parent with the child.

The court may not use one factor to the exclusion of all others. The primary caretaker factor may not be used as a presumption in determining the best interests of the child. The court must make detailed findings on each of the factors and explain how the factors led to its conclusions and to the determination of the best interests of the child.

Like Minnesota, many states attempt to give judges guidance in applying the best interest standard by providing a list of factors to consider. The states also provide some uniformity and open the door to appellate review by requiring the judge to make detailed findings of fact. *See* Uniform Marriage and Divorce Act § 402, 9A U.L.A. 147 (1987). It is also worth noting that usually these statutes are not intended to be exclusive. The basic inclusiveness of the best interest standard asserts itself in the phrase "all relevant factors" at the beginning of the Minnesota Statute.

(2) Legal Effects of the Best Interest Standard. While it is obvious that the best interest standard makes the welfare of the child the highest priority, the principal case makes it clear that there are a number of other important legal aspects of the standard:

(a) The standard gives the trial court great discretion. The parties may find that the fate of their children is decided by a person with very different values from their own.

(b) Appellate courts will give the decision of the trial court great deference. The trial court cannot be overturned unless a high standard is met: abuse of discretion, gross abuse of discretion, or, as the principal case states, manifestly erroneous. In fact, appeals are not common in this area.

(c) The standard may encourage litigation since the decision must be made on a case-by-case basis.

(d) The standard makes custody cases fact-intensive, and the outcome is difficult to predict.

(3) **Human Decision.** It is difficult to imagine that this flexible standard could be supplanted by a formula or even by a bright-line legal standard. The best interest standard insures that the decision is made by a thinking, feeling human being who looks at all the relevant facts. *But see* Otto & Butcher, *Computer-Assisted Psychological Assessment in Child Custody Evaluations*, 29 Fam. L.Q. Spring 1995 at 79.

(4) **Court-Ordered Evaluation.** Often the best interests of the child will be determined by the court with the assistance of an outside evaluator, for example a social worker or psychologist. The evaluator interviews the parties, children, and others, inspects the homes of both parents, and ultimately writes a report which usually includes a recommendation. The reports are especially helpful to judges in evaluating the relationship between the parent and child. The frequency of these reports varies greatly from state to state. For a representative evaluation scheme, see Minn. Stat. Ann. §§ 518.167, 518.17.

[B] The Gender of the Parents

PUSEY v. PUSEY
Utah Supreme Court
728 P.2d 117 (1986)

Durham, Justice.

. . . .

The parties were married twelve years and had two sons, aged twelve and nine at the time of trial in 1984. . . .

The trial court conversed with the parties' two minor children in chambers and learned that the older boy expressed a marked preference for living with his father, whereas the younger boy indicated equal attachment of both parents. In spite of recommendations by a social worker that the parties be awarded joint custody and by plaintiff's brother, who had given the family professional counseling, that plaintiff would be the better parent to have custody of both children, the trial court awarded custody of the older boy to defendant and custody of the younger to plaintiff, with reasonable visitation rights in both parties.

III.

Plaintiff cross-appeals from that portion of the divorce decree awarding custody of the older son of the marriage to defendant and requests that both children be awarded to her. This Court's judicial preference for the mother, reaffirmed in *Nilson v. Nilson*, 652 P.2d 1323 (Utah 1982), and *Lembach v. Cox*, 639 P.2d 197 (Utah 1981), is cited in support. We acknowledged in dictum the continued vitality of the preference in *Jorgenson v. Jorgenson*, 599 P.2d 510, 511 (Utah 1979), "all other things being equal." We believe the time has come to discontinue our support, even in dictum, for the notion of gender-based preferences in child custody cases. A review of the cases cited by plaintiff shows that "all other things" are rarely equal, and therefore this Court has not treated a direct challenge to the maternal preference rule in over five years. In the unlikely event that a case with absolute equality "of all things" concerning custody is presented to us, the provisions of article IV, section 1 of the Utah Constitution and of the fourteenth amendment of the United States Constitution would preclude us from relying on gender as a determining factor.

Several courts have declared the maternal preference, or "tender years presumption," unconstitutional. As early as 1973, the New York Family Court, Kooper, J., held that "application of the 'tender years presumption' would deprive [the father] of his right to equal protection of the law under the Fourteenth Amendment to the United States Constitution." *State ex rel. Watts v. Watts*, 77 Misc.2d 285, 350 N.Y.S.2d 285, 290 (1973). Citing several studies which determined that a child needs "mothering" rather than a mother, the court determined that the presumption does not serve a compelling state interest. Although *Watts* used a strict scrutiny test, it is equally doubtful that the maternal preference can be sustained on an intermediate level of review. This is particularly true when the tender years doctrine is used as a "tie-breaker," as it is in Utah, because in that situation the Court is "denying custody to all fathers who . . . *are as capable as the mother. . . .* [W]hile over inclusiveness [sic] is tolerable at the rational basis level of review, it becomes problematic at the heightened level of scrutiny recognized in gender discrimination cases." [*See* Hyde, *Child Custody in Divorce*, 35 Juv. & Fam. Ct. J. 1, 11 (1984)].

Even ignoring the constitutional infirmities of the maternal preference, the rule lacks validity because it is unnecessary and perpetuates outdated stereotypes. The development of the tender years doctrine was perhaps useful in a society in which fathers traditionally worked outside the home and mothers did not; however, since that pattern is no longer prevalent, particularly in post-separation single-parent households, the tender years doctrine is equally anachronistic. Further, "[b]y arbitrarily applying a presumption in favor of the mother and awarding custody to her on that basis, a court is not truly evaluating what is in the child's best interests." *Id.* at 10.

We believe that the choice in competing child custody claims should instead be based on function-related factors. Prominent among these, though not exclusive, is the identity of the primary caretaker during the marriage. Other factors should include the identity of the parent with greater flexibility to provide personal care for the child and the identity of the parent with whom the child has spent most of his or her time pending custody determination if that period has been lengthy. Another important factor should be the stability of the environment provided by each parent.

In accord with those guidelines, we disavow today those cases that continue to approve, even indirectly, an arbitrary maternal preference, thereby encouraging arguments such as those made by the cross-appellant in this case.

In *Jorgenson*, 599 P.2d 510 (Utah 1979), we affirmed a split custody award made by the court. "While it is true that a child custody award which keeps all the children of the marriage united is generally preferred to one which divides them between the parents, that preference is not binding in the face of considerations dictating a contrary course of action." *Id.* at 512.

Although the trial court in this case found both parties to be fit custodial parents, its ultimate judgment on custody required an assessment of the complex situation before it. The court did not follow the recommendations made by the social worker or the plaintiff's brother. As child custody determination turns on numerous factors, however, that choice was within it discretion. The evidence indicated that the twelve-year-old son manifested a strong preference for his father, which had caused friction and ill feelings between him and his mother. The father also appeared to show a preference for the older son, which fact supports the trial court's decision to split the custody of the children between the parents. Certainly these were factors dictating the course of action taken by the trial court. We find no abuse of discretion in the custody award.

The judgment is affirmed, the parties to bear the costs incurred in their respective appeals.

NOTES AND QUESTIONS

(1) **Common Law.** Gender as a factor in child custody decisions originally favored fathers. The common law rule was that the father had to be awarded custody unless he was, in modern terms, unfit. *See* Brown, Comment, *The Custody of Children*, 2 Ind. L.J. 325 (1926).

(2) **Tender Years Presumption.** In more recent years, courts have favored the mother as a custodial parent. Often this preference was stated as a presumption: all things being equal, the court will presume that the child of tender years should be placed with the mother. *See, e.g., Hammac v. Hammac*, 19 So. 2d 392 (Ala. 1944) (stating that the tender years presumption was not a classification based upon gender, but merely a factual presumption based upon the historic role of the mother); *Daigle v. Daigle*, 222 So. 2d 318, 321 (La. Ct. App. 1969) (holding that "[i]t is in the best interest of small children to be placed in the custody of their mother"); *Morrow v. Morrow*, 218 So. 2d 393, 395 (La. Ct. App. 1969) (finding that "[c]ertainly there are cases when it is, 'for the greater advantage of the children' that infants be removed from the custody of their mother and placed in the custody of the father; those cases, however, are rare"); and, even recently, *Silvestri v. Silvestri*, 309 So. 2d 29, 31 (Fla. Dist. Ct. App. 1975) (stating that "[w]here all else is equal, children of tender years should be awarded to mother").

(3) **Constitutional Aspects.** In *Ex parte Devine*, the Alabama Supreme Court also concluded that the tender years presumption was unconstitutional gender-based discrimination:

> Having reviewed the historical development of the presumption as well as its modern status, and having examined the presumption in view of the holdings in *Reed, Frontiero, Orr* and *Caban*, we conclude that the tender years presumption represents unconstitutional gender-based classification which discriminates between fathers and mothers in child custody proceedings solely on the basis of sex. Like the statutory presumption in *Reed* [preferring men over women for appointment as estate administrators], the tender years doctrine creates a presumption of fitness and suitability of one parent without any consideration of the actual capabilities of the parties. The tender years presumption, like the statutory schemes in *Frontiero* [presumption of dependency for spouses of male military personnel but not for spouses of females] and *Orr* [husbands but not wives could be required to pay alimony], imposes legal burdens upon individuals according to the "immutable characteristic" of sex. By requiring fathers to carry the difficult burden of affirmatively proving the unfitness of the mother, the presumption may have the effect of depriving some loving fathers of the custody of

their children, while enabling some alienated mothers to arbitrarily obtain temporary custody.

Ex Parte Devine, 398 So. 2d 686, 695–96 (Ala. 1981)

(4) **Practical Effects.** Rules against the use of the tender years presumption ultimately affect situations in which a trial court enunciates that a gender preference is the basis of the custody determination. Do you think that judges, merely because of their upbringing in our society, may have a preference for placing young children with mothers if all other things are equal? Do you have such a preference? How would you resolve a case involving a two-year-old in which all things are genuinely equal: both parents are loving, both have acted as a primary caretaker for some period, both have professions and would require some child care assistance, and both have the financial resources which will allow them to raise the child?

(5) **Gender As One Factor among Many.** Some modern cases have permitted the sex of the parents to be included as a factor to be considered among others in custody proceedings. *See Mercier v. Mercier*, 1998 WL 409478 (Miss. 1998); *Baneck v. Baneck*, 455 So. 2d 766, 767–68 (Miss. 1984); *Davis v. Davis*, 422 So. 2d 680, 681–82 (La. Ct. App. 1982); *Robertson v. Robertson*, 415 So. 2d 1085, 1088 (Ala. Civ. App. 1982).

(6) **Tender Years Revisited.** Some recent feminist commentators have defended the tender years presumption. *See, e.g.*, Mary Becker, *Maternal Feelings: Myth, Taboo and Child Custody*, 1 S. Cal. Rev. L. & Women's Stud. 133, 203-22 (1992) (proposing a "maternal deference" standard that would defer to a mother's judgment regarding custody, so long as the mother is fit). *Query*: Would this standard be constitutional?

(7) **Tie Breaker.** Perhaps the best that can be said for the tender years presumption is that it provided judges with a way out when all things really were equal. However, even this view has been severely criticized: courts have come to rely upon the presumption as a substitute for a searching factual analysis of the relative parental capabilities of the parties, and the psychological and physical necessities of the children. The presumption has thus become what one writer refers to as an "anodyne" for the difficult decisions confronting the court. *See* Roth, *The Tender Years Presumption in Child Custody Disputes*, 15 J. Fam. L. 423, 438 (1976); *see also Ex parte Devine*, 398 So. 2d 686, 696 (Ala. 1981).

(8) While the vast majority of children live with their mother following a divorce, (*see* Reiboldt & Seiling, *Factors Related to Men's Awards of Custody*, 15 Fam. Advoc., Winter 1993, at 42), there is some evidence that women suffer gender based discrimination in litigated child custody cases:

> It is now widely believed that only fathers face gender bias in custody decisions. However, statistics show that when custody disputes end up in court, fathers are successful seventy percent of the time. Women are often deprived of custody due to choices and lifestyles that are held acceptable for men, such as frequent sexual activity and ambitious career goals. This is particularly true for women who work or are active outside of the home. The cultural stereotype of the good mother is the unselfish woman who is at home taking care of her children. As a result, the courts' stereotyped thinking about the role of women can disadvantage mothers in their attempts to gain custody.

Carpenter, Comment, *Why Are Mothers Still Losing: An Analysis of Gender Bias in Child Custody Determinations*, 1996 Det. C.L. Rev. 33, 42 (1996). This view is supported by

Maccoby and Mnookin, although they find that the litigated cases in their study split 50-50 between mothers and fathers. *See* Maccoby & Mnookin, *Dividing the Child, Social and Legal Dilemmas of Custody* 273 (1992). Doing research for this chapter led the author of this section to a non-scientific conclusion that the seventy percent figure is more accurate for cases which reached the appellate level. In recent times, there seem to be many more cases in which custody is awarded to the father.

(9) For further discussion of the tender years presumption, see Ahl, *A Step Backward: The Minnesota Supreme Court Adopts a "Primary Caretaker" Presumption in Child Custody Cases: Pikula v. Pikula*, 70 Minn. L. Rev. 1344 (1986); Strom, Comment, *The Tender Years Presumption: Is It Presumably Unconstitutional?*, 21 San Diego L. Rev. 861 (1984); Neely, Comment, *The Primary Caretaker Parent Rule: Child Custody and the Dynamics of Greed*, 3 Yale L. & Pol'y Rev. 168 (1984); Klaff, *The Tender Years Doctrine: A Defense*, 70 Cal. L. Rev. 335 (1982).

[C] The Primary Caretaker

PIKULA v. PIKULA
Minnesota Supreme Court
374 N.W.2d 705 (1985)

WAHL, JUSTICE.

This matter concerns the propriety of the custody award of two minor children in the judgment and decree dissolving the marriage of Kelly Jo Pikula and Dana David Pikula. Both parents sought custody of their daughters, aged 4 and 2. After a two-day trial, the trial court awarded custody to Dana, the father. On Kelly's appeal, the Court of Appeals reversed, concluding that the evidence, considered in light of the statutory factors set forth in Minn. Stat. § 518.17, subd. 1 (1984), was insufficient to support the award of custody. The Court of Appeals remanded the matter with direction to the trial court to enter judgment granting custody to the mother. We granted discretionary review.

Kelly and Dana Pikula were married on March 29, 1980, when Kelly was 17 and Dana 20. At the time of their marriage, their older daughter, Tiffany, was 8 months old. Prior to Tiffany's birth, Kelly and Dana had lived with Kelly's sister, Denise, in St. Paul. After the baby was born, the family moved to Brainerd, Dana's hometown, where they had frequent contact with Dana's parents and sisters. The Pikula family is closely knit, with Dana's parents at the center of the family. The family members visit each other frequently and spend holidays together. Two of the three adult Pikula children work for their father, and the parents continue to assist the adult children financially. Dana took a job with his father's trucking company, working a split shift as a driver. Kelly had a second daughter, Tanisha, in 1981, and finished high school while taking care of the children and managing the home.

As the Court of Appeals observed, it appears from the evidence that both Kelly and Dana were imperfect parents. Dana and members of his family testified Kelly occasionally had trouble controlling her temper with the two girls, was somewhat ambivalent about her role as mother, and was a poor housekeeper. Kelly did not dispute she was sometimes dissatisfied and frustrated, but by her own account and by the testimony of Dana and his family, she was a good mother. She testified her dissatisfactions were rooted in her relationship with

Dana and in Dana's problems with alcohol which at times resulted in physical displays of temper and verbal abuse. These problems persisted throughout the marriage and became particularly severe after Tanisha, their second child, was born. Dana was hospitalized during this period after injuring his hand by putting his fist through a door. He initially agreed to undergo counseling at that time, but soon stopped attending because he "didn't feel he had a problem with other people." He did attend AA meetings for a period, but began drinking again after five or six months. According to the report prepared by the custody evaluator, Dana continues to have problems with chemical dependency.

Kelly and her sisters also testified Dana's drinking in part precipitated the couple's separation. At the time Dana began drinking again, Dana forced Kelly and the children to leave her sister Renee's home in St. Paul where Kelly had been visiting with the children. Dana appeared at the house at around 9 p.m. and insisted Kelly and the girls leave immediately with him. When Kelly resisted, he took the children, put them in the car, and then dragged Kelly out of the house. In the meantime, Renee's boyfriend came out of the house and hit Dana on the arm with a baseball bat. Kelly said the children were watching this scene from the car, and once they were underway, Dana drove recklessly, shouted at her, and prevented her from comforting the children. Dana denies he used physical force, had trouble operating the car, or kept Kelly from the children. Kelly's sisters stated, though, they were sufficiently concerned to report the incident to the police.

Kelly did not remain in the home long after their return from St. Paul. She said Dana told her he was going to keep her there and he intended to take the children away so she would know what it was like to be alone. He was angry at her for not taking his side against her sister's boyfriend. Kelly then left the home and moved into the Women's Center of Mid-Minnesota, a shelter for battered women, where she continued to live until the time of the trial.

During this time, the couple agreed to a joint custody arrangement until custody was judicially determined. The arrangement was an uneasy one. For a time, the children remained in the family home while Kelly and Dana alternated living there on a four-day rotation schedule. Kelly began bringing the children to the shelter for her custody period, however, when tensions between Kelly and Dana escalated.

The recommendations of three professional social workers were also before the trial court. All three recommended that custody be awarded to Kelly. Social worker Jean Remke met with Kelly and Dana together or separately four times. In her view, both Kelly and Dana are somewhat emotionally immature. In Remke's opinion Kelly is "decidedly the most functional parent," because she seemed more capable of "putting herself aside to attend to the physical and emotional needs of others," while Dana repeatedly used the children in efforts to control their mother," and showed "no signs of really understanding this and no signs of altering his behavior."

Social worker Louise Seliski had extensive contact with Kelly at the shelter, both through individual counseling and observation. Seliski also found Kelly had been a fit mother to the two girls and believed she would continue to provide a loving and supportive environment for them. She said she observed affection between Kelly and the children, that Kelly never used excessive discipline, and that the children were always clean. Seliski terminated therapy with Kelly because Kelly was "handling her life as well as anyone could expect her to handle it" and had no significant psychological problems or chemical dependency. It was Seliski's recommendation that custody be given to Kelly.

The reports prepared by Remke and Seliski were included in the custody evaluation prepared by social worker Nancy Archibald. The evaluation also included reports of interviews with the parties, their families, neighbors and friends, a church premarital evaluation, and letters of recommendation. In Archibald's opinion, the views expressed by Remke and Seliski were supported by her interviews with Kelly and Dana. She also recommended, based on all the data, that custody be awarded to Kelly with reasonable visitation provided to Dana.

Evidence was also introduced at trial concerning the custodial environment each parent would provide the children. Kelly testified she intended to move with the children to her sister's home in Maplewood until she could find employment and move into her own apartment. Dana objected to this plan, and testified that Kelly's sister had used marijuana and characterized some of her sister's friends as "bikers." Dana testified that he intended to remain in Brainerd if he were awarded custody of the girls. He continued to work a split shift at the time of trial, and his schedule required him to leave Brainerd at 3:00 a.m. for Wadena, lay over in Wadena from 7:00 a.m. until 3:00 p.m., and return to Brainerd at 7:00 p.m. Occasionally, he would return to Brainerd during his layover, permitting him to spend several hours at home. The child care responsibilities were principally borne by Dana's mother, however, and the children frequently spent the night with her and were cared for by her during the day.

Based on this record, the trial court initially made two key findings of fact in awarding custody to Dana. . . .

Amended Finding 11. That there is a strong, stable, religious family group relationship within the Pikula family, including respondent and the children, that has been developed, nurtured and cultivated over the years. It has stood like a bedrock through the depression years and post-war years of plenty and permissiveness. This environment has inbred in the family, including respondent, a unity, respect, loyalty and love that for the most part has been destroyed and lost in most modern American families. It is in the best interests and welfare of the children that their custody be awarded to respondent, who shares these attributes and who will assure that these children will be raised in the present cultural, family, religious and community environment of which they have been and are integral parts, which environment affords them stability, appropriate socializing and family orientation. The children are properly adjusted to their current home situation, broadly defined, and to the greater community within which they have lived virtually their entire lives, the children behave well and have extensive and qualitative contacts with significant persons within this environment, respondent's personal environment continues to stabilize and improve and is presently satisfactory, as well as gives indications of continuing stability, and it is desirable that the children's continuity with respondent and significant other persons and institutions here be maintained, respondent offering a permanent, well-established, concerned and involved, as well as supporting home for the children, the overall health of those who likely will here affect the mental, physical, emotional, educational, cultural and religious growth of the children is good, and respondent is inclined to, has and likely will continue to care for the children and raise them in their religion, creed and culture.

Amended Finding 12. That the environment in which petitioner finds herself is almost the exact opposite of that in which respondent lives and will raise the children, it would subject the children to considerable uncertainty and instability in home, community, culture, persons and religion, should custody be awarded to petitioner, and further, such an award would disrupt, curtail and likely end the children's nurturing and constant contacts with the environment, persons and institutions now significantly and positively affecting their lives, petitioner's behavior and practices of child rearing as well as her interest in her children are at least subject to serious question and doubt, and it would not be in the children's best interest to award their custody to petitioner.

The Court of Appeals, in reversing, held that the trial court had abused its discretion in awarding custody of the children to Dana on the facts of this case. The Court of Appeals noted little reference was made by the trial court to the statutory factors set forth in Minn. Stat. § 518.17, subd. 1 (1984) in fashioning its findings, that the trial court had instead emphasized the desirability of Dana's extended family, and had dismissed the expert opinions of three social workers. Moreover, the court observed it appeared the trial court had penalized Kelly for the divorce and remarriage of her parents, for actions and attitudes of other close relatives, and for her involvement with persons concerned with women's issues, without finding that any of these factors affected the relationship between children and mother. . . .

We conclude, however, that the trial court erred in determining that custody of the children should be awarded to Dana on the basis of the facts that were found. . . .

In *Berndt v. Berndt*, 292 N.W.2d 1 (Minn. 1980), we held the enumerated statutory criteria, even absent consideration of other relevant factors, mandate that, when the evidence indicates that both parents would be suitable custodians, the intimacy of the relationship between the primary parent and the child should not be disrupted "without strong reasons which relate specifically to the [primary] parent's capacity to provide and care for the child." *Berndt*, 292 N.W.2d at 2. Awarding custody to the non-primary parent without such strong reasons, when the primary parent has given the child good care, may constitute reversible error.

The guiding principle in all custody cases is the best interest of the child. The importance of emotional and psychological stability to the child's sense of security, happiness, and adaptation that we deemed dispositive in *Berndt* is a postulate embedded in the statutory factors and about which there is little disagreement within the profession of child psychology. For younger children in particular, that stability is most often provided by and through the child's relationship to his or her primary caretaker—the person who provides the child with daily nurturence, care and support. As we further noted in *Berndt* a court order separating a child from the primary parent could thus rarely be deemed in the child's best interests. Courts in three other states have reached similar conclusions in construing their custody statutes and rules. We follow the reasoning of those states in adopting the rule that when both parents seek custody of a child too young to express a preference, and one parent has been the primary caretaker of the child, custody should be awarded to the primary caretaker absent a showing that that parent is unfit to be the custodian. . . .

While it is difficult to enumerate all of the factors which will contribute to a conclusion that one or the other parent was the primary caretaker parent, nonetheless, there are certain obvious criteria to which a court must initially look. In establishing which natural or adoptive parent is the primary caretaker, the trial court shall determine which parent has taken primary responsibility for, *inter alia*, the performance of the following caring and nurturing duties of a parent: (1) preparing and planning of meals; (2) bathing, grooming and dressing; (3) purchasing, cleaning, and care of clothes; (4) medical care, including nursing and trips to physicians; (5) arranging for social interaction among peers after school, i.e., transporting to friends' houses or, for example, to girl or boy scout meetings; (6) arranging alternative care, i.e., babysitting, day-care, etc.; (7) putting child to bed at night, attending to child in the middle of the night, waking child in the morning; (8) disciplining, i.e., teaching general manners and toilet training; (9) educating, i.e., religious, cultural, social, etc.; and, (10) teaching elementary skills, i.e., reading, writing and arithmetic.

Garska, 278 S.E.2d at 363. When the facts demonstrate that responsibility for and performance of child care was shared by both parents in an entirely equal way, then no preference arises and the court must limit its inquiry to other indicia of parental fitness. Once the preference does arise, however, the primary parent should be given custody unless it is shown that the child's physical or emotional health is likely to be endangered or impaired by being placed in the primary parent's custody. . . .

Turning to the facts of this case, we conclude that the matter must be remanded for a determination of which, if either, parent was the primary caretaker of the children at the time the dissolution proceeding was commenced. Any disruption in the relationships between the children and their parents occasioned by the events leading to the divorce is irrelevant to that determination. If either parent was the primary caretaker, custody should be awarded to that parent absent a strong showing of unfitness.

NOTES AND QUESTIONS

(1) **Certainty.** In *Pikula* the court clearly appears to yearn for some sort of certainty in child custody decisions, and appears to find that certainty in the concept of continuity of care and the primary caretaker presumption. Yet even applying these concepts does not prevent the court from making hard choices. For example, what if the primary caretaker at the commencement of the trial is different from the one at the time the matter is reconsidered after appeal? In *Pikula*, what if on remand the trial court determined that the mother had been the primary caretaker of the children up to the date of the trial and that because of the trial court's ruling, the children had been cared for primarily by the father for the three or four years immediately prior to the Minnesota Supreme Court's decision? Or what if after the trial the primary caretaker was the paternal grandmother of the children?

(2) **Presumption.** Garska v. McCoy, 278 S.E.2d 357, 357 (W. Va. 1981), first established the primary caretaker presumption. While the need for certainty in child custody matters seems to be the main consideration in *Pikula*, *Garska* exhibited more concern for the plight of caretaker parents who usually had lower incomes than the non-caretaker parents. According to the court in *Garska*, the caretaker parent who fears loss of custody, under the case-by-case method created by the best interest standard, often trades support and property rights in order to avoid a custody battle.

(3) **Tie-breaker.** The court in *Pikula* states that the primary caretaker presumption will prevail unless it can be shown that the primary caretaker is unfit. Another approach might be to apply the presumption where both parents are found to be fit so that the presumption becomes, in effect, the tie-breaker. Are these two approaches significantly different? Perhaps the only difference would be the effect the approaches have on the burden of proof.

(4) **Criticism.** *Pikula* has been severely criticized because it replaced the legislatively established best interest standard and the list of factors in the Minnesota statute with the primary caretaker standard and the list of factors from *Garska*: "Thus the *Pikula* ruling essentially instructs the custody court judges to substitute a list of homemaking duties for the best interests factors expressly provided by the Minnesota Legislature in section 518.17." Ahl, Comment, *A Step Backward: The Minnesota Supreme Court Adopts a "Primary Caretaker" Presumption in Child Custody Cases: Pikula v. Pikula*, 70 Minn. L. Rev. 1344, 1359 (1986). This article points out that *Garska* was decided in the absence of a legislatively established custody standard. The only justification for this judicial activism would seem to be that the primary caretaker presumption is vastly superior to the best interests standard in that it provides stability and certainty and protects the primary caretaker from the threat of loss of custody. Are these factors so important that all the other factors should be disregarded? Why not have a system in which the primary caretaker is one consideration among many in determining the best interests?

(5) **One Factor Among Many.** While there is controversy over the fact that the consideration of primary caretaker has been elevated to the level of a presumption, few would quarrel with the fact that it is a factor which should be considered in the decision to determine what the best interests of the child really are. The Supreme Court of North Dakota stated, "[w]hat is in the child's best interest is the single issue to be determined. . . . In North Dakota the primary caretaker factor is not a presumptive rule but only one of the many considerations to be evaluated by the trial court in making its finding as to the best interests of the child." *Wolf v. Wolf*, 474 N.W.2d 257, 258 (N.D. 1991). *See also* Cochran, Jr., *The Search for Guidance in Determining the Best Interests of the Child at Divorce; Reconciling The Primary Caretaker and Joint Custody Preference*, 20 U. Rich. L. Rev. 1 (1985) (recommending that between fit parents who cannot agree on a parenting plan, the court should give joint physical custody with majority of time with primary caretaker and sole custody to primary caretaker).

(6) **Minnesota.** As mentioned in the *Maxfield* case, Minnesota has downgraded primary caretaker from presumption to one factor among many. *See Maxfield v. Maxfield*, 452 N.W.2d 219, 224 (Minn. 1990).

[D] **Child's Preference**

YATES v. YATES
Wyoming Supreme Court
702 P.2d 1252 (1985)

BROWN, JUSTICE.

. . . .

The parties here were divorced in December, 1980. The divorce decree awarded appellant [mother] custody of the parties' three minor daughters, and awarded appellee [father] visiting privileges. Appellant was awarded alimony in eighty monthly installments. The divorce decree recited that the parties had stipulated regarding a property settlement. The court approved such settlement.

After the divorce the parties had a multitude of problems regarding visitation rights. A phenomenon rarely seen by a trial judge, if ever, is a post-divorce squabble where all the equities are on one side. This case is no exception.

In February, 1983, appellee filed a petition to modify the divorce decree with respect to alimony and visitation. An amended petition to include changing the custody of Amy Yates was filed July 14, 1983, during the time Amy was visiting her father. On August 23, 1983, the district court entered an ex parte order granting temporary custody of Amy Yates to appellee. A trial to the court on appellee's amended petition was had on June 21 and 22, 1984. The court entered an order on July 24, 1984, awarding custody of Amy Yates to appellee, and modifying the alimony provisions of the divorce decree.

I.

. . . .

At the June 21-22, 1984 trial, appellee called several witnesses to testify in support of his petition to modify the divorce decree. One of his witnesses was Amy Yates, who was cross-examined by appellant's attorney. Appellant called two expert witnesses and also testified on her own behalf. After the recross-examination of appellant, both appellant and appellee told the court that they had nothing further. . . .

The following afternoon, the judge talked to the three minor daughters of the parties in chambers. Only the judge, the three daughters, and the court reporter were present. During this in-chambers discussion with the children, the judge said that he was going to let Amy stay with her father.

It should not come as a great surprise to counsel that sometimes a trial judge decides the outcome of a case before the last word of testimony goes into the record. It would be somewhat unusual, however, for the judge to reveal his decision before all the testimony is in the record. In the context of the trial judge's interview with the three minor children, an early indication of his custody determination was logical and was important to the main purpose of the interview, that is, preparing the minor children for the changes affecting their lives.

The kindly trial judge had an informal, fatherly talk with the three girls. He assured them that both parents loved them. He explained to them the purposes of the trial, and tried to condition them to the fact that Amy would be living in Wyoming and the other two girls in California. The judge talked to them about Amy's visitation in California and Julie's and Molly's visitation in Wyoming. The judge tried to find out about problems the girls had with each other, with their parents and with their stepmother. The judge's final order modifying the decree of divorce reflected some of the problems expressed by the girls during the in-chambers interview. . . .

II.

[A]ppellant contends that the trial court abused its discretion when it changed the custody of Amy Yates from appellant to appellee. The statutory authority for a judge to change the custody of minor children is § 20-2-113, W.S.1977:

(a) On the petition of either of the parents, the court may revise the decree concerning the care, custody and maintenance of the children as the circumstances of the parents and the benefit of the children requires. . . ..

Here, some of the changes in circumstances since the original divorce decree are: 1) Appellee purchased the family home in Green River; 2) appellee married Anita Yates who loves and has a good relationship with Amy; 3) appellee experienced difficulty with appellant in visiting and communicating with Amy; and 4) Amy has been in three different schools. In addition to the identifiable changes in circumstances the trial court must also consider the effect these changes have had on the child. Here, there was evidence of more stability in Amy's life since living with her father. Although the Green River school is more difficult than the California school, Amy makes the honor roll. She is happy and exhibits more confidence, and the increased stability has contributed to increased self-esteem. Additionally, Amy has expressed a strong preference to living with her father, and is now back with former childhood friends.

In a custody hearing a minor child will ordinarily favor the parent he or she lived with just before the hearing. In this case appellant suffered some disadvantage because Amy had lived with her father for almost a year before the change of custody hearing. Despite appellee's protestations to the contrary, we would be surprised if he did not try to ingratiate himself with Amy during the time just before the hearing. Ideally, a child should be in a neutral environment before he or she states a preference concerning custody.

However, the trial judge has had long experience in custody matters and no doubt scrutinized Amy's testimony carefully when she said her father had not tried to influence her, and when she expressed a desire to live with him. The preference of a child of sufficient age and maturity is a factor to be considered by a court in ascertaining what is in the child's best interests. . . .

Courts in other jurisdictions have taken into consideration the wishes of children when determining custody. *See DuPont v. DuPont*, 59 Del. 206, 216 A.2d 674 (1966); *State ex rel. Waslie v. Waslie*, 274 Minn. 564, 143 N.W.2d 634 (1966); *In re Marriage of Kramer*, Mont., 580 P.2d 439 (1978). In *Kramer* the court held:

> We are committed to the view that the welfare of the children is the paramount consideration in awarding custody. [Citations.] We believe the welfare of the children, particularly children of the ages involved here [the ages of the children involved were 11, 13, and 15] is not being served if their wishes are not considered by the trial court. *Id.* at 444.

The older a child becomes, greater weight should be given his preference; and as a child grows older, it is much more difficult to require him to remain in the custody of a parent he does not prefer. In addition, the preference which has a stated basis and is expressed in a plain manner should be accorded greater weight than one whose basis cannot be described. This is not to say that the preference of a minor child is controlling upon the court. *See Douglas v. Sheffner* [79 Wyo. 172, 331 P.2d 840 (1958)].

In determining the weight to be given a child's preference several factors should be considered: the age of the child; the reason for the preference; the relative fitness of the preferred and non-preferred parent; the hostility, if any, of the child to the non-preferred parent; the preference of other siblings; and whether the child's preference has been tainted or influenced by one parent against the other.

Although custodial preference is not conclusive, the court here was entitled to give more consideration to a fifteen-year old girl's preference than say, the preference of a six-year old child. Also, it should not be overlooked that Amy had stated a preference to live with her father as far back as the divorce in 1980, and had not changed that preference.

The judge's finding that there had been a substantial change in circumstances is principally a factual determination. We accord great deference to a trial judge's factual determination. The judge hearing a modification petition is in a better position to determine the credibility of a witness and the value of the testimony. *Stirrett v. Stirrett*, 35 Wyo. 206, 248 P.2d 1 (1926). . . .

The trial judge here could reasonably conclude that appellee should have primary custody of Amy, and under the circumstances of this case, the judge's determination did not exceed the bounds of reason. We hold that there was no abuse of discretion in the judge's determination.thinsp;. . .

NOTES AND QUESTIONS

(1) **Key Issues.** The key issues regarding the child's preference are: 1) at what age is a child sufficiently mature to state a preference for one parent over another; 2) what weight should be given to the child's preference; and 3) how should the child's preference be determined.

(a) *Age and Maturity.* As to the age issue, the court in *Yates* appears to use a sliding scale approach: "the court was entitled to give more consideration to a fifteen-year-old girl's preference than say, a six-year old child." Most jurisdictions apply a similar flexible approach. For example, the Minnesota Marriage Dissolution Act states that the court may consider "the reasonable preference of the child, if the court deems the child to be of sufficient age to express preference." Minn. Stat. Ann. § 518.17(b) (West 1989). *See also* Cal. Fam. Code § 3042 (1998) and Conn. Gen. Stat. Ann. § 46b-56 (West 1986).

In using the flexible standard, what factors should the court consider? One article suggests the following list of things to look for: "an understanding and willingness of the child to speak the truth; adequate memory; verbal capability including the ability to make understandable responses; maturity, evincing an ability to make a rational judgment concerning his or her welfare; and general intelligence." Newman & Collester, Jr., *Children Should Be Seen and Heard: Techniques for Interviewing the Child in Contested Custody Proceedings*, 2 Fam. Advoc., Spring 1980, at 8.

Some jurisdictions apply a fixed age standard, which can be a minimum age for consideration. Ga. Code Ann. § 19-9-1(3), states as follows:

> In all cases in which the child has reached the age of 14 years, the child shall have the right to select the parent with whom he or she desires to live. The child's selection shall be controlling, unless the parent so selected is determined not to be a fit and proper person to have the custody of the child.

(b) *Weight.* What weight should be given to the child's preference? At some point a mature child's decision alone may be given great weight, and, if all other factors are equal, the child's preference may serve as a suitable tie breaker. However, there may be situations where the child's preference should not be determinative even if the child is older. In determining the weight of a child's preference, how should the court make sure that the preference has not been tainted by the intimidation or cultivation of one parent? What if it appears that the preference is based on the fact that one parent is more lenient? Or should the preference of a child feeling the stresses and strains of adolescence be considered as grounds to be given significant weight? *See Tomlinson v. Tomlinson*, 374 A.2d 1386, 1389 (Pa. Super. Ct. 1977).

(c) *Determining the child's preference* would seem like a rather straightforward matter. However, a number of important factors involving the manner in which the determination is made may influence the decision. Most important is the child's feelings. Who can doubt the possibility of mental and emotional trauma from having to pick one parent over the other, especially in open court? It would seem easy to prevent this trauma: the child could state his or her preference to a friendly third party or to the judge who would promise to keep the child's decision secret. It can be included in a family evaluation by a social worker who, as a part of the evaluation, interviews the children. But other factors impinge. The child's preference is evidence. If the child states a preference to a third party, such as a phychotherapist or a mediator, the preference is hearsay when the third party relates it in court. The most common alternative is for the court to take the child's testimony in chambers. For example, Missouri Annotated Statutes § 452.385 states "the court may interview the child in chambers to ascertain the child's wishes as to his custodian and relevant matters within his knowledge." Problems still arise. Should a court reporter record the conversation for possible appeal? Does due process require that counsel for the parties be present? If they are present, do they have the right to cross-examine the child?

For additional discussion, see Parker, *The Rights of Child Witnesses: Is the Court a Protector or Perpetrator?* 17 New Eng. L. Rev. 643, 661 (1982); and Dubin, *Child's Preference Legal Issues*, 10 Fam. Advoc., Winter 1988, at 35.

(2) It is clear that courts view the child's preference within the context of all the factors which must be weighed together. Often, courts will reach differing conclusions about a child's ability to make a mature decision, even when the children are the same age, depending on the context in which the decision must be made. For two interesting cases in an international setting, both involving 10-year-olds, see *Schleiffer v. Meyers*, 644 F.2d 656, 664 (7th Cir. 1981), *cert. denied*, 454 U.S. 823 (1981) (holding that the Swedish mother regain custody of son despite preference for staying with father in the United States; son was returned to Sweden); *Goldstein v. Goldstein*, 341 A.2d 51, 53 (R.I. 1975) (allowing the Israeli father to retain custody of daughter in Israel because of daughter's preference, despite physical danger in terrorist-threatened Israel).

[E] Religion

PATER v. PATER
Supreme Court of Ohio
588 N.E.2d 794 (1992)

WRIGHT, JUSTICE.

Today we reaffirm that a domestic relations court may consider the religious practices of the parents in order to protect the best interests of a child. However, the United States Constitution flatly prohibits a trial court from ever evaluating the merits of religious doctrine or defining the contents of that doctrine. Furthermore, custody may not be denied to a parent solely because she will not encourage her child to salute the flag, celebrate holidays, or participate in extracurricular activities. We reverse the trial court's custody and visitation orders because these decisions were improperly based on Jennifer Pater's religious beliefs.

Our analysis of this case begins with the child custody statute and our standard of review in custody disputes. Former R.C. 3109.04(C) (now 3109.04[F] [1][c], [d] and [e]) provided that to determine the best interests of a child, a domestic court judge must consider all relevant factors, including:

. . . .

"(3) The child's interaction and interrelationship with his parents, siblings, and any other person who may significantly affect the child's best interest;

"(4) The child's adjustment to his home, school, and community;

"(5) The mental and physical health of all persons involved in the situation."

The statutory standard is written broadly and requires the domestic relations judge to consider all factors that are relevant to the best interests of the child. The purpose of a far-reaching inquiry is to allow the judge to make a fully informed decision on an issue as important as which parent will raise the child. "The discretion which a trial court enjoys in custody matters should be accorded the utmost respect, given the nature of the proceeding and the impact the court's determination will have on the lives of the parties concerned. The knowledge a trial court gains through observing the witnesses and the parties in a custody proceeding cannot be conveyed to a reviewing court by a printed record." (Citations omitted.) *Miller v. Miller* (1988), 37 Ohio St.3d 71, 74, 523 N.E.2d 846, 849. A reviewing court will not overturn a custody determination unless the trial court has acted in a manner that is arbitrary, unreasonable, or capricious.

It is against this standard of broad discretion that we must review the scope of a trial court's inquiry into the parents' religious practices. The other starting point for our analysis is that a court may well violate the parent's constitutional rights if its decision is improperly based on religious bias. The United States Constitution and the Ohio Constitution forbid state action which interferes with the religious freedom of its citizens or prefers one religion over another. To the extent that a court refuses to award custody to a parent because of her religious beliefs, the court burdens her choice of a religion in violation of the Free Exercise Clause of the United States Constitution.

In addition to their free exercise rights, parents have a fundamental right to educate their children, including the right to communicate their moral and religious values. . . . In a custody dispute, the parents' rights must be balanced against the state's need to determine the best interests of the child. This balancing requires more than a rote recitation that a domestic relations judge may consider any factor relevant to the best interests of a child, especially if the best-interests test is read broadly to encompass all aspects of child-rearing.

Courts have repeatedly held that custody cannot be awarded solely on the basis of the parents' religious affiliations and that to do so violates the First Amendment to the United States Constitution.

On the other hand, a parent's actions are not insulated from the domestic relations court's inquiry just because they are based on religious beliefs, especially actions that will harm the child's mental or physical health. See *Prince v. Massachusetts* (1944), 321 U.S. 158, 64 S.Ct. 438, 88 L.Ed. 645; *Birch v. Birch*, [11 Ohio St.3d 85, 463 N.E.2d 1254 (1984)).

In *Birch*, we held that courts can examine the parent's religious practices to determine the best interests of the child because ". . . the law does not require that a child be actually harmed or that a parent's unsuitability to have custody of her children be disregarded because the parent claims that the bases of her unsuitability are religious practices." *Birch*, 11 Ohio St.3d at 88, 463 N.E.2d at 1257. The state's compelling interest in protecting children from physical or mental harm clearly allows a court to deny custody to a parent who will not provide for the physical and mental needs of the child. . . . .

Appellee claims that Jennifer will not allow their son to celebrate birthdays and holidays, sing the national anthem, salute the flag, participate in extracurricular activities, socialize with non-Witnesses, or attend college. Appellee is concerned that the child will be socially ostracized and not adequately exposed to ideas other than those endorsed by the Jehovah's Witnesses. We can sympathize with his parental concern for his child, but are concerned that the state not exceed its proper role in resolving what is essentially a dispute between the parents' religious beliefs. Although the listed activities are those that most people may consider important to the socialization of children, we need to separate the value judgments implicit in the so-called norm from any actual harm caused by these practices.

Even if we accept the premise that Jennifer will actively forbid Bobby to celebrate holidays, be involved in extracurricular activities, or salute the flag, these practices do not appear to directly endanger the child's physical or mental health. A showing that a child's mental health will be adversely affected requires more than proof that a child will not share all of the beliefs or social activities of the majority of his or her peers. A child's social adjustment is very difficult to measure, and the relative importance of various social activities is an extremely subjective matter. For these reasons, a court must base its decision that a particular religious practice will harm the mental health of a child on more than the fact that the child will not participate in certain social activities. A parent may not be denied custody on the basis of his or her religious practices unless there is probative evidence that those practices will adversely affect the mental or physical health of the child. Evidence that the child will not be permitted to participate in certain social or patriotic activities is not sufficient to prove possible harm.

The evidence offered by appellee to prove that these practices would harm Bobby consisted of two expert witnesses. Dr. Bergman testified, on the basis of a dissertation he had written, that mental illness was more common among Jehovah's Witnesses than among the general population. This testimony was a blatant attempt to stereotype an entire religion. Regardless of the rate of mental illness among an entire group, that evidence does not prove that the religion in question will negatively affect a particular individual. Furthermore, this one piece of statistical evidence is meaningless. To follow this evidence to its "logical" conclusion, a court would need to compare this rate to the same rate for all faiths and for people who are not associated with any particular religion. If the latter group has the lowest incidence of mental illness, then under this reasoning we would have to forbid all parents from exposing their children to their religious beliefs.

Dr. Denber testified that generally extracurricular activities are beneficial to a child's socialization. Neither Dr. Denber nor Dr. Bergman had interviewed Bobby. No proof was offered that this particular child was suffering or would suffer any ill effects from being exposed to his mother's religious practices. In the absence of any probative evidence that a child will be harmed by a parent's religious practices regarding social activities, the court may not use those beliefs to disqualify the parent as the custodial parent.

We feel it is appropriate to question a parent about her general philosophy of child-rearing. However, the scope of this inquiry into the religious beliefs and practices, not just of the mother, but of an entire religion was improper and an abuse of discretion. The isolated statements of the trial judge that he would not decide custody on the basis of the mother's religious beliefs will not insulate the court's decision from review.

The trial court appears to have awarded custody to Robert because of Jennifer's religious affiliation. There is no dispute that both parents are excellent parents and we must begin from the assumption that both are equally competent to care for this child. However, at the time of the hearing, Jennifer had been Bobby's primary caretaker for the first three years of his life. She also testified that she would have more time during the week to devote to the child because she worked on only one or two weekdays. Jennifer deserves a custody hearing free from religious bias.

The visitation order in this case also indicates that the court's decision was based on Jennifer's religion. The order demands that Jennifer "shall not teach or expose the child to the Jehovah[']s Witnesses' beliefs in any form." This order is so broad that it could be construed as forbidding any discussion of the Bible. It is equally unclear whether Jennifer is permitted to discuss moral values because these values are influenced by religious beliefs.

[T]he rule appears to be well established that the courts should maintain an attitude of strict impartiality between religions and should not disqualify any applicant for custody or restrain any person having custody or visitation rights from taking the children to a particular church, except where there is a clear and affirmative showing that the conflicting religious beliefs affect the general welfare of the child." *Munoz v. Munoz* (1971), 79 Wash.2d 810, 813, 489 P.2d 1133, 1135. This rule has been adopted to protect both parents' right to expose their children to their religious beliefs, a right that does not automatically end when they are divorced. The courts should not interfere with this relationship between parent and child unless a child is exhibiting genuine symptoms of distress that are caused by the differences in the parents' religious beliefs. Today, we adopt the majority rule that a court may not restrict a non-custodial parent's right to expose his or her child to religious beliefs, unless the conflict between the parents' religious beliefs is affecting the child's general welfare. Because a divorce is a stressful event for a child, a court must carefully separate the distress caused by that event from any distress allegedly caused by religious conflict.

. . . . *Judgment reversed and cause remanded.*

NOTES AND QUESTIONS

(1) Many courts are in accord with the principal case. In *Quiner v. Quiner*, the California Court of Appeal stated that:

> courts have no power to tell parents who teach nothing secularly immoral, unlawful or against public policy, how to shape the minds of their children, particularly on the subject of accepted religious belief. Evidence must be produced which will sustain a finding that there is actual impairment of physical, emotional and mental well-being contrary to the best interests of the child.

Quiner v. Quiner, 59 Cal. Rptr. 503, 516 (Cal. Ct. App. 1967). *See In re Marriage of Hadeen*, 619 P.2d 374, 382–83 (Wash. Ct. App. 1980); *Funk v. Ossman*, 724 P.2d 1247, 1250 (Ariz.

Ct. App. 1986); Annot., *Religion as a Factor in Child Custody and Visitation Cases*, 22 A.L.R.4th 971 (1983); *see also* Mangrum, *Exclusive Reliance on Best Interest May be Unconstitutional: Religion as a Factor in Child Custody Cases*, 15 Creighton L. Rev. 25 (1981).

(2) Should religion be a factor when one parent is an atheist? For example, should a court be allowed to award custody based upon the court's belief that the best interests standard requires that, all other things being equal, the child should be raised in a home by the parent who would provide some religious training rather than in the home of the atheist parent who would train the child to avoid all organized religion? *See* Pfeffer, *Religion in the Upbringing of Children*, 35 B.U. L. Rev. 333 (1955).

(3) Should the court consider the fact that one parent's religion denies medical treatment to its adherents? In *Osier v. Osier*, 410 A.2d 1027, 1029 (Me. 1980), the court answered this question in the affirmative. After making a decision as to which parent is the better custodian, independent of religious grounds, the court can consider religious practices of the favored parent which might affect the health of the child.

(4) **Agreements.** Should parental agreements regarding the a child's religious upbringing be enforced? Traditionally the answer has been no. For example, in *Zummo v. Zummo*, 574 A.2d 1130 (Pa. Super. Ct. 1990), the Pennsylvania Superior Court refused to enforce a oral agreement regarding the child's religious training and stated,

> The great weight of legal authority is against enforcement of such agreements over the objections of one of the parties. Without exhausting all of the arguments suggested in the cases and commentaries in support of this position, we find we are fully persuaded of its correctness. We note that in recent years psychologists and theologians have specifically questioned the wisdom of such agreements and attempts at their enforcement. We also note that the trend is away from the use of such agreements.
>
> *Id.* at 1148.

However, thoughtful commentators have argued strenuously for the enforcement of such agreements. *See* Korzec, *A Tale of Two Religions: a Contractual Approach to Religion as a Factor in Child Custody and Visitation Disputes*, 25 New Eng. L. Rev. 1121 (1991) (arguing that written agreements regarding a child religious training after the parents divorce should be enforced if enforcement can be based upon the application of neutral contract principles as in such cases as *Avitzur v. Avitzur*, 58 N.Y.2d 108, 446 N.E.2d 136, 459 N.Y.S.2d 572, *cert. denied*, 464 U.S. 817 (1983)); Weiss and Abramoff, *The Enforceability of Religious Upbringing Agreements*, 25 J. Marshall L. Rev. 655 (1992) (also arguing that such agreements should be enforced because the do not violate religious freedom and often prevent a child being raised in two religions simultaneously to the child's detriment).

[F] Race

PALMORE v. SIDOTI
United States Supreme Court
466 U.S. 429 (1984)

CHIEF JUSTICE BURGER delivered the opinion of the Court.

We granted certiorari to review a judgment of a state court divesting a natural mother of the custody of her infant child because of her remarriage to a person of a different race.

I

When petitioner Linda Sidoti Palmore and respondent Anthony J. Sidoti, both Caucasians, were divorced in May 1980 in Florida, the mother was awarded custody of their 3-year-old daughter.

In September 1981 the father sought custody of the child by filing a petition to modify the prior judgment because of changed conditions. The change was that the child's mother was then cohabiting with a Negro, Clarence Palmore, Jr., whom she married two months later. Additionally, the father made several allegations of instances in which the mother had not properly cared for the child.

After hearing testimony from both parties and considering a court counselor's investigative report, the court noted that the father had made allegations about the child's care, but the court made no findings with respect to these allegations. . . .

The court then addressed the recommendations of the court counselor, who had made an earlier report "in [another] case coming out of this circuit also involving the social consequences of an interracial marriage. *Niles v. Niles*, 299 So. 2d 162." From this vague reference to that earlier case, the court turned to the present case and noted the counselor's recommendation for a change in custody because "[t]he wife [petitioner] has chosen for herself and for her child, a life-style unacceptable to the father *and to society*. . . . The child . . . is, or at school age will be, subject to environmental pressures not of choice." Record 84 (emphasis added).

The court then concluded that the best interests of the child would be served by awarding custody to the father. The court's rationale is contained in the following:

> The father's evident resentment of the mother's choice of a black partner is not sufficient to wrest custody from the mother. It is of some significance, however, that the mother did see fit to bring a man into her home and carry on a sexual relationship with him without being married to him. Such action tended to place gratification of her own desires ahead of her concern for the child's future welfare. *This Court feels that despite the strides that have been made in bettering relations between the races in this country, it is inevitable that Melanie will, if allowed to remain in her present situation and attains school age and thus more vulnerable to peer pressures, suffer from the social stigmatization that is sure to come.* App. to Pet. for Cert. 26 27 (emphasis added).

The Second District Court of Appeal affirmed without opinion, 426 So. 2d 34 (1982), thus denying the Florida Supreme Court jurisdiction to review the case. We granted certiorari, 464 U.S. 913 (1983), and we reverse.

II

The judgment of a state court determining or reviewing a child custody decision is not ordinarily a likely candidate for review by this Court. However, the court's opinion, after stating that the "father's evident resentment of the mother's choice of a black partner is not sufficient" to deprive her of custody, then turns to what it regarded as the damaging impact on the child from remaining in a racially mixed household. This raises important federal concerns arising from the Constitution's commitment to eradicating discrimination based on race.

The Florida court did not focus directly on the parental qualifications of the natural mother or her present husband, or indeed on the father's qualifications to have custody of the child. The court found that "there is no issue as to either party's devotion to the child, adequacy of housing facilities, or respectability of the new spouse of either parent." [App. to Pet. for Cert] at 24. This, taken with the absence of any negative finding as to the quality of the care provided by the mother, constitutes a rejection of any claim of petitioner's unfitness to continue the custody of her child.

The court correctly stated that the child's welfare was the controlling factor. But that court was entirely candid and made no effort to place its holding on any ground other than race. Taking the court's findings and rationale at face value, it is clear that the outcome would have been different had petitioner married a Caucasian male of similar respectability.

A core purpose of the Fourteenth Amendment was to do away with all governmentally imposed discrimination based on race. Classifying persons according to their race is more likely to reflect racial prejudice than legitimate public concerns; the race, not the person, dictates the category. Such classifications are subject to the most exacting scrutiny; to pass constitutional muster, they must be justified by a compelling governmental interest and must be "necessary to the accomplishment" of their legitimate purpose, *McLaughlin v. Florida*, 379 U.S. 184, 196 (1964).

The State, of course, has a duty of the highest order to protect the interests of minor children, particularly those of tender years. In common with most states, Florida law mandates that custody determinations be made in the best interests of the children involved. Fla. Stat. § 61.13(2)(b)(1) (1983). The goal of granting custody based on the best interests of the child is indisputably a substantial governmental interest for purposes of the Equal Protection Clause.

It would ignore reality to suggest that racial and ethnic prejudices do not exist or that all manifestations of those prejudices have been eliminated. There is a risk that a child living with a stepparent of a different race may be subject to a variety of pressures and stresses not present if the child were living with parents of the same racial or ethnic origin.

The question, however, is whether the reality of private biases and the possible injury they might inflict are permissible considerations for removal of an infant child from the custody of its natural mother. We have little difficulty concluding that they are not. The Constitution cannot control such prejudices but neither can it tolerate them. Private biases may be outside the reach of the law, but the law cannot, directly or indirectly, give them effect. "Public officials sworn to uphold the Constitution may not avoid a constitutional duty by bowing to the hypothetical effects of private racial prejudice that they assume to be both widely and deeply held." *Palmer v. Thompson*, 403 U.S. 217, 260–261 (1971) (White, J., dissenting).

This is by no means the first time that acknowledged racial prejudice has been invoked to justify racial classifications. In *Buchanan v. Warley*, 245 U.S. 60 (1917), for example, this Court invalidated a Kentucky law forbidding Negroes to buy homes in white neighborhoods:

> It is urged that this proposed segregation will promote the public peace by preventing race conflicts. Desirable as this is, and important as is the preservation of the public peace, this aim cannot be accomplished by laws or ordinances which deny rights created or protected by the Federal Constitution. *Id.*, at 81.

Whatever problems racially mixed households may pose for children in 1984 can no more support a denial of constitutional rights than could the stresses that residential integration was thought to entail in 1917. The effects of racial prejudice, however real, cannot justify a racial classification removing an infant child from the custody of its natural mother found to be an appropriate person to have such custody. *The judgment of the District Court of Appeal is reversed.*

NOTES AND QUESTIONS

(1) The court speaks definitively in *Palmore*, and, although *Palmore* is a modification of a custody case, it applies equally to initial custody proceedings. It is difficult to imagine any other factual situation in which race would be a factor in a custody dispute between natural parents. But would it make a difference if the proceeding were between a natural parent of the same race and a non-parent of a different race from the child? Such a factual scenario could occur, for example, in an adoption proceeding. For additional discussion of the role of race in adoption, see § 8.05[A], *above.*

(2) As Jonas and Silverberg described in an article written approximately at the same time as *Palmore*, the cases that considered the role of race in child custody proceedings can be divided into three categories: "(1) cases considering race as one of several factors in awarding or modifying custody; (2) cases holding that race can be considered as a factor but cannot be the determinative factor; and (3) cases holding that race cannot be considered at all." Jonas & Silverberg, Comment, *Race, Custody and the Constitution: Palmore v. Sidoti*, 27 How. L.J. 1549, 1559–60 (1984). This article also includes an interesting account of the oral argument before the Supreme Court. *See id.* at 1567.

(3) In *Palmore*, should the Court have remanded the case to the trial court for further consideration of the best interests of the child without reference to race? Or would such a decision have merely allowed the trial court, if it wanted to, to reach the same conclusion with race as an unstated rationale? On the other hand, perhaps race was just used as a tie-breaking factor, and the trial court without the factor of race might reconsider the entire matter, looking for new factors to make its decision to be in the child's best interest.

(4) The Supreme Court of South Dakota allowed consideration of the children's Native-American heritage in a custody decision. In *Jones v. Jones*, 542 N.W.2d 119 (S.D. 1996), the mother argued that:

> [T]he trial court awarded the children to [the father] for the principal reason that, as a Native American, he has suffered prejudice and will therefore be able to better deal with the needs of the children when they are discriminated against because, although they are biracial, they have Native American features.

Jones, 542 N.W.2d at 122.

The Supreme Court responded:

> While the trial court was not blind to the racial backgrounds of the children, we are satisfied that it did not impermissibly award custody on the basis of race. As noted, [the father] showed a sensitivity to the need for his children to be exposed to their ethnic heritage. All of us form our own personal identities, based in part, on our

religious, racial and cultural backgrounds. To say, as [the mother] argues, that a court should never consider whether a parent is willing and able to expose to and educate children on their heritage, is to say that society is not interested in whether children ever learn who they are.

Jones, 542 N.W.2d at 123.

(5) For further discussion, see Weinstock, *Palmore v. Sidoti: Color-Blind Custody,* 34 Am. U. L. Rev. 245 (1984); *see also* Blackwood, Note, *Race as a Factor in Custody and Adoption Disputes: Palmore v. Sidoti,* 71 Cornell L. Rev. 209 (1985), and Shernow, Comment, *Recognizing Constitutional Rights of Custodial Parents: The Primacy of the Post-Divorce Family in Child Custody Modification Proceedings,* 35 UCLA L. Rev. 677, 685–87 (1988).

[G] **Parental Fitness**

[1] **Sexual Conduct**

HANHART v. HANHART
Supreme Court of South Dakota
501 N.W.2d 776 (1993)

WUEST, JUSTICE.

Karel Anthony Hanhart (hereinafter "Father") appeals a judgment and decree of divorce which granted child custody to Donna Rochelle Hanhart (hereinafter "Mother"). We affirm.

FACTS/PROCEDURAL HISTORY

Father and Mother were married in 1976 and had three children: Liesl (DOB: 8/31/80); Melissa (DOB: 5/10/82); and, Michael (DOB: 7/28/83). A fourth child (Nathan (DOB: 8/8/90)) was born during this marriage but is not Father's biological son.

Father has worked for Shopko for approximately four years. He has traditionally worked approximately 60-65 hours per week. It is Shopko's standard policy that employees move every two to three years. However, there was testimony that Father may apply to be a "resident area manager" which would enable him to stay indefinitely in one location. Mother is a music teacher and has worked part-time over the last several years.

On November 1, 1990, Father filed for divorce on the grounds of extreme mental cruelty and alleged Mother was openly carrying on an adulterous relationship with the next-door neighbor, Robert Rochelle. The trial court entered a temporary order granting Father custody of the three eldest children. Nathan remained with Mother because he was still being breast fed. Mother answered Father's complaint, denied Father's allegations of adultery, alleged extreme mental cruelty, and requested custody of all four children.

At trial, Mother denied having sexual contact with Robert Rochelle during her marriage with Father, although she admitted having sexual contact with him during her separation from Father. The trial court held a full evidentiary hearing and then determined it was in the best interests of the children for Mother to have custody. Father was given liberal visitation rights. Father appealed to this Court.

During the pendency of that appeal, Mother admitted committing adultery during their marriage and told Father Nathan was not his biological son. Blood tests confirmed that

Father is not Nathan's biological father. At Father's request, this Court remanded jurisdiction to the trial court so as to present this newly discovered evidence.

The trial court held a second trial. The evidence at the second trial was essentially the same as at the first trial except Mother admitted she lied at the first trial about committing adultery. The trial court re-interviewed the children and found them better adjusted and more outgoing after being in Mother's custody. The trial court issued a new divorce decree again giving Mother custody. . . . Father appeals.

DECISION

The facts of this case are essentially undisputed. . . . Therefore, the main issue is whether the trial court abused its discretion in concluding it was in the best interests of the children for Mother to have custody.

The trial court considered each of Father's arguments and concluded, in a well-reasoned decision, that the best interests of the children would be served by giving Mother custody, with liberal visitation by Father. A trial court's decision on a custody question will only be reversed if there was a clear showing of an abuse of discretion. The following factors support the trial court's decision.

1. Fault is not considered in determining custody, except to the extent it is relevant to prove unfitness of the parent. Although Mother had committed adultery, the trial court did not find her affair had any detrimental impact on the children. Liesl, the eldest daughter, told Judge Gilbertson she saw Mother kiss Bob Rochelle once. Otherwise, there was no evidence the children were aware of Mother's extramarital affair.

2. Siblings should not be split unless there are "compelling circumstances." *Mayer v. Mayer*, 397 N.W.2d 638 (S.D.1986). Nathan is an infant and is not Father's biological son. It appears Father did not seek custody of Nathan after this was discovered. There was significant evidence that all four children are bonded and love one another.

3. Frequent moves and transient lifestyles are not in children's best interests. Father's job requires him to work long hours and to move often. As a result, if Father had custody a significant amount of the children's day would be spent with a child care provider.

4. If Father was given custody he would have to expend a significant amount of money hiring child care providers. The trial court determined that would be an unnecessary strain on the limited finances available to this family.

5. The trial court interviewed the children and indicated that they were more outgoing and talkative than when Father had custody. Two of the three children interviewed indicated they wanted to live with Mother. The trial court specifically found the children had not been coached. In appropriate circumstances the choice of the children can be considered.

The trial court had significant articulable reasons for granting custody to Mother. The trial court's custody decision is affirmed. . . .

HENDERSON, JUSTICE (dissenting).

. . . .

Mother is an adulteress having taken up a life of adultery with a neighbor across the street. Mother committed perjury in the first trial. A second trial was held because of her perjury at the first trial.

The neighbor, who sired an illegitimate child with Mother, during the course of her marriage to Father, has a record with several felony convictions. He is a multiple convict. Witnesses testified before the trial judge that he was abusive to his own wife, had a violent temper, and abused his children, inter alia, by using vulgar, filthy language to them. Apparently, the trial judge paid no heed whatsoever to this testimony of independent witnesses. Mother described him, at the second trial, as being "quite a nice person, very compassionate and a good listener as well, but when pushed to the wall, he can be—can be hot tempered and he can also be somewhat rude." It is obvious that Mother has a poor value system.

Testimony reveals in this trial that Mother's adulterous relationship was such that neighbors saw him going in and out of the window, saw him partially unclad, and made no effort to hide his relationship from the children. It portrayed an immoral, unethical, and bad impression upon the children. The lovers were concerned with what the neighbors saw. Hence, the sneaking in and out of the window. But the neighbors saw. Mother not only committed adultery in this home, while Father worked, she also secretly discussed her relationship with the oldest girl. A child therapist testified that the conduct of the Mother, concerning her illicit relationship with the felon and the matters pertaining to the divorce, was very detrimental to the oldest girl and placed this young girl in the position of being a "parentified child." This therapist testified that this caused the young girl to take on an adult role, a role she was not equipped to handle. By taking the child into her confidence, this adulteress was trying to win the child over on her side. Trial judge had testimony before him that Mother's actions and deeds were contrary to the best interests of the children. At one time, the felon was released from jail and Mother had children prepare a bed for the felon in the basement of the family home. Society in this age—sinks deep and deeper. How can these children approach problems in life and try to solve them with any sense of pride and responsibility when adults set this kind of example?

There is no doubt in the wide, wide world that these children were openly exposed to this adulterous relationship. The children's therapist testified that this adulterous conduct, in their presence, harmed them. Notwithstanding, the trial judge opined it was in the best interests of the children to be with the Mother. The children's therapist, who worked with these children as the result of the Mother's terrible conduct, testified that the Father was a competent parent to have care, custody and control of these children.

It is obvious that the relationship between the Mother and the felon affected the children's development of what is right and wrong in this world. During the course of all of these proceedings, at one time Father had custody of these children, namely from January 1991, until on or about May 15, 1992. Teachers and witnesses came to the trial court and testified that the children were clean, well-dressed, well-nourished and were getting along in school and socially quite well. There is nothing to suggest that at any time the Father did not provide a stable and good environment for these children. With him, the children had positive experiences; with the Mother, the children had negative experiences. An example of this conclusion is illustrated in the transcript by the testimony of Karen Hanson, a neighbor. Ms. Hanson testified she saw the convict and adulteress Mother together frequently and listened to violent language of the convict. In the presence of his children, she heard him say: ". . . 'you fucking little sons of bitches'—that's what he (Bob Rochelle) said to his kids."

The record is replete with the fact that the Father is an extremely hardworking man who makes approximately $26,000 per year. He works approximately 45 to 55 hours per week. While he had temporary custody of the children, a next door neighbor, well known to the children, took care of the children and Father would pick them up at approximately 6:30 p.m. The children were in the care of the next door neighbor for approximately 3 1/2 hours per day while Father was working.

An expert testified that the Father puts the needs of the children first. Further, he did not manipulate the children by saying terrible things about the Mother. Testimony reveals that the Mother talked against the Father to the children, ran him down, and discussed the problems of her marriage. She had utter contempt for her husband. Obviously, this conduct emotionally tore the children apart. And testimony so established. In *Palmer v. Palmer*, 316 N.W.2d 631 (S.D.1982), we held that the trial court's findings reflected that the mother's utter contempt for the father may have, in some measure, have been transferred to the child. We held the trial court was justified in finding that she was a negative role model for a child. We held that the trial court did not abuse its discretion in awarding custody of the four year old daughter to the father. Here, this trial judge has clearly abused his discretion.

. . . . Accordingly, I dissent.

NOTES AND QUESTIONS

(1) **The Principal Case.** Perhaps because of the rage of Justice Henderson, the *Hanhart* case frames the issue well. Should the court have awarded the custody to the mother, who had an open and adulterous affair with a convicted felon, or to the father, who worked between 45-55 hours per week, who would have had to place the children in extensive day care, and who may have to move often in his job. Other factors are that the children wanted to live with their mother, and the court did not want to split up the four children. In addition, the mother perjured herself at the first trial. As to the mother's parenting skills, even Justice Henderson does not question them other than to mention that she discussed her affair with the oldest daughter. In the end, the trial court and all but one of the Justices of the Supreme Court were convinced that the mother should have custody.

(2) **The Issue.** Does adultery or other sexual conduct make the parent per se unfit because of the moral effect on children or must the court look to the actual adverse impact that the conduct has on the children's welfare? In a case where the mother was cohabiting with another man, the Supreme Court of Illinois upheld an award of custody to the father and said that the mother's "disregard for existing standards of conduct instructs her children, by example that they, too, may ignore them . . . , and could well encourage the children to engage in similar activity in the future." *Jarrett v. Jarrett*, 400 N.E.2d 421 (Ill. 1979), *cert. denied*, 449 U.S. 927 (1980). The problem with this view is it substitutes the court's values for that of the parent. The mother in *Jarrett*, like may Americans, may have viewed cohabitation as morally acceptable and may even have believed it was permissible for her children when they grew up. On the other hand, a New York court, finding a mother's swinging lifestyle was not known to the children and did not have a negative effect on their welfare, stated in the early 1970's "amorality, immorality, sexual deviation, and what we conveniently consider to be aberrant sexual practices do not ipso facto constitute unfitness for custody." *Feldman v. Feldman*, 358 N.Y.S.2d 507, 510 (N.Y. App. Div. 1974).

The danger of this view is that it places no weight on moral values, an approach many people are reacting to today.

(3) **The Trend.** The principal case represents the clear trend not to consider the sexual conduct of the parents in a custody dispute as long as the conduct does not directly impact the children. While this trend does not appear to have stopped, it is being questioned by a new movement to return the concept of fault in divorce. There are many cases in support of this trend. *See Slack v. Slack*, 641 So. 2d 1059, 1061 (La. Ct. App. 1994) (holding that proof of adultery does not necessarily render a parent unfit; numerous other factors supported the award of physical custody to mother); *Kenneth L.W. v. Tamyra S.W.*, 408 S.E.2d 625, 628 (W. Va. 1991) (stating that adulterous behavior of mother should not be considered where there is no evidence of deleterious effect upon children; the mother was therefore entitled to the primary caretaker presumption); *Leszinske v. Poole*, 798 P.2d 1049, 1055 (N.M. 1990) (affirming custody award to the mother despite marriage to uncle, as long as marriage is valid, and there are no harmful moral or legal effects on children); *Hanson v. Hanson*, 562 A.2d 1051, 1053 (Vt. 1989) (remanding trial court decision to award custody to father because of mother's continuing affair which caused break up of the marriage where there was no finding of adverse impact on the children); *Truitt v. Truitt*, 431 N.W.2d 454, 458 (Mich. Ct. App. 1988) (custody award to mother remanded where trial court showed bias toward father's cohabitation); *Stacy v. Stacy*, 332 S.E.2d 260, 261 (W. Va. 1985) (reversing and remanding custody award in favor of father; lower court failed to consider the primary caretaker presumption, and erred in considering adultery of mother where there is no finding of deleterious effect on children).

(4) **The Traditional View.** There are of course cases to the contrary which use adultery or sexual conduct as the basis of denying custody. Older cases tend to be based upon moral fault. More modern cases waver between moral fault and impact. Recent examples are *Adam v. Adam*, 436 N.W.2d 266, 268 (S.D. 1989) (finding the trial court did not abuse its discretion in awarding custody to the father where the child was exposed to mother's affair and there was evidence that the misconduct had a harmful effect on the child); *Grant v. Grant*, 510 So. 2d 271, 272 (Ala. Civ. App. 1987) (trial court considered evidence that mother was having an "adulterous relationship" in awarding father the custody of four small children); *Reynaud v. Reynaud*, 484 So. 2d 294, 296 (La. Ct. App. 1986) (finding that the trial court abused its discretion in awarding joint custody in the face of evidence that the mother engaged in an adulterous relationship and did not provide a stable environment for the children); *Santmier v. Santmier*, 494 So. 2d 95, 96 (Ala. Civ. App. 1986) (upholding trial court award of custody to the father; no abuse of discretion considering mother's affair with a married man and conduct toward children during course of affair); *Dockins v. Dockins*, 475 So. 2d 571, 573 (Ala. Civ. App. 1985) (finding that the moral misconduct of a parent must be such as to have direct bearing on the welfare of the child; adulterous conduct of mother was considered in upholding custody award to father); *Larson v. Larson*, 294 N.W.2d 616, 618 (N.D. 1980) (court considered moral fitness of mother who had several live-in paramours).

(5) **The Double Standard.** Regardless of what conclusion you draw, almost all of the cases dealing with heterosexual conduct or misconduct involve women. Does this mean that men never engage in sexual misconduct, that sexual misconduct of fathers is accepted, that courts are biased against the sexual conduct of mothers which exceeds the bounds of

traditional norms, or that fathers tend to use sexual conduct of mothers as leverage in custody battles more than mothers? One last thought, which relates to this double standard: Maccoby and Mnookin point out that one of the common elements of high conflict divorces, those that require adjudication, was the degree of hostility that the father had toward the mother. In other words, a high degree of hostility by the father was more likely to lead to litigation than a high degree of hostility by the mother. *See* Maccoby & Mnookin, *Dividing the Child, Social and Legal Dilemmas of Custody* 272 (1992). Fathers, angry about the mothers' sexual conduct, may be much more willing to fight it out, and in some cases they find judges who support them. Indeed, Justice Henderson in *Hanhart* seems to assume and to express this anger.

[2] Sexual Preference

BOTTOMS v. BOTTOMS
Court of Appeals of Virginia
444 S.E.2d 276, *reversed*, 457 S.E.2d 102 (Va. 1995)

COLEMAN, JUDGE.

In this child custody appeal, we find the evidence insufficient to support the trial court's decision to remove custody of a three-year-old child from his natural parent, the mother, and to grant custody to a third party, the child's maternal grandmother. As in all child custody cases, we are governed by the constant that a child's best interest controls. A child's best interest is presumed to be served by being in the custody of the child's natural parent, rather than a non-parent. A non-parent is granted custody over a parent only when the parent is unfit to have custody of the child or when continued custody with the parent will be deleterious to the child.

In this case, the evidence fails to prove that Sharon Bottoms, the child's mother, abused or neglected her son, that her lesbian relationship with April Wade has or will have a deleterious effect on her son, or that she is an unfit parent. To the contrary, the evidence showed that Sharon Bottoms is and has been a fit and nurturing parent who has adequately provided and cared for her son. No evidence tended to prove that the child will be harmed by remaining with his mother. We hold, therefore, that the trial court abused its discretion by invoking the state's authority to take the child from the custody of his natural mother, Sharon Bottoms, and by transferring custody to a non-parent, Kay Bottoms, the child's maternal grandmother.

I. THE EVIDENCE

In 1989, Sharon Bottoms married Dennis Doustou. They separated when Sharon was pregnant with their son, who was born in 1991. The 1991 divorce decree awarded custody of the child to Sharon Bottoms. Doustou has not been actively involved in his son's life since the divorce. During the three years following the divorce, Sharon Bottoms dated another man, lived with her cousin, lived with two lesbians, and in 1992, began living with April Wade. During this time, Sharon Bottoms had legal custody of her son, but she frequently relied on her mother, Kay Bottoms, to keep and care for the child. Kay Bottoms estimated that she had kept the child most of the time after his birth.

In January 1993, Sharon Bottoms informed her mother that her son would be spending less time at her mother's house because of Tommy Conley's presence there. Tommy Conley was Kay Bottoms' live-in male companion. The two had lived together and reared Sharon Bottoms from the time Sharon was a child. Sharon Bottoms explained to her mother that she was taking her son out of the household because while she, Sharon, was growing up, Tommy Conley had sexually abused her over 800 times. Kay Bottoms was shocked and upset by the accusations, but she later decided that the accusations were not altogether unfounded.

Shortly after the conversation between Sharon and Kay Bottoms, Kay filed a petition with the juvenile and domestic relations district court seeking custody of her grandson. She asked Tommy Conley to move out of the house during the custody dispute because her lawyer "thought it would be best." The circuit court ultimately granted Kay Bottoms custody of her grandson, and this appeal followed.

Sharon Bottoms acknowledges that she is a lesbian and that she shares a residence with April Wade, her lesbian companion. Sharon Bottoms admits that she and April Wade engage in consensual sexual acts in the privacy of their residence. She testified that they share the same bed and engage in oral sex once or twice a week. For a period of time, when the child was very young, the child's crib was in the bedroom where they slept. Sharon Bottoms testified that she and April Wade have never engaged in any type of sexual activity in her son's presence, nor has she exposed him to sexual conduct of any type. She admits that she and April Wade have displayed some affection in the child's presence by hugging, kissing, or patting one another on the bottom. All the psychological evidence introduced on this issue was to the effect that Sharon Bottoms' open lesbian relationship has had no visible or discernible effect on her son.

While the child has spent considerable time with his grandmother, Kay Bottoms, the evidence proved that he and his mother, Sharon Bottoms, have had a close, loving mother-child relationship. Sharon Bottoms has adequately provided him with the basic necessities of life, including food, clothing, and shelter.

On two occasions, Sharon Bottoms spanked the child on the leg "too hard." The evidence did not show that the spankings bruised or injured the child. The evidence showed that Sharon Bottoms had punished the child by making him stand in a corner and had on occasion cursed in the child's presence. However, she has not physically abused the child, neglected him, or endangered or threatened his life, physical safety, or well-being. The psychological evaluations stated that Sharon Bottoms is "warm" and "responsive" with her son, and that he "behave[s] as if entirely secure and at ease with his mother, it being a very familiar and comfortable situation for him."

Kay Bottoms testified that on one occasion, Sharon Bottoms left the child at Kay's home for a week without telling her how she could be reached. No evidence showed that Sharon Bottoms had ever left the child with an irresponsible person or unattended. Until recently, Sharon Bottoms had been unemployed. She has been receiving Aid to Dependent Children benefits. The evidence shows that April Wade is a recovering alcoholic. The child's father, Dennis Doustou, pays no child support.

II. THE TRIAL COURT RULING

The trial court ruled that because Sharon Bottoms lives in a sexually active lesbian relationship and engages in illegal sexual acts, she is an unfit parent as a matter of law. The trial court held as follows:

> Sharon Bottoms has . . . admitted . . . that she is living in an homosexual relationship. . . . She is sharing . . . her bed with . . . her female lover. . . . Examples given were kissing, patting, all of this in the presence of the child. . . . There is no case directly on point concerning all these matters. In the case of *Roe v. Roe*, it's certainly of assistance to me in reaching a decision here today. I will tell you first that the mother's conduct is illegal. . . . I will tell you that it is the opinion of the court that her conduct is immoral. And it is the opinion of this court that the conduct of Sharon Bottoms renders her an unfit parent. However, I also must recognize, and do recognize, that there is a presumption in the law in favor of the custody being with the natural parent. And I then ask myself are Sharon Bottoms' circumstances of unfitness . . . of such an extraordinary nature as to rebut this presumption. My answer to this is yes [under] *Roe v. Roe*. . . . I further find that in addition to this, there is other evidence . . . which is unrebutted of the cursing, the evidence of the child standing in the corner.

The trial judge granted custody to Kay Bottoms and visitations on Mondays and Tuesdays to Sharon Bottoms, provided that no visitations be in the home shared with April Wade or in April Wade's presence.

III. THE LEGAL PRINCIPLES

Virginia law presumes a "child's best interests will be served when in the custody of its [natural] parent." *Judd v. Van Horn*, 195 Va. 988, 996, 81 S.E.2d 432, 436 (1954). The parental presumption arises when a third party undertakes to deprive a natural parent of the custody of his or her child. Although a child custody award may be temporary and subject to modification as circumstances change, the relationship between a child and its parent is one of the most jealously protected rights in Anglo-Saxon jurisprudence. . . .

The custody dispute between Sharon and Kay Bottoms is not governed by the same principles that control a dispute between two parents. When natural parents are contesting for custody of their child, the court balances the equities between the parents and determines with which parent will the child's best interests be served. The court determines which parent will be the more fit and suitable custodian to care for the child's needs based on the current and foreseeable circumstances.

However, unlike parental custody disputes wherein the parents stand on equal legal footing, when a third party attempts to divest custody of a child from a natural parent, the presumption of parental fitness must be rebutted before a court may consider whether a third party would be a fit or proper custodian. . . .

. . . No credible evidence proves that Sharon Bottoms is an unfit parent or that her having custody of her son will be harmful to his physical, emotional, or psychological well-being.

The most that can be said against Sharon Bottoms, insofar as her parenting is concerned, is that on two occasions she spanked her son "too hard," on occasion she swore in his presence, she had him stand in a corner, and on occasion she had failed to change his diaper as soon as conditions required. Sharon Bottoms had lived in four different residences in different relationships in a three-year period, and she had not been regularly employed. On one occasion, Sharon Bottoms had left her son with Kay Bottoms, the grandmother, for a week without informing the grandmother how she could be reached.

Although Sharon Bottoms' parenting during this three-year period was far from ideal, she was not indifferent to her child's well-being. Her disciplining of the child, even if by some standards considered intemperate or inappropriate, was not abusive. Her lifestyle in moving several times in a short period, in being unemployed for a time, and in failing to inform her mother of her whereabouts for a week were not acts of neglect or abuse sufficient to render her an unfit custodian. At all times, Sharon Bottoms either cared for the child or assured that proper care was provided for the child. No evidence suggested that any of Sharon Bottoms' actions resulted in psychological, emotional, or physical harm to the child or that her actions constituted neglect or abuse.

The psychological evaluations admitted into evidence indicated that Sharon Bottoms' son is a "happy, well-adjusted youngster" with an "out-going, engaging manner . . . capable of forming and sustaining both emotional and social attachments to others." The psychological reports concluded that Sharon Bottoms is "warm" and "responsive" with her son and that "[he] behave[s] as if entirely secure and at ease with his mother, [being with her is] . . . very familiar and comfortable . . . for him."

The trial judge based his finding of Sharon Bottoms' parental unfitness on the fact that she is living in an open lesbian relationship with April Wade and that the two engage in sodomy, an illegal sexual act, in the home where the child would reside. Certainly, those facts, which define the nature of the relationship between a custodial parent and a resident of the household where the child would reside, are the most critical and significant factors in this case for determining whether this parent is unfit or whether continued parental custody will be harmful or deleterious to the child. All factors must be considered, but in this instance, the open lesbian relationship and illegality of the mother's sexual activity are the only significant factors that the court considered in finding Sharon Bottoms to be an unfit parent.

We agree with the trial court that the nature of the relationship between a parent and the parent's live-in companion where the child resides may affect the type of conduct and behavior to which a child will be exposed and, thus, profoundly affect the child. The Supreme Court of Virginia has expressly said that a lesbian "lifestyle" is one factor "to [be] . . . considered in determining [a woman's] fitness as a mother." *Doe v. Doe*, 222 Va. 736, 748, 284 S.E.2d 799, 806 (1981). A parent's behavior and conduct in the presence of a child influences and affects the child's values and views as to the type of behavior and conduct that the child will find acceptable.

The fact that a parent is homosexual does not *per se* render a parent unfit to have custody of his or her child. Thus, the fact that a mother is a lesbian and has engaged in illegal sexual acts does not alone justify taking custody of a child from her and awarding the child to a non-parent, even though an award of custody may be only temporary. The fact that a parent has committed a crime does not render a parent unfit, unless such criminal conduct impacts upon or is harmful to the child, or unless other special circumstances exist aside from the parent's conduct that would render continued custody with the parent deleterious to the child.

A parent's sexual behavior, particularly a parent's sexual indiscretions, in a child's presence is conduct which may render a parent unfit to have custody of a child. A parent's private sexual conduct, even if illegal, does not create a presumption of unfitness. In order for the state or a third party to take custody of a child from its natural parent, more is required than simply showing that a parent has engaged in private, illegal sexual conduct, lacks ideal parenting skills, or is not meeting society's traditional or conventional standards of morality. A court will not remove a child from the custody of a parent, based on proof that the parent is engaged in private, illegal sexual conduct or conduct considered by some to be deviant, in the absence of proof that such behavior or activity poses a substantial threat of harm to a child's emotional, psychological, or physical well-being.

Of course, courts must not delay in granting a remedy until a parent's conduct or behavior has harmed the child; the rule of law does not require that the damage sought to be avoided must occur before a court may act to prevent injury or to remedy a harmful situation. However, before courts may deprive a parent and child of their fundamental rights to be together and to associate with one another, the evidence must show that the parent is unfit and that the child is subjected to conduct and behavior that will harm the child. A court may not simply surmise, speculate, or take notice that because a parent engages in private, sexual conduct, even that which is illegal or conduct that is perceived by some as immoral or antisocial and to which the child is not subjected and which does not affect the child, the parent is unfit or the child is being harmed. . . ..

In Sharon Bottoms' case, the trial court found that Sharon Bottoms engaged in illegal sexual activity and that her open lesbian relationship rendered her an unfit parent "as a matter of law." The trial court erroneously adopted a *per se* approach in finding Sharon Bottoms to be an unfit parent without finding that she engaged in conduct or exposed her son to conduct that would be harmful to him. In declaring as a matter of law that Sharon Bottoms is an unfit parent, the trial court misapplied the Supreme Court's decision in *Roe v. Roe*, 228 Va. 722, 324 S.E.2d 691 (1985). . . .

The Supreme Court of Virginia has held that adverse effects of a parent's homosexuality on a child cannot be assumed without specific proof. "There is no evidence that children who are raised with a loving couple of the same sex are any more disturbed, unhealthy, or maladjusted than children raised with a loving couple of mixed sex." [*Doe v. Doe*,] 284 S.E.2d [799,] 806 [(1981)] (quoting *Bezio v. Patenaude*, 381 Mass. 563, 410 N.E.2d 1207, 1215–16 (1980)). The psychological testimony presented in this case was to the effect that a parent's homosexual relationship alone does not harm a child emotionally or psychologically or make the parent an unfit custodian. The social science evidence showed that a person's sexual orientation does not strongly correlate with that person's fitness as a parent. No evidence was presented to refute these studies. No evidence was presented that tended to prove that Sharon Bottoms' living arrangement with April Wade and their lesbian relationship have harmed or will harm Sharon Bottom's son.

For these reasons, we hold that the trial court erred in finding that Sharon Bottoms' lesbian relationship alone constituted clear and convincing evidence of parental unfitness. The trial court erred in holding that the evidence "of the cursing [and] . . . of the child standing in the corner" and the fact that Sharon Bottoms is a lesbian who lives with her lesbian companion are "of such an extraordinary nature as to rebut the presumption [of parental fitness]."

Because we hold that the presumption favoring Sharon Bottoms in this case was not rebutted, we do not decide whether the grandmother, Kay Bottoms, could best provide for the child's needs. Accordingly, we hold that Sharon Bottoms is not to be deprived of custody of her son upon the present record. We reverse and vacate the circuit court's order and remand the case with directions that the circuit court enter an order effectuating the resumption of custody by the mother of her son. *Reversed and remanded.*

NOTES AND QUESTIONS

(1) **Virginia Supreme Court.** The *Bottoms* case became nationally known and to some degree a *cause celebre* for gay and lesbian rights. The Virginia Supreme Court overruled the appellate decision; construing the facts differently. The intermediate court case is presented here because it is difficult to determine the legal standard being used by the Supreme Court of Virginia. The latter court concluded:

In the present case, the record shows a mother who, although devoted to her son, refuses to subordinate her own desires and priorities to the child's welfare. For example, the mother disappears for days without informing the child's custodian of her whereabouts. She moves her residence from place to place, relying on others for support, and uses welfare funds to "do" her fingernails before buying food for the child. She has participated in illicit relationships with numerous men, acquiring a disease from one, and "sleeping" with men in the same room where the child's crib was located. To aid in her mobility, the mother keeps the child's suitcase packed so he can be quickly deposited at the grandmother's.

The mother has difficulty controlling her temper and, out of frustration, has struck the child when it was merely one year old with such force as to leave her fingerprints on his person. While in her care, she neglects to change and cleanse the child so that, when he returns from visitation with her, he is "red" and "can't even sit down in the bathtub."

Unlike *Doe*, 222 Va. at 747, 284 S.E.2d at 805, relied on by the mother, there is proof in this case that the child has been harmed, at this young age, by the conditions under which he lives when with the mother for any extended period. For example, he has already demonstrated some disturbing traits. He uses vile language. He screams, holds his breath until he turns purple, and becomes emotionally upset when he must go to visit the mother. He appears confused about efforts at discipline, standing himself in a corner facing the wall for no apparent reason.

And, we shall not overlook the mother's relationship with Wade, and the environment in which the child would be raised if custody is awarded the mother. We have previously said that living daily under conditions stemming from active lesbianism practiced in the home may impose a burden upon a child by reason of the "social condemnation" attached to such an arrangement, which will inevitably afflict the child's relationships with its "peers and with the community at large." *Roe v. Roe*, 228 Va. 722, 728, 324 S.E.2d 691, 694 (1985). We do not retreat from that statement; such a result is likely under these facts. Also, Wade has struck the child and, when there was a dispute over visitation, she has threatened violence when her views were not accepted.

Bottoms v. Bottoms, 457 S.E.2d 102, 108 (Va. 1995). *See* Parsons, *Bottoms v. Bottoms: Erasing the Presumption Favoring a Natural Parent Over Third Parties—What Makes This Mother Unfit?*, 2 Geo. Mason L. Rev. 457 (1994).

(2) **Different Approaches.** It is difficult to categorize the cases dealing with sexual preference simply because sometimes it is impossible to tell if the court is using homosexuality as the sole criteria or if the court is viewing it as one factor among many. The Supreme Court of Virginia decision in *Bottoms* mentioned above is an example of a decision whose rationale is difficult to categorize. Another example is *G.A. v. D.A.* in which the Missouri Court of Appeals stated that the mother's lesbian relationship "tipped the scales" in favor of the father. *G.A. v. D.A.*, 745 S.W.2d 726, 727 (Mo. Ct. App. 1987).

Despite this difficulty in categorization, cases which have a well developed rationale can be divided into three categories: per se unfitness, presumption of unfitness, and nexus.

(a) *Per Se Unfitness.* The trial court in *Bottoms* epitomizes this position. The trial court states out right: "I will tell you that the mother's conduct is illegal. . . . I will tell you that it is the opinion of the court that her conduct is immoral. And it is the opinion of the court that the conduct of Sharon Bottoms renders her an unfit parent." The per se approach is usually based upon one of the two reasons—illegality and immorality—stated in this quotation; however there are other reasons sometimes given:

> Courts also base the per se approach upon judicial perception that the child of a homosexual parent "may have difficulties in achieving a fulfilling heterosexual identity of his or her own in the future," [*S.v S.*, 608 S.W.2d 64, 65 (Ky. Ct. App. 1980)] or that a child would bear an "intolerable burden" because of the perceived "social condemnation" attached to homosexuality which would "inevitably harm" the child's relationship with his or her peers and with the community at large. [*Jacobson v. Jacobson*, 314 N.W.2d 78 (N.D. 1981); *M.J.P. v. J.G.P.*, 640 P.2d 966 (Okla. 1982); *Kallas v. Kallas*, 614 P.2d 641 (Utah 1980).]

Swisher & Cook, *Bottoms v. Bottoms: in Whose Best Interest? Analysis of a Lesbian Mother Child Custody Dispute*, 34 U. Louisville J. Fam. L. 843, 849 (Fall, 1995–96). Regarding per se approach, see Strasser, *Fit to be Tied: On Custody, Discretion, and Sexual Orientation*, 46 Am. U. L. Rev 841 (1997).

(b) *Rebuttable Presumption of Unfitness.* Some courts take a middle ground; homosexuality in a parent or merely the presence of a gay or lesbian lover creates a presumption that it is in the best interest to place the child with another parent. This view is rejected in the appellate court decision in *Bottoms*: "[a] parent's private sexual conduct, even if illegal, does not create a presumption of unfitness." *Bottoms*, 444 S.E.2d at 283. Other courts have embraced this approach. In *Constant A. v. Paul C.A.*, 496 A.2d 1, 5 (Pa. Super. Ct. 1985), the court stated, "We submit the law is and should be that, where there is a custody dispute between members of a traditional family environment and one of homosexual composition, *the presumption of regularity applies to the traditional relationship* and the burden of proving no adverse effect of the homosexual relationship falls on the person advocating it." *Id.* at 5. (emphasis in original). *See also Conkel v. Conkel*, 509 N.E.2d 983, 986 (Ohio Ct. App. 1987).

(c) *Nexus.* The nexus theory or test holds that "a parent's gay or lesbian sexual orientation or sexual conduct should have no bearing in a child custody determination unless credible evidence is presented to show such orientation or conduct has a detrimental or adverse affect on the child." Swisher & Cook, *Bottoms v. Bottoms: in Whose Best Interest? Analysis of a Lesbian Mother Child Custody Dispute*, 34 U. Louisville J. Fam. L. 843, 853–54 (1995–96). There must be a positive showing of mental or psychological harm. Rather than focusing on the fact that a parent is gay or lesbian, the court applies the best interest standard. If there is actual harm or detriment to the child caused by the parent's conduct, then it is factored into the best interest test as one factor among many. If the harm is substantial, it could become very important in the court's decision; if the harm is nonexistent, other factors determine the courts decision entirely. Many jurisdictions follow this approach: *Nadler v. Superior Court*, 63 Cal. Rptr. 352 (Cal. Ct. App. 1967); *M.P. v. S.P.*, 404 A.2d 1256 (N.J. Super. Ct. App. Div. 1979); *DeBoise v. Robinson*, No. C-9104 (Del. Fam. Ct. 1980); *D.H. v. H.*, 418 N.E.2d 286 (Ind. Ct. App. 1981); *Medeiros v. Medeiros*, 8 Fam. L. Rep. (BNA) 2372 (Vt. Super. Ct. 1982); *Doe v. Doe*, 452 N.E.2d 293 (Mass. App. Ct. 1983); *In re Marriage of Cabalquinto*, 669 P.2d 886 (Wash. 1983); *Guinan v. Guinan*, 477 N.Y.S.2d 830 (N.Y. App. Div. 1984); *S.N.E. v. R.L.B.*, 699 P.2d 875 (Ala. 1985); *Rowsey v. Rowsey*, 329 S.E.2d 57 (W. Va. 1985); *Stroman v. Williams*, 353 S.E.2d 704 (S.C. Ct. App. 1987); *M.P. v. S.P.*, 552 N.E.2d 884 (Ohio 1990); *In re Adoption of Charles B.*, 552 N.E.2d 884 (Ohio 1990); *A.C. v. C.B.*, 829 P.2d 660 (N.M. Ct. App. 1992); *Blew v. Verta*, 617 A.2d 31 (Pa. Super. Ct. 1992). *See also Johnson v. Schlotman*, 502 N.W.2d 831 (N.D. 1993) (Levin, J., concurring).

However, one commentator has argued that even courts which follow the nexus approach show signs of homophobia. Ronner, *Bottoms v. Bottoms: The Lesbian Mother and the Judicial Perpetuation of Damaging Stereotypes*, 7 Yale J.L. & Feminism 341 (1995).

(3) **Research.** The literature regarding empirical research into parenting skills of lesbian and gay parents can be summarized by the following quotation:

The social science literature reviewed here demonstrates clearly that lesbians and gay men can and do raise psychologically healthy children. In fact, no evidence has emerged to date which suggests that homosexual parents are inferior to their heterosexual counterparts, or that their children are in any regard compromised. Taken as a whole, these findings have important implications in the legal arena. First, because no significant differences have been found between heterosexual and homosexual parent families, there exists no empirical support for the dissimilar treatment of lesbian and gay families under the law. Specifically, the literature does not support blanket policies or presumptions denying lesbian or gay couples the right to adopt children, become foster parents, retain child custody or visitation after divorce, or utilize reproductive technology. On the other hand, the social science literature also does not support the position that every individual, heterosexual or homosexual, is suitable to raise children. Rather, what the evidence suggests is that courts determining parental fitness among lesbian and gay individuals need not apply special presumptions, nor require expert evaluations, which depart from typical methods of psychosocial assessment. Instead, the literature is consistent with appropriate case-by-case evaluations of lesbian and gay families based on the same criteria employed with heterosexual parent families. Moreover, once lesbian and gay families are formed, the available evidence offers no justification for withholding from them the same legal protection and benefits offered to heterosexual-parent families. Specifically, they provide no basis upon which to deny same-sex parents full parental status, either during the couple's relationship, or afterward—should it end. Although further research is necessary to fully understand the functioning of families headed by lesbians and gay men, there already exists sufficient evidence to support judicial reassessment of the disparate treatment sometimes afforded lesbian and gay families within the American legal system

Flaks, *Gay and Lesbian Families: Judicial Assumptions, Scientific Realities*, 3 Wm. & Mary Bill Rts. J. 345, 371 (1994).

(4) **Parental Preference Presumption.** *Bottoms v. Bottoms* 457 S.E.2d 102, 107 (Va. 1995) is especially interesting because the Supreme Court of Virginia upheld a trial court decision to award custody to a grandmother instead of a lesbian mother despite the fact that there is a presumption in Virginia, as in most states, in favor of the parent. Although the court in its discussion considered many factors in determining the best interest of the child, the fact that the parental presumption was overcome may indicate that the supreme court was not following the nexus approach. Two other courts have done the same recently. *See Mcginnis v. McGinnis*, 567 So. 2d 390, 392 (Ala. Civ. App. 1990) (the mother at one point signed voluntary relinquishment); and *White v. Thompson*, 569 So. 2d 1181, 1184 (Miss. 1990) (the lesbian mother used marijuana and neglected the children somewhat).

(5) Custody disputes can also arise between two gay parents. *See In re Custody of H.S.H.-K.*, 533 N.W.2d 419 (Wis. 1995); *see also* § 3.02 *above*, Note (5).

(6) Many law review articles have dealt with this subject: Wolfson, *Crossing the Threshold: Equal Marriage Rights for Lesbians and Gay Men and the Intra-Community, Critique*, 21 N.Y.U. Rev. L. & Soc. Change 567 (1994–95); Strasser, *Fit to Be Tied: On Custody, Discretion, and Sexual Orientation*, 46 Am. U. L. Rev. 841 (1997); Wardle, *The Potential Impact of Homosexual Parenting on Children*, 1997 U. Ill. L. Rev. 833 (1997); Eichinger-Swainston, *Fox v. Fox: Redefining the Best Interest of the Child Standard for Lesbian Mothers and Their Families*, 32 Tulsa L.J. 57 (1996); Shapiro, *Custody and Conduct; How the Law Fails Lesbian and Gay Parents and Their Children*, 71 Ind. L.J. 623 (1996); Symposium, *Defining Family: Gays, Lesbians, and the Meaning of Family*, 3 Wm. & Mary Bill Rts. J. 289 (1994); Tamayo, *Sexuality, Morality and the Law: the Custody Battle of a Non-Traditional Mother*, 45 Syracuse L. Rev. 853 (1994); Parsons, Note, *Bottoms v. Bottoms: Erasing the Presumption Favoring a Natural Parent over Third Parties—What Makes this Mother Unfit?*, 2 Geo. Mason L. Rev. 457 (1994); Rosenblum, Comment, *Custody Rights of Gay and Lesbian Parents*, 36 Vill. L. Rev. 1665 (1991).

[H] Physical and Mental Health

IN RE MARRIAGE OF CARNEY
California Supreme Court
598 P.2d 36 (1979)

MOSK, J.

Appellant father (William) appeals from that portion of an interlocutory decree of dissolution which transfers custody of the two minor children of the marriage from himself to respondent mother (Ellen).

In this case of first impression we are called upon to resolve an apparent conflict between two strong public policies: the requirement that a custody award serve the best interests of the child, and the moral and legal obligation of society to respect the civil rights of its physically handicapped members, including their right not to be deprived of their children because of their disability. As will appear, we hold that upon a realistic appraisal of the present-day capabilities of the physically handicapped, these policies can both be accommodated. The trial court herein failed to make such an appraisal, and instead premised its ruling on outdated stereotypes of both the parental role and the ability of the handicapped to fill that role. Such stereotypes have no place in our law. Accordingly, the order changing custody on this ground must be set aside as an abuse of discretion.

William and Ellen were married in New York in December 1968. Both were teenagers. Two sons were soon born of the union, the first in November 1969 and the second in January 1971. The parties separated shortly afterwards, and by written agreement executed in November 1972 Ellen relinquished custody of the boys to William. For reasons of employment he eventually moved to the West Coast. In September 1973 he began living with a young woman named Lori Rivera, and she acted as stepmother to the boys. In the following year William had a daughter by Lori, and she proceeded to raise all three children as their own.

In August 1976, while serving in the military reserve, William was injured in a jeep accident. The accident left him a quadriplegic, *i.e.*, with paralyzed legs and impaired use of his arms and hands. He spent the next year recuperating in a veterans' hospital; his children visited him several times each week, and he came home nearly every weekend. He also bought a van, and it was being fitted with a wheelchair lift and hand controls to permit him to drive.

In May 1977 William filed the present action for dissolution of his marriage. Ellen moved for an order awarding her immediate custody of both boys. It was undisputed that from the date of separation (Nov. 1972) until a few days before the hearing (Aug. 1977) Ellen did not once visit her young sons or make any contribution to their support. Throughout this period of almost five years her sole contact with the boys consisted of some telephone calls and a few letters and packages. Nevertheless the court ordered that the boys be taken from the custody of their father, and that Ellen be allowed to remove them forthwith to New York State. Pursuant to stipulation of the parties, an interlocutory judgment of dissolution was entered at the same time. William appeals from that portion of the decree transferring custody of the children to Ellen.

It is settled that to justify ordering a change in custody there must generally be a persuasive showing of changed circumstances affecting the child. And that change must be substantial: a child will not be removed from the prior custody of one parent and given to the other "unless the material facts and circumstances occurring subsequently are of a kind to render it essential or expedient for the welfare of the child that there be a change." (*Washburn v. Washburn*, (1942) 49 Cal. App. 2d 581, 588 [122 P.2d 96].) The reasons for the rule are clear: "It is well established that the courts are reluctant to order a change of custody and will not do so except for imperative reasons; that it is desirable that there be an end of litigation and undesirable to change the child's established mode of living." (*Connolly v. Connolly* (1963), 214 Cal.App. 2d 433, 436 [29 Cal.Rptr. 616], and cases cited.)

. . .

Finally, the burden of showing a sufficient change in circumstances is on the party seeking the change of custody. In attempting to carry that burden Ellen relied on several items of testimony given at the hearing; even when these circumstances are viewed in their totality, however, they are insufficient for the purpose. . . .

Ellen next pointed to the fact that William's relationship with Lori might be in the process of terminating. . . .

Ellen first raised the issue in her declaration accompanying her request for a change of custody, asserting that because of William's handicap "it is almost impossible for [him] to actually care for the minor children," and "since [he] is confined to a hospital bed, he is never with the minor children and thus can no longer effectively care for the minor children or see to their physical and emotional needs." When asked at the hearing why she believed she should be given custody, she replied *inter alia*, "Bill's physical condition." Thereafter she testified that according to her observations William is not capable of feeding himself or helping the boys prepare meals or get dressed; and she summed up by agreeing that he is not able to do "anything" for himself.

The trial judge echoed this line of reasoning throughout the proceedings. Virtually the only questions he asked of any witness revolved around William's handicap and its physical consequences, real or imagined. Thus although William testified at length about his present family life and his future plans, the judge inquired only where he sat when he got out of his wheelchair, whether he had lost the use of his arms, and what his medical prognosis was. Again, when Lori took the stand and testified to William's good relationship with his boys and their various activities together, the judge interrupted to ask her in detail whether it was true that she had to bathe, dress, undress, cook for and feed William. Indeed, he seemed interested in little else.

The final witness was Dr. Jack Share, a licensed clinical psychologist specializing in child development, who had visited William's home and studied his family. Dr. Share testified that William had an IQ of 127, was a man of superior intelligence, excellent judgment and ability to plan, and had adapted well to his handicap. He observed good interaction between William and his boys, and described the latter as self-disciplined, sociable, and outgoing. On the basis of his tests and observations, Dr. Share gave as his professional opinion that neither of the children appeared threatened by William's physical condition; the condition did not in any way hinder William's ability to be a father to them, and would not be a detriment to them if they remained in his home; the present family situation in his home was a healthy environment for the children; and even if Lori were to leave, William could still fulfill his functions as father with appropriate domestic help.

Ellen made no effort on cross-examination to dispute any of the foregoing observations or conclusions, and offered no expert testimony to the contrary. The judge then took up the questioning, however, and focused on what appears to have been one of his main concerns in the case *i.e.*, that because of the handicap William would not be able to participate with his sons in sports and other physical activities. Thus the court asked Dr. Share, "It's very unfortunate that he's in this condition, but when these boys get another two, three years older, would it be better, in your opinion, if they had a parent that was able to actively go places with them, take them places, play Little League baseball, go fishing? Wouldn't that be advantageous to two young boys?" Dr. Share replied that "the commitment, the long-range planning, the dedication" of William to his sons were more important, and stated that from his observations William was "the more consistent, stable part of this family regardless of his physical condition at this point." The judge nevertheless persisted in stressing that William "is limited in what he can do for the boys," and demanded an answer to his question as to "the other activities that two growing boys should have with a natural parent." . . .

We need not speculate on the reasons for the judge's ensuing decision to order the change of custody, as he candidly stated them for the record. First he distinguished a case cited by William, emphasizing "There was no father there or mother that was unable to care for the children because of physical disabilities. . . ." Next he found William and Ellen to be "both good, loving parents," although he strongly chided the latter for failing to visit her sons for five years, saying "She should have crawled on her hands and knees out here if she had to to get the children. . . ." The judge then returned to the theme of William's physical inability to personally take care of the children: speculating on Lori's departure, the judge stressed that in such event "a housekeeper or a nurse" would have to be hired overlooking the admitted fact that Ellen would be compelled to do exactly the same herself for nine hours a day. . . .

More importantly, the judge conceded that Dr. Share "saw a nice, loving relationship, and that's absolutely true. There's a great relationship between [William] and the boys." Yet despite this relationship the judge concluded "I think it would be detrimental to the boys to grow up until age 18 in the custody of their father. *It wouldn't be a normal relationship between father and boys.*" And what he meant by "normal" was quickly revealed: "It's unfortunate [William] has to have help bathing and dressing and undressing. *He can't do anything for the boys himself except maybe talk to them and teach them, be a tutor, which is good, but it's not enough.* I feel that it's in the best interests of the two boys to be with the mother even though she hasn't had them for five years." (Italics added.)

While it is clear the judge herein did not have the totally closed mind exhibited in *Richardson*, it is equally plain that his judgment was affected by serious misconceptions as to the importance of the involvement of parents in the purely physical aspects of their children's lives. We do not mean, of course, that the health or physical condition of the parents may not be taken into account in determining whose custody would best serve the child's interests. In relation to the issues at stake, however, this factor is ordinarily of minor importance; and whenever it is raised whether in awarding custody originally or changing it later it is essential that the court weigh the matter with an informed and open mind.

In particular, if a person has a physical handicap it is impermissible for the court simply to rely on that condition as *prima facie* evidence of the person's unfitness as a parent or of probable detriment to the child; rather, in all cases the court must view the handicapped person as an individual and the family as a whole. To achieve this, the court should inquire into the person's actual and potential physical capabilities, learn how he or she has adapted to the disability and manages its problems, consider how the other members of the household have adjusted thereto, and take into account the special contributions the person may make to the family despite—or even because of—the handicap. Weighing these and all other relevant factors together, the court should then carefully determine whether the parent's condition will in fact have a substantial and lasting adverse effect on the best interests of the child.

The record shows the contrary occurred in the case at bar. To begin with, the court's belief that there could be no "normal relationship between father and boys" unless William engaged in vigorous sporting activities with his sons is a further example of the conventional sex-stereotypical thinking that we condemned in another context in *Sailer Inn v. Kirby* (1971), 5 Cal. 3d 1 [95 Cal. Rptr. 329, 485 P.2d 529, 46 A.L.R.3d 351]. For some, the court's emphasis on the importance of a father's "playing baseball" or "going fishing" with his sons may evoke nostalgic memories of a Norman Rockwell cover on the old Saturday Evening Post. But it has at last been understood that a boy need not prove his masculinity on the playing fields of Eton, nor must a man compete with his son in athletics in order to be a good father: their relationship is no less "normal" if it is built on shared experiences in such fields of interest as science, music, arts and crafts, history or travel, or in pursuing such classic hobbies as stamp or coin collecting. In short, an afternoon that a father and son spend together at a museum or the zoo is surely no less enriching than an equivalent amount of time spent catching either balls or fish.

Even more damaging is the fact that the court's preconception herein, wholly apart from its outdated presumption of proper gender roles, also stereotypes William as a person deemed forever unable to be a good parent simply because he is physically handicapped. Like most stereotypes, this is both false and demeaning. On one level it is false because it assumes that William will never make any significant recovery from his disability. There was no evidence whatever to this effect. On the contrary, it did appear that the hearing was being held only one year after the accident, that William had not yet begun the process of rehabilitation in a home environment, and that he was still a young man in his twenties. In these circumstances the court could not presume that modern medicine, helped by time, patience, and determination, would be powerless to restore at least some of William's former capabilities for active life.

Even if William's prognosis were poor, however, the stereotype indulged in by the court is false for an additional reason: it mistakenly assumes that the parent's handicap inevitably handicaps the child. But children are more adaptable than the court gives them credit for; if one path to their enjoyment of physical activities is closed, they will soon find another. Indeed, having a handicapped parent often stimulates the growth of a child's imagination, independence, and self-reliance. Today's urban youngster, moreover, has many more opportunities for formal and informal instruction than his isolated rural predecessor. It is true that William may not be able to play tennis or swim, ride a bicycle or do gymnastics; but it does not follow that his children cannot learn and enjoy such skills, with the guidance not only of family and friends but also the professional instructors available through schools, church groups, playgrounds, camps, the Red Cross, the YMCA, the Boy Scouts, and numerous service organizations. As Dr. Share pointed out in his testimony, ample community resources now supplement the home in these circumstances.

In addition, it is erroneous to presume that a parent in a wheelchair cannot share to a meaningful degree in the physical activities of his child, should both desire it. On the one hand, modern technology has made the handicapped increasingly mobile, as demonstrated by William's purchase of a van and his plans to drive it by means of hand controls. In the past decade the widespread availability of such vans, together with sophisticated and reliable wheelchair lifts and driving control systems, have brought about a quiet revolution in the mobility of the severely handicapped. No longer are they confined to home or institution, unable to travel except by special vehicle or with the assistance of others; today such persons use the streets and highways in ever-growing numbers for both business and pleasure. . . .

. . . Although William cannot actually play on his children's baseball team, he may nevertheless be able to take them to the game, participate as a fan, a coach, or even an umpire and treat them to ice cream on the way home. Nor is this companionship limited to athletic events: such a parent is no less capable of accompanying his children to theaters or libraries, shops or restaurants, schools or churches, afternoon picnics or long vacation trips. Thus it is not true that, as the court herein assumed, William will be unable "to actively go places with [his children], take them places."

On a deeper level, finally, the stereotype is false because it fails to reach the heart of the parent-child relationship. Contemporary psychology confirms what wise families have perhaps always known that the essence of parenting is not to be found in the harried rounds of daily car-pooling endemic to modern suburban life, or even in the doggedly dutiful acts of "togetherness" committed every weekend by well-meaning fathers and mothers across America. Rather, its essence lies in the ethical, emotional, and intellectual guidance the parent gives to the child throughout his formative years, and often beyond. The source of this guidance is the adult's own experience of life; its motive power is parental love and concern for the child's well-being; and its teachings deal with such fundamental matters as the child's feelings about himself, his relationships with others, his system of values, his standards of conduct, and his goals and priorities in life. Even if it were true, as the court herein asserted, that William cannot do "anything" for his sons except "talk to them and teach them, be a tutor," that would not only be "enough" contrary to the court's conclusion it would be the most valuable service a parent can render. Yet his capacity to do so is entirely unrelated to his physical prowess: however limited his bodily strength may be, a handicapped parent is a whole person to the child who needs his affection, sympathy, and wisdom to deal with the problems of growing up. Indeed, in such matters his handicap may well be an asset: few can pass through the crucible of a severe physical disability without learning enduring lessons in patience and tolerance. . . .

We agree, and conclude that a physical handicap that affects a parent's ability to participate with his children in purely physical activities is not a changed circumstance of sufficient relevance and materiality to render it either "essential or expedient" for their welfare that they be taken from his custody. This conclusion would be obvious if the handicap were heart dysfunction, emphysema, arthritis, hernia, or slipped disc; it should be no less obvious when it is the natural consequence of an impaired nervous system. Accordingly, pursuant to the authorities cited above the order changing the custody of the minor children herein from William to Ellen must be set aside as an abuse of discretion. . . .

SCHUMM v. SCHUMM
Court of Appeals of Minnesota
510 N.W.2d 13 (1993)

LANSING, JUDGE.

This custody appeal raises issues on the adequacy of findings on the factor of the mother's mental health and the exercise of the court's discretion in placing custody with the father. The trial court's detailed findings are supported by the record and meet the requirements that apply to factors listed in Minn.Stat. § 518.17, subd. 1(a). We affirm.

FACTS

Brenda and August Schumm are the parents of two children, ages 12 and 9. Both parents actively cared for the children when the children were young, but Brenda Schumm has had primary responsibility for the children since 1985 when August Schumm began working as an over-the-road truck driver. Both parents are currently employed and maintain a close relationship with the children.

Brenda Schumm has a major mood disorder and a history of vascular headaches, both of which have interfered with her ability to function. She has encountered problems with slurred speech, falling asleep at unusual times, and dropping lighted cigarettes on the floor. She has expressed a fear of crossing the center line while driving and in September 1991 ran into another car while driving with one of the children. She has received ongoing medical care and medication to deal with her mood disorder and headaches. In February 1992 she began to take lithium, and her mental health has improved.

As part of the custody study, Brenda Schumm participated in a chemical dependency evaluation. This evaluation noted potential chemical dependency and recommended a more intensive evaluation. Schumm indicated she did not have the financial resources to obtain the additional evaluation. There was also evidence at trial that Schumm's use of medication containing codeine has created problems. Schumm lost her L.P.N. license and two jobs because of failure to properly account for medication. Schumm's doctor has now prescribed headache medication that does not contain codeine.

The custody evaluator recommended that August Schumm have physical custody of the children. August Schumm has transferred from over-the-road driving to a day job to provide a stable home for the children. He has arranged for after-school child care with his brother's family. His brother's children are close in age to his younger child and they enjoy spending time together. The trial court granted sole physical custody to August Schumm. Brenda Schumm appeals both the judgment and the denial of her posttrial motions.

ANALYSIS

I

A child's best interests serve as the focal point in custody decisions. In considering a child's best interests, the trial court must make findings reflecting the trial court's consideration of the statutory factors listed in Minn.Stat. § 518.17, subd. 1(a). The court may not use one factor "to the exclusion of all others," and, although the "primary caretaker factor" is significant, it cannot be used as a presumption in determining a child's best interests. An appellate court will not reverse a custody determination unless the trial court has abused its discretion by setting forth findings that are unsupported by the evidence or by improperly applying the law.

Brenda Schumm argues both that the findings do not satisfy the statutory requirements and that they are unsupported by the evidence. Her challenge to the adequacy of the findings focuses on the specific language added to the mental and physical health factor of Minn.Stat. § 518.17, subd. 1(a)(9) in 1992. This new language requires consideration, if relevant, of "the mental and physical health of all individuals involved" and states that "a disability, as defined in section 363.01, of a proposed custodian . . . shall not be determinative of the custody of the child, unless the proposed custodial arrangement is not in the best interest of the child . . . ." *Id.*

Minnesota law defines disability as "any condition or characteristic that renders a person a disabled person." Minn.Stat. § 363.01, subd. 13 (1992). This section defines a disabled person as "any person who (1) has a physical, sensory, or mental impairment which materially limits one or more major life activities; (2) has a record of such an impairment; or (3) is regarded as having such an impairment." *Id.*

Brenda Schumm's mental health problems raise a prima facie case of disability under Minn.Stat. § 363.01, subd. 13. Brenda Schumm was unable to work for several years as a result of depression. The trial court made detailed findings on all statutory factors, including the children's preferences, the children's relationship with their parents, the children's primary caretaker, and the children's integration into home, school, and community. The trial court also made findings on Brenda Schumm's major mood disorder, her positive response to lithium, and her vascular headaches, which can last two to three days and prevent her from most activity. The trial court found that Brenda Schumm was under the care of a psychiatrist, that she was improving with treatment and had a good prognosis, and that she would need ongoing treatment to maintain improvement. The trial court also made findings on Brenda Schumm's possible chemical dependency, her September 1991 car accident, and her problems of falling asleep while talking or while smoking cigarettes.

The trial court addressed the effect of Brenda Schumm's mental health on the children's best interests in a separate memorandum. The court indicated that there have been occasions when the two children "were their own caretakers as well as their mother's." The court also considered several examples of Brenda Schumm's inability to care for her children, and the children's concern for both their own safety and their mother's health and safety.

These findings satisfy the specific requirements of Minn. Stat. § 518.17, subd. 1(a). The findings directly address Brenda Schumm's disability and the effects of the disability on the children and their environment. The court properly considered the disability only to the extent it was relevant to the best interests of the children. See Minn. Stat. § 518.17, subd. 1(a)(9).

The trial court's findings on Brenda Schumm's mental and physical health as well as the other statutory factors are supported by the record. An appellate court will affirm the trial court's findings unless clearly erroneous. *Pikula*, 374 N.W.2d at 710. The findings are not erroneous. . . . .

The trial court made detailed findings supported by the record on the statutory factors, including Brenda Schumm's mental health, and determined that awarding August Schumm physical custody is in the best interests of the children. We affirm.

NOTES AND QUESTIONS

(1) Do the courts in *Carney* and *Schumm* disagree? Under statutes like Minnesota and the Uniform Marriage Act, courts may consider the "mental and physical health of all the individuals involved." 9A U.L.A. 561 (1987). But note that *Schumm* makes it clear that health is only one factor among many.

(2) **Physical Health.** *Moye v. Moye*, 627 P.2d 799, 800 (Idaho 1981), is in accord with *Carney*. Should the court consider the physical health of the parent in situations in which the physical condition is less debilitating than those in *Carney*? See *In re Marriage of Benevento*, 454 N.E.2d 766, 768 (Ill. 1983) (the physical health [hypertension and arthritis] of the father who received custody was just one of the many factors to be weighed by the trial court in determining the custody issue in a marriage dissolution case).

(3) **AIDS.** What effect should the fact that one parent has AIDS have on the custody decision? Should AIDS be treated like any other debilitating and fatal disease? At first the courts acted somewhat hysterically and treated both HIV infection and AIDS as an absolute factor against custody. They soon came to their senses and began to limit the inquiry to whether or not the parent with HIV or AIDS could care for the child. See *Stewart v. Stewart*, 521 N.E.2d 956, 963 (Ind. Ct. App. 1988); *Doe v. Roe*, 526 N.Y.S.2d 718, 725 (N.Y. Sup. Ct. 1988); *Jane W. v. John W.*, 519 N.Y.S.2d 603 (N.Y. Sup. Ct. 1987); see also Mahon, Note, *Public Hysteria, Private Conflict: Child Custody and Visitation Disputes Involving an HIV Infected Parent*, 63 N.Y.U. L. Rev. 1092 (1988).

(4) **Mental Fitness.** See *In re Marriage of Lewin*, 186 Cal. App. 3d 1482, 231 Cal. Rptr. 433, 437 (Cal. Ct. App. 1986) (custody of minor daughter awarded to father where mother had engaged in outrageous conduct of making unfounded drug charges against father); *In re Marriage of Nordby*, 705 P.2d 277, 278 (Wash. Ct. App. 1985) (award of custody to mother could not be made on the grounds that court thought that there would be remission in the mother's mental illness; the test for fitness for custody should be present condition of parent and not any future or past conduct); *Jones v. Jones*, 377 N.W.2d 38, 41 (Minn. Ct. App. 1985) (primary parent caretaker doctrine was inapplicable where record indicated mother was incapable of being adequate parent at all times due to irregular episodes of mental illness); *Bukovic v. Smith*, 423 N.E.2d 1302, 1307 (Ill. App. Ct. 1981) (past mental instability on part of mother, where there is no indication of probable future difficulties, is not a proper basis for denying custody to her).

(5) **Smoking.** An interesting case regarding health is *Gilbert v. Gilbert*, 1996 WL 494080 (Conn. Super. Ct. 1996). The court awarded custody of an asthmatic 9-year-old boy to his father despite his request to be placed with his mother because his mother and her husband were smokers. See generally Sobie, *Second Hand Smoke and Child Custody A Relevant Factor or Smoke Screen?*, 18 Pace L. Rev. 41(1997); Hall, *Secondhand Smoke as an Issue in Child Custody/Visitation Disputes*, 97 W. Va. L. Rev. 115 (1994)

[I] Working Parents

IRELAND v. SMITH
Supreme Court of Michigan
547 N.W.2d 686 (1996)

PER CURIAM.

. . . .

I

In their mid-teens, plaintiff Jennifer Ireland and defendant Steven Smith conceived a child, Maranda, who was born in 1991. The parties did not marry, but continued living with their respective parents while they completed high school. After initially planning to put the baby up for adoption, Ms. Ireland decided instead to keep her. The child lived with Ms. Ireland and her mother in Mount Clemens.

After a time, Mr. Smith began visiting the child and providing a few items for her care. However, Maranda continued to live with her mother and maternal grandmother, who provided nearly all the necessary support.

In January 1993, Ms. Ireland began an action to obtain child-support payments from Mr. Smith. She also obtained an ex parte order that granted her continuing custody of Maranda.

Ms. Ireland enrolled as a scholarship student at the University of Michigan in Ann Arbor for the fall semester of 1993. She and Maranda lived in the university's family housing unit. On weekdays, Maranda attended a university-approved day-care center.

During this period, Mr. Smith remained at his parents' home. He evidently continues to live with them.

In May and June 1994, the circuit court conducted a trial regarding the issue of custody. It would be difficult to exaggerate the extent to which the parties disagreed with regard to the proper setting for Maranda. Each produced witnesses who spoke very disparagingly of the other, and there was little agreement about the facts of this matter.

Following the hearing, the circuit court issued an opinion in which it discussed each of the statutory factors for determining the best interests of the child. The court found that each of the statutory factors weighed evenly between the parties, except factor *e*, which concerns: "The permanence, as a family unit, of the existing or proposed custodial home or homes."

The circuit court found that factor e "heavily" favored Mr. Smith. It contrasted the stability of continued residence with Mr. Smith and his parents with the occasional moves that were likely as Ms. Ireland continued her education. In an extended discussion of this factor, the court also noted the demands that would be imposed on Ms. Ireland as she sought both to raise a child and attend the university.

For those reasons, the circuit court ordered that Mr. Smith be given custody of Maranda. Ms. Ireland appealed, and the Court of Appeals entered a stay. . . .

II

In the central portion of its analysis, the Court of Appeals first explained its conclusion that the evidentiary record did not support a factual finding that factor e favored Mr. Smith:

> We find no support in the record for the trial court's speculation that there is "no way that a single parent, attending an academic program at an institution as prestigious as the University of Michigan, can do justice to their studies and to raising of an infant child." The evidence shows that the child has thrived in the university environment. Defendant concedes that he has no complaint about the university day care, and the trial court recognized that the child has had a "meaningful experience" there. The trial court found plaintiff's day-care arrangements "appropriate," but concluded that defendant's plan to have his mother baby-sit was better for the child because she was a "blood relative" rather than a "stranger." Both parties will necessarily need the help of other people to care for their child as they continue their education and employment, and eventually their careers. In light of undisputed evidence that plaintiff's child-care arrangements are appropriate and working well, the evidence does not support the trial court's judgment that defendant's proposed, but untested, plans for the child's care would be better. [214 Mich.App. at 245–246, 542 N.W.2d 344.]

The Court of Appeals then explained that the circuit court had committed an error of law in its application of factor e. Observing that the factor concerns "permanence" of the custodial home, not its "acceptability," the Court stated:

> Moreover, an evaluation of each party's arrangements for the child's care while her parents work to go to school is not an appropriate consideration under this factor. We find the trial court committed clear legal error in considering the "acceptability" of the parties' homes and child-care arrangements under this factor, which is directed to the "permanence, as a family unit," of the individual parties. "This factor exclusively concerns whether the family unit will remain intact, not an evaluation about whether one custodial home would be more acceptable than the other." See *Fletcher v. Fletcher*, 200 Mich.App. 505, 517, 504 N.W.2d 684 (1993). . . .

Finally, the Court of Appeals provided direction for the proceedings on remand:

> On remand, the trial court is to consider "up-to-date information" regarding this factor, as well as the fact that the child has "been living with the plaintiff during the appeal and any other changes in circumstances arising since the trial court's original custody order." The trial court is not, however, to entertain or revisit further "evidence" concerning events before the trial in May and June 1994.

III

We affirm the decision of the Court of Appeals to remand this case, and we agree that the circuit court erred in finding that factor e heavily favored Mr. Smith. However, we write to clarify the analysis and modify the terms of the remand.

A

First, there is the issue how properly to understand factor e. As the Court of Appeals observed, we discussed this factor in *Fletcher*, where we explained:

Factor e requires the trial court to consider "[t]he permanence, as a family unit, of the existing or proposed custodial home or homes." In the instant case, the trial court focused on the "acceptability of the custodial home," as opposed to its permanence. It stated its findings as follows:

> "The Court is satisfied that either parent would provide permanence, as a family unit, and would offer acceptable custodial homes. It is undisputed that plaintiff as a father is accustomed to and willing to preform [sic] the day to day jobs to maintain a household. The Court feels that some weight should be assigned in favor of plaintiff because the evidence shows that defendant had been out of the home in the evening many times and thus not caring for the family while plaintiff has been present on those occasions." Because acceptability of the home is not pertinent to factor e, the panel found that it was legal error for the trial court to consider it. We agree with the Court of Appeals. The facts relied upon and expressed by the judge relate to acceptability, rather than permanence, of the custodial unit. Therefore, the trial court's error seems to go beyond mere word choice. [447 Mich. at 884-885, 526 N.W.2d 889.]

We adhere to that explanation. . . .

In this instance, we discern no significant difference between the stability of the settings proposed by the two parties. Ms. Ireland likely will continue to spend time both at the University of Michigan and at her mother's home in Mount Clemens (two settings that are now familiar to the child). It is also possible that she will change residences at the university, and that she will move again after completing her education. Such changes, normal for a young adult at this stage of life, do not disqualify Ms. Ireland for custody.

Neither are such changes to be ignored, however. While a child can benefit from reasonable mobility and a degree of parental flexibility regarding residence, the Legislature has determined that "permanence, as a family unit, of the existing or proposed custodial home or homes" is a value to be given weight in the custodial determination.

In some respects, Mr. Smith's proposed custodial home appears more stable. However, that stability may be chimerical. He will not live with his parents forever, and until the likely path of his life becomes more apparent, it is difficult to determine accurately how stable a custodial home he can offer. It would be ironic indeed if the uncertainty of Mr. Smith's plans regarding education, employment, and the early years of adulthood worked to his benefit as a court considered factor e.

In all events, however, the best interests of Maranda, not of Ms. Ireland or Mr. Smith, are central. As in every case, the circuit judge is to give careful consideration to the whole situation. When the court turns to factor e, it must weigh all the facts that bear on whether Ms. Ireland or Mr. Smith can best provide Maranda the benefits of a custodial home that is marked by permanence, as a family unit.

B

Second, we need to confirm that actual and proposed child-care arrangements—whether in the custodial home or elsewhere—are a proper consideration in a custody case. Many children spend a significant amount of time in such settings, and no reasonable person would doubt the importance of child-care decisions. While not directly within the scope of factor e, a parent's intentions in this regard are related to several of the statutory factors:

(b) The capacity and disposition of the parties involved to give the child love, affection, and guidance and to continue the education and raising of the child in his or her religion or creed, if any.

(c) The capacity and disposition of the parties involved to provide the child with food, clothing, medical care or other remedial care recognized and permitted under the laws of this state in place of medical care, and other material needs.

. . . .

(h) The home, school, and community record of the child.

Having said that child-care arrangements are a proper consideration, we then encounter the issue that brought sixty-one amici curiae to the Court of Appeals (all in support of Ms. Ireland): *How* are such arrangements to be considered? Does a parent seeking custody lose ground by proposing to place a child in a day-care center while the parent works or goes to school? Is in-home care from parents and other relatives better than day care with other children under the supervision of licensed care givers? Is day care better?

Such questions are not susceptible of a broad answer. Certainly, placement of a child in a good day-care setting can have many benefits and is in no sense a sign of parental neglect. Both single and married parents have many obligations, and day care generally is an entirely appropriate manner of balancing those obligations.

At the same time, it requires no stretch of imagination to produce hypothetical situations in which a parent's unwise choices in this regard would reflect poorly on the parent's judgment. More fundamentally, every child, every adult, and every custody case is unique. There can be no broad rules that dictate a preference for one manner of child care over another. The circuit court must look at each situation and determine what is in the best interests of the child. . . .

IV

With the clarifications and modifications noted in this opinion, we affirm the judgment of the Court of Appeals, remanding this case to the circuit court for further proceedings.

NOTES AND QUESTIONS

(1) The issue in the principal case is not uncommon. It usually arises between the working mother or student mother and a father who lives with his new wife or his parents. The father's argument is usually that the loving care of his family or of his new wife is better than the impersonal day care offered by the mother. This argument may be unfair to working mothers and it may be clearly untrue. Grandparents may or may not be good caretakers; they may be too old to do the job properly. Stepparents often have a rocky relationship with children. Day care may have its own positive benefits; children become socialized by playing and learning with other children. The court in the principal case takes a case by case approach. Placing children in day care is not a per se factor nor does it give rise to a presumption. What do you think of the case by case approach? Should it be considered at all?

(2) In a fascinating article, D. Kelly Weisberg, *Professional Women and the Professionalization of Motherhood: Marcia Clark's Double Bind*, 6 Hastings Women's L.J. 295 (1995),

Professor Kelly Weisberg has traced this problem as it relates to the public drama involving Marcia Clark, the prosecutor in the O.J. Simpson case. In the course of this long and arduous trial, Ms. Clark's husband sought to change custody because of her work schedule:

> In the background of the O.J. Simpson trial lurks a mini-drama. This drama will have long-lasting consequences but not for O.J. Simpson. Rather, it will affect the lives of two small boys who are the focus of a custody dispute involving Simpson's chief prosecutor Marcia Clark. Marcia Clark is one of a number of professional women who are victims of a "double bind"; their successful careers become a weapon used against them by their ex-husbands in custody disputes. . . . [*Id.* at 296]
>
> . . . .
>
> The issue of Marcia Clark's child care resurfaced at the end of February. When Judge Lance Ito attempted to schedule a late Friday session, the prosecutor requested that the session be canceled because of her problem arranging child care. The following Monday, she was forced to defend herself against charges by defense attorney Johnny L. Cochran, Jr., that she had used the issue of child care as a ruse in order to delay the testimony of Simpson's alibi witness Rosa Lopez. Clark countered that she was "offended as a woman, as a single parent, as a prosecutor and as an officer of the court."
>
> That same day, Gordon Clark filed a petition seeking temporary primary custody. He alleged that his ex-wife's work schedule was harming the children. He claimed that, at most, she saw the children an hour a day during the week. "[She] is never home and never has any time to spend with them," he asserted. "I have personal knowledge that on most nights she does not arrive home until 10 p.m. and even when she is home, she is working," he also claimed. He continued, "[w]hile I commend [Marcia Clark's] brilliance, her legal ability and her tremendous competence as an attorney, I do not want our children to continue to suffer because she is never home, and never has any time to spend with them."
>
> In contrast, he said "I work regular hours from 8 to 6," and claimed to arrive home by 6:15 almost every night. He argued that "[t]here's no reason why they [the children] shouldn't be with me instead of constantly being with baby-sitters." [*Id.* at 299-300]

On June 14, 1995, the Superior Court, Commissioner Keith M. Clemens, granted a request by Marcia Clark to seal the record, forbidding the attorneys to discuss the case, and serving, in effect, as a "gag order" on her custody dispute. *Id.*, at 300.

Professor Weisberg draws several important conclusions. Gender bias does exist in these cases; this bias is shown both by empirical evidence and by subjective statements of judges that they think women should be home with children. She believes this bias can be remedied by consciousness-raising about the gender bias and by the use of non-litigation means such as mediation to resolve these disputes. Parent availability as a factor should be used with caution; it is not a matter of totalling up the hours. Courts should be watchful of parents using parent availability as a leverage to gain joint custody for the purpose of lowering support obligations. Finally there is a strong need for workplace day care accommodations. *See Fitzsimmons v. Fitzsimmons*, 722 P.2d 671, 675 (N.M. Ct. App. 1986) (holding that "[a] mother's employment should not be accorded a different or negative effect when compared with a father's employment"); *Landsberger v. Landsberger*, 364 N.W.2d 918,

919 (N.D. 1985) (stating that a "career mother" should not be disqualified for custody of her children any more than a working father); *Tasker v. Tasker*, 395 N.W.2d 100, 103 (Minn. Ct. App. 1986) (court may not consider a stable job as indicative of emotional stability in the context of a child custody relationship); *Maloblocki v. Maloblocki*, 646 N.E.2d 358, 362 (Ind. Ct. App. 1995) (holding that father should receive custody where mother did not have an adequate plan for child care during her erratic work schedule).

(3) Other law review articles on this subject include: Carpenter, Comment, *Why Are Mothers Still Losing: an Analysis of Gender Bias in Child Custody Determinations*, 1996 Det. C.L. Mich. St. U. L. Rev. 33 (1996); Field, *Damned for Using Daycare: Appellate Brief of Jennifer Ireland in Ireland v. Smith*, 3 Mich. J. Gender & L. 569 (1996); Genasci, *Increasingly Working Mothers Lose in Custody Fights*, L.A. Times, Jan. 20, 1995, at D8; Jacobs, Note & Comment, *The Hidden Gender Bias Behind "The Best Interest of the Child" Standard in Custody Decisions*, 13 Ga. St. U. L. Rev. 845 (1997); Raymond, Annotation, *Mother's Status as "Working Mother" as Factor in Awarding Child Custody*, 62 A.L.R.4th 259 (1988); Swank, Comment, *Day Care and Parental Employment: What Weight Should They be Given in Child Custody Disputes?*, 41 Vill. L. Rev. 909 (1996); Wood, Note, *Childless Mothers?—The New Catch-22: You Can't Have Your Kids and Work for Them Too*, 29 Loy. L.A. L. Rev. 383 (1995).

One author commented:

> Mothers may be penalized for not staying at home, while fathers, who may participate more than in the past, may be looked on more favorably even if they are not the primary caretaker. Perhaps, "working mother" has replaced "moral unfitness" as a criteria for granting custody to fathers.

Mason & Quirk, *Are Mothers Losing Custody? Read my Lips: Trends in Judicial Decision-Making in Custody Disputes—1920, 1960, 1990, and 1995*, 31 Fam. L.Q. 215, 235 (1997).

(4) **Relative Economic Position of the Parties.** The California Supreme Court has succinctly stated the approach to using disparate wealth and income as a factor in custody disputes:

> The trial court's decision referred to William's better economic position, and to matters such as home ownership and ability to provide a more "wholesome environment" which reflect economic advantage. But comparative income or economic advantage is not a permissible basis for a custody award. "[T]here is no basis for assuming a correlation between wealth and good parenting or wealth and happiness." Klaff, *The Tender Years Doctrine: A Defense*, 70 Cal. L. Rev. 335, 350 (1982); *see* Mnookin, *Child Custody Adjudication: Judicial Function in the Face of Indeterminacy*, 39 Law. & Contemp. Probs. 226, 284 (1975). If in fact the custodial parent's income is insufficient to provide a proper care for the child, the remedy is to award child support, not to take away custody. *See Burchard v. Garay*, 724 P.2d 486, 491 (Cal. 1986).

Other cases have supported this view. *See Boyd v. Boyd*, 647 So. 2d 414 (La. Ct. App. 1994).

[J] Child Abuse and Domestic Violence

ALLEN v. FARROW
New York Supreme Court, Appellate Division
197 A.D.2d 327 (1994)

Ross, Justice.

In this special proceeding commenced by petitioner to obtain custody of, or increased visitation with, the infant children Moses Amadeus Farrow, Dylan O'Sullivan Farrow and Satchel Farrow, we are called upon to review the IAS Court's decision which, *inter alia*, awarded custody of the three children to the respondent, denied the petitioner's requests regarding visitation and awarded counsel fees to the respondent. Upon such review we conclude, for the reasons set forth below, that the determination of the IAS Court was in accordance with the best interests of these children, and accordingly, we affirm.

The petitioner and the respondent have brought themselves to this unhappy juncture primarily as a result of two recent events. These are, Mr. Allen's affair with Soon-Yi Previn and the alleged sexual abuse of Dylan O'Sullivan Farrow by Mr. Allen. While the parties had difficulties which grew during Ms. Farrow's pregnancy with Satchel, it was the discovery of the relationship between Mr. Allen and Ms. Previn that intensified Ms. Farrow's concerns about Mr. Allen's behavior toward Dylan, and resulted in the retention of counsel by both parties. While various aspects of this matter remain unclear, it is evident that each party assigns the blame for the current state of affairs to the other.

The parties' respective arguments are very clear. The petitioner maintains that he was forced to commence this proceeding in order to preserve his parental rights to the three infant children, because the respondent commenced and continues to engage in a campaign to alienate him from his children and to ultimately defeat his legal rights to them. The petitioner contends, *inter alia*, that the respondent seeks to accomplish her goals primarily through manipulation of the children's perceptions of him. He wishes to obtain custody, ostensibly to counteract the detrimental psychological effects the respondent's actions have had on his children, and to provide them with a more stable atmosphere in which to develop. Mr. Allen specifically denies the allegations that he sexually abused Dylan and characterizes them as part of Ms. Farrow's extreme overreaction to his admitted relationship with Ms. Previn.

The respondent maintains that the petitioner has shown no genuine parental interest in, nor any regard for, the children's welfare and that any interest he has shown has been inappropriate and even harmful. Respondent cites the fact that the petitioner has commenced and maintained an intimate sexual relationship with her daughter Soon-Yi Previn, which he has refused to curtail, despite the obvious ill effects it has had on all of the children and the especially profound effect it has had on Moses. It is also contended that petitioner has at best, an inappropriately intense interest in, and at worst, an abusive relationship with, the parties' daughter Dylan. Further, the respondent maintains that petitioner's contact with the parties' biological son, Satchel, is harmful to the child in that petitioner represents an emotional threat and has on at least one occasion threatened physical harm. Respondent contends that the petitioner's only motive in commencing this proceeding was to retaliate against the allegations of child sexual abuse made against him by Ms. Farrow.

Certain salient facts concerning both Mr. Allen's and Ms. Farrow's relationships to their children and to each other are not disputed. Review of these facts in an objective manner and the conclusions that flow from them, demonstrate that the determination of the IAS court as to both custody and visitation is amply supported by the record before this Court.

From the inception of Mr. Allen's relationship with Ms. Farrow in 1980, until a few months after the adoption of Dylan O'Sullivan Farrow on June 11, 1985, Mr. Allen wanted nothing to do with Ms. Farrow's children. Although Mr. Allen and Ms. Farrow attempted for approximately six months to have a child of their own, Mr. Allen did so apparently only after Ms. Farrow promised to assume full responsibility for the child. Following the adoption however, Mr. Allen became interested in developing a relationship with the newly adopted Dylan. While previously he rarely spent time in the respondent's apartment, after the adoption of Dylan he went to the respondent's Manhattan apartment more often, visited Ms. Farrow's Connecticut home and even accompanied the Farrow family on vacations to Europe. Allen also developed a relationship with Moses Farrow, who had been adopted by the respondent in 1980 and was seven years old at the time of Dylan's adoption. However, Allen remained distant from Farrow's other six children.

In 1986 Ms. Farrow expressed a desire to adopt another child. Mr. Allen, while not enthusiastic at the prospect of the adoption of Dylan in 1985, was much more amenable to the idea in 1986. Before the adoption could be completed Ms. Farrow became pregnant with the parties' son Satchel. While the petitioner testified that he was happy at the idea of becoming a father, the record supports the finding that Mr. Allen showed little or no interest in the pregnancy. It is not disputed that Ms. Farrow began to withdraw from Mr. Allen during the pregnancy and that afterwards she did not wish Satchel to become attached to Mr. Allen.

According to Mr. Allen, Ms. Farrow became inordinately attached to the newborn Satchel to the exclusion of the other children. He viewed this as especially harmful to Dylan and began spending more time with her, ostensibly to make up for the lack of attention shown her by Ms. Farrow after the birth of Satchel. Mr. Allen maintains that his interest in and affection for Dylan always has been paternal in nature and never sexual. The various psychiatric experts who testified or otherwise provided reports did not conclude that Allen's behavior toward Dylan prior to August of 1992 was explicitly sexual in nature. However, the clear consensus was that his interest in Dylan was abnormally intense in that he made inordinate demands on her time and focused on her to the exclusion of Satchel and Moses even when they were present.

The record demonstrates that Ms. Farrow expressed concern to Allen about his relationship with Dylan, and that Allen expressed his concern to Ms. Farrow about her relationship with Satchel. In 1990 both Dylan and Satchel were evaluated by clinical psychologists. Dr. Coates began treatment of Satchel in 1990. In April of 1991 Dylan was referred to Dr. Schultz, a clinical psychologist specializing in the treatment of young children with serious emotional problems.

In 1990 at about the same time that the parties were growing distant from each other and expressing their concerns about the other's relationship with their youngest children, Mr. Allen began acknowledging Farrow's daughter Soon-Yi Previn. Previously he treated Ms. Previn in the same way he treated Ms. Farrow's other children from her prior marriage, rarely even speaking to them. In September of 1991 Ms. Previn began to attend Drew

College in New Jersey. In December 1991 two events coincided. Mr. Allen's adoptions of Dylan and Moses were finalized and Mr. Allen began his sexual relationship with their sister Soon-Yi Previn.

In January of 1992, Mr. Allen took the photographs of Ms. Previn, which were discovered on the mantelpiece in his apartment by Ms. Farrow and were introduced into evidence at the IAS proceeding. Mr. Allen in his trial testimony stated that he took the photos at Ms. Previn's suggestion and that he considered them erotic and not pornographic. We have viewed the photographs and do not share Mr. Allen's characterization of them. We find the fact that Mr. Allen took them at a time when he was formally assuming a legal responsibility for two of Ms. Previn's siblings to be totally unacceptable. The distinction Mr. Allen makes between Ms. Farrow's other children and Dylan, Satchel and Moses is lost on this Court. The children themselves do not draw the same distinction that Mr. Allen does. This is sadly demonstrated by the profound effect his relationship with Ms. Previn has had on the entire family. Allen's testimony that the photographs of Ms. Previn ". . . were taken, as I said before, between two consenting adults wanting to do this . . ." demonstrates a chosen ignorance of his and Ms. Previn's relationships to Ms. Farrow, his three children and Ms. Previn's other siblings. His continuation of the relationship, viewed in the best possible light, shows a distinct absence of judgment. It demonstrates to this Court Mr. Allen's tendency to place inappropriate emphasis on his own wants and needs and to minimize and even ignore those of his children. At the very minimum, it demonstrates an absence of any parenting skills.

We recognize Mr. Allen's acknowledgment of the pain his relationship with Ms. Previn has caused the family. We also note his testimony that he tried to insulate the rest of the family from the "dispute" that resulted, and tried to "deescalate the situation" by attempting to "placate" Ms. Farrow. It is true that Ms. Farrow's failure to conceal her feelings from the rest of the family and the acting out of her feelings of betrayal and anger toward Mr. Allen enhanced the effect of the situation on the rest of her family. We note though that the reasons for her behavior, however prolonged and extreme, are clearly visible in the record. On the other hand the record contains no acceptable explanation for Allen's commencement of the sexual relationship with Ms. Previn at the time he was adopting Moses and Satchel, or for the continuation of that relationship at the time he was supposedly experiencing the joys of fatherhood. . . .

As we noted above, Mr. Allen maintains that Ms. Farrow's allegations concerning the sexual abuse of Dylan were fabricated by Ms. Farrow both as a result of her rage over his relationship with Ms. Previn and as part of her continued plan to alienate him from his children. However, our review of the record militates against a finding that Ms. Farrow fabricated the allegations without any basis. Unlike the court at IAS, we do not consider the conclusions reached by Doctors Coates and Schultz and by the Yale-New Haven team, to be totally unpersuasive. While the tendency of Dylan to withdraw into a fantasy and the inconsistencies in her account of the events of August 4, 1992, noted particularly by the Yale-New Haven team, must be taken into account in the evaluation of these serious allegations, the testimony given at trial by the individuals caring for the children that day, the videotape of Dylan made by Ms. Farrow the following day and the accounts of Dylan's behavior toward Mr. Allen both before and after the alleged instance of abuse, suggest that the abuse did occur. While the evidence in support of the allegations remains inconclusive, it is clear that the investigation of the charges in and of itself could not have left Dylan unaffected.

Any determination of issues of child custody or visitation must serve the best interests of the child and that which will best promote the child's welfare. The existence of a prior arrangement of custody agreed upon by the parties, should be given weighty but not absolute priority in the absence of extraordinary circumstances. Such priority is afforded in the belief that stability in a child's life is in the child's best interests. The court, however is not bound by the existence of a prior agreement and has the discretion to order changes in custody as well as other modifications when the totality of circumstances warrants its doing so in the best interests of the child. Primary among those circumstances is the quality of the home environment and the parental guidance the custodial parent provides for the child. It has long been recognized that it is often in the child's best interests to continue to live with his or her siblings. "While this, too, is not an absolute, the stability and companionship to be gained from keeping the children together is an important factor for the court to consider." . . .

It was noted by the IAS court that the psychiatric experts agreed that Mr. Allen may be able to fulfill a positive role in Dylan's therapy. We note specifically the opinion of Dr. Brodzinsky, the impartial expert called by both parties, who concluded that contact with Mr. Allen is necessary to Dylan's future development, but that initially any such visitation should be conducted in a therapeutic context. The IAS court structured that visitation accordingly and provided that a further review of Allen's visitation with Dylan would be considered after an evaluation of Dylan's progress.

Although the investigation of the abuse allegations have not resulted in a conclusive finding, all of the evidence received at trial supports the determination as to custody and visitation with respect to this child. There would be no beneficial purpose served in disturbing the custody arrangement. Moreover, even if the abuse did not occur, it is evident that there are issues concerning Mr. Allen's inappropriately intense relationship with this child that can be resolved only in a therapeutic setting. At the very least, the process of investigation itself has left the relationship between Mr. Allen and Dylan severely damaged. The consensus is that both Mr. Allen and Ms. Farrow need to be involved in the recovery process. The provision for further review of the visitation arrangement embodied in the trial court's decision adequately protects the petitioner's rights and interests at this time.

With respect to Satchel, the IAS court denied the petitioner's request for unsupervised visitation. While the court stated that it was not concerned for Satchel's physical safety, it was concerned by Mr. Allen's "demonstrated inability to understand the impact that his words and deeds have upon the emotional well being of the children." We agree. The record supports the conclusion that Mr. Allen may, if unsupervised, influence Satchel inappropriately, and disregard the impact exposure to Mr. Allen's relationship with Satchel's sister, Ms. Previn, would have on the child. . . .

The record indicates that Ms. Previn when not at college spends most of her time with Mr. Allen. Contact between Ms. Previn and her siblings in the context of the relationship with Mr. Allen would be virtually unavoidable even if Mr. Allen chose to insulate his children from the relationship. Expert medical testimony indicated that it would be harmful for Ms. Previn not to be reintegrated into the family. However, the inquiry here concerns the bests interests of Dylan, Moses and Satchel. Their best interests would clearly be served by contact with their sister Soon-Yi, personally and not in Mr. Allen's presence. Seeing both Ms. Previn and Mr. Allen together in the unsupervised context envisioned by Mr. Allen would, at this early stage, certainly be detrimental to the best interests of the children.

It has been held that the desires of the child are to be considered, but that it must be kept in mind that those desires can be manipulated. In considering the custody and visitation decision concerning Moses, who is now a teenager, we cannot ignore his expressed desires. The record shows that he had a beneficial relationship with the petitioner prior to the events of December 1991. However, that relationship has been gravely damaged. While Moses' feelings were certainly affected by his mother's obvious pain and anger, we concluded that it would not be in Moses' best interests to be compelled to see Mr. Allen, if he does not wish to.

Therefore, we hold that in view of the totality of the circumstances, the best interests of these children would be served by remaining together in the custody of Ms. Farrow, with the parties abiding by the visitation schedule established by the trial court. . . .

Accordingly, the judgment of Supreme Court, New York County (Elliot Wilk, J.), entered July 13, 1993, which, *inter alia*, denied the petitioner Woody Allen's request for custody of Moses Amadeus Farrow, Dylan O'Sullivan Farrow, and Satchel Farrow, set forth the terms of visitation between the petitioner and his children and awarded Ms. Farrow counsel fees, is affirmed in all respects, without costs.

NOTES AND QUESTIONS

(1) **Generally.** Domestic violence is the subject of extensive discussion in Chapter 6. The use of abuse as a factor in child custody cases assumes a variety of forms. First, there is the physical or sexual abuse of the child which is the subject of the custody dispute. This form of abuse is of course a basis for determining child custody; it can even be a per se factor. There is also the abuse of a sibling and the abuse of a spouse. Not all states have recognized abuse of a sibling or abuse of a spouse as a factor in child custody; however, the trend is clearly in that direction, and it is gathering strength since the O.J. Simpson trial. *See Bruner v. Hager*, 534 N.W.2d 825, 826 (N.D. 1995); *Krank v. Krank*, 541 N.W.2d 714, 716 (N.D. 1996) (holding that where both parents have committed violence there is a presumption against parent who has committed the greatest violence); *In re T.M.B.*, 491 N.W.2d 58, 61 (Neb. 1992); *Knock v. Knock*, 621 A.2d 267, 273 (Conn. 1993); *Bunch v. Bunch*, 469 So. 2d 1191, 1198 (La. Ct. App. 1985) (finding that allegations by father that mother had murdered previous child and court's own conclusion that mother had been at least remiss in not caring for the child who had died did not justify removal of the child from physical custody of mother); *see also Uhl v. Uhl*, 395 N.W.2d 106, 110 (Minn. Ct. App. 1986) (holding that the trial court erred in awarding custody to the mother based on a custody evaluation which did not encompass careful examination of allegations of physical abuse by the mother). *But cf. Hack v. Hack*, 695 S.W.2d 498, 500 (Mo. Ct. App. 1985) (stating that the mother's use of physical force against her minor son was minimal and within a mother's common law right to discipline a child).

(2) Many states are making all forms of domestic violence and abuse factors in child custody disputes. *See, e.g.,* Nev. Rev. Stat. § 125.480 (1995); Mont. Code Ann. §§ 40-4-212,

217 and 219 and also § 45-5-304 (1995) (stating that there is a rebuttable presumption against custody where there has been abuse); Fla. Stat. Ann § 61.13(b) (1994); La. Rev. Stat. Ann § 9:364 (Supp. 1994); N.D. Cent. Code § 14-09-06.2 (1993); Va. Code Ann. § 20-124.3 (Supp. 1994). *See also* Keenan, Note, *Domestic Violence and Custody Litigation: The Need for Statutory Reform*, 13 Hofstra L. Rev. 407 (1985); Michaels & Walton, *Child-Abuse Allegations: How to Search for the Truth*, 10 Fam. Advoc., Fall 1987, at 35.

(3) ***Allen v. Farrow***. The notorious principal case involving Mia Farrow and Woody Allen has a tabloid quality to it. There are allegations both of child abuse and something which is akin to sibling abuse, although the sibling in this case in no longer a minor and the term abuse my not be technically appropriate. It is interesting that although the court did not conclude that there had been direct sexual abuse of the children involved, the visitation allowed Allen was supervised.

(4) **False Allegations of Abuse.** A parent who has made a false allegation of child abuse may be disfavored in a custody dispute. It is often difficult to tell if the parent is being punished or if the false allegation is a sign of instability or lack of cooperation on the part of that parent. *See In re Marriage of Liebich*, 547 N.W.2d 844, 848 (Iowa Ct. App. 1996). "A wave of false allegations, filed by persons in the midst of custody and visitation disputes, is flooding the police and the courts." Thomas D. Lyon, *False Allegations and False Denials in Child Sexual Abuse*, 1 Psychol. Pub. Pol'y & L. 429 (1995); Roopenian, *Family; False Allegations of Child Abuse*, 27 Pac. L.J. 794 (1996); *The Sexual Abuse Allegations Project, Final Report* (Nancy Thoennes, ed. 1988); *see also* Thoenne & Tjaden, *The Extent, Nature, and Validity of Sexual Abuse Allegations in Child Custody/Visitation Disputes*, 14 Child Abuse & Neglect 151–63 (1990).

For a case discussing false allegations of abuse, see, e.g., *Young v. Young*, 628 N.Y.S.2d 957, 966 (N.Y. App. Div. 1995) (granting custody to the father because the mother made false allegations of child abuse).

(5) **Miscellaneous Factors.**

(a) *Cooperative Parent*. Courts have tended to favor custody with parent who is most open to visitation or at least would not block visitation by the other parent. *See In re Marriage of Hart*, 547 N.W.2d 612, 614 (Iowa Ct. App. 1996); *Hakas v. Bergenthal*, 843 P.2d 642, 644 (Alaska 1992); *Campbell v. Campbell*, 604 A.2d 33, 34 (Me. 1992).

(b) *Parental Alienation Syndrome*. A popular theory developed in the early nineties that many allegations of abuse were due to concerted efforts by one parent (usually the mother) to brainwash the child against the other (usually the father). A book was published based upon the work of a psychiatrist. *See* Gardner, *The Parental Alienation Syndrome* (1992); *see also Karen B. v. Clyde M.*, 574 N.Y.S.2d 267, 270 (N.Y. Fam. Ct. 1991); Wood, Comment, *The Parental Alienation Syndrome: A Dangerous Aura of Reliability*, 27 Loy. L.A. L. Rev. 1367 (1994) (arguing that evidence of Parental Alienation Syndrome should not be admitted as being scientifically unreliable); *In re Marriage of Rosenfeld*, 524 N.W.2d 212, 215 (Iowa Ct. App. 1994).

(c) *Family Unity*. Often the desire to keep siblings together becomes a factor. *See Wiskoski v. Wiskoski*, 629 A.2d 996, 998 (Pa. Super. Ct. 1993); *Dowdy v. Dowdy*, 864 P.2d 439, 440 (Wyo. 1993).

(d) *Continuity of Care.* Goldstein, Freud, and Solnit in Beyond the Best Interests of the Child; argue that continuity of care is essential in custody proceedings. This means that the present care-taker should be favored, that the decision should be made swiftly, and once it is made it should not be changed. *See* Goldstein, Freud, and Solnit, Beyond the Best Interests of the Child 37 (Macmillan Publishing Co. 1973).This book has been criticized as being based upon an outmoded psychoanalytical paradigm. *See* Batt, *Child Custody Disputes and the Beyond the Best Interests Paradigm: A Contemporary Assessment of the Goldstein/Freud/Solnit Positions and the Groups Painter v. Bannister Jurisprudence*, 16 Nova L. Rev. 621 (1992).

(e) *Criminal Record. See In re Ditter*, 322 N.W.2d 642, 645 (Neb. 1982) (holding that "A parent's inability to perform his parental obligations because of imprisonment, the nature of the crime committed, as well as the person [natural mother] against whom the criminal act was perpetrated are all relevant to the issue of parental fitness and child welfare, as are the parent's conduct prior to imprisonment and during the period of incarceration"); *In re Marriage of Cole*, 729 P.2d 1276, 1281 (Mont. 1986) (finding that the trial court's exclusion of evidence concerning accusation by mother's employer that she had committed theft and mother's inability to balance checkbook as irrelevant to custody determination was not abuse of discretion because evidence did not affect relationship of wife with children); *In re Abdullah*, 423 N.E.2d 915, 918 (Ill. 1981) (holding that in proceeding to terminate parental rights, fact that natural father murdered the mother justified termination and adoption of minor child by third party without father's consent even though an appeal was pending on father's conviction); *see also Rector v. Rector*, 947 S.W.2d 389, 394 (Ark. Ct. App. 1997) (stating that criminal record and alcohol abuse is relevant to custody determination); *Dordell v. Dordell*, 651 N.Y.S.2d 258, 260 (N.Y. App. Div. 1996) (taking mother's criminal record into account in denying her request for change of custody); *Wilcox-Elliott v. Wilcox*, 924 P.2d 419, 421 (Wyo. 1996) (granting modification in favor of father in light of mother's criminal record); Ackerman & Ackerman, *Child Custody Evaluation Practices: A 1996 Survey of Psychologists*, 30 Fam. L.Q. 565, 576 (1996) (rating sole/single parent custody decision-making where a parent has a criminal record).

(f) *Alcohol and Drug Abuse. See Rector v. Rector*, 947 S.W.2d 389, 394 (Ark. Ct. App. 1997) (stating that criminal record and alcohol abuse is relevant to custody determination); *Becton v. Sanders*, 474 N.E.2d 1318, 1325 (Ill. App. Ct. 1985) (stating that the extent of a parent's use of marijuana is relevant to the issue of custody, but only if parent's use of substance can be shown to affect that parent's mental or physical health or relationship with child); *Storlien v. Storlien*, 386 N.W.2d 812, 814 (Minn. Ct. App. 1986) (finding that the award of custody to mother was not an abuse of discretion where mother provided for children's discipline, health, education and religious training and the father had an alcohol dependency problem).

(g) *Educational Needs.* In *Miller v. Mangus*, 893 P.2d 823, 826 (Idaho Ct. App. 1995), a father was awarded custody where he was in the best position to meet the child's educational needs.

(9) **Problem.** Wilma and Hal had been married for nine years when Hal was diagnosed as having multiple sclerosis. At that time they had two children, Lynn aged 3 and Kelly aged 7. During the marriage, Wilma had not worked outside the home; but because of Hal's

illness the couple decided that Wilma would now return to her former job selling Main Frame Computers. Hal would stay home and take care of the children. In her new job, Wilma had to travel away from home about three or four nights a week. Hal, who is 30 years old, has a life expectancy of about 40 years. His disease is degenerative, and he has already lost some of his motor control especially his ability to walk. Over the years he will go from crutches to a wheelchair, and ultimately he will be bedridden.

Two years later, Hal brings an action for divorce and custody of the children. While the divorce action is pending, the parties separate, with the children staying with Hal.

Both parties want child custody. Wilma's job still requires her to travel, but her mother is available to take care of the children when she is not at home. Wilma makes about $70,000 per year. Hal spends most of his time with the children, who have been well taken care of, and makes about $15,000 a year as a computer programmer in the home. Hal is now on crutches and he has difficulty sleeping. He admits that he often smokes marijuana at night before going to bed. He says that it is to help sleep and release him from the pain. The children do not know about the marijuana. When asked, Kelly says that she wants to stay with her dad; Lynn only says "I want my mommy." Both parents love the children very much. The parties hotly contest the issue of child custody. What will be the result?

§ 12.03 Visitation

STERLING v. STERLING
Court of Appeals of Ohio
519 N.E.2d 673 (1987)

PER CURIAM.

This cause came on to be heard upon an appeal from the Court of Common Pleas of Clermont County.

On November 6, 1979, a decree of dissolution was filed in the Clermont County Court of Common Pleas, ending the marriage of Mark K. Sterbling and Susan K. Sterbling. A separation agreement incorporated into the decree granted, among other things, custody of the couple's only child, Christina, born April 26, 1978, to Susan. Mark was awarded reasonable visitation rights with the child. The next six years, as reflected in the transcript of docket and journal entries, were marked by a continuing animosity between the parties, at times escalated by both parties' filing motions to increase or decrease child support and to modify visitation rights.

In October 1985, Susan, who had remarried, moved from Highland Heights, Kentucky, to Centerville, Ohio. The relocation was the result of Susan's husband's receiving a new job. The move significantly increased the travel time and distance involved in transporting Christina to and from Mark's home in Cincinnati, Ohio, for visitation.

On November 6, 1985, the parties prepared and filed an agreed entry which ostensibly settled their pending differences on the issues of support and visitation. . . .

The entry further established a specific visitation schedule for Mark during weekends, holidays and summer vacations, and also provided for weekly telephone visitation with the child. The entry was signed by the trial court, the parties and their attorneys.

Within a week, Mark filed a motion which alleged that Susan had interfered with his weekend and telephone visitation rights. The motion asked that Susan be held in contempt for violating the November 6 entry and further requested that Mark be granted increased visitation with his daughter. Susan responded by filing her own motion in which she alleged that Mark had failed to pay one half of the expenses required to send Christina to a clinical psychologist for evaluation and treatment.

These motions were heard by a referee who issued a report on April 1, 1986. The referee advised against any changes in the visitation schedule but did recommend that Mark be permitted to make up missed visitations on holidays and weekends. The referee, in response to another request by Susan, refused to order Mark to submit to counseling as a prerequisite to retaining his visitation rights, but encouraged counseling to help to develop a better relationship with the child. The referee also recommended that the costs of psychological treatment for Christina were not subject to reimbursement by Mark. Finally, the referee recommended that Susan share responsibility for Christina's visitation transportation and ordered her to pick the child up at Mark's residence upon the conclusion of each visit.

Susan timely filed objections to the referee's report. The trial court reviewed a transcript of the testimony presented to the referee and heard arguments regarding Susan's objections. In a decision dated June 23, 1986, the trial court overruled all of Susan's objections except for the one pertaining to the expenses for Christina's psychological counseling. The court determined that such treatment qualified as a medical expense for which Mark should pay one half of the cost not reimbursed by insurance. A judgment entry, reflecting the court's decision, was journalized on July 23, 1986. Mark timely appealed the judgment entry and Susan then cross-appealed the same entry. . . .

The first assignment of error in Susan's cross-appeal claims that the trial court erred by not ordering Mark to undergo counseling in order to maintain his visitation rights. At the hearing before the referee, Daniels opined that both parties should undergo therapy with Christina and that a good relationship between father and daughter would only be accomplished through such therapy. Daniels further advised against an increase in visitation until Mark's relationship with his daughter improved.

We have previously held that the trial court has considerable discretion in determining the visitation rights of a parent who is deprived of the care and custody of his or her child. The court can grant and formulate such visitation rights as are in the best interests of the child. A noncustodial parent's right of visitation is a natural right and should be denied only under extraordinary circumstances, which would include, among other things, a showing that the visitation would harm the child. The burden of proof in this regard is on the party contesting the visitation privileges.

Daniels testified that he believed therapy was necessary to improve Mark's relationship with his daughter. Daniels acknowledged, however, that he had never met or interviewed Mark, but based his conclusions solely upon information he had received from Susan and the child. While therapy was recommended, Daniels did not state that all visitation should be terminated unless Mark received treatment. However, Daniels steadfastly advised against any increase in visitation unless Mark received counseling and therapy.

The court's decision in regards to visitation must be unreasonable, arbitrary or unconscionable in order to constitute an abuse of discretion. Given the facts and circumstances herein, we find no abuse of discretion by the trial court in refusing to make Mark's visitation rights contingent upon his receiving psychological counseling. Susan's first assignment of error on the cross-appeal is therefore overruled.

For her second assignment of error, Susan claims that the trial court erred in ordering her to share in the cost and responsibility of transporting Christina to and from Mark's home for visitation. Susan's argument is primarily based upon economic considerations. Because of her family's relocation to Centerville, Susan was forced to give up her part-time employment in Cincinnati and currently has no source of income. Mark, on the other hand, is gainfully employed and is capable of providing both transportation and paying the expenses necessary for visitation. In addition, Susan claims that she suffers from "night vision" and can only drive during daylight hours, making it difficult, if not impossible, to fulfill her obligation to transport Christina for visitation.

As with the previous assignment of error, we find no abuse of discretion by the trial court in ordering Susan to share the transportation expenses and responsibilities associated with visitation. Although Susan may have surrendered her employment by moving to Centerville, we find it difficult to accept her argument that she is without any source of income. The move was for economic reasons, i.e., Susan's husband's job, and it is rather incomprehensible that she does not receive some stipend from her husband if she is in fact not working. Nor is it unreasonable for her to assume some responsibility for the increased travel obligations arising from the relocation to Centerville. Having found no abuse of discretion, we accordingly overrule Susan's second assignment of error.

The assignments of error properly before this court having been ruled upon as heretofore set forth, it is the order of this court that the judgment or final order herein appealed from be, and the same hereby is, affirmed.

NOTES AND QUESTIONS

(1) **Visitation Rights of the Noncustodial Parent.** The basis for visitation is commonly expressed in terms of a right which attaches to the noncustodial parent:

> A noncustodial parent's right of visitation is a natural right and should be denied only under extraordinary circumstances, which would include, among other things, a showing that the visitation would harm the child. The burden of proof in this regard is on the party contesting the visitation privileges."

Sterbling v. Sterbling, 519 N.E.2d 673, 676 (Ohio Ct. App. 1987).

Nevertheless, this right is exercised within the limitations of the best interests standard:

> A parent posesses certain natural rights with respect to his child whose custody is given to the other parent, one of which is the right to visit the child. . . . The right of visitation is not without its limitations. The rights of any parent are always subservient to the best interest of the child.

Reed v. Hagroder, 525 So. 2d 661, 663 (La. Ct. App. 1988).

(2) **Welfare of the Child.** *Sterbling, above*, highlights a common problem regarding visitation. The child "displayed certain behavioral disorders upon returning from visits with Mark . . . [such as] excessive restlessness and anxiety, nightmares, nail biting, and marked deterioration in the child's school performance." *Sterbling*, 519 N.E.2d at 675. A custodial

parent who is acting in good faith may be genuinely concerned that the noncustodial parent is doing something to aggravate the child's trauma or that the visitation schedule exacerbates the trauma of a divorce; a custodial parent with an axe to grind may seize upon this behavior as a basis to end all visitation.

Query: Should this behavior ever be the grounds for terminating visitation, at least where the noncustodial parent has not actually engaged in misconduct?

As the psychologist in *Sterbling* mentions, this behavior is "not uncommon in the early stages of a divorce setting." And wouldn't you expect the child to feel the effect of divorce perhaps the most upon the return from vistation? After all, the child to some degree has lost the noncustodial parent, and each time the child returns from the visitation there is a chance that the child will re-experience that loss. A custodial parent who sees the child depressed or misbehaving because of the sense of loss or other psychological reactions may conclude that visitation is bad for the child. But if the child's feelings upon returning from visitation are used as grounds to end visitation, then the child runs the risk of an even greater loss, the complete end to the child's relationship with the noncustodial parent, simply because of the child's normal response to the divorce.

(3) **Visitation Schedule.** Depending on how cooperative the parents are, the visitation schedule may be stated in general terms or in very specific terms. If the parties are very cooperative, they may have an agreement which just allows for reasonable visitation. However if there is a falling out between the parents or if they cannot agree on what is reasonable, courts will order a specific visitation schedule like the following:

> The visitation schedule contained in the final decree is unworkable and must be amended. As the father has not seen the children for some time, visitation shall be structured as set out below to allow him a gradual reacquaintance with the children. [It] is thereby ordered that he shall not, at any time, allow the children to be in the company of his brother, John Fanning. The final decree is hereby amended to change visitation to be as follows:
>
> A. Beginning June 1, 1986, the defendant can visit the children the first and third Sundays of each month at the plaintiff's home from 1:00 P.M. until 5:00 P.M.
>
> B. Beginning September 7, 1986, the defendant may take the children with him for visitation on the first and third Sundays of each month from 1:00 P.M. until 6:00 P.M. and from 9:00 A.M. December 26 until 6:00 P.M. December 28.
>
> C. Beginning January 1, 1987, visitation shall be:
>
> (1) The first and third weekends of each month from 6:00 P.M. Friday until 6:00 P.M. the following Sunday.
>
> (2) Each Christmas Day from 3:00 P.M. until 3:00 P.M. on the following New Year's Day.
>
> (3) Four weeks during the summer in two week intervals selected by the defendant, but upon written notice to the plaintiff at least thirty (30) days in advance of such visitation.
>
> (4) Every other Thanksgiving Day from 10:00 A.M. until 6:00 P.M. of the same day beginning with the defendant having visitation on Thanksgiving of 1987.

5) Alternate AEA Spring Holidays when the children are not in school commencing 6:00 P.M. Friday preceeding the week of Spring Vacation through 6:00 P.M. Sunday, the day before resumption of school beginning with the defendant having visitation during Spring Holidays of 1988.

Other and different times of visitation may be exercised by agreement of the parties, without prejudice to the other periods of prescribed visitaiton.

Fanning v. Fanning, 504 So. 2d 737, 738 (Ala. Civ. App. 1987). This visitation schedule is a very common one; a variation on the old theme: every other weekend, alternating holidays, and an extended period in the summer.

If a couple determines a parenting plan through negotiations or mediation, they may have great discretion in adjusting the visitation schedule to meet the needs of all concerned. Nevertheless, courts can and sometimes will order something different once the matter comes before them. *See In re Truitt*, 863 P.2d 1287, 1289 (Or. Ct. App. 1993), and *Schwab v. Schwab*, 505 N.W.2d 752, 758 (S.D. 1993).

(4) Special Restrictions on the Noncustodial Parent. Courts do have the power to place special restrictions on the conduct of parents during times of visitation. The restrictions often occur when one parent engages in sexual conduct which the other parent does not approve of, and therefore have the effect of allowing one parent to control the behavior of the other.

In cases dealing with restrictions on visitation because of the noncustodial parent's sexual conduct or preference, the courts base their decisions on the best interest standard. In *Repetti v. Repetti*, 377 N.Y.S.2d 571, 573 (N.Y. App. Div. 1975), the court refused to condition weekend visitation with the father in the absence of another woman; and, in *Snyder v. Snyder*, 429 N.W.2d 234, 236 (Mich. Ct. App. 1988), the court refused to enjoin a father from having his children in the presence of the woman with whom he was living but to whom he was not married. Other courts have been willing to place conditions upon visitation which limit the presence of persons of the opposite sex. *See e.g., J.L.P. v. D.J.P.*, 643 S.W.2d 865, 869 (Mo. Ct. App. 1982) (denying gay father overnight visitation and right to take son to gay rights church); *DeVita v. DeVita*, 366 A.2d 1350, 1351 (N.J. Super. Ct. App. Div. 1976). *Fulwiler v. Fulwiler*, 538 P.2d 958, 960 (Or. Ct. App. 1975). The courts seem especially willing to place conditions on the rights of gay and lesbian parents. *See, e.g., S.E.G. v. R.A.G.*, 735 S.W.2d 164, 167 (Mo. 1987); *Kelly v. Kelly*, 524 A.2d 1330, 1335 (N.J. Super. Ct. Ch. Div. 1987); *In re Jane B.*, 380 N.Y.S.2d 848, 857–60 (N.Y. Sup. Ct. 1976); With cases involving gays and lesbians, the courts have the same dilemma regarding presumption versus nexus. *See North v. North*, 648 A.2d 1025, 1030 (Md. Ct. Spec. App. 1994) (refusing restrictions based upon positive HIV status of noncustodial parent unless there was actual danger to child's health) and *Hertzler v. Hertzler*, 908 P.2d 946, 951 (Wyo. 1955) (allowing restrictions based on the sexual preference of the noncustodial parent).

The issue of restrictions comes up in other areas. In *Johns v. Johns*, 918 S.W.2d 728, 730 (Ark. Ct. App. 1996), a father was ordered to take his children to church and Sunday school, and this order was held not to violate his First Amendment rights. *See In re Marriage of Rykhoek*, 525 N.W.2d 1, 4 (Iowa Ct. App. 1994) (refusing to prohibit the use of alcohol or the use of profanity unless there was a showing of actual detriment).

(5) Visitation and Support. The general rule is that the duty to pay support and the duty to allow visitation are independent of each other. The duty to support continues even when there is interference with visitation, and the custodial parent or court is not justified in cutting off visitation if the support is not forthcoming. However, there has been a willingness to change this rule in cases where there is a willful refusal to pay support or to allow visitation. In *Peterson v. Jason*, 513 So. 2d 1351, 1352 (Fla. Dist. Ct. App. 1987), the Florida District Court of Appeal dealt with an exception which would allow the court to sever visitation for the willful refusal to pay support. The court stated:

> However, there are some cases holding that, while the right to visitation does not terminate upon an excusable failure to pay support, in the face of a willful and intentional refusal to pay child support which is detrimental to the welfare of the child, the right to visitation may be terminated. *Acker v. Acker*, 365 So. 2d 180, 181 (Fla. 4th DCA 1978). Therefore, it appears that a trial court can terminate a parent's right to visitation with a minor child for nonpayment of support only when the nonpayment has been willful and intentional and detrimental to the welfare of the child so that termination would be in the child's best interest.

Peterson, 513 So. 2d at 1352. There are also cases in which courts have refused to allow a custodial parent who has hidden the child to collect arrearages. *See Szamocki v. Szamocki*, 47 Cal. App. 3d 812, 121 Cal. Rptr. 231, 235 (1975). For a general discussion of the relationship between visitation and support, and a critque of prevailing approaches, see Karen Czapanskiy, *Child Support and Visitation: Rethinking the Connections*, 20 Rutgers L.J. 619 (1989).

(6) Grandparent Visitation. The traditional view was that grandparents had no independent right to visitation; they could visit grandchildren when their children had visitation. A few courts did award visitation to grandparents at least where the parents did not object. *See Odell v. Lutz*, 177 P.2d 628 (Cal. Ct. App. 1947); Rydstrom, Annotation, *Visitation Rights of Persons Other Than Natural or Adoptive Parents*, 98 A.L.R. 325 (1968). However, loving grandparents make a strong case for their rights both in courts and in legislative lobbies. In the early 1980's, there was a trend in favor of an independent grandparent right to visitation especially where the child/parent was dead or had been denied visitation. The result was that all states passed legislation allowing courts to award visitation to grandparents. *See* H. Clark, *The Law of Domestic Relations* 536 (2d ed. 1987).

These statutes recognize that grandparents have an interest to be protected; however, the standard is still the best interest of the child. Even though this legislation seems to favor grandparent visitation, courts using the broad discretion that comes with the best interest standard have denied visitation. For example, in *Kudler v. Smith*, 643 P.2d 783 (Colo. Ct. App. 1981), *cert. denied,* 459 U.S. 337 (1982), the grandparents (Kudlers) who once had custody sought to visit the children of their daughter, who had committed suicide. The father (Mallory Smith) was remarried and living in another state. The court denied the visitation because of the tension that existed between parent and grandparents. *Id.* at 785; *see also Daughery v. Ritter*, 652 N.E.2d 502, 503 (Ind. 1995).

To a small degree the trend toward grandparent visitation may be ebbing. Professor Clark has been genuinely critical of this trend:

> In fact the movement for wider grandparent visitation is in large part based upon a desire to vindicate the claims of the grandparents rather than to benefit the children. The institution of this sort of a lawsuit alone imposes heavy financial burdens on the custodian, who in most cases will have inadequate financial resources even to meet

the daily demands for support. In addition, the lawsuit imposes serious psychological stresses on the children at a time when they are least able to sustain them. If the grandparent's claim is upheld, the custodian, who is often a hard-pressed single parent, will be subjected to deadlines and requirements which will interfere with her own relationship with the child. For all these reasons the statutes and the decisions dependent upon them are singularly ill advised. The law should return to the position taken before grandparent visitation statutes were enacted.

H. Clark, Law of Domestic Relations 542–43 (2d ed. 1987). Is professor Clark's criticism justified if the best interest standard is used to determine when grandparents have visitation rights? *See* Harpring, Comment, *Wide-Open Grandparent Visitation Statutes: Is the Door Closing?*, 62 U. Cin. L. Rev. 1659 (1994).

Some recent cases have taken a step back from grandparent visitation. In *Beagle v. Beagle*, 678 So. 2d 1271, 1276 (Fla. 1996), a statute authorizing grandparent visitation over the objection of parents in an intact family was held unconstitutional because it violated parents' right to privacy. In another case, *Brooks v. Parkerson*, 454 S.E.2d 769, 773 (Ga. 1995), *cert. denied,* 133 L. Ed. 2d 301 (1995), such a statute was not unconstitutional, but the court held that an award could not be made unless the grandparents met the burden of showing that the failure to allow visitation would be detrimental to the children. Also, how about great-grandparent visitation? One court has denied it: *David "M" v. Lisa "M"*, 615 N.Y.S.2d 783, 784 (N.Y. App. Div. 1994).

(7) **Third-Party Visitation.** Some of the statutes which authorize grandparent visitation actually give broad discretion to order visitation to anyone who meets the statutory criteria. The Connecticut statute is extremely broad; the court may award visitation to "any person, upon an application of such person." Conn. Gen. Stat. Ann. § 46-b-59 (1986). The standard is of course the best interest of the child. California is a little more explicit: "any other person having an interest in the welfare of the child." Cal. Fam. Code § 3100(a) (1998). However, the Oregon statute is a good example of the real reason these statutes have been passed; it allows the court to order visitation to a person "who has established emotional ties creating a parent-child relationship with a child." Or. Rev. Stat. Ann. § 109.119 (1991).

(8) **Step-parent Visitation.** Because of the parental preference presumption, courts almost always award custody to a biological parent over a step-parent. Once custody is awarded, they have traditionally been reluctant to award any visitation rights at all to step-parents. The statutes mentioned above and others like them have greatly helped step-parents continue their relationship with children for whom they may even have been the primary caretaker. Here are some recent cases which have favored step-parents who were the psychological parent of the child: *In re Shofner*, 905 P.2d 268, 273 (Or. Ct. App. 1995); *In re Carl S.*, 637 N.Y.S.2d 607, 609 (N.Y. Fam. Ct. 1995). One step-parent was even allowed to intervene in a custody dispute between parents; the court opened the door for her to receive custody if it was in the best interest of the child. *See In re Sorenson*, 906 P.2d 838, 841 (Or. Ct. App. 1995); *see also* Davis, *The Good Mother: A New Look at Psychological Parent Theory*, 22 N.Y.U. Rev. L. & Soc. Change 347 (1996).

(9) **Equitable Parent.** Some cases have allowed men visitation as equitable parents even though it was shown that they were not the biological parent. Usually the wife represented to the husband that the child was his, and he raised the child as his for a number of years.

See Francis v. Francis, 654 N.E.2d 4, 6 (Ind. Ct. App. 1995). *But cf. In re Marriage of Roberts*, 649 N.E.2d 1344, 1349 (Ill. App. Ct. 1995).

(10) **Gay and Lesbian Partners.** Gay and Lesbian partners often raise children together. The children may be from a former marriage of one partner, or the couple may decide to have children through the use of artificial insemination or surrogacy. In these situations there is no doubt that the non-biological parent could be the psychological parent of the child. The Supreme Court of Washington has held that courts may use their equitable powers to grant visitation to a former live-in partner of a lesbian parent if she is able to show a parent-like relationship. However, in most cases which have been decided, the courts have clearly favored the biological parent who has opposed visitation. *See, e.g., Nancy S. v. Michele G.*, 279 Cal. Rptr. 212, 217 (Cal. Ct. App. 1991); *Alison D. v. Virginia M.*, 572 N.E.2d 27, 28 (N.Y. 1991); *Music v. Rachford*, 654 So. 2d 1234 (Fla. Dist. Ct. App. 1995).

(11) **Tardiness.** Late pick-ups and deliveries for visitation are a common problem. Both custodial and noncustodial parents are culprits. It is often difficult to tell if the tardiness is deliberate. Parents claim that they are just disorganized, but they may also be acting out their dissatisfaction with the custody/visitation arrangement or some other matter. Oklahoma has established a Child Visitation Registry which requires listing of all persons who may have visitation rights and the scheduled times of pick up or delivery. The law is intended to prevent child stealing; however, part of this law is also designed to stem tardiness regarding pick up and delivery: "If a parent, or other person with custody, is habitually late to pick up or deliver the child or children, the court may, upon proper notice, consider reducing or canceling visitation temporarily or permanently." 43 Okl. St. Ann. § 424(B) (1995).

(12) **Supervised Visitation.** Even in the case of child abuse, courts may award visitation if there is proper supervision. *See Moore v. Moore*, 456 S.E.2d 742, 743 (Ga. Ct. App. 1995) (ordering supervised visitation with father after mother's allegation of child abuse was substantiated). In *Allen v. Farrow*, 611 N.Y.S.2d 859, 860 (N.Y. App. Div. 1994), reprinted above, there was an order of supervised visitation where the father was having an affair with child's sibling who was over 18.

(13) **Prison Visitation.** Visitation can also take place in prison. *See Knight v. Knight*, 680 A.2d 1035, 1038 (Me. 1996). However, most courts have been hesitant to order such visitation. The stated reason is usually that the visitation is not in the best interest of the child. *See In re Gallego*, 133 Cal. App. 3d 75, 183 Cal. Rptr. 715, 720–22 (Cal. Ct. App. 1982). Some courts even say it is presumptively not in the best interest of the child. *See In re Erica*, 640 N.E.2d 623, 624 (Ohio Comm. Pl. 1994) (disallowing prison visitation where the father murdered daughter's mother). Sometimes prison officials will block visitation for security reasons. *See Bills v. Dahm*, 32 F.3d 333, 335 (8th Cir. 1994) (holding that father did not have a right to overnight visit with infant even though state allowed mothers such visits because security concerns in men's prison were substantially greater).

(14) **Enforcement.** Enforcement of visitation rights is often a difficult thing. There are remedies available, but all seem to have their downside too. At least one recent case has held that contempt may be a remedy for a parent who has not fulfilled his obligation under a parenting plan. *See In re James*, 903 P.2d 470, 473 (Wash. Ct. App. 1995). However, if it involves jail time, it deprives the children of their custodial parent. *See Smith v. Smith*, 434 N.E.2d 749, 752 (Ohio Ct. App. 1980). Fines are also available, but often the custodial

parent has so little money that the impact is negligible; the children may be deprived of necessities. *See* Alaska Stat. § 25.20.140 (1997). Some jurisdictions implement detailed supervision. *See* Mich. Comp. Laws Ann. § 552.642 (1997). Change of custody is also a remedy where there is a deliberate attempt to prevent visitation, but this would seem to be appropriate only where custody goes to a parent who is both fit and wants to be the primary custodian. *See Egle v. Egle*, 715 F.2d 999, 1016 (5th Cir. 1983).

§ 12.04 Joint Custody and Parenting Plans

Until recently, the most common post-divorce parenting arrangement, in both contested and uncontested cases, was sole custody to one parent (usually the mother) with reasonable visitation to the other parent. Over the past two decades, this model has come under attack as unfair to the non-custodial parent and as inconsistent with a child's interest in maintaining a substantial relationship with both parents after divorce. *See Generally* Joint Custody and Shared Parenting, 2d ed. (Jay Folberg, ed. 1991). Critics of the traditional, sole custody model have proposed joint custody or shared post-divorce parenting as an alternative. Despite its growing popularity, "joint custody is not a precisely defined term and statutes and cases are often not clear as to the way in which the term is being used." Marygold S. Melli, Patricia R. Brown & Maria Cancian, *Child Custody in A Changing World: A Study fo Postdivorce Arrangements in Wisconsin* Ill. L. Rev. 773, 776 (1997).

Many courts and commentators distinguish two aspects of joint custody: legal custody and physical custody. Joint legal custody generally means that parents have shared and equal authority to make significant decisions involving a child's health, education, and welfare. Joint physical custody, by contrast, refers to a residential arrangement under which a child spends substantial periods of time living with, and being cared for by, each parent. *See* Jana Singer & Williaim B. Reynolds, *A Dissent on Joint Custody*, 47 Md. L. Rev. 497, 499 (1988). Although some joint custody arrangments involve both joint physical custody and joint legal custody, many other awards entail joint legal custody only. Indeed, several recent empirical studies suggest that joint legal custody with physical custody to the mother is now the dominant custody arrangement in several parts of the country. *See* Eleanor E. Maccoby & Robert H. Mnookin, Dividing the Child, Social and Legal Dilemmas of Custody 73-75, 106-07 (1992) (study of post-divorce parenting arrangements in California shows that while most children continue to live with their mothers, "joint legal custody" has become the norm."); Marygold S. Melli, Patricia R. Brown & Maria Cancian, *Child Custody in A Changing world: A Study of Postdivorce Arrangments in Wisconsin*, 1997 U. Ill. L. Rev. 773 (reporting that joint legal custody with mother maintaining physical custody now accounts for 81% of custody awards in Wisconsin).

Almost all jurisdictions, whether by statute or by case law, now authorize a court to award joint custody at the time of divorce. Courts and comentators disagree, however, about whether a court should award joint custody over the objection of one (or both) parents and about whether there should be a preference or presumption in favor of some form of joint custody.

SQUIRES v. SQUIRES
Supreme Court of Kentucky
854 S.W.2d 765 (1993)

LAMBERT, JUSTICE.

This Court granted discretionary review to address the proper construction and application of KRS 403.270(4).[1]

With its 1980 enactment of the foregoing statute, the General Assembly expressly declared the right of trial courts to grant joint custody to the parents of a child with the only standard being "best interest." Heretofore this court has not provided any guidance to trial courts in exercise of their broad discretion. As the appropriate use of joint custody is the subject of considerable debate and there appears to be little uniformity among the trial courts of Kentucky in its application, we took review of this case as it contains the elements of the classic dilemma.

Of the parties' four-month marital cohabitation was born a son. Upon commencement of proceedings to dissolve the marriage and the appearance of a dispute over child custody, inter alia, the case was assigned to the Domestic Relations Commissioner who heard extensive testimony and rendered proposed findings of fact and conclusions of law. The Commissioner found that both parties would be good parents who would place the interest of their child first. This, he believed, made them likely candidates for joint custody. However, he also found that the parties were not sufficiently cooperative to accommodate joint custody and recommended that it not be granted. On exceptions to the Commissioner's report, the trial court acknowledged the hostility between the parties, but concluded that this alone did not prevent an award of joint custody. The court emphasized that the parties were "good parents" and in reliance on its "policy" to grant joint custody and the statutory standard of the child's best interest, determined that the benefits of joint custody outweighed the detriments. The court also recognized the availability of subsequent custody litigation when joint custody has been granted, and the extreme difficulty of such litigation when sole custody has been granted. Upon the foregoing, judgment was entered granting the parties joint custody.

A divided panel of the Court of Appeals affirmed the trial court. The majority emphasized the positive aspects of joint custody such as shared decision-making, parental involvement in child rearing and encouragement of parental cooperation. It also noted the availability

---

[1] For convenient review, KRS 403.270 is here reproduced in its entirety.

Custody—Best interests of child shall determine—Joint custody permitted.

(1) The court shall determine custody in accordance with the best interests of the child and equal consideration shall be given to each parent. The court shall consider all relevant factors including:
   (a) The wishes of the child's parent or parents as to his custody;
   (b) The wishes of the child as to his custodian;
   (c) The interaction and interrelationship of the child with his parent or parents, his siblings, and any other person who may significantly affect the child's best interests;
   (d) The child's adjustment to his home, school, and community;
   (e) The mental and physical health of all individuals involved; and
   (f) Information, records, and evidence of domestic violence as defined in KRS 403.270.
(2) The court shall not consider conduct of a proposed custodian that does not affect his relationship to the child. If domestic violence and abuse is alleged, the court shall determine the extent to which the domestic violence and abuse has affected the child and the child's relationship to both parents.
(3) The abandonment of the family residence by a custodial party shall not be considered where said party was physically harmed or was seriously threatened with physical harm by his or her spouse, when such harm or threat of harm was causally related to the abandonment.
(4) The court may grant joint custody to the child's parents if it is in the best interest of the child.

of subsequent litigation if joint custody proved to be unworkable. The dissenting opinion expressed the view that prior to an award of joint custody, the court must be satisfied that the parties possess sufficient maturity to suppress their enmity toward one another and avoid having their personal animosity destabilize the upbringing of the child.

From the foregoing facts . . . the issue which emerges is whether parties who are found to be good parents who will endeavor to place the interest of their child uppermost should be denied joint custody due to their hostility and refusal to cooperate with one another.

At the outset, we must consult the statute. A cursory examination of KRS 403.270 manifests the overriding consideration that any custody determination be in the best interest of the child. It is equally clear that neither parent is the preferred custodian and the parents' wishes, while appropriate for consideration, are not binding on the trial court. While the focus of this case is on joint custody as authorized in section (4) of KRS 403.270, the decision to grant or deny joint custody cannot be determined without reference to the entire Act. As such, the broad array of factors contained in the Act must be considered appropriately prior to a determination of joint custody or sole custody.

We begin with the assumption that it would be in a child's best interest to be reared by two parents who are married to each other. With the occurrence of divorce, however, such a circumstance is not possible and trial courts are faced with the task of formulating a custody arrangement which will as nearly as possible replicate the ideal and minimize disruption of the life of the child. As such, and prior to any particularized assessment of the parents and child, joint custody would appear to be the best available solution. In theory, the child would continue to be reared by both parents and have the benefit of shared decision-making with respect to important matters, with neither parent being designated as the primary custodian and the other relegated to a secondary status. Clearly, it was this ideal which motivated the General Assembly to declare that trial courts may grant joint custody, but place it within the context of the entire custody statute, KRS 403.270, and limit it by the best interest test.

It is now widely recognized that in many cases, embittered former spouses are unwilling to put aside their animosity and cooperate toward their child's best interest. Often joint custody merely prolongs familial conflict and provides vindictive parties with a convenient weapon to use against one another. Of course, the same is true of a custody and visitation arrangement. As such, some contend that it is better to have a clean break between spouses and award one or the other sole custody to bring about the child's most rapid adjustment to post-divorce circumstances. While the logic of this position is not unappealing, if it were fully applied, the role of the noncustodial parent would be diminished to a point of insignificance.

Even if this Court were so inclined, it is not our prerogative to eradicate the concept of joint custody from the law of Kentucky. The General Assembly has determined that it is viable and it is our duty to apply the statutory framework in a manner which gives effect to legislative intent. From the language used, we believe the General Assembly intended to inform courts of their option to award joint custody in a proper case without mandating its use in any case. Implicit in the authorization to award joint custody is that the court do so after becoming reasonably satisfied that for the child the positive aspects outweigh those which are negative. We see no significant difference between the analysis required with respect to joint custody than the analysis required when the court grants sole custody.

In either case, the court must consider all relevant factors and formulate a result which is in the best interest of the child whose custody is at issue. Legislative authorization of joint custody merely gives the trial court another alternative if such appears to be appropriate.

The parties have debated the significance of parental agreement and willingness to cooperate at the time of the custody determination. While we have no doubt of the greater likelihood of successful joint custody when a cooperative spirit prevails, we do not regard it as a condition precedent. To so hold would permit a party who opposes joint custody to dictate the result by his or her own belligerence and would invite contemptuous conduct. Moreover, the underlying circumstance, the parties' divorce, is attended by conflict in virtually every case. To require goodwill between the parties prior to an award of joint custody would have the effect of virtually writing it out of the law.

By what standard then should a trial court determine whether joint custody should be granted? Initially, the court must consider those factors set forth in KRS 403.270(1). By application of these, the child whose custody is being litigated is individualized and his or her unique circumstances accounted for. In many cases, appropriate consideration of KRS 403.270(1) may reveal the result which would be in the child's best interest. Thereafter, we believe a trial court should look beyond the present and assess the likelihood of future cooperation between the parents. It would be shortsighted to conclude that because parties are antagonistic at the time of their divorce, such antagonism will continue indefinitely. Emotional maturity would appear to be a dependable guide in predicting future behavior. By cooperation we mean willingness to rationally participate in decisions affecting the upbringing of the child. It should not be overlooked that to achieve such cooperation, the trial court may assist the parties by means of its contempt power and its power to modify custody in the event of a bad faith refusal of cooperation. . . .

Perhaps no decision which confronts circuit courts is more difficult than a contested child custody case. In such cases, the court is called upon to decide who shall have what the parties often perceive as their most precious "possession." With the enactment of KRS 403.270(4), this burden was enhanced, but the duty of the court remains the same. Just as it is impermissible to prefer one parent over the other based on gender, it is now impermissible to prefer sole custody over joint custody. In every case the parties are entitled to an individualized determination of whether joint custody or sole custody serves the child's best interest. That the court possesses broad discretion in this regard cannot be gainsaid.

Based upon these authorities, we discover no error in the trial court's handling of the case at the exceptions phase.

We affirm. . . .

LEIBSON, JUSTICE, dissenting.

Respectfully, I dissent.

The decision in this case will profoundly affect the future of countless children. The subject is how to interpret and apply KRS 403.270(4), which states: "The court may grant joint custody to the child's parents if it is in the best interest of the child."

Under this statute, including subsection (4), the "best interest of the child" is not just another thing to be considered along with the sensibilities of the parents in awarding custody. It is not just the most important thing. It is the only thing.

The Majority Opinion states: "In such cases, the court is called upon to decide who shall have what the parties often perceive as their most precious 'possession.'"

Children are "precious" but not as their parents' "possession," and parents must not treat them as such. Social science data amassed since the advent of the joint custody experiment some 20 plus years ago studying the effects of joint custody awards demonstrates overwhelmingly that except for "those few, exceptionally mature adults who are able to set aside animosities in cooperating for the benefit of their children," joint custody is not a problem solver, but a pernicious problem causer. J. Rainer Twiford, J.D., Ph.D., Joint Custody: A Blind Leap of Faith?, Behavioral Sciences & the Law, Vol. 4, No. 2, p. 157–68 (1986). . . .

The Majority Opinion acknowledges the existence of this empirical data, and cites no data to the contrary. None is cited to us. Yet the Majority disregards its significance.

A report prepared in February 1983 by the Ad Hoc Committee on Family Dissolution of the Kentucky Psychological Association, entitled "Custody and Visitation Patterns in Children of Divorce," sums up as follows:

> It should be recognized that joint custody is not a panacea. It requires that the parents have the emotional capacity and the psychological commitment to resolve their differences and engage in communication, cooperation, and compromise. Obviously, it cannot be imposed on a fighting couple as a way of resolving their dispute. It is also not for those who have not thought through its implications. . . . It should not be used as a "cop-out" by the court to avoid the careful weighing of all of the variables determining the child's best interests . . . .

The Trial Commissioner in this case was tuned in to reality. His findings, after a lengthy, video-taped hearing were as follows: "cooperation and communication between the parties is required for an award of joint custody. . . . In this case, it is obvious to the Court [Commissioner] that the parties cannot agree or cooperate to the extent necessary to accommodate a joint custody award. "

The trial court neither heard the evidence nor reviewed the tapes, but awarded joint custody contrary to this finding, stating it was the court's "policy" to "grant joint custody of children whenever possible to do so," and that "the national trend is for joint custody." The trial court was mistaken as to "policy" and the present direction of the "national trend." Neither reason suffices to support a finding in favor of joint custody in this case.

Obviously there are cases where, based on the evidence presented (not policy or trend), joint custody is an appropriate arrangement, and the custody statute makes it available for such cases. But the decision to award it should turn on individualized fact-finding, not inappropriate policy considerations. . . . The trial court could not accept the facts found by the Commissioner as to the parents' suitability to share custody, yet disregard his decision on the ultimate fact based on policy considerations. These policy considerations are not part of the law, and disregard the empirical data undermining their cogency.

Before awarding joint custody the trial court should be required to find that these parties are presently emotionally mature adults capable of cooperating and sharing in the decision-making involved in raising this child, not that "hopefully" they will become so. The final order of the trial court in this case is to the contrary:

The Court recognizes that this has been another very bitter divorce in which the parties and their attorneys have hotly contested nearly every issue. . . . Hopefully, after this divorce is finalized, the parties, who are mature individuals and not teenagers, will cooperate with the give and take that is in the best interest of the child.

This is not good enough. Rather than finding what the record shows is in the best interest of the child, it evades the issue.

At the least, this case should be remanded to the trial court with instructions for the trial court to determine the custody issue based on a review of the evidence firsthand. . . .

. . . Without exception, the social science data amassed on this subject proves that the joint custody arrangement is a vehicle peculiarly unsuited to resolve quarreling over a child; indeed, it is counterproductive to this end. The worst interest of the child rather than the best interest of the child is served by fostering a continuing instability in the child's custodial arrangements . . ..

A recent article in the Wall Street Journal (July 15, 1991, p. 81) quoted by Judge Huddleston in his Court of Appeals Dissent in this case brings us up-to-date on the impact of joint custody. We quote, in part:

> Joint custody, once hailed as the ideal child-rearing arrangement for divorced couples, is coming under fire from psychologists, lawyers and embittered parents. . . .
>
> Robert Mnookin, Director of the Stanford Center on Conflict and Mediation, which conducted a child-custody study of 1,100 families in California, says, "Where parents are fighting and remain locked in conflict, joint physical custody can be like carrying out King Solomon's threat. A child can be torn apart psychologically."
>
> . . . [A] study of 700 divorce cases in Cambridge by the Middlesex Divorce Research Group found that couples with joint legal custody were more than twice as likely to relitigate their child-care agreements as couples with sole custody.
>
> Moreover, joint legal custody "makes no difference in terms of the amount of parents' contact with their kids, the quality of communication between parents, or the rate of compliance with child-support payments," says Stanford's Mr. Mnookin.
>
> Researchers say joint custody hasn't lived up to its promise because most parents haven't embraced the concept willingly . . .

I fear for the future. I fear for the children whom joint custody decrees will force to live in unstable relationships, subject to uncertain authority. I fear for the emotional damage to children who will be the noncombatant casualties in future courtroom battles. . . .

NOTES AND QUESTIONS

(1) **The Ongoing Debate.** The traditional form of custody was to give one parent sole custody, meaning sole legal and physical custody, and allow the other parent visitation in order to maintain the relationship between the child and the non-custodial parent. Not only did the child live with the custodial parent, but that parent also made all the important decisions regarding the child's upbringing. The rationale was that if the parents could not manage to avoid the battles between them which led to the divorce, they should not be allowed to continue to fight over the raising of their children. Therefore, the best interests

of the child required that one person alone should be in control of the child's destiny. The assumption was that people who cannot stay married cannot cooperate sufficiently to raise their children. Do you think that this assumption is true? Do you think this approach fostered a close relationship between the child and the non-custodial parent or do you think that it helped to sever what ties still existed? Do you think that the sole custody approach could have been fostered by the belief that fathers played a minor role in the day-to-day care of the child?

(2) **"Toss a coin."** Support for sole custody comes from a significant book authored by Goldstein, Freud and Solnit, arguing that continuity of care and certainty as to the identity of the psychological parent are the most important factors in resolving custody disputes. See J. Goldstein, A. Freud, and A.J. Solnit, Beyond the Best Interests of the Child 37 (1973). Their position is well summarized by the following passage by Deborah Anna Luepnitz:

> The most disparaging view of shared custody is offered by Goldstein, Freud, and Solnit in Beyond the Best Interests of the Child. The authors posit that because of the children's need for "unbroken continuity" of affectionate relationships with "an adult," courts should make custody determinations with utmost dispatch. Drawn-out custody battles wherein children's placement is indefinite for a period of time are to be avoided at all costs. They point out that the child's sense of time is different from that of adults; that is, one month to a seven-year-old can seem an eternity. The authors contend further that the psychological tie between a parent and a young child can be severed by even a brief separation. Much more controversial than the preceding statements is the authors' emphasis on establishing one and only one permanent custodian. How can the courts make fast decisions in cases where two fit parents each desire custody? Goldstein, Freud, and Solnit advise that in such cases a "drawing of lots" would be the optimal way of choosing the child's custodian. (Interestingly, they do not make a special case for the mother). Once that determination is made, moreover, it should be the custodian who decides if and when the other parent should visit the child. Weiss (1978) has pointed out that the merit of this particular proposition would be in ending the helplessness of custodial parents in dealing with vindictive noncustodial parents. Indeed, the spirit of the Goldstein, Freud, and Solnit recommendations is not controversial. It is aimed at reducing the possibility of a parental tug-of-war in which each parent claims his or her legal rights while tearing the child apart. Goldstein, Freud, and Solnit fail to demonstrate, however, that joint custody actually increases the probability of such struggles. Without citing even an illustrative case history, the authors dismiss joint custody as "an official invitation to erratic changes and discontinuity in the life of the child."

Luepnitz, Child Custody: A Study of Families After Divorce; 11–12 (1981).

(3) **Joint Custody Statutes.** There can be no doubt that there is strong statutory recognition of joint custody. In 1996, Linda Henry Elrod and Robert G. Spector, in their annual review of family law, reported that "states continue to indicate a preference for joint custody." Elrod & Spector, *A Review of the Year in Family Law: Children's Issues Take Spotlight*, 29 Fam. L.Q. 741, 755 (1996). In the following year, Ms. Elrod and Mr. Spector reported that all states have some sort of joint-custody law except for Arkansas, Delaware, Hawaii, Maine, New York, North Carolina and Washington. *See* Elrod & Spector, *A Review of the Year in Family Law: of Welfare Reform, Child Support, and Relocation*, 30 Fam.

L.Q. 765, 805 (1997). The statutes supporting joint custody can be divided into two groups: those statutes which create a presumption in favor of joint custody and those which merely authorize joint custody when it is in the best interests of the child. The latter appear to be in the majority.

(a) *Statutes Creating a Presumption or Preference in Favor of Joint Custody.* There are about fourteen states which create a presumption in favor of joint custody come in several different forms. Some statutes create a presumption directly in favor of joint custody. The following Texas statute is an example of this type, although it uses a different name:

§ 153.131. Presumption that Parent to be Appointed Managing Conservator.

(a) Unless the court finds that appointment of the parent or parents would not be in the best interest of the child because the appointment would significantly impair the child's physical health or emotional development, a parent shall be appointed sole managing conservator or both parents shall be appointed as joint managing conservators of the child.

(b) It is a rebuttable presumption that the appointment of the parents of a child as joint managing conservators is in the best interest of the child.

Tex. Fam. Code § 153.131 (1995); *see also* Fla. Stat. Ann. § 61.13.2 (West 1985 & Supp. 1993), and La. Rev. Stat. Ann. § 9:335 (West 1993) (stating a preference that custody be shared equally).

(b) *Presumption Where Both Parties Seek Joint Custody.* Other states merely create a presumption in favor of joint custody where the parties seek it, a position which at least requires a modicum agreement before child custody will be awarded. For example, here is the California version:

§ 3080. Presumption of joint custody

There is a presumption, affecting the burden of proof, that joint custody is in the best interest of a minor child . . . , where the parents have agreed to joint custody or so agree in open court at a hearing for the purpose of determining the custody of the minor child.

§ 3081. Application by parents; custody investigation

On application of either parent, joint custody may be ordered in the discretion of the court in cases other than those described in Section 3080 . . . . For the purpose of assisting the court in making a determination whether joint custody is appropriate under this section, the court may direct that an investigation be conducted . . . .

Cal. Fam. Code §§ 3080–3081 (1998).

(c) *Statutes Authorizing Joint Custody but Without Preference or Presumption.* A good example of a neutral statute is the Kentucky statute set forth in foonote one of the principal case. *See also* Ok. Stat. Ann. § 109 (1997); Va. Code Ann. § 20–124.1 (Michie Supp. 1994) (authorizing but not requiring joint custody); Utah Code Ann. § 30-3-10.3 (Supp. 1994) (requiring that parents receiving a joint custody decree must attend a special parenting course). The majority of states fall into this last catergory.

(4) **Case Law.** While statutory law either favors or is neutral about joint custody, most of the custody cases, at least on the appellate level, deny joint custody or modify joint

custody to sole custody. Of course it must be noted that most couples who choose joint custody do so without a published appellate ruling and that a successful joint-custody arrangement will probably never return to court for modification. Nevertheless the following cases are interesting.

(a) *Cases denying or modifying joint custody*: See *Wolf v. Wolf*, 666 So. 2d 17 (Ala. Civ. App. 1995); *In re Marriage of McCoy*, 650 N.E.2d 3 (Ill. App. Ct 1995); *Ulsher v. Ulsher*, 867 P.2d 819 (Alaska 1994); *In Interest of S.D.J.*, 452 S.E.2d 155 (Ga. Ct. App. 1994); *Darnall v. Darnall*, 657 So. 2d 387 (La. Ct. App. 1995); *Davis v. Kostin*, 617 N.Y.S.2d 229 (N.Y. App. Div. 1994); *Drummond v. Drummond*, 613 N.Y.S.2d 717 (N.Y. App. Div. 1994); *Cranston v. Cranston*, 879 P.2d 345 (Wyo. 1994); *In re Pfaff*, 619 N.E.2d 875 (Ill. App. Ct. 1993); *T.M.C. v. S.A.C.*, 858 P.2d 315 (Alaska 1993); *Laura A.K. v. Timony M.*, 611 N.Y.S.2d 284 (N.Y. App. Div. 1994); *Boyd v. Boyd*, 867 P.2d 492 (Okla. Ct. App. 1994); *Caraballo v. Hernandez*, 623 So. 2d 563 (Fla. Dist. Ct. App. 1993).

(b) *Cases favoring joint custody*: See *Periquet-Febres v. Febres*, 659 N.E.2d 602 (Ind. Ct. App. 1995); *In re A.R.B.*, 433 S.E.2d 411 (Ga. Ct. App. 1993); *Luther v. Vogel*, 863 S.W.2d 902 (Mo. Ct. App. 1993); *In re D.F.D.*, 862 P.2d 368 (Mont. 1993); *In re Richmond*, 855 P.2d 1132 (Or. Ct. App. 1993).

(c) *Miscellaneous*: See *Brook v. Brook*, 881 S.W.2d 297 (Tex. 1994) (awarding joint custody to mother and grandmother over objection of mother).

(5) **Effects of Joint Custody.** The research into the effects of joint custody is inconclusive. Here are some samples of research in this area over the last two decades.

(a) Deborah Anna Luepnitz, Child Custody: A Study of Families after Divorce 150–51 (1982):

> My conclusion, based on these fifty families, is that joint custody at its best is superior to single-parent custody at its best. My prediction is that more families will elect joint custody in the near future. . . . When more families begin coparenting, there will be more available examples of how it is done. Its social acceptability will probably rise accordingly.
>
> One important finding from the joint families in this study is that they had had to change their arrangements over the years to suit their changing conditions . . . .

(b) Steinman, *Joint Custody: What We Know, What We Have Yet to Learn, and the Judicial and Legislative Implications*, 16 U.C. Davis L. Rev. 739, 748 (1983):

> The evidence we currently have does not support a legal presumption in favor of joint custody, particularly where parents are in dispute. Rather, a legal presumption would be based on hope: the hope that the hostility and conflict between the disputing parents will die down, the hope that parents can be forced by a court order to cooperate in the best interest of the child, and the hope that a joint physical custody arrangement will still be beneficial to children under these circumstances.

(c) Singer & Reynolds, *A Dissent on Joint Custody*, 47 Md. L. Rev. 497, 506 (1988):

> Despite the popularity of "joint custody" as a legal concept, few empirical studies have actually examined how joint custody works in practice. The studies that do exist fail to support either court-imposed or presumptive joint custody. First, virtually

all the studies invoked by proponents of court-imposed joint custody involve voluntary joint custody arrangements, that is, joint custody arrangements initiated and agreed upon by the parties outside of court. The success of self-initiated arrangements (assuming they are successful) tells us little about the likely success or potential benefits of court-imposed joint custody. Parents who agree voluntarily, outside of court, to share custody of their children after divorce are generally highly motivated and cooperative, at least when dealing with their children. To extrapolate from the success of these voluntary arrangements to the desirability of imposing joint custody on parents who oppose it is both factually and logically flawed; it is equivalent to suggesting that the benefits associated with a healthy marriage justify court-imposed marriages regardless of "spousal" consent.

(d) Maccoby & Mnookin, Dividing the Child, Social and Legal Dilemmas of Custody 277–78 (1992):

While our study did not attempt to measure the impact of co-parenting relations on the well-being of children, the results of the follow-up study of the adolescents in our sample families, as well as the research of others, make us confident that there are important effects. Children derive real benefits—psychological, social, and economic—when divorced parents can have cooperative co-parenting relationships. With conflicted co-parental relationships, on the other hand, children are more likely to be caught in the middle, with real adverse effects on the child. Where there is spousal disengagement, the effects on children are intermediate: better than conflicted but less good than cooperative (Buchanan, Maccoby, and Dornbusch, 1991).

Contrary to what might have been expected, we found roughly equal proportions of the three types of co-parental relationships in each of the residential arrangements. In other words, the proportion of families with conflicted co-parental relations was as high with dual residence as with mother residence or father residence. We believe that conflicted co-parental relations are a function of anger arising from the spousal divorce and from the extent of legal conflict. It does not appear to be the case that parents with cooperative relationships will more frequently choose dual residence; nor is it true that once dual arrangements are adopted, conflicted parents become cooperative.

In sum, we found that former spouses obviously have a great deal of difficulty doing business together with respect to the children. Although conflict declines over time, avoidance is commonplace. Many parents would prefer not having to deal with the other, and mothers and fathers with sole residence both indicate that in some ways it is easier for them, now that they are separated, to raise the children according to their own values, with less need to consider those of the other parent.

(6) **Negotiations.** To some degree the existence of joint custody as a possible outcome strengthens the father's hand in negotiating a divorce settlement. Under a system in which sole custody tended to be awarded to the mother because of the tender-years presumption or under the primary-caretaker presumption, *see* Gregory, Swisher & Scheible, Understanding Family Law § 10.03[B] (Matthew Bender 1995), the father had little chance to gain custody absent some showing of maternal unfitness. Under joint custody the father has a real bargaining chip which could be used to get property and support concessions from the wife. *See* Scott & Derdeyn, *Rethinking Joint Custody*, 45 Ohio St. L.J. 455, 478 (1984).

(7) **Conclusion.** Perhaps a good statement to conclude this section on joint custody is the following:

> We have argued that the co-parental relationship between divorced parents is something that needs to be constructed, not something that can simply be carried over from pre-separation patterns. It takes time and effort on the part of both parents to arrange their lives in such a way that the children can spend time in both parental households. The dual-residence arrangement, although it offers parents some benefits in terms of time off from parental duties, is nevertheless particularly demanding—the need to negotiate with the other parent over schedules arises frequently, more trips must be made to take the children back and forth, and it is especially difficult to maintain the arrangement if a parent moves and the driving distance increases. We have found that parents are less likely to adopt a dual arrangement if they have more than one child, or if one of the children is very young; in addition, they are less likely to maintain such an arrangement in the face of intense hostility between the former spouses. We believe these facts imply that any factor that increases the overall time and effort involved in parenting will make it less likely that parents will take on the additional demands of a dual-residence arrangement.

Maccoby & Mnookin, Dividing the Child, Social and Legal Dilemmas of Custody 276 (1992).

(8) **Joint Custody and Domestic Violence.** A number of courts and commentators have expressed concern that joint custody awards may endanger victims of domestic violence. *See, e.g.,* In re Marriage of Hickey, 689 P.2d 1222 (Mont. 1984) (reversing joint custody decree bacuase of father's history of violent temper and threats against wife); Margaret Martin Barry, *The District of Columbia's Joint Custody Presumption: Misplaced Blame and Simplistic Solutions* 46 Cath. U. L. Rev. 767, 798-801 (1997); Joan Zorza, *"Friendly Parent" Provisions in Custody Determination*, 26 Clearinghouse Rev. 921, 924-25 (1994). These commentators argue that perpetrators of domestic violence often use access to children to continue to control or harass their victims andthat joint custody arrangements may require victims to "cooperate" with their physically abusive former spouses. Joint custody statutes in several states respond specifically to these concerns by listing domestic violence as a factor that precludes or disfavors a joint custody award. *See e.g.* Fla. Stat. Ann. § 61.13.2(b)(2) (1997) (directing court to consider domestic violence as evidence that shared parental responsibility would be detrimnetal to the child) (1997). Morevoer, at least a dozen states have reently enacted statutory presumptions against awarding either joint or sole custody to a parent who has engaged in domestic violence. *See* Lynee R. Kurtz, *Protecting New York's Children": An Argument for the Creation of Rebuttable Presumption Against Awarding A Spouse Abuser Custody of a Child,* 60 Alb. L. Rev. 1345 (1997).

(9) **Disputes Between Joint Custodians.** In a growing number of cases, courts have been asked to resolve post divorce parenting disputes between joint legal custodians who disagree about a particular decision involving their child. *See e.g., Brozozowski v. Brozozowski*, 625 A.2d 597 (N.J. Super. 1993) (court asked to resolve dispute over whether child should undergo surgery); *Lombardo v, Lombardo*, 507 N.W.2d 788 (Mich. Ct. App. 1993) (disagreement between parents with joint legal custody over whether to enroll child in educational program for gifted and talented children); *Hight v. McKinney*, 627 N.Y.S.2d 271 (N.Y.Fam. Ct. 1995) (court asked to resolve disagreement over whether 13-year old

child should attend sex education classes); *cf. Pogue v. Pogue*, 370 A.2d 539 (N.J. Super. Ct. 1977) (where no custody order had been entered, nonresidential parent requested that court enjoin child from playing on school basketball team). In some of these cases, the court has refused to resolve the underlying dispute, and has instead granted final decision-making authority over the issue to the parent with primary physical custody. In other cases, the court has resolved the dispute directly, using a best interest of the child standard. Which approach do you think is prefereable? Does the fact that divorced parents have been unable to resolve their differences without further judicial intervention indicate that their joint legal custody arrangment has become unworkable? Why or why not?

(10) **Parenting Plans.** Parenting plans are the subject of legislation in many states; indeed, it is safe to say that there is a well-established legislative movement in favor of parenting plans. A parenting plan can be described as follows:

> Simply put, a parenting plan is a detailed articulation of postdivorce parenting responsibilities. It goes far beyond the usual, basic custody order that specifies which parent will have custody and when the other parent will have access to the children. It addresses the specific functions of parenting and distributes responsibility for those functions to either one parent or the other, or both. Before we examine the concept of parenting plans in detail and how they operate, we should enumerate the assumptions behind the concept.

Tompkins, *Parenting Plans: A Concept Whose Time Has Come*, 33 Fam. & Conciliation Cts. Rev. 286 (1995). Following the lead of the state of Washington (Wash. Rev. Code Ann. § 26.09 (1997), many other states have either adopted legislation or are considering legislation requiring that a parenting plan be filed with the court in every divorce where there are children. The following jurisdictions have adopted legislation requiring parenting plans: District of Columbia, D.C. Code 1981 § 16-911 (1998); Illinois, Ill. Stat. Ann. Ch. 750 § 5/602.1 (West 1998); Kansas, Kan. Stat. § 60–1610 (1997); Montana, Mont. Stat. § 40–4 (1997); Nebraska, Neb. Rev. Stat. § 43–2912 (1997); New Mexico, N.M. Stat. § 40-4-9.1 (1997); Oregon, Or. Rev. Stat. §§ 107.101–102 (West 1997); Tennessee, Tenn. Code Ann. § 36–6–400 (1997). The following states are considering the adoption of legislation requiring parenting plans: Arizona, California, Colorado, Kentucky, Michigan, Minnesota, Missouri, New Jersey, New York, South Carolina, Pennsylvania, and Virginia.

Parenting plans are also an important tool even where there is no legislation. When parents go to a lawyer, the lawyer, in the process of helping them resolve their legal issues of custody, visitation, and support, also molds their thinking and to some extent narrows their focus to those issues. The parents may begin to think only in terms of those legal issues, and they may forget to fully consider the practical matters of their day-to-day lives with their children. They may not have considered how complicated their schedules will become; they may not have considered who will take responsibility for certain tasks, such as taking the children to the doctor or dentist. They may not have worked out how to maintain the children in sports programs. If the parents attempt to work out a detailed parenting plan, it forces them to think about the practical aspects of their children's future. While attorneys can help their client to work on the parenting plan, mediation is also especially helpful because it give the parties a greater oppportunity to speak directly with each other.

(11) **Problem.** While Henry and Wilma were married they both took a strong interest in their children. In fact you could say that the children were the center of their lives, perhaps

because their marriage had serious problems in other areas. All the important decisions regarding the children's lives were made by Wilma and Henry together. Although they would discuss important decisions regarding their children, they rarely disagreed over these decisions. Wilma was the primary caretaker of the children, but Henry, who was great at teaching the children all kinds of skills, spent many active hours with them. In every respect Henry and Wilma were good parents.

Wilma decided to get a divorce because Henry was having an affair. Henry, because he feared the loss of his children, sought reconciliation, which was rebuffed by Wilma. In fact one day Wilma tearfully told the children about Henry's adultery, to explain why their parents were splitting up. Wilma's rebuff and the fact that she told the children made Henry bitterly angry.

During the divorce the children stayed with Wilma during the week and spent the weekends not far away with Henry. Both parents advised and disciplined the children. Since the parents have similar values regarding child raising, there are not many substantive disagreements between them; however, many of the conversations between the parents end in acrimonious disputes.

A court-appointed social worker investigated the case, and seeing what good parents both Wilma and Henry are, and how much reciprocal love exists between the children and their parents, recommended joint custody with the time divided between the parents: weekdays with Wilma, weekends with Henry. Indeed, the social worker stated that except for the bitterness between the parents, they were the ideal couple for joint custody. However, Wilma and Henry refuse to agree to this; both of them want sole custody of the children with limited visitation for the other parent. If this case proceeds to a hearing and you are the judge, how would you resolve this dispute?

§ 12.05 Modification

[A] Changed Circumstances or Best Interest?

BURCHARD v. GARAY
California Supreme Court
724 P.2d 486 (1986)

BROUSSARD, JUSTICE.

This case concerns the custody of William Garay, Jr., age two and one-half at the date of trial. Ana Burchard, his mother, appeals from an order of the Superior Court awarding custody to the father, William Garay.

As a result of a brief liaison between Ana and William, Ana became pregnant. Early in her term she told William that she was pregnant with his child, but he refused to believe that he was the father. William, Jr., was born on September 18, 1979.

After the birth, Ana undertook the difficult task of caring for her child, with the help of her father and others, while working at two jobs and continuing her training to become a registered nurse. William continued to deny paternity, and did not visit the child or provide any support.

In the spring of 1980 Ana brought a paternity and support action. After court-ordered blood tests established that William was the father, he stipulated to paternity and to support in the amount of $200 a month. Judgment entered accordingly on November 24, 1980. In December of that year William visited his son for the first time. In the next month he moved in with Ana and the child in an attempt to live together as a family; the attempt failed and six weeks later he moved out.

William asked for visitation rights; Ana refused and filed a petition for exclusive custody. William responded, seeking exclusive custody himself. The parties then stipulated that pending the hearing Ana would retain custody, with William having a right to two full days of visitation each week.

At the onset of the hearing Ana requested a ruling that William must prove changed circumstances to justify a change in custody. William opposed the motion, arguing that the court need only determine which award would promote the best interests of the child. The court deferred ruling on the motion. The evidence at the hearing disclosed that William, Jr., was well adjusted, very healthy, well mannered, good natured, and that each parent could be expected to provide him with adequate care.

After hearing the evidence, the court issued a statement of decision in which it impliedly ruled that the changed-circumstance rule did not apply because "there has been no prior *de facto* nor *de jure* award of custody to either parent." Applying the "best interests" test, it awarded custody to William. Its decision appears to be based upon three considerations. The first is that William is financially better off, he has greater job stability, owns his own home, and is "better equipped economically—to give constant care to the minor child and cope with his continuing needs." The second is that William has remarried, and he "and the stepmother can provide constant care for the minor child and keep him on a regular schedule without resorting to other caretakers"; Ana, on the other hand, must rely upon babysitters and day care centers while she works and studies. Finally, the court referred to William providing the mother with visitation, an indirect reference to Ana's unwillingness to permit William visitation.

Pursuant to the court order William took custody of the child on August 15, 1982. Ana appealed from the order, and sought a writ of supersedeas. The Court of Appeal, however, denied supersedeas and subsequently affirmed the trial court's order. We granted a hearing in August 1984. Ana did not seek supersedeas, and William, Jr., remained in his father's custody pending this appeal.

We begin with a brief summary of our decision. The petition for hearing raised the question whether the changed-circumstance rule applies in a case such as this. We conclude that it cannot apply. The rule requires that one identify a prior custody decision based upon circumstances then existing which rendered that decision in the best interest of the child. The court can then inquire whether alleged new circumstances represent a significant change from preexisting circumstances, requiring a reevaluation of the child's custody. Here there is no prior determination; no preexisting circumstances to be compared to new circumstances. The trial court has no alternative but to look at all the circumstances bearing upon the best interests of the child.

But although we conclude that the trial court correctly ruled that the case was governed by the best-interest standard, we find that it erred in applying that standard. The court's reliance upon the relative economic position of the parties is impermissible; the purpose of child support awards is to ensure that the spouse otherwise best fit for custody receives adequate funds for the support of the child. Its reliance upon the asserted superiority of

William's child care arrangement suggests an insensitivity to the role of working parents. And all of the factors cited by the trial court together weigh less to our mind than a matter it did not discuss—the importance of continuity and stability in custody arrangements. We therefore reverse the order of the trial court.

Upon beginning a more detailed analysis, we first consider the function of the changed-circumstance rule in child custody proceedings. In deciding between competing parental claims to custody, the court must make an award "according to the best interests of the child" (Civ. Code, § 4600, subd. (b)). This test, established by statute, governs all custody proceedings. The changed-circumstance rule is not a different test, devised to supplant the statutory test, but an adjunct to the best-interest test. It provides, in essence, that once it has been established that a particular custodial arrangement is in the best interests of the child, the court need not reexamine that question. Instead, it should preserve the established mode of custody unless some significant change in circumstances indicates that a different arrangement would be in the child's best interest. The rule thus fosters the dual goals of judicial economy and protecting stable custody arrangements. (*In re Marriage of Carney*, (1979) 24 Cal. 3d 725, 730;; *Connolly v. Connolly*, (1963) 214 Cal. App. 2d 433, 436.)

"The change of circumstances standard is based on principles of *res judicata.*" (Sharp, *Modification of Agreement-Based Custody Decrees: Unitary or Dual Standard?*, (1982) 68 Va. L. Rev. 1263, 1264, fn. 9.) The rule established in a majority of jurisdictions, which we here endorse, applies that standard whenever custody has been established by judicial decree. A minority of states limit the standard further, applying it only when custody was determined through an adversarial hearing. No state, so far as we have ascertained, applies the changed-circumstance standard when there has been no prior judicial determination of custody.

Ana argues that the trial court erred in failing to apply the changed-circumstance rule in the present case. But on close review of her argument it becomes clear that Ana does not claim that there has been a prior custody determination, and that the court should have examined only events which occurred subsequent to that determination. Instead, she argues simply that because she has had custody for a significant period, she and William do not start on an equal basis; instead, he should have the burden of persuading the court that a change in custody is essential or expedient for the welfare of the child. We agree in substance with this argument: in view of the child's interest in stable custodial and emotional ties, custody lawfully acquired and maintained for a significant period will have the effect of compelling the noncustodial parent to assume the burden of persuading the trier of fact that a change is in the child's best interest. That effect, however, is different from the changed-circumstance rule, which not only changes the burden of persuasion but also limits the evidence cognizable by the court. . . .

In most cases, of course, the changed-circumstance rule and the best-interest test produce the same result. When custody continues over a significant period, the child's need for continuity and stability assumes an increasingly important role. That need will often dictate the conclusion that maintenance of the current arrangement would be in the best interests of that child. But there will be occasional cases where it makes a difference. Consider, for example, a case in which a couple separate, and in the emotional turmoil of the separation the less suitable spouse takes custody of the child. In a later custody proceeding, the noncustodial parent may be able to prove that the custodial parent is unable to provide proper care, but not that his or her ability to do so has deteriorated since the separation. In such a case the changed-circumstance rule might require the court to confirm a custody not in the best interest of the child. Or, to take another example, a child may be born out of wedlock to a woman who for some reason is not able to give it suitable care. The changed-circumstance rule would require the father, when he seeks custody, to prove not only that the mother is unsuitable, but that she has become more so since the baby's birth. In this example, the changed-circumstance rule again might require the court to endorse a custodial arrangement harmful to the child.

We conclude that custody in the present case should be decided on the basis of the best interests of the child without requiring William to prove in addition that changed circumstances render it essential that he receive custody. We therefore turn to examine the decision of the trial court to determine whether it abused its discretion in deciding that the best interests of the child required it to award custody to William.

The trial court's decision referred to William's better economic position, and to matters such as homeownership and ability to provide a more "wholesome environment" which reflect economic advantage. But comparative income or economic advantage is not a permissible basis for a custody award. "[T]here is no basis for assuming a correlation between wealth and good parenting or wealth and happiness." (Klaff, *The Tender Years Doctrine: A Defense* (1982), 70 Cal. L. Rev. 335, 350; *see* Mnookin, *Child Custody Adjudication: Judicial Function in the Face of Indeterminacy* (1975), 39 Law & Contemp. Probs. 226, 284.) If in fact the custodial parent's income is insufficient to provide a proper care for the child, the remedy is to award child support, not to take away custody.

The court also referred to the fact that Ana worked and had to place the child in day care, while William's new wife could care for the child in their home. But in an era when over 50 percent of mothers and almost 80 percent of divorced mothers work, the courts must not presume that a working mother is a less satisfactory parent or less fully committed to the care of her child. A custody determination must be based upon a true assessment of the emotional bonds between parent and child, upon an inquiry into "the heart of the parent-child relationship—the ethical, emotional, and intellectual guidance the parent gives to the child throughout his formative years, and often beyond." (*In re Marriage of Carney, supra*, 24 Cal. 3d 725, 739.) It must reflect also a factual determination of how best to provide continuity of attention, nurturing, and care. It cannot be based on an assumption, unsupported by scientific evidence, that a working mother cannot provide such care–an assumption particularly unfair when, as here, the mother has in fact been the primary caregiver. . . .

All of these grounds, however, are insignificant compared to the fact that Ana has been the primary caretaker for the child from birth to the date of the trial court hearing, that no serious deficiency in her care has been proven, and that William, Jr., under her care, has become a happy, healthy, well-adjusted child. We have frequently stressed, in this opinion and others, the importance of stability and continuity in the life of a child, and the harm that may result from disruption of established patterns of care and emotional bonds. The showing made in this case is, we believe, wholly insufficient to justify taking the custody of a child from the mother who has raised him from birth, successfully coping with the many difficulties encountered by single working mothers. We conclude that the trial court abused its discretion in granting custody to William, Sr., and that its order must be reversed.

We acknowledge the anomalous position of an appellate court, especially a supreme court, in child custody appeals. Over four years have passed since the trial court awarded custody to William. Our decision reversing that order returns the case to the trial court which, in deciding the child's future custody, must hold a new hearing and determine what arrangement is in the best interests of the child as of the date of that hearing. Thus, the effect of our decision is not to determine finally the custody of William, Jr., but is to relieve Ana of the adverse findings of the trial court and of the burden of proving changed circumstances since the trial court order, and to make clear that in deciding the issue of custody the court cannot base its decision upon the relative economic position of the parties or upon any assumption that the care afforded a child by single, working parents is inferior.

The order is reversed. . . .

Mosk, J., concurring.

I concur in the reversal of the trial court order, but strongly disagree with the manner in which the majority reach that result, especially their tacit and far from candid overruling of *In re Marriage of Carney*, (1979) 24 Cal.3d 725, and their denial of needed protection to an entire class of children solely because custody was not originally established by judicial decree.

In *Carney* a unanimous court held that regardless of how custody was originally established, a child will not be removed from the custody of one parent and given to the other unless the noncustodial parent shows that material facts and circumstances occurring subsequently are of a kind to render a change essential or at least expedient for the welfare of the child. (*Id.*, at pp. 730–731.) Put simply, the rule requires the proof of two ultimate facts: (1) a change in circumstances and (2) the present necessity for a change in custody.

In its two requirements the changed-circumstances rule serves two distinct objectives: the finality of judgments and the best interests of the child in particular, his well recognized right to stability and continuity. . . .

The majority's reading of *Carney* as not extending the protection of the changed-circumstances rule to so-called "de facto" as well as "de jure" custody is sheer sophistry. In *Carney* we expressly held that the rule applied "regardless of how custody was originally decided upon . . . ." (24 Cal. 3d at p. 731, fn. 4.) We imposed on the noncustodial mother the burden of proving that a substantial change in circumstances had occurred. (*Id.* at p. 731.) And we concluded that she had not carried her burden. (*Id.* at p. 740.) It is difficult for me to conceive how we could have established the point more clearly. . . .

More troubling, the majority's tacit overruling of *Carney* and its consequent limitation of the changed-circumstances rule to cases in which custody was originally established by judicial decree have untoward consequences and are unsound.

First, the limited application of the changed-circumstances rule that the majority adopt is in conflict with the primary purpose of the rule. The child whose custody was established by means other than judicial decree has the same need for and right to stability and continuity and accordingly the same entitlement to the protection the rule is intended to provide as the child whose custody was established by judicial decree. Because it is not unreasonable to assume that the children of two-parent and relatively more affluent families are disproportionately represented in the class of children whose custody was originally established by judicial decree, the majority's holding, I fear, will effectively deny needed protection disproportionately to children of single-parent and less affluent families.

Second, most states including, until today, California appear to require "changed circumstances" to modify custody regardless of how custody was originally established. (*See* Sharp, *supra*, 68 Va. L. Rev. at pp. 1265, 1268–1271, and cases and other authorities cited.) The rationale for this position was explained in *Carney*: "regardless of how custody was originally decided upon, after the child has lived in one parent's home for a significant period it surely remains 'undesirable' to uproot him from his 'established mode of living,' and a substantial change in his circumstances should ordinarily be required to justify that result." (24 Cal. 3d at p. 731, fn. 4; *accord*, Sharp, *supra*, at p. 1270.) That the cases with the notable exception of *Carney* involve a custody decree is plainly fortuitous: the fundamental question they all address is not whether to modify a decree but whether to change custody. No state, so far as I have ascertained, declines to apply the changed-circumstances rule when custody was not originally established by judicial decree. The majority, alone in the country, take that retrogressive step.

The majority claim that the *Carney* rule is "unsound, unworkable, and potentially harmful." Their argument in support, however, is hollow.

Their first point is that the *Carney* rule "is unsound because, absent some prior determination of the child's best interests as of some past date, the courts have no warrant to disregard facts bearing upon that issue merely because such facts do not constitute changed circumstances." But if the *Carney* rule is unsound for this reason, so is their newly created rule: even in cases in which custody is established by judicial decree, such a determination is seldom made.

In virtually all cases, it appears, the parents decide on custody in a negotiated settlement and thus do not dispute the question at a hearing. And in these cases "courts usually 'rubber-stamp' such agreements . . . ." (Sharp, *supra*, at p. 1279.) The percentage of cases in which a trial court initially determines custody in a contested manner is minuscule.

But the fact remains that even when custody is not adjudicated and indeed even when it is not established by judicial decree, we may nevertheless presume that such custody is in the child's best interest and as a result require the noncustodial parent to show that a material change of circumstances has subsequently occurred.

Such a presumption is justified when custody is established by agreement. "First, most parents genuinely love their children, and it is reasonable to assume that the children's welfare is a vital consideration in the parents' decision to resolve their dispute by agreement. . . . Second, parents have a better informational base upon which to make a decision about custody. The adversarial process is an inadequate means to assemble sufficient 'facts' to resolve custodial disputes satisfactorily. Third, it is difficult to protect a child from the painful pull of divided loyalties when his parents fail to agree. Parental agreements help to preserve an atmosphere of at least superficial peace between parents and thereby facilitate a much easier and more meaningful future relationship between the child and the non-custodial parent." (Sharp, *supra*, 68 Va. L. Rev. at p. 1280, fn. omitted.)

Such a presumption is also justified when, as here, custody is established by default rather than by decision. First, as between the parent who undertakes to provide care and the parent who fails or refuses to do so, custody with the former must be deemed to serve the child's best interests. Thus, it is altogether reasonable to require the latter to demonstrate changed circumstances should he subsequently attempt to obtain custody. Second, as Dr. Andrew Watson, psychiatrist and professor of law, has observed, stability is "practically the principal element in raising children" and "a child can handle almost anything better than he can handle instability." (Proceedings of Special Com. on U. Marriage and Divorce Act, Nat. Conf. of Comrs. on U. State Laws 98, 101 (Dec. 15–16, 1968); . . .).

The majority's second point is that the *Carney* rule "is unworkable because, absent such a prior determination the courts have no established basis on which they can assess the significance of any change." But "Identification of a base line against which to measure a subsequent change of conditions is not as difficult as the [majority] suggest. The simple fact is that a demonstration of changed conditions does not normally require a preexisting record of all the facts that prevailed at the time [custody was originally established] . . . . It is plausible therefore to suggest that the concern about the necessity for a prior record is somewhat of a red herring." (Sharp, *supra*, 68 Va.L.Rev. at pp. 1285, 1287.)

The majority's final point is that the *Carney* rule "is potentially harmful because it could compel the court to make an award inconsistent with the child's best interest." But the concern that application of the changed-circumstances rule in cases in which custody was not judicially established might leave a court helpless to intervene where there was no change in circumstances but the welfare of the child required a change in custody does not justify a limitation of the rule such as the majority have adopted. To begin with, the rule could theoretically leave the court helpless in any case in which it is applied whether or not custody was originally established by judicial decree. The concern, therefore, is rooted not in the use of the rule in any particular class of cases but rather in a mechanical and formalistic use of the rule itself. In any event, "Nothing in the case law of the majority states, or in any of the literature in this area, suggests such a rigid application of the changed circumstances standard. . . . Clearly, courts can easily accommodate the 'worst case' hypothetical within existing law." (Sharp, *supra*, 68 Va. L. Rev. at p. 1288, fn. omitted.) . . .

In sum, the *Carney* rule rightly protects all children against needless change in custody and against the threat of such change. Whatever harm a mechanical application of the rule poses in unusual circumstances which are not present here can readily be prevented by permitting a pragmatic exception. The rule therefore should not be discarded; it should simply be modified if and when the need arises. . . .

NOTES AND QUESTIONS

(1) **Standard for Modification.** Custody awards are modifiable in all states. *See* Wexler, *Rethinking the Modification of Child Custody Decrees*, 94 Yale L.J. 757 (1985). The real question is: what is the standard? The opposing standards are set out in *Burchard*: the changed circumstances test and the ubiquitous best interest standard. These two standards embody the inherent tension in the law regarding modification of custody decrees. On one hand, there is the need for the finality of judgments. The principles of res judicata apply to all judgments, but they are even more important in the area of custody since the uncertainty of repeated litigation takes a psychological toll on the child involved and saps the financial resources of the parents. On the other hand there is a need to provide for the welfare of children, a need which the courts can never ignore.

(a) **The Changed-Circumstances Test.** The changed-circumstances test discussed so articulately in *Burchard* represents the interest in certainty and finality. Theoretically, when one party moves for a modification of custody in a state which has adopted the changed-circumstances test, only evidence of circumstances which have arisen since the original decree can be admitted. Thus, finality is preserved because the parties cannot relitigate the facts upon which the original award was based. Once it is established that there has been a change of circumstances since the original decree, the court will redetermine who should have custody based upon the best interest standard. Sometimes the courts will require that the changed circumstances be "substantial." But the addition of this word does not change the threshold of proof. In truth, the degree of change must merely be great enough to get a trial court to think that the child's welfare may be at stake. *See Nabors v. Nabors*, 418 So. 2d 143, 143–45 (Ala. Civ. App. 1982); *Vaughn v. Vaughn*, 418 So. 2d 155, 156–57 (Ala. Civ. App. 1982); *In re Marriage of Simmons*, 487 N.E.2d 450, 453 (Ind. Ct. App. 1985); *Ryan v. Ryan*, 652 S.W.2d 313, 315 (Mo. Ct. App. 1983); *Pact v. Pact*, 332 N.Y.S.2d 940, 949 (N.Y. Fam. Ct. 1972); *State ex rel. Reitz v. Ringer*, 510 N.W.2d 294, 299 (Neb. 1994); *Blotske v. Leidholm*, 487 N.W.2d 607, 609 (N.D. 1992); *Agati v. Agati*, 492 A.2d 427, 432 (Pa. Super. Ct. 1985).

(b) **Best Interest Standard.** If courts apply the best interest standard, it means in effect that they will not only consider facts which have arisen since the original decision but also those facts which were in existence at the time of the decree. While there may be an attempt by the individual trial court to limit the evidence to new facts, a skillful attorney can probably have a de novo hearing of all the facts, especially where a case can be made that the original decision was misguided and the child is suffering because of it. *See Kateley v. Kateley*, 374 A.2d 1049, 1050 (Conn. 1977); *In re L.J.T.*, 608 A.2d 1213, 1214 (D.C. 1992); *Griffith v. Griffith*, 627 So. 2d 527, 528 (Fla. Dist. Ct. App. 1993); *Mirras v. Mirras*, 202 So. 2d 887, 892 (Fla. Dist. Ct. App. 1967); *Valencia v. Valencia*, 375 N.E.2d 98, 100 (Ill. 1978); *Borys v. Borys*, 386 A.2d 366, 377 (N. J. 1978); *Brooks v. Brooks*, 530 P.2d 547, 551 (Or. Ct. App. 1975).

(2) **UMDA.** The framers of the Uniform Marriage and Divorce Act have taken a strong stand in favor of finality in child custody decrees, not only by adopting the changed-circumstances test, but also by requiring a two-year waiting period for modification (except in dire circumstances) and by limiting evidence of conditions previous to the award so that the court cannot simply readjudicate the original issues. Uniform Marriage and Divorce Act, 9A U.L.A. 211 (1987); *see Naylor v. Kindred*, 620 N.E.2d 520 (Ill. App. Ct. 1993). *See also* Wexler, *Rethinking the Modification of Child Custody Decrees*, 94 Yale L.J. 757, 760 (1985).

This provision is an attempt to prevent any circumstance which was in existence at the time of the original decision from playing a role in the modification process. However, does it allow evidence of prior conditions in by the back door in the sense that the court cannot know if there has been a changed circumstance unless it knows the previous condition? *See* Wexler, *Rethinking the Modification of Child Custody Decrees*, 94 Yale L.J. 757, 760 (1985).

(3) **Consensual Child Custody.** There are other cases which agree with the principal case that changed circumstances may not be required where the original custody arrangement was merely de facto or a matter of agreement. *See Hill v. Hill*, 620 P.2d 1114, 1119 (Kan.

1980); *Friederwitzer v. Friederwitzer,* 432 N.E.2d 765, 766–69 (N.Y. 1982); The California approach was applied again in *Catherine D. v. Dennis B.,* 269 Cal. Rptr. 547, 552 (Cal. Ct. App. 1990).

(4) **Burden of Proof.** It is widely recognized that the burden of proof is on the party seeking to modify the custody arrangement. *See* H. Clark, *The Law of Domestic Relations in the United States* § 20.9 at 549. This is true in jurisdictions which use the changed-circumstances test (*e.g., T.M.C. v. S.A.C.,* 858 P.2d 315, 317 (Alaska 1993)), as well as those applying the best interests test (*e.g., Treutle v. Treutle,* 495 N.W.2d 836, 837 (Mich. Ct. App. 1992)).

(5) **Basis for Change.** What kinds of things lead to change of custody and visitation? Here are some recent examples:

(a) Domestic violence: *Anderson v. Hensrud,* 548 N.W.2d 410, 412 (N.D. 1996).

(b) Child preference: *McDonough v. Murphy,* 539 N.W.2d 313, 316 (N.D. 1996). *But see Mulkey-Yelverton v. Blevins,* 884 P.2d 41, 43 (Wyo. 1994).

(c) Mental disability of custodian: *A.H. v. W.P.,* 896 P.2d 240, 244 (Alaska 1995); *Evenson v. Evenson,* 538 N.W.2d 746, 749 (Neb. 1996); *but see Kamholtz v. Kovary,* 620 N.Y.S.2d 576, 577 (N.Y. App. Div. 1994).

(d) Interference with visitation: *Brown v. Brown,* 552 So. 2d 271, 273 (Fla. Dist. Ct. App. 1989); *Dabill v. Dabill,* 514 N.W.2d 590, 595 (Minn. Ct. App. 1994); *Sigg v. Sigg,* 905 P.2d 908, 912 (Utah Ct. App. 1995); *Ready v. Ready,* 906 P.2d 382, 385 (Wyo. 1995).

(e) Custodial parent's gay or lesbian relationship: *H.J.B. v. P.W.,* 628 So. 2d 753, 754 (Ala. Civ. App. 1993); *In re Marriage of Martins,* 645 N.E.2d 567, 573 (Ill. App. Ct. 1995)(using nexus approach); *but see Fox v. Fox,* 904 P.2d 66, 69 (Okla. 1995).

(f) Substance abuse: *Ludwig v. Burchill,* 514 N.W.2d 674, 675 (N.D. 1994); *In re LeGrand,* 495 N.W.2d 118, 120 (Iowa Ct. App. 1992).

Some interesting circumstances have not been grounds to modify: mother's drug rehabilitation: *In re Weber,* 619 N.E.2d 768, 771 (Ill. App. Ct. 1993); mother's cohabitation: *In re Nolte,* 609 N.E.2d 381, 385 (Ill. App. Ct. 1993); failure to provide for child's college expenses: *Smith v. Smith,* 553 N.Y.S.2d 243, 244 (N.Y. App. Div. 1990); *Zummo v. Zummo,* 574 A.2d 1130 (Pa. Super. Ct. 1990).

(6) **Age.** How minimal can the change of circumstances be? Will a change in the child's age be a sufficient change of circumstance? A change in age from four to six was sufficient to change the primary residence in a joint custody situation from the mother's home to the father's. The Supreme Court of Rhode Island stated:

> It is, then, our opinion that a substantial increase in the age of a child during some critical period in his life, standing alone, constitutes a change of circumstance sufficient to warrant the trial court in reopening the prior order awarding custody. There is apparently a dearth of decisions on this particular question, but in two cases decided by the Missouri Court of Appeals such an increase in the age of a child, standing alone, has been held to constitute a sufficient warrant for the reopening of the previous custody order. *Blair v. Blair,* 505 S.W.2d 444, 447 (Mo. Ct. App. 1974); *Cascio v. Cascio,* 485 S.W.2d 857, 859 (Mo. Ct. App.1972).

King v. King, 333 A.2d 135, 138 (R.I. 1975); *see also Butler v. Butler*, 669 N.E.2d 291, 293–94 (Ohio Ct. App. 1995).

(7) **Continuity of Care.** As you can see, the concepts of continuity and stability are important aspects of the changed-circumstances test. Goldstein, Freud, and Solnit go one step beyond the changed-circumstances test:

> Child placements in divorce and separation proceedings are never final and often are conditional. The lack of finality, which stems from the court's retention of jurisdiction over its custody decision, invites challenges by disappointed parties claiming changed circumstances. This absence of finality coupled with the concomitant increase in opportunities for appeal are in conflict with the child's need for continuity. As in adoption, a custody decree should be final, that is, not subject to modification.

J. Goldstein, A. Freud, and A.J. Solnit, Beyond the Best Interests of the Child 37 (1973).

(8) **Problem.** Reread the Problem in § 12.02[J], *above*. Assume that Hal got custody of the kids. A number of years have passed and there is no bitterness between Wilma and Hal. Wilma is no longer traveling and settled down in the same city where Hal and the children live. She is married to a new husband. The kids visit her regularly at her house, and she has a good relationship with both of them. Hal has a great relationship with both children, and the children have been well taken care of over the years. Hal is now confined to a wheelchair and often he is bedridden for many days at a time. The household is well managed. The children, now aged 10 and 14, take orders from their father and by and large run everything. When asked, both children say they love their mother very much, but they are adamant that they want to continue to live with their father. There is every indication that Hal's physical condition will only get worse. Wilma brings an action to change custody out of genuine concern for the kids' welfare; she is afraid they overextend themselves to help their dad. She promises to make sure the kids will have ample contact with their father. What will be the result of the custody action?

[B] Relocation

TROPEA v. TROPEA
Court of Appeals of New York
665 N.E.2d 145 (1996)

TITONE, JUDGE.

I.

The parties in this case were married in 1981 and have two children, one born in 1985 and the other in 1988. They were divorced in 1992 pursuant to a judgment that incorporated their previously executed separation agreement. Under that agreement, petitioner mother, who had previously been the children's primary caregiver, was to have sole custody of the children and respondent father was granted visitation on holidays and "at least three . . . days of each week." Additionally, the parties were barred from relocating outside of Onondaga County, where both resided, without prior judicial approval.

On June 3, 1993, petitioner brought this proceeding seeking changes in the visitation arrangements and permission to relocate with the children to the Schenectady area.

Respondent opposed the requested relief and filed a cross petition for a change of custody. At the ensuing hearing, petitioner testified that she wanted to move because of her plans to marry an architect who had an established firm in Schenectady. According to petitioner, she and her fiance had already purchased a home in the Schenectady area for themselves and the Tropea children and were now expecting a child of their own. Petitioner stated that she was willing to cooperate in a liberal visitation schedule that would afford respondent frequent and extended contact and that she was prepared to drive the children to and from their father's Syracuse home, which is about two and a half hours away from Schenectady. Nonetheless, as all parties recognized, the distance between the two homes made midweek visits during the school term impossible.

Respondent took the position that petitioner's "need" to move was really the product of her own life-style choice and that, consequently, he should not be the parent who is "punished" with the loss of proximity and weekday contact. Instead, respondent proposed that he be awarded custody of the children if petitioner chose to relocate. To support this proposal, respondent adduced evidence to show that he had maintained frequent and consistent contact with his children at least until June of 1993, when the instant proceeding was commenced. He had coached the children's football and baseball teams, participated in their religion classes and had become involved with his older son's academic education during the 1992-1993 school year. However, there was also evidence that respondent harbored a continuing bitterness toward petitioner which he had verbalized and demonstrated to the children in a number of inappropriate ways. Respondent admitted being bitter enough to have called petitioner "a tramp" and "a low-life" in the children's presence and, in fact, stated that he saw nothing wrong with this conduct, although he acknowledged that it had a negative effect on the children. Respondent's mother confirmed that he had spoken negatively about petitioner in the children's presence and that this behavior had not been helpful to the children.

Following the hearing, the presiding Judicial Hearing Officer (JHO) denied petitioner's request for permission to relocate. Applying what he characterized as "a more restrictive view of relocation," the JHO opined that whenever a proposed move "unduly disrupts or substantially impairs the [noncustodial parent's] access rights to [the] children," the custodial spouse seeking judicial consent must bear the burden of demonstrating "exceptional circumstances" such as a "concrete economic necessity." Applying this principle to the evidence before him, the JHO found that petitioner's desire to obtain a "fresh start" with a new family was insufficient to justify a move that would "significantly impact upon" the close and consistent relationship with his children that respondent had previously enjoyed.

On petitioner's appeal, however, the Appellate Division reversed, holding that petitioner had made the necessary showing that the requested relocation would not deprive respondent of "regular and meaningful access to his children." . . . Further, the Court noted, petitioner's proposed visitation schedule afforded respondent the opportunity for frequent and extended contact with his children. Finally, the Court found that the move would be in the best interests of the children. Accordingly, the Court ruled that petitioner should be permitted to move to Schenectady and remitted the matter to Family Court for the establishment of an appropriate visitation schedule. The final Family Court judgment from which respondent appeals awards respondent substantial weekend, summer and vacation visitation in accordance with the Law Guardian's recommended schedule. . . .

II.

Relocation cases such as the [one] before us present some of the knottiest and most disturbing problems that our courts are called upon to resolve. In these cases, the interests of a custodial parent who wishes to move away are pitted against those of a noncustodial parent who has a powerful desire to maintain frequent and regular contact with the child. Moreover, the court must weigh the paramount interests of the child, which may or may not be in irreconcilable conflict with those of one or both of the parents.

Because the resolution of relocation disputes is ordinarily a matter entrusted to the fact-finding and discretionary powers of the lower courts, our Court has not had frequent occasion to address the question . . . .

[T]he lower courts have evolved a series of formulae and presumptions to aid them in making their decisions in these difficult relocation cases. The most commonly used formula involves a three-step analysis that looks first to whether the proposed relocation would deprive the noncustodial parent of "regular and meaningful access to the child" (e.g., *Lavane v. Lavane*, 201 A.D.2d 623, 608 N.Y.S.2d 475; . . . .) Where a disruption of "regular and meaningful access" is not shown, the inquiry is truncated, and the courts generally will not go on to assess the merits and strength of the custodial parents' motive for moving. On the other hand, where such a disruption is established, a presumption that the move is not in the child's best interest is invoked and the custodial parent seeking to relocate must demonstrate "exceptional circumstances" to justify the move. Once that hurdle is overcome, the court will go on to consider the child's best interests.

The premise underlying this formula is that children can derive an abundance of benefits from "the mature guiding hand and love of a second parent" and that, consequently, geographic changes that significantly impair the quantity and quality of parent-child contacts are to be "disfavored." While this premise has much merit as a tenet of human dynamics, the legal formula that it has spawned is problematic and, in many respects, unsatisfactory (see, Miller, Whatever Happened to the "Best Interests" Analysis in New York Relocation Cases?, 15 Pace L Rev 339).

One problem with the three-tiered analysis is that it is difficult to apply. The lower courts have not settled on a uniform method of defining "meaningful access," and even the distance of the move has not been a reliable indicator of whether the "meaningful access" test has been satisfied (*compare*, *Rybicki v. Rybicki*, *supra* [disapproving 84-mile move], *with Matter of Schouten v. Schouten*, 155 A.D.2d 461, 547 N.Y.S.2d 126, *supra* [approving 258-mile move]; *Murphy v. Murphy*, 145 A.D.2d 857, 535 N.Y.S.2d 844, *supra* [approving 340-mile move]).

On a more fundamental level, the three-tiered test is unsatisfactory because it erects artificial barriers to the courts' consideration of all of the relevant factors. Most moves outside of the noncustodial parent's locale have some disruptive effect on that parent's relationship with the child. Yet, if the disruption does not rise to the level of a deprivation of "meaningful access," the three-tiered analysis would permit it without any further inquiry into such salient considerations as the custodial parent's motives, the reasons for the proposed move and the positive or negative impact of the change on the child. Similarly, where the noncustodial parent has managed to overcome the threshold "meaningful access" hurdle, the three-tiered approach requires courts to refuse consent if there are no "exceptional circumstances" to justify the change, again without necessarily considering whether the move would serve the child's best interests or whether the benefits to the children would outweigh the diminution in access by the noncustodial parent. The distorting effect of such a mechanical approach may be amplified where the courts require a showing of economic necessity or health-related compulsion to establish the requisite "exceptional circumstances."

In reality, cases in which a custodial parent's desire to relocate conflicts with the desire of a noncustodial parent to maximize visitation opportunity are simply too complex to be satisfactorily handled within any mechanical, tiered analysis that prevents or interferes with a simultaneous weighing and comparative analysis of all of the relevant facts and circumstances. Although we have recognized and continue to appreciate both the need of the child and the right of the noncustodial parent to have regular and meaningful contact, we also believe that no single factor should be treated as dispositive or given such disproportionate weight as to predetermine the outcome. There are undoubtedly circumstances in which the loss of midweek or every weekend visits necessitated by a distant move may be devastating to the relationship between the noncustodial parent and the child. However, there are undoubtedly also many cases where less frequent but more extended visits over summers and school vacations would be equally conducive, or perhaps even more conducive, to the maintenance of a close parent-child relationship, since such extended visits give the parties the opportunity to interact in a normalized domestic setting. In any event, given the variety of possible permutations, it is counterproductive to rely on presumptions whose only real value is to simplify what are necessarily extremely complicated inquiries.

Accordingly, rather than endorsing the three-step meaningful access exceptional-circumstance analysis that some of the lower courts have used in the past, we hold that each relocation request must be considered on its own merits with due consideration of all the relevant facts and circumstances and with predominant emphasis being placed on what outcome is most likely to serve the best interests of the child. While the respective rights of the custodial and noncustodial parents are unquestionably significant factors that must be considered, it is the rights and needs of the children that must be accorded the greatest weight, since they are innocent victims of their parents' decision to divorce and are the least equipped to handle the stresses of the changing family situation.

Of course, the impact of the move on the relationship between the child and the noncustodial parent will remain a central concern. Indeed, even where the move would leave the noncustodial parent with what may be considered "meaningful access," there is still a need to weigh the effect of the quantitative and qualitative losses that naturally will result against such other relevant factors as the custodial parent's reasons for wanting to relocate and the benefits that the child may enjoy or the harm that may ensue if the move is or is not permitted. Similarly, although economic necessity or a specific health-related concern may present a particularly persuasive ground for permitting the proposed move, other justifications, including the demands of a second marriage and the custodial parent's opportunity to improve his or her economic situation, may also be valid motives that should not be summarily rejected, at least where the over-all impact on the child would be beneficial. While some courts have suggested that the custodial spouse's remarriage or wish for a "fresh start" can never suffice to justify a distant move (*see, e.g., Elkus v. Elkus*, 182 A.D.2d 45, 48, 588 N.Y.S.2d 138; *Stec v. Levindofske*, 153 A.D.2d 310, 550 N.Y.S.2d 966), such a rule overlooks the value for the children that strengthening and stabilizing the new, postdivorce family unit can have in a particular case.

In addition to the custodial parent's stated reasons for wanting to move and the noncustodial parent's loss of access, another factor that may well become important in a particular case is the noncustodial parent's interest in securing custody, as well as the feasibility and desirability of a change in custody. Obviously, where a child's ties to the noncustodial parent and to the community are so strong as to make a long-distance move undesirable, the availability of a transfer of custody as realistic alternative to forcing the custodial parent to remain may have a significant impact on the outcome. By the same token, where the custodial parent's reasons for moving are deemed valid and sound, the court in a proper case might consider the possibility and feasibility of a parallel move by an involved and committed noncustodial parent as an alternative to restricting a custodial parent's mobility.

Other considerations that may have a bearing in particular cases are the good faith of the parents in requesting or opposing the move, the child's respective attachments to the custodial and noncustodial parent, the possibility of devising a visitation schedule that will enable the noncustodial parent to maintain a meaningful parent-child relationship, the quality of the life-style that the child would have if the proposed move were permitted or denied, the negative impact, if any, from continued or exacerbated hostility between the custodial and noncustodial parents, and the effect that the move may have on any extended family relationships. Of course, any other facts or circumstances that have a bearing on the parties' situation should be weighed with a view toward minimizing the parents' discomfort and maximizing the child's prospects of a stable, comfortable and happy life.

Like Humpty Dumpty, a family, once broken by divorce, cannot be put back together in precisely the same way. The relationship between the parents and the children is necessarily different after a divorce and, accordingly, it may be unrealistic in some cases to try to preserve the noncustodial parent's accustomed close involvement in the children's everyday life at the expense of the custodial parent's efforts to start a new life or to form a new family unit. In some cases, the child's interests might be better served by fashioning visitation plans that maximize the noncustodial parent's opportunity to maintain a positive nurturing relationship while enabling the custodial parent, who has the primary child-rearing responsibility, to go forward with his or her life. In any event, it serves neither the interests of the children nor the ends of justice to view relocation cases through the prisms of presumptions and threshold tests that artificially skew the analysis in favor of one outcome or another.

Rather, we hold that, in all cases, the courts should be free to consider and give appropriate weight to all of the factors that may be relevant to the determination. These factors include, but are certainly not limited to each parent's reasons for seeking or opposing the move, the quality of the relationships between the child and the custodial and noncustodial parents, the impact of the move on the quantity and quality of the child's future contact with the noncustodial parent, the degree to which the custodial parent's and child's life may be enhanced economically, emotionally and educationally by the move, and the feasibility of preserving the relationship between the noncustodial parent and child through suitable visitation arrangements. In the end, it is for the court to determine, based on all of the proof, whether it has been established by a preponderance of the evidence that a proposed relocation would serve the child's best interests.

III.

Turning finally to the case before us, we conclude that the orders of the courts below, which approved the petitioners' requests to move, should be upheld. In *Tropea*, petitioner sought permission to relocate from Onondaga County to the Schenectady area so that she could settle into a new home with her fiance and raise her sons within a new family unit. The Appellate Division found that the move was in the children's best interest and that the visitation schedule that petitioner proposed would afford respondent frequent and extended visitation. We find no reason derived from the record to upset the Appellate Division's determinations on these points. It is true that the Court considered whether the relocation would deprive respondent of "meaningful access" to his children. However, it is apparent from the remainder of its writing that the Court did not treat that factor as a threshold test barring further inquiry into the salient "best interests" question. . . .

Accordingly, in *Matter of Tropea v. Tropea*, the judgment of the Family Court and the prior nonfinal order of the Appellate Division brought up for review should be affirmed, with costs. . . .

NOTES AND QUESTIONS

(1) **When Good Parents Fight.** The issue of relocation often involves two parents who may have successfully resisted litigation in the past, who have determined their own custody arrangement, and who have both developed a relationship with their children after divorce. Nevertheless, external factors impinge upon their lives plunging them into controversy. Often the outside factors are things which would normally be considered a blessing: a job promotion or a new relationship for the custodial parent. However, with the blessing comes a need to move. The necessity of moving for a job promotion is an especially touchy issue for custodial mothers. Life for a single parent is difficult enough, and when the parent manages to get a significant promotion, often by overcoming gender bias and the "glass ceiling", the promotion is especially important. Also, when a custodial parent of either sex finds a new partner, it can be threatening to the noncustodial parent. Most importantly, regardless of other emotional factors, the move itself poses a threat to the noncustodial parent; the threat of losing the relationship with the child. The result makes relocation the most common modification controversy for the courts, at least in recent years.

In a sense, relocation cases are also the most confusing, if for no other reason than the wide variety of approaches which developed among the states. As one court has stated:

> At the outset we note that our research has failed to reveal a consistent, universally accepted approach to the question of when a custodial parent may relocate out-of-state over the objection of the non-custodial parent. In fact, the opposite is true. Across the country, applicable standards remain distressingly disparate.

Gruber v. Gruber, 583 A.2d 434, 437 (Pa. Super. Ct. 1990).

(2) **Modification.** Relocation cases are treated here as modification cases. There are many states which require the party seeking the relocation to apply to the court for permission to relocate. *See, e.g.*, N.D. Cent. Code § 14–09–07 (1991); Nev. Rev. Stat. § 125A.350 (1991). However, the real issue is modification of the custody arrangement. While the courts

in relocation cases may issue an order prohibiting the relocation, they do not have the power to prevent the custodial parent from moving. *See Kerkvliet v. Kerkvliet*, 480 N.W.2d 823, 829 (Wis. Ct. App. 1992). The court's real power lies in the ability to modify the custodial arrangement in one of two ways. First, the court can modify the agreement by awarding custody to the noncustodial parent. Second, the court can make retention of custody contingent on remaining in the same location. Whether the noncustodial parent brings the action to block the move or the custodial parent brings the action for permission to relocate, the modification issue remains.

(3) **The Best Interest Standard.** *Tropea* was to some degree considered a controversial case, perhaps because it changed the approach which had been established by the New York intermediate courts. Nevertheless, it is a moderate decision; it refuses to tip the scales of justice in favor of either the custodial or noncustodial parent. In fact, it is also a traditional approach. While the case does not mention the changed-circumstances test, the relocation is the changed circumstance, which, once found, opens the door for application of the best-interest standard in modification proceedings. This approach is very well stated in the dissent in another case receiving great publicity, *In re Marriage of Burgess*:

> I also agree with the majority that when a relocation dispute arises after an initial award of custody has been made, the usual "changed circumstances" rule should apply. A child's welfare is not served by casual changes in care giving arrangements, and the law abhors the endless relitigation of matters already determined. Hence, the parent who seeks a change in formal custody based on "changed circumstances" (including a parental relocation) bears the burden of persuading the court that in light of the new circumstances, an alteration of the existing award is in the child's "best interest."

In re Marriage of Burgess, 913 P.2d 473, 484–86 (Cal. 1996) (Baxter, J., dissenting). Other cases which follow a best interest approach include: *House v. House*, 779 P.2d 1204, 1207–08 (Alaska 1989); *Blake v. Blake*, 541 A.2d 1201 (Conn. 1988); *Seessel v. Seessel*, 748 S.W.2d 422 (Tenn. 1988).

(4) **Tipping the Scales in Favor of the Custodial Parent.** There are a number of states which have stated that there is a presumption in favor of the custodial parent. The custodial parent therefore has the right to move with the child unless the noncustodial parent can show that the move is not in the best interest of the child. *See Mize v. Mize*, 621 So. 2d 417, 419 (Fla. 1993); *Russenberger v. Russenberger*, 669 So. 2d 1044, 1046 (Fla. 1996); *Lorenz v. Lorenz*, 788 P.2d 328, 331 (Mont. 1990); *Fortin v. Fortin*, 500 N.W.2d 229, 230–36 (S.D. 1993); *Fossum v. Fossum*, 545 N.W.2d 828, 832 (S.D. 1996); *In re Marriage of Paradis*, 689 P.2d 1263, 1265 (Mont. 1984).

In a case which overruled a scheme favoring noncustodial parents created by the appellate courts, the California Supreme Court adopted a presumption in favor of relocation:

> In addition, in a matter involving immediate or eventual relocation by one or both parents, the trial court must take into account the presumptive right of a custodial parent to change the residence of the minor children, so long as the removal would not be prejudicial to their rights or welfare. . . . The showing required is substantial. We have previously held that a child should not be removed from prior custody of one parent and given to the other " 'unless the material facts and circumstances occurring subsequently are of a kind to render it essential or expedient for the welfare of the child that there be a change.' "

In re Marriage of Burgess, 913 P.2d 473, 482 (Cal. 1996). This presumption can also be created by statute. *See, e.g.,* Wis. Stat. Ann. § 767.327(3)(a)(2)(a) (West 1993).

In addition there are cases which do not create a presumption in favor of the custodial parent but which have a relocation standard which appears to favor the custodial parent or at least which favors the policy of stability of primary care and/or the policy of continuous and frequent contact with both parents. In some cases, the method requires the noncustodial parent to show that the change in custody is necessary. *See Barstad v. Barstad*, 499 N.W.2d 584, 587–90 (N.D. 1993); *Lane v. Science*, 614 A.2d 786, 791 (Vt. 1992).

Some scholars have come down heavily in favor of approaches which favor the custodial parent. *See* Bruch & Bowermaster, *The Relocation of Children and Custodial Parents: Public Policy, Past and Present*, 30 Fam. L.Q. 245 (1996); LaFrance, *Child Custody and Relocation: A Constitutional Perspective*, 34 Fam. L.Q. 1 (1996). A particularly important scholarly article is Wallerstein & Tanke, *To Move or Not to Move: Psychological and Legal Consideration in the Relocation of Children Following Divorce*, 30 Fam. L.Q. 305 (1996). This article, which originated as an amicus brief in the *Burgess* case, concludes:

> Our research at the Center for the Family in Transition ("the Center") has revealed several factors associated with good outcomes for children in post-divorce families. These include: (1) a close, sensitive relationship with a psychologically intact, conscientious custodial parent; (2) the diminution of conflict and reasonable cooperation between the parents; and (3) whether or not the child comes to the divorce with pre-existing psychological difficulties.
>
> All of our work shows the centrality of the well-functioning custodial parent-child relationship as the protective factor during the post-divorce years. When courts intervene in ways that disrupt the child's relationship with the custodial parent, serious psychological harm may occur to the child as well as to the parent. We have mounting evidence that children are in terror during court proceedings, especially those proceedings that involve evaluation of the child, separation from custodial parents, and disruption of the family unit.
>
> Following divorce, a second or third disruption in the child's life has a serious potential for not only creating more suffering, but for doing lasting psychological damage to a child who has already been traumatized by the divorce, and for whom repeated disruptions in relationships represent an experience which the hapless child dreads.
>
> Additionally, our studies of divorce have taught us the significance of the parents' relationship with each other for the child's moral and emotional development. Parent-to-parent relationships continue to be important following divorce. The cooperative interaction of the parents is critical to the child's healthy development and peace of mind. The high potential for continued or re-opened conflict, as in the relocation issue, can severely threaten the child's sense of security, confirming a view of the world as an armed camp in which the child can trust no one.

Id. at 310–11.

(5) Tipping the Scales in Favor of the Noncustodial Parent. The scheme developed by the appellate courts of New York, rejected in *Tropea,* exemplifies the approach which appears to favor the noncustodial parent. Other courts have followed a similar approach.

The appellate courts in California, had a similar approach which was rejected in *In re Marriage of Burgess*:

> [The Court of Appeal] formulated the following test for relocation cases. The trial court initially must determine whether the move "will impact significantly the existing pattern of care and adversely affect the nature and quality of the noncustodial parent's contact with the child. The burden is on the noncustodial non-moving parent to show this adverse impact." If the impact is shown, the trial court must determine whether the move is "reasonably necessary," with "the burden of showing such necessity fall[ing] on the moving parent." If it concludes that the move is "necessary"—either because not moving would impose an unreasonable hardship on the custodial parent's career or other interests or because moving will result in a discernible benefit that it would be unreasonable to expect the parent to forgo—the trial court "must resolve whether the benefit to the child in going with the moving parent outweighs the loss or diminution of contact with the nonmoving parent."

In re Marriage of Burgess, 913 P.2d 473, 477 (Cal. 1996).

Requiring the custodial parent to prove the necessity of the move emphasizes the policy in favor of the continuous and frequent relationship of the child with the noncustodial parent and other factors such as the child's relationship to community, schools, friends and family. This view seems to be in decline. However it is not without its supporters. *See* Adams, *Child Custody and Parental Relocations: Loving Your Children from a Distance*, 33 Duq. L. Rev. 143 (1994).

(6) **Joint Custody.** Several cases have determined that a presumption in favor of the relocating custodial parent does not apply where there is court-ordered joint custody. *See Ayers v. Ayers*, 508 N.W.2d 515, 520 (Minn. 1993). In California, which does favor the relocating parent but which does not have a presumption, the Supreme Court has indicated that the prevailing approach, which provides that the parent opposing relocation must show that the denial of the move is expedient and essential to the best interest of the child, does not apply when the parents share joint physical custody. *See In re Marriage of Burgess*, 913 P.2d 473, n.12 (Cal. 1996). *Query:* Does this approach unduly encourage divorcing parents to fight for joint custody at the time of divorce?

(7) **Additional Reading.** *See generally* Holtz, *Move-Away Custody Disputes: The Implication of the Case-by-Case Analysis & the Need for Legislation*, 35 Santa Clara L. Rev. 273, 319 (1994); Baron, *Refining Relocation Law—The Next Step in Attacking the Problem of Parental Kidnaping,* 25 Tex. Tech. L. Rev 119 (1993) (pointing out a connection between relocation and jurisdiction disputes).

§ 12.06 Child Custody Jurisdiction

[A] Introduction

The subject of child custody jurisdiction has been chaotic, to say the least. The only theme that runs through this area of the law is that state courts have been unhesitatingly willing to exercise their own jurisdiction to decide initial child custody issues and to modify the decisions of other state courts. As with most aspects of family law, jurisdiction to resolve child custody matters has traditionally been the domain of the state courts. Once state courts began to assert their power to resolve child custody matters, they gradually expanded the limits of their own jurisdictional requirements. Many states originally required the child to be domiciled in the state but later adopted a multi-factor approach, which included mere presence of the child as a factor. This expansion greatly exacerbated the problem of interstate custody disputes. In addition there was very little constitutional limitation on the jurisdictional rights of the states to resolve these disputes. The Full Faith and Credit Clause, U.S. Const. Art IV, § 1, was interpreted in a manner which did not limit interstate custody disputes: states were not required to give the custody judgments of other states any more deference than they gave their own decrees.

In an effort to bring order to the law of child custody jurisdiction, the Uniform Child Custody Jurisdiction Act (UCCJA) was promulgated and adopted by all fifty states, although the individual states made many modifications in the act when they adopted it. However, in the eyes of many this act was not successful, and so Congress passed the Parental Kidnaping Prevention Act (PKPA), which mirrored the UCCJA in many ways but which attempted to fill significant loopholes in the UCCJA. Finally, the UCCJA has now been modified to reflect the changes in the PKPA and renamed the Uniform Child Custody Jurisdiction and Enforcement Act, which as of this writing, had only been adopted by one state.

The result is that there has been a great deal of change in the law of child custody jurisdiction. The material in this section is organized chronologically to show the historical change that has taken place. The first part deals with the traditional basis for jurisdiction. This material is included because the issues which plagued the system in the past are still issues today. The following subsections deal with the state legislation (the UCCJA and the modifications in the UCCJEA), federal legislation (PKPA), and the Hague Convention. As to whether all this legislation has brought order out of chaos, the authors will leave it to the individual readers to decide.

[B] Traditional Jurisdiction

The historical background leading to our present child custody jurisdiction laws can be better understood by reviewing the following important statements seeking to resolve interstate disputes. The tension between competing objectives, to consider the best interest of the child and to discourage child snatching, continues.

(a) **First Restatement—Domicile.** The first Restatement of Conflict of Laws stated the jurisdictional requirement for custody matters as follows:

> § 117. Guardianship of the Person.
>
> A state can exercise through its courts jurisdiction to determine the custody of children or to create the status of guardian of the person only if the domicile of the person placed under custody or guardianship is within the state.
>
> Restatement of Conflict of Laws § 117 (1934).

This provision severely limited the power of states to decide custody cases and to modify the custody decisions of other states. However, the rule was severely criticized because it did not allow states to provide for the best interests of children. *See* Stumberg, *The Status of Children in the Conflict of Laws*, 8 U. Chi. L. Rev. 42 (1940), and Stansbury, *Custody and Maintenance Across State Lines*, 10 Law & Contemp. Probs. 818 (1944). For an historical account of this period of the law, see Blakesley, *Child Custody Jurisdiction and*

Procedure, 35 Emory L.J. 291 (1986), and Coombs, *Interstate Child Custody: Jurisdiction, Recognition, and Enforcement*, 66 Minn. L. Rev. 711 (1982).

(b) Second Restatement and Case Law—Multiple Bases of Jurisdiction. The position of *Sampsell* was so pervasive that it was adopted by the Second Restatement.

> § 79. Custody of the Person;
>
> A state has power to exercise judicial jurisdiction to determine the custody, or to appoint a guardian, of the person of a child or adult (a) who is domiciled in the state, or (b) who is present in the state, or (c) who is neither domiciled nor present in the state, if the controversy is between two or more persons who are personally subject to the jurisdiction of the state.

Restatement (Second) of Conflict of Laws § 79 (1971).

(c) United States Supreme Court. One might think that, if the *Sampsell* approach to jurisdiction created uncertainty as to the finality of custody decisions, this uncertainty would be curbed to some degree in interstate disputes by the Full Faith and Credit Clause, U.S. Const. Art. IV, § 1. However, two decisions by the United States Supreme Court limited the effect of the Full Faith and Credit Clause.

The first held that the Full Faith and Credit Clause does not prevent a state from modifying a child custody decision of another state. In other words a state has the same power to modify the child custody decrees of a foreign state as it does to modify its own decrees. *See Reynolds v. Stockton*, 140 U.S. 254 (1891); *Halvey v. Halvey*, 330 U.S. 610 (1947). As stated in *Halvey*, Article IV, § 1 of the Constitution provides that:

> "Full Faith and Credit shall be given in each State to the public Acts, Records, and judicial Proceedings of every other State. And the Congress may by general Laws prescribe the Manner in which such Acts, Records and Proceedings shall be proved, and the effect thereof" . . . . But a judgment has no constitutional claim to a more conclusive or final effect in the State of the forum than it has in the state where rendered. Whatever may be the authority of a State to undermine a judgment of a sister State on grounds not cognizable in the State where the judgment was rendered, *it is clear that the State of the forum has at least as much leeway to disregard the judgment, to qualify it, or to depart from it as does the State where it was rendered.*

Halvey, 330 U.S. at 615 (emphasis added). Since standards for modification of a custody jurisdiction, traditionally the changed-circumstance test or more recently the best-interest test, allow states great discretion to modify their own decisions, states have a similar broad power to modify the decisions of other states.

The second important decision of the Supreme Court, *May v. Anderson*, 345 U.S. 528 (1953), held that the Full Faith and Credit Clause and the federal legislation implementing it require that there be in personam jurisdiction over a parent before a judgment adversely affecting the parent is entitled to full faith and credit. In *May* the father had a Wisconsin decree awarding custody to him, but enforcement in Ohio against the mother was denied by the Supreme Court despite the children's domicile in Ohio:

> In the instant case, the Ohio courts gave weight to . . . [the father's] contention that the Wisconsin award of custody binds . . . [the mother] because, at the time it was

issued, her children had a technical domicile in Wisconsin, although they were neither resident nor present there. We find it unnecessary to determine the children's legal domicile because, even if it be with their father, that does not give Wisconsin, certainly as against Ohio, the personal jurisdiction that it must have in order to deprive their mother of her personal right to their immediate possession.

Id. at 534.

The effect of *May* was confusing at best. While it would appear to make personal jurisdiction the required basis for custody decisions, this aspect of the decision has been largely ignored even in matters of full faith and credit. Instead, it opened the door to the relitigation of custody cases since many of them, under the multiple-basis approach, were not based upon in personam jurisdiction. And even if there was personal jurisdiction for the original decree, courts were willing to just ignore *May* and relitigate the child custody issue either as a matter of modification or simply because the best interest of the child demanded it.

The result was a system in which a parent who did not appreciate a child custody award would simply take the child to another jurisdiction and seek to modify the award there: "at the time the [Parental Kidnapping Prevention Act] was enacted, sponsors of the Act estimated that between 25,000 and 100,000 children were kidnaped by parents who had been unable to obtain custody in a legal forum." *Thompson v. Thompson*, 484 U.S. 174 (1988); *see* Foster and Freed, *Child Snatching and Custodial Fights: The Case for the Uniform Child Custody Jurisdiction Act*, 28 Hastings L.J. 1011 (1977); Bodenheimer, *The Rights of Children and the Crisis In Custody Litigation: Modification of Custody In and Out of State*, 46 U. Colo. L. Rev. 495 (1975); Hudak, *Seize, Run and Sue: The Ignominy of Interstate Child Custody Litigation in American Courts*, 39 Mo. L. Rev. 521 (1974). These abuses continue even today despite the attempts of both state and federal legislators to solve the problems with the statutes discussed below.

[C] State Legislation

THE UNIFORM CHILD CUSTODY JURISDICTION ACT
9 U. L. A. 123 (1988)

. . .

§ 2. [Definitions].

As used in this Act:

. . . .

(5) "home state" means the state in which the child immediately preceding the time involved lived with his parents, a parent, or a person acting as parent, for at least 6 consecutive months, and in the case of a child less than 6 months old the state in which the child lived from birth with any of the persons mentioned. Periods of temporary absence of any of the named persons are counted as part of the 6-month or other period;

. . . .

§ 3 [Jurisdiction]

(a) A court of this State which is competent to decide child custody matters has jurisdiction to make a child custody determination by initial or modification decree if:

    (1) this State (i) is the home state of the child at the time of commencement of the proceeding, or (ii) had been the child's home state within 6 months before commencement of the proceeding and the child is absent from this State because of his removal or retention by a person claiming his custody or for other reasons, and a parent or person acting as parent continues to live in this State; or

    (2) it is in the best interest of the child that a court of this State assume jurisdiction because (i) the child and his parents, or the child and at least one contestant, have a significant connection with this State, and (ii) there is available in this State substantial evidence concerning the child's present or future care, protection, training, and personal relationship; or

    (3) the child is physically present in this State and (i) the child has been abandoned or (ii) it is necessary in an emergency to protect the child because he has been subjected to or threatened with mistreatment or abuse or is otherwise neglected [or dependent]; or

    (4) (i) it appears that no other state would have jurisdiction under prerequisites substantially in accordance with paragraphs (1), (2), or (3), or another state has declined to exercise jurisdiction on the ground that this State is the more appropriate forum to determine the custody of the child, and (ii) it is in the best interest of the child that this court assume jurisdiction.

(b) Except under paragraphs (3) and (4) of subsection (a), physical presence in this State of the child, or of the child and one of the contestants, is not alone sufficient to confer jurisdiction on a court of this State to make a child custody determination.

(c) Physical presence of the child, while desirable, is not a prerequisite for jurisdiction to determine his custody.

. . . .

§ 8 [Jurisdiction Declined by Reason of Conduct].

(a) If the petitioner for an initial decree has wrongfully taken the child from another state or has engaged in similar reprehensible conduct the court may decline to exercise jurisdiction if this is just and proper under the circumstances.

(b) Unless required in the interest of the child, the court shall not exercise its jurisdiction to modify a custody decree of another state if the petitioner, without consent of the person entitled to custody, has improperly removed the child from the physical custody of the person entitled to custody or has improperly retained the child after a visit or other temporary relinquishment of physical custody. If the petitioner has violated any other provision of a custody decree of another state the court may decline to exercise its jurisdiction if this is just and proper under the circumstances.

(c) In appropriate cases a court dismissing a petition under this section may charge the petitioner with necessary travel and other expenses, including attorneys' fees, incurred by other parties or their witnesses. . . .

NOTES AND QUESTIONS

(1) **Public Policy.** The Uniform Child Custody Jurisdiction Act (UCCJA) seeks to implement rather comprehensive goals as set out in § 1 to provide a uniform basis for child custody decisions that is not as inflexible as the old domicile standard, to prevent conflicts between courts in various states, and to prevent relitigation of custody matters by courts other than the one which originally rendered a judgment. Do you see any tension among the goals? For example, is the goal of providing a basis which has some flexibility (so that the best interests of the child in a mobile society can be met) always going to be at odds with the goal of resolving conflicts between courts? Is the balance struck by the legislation the proper one?

(2) **Scope.** UCCJA § 2(1) applies the statute broadly to any "person, including a parent, who claims a right to custody or visitation" and § 2(2) establishes that the Act covers a wide variety of custody proceedings: initial custody, visitation, modification following divorce, and dependency in child neglect cases. A putative father has been included as a parent under the act. *See In re Paternity of R.L.W.*, 643 N.E.2d 367, 369 (Ind. Ct. App. 1994). However a proceeding to terminate parental rights does not fall under the UCCJA.

(3) **Basis of Jurisdiction.** UCCJA §§ 3(a)(1) and (2) play the most important roles in most custody disputes. The "home state" provision of § 3(a)(1) establishes jurisdiction in the vast majority of child custody decisions. "Home state" is defined in § 2(5). The concept of home state in a sense serves as a substitute for domicile, one that is less rigid than domicile but which provides a firmer foundation for jurisdiction than presence. In fact the UCCJA has expressly rejected presence as the sole basis for jurisdiction in § 3(b). Although presence is not required for jurisdiction, when presence does reach six months, presence will trigger a home state determination. In other words home state does not require residence; it is sufficient for the child to be present for six months. *See Hangsleben v. Oliver*, 502 N.W.2d 838, 843 (N.D. 1993). Also a child does not have to be present in a state with a parent; presence with any person acting as a parent is sufficient. For example, living with a grandparent is sufficient. *See Mark L. v. Jennifer S.*, 506 N.Y.S.2d 1020, 1023 (N.Y. Fam. Ct. 1986); *In re B.R.F.*, 669 S.W.2d 240, 245–46 (Mo. Ct. App. 1984).

The "significant connection" test of § 3(a)(2) provides the major alternative to the home-state provision and adds flexibility to the Act. However most interstate custody disputes will be based upon a conflict between the home-state and the significant-connection provision. Although the significant-connection provision is not treated as an exception to the home-state section, it can be used that way. Is this exception too much of a loophole? Won't every parent seeking to establish jurisdiction in a state other than the home state muster all the possible facts to establish a significant connection? And if there is no hearing pending in the home state, won't the forum court have great discretion to adjudge itself the state with significant connections? *See Pomraning v. Pomraning*, 682 S.W.2d 775, 778–79 (Ark. Ct. App. 1985); *Allison v. Superior Court of Los Angeles*, 160 Cal. Rptr. 309, 311–12 (Cal. Ct. App. 1979); *Smith v. Superior Ct. of San Mateo Cty.*, 137 Cal. Rptr. 348, 352–53 (Cal. Ct. App. 1977) (UCCJA concerns subject-matter (child custody) jurisdiction and is not concerned with personal jurisdiction over parents).

(4) **Simultaneous Proceedings.** The UCCJA has several methods of dealing with custody proceedings in other states. Section 6(a) requires a court to refrain from asserting its jurisdiction when there is a proceeding pending in another state as long as that proceeding is based on jurisdictional grounds similar to those in the UCCJA. Section 6(b) requires judges to make inquiries regarding the pendency of another hearing, which must be revealed in filing papers (under § 9), or which may be disclosed by referral to the child custody registry (established by §16), and § 6(c) mandates that a court stay a proceeding when it discovers a proceeding in another state which was already pending. In this situation, the courts should communicate directly with each other and exchange information in order to determine which court should go forward.

The vehicle for determining which court should hear and decide the case is the inconvenient forum provision, § 7. This section uses a multi-factor approach to determine which forum should hear the case. These factors are set out above, but it is worth noting that the "interest" of the child is to be considered. For an example of the application of the multi-factor approach, see *Brossoit v. Brossoit*, 36 Cal. Rptr. 2d 919 (Cal. Ct. App. 1995), in which a California court rejected Tennessee as a more convenient court:

> In the present case, at the time of the hearings in January 1994 the children were 12 and 10 years old, respectively, and had lived with the grandmother for some seven years. They had been in Tennessee less than a year, having lived all the rest of their lives in California. The parents were divorced in California and both remain residents of this state. Until March of 1993, the grandparents also lived in California.
>
> One of the main issues raised by appellant's request for modification of the custody order is appellant's ability to care for the children. In urging Tennessee as the more convenient forum, the grandmother argues that the following witnesses in Tennessee could provide the court with information about the children's present or future care, protection, training and personal relationships: The grandparents with whom the children reside; the children; the children's teachers and athletic coaches; the children's aunts and uncle, who apparently also moved from California to Tennessee; a family friend from California who lived near the grandparents in Tennessee, and the parents of the children's friends. . . . [T]he connections upon which the grandmother relies were established after her removal of the children to Tennessee and their short-term nature renders them insignificant as compared to the connections established with California during the many years all the parties lived in this state.

Id. at 927.

(5) **Wrongful Conduct.** Wrongfully taking a child from another state and improperly removing a child from the custodial parent are both grounds for a court to decline to exercise jurisdiction in § 8, although the court is not bound to do this and indeed is cautioned to decline jurisdiction only where it is "just and proper under the circumstances" for initial decrees in § 8(a) and when the "interest of the child" does not demand the court to exercise its jurisdiction for modifications in § 8(b).

(6) **Out-of-State Judgments and Decrees.** The UCCJA requires the recognition and enforcement of out-of-state custody decrees if they are in substantial compliance with the jurisdiction requirements of the UCCJA in § 13; however, under § 14, the out-of-state decree can be modified if the rendering court no longer has jurisdiction or declines to assume it and the forum state does have jurisdiction.

(7) One of the stated goals of the UCCJA is to create uniformity among the states. All states have adopted the Uniform Child Custody Jurisdiction Act in some form. For a complete listing of the state statutes, consult the Table of Jurisdictions in 9 U. L. A. 115. Consulting this list will lead to the conclusion that the states have greatly modified the act.

(8) For further reading on the aftermath of wide-spread adoption of the UCCJA, see the following: Note, *UCCJA: Coming of Age*, 34 Mercer L. Rev. 861 (1983); Comment, *The Due Process Dilemma of Uniform Child Custody Jurisdiction Act*, 6 Ohio N.U. L. Rev. 586 (1979); Bodenheimer, *Progress Under the Uniform Child Custody Jurisdiction Act and Remaining Problems: Punitive Decrees, Joint Custody, and Excessive Modifications*, 65 Cal. L. Rev. 978 (1977).

MATTER OF CUSTODY OF ROSS
Oregon Supreme Court
630 P.2d 353 (1981)

PETERSON, J.

This case involves the abduction and subsequent concealment of a child by her father in anticipation of pending divorce proceedings in Montana, in order to obtain de facto custody and exclude the mother from any custody. When the present custody action was commenced in May, 1979, the child was a little over three years of age; at the time of her abduction by her father, she was 19 months old. The case squarely presents the problem of determining the jurisdictional limitations that ORS 109.840 section 14 of the Uniform Child Custody Jurisdiction Act (the "UCCJA," or, herein, the "Act") imposes on a forum state in applying the provisions of the Act where modification of a custody decree from another state is involved.

In this opinion we will refer to the parties as "father" and "mother," to the state where the original custody decree was made in this case, Montana as the "decree state," and to the state where modification is sought in this case, Oregon as the "forum state."

We draw upon the opinion of the Court of Appeals for the facts:

The child was born in Billings, Montana, January 19, 1976. Her parents were married [four] months later. The parties separated August 26, 1977. Two days later, while father had the child temporarily in his custody, he left Billings with the child and an 18-year old woman he had known about a month. He married this woman shortly before the Oregon custody hearing.

Mother filed for divorce in Montana on August 30, 1977. Service was made by publication, father's whereabouts being unknown. [Father continued to reside in Montana for nearly two months following the abduction.] Mother was granted a divorce by default and awarded custody of the child on October 26, 1977. Unable to locate the child, mother, in December, 1977, initiated criminal charges against father for custodial interference.

Meanwhile father, his girlfriend and the child had settled in Milton-Freewater, Oregon, in October, 1977. Father had contacted mother to assure her of the child's safety and to tell her he intended to keep the child with him. He was aware the mother was taking steps to gain physical custody of the child, but he made no move to seek lawful custody himself.

Father continued to make occasional phone calls to mother to assure her of the child's welfare, but he never disclosed the child's location. Mother had no knowledge of the child's whereabouts until May 15, 1979, when father was arrested in Milton-Freewater for custodial interference.

Mother then filed this suit in Umatilla County Circuit Court, petitioning for enforcement of the Montana decree. Father's answer prayed the Oregon court to assume jurisdiction and hold a full hearing to determine custody of the child and asked that custody be awarded to him.

Following a hearing on May 18, 1979, the court concluded that Oregon has jurisdiction and that an Oregon court should exercise its jurisdiction and hold a custody hearing. The court denied mother's petition for enforcement of the Montana decree. The custody hearing was held on July 11 and 12, 1979, and on July 23, the court awarded custody of the child to father.

The Court of Appeals affirmed. . . . Because of the public importance of the problems presented by this case and the national recognition being accorded the problem of parental seizure, restraint, concealment and interstate transportation of children with concomitant disregard of court orders and excessive relitigation, because of the harm to children that "seize-and-run" tactics may engender, . . . we granted the mother's petition for review.

DISCUSSION OF PERTINENT SECTIONS OF THE UCCJA

Relevant jurisdictional provisions of the Act include ORS 109.730 and ORS 109.840. ORS 109.730 provides, in part, as follows:

(1) A court of this state which is competent to decide child custody matters has jurisdiction to make a child custody determination by initial or modification decree if:

(a) This state is the home state of the child at the time of commencement of the proceeding, or had been the child's home state within six months before commencement of the proceeding and the child is absent from this state because of his removal or retention by a person claiming his custody or for other reasons, and a parent or person acting as parent continues to live in this state; [or]

(b) It is in the best interest of the child that a court of this state assume jurisdiction because the child and his parents, or the child and at least one contestant, have a significant connection with this state, and there is available in this state substantial evidence concerning the child's present or future care, protection, training, and personal relationships.

It is probably fair to say that the purpose which pervades the Act is to provide that child custody determinations will be made in the state where there is optimum access to evidence. ORS 109.720(1)(c) states that one of the general purposes is to "agree that litigation concerning the custody of a child takes place ordinarily in the state with which the child and his family have the closest connection and where significant evidence concerning his care, protection, training, and personal relationships is most readily available." Consistent with this premise, forum state jurisdiction exists when the forum state is the "home state" of the child at the time of commencement of the proceedings. "Home state" is defined in ORS 109.710(5) as "the state in which the child, immediately preceding the time involved, lived with his parents, a parent, or a person acting as parent, for at least six consecutive months." Therefore, even in cases involving abductions of over six months in length, where the parent has been in the forum state for six months or longer, jurisdiction would exist under ORS 109.730(1)(a) unless barred by another section of the Act. As a corollary, in such cases jurisdiction would seem to exist, as well, under ORS 109.730(1)(b), for with the passage of time, the abducting parent and the child develop "a significant connection" with the state, and "substantial evidence concerning the child's present or future care, protection, training, and personal relationships" thereby becomes available in the state. Therefore, successful long-term concealment following an abduction may result in the vesting of jurisdiction in the forum state under section 3 of the Act, ORS 109.730(1). That was the holding of the trial court and the Court of Appeals in this case (47 Or. App. at 635), and that was the holding of this court in *Settle, supra*, 276 Or. at 759, 764, 767. Here, as in *Settle*, Oregon satisfies the jurisdictional prerequisites of either or both ORS 109.730(1)(a) and (b), and is empowered to act unless the exercise of that modification jurisdiction is prohibited by ORS 109.840(1) or some other section of the Act.

Section 14 of the Act, ORS 109.840, limits the power of a forum state court to modify a custody decree of another state. ORS 109.840(1) provides:

> If a court of another state has made a custody decree, a court of this state shall not modify that decree unless it appears to the court of this state that the court which rendered the decree does not now have jurisdiction under *jurisdictional prerequisites substantially in accordance with ORS 109.700 to 109.930* or has declined to assume jurisdiction to modify the decree and the court of this state has jurisdiction. (Emphasis added.)

Section 14 is designed to attain the general purpose set forth in ORS 109.720(1)(a) (to avoid jurisdictional competition and conflict) and to deter abduction of children, ORS 109.720(1)(e).

The trial court apparently concluded that jurisdiction existed solely by virtue of ORS 109.730 because Oregon had a "more substantial connection" than Montana. The Court of Appeals, however, considered ORS 109.840(1) and decided this case consistent with the ruling in *Settle, supra*. We turn then to a discussion of the modification jurisdiction of the Montana courts under ORS 109.840(1) in May of 1979, "under jurisdictional prerequisites substantially in accordance with [the Act]."

CONTINUING JURISDICTION OF DECREE STATE WHERE CHILD IS IMPROPERLY REMOVED AND CONCEALED

Even though father removed the child prior to the time mother filed her suit, there is no dispute that the child was improperly retained, and there is no claim that the Montana court lacked jurisdiction to enter its initial decree. Apart from section 3 of the Act (ORS 109.730(1)), in May of 1979 Montana would probably have had jurisdiction to modify its decree. It had jurisdiction at the time the original decree was entered. All parties resided there at the time the complaint was filed. The mother continued to reside there, and Montana has an interest in maintaining the integrity of its decree. But in determining whether Montana has jurisdiction under the Act we do not look alone to historical standards of procedural due process. The issue now before us whether Oregon has modification jurisdiction under ORS 109.730(1)(a) and/or (1)(b) depends upon whether Montana, in May of 1979, continued to have jurisdiction "under jurisdictional prerequisites substantially in accordance with [the Act]." Montana has adopted the UCCJA. It became effective on July 1, 1977.

Although the term "in the best interest of the child" is used in ORS 107.730(1)(b) and R.C.M. 40-4-211(1)(b) as one jurisdictional premise for initial or modification jurisdiction to exist under the Act, the determinative factors under ORS 109.730(1)(b) and R.C.M. 40-4-211(1)(b) actually are these:

   1. The child, and at least one contestant must have a significant connection with the state whose jurisdiction is at issue; and

   2. There must be available, in the state whose jurisdiction is at issue, "substantial evidence concerning the child's present or future care, protection, training, and personal relationships."

Therefore, in determining whether Montana continued to have jurisdiction "under jurisdictional prerequisites substantially in accordance with the [Act]," we look at those two factors, as they relate to Montana.

As to the second factor, the evidence shows that the child had lived in Billings since birth, the child's mother had lived there since 1967, both the mother and father were employed in Billings, and they lived together with the child and her older sister following the child's birth until the child's abduction. There is substantial evidence in Montana concerning the type of care, training and love given to this child by both parents while the child was in Montana, and the record shows that evidence is available from other persons in Montana relative to the parental attitudes toward the child. Furthermore, evidence is available in Montana of the father's and mother's character, and finally, the record shows that there was substantial evidence in Montana as to the child's medical history.

The more difficult problem is to determine if the first requirement is met, whether "the child and at least one contestant, have a significant connection with [Montana]." There is no question as to the relationship between the "one contestant" the mother and Montana. She continues to live there, in the same home as when the child was with her, and continues to work in Montana. So far as the mother is concerned, clearly Montana is the state with which she has the most significant connection.

But did the child, in May of 1979, continue to have a significant connection with Montana? Although the child then lived in Oregon, and although the child's father was in Oregon, it cannot be said that Montana lacked any connection with the child. The mother still lived there, and the relationship between mother and child is itself a significant one. Beyond that, although the child was forcibly removed at an early age, the child had other significant connections with the state. Her older sister continued to reside in the family home with the mother, and other friends and neighbors, who had also been involved in the child's upbringing also continued to live nearby.

It is clear from the purposes set forth in the Uniform Act, ORS 109.720, and from the commentary to the Act, that the framers aimed to deter abduction of children, so as to prevent the proliferation of custody jurisdiction in the cases of abducted children. It could not have been intended that unilateral removal of the child results in the deprivation of decree state jurisdiction upon the expiration of six months (the time necessary for a new state to become the "home state" of the child). Yet, it is inescapable that, with the passage of each day, the relationship of the abducted child to the decree state becomes a little less substantial. Ultimately, perhaps, decree state jurisdiction would cease to exist under ORS 109.730(1)(b). However, we remain convinced that we should construe the Act in favor of decree state jurisdiction for a reasonable period of time following the abduction of the child. We therefore conclude that Montana, in May of 1979, continued to have jurisdiction "under jurisdictional prerequisites substantially in accordance with [the Act]," and that Oregon therefore could not modify the Montana decree, ORS 109.840(1).

It is never in the best interest of the child to be subjected to the turmoil and disruption that often attends custody abduction schemes perpetrated by warring parents. Rather, it is in the child's best interest that courts act as strongly as possible to discourage such child abusive actions. On the interrelationship of ORS 109.730 and ORS 109.840(1) (sections 3 and 14 of the Act), the Reporter for the Act stated:

> The Uniform Act gives jurisdiction to the child's "home state", defined as the state in which the child has resided for the preceding six months. When a child stays in a state for six months or more as a visitor or a victim of abduction, the question arises whether the new state has power to modify the custody decree. The answer is that the Act does not permit the second state to take jurisdiction because the paramount jurisdiction of the prior state continues. Section 3 of the Act, the basic provision on subject matter jurisdiction, must be read in conjunction with section 14, which does not permit modifications by another state as long as the prior state's exclusive jurisdiction continues. This is true whether or not another state has technically become the child's home state. Any other reading of the Act would subvert its purposes by permitting a kidnapper to go into hiding for 6 months and then seek modification, and by encouraging a visited parent to prolong the period of visitation with or without consent of the custodial parent in order to seek modification in the visited state. *The Act does not support an interpretation which would encourage the very evils the Commissioners on Uniform State Laws intended to eradicate.*

(Emphasis added; footnotes omitted.)[2]

"Child-snatching" has become a serious societal problem. The literature, lay literature as well as legal literature, is filled with reports of angry parents who, afraid of losing custody of their children and encouraged by state laws, take matters into their own hands, often with disastrous consequences to the children. In many states child-snatching is not regarded as a crime, and the parent whose child is abducted by the other parent often gets little or no help from law enforcement authorities in locating the abducted child or children.

We believe that this holding is within the clear meaning of the Act, helps to attain the goals listed above, and will further one of the main purposes of the Act, without doing violence to other purposes of the Act.

We should (and do) emphasize that our holding in this case is limited to its facts. Perhaps a case will one day arise when the abduction has been of such a long duration and the child of such an advanced age that the decree state would cease to have jurisdiction under

---

[2] Bodenheimer, *Progress Under the Uniform Child Custody Jurisdiction Act and Remaining Problems: Punitive Decrees, Joint Custody, and Excessive Modifications*, 65 Cal. L. Rev. 978, 988 (1977).

section 14, ORS 109.840(1). An abduction and concealment of but 21 months does not divest the decree state of jurisdiction. Any other holding "[puts] a premium upon an improper removal of Children from their state of original residence." . . .

Reversed and remanded with instructions to (1) vacate the order denying mother's petition for enforcement of the Montana decree, (2) vacate the July 23, 1979, decree of custody determination, and (3) enter a decree recognizing and enforcing the Montana decree pursuant to ORS 109.830 (including the immediate transfer of physical custody of the child to mother).

Costs to mother.

NOTES AND QUESTIONS

(1) **The Significant-Connection/Substantial-Evidence Test.** More often than not the significant-connection/substantial-evidence test of § 3(a)(2) is used to expand the number of forums that may have jurisdiction. Some courts have taken an extremely broad view of UCCJA § 3(a)(2), placing the greatest emphasis on the substantial evidence which is in the forum state. *See, e.g., Allison v. Superior Court of Los Angeles Cty.*, 160 Cal. Rptr. 309, 311–12 (Cal. Ct. App. 1979); *Schlumpf v. Superior Court of Cty. of Trinity*, 145 Cal. Rptr. 190, 193–95 (Cal. Ct. App. 1978).

(2) **Wrongful Conduct.** Should subsection 8(a) have played a greater role in *Ross*? In subsection 8(a), what does "wrongfully taken the child" mean? Can a parent who has physical custody of a child, where there is no outstanding award of custody to the other parent, wrongfully take his or her child? Does it make a difference if the child is hidden from the other parent? In *Morgan v. Morgan*, 666 P.2d 1026, 1029 (Alaska 1983), the Supreme Court of Alaska held that Virginia had properly exercised jurisdiction under the act where it had not declined jurisdiction and where a father had taken the child from Washington during a period in which there was no court order pending; the father had not "wrongfully" transported the children from Washington to Virginia. Custody proceedings were not instituted until after the father returned to Virginia. Thus, at the time he left Washington with the children, no court had taken jurisdiction over the dispute, and both parents were equally entitled to custody. The father's conduct was therefore not "wrongful." However, the Alaska Supreme Court did decline jurisdiction where the mother dismissed a custody action in another state in order to avoid loss of custody due to a temporary order. *See Stokes v. Stokes*, 751 P.2d 1363, 1365–66 (Alaska 1988).

(3) **Continuing Jurisdiction.** One issue created by the UCCJA involves the continuing jurisdiction of the decree-granting state. In *Ross*, the court had to resort to the significant-connection/substantial-evidence test simply because there is no specific provision for Montana to have continuing jurisdiction. It is clear that the decree-granting state does not have continuing jurisdiction where all the parties have moved out of the jurisdiction and the child has a new home state. *See Nelson v. Nelson*, 910 P. 2d. 319, 321 (N.M. 1995). However, what happens when there is a new home state, but one parent still lives in the decree-granting state? Some courts have said that the decree-granting state must affirmatively reserve continuing jurisdiction. *See Manley v. Hoag*, 917 P.2d 1011, 1013–14 (Okla. Ct. App. 1996). However, other courts have found continuing jurisdiction implicitly in the UCCJA. The court in the following case is a good example of the latter.

GREENLAW v. SMITH
Supreme Court of Washington
869 P.2d 1024 (1994)

ANDERSEN, CHIEF JUSTICE.

FACTS OF CASE

This is a child custody dispute. The mother, who is custodian of the child, challenges the subject matter jurisdiction of a Washington trial court to modify its own custody decree once the child and custodian have moved from the state of Washington and established a new "home state" under the Uniform Child Custody Jurisdiction Act, RCW 26.27.

Rosemary B. Greenlaw (the mother) and Daniel Smith, III (the father) were married in January 1978. Their son, Alexander Geoffrey Smith (Alex), the child who is the subject of this proceeding, was born October 14, 1978. He is now 15 years old. The marriage was dissolved on March 11, 1982, when Alex was 3 1/2 years old. Under the decree of dissolution, the mother was granted custody of the child and the father apparently was granted reasonable visitation.

The parents have a history of conflict which is reflected in the Pierce County Superior Court dissolution file. Correspondence between the parents apparently was regularly copied to the court file following the dissolution.

In May of 1985, the mother accepted a 3-year job assignment with the United States Army in Frankfurt, Germany. The mother's job required her to travel frequently and she placed Alex in a German-speaking boarding school for 3 years, from approximately age 7 to age 10. During this time Alex saw his mother only irregularly on weekends and on holidays.

In 1988, Alex and his mother returned to the United States and began living in California, and Alex resumed regular visitation with his father in Tacoma. From 1988 to 1990, Alex and his mother moved four times; Alex attended three different schools during that 2-year period. In 1990, the mother began attending law school in San Jose and Alex spent the school year living with his mother's former boyfriend in Berkeley, California. During the 1990–91 school year, Alex apparently saw his mother on weekends and saw his father during school vacation periods.

While Alex was in Tacoma with his father during visits in 1990 and 1991, the child began seeing a counselor who ultimately recommended a change in custody from the mother to the father. The counselor concluded:

> In summary, the emotional and mental needs of Alex, including needs of warmth, love, nurturing, caring and involvement in the social, cultural and family development have not been met or provided by his mother in the years that she has been charged with the custodial relationship of Alex. Similarly, these needs have not been met by the surrogate caretakers which Alex's mother has placed him with during several of these years. Alex has inappropriately been put in the position of self-parenting as a result of the neglect and virtual parental abandonment by his mother, his custodial parent. This situation is injurious to Alex and in my opinion there is an immediate need for corrective intervention to avoid additional injury and to assist Alex in a program of normal childhood development.

. . .

In July of 1991, the father filed a petition in the Pierce County Superior Court, asking that he be granted custody of Alex.

The mother responded by asking the court to decline jurisdiction over the matter and to transfer the case to the State of California, claiming California more properly had jurisdiction to determine the issues.

The superior court commissioner set the matter for hearing and appointed a guardian ad litem to investigate the request for modification. The hearing on the mother's motion was held after the guardian ad litem had filed his initial report and after the commissioner had interviewed the child in chambers. The commissioner, in an order entered September 20, 1991: (1) determined that it had jurisdiction to hear the case because Washington had significant contacts with the child and because an emergency existed; and (2) changed the residential placement of the child pending a final hearing on the father's petition.

Following entry of the commissioner's order, the mother moved to revise the decision with respect to the jurisdictional issues. The motion for revision was denied by the Superior Court on December 13, 1991, and the mother appealed. The Court of Appeals reversed, holding that Washington did not have subject matter jurisdiction. We reverse the Court of Appeals. . . .

The principal issue in this appeal is whether a Washington court has continuing jurisdiction to modify its own decree after the child and custodial parent move away from Washington and establish a new "home state", but while the noncustodial parent continues to live in Washington and the child continues to have some connection with this state. . . .

Our resolution of this issue depends on an analysis of two laws, (1) the UCCJA, RCW 26.27 (hereinafter the Act), a uniform law that has been adopted by all 50 states and the District of Columbia, and (2) the Federal Parental Kidnaping Prevention Act of 1980. 28 U.S.C.§1738A.

The UCCJA was a response to an increasing tendency of courts to assert jurisdiction over the custody of children within their state's borders, without regard to the length of time the children lived within the state and without regard to the quality of contacts the children had with the state.

The Act . . . sets forth the bases upon which a court may initially assume jurisdiction to enter a custody order. The Washington Act provides: . . . [The court quotes the provision which is the same as § 3 of the Uniform Custody Jurisdiction Act reprinted above.]

These bases for assuming jurisdiction are not so much a grant of jurisdiction as they are a limitation upon a court's assumption of jurisdiction. When a court is asked to modify an existing custody decree, the above quoted section is to be read in light of the additional restrictions contained in RCW 26.27.140 (UCCJA§14).

RCW 26.27.140 provides:

> (1) If a court of another state has made a custody decree, a court of this state shall not modify that decree unless (a) it appears to the court of this state that the court which rendered the decree does not now have jurisdiction under jurisdictional prerequisites substantially in accordance with this chapter or has declined to assume jurisdiction to modify the decree and (b) the court of this state has jurisdiction . . . .

The official comment to the parallel section in the UCCJA states:

> Courts which render a custody decree normally retain continuing jurisdiction to modify the decree under local law. Courts in other states have in the past often assumed jurisdiction to modify the out-of-state decree themselves without regard to the preexisting jurisdiction of the other state. In order to achieve greater stability of custody arrangements and avoid forum shopping, subsection (a) declares that other states will defer to the continuing jurisdiction of the court of another state as long as that state has jurisdiction under the standards of this Act. *In other words, all petitions for modification are to be addressed to the prior state if that state has sufficient contact with the case to satisfy section 3. The fact that the court had previously considered the case may be one factor favoring its continued jurisdiction. If, however, all the persons involved have moved away or the contact with the state has otherwise become slight, modification jurisdiction would shift elsewhere.*

(Citations omitted. Italics ours.) UCCJA §14, comment, 9 U.L.A. 292 (pt. 1) (1988).

Although all states are bound to the same jurisdictional mandates, there has been considerable confusion about which of two or more states has authority to act when a state is asked to modify its own custody decree or the custody decree of another state.

Professor Clark writes:

> With advent of the UCCJA . . . the analysis of the continuing jurisdiction problem has changed but the uncertainty and unpredictability of result in the case law has not been reduced. Although the problem was recognized by all who dealt with interstate custody, for some unexplained reason it was not explicitly covered by the UCCJA. The crucial section of that Act is section 14 . . . . The language of this section must of course be construed with the statutory purposes in mind, particularly those purposes related to the avoidance of the re-litigation of custody disputes and to the elimination of continuing controversies over custody. The Commissioners' Comments to section 14 assert that in order to achieve those purposes petitions for modification must be submitted to the state rendering the initial decree so long as that state meets the requirements for jurisdiction imposed by section 3 of the Act. Unfortunately those requirements are often so difficult to apply to specific situations that the Commissioners' precepts are not helpful in most instances.

(Footnotes omitted.) 1 H. Clark, Jr., Domestic Relations in the United States §13.5, at 808–09 (2d ed. 1987).

Professor Donigan states:

> The Commissioners' Note to section 14 of the UCCJA indicates the original state must satisfy section 3 in order to have continuing jurisdiction. This requirement usually involves an inquiry into whether the original state is still the home state, and if not, whether it has lost significant connections with the child. The Note[s] to section 14 specify that the first state loses its continuing jurisdiction once "all the persons involved have moved away or the contact with the state has otherwise become slight . . . ." While it has generally been accepted that the decree state loses its jurisdiction once all parties have moved away, the troublesome question is whether the decree state loses its jurisdiction prior to that time. . . .

> The Act was intended to create exclusive continuing jurisdiction in the decree state, but the interpretations of continuing jurisdiction have been . . . inconsistent . . . .

(Footnotes omitted . . . .) Donigan, Child Custody Jurisdiction: New Legislation Reflects Public Policy Against Parental Abduction, 19 Gonz. L. Rev. 1, 15–18 (1983–1984).

Professor Bodenheimer, a draftsman of and the reporter for the UCCJA, in an often quoted explanation of section 14 of the Act, states:

> In other words, the continuing jurisdiction of the prior court is exclusive. Other states do not have jurisdiction to modify the decree. They must respect and defer to the prior state's continuing jurisdiction. Section 14 is the key provision which carries out the Act's two objectives of (1) preventing the harm done to children by shifting them from state to state to relitigate custody, and (2) preventing jurisdictional conflict between the states after a custody decree has been rendered. . . .
>
> Exclusive continuing jurisdiction is not affected by the child's residence in another state for six months or more. Although the new state becomes the child's home state, significant connection jurisdiction continues in the state of the prior decree where the court record and other evidence exists and where one parent or another contestant continues to reside. Only when the child and all parties have moved away is deference to another state's continuing jurisdiction no longer required.

(Footnote omitted.) Bodenheimer, Interstate Custody: Initial Jurisdiction and Continuing Jurisdiction under the UCCJA, 14 Fam. L.Q. 203, 214–15 (1981). . . .

In part because of the confusion resulting from conflicting state court decisions regarding child custody jurisdiction, Congress enacted the Parental Kidnaping Prevention Act of 1980 (PKPA), 28 U.S.C.§1738A. The PKPA requires states to give full faith and credit to the custody decrees of other states which are consistent with the federal law. The PKPA also attempts to more clearly limit the circumstances under which a court may modify the custody decree of another state. In addition to the jurisdictional bases set forth in section 3 of the UCCJA, the federal law includes the following basis:

> The jurisdiction of a court of a State which has made a child custody determination consistently with the provisions of this section continues as long as the requirement of subsection (c)(1) of this section continues to be met and such State remains the residence of the child or of any contestant. 28 U.S.C.§1738A(d).

Subsection (c)(1), which is referred to, requires that a state have jurisdiction to modify a custody decree under that state's own laws.

The PKPA should be considered whenever the court is asked to determine which of two or more states has jurisdiction to decide a custody dispute.

Much of the confusion generated by the language of the two laws can be eliminated if a trial court which is asked to determine custody clearly distinguishes between jurisdiction to determine the initial custody of a child and jurisdiction to modify a prior custody order.

In the present case that distinction was not made. The trial court and the Court of Appeals both failed to consider the presumption created by the UCCJA and the PKPA that the decree state—Washington—had continuing jurisdiction to modify its own order and other states must decline to modify until the decree state loses or declines jurisdiction.

It appears that the majority of appellate courts which have addressed the issue presented here hold that the state in which the initial decree was entered has exclusive continuing jurisdiction to modify the initial decree if: (1) one of the parents continues to reside in the decree state; and (2) the child continues to have some connection with the decree state, such as visitation.

We agree that this approach best advances the purposes of the law and provides the most security for children who are subject to these decrees.

We now apply this law to the present case. Washington is the decree state and the father continues to reside in Washington. There is no dispute that Washington had jurisdiction to enter the initial decree. Washington law provides that a custody decree may be modified under certain circumstances.

The remaining question is whether Alex has continued to have a sufficient connection with the State of Washington to result in continuing jurisdiction over his welfare. We conclude that he has. First, the Pierce County Superior Court file reflects the correspondence between the parents for a number of years, and reflects the history of this litigation. Second, the child has had consistent visits with his father when the child has been in the United States. Third, the child's extended family on both the mother's side and the father's side, live in Washington in the Tacoma area. Fourth, the child's counselor at the time the petition was filed is in Washington. Fifth, Alex, at age 15, is mature enough to have an opinion about his custody and has expressed that he wants to live with his father. Substantial evidence regarding the child's future care, education, social development and family and other personal relationships exists in the state of Washington. Thus the child's contact with the state of Washington continues to be more than slight. . . .

Interpreting the UCCJA to allow an automatic shift in modification jurisdiction simply because a child establishes a new home state would not further the purposes of the Act as it would permit forum shopping and instability of custody decrees.

We thus interpret the UCCJA and PKPA to mean that jurisdiction to modify a custody decree continues with the decree state so long as: (1) that state's decree is entered in compliance with the UCCJA and PKPA; (2) one of the parents or other contestants continues to reside in the decree state; and (3) the child continues to have more than slight contact with the decree state. The child's continued visitation with the parent who remains in the decree state may constitute more than slight contact with the decree state. . . .

The Court of Appeals is reversed and the case is remanded for trial on the merits. . . .

NOTES AND QUESTIONS

(1) **Continuing Jurisdiction Revisited.** If you were to read the UCCJA and interpret it according to the plain meaning of the words used in the text and without the benefit of the scholars quoted in *Greenlaw*, would you reach the same conclusion as the court in *Greenlaw* regarding the continuing jurisdiction of the decree-granting state?

(2) **The Uniform Child Custody Jurisdiction and Enforcement Act.** In the summer of 1997, the National Conference of Commissioners On Uniform State Laws completed a new version of the UCCJA called the Uniform Child Custody Jurisdiction and Enforcement Act (UCCJEA). The expanded name takes into account the NCCUSL's addition of

provisions of the Uniform Child Visitation Act. At the time of this writing the UCCJEA has not been presented to the state legislatures. A summary of the proposed UCCJEA is available at <http://www.nccusl.org/summary/uccjea.html>.

Here are two of the most significant changes.

(a) *Jurisdiction.* The UCCJEA adopts the position of the PKPA, in which the significant-connection/substantial-evidence test is used only where there is no home state:

> SECTION 201. INITIAL CHILD-CUSTODY JURISDICTION
>
> (a) Except as otherwise provided in Section 204, a court of this State has jurisdiction to make an initial child-custody determination only if:
>
> > (1) this State is the home State of the child on the date of the commencement of the proceeding, or was the home State of the child within six months before the commencement of the proceeding and the child is absent from this State but a parent or person acting as a parent continues to live in this State;
> >
> > (2) a court of another State does not have jurisdiction under paragraph (1), or a court of the home State of the child has declined to exercise jurisdiction on the ground that this State is the more appropriate forum under Section 207 or 208, and:
> >
> > > (A) the child and the child's parents, or the child and at least one parent or a person acting as a parent, have a significant connection with this State other than mere physical presence; and
> > >
> > > (B) substantial evidence is available in this State concerning the child's care, protection, training, and personal relationships;
>
> . . . .

It is worthy of note that this provision also is entitled "Initial Child-Custody Jurisdiction," perhaps in order to distinguish it from a proposed modification of an existing order.

(b) *Continuing Jurisdiction.* The UCCJEA also clarifies the issue of continuing jurisdiction by expressly providing that the state which has made the initial custody determination should have continuing jurisdiction at least until all parties and the child are removed from that state:

> SECTION 202. EXCLUSIVE, CONTINUING JURISDICTION
>
> (a) Except as otherwise provided in Section 204, a court of this State which has made a child-custody determination consistent with Section 201 or 203 has exclusive, continuing jurisdiction over the determination until:
>
> > (1) a court of this State determines that neither the child, the child's parents, and any person acting as a parent do not have a significant connection with this State and that substantial evidence is no longer available in this State concerning the child's care, protection, training, and personal relationships; or
> >
> > (2) a court of this State or a court of another State determines that the child, the child's parents, and any person acting as a parent do not presently reside in this State.

(b) A court of this State which has made a child-custody determination and does not have exclusive, continuing jurisdiction under this section may modify that determination only if it has jurisdiction to make an initial determination under Section 201.

---

(3) **Problem.** Mary and David married in the state of Washington in 1986. Shortly thereafter they purchased a home in Washington near Mary's parents. They had two children, Erika in 1988 and Dennis in 1990. Unfortunately Mary developed a drug problem, subsequently losing interest in her family and her marriage. After many attempts to help Mary, David gave up on the marriage.

In 1994, he moved to Arizona, where his family was located, and took the children with him. In Arizona he enrolled the kids in school and got a new job. David waited a year to see if Mary would turn her life around, but, when she did not, he went ahead with the divorce, which was granted in 1995. Mary did not oppose the custody settlement which David offered. He would have legal and physical custody and she would have visitation for 2 months each summer starting in 1996 if she successfully completed a drug rehabilitation program. This agreement was incorporated into the Arizona decree.

Six months later David remarried to a woman with three kids. David and his new wife moved with their kids to a new home in Arizona. Mary, realizing that she might lose contact with her children, entered the drug rehabilitation program and completely turned her life around.

When the summer of 1998 came, Mary was ready for the kids. She was off drugs and working part time. She was receiving additional support from her parents and living in the family home in Washington. Things had gone so well for her that she asked David if she could have the kids for three months. He agreed to this request because there was some tension between the combined families in Arizona.

After the kids arrived in Washington, they moved into their old bedrooms, renewed all their old acquaintances, and spent many hours with their maternal grandparents. They started going back to their old church and enrolled in summer programs at their old school. By the end of summer the kids were genuinely ambivalent about returning to Arizona. They missed their father and their paternal grandparents, but they really liked being in Washington. If pressed, Erika would say that she would prefer to be with her father, but Dennis would say that he wanted to stay with his mother.

One week before the kids were scheduled to return to their father, Mary brought an action in Washington to modify the Arizona child custody order so that the children would live with her during the school year and have three months visitation with their father in the summer. Mary alleged that the changed circumstances were her drug rehabilitation and David's remarriage. At the time she brought the action she requested temporary custody pending the court's decision following a hearing. Temporary custody, pending a hearing, was granted ex parte, and Mary enrolled the children in school.

David challenges the jurisdiction of the Washington court. Both Washington and Arizona have adopted the UCCJA. Can the Washington court assert jurisdiction? If it can, should the court do so? If the Washington court modifies custody as Mary requests, will the court of Arizona have jurisdiction to modify the Washington judgment if the next summer David brings an action to modify there? Will the significant connections with Arizona be any less than they were with Washington?

[D] Federal Legislation

PARENTAL KIDNAPPING PREVENTION ACT OF 1980

28 U.S.C. § 1738A

§ 1738A. Full faith and credit given to child custody determinations.

(a) . . .

(b) As used in this section, the term—

   . . .

    (4) "home State" means the State in which, immediately preceding the time involved, the child lived with his parents, a parent, or a person acting as parent, for at least six consecutive months, and in the case of a child less than six months old, the State in which the child lived from birth with any of such persons. Periods of temporary absence of any of such persons are counted as part of the six-month or other period;

   . . .

(c) A child custody determination made by a court of a State is consistent with the provisions of this section only if—

    (1) such court has jurisdiction under the law of such State; and

    (2) one of the following conditions is met:

        (A) such State (i) is the home State of the child on the date of the commencement of the proceeding, or (ii) had been the child's home State within six months before the date of the commencement of the proceeding and the child is absent from such State because of his removal or retention by a contestant or for other reasons, and a contestant continues to live in such State;

        (B) (i) it appears that no other State would have jurisdiction under subparagraph (A), and (ii) it is in the best interest of the child that a court of such State assume jurisdiction because (i) the child and his parents, or the child and at least one contestant, have a significant connection with such State other than mere physical presence in such State, and (ii) there is available in such State substantial evidence concerning the child's present or future care, protection, training, and personal relationships;

        (C) the child is physically present in such State and (i) the child has been abandoned, or (ii) it is necessary in an emergency to protect the child because he has been subjected to or threatened with mistreatment or abuse;

        (D) (i) it appears that no other State would have jurisdiction under subparagraph (A), (B), (C), or (E), or another State has declined to exercise jurisdiction on the ground that the State whose jurisdiction is in issue is the more appropriate forum to determine the custody of the child, and (ii) it is in the best interest of the child that such court assume jurisdiction; or

    (E) the court has continuing jurisdiction pursuant to subsection (d) of this section.

(d) The jurisdiction of a court of a State which has made a child custody determination consistently with the provisions of this section continues as long as the requirement of subsection (c)(1) of this section continues to be met and such State remains the residence of the child or of any contestant. . . .

NOTES AND QUESTIONS

(1) **Creation.** When the PKPA was first drafted, only about half the states had adopted UCCJA, and when it was becoming apparent that the states were adopting it with variation which could lead to inconsistent results. *See* Coombs, *Nuts and Bolts of the PKPA*, 22 Colo. Law. 2397 (1993). By the time PKPA was adopted, 43 states had adopted UCCJA in some form. *See* Goldstein, *The Tragedy of the Interstate Child: A Critical Reexamination of the Uniform Child Custody Jurisdiction Act and the Parental Kidnaping Prevention Act*, 25 U.C. Davis L. Rev. 845 (1992). This federal legislation was also revolutionary because family law had traditionally been the domain of the states. *See* Coombs, *Progress under the PKPA*, 6 J. Am. Acad. Matrim. Law 59 (1990)

(2) **Policy.** The stated purposes of the Parental Kidnapping Prevention Act, similar to § 1 of the UCCJA, are not included in the code itself but rather are included with other legislative documents contained in the "Historical and Statutory Notes" following the statute:

    (c)(1) promote cooperation between State courts to the end that a determination of custody and visitation is rendered in the State which can best decide the case in the interest of the child;

    (2) promote and expand the exchange of information and other forms of mutual assistance between States which are concerned with the same child;

    (3) facilitate the enforcement of custody and visitation decrees of sister States;

    (4) discourage continuing interstate controversies over child custody in the interest of greater stability of home environment and of secure family relationships for the child;

    (5) avoid jurisdictional competition and conflict between State courts in matters of child custody and visitation which have in the past resulted in the shifting of children from State to State with harmful effects on their well-being; and

    (6) deter interstate abductions and other unilateral removals of children undertaken to obtain custody and visitation awards.

(3) **Jurisdiction.** Subsection (c)(2) contains the provisions dealing with jurisdiction which are substantially the same as the provisions of UCCJA § 3, with one very important difference. Under the PKPA the significant-connection/substantial-evidence test only comes

into play if there is no home state. This greatly limits the possibility that two states can have jurisdiction at the same time.

(4) **Clean Hands.** While the PKPA, like UCCJA, prohibits jurisdiction where there is a pending case in another forum which has jurisdiction under the Act, the PKPA does not have a provision preventing the exercise of jurisdiction where the child has been wrongfully taken. However, this clean hands criterion for denying jurisdiction may still be valid under the UCCJA. In *Patricia R. v. Andrew W.*, 121 Misc. 2d 103, 467 N.Y.S.2d 322, 325–26 (Fam. Ct. 1983), the court applied section 7 regarding inconvenient forum of the UCCJA in a case covered by the PKPA despite the fact that PKPA did not have a similar provision.

(5) **Modification.** The PKPA controls the issue of whether a court must enforce a judgment rather than modify it. Under the PKPA, subsection (a) requires a court to enforce rather than modify a custody judgment of another state, unless the special requirements of subsection (f) are met. Subsection (f) allows modification where the court "has jurisdiction to make such a child custody determination" and "the court of the other State no longer has jurisdiction, or . . . has declined to exercise such jurisdiction to modify such determination." Although this provision will be controlling, it is not significantly different from UCCJA § 14(a) as adopted by most states.

(6) **Federal Cause of Action.** In *Thompson v. Thompson*, 484 U.S. 174, 187 (1988), the United States Supreme Court dealt with an argument that PKPA created a cause of action in federal court:

> In sum, the context, language, and history of the PKPA together make out a conclusive case against inferring a cause of action in federal court to determine which of two conflicting state custody decrees is valid. Against this impressive evidence, petitioner relies primarily on the argument that failure to infer a cause of action would render the PKPA nugatory. We note, as a preliminary response, that ultimate review remains available in this Court for truly intractable jurisdictional deadlocks. In addition, the unspoken presumption in petitioner's argument is that the States are either unable or unwilling to enforce the provisions of the Act. This is a presumption we are not prepared, and more importantly, Congress was not prepared, to indulge. State courts faithfully administer the Full Faith and Credit Clause every day; now that Congress has extended full faith and credit requirements to child custody orders, we can think of no reason why the courts' administration of federal law in custody disputes will be any less vigilant. Should state courts prove as obstinate as petitioner predicts, Congress may choose to revisit the issue. But any more radical approach to the problem will have to await further legislative action; we "will not engraft a remedy on a statute, no matter how salutary, that Congress did not intend to provide." . . .

ATKINS v. ATKINS
Supreme Court of Arkansas.
823 S.W.2d 816 (1992)

DUDLEY, JUSTICE.

We have accepted appellate jurisdiction of this case because it is a significant case involving the construction and interpretation of state and federal statutes setting out the jurisdictional requirements for interstate child custody disputes, and additionally, it involves interpretation of the federal statute which sets out the requirements for according full faith and credit to a foreign child custody decree. In interpreting the applicable statutes, we affirm the Chancellor's refusal to accord full faith and credit to a foreign custody decree.

Appellant Linda Atkins and appellee Sterling Atkins were married on December 27, 1985, in Linda's hometown of Bastrop, Louisiana, and immediately returned to Sterling's hometown of Hamburg, Arkansas, where they resided until they were separated. Bastrop, Louisiana, and Hamburg, Arkansas, are only thirty (30) miles apart. The couple had one child, Lindsey, who was born in a Bastrop hospital on December 29, 1989.

On August 15, 1990, while still living in Hamburg, the mother, Linda, and the father, Sterling, separated, and the mother took the child to her parent's home in Bastrop. On August 28, 1990, she filed a petition for separation in Morehouse Parish, Louisiana, the Parish in which Bastrop is located. On September 4, 1990, service of process was had on the father under the Louisiana long-arm statute.

Three days later, on September 7, 1990, the father filed a suit for divorce in the Chancery Court of Ashley County, Arkansas, which is the County in which Hamburg is located. Service of process was had on the mother under the Arkansas long-arm statute on October 22, 1990.

On October 11, 1990, a hearing was held in the Louisiana proceeding. The father objected to the jurisdiction of the Louisiana court and requested a stay of the proceedings. The trial court overruled the father's objections and heard the case on its merits. The trial court awarded temporary custody of the child to the mother and ordered the father to pay temporary alimony and child support. The father appealed to the Court of Appeal of Louisiana. The appellate court reversed that part of the decree that ordered the father to pay temporary alimony and child support because they found there was no personal jurisdiction over him. The father did not appeal from the award of custody of the child to the mother.

On November 13, 1990, the mother moved to dismiss the proceeding in Ashley County, Arkansas, because Ark. Code Ann. § 9–13–206(a) (Repl.1991), which is a part of the Uniform Child Custody Jurisdictional Act (UCCJA) as adopted by the Arkansas General Assembly, provides:

> A court of this state shall not exercise its jurisdiction under this subchapter if at the time of filing the petition a proceeding concerning the custody of the child was pending in a court of another state exercising jurisdiction substantially in conformity with this subchapter, unless the proceeding is stayed by the court of the other state because this state is a more appropriate forum or for other reasons.

On February 12, 1991, the Arkansas trial court denied the mother's motion to dismiss and on March 25, 1991, refused to accord full faith and credit to the Louisiana decree, granted the father a divorce, and awarded custody of the child to the father, with the right of visitation being granted to the mother. The mother subsequently filed this appeal.

The mother argues that the Louisiana proceeding was never stayed, and therefore, the Arkansas trial court exercised jurisdiction in violation of Ark. Code Ann.§ 9–13–206(a), quoted above. She admits that the quoted statute is a part of the UCCJA and that, under it, the Arkansas court could exercise jurisdiction if the Louisiana court had not acted "substantially in conformity" with the UCCJA. (Both Louisiana and Arkansas have adopted the identical uniform act. See La. Rev. Stat. Ann. § 13:1700–1724 (1983) & Ark.Code Ann. § 9–13–203 to–27 (Repl. 1991)). But, she argues, the Louisiana court acted substantially in conformity with UCCJA, and as a result, the Arkansas court erred in exercising jurisdiction. The argument concerning the UCCJA is most likely without merit, and although we discuss the argument, we do not decide it, because this case is governed by a preemptive federal statute, the Parental Kidnaping Prevention Act of 1980, 28 U.S.C. § 1738A (1982), and the trial court's ruling was correct under that federal act.

The UCCJA outlines when a court has jurisdiction to determine child custody upon the finding of one or more of four facts:

> (a) A court of this state which is competent to decide child custody matters has jurisdiction to make a child custody determination by initial or modification decree if: (1) This state (i) is the home state of the child at the time of commencement of the proceeding, or (ii) had been the child's home state within six (6) months before commencement of the proceeding and the child is absent from this state because of his removal or retention by a person claiming his custody or for other reasons, and a parent or person acting as parent continues to live in this state; or (2) It is in the best interest of the child that a court of this state assume jurisdiction because (i) the child and his parents, or the child and at least one (1) contestant, have a significant connection with this state and (ii) there is available in this state substantial evidence concerning the child's present or future care, protection, training, and personal relationships . . . .

Ark.Code Ann. § 9–13–203(a)(1)–(4) (Repl. 1991).

"Home state" is defined as "the state in which the child immediately preceding the time involved lived with his parents, a parent, or a person acting as a parent, for at least six (6) consecutive months[.]" Ark.Code Ann. § 9–13–202(5) (Repl. 1991). Under this definition Arkansas was the home state of the child, and therefore, the Louisiana court could not have exercised jurisdiction under subpart (1), quoted above. Subparts (3) and (4) of the above quoted statute are not applicable, and the Louisiana court could not have exercised jurisdiction under either of them. Subsection (2) quoted above, the "significant connection" and "substantial evidence" provision, is the only provision under which the Louisiana trial court could have possibly exercised jurisdiction, but there is no record of findings of fact by the Louisiana court to support such jurisdiction.

In discussing subsection (2) we have said: "[T]hat provision, while broad, must be judiciously applied, and it should not be regarded as giving a court only recently involved an excuse to act precipitously, in an ex parte proceeding, by disregarding the remainder of the act, so plainly aimed at promoting cooperation between courts." Norsworthy v. Norsworthy, 289 Ark. 479, 485, 713 S.W.2d 451, 455 (1986). Further, we reversed an Arkansas trial court for exercising jurisdiction under subsection (2) under facts almost identical to those which were before the Louisiana court in this case.

However, we need not decide whether the Louisiana court did find, under subsection (2), that the child had a "significant connection" with Louisiana and that there was "substantial evidence" there because, even if the Louisiana court did so find, the result would be that under the UCCJA there was concurrent jurisdiction in the two states.

The Parental Kidnaping Prevention Act of 1980 (PKPA) was passed by Congress for cases just like this one because the states' UCCJA's flexible provisions, especially those involving "significant connection" and "substantial evidence," can be interpreted to permit two states to assert jurisdiction concurrently. The existence of concurrent jurisdiction under the UCCJA continued to allow forum shopping. In response, Congress enacted the PKPA. In Thompson v. Thompson, 484 U.S. 174, 177, 108 S. Ct. 513, 515, 98 L. Ed. 2d 512 (1987), the opinion of the Court explained: "As the legislative scheme suggests, and as Congress explicitly specified, one of the chief purposes of the PKPA is to 'avoid jurisdictional competition and conflict between State courts.' Pub. L. 96–611, 94 Stat. 3569 § 7(c)(5), note following 28 U.S.C. § 1738A." We stated in Garrett v. Garrett, 292 Ark. 584, 732 S.W.2d 127 (1987), that the principal distinction between the UCCJA and the PKPA is that the PKPA gives exclusive jurisdiction to the child's home state. "Home state" is defined as the state in which the child lived with his parent or parents for "at least six (6) consecutive months." 28 U.S.C. § 1738A(b)(4) (1982). Accordingly, under the PKPA, the Arkansas court had exclusive jurisdiction since it was the home state, while under the UCCJA there might have been concurrent jurisdiction because of the "significant connection" and "substantial evidence" provision. When the UCCJA and the PKPA conflict, the preemptive federal PKPA controls. Norsworthy v. Norsworthy, 289 Ark. 479, 713 S.W.2d 451 (1986).

Although the PKPA only applies directly to modification proceedings, it also indirectly governs initial custody determinations. This is due to the fact that if a custody decree fails to conform to the requirements of the PKPA, it will not be entitled to full faith and credit in another state. See 28 U.S.C. § 1738A(a) (1982) . . . .

Accordingly, we affirm the exercise of jurisdiction by the Arkansas trial court and affirm its refusal to afford full faith and credit to the decree of the Louisiana court

NOTES AND QUESTIONS

(1) **UCCJA and the PKPA.** The relationship of the PKPA of 1980 and the UCCJA is complex, to say the least; and to some degree it is safe to say that this relationship was not fully thought out by Congress. There are two main views of this relationship.

   (a) *Initial v. Subsequent Jurisdiction.* This view holds that since the UCCJA is state law it controls situations of initial state jurisdiction, but, when there is an issue of conflicting state jurisdiction or an issue of modification, then the PKPA controls. On its face the PKPA specifically states that it is to govern full faith and credit, and it is worthwhile to note that Section 201 of the UCCJEA states that it deals with "Initial Child-Custody Jurisdiction." There is a role for both the UCCJA and the PKPA. However as noted in *Atkins*, the PKPA can influence initial jurisdiction: if a state wants its judgments to stand up to attack in other jurisdictions, it had better use the jurisdictional standards of the PKPA.

   (b) *Preemption.* The other view is that the PKPA preempts the UCCJA under the Supremacy Clause. U.S. Const. Art. VI. This view is expressed in what might be called the simple version and the complex version. The simple version is that wherever the two statutes conflict, the PKPA will prevail. There are many cases which recite this view, although many of these cases do not deal directly with preemption issues. The more complex approach works hand in hand with the initial

v. subsequent jurisdiction theory. This approach holds that PKPA preempts UCCJA whenever they are in conflict at least as to subsequent jurisdiction. In other words, because the PKPA specifically deals with full faith and credit, it preempts only as to matters related to questions beyond initial jurisdiction. *See* Coombs, *Interstate Child Custody: Jurisdiction, Recognition, and Enforcement*, 66 Minn. L. Rev. 711 (1982).

(2) **Wrongful Conduct.** An interesting exercise is to imagine how the PKPA would handle the situation presented in *Matter of Custody of Ross,* 630 P.2d 353 (Or. 1981) (reprinted above) in which the father wrongfully abducted the child from Montana for a period of time which was long enough for Oregon to become the child's home state. The application of the significant-connection/substantial-evidence test would not work because there is a home state, but Montana would still have jurisdiction under the continuing jurisdiction provision of the PKPA.

However, a more difficult problem for the PKPA lurks in the facts of *Ross*. What if the mother in *Ross* had never obtained a custody order in Montana? Under the PKPA there would be no jurisdictional base for Montana to exercise jurisdiction. Montana was not the home state; Oregon was. Montana cannot obtain jurisdiction under the significant-connection/substantial-evidence test because there is a home state; finally, Montana does not have continuing jurisdiction because there was no original decree. Under this analysis, it appears that if PKPA is used, the father would have successfully robbed Montana of jurisdiction.

This problem has been confronted in a West Virginia decision. In *Sams v. Boston*, 384 S.E.2d 151, 162 (W. Va. 1989), the West Virginia Supreme court held that, where West Virginia had not issued a decree and the father had abducted the child to Florida for three and one half years, West Virginia remained the child's home state for a "reasonable period of time" due to the child's abduction. This decision has been severely criticized by Professor Russell Coombs, under the heading "egregious misinterpretations," as being unsupported by the language of the PKPA. *See* Coombs, *Progress Under the PKPA*, 6 J. Am. Acad. Matrim. Law 59 (1990). However, this approach cures an egregious loophole in the PKPA, one that would allow a child-stealing parent to deprive a non-decree-granting home state of jurisdiction. If Professor Coombs is correct that the decision in *Sams v. Boston* is contrary to the PKPA, a parent who is a victim of child stealing must act within six months, while jurisdiction remains in the home state, to initiate a process which will lead to a mandatory home-state decree to which other state courts must then defer. Otherwise, home state jurisdiction changes to the state of abduction.

(3) **Adoption.** One area in which commentators almost uniformly agree is the misapplication of UCCJA and the PKPA to adoption proceedings. *See* Waller, Note, *When the Rules Don't Fit the Game: Application of the Uniform Child Custody Jurisdiction Act and the Parental Kidnaping Prevention Act to Interstate Adoption Proceedings*, 33 Harv. J. on Legis. 271 (1996).

(4) **Relocation.** The growing trend to allow custodial parents to relocate with their children, may create interstate custody problems. A relocation case is a jurisdictional dispute waiting to happen. As Roger M. Baron has stated, "The time has come for courts and legislatures to realize that the events which trigger a state's relocation laws are also precursors of jurisdictional disputes. An ounce of prevention in the relocation laws may

very well be worth the pound of cure found in the PKPA." Baron, *Refining Relocation Laws—The Next Step in Attacking the Problem of Parental Kidnapping,* 25 Tex. Tech L. Rev. 119, 136 (1993). Under the PKPA it seems pretty clear that the state of origin will remain the jurisdiction with the power to modify the custody order as long as the non-custodial parent remains there, under the continuing jurisdiction section of the PKPA. Professor Baron has also suggested that the parties consent to the continuing jurisdiction of the original home state to avoid any confusion which may result:

> It is simply suggested that notice to the other contestants [those other than the relocating custodial parent] and an acknowledgment [by the relocating parent] of the continuing exclusive jurisdiction of the forum be required prior to relocation. Consent, either of the other contestants or of the appropriate court, would also be required only insofar as it would have already been required in accordance with the substantive law of the state and as a mechanism to insure the acknowledgment. The simple acknowledgment itself may be excused by the court for any appropriate reason, including a declination of future jurisdiction.

Id.

(5) **Repeal.** There have been some suggestions in the literature that the UCCJA and the PKPA be repealed. For example, Professor Anne Goldstein has made the following argument:

> This article's thesis is that the UCCJA and the PKPA have not eliminated jurisdictional competition because a federal system such as ours cannot achieve both of the Acts' two main instrumental goals—preventing or punishing "child-snatching" and promoting well-informed decisions. Our system commits custody decisions to sovereign states, which make and modify the decisions according to indeterminate precepts. Such a system will inevitably create some version of the problem of the interstate child; so long as these features of our system persist, legislation cannot solve the problem. Therefore, although this article proposes amendments to the UCCJA designed to increase its effectiveness, in the alternative, it urges legislatures to repeal both the UCCJA and the PKPA, in order to eliminate the superfluous delays and transaction costs that impede the courts' search for justice in individual child custody cases.

Goldstein, *The Tragedy of the Interstate Child: A Critical Reexamination of the Uniform Child Custody Jurisdiction Act and the Parental Kidnaping Prevention Act,* 25 U.C. Davis L. Rev. 845, 851 (1992).

(6) **Personal Jurisdiction.** Neither the UCCJA nor the PKPA require personal jurisdiction over the respondent. Although *May v. Anderson,* 345 U.S. 528, 533–34 (1952) (discussed in § 12.06[C], *above*), a plurality opinion, literally stands only for the proposition that full faith and credit will not be given to a custody decree unless there is personal jurisdiction over the respondent, one viable extension of this case is that all such decrees are void without personal jurisdiction. However, this interpretation of *May* has been ignored by the framers of the UCCJA and the PKPA. *See* Hazard, *May v. Anderson: Preamble to Family Law Chaos,* 45 Va. L. Rev. 379 (1955). As the authors of one article pointed out:

> Irrespective of whether *May v. Anderson* has been disavowed by the Supreme Court, it seems inconceivable that the present United States Supreme Court, which has demonstrated increasing concern for children in recent years, would subscribe to the

rationale of the [plurality] opinion. None of the Justices could be expected to support the antiquated notion of parental rights in and to children analogous to property rights which may be adjudicated without regard to the children's interests. Rather, once the question of custody jurisdiction reaches the Supreme Court again, perhaps a generation after *May v. Anderson*, the Court can be expected to take note of such subsequent developments as the particularized jurisdictional rules enacted in the majority of states by the adoption of the Uniform Child Custody Jurisdiction Act, and the rules of the Second Conflicts Restatement applicable in the remaining states.

Bodenheimer and Neeley-Kvarme, *Jurisdiction Over Child Custody and Adoption After Shaffer and Kulko*, 12 U.C. Davis L. Rev. 229, 251–52 (1979). Perhaps following this rationale, many courts have either limited *May* or simply ignored it. *See, e.g.In re Marriage of Leonard*, 175 Cal. Rptr. 903, 911–12 (Cal. Ct. App. 1981); *Balistrieri v. Maliska*, 622 So. 2d 561, 563–64 (Fla. Dist. Ct. App. 1993); *Goldfarb v. Goldfarb*, 268 S.E.2d 648, 651 (Ga. 1980); *Morrell v. Giesick*, 610 P.2d 1189, 1191–92 (Mont. 1980).

One way to circumvent the personal jurisdiction requirement may be to say that a child custody hearing merely determines custody status, which does not require in personam jurisdiction according to *Shaffer v. Heitner*, 433 U.S. 186, 212 (1977). *See In re Marriage of Schuham*, 458 N.E.2d 559, 561 (Ill. App. Ct. 1983); *see also* Bodenheimer and Neeley-Kvarme, *Jurisdiction Over Child Custody and Adoption After Shaffer and Kulko*, 12 U.C. Davis L. Rev. 229 (1979).

On the other hand, a United States Supreme Court decision may indicate that the issue of personal jurisdiction is not dead in the area of child custody. In *Burnham v. Superior Court,* 495 U.S. 604 (1990), Justice Scalia, writing for a three-justice plurality, perhaps inadvertently supported a requirement of personal jurisdiction for child custody when he assumed that personal jurisdiction was required to determine child custody. The opinion is weak authority on this issue, not only because it represented the views of only three justices, but because the statement in question is dictum. For a full discussion of this issue see Atwood, *Child Custody Jurisdiction and Territoriality*, 52 Ohio St. L.J. 369 (1991). Finally, for an argument that a rule which does not require personal jurisdiction over a parent in a child custody dispute deprives the parent of procedural due process, see Garfield, *Due Process Rights of Absent Parents in Interstate Custody Conflicts: A Commentary on In re Marriage of Hudson*, 16 Ind. L. Rev. 445 (1983).

Resolution of this complex issue requires addressing situations in which the interests of children would be ill-served if courts could not make or modify custody orders because a parent is not around. Should the issue of personal jurisdiction be "circumvented" as based only in "an antiquated notion of parental rights . . . analogous to property rights?" Is it an answer to approve a parent's move away with a child conditioned on a waiver of personal jurisdiction in a state that has asserted initial jurisdiction and is maintaining continuing jurisdiction? Or, should a parent who moves away with the child without court sanction be deemed to have waived personal jurisdiction issues, as could a parent who moves away without the child. But what is the recourse of a parent left behind, without the child, in the event that the move-away parent finds a statutory basis to seek a modification (or an initial decree) in the new state?

(7) Law Review Literature. The vast amount of law review literature regarding the PKPA is testimony to the complexity of the issues and the importance of child custody jurisdiction. The following law review articles, notes, and comments address the Parental Kidnaping Prevention Act separately or in conjunction with the Uniform Child Custody Jurisdiction Act: Shapiro, *Uniform Child Custody Jurisdiction Act (UCCJA) and the Parental Kidnapping Prevention Act (PKPA): A Comparative Study*, 11 Wis. J. of Fam. Law 1 (1991); Coombs, *Progress under the PKPA*, 6 J. Am. Acad. Matrim. Law 59 (1990);. Note, *Thompson v. Thompson: The Jurisdictional Dilemma of Child Custody Cases Under the Parental Kidnaping Prevention Act*, 16 Pepperdine L. Rev. 409 (1989); Finch and Kasriel, *Federal Court Correction of State Court Error: The Singular Case on Interstate Custody Disputes*, 48 Ohio St. L. J. 927 (1987); Blakesley, *Child Custody-Jurisdiction and Procedure*, 35 Emory L. J. 291 (1986); Lewis, *A Brave New World for Personal Jurisdiction: Flexible Tests Under Uniform Standards*, 37 Vand. L. Rev. 1 (1984); Krauskopf, *Remedies for Parental Kidnaping in Federal Court: A Comment Applying the Parental Kidnaping Prevention Act in Support of Judge Edwards*, 45 Ohio St. L. J. 429 (1984); Donigan, *Child Custody Jurisdiction: New Legislation Reflects Public Policy Against Parental Abduction*, 19 Gonz. L. Rev. 1 (1983–84); Coombs, *Interstate Child Custody: Jurisdiction, Recognition, and Enforcement*, 66 Minn. L. Rev. 711 (1982); Sherman, *Child Custody Jurisdiction and the Parental Kidnaping Prevention Act-A Due Process Dilemma?*, 17 Tulsa L.J. 713 (1982); Foster, *Child Custody Jurisdiction: UCCJA and PKPA*, 27 N.Y.L. Sch. L. Rev. 297 (1981).

[E] International Law

FEDER v. EVANS-FEDER
United States Court of Appeals
63 F.3d 217 (3d Cir. 1995)

MANSMANN, CIRCUIT JUDGE.

In this case of first impression for this circuit, we have before us a petition filed by one parent against the other under the Hague Convention on the Civil Aspects of International Child Abduction. Edward M. Feder asserts that Melissa Ann Evans-Feder "wrongfully retained" their son, Charles Evan Feder ("Evan"), in the United States and requests that Evan be returned to him in Australia. Concluding that the United States was Evan's "habitual residence", Hague Convention, Article 3a, the district court held that the retention was not wrongful and denied Mr. Feder's petition.

We, however, conclude that Australia was Evan's habitual residence and hold that Mrs. Feder's retention of Evan was wrongful within the meaning of the Convention. We will therefore vacate the district court's denial of Mr. Feder's petition and remand the case for a determination as to whether the exception that Mrs. Feder raises to the Convention's general rule of return applies to preclude the relief Mr. Feder seeks.

I.

We begin by reviewing the evidence presented in this case. The facts as found by the district court leading to Mrs. Feder's retention of Evan are not in dispute.

Mr. and Mrs. Feder are American citizens who met in 1987 in Germany where each was working: she as an opera singer, and he as an employee of Citibank. Evan, their only child, was born in Germany on July 3, 1990.

In October, 1990, the family moved to Jenkintown, Pennsylvania, because Mr. Feder had accepted a management position with CIGNA in Philadelphia. When CIGNA terminated Mr. Feder's employment in June of 1993, he began exploring other employment opportunities, including a position with the Commonwealth Bank of Australia. Although Mr. Feder greeted the possibility of living and working in Australia with enthusiasm, Mrs. Feder approached it with considerable hesitation. Nonetheless, that August, the Feders traveled to Australia to evaluate the opportunity, and while there, toured Sydney, the city where Mr. Feder would work if he were to accept the position with Commonwealth Bank. They spoke with Americans who had moved to Australia, consulted an accountant about the financial implications of living in Australia and met with a relocation consultant and real estate agents regarding housing and schools. Mrs. Feder also spoke with a representative of the Australia Opera about possible employment for herself.

In late August or early September of 1993, the Commonwealth Bank offered Mr. Feder the position of General Manager of its Personal Banking Department. Finding the offer satisfactory from a professional and financial standpoint, Mr. Feder was prepared to accept it. Mrs. Feder, on the other hand, was reluctant to move to Australia. She had deep misgivings about the couple's deteriorating marital relationship; in October, 1993, she consulted with a domestic relations attorney regarding her options, including a divorce. Nevertheless, for both emotional and pragmatic reasons, Mrs. Feder decided in favor of keeping the family together and agreed to go to Australia, intending to work toward salvaging her marriage.

Upon Mr. Feder's acceptance of the bank's offer, the Feders listed their Jenkintown house for sale and sold numerous household items that would not be of use in Australia. Toward the end of October, 1993, Mr. Feder went to Australia to begin work. Mrs. Feder remained behind with Evan to oversee the sale of their house in Jenkintown; Mr. Feder, in the meantime, looked for a house to buy in the Sydney area, sending pictures and video tapes of houses to Mrs. Feder for her consideration. In November of 1993, Mr. Feder purchased, in both his and Mrs. Feder's name, a 50% interest in a house in St. Ives, New South Wales, as a "surprise birthday present" for his wife.

Mr. Feder returned to Pennsylvania on December 13, 1993. Even though the Jenkintown house had not sold, Mr. Feder arranged for a moving company to ship the family's furniture to Australia and bought airline tickets to Australia for Mrs. Feder and Evan. The Feders left for Australia on January 3, 1994, where they arrived on January 8, 1994, after stopping briefly in California and Hawaii. Mrs. Feder was ambivalent about the move; while she hoped her marriage would be saved, she was not committed to remaining in Australia.

Once in Australia, the Feders finalized the purchase of their St. Ives house, but lived in a hotel and apartment for about four and one-half months while Mrs. Feder supervised extensive renovations to the house. Evan attended nursery school three days a week and was enrolled to begin kindergarten in February, 1995. Mrs. Feder applied to have Evan admitted to a private school when he reached the fifth grade, some seven years later. Although Evan is not an Australian citizen and was not a permanent resident at the time, Mrs. Feder represented to the contrary on the school application.

In an effort to acclimate herself to Australia, Mrs. Feder pursued the contacts she had made during the Feders' August, 1993, trip and auditioned for the Australian Opera

Company. She accepted a role in one of the company's performances set for February, 1995, which was scheduled to begin rehearsals in December, 1994.

Mr. Feder changed his driver's license registration from Pennsylvania to Australia before legally obligated to do so and completed the paperwork necessary to obtain permanent residency for the entire family; Mrs. Feder did not surrender her Pennsylvania license nor submit to the physical examination or sign the papers required of those seeking permanent residency status. All of the Feders obtained Australian Medicare cards, giving them access to Australia's health care system.

According to Mrs. Feder, her marriage worsened in Australia. In the early spring of 1994, she and Mr. Feder discussed her unhappiness in the marriage as well as her desire to return to the United States. Mr. Feder attributed the couple's difficulties to the stress of his new job and requested that Mrs. Feder stay in Australia, anticipating that their problems would subside once the family moved into their new home. Once again, for both personal and practical reasons, Mrs. Feder agreed.

The family moved into the St. Ives home in May, 1994; the Feders' relationship, however, did not improve. Ultimately, Mrs. Feder decided to leave her husband and return to the United States with Evan. Believing that Mr. Feder would not consent to her plans if her true intent were known, Mrs. Feder told Mr. Feder that she wanted to take Evan on a visit to her parents in Waynesboro, Pennsylvania, in July. Mr. Feder made arrangements for the trip, buying two round-trip tickets for departure to the United States on June 29 and returning to Australia on August 2.

Mrs. Feder and Evan left Australia as scheduled and upon their arrival in the United States stayed with her parents. In July, 1994, Mr. Feder traveled to the United States on business, and arranged to meet his wife and son at their still unsold house in Jenkintown. When Mr. Feder went to the house on July 20, 1994, he was served with a complaint that Mrs. Feder had filed in the Court of Common Pleas of Montgomery County, Pennsylvania on July 14, 1994, seeking a divorce, property distribution, custody of Evan and financial support. Shortly thereafter, Mr. Feder returned to Australia and Mrs. Feder and Evan moved into the Jenkintown house.

In September, 1994, Mr. Feder commenced a proceeding in the Family Court of Australia in Sydney, applying for, inter alia, declarations under the Hague Convention on the Civil Aspects of International Child Abduction. On October 4, 1994, the Judicial Registrar of the Family Court of Australia heard argument and issued an opinion declaring that Evan, Mr. Feder and Mrs. Feder were habitual residents of Australia immediately prior to Mrs. Feder's retention of Evan in the United States; that Mr. Feder had joint rights of custody of Evan under Australian law and was exercising those rights at the time of Evan's retention; and that Mrs. Feder's retention of Evan was wrongful within the meaning of the Convention.

On September 28, 1994, Mr. Feder commenced this action against Mrs. Feder by filing a petition pursuant to the Convention in the United States District Court for the Eastern District of Pennsylvania, alleging that his parental custody rights had been violated by Mrs. Feder's "wrongful removal and/or retention" of Evan and requesting the child's return. Mrs. Feder opposed the petition, denying that Evan's removal from Australia and retention in the United States were wrongful and asserting that even if they were, Evan cannot be returned to Australia because there is a "grave risk" that his return will expose him to "physical or psychological harm" or place him in an "intolerable situation."

On October 14, 1994, the district court conducted an evidentiary hearing and on October 31, 1994, issued an opinion and order denying Mr. Feder's petition. Feder v. Evans-Feder, 866 F. Supp. 860 (E.D. Pa. 1994). Concluding that Mr. Feder failed to prove that "Evan's habitual residence in the United States as of January 8, 1994, had changed to Australia by the time Mrs. Feder refused to return him from Pennsylvania in the summer of 1994[,]" the court held that "the habitual residence of Charles Evan Feder is in the United States and that his mother has not wrongfully retained him here." *Id.* at 868. The court's holding was based on the view that although "Mr. Feder may have considered and even established Australia as his habitual residence by June of 1994 . . . , Mrs. Feder assuredly did not[,]" as "she never developed a settled purpose to remain [there]." *Id.* Because of its decision regarding Evan's habitual residence, the court did not reach the merits of Mrs. Feder's claim that Evan's return to Australia would place him at risk. *Id.* This appeal followed.

II.

The Hague Convention on the Civil Aspects of International Child Abduction reflects a universal concern about the harm done to children by parental kidnapping and a strong desire among the Contracting States to implement an effective deterrent to such behavior. Hague Convention, Preamble; 42 U.S.C. §11601(a)(1)–(4). Both the United States and Australia are signatory nations. The United States Congress implemented the Convention in the International Child Abduction Remedies Act, 42 U.S.C. §11601 et seq., expressly recognizing its "international character" and the "need for uniform international interpretation" of its provisions. 42 U.S.C. §11601(b)(2), (3)(B). In Australia, the Convention was implemented by the Family Law (Child Abduction Convention) Regulations made pursuant to §111B of the Family Law Act 1975.

The Convention's approach to the phenomenon of international child abduction is straightforward. It is designed to restore the "factual" status quo which is unilaterally altered when a parent abducts a child and aims to protect the legal custody rights of the non-abducting parent. Thus, the cornerstone of the Convention is the mandated return of the child to his or her circumstances prior to the abduction if one parent's removal of the child from or retention in a Contracting State has violated the custody rights of the other, and is, therefore, "wrongful". Hague Convention, Article 12. The general rule of return, however, has exceptions. If, for example, "there is a grave risk that [a child's] return would expose the child to physical or psychological harm or otherwise place the child in an intolerable situation[,]" return is not mandatory. Hague Convention, Article 13b.

Under Article 3 of the Convention, the removal or retention of a child is "wrongful" where:

a. It is in breach of rights of custody attributed to a person, an institution or any other body, either jointly or alone, under the law of the State in which the child was habitually resident immediately before the removal or retention; and

b. at the time of removal or retention those rights were actually exercised, either jointly or alone, or would have been so exercised but for the removal or retention.

The rights of custody mentioned in sub-paragraph a above, may arise in particular by operation of law or by reason of a judicial or administrative decision, or by reason of an agreement having legal effect under the law of that State.

Hague Convention, Article 3.

For purposes of the Convention, " 'rights of custody' shall include rights relating to the care of the person of the child and, in particular, the right to determine the child's place of residence[.]" Hague Convention, Article 5a. . . .

Pursuant to the International Child Abduction Remedies Act, state and federal district courts have concurrent original jurisdiction of actions arising under the Convention. 42 U.S.C.§11603(a). Any person seeking the return of a child under the Convention may commence a civil action by filing a petition in a court where the child is located. *Id.*§11603(b). The petitioner bears the burden of showing by a preponderance of the evidence that the removal or retention was wrongful under Article 3; the respondent must show by clear and convincing evidence that one of Article 13's exceptions apply. *Id.*§11603(e)(1)(A), (2)(A).

III.

A.

The question of Evan's habitual residence immediately prior to the retention is the threshold issue we must first address. The Hague Convention on the Civil Aspects of International Child Abduction does not provide a definition for habitual residence; case law analyzing the term is now developing. We are not, however, without guidance. . . .

In re Bates, No. CA 122–89, High Court of Justice, Family Div'l Ct. Royal Courts of Justice, United Kingdom (1989), a mother petitioned the court under the Convention for the return of her child, Tatjana, asserting that Tatjana had been wrongfully removed from New York to London by the child's nanny at the father's request. The father, born and raised in England, was a successful musician who enjoyed international fame; the mother was a United States citizen who shared her husband's life of world-wide public engagements, rehearsals and recording sessions. The father owned a home in London which served as the family's "base". In the early part of 1989, the father's band was about to embark on a tour, starting with the United States, going next to the Far East, and ending with a stay of indefinite duration in London. The parents rented or borrowed a friend's New York apartment, having decided that Tatjana and her mother would live in New York while the father was on tour. Because Tatjana's speech skills were deficient for a two-and-a-half year old child, the mother consulted a New York speech therapist with whom she discussed arrangements for therapy sessions for Tatjana during their stay. Toward the end of January, 1989, the family moved into the New York apartment. After accompanying the father on various engagements in British Columbia and the United States during the first week of February, 1989, Tatjana, her mother and her nanny returned to New York, even though her father only reluctantly agreed to that course, preferring to have Tatjana return with the nanny to the London home. Two days after the father's departure for the Far East, Tatjana's nanny telephoned him to report a heated argument with Tatjana's mother. The father authorized the nanny to take Tatjana immediately to England, which she did.

In her petition, the mother alleged that Tatjana's habitual residence was New York and that her rights of parental guardianship under New York law had been breached by the child's removal. In deciding the question of habitual residence, the court initially observed that the concept is fluid, fact-infused and largely free from technical rules and presumptions, *id.* slip op. at 9, and recognized that although "[t]he residence whose habituality has to be established is that of the child[,] [i]n the case of a child as young as Tatjana, the conduct and the overtly stated intentions and agreements of the parents during the period preceding the act of abduction are bound to be important factors and it would be unrealistic to exclude them". *Id.* slip op. at 10.

In its opinion, the court set forth a governing principle for ascertaining the elements of habitual residence, which we find instructive:

> [T]here must be a degree of settled purpose. The purpose may be one or there may be several. It may be specific or general. All that the law requires is that there is a settled purpose. That is not to say that the propositus intends to stay where he is indefinitely. Indeed his purpose while settled may be for a limited period. Education, business or profession, employment, health, family or merely love of the place spring to mind as common reasons for a choice of regular abode, and there may well be many others. All that is necessary is that the purpose of living where one does has a sufficient degree of continuity to be properly described as settled. *Id.*

Applying this principle to the facts, the court concluded that because New York had acquired a "sufficient degree of continuity to enable it properly to be described as settled[,]" it was Tatjana's habitual residence within the meaning of Article 3 of the Convention. . . .

Guided by the aims and spirit of the Convention and assisted by the tenets enunciated in Friedrich v. Friedrich and Re Bates, we believe that a child's habitual residence is the place where he or she has been physically present for an amount of time sufficient for acclimatization and which has a "degree of settled purpose" from the child's perspective. We further believe that a determination of whether any particular place satisfies this standard must focus on the child and consists of an analysis of the child's circumstances in that place and the parents' present, shared intentions regarding their child's presence there.

When we apply our definition of habitual residence to the facts, we conclude that Australia was Evan's habitual residence immediately prior to his retention in the United States by Mrs. Feder. Evan moved, with his mother and father, from Pennsylvania to Australia where he was to live for at the very least the foreseeable future, and stayed in Australia for close to six months, a significant period of time for a four-year old child. In Australia, Evan attended preschool and was enrolled in kindergarten for the upcoming year, participating in one of the most central activities in a child's life. Although Mr. and Mrs. Feder viewed Australia very differently, both agreed to move to that country and live there with one another and their son, and did what parents intent on making a new home for themselves and their child do—they purchased and renovated a house, pursued interests and employment, and arranged for Evan's immediate and long-term schooling. That Mrs. Feder did not intend to remain in Australia permanently and believed that she would leave if her marriage did not improve does not void the couple's settled purpose to live as a family in the place where Mr. Feder had found work.

We thus disagree with the district court's conclusion that the United States, not Australia, was Evan's habitual residence and with its analysis of the issue in several respects. In rejecting Australia, the court placed undue emphasis on the fact that the majority of Evan's years had been spent in the United States, ignoring the approximately six months that Evan lived in Australia immediately preceding his return to the United States and the circumstances of his life in Australia. Moreover, the court disregarded the present, shared intentions of both Mr. and Mrs. Feder with regard to Evan's stay in Australia, focusing instead on Mrs. Feder exclusively and on the facts which indicated that she did not intend to remain in Australia if her marriage ended at some future date. . . .

We thus hold that Evan was habitually resident in Australia immediately prior to his retention by Mrs. Feder in the United States.

B.

Our analysis, however, does not end here. Having concluded that Evan was a habitual resident of Australia, we must now determine whether his retention by Mrs. Feder was wrongful under Article 3 of the Convention. This determination involves two inquiries: whether the custody rights Mr. Feder enjoyed under Australian law were breached by the retention and whether Mr. Feder was exercising those rights at the time. . . .

Thus, Mr. Feder's custody rights are determined by Australia's Family Law Act 1975, of which we may "take notice directly . . . without recourse to the specific procedures for the proof of that law . . . ." Hague Convention, Article 14. Under the Act, in the absence of any orders of court, each parent is a joint guardian and a joint custodian of the child, and guardianship and custody rights involve essentially the right to have and make decisions concerning daily care and control of the child. Family Law Act 1975 26§63(E)(1)–(2), (F)(1).

Turning next to the Convention's requirement that Mr. Feder was actually exercising the custody rights he had at the time of the retention, Hague Convention, Article 3b, we observe that Mrs. Feder conceded both in the district court and before us on appeal that Mr. Feder had and was exercising joint custody with respect to decisions concerning their son. Accordingly, we hold that Mrs. Feder's unilateral decision to retain Evan in the United States was wrongful within the meaning of Article 3 of the Convention.

IV.

As we recognized, there are exceptions to the Hague Convention on the Civil Aspects of International Child Abduction general rule that a child's return is mandatory where he or she has been wrongfully retained by a parent. Hague Convention, Article 13. Here, Mrs. Feder raised one of the exceptions, asserting that Evan's return would expose him to a grave risk of psychological or physical harm or otherwise place him in an intolerable situation. Hague Convention, Article 13b. In light of its conclusion that Mr. Feder failed to satisfy his burden of proof on the threshold question, the district court did not reach this issue.

This case, therefore, must be remanded for the district court to consider in the first instance whether as the International Child Abduction Remedies Act requires, Mrs. Feder can establish the exception by clear and convincing evidence. . . .

SAROKIN, CIRCUIT JUDGE, dissenting.

I respectfully dissent, not necessarily because I disagree with the majority's analysis of the facts, but rather with the standard by which these facts are reviewed. The issue presented to the district court was the determination of a four year-old boy's "habitual residence," either Jenkintown, Pennsylvania, where he has lived almost his entire life and where his mother now resides, or Sydney, Australia, where he stayed for five months in 1994 and his father now resides. Resolution of this issue determines where the child shall reside pending conclusion of his parents' custody dispute.

In my view the issue of habitual residence is essentially a factual one, and the findings of the district court should not be disturbed unless they are clearly erroneous. Because I respectfully believe that the majority has established an incorrect standard of review, and because I would affirm the district court's finding as supported by the evidence and not clearly erroneous, I dissent. . . .

NOTES AND QUESTIONS

(1) **Habitual Residence.** Does the "settled purpose" test for habitual residence as used in *Evans* provide enough guidance? Is the application here appropriate: a four-year-old child who has lived most of his life in the United States, who is a U.S. Citizen, whose parents are U.S. citizens, whose mother resides in the U.S., whose extended family and family home are in the U.S. is subject to the jurisdiction of the Australian courts after a five-and-one-half-month stay in Australia. By U.S. standards, Australia would not have even qualified as the child's home state.

The habitual residence standard is better exemplified by its application in *Friedrich v. Friedrich*, 983 F.2d 1396, 1401 (6th Cir. 1993), where the court made the following statement:

> Thomas was born in Germany to a German father and an American mother and lived exclusively in Germany except for a few short vacations before Mrs. Friedrich removed him to the United States. Mrs. Friedrich argues that despite the fact that Thomas's ordinary residence was always in Germany, Thomas was actually a habitual resident of the United States because: 1) he had United States citizenship; 2) his permanent address for the purpose of the United States documentation was listed as Ironton, Ohio; and 3) Mrs. Friedrich intended to return to the United States with Thomas when she was discharged from the military. Although these ties may be strong enough to establish legal residence in the United States, they do not establish habitual residence.

Id. at 1401. The settled-purpose test was also applied in *Ponath v. Ponath*, 829 F. Supp. 363, 367–68 (D. Utah 1993). *See also Meredith v. Meredith*, 759 F. Supp. 1432, 1436 (D. Ariz. 1991); *Levesque v. Levesque*, 816 F. Supp. 662, 666 (D. Kan. 1993).

(2) **Wrongful Removal.** Article 3 governs wrongful removal. The test is twofold: first, there must be a "breach of rights of custody"; and second, those rights must be "actually exercised." As discussed in the principal case, the law of the state of habitual residence governs these issues. *See* Dyer, *The Internationalization of Family Law*, 30 U.C. Davis L. Rev., 625, 637–39 (1997).

(3) **Return Remedy.** In a sense, the remedy aspect of the Hague convention is very simple. The child is to be returned to the country of habitual residence if there has been a wrongful removal of the child. The return remedy is mandatory if the proceeding was brought within one year of removal and discretionary if the action was brought after a year from the date of removal. *See* Silberman, *Hague Convention on International Child Abduction: A Brief Overview and Case Law Analysis*, 28 Fam. L.Q. 9, 10–12 (1994).

(4) **Defenses.** The convention allows defenses to be asserted to the return of the child. Article 13b bars return where it "would expose the child to physical or psychological harm or otherwise place the child in an intolerable situation." This provision was applied in *Friedrich v. Friedrich*, 78 F.3d 1060, 1069 (6th Cir. 1996), the second appellate opinion in the case cited in Note (1), *above*:

> [W]e hold that the district court did not err by holding that "[t]he record in the instant case does not demonstrate by clear and convincing evidence that Thomas will be exposed to a grave risk of harm." Although it is not necessary to resolve the present appeal, we believe that a grave risk of harm for the purposes of the Convention can exist in only two situations. First, there is a grave risk of harm when return of the child puts the child in imminent danger prior to the resolution of the custody dispute—e.g., returning the child to a zone of war, famine, or disease. Second, there is a grave risk of harm in cases of serious abuse or neglect, or extraordinary emotional dependence, when the court in the country of habitual residence, for whatever reason, may be incapable or unwilling to give the child adequate protection.

Id. at 1069. The court in *Friedrich II* rejected the mother's argument that the return would be "traumatic and difficult." The court also noted that the courts in the other contracting countries had adequate provisions for the protection of children. For a similar result, *see Nunez-Escudero v. Tice-Menley*, 58 F.3d 374, 377 (8th Cir.1995) (recognizing that Mexican authorities can protect a child from abusive parent).

(5) **Choice of Law.** Under the Convention, the underlying custody dispute and other custody issues which arise under the Convention (such as who has custody rights or whether they are being exercised) will be resolved by the law of the habitual residence. *See* Silberman, *Hague Convention on International Child Abduction: A Brief Overview and Case Law Analysis,* 28 Fam. L.Q. 9, 11 (1994).

(6) **The Principal Case.** After reading the *Evans* case, how would you advise one of the millions of American nationals working and living abroad about child custody jurisdiction? When a marriage becomes troubled, one party may naturally want to return home to the U.S.; and if that person is the primary caretaker, he or she may want to take the children home, too. What happens under the Hague convention, especially if the parent living abroad has made a decision to remain abroad?

Also, what would you think of the principal case (or, better yet, how would you feel about the case) if, instead of Australia, the children were to be sent to a country which did not value women's rights or which automatically favored a father's claim to his children?

(7) The United States Congress addressed international child abduction in 1993, by enacting the International Parental Kidnapping Act (IPKA), 18 U.S.C. § 1204 (1994), which makes it a federal felony for a parent wrongully to remove or retain a child outside the United States.

CHAPTER 13

MARITAL CONTRACTS: PREMARITAL AND SEPARATION AGREEMENTS

SYNOPSIS

§ 13.01 Introduction
§ 13.02 Breach of Promise-to-Marry Contracts and Premarital Gifts
§ 13.03 Premarital Agreements
    [A] Introduction
    [B] Traditional Premarital Agreements: Estate Planning
    [C] Divorce Planning in Premarital Agreements
    [D] Waiver of Spousal Support
    [E] The Uniform Premarital Agreement Act
§ 13.04 Separation or Property Settlement Agreements
    [A] Introduction
    [B] Necessary Elements for a Valid Separation Agreement
    [C] Subsequent Attack on a Separation Agreement Based Upon Nondisclosure of Marital Assets: Intrinsic vs. Extrinsic Fraud
    [D] Drafting a Separation Agreement
        [1] A Recommended Checklist Approach
        [2] Separation Agreement Problem
§ 13.05 State Recognition of Religious Contracts

§ 13.01 Introduction

Marital property rights and support obligations normally devolve upon the spouses by operation of law at the time of the marriage (*see* §§ 2.03 and 2.04, *above*), whereas property and support rights on divorce are governed by state statutory and judicial authority at the time the marriage is dissolved (*see* §§ 2.03 and 2.04, *above*) (Property and support rights in nonmarital relationships and domestic partnership alternatives to marriage are discussed in Chapter 3, *above*.)

However, the parties may also create binding economic rights and obligations by contract: prior to their marriage in the form of a premarital or antenuptial agreement; when a marriage engagement is contracted for and subsequently broken in a minority of states; or in the form of separation agreements or property settlement agreements at the time of divorce or the dissolution of the marriage. Indeed, some commentators have estimated that over

80% of all divorces or dissolutions involve some form of a contractual agreement which may affect the parties' spousal support rights (or waiver of such rights); a division of the parties' marital property; and child support and child custody (subject to court approval).

The courts therefore have increasingly been asked by the parties to evaluate and enforce these marital contracts, either oral or written, actual or implied, that deal with the economic rights and obligations between marital partners. For example, in the past, premarital agreements were primarily made by older couples—normally widows and widowers—who were about to be remarried, and who had acquired considerable property from a prior marriage that they wished to control and pass on to the children of their first marriage. However, premarital agreements today are increasingly being utilized by younger Americans who have acquired, or will acquire, substantial property and, due to a higher probability of divorce or marriage dissolution than in past decades, desire to retain such property as separate rather than marital property.

Premarital agreements may also be utilized by the prospective spouses to provide *more* sharing of income and assets during marriage or after divorce than the statutory rules would otherwise require. *See, e.g.,* Leah Guggenheimer, *A Modest Proposal: The Feminomics of Drafting Premarital Agreements*, 17 Women's Rights L. Rep. 147, 204 (1996) (arguing that drafting norms for premarital agreements should move away from an exclusive focus on competing interests and claims and move "toward a vision of private ordering that is governed by conjoining interests and distributional needs"). In addition, some commentators have suggested that premarital contracts have the potential to improve communication and enhance commitment, both before and during a couple's marriage. *See, e.g.,* Allison A. Marston, *Planning for Love: The Politics of Prenuptial Agreements*, 49 Stanford L. Rev. 887, 916 (1997): "Prenuptials do not deserve their reputation as the bastion of greed and selfishness in marriage. They can offer more than protection against scheming second wives or social climbing husbands. Rather, prenuptial agreements can promote greater love, communication, and, ultimately, happiness in marriage. A legal framework incorporating an independent counsel requirement would promote fairness and full knowledge by both parties, which increases the potential for prenuptials to be a positive, relation-enhancing experience." *See also* Robert E. Burger, The Love Contract: Handbook for a Liberated Marriage (1973).

Not all commentators applaud the increased use of marital contracting. Some scholars oppose the "contractualization" of marriage and divorce because of "the unique nature of the marital relationship, the possibility of irrational and uninformed decision-making at the time of contracting, the likelihood of unforeseen changes in circumstance over the life of the marriage, and the real risk of disadvantage to the economically weaker spouse." Barbara Atwood, *Ten Years Later: Lingering Concerns About the Uniform Premarital Agreement Act*, 19 J. Legis. 127, 131 (1993). *See also* Sally Sharp, *Fairness Standards and Separation Agreements: A Word of Caution on Contractual Freedom*, 132 U. Pa. L. Rev. 1399 (1984) (urging greater substantive and procedural fairness review for marital agreements); Jana Singer, *The Privatization of Family Law*, 1992 Wis. L. Rev. 1443 (discussing the advantages and disadvantages of a shift from public to private ordering in family law). Moreover, some feminist scholars have argued that premarital agreements invariably harm women by waiving legal and financial protections offered by state law, and by magnifying an unequal distribution of wealth along gender lines. *See, e.g.,* Gail Frommer Brod, *Premarital*

Agreements and Gender Justice, 6 Yale J. L. & Feminism 229 (1994); and Patricia Tidwell and Peter Linzer, *The Flesh-Colored Band Aid Contracts, Feminism, Dialogue, and Norms*, 28 Houston L. Rev. 791 (1991). Other scholars, however, have challenged this view, arguing that "emphasizing women's inferior status and bargaining power over women's autonomous right to structure their relations as they see fit reifies the perception that women are the weaker sex and justifies the view that the law—and men—need to protect women from themselves." Leah Guggenheimer, *A Modest Proposal: The Feminomics of Drafting Premarital Agreements*, 17 Women's Rights L. Rep. 147, 155 (1996). These scholars suggest that a better approach to empowering women would be to enact procedural and substantive reforms designed to make premarital agreements fairer from the outset, rather than allowing judges to invalidate such agreements on ad hoc grounds of fairness or equity. *Id.* at 204–07. *See also* Marston, *above*, at 909–16.

Likewise, separation agreements or property settlement agreements on divorce or dissolution of marriage that were once looked upon by some courts with suspicion for allegedly being in derogation of marriage, or for allegedly "promoting" the procurement of divorce, are now highly favored by most courts in almost all jurisdictions. *See, e.g. Reynolds v. Reynolds,* 415 A.2d 535, 537 (D.C. 1980) ("This jurisdiction encourages the parties in any marital dispute to resolve by agreement their joint marital interests"); *Drawdy v. Drawdy*, 268 S.E.2d 30, 31 (S.C. 1980) (stating that marital agreements "are praiseworthy products of cooperation between parties seeking a divorce. They also serve to decrease the workload on family courts and thereby enhance judicial efficiency."). *See generally* A. Lindey & L. Parley, Lindey on Separation Agreements and Antenuptial Contracts (Matthew Bender 1997 rev. ed.); S. Schlissel, Separation Agreements and Marital Contracts (1986); S. Green & J. Long, Marriage and Family Law Agreements (1984).

Marital agreements— whether they be premarital, postmarital, or separation agreements— thus allow the parties to agree upon, and privately control, many important aspects of their own marriage or divorce. While such agreements have traditionally been used to limit economic rights and obligations arising from marriage, they are increasingly being viewed as vehicles to enhance both the economic and non-economic benefits of marriage. In assessing the desirability of such agreements, and in evaluating their validity in any particular case, it may be useful to keep in mind the alternatives to relying on such private ordering of marriage and divorce. As Professors Michael Trebilcock and Rosemin Keshvani aptly observe:

> [W]hatever the deficiencies of the private ordering process, in every context the hard question must be, compared with what? And the "what" with which actual private ordering regimes must be compared should not be some idealized alternative form of legal ordering, but the available alternative forms of legal ordering as they are actually likely to operate in the real world. Comparing flawed real-world alternatives is often a useful antidote for naive idealism . . . [T]he preferences of legislators, judges, bureaucrats, experts', and academics, with all their sundry biases and subjectivities, must be compared with the flawed self-understandings and preferences of individuals attempting to determine their life plans for themselves.

Michael J. Trebilcock & Rosemin Keshvani, *The Role of Private Ordering in Family Law: A Law and Economics Perspective*, 41 U. Toronto L. Rev. 533, 589–90 (1991). *See also* Carol Weisbrod, *The Way We Live Now: A Discussion of Contracts and Domestic Relations*, 1994 Utah L. Rev. 777 (1994).

§ 13.02 Breach of Promise-to-Marry Contracts and Premarital Gifts

An action for breach of promise to marry has existed under the common law for over three hundred years. In such a breach of promise action, the plaintiff was entitled to recover damages in contract or tort for injury to his or her feelings, health, and reputation; and such damages could be awarded based upon the defendant's wealth, income, and social position. Seduction could also be argued as an "aggravation of damages."

Proof of a breached promise to marry would often be by means of circumstantial evidence, and in this highly emotional area it thus "afforded a fertile field for blackmail and extortion." W. Keeton, Prosser and Keeton on the Law of Torts, § 124 (5th ed. 1984). Thus, many critics over the past fifty years have advocated the abolition of this anachronistic common law action, and most states have now abolished breach-of-promise-to-marry actions through so-called state "anti-heart-balm" statutes. *See* H. Clark, The Law of Domestic Relations in the United States 1 pp. 1-30 (2d ed. 1987). To date, only small minority of states still recognize an action for breach of promise to marry. *E.g. Stanard v. Bolin*, 565 P.2d 94 (Wash. 1977). Nevertheless, as Professor Clark concedes—and as the following case demonstrates—"the enactment of these statutes has not ended litigation in [this] area" Clark, *above*, at 22. Moreover, there has been some recent scholarship suggesting that the action for breach of promise to marry and related "heart balm" statutes may *not* be as "anachronistic" as conventional wisdom apparently holds, particularly for women. *See, e.g.,* Jane Larson, *"Women Understand so Little, They Call My Good Nature Deceit' ": A Feminist Rethinking of Seduction*, 93 Colum. L. Rev. 374 (1993).

BROWN v. THOMAS
Wisconsin Court of Appeals
379 N.W.2d 868 (1985)

WEDEMEYER, J.

Dennis Brown appeals from a judgment dismissing his claim for the return of an engagement ring given to Terry Thomas. Brown argues that the trial court erred as a matter of law in ruling that recovery of the ring was barred by the statutory abolition of actions for breach of contract to marry. *See* ch. 768, Stats.

The essential facts are concise and clear. In September, 1983, Brown and Thomas became engaged to be married and Brown gave Thomas an engagement ring. Although a specific date for the wedding was not set, it is uncontroverted that both parties considered the ring to be an engagement ring. In December, 1983, the engagement was terminated. Brown subsequently sued Thomas for return of the ring. At trial both parties alleged that the other broke off the engagement, but a jury finding on this factual issue was precluded by the trial court's decision to grant Thomas's motion for a directed verdict dismissing the complaint on the merits.

The trial court stated that the clear legislative mandate of ch. 768, Stats., was to prohibit all actions arising from a breach of contract to marry except where property was obtained by fraud. *See* §§ 768.01,.02 and.06.[1] Because Brown neither alleged nor proved that Thomas

---
[1] 768.01 . . . All causes of action for breach of contract to marry, alienation of affections and criminal conversation are hereby abolished, except that this section shall not apply to contracts now existing or to causes of action which heretofore accrued.

fraudulently induced him to give her the engagement ring, the trial court concluded that Brown had no remedy under Wisconsin law. We disagree....

It is well settled that statutes in derogation of the common law must be strictly construed. *LePoidevin v. Wilson*, 330 N.W.2d 555, 562 (Wis. 1983). This maxim of construction provides that if a statute would change the common law doctrine relevant to the issue presented by the parties, the legislative intent must be clearly expressed. 330 N.W.2d at 562. The ultimate goal is to construe the statute as far as possible in harmony with the common law. *Bob Ryan Leasing v. Sampair*, 371 N.W.2d 405, 406 (Wis. Ct. App. 1985).

Prior to 1959, the common law action for breach of promise to marry was recognized in Wisconsin as an action on contract, with damages determined as if the action sounded in tort. *Dauphin v. Landrigan*, 205 N.W. 557, 558 (Wis. 1925). As explained by the supreme court in *Klitzke v. Davis*, 179 N.W. 586, 588 (Wis. 1920), the "usual elements of damages in actions of this character" included compensation for disappointment in the "reasonable expectations of pecuniary advantage from marriage with defendant," injury to feelings, mortification and mental suffering. *See also Wallin v. Sutherland*, 31 N.W.2d 178, 180 (Wis. 1948) ($12,000 jury award upheld because the "benefits and advantages" to plaintiff of the canceled marriage included a permanent home and the right to share defendant's property, earnings, and situation in life).

In the mid 1930's, several state legislatures began to question the continued viability of actions for breach of promise and other actions alleging interference with domestic relations, such as alienation of affections and criminal conversation, because all of these actions have afforded a fertile field for blackmail and extortion by means of manufactured suits in which the threat of publicity is used to force a settlement. There is good reason to believe that even genuine actions of this type are brought more frequently than not with purely mercenary or vindictive motives [and] that it is impossible to compensate for such damage with what has derisively been called "heart balm"....Prosser and Keeton on the Law of Torts § 124 at 929 (5th ed. 1984)....

In 1959, our legislature abolished breach of promise suits by enacting ch. 248 (now ch. 768)....

A question remained, however, as to the intended scope of this statutory abolition of common law rights. In *Lambert v. State*, 243 N.W.2d 524, 529 (Wis. 1976), the supreme court concluded: "In abolishing the action for breach of contract to marry, it is apparent that the legislature intended to abolish only the common-law suit for damages based on the emotional harm caused by the breach."

The trial court's analysis of the legislative intent behind ch. 768, Stats., is contrary to that of the *Lambert* court. The trial court construed ch. 768 to abolish all common law

---

768.02 No act hereafter done within this state shall operate to give rise, either within or without this state, to any of the causes of action abolished by this chapter. No contract to marry, which shall hereafter be made in this state, shall operate to give rise, either within or without this state, to any cause of action for breach thereof, and any such acts and contracts are hereby rendered ineffective to support or give rise to any such causes of action, within or without this state.

768.06 Actions for the recovery of property received by one party from the other after the alleged contract to marry and before the breach thereof, which was procured by such party by his or her fraud in representing to the other that he or she intended to marry the other and not to breach the contract to marry, are not barred by this chapter; but such actions must be commenced within the time provided by § 893.41 or be barred. The cause must be shown by affirmative proof aside from the testimony of the party seeking the recovery.

suits related to breach of contract to marry, except for actions based on fraud, § 768.06, and stated: "One would assume that if the legislature had intended to accept [sic] conditional gifts or engagement gifts from the purview of Chapter 768 it would have so indicated." We are not persuaded.

The language of § 788.06, Stats., does not imply the exclusive remedy suggested by the trial court. It simply provides that "[a]ctions for the recovery of property . . . procured by . . . fraud . . . are not barred by this chapter . . ." To transform this negatively phrased statute into an exclusive remedy is to violate a cardinal rule of statutory construction. Rules of the common law are not to be changed by doubtful implication. *State v. Klein*, 130 N.W.2d 816, 820 (Wis. 1964), *cert. denied*, 380 U.S. 951 (1965). *See* Comment, *Abolition of Breach of Promise in Wisconsin Scope and Constitutionality*, 43 Marq. L. Rev. 341, 353 (1959) ("It is doubtful construction to imply a legislative purpose to allow an unjust enrichment, merely because fraud cannot be proven."). . . .

Most jurisdictions recognize the rule that an engagement gift made in contemplation of marriage is conditional upon a subsequent ceremonial marriage. *Piccininni v. Hajus*, 429 A.2d 886, 888 (Conn. 1980); *see* Annot., 46 A.L.R. 3d 578, § 3 at 584. To invoke the picturesque metaphor of Justice Musmanno in *Pavlicic v. Vogtsberger*, 136 A.2d 127, 130 (Pa. 1957):

> A gift given by a man to a woman on condition that she embark on the sea of matrimony with him is no different from a gift based on the condition that the donee sail on any other sea. If, after receiving the provisional gift, the donee refuses to leave the harbor, if the anchor of contractual performance sticks on the sands of irresolution and procrastination the gift must be restored to the donor.

Wisconsin, too, has long acknowledged the distinction between absolute and conditional gifts. Where a gift of personal property is made with the intent to take effect irrevocably, and is fully executed by unconditional delivery, it is a valid gift inter vivos. *Will of Klehr*, 133 N.W. 1105, 1107 (Wis. 1912). Such a gift is absolute and, once made, cannot be revoked. *Guenther v. Guenther*, 12 N.W.2d 727, 730 (Wis. 1944). A gift, however, may be conditioned on the performance of some act by the donee, and if the condition is not fulfilled the donor may recover the gift. *Conway v. Town of Grand Chute*, 155 N.W. 953, 954 (Wis. 1916).

We find the conditional gift theory particularly appropriate when the contested property is an engagement ring. The inherent symbolism of this gift[2] forecloses the need to establish an express condition that marriage will ensue. Rather, the condition may be implied in fact or imposed by law in order to prevent unjust enrichment. *Gikas v. Nicholis*, 71 A.2d 785,

---

[2] Commenting on the symbolic nature of engagement rings in a case similar to the one before us, a New York trial court observed:

> The ring is employed in rites of courtship and marriage in many cultures, primitive and sophisticated; in widely dispersed regions of the earth; persisting through the centuries, in fact millienia [sic]. In our culture, the ring generally is placed on one of the fingers, in others it may be attached to other positions of the anatomy, at intermediate points from the top of the head to the tip of the toes. It is a universal symbol of deep seated sexual and social ramifications, a seminal area of research for behavioral scientists. Is it any wonder that it presents such complicated problems for mere lawyers?

Goldstein v. Rosenthal, 288 N.Y.S.2d 503, 504 (Civ. Ct. 1968).

785-86 (N.H. 1950).³ In Wisconsin, the undergirding theory for recovery on the basis of unjust enrichment is quasi-contractual:

> A quasi contract means that there is no contract in fact but the parties will be treated under the circumstances as if there had been a contract: Recovery is based upon the universally recognized moral principle that one who has received a benefit has the duty to make restitution when to retain such benefit would be unjust. . . .

The essential elements of a quasi contract entitling one to judgment for unjust enrichment are: (1) A benefit conferred upon the defendant by the plaintiff; (2) appreciation by the defendant of the fact of such benefit; and (3) the acceptance or retention by the defendant of such benefit under circumstances such as it would be inequitable to retain the benefit without payment of the value thereof . . . [citations omitted] We therefore conclude that Brown has a cause of action based on the theory of conditional gift and unjust enrichment which is not precluded by ch. 768, Stats.

We acknowledge that most jurisdictions allow recovery of conditional engagement gifts only if the party seeking recovery has not unjustifiably broken off the engagement. *See Wilson v. Dabo*, 461 N.E.2d 8, 9 (Ohio App. 1983), Restatement of Restitution § 58 comment c (1937). We decline to join them. As the record of this two-day jury trial demonstrates, the answer to the multiple question "who broke off the engagement, when, and was he/she justified?" is often lost in the murky depths of contradictory, acrimonious, and largely irrelevant testimony by disappointed couples, their relatives and friends. The better approach was persuasively stated by the high court of New York in *Gaden v. Gaden*, 29 N.Y.2d 80, 323 N.Y.S.2d 955, 961-62 (1971):

> In truth, in most broken engagements there is no real fault as such one or both of the parties merely changes his [or her] mind about the desirability of the other as a marriage partner. Since the major purpose of the engagement period is to allow a couple time to test the permanency of their feelings, it would seem highly ironic to penalize the donor for taking steps to prevent a possibly unhappy marriage.

> Just as the question of fault or guilt has become largely irrelevant to modern divorce proceedings, so should it also be deemed irrelevant to the breaking of the engagement. [Citation and footnote omitted]. . . .

Accordingly, we conclude that the public policy embodied in Wisconsin's no-fault divorce law, ch. 767, applies to actions for recovery of gifts conditioned on marriage. Thus, an inquiry as to how the engagement was dissolved is not necessary in a common law action based on the theory of conditional gift and unjust enrichment. In commenting on the public policy decisions that led to the adoption of no-fault divorce in Wisconsin, our supreme court stated:

> Establishing blame for the failure of a marriage was a primary function under the prior divorce law. It was also the primary basis for criticism of that law and led to its repeal. The proponents of no-fault divorce pointed out, and the legislature apparently agreed,

---

³ The *Gikas* court, in allowing recovery of an engagement ring, clearly distinguished the ring from several miscellaneous gifts made by the spurned suitor. The latter were "personal gratuities upon which the law imposes no condition of return and are more nearly akin to a Christmas present." *Gikas*, 71 A.2d at 786. In the instant case, the interrogatories established that Brown gave Thomas several items of jewelry during their courtship. No action for their recovery, however, was initiated, and the trial court properly limited testimony in this area.

that usually the conduct of both spouses contributes to the failure of a marriage [and] that establishing guilt and innocence is not really useful. . . .

Dixon v. Dixon, 319 N.W.2d 846, 851 (Wis. 1982). This persuasive policy statement, which governs our approach to broken marriages, is equally relevant to broken engagements. We therefore apply the no-fault policy inherent in ch. 767 to common law actions maintainable under ch. 768. The former chapter deals with unhappy results, the latter with unhappy preliminaries. The subject matter, however, is essentially the same, and statutes relating to the same subject matter may be considered in construing a statutory provision. *Kollasch v. Adamany*, 313 N.W.2d 47, 53 (Wis. 1981).

We now turn to the specifics of the instant case. Brown initiated this suit as an action in replevin, alleging that Thomas had "wrongfully detained" the engagement ring. He sought not only the return of the ring, but also "interest" and "damages." These latter two remedies are contrary to the purpose of ch. 768 and generally inappropriate in cases of this kind, especially when we consider that "loss of use" and punitive damages may also be sought in replevin actions. *Durham v. Pekrul*, 311 N.W.2d 615, 616 (Wis. 1981).[4] Brown's recovery, therefore, should be limited to in specie restitution, *i.e.* return of the conditional gift or its equivalent value. . . .

Judgment reversed and cause remanded.

NOTES AND QUESTIONS

(1) According to Green & Long; Marriage and Family Law Agreements 102-07 (1984) a common law action for breach of promise to marry still exists today in a small minority of jurisdictions, including Georgia, Hawaii, Kansas, Nebraska, North Carolina, Texas, and Washington State. Illinois retains this action by statute, but the statute limits recoverable damages only to actual damages. However, the vast majority of American states have abolished a breach of promise to marry through state "anti-heart balm statutes." *See generally Askew v. Askew*, 28 Cal. Rptr. 2d 284 (Cal. Ct. App. 1994), which provides an excellent background discussion of breach of promise to marry actions and state "anti-heart balm" statutes.

---

[4] It is only when the plaintiff alleges fraud pursuant to § 768.06, Stats., that the full panoply of tort damages may be available. *See Glydenvand v. Schroeder*, 280 N.W.2d 235, 239 (Wis. 1979) (plaintiff in deceit action may recover both consequential and general damages), *Jeffers v. Nysse*, 297 N.W.2d 495, 499 (1980) (punitive damages may be awarded in cases of fraudulent inducement).

This distinction between available remedies brings §§ 768.01,.02 and.06, Stats., into harmony. Sections 768.01 and.02 abolish common law actions aimed at recovering damages for the alleged emotional harm caused by the breach of promise to marry. Section 768.06, in allowing the recovery of property obtained by fraud, is not the exclusive remedy suggested by the trial court, but rather is declaratory of the common law. Such a declaration is a useful guide to our courts since other jurisdictions have split sharply on the issue of whether the statutory abolition of breach of promise actions precludes a suit based on fraud or deceit. In *Piccininni*, 429 A.2d 886 (Conn. 1980), the plaintiff alleged that he spent $40,000 to renovate his home due to the defendant's promise to marry him and occupy the refurbished house. His action was based on counts of breach of contract, false representation and unjust enrichment, but the trial court dismissed the fraud claim. Although a majority of the Connecticut Supreme Court reversed, a vigorous dissent insisted that the conditional gift/unjust enrichment theory of recovery was the only valid claim because "a cause of action in deceit carries with it the capacity to generate claims for mental distress and punitive damages that will only exacerbate the opportunity for blackmail that the Heart Balm Act was intended to prevent." *Id.* at 889 (Peters, J., dissenting) (citations omitted)

(2) The *Brown* case, *above,* is not an isolated case, and many other state courts are still grappling with the problem of determining the applicability of state "anti-heart balm" statutes to gifts conditioned on marriage, and related marital actions in tort and contract. *See, e.g., Dixon v. Smith,* 1997 Westlaw 199049 (Ohio Ct. App. 1997) (holding that the recovery of property transferred in reliance on a promise to marry is not related to a breach of promise action which is barred by a state anti-heart balm statute, and recovery is permitted upon the equitable theory of preventing unjust enrichment); *Miller v. Ratner,* 688 A.2d 976, 990–91 (Md. Ct. App. 1997) (holding that nonmarital partners can still be subject to a suit for contractual promises that are made independent of promises to marry which would be barred by the state's anti-heart-balm statute); *Patterson v. Blanton,* 672 N.E.2d 208, 210 (Ohio Ct. App. 1996) (holding that gifts made in contemplation of marriage may be recovered if the marriage does not occur, even if the donor was married to someone else at the time of the gift); *Jackson v. Brown,* 904 P.2d 685, 687–88 (Utah 1995) (holding that although breach-of-promise-to-marry actions are abolished in Utah, damages could still be maintained based upon reliance and intentional infliction of emotional distress). Although the Wisconsin Supreme Court in a subsequent decision questioned the *Brown* court's interpretation of the relevant statutory law, the *Brown* holding is nevertheless consistent with the modern approach to gifts conditioned on marriage in a growing number of states. *See Koestler v. Pollard,* 471 N.W.2d 7 (Wis. 1990).

(3) *Brown* is one of a number of cases discussing who is entitled to an engagement ring or other marital gift once a marriage engagement is terminated. A number of courts apply the traditional rule holding that the donor of the engagement ring can recover the gift *only* if the engagement is dissolved by mutual agreement, or if it is unjustifiably broken by the donee. *See, e.g., White v. Finch,* 209 A.2d 199 (Conn. 1964); *DeCicco v. Barker,* 159 N.E.2d 534 (Mass. 1959). The modern majority view, however, is that in the absence of an agreement to the contrary, the engagement ring must be returned to the donor upon termination of the engagement, regardless of fault. *See, e.g., Fanning v. Fanning,* 535 N.W.2d 770 (S.D. 1995); *Spinnell v. Quigley,* 785 P.2d 1149 (Wash. Ct. App. 1990); *In re Estate of Lowe,* 379 N.W.2d 485 (Mich. Ct. App. 1985). Which legal theory is more persuasive to you? Based on what underlying public policy arguments? Which view did the *Brown* court adopt?

(4) What should be the general rule with other premarital gifts and expenses in addition to engagement rings? *See Gerard v. Costin,* 215 P. 1011 (Kan. 1923) (conveyance of land); *Fortenberry v. Ellis,* 217 So. 2d 792 (La. Ct. App. 1969) (stereo set as a premarital gift); *Earl v. Saks Co.,* 226 P.2d 340 (Cal. 1951) (fur coat gift induced by fraud). For engagement ring and other premarital-gift disputes, see generally Annotation, *Rights in Respect of Engagement and Courtship Presents When Marriage Does Not Ensue,* 46 A.L.R.3d 578 (1972).

(5) **Fraudulent Inducement into a Marriage Contract.** According to the *Brown* court, Dennis Brown's recovery of his engagement ring was not limited by Wisconsin law only to property acquired by fraud. However, in footnote 5 of its opinion, the court also stated that if the plaintiff alleged and proved fraud, then "the full panoply of tort damages may be available" including consequential, general, and punitive damages.

Thus, even though a breach of promise to marry action has been abolished in the vast majority of states, a party may still have an action for fraud against another party, specifically for a "fraudulent inducement into a marriage contract." For example, when a man fraudulently conceals the existence of his prior marital status at the time of his bigamous marriage to yet another woman, that woman may seek compensatory and punitive damages against the man under a fraudulent-inducement-to-marry action based upon this fraud, for her mental pain and suffering, as well as for lost wages and property, and other enumerated damages. *See, e.g., Holcomb v. Kincaid,* 406 So. 2d 650, 652–53 (La. Ct. App. 1981) (awarding damages in excess of $100,000 against a defrauding husband in a fraudulent-inducement-to-marry action). *See also Buckley v. Buckley,* 184 Cal. Rptr. 290 (Cal. Ct. App. 1982); *McGhee v. McGhee,* 353 P.2d 760 (Idaho 1960); *Humphries v. Baird,* 90 S.E.2d 796 (Va. 1956); Annotation, 72 A.L.R.2d 956, 981 and Later Case Service.

(6) **Contracts Restraining Marriage.** A contract in general restraint of marriage is void as against public policy. Restatement (Second) of Contracts § 189 (1981). The rationale behind this rule is that "the sanctity of the marriage relationship is at the foundation of the welfare of the State," 15 Williston on Contracts § 1741 (3d Jaeger ed. 1972), and that the right to marry is a fundamental right. *Zablocki v. Redhail,* 434 U.S. 374, 383 (1978). However, the law has regarded agreements in partial restraint of marriage to be valid if the specific restraint is shown to be "reasonable" under the circumstances. *See, e.g., Perreault v. Hall,* 49 A.2d 812 (N.H. 1946), and 6A Corbin on Contracts § 1474 (1962). The problem, however, is to identify what would constitute a "reasonable restraint" on marriage. Consider the following situations:

(a) A father contractually promises his 25-year-old son that he will give the son $250,000 in return for the son's promise not to marry for at least ten years. A reasonable restraint on marriage?

(b) A female school teacher must under her employment contract resign from her teaching position upon marriage. A reasonable restraint on marriage? What about a similar employment contract applied to airline flight attendants? What about a similar employment contract applied to employees of a dating service?

(c) An ailing 78-year-old uncle contractually promises to give his 45-year-old niece certain real and personal property in his will if she will remain unmarried, live with him, and take care of him until he dies. A reasonable restraint on marriage?

(d) A paragraph in a will gives testator's niece "all my real and personal property so long as she remains single and unmarried." But if she marries, the bulk of the property would go to another niece and nephew. A "general" restraint on marriage, or a "reasonable" restraint on marriage?

See generally Annotation, *Conditions, Conditional Limitations, or Contracts in Restraint of Marriage,* 122 A.L.R. 7 (1939); Browder, *Conditions and Limitations in Restraint of Marriage,* 39 Mich. L. Rev. 1288 (1941); and Illustrations to Restatement (Second) of Contracts § 189 (1981).

(7) **Contracts Promoting Marriage.** The business of a "matchmaker" or a "marriage broker" is illegal in a number of states, and therefore no action will lie for the collection of a marriage broker's promised fees for procuring a husband or wife. *See, e.g., Duvall v. Wellman,* 26 N.E. 34 (N.Y. 1891); *Morrison v. Rogers,* 46 P. 1972 (Cal. 1896); *Jangraw v. Perkins,* 56 A. 532 (Vt. 1903); 10 Williston on Contracts § 1289A p. 1031 (3d Jaeger ed. 1967). Under what public policy rationale? What effect, if any, does this law have on commercial dating referral services and "computer match" services?

(8) **Third Party Interference with Marriage.** It is well-settled commercial law that inducing the breach of a business contract can be actionable in tort. *See* W. Keeton, Prosser and Keeton on the Law of Torts § 129 (5th ed. 1984). Nevertheless, the courts have been unwilling to apply this commercial business action to a third-party-induced breach of promise to marry. One rationale for denying this relief in a family-law context is that such an action would prevent parents, relatives, and friends from giving advice to the prospective spouse. Another is that it would allow an unsuccessful suitor to sue his rival for damages. *See generally* 1 H. Clark, The Law of Domestic Relations in the United States 33–34 (2d ed. 1987).

Likewise, in the vast majority of American states there is no longer a common-law action for "alienation of affections" by a jilted suitor or a spurned spouse, based upon the conduct of a third party. *See* Brown, *The Action for Alienation of Affections*, 82 U. Pa. L. Rev. 472, 476 (1934). *But see Cannon v. Miller*, 327 S.E.2d 888 (N.C. 1984) *vacating* 322 S.E.2d 780 (N.C. Ct. App. 1984), where the North Carolina Supreme Court vacated an appellate court decision that attempted to abolish alienation of affection actions in North Carolina in disregard of the North Carolina Supreme Court's prior decisions. In August 1997, a North Carolina jury awarded jilted wife Dorothy Hutelmyer one million dollars in damages against Margie Cox, now Lynne Hutelmyer, her husband's paramour and subsequent wife who allegedly "stole" Dorothy's husband away from her. The husband whose affections wandered, insurance executive Joseph Hutelmyer, wasn't ordered to pay anything. *See* MSNBC, August 13, 1997, http://www.msnbc.com/news/105058.asp.

(9) **Problem.** Sharon Wildey and Richard Springs became acquainted in 1992. Sharon is an attorney in Chicago, and Richard is an Oregon cattle rancher. Introduced by a mutual friend, the two began a long distance relationship over the telephone. After a number of telephone calls, Richard visited Sharon in Chicago, and the parties decided that a Florida vacation was in order. At the end of their five-day Florida vacation, the parties decided to be married. While waiting for an airplane in the Orlando airport, Richard agreed to marry Sharon, but he expressed concern about their long distance relationship. Sharon wanted to stay in Chicago until her children got out of school, and Richard did not want to leave his Oregon ranch. The parties eventually decided on a "commuter type" marriage for a five-year period, leading to an eventual relocation for both in Florida or the Caribbean. They then flew back to Chicago, and Richard returned to Oregon. One month later, Richard again visited Sharon in Chicago and bought Sharon an engagement ring. He got down on one knee and proposed to Sharon, and the couple planned a Chicago wedding ceremony.

Two months later, however, Richard had second thoughts about the marriage. On a flight to Florida after visiting Sharon in Chicago, Richard decided to break his engagement to Sharon. He composed a letter of Sharon explaining his doubts about the marriage, and suggested that she keep the engagement ring and some money he had placed in a Chicago bank account. He mailed his letter to Sharon in Florida. Sharon replied with a letter from Chicago. She stated that the broken engagement had caused her to become "extremely depressed and anxious." Sharon said that she had spoken with an attorney, and she intended to file suit against Richard under the Illinois Breach of Promise to Marry Act. Sharon stated that she had been willing to marry Richard and she gave him the option of discussing the matter with her. Sharon did not, however, include any of the dates upon which the parties had exchanged their mutual promise to marry, as required under the Illinois Breach of Promise to Marry Act.

Sharon filed suit soon afterwards. Sharon contended, among other things, that her broken engagement had necessitated large expenditures on her medical care, and had caused her to lose business income. She additionally sought recovery for pain and suffering. The jury returned a verdict in Sharon's favor, and against Richard, totaling $178,000. Of this amount, $25,000 was awarded for past and future medical expenses, $60,000 was awarded for lost business profits; and $93,000 was awarded for pain and suffering. Richard's attorney appealed this jury verdict, arguing the following, among other things: (1) Illinois law should not apply, since the state laws of both Oregon and Florida have abolished breach of promise to marry actions; (2) Sharon should not recover for her lost business profits; and (3) Sharon did not strictly comply with the notice requirements of the Illinois Breach of Promise Act, and "substantial compliance" with these statutory requirements is not enough. How should the appellate court rule in this case, and why? *See Wildey v. Springs*, 47 F.3d 1475 (7th Cir. 1995).

§ 13.03 Premarital Agreements

[A] Introduction

Premarital agreements (also called prenuptial agreements or antenuptial contracts) are generally favored by state law when prospective spouses privately contract to vary, limit, or relinquish certain economic rights which they would otherwise acquire in each other's property or estate by reason of their impending marriage. *See* Gregory, Swisher & Scheible, Understanding Family Law § 3.05 [A] (Matthew Bender 1995). Alternatively, premarital agreements may contractually provide for *more* economic and non-economic benefits for the prospective spouses. *See generally* §13.01, above.

Typically, premarital agreement provisions might include a release of the distributive shares in each other's estate; the mutual bar or waiver of dower and curtesy rights or their statutory equivalent under state augmented estate statutes; the surrender of a right of election to take against the other's estate or will; an agreement to keep certain property acquired before or after the marriage as separate property rather than as marital property; an agreement to limit or waive spousal support rights and obligations on marriage or thereafter; and any other transfer of money, gifts, or property to the other spouse, either before or after the marriage. *See generally* Gamble, *The Antenuptial Contract*, 26 U. Miami L. Rev. 692 (1972); Clark, *Antenuptial Contracts*, 50 U. Colo. L. Rev. 141 (1979); 2 A. Lindey and L. Parley, Separation Agreements and Ante-Nuptial Contracts § 90 (Matthew Bender 1997 rev. ed.)

Traditional premarital agreements could only validly affect property rights on the death of a spouse. *See, e.g., Crouch v. Crouch*, 385 S.W.2d 288 (Tenn. Ct. App. 1964). *See also* Annotation, *Validity, Construction, and Effect of Provision in Antenuptial Contract Forfeiting Property Rights of Innocent Spouse on Separation or Filing of Divorce or Other Matrimonial Action*, 57 A.L.R.2d 942 (1958). However, recent cases have held that contingent divorce planning provisions in premarital agreements should not be invalid *per se* and must be tested by the objective intent of the parties themselves. *See generally* Swisher, *Divorce Planning in Antenuptial Agreements: Toward a New Objectivity*, 13 U. Rich. L. Rev. 175 (1979); Note, *For Better or For Worse . . . But Just in Case, are Antenuptial Agreements Enforceable?*, 1982 U. Ill. L. Rev. 531 (1982); and Oldham, *Premarital Agreements are Now Enforceable Unless . . .*, 21 Hous. L. Rev. 757 (1984). The Uniform

Premarital Agreement Act, enacted in 1983 and adopted by a growing a number of states, hopefully may resolve many of these troublesome problems with the drafting and the enforceability of premarital agreements generally. *See also* Jeffrey Evans Stake, *Mandatory Planning for Divorce*, 45 Vand. L. Rev. 397 (1992) (arguing that American family law should *require* couples to enter into premarital agreements); Alliston Marston, *Planning for Love: The Politics of Prenuptial Agreements*, 49 Stan. L. Rev. 887 (1997) (reviewing the history and current status of premarital agreements, and recommending that they be more widely utilized as long as each party has independent legal counsel).

[B] Traditional Premarital Agreements: Estate Planning

IN RE ESTATE OF BENKER
Michigan Supreme Court
331 N.W.2d 193 (1982)

WILLIAMS, J.

I. FACTS

On December 15, 1976, Charles Benker died intestate leaving as his sole heirs at law his widow, Elizabeth Benker, and Ruth Counts, a daughter from a previous marriage, who was appointed administratrix of his estate. Three days prior to the marriage, Mrs. Benker, defendant in this case, and the decedent entered into an antenuptial agreement, the subject of this litigation.

The decedent and his widow each had been married once before, and each had one child from the previous marriage. The couple was married in 1963 after knowing each other for over 20 years through employment at Ex-Cell-O Corporation. Decedent was in charge of maintenance prior to retiring in 1959, and defendant worked in maintenance and later in the inspection department. Decedent was 71 years old when the marriage took place, and defendant was 60 years old.

Decedent left a very substantial estate when he died, $640,500, of which $221,500 was in a trust account at First Federal Savings and Loan Association for the benefit of his daughter. Despite the worth of his estate, decedent had a modest lifestyle. He did not display his wealth at all and was somewhat secretive about it. He lived in a most modest neighborhood in Highland Park, his house was valued at $3,000, and he drove a car worth approximately $500. His daughter testified that she did not realize the extent of her father's estate. . . .

The antenuptial agreement at issue here was signed by Elizabeth Stewart and Charles Benker on May 29, 1963. The agreement contains no reference to the assets of either party, generally or specifically, nor does it make any statement at all regarding disclosure of assets by the parties to the agreement. The agreement provides for a complete waiver of rights by the widow to take by the laws of descent and distribution, provided by the following language of the contract:

> (8) The party of the second part likewise waives all right of inheritance, under the laws of descent and distribution of property of any jurisdiction in or to any estate or property of the party of the first part dying intestate, and does also waive all rights as a widow, in the event of death of the party of the first part, to elect to take against

or contrary to any last will and testament or codicil executed by the party of the first part and admitted to probate.

But the agreement failed to state whether there was an understanding on her part that the husband's rights in her estate were far less substantial than the wife's rights in his estate and that therefore she was waiving far more than he was.

The attorney who prepared the agreement, Mr. William Dye, testified in a deposition on September 12, 1977. He could not recall specifically the steps taken for this particular agreement, but testified as to his "normal procedure" in such a situation which would include a discussion of assets. Mr. Dye later testified as follows in response to a question asking how he insured that there was full disclosure of assets by each party:

> Well, I didn't press the full disclosure matter, for the simple reason that once you outline to your clients the purpose of a prenuptial agreement, then they disclose their assets to you. You don't press them for undisclosed assets, or at least I didn't.

Mr. Dye also stated that the main objective of an antenuptial agreement, in general, was to retain the status quo of each party, and that he was not concerned with what Mrs. Benker would receive upon Mr. Benker's death. He represented both parties in executing this agreement and felt that he had an obligation to make sure that this was "an arm's length transaction" between the two of them. He was acquainted with Mr. Benker through his father's association with Ex-Cell-O Corporation as general counsel. Mr. Dye could not recall much of the events leading up to the execution of the subject agreement.

The antenuptial agreement became the subject of controversy when plaintiff, as administratrix of her father's estate, petitioned the probate court to determine the validity of the antenuptial agreement and to instruct as to the assignment of the residue of the estate. After hearing testimony on the issue, the probate court allowed the parties to submit briefs as to which party had the burden of proof and whether there was a presumption of non-disclosure on the part of the deceased husband in light of the facts presented. On January 9, 1978, the probate court, without deciding which party had the burden of proof in attacking the validity of antenuptial agreements for failure of disclosure, held that there was a presumption of non-disclosure and that the evidence presented was not sufficient to rebut the presumption. Therefore, the agreement was held to be invalid. This decision was appealed to the circuit court which summarily affirmed. The Court of Appeals reversed and remanded, holding that the trial court erred by not allocating the burden of proof to defendant widow, the party seeking to invalidate the antenuptial contract. 97 Mich. App. 754; 296 N.W.2d 167 (1980). We granted leave to appeal.

II. ANTENUPTIAL AGREEMENT AND THE DUTY OF DISCLOSURE

It is now generally recognized that antenuptial agreements which relate to the parties' rights upon the death of one of the parties are favored by public policy. MCL 557.28; MSA 26.165(8) recognizes such contracts and provides that:

> A contract relating to property made between persons in contemplation of marriage shall remain in full force after marriage takes place.

Such agreements, while recognized as valid instruments, are of a special nature because of the fact that they originate between parties contemplating marriage.[5] This relationship

---

[5] Marriage alone is sufficient consideration for the antenuptial agreement, and it need not be recited in the agreement. *Richard v. Detroit Trust Co.*, 269 Mich. 411, 413-414; 257 N.W. 725 (1934).

is one of extreme mutual confidence and, thus, presents a unique situation unlike the ordinary commercial contract situation where the parties deal at arm's length.

In order for an antenuptial agreement to be valid, it must be fair, equitable, and reasonable in view of the surrounding facts and circumstances. It must be entered into voluntarily by both parties, with each understanding his or her rights and the extent of the waiver of such rights. *Hockenberry v. Donovan*, 136 N.W. 389 (Mich. 1912). Antenuptial agreements give rise to a special duty of disclosure not required in ordinary contract relationships so that the parties will be fully informed before entering into such agreements. . . .

The duty of disclosure is recognized by numerous jurisdictions and is succinctly described in Anno.: *Setting Aside Antenuptial Agreement Based on Non-Disclosure*, 27 ALR2d 883, 886, as follows:

> Where, as is usually the case, the parties to an antenuptial property settlement occupy a confidential relationship toward one another, and the agreement substantially affects the property interests which one or the other would otherwise acquire by the marriage, each is under an affirmative duty to disclose to the other the nature of his property interests so that the effect of the agreement can be understandingly assessed, and in the absence of such a full and frank disclosure, the courts will refuse to give effect to such an agreement attacked by the spouse to whom disclosure should have been made. (Footnotes omitted.)

III. BURDEN OF PROOF IN CHARGING NON-DISCLOSURE

It is clear that there is a duty to disclose one's assets to the other party entering into an antenuptial agreement 41 Am Jur 2d, Husband and Wife, § 297, pp. 244-245. The Court of Appeals here properly interpreted the law of this state as placing the burden of proof on the party seeking to invalidate the agreement on the basis of fraud. . . .

We reaffirm, therefore, that the burden of proof rests on the party seeking to invalidate the antenuptial agreement because of non-disclosure by the other party. However, this does not end our analysis. We must, as the Court of Appeals failed to do, address the question whether there is a presumption of non-disclosure in certain cases, specifically the case at hand.

IV. PRESUMPTION OF NON-DISCLOSURE

Even if the burden of proof is on the party seeking to invalidate the antenuptial agreement on the basis of non-disclosure, there will be instances where there is sufficient evidence to raise a rebuttable presumption of non-disclosure. Many jurisdictions apply such a presumption when the antenuptial agreement provides a disproportionately small allowance for the wife.

> Where a confidential relationship exists between the parties to an antenuptial contract requiring the exercise of the utmost good faith in dealings between them, if no provision is made for the wife therein, or if the provision secured for her is inequitable, unjust, and unreasonably disproportionate to the means of the intended husband, taking into consideration the rights given her by law in the property of her husband in the event of his death prior to her death, then a presumption arises that the intended wife was not fully informed as to the value and extent of her prospective husband's property, and the courts will refuse to give effect to the contract, in the absence of proof

affirmatively disclosing that proper disclosure was in fact made. 27 ALR2d 891. *See* 27 ALR2d 873 and cases cited therein.

We do not here adopt a presumption of non-disclosure based merely on a disproportionately small allowance for the wife, but hold that the presumption is properly invoked when the facts are, in general, as follows: One, the antenuptial agreement provides for a complete waiver of all rights of inheritance and rights of election by the widow and does not make any provision for her upon her husband's death. Two, the husband's estate is very ample in comparison to the wife's. Three, the decedent was shown to be rather secretive about his financial affairs, lived very modestly, and gave no outward appearance of his wealth. Four, the agreement makes no reference whatsoever, in general or specific terms, to whether the parties had been fully informed of the property interests held by each other. Five, the widow was not represented by independent counsel. Six, the attorney who drafted the subject agreement testified in a deposition as to his normal procedure in such a matter and stated that he normally would discuss the assets of the parties, but that he did not press the full disclosure matter. Seven, the scrivener testified that he was not concerned with what the widow would get. These factors support the trial judge's decision to invoke the presumption of non-disclosure. . . . [The court then applied these seven factors to the facts of the case]. . . .

CONCLUSION

We hold: (1) that the burden of proof of breach of fair disclosure falls upon the party charging it, and (2) that under the facts of this case the required proof by the party charging breach of fair disclosure was supported by a rebuttable presumption of non-disclosure. We further find that there were not sufficient facts to rebut this presumption of non-disclosure of assets. Therefore, we hold that the probate court properly held the antenuptial agreement to be invalid.

The judgment of the Court of Appeals is *reversed*.

NOTES AND QUESTIONS

(1) The *Benker* court stated the general rule that: The burden of proof is initially placed upon the party alleging the invalidity of a premarital agreement; but since claims of nondisclosure of assets in marital agreements are not limited only to fraud claims, therefore sufficient evidence may raise a *presumption of nondisclosure* (alternately referred to as "overreaching" or "designed concealment") which, if not rebutted, may void the premarital agreement. *Query*: Why wasn't this a typical "arm's-length" contract, which would be voidable only upon proof of actual fraud or duress?

(2) Will nondisclosure of assets *always* void a premarital agreement? Some courts have adopted an alternative test: "To render an antenuptial agreement valid, there must be a fair and reasonable provision for the wife [or husband] or in the absence of such provision there must be a full and frank disclosure of the husband's [or wife's] worth or adequate knowledge thereof on her part independently of disclosure. [T]he question of reasonableness arises only if the man [or woman] has failed to make proper disclosure, or if the woman [or man] has not had independent knowledge. Conversely, where the provision for the wife [or

husband] is reasonable, disclosure or knowledge is of no consequence." *See* 3 A. Lindey and L. Parley, Separation Agreements and Ante-nuptial Contracts §§ 90-52 to 90-58 (Matthew Bender 1997 rev. ed.), *See also Battleman v. Rubin*, 98 S.E.2d 519, 521 (Va. 1957) (holding that a valid premarital agreement requires a fair provision or full disclosure and independent legal advice); *Friedlander v. Friedlander*, 494 P.2d 208, 214 (Wash. 1972) (same holding as *Battleman*). *Query:* What would constitute a "reasonable provision"?

(3) Does a premarital agreement have to be "fair" to both parties? The *Benker* court admittedly did not adopt a presumption of nondisclosure "based merely on a disproportionately small allowance for the wife." Indeed, unless overreaching or fraud is found, an apparently unreasonable provision for the wife would not in itself afford a basis for voiding the premarital agreement. *See, e.g., Estate of Moss*, 263 N.W.2d 98 (Neb. 1978). *See also Del Vecchio v. Del Vecchio*, 143 So. 2d 17, 20 (Fla. 1962) (holding that where full disclosure has been made, the premarital agreement is binding on the parties, regardless of fairness); and *Newman v. Newman*, 653 P.2d 728, 731 (Colo. 1982) (holding that once the tests of full disclosure and lack of fraud or overreaching are met, the parties are free to agree in a premarital agreement to any arrangement for the division of their property, including a waiver of any claim to the property of the other). *See also Pardieck v. Pardieck*, 676 N.E.2d 359, 363 (Ind. Ct. App. 1997) (holding that if a premarital agreement is clear on its terms, and is not unconscionable, it will be enforced as written); *Moore v. Gillis*, 391 S.E.2d 255, 256–57 (Va. 1990) (similar holding); Jeffrey Evans Stake, *Mandatory Planning for Divorce*, 45 Vand. L. Rev. 397 (1992) (arguing that American family law should *require* couples to enter into premarital agreements); Alliston Marston, *Planning for Love: The Politics of Prenuptial Agreements*, 49 Stan. L. Rev. 887 (1997) (reviewing the history and current status of premarital agreements, and recommending that they be more widely utilized as long as each party has independent legal counsel).

(5) A premarital agreement must be in writing to comply with the Statute of Frauds. *See, e.g.*, Va. Code Ann. § 11-2(5) (1976). But an oral premarital agreement may be taken out of the Statute of Frauds by detrimental reliance and part or full performance. *See, e.g., In re Lord's Estate*, 602 P.2d 1030 (N.M. 1979); *Herr v. Herr*, 98 A.2d 55 (N.J. 1953). *Cf. Jackson v. Jackson*, 933 P.2d 1353, 1371–72 (Haw. Ct. App. 1997) (in the absence of detrimental reliance by a party, there would be no valid oral premarital agreement).

(6) **Problem.** Laura was an employee and a bookkeeper in Jim's Widget Company. Prior to their marriage, Jim asked Laura to sign a premarital agreement waiving Laura's rights to all of Jim's property, which was substantially tied up in his widget business. There was no full disclosure of Jim's assets, and Laura was not represented by independent legal counsel. The property distribution in the premarital agreement was grossly disproportionate in favor of Jim. Would this be a valid, or an invalid, premarital agreement? *Compare Knoll v. Knoll*, 671 P.2d 718 (Or. Ct. App. 1983) *with Matson v. Matson*, 705 P.2d 817 (Wash. Ct. App. 1985).

(7) **Problem.** Wife sought to set aside a premarital agreement which was executed by the parties two days before they were married, on the basis that the agreement was signed under duress, that it was prepared by husband's attorney and that she was unrepresented when she signed it, that it failed to provide adequate disclosure of the parties' assets, and that the premarital agreement was "not fair." What result? *See Coulbourn v. Lambert*, 1996 Westlaw 860586 (Del. Fam. Ct. 1996). What if wife, represented by legal counsel,

reluctantly signed a premarital agreement because husband threatened not to marry her unless she signed the agreement. Undue influence? *See In re Marriage of Spiegel*, 553 N.W.2d 309 (Iowa, 1996).

[C] Divorce Planning in Premarital Agreements

OSBORNE v. OSBORNE
Supreme Judicial Court of Massachusetts
428 N.E.2d 810 (1981)

HENNESSEY, CHIEF JUSTICE.

This is an appeal from Probate Court judgments entered in connection with reciprocal divorce actions by husband and wife, and in connection with an equity action brought by the husband to establish an ownership interest in certain real estate and personal property. The husband also seeks an award of alimony and a division of property . . . The alimony and property claims were referred to a master, who, after a hearing, filed a report concluding that the husband should receive neither alimony nor an equitable division of property. . . .

The husband claims that the probate judge erred in adopting the master's report because (1) the master failed to apply properly the factors enumerated in G.L. c. 208, sec. 54, relating to the needs of the parties and their station in life, (2) he master's findings relating to the husband's ownership interest in the personal property were against the weight of the evidence, and (3) the master improperly admitted certain prejudicial evidence relating to the postseparation conduct of the husband. On cross-appeal, the wife contends that the probate judge erred in . . .failing to give full effect to an antenuptial contract entered into by the parties in which both parties waived their rights to alimony or to any portion of the other's estate. . . .

The relevant facts as found by the master are summarized. The parties, Barbara E. Mallinckrodt (Barbara) and David P. Osborne, Jr. (David) met and became engaged while they were both attending medical school. They were married on August 19, 1967. Barbara is an heiress to a large family fortune amounting to nearly $17,000.000, most of which is held in trust. Barbara's income from these funds was approximately $540,000 in 1976. At the time of their engagement, David had no assets of significant value. A few hours before their wedding they executed an antenuptial agreement containing, among other things, the following pertinent provisions: "Barbara now has sufficient property to provide adequate means for her own support and David, by reason of his becoming a member of the medical profession, contemplates that he will have adequate earning power for his own support": "Barbara and David intend this agreement to be in full discharge of all . . . statutory marital property rights under the statutes or law of any state in which they are now or may hereafter be domiciled"; "neither, upon or subsequent to said marriage, shall acquire any interest, right or claim in or to the property, real and personal, of whatever kind or wherever situated, which the other now owns . . .or which the other may own. . . ; that if their "marriage is legally terminated in accordance with the laws of any jurisdiction in which they or either of them may be domiciled, then . . . neither shall be entitled to any alimony, support money, costs, attorneys fees, or to any other money by virtue thereof. . ." Attached to the agreement was a schedule accurately showing Barbara's wealth and expectation of inheritance. David read the agreement before he signed it.

Two children were born of the marriage. During the marriage the parties maintained a high standard of living which was financed completely by the income from Barbara's trust accounts. Barbara maintained joint checking accounts upon which either party could draw funds. These accounts were funded with monies from her separate trust accounts. During the marriage the parties acquired furniture fixtures worth approximately $15,000, jewelry valued at approximately $225,000, art valued at approximately $428,545, a wine collection worth $60,000, and three parcels of real estate valued at $100,000, $60,000, and $40,000. The husband claims an ownership interest in all these items of property. Both parties are now practicing physicians and earn respectable salaries. . . .

Validity of the Antenuptial Agreement

We must first determine the validity of the antenuptial agreement. This court has not previously passed on the validity of an antenuptial agreement that attempts to regulate the rights of the parties in the event of their subsequent divorce. The majority of Massachusetts cases dealing with the validity of antenuptial contracts concern the rights of the parties to modify those property rights that would otherwise arise during the marriage or upon the death of one of the parties. *See, e.g., Rosenberg v. Lipnick*, 377 Mass. 666, 389 N.E.2d 385 (1979) . . . These contracts have generally been upheld where there has been no fraudulent conduct on the part of either party, or, more recently, where the parties have acted honestly and fairly and have fully disclosed their assets one to the other. *Rosenberg v. Lipnick, supra*. Antenuptial contracts are recognized by statute and at common law. . . .

In many jurisdictions it has been held that an antenuptial contract made in contemplation of divorce is void as against public policy. *See generally* 2 A. Lindey, Separation Agreements and Ante-Nuptial Contracts Sec. 90 at 90-33. . . . The reasons most frequently given for invalidating such contracts are (1) they are not compatible with and denigrate the status of marriage, (2) they tend to facilitate divorce by providing inducements to end the marriage, and (3) a contract waiving or minimizing alimony may turn a spouse into a ward of the State. . . .

In *Fox v. Davis*, 113 Mass. 255, 257-258 (1873), this court stated: "The great weight of authority sustains the validity of such contracts, where the separation has taken place, or is to take place immediately. But where the agreement is made in contemplation of future separation, the current of authority is against its validity." Had the issue come before this court several decades ago, the law as stated in *Fox* might well have been held to be controlling. In *French v. McAnarney*, 290 Mass. 544 (1935), it was held that an antenuptial contract wherein the wife agreed not to make any claim for support against the husband was void as against public policy. The facts of the case are distinguishable in that there the parties were not divorced; yet the rationale is applicable. The court in *French* concluded that certain rights and duties incident to the marital relation, including the duty of the husband to support his wife, could not be avoided by an antenuptial contract. Under the case law of the time, this same reasoning would have applied to the rights of the parties upon divorce, since the obligation of the husband to pay alimony was also based on the husband's legal duty to support his wife . . . .

In 1970 the Florida Supreme Court took the lead in departing from this approach. In *Posner v. Posner*, 233 So.2d 381 (Fla. 1970), the court held that antenuptial agreements settling alimony and property rights upon divorce are not void *ab initio* as contrary to public policy. The court disagreed with the traditional assumption that such agreements tended to facilitate divorce, suggesting that such contracts are no more likely to encourage divorce than antenuptial contract in contemplation of death. *Id.* at 383-384. With respect to public policy, the court stated: "We know of no community or society in which the public policy that condemned a husband and wife to a lifetime of misery as an alternative to the opprobrium of divorce still exists. And a tendency to recognize this change in public policy and to give effect to the antenuptial agreements of the parties relating to divorce is clearly discernible." *Id.* at 384. A number of jurisdictions have followed the approach of the *Posner* case. . . .

We conclude that we shall follow the reasoning of the *Posner* case and its progency and uphold the contract. While the matter is not free from dispute, it is apparent that the significant changes in public policy during the last decade in the area of domestic relations warrant a tolerant approach to the use of antenuptial contracts as vehicles for settling the property rights of the parties in the event of divorce. In recent years the Legislature has abolished the doctrine of recrimination and recognized irretrievable breakdown as a ground for divorce. . . . The Legislature itself has thus removed significant obstacles to unhappy couples wishing to obtain a divorce. There is little reason not to allow persons about to enter into a marriage the freedom to settle their rights in the event their marriage should prove unsuccessful, and thus remove a potential obstacle to their divorce. W therefore hold that an antenuptial contract settling the alimony and property rights of the parties upon divorce is not *per se* against public policy and may be specifically enforced. We express no opinion on the validity of antenuptial contracts that purport to limit the duty of each spouse to support the other during the marriage.

Legal Limitations Upon Antenuptial Agreements

We note that the freedom of the parties to limit or waive their legal rights in the even of a divorce is not appropriately left unrestricted. We therefore set forth some guidelines to be used in determining the extent to which such agreements should be enforced, observing at the same time that none of these comments are relevant or applicable to the decision in the case before us. At the outset, the validity of such agreements should be judged by the same "fair disclosure" rules set forth by this court in *Rosenberg v. Lipnick*, 377 Mass. 666, 389 N.E.2d 385 (1979). . . .

In addition, antenuptial agreements that settle the alimony and property rights of the parties in the event of a divorce should be binding on the courts to the same extent as postnuptial separation agreements. The public policies that underlie the laws regulating separation agreements are equally applicable whether the agreement is entered into before the marriage or after the marriage and in expectation of separation or divorce. Accordingly, the agreement must be fair and reasonable at the time of entry of the judgment nisi, and it may be modified by the courts in certain situations, for example, where it is determined that once spouse is or will become a public charge, or where a provision affecting the right of custody of a minor child is not in the best interests of the child. See generally *Knox v. Remick*, 371 Mass. 433, 358 N.E.2d 432 (1976). See also Restatement (Second) of Contracts Sec. 191 (1981). In any case where the issue is whether payment shall be ordered in excess of that provided in the agreement, the agreement can be raised as a potential bar in the same proceeding. . . . Finally, we recognize that certain contracts may so unreasonably

Duress

David alleges that the antenuptial contract is invalid because it was entered into under duress. [There was no claim of fraud made, since David was fully aware of the extent and nature of Barbara's assets from the full disclosure of Barbara's property attached to the antenuptial contract that David read before he signed the contract.] David saw the contract for the first time a few hours before the wedding ceremony when it was presented to him by Barbara's attorney for signing. However, the master whose report was adopted by the Probate Court found that on several occasions before the marriage Barbara had told David that she intended to have her money pass to her legitimate descendants and their descendants. The master also found that at some point after their engagement and before the wedding they had discussed the antenuptial agreement. The master concluded that the husband had entered into the agreement "of his own free will . . . without any fraud, coercion, undue influence or duress." On review of the record, we conclude that there was ample evidence to support the master's findings and that they are therefore not clearly erroneous. . . .

NOTES AND QUESTIONS

(1) Prior to the 1970 Florida case of *Posner v. Posner*, discussed in *Osborne v. Osborne*, it was a public policy rule in almost all states that premarital agreements which attempted to govern the rights and duties of the parties on divorce were void because such agreements were thought to "promote" or "induce" divorce. Moreover, judicial practice was to void any divorce contingency provisions in premarital agreements that might "encourage" or "promote" divorce, rather than looking at the actual intent of the contracting parties themselves. *See, e.g., Fricke v. Fricke*, 42 N.W.2d 500 (Wis. 1950); *In re Marriage of Gudenkauf*, 204 N.W.2d 586 (Iowa 1973). *See also* Annotation, *Validity of Antenuptial Agreement, or "Companionate Marriage" Contract, Which Facilitates or Contemplates Divorce or Separation*, 70 A.L.R. 826 (1931); Annotation, *Validity, Construction, and Effect of Provision in Antenuptial Contract Forfeiting Property Rights of Innocent Spouse on Separation or Filing of Divorce or Other Matrimonial Action*, 57 A.L.R.2d 942 (1958); Swisher, *Divorce Planning in Antenuptial Agreements: Toward a New Objectivity*, 13 U. Rich. L. Rev. 175, 177–83 (1979).

For example, the Tennessee Court of Appeals in *Crouch v. Crouch*, 385 S.W.2d 288, 293 (Tenn. Ct. App. 1964) defended the traditional rationale for prohibiting divorce planning in premarital contracts in this manner:

> Such [a] contract could induce a mercenary husband to inflict on his wife any wrong he might desire with the knowledge [that] his pecuniary liability would be limited. In other words, a husband could through abuse and ill treatment of his wife force her to bring an action for divorce and thereby buy a divorce for a sum far less than he would otherwise have to pay. *Id.*

Query: Is this rationale persuasive to you? Why or why not? How did the *Osborne* court justify the need for divorce planning in premarital contracts? Was Mrs. Osborne a "mercenary wife" who inflicted such wrongs on her husband? Why or why not? Why didn't Barbara allow David to have his own independent legal counsel before he signed the premarital agreement only hours before the wedding? *See* Allison Marston, *Planning for Love: The Politics of Prenuptial Agreements,* 49 Stan. L. Rev. 887 (1997) (arguing that the courts should require that each party entering into a premarital agreement have the benefit of consulting with independent legal counsel prior to signing the agreement in order to prevent allegations of coercion and duress that are possible in the highly-charged atmosphere of an impeding wedding).

(2) A number of states have not yet reassessed their traditional public policy rule prohibiting divorce planning in premarital agreements in light of present societal needs, as the *Osbourne Frey* court did; and other judicial decisions continue to adhere to the traditional prohibition against any divorce planning in premarital agreements. *See, e.g., Duncan v. Duncan,* 652 S.W.2d 913 (Tenn. Ct. App. 1983). But as more states adopt the Uniform Premarital Agreement Act (*see* § 13.03[E], *below*) much of this legal uncertainty hopefully may be alleviated. In addition to the *Posner* and *Osborne* decisions, *above*, a number of other courts also recognize the concept of divorce planning in antenuptial contracts. *See, e.g. Newman v. Newman,* 553 P.2d 728 (Colo. 1982); *Volid v. Volid,* 286 N.E.2d 42 (Ill. App. Ct. 1972); *Unander v. Unander,* 506 P.2d 719 (Ore. 1973); *Frey v. Frey,* 471 A.2d 705 (Md. Ct. App. 1984).

[D] Waiver of Spousal Support

RIDER v. RIDER
Supreme Court of Indiana
669 N.E.2d 160 (1996)

SELBY, JUSTICE.

Charles Rider petitioned for dissolution of his marriage and sought to enforce an antenuptial agreement that he and his wife had executed just prior to marriage. The trial court enforced part, but not all, of the antenuptial agreement, and the Court of Appeals affirmed. We granted transfer, and we now hold that the trial court erred by not enforcing this agreement in its entirety.

FACTS

On February 8, 1988, Leslie Ann Sears and Charles Russell Rider entered into an antenuptial agreement. The agreement provided that "by virtue of the said marriage, neither one shall have or acquire any right, title, or claim in and to the real and personal estate of the other", and that "each party, in the case of a separation of the parties hereto, shall have no right as against the other by way of claims for support, alimony, attorney fees, legal and court costs, or division of property." The couple married on February 14, 1988. They lived in the house owned by Leslie, along with Leslie's teenage daughter from a prior marriage. They separated on August 13, 1992, and Charles sued for divorce on October 27, 1992.

Prior to marriage, Leslie worked as an auditor and Charles was employed by Delco Remy. Leslie owned her home, and each owned a car, but neither had any other property of significance. During their four-and-one-half year marriage, Leslie's health deteriorated, and she was diagnosed with inflammatory neuropathy. Her condition is incurable and causes considerable pain. As a result, Leslie quit her job and is now unable to work. . . .

PROCEDURAL HISTORY

During divorce proceedings, Leslie asked the trial court to enforce the antenuptial agreement with respect to property, but because of her condition and her inability to support herself, she asked the court to find the agreement to be invalid with respect to maintenance [spousal support]. The trial court agreed . . . [and] ordered Charles to pay Leslie $225 per month. . . .

Charles appealed from the trial court's award of maintenance, raising the issues of whether the trial court's decision amounted to an unconstitutional impairment of contract and whether the trial court erred by refusing to enforce the no-maintenance provision of the antenuptial agreement. . . . We granted transfer in order to examine the issue of when a trial court may choose to disregard all or part of a no-maintenance provision of an antenuptial agreement . . .

DISCUSSION

Antenuptial agreements are legal contracts which are entered into prior to marriage which attempt to settle the interest each spouse has in property of the other, both during marriage and upon its termination. This court has long held antenuptial agreements to be valid contracts, as long as they are entered into freely and without fraud, duress, or misrepresentation, and are not unconscionable. *See Mallow v. Eastes*, 179 Ind. 267, 100 N.E. 836 (1913); *Kennedy v. Kennedy*, 150 Ind. 636, 50 N.E. 756 (1898). . . . These early cases drew a distinction between agreements which took effect upon the death of a spouse as opposed to those which took effect upon dissolution of the marriage. . . .

Since these turn of the century cases, the number of subsequent marriages in our society has increased substantially. *See In re Marriage of Boren*, 475 N.E.2d 690, 693 (Ind. 1985). Individuals, especially those who have children from previous marriages, may wish to protect their property interests upon entering into a marriage. *Id.* at 694. In *Boren*, we concluded that policy reasons no longer compel us to find antenuptial agreements which take effect upon divorce to be void per se. Further, we held that the same traditional contract tests which apply to antenuptial agreements which take effect upon the death of a spouse also apply to antenuptial agreements pertaining to the dissolution of marriage. *Id. Boren* was the last time we addressed the issue of the validity of antenuptial agreements.

Since *Boren*, our Court of Appeals has had several occasions to address this issue. The leading case is *Justus v. Justus*, 581 N.E.2d 1265 (Ind. Ct. App. 1991) *trans. denied*. In *Justus*, the Court of Appeals was presented with a situation where the couple entered into an antenuptial agreement freely, without fraud, duress, or misrepresentation. However, during the course of the marriage there was a change in circumstances, and the trial court would not enforce the agreement in its entirety. The Court of Appeals . . . [discussed] cases from other jurisdictions, focusing primarily on *Newman v. Newman*, 653 P.2d 728 (Colo. 1982). In *Newman*, the Supreme Court of Colorado applied the general contract analysis for property division, but would not do so for maintenance. For the latter, the *Newman* court found that such provisions may become voidable as unconscionable due to circumstances existing *at the time of dissolution*. 653 P.2d at 734-35.

In *Justus*, the Court of Appeals noted that we, in *Boren*, had cited approvingly to *Newman*. Further, the *Justus* court found that where enforcement of an antenuptial agreement would leave a spouse in the position where he [or she] would be unable to support himself [or herself], the state's interest in not having the spouse become a public charge outweighs the parties' freedom to contract. *Justus*, 581 N.E.2d at 1273. Therefore, the *Justus* court agreed that a court may look to circumstances at the time of dissolution to determine unconscionability of an antenuptial agreement.

This view, that traditional contract law applies to antenuptial agreements unless unconscionable at the time of dissolution, is a growing trend in this country. Many states have codified this view by adopting the Uniform Premarital Agreement Act (1984) ("UPAA"). The UPAA reads in part:

> If a provision of a premarital agreement modifies or eliminates spousal support and that modification or elimination causes one party to the agreement to be eligible for support under a program of public assistance at the time of separation or marital dissolution, a court, notwithstanding the terms of the agreement, may require the other party to provide support to the extent necessary to avoid that eligibility.

UPAA Sec. 6(b). In addition to the states which have adopted the UPAA, courts in a number of other jurisdictions have adopted a similar view . . . . Although the courts in most of these cases apply traditional contract law, they modify it to take account of unconscionability at the time of divorce. Along with the state's interest in keeping the spouse off of public assistance, reasons for modifying traditional contract law [with regard to spousal support needs] include the fact that the state has a special interest in marriage, *see, e.g., MacFarlane v. Rich*, 132 N.H. 608, 567 A.2d 585 (1989); that there is substantial likelihood that the contracting parties were not dealing at arm's length, *see, e.g., Burtoff v. Burtoff*, 418 A.2d 1085 (D.C. 1980); and that the state is a third party to any marriage contract, *see, e.g., Gant v. Gant*, 174 W.Va. 740, 329 S.E.2d 106 (1985). Only a few states have adopted a contrary view [that an antenuptial agreement waiver of spousal support or maintenance is contractually enforceable, even if a spouse would become a public charge. *See, e.g., Baker v. Baker*, 622 So.2d 541 (Fla. Ct. App. 1993)].

We are asked in this particular case to examine an antenuptial agreement which was not unconscionable when made, but due to a change of circumstances would operate to create a financial hardship for one spouse. We note that in 1995, Indiana joined the growing list of states which have adopted the UPAA. . . . The Indiana statute did not take effect until July 1, 1995, and is therefore not applicable to this case. Still, the adoption of the UPAA provides useful guidance regarding the question of unconscionability and supports the trend of applying traditional contract law unless the agreement is unconscionable at the time of dissolution.

In this case, there is no evidence of fraud, duress, misrepresentation, or unconscionability at the time the contract was made. . . . [and] the agreement was silent regarding support in the event that one spouse would become disabled. Given these circumstances, if such support had been important to either of the parties, surely it would have been included in the agreement. Rather, the agreement specifically stated that if the parties separated, neither would be entitled to support.

As discussed above, the trial court found that Leslie has assets worth between $65,000 and $85,000. However, due to her illness and her inability to work, she is not capable of supporting herself. Thus, the trial court found that the agreement is "not binding" with regard to maintenance, and awarded Leslie $225/mo. The Court of Appeals agreed, finding that "an antenuptial provision limiting or eliminating spousal maintenance is unconscionable and will not be enforced when it would deprive a spouse of reasonable support that he or she is otherwise unable to secure". *Rider,* 648 N.E.2d at 665.

However, both the trial court and the Court of Appeals failed to consider the relative financial positions of the spouses. Unconscionability involves a gross disparity. *See Justus,* 581 N.E.2d at 1272. Thus, while an antenuptial agreement which would force one spouse onto public assistance may be unconscionable, we believe that a finding of unconscionability requires a comparison of the situations of the two parties. At the time of divorce, Leslie's assets were worth at least $65,000 and she received $645/mo. child support from a former spouse. Charles had personal assets which were worth only several thousand dollars and a pension which paid a gross $1,247/mo. . . . Given Charles' limited financial position, we do not find enforcement of the parties' own agreement to be unconscionable.

We agree with the trial judge that Leslie should continue to pursue her claims for disability and social security. While we sympathize with her, and we understand that enforcement of this contract eventually may force her to sell her home, we cannot find enforcement of this antenuptial agreement to be unconscionable. Finally, we note that this case does not involve a situation where, following divorce, one spouse is left with considerable assets while the other spouse is left virtually penniless, with no means of support. Rather, in this case, one party is left with a modest income stream, while the other party is left with a modest amount of real and personal property.

CONCLUSION

This antenuptial agreement is enforceable. We remand to the trial court for action consistent with this opinion . . .

NOTES AND QUESTIONS

(1) Courts applying a more traditional approach to the waiver of spousal support in premarital agreements point out that although the parties themselves may validly limit or waive alimony on divorce in a separation agreement, at the time such a separation agreement is drafted the parties presumably understand their immediate economic needs and their ability to provide for them. But if the parties waive or limit their respective rights to alimony in an antenuptial agreement, many years later upon divorce their economic needs and abilities may have drastically changed. Thus

> [t]he real reason for invalidating such antenuptial contracts seems to be that although the [spousal support] provisions may be fair at the time they are made, they may not be later when the separation or divorce occurs. The wife may thus be left with entirely inadequate support, or the husband with an excessively heavy liability to his wife [or vice versa]. . . . Thus, the difficulty of forecasting the parties' circumstances so far in the future has led the courts to disallow antenuptial contracts which attempt to do this with respect to support.

Reiling v. Reiling, 474 P.2d 327, 328 (Or. 1970), *quoting* H. Clark, The Law of Domestic Relations in the United States 28–29 (1968).

What is a possible solution to this problem? Using an objective case-by-case evaluation, alimony or spousal support provisions—or provisions waiving such support—in antenuptial agreements would be upheld by the court if the terms were fair and made with full disclosure. Otherwise, like separation agreements in most states, these provisions might be modified or reformed under the court's equitable powers. Perhaps the party's circumstances should be evaluated at the time enforcement of the agreement is sought, as the Oregon Supreme Court has stated:

> We have now come to the conclusion that antenuptial agreements concerning alimony should be enforced unless enforcement deprives a spouse of support that he or she cannot otherwise secure. A provision providing that no alimony shall be paid will be enforced unless the spouse has no other reasonable source of support. If the circumstances of the parties change, the court can modify the decree just as it can modify a decree based upon [a separation] agreement made in contemplation of divorce which has a provision regarding payment of support.

Unander v. Unander, 506 P.2d 719, 721 (Or. 1973), *overruling in part Reiling v. Reiling, above.*

(2) *Query.* How does the Uniform Premarital Agreement Act address this spousal support problem? How did the *Rider* court, *above*, address this problem?

(3) Some other courts, however, insist on applying classical contract principles to separation agreements and to premarital agreements, and will not modify any waiver or limitation of alimony or spousal support provisions in the agreement, absent clear evidence of fraud, duress, unconscionability, or designed concealment. *See, e.g. Baker v. Baker*, 622 So. 2d 541, 543–44 (Fla. Dist. Ct. App. 1993) (holding that premarital agreements waiving spousal support are enforceable even if one spouse would become destitute and a public charge); *Simeone v. Simeone*, 581 A.2d 162, 165–66 (Pa. 1990) (holding that a premarital agreement's alleged unconscionability should be determined at the time of execution; that virtually all marriages involve a change of circumstances; and that this fact alone should not otherwise invalidate an otherwise valid contract). *Cf. Moore v. Gillis*, 391 S.E.2d 255 (Va. 1990). Which approach, in your opinion, is the better reasoned approach in evaluating a waiver or limitation of spousal support in premarital agreements? Why?

[E] The Uniform Premarital Agreement Act

UNIFORM PREMARITAL AGREEMENT ACT (1983)
9B U.L.A. 369
Drafted by the National Conference of Commissioners on Uniform State Laws

PREFATORY NOTE

The number of marriages between persons previously married and the number of marriages between persons each of whom is intending to continue to pursue a career is steadily increasing. For these and other reasons, it is becoming more and more common for persons contemplating marriage to seek to resolve by agreement certain issues presented by the forthcoming marriage. However, despite a lengthy legal history for these premarital agreements, there is a substantial uncertainty as to the enforceability of all, or a portion, of the provisions of these agreements and a significant lack of uniformity of treatment of these agreements among the states. The problems caused by this uncertainty and nonuniformity are greatly exacerbated by the mobility of our population. Nevertheless, this uncertainty and nonuniformity seem reflective not so much of basic policy differences between the states but rather a result of spasmodic, reflexive response to varying factual circumstances at different times. Accordingly, uniform legislation conforming to modern social policy which provides both certainty and sufficient flexibility to accommodate different circumstances would appear to be both a significant improvement and a goal realistically capable of achievement.

This Act is intended to be relatively limited in scope. Section 1 defines a "premarital agreement" as "an agreement between prospective spouses made in contemplation of marriage and to be effective upon marriage." Section 2 requires that a premarital agreement be in writing and signed by both parties. Section 4 provides that a premarital agreement becomes effective upon the marriage of the parties. These sections establish significant parameters. That is, the Act does not deal with agreements between persons who live together but who do not contemplate marriage or who do not marry. Nor does the Act provide for postnuptial or separation agreements or with oral agreements.

On the other hand, agreements which are embraced by the act are permitted to deal with a wide variety of matters and Section 3 provides an *illustrative* list of those matters, including spousal support, which may properly be dealt with in a premarital agreement.

Section 6 is the key operative section of the Act and sets forth the conditions under which a premarital agreement is not enforceable. An agreement is not enforceable if the party against whom enforcement is sought proves that (a) he or she did not execute the agreement voluntarily or that (b) the agreement was unconscionable when it was executed and, before execution of the agreement, he or she (1) was not provided a fair and reasonable disclosure of the property or financial obligations of the other party, (2) did not voluntarily and expressly waive, in writing, any right to disclosure of the property or financial obligations of the other party beyond the disclosure provided, *and* (3) did not have, or reasonably could not have had, an adequate knowledge of the property and financial obligations of the other party.

Even if these conditions are not proven, if a provision of a premarital agreement modifies or eliminates spousal support, and that modification or elimination would cause a party to be eligible for support under a program of public assistance at the time of separation, marital dissolution, or death, a court is authorized to order the other party to provide support to the extent necessary to avoid that eligibility.

These sections form the heart of the Act; the remaining sections deal with more tangential issues. Section 5 prescribes the manner in which a premarital agreement may be amended or revoked; Section 7 provides for very limited enforcement where a marriage is subsequently determined to be void; and Section 8 tolls any statute of limitations applicable to an action asserting a claim for relief under a premarital agreement during the parties' marriage.

SECTION 1. DEFINITIONS

As used in this Act:

(1) "Premarital agreement" means an agreement between prospective spouses made in contemplation of marriage and to be effective upon marriage.

(2) "Property" means an interest, present or future, legal or equitable, vested or contingent, in real or personal property, including income and earnings . . .

SECTION 2. FORMALITIES.

A premarital agreement must be in writing and signed by both parties. It is enforceable without consideration. . . .

SECTION 3. CONTENT.

(a) Parties to a premarital agreement may contract with respect to:
  (1) the rights and obligations of each of the parties in any of the property of either or both of them whenever and wherever acquired or located;
  (2) the right to buy, sell, use, transfer, exchange, abandon, lease, consume, expend, assign, create a security interest in, mortgage, encumber, dispose of, or otherwise manage and control property;
  (3) the disposition of property upon separation, marital dissolution, death, or the occurrence or nonoccurrence of any other event;
  (4) the modification or elimination of spousal support;
  (5) the making of a will, trust, or other arrangement to carry out the provisions of the agreement;
  (6) the ownership rights in and disposition of the death benefit from a life insurance policy;
  (7) the choice of law governing the construction of the agreement; and
  (8) any other matter, including their personal rights and obligations, not in violation of public policy or a statute imposing a criminal penalty.
(b) The right of a child to support may not be adversely affected by a premarital agreement. . . .

SECTION 4. EFFECT OF MARRIAGE.

A premarital agreement becomes effective upon marriage. . . .

SECTION 5. AMENDMENT, REVOCATION.

After marriage, a premarital agreement may be amended or revoked only by a written agreement signed by the parties. The amended agreement or the revocation is enforceable without consideration. . . .

SECTION 6. ENFORCEMENT.

(a) A premarital agreement is not enforceable if the party against whom enforcement is sought proves that:
  (1) that party did not execute the agreement voluntarily; or
  (2) the agreement was unconscionable when it was executed and, before execution of the agreement, that party:
    (i) was not provided a fair and reasonable disclosure of the property of financial obligations of the other party;

(ii) did not voluntarily and expressly waive, in writing, any right to disclosure of the property or financial obligations of the other party beyond the disclosure provided; and

(iii) did not have, or reasonably could not have had, an adequate knowledge of the property or financial obligations of the other party.

(b) If a provision of a premarital agreement modifies or eliminates spousal support and that modification or elimination causes one party to the agreement to be eligible for support under a program of public assistance at the time of separation or marital dissolution, a court, notwithstanding the terms of the agreement, may require the other party to provide support to the extent necessary to avoid that eligibility.

(c) An issue of unconscionability of a premarital agreement shall be decided by the court as a matter of law.

COMMENT

Nothing in Section 6 makes the absence of assistance of independent legal counsel a condition for the unenforceability of a premarital agreement. However, lack of that assistance may well be a factor in determining whether the conditions stated in Section 6 may have existed (see, e.g., *Del Vecchio v. Del Vecchio*, 143 So. 2d 17 (Fla. 1962).

Even if the conditions stated in subsection (a) are not proven, if a provision of a premarital agreement modifies or eliminates spousal support, subsection (b) authorizes a court to provide very limited relief to a party who would otherwise be eligible for public welfare (see, e.g., *Osborne v. Osborne*, 428 N.E.2d 810 (Mass. 1981) (dictum); *Unander v. Unander*, 506 P.2d 719 (Ore. 1973) (dictum). . . .

SECTION 7. ENFORCEMENT: VOID MARRIAGE.

If a marriage is determined to be void, an agreement that would otherwise have been a premarital agreement is enforceable only to the extent necessary to avoid an inequitable result . . .

SECTION 8. LIMITATIONS OF ACTIONS.

Any statute of limitations applicable to an action asserting a claim for relief under a premarital agreement is tolled during the marriage of the parties to the agreement. However, equitable defenses limiting the time for enforcement, including laches and estoppel, are available to either party. . . .

SECTION 11. SEVERABILITY.

If any provision of this [Act] or its application to any person or circumstance is held invalid, the invalidity does not affect other provisions or applications of this [Act] which can be given effect without the invalid provision or application, and to this end the provisions of this [Act] are severable.

NOTES AND QUESTIONS

(1) At present, the Uniform Premarital Agreement Act has been adopted in 24 states, including: Arizona. Arkansas, California, Hawaii, Idaho, Illinois, Indiana, Iowa, Kansas, Maine, Montana, Nebraska, Nevada, New Jersey, New Mexico, North Carolina, North Dakota, Oregon, South Dakota, Rhode Island, Texas, Utah and Virginia.

(2) How does the Uniform Act address the problem that a spouse who initially waives the right to spousal support in a premarital agreement might in fact require spousal support a number of years in the future? How does the Act affect child support obligations? *See* Annotation, *Opening or Modification of Divorce Decree as to Custody or Support of Child Not Provided for in the Decree*, 71 A.L.R.2d 1370, 1396 (1960) and Later Case Service; 1 H. Clark, The Law of Domestic Relations in the United States 48–63 (2d ed. 1987) (both stating the general rule that child support provisions—and child custody provisions—in marital agreements are always modifiable, no matter what may be provided to the contrary in the marital agreement). *Query:* Why is this important distinction made between spousal support provisions and child support provisions in premarital and postmarital agreements?

(3) Does the Uniform Premarital Agreement Act expressly require independent legal counsel for each party? Is independent legal counsel still advisable? Why or why not? *See* Allison Marston, *Planning for Love: The Politics of Prenuptial Agreements*, 49 Stan. L. Rev. 887 (1997) (arguing that the courts should require each person entering into a premarital agreement have independent legal counsel). In your jurisdiction, could an attorney ethically represent both parties to an antenuptial agreement, as the attorney in *In re Estate of Benker*, reprinted in § 13.03[B], *above*, purported to do?

(4) Regardless of whether a particular state applies traditional contract principles, a hybrid "divorce-planning" view, or the Uniform Premarital Act approach to premarital agreements, the increased use of antenuptial contracts has had a mixed reception, as demonstrated by this letter to, and answer from, a popular newspaper columnist:

DEAR ABBY: I read with interest the letter from "Parents of the Bride," whose daughter had been manipulated into signing a prenuptial agreement on her wedding eve. Some years ago, I married a very wealthy man who asked me to sign a prenuptial agreement. He said he "couldn't" marry me unless I signed it. The agreement not only protected his premarital assets, it prevented me from sharing in any income he earned during our marriage, stipulating what I would receive should we be divorced and it guaranteed me only a pittance in his will. I hated the agreement, but I loved the man, so I signed it against the advice of an attorney. I was convinced that I was marrying a fair and generous man, and felt confident that after we were married, he would trash the document. I was wrong. After many years of marriage, he refused to alter or destroy the agreement, all the while proclaiming his great love for me. He gave me a modest allowance for my personal needs. I bought most of my clothes and even my new car with my earnings. (Yes, I continued to work after my marriage. I was afraid to quit because I felt financially insecure.) When I finally caught him with another woman (I later learned there had been many), I had the choice of putting up with his philandering, or I could leave empty-handed. I chose to leave while I was still able to support myself rather than having him dump me in my old age. I got exactly what the prenuptial agreement stated except that due to inflation, my pittance of alimony barely pays for my birdseed. My advice to any woman who is asked to sign a prenuptial agreement is to run as fast as she can from the stingy bum. Women, everywhere, should refuse to sign them. A well-known divorce lawyer once said: "Prenuptial agreements serve only to deny a woman the rights she has under the law, to property accumulated during her marriage. I have never seen a marriage work that required a prenuptial agreement." CHEATED IN SAN FRANCISCO

DEAR CHEATED: Whatever happened to "equal rights"? Prenuptial agreements can benefit (and/or protect) women as well as men. But each party should retain his or her own attorney.

Query: Do you agree with this negative assessment of antenuptial agreements generally? Why or why not? *See* Gail Frommer Brod, *Premarital Agreements and Gender Justice*, 6 Yale J.L. & Feminism 229 (1994) (arguing that premarital agreements invariably harm women by waiving various legal and financial protections offered by state law, and magnifying an unequal distribution of marital wealth along gender lines). *But see also* Leah Guggenheimer, *A Modest Proposal: The Feminomics of Drafting Premarital Agreements*, 17 Women's Rights L. Rep. 147 (1996) (arguing that emphasizing women's alleged "inferior status and bargaining power" in premarital agreements only reinforces the perception that women are the "weaker sex", and justifies the view that the law—and men—need to "protect women from themselves").

(5) **Problem.** Assume that you are a family law practitioner in your particular state, and Sarah Green comes to you for legal advice and counsel. Sarah and Michael McGuire are currently in their last year of law school, and they are planning to be married. They have been dating each other for the past two years, and they believe there is a strong foundation on which to build a martial relationship. Because Sarah's parents were divorced when she was nine years old, however, Sarah wants a written premarital agreement spelling out the nature of their marital relationship, and the marital sharing benefits and obligations that each shall have upon marriage. Michael, however, comes from a more stable and loving family relationship, where his parents have been married for over thirty years, and Michael has three brothers and two sisters. Michael tells Sarah that they do *not* need any premarital agreement between them, because Michael strongly believes that marriage is much more than a written contract, and that their love will endure--like Michael's parents--for better or for worse

Sarah has a good job offer with a large metropolitan law firm after graduation. She was Articles Editor for the Law Review, and she was the recipient of a law school scholarship for the past three years. Michael's law school grades are fairly good, and he was on the school's Moot Court Board and intercollegiate moot court team, but he is still looking for employment. Michael does have a job offer with a large interstate bank, but it is in a nonlegal capacity. Michael has substantial student loans from law school; Sarah does not.

Sarah is looking forward to her new job with the large metropolitan law firm. In a "few years," though, Sarah and Michael would like to raise a family, preferably having one or two children (Sarah wants at least one child, Michael wants at least three). Sarah is Jewish, and although her religion is very important to her, she does not attend temple on a regular basis. Michael is devout Roman Catholic and he attends church on a regular basis. Although Sarah and Michael are aware of their familial and religious differences, they love each other very much, and they are planning to be married soon after they take the state Bar Exam.

What realistic legal advice would you give Sarah? *See, e.g.* Lenore Weitzman, *Legal Regulation of Marriage: Tradition and Change*, 62 Calif. L. Rev. 1169 (1974); Jana Singer, *The Privatization of Family Law*, 1992 Wis. L. Rev. 1443 (1992); Leah Guggenheimer, *A Modest Proposal: The Feminomics of Drafting Premarital Agreements*, 17 Women's Rts. L. Rep. 147 (1996). *But see also* Gail Frommer Brod, *Premarital Agreements and Gender*

Justice, 6 Yale J.L. & Feminism 229 (1994), and Patricia Tidwell & Peter Linzer, *The Flesh-Colored Band-Aid: Contracts, Feminism, Dialogue, and Norms*, 28 Houston L. Rev. 791 (1991).

(6) **Problem.** Nancy and Charles plan to be married in the near future, and come to your law office for advice. They want you to draft a premarital agreement for them regarding certain financial and property matters as well as other specified rights and obligations.

Nancy and Charles met at Seawash University, where Nancy was obtaining an M.B.A. degree, and Charles was attending medical school. Both are presently employed in the City of Metropolis, State of Brandeis. Nancy is employed with a brokerage firm an annual salary of $100,000 a year, and Charles is a neurosurgeon, earning approximately $350,000 a year in private practice.

Both Nancy and Charles have accumulated certain real and personal property that they wish to retain as separate property. Charles also inherited a country estate, Blackacre, from his maternal grandparents. He desires to give Blackacre to Nancy as a premarital gift, but in the event of divorce, for whatever reason, Nancy must return Blackacre back to Charles.

They both desire to retain their present and future salaries as separate property, and as far as their household and "other marital expenses," Charles and Nancy agree to pay for them on a 3:1 ratio, according to their present salary scale. In the event of divorce or legal separation, neither Charles nor Nancy desire spousal support, and both agree to waive any future spousal support rights in their premarital agreement.

Charles and Nancy further agree that they will not have any children for at least three years, and at the end of that time they will have one or two children. During this time, sexual relations will only occur upon mutual consent and Charles will be responsible for birth control measures during these first three years. Nancy will continue to work as a stockbroker except for brief periods during pregnancy and childbirth. They will hire a housekeeper who will take care of the children, and they will equally provide for the children's education in private schools and college.

(a) What would you advise Nancy and Charles regarding their proposed premarital agreement? Are all their intentions contractually enforceable? Could you represent both of them in drafting this premarital agreement, or only one of them?

(b) *Scenario six years later*. After signing the premarital agreement and after the parties' subsequent marriage, a few unexpected events occurred. Charles was negligent one night in maintaining proper birth control measures, and the result was twins. Nancy had a difficult pregnancy and was forced to leave her job for an extended period of time. She finally lost her job when her brokerage company collapsed due to an insider trading scandal and a subsequent company merger, and although Nancy was blameless, no one in Metropolis wants to hire her. However, Nancy is happy and fulfilled as a homemaker and caretaker of her two minor children without the help of a housekeeper.

Meanwhile, Charles had decided to give up his lucrative medical practice where he is now making $525,000 a year and join the medical school faculty at Seawash University to do research at $100,000 a year. Subsequently, Charles met Wanda, a sociology professor at Seawash, and Charles developed an intimate relationship with Wanda. Charles now intends to divorce Nancy and marry Wanda.

What effect, if any, do these subsequent facts have on Nancy and Charles' premarital agreement? *See also* Carol Weisbrod, *The Way We Live Now: A Discussion of Contracts and Domestic Relations*, 1994 Utah L. Rev. 777 (1994).

§ 13.04 Separation or Property Settlement Agreements

[A] Introduction

Separation agreements, also called property settlement agreements, were once looked upon by many courts as illegal contracts and void as against public policy, since such agreements between a husband and wife to live separate and apart in the future were believed to be in derogation of marriage, in effect promoting the procurement of divorce. Historically, however, separation agreements between a husband and wife were generally upheld as valid if the separation took place prior to the time of the agreement, or immediately following it. *See* J. Madden, Handbook of the Law of Persons and Domestic Relations 331–35 (1931).

Today separation agreements, are favored by the law, thus allowing a husband and wife, with the help of their respective attorneys, to contractually agree upon a division of marital property and other marital assets and debts, spousal and child support, child custody matters, pension and retirement plans, life and health insurance coverage, tax planning, and the like prior to divorce.

The benefits of a voluntary contractual separation agreement between a husband and wife over an adversarial court-imposed order are numerous:

> The parties to a marriage in a separation situation can usually better resolve disputed matters by agreement worked out between themselves than can any divorce judge dealing with the same matters. The parties know themselves, their problems, their children, their assets, their liabilities, and their needs better than any judge, who at best has only limited knowledge of these matters.

> The experience of most practitioners and the courts demonstrates that a voluntary separation and property settlement agreement, with fair and reasonable compromise on both sides, usually results in the parties voluntarily abiding by the solutions contained in such agreements. Court-imposed solutions are often ignored or flouted and more often require court enforcement. Moreover, in most jurisdictions there are very serious delays before the parties can go to trial on the contested calendar. This factor should be weighed by the parties in seeking compromises that permit reaching an agreement.

S. Green & J. Long, Marriage and Family Law Agreements, 213 (1984). *See also Drawdy v. Drawdy*, 268 S.E.2d 30, 31 (S.C. 1980): "Property settlement agreements are praiseworthy products of cooperation between parties seeking a divorce. They also serve to decrease the workload on family courts and thereby enhance judicial efficiency."

However, if a husband and wife for various reasons are unwilling or unable to contractually settle their support and property rights prior to divorce, or if one of the parties is represented by an unethical attorney (a so-called "bomber" in the profession) who intentionally refuses any reasonable settlement in order to "keep the meter running," then a separation agreement may not be possible, and the only alternative may be costly and time-consuming litigation in court. The vast majority of marital dissolution or divorce actions today, however, involve some kind of separation or property settlement contractual agreement between the parties.

Nevertheless, since the parties in a divorce proceeding often experience a great deal of anger, hurt, and other strong emotionals, the family law practitioner often must affirmatively act as his or her client's legal counselor in explaining the many benefits inherent in a fair separation agreement as a reasonable compromise, even though his or her client may not initially be predisposed to such a contractual settlement. *See generally* A. Lindey & L. Parley, Lindey on Separation Agreements and Antenuptial Contracts, (Matthew Bender 1997 rev. ed.).

Alternatively, as with premarital agreements, the parties may desire to provide *more* economic and marital benefits than would ordinarily be required by state statute, involving enhanced child support, spousal support, division of property on divorce, and enhanced educational, medical, or insurance benefits for the parties' children.

[B] Necessary Elements for a Valid Separation Agreement

A separation or property settlement agreement, as with most other marital contracts, will be enforced by the courts if the agreement is viewed as "fair." *See, e.g., Reynolds v. Reynolds*, 415 A.2d 535, 537 (D.C. Ct. App. 1980): "This jurisdiction encourages the parties in any marital dispute to resolve by agreement their joint marital interests. In the absence of fraud, duress, concealment or overreaching, an agreement is binding no matter how ill-advised a party may have been in executing it." *But see also* Sally Burnett Sharp, *Fairness Standards and Separation Agreements: A Word of Caution on Contractual Freedom*, 132 U. Pa. L. Rev. 1399 (1984). But how will this "fairness" requirement for a valid separation agreement be interpreted by the courts? The following case presents one illustration.

GOLDER v. GOLDER
Idaho Supreme Court
714 P.2d 26 (1986)

DONALDSON, C.J.

This appeal stems from an independent action by a former wife to reopen a judgment and decree of divorce in order to obtain equitable relief from the property settlement agreement incorporated in the decree. James and Diane Golder were married on September 5, 1970. They subsequently adopted one child, Tara, on April 9, 1975. James Golder is a stockbroker and was elected to the Idaho Legislature in 1976. He continued as a legislator throughout the course of proceedings in the present action. Diane is currently employed as a secretary and was so employed throughout most of the marriage. During their marriage, the parties owned and managed various rental properties. In 1978 they purchased a chrome plating business which was subsequently sold on June 1, 1979.

The marriage began to deteriorate in 1978 and by early 1979, the Golders decided that divorce was inevitable and began to discuss a division of their community property. On July 5, 1979, Diane signed her interest in eight deeds of trust in community real property over to James. On July 6, 1979 the parties entered into a property settlement agreement. The agreement provided that Diane was to receive one-half of the household furniture (stipulated value $2,500), a 1971 Plymouth automobile (stipulated value $800), the funds in their joint checking account ($77 on July 6, 1979), and the funds in her credit union account ($441 on July 6, 1979). In addition, James agreed to give Diane $20,000, payable in $100 monthly installments without interest. The remainder of the community property was declared to be James's sole and separate property. Such remainder was not itemized except to state that it included "certain stocks and bonds and real property which husband has acquired."

The agreement gave Diane custody of Tara, allowing James visitation two nights a week, every other weekend and every other holiday and summer. James agreed to pay Diane $75 per month as child support.

James filed for divorce the same day the agreement was signed. A hearing was held on August 9, 1979. Diane did not appear at the hearing and a judgment granting the divorce and incorporating the property settlement agreement was entered on that date.

The property settlement agreement was drafted by James's attorney. Diane was not represented by counsel at the property negotiations nor at the time of the granting of the divorce. In the action to reopen the divorce, the parties stipulated that the value of the Golders' community property was $352,675.00 on July 6, 1979, the date the property settlement agreement was signed, and $355,566.00 on August 9, 1979, the date the divorce was granted. The present value of the property Diane received in the divorce settlement was $13,536.04.

On August 8, 1980, Diane initiated an independent action seeking to reopen the judgment and decree of divorce. . . .

Trial on the property issues was held on September 19-23, 1983. The district court determined that the property agreement had merged into the divorce decree and therefore that the action was before the court as an equitable independent action to relieve a party from judgment pursuant to I.R.C.P. 60(b). The court found James guilty of fraud and overreaching and ordered equitable redivision of the community property. The court determined that the community property had a value in excess of $355,000.00 at the date of divorce of which Diane had already received $10,875. It therefore awarded her an additional $166,125.00. James appeals from this award. Diane has cross-appealed asserting that the trial court erred in refusing to award her attorney fees and punitive damages.

I.

We begin our analysis by noting that an independent action to relieve a party from a judgment is a most unusual remedy. It is available only rarely, under the most exceptional circumstances. *Compton v. Compton*, 101 Idaho 328, 335, 612 P.2d 1175, 1182 (1980). Such an action will lie only in the presence of extreme fraud. Absent overreaching, the burden is on the claimant to prove each element of fraud by clear and convincing evidence. *Id.* The presence of overreaching, however, "automatically shifts the burden to the party benefited by the unequal agreement to show that the community should not be reapportioned." *Id.* at 336, 612 P.2d at 1183.

In the instant case, the trial court, applying the standards set out in *Compton*, found that James Golder was guilty of both fraud and overreaching in negotiating the property settlement agreement. On appeal, James asserts that these findings are not supported by the record.

The determination of whether the degree of fraud in a particular case rises to the level justifying relief from a judgment requires an assessment of both the relationship between the parties and the actual conduct involved. *Compton, supra* at 335, 612 P.2d at 1182. The courts must strike a balance between competing interests. On one side rests the need for finality of judgments. On the other lies justice the courts' reluctance to serve as a shield in the perpetration of a fraud.

The marital relationship imposes the high duty of care of a fiduciary on each of the parties. This duty continues until the moment of the marriage's termination.

> This fiduciary duty extends to the parties' negotiations leading to the formation of the property settlement agreement during marriage, and requires, at least, a disclosure by both parties of all information within their knowledge regarding the existence of community property and of pertinent facts necessary to arrive at a reasonable valuation of the property. Like a business partner, each spouse is free to adopt a position favorable to himself or herself regarding the property's valuation, its inclusion in the community, or other such issues. They are not free, however, to resolve such issues unilaterally by concealing the very existence of particular items or amounts of property.

Id. at 336, 612 P.2d at 1183. In the instant case, the trial court found that James had concealed the equity values of the parties' property.

> James made false representations to Diane as to the value of community assets and liabilities. His concealment of the substantial equity values of the parties' property to the degree indicated here constituted an extreme degree of fraud. . . .

> He had $26,000.00 in a money market fund that he never disclosed to Diane [and] in loan documents at Idaho First as of September 1, 1978 a net worth of $313,030.00 was shown. . . .

Diane was without legal representation throughout the course of the property settlement negotiations and divorce. The district court found that James had threatened Diane with custody litigation if she secured legal representation or disputed the property settlement agreement, and concluded that James was guilty of overreaching. This Court noted in *Compton* that "[o]verreaching often appears where one of the parties is not represented by independent counsel." *Id.* at 336, 612 P.2d at 1183.

The district court carefully followed the mandate of *Compton* and in a well-reasoned memorandum decision found that Diane had proven both fraud and overreaching under the strict standards set out in that opinion. Findings of fact by a trial court will not be disturbed on appeal unless they are clearly erroneous. I.R.C.P. 52(a). We have carefully reviewed the record in this case and we conclude that it supports the trial court's findings that James Golder was guilty of both fraud and overreaching. Accordingly, we affirm the trial court's decision reopening the judgment and decree of divorce and equitably redividing the parties' community property.

II.

Diane has cross-appealed asserting that the trial court erred in denying her motions for punitive damages and attorney fees. Punitive damages are not favored in the law and should be awarded only in the most unusual and compelling circumstances. *Cheney v. Palos Verdes Inv. Corp.*, 104 Idaho 897, 904-05, 665 P.2d 661 (1983). In the instant case, the trial court concluded that the harsh remedy of punitive damages was inappropriate. An award of punitive damages is within the province of the trier of fact and the trial court is granted wide discretion in determining when such an award is appropriate. *Id.* at 904, 665 P.2d at 668. Absent an abuse of discretion, the trial court's decision will not be disturbed on appeal. We hold that the trial court did not abuse its discretion in denying an award of punitive damages in the present case.

Similarly, we hold that the trial court did not abuse its discretion in refusing to award attorney fees. . . .

Such an award is not appropriate where a party has the financial resources necessary to prosecute or defend the action. . . . In the instant case, Diane was awarded an additional $166,000 as her share of the parties' community property. In light of this award, it cannot be said that Diane was without sufficient funds to pay her attorney fees. We therefore hold that the trial court did not abuse its discretion in failing to award attorney fees. . . .

BISTLINE, J., concurring in part, dissenting in part.

I concur in all of the majority's opinion except its holding that the district court did not abuse its discretion in refusing to award punitive damages. If ever there were a case justifying imposition of such damages, and if ever there were a case where the district court abused its discretion in not awarding them, this is it. The test for justifying an award of punitive damages was established in *Cheney v. Palos Verdes Investment Corp.*, 104 Idaho 897, 905, 665 P.2d 661, 669 (1983), wherein this Court stated:

> An award of punitive damages will be sustained on appeal only when it is shown that the defendant acted in a manner that was "an extreme deviation from reasonable standards of conduct, and that the act was performed by the defendant with an understanding of or disregard for its likely consequences . . . ." The justification for punitive damages must be that the defendant acted with an extremely harmful state of mind, whether that state be terms "malice, oppression, fraud or gross negligence." (Citations omitted.)

Here we have Mr. Golder defrauding his wife out of $166,000 through acts of deceit, threats, and grand-scale bullying. It is inconceivable to view Mr. Golder's acts as being anything but unreasonable; they extremely deviate from any "reasonable standards of conduct." *Id.* Only an individual possessing "an extremely harmful state of mind," could have committed the acts of fraud Mr. Golder committed in this case.

Mr. Golder deserves to be punished, on of the purposes of punitive damages. As this Court has stated, "the public purpose behind punitive damages is both to punish and to deter." *Abbie Uriguen Oldsmobile Buick, Inc. v. United States Fire Ins. Co.*, 95 Idaho 501, 504, 511 P.2d 783, 786 (1973); *see also Shields v. Martin*, 109 Idaho 132, 706 P.2d 21, 27 (1985) ("Punitive damages are not awarded for purposes of compensating the plaintiff, but to punish the defendant and deter others from following defendant's example.").

As this Court stated in *Boise Dodge, Inc. v. Clark*, 92 Idaho 902, 909, 453 P.2d 551, 558 (1969): "Exemplary damages are more likely to serve their desired purpose of deterring similar conduct in a Fraud case . . . than in any other area of tort." Quoting *Walker v. Shelton*, 223 N.Y.S.2d 488, 492, 179 N.E.2d 497, 499 91961), cited with approval in *Cheney, supra*, 104 Idaho at 905, 665 P.2d at 669.

The facts in this case speak for themselves. Punitive damages should have been imposed. I would therefore affirm, but remand to the district court for a hearing on the amount of deterrence which might reasonably be expected to deter such future conduct. . . .

NOTES AND QUESTIONS

(1) **Full Disclosure of the Parties' Worth.** As the *Golder* court emphasized, the marital relationship imposes a fiduciary duty on each of the parties which requires, at the very least, full disclosure and fair dealing by each party regarding his or her financial assets. If full disclosure of the parties' assets is not made, the separation agreement may be voided for fraud, overreaching (taking unfair advantage of the other spouse), or designed concealment. *See also Cook v. Cook,* 912 P.2d 264 (Nev. 1996); *Creeks v. Creeks,* 619 A.2d 754 (Pa. Super. Ct. 1993); *Williams v. Williams,* 508 A.2d 985 (Md. 1985); *Koizim v. Koizim,* 435 A.2d 1030 (Conn. 1980). In the *Creeks* case, wife's attorney alleged that husband had breached the disclosure clause of the parties' separation agreement, and successfully sought to have a constructive trust imposed by the court on the concealed and undisclosed marital assets.

If the marital assets are modest or easily discoverable, then the full disclosure schedules made by husband and wife in their separation agreement may be prepared informally, as representing a reasonable approximation of the parties' assets and liabilities. However, in cases involving more substantial marital assets, or when the possibility of designed concealment may occur, it is strongly recommended that certified public accountants prepare the full disclosure financial statement for each party.

(2) **Independent Legal Advice.** In another part of the *Golder* opinion, the court stated that "overreaching often appears where one of the parties is not represented by independent legal counsel." *Query:* Does this mean that the lack of independent legal counsel for both parties will always render a separation agreement invalid and unenforceable? Not necessarily, although almost all courts and legal commentators recommend that each party to a separation agreement should indeed have independent legal advice before signing the document. For example, in *Croft v. Croft,* 478 So. 2d 258, 263 (Miss. 1985), the court emphasized that since both husband and wife were represented by independent legal counsel, this fact alone constituted strong evidence that each party was advised of his or her respective rights and responsibilities under the separation agreement, and that each party knowingly and voluntarily agreed to be bound by that agreement. On the other hand, in *Whitney v. Seattle-First Nat'l Bank,* 579 P.2d 937, 940 (Wash. 1978), the court stated that since "the [separation] agreement here was fair and reasonable, and because petitioner has not shown fraud or overreaching, there is no absolute requirement that the wife have acted upon the competent, independent advice of counsel, or that she specifically be informed of her right to seek the same. This holding [however] is not meant to dissuade counsel from recommending that independent legal counsel be consulted in appropriate cases."

Thus, when only one party in a separation agreement has an attorney, the courts will closely examine the circumstances that led to the other party not being represented, including the unrepresented party's awareness of the financial circumstances surrounding the agreement, and the unrepresented party's ability to understand the agreement and to waive counsel. *See, e.g., Levine v. Levine,* 451 N.Y.S.2d 26 (N.Y. 1982); *McClellan v. McClellan,*

451 A.2d 334 (Md. Ct. App. 1982), *cert. denied*, 462 U.S. 1135 (1982). *And see also* 1 A. Lindey & L. Parley, Lindey on Separation Agreements and Antenuptial Contracts §§ 6.01-6.06 (Matthew Bender 1997 rev. ed.)

Comment. The reality in many uncontested divorce situations is that one party may be easily manipulated by the other. Sometimes one spouse feels guilty about his or her role in ending the relationship, especially (but not only) if an affair was involved, or if there are children in the family. Often a spouse wants to "put this behind me and move on" as fast as possible, feels a need to try to retain the friendship and good will of the other, or is otherwise so inclined to avoid conflict that he or she cannot effectively look out for his or her long-term interests. Situations where one party is subject to the other's manipulations or strong wishes arise surprisingly often and are not easily recognized by the inexperienced or unattuned attorney. In this situation, a spouse willing to take advantage of the other might privately urge that separate counsel not be retained, to save money and "so the lawyers don't get us fighting just so they can have some work to do." To counter this, strong and sincere urging by counsel for the represented party that the other spouse at least retain counsel to look over the draft agreement, or even refuse to proceed unless legal counsel will be retained, is arguably the most appropriate course of action, even if it is not mandated by the law or by formal professional ethics.

(3) *Query.* May an attorney represent both parties in drafting a separation agreement? If there are any existing disputes between the parties regarding spousal or child support, child custody, division of marital property, and the like, then the answer would be that an attorney cannot ethically draft a separation agreement for both parties. Why not? *See generally* § 15.04 [B], *below.*

However, if an attorney is able to maintain his or her neutrality in the matter, and the separation agreement is fair and equitable to both parties, then some courts have held that the agreement would not be invalid *per se* if the attorney who drafted the agreement represented both parties. *See, e.g., Perry v. Perry*, 64 A.D.2d 625, 406 N.Y.S.2d 551, 552 (1978) ("While the practice of one attorney representing both parties in the preparation of a separation agreement has been criticized, we agree with the trial court that, in this instance, the attorney managed to preserve neutrality and that the agreement was arrived at fairly, without overreaching by either spouse. Furthermore, the substantive provisions of the agreement are, in toto, fair and equitable."); *accord, Levine v. Levine*, 436 N.E.2d 476, 478–79 (N.Y. 1982). *But see also Hale v. Hale*, 539 A.2d 247, 254 (Md. 1988) ("We feel that when a husband and wife are contemplating a separation agreement, it should be obvious to an attorney that he [or she] cannot adequately represent the interests of both parties").

Query: How can an attorney representing both parties realistically "second guess" if a court will ultimately determine that such representation is in fact "neutral," and if such an agreement in fact is "fair and equitable"? Conclude Green and Long, "This trend in case law does not diminish the importance of the obvious fact that separate representation by retained counsel can go far to protect each side from a variety of possible claims advanced for the purpose of having a separation agreement set aside." S. Green & J. Long, Marriage and Family Law Agreements 217 (1984). So applying the hoary adage "better safe than sorry," independent legal advice of counsel for each party is strongly recommended whenever a separation agreement is drafted, especially since the specter of a substantial legal malpractice suit increasingly looms over the family law practitioner in today's litigious society.

The growth of alternative dispute resolution in the family law field is raising a related question in some jurisdictions where attorneys are permitted to serve as mediators. Some attorney-mediators are willing to assist divorcing couples in resolving disputed issues and draft a separation agreement that will become binding when approved by the court. Some of these practitioners tell clients that they will provide legal information that would apply should a judge have to decide the case, but disclaim giving legal advice and make it plain that they are representing neither one party, nor the other, nor both. Most mediators insist that both parties retain independent outside legal counsel.

Query: Is this any different from the ethically proscribed practice of representing two parties with adverse interests? If so, how? What considerations should govern in deciding the propriety of such an arrangement? Are there situations where the mediator should conclude that mediation is inappropriate, at least without counsel for the parties in the room?

(4) What happens when an attorney attempts to represent one spouse in negotiating a separation agreement, but the other spouse refuses to retain independent legal counsel to represent his or her own interests? According to a Virginia State Bar advisory opinion, when one of the parties to a separation agreement is unrepresented, the attorney for the represented spouse has the following obligations: (1) advise the unrepresented spouse to secure independent counsel; (2) do not state or imply disinterest; (3) advise the unrepresented spouse that you represent the interests of your client only; (4) advise the unrepresented spouse that his or her interests are, or may be, adverse to those of your client. Virginia State Bar Committee on Legal Ethics, Opinion No. 876, reprinted in 13 Fam. L. Rep. 1284 (Feb. 2, 1987). It would be a wise practice to give such advice to the unrepresented spouse orally and in writing, with a copy for your files.

(5) **Problem.** In March of 1996, Julie and Gary, husband and wife, signed a property settlement agreement prior to their divorce in order to reach a mutual agreement regarding the division of their marital assets. This agreement stated that each of the parties warranted that there was a full disclosure of their assets. Although an attorney prepared the agreement, neither Julie nor Gary received any legal advice from the attorney. In November of 1998, Julie moved to set aside the property settlement agreement, alleging that Gary had committed fraud or misrepresentation in his disclosure-of-assets statement, since she was not informed in the agreement about his retirement program, his shares of stock in the company he worked for, or his actual income. Gary presented evidence, however, that Julie had actual knowledge of his income, stock options, and retirement plan, even though Gary made no mention of these assets in the parties' separation agreement.

How should the court rule in this case? Should Julie's and Gary's separation agreement be upheld or voided by the court? Why? *See In re Marriage of Gerleman*, 741 P.2d 426 (Mont. 1987). *Cf. Eltzroth v. Eltzroth*, 679 P.2d 1369 (Ore. Ct. App. 1984). Assuming *arguendo* that the separation agreement was upheld by the court, would Julie have a valid cause of action against the attorney? Why or why not? See also *Williams v. Williams*, 508 A.2d 985 (Md. 1986) and *Derby v. Derby*, 378 S.E.2d 74 (Va. Ct. App. 1989), both cases allowing a husband to successfully set aside a separation agreement on the grounds of unconscionability.

[C] Subsequent Attack on a Separation Agreement Based Upon Nondisclosure of Marital Assets: Intrinsic vs. Extrinsic Fraud

As illustrated in the *Golder* case, *above*, a spouse who believes that the other spouse was guilty of designed concealment or nondisclosure of marital assets, overreaching, or fraud in the separation or property settlement agreement may subsequently attack such a marital agreement based upon a state rule, statute, or procedure similar to Federal Rule of Civil Procedure 60(b). Rule 60(b) is itself an exception to the general rule of *res judicata* and generally states that a case may be reopened in exceptional circumstances involving fraud, mistake, or newly discovered evidence. *See, e.g., Cook v. Cook,* 912 P.2d 264, 267 (Nev. 1996) (holding that, under Nevada Rule of Civil Procedure 60(b), part of a divorce decree relating to a property settlement agreement could be vacated because of fraudulent nondisclosure of marital assets by the husband, without disturbing the dissolution of the parties' marriage itself).

However, not all separation agreements involving a party's fraudulent non-disclosure of marital assets have been set aside by the courts, either under a Rule 60(b)-type action or a similar state statutory remedy, or under a common-law fraud action. When a spouse's fraudulent conduct constitutes "intrinsic fraud" rather than "extrinsic fraud," there may be no remedy, as the following case illustrates.

CERNIGLIA v. CERNIGLIA
Supreme Court of Florida
679 So. 2d 1160 (1996)

HARDING, JUSTICE.

We have for review the decision in *Cerniglia v. Cerniglia,* 655 So.2d 172, 175 (Fla. 3d DCA 1995), which certified conflict with the opinion in *Lamb v. Leiter,* 603 So.2d 632 (Fla. 4th DCA 1992) on the issue of whether allegations of coercion and duress constitute extrinsic fraud or intrinsic fraud . . .

The Cerniglias were married in 1970. Joseph Cerniglia (the husband) filed a petition for dissolution of marriage on July 11, 1990. The parties signed a marital settlement agreement on the same day. At the August 20, 1990 dissolution proceeding Donna Cerniglia (the wife) informed the court that she had voluntarily signed the settlement agreement, had received advice from her attorney, and was satisfied with the husband's disclosure of assets. [In a related footnote, the court declared "The wife's attorney actually counseled her against signing the agreement. The attorney refused to allow her name to be associated with the agreement and stated on the record her opposition to the agreement. Despite this legal advice, the wife still informed the court that she was satisfied with the agreement and that she had freely and voluntarily signed the agreement."] The court entered final judgment dissolving the marriage and incorporating the July 11 settlement agreement.

In 1993, the wife brought a five-count civil action against the husband. Counts I through IV were damage claims for assault and battery, intentional infliction of emotional distress, common-law fraud, and breach of contract. Count V alleged extrinsic fraud or fraud on the court and sought to set aside the marital settlement agreement [based upon husband's failure to make a complete financial disclosure in the agreement]. The wife also filed a contemporaneous motion for relief in the dissolution action pursuant to the 1993 amendment to Florida Rule of Civil Procedure 1.540(b). [Prior to a statutory amendment in 1993, Florida Rule of Civil Procedure 1.540(b) provided that a court may relieve a party or his legal representative from a final judgment, decree, or order for fraud, misrepresentation or other misconduct of an adverse party provided that such a motion shall be made within a reasonable time, and for fraud or misrepresentation not more than one year after the date of the judgment. This rule was amended in 1993 to provide that "there shall be no time limit for motions based on fraudulent financial affidavits in marital cases."]. . . .

The trial court denied the wife's motion for rule 1.540(b) relief, finding that the 1993 amendment did not have retroactive application. For the same reason, the trial court also denied her motion to amend Count V to assert a claim based on the filing of false financial affidavits. The court further concluded that the issues of voluntariness, duress, and full disclosure had been tried in the dissolution proceeding and had to be brought within the one-year time limit prescribed by rule 1.540(b). Accordingly, the court entered summary judgment for the husband and denied rehearing.

On appeal, the district court affirmed the trial court's summary judgment for the husband on all counts. . . . However, the court certified conflict with *Lamb v. Leiter* on this issue. . . .

Lamb v. Leiter, which the district court certified to be in conflict with the instant case, involved a wife's attempt to vacate a final judgment of dissolution and set aside a separation and property settlement agreement three years after final judgment was entered. 603 So.2d at 632. The wife claimed that the husband had forced her to give up any defense to the dissolution action and procured the agreement through coercion, duress, and deceit. *Id.* at 632-33. The trial court found that the wife's claims constituted intrinsic fraud and that a motion to set aside judgment on this basis had to be filed without one year of final judgment. *Id.* at 634. On appeal, the district court reversed, finding that the circumstances alleged by the wife amounted to extrinsic fraud or fraud on the court for which an action to vacate judgment could be brought at any time. *Id.* at 635.

In *DeClaire v. Yohanan*, 453 So.2d 375 (Fla. 1984), this Court explained the difference between extrinsic fraud and intrinsic fraud. Extrinsic fraud, which constitutes fraud on the court, involves conduct which is collateral to the issues tried in a case . . . . "[E]xtrinsic fraud occurs when a [party] has somehow been prevented from participating in a case" *Id.* [at 377]. "Intrinsic fraud, on the other hand, applies to fraudulent conduct that arises within a proceeding and pertains to the issues in the case that have been tried or could have been tried" *Id.* The distinction is important because while rule 1.540(b) imposes a one-year time limit on motions based on fraud, it also provides that the rule "does not limit the power of a court to entertain an independent action to relieve a party from a judgment, decree, order, or proceeding or to set aside a judgment or decree for *fraud upon the court*." Fla. R. Civ. P. 1.540(b) (emphasis added); *see also DeClaire*, 453 So.2d at 378.

DeClaire involved a wife's attempt to set aside a final judgment of dissolution based upon the husband's fraudulent misrepresentation of his net worth in a financial affidavit submitted to the court. 453 So.2d at 376. This wife alleged that the husband's fraudulent affidavit constituted fraud on the court and thus the final judgment could be set aside three years after the entry of final judgment. *Id.* Because the false financial affidavits submitted by the husband were part of the record in the case and the husband's net worth was a matter before the court for resolution, this Court found the conduct to be intrinsic fraud, not fraud on the court, and thus subject to the one-year limitation in rule 1.540(b). *Id.* at 380. . . .

Applying the *DeClaire* standard to the facts of the instant case, we conclude that the wife's allegations of coercion and duress, enticement, and fraudulent financial disclosure constitute intrinsic fraud and were thus subject to the one-year limitation for seeking relief from the final judgment of dissolution. As in *DeClaire*, the issue of the husband's net worth was a matter before the court for resolution and, prior to the 1993 amendment of rule 1.540(b), subject to the one-year limitation. . . .

We further note that the 1993 amendment to rule 1.540(b) was inapplicable in the present case. As we explained in *Mendez-Perez v. Mendez-Perez*, 656 So.2d 458, 460 (Fla. 1995), rules of procedure are prospective unless specifically provided otherwise, and the amendment to rule 1.540(b) became effective on January 1, 1993, which precluded retroactivity . . .

The final issue that we address relates to the summary judgment on counts I through IV, involving a number of tort and contract claims. The district court agreed with the trial court's determination that the release contained in the marital settlement agreement was intended by the parties to serve as a complete bar to all claims arising from the marriage. *Cerniglia*, 655 So.2d at 174. Thus, the court concluded that summary judgment was proper as to these counts. *Id.* . . .

For the reasons discussed above, we approve the decision below and disapprove the opinion in *Lamb v. Leiter*.

It is so ordered . . .

NOTES AND QUESTIONS

(1) The important distinction in the *Cerniglia* case between extrinsic fraud on the court, which is seldom time barred, and *i*intrinsic fraud, which is often time barred, frequently is raised by defendant's attorney whenever plaintiff's attorney attempts to reopen a dissolution decree or judgment based upon the fraudulent concealment of marital assets in the parties' separation agreement. For example, in the case of *Schorr v. Schorr*, 1996 WL 148613 (Tenn. Ct. App. 1996), the husband fraudulently concealed over $500,000 of marital assets in a division of the parties' marital assets in a separation agreement. But when, three years later, based on newly discovered evidence, the ex-wife requested "a fair and equitable division of marital based upon the truthful disclosure and accurate total of the parties marital assets as of the date of the divorce", the ex-husband's attorney countered that the divorce proceeding was now *res judicata*, and no remedy was provided under Rule 60 of the Tennessee Rules of Civil Procedure for one-year time-barred intrinsic fraud, rather than extrinsic fraud on the court, that would allow the final decree of divorce and its separation agreement to be set aside. Declared the Tennessee Court of Appeals,

> Although the characteristics of intrinsic and extrinsic fraud are somewhat amorphous, it is generally held that extrinsic fraud "consists of conduct that is extrinsic or collateral to the issues examined and determined in the action," *Thomas v. Dockery*, . . . 323 S.W.2d 594, 598 [Tenn. Ct. App. 1950], while intrinsic fraud is fraud within the subject matter of the litigation, such as forged documents produced at trial or perjury by a witness. *Id.* at . . . 598.
>
> . . . [W]e think it is settled beyond controversy that a decree will not be vacated merely because it was obtained by forged documents or perjured testimony. The reason for this rule is that there must be an end of litigation; and when parties have once submitted a matter, or have had the opportunity of submitting it, for investigation and determination, and when they have exhausted every means for reviewing such

determination in the same proceeding, it must be regarded as final and conclusive, unless it can be shown that jurisdiction of the court has been imposed upon, or that the prevailing party has, by some extrinsic or collateral fraud, prevented a fair submission of the controversy.

Id. Query: Does this traditional legal distinction between "intrinsic" and "extrinsic" fraud allow an unintended legal consequence that a husband or wife may intentionally and fraudulently conceal from the other spouse the true nature of the parties' marital assets in drafting their separation agreement, knowing full well that after one year an unsuspecting innocent spouse may lose his or her legal right to relitigate their marital dissolution or the fraudulent terms of their separation agreement? And was this the primary reason why the Florida legislature subsequently amended its procedural rules in 1993 to provide that "there shall be no time limit for motions based on fraudulent financial affidavits in marital cases"? Other courts, however, apparently have not been limited by these traditional parameters of "extrinsic" and "intrinsic" fraud. *See, e.g., Wood v. Wood,* 1997 WL 467338 (Ohio Ct. App. 1997) (holding that "A separation agreement which does not fully disclose the [marital] property [and the value of such property] . . . can constitute a fraud upon the court" entitling a party to judgment under Ohio R. Civ. Pro. 60(B)(5), it;Golder v. Golder, *above,* §13.04[B].

(2) **Problem.** How can you reconcile—or distinguish—the holdings in *Cerniglia v. Cerniglia* and *Schorr v. Schorr, above,* with the holding of *Golder v. Golder* in § 13.04 [B], *above*? *See also Cook v. Cook,* 912 P.2d 264, 267 (Nev. 1996) (similar holding to *Golder v. Golder,* applying Nev. Rule of Civil Procedure 60(b), and making no distinction between "intrinsic" and "extrinsic" fraud). Which judicial decisions are more persuasive to you? Based upon what underlying public policy arguments? What is the procedural rule in your own state regarding "intrinsic" and "extrinsic" fraud as grounds for subsequently attacking the validity of a separation agreement incorporated into a prior divorce decree?

(3) Some courts have ameliorated various time-barred statute of limitations for "intrinsic" fraud by holding that such time-barred limitations for fraud begin to run from the date that such fraud could reasonably have been discovered rather than from the time the fraud was committed. *See, e.g., Murphy v. Murphy,* 622 N.Y.S.2d 755, 756–57 (App. Div. 1995) (The trial court judge described defendant husband as an "artful dodger" and stated that "it would be impossible for me, or anybody who has been in the court system, to determine anything of what Mr. Murphy did, until, at the minimum,'84, probably'89." The New York appellate court agreed that the statute of limitations for a cause of action sounding in fraud in New York is six years from the date of the wrong, or two years from the date the fraud could reasonably have been discovered, whichever is later.). *See also Harker v. Harker,* 1995 WL 127945 (Conn. Super. Ct. 1995) (holding that the husband's fraudulent concealment of marital assets was a valid ground to reopen a decree for dissolution of marriage and its incorporated separation agreement five years later under Connecticut's "discovery rule").

(4) **Problem.** In 1995, ex-wife filed a petition for special relief in Pennsylvania, alleging that her ex-husband in the parties' 1981 separation agreement "wrongfully, intentionally and maliciously" engaged in a course of conduct to defeat the wife's claim to the equitable distribution of his pension property by "wilfully concealing" such marital assets. To rectify this alleged fraud, the ex-wife sought a constructive trust on the marital assets. The trial court found that the ex-wife had a valid cause of action, and granted the ex-wife 50% of

the undisclosed pension plan, citing as authority *Creeks v. Creeks*, 619 A.2d 754 (Pa. Super. Ct. 1993) (*see* § 13.04[B], Note (1), *above*).

The ex-husband appealed this trial-court decision, arguing that: (1) such alleged fraud had never been adequately proven by the ex-wife, since this non-disclosure was due to a "mutual mistake" of the parties; and (2) the ex-wife's action to relitigate this marital-property dispute was time barred under 23 Pa. Cons. Stat. Ann. § 3332, which provides a statute of limitations in Pennsylvania restricting the opening or vacating of a divorce decree for the following reasons: Where intrinsic fraud or new evidence attacking the validity of a divorce decree is alleged, a motion to open must be filed within 30 days after the entry of the decree; and, where extrinsic fraud is asserted as a basis to vacate the decree, action must be initiated within five years. What should be the decision on appeal? *See Hassick v. Hassick*, 695 A.2d 851 (Pa. Super. Ct. 1997).

(5) In considering fraudulent nondisclosure as a ground for setting aside an agreement, note that the distinction between intrinsic and extrinsic fraud continues to bedevil some courts while it is apparently ignored by others, depending on applicable state law and the ability of legal counsel to make such an argument. In most jurisdictions, a separation agreement or property settlement agreement on divorce or dissolution of marriage will be held contractually valid and enforceable if it meets the following criteria: (1) its terms are fair and just; (2) its making is untainted by fraud, duress, illegality, or undue influence; (3) it was entered into by competent parties with full knowledge of their rights and all the material circumstances; (4) there was full and fair disclosure of the parties' assets and liabilities: and (5) it was executed after the separation of the parties or in contemplation of an imminent separation by the parties. *See generally* 1 A. Lindey & L. Parley, Lindey on Separation Agreements and Antenuptial Contracts § 6.01 (Matthew Bender 1997 rev. ed.).

(6) **Related Ground for Invalidity: Illegal Consideration.** In addition to fraudulent nondisclosure of marital assets, duress and coercion, marital agreements may also be declared invalid if they are based on extortion or illegal consideration. For example, the case of *Quirling v. Quirling*, No. 23353 (Sept. 2, 1997), 23 Fam. L. Rptr. 1537 (Idaho 1997) involved a separation agreement and a quitclaim deed executed by the estranged husband and wife, where the husband relinquished his interest in the marital home, and the wife promised not to inform law enforcement officials about their daughter's allegations that the husband had committed sexual improprieties with her. The Idaho Supreme Court held that such a marital agreement and quitclaim deed were both unenforceable and void as against state public policy. Explaining that the wife had a statutory duty to report these sexual abuse allegations, the Idaho Supreme Court found that she could not legally contract to refrain from doing so, and the court further stated that this transfer of marital property by threat of arrest—whether lawful or unlawful—and threatened community exposure amounted to theft by extortion. The court concluded that the parties' separation agreement was therefore illegal, and the quitclaim deed was premised on such illegal consideration. The court remanded the case back to the trial court for an equitable division of the parties' property. Contrast this case with *Upton v. Ames & Webb Inc.,*, 18 S.E.2d 290, 293 (Va. 1942) where the Virginia Supreme Court upheld a marital agreement based on the consideration that the wife contractually agreed not to prosecute a valid divorce claim against the husband for a stipulated amount of money. *Query:* How can these two cases be reconciled?

[D] Drafting a Separation Agreement

[1] A Recommended Checklist Approach

There are a number of legal form books and practice treatises in most law libraries that contain various sample forms and checklists for drafting a separation agreement or property settlement agreement. *See, e.g.*, 1A. Lindey & L. Parley, Lindey on Separation Agreements and Antenuptial Contracts (Matthew Bender 1997 rev. ed.); Schlissel, Separation Agreements and Marital Contracts (1986); Green & Long, Marriage and Family Law Agreements (1984); West's Legal Forms 2d, Vol. 7, pgs. 339–740 (1995); and a multitude of state publications.

For further reading, see Grisham, *A Fiduciary Relationship Between Divorcing Spouses: Impact on Property Settlements*, 13 Community Prop. J. 58 (1986); Haas, *The Rationality and Enforceability of Contractual Restrictions on Divorce*, 66 N.C.L. Rev. 879 (1988); Koritzinsky, *Setting up a QDRO* [Qualified Domestic Relations Order], 8 Fam. Advoc. 27 (1985); Kozub & Davis, *Structuring Separation Agreements and Divorce Settlements after the Tax Reform Act of 1986*, 16 Tax'n for Law 82 (1987); Lepow, *Tax Policy for Lovers and Cynics: How a Divorce Settlement Became the Last Tax Shelter in America*, 62 Notre Dame L. Rev. 32 (1986); Sally Sharp, *Fairness Standards and Separation Agreements: A Word of Caution on Contractual Freedom*, 132 U. Pa. L. Rev. 1399 (1984); Smith, *Client and Pension Plan Data Form*, 8 Fam. Advoc. 33 (1985).

Although reasonable attorneys may differ as to the format and substance of a separation or property settlement agreement, and although each separation agreement must address a unique factual situation for each individual client. There are nevertheless some general principles and legal drafting concepts common to most separation agreements. A family law practitioner often utilizes a checklist that serves as a valuable aid in drafting separation agreements, such as the following legal drafting checklist:

1. *Document Title* [E.g., Separation Agreement, Property Settlement Agreement, or Marital Settlement Agreement]

2. *Preamble* [also called Introduction or Recitals] which often includes:

   a. The name and address of Husband.

   b. The name and address of Wife.

   c. When and where the parties were married.

   d. Children of the marriage, adopted children, and other children requiring a support obligation, their date of birth, and present age.

   e. Purpose of the Agreement [that due to irreconcilable differences the parties have separated, and intend to define their respective support, property, and custody rights and obligations through this agreement].

(Contrary to popular belief, *WITNESSETH* is not a necessary part of this, or any other, modern legal document.)

3. *Full Disclosure of Husband's and Wife's Assets and Liabilities*

This is a necessary part of any marital agreement, unless a party voluntarily waives full disclosure of such assets and the law of that state permits an informed waiver. Should these full disclosure provisions be informally prepared without documentation, or should they be formally prepared by a C.P.A.? Once again, an absence of full disclosure of the spouses' assets may result in the marital agreement being invalidated by the court.

4. *Spousal Support Provisions, or Waiver of Spousal Support*

a. Are these spousal support provisions fixed or to be modifiable in the future after judgment? In some jurisdictions, if the parties do not expressly state that spousal support is modifiable, then the court cannot modify the parties' spousal support provisions. Other jurisdictions, however, provide by statute that a court may modify spousal support in a separation agreement if it would be inequitable not to do so.

b. If spousal support is modifiable, should it be determined solely on a bona fide change of circumstances, or may cost of living increases be factored into the agreement based upon a relevant consumer price index?

c. Duration of spousal support. Traditionally, "permanent" spousal support based on long-term marriages generally was awarded until the death or the remarriage of the payee spouse, or the death of the payor spouse, whichever came first. "Rehabilitative" spousal support has gained favor by encouraging a transition by the recipient to independent, self supporting status. *See* Gregory, Swisher & Scheible, Understanding Family Law § 8.04[C] (Matthew Bender 1995). However, spousal support may contractually be for a temporary period of time, or it may be waived by one or both of the parties. Another contractual option provides that spousal support may be terminated when the payee spouse lives with another person "as though married" for a specified period of time. In addition, spousal support may be extended beyond the death of the payor, as an obligation of the payor's estate. A party may also reserve the right to request spousal support at a future time, should circumstances so warrant.

5. *Division of the Marital Residence*

Will the parties sell the marital residence within a specified period of time and divide the assets, or will the payee spouse and children be permitted to live in the marital residence for a specified period of time? If this latter approach is taken, who will make the mortgage payments, and pay for related utilities, maintenance, and repairs to the marital residence?

6. *Division of Marital and Separate Property*

The division of the parties' real and personal property, whether marital or community property, separate property, or a hybrid mix of both martial and separate property, is often made in a number of property-division schedules that are attached to the separation agreement. A number of property-settlement agreements incorporate an additional contractual provision regarding "after-discovered property" that a party might have initially "overlooked" in negotiating the marital agreement.

7. *Division of Pension, Profit-Sharing, and Other Retirement Plans*

Deferred compensation pension and retirement plans constitute marital property in most states, and a separation agreement must provide for their division or a waiver of the non-owner's rights to his or her shares. An attorney will often require the assistance of a financial expert to do this. *Important Note*: If a spouse is receiving any retirement or pension rights from the other spouse, there must be an enforceable order pursuant to the Retirement Equity Act of 1984, 29 U.S.C. § 1002 and I.R.C. § 414(p), that will qualify as a qualified domestic relations order or QDRO. *See e.g.* Koritzinsky, *Setting Up a QDRO*, 8 Fam. Advoc. 27

(Fall 1985). Generally, the QDRO will be prepared as a separate document, to be approved by the pension plan administrator, in addition to the the separation agreement and final divorce decree. The Internal Revenue Service recently issued I.R.S. Notice 97-10 to provide guidance in the drafting of QDROs to comply with the Internal Revenue Code and ERISA sections.

8. *Child Support Provisions*

a. How much child support will be paid, and which party or parties will make such payments? However, child support provisions cannot be *less* than child support awards mandated by state child support statutes. [Normally child support ceases at the child's age of majority, death, marriage, or legal emancipation, whichever occurs first. However, the parties may also contractually agree to pay child support past the age of the child's majority.]

b. Will the payor's estate be bound to make such payments if the payor dies prior to the child attaining the age of majority?

c. Will the payor, or the payor's estate, pay for private school or college expenses for each child? Should an educational trust fund be established for each child?

d.. Are there any other expenses not covered by child support, with which the payor will be obligated to help (e.g., unusual medical expenses, summer programs)?

9. *Child Custody Provisions*

a. Shall one of the parties have sole custody of the minor children, or shall both parties have joint legal and physical custody? *See* Gregory, Swisher & Scheible, Understanding Family Law § 10.04 (Matthew Bender 1995).

b. If one parent has sole custody of the children, what visitation rights will the other parent have? And if custody is shared, what is the schedule or how is it to be determined? Should grandparents and other family members have visitation rights?

c. The parties should agree to exert reasonable efforts not to alienate the affections of the children toward each other.

d. Will notice be given to the non-custodial parent concerning any illness, injury, or other emergency regarding the children?

e. What happens if either party moves out of the state?

[*Important Note*: In the vast majority of jurisdictions, the parents cannot permanently "fix" child support or child custody provisions in a separation agreement. The court will decide whether to initially approve the arrangements, basing its decision on the best interests of the child; and it will retain jurisdiction to modify the plan if circumstances change.]

10. *Dental and Medical Expenses and Health Insurance Provisions*

Who pays the dental and medical expenses of the payee spouse and minor children? For how long? What is the applicable health insurance coverage, if any? Prior to 1985, a husband or wife who had relied on group health care coverage provided by the other spouse's employer often lost this health insurance coverage upon divorce, dissolution of marriage, or legal separation. Pursuant to Consolidated Omnibus Budget Reconciliation Act of 1985 (COBRA), a divorced spouse and children may continue to be covered by the employed spouse's group health plan for a certain period of years. 29 U.S.C. §§ 1161–68; I.R.C. § 162(k). *See also* DTE Digest Series, COBRA: Health Benefits after Divorce (1988). Under the Omnibus Budget Reconciliation Act of 1993, an employer group health plan must also comply with a Qualified Medical Child Support Order (QMCSO) if a plan participant is required to provide coverage to a dependent child as a result of divorce. 29 U.S.C. § 1169(a). *See generally* Linda Elrod, *Child Support Reassessed: Federalization of Enforcement Nears Completion*, 1997 U. Ill. L. Rev. 695 (1997).

11. *Life Insurance Provisions*

If the payor spouse makes a life insurance policy in favor of the payee spouse or children as beneficiaries, family law practitioners often ensure that the payor spouse gives up all ownership rights and the right to assign the policy to any third party, and ensure that such beneficiaries are irrevocable beneficiaries. Also, the beneficiaries should receive notice from the insurer that all premiums are being paid, so the insurance coverage is not in danger of lapsing. *See* Annotation 31 A.L.R. 4th 59.

12. *Debts and Obligations*

Who pays the debts and obligations incurred during the marriage? What about the debts and obligations incurred after signing the agreement that are not expressly mentioned in the agreement? The parties should specify which separate and marital debts will be paid by each spouse

13. *Mutual Release Clause*

This clause covers the mutual release from dower and curtesy rights or their statutory augmented estate equivalent, and the mutual release from all other marital rights, debts, and obligations except for those expressly set forth in the separation agreement. Specificity is greatly recommended in describing exactly what rights and obligations are waived or releases, since this separation agreement provision has been subject to much litigation if poorly drafted.

14. *Tax Considerations*

This provision can cover the tax implications of filing prior to and after divorce, including spousal support, if any, that is includable and deductible to each party; which parent gets the child dependency exemption; deductibility of legal fees, *etc. See, e.g.,* 26 U.S.C. §§71, 215, 152(e), respectively. *See also* Annotation, *Divorce or Separation: Consideration of Tax Liability or Consequences in Determining Alimony or Property Settlement Provisions*, 51 A.L.R. 3d 461 (1973). *Caveat*: Various Tax Reform Acts have made many important changes in federal tax law involving divorcing parties; therefore do not rely on older legal forms, cases, and statutes to do your tax planning. An independent tax expert may be necessary when substantial marital assets are involved.

15. *Non-molestation and Mutual Cooperation Provisions*

This important provision reemphasizes the fact that the parties agree to fully cooperate in fulfilling the terms of this marital agreement, and agree not to harass or molest the other spouse.

16. *Incorporation Provision*

Does the client want the separation agreement incorporated, but not merged? That is, what provisions should be merged into a final divorce decree so that a court would have contempt powers over a breaching party? Or, do you wish to incorporate those provisions for which the parties desire civil, or alternate dispute resolution, remedies?

17. *Miscellaneous Provisions.* This is the place to put other matters which the parties' unique circumstances require them to cover in their agreement.

18. *Sanctions and Penalties for Breach of Agreement*

This provision normally provides that the non-breaching prevailing party may obtain court costs, attorneys fees, and other specified damages from the breaching party regarding any breach of performance in the separation agreement.

19. *Optional Mediation or Arbitration Clause*

The parties may alternately agree that should any dispute arise out of the interpretation or performance of the agreement, that the parties agree to settle such a dispute through alternative dispute resolution, including divorce mediation or arbitration, rather than through court litigation. *Caveat*: Although most courts will recognize the parties' contractual right to mediate or arbitrate their own property or support disputes, many courts refuse to be bound by a mediated or arbitrated settlement regarding child support and child custody matters under their state's *parens patriae* doctrine.

20. *Entire Agreement Provision*

This provision protects both parties against various parole evidence problems.

21. *Modification of Agreement Provision*

This clause allows the parties to make subsequent modifications in the separation agreement, but requires that any such modification be in writing and signed by both parties, with the same formality as the original agreement.

22. *Governing Law of Agreement.*

Here the parties agree that the separation agreement shall be interpreted and performed according to the laws of a particular state that has a significant connection with the parties and their marital agreement. This provision helps to alleviate possible uncertainties in applicable law, especially if one or both of the parties move out-of-state subsequent to signing the agreement.

23. *Binding Agreement Clause*

This clause serves to contractually bind the parties, their heirs, administrators, personal representatives, and assigns.

24. *Severability Clause*

This provision provides that if any part of the agreement is declared to be invalid by a court of competent jurisdiction, the rest of the agreement shall nevertheless remain in effect and valid.

25. *Provision Regarding Independent Advice of Counsel*

This crucial provision provides that each party has obtained independent legal advice from legal counsel of his or her choice, that each party has read the agreement and has been fully informed by his or her legal counsel of all legal rights and liabilities in the agreement, and that after such advice and knowledge, each party believes the agreement to be fair and signs the agreement voluntarily.

26. *Counterparts*

In order to avoid problems with the "best evidence rule" it is also wise to provide that the agreement may be executed in two or more counterparts, each of which shall be an original, but all of which shall constitute one and the same agreement.

27. *Parties' Signatures and Notarization*

[2] Separation Agreement Problem

You are an attorney practicing family law in your state of choice, and Betty Sinclair Jones has come to your law office, asking you to represent her in a divorce action. Since Betty and her husband Ralph are already living separate and apart from each other, and since they both desire to settle their property and support rights and obligations "as soon as possible," you have recommended to Betty that a written separation agreement signed by both parties would be appropriate in this case. You have further learned that Betty's husband, Ralph Edward Jones, will be represented by Mitchell Aardvark, a discreet and competent attorney at law.

The facts of this particular case are as follows:

Ralph E. Jones and Betty S. Jones were married in the state of Jeffersonia on June 10, 1986. Due to unhappy circumstances and irreconcilable differences, Ralph and Betty have decided to obtain a no fault dissolution of their marriage. They have already separated on October 5, 1998.

Betty currently lives at 5440 Oregon Avenue in your city and Ralph currently lives at 1066 Hastings Road, in the same city. The Oregon Avenue house is presently owned by both Betty and Ralph as tenants by the entirety. The current fair market value of their house has been appraised at $460,000 with an existing mortgage of $150,000. The monthly mortgage payments are approximately $2,060, which includes principal, interest, property taxes, and homeowner's insurance. There are 15 years left on the mortgage. Ralph is willing to let Betty have title to this house in her own name if she assumes the mortgage and all other related obligations, and if she signs over her interest to Ralph in a beachfront condominium, "Sand Pebbles," which was bought in 1986 for $150,000 in cash from one of Ralph's company bonuses and which is titled in both their names.

Betty would agree to Ralph's offer, but currently Betty is a housewife and she is not employed outside the home. To be employed as a secondary school teacher, Betty estimates that in order to obtain her secondary school teaching certificate and a public school teaching position at Newburg High School would require three more years as a full-time student at State University, or five to six years as a part-time student. Betty is confident that she can return to the full-time job market as a teacher, but she needs support from Ralph until that time.

Betty and Ralph have two children: Bobby, age 11, and Cynthia Ann, age 7. Both children are currently living with Betty under a temporary *pendente lite* court order, but Ralph wants liberal visitation rights with Cynthia Ann, especially during the summer months. Ralph also wants sole custody of Bobby, which Betty objects to because of Ralph's new "bachelor" lifestyle, with his dating and drinking habits, which are both excessive. No matter who gets custody, however, Ralph and Betty have agreed that they desire to pay for Bobby and Cynthia's undergraduate college education, at least four years at a public university, with Ralph contributing at least 75% of the total cost.

Ralph is currently a principal partner with a small regional advertising company, Acme Unlimited, Inc., with an average annual salary of approximately $175,000 per year over the past five years, although his yearly salary has been in the range of $125,000 to $250,000. However, you have learned that Ralph's advertising business has recently suffered a number of financial setbacks, and Ralph has been looking for additional capital. He has suggested to Betty, for example, that they put a second mortgage on the Oregon Avenue home, and a mortgage on the beachfront condominium "only temporarily" until Ralph can "land" a big client he has been working on for the past two years, which will "allow my advertising firm to expand as a nationally-recognized company and relocate to Los Angeles or New York City, where the real money is."

Ralph has no retirement plan with Acme Unlimited, Inc., *per se*, but he has been involved with a profit-sharing, stock-option program since 1976, before he married Betty. Ralph has since acquired company stock currently worth approximately $725,000 which, in ten more years, his financial accountant estimates will be worth triple that amount if the company successfully expands nationally as originally planned. However, if Ralph's firm doesn't "land" its big client, the stock will be worth approximately $350,000.

Since Ralph has heavily invested most of his assets back into Acme Unlimited stock, he has no life or disability insurance coverage to speak of. He had "meant to get some good insurance coverage" but "never had the time." The Jones family, however, currently is covered by Acme's medical and dental group insurance plan from the Zeno Health Insurance Company.

As far as personal property, Ralph has moved most of his personal effects out of the Oregon Avenue house, except for his rather extensive library, his Sony and Sansui stereo sound systems, and his library of compact discs. He also wants the family's antique English mahogany dining room set and sideboard, and the antique Wedgewood china set that he inherited in 1980 from his grandmother. He will give the rest of the furniture to Betty, along with the family 1990 Volvo Station Wagon, if he can keep his 1998 Mercedes. Ralph and Betty currently have a joint checking account with assets of $12,430, and they owe $8,538 on a Visa card and $6,344 on a Mastercard.

Ralph has called Betty on the telephone at all hours of the day and night to demand all the furniture, books, and stereo equipment that he has identified as his or that he wants in his proposed division of property. Betty says this harassment often has resulted in shouting matches over the telephone. Based on Ralph's drunken threats to "come over, kick your ___, and take what's mine," Betty has changed all the locks on the Oregon Avenue house, but she still lives in fear of what Ralph might do to her and the children "especially when he's been drinking." Finally, you have learned that during their separation, Ralph has been seen in the constant company of Wanda Rustic, and Betty has been seen recently in the company of her old high school sweetheart Jack Armstrong.

You have further learned that Wanda Rustic has two children from a prior marriage and divorce that Ralph plans to support, and that Ralph may therefore request a deviation or departure from your state's child support statutory guidelines. *And query*: Would your proposed separation agreement be drafted any differently if Ralph (or Betty) were primarily responsible for the breakdown of their marriage on particular fault grounds?

Immediate Problem: As Betty's attorney, your task is now to draft a separation agreement that will be mutually acceptable to Betty, Ralph, and Ralph's attorney Mitchell

Aardvark. From the fact situation above, what possible problems do you foresee in attempting to draft such an agreement? How might these problems be resolved? What additional problems do you anticipate?

Legal Drafting Exercise: Utilizing the above fact situation, selected legal form books, outlines, and appropriate checklists, draft an appropriate separation agreement as the attorney for Betty Jones. (Feel free to use poetic license to create any additional facts you believe might be necessary or useful in drafting your agreement.)

Remember that although you are representing Betty to the best of your ability as her legal counsel and advocate, some compromise will nevertheless be necessary if Ralph is to sign your agreement, based on the advice of *his* legal counsel. Thus, a separation agreement is meant to be a realistic "win-win" endeavor, rather than an unrealistic (and probably unsigned) "win-lose" proposition. *See generally* R. Fisher & W. Ury, Getting to Yes: Negotiating Agreement Without Giving In (1981). *See also* R. Dickerson, Fundamentals of Legal Drafting, (2d ed. 1986), and R. Dick, Legal Drafting (2d ed. 1985). *And see* P. Swisher, *Techniques of Legal Drafting: A Survival Manual*, 15 U. Rich. L. Rev. 873 (1981), reprinted in 31 Law Rev. Digest 4 (1982).

Future Problem: Assume further that three years after the parties' separation agreement has been incorporated into a final divorce or dissolution of marriage decree, Betty discovers that Ralph has fraudulently concealed over $950,000 in marital assets that he did not disclose while negotiating the parties' separation agreement. *Query:* Does Betty have a legal right to reopen this proceeding and attack the validity of the parties' separation agreement according to the procedural law of your particular state? Why or why not?

§ 13.05 State Recognition of Religious Contracts

Although marriage, annulment or dissolution of marriage, and other family law matters were originally controlled and regulated by the ecclesiastical courts and canon law of Medieval Europe, American family law has always been subject to the control of secular state law. *See, e.g., Maynard v. Hill*, 125 U.S. 190, 205 (1888). Nevertheless, in most American jurisdictions, a state will still recognize religious marriages performed by authorized priests, rabbis, ministers, or other religious leaders as long as the parties, and the religious officials, comply with the state's secular statutory marriage requirements.

Likewise, when a person seeking a divorce or dissolution of marriage is domiciled within an American state, only secular divorce law would control, and any religious divorce laws would have no effect on that state's sovereignty. *See, e.g., Chertok v. Chertok*, 203 N.Y.S. 163 (1924) (refusal to recognize a Jewish *Get* divorce, when New York divorce statutes were not utilized); *Hilton v. Roylance*, 69 P. 660 (Utah 1902) (refusal to recognize a Mormon religious divorce when Utah divorce statutes were not utilized). Conversely, although a state statutory divorce may not be recognized by a religious denomination such as the Roman Catholic Church unless it also complies with church canon law, such a divorce or dissolution of marriage is nevertheless legally valid for all civil purposes.

However, should a state court be bound by a religious covenant or religious agreement that affects secular marital obligations? The following case addresses this issue.

AVITZUR v. AVITZUR
New York Court of Appeals
446 N.E. 2d 136 (N.Y.),
cert. denied, 464 U.S. 817 (1983)

This appeal presents for our consideration the question of the proper role of the civil courts in deciding a matter touching upon religious concerns. At issue is the enforceability of the terms of a document, known as a Ketubah, which was entered into as part of the religious marriage ceremony in this case. The Appellate Division held this to be a religious covenant beyond the jurisdiction of the civil courts. However, we find nothing in law or public policy to prevent judicial recognition and enforcement of the secular terms of such an agreement. There should be a reversal.

Plaintiff and Defendant were married on May 22, 1966 in a ceremony conducted in accordance with Jewish tradition. Prior to the marriage ceremony, the parties signed both a Hebrew/Aramaic and an English version of the "Ketubah." According to the English translation, the Ketubah evidences both the bridegroom's intention to cherish and provide for his wife as required by religious law and tradition, and the bride's willingness to carry out her obligations to her husband in faithfulness and affection according to Jewish law and tradition. By signing the Ketubah, the parties declared their "desire to . . . live in accordance with the Jewish law of marriage throughout [their] lifetime" and further agreed as follows: "[W]e, the bride and bridegroom . . . hereby agree to recognize the Beth Din of the Rabbinical Assembly and the Jewish Theological Seminary of America or its duly appointed representatives, as having authority to counsel us in the light of Jewish tradition which requires husband and wife to give each other complete love and devotion, and to summon either party at the request of the other, in order to enable the party so requesting to live in accordance with the standards of the Jewish law of marriage throughout his or her lifetime. We authorize the Beth Din to impose such terms of compensation as it may see fit for failure to respond to this summons or to carry out its decision."

Defendant husband was granted a civil divorce upon the ground of cruel and inhuman treatment on May 16, 1978. Notwithstanding this civil divorce, plaintiff wife is not considered divorced and may not remarry pursuant to Jewish law, until such time as a Jewish divorce decree, known as a "Get," is granted. In order that a Get may be obtained, plaintiff and defendant must appear before a "Beth Din," a rabbinical tribunal having authority to advise and pass upon matter of traditional Jewish law. Plaintiff sought to summon defendant before the Beth Din pursuant to the provisions of the Ketubah recognizing that body as having authority to counsel the couple in the matter concerning their marriage.

Defendant has refused to appear before the Beth Din, thus preventing plaintiff from obtaining a religious divorce. Plaintiff brought this action alleging that the Ketubah constitutes a marital contract, which defendant has breached by refusing to appear before the Beth Din, and she seeks relief both in the form of a declaration to that effect and an order compelling defendant's specific performance of the Ketubah's requirement that he appear before the Beth Din. Defendant moved to dismiss the complaint upon the grounds that the court lacked subject matter jurisdiction and the complaint failed to state a cause of action arguing that resolution of the dispute and any grant of relief to plaintiff would involve the civil court in impermissible consideration of a purely religious matter. Plaintiff, in addition to opposing the motion, cross-moved for summary judgment.

Special Term denied defendant's motion to dismiss, noting that plaintiff sought only to compel defendant to submit to the jurisdiction of the Beth Din, an act which plaintiff had alleged defendant bound himself to do. That being the only object of the lawsuit, Special Term was apparently of the view that the relief sought could be granted without impermissible judicial entanglement in any doctrinal issue. The court also denied plaintiff's motion for summary judgment, concluding that the issues concerning the translation, meaning, and effect of the Ketubah raised factual questions requiring a plenary trial.

The Appellate Division modified, granting defendant's motion to dismiss. Inasmuch as the Ketubah was entered into a part of a religious ceremony and was executed, by its own terms, in accordance with Jewish law, the court concluded that the document constitutes a liturgical agreement. The Appellate Division held such agreements to be unenforceable where the State, having granted a civil divorce to the parties, has no further interest in their marital status.

Accepting plaintiff's allegations as true, as we must in the context of this motion to dismiss, it appears that plaintiff and defendant, in signing the Ketubah, entered into a contract which formed the basis for their marriage. Plaintiff has alleged that, pursuant to the terms of this marital contract, defendant promised that he would, at plaintiff's request, appear before the Beth Din for the purpose of allowing that tribunal to advise and counsel the parties in matters concerning their marriage, including the granting of a Get. It should be noted that plaintiff is not attempting to compel defendant to obtain a Get or to enforce a religious practice arising solely out of principles of religious law. She merely seeks to enforce an agreement made by defendant to appear before and accept the decision of a designated tribunal.

Viewed in this manner, the provisions of the Ketubah relied upon by plaintiff constitute nothing more than an agreement to refer the matter of a religious divorce to a nonjudicial forum. Thus, the contractual obligation plaintiff seeks to enforce is closely analogous to an antenuptial agreement to arbitrate a dispute in accordance with the law and tradition chosen by the parties. This agreement the Ketubah should ordinarily be entitled to no less dignity than any other civil contract to submit a dispute to a nonjudicial forum, so long as its enforcement violates neither the law nor the public policy of this State.

Defendant argues, in this connection, that enforcement of the terms of the Ketubah by a civil court would violate the constitutional prohibition against excessive entanglement between Church and State, because the court must necessarily intrude upon matters of religious doctrine and practice. It is urged that the obligations imposed by the Ketubah arise solely from Jewish religious law and can be interpreted only with reference to religious dogma. Granting the religious character of the Ketubah, it does not necessarily follow that any recognition of its obligation is foreclosed to the courts.

It is clear that judicial involvement in matters touching upon religious concerns has been constitutionally limited in analogous situations and courts should not resolve controversies in a manner requiring consideration of religious doctrine. . . . In its most recent pronouncement on this issue, however, the Supreme Court, in holding that a State may adopt any approach to resolving religious disputes which does not entail consideration of doctrinal matters, specifically approved the use of the "neutral principles of law" approach as consistent with constitutional limitation (*Jones v. Wolf, supra,* 443 U.S. at p. 602). This approach contemplates the application of objective, well-established principles of secular law to the dispute thus permitting judicial involvement to the extent that it can be accomplished in purely secular terms.

The present case can be decided solely upon the application of neutral principles of contract law, without reference to any religious principle. Consequently, defendant's objections to enforcement of his promise to appear before the Beth Din, based as they are upon the religious origin of the agreement, pose no constitutional barrier to the relief sought by the plaintiff. The fact that the agreement was entered into as part of a religious ceremony does not render it unenforceable. Solemnization of the marital relationship often takes place in accordance with the religious beliefs of the participants, and this State has long recognized this religious aspect by permitting duly authorized pastors, rectors, priests, rabbis, and other religious officials to perform the ceremony. Similarly, that the obligations undertaken by the parties to the Ketubah are grounded in religious belief and practice does not preclude enforcement of its secular terms. Nor does the fact that all of the Ketubah's provisions may not be judicially recognized prevent the court from enforcing that portion of the agreement by which the parties promised to refer their disputes to a non-judicial forum. The courts may properly enforce so much of this agreement as is not in contravention of law or public policy. . . .

Accordingly, the order of the Appellate Division should be reversed with costs, and defendant's motion to dismiss the complaint, denied.

NOTES AND QUESTIONS

(1) In *Avitzur v. Avitzur*, 449 N.Y.S.2d 83 (App. Div. 1982), the Appellate Division held that it could not assume jurisdiction to specifically enforce the parties' agreement, since it was a religious agreement, and the state had already granted a secular divorce. Why did the New York Court of Appeals reverse this lower court decision?

(2) In *Aziz v. Aziz*, 488 N.Y.S.2d 123 (Sup. Ct. 1985), a New York court ruled that a Muslim premarital agreement called a *sadaq* entered into under Islamic Law would be fully enforceable as to its secular terms, as long as the contract's religious aspects were not subject to court scrutiny. *See also Swartz v. Schwartz*, 583 N.Y.S.2d 716, 718 (Sup. Ct. 1992) (also holding that courts may use "neutral principles of law" to resolve disputes touching on religious concerns).

(3) *Query*. What if the parties had a premarital or postmarital agreement which provided that during the marriage or upon its dissolution, any children born of that marriage shall be raised in the Roman Catholic faith? *See Hackett v. Hackett*, 150 N.E.2d 431 (Ohio Ct. App. 1958); *Stanton v. Stanton*, 100 S.E.2d 289 (Ga. 1957). *Cf. Lundeen v. Struminger*, 165 S.E.2d 285 (Va. 1969); *Carrico v. Blevins*, 402 S.E.2d 235 (Va. Ct. App. 1991). On what criteria should the court base its determination as to the enforceability of such contractual provisions? *See generally* Annotation, *Religion as a Factor in Child Custody and Visitation Cases*, 22 A.L.R.4th 971 (1983); Comment, *You Get the House. I Get the Car. You Get the Kids. I Get Their Souls: The Impact of Spiritual Custody Awards on the Free Exercise Rights of Custodial Parents*, 138 U. Pa. L. Rev. 583 (1989). *Cf.* Susan Higginbotham, *"Mom, Do I Have to Go to Church?": The Noncustodial Parent's Obligation to Carry Out the Custodial Parent's Religious Plans*, 31 Fam. L.Q. 585 (1997).

(4) **Problem.** June and David were married in a religious ceremony approximately one year ago. At the time of the ceremony, both June and David were Jewish, and in front of the rabbi, at a pre-marriage ceremony, they both faithfully promised to attend regular sabbath services. The rabbi made clear to them that absent such a promise from them, he would not marry them in accordance with Jewish Law as interpreted by the conservative synagogues. Both June and David agreed to this and repeated their promise in front of the rabbi, both their parents, and their matron of honor and best man. They also signed a document produced by the rabbi which indicated that the parties had been counseled and had agreed to attend services on a regular basis. Subsequently, after the marriage, June refuses to attend services as she had previously promised to do. Attendance at services had always been a very important part of David's life. David has come to you for advice, especially as to how he might force June to honor her promise to attend religious services. In light of *Avitzur, above,* what advice might you give David, and what legal remedies, if any, would David have? *See Minkin v. Minkin,* 434 A.2d 665 (N.J. Super. Ct. 1981).

See generally Barbara J. Redman, *What Can Be Done in Secular Courts to Aid the Jewish Woman?*, 19 Ga. L. Rev. 389 (1985); Lieberman, *Avitzur v. Avitzur: The Constitutional Implications of Judicially Enforcing Religious Agreements*, 33 Cath. U. L. Rev. 219 (1983).

(5) **Problem.** Husband and Wife, both devout Muslims, were married in Tampa, Florida, in 1991. One day prior to their marriage, they signed an Islamic premarital agreement or *sadaq* which stated, "The *sadaq* being fifty thousand and one dollars, of which one U.S. dollar advanced and fifty thousand dollars postponed." The parties were subsequently divorced, and the wife petitioned a Florida court to enforce the parties' *sadaq* for the deferred payment of fifty thousand dollars. The wife and her Islamic expert witness testified that a *sadaq* is similar to a dowry, and that a wife's right under Islamic law to receive the *sadaq* would not be negated if the wife filed for divorce. The husband testified, however, that he believed that the postponed portion of a *sadaq* was forfeited if a wife chose to divorce her husband, based upon his sister's experience with an Islamic court in Lebanon. The trial court judge held that this agreement was unenforceable based on lack of consideration and a "meeting of the minds." How should the appellate court rule, and why? *See Akileh v. Elchahal,* 666 So. 2d 246 (Fla. Dist. Ct. App. 1996).

CHAPTER 14

TAX CONSEQUENCES AND BANKRUPTCY

SYNOPSIS

§ 14.01 Introduction
§ 14.02 Tax Consequences of Marriage and Divorce
    [A] Child and Spousal Support
    [B] Tax Aspects of Property Division
§ 14.03 Bankruptcy and Divorce

§ 14.01 Introduction

As everyone knows, taxes permeate every aspect of American life. Family law is no exception; it is simply impossible to practice family law without a knowledge of the tax law. The discussion here does not attempt to summarize the tax laws which affect the American family. The emphasis here is on the federal tax consequences of divorce. In many states, the state income tax system duplicates the federal system, but this is not true everywhere. Fortunately, bankruptcy is not as pervasive as taxation in American life; nevertheless, bankruptcy does pose some important traps for the unwary family law practitioner. Also, important new changes have occurred in the bankruptcy law, changes which have been proposed by commentators on divorce and bankruptcy for years.

§ 14.02 Tax Consequences of Marriage and Divorce

[A] Child and Spousal Support

ROOSEVELT v. COMMISSIONER OF INTERNAL REVENUE
United States Tax Court
70 T.C.M. (CCH) 612, T.C.M. (RIA) 95,430 (1995)

NAMEROFF, SPECIAL TRIAL JUDGE:

. . . Respondent determined deficiencies in petitioner's 1990 and 1991 Federal income taxes in the amounts of $3,903 and $3,323, respectively. . . .

The sole issue for decision is whether payments received by petitioner from her former husband constituted alimony as defined by section 71. The parties submitted this case fully stipulated, and the stipulated facts are so found. The stipulation of facts, supplemental stipulation of facts, and attached exhibits are incorporated herein by this reference. . . .

Petitioner, an accountant, was formerly married to T. Steven Roosevelt (Mr. Roosevelt). Two children, Theodore Kevin Roosevelt and Alexis Ann Roosevelt, were born of the marriage. Pursuant to the divorce judgment and order (the divorce judgment) executed and entered on November 4, 1981, by the Superior Court of the County of Los Angeles, Mr. Roosevelt was ordered to pay petitioner

> as and for unallocated family allowance and support, the sum of $2,700.00 per month, . . . commencing October 1, 1980, and continuing at said rate for forty-two (42) months, after which said family allowance and support shall be reduced to $2,000.00 per month, . . . continuing at said rate until [petitioner's] remarriage, death of either party or further order of Court, whichever shall first occur.

In the event that the family allowance and support ceased by operation of law or further order of the court, the divorce judgment provided that Mr. Roosevelt was to pay petitioner "as and for child support . . . the sum of $700.00 per child, per month, for a total of $1,400.00 per month" until each child "reaches the age of majority, marries, becomes emancipated, or by further order of the Court, whichever shall first occur."

During 1990, petitioner received $23,000 from Mr. Roosevelt. On her Form 1040 for taxable year 1990, petitioner reported alimony received in the amount of $6,200. During 1991, petitioner received $25,000 from Mr. Roosevelt. On her Form 1040 for taxable year 1991, petitioner reported alimony received in the amount of $7,200. Petitioner contends that $16,800 received in each year represents nontaxable child support payments in the amount of $700 per child per month. Respondent contends that the entire amounts of $23,000 and $25,000 for the taxable years 1990 and 1991, respectively, represent taxable alimony.

The parties agreed in the Supplemental Stipulation of Facts that if the Court found that $16,800 received each year represented child support, then petitioner received taxable alimony of $6,200 in 1990 and $8,200 in 1991. The parties also agreed that if the Court finds that $16,800 received each year was not child support, petitioner received taxable alimony of $23,000 in 1990 and $25,000 in 1991.

Petitioner bears the burden of proving that respondent's determinations are erroneous. Rule 142(a). Pursuant to section 71(a)(1), as in effect for 1981, the year in which the divorce judgment was entered into, gross income includes amounts received as alimony or separate maintenance payments. However, section 71(b) provides as follows:

SEC. 71(b). Payments to Support Minor Children.—Subsection (a) shall not apply to that part of any payment which the terms of the decree, instrument, or agreement fix, in terms of an amount of money or a part of the payment, as a sum which is payable for the support of minor children of the husband. . . .

The word "fix," as used in section 71(b), has been interpreted to mean that in order for child support to be excluded from gross income, the allocations to child support must be specifically designated in a written agreement and "not left to determination by inference or conjecture." *Commissioner v. Lester*, 366 U.S. 299, 306 (1961). The regulations further provide that if periodic payments are received by the wife for the support and maintenance of herself and of minor children, without a specific designation of the portion for support of such children, then the entire amount of the payment is includable in the income of the wife as provided in section 71(a). Sec. 1.71-1(e), Income Tax Regs.

Petitioner's principal argument is that section 71(c)(2) is applicable in the present situation. In essence, petitioner argues that section 22(k) of the Internal Revenue Code of

1939, the predecessor to section 71, controlled the result in *Commissioner v. Lester, supra*. Since the Internal Revenue Code of 1954 was amended to include section 71(c)(2), petitioner's argument continues, *Lester* was overruled and is inapplicable to the divorce judgment at issue. Accordingly, petitioner argues that the divorce judgment provides for the payment of $700 per child in the event of certain contingencies. Thus, petitioner argues, the divorce judgment "fixes" child support as required by section 71(c)(2).

However, petitioner's reliance on section 71(c)(2) is misplaced. In the Deficit Reduction Act of 1984, Pub.L. 98-369, sec. 422(a), 98 Stat. 494, 795-796, section 71 was amended by the addition of section 71(c), providing that the terms of a divorce or separation agreement for the support of children will be "treated as an amount fixed as payable for the support of children" where any amount of the support payable in the instrument will be reduced, generally, on the happening of a contingency related to the child, such as the child's attaining a certain age, marrying, dying, or leaving school. The effect of section 71(c)(2) is to legislatively overrule the decision in *Lester*. *Gable v. Commissioner*, T.C.Memo. 1985-423.

However, section 71(c)(2) is applicable for decrees or separation agreements made or in certain respects modified after 1984. In this case, the divorce judgment was issued during 1981 and was not modified after 1984; therefore, section 71(c)(2) is inapplicable. Section 71, as in effect prior to 1984, and the case law interpreting this section, including *Lester*, control the result in this case. Thus, petitioner's argument must fail.

Petitioner asks us to infer from the language of the divorce judgment that $1,400 of the monthly payment represents child support and is excludable from her gross income. This approach was rejected by the Supreme Court in *Lester* and by this Court on many occasions.

The divorce judgment provides for an unallocated family allowance of $2,700 per month, subsequently reduced to $2,000 per month. No portion of either of these amounts is specifically designated as child support. In order to satisfy the requirements of section 71(b), the amount of child support must be fixed by the separation or divorce agreement. "[W]e have repeatedly refused to allow inference, intent, or other nonspecific designation of payments as child support to override the clear rule of section 71(b)." *Mass v. Commissioner*, *supra* at 123. Based upon the record presented, we must conclude that the divorce agreement does not "fix" any amount of the monthly payment as child support. Accordingly, we sustain respondent on this issue.

Decision will be entered for respondent for the deficiencies and for petitioner for the accuracy-related penalties.

FOSBERG v. COMMISSIONER OF INTERNAL REVENUE
United States Tax Court
64 T.C.M. (CCH) 1527, T.C.M. (RIA) 92,713 (1992)

MEMORANDUM OPINION

DINAN, SPECIAL TRIAL JUDGE:

. . . Respondent determined a deficiency in petitioner's 1987 Federal income tax in the amount of $4,463.

Concessions having been made by petitioner, the issue remaining for decision is whether petitioner is entitled to deduct $7,800 as payment of alimony to Ingrid S. Fosberg in 1987.

Some of the facts have been stipulated. The stipulations of fact and accompanying exhibits are incorporated herein by reference. Petitioner resided in Farmington, Connecticut, at the time this petition was filed.

Petitioner was divorced from Ingrid S. Fosberg on December 9, 1985. As required by the divorce judgment, petitioner paid Ingrid S. Fosberg $7,800 in 1987 and deducted that amount on his return as alimony. Paragraph IV of the divorce judgment states:

> The Defendant husband is ordered to pay the Plaintiff wife as alimony, the sum of $175.00 per week until the wife is employed either part-time or full-time, or in any event, until December 31, 1986, and then said alimony shall be reduced to $150.00 per week and shall continue until her death, remarriage or until the youngest child reaches the age of 18 years, whichever first occurs. Thereafter said alimony will cease, and the wife will have no further right to same.

Paragraph III states:

> A. It is ordered that the Defendant pay the amount of $75.00 per week per child. B. It is further ordered that in the event the Defendant is more than 30 days in arrears, the Plaintiff wife will be allowed to bring a wage garnishment for said support in accordance with Connecticut General Statutes Section 85-548. C. Further, the Defendant is ordered to maintain medical insurance for the minor children. Any unreimbursed or uninsured medical expenses with respect to said minor children is to be shared by the parties equally. . . . F. The Defendant is entitled to the dependency exemptions for the two minor children for so long as he is current on his support payments.

Section 71(a), provides that there shall be included in gross income any amount received as alimony or as separate maintenance. There is a corresponding deduction allowed under section 215 for payments of alimony or separate maintenance made by an individual. On the other hand, payments made for child support are neither includible under section 71 nor deductible under section 215.

Alimony does not include that part of a payment which is payable for child support. Sec. 71(c). Section 71(c)(2) sets forth the treatment of reductions in payments relating to contingencies involving a child. Generally, if any amount will be reduced as a result of a contingency relating to a child, then the amount of the reduction will be treated as child support. . . .

Because the alleged alimony payments in this case will be reduced to zero when petitioner's youngest child reaches the age of 18 years, in accordance with Paragraph IV of the divorce judgment, the provisions of section 71(c)(2)(A) are applicable. Accordingly, we hold that petitioner is not entitled to the alimony deduction of $7,800 claimed by him on his 1987 return.

Decision will be entered for the respondent.

NOTES AND QUESTIONS

(1) **Marriage Penalty.** The term "marriage penalty" usually refers to the belief that the federal tax rate system favors single people over married couples. It is commonly believed that married people pay a greater share of their income to federal income tax than do single

people, and that if two people get married they will end up paying more taxes than they would if they both remained single. A more accurate statement of the concept of marriage penalty is that some people will pay more taxes if they get married. However, others will actually pay less. For some couples, there is actually a marriage bonus. A recent article offers the following example of a marriage penalty:

> If individuals A and B are single and each earns $30,000 in 1996, they each will pay federal income taxes of $3,517.50 for a total of $7,035. If they marry, however, their total tax liability will be $8,283. That results in a marriage penalty of $1,248: the tax liability of A and B as a married couple ($8,283) is $1,248 greater than the total of their respective liabilities if they are single.

Jonathon B. Forman, *What Can Be Done About Marriage Penalties*, 30 Fam. L.Q. 1, 5 (1996) (footnotes omitted). This same article also gives a good example of a marriage bonus:

> On the other hand, if individuals C and D are single but share the same household, and C earns $60,000 and while D earns nothing in 1996, C will pay $11,846 in federal income tax while D will pay nothing, for a total tax of $11,846. If they marry, their total tax will be just $8,283. This marriage bonus for C and D together is $3,563.

Id. at 6. Nevertheless the tax penalty for two income married couples is an issue of general concern and, along with other provisions of the tax system which are not marriage neutral, may be subject to tax reform. The Forman article suggests a comprehensive plan for reform which would lead to couple neutrality.

(2) **Spousal Support.** As the principal case states, alimony or separate maintenance payments are includable in the income of the payee; they are also deductible by the payor. I.R.C. § 71(a) states, "Gross income includes amounts received as alimony or separate maintenance payments"; and I.R.C. § 215(a) states, "In the case of an individual, there shall be allowed as a deduction an amount equal to the alimony or separate maintenance payments paid during such individual's taxable year." Alimony or separate maintenance are defined by the tax code, and this definition provides the prerequisites for includibility by the payee. However, the real reason for these requirements and indeed almost all the rules in this area is to govern when the payor can deduct the support payments. The rules are based upon the assumption that the payor will be in the higher tax bracket than the payee and that there can be a net tax savings (which can even be split between the parties) by shifting income from payor to payee. The temptation is to label payments for child support or for property settlement as spousal support. Here are some of the requirements for deducting spousal support; others are mentioned under the subjects of "Child Support" in note (3) and under "Anti-Front-Loading Rules" in note (4) below.

(A) *Cash Payments.* The support payments must be made in cash, which includes payments by check or money order and rent or mortgage payments. *See* I.R.C. § 71(b)(1) (1998); T.D. 7973, 1984-2, C.B. 174 (1998).

(B) *Decree or MSA.* The payments must be made pursuant to a divorce decree or marriage settlement agreement, I.R.C. § 71(b)(1)(A) (1998), which must be in writing. *See* I.R.C. § 71(b)(2) (1998).

(C) *No Contrary Intent.* The divorce decree or the agreement reached by the parties must not expressly "designate such payment as a payment which is not includible in gross income under this section and not allowable as a deduction under section

215. . . ." I.R.C. § 71(b)(1)(B) (1998). This provision, while couched in terms of a requirement for deductibility and includibility, also means that the parties are free to structure the tax aspects of their divorce as they choose.

(D) *Living Separately.* Spouses must not be members of the same household at the time the payments are made. *See* I.R.C. § 71(b)(1)(C) (1998). However, if the parties are not yet divorced but are living separate lives although still living in the same dwelling, the payments are deductible by the payor and includible by the payee. Once the divorce is granted, the couple must be living in different dwellings for the standard rules to apply. *See* Tres. Reg. § 1.17-1T, A-9. This exception is apparently designed to encourage reconciliation on the part of couples who are still living in the same household.

(E) *No Post-Death Liability.* In order to discourage the use of alimony as a substitute for property settlement, there cannot be a requirement that the payments continue after the death of the payee. *See* I.R.C. § 71(b)(1)(D) (1998) states as a requirement, "there is no liability to make any such payment for any period after the death of the payee spouse and there is no liability to make any payment (in cash or property) as a substitute for such payments after the death of the payee spouse." The assumption is that if the payments continue after the death of the payee, or if a lump sum is paid to the payee's estate, these payments are not really support but rather property settlement payments which are not deductible by the payor.

(F) *No Joint Tax Returns.* The provisions for includibility and deductibility do not "apply if the spouses make a joint return with each other." I.R.C. §71(e) (1998).

(3) **Child Support.** For child support the rule is just the opposite: child support payments are not deductible by the payor and not includable in the income of the payee. *See* I.R.C. § 71(c)(1) (1998). As mentioned above, if the parties are in different tax brackets, the temptation is for them to treat child support payments as spousal support so that the federal income tax will be paid at a lower level. "Temptation" may be the wrong word to use here. "Strategy" might be better because this practice of shifting the funds to the lower tax bracket is perfectly legal if the stringent requirements of the tax code are met.

In fact, this practice was expressly sanctioned by the United States Supreme Court. In *Commissioner v. Lester*, 366 U.S. 299 (1961), the Court held that all the support payments could be treated as alimony as long as the decree or marriage settlement agreement did not fix an amount as child support. The term "fix" was interpreted to mean "specifically designate." However, there is some evidence in the case that the Supreme Court did not fully understand the implications of what it was doing:

> the Congress was in effect giving the husband and wife the power to shift a portion of the tax burden from the wife to the husband by the use of a simple provision in the settlement agreement which fixed the specific portion of the periodic payment made to the wife as payable for the support of the children.

Id. at 404. The Court's ruling really gave the husband and wife the power to shift a portion of the income to the lower tax bracket. *Lester* created a major strategy for tax planning after divorce.

This strategy was severely limited in the Deficit Reduction Act of 1984, which created the rules which are controlling today. Support payments will be considered non-deductible/non-includible child support if they cease or are reduced

> (A) on the happening of a contingency specified in the instrument relating to a child (such as attaining a specified age, marrying, dying, leaving school, or a similar contingency), or
>
> (B) at a time which can clearly be associated with a contingency of a kind specified in subparagraph (A), an amount equal to the amount of such reduction will be treated as an amount fixed as payable for the support of children of the payor spouse.

I.R.C. § 71(c) (1998). This provision is based upon the assumption that a payor will not want to pay child support to an ex-spouse when there is no longer an obligation to do so, and that an alimony award which contains a child support component will be structured to step-down when the child reaches maturity. For example, an agreement could be written to allow for two reductions: the wife receives $3000 per month until the first child turns 18, when the amount will be reduced to $2000; she will continue to get that amount until the second child leaves school, when the support will again be reduced, this time to $1000. Under this agreement, only $1000 will be deductible and includible.

The IRS has taken steps to further shore-up Section 71(c) by establishing two important presumptions:

> There are two situations . . . in which payments which would otherwise qualify as alimony or separate maintenance payments will be presumed to be reduced at a time clearly associated with the happening of a contingency relating to a child of the payor. . . . The first situation referred to above is where the payments are to be reduced not more than 6 months before or after the date the child is to attain the age of 18, 21, or local age of majority. The second situation is where the payments are to be reduced on two or more occasions which occur not more than one year before or after a different child of the payor spouse attains a certain age between the ages of 18 and 24, inclusive.

Tres. Reg. § 1.17-1T, A-18. Both of these presumptions are rebuttable "by showing that the time at which the payments are to be reduced was determined independently of any contingencies relating to the children of the payor." *Id.* The first of the presumptions is very straightforward, but the latter may require some explanation; the Regulations give this complicated example to elucidate the rule:

> A and B are divorced on July 1, 1985, when their children, C (born July 15, 1970) and D (born September 23, 1972), are 14 and 12, respectively. Under the divorce decree, A is to make alimony payments to B of $2,000 per month. Such payments are to be reduced to $1,500 per month on January 1, 1991 and to $1,000 per month on January 1, 1995. On January 1, 1991, the date of the first reduction in payments, C will be 20 years 5 months and 17 days old. On January 1, 1995, the date of the second reduction in payments, D will be 22 years 3 months and 9 days old. Each of the reductions in payments is to occur not more than one year before or after a different child of A attains the age of 21 years and 4 months. (Actually, the reductions are to occur not more than one year before or after C and D attain any of the ages 21 years 3 months and 9 days through 21 years 5 months and 17 days). Accordingly, the reductions will be presumed to clearly be associated with the happening of a contingency relating to C and D.

Id.

Both presumptions can be rebutted by a showing that the time chosen to reduce the support was determined independently of a child-related date, according to a customary or statutory practice of a local jurisdiction, or actually a complete cessation of spousal support occurring during the sixth post-separation year or at the end of a six-year period.

(4) **Anti-Front Loading Requirements.** As noted above, the tax code also seeks to discourage the parties from disguising property settlement payments as alimony. The advantage to taxpayers of so disguising their settlement was twofold. First, the high income payor could get a deduction for the transfer of property; second, the payee would be free from the threat of bankruptcy on the part of the payor because, under former law, periodic payments of a property settlement were a debt dischargeable in bankruptcy while alimony payments were not dischargeable. The anti-front loading provisions are based upon the assumptions that the payor is going to want a large tax break in the years immediately following the divorce and that the payee does not want to spread the payments over many years. Therefore, the parties want to "front load" the support payments with property settlement money during the first few years after divorce. The provisions are stated in I.R.C. § 71(f) (1998), summarized as follows:

(A) Payments exceeding a total of $15,000 per year must be spread out over three years. This means that the payments must span three years; technically the minimum number of payments is not thirty-six but rather fourteen.

(B) Excess payments can be recaptured to the payor's income according to a statutory formula. Basically, if the payments the first year exceed the average of years two and three by more than $15,000 the excess amount is recaptured (includible) in the third year. And if the amount in the second year exceeds the amount in the third year it is recaptured in the third year.

(5) **Miscellaneous Child Support and Custody Issues.** As mentioned in the introduction, it is impossible in the space allocated to tax matters in this casebook to cover all the tax aspects of divorce. Here are just a few other tax issues relating to child custody and support:

(A) *Dependency Exemption.* The parent who has the child the majority of the time may claim the dependency exemption. However, the parent with the right to the exemption may trade the exemption to the other parent, presumably in return for a higher support payment. In other words, the exemption can be traded to the higher earning noncustodial parent for a net tax savings which will be split between the parents. The only requirement is a signed written statement waiving the right to claim the exemption. There is a non-mandatory official form for this waiver, and the form or statement must be attached to the return of the non-custodial parent who claims the exemption. *See* I.R.C. § 151(e) (1998).

(B) *Filing Status.* The custodial parent usually will qualify as a "head of household" and can take advantage of tax rates which are more favorable than those for "single" taxpayers. To qualify, the taxpayer must pay more than half of the costs of the household and maintain it as the principal place of residence of an unmarried minor child. It is not necessary that the child be a dependent. If the parties have joint custody, the parent who has the child the majority of the time can claim head of household status. Head of household filing status is also available if the residence is the principal abode for a dependent married child or parent. *See* I.R.C. § 2(b)(1)(A) (1998).

(C) *Child Care Expenses.* Parents who maintain a household may receive a tax credit for a percentage of the costs of child care expenses for a dependent child under thirteen (13) when the expenses enable the parent to be gainfully employed. If the parties are legally separated, only the parent who has custody the majority of the time can claim the credit. *See* I.R.C. § 21(e)(5) (1998). If the parties are merely living separate and apart without a decree and file separate returns no credit can be claimed, unless the other spouse has been absent from the household for six months. *See* I.R.C. § 21(e)(2), (4) (1998).

(D) *Medical Expenses.* Both parents can treat a child as a dependent for purposes of deducting medical expenses as long as the parents have actually paid the medical expense and the other requirements to take the deduction are met.

(6) **Support Trusts.** The use of a trust can be an important tax planning tool, at least for those who are wealthy enough to fund a trust. The payor of a support obligation creates and funds a trust; the proceeds of the trust will be used to make the monthly spousal or child support payments. The payee gets added security for the support payments, and there can be tax advantages for both parties. The basic tax treatment of this trust income does not differ from the normal pattern of includibility. If the trust income is used to satisfy spousal support obligations, then the income is includible in the income of the payee. The payor does not deduct it, but the result is ultimately the same because the income is not includible for the payor. If the trust income satisfies a child support obligation, the payments are includible in the income of the payor. *See* I.R.C. § 682 (1998). There are still a number of tax advantages. It is possible to have tax-free support if the trust income is not taxable. For example, if the trust income is from tax-free municipal bonds, the support payments from this income will be tax-free. *See* I.R.C. § 643(a) (1998); *Ellis v. United States*, 416 F.2d 894, 895 (6th Cir. 1969). Also, because the trust is governed by I.R.C. § 682 and not by I.R.C. § 71, the requirements of includibility in Section 71 mentioned above in note 2 do not apply. Also, the Section 71 rules of recapture probably do not apply, although at the time of this writing this issue has not been ruled upon by the IRS.

(7) **Attorney Fees.** Attorney fees and other costs related to divorce, such as those for accountants, appraisers, and other experts, are generally not deductible. The tax code draws a distinction between personal and family expenses and expenses that "arise in the connection with a taxpayer's profit-seeking activities," and most divorce related expenses fall into the former category. *See United States v. Gilmore*, 372 U.S. 39, 49 (1963). The practical effect is that all of the following fees, which are considered personal and marital are not deductible: fees related to child custody, *Karelas v. Commissioner*, 56 T.C.M. 832 (P-H); fees incurred for obtaining or collecting child support, *Smith v. Commissioner*, 49 T.C.M. 395 (1980), *Swenson v. Commissioner*, 43 T.C. 897 (1965); and, finally, fees incurred regarding property division, *United v. Gilmore*, 372 U.S. 39 (1963). The two main areas of deductibility are spousal support and tax planning. Attorney fees and costs to obtain, collect, modify support upward, or to resist modification of support downward are all deductible. *See* I.R.C. § 212(1) (1998). The rationale is that these activities are expenses incurred for the production of income. Fees incurred seeking support are distinguished from those incurred resisting support, which are not deductible, because the latter are not directly income producing. Fees for spousal support are also distinguished from fees for child support, which are not deductible, because the latter are not includible as income. A wide

variety of tax advice and tax planning related to divorce can be deducted, including advice and planning fees related to child support, dependency exemption, spousal support (even by the resisting party), and the division of property. *See* I.R.C. § 212(3) (1998); *Carpenter v. United States*, 338 F. 2d 366, 367–69 (Ct. Cl. 1964). Finally, it should be remembered that these deductions are subject to the 2% floor for miscellaneous itemized deductions; that is, they are deductible only to the extent they exceed 2% of the adjusted gross income. *See* I.R.C. § 67 (1998).

PROBLEMS

(1) At the time of their divorce, Wilma and Henry had been married sixteen years and had one child who was ten years old. Henry and Wilma live in a jurisdiction which has a statutory presumption that spousal support should be paid for a period equal to half the length of the marriage. Henry agrees to pay Wilma family support for eight years. The amount of the support is twice that of the child support guideline. At the end of eight years the support will cease completely. Will Henry be able to deduct the full amount of the support?

(2) Winnie and Harry have two children, Dorothy, born July 4, 1980, and Sam, born Jan 1, 1982. At the time of their divorce in 1998, Winnie agreed to pay Harry spousal support for ten years until 2008 and to pay child support which would continue for four years of higher education. In order to maximize tax savings, the support payments were merged in the MSA into one payment of $2000 per month, designated as family support as permitted by local law. The $2000 payment was to be reduced by $600 in June of 2002 and again by $600 in June of 2004. Winnie would continue to pay Harry $800 per month until 2008. Will Winnie be able to deduct the full amount of the support payments each year?

[B] Tax Aspects of Property Division

ARNES v. UNITED STATES [ARNES I]
United States Court of Appeals
981 F.2d 456 (9th Cir. 1992)

Hug, Circuit Judge:

The issue in this case is whether a taxpayer must recognize for income tax purposes the gain that she realized when, pursuant to a divorce settlement, a corporation redeemed her half of the stock in the corporation, the remaining stock of which was owned by her former husband. The district court, ruling on cross-motions for summary judgment, held that Section 1041 of the Internal Revenue Code of 1986 (I.R.C.) relieved the taxpayer of having to recognize the gain, and awarded the taxpayer a refund of $53,053 for 1988. . . . We affirm.

II.

Joann Arnes, the Taxpayer-Appellee, married John Arnes in 1970. In 1980, they formed a corporation, "Moriah," to operate a McDonald's franchise in Ellensburg, Washington. That corporation issued 5,000 shares of stock in the joint names of John Arnes and Joann Arnes. In 1987, the couple agreed to divorce. McDonald's Corporation required 100%

ownership of the equity and profits by the owner/operator, and informed John Arnes that there should be no joint ownership of the restaurant after the divorce.

Joann and John Arnes entered into an agreement to have their corporation redeem Joann Arnes' 50 percent interest in the outstanding stock for $450,000. The corporation would pay that money to Joann Arnes by forgiving a debt of approximately $110,000 that she owed the corporation, by making two payments of $25,000 to her during 1988, and by paying the remainder of approximately $290,000 to her in monthly installments over ten years beginning in February 1988. The agreement was incorporated into the decree of dissolution of the marriage, dated January 7, 1988. Joann Arnes surrendered her 2,500 shares to the corporation on December 31, 1987, and the corporation canceled her stock certificate on May 4, 1988, then issuing another 2,500 shares to John Arnes.

On her federal income tax return for 1988, Joann Arnes reported that she sold her stock in Moriah on January 2, 1988, for a price of $450,000, and that her basis was $2,500, resulting in a profit of $447,500. She received $178,042 in 1988 as part of the sales price. Using an installment method, she treated $177,045 as long-term capital gain and the remainder as recovery of a portion of her basis.

On December 27, 1989, she filed a timely claim for refund of $53,053 for 1988 on the ground that she was not required to recognize any gain on the transfer of her stock because the transfer was made pursuant to a divorce instrument. The IRS did not allow the claim for refund, and Joann Arnes initiated this suit.

The district court found that the redemption of Joann Arnes' stock in Moriah was required by a divorce instrument, and that John Arnes had benefitted from the transaction because it was part of the marital property settlement, which limited future community property claims that Joann Arnes might have brought against him. The court, in applying the IRS regulations, found that, although Joann transferred her stock directly to Moriah, the transfer was made on behalf of John and should have been treated as having been made to John. Therefore, the transfer qualified for nonrecognition of gain pursuant to the I.R.C. exemption for transfers made to spouses or former spouses incident to a divorce settlement. *See* 26 U.S.C. §1041 (1988). Summary judgment was granted in favor of Joann Arnes.

The Government appeals. Meanwhile, in order to insure that the capital gain will be taxed, the Government has asserted a protective income tax deficiency against John Arnes, who has contested the deficiency by filing a petition with the Tax Court. His case is pending but not before this court. The Government maintains that, although Joann Arnes is the appropriate party to be taxed for the gain, John Arnes should be taxed if the district court's ruling is upheld. If neither John nor Joann is taxed, the $450,000 used to redeem Joann's appreciated stock apparently will be taken out of the corporation tax-free. . . .

III.

The Government contends that the gain resulting from Moriah's redemption of Joann Arnes' stock does not qualify for exemption under section 1041, which is limited to transfers made directly to one's spouse or former spouse, or transfers made into trust for that person. Joann Arnes' transfer to Moriah, the Government contends, is outside the scope of the exemption.

Joann Arnes contends that her transfer of stock to Moriah should be considered a transfer to John, resulting in a benefit to John, and absolving her of the obligation to bear the burden of any resulting tax.

Section 1041 provides in part:

> (a) General rule. No gain or loss shall be recognized on a transfer of property from an individual to (or in trust for the benefit of)
>
> (1) a spouse, or
>
> (2) a former spouse, but only if the transfer is incident to the divorce.
>
> (b) Transfer treated as gift; transferee has transferor's basis. In the case of any transfer of property described in subsection (a)—
>
> (1) for purposes of this subtitle, the property shall be treated as acquired by the transferee by gift, and
>
> (2) the basis of the transferee in the property shall be the adjusted basis of the transferor. 26 U.S.C. §1041 (1988) ("Transfers of property between spouses or incident to divorce").

The purpose of the provision is to defer the tax consequences of transfers between spouses or former spouses. Property received in such a transfer is excluded from the recipient's gross income. The recipient's basis is then equal to the transferor's basis. Later, when the recipient transfers the property to a third party, the gain or loss must be recognized.

After section 1041 was enacted, the Treasury Department published a temporary regulation to implement the statute. Temp.Treas.Reg. §1.1041-1T (1992). The regulation explains that in certain cases a transfer of property to a third party "on behalf of" a spouse or former spouse should be treated as a transfer to the spouse or former spouse. *Id.* at Q-9, A-9. One example supplied in the regulation is the case where the transfer to the third party is required by a divorce or separation instrument. Such a transfer of property will be treated as made directly to the nontransferring spouse (or former spouse) and the nontransferring spouse will be treated as immediately transferring the property to the third party. The deemed transfer from the nontransferring spouse (or former spouse) to the third party is not a transaction that qualifies for nonrecognition of gain under section 1041. Temp.Treas.Reg. §1.1041-1T, A-9 (1992).

The example suggests that the tax consequences of any gain or loss arising from the transaction would fall upon the nontransferring spouse for whose benefit the transfer was made, rather than upon the transferring spouse. Consistent with the policy of the statute, which is to defer recognition until the property is conveyed to a party outside the marital unit, the regulation seems to provide for shifting the tax burden from one spouse to the other, where appropriate.

Thus, a transfer by a spouse to a third party can be treated as a transfer to the other spouse when it is "on behalf of" the other spouse. Whether the redemption of Joann's stock can be construed as a transfer to John, pursuant to the regulation example in A-9, depends upon the meaning of "on behalf of." The district court interpreted the regulation as meaning that a transfer was made "on behalf of" John Arnes if he received a benefit from the transfer. The court then concluded that John did receive a benefit, because the transfer was part of the marital property agreement which settled any future community property claims that Joann Arnes could have asserted against John.

Although no case is directly on point, many tax cases concern transfers made on behalf of other persons. Generally, a transfer is considered to have been made "on behalf of" someone if it satisfied an obligation or a liability of that person. If an employer pays an employee's income tax, that payment is income to the employee. If a corporation assumes a shareholder's bank note in exchange for stock, the shareholder receives a taxable constructive dividend. *Schroeder v. Commissioner*, 831 F.2d 856, 859 (9th Cir.1987). . . .

John Arnes had an obligation to Joann Arnes that was relieved by Moriah's payment to Joann. That obligation was based in their divorce property settlement, which called for the redemption of Joann's stock. Although John and Joann were the sole stockholders in Moriah, the obligation to purchase Joann's stock was John's, not Moriah's. Furthermore, John personally guaranteed Moriah's note to Joann. Under Washington law, Joann could sue John for payment without suing Moriah. *See* Wash.Rev.Code Ann. §62A.3-416(1) (West 1979). Thus, John was liable, with Moriah, for the payments due Joann.

We hold that Joann's transfer to Moriah did relieve John of an obligation, and therefore constituted a benefit to John. Joann's transfer of stock should be treated as a constructive transfer to John, who then transferred the stock to Moriah. The $450,000 was paid to Joann by Moriah on behalf of John. The transfer of $450,000 from the corporate treasury need not escape taxation, if we hold, as we do, that Joann is not required to recognize any gain on the transfer of her stock, because it is subject to section 1041. The tax result for Joann is the same as if she had conveyed the property directly to John. . . .

The judgment of the district court is AFFIRMED.

NOTES AND QUESTIONS

(1) **Non-recognition.** As the principal case mentions, the transfer of property from one spouse to another pursuant to a marriage settlement agreement or a divorce judgment does not trigger the recognition of taxable gains or of losses. *See* I.R.C. § 1041 (1998). This rule in effect means that transfers which occur in the dissolution process are not a taxable event.

This has not always been the case. In 1962, the United States Supreme Court held that such transfers were a taxable event. When the property was transferred, the recipient would pay tax on the gain and then receive a new basis based upon the value at the time of transfer. *See United States v. Davis*, 370 U.S. 65 (1962). In *Davis*, the husband's "cost basis for the 1955 transfer was $74,775.37, and the fair market value of the 500 shares there transferred was $82,250." *Id.* at 67. Because the court held that his transfer was a taxable event, the husband was required to pay capital gains tax on $7,474.63. Professor Asimov has commented on the impracticality of this rule:

> While the *Davis* decision made theoretical tax sense, it made no practical sense. It frequently imposed a heavy tax burden at the worst possible time—when a couple's finances were in disarray and every available dollar was needed to finance the transition from one household into two. The taxable transfer was essentially involuntary because it was compelled by marital property law. Finally, the transfer produced no cash with which to pay the tax.

Michael Asimov, *The Assault on Tax-Free Divorce: Carryover Basis and Assignment of Income*, 44 Tax L. Rev. 65, 67 (1988). Under the *Davis* case, however, the recipient spouse received a new and higher basis for the property, the value at the time of the transfer. The basis to the wife would be $82,250.

I.R.C. § 1041, enacted in 1984, legislatively overruled *Davis*. Under this provision, gain on the transfer of property between spouses or between former spouses "incident to divorce" is not recognizable and therefore not taxable. It is worth emphasizing that this provision applies to all transfers between spouses, not just spouses that are divorcing. If the parties are divorced, then the transfer must be made "incident to divorce," which means within one year of the date the marriage ceases or it must be "related to the cessation of marriage." Regulations have defined this latter concept to mean that the transfer was made pursuant to a divorce or separation instrument and occurs within six years after the marriage terminates. A modification of the terms of divorce by decree or agreement will qualify for non-recognition under this rule if it fits within the six-year period. *See* Tres. Reg. § 1.1041-1t, A-7.

The recipient of a transfer under I.R.C. § 1041 receives the property with its original basis. As a result of this "carryover basis," the tax liability on the property is ultimately borne by the recipient spouse. For example, in the *Davis* case in which the husband transferred stock to the wife with a basis of $74,775.37 and a fair market value of $82,250, the husband would not pay tax on the gain and the wife would take the shares with a basis of $74,775.37. If the shares do not lose their value, the wife will ultimately pay the tax on the $7,474.63 gain when she sells the shares.

Finally, just because the transfer of property incident to divorce is not a taxable event, it does not mean that tax consequences of a transfer should not be taken into consideration at the time of divorce. For example, if the husband is awarded stock with a basis of $50,000, which is worth $100,000, and the wife is awarded a $100,000 in cash, this division is not equal. The present value of the stock is actually much less because it has a potential tax liability attached.

(2) The Family Home. The Taxpayer Relief Act of 1997 made important changes in the law governing taxation of gain on the sale of family homes. These changes solved many problems that faced divorcing couples in dealing with this important piece of property. Perhaps the major change is that for most families the Act provides for a tax-free sale of the family home. After May 7, 1997, gain on the sale of a family home is taxable only to the extent that gain exceeds $250,000 for an individual or $500,000 for a couple if the home is sold in a year that the couple files a joint return. *See* I.R.C. § 121(a), (b)(2)(A) (1998). In order to qualify for this exclusion, the home must have been the couple's principal place of residence for an aggregate of two years during the last five years. *See* I.R.C. § 121(a) (1998). The Act also facilitates divorce arrangements in which one spouse is granted exclusive use of the house until a later time when the house is sold and the proceeds divided. The spouse who is out of possession will still get the benefit of the exclusion because the property will be treated as his or her principal residence "while such individual's spouse or former spouse is granted use of the property under a divorce or separation instrument." I.R.C. § 121 (d)(3)(B) (1998). Finally, this exclusion can be used every two years. *See* I.R.C. § 121 (b)(3)(A) (1998).

(3) Retirement Plans. It is well beyond the scope of this note to describe the taxation of pension and retirement plans. There are, however, a few basics that are important to know for purposes of divorce. The Retirement Equity Act of 1984, Pub. L. 98-397, 98 Stat.

1426, created a system in which a pension benefit may be assigned to an alternative payee, usually a former spouse or a child, following divorce. The alternative payee is taxed in the same manner as the original participant would be and no additional tax liability is incurred by virtue of the assignment to the alternative payee. The assignment must be made pursuant to a Qualified Domestic Relations Order (QDRO). Although the Employment Retirement Security Act (ERISA) contains an anti-alienation provision that can create income consequences, these consequences will not be triggered by a QDRO. For a full discussion of the taxation of retirement and pension plans, see Marjorie A. O'Connell, *Taxation of Employee Benefits: Qualified and Nonqualified Retirement Plans and Deferred Compensation Arrangements*, 30 Fam. L.Q. 91 (1996).

Here are a few other things to remember. Annuities are taxed at the time of distribution. If the distribution is made in payments, a portion of each payment is considered to be repayment of the original nondeductible contribution, which was already taxed and therefore is excluded from income at the time of distribution. A formula in the form of a ratio is used to determine the excludable portion: "[t]he nontaxable portion is the payment times the ratio of the investment in the contract over the expected return from the contract." *Id.* at 92 (citing I.RC. § 72(c)(1)). This formula is available for use by an alternative payee. *See id.* at 94 (citing I.RC. § 72(m)(10)). There are some annuities that are funded with tax-deferred income, such as those for employees of educational institutions and certain tax-exempt organizations under I.R.C. § 403(b) in which the entire payout for either the recipient or the alternative payee is taxable.

As to lump-sum payments, the same basic concept applies: the recipient is not taxed on the original non-deductible contribution. This applies to the alternative payee as well. There are also some special rules which avoid the harsh tax consequences of a single-year payment on a lump-sum distribution. The taxes may be averaged for a five-year period. *See* I.R.C. § 402(e)(1)(B) (1998). Alternately, the lump-sum payment can be rolled over into an IRA or into some other qualified tax deferred retirement plan. *See* I.R.C. § 402(c)(3) (1998).

Often the IRA rollover is extremely important for the alternative payee. It is not uncommon for some pension and retirement fund contracts to require a lump-sum payment to the alternative payee. The alternative payee is treated very much like an employee who has severed employment. The IRA rollover not only allows the alternative payee to avoid lump sum taxation but also early payment penalties. Income averaging is also available. *See* O'Connell at 95 (citing I.R.C. § 402(c)).

(4) **Stock Transfers and Redemptions.** Under I.R.C. § 1041, the transfer of stocks and bonds incident to divorce does not trigger tax consequences. Regardless of whether community or separate, jointly held or in the name of one party, stocks may be transferred and capital gains tax will not be incurred until the time that the recipient sells the stock. The original basis of the stock is carried over. This rule is applied to transfers of stock in closely held corporations.

A special problem arises with family businesses because the usual approach is for the business to be awarded, by agreement or decree, to the proprietor. If this award is offset with other marital or community assets, that transfer is non-taxable. If the community does not have enough assets to balance out the division of property, then the proprietor spouse may buy out the non-proprietor spouse with separate property. This buy-out is non-taxable.

If there is insufficient marital or separate property to equalize the transfer of business, then it is not uncommon for the proprietor to buy out the other spouse with a note.

The problem is more complicated if the business is a closely held corporation. The temptation is to buy out the non-proprietor with corporate funds. This transaction is called a stock redemption. The benefit is that the corporation's funds may be used for the buy-out. Despite the principal case, there is still confusion regarding the tax consequences of a stock redemption. The problem is that the stock is transferred to the corporation by the non-proprietor spouse. The transaction is not between the divorcing couple. The proprietor is not a party; he or she receives no dividend or gain. Thus, the sale would clearly be taxable to the spouse selling the stock back to the corporation as a capital gain if the sale was not required by the marriage settlement agreement. See Priv. Ltr. Rul. 90-46-004. There is a private ruling which has upheld taxation of the non-proprietor even where the transaction was required by the marriage settlement agreement. See id. This is of course contrary to *Arnes v. United States [Arnes I]*, 981 F.2d 456 (9th Cir. 1992), the principal case.

In *Arnes I*, the Ninth Circuit held that the transaction was not taxable to the non-proprietor if the transaction was "on behalf" of the proprietor, which would seem to mean that the transaction was required by the property award or settlement, requested by the proprietor, or for his or her benefit.

The next question is whether the transaction is taxable to the proprietor. This question remains unanswered.

In *Arnes v. Commissioner [Arnes II]*, 102 T.C. 522 (1994), the tax court took up the issue of taxing the husband in the *Arnes* case based upon the ruling in the action of the Ninth Circuit in *Arnes I*. The tax court held that the husband-proprietor had not received any dividend in this transaction, and so the transaction was not taxable to him. *Id.* at 522. The private ruling referred to above, Priv. Ltr. Rul. 90-46-004, also indicated that the transaction is not taxable to the proprietor. The effect of the two *Arnes* decisions was to whipsaw the government; that is, neither of the spouses incurred a tax liability.

If there is going to be a change in the law, the most likely approach will be to change the rule of *Arnes I*. At about the same time as *Arnes II*, another Private Letter Ruling was issued which supported the pre-*Arnes* view that the redemption was taxable to the non-proprietor, at least to the extent that it was the result of an arms-length negotiation. *See* Priv. Ltr. Rul. 94-27-009. Also in 1984, another tax court case, *Blatt v. Commissioner*, 102 T.C. 77 (1994), disapproved of *Arnes I*.

The issue of redemption remains unsettled at the time of this writing. For a full discussion of this issue, see Paul J. Buser and Thomas S. White, *Stock Redemption in Marital Separation Agreements: Unsteady Steps for the Unprepared*, 30 Fam. L.Q. 41 (1996), in which the authors disapprove of the approach of *Arnes I*.

(5) **Estate and Gift Tax.** Federal gift tax applies to transfers of property that are for "less than an adequate and full consideration in money or money's worth." I.R.C. § 2512(b) (1998). Transfers for purpose of spousal or child support are for "adequate and full consideration" so they are not subject to gift tax. *See* Rev. Rul. 68-379, 1968-2 CB 414. Transfers which are the result of a judicial decree are not subject to gift tax. *See Commissioner v. Harris*, 340 U.S. 106 (1950). Perhaps most importantly, transfers of property in a written agreement relating to "marital and property rights" are not transfers

if the agreement is entered into within a three-year period beginning one year before the divorce. *See* I.R.C. § 2516 (1998). Finally, transmutations of community property to separate property are not considered gifts subject to the gift tax, and, presumably, this rule would apply to transmutations of marital property to separate property. *See Commissioner v. Mills*, 183 F.2d 32 (9th Cir. 1950). Similar rules apply to transfers from a decedent's gross estate made pursuant to a decree or property settlement agreement if the agreement meets the standards of Section 2516.

PROBLEMS

(1) Winona and Hank purchased a house when they were first married for $50,000. At the time of divorce, the house was worth $100,000. In their marriage settlement agreement, Winona and Hank agreed that Winona would have the right to live in the family home rent-free, with the parties to split the proceeds when the house was eventually sold. After three years, Hank agreed to transfer the house to Winona. Will Hank have to pay taxes on this transfer?

(2) Husband and Wife enter into a premarital agreement in which he will give her half of his salary as her separate property. How will this income be taxed?

§ 14.03 Bankruptcy and Divorce

IN RE OSTERBERG
United States Bankruptcy Court
109 B.R. 938 (D.N.D. 1990)

WILLIAM A. HILL, BANKRUPTCY JUDGE.

This adversary proceeding was commenced by Complaint filed June 7, 1989, by which the plaintiff, Julie Streich, seeks a determination that divorce decree provisions by which the defendant/Debtor, Scott Osterberg, would remain responsible for certain marital obligations are in the nature of alimony and support and thus nondischargeable under section 523(a)(5) of the United States Bankruptcy Code. Trial of the matter was held on January 10, 1990. . . .

Findings of Fact

The parties were married in August 1979. After several years of marriage and two children (Farrah, born November 10, 1976, and Justin born May 13, 1980) they were divorced on January 13, 1987. In contemplation of the divorce the parties entered into a Stipulation and Property Settlement Agreement in December 1986. This agreement was incorporated into the divorce judgment. As relevant to the issues presented the agreement in part provides: . . .

(3) Alimony. Neither party shall receive alimony from nor pay alimony to the other party. . . .

(5) Child Support. Husband shall pay Wife the sum of One Hundred Dollars ($100.00) per month per child until each child attains the age of eighteen (18) years or graduates from high school. . . .

(7) Division of Property—Property Apportioned to Wife. There is hereby apportioned, set aside, transferred, and confirmed to Wife, free of all claim and demand of Husband, the following items of property that are set aside and transferred to Wife and taken by her with all encumbrances and other obligations to which such items may be subject. The items include the 1984 Chevrolet Cavalier, Christmas tree and household decorations, and Wife's high school memorabilia. Wife will be responsible for the upkeep and insurance on the automobile, and Husband shall make the payments on said vehicle as they become due. . . .

At the time of the divorce both parties were 31 years of age and in good health. Julie, a high school graduate, had an approximate monthly net income of $430 from her employment at a hospital. Scott farmed two quarters of land and worked for an oil field construction company earning $7.00 per hour when work was available. He testified that his income from farming alone was around $11,000.00 per year and was approximately $700 to $800 net per month from all sources.

Although not specifically mentioned in the decree, the parties owned a mobile home which was pledged as security to Midwest Federal. The debt owing Midwest was a joint obligation of the parties upon which they were obligated to make payments of $234.00 per month. At the time of the divorce Julie and the children were no longer occupying the mobile home, having moved to an apartment in Mohall, North Dakota due to marital discord. According to Julie, she never went back to the mobile home after leaving in August 1986. Scott continued to occupy the mobile home until it was repossessed by Midwest Federal who asserted a claim against the parties for a deficiency of $8,985.10. Scott has listed this claim as an unsecured debt in his bankruptcy schedules. Julie is now being dunned by the bank. . . .

The 1984 Chevrolet awarded to Julie was necessary for her daily transportation. When Scott failed to maintain the payments on the vehicle Julie and her present husband, in order to prevent its repossession, took out a bank loan and paid Ford Motor Credit Company the payoff balance of $3,622.22. They then commenced an action in state court for this amount and on April 18, 1988, received a default judgment against Scott in the sum of $3,727.42 inclusive of court costs.

Julie testified that the vehicle was necessary for transportation and that she could not make the payments by herself. Until her remarriage, her income was insufficient to provide for the complete support of herself and children necessitating her use of AFDC payments and food stamps. Scott agreed at trial that Julie could not have supported herself or the children on her income alone but he felt that her income would have been sufficient when the $200 per month child support payment was taken into consideration.

Julie acknowledged that alimony was never discussed with Scott because she knew he would never pay it and she felt she could not rely on it. She simply wanted her transportation provided for and all other debts, including the Midwest obligation, taken care of by Scott so that there would be more money available for the living expenses of herself and the children.

Scott not only failed to maintain the automobile and mobile home payments but also failed to pay one-half of the attorney's fees as required by the decree and is $950.00 in arrears on his child support obligation.

Conclusions of Law

Julie takes the position that given the circumstances at the time of the divorce, the state court judgment of $3,727.42 resulting from the satisfaction of the automobile loan and the balance due in consequence of the mobile home deficiency are in the nature of alimony, maintenance and support, and thus nondischargeable under section 523(a)(5) of the Bankruptcy Code. Scott, pointing to the language of the Agreement itself says that the parties' intent was nothing more than a division of property. Section 523 excludes from discharge debts:

To a spouse, former spouse, or child of the debtor, for alimony to, maintenance for, or support of such spouse or child, in connection with a separation agreement, divorce decree or other order of a court of record, determination made in accordance with State or territorial law by a governmental unit, or property settlement agreement, but not to the extent that. . . .

11 U.S.C. §523(a)(5).

This court in previous decisions has held that the designation and labeling of the obligation in the agreement itself are not determinative of the nature of the award in a bankruptcy context. Of primary consideration is the intent of the parties or the divorce court in creating the obligation. That is, what function was the obligation or award intended to serve at the time? *In re Yeates*, 807 F.2d 874 (10th Cir.1986). This determination is made by looking not at the language of the agreement but at its substance in light of surrounding circumstances. Various courts have endeavored to list those circumstances which are indicative of whether a particular obligation is a property division or nondischargeable support. This court has also commented upon those factors relevant to such a determination. From a review of its own decisions and those of other courts, the following are appropriate consideration:

(1) The age, health, educational level, skills, earning capacity and other resources of the respective parties;

(2) Whether there were minor children involved;

(3) Whether the obligation balances disparate incomes of the parties;

(4) Whether there was a need for support at the time necessary to provide for the daily needs of the recipient and any children;

(5) Whether a support or maintenance obligation also exists;

(6) Whether any other support award would be inadequate absent the obligation in question;

(7) Whether one party relinquished a right to support under state law in exchange for the obligation;

(8) Whether the obligation terminated upon death or remarriage of the recipient;

(9) Whether the obligation extended over time or is in a lump sum;

(10) How the obligation is characterized under state law;

(11) Tax treatment of the obligation.

In *Yeates, supra*, the court said that a very important factor was the spouse's need for support at the time of the decree. In that case the court had before it a settlement whereby the parties waived any right to alimony but the debtor was to assume and pay a mortgage on a home awarded to the wife. The court concluded that the wife was in dire financial circumstances at the time and the payment by the debtor was necessary for her to retain one of her basic necessities, hence the obligation was regarded as nondischargeable. . . .

The agreement presently before the court is in itself not a model of clarity for, in paragraph four, the parties state the purported purpose of the agreement to be a settlement of all claims Julie may have against Scott for alimony, spousal support, maintenance and similar payments intended to provide fairly and adequately for her support. The parties then in a later paragraph agree that neither should receive alimony. Reading these two provisions together one may infer that any obligation agreed to was meant by the parties to stand in recognition of Julie's right to alimony and support. The only substantial property awarded to Julie was the 1984 Chevrolet, all other property, including the mobile home, was given to Scott who expressly agreed to assume all debts of the marriage including the balance due on the car. At the time this agreement was entered into Julie's monthly income was approximately one-half of that of Scott. Scott knew this was insufficient to take care of her necessities. But when her income was coupled with the anticipated $200.00 per month child support bringing her monthly net income to approximately $600.00 per month, he felt she would have sufficient financial resources to take care of her and the children's needs. Obviously Scott could not have reached such a conclusion if in calculating Julie's net income, she were to remain obligated for a $234.00 per month mobile home payment as well as car payments. Even with child support, her monthly net income would be effectively wiped out leaving her with no means at all with which to provide for herself and the two minor children. Indeed, as Julie testified, the income was insufficient as she has to resort to AFDC and food stamps. Clearly, the $200.00 per month child support would have been grossly inadequate if she had also remained obligated on the automobile and mobile home obligations. The court believes that Julie, in anticipation of Scott assuming all mutual debts, relinquished her rights to alimony and support and that both of the parties intended such assumption to be critical to her financial stability. The court believes that the unequal division of debts was intended by the parties at the time as a means of balancing the disparity in incomes and alleviating the impossible financial strain that would be created for the family if Julie had remained liable for those debts. Our own Circuit has noted with similar effect that undertakings by one's spouse to pay the other's debts can constitute support where, under the circumstances, it was necessary to help meet monthly living expenses.

Scott suggests that Julie's need for the support and her indicated income levels were artificial because she remarried shortly after the divorce. Nothing in the evidence convinces the court that Scott was misled into signing the agreement or that he felt Julie had nondisclosed financial resources. The parties were granted a divorce on the grounds of irreconcilable differences with neither the agreement nor the decree fixing blame. What subsequently occurred in Julie's life is irrelevant to the issue before the court, it being inappropriate to expand a dischargeability issue into an assessment of subsequent financial circumstances.

The court concludes from the facts and circumstances that Scott's assumption of the marital debts was essential to Julie's economic security and thus were in the nature of maintenance and support. Accordingly, the State Court Judgment in the sum of $3,727.42 and the $8,985.10 balance due in consequence of the deficiency on the mobile home loan are nondischargeable support obligations under section 523(a)(5) of the United States

Bankruptcy Code. Judgment may be entered in accordance herewith in favor of the plaintiff, Julie Streich, and against the defendant/Debtor, Scott Osterberg.

IN RE PATTERSON
United States Court of Appeals
132 F.3d 33 (6th Cir.1997)

Unpublished Disposition[1]

PER CURIAM.

This case involves a single bankruptcy issue: whether the bankruptcy court erred in finding nondischargeable a court-ordered debt owed by an ex-husband to an ex-wife. Finding that the bankruptcy court committed no reversible error, we affirm for the following reasons.

I. FACTUAL AND PROCEDURAL HISTORY

The appellant, Paul A. Patterson ("debtor" or "appellant"), is a debtor in Chapter 7 bankruptcy. Appellee Janie M. Patterson, the former wife of the debtor, filed a complaint for a determination of nondischargeability of the debtor's obligation to pay her $31,606.88, an obligation pursuant to a state court's order in the parties' divorce action. The sum represents $25,000 for one-half of the value of their marital business and $6,606.88 for one-half of the marital credit card debt. The bankruptcy court found the debt to be nondischargeable.

The district court affirmed the bankruptcy court. The debtor-appellant now appeals to this court, arguing that the bankruptcy court erred in its nondischargeability determination by miscalculating the debtor's excess income and also by erroneously performing the statutory balancing of relative detriments test.

II. DISCUSSION

The appellant appeals to this court arguing (1) that the bankruptcy court erred in its application of 11 U.S.C. §523(a)(15), the provision addressing the nondischargeability of debts incurred in the dissolution of a marriage; and (2) that the bankruptcy court clearly erred in the factual determinations underlying its decision.

Congress amended the Bankruptcy Code in 1994 to add a new section, 11 U.S.C. §523(a)(15), that provides that debts incurred in a divorce proceeding are now generally nondischargeable in bankruptcy. While §523(a)(15) provides that divorce property settlements are generally nondischargeable in bankruptcy, §523(a)(15) does include two exceptions.... Section 523(a)(15) was enacted to protect spouses who had agreed to reduced alimony in exchange for being held harmless on joint debts or for accepting a larger property settlement. Under the new 11 U.S.C. §523(a)(15), a debtor is not discharged from any marital debt that is not in the nature of alimony, maintenance or support unless (1) the debtor is unable to pay the debt, or (2) the benefit to the debtor of discharging the debt would outweigh the detriment to the debtor's former spouse. 11 U.S.C. §523(a)(15)....

---

[1] Available in 1997 WL 745501. Sixth Circuit Rule 24(c) states that citation of unpublished dispositions is disfavored except for establishing res judicata, estoppel, or the law of the case and requires service of copies of cited unpublished dispositions of the Sixth Circuit.

A. Ability to Pay Test

The bankruptcy court found that the debtor did not meet his burden of proving an inability to pay his debt to the appellee, one of the two exceptions to nondischargeability under §523(a)(15). The appellant argues that the bankruptcy court erred because his submitted schedules reflected that his expenditures and child support payments exceeded his income and because he presented evidence regarding a hand injury that restricts his working hours and earnings. The bankruptcy court found the evidence regarding the hand injury to be incomplete and unpersuasive. It also found that the itemized expenditures were for past expenses and that the debtor's expenses had decreased so that the debtor indeed had excess monthly income and thus had an ability to pay the court-ordered debt.

The appellant has presented no evidence of clear error. The bankruptcy court relied on documentation of a decrease in expenditures and conducted a detailed review to find that the debtor had excess monthly income. In addition, the bankruptcy court found the evidence and testimony regarding the debtor's hand injury and its effect on his income to be unpersuasive. We affirm the bankruptcy court as to this issue.

B. Balancing of Detriments Test

Section 523(a)(15)(B) contains a second possible exception to nondischargeability: a balancing test that allows discharge of a marital dissolution debt if discharging such debt would result in a benefit to the debtor that outweighs the detrimental consequence to a spouse, former spouse, or child of a debtor. §523(a)(15)(B). The bankruptcy court adopted the approach to the §523(a)(15)(B) balancing test outlined in *In re Smither*, 194 B.R. 102, 111 (Bankr. W.D. Ky.1996). There, the bankruptcy court applied the balancing test by reviewing the financial statuses of the debtor and the creditor and comparing their relative standards of living to determine the true benefit of the debtor's possible discharge against any hardship the former spouse and/or children would suffer as a result of a discharge.[2]

If, after making this analysis, the debtor's standards of living will be greater than or approximately equal to the creditor's if the debt is not discharged, then the debt should be nondischargeable under the 523(a)(15)(B) test. However, if the debtor's standard of living will fall materially below the creditor's standard of living if the debt is not discharged, then the debt should be discharged. In this case, the bankruptcy court compared the relative detriments of discharge to the two parties' standards of living and found that the appellee had demonstrated extreme detriment to her and the parties' child if the debt was discharged. The bankruptcy court additionally found that the debtor had dealt with his ex-spouse in bad faith, running up $45,000 in credit card charges (15 cards) since the divorce, failing to pay child support, buying and selling four cars and a timeshare and putting down $8000 on a boat immediately before filing for bankruptcy. In addition, this bankruptcy was the debtor's third bankruptcy and he was in arrears in his child support payments. Based on all of these factors, the bankruptcy court concluded that the balancing test favored the appellee.

---

[2] The *Smither* court listed 11 non-exclusive factors to be considered in a §523(a)(15)(B) balancing test. They are summarized as follows: (1) the amount of debt and payment terms; (2) all parties' and spouses' current incomes; (3) all parties' and spouses' current expenses; (4) all parties' and spouses' current assets; (5) all parties' and spouses' current liabilities; (6) parties' and spouses' health, job training, education, age, and job skills; (7) dependents and their ages and special needs; (8) changes in financial conditions since divorce; (9) amount of debt to be discharged; (10) if objecting creditor is eligible for relief under the Code; and (11) whether parties have acted in good faith in filing bankruptcy and in litigation of §523(a)(15). *In re Smither*, 194 B.R. at 11.

We have reviewed the record and can find no indication that the bankruptcy court either applied the statute incorrectly or committed clear error in its factual findings. Accordingly, the appellant's argument regarding this issue fails as well.

III. CONCLUSION

For the foregoing reasons, we AFFIRM the bankruptcy court.

NOTES AND QUESTIONS

(1) **Background.** As you know, bankruptcy is a matter of federal law, 11 U.S.C. §§ 101-1330 (1998), and divorce law is usually a matter of state law. The subject of this section is really the conflict between these two areas of the law which arises because they both attempt to resolve some of the same problems:

> Both divorce and bankruptcy law attempt to balance an individual's interest in a fresh financial start with the obligation to honor family commitments. Modern divorce law does this by allowing easy exit from marriage, but requiring divorcing spouses to support their children and to apportion equitably between themselves the economic gains and losses attributable to their marriage. Federal bankruptcy law currently strikes this balance by allowing debtors to discharge divorce-related financial obligations unless a court determines that particular obligation is "in the nature of alimony, maintenance or support" [or otherwise dischargeable.]

Jana B. Singer, *Divorce Obligations and Bankruptcy Discharge: Rethinking the Support/Property Distinction*, 30 Harv. J. on Legis. 43, 45 (1993).

More specifically, the two areas come into conflict over the subject of dischargeability. Federal bankruptcy law allows financial obligation to be discharged, which means that the creditor is prohibited from collecting the debt from the debtor. *See* Margaret Howard, *A Bankruptcy Primer for the Family Lawyer*, 31 Fam. L.Q. 377, 390 (1997). Some of these debts are ones imposed by family law courts or agreed to in the settlement. Traditionally, the bankruptcy statute said that only the support obligation was nondischargeable, 11 U.S.C. § 523(a)(5), and all other debts and obligations imposed by the family court were dischargeable. In 1994, the law was modified to allow other debts related to marital dissolution to be nondischargeable in certain circumstances. Nevertheless, there is still an opportunity to discharge marital debts due to the nature of the law as it now stands.

(2) **Automatic Stay.** Although the main focus of this subchapter is dischargeability of debts related to marital dissolution, family law-related cases may be affected before the issue of dischargeability is ever reached because there is an automatic stay placed upon all actions to collect a debt when the debtor files for bankruptcy. This stay is applicable even to a creditor who has not been given notice of the bankruptcy. *See* 11 U.S.C. § 562(a) (1998). However, many actions related to family law are treated as exceptions to the automatic stay. Under Section 362(b)(2)(A), the filing does not operate as a stay in action for "(i) the establishment of paternity" or "(ii) the establishment or modification of an order for alimony, maintenance, or support" and under Section 362(b)(2)(A) for "the collection of alimony, maintenance, or support from property that is not property of the estate."

(3) **Statutory Discharge.** Here is the full text of the statutes on discharge referred to in the cases above:

> (a) A discharge under section 727, 1141, 1228(a), 1228(b), or 1328(b) of this title does not discharge an individual debtor from any debt—

. . .

(5) to a spouse, former spouse, or child of the debtor, for alimony to, maintenance for, or support of such spouse or child, in connection with a separation agreement, divorce decree or other order of a court of record, determination made in accordance with State or territorial law by a governmental unit, or property settlement agreement, but not to the extent that—

(A) such debt is assigned to another entity, voluntarily, by operation of law, or otherwise (other than debts assigned pursuant to section 408(a)(3) of the Social Security Act, or any such debt which has been assigned to the Federal Government or to a State or any political subdivision of such State); or

> (B) such debt includes a liability designated as alimony, maintenance, or support, unless such liability is actually in the nature of alimony, maintenance, or support;

. . .

(15) not of the kind described in paragraph (5) that is incurred by the debtor in the course of a divorce or separation or in connection with a separation agreement, divorce decree or other order of a court of record, a determination made in accordance with State or territorial law by a governmental unit unless—

(A) the debtor does not have the ability to pay such debt from income or property of the debtor not reasonably necessary to be expended for the maintenance or support of the debtor or a dependent of the debtor and, if the debtor is engaged in a business, for the payment of expenditures necessary for the continuation, preservation, and operation of such business; or

(B) discharging such debt would result in a benefit to the debtor that outweighs the detrimental consequences to a spouse, former spouse, or child of the debtor. . . .

11 U.S.C. §523 (1998).

(4) **Mutual Exclusion.** These provisions are mutually exclusive. Before a debt may be considered under § 523(a)(15), it must be found to be "not of the kind described in paragraph [§ 523(a)](5)." This means that a threshold determination may have to be that the debt is not support, and then a second determination may be made that the debt is nondischargeable. A creditor may first have to argue that the debt is support and then to argue that it is not.

(5) **Support.** Traditionally, the only protection provided to a former spouse in bankruptcy was 11 U.S.C. § 523(a)(5), which basically states that spousal and child support are nondischargeable in bankruptcy. This provision was codified in 1903; however it originally stemmed from three United States Supreme Court cases: *Audubon v. Schufeldt*, 181 U.S. 575 (1901); *Dunbar v. Dunbar*, 190 U.S. 340 (1903); and *Wetmore v. Markoe*, 196 U.S. 168 (1904).

The issue which, of course, arises most commonly is whether debts (periodic or lump sum payments which are already overdue—arrearages—or due in the future) qualify as support, or whether they are debts owed for other reasons such as property distribution, which may be dischargeable. Despite the apparent certainty of the court in the principal case, *In re Osterberg*, the test for whether debts are support is not well formulated.

The way a debt was characterized (as support or property settlement) in an agreement or court order, is always relevant to the issue of dischargeability, *Long v. West* (*In re Long*), 794 F.2d 928, 931 (4th Cir. 1986), and in many cases this characterization is determinative, especially where the language is clear and unambiguous. *See Clark v. Clark* (*In re Clark*), 113 B.R. 797, 801 (Bankr. S.D. Ga. 1990), *rev'd in part*, 925 F.2d 1476 (11th Cir. 1991). However, some debts which were not designated as support have held to be support and thus non-dischargeable as in *Osterberg, above.*

Courts have also chosen to follow the intent of the parties in an agreement or the court in an order if that intent is clear and unambiguous as to whether obligation is support or some other debt. *See, e.g., Yeates v. Yeates* (*In re Yeates*), 807 F.2d 874 (10th Cir. 1986); *Smith v. Smith* (*In re Smith*), 131 B.R. 959 (Bankr. E.D. Mich. 1991).

However, courts have also been willing to look at the actual function of the payments. Do the payments in fact function as support? Courts have been willing to infer this function from all the surrounding circumstances. The ten-part test provided in *Osterberg* is an attempt to fully articulate this function approach. The criteria for determining if a debt is support in *Osterberg*, have been applied by other courts. *See, e.g., In re Tatge*, 212 B.R. 604 (Bankr. 8th Cir. 1997); *Kubik v. Kubik*, 215 B.R. 595 (Bankr. D.N.D. 1997).

(6) **Other Debts, Pre-1994.** 11 U.S.C. § 523(a)(15) was added to the Bankruptcy Code in 1994 in response to a number of commentators who had been critical of the code for not going further to protect former spouses. *See* Jana B. Singer, *Divorce Obligations and Bankruptcy Discharge: Rethinking the Support/Property Distinction*, 30 Harv. J. on Legis. 43 (1993). Prior to this legislation, only marital debts which could be characterized as support were nondischargeable; all other debts could be discharged. There were two very common situations where debts were discharged: first, future payments on property settlements or divisions and, second, agreements to pay off marital debt. Often agreements were negotiated in which there would be a quid pro quo for the future payments or for the acceptance of marital debt. Perhaps the most egregious situation was where the husband would negotiate a waiver of spousal support or a lower amount of spousal support in return for either (1) a large property settlement, with a portion of the settlement to be paid in the future, or (2) a settlement agreement in which the husband assumed the wife's share of the marital debt. After the judgment became final, the husband would declare bankruptcy, and the debt to the wife would be discharged, or the husband's obligation to pay the marital debts would be discharged and the creditor would attempt to collect from the wife. The wife, who, because she was to receive support, was probably the low income partner, would now be stuck with less support and all of the marital debt. Usually this meant bankruptcy for the wife too.

Moreover, the old law negated the use of the "hold harmless clause." Where one spouse agreed to assume the marital debt in return for some benefit, one might think that the other spouse could be protected from creditors by a hold harmless clause in the marriage settlement agreement. In other words, the spouse who assumed the debt would promise to reimburse the other spouse for payments to creditors attempting to collect on the marital debt. This approach would not work because the hold harmless clause itself was a debt which, because it was not spousal support, was dischargeable in bankruptcy.

(7) Other debts, Post-1994. In 1994, the bankruptcy statute was amended to add Section 523(a)(15) which appears not to be retroactive, applying to all bankruptcies filed after October 22, 1994. *See Bodily v. Morris (In re Morris)*, 193 B.R. 949 (Bankr. S.D. Cal. 1996). While it cannot now be said that all other debts related to marital settlements are nondischargeable, it can at least be said "that all marital debts are presumed to be nondischargeable." Bernice B. Donald & Jennie D. Latta, *The Dischargeability of Property Settlement and Hold Harmless Agreements in Bankruptcy: an Overview of § 523(a)(15)*, 31 Fam. L.Q. 409 (1997).

This change took place for several reasons. First was the bare-faced injustice which occurred when courts allowed one former spouse to completely revise the marital settlement agreement in a way which caused a great detriment to the other former spouse. Second, it was widely recognized that there was an important change in the family law system with which the bankruptcy scheme was out of sync. At one time in most states support or alimony was the primary method of protecting low or non-income earning spouses; however, with the shift to marital property regimes in most states, a change which allowed both spouses to share in the marital property, the property division became the primary method of protecting low or non-income generating spouses. Under former law, marital property debts were fully dischargeable, but it was argued that the bankruptcy law should reflect the change in the family law. *See* Jana B. Singer, *Divorce Obligations and Bankruptcy Discharge: Rethinking the Support/Property Distinction*, 30 Harv. J. on Legis. 43 (1993). Finally, the whole problem was exacerbated by the rise in both divorce and bankruptcy; far more people were being affected by the law. *See* Allen H. Parkman, *The Dischargeability of Post-Divorce Financial Obligations Between Spouse: Insights from Bankruptcy in Business Situations*, 31 Fam. L.Q. 493, 495 (1997).

There are three basic elements required to show that the debt is nondischargeable under § 523(a)(15). First, the proponent of nondischargeability must establish that the obligation arises out of a divorce-related separation agreement or order but that it is not support. If this first requirement is met, the debt will be nondischargeable unless it is shown, secondly, that the debtor does not have the ability to pay and, thirdly, that the "benefit to the debtor . . . outweighs the detrimental consequences" to the creditor, the former spouse or child. The latter two requirements are usually characterized as affirmative defenses. This characterization and the wording of the statute would seem to indicate that the debtor would have the burden of proving the last two elements, that the debtor has the inability to pay and that the benefit to the debtor outweighs the detriment to the creditor; however, there is currently much confusion among various district courts as to who has the burden as to each element of the case for nondischargeability, even as to the affirmative defenses. Bernice B. Donald & Jennie D. Latta, *The Dischargeability of Property Settlement and Hold Harmless Agreements in Bankruptcy: an Overview of §523(a)(15)*, 31 Fam. L.Q. 409, 420–21 (1997).

The last two elements also add greater uncertainty as to just when a debt will be discharged. The ability to pay test includes consideration of both assets and income from which monthly installment payments can be made. *See id.* at 422. However, the courts are split as to whether the income of the debtor's new spouse may be considered. *See id.* at

424. The benefit/detriment test is a multiple factor balancing test not unlike the test used to determine spousal support in many jurisdictions.

(8) **Partial Discharge.** Some courts in response to the balancing test applied under 11 U.S.C. § 523(a)(15) have responded by allowing a partial discharge of the debt. *See, e.g., In re Greenwalt*, 200 B.R. 909, 914 (Bankr. W.D. Wash. 1996); *In re Comisky*, 183 B.R. 883, 884 (Bankr. N.D. Cal. 1995). However, this view has been rejected in other cases which have held that since there is no mention of the possibility of partial discharge in the code, the courts have no power to implement this remedy. *See In re Haines*, 210 B.R. 586, 592 (Bankr. S.D. Cal. 1997); *In re Florez*, 191 B.R. 112, 115 (Bankr. N.D. Ill. 1995).

(9) **Hold Harmless Clause.** The addition of Section 523(a)(15) to the Bankruptcy Code has strengthened the hold harmless clause in marital settlement agreements. Now there is a chance that this debt will not be discharged in bankruptcy. This is important because it is very common for the parties to divide marital debts along with marital property. An effective hold harmless clause is one of the few ways in which this division of debts can be made to stick. A typical clause might read "Husband (or Wife) shall assume the following community debts and shall hold Wife (or Husband) indemnified and harmless therefrom." Unfortunately, because of the affirmative defenses in the bankruptcy law, there is still the possibility that this promise will be discharged. If there is no hold harmless or indemnity clause, the party in bankruptcy has an obligation only to third parties and not to the former spouse, and so the debt is dischargeable as to that party. *In re LaRue*, 204 B.R. 531(Bankr. E.D. Tenn. 1997). But the former spouse may still be liable.

(10) **Future Legislation.** The future of 11 U.S.C. § 523(a)(15) as it is presently written is uncertain. Some critics want to abolish this provision entirely, some on the grounds that it cause a relitigation of divorce issues:

> The problem with that section is that it requires bankruptcy courts to revisit, in excruciating detail, the anger, the bitterness, and the pain which the Debtor and the Debtor's former spouse have felt and now feel. In the instant case, one could almost see the old wounds being reopened and new and more expensive scars being inflicted upon both Parties.

Silvers v. Silvers (In re Silvers), 187 B.R. 648 (Bankr. W.D. Mo. 1995). Other critics take the position that Congress should make the marital debts absolutely nondischargeable because the marital debt is not essentially different from other debt. *See* Brian P. Rothenberg, Comment, *The Dischargeability of Marital Obligations: Three Justifications for the Repeal of § 523(A)(15)*, 13 Bankr. Dev. J. 135 (1996). Others merely bemoan the extensive procedural difficulties that this law has created and the fact that the ability to pay and the greater benefit defenses are fact intensive which makes it difficult to predict the outcome of a particular case, thus encouraging litigation. Michael M. White, *The Procedural Plight of the Property Settlement Creditor*, 31 Fam. L.Q. 463 (1997). But for many, the argument for absolute dischargeability which existed before the 1994 amendment are still valid. *See* Allen M. Parkman, *The Dischargeability of Post-Divorce Financial Obligations Between Spouse: Insights from Bankruptcy in Business Situations*, 31 Fam. L.Q. 493 (1997).

(11) **Effect of Bankruptcy on Future Support.** One interesting twist is that bankruptcy and the subsequent release from debt and debt payments may constitute sufficient change circumstances to justify a change in support either for the child or for the former spouse. *See Dickson v. Dickson*, 474 S.E.2d 165, 171 (Va. Ct. App. 1996). Perhaps a more effective

approach to spousal protection would be to include a provision in the marriage settlement agreement to make the discharge of marital debts the basis for the initiation of a spousal support award or for an increase in spousal support. For example, the husband could assume the marital debts and promise to pay the wife support in an amount which compensates her for any losses due to his default on the marital debt.

Problem. After a seven-year and sometimes troubled marriage, the parties were divorced in December 1995 on the grounds of irreconcilable differences.

At the time of the divorce, Dee was 40 and Klay was 37. Dee had a four-year nursing degree and had worked as a registered nurse from 1987 to 1994. In 1994, difficulties with alcoholism and the falsification of patient records caused her to lose her nursing license. After extended inpatient treatment, she recovered from her alcoholism and remained sober. Her recovery allowed her to start a home-based day care business. At the time of the divorce she was earning $8,000 per year from the day care operation.

Klay grew up on his family farm and has considerable farm-related job experience. He graduated with an associate's degree in business management from North Dakota State School of Science and has both training and experience as an insurance salesman. In 1993, he started bartending part-time, which lead to a general manager position at a restaurant. During the marriage, most of his time and finances, as noted by the state court, were devoted towards saving the Kubik family farm in Dunn County and a bar owned by his father in Manning, North Dakota. Both of these businesses eventually failed despite considerable cash infusions and debt forgiveness.

In 1994, the parties purchased a home, now occupied by Dee, for $80,000, with the bulk of the funds coming from proceeds of a sale of land Dee had received as a gift from her parents. The home was acquired debt-free and remained so until Klay's farming difficulties came to a head in 1994, when as part of an FmHA loan buy down, Klay needed collateral to secure a loan from the Security Bank of Hebron. In August of that year the bank made a $76,000 loan to the parties, secured by a mortgage on the formerly debt-free family home.

Following an extended trial, the state district court made detailed findings and conclusions of law whereby Dee was awarded custody of the three minor children born of the marriage, as well as a minor child born of a prior marriage, the court believing it important that they retain continuity in their home, school and community environment. In awarding child support of $450 per month, the state court discussed at some length the couple's financial difficulties and Klay's struggles to preserve several business ventures. The court concluded in its opinion that Klay, being possessed of vocational talents, had the ability to provide substantial support for himself and the children. Although the decree specifically states that neither party will be obligated to provide any form of spousal support, it does purport to make a distribution of the real and personal property of the parties. In making its determination to award Dee sole title to the home and, in turn, make Klay responsible for the mortgage, several factors were significant to the state court, to wit: "It seems important to try to preserve for Dee and the children the marital home they have established in Dickinson. Both parties recognize that they have a substantial home for the children to live in only because of the substantial gift made to them by Dee's parents of approximately $55,000." Klay was ordered to obtain a satisfaction of the mortgage by January 15, 1996, **and failing to do so, his remaining assets would be liquidated with the proceeds applied** to reduce the mortgage. Any unsatisfied balance remained Klay's obligation as a part of the property division and he was to hold Dee harmless therefrom.

Since the divorce, Dee has remained in the family home with the four minor children. She presently runs the home-based day care facility, earning approximately $1,800 per month gross on average. Her net income is about $1600 per month. In addition to day care income, she has received child support income of $5400 per year. Thus, for 1997 her net cash income from these two sources was about $24,600. Monthly living expenses for herself and the children total $2,000 per month or $24,000 per year.

Klay presently works part-time as a corrections officer earning $8.50 per hour. He hopes this will develop into a full-time position but is unsure of that prospect. In addition to his corrections officer job, he receives minimal income from his Amway business and insurance residuals. From January to October 1997 his total net income was $4,573—an amount he acknowledges he cannot live on. He is presently residing with his parents to reduce living expenses which he estimates at $1,800 per month inclusive of the child support obligation and health insurance which he is not presently paying. Klay acknowledges that he is in good health, able-bodied and capable of physical work. In the past he has held a variety of jobs, as before noted, but enumerates a litany of reasons why he has been so remarkably unsuccessful. He does not want to live too far from his children and wants to be around on weekends for visitation. He does not want to pursue the insurance business because it is too time-consuming, in his opinion. He professes to have faith in the Amway business and feels it could generate around $40,000 per year if he could stock products properly.

As circumstances developed in early 1997, the mortgage was not satisfied by the court-established deadline, prompting a liquidation of Klay's remaining assets. After applying the proceeds to the debt, there remained an unsatisfied balance of $29,122.16 owing to the mortgagee, Security Bank of Hebron. Faced with foreclosure, Dee paid the balance through a loan from her parents (to whom she remains indebted) and then sought and obtained from the state court a supplemental money judgment against Klay in the sum of $29,561.76. In late 1997, Klay filed for bankruptcy. The sum of $29,561.76 remains unsatisfied and is the claim upon which Dee rests the instant proceeding. Is the debt dischargeable?[3]

---

[3] Most of these facts are actually quoted in a significantly rearranged fashion from *Kubik v. Kubik*, 215 B.R. 595 (Bankr. D. N.D. 1997), which answers the question posed but does not discuss all the possible issues raised.

TABLE OF CASES

[Principal cases appear in capital letters; References are to pages.]

A

Abdullah, In re	1154
A.C. v. C.B.	215; 1132
Accent Serv. Co. v. Ebsen	603
Adam v. Adam	1124
Adam, In re Paternity of	388
Adams v. Adams	813
Addis v. Addis	927
Adoption/Guardianship No. 3598, In re	662
Adoption No. 92A41, In re	757
Adoption of (see name of party)	
Agati v. Agati	1182
A.H. v. W.P.	1182
Ainscow v. Alexander	30
Ainsworth, In re Marriage of	1035
Akileh v. Elchahal	1287
Akron v. Akron Ctr. for Reproductive Health	255
Albemarle Paper Co. v. Moody	158
Aldrich v. Aldrich	96; 784
Alexander v. Alexander	355
Alison D. v. Virginia M.	215; 1162
Alleged Contempt of (see name of party)	
Allen v. Allen	927
ALLEN v. FARROW	1148; 1162
Allison v. Superior Court of Los Angeles Cty.	1197; 1204
Allocco v. Allocco	911
Alma Soc'y, Inc. v. Mellon	751
Alston v. Alston	934
Altman v. Altman	799
Amanda M., In re	539
Amato v. Amato	903; 904
American Export Lines, Inc. v. Alvez	150
Americana Healthcare Center v. Randall	138
Anderson v. Anderson	819; 915
Anderson v. Hensrud	1182
Andrew R., Matter of	602
Angel Lace M., In re	717
Angela M.W., State ex rel. v. Kruzicki	551
Ankenbrandt v. Richards	456
Anonymous v. Anonymous	57; 63
Anonymous, Ex parte	595
Anonymous, In Matter of	1056
Anonymous, In Petition of	594
Ansay, In re Marriage of	1040
Anthony v. Anthony	884
Appeal of (see name of party)	
Appeal of Estate of (see name of party)	
Application of (see name of applicant)	
A.R.B., In re	1171
Archer v. Archer	906
Archer v. Roadrunner Trucking Inc.	151
Argersinger v. Hamlin	1069
Aristotle P. v. Johnson	626
Arkansas Dep't of Human Servs. v. Couch	626
Arnelle v. Fisher	45
Arnes v. Commissioner [Arnes II]	1304
ARNES v. UNITED STATES [ARNES I]	1298; 1304
Artibee v. Cheboygan Circuit Judge	370
Askew v. Askew	1238
Assalone, In re	751
Aster v. Gross	819; 948
Astonn H., In re Guardianship of	226
ATA v. City and Cty. of San Francisco	230
Atassi v. Atassi	786
Atherton v. Atherton	4; 781; 797
ATKINS v. ATKINS	1214
Atlanta, City of v. McKinney	231
Atlanta, City of v. Morgan	231
Attorney General v. Desilets	225
Aud, In re Marriage of	940
Audubon v. Schufeldt	1312
AVITZUR v. AVITZUR	1284; 1286
Ayers v. Ayers	1192
Aziz v. Aziz	1286

B

B. v. B.	57
BABY BOY C., IN RE	678; 689; 692; 693; 741
Baby Boy R., In re	662; 663
BABY DOE, IN RE	309
BABY E.A.W., IN RE ADOPTION OF	669; 693
BABY M, IN THE MATTER OF	285
Baby Girl C., In re Adoption of	661
Baby Girl D., In re	710; 711
Baby S., In re Adoption of	752
Bachman v. Bachman	806
BAEHR v. LEWIN	46; 223; 231
Baehr et al. v. Miike, No. 91-1394	53
Bailey v. Bailey	1052
BAKER v. BAKER	436; 950; 1256
Baker v. Nelson	55; 56
Baker, In re Marriage of	1056
Bales v. Hack	802
Balistrieri v. Maliska	1220
Bandow v. Bandow	904
Baneck v. Baneck	1102
Bang v. Park	786
Banton v. Mathers	1086
Barbarine v. Barbarine	1000
Barber v. Barber	773
BARIL v. BARIL	1048
Barlow; State v.	1069; 1076
Barone v. Barone	915
Barr v. Barr	900
Barriger v. Barriger	939
Barrons v. United States	26
Barstad v. Barstad	1191

TABLE OF CASES

Basiouny v. Basiouny 793
Batcheldor v. Boyd 355
Batey v. Batey 23
Battersby v. Battersby 1044
Battleman v. Rubin 1247
Beagle v. Beagle 1161
Beal v. Doe 254
Beasley v. Beasley 926
Becton v. Sanders 1154
Belcher v. Terry 1071
Belle Terre, Village of v. Boraas 222
Bellotti v. Baird 254; 588
Belsito v. Clark 303
Belt v. Belt 896
Benevento, In re Marriage of 1141
BENKER, IN RE ESTATE OF 1243
Bensen, In re 972
Bergeron v. Bergeron 806
Berman v. Allan 282
Berry v. Davis 281
B.G.C., In re 417; 694
Bieluch v. Bieluch 941
Bills v. Dahm 1162
Bilowit v. Dolitsky 80
Bishop v. Bishop 83; 86
Blackman v. Blackman 939
Blackwelder v. Safnauer 506
Blair v. Blair 793
Blake v. Blake 1190
Bland v. Larsen 1069
Blankenship v. Blankenship 25
Blatt v. Commissioner 1304
Blaw-Knox Construction Co. v. Morris 17
Blazel v. Bradley 436; 442
Blew v. Verta 1132
Blotske v. Leidholm 1182
Blum v. Blum 829
Blumenfeld v. Borenstein 159
B.L.V.B. AND E.L.V.B., ADOPTIONS OF . . 713; 717
Boaden v. Department of Law Enforcement 159
Board of Regents v. Roth 610
Boddie v. Connecticut 779
Boerne, City of v. Flores 505
Bold v. Bold 989
Bone v. Allen 224
Bonte v. Bonte 482
Bonura v. Bonura 809
Booth v. Booth 938
BORELLI v. BRUSSEAU 139
Borys v. Borys 1182
Boseman, In re Marriage of 822; 941
Bosserman v. Bosserman 930
Botner v. Botner 1056
BOTTOMS v. BOTTOMS 1125; 1131; 1133
Bowen, Matter of 841
Bowerman v. MacDonald 370
Bowers v. Hardwick 243
Boyd v. Boyd 1147; 1171
Boyer v. Boyer 801
Boyt v. Romanow 1045

Boyton v. Boyton 786
Brabec, In re Marriage of 819; 948
Brack v. Brack 19
BRADWELL v. ILLINOIS 107
Brady v. Brady 799; 806
Brannon v. OshKosh B'Gosh, Inc. 179
Braschi 232
BRASCHI v. STAHL ASSOCIATES COMPANY . . 218
Bray v. Alexandria Women's Health Clinic 269
B.R.F., In re 1197
BRIDGET R., IN RE 730; 740; 741
Brinkley v. Brinkley 877
Briton v. Briton 1068
BROADBENT v. BROADBENT 473
Brook v. Brook 1171
Brod, Sherman M., In re Adoption: . . . 710
Brooks v. Brooks 1182
Brooks v. Parkerson 1161
Brooks, In re 926
Brossoit v. Brossoit 1198
Brown v. Board of Education 490
Brown v. Brown 31; 134; 904; 1182
BROWN v. THOMAS 1234
Bruce v. Bruce 813
Bruneau v. Bruneau 794
Brunell v. Wahl 481
Bruner v. Hager 1152
Bruno v. Codd 426
Brunswick v. LaPrise 134
Bryan; State v. 443
Brzonkal v. Virginia Polytechnic 448
Buck v. Bell 271; 280
Buckley v. Buckley 80
Bukovic v. Smith 1141
Bunch v. Bunch 1152
Burch v. Burch 1040
Burchard v. Garay 1147; 1175
Burger King v. Rudzewicz 1082
Burgess, In re Marriage of 1190; 1191; 1192
Burr v. Board of County Commissioners 764
Burroughs, Estate of, In the Matter of the 17
Burroughs, In re Marriage of 1061
Burt, In re Marriage of 904
Burton v. Burton 799
BUSH v. STATE 630
Butcher v. Robertshaw Controls Co. . . 151
Butler v. Butler 1184
Byers v. Mount Vernon Mills, Inc. 17
Byrd v. Byrd 806
Bywater v. Bywater 904

C

Cabalquinto, In re Marriage of 1132
Caban v. Mohammed 398; 650
Caldwell v. Caldwell 31; 795
Calhoun v. Eagan 481
Califano v. Webster 120
California v. Copus 137
CALIFORNIA FEDERAL SAVINGS & LOAN ASSOCIATION v. GUERRA 161

Callaghan, Marriage of, Matter of	1024
Callahan v. Callahan	828
Campbell v. Campbell	1153
Campbell v. Moore	83
Campbell, In re Marriage of	781
Campion v. Campion	894
Cannon v. Miller	149
Caraballo v. Hernandez	1171
Carbonell v. Carbonell	1052
Carey v. Population Services International	239; 240; 596
Carl S., In re	1161
CARNEY, IN RE MARRIAGE OF	745; 1134
Carpenter v. Bishop	473
Carpenter v. United States	1298
Carr v. Carr	781
Carrico v. Blevins	1286
Carrington v. Townes	370
Carter v. Carter	885
Cassano v. Cassano	1045
Cassiday v. Cassiday	891
Catalano v. Catalano	68
Catalano, In re Marriage of	1061
Cates v. Cates	473
Catherine D. v. Dennis B.	1182
C.C. v. A.B.	389; 667
C.C.R.S., In re Custody of	668
CERNIGLIA v. CERNIGLIA	1271
Chambers v. Omaha Girls Club, Inc.	171
Charles B., In re Adoption of	746; 1132
Charrier v. Charrier	915
Chatman v. Ribicoff	17
CHENAULT v. CHENAULT	886
Cherry v. Cherry	934
Chertok v. Chertok	1283
Cheryl E., In re	662
Chihak, In re Marriage of	948
CHILDERS v. CHILDERS	1053
Children's and Parent's Rights Ass'n of Ohio, Inc. v. Sullivan	1009
Chipp v. Murray	131
Chivers v. Couch Motor Lines	19
Church v. Church	898
Cihak, In re Marriage of	819; 941
City v. (see name of defendant)	
City and County of (see name of city and county)	
CLARK v. ALEXANDER	847
Clark v. Clark	802; 917
CLARK v. JETER	343
Clark, In re	1313
Claunch v. Claunch	931
Cleverly v. Cleverly	948
Coe v. Coe	809
Colabianchi v. Colabianchi	821
Colby v. Colby	785
Cole v. Cole	773
Cole, In re Marriage of	1154
Comer, In re Marriage of	1069
Comisky, In re	1315
Commission v. (see name of opposing party)	
Commissioner v. (see name of opposing party)	
Commissioner of Internal Revenue (see name of defendant)	
Commissioner of Soc. Servs. of City of New York v. Nieves	1039
COMMITTEE ON PROFESSIONAL ETHICS AND CONDUCT OF THE IOWA STATE BAR v. HILL	841
Commonwealth v. (see name of defendant)	
Commonwealth ex rel. (see name of relator)	
Compos v. McKeithen	728
Compton v. Davis Oil Co.	37
Conduct of Jayne, In re	838
Conkel v. Conkel	1132
CONNELL v. FRANCISCO	207; 232
Connolly v. Connolly	898
CONNOR v. SOUTHWEST FLORIDA REGIONAL MEDICAL CENTER	127
Conservatorship of (see name of party)	
Constant A. v. Paul C.A.	1132
Cook v. Cook	1268; 1271; 1274
Cooper v. Cooper	773
Cooper, In re Estate of	224
Cooper, State by, v. French	225
Cooperman, In re	844
Coulbourn v. Lambert	1247
COULSON v. COULSON	829
County v. (see name of defendant)	
County Dep't of Soc. Servs. v. Williams	370
County of (see name of county)	
Courtney v. Compaleo	482
Covington v. Covington	903
Cox v. Florida Dep't of Health & Rehabilitative Servs.	746
Cranston v. Cranston	1171
Craven, In re Marriage of	948
Creeks v. Creeks	1268; 1275
Crocker v. Crocker	906
Croft v. Croft	1268
CROSSON v. CROSSON	15
Crouch v. Crouch	877
Crowe v. DeGioia	200; 214
Cruise v. Cruise	901
Cullman, In re Marriage of	893
Culmo; State v.	443
Cupp, In re	906
Curtis v. Kline	1056
Curtis v. School Comm. of Falmouth	240
Custody of (see name of party)	
Cutlip v. Cutlip	808
Cutts v. Fowler	158

D

D. v. D.	77
Dabill v. Dabill	1182
Daigle v. Daigle	1101
Dalessio v. Dalessio	904
Dalip Singh Bir's Estate, In re	23; 62
Dalton v. Clanton	1014
Damico, In re Marriage of	1069
Dandy v. Dandy	17

D'Arc v. D'Arc	819
Darnall v. Darnall	1171
Daugherty v. Daugherty	941
Daughery v. Ritter	1160
David "M" v. Lisa "M"	1161
Davis v. Davis (Conn. 1934)	88
Davis v. Davis (La. Ct. App. 1980)	1102
Davis v. Davis (Miss. 1984)	210
DAVIS v. DAVIS (Tenn. 1992)	317
DAVIS v. DAVIS (Tenn. 1983)	457
Davis v. Davis (Tex. 1975)	37
Davis v. Davis (La. Ct. App. 1980)	806
DAVIS v. DEPARTMENT OF EMPLOYMENT SECURITY	216
Davis v. Grover	490
Davis v. Kostin	1171
Davis; United States v.	1301; 1302
Day v. Day	806
De Castro v. De Castro	948
De Santo v. Barnsley	56
Dean v. Dean	894
Dean v. District of Columbia	56
DeBoer v. Schmidt	664
DeCicco v. Barker	1239
Del Vecchio v. Del Vecchio	1247
DeLa Rosa v. DeLa Rosa	914; 989
DELOZIER v. DELOZIER	977
DeMasi v. DeMasi	926
DeMedio v. DeMedio	12
Denton v. Denton	911
DESHANEY v. WINNEBAGO COUNTY DEP'T OF SOCIAL SERVICES	553
Deukmejian, People ex rel. v. Brown	835
Devaux v. Devaux	369
Devine, Ex Parte	1102
DeVita v. DeVita	1159
DEWEES v. STEVENSON	723; 727
D.F.D., In re	1171
D.H. v. H.	1132
Dibble v. Dibble	38
Dick, In re Marriage of	781
Dickson v. Dickson	1315
Dinon v. Board of Zoning Appeals	223
Diogo; United States v.	86
DiSandro, In re the Matter of	841; 843
Ditter, In re	1154
Dixon v. Smith	1239
Dockins v. Dockins	1125
Doe v. Bolton	253
DOE v. CLARK	650; 653
Doe v. Commissioner of Corrections	43
Doe v. Doe	1132
Doe v. Holt	481
Doe v. Kelly	296
Doe v. Roe	1141
DOE v. SUNDQUIST	747
Doe, In re	664; 667
Dominque; People v.	282
Donovan v. Workers' Compensation Appeals Bd.	224
Dooley v. Dooley	809
Dorbin v. Dorbin	883
Dordell v. Dordell	1154
Dothard v. Rawlinson	158
Doucet v. Fontenot	882
Douglas v. Douglas	940
Dowdy v. Dowdy	1153
Downs v. Downs	914
Downs v. Wortman	663
Drahos v. Rens	883
Drawdy v. Drawdy	1233; 1263
Drummond v. Drummond	1171
Drummond v. Fulton County Dep't of Family & Children's Servs.	728
DUGAN v. DUGAN	919; 926
Dugue v. Dugue	911
Duley v. Duley	73
Dunaway v. Dunaway	998
Dunbar v. Dunbar	1312
Duncan v. Duncan	927; 1252
Duncan v. Harden	663
Dunn v. Dunn	781; 821
Durnell v. Durnell	823
Duspiva v. Duspiva	911
D.W. v. D.W.	626

E

E, In re Adoption of	745
Earl v. Earl	939
Eastis v. Bredehoft	1056
Eaton v. Johnson	877
Ebbert v. Ebbert	821
Edmund v. Edwards	76
Edwards v. Edwards	841
EEOC v. Rath Packing Co.	159
E.G., IN RE	582
Egle v. Egle	1163
Eisenstadt v. Baird	239
EKLUND v. EKLUND	1016
Elkind v. Byck	1086
Ellam v. Ellam	813
Elliot v. Willis	151
Ellis v. United States	1297
Eltzroth v. Eltzroth	829; 1270
Employment Div'n, Dep't of Human Resources of Oregon v. Smith	504
Endy v. Endy	823
English, State ex rel. v. Troisi	1040
Enlow v. Fire Protection Sys., Inc.	18
Epp v. State	1069; 1076
Epperson v. Epperson	144
Erica, In re	1162
Eriksen, In re Estate of	201
Erlandson v. Erlandson	941
Esenwein v. Commonwealth	785
Est. of (see name of party)	
Estate of (see name of party)	
ESTEVEZ v. SUPERIOR COURT	1040
Estin v. Estin	798
ETHERIDGE v. SHADDOCK	67

Evans v. Asphalt Roads & Materials, Inc.	796
Evenson v. Evenson	1182
Everett v. Everett	30; 795; 802; 809
Ex parte (see name of applicant)	
Ex rel. (see name of relator)	
Eyler v. Eyler	929

F

F., In re Adoption of	661
Fain, In re Marriage of	1024
Fanning v. Fanning	1159; 1239
Farah v. Farah	17
Farrah v. Farrah	95
Farrell, In re Marriage of	914
Farris v. Farris	950
Feathler v. Feathler	898
FEDER v. EVANS-FEDER	1221
Fehlhaber v. Fehlhaber	799
Feldman v. Feldman	1124
Ferrin v. New York Dep't of Correctional Servs.	43
Fields, In re Marriage of	904
Finnerty, Matter of	847
Fischer v. Fischer	882
Fischer, In re Estate of	14
Fisher v. St. Paul, City of	270
Fishman v. Fishman	37
Fiske v. Fiske	773
Fitzsimmons v. Fitzsimmons	1146
Flanagan v. Flanagan	1035; 1039
Fleek v. Fleek	781
Florez, In re	1315
The Florida Bar v. Patarini	847
Fonger v. Fonger	806
Forbes v. Forbes	1024
Forbis v. Forbis	74
Ford v. Whelan	781
Forsythe v. Forsythe	893
Fortin v. Fortin	1190
FOSBERG v. COMMISSIONER OF INTERNAL REVENUE	1291
Fossum v. Fossum	1190
Fowler v. Jones	215
Fowler, In re Ex parte	663
Fox v. Fox	1182
FRANCIS, IN RE MARRIAGE OF	823; 983; 1162
Frausto v. Frausto	906
Frederick, In re Marriage of	939
Fricke v. Fricke	1251
Friederwitzer v. Friederwitzer	1182
Friedlander v. Friedlander	1247
Friedman v. Friedman	214
Fulwiler v. Fulwiler	1159
Funk v. Ossman	1116
Funk v. United States	151

G

G.A. v. D.A.	1131
Gabel v. Lores	1056
Gallego, In re	1162
Gan v. Gan	903
Garrison v. Garrison	773
Garska v. McCoy	1107
Gaughan v. Gilliam	662; 663
Gaulkin, In re	161
Gause v. Gause	838
G.D.L., In re	757
GEITNER v. GEITNER	74
General Electric Co. v. Gilbert	169
George v. Associated Stationers	179
George v. King	797
Gerard v. Costin	1239
Gerdel v. Gerdel	781
Gerleman, In re Marriage of	1270
Gerlich v. Gerlich	905
Ghali v. Ghali	893
Gibson v. Gibson	806
Giedinghagen v. Giedinghagen	902
Giha v. Giha	902
Gilbert v. Gilbert	1141
GILMAN v. GILMAN	991
Gilmore; United States v.	1297
Girl C., In re	662
Glasgow Educ. Assoc. v. Board of Trustees	159
Glass v. Glass	101
Glassboro v. Vallorosi	223
Glona v. American Guarantee & Liability Insurance Company	343; 400
Glover v. Glover	38
GOLDBERGER v. GOLDBERGER	1030
GOLDER v. GOLDER	1264
Goldfarb v. Goldfarb	1220
Goldstein v. Goldstein	1112
Goldstein v. Lees	837
Golub v. Golub	913
Gomez v. Perez	371
Gottlieb v. Gottlieb	806
GRADY, IN RE	273
GRAHAM v. GRAHAM	108; 1061
Graham, In re Marriage of	906
Grant v. Grant	1124
Grant v. Superior Court	18
Grant v. Zich	884
Graves; State v.	73
Green, In re	581; 582
GREENLAW v. SMITH	1205
Greenwald v. H & P St. Assocs.	224
Greenwalt, In re	1315
Greenwood, In re Estate of	355
Griffith v. Griffith	1182
Griggs v. Duke Power Co.	158
Grimmeisen v. Grimmeisen	806
GRISWOLD v. CONNECTICUT	; 426
Groat v. Glenville, Town of	151
Gross v. Lamb	840
GROSSKOPF v. GROSSKOPF	814
Grotelueschen v. Grotelueschen	819
GROVES v. CLARK	752
Gruber v. Gruber	1189

TABLE OF CASES

Guardianship of (see name of party)
Gudenkauf, In re Marriage of 1251
Guidubaldi v. Guidubladi 939
Guinan v. Guinan 1132
Gullo v. Brown 797
Gussin v. Gussin 934

H

Haas v. Haas 773
Habelow v. Traveler's Insurance Co. 151
Hack v. Hack 1152
Hackett v. Hackett 1286
Haddock v. Haddock 783
Hadeen, In re Marriage of 1116
Hadinger; State v. 224
Hager v. Hager 62
Haight v. Haight 133
Haines, In re 1315
Hakas v. Bergenthal 1153
Haldemann v. Haldemann 892
Haley v. Boles 160
Hall v. Hall 890
Hall v. Tawney 521
Halpern v. Halpern 891
Halvey v. Halvey 1194
Halvorson v. Halvorson 939
Hammac v. Hammac 1101
Hammett v. Woods 1024
Hammond v. North Am. Asbestos Corp. 151
Hammonds v. Hammonds 805
HAMPSHIRE; UNITED STATES v. 1071
Hand v. Berry 88
Hangsleben v. Oliver 1197
HANHART v. HANHART 1120
Hanify v. Hanify 903; 905
Hanson v. Hanson 926; 1124
Hanson, In re Marriage of 948
Hardiman, In re Marriage of 1035
Hardin v. Davis 25
Hardy v. Hardy 904
Harker v. Harker 1274
HARPER v. HARPER 878
Harris; Commissioner v. 1304
Harris v. Harris 31; 917
Harris v. McRae 254
Hart, In re Marriage of 1153
Hartman v. Hartman 774
HARVEY v. ROBINSON 1028
Hashimoto v. Hashimoto 934
Hassick v. Hassick 1275
HASTY v. HASTY 1036
Hathaway v. Worcester City Hosp. 282
Hatzopoulos, In re 226
Hawkins v. United States 151
Haynes v. Lapeer 281
Haywood v. Haywood 914
H.B. v. Wilkinson 594
Head v. Head 940
Hecht v. Superior Court 317

Heilman v. Heilman 822; 903; 941; 947
Helm v. Helm 906
HENDERSON v. SMITH 1025
Hendrickson, In re 281
Hernandez v. Hernandez 906
Herr v. Herr 1247
Herr, Marriage of 891
Hertzler v. Hertzler 1159
Hesington v. Hesington, Estate of 18
Hess, In re Adoption of 757
HEWITT v. FIRESTONE TIRE & RUBBER CO. 32
Hewitt v. Hewitt 213
Hicklin v. Hicklin 19; 22
Hickman v. Hickman 808
HICKS v. FEIOCK 1063
Hight v. Hight 134
Hill v. Hill 1182
Hilton v. Guyot 786
Hilton v. Roylance 1283
Hinman v. Department of Personnel Admin. 225
Hisquierdo v. Hisquierdo 896
H.J.B. v. P.W. 1182
H.L. v. Matheson 254; 595
Hoak v. Hoak 906; 989
Hockett, In re 832
Hodge v. Hodge 906
Hodgson v. Minnesota 254; 596
Hoffman v. Hoffman 877; 883; 884
Hogue v. Hogue 133
Holbert v. West 69
Holbrook v. Holbrook 926
Holcomb v. Kincaid 80
Holder v. Holder 885
Hollis v. Hollis 806
Holston v. Holston 931
Holtzman v. Knott 215
Homan v. Homan 74
Hooker v. Hooker 813
Horn, In re Marriage of 1032
House v. House 1190
HOYE v. HOYE 146
H.P.A. v. S.C.A. 1056
H.S.H.-K., In re Custody of 1133
Hubbard v. Hubbard 914
Hubner., Marriage of, In re 1044
Hudson v. Aetna Life Ins. Co. 1053
Hudson v. Hudson 800
Hughes v. Walker 357
Hull v. Hull 894
Humphreys v. Baird 80
Hunter v. Hunter 809; 1052
Hursey v. Hursey 874
Husband v. Pierce 73
Hussey v. Hussey 893
Husting v. Husting 821
Hutchinson v. Hutchinson 133
Hyde v. Hyde 794; 1036

I

Igo v. Igo	938
Ilhardt v. Sara Lee Corp.	180
In re (see name of party)	
International Union, UAW v. Johnson Controls, Inc.	170
IRELAND v. SMITH	1142
Isabella County Dep't of Soc. Servs v. Thompson	357
Ishmael v. Millington	827
Israel v. Allen	43
Ivancovich v. Ivancovich	822; 941

J

Jackson v. Benson	489
Jackson v. Brown	1239
Jackson v. Jackson	883; 1035; 1247
Jackson; People v.	160
Jackson v. Rapps	1010
Jackson v. State	764
Jacob, In re	717
Jacobs v. Jacobs	769
J.A.L. v. E.P.H.	215
James, In re	1162
Jameson v. Jameson	1056
Jamison v. Jamison	809
Jane B., In re	1159
Jane Doe, In re	594
Jane W. v. John W.	1141
Janni v. Janni	801
Jarrett v. Jarrett	1124
Jason C., In re	746
J.E.B. v. Alabama	120
Jeffrey v. O'Donnell	505
Jeffry v. Pounds	835
Jennifer A., In re	745
Jennings v. Hurt	19
Jensen v. Jensen	828; 882; 885
Jersey Shore Med. Ctr.-Fitkin Hospital v. Baum, Estate of	112; 121; 131
JESSICA G. v. HECTOR M.	365
Jessica N., In re Adoption of	746
J.H.G., In re	709
JHORDAN C. v. MARY K.	310
Jiminez v. Weinberger	400
J.J.B., In re Adoption of	667
J.L.P. v. D.J.P.	1159
J.M., In re	370
Johl v. United States	87
Johns v. Johns	1159
JOHNSON v. CALVERT	297
Johnson v. Johnson	12; 781; 891; 916; 1024
Johnson v. Muelberger	796
Johnson v. Schlotman	1132
Johnson, In re Marriage of	894; 895
Johnston v. Johnston	101
Jolis v. Jolis	891
Jones v. Chandler	371
Jones v. Hallahan	56
Jones v. Jones	133; 160; 911; 1119; 1141
Jones, In re Marriage of	806
Jordan v. Jordan	885
J.P., IN THE INTEREST OF	508
J.S. v. F.V. (In re R.D.S.)	757
Jurek v. Jurek	904

K

Kamholtz v. Kovary	1182
Kaplan, In re Marriage of	939
Karelas v. Commissioner	1297
Karen B. v. Clyde M.	1153
Karp v. Karp	876
Kaslinski v. Questel	939
Kass v. Kass	327
Kateley v. Kateley	1182
Katterhagen v. Meister	882
Kay v. Vaughan	1069
Kaye v. Kaye	929
Kelderhaus v. Kelderhaus	18
Kelley v. Kelley	781
KELLY v. CROSFIELD CATALYSTS	174
Kelly v. Kelly	1159
Kelm, In re Marriage of	1024
KELSEY S., IN RE ADOPTION OF	402
Keltner v. Keltner	1068
Kendall v. Kendall	799
Kennedy v. Nelson	145
Kenneth L.W. v. Tamyra S.W.	1124
Kerkvliet v. Kerkvliet	1190
Kessler v. Fauquier National Bank	785
Kilbourne, In re	902
Kilbride v. Kilbride	898
Kinast, In the Matter of	839
King v. King	1184
King v. Smith	224
Kingsley v. State	711
Kleinfield v. Veruki	87
Klemm v. Superior Court	828
Kline v. Kline	893
K.M. and D.M., In re petition of	717
Knight v. Knight	1162
Knock v. Knock	1152
Knoll v. Knoll	1247
Kober v. Kober	78
Koizim v. Koizim	1268
Kothari v. Kothari	940
Kottke v. Kottke	890
Kowalski, In re Guardianship of	226
Kozich v. Kozich	904
Kozlowski v. Kozlowski	200
Kramer v. Kramer	897
Krank v. Krank	1152
Kranz v. Kranz	1061
Krause v. Krause	911
Kubik v. Kubik	1313; 1317
Kudler v. Smith	1160
Kugler v. Haitian Tours Inc.	793
Kujawinski v. Kujawinski	1052

TABLE OF CASES

KULKO v. SUPERIOR COURT	801; 1077
Kuvin v. Kuvin	916
Kwiatkowski; Commonwealth v.	443

L

L. Pamela P., Matter of v. Frank S.	374
Lacey P., In re	239
Lach v. Welch	355; 356
Lackey v. Lackey	780
Ladue, City of v. Horn	223
LaForge v. LaForge	1035
Lagars v. Lagars	823
Lalli v. Lalli	332; 343
Lambert v. Lambert	891
Landay v. Landay	883
Landrum v. Gomez	25
Landsberger v. Landsberger	1147
Lane v. Science	1191
Lannamann v. Lannamann	88
Larroeque, In re Marriage of	972
Larson v. Larson	77; 1125
Larson v. Scholl	371
Larson, In re Marriage of	938
LaRue, In re	1315
Latham v. Latham	200
Laura A.K. v. Timony M.	1171
Lawrence v. Lawrence	93
Lawson v. Brown	603
Layton v. Layton	785
LeClair v. LeClair	1057
Lee, In re Estate of	37
Lee, In re Marriage of	1024
Legg; State v.	532
LeGrand, In re	1182
Lehr v. Robertson	169; 302; 390; 650; 694
LEMLEY v. BARR	664; 667; 668; 693
Leonard, In re Estate of	37
Leonard, In re Marriage of	1220
Lester; Commissioner v.	1294
Leszinske v. Poole	68; 1124
Levesque v. Levesque	1228
Levine v. Levine	828; 1268; 1269
Levinson v. Washington Horse Racing Comm'n	44
Levy v. Louisiana	400
Lewin, In re Marriage of	1141
Licciardi v. Collins	839
License of (see name of party)	
Liebich, In re Marriage of	1153
Liff v. Schildkrout	151
Linsay v. Linsay	939
Lipham v. State	796
Little v. Streater	370
L.J.T., In re	1182
L.M.S. v. S.L.S.	316
Lochner v. New York	266
Loeb v. Loeb	799; 800
Long, In re	1313
Lord v. Lord	931
Lord's Estate, In re	1247
Lorenz v. Lorenz	1190
Loving v. Virginia	73
Lowe, In re Estate of	1239
Lowery v. Lowery	906; 914
Lucas, In re Marriage of	918
Ludwig v. Burchill	1182
Luna v. Luna	897
Lundeen v. Struminger	1286
Luther v. Vogel	1171
Lutwak; United States v.	83; 86

M

M., In re Matter of	354
MacPHERSON v. MacPHERSON	96
Madsen v. Women's Health Center, Inc.	270
Mahaffey, In re Marriage of	902
Maher v. Roe	254
Mahoney v. Commonwealth	443
Mahoney v. Mahoney	906; 989
Mallet v. Mallet	913
Malmquist v. Malmquist	883
Maloblocki v. Maloblocki	1147
Manasseri v. Manasseri	786
Manley v. Hoag	1204
Mansell v. Mansell	897
Maples, In re	751
Marchman v. Marchman	1060
Marion v. Marion	934
Mark L. v. Jennifer S.	1197
Markham v. Colonial Mortgage Serv. Co.	225
Markham v. Markham	822; 947
Marquette v. Marquette	442
Marriage of (see name of party)	
Marsh v. Marsh	904
Martins, In re Marriage of	1182
MARVIN v. MARVIN	191; 196; 202; 232
Mary P., Matter of	596
Mathews v. Eldridge	610; 611
Matson v. Matson	1247
Matter of (see name of party)	
MATTER OF CUSTODY OF ROSS	1199
MATZA v. MATZA	844
Maui Land & Pineapple Co. v. Naiapaakai Heirs	648
MAXFIELD v. MAXFIELD	1093; 1108
May v. Anderson	1082; 1194; 1219
May v. Leneair	76
MAYER v. MAYER	787
MAYNARD v. HILL	3; 1283
May's Estate, In re	68
Mazaenic v. North Judson-San Pierre Sch. Corp	505
McAlprin v. McAlprin	933
McCarty v. McCarty	896
McClellan v. McClellan	1269
McConkey v. McConkey	101
McCORD, IN RE THE MARRIAGE OF	1057
McCoy, In re Marriage of	1171
McDonough v. Murphy	1182
McFarland v. McFarland	781
McGee v. International Life Ins. Co.	1082

Case	Page
McGhee v. McGhee	80; 144
McGill; State v.	443
Mcginnis v. McGinnis	1133
McGowan v. McGowan	914
McGuffin v. Overton	226
MCGUIRE v. MCGUIRE	124
McIver v. McIver	877
MCKINNEY v. STATE	758; 764
McMillan, Matter of	504
McMinn v. Oyster Bay, Town of	223
McNabney v. McNabney	934
Meacham; State v.	370
Mead v. Batchlor	1069
Meason v. Meason	890
Meehan v. Hopps	837
Menge v. Menge	809
Mercier v. Mercier	1102
Meredith v. Meredith	1228
Meredith v. Shakespeare	88
Merrick v. Merrick	808
Messerle, In re Marriage of	928
Metropolitan Life Ins. Co. v. Holding	18
MEYER v. NEBRASKA	486
M.H. v. Caritas Family Servs.	764
MICHAEL B., IN THE MATTER OF	612
Michael H. v. Gerald D.	242; 379; 741
MICHAEL H., IN RE ADOPTION OF	410
Michael M. v. Superior Court	170
Michele T., In re Adoption of	745
Michels v. Weingartner	1061
Michigan v. DeJonge	506
Mickle v. Heinrichs	281
Miller v. Johnson	282
Miller v. Mangus	1154
Miller v. Miller	134; 378; 809; 865
Miller v. Ratner	1239
Miller v. Schou	1044
Mills; Commissioner v.	1305
Minkin v. Minkin	1287
Mintz & Mintz, Inc. v. Color	226
Mirras v. Mirras	1182
Miskimens; State v.	569
Mission Ins. Co. v. Industrial Comm'n	18
Mississippi University for Women v. Hogan	120
Mistler v. Mistler	902; 904
Mitchell v. Davis	473
Mitchell v. Mitchell	927
Mize v. Mize	1190
M.J.B., IN RE PATERNITY OF	348
M.M.D. & B.H.M., In re	717
MOE v. DINKINS	70
Mohorn v. Ross	473
Molien v. Kaiser Foundation Hospitals	151
Moll, In re	915
Molloy v. Molloy	808
Mong; Commonwealth v.	137
Monihan v. Monihan	800
Moore v. East Cleveland, City of	223; 611
Moore v. Gillis	1247; 1256
Moore v. Moore	883; 900; 937; 1060; 1086; 1162
Morgan v. Morgan	1204
Morone v. Morone	201
Morphet v. Morphet	799
Morrell v. Giesick	1220
Morris v. Geer	833
Morris v. MacNab	80
Morris, In re	1314
Morrissey v. Brewer	610
Morrow v. Morrow	1101
Morse, In re Marriage of	892
Morton v. Mancari	741
Mosbarger v. Mosbarger	819; 822; 941; 948
Moscheo v. Moscheo	1056
Moschetta, In re Marriage of	296; 315
Mosley v. Mosley	901
Moss, Estate of	1247
Moye v. Moye	1141
M.P. v. S.P.	1132
M.T. v. J.T.	57
Mulkey-Yelverton v. Blevins	1182
Mullane v. Central Hanover Bank & Trust Co.	610; 797
Muller v. BP Exploration, Inc.	159
Munger v. Munger	96
Murphy v. Arkansas	506
MURPHY v. MEYERS	371
Murphy v. Murphy	797; 903; 1274
Music v. Rachford	1162
M.V.R v. T.M.R.	802

N

Case	Page
Nabors v. Nabors	1182
Nadler v. Superior Court	1132
Nancy S. v. Michele G.	214; 1162
Nash County Dep't of Soc. Servs. ex. rel. Williams v. Beamon	357
Nassau County Dep't of Social Servs. v. Laquetta H.	550
National Org. for Women v. Operation Rescue	269
Naylor v. Kindred	1182
Neal v. Neal	149
Nearhoof, In re	757
Needham v. Needham	69
Nehorayoff v. Nehorayoff	930
Nelms v. Nelms	781
NELSON v. MARSHALL	10
Nelson v. Nelson	1204
Nemeth v. Nemeth	809
New Jersey Welfare Rights Org. v. Cahill	224
New York v. Heckler	597
Newman v. Newman	876; 1247
NEWMARK v. WILLIAMS/DCPS	569
Nicholson v. Hugh Chatham Mem. Hospital	150
Nicole G., In re	539
Nisos v. Nisos	898
Noble v. Fisher	1056
Noble v. Noble	905
Nodgren v. Mitchell	370
Nolan v. Nolan	891

TABLE OF CASES

Case	Page
Nolte v. Nolte	1061
Nolte, In re	1182
Nordby, In re Marriage of	1141
North v. North	1159
North Carolina Ass'n for Retarded Children v. North Carolina	280
North Ottawa Community Hospital v. Kieft	121
Northampton Brewery Corp. v. Lande	145
Null v. Board of Educ.	505
N.M.W., IN THE INTEREST OF	534
Nyberg v. Virginia, City of	254; 282

O

Case	Page
Oberhansly v. Oberhansly	822
O'Brien v. O'Brien	145; 819; 907; 948
O'Connell, In re Marriage of	1052
Odell v. Lutz	1160
Ohio v. Akron Ctr. for Reproductive Heath	254
Ohio ex rel. Popovici v. Agler	773
Olah v. Olah	911
Olar, In re Marriage of	914
Old Colony Trust v. Porter	796
Olinger, In re	885
O'Loughlin v. O'Loughlin	819; 823; 941; 948
Orr v. Orr	120; 954
Ortiz v. Ortiz	1068
ORZECHOWSKI v. PERALES	741
OSBORNE v. OSBORNE	1248
Osier v. Osier	1116
OSTERBERG, IN RE	1305; 1313
OTIS, IN RE MARRIAGE OF	956

P

Case	Page
Pact v. Pact	1182
Pahlke, In re Marriage of	939
Palmore v. Sidoti	728; 1117
Paradis, In re Marriage of	1190
Pardieck v. Pardieck	1247
PARHAM v. HUGHES	339
Parker v. Parker	17
Parker v. Stage	134
PARKS v. WARNER ROBBINS, City of	153
Partyka, In re Marriage of	939
Pastore v. Pastore	915
PATER v. PATER	1112
Patricia B. v. Steven B.	934
PATTERSON, IN RE	1309
Patterson v. Blanton	1239
Patzer; State v.	506
Paul v. Paul	818
PAULIN, IN RE THE MARRIAGE OF	1026
People v. (see name of defendant)	
People ex (see name of defendant)	
People ex rel. (see name of defendant)	
Periquet-Febres v. Febres	1171
Perlberger v. Perlberger	819; 941
Perlstein v. Perlstein	96
Perrin v. Perrin	794
Perry v. Dowling	375
Perry v. Perry	1269
Petachenko v. Petachenko	813
Peterson v. Jason	1160
Petition, Adoption to Release Records Pursuant to, In re	751
Petition of (see name of party)	
PETRIE, IN RE	702
Petrini v. Petrini	903
Pettit, In re Marriage of	1024
Pfaff, In re	1171
Phillips v. Wisconsin Personnel Comm'n	225
Picarella v. Picarella	12; 73
Pickering v. Pickering	389; 469
PIERCE v. SOCIETY OF SISTERS	487
PIETROS v. PIETROS	375
PIKULA v. PIKULA	1103
Pilcher; State v.	842
Pima County Juvenile Action, In re Appeal of	746
Pimm v. Pimm	1000
Pitts v. Pitts	813
Plank v. Hartung	226
Planned Parenthood Association v. Ashcroft	254; 255
Planned Parenthood Fed'n of Am. v. Heckler	239; 597
Planned Parenthood of Missouri v. Danforth	253; 374
Planned Parenthood of Southeastern Pennsylvania v. Casey	242; 253; 256; 374
Platt v. Platt	819
Plemel v. Walter	353
Plessey v. Ferguson	266
PLUMMER, IN RE MARRIAGE OF	1054
Poelker v. Doe	254; 282
Poindexter v. Willis	801
Pointer; People v.	282
Pomraning v. Pomraning	1197
Ponath v. Ponath	1228
Ponder v. Graham	4
P.O.P.S. v. GARDNER	1004
Posey v. Tate	1024
Posner v. Posner	1251
Postema v. Postema	911
POTTER v. MURRAY CITY	58
Pouliot v. Kennedy	371
Powell v. Powell	435
Prahinski v. Prahinski	918
Preece v. Preece	939
Price v. Price	890; 892
PRICKET v. CIRCUIT SCIENCE, INC.	181
PRINCE v. COMMONWEALTH OF MASSACHUSETTS	491
Prudential Ins. Co. v. Lewis	30
Pullman v. Pullman	890
PUSEY v. PUSEY	1099
Putnam v. Putnam	930
Pyeatte v. Pyeatte	914

Q

Case	Page
Queen v. Queen	905
Quesnel v. Quesnel	950

Quilloin v. Walcott 302; 398
Quiner v. Quiner 1116
Quinn v. Quinn 890
Quirling v. Quirling 1275

R

R. J. D. v. VAUGHAN CLINIC, P.C. 597
Rabourn v. Rabourn 31; 795
Raccio v. Raccio 903
Ragouzis v. Ragouzis 801
Rahn v. Rahn 916
Ramirez, In re Marriage of 1061
Ramos, In re Marriage of 1069; 1076
Rand v. Rand 131
RANDALL v. RANDALL 93
Ransom v. Ransom 839
Rawlings v. Rawling 1032
Raybin v. Raybin 773
Ready v. Ready 1182
REBOUCHE v. ANDERSON 20
RECKNOR, IN RE MARRIAGE OF 26
RECODO v. STATE 636
Rector v. Rector 1154
Rediker v. Rediker 29
Redmann v. Redmann 101
Reed v. Flournoy 370
Reed v. Hagroder 1157
R.E.G. v. L.M.G. 947
Regan v. Taxation with Representation 780
Reid v. Reid 915
Reiling v. Reiling 1255
Reitz, State ex rel. v. Ringer 1182
Renshaw v. Heckler 14; 18
Repetti v. Repetti 1159
Respole v. Respole 25
Rexrode v. Rexrode 819; 931; 947
Reyna v. Reyna 1024
Reynaud v. Reynaud 1124
Reynolds v. Kimmons 370
Reynolds v. Reynolds 77; 1233; 1264
Reynolds v. Stockton 1194
Reynolds v. United States 61
Rezac v. Rezac 885
RHODES; STATE v. 424
RICE v. STATE 523
Rich v. Rich 904
Richardson, Adoption of 745
Richmond, In re 1171
Rickard v. Trousdale 17
Rickards v. Rickards 77
Riddle v. Riddle 904
RIDER v. RIDER 1252
Rinderknecht, In re Marriage of 780
Risinger v. Risinger 133
Rivera v. Minnich 369
R.M.G., In re Petition of 728
Roatch v. Puera 201
Robert F. Dippio, In the Matter of 841
Roberts, In re Marriage of 1162

Robertson v. Robertson 821; 934; 947; 1102
Robinson v. Robinson 819; 823
Rodgers v. Davenport 833
Rodgers v. Rodgers 874; 890
ROE v. IMMIGRATION & NATURALIZATION SERVICE
.... 83
Roe v. Wade 241; 243; 252
Rogers v. Rogers 1035
Rogers, In re Estate of 355; 356
Rogers, In re Marriage of 917
ROLFE v. ROLFE, IN RE 899
Roller v. Roller 473
Romanski's Estate 31
Romeo v. Romeo 144
ROOSEVELT v. COMMISSIONER OF INTERNAL REVENUE
.... 1289
Rose v. District Court of Eighth Judicial District .. 370
Rose v. Rose 1024; 1071
Rosenberg v. Rosenberg 891; 939
Rosenbluth v. Rosenbluth 797
Rosenfeld, In re Marriage of 1153
Rosenstiel v. Rosenstiel 794
Ross v. Denver Dep't of Health and Hosps. 224
Ross v. Moore 370
Ross v. Ross 801
Ross v. Stouffer Hotel 159
Ross, In re Marriage of 389
ROSS, MATTER OF CUSTODY OF 1199
Roussos v. Roussos 808
Rovira v. AT&T 224
Rowsey v. Rowsey 1132
R.S. v. R.S. 316
Rubenstein; United States v. 83; 86
Ruiz v. Ruiz 73
Russell v. Russell 927
Russenberger v. Russenberger 1190
Rust v. Sullivan 254
Ryan v. Ryan 4; 1182
Rykhoek, In re Marriage of 1159

S

Salenius v. Salenius 874
SAMPSON, IN RE 577; 581
San Antonio Indep. School District v. Rodriguez .. 490
Sanders v. Shephard 442
Sanders, In re 356
Sanderson v. Sanderson 79
Santa Clara County v. Hughes 133
Santmier v. Santmier 1124
Santosky v. Kramer 370
Sara K v. Timmy S. 663
Saunders v. Clark County Zoning Department 223
Sawada v. Endo 121
Saylor v. Board of Education for Harlan County ... 521
Schenck v. Pro-Choice Network of W.N.Y. 270
Scherer v. Scherer 795
Schibi v. Schibi 83; 86
Schinker v. Schinker 78
Schleiffer v. Meyers 1112

TABLE OF CASES

Schlumpf v. Superior Court of Cty. of Trinity ... 1204
Schmidt v. Schmidt ... 883
Schorr v. Schorr ... 1273
Schuenman v. Schuenman ... 898
Schuham, In re Marriage of ... 1220
SCHUMM v. SCHUMM ... 1139
Schwab v. Schwab ... 1159
Schwebel v. Unger ... 92
Sclamberg v. Sclamberg ... 68
Scott v. Family Ministries ... 745
Scott, In re Marriage of ... 876
S.D.J., In Interest of ... 1171
SEATON v. SEATON ... 449
Seemar v. Seemar ... 802
Seessel v. Seessel ... 1190
Sefton v. Sefton ... 101
S.E.G. v. R.A.G. ... 1159
Seidle v. Provident Mutual Life Insurance Company ... 180
Seizer v. Sessions ... 4; 89; 92
Shaffer v. Heitner ... 779; 780; 1082; 1220
Sharon Clinic v. Nelson ... 131
Sharp v. Sharp ... 939
Sharp, In re ... 1061
Sharpe Furniture Inc.. v. Buckstaff ... 131
Shepherd v. Shepherd ... 134
Sherbert v. Verner ... 61
Sherer v. Sherer ... 795
Sherlock v. Stillwater Clinic ... 282
Sherrer v. Sherrer ... 784
Shippy, In re Estate of ... 63
Shirley D. v. Carl D. ... 371
Shockley v. Prier ... 150
Shofner, In re ... 1161
Shuraleff v. Donnelly ... 214
Siecht v. Siecht ... 78
Sielski v. Sielski ... 435
Sigg v. Sigg ... 1182
Sigler, In re Marriage of ... 1024
Silver v. Shebetka ... 1069
Silvers, In re ... 1315
Silvestri v. Silvestri ... 1101
Simeone v. Simeone ... 1256
Simmons v. Simmons ... 948
Simmons, In re Marriage of ... 894; 1182
Simms v. Simms ... 773
Simons v. Miami Beach First National Bank ... 800
Singer v. Hara ... 54
SINHA v. SINHA ... 810
Skinner v. Oklahoma ... 272; 281; 295
Skipper v. Skipper ... 1024
Skipworth v. Skipworth ... 19
Slack v. Slack ... 1124
Slayton v. State ... 56
Smith v. Commissioner ... 1297
Smith v. Fair Employment and Housing Commission ... 225
Smith v. Lewis ... 832; 833
Smith v. Organization of Foster Families [O.F.F.E.R.] ... 398; 605; 741
Smith v. Smith (6th Cir. 1954) ... 1068
Smith v. Smith (N.Y.A.D. 1990) ... 920; 1182
Smith v. Smith (N.Y.A.D. 1948) ... 78
Smith v. Smith (Ohio Ct. App. 1980) ... 1162
Smith v. Smith (Ohio Ct. App. 1943) ... 796
Smith v. Smith (Okla. Ct. App. 1993) ... 822; 941
Smith v. Smith (Tenn. Ct. App. 1985) ... 926
Smith v. Superior Ct. of San Mateo Cty. ... 1197
Smith, In re ... 596; 884; 1313
Smith, In re Marriage of ... 939
Smoot v. Smoot ... 819; 884; 948
S.N.E. v. R.L.B. ... 1132
Snyder v. Snyder ... 1159
Soden, In re Marriage of ... 1025
Solomon v. District of Columbia ... 224
Sommers, In re Marriage of ... 948
Soos v. Superior Court ... 304
Sorenson; People v. ... 316
Sorenson, In re ... 1161
Sosna v. Iowa ... 4; 774
Spaeth v. Warren ... 389
Spalding v. Davis ... 832
Sparks v. Sparks ... 819; 931; 943; 951
Spellens v. Spellens ... 28; 794
Spiegel, In re Marriage of ... 1248
Spindel v. Spindel ... 773
Spinnell v. Quigley ... 1239
SQUIRES v. SQUIRES ... 1163
St. Mary's Hospital Med. Ctr. v. Brody ... 131
Stacy v. Stacy ... 1124
STAKELUM v. TERRAL ... 81
Stallworth, In re Marriage of ... 939
Stambaugh v. Stambaugh ... 799; 800
Stanard v. Bolin ... 1234
Stanford v. Stanford ... 1053
Stanley v. Illinois ... 397; 668
STANTON v. STANTON ... 120; 1045; 1051; 1286
State v. (see name of defendant)
State by Cooper v. French ... 225
State ex (see name of state)
State ex rel. (see name of state)
State of (see name of state)
States v. Hampshire ... 780
States v. Marashi ... 153
Statter v. Statter ... 96
Steckler v. Steckler ... 436
Steffes, In re Estate of ... 213
Steffke, In re Estate of ... 30
Stephen, In re Adoption of ... 710
STERBLING v. STERBLING ... 1155; 1157
Stevens v. Stevens ... 906
Stewart v. Stewart ... 1141
Stewart, In re Marriage of ... 940
Stice, In re Marriage of ... 933
STILES, IN RE ESTATE OF ... 65
Stokes v. Stokes ... 1204
Stone, In re ... 927
Storlien v. Storlien ... 1154
Stover v. Stover ... 948; 1056
Straub v. Todd ... 374

Stroman v. Williams	1132
Stroop v. Stroop	890
Sturgis v. Sturgis	885
Sudwischer v. Hoffpauer, Estate of	355
Suppressed v. Suppressed	841; 843
Surrogate Parenting v. Commissioner ex rel. Armstrong	295
Suster v. Arkansas Dep't of Human Servs.	758
Suter v. Artis M.	628
Sutton v. Leib	101; 785
Swanner v. Anchorage Equal Rights Comm'n	225
Swartz v. Schwartz	1286
Swenson v. Commissioner	1297
Syijuberget, In re Marriage of	931
Syrkowski v. Appleyard	295
Szamocki v. Szamocki	1160

T

T. v. M.	77
Tacchi v. Tacchi	78
Tagalicud; United States v.	87
Talent v. Talent	939
Tammy, Adoption of	717
TANDRA S. v. TYRONE W.	358
Tarr v. Tarr	898
Tarro v. Tarro	819; 931; 947
Tasker v. Tasker	1147
Tatge, In re	1313
Tatum v. Tatum	38
Taylor v. Taylor	904
Tennessee Dep't of Human Servs. v. Hooper	357
Thames v. Thames	819; 823; 941
THOMAS v. LAROSA	202; 206
Thomas v. Metroflight, Inc.	158
Thomas v. Thomas	813
Thomasson v. Johnson	1032
Thompson v. Thompson	801; 839; 1195
Thornton, In re Marriage of	781
Thurman v. Torrington, City of	426
Tinsley v. Tinsley	781
Titchenal v. Dexter	214
Tjaden, In re Marriage of	941
T.M.B., In re	1152
T.M.C. v. S.A.C.	1171; 1182
T.M.M., Adoption of, In the Matter of	662
Tobon v. Sanchez	80
Tomblin v. Hill	837
Tomlinson v. Tomlinson	1112
Tompkins v. Tompkins	77
TORRES v. TORRES	23
Tourville v. Kowarsch	201
Towery v. Towery	134
Trammel v. United States	151; 152
Treutle v. Treutle	1182
TRIMBLE v. GORDON	334; 400
TROPEA v. TROPEA	1184
Troy D, In re	550
Truitt v. Truitt	1124
Truitt, In re	1159

Trust Estate of (see name of party)	
Tubbs v. Tubbs	893
Tuck v. Tuck	80
Tukker M.O., In re Paternity of	1045
Tullock v. Flickinger	1024
Turner v. Safley	43
TWITCHELL; COMMONWEALTH v.	563
TWYMAN v. TWYMAN	457

U

Uhl v. Uhl	1152
Uhls, In re Marriage of	813
Ulsher v. Ulsher	1171
Unander v. Unander	1256
Union Grove Milling & Mfg. Co. v. Faw	121
United v. Gilmore	1297
United States v. (see name of defendant)	
United Steelworkers of Am. v. Weber	169
University of Alaska v. Tumeo	226
Unkle v. Unkle	903
Upton v. Ames & Webb Inc.	1275
U.S. v. Bailey	457
U.S. v. Gluzman	457
U.S. v. Wright	457

V

Valencia v. Valencia	1182
Valerie D., In re	550
Van Bussum v. Van Bussum	914
Van de Loo v. Van de Loo	904
VAN KLOOTWYK v. VAN KLOOTWYK	960
Vandenburgh v. Vandenburgh	828
Vanderbilt v. Vanderbilt	785; 798
Vann v. Vann	773
Vaughn v. Vaughn	1182
Ver Dught, In re	847
Vermont v. Lorrain	130
Vigars v. Valley Christian Center of Dublin, California	171
Virginia; United States v.	120
V.J.S. v. M.J.B.	78
VOISHAN v. PALMA	1010
Voishon v. Palma	1044
V.R.W. Inc. v. Klein	121

W

Wade v. Wade	883; 931
Wahlberg v. Wahlberg	972
Walden v. Hoke	829
Walker v. Superior Court	568; 569
Ward v. Terriere	19
WARREN v. STATE	444
Warren v. Warren	473; 482
Warren, In re	847
Wasserman v. Wasserman	773
W.A.T., Adoption of, In the Matter of the	745
Waters v. Gaston County	158

TABLE OF CASES

Watson v. Watson ... 939
Wawrykow v. Simonich ... 355
Weakley v. Weakley ... 905
Weaver v. G. D. Searle Co. ... 56
Weaver v. State ... 14; 22
Webb v. Webb ... 847
Weber v. Aetna Casualty & Surety Co. ... 332; 400
Weber v. Weber ... 31
Weber, In re ... 1182
Webster v. Reproductive Health Servs. ... 255
Weeks v. Weeks ... 68
Weidenbacher v. Duclos ... 388
Weinstein, In re Marriage of ... 906
Weintraub v. Weintraub ... 101
Weisel v. National. Transp. Co. ... 17
Weisenberger v. Wiesenfield ... 121
Weisfeld v. Weisfeld ... 904
Welder v. Lambert ... 883
WELSHER v. RAGER ... 1083
Wesley, Marriage of, Matter of ... 1036
West v. West ... 885
Westbrook v. Westbrook ... 885
Western Community Bank v. Helmer ... 214
Western State Constr., Inc. v. Michoff ... 214
Westervelt v. Westervelt ... 802
Wetmore v. Markoe ... 1312
Whaley v. Whaley ... 928
Wheeler v. Wheeler ... 1000
Wheeling Silver Dollar Sav. & Trust Co. v. Singer ... 648
Whitaker v. Colbert ... 1024
White v. Finch ... 1239
White v. Marciano ... 1044
White v. Thompson ... 1133
WHITNER v. STATE ... 540
Whitney v. Pinney ... 695
Whitney v. Seattle-First Nat'l Bank ... 1268
Wierman, In re Marriage of ... 111
Wilcox-Elliott v. Wilcox ... 1154
Wilder v. Bernstein ... 744
Wildey v. Springs ... 1242
Wilen v. Wilen ... 877
Wilkins v. Zelichowski ... 73
William M. v. Superior Court ... 356
Williams v. North Carolina [I] ... 96; 773; 781; 783; 798
Williams v. North Carolina [II] ... 62; 773; 779; 754
WILLIAMS v. WILLIAMS ... 802; 819; 1268
WILLIAMS, IN RE MARRIAGE OF ... 969
Williams, State ex rel. v. Marsh ... 442

Williquette; State v. ... 532
Wills v. Jones ... 1032
Wilson v. Wilson ... 926; 1061
Wilson, In re Estate of ... 648
Winegard, In re Marriage of ... 792
Winter v. Winter ... 893
Wisconsin v. Yoder ... 61; 494
Wiskoski v. Wiskoski ... 1153
Witchey; State v. ... 153
Witt v. Witt ... 96
Wolf v. Wolf ... 1108; 1171
Wolfe v. Wolfe ... 79
Wolter v. Wolter ... 999
Wood v. Wood ... 809; 1036; 1274
WOOD, IN RE THE MARRIAGE OF ... 1032
WOODS v. SUPERIOR COURT OF TULARE COUNTY ... 834
Woodworth v. Woodworth ... 911
Worth, In re Marriage of ... 902
Worthington v. Worthington ... 82; 96; 891
Wright v. MetroHealth Med. Ctr. ... 158

Y

Yarborough v. Yarborough ... 1086
Yates v. Keene ... 296
YATES v. YATES ... 1108
Yeates, In re ... 1313
Yeatman v. Gortney ... 1061
Yeldell v. Yeldell ... 882
Yoder v. Yoder ... 794
YOPP v. BATT ... 653; 663; 752
Young v. Colorado Nat'l Bank ... 74
Young v. Young ... 1153

Z

ZABLOCKI, MILWAUKEE COUNTY CLERK v. RED-HAIL ... 39; 73
Zachery v. Zachery ... 898
Zaent, In re ... 902
Zecchin v. Zecchin ... 948
Zeigler v. Zeigler ... 939
Zeilinger; People v. ... 841
Zenker v. Zenker ... 797
Zimin v. Zimin ... 883
Zipf v. Zipf ... 930
Zullo v. Zullo ... 999
Zummo v. Zummo ... 1116; 1182
Zummo, In re Marriage of ... 917
Zwerling v. Zwerling ... 794

INDEX

[References are to pages.]

A

ABANDONMENT BY PARENT, TERMINATION OF PARENTAL RIGHTS ON (See ADOPTION, subhead: Involuntary termination of parental rights)

ABORTION
Generally . . . 243–252; 267
Demonstrations . . . 269–270
Fathers' rights . . . 253
Freedom of Access to Clinic Entrances Act of 1994 (FACE) . . . 269–270
Minors, abortions for
    Generally . . . 254
    Disagreements between minors and parents, effect of . . . 588–597
    Mature minor doctrine . . . 585–586
Partial Birth Abortion Act of 1996 . . . 270
Public funding and use of public facilities . . . 254
RU486 . . . 240; 268–269
Violence at abortion clinics . . . 270

ABUSE
Alcohol abuse (See ALCOHOL ABUSE)
Child abuse (See CHILD ABUSE)
Domestic violence (See DOMESTIC VIOLENCE)
Drug abuse (See DRUG ABUSE)

ADDICTION TO DRUGS (See DRUG ADDICTION)

ADOPTION
Generally . . . 627–646; 647–650; 695; 746–747
Abandonment by parent, termination of parental rights on (See subhead: Involuntary termination of parental rights)
Adoption and Safe Families Act of 1997 629–630
Adoption Assistance and Child Welfare Act (AACWA) . . . 627–629; 649
Advertising restrictions . . . 710
Age as criterion in selection of adoptive parents . . . 745
Agency adoptions
    Generally . . . 648–649; 696; 699
    Adoptive parents, services for . . . 697–698
    Birth parents, services for . . . 696–697
    Children, services for . . . 697
    Home studies . . . 702
    Independent adoptions distinguished . . . 663
    Religious organizations, private adoption agencies affiliated with or sponsored by . . . 744–745
American Indian children, adoption of (See subhead: Indian Child Welfare Act)

ADOPTION—Cont.
Attorneys (See subhead: Lawyers)
Best interest of child
    Custody determination when adoption denied or set aside for lack of valid parental consent . . . 667–668
    Home study to find circumstances contrary to . . . 702
    Revocation of consent to adoption 664; 667–668
    Termination of parental rights (See subhead: Involuntary termination of parental rights)
Confidentiality of adoption records
    Generally . . . 747–752
    Open adoption (See subhead: Open adoptions)
Consent
    Generally (See subhead: Consent to adoption)
    Meetings between adoptees and birth relatives, facilitation of consensual . . . 751–752
    Mutual consent registries . . . 751–752
    "Search and consent" procedures . . . 751–752
Consent to adoption
    Generally . . . 650
    Minor parent, consent of . . . 663
    Ratification of pre-birth consent . . . 653
    Revocation of consent (See subhead: Revocation of consent)
    Timing and validity of consent . . . 650–664
    Unwed fathers, consent of . . . 668–695
Constitutional issues
    Due process (See subhead: Due process)
    Indian Child Welfare Act, limitations on scope of . . . 734–738
    Open adoptions, constitutional challenges to sealed records system by advocates of . . . 752
    Race-matching policies, constitutionality of . . . 728
Co-parents, adoptions by . . . 713–718
Custody determination when adoption denied or set aside for lack of valid parental consent 667–668
Defined . . . 647
Direct placement adoptions (See subhead: Independent adoptions)
Disclosure requirements
    Generally . . . 758–766
    Family information on child placed for adoption, disclosure of . . . 699; 758–766
    "Good cause" for release of identifying information . . . 750–751

ADOPTION—Cont.
Disclosure requirements—Cont.
    Identity of father, effect of mother's refusal to disclose . . . 694
    Medical information on child placed for adoption, disclosure of . . . 699; 758–766
    Privacy concerns of birth parents . . . 766
    "Search and consent" procedures . . . 751–752
Due process
    Indian Child Welfare Act, limitations on 734–737
    Unwed father's parental rights, involuntary termination of . . . 668–695
Duress, revocation of consent obtained by 662–663
Equitable adoption . . . 648
Estoppel, adoption by . . . 648
"Facilitative accommodation" of racial preferences of prospective adoptive parents . . . 729
Family information on child placed for adoption, disclosure of . . . 699; 758–766
Foreign-born children, adoption of . . . 649
Fraud or duress, revocation of consent obtained by . . . 662–663
"Good cause" for release of identifying information . . . 750–751
Grandparents, post-adoption visitation by 757–758
Gray market adoptions (See subhead: Independent adoptions)
Historical perspectives on . . . 648; 746–747
Home studies, use of . . . 702
Homosexual parents
    Co-parent adoptions . . . 713–718
    Criterion in selection of adoptive parents, sexual orientation as . . . 746
ICWA (See subhead: Indian Child Welfare Act)
Independent adoptions
    Generally . . . 648–649; 696
    Advantages of . . . 700–701
    Advertising restrictions . . . 710
    Agency adoptions distinguished . . . 663
    Conflict of interest . . . 698; 702–712
    Court procedures for . . . 702
    Disadvantages of . . . 698
    Dual representation problems . . 698; 702–712
    Home studies for . . . 702
    Lack of objective counseling for birth parents . . . 699
    Legality of . . . 699–700
    Prevalence of . . . 700
    Reasons birth parents choose independent placements . . . 700–701
    Risks of . . . 701
    Role of intermediaries . . . 701

ADOPTION—Cont.
Independent adoptions—Cont.
    Separate legal counsel . . . 701
    Services available . . . 701
    Shortcomings of . . . 698
Indian Child Welfare Act
    Generally . . . 649; 729–741
    Constitutional limitations on scope of act . . . 734–738
    Definition of Indian child . . . 732
    Due process limitations . . . 734–737
    Equal protection considerations . . . 737–738
    'Existing Indian family" doctrine . . 733–734; 738–740
Interethnic Adoption Provisions of 1996 . . . 649; 723–724; 727–728
Intermediaries
    Independent adoptions, use of intermediaries in (See subhead: Independent adoptions)
    Meetings between adoptees and birth relatives, facilitation of . . . 752
International adoptions . . . 649
Interstate Compact on Placement of Children (ICPC), violation of . . . 662
Invalid consent, revocation of (See subhead: Revocation of consent)
Involuntary termination of parental rights
    Generally . . . 668–695
    Counsel provided for parents in termination proceedings . . . 718–720
    Court costs, effect of inability to pay 718–720
Lawyers
    Independent adoptions, use in (See subhead: Independent adoptions)
    Termination proceedings, counsel provided for parents in . . . 718–720
Licensed private adoption agencies (See subhead: Agency adoptions)
Marital status as criterion in selection of adoptive parents . . . 745–746
Medical information on child placed for adoption, disclosure of . . . 699; 758–766
Mistake, revocation of consent based on . . . 663
Multiethnic Placement Act of 1994 . . . . . . 649; 727–728
Mutual consent registries . . . 751–752
Native American children, adoption of (See subhead: Indian Child Welfare Act)
Non-agency adoptions (See subhead: Independent adoptions)
Non-presumptive parents, rights of . . . 389–417
Non-profit adoption agencies (See subhead: Agency adoptions)
Open adoptions
    Generally . . . 648; 752

[References are to pages.]

ADOPTION—Cont.
  Open adoptions—Cont.
    Constitutional challenges to sealed records system by advocates of open adoptions . . . 752
    Visitation after adoption (See subhead: Post-adoption visitation)
  Payments
    Allowable payments . . . 711–712
    Prohibited payments and activities . . 710–712
  Physical ability as criterion in selection of adoptive parents . . . 745
  Post-adoption visitation
    Generally . . . 752–758
    Grandparents, visitation by . . . 757–758
  Private adoption agencies (See subhead: Agency adoptions)
  Private adoptions (See subhead: Independent adoptions)
  Public adoption agencies (See subhead: Agency adoptions)
  Putative father registries . . . 694
  Race
    Constitutionality of race-matching policies . . . 728
    "Facilitative accommodation" of racial preferences of prospective adoptive parents 729
    Indian Child Welfare Act (See subhead: Indian Child Welfare Act)
    Role of race in adoption . . . 720–723
    Transracial adoption (See subhead: Transracial adoption)
  Ratification of pre-birth consent . . . 653
  Registries
    Mutual consent registries . . . 751–752
    Putative father registries . . . 694
  Religion
    Matching provisions of adoption laws 741–746
    Private adoption agencies affiliated with or sponsored by religious organizations . . 744–745
  Relinquishment of child (See subhead: Consent to adoption)
  Revocation of consent
    Generally . . . 653–664
    Best interest of child . . . 664; 667–668
    Consequences of invalid consent . . . 664–668
    Failure to comply with statutory requirements . . . 661–662
    Fraud or duress, consent obtained by 662–663
    Interstate Compact on Placement of Children (ICPC), violation of . . . 662
    Mistake, revocation of consent based on 663

ADOPTION—Cont.
  Revocation of consent—Cont.
    Time period, revocation within statutory 661
  Sealed adoption records (See subhead: Confidentiality of adoption records)
  "Search and consent" procedures . . . 751–752
  Second parent adoptions . . . 713–718
  Sexual orientation as criterion in selection of adoptive parents . . . 746
  State adoption agencies (See subhead: Agency adoptions)
  Stepparent adoptions . . . 713–718
  Termination of parental rights
    Generally . . . 630–646
    Involuntary termination (See subhead: Involuntary termination of parental rights)
    Stepparent exception to . . . 713–718
    Voluntary termination (See subhead: Consent to adoption)
  Tort cause of action for wrongful adoption (See subhead: Wrongful adoption actions)
  Transracial adoption
    Generally . . . 720–723; 724–727
    Constitutionality of race-matching policies . . . 728
    Indian Child Welfare Act, effect of (See subhead: Indian Child Welfare Act)
    Interethnic Adoption Provisions of 1996 . . . . 649; 723–724; 727–728
    Multiethnic Placement Act of 1994 . . . . 649; 727–728
  Unfit parent, termination of parental rights of (See subhead: Involuntary termination of parental rights)
  Uniform Adoption Act
    Generally . . . 416; 650
    Consent requirements (See subhead: Consent to adoption)
    Disclosure requirements (See subhead: Disclosure requirements)
    Payments permissible under act . . . 711
    Post-adoption visitation . . . 758
    Race, provisions regarding . . . 728
    Shortcomings of independent adoption, act addressing . . . 699
    Stepparent adoptions, effect on . . . 718
  Unwed fathers, consent of . . . 668–695
  Visitation after adoption (See subhead: Post-adoption visitation)
  Voluntary termination of parental rights (See subhead: Consent to adoption)
  Wrongful adoption actions
    Generally . . . 758–766
    Consumer remedy, action as . . . 766

[References are to pages.]

ADOPTION ASSISTANCE AND CHILD WELFARE ACT (AACWA)
Generally . . . 539; 627–629; 649

ADR (See ALTERNATIVE DISPUTE RESOLUTION)

ADULTERY
Divorce, grounds for (See DIVORCE)

ADVERTISEMENTS
Adoption, restrictions on advertising for . . . 710

AGE
Adoptive parents, age as criterion in selection of . . . 745

AGENCY ADOPTIONS (See ADOPTION)

AID TO FAMILIES WITH DEPENDENT CHILDREN (AFDC)
Cooperation requirements . . . 374–375

ALCOHOL ABUSE
Child custody disputes, factor in . . . 1154
Maternal alcohol abuse . . . 549

ALIENATION OF AFFECTIONS
Actions for . . . 147–149; 1241

ALIMONY (See SPOUSAL SUPPORT)

ALL-PROPERTY EQUITABLE DISTRIBUTION (See DISTRIBUTION OF PROPERTY, subhead: Equitable distribution)

ALTERNATE PAYEES (See QUALIFIED DOMESTIC RELATIONS ORDERS (QDRO))

ALTERNATIVE DISPUTE RESOLUTION
Arbitration (See ARBITRATION)
Mediation (See MEDIATION)

AMERICAN INDIANS (See NATIVE AMERICANS)

AMISH RELIGION
Generally . . . 494–504

ANNULMENT
Defenses . . . 97–98
Estoppel by judgment as defense . . . 98
Grounds for . . . 97–98
Jurisdiction . . . 96–97
Laches as defense to action . . . 98
Property rights on annulment . . . 98–102
Ratification of marital defect as defense . . . 97
Res judicata as defense to . . . 98
Spousal support rights on annulment . . . 98–102
Statute of limitations for action . . . 97

ANTENUPTIAL AGREEMENTS (See PREMARITAL AGREEMENTS)

ARBITRATION
Distinguished from mediation . . . 856; 864–865
Mediation distinguished . . . 856; 864–865
Provisions for binding arbitration of custody disputes . . . 864–868

ARREARAGES, CHILD SUPPORT (See CHILD SUPPORT)

ARTIFICIAL INSEMINATION
Generally . . . 309–317
Defined . . . 310
Frozen sperm, custody of . . . 317
Surrogacy (See SURROGACY)

ASSIGNMENT OF WAGES
Child support, collection of . . . 1070; 1075–1076

ATTORNEY-CLIENT PRIVILEGE
Generally . . . 834
Criminal act, attorney's release of confidential information to prevent client from committing . . . 834; 844
Fraud
    Client's fraud, attorney's knowledge of . . . 838; 844
    Third-party fraud, attorney's knowledge of . . . 838–839
Past and future conduct of client . . . 839
Third-party fraud, attorney's knowledge of . . . 838–839
Waiver of privilege on dual representation . . . 828

ATTORNEYS
Adoptions, role in (See ADOPTION, subhead: Lawyers)
Attorney-client privilege (See ATTORNEY-CLIENT PRIVILEGE)
Behavior in court . . . 844
Children, representation of
    Generally . . . 847; 855
    Comparison of attorney's role and guardian ad litem's role . . . 847–856
Competency of lawyer . . . 832–833
Confidentiality (See ATTORNEY-CLIENT PRIVILEGE)
Conflict of interest (See subhead: Dual representation by attorney)
Consent
    Confidential information, consent to release of . . . 834
    Dual representation, consent to . . . 828–829
Disqualification of attorney
    Former client, interests materially adverse to . . . 834
    "Substantial possibility" test . . . 834–838
Dual representation by attorney
    Generally . . . 827–834

[References are to pages.]

ATTORNEYS—Cont.
Dual representation by attorney—Cont.
    Adoptions, independent . . . 698; 702–712
    Consent by clients . . . 828–829
    Disadvantages of . . . 828
    Fraud upon court . . . 830–834
    Waiver of attorney-client privilege . . . 828
Ethical considerations
    Generally . . . 827
    Dual representation (See subhead: Dual representation by attorney)
    Fraud upon court . . . 830–834
    Migratory divorces, advice on . . . 839
    Privileged communications (See ATTORNEY-CLIENT PRIVILEGE)
    Sexual relationship with client . . . 840–843
Evidence, attorney's presentation of false 846–847
False evidence, presentation of . . . 846–847
Fees (See ATTORNEY'S FEES)
Fraud
    Court, fraud upon . . . 830–834
    Privileged information (See ATTORNEY-CLIENT PRIVILEGE)
    Withdrawal of attorney . . . 844–847
Guardian ad litem (See subhead: Children, representation of)
Mediation, role in . . . 862
Own divorce, attorney's misconduct in . . . 847
Paternity case, indigent defendant's rights to counsel in . . . 370–371
Privileged communications (See ATTORNEY-CLIENT PRIVILEGE)
Pro se divorces . . . 840
Representation by attorney (See subhead: Dual representation by attorney)
Sexual relationship with client . . . 840–843
"Substantial possibility" test, disqualification of attorney based on . . . 834–838
Unrepresented spouse and role of attorney 833–834
Waiver of attorney-client privilege on dual representation . . . 828
Withdrawal of attorney
    Generally . . . 844–847
    Fraud by client . . . 844–847
    Sexual relationship with client . . . 840–843

ATTORNEY'S FEES
Contingency fee agreements, use of . . . 839–840
Divorce action . . . 839–840
Tax deductibility of fees related to divorce 1297–1298

B

BANKRUPTCY
Generally . . . 1311
"Ability to pay test" exception to nondischargeability of debt . . . 1310; 1312; 1314
Automatic stay of all actions to collect debt 1311
"Balancing of detriments test" exception to nondischargeability of debt . . . 1310; 1312; 1314
Exceptions to nondischargeability of debt . . 1310; 1312; 1314
Future legislation . . . 1315
Future support, effect of bankruptcy on 1315–1316
"Hold harmless" clauses . . . 1313; 1315
Nondischargeability of debt
    Generally . . . 1305–1317; 1312
    Exceptions to nondischargeability of debt . . . 1310; 1312; 1314
    Text of statutes on discharge . . . 1312
Partial discharge of debt . . . 1315
Post-1994 non-support debts, effect on . . . 1314
Pre-1994 non-support debts, effect on 1313–1314
Stay of all actions to collect debt . . . 1311
Text of statutes on discharge . . . 1312

BATTERED WOMEN (See DOMESTIC VIOLENCE)

BEST INTEREST STANDARD
Adoption (See ADOPTION)
Attorney, child's representation by . . . 847
Custody of child (See CHILD CUSTODY)
Visitation restrictions . . . 1159

BIGAMY
Generally . . . 57–63

BIRTH CONTROL (See REPRODUCTIVE ALTERNATIVES)

BLOOD TESTS
Marriage, requirement for . . . 10
Paternity, establishment of . . . 347–353

BONDS
Child support payments, security for future 1070; 1075

BREACH OF CONTRACT
Marry, breach of promise to . . . 1234–1242

BURDEN OF PROOF
Custody arrangements, modification of . . . 1183
Tracing of property . . . 890

BUSINESSES
Distribution on divorce or dissolution of marriage (See DISTRIBUTION OF PROPERTY)

BUY-SELL AGREEMENTS
Generally . . . 928–929

C

CAPACITY
Marriage (See MARRIAGE)

CHILD ABUSE
(See also CORPORAL PUNISHMENT)
Adoption Assistance and Child Welfare Act (AACWA) . . . 539; 627–629
Alcohol abuse by pregnant woman . . . 549
Child Abuse Prevention and Treatment Act of 1974 . . . 568
Controlled substance use during pregnancy 540–552
Custody disputes, abuse as factor in . . 1148–1155
Distinguishing between abuse and discipline 507–522
Drug use during pregnancy . . . 540–552
Failure of parent to protect child from abuse 522–533
Fetus, abuse or neglect of . . . 540–552
Foster care (See FOSTER CARE)
Government responsibility to protect children . . . 553–562
Medical care for children (See MEDICAL CARE FOR CHILDREN)
Neglect
    Adoption Assistance and Child Welfare Act (AACWA), reasonable effort requirements of . . . 539; 627–629
    Defining and responding to neglect 534–540
    Fetus, neglect of . . . 540–552
    Foster care (See FOSTER CARE)
    Homelessness, effect of . . . 539–540
    Medical neglect . . . 569–582
    Minimum intervention approach to . . 537–539
Number of incidents of abuse and neglect 518–519
Prenatal child abuse . . . 540–552
Reporting statutes . . . 518
Supervised visitation . . . 1162
Tort remedies for failure to protect children . . 561

CHILD CARE
Generally . . . 184–186
Spousal support, effect of child care responsibilities on . . . 968–969
Tax credit for percentage of dependent's child care expenses . . . 1297

CHILD CUSTODY
Generally . . . 1092–1093
Adoption denied or set aside for lack of valid parental consent, determination of custody when 667–668
Alcohol abuse as factor . . . 1154
Arbitration of disputes (See ARBITRATION)
Attorney's representation of child (See ATTORNEYS)
Availability of parent as factor . . . 1142–1147
Best interest standard
    Generally . . . 1092; 1093–1099
    Modification of custody . . . 1175–1184
Burden of proof for modification of custody 1183
Changed circumstances, modification of order due to . . . 1175–1184
Child abuse as factor . . . 1148–1155
Child-care arrangements as factor . . . 1142–1147
Child's preference as factor . . . 1108–1112
Cohabitants, custody disputes between unmarried . . . 214–215
Continuity of care as factor . . . 1154; 1184
Cooperation of parent as factor . . . 1153
Criminal record of parent as factor . . . 1154
Double standard regarding sexual conduct . . 1125
Drug abuse as factor . . . 1154
Educational needs as factor . . . 1154
Evaluation ordered by court . . . 1099
Exclusive use and possession of marital home to custodial parent, award of . . . 915–918
Family unity as factor . . . 1153
Fitness of parent
    Mental fitness of parent . . . 1134–1141
    Physical fitness . . . 1134–1141
    Sexual conduct of parent . . . 1120–1125
    Sexual preference of parent . . . 1125–1133
Gender of parent as factor . . . 1099–1103
Hague Convention on the Civil Aspects of International Child Abduction . . . 1221–1229
International child abduction . . . 1221–1229
Investigation and report concerning custodial arrangements, court-ordered . . . 1099
Joint custody
    Generally . . . 1092–1093; 1163–1175
    Child support, effect on . . . 1020–1021
    Effects of . . . 1171–1172
    Negotiation of divorce settlement, use of joint custody in . . . 1172–1173
    Statutes for . . . 1169–1171
Jurisdiction
    Generally . . . 1193
    Federal legislation . . . 1212–1221
    International law . . . 1221–1229
    State legislation . . . 1195–1212
    Traditional jurisdiction . . . 1193–1195

[References are to pages.]

CHILD CUSTODY—Cont.
Legal effect of best interest standard . . 1098–1099
Mediation of disputes (See MEDIATION)
Mental fitness of parent as factor . . . 1134–1141
Modification of custody
    Best interest standard . . . 1175–1184
    Burden of proof . . . 1183
    Changed circumstances . . . 1175–1184
    Continuity of care as factor . . . 1184
    Relocation . . . 1184–1192
    Uniform Marriage and Divorce Act requirements for . . . 1182–1183
Parental Alienation Syndrome . . . 1153
Parental Kidnapping Prevention Act (PKPA) 1193; 1208–1209; 1212–1221
Physical fitness of parent as factor . . . 1134–1141
Primary caretaker presumption . . . 1103–1108
Race as factor . . . 1117–1120
Religion as factor . . . 1112–1116
Relocation, modification of custody due to 1184–1192
Sexual conduct of parent as factor . . . 1120–1125
Sexual preference of parent as factor 1125–1133
Spousal support, effect of child care responsibilities on . . . 968–969
Tax consequences of (See TAXATION)
Tender years presumption . . . 1099–1103
Uniform Child Custody Jurisdiction Act (UCCJA) . . . 1193; 1195–1212; 1217–1221
Uniform Child Custody Jurisdiction and Enforcement Act (UCCJEA) . . . 1193; 1210–1211
Uniform Marriage and Divorce Act requirements for modification of custody . . . 1182–1183
Visitation rights (See VISITATION)
Working outside of home as factor . . . 1142–1147

CHILDREN AND MINORS
Abortions for (See ABORTION)
Abuse of (See CHILD ABUSE)
Adoption of (See ADOPTION)
Attorney's representation of (See ATTORNEYS)
Best interest of (See BEST INTEREST STANDARD)
Cohabitants, co-parenting agreements between unmarried . . . 214–215
Condom-availability programs in schools . . . 240
Constitutional framework for raising children 486–507
Contraceptives for (See CONTRACEPTION)
Custody of (See CHILD CUSTODY)
Disobedient children . . . 597–604
Divorce from parents . . . 603
Divorce's negative impact on children . . 771–772
Education of (See EDUCATION)
Emancipation of (See EMANCIPATION OF MINORS)

CHILDREN AND MINORS—Cont.
Foster care (See FOSTER CARE)
Illegitimate children (See NONMARITAL CHILDREN)
Incorrigible children . . . 597–604
Juvenile court proceedings to reinforce parental authority over children . . . 602
Medical care (See MEDICAL CARE FOR CHILDREN)
Neglect of (See CHILD ABUSE)
Nonmarital children (See NONMARITAL CHILDREN)
Parent-child tort actions . . . 473–483
Sale of contraceptives to minors . . . 239
Tort actions between parents and children 473–483
Unruly children . . . 597–604
Visitation rights (See VISITATION)

CHILD SUPPORT
Generally . . . 1003–1004
Actual income, calculation based on . . 1025–1032
Adult child, support for . . . 133–134; 1057
Assignment of wages . . . 1070; 1075–1076
Bankruptcy's effect on support obligations (See BANKRUPTCY, subhead: Nondischargeability of debt)
Bond as security for future payments . . 1070; 1075
Capacity to earn, calculation based on 1025–1032
Child Support Act of 1988 . . . 1075–1076
Child Support Enforcement Amendments of 1984 . . . 1075
Child Support Recovery Act of 1992 1075–1076
College, support for . . . 1053–1057
Contempt to enforce payment of . . . 1069–1070
Death of supporting parent . . . 1052–1053
Disability benefits used to satisfy support obligations . . . 1071
Duration of support
    Age of majority of child . . . 1045–1053
    College, support for . . . 1053–1057
    Emancipation of child . . . 1052
During marriage . . . 131–134
Earning capacity, calculation based on 1025–1032
Emancipation of child, support until . . . 1052
Employer conspiring with support obligor to evade automatic withholding, cause of action against . . . 1071
Enforcement of orders
    Generally . . . 135
    Federal enforcement . . . 1071–1077
    Interstate enforcement . . . 1083–1089

[References are to pages.]

CHILD SUPPORT—Cont.
Enforcement of orders—Cont.
    State remedies for . . . 1063–1071
Escalator clauses for modification of support, use of . . . 1061–1062
Family expense statutes . . . 131–134
Family Support Act of 1988 . . . 1009
Federal mandates . . . 1004–1010
Flat percentage of income model . . . 1019
Full Faith and Credit for Child Support Orders Act of 1994 . . . 1076; 1086
Garnishment of wages . . . 1070
Guidelines for determining basic support obligations . . . 1010–1016
History of federal involvement . . . 1008–1009
Income of parents, calculation of
    Actual income or capacity to earn 1025–1032
    Extraordinarily high income, effect of 1040–1045
    Gross or net income, use of . . . 1022–1025
    Other children, support obligations for 1036–1040
    Spousal income . . . 1032–1036
    Subsequent spouse or nonmarital partner, income of . . . 1032–1036
Income shares model for determining support . . . 1010–1016
Income withholding statutes . . . 1075
Interstate enforcement of orders . . . 1083–1089
Jurisdiction for support . . . 1077–1083
License, revocation or suspension of state 1070–1071
Liens on property to collect arrearages . . . 1075
Maternal cooperation requirements . . . 374–375
Maximum child support . . . 1044
Melson formula as variation on income shares method . . . 1014–1015
Mentally disabled child receiving support beyond age of majority . . . 134
Modification of support . . . 1057–1063
Omnibus Budget Reconciliation Act of 1993 1076
Overtime, impact of . . . 1024–1025
Parent Locator Service . . . 1074–1075
Paternity, establishment of . . . 371–378
Pendente lite statutes . . . 134
Percentage of income model for determining support . . . 1016–1021
Personal jurisdiction for support . . . 1077–1083
Personal Responsibility and Work Opportunity Reconciliation Act of 1996 . . . 1076–1077
Physically disabled child receiving support beyond age of majority . . . 134
Potential income, calculation based on 1025–1032

CHILD SUPPORT—Cont.
Retroactive child support . . . 1053
Revised Uniform Reciprocal Enforcement of Support Act (RURESA) . . . 1085–1088
Revocation of state license for failure to pay support . . . 1070–1071
Security for future payments . . . 1070; 1075
Shared custody, effect of . . . 1020–1021
State remedies for enforcement of orders 1063–1071
Suspension of state license for failure to pay support . . . 1070–1071
Tax consequences of (See TAXATION)
Termination of support (See subhead: Duration of support)
Title IV-D program for enforcement of support . . . 1008–1009; 1074–1075
Uniform Interstate Family Support Act (UIFSA) . . . 1077; 1086–1089
Uniform Marriage and Divorce Act
    Death of supporting parent, effect of 1052–1053
    Modification of support . . . 1060
Uniform Reciprocal Enforcement of Support Act (URESA) . . . 1085
Varying percentage of income model . . . 1020
Visitation and support payments . . . 1159–1160
Wage garnishment . . . 1070

CHRISTIAN SCIENTISTS
Criminal prosecution for parental failure to seek medical care . . . 563–569
Entrapment by estoppel . . . 567
Medical neglect by . . . 569–582

CIVIL RIGHTS REMEDIES FOR GENDER-MOTIVATED VIOLENCE ACT
Generally . . . 448–457

CLONING
Generally . . . 329–330

COHABITATION
Generally . . . 189–191
Benefits to unmarried cohabitants, availability of . . . 190–191; 223–226
Child custody and visitation disputes between unmarried cohabitants . . . 214–215
Creasman presumption . . . 208
Custody and visitation disputes between unmarried cohabitants . . . 214–215
Danish Act . . . 233
Death or disability of one member of couple, disputes between unmarried cohabitants and other family members upon . . . 226
Domestic partnership legislation . . . 191; 228–233
Modification of spousal support, effect on 991–998; 999–1000

[References are to pages.]

COHABITATION—Cont.
Palimony . . . 204
Partnership theories . . . 206–216
Property and partnership theories . . . 206–216
"Rational relationship" test of legislation 217–218
"Reciprocal beneficiaries" in Hawaii, registration as . . . 230–231
Role of contract in disputes between unmarried cohabitants . . . 191–206
Single-family zoning ordinances, effect of . . . 223
Spousal support, effect on modification of 991–998; 999–1000
Status relationship or contract, cohabitation as . . . 190
Third parties and cohabitants, disputes between . . 216–227
Visitation and custody disputes between unmarried cohabitants . . . 214–215
Western countries, domestic partnerships in other . . . 232–233
Zoning ordinances, effect of restrictive application of single-family . . . 223

COLLATERAL ATTACKS
Divorce . . . 795–797

COLLEGES AND UNIVERSITIES
Divorce, classification of professional degrees on . . . 906–915
Support beyond age of majority for child's college education . . . 1053–1057

COLLUSION
Divorce, defense to . . . 807–808

COMITY
Divorces in foreign countries recognizable in United States under discretionary principle of . . . 786

COMMON-LAW MARRIAGES
Generally . . . 14–19

COMMUNITY PROPERTY
Generally . . . 119; 123
Distribution of (See DISTRIBUTION OF PROPERTY)
Transmutation of property (See TRANSMUTATION OF PROPERTY)

CONCILIATION
Divorce, court-ordered conciliation prior to . . 821

CONDOM-AVAILABILITY PROGRAMS
Generally . . . 240

CONDONATION
Divorce, defense to . . . 808

CONDUCT
Attorneys, ethical misconduct by (See ATTORNEYS)
Distribution of marital property, misconduct as factor in (See DISTRIBUTION OF PROPERTY)

CONFIDENTIALITY
Adoption records (See ADOPTION)
Mediator's confidentiality . . . 862–863
Privileged communications (See PRIVILEGED COMMUNICATIONS)

CONFLICT OF INTEREST (See ATTORNEYS, subhead: Dual representation by attorney)

CONFLICT OF LAWS
Marriage considerations . . . 88–96

CONNIVANCE
Divorce, defense to . . . 807

CONSENT
Adoption (See ADOPTION)
Attorney, consent given to (See ATTORNEYS)

CONSIDERATION
Separation agreement based on illegal consideration, invalidity of . . . 1275

CONSORTIUM
Rights of . . . 150–151

CONSTITUTIONAL ISSUES
Adoption, effect on (See ADOPTION)
Children, raising of . . . 486–507
Due process (See DUE PROCESS)
Illegitimate children . . . 334–347
Marriage as constitutional right . . . 39–44
Nonmarital children . . . 334–347
Paternity (See PATERNITY)

CONTEMPT
Child support payments, enforcement of 1069–1070
Domestic violence cases, use of contempt to enforce protective orders in . . . 443

CONTRACEPTION
Generally . . . 235–243
Access by minors to contraceptives . . . 596–587
Condom-availability programs in schools . . . 240
Norplant device . . . 239–240
Privacy, right to . . . 241–242
Sale of contraceptives to minors . . . 239
Tort litigation regarding safety of new contraceptives . . . 240

CONTRACTS
Breach of (See BREACH OF CONTRACT)
Buy-sell agreements . . . 928–929

[References are to pages.]

CONTRACTS—Cont.
Cohabitation contracts (See COHABITATION)
Co-parenting agreements between unmarried cohabitants . . . 214–215
Marital contracts (See MARITAL CONTRACTS)
Marriage as contract . . . 3–10
Premarital agreements (See PREMARITAL AGREEMENTS)
Separation agreements (See SEPARATION AGREEMENTS)
Surrogacy contracts (See SURROGACY)

CORPORAL PUNISHMENT
(See also CHILD ABUSE)
Attitudes toward punishment . . . 519–520
Home, punishment at . . . 507–522
International perspectives on . . . 520–521
Schools, punishment in . . . 521–522

COUNSELING (See PREMARITAL COUNSELING)

COUNSEL, RIGHT TO
Paternity case, rights of indigent defendant in . . . 370–371

COVENANT MARRIAGES
Generally . . . 6–7

CRIME
Attorney's release of confidential information to prevent client from committing criminal act . . 834; 844
Child custody disputes, criminal record as factor in . . . 1154
Divorce, conviction of crime as grounds for 769; 807
Domestic violence, generally (See DOMESTIC VIOLENCE)
Medical care, criminal prosecution for parental failure to seek . . . 563–569
Violence Against Women Act (See VIOLENCE AGAINST WOMEN ACT)

CRIMINAL CONVERSATION
Generally . . . 147–149

CRUELTY
Divorce, grounds for . . . 769; 806

CURTESY
Generally . . . 121–122

CUSTODY OF CHILD (See CHILD CUSTODY)

D

DEATH
Child support, death of parent providing 1052–1053

DEATH—Cont.
Cohabitants and other family members in dispute upon death of one member of couple, unmarried . . . 226
Property rights on death of spouse . . . 121–122
Spousal support, termination of . . . 998

DEFENSE OF MARRIAGE ACT
Generally . . . 56

DEFENSES
Annulment . . . 97–98
Divorce (See DIVORCE)

DEFERRED COMPENSATION BENEFITS
Distribution of benefits on divorce . . . 901–902

DEFICIT REDUCTION ACT OF 1984
Generally . . . 1294–1296

DEFINITIONS
Adoption . . . 647
Annulment . . . 97
Artificial insemination . . . 310
Collusion . . . 807–808
Comity . . . 786
Condonation . . . 808
Connivance . . . 807
Divorce . . . 768
Domestic violence . . . 420–421
Domicile . . . 773
Fair market value . . . 928
Foster care . . . 605
Income for purposes of child support 1022–1023
Indian child under Indian Child Welfare Act 732
Marriage . . . 2
Mediation . . . 856
Partial birth . . . 270
Putative marriage . . . 19
Serious health condition under FMLA . . 179–180
Sham marriage . . . 83
Stalking . . . 443
Voidable marriage . . . 45
Void marriage . . . 45

DELAY
Divorce action (See DIVORCE)

DESERTION
Divorce, grounds for . . . 769; 806–807

DIRECT PLACEMENT ADOPTIONS (See ADOPTION, subhead: Independent adoptions)

DISABILITY BENEFITS
Child support obligations, benefits used to satisfy . . . 1071

[References are to pages.]

DISABLED PERSONS
Mentally disabled (See MENTALLY DISABLED)
Physically disabled (See PHYSICALLY DISABLED)
Unmarried cohabitants and other family members in dispute upon disability of one member of couple . . . 226

DISCHARGE OF DEBT (See BANKRUPTCY)

DISCIPLINE, CORPORAL PUNISHMENT AS MEANS OF (See CORPORAL PUNISHMENT)

DISCLOSURES
Adoption (See ADOPTION)

DISCOVERY
Divorce actions . . . 808

DISCRETION
Attorney's fees, court's determination regarding reasonableness of . . . 839–840
Distribution of property on divorce, judicial discretion in . . . 950–952

DISQUALIFICATION OF ATTORNEYS (See ATTORNEYS)

DISSOLUTION OF MARRIAGE (See DIVORCE)

DISTRIBUTION OF PROPERTY
Generally . . . 871–878; 930–931
Active appreciation of separate property, effect of . . . 890–893
All-property equitable distribution (See subhead: Equitable distribution)
Alternate payee, assignment of pension benefits to . . . 897
Appreciation of separate property, effect of 890–893
Bibliography on equitable distribution . . 952–953
Book value of businesses and professional practices . . . 928
Burden of proof when tracing property . . . 890
Businesses and professional practices, valuation of
    Generally . . . 927–929
    Book value . . . 928
    Buy-sell agreements, use of . . . 928–929
    Capitalization of excess earnings . . . 928
    Goodwill, classification and valuation of 918–927
    Minority interest in enterprise, discount for . . 929
Buy-sell agreements used in valuation of businesses . . . 928–929
Capitalization of excess earnings as method of valuation . . . 928
Closely held businesses, valuation of (See subhead: Businesses and professional practices, valuation of)

DISTRIBUTION OF PROPERTY—Cont.
Community property
    Generally . . . 123; 872–873
    Equitable distribution of (See subhead: Equitable distribution)
    Inception of title theory . . . 880–885; 883–884
    List of states . . . 872–873
    Overview of . . . 876–877
    Pro tanto community property interest . . 881; 883
    Source of funds theory . . . 881–882; 883–884
    Transmutation of property . . . 885–886
Deferred compensation benefits . . . 901–902
Deferred distribution of pension or retirement benefits . . . 898–901
Degrees and licenses, professional . . . 906–915
Discretion of judge, role of . . . 950–952
Dissipation or waste of marital assets, effect of . . 938–940
Dual-property equitable distribution (See subhead: Equitable distribution)
Employee Retirement Income Security Act, effect of . . . 897
Enhanced earning capacity from professional degrees and licenses . . . 906–915
Equitable distribution
    Generally . . . 873–875
    All-property equitable distribution
        Generally . . . 874–875; 930
        Dual-property equitable distribution compared . . . 875–876
        Gifts, status of . . . 893–894
        List of states . . . 875
    Bibliography on equitable distribution 952–953
    Classification of property . . . 877–882
    Dual-property equitable distribution
        Generally . . . 874; 930
        All-property equitable distribution compared . . . 875–876
        List of states . . . 874
    Fault, role of (See subhead: Fault, role of)
    Long-term marriages, recharacterization and distribution of property based on . . . 936–938
    Overview of . . . 876–877
    Presumption of equal division versus equal division starting point . . . 933–935
    Statutory factors for distribution of property . . . 931–933
    Tracing and transmutation of property 885–886
ERISA, effect of . . . 897
Exclusive use and possession of marital home to custodial parent, award of . . . 915–918
Factors for distribution of property, statutory 931–933

[References are to pages.]

DISTRIBUTION OF PROPERTY—Cont.
   Fair market value defined . . . 928
   Family home
      Generally . . . 915–918
      Fraudulent sale of . . . 939
   Fault, role of
      Generally . . . 938
      Dissipation or waste of marital assets 938–940
      Economic fault . . . 938–940
      Misconduct as factor (See subhead: Misconduct during marriage as factor in property division)
      Spousal support (See SPOUSAL SUPPORT)
   Federal pension and retirement benefits, division of . . . 896–897
   Finality and non-modifiability of awards . . . 871
   Fraudulent sale of marital home . . . 939
   Gifts as separate property (See subhead: Separate property)
   Goodwill, classification and valuation of 918–927
   Immediate offset method for distribution of pension or retirement benefits . . . 898
   Inception of title theory . . . 880–885; 883–884
   Inheritances as separate property (See subhead: Separate property)
   Joint gift presumption . . . 893–894
   Judicial discretion, role of . . . 950–952
   Licenses and degrees, professional . . . 906–915
   Long-term marriages, recharacterization and distribution of property based on . . . 936–938
   Military retirement benefits, division of . . . 897
   Minority interest in enterprise, discount for . . 929
   Misconduct during marriage as factor in property division
      Generally . . . 940
      Rejection of fault factors, arguments for 940–941
      Retention of fault factors, arguments for 941–950
   Passive appreciation of separate property, effect of . . . 890–893
   Pensions and retirement benefits
      Complexity of dividing benefits . . . 895–897
      Federal pension and retirement benefits, division of . . . 896–897
      Private pensions governed by ERISA, division of . . . 897
      Valuation and division of benefits . . 898–900
   Personal injury awards . . . 902–906
   Presumptions
      Equal division presumption versus equal division starting point . . . 933–935
      Joint gift presumption . . . 893–894
   Professional degrees and licenses . . . 906–915

DISTRIBUTION OF PROPERTY—Cont.
   Professional practices (See subhead: Businesses and professional practices)
   Pro tanto community property interest . . 881; 883
   Qualified domestic relations orders (QDRO), effect of . . . 897
   Railroad Retirement Act, effect of . . . 896–897
   Reimbursement, award of property based on equitable . . . 914–915
   Relative-time method for distribution of pension or retirement benefits . . . 898–901
   Relative-value method for distribution of pension or retirement benefits . . . 898
   Research bibliography on equitable distribution . . . 952–953
   Residence of family (See subhead: Family home)
   Retirement benefits (See subhead: Pensions and retirement benefits)
   Retirement Equity Act of 1984 . . . 897
   Sale of family home (See subhead: Family home)
   Separate property
      Generally . . . 874–876; 877
      Active appreciation of property . . . 890–893
      All-property equitable distribution, effect of (See subhead: Equitable distribution)
      Dual-property equitable distribution, effect of (See subhead: Equitable distribution)
      Inception of title theory . . . 880–885; 883–884
      Long-term marriages, recharacterization and distribution of property based on . . . 936–938
      Passive appreciation of property . . . 890–893
      Pro tanto community property interest . . 881; 883
      Source of funds theory . . . 881–882; 883–884
      Status of property acquired by gift or inheritance . . . 893–894
      Tracing and transmutation of property 885–886
   Source of funds theory . . . 881–882; 883–884
   Spousal support (See SPOUSAL SUPPORT)
   Standard of proof when tracing property . . . 890
   Statutory factors for distribution of property 931–933
   Tort claims for marital misconduct . . . 942–943
   Tracing of property . . . 885–890
   Transmutation of property . . . 885–890
   Uniformed Services Former Spouses' Protection Act (USFSPA) . . . 897
   Uniform Marriage and Divorce Act (UMDA)
      Generally . . . 874; 952
      Equitable distribution, statutory factors for . . . 931–933
   Waste of marital assets, effect of . . . 938–940
   Workers' compensation awards . . . 902–906

[References are to pages.]

DIVISIBLE DIVORCE DOCTRINE
Generally . . . 797–801

DIVORCE
Generally . . . 768–769
Addiction to drugs as grounds for divorce . . 769; 807
Adultery
    Grounds for divorce . . . 769; 802–806
    Statute of limitations in bringing action based on . . . 808
Arbitration of issues (See ARBITRATION)
Attorneys (See ATTORNEYS)
Attorney's fees in divorce action . . . 839–840
Bilateral migratory divorces . . . 784–785; 796
Children divorcing parents . . . 603
Coexistence of financial factors with nonfinancial factors in determining financial issues in divorce . . . 824–825
Collusion as defense to fault-based divorce 807–808
Comity, recognition of foreign-country migratory divorces under discretionary principle of . . . 786
Conciliation ordered by court . . . 821
Condonation as defense to fault-based divorce . . . 808
Connivance as defense to fault-based divorce 807
Conviction of crime as grounds for divorce . . 769; 807
Court-ordered conciliation and mediation . . . 821
Cruelty as grounds for divorce . . . 769; 806
Current divorce statistics and concerns . . 770–772
Custody of children (See CHILD CUSTODY)
Defenses
    Collusion as defense to fault-based divorce . . 807–808
    Condonation as defense to fault-based divorce . . . 808
    Connivance as defense to fault-based divorce . . . 807
    Delay in bringing divorce action as defense to fault-based divorce . . . 807
    Estoppel defenses in attacking void divorce . . . 794–795
    Recrimination as defense to fault-based divorce . . . 808
Defined . . . 768
Delay in bringing action
    Adultery, action based on . . . 808
    Defense to divorce . . . 807
Desertion as grounds for divorce . . . 769; 806–807
Discovery . . . 808
Disqualification of attorney (See ATTORNEYS)
Distribution of property (See DISTRIBUTION OF PROPERTY)

DIVORCE—Cont.
Divisible divorce doctrine . . . 797–801
"Domestic-relations exception" to federal courts having jurisdiction . . . 773
Domiciliary requirement . . . 772–782
Drug addiction as grounds for divorce . . 769; 807
Drunkenness as grounds for divorce . . . 769; 807
Economic fault . . . 822
Economic impact of no-fault divorce . . . 771–772
Emotional distress claims arising out of divorce . . . 457–473
Equitable distribution of property (See DISTRIBUTION OF PROPERTY)
Estoppel defenses in attacking void divorce 794–795
Ethical issues for family lawyers (See ATTORNEYS)
Fault-based divorce
    Generally . . . 769–770; 801–809; 821–824
    Defenses (See subhead: Defenses)
    Distribution of marital property, effect on (See DISTRIBUTION OF PROPERTY)
"Feminization of poverty" resulting from divorce . . . 771
Foreign-country migratory divorces . . . 786–795; 796
Grounds for divorce
    Fault-based divorce . . . 769–770; 801–809
    No-fault divorce . . . 769–770; 809–821
Habitual drunkenness as grounds for divorce 769; 807
Hague Convention on the Recognition of Divorce and Legal Separations . . . 795
Historical background . . . 768–769
In propria persona, divorces filed . . . 840
Insanity as grounds for divorce . . . 769; 807
Irretrievable breakdown of marriage as grounds for divorce . . . 770; 814–821
Jurisdictional requirements
    Collateral attack of divorce . . . 795–797
    Divisible divorce doctrine . . . 797–801
    Domiciliary requirement . . . 772–782
    Long arm statutes . . . 801
    Migratory divorces
        Generally . . . 782–783
        Foreign-country migratory divorces 786–795; 796
        Sister-state migratory divorces 783–786; 795–796
Living separate and apart as grounds for 809–813
Long arm statutes . . . 801
Mediation of issues (See MEDIATION)
Mexican divorces . . . 787
Migratory divorces
    Attorney's advice regarding . . . 839

[References are to pages.]

DIVORCE—Cont.
Migratory divorces—Cont.
    Jurisdictional requirements (See subhead: Jurisdictional requirements)
No-fault divorce
    Generally . . . 769–770; 809–821; 821–824
    Children, negative impact of no-fault divorce on . . . 771–772
    Equitable distribution proceedings, arguments for rejection of fault factors in . . . 940–941
    Spousal support, effect on (See SPOUSAL SUPPORT)
Premarital agreements, divorce planning in (See PREMARITAL AGREEMENTS)
Property distribution (See DISTRIBUTION OF PROPERTY)
Property settlement agreements (See SEPARATION AGREEMENTS)
Pro se divorces . . . 840
Recrimination as defense to fault-based divorce . . . 808
Rejection of fault factors in no-fault divorces, arguments for . . . 821–822
Relevance of fault factors in no-fault divorces . . . 821–824
Religious divorce laws, state recognition of 1283–1287
Retaining fault factors in no-fault divorces, arguments for . . . 823–824
Separation agreements (See SEPARATION AGREEMENTS)
Service of process . . . 782
Sister-state migratory divorces 783–786; 795–796
Spousal support (See SPOUSAL SUPPORT)
Statistics on . . . 770–772
Statute of limitations in bringing action based on adultery . . . 808
Support (See CHILD SUPPORT; SPOUSAL SUPPORT)
Tax consequences of (See TAXATION)
Third party's attempt to collaterally attack divorce . . . 796–797
Tort claims arising out of divorce . . . 457–473
Uniform Marriage and Divorce Act, effect of . . . 770
Venue . . . 781–782
Visitation rights (See VISITATION)
Void divorce
    Collateral attack on . . . 795–797
    Estoppel defenses in attacking divorce 794–795
Williams I and *Williams II* doctrines . . . 784–785; 795–796
Withdrawal of attorney (See ATTORNEYS)

DNA TESTING (See PATERNITY)

DOMESTIC VIOLENCE
Generally . . . 419–422
Anti-stalking statutes . . . 443
Arrest policies, mandatory . . . 426–435
Child abuse (See CHILD ABUSE)
Civil protection order process . . . 435–443
Compensation of victims for economic costs of domestic violence . . . 435
Contemporary approaches to domestic violence . . . 426–447
Contempt as mechanism for enforcement of civil protection order . . . 443
Criminal prosecution of batterer . . . 426–435
Defined . . . 420–421
Enforcement of civil protection orders . . . 442–443
Ex-parte protection orders . . . 435–441
Intrafamily tort liability (See INTRAFAMILY TORT LIABILITY)
Leaving batterer, reasons for not . . . 422–423
Mandatory arrest policies . . . 426–435
Marital rape . . . 443–447
Mediation in cases involving domestic violence . . . 860
No-drop prosecution policies . . . 426–435
Protective orders . . . 435–443
Rape of spouse or intimate partner . . . 443–447
Sexual assault as form of domestic violence 443–447
Stalking, statutes criminalizing . . . 443
Temporary protection orders . . . 435–443
Tort liability (See INTRAFAMILY TORT LIABILITY)
Traditional response to domestic violence 423–426
Violence Against Women Act (See VIOLENCE AGAINST WOMEN ACT)

DOMICILE
Defined . . . 773
Divorce, requirement for . . . 772–782

DOWER
Generally . . . 121–122

DRUG ABUSE
Child custody disputes, abuse as factor in . . 1154
Fetus, abuse or neglect of . . . 540–552

DRUG ADDICTION
Divorce, grounds for . . . 769; 807
Prenatal maternal drug addiction . . . 540–552

DRUNKENNESS
Divorce, habitual drunkenness as grounds for . . . 769; 807

[References are to pages.]

DUAL-PROPERTY EQUITABLE DISTRIBUTION (See DISTRIBUTION OF PROPERTY, subhead: Equitable distribution)

DUAL REPRESENTATION (See ATTORNEYS)

DUE PROCESS
Adoption (See ADOPTION)

DURESS
Adoption, revocation of consent for . . . 662–663
Marriage under duress . . . 80–82

E

EDUCATION
Amish students, effect of compulsory school-attendance laws on . . . 494–504
Bilingual education of children . . . 486–487; 489
Child custody disputes, educational needs as factor in . . . 1154
Colleges and universities (See COLLEGES AND UNIVERSITIES)
Compulsory education laws . . . 487–488; 494–504
Condom-availability programs in schools . . . 240
Constitutional issues regarding education of children . . . 486–507
Corporal punishment in schools . . . 521–522
Home schooling . . . 505–506
Mediation, parent education program as prerequisite to . . . 863
Voucher programs, constitutionality of . . 489–490

EDUCATIONAL DEGREES
Divorce, classification of professional degrees on . . . 906–915

ELECTIVE SHARE STATUTES
Generally . . . 122
Augmented estate elective shares . . . 122

EMANCIPATION OF MINORS
Generally . . . 603–604
Child support, effect on duration of . . . 1052

EMBRYO STATUS
Generally . . . 317–329
Donation of embryo . . . 328
Protection of embryo . . . 327–328

EMOTIONAL DISTRESS
Marriage and divorce, claims arising out of 457–473

EMPLOYEE RETIREMENT INCOME SECURITY ACT (ERISA)
Generally . . . 897; 1303

EMPLOYER AND EMPLOYEE
Child support obligor evading automatic withholding, cause of action against employer for conspiring with . . . 1071

ENFORCEMENT
Child support (See CHILD SUPPORT)
Domestic violence cases, protective orders in 442–443
Visitation rights . . . 1162–1163

ENOCH ARDEN STATUTES
Generally . . . 63

EQUITABLE DISTRIBUTION OF PROPERTY (See DISTRIBUTION OF PROPERTY)

ESTATE TAXES
Generally . . . 1304–1305

ESTOPPEL
Adoption by estoppel . . . 648
Annulment action, estoppel by judgment as defense to . . . 98
Divorce, estoppel defenses in attacking void 794–795
Entrapment by estoppel . . . 567
Marriage by . . . 26–32
Paternity actions . . . 375–378

ETHICAL ISSUES
Attorneys (See ATTORNEYS)
Mediation, use of . . . 861–862

EVIDENCE
Divorce attorney's presentation of false evidence . . . 846–847
Privileged communications between spouses 151–153

EX-PARTE PROCEEDINGS
Domestic violence cases, protective orders in 435–441

EXTORTION
Separation agreement based on extortion, invalidity of . . . 1275

F

FAITH HEALING
Generally . . . 563–569

FAMILY AND MEDICAL LEAVE ACT (FMLA)
Generally . . . 172–188
Federal legislation and FMLA, interaction of 179
Litigation under act . . . 179
State family leave laws and FMLA, interaction of . . . 178–179

[References are to pages.]

FAMILY AND MEDICAL LEAVE ACT (FMLA)—Cont.
Text of . . . 172–174

FAMILY HOME
Distribution on divorce (See DISTRIBUTION OF PROPERTY)
Sale of home
    Generally (See DISTRIBUTION OF PROPERTY, subhead: Family home)
    Taxation of gain on sale of home . . . 1302

FAMILY SUPPORT ACT OF 1988
Generally . . . 1009

FAULT, EFFECT OF (See DIVORCE)

FEDERAL TAXES (See TAXATION)

FITNESS OF PARENT (See CHILD CUSTODY)

FMLA (See FAMILY AND MEDICAL LEAVE ACT (FMLA))

FOREIGN COUNTRIES
Adoption of foreign-born children . . . 649
Divorces, migratory . . . 786–795; 796
Surrogacy in . . . 308

FOSTER CARE
Generally . . . 604–624; 627–628
Adoption and Safe Families Act of 1997 629–630
Adoption Assistance and Child Welfare Act (AACWA) . . . 539; 627–629
Defined . . . 605
Equitable adoption, effect of doctrine of . . . 648
Extended family members, foster care provided by . . . 624–627
Family members, foster care by . . . 624–627
Homosexuality as factor in selection of adoptive parents . . . 746
Interethnic Adoption Provisions of 1996 . . . . . . 723–724; 727–728
Kinship foster care . . . 624–627
Psychological parenting theory . . . 622–624
Relatives, foster care by . . . 624–627
Removal of children from foster homes 604–624
Sexual orientation as criterion in selection of adoptive parents . . . 746
Sibling groups, placement of . . . 626

FRAUD
Adoption, revocation of consent for . . . 662–663
Attorney-client privilege, effect on (See ATTORNEY-CLIENT PRIVILEGE)
Attorney, representation by (See ATTORNEYS)
Collusion (See COLLUSION)

FRAUD—Cont.
Economic fault, fraudulent sale of marital home as . . . 939
Marriage (See MARRIAGE)
Separation agreement subsequently attacked based on fraudulent nondisclosure of assets . . 1270–1275

FREEDOM OF ACCESS TO CLINIC ENTRANCES ACT OF 1994 (FACE)
Generally . . . 269–270

FULL FAITH AND CREDIT FOR CHILD SUPPORT ORDERS ACT OF 1994
Generally . . . 1076; 1086

G

GARNISHMENT OF WAGES
Child support, collection of . . . 1070

GERMAN MEASLES (See RUBELLA TEST)

GESTATIONAL SURROGACY (See SURROGACY)

GIFTS
Distribution of property, effect on (See DISTRIBUTION OF PROPERTY, subhead: Separate property)
Premarital gifts, return of . . . 1234–1242

GIFT TAXES
Generally . . . 1304–1305

GOODWILL
Professional practices and businesses, goodwill of . . . 918–927

GRANDPARENTS
Adoption, visitation after . . . 757–758
Foster care provided by . . . 624–627
Visitation rights of (See VISITATION)

GRAY MARKET ADOPTIONS (See ADOPTION, subhead: Independent adoptions)

GUARDIAN AD LITEM (See ATTORNEYS, subhead: Children, representation of)

H

HAGUE CONVENTION
Child Abduction, Hague Convention on the Civil Aspects of International . . . 1221–1229
Divorce and Legal Separations, Hague Convention on the Recognition of . . . 795

"HOLD HARMLESS" CLAUSES
Bankruptcy, effect of . . . 1313; 1315

HOME SCHOOLING
Generally . . . 505–506

[References are to pages.]

HOME STUDIES
Adoptions, use in . . . 702

HOMOSEXUALITY
Adoption, effect on (See ADOPTION)
Child custody disputes, parent's sexual preference as factor in . . . 1125–1133
Cohabitation (See COHABITATION)
Domestic partnership legislation . . . 191; 228–233
Domestic violence between homosexual partners (See DOMESTIC VIOLENCE)
Foster parents, homosexuality as factor in selection of . . . 746
Marriage, homosexual . . . 46–57
Visitation rights for parents and partners (See VISITATION)

HUMAN LEUKOCYTE ANTIGEN (HLA) BLOOD TEST
Paternity, establishment of . . . 347–353

HUSBAND AND WIFE (See MARRIAGE)

I

ICWA (See ADOPTION, subhead: Indian Child Welfare Act)

ILLEGITIMATE CHILDREN (See NONMARITAL CHILDREN)

IMMIGRATION
Marriage for immigration purposes . . . 83
Sham marriages for immigration purposes . . . 83

IMMIGRATION MARRIAGE FRAUD AMENDMENTS ACT
Generally . . . 87–88

IMMUNITY
Intraspousal tort immunity . . . 457–459
Parental tort immunity doctrine . . . 473–483

INCEPTION OF TITLE THEORY
Generally . . . 880–885; 883–884

INCESTUOUS MARRIAGES
Generally . . . 63–69

INCOME
Child support, determination of (See CHILD SUPPORT)

INDEPENDENT ADOPTIONS (See ADOPTION)

INDIAN CHILD WELFARE ACT (See ADOPTION)

INDIANS (See NATIVE AMERICANS)

INFORMAL MARRIAGES (See MARRIAGE)

INHERITANCE
Distribution of property, effect on (See DISTRIBUTION OF PROPERTY, subhead: Separate property)
Illegitimate children, rights of . . . 334–343
Nonmarital children, rights of . . . 334–343

INMATES AND PRISONERS
Marriages of . . . 43
Visitation with children while in prison . . . 1162

IN PROPRIA PERSONA
Divorces filed . . . 840

INSANITY
Divorce, grounds for . . . 769; 807

INTERETHNIC ADOPTION PROVISIONS OF 1996
Generally . . . 649; 723–724; 727–728

INTERSTATE COMPACT ON PLACEMENT OF CHILDREN (ICPC)
Generally . . . 662

INTRAFAMILY TORT LIABILITY
Divorce and marriage, tort claims arising out of . . . 457–473
Emotional distress claims arising out of marriage and divorce . . . 457–473
Married Women's Property Acts, effect of . . . 457
Parent-child tort actions . . . 473–483
Spousal immunity . . . 457–459

IN VITRO FERTILIZATION
Generally . . . 317–329
Gestational surrogacy (See SURROGACY)
Status of embryo (See EMBRYO STATUS)
Surrogacy (See SURROGACY)

INVOLUNTARY TERMINATION OF PARENTAL RIGHTS (See ADOPTION)

J

JEHOVAH'S WITNESSES
Generally . . . 491–494
Blood transfusions, refusal to consent to 577–581; 583–587

JOINT CUSTODY (See CHILD CUSTODY)

JUDAISM
Marriage contracts, state recognition of religious . . . 1283–1287

JUDICIAL DISCRETION (See DISCRETION)

JURISDICTION
Annulment . . . 96–97
Child custody jurisdiction (See CHILD CUSTODY)

[References are to pages.]

JURISDICTION—Cont.
Child support, personal jurisdiction for 1077–1083
Divorce (See DIVORCE)
Paternity actions, personal jurisdiction in . . . 371

JUVENILE COURT
Parental authority over children, proceedings to reinforce . . . 602

L

LACHES
Annulment action, defense to . . . 98

LAWYERS (See ATTORNEYS)

LICENSES
Adoption agencies (See ADOPTION, subhead: Agency adoptions)
Child support, revocation or suspension of state license for failure to pay . . . 1070–1071
Divorce, classification of professional licenses on . . . 906–915
Marriage licenses . . . 10–13

LIENS
Child support arrearages, liens on to collect 1075

LIMITATIONS, STATUTE OF (See STATUTE OF LIMITATIONS)

LONG ARM STATUTES
Divorce actions . . . 801

M

MAINTENANCE (See SPOUSAL SUPPORT)

MARITAL CONTRACTS
Generally . . . 1231–1233
Breach of promise-to-marry contracts and return of premarital gifts . . . 1234–1242
Fraudulent inducement into marriage contract . . . 1239–1240
Premarital agreements (See PREMARITAL AGREEMENTS)
Religious contracts, state recognition of 1283–1287
Restraint of marriage, contract in . . . 1240
Separation agreements (See SEPARATION AGREEMENTS)
Third party's interference with marriage . . . 1241

MARITAL HOME (See FAMILY HOME)

MARRIAGE
Generally . . . 1–3; 105–106

MARRIAGE—Cont.
Adverse spousal testimony rule . . . 151–153
Alienation of affections actions . . . 147–149; 1241
Annulment (See ANNULMENT)
Anti-nepotism rules . . . 154–161
Bigamous and polygamous marriages . . . 57–63
Blood test requirement . . . 10
Breach of promise to marry actions . . 1234–1242
Capacity and intent to marry
   Generally . . . 44
   Voidable marriages (See subhead: Voidable marriages)
   Void marriages (See subhead: Void marriages)
Cohabitation as alternative to (See COHABITATION)
Common-law marriages . . . 14–19
Community property (See COMMUNITY PROPERTY)
Conflict of laws . . . 88–96
Consortium, rights of . . . 150–151
Constitutional right of individual to marry 39–44
Contemporary perspectives on marriage 112–119
Contract or status relationship, marriage as 3–10
Counseling before marriage . . . 7–8
Covenant marriages . . . 6–7
Criminal conversation . . . 147–149
Curtesy . . . 121–122
Death of spouse, property rights on . . . 121–122
Defense of Marriage Act (See DEFENSE OF MARRIAGE ACT)
Dissolution of marriage (See DIVORCE)
Divorce (See DIVORCE)
Dower . . . 121–122
Duress, marriage under . . . 80–82
Economic transactions between spouses 139–145
Elective share statutes . . . 122
Emotional distress claims arising out of marriage . . . 457–473
Enoch Arden statutes . . . 63
Estoppel, marriage by . . . 26–32
Evidentiary privileges . . . 151–153
Family expense statutes . . . 131–134
Federal Defense of Marriage Act (See DEFENSE OF MARRIAGE ACT)
Formal statutory requirements . . . 10–13
Fraud
   General discussion of fraudulent marriages . . 77–80
   Inducement into marriage contract, fraudulent . . . 1239–1240
Homosexual marriages . . . 46–57

[References are to pages.]

MARRIAGE—Cont.
Immigration Marriage Fraud Amendments Act . . . 87–88
Immigration purposes, marriage for . . . 83
Incestuous marriages . . . 63–69
Informal marriages
    Generally . . . 14
    Common-law marriages . . . 14–19
    Estoppel, marriage by . . . 26–32
    Proxy marriages . . . 23–26
    Putative marriages . . . 19–23
Inmate's marriage . . . 43
Intentional interference with marriage . . 147–149
Intent to marry (See subhead: Capacity and intent to marry)
Invalidity of marriage, effect of . . . 2
Jest, marriage in . . . 83; 88
Last-in time marriage presumption . . . 32–39
Lex loci contractus rule . . . 88
License requirements . . . 10–13
Married Women's Property Acts . . . 119–121
Mental incompetence, effect of . . . 73–77
Modern theory of marriage as partnership of equals . . . 111–112
Necessaries, common law doctrine of . . 127–131
Nepotism, policies against . . . 154–161
Partnership of equals, modern theory of marriage as . . . 111–112
Physical incompetence, effect of . . . 73–77
Plural marriages . . . 57–63
Polygamous marriages . . . 57–63
Premarital counseling requirements . . . 7–8
Prisoner's marriage . . . 43
Privileges, evidentiary and testimonial . . 151–153
Property rights during marriage (See PROPERTY RIGHTS)
Proxy marriages . . . 23–26
Putative marriages . . . 19–23
Roles and responsibilities during marriage
    Contemporary perspectives on marriage 112–119
    Modern theory of marriage as partnership of equals . . . 111–112
    Traditional view of . . . 106–111
Rubella test requirement . . . 10
Same sex marriages . . . 46–57
Sham marriages . . . 83–88
Spousal support (See SPOUSAL SUPPORT)
State regulation of . . . 39–44
Statutory requirements . . . 10–13
Testimonial privileges . . . 151–153
Third party interference with marriage . . 147–149
Tort claims arising out of marriage
    Generally . . . 457–473

MARRIAGE—Cont.
Tort claims arising out of marriage—Cont.
    Intentional interference with marriage 147–149
    Misconduct during marriage . . . 942–943
Traditional view of roles and responsibilities during marriage . . . 106–111
Transsexual marriage . . . 57
Underage marriage . . . 69–73
Uniform Marital Property Act (See UNIFORM MARITAL PROPERTY ACT)
Uniform Marriage and Divorce Act . . . 64–65
Validity of marriage, effect of . . . 2
Voidable marriages
    Generally . . . 44–46
    Annulment (See ANNULMENT)
    Defined . . . 45
    Duress, marriage under . . . 80–82
    Fraudulent marriages . . . 77–80
    Jest, marriage in . . . 83; 88
    Mental and physical incompetence, effect of . . . 73–77
    Sham marriages . . . 83–88
    Underage marriage . . . 69–73
Void marriages
    Generally . . . 44–46
    Annulment (See ANNULMENT)
    Bigamous and polygamous marriages . . 57–63
    Defined . . . 45
    Incestuous marriages . . . 63–69
    Same sex marriages . . . 46–57

MARRIED WOMEN'S PROPERTY ACTS
Generally . . . 119–121
Spousal immunity doctrine, effect on . . . 457

MATERNAL LEAVE (See PARENTAL LEAVE)

MEDIATION
Generally . . . 821; 856–858; 1093
Arbitration distinguished . . . 856; 864–865
Concerns about mediation . . . 858–860
Confidentiality . . . 862–863
Court access and mediation . . . 863
Defined . . . 856
Distinguished from arbitration . . . 856; 864–865
Domestic violence, mediation in cases involving . . . 860
Ethical considerations . . . 861–862
Parent education programs as prerequisite to 863
Role of attorneys in . . . 862
Standards for divorce and family mediators . . 858

MEDICAID
Generally . . . 137–138

[References are to pages.]

MEDICAL CARE FOR CHILDREN
Abortions (See ABORTION)
Child Abuse Prevention and Treatment Act of 1974 . . . 568
Children as decision-makers . . . 583–587
Criminal prosecution for parental failure to seek medical care . . . 563–569
Faith healing exemption . . . 563–569
Jehovah's Witnesses' refusal to consent to blood transfusions . . . 577–581; 583–587
Mature minor doctrine . . . 585–587; 588
Neglect, medical . . . 569–582
Parens patriae doctrine . . . 573; 579; 586
Tax deduction for dependent child's medical expenses . . . 1297

MEDICARE
Generally . . . 137–138

MENTALLY DISABLED
Child custody disputes, parent's mental fitness as factor in . . . 1134–1141
Child support beyond age of majority for . . . 134
Marriage, effect of incompetence on . . . 73–77
Sterilization of (See STERILIZATION)

MIGRATORY DIVORCES (See DIVORCE)

MILITARY RETIREMENT BENEFITS
Division of . . . 897

MINORS (See CHILDREN AND MINORS)

MISCONDUCT (See CONDUCT)

MISTAKE
Adoption, revocation of consent for . . . 663

MODIFICATION
Child support . . . 1057–1063
Custody orders (See CHILD CUSTODY)
Spousal support (See SPOUSAL SUPPORT)

MULTIETHNIC PLACEMENT ACT OF 1994
Generally . . . 649; 727–728

N

NATIVE AMERICANS
Indian Child Welfare Act (See ADOPTION)

NECESSARIES
Generally . . . 127–131

NEGLECT OF CHILDREN (See CHILD ABUSE)

NEPOTISM
General discussion of policies against . . . 154–161
State civil rights statutes, challenges to anti-nepotism rules under . . . 159

NEPOTISM—Cont.
Title VII challenges to anti-nepotism policies 158–159

NO-FAULT DIVORCE (See DIVORCE)

NON-AGENCY ADOPTIONS (See ADOPTION, subhead: Independent adoptions)

NONDISCHARGEABILITY OF DEBT (See BANKRUPTCY)

NONMARITAL CHILDREN
(See also PATERNITY)
Constitutional considerations . . . 334–347
Current perspectives on . . . 332–334
Historical background for establishment of legal parenthood . . . 331–332
Inheritance rights of . . . 334–343
Uniform Parentage Act, effect of . . . 332

NONMARITAL COHABITATION (See COHABITATION)

NON-PROFIT ADOPTION AGENCIES (See ADOPTION, subhead: Agency adoptions)

NORPLANT DEVICE
Generally . . . 239–240

O

OMNIBUS BUDGET RECONCILIATION ACT OF 1993
Generally . . . 1076

OPEN ADOPTIONS (See ADOPTION)

P

PALIMONY
Generally . . . 204

PARENS PATRIAE DOCTRINE
Generally . . . 573; 579; 586

PARENTAL ALIENATION SYNDROME
Generally . . . 1153

PARENTAL KIDNAPPING PREVENTION ACT (PKPA)
Generally . . . 1193; 1208–1209; 1212–1221

PARENTAL LEAVE
Maternal leave
    Generally . . . 161–171; 168–169
    Availability of . . . 187
    Financing of . . . 187–188
Paternal leave
    Generally . . . 167–168; 186–188

[References are to pages.]

PARENTAL LEAVE—Cont.
Paternal leave—Cont.
    Availability of . . . 187
    Barriers to use of leave . . . 188
    Financing of parental leave . . . 187–188
    Hostility in workplace to . . . 188
    Workplace hostility to . . . 188

PARENTAL TORT IMMUNITY DOCTRINE
Generally . . . 473–483

PARENT EDUCATION PROGRAMS
Mediation, prerequisite to . . . 863

PARENT LOCATOR SERVICE
Generally . . . 1074–1075

PARENTS
Mediation, parent education program as prerequisite to . . . 863
Relative responsibility statutes . . . 135–138
Stepparents (See STEPPARENTS)
Tort actions between parents and children 473–483

PARTIAL BIRTH ABORTION ACT OF 1996
Generally . . . 270

PARTNERSHIPS
Cohabitation cases, use of partnership theories in . . . 206–216

PATERNAL LEAVE (See PARENTAL LEAVE)

PATERNITY
(See also NONMARITAL CHILDREN)
Blood tests to establish paternity . . . 347–353
Child support obligations, establishment of legal parenthood to impose . . . 371–378
Constitutional issues
    Court-ordered paternity tests, constitutionality of . . . 370
    Statute of limitations on paternity actions, constitutionality of . . . 343–347
Counsel in paternity actions, right to . . . 370–371
Court-ordered paternity tests, constitutionality of . . . 370
DNA testing
    Generally . . . 353–356
    Privacy concerns . . . 356
Equitable estoppel . . . 375–378
Federal involvement in paternity establishment . . . 357
Genetic testing . . . 347–358
HLA typing . . . 347–353
Human Leukocyte Antigen (HLA) blood test 347–353
Jurisdiction in paternity actions . . . 371

PATERNITY—Cont.
Maternal cooperation requirements . . . 374–375
Non-presumptive parents, parental rights of 389–417
Payment for scientific tests, state's obligation to provide . . . 370
Personal jurisdiction in paternity actions . . . 371
Preponderance of evidence standard of proof 369–370
Presumptions
    General discussion of presumptions to be used in paternity actions . . . 387–389
    Parental rights of presumptive parents 379–389
    Scientific evidence, presumptions based on . . 356–357
Procedural issues in paternity cases . . . 369–371
Rebuttable presumptions to be used in paternity actions . . . 387–389
Relitigation issues . . . 358–369
Res judicata issues . . . 358–369
Right to counsel in paternity actions . . . 370–371
Scientific testing to establish paternity . . 347–358
Standard of proof . . . 369–370
State's obligation to pay for scientific testing 370
Statute of limitations on paternity actions, constitutionality of . . . 343–347
Support obligations, establishment of legal parenthood to impose . . . 371–378
Surrogacy cases, establishment of paternity in . . . 295
Uniform Adoption Act, effect of . . . 416
Uniform Parentage Act (See UNIFORM PARENTAGE ACT)
Venue in paternity actions . . . 371
Voluntary acknowledgement of paternity . . . 357

PENDENTE LITE STATUTES
Generally . . . 134

PENSION AND RETIREMENT PLANS
Distribution of benefits (See DISTRIBUTION OF PROPERTY)
Military retirement benefits . . . 897
Taxation of benefits . . . 1302–1303

PERMANENT SPOUSAL SUPPORT (See SPOUSAL SUPPORT)

PERSONAL INJURIES
Distribution of awards on divorce . . . 902–906

PERSONAL RESPONSIBILITY AND WORK OPPORTUNITY RECONCILIATION ACT OF 1996
Child support, effect on . . . 1076–1077

PHYSICALLY DISABLED
Adoptive parents, physical ability as criterion in selection of . . . 745
Child custody disputes, parent's physical fitness as factor in . . . 1134–1141
Child support beyond age of majority for . . . 134

PKPA (See PARENTAL KIDNAPPING PREVENTION ACT (PKPA))

POLYGAMY
Generally . . . 57–63

PREGNANCY DISCRIMINATION ACT OF 1978
Generally . . . 161–171

PREMARITAL AGREEMENTS
Generally . . . 1231–1233; 1242–1243
Divorce planning in premarital agreements
    Property provisions . . . 1248–1252
    Spousal support provisions . . . 1252–1256
Estate planning, use of agreements for 1243–1248
Uniform Premarital Agreement Act
    Generally . . . 144; 1242–1243; 1256–1263
    Text of . . . 1256–1263

PREMARITAL COUNSELING
Generally . . . 7–8

PRENUPTIAL AGREEMENTS (See PREMARITAL AGREEMENTS)

PRESUMPTIONS
Distribution of property (See DISTRIBUTION OF PROPERTY)
Last-in time marriage presumption . . . 32–39
Paternity (See PATERNITY)

PRISONERS (See INMATES AND PRISONERS)

PRIVACY, RIGHT TO
Abortion (See ABORTION)
Contraceptives, use of . . . 241–242

PRIVATE ADOPTIONS (See ADOPTION)

PRIVILEGED COMMUNICATIONS
Attorney-client privilege (See ATTORNEY-CLIENT PRIVILEGE)
Marital communications privilege . . . 151–153
Spouses, communications between . . . 151–153

PROFESSIONAL PRACTICES
Distribution on divorce or dissolution of marriage (See DISTRIBUTION OF PROPERTY, subhead: Businesses and professional practices, valuation of)

PROPERTY RIGHTS
Annulment of marriage, rights on . . . 98–102

PROPERTY RIGHTS—Cont.
Cohabitation cases, use of property theories in . . . 206–216
Death of spouse, rights on . . . 121–122
Distribution of property on divorce or dissolution of marriage (See DISTRIBUTION OF PROPERTY)
Marriage, rights during
    Generally . . . 119
    Community property . . . 119; 123
    Married Women's Property Acts . . . 119–121
    Tenancy by the entirety . . . 121
Uniform Marital Property Act (See UNIFORM MARITAL PROPERTY ACT (UMPA))

PROPERTY SETTLEMENT AGREEMENTS (See SEPARATION AGREEMENTS)

PRO TANTO COMMUNITY PROPERTY INTEREST
Generally . . . 881; 883

PROTECTIVE ORDERS
Domestic violence . . . 435–443

PROXY
Marriage by . . . 23–26

PUTATIVE MARRIAGES
Generally . . . 19–23

Q

QUALIFIED DOMESTIC RELATIONS ORDERS (QDRO)
Generally . . . 897; 1303
Alternate payees
    Generally . . . 897
    Taxation of pension benefits assigned to 1303

R

RACE
Adoption, effect on (See ADOPTION)
Child custody disputes, race as factor in 1117–1120

RAILROAD RETIREMENT ACT
Generally . . . 896–897

RAPE
Marital rape . . . 443–447

RATIFICATION
Adoption, ratification of pre-birth consent for . . . 653
Annulment, ratification of marital defect as defense to . . . 97

[References are to pages.]

RECRIMINATION
Divorce, defense to . . . 808

REGISTRIES
Adoptions, use in (See ADOPTION)

REHABILITATIVE SPOUSAL SUPPORT (See SPOUSAL SUPPORT)

REIMBURSEMENT ALIMONY (See SPOUSAL SUPPORT)

RELATIVE RESPONSIBILITY STATUTES
Generally . . . 135–138
Medicaid funds used for parents, adult children's reimbursement of . . . 137–138

RELIGION
Adoption, effect on (See ADOPTION)
Amish religion . . . 494–504
Child custody disputes, religion as factor in 1112–1116
Christian scientists (See CHRISTIAN SCIENTISTS)
Contracts of marriage, state recognition of religious . . . 1283–1287
Jehovah's witnesses (See JEHOVAH'S WITNESSES)
Jewish marriage contracts, state recognition of . . . 1283–1287
Marriage contracts, state recognition of religious . . . 1283–1287

REPRODUCTIVE ALTERNATIVES
Abortion (See ABORTION)
Artificial insemination (See ARTIFICIAL INSEMINATION)
Cloning (See CLONING)
Contraception (See CONTRACEPTION)
In vitro fertilization (See IN VITRO FERTILIZATION)
New reproductive technology . . . 309
Status of embryo (See EMBRYO STATUS)
Sterilization (See STERILIZATION)
Surrogacy (See SURROGACY)

RESIDENCE OF FAMILY (See FAMILY HOME)

RES JUDICATA
Annulment action, defense to . . . 98
Paternity judgments . . . 358–369

RETIREMENT EQUITY ACT OF 1984
Generally . . . 897

RETIREMENT PLANS (See PENSION AND RETIREMENT PLANS)

REVISED UNIFORM RECIPROCAL ENFORCEMENT OF SUPPORT ACT (RURESA)
Generally . . . 1085–1088

REVOCATION
Adoption, consent to (See ADOPTION)
Child support, revocation of state license for failure to pay . . . 1070–1071

RU486
Generally . . . 240; 268–269

RUBELLA TEST
Marriage, requirement for . . . 10

RURESA (See REVISED UNIFORM RECIPROCAL ENFORCEMENT OF SUPPORT ACT (RURESA))

S

SALE OF FAMILY HOME (See FAMILY HOME)

SCHOOLS (See EDUCATION)

SEALED ADOPTION RECORDS (See ADOPTION, subhead: Confidentiality of adoption records)

SEPARATE PROPERTY
Generally . . . 123
Distribution of (See DISTRIBUTION OF PROPERTY)
Transmutation of property (See TRANSMUTATION OF PROPERTY)

SEPARATION AGREEMENTS
Generally . . . 1231–1233; 1263–1264
Arbitration of disputes (See ARBITRATION)
Attorneys, use of (See ATTORNEYS)
Bankruptcy's effect on property settlements (See BANKRUPTCY)
Checklist for drafting agreement . . . 1276–1281
Consideration, invalidity of agreement based on illegal . . . 1275
Drafting considerations . . . 1276–1283
Extortion, invalidity of agreement based on 1275
Fraudulent nondisclosure of assets, subsequent attack on agreement based on . . . 1270–1275
Illegal consideration, invalidity of agreement based on . . . 1275
Mediation of disputes (See MEDIATION)
Necessary elements for valid agreement 1264–1270
Statute of limitations for fraudulent nondisclosure . . . 1274
Tax consequences of division of property (See TAXATION, subhead: Property division)

SERVICE OF PROCESS
Divorce or dissolution of marriage actions . . . 782

SHAM MARRIAGES
Generally . . . 83–88

[References are to pages.]

SOURCE OF FUNDS THEORY
Generally . . . 881–882; 883–884

SPANKING (See CORPORAL PUNISHMENT)

SPOUSAL ABUSE (See DOMESTIC VIOLENCE)

SPOUSAL SUPPORT
Generally . . . 870–871; 953–954
Annulment of marriage, support rights on 98–102
Bankruptcy's effect on support obligations (See BANKRUPTCY, subhead: Nondischargeability of debt)
Child care responsibilities, effect of . . . 968–969
Cohabitation, effect of . . . 991–998; 999–1000
Compensation for loss . . . 969–977; 983
Death of either party, termination of support on . . . 998
Economic needs test for modification of support . . . 996; 999–1000
Equalization of parties' incomes . . . 977–982
Family expense statutes . . . 131–134
Foregone economic and career opportunities as justification for support . . . 969–977; 983
Gender as traditional rationale for support 954–956
General discussion of link between alimony and distribution of property . . . 983–991
Income sharing, alimony as . . . 977–982
Loss-compensation theory for award of support . . 969–977; 983
Marital support obligations . . . 124–138
"Michoff marriage'," effect of . . . 996–998
Modification of awards
    Generally . . . 871; 991–1001
    Cohabitation, effect of . . . 991–998; 999–1000
    Obligor's circumstances, effect of changes in . . . 1000
    Retroactive modification of arrearages . . 999
Necessaries, common law doctrine of . . 127–131
Need as traditional rationale for support 954–956
Non-intervention principle for support during marriage . . . 124–127
Obligor's circumstances, effect of changes in 1000
Pendente lite statutes . . . 134
Permanent spousal support
    Generally . . . 962
    Rehabilitative spousal support distinguished . . . 962
Premarital agreement, support provisions in 1252–1256
Rehabilitative spousal support
    Generally . . . 956–969; 983–991

SPOUSAL SUPPORT—Cont.
Rehabilitative spousal support—Cont.
    Permanent alimony distinguished . . . 962
    Remarriage, effect of . . . 999
Reimbursement alimony
    Generally . . . 871; 983–991
    Non-student spouse, payable to . . . 914
    Remarriage, effect of . . . 999
Remarriage, termination of support on . . . 999
Ruff-Fischer guidelines, use of . . . 962–964
Self-sufficiency, promotion of (See subhead: Rehabilitative spousal support)
Tax consequences of (See TAXATION)
Termination of support
    Death of parties . . . 998
    Remarriage of obligee . . . 999
Traditional rationales for support based on need and gender . . . 954–956
Uniform Interstate Family Support Act (UIFSA) . . . 1086–1089
Uniform Marriage and Divorce Act (UMDA)
    Modification of support . . . 999
    Remarriage, effect of . . . 999
    Termination of support . . . 999
Uniform Reciprocal Enforcement of Support Act (URESA) . . . 1085
Voluntary reduction of income, effect of . . . 1000

STALKING
Domestic violence, anti-stalking statutes protecting victims of . . . 443

STATUS OF EMBRYO (See EMBRYO STATUS)

STATUTE OF LIMITATIONS
Annulment action . . . 97
Divorce action based on adultery . . . 808
Paternity actions . . . 343–347
Separation agreements, fraudulent nondisclosure of assets in . . . 1274

STAY OF ACTIONS
Bankruptcy, effect of . . . 1311

STEPPARENTS
Adoption by . . . 713–718
Visitation rights of . . . 1161

STERILIZATION
Generally . . . 270–284
Voluntary sterilization of mentally handicapped or mentally ill . . . 272

SURROGACY
Generally . . . 284
Foreign countries, legislation in . . . 308
Gestational surrogacy
    Generally . . . 284; 297–309

[References are to pages.]

SURROGACY—Cont.
Gestational surrogacy—Cont.
    Maternity, establishment of . . . 358
Traditional surrogacy
    Generally . . . 284–296
    Paternity, establishment of . . . 295

SUSPENSION OF LICENSE
Child support, suspension of state license for failure to pay . . . 1070–1071

T

TAXATION
Generally . . . 1289
Alimony (See subhead: Spousal support)
Alternate payee, taxation of pension benefits assigned to . . . 1303
Annuities, taxation of . . . 1303
Anti-front loading requirements . . . 1296
Attorney's fees and other costs related to divorce, deductibility of . . . 1297–1298
Child care expenses for dependent child, tax credit for percentage of . . . 1297
Child support
    Arrearages, use of tax refund intercepts to collect . . . 1075
    Exclusion from gross income . . . 1290–1291
    Gift tax, transfers for purposes of support not subject to . . . 1304–1305
    Nondeductibility of payments . . . 1294–1296
    Trust income used for payments . . . 1297
Deficit Reduction Act of 1984, effect of 1294–1296
Dependency exemption, claim of . . . 1296
Division of property (See subhead: Property division)
Employee Retirement Income Security Act (ERISA), effect of . . . 1303
Estate taxes . . . 1304–1305
Family home, taxation of gain on sale of . . . 1302
Filing status of custodial parent . . . 1296
Gift taxes . . . 1304–1305
"Head of household" filing status for custodial parent . . . 1296
IRA rollovers . . . 1303
Lump-sum distributions, treatment of . . . 1303
"Marriage penalty" . . . 1292–1293
Medical expenses of dependent child, deduction for . . . 1297
Nonrecognition of gain for qualified transfers . . . 1298–1305
Pension plans, taxation of . . . 1303
Property division
    Estate and gift taxes . . . 1304–1305
    Family home, taxation of gain on sale of . . . 1302

TAXATION—Cont.
Property division—Cont.
    Nonrecognition of gain for qualified transfers . . . 1298–1305
    Retirement plans . . . 1303
    Stock transfers and redemptions . . . 1303–1304
Qualified Domestic Relations Order (QDRO), assignment of pension benefits made pursuant to 1303
Redemption of stock . . . 1303–1304
Refund intercepts to collect child support arrearages . . . 1075
Retirement Equity Act of 1984, effect of 1302–1303
Retirement plans, taxation of . . . 1303
Separate maintenance (See subhead: Spousal support)
Spousal support
    Anti-front loading requirements . . . 1296
    Attorney's fees, deductibility of . . . 1297–1298
    Deduction for payment of 1291–1292; 1293–1294
    Gift tax, transfers for purpose of support not subject to . . . 1304–1305
    Income of payee, includable in . . 1291–1292; 1293–1294
    Property settlement payments disguised as alimony . . . 1296
    Trust income used for payments . . . 1297
    Unallocated family allowance . . . 1289–1291
Stock transfers and redemptions . . . 1303–1304
Taxpayer Relief Act of 1997, effect of 1302–1303
Tax planning
    Fees, deductibility of . . . 1297–1298
    Trusts as tax planning tools . . . 1297
Transmutations of community property to separate property . . . 1305
Trust income used for support payments . . . 1297
Unallocated family allowance . . . 1289–1291
Waiver by custodial parent of right to claim dependency exemption . . . 1296

TAX REFUND INTERCEPTS
Child support arrearages, collection of . . . 1075

TEMPORARY ASSISTANCE TO NEEDY FAMILIES (TANF)
Cooperation requirements . . . 374–375

TENANCY BY THE ENTIRETY
Generally . . . 121

TERMINATION OF PARENTAL RIGHTS
Generally (See ADOPTION)
Abuse, parental failure to protect child from 532–533
Divorce from parents, child's . . . 603

[References are to pages.]

TERMINATION OF SUPPORT
Child support (See CHILD SUPPORT, subhead: Duration of support)
Spousal support (See SPOUSAL SUPPORT)

THIRD PARTIES
Attorney's knowledge of fraud by third party . . . 838–839
Cohabitants and third parties, disputes between . . . 216–227
Divorce, third party's attempt to collaterally attack . . . 796–797
Fraud by third party, attorney's knowledge of . . . 838–839
Marriage, third party's interference with . . . 147–149; 1241
Paternity, DNA testing of third parties to establish . . . 355–356
Visitation rights of . . . 1161

TITLE IV-D PROGRAM
Generally . . . 1008–1009; 1074–1075

TITLE VII OF CIVIL RIGHTS ACT OF 1964
Childrearing leave . . . 167–168
Nepotism policies, challenges to . . . 158–159
Pregnancy and childbearing and employment . . . 161–171

TORTS
Abuse, state remedies for failure to protect children from . . . 561
Adoption, wrongful (See ADOPTION, subhead: Wrongful adoption actions)
Contraceptives, litigation regarding safety of . . . 240
Intrafamily tort liability (See INTRAFAMILY TORT LIABILITY)
Marriage, claims arising from (See MARRIAGE)

TRACING OF PROPERTY
Generally . . . 885–890

TRADITIONAL SURROGACY (See SURROGACY)

TRANSMUTATION OF PROPERTY
Generally . . . 885–890
Gift tax inapplicable to transmutations . . . 1305

TRANSRACIAL ADOPTION (See ADOPTION)

TRANSSEXUALITY
Marriage, transsexual . . . 57

TRUSTS
Tax treatment of support trusts . . . 1297

U

UCCJA (See UNIFORM CHILD CUSTODY JURISDICTION ACT (UCCJA))

UCCJEA (See UNIFORM CHILD CUSTODY JURISDICTION AND ENFORCEMENT ACT (UCCJEA))

UIFSA (See UNIFORM INTERSTATE FAMILY SUPPORT ACT (UIFSA))

UMPA (See UNIFORM MARITAL PROPERTY ACT (UMPA))

UNEMPLOYMENT BENEFITS
Work-family conflicts and benefits . . . 181–183

UNFIT PARENT, TERMINATION OF PARENTAL RIGHTS OF (See ADOPTION, subhead: Involuntary termination of parental rights)

UNIFORM ADOPTION ACT (See ADOPTION)

UNIFORM CHILD CUSTODY JURISDICTION ACT (UCCJA)
Generally . . . 1193; 1195–1212; 1217–1221

UNIFORM CHILD CUSTODY JURISDICTION AND ENFORCEMENT ACT (UCCJEA)
Generally . . . 1193; 1210–1211

UNIFORMED SERVICES FORMER SPOUSES' PROTECTION ACT (USFSPA)
Generally . . . 897

UNIFORM INTERSTATE FAMILY SUPPORT ACT (UIFSA)
Generally . . . 1077; 1086–1089

UNIFORM MARITAL PROPERTY ACT (UMPA)
Generally . . . 123

UNIFORM MARRIAGE AND DIVORCE ACT
Generally . . . 64–65; 770
Child support, effect on (See CHILD SUPPORT)
Custody order, requirements for modification of . . . 1182–1183
Distribution of property, effect on (See DISTRIBUTION OF PROPERTY)
Modification of custody order, requirements for . . . 1182–1183
Physical incompetence, effect of . . . 73–74
Spousal support, effect on (See SPOUSAL SUPPORT)

UNIFORM PARENTAGE ACT
Generally . . . 332
Evidence related to paternity . . . 347–348
Presumption of paternity . . . 387–389

UNIFORM PREMARITAL AGREEMENT ACT (See PREMARITAL AGREEMENTS)

[References are to pages.]

UNIFORM RECIPROCAL ENFORCEMENT OF SUPPORT ACT (URESA)
Generally . . . 1085

UNIVERSITIES (See COLLEGES AND UNIVERSITIES)

UNMARRIED COHABITATION (See COHABITATION)

URESA (See UNIFORM RECIPROCAL ENFORCEMENT OF SUPPORT ACT (URESA))

V

VALUATION OF PROPERTY, GENERALLY (See DISTRIBUTION OF PROPERTY)

VAWA (See VIOLENCE AGAINST WOMEN ACT)

VENUE
Divorce actions . . . 781–782
Paternity actions . . . 371

VIOLENCE AGAINST WOMEN ACT
Generally . . . 447–457
Civil Rights Remedies for Gender-Motivated Violence Act . . . 448–457

VISITATION
Generally . . . 1155–1163
Adoption, visitation after (See ADOPTION, subhead: Post-adoption visitation)
Arbitration of disputes (See ARBITRATION)
Cohabitants, visitation disputes between unmarried . . . 214–215
Enforcement of visitation rights . . . 1162–1163
Equitable parents, visitation rights for . . . 1162
Grandparents' visitation rights
    Generally . . . 1160–1161
    Adoption, visitation after . . . 757–758
Homosexuals
    Partners, visitation for gay and lesbian 1162
    Restrictions on rights of noncustodial gay and lesbian parents . . . 1162

VISITATION—Cont.
Mediation of disputes (See MEDIATION)
Prison visitation . . . 1162
Restrictions on noncustodial parent . . . 1159
Schedule for . . . 1158–1159
Stepparents' visitation rights . . . 1161
Supervised visitation . . . 1162
Support payments and visitation . . . 1159–1160
Tardiness in picking up or dropping off child . . . 1162
Third parties' visitation rights . . . 1161

VOID AND VOIDABLE MARRIAGE (See MARRIAGE)

VOID DIVORCE (See DIVORCE)

W

WAGES
Assignment of wages to collect child support . . . 1070; 1075–1076
Garnishment of wages to collect child support . . . 1070

WAIVER
Attorney, waiver of attorney-client privilege on dual representation by . . . 828
Dependency exemption, custodial parent's waiver of right to claim . . . 1296

WIFE (See MARRIAGE)

WITHDRAWAL OF ATTORNEY (See ATTORNEYS)

WORDS AND PHRASES (See DEFINITIONS)

WORKERS' COMPENSATION
Distribution of awards on divorce . . . 902–906

WRONGFUL ADOPTION (See ADOPTION)

Z

ZONING
Cohabitants, effect of single-family zoning ordinances on unmarried . . . 223